AT WATER'S EDGE

Joy L. Esterby, Editor

THE NATIONAL LIBRARY OF POETRY

At Water's Edge

Library of Congress
Cataloging in Publication Data

ISBN 1-56167-271-8

Proudly manufactured in the United States of America by
Watermark Press
11419 Cronridge Dr., Suite 10
Owings Mills, MD 21117

Editor's Note

The power of a poem is in its ability to make the reader see, feel, and experience the moments and thoughts which give meaning and purpose to life. A poet's talent lies in the way he accomplishes this feat in an often restricted amount of space. Words and images must be chosen with the utmost care, as each contains subtle nuances that in some way affect the work as a whole. The following collection is a wonderful tribute to all the talented poets, young and old and from all walks of life in the world. As an editor, I truly enjoy the variety of poems we receive each day and the challenge which they present when it is time to select the final winners.

After careful consideration, the editors chose Desmond Sequeira's "Full Moon At Balupet" as the Grand Prize winner of the contest. Sequeira's chilling concrete imagery relentlessly pulls you into the horror of war. The narrator's surroundings are almost surreal as he wages war internally for the elusive hope of escape, represented by the train. In his estranged world, the train tracks appear as "parallel flames metal bright...curving away uphill;" the red train signal is "drowning in its own blood;" and the darkness "leak[s] from a perforated sky." As they try to cope with this skewed reality, the narrator and his fellow soldiers must focus on the moment, on each "elastic" stride they take, on the only thing they have control over - their own physical movements. Sequeira illustrates this need for simplicity by setting off three abrupt, simple sentences in the middle of the poem:

> *Talk was inconsequential*
> *We kept silent*
> *We forged chains*

The men "forge chains," or bonds, with each other as they look for the train to carry them to safety:

> *We erected laughter against a dread certainty*
> *that everything was possible: that most of all,*
> *later, alone, in a distant land, the forged chains*
> *biting into flesh would pull and pull again.*

Sequeira shows us that the experience of war can never be left behind, that each new day, each new memory, is an extra link forged in the chain which will pull at the men again and again as long as they live. I urge you to read Sequeira's "Full Moon At Balupet" several times, as there are many layers of meaning in his words.

There are a variety of other poems worthy of special attention as well. "The Botanist" (p. 378) by Sha'va Saint-Jean illustrates the importance of the poem's first lines which must hook the readers' attention and reel them into the action:

> *Cold shadows, red clay, gray grass, connection*
> *Like sex, or like waking.*

Though her subject initially remains concealed, Saint-Jean immediately focuses in on her theme of "connection," the bold description setting the tone for the action to come. The botanist in the poem, while watching a seemingly dull, static plant, suddenly connects with its movement, its life-affirming thrust toward the sun:

> *It happened to her then: the brain snapping on*
> *Like a bulb, adrenalin tides, chemical burning.*
> *Palms raised, dendrites for fingers, basking in light...*

In this moment, the botanist has found her place in the universe; she is grounded by the roots of her origin, yet will always strain to reach the stars, becoming "part of the signal" or connection between nature and humankind. Perhaps until now, we readers have been like the tourists, who, in an amazing display of irony, believe the botanist to be "So far from what's really happening in the world."

In another poem about nature's example for humankind, Robyn Condit's "Jealous of the Holly Tree" (p. 49) addresses the universal topic of the changing of seasons and gives it a fresh, highly creative sound. First she describes the relatively calm exchange of seasons in the south:

> *...greasy puddles may grow out of the asphalt, nurtured by a charcoal sky,*
> *and the palms may have some romance torn away by a vagrant wind.*

The leaves in the north, however, face a violent battle over life and death:

> *The veins of every leaf cry for the thick plastic vibrancy*
> *they used to be....Broken by the grimace of cloud, each stem*
> *exerts a double strength, stretching the thinnest fibers,*
> *willing life back into the branch.*

By dramatizing the prevalent image of leaves dying in autumn, Condit makes an effective statement on the human fear of death.

Other poems make considerable use of the extended metaphor to convey their messages. "To My Father" by Lydia Vine (p. 75) poignantly compares the narrator's father to a great oak, always strong and protective, even when "bowed and bent" with age. "I Name My Song" by Peggy Davis (p. 213) compares her child alternately to a flower and to music in this bitter poem about a mother's fierce love and possessiveness. Betty Harmon's "The Quilters" paints a beautiful picture of earth and the heavens as a never-ending patchwork quilt.

There are several other outstanding poems you won't want to miss: "A Sonnet" by John Loprieno (p. 336); the romantic "Your Pillow" by Richard Ochoa (p. 569); Pamela Morrison's touching "If Home Is Where The Heart Is" (p. 179); and "His Hands" by Ann Brabant (p.442).

There are so many more noteworthy poems, I could not possibly name them all. I invite you to delve deeply into the pages that follow and enjoy all the different topics, styles, and themes as I have. All of the poets displayed in *At Water's Edge* should be proud of their accomplishments.

Joy L. Esterby
Editor

Grand Prize

Desmond Sequeira / Palm Beach, FL

Second Prize

Arnette Bradley / South Holland, IL
Barbara Rose Brooker / San Francisco, CA
Mary Clancy / Copperopolis, CA
Robyn Condit / Tacoma, WA
Peggy Davis / Mogadore, OH

Vicky Dill-Schreiner / Kerrville, TX
John Loprieno / Elk Grove Village, IL
Sha'va Saint-Jean / Dorchester, MA
Keith Sobraske / Scottsdale, AZ
Gordon Steele / Alexandria, VA

Third Prize

Mona Abdelaziz / Albany, CA
Amanda Austin / Wilbraham, MA
John Bargetto / Scotts Valley, CA
Vonna Bechtel / Tonopah, NV
Ann Brabant / Jacksonville, FL
Arletha Brewer / Lansing, MI
Heather Brown / Chicago, IL
David Busby / Las Vegas, NV
Marianne Cable / New Milford, CT
Lori Cameron / Los Alamitos, CA
Donald Capoldo, Jr. / Marathan, FL
Charles Clary / Santa Rosa, CA
Johnny Cuesta / San Francisco, CA
Lynne Dammer / Katy, TX
Victor David / Berkeley, CA
Leslie Deaton / Franklin, OH
Marie Deavereaux / El Cerrito, CA
Dianna Depenbrock / Arlington, VA
Taysha Dishman / Atchison, KS
Catherine Draycott / Jamaica Plain, MA
Catherine Drougas / Chicago, IL
James Dwyer / Framingham, MA
David Egan / Mount Sinai, NY
Don Eischen / Santa Cruz, CA
Alberto Factora / San Francisco, CA
Mary Foster / Los Gatos, CA
Matthew Gaddy / Cedar Rapids, IA
John Gallar / San Jose, CA
Joseph Gibbs / Bogota, NJ
Betty Harmon / Kittanning, PA

Evelyn Holden / Lebanon, OR
Kathy Hudson / Taos, NM
Jim Hunter / Philadelphia, PA
Marjorie Hyman / San Mateo, CA
Rosemary Jones-Wylde / Spokane, WA
Bridget Keller / San Francisco, CA
Joshua Locantore / Sayville, NY
Shirley Matthews / Catonsville, MD
Simone Mavrodineanu / W. Palm Beach, FL
Gabriel Meister / Owings Mills, MD
Roy Merritt / Westwood, MA
Pamela Morrison / Orlando, FL
Richard Ochoa / Covington, LA
Linda Quillian / Upper Marlboro, MD
Robert Raingruber / Lodi, CA
David Rekrut / Venice, CA
Scott Roberts / Ft Myers, FL
Charlotte Rotkin / Pelham Manor, NY
Sanghamitra Roychowdhury / New York, NY
Richard Schaub / Lookout Mountain, CO
Samuel Schulman / Arlington, VA
Elaine Schwager / New York, NY
Michael Sorg / Anderson, IN
Merlevic Tamondong / Tempe, AZ
Lawrence Toole / Buffalo, NY
Lydia Vine / Farmington, CT
Misty Watrous / Harrisonburg, VA
Scott Williams / Decatur, AL
Patzi Zlakovski / Tecumseh, MI

Grand Prize Winner

Full Moon At Balupet

Our stride was elastic: Stretched and shrank
to put each foot unfailing smack
on each dew-dunked-sleeper.
With peripheral vision we saw parallel flames
metal bright, run curving away uphill each rise
and come sliding back, as sure, every fall, on and on.
Once we paused, turned and looked at red eye
drowning in its own blood. Glory as ever
recurring at each death.

Talk was inconsequential
We kept silent
We forged chains

Then with darkness leaking from a perforated sky
anxious, fending, we talked: If a train should come,
how grope blindly without the surety of blindness
up Balupet hill! And if the moon should not rise!
We erected laughter against a dread certainty
that everything was possible: that most of all,
later, alone, in a distant land, the forged chains
biting into flesh would pull and pull again.

—Desmond Sequeira

The Sky

Open space.
A blue-black world with unfathomable distance
Known only by spirits and gods.
Sparkling lights of pearl dance and sing.
An ever-changing painting.
Undefinable, yet framed by earth's horizons.
Defining negative space
Connecting grounded beings with Heaven.
Sparks of earth crackle and fly
Becoming one with the stars
Whispering, watching
I become wind, flying over brimstone and flame.
Its heated breath warming my soul
Comforting my translucent body.
I fly higher and become the sky,
The undefinable space.
Life is twinkling stars, wind my breath.
I am gentle, free.

Jeremy Scott Hanlon

Choice Of Freedom

As I grow there are children surrounding me
and the factors of life: politics; economy;
ecology; and of course religion, mold
my being into what society dictates.
Can I truly do what I want?
Can I make a difference in this world?
Will another doctor, lawyer, writer, or salesman
create a utopia for someone, somewhere?
Think each day of the influence you possess.
Take a chance on bettering yourself.
Your purpose is undefined, but it is understood,
that anyone with drive and desire
will cause change to themselves and others
each moment of existence.
For now, change me, cover me, and
give me my bottle; it's time for my nap.
When I awake, my next attempt at
exiting my crib could create
the freedom of tomorrow!

John R. Diggs

Night Life

I woke in the night,
a door accidentally closed hiding inner house glow.
Only light from a three quarter moon filtered through shutter slats

Where was I? Where was the light filled day-the cheerful bird songs?
The empty night sounds were unbroken. Silence matched loneliness.

The empty void was mine alone. Stretching ahead, endlessly
Could I last the growing moon? Could I last the night?

Was there another tomorrow? Would my dreams return
And make the dark passage a thing to be forgotten?

I must fall asleep again and forget the timeless passage
It was only a passing moment. I will live again.

Brian Finley

Mockingbird In A Honeysuckle Vine

I heard you singing joyfully in the bright moonlight,
I heard you singing lullabies in the dark of night.
I heard your quarrelsome voice and I looked out to see,
You warning off another bird that sat in a nearby tree.
Back and forth you flittered, as busy as could be,
Darting into a mass of vines, behind an old pine tree.
Then I discovered, just today your joy and anxiety,
A nest in a honeysuckle vine, with babies numbering three.

Frances R. Sparks

"Today She Got Her Wings"

In your time of sorrow and pain, take to heart this thought,
Sunshine appears after the rain, and peace when a battle's been fought.

Think not of what might have been, but of what is yet to be.
God's plan was never to condemn, he just set an angel free.

And know that in a future time, there will come a day,
When once again, you can hold your child in glorious array.

So close your eyes and say a prayer, then listen for the sound of wings.
Your daughter is there and in God's hands, while all of heaven sings.

T. J. Merritt

"Happy Anniversary, Dear!"

Way last spring, what did I find?
A beautiful card, very special kind.
In a secret place I hid it away....
Just waiting for this special day.

Lovely flowers on the cover spread...
"I LOVE YOU!" the message read.
It said "I NEED YOU!" how much I care..
I'd be very lonely if you weren't here.

You're very special in so many ways....
We've grown closer these 15,000 days,
We've stuck together, through thin and thick,
You've been beside me when I was sick.

No day goes by without a prayer for you...
And I thank God for all that you do.
You're very special in your special way...
"I LOVE YOU, MY DEAR!" what more can I say

Needless to say, and I must admit.....
My memory is not so brightly lit...
I can't find the card, that I hid away—
Maybe I'll find it for another special day.

Floyd A. Dailie

Rose Bouquet

Early in spring I planned to send
  A bouquet to an ailing friend
Her heart could hum so happily
  While roses whispered love from me
Each golden dawn I hoped to go
  And visit her a while or so
Though each tomorrow quickly fled
  There still were days and weeks ahead
Then autumn leaves waved their goodbyes
  As sorrow stalked my weeping eyes
For tears now hugged a floral spray
  Instead of smiles...a rose bouquet
And silence shouted from her door
  Since her heart hums...on Heaven's shore...

Dorothy Frank Ferguson

"On Being Shy"

A silent heart may find no love;
A bridled tongue may speak no peace;
A quiet mind keeps "thinking of,"
But yet [again] finds no release.

With you I've learned these things for sure:
The silent heart.., the quiet mind..,
An anticipation without a cure
Because of words I fail to find.

A silent heart may sometimes ache,
When a bridled tongue may long for speech,
As a quiet mind begins to wake,
Aroused by another it yearns to reach.

James D. Padgett

When I Look Into Your Eyes

When I look into your eyes I feel
a calm that turns the world to quiet peace,
like power God must have to make storms cease.

When I look into your eyes I see
impatient anger waiting to be free,
like storm clouds gath'ring dormant energy.

When I look into your eyes I sense
a love that warms the world with gentle light,
like faithful dawn that God lays onto night.

When I look into your eyes I muse.
What little imp of mirth gives you your glee,
like bubbles giggling past a shell at sea?

When I look into your eyes I feel
your soul, its thirst alive, a magnet for the truth,
in contest with the unkind thief of youth.

When I look into your eyes I am
in awe that God has given me a great surprise,
the precious gift of looking in your eyes.

Carol L. Thompson

"The Gift"

Once in a while the Lord will look down, and bless you with
a child or two;
You can love them or hate them, he leaves that up to you;
I'm a very blessed man and this you should know,
If you're smart you'll take time, and watch your children grow;
You should teach them, protect them, and love them I'm sure;
'Cause the love you get back, is so good and so pure;
They grow up so quick it doesn't seem to last;
'Cause the time you have with them goes by way too fast;
If they know that you love them, and your love is true;
their love is forever, and they'll forever love you;
But you better be careful and don't live a lie;
'Cause the good Lord can take them in the blink of an eye;

Dennis R. Yocom

Me

As the wind blows, the oceans spray.
    A comfort comes upon me.
The smell of salt, the coolness of the rocks, the warmth of the sun.
    A comfort comes upon me.
As the baby's born, the first cry,
    a comfort comes upon me.
A child at play, the sigh before they sleep
    a comfort comes upon me.
When I'm in your arms, the need is to be complete,
    a comfort comes upon me.
My eyes closed, my body so quiet, not even the sound of my heart beat.
    A comfort comes upon me.
THE DARKNESS, a comfort comes upon me....

JACs

Yesterday

These shadows of yesterday are still lurking around me.
A face, then nothing; a heartbeat, then silence;
a silence, then chaos.
Do I think that I am fine, it might be that I am,
the question is, do I want to be?
Cursing the ground of the demigods I have known,
nothing helps.
Like a seashell, the water comes crashing in around me,
I am drowning in my thoughts,
of yesterday.

Jodi Alfieri

Special Words

If I could be granted, but just a single day.
A day my mind and heart, and every thought
Could inspire me to write words so stirring
To move your heart, your mind, your soul.
To inspire awe at the first and every reading of my toil
To give you such clarity of thought and peaceful calm
All of your doubts and fears could be cast away
And together - we would find eternal peace and joy.
If I were immortal, I would surely give it all away...
A fair and honorable exchange for this gift - this dream
And for what time is left me
I would bask in the glory of our togetherness.
I would be saddened, not
For brevity of life as a mortal with you
Is doubtless superior to eternity without you.
Forever to you I give my life, my heart, my soul.
You are the definition of my existence, the meaning of Love
You are what dreams are made from
And the reason for eternal hope
I Love you, and you alone.

Edward D. Hugus

I Am Woman

My breathing is very still as the air in
a deep ravine at daybreak, yet in an
instant as labored as eagle wings stirring forces
that set his ascent into being.
My smell is as enveloping as poisonous fumes
yet gentle as unknowing substances that
have the power of life and death

My laughter is lilting and magical. It
has the power to make your day and is as
haunting as a spirit with power to disturb
your night

My smile is pleasant and may tell you
many things about me what you need to
fear is the things it does not portray.

I can be mysterious and deadly
I can be simple yet fascinating
I rise to the occasion what is your
desire?? I am woman

Betty Starnes McDavid

"Island Lake"

A year ago I came to see
a double wide trailer, perfect for me.
It's got three bedrooms and bathrooms, two,
to keep it clean, there's plenty to do.

A wood burning fireplace, "Oh boy, what fun."
A brick patio for sitting in the sun.
A front porch, a kitchen that seats at least four,
and off my family room, a big sliding door.

Big dining room where I've got a Ficus tree,
and a white wicker bedroom just for me.
Big back yard for my dog to run,
Deck in the back where we've all had fun.

I made this big move after twenty-nine years,
"Did I make a mistake?" Was one of my fears.
Staying out here I've had to adjust,
I've already bought it so "Stay, I must."

The summer out here is lots of fun,
the weather's so nice I'm always on the run.
Winter has come, all ice and snow,
"Do I like it or not?" "I just don't know."

Joyce Rice

4

My Dream

I had a dream
a dream I've never had before.
I dreamed of the sky turning red
and the moon turning blue.

I said to myself what is going on,
is the world ending before my eyes?
As I turned to the ocean
I saw that it was flaring red with blood,
I walked to the ocean and as it pulled me in,
I said to myself the world is ending and
there's a time when you have to go and this time
is mine.

As the ocean pulled me in, I began to awake
in a puddle of sweat.
I hope I never have a dream like I had
because that dream I dreamed should never come back.

Joyce Nicole Simmons

Heavenly Walk

Lord let me walk on heavenly ground, let your
angels guide me all around.

Let me walk each day with thee. So that I might
live safe and free.

Lord I will never get tired if you'll only be my guide.

Lord let me walk daily in thy light because
your pathway is so lovely and bright.

Carrie Manuel

My Favorite Girl

She is the only one that rules this heart of mine.
A girl that is sweet, cute, sincere and kind.

She gives me self-esteem and has made me what I am today.
She gives me hope and molds me in her own special way.

She fills me with joy, something I didn't always have inside.
Now, ever since I met her, it's a feeling I can no longer hide.

If I could give her everything she wanted today,
she knows that I would.
But instead I give her my heart, my soul and my love,
just like I should.

I'm thankful every day that she is a part of my world.
Because she knows, that without a doubt, she is my favorite girl.

Damon Wadley

No Trace

From across the room I saw you there
a glance or two I did not stare.
I lift my eyes to catch a glance
and there you are I take a chance.
I close my eyes to dream of you
to dance and dance the whole night through.
I often speak to you on daily basis
and yet again I leave no trace,
of how I feel inside of me
the spark of love that wants to free.
We often speak of things to come
and how we want things to be done.
And yet I long for your sweet lips
and just one night of romantic bliss.
I yet to long for your embrace and
yet again I leave no trace.

Anna M. Currao

God Sent An Angel

An unselfish love and generosity flow deep as the sea
A heart of mercy and kindness, waves upon the shore
Humility and patience, a shore of pebbles so wee
Spontaneity and faith, a tropical breeze and more

Joyful wit shared in countless ways
Her humor turns a frown upside down
Refreshing the soul all our days
Cherished memories forever stay around

A smile, warm as the sun
Eyes that twinkle bright as stars
Her love, radiates like the sound of a drum
A loyalty that reaches Mars

Adored by those who love her
Integrity and goodness her gift to us
Loved by those who know her
Joy and happiness she left in trust

Yes! God sent an angel
He called her Angela
Yes! God sent an angel
We call her Angie

Carol A. Sikorski

The Feeling

Around the eyes the darkness showed
A hidden feeling, the heartbeat slowed
The empty happiness; the full aggression
Why does it always have to end with deep depression?
A friend came by, a friend to talk
I turned around and started my walk.
The mind was heavy with long asked questions
No answers, just hate, and fake pretensions.
I passed by trees, houses, and distant places
Nowhere to go, wanting to see familiar faces.
The sky darkened as the thoughts persisted
In my mind, in my soul, in nothing existed.
Retrieving the happiness I once misplaced;
It comes to this: it must be faced.

Javier Gayo

"This Husband Of Mine"

I looked and I looked, and no where could I find
A Husband as wonderful as the one I call mine.

He's thoughtful and caring, loving and sincere
This Husband of mine, who's so very dear.

I know I'm as lucky as I can be
To have a Husband who cares so for me.

This Husband of mine is loved more each day
He's perfect to me, in every way.

Husband, I'm so very thankful for all you do
But most of all, I'm thankful for you.

I wish you a very Happy Valentine
This Husband I cherish, this Husband of mine.

Adrienne Kahn

"The Night Before"

The stars of night glisten so softly in the black sky.
A gentle whisper of sound from the wind moving through the trees.
The silver glow of the moon smiling down on mankind to light his path.
The silence of the hustle and bustle of people rushing to get somewhere.
The quiet wail of a distant train moving through the long night to an
unknown destination.
Again I watch and wonder, trying to understand what brings us to that
inevitable - MONDAY!

Joseph P. Ferrera

A Sun That Cannot Rise Above a Glow

A sun that cannot rise above a glow
A kind of cold that only stones can know
Aurora's reach beyond the finity
Alaska's .. winter trinity

But, when the vernal equinox bird sings
Generative forces drive to charge such springs
As cannot find their counterparts elsewhere
As life explodes on water, earth and air

The summer solstice converts night .. to day
Inviting warmth, as if a guest, to stay
The lowland flower and mountain lichen prosper
While procreating animations phosphor

A gossamer of ending chills the air
Autumnal colours range from here to there
Anticipating change as if to know
A sun that cannot rise above a glow

Gary Valentine Hansen

"Wings Of Flight"

Pressed close to the window pane
a little boy's face glared into space,
as he looked into an unknown galaxy
with stars, rainbows, sun and moon.
His imagination stretching into a universe
Visualizing his small frame compared to a world so vast so large...
He imagined wings penetrating through his
Shoulders as he gained ability to fly; to explore.
Lifting upward, seeing beyond his room...his window...being in flight
Soaring to heights only astronauts devices require in this universe
so full of life.
He saw where the snow is stored, where the wind blows from,
the gates of hell, the windows of heaven,
The famous black hole, the ozone layers,
Rotation of the earth on its axis.
He heard the morning stars sing.
He walks the path of the thunderbolts
Wisdom has been laced in his mind understanding in his heart
I have seen and imagined beyond my years
Wisdom...understanding produces wings of flight.

Carolyn Ann Fortner

Dream Ship

A fleecy cloud sailed in the blue,
A phantom ship all dripping dew;
Like migrant swan upon the wing,
It drove along—a lovely thing.

Then as I drowsed, strange things took place.
The ship I'm sure had changed its pace.
It veered to lee, it turned around,
As if its bow had run aground.

It warped and twisted, went askew.
The decks fell in, the timbers too;
The sails grew limpid in the sun;
I knew at once the voyage was done.

Enthralled I watched that shipwreck fade;
The cloud showed bright, another shade.
Its changing, writhing, in the breeze
Brought forth the form of living trees.

It changed once more above my head,
Disturbed my rest in grassy bed.
My reverie was spoiled again,
It tumbled down as cooling rain.

Alexander Clark

My Unknown Love

So very tiny that's how you start out,
A little life inside me that's what this is about.
Just knowing you could be my little girl,
Sends my heart in a frantic whirl.
How I wish there was some way, somehow,
But there's no one that will help me now.
I couldn't even give you his name,
For you were created in a cheating game,
My stomach's in constant knots,
I see a part of me as it wroughts,
Indeed I find myself very scared,
I wish there was someone who cared,
So many things I'll never know,
Forever and ever it will hurt so.
Tried to be so grown-up, Damn!
Now I've learned a child myself I am.

Dorie Lawhorn

A Lost Love

Never have I known such a man as he
A lonely heart of lust, desire, and passion.
Riding on his steed, might mistaken for a prince;
But no prince was he, nor a noble of men.
A rouge, a rake, a rebel of the converted cause,
A quest no one could name, one no one dares.
He sailed alone into the Seven seas, east, north, south
And to the west he had searched
He'd done battle and war
Encountered scourge and angels, won and lost.
Tasted love and peace, hate and blood
For the purpose unfathomed to the common.
Then one day, eons later, an end to his journey
An end to his longed for search.
For love, trust, honor, and peace, once so distanced;
For his most treasured, he found his lost angel,
An one who understood; his desire, his hardship
His dreams...
And this is I...
His wife, his love. His angel...

Samantha J. Kyles

Nature's Pitiful Song

As I stumbled into the garden
A picture came bright and clear
I hoped the creatures would give me pardon
from their quiet home frontiers.

I saw an eagle soaring
the wind beneath his wings
A caterpillar mourning
in all the songs she sings.

A rabbit thumped right over
and sat below my toe.
A lion hung in the clover
to sit and watch the show.

All the creatures of the world
drifted to my side.
Chickens clucking, ducks a quacking,
I had nowhere to hide.

Then pitifully, sorrow came
Upon my heavy heart-
and nature showed me who was to blame
For driving us apart.

Jenn Kummer

Only A Dream

Out on the Pacific Ocean where the sky is always blue,
A lonely ship is sailing; sailing just for you.

Why is this ship a sailing? Why is it at sea?
This ship is on a mission; a mission headed by me.

I am the captain, the commander, and the boss.
I give the orders, so that no soul will be lost.

I'm on the bridge, looking over the bow.
I'm behind the wheel, steering the best I know how.

If only this was real, how sweet it would be;
Having my own crew kneeling and bowing to me.

I would sail the world all over; once and twice again.
I would sail the ship and sail the ship; never bringing
it to an end.

I'll sail here, I'll sail there, I'll sail——-
    "Hey! Wake up, it's time for breakfast."

Argusta McDuffey

Sedated

The phone rings incessantly from the other room
A lonely woman from a drunken affair hoping for fulfillment
The tele flashes images of the bloody collage
Left from the massacre of yesterday's war
An obnoxious deejay spews his worthless opinions
On the issue of child abuse while cuing the next single
From an overrated band from Seattle
The dog peers through the fence to the street
Joining his breed in a ghostly howl to the sky
The clock ticks with methodical chimes
Recording and erasing the precious loss of time
From somewhere, below, a woman screams in torment
As her drunken lover slams her down the stairs
A jackhammer tears open the earth with such brutality
That chips of asphalt sail out of sight, out of mind
And a small river of blood runs along the floor
From the slit wrists of a lonely man.

Jason Michael Wiswell

Until The End Of Time

The sky shimmered a golden apricot in the autumn twilight.
A myriad of fiery leaves waltzed gaily on the brisk wind,
Swirling round and round,
Before cascading to the ground with a graceful flourish.
The thin, high clouds had already changed
From the pristine white of day to the bluish-grey of night.

The Sun sank lower with each passing moment
And in its wake,
A crimson stream slowly spread across the evening sky.
The Sun was grieving for his beloved,
And his heart lay bare and bleeding
For the world to see,
While a mournful sigh escaped his lips.

Before he finally succumbed to the all-consuming darkness of
Night,
His flame burned brightly
For one last instant.
A farewell kiss,
To the dear one
That would remain firmly locked in his heart,
Until the end of time.

Daniella Bernett

"A Poet Without A Muse"

I have knowledge that no one will hear,
A mind that thinks and a heart that feels;
True thoughts, wisdom that verily heals:
A beacon of light that comforts fear.

A glassy visage of yellow hides Raster:
Friction of faith contradicting the master.
Difficult to remove but easily found,
The thick cloud hides an airship that's knowledge bound.

Where behind lies a kind face wrinkled by sin
And a voice that proclaims the thoughts from within.
Eyes that see more clearly with every trial
To discern the thin line between good and vile.

I've a gift, this I cannot refuse
Choice of desire I secretly hide
That which's within these worlds I confide:
I am a poet without a muse.

Art Raster

Winds Of Winter

The winds of winter howled outside the citadel.
A mist hung over the landscape like a widows veil.
She stood by the fire, but the glacier within
Covered the spot where her heart had been.
She realized the madness of unshed tears
Took the journey put off for years,
To the cold gray fortress by the sea
Where he lived protected from painful memories.
She passed his guard with a casual wave
Entered the chamber he favored by day
Through new eyes se saw him, charming — self centered, a bore.
Gone was the knight of ancient Grail lore.
She took back her heart placed it in the cold,
Leaving Camelot to myths — gave back his gold.

Joan Rainwater

"Mystical Look"

A Unicorn with his spiral horn,
A mystical look to be adorned.
He's a free running spirit,
So sleek and so bold,
And his magical story
Has been told and retold.
He's oh so white with a golden horn,
And you may have seen him on a misty morn.
If he sees you he'll probably turn and run,
But don't worry it's nothing you have done.
It's just that he's so gentle and shy,
He doesn't feel comfortable when someone is by.
So if you're lucky enough to catch a quick glance,
Be thankful, for most of us never get the same chance.

Jacci Clapper

"The Man Of Men"

The man of men can only be one
A man that lost, but eternity won
A man that continues through a daughter and sons

The man of men can only be
A man that helped plant that special seed
A seed that started the family tree

Through his life a message will send
He struggled for us until the end
For this is why he is "The Man Of Men."

David R. Carter

Precious Child

Into their hands a child was placed.
A precious gift of God's loving grace.
Although Olivia's life was but for a short while.
To those who knew her she brought many a smile.

She was a tiny and very weak child.
Who struggled for life all the while.
Her parents tended to her every care and need.
While in sorrow their hearts truly did bleed.

Through all her sorrow and pain,
Every day that passed, was another gained.
Heidi told me about Olivia's first wave,
How she jumped up and down for the triumph she made.

The last day I saw her she was tired and weak.
But still she played with my hair and rubbed my cheek.
I guess this was her way of telling me good-bye,
For you see, any other time she would only cry.

On the last day with her mother and father,
As she lay in Heidi's arms, Heidi told her,
"Go on baby, Go now to Jesus's arms.
Go up now and be a new baby's guardian angel."

Donna Duarte

God's Child, My Child, Our Child...

God has lent to me awhile
a priceless treasure, a precious child.
Mine for a time, not forever
but for whatever reason, God has
brought us together.
A child for me to call my own
'til God is ready to call him back home.
I'll stand beside my child when the
day is long and do my best to teach him right
from wrong.
And in the darkness I'll show him there is light
and hold him in my arms to help him through the night.
I'll answer his questions and help him to understand
I'll always be there when he needs a helping hand.
And I thank you God for this wonderful loan
I promise to love and take care of him
'til you call him back home.

Brenda Lawson

"Little Things"

Thank you, Lord, for little things —-
A robin's song on a warm spring day,
A stranger's smile along the way.
The muffled quiet of new-fallen snow
and dancing shadows of a firelight's glow.
For emerald oceans, and sapphire skies,
and children's laughter and babies' cries.
For sandy beaches and wooded glen,
and memories I've made, and places I've been.
On a mountain - top at midnight's hour
that lets me feel a Greater Power.
For a special friend, with miles between,
but connected by some bond unseen.
The solitude of a summer day, and
fresh-cut grass, and new-mown hay.
For a harvest moon in an autumn sky,
and a distant whippoorwill's lonely cry.
For whatever the dawn of tomorrow brings
Thank you, Lord, for little things.

Joyce B. Shaw

Blue Lady, I'm Still Here

Madonna Maria,
A role model since a small child.
I knelt before you,
Your cape of blue,
Golden crown on your head,
Hands folded gracefully
held upright in prayer.
An image, now, imprinted inside my soul.

When predominate fear
perpetuated the night,
Your cloak held me safe.
Wrapped over my shoulders
covering, comforting, consoling me
through the fragmented, intrinsic stages of life's challenges.

Kneeling, Dear Lady, today in prayer.
Your presence enfolds me
Your child forever, mother to us always.
Hope you give, with love, to this troubled world.
Your heavenly petitions,
Like mother, like daughter, I channel your word.

Elizabeth Allendorf

Eel River

She moves through the mountainscape. Her journey towards the sea
A series of meandering curves glistening in the sunlight green,
Mysterious under the canopy of cloud cover blue.

Like an anthem of freedom, she nurtures the spirit of all things
Living in a forest of swirling colorpaints and giant redwoods,
Undulating through passageways descending, revealing intimate secrets
Hidden in springs born of thunderclouds and rainfall.

The wind, swishing through the leaves of trees gently swaying,
Dances lightly across the water's surface, creating the illusion
Of moving in all directions at once, playfully fooling my mind
Into thinking the river flows one way instead of the other.

Looking into the rippling water glass, I become mesmerized by
Thousands of sunbeams twinkling like miniature stars, enticing me
To surrender to the natural wonder of her embrace.

Oh, but to know your secret.
Oh, but to actually believe in God.

The lamprey eel watches silently as I dive into the water a broken
Man and emerge completely healed.

Dan Guaraldi

Seasons

Do you have a favorite season
A special time during the year
When your heart is a little lighter
And each day is filled with cheer?

SPRING is a delightful time
When everything begins to grow
The trees and grass all turn to green
While daffodils and tulips have colors to show.

SUMMER appears ever so gently
With warm days and sudden showers
There are picnics, parties and days at the park
With warm evenings and time for quiet hours.

FALL, such a spectacle of beauty and color
And it varies from city, state and nation
It's beautiful, it's warm and secretly inviting
As it fills one's heart with so much expectation.

WINTER signals an end to the year
And it brings wind, ice and snow
As our hearts fill with excitement
For it's Christmas, a time for love, hope and candle glow.

Jane Johnson

Shadows

I awoke startled, in a cold sweat
A shadow danced on the wall
As if to threaten me
Just my imagination, but all too real
The shadow slowly disappeared

Footsteps on the stairs
I jumped to lock the door
It was too late
I felt myself being carried to an unknown place
Cold fingers dug into my arms as I went limp
I felt myself floating through the air

A shadow danced on the wall
My cold fingers squeezed someone's arm
Waiting, waiting for it to go limp
I now lived in a dark, shadowy world
Held against my will

Jennifer Schonvisky

Untitled

Keep it simple. 'Twas put forth mildly
A soft new idea, more like a gesture, I think.
A subtle gesture, as the subconscious tugging
of a garment.
Removing the wrinkles of doubt.
A new feeling, that of fresh pressed progress,
and know how.

But nothing ever comes that easy.
So said the quivering masses.
Now tired of walking, they look down their acne
scarred noses at Mother Earth.
So complicated, complex. There could be no simplicity.
There would be none. Damn your new and blasphemous ways.
Send forth the machines of our times.
Our ramrods of complexity, and stop this simple madness.
Raise the banners, colorful and confusing
and let them wave in the light of our anger....

In the end, there are only ashes upon earth.
Ashes are simple, aren't they.

James B. Stiritz

Autumn Dancers

Autumn Dancers those with such
a style. Each with the steps of
a different dance, not one familiar
in any graceful flutter.

They wait for a lifetime in their
green silken garments hovering without
a grumble or complaint, peaceful and
solemn they float.

Until autumn the dancers become
restless, they slowly slide their multi-
golden costumes over their silken garments.

Then a sudden burst of relief the
wind comes, The dancers quiver with anxiety
then with all their might, they wrench free
from the trees' grasp. They begin to perform
their hypnotic dance, Their movements are
perfect, then they lightly settle on the
ground, They lie there, it's over.
The dance has ended until the next....
Autumn Dance

Daniel Sherrill

Christmas Is

Christmas time will soon be here;
A time of shopping, a time of cheer.

A time for greetings with a smile,
A time to make the season all worthwhile.

A time to love and a time to give
And a time to share the way we live.

A time for kindness and compassion
And a time to do it in our own fashion.

A time to amend the harsh spoken word
And a time to forget the rumor you heard.

A time to remember those who have gone
And a time to accept and not prolong.

A time to share a very small portion
Of the goodness in us that is our fortune.

A time to give of yourself by sharing
And meet the spirit of Christmas caring.

A time to give the best that's in you
So a peaceful new year will continue.

Bette V. Reason

The Hour Of The Day

The old clock he sits as time ticks by,
A time to laugh, a time to cry,
A time to live, a time to die

He shows no emotion as time passes away,
For his only chore,
is to keep the hour of the day

And although he keeps watch,
over the most powerful force on earth,
He really doesn't seem to value his worth

The old clock he sees us as through life we pass,
peering from numbers behind a glass,
As babes, and in twilight as our light grows dim,
It all seems to be in futility to him

For no matter tomorrow, or the world's last day,
The clock's only chore will still be
to keep the hour of the day.

Gary Parsons

Thought

Bubble, Bubble, in the river
a tiny breeze will make it quiver,
while keeping safe, secrets which hide beneath its darkest depths...
so warm and wet, so warm and wet.
The mud that lies under the surface has been aroused I must confess,
but we know it may cause us trouble
when midnight creatures make it Bubble.
The surface must stay strong and keep its contents hidden,
keep the mud inside forbidden.
Bubble, Bubble, they keep on rising and the water starts its
  compromising.....
"Let me play with the midnight creatures,
they play so very well when they ripple me, tickle me, and tease."
I must tell the water, "Play only a little and always be nice,
for when waves start to ripple the mud is turned loose
and clouds up the beauty inside, no water likes to be grim.
Even though it may Bubble, mud causes trouble,
so let's keep it quiet within..."

Chelsi Stahr

Christian Cowboy

Gather round folks and I'll tell you a story
About an old cowboy who died and went to glory.

He's just biding his time, till he rides that heavenly range;
On a beautiful quarter horse with a long silver mane.
He'll ride the length of the Milky Way;
And round up the stars that have wandered away.

He'll unsaddle his horse at the end of the day;
And turn him in the corral where there's plenty of hay;
In his blankets he'll dream about pards left behind;
And he hopes they all make it while there's still time.

There'll be a cowboy reunion at the golden gate;
They'll come riding in from every state.
They'll get down on their knees and give thanks to the Lord;
For giving them new bodies that won't ache and hurt.

Now the Lord is my Savior, I love Him through and through;
'Cause He died on the cross for me and for you.
So heads up cowboys and take a good look;
Be sure to get your name in the big tally book.

You better get branded with the Lord's brand;
'Cause if you don't, you'll wind up a stray in no man's land.

Everett G. Jones

Recollections Of My Youth

To express some thoughts I'm writing this poem,
   about some memories of my childhood home.

The house was not by the river nor by a hill,
   just a house in the city a few blocks from the mill.

The yard was small like most yards in the city,
   with a tall full maple and fall leaves so pretty.

A branch held our swing and a tree house we made,
   we played hopscotch below, so cool in the shade.

We shared this house with our grandparents you see,
   Grandpa hammered and sawed making 2 apartments with each a key!

Sunday morning meant breakfast at Grandma's so good!
   And a ride in her hammock while waiting we would.

Mondays were wash days with lines crowded full,
   neighbors would chat as clothes came off with a pull.

In winter clothes froze as stiff as a board,
   thawed on radiators while hot chocolate we poured.

Upstairs bedrooms had no electricity to light the way,
   going up after dark meant burning candles for our night's stay.

These are just a few memories I like to recall,
   as a little girl winter, spring, summer, fall.

Elaine Smith

To A Friend

If you should need a listening ear,
A shoulder on which to drop a tear,
Or just the presence of a friend,
I'll be there, just tell me when.

If you should feel down and out,
Nowhere to turn and full of doubt,
Do not despair, for it is not the end.
I'll be there, just tell me when.

If you should feel all alone,
As if you've been abandoned, and left on your own
There is only one thing I can say, my friend
I'll be there, until the end.

H. M. Hollis

God's Creation

I search myself for the right things to say
   About this lovely creature that God created one day.
He saw that Adam was in need of a friend,
   So a rib He took from the side of this man.
Her virtues are many; her love has no end;
   What a beautiful thing - God's creation from man.
She rises early to meet the needs of her household and friends
   And she still has not finished after a long day's end.
Her tasks are great; her chores are many;
   She has little time for herself - very little if any.
She's the greatest of all creatures; you can compare her to none.
   When she enters a room, it's like a ray of bright sun.
It's an honor to be a woman for she is chosen alone, and made so
   perfect that she can give of herself to bring new life from her own
She instills in its heart the ways of life's goals,
   And teaches and trains it miracles untold.
Her wealth is in giving so greatly of herself unto others;
   She's a rare precious jewel; there really is none other.
For her price is above rubies; her value is priceless in rate.
   Yes, this creature called woman - yes, woman, man's mate.

Brenda Whitlock

I Kept

I've been thinking about my life nowadays;
About what is about to come and long gone;
Thinking about who am I, hiding, invisible;
In a world created by others.
Thinking about how I've truly met poets and
others artists digging up mouths like holes in the world, and
those who do it with their bare hands.
I've been thinking about life nowadays,
About how it relates to creation and God.
I've heard about Him; So,
I now have a space for Him in my realm.
Nothing touches me but the spirit which I became aware of;
'Cause the world split open.
What can I give anyway, if we are tied up to this world;
Grazing like herbivores, looking down to the short;
Perhaps the spirit can give a clue on the spot;
Beware that nobody is asking you for it.

Felipe Hinrichsen

To The Family Doctor

In the dead of the midnight when a baby cries
After going to bed but not closing his eyes
The good doctor arises and dons his clothes
And in the midst of the ghetto of human woes
He examines, listens, prescribes and is gone
On to another patient's home.

Shackles of ignorance fall to the floor
As he teaches and reaches to those who adore
And have loved him for years as he makes his rounds
To patients whose lives encompass this town.

Greater are those who minister and serve
To the mass of humanity who doesn't deserve
Sometimes, the compassion that equals the pills
That helps cure all our every day ills!

Gratitude from the heart is directed his way
As we arise to the task of each new day
Not only in the ghetto where the baby cries
For his service has blessed and enriched all our lives!

Clarece D. Hunt

Listen, Listen And You May Hear

Beyond the night
Above the clouds
Distant sound of angels' wings
Flying above in celestial realm
Searching below for captainless helm
Draped in a shimmering brilliant white gown
Singing God's praises and beaming them down
Messages telegraphed down from above
Speak of the light and redeeming true love
Bursting with joy, our hearts awaken
Timidly reaching our hearts and souls taken
Peace, rest, tranquility, calm, contentment,
security
Love's soothing balm
Listen. Listen.. and you may hear
The distant song of angels drawing near.

Chris Beloat

I Am What I Am

Love me for what I am, not what I can or cannot be.
Accept me for who I am, not what you want for me.
For I am a unique individual in every way.
You can't mold me into someone, just because you want me that way.
I am who I am, with strengths and characteristics all my own.
I'll live life to my choosing, when I'm gone from home.
Don't try to force me to be someone that I'm not!
To change the essence of MYSELF is asking a lot.
For I am what I am, that's all I can be.
I can't be anyone, other than me.

Carla E. Gillis

Afterwards

   While the flowers withheld the scent of their technical
advice he began to feed the pigeons at his feet with scraps
of recall from the way once the summers were as sparrows
argued over the formulas for forever by their analysis
of the dust unto dust he could hear reminiscences
consulting their resources from the towers tolling
every ivory reason to calculate the inexplicable truth
by the compass bearing of a swallow's flight
   as on and on and out of sight it flew
he ventured to diagram the sentence of
the afternoon by the annulment of its height
   as by and by and into the night it grew
the gears of his eyes ground the shadows of light
into splinters of right on the fault line in the temple
of his mind he could hear the inaudible truth
bellowing to come in while the quaking
leaves withheld their timing on when
in autumn to fall.

Gordon Steele

The Wanderer

The Pig and Whistle was her home.
After living there fourteen years,
She decided to roam.
Night time in the desert,
A bed in the sand,
Back pack for a pillow,
She kept searching for that
Dark eyed handsome man.
One day in desperation and despair,
She stopped by a neighborhood bar.
She looked around and he was there!
Tall, handsome with dark eyes and kind face.
Seemed as if she had ended her journey,
When she stopped at this place.

Jessie Taylor

Growing Up

When I think of giraffe
Africa comes to mind.
The small and the quick running from lions,
like blood running down hill.
Oceans and natives and birds —
   an eagle on a mountain
as I see through my mind's eye.
Foreign wars, death; innocent children mourning
somebody's death.
That's strength and power weeping a kind of loss
in a lion's belly.
Growing up is another kind of coming to power.
A coming into an ability to command people
   much like a mother over a brood.
Training to walk on air without wings.
Or taming the lion at the mount of his own den.

Christopher Deer

I Remember

I remember a camp called K.P. Cienaga with late
   afternoon sunshine trembling on aspen leaves;

I remember a lone and majestic Valley oak silhouetted
   against a summer sunset;

In that same dry and dusty valley I remember the early
   morning smell of dew, the sky shading to purple
   before sunrise.

I remember crossing snowfields below Muir Pass; we
   were so tired we did not think of the treachery
   of the ice, but only the sunset splashes of purple
   and orange on the snow, on the rocks.

Just at nightfall we came to the first Whitebark pines.
   A stream rushed by both sides

And a full silver moon rose.

I remember another moonrise over Casa Grande, a
   mysterious light outlining the edges of the rock,
   finally a great golden ball balanced on the top.

I have often thought that when I am dying I will want
   all these images in my mind

But I wonder. They make living so sweet and precious.

Arlene Roos

Happiness

I wish I had the words to express
All the wonderful things that define happiness,
It doesn't have to do with the money we make
But knowing how to give and not just to take;
Realizing the little things that mean so much
The sunshine, the rain, a smile, a touch;
The blessing of rising to greet each new day
And every new friend we meet along the way.
The stars, the moon, the sky so blue
All these things can bring happiness to you,
If only you take the time to enjoy
It will be worth every effort you employ.
And through it all take time to pray
Thanking the Lord, that life is that way.
Then always take the time to share
And show someone you really care.
For some, even the greatest dream
Is to sit with a friend beside the stream.

Daisyann B. Fredericks

Nightmares

My heart quickens,
Again and again they continue to plague me.
Night after night, there seems no end to this madness.
A force within me can no longer be controlled.
STOP! STOP! I cry out to no avail.
My arms fling outward at the still, dry air.
I am denied rest once more.
Tired, very tired, I fight the much needed sleep,
Remembering the dreams, the dreadful terrorizing dreams.
Even awake, I cannot escape them,
As they play havoc on my mind.
Exhausted and baffled by their continuity,
Sleep becomes the victor.
The nightmares at its throne
Whose reign seems to have no end.

Carol Rosenblatt

Alive

Alive are the feelings I feel.
Alive with strength and power of wanting to
give the best of me to work this love until the end.
Alive though my heart is not made of stone.
Alive crying over pain.
Alive with sorrow inside my heart.
Alive, alive just alive wanting to find someone
That will make me feel alive without making me cry.

Adriana Vasquez

Our Futures

As I walk through the door of time.
All I see is darkness.
This darkness invades every corner of my mind, body,
and my very being.
With that darkness comes fear.
The fear that strikes a note in even the strongest man.
The fear that you are insignificant.
That your life is to amount to nothing.
But as I keep walking I notice a brilliant light.
This is what is to become.
My future and as you note it is to become a brilliant one.
It could be yours, too. If you want it bad enough.

Jessica Fiorini

"The Fourth Wall"

I can picture a room where everyone in the crowd is being "force-read"
all tied, gagged and bound to their seats, like amnesty dissidents,
while the pet from hell reads confessional whining disguised
under the archaic name of "poetry."

I can imagine a perennial exhibitionist get his due bullet in the head.
A conspiracy by consenting voyeurs turned snipers;
facing his room, tired of his ritual acts, of seeing him expose
his pubics in public. An unwanted symbiotic relationship put to a close.

I can imagine the worst case scenarios: Where a boy and girl are both
born deaf, blind and thalidomide, with missing limbs and fingers;
so neither could even sign nor read in braille. Or where
a coat check girl, rushing to get to work, hoping it will be busy,
crashes her car against barrier walls and dies due
to slippery roads and conditions dreary, icy, cold, and bad.

I can picture a room with two people sitting, tender strangers and
cruel lovers facing each other, not saying a word,
neither looking nor acknowledging each other's existence.
One chewing his nails, so fixed in his cold read;
looking past the other, past facades and masks,
beyond touch or love, beyond recognition, miles apart.

Joselito Gamalinda

My Autumn Time

My world, my season, my autumn, its crisp alerted leaves,
Already in a splendor of kaleidoscopic trees.

It's long in preparation, with spring and summer slow,
Those endless months of waiting for her cataclysmic show.

It's as a festive banquet, all too grand to be believed,
A carnival's excitement, a canvas yet conceived.

How awe-full is its wonder, the colors blend and bleed,
To me all other seasons are mere servants to her need.

Now as a nova, brilliant, a splendid burst beheld,
So now is Autumn's grandeur, all a sudden on us, fell.

Too soon excitement done with, chill winter sets the scene,
And lulls my world, my season, in a silent dreamer's dream.

And there in sleep, quiescent, all needs aside now lain,
There beats a breathless waiting for my autumn time again.

John William Beckett

"Eternal's My Name"

I come from the stars, I come from the earth,
Although I'm not mass, I can cover the dirt,
I see all that's been, I see all that will be,
I'm like a raging bull, I'm like a tranquil sea,
I was present when you triumphed, also when you failed,
When you were jeered, when you were hailed,
I have the power, the truth and the way,
To help you if you wish, each and every day,
Your choices are many, the right one's so few,
Be careful my child, in all that you do,
So when troubles abound, and vision's are not clear,
Remember your contemplations, your time may be near,
So worry not about your future, or troubled past,
For I am the rod, that helps you stand fast,
So awaken this morning, to the warmth of my light,
I will shine down radiant on you, so brilliant and bright,
For I hear all your cries, I know all your pain,
I will dry all your tears, for "Eternal's My Name."

Joseph McCormack

My Faith

Did you ever feel a pat on your back?
Although there's no one there
Well, I have, that's a fact
When I feel badly, I know that someone cares
I can't see my Lord
But He's there I know
That's my Faith!
I see the world changing
Not for the good, but for the bad
Although it's not the world I'm blaming
It's the people in it, and that's sad
I wish with all my heart there would be more faith
There's someone higher than we are, right?
Mostly everyone has forgotten the values of life
That's why we hurt
Please look to the Lord.
He will comfort you in despair
Just believe in the Lord, because He cares
Live the righteous way,
Before it's too late.

Alice Vendetto

The Military Child

Traveling to distant places.
Always seeing unknown faces.
People coming to say hello,
Then as time passes by, you watch them go.
There is a sadness to leaving familiarity behind,
But at least there's a chance of a new life to find.
You try to survive all the changes in life,
But each time it gets harder to face all the strife
And the ignorance of the people who do not see
That there is likeness between them and me.
At least there are people that seem to know
That the differences inside, the outer ones don't show.
I have a homeland but I don't know it well,
I have a birthplace, but about it, I can't tell.
At least I've been given a chance to collect
A sample of all cultures and lives I can possibly get.

Hazell Wi Bareng

Among The Trees

Among the trees, stood one of awesome strength,
Among the rivers, flowed one of incredible length.
Among the hilltops, stood one of great steepness,
Among the oceans, there was one of remarkable deepness.
Among the good, was one that was great,
Among the seven wonders, arose number eight.
Among the birds, flew one of immense grace,
Among the greatest artists, one beheld exquisite taste.
Among the wind, blew one soothing breeze,
Among the pleasures, there was one that was sure to please.
Among the bells, rang one of unmatched clarity,
Among the poetry, was one of undeniable sincerity.
Among the lies, up came the truth,
Among the old, was the birth of the youth.
Among the masses, stood one so grand,
Among the world, you stood, and there you still stand.

Jon Jackson

Understanding

It is a simple concept to convey,
Among two people it is shared with care,
Not even a difficult word to say,
Needs no explanation, it is not rare,
Understanding is a long-lasting peace,
Love expresses this in such a fine way,
Always finding a time to be at ease,
So many things that one wants and can say,
It cannot be bought with large sums of wealth,
Nor is it a gift or some donation,
Understanding begins within one's self,
Do not turn from a hard situation,
Take time of your day and spend it to say,
I understand you my own special way.

Jessica Marks

Happy Birthday To Me

I look in the mirror, what do I see.
An old woman, staring back at me.
Oh! How can that be!
It was just yesterday I was young and carefree
Happy birthday to me.
There is so much of me to share,
but no one seems to care
I am so lonely with despair,
It doesn't seem fair
No one cares to say
Happy Birthday to me.

Doris Timberlake

The Imprisoned Soul

A tear of sweat,
An aching back
A goal set
to make sure I don't slack

To see the endless rows
would make one cringe.
I bend over like and old man
all worn and singed

The coolness of the night
helps the soreness and the blisters to subside
only to replace the hunger felt inside.

To be free from this imprisonment
is what we wish
Upon that northern-most star
I always worship

A struggle is what we must overcome
People versus people
What has this become?

Brett Salmonson

Guardian Angel!

What is an angel?
An angel is a supernatural being
that looks over your life,
leading and guiding you,
making sure everything is going just right.

My guardian angel watches over me,
protecting me from dangers
that my eyes cannot see.

My guardian angel is always around,
watching and waiting, but never making a sound
Just when something's about to go wrong,
my guardian angel comes along.

So remember that while on this earth you abide,
you are never alone
for "your" guardian angel
is by your side!

Denise A. Kelley

The Yearning

How can I explain this need that's all consuming.
An end to this need is my searching goal,
To fill the empty place in heart and soul;
  The yearning.

This thing called love is what I'm craving.
Someone to fill the empty void within me,
A special person is this man who will see;
  The yearning.

He'll take away all loneliness and hurting.
I'll then be filled with love and paradise,
The emptiness filled as the loneliness sighs;
  The yearning.

How can I explain this need that's all consuming.
The joy and happiness that turns all to pleasure,
Now my heart and soul are full of this treasure;
  The yearning.

Janet Cedras

Children Of Darkness

They "awoke" filled with "Light."
An essence of joy, love and trust.
Harmless.
Not harmful.
The tiny infants viewed the world
   through ageless eyes.

Unbeknownst to them
   a monstrous shadow began to cover the "Light;"
   a demoniacal, heinous plan speeding its growth
   so the children could no longer see.
Until the innocent appeared "old" while still babes.

Unable to see the "Light" by which they "awoke"
   they stumbled and fell in the darkness
   with no one to hear their cries.

Will you light their way?
     Jeanne-Helene Wattel

Image

As I sit alone, I look at a mirror image of ourselves,
An image that outlines two beings, yet one of feeling.

Bodies embraced...They feel the passion of a warm and gentle
love that they share.

A love, the kind that makes two beings together, as one.

The image portrays the way I feel. If only he knew how
I longed to be as one.

As I gaze across the room I hear his breathing.
I feel his heartbeat.

Our breaths are yet one in the same.
My heart beats steadfast with his.
Yet, can he not know how I feel?

Let it remain on the wall as an image, or simply a daydream of
being man and wife.
     Cynthia J. Coggins

Tears And Broken Hearts

I heard a mother died last night
An overdose of drugs
She left behind a family, was she thinking right?

I'd say no, selfish I think
Her thoughts were on herself
God gave her the children
To nourish and love since birth.

Now they're with their father
Whose brain is also fried
So what's become of the children
Whose mother has gone and died.

I wish I could have talked to her, mother to mother
Would she have listened to my plea?

I kinda wish she would have
The tears would not be flowing
The hearts would not be broken
Instead hugs and kisses, children.

I feel sorry for the little ones
I wish I could hold them all
But I'll say a prayer for the mother, who has lost the war.
     Josephine Martino

The Day Ends

The majestic sun has set long ago,
and all the lights around me have faded to dark.
My tired head rests upon my sinking pillow,
as my body lay still on my lazy bed.
I recall all the things I did today
and all I forgot to do
and as the day ends the night takes over the former sky of blue.
Memories I made today come rushing vividly to my eyes,
and even though my eyes are closed I can still see quite clearly.
I wish the day would never end,
so I could stay right where I am,
in my relaxed state of comfort and security,
and stay this way for eternity and beyond.
But no, I must drift away,
so tomorrow I can live yet another day.
So as my thoughts give way to dreams
I slowly mold into the blackness that surrounds me,
and the day ends.
     Justin Rogers-Cooper

"When We're Apart"

I miss your touch, your warm embrace.
And all the things words can't replace,
Like looking in your eyes and seeing your smile,
For these things my love, I'd walk a mile.

I want to be right by your side,
With no feelings of fear or reasons to hide.
Just being together is what I dream of.
And for this I pray to the Lord above.

I cherish every moment that we have spent,
Holding each other close and feeling content.
It is in your arms where I feel at peace,
Where all my loneliness and sorrows cease.

But even though for now we must be apart.
I know deep down inside my heart.
That our special love will see us through,
And the someday we've both waited for will
finally come true.
     Donilee Neeley

The Primal Call

The old hen wandered the chicken yard
   And came to the garden gate.
She had rough scaly legs, but her comb was red.
   She was old — but it was not too late.

She tipped up her head and gazed at the sky
   Where Winter was chasing out Fall.
The other hens sheltered out of the wind
Alert to the rooster's call.

But the old hen felt as she clucked to herself
   The urge of what she must do.
She pecked all around past the break in the fence
   And suddenly darted through.

She clucked and muttered as she hunted outside.
   These eggs must be laid in a nest.
The lives that she cherished must now have a home
   Before she could take Nature's rest.

We caught the old hen—fool that she was
   Running off there in the Fall.
In stewpot with dumplings she made a good feast
—and nothing was known of her call.
     Evelyn Holden

Nobody's Child

They are ridiculed and made fun of,
and are left alone out on the streets.
A few rags cover their thinning bodies,
and they walk with no shoes upon their feet.

A woman rummages in the garbage,
searching for the treasure of a crust of bread.
She has no home to go to,
a cardboard box is the only place to rest her head.

We pass by them on the street,
but our eyes they do not see.
Instead we decorate ourselves with glitter and gold,
in our world there is only me.

Do they ever feel any happiness?
Will they ever have anything of their own?
Are they destined to wander the streets-
until the day comes when they die, all alone?

Jada Anne Robertson

Mom And Dad

You give me everything that you have
And ask for nothing in return
You taught me the difference from right and wrong
So when I am faced with decisions I can discern

You taught me a lot of different things
You taught me how to love
And that when I cannot see what is ahead
I can always look up above

When my friends cannot be there for me
When I need someone to see me through
You guided me to a very special friend
Who always knows what to do

When I wanted to stay out late at night
You made me stay inside
I did not understand it then
But now I know that you were right

I will not always be there for you
You say from day to day
There are many paths in life to choose
So you must begin to find your way.

Jason D. Hardy

A Black Woman

I'm a black woman of which I'm proud,
And glad to be just who I am.
I'll say it often and I'll say it loud,
So all can know that I'm black and I'm proud.

Today's woman has many more advantages,
And this kind of strength and courage doesn't just come by chance,
Sometimes it stems all the way back to our heritage,
It's in our inner being and it has to be enhanced.

We're black, we're proud, and yes we're strong,
I'm talking about strength that comes from within,
Not from fighting and fussing, don't get me wrong,
But soul strength that helps us, our everyday battles to win.

From the Motherland, I grant you can do what we do,
We can develop a career, and manage a home,
We can get in the kitchen and cook up a stew,
We can raise our children with not a one to roam.

Hey, that's not easy in these days and times,
But in my house, I put down the law and lay it on the line,
I rebuke drugs and hustlers from stealing their minds,
'Cause this black woman won't have it, No! No child of mine.

Correne S. Cannon (Jackie)

Whooppie!——Here's Aunt Lil!

Aunt Lil visits 'round with kin
And bears the latest "news" of all——
Relates the stories 'til they're thin
And never fails to make them "tall."
"Oh, here's Aunt Lil," with glee we cry—
And sit gape-mouthed and ears alert.
But when she's gone, "'Tis shame," we sigh
"The way Aunt Lil digs up such dirt."

Next week our cousins, on the phone
Tell "juicy" tales Lil did discuss———
Sure made us all to moan and groan—
When slipped the ones she told on us!
"What we won't do when she comes back!"
We shout in huddle——void-of-cheer,
And yell it out, "No joy we'll lack
When Auntie dear gets kick-in-rear!"

Daisy E. Brown

"Once"

My grandma had the prettiest clothes
and beautiful jewelry.
She had a pair of shoes for almost
every outfit she owned.
She could have had any man
she wanted.
She picked my grandpa. He worked
as hard as he could every day of his life.
My grandma also had a lot of friends.
She would go all over the place with them.
Her best friend was Jen. No matter
what happened to my grandma she was
there for her.
Anything can happen to anyone.
My grandma had a stroke, but now
what she's got is more important
than any of those things she had before.
Now she has love! I love you grandma

Amber McMann

The Seasons

The wind kisses the snow,
and lifts it onto feathery wings in the air.

Swirling masses of white spin
around in late December. It is Winter.

Flowers open to reveal their scents,
and petals cascade the lush grass.

Birds learn to fly on a warm
April breeze. It is Spring.

Scorching heat is applied to
the baking hot land.

Trees beg the sun for mercy
on their drooping branches in July. It is Summer.

Crisp leaves fall gently off
a golden-red tree.

The flavor of snow is in
the air of October. It is Autumn.

The wind kisses the snow,
and lifts it onto feathery wings in the air.

Swirling masses of white spin
around in late December. It is Winter.

Jenny Duggan

Miss Mattie, Mister Danny

He used to sit up and draw pictures of naked women
and do crossword puzzles, both always in ink.
She used to pick, wash, and cook greens. And boy
could she dip some snuff and chew some tobacco.
They used to try to out-give each other when
it came to me.
He'd give me fifty cents, she'd give me a dollar—-
He'd give me three pieces of candy—
She'd give me five pieces.
They were practically my grandparents.
I was just beginning to understand
their love for me,
When a ferocious monster came to put a spell on him
and took him away.
It came back for her, too.
In my lonely moments of despair
I long for naked ladies and the scent of tobacco.

Arletha Brewer

Love Has To Wait

As I stand at the window looking out at the rain.
And each drop that falls fills my heart with pain.
Because my heart knows we will always be apart.
I really should have known this from the very start.
Me from one world, you from another.
I have to be careful, because now I'm a mother.
It is a secret I must keep to myself, because some might
    say I am crazy or obsessed.
So all the dreams I have, I must keep from the rest.
Some say you're moody and sometimes cold.
I want to be there as you're growing old.
No matter how my life works out, I always seem to loose.
While every day I monitor your every move.
May you always be happy and have continued success,
You may not think so now, but you'll get out of this mess.
The faces you see may all look the same.
One day mine will be out there, you won't know my name.
How could I have never met you and be this in love?
Maybe another life? Maybe another time, I realize now that you
are my soul mate, but for now, love has to wait...

Jacqueline B. Lee

Happy Valentines Day

V——is for the Value, I put on our love,
    and for which I'd like to thank, our Father up above.

A——is for the Angels, that watch o'er us every day,
    to help us and to guide us, in their special way.
L——is for the Love, which my heart is full for you,
    and I hope that I can show it, in everything I do.
E——is for the Emotion, you stir up, within my heart,
    just like little ole Cupid, when he shot that dart.

N——is for the Noise, you make, when you nibble on my neck,
    oh well, we're both old enough, so what the heck.

T——is for the Teamwork, you and I worked out together,
    oh yes, we always get along, no matter what the weather.

I——is for the Influence, you've had upon my life,
    you've taken away the heartaches and all the strife.

N——is for the Nighttime, which I treasure very dear,
    for whenever I reach for you my love, you're always near.
E——is for the Endless, time you have for me,
    and I pray to God, let it forever be.

Jan Schock

"The Art Of Listening"

If friends were to gather, say in a group of five
And each one tries to keep the conversation alive,
This could really develop into a verbal contest
Between those who assume their comments are best.

But who'll do the listening, it's hard to say
As all five strive to have their own way?
Their words of gossip, comedy or just some advice
Will need ears that will listen...it would be nice.

Two ears and one mouth at birth we all get,
Perhaps thus to "listen" twice - speak once, and yet
We could all curb our conversational drive,
And not be loquacious...like the talkative five!

Joseph A. Betancourt Jr.

"That's Life"

If life to you seems cruel without a cause,
And efforts you expend seem all in vain;
    I beg of you, do not bemoan your fate,
As though, alone, adversity to know.
    No need to spend long hours in a search
For other souls on whom misfortune feeds;
    Just take a look around to left or right
To find a soul who's all the more bereft.
    Consider then the strength of your complaint
Against the cumbrous burdens others bear.
    Recall the times when in the past you sensed
Discouragement surrounding as a cloud;
    How bolstered traits emerged, to your surprise
And helped you over circumstance to rise.

Don Dunning

Memoir

It grows a scab, this wound so deep,
and for a frozen moment, pain disappears.
Like the false dawn that shimmers
before the dark of night engulfs the struggling light.
I feel the burden lift, then
a chord is struck, the pain begins again.
My child is gone. It was so long ago.
I held her in my arms, I kissed her toes.
I kissed each finger, then her slumbering form.
It was goodbye, not just good night.
Since then, the world has not been right.
A stranger missing cues, so out of place
While other couples grew, we two froze in space.
Morbidly re-living the agony so cruel
Nothing in common; just a pair of fools.
Still not a sparrow falls, and every hair is counted;
while the eye of God, surveying over all
the land and seas and space knows all
So where to turn? Sweet spirit, fill my heart with balm
I'm so tired of passion, I need the calm.

Elizabeth Dodd

Love

Ask, "What is meant by the word love?"
And for each soul, you would find a new meaning.
Say, "Let's create our own vision of love,
And for each moment, you will find a new feeling.
Whisper, "Let's never forget this day, and how we feel,"
And for each year, you will find a new healing.
Love and Grow within each other's arms.
Create the joy, release the tears,
Embrace and glow within each other's dreams.
Keeping the fire, and the faith,
And the courage to nurture your souls.

Alisa Cook

Daddy's Girl

For my little girl, with big eyes of brown
And for as long as I live, hope I'll never let down
Life will sometimes throw curves, that you won't deserve

But I will always be there, to show you I care
If anything makes you sad, you don't have to feel bad
I'll try to come with a plan, to help you understand
See I owe you this much, cause you've helped me to grow up
The day you came to this land, you changed a boy to a man
My first sight of your smile, made my heart grow a mile
As you grow up so fast, I sometimes look back to the past
Back when you took to me, even mommy will agree
You've always been daddy's girl, his first prize in the world
Now today you turn seven, your hugs still put me in heaven
Just like they will, when I'm over the hill!!!

Frank M. Scott

"Memories Of A Rose"

The memories of you are oh! So sweet,
And for what you've taught us children, we kneel at your feet.

You've been the best grandmother anyone could've had,
You were always smiling through the good times and the bad.

You were an inspiration to everyone here,
And we know you're rejoicing, though we shed our tears.

Your little rose garden is full A'bloom,
And that same sweet scent fills the whole room.

As we look up into the sky and the clouds part away,
We children can't wait until we're with you someday.

But as for now all we have are memories of a Rose,
And I guess we will have to survive on those.

Chris Beathard

My Best Friend

At six she blew bubbles in the sun
and danced at night.
But by ten she had forgotten
because her father wasn't there.
He was working or drinking and
even when he was there - he wasn't.
(But he did love her - he had just forgotten.)
He had taught her to forget.
But when he made his final exit
and her world was painted in black,
when we thought those memories
were gone forever, she remembered.
And she saw more colors in the bubbles
in the sun than she had seen at six
or three or nine and her life
became a dance and she didn't forget.
She never forgot again.

Erin Lavery

Images In The Sand

I, a traveler in the desert,
and he, only a mirage.
He comes and goes —
fades in and out.
My longing only leaves me in despair.
My mirage —
short lived, yet thoroughly enjoyed.
Working hard but realizing it is fading as the sun sets.

Now I am deserted in the desert,
alone and barren,
Waiting 'til the sun of tomorrow

Angela Marie Sacchet

Perspective

Sometimes we say words that come from our own hurt
    and frustration
or we decide to say nothing to avoid
    a confrontation.
Sometimes when we feel a sense of confusion
    we allow our minds to play tricks on us
we question if what we are seeing is real or
    just an illusion.
There are times when we get so caught up in
    making excuses to save ourselves, feeling distraught
we shift the blame onto someone-else.
We tend to hesitate at saying sometimes what we
    really want to
so we intimidate ourselves when we contradict
    what we do.
Eventually, we discover sometimes all it takes to
    make a difference in any situation
is an adjustment in our own attitude.

Cathy Brandt

Heaven Can Wait

You have given me all the love my earthly soul could ask for....
    And Heaven can wait
When lonely, you've given me company and companionship
When in doubt, you've opened the door and shown me the right path
When weak, you've given me your strength to feed upon and use as I
    so needed....
When in sorrow, you've lifted me up, enabling me to see the good in
    the world— separate from my smallness
When happy, you've enjoyed my gaiety, making me even happier
When worried, you've taken over the burden, thus setting me free and
    my mind at rest...
And when strong of will, you have made me see reason...
For all these things and many more, I love you....
I love you with every part of me, and when away from you, my soul
    reaches out to clasp and mingle with yours so that we are never
    really apart.
To have, to hold and to return your love is the very essence of Life.
    And I shall ask for nothing more.

Joyce R. Dalmas

Wheelchair Blues

I am sick and tired of being sick and tired,
And I'm weary from the pain that I feel.
It seems like in quicksand my feet are mired,
And I have been offered a raw deal.

A wheelchair for me, oh no, not at all,
I'm used to standing up, I'm five feet seven inches tall.
If I'm in a wheelchair I'll be so short, you see,
That everyone will undoubtedly walk into me

Alright, Doc, I know what you mean,
A wheelchair I'll use, but I don't want to be seen.
Instead of the grocery store, I'll go to the mall,
Where I'm sure no one there will know me at all.

I could leave the confinement of my house and home,
To go to church, to shop, sight see, visit and roam.
The invention of the wheelchair is a godsend,
For me to pick up the pieces and start to mend.

The use of the wheelchair is a great thing,
To use it to the best of my ability makes my heart sing.
I can do my duties as a mother, grandmother and wife,
No! I won't let this disease I have ruin my life.

Janice E. Rhineberger

A Chance

I will always miss you (more than you know),
and I cry and want to ask you why you had to go.
(You said I had A Chance.)

A Chance for me to know you and for you to understand me
has passed before my eyes, it disappeared — so suddenly.

A Chance for me to evolve through your wisdom and wanderings
is never to be challenged — it stays part of my dreams.

A Chance, my chance, to love you and show you how I've grown —
A Chance for you to love me — if only we'd have known.

Oh, yes, I love and miss you (much more than you know),
and I cry and can't stop wondering why you had to go.
('Cuz you said I had A Chance.)

Golden Felice

Untitled

I have made it to this wonderful place
And I have met this beautiful face.
I have lived, died, and was reborn again
And in each life you have always remained a friend.
I crossed the waters and walked the sands
And you were there to guide and hold my hand.
I was sick and you my only cure,
I love you, that is for sure.

Corey Raymond Brey

Everybody Asks Me What's Wrong

Everybody asks me what's wrong,
And I reply with a nothing,
But in my head I'm the only one who knows
There's a something.
I'm not acting myself lately,
And people say I've changed.
I really don't know why but I feel like being hanged.
Every night I feel like crying
And I never can get any sleep.
So at night all I do is sit and weep.
I have no reason for crying.
I guess it's just a fourteen year old thing,
People expect me to be happy
And always in the mood to sing.
So when people ask me what's wrong,
I'll still reply with a nothing,
But maybe soon sometime someone
Will know there's a something.

Dana Douglas

Under The Tree

What are those things under the tree?
All of those things can't be for me!!
Well, here is one that says my name.
I open it up, inside is a game!!

There is another one that says Andrew.
Inside's a puppy, not one but two!!
How many 'these things do I get?
Here's one with a
Basketball, hoop, and net!!

All this excitement, it's driving me insane!!
I'll open another one, inside is a train!!
Here's one that says "To father and mother."
I found about five that are to my brother!

All of them say from "Santa Claus."
I think a minute while I pause.
I ask myself who in the world's he?
He's a great person definitely!!!!!

Andrew S. Hemler

Time Passes

Time passes like lightning
And if you want to surpass it... do one thing
Don't do good... don't do bad...
Free your mind... and all that you had
If you do it... then you have the wit
And for this life... you are fit
Ethics inspired my precious heart to be polite
To work... to accept the will of the divine might
But the clouds of my days became black and unbudging
Like the gypsic hair of my beloved...
When she appeared with pinky gown
She cried and sobbed with groan:
"Tomorrow I will marry,"
And like a deer... she ran in hurry
I wept... yelled and said while my hand gave a farewell wave:
"God is to bless your life... and your soul to save;
But please... before you go... take the love you gave
Come... come and put me in the grave."
I killed myself... I was brave
And still... time passes.

Al-Shorbajee Abd-Al-Naser

Another Autumn

I watched the silver-green of youth, the spring,
    And in it found a measure of delight.
Though when it passed on lightly feathered wing,
    I made no move to halt its errant flight.

The summer years like rose and golden fruit-
    Have ripened; fallen from the bough, are gone.
This I beheld; yet moved not in pursuit,
    As time flew. I had time to draw upon.

The brown and russet tones of autumn bring
    A hint of winter in her snowy shroud;
Though I may taste no more the youth, the spring-
    One favor; small, I would that time allowed:

That I might look upon your lovely face
    Another autumn in some other place.

John R. Stevens

Country X'mas Tree

We're bringing home a country X'mas tree
And it means an awful lot to me
I cut it down today myself, you see,
So we're bringing home a country X'mas tree.

I know it's just an old pine tree for sure
But once inside it will mean a whole lot more
We'll dress it up so fine you wait and see
And then it won't be just an old pine tree.

So we're bringing home a country X'mas tree
And it means an awful lot to me
I cut it down today myself, you see,
We're bringing home a country X'mas tree.

The gifts will be underneath the tree
Sitting there for all the kids to see
And when we turn on those X'mas lights
Then everyone will start to feel alright!

On X'mas morn we'll gather around the tree
And I'll open my gift from you to me
Then we'll sit down to have a bite
And talk about the things in our life.

Dan DiNicola

Tollage Of The Soul

Be quiet, my troubled heart,
  and leave my mind at ease.
I must not let my tears and fears
  run rampant as they please.

The years take tollage of the soul
  for strength and courage wane.
The efforts spent through fleeting time
  so often end in vain.

The battle to the swift must go
  to those who falter not,
who lift their chins and grit their teeth,
  accepting life's sad lot!

Bess Huber

If

If we can read good books and sing good songs
and listen to the birds high in the trees,
If we can strive for rights to make us free,
and keep a gracious smile when things go wrong,
If we can talk sincere and not headstrong,
and laugh with joyous mirth and keep our pride,
If holy blessings reign o'er us on high,
and grant us grace and strength as we go 'long
Our lives will then be worth the test to live,
To give ourselves the chance to prove and do
each little deed that comes along the way,
Then God overhead supremely blesses and gives
Rewards to us for trying to be true,
and brings us safely home to rest and stay.

Audree S. Alexander

My Fellow Man

There are men of this world who think themselves so supreme
And look upon all others as much lower and unclean
They hold their heads up so very high and look over across a frown
For fear of catching another's eye who may be unfortunately down

And then there are so many who go by the color of the skin
To justify their supremacy over their fellow men
And strut off to church on Sunday to be seen in their holiness
Or is it merely a cover up of their week day lowliness

Now I like to see a man of great accomplishment and renown
A man who's life is worthy of respect from all around
His face, creed, or color has no bearing at all to me
For I feel his accomplishments in life are all that's necessary to see.

Louis Raymond Mustian Sr.

Hope

To live with a goal,
  A light at the end of the tunnel,
    Purposes revealed and understood.
      This is hope!

To be without self pity,
  Forge ahead for living,
    Savor life's rich rewards.
      Remember your hope!

Listen to other's problems,
  Share life's rich rewards,
    Give others your trust and feelings.
      Pass hope on!

Think fondly of fellow people,
  Make amends for past wrongs,
    Keep the light of lights in your heart.
      NEVER FORGET HOPE!!!

Harry Ellis Brawley III

Mind Machine, Time Machine

I seclude myself in my private room
And lose myself in my own world of thought.
It's where I rise above the here and the now
As off into timeless space I depart.

It's as though I'm in a time machine
For memories take me way back in time.
And I collect the relics, the reminders
From the deep recesses of my mind.

Next hopes and dreams thrust me into the future,
That time period which is beyond compare
Because in future land I control my destiny.
And oh! How I fantasize whenever I'm there.

Through my mind my time machine makes its way
And back to the present I return.
Thus once more reality becomes my focus,
Though not forgetting future and past lessons learned.

Yes! it takes both reality and fantasy
To propel my mental time travel.
And with success I weave together the past, present and future
As the World outside my room seems to unravel.

Clarence H. Fitchett Jr.

The Old, The New

Guilt heavy on my shoulder
and my heart saturated with fears
Everyday another day older,
I speak out with truth, no-one hears.

No-where does a glimpse of hope appear.
Will guilt and fear ever go away?
I can see, but not quite clear,
Seems like night, twenty-five hours a day,

Guilt laden and full of fear,
I now fly to you, my savior Lord,
No-place does a glimpse of hope appear.
Except on the pages of your written word.

On those pages, a field hidden lies,
A gem of price unknown.
A person becomes divinely wise
in making this Gem their own.

Where my cunning and reason did fail
You Lord are now my guide to life, through all its gloomy vale.
Old guilt, old fear, no-longer cut upon me like a double-bladed knife.
Thank you for having freed me and given New Life.

Edward B. Wilkes

1993

In the year 1993,
A strange thing happened to my family,
When my younger sisters born two years apart,
Became the same age and gave everyone a start!

Mom and Dad could only stare,
And bite their nails and grow grey hair,
As sister Jenni turned 22,
Sister Jessi turned 20, too.

And Mom and Dad did wonder,
About their youngest daughter,
When Jenni becomes 32,
Will Jessi become 30, too?

But they need not worry more,
For when Jenni becomes 24,
Jessi won't be older, too,
She'll still be just 22.

Joyce A. Summer

My Neighbor's House

Tho never dreamed by architect, nor prized for stately halls,
And never masterpiece of art has covered its bleak walls;
Tho never silver slippered feet have touched the aging stairs,
And never wealth enough there was to dull the work day cares;
Tho often have I bode my ease to talk of thens and nows,
I'm never tired of visiting when in my neighbor's house.

Tho aging now, and weathered black, and falling in decay,
Each tattered room may hold a dream of memory's happy day;
Tho sill be worn to almost naught by many feet that crossed,
And sagging doors and scrubbed-white floors show time and
    labor's cost;
The smile I see on time-tired face when coming from his ploughs
Is all I need to gladly greet my neighbor in his house.

Harry L. Bingaman

Pocket Full Of Keys

Key to life is being someone special
and nice without being selfish and self-serving.

Key to being a great Lion is
to be hard working, friendly,
ethical and willing to put something
back into the community.

Another key is attitude, charm,
and learning to listen.
Instill community pride, extend
yourself, give recognition.

The key to success is strictly hard
work and you're the only one
who can make the difference.
Nothing happens until you make it happen.
Most important have Faith in Yourself.
That's the key that opens all doors.

Henry Latas

So Long

It's been so long and you're far, far gone.
And now I am lying on my bed with nothing
but your likeness in my head and
I start to think...
    Waiting, why am I waiting?
Wishing you were here maybe catching the
tear your imbedded memory has incited. Why did
you leave, why don't you care, can't you see it's my
heart you handling without care? And I think...
    Waiting, why am I waiting?
Well the feel of your touch is what I am
missing so much and the style of your matter,
Is what made me flattered too much to omit my
anticipation. Then I think.....
    Waiting, why am I waiting?
Even though it's been so long and you're
far, far gone, my love for you is forever.

Honey E. Dixey

The Eyes Of A Woman

As the eyes are the window of the soul,
And say so much without being told.
Individual struggles from elation to strife,
Emotions endured through the heartbreak of life.
Wishing the focus on all beautiful things,
The sweet teardrops of joy are what hold the key.
The sparkle within, a subtle glint of delight,
Her stunning eyes, the shade of midnight.

Anthony Michael Avanzo

The Woodshed

The Woodshed's a vestige of life long ago
and Oh, the secrets she holds....
of fugitive slaves and kid's escapades
and chickens decapped in the cold.

The shed played a role in discipline too,
when youngsters misbehaved.
Mom's open palm was the first response,
but for situations grave
Dad ushered the culprit to the shed
his dignity to be saved.
We innocent ones waited on edge
to hear the suffering cries.
But cries never came, and when they returned,
(to our great surprise)
Dad and the boy walked hand in hand,
contentment and joy in their eyes.

Never would the naughty one tell
the secrets Woodshed hid.
It was years before the truth leaked out...
Dad just talked to the kid!

Catherine D. Smith

River Of Tears

I will walk on through this river of tears,
And put aside all my worldly fears.
I will stand up and gather some pride,
To trudge on through to the other side.

With the help of those who truly care,
I'll defeat my demons and surface somewhere.
And although many may try to defeat my cause,
I will keep on fighting and never pause.

Sometimes the current seems too strong,
And it seems that I won't stand for long.
Just when it seems I'll lie down and die,
Something happens that gives me courage to try.

This river of tears has run my whole life,
And sometimes the pain cuts like a knife.
But with prayers and a helping hand,
One day on the other shore I'll stand.

Crystal Havner

Understanding What You See

Here I sit, on a brown seat, staring out at nothing.
And seeing everything.
The world.
Its future.
My future.
Everyone's future.
For the life, we live.

While I sit, here, I think of things most people don't,
Anymore.
They think only of themselves.
They think what they can get from that person.
They use a person like a tissue paper.
And only for their pleasure.
They are selfish, and don't understand the world.

As I sit here, looking at the buildings going by,
I begin to understand the world.
And why people do the things that they do.
But not fully.
Because only the person that created life can.

Erika Brumbeloe

I'm On My Way

I heard you the first time when you yelled
and said, "Don't watch TV, Go straight to bed."

I was walking slow but I was on my way
to be like a bear and hibernate.

I heard you once but you said it twice I
guess you thought three times would be nice.

What's the rush it's only eight o'clock at
least that's what it says on my alarm clock

Walking slow without any speed I guess
like a turtle I thought I'd be.

You said it again a fourth and fifth time
You must of got tired because you beat my behind.

Jessica S. Travis

We'll Do It Our Way

You've done it your way, and I've done it mine,
And several times our paths intertwined.

As days grow short and nights grow dim,
I think of you, and have a whim.

If we could recapture the love we once had,
We'd have each other and surely be glad.

We've done it all - had great loves in our days,
Let's live life for now - as the poet says.

We had a true love, we did, you and I,
And parted company, not knowing why.

Let's run off together, just you and me,
Think of tomorrow and what our love could be.

A love like ours that has lasted this long,
Will bring us together, where we belong

Our spouses have died, and our children are grown,
It's silly and lonely to live life alone.

When we love each other the way that we do,
We'll live life as one instead of as two.

So give me your answer and enrich my life,
We'll do it our way as husband and wife.

Donna Semega Schaffer

He Created All

The cattle on a thousand hills are his,
And so is the green forest glen.
We marvel at all these wonders.
And the coolness at the river's bend.

The azure blue of the sky,
And the refreshing summer shower.
The dewdrop on the petal of a rose,
Are all a display of his great power.

Our lives are but a vapor in his sight.
And our age, to him, he knows.
So live each day, the best that you can
Counting your blessings, his kindness to show:

If God sees the sparrow's fall,
And paints the lilies short and tall.
He gives the sky its brightest blue
Will he not then care for you?

Dorothy H. Fritz

Tender Of Age And Tender Of Heart

You left us at such an early time in our lives,
And so unexpectedly, too.

We never had a chance to say goodbye,
Or reconcile our feelings with you.

Tender of age and tender of heart, your death left us broken inside,
Years come and go but the ache in our souls never completely subsides.

Time heals all wounds so I am told, but I beg to differ with that,
Time only makes us learn to live with a sorrow we cannot combat.

For nothing can heal a young heart that is broken by losing someone
 so dear,
Time only makes us miss you more, and wish every day you were here.

Janice Henderson

How Many Times?

How many times can a heart be broken
And still be willing to try
To have faith in words that someone has spoken
When it seems that they've all been a lie?
How many times can a heart forgive
And forget the pain it has felt
Then just go on and continue to live
Wait for love that will make it melt?
How many times can a heart be mended
By the hope that the words will be true
Believe in the love that is intended
To be shared by me and you?

Beverly Smith

Forrest Gump

I will go back as far as I can,
and tell you my whole story.
To tell you the facts would be easy.
But to tell the truth, the why,
without distortion, and without being subjective,
would be harder for a smart man
than it would be for a camel
to pass through the eye of the old needle.
Truth is like a feather.
When it lands-if it lands-
it hardly touches down, and it is barely felt.
It has no root,
no attachment, favors no one,
and is not possessed.
So I will tell you the truth,
because I haven't hid it
like a smart man,
but have let it be.
And so it is mine to tell.

John B. Hayes

Cats

Purr so sweet.
And lick their feet.
Some are graceful.
I don't think they would be very tasteful.
They love to be pet.
If you don't have one you'll regret
When you come home they're there to greet you.
I bet you never knew how much they like to meet you.
Cats are usually nice.
They really like mice.
Cats are cute.
Especially in a boot.
They have furry little paws.
And I love them just because.

Autumn Crider

Twins

I was blessed before I was born
And that blessing is here today.
It was the spirit of God in my mother's womb
So fragile it could not survive.
But we were one and I needed her
So I taught her to fight and endure.
That spirit was born so tiny and weak
But with a strong will that she learned from me.
I was blessed before I was born
And that blessing is here today.
My twin lives with the spirit of God
In her heart and keeps me always near.
I need her and her inner strength teaching
Me to have faith in God and in my family.
I need her! She needs me! We are one
Because the spirit in the womb made us one.
I will survive this terrible ordeal, I know, because
I was blessed before I was born
And that blessing is still with me today!

Cheryl A. Hoffman

Ballet Exercises

like the ticktock of the studio clock
and the floor tapping of the wooden cane
first it's this way, then it's that way
then it's begin again
then it's this way, then it's that way
then it's begin again
the rhythmic piano notes
exercises the dancer
first it's that way, then it's this way
then it's begin again
the rhythmic dancer moves
exercises the piano
first it's this way, then it's that way
then it's begin again
the dancer dances, the piano plays
the can taps and the clock ticks
then it's this way, then it's that way
then it's begin again

Earl Bellack

Mine Enemy, Mine Friend

That bellowing heard inside my head... it calls me to do evil things.
And the devil sits... sits upon my right shoulder.
And the little angel... the little angel lies defeated... defeated on the floor.

I look over... carefully and cautiously to my left shoulder
ever so hopeful
And I see a grave emptiness... feelings strong of anxiety overcome me
Thus I slowly turn... my head faces its direction original,
Proceeding... my countenance independently seeks the other side
shadowed only by itself.

My dependence is with mine enemy... mine enemy, mine friend;
Looked all over... to the left and to right the same,
But now... there is nowhere left to turn.

Inside my echoing skull so loudly... like African drums beating in the
night dark enchanted,
Evil rebounds from side to side... more yet more, energy to it
My heart fears its potential... of this evil which grows inside my skull.
And the devil sits... sits upon my right shoulder wearing a grin wider
than the sky high
And the angel little in its silence... lies still defeated... upon the
cold floor with eyes closed painful.

Derek Dailey

Destiny

I've come to the place from which life came,
  and the magnitude casts a spell.
The endless waves rush the constant shore
  while whispering to me "all's well."
Where the secrets of space with the depths
  intertwine.
My grieving heart seeks the answers evading
  mankind, all through time.

As swiftly as I asked, peace rushed
  through my mind.
While crying sea gulls flew gently on high,
  a voice inside me I softly heard sigh:
"Don't worry of things you don't
  understand.
The one who made you still has you
  in hand."

DeAnn Tompkins

"Come To Me"

Come to me when the stars go out-
  and the moon no longer sends pail light,
I'll open my door to you-
  as the soft dawn colors night...

Come to me when the rising sun
  warms the glittering dew,
And as you step into my life-
  I'll open up my arms to you...

Come to me when the noonday sun-
  blazes through leafy trees,
I'll open up my heart to you-
  and hand you its only keys...

Come to me when twilight
  is weathered in smoky haze,
I'll open up my soul to you-
  and there will be no more lonely days.

Carolyn D. Rodriguez

Five And Growing

He was just a little tot, his age was barely five,
and the questions that he asked, took his mother by surprise.
Then slowly she sat down beside her little man,
and answered all his questions as only a mother can.

Will I get big like daddy, just as big and strong?
And Mom I really hope that it won't take too long.
But I seem to grow so slow, and it's awful hard to wait.
I wish that I could grow up fast, before it gets too late.

Does Daddy work real hard when he's gone most every day?
Does he miss us, Mom, the time that he's away?
He buys my favorite candy every time we go to town,
and sometimes when I get tired he carries me all around.

I'd like to have a brother. That really would be fun,
and he could use my toys as soon as I am done.
I don't know where you'd find him, but I hope that you will try
Just a little one will do, Mom, cause he'd get bigger by and by.

As she hugged her son that night and tucked him into bed,
she gently tucked the covers around his little head.
She thought about her family and she knew that she'd been blessed.
God had been so good to her, he had given her the best.

Eugene C. Webb

Sunshafts And Joybeams

The mornings of the earth are canticles of praise
and the rainbows of the morning
  bind the earth with gladness

As we watch with solemn wonder
You come to us in splendor
and silent echoes of holy joy
  flutter from heart to heart

The customs of the Lord
are as wondrous as the beams of joy
that dazzle the hearts of men
for the sunshafts have pierced the corners
  and amazed the humble ones

Georgia Gunzenhauser

Angeles

When day turns to dusk
And the sky is crimson and gold
An angel comes to her keep
She walks the sea calming the storm
Her lullaby keeps the earth in silent slumber
She kisses each child with pleasant dreams
And then returns to the sandy shore
With a golden key she unlocks the majesty of morn
And chains the ebony covering the land
The sound of her trumpet awakes the sleeping
At last she showers the earth with her tears
With one final goodbye she leaves with a
  prayer in the wind

Allison McClure

Untitled

You're the truest one I've known to be,
And the way you make me feel,
How loving and friendly you are to me.
I don't believe you're real.
The way you make me laugh with your humor so fine,
I'm just glad that you are mine.
The way you joke around and your sweetness too,
I love your personality and I love to be with you.

Caryn Briggs

Just To Let You Know

Just to let you know that I love you tooooooooo much
And think of you every single day.
It seems so long ago, since you were home, or that
We had anything to say.

I know you've been studying hard and taking exams,
But I hope you think of me, as well.
'Cause if you don't I will just scream and put you
Under some kind of a spell.

Hey, your ole dad's just kidding! For the time being,
Anyway, your mind should be on your books.
After all, there is no such thing as being in this
Game of life just for your looks.

Then too, just think! In a few more days you will soon
Be through with all those tests.
Before you know it, we will be headed south to Florida
For a week of fun and rest.

So, just to let you know, that you're being thought of
In a special kind of way.
I love you tooooooooooooooooooo much and hope you have
A great and wonderful day.

James L. Ellis

God's Creatures

I love God's creatures that live by me -
And to watch the squirrels playing from tree to tree.
Early in the morning the birds begin to sing,
How joyful the sound of their melody rings.
First Jenny Wren, the robins, the mocking birds —
Take turns in the chorus so each can be heard.
The barn swallows come back year after year
To build in the barn where there's nothing to fear.
To my amazement who should share with them
A family of groundhogs building a den.
Late in the evening when the suns going down,
I so often see the bunnies scampering around.
They're so joyful and carefree,
Because God's watching ore them
The same as you and me.
God's gift of these creatures make my life worthwhile.
I'll rejoice and thank Him and wear a smile.

Arline Turner

What Kind Of Vessel?

Now that the Lord of the earth has found me
And visited me with a joy that I find complete
I am faced yet with another valley
As I ponder, what kind of vessel lingers with me.

Down the history lane, human decadence is told
How folks lost hold of their new found states;
How the beautiful in the start, turned grotesque at last
I start to wonder, what kind of vessel lingers with me.

I want to anchor my vessel in the rays of the sun
Far above the earth, as long as I draw a breath
Where my vessel shall remain preserved, and renewed;
The kind that shall stay untainted by the fall of man.

Take away my valley, O Lord of the earth
Let the vessel that now lingers, serve me with faith
As the slumbering lion within me boldly awakens
To its mission of ascent to the luminous heights.

Ijedimma Bernard Oparah

Valentine's Day

I was thinking of gifts for Valentine's Day
and was examining what the stores had on display.
It was enough to blow my mind!
Candy, candy, everywhere and cards of all kinds.

I quietly purchased some candy and cards
and thought this shopping would really not be hard.
I was rather pleased with what I had bought,
but then I had a very troubling thought.

For that very special one what would it be?
Something more than candy or a card, you see.
While candy and cards have a place
It was not what I wanted in this case.

Not knowing what to get troubled me to no end
as I was thinking of a very special friend.
And then suddenly a thought came to mind,
Why not simply say, Be My Valentine?

Now, that sounds so simple and real,
and could express what I really feel.
So, I'll not write another line,
but, truthfully ask - - will you Be My Valentine?

Charles E. Lawrence

The Wall

The wall was invisible, but sturdy
and was finished within a day.
It took minimal time to build
and had an incredible will to stay.
As her emotions were freed, the wall dissolved
until her heart was exposed at last.
But the wall quickly appeared again...
If only trust could be built so fast.
She molds the wall around her
with a firm but weary hold;
inside, she's still the same,
but the fortress is rigid and cold.
The wall must be chipped away
to start with a brand new slate;
the interim is hard to endure,
but the results will be worth the wait.
Even when the wall is tossed aside,
it won't be hard to find -
all it takes is an ounce of hurt
and a simple command of the mind.

Jacquelyn A. Orender

Dear Jimmy

Dear Jimmy, Dear Jimmy, we know of your pain
And we all say that she is to blame.
Whether it is right or wrong, I cannot say,
But if it weren't for her, it wouldn't have ended this way.

No matter what you did, it seemed you just couldn't win.
You worked hard for those you loved.
Your boy Tanner, her, and the unborn, too.
She hurt you bad when she took them from you.

The hurt was so bad you took fate in your hands,
Speeding to the tunnel of a safe, happy place.
One final call to all your close friends,
Leaving one final good-bye on their memories.

Death and birth are one and the same.
Your daughter was born as you passed away.
As your souls passed in heaven, what did you say?
"Hello," "Good-bye," "I wish it weren't this way?"

In your letters, you said you just wanted to sleep,
Still, here today, it is for you that we weep.
Sleep peacefully, Dear Jimmy, you've escaped the pain,
And hopefully one day we will meet again.

Amanda Scampini

Invited Or Un-Invited Guest?

Summer days have come and gone,
And we spent every day on the phone.
We grew as friends and even more,
Before I knew it love knocked on my door.
"Let me come in," he seemed to call,
But I put him off and then came the fall.
"How can I let you in?, I said,
"The love I once felt must be dead!"
It had to be from that broken heart,
But maybe if I try I can make a new start.
Then it happened one unsuspecting day,
I fell asleep and love came my way.
Love didn't knock on my door,
He came right in like he had before.
When I woke up, I felt kind of strange,
"While I was asleep, did someone re-arrange?"
What had happened, did love go away?
Or was he in my house to stay?
I hope he stays to be my guest,
and does not leave like all the rest!

Elizabeth J. Wentzky

Weave Yourself A Dream

Gather up some golden thread
and weave yourself a dream.
About times past, or days ahead,
Whatever your life's scheme.

Just spin the thread and it will come,
The things you'd like to do.
Where you're going, where you've come from,
What is most dear to you.

Fill your dream with lifelong wishes,
And plenty of peace and love.
Lots of hugs and gentle kisses,
'Cause that's what dreams are made of.

And for those fleeting seconds
To dreamland you have whirled,
Life's troubles will not beckon,
You're in a perfect world.

Helen Wammes

Just Me.....Just Me...

The love of my dad was very strong.
And when he passed.....I was all alone.
He lay in his bed and he didn't ....complain of the pain,
    that would come and go.

The love of my dad was all.....I had.......I knew in his heart
That he loved me so. Just me...
And now his life is gone.......and, I am all alone,
    Just me.... Just me.
I will always be glad......of the Dad.....that.....I once had.
    For just...me.... Just me.

My family was there......they help me.....to share......
The great love of my.....great dad and just me...just me.

Bertha Johnson

Neglect

Once we touched hands
And wrapped our souls into one.
We pressed our lips
Together and breathed each other's chemistry.
Once I ran my hands down your hips
And felt the fire inside my heart.

But then you dropped the ball,
Threw a damp blanket on my flaming heart,
Ignored my pleas,
And drifted out of my life,
To do whatever you pleased.

You held up no signs,
Made no announcements,
But quietly stabbed me in the back
With neglect.

Brian Carnes

Beach

The bright sun blazed upon the ocean blue,
And sea gulls in the sky were flying high;
Beating out a rhythm as they flew,
Looking for a silent place to die.
The wind blew gently over the white sand.
The horrid waves crashed on the barren shore.
The lovers that walked here holding hands,
Have split apart, love lost forevermore.

Night has come and all the birds have gone,
Their rhythm following them to their new home.

Jameka Wrisbon

Big Dago

It was never really his (my father's) nickname

It's what they called another Italian demi-hero of his time,
another longshoreman who never entered my mind
save for the name and the rough myths

My father was Big Dago to his first born son
(as a child) — and, briefly, hero...

This simple, steady and plain edged "I"talian, who
clumsily loved his family without thinking,
and mistook pale gestures for respect

I never spoke of my child-like disappointment
when he stopped being Big Dago

His last words to me were of his fatherly
disappointment with me

We no longer speak as we spend the short end of our lives,
and never will get to know each other
(or forgive the disappointments)
Strangely, we both did our best
I love you
Dad

Alex Cortlund

"A Vision Of My True Love"

Infinite thoughts of her enters my mind so intricately sweet I'm
anticipating on the moment we can finally meet.... In the

extragalactic mist of my most romantic dreams which only transpire in
the still of the night, comes to me a vision of us embracing
passionately under God's silver moonlight ... I often visualize us

strolling along the shores of our own island of paradise, how it would
be so nice, our arms entwined, our love would be ultimately divine for
all time... This woman I would compare to a rose, my flower of all

God's seasons the exquisite characteristics of its beauty inspires me
for this reason...

To elaborate on her loveliness it would take all of eternity, all the
while it's stirring my emotions like God stirs the sea, she means so
much to me. Like water to a stream and a vision to a dream, with one
tender caress she can bring under arrest the loneliness that surrounds
me, forever by my side is where she will always be... For this woman

I have prepared an eternal place with in my heart When God joins us
together, I will pray to him forever, to never let us grow apart... I
will promise to give her all of my undying love, with the essence

Of true romance, while I wait here in reality contemplating all my
Possibilities of chance...

Darrell Stringer

The Zoo

I like to walk through and through
And gaze at the animals in the zoo.

The lions and tigers are my inspire,
But the cute little monkeys are Nancy's desire.

Penguins, elephants, and kangaroos too,
Are all just a few,
Of the animals we share between me and you.

The hyenas and bears are such a treat,
When I look at them as I walk down the street.

As I close this poem with a wave of goodbye,
I must not lie,
The zoo has a definite catch to my eye.

Audrey L. Swartz

Growing Pains

The blocks are gray, big and square,
  Anything in them cannot breathe,
And they're going to suffocate a little pink house
  To fulfill their greedy need.

So one by one the big square blocks
  Paint their own gray picture.
Suffocating this simple beauty
  With the brush of a poisonous mixture.

And as the brush moves along
  With upward and downward strokes,
A faint cry is heard
  As the pink house is covered within its cloaks.

Though the cry was weak,
  It wasn't in total vain,
For an open heart had heard it
  And will remember its growing pains.

Now somewhere in the distance,
  On a not well travelled road,
Sits a pretty little pink house
  Where a story is forever told.

Jane Ann Defiel

No More War Games

Are we synthetic soldiers hollow and unreal?
Are we symbolic warriors who would rather yield?
Are we unfeeling Christians callous and waxed cold?
When do we get serious, when do we get bold?

Are we half-hearted church folk jangling in vain?
Are we the real thing to God, have we faith unfeigned?
Are we not all taught to fight in our Lord's great name?
Jesus spelled it out for us so precise and plain.

No more, no more war games.
No more, no more war games.
No more, no more war games.
No Lord, no more, let your glory reign!

Growing stronger everyday, God's own on the move,
newly recruited trainees look to seasoned troops.
Heaven's Angelic Army stand on alert,
a fresh anointing pours out on His saints of Earth.

Holy disciples of God loyal and prepared,
await mighty miracles in response to prayer.
Inside God's throne room is heard the decree, "No more!"
Father's promise is fulfilled, "Behold! Christ your Lord!"

David Henry Sarauer

Granny

It's Granny's graduation day,
  And all the saints are cheering.
They've all been looking forward to
  The day of her appearing.
From every corner of the earth
  They've gathered up in glory
To meet the one whose mission zeal
  Helped them to hear the story.
Old friends and relatives are there,
  And the joy is overflowing,
As granny greets them one-by-one
  Her face is radiantly glowing.
And then she sees her dearest friend,
  And smiles through happy tears,
As she hears the voice that has guided her
  For more than 90 years?

Amy Moore

Deep In My Heart

Deep in my heart, so far away, I dream of a cottage
  around a glistening bay
Deep in my heart, so far away, I dream of a waterfall
  so colorful and tall
My waterfall, so great and tall, that will flow into the bay
  around the cottage so far away
Deep in my heart, so far away, as the birds wake me up
  with their sweet little call
(I think they're telling us it's finally fall)
Deep in my heart, so far away, winter brings snow
As we slide down the hill, I said with a flash,
"I'll race you down. Ready, set, go!"
Back in New York, I woke up really fast; I listened to hear
  a new song the birds did sing
Time goes by so fast; one day of Fall, one day of Winter,
  then it's already Spring
Deep in my heart, so far away, as I gazed at the fading of
  the wandering stream
It was deep in my heart and deep in my heart,
  it's all been a dream!

Danielle & Brianna Sinclair

For The Old One Asleep

Rock gently, Soul, within the sleeve of sleep
As foggy vapors twinkle in the night.
Let snowdrifts in the aging mind grow deep.

Escape day's tangled trails that can keep
The mental curtains flapping in a fright.
Rock gently, Soul, within the sleeve of sleep.

Forget obnoxious moments when you weep.
Turn tears into the snowflakes soft and white.
Let snowdrifts in the aging mind grow deep.

The magic of the ages can o'er leap
The fences of resentments that you fight.
Rock gently, Soul, within the sleeve of sleep.

The howling winds of winter's storm do reap
An avalanche of woes with awesome might.
Let snowdrifts in the aging mind grow deep.

Pull covers tighter as the dreams all creep
Up closer to behold you in your plight.
Rock gently, Soul, within the sleeve of sleep.
Let snowdrifts in the aging mind grow deep.

Betty Jane Sachara

The Cowboy

A flicker of a match interrupts the night
as he lights a cigarette,
and a cloud of smoke rises and hovers above his Stetson.
His golden hair just reaches the collar
of his worn flannel shirt,
the beat-up boots on his feet
rest just outside the stirrups of his mount.
His strong frame silhouetted against the moon,
he sits silently atop his horse.
He has first watch tonight,
guarding the herd of cattle
moving across the plains.
He looks natural in the saddle,
as if born and nurtured there;
perhaps he was...
he is content out here,
relying on no one but himself
and the good Lord.
A lone star emerges from the open sky,
still, quiet, never blinking... a metaphor.

Christine L. McGuinn

The Kingdom In The Sky

The light shines down upon the earth
As he makes final preparations to welcome her.
He's been preparing for this day since her journey of life began,
Hoping she would be able to call a place home once again.
It's been hard on everyone as he can see,
But her pain will be gone and her soul will be free.
He knows she, as well as loved ones, have enjoyed her stay,
No one will ever forget all the love she gave.
She is a wonderful wife, mother,
and grandmother full of happiness and love,
Always having a smile sent from above.
She'll always be in the hearts and minds of friends and loved ones,
She's left her mark on life as well as on the young.
It's time to not forget, but say goodbye,
For she's gone home to the kingdom in the sky.

Christina Laethem

Come Back

Tears run down my cheeks,
as I stand in the rain.
It's been another week,
another week in pain.
My heart is asking for you,
my body hungers for your touch.
I've been waiting for you for so long,
I want you so much.
I miss the touch of your hands
as we make love on the dock.
We've been apart too long on different lands,
lands that time ticks and tocks.
Waiting for your luscious kisses
and waiting for your hands to touch me,
where only you have. I miss
the way we were, the way
we loved each other.
I want you back so bad.

Amanda Riedel

Saying Good-bye

The day came when he had to die and I feel
as if I should cry. It has been but two years, but
still fall my tumbling tears.

For now I feel in my heart that we will always be apart.
That day will come as I reach my destiny. Then I will
Find that one who loves me.

One Grandfather and Granddaughter being united.
Then joy and love will be sighted. One child's
dream may come true, always remember someone loves you.

Above the world and in the skies, is heaven that
holds the greatest man alive. He knows when
you're sleeping good or bad so shape up ladies and lads.

The day will come when you will reach your
destiny and you will see the ones who love
you and me.

My grandfather will always have a huge place in my
heart and we shall never be apart.

I still have his words to me before received. He
says, "Be good, take care, I love you." I love you
too, good-bye.

Janelle Ebaugh

Snow

Each tiny crystal dances and spins
    As if to a silent tune, it begins
To an endless melody, they dance and whirl -
    So unaware of their purity they bring to the world;

As each one descends without a sound
    It gracefully bows and settles to the ground
When this magnificent orchestra and its flawless members perform
    I need not ask who this conductor may be
For the Creator, in all His Glorious Majesty,
    Has performed for all to see;

As I watch in wonder and awe
    Such blessings of beauty are free for all
A sweet kind of peace warms my heart
    For I know that God is the creator of this work of art!

Jo Ann Edwards

White Moon, Black Sky

The sun goes down behind the land.
As it does, you take my hand.
Pinks and purples fade to night.
the full moon rises making it bright.
It looks as though we could touch it now,
like it's slowly getting closer to Earth somehow.
We stare at a white moon in a black sky.
I let go of your hand and begin to fly.
Above the clouds and above the storm.
The night is cold, but I am warm.
From this height I can see you there
starring at me, running a hand through your hair.
I see a certain look in your eyes,
I hear your voice... distant cries.
And now I realize why you're crying for me.
We've grown apart from what we used to be.
But you stop crying, you forget to care.
The love we felt is no longer there.
As I watch a white moon in a black sky.
I think of our love and begin to cry.

Jennifer Robins

"The Shore"

Harken, rest and listen, to the gentle pound of the blissful sound,
As it gurgles and splashes around and around,
Slapping and lapping pebbles and brush,
Tread on by rabbit, squirrel and thrush.
Hot summer sun, lighting the dew laden clear air of morning
hours,
Bathed with salt spray, blossom and flowers.
Far from the beaten path in seclusion,
Proboscis of Long Island's north shore protrusion.
Mystified by echoes of Indians and pirates bold,
Many legends can be told.
Rarefied, pure, lure to shark, wild gulls and tern,
The sound, violent and angry, at times stern.
Swelling over the narrow beach to beat its fury against the cliff
tested,
When pacified, its uncontrolled passions arrested.
It gently laps the thin edge of the shore lines rook,
Babbles quiet as a meandering meadow brook.
For those willing to brave the storm, there are indescribable
cheerful times.
Where the world as most know it is sublime.

Emil Hess

Gift Of Love

Love is a gift from God above,
As pure and lovely as a turtle dove.
A turtle dove who woos and coos
To show his affection to the one he will choose.
This wonderful gift of true affection
Is, no doubt, not without perfection.
This wonderful, beautiful gift of love
Must always be handled with kid gloves.
It must be attended to day and night
So that everything will be all right.
Love involves both taking and giving
All in all, it makes life worth living.
Life will become full and complete
When two loving people chance to meet.
They give and take, share and love
And then give thanks to God above
For having the opportunity to enjoy
The wonderful gift of a baby boy!

Carolyn Lucas Hillocks

Sister's Piano

Years...   the first seven come upon her revealed
                  as silent music and shame
                  lovingly woven tendrils over therapists' heads

Silent sounds... summoning dread, past fragments forgotten
                  now remembered, but
                  discordantly stuck

Conflicts...   ticking short staccato notes
                  engaging family discord with rage.

Ideas...   decrescendo and slide
                  as age into seclusion
                  and life fears to come

Denials...   an unspent life, mine or hers?
                  ours!...vivace gone dead

Are we...   deaf to her charms?
                  piano excepted...etude upon etude

Waves...   vibrating...caging silence
                  of waxed eloquence
                  stunning to all, save her own.

Cynthia Mills

"Is Life Fair"

I wonder sometimes if Life is really fair.
As some problems we face are so hard to bare
You work so hard each and every day.
And all of a sudden a Loved one is taken away.
So with all the heartaches and worry we do
Is it all worth what we have to go through?

Remember back when our Grandparents were here.
We thought Life was great and had nothing to fear.
But now with all the Drugs and crime taking place,
We have so much more in our Lives to face.
It's no longer safe to walk down the street,
And someone may attack you-and drop you to your feet:
So remember my friends-whatever you do,
Just keep on striving until your Life is through.
The day will come when your Life will end.
So remember God is your best friend.
Then you will be in Heaven above,
Along with all the people that you Love.

Dale D. Gould

Chameleons

The Cayman breeze beckons us
as stardust sand snoozes
at the feet of palms
and a sea lies lapping,
its crests of lace unfurling
shimmering specks of diamonds and silver slivers.

Champagne bubbles swirling
are invitations to indulge
as we sway from beneath thatched roofs
swinging to the steel drum rhythms
and hypnotized by constellations
woven into patterns of seduction.

As our sunbeaten skins
familiar with the other's feel, touch,
and the heat licks at our senses
a titillating tongue tempting us to come, to play
we witness a weeping of stars
and before they disappear past the dipper into the dawn
we wish we could cease shading skins,
unafraid of life's lurking predator

Dianna Depenbrock

Untitled

A light can be seem from the village below.
As the miser Silas Marner recounts his gold
The clicking of coins and the smile on his face
As he puts back his gold in his safe hiding place.
But little does he know that Dunston is there
And puts it always with the greatest of care

Down to the village he beg his door wide open he doesn't lock
Straight to the gold Dunston did run removing the tiles with the
Greatest of fun running the gold through the palms of his hands,
Imaging it was the rich smooth sand up he stood and to the door he ran
His hands filled with the rich smooth sand

Back to the cottage Silas did walk
to that door he had left unlocked
Smelling the roast on the warm fireplace
Caused a smile to come over his face.
Quickly noticing the tiles unplaced
Caused quite a change to come over his smiling face

First a shriek and then a shout then the small dim candle did go out
Up he got and to the door he ran
Crying and sighing like an insane man.

Faheme J. Honna

Help Me

You hear me speak, my words are unheard
As I try to tell you, in just the right words
I cry listen to me, hear me as I speak
Will someone try to understand

I need guidance, help through this maze
My cries fall upon ears that are deaf
I call for help that is not there
Help me please help me

Begging you hear me as I speak
Give the understanding that I seek
There's no one to hold my hand
Help me please help me

I sit bewildered filled with despair
Scratching, hoping, ever groping
Will someone hear my plea
Help me, someone, please help me

C. Robert Baker

The Battle

His majestic crown grazes the green canopy,
As the smothering silence tells a corrupt tale
Of a war where evil triumphs and the strong fall.
He recalls the evil victor's exultant cry
As it echoed off the far walls of the valley.
Man has won, leaving only one other standing.
Alone the other watches with defeated pride.
The Hunter moved on satisfied with his slaughter.
The lone buck sadly goes on to another day.
The eyes of nature release their grief from above.
Her tears stain his path and her arms lend their shadow.
The torrent erases the evidence of war;
The remainders of a triumph and tragedy.

Jenne Hughes

Wind In My Heart

As I awoke, my mind all aglow, the window burst forth,
as the wind did blow

Thoughts of my love kept me still dreamy, oh take to
the wind, if she could but see me

As truth of old lies are unveiled, the light of my
feelings flickers unhailed

Try as I might, though graceless, not crude, I threw
out my heart, but still I did brood

Give love a chance, I confess, it can bring back such
loveliness

Then back to dreams surely I'll go, hoping once more
to be all aglow

David B. Hallford

Last Sorrow

The wind cleanses a heart,
As water does soiled hands.
Tears rippling down blushed cheeks,
As a stream over polished stones.
Screams release the wicked soul,
As clouds pass in front of the moon.
No light upon this dark world.
Haunted eyes seek revenge.
Feet stumbling over rugged terrain.
A heavy breath passes through an open mouth.
Waves crashing upon the rocks below.
A deep sigh whispers to the moon,
One last stumble, one last scream,
Vengeance is merciless.

Amy Rana Wolfe

Mother

The first arms to hold me and wrap me with care, for one reason or
another are no longer there. To heal the wounds with time you see,
the scares forever there will be.
In the river where red runs, hate can be a steady burn, look into my
eyes and you will see just what the pain has done to me. I try to
say but you don't hear, why do you always disappear?
When I needed, you weren't around, I search for memories but none to
be found, of happy feelings or a hand to hold,
a shoulder to cry on young or old.
I know you love me and all this hurts but I surely couldn't feel
any worse, show you care by calling sometime, to see what's up or
just chat awhile. The distance between make us miles apart, but
communication comes from the heart. In your place there is no
other, you are my first, you are my mother......

Candy Meade

To Teach

To teach is a marvelous feeling,
    As we show 'n tell someone the way.
Everyone is a student of learning,
    As we communicate night 'n day.

To teach is not a brainwashing,
    As we create the proper stage.
The secrets of knowledge are endless,
    For learning knows no age.

To teach is to encourage curiosity
    In your audience for the unknown.
Because open minds will prevail,
    As the learning process becomes their own.

To teach is a wonderful privilege,
    As we seek to impel desire.
But, it's not enough to see 'n hear,
    First we must strive to inspire.

Elmer A. Rasmussen II

The Greatest Gift

A beautiful singing voice
As well as physical beauty,
These are wonderful gifts.
The ability to run very fast
Or possessing other superior athletic abilities,
These are wonderful gifts.
There are many wonderful gifts in our lives
But, when someone is willing
To give you their love,
That is the greatest gift in the world.

Jason M. Demkowicz

Sober At Midnight

I love my real friends
At good ole "A.A."
I always try to do my part
Practicing the 12 steps each and every day

If it weren't for each and every one of you
Hard telling where I'd be
But, one thing for sure I'm sober today
And I couldn't do it, without the good Ole "A.A."

If we take it seriously "How It Works"
We will be well along the way
And be a recovering member of the good Ole "A.A."

If you want to take it seriously
And don't know what to do
Just call the number of "A.A."
And we will be on our way to you

Without God or our Higher Power
We don't know what to do
But, one thing for sure
Just open up your heart and "A.A." will come to you

Betty L. Barrett

Holocaust

Those of you who feel you are not affected,
    are affected the most,

Those of you who feel it did not happen to you,
    will experience it the most,

Those of you who don't want to remember,
    will have the most terrifying nightmares,

Those of you who think it never happened.
    will live through it again.

Ann Schonwetter Arnold

The Diagnosis-Die Diagnosis (A Pun Poem)

This is a little ditty for to tell
At last, the diagnosis for poor little El.

Oh, my tummy! Oh, my tummy!
Just your nerves, just your nerves - my dear honey.

"It seems to be just in your head.
Now take this medicine," the doctor said.

Oh, my tummy! Oh, my tummy!
So please don't worry, please don't worry - my dear honey.

As the years they passed, so did the pills
Prescribed to cure all little El's ills.

Oh, my tummy! Oh, my tummy!
Wretched one, wretched one - my dear honey.

'Lazy-chitis' still some others would say
But there was coming a brand new day.

Oh, my tummy! Oh, my tummy!
Diet special, diet special - my dear honey.

Doctor Gutensohn wise internal medicine man
Food allergies, milk and wheat, so you must plan.

Great, my tummy! Great, my tummy!
Die diagnosis, die diagnosis - my dear honey.

Ellen K. Davison

What Is A Mother?

I think I know what a mother should be,
At least I can feel it in my heart.
But, how do I get there from here?
I love my kids, I think they know that.
Does it show in my actions?
I'm afraid not always.
Will they forgive me? I hope so.
I try to do my best. It doesn't always show.
I do things for them. I take them here and there.
But the best gift I can give them,
Is to show that I care.

Denise A. Skiba

Nature At Peace

On the Mountain top I was looking down
at Nature's fairest glory, a sight unseemly to behold.
The moonlight glittered through the forest like
a sensuous rainbow set upon sockets of fine gold.

As the water rushed gloomily down the river,
I could hear the night creatures bellowing their
approval as though they knew what I was feeling.

Yes they knew, even they did,
Because only a heartless person would doubt
that there's an invisible hand that forms
and fashions our beautiful land;
Yea, it all together lovely.

Dezrene Gunn

My First Kiss

Kissing tag is what we played
at recess on those nice warm days
we thought we never would be caught.
But so much for that foolish thought.
We grabbed each other and swung round and round
We feel off balance to the ground.
A sweet, soft kiss is what we gave
and then her family moved away.
I thought that girls were really gross
But now they're what I think of most.

Freddie Reed

Enlightening Hope

I looked when the sun came out
at the herald, huge weeping willow tree.
The drops of water still dropping,
crying, as soon, it would not be.

Then I compared it to myself as
it harbored birds and squirrels.
And I, the children who would soon
be adults into an unnerving world.

Between the two of us there was a bond
of living the life we were destined.
Each in our own way and with whom
giving shade and comfort to life as mentioned.

You and I for years have given our thoughts
and values by withstanding a wind of madness
that is weeping the world over and under us.
We sigh and weep with sadness.

But life is awe inspiring we have known.
Even though we are gnarled and scrawny we can
see changes happening, spring and a new era
is coming. The youth, I and the tree will have a tan!

Jean K. Mathis

The Wish

Each night I stare into the sky,
At the stars so bright and bold,
For the star that holds my wish untold.

The wish that I hold close to me,
The wish that will always be.

Each night I whisper my wish to that star,
Each night it whispers back,
Keep that wish alive in you heart,
So that it will always last.

Brenda Rohrbeck

Ukraine, Our Ukraine

You're like a child bewildered
    at the sudden change of pace.
Thank God you've built your strength
    through painful chain and chase.
So long you've waited to embrace your land
    and feel free soil in your hand.
The winds that used to blow upon the fields of green.
The warmth of the sun upon your face.
The calmness of the waves at sea, beneath the sky of blue.
Could this be true? A free Ukraine!
Freedom, yes, was long in waiting.
Return you people, appraise the land.
The hands of God will help to plant
    the seed of honor and respect.
New leadership to the young,
    abiding glory to the old.
Stand proud! Sound the trumpet loud!
    For our Ukraine.

Irena Turiansky Johnson

Untitled

I'm sending my love special delivery
    because we are so far apart.
Since we are apart it's been hard on my heart.
So, I'm sending my love special delivery
    so it gets there with speed from the heart.
Please accept my love special delivery
    then we will no longer be so far apart.
I'm sending my love special delivery
    straight from my heart, Sweetheart.

Bud McKenzie

The Creative Cosmic Clowns

LIFE? A comedy enfolding tragedy: A tragedy unfolding comedy
Awakening more experiences and newer options to Harmony.
A reflexive-reflective mirror.

DEATH? We are born to die. In dying we are born to endless life,
Balancing Earth with Heaven-and-Hell: Yin-Yang.
A narrow opening to Infinity.

ETERNITY? Within-beyond absence and presence
Centering on Fullness and Nothingness as Possibility.
A conscious paradigm shift.

WISDOM? That we know is known. What we know is unknown.
Beyond the mysterious paradox, light at the end of the tunnel.
Delight.

HUMOR? Laughter and action with compassion,
Niente ti turbi. Hakuna matata. Take it easy.
Playfully-Painfully: The clown.

HARMONY? Justice, Peace. A transparent consciousness
Unfolding-enfolding sustainable growth and happy miracles
Creatively Cosmic and Fully Alive here-and-now.
YOU and ME!

Ariosto J. Coelho

"Stones Cut The Dreamer"

Stones cut the dreamer, his voice passing by
baggy clothes, wore the believer, his meekness outside
As morning rain, felt like sleep, softly more.
a long pause, in valleys lean exploring shores.
Where solid whispers, lived in street lamps, dividing days,
Little goliath lay dead, where children played.
Broken glass at his feet, just beyond the shade.
A scratch, on his knee, that was left to age.
While a frozen leaf, startles a rain-coat señor:
He cries "cuba be free" the rebel snores.
A woman laughs then sneezes, her blond hair adored.
By the light of evening, their shadows in accord.
as a ball rolls slowly, an old man Threw.
His relation chasing after, what he already knew.
He's wearing baggy clothes, an a base-ball hat.
A scar on his chin, some friend did that.
Well, stones cut the dreamer: from a void unsung.
Now folks make-believe, that a bruise, leaves no lumps,
My life above me, if I could jump.

James C. Olivera

Gianna Now Smiles

Upon our anxious lives this child bursts upon our fate,
beams of pure white light, eyes fixed upon birth's gate.
Silent music sounds, my spirit unseats,
with selfless wonder, my heart skips beats.

And rushed I am with youthful reminiscing,
from the shadows come memories still rekindling.
Fondness grows for times since forgotten,
a youth once lived, sweet memories begotten.

So weak, yet so strong, inspires us still,
the One more powerful, has moved to fulfill.
What little we did, to create such a wonder,
in spite of ourselves, life moves in quiet thunder.

Unwrapped are the ropes, in bondage we'd laid,
ego and pride, only We could have made.
We mortal fools, how humble, called we are to be;
Gianna now smiles, and yes, finally we see.

Conscience calls us, life finished not yet,
challenges await us, countless goals to be met.
Thus, a glorious Alleluia now said,
Temptation beaten, we move humbly ahead.

John Bargetto

Love's Remembered Pain

I harvest Love with great rapture, without chore..
because Love seeded itself deep within my Heart.
Now I soweth Love seeds in the Hearts of those I adore
Everyone knows of Hate, which tears all things apart.
When I love, I love with such fullness, as to overflow
My heart swells and bursts like clouds and pours like rain
And the rain forms a pool of remembrance, so Hate must go.
Hate drowns on the threshold in a pool of Love's Remembered
pain
If Hate can, it will enter and refrigerate the Heart.
But Love remembers the pain, so Hate never gets a start.

Benjamin L. Jones

Dearest Children

Much of my life has been beautiful
Because of you, my children
I have known the beauty of burping
The pain of your all night colics
The aches of sore throats and cutting teeth
I have known the stink of messy diapers
The sweetness of milk breath, your first steps
Your first day of school, the misery of acne
The giddiness of your first date
The joys and sorrows of your adult life
I have always been your sounding board
When you are upset with each other
You try to sway me to your side
There is no side for me, just middle ground
Giving advice, praising good points
Be proud of yourself and your family
Love each other, give help when needed
Watch and listen for your ship
It's out there, somewhere, until then
Be happy and think of your Mother

Jean P. Jones

Untitled

I am questioning people's ability to judge.
Because the court room I am familiar with
we are all nothing but fudge.
And Jesus Christ will be the Judge.
So watch out you piece of fudge.

Love and forgiveness shall prevail.
And Jesus is ready to step in and
take us away to heaven. And send
the Devil to hell. Where the pit
will belch and put out a bad smell.

James A. Meyer

Empty Boots

I hope you never find my empty boots
    black and dull dusty
    or study the flashing light
    blue and screaming

    tears desperate gasp
    heart legs pumping
    tragic dog

What do you think you will see?

People don't die like they used to like that picture
in our 8th grade history book with friends and family
gathered round the bed and the final breath
expected performed

Today you'll be lucky to find
    my empty boots.

Donald L. Michaels

Life Must Go On

Feeling sorry for yourself
Because you're all alone
Like an old book upon a shelf
You must make a world of your own

To always be alone, not easy to do
When you feel so lost, sad and blue
That empty chair that stares back at you
You are alone, so all alone

We must Smile and help one another
There are others out there, just like you
God must have left us with a job yet to do
So keep busy, the days may be few

The children from our Love
The precious jewels, God gave us from above
To our life they will fulfill
So we must follow God's will

So try not to waste time for sadness
Our days must be filled with gladness
Remember the good times we had.
Do not let our days be lonely and sad.

Helen Ulm

The Blind Shepherd

I felt it first last night
Before the dawn of holy light
Awoke the wonder of their sight
I felt the joy.
I did not hear, but rather did resound
With that great universal sound
Of praise, spilled out upon the world.
Before the blessing was to them unfurled,
I knew the wonder of the Holy Word;
The world's excitement at the new-born Lord.

They tell me of the angels, of the glory of the light;
How blest they were in seeing all that bright and wondrous sight...

And yet their eyes could hold no more than my o'er flowing heart...
I cannot help but think that I received the better part.

I felt it still, last night,
When all had gone to find -
And I was left, with bleating sheep, behind.
They sought afar a sign that they could see; I felt within the
    blessing they might find,
The birth of One Who came to save the blind!

Earl Leonard Langguth

Faith In A Relationship

When in a long and loving relationship faith becomes like a religious
belief.
When in a relationship faith means loyalty not grief.
To know and believe that the faith is there can be a tremendous relief.
But when that faith is taken by adultery, will your life, body and
mind perform as if they had limited boundaries?
If so, as time goes on will it seem like a century?
If it does...remember your mind controls everything, so dwelling you
might do.
Dwell...and like your mind, your body and soul will not be well.
But if you must...dwell on faith and relationships in a positive way.
Dwell on the thoughts that faith also means complete trust and
confidence.
Have this with yourself, and the apprehensive faith you have with your
mind, body and soul will be free.
Because faith in a relationship is what every person should see.
Just remember...two makes a relationship not three!!!

Jamila Cross

31

Until That Time

Never say good-bye, but just until that time when life's sun
begins to set, and chapel bells begin their chime,
gaze upon the mist above the valley of the moon;
Dream your childhood dream, of a kingdom, Brigadoon.

It is there, as you lie among the Heather, on the hill and in the glen.
That you dwell upon the Fables and the beauty,
as drawn by the poet's pen.

So never say good-bye, say just until that time when life's sun
begins to set, and the chapel bells begin their chime.

Take time, to look across the meadow, and the valley filled with
weeds and multi-colored flowers.
Take but a moment, and enjoy the white majestic mountains and
refreshing spring time showers.

Cherish all the fantasies housed in the castle of your mind.
Enjoy all that is today, and life's treasures that you find.

Remember, that nothing is for sure, and there are no guaranties.
For life is but a forest, with a multitude of trees.

So never say good-bye, but just until that time, when life's sun
begins to set, and the chapel bells begin their chime.

Arnold L. Johnson

A Poet's Darkness

Darkness is not so much as a small and
beguiling thing, of rosy lips, sensuous hips, and
death's little sting.

Abstraction of affection, this wondrous
applause. It is two souls who seek, two souls that
meet, and two souls who now shall share.

An avatar of beauty, be calming my wild
heart, feral in its desire.

Care worn I carry on. Life is love,
life is what beats and breathes in the heart of
poets. Caustic caro, oh how you burn me.
To taste life in all its senses. That is what
the darkness is made of. Dreams and pain
defeat and pleasure. That is what beats that
is what breathes. That is the heart of a poet.

James W. Cashatt III

One More Road To Travel

One more road to travel
Another mountain to climb
Another world to discover in this age
and time

The choice to decide what is right
And wrong
To face the good and the bad as it
Comes along

To help someone who has lost their way
To brighten it up and help them along the
Way

To comfort a love one who is down and
Feeling blue
To look them in the eye and say "I love
And need you"

So another road to travel
Another mountain to climb
Another world to discover in this age
And time

Bobbi J. Hager

The Eye Of The Beholder

In a dream I saw an eye.
Believe me when I say this,
Very rarely do I lie.

It was an eye of pain,
     of fear,
     and of agony.

It had no color,
     nor was it black or white.
It was full of emotions,
     and had amazing light.

That burning memory I did keep,
To find I had been crying in my sleep.

Was it my eye I had seen?
Or maybe - maybe it was the eye of the earth?
Perhaps even it belonged to the overseer?

As far as I can see,
It was the eye of its beholder.

Its beholder-
Whom?
I do not know.

Hanser Pimentel

End Of Dreams

Death waits for the young, where do I
belong. I got no friends, no pride, no love,
everything is wrong. The devil sings his song
He keeps me near to feel my fear
Believes in a life of hopelessness, My hair's in
flames, A shame to complain, In a place I
don't belong. The heavens strive to keep
still searching for your light, I float around
in seas. Oceans to overcome, Mountains I
will never see, you washed away my dreams
You tried to bury me. The pain leaked out the
cracks, you filled the rest with me, a mask
of disguise, you tried to hide, in a dream I
can't control, my past consumes the new
I hate everything I want, I lose everything I
have, I'm leaving this hate at last, But first
let me sort the past, I need no one else but
me, forget all those prayers you read
I need no one else but me
To live this life I lead.

Anthony Mata

Guardian Angel

Heavenly messenger transcendent, from far
beyond the deep blue sky.

Amiable guardian of my soul, my very being
personified.

With silent persuasion guide my footsteps, from
life's predestined course let me not stray.

Be ever present, ever vigilant, escort me as I
sojourn through each day.

Should I fall short of expectations, drift beyond the
bounds prescribed.

Life me up, give me direction, always keeping by
my side.

Shield me evermore from danger, comfort my soul
with peace and love.

Until my numbered days have ended, and you
return to the heavens above.

Carole Y. de Ibern

Untitled

Storm of broken dreams ... Last tomorrow...
Black hides the hope of hearts...
A fairy tale ending...Within the light of dark...
Full moon rising...
In the brightness of that which is night...
Hole in the horizon...
Last warrior of a never-ending tale...
A God of black, a God of light...
Crimson red the rivers flow...
An ocean mighty, swallowed by the earth...
An immortal soul devoured whole...
Sin that steals all we are...
But how can we be when we are not...
A soldier to the battle calls...
Lost hope and broken knows...
Feel the pain and sorrow...
When you know there's no tomorrow...
I can hear them knocking...Death is at the door...
So beyond I pass...A quiet death...
Where vultures take their toll

Jon Beckmon

Conversation With The Beast

"Daddy, you've poured salt in the wound..." "Why?"

    The question is asked tonelessly.
     Bland, flat curiosity
     tastelessness bred from monotony.

"You just want to give me a hug?" "Promise?"

    Hope is felt, fleeting and brilliant.
     the illusion magnificent
     but the child halts, hesitant.

"Do you really promise this time?" "Really?"

    Feet move in patterned drudgery.
     propelled towards catastrophe
     mind slips to altered reality.

Silence, stillness, as the beast comes. Once More.

    Throat swallows thick and sticky.
     gasp for breath, fleeing death
     gathering shreds of sanity.

"Daddy, you've poured salt in the wound."

J. Prescott

Eye To Eye

Breaking from the heavens came a thunderous blast
Blinding light announcing its calling
The round blue world arrived in its wake
With healing waters and a sheltering sky

Indigenous beings rose in a flash
Differently, beautifully, all from the same seed
Learning, surviving, thriving, conquering with greed
Annihilating most, for the pleasure of "I"

From mother and path, astray with evil some dwelled
Down Father, down Brother, down Friend, all fell
From different to same, the question remained
Oh why, oh why, why, why

Race killing race, blood killing blood, all in despair
Parents killing children, no degree of evil compares
Evil, seeks praise, as the blue world greys
Smothering the sheltering sky

Oh thunderous blast, return with your light
Destroy evil, with a merciless cry
Because only then, in the end
Will all finally see Eye to Eye

Frederick Frelot

Fear Of The Galaxy

The stars, in empty cold, burn fierce.
Blazing gaseous masses of power.
Till death their shining rays do pierce
Our envelope sky, in darkness hour.
In void of space they flare within.
Atomic structures bond their fate.
With each new birth, a sun begins
Transitions toward a nova state.
Worship in the morning time, a god so vast and proud.
Whose mightiness of upward climb, is dust to dissension fire,
Crimson earth and cloud.
Fear the future, our children's, children's demise,
When eight minutes past, calamity
Reigns down on unsuspecting skies.
Then soil, sea, and all that is, shall instantly cease to be.
These suns, whose deaths rive the universe, depart in form, then
Contract to control.
As unseen thieves, silent and terse, they condemn the light to
Blackest hole.
The stars, in empty cold, burn dim.
In age they melt away.
Till galaxy heart to farthest rim,
Can no longer lay claim, to having seen the warmth and light of day.

Brian Thomas Maher

Sunday Morning By The River

Walking slowing by the river with the cold wind
blowing gently in your face, and a cold chill at
your back, holding the warm hands of a man that
you have loved over half of your life, this is
such a wonderful and delightful feeling. As we
walked I could feel his warm eyes looking at me.
And his touch was as gentle as it was all those
years ago, when we first fell in love! All the
trees were naked looking at us, and perhaps saying
we will see you in the spring! The dead leaves
under our feet were making soft noises, the ground was
semi-frozen, and the river was magnificent,
and the tide was high. Oh! The sky was beautiful,
and my love and I were caught up in that moment
of time. Together with the thoughts of no one
but ourselves, our souls were connected at that
beautiful moment as we stood, and walked hand
in hand that morning with the cold wind, and the
bright sky on that wonderful Sunday morning by the river!

Jeanette Jackson Jones

Winter

The many splendored grandeur of autumn is long gone
Blue-gray days of winter stretch on and on and on
I'm told cabin fever abounds everywhere
With lots of mothers ready to pull out their hair
Those garden seed catalogs are arriving almost daily
Outside the downy snow is falling, falling gaily
Settling on each limb of the trees
Stacking knee deep on sidewalks only to freeze
And to be wearily trudged through without ease
So pure, so white, so many flakes
A variety of shapes, what a master it would take
To manufacture thousands and thousands of these
Would require quite a marvelous expertise
The snow shovels don't even begin to repel
As on the roughened edge snow congeals
To shake it off you must become adept
Some people their walks may only have swept
To continually clean off these walks
Day after day, reluctantly, out the door my hubby stalks

Eva Nell Wilmeth

Daydreams

I would love to be my four-legged friend,
born with grace and beauty
fragile yet wild and free,
with trust in my eye
and bond with my home,
with gaits smooth and effortless,
chasing butterflies and brilliantly bright stars
across wondrous fields,
while my mane
blows in the rhythm of the wind,
taking magnificent leaps over gates and walls,
with the coolness
of the spring air filling my nostrils.
When I am old and wise,
I will love to watch the graceful young
grow to love land I love.

Amy Aschinger

A Father And His Boy

Both together one on one.
Both enjoying all the fun.

They laugh, they talk, they both compete
To see which one of them will beat.

The father is easy on his son,
For all he remembers is the fun.
The son just enjoys the times with DAD
And never forgets the times they had.

The games, the talks,
The hunts, the walks
All the times where love was just a part
Of the special bond of each their hearts.

The father has a wish and only one
and he prays to the LORD his wish be done.
That his son is happy and grows to be
A man who is strong and caring as he.
This is the one wish that would bring such joy
To the fortunate father and his boy.

Jill C. Hudson

Summer Sky

What do I see when I look up
Bouquet of flowers moving with ease
In some distance lands
Where birds soar high on summer current winds
And airplanes fly overhead on sonic wave sent

Balloons drifting by in sky so blue
Dressed in rainbow colors of springtime
Kites spinning like a top, jump, dip, bend
And fall to the earth from which it started
Back up again in the hot summer rays
Of sunshine brightness.

What do I see when I look up
Moonlit nights turning into sparkling starlights
which slowly move along into tomorrow

Cynthia Rochester

Light Of Life

Bright, dazzling, shimmering rays
Burst through a hole in the cloudy, gloomy sky;
More blinding than the shine of gold
That raised not the pale down-turned leaf.
whereas, there rays seeped through and into the leaf
Enlightening, reviving...
The leaf twisted up,
Gleaming in green.

Irwyn Ng Wun Kit

This Little Girl Of Mine

She went out to play, on a bright sunny day.
but couldn't help the mud that was in her way,
so there she decided to play.

This little girl of mine, so lovely and sweet,
with mud all over her feet.

She runs and plays from morning until dark,
not even one sadness for her does lark.

This little girl of mine, so untamed
life to her is one big game.

She has grace and beauty given from above,
and the mischief in her eyes, is full of love.

This little girl of mine, so lovely and sweet,
will make your heart skip a beat.

As she walks down the isle, with me by her side
my sadness I will try to hide,
for as I give her hand to you, my son
It's the hardest thing I've ever done.

This little girl of mine, is now your wife,
and I pray she will be happy for the rest of her life.

Janette Moore

Love And Wind

You cannot see the love you feel
But, even so it is very real
Just as it is with the mighty wind
When you open the door and it rushes in.
We try to stop it or push it away,
But it goes where it will and stops to play.

Just pray you're no victim to its cruel side
Like the wind when it blows against the tide
For it is fierce when it blows you to and fro
To that side of love we do not wish to go.

We long to go where love's a gentle breeze
Where it flows through us with the greatest of ease.
And when the gusts of life come about
You take a deep breath, and then let it out.
And continue on through the darkest times
Knowing well that again the sun will shine.

You must respect the wind for what it is
And a chance at love you must not miss
For in both we can hope by harnessing it
That all whom it touches will benefit.

Angela K. Lay

To The Man I Love...

You are who you are, this is true,
But, I am who I am because of you.
When I met you I knew from the start.
You would always hold a piece of my heart.
You brighten my days and lighten my nights.
Even when we are mad and having our fights.
Sometimes to see you makes my heart skip a beat.
Other times you make me melt from my head to my feet.
I'm glad you are a part of my life.
And I am blessed to have become your wife.
After so many years spent with you.
I cannot believe our love is still true.
You and I are meant to be together.
Not just for now, but always and forever.
I Love You from now till the end of time.
And now my love this is the end of my rhyme.

Jackie McVeigh

Where Do I Belong?

A bird does not always stay on the right path,
But eventually he gets to where he is going.
  The bird may swoop down into muddy waters,
  Cross high mountains on the way,
Or even hurt other creatures,
Still not knowing the pain.

As the bird finds his flock again
He ventures among them, not knowing how to act,
  For he has drifted long and hard
  To only be left out in the cold.
He is with his flock, yet all alone in part,
For his adventure tore him away at the heart.

Now the bird must venture on to near and far places,
For the ones he loved, he has left behind
  To find a new path to follow.
  With his heart as his guide,
He finds himself where he is meant to be —
With his own unique flock, where he began.

Glynnis Fellers

The Blind Man

The path of the blind man is long and dark,
But he judges people by their heart,
And by what they do and say.

In the dark and sinister world of today,
A blind man can teach you how to see,
The blind man has the right of way.

He can't judge people by their skin,
It's really all the same to him,
Sometimes he may wobble,
Sometimes he may sway,
But the blind man has the right of way.

Andrea Crouse

Untitled

You never know what will come up next,
But he will always watch over you and do his best.
He watches and knows how we act,
You know in your heart that's a fact.
When I'm in doubt or in need,
he always makes sure that I can see,
The good things in life for he planned,
Sometimes as I'm listening
Tears drip into my hands.
But I feel his love bubbling in me,
Why can't you non-believers look and see?
I know when he comes for the final time,
Life will end but believers won't die.
So when it comes to the final end,
I know my fate, how 'bout you friend?

Donnita Nygren

Seasons Of Two

Two sit in the shade of a tall oak amidst fields of spring wildflowers
and watch the drifting clouds that float above colored dreams.

Two run into the torrent of oncoming surf over castles of summer sand
and survive the swirling ebbed tide that consumes jubilant innocence.

Two walk within shadows on a leafy path under branches of autumn bareness-
and wonder upon a crisp breeze that whispers through mindless time.

Two lay in the darkness of hollowed earth below crystals of winter silence-
and arise to warm bright sunlight that awakens a forgotten memory...

Daniel J. O'Connor

Reflections

There are those who say looking back is bad.
But how else can one measure growth or progress?
Since you took me by the hand and waited patiently
  for me to grow.
I can look back with objectivity and without longing.

After five years knowing you, it's rare
When things grab the frayed emotional edges.
Unpleasant memories of my past are minimized
With love shared in subtle unspoken ways.

I'm more content with "me"; understand more;
Resent less; and hold new hopes inside.
Some lives touch us briefly, but ours,
(I'm glad) is new with each encounter.

I'm aware of your influence, however slight
It appears, and marvel at your patience.
You've given strength and direction, much happiness
And love. I want this to say, "Thank you".

Betty J. Udy

"A Place Called Heaven"

It is a place someday I want to go,
But how to get there, I really don't know.
You can't fly or take a boat,
Because you see, it is so remote.
That God will take us by the hand,
And lead us to his promised land.
Depending on how your life has been,
Living with God's love or in sin.
If in sin, God will turn away,
And say be lost forever and a day.
But if you love him as I do, he will surely take care of you.
In sickness or in health, no matter how hard,
All you do is pray, he is never too far.
I was away from God you see, but still he took care of me.
Then one night I thought and prayed,
And knew I would see my Lord on judgement day.
It's such a relief for me to know,
Which way I am going to go. To stand with my Lord, and loving him,
Or forever be lost in sin. To be in heaven with my Lord,
Is all I ask for my reward.

Don Lockwood

Good-Bye, My Love

I thought I was ready for you to go,
  But I find that it was not so.
Even though I knew it was going to be,
  It still came as a shock to me.

For a long time now, I have cared for you
  In a very special way,
And I could see that the help you needed from me
  Was more and more each day.

Then lately, things grew so much worse;
  You ceased to be the real you.
Even so, I still felt that it was truly you
  And that such care was your wifely due.

Then of a sudden one day, you needed no help.
  Your soul had departed this life.
So where is the relief I was supposed to feel
  When freed of the care of my wife?

I feel empty. I feel choked. I feel all alone.
  Pangs of pain from the loss do I feel.
Sobbing and tears I cannot escape.
  All this pain, time alone must heal.

Edward W. Clautice

Renee

After nine long months, I'm finally here
But I'm going to require a lot of care

Feeding myself, of that I'm not yet sure
But that's what Mommy and Daddy are for

Changing my diaper, I know it's not fun
But if I don't cry, then it might not get done

Everything to me in this world is new
That's why I need to depend on you

We still have a lot to get used to, you and I
But just wait and see, because the time will fly

Before you know it I will be running and playing
There will be a new word each day I'll be saying

My first day at school, you make sure I'm prepared
Give me a kiss, tell me not to be scared

Next thing you know graduation day is here
You wave from the stands as you wipe away tears

I'll make you so proud, just wait and see
I'll be the good person you both taught me to be

But we better not jump ahead too fast
Let's make this special time together last.

Diane Orcione

Lifeless

Nowhere to go,
but in a corner to be left alone.
Trying to live a meaningless life,
isn't going to make you happy.
Climbing in a coma with no thoughts of
being contented,
not being contented is a very important part
You need someone to make you feel needed,
you are down a dead end road with nowhere to go.
You can only turn back,
and make a new path for yourself.
Make that certain block disappear,
to make your life happy again.
You will begin your journey through a field of thoughts.
With no turning back with a hopeless face.
Find your dreams and lift them high into the sky.
You had me where I didn't want to be,
I am now gone and you have no one to
make a disaster out of.
So for now I am happy with myself.

Amy Jenkins

"People" "Who And Why"

I guess some people can pass a test!
But those people may never be the best?
Those people to abolish the rest!
When they should really take a rest?

Some people who really tried!
Other people will never be satisfied?

People who try to analyze?
Those people keep their head full of ties!
Will people ever realize?
There's people who also antagonize!

Some people are willing to try to fit!
While other people may be counterfeit!
But who is the hypocrite?

Some people pretend to be nice?
While other people really pay the price.
Maybe people should try to be their twice?

James E. Hittle II

The Way Life Is

Life is hard, sometimes fun,
but it's all our doing for what we've done.
Rather right or rather wrong,
the time we've spent is forever gone.

Life goes on and on and on, but life itself is a bond.
It holds us tight, sometimes wrong,
but for sure the time is gone.

We've just one life, it's full of curves,
we run on love, and sometimes nerve.
With bumps and grinds the way life goes,
sometimes no choice with the seeds it sows.

You can say life's not fair, but who are we, and do we dare?
Let's be honest, the way we are, the life we want is like a star.
Standing tall, full of light, but let's be real, it's not all bright.

Life is meant to share, to give, to love.
It's for two, not for one.
It's to touch, it's to hold, it's for joy, it's for fun.
It's the way I feel life should run.

Jon V. Zook

Untitled

Everything I've been through seems as though it was a dream,
but not when I'm with you. When I'm with you it seems real.
You see, my dreams are not just dreams but nightmares, yet
when I am with you, you make every nightmare go away. You are
like a ray from the sun's body, warming my every move. For
you I would give the last drop of water left and cry just so
you can drink my tears so you wouldn't have to go thirsty.
You are a worthy person and I must take care of you. I must
make everything I do for you special because you are special.
You are who you are and no one else can come close to being
as special as you. That's why I love you so much.

Jennifer Karen Cossu

The Old House

The Old House reminiscent of all that used to be,
but now is cold and damp and shrouded in mystery.
It had its day when I was young,
it echoed every song that was sung.
And though this was but yesterday
nothing on earth is here to stay.
The old house was very strong,
but 'til it falls will not be long.
Old house, you have had your time
just the same as I've had mine.
And what was, again will never be,
this is true old house, for you and me.

Clifford J. Queen

Slavery

Slaves are people like me and you,
but they're mistreated and so abused.
They think like human beings do,
So what makes them different, I ask you?
You say they're stupid,
as most white men do.
You'd say all these things,
but what about you?
You have no answer, as I can see,
'cause you have no excuse, that's apparent to me.
How would you like it every day,
if you worried about your life in every way.
I don't know about you,
but I know about me.
I think slavery's ignorant,
as ignorant can be!

Ricky Adams

It Seems Like Time Has Got Us By The Souls

It seems like only yesterday I shaved,
But now my face is carpeted again.

It seems like only yesterday we waved,
But now I reach you only with my pen.

It seems like only yesterday we joked
About our distant trials and days of old.

It seems like only yesterday we spoke
But now to sheeted wood my words are told.

It seems like only yesterday we gazed
Together, out upon the rolling green.

It seems like only yesterday we blazed
Our precious youth like fire through out teens.

It seems like only yesterday we heard
Of how a man and woman meet and wed.

It seems like only yesterday we learned
Of love, but all cliches have now been said.

It seems like only yesterday we tried
To stifle grim attempts to silence us.

It seems like only yesterday we died
But look, our bodies have since turned to dust.

 Gian E. Saja

Everything And Everybody

February, usually gloomy and cold,
but often, here, we see a little of nature's gold,
Early blooms and early blossoms,
but nature never lies,
And everything and everybody dies.

Looking down on a once strong man,
A man who long-stood at the head of our clan,
The observer stands and looks on and cries,
Remembering that nature never lies,
And everything and everybody dies.

The realization of the brevity of life never stronger,
Believing all along somehow it should be longer.
What a worn out cliche', "How time flies,"
But, indeed, nature never lies,
And everything and everybody dies.

Nothing left but to sit and ponder,
With the knowledge that I am powerless,
is there any wonder,
that I believe nature never lies,
And everything and everybody dies.

 Denny Dial

Fair Share

They all work hard day and night.
But to get their share it is a hard fight.

They work from dawn until dusk.
They do their jobs, work hard they must.

But bosses say not good today.
And then with that they cut their pay.

They do this not 'cause they are mean.
They do it because of something unseen.

They do it to people black or white.
It is all we can do to put up a fight.

Male or female they see you,
just as someone who can be under their shoe.

 Barbara Urquhart

A Tear In The Sand

Life there was so true to me,
But over here how could it be?
Over here I wake or call,
When over there I had it all,

Behind these gates of hell and madness,
All that's inside of me is sadness,
I dream of tomorrow a time of joy,
But I fear today, I'm only a boy,

How can they take me from a life so grand,
And place me in a cold war in a foreign land?
When all I know are books and dreams,
Now all I hear are shots and screams.

To God I pray, you guide my way,
So I may live another day,
Though in my mind I can never see,
What really may become of me.

 Eric J. Parisano

Untitled

You left us without warning,
but sadly we move on
sharing love and memories
of the part of us that's gone

As we sit within the loneliness
the memories come pouring in
like the blood of wounds that just won't heal
and the pain comes back again
There's nothing that can bring you back
and there's little I can do
But there's one thing that will never leave
the memories we share of you
There's one thing left for all of us
there's one thing left to say
it's time for us to say goodbye
and let God show you the way

 Brett Scott

Colorblind

A rainbow has beautiful colors indeed,
But the promise from God is all that I see.

The colors of flowers do set them apart,
Tho' the oxygen they produce is what helps the heart.

Remember with people, real beauty is found within
It's not the color of the face, but the warmth of the grin.

 Dave Crawford

New Amsterdam

Laggard knaves purloin your Inquietude.
But there are also poets, prophets, and Martyrs amongst your
Verdant and primeval architecture.
A twilight sky's acculturated, jagged edge, silhouettes the
Pinpricks of concrete Tenants.
I want to be there now.
Their spurious needles pointing to the sky; the sun dancing
Lazily off them, flashing brilliant, minute flashes across a
Truculent Hudson, like someone sending Morse code.

How I long to join the aberrant vessels of Forty-Second Street.
To dance amongst the maddening crowds.
To smell the odor of dead cement and diseased insects,
To wander amongst a dense wilderness of steel,
To wallow like a mole underneath this vibrant and cohesive
Pleasure palace,
Speeding along in man-made carcasses.

 Joseph G. Gibbs

The Edge

Climb to the edge and you see quite a view
But there's more to be seen from behind
Look through a camera and see half a world
Turn around, see the picture denied

Look in a mirror and see half a man
Look again, looking deep down inside
Be who you are by the way that you be
And not someone your picture can't hide

Climb to the edge of that story book tree
that grows weaker the higher you climb
flee from the branch, searching in not around
and your spirit shall flourish and fly

John Chadwick

Be Glad You're You

I am just a puppy dog, I'm friendly as can be
But there's one problem that I have, I don't like being me.

I'd like to be a puppy-bird and fly all over town,
But wait a minute, I can't fly and so I would fall down.

Well, I can be a puppy-cat, that may be lots of fun,
But then the dogs would follow me and I would have to run.

A puppy-tiger may be nice, I think that just might do,
But then I'd have to be caged up and live in some big zoo.

I could be a puppy-fish, blow bubble after bubble,
But I can't swim and so I think I may end up in trouble.

I should be a puppy-bear, be big and weigh a ton,
But I'd have to sleep all winter and I'd miss a lot of fun.

I'll be a puppy-lion, imagine how I'll roar
Inside a scary jungle, Oh! I must think some more.

So after thinking one more time, I'm standing proud and tall
Because to be a puppy dog is a good thing, after all!

Elizabeth Newlon

This Picture

They say a picture's worth a thousand words.
But to me this picture's worth so much more.
This picture's a memory of what we used to be.
Of the fun we had and the love we shared.
This picture's a time when life was lived.
And when you shared your dreams with me.
This picture showed how much you really cared.
And how much our relationship meant to me.
But now this picture is all I have left.
It's all I can hold when times get tough.
And now that you're gone, I just don't know.
If my love will ever again be able to grow.

Gina Strand

Orange Clouds

When the sun sets,
and the clouds are turned orange,
it is the most beautiful sight
I have ever seen.
My dreams are in those orange clouds,
but the clouds disappear in a few seconds,
so do my dreams.
My mother is in those orange clouds
making them so beautiful.
I live in those clouds and the memory of
my mother's beautiful smile.

Amelia Martin

My Dream

I went to bed last night to dream of my childhood,
but walked into the future instead.
I strolled up the street where the woods once were growing;
where the path of my childhood once led.

I found a hugh fence, and walked through the gate
that by chance did not have a lock.
With my eyes all a-light, I took in the sight;
I didn't realize I was in for a shock.

Instead of two miles, it was just a short stroll,
I came into a teeming shop mall.
I rubbed both my eyes which were wide with surprise;
"Lord, what have you done to it all.

Where are the sand slides, the old willow tree,
the spring where we used to hunt snakes.
The creek in the hollow that we used to follow
to catch craw-dads behind Uncle Jake's."

I woke with a start, a pain in my heart,
and a longing for my youth once again.
I slowly crawled out of bed to face the sunrise,
and looked to the future instead.

John J. Senger

"Mom Please"

Sticks and stones won't even touch me,
but words will make me cry.

I feel your hatred, why was I born,
my mother said that I.

Was in her way so please just fade
and do just what her heart would say.

If you'll just die, the money will flow.
I see you want me dead.

I hate you most for being mine,
I hate you now for all the pain.

Mom, don't say that, I promise I will change!

Is it my fault for being young,
my tears will drown my sorrow.

If I'm not dreaming or falsely hearing,
I hope to die tomorrow...

(PLEASE WATCH THOSE WORDS,
THEY CAN REALLY MAKE DAMAGE
TO A YOUNG MIND)

Jose Luis Garcia

The Child Inside

I saw a child, looking in a mirror;
A child so lonely, so scared, so dear;

I sat and wondered, what it all meant;
A child, who sat in a corner, where all her time was spent;

No one could hurt her;
See the pain, or all her fears:

No one was to see her tears, or hear her cries for help;
So was told to keep them silent, because
no one wanted to hear;

So she sits in her corner, only a small light shining;
Silent tears flowing, hoping no one would see:

That child in the mirror;
That child was me.

Lisa Elsing

From A Son To His Father

Did you love me? I long to know
but you are dead and the dead are silent.

You lie there cold within your grave,
impenetrable as you were in life,
with nothing but a plaque and me to mark your living.
You never let me understand the you inside that stony man,
withholding both your self and your affection.

One night you told me in a dream you were all right and not to worry.
Your manner was both sad and peaceful, the hardened edges softened.
Your voice expressed a tenderness and feeling,
the words were charged with such emotion,
you caused me to awaken, crying.

Your presence was so real and lifelike I felt you even after waking,
and I took a passing comfort in this visit you had paid me.
Was this your way of finally saying all that had been left unspoken?

Or were you just an apparition drawn by my imagination
fuelled by painful memories and voiced by my regrets?

Did you love me? I'll never know
for you are dead and death is silence.

Joseph P. Wechselberger

Untitled

My love for you is so true.
But you make me feel blue.
You know you got me wrapped around your little finger.
When we're alone I'm happy, but behind you and your friends I linger.

I love you with all my heart.
But with your girlfriend, you'll never part.
I know I tried to find somebody new.
But now I realize nobody is better than you.
I love you more than you'll ever know
I give to you my heart and soul.

This might not mean a thing to you
but you have to know my love is true
my love for you will always endeavor
because I want you in my life forever.
but yet through you I see
you didn't really care for me.

I'm doing all I can to make you see
that you're the one, the only one for me
maybe one day we will be together
I'll wait because I will love you forever.
To my heart you have the key
I'll never give up, until you love me.

Dana M. Collins

They Tell Me A Friend Was Killed Today

They tell me a friend was killed today,
A brother who shared with my heart,
Can someone tell me just what is real,
My senses are dulled in the dark.

David I'll love you forever,
Your beauty is in your smile,
Freedom's your only lover,
You chased her over many a mile.

They tell me a friend was killed today,
He was found in a wreck on the highway,
I know he was chasing his mistress the wind,
He'd sing how he'd soon catch her one day.

David I'll love you forever,
Nothing I guess stays the same,
I know now you've found your true love,
'Cause I hear the wind whisper your name.

Preston E. Presley

Mom

A year ago impatience tinged my voice
but You were determined to go ahead.
My unwillingness showed, as this was not my choice.
I wonder now what prodded You along,
a knowledge that Your time was short?
Your enthusiasm began to gnaw at my reluctance,
and excitement slowly grew as I watched the joy and
pleasure which You knew.
When all was done Your happiness renewed my spirit.

Janet Hazen

Hope I'm Not Too Late??

The road is rough, the road is long,
But your love for me, is oh, so strong **
Still I linger and I don't know why??
Because it was for me, that you had to die **
So time's been wasted, and days gone by !!

When my Jesus, will soon, very soon arrive !!!
Hope I'm not too late, to go with you my Friend !!
For my blessed Savior, will be there 'till the end ***
So hold me tight, as I know you care,**
Because my Lord and Savior is always there ***

Florence L. Cole

From The Series "Of The Silence"

To think of you is the same as to invent you.
A challenge to the unbelievable of remembrance.

To say your name and paper china moons soaring
onto the wind is one in the same thing.

Or that for example the world swivel stiff with mist
surrounding white doves invented in the exile.

Why does your name always sponge up and grow?
of what forgotten bound does it approach near
the vertically of my memory?

I ask and there is no answer.
There are, Oh! yes, white ants walking on my epidermis.
Inventions of clouds and little lambs
scattered through the twirls of the wind.

And Penelope was no longer in the season of time.
The war had taken her away.
She was the recluse in the charcoal tunnels
from a village whose houses had spiral windows
closed to the memory of firefly for ever.

Mayamerica Cortez

Collective Wisdom

Aisle upon aisle conquered
A cart full of necessities
Tender youth in tow
A small urgent cry from Mother Nature
Startles present state of mind
As feet and cart speed with urgency
To master the impending task
The tiny wonder gazing upon a porcelain well
Pondering a dutiful performance
Exclaims... "There's a penny in there..."
  Dropped from a pocket?... or
"Maybe someone wants to make a wish"

J. Clark

My Kingdom Of Safety.. The Ocean

Cradled in a fathomless blue, safe to be me, I am now free.
I know it will always be here around me..
Here to support me
Behind me, beyond me
The surface is so far up I have forgotten it's there.
The inhabitants have noticed me; I noticed they care.
Organisms of tremendous diversity..
Porifera, Cniderians, Mollusks, and Crustaceans surround me.
They have acknowledged my presence, and granted my acceptance..
To swim with them, live among them, and intertwine our lives.
Extreme pain, deep suffering, and salty tears
I can hear their cries.
Try and absorb their vivid spirits, we all have a lot to learn..
With time and dedication, their habitats will return.

Marcella Angela Garcia

Hourglass

An irregular web on a tough silk
strand supporting a cotton-like sac of eggs
lies hidden in a dark nook under
a decaying woodpile. There
standing watch is
a shiny black
spider
whose globular
abdomen is bedaubed
with a rouge hourglass. She
appears serene, her soon-hatching
young safe from the lesser absent mate, a
venom victim, his time being up.

Robert Raingruber

Countdown

10 children playing in the mud with faces so dirty.
9 for all the times you said come to me.
8 the way they circled scared us all.
7 preying on the little to feed the gorge.
6 fire on the hill.
5 ways to find the hidden link.
4 seeing no way out but through.
3 holding on to the thread with a needle.
2 the unit finds a way.
and then there was 1.
he slowly faded away with no light from the past.

Michelle C. Roberts

Farewell My Love

Love
a betrayal of the soul
Your Heart yearns for it
Your mind screams out against it
A knife in the back
A strangle hold on my life
You got too close, I let you
You hold my heart in the palm of your hand
My fate rests with you
Am I visible?
Or do you choose to ignore me?
I once thought of you
As the most beautiful orchid I had ever seen
Now you are a dried and withered remnant
Slashed and burned long ago
How blind I must have been
You did it to yourself
Don't drag me down
Give me back my heart
So I can finally say Goodbye.

Troy M. Federico

Courage

When you seem to feel a trifle blue,
A bit discouraged and distracted too;
When patience is lost and things go wrong,
Don't think of sadness, but of laughter
and song.

Never give up when only once you've tried,
but keep up your courage - think, Great
men have died;
Men who once traveled the same path as you,
These are our Gods - Those who dare and do.

Think of the cripples and blind ones too,
Those who are lame and have cause to be blue;
Then look at yourself and make things look gay,
Do a good deed when the chance comes your way.

Give someone a smile and someone a cheer,
Give someone courage each day of each year;
And when you begin to feel lonely and blue,
Just think of the ones far worse off than you.

Virginia Spangler McCary

My Thoughts Spoken Aloud

I watch the racing world go by-
A blur of crumpled hats and coats;
Never stopping to watch the sky
Or the clouds bound in it float.
I walk outside to make them stop-
Instead they pull me in;
The time ticks faster on the clock
As I struggle to breathe within the den.
I finally break free from the crippling strife-
Now I am old and gray;
I have wasted my entire life
Living it the normal way.
I miss the way things used to be-
So young, beautiful and carefree.

Sara Horst

Untitled

Tonight I saw a moon
A moon anyone saw
An indiscriminate moon
For anyone and all to see
A caffinated moon
A detox moon
An indiscriminate moon
That will exist the night after ever
A local moon a foreign moon
an insignificant part of the day
The day to be Valentines Day of ninety-five
A day like any other
An indiscriminate day
Everyone gets a day
Everyone gets a glance,
At the moon
The indifferent security of the moon

Rachel Belisle

Torn Love

Love so precious and undying,
but yet two hearts torn apart that once loved as one.
Two hearts that once loved as one love apart.
Feelings, dreams, fears, closeness that
were all shared were torn apart.
Tears falling down your eyes...Love torn apart.
From a distance I love you, from near I hate you.
Two hearts torn apart that once loved as one love apart.

Anita Diaz

If I Had Lived In The Long Ago

Who would I have been if I had lived in the long ago?
A child of the Pueblos running to and fro?

I would have looked and found things that lived in the lane.
Something for my mother made clean by the rain.

Would I find a leaf, a piñon cone or a feather?
Perhaps a piece of clay made soft by the weather?

I would have liked it living long ago.
A child of the Pueblos running to and fro.

What if I had lived in the long ago?
Would I have learned to weave a basket or to fetch my father's bow?

Would I have gathered corn; blue, yellow or red?
To grind for my grandmother so she could make it into bread?

My house would be warm and so would my bed.
A deer skin would cover me from my toes to my head.

The best of life would be there for all three.
All of my family - FATHER, MOTHER and ME.

Mercedes Conner

Flight

I was not alone on the hillside -
A child was there who watched a plane,
And dreamed, as small boys do.

As if he were really on that plane,
The small boy laughed and headed
For lands of enchantment.

A gesture with his arm, and the plane
Went swooping smoothly through the blue sky
Just like magic.

Now, on his back, bright eyes fixed aloft,
He made loud putt, putt engine sounds.
The plane was his -

He was the ace pilot, the polite steward,
The passenger belted in seat seven A.
Two arms stretched skyward, far as they could go,
Trying to grasp his plane and hold it
Close to his heart.

But it disappeared into the blue
Without noticing a small boy
On the hillside.

Lucille J. Oosterhous

Just Counting My Blessings

True loneliness is to have a heart like outer-space
A cold vacuum full of "Black-holes" that suck the light out
of every star that shines too near its grasp

I've known loneliness that made me cry out in deepest pain
But never the loneliness of an evil heart

Unending agony of the mind, the body and soul, even as one
sleeps, is my vision of not only true loneliness
But of hell itself as well
I though my sorrow knew no end my tears would never cease
Till the moment I realized I'm blessed for I can love and love
is like a double-edged sword. It cuts both ways
To be loved you must be able to love
To find compassion, you must possess it

Yes, I am blessed for I posses something the truly lonely do not
HOPE,... THANK YOU GOD!

Karen Denise Bynum Jones

I Looked...

I looked into the eyes of God and saw the heavens,
A clock of beauty — brilliant, unsurpassed.
A voyage into worlds of wonder,
Mystery upon mystery amassed.

I looked into the eyes of God and saw a tear drop,
A meteor so bright against the sky!
Its fractured beauty through the heavens
Made one think aloud and wonder why.

I looked into the eyes of God and heard a snow flake
Earthward bound on driven path,
Missioned to form a blanket of concealment.
A beauty to behold in aftermath.

I looked into the eyes of God and saw a feather
Plumaged with forethought on a crested head.
A dab from Nature's pallet..living;
A life of purpose before it quietly lay dead.

I looked into the eyes of God and saw His pleasure,
Beauty, music, color, love and plan.
Would that all below could truly treasure
And through the eyes of God man know man.

E. Lee Schneider

The Bike Ride

I thought - Life to me is like riding my bike. I had wrecked
a couple years ago. I had tried to ride again and was too
scared. The other week it was still scary, especially
through the rocks. So I rode the brakes and went real slow.
Today I picked up a little more speed. I still rode the
brakes a little bit, I mainly coasted. I picked up speed
here and there then slowed down in the rough spots - It was
great. It gets easier and easier every time I ride, somewhat
like life - Go slow and gentle through the rough spots and
speed up and enjoy on the smooth spots.

Oh what a release - OOOH AAAH!!

Kelley Middleton

A Broken Dream

The windows are broken, all smashed to the floor
A creek can be heard as only one hinge still holds the door

NO furniture can be seen, was moved long long ago
The house leans some now as the weather continues to take its tow

The wallpaper is torn and shredded as the rain runs down the wall
The house is now totally empty and seems so very very small

The paint on the outside is faded making it look cold and bare
The house has long been deserted and without tender loving care

The wind is in control, with its howling and whistles
The once green grass outside is now full of weeds and thistles

This house once was full of life, was a home with purpose and a dream
Which must have fallen and evaporated like raindrops in a swollen
stream

Marjorie Kolthoff

A Spring

A spring is not a spring without trees, trees without
branches, or branches without leaves.
A spring is not a spring without a beautiful sky,
a sky without clouds, or clouds without a sun.
A spring is not a spring without wonderful
families, families without relatives, or relatives
without friends.
Spring would not be spring without all these
wonderful things

Courtney Olivier

Survival In Time

At home in the house of my labyrinth mind,
   A crisis remained in the Passage of Time.
Memories shadow an uncertain face
   Elusively hovering ... what was erased?

Unbidden glimpses of yesterdays past;
   Gossamer frailties, disjointed grasp.
Kaleidoscope presence, encompassing eyes
   Revealing compulsions in silent reprise.

Plurality struggles in uneven gait,
   Broken pubescence cognition awaits.
Riven wounds webbing on deep feelings scarred;
   Tokens of promise deceitfully marred.

Angry yet fearful a child in the haze
   Now adult confronting the passage to gaze;
Hopelessly grooving repetitive band,
   Orphaned and desolate ... what price this land?

Dismantled counterpane yielding a view;
   Internal compass adjusted, renewed.
Identity unified disarms the grief;
   Experience owned, surprising relief.
   M. Elizabeth Thompson

Veterans Day

This is the eleventh of November
A day in history we should remember;
We were at war and on this day
Joy came to men dressed in khaki, white, blue and gray.

Men in khaki-Army ground troops;
At the front with guns or cannons in groups.
Some were medics for the wounded men
Who gave their lives as good Americans.

Men in white or Blue of the navy
Were sailors of the sea, some in submarines
Some on ships protecting harbors and waters rough and wavy
While guns or bombs tore into a troubled terrain

Men in gray - the Air Force clan
Roaming the war torn skies
Protecting our country and land
From such devastation as beneath them lies

Race or color were never a part
Of the patriotism in their heart.
They gave of their lives - a way
Of love, something which we can never repay.
God Bless All Veterans!
   Rowena A. Smith

If I Had Wings

If I had wings, I would have
A different perspective of the world.
I would see things no one else could;
I would do things no one else would.
If I had wings, I would fly to the heavens.
I would stop in the heavens and visit
my late friends and family.
I would fly to a place yet unseen,
I would go beyond my wildest dreams,
Like an eagle I would fly. I would soar to mountain tops and
survey the land.
If I had wings I would have a better perspective of the world.
If I had wings I wouldn't see all the violence and unrest in the world.
I would leave all my problems, worries and troubles behind;
I would leave them behind and hope they will be gone.
If and when I return
All the people that worry about me, would worry no longer.
If I had wings...
I would be free!
   Steven Lopez

Untitled

Who's that knocking on my window pane
A few drops of glistening rain
Pull back my blinds just in time
Lightening paints the sky
while clouds begin to cry
Tears of life hit the ground
with a calm pleasant sound
Quenching the thirst of every living thing
sparrows and robins begin to sing
   Tim Fish

The End

The gavel strikes and all is quiet in the room
A few last words are spoken and what once was is no more
How can you encompass thirty years of life
The picture in your mind is not a painting,
It is the word "Final" and nothing else.
You look around and all you see is what you left behind
A child once warm against your bosom stands silently
As teardrops fill his worried eyes
He is grown now, but comprehension of the end is still
A foreign thought to him.
How can one choose between a mother and a father
Which one shall he visit more?
There was always love there for him
In equal parts, not one part less or more
His brother's thoughts are just the same
The love no less for one parent or the other
The end has to be the beginning of a new life
A life of chance but just as filled with love
It is the end of togetherness and not the end of love
   Marianne Williams

Man's Creation

Wars are man's creation;
A force of evil destruction.
Armies trained to annihilate,
Changing gentle minds to hate.

Strategy of wars are mapped and planned
For acquisition of power and land.
Whether the cause be wrong or right,
Mother's sons bear arms to fight.

Opponents respond in defense,
Separating themselves by an imaginary fence.
Innocent victims caught in the violence;
In death, sealing their lips in silence.

Wars maim or kill the living,
Whether it be beast or being.
Mother Earth scorched by weapons,
Searing land with its possessions.

Man should take leave of war's evil ways,
And have thoughts for constructive beautiful days.
Those responsible must tell
Future generations: "WAR IS HELL!"
   Toine Fischman

Photograph Of Memory

In a photograph of memory I'll see you there:
   A place in time only you and I can share.
Together we will soar,
   Until there is no more,
But the essence,
   and the photograph of memory.
   Susan Chrysanthus Konnick

I Remember

I remember,
    A glance, across a crowded room

    A touch, as your fingers glaze my cheek
    A smell, as you slowly walk pass

I remember,
    The sparkle, in your eyes

    The warmth, in your smile
    The laughter, in your voice

I remember,
    A whisper, in the dark

    A longing, to touch you
    A tear, piercing my heart

I remember,
    Empty nights, thinking of you

    My body, aching to be touched
    My heart, crushed without your love

I remember...

Mary Hillman

My Mother's Field

My mother had a gentle way,
A kind and loving heart;
Should friend or foe but need her help,
She always did her part.

Alas, one day, death came to our door,
He took my mother's hand.
We watched as she slowly slipped away with him,
Though his victory we tried to withstand.

God let my mother see, before her death,
A place of peace and rest;
A sunny, quiet, field of green,
Among the Godly blessed.

Now, some folks say that Heaven's streets are made of gold,
And on these streets are mansions with riches yet untold;
But I believe the God himself opened Heaven's door,
In my mother's peaceful, field.

Margaret A. Hunter

I Found The Lily

I walked through the valley and there I did find
A lily, so pretty, my heart was inclined
To smell the fragrance to know it was real
When to my amazement, the lily could feel!

It was not a lily that grows by the way
For it was so different, so lovely and gay.
As I reached to touch it, it reached out to me;
My eyes were then opened, Alas! I could see!

This lily was Jesus who stood there alone;
He knew through this valley, soon I must roam.
So there in the valley, He touched me anew;
He strengthened my spirit with peace, hope and truth.

Then He gave me courage, the mountain to climb;
He led the way; I followed behind.
As I followed real closely, with help from my friend,
My mountain so rugged soon came to an end.

Marjorie Allen

Sea Shell

Sand along the endless edge of sea;
A lost and bewildered sea shell.
Only to be found and kept once.
Better than the rest, for now you can tell.

Only for short, cherished moments,
It is to be showed off to all strangers.
While being saved from the sea's ferocious pull,
And all other seaside dangers.

Dragged into the sunlight,
From the sand's dark shadow.
Blinded by the life never seen,
Deep down below.

Forgotten hardships of all the bad times,
Simple struggles to keep what is good.
It is time for all dreams to meet new reality;
Look back upon where hope once stood.

Onto a new place to be virtually free.
But to only be added to shells of the same.
Again a lost and bewildered sea shell,
Hidden within the others who have lost all fame.

Sarah Wedow

Little Boy Lost

A child for so short a time
A man grown too soon.
Responsibility so unwanted
Stark fear of the surfacing pain.
Loved but for a moment
Then a void unfulfilled.
Where has she gone?
"Why?" goes unanswered.
Warmth and protection disappear with a sob.
He must now be strong
His eyes shade the hurt deep inside
A cry echoes in blind anger
No one hears the call.
A house built on love has tumbled and
    fallen.
He erects a great wall
Hides all the doubting inside.
Expect not too much
Love is not always perfect
He'll just throw it away.

Marcia Goodman

Valentine Medicine

Lollipops and nerds, setting on the TV stand,
A memory of little boy blue
Here today, tonight bland.

One is cherry coated, filled with sticky gum,
One is yellow and red
"Sour medicine" says little-one.

I think about him often, separated from his days,
Funny how candy can be
A foreshadowing in the haze.

Mommy is gone again, to the lonely star state,
Looking for her cherry candy
And her heart-filled mate.

Selfish and adulterated, like a mix of yellow and red,
Little one you're so right
Sour medicine for the soul-dead.

We will always be here son, steadfast and few words,
And some day daddy will tell you
About the lollipop and the nerd.

Michael P. Ryan

What Is Life?

What is life but to live and die
A mere creature created to pursue the goals we create for ourselves
To somehow mature and grow within ourselves
To make our own decisions but yet always listen when others give orders
To live a life filled with happiness and joy
Yet it is unknown how to achieve these easy but difficult emotions
within ourselves
How do we express ourselves when we are taught to keep it inside?
Is there any meaning in this word Life?

Why do we live a life filled with pain and sorrow?
Why do we purposely and continuously hurt one another?
Do we really know what happiness is ?
How do we know when we've reached it?
Is it a warm embrace, a gentle touch, a soft word or a mere smile?
Will we ever be truly happy?

Trapped in a world I do not belong
Yet not knowing if there is a world where I do belong
If there is, how do I reach it; if there is not, where do I go
I wander aimlessly unknowing my destination

Madeline Martinez

A Mother's Vision

A mother's vision is when a child is born,
A mother's heart is being torn.
She doesn't know what their future will be
She will have to wait and see.
She can be a singer, or teacher
He can be a politician, president, or a preacher
Her life will always be in fear.
For what about she might hear.
He could be in a competition
She could read it in the next edition
A daughter is a daughter all her life
But a son is a son till he gets a wife.
His marriage could be bad,
He might be miserable or sad.
He or she could commit a crime
And serve a long sentence and time
So a mother's heart is torn.
When a child is born
She doesn't know, what his life is about
Whether his marriage will work out.

Mary Sysko

A Mother's Heart

Tolerant with tear and shuddered thoughts,
A mother's prayer has always brought:
Hopes and wishes fraught with care,
Where trifles and gold nay compare.

Her sacrifice constant yet constrained;
Led by faith and duty nor complain,
She works and toils with daily load,
Nor thinking her choice a task too bold.

She plans and schemes of ways to lead;
Her offspring fettered from misdeed,
She bathes them all in kindly light;
With nary a sway from left to right.

Great pleasure in each is her delight;
With patience cradled their first night,
A mothered care transformed her airy,
A rose or deed can never compare.

A. J. Thornton

Sista, Sista

Sista, Sista
a mountain you have climbed to show the world
your beauty which comes from inside.
You are intelligent, a woman who can stand
next to anything with pride
a woman never loosing your stride.

Sista, Sista
you have accomplished all that you desire,
the word defeat cannot touch what you aspire.

Sista, Sista
you are loving, a jewel to your friends
and a good woman for any man
who will love you to the end.
You are a role model for all to see
exactly what a woman is supposed to be.

Sista, Sista
I pray that you never loose your faith
for it is God who has made what you are today.
So continue being exactly who you are;
a classy woman with heart and Sista with charm.

Mitzi Greshawn Smith

Above And Beyond The Sun

Erupted from a tiny speck.
A new life had begun.
Shoved through the crust
Like a small mountain.

Upward and thicker
While leaves began to grow.
The branches stretched
For long were they asleep.

Above and beyond
While the pods began to evolve.
Slowly plunking to the ground
In smoky autumn.

Buried beneath the orange, yellow, and red
Quilted by Mother
To dream
Of beginnings.

Kate Pientka

Prisoner Of Ignorance

I sit here and watch the children
A new world of perception
Begins to unfold before my eyes

I being an able bodied person
Begin to see what I had taken
Advantage of so many times before.

The excitement I feel in my heart
As I witness these disabled children
Blossom and grow within this their world

I look at myself, to these children
I am not normal.
To myself they aren't either.
Where is the tie that could forever
bind us together?

Desperately I want to help these children
I want to be their miracle angel.

For now I am aware of how lucky
I am to be free from the disabilities.
I realize I am a prisoner
In this world of ignorance.

Kandie Davies

"Quiet Whisper"

Only in this opening dawn.
A new year begins, as the old one is gone.
I hear the rushing winds, bringing
in a new song.
A quiet whisper, that only you belong.
You give me a melody, that serenades
my heart.
It's as nothing, could tear us apart.
In this new beginning, we have
worlds, to conquer.
Love to spread, as its only weapon.
Where peace, would be completely accepted.
In a world gone mad, you're the best,
I ever had.
Only in this opening dawn. A new
year begins.
As the old one is gone.
I hear the rushing winds, bringing in
a new song.
A quiet whisper, that only you belong.
Michael Meade

"Mystery"

Mystery titillates a lake below
A parachute of mist
Suspicious are the waters' waves
A friend of nature daring a return to faith
A bird, a rabbit, and a deer
Listen to a silent song
A small sacrifice for sublime devotion
A ruthless game to begin
Illusive remains the Phantom
The pawn is moved to bewilder
Hoping the water is pure
An innocent diver
Surrender to Infinity…
Susanna Maier

Oswald's Grave

A journey and a morbid fascination;
A party of one and a Texas highway;
A tank of Gas and questions without answers.

A map and a mile from Oswald's grave.

The keeper; an old, old man.
As old as I hope to be some day.
2 weathered eyes and 6 hands that tell the story.

2 hands on the Bible.
2 hands on a clock, forever in motion.

Another clock; 2 hands stilled at 12:55 p.m.

Past the gate, to Oswald's grave.
Richard L. Street

"Someone I Hurt"

When I look in his eyes I see
a picture of her, when I look into
him I see a heart that's broken. I forgot
I did that. He was the joy of my life, till
I died. Now he doesn't see me 'cuz I'm
a ghost. If I could say one more thing
to him it would be "I love you, and I
always will." I could tell he still loves me. Because
he isn't havin' any fun. But I'll be waitin' for
him when he comes. The one I hurt,
my baby.
Kimberly Beem

"My Heart"

Someday in time,
a place for you,
for me,
separate…together,
don't be angry for what I've done to you,
to me,
I've loved before,
alone…together -
that certain time will come,
when we are one,
alone…together.
J. Averil Nicewarner

"My Little One"

Where have you strayed to, My Little One?
A place where clouds always hide the sun.
You are trying to win, but you always lose,
I fear you are lost in the Land of Booze.
Drifting back in time, your childhood years,
There is no way to stop the flow of tears.
My sweet, innocent child, gone for so long,
Was it my fault, did I do something wrong?
Always looking for an answer, why you put up that wall,
You are beyond my reach, in a haze of alcohol.
Things that used to matter, your family, your pride,
Are lost to you now, you choose to run away and hide.
The lies and deceit have already begun,
How can he trust you, your wonderful son?
You think he's not affected, so you just ignore,
Any signs that he's hurting, this child we all adore.
I can no longer watch you on your road to self-defeat,
Listening to your tales of feeling incomplete.
But if one day you wake up and suddenly see the sun,
I'll be here waiting, for I love you, My Little One.
Lindy Rickson

My Secret Place

I know a place - a very secret place
A place where warm, golden rays melt into deep orange
And then are consumed by fiery reds
Until there is only a burning white heat

I know a place where passion runs wild
Where kisses are long and lips are sweet
Where a touch knows no boundaries
And hands are free to explore

I know this place, and it's not very far
It's just beyond the moon on the other side of the sun
Nestled between two stars that left their glow to lead the way
We can get there in an instant or we can take our time
Let me know when you're ready, and we can share in my secret place
Stephenie E. Frazier

From The Mind Of A Curious Child

Whose child is this?
A child blithe, exuberant, and
Who is always asking questions, so many, to no end
Why is, what is, when will, where are and how did?
All these many forms that percolate and bubble up
From the mind of a curious child
A child young and immature
But with a mind alert, and observant, I am sure
As we respond clearly, to every posed query
The child, stimulated, will grow mind awakened
And mature, for sure, keen and well kenned
This child with a curious mind
Is mine.
Yoshiyuki Otoshi

A Rose

My first glance upon your beauty, so kind.
A rose. It transgress the boundary of my mind.
Extremely beautiful, fragrant flower.
Transpired from heavenly showers.
Tears of angelical beings, from heaven above.
Gracefully sprinkled it with beauty and love.
Intensified, the thought of you, a rose.
That you are, I had to look again.
The aroma from your love. Heaven I am in.
Such an overwhelming affect.
A rose.
You!!!
Beauty at its best....

Myron DeWarren Richardson Sr.

Another Angel Just Fell

They carry their weapons to prove themselves.
A shot rings out like the sound of a bell.
One is hit with a bullet; another is stabbed,
And God weeps, for an angel just fell.

For love of money, he pushes drugs all day.
He'll do anything to make the sell
To strangers or children. He doesn't care
That another angel just fell.

She drinks with her friends or alone at home.
Her parent's bar could fill a small well.
She just passed out behind the wheel, and
With four others, five angels just fell.

He ran from home when he was very young.
Now he lives on the streets of hell.
He sleeps in a box and eats what he can find,
And another angel just fell.

She's a user, an abuser, who's tried it all.
How often each day? Who can tell?
She doesn't even know she's conceived a child,
Or that because of her, God's tiniest angel just fell.

Karla R. M. Osborne

Oho - K!

The stride simple,
A steady gait. Supple spine,
my roots atendriled: water-grounded
Suckling nourishment and nurture... from almond-blossomed staffs,
regal nature's scepters: and wonted staves for my reed's rhythmic
cavorts.

Amidst tonal-directives, mystic huffs in synchronization.
My Being - kindred, inalienable; this way; that a sways:
experience unfolding - puffing - turns mine nectar laden vessel:
As the Breezes will and may. i, skipper,
Inspirited by Salt in frothy sprays,
glide the keel through an ambuscade of lethal, jagged stays.

With sea and sky, day and night, Peace abiding;
in meek and prudent measure; malleable - i - emancipated
from grand expectations - heartbreak's the pay... oh, how we slave
for devious delusions, paradigms opposing
amused Intuition's play. The way to do is to Be;
trust joys, raptures, pains...
As forms indispensable - integral - of sun and moon, rest and labor's
eons-old game.

Life's not a tussle: not by far - nay! 'Tis ever-growing
myriad-adventure; a rainbow-hued, chiaroscuro, total spectrum:
an imp's trek within a privileged, oft dreamt domain!
Kipling's "If...," with a host of others, leaping at you from a page,
along with Maturity's morn-dew, unveilers of Truth, shall footprint
the
Way.

J. L. Gonzalez

Life

Life is such a precious thing. As it starts it's
a small fragile thing with eyes wide open and mind
So free it begins each day to test its wings.
As days and years go by it finds its loves, hates,
and sometimes just sits and meditates on its past,
present and future things.
To wake one day and realize it is nothing more than
Just a borrowed thing, with this in mind, it sets
out every day trying new and exciting things each
time doing more dangerous things, its dreams
start to become obsessions and finds it knows no
fear and has no limitations.
With all that it has going for it, it looks in
the mirror and says to itself, it lives each
day to the fullest. With no regrets, no sorrow
and after all is said and done we realize...
Life is such a Precious thing.

Lana C. Cressler

"The Life Of A Rose"

A delicate little rose has been planted today
A soft and bright little bud just emerged right now.
For this rose is about to be unveiled of its beauty.

Those little red petals slowly emerge and the rose starts to express itself
In a few days, it will be a rose and fully matured
Now it is a beautiful rose, glaring at the sun

A few days later the rose is all worn out
Now its petals are beginning to fall off.
The beauty of this rose has vanished forever.

It is not looked at for beauty and radiance anymore
It is left as a reminder to us all
That we too have the same thing coming, age!

Lisa Dominic

"Gray Enlightenment"

Raw flesh and bone, an intricately complex chemical composition.
A soul, a heart/body and intellect bound together, forming a singular
part of humanity.
Immersed in a whirlpool of one's own ideals, culture and tradition.
Diversity but yet intolerance born of egocentricity and one's own vanity.
Why all this pain and sorrow bearing weight of misfortune and sedition?
Our greater power by any name, His plan for us surely was not this
prevailing insanity.
Minimization...a perception of ignorance born by indifference and
mistrust towards those not cloned like us, but having a different tradition.
Oh, human existence, look ye past bodies into culture and celebrate
acceptance, for only by doing thus can we be bound to one another in
love and humility.

LaVon Rigsby M.S.

Time

Time is a valuable commodity
A more precious element than gold
It has no shape or form
　It just exists.
Time cannot be manufactured, stored or stockpiled
Free time is not always free
It cannot be owned, yet it can be stolen.
When time is lost, it is gone forever
　never to be recovered
Our lives are scheduled to meet time frames
When it's time one must go
There is no control
It's just time.

Lois Gehrig

The Spark

Within the human BodyMind, what is the purpose of a spark?
A sparks ignites, if understood.
If fired up fierce passion plays upon the face of God,
within the heart of God.
MotherFather, light this realm.
Tend this carefully laid-out plan to fan these sparks to brilliant flame.
A spark is here in everything. Why be distracted by so much.
Illusions all - not well and good, not this or that, not us or them -
but just One Thing.
Yet, one is all - and all have sparks that must ignite.
Vast fires rage, yet can be held within the conscious, understood.
Held safely, held gently, even used to love and heal.
Within the human BodyMind, Matter is magnetic fire,
Spirit is electric fire. Wed together sparks the flame.
Let this Inner Light explain how to ignite Divine Flame.
Unify the BodyMind. Integrate the Heart and Mind.
Illuminate the Cosmic Mind.
Allow the fire to exclaim the Gods within,
Their Presence plain.

J. Bruce Wilcox

A Testament Of Solitude

A time to give, a time to live,
A time to share, a time to care.
A moment of peace, a moment to rejoice
A time out for prayer, with the church
    of one's choice.
Peace and tranquility are within one's
reach, along with the encouragement
from Jesus Christ, the one who can
    teach.
Life is a mystery, and we are given
choices along with a path,
For either the Lord's love or His wrath.
Life will teach us and prepare us for
either a life of pleasure or a life of pain
The choice is ours on whether we live
our lives in love or in vain. This
testament is not meant to be rude or
shrewd. This is just my
"Testament of Solitude."

Sherri Fletcher

Destiny

    With a flare of her nostrils, and
a twitch of her ears; the chestnut mare stars running.
    Her destiny unknown to anyone, she
throws up her delicate head and let's her mane fly in the wind.
    She runs for days, stopping for only a few hours of rest at night.
Her coat is no longer the color of copper.
It is dirty, and full of pine needles and burrs.
    So long she has run, so far away is her home and loving owner.
    Suddenly, her roof hits something hard and black.
Something she has never felt before.
    Curious, she walks onto the strange surface.
Only a moment later, she sees two large lights shined in her eyes,
and a strange noise pierces the air.
Paralyzed with fear, she doesn't move.
A split second later, her body lies lifeless on the side of the road.
She is a horrible sight. There is blood on her coat,
and she has broken bones.
    Finally, she has found her destiny.

Trina Steinmaker

Drifters

Drifters on an open sea.
A vast sea, full of waves
That can turn a man into a beast-
Ruthless waves, exhibiting no mercy on their prey.

And yet these same raging waves
Can be calm and gentle,
Surprising even the most hard-bent sailors-
At her chameleon change, and now placid face.

Suddenly the ever-changing sea is again on a rampage,
Against who or whom it is yet unknown,
But this hard-bent sailor recognizes the threat-
And makes ready for a trip into the furies.

As rapidly as the madness came, it is gone-
But not without undue harm,
For this hard-bent sailor is no more-
He is now one of the seas' many drifters forevermore.

Tatiana Tarbutton

Untitled

Life Gushes Without Restraint.
A waterfall of energy, emotion pours endlessly,
The rage of feelings swimming toward self-discovery.

Drenched in reality.
Intrigued by the beauty, bewildered by the pain.
A distant observer, riding turbulent waves.
Soaking with experience, the shore is still unknown.
Vast clear blue surrounds and encompasses.

A magnificent view of the world.
No charted destination, floating through lonely isolation.
Shifting tides - the whirlpool of fate.

Thoughts drift, dreams set sail.
Open arms stroke toward change - relentless faith.
The soul navigates journeys of the heart.
From the surface not much can be heard or seen.
Trickling sensitivity cleanses internally.

Uncompromising wildlife.
Suspended between the land and sky.

Kortney Oates

Your True Reflection In The Mirror

    A person looks in the mirror and sees
a whole lot more than what people expect her to see.
    Besides a pretty face, not thinking of such
things as its style and grace
    Unaware of either big eyes or lips, no
recognition of any tooth chips.
    She yearns for her true side to show forth,
desperately wanting to know the real insides, of course.
    Totally convinced there's something more than
just a twinkle in an eye, relies on the fact that the one
Mind can't lie
    Which brings knowledge of herself:
purity, goodness has been surrounding her in wealth.

Rebecca Sue Maurer

My Name Is Tudy - I Am An Alcoholic

    My name is Tudy. I am an alcoholic. My daddy was an
alcoholic. He was also a horrible person. Am I a horrible
person, too? I don't want to be a horrible person. I don't
want to be an alcoholic. Please, God, don't let me be an
alcoholic. Don't let me be a horrible person.
    I hate my daddy. I also hate myself. My daddy is dead.
I am dead also. I have a family. They love me. I love them.
My name is Tudy. I am an alcoholic.

Tudy McNabb

47

Untitled

Start now,
a world joined together, holding hand in hand,
happiness surrounds me, all throughout the land,
children playing safely, walking down the street,
talking to each other, the kind I like to meet,
a peaceful land of dreamers, a wondrous place to be,
I don't think you see it, but it comes clear for me,
watching out for others, isn't hard to do,
you be nice to me, and I'll be nice to you,
keeping in my heart, what the future brings,
maybe we can fix all the terrible things,
maybe we can stop the violence, maybe we can love each other,
I will be your sister, and you can be my brother.

Kelli Thunell

We Live In A World

We live in a world, a world of pain,
a world of anger, a world of shame
where color's what matters
and hearts become shattered
by our pitiful minds, that are against different kinds.

We live in a world, a world to blame,
for all of the problems that still remain
in a society of prejudice, in which we can't face;
prejudice against the other race.

We can change our world, to a world of peace,
where equality's what matters and all problems cease.
We must ignore the color of another person's skin,
when we should be thinking of how to begin
a new friendship with someone of a different background,
when in fact the world's turning 'round.

We live in a world of different faces,
a world of people from different places.
Everyone's special and has their own mind in which
they should use to treat others who are kind,
in a way in which they wish to be treated.

Kimberly Pflueger

Time

Have you often wondered
about this particular word
That lives with us throughout our lives
each and every day

Time, time is not just a number
Nor is it a simple phrase
Neither is it a word, that can be toss away.

Time, is for all seasons, that comes each year
Time, is morning, noon, and night.
For time is always here
Time, is happiness, sadness, also our fears

It's our lives that's basis on time
And how we live it from day to day
For time is the essence of what we do
As well as what we say

Time, is for sickness, as well as to heal
Time, is our do's and don't
For only time will be fulfilled
It's our lives that's basis on time
so live it with tranquil.

Linda J. Anthony

The Edge Of Insanity

My mind is built like the largest empire,
Absorbing all the knowledge it can acquire,
And when a part of it does expire,
It gets soft and wet like a quagmire.

The headache rages through me like wildfire,
Burning into my mind a boisterous bonfire,
At night when I lay down to retire,
My nightmares wake me with torrential ire.

There are no voices singing in a choir,
Only my wakening screams telling a sad satire,
The results of these traumas are very dire,
From all the mental anguishes that transpire.

They stay with me burning like a roaring fire,
Like an open wound with no attire,
Leaving my sanity without any desire,
I shall destroy these memories before I expire.

Man and the Devil they try to conspire,
To place my brain, mind, and sanity on an open byre,
But with all the strength that I can acquire,
I will once again build the largest empire.

Karen A. Blackmer

Orpheus at Dachau: Reflections While Visiting the Holocaust Museum

(for mh)

Sepia photos, hard wood bunks, pocked ceramic soup bowls,
actual footage; whole towns vanished, tattooed survivors,
tactical maneuvers, several heroes.

Rooms deep in dust and leather splay each foot's outline;
recognizable heel prints remember each ankle, describe each toe
and name names.

Like my little Moses boy's pajamas cast in wool and hanging
from a hook with the elbows round, knees and toes waiting —
no doubt which "ghost" owns these!

"Brush your teeth," I tell him. "Have your bath; put on your
jammies with that little dance you do: first one leg, now the other.
I'll help you keep balance. Now come lie down beside me;
We'll read a story worth your haste."

Orpheus played his lute and became almost charming, nearly
regaining what Hades once stole. Orpheus, dance faster!

Quick! Where are our night clothes? Time to bathe quietly,
to dance in and wrap up all that's pounding in the arms of a story —
one that tenderly comforts Holocaust eyes
washed brighter by tears.

Vicky Dill-Schreiner

Flow Of Life

God I see as He smiles from a child
Again Him I see as one struggles for life
Should not this make me meek and mild
The thrill of the living - peace, love, and no strife

Then of a sudden am I smote with a sting
A bolt from beyond was thrown by a sling
Between sunrise and sunset a storm does brew
It vents its fury - will I make it through

Ever onward go I in my path
Fear I my God and His Righteous Wrath
Life courses its way from head to heel
A strengthening surge from Him I feel
Giving newness and direction as I respond
For this flow of life comes from beyond

Richard D. Cagg

Jealous Of The Holly Tree

Seasons in the south are more discreet.
After the last turkey sandwich is tugged with sticky fingers
from its bag, before Caesar's ghost cringes at a lost warning,
greasy puddles may grow out of the asphalt,
nurtured by a charcoal sky,
and the palms may have some romance torn away by a vagrant wind.

Seasons in the north terrify.
After the homecoming crowd has evaporated
king and queen huddle in a flood of starlight,
misplacing curfews, hypnotized by the towering pines.
The veins of every leaf cry for the thick plastic vibrancy
they used to be. Settled into their winter hues
pumpkin, gold and deep amber, sunset fragments lining the rooftops,
a frost churns through the satin air, threatening the tissue paper
they have become. Broken by the grimace of cloud, each stem
exerts a double strength, stretching the thinnest fibers,
willing life back into the branch. They feel others release
only to crumble under the heel of a child.

In the rich wet ground beneath the tree
they might sink and feed and sprout into warmth again
but they shudder at the risk, and hold on.

Robyn Condit

"Poor Old Mr. Possum"

Well, Mr. Possum's lying dead in the middle of the road,
All flattened out like a big fat toad.
Thinking he just had to get to the other side,
He never thought he might lose his hide.

Was he crossing for fun, or going for food?,
It does not matter, he is no longer in the mood.
If Mr. Possum had stayed in the persimmon tree,
He would still be as well off as you or me.
But Mr. Possum never counted on an old Ford van,
Driven by an eighty year old nearsighted man,
Coming out of nowhere, and coming mighty fast,
But when he saw it, he knew it was the last.

One of the last thoughts on Mr. Possum's mind,
Was, "how can anything be so unkind?"
And the last thought he had just before he died,
Was, "I sure wish I knew what is on the other side."

Poor old Mr. Possum. Good-bye Mr. Possum.

Robert E. Tew

Concern For Others

Life is sort of funny with
all its twists and turns
If you pay a little attention it's
amazing what one learns
Some of the most intriguing truths
are not learned while in school
Many come from just practicing
the good old Golden Rule
The more one socializes and reaches
out to their fellow man
The more you understand that people
haven't changed much since the world began
Love is so sorely needed and yet it's
the easiest thing to give
It makes no sense at all to withhold it
from those with whom you live
You don't have to say "I Love You"
but simply show you care
This concern for others can be practiced,
very easily, almost anywhere

Thomas S. O'Donoghue

The One I Love

Sexy smiles and dancing eyes
All of this makes me realize
That when I'm lost in this foray,
It makes me want to live for today
Then I pray to the heavens above
To help me find the one I love.

Heart of Gold and a precious soul
Please, God, help me achieve this goal.
Emptiness and confusion lie all around
It's hard to keep my feet on solid ground.
Save me from what I'm dreaming of,
Please bring to me the one I love.

And now it's dark and I'm alone,
And I think of how I've grown.
Now she's dead, and I am lost.
I think to myself, what was the cost?
Bring to me the peace of the dove.
Oh, God, please protect the one I love.

Nick C. Grayem

To Brian And His Fight With AIDS

In the absence of light, a flower fades away;
Alone and in the dark, it pulls away and frays.
In a matter of seconds, his roots could start to dry;
Echoing only a whisper, sad, empty, cry.
Even after a shower, steady, pouring rain;
The mark of death lingers, stopping all the pain.

In a matter of minutes, the wilting could begin;
Falling, falling, quickly, shriveling his skin.
Even after one second, an echo of a voice;
Once spoke of nurture, then took away the choice.

The flower once felt passion of care, then it began to fade;
He withers his existence, lies in the grave, for him, was made.
He 'drank' the wrong supplier, looking for his food;
Now he slowly crumbles over, dangling oh so crude.
But it would never happen, in love he once said;
Then his existence as a flower, was pronounced dead.

Forever in the past, what he felt in a second of love;
Now the flower eats his anger, in a land above.
Living dies out helplessly, the flower is bereft;
And one lonely, shattered petal, lies on the ground he left.

Kathryn Long

Farewell From Sophie - And To A Beloved Puss!

No "meows" today, Mama
Although I love you so.
No "meeows" today, Mama
Because I've gone away!

No "meeows," my darling Boss
Although I love you too!
No "meeows" today, my friends
But I'll always be with you!

No "meeows" today, Mama
But try to look for me
In every blossom, plant and flower
In every leafy tree.

No "meeows" today, Mama
But I am by your side
And God in all His mercy
Will let me be your guide.

Marilyn H. Curry

Keep The Faith

When your life seems to be going nowhere, don't give up
always care, the one up above won't give you more than you
can bare, keep the faith, remember tomorrow will be a
better day. If for some reason it's not, just pray, you will
soon see all your troubles will go away, keep the faith.

Time will heal, just believe in the power it's real, there
are times when despair we all feel, keep the faith, your
zeal! Follow your dreams, no matter how hard it may seem,
keep the faith, your dreams will come true, tell yourself
there's nothing you can't do.

Success is within your reach, apply yourself, express
your thoughts, always keep in mind what was taught, keep
the faith. The day will come to taste the juices of the
peach, there are mountains, and hills to climb, but you'll
get there it's just a matter of time. If someone should reach
the top before you, keep the faith, don't feel left behind.

Phyllis Mobley

Dawning Of A Heart

His warmth and light caressed the dawn to greet the birth of day
Amid the paths we'd chosen to guide us on our way

Where angelic cooing shadows danced upon our cheeks
As if to say..come this way..it's love's crossroad that man seeks

Loosed from our memory's bonds springs forth a captive list
Of life and love and beauty lost, of treasures we had missed.

In retrospect we failed to pause to greet the gentle breeze
The creator's gift of life and breath for man and beast and trees

We might have shared that single word or gestured with a smile
And erased the tears from someone's heart and made our life
worthwhile

We should have been more caring but in our youth we did not see
Who helms the ship in which we will sail for all eternity

Time teaches that the beauty found in every passing day
Is measured not in what we have but give along the way

Be faithful in believing that the signs sent from above
Are saying to your heart and soul there's no greater gift than love

Michael James Soroka

Christian Call

Can't you hear them cry, a waning tear
among so many
The children numbered days, if any
The once proud peoples' agony, anguish again
Listen all ye sovereign souls, cries, now death they win

We of plenty, rich and rare
Can't you see us losing there
Lest we hope and try in vain
Scattered souls upon the plain

Patrick E. Yore

I Wish.....

I wish I were as the trees
and could blow free with the breeze.
I wish I were as the bees
so across the whole land I could see.
I wish I were as the deer
so every little sound I could hear.
I wish I were as the cat
so on my back I would receive a pat.
But as for now these wishes can't be
so I guess I have to settle for just being me.

Melena Jean Adams

Mystics Incorporated

Is this where my God hides?
Among the eucalyptus and the desolation
Kakadu's awakening, and its morning cry steals
the heart of the phantom dawn
does it hide in the dance of the wind
or in the patterns of the fallen dying leaves
does it hide from me at all?
Or I from it?
Broken velvet breeze, whisper your name
and I'll bow down
silent stone fences, show me its path
we beat upon the sun, yet peace doesn't come
SHOW ME YOUR FACE!
I'll stare at the lines upon it
and think out loud..
I'll ease your pain (if it can be done)
Reigning visions of rain will sweep away this bareness
are you all eyes and no face...
or no eyes...all face?
Shadows' rage, ignorance...Hope...

Lawrence Toole

Emptiness

My life is a hole,
An emptiness in my soul
I hope I can disappear soon,
Because I feel like a caterpillar in a cocoon
Nothing good happens around me,
But soon I will grow, grow like a tree
Beautiful, natural, ordinary, and new,
People will love me and they could love you too
If you give life a chance goodness will turn your way,
If you don't want it to happen you can just sit around and lay,
lay, lay
But do give it a chance please do, really do,
Because I love you and others do too
If you're black, white, a mix, or all three,
I am just telling you to be all you can be.

Star DiFilippo

To Be Me

I wish I was a candle, then I could show the way.
An eternal flame burning, a flame that has power.

I wish I was a rose, with folding petals of love,
to take an ugly wall, and make it beautiful
To creep through each crevice, climbing toward the sun,
embraced by light.

I wish I was a dancer, whose presence could stutter your heart beat,
whose grace could open a flower, whose strength greater than any man.

I wish I was a painting, taught all the secrets, colorful and bright,
dull and gray.

I wish I was a canyon that could home a mighty river,
or move a grand mountain
Where you could see beauty in each layer of my earthen years.

I wish I was an owl, with great big eyes to see whose call could
make you think.
Holding so much knowledge, passing it on without consent.

I wish I was a child, whose tears could make you laugh,
Whose smile could make you cry, whose giggles filled you with joy;
whose possibilities were endless, who held the key to your dreams.

But maybe I am all these things, and if I am not,
Maybe it doesn't matter. Maybe I am enough.

Patricia Siudut

Fallen Memories

Frail child, laughing in the shade of
an oak tree, staring up, grasping at
the life in the branches, spinning
in circles, falling down, drunken with
dizziness. Laughing in those lazy days
of summer.

Small hand raised to block the sun, tiny
eyes peering from behind, a broken string,
her kite still fluttering in the wind,
falling quickly, pelting the ground with
rain, the sky cracks and moans. She stands,
engulfed completely by storm.

Damp hair falling in around her face, tear
stained cheeks, puffy eyes and a lost voice.
Time is an unreliable companion, the weight
of a year lies upon her heart. Her kite has
fallen, her summer has faded to autumn, and
her mother has died.

Leslie Deaton

Renovation Time

Just as the construction crew tears down
an old abandoned building to replace it
with a new one.

That very same thing is happening to me, so
please be patient because God's work has just begun.

Just like that old building where everything
has to be replaced with better things.
Well, I'm like that old building and everything
has to be replaced from the heels of my feet
to the roots of my hair strings.

So when God is finished with me I know
I will outshine that newly renovated building.

Because unlike that building, I can and I will
continue to grow from my Master's work of renovation.

Sharon Mahaffey

The Golden Heart

Do I see a heart of gold?
An unsolved mystery,
A story untold.
My love for you as it is today
Will it last forever?
Only this I pray.
Is this real, or is this not?
It's been so long
that I forgot.
My love for you grows each day.
I can only show you
In my special way.
My heart has been broken time and time again
I need your love
To heal me, my friend.
All I need is your magic touch
To heal my heart
It doesn't take much.
The secret is, it has to be true
Before I say the words "I love you."

Tammy Collier

The Dance

All it took was one short glance
And a question, "May I have this dance?"
A movie, some talk who would have thought
That such small things could tie a lover's knot?
Roses, candy, and joyful smiles;
Loving to talk, and meet for awhile
Those sparkling gems on black velvet above
Helped to weave the miracle of love,
And shimmering sand bathed in moonbeams
Provided a scene for whispering dreams.
Then one day, a look so imploring,
Pulling timidly at the very heartstrings-
All it took was one reply:
"I'll dance with you until the end of time."

Karena Dawnwood

The One

The one I care for,
and always think about.
Sweet and sensitive,
understanding to my feelings.
Who is always there for me when I need him.
Listening to my problems,
letting me cry on his shoulder.
The one I need.
Always a problem here and there,
never one that goes unsolved.
The one I love.
My feelings are hard to express,
the words aren't there.
Even though I'm unable to express in words,
he knows how much I care.
The one,
I grow closer and closer to every day.

Sherry Van Bramer

Ambivalence

We humans are very complex
and ambivalence does us vex.
We do not resent a wooden post,
but always the one we love the most.
The whore often turns a trick,
but hates every Harry and Mick.

When I am the household host,
I want to be nice the most,
but I also wish our talkative dinner guest
would see the clock and leave us at rest.
I do not want to live forever,
but the time for death is never.

When boredom is in our range
our condition we would exchange.
But we also want the security
that comes only from continuity.
If urges were of one kind,
we would have more peace of mind.

But only if human nature has a revision
will we shed our inner division.

Vincent A. Camarca

Rose

Every time I reach for that Rose
An ouch is heard as the thorn
Of pain inflicts a wound upon my hand
And once again I withdraw
But, thoughts are there forever
Forever, reaching for that Rose

Robert J. Morrow

"All That Time It Was The Art Of Noise"

"Moments In Love."

Hot was the night
And as tense as it could be.
Light only from television appeared.

At first, movement was made.
Then shadows appeared, it came.
Down it went, but up again it came,
higher than before.

Sounds are around but not clear to make out.
Against the wall it seems.
Hotter it became, closer it got
stern it was.
In and out... In and out.
Wet? Maybe from the rain.
But no rain coat to obtain.

Sticky it was as the heat dried the
wetness up so quickly.
Hot was the night
and as tense as it could be.

Ms. Nathlon N. Jackson

Jean Marie

A rose in winter never dies
And as we sparrows roost, grounded
Her effervescent spirit flies.

She is watching us from that tranquil place
That we who are earthbound will always chase
And cannot attain until called.

She knows what's in our hearts
What we always meant to say
She knows all of our thoughts on any given day.

She also weeps for our grief and our sorrow
Yet, for her, like us
There is the promise of tomorrow.

She embraces our pain and yet it will ebb, then one day
We shall meet face to face
In that lovely, peaceful and tranquil place.

A rose in winter cannot ever die
And never forget that while we cry,

Jean Marie is as soulfully free
As we are all intended to be.

Mary Elizabeth Hooghuis

West Texas Delight

West Texas delight, I love your day
and crave your night.
Your wind feels good;
It burns with sand.
How can they scorn this awesome land.

West Texas, sprawling, sun scorched, dry baked,
a million mini-universes within your great expanse,
Is your magnificent beauty veiled, or hidden?
Does a man's eye see West Texas delight by chance?

You are energized with life, West Texas;
You are quieter than the whisper of a sparrow,
Desolate, sparse, spare, a hundred miles I view,
Active, busy, in transition of life, wide narrow.

A tumbleweed, once green, gives up the ghost,
Begins to tumble, roll and roast
Under the burning, blistering, glorious sun.
West Texas delight, I love your day
And crave your night.

Nancy McCann

When I Was Down With Deep Despair

When I was down with deep despair
and asked the Lord why no one cared,

A gentle hand had touched my tears
and washed away those awful fears.

I felt a wing, an "angel's touch,"
a compassion and strength that meant so much.

And then so softly, I barely heard
the sound of an angel in every word.

"Oh, you say I've not been there,
to embrace and comfort your every care?

But you always had the ability
to open your eyes and look at me!

For I've kept a vigil upon your life,
with every tear and every strife.

My wings have covered your very soul
and kept your life within its goal.

So, when you think that no one cares,
just look around and I'll be there."

Your Guardian Angel

Sharon A. Woss

To One Who Cared

That day when wings of dusty darkness passed
   And brushed my soul, a truth I learned to face:
   Compassion is a gem of narrow space
Indifference is infinite and vast.

Though some there were who half had feigned to care,
   When grief arrived, they modified their tune.
   They had no heart for shadows in the noon,
And Sympathy was unaccustomed fare.

But thou, my ever-faithful one of all,
   A challenger alone upon the lists
   Thou came among the wan and weary mists,
And heard the heart and hollow of my call.

When earth was blasted with disordered tone,
   I heard thy comfort's pure melodious sound;
   I searched the cold and touchless void, and found
One hand in all the world, and thine alone.

R. William French

Basketball

If I could be a boy again, I would set these reading glasses aside
And close this worn leather briefcase.
I would shut my office door behind me and slip on a pair of high top sneakers
The black canvas kind that smells of dirty socks
Not white leather that look like success.

We would run out on that court together and hear the squeaking of our soles
Against the waxed wood and feel the warmth of the rigid leather in our hands
I would feel the air rush near my face as you came driving, blocking running, past me.
When you stretched your lean body taut and straight
My fingers would be next to yours and
We would tip the ball into the orange metal hoop together.
The walls of the gymnasium would echo with cries of victory
And the shouts and cheering for you would be for me too and
I would be your friend.

If I could be a boy again
And not your father.

Meryl L. Martin

Buggies And Beaus

I'm glad I grew up in the olden days
And did my chores in the old fashioned ways.
We worked with things that no longer exist,
'twas the happiest time of my life, I would insist.

The horses and harness and headers and harrows,
The sickle and sows and stubble and sparrows-
Our work had to be done then put away the hoes,
The time was not yet for the buggies and beaus.

The pitchforks and posts and plows and planters,
The rakes and the rabbits, the roofs and the rafters-
All needed attention plus shoot all the crows,
Before we took time for the buggies and beaus.

Clean out the baler the barn and the bin,
Take care of the team the tank and the tin-
Open the road from all of the snows,
We'll soon be off with our buggies and beaus.

After the work was all said and done,
Came the time we could have our fun.
Hurrah! Get ready for the So La Te Do's,
At last it is time for the buggies and beaus!

Marjorie Andrasek

My Upbringing Was Firm And Stable

Living a Christian life - the Lord always made us able;
And early in life, I was known for my creation
That was the beginning, of my quest called "Determination;"

A decision to continue, to keep on living
I have great testimony, for this more than abundant, giving;

In my hands was put the life of two
God saved all three of us - now I know I have something to do;

Trust in the Lord with all thine heart - Proverbs 3:5
And towards a more sacred place - I do strive;

I must confess and believe myself - that Jesus rose for me
And at the day of judgment - it is God's face that I will see;

God sent his angels down to protect each of us
And I can picture satan now - making a big fuss;

Although I was determined to stay alive
At my door of judgment - Jesus did arrive;

When my work is through - to God be the glory
And with praise and true worship - I'll end this "Determination"
  story.

Melanie A. Smith

Crying In The Shadow

And if I'm crying in the shadow, over losing my best friend,
And feeling nothing less than her could let me love again.
With nothing left to show her, and nowhere left to turn,
In silence I'll adore her -
In my heart she'll always burn.

If one word could tell of heartache, like I have over you,
I'd softly speak just once forever, that's all I'd have to do.
You see, I tried so hard to tell you -
But the words just never seem to describe the way I'm feeling
and what this lady means to me.

So, if forever means without you - it has no place for me.
Just leaves me crying, in the shadow, of a Love -
To never be.

E. Blake

A Magical, Mystical Morn

Clothed in light and beauty, Aurora slowly rose,
And flung her robes across the sky,
And a new beginning was born
On a magical, mystical morn.

She dispelled darkness with a blaze of light.
And warmth encircled the world.
So, the curtain of darkness now was torn.
On a magical, mystical morn.

"For light is love," she whispered,
"And its radiance helps you grow.
With hearts no more forlorn"
On a magical, mystical morn.

"You are all heirs of the giver of love.
And beautiful children of light
Now, let light and love in your hearts be born.
On this magical, mystical morn."

Peggy Litz

A Poem To My Mother

For this the season to be together me and my mother always
and forever. She is always here to love, always here to care.
I'll always have my mother and the special love we share.

She does everything she can for me so i know her love is true.
Our love will always stand strong no matter what we will go through.

This is my way to give you praise and grace my one and only
mother and my heart is your righteous place. I miss you when
you're gone, I love you when you're here. I hope you know
when I say this that I am truly sincere. I'll always be her
daughter, she'll always be my mother and one thing is for
certain that I'll never forget how to love her.

Valentine Toohey

The Boy In The Loft

The children heard their mother singing praises to the Lord
And heard their Father praying to God for the family he adored.

They told the children of one who came from heaven many years ago
The reason He came, they told them, was because He loved them so.

Howard, one of the boys, listened and in his heart he knew
he had sinned and disobeyed God - but he knew what to do.

He took his Gospel of John to the barn - climbed into the loft,
There he heard God's voice speaking to his heart ever so soft.

As he read, his heart was touched with God's love
And that day in the loft, another name was written in The Book above.

As Howard grew to manhood, God's word became more dear,
And he witnessed to many, making the message of God clear.

Life wasn't always easy with temptations,
trials and times that were tough,
But he faithfully followed Jesus - He was always enough.

He was pastor of a church - weddings, funerals, visiting,
doing his best.
And over 28 years many hearts and lives have been blessed.

Howard was faithful and dependable, his preaching fervent.
Surely someday he'll hear the words "Well done,
good and faithful servant."

He has told us the message of God's love so oft,
It's blessed to look back and see how God used that boy in the loft.

Lucille Martens

The Divine Life Within

The all-powerful life of God moves in and through me,
And I am whole, well and strong
Energy and vitality of God lies within me
Through my mind and body where it does belong.

I am not always consciously aware
Of the divine life within,
But it is always there at work
Healing cell and organ, again, again.

God created me to be whole and strong
So that I can participate fully in life
I can claim my wholeness now
And do away with all my strife.
Because I am sustained and upheld
By deep inner faith and love
I radiate the life and vitality
Granted by my father up above.

Vivian Young

Rain

Rain - Full of repose
And I can hear the pulsation of drops on
the roof
I must refrain from falling asleep
From being slowly lured by the vehement cloud
of rain
Beneath its profound darkness
It has the audacity to laugh hypocritically
It's my supposition that rain will vex me
again today
Speaking cunningly as if in triumph over me
Rain - It must be stopped
And today I will dismember it from my thoughts

Steve Andersen

If To Fly

From this mountain, we can see everything.

In the distance I see a fountain.
And I can only imagine how it sings.

There is a long, deep lake nearby,
but to get there we must learn to fly.
The first thing is to be confident and ready.
The next is to keep your imaginary wings steady.

Under this lake and through some caves,
there is a special and serene place.
It's a place of fantastic illusion.
It is absent of death and confusion.

Of this place, only I know.
And to one ever have I shown.
So if you'd like to give this place a try,
You must find some wings and learn to fly.

Mark Ramsey

Flowers Plucked Too Soon

The cannons have thrust their last fusillade
And the snapping sounds of rifles have abated
After dispatching their lethal messages.
Bodies, still strewn in their grotesque forms,
Profane the earth where once pristine fields
Flattered the eye to the far horizon.
Now a deathly silence falls heavy here
Upon a ghastly sight too often seen,
Repeated ceaselessly from ancient times.
In the silence of this numbing sight,
We can hear the pleading echoes across time:
Why? We were all of us flowers plucked too soon.

H. Nelson Fitton

It's You Lord

When the day's gone wrong with no luck in sight,
And I come home late from my work at night,
there's only one that can make things right,
It's you Lord.

Problems melt away with your cheerful smile,
and you show that you care in you own quaint style,
For all these things I would walk a mile,
Just for you, Lord.

There are many rules from which to choose
but the rule I follow is not new
I keep only the ones you want me to,
I love you Lord.

When I come at last to that river so wide
I will not fear at the rising tide
If I can but see your face on the other side
It's you Lord.

Rose Ann Thomas

He Winked At Me Today

He winked at me today
And I was walking on air,
I started staring dreamily out the window,
And absently twirling a lock of my hair.

I became so happy,
I put a smile on my face,
I floated down the hallway,
Instead of going at my usual pace.

The weather may be cloudy,
And the sky may be gray,
But nothing else matters,
Because he winked at me today.

Tracy Dudek

Grandma's Curtains

I stand at the door,
And I watch the sun,
Splashing down on the hardwood floor.

Daisies sitting on the table,
Some hanging, drooping from the jar.
Moving in the breeze as much as they are able.

The bed is made now,
And the pillows all plumped up.
The rustling bedspread fringe takes a carefree bow.

Waving in the room,
The curtains move with the wind.
Dancing over the sadness and gloom.

This was grandma's place,
This is where she rested.
Where I last saw her smiling face.

She still occupies this room.
I know because,
Her curtains wave at me.

Roselle E. Rappette

I Imagined

I came upon an open field,
and imagined it a forest.
I came upon a desert,
and imagined it an ocean.
I came upon a patch of weeds,
and imagined it a rose garden.
Then I came upon you,
and you were more than I could imagine you to be.

Stacey L. Miller

54

Teacher

Give me hope,
and I will fly.

Give me courage,
and I will rise once more.

Give me faith,
and I will always love.

Give me strength,
and I will not fail.

But give me evil,
and I will find the courage to fight back.

Give me pain,
and I will find the faith to carry me through.

Give me hate,
and I will find the hope to withstand.

Give me wounds,
and I will find the strength to heal.

Theressa Billings

Combined Spirits

One Selfish Prayer Warrior

I was blessed with the armor of God
and I can do all things, through Christ
Who strengthens me.
Now I command you, Satan, Get Thee behind Me
In the Name of Jesus.
Victory is mine, all mine!
Praise the Name of the Lord!
Amen.

One Lamb Astray

Hear my voice, over the wind-blown leaves.
I see through the eyes of an alien.
I wander on, though weakness sets in.
Buzzards swarm the air, as patience is a virtue.
To find my Shepherd... as to move a mountain.
I have lost my way... as a road to Nowhere.

Inspiration

Warrior Spirit passed through the Lamb,
Like a plow in the field.
Fertilized with Love, words form
as though seeds were sprouting.
Inheritance of artistic talents
harvested.

Ronald A. Strong

"Surrender"

Break the dried stem of the basil plant
  and it gives forth its fragrance
The fragrance of the gardenia blossom
  is more intense as it darkens and begins to die-
Nature shows us that oft times when
  it's in stress it gives forth its sweetest aroma-
The lessons of the Spirit life is much
  like those of the natural life
In brokenness we reach forth for the
  love and peace of Jesus
In dying of self we give forth the
  sweet aroma of compassion
In the surrender of our life itself
  we give forth joy
So in brokenness, dying and surrender,
  We gain the only true life - Jesus Christ

Maxine Gollberg

"Love"

Love is a precious thing, that springs from the heart of God.
And is shown toward every one of us, who walk upon this sod.
Yes! Love is eternal, and is extended by God, to every man.
It strikes a resounding note in his heart, and reverberates back again.

We know it was God's love expressed to us, through his Son.
Fulfillment of our redemption, designed by God,
before the world begun.
The love of God is powerful, it cannot be broken, even by sin.
Love sent Christ to die on the cross, to buy man back again.

And when we accept him into our heart, God's love is shed abroad.
It overflows and reaches out, to other souls upon this sod.
For God so loves the people of this world, he gave his only Son.
That whosoever believes in him, a new life has begun.

H. Fitzgerald Durbin

Future Holdings

A son was born, bringing bag-loads of joy! Cute, cantankerous, smart and sassy, all after six months What does his future hold?

His parent hold grandeur of great athleticism, wit, charm, humbleness and intelligence, traits found in the heroes of the 90's like Andre Agassi, David Robinson, Julie Krone, or Coach K.

In touch with today's adolescence, his grandparents speak of the issues youths. Funny how the spoked wheel of history comes around. Race issues. America remembered the Civil Rights movement of Selma Alabama twenty years back. Today in Michigan, people of color, who are looked up to, threaten work stoppages to protest whitey's role in ceasing undesirable behavior exhibited publicly by a person teaching and unfortunately, influencing children whose minds have yet to develop such prejudice....

In touch with today's world, his great-grandfather speaks of issues on lifestyle. "When I was twenty the word stress was not in existence. Now, I here about being stressed out and chuckle to myself. "Working 50-70 hours weekly, feeding family, fixing frozen pipes, up-rooting often for the job and still able to find some semblance of self esteem, assuredness and motivation to continue forward. It is certain he never imagined today's world and what it stored us grandchildren as we continue forward.

Investing today is not a sure thing, unless you take out risky variables such as prejudice, nouveau excuses.

Take stock in Future Holdings like our children and ourselves, changing things we can, attitudes and behavior. Be loving, accountable, open-minded, willing to accept change and communicate. Only then can we be as whole as the sports heroes mentioned and collect the interest on our Future Holdings.

Thomas Lilly

My Dad

I can still picture you in the yard-
And in my mind's eye, I still see you holding the cat
Or feeding the birds and chasing the squirrels away.

When I close my eyes tight,
I can almost hear that chair squeaking
And when I sit at your desk, I feel your presence.
There's a part of you everywhere.

I still feel the ache when I recall the words
"Your father is gone."
Because the Lord called you home without warning,
I never said "Good-bye."
But because you lived your life for the Lord
And showed me how to,
I know a calm assurance that I will see you again one day.

....I didn't need to say "good-bye" after all.

Shirley Young

55

You Too Are Very Rare

I Often ponder my existence,
And know a God there must be.
For in all the universe there is no other like you or me.

He made the birds that fly,
And each heavenly body in the sky.
And each as you can see is made quite differently.

So always remember that God made you with love and care,
And like each bird and flower,
You too are very rare.

Lucille D. Dula

I Would Like To See My Mom

Dear God, can you let me see my Mom? I just want to talk to her,
and let her know that forever in my heart she'll have a place.
If I have to die this moment so I can see her today,
I will give my life with pleasure, just to hug her once again.

If I don't make it to heaven, please take good care of her,
because she was the kindest person with all the people close to her.
With courage, sweetness and wisdom, she brought me up by herself,
and taught me how to be humble, to be honest with myself.

She wasn't only my mother, she was my father, my friend,
because of her today I'm here; she was in my life the best.
Dear Mom if you can hear me, I wrote this poem to say
that I will love you forever, I'll miss you every day.

Wilfredo Fraticelli

Moods

A mood is like day to night
and like minutes to seconds.
One moment things are fine,
but with a blink of an eye,
everything has gone so wrong.
You ask why, but there are no answers.

Everything looks bright and clear
like the sun shining on the water.
You laugh, you joke, and you talk
like there was no sorrow.
But deep inside of you-
there's a bomb ready to explode.
You keep in control, not to blow,
showing a different face as you go.
Hoping that soon, everything will turn out right.

Leticia M. Guajardo

Equality

Strong as an ox and made of steel,
a powerful beast, a man must feel.
A women that's strong and toys with a male,
is a heartless witch, with horns and a tail.

Men call the shots and women accept.
Blindly she loves and never protests.
He'll promise her heaven, then deliver hell,
but she offers him chances to redeem himself.

He'll cut her down and make her fell low,
but then his smile will make her eyes glow.
He'll hand her flowers and apologize,
she'll accept this gesture and defend his pride.

He'll make her feel special by pulling her close,
then with a dagger, behind her back boast.

"She doth protest too much,"
I wish it were true
but I am afraid it is not
in the eyes of the world.

Nicole J. Fouliard

God's Rocking Chair

God has a rocking chair He is ready to share
And most anytime you can find me there

When I have trials and troubles, cannot sleep at night
He is always there to pick me up and hold me tight

When he calls my name and says peace
Then with love He rocks me to sleep

I sure do feel safe in His strong arms
Knowing with Him I'm safe from all harm

I just turn to God with troubles and cares
for I know they'll disappear in His rocking chair

In God's arms you can feel so much love
That's shown only by our God up above

He is always there when we call His name
With the same measure He loves everyone the same

If you have a need in your life today
Tell God all about it, take time to pray

If we will seek shelter under the wings of prayer
We can rest forever in God's rocking chair

Mildred Spain

Between Yesterday And Tomorrow

Whenever I wake to a brand new day,
And my mind is open for dreams;
The plans and purposes I had yesterday
Are forgotten, and replaced by new themes.

Today I'll smile at the first person I meet,
And I'll try to make him smile at me.
A smile costs nothing, but it adds to face value.
So to be fully dressed I must wear one you see.

A hug is a timely and perfect gift,
There's no problem, one size fits all.
It affords both the giver and receiver a lift.
And may prevent or soften a fall.

The best preparation for tomorrow, they say,
When I seek to do something good,
Is to make proper use of opportunities today.
Maybe some are in my own neighborhood.

Today I will try to do what I need to,
Overcoming my worries and accepting my fate.
I will say to a friend, "It's so good to know you."
Tomorrow may already be too late.

Lois B. Smith

The Muslim

The Muslim is known by his heart
And not the A's and B's of being smart
He is kind, generous, merciful and wise
His thoughts are revealed through truth and not lies.
His deeds may be great, but if it's just for show
Allah will soon reveal it
So the world will know.
His actions are sincere, courageous and bold
He never disrespects the young or the old.
His intelligence is respected by all mankind
He was once an addict or a drunk
Drowning in ignorance and wine.
He now stands tall for the world to see
Yes, the ex-slave and descendants of you and me.

Lavern Bilal

56

Love

Some people say that they love you,
And others run off with your heart,
Some will love you for whatever you do,
While others just want to part,
You may think you're in love,
Or that you're looking in all the right places,
And it may seem no matter what you do,
You're always looking into strange faces,
But you're not the only one who feels pain and sorrow,
So hold your head up and expect a better tomorrow,
And now with your new confidence and your head
Held up high above,
You hope the next one will be true love.

Leigh-Ann Powers

Monetary Disease

I saw the fungus on the trees,
And prayed to Heaven, "Dear God, please."
We need these trees for future good
As we believe Thou thought We should.

And then I thought about inflation,
A dastardly blight upon our nation;
A tragic monetary disease so steep
So that all of us should weep.

But we all go on our merry way
In disregard of the hell to pay;
For when we think of erosion of the dollar
We all should gripe and start to holler.

Once a dollar down and a dollar a week
Could get us an item we sought to seek;
But now there is hardly room in the blank
of the check for the price of a water tank.

Part of the problem of our national debt,
Our politicians have been too well kept.
We had better start taking the alternate route
by keeping right on at turning them out.

Robert John Hamilton

To Paul Hill

I believe in life, Mr. Hill,
And I've heard that you do, too.
How then can it be that you've taken a life
And claim it in the name of truth?

You say he will never kill again
And I suppose that that is true.
But what of HIS life, Mr. Hill?
And what does that make you?

Before, when I reached out to help, Mr. Hill,
Those who were lonely, confused and afraid,
We would fall to our knees and pray, Mr. Hill,
And with God, we would find a way.

I know that you know all of this, Mr. Hill.
For once you were a believer, too.
What happened to make you think, Mr. Hill,
It's alright to do as they do?

Do you know what you've really done, Mr. Hill?
They now fear ME and GOD, too.
Those who once might have stopped to pray, Mr. Hill,
Now, don't know how to trust - or who.

Madeline D'Agostino

The Dream...

This narrow path I walk along seems strange
and quite unreal.
Its edges are jagged and though on bare feet,
the pain I cannot feel.
The path is tiresome so I stop to rest
and slowly catch my breath.
I close my eyes and gently struggle to free
myself from death.
Its grip is fierce and takes my soul to play
against my heart.
As I grow weary, one must win.
For death and life must part.
I free myself from non-existence and
fight once more to live.
Death is at anger, for its hunger not quenched
by a soul I will not give.
I rise by will to escape the darkness and
struggle through its wrath.
I will follow the light that truly guides me and
once again walk down the path.

Kimala Hunt

Life

Life is an unwanted jungle, for us to live
and share; when life is taken from someone, it
leaves us in despair.
Life is an unwanted sorrow, that leaves us here
to mourn; but when the love is added, it keeps
us safe and warm.
Then when love has swiftly crumbled, we wait for
at least one day; when another love-lost mourning
soul, will desperately come our way.
Then there are those happy times, that keep us live
and joyful; those days when we're so happy, when
life is complete and full.
Something is always on your mind, to keep
you sad and down; but you have to overcome these
things, the sadness and the frown.
Life is an unwanted jungle, though changing
all the whiles; if love is in and by your life,
you'll always end up in smiles.

Tiffiny Meyer

The Men In My Life

Four men are a part of my life
and they cause either warmth, joy, misery or strife.
Each one plays a different part
and each has a significant place in my heart.

My husband was a man who wanted control.
He didn't believe that I could reach my goal.
After years of marriage, I had to leave
I had to be myself in order to achieve.

A son was conceived by the first that I adored.
He is kind and gentle, and cannot be ignored.
He is unsure of what he wants, but he will survive,
He knows that self endurance will keep him alive.

I now have a friend, who is as good as can be.
He knows what to say and has faith in me.
He believes in God and that's what it takes.
I know that he loves me and what a difference that makes.

My heavenly father is the most important to me
for without him, there wouldn't be the other three.
He has given me wisdom, strength and a loving heart
and I will honor him always till this earth I depart.

Virginia Parker

To Barrow School, Staff And Friends

Some days I felt very lonely,
And some days I felt so sad,
But whenever I came into this school,
You always made me feel so glad.

You always had a smile on your face,
That I never wanted to leave this place.
And if I needed a helping hand,
You always tried to do the best you can.

You made me feel so welcome,
With all the laughs and smiles,
That I forgot all my troubles,
And was happy for a while.

You gave me plenty of things to do,
That put my mind at rest,
And I felt as if you were all my family,
So I just wanted to do my best.

So I say this to all of you,
Barrow school, staff, and friends
If I haven't said it enough times before,
To you many, many thanks again.

Nancy Lewandowski

Kansas Citizen

Kansas is a state of prairies and plains, with summers of sage brush
and springs of fresh rains.
It is a land of harshness and hope, where nature still dictates the
wild antelope.
Its people are honest, hard-working, and strong, they know the
difference between right and wrong.
Here, there are people unlike other places, who don't see the
difference between the races.
They respect one another by word and by deed, sometimes they
follow, sometimes they lead.
With a sense of community they become as one to accomplish their
tasks and have lots of fun.
The laws they make protect our right to live together both day and night.
Who are these people about whom I speak, who live each day both
strong and meek?
Who carry on lives of service and caring, for family and friends
and others worth sharing?
These people I talk of are not queens and kings, with servants and
jewels and luxurious things.
They're actually quite common with much to give as citizens of
Kansas, the state where they live.
They're each one of us who tries to make a difference for our
community's sake.
Who support the laws and speak what's true, whether it's popular
or fashionable to.
So, we are the citizens who are demanding that each and every one
of us become outstanding!

Shawn Murphy

Progression

One day it glistens brightly on our faces
And our cares are far and few between,
Footsteps like the sands of time,
Crystals are the jewels that adorn the mind.

Through the years the winds silently blow.

One evening the sun may set
In a land not strange to all,
Where the running water runs warm under your feet,
Sharing stories of yesterday to keep today complete.

Through the night the sun still shines
Brightly through the window pane,
One more chance to enhance life,
For through us a world is sustained.

Kellie R. Fair

Crime

God, what's happening to our children. They are robbing, killing,
and stabbing each other, God.

They are babies wanting to be grown, but their minds are still
young, and the crimes they commit are adult crimes with children
getting adult time.

God, what happened with our children? Parents crying all the time,
not knowing what went wrong. Saying, "Oh God, this child is just
a baby, my baby got to do time."

Children, our tears are so heavy they can't do anything but fall
down our face, for the crimes you do calls for big time.

Children please listen, parents saying, they can't go on because
their child has to do time.

The stabbing, robbery and killing can't keep going on, our babies
are giving their lives to crime and are getting big time.

Sharon Swidecki

Hallucinations

The sky is gray outside on the grass
and the cars go by on the road
as the building with the bricks
keeps growing up and up
shattering the dull glass plate
that the sky sits on
(And everything just keeps going in a circle
with the peppermint stick in front
of the barber shop window)
while the dogs line up to piss
on the red fire hydrants that God set up
along the sidewalk
in case of an emergency.

Kerry Hinkson

My Thoughts

The dead are the dead,
and the living become the dying.

The motions of life are just motions,
thus actions and emotions can become illusions.

For the reality of life is stifling,
and the creation of an illusion brings relief.
To endure this cycle we call life,
one must drift from one world to the other.

Thus creating a balance, to insure
any normalcy to our existence.

Timothy N. Norton

"Hidden Morning"

Time stands still on solemn sorrow
And the shadows are alive in the night
Once there was a time to borrow
And this brought home the darkened fright

Now all the pain has gone
Like the dew in midmorn
As all the clouds pass so slowly across a blackened sky
And the flowers turn in their petals to hide
So the tear of forgotten misses my avid eye

The tears are finally silent, the leaves sing no more
How the waves seem to have forgotten their mother shore
And why are there no more clouds in the sky?
Have they finally found a place on earth to hide?

The sun has not been around for a year
And a day, on the horizon, I fear
Sunrise will be somewhat of a memory
But I can't seem to recall its poetry

Lance Boudreaux

My Favorite Sounds

Whispering pines on a warm summers eve
And the singing birds in the nearby trees

Rain on the roof on a dark dreary day
The grouchy old bull frog croaking away

A motor-boat's hum on the placid lake
Then listening on shore to its lapping wake

A tumbling waterfall cascading down
And small evening crickets chirping their sound

The tinkling wind-chimes in a soft cool breeze
A babbling brook sounding...only to please

A fountain of water dances then falls
A distant ship's horn sends its woeful calls

The soft cooing doves awake to the light
A train's far-off whistle fades in the night

A cracking fire in a warm cozy room
My favorite sounds...may I hear them soon!

Shirley Michelson

Untitled

I am glad, the world is not all flat
And the sky is not always blue
And if we had all sunshine and no rain
The flowers would be so few.

We would miss all the beauty of the mountains
And the lush valleys, so lovely and green
And all the great, water falls
Throughout the earth, can be seen

We could not climb a mountain
And sit under a cool green tree
And watch the rainfall flow down
Helping to form a great sea

We have our mountains to climb in life.
We have our valleys, to go down to rest.
Mountains make us strong if we overcome
Valleys make us humble and feel blest

So when you are down in the valley
Take the time to look at the mountain above.
And all around the beauty of the earth,
And the one who gave it to us with love.

Venice Waugh

For All Those We Loved

For all those we loved who gave us sunshine in their smiles
and the sounds of their laughter
For all those we loved who filled our hearts with everlasting joy
For all those we loved who taught us lessons in life
The values of living and being the best we can
For all those we loved with whom we shared our hopes and our dreams
Our secrets and our tears
As the sun shines
As the stars glow
As the streams flow
For the young and the old
As the seasons change
As the leaves turn their radiant colors
As the rain sprinkles down and the snow falls
For all those we loved who watch over us now from the heavens above
For all those we loved who with all our hearts will always be
remembered and always be loved by us

Lu Ann Bohon

Evening's Silence

I sit in evening's silence, my child to me I press,
and think of all God's creatures and of all the wonderness.

A miracle I hold so close, to stroke her silken hair,
and in the Evening's Silence God's presence we can share.

And as the World turns on and on with all its toil and strife,
to sit in Evening's Silence brings perspective to my life.

Such Blessings as an Eternal Family, they are all mine to enjoy,
As I sit Evening's Silence, my soul it fills with joy.

To contemplate my place on Earth, the pathway I should trod,
To sit in Evening's Silence, at peace to think of God.

And now perhaps was meant to be, the Father and the Son,
Did sit one Evening's Silence and say "The work is done."

I kneel now in Evenings Silence, my eyes are closed in prayer,
in humble supplication for the Spirit to join me there.

A glimpse of my home, with all I love close by me at the end,
As my soul reaches Evening's Silence, my new life will begin...

So long the path ahead to Evening's Silence.

Maryellen Fuller Stoker

The Night Before And Now

My thoughts did soar, the night before, that lovely afternoon.
And though the winter chill was real, all things were set to bloom.

The trees were still, in winter's chill, all seemed void of motion.
Except my mind, that raced my heart, just bursting with emotion.

The sky so blue, in lapis hue, beyond all comprehension.
But still the chill of winter caused a note of apprehension.

A momentary falter, as I thought of how to alter,
the things we set in motion by emotions of the day.

My mind was set to scramble, and as I began to ramble,
I devised a plan of action and exactly what to say.

But then I heard a whippoorwill, and winter's wind gave rise to chill
my heart that seemed to just still....

And gave my mind some time, to contemplate my thoughts of late,
and realize the winter's cold was beckoning the blooms of spring.

Then love began to rise again and warmed that winter's solitude.
I realized with open eyes the pros that must be viewed.

The blooms of love just opening, like flowers in an early spring,
to fill the heart, and warm the soul, the petals one by one unfold.

And so it goes, just one by one, the pleasures and the sorrows.
And all that fear, that holds me here, melts into all tomorrows.

Vivian M. Jones

When Lightning Strikes The Grassland Plain

When lightning strikes the grassland plain
And thunder roars, it soon will rain.

With harsh winds blowing back and forth,
Slowly drifting to the north.

The sky is cloudy dark and gray.
It's going to be a stormy day.

All the animals run and hide,
The skies are showing their angry side!

When skies clear up they'll go and play.
Then it will be a happy day!

But when skies are ugly, dark and gray,
And lightning strikes "the grass-like hay,"
And thunder roars at home they'll stay.
Because it's going to be a stormy day!

Tracy E. Evan

The Battle

The sun glows like a radiant fire on the churning sea of foam
and mist.
The waves turn with agony and pride.
A soldier rises from the battlefield.
The waves peak and crest,
shimmering in the light.
The soldier stands and holds his head high and proud
in the morning sun.
The waves dreamily creep along, slowly rising and falling,
gliding noiselessly towards the bumpy shore.
The soldier lifts his head to the sky, chest heaving,
and lays down his weapon.
The waves soar smoothly like a deep green prayer
and crash down upon the rocky earth.
The soldier falls to his knees,
thankful for his life.
The sun shines down upon its victors.

Lauren Urbanek

Seasons

In the winter I have fun,
and sleigh ride till the day is done.
I like to skate out on the lake,
after we're sure the ice won't break.
Spring is when the flowers sprout,
and all the animals run about.
All the trees start to bud,
and all the rain turns dirt to mud.
In the summer I swim in the pool,
I can swim all day 'cause we have no school!
I like to go camping in the park,
and build a fire after dark.
Fall is when the leaves turn yellow,
and the wind is cool and mellow.
All the leaves fall in a big pile,
and all the children start to smile.
These are just some of the reasons,
why I like the different seasons.

Marissa Alp

Winter's Death

Moon beams on hot ice where my fire burns,
and turning up, I lay flat.
Merciful stars, in darkness turn also,
and cry your light to my eyes.
Winds of earth, you may bend the trees,
yet I am land, and will not die.
The clouds may ride your tempest train,
an owl shiver at your wrath.
But I inside this frame—small me,
live for light.
Think no ill of me, Father Spirit,
that I lay upon the snow.
Die winter, for the sun is my star,
and my lover in need of rain.

Mark Czaja

March Beach

I yearn to dance upon the shore
and feel the driven mist upon my cheek.
The vibrancy of life recaptured from the wind
allows my heart to sing with life and joy.

Cares recede, sorrows on hold, life renews.
The wild sonance of the sea gulls' cry,
stirs freedom rising from hidden recesses.
Total abandonment, utter joy, dancing on the beach.

Ruby Swayze

The Sea Gull

Feathered wings float quiet 'round the sail
   and to the sea,
Finger-dance on waves that swell and fall;
They swoop below and dip with silent energy
And only when the prey is gulleted they call....
   ...and flap in fearsome victory.

Marcy Magnus

Untitled

Did you ever wake with a start in the middle of the night
And to your surprise hear a soft, muffled cry?
Hold your breath, listen carefully, it's the sound of the
Babies never born.
Unwanted children put to death, even before their very
First breath.
It might have been hard,
You might have been scared.
But would it have mattered if one life had been spared?
I hear it now one more soft, muffled cry,
Another little baby who had to die.

Kristy Marie Lucia

Life's Greatest Secret

Out of all the world's gifts
and treasures, pain and sorrow,
People miss out on the best and sometimes
worst treasure
man has to give to one another,

LOVE
At times this is the best gift,
other times this can be the worst gift
but something love always is,
is a very precious gift.
And this is the gift that I give to you.

What makes this gift more precious
than any other?

This gift lasts forever
unlike any gold or silver.
This gift will always continue to come
no matter what your faults and troubles are.

This gift needs no repair of lifetime
for this gift I give to you lasts
all eternity.

Kevonya Renee Elzia

First Birthday

She smiles so sweetly
and trusts completely - this child of one.

She's learning to walk, waddling to and fro
seldom afraid to let go - this child of one.

Ever pursuing her puppy's tail
knowing he will never fail to entertain - this child of one.

Each day a new challenge to learn
what makes a ball spin, a top turn - this child of one.

Pink and pretty, charming and smart
able to capture even a pirate heart - this child of one.

So loving and giving, an inspiration
to all who are living with - this child of one.

Just watching her grow and love and play
is having a valentine every day - in this child of one.

She's proof that God's work is never done
for he created a miracle in this child of one.

Sandra Lee Cahill

"A Smile Or Two"

There are many folks who go through life
 and very seldom smile
They wear a scowl upon their face
 as if it were in style

We should brighten up each day with smiles
 and not always look so stern
For if we greet a person with a smile
 we'll then receive one in return

As we go through life each one of us
 has burdens we must bear
And all the people on this great earth
 seem to have their share

Everyone should all help
 to spread a little cheer
For life is short and we may as well
 enjoy it while we're here

So from this day on enjoy yourself
 and give a smile or two
It will extend happiness to others and
 make life much more enjoyable for you!

Mary Alice Warwick

These Hands

My hands have grown old my tired eyes see
and when did this happen — so long ago —
it seems it; being old takes such a long time
to get over with.

The days with you flourished laughter's life
and each time we noticed getting older, well,
tomorrow we'll be older, enjoy today.

So we realized each other's smiles
toted each child and watched them marry
as we watched another's hair grey
- and I miss you, my wife,
that if you were here
holding my hand — oh it's grown so old,
and my eyes still shine;
you'd look at me and still say:
I still miss you, too —-
after all these years.

Michael Lim

A Break?

Sooner or later. We all make a mistake.
And when we do, we all hope for a break.

No matter how hard we try, the pattern is set.
For no one is perfect, at least not yet.

Don't you kinda wonder why, when we see someone err,
We hesitate to lend a hand, or let them know we care?

Just think for a moment - what a nice world this could be.
If I did my best, to bless your life - and you did the same, for me.

Robert H. Rodgers

"Life Holds Many Treasures"

In life there are many treasures, which one sees with one's eyes,
and with one's mind, and yet the truth to the rarest of all, is
truly the one to one's own heart, for to understand a thing, or a
treasure, is to first understand your heart, and your heart is to
know, that the only rarest treasure of treasures, is of your
heart, and within yourself, so that you may see it all, have it all,
and love with all your heart, and soul.

Samuel Cohen

Love Lost

I think I may have lost a good thing,
 But I cannot hold onto the past.
I know deep down that I honestly believed,
 That someday our love would last.
Do we go our separate ways hoping
 That one day, our paths will cross?
Or do we salvage a relationship where
 Temporarily, our love was lost?
I'll never forget all those times we shared,
 We each had so much to give.
I made a decision in which one heart was spared,
 And the other just wanted to live.
Those cold, dark nights when I thought I was alone,
 You opened your arms and welcomed me home.
I miss you, I love you - God, what shall I do?
 I've misplaced true love and I feel like a fool.
We'd been through so much and had lots of fun,
 But how was I to know that You were the one?
I want you to love again, to feel happy and free;
 Find someone to love you the same way you love me.

Michele R. Smith

Untitled

It's seven in the morning, I guess it's time to go to work
But I can't find my black briefcase, man I feel like such a jerk

The toothpaste tube is empty, the handle's broken on my brush
The percolator's overflowing, and I missed the morning bus

My new silk suit is wrinkled, my deodorant is gone
The dog ate my leather pumps that now decorate the lawn

As I am running out the door, I see a book upon the table
I want to stop and pick it up, but my watch says I'm not able

It seems like nowadays I don't find anything reliable
Maybe I should set some time aside to just stop and read the Bible

This thought passes through my head as I go about my day
I guess I just conveniently forgot I thought the same thing yesterday

Michelle N. Espada

The Power Of Belief

I don't know where you come from
But I come from a world of believers.

We don't stop. We don't stare.
We don't abuse. We are achievers.

I don't know where you are going
But my destination is forever.

I have set my sights straight ahead
And I will look back never.

I won't say how I'll get there for
even that mystery will have to un-fold.

But it's up to me seek the wisdom
and decipher life's secret codes.

I will endure no matter what
Even if you think I've come to a stop.

You'll look around. I won't be sitting
down. I'll be standing with Him at the top.

I will give thanks to the real powers that be —
the power of belief that is in you—
that is in me.

Loretta Johnson

I'm Your Friend

Where do you turn when you're down and out
  And you don't know how you'll go on,
Where do you turn when you're full of doubt
  And you need some help to be strong.

Where do you turn when your troubles don't end
  And you dread the dawn of each day,
Where do you turn when the heartaches won't mend
  And you can't find the right words to say.

Where do you turn when things go all wrong
  And nothing you do turns out right,
Where do you turn when your days seem so long
  And you hide from your thoughts every night.

Where do you turn when you've lost all hope
  And you've finally reached your wits end,
Where do you turn when you need help to cope
  Just turn to me.... I'M YOUR FRIEND.
    Marty L. Darden

Gaze Upon Your Wedding Ring

When you're feeling sad and blue,
and you just don't think you can make it through,
just gaze upon your wedding ring and know that I
am there for you.

When your days seem dark and cloudy, with no sight
of sunshine coming through, just gaze upon your
wedding ring and feel the glow my love has for you.

Yes, gaze upon your wedding ring, for it units us
as one, you see, when things aren't right for you, that
gaze will remind you, that you are not alone,
for God graciously gave you me.

Though through the day we are far apart, our love,
is as close to each of us as our hearts.

So gaze upon your wedding ring, a symbol of
eternity it should bring joy and warmth to the
thoughts that you have.

Gaze upon your wedding ring.
    Phillip Lee Myers

Shelley, "A Lamb"

Who is this little person in pink?
Angelic, perfect, a cherub I think.
Rosebud nose, delicate skin-
A chunk of a diamond, flawless within.

How will I nurture this person in pink?
I will love her, I'll guide her, and lead her to drink
From the waters of life that refresheth the soul,
This little angel, my first baby, in pink.

She possesses a spirit that is trusting and sweet,
An inner joy; and she has happy, fat feet.
She is sensitive, aware, of each little thing
That each day in her life brings to her delight.

For this little person adorned in lace and in pink,
I wish for her, happiness clothed in light;
And her soul, in diamonds, priceless and pure,
The finest for her; a life rich and secure;

For this little girl, this baby in pink.
    Sue Shambaugh Hinkle

A Mother's Anger

Mother nature's hands shave the earth in anger
Anger at the deafness of society to hear her
  Daughter's Pleas
Her mouth yells out in hurricanes
At a world that would see her daughter
Dictated to, harassed, and altogether tormented
For their supposed sin of loving a part
Tears pour out in floods
For the shots that echo out at the innocent
Who simply asked for the right to choose
But instead were chosen
Society easily excuses those violations of women
But a mother does not
To show her disdain she ravages abuse on all
She randomly calls up her weapons
To show the Abusers the way it feels
To be a powerless victim
To be violated, abused, and destroyed
The innocent do not escape her wrath
Because the innocent never escape anyone's wrath
    Laura Grand-Jean

"Just A Dream"

Death with no reason.
Anger with no end.
The bottling up of feelings,
Wanting so much to pretend;
That all is just a dream....

Then, to your surprise,
Without any warning;
Another death with no reason,
Causing anger with no end.
Then you realize it isn't just a dream....

Death with no reason.

Anger with no end.
Now realizing the truth;
Unable to pretend,
That all is just a dream...
    Tammi C. Redd

I Am The Words

Broken hearts — sleepless nights
  Angered words — senseless fights
    Painful thoughts disagree
I am the words called misery.

Whispers soft — a gentle touch
  Words that say we care so much
    A soft caress — a pure white dove
I am the words you call love

Another day — another try
  A few kind words — a reason why
    Another day we try to cope
I am the words you call hope

Accomplishments — knowledge too
  The way you dress — the things you do
    The hurt you feel — the tears you hide
I am the words you call pride

All the words I've written here
  All the lines I'll pen next year
    All the rhymes that came from me
I am the words called poetry.
    T. Jade Bessette

One's Search

Inward? Outward? Where does one turn?
Applause? A cause? For what to yearn?
Something of value.

For self? Or pelf? What's the concern?
One's birth - What worth? Can merit earn
Something of value?

Hoping, Groping ... Traditions? Burn!
Preacher? Teacher? Who dares to learn
Something of value?

Confusion? Illusion? Mind foment, churn.
Shifting. Drifting. Wise men discern
Something of value?

The quest - a jest? Why faith to spurn?
Wanderer. Ponderer. Will you return to
Something of value?

Louisa P. Salmon

Visit To A Graveyard, Roxana, Delaware

It's been six weeks without rain, but the waves
are as long as daylight. Here, in late December,
twenty miles from shore, the grass still grows.
In the car you said it's about time you met him,
switched the radio dial and drove. Your breath
still smelled like coffee. Now you're lost in this
stubble of weeds and granite trying to show
me: the tattoos, the charcoal half-moon worn
into his finger by the pistol range, the way his
bottom lip turned dark and quivered, like yours.
You're still talking, long after high tide. A rusty
muffler passes on the road behind us; the sun
is wearing a paper bag. Sometimes it's too late
for introductions; you voice is to the wind. But
you knead you olive sweater and try to tell me,
until you sink like an abandoned barn, burning.
So I hold you in the grass, over your father, and
watch the winter crocus.

J. K. Gilligan

The Sword Of Life (Tsuguri Ken)

This is the place where swords
Are forged with compassion
And tempered in love.
Here, truth is the air
From the bellows stoking
The refining fire in the heart.

The blade is life. The heart,
The spirit, and the soul
Of every true warrior.
Practice is the understanding
Of this sword of life.

The sword cuts its path.
In its wake, many of the ten thousand
Things are united, leaving one more fold
Of the universe revealed.

We follow its path: This is practice.
To understand the sword is to fully realize
One's own self; perfect, just as you are.

May the sword of life
Cut you well.

Sandifer Deer

Untitled

Those who conform to the ways of the world
    are lost to the dogs of prey.
No sense of direction to turn around
    as destined they will stay.

Imprisoned in their body and mind,
    their souls are at constant loss.
Mangled thoughts with nowhere to turn
    never to get their point across.

While the strong of heart outsmart the beasts,
    they know their time will come,
To direct their attention to the worse of fate;
    to save the troublesome.

Wrapped up in the continuous game
    wondering what to do.
Are you the beast who preys on others,
    or do the beasts prey on you?

Rachel Janzen

Voices

The voices in my mind
Are very unkind
They force me to kill
Innocent women against my will
I do it so carefully
So no one will see
I take a trip to their home
When I know she will be all alone
I throw a towel upon her head
Knowing that soon she will be dead
Then I bring the hammer crashing down.
Load her up and drive out of town
To this cave that looks more like a grave
I work from night till dawn
Burying the body so the voice will be gone
But soon the voice will return
And it will be another's turn

Randa Gage

Worship

Most precious Holy Father is this quiet morning hour,
As I see the day beginning, as I see thy Mighty Power,

You are the fairest to my soul, you are the bright and morning star,
The God of all creation, tallest tree to brightest star,

You are the King of Kings, you are the Lord of Lords,
You are the Alpha and Omega, I love your precious words.

You are the great I am, our glorious majestic God,
Creator of the Universe and the Earth where Christ hath trod.

I love your glorious attributes, we know but just a few,
Your attributes are innumerable, I love and worship you.

I praise thee oh my Father, for thy greatness and thy power,
For your Mercy, Grace and Love, and blessings every hour.

My heart is full of worship, adoration and thanksgiving
To the God of my salvation, who within my heart is living.

Oh! Precious Holy Father, accept the praise I bring,
And through this day as I walk with you, your glories I will sing.

All praise to the Father, all praise to the Son,
All praise to the Spirit, all glorious three in one.

I give thee praise and honor, our gracious Almighty King,
I want to live for you today and to your heart joy bring.

Kathy Kumar

Sleep

Sleep wraps its luring tendrils
Around your heart and mind.
Pulling you slowly and gently,
And ever so sweetly downward.
Down into its dark and swirling grayness.
Relax!
Let your body forget the cares,
And the troubles,
That burden your waking hours.
Let go your grasp,
On the edge of your awareness
Of reality,
And slip softly,
Sweetly,
Silently,
Into peace.

Mellenie L. Hilpert

Within The Realm

A stirring in my soul takes me far away to a place and fair,
as comfortable and familiar as old faded blue jeans
that know by heart the lines and curves
of the one who values their worth.

I am filled by the grandeur that lies before me...
Pine trees, tall and regal;
grasses soft as lamb's wool, yet cool as crisp clean sheets;
skies ten times more blue than the lakes below that reflect them.

Warm breezes, tracing their path through majestic pines,
sing in harmony with cool waters coursing swiftly across
snags of a mountain stream.
Their song, whispered low and deep, echoes a dedication
to what has been.

My own steps have worn a path that follows every turn of the stream
like a heavy crayon outline made by stubby fingers in a coloring book.
Sometimes straight, often steep, the path is
no more, no less than what I have made of it.

In this place where time never was, I find rest.
I find comfort. With slow, deep breaths I find peace.
In the solitary realm of my mind, where paradise begins and ends,
I am.

Melanie Kennedy

To Life

Seven numbers go through my fingers
As dreary atmosphere lingers
Could not hear anybody from the other side
Please pick up for pain cannot hide

And darkness but light through window
As shown through heart so hollow
When will I hear what you say?
Thrown forth tomorrow or yesterday.

What I say you better believe
Or you shall see my sharpness of leave
Are you with your other world or me?
While my short visit it when I cannot see

Significant other than me?
For that thought I cannot even perceive
Another ring for a chance to say hello
Frightening thoughts are still at flow

For I have cried but I do not bleed
For that will soon change as life I leave
What do you want? Do you want my love?
Which ones true? Which ones above?

Ryan Wiebel

Anticipation

The wind dies down
As fewer rays reach the ground.
The amber clouds become still,
While the sun sets over the hill.

Its golden beams glisten
In a silent array of crimson.
With the night on its way,
They mark the end of the day.

It is time for the day star to part.
The twilight casts a shadow on its fading heart.
So the sun disappears in the night,
Ready to come up at dawn just as bright.

Nicole Palmer

Uncle Zert

Zert he was called, what an odd name
As he strutted around in his tall thin frame.
I remembered him best when I was very small,
To me his six feet seemed extremely tall.

He would pay quick visits to my grandmother's home,
Hurriedly he'd leave her for the streets to roam.
Grandmother smiled brightly at his entree,
Sobbing loudly each time he went away.

His reasons for leaving were mostly lies
But she continued to treat him like a special prize.
Grandmother never questioned him about his life
Even though she knew he lived with strife.

All of her children she loved, each and everyone,
But none made her feel like uncle zert, her special son.
In grandmother's heart she felt there was no other like him,
Her love for him ceased, only when her lights shone dim.

Lois Waterhouse

Broken Heart

I think of you
    As hours pass away
Wishing I was in your arms
    And you never let me go away
My love for you is the strongest feeling I know
    I wish you felt this way

I think of you from night to day
    Wishing you were beside me but knowing you're far away
I feel our love is standing still
    You know we need to move on
I know my heart is broken
    Without your love beside me
I know how I feel
    I need to know how you feel

I think of you as hours pass away
I think of you from night to day
    I'll always think of you
        Because I LOVE YOU

Melissa Marie Gentry

In Loving Memory Of Earl And Joanne Travis

The tears I'm crying for you,
Are so hard to see through.
The tears are like rain falling from the sky,
I have nothing here to do but cry.
There's still so much we wanted to do,
Still so much I needed to learn from you.
You were there for me through my pain and fears,
And I wish you were here to help me through the tears.
I'll always have good memories,
Because that's all that's left between you and me.

Megan Langfitt

64

Untitled

When I pray for you
  as I frequently do
I don't pray for large miracles
  just the small ones.
I pray for courage and the
  strength for you to do all you need to do
For your kids and your man
  and for yourself.
When I think of you
  as I frequently do,
I see the strength and the
  courage.
I see God's little miracles
  in you.

  Nan Gabet

"Unity"

In all of our hatred, anger and destruction in the past,
As I look and hear around me the evil that seems to last,
When history has been written of all our mistakes,
We all are unable to change because of the sense it makes.
Why does mankind continue to live in his evil ways
Even though God's Word warns us of our limited days.
Throughout my years I've seen the hatred of a few
cause many to die,
Without regard to the children who are left to suffer and cry.
Everyone has been more concerned about their own identity,
And ignored God's purpose for mankind to live in unity.
Our world and its resources have been constantly
depleted by man,
We have done everything possible to ignore God's perfect plan.
From the garden of creation, to present time,
to our eternal destiny,
We who are created images of God have yet to live
in perfect unity!

  Wilkie L. Sanders Sr.

A True Story

Once upon a midnight dreary
As I toiled alone and weary
Sweeping up the kitchen floor
Clearing counters forevermore
Suddenly I heard a turning —
THE PANTRY DOORKNOB WAS SLOWLY TURNING!!!

I dashed upstairs for my Lord and Master
A tough Marine who feared no disaster
Down he flew with cudgel in hand
Went to the door and in manner grand
Flung it open, was ready to strike —
When lo and behold there sat our cat "Mike"
Who sauntered out with feline grace
Looked around and with unhurried pace
Went to a corner to resume his grooming
While hubby snarled and went out fuming.

  Lottie J. Pidgeon

Purple Rain

Purple rain
As the clouds roll in I run for cover but it is too
late, my hands are covered with water, my face not.
My fears, troubles, and my strength leave my body.
My body feels clean, like freshly picked out of the garden.
I feel relaxed.
As I walk to the place from which I came. My Body
will soon be filled again with my fears, troubles, and my strength.

  Stephanie Davick

Racial Acknowledgement Comes Easily

Am I you?
Are you me?
I think not, yet perhaps.
We have come from all around the world;
To unite from a melange of culture into a solitary nation.
Is there any disparity between you and me?
Why must we be blind with xenophobia?
Some come from afar:
A place in which is esoteric and strange,
A land where a dearth number of meals and life may be discovered.
Despite that, is it necessary to bring animosity within one's content
  sole?
I am not able to change you,
You are not able to change me.
We shall do what we must;
To accept,
to join hands,
To be as one.
It's not easy,
Yet is it hard?

  Naihin Saephan

Friend And Foe

If all the people of your town
are your friends, it's not enough,
If one of them is your enemy he is too much.
The mother said to her son;
"Before leaving home your shoes should shine
A friend looks at your eyes
Your enemy stares at your shoes."
When in battle your foe feels the same as you fear,
Endured he that conquers his fear.
A foolish friend will pull you down
But a wise enemy will lift you up.
If hurt you become,
do not be a beaten dog,
who pushes between his legs his tail,
Running around barking in wail.
Be a lion who turns to his den,
leaks his wounds and waits for the day.
Remember the king when was old, to his son he said
To punish the ones by whom he was betrayed.

  Samuel Shoshani

Fellowship

Her eyes are as wide as the rivers and creeks that flow around her.
As she bows her head to greet you, her hair flows like moss hanging
gently from an oak tree. You can't help noticing the soles of her
shoes, the way they are slightly worn. She smiles with embarrassment
and explains that they are constantly being repaired. As you begin
to walk down the street, you notice her wearing apparel. She wears
a sundress filled with blooming flowers that seem to enhance her
beauty. Though she complains of her chest being congested during
the morning and most afternoons, she assures you that by sunset she
can breathe freely once again. Though she walks with pride that
extends beyond the rails of the Mississippi River bridge, in her eyes
you sense something is wrong, as her beautiful smile disappears.
She notices you watching, shrugs her shoulders and exclaims,
"Everyone has problems at one time or another." Her smile
returns as you continue you walk together. She lets you in on
some of her favorite pastimes, like sitting along the levee and
watching the traffic of the barges and ferry boats. And on
Thursdays, she shows her hospitality to visitors as they are getting
off the Riverboat Delta Queen. As she greets her guests, her smile
disappears. She's worried about her family and their problems.
And like the early morning sunrise, the smile returns as she is
reminded that her faith is what keeps her home together.
She is your community.

  Tammy Moore

Silent Cries

This night I sit here thinkin' with my classroom on my mind -
As I visualize their streets, troubled lives are there to find.
I see the little faces that my heart holds so dear -
The little children's silent cries are what my ears now hear.
"My daddy hit my mommy, he was drunk again last night.
I shivered in the corner and held my sister tight."
"A little love is all I want. Is that too much to ask?
It seems as though a little hug is far too great a task."
As I put my arms around them, their trouble softly lies -
The anger that they hold soon turns to silent cries.
Life on the streets is what they know - their "Homies" by their side -
They say their gang is all they need to keep them satisfied.
If you look below the surface though, you'll see they long for more -
A way to reach their childhood dreams is what they're searching for.
They soon become a part of me - forever in my heart -
And I'm saddened as I start to think - soon we, too, must part.
I hope the things I've taught them will help to see them through,
And I lay awake and think at night, "Is there more that I can do?"
Lord let me never pass a child with that longing in their eyes,
And listen on with deafened ears, and miss their silent cries.

Krissandra P. Gatz

Soldier's March

Viet Nam

Up the dusty road they went, their left,
As if to war they were sent, their right,
With uniforms pressed and starched, left, right,
Stepping proudly as they marched, left, right.

Into war they moved their stride, there left,
Feeling fears they could not hide, that's right!
Soldiers dropping by their side, they fight,
Sinking feelings deep and wide, they're left.

Victory for us they sought, that's right,
Shooting, spilling blood they fought, what's left?
Remembering, all that they were taught, who's right?
Bleeding for the ticket bought, what's right.

On the foreign fields their dreams, they left,
Growing up or so it seems, not right,
While the gold at home still gleams, it's left,
Inner voices left to scream, what's right!

Home they came from where sent, their left,
Stepping proudly as they went, their right,
Going to familiar places, left, right,
Seeing people hide their faces, not right!

Robert S. Baldwin

Remember?

Winding the white string
around the wooden wheel
and splinting the red woven plastic
taking shape we're ready and we run together
and run holding Red above us
and running Wind catches up with us and
chooses the lighter one as we scream
together breathing and laughing
and the white string begins to unravel and
unravel and unwind its roped body
stiffening so tight that when we pluck it
it makes a funny noise
and holding on tight just staring at the thing flying
that used to be Red only it's not now
it's just how we remember it
and I think that we might lose it now
because String is so tight and Wind is so strong
and it's getting dark
and I don't think we are able to bring it
down.

Laurel Williamson

Balloon Flight

We floated
As if we were the early morning fog itself.
We became one
With the sun, the mist, the tops of trees.
We sailed in silence,
Our experiences not providing adequate words.
Slipping softly over an unsuspecting deer,
  a private life, reflecting water.
Out a time, out a space,
  within our limitations …
To share one moment with the eyes of God.
Only we, who shared this gift together,
Know.

Stan Price

In A Cavern

Inside I'm crying out,
  as in a cavern deep.
But who can hear, except my God,
  and He appears asleep.
My need seems more than I can bear!
  Within I cry, "It's just not fair!"
And yet I know I must not dwell
  where woes are exalted down to hell.

Will I, in time, have peace of mind?
  (I seek release through prose and rhyme.)

My eyes look up, and there I see
  a challenging climb awaiting me.

Linda Everson

Moments

Moments dancing by the windows of my eyes,
as lightning is to the heaven and skies.
Moments are but a wrinkle in time, not a chapter,
each etched with hope, dreams, fear or laughter.

Moments of our lives happening as on a lighted stage,
moments that thrill us, satisfies us, or moves us to rage.
Moments of a pleasant time can set a day apart,
by giving it a special place within our heart.

Moments that define the happenings of our history,
as transitions in the dark for all to see.
Every smile and hug small moments that last,
represent precious moments, pieces of the past.

The wonder of a miracle from which these moments began,
there is much to be found in the eyes, or the touch of a hand.
The moments of tomorrow and the hope of dreams come true,
a reminder of the moments frozen in time, or still due.

Moments that are unique to me - dwindle away,
defining moments that are here to stay.
If we could forward a few words from our heart,
cherish every moment right from the start.

Lucille Brown Roberts

Peace

As soft as a rose petal in my hand,
As secretive as a shell hiding underneath the sand.
As magical as the heavens above,
As wonderful as a flying dove.
The earth is quiet,
No sounds of worry I can hear,
I can't even see one single tear.
Peace is such a delightful thing
Such as flowers blooming in the spring.
Peace is love, warmth, and kindness,
And peace gets rid of everyone's blindness.

Stacy Martin

"The Unconquerable Glare"

Late one evening
As my brother sailed the oceans bay,
An unconquerable glare...
Reversed night into day.

Brought on by this glare
Came a thundering roar,
The sound came from our Lord...
He was slamming his door.

I was trembling and worried
About this great light
And the Lord, he was pissed,
'Cause this light was so bright.

I explained to the Lord...
"This glare's not from candles' of my birthday cake...
I'm on a diet,
So instead we had steak!"

Man...I was shaking
Until the Lord said, "Fear not,
It's the full moon reflecting...
From your brother's bald spot!"

Robin J. Blanquera

another blossom fell...

i drift into sleep
as soft sounds of the night
are like those of a summer breeze
gently caressing the dogwood leaves
blossoms, wildflowers, tall grass
just you and me
embraced in the cozy shade
of that dogwood tree
with our desires content
we lay back to rest
then a blossom fell
and kissed your breast
the aroma of making love enhances
earthly fragrance of meadowland
and i savor the comfort
of your tender lips upon my hand
another blossom fell
to kiss the spot that 'he' just knew
and with that kiss 'her' sweetness grew
along with the all-over-lovely
sweetness of you ...
(my lover, friend, companion, support
and security through all the years)
(sweet Alzheimer's lady, Pearl)
another blossom fell ...

will slocum

Riding On Moonlit Dreams

The moon in the sky was half its size,
as the bright brilliant light
lit up the dark night.
Then whisking through the magical moonlit sea,
the wind whispered softly his gentle breeze,
into the ear of a youthful soul
to be free; strong; bold;
Ride the wind, once again;
Run your hand, through the warm soft sand,
live each moment to no end;
Celebrate life; How great; How grand,
for you are only young once little man!
So hold on tight to this ride called life,
though it may throw you once or twice,
saddle back up, however impossible it may seem;
Clench tight the reigns and follow your dreams.

Tamara J. Doskocil

Epitaph For A Small Town Misery

As darkness envelopes me, the demons are calling.
As the closeness of death whispers, my shield is falling.
I see them through the windows of my soul:
I am jerked from silence into a violet black hole.

To describe them... I have no words to say.
To defeat them... Does no good to pray.
You can't help me. So leave me alone.
You also have sins for which you must atone.

Night's cool breeze whispers up a hill.
I stand at the edge of hell's windowsill.
In the distance, I see No Future City's orange glowing fire.
A lost figure bestowed a title of night's squire.

My demons live in a world so far away. Yet, too near.
I stand on a lone hill. Train whistle cry is all I hear.
I have an angel beside me. Echoing heaven's mourns:
Her song of life thrashes through my home thistle and thorns.

Can't outrun that small orange glow.
Does she see the demons through my soul's window?
If so, Beauty run. And leave me alone.
I have sins for which I must atone.

Patrick Blake Carnley

A Misty Morning

The hills lie silent
as the fog moves in to hide
their view,
Beneath a featherbed of golden leaves
that have fallen softly with the dew.

The misty morning speaks in tones unruffled
to high flying creatures,
To man and beast alike -
And the hills lie silent
giving sanction to migrants,
Through the light of day or dark of night.

Ruth Atchison Bradshaw

The Falling Of A Star

I gaze upon the midnight sky,
as the moon and stars dazzle my eye.
The sheltering of their light
looks upon me, as I wonder in fright....
Would it burst into flames, if I were to
reach out my hand and scream out my name?
How I would love to see the power it holds,
when the falling of a star leaves me cold.
  I shiver and I shake,
  as the earth begins to quake,
  while the ocean roars,
  as the waves find the shore,
  I look to see the earth no more....

Naona Rae Doty

Each Day On Earth

Each day we walk upon this land,
Be grateful for each thing we can,
So many people complain and cry,
Never realizing all they had to do was try.

When life is o'er and we're laid to rest,
May all who knew us, say, they did their best,
The only way to be assured of this,
Is to learn to live and love in bliss..

Mary B. Costner

The School Bus

Thirty some years I waited for that Bus to round the bend...
As the squeal of the brake announced its approach each morn
at about 8:10... Children across the road, and down the road, and
up the road a bit... Would gather here to board that bus decked out
with hats and mitts... My own sweet ones, the neighbors near, and
then my grandson too... would all be rushing down the walk before
the bus horn blew... Some I would cheer up, others calm down, and
perhaps even tie a shoe... Yes, those happy times will stay with
me, oh, the years were just too few... Some moved away, the others
are grown, the bus stops here no more... But when I hear that old
sweet sound I still rush to the door... And then I miss those
precious times of hugs and kisses and 'byes... But deep within my
memory that picture forever lies... I hope their lives are happy
now... Will my broken heart e'er mend?... For now I'm sad and
lonely when that school bus rounds the bend.

Martha Walters Carroll

The Sea

The whistling of the waves
as they abruptly end on the seashore
Brings that feeling of comfort and peace
one finds only in such primordial natural settings.
Along with all the wonders of this vast creation
comes the transcendent effect of nature
And all the marvels that lie in
the depths of the obscure, A world of its own!
Unpredictable events occur in the midst
of the unknown,
Even to those who proclaim so much
knowledge.
With that look of exquisite beauty and
peaceful innocence
Hides a furious briny and
inexplicable fortuity.
With the bewildering circumstances and
the suppressed force that lies for miles and miles,
Just as the tempestuous future
that lies ahead in our lives.

Rita Llinas

Earth's Fury

Her cry went unanswered,
As they burnt and raped her being.
Her body erupted from within,
Sending fires of rage throughout the land.
Spitting out vapors of pain across the skies.

The colors of her spirit became subdued,
As they blended into darkness.
Her blood ran cold and exploded,
Propelling shock waves within her soul.
Plunging forth a tumultuous liquid.

And as she twirled faster and faster,
Her creator watched with tearful eyes.
Indeed the human factor destroyed it all.
So, with a wave of his hand,
She vanished, giving rise to the new millennium.

Teresa Donoher-Ryan

When Last We Meet

When last we meet it shall be upon a plain
Bereft of trees and grass and rolling hills.
You shall look at me and not recall my name
Nor I the time we spent when lie was still
Meted out in hours, days and weeks
Clothed in seasons full but bittersweet.

Mary L. Sullivan

Revolution

A prisoner, newcomer, crying in his cell,
Asking who am I to trust...
Silence!
For he does not speak the native tongue.
Those appointed to guard him and keep him, abuse him.
So... shall the poor wretch starve and want for nurture.
Others look on with disgust, not at his torture but the gruesome
   result,
A decaying human nature.

Day after day he consumes what is given,
For any hungry enough will feed on the most vile of victuals for
   survival sake.
So let it be the violence and abuse that are the nourishment for
   his pang of hunger.

Years later...
He takes a prisoner of his own.
He feeds the newborn the only way he knows how.

Susan A. Harakall

Sundry Thoughts Surfacing At Random

Energy and Mass as One did radiate
   At dawn created eons of time ago
   Now in its plan they both do separate
   Into the Cosmos throughout space dilate

To the far reaches of the Universe
   Probes Man his curiosity to assuage
   Coy Wisdom to Her bosom he would nurse
   But never satisfied that remains his curse

Far beyond the googol leading to the googolplex
   I struggled on through muddied fields of cyphers
   Saw many a mystery there that made me sorely vex
   God Gravity Cosmic Force each fact did me perplex

Humanity corrupt and arrogant day by day doth show
   To what degraded state It falls with ease
   And shrugs Its shoulders at morality and so
   What direful baneful harvest shall It mow?

Old World doth spin in infinite domain
   A speck upon its axis turns eternal
   Follows its path around the Sun amain
   Among the spheres it chants its own refrain

Nicholas W. Carter

Great-Grandma

The death of my Great-Grandma was a living hell.
At first I was told she was getting well.
But when my Mom called from work and said she was dead
So many things were running through my head.

One moment she was here and the next she was gone.
And what hurts most is I didn't even get to say so long.
Although it's almost been a year,
Thinking about her still makes me shed a tear.

In my prayers I pray that she's okay
Since I won't see her because she's so far away.
Every night before I'm asleep
I lay on my pillow and begin to weep.

When I see pictures of her and I,
I get all watery-eyed and get ready to cry.
And now I think about the good times we had,
It makes me very sad and at the same time a little mad.

I try to raise enough courage to go to see her grave
But I would rather be alone in a deep, dark cave.
As I remember her wrinkled hand
I wonder, Was her soul really in demand?

Megan C. Lawther

His True Love

He opened the door and stared a while
At how her lips almost seemed to smile.
A few strands of hair had wandered onto her face,
And he brushed them away with tenderness and grace.
He felt the smoothness of her skin
And thought of all the memories she had given him.
He remembered the summer they spent together.
The one he thought would last forever.
The ring he held in the palm of his hand
Was one that would wed them, woman to man.
He lifted her hand and slid the ring on her finger.
He said, "In my heart, our love will always linger."
As he leaned over her body and gave her one last kiss,
A single tear fell to her cheek from his.
He closed the door and turned to go,
Realizing her love he would never again know.
He wanted the perfect love but waited too long.
Now it's too late; his true love is gone.

Keiva McCain

The Power Of Her Memory

Light phasing through the chasms of my brain
Awaken sleeping eyes for an eternal instant.
Raindrops fall in perfect harmony and subtle refrain,
Leading dull ears to hear what once was distant.
Winds speak in passionate, poetic tenses,
Giving me the gift of oral mastery.
The magic of the storm has unleashed my senses,
Releasing my soul from the abyss of life's diabolical mystery.
My heart is cleansed in the waters of salvation,
Springing renewed thoughts of love to my head.
If only she could witness nature's newest creation,
Bringing life to that which was dead.
But, alas, she is hopelessly gone and my miracle is done.
For in seconds comes the morn and these eyes fear the sun.

Mitch Girdler

Merry Christmas 1994

Jesus was born on Christmas day.
Away in a manger, his bed was hay.

He was born a spiritual birth.
As he grew in stature, he walked the earth.

He healed the ill, the blind did see.
This great leader of Galilee.

He walked on earth, among sin and decay.
Help us Jesus, it grows more wicked, day by day.

He ascended into Heaven, he said a comforter he would send.
This Holy Spirit will guide us, till we reach journey's end.

If we go to Jesus in our time of distress.
At the end of our journey, we will find sweet rest.

When life on earth, shall ever cease.
We can dwell with Jesus, in joy and peace.

Family, friends, loved ones, keep this ever in your minds.
Do good to the needy, joy and happiness you will find.

Jesus bless the ill, the weak and the strong.
Put joy in the hearts of everyone.

As we celebrate the birth of God's only begotten son.
May joy and peace abide, in the hearts of everyone.

Pauline Nix Patterson

Ode To Our Military

Mighty machines tumble out of the sand like ants.
Awesome yet as frail as the skills of those entranced
In the mechanized toys of war.

Onward they march braving weather, the enemy and fear.
Dreaming of home, and of loved ones far from here,
And the country they're fighting for.

Conquer the foe, keep your mind on the task at hand!
Remember you've come to bring freedom to this land!
This tiny land stricken sore.

With courage and bravery, their task has come to an end.
Yet these men will return without many of their old friends,
Who were downed by the terrible toys of war.

Reva A. Jackson

Untitled

Babies are such precious little creatures.
Babies have tiny little fingers and
tiny little toes.
Babies have skin so soft and so natural,
it's like nothing I've ever felt
Hearing his baby noises and seeing
beautiful expressions he makes so sweet
Watching him grow, so fast, I treasure
every moment he experiences life and,
One day he learns to walk with a
Smile that says, "I did it!"
When he's a little older he gets so
hungry for knowledge, he always wants
to know "why mommy?"
There are so many joys to having a baby
of your own, watching him grow
from a tiny baby to a mature handsome
young man. And soon he will have a
baby of his own and get to
experience the same joys I did with him.

Teresa J. Calderon

My Children -My Birdies 1994-95

Greg sits atop a mountain in the crisp coldness of white snow under barefeet, draped only in his gi- one with the forces of nature, his spirit ethereal in movement thought and stride. Powerful in his gentleness, strengthened by the force within, his soul searching for the answers

Daren wrapped in the warmth of love, fickle yet real for the moment, lusting after life's offerings- giving self and more, his energy source good humour, logic with vision, wonderment forcing him on, the inner man still unresolved

Amy bursting, blossoming, reborn again. Pressing against the wind- lifting from the ground, laughing, whirling, beautiful again recovering and discovering her soul

Lea gathering her self, living reality with the freshness of curiosity and innocence, a treasure of feelings and emotions- peeking through the velvet fronds of nature's way mirroring the ripples of the water as the pebble nestles softly, comfortable on the sandy floor of life's experiences

My children- MY BIRDIES- treasures to be marvelled at, not measured or weighed, but felt within as a force that regulates the rhythm of one's breath, the warmth of a tear on a cheek, the touch of lashes lowering to protect, the smile and tinkle of laughter, the love in the glance knowingly from Mom to Pop

Marion Hallert

Misunderstood

Why is it that our history books are only filled with
bad things? I sit here and listen to my teacher talk
endlessly about a subject I never knew.

All those wars, deaths, and murders! Why didn't people
then know what pain they'd cause for today?

The students around me are awake, but only in worlds
where they wish to be. They aren't here, where I am.
Here where I can't understand the motivations behind
those lost peoples' wars.

Do my friends and enemies who now sit sleepily beside me
understand? Do they care? I do.

And I want to know if I am going to become history. I
hope not. Not if it means that I too am bad....

Kathryn Marie Wilson

The Coachman

I have heard the horses coming,
   but I drove them back with hate.

I have seen the carriage coming,
   but I drove it back with anger.

I have heard the coachman speak,
   but I drove him back with pain.

I have seen the curtains moving,
   but I drove them back with fear.

I have heard the doorbell ring,
   but I drove it back with worry.

I have seen the coachman at the door,
   but I have driven him back with sorrow.

I have heard the rust of the hinge,
   but I drove it back with denial.

I have seen the dark claim the light,
   but I drove it back with pleading.

I have heard the rattle of death,
   and I accepted it with love.

Mary Elizabeth Tillman

Montana Roots

It was the time of the traditional revival
But he had been interpreting the early players
Long before they gave Bunk Johnson new teeth
Anointing him among jazz soothsayers.

A piano player moving through the west
Playing 'Jelly Roll' and swinging like 'Father'
A "Peck's Bad Boy" often unreliable
He seemed not to care or bother

In truth, he was both tolerant and patient
Allowing the untrained to sit in and play
Straining the endurance of his many fans
But some learned to play and returned another day

A jazz man of dedication and talent
X-ray eyes - an improvisor's vision
of a musical history
evolving eclectic fission

A revival fixture in San Francisco
with Waters and Murphy and on the pier
A living legend for 30 more years
To his many friends he was very dear.

Robert F. Michaud

Perfect Touch

Long black waves pulled back
Beautiful sparkling oceans
Wide grinning white
Soothing comforting tones
Gentle caring caress
Warm soft skin next to mine
So kind and real
Touch of silk
No harm in sight true and honest
The perfect touch our bodies next to each other
Firm embrace so kind and gentle
His arms around me my arms around him
Kiss on my lips
His hands caressing my body
My hands running through his hair
Down his back and up his chest
To his face bringing it closer to mine
Looking into each other's eyes
Our eyes close and our lips touch.

Shelly Lynn Pierce

Grace

Grace is Grace under pressure, Grace is
beauty that can't be measured, Grace is
a woman in a dress walking down the street

Grace is when she looks like somebody that
you want to meet.......... it is a bird gliding
across the sky

Watching its long wingspan makes you
wonder why....... it is day rolling into night
it is a relationship that you can get into
and find out later on that it's right

Grace is the way your girl looks the way
your girl talks........ it is the way that she comes
to you when you are hurt

Grace is a baby boy or girl, all of the snow
on the ground that you can see........

When you have a little woman and a family
by a Christmas tree........

Steven Wilson

Dedication To Alene, My Godmother

I have thought about the times we've had, the memories of good
and bad.
The reminiscing of old, and the stories that were left untold.
How can I go back to relive the past, when in between there's an
enormous gap?
Why is this so hard to do, when all I do is think of you?
There's an unbearable pain inside, telling me to run and hide.
Will my troubles follow me, or will they cease to proceed?
I can't take much more of this, I would like just one last wish.
Even though you are gone, my life on earth is not yet done.
I hope to see you again, when my days also come to an end.
I'm sorry I couldn't say good-bye,
it was all because of my foolish pride.
I just wanted you to know, that I really loved you so.
I must now compose my love for you, it shows my love through
and through...
You were a very nice person, your soul will move on.
I don't worship these days, when our loved ones are gone.
So remember the memories, they'll always live on!

Lisa Gooley

Individualism

One should not be looked upon with scorn
Because he or she violates the norm
We all have different ways of expression
Different ways of answering our own questions.
Life is but a short span soon to pass
Make the most of it while it lasts
Always be yourself.

Some might question your fashion
But I ask you to just imagine
What it would be like if we were all the same
In life's unpredictable game
Wouldn't it be somewhat lame?
You have a right to freedom of expression
So when they ask, give them this suggestion,
Always be yourself.
Kelechi Kalu

My Cat Symbony

This poems is dedicated to my special cat Symbony,
Because his meowing has a sound of a beautiful symphony.
His dark, black, and soft fur coat is shiny,
As his bright golden eyes reflect from the moon in the sky.
When I come home from work all sad and blue,
He comes and cheers me up, making me feel like new.
At night, when I go to bed, he lies with me like a teddy bear,
Because he likes to show me that he does care,
Symbony is more than a pet to me;
I feel he is a part of my family.
When he plays with the other cats in the front yard,
I make sure that they do not treat him wrong.
We both love each other as best friends,
And nothing can stop our friendship or make it end.
Laura Cathleen Montague

The Golden Years

What are the golden years? I'd really like to know.
Because the time has come for me and mine
And we're waiting for the "Golden" ray
To shine on us and show,
That glorious time that's talked about
Before it's time to go.

We planned all kinds of things to do
And places we would go.
But now that the time is here,
Our plans are going to show,
We cannot do all this, you see
Because none of it is free.

I guess we'll have to take it in stride,
And know that we have tried
To appreciate the "Golden Years"
And in all the rules abide.
We have each other and good health, too
Isn't that enough to get us through?
Lorraine M. Youngbar

Christmas

Christmas is a time of fun
Because you get presents from everyone
We stay by the fire to keep real warm
Because outside there is a big snow storm
On the roof top we hear jingle bells
It's Santa with his little elves
Reindeer flying in the skies
While children are sleeping in their beddie-byes
In time to wake up Christmas morn
Because it's the day Jesus Christ was born
Lauren Moreno

Deputy Section Blues

It's pathetic to see people unemployed, waiting in comp lines and
becoming annoyed.
Gazing at their numbers and wondering who's next, at the least
little sound
They all get vexed. Smelling of stale liquor and tobacco smoke.
Man standing in the comp lines ain't no joke!!

Some wear the remnants of their work, from brogan boots to
cashmere
shirts. Young folks, old folks and father young kids,
People from all levels who've lost their gigs,
But the claim searchers, in the files seldom poke.
Man standing in the comp lines ain't no joke!!

Folks guts are growling haven't eaten since six,
Been here since eight and they've got to wait.
Folks are cussin' and it's close to three,
But the sisters in the claim booth think it's funny.
They're watering flowers, reading cards, eating cookies and
Flirting with hearts.
Newspapers are lying all around and the folks are reading of other
let downs. Hail, to the folks!! Who'd rather be broke!!!

'Cause man, standing in the comp lines ain't no joke!!
Zyangquelyn A. Poe

"Aged To Perfection In '95"

Four boys came into this world
Before my parents had a little girl.

February 5, 1915 was the arrival date
For a little girl they no longer had to wait.

The things I have seen in 80 years you won't believe.
It's almost more than the mind can conceive.

Horse and buggy days, Model T's, fast cars and jets
So much more I tend to forget.

Indoor plumbing, electric lights, and telephone
Imagine talking around the world from your home.

What about the fireplace in days of old?
Your front was hot and your back was cold.

Listen to the radio and then watch TV
Music in the air, pictures you could see.

A man on the moon seemed out of the question
It has all happened while aging to perfection.

Now, tell the truth, which would you rather be,
A teenager, middle age, or old like me?

To me it is simple and not a question
I think in my years I have "Aged to Perfection."
Merial G. Preston

Soul Baring

Everyone wants freedom, but everyone doesn't want to
  be alone
Every time I look at someone; I wonder what they
  feel or think?
Are they happy, sad, content?
Sometimes I wonder what it would be like to be
  in someone else shoes.
Would it make me happy or different; maybe?
I guess I should try to make my shoes worthwhile.
Looking past the wear and tear. Maybe splurge on a polish!
I guess God made us fit into each sole in our
  own unique ways.
To challenge us from getting bored. To come to the
realization that, "If the shoe fits, wear it!"
So don't be concerned if it's too big or too small
Just be happy you have a pair at all!
Lisa Schleupner

Heaven's Rose

A mother holds her promised child
Before the eye can see.
A butterfly's dance in memory filed
She loves this life to be.

For now they share a quiet time
Whispered dreams between the two.
Then Christmas books with nursery rhymes
And teddy bears just for you!

You can choose the Christmas tree
I'll buy you a palace grand!
We'll find a beach where kites fly free -
I'll hold your soft warm hand.

Some petals fall with fragrance sweet
To fill this world with love.
The promised child she couldn't meet
Is held by God above.

The barren stem gives no clue
Of color meant to be.
A tiny bud touched by heaven's hue
Now a rose for His eyes to see.

Mary Allene Kirry

"A Starksfield Winter"

Even before the wind rips through me and my hands
begin to shake in the bitter cold,
I imagine I hear sound of the sleigh
slicing across the hard-packed snow.
It is a sound I have heard on nights colder than this,
but never so cleanly, so clearly as this one.

In the distance, I can see the church I was married in,
where I once sat quietly as a child, listening to the story
of a man named Job, trying desperately to forget the pain
of my too-tight shoes. I remember, too, the pain of admonition,
the pinches and jerks that came when I did not have the strength
to walk away on my own.

In moments I will lift my thick boots to this sleigh, but not before
two slender arms snake their way around my chest,
calming my fears and lending reason to this strange trip.
And even as the wind steals my breath away, she will hold me to steel,
her arms and legs like ropes that pull us downhill and into the night,
together towards something sweet and stolen,
some dim flicker snuffed out years ago
in the darkness of these Starksfield winters.

Misty D. Watrous

"No Control"

A nuclear missile
Behind the clouds, Covering the fog,
Darting forward as the Earth panics.
Fiercely, as they Gather together,
Hoping they will survive,
Idealistically, Justified faces,
Kindness to everyone.
Loving the last Minutes of time,
Never seeing each other again On this wide, circular earth.
Praying for lives, Quietly,
Running in the Streets Toward any protection, at doubt.
Underground, possibly,
Verging, While looking up,
Xenon is in the air.
Yelling, now running in terror, as the Zoom has begun.

Mendy Bennett

The Forest Deep

   Still was the night in the Forest Deep... I heard the willow
bend and weep... and the wind it blew against my face,
the scent of pine in a hallowed place... I heard the
sound of the owl's hoot, and the rustling leaves beneath
my foot... the sound of silence so still and calm, the
fragrant essence of a summer's balm... the whistling
wind played me a tune, the light was bright in the new
full moon... birds were asleep in their tree-top nest,
the crickets leaped without a rest... an elk scurried
amidst the trees, the branches swayed in the gentle
breeze... stars twinkled in the midnight sky, the
fluorescent glow of a firefly... the leaves whispered
in deep commune, the sparkling eyes of a ring-tailed
raccoon... a fox at large on a midnight prowl, the
eerie sound of a grey-wolf's howl... the creek trickled
with every drop, the bounding leaps of a rabbit's hop...
a warbler purred with sleepy eyes the anxious anti-
cipation of a new sunrise... Still was the night in the
forest deep, now I lay me down to sleep... Awaken
I will to another day... where in the forest I will stay.

Peter Mastropolo

Prairie

Gold upon the grain, long, slender,
Bending gingerly in the ticklish breeze;
Hills fluffed up like golden pillows
Beneath sheets of broccoli green.
The cedar tree is cemented in the soil,
Stiff and solitary among the waving wheat.
Twisted, knotted limbs, hang low
And are warmed by the persistent sun;
Each leaf follows its shadow - moving time.
Unending horizon holds the outstretched
Hand of an aqua sky.
Bread is on the wind.
There is distance everywhere.
The air gives way to cinnamon dust.
Dragonflies glisten green and blue;
Long and slender, they hover gently
Over flowers ripe with prairie cologne.

Mark Beal

One Last Kiss

A serenade of love has left,
beneath the sea the secret gift.
Upon a rock gathering the frayed,
together here you could have stayed.
A time so short but a time so true,
blood through my veins, an apocalypse for you.
My heart has died a thousand deaths,
a tear for every eternal theft.
A life alone, no time to spare,
she stole from me, but do you care?
A final kiss, a breathless pain,
a tear from my heart, like a drop of rain.

Kimberly Meek

Rain Time Slumber

When I hear the wind blow softly through the trees,
And the soft pitter-patter of rain through the breeze,
I slip away to a far off place and dream of other things.
I have nothing there to hide from, no fear of what life brings.
So beautiful and perfect everything seems to be,
Far off from reality, from things I don't wish to see.
Dreaming of the perfect things, especially romance.
Feeling the rain on my back when I choose to dance.
But when the rain is over and the winds all disappear,
I come back reluctantly and in real life I reappear.

Mary Gentili

While

The sun slowly drops its last tired ray
beneath the stubborn seas
while I drown in the depths of your eyes

You hold me safe as a bird flying free
and I dream dreams only angles could
while I sleep the sleep eternal

Raging storms thrash over the land
cleansing the earth for the spring buds
while I wilt in your glowing love

Volcanoes spewing stones across oblivion
and ash drifts over the majestic world
while I suffocate in the strength of your love

Be with me until the earth is reborn
for our love will forever prevail
through all existence.

Stacey Hammons

A Man

A New England farmer's life is demanding all year long,
beside him stood his wife, and family, keeping him strong.
Though never officially introduced, I saw him as a man,
dairy products they produced, on schedule, according to plan.
Through bitter cold and snowfall, sparing no time for fun,
with chain saws, axes, and splitting mauls, to the woods
went father and son.
Planting fields, no time to relax, cows being milked each day,
repairs, improvements, and property tax, a typical farmer's way.
Strenuous chores in sizzling heat, filled their barns with hay,
his son trudging the same beat, leaving no time for play.
Harvest, eternally saddened the farm, while chopping acres of corn,
this man encountered physical harm, his life was suddenly gone.
He worked for years with equipment, accidents are events unplanned,
just one unsightly moment lost a respected man. Invincible spirit
all along, determined to survive, he clung to life that fatal morn,
needing his wife by his side. For their father profound
admiration, his children were always his pride. I saw him, in
the heart of his son, looking deeply beyond his eyes.

Linda Lillibridge

Life

Life has IF in the middle, it is true
But don't let it make you feel blue.
   Love, laughter, lusty, longing
   Ignore, irate, irresistible
   Fair, flat, fabulous, funny
   Endure, elated, embrace, enjoy

Some people have dreams that go no further,
others, life gets snuffed out, due to another.
What right do they have?
NONE I SAY, BUT FOR THEM I MUST PRAY.

Why, only God knows. We must go on
even when our hearts ache
Memories ah, sweet memories so
dear to our loved one.

Yes, life can be one huge IF-draw
strength embrace it, fill life with
laughter. Ignore, but never forget-life
is not always fair, it can leave you
flat. Our life on earth is short, so
remember to embrace all the times are for a reason.

Nancy Gilbert

"Best Friends"

Can someone tell me what these two words mean?
Best is an adverb that tells to what extent
Best is a phrase that only one friend is sent
Best is a feeling that gives us a sense of pride
Best is a word that makes us smile real wide
Best is a narration recounting the events we've endured
Best is an illustration depicting the dreams we've shared
Best is an expression of the experiences we've walked
Best verbally represents the conversations we've talked
But why is Best accompanied by Friend?
Because Friend is a lonesome character when wandering alone,
but Friend is the most beautiful miracle when it has someone to
call its own
Friend is the part that sticks with no strings attached
Friends is the part that could care less if Best is mismatched
Friend is the part that strives to make everything right,
but yet when threatened, won't hesitate to fight
Put Best and Friends together transposed, scrambled, or even revised
and you still have two words that are easily recognized.

Lisa M. Brown

Stairway To Maturity

No longer a boy, yet not a full man,
Betwixt and between I don't understand!
Do I reach for a star or hold on to my youth,
Think I'll journey on, my search is for the truth.
I'm twenty now and time has passed so fast,
I reach for everything, but nothing seems to last!
I'll pinch myself and say, "This is not true,"
I'm still a young boy, nothing less will do!
I hear a little clatter somewhere in my brain,
The voice of someone loving, is this for my gain?
The words are quite persuasive, have I yet to learn,
That growth is but a stairway which rises at each turn.
I'm rising, I'm rising, with steps sure and true,
To wear the robe of man, I leave my youth to you.

Robert S. Cassell

Unknown

I must go seek for a love, a love I've yet to find.
Beyond the clear waters or the dirty skies;
There is one so perfect yet unknown,
Help me identify him for he shall be mine.

I must go seek for my feelings, yet unfolded.
I am a story, a story untold;
Bring out the best and the worst of me,
Then I'll help you for he shall be mine.

I must go seek for the words, my words only.
They have so much to say with little said;
and all I ask is for you to bring Him to me,
for He shall be mine.

Shana Pealer

Untitled

And now comes the thought of the rough seas
Beating heavily against the shores
The wind making haste, and yet,
Music and song to one's ears

The clouds rolling by into space
And the sun trying to peep through
To smile down upon my discovered treasures
And what are my discovered treasures?
'Tis love, life and beauty
For beauty is life and the Beauty of life is love
All this and heaven too
Lets me write this poem to you.

Vincent Nanni

Nepenthe

Evil miseries lurk tonight
Bitter thoughts abound
A gust of horror blows this way
and Sorrow felled by honest rite

To everything, a touch of blackness
To everywhere, a taste of shadow
A pitiful moan alights on ears
mad phantoms dance to convert the Sadness

Immoral, green and slimy creatures
Dark and damp things smell of rot
A visage of death stares out of the fog
and Failure reflected in horrible features

Tortured and twisted and savage by name
The power of poison and anger is nigh
Murderous demons play cut-throat this night
bright-eyed lunatics follow closely the Pain

Deadly slashes streak from above
Spiteful eyes glare and hateful mouths laugh
A nightmare at midnight is haunting outside
these monsters come forth to heal the lost Love

Robert Rembecki

Rain

Clouds tumbling along in the sky, first whites, greys, dark blues
and black, a storm is forming, that is why.

The earth smells sweet and moist, and eager with thirst;
for rain is life-giving to all the Universe.

Sweet gentle drops, kissing earths' brow,
Washing away the old, that was then, and shaping the new that is now.

Rain is sometimes like love, coming and going,
Violent with passion, then lulling to compassion.

Sometimes sad, its drops like tears,
Crying and weeping, for all to hear.

Full of fury, destruction and hate,
Often destroys, regretting too late.

When the storm ends, and the mists clear away,
The earth is refreshed, and it's a glorious day.

Over the horizon, a rainbow is seen,
With the beauty and promise that will come with the spring.

So thank God for rain, in all its forms,
For without it, we would be no more.

Tonia J. Elk

Ah Lin

China Woman, my Amah with her pigtail,
Black and white shadow
Carting cleaning rags and pail.

China Woman! I've come to say goodbye.
Thanks for all you've done
And never asking why.

China Woman, do not look so sad.
Mistresses come and go,
A new job will be had.

China Woman, turn your misting eyes from me.
(My pain and loss in parting
Is not for you to see.)

China Woman! So long, farewell, goodbye.
(Beloved surrogate mother
Without you I shall die!)

Nancy Morris

People

Rich people, poor people,
Black, red, white people.
Fat, tall, short, small,
Size differs within them all.

Young people, old people,
Newborns and dead people.
Lifeless, sightless, careless people,
Frail, braille, deaf people.

Fragile, broad, stout,
Did I leave any people out?
Angry people, kind-hearted people,
Messy, neat, on the spot people.
In this world, there are so many different kinds of people.
Just open your eyes and see.

Lisa Marie Rosini

Untitled

A man is of God, Jesus Christ, I'm sorry, I'm a bad.
  :Black snakes, good, eats man:, I'm naked woman
Remember, O most gracious Mary Virgin, I love Jesus Christ.
  A cuts of apple red good, good, good, pie, 8, see light.
Penn state polcine, pals of mine, I love all yea. Law of God.
  Good a man a land, freedoms, $.25, phone. Happicat, crap.
North American, so thee two and for cup kaffe, coffee $.65
  Volunteer job, U.S.A. a see swichic I tummy, I sorry stroke.
A man Smith Ben France, I love yall, Pope, world.

Leonard W. Dessify

The Phoenix

In my darkest nightmares
black wraiths with their stinging fingers
taunt me with their icy cackles
echoing in my mind's shadowy corner.

Their sneering faces cloud my vision
obscuring all but evil songs
that strike a deep and terrible rhythm
in some unprotected part of my heart.

With swords and knives of torment and scorn
they slash me, stab my soul
leaving raw, nagging incisions
that will not heal, but lead to scars.

Yet with these scars comes a new strength
rising from the flames of pain
like the mighty bird the Phoenix
my tortured soul will rise again
and triumph.

Lauren Moran

Daughters Prayer

Heavenly Father full of grace,
Bless my mother's pretty face.
For now is the first time for which I've said,
"Thank you for letting me be your kid."
Bless her for being my friend,
I know our friendship will never end.
Bless her arms that comfort me.
Bless her for showing me things I would've never seen.
If she happens to read this poem of mine,
I hope she realizes I treasure all of our time.
Bless her for beginning my life,
For my father says she is the perfect wife
Bless her for letting me feel
For now I know what is real.
If I don't love her like I should,
Forgive me Father for I have just committed a sin.

Ryan Elizabeth Savage

Searching For Vera Cruz

They succumbed at Auschwitz,
blindly and dazed.
Their strife was a people's mourning,
recognized but not explicit.
Many a people left tears trailing on their
road to mortality.
From the arid haunches ridden by Cortes,
to the frigid ideals melted by Stalin.
Pillars and skins rolled over Europe with
imperial negligence,
And not a drop of emotion is shed for
these indecencies.
The great lands here produced at the expenses of a race,
but never discussed, though heartily ignored.
If consecration of the chosen people hallows their innocence,
then all races must be acknowledged,
And all suffering must pass.
As the pains subsist, so looms the threat of
repeat.

Sean Flannery

Life

Birth such a wonder, The miracle of life
Born without worries, born without strife

But change comes so quickly,
and time goes so fast
We only get started,
We blink, it's passed.

When young we're immortal
With time on our side
No thoughts of the future
Just enjoying the ride

Then just when we're thinking
We're under control
age slips upon us, were suddenly old.

But just growing older
Doesn't mean we are through.
As long as there's breath,
There's living to do.
So learn to enjoy it,
This gift we were given
Take each precious moment and use it for livin!

Johnny J. Davidson

To My Father

Great Oak
   Bowed and bent
      With
Scabrous branch
   Straining under winter's heavy load
      I
Cannot cloak your shivering limbs
   Nor
Stay the bleeding from within

The wind carries you to me
   In the far away places of my heart
      I
Have been a witness to you in better times
   Have leaned against you
      On a warm spring day

I am beside you now as always
   A fragile vessel
      Slight and small
In awe of the gnarled roots
   Reaching deep into the hard unyielding ground

Lydia C. Vine

Autumn In Texas

I love the autumn, in all its colors;
   Brilliant reds, golds, yellows and all the others.
The crisp, cool air finally reaches the south,
   The smells of fall, tease my nose and my mouth.
The squirrels are busy, storing their winter food,
   A colt in the pasture romps, in his giddy mood.
We open windows wide, and welcome fresh air;
   Being tired of summer, Texas heat hard to bare.
Hummingbirds head south with the ducks and geese;
   Coming back next spring, after winter's release.
Pumpkins and pecans will be ready real soon;
   The harvest takes place at the full of the moon.
The turkeys are fat, what a feast they will make;
   With cornbread dressing, and the pies we'll bake.
Autumn means football, our super-bowl-team,
   Bar-B-Que and hot dogs, home-made chili——I mean!
The first frost is early, winters on its way,
   I love autumn in Texas, I think I will stay.

S. Brownlee Cobb

Sweet Memories

Sweet memories, of days gone by...
Bring back visions of friends by your side.
   Sweet Memories
Visions of the things you loved
When your youth you were full of....
Fly through your mind as you smile, sweetly.
   Sweet Memories
The thoughts of youth come and go...
That couldn't have been so long ago?
The smells of fresh spring winds
Floating past, as you dream of pleasant days,
pleasant ways...
   Sweet Memories
The sounds are sweet and mellow...
Sweet and mellow.
Quiet, smooth, and calm,
They linger, long in your memories.

Patsy L. Samanski

Sunset Over Mecox Bay

His old skin is wrinkled -
brown, weathered, and dry.
The setting sun casts a glint in his eye.
A flock of sparrows flitter by.

Walking the sand that time won't leave still,
he looks from the shore to his house on the hill.
Leafless trees blow in a cold winter chill.
He remembers the bushels he used to fill.

Home before dusk; dawn saw him awake
to ready his waders and load up the rake -
ten, fifteen baskets - a good day's take.
Kept his home warm with the toil he'd make.

His wind battered boat is now hauled ashore -
no longer seaworthy, she will sail no more.
Salt rusted rake now holds an allure
for sand crabs and terns, no clams as of yore.

Gulls fly high as the clouds start to blow.
"Birds in a flurry. We'll be getting some snow."
I reach for his hand as the sun sets low.
A kiss on the cheek, "Come on, Dad. Let's go."

Marjorie Squires Johnston

The Child Within

The pain of abuse, too great for a child
Buried so deep, it now appears mild
The pain grows with them, day after day
If anyone knew, what would they say
No one to listen, no one to care, never to tell, they wouldn't dare
Silent screams that can't be heard
It must stay a secret, they can't breathe a word
They drift off to sleep, in a state of fright
Dreams of peace get them through the night
Restless with fear, feeling deranged
A new day upon them, yet nothing has changed
Never learning love and tenderness, only fear and violence
They carry the guilt, they can no longer hide
A burden too great to be held inside
To open their hearts, and let the child out
Would bring too much grief, without a doubt
A life of confusion, filled with despair
While society continues to perceive it as rare
We must put an end to this tragic route
The child within must be let out

Shelly Hill

"Eyes Of Faith"

They tell me spring is coming just two weeks from today.
But after Monday's ice storm it seems very far away.
The trees, their branches frozen, they are a pretty sight.
But as far from showing springtime as day is far from night.

The calendar says Easter is next on down the road,
Portraying Jesus' rising and lifting of our load.
I wasn't there to see it - they say 'twas quite a sight!
The stone rolled back from Jesus' grave -
by God's own awesome might!

They said if I would trust Him, believe He died for me,
I wouldn't have to see it, but He would make me free!
I said that I would do it and everything looked new.
His words took on new meaning and all of them are true!

Just as sure as new life's given is the cycle of the year.
And though we may not see it, the sun's in the atmosphere.
They say the King is coming as Lord of everyone.
So put your eyes of faith on - we're going to see the Son!

Kathie Merrill

Lost

I walk through the streets looking for that face,
But all I ever meet is my destined place.
Friends say I'm not alone,
They will be there throughout the years.
Yet no answers on the phone,
When silence brings my tears.
On the screen at which I stare,
Lovers embrace in a hug.
Oh why can't I be there,
I just lie solely on this rug.
Once I crawled beneath covers for warmth and care,
Time has passed, now I do not even dare.
I'm tossing and turning, so by the window I sit.
Are you ever returning, hoping my candle is always lit.
A starry sky shines so bright,
My wish is cast for you.
I can wait if I might,
For in my dreams one has found two.

Paula Starr

Without Love!

Love what a wonderful word
But can you believe
It's one some have never heard
Life is short, sometimes long
But without love it's always wrong
Imagine, if you can
Not having that girl or special man
Not having someone to yell at when you're mad
Not having a shoulder when you're sad
Not having someone who would go that extra mile
Not having someone to make you smile
Without love it's like the summer with sunshine lost
Like the winter without the frost
So if you're lonely I hope you see
Love is around you and me
If you open your arms to accept
You'll find love with no regret

Rowland L. Trent Jr.

Farewell To A Friend

It's hard to accept when you lose a good friend,
But he won't be away for too long.
Perhaps around the corner, perhaps around the bend,
God has his way of uniting us again.

Well miss his laughter, we'll miss the fun,
of watching his reaction when I'd
Tell him the band won.

He loved what the band stood for, and likewise
So do we, to watch him march and play
his music, it wasn't hard to see.

We'll see you again, another season,
Another Street.
And if God leads a band in heaven,
You'll never miss a beat.

Kevin J. Gibbons

Mumbling Ducks

I heard some mumbling ducks today
Beside a lake where children play
And a sea gull grinned and caught my eye
As a butterfly swirled and twirled merrily by
And the birds chattered happily up high in the trees,
While the flowers tried to playfully catch the bees
And amidst such natural expressions of delight
I found there was no way that I could write
So I had to put my pen away
And go to join the children play

Vicki L. Volkman

Except You

I am writing you this poem I
doubt you'll ever see. To explain things,
are more different than I even thought they'd be.
I handed you my heart with every bit of love,
then I felt it coming back with a push
and then a shove.

Not even then would I give up. I tried
to keep you near but yet still then you went
away and did not shed a tear. Things became
so different and we got so out of hand. The
time was then I needed you most and you
wouldn't understand. Whoever said love
hurts needs to know the truth. Love hurts to
everyone, everyone but you.

Erica Wigginton

Majestic Ruin

Henry VIII killed wives, lovers, friends, enemies - BEHEADED
By his command. Not all were mortals.
Stretching high towards God's heaven, NAKED, stripped of
Gold, jewel, sculpture (all of value long gone
With Henry's men) stands Tintern Abbey, roofless -
   BEHEADED !
With paneless windows, walls less high (some not there),
Steeples, towers gone - Tintern Abbey stands proud, stands tall:
Still visited by legions, who stare in awe,
And leave a piece of their hearts here.
A silent laugh may be heard, by those who listen with
Their HEARTS, made by this proud house of God.
   SHE KNOWS !
Henry is unloved, dead, gone,
While within the hearts of Wordsworth, Englishmen,
The legions, our beloved Tintern Abbey LIVES ON !

   Joan Busic Hey

Incense Of Insanity

The tears filled the mind,
By the black twisted spoon.
All of which fell red,
Stained the heart of death.
Laced with deception,
Spots of green appeared.
The patches of life faded,
Overcome with the angels of Hell.
Dreaming against the ropes of the destined.
With goats as their rulers,
None of whom sleep,
Amongst the stars of day.

   Jennifer Yim

Heralding Spring

The sun of this late February day has warmth equaled only
by the warmth I feel when I am near to you.
I basked in that warmth all this lazy afternoon, iced tea at
my elbow, footstool at my feet.—pen in hand, to record the
wonderful splendor of your friendship.

Tomorrow it may snow.—and the hungry little birds, devouring
my humble offerings, will hide away—waiting to return when
spring is ever closer.

But I have absorbed enough heat today, from God's nature,
and your special kindness, to last me through the coldest
of hours.

Blessings flow. Praise God from whom they have been sent.
For he truly has blessed our warm and gentle friendship.

   Jo Piper

Seven To Three-Thirty, Five Days A Week

Calloused fingers,
Calloused brain.
No break in the monotony of the day.

The hum of the machines
becomes my own jungle of dreams.
drifting...drifting...
I become one with my thoughts...

Snapped back to reality by a sharp buzz,
we all trudge,
ONE PEOPLE, thepuertoricanspolishandme.
Language is our only barrier
as we moan and complain.

Such is the life of the Holyoke factory worker,
Such is the life of me.

   Beth Babski

The Leaf

The leaf sits on the tree
Calmly, Patiently
Waiting for something
Perhaps a light breeze for it to sway slightly with
Or maybe a drop of rain to rest in its sheltering green palm
Until then, the leaf waits patiently, patiently
For something to happen
Maybe death
When it floats softly down to the ground
And ends its life.

   Florence Kizza

God

Can He who created all eyes, not see?
Can He who created all emotions, not feel?
Can He who created all ears, not hear?
Can He who created all minds, not understand thoughts?
Can He who created all muscle, not move?
Can He who created all noses, not smell?
Can He who created humor, not laugh?...

Let me then, bow at my knees to the Majestic
King who created all.
Let me then, give praise and worship from
the mouth and lips that He created.

   Juliana Anfeldt

Day Of Sorrow

Oh, wretched day of despair
Can hope show its face to meet this dreadful requiem.
Could I, if need to, brace my courage to its hilt
Thereby not seeing, and hide my tears of deep pain
   and desperate gloom.

Somewhere lies trust dormant, but not within me.
My anger with my fate dwells and sours my being
And yet, I strive within me to comprehend this
   that plucks the joy from my life.

My courage has waned leaving my bare nerves exposed
   and vulnerable.
The weight of my destiny lies hard and heavy.
But only I can resolve what must to bring about the
   ultimate end.

   Barbara S. Ninness

Adversity

Wake me up from this nightmare.
   Can I not have any relief from
This pain and frustration.

Wake me up from this nightmare.
   Or is this just life, and I am thrown
In the middle of this confusion.

Wake me up from this nightmare.
   Even though, the alternative is
Far more devastating.

Wake me up from this nightmare.
   However, this constant adversity has changed me;
Made me stop and look at life from a different perspective.

Wake me up from this nightmare.
   Although, this nightmare emphasized certain desires.
And a passion to see them through.

Wake me up from this nightmare.
   But, I can see a deeper purpose for certain
Actions, and a reason for continuing.

Wake me up from this nightmare.
   Maybe not.

   Dena Campbell

Friends In Flight

Carefree
Floating freely
In the sky blue height;
Gentle breezes
Guiding our flight;
Winged mocking birds
Singing blithe;
Alighting together
In the moonlit twilight.

William F. Hoffman

New Horizons

Staring into the darkness
A blank thought on a piece of paper
Broken dreams an open future
left for my own fixed destiny

Peering into the sunlight
warm rays on my skin
inquisitive eyes gaze
at the pool of corn flower blue
some call the sky

Wondering, thinking deeply
is the earth really such a large place,
or is it that the human race is so small

A big open world around me
new experiences at my reach
to be taken advantage of
new growth and development
to take to the limit to live on the edge
interesting people to meet, places to see
friendly faces
Each star sparkles just for me

Katherine McGuire

A New Life

In the spring of a morn
A child is born
So soft and so fresh
A child to caress

It gives life new meaning
Simplicity Seething
A purpose in life
To face all the strife

A fresh breath of air
A reason to care
New hopes and new dreams
A future it seems

Life's outlook gets brighter
Our hearts feel much lighter
In the spring of a morn
A child is born.

MaryLynne Swetland

Sleeper's Insomnia

Sleep is, as it asks,
a cure for some wounds.
A temporary task,
to hide in our womb.
A time to live dead,
the anatomy lies.
While subconscious, instead,
reveals truths, denied.

Theodore T. Owen

Love

A gorgeous summer day,
A delightful park in Maine,
A bottle of wine,
A pair of goblets,
A book,
A bag of chips,
A cool breeze,
A moment in time,
A memory of love,
A romance,
A handsome man,
A beautiful woman,
A cuddle,
A caress,
A kiss,
A love,
One love,
Our love,
Forever...........

Loretta McLean

A Dream

A dream is a picture of what could be
A dream is a memory of what used to be
A dream is a hope
A dream is a wish
A dream is your thought of what life is

Some dreams are happy
Many are sad
To dream a dream is better
Than to never have

To be able to dream
Is a wonderful thing
To know what you want
To be what you want to be

To never dream is such a loss
To imagine, to escape
To be your own boss
To be in control you will never know
A dream is a dream you know

Kimberly A. Moniz

Garden Of Lies

I planted a garden
A garden of lies
I planted it years ago

It survives by disguise
and false alibis
Still it continues to grow

The truth becomes lost
as I stop at no cost
to protect my garden from fact

And the lies that I've used
have made the truth seem confused
and now rendered my life just an act

If I go to my grave
with the lies that I gave
please don't consider me wise

When they write on my stone
beneath this ground lies alone
A fool in his garden of lies

Paul Spinola

The Past's Pleasantness

Tomorrow is a reach for the future
   a goal to conquer.
Yesterday is a well worn
   memory book
   not given a second look.
The future is a street
   of discoveries to be reached.
Very few look back
   to review the past.
It's filled with golden moments
   and pleasantness.
When faced with life's differences
   it brings on a ray of hope
   and new light.
Too bad, the world is moving too quick,
   to once look back....
      to see,
What peace the past has brought.

Lara Bartlett

One Perfect Moment

It lasted so short a time;
A lifetime lived in that moment.
I wished to suspend, to grasp, to control
That single instant.

The perfectness of time was contained;
The vividness of reality shown.
A moment of truth -
All illusion gone.

Never was life so sweet
Than in that single instant,
Yet I could not reach to grasp
Nor manage to suspend or control.

It slipped
   and fell -
Like a rock shattering glass.

Tami L. Hite

An Elusive Dream

Fond memories of the past,
a longing to hold,
for them to last.
Recaptured moments in our dream,
short and fleeting,
though they seem.
A love long gone,
a hint of song.
Momentarily a face
of my beloved.
A special place,
that haunting need,
lost heart to feed.
A word, a touch
to mean so much.
A shadowy form
to yet remain,
to ease the ache,
to soothe the pain.

Louise Witherspoon

Looking Down

Colored lights shine in
   an endless path
Never ceasing
   till morning arises.

Sara Mayo

A Simple Love Poem

I hope that I will someday see
a Love as true as it can be.

A Love so true that it would Share
and Love and Give and Love and Care.

There's nothing else of equal worth
and I must find it here on Earth.

'Cause in the Afterlife I know
exists that Love where some will go.

The requisite for getting in?
A hope to find that Love and Win.

Thomas Owen Maxwell

There's A Love Burning Deep

Way down inside.
A love so intense,
   It won't be denied.

It's a love that's meant,
   for two alone to share.
A love so great,
   none other could compare.

But there's a barrier there,
   That's been meant to be.
And until it is broken,
   I'll never be free.

I've tried and I've tried,
   but I can't let it go.
All it wants it says,
   Is a chance to grow.

Tammy T. Murray

Love Curse

A curse is an infliction on the soul,
a madness in the brain,
Which causes emotions to stir-
and often feelings of pain.
Is love evil, is that what I feel;
being away from you
Hurts the fibers of my essence,
tears at my mind,
Causes my fingers to tremble
with rage and excitement
at the same exact time.
I wish I knew what to say,
I wish I knew what's in my head,
I lay tossing and turning
all along in my bed!

Keith L. Stanley

My Mother's Garden

My mother's garden was really
A sight to see. All the beautiful
Vegetables growing she cared
For so tenderly. She really loved
Her garden and she tended it each
Day; she tended it with loving care
Just before God called her away.
And through the middle of her
Garden she always planted a row of
Flowers. She loved to watch them
While she worked away the hours.
Now her garden is no longer
Growing for the Lord has called
Her home. But I can still see
In my memory that garden stands
Alone.

Royce E. Alley

Homeless

I'm a homeless person.
A man gave me a wastebasket today.
When he looks at me
does he see waste to be thrown away?

My jacket has holes.
My blanket is holes.
My shoes are so holey
they have attained nirvana
and ceased to exist.
Drink keeps me warm
where my blanket does not
and puts holes in my life.

I can't decide if it's better
to live in the holes,
which are blank,
or to live in the pieces
around them.
Which part should I throw away
in the wastebasket?

Maria A. Boyd-Paddock

I Tried

Every time I close my eyes
A picture of you forms in my mind
I cannot sleep
I cannot hide
These secret feelings I have inside
I slowly bow my head and cry
My heart is tired and mystified
I heard your thoughts
I knew
I tried
The only way
True suicide
One final time, I close my eyes
Take a breath
Fall and rise
Nothing is true
When someone dies
I near the end
Not proud
Inside

Mavilen Silva

This Sinner's Prayer

My God, My God, My Lord, My Christ
A sinner's prayer I pray.
Thee died to set the sinner free
Please heed my cry today.

Thee died, three days returned to life
This I believe is true,
And with thy death unloosed the chains
And gave us life anew.

Satan has lost, My God, My Lord
His hold because of thee.
Dear Jesus come into my life
And set this sinner free.

Jesus, my wretchedness thou see
But I know thee still care
My God, My God, My Lord, My Christ
Please hear this sinner's prayer.

Raven Forest

The Temple

I love to see the temple
A special place of God
He knows that I will listen
And hold strongly to the rod

A peaceful house of love
That it will always be
When I go inside the temple
I will see all I can see

I'll fast and pray and listen
And when it's time to go
I'll hear a holy whisper
And I will always know

It's time to go inside the temple
To marry to my mate
I know that God will be there
To seal us on this date.

Tammy Craven

Easter

Ash Wednesday comes and with it, Lent
A time for preparation
When Christians of their sins repent
In prayer and meditation

The season passes swiftly by
Palm Sunday soon is here
The multitudes "Hosanna!" cry
When Jesus passes near

Maundy Thursday - one last time
To break bread with the Lord
Before Good Friday's vile crime
Fulfills God's holy word

Saturday, the darkened tomb
A symbol of our sin
Like caterpillar's webbed cocoon
Holds wondrous joy within

For as the butterfly is born
Released from his dark prison
So Christians sing on Easter morn
"Alleluia! Christ is risen!"

Marjorie Lawrance

A Time For Children

Christmas is a time for children
A time to be happy and gay
Christmas is a time for children
When Santa comes on his sleigh
To open their presents with joy
To receive that very special toy
For laughing and for playing
To learn of loving and of praying
To dress up in a special way
To gather with all on this magical day
Christmas is a time for children
A time of love and hope and cheer
Christmas is a time for children
And it comes just once a year
Christmas is a time for children
Christmas is a time
Christmas is
And it comes again next year.

Ronald J. D'Elia

Winter

Winter is gray
A time to pray
The snow falls hard
Upon the bard.

The flowers are dead
We get ahead
By enjoying the view
From the church pew.

I look to God
For power and might
I find a mode
Of strength and light.

I see a vision
Of non-derision
A look of emotion
And true devotion.

Marie Merenhole

"To Bob and Sleep"

It would have been
a tragic twist of fate
had I arrived
a minute later.

Greater
would have been the risk
to have missed
a single kiss
if I had tarried.

Ferried deep
to bob and sleep
alist in liquid dreams
immersed.

Thirst sated
saturated
in this
cavernous
abyss
of bliss.

Lisa D. Hoberg

Who Will Be Next

When God looks down and sees
All these people who have paid their fees
They have earned their tickets out of here
To live in a place without fear

How does he choose
Who will be the next one we will lose
Will it be my best friend
Whose life has to end

How can he tell if they are ready yet
We will never find the answer, I bet
Does he just guess
Some say no, some say yes

But, the greatest question has to be
When will he take me
Will he just pass me by
Just take my friends, and watch me sigh

He probably has a plan
For every child, woman, and man
I guess we will never have a clue
Will it be me, or will it be you

Trisha M. Smith

My Loved One Is Waiting For Me

My loved one is waiting for me
A way up in the sky
Far above the clouds so high.
One day I will be there,
Though the waiting is hard to bear,
Just to know, that I will see
My loved one waiting for me.

The days and nights are long,
But, with the Lord, I am strong.
Oh I do miss my loved one so,
I'm sure he must know
That I have to wait
Till I can go through the gate.
My loved one is waiting for me.

Vera L. Moody

A Child's Tear!

A tear of a child,
A wisp of blond hair,
Piercing blue eyes,
A heart full of fear.

A heart stricken song,
Of whimpers and whines,
A clenched little hand,
Full of so much time.

A sad little song,
Expressing so much,
Escaping from the world,
Without even a touch.

Meghan Paquette

"A Wonderful Mother"

God made
  a wonderful mother,
One whose soul
  Never grows old.
He made her smile
  Of the sunshine,
And he molded her
  heart of pure gold.
In her eyes he placed
  bright shining stars,
In their cheeks
  Fair roses you'll see.
God made
  A beautiful mother
And he gave that
  Dear mother to me!
  With all my love,

Robyn Jean Gary

Alone

A path that is like
A maze
Each opening a
Closing
Lost in the middle
You turn, see a mirage
An image so clear
No one really there
Leaves whispering
Bringing another end
Helpless tears
Running down a face
Knowing
Alone.

Lynnette R. Hamm

Dream

I never dream
About the waving of the trees
And the breeze in the leaves.
I never dream
Of the spray from the sea
And the sand on my knees -
So, I go sit in the forest
Where the leaves flourish,
Or travel to the ocean
To lie on the sand -
Follow the trail of a tern
While the sun constantly burns.
Because what I do dream
Is of a surrealistic hell
Where there is no sense of smell -
What pleasure is there then?
Like being stuck on an isolated river bend.
In what of dreams do people see
When all I desire is in reality.

Thomas M. Powers

New Beginning

Today I'm writing, for you,
About what is going to be,
Together, forever,
Just you and me.

Time seems to be nothing,
If you're not near to share,
And the days seem forever,
If you're not there.

But, when we are together,
The time just slips away,
Nights never last long enough,
Before it's a new day.

We've taken so much for granted,
But that's all going to end,
Now that we're starting to realize,
It's time to begin again.

From this day on,
It will be the way it's meant to,
No more tears or pain,
For my darling, I love you.

Michelle Baker

Bread And Water

Bread and water, bread and water;
All our bread was made with water.
And, water also made our gravy
Though passing years have made it hazy.

Times back then were very bad,
I know it made my Mother sad
Not to set a better table
But doing all that she was able.

Stomachs to our backbones touched
From skipping lunch to make enough
For Mom to make that night time meal.
And all those empty stomachs fill.

Things were tough but we were fighters,
Laughter and singing made hearts lighter
And always, there, was my Mother's love
And her loving trust in our God above

Bread and water, bread and water,
Both bread and gravy were made with water.
The years have passed, and Mom is gone;
But still the memories linger on.
Mom I love you.

Wanda Matlock Compton

"A New Start"

As you walk right in the door,
again I'll try to even the score.
You've taken my love and thrown it away,
and now it's too late for me to stay.
Life used to be 'oh so grand,'
until upon me, you laid your hand.
What ever happened to all the flowers,
and all the other happy hours.
Once I thought our love forever,
but now I know, it was for never.
This letter I write to say 'goodbye,'
for all the if's, when's and why's.
With my life, that you've torn apart,
I think it's time, I made a new start!

Sue Widdowson

The Rock

I'm standing on the Rock,
against the raging sea;
   the waves are rolling in
   pounding against me.

The sand all around me
seems to wash away;
   but that Rock that I'm standing on
   is always there to stay.

As the wind starts whirling,
whirling all around,
   with the Rock as my foundation
   I won't be blown, down to the ground.

The Rock in my life
the one that is my brace,
   it is the love of God
   and I've been saved by grace.

Kristina Smith

Living Water

Rough water crashes,
against the rocks,
rushing to be first place,
and to win their love.

The seas are burning,
for their one true love.
Before the tide runs out,
and all the love of one person,
dies.
All the love in the world,
reaches the tide,
on the earth.

Rough water crashes,
Against the rocks,
all have gained first place,
all have won their one true love.

Seth Mead

Tribute

Listening, hearing,
A smile on my face,
Or a tear in my eye.

When I celebrate,
The music lets me dance and sing.
When my soul is crying out,
It is comforted by song.

Without music, there is no release,
And emotion is trapped in the soul.

Shelly L. Loutzenhiser

My Children

As I watch my children's faces,
ages 10-2 and 1,
I see so much love, so much beauty.
No ugliness, no anger, just questions...

How do I answer the questions
That I know will come.
How do I say "he loved you, he just
Loved himself more."
How do I say "You are special, there's
No one else in the whole world like you."
How do I say "I'm sorry I made the
wrong choices, but I'm glad I did
or I wouldn't have you."
How do I say "It's not my fault."

Victoria Sanders

God's Friend

Mommy, did God have a little ole dog
All shaggy and good like mine
With warm, soft fur and a cold, wet nose
And a waggly tail all the time?

Yes, Son, I'm sure as He knelt to pray
In the garden when He was alone,
Resting quietly at His feet
Was a little dog all His own.

And too I'm sure if it were known
When Jesus was a boy like you,
Trotting behind wherever he went
Was his little dog...faithful and true.

And when He carried that heavy cross
To the hill where He died that day,
I have no doubt that His little friend
Followed not far away.

I believe as Jesus forgave them all
He looked down at His little friend
"Stay here and carry on for me,
Until I come again...."

W. Robert Hylton

Love

Oh, Love-Spirit so sweet and pure,
All sickness and pain Thou can cure.
But just the thought of Thou so great,
Will make us know we are to mate.
That someday, somehow, somewhere,
Along the ground, the water or the air,
We shall rest forever in each other arms,
And to us the world will do no harm.
For Holy, Holy, Holy are we -
Your love, my wife and me.

K. K. Kenny

Aloneness

The earth has stopped its spinning.
All is dark and still.
I await a movement, a light, a sound
But, it is silence still.

All is dark and lying
The wind no longer can you hear.
A dread, a fear, rises in my chest
As big as the world is wide.

I am left outside the show of life
With no one by my side.

Norma P. Barger

Dream's Reality

I dreamed we were strolling...
   along a white sandy beach...
Where the stars were like diamonds...
   sparkling far beyond reach.
And as we listened to the ocean...
   gently caressing the shore...
We were caught in the rapture...
   of the moon's lusty lure.
It was a beautiful fantasy...
   I wished to come true...
Shared by two lovers...
   beneath a sky of deep blue.

But as the soft evening breeze...
   echoed our sighs in the night...
The dream slowly faded...
   into dawn's morning light.
Then suddenly you appeared...
   as clear as could be...
And what I thought was a dream...
   was reality.

Pauline Selby

My Desire

Hidden within my hearts desire
an ember waiting to become a fire.
There in my mind for me to see
oh won't you be a part of me.
My head is full of a glorious time
when you will share my simple rhyme.

My desire for you is all I know
it picks me up and makes me go.
A heart is breaking within me now
you are the cure let me tell you how.
For I know that when and if we meet
my desire for you no one can beat.

The future I see and it is oh so clear
will have you with me my darling dear.
I'll hold you in my arms so tight
give me a chance I'll make it right.
My desire is enough to feed my soul
but you are my love the eternal goal.

J. A. Emerson

A Rose

One day I received a rose,
A very beautiful red rose.
The card read:
"I Love You So"
But with no signature.

The next day I received a rose,
A very beautiful white rose.
The card read:
"I Love You Even More So"
Again with no signature.

The following day,
Valentine's Day,
I received a rose,
A very beautiful peach rose.
The card read:
"I Love You Just The Same"
But this time with a signature...
But one I could not read!

Melissa Ann Feder

"Old Tired Man"

There in front of me
An old tired man sits
He stares as if he cannot see me
Not a word from his tired lips

Together we sit in silence
Not a word do we speak
As if in case of violence
Not a word does he speak

Reminding me of a man
Who never showed he cared
A man, who never even held my hand
So the silence is all we shared

Break the silence
Leave and be gone
Never saw any violence
No good-bye and I was gone

The old man reminds me of
one I had known
Silence we shared together
No emotions had he ever shown
The old man in front of me, had been my
father

Marla King

Each Cherished Kick

I felt your first kick,
    an was overjoyed,
        Your first hello.
            Mommies always cherish
                each of their children's
                "Firsts."

With you, I cherished
    each kick. They were
    few and far between.

One happy Saturday night,
    not only did I feel your kick,
        but I saw it to.
            Again I was overjoyed.

Three days later, sadly
    I gave birth
        to you silent, still form.
            Now I know,
                and cherish even more,
                    that last kick.
                        Your only goodbye.

Rogers

My Mother

Mother a soft and gentle touch,
A word spoken that means so much,
Teacher, friend, homemaker, and often
a prayer maker,
Most of all she is a real caretaker.

What would the world be without this
person so lovely,
Lonely and cold are the words to me
Without this woman to mold our family.
Aches and pains are many for her
None so big she can't conquer.

A hug and a kiss mend the heart,
And she's always ready for a new start.
This is what a mother is to me,
Blessed by God may she always be.

Vicki Booth

Farewell

Only these few short hours, my darling,
And all my life long
I must feed my secret dreams
Upon the bare remembrance of your face
What shall I do, my dearest,
When the age-old longing for your kiss
Returns?

What shall I say when,
In the dull monotony of years,
I hear a voice like yours?
And like a wounded bird,
The wing beats of my heart
Grow frantic at the sound
And die again, seeing a stranger speaks.
Let me remember this:
That though for others many years
Cannot suffice,
In these few hours, we, knowing they were all,
Lived out our lives.

Louise Moon

Soldier Boy

When shadows fall upon the earth,
And birds hop from tree to tree,
And cattle feed upon the turf,
Then it's home I long to be.

When peepers call from out the deep
And bobolink calls me too;
Then it's back home I long to be
Where the sky is clear and blue.

Back to my sweetheart, and the folks
Back to a country that's free;
It's living in peace at my home
That lives in my memory.

I wish I could sleep in my bed
All downy and soft and white,
And have lots of good books to read,
And a room flooded with light.

Oh! For a place to hang my hat
And plenty of food to eat,
A catcher's glove, a ball, and bat,
And the whole world at my feet.

Marjorie Miller

Fall Away

The moon lights your face
and I wonder
if you have yet
to notice me
in the shadows
watching you
dance amongst the candles.

The candles dim
one by one
and all go out
at once
leaving you to guess
where the headstones are.

I decide to leave
hoping you'll follow me.
Maybe you did.
How should I know?
I jumped the bridge
on the way home, thinking you loved me
enough to catch me if I fell.

Victoria Lelaina & Kate L. Debnar

My Little Tammy

Pink and soft
and delectably sweet
from her perfect head
to her tiny little feet

Tammy's her name
and it's nearly a week
since she came to us
to protect and to keep

I'll kiss away her hurts
as much as I can
and when she needs me
I'll hold her little hand

I'll spoil her a little
but not too much
this little girl
I love to touch

My little Tammy
I want you to know
out of Grandma's heart
love will forever flow

Mary L. Alex

Change

Where nature's trees once stood
And fruitful orchards grew,
There's now a dearth of grass;
Flowers and shrubs are few.

Entombed is fertile earth
In concrete covered grave,
Headstoned with structures
In nature-altering wave.

Fields of corn and other crops
Nourished abundantly from soil today
Grow less, and alarmingly fade away
As concrete and building interplay.

God gave us light, soil, and drink—
this earth of life and beauty;
He also gave wherewith to think,
Memory, and sense of duty.

Are not gratitude and vision,
Using endowments prudently—
Nothing of nature destroying—
Each man's responsibility?

M. Dail Riggs

"April"

Scores of daffodil,
And gentle breezes blowing;
Green grass and blue skies,
Our senses glad in knowing.

Tired winter has to concede
To the brilliant burst of life;
Cascading drops on verdant hills,
The sky takes the earth for a wife.

Diamonds cannot be compared
To the radiant jewels of spring;
A heavenly choir seems to accompany
A fledgling's first attempts to sing.

Unfettered we go into the summer,
Having known the better part.
Our freshly-washed world
Is April's most eminent work of art.

Marilyn Follis

Save Us Some Land

Save us some land,
And give us a hand.
We're endangered species.
Please help us if you can.
We're like a human.
Oh, please, please understand,
We need a helping hand.
Please don't be prejudiced,
You have to understand this.
We really need a helping hand.
So, please save us some land.

Stephanie Rivera

Then And Now

Inspired by Diane Ward
God gave me to you
And God gave you to me,
But we couldn't Love the way we ought
We were too blind to see.

You couldn't be that woman
And I couldn't be that man,
Who could love each other perfectly
Throughout our whole life span.

Through God's grace our eyes were
opened,
Open wide enough to see,
That the kind of love we needed
Comes through Christ who set us free.

Now we run this race together
With true love and life anew,
And we thank and praise our Savior
That now we walk as one
And no longer strive as two

Sherwood L. Ward

My Love

My love is here
And here it will stay
Your love is gone
And it will never be the same
You said you love me
And I thought it was true
But time has passed
Not a word from you
Being apart day by day
Makes the pain in my heart never go away
Without our love I can't forget
The good times we shared
The laughter, the romance we once had
Now time has moved on
Although our good-byes was never said
I knew in my heart your love was dead

Monica R. Waller

My God And I

Today I will sit before my Lord
And I will meditate upon His word
My God is patient, just and kind
The Lord dwells deep within my mind.

And so, I seek God early in the morning
As I wait for the new day's dawning
Then we will walk together
Hand in hand, my God and I.

Stella Chmell

Dreams

I look at my life and what I have done
and I think of what I dreamed.
I think of how naive and young I was
and how easy those dreams seemed.

I dreamed about the wildest things,
how grand and glorious they were.
I sailed the ships of the Seven Seas,
and in the Northland, trapped for fur.

I rode the Western Plains, of course,
and my stead was a kingly mount.
And, fighting for my true love's sake,
I beat the crooked Count.

Those dreams are all just memories now,
of a life both bright and new,
Washed away with the toils of the day
as life is so apt to do.

But, in another way, the dreams remain,
to come at my beck and call,
For a human being devoid of dreams
is a human with nothing at all.

R. F. Hulbert

Cold Grey Light Of Dawn

She was just a fantasy
and I was but a pawn
In a game two lovers play
in the cold grey light of dawn

I knew she couldn't stay with me
she had just come by to have fun
The dreams became reality
in the cold grey light of dawn.

I know that it was destiny
No one could call it wrong
To live in a world of fantasy
'til the cold grey light of dawn

She was something special
Her memory still lingers on
It helps to get me through
the cold grey light of dawn.

Ronnie Dean Phillips

Anticipation Of Love

I think about your kiss
    And I'm starry-eyed and dreamy.
I anticipate your love
    As I wait for you.

My heart is longing
    For that magical moment
When you will come to me
    And make me yours alone.

I'm no good without you;
    I want and need you so.
My life has been meaningless;
    Why did you have to go?

I've lived for your return
    When again your arms enfold me
So gently, tenderly,
    In your warm embrace.

Now is that magical moment
    When two hearts are yearning,
Hungrily desiring the ecstasy of love
    That we alone can share.

Margaret F. Richardson

A Smile - A Tear

Just as the sun shines through the rain
And Joy sometimes comes with pain
A smile can mingle with a tear
To soften hearts of all those near.

A smile is such a little thing
To pass along the way
It strikes a Light and leaves its mark
On young and old alike.

Yes, a smile is a little thing
Given to a man or child
Or to a cat or dog, don't you agree
A smile must surely come from God.

And a tear,...
A tear may be a sign
Of heartbreak or of joy
Coming from a girl and also from a boy.

It's such a gentle little thing
That rolls down on the cheek
And somehow, it seems to find its way
To both the strong and weak.

Phyllis Blanche Disney

Illusion Of Reality

As I flew above the deep blue sea
And looked into you hollow soul
Tranquility devoured me
Your evil took a hideous toll

As I walked upon the crimson moon
Smiling at the face of death
Life was but a simple tune
Singing with its final breath

As I laid beneath the mystic mire
I wept a tear for every sin
Fantasies eluded desire
Happiness was ravaged within

As I close my eyes and bury my soul
Within the comfort of this coffin
I say farewell to my life as a whole
And my shield begins to soften

Lori Neil

Manifest Destiny

They came in search of new life;
and most likely would have died
Had it not been for the natives who
roamed this land with pride.
Then when sufficient numbers,
arrived on eastern shores.
They took their land and shot them dead,
to open western doors.

Lee Odies Ellison

God's Setting

I cast my eye to the sky
    and not forgetting
that it's God's setting.
    In early morn, I was torn,
times so few, but such a view;
    the morning star
out so far, placing the moon
    to the perfect tune
all in place with such grace
    and not forgetting
it's God's setting.

A. T. Neville

No Fate

Through candy-filled dreams
    and nightmarish screams
There lives a girl who has no
    nightmares
He will come home late and yell at her
    never ending fate,
    she still ALIVE
He goes to bed easily
    but she lies awake
    thinking of tomorrow, of no fate
Repetitious he comes home
    thinking of new and creative ideas
Pots, pans, dishes of every sort
    missing and if not lucky hitting
Excuses having to be made of why?
    The usual falling down a tree
    and scraping her knee
She leaves her home at the age of eight
    dreaming of tomorrow
    of someday FATE

Sara Vanderleest

"An Angel Looking Over You"

When life gets you down
and no answers can be found
Right over your shoulder
I am always around

For I have been chosen to look
after you
Your guardian angel this is true
I travel with you every day
Watching over you as I pray

And when you feel things are
too hard to bear
Never forget I'm always near

God sent me to be your
number one friend
I am to be with you
to the very end

Do not hesitate to ask me
for help, in my arms it is you
I have always held

It is I, your Guardian Angel!

Sandra Riddle

Dreams

When a tear falls from my eye
And pain is all around;
When silent screams of yesterday
Are deafening with sound.
When sadness fills my lonely heart
And hopes are fading fast;
When turmoil clings unto my soul
With nightmares from my past.
When bitter winds blow icy cold
And I dread the coming night;
When I lie alone in fear
And no one holds me tight.
I reach deep down into my soul
And find my fondest dreams;
And light begins to find my strength
Though hopeless as it seems.
Never lose your dreams my friend
And you'll always find a way;
To find the strength you need to keep
To make a better day.

Linda E. Henslee

Heal Me With Love

Heal me with love,
And not with your ego.

I want to get well.
(This lifestyle is hell.)
So I've chosen you,
To help me along-
Help me get strong.

But I want you to know,
What I already know-
That you're not my God,
Or omnipotent master.

Together on our knees,
We can maybe find an answer.
But I'm not here to worship you,
Revere you,
Adore you.

I'm here to heal myself,
With your help.

For I am a fellow sojourner,
And truth is nobody's corner.

Memrie A. Gaddis

Your Guardian Angel

With thoughts of concern
And prayers up above,
She sits ever near you
With sweetness and love.

As you may lay crying
With worries or fears,
A brush of her wing
She's calmed your tears.

"Dear Heavenly Father,"
She prays without end,
"Give to her peace,
My companion, my friend."

At that you feel stillness
And glance over to see
A little white feather
As it falls to your feet.

You smile to yourself
As joy starts to soar,
You know you've been touched
By an angel of the Lord.

Sandra Robinson

The Guiding Light

We wake with the morning,
And there is a light.
The light shines to show us
Wrong from right.
If we heed the warning
And follow the light,
It will separate
Day from night.

Your life may be filled
With sorrow and fear,
But open your eyes
Because the light is near.
Let is lead you.
Let it guide you.
It will never lie to you,
Because, you see, Jesus is that light.

Rita L. Smith

Awakenings

Bright red, sunset skies,
and quiet, moonlight glow,
and shining stars, late at night,
all lift our weightless soul.

Tides that tug the mighty seas,
and lightening and its thunder,
and strong winds, that bend big trees,
stir thoughts of power and wonder.

Auroras, and their shimmering arrays,
dart about the polar skies;
and when observed, they do amaze,
our unbelieving eyes.

Rainbows, so radiant,
in delights of brilliant color,
brings to mind God's covenant,
His justice, and His power.

Aroused by such displays,
we see a kind of majesty divine;
a sense of divinity ablaze;
a touch of eternity in time.

Robert A. Welcome

Angel In The Sky

Suzie came to me last night
And said "Sis, I'd like to talk,"
I can't remember getting up
But we began to walk

The path was warm and peaceful,
She spoke of things she's done
But Mom and Dad please don't be sad
Her fun had just begun

Before she left me for the night
One thing she asked of me
To take her message to both of you
And try to make you see

Her words were plain and very clear
"Please Mom and Dad don't cry
For I am very happy now
I'm an angel in the sky."

Lillian Marchant

Sad Times

I've tended stock most all my life
and seen some awful sights.
Like cows a lyin' dead from bites
and horses put to sleep,
and calves that just can't make it
'cause the snow'd got too deep.

I've watched the pasture burning up
'cause the rains they just won't come.
The cows are all a dryin' up,
the calves can get about as much
by sucking on my thumb.

The people's even changing,
ain't like it used to be.
Those were the days when I helped you,
and the next day you helped me.

But I think the saddest thing I've seen
while looking through these peepers
is when my old compadre Bill
had took to wearing sneakers!

Monty Patton

Someday

I wish I could have traveled more,
And seen this land of ours.
I wish I could have done so much,
And not have wasted the hours.
  Someday.
I wish I was a better friend,
Like I knew I should.
I wish I was full of love,
And did the things I could.
  Someday.
I wish I had lived my life,
To never have regrets.
I wish I had done everything
To make my heart forget.
  Someday.
The time will come,
When I can say,
I'll do it now,
And not SOMEDAY!

Odessa A. Szumita

The Alpha And Omega

Turn the world around for me
  and show me where's the end.

Stride across a new found land.
  and stand around the bend.
Glide on waters wide and smooth
  to soothe your restless trend.
Sail on slipp'ry streams of air,
  and share your tales about.

Scale the mountains far and high,
  and sigh for souls without
A star, light and bright to guide,
  in side, around, and out...
Now, shout loud a joyous cry.
  let fly your soul, and then,
Send your spirit's love to be,
  in me, a loving friend.

Turn the world around with me,
  and know me as a friend.
Turn the world around and see
  the beginning's in the end.

Michael L. Farahay

The Message

The fire was quaking
And speaking in an ancient tongue.
My thoughts took over,
As I wondered what must be done.

For, that very moment
I had fallen apart
With questions inside me
And dreams in my heart.

Then at once I could hear her,
A voice so unique.
She gave me a feeling,
'Twas one that was bleak.

She asked me to help her,
And I begged her to tell
The voice had no body,
But its shape I knew well.

If you listen deep inside,
You too may hear.
The voice is Mother Earth's,
And she is stricken with fear.

R. Conrad Howell

To My Daughter

You are my one and only daughter-
and that you will always be
So you hold a special place in my
heart - for all eternity
And with all the love I can
show you - and all the love you
just don't see - just remember
all through your life - you will
always be a part of me.

Sandie Saxon

Brave It!

Mountains serene,
and the lake's at peace.
But there's a storm brewing in the sky.
The thunder starts,
and people run...
But not I;
I stay outside. -
To watch the clouds get darker,
and the rain will
pour on me -
But, soon the sun will
shine again,
and the children,
they'll run free.

So, I can say,
I stood through the storm,
didn't run, nor did I hide.
But I sat out there,
in the mist of it all -
With you, by my side.

Sarah E. Martinus

Untitled

I Look Back Over My Shoulder
and there I see
The boy I once was
and the man he meant to be

And I wonder how it happened
that the boy I see,
Became the man I now am -
not the man he meant to be.

I remember him well-the boy I once was;
I remember the man he dreamed I would be
now the dreams are forgotten by
the boy and me -
For I'm not the man I dreamed I would be

William Botts Walker

Teardrops In The Ocean

Tonight I kissed a teardrop
And released it into the ocean.
Hoping that it would bring you
All my love and devotion.

I prayed that the waves
Would tell you of my loneliness.
So you would come back home
And straighten out this mess.

I wished upon a star,
To seal these dreams up tight.
Then I sat and waited
under the pale moon light.

Vicki Garig

Time

Time is ticking,
And things of the past,
Are washed away forever
And heartache is gone at last.

New things begin,
Old things go away,
To be put in your memory,
And take out another day.

Time ticks on,
As we grow old,
To leave us longing
For something to hold.

The long awaited fate,
Is finally met,
To rid our heart,
Of any regret.

So now we sleep
In comfort and grace
And hope that heaven
Is our final resting place.

Mary A. Ritchie-Worstell

Untitled

"Absence makes the heart grow fonder"
And this I know is true,
For every time that we're apart
My heart yearns for only you.

I think of all the times we've shared,
Both the happy and the sad;
But a stronger love is not compared
To the one that we have had.

Your duty takes you far from me
And this I understand,
So it makes me cherish what I feel
When you're here to hold my hand.

A greater love you could not find
If you searched both near and far;
For ours has stood the test of time
And of loving from apart.

Rayna Kesecker

The Quest

We live a rather structured life;
And put our dreams "on hold,"
Thinking, soon, we'll follow them
Before we grow too old.

But, time's a thief, as someone's said
And the years go flying by;
And sometimes dreams go up in smoke
Into the endless sky.

Though some of mine have not come true,
I've no regrets, you see;
For I have had much love and joy —
God's been good to me.

For if you never dare to dream
How empty life would be;
So I'll continue on my quest
Toward things I cannot see.

For I believe that life's a quest
And dreams a vital part;
So dream your dreams and dare to hope
And keep them in your heart.

Shirley Morgan Branch

She Asks Nothing

She asks nothing
and tho' she weeps
she weeps not that she receives nothing
but that you
offer nothing
nor know
what to give.

You scream something
and then you swear
you swear not that you own nothing
but that she weeps
and asks
nothing.

Larry Carter

Away From Home

Times, when I am lonely
and times when things are bad.
Sometimes, when I am only
resigned to feeling sad.

Then times when thoughts of home
remind, and thoughts are bent
to times when love was shown.
The kind that's heaven sent.

Then time seems not so long
and rhyme conceived in poem,
designed for joyful song.
It's time. I'm going home.

Larry D. Bright

My Lord Spoke To Me!

Do you really long to be My child
    and truly bear My name?
And walk the way I would have you go
    free from sin and blame?

Then, My child, come unto Me
    and give Me all your care
And know that truly My Father and I
    all your trials and grief do share.

Stand upon My Father's word
    and ask of Him only in My name
And praise Me before all men
    even those who would bring Me shame.

Remember, there is no problem
    for My Father too big or too small,
But only by your own true faith can
    He answer them at all.

So if you doubt My love for you is free
    and that all that I speak is true
Remember My death as I hung nailed to a tree
    and the blood I shed for you.

Virginia D'Isa Davidson

Lost

It's not the time or place
and now our minds separate
my heart remains the same
though you're away
I'll always be right here
love what is worth loving
and with a tear drop
blow the rest away.

Russell Kirton

Shades Of Love

I have seen Love in all its shape, size
and vagary.
The discipline of its staid devotion,
And the capricious twist of its
opposite side.
Others wondered; I searched.

I have applauded love in all
its sweet splendour.
The egoistic ignorance
of its vain lovers;
And the tender dignity
of its gentle ones.
Others tasted, yet I searched.

Now I finally know,
That what my mind could not conceive
My heart knew for so many years;
That what I was searching for
was you love.
And finally,
I have found you.

Leni Singh

The One I Most Fear

I sleep alone as nights go by
and watch the moon glow in the sky
and dream the dreams not dreamt before
and think of things not thought of more
and wonder why some things are so
and thinking 'bout how far I'll go
and wond'ring whether life's worth while
and thinking of death, no certain style
and want to change the way I sleep
a way so that you hear no peep
then think my dreams are not so bad
and make myself feel not that sad
and then can't sleep on the idea
That I'm the one I really fear.

Paula Bergeron

Apothegm

I write a line, an ode, a poem
And with it reveal my being;
But other eyes see not the fact,
And think it only dreaming.
To them the poet vanishes
In mists of rhyme and rhythm;
Yet poetry is not in things,
Would they could see it's in them.

Wayne Alholm

The Music Of The Heart

Listen to the music of the heart,
And think of me.
Listen to the music of the heart,
And know of my love for thee.

The music of the heart,
Tells of my undying love,
Tells of how my love soars,
Like the flight of a dove.

The music of the heart,
Whispers words of your beauty,
Listen to the music of the heart,
And think of me.

Trever Bierschbach

"A Shadow Of Myself"

"I see a shadow on the ground
and wonder who she is?
Is the shadow, my inner
soul in disbelief.
My shadow keeps me
company as long as we
keep in step."
"I talk to my shadow
as to a friend, and wonder
if someday I will hear an
answer from my shadow
in return."

"My shadow lingers with me,
when the sun is shining
bright, and slowly diminishes
when the sun is gone
and out of sight."

Mildred L. De Marco

Endless Weekend

French doors-
and you say
down the slide we go
it's easy
no effort
down the slide
through
the final curtain

Through french doors
the olive tree
illuminated
silver leaves disappearing
in illuminated space

Through the curtain
you wonder
the cosmic explosion

I feel so close.

Amido

Love

It's soft and delicate,
and you'll never forget it.
You'll know when it comes,
you get kind of numb.
You can feel it.
It's real.
As real as you and me.
Love will never happen
if it's not meant to be.
When you and another person share it,
you'll always care for it.
So when love hits you,
there is no limits for what you'll do.

Lisa Berry

It's Valentine's Day

It's valentine's day
As it goes by we play and play
Giving out cards and reading them too
Some will say I love you!
Red white and pink.
Some written in ink.
Some bought, some from thought
All that's left to say is
"Happy Valentine's Day"

Tiffany Dover

The Sun

Lustre of gold on the sky,
Anybody can get you beauty of shine.
He knows best the world-history,
Sunbeam see how I struggle with the life.
Common fate for us,
We together go to sleep.
Always he wakes up first,
Laughs at me, if I'm late.
What happens with us people,
When one day he doesn't come up?
Eternal fire ceases burning,
And all kinds of life die.
We are the reason the people,
Who live without God,
Punishment will be rightful for us.

Laszlo Szuromi

"On Storm's Edge"

A storm out at sea...
   approaching
Causes the waves to crash
mercilessly
   against the beach
   where we lie
Soulful and sandy soft, in silence
Though both feeling a bit on edge,
   while we say nothing
Sea gulls...
   grace the sky above

Lee Wilson

Etchings

The Etchings of my life
Are buried deep
In my mind
Pictured at times
As
Times of joy/times of sorrow
Of loves won/loves lost
Glorious times/struggles to live
So vivid and colorful a picture
Never to return

San Carmen Dodd

The Burden

The burden's of our life
are not always easy to bear
Sometimes we become very lonely
when we have no one with whom to share.

It is time like these
that make us to realize
It was our own wrong-doing
that ruined our lives.

The lessons we learn are sometimes
very painful indeed.
But it is what we have done to other's
that makes our heart grieve.

Life is not always easy
But we must give it our best.
We learn far more from failure
than we ever will from success.

On this precious day
My love I do send.
Asking your forgiveness
hoping and praying to begin again.

William Kirkland

My Garden Of Life

Born to us
Are Sons and Daughters,
Making us parents,
Mothers and Fathers.

Trying our Patience
As they go through their stages.

Our daughters marry
We have a new son,
Our sons marry
And we still are not done.

Once they get there
Married - Well then,
We become Grandparents
And it starts all over again.

We've been pretty lucky,
This family of ours.
I'd not trade a one
Of my various Flowers!!

A. S. Cothran

The Woodscolt

Eyes reflected by my mirror
are very rare I see.
I gave them to my children
but who gave them to me?
A misty man of shadows,
A name without a face.
He came to make my life start
then left without a trace.
For I am but a woodscolt,
with shadows on my name.
I do not know my bloodlines,
nor from whence I came.
My father is a poor man,
My father is a king,
My father is whatever
I might wish or dream.
It's nice to be a woodscolt,
so wild, untamed and free.
For I can be whomever,
I might want to be.

Marilyn Carol Juel Rake

My Life...Only As I Know It.

My walls are covered with memories
as any walls would be,
Each souvenir has a story
Each one special to me.

My eyes see where I'm going
My heart knows where I've been,
I don't know when my life began
or when my life will end.

I know my life, I know it well
Each memory to a "T,"
No one can take my memories away
They'd be taking away me.

They say I'm just a kid
Too young to know a thing,
But I swear, 'tis true, what I say to you
My, memories, a smile do bring.

It's not a bed of roses
A bowl of cherries...each one a pit,
But it's what God gave me
My life...Only as I know it.

Maria Dominguez

Little Footsteps In The Air

In the early morning light
as dawn takes over for the night,
I think I see you dancing there,
- little footsteps in the air -
My heart begins to break in two,
as I realize it isn't you -
but only wisps of memory
are all that's left of you for me.
Oh precious, sweetest little boy.
You always were my greatest joy.
And though my love for you was deep,
He told me you weren't mine to keep.
So as I look into the light,
He promises He'll hold you tight;
and let you do your dancing there,
- little footsteps in the air -

Sandra L. Berry

Lady Of Night

Lady of night, she wears the fog
as her cloak and the stars for jewelry.
The moonlight smiles in her deep eyes
and sounds out diamond in her hair.

Her lips curve in a forgotten smile
and the fluidity with which she moves
was stolen from a dying stream.

She the mysterious mother gypsy
whose mountain soul is masked
with a dancers' slim perfection.

She is a poem which must be performed,
a dance which must be written.
Unquestionable, for to question
is to close doors on the answers.

Lynda Ferrell

A Prayer For Mother

Dear Jesus are you listening,
As I kneel down here to pray
Please watch out for my Mother,
For she's headed up your way.

Please wrap your arms around her
And hold her tight for me,
For I will surely miss her
When she comes to live with thee.

Please make her legs strong again,
And give her wings so she can fly.
Make her eyes to see real clear
So she can watch us from on high.

Please give her back her memories
Through the years they tend to fade,
Of all her friends and family
And the life that she has made.

Please tell her how we love her,
And will miss her when she's gone.
Our love will live eternal,
For she's our hero, she's our mom.

Linda Mugrage

Care

When I am here
And you are there
I find it hard for me to care
But when you come back
   from where you were
I start to care like I did before

Violet L. Trice

The Moon...

I wondered if you thought of me
As it shone brightly on that first snow.
I wondered where you were
And how I could possibly know.
I felt excited as I thought
How fresh and new the feeling
This new snowfall, the full moon, too.
Peacefulness, so revealing.
The little time we'd had
Meant so much - without a doubt.
My world had been so jumbled.
Was your friendship my way out?
I saw a star, and then another
Counting so many as before.
That one seemed so much brighter.
I wanted to see you more.
I knew it was shining over you
At that moment, as it was me.
Just hoped the feeling was real
And like the moon, it'll always be.

Myra Hampton

On Wings Of An Angel

The wind was blowing to and fro.
As I watched I knew it was
Your time to go.
On Wings of an Angel, by earth's
Early dawn.
I received Mother's message that
Daddy was gone.
I ran to your rescue, but to my
Surprise,
You were lifeless but smiling
For your Soul had taken Flight.
I saw on your lap God's holy word,
And I knew in an instant the
Voice you had heard.
Now in my heart I'm rejoicing,
For someday we shall sing.
Together in God's presence
Delivered on Angel wings.

Melody L. Hamilton

A Son's Love

The day came when you gave birth,
Birth to a growing son.
This son has grown now,
Grown into a young man.

Though there were tough times,
You have stood beside him.
Even through times of conflict,
You were always there.

There were times of confusion,
Confusion in both lives.
Yet both stood by one another,
Stood by with such tender love.

There was even times when words,
Words that should have been said.
Though they were never said,
They were always felt.

So today when you think about him,
There is one thing you should know.
That through time and time again,
That he love you with all his heart.
I love you mom.

Kemp G. Skidmore

"God's Beauty"

Listen to the rain
As it's falling down,
Tipping on the roof
What a peaceful sound
If you find I'm not stirring around,
In my bed is where I'll be found.
If I'm sleeping, please don't wake me,
For the best time to sleep is
When it's raining.
When it's all over,
And the sky is clear,
I'll go out and smell the fresh clean air.
Then I'll bow my head in Prayer,
Thanking God for the beauty he shares.

Shelia Bax

"Renewal"

Springing forth from the earth
    As since time began,

The blossoms and plants are wakening
    For the pleasure of man.

Though God has created all
    Through his almighty power,

Man creates his own delightful
    Botanical bower.

Gathering the plants, flowers,
    Shrubs and some soil;

Man comes together with
    Nature and begins his toil.

A moment in time,
    As many times before;

Yet it awakens the awe and
    Wonder of life's central core.

Man is part of nature,
    Yet sometimes forgets his place.

But his awareness is apparent
    Upon his tired reverent face.

A time of renewal for flora, fauna and man;

A jubilant time since time began.

Mary R. Smith

Saying Goodbye

I stood upon the altar
As tears ran down my cheeks
It was hard for me to say what I felt
For inside I was so weak
The anger that ran through me
the pain was so intense
everything I managed to say
seemed to make no sense
But as I continued talking
I walked over to where she lay
My grandmother whom I loved so much
Was now a million miles away
As she lay there so unmoving
I whispered I loved her in her ear
And everyone who heard me
had to force away a tear
I kissed her fragile cheek
And as I turned to walk away
I said "Wait for me in heaven,
for I'll be there with you one day."

Natalie Rios

Our Secret

Softly the wind blows,
as the sun is setting slow.
The bullfrogs bellow their tune,
the sun is gone.

The crickets serenade.
and moonlight takes over.
As we sit,
at the waters edge.

You whisper you love me.
I hope that it's true.
You reach to hold me
I snuggle close too.

You're my warmth, you're my man,
you're rugged like steel,
The strength in your body,
I desire to feel.

The wind blows my hair,
puts a chill in the air.
The night,
I love the night

Terry L. Martin

Untitled

The seals they lie in silence,
As the waves wash near by;
There is a sense of sadness,
In the eyes of all who try;
The past comes back to mind,
And two hearts that still can find,
The beating of a love
So gentle and so kind;
Just one more kiss
I wish that we could share;
And let time capture, a love
That's still there;
The warmth of your kiss, I
Hold deep within;
And how I always treasure,
Your touch upon my skin;
A love that stays inside,
In our memories
That we keep, and hold it
Tight within us, and in dreams as we sleep!

Teresa Lynn Turnage

Wake-Up Call

How many children have to die
Before the world awakes?
How many mothers have to cry?
How many does it take?

How many bullets have to fly
Like a demon Cupid's darts?
How many sad, heartbroken sighs
Will echo from our hearts?

Laneta, Marcus, Sonya, Don
Their eyes reflect our pain.
Tameka, Bryan, Tonya, Ron—-
The roll call of the slain

Before our nation's seeds of hope
Lie lifeless in the sod,
Before we drown in death and dope,
Wake up, you men of God!

Wake up and sound the rallying cry
Of peace and harmony;
For if we let our children die,
Their blood's on you and me!

Rose Camille Parrish

Through Grandma's Eye's

A little girl was born
As tiny as a bird
But when she wanted mommy
She could surely be heard

She'll grasp her Daddy's finger
with a sigh and big smile
knowing he'll pick her up
And hold her awhile

She holds the key
That will unlock the door
To daddy and Mommy's future
forever more

The love these three share
can never be replaced
After seeing all the love
In this little girls face

Mary E. Jacobs

Wondrous Light

Speak to me bright one
As you stare at me from above.
Explain to me the pains of life
And why everything is so...
Why is it that my heart
Must leave me in the cold?
Too often do I feel alone
And comfort so far from home.
The very core of me is torn away
But still part of it remains
Crushed, never to move until
My love returns again.
I'll never be complete with
My heart at such a distance.
Why not stop cruel world
And return to me what belongs?
The bright ones inside of me
Have lost their effervescent glow
Who knows why life is so cruel
And why everything is so...

Nicole McAuley

"The Shadow"

One day we were walking together
and I was looking down
you told me,
that is the reflection of my shadow.
I did not respond anything
I thought to myself,
that is not your shadow
that is my shadow
walking beside you
following you
everyday, every place
until the end of my life.

Lilly Wheeler

I Wish I Could Be Her

I see him holding her hand
As their lips start to join
I wish I could be her
His one and only true love.
But since I'm not
the only thing I can do
is to wish and hope that
one day my wish comes true.
But until then
I will just dream that we were together.

Noelle Richards

Grades

Outstanding
at
first
then
dropping
to
just
high
after
some
months
it's
down
to
an
o.k.
then it gets
worse
Eek! an
Interim Report

Katherine Miller

Stage 4

Crouched in alleyways
at midnight, he smelled
musty clothes thrown out
in large canisters. A cat
crept past, quiet, watched

Each move carefully. Crusty
palms stayed empty as others'
selfishness increased. His
endless travels were monotone,
warm street vents became cold.
He searched through trash, starved
with fear like a forgotten child

Left in the dark. He pulled a torn
overcoat close around his frigid
mass, for warmth and protection
against winds. Curled tight, time
passed slowly, he wished to be in
a dream state.

Mary Elizabeth Varn

Expression Of Love

Today I want to express my love
But I cannot send you a flower
However I'd like for you to know
My love is with you every hour

Just as I see your heart run free
Spreading friendship to those you know
I choose to leave the flower unplucked
So it may flourish and unpotted grow

To spread its seeds of life at random
And reign as the beauty of the wild
To be innocent and untainted by man
As free and pure as a new born child

Adorning the hills and lining the brooks
With loveliness to fill one with awe
To appear every year in a different array
More beautiful than the one you last saw

I know you share my friendship and love
And I hope with each wildflower you see
You'll think of me and knowingly smile
Because flowers, friendship, and love are free

TAT

Memphis

Memphis, Tuscaloosa,
Atlanta.
Somewhere it rolls off the tongue,
Hot and Humid.
Troubled,
Like troubled rain.
Showering the people
With pride and hardship,
Stubbornness and faith.
The Promised Land.
O, Martin Luther King!
Your shoes trudged the
Land in these paths,
Trampled with the blood of many
And the love of a few.

Safika ErSelcuk

Eternal Spirit

I woke up sad this morning,
Aware that you were gone.
Yet as I lay there grieving
Despair somehow seemed wrong.
For through your greatest battles
Against all odds you fought,
Providing inspiration
Which pain and courage bought.

Though your body lies so still now
Beneath the hollowed sod,
Your soul lives on in Heaven
So proudly claimed by God.
And as each new tomorrow
Brings forth unwanted strain,
The memory of your spirit
With me shall e'er remain.

Marilyn J. Noll

Pada Cake

Pada Cake
Bakers Girl
Bake me a cake
As big as the world
Roll them up
Roll them up
Put them in a pan
Yummy Yummy Yummy
She eat all that she can

Velma Dunn Pickard

Longing

Pink-tinged clouds turn gray behind
Bare limbed sullen branches
And dusky sky gives way to night
As moon then stars start dancing

Roaring silence caving in
Window icy to the touch
Loneliness faithful companion
Heart compressed as if crushed

I close my eyes and in my mind
You're loving me again
Sitting by my side
You take my hand and then

A bird's first song brings me back
From bittersweet enchantment
And gray-tinged clouds turn pink behind
Bare limbed sullen branches

Karen Sniegon

Tongues

Swaggering
bare to me
closed to me
skin of glass
a secret well tended and ready
self-assured she knows
she needs
I said once "To be conquered
is everything…"
… and she speaks the tongues of animals
…of marrow
…raw and fresh
she needs the covetous to breathe
to feed
she mourns more than she wants to
…and when the sun goes down
she weeps alone
for the cancer
to end

Zachariah B. Singleton

To My Guardian Angel

Guardian Angel, please help me
be all I wish that I could be
and when my soul is feeling low
show me how to make it glow
with warmth and love,
that all can see,
for God and Earth and Man and Me.

Holy Angel, know I care.
It comforts me to know you're there
watching and listening to all I say
and lighting the candle
to show me the way.

Mariann Noller

My Love For Him

My love for him is more
beautiful than the bright shimmering
stars silhouetted against the
black night sky.

My love for him is
more beautiful than the late
afternoon sun showing a
path of love just before it dips
beyond the horizon.

My love for him is
more beautiful than a full
moon's silver streaks
showing a few rays of hope.

My love for him is
more beautiful than a
Christmas tree in the glow
of a child's face on Christmas morning.

Marsha Renee Hall

Used Black Warrior

Be the best.
    Blacks fight.
        Blacks die.
            The wars are over.
                Who has won?
                    Go back to nothing,
                        Used Black Warrior.
                            You're Done.

Robert E. Allen

Love Shines Through

Wonderful and wise,
Beauty and full of surprise.
Laughs, yet knows how to cry.
Loves without expectations,
Respected with devotion.
Listens with her heart,
Smiles with her eyes.
Shines through and through,
It's no wonder how much
We love you!

Susan L. Lundstrom

D-r-u-g-s

A word you hate to hear
Because of all the fear
It isn't just the dope
But a fear there is no hope

The children are pressured by peers
And the parents close their ears
The parents make a mistake
By thinking "My child won't take"

Now we must take a walk
And ask our children to talk
So we can get their feeling
In hope they won't start stealing

We have to get involved
Or our hope will be dissolved
If our children are to go about
the D-R-U-G-S will have to go out!

Warren D. Sawyer

Special Friend

The room is dark, but I'm not afraid,
because you're there to guide me.
You are my own special friend.
I share my deepest thoughts with you,
and without a word, you smile back.
you never say anything bad
you never say anything at all.
Sometimes I wonder If you're still there
But then again, what do you expect from
a star?

Lisa Marie Hasenpat

Eternity Trails

Count us all
beginning with the very first
called man.
In the vastness of the universe
We're each one grain
of sand.

Tiny trails in all directions
from the depths up to the shore,
in a great and endless ocean
of men now
and those before.

So, count us all and consider,
though just one grain
are we,
the trails we leave behind us
will change
The Mighty Sea.

Melvia Mullins

A Friend

Someone you …
Believe in totally,
Trust in completely,
Follow unquestionably,
Would die for undoubtedly.

Others will find their …
Love unconditional,
Trust uncontestable,
Loyalty unshakable,
Dedication undeniable.

In you I have found a
Friend
Who I've never found
Before.

Tressa Ann Price

"The Sea"

Beautiful waves
bending and breaking,
Swirling foam
washing to and fro,
Salty spray
splashing through the air,
That is my home,
The sea.

Rebecca Hamil

Treasure

Tonight I awakened to find you still
beside me.

My thoughts keep myself wondering
how long our love will be.

As a treasure of gold, the value is too
deep and you're left wondering how
long it will last.

Maybe a lifetime or not, it's just
Something you have to chance.

Tomorrow may find me with a different
answer, for I don't know what the
value will be.

It may be a day filled with love or a
love forgotten,

Tonight I will just treasure my gold
and hope for a life time dream.

Sandy Scarlett

Heart Sore

Two youngsters stand
Beside me, laughing
At the paper hearts,

Especially
The one with Cupid
Shooting golden darts.

And while they're poking
Fun at "such a
Corny Valentine"

Here I stand,
Their grandma…
Wishing it were mine.

Shane A. Ewell

Decision Of Death

Death is but a choice
between heaven or hell.
The horns of the devil
or the white glistening bell.

Each force states the reasons
of why I should go;
to the pit of despair
or to the angels that glow.

They impatiently wait
as I helplessly stall,
though deep in my soul
there is no doubt at all.

'Tis the devil I want
though I know it is wrong,
to chant and to dance
and to join in his song.

So the angels retreat
slowly and wretched,
as I rest my head
in the fiend's arms outstretched.

Kimberly Erica Colbert

In Tears I Drown

Roses are everywhere,
Blood is on the ground.
Mama said leave him alone,
Now here in tears I drown.
Comforting and preaching to our souls
He stands over you,
All dressed in black
He stands over you,
Stealing away your soul.
Roses are everywhere,
Blood is on the ground.
Mama said leave him alone,
I didn't listen,
So now here in tears I drown.

Marquita D. Neal

Love

Love is like a flower
blooming in the spring,
behind a peach bloom
as the little birds sing.

K. A. Dowell

Childhood Memories

Dogwoods in bud
As I walk in thought
Of childhood memories
Too long forgotten.

Such a pretty picture
Is a child at play
Dancing around
With clothes
All dirty and torn

Playing hopscotch
On the walk
Then made out of clay.

With expressions on a face
Of a child that knows
Only love.

Wanda Horner

Portrait

Tall man, wearing plaid,
Blue eyes, distant sad.
Shoulders squared, chest lean,
Handsome man, wearing green.
Long-sleeved, dress maroon,
Grey eyes like a full-moon.
Mature man, wearing blue,
The epitome of virtue.
Gentle man, wearing gray,
Eyes reflect what colors say.
Sporting ties that never match,
Over his heart, keeps careful watch.
Complex man, wearing black
Committed to never turning back,
Lest he repeat sins of the past,
Unable to move forward too fast.
Seeking pureness of his soul,
Finding peace in the spiritual.
He could have heaven and earth
If he only knew his worth.

Patricia Ann Kerr

Color

Green grass,
Blue sky,
Gold brass,
brown eye,
Gray sidewalk
Purple cars
Clear talk,
yellow stars
Red cherry,
White notebook,
Black berry,
Silver hook.

Misty A. Joseph

Lint

I am lint.
Born on a flannel shirt.
Grew in a dryer.
Harvested by humans on a
lint screen.

Then thrown away,
where I see food, garbage,
and a few distant relatives.
I am told I don't have
much of a life,
but I live proudly because...
I am lint.

Sarah Gardner

Loving You

The stars all shining
bright tonight, you can
sit and think and admire
the site. The moon is
shining, the breeze is calm,
but I still sense that
something's wrong. There's
something missing. Is that
why I'm blue? Could it be
that it is you? The stars
are bright in the sky so
blue, it's the perfect time
to tell you, I love you!

Sharon Martinez

Sit Quietly In Morning Sun

Let dreams escape
Bring fields of flowers to the senses
Tell secrets to the air
Melt years together and
paint pictures with memories
Open gates
Venture to lost places

Sit quietly in morning sun

Regina Meatris

Bugs

Bugs
Bugs,
Bugs.
Brown bugs,
Black bugs,
Hideous, frightening, ugly bugs,
Horrible, vulgar, vile bugs,
Those are just a few.

Dreadful bugs,
Awful bugs,
Disgusting, terrible, disgraceful Bugs,
Gross, Slimy, Poisonous Bugs,
Round bugs too.

Fat bugs,
Skinny bugs,
Don't forget Ladybugs,
Last of all...Best of all...
Baby bugs.

Kristan F. R. Jones

"Live To Die"

Born with disease not chosen by he-
burdened the world...
a future non-seen.

Struggle the body invaded by death-
by no choice of his...
he's here...he exists.

Drug addict mother abandoned his soul-
back to the streets...
she's lost all control.

Cry, not of pain, nor pity, nor shame-
a world brought abruptly...
he'll see never again.

10 minutes of life lasted awhile-
dark road towards death...
he managed to smile.

Death was a blessing, honored by innocence-
smiling angelically...
he died with no sin.

Noed B. Lugo

4:05

4:05 bay metro now boarding.
Bus tokens, the old lady is hoarding.
She's wary of everyone who casts a smile,
as friendly to others as a crocodile.
She will die a lonely, cold death,
bitterness is all she has left.
I try to brighten her day
    with a laugh,
but she puts her head down and
    walks on past.

Vincent G. Paige Jr.

Life.....Or Death!

Life is nothing,
But chaos and confusion.
Death is the complete opposite,
But not a wise solution.

To die is to be non-existent,
And definitely more peaceful.
But living is a greater task
That can possibly be wonderful.

Life is what you make of it,
Happiness or a waste of time.
But don't allow anyone to ruin it,
To waste your life would be a crime.

Though at times
Death may seem a reasonable way out.
Especially when life is full,
Of heartache and doubt.

When you're feeling suicidal,
Think about things that happen and why.
Concentrate on this single thought:
No one really wants to die.

Shannon R. Gum

Sleepless Night

Darkness reigns in the bedroom
  But for a streak of light that
  Seeps through the window shade
Raindrops are falling, tapping
  The window pane
Sleep evades me
I toss, turn in bed
Like overflowing rivers' waters
  Memories cascade
  Opening wounds long healed, dead
I cry a little, laugh a little
  At the travesty of it all
Turning the light on, read
  Write
The clock marks three
Wondering when sleep will come
  Be it dawn or morn
  I drop the pen, turn off the
  Light, past
  Pray sleep will come at last.

Veola Victoria Barnes

Thanksgiving For Spring

I have been asleep, but I have
Awakened this day.
The morning dawn, so beautiful
Birds chirping, dew on flowers
Like teardrops on joyful faces.
Sparkling sunshine through the
trees.
It's heavenly to be greeted
this way; by friends of nature
and caring family.
Softness of light and
Strength of love.
Little children with angel
voices, adults speaking calmly
A good breakfast, warm hugs
Then off to school and work
they go.
Thanks God, family and friends
for another day like spring
and for dreams come true.

Ray O'Neal

Blessed

One I couldn't fly.
But God came in,
And now I walk in pastures green.
I stroll by the River side,
Then the love of my soul comes by.
And I can Fly, Way up High,
Like an Eagle in the sky,
I can feel the breeze in my soul.
Thank God, I can fly, I can fly.
Since Jesus came in my soul.
Now I can feel him near.
Yes I can fly, I can fly.

Peggy Albert

The Creation Of Death

We create
but have learned to destroy.
Death knocks
opened doors.
Chemicals controlling
actions.
Thoughts of suicide.
Exploding bullets
Shattering dreams.
Innocent life of a womb;
forced nonexistence.
Free love
to disease.
A button is pressed
for life is of no value.
We are blown away
by burning radiation.
We have succeeded in death.
We create it.

Kimberly Joyce Heaton

The Mirror

I see him in the mirror,
But he isn't really there.
I can see his bright blue eyes,
And his rusty colored hair.

He scares me just a little,
When he smiles at me.
But I can't understand.
Why it's such a mystery.

Why can't he just go away?
And yet I don't want him to leave.
Because if he wasn't there,
It would be like a death to grieve.

So one night I got real angry,
And I screamed and hit the door.
And now I'm just sad and lonely,
For the mirror lays shattered on the floor.

Wanda Romkema

What Is Fear?

Fear is nothing more than a gear,
For fear cannot be set in motion,
Without some sort of notion.
Fear is not an involuntary source,
It must be set by force.
To overcome your fear
Is to not hear
The mere workings
Of your imagination.

Zak Allen

No One

I don't know where I 'm goin'
  but I surely know where I've been.
I've been down this road before
  and I know that I have sinned.

I'm out here all alone
  and no one seems to care,
No one is a friend of mine
  No one's always there.

I was brought here for a reason
  but that reason is unknown
You live life to the fullest
  and you leave the rest alone.

There's one thing I don't understand,
  why is no one here?
The only time I need someone
  No one really cares.

When I stop to think
  and then I start to cry
Seeing how things are today
  I just want to die.

Rena' Gail Acree

I Am The Future

K-I-D is my name
But I'm not insane
I roam the streets
I feel the pain of poverty

The faceless Kid that you curse and say
It's a damn shame they destroy this way
But I am the future.....
I am the future.....

Playing ball in an empty lot
Living in a building time forgot
Dodging cars to play stick ball
Me and my friends up against a wall

When you see me coming you turn and say
It's a damn shame they destroy this way
But I am the future.....
I am the future.....

Marice Baker

Faith

Faith is something I cannot see,
But it's something deep inside of me.
Faith is something I cannot feel,
But it's something I know is very real.
Faith is something I cannot touch,
But it's something I need so very much.
Faith comes to me when I trust my Lord,
When I obey what I find within His Word.

Margaret Good

Yo-Yo

Up and down
Down and around
High is high
Low is low
With a flip it's up again
Then it's down again
Up and down
Up and down
Snap!
The yo-yo string broke

Robert Janeski

Lonely Heart

The ocean might be big,
but my heart for you
is bigger. The day
I saw you, was the
day I felt true love.
Your beauty is fine
like a dozen of roses.
I was the fool for not
telling you. You are
the one who's right
for me, but the shyness
within me is the thing
you see.

Lee Moua Chongtua

I Used to Love

I used to love you,
But now I hate you.
All of my feelings are gone,
My heart is completely numb.
The things that you did to me,
Never to be forgotten.
The pain is so strong,
Burning through my soul.
The angry words you yelled,
Still ringing through my ears.
All of the mental anguish,
Hurting my delicate soul.
Yeah, I used to cherish you,
But now I want you to pay.
I want you dead, without life,
Like my broken heart and soul.

Toni Ruzga

I Seem To Be

I seem to be a towering pyramid
But really I am an old granite tombstone

I seem to be a wide expanse of desert
But really I am a child's sandbox

I seem to be an intricate computer
But really I am a child's abacus

I seem to be a powerful, restless ocean
But really I am a trickling stream

I seem strong to those around me
But really I am just like them

Kristy Wells

The Girl

Her eyes shed a single tear,
But she will never, ever fear.
She stays at home, all alone.
She claims she will be there
for very long.
But we hope this won't last,
That this phase will be over
very fast.
We hope, we pray,
That she won't stay.
Could a person act like this,
Without receiving a single kiss.
Is there really such a girl,
Throughout this whole entire world?

Lisa Famiglietti

Untitled

I tried to write a poem today...

I tried to write a poem today,
but then I didn't know
what to say...

I tried to write with rhyme
and reason, I even thought
about the season...

It's hard to write for a contest
it's true, but this is the best
that I can do...

I tried to write a poem today...

Robert Walthers

"That Old Book"

If you take a real good look,
At what they call "that old book,"
You can really look and see
That book was made for you and me.

"That old book" is the bible,
It was first written on scrolls,
It really is reliable,
And it tells us of our tolls.

So if you go walking around,
And you see this nice book,
Do not keep walking on,
Stop and take a look.

Kayla Lee Music

Beware

It is there,
But we don't see it.
It can spread fast,
But we feel it last.

You don't know it yet,
But it's in your hearts.
For some, it comes and goes,
For others, it stays forever.

It's not love, but can bring out hate.
With it, you could begin your fate.
It never ends, nor begins,
It may thicken, but never thins.

It's in the sky on a dark, gray night,
It fills us with more than just fright.
It's all around, including here,
I dare YOU to discover fear.

Ryan Pretzer

"I Don't Want To Lose You"

I sit here feeling
blue 'cause I keep
thinking that I'm
losing you. I don't
know what I will
do if I lose you.
I hope you really
see that I don't
want to lose you,
but if I do lose
you all I can do
is get over you.

Mary Herman

She's Stuck In These Walls

She sits by the window crying, pleading.
But yet no one hears her crying,
Her father so far away can't ever
hear her crying.

Her family doesn't see her,
They act like a she's a nobody.
All they do is yell, around her.
Her sisters could get away with
murder if they could.

She lives in those walls,
She wishes she were dead!
Surely not,
She lives in a human form,
but her family thinks
She was dead.

But again she lives
in these walls.

Tashina Jo McClain

"A Burning Fire"

When you have been warmed
By a burning fire
And the flames has been so
Beautiful to look at

And you have shared your dreams
With that one you called your queen

And that one refused to keep
This fire going and knowing
It would go out

The creeping cold is chilling
Your bones
For the lack of enough fuel
The fire has died out
In your home

O. D. Smith

Tranquility

When I was young, I wandered far
By country lane and stile;
And one green pathway bore a sign
"Tranquility-1 MI."

The hour was late, my feet were tired,
I needed some surcease;
And so I never did explore
That place of promised peace.

I've wandered quite a lot since then
On land, and by the sea;
But never-EVER- have I chanced
Upon tranquility.

The world is in a mess today -
Our lives are so intense;
With rioting in city streets
And campus violence.

Now I am old, and years are few,
I sit, and wryly smile -
To think that once I was So close -
"Tranquility-1 MI."!

Marian Gage

Our Mom And Dad

Mom and dad were precious stones
By time and trouble softly honed
Until each facet on its own,
Gave forth a glow before unknown!

Though simple folk, be not deceived,
They lived by faith, on God believed
That he would help them with his might,
Forever walking in his light!

Their children though, not good as they,
The best they can; their only way
We know by standards we fall flat,
Weaker, wiser, comes down to that!

I pray when God unfurls his scrolls,
The lightning flashes; thunder rolls
Mom and Dad's whole family's names
Will there be written all the same!

As children, though, with feet of clay
We struggle bravely on our way;
Still trying to attain the best
God's own reward, eternal rest!

Louise B. Davis

Bosnia

Who will hold the light
calm those frightened by guns
comfort those
lost in grief

Will they remember
the goodness within
for they have lived
the sidelines of death
caught in cross fires
of civil war

How will they reach
the star that is the light
or are they too desperate
to pray

Perhaps
we could be their memory
on this silent night
this holy night
and save their hearts
from turning to stone

Mimi Eagan

Eloy

The wind is bitter
cold against
the blazing sun, half-mast
in the sky.

A few leaves cling
to their source of life,
a bare tree
at the side of the path.

He stands in black,
his collar turned up against
the cold wind
and his back toward the path
and the sun.

Rain begins to fall
as the heavens weep
for the lost one.

This time the Father cries
Eloy, Eloy lama sabachthani.

Katie Martineau

"Brother"

Brother can you hear us,
can you feel our pain?

Brother are you listening?
life will never be the same.

So suddenly you left us,
and God took you home.

But please don't be frightened;
because you didn't go alone.

For on your final journey
our hearts went with you.

We loved you dearly
more than you ever knew.

Life is so precious
but, can be so unfair.

Till we meet again dear brother
your memories we will share.
                              "Sisters"

Sandra Peterson

Dragons

Some are sweet
careful and neat.

Some are mean
gruesome and green

Some are smart
and loving at heart.

You may think
they're imaginary or really really
scary.

But they're my
friends and I will love
them till the end.

Shannah Rose O'Meara

Noise Pollution

Annoying harmful noise
Can be pollution,
Endangering the environment,
Cars, boats, planes;
Noise pollution!

Noah Kieren

Untitled

Hustle
Bustle
Rustle of papers
Bureaucrats
Are up to their capers
Whirring
Humming
Spinning drives
Technocrats
From nine to five
At ease
Please
My mind relaxes
It's April Fool's day, and
I've paid my taxes

Robert A. Lange

Untitled

Rain falls upon the flowers,
Casts a spell beyond our power.
Kissed by magic from within;
Fills lonely hearts enraged with sin.

Swept in tears as they fall and settle;
Caressed within each scarlet petal.
Filled with mysteries left untold;
Beauty is born as blooms unfold.

Fantasies wished but left unspoken;
Dreams remain only those
Secrets kept within the Rose.

Linda Walden

Remembering You

I have a pain in my heart
Caused from loving you
Sometimes it's not fair
Because our love won't do.

It hurts when I think of you
Lying there with your smile
When I see you again
It will be all worth while.

I remember the things about you
The way you touched me with your heart
But I will always remember you
Even though were far apart.

Things have changed
Between you and me
Though I know in my heart
You will always be.

Manda M. Klarer

Transformation

The closeness between us
causes a friction
My face becomes as lucent
as the cracking of dawn
My arms outstretched
as the branches of a tree
My heart races
as a greyhound world
My eyes begin to sparkle
as the stars in the sky
My body is burning
as the fires of hell.

Kara D. Oliver

Michael's Apartment

Tapestries and Turpentine
   Canvas watching —
Patterned Schizophrenia
   dance around the Virgin Statue
   and gaze into your soul.
Indifferent white wine
   sifting sound.
And hard wood swaying
   with tired but eager feet.
Cobbler's ghost grinning
   that it sweats no more
As silent hammers
   echo in the dawn.
Pappa searches truth
   on inadequate sheets
As tomorrow and yesterday
   flow together for a sweet while.

Jo Hamilton

Invisible Chains

I'm bound by invisible chains,
Chains that will not break;
I've never been afraid of death,
Its life I cannot take.

You may sometimes hear me say,
In a calm and sacred voice,
To choose life over death
Is to make a foolish choice.

I'm too scared to live,
And too unfortunate to die;
Too scared to take chances,
And too eager to cry.

I always look for a way out,
So I have no need to pretend;
I scream to inform the world
That I look forward to the end.

I look forward to the day
When I take my final breath;
And only then will I know
If the only peace in life is death.

Larry R. Muncy II

Misty Sunrise

As the rue of the ocean
changes from green to blue
Tides eradicate testimony
of all evidence.

Waves wreak havoc
While gulls soar
fluttering above
to seize sea urchins.

Sea crabs glued
to wet sand
sand dollars awash
with each wave

Each rush reaching
for sand anew
creating minuscule
riddles and ridges

Pillage of drifts
lay dispersed
as morning dew
inhabits its shore.

Lorelei Hodges

Bushwhacked

Recalled to mind was a pleasurable,
childhood memory, riding on the
running boards of dad's car.
Often, my brother and I stood by
the driveway, in readiness, watching
for a glimpse of dad's car.

Dad's car in sight, simultaneously,
with a jump and leap, we landed
on the running boards.
Places taken, my brother grabbing
the driver side, and I the passenger
side, near a line of bushes.

Underway, enjoyable was the ride.
Until, my head bumps against a bush.
Whack! My hair tangles in a branch.
Dad stops the car to untangle my
hair, provide a scarf, and save me,
from being bushwhacked again.

Pat Bordner

"Children Of Today"

What has gone wrong with the
children of today?
It seems a lot of them gave up
and gone astray.
The future will determine if
there's a bitter past.
Something must be done, and
it has to happen fast!
They stand behind their gangs,
with no self respect of pride.
Someone needs to reach out,
and tell them not to hide.
To reach within their soul, and
find out what is wrong.
Bring it to the surface, and show
them they belong.
The joy is in the hope of knowing,
you can tame a wild heart!
But the saddest part of all...
is not knowing where to start.

Susan R. Myhre

Traeci's Goodbye

Open me
Close me
You've memories
reply, but
Don't ever
forget me or
never deny.
Shed a tear,
or treasure
a smile, but
Never forehold
A chunk
of denial. Don't
rely solely
on the future
Nor on the past,
But forget me
Nonetheless.

Traeci Orndorff

Yielded

Oh, my lord, I ask of you
Come to my soul's rescue.
Conquer my stubborn, selfish will,
Continuing until I yield.

Don't retreat upon my sigh
My flesh does not want to die.
Although I say, "Go away!"
Oh, my lord, in mercy stay.

And bar the world from our abode
That causes hurt and many woes.
Although a fleeting glance I give,
May I in you forever live.

And all I love more than you,
Place them in their proper view.
For then I know that all is well
And only then with you I dwell.

Nancy G. Pribble

Thoughts Of Thelma

Thoughts of my mother keep
coming to my mind. Her gentle
spirit was like the cool winter breeze.
I live in a world of ages ago,
how I got there only my mother
knows. Talks of the future
she would say are just hopes and
dreams of another day. Now
hopes and dreams are just a
reflection in my mind of years
ago when she was still alive

Rosemary Lester

Desert Sage

A small white dove
coos softly to
dawn's newly crowned
morning,

Beckoning blue feathered
herons bedded in stalks of
ecru buffalo grass,

While butterflies dance
in circles of cottonwood
trees blanketing
earth's fleece, cooling
the thirsty land with
shades of shifting shadows
on the edge of an ancient
and winding river.

As calm ripples ebb in
golden splendor under
evening's pink horizon.

Ursula Swansun Stillwell

Solitary Dancer

Couples come
Couples go
The music plays on
Romantic, sultry, spirited, evocative

The man sits
One at a table for four
Following the mood of each tune
With barely noticeable moves
A hand, a foot, a shoulder
In flow with some absent partner
Herself graceful, responsive
Each feeling the beat
Each sensing the other
He sits alone
And dances with her

Louis DuBois

101 South, To The Bridge

Surfing the rock stations
cresting on ZZ Top
Nationwide —
clouds are layered lace
through which lowers the Sun.

Pink-gold torches diffuse
above vertical vermilion
through which shimmers in dark,
electric blue middle distance
the lit City's glittering edge —
a faceted seam
of the deepening sapphire sky.

Linda C. Himes

Remembrance

A crisp, sparkling day
   Crunching through the snow
Misty breath precedes my warmth
   Sifting through the snow

Cool winds smoothing my face
   Breathing thoughts of the past
Frosted trees swing fluently
   Savoring times of the past

An icy stream flows happily
   Gurgling a chorus of nature
My eyes soak in the splendid scenery
   Filled with the spirit of nature

Tears trickle down my cheeks
   A wish for a life that is gone
I turn away from this picture of peace
   Feeling a part of me that's gone
      Mark Theriault

Untitled

The children playing
Cute clothes on
Singing, hoping
All day long.
Where have the children gone?

Where have the children gone?
Off to parts unknown, beyond.

In search of truth life answers none.
To school-war. They've died.
They are done. Soot.

The children playing
Same clothes on running, hiding
All day/night long.
Where have the children gone?

To peace and joy
Life's answers now. No work.
They're safe and happy now.
Celestial freedom.
      Richard H. McElroy

Seasons Of Love

Her lips of satin hue
danced on face of pink.
Eyes of mischief sparkle
encircled by auburn strand.

Graceful movements make
about my heart entangled.
Arms which yearn to hold
my love of childhood dream.

Heat of summer wilting,
romance once, now passing.
Winter's cold surrounds
with chill upon my heart.

Spring's engendered breeze
brings vestige of opportunity.
To rekindle flame, smoldering
of love oft left unspoken.

Heat of passion blazing
now forever in my soul.
With tide is swept away
if ever it is slighted.
      Steve Neher

"Snowflakes"

Tiny dancers float around,
Dancing, drifting, toward the ground.
The wind is you music,
The sky is your stage.
Flowing as easy as a turn of the page.
Tiny dancers flit and fly,
Landing softly, left to die.
The song of the wind has long since gone,
Leaving you left to melt on the lawn.
Tiny dancers take a bow,
Your death was not in vain,
For the standing ovation of flowers,
Greet you now as rain.
      F. J. McGraw

Song For Kelly

Who is my grandchild?
Dawn gold and blue
Bird song and laughter
Tears bright as dew
Running, arms outstretched
To clasp all the world
Curled up in sleep
With hands petal furled.

Who is my grandchild?
How came she to be
Born of love into loving
And bringing to me
Joy beyond singing
And loves yet to be.
      Olive Kefauver

Our Wedding Day

As I give myself to you on this
Day.

I find that I am ready to live
The rest of my life with you.

You have showed me that being in
Love is very special.

The one thing that will stay in
My heart is how true are love is.

And how I really love you with
My undying heart and soul.
      Ruby Acup

Risks

An open hole - I stare
Down into the Darkness.
   "Hello."
      It echoes into
The desolate moisture.

I smell the soil - many
Layers going miles into the
Earth. No Sound. Darkness
Calling - A Whisper.
      What was that?
   "Jump!"

Somehow Reassuring -
Somehow frightening. Maybe...
I'll tie a Rope to that
Tree - have a support
Cable - Maybe I'll just
   Jump head first -
      Take the Risk.
      Randall O'Neill

"Days Of Thunder"

Days of Thunder,
Days of Thunder,
It's more than you and me,
It's more than you can see,
Days of Thunder,
Days of Thunder,
It's more than singing birds,
It's more than dancing clouds,
Days of Thunder,
Days of Thunder,
It's more than friends could see,
It's more than love could be,
Days of Thunder,
Days of Thunder,
It's more than lightening bugs,
It's more than a storm,
Days of Thunder,
Days of Thunder,
It's more than you and me,
It's more than you can see, I Days Of
Thunder!
      Lisa Kauffman

A Prayer Without Words

   The world is very still
Dear God
   I'd like to softly
pray
   I have some lovely
thoughts of you,
   But thoughts are hard
to say
   Yet, you can even
hear my thoughts
   The thoughts I
cannot say
   And you can love
a little child
   Who finds this
way to pray.
      Leslie Flanigan

Moment To Moment

We're all soft sculptures
but some hack away
by judgments and criticism
and things that they say

Only God knows what lies
in the secret abyss
and can heal and fill
the things that are amiss

Like a river into
its tributaries spilling
God's love is life-giving
and all fulfilling

And if all of our sufferings
brought us to God's breast at last
we must surrender to Him all
that's in the past

The future is veiled
from our eyes
but it's in this moment
that eternity lies
      Michelle Schell

Living For Jesus

Living for Jesus
Dear God that's my plea
Trying my very best
To be more like Thee

Living for Jesus
That's my real concern
Giving my all and
Expecting nothing in return

Living for Jesus
In each and every way
Not just on Sunday
But day after day

Living for Jesus
So when my eyes are closed
Let me with you Father
In your Heavenly Abode

Amid tears of celebration
Let them all say
She lived for Jesus
And she is with Him today
Lillie F. Lee

Untitled

My love for you is higher than the sky;
Deeper than the ocean;
brighter than the sun; and
Purer than the white snow.
You give me warmth and security.
You put joy into my heart and soul.
My heart and soul are dancing with
joy in the flames that you have created.

You are the man I have
always dreamed of sharing my life with.
My love for you is richer than
chocolate and sweater than sugar.
You mean the world to me.
Tina F. Schroyer

Loneliness

No confusion hot,
Desolation of the winter, neither.
Floating on the blue river:
A burning colorful heart.
Waving leaves flow the wondering clouds.
Spring wind allures the World.
Xiaosheng Liao

Inside * Outside

My inside self and outside self are
different as can be

My outside self wears neat clothes
and is average height for her age
she has short brown hair
and blue eyes
and is very funny.

My inside self is interesting

My inside self is a
Marine biologist playing
with dolphins
she's tall and pretty
and very nice.
and loves all mammals.
Tracy Jenkins

Confused About Our Separation

A comma separates the Jr. from my name,
Distances me from my father.
Now it's bent metal,
A walker that needs to be pushed,
Like a comma that blocks hugs.

Should I ask that it be moved aside?
Should I grab your hands—
Cold on the walker side,
Warm on the free—
And dance around the house with you,
Holding up your limp arms
As you held my
Little arms at weddings past?

Or should I put a
Magazine in your new nylon bag,
Pat you on your knee
And leave your
Home?
Ted Holsteen

Until I Know

Does he feel what I feel?
Does it make it so?
The hair on my arms salute him,
My lips they tingle so.
The aura that surrounds him,
I want to make it glow.
The electricity inside him,
I want to spark it so.
His smell is his and his alone,
It's like fresh fallen snow.
When beside him,
I cannot think.
I dare not let it show,
Until I know.
Does he feel what I feel?
Does it make it so?
Rochelle Ann Wilsey

Just Because You're Elderly

Just because you're elderly
Doesn't mean you quit
Tell a joke, have a laugh
It doesn't hurt a bit

People just aren't interested
Hearing about your woes
They'd rather hear a funny joke
And that's the way it goes

And when you think about it
I think we'll all agree
We'd rather hear the brighter side
Than all that misery

We have our friends and relatives
Who know of our frustrations
Of all our aches and all our pains
And all our operations

So give a break to the public
You can do it if you try
Then you'll get lots of waves and smiles
As you go walking by
Kay Ringie

Alive In Me

I see the tears welling in your eyes,
Don't be sad, please don't cry.
Someday we shall meet again,
Then our new lives will begin.
I knew, in time that you would pass,
I didn't know it would come so fast.
I'll keep you in my heart and mind.
And when I look there I will find,
The memories of our friendship true.
The special times between me and you.
So, you see, I'll always remember,
The life and love we had together.
So to you friends I'll say good-bye,
I won't be sad, I will not cry.
Alive in me, you'll never die.
Kristen Massman

"Regurgitations Of The Holy Man"

Flowers are evil
Doth say the grind
Rivers of hope
Polluted and dry

Tell your truths
Social suicide
Swallow this world
With your eyes

Spit it out!
Spit it out!
Makes you sick

When asked of why
We will answer this:
Checkerboard Politics....
Rye Mattson

Inside

So small the outline of her frame
Down deep inside she feels so shamed

No one knows the pain she feels
Her mind destroyed, her lips are sealed

She glazed into a mirror on her wall
Her dark brown eyes filled with tears

Battered and abused
How could he misuse

Eyes filled red with fire
Loves is what she desires

Low self esteem
Blood boils through her stream

Death is near to end
There's no way out but to sin

Alone it seems so wrong
Wasted and now she's gone
Nina Faith Woods

"Dreams"

Dreams for me, dreams for you,
dreams for everybody, too.
Dreams here dreams there,
I see dreams almost everywhere.
Awake or asleep I don't care
as long as my dreams are there!!
Maggie Sullivan

Crystal Blue

Crystal blue was the water that rained
down on me and you.
Crystal blue are my feelings when
I say I love you.
Crystal blue was the color of your
eyes when I next saw you.
Crystal blue was the color of my
tears when you asked me to marry you.
Crystal blue were the color of the
balloons you bought after the birth
of our children.
Crystal blue was the sky when you
looked at me and said good-bye.
Crystal blue were the tears that
fell from my eyes.
Crystal blue was the color of your
suit the day I had to bury you.

Michelle Wilson

Variety

Some of us
Drink coffee, black
Cheat at cards
Hate blackjack.

Some of us
Hate chocolate cake
Like foggy days
Hate milk shake.

Some of us
Like to smoke
Walk in the rain
Can't tell a joke.

Some of us
Like stormy nights
Hate warm beer
Have fear of heights.

What a bore in this "rat race"
If we all liked the same pretty face
Had the same friends
Liked the same place.

Rebecca P. Bell

A Cry For Peace

Where is peace?
Did it leave and go away to stay?
Was it here yesterday?
Babies crying
Children dying
Gunshots bang,
Teardrops upon barricade windowpanes
Weeping widows
Childless mothers
Cry out to the streets:
PEACE! PEACE! Where are you?
PEACE is dead, someone cried
Our mates took it away
When they fought and died.
Go to bed, someone said
Rest your weary head
Melt your spirit around peaceful streams
Dance upon your dreams...then
Peace will come like a quiet flowing river.
NO ONE will be there to make you quiver.

Rosa Baldwin

You

The BOREDOM in my head
drowns my brain;
The candle light in my eyes
burns my pupils;
The ringing in my ears
pounds in my head.

BUT YOU...

you kill the silence in my heart.
Your rude breath,
and your stabbing hand
bruise my soul.

LEAVE ME...

Leave like the trace of your sword.
Go or lie in a puddle
of cold, running blood,

BECAUSE YOU.

Tracy Compton

September Aubade.... Berkeley

New light brings incense..
Drying apples with
Eucalyptus fire
On altars
There in the expansive
Air.

A sachet room
Rattles as dry leaves
With the
Sombrescented
Crackle of the
Air fire.

Awakening ..
Still aware of
Love's embers....
We uncover apple-scented
Autumn in the
Cool wooing air of
Colder days to come...

L. Campbell

My Friend, The River

Drawn to the water's of the river
during my darkest hour,
I longed for peace and contentment
from my Lord's Holy Power

I was heavy hearted,
and all torn inside
from the pressures of the world
that had served as my guide

So to my friend the river
with all it's mysteries and bins,
I extended my hands
in gesture of a friend

And like two minds meeting
we joined together as one,
and I knew nothing on God's Earth
could weaken the bond

So true to the story
told long, long ago,
I found peace and contentment
with friend river below.

Nancy Baylis Shepard

What About You

What do you do
each day with your life?
Do you spread joy and goodwill
or create hatred and strife?

You have a choice, you know,
and it's all up to you
You present your own image
by the things that you do.

You can be kind to your neighbor
and help if he asks
If you just look around
there are so many tasks.

Sometimes just a smile
can help someone who's down
Even you'll feel better
when you wipe off your frown.

So just take a good look
at the way that you live,
You'll be very surprised
how much more you can give.

Lois Adams

Hand In Hand

Through each trial and triumph,
Each joy or cross to bear,
Through calm or stressful waters,
My love will always be there.

When dark clouds surround me,
I'd leave my fears behind,
I find a bright horizon,
As you place your hand in mine,

I trust each new tomorrow,
To your unerring care,
Knowing that tomorrow,
Your love will still be there.

Margaret Floyd

My Lover My Friend

You are my lover
Each night and day
But you are also much more
Which I am proud to say
Because you are also my friend

I not only share my body and soul
Also my feelings and mind
Which I am able to do
Because you are so kind
To feel the way you feel
And be honest and open
About the feelings that are real
Plus, all that we are hoping

You are my lover
Through good and bad times
We talk things out
Which we always seem to find
That's also what our friendship is
all about!

Paula J. Wolfe

"Innocent Child"

Every word spoken
Echoes memories askew.
Unraveling messages
of what's next to undo.

Troubles all around
Fights and screams
Stares and frowns
Beatings abound.

Don't mind me
Little and loyal
Loving and innocent
Silence is a given.

Frozen in fears
God no tears
Strength is a virtue
No need for nurture

Trust and love
Words to me
Unjust avenues
Never walked through.

Marylou Baier

Valentine Snowflake

The February wind gently swirls and
eddies. A snowflake suddenly appears
before us.

It's a small, white, lace Valentine
flurrying down on Cupid's arrow.

His frozen heart has fallen as a
snowflake and it is callin' —

The cold wintry wind which howls now
more bold —

We huddle close together in the
freezing cold.

Suddenly, the Valentine Snowflake
disappears upwards —
on another mission of love.

Virginia Hewitt

Breakfast Time At Grandma's

Bacon fried golden brown,
Eggs done sunny side up,
Yellow and round.
Biscuits fluffy, full of steam,
Good strong coffee, sugar and cream.
Breakfast time at Grandma's.

Homemade butter in a mould,
Milk in a pitcher, good and cold.
Jams and jellies,
Sweetness in jars,
Breakfast time at Grandma's.

Grandma just a-stewin,
Her apron's all a-flutter,
Makin' sure our biscuits
Are spread with tasty butter.
Makin' sure our plates are full
Of bacon and the rest.
Of all my memories, this was the best.
Breakfast time at Grandma's.

Donald Paul Whitted

Ode To A Goalie

In net, you have the
elegance of a
dancer in a grand
spotlight; a sentry
with commanding
power and allure.

Oh, to be snagged with
your cat-like quickness...
to be protected
with such urgency...
to be nestled
within those padded
arms of yours.

Oh, to be a puck.

J. L. Hutchison

Rage, Brain Damage, Death

Encased within a body; like a body
  encaged within a cell.
Always on edge.
Just bordered with hatred.
Just above anger.

If such a mind should falter,
A cell damaged beyond reprieve.
Plasmatic body out of sync,
Limbs all but wasted away.

If such a mind should falter,
If it would happen to cease.
All of man would come to a halt, or,
Just be classified as deceased.

Lisa Kern

The Stalker

The fog covers the shore like a glove,
Encircling the pines,
Sitting silent and hushed
So the moon cannot find
A crevice in which to slide
And brighten the darkened sand.
The fog clenches the water
With its hands.
It crawls under the dock
Wrapping its arms around the sea grass.
The fog tiptoes along the damp earth
Leaving no footsteps behind.
Stopping to rest,
It sleeps.
The moon breaks through,
A soft, glowing light on the beach.
The fog retreats
Waiting to return
Another night.

Karen Young-Burns

Dreams

Dreams make us laugh
Dreams make us cry
Some dreams even let us fly
What is a dream?
Does it come from our imagination?
Or do we go to another world
like my mother always says
For, I, do not know
But when I do I will
tell you.

Tiffanie Bukowski

"The Beauty Of Nature"

As I sit here all alone,
Enjoying the beauty of my home.
Watching the cardinal's blue birds,
finch, and doves,
eat from the feeders and fly up above.
Watching the wild life graze
From the meadows below,
making my heart feel all aglow.
Overlooking the catfish pond,
Where we sometimes go fishing.
and have fun.
Watching the rain fall on the deck,
So we say, oh what the heck.
Tomorrow the sun may shine.
So we enjoy nature, and have a good time.

Virginia C. Bolton

Desire

   Life is a black hole that
everybody tries to avoid. When the
hope and drive is gone you get sucked
into a blackness of lonely, disheartened
hatred. The stubborn ignorance that
roams the wasteland is like the
pounding of a cold rain. The sun
washes over the destitution to show
A glimmer of hope.

Rebecca Breckler

Untitled

Up, forever, in the sky
Everything is possible.
Immortality
Lives in me and for me
Forcing uncommon laws to occur.
Plaid breathe comes off your tongue.
Windows of redness bleed for us.
Desks climb the walls
Begging for freedom.
Dinosaurs fly under
Wings of chaos,
Moons shine along
The knife of the butcher.
This will never end.
I fall over and stop.
This continues.

Kellie Walters

What Is Your Message

There is a message in
Everything you say or do.
These are the stepping stones
In life for you.
So, be careful of the kinds
Of words you use.
Your mode of dress, actions too
Reveal the kind of life you choose.
The way you do express yourself
Will determine work, determine wealth,
Reflects your mood, the way you live.
Remember too, it affects your health.
Take time to think and plan your life
To bring about the best in you.
Fun today may bring only grief
And let you wonder what to do.
Every action you portray
Are signals of your inner self.

Laura Belle Martin

Widower's Lament

Relatives, relatives
Everywhere!
But, very few relatives
Who really care.

A very few friends,
A few friends remain;
They are the ones who
Will help me sustain.

A few good relatives
A few true friends;
They are the ones who
Share in my sorrow,
They are the ones I can
Turn to tomorrow.

Thomas L. Beaner

Blood

The stars in the sky
Explode without warning
I match the night
For I am in deepest mourning
I have savored the blood
That pools at your feet
A bitter taste
That I find so sweet
I sink my sharp teeth
Into your soft neck
Sipping out the blood
Beautifully wet
Your tears mean nothing
For I cannot cry
Nor does your death
For I've already died
Yet I needed your affection
Your trusting love
It was the only way
To get to your blood

Melanie Walsh

A Christmas Poem

Christmas is a time for
Extra special gifts for our
Loved ones and friends.

No matter what it may be
As long as it's given from
The heart.

This time of year also brings
Sadness to those who can't give.

But, if it's only a simple
Phrase as, "I love you
And thank God for you and I,"

That's more than any gift
Could ever hold.

Velma L. Flowers

Color Of A Bruised Heart

Purple, black, blue
Empty, sad, forbidden
Angered, broken, mistakened

   The Color of A Bruised Heart
Lifeless, bleeding, dropping
   Gone
The color of a bruised heart

Michelle Rae Edwards

South Azania

Hear the cry in the summer
Feet pounding, hands clapping,
Voices shouting
"Freedom is coming tomorrow"
Blood spills, children squeal
The police guns aimed to fire
People fall for no cause
Innocent bodies lie on the ground
Backs torn open, life ebbing away
"Freedom is coming tomorrow"
But how many more must die
Before their cry is heard
"Freedom is coming tomorrow!"

Sheldon W. Rice

Frigid Crime

Shades of darkness
fill the mind
to shatter dreams
of endless ties
broken heart
filled with lies
falls from grace
with tattered sighs
lust burned hot
now fades and dies
love lost to
frigid crime
shattered dreams
and broken ties
now fill
the darken sight
hear the cry
of tortured mind
and lay to rest
the frigid crime

William D. Krueger

Opening Memories

I opened up the year book for the
first time in so long,
Turning through each page to find
that the memories were not gone.

I glanced at old classmates in which
I shared my hopes and dreams;
Now they are all grown up, and have
families just like me.

Some faces I remember while others
lie deep within my mind;
I wiped the dust from the year book
which had a beautiful golden bind.

A tear fell from my check as I longed
to go back in time.
When I had not experienced the world
and innocence was mine.

I guess time doesn't stop, not even
for a second to stand still;
Memories will not let me forget
And in many ways they never will.

Stacy Boyd

A Fishing Miracle

Waters deep, icy cold
Fishing boat getting old
Gusting winds, angry sea
Hungry sharks haunting me
Sinking sun dims the light
Darkness comes, moonless night
Fearful hearts beating fast
Crashing waves, forceful blast
Dampness felt chilling feet
Sea and men soon to meet
Kneeling now, heads are bared
Praying we will be spared
Suddenly, welcomed sound
Foghorn wails, lost crew found.

Shirley J. Mason

The Banquet Table

See Saffron pansies,
flowers floating in Harrison's Banquet.
He prohibited trout as an appetizer,
and everything stayed off the linen.
A necessary evil even for the enemy,
eating to live,
Supporting life.
This is Harrison's Decision.

Kathleen Sullivan

Excitement

Power, jumping
flying
With blood pumping
prying
Running to stop
insane
Going to pop
death bane
Faster
spring
Caster
ring
No more time
Blink
Past sublime
Brink
Dying
Strife
Trying
Life

Kevin S. Doyle

The Birth

All ending search
For its beginning
Who am I
Truth is forth seen in the reflection
Of the midnight moon
Thrust into a tunnel of light
My knees folded shape
In grace with all mercy
Taken as a rising star
From my world
Risen to the morning glory
Tears silently fall
On this graven soul
Awaken in Quickness
For as much of my tears
Spill on this ink
To find I am
LIFE...

Rene Hinojosa

March

I like March
for I know it'll bring
A kite on a string
And the beginning
Of Spring.
Sheena Beale

My Heart And My Soul

Keep me Oh Lord, Please do!
For my heart and my soul I
Give to you
And walk with me each step
That I take
Be near me each morning when
I awake
Be the sunshine that warms
My heart
And the light that shines as
My day starts
Give me wisdom to do your
Will
And when I hear gossip hold
My tongue still
And let my love show
As yours long ago
For I give to you my
Heart and my soul
Ruby Andes

History

Waves of grain
Drops of rain
Oklahoma winds blow
People come and go
Through a town so small
Can't you hear the call
Of something you can't see
This thing called History
If you look carefully
Pictures and story
Of the History of the town
And places now run down
One day the sun will rise
And another small town dies
Sheldon Scott Stout

Tragedy?

Jane's husband married her
for her chest.
He called them "Boobs."
He could not say "breasts."
It is too bad they fell
down flat.
How do you cope with
a thing like that?
Shirley Male

Blue Eyes Behind Glasses

Genuine and glowing as youth
Expressing sincerity, wisdom, and truth
Portray how one feels within
Are glasses hiding secret or sin?
Do they cover up shyness or lies...
Or just two innocent blue eyes?
Deborah Rose Meyerstein

Intangible Heed

One day I saw a butterfly
    descend upon a star
That fell to earth and fell
    apart to a thousand
    different shines
    And the butterfly was
    glowing
The star was hurt
    "but still"
As long as the butterfly
    was there
The star remained
    "tranquil."
Phyllis Erris

Frostbite

Do you feel cold?
Do you feel lost?
Do you feel spaced?
Do you feel frost?

Are you kinda high?
Are you kinda numb?
Are you kinda sly?
Are you kinda dumb?

If you don't see,
If you don't know,
The reason you're cold,
You're standing in snow.
Rhonda S. Blomberg

Are You Proud Of Me Today

Mom are you proud of me today?
As I go to school, I wonder all the way.

As I help the children
To keep them out of way

Oh mom are you proud of me today?

I need the hugs and kisses
That only moms can give.

I need a special moment
To make me grow and live.

I never felt my mother's hug
Or kiss upon my cheek.

I never knew that I was loved
Those days it wasn't chic.

As I kneel here to pray,
Oh mom are you proud of me today?
Etta N. Kowalski

Till We Meet Again

His life ebbed away
as I held his head in my hands,
disbelief and shock took over.
Mechanically, events whirled.
    Friends came.
    Family arrived.
    Arrangements were made.
Loving memories surfaced,
to cut through the wall of grief.
Torrents of tears in private.
Laughter and life are alive.
Adventures in the future.
My love for Jim
will forever undiminish.
Gertrude C. Stevens

Face Value

When someone sheds a smile
and you don't know why,
Just be glad they did
Because it's better then seeing ya cry.
A smile increases your face value
but makes a friend or two.
When someone smiles you feel good
and you smile, that's what you do.
Now don't say you don't and
then go ahead and do it,
Come on you cute kid
where is the gleaming of your spirit?
Giggle if you have to
no matter who's around,
because when you do
people don't walk around with a frown.
So next time you feel grumpy,
or you feel you have to hate,
Just put on a smile
and you'll feel great.
Doug Cohen

There's No Difference

Roses are all color's
And you know you love them all,
There's no difference in your heart
If one is large or small.

Violets are found all over this world
In some of the most amazing places
And there's no difference in your heart
About its origin or destination

There's no difference
In all our universal creation
Love it all, be it great or small
There's no difference
Jessie Grinstead

"Space"

Space, Where gravity is gone
    and you never see dawn.
Space, a mysterious place
    Which will put a smile on your face
Space, nothingness surrounds
    and blackness abounds
Space, where future might be
    but some disagree
Amber Boyce

Wet Dream

I reach out for you,
And you reach out for me,
Our fingers touch,
Slide together,
So that our palms are pressed
    to one another,

You draw me into your arms,
As I pull you close to me,
Our lips join,
Our fingers touch,
I move my hands
    to feel your body,
I let my legs
    straddle your hips,

And then...
    the dream ends.
Jeannette Street

Lost In Clouds

A grayness the sky portrays
  Cannot hide the suns laughter;
    Cannot deeper within flickering rays of light;
    Cannot speak to me the way you do.

Gathering clouds, passively mention rain,
  But leave me wondering
    Whether I'll ever see your face again,
    And why I even think of you at all.

I know there was a time.
  In spring, so long ago -
    That we breathed each others lives.

When we gave without vain,
  Where we loved with no pain -
    And we could deny the word with our ecstasy.

Now I look,
  And there is naught -
    But the grayness of clouds.
  Jacque Walker

At One With The Earth

Reverently she steps through the silent forest
  careful not to disturb one leaf or stem
She stops to enjoy the peaceful silence of the spring morning,
  feeling at one with the earth.

Surrounded by the green forest
  she looks up at the ceiling of leaves
    that hides the sky from her view.
Bathed in the beauty,
  she sits at the foot of an ancient oak tree
    and feels it breathing with her.

A bird flies by and, not noticing her,
  dips and swoops in its ritual mating dance.
The long forgotten dance that was born when the earth was,
  and was made for all creatures who are connected
  through the power of the spirit of life.

This special woman is one of the last
  who appreciate the beauty of the earth -
  and how sacred it is to keep it alive.
  Eleni Delopoulos

In Tribute To The Gallantry Of The Crew

And The Battleship "Arizona"

Behold serene now cloudless skies,
Cast too thine eyes upon the sea,
Of which the past, the tragedy,
When slipped beneath its saddened waves,
A noble ship to watered graves,
Its Captains Courageous, and mariners too,
Of sainted youth, to manhood grew,
As shield did they, this land of ours,
Amid attack, those fatal hours,
Yet though in shallow waters lie,
The valiant men who did but die,
For love of peace forevermore,
To still the beastly cannon roar,
Although divine but to forgive,
Forget we not that free men live,
Because of those who gave that day,
On distant seas, so far away.

*Dedicated to the valiant men and women of our country's
armed forces, and to all of those who gave of themselves
during the sneak attack on Pearl Harbor, December 7, 1941.*
  Anthony Monteleone

"Mountains"

Explore me from head to toe;
Caress my Ridges with your limbs, so softly.
See my Deep Dark Creases Growing stronger;
Your eyes are the window to my soul;
Drown your limbs in the Cool Spring Water;
Divide the hills with Grass So Green;
Your limbs so warm and tender;
The Valley so Deep and Wide, come inside?
Come and Explore me.
The Eagle so very rare: flies down
and touches the mountains so proud.
and screams out its name.
The Mountains peaks; as the Darkness grows near.
The Strong Wind lashes out through the
Deep, wide, and Dark Valley.
Suddenly, Thunder!
Lightning! The mountain quakes!
  Cynthia Stringfield

Maine In The Twilight Of The Year

Winter's sky hangs heavy above the sea,
Casting on it a thousand shades of gray.
A tall, gaunt, barren evergreen tree
Holds with long gnarled fingers, tenaciously,
To the rocky cliff of the deserted bay.

The water pounds the rocks below.
And, sucking the marrow from their bones,
Backs up to deliver a stronger blow,
While white-caps froth a fluorescent glow,
Upon the corpses of the stones.

Brackish seaweed crawls up the shore,
Gaining ground with every whispering wave.
Waves push forth shells from Neptune's secret store,
Exchanging more for less, and less for more,
Then drag debris down to a watery grave.

Gulls watch in silence for signs of food,
Ducks and loons bob about on their cold, wet bier.
Even seals, those harbor clowns, seem subdued,
As if they sense the changing mood,
Knowing winter's near.
  Allison Lembo

Untitled

The special times we've shared, are very important to me.
'Cause every time we share one, it adds a branch to my tree.

That tree is made of memories, to be cherished for years.
Some of them are made of happiness, some of them are made of tears.

Sometimes I just like to sit and reminisce, of all the fun we've
had in the past; and how a lot of those memories I really do miss,
and how I wish they could forever last.

We've gone through things that other's couldn't comprehend.
Yet, we make the best out of the happiness that it brings.
We've gotten this far, and we won't stop now, because together,
we can do anything.

But, if you think about it, life isn't all that bad.
There's an old saying that I hear a lot... and that's "not to
complain about what you don't have, and be grateful for what
you've got."

'Cause the special times we've shared, are a major part of me.
And through the years, more memories will come, adding branch,
by branch to my tree.
  Jessica Chapman

"Desert"

The wind races across the desert floor,
  chasing bits of fine sand.
The piercing blue sky is contrasted by the
  dazzling orb which has begun its descent.
Shapes become obscure and distorted and,
  therefore, become meaningless.
In the distance, the shadow-cast mountains
  give conceptual knowledge of man's beginning

Brian Mitchell

Cherished

Cherished are you to me,
Cherished is the time I have with thee.
Cherished is your heart and soul,
Cherished are your tender lips that touch my skin.

Cherished is your gentle caress
Cherished is your kindness that you give to me,
And your patience, and your love,
That sings more beautifully than anything on earth.

Cherished are your eyes that look upon me with warmth,
Cherished is our love so rare,
That only God could tear it apart.
Cherished is the moment that you hold me, oh so close!

Cherished is the happiness that you have given to me,
For without you there would be nothing to cherish,
Except the time it took me to find you.

Angel Woods

"Winter Scenes"

Ice skaters skating on a frozen pond
Children bundled up in warm clothing
Sledding down a snow covered hill
Logs blazing in an open hearth.
My Grandmother at the old wood stove
Cooking chicken and dumplings
Biscuits and cornbread warm from the oven.

Old Nellie pulling the home-made sled
filled with logs for the fire,
With my Grandfather at the reins.
All the grandchildren rosy-cheeked
in from the cold, setting around the
large, wooden table, filled with
mounds of home-made food.
Everyone laughing and talking with
love for one another.

These are the Winter Scenes
from my childhood memories
My heart will never forget.

Georgia Roberts

Winter

Lonesome hours dreary days
Cloudy skies of darkest grays
Chilliness in the wind that blows
That touches heart as well as toes
Everything as dead as nails
Gloom as dark as night prevails
Come my love and smile at me
And make the sun shine merrily
The dark no longer will be gloom
But tender mystery in the room
The cold would be a sweet command
to sit so close and hold your hand.
Then the sun would shine and the birds sing too
For the only sun I need is you.

Katherine T. Craddock

Untitled

Scenes of disaster
cold laughter
and
fear
They come to you now, are the memories clear?
Small children on swingsets
black music inside;
the shadows put lines on their faces in time.
Helpless and pure
and too young to know
the Evil that lurks in a stranger's dark soul.
The pain we conceal
and hide from ourselves,
keeps others at bay and love on the shelf.
The Fragmented Child
who smiles when she cries
is fearful of love
but doesn't know
Why.

Barbara L. Masi

Atropos

Betwixt twilight hour and dawn's early glow,
Comes solitude's balm over long day's rake;
Like tranquil sea mutes cosmic break,
Merging silent tide with earth's rhythm slow.

Granite walls secret time's vernal sound
Veiled from eternity's supernal ring;
Light hearts succumb to polemic string
Enthralled for the ages by Atropos bound.

The timeless hour, long gone from history's sphere—
Melded into universal aeon's cold keep—
Entombs infinity - sterile in moldering sleep,
Life's vital winds wither the eternal year.

Re-creations of universe on earth's lowly plane
Are the sacraments bestowed on graceful life—
Grains of emotions bearing motility's strife—
Compositions of multitudes, tranquil and sane.

Resurrection of mankind's genetic bent
Betrays modernity's morbid strain
Of cultures deep rooted in millennia's pain—
A lending of virtues to humanities spent.

Alex V. Christoff

At Long Last

A promise of forever is unconditional.
Completeness within itself is its passion.
For passion to live, there must be affection;
for affection gives birth to love.
For love to be lasting, it must be free;
As it is priceless.
For freedom to sustain, it must be boundless;
In its essence it has no limits, only choices.
Choices determining our pursuit of happiness;
for our happiness lies in our own beauty.
Beauty, hidden deep within;
Evasive, until the search is surrendered.
for discovery of potential is seized
through retreating advances.
Potential is fulfilled with a commitment
to trust, trust in the commitment.
Belief in ourselves, mastered through
the art of honesty, the final resort.
Honesty, fully realized through acknowledgement;
We are only immortal for a limited time.

Chris P. Peppers

Pass It On

Focus in your chance has come;
Consider others lest your work is undone;
Abound in life by investing your best
To uphold the foundation where our future rest.

Let not one hour slip away
That you can break ground for a better day.
Each wasted moment narrows the chance,
Each overlooked door lessens the advance.

By fate you'll be the only star in the night,
The truest thing near, the only real right;
The last thread of hope dangling in sight;
The final reason to increase another's might.

Set out seeds where your roses will grow
And beautify the road where the travelers go,
And can sniff the fragrance that fills the air,
And know for sure that love is planted there.

More abiding hope will bud each day
When we can walk the path that paves the way;
Where petals of courage keep drawing men back,
Retreading the road they won't lose the track.

Dorothy J. Ross

Yearning

Yearning!
Constant companion
of my days and of my nights
a yearning of the slow routine of the country
progressive shadow in the direction of oldness
a yearning for the world that I had
small town without many options
only talk and dreams
a yearning for my parents
a yearning for the innocence and simplicity of people

Submerged in this absolute state
I keep living my life
carrying the days like sacs of potatoes
over my shoulders
obstinate, I will carry on with my objectives
to work and to study in the big city
determined to live in this state
for some long years
for the real friends
I will be only yearning

Geraldo F. De Souza

Seashore Moments

Sunshine glistening across the sea
Cool misty breezes caress me
Walking on the cool wet sand
The seashore - in the morning

Seashells gathered on the beach
Kites flying out of reach
Children building castles in the sand
The seashore - in the afternoon

Boardwalk noises coming my way
Boats settled quietly in the bay
Waves sweep clean the beaches at night
The seashore - in the evening

The lighthouse majestically reaches for the sky
Sea gulls searching and soaring high
Spring, summer, winter, or fall
Any season is special at the shore

Eleanor Farenga

The Goddess Of Love

As I sit in complete darkness, silently, missing you,
Constantly on my mind, everything we have been through.

I often wonder, why Margaret, did you have to leave?
You never answered my question, please tell me please?

We spent a long, amazing eighteen years together,
The memories we shared, will be remembered forever.

When I needed you, you always lent your hand,
And here in my heart, now and forever, lies "Margaret's Land."

You were built with perfection in the eyes of family and friends,
The question still asked by everyone is "WHY" again?

You lit up everyone's life in so many different ways,
Then brought sadness on the rainy days.

We all knew in our mind, that you would have to leave us soon,
Your face was round and beautiful as the nightly moon.

I feel so helpless, like I don't know what to do,
But I know one day, we will reunite and I will be with you.

When you were in the hospital, I had wished you the best,
Now you're in heaven and now you must rest!!

Anika Simone Belnavis

The Gap

He sits quietly and waits for things to come
Content or discontent, no expression shown
Living life to survive:
   Repairs and maintains the engine
   Wife fuels it, kids run it
Body deteriorates, but mind lives on
A walking encyclopedia of our history
Vivid memories alive and kicking
Just waiting to be released at the right moment
When someone sparks interest
Like a bottle filled to the top, but once it's opened
Stories of life leak out
Pouring into our cups old wisdom
I need to learn, before it's too late
How to open the door to my past and future
Some days only one word is exchanged
A friendly hello, like to an old acquaintance
But there's more boiling inside me
The lid is tight
So I reach to kiss him good-night and he kindly thanks me.

Doris Fuad Hanhan

"Just Do It Now!"

It's called a bad habit, but I'm not so sure
Could be a weakness, sickness, laziness, or more
Put it off here, put it off there
Excuses, excuses, everywhere
Procrastination is a pet peeve of mine
Just Do It Now! Quit wasting time
While you're in seclusion, the deadline draws near
Is it the lack of self-confidence you fear?
You're very aware of what needs done
But meeting it face to face, you begin to run
Is your brain on "pause", trying to "rewind"
Well, nudge it to "fast-forward," while there's still time
Is there a remedy? I sure hope so
While your mind's on "hold", mine's ready to blow!
Everyone may do it once in a while-but for every little thing—
That's just not my style.
Yes, I have bad habits, but I do believe
You have to tackle a task in order to achieve
Next time before procrastinating, heed what I've said
Just Do It Now!! You'll be further ahead.

Joy Smith

Brown Ballet Dancers

Madame C. J. Walker and Overton's High brown, Nut brown
  cosmetic dainties dusted their
  curious dark expressions poised on
  regal Ebony shoulders
  held captive by rigid Ghetto corsets.

Their ballet dreams
  trashed stained Earth weary peds
  from dilapidated shacks, rodent projects, broken glass alleys,
  and steamy kitchens
  from Capezio cotton candy pink satin toe shoes.

Limbre and rhythmically chiseled
  Hallelujah Brothers and Sisters
  nurtured by royal Egyptian primordial origins
  painted their satin toes bronze,
  to choreograph and pas de bourree The Fire bird, Giselle and others
  to pull walls down.

They captured the stars in
  clouds of baby breath tulle, tutus, and leotards
  to bow to applause from
  Harlem to Paris, and beyond to dance upon heaven's stage.

Arnette V. Bradley

Could It Be Little Star?

As I gaze upon Thee little star, bringer of light from afar
Could it be that you, a burning flame, are really the same as I
As I look upon the twinkling sky?

Could it be that a soft meadow of summer morn
The blue sky comes up as the new day is born
Are really the same as I, the spring to live, the winter to die?

Could it be that the oceans deep and the forests of night
With all their power and their might
Majesty and beauty from afar, are what you are you bright twinkling
  star?

Could it be all are rapidly bound to this whole vast array
Born to glory but then fade away
Leaves that are falling, the night into day
Man from the child, returning to clay

Could it be little star that one day I'll be you
Taking my place amongst the galaxied star'd view
Beyond the reach of the planets and Mars
And looking down I'll see my son
Through the green fields and meadows there he will run

And looking up he'll see a bright twinkling star
His father with love gazing off from afar

Gene Evers

Caring Means Sharing

Caring means sharing the good and the bad.
Caring means sharing the happy and sad.

It multiplies our joys, and divides our sorrows;
Gives us strength for today and hope for tomorrows.

Sharing our love was better than being alone.
With blessings from above, God made our house a home.

But now that you're gone, what will I do?
I'll have to share my memories of you.

I'll share with our children the love that we had.
It lasted a lifetime and that's not so bad.

Caring means sharing the love that we knew
It lasted a lifetime, a lifetime with you.

Doris F. White

Three bears

I lived with a man who couldn't dream.
could not — unable
He'd discarded his sense of imagination in a cloak room some-
  where
downtown.
long before I'd met him

We once saw an image:
a door ajar … an over-tottled chair…an unfinished meal …
Uncaptioned, for him at least it wasn't the fairy tale;
No association —
(to me).

Young curly girl stepping outside ego;
touching worlds hitherto secret:
(learning arousal).

Or, young man discovers female, not mother,
in between his sheets.

Or, the amazing first encounter of foreigners.

Or, the violating intrusion of a stranger.

Or,

Or even,

- Why it's an empty room; possibly someone left in a hurry,
ventured my undreaming man on the last image we never saw
together.

Bridget Keller

Snow

  Snow,
Covering my heart as it does my window pane.
  Snow,
Cold, wet, like the tears falling from my eyes.

  Snow,
Creating patterns on the glass as it
  (snows),
Creates memories real and yet to be in my heart.

  Snow,
White, soft, gentle, covering my body as
  (snow),
Your lips, soft and caressing, cover mine.

  Snow,
Drifting, floating aimlessly to the earth.
  Snow,
Like me, floating, the dizzy way you make me feel.

Jennifer L. Schulz

Father

A father is someone who will always be a part of his children's life
Even though he is not with his wife
He will be there for them Winter Spring Summer and Fall
And even when they call
He will tuck them in their bed at night
And give them a hug and kiss goodnight
He will never let them down
Because he will always be around
A father is good to have
Because when you are sad, he will make you laugh
And at times when he can't be there for you
You know his love will always be true
Even when he has to go away
His love will always stay

This is dedicated to John Rutherford III, the man I love

And the one I will always cherish and be proud of.

Angela Tucker

America Speaks

Once I was a beautiful land of sweeping grasses,
Crystal blue lakes, and mountains that touched the sky.
Now I am a stagnant wasteland.

Once American Natives roamed freely all over me,
Respecting and loving and admiring my thoughts and feelings.

Now they have been pushed onto minuscule pieces of land
Or were unjustly murdered by people who thought they
Could own me.

Once I was thought to be a place of escape,
A chance to start anew.
Free from persecution and hatred towards foreign ideas.
Now I have become exactly what they were running from.
A nation that tells you how to think, live, and feel.

Why have you done this to me!
I did nothing but love and accept you, and you took
Advantage of me. You ruined me!
How could you do this to someone you profess to love!
Oh, I weep for the future.

Amanda Maunus

What I have Held In

Things hurt so bad and
  cut so deep.
I don't know why things
  look so bleak
Sometimes I want to cry
I sit and wonder why -
  Things don't change
I sit and wonder who's
  really to blame; is it me, or is it them?
Can any body see what I have held in?
My anger explodes and I have to fight.
What if this is the last day of my life.
It's hard to let go of the
  things that I have known
The pain and anger I have felt
It's hard to love and trust
  and feel content
Will the pain ever stop
  or the hurt just quit?
I don't know; I'll just turn numb and sit.

Barbara M. Garner

Father

The burning in my heart grows
Deeper still
Waiting for you to return the love
You shall never feel
Deep in the pit of my soul I cry...
A tear is shed...
But you shall never see
The grievance which stirs in me
You shall never know the pain that I feel
For you could not bear a pain that is so real...
A life filled with sorrow...
Pain and misery are what I know best
I wanted you to be different, not like the rest.

Rip open my unhealed wounds,
Let me bleed upon your hand.
Feel the wrath you have created,
For I cannot love the man whom
I have always hated.

You rip my heart to pieces
But you feel no shame.

Heather D. Sturgill

Untitled

Would the tears stop when they're finally laid to rest?

When would the pain stop eating my heart away?
Darling, I don't have the answers but you can count
That I'll be here in case that you dismay.

The battle is on, the flags are down, no truce,
No mercy, bend your knees or fall down,
There's no turning back now!!!

Fight to the end, giving it all until there is no more.
This is our battle zone...

The victorious winner takes all, pride, honor, love.

Would the pain go away when the tears stop?
Maybe, but from the bleeding heart; the wounds must heal,
Perhaps when winner and the loser take each their share

Only when casualties are counted.
Only when the fields are washed.
Only when the prayers are answered.
Only when the trophy is held high above.
Only when winners and losers consider love.

Only then the tears will stop!!!

Harold Briones

Daughters In The Sun...

Daughters in the Sun get burned.
Daughters in the light of love get burned.
Daughters like me are blinded by fantasies,
Of broken dreams; of dying many times
And living to speak of it.

The darkness is the light to us.
Though we cannot see, we move closer to it —
Still trusting the darkness to save us.
Still trusting the first love that betrayed us.

Herschey McGhee

Dawn

Dawn is the world's way of giving warmth to life
Dawn is the beginning of living—waking up the world to begin again
Dawn allows teardrops to feed the Soul, nurturing all that hungers
Dawn is the beginning of time—giving space for things to grow
Dawn welcomes the smile of the morning light bringing along happy
  songs of birds in flight
Dawn warms the heart giving hope for us to know love
Dawn chases away the "screamin' demons" inside—helping us
  not to fear but to live
Dawn cares for the child within, telling us to come out and play
Dawn opens our eyes to show others that window to our Soul
Dawn, your gift to life is to live free of darkness
Dawn, I feel love and want to be growing with it
Dawn, I want to be alive to share the light you bring
Dawn is my favorite time in this world—love to see and be with
  it every time
Dawn—thank you for my life:

David Kruljac

Lost Friends

I don't know what I've done,
  but I do know what I've lost,
    my one and only loving friends,
      one gone and none to come,
        I wish and wish upon a star to pass,
        but for so long my life may never
          last.

Serenity Hamm

New Birth

Sleeping passively under the blanket of
Death's whisper, which robbed the restless air.
Wandering soul's teetering neither here,
Not yet there.

Silenced cries lost in the essence of
Rhythmic rains.
Clutches of hope in search of but
Not soothing merciless pain.

In God's preparation, wondrously, He'd
Forewarned us earlier in the day,
Through fluttering of a sparrow's wings
Brushing past the windowpane.

His ultimate ushering of archangels
Worthy to reclaim. And when they came

— Hallelujah! Singing praises —

Gathering precious jewels from this earth,
Most holy spirits abundantly comforted me
In parting sorrow of my son's rebirth.

Audrey Lipscomb

Education

Enlightenment- Emancipation which liberates the mind.
Dedication- Devotion- without which achievement and progress are
   nullified.
Universality- which education brings, thereby fostering a certain
   amount of kinship and oneness among all people.
Collectivism- Collegiality, which brings about cooperation,
   annihilating the corrosive effects of competition.
Activism- which engenders excitement, which in its turn creates,
   proselytizers, who preach fervently about the gospel of education
   and its curative powers.
Temperance- the ability to be critical without engaging in any kind
   of futile polemics. Most of all, respecting the opinion and
   judgment of others, no matter how flawed they may be.
Intellectuality- the ability to be a learned, dispassionate observer.
   An observer who analyzes, dissects and critiques like most eminent
   surgeons would with their experienced scalpels. It also means, not
   accepting anything at face-value.
Omnipresence- being in the moment. Participating actively in this
   most majestic of processes in the human experience.
Nature- learning is a process that nature forces upon us, challenging
   us to demystify its mysteries, thereby creating a symbiotic and
   respectful relationship.

Alain J. Vielot

My Brother's Room

My brother's room
dark with gloom
messy and musty and very dusty,

Papers and pencils
ball cards and books
old chess pieces like bishops and rooks
if someone were robbing our house
it would trap the crooks.

My mom went in she said, "clean this pit!!"
but he was gone lickety-split
somewhere outside throwing a fit,

I lost a shoe in there last summer
it is buried down deep in all the clutter
My God!! on his pillow there is a pat of butter,

It is deep
it is dark,
go take a peek.

Brad Betschart

Untitled

So long ago, a lost soul ran crippled- yet convinced!
Delusional of the facts of importance needed to guide
The evolutional circle she must now consider since
That kindred creature abolished the dark cloak from where
she'd hide.

One continual battle to locate a gentle peace all her own
The lone Rangerette would rebelate any conquests there were to be.
Yet how could this be, for that true companion she WAS prone
A deep nurturing ache to connect, authentically tied to fly
free.

'Tis over at last, solid proof has been shown
Your crusades are no longer needed.
What a joy to apply lasting efforts of love never known
Finally tasting of the existence for which you've so pleaded.

At once she's realized how it ends NOT with her.
Our precious circle brings others to attempt paths all THEIR own.
Time now taken to ponder bountiful assets, one could conquer
However, BEGINNING with true love to HERSELF, first must
be shown!

Carly Gerchov Dennis

That Deception

That deception- in your life
   did it weave peace, or love, or might?
That deception- in your heart
   did it offer freedom from pain, or fright?
That deception- in your eyes
   did it make promises to improve your sight?
That deception- in your veins
   did it get you through life, or just one night?

   but what did it take -That deception
that crawled like a snake through your soul?
   but what did it invade -That deception
that holed through your life like a mole?
   but where did it leave you -That deception
that highwayed you penniless to the toll?
   but who did it sell you to -That deception
that greeted you on the thorny knoll?

do you know who you are, where you're going, where you've been?
are you pained and lonely, lost, tangled up in sin?
or, tell me, my friend -That deception, did it win?

Donna Malsom

When The Dolls Go Dancing

Dolls; are they really what they seem to be?
Do they seem to move, or is it just me?
Are they just stuffing and pretty painted faces?
Maybe they're watching and wanting to go places.

Sometimes I wonder in bed at night,
Do dolls like to have fun; maybe fly a kite?
When I'm asleep, do they go dancing,
With a body of energy and endless prancing?

They're all dressed up and nowhere to go,
Or are they going somewhere; I really don't know.
Do dolls have a special kind of magic unknown to mankind?
Do they have special powers, or can they read minds?

Will we ever know these hypothesized answers?
Or do dolls know more, such as cures to cancers?
Do they have senses and are they alive?
If they are, how would they survive?

Will they save the world from the evil hate?
Maybe dolls aren't alive; we'll have to debate.
So, do they have fun; I guess we'll never know,
But with our imaginations, the places we'll go!

Brooke Neeley

The World We Live In

Did you hear the gunshots this morning
Did you hear the screams from the ghetto
Did you hear the sirens from the policemen
And did you hear the dirt from the digging of the new grave
Do you hear the cries of the babies
Do you hear the hunger in their bellies
Do you hear the teardrops of mommy and daddy
Because they have three hungry mouths to feed
    and America sold their jobs
Ladies and gentlemen, this is the world we live in
The problems are more serious than what you're going
    to watch on T.V.
So don't turn away, we've got to think about the economy
Just look around you and try to help someone else
Because this is the world we live in and pain and suffering
    are all around
This is the world we live in
Can't we help somebody up off of the ground?

Catina Davett Perez

Goodnight Mom

What were you thinking about when you died?
Did you think about us and the times that we cried?
Were you scared, were you frightened,
did you wish you could run?
Were you glad it was over,
did you think it was fun?
Did you think about your husband,
what your love had become?
Did you think about your children,
your daughters, your son?
Or maybe your grandchildren,
the ones you didn't know.
Were you sad when you knew it was your time to go?
So now that it's over do you know why we're here?
If you did would you tell me,
would you whisper in my ear?
Like you did when I was little,
when you turned out the light.
Then in the dark you leaned over
and you kissed me goodnight.

Daniel J. McDermott

Yesterday

Yesterday, I walked by your side,
    didn't say a word, just looked in your eyes.
You passed me by, as the icy rain,
    and you left in my soul all this pain.

I'm walking fast hiding my broken heart,
    picking up the pieces that are falling apart,
but I know the sun will be shining tomorrow,
    and all this pain will subside and the sorrow.

Abimeleth Roman

Moments

Works of splendor weave through each corridor of my mind seeking to
displace every painful picture mounted deep within.

Cerebral canvas renewed by life's sunrise is readied for new
impressions to place within its galleries. Reflecting on past works,
styles used, hoping to refine and improve the day's painting.
Worthy of the walls or placed in storage, each has its value.

Moments created, recorded on the media of my mind. Placed within
life's gallery, each one yearning to be a masterpiece, many falling short.

Continuing to paint, placing strokes from life onto the canvas until
the works are finished, the painter lays down the brushes and the
gallery doors are closed.

Howard Woodward

Mystery Mountain

The mountain loomed out my window,
Distracting. Deceiving.
It pulled my attention,
"Look at me. Where are you? Who am I?
The mountain beckoned.
My eyes longingly searched over each curve.
"What is it about you? Yes. You draw
me in." I thought.
I want to feel your soil sift
through my fingers.
Oh, that I could walk through your solidness.
To feel not your coldness like a grave,
but your warmth like a womb.
Your age, your beauty, your knowledge
intrigues my young mind,
my old spirit.
Our energies mesh. We are but light
dancing a sweet song.
How strong the melody
How faint the memory.

Brighton Mangini

Silhouettes Of Passion

Dear sweet memories and yesterday's dreams...
Do me favor... and die not on the vine of my illusive reality...
I relish in the pleasure of your stinging bite,... and always
welcome you with warm anticipation...
Though sometimes bitter,... you are all that I live for...
Cast out your call and guide me to your sacred place...
Help me to create a different song for my life...
Open my eyes to all of your sensuous beauty...
and your timeless faults...
Help me to understand who and what I am...
Help me to believe in me...
Teach me to return the kind favors that you have recorded
upon my heart...
Take me as your solemn prisoner and change me...
Comfort me in your rapture and beg my departure...
Push me back through reality's doorway... that I may learn to
survive in this world alone...
Without you...
For me... there is no mercy for my dreams...
And I can only awaken to face reality once more...

Clarence H. Parks Jr.

To Have Hate In Your Heart

Dear Father their hearts are filled with much hate
Do not they know for what to themselves they create
I am saddened for the truth that my eyes see
The hate they create and what it has done to me
I ask you my dear Father. Why?
have you given me the answer with each tear I cry
With each tear my soul feels a release
What follows is a wonderful peace
The hate that was sent can harm not
The children of God with even a thought
He loves all His children for to Him they belong
The hate will never defeat for through Him they are made strong
The hate you send will fill your own eyes with despair
You will plead for His grace when He takes away your air
Upon your departure you will move before Him
it is then you will feel the pain of your own hate and sin
So, for the sake of your own soul this hate must stop
For he says to have hate in your heart is to know him not.

Jule Marie Glavach

Mother Of Aztlan

Mother of Aztlan!
Do you hear your children's voices?
Take a walk into the streets.
Your children beckon in the distance.
Gather them into your embrace.
Tell them that you love them.
You'll hear their confused, hurting heart but.
Our children are getting lost!
Reunite your hearts with theirs.
Do you hear the bullet's sound?
Our children dying on the streets.
Killing each other, without mercy.
Help me!
By joining our efforts.
We will be victorious.
At last we must realize,
that on the highest mountain.
A new nation will be born!

Isabel Gallegos Byrd

Untitled

When you were small...
do you remember the stars?
I remember the stars:
They were like pinholes into heaven,
but they were just stars,
keeping us company,
teaching us a place,
while spinning out there
defining the universe and space.
Maybe our hearts are the pinholes into heaven,
or maybe they're just little lights, too,
shining a path to Jesus,
defining a love that's true.

Judith E. Stinson

Pro-Life?

There's a roach in my cupboard should I kill it or not
Does it have a life beyond my cupboard or not.
It's a living creature alive just like me but it's just a
Roach that's annoying me. Behind that cupboard is there
A family tree, am I killing a father or a mother to be
Or is it somebody's sister or best friend, don't you
See? Am I crazy to think or compare its life to mine,
Because it was created I think? Now that it comes to
Mind. I decided to leave this roach alone, and I went
On a trip to the forest all alone, I lay in my tent
And I thought about the roach, then I went for a walk
When a bear approached, I ran like hell, because now
I am thinking again, does this bear feel that I'm
Alive or just another meal to him!

Bernadette Fowlkes-Bridges

The Most Precious Of Emotions

Friendship limits not by sex,
Color, creed or origin.

It only offers peace; peace of mind, calmness of
Spirit...

A shared depository for
Innermost confidences.

Treasure each of your precious
Friendships
'Tho they may number only
One, for one...
May be the sole enjoyment
Of your life.

Donald L. Crosson

Love's Darker Side

Heartache, another sleepless night,
'doesn't matter who's wrong or right.
The relationship has ended, forget the blame,
My world it seems, will never be the same.

By the phone, I hopefully wait for your call,
a picture of us hanging from the wall
They say love is perennial as the grass,
These words are like a eulogy for a funeral mass.

Objects of affection, I put aside,
tears of hurt, from the world I hide.
There's someone, for everyone;
Fun-filled memories, we share under the sun.

Our dreams seemed to go in the right direction
Have you given another your sweet affection?
Do you still have feelings for me?
or am I another fish in an endless sea?

On the street, will you look the other way?
The perfect couple, people would say.
This broken heart, will it mend?
Lovers once, I can't be a friend.

Jon Jay Uebel

Blessed Am I

How can I repay thee for all that you have
Done?
For you have given everything - including your
Son.

You have given me salvation, even though I went
Astray,
But you had everlasting patience and you waited
One more day.

You called out my name though I neglected to
Hear,
How your love and your presence was so very
Near.

How can I repay thee? No gift will ever
Do,
But I take all my blessings and I give them
Back to you.

Carol Bowersock

"Dreams To Shine"

Be yourself, be yourself, that's all you can be.
Don't dream of being a flower or even a sun,
that is not why you are free. Shine the
way you want to shine, don't look
behind at the other stars. Make the
best with what you have and your own
heart will smile. One day you'll realize
you're just as big and bright. Don't act to
impress or to be what you're not, just be
your true self. Trying to be what is not
there will not get you through on your
own. Just look and smile at the others
around, knowing you're the best that you
can be. One day we'll all look back with
our future lives beside us. Remember the path
you are to follow, the road to your own success.
Someday we'll all be together, for God made you,
God made me. One day we'll all fly away, wondering
if our lives were fulfilled. If you loved and believed in
others as well as yourself, I assure you that's all that matters!

Carrie Mills

You Want To Be Cool, Don't Be A Fool

It's not cool to be nobody's fool
Don't follow them, let them go with you
'Specially if you know what's right and what to do,
Don't be a fool
stay and finish school, that's cool
Don't smoke, it's no joke, don't drink, alcohol stinks
Don't be no fool, be true cool
Let dope alone or you'll be dead and gone
Don't play with guns, they're no fun
Mess with them and you or someone might end up dead
And that's sure not using your head
Don't be a fool, be cool
Don't follow them who you feel are wrong
If they mess up, you are also gone
The police ain't gonna have no mercy on you
So do what you know is right to do, then you'll be cool
And you're certainly no fool
Don't beat up on others
That ain't cool, 'cause this is something
For stupid fools, so now - be cool don't - be a fool cool!

Bob Hunt

Corridors

The corridors;
    Door after door stood welcoming
    I looked inside each door, vast rooms beyond, and fantasized.
    But I never believed any one room could fulfill my many desires.

The corridors;
    Door after door stood open.
    I charged from one another, looking into the first as I stepped
        into the second.
    But I never stayed in one long enough to appreciate the dedication
        necessitated in its construction.

The corridors;
    Door after door stood ajar.
    I peeked at what each had for me, judging them from a far.
    But I never allowed them to reveal their true merit,
        fearing another might offer a better future.

The corridors;
    Door after door stood bolted.
    I sat silently in the center of the hall, weeping into empty hands
        as I dreamt of the lost treasures.
    But I never thought I would run out of time.

Alan Gramont

Victoria

Long golden sun-kissed strands
Down it falls like soft breaking waves
Against a shore made of silk and amber sand

The sky a pale thin baby blue
Victorian eyes alive with light
Reflecting upon two small oceans
Of bright coral
Her lips are defined and full
Coloured bordeaux simply
Irresistibly beautiful
Her touch is a soft caress
A victorian kiss captivates
All senses holds them in gentle tenderness
Her figure too defined, too pure to be clothed
By a simple dress
Victoria is love epitomized
Beauty personified
Passion amplified
Victoria is femme fatal
Beautified

Dan Rodriguez

Fly Birdy Fly

Growing up in a Christian home, why do I feel all alone?
down through the years mamma said he would be there
But now I am at college, where is he now?
Has he lost me in the mix or does he care at all?
I remember a song long ago about how he keeps his
eye on the sparrow
Am I not greater than a sparrow?
The day I left for college mamma said, "fly birdy, fly"
What did she mean and why?
As I compare every day as another flight it seems
as if I will never win a fight.
Some days I glide and sometimes, as if I want to fall
But all in all I must remember "fly birdy, fly."

Donald Douglas

Arabia

I wandered up the road, scarce knowing where I went -
Dreaming of a far-off land where younger years were spent,
The streets I walked, not these, but paths that scaled the dunes,
And reached down to the deep in land of ancient runes.

I watched the dhows once more before the setting sun;
Sails, so still and lank, the mast, and they, were one
I saw the Arabs gather their plethora from the sea,
As mists began to settle on sand and sea and me.

Then, in steady plod and flow, come camel trains at twilight.
While, beyond a distant rise, gases, burning in the night,
Send acrid odors drifting across the vast and quiet sand
As wounds of "Call to prayer" come surging o'er the land.

They mysteries of the Orient, and desires that still must burn,
Have set my heart and mind to this dreaming of return
To that great disparate realm of camel, pearl, and King,...
Of flares that light a desert,...of falcon on the wing.

Jean B. Cremidas

Dreamscape

Walking through the window of my mind, asleep yet awake,
dreams rush by me as if clouds in the sky.
Showing pictures of the past and perhaps the future.
Thoughts explode all around me.
Sweet memories whirl about me, shining warmth, as if the summer
sun had just bent down and blew a sunset kiss.
Dreamscape forever with me.

Bernadette P. Beckmann

The Purple Grape Disaster To Triumph

One purple grape doomed by its shape
Dropped through the air plopped on the chair
Sneaked under a dame as she shifted her frame
Its fate was to crush between chair and tush
Made a purple stain like a varicose vein
On the left-hand cheek it caused her to shriek
She swabbed the spot made a polka dot

She without pause wanted to cause
The stain to erase and leave no trace
She rose from her seat and beat a retreat
To the ladies' loo to wipe off the goo
With might and main she attacked the stain
It wouldn't wash out but faded about
To a violet Rorschach* all over her back
When she tried to explain her friends would exclaim
On the clever design they said it was fine
But we know where it came it was the stain
Of an errant grape splotched onto her shape
Between seat and rear not worth a tear.

Don Eischen

Love Life

Does love ever run out?
Dry up in a drought?
Does it merely survive
Each day with no drive?

Will the people you meet in your lifetime,
Tickle you with their humor sublime?
As you enjoy the sun's welcoming rays,
Are these people by your side to stay?

Are their feelings left like castaways?
Do their memories unravel and start to fray?
Do the lives we have touched carry us through
on the journey with many, ending with few?

Does your love make you want to shout?
Carry on, jumping, spinning wildly about?
Must we always embark on a search to find
The love of so many in so short a lifetime?

Can't we be happy with just who we are?
Sharing this happiness with those near and far.
And truly make this world a great place
For those who are called the human race.

Cindy Bandur

Loving You

Each day lost is a day without you.
Each day gained is a day of me waiting and wanting you.
My life is lost without you.
When you're near all of my fears are gone.
I want to hold you close in my arms, but you won't let me.
Are you afraid to be loved?
Love is an endless river that flows inside your heart.
It is a flower that blooms each day.
Only if you loved me the way I love you.
My heart beats for you, my tears fall from my eyes.
Can I put my arm around you to show you how much I care?
If you only knew how great my love was for you.
My love for you can knock down barriers and overcome your greatest
   obstacles.
Love is the greatest thing in life, it conquers all.
I dedicate this poem to the one I love.

Felicia M. Johnson

Untitled

In the beginning there was illumination
elegance and beauty mingled in the sunlight

In the beginning there was brilliance
angelic and exquisite entwined in the flames

In the beginning there was light
stunning and sublime floating among the heavens

In the beginning there was hope
sparkling and warm in the glowing embers

In the end there was dusk
broken and demented under the falling stars

In the end there was gloom
swaying and laughing maniacally in the shadows

In the end there was darkness
twisted and mangled beneath the tormented sky

In the end there was nothing

Charrisse Truax

Keep The Fire Burning

Imagine walking along a bridge in the forest, the warmth of the sun
embraces you.
Birds are singing, trees swaying, and flowers blooming.
Your steps become lighter as a new power beings to flow in.
You begin to enjoy peace of mind, for this is the place where dreams
are dreamt.
This is the place where the fire within begins to burn brighter and
brighter, emitting flames of passion, ambition, confidence, and
determination.
A slight breeze glides through the trees, as your cares begin to
melt away.
Dreams are what bring hope, dreams create the future.
Embrace your dreams, feed the fire, as joy and happiness fill the air
and your very spirit is renewed.

Juanita Montechello

Untitled

   As I lay here, the emptiness of this room
enclosing on me ...
      I feel afraid

   The vastness of this dark empty space is
all encompassing ...
      I feel terrified

   As I lay here trembling, afraid of the emptiness.
I curl into a ball to protect myself from the darkness...
      I close my eyes ... Not to be afraid
I think of soft and gentle things, warm things

   Now I can feel your soft, gentle touch, the warmth
of your body so very close.

   Your warm breath on the back of my neck, tenderly
kissing my shoulders, and rubbing your moist naked body
slowly and very close to mine ...
As you turn me to you ... The darkness clears

   As I imagine you touching, kissing, and holding
me tight ...
      The emptiness vanishes

Georgene Messina

Our Gifts

Our gifts are many for which we give thanks -
Enduring love of family and friends,
Pleasant memories, beautiful tomorrows -
All these seem to have no end.

Beauty of the earth, the bountiful harvests,
The successes in life, the joy and peace;
The freedom, the hope, good health and happiness,
The serenity that gives our souls release.

Sincere thanks to all who have touched our lives;
The close and caring friendships we cherish each day.
Gifts that abound for us, we wish for you
As daily you travel on life's highway.

Now as we ponder these precious gifts
In the garden of life we sincerely treasure;
Special thanks we give to God who provides
The way to enjoy our gifts in full measure.

Evelyn Copple Widner

Steam Engine

The train traces the abyss of the green mountain slicing swiftly
engine singing triumph beside streams
and across land between long shadows of weeping trees
its gray steam permeates the air in billowing chains
train tracks thread through the mountain
tying up nature without a bow

The train traces the rivers that now run indifferently
unraveling the lace of the flowers
the knot is tied teutonically yet the flowers fight not
and only a thread remains to be trampled
gray mountains stand destitute
the river catches tears

Emily Suzanne

Intricate Passage

I stand alien and observe the cobwebs of youth
entanglements of friends, family and the idiom-

The evolution passage ensnared by
blissfulness and aloofness-

Mesmerized by wanting and afraid
Burrowing into the arms of Morpheus
transcending through the universal star wars of knowledge-

Hurdles of bygones surpassed the intricate passage
Cobwebs of youth brushed aside
Unfolding salvo of cheers, jovial warmth of
friends, family, celebrating GRADUATION DAY-

Jessica C. Van Benthuysen

Life's Eternal Song

Lift the veil of all your sorrows
Enter the chambers where I dwell in you
Let the tears of your yesterdays be no
   More tomorrow
Dance in my garden of cascading flowers
Bathe in my streams of purifying love
Let my music lift your spirit and fill
   Your soul with ecstasy
I will light your darkness with candles
   Of passion
Come dwell in me to savor the nectar of life
   That fills your being
As In enfold you in my arms, your pain
   Becomes mine
No longer a prisoner unto yourself
Free to dwell in the rapture of life's
   Eternal song

Bea Hayes

Feign Love

   They left me in abasement; still to come back in retort
even after feeling ignominy; they tried to place me in the
nativity of a God
There mendacity would cause them to be afflicted
there presuming my severance would leave their death uncanny
For I am sublimity even in Feign Love; my manifold love for you
soul of my soul; Indecent amenity for you
Christ bleeds on my life; sanguinary life
humerus victims, "Kill Them"
Sever them eloquently
Look at them pirouette
their minds are pregnant
Like a liar at a witch's trial
They try to inject my mind;
my mind, with waning stagnant life
I am enisled in mental reality, I am a caitiff
God forgive me.

April Rose

The English Language

The English Language can be confusing,
   Even to the point of being bizarre
Colonel, for instance...look at its spelling
   ...It sounds like kernel, but where is the R?
Ever notice what a letter can do...?
   In "one" you'll see a good illustration
Abracadabra...Now right before you,
   With a G...it's "gone," like a magician!

What about "bomb," or "comb" for that matter..
   If you use a T, it becomes a grave!
The whole meaning can change on a letter
   ...When you meant "naive" you may have typed "waive"

Sometimes the letters are not even changed,
   But the word itself is used different ways:
"Present," as to give can be rearranged
   To mean the gift we get on our birthdays
And not only that..it can be today,
   Not the past or future...but the "present."
Confusing, perhaps...but its unique way
   is widely acclaimed to best represent.

Bob G. Martinez

"The Resurrection"

Jesus' love was sinless and free
Even while He walked up to Calvary.
Jesus healed the blind, cured the sick, and rose the dead.
The Roman Soldiers mocked Him, spit upon Him, and whipped
Him 'til He bled.
Caiaphas paid Judas thirty pieces of silver
And Jesus was who Judas was to deliver.
Jesus and Judas paid a price and were somewhat in the same position.
But the price Jesus had to pay was not a decision.
The people who loved Him, their hearts were torn
As Jesus was served with a crown of thorns.
He was put upon the cross and as he died
Everyone that loved, cared, and followed Him just sat there and cried.
Jesus died and was buried in a tomb
For the next three days all there was, was gloom.
Satan was happy because he thought he won the fight
Then an angel appeared and showed him that "Jesus is the Light."
The next thing you know the stone was rolled away
All of the Christians began rejoicing that day.
The end is coming soon, when, nobody knows
But up from the Grave, Jesus Christ Arose!

Ann Marie Starkey

My Best Friend

He was the best son, the best brother anyone could
ever have. He died. He died because of drugs.

Because of his weakness, because he couldn't or didn't
know when or how to say NO! - He Died.
My best friend died.

Now, because of his death today I mourn, he left a big
emptiness in everyone's heart. - He was my best friend -

He was addicted. Addicted to drugs.
He never knew how to stop. He never took the time to think,
never took the time to pray and ask God for help.
Drugs was his everything, it was his soul and only world.

He lost everything, he lost everyone,
his addiction was more important than himself.

A dime here, a dime there,
drugs was all he cared about.

Let's not lose our souls, our minds, our bodies,
our families and our friends to drugs.

Carmen Viloria

It Was Love That Caused God

It was love that caused God to create this world and put in it
every nation, man, woman, boy, and girl.

It was love that caused God to make man from the dust of the land
and give him a beautiful garden home to live in.

It was love that caused God to make woman for man, so that man
would have a helping hand.

It was love that caused God to make every tree and lead the
children of Israel through the Red Sea.

It was love that caused God to save the animals and Noah from the
flood, and years later Jesus shed his blood.

It was love that caused God to give his only begotten Son for the
sins of everyone.

It was love that caused God's Son Jesus to die on the cross of
Calvary just for sinners like you and me.

It was love that caused God's Son Jesus to lay down his life, now
the believers and Christians can live with him in paradise.

It was love, It was love from our heavenly Father above.

Brenda Hardani

I?

Alone in a cold, dark world
Everyone and everything has disappeared
Escape the pain they left behind
Where have they gone?
Or did I leave and with me came the pain?
I feel the pain is me, myself.
I am the pain to me and to you
And to the dog pissing on the fire hydrant across the street
Am I pain in flesh? Or are you and the rest of you the pain I feel?
Pain, everything, us, I am numb to
Maybe the pain is love?
Love I have not received
Maybe the pain is the love I have received- or have I?
Show me kindness, like I to you.
Don't I deserve it? Do I want kindness?
Rejection feels good. Do I know rejection?
Have I met it? Or Am I it?
Pain, love, rejection- are these all the same?
Phantom of the opera, mask- to hide his physical pain
Happiness to hide emotional pain.

Angela Cornett

The Runner

Everything in life is so evil.
Everything destroyed by mankind.
Memories of the past forgotten,
Lost forever, somewhere deep in time.

Why have I been running?
What is it that I fear?
Nothing the way it used to be,
Gone, everything that was dear.

Everyone now is running,
Looking for a place to hide.
Someone will be left behind,
Frozen, forgotten by the people at his side.

One day I will stop running,
And I will not run anymore.
I will remember what has happened,
And I will remember life, the way it was, before . . .

Jessica Vitak

The Mountain's Call

It's a funny world to be in when there's nothing left to win
Except some poker chips on the table and a friendly smile again,
You need someone to hold you, someone to let you in
Where angels will tread lightly, and you feel beneath your skin.
It's time to ask for the check and lie down alone for the night,
You wonder if you should let the waitress go and fade away from sight,
Your heart starts to weigh heavy as you look for words to say,
But all you find the courage to do is reach for your wallet and pay.
If the motel room TV were any bigger you'd try to fit inside,
If people were out to get you it wouldn't be a bad place to hide,
But nobody would be following you with so precious little to find
Between the clothes stuffed in your backpack and the thoughts
    haunting your mind.

Your deck of cards is missing the queen of hearts,
You feel the pain, it stops and then starts,
For living in a world full of lessons to teach
About love that is here, then lingers out of reach.
The joke may be on you, life is not as it seems
Like time locked in a jar in nonsensical dreams,
You're fighting to get out of other people's schemes
Until you only hear the sound of mountain streams.

Eric Bonaventura

1939?

Sticky fog patches bedew squinty eyes,
Faint wail of skylark falls deep into heart...
Smoke from burned quitch grass licks face with a tart,
Leaves whisper prayers falling from the skies....
    Autumn begins its mystery design.....
    What autumn is it? Is it 39?

Innocent shadows crawl over the trees,
Children catch sun spots in a morning play;
Suddenly rattling .... Bullets spatter clay....
Do they pretend that they gasp for the breeze?
    Who are these children? No, they are not mine.....
    What autumn is it? Is it 39?

Panic and anguish; Alone, all alone!
Blotted wings bursting with flickering flames.....
Hundreds - all running in last mortal games.....
The skies are empty; the shadows are gone.....
    Autumn is dandling a baby from whine......
    What autumn is it? Is it 39?

Sunset turns misty, chills run down the spine,
Stubborn time trickles .... Why?.... Why 39?

John J. Gallar

"Farewell"

Farewell my love!
Farewell I'll be!
Farewell my love!
Like a big oak tree.
Farewell my heart!
Farewell like an ark!
I know, I'll never see you again in history.
Century after century.
I know and you know, we'll never see each other again!
You live your life!
And I'll live mine!
You'll live. You'll die.
And I'll do the same with mine.
Still, I'll never see you again!
Yes, farewell my love!
Farewell I'll be.
Farewell my love!
Like a big oak tree.
Farewell!
Farewell!

Judy A. Boyett

Fear: Failure Against Freedom

Fear is the father of all feelings,
Fear follows fugitives to freedom,

Fear does not end with freedom for
the fugitives fear for their families,

Fear is like chewing gum on freed slaves
Feet; it sticks with them wherever they go,

Harriet hates fear for it almost kept her
from freedom,

Fear failed in keeping Harriet from
freeing slaves,

Fear failed; for slaves won the fight for
freedom,

Fear a failure in freedom fighters

Gregg Robinson

Untitled

Hidden emotions that can never be revealed.
Feelings that can never be shared.
Wantings that can never be satisfied.
Lives that can never touch.
Two people who see but can never
look in each other's direction.
While the world goes on, their
souls go on touched by each
other without ever touching.
If emotions were revealed, and feelings shared,
people wouldn't understand.
If wanting were satisfied, their lives would be
touched with the simplicity of love.
And if their love was shared they
would love in a way different from all other.

Amy McClam

Nature And Corruption

Flood waters rising
Fire coats the land with bright red icing
Winds that whip through the air
Fighting against the hills so bare
A slashing, rushing tide
I wonder how nature can hide the trauma and terror
The building pressures that grow
Before the storm starts to flow
Over land and sea, I just know what will be
Left when the disruption is over
Nothing but chaos, explosions, and dust
Cities abandoned to rot and rust
Mother Earth ... she grips our hopes tight
Like pulling on a saddle and girth
Yet we struggle and fight for life
To claim what is left of our havoc-stricken strife

Carrie Cato

The Abyss

death becomes all but hope in an endless surreality of
despair and unwillfulness...
Feelings are stolen by an unholy void that seeks to devour
my soul from end to end.
Ripping out all my internal hopes and dreams, he feeds on my
inner most thoughts and mocks me as I cry in pain...
An ungodly scream tears through the dense air and causes
every fiber of my being to loose all will to live on...
Soon all will be replaced by an eternal, black void that
will surcomb all which made me whole and all which condemned
my soul to this wretched place as reality and self-state-of-mind
slip away into an eternal, heartless darkness...

Bron Rogers

Basic Instinct

There is a way that seems right to all men, and they always go there
    first
Only to find it leads to shame, and no one need rehearse
Men are like the beast, they all die and turn to dust
So our prayers should be to God, that he forgive for our lust

As time is surely the one true enemy of all human soul
Beauty is to each eye, if only the heart can behold
For to laugh is to cry, and to cry is to feel
And to share a heart of pain, in itself, is to heal

To eat in a timely fashion is to control the inner man
For how can one succeed without direction-without plans
Basic is the instinct of humans to take without giving
But basic instinct without love is a life not worth living.

Ivory Jazz Shields

This Flag Waves For Texas

While sorting through some rubble I found to my dismay; some
Texas flags that were buried there, all tattered, worn, and gray.
To my surprise when I asked a man "what should I do with these?"
his reply to me was "just toss them out, or do whatever you
please." Now I descend from Ireland, a poor family with lots of
pride who could never dishonor any flag much less toss it aside.
After thinking on this matter there is just one thing I would like to
say: "There are still countless ones of us who have seen our better
days and friend, this flag waves for Texas. This flag waves for
Texas, and has for many years; it stands along side old glory
through battles, blood and tears. Though she may be worn and
tattered; she'll still catch the wind with pride. To keep her waving
bravely; fearless men have fought and died. No, I am not a Texan
I came as a stranger to her land, but I am now part of her big
family through the help of her native's hands. So if you should
think to dishonor her; there's one thing you should know. There
are still many who will defend her; remember the Alamo? Now
listen carefully partner; I'll tell you once again; in case you're
having second thoughts, on this you can depend. Let no one try to
defame her, or think to spurn her name; you'll find that you are
outnumbered, and there's nothing you can gain. "BECAUSE
THIS FLAG STILL WAVES FOR TEXAS!"

Faye H. Dixon

Deception

Walking down a long hallway
floor—dusty and cracked with age,
walls—gloomy and victims of graffiti,
—trapped in an inner world. Deception.

Seeing the light ahead leading to the outer world.
Wanting to reach the light,
is it impossible or not to come upon? Deception.

Walking for miles and miles,
floor—never coming to an end,
frustration —going through the body. Deception.

Internally screaming with pain
but external appearance
feigns control.

The LIGHT! The LIGHT!
there it goes — A BRIGHT RADIATING LIGHT!
diminished to a speck of brightness.

Was the light really glowing
    or an elusive pulsation
        within the mind?
DECEPTION!

Debbie Crowley

Awareness

Awareness,
fluttering butterflies in my stomach as
the surface of my skin moves with indentations as you move inside
and stretch and grow.
My navel protrudes even with my skin as though it was never any
different than the rest, now joined;
technology pounding on arrhythmia strips as your heartbeat is
recorded-
I see your tongue stick out from your mouth in a gesture of defiance,
and your finger throws caution to the wind as if I told you so.
Character formed, where did you learn these gestures inside
or were they beyond your existence in another atmosphere of
inanimate bodies
Scientists debate on learned and natural responses but yes, I know you
Know, just know that we're playing a waiting game and you're
toying with us
so anxious to see your sweet, sweet face
as you have these early contractions in mockery
as we play the delivery game.

Debra Carter Yalin

Nobody Is Around

Silence sets in,
Followed by night,
Thousands of stars appear in the sky.
The moonlight shines through,
Setting shadows upon the ground.
Nothingness spreads through the child-like minds.

Soon it will be gone,
Followed by tears,
The door will close up
Locking in all the fears,
Of children left alone
Far into the night.
Nobody is around.
Nothing is in sight.
Nobody can hear,
The children's sad sighs,
As they float through the night.

Amanda Jean Hancock

Untitled

This pen I hold / is so bold / taking a part of my heart /
for a line of rhyme.

It is me that moves the quill / it is he who holds the will

All this time / I was unaware he was there / inside /
A smile, a tear, a fear and more he held in store /
filling a deep and inky well.

I felt him say "your heart is full and I the key / let go
your soul / follow me."

I have been a friend of paper and pen / but only just met
this one in hand / leading me now / to this land.

This glen of dreams / safe and free / where all or none /
may want or not / hear me.

When startled of late, I hesitate / as a thought or phrase /
reveals a sorrow or rage.

I may not be this free / what of regret and sin also / are
they to be parts I extol ? "Yes," said he. "They too will
flow."

This treachery / crushing me / for to leave this land / will
still my hand.

This pen I hold / is so bold / slowly he dips into my soul.

Dianne Damico

Heartbroken

We've seen each other so many times, yet we have never met
For a long time I've been in love with you
but I know we can never be
We don't know each other, and you love someone else
Which hurts me even more
You two have happiness
And I have shattered hopes
You are always on my mind and in my dreams
But mostly in my heart
It pains me to know you can never feel the same way
You don't know how I feel about you, but I wish you did
I shed a tear or two thinking about you
Knowing your mind and love is with someone else
Someone out there will always love you
You may never guess it's me
You and I are a dream that can never come true
But you will always remain secretly in my heart
And I will always love you no matter how much it hurts
And that I guess that you'll never know

Jasmine Magtira

For A Time When...

For a time when we stand in today.
    For a time when we stand for now!
For a time when, time after time a small reminder
    comes our way.
For a time when history has its moments and movements.
For a time when one puts others beneath themselves.
    For a time when the color of someone's skin meant something!
For a time when a black man was called "boy."
    For a time when the crack of a whip splits skin in two!
For a time when his black face flinches with pain.
    For a time when a man of the cloth preaches by day,
    and "KKK" by night!
For a time when salt blends with blood to burn the sting.
    For a time when a young white boy sees a cross burning red!!
For a time when a "colored" becomes a blackman,
    For a time when a whiteman sees blood in a wound,
    not the color around the wound!
For a time when we stand together "white," "black," "asian,"
    "gay," "straight," "man," and "woman."
    For a time when it becomes the "Human Race!!!"

Douglas M. Smith

Untitled

I want you,
For all the time fate has to give me.
I need you,
For all the breath the living takes.
I love you,
For every mark The Artist makes;
For every crease, for every line He creates.

Fully, with a warmth from within
Closer than men at tragedy,
Open, like a blossom
For all the land to see.

With no wing,
No apologies or questions,
No heaps of broken images,
No nostalgia or compromise.

I love you... now.
With no changes,
Deeper than my blood runs,
Father of my soul.

Gina Tenore

The Final Curtain

Death—life's black hole.
For Christians it's life's ultimate goal.
For others an opportunity,
To improve one's status on this earthly journey.
Death—the final frontier.
There are those who anticipate it with great fear,
But for those who believe in the Truth and the Light,
Death will be the end of a long, hard fight.
The end of despair, the end of pain,
The end of misery, the end of strain.
Death brings much sorrow to the living,
But to the dead, a new beginning.
Some will enter the fires of hell.
Others will hear a heavenly bell,
Calling them to the Promised Land,
Where glorified bodies walk hand in hand.

Alexandra Courtis

Godspeed, Little Baby, Godspeed

Godspeed, Little baby, Godspeed,
For God awaits,
For created in his image you were
   Certainly made,
Giving your soul a soft breath of light,
In order to help you fight the good fight,
For God preserves our precious souls,
Through his love and might,

Godspeed, Little Soul, Godspeed,
Carried by angels,
Until you learn to fly,
Please don't cry,
It's all right to suck your thumb and sigh,

Through an act of fate,
Your life was cut short,
Not allowed to live, but only to die,
Sh, sh, sh, do not be disturbed or afraid,
Goodness, love and peace await,
With tears and pain, we say Good-Bye.

Godspeed, Little Angel, Godspeed!

Elizabeth L. Flores

She Lay In A Nursing Home Bed

She lay in a nursing home bed
Frightened of the nurse with the needle
While her family bickers
Over her dwindling fortune.

Her eyes roam her drab room
Searching for something to connect to
While her family cannot stand
The sight of what she has become.

She is fed with a tube
Through a diseased hole in her stomach
While her family frets
That she may die at an inconvenient time.

She no longer recognizes her family
The ones she fed, cuddled and played with
While they visit her for a few moments
And complain of her lingering on for so long.

She lay in a nursing home bed
Frightened of life, not able to die
While her family lives out in the world
Frightened of death, not able to live.

Eileen Holland

A Knight Of Love

A knight in his loneliness was ill-pleased,
For he could not change a lady's fate.
She would not call upon him,
The one who could give only happiness.

The Knight had known the softness of her
touch,
Her heart's warmth, even the need in her
sad eyes.
Yet, he stood alone in his watch
O'er her estate until the day he died.

Charles A. Blue

"Engagement"

Unto God our Lord in the Highest.
   For His love reins inside us.
Lest we take, we shall not receive,
of and through Him we must surely believe.
Within the old and the new, His message perceive.
Lay it down this hand, let's all stand.
For of these things some will see, blessed art those that believe.
Do unto Him, this His call of all men; do not be deceived.
For what is there of right, comes from the light; take heed.
Do not look astray lest we fall away, with vengeance we receive.
   For His love reins inside us, cannot you see?
Of the heart and the mind one may be blind.
Pray for ye that of me, you may conceive.
For unto all I do call; Do not flee.

David G. Graber

The Droop

Now there is something that I dread, the bane of my old age
For it attacks the muscles and puts me in a frightful rage
DROOP it is that surrounds me now, droop of lid of eye
Droop is there in jaw and arms, Why O God, O Why?

I see it in my ankles, in the part above the bone
I see it in my calves, oh where's my muscle tone?
But the droop that is the worst of all is there about my breast
Parts are not where once they were but sag below the crest.

So how to stop this cursed invader, how to slow this change?
Even if I square my shoulders, is there a roundness range?
Can I be there in the loop with those who know just how
To slow the droop of lid and limb with creams and make-up now?

Oh, to be among the graceful troop of those who aren't old
Where bikinis hold the tush in place and midriffs aren't rolled
That dreaded force called gravity has made me take the count
Alas, the years have shown their mark, and droop is paramount.

So get me back out of this soup, back with those youthful troops
That bend and swoop along the loop and whoop it up in groups
Poop on droop, do go away, leave me lean and straight
For I have much so much to do, droop will have to wait.

Eileen Mehan Christian

Moonlight And Roses

We walk along a beach so long.
Colored silver by the moonlight above,
So red the rose we hold in our hands,
To remember a night like grains of sand.

The moon above to the ocean below.
Shines a sparkling silvery glow.
Stars so beautiful as they shine in the sky.
They speak of a future to which one will try.

The bed of roses once walked,
Their petals are now floating off;
To the ocean, far out to a destiny.

Brad Beck

Good-Bye My Friend

There comes a time in life, when you have to put love to rest.
For it hurts and you may cry, but it is for the best.

This is the end, my dear friend, the journey has been long.
So let's say good-bye and go our ways and hold on to yesterdays.

Before I go, I must stay, I loved you 'til the end.
Is that a tear in your eye? Please don't cry, my friend.

One more thing before I go, I just want you to know,
Maybe someday our paths will cross and we will find the love we lost.

So hold up your chin and say, It's not so bad today.
The sun is out, the sky is blue, you just have to sing and shout,
Hello to you and you.

I find it hard to say good-bye without a tear in my eye.
For really my friend it's not the end
It's just a stepping stone, that we must cross so we may grow
Sometimes one cannot know.

Go ahead but don't look back, I will do the same.
For the road ahead is shorter now
I know it is but don't ask how.

Good-bye my friend, good-bye.
Diane Marie Sly

The Heavenly Choice

My Spirit was free and in a heavenly place
For it lived with God in his vast open space.
But my heart yearned for the next best thing,
A Mother and a Father on the earthly scene.
So God and I looked the whole world over and excitedly agreed,
That the two of you were perfect for me.
God marked his calendar and put his miracle in motion,
And I came to earth with the strongest of potions.

The home was more than expected,
The love enough to astound.
I am so thankful for the parents that God and I have found.
As time passed by, I knew I had to leave,
To share with others this fabulous family tree.
I left the home but yet I knew I didn't,
For we were joined by love to form a special "unit."
We have grown so in numbers that I just knew your hearts would break,
But they just opened wider to make the extra space.

Thank you my loves for all that you have done,
And for making my life such a pleasant one.
I love you Mom and Dad!
Judy Beattie

Twins

Two urns stood high on a window shelf
   For all the world to see.
They were perfectly matched, I know 'tis so,
   In form, in grace and beauty.

Then it happened to one, a pain so bad,
   A cruel, insidious thing;
She fell - was shattered in pieces,
   Her life's breath had taken wing.

The other stood trembling and shaken,
   Wishing and wailing in tears
For quick release from life on the shelf,
   E'en though she was filled with fears.

A careless hand then her wish fulfilled
   As she fell from the shelf to the floor.
Her grace and beauty then was stilled
   And wishing for her was o'er.
Helen M. Fischer

Still At Peace

For I am happy, I have met and married my true, true love.
For now my word is humble and my life is at peace.
For as we walk along the sandy beaches holding hand in hand,
I look into his heavenly eyes; and I am wondering if I have died
and gone to heaven. For my soul was one and now together we are two.
I ask myself, can I really be this happy? And yet, here we still are,
holding hands, wrapped in each other's love.

For my days are fulfilled and my nights as well. If I'm dreaming dear
Lord, please let me sleep. For I am happy and my life is still at
peace. For I have awakened into what would be the next day to find
that my true love was here to stay. For now I must confess,
I am truly happy and my life is complete and my world is humble and
still at peace.

Now as time goes by and our golden years have come and passed,
I must now lay to rest my true, true love. For now my life would
never be the same, since my true love has passed away. So may he
lie in peace knowing that I will forever be his and my heart is
fulfilled and my soul is still at peace.

So remember my dearest love, my life may not be complete, but our
world is humble and still at peace. So rest my dear sweet,
sweet love, rest in peace.
Angela Denise White

Trapped

Somewhere over the horizon is where I wish to be,
for that is where my love is waiting patiently.

I remember when, I couldn't wait to leave,
now my desire to return is one I can't believe.

I never knew it hurt this much to leave someone you love,
but now that I have realized, it's you I'm thinking of.

In this state of mind, the thing that I most fear,
is that your love for me will slowly disappear.

Although I feel this way, there is nothing I can do,
I'm trapped inside this loneliness until I return to you.

The recent time passed has been so very tough,
the day we stand there face to face won't come too soon enough.
James Spence III

Moments Of Longing

In his eyes I can see beyond myself,
for the mirrors of the soul cannot hide the truth.
In bewilderment I glance at my reflection,
seeking what is yet to come.

Emotions surface as I awake the perils of the past.
Remembered are the moments of affection and delight,
forgotten those of anger and tears.

I begin to define those images of Life,
challenging my honesty and self esteem.
Slowly, I reveal the path of my being
for what we seek is destined within ourselves.
Gabriele C. Woodhall

Every day Of Your Life

Every day of your life you will learn something new,
Every day you will find something better to do.
Your life is full of the extreme ups and downs,
That fills the day with smiles and frowns.
As each and every day passes by,
Another dream will soar into the sky.
Do not hurry to take the next day in line,
Take every day of your life, one day at a time.
Amber Jacoby

My Life Is Like An Andy Warhol Film

My life is an Andy Warhol film
for the simple reason that those beautiful pastel
colors
that appear so fluently and regularly in the lives of everyone else
do not exist in mine
instead I live on a giant silk screen
canvas
of chartreuse and violet raw umber and little splashes of
indigo
not that I mind
my canvas is filled with recurring themes of love and desperation and
of course nothing
seems to work out quite like it should but everyone loves it anyway
I know words of men that reach the gods in golden
phrases but mine reach the souls of all
angels
in pictures of green cows flying hot dogs
and
the occasional pair of lips belonging to Marilyn
Monroe

Amanda Austin

My Brother's Love

For my eyes have seen my brother
    for the very last time
Nor shall my mind escape from thee
My heart will always beat twice,
    one for you and the other for me
You have not perished from me,
    you have just left me for awhile
We have always been of one soul,
    no matter how we differ
I, the oldest, you the only boy
I'll never forget how you were my protector
I can hear you all around me
When I'm alone, you make me laugh
    only to cry later, "How I miss you"
How I wish to see you smile again
In my house, shadows of your being,
    are all around
For I know within me, will always be
My brother's love

Janine Cori Glasco Carter

A Song For Anastasia

The scion of Pythagoras and Euterpe
For you, Anstice, is the song

The times your geometric tonals
    have tickled my ear
I return to you what gave you me

Your elegant neck welcomes my callow touch
A tender embrace about your waist
To feel the breathless voice of an angel

Albert Valenciano Desonia

My Rainbow

I give you my rainbow, that you loved so much
For you to admire, feel and touch

It's only a teardrop of crystal you see,
But with you, it meant more than the world to me

It was our rainbow, to catch and to follow,
And now it is yours, for all your tomorrow

So hang it up high, let the bright sun shine through,
Remember this rainbow is my love for you.

Charlene F. Medley

Impressions

To live to die eternal,
forever yours yet truly mine,
who can say, but on a whisper
of a breath, the future flutters.

My heart yearns for expression,
freedom like a butterfly, elusively flies
'twixt here and now - but what's to grasp?
Where to go and how to see. The quest
lies there, here and far behind.

Expression of thought, love
and intimacy, blend together to create
a unified haven. Safe, timeless yet momentary,
the butterfly sallies to and fro.

Our destinies shimmer in the translucent
light, beckoning, calling, waiting to be fulfilled -
can destiny be averted? Like the butterfly,
it tempts us to let go, to be, to fly effortlessly,
to dance in the radiance of life -
laughing and fulfilled!

Janine Gardner

Windmaster

You blow your soft breath around our shoulders,
freezing us to death.
Your warmth is spread for us to share, little by little
we warm.
Your chilled air makes us shiver from thoughts, from the
unknown.

Windmaster! Stop haunting me.
Let me live, let me stay!
I will be your servant, showering you with gifts.
W-o-o-o-s-h! Your temper is growing.
Believe in me, oh great one, for I can help.

Love! Hope! Dreams! Surround me, make him understand.
The breeze in which he blows is harmful.
Warm him, love him, show him. He shall learn to care.

Whisper your sorrow, whisper your hope!
Let me learn to love you.
I, your servant, will reach you, showing you I care.

Silence, fills the air, a deepening warmth is felt.
I have succeeded.
The Windmaster is at rest.

Julie Frey

To Be Born Lucky

I remember those days,
fresh fruit, the milk, a small market.
The smell of the salty lagoons;
sitting in a corner, green adobe walls,
cutting paper cartoons.

A quart of milk for breakfast and dinner
white rice is my side dish,
the food tastes good and we have island bananas,
five rolls of bread to last until next day
and Grandma will do the oatmeal.

I was sad, I was happy,
I had friends, I had none,
tears, smiles, time to wait.

I can see in the daylight,
only the stars during the night,
it was so natural and simple,
those days I remember. It's a small
part of me, I am lucky I remember!
It feels good; It was me.

Gianina Opris

The Blue Fish

A dozen of little Gold fish swam in a
fresh tank full of clean water, that a boy had purchased.
  Soon a big blue fish was introduced
to the others.
  The blue fish was getting very
lonely because he was teased and picked on
by the other fish because he was different.
  Soon he realized he didn't have
to take that kind of punishment. He would
stand up for himself since he was the
biggest fish in the tank.
  So whenever one of the smaller
fish picked on him, he ate them.
  After all the little fish were gone,
the boy purchased two more blue fish and
a brown fish much larger than the
other fish. And the blue fish thought to
himself, and told the other blue fish, "What-
ever you do don't tease the brown one,
I don't want to become tuna on weed."

  Catherine Carter

Friends

Friends are for feastings, fun and sharing feelings.
Friends are treasures to have, hold and caress gently.
Friends are often many or few in number.
The quantity does not so much matter but the quality
gives meaning to each day's existence.

To have someone care, to know a deep, lasting relationship,
Someone to stand by, reach out and give freely is the joy of
warmth,
freedom and security.

For we are only as secure as our trust allows us to be,
Only as whole as others allow us to be ourselves and
accept us as we truly are.
Allowing us to fail, bend and disagree.
Allowing us to be who we are meant to be
Though imperfect but trying to achieve the goodness of
the "MASTER'S" qualities.

  Jan Simon

One Hundred Eighty Degrees

Arise! Arise with energy
  give up the lazies, O, my soul.
Give us the chance to feel the sun
  and see the ages roll, and roll, and roll.

Erase! erase methodicals;
  let up the crazies to come forth.
The time is now, is new, is blue
  and hope will render south as north.

Give up! give up the real mundane,
  let joy be unrefined.
When streets and gutters all run rain
  and we just gently, gladly, wildly lose our minds.

And you! out there, somewhere,
  to tune into the fray.
Just give up, let up, get up square,
  and face the true, the blue, new way.

Relax, release, reload, relocate,
  the way is clear to find new goals.
Define, refine, realign and rotate,
  to leave the depths and seek the shoals.

  Gerald W. Erwin

Untitled

A Lily she may be, a flower in bloom. Soaking up the rays
from above. The warmth she gathers from above filters
through the clouds, leaving only the wonderment of HIS
creations. The gifts she has to offer are gifts that have
been given to her from someone whom watches over her. She
shines in HIS glory as the sun arises, looking as beautiful
as she was meant to be. Give her love, talk to her, take
pride, of her beauty. Show her to everyone. Tell of all her
gifts, of her beauty, and take pride in what you have. Take
the gifts she gives you and reunite them in her heart. Talk
to her tenderly, watch over her in genuine care. Your warm
love will open her petals, to which she may now see you in
whole. Feed her with the tender moments that you both may
hold in your hearts forever, Just as we are made to be
unique and special, so is this sweet wonderment of
nature. Allow her top grow in your rich soils of love. Guard
her with your rays of peace. And capture her beauty in your
heart like no other, for this is your MOTHER.

  Donna Wilson

Real Love

It starts out like a whisper
  from deep inside your soul...
An urging from an emptiness,
  a yearning to be whole.
You wake up in the morning
  and hear it call your name...
Then somehow in the heart of you,
  you'll never be the same.
The past is far behind you,
  there are changes from within...
It started not so long ago
  when you found him there again.
When you look into those eyes of his,
  you see a gentle man so kind...
He was your friend through thick and thin,
  could you have been so blind?
It's within his sweet acceptance
  that I ask myself this question now...
Is his the love I've longed for
  appearing through the clouds somehow?

  Becky J. Jackson

The Only One

You're the only one for me,
From earth to sky; from land to sea,
One of these days; I'll have you for my own,
Then I would say; "That's a job well done."

I've tried so hard, over all of the years,
To win you over; to fight the tears,
That come into my eyes, each time I turn around,
It always ends up, that you let me down.

Ever since we were kids; I have loved you so,
But as always, you were on the go,
Never stopping or looking to see,
That I had enough love for you and me.

One of these days, you just wait and see,
You just might happen to fall in love with me,
And when you do, I want you to become my wife,
Then we'll be together for the rest of our life.

The only one, yes, the only one,
When I get you, my work will be done,
The only one, yes, the only one,
To change your name to mine, will be a job well done.

  Dolores P. Nosser

Luciana (A Cerebellum Meringue)

It's four o'clock in the morning.
From my second story perch, I see the cyclists go by.
A tranquil rain, cleansing for a gracious few,
is pelting those who argue.
Between the storm, and, through the darkness,
I can still see your face.
The sporadic lightning and the stoic streetlight do not
    assist me,
for you are eighteen-hundred miles away.
My soul is free, but memories continue to serve.
Another day has come.
Another plane flies above my head.
Memories are fed, clothed, and nurtured.
I hear things.
Whispers say, "go to her."
Screams, beating their drums, tell me to feast.
I will not fight.
I am tired of fighting.
If memories cease to operate, a cerebellum meringue perhaps,
all will be well.
Until then, I will wait for you to pedal by;
I will watch you sigh.

Donald Capoldo, Jr.

The Forest

The forest floor is black at night
From the distance it looks quiet
But if you look closer you see much activity

In the darkness they creep about
    doing that which is unseemly
      alone
        with each other
          to their children

When can't be seen didn't happen
Words no one heard weren't uttered

Some people can't see the forest
    for the trees

Joann Griggs

Through

Through the woods I run,
From the many bad people and places.
I am afraid and don't know where
I am supposed to stop.
Through the woods I run.

Through the water I swim,
From the many diseases and sicknesses.
I am dying and don't know where
I am supposed to live.
Through the water I swim.

Through the air I fly,
From the pollution and smog.
I am choking and falling and don't know where
I am supposed to land.
Through the air I fly.

Through the space I float,
From the hazardous planet they call
EARTH.
Through the woods I run....

Colin M. Cramer

The Sense Of Time

Time isn't time unless change is seen
    from tick to tock as the pendulum swings.
An inch of growth ... a wrinkle formed there
    give proof to the spectacle which we all share.
What if we were numb, deaf, unable to see,
    unable to feel the time-consuming sea breeze?
Without a gauge to tell present from past
    no measurement to tell what happened last
Would time exist or would time stand still
    or would it proceed with an angel's appeal?
We wouldn't know ... knowing nothing at all
    living life for life, not knowing thought for thought.
Senses we have to decipher all this
    four remain in case one we should miss
To take in the passage of time in a stream
    because time isn't time unless change is seen.

Alston Sendoll Blenman II

"Changes"

I'm not retired, just changed my life
from working hard both day and night
to doing things I really like.

When snow is falling and the windshield is iced,
I sit by my window and watch the sights.

My days are spent doing things I like,
from reading my books to riding my bike.

God has blessed me in so many ways,
I just can't began to say.

Now, the only thing that might be necessary,
I think I might need a secretary.

Jo Ann Schneider

Good Friday

The black umbrellas move up Summer Street toward the park.
Full of hardy north Atlantic wind, some fold inside out
some snap and blow into a corner, and what can you trust.
I am there under one of them, looking down,
believing strongly in the hardness of the pavement
how the gravel in my shoe grates like a memory.
And if I fall, who in this determined parade would stop,
pick me up, carry my broken bag.

J. M. Clermont

Mother

You are the sunshine of my morning, my moon at night.
Full of love that holds me tight.

You are the coat that keeps me secure,
You are my mother so sweet and pure.

You are my happiness through each and
every day, giving me beauty inside to stay.

You are my wisdom, which I hold
inside, you are my confidence, I dare not hide

You are my trust, which is in my heart,
together forever we shall not part.

You are my respect, which I see in my eye.
The love and closeness shall never die.

Through everything you have taught me
and I have learned, I hope someday I can return.

No matter what we go through, or how hard it may get,
please try to never forget.
How much you mean to me as a person,
best friend and mother.

Faith Wensel

Dreamer

Sometimes I wish I were not such a dreamer....
gathering fantasies in my mind's basket,
like candid pieces of precious moments to be
explored.

Searching the depths of—sometimes-seemingly—
a childish heart—yet, containing the burning
coals of a woman's desires.

Sometimes I can see myself flying away in a
world so free—dancing upon the moonlight...
feeling the warm fluid air upon my face...
caressing every inch of my entire body—
making me feel as if I were a particle cast
into space....
Sometimes I can see myself in a distant place—
picking love flowers—to spread over the deep
blues seas—a nymph like gesture—a reminder that
I had been there—in hopes of leaving a bit of
me.

Yet, when I settle myself—again—gently—
I smile because I hold a bouquet of such sweet memories.

Irene Dennie

To My Daughter, Karleen, On Her 40th Birthday:

Another moment, I'll never forget, was a bouquet all white and pure.
Given to me on your birthday, a loving gesture - that's for sure.

The note attached, was a tender one, "Thank you for giving me life."
How many daughters are that considerate, in this world filled with
  strife?

You have only given me happiness, never a day of despair.
Any time that I have needed help, you have always been there.

Now at this time of your life, you have opened another door.
You are happier and more beautiful than you have ever been before.

Elaine Rockow

Heaven Bound

In times of worried souls,
God is always there to comfort thee
High in the heavens awaiting your plea.
When grief and sorrow encase your heart,
He will comfort you from the start.
So, turn to him not only when all is midst,
He will free your soul and give you his gift.
Help thy neighbor and forgive thy foe
For in the end, together hand in hand
To heaven you may go.
Life is so short for the time we are here.
Eternal salvation is ever so dear.
To the children of today: make this world
A better way. So teach the babes that the Lord
Is within, to free their future from certain sin.
Together amongst the clouds we pray we will rise:
My Lord, my love, my children and I.

Christine Seaholtz

He's Always Near

In the midst of deepest drear,
  God our father is always near.
With him in our presence we have the whim,
  a sudden urge to be with him.
And if we ponder on His love,
  His heavenly grace will fall from above.
He will touch us with His comforting hand,
  His love for us we can't understand.
So if you're down, don't shed a tear,
  just look to God he's always near.

Josh Ingram

The Interrogation

A baby was murdered today.
God, were you there?

Two men killed in an alleyway.
God, were you there?

An elderly woman brutally slain.
Oh God, were you there?

Child molestation; illegal sex games
Dear God, were you there?

People abusing crack, alcohol and PCP.
My God, were you there?

Constant poisons and dangers we cannot see
Tell me God, were you there?

Babies having babies; husbands beating wives;
sons killing mothers —-

God, were you there?

Annette J. Chisolm

In A Child's Cry

Born of the love a true intimacy shares.
God's hand has given enrichment to life,
and with it the joys and sorrows one bears.
Love can be heard in a child's cry.

Rolling, crawling, steps are taken
away from the arms that held them tight.
The world is fantastic, but they can stumble again.
Fear can be heard in a child's cry.

Feeling their need for warmth, they reach.
The warmth of a blanket is something to try,
but is not preferred to a hug, they beseech.
Discomfort can be heard in a child's cry.

The world awaits for the child to learn.
Endless appetites for knowledge and what's why.
Eager to experience at every turn.
Hunger can be heard in a child's cry.

In a child's cry you can find it.
Just listen close. Dry the tears.
Nourishment, warmth, assurance and love.
These are needed for a child's first years.

Christopher M. Sailar

Reflections

As we swim our way toward the shore
God's the one who's keeping score.
As we struggle against wave after wave
We are tossed about and pray to be saved.
When the water gets shallow and our feet touch down
We take some time to look around. Are we ready to
walk upon the shore or would we rather live a
little more? As we look back at where we've been
We wonder if we could do it again. We've reached
a time when we can rest. We ask ourselves if
we've done our best. We've all made mistakes
along the way; for some we've already had to pay.
We've been through hardships big and small.
We've learned to get up and walk on tall.
Should we pass these lessons to younger folks,
You know, the ones who think we're jokes?
Why not? They won't listen you see.
They know more than you and me.
We'll tell what we've learned and someday they'll know
Why we told them to take it slow.

Charlene Berry

Grandpa Is Sick!

Guess what?
Grandpa is sick and when he is sick no one else has his ills.
"Grandma this and grandma that," he roars, "I need some water
And my pills!"
"Make it stat!"
Grandma, bless her soul, just takes her time and follows through
His every whim!
Even plants a kiss, just above his chin!
Must be love that she has for him!

Frances G Nash

The Seed

I kept the seed of which did plant and with God's grace He did
grant. As the seed began to bloom, I could feel it move within my
womb.

I gave it daily loving care and nightly prayed a new life I would
bare. As time did pass the seed had changed and its position had
rearranged.

Then, July 13, '69 a miracle came down to earth; unto an infant
female child I gave birth.

I praised the Lord for His graciousness and asked Him; Jodie
Loyal, He would bless. I made a promise to Him then; to love and
cherish her until the end.

Jill Chaves

Earthquakes

In the darkness of the night, families are curled
Grumbling, rumbling, shaking of the world.
People left homeless, no where to turn
Loneliness and despair is learned.
Innocent victims feeling helpless
Fires and floods leave nothing but sadness.
Destroys homes of families
Momentous memories lost in debris.
Nothing will ever be the same
The former picturesque scenery is now sorrow and
pain.

Briana Berg

Hindsight

We dance blissfully unaware, through lives made of porcelain, through
   halls so fragile.

   Vision blurred by soft lights of lost love
   That warm our beings; they make us feel so safe.
   And they speak…whispering…gently,
   About "a glow that lasts forever,"

   But they lie…

(These are ripe, plush lies, swelled and soon to burst, but still we
   believe them.)

   A sudden scream tears through the halls!
   Rebounding off corridors yet unseen.

   It's our own.

   And it all comes down. And it all comes down.
   And there's nothing we can do or say.
   When our eyes are clouded, (And they're always clouded,)

   Until we gaze through darkened glasses—
   A false veneer to hide our pain,
   At this Kaleidoscope of debris…

Hindsight is 20/20
Twilight hours, the only thing to light our way.

David Busby

Life

Life is like a tale
Handed down from one generation to another.
Ever changing,
Always exaggerated,
Our lives are mere chapters,
Small but significant
In the grand design of the plot.
The writers are our conscience,
Urging us to follow the pre-written chapters
For they are our lives as they should be.
However, as it gets passed down,
Things are inevitably forgotten
And people die,
Or stray from otherwise preset and happy lives.
But even in death there is life,
for no story merely ends but does something to make itself even more
   memorable than any other part of life.

Ben Wolfson

Cold Death

Cold death
harsh and scratching
scratching at you
your mind, your heart and your soul
scratching 'til you bleed insanely, unnoticeably
unnoticeable to all but you and you alone
you bleed 'til you are drained and can bleed no more
then you wither up dry and empty of mind heart and soul
empty of all
cold death

John Turner

"I Am Numb"

I am numb, for I have lost love.
Have not been able to retrieve it, for it has flown away
like a pure and innocent dove.
Without hesitation I gave my soul.
To have it denied and dismissed with no purpose or goal.
You have hurt me, this is true.
But most of all I've hurt myself for thinking love was only you.
You could never imagine the sense of emptiness
that runs through my veins.
The shortness of breath when I hear your name.
Because of you my world has been turned upside down.
Now I must get my emotions back on solid ground.
You mean the world to me, but I guess your world wasn't
large enough, I now see.
You captured my light in your eyes, but the only thing
you saw was goodbye.
The pain I feel is so hard to describe, all the happiness
and love I used to own has now died.
Getting over you will be hard, but that's a path I must cross.
I am numb, for I have lost love.

Briana M. Davis

From Hand To Hand

When I come into your store and place my hard earned money in your
hands, you throw the change done on the counter avoiding
touching my hand!
Do you despise me that much?
There's no reason for it!
I'm just as human as you!
Yet, you won't admit it!
The hatred must stop now, of course, from both ends!
We can respect each other.
It's never, never too late!

Andrea Lawson Robinson

"Lost And Found"

I wandered around aimlessly
Having no idea I was lost.
Living my life, without counting any cost.
I never even realized
How misled I had been
That I was being encouraged, by the ruler of Sin
Then one day I wandered, to a little Country Mission
I bowed to my knees, in total submission,
Oh Lord please forgive me
In a moment he replied
Rise up my child, for I have come inside
I'm in your heart and soul, forevermore
I'll live my life in you
Till your life is no more.
Your hands, in my hand
Your face in me, my child you can hide
I'll even walk with you, across the heavenly tide
There you'll live, in my Mansion on high
Waiting for your loved ones
In the sweet by and by.

Judy C. Weaver

Holy Puzzle

He guides me in all that I do.
He allows me to find his word to be true.
He lifts my spirits when I am sad.
He's everlasting not like a now-a-day fad.
In making decisions I'm allowed to make my own choice.
But I've been taught to patiently wait and listen for his voice.
When I fail, and believe me I do.
He is always there, and I'm not made to feel like a fool.
He always keeps his promise he has made to me.
He has even broke the chains that once bound me, now I am free.
I hope you'll consider him as your friend too.
I'll tell you his name after one more clue.
His ultimate gift was his son's death sacrifice.
Accept him in your heart now, don't think twice.
God is the answer and Jesus is his son.
Living within is the Holy Spirit together they are one.
This is the end of my puzzle and poem.
Someday I Hope to see you in my heavenly home.

Dori J. Keene

Live To Dream

A dreamer has the strength to breathe
he has the ability to teach another.
A dreamer sees life as no other
he can lift your spirits and take you through
life with a smile.

A dreamer can show you his world
he can ask what you see when you're there.
A dreamer feels as if he were all
he longs for hearts that can follow
A dreamer won't let himself fall
but yes, there are times when he does crawl.

One search of his soul
tells a story so deep and true
He reaches for his dream
and knows he has something to give you.

A dreamer senses when misery is near
he breathes form wiping away your tear
a dreamer will tell you
no matter how hard life may seem
you can always reach for a dream.

Gabriella Hartwell

The Center That Holds

Thanks be to God and his new physics
He invented a center that holds
Though they yet abort our bodies
No longer do they abort our souls
With love as the essences
Of his new creation
The center is the vessel
That hold the seed of manifestation
And like the sun, it gives life to the soul
For love is the only light
That can shine in a black hole

Edna Beard

I Am Your Shelter

He cannot go, I will not let him
He is going to stay with me today
This is what has to be, this is my way.

I am going to hold on tight, never letting go,
it's a mother's will, a mother's fight

I will take care of him, he needs only me
I knew him before he was born
I know his every need

I am his shelter from the rain
I am the guardian of his pain

I am to be his shield in whatever he must face
But slowly I didn't realize that
God had taken my place.

Bonita S. Martin

At The Drop Of A Hat

I have a friend whose name is Nat
He knows where the action's at
He'll never fail to start a spat
At the slightest drop of a hat.

We'll be having a friendly chat
Chewin' the fat 'bout this 'n that
When all of a sudden, my pal Nat
Steps up to the plate, and goes to bat.

"Clinton's a phony, he declares
How can you be unawares?
The New York Jets are sure to lose
Why don't you just read the News?"

"The car you're driving is a pup 'bout time you gave it up
And that suit went out years ago I'm surprised you don't know."

I defend my views as best I can
But Nat's not a very reasonable man
He raises his voice in impassioned tones
Sure he's right, and makes no bones
He seems to enjoy our weekly chat
Nat's in the ring at the drop of a hat.

Albert Dillof

Untitled

Love does burn within my heart
as no other love has known.
Love burns as a fire
in a heart on a winter's eve.

As thou hath been on a journey,
my love stayed a flame.
But thou hast been gone
for a half a lifetime.
No flame burns again,
for you my love has ceased.

Janel Hickey

John Girdler

John Girdler earned his life at sea.
He spent it bit by bit with friends,
And with his well loved family
About his hearth at voyage ends.

He sailed the Dixie round the Horn
With cargoes for our Western shore.
Before the gold rush towns were born,
He learned the California lore.

New England tinware, woven cloth,
He'd trade for Western fur and hide.
And then he'd sail through crest and through
For Marble head, which was his pride.

He'd stop at ports along the way
To trade a bit and get supplies.
He learned a lot at every stay
Because he used his ears and eyes.

So, at his hearth, his yarns he'd spin
And they like driftwood fire would be.
The warmth came from the man within,
The color from the salty sea.

Howard M. Fitch

No Vacancy

Arthritis was roaming the streets looking for a body to invade.
He started past my house, stopped, came in to visit and stayed.

"What a nice body," he said, and he moved right in.
I've tried some of everything and I can't get rid of him.

So I doubled my efforts and prayed morning, noon, and night.
I wanted old Arthur completely out of my sight.

One day when I was not aware of it he left my residence.
Guess what he did? He invited Sis Gout to fight in his defense.

I thought old Arthur was bad. Sis Gout takes the cake.
She hit me with a pain and said, "I'm in charge, of that make no mistake."

So I took time out and to the doctor I did go.
Hobbling alone and walking very slow.

Sis Gout smiled with satisfaction when the medicine made me sick.
She said, "I told you I'm in control and I see you did forget."

Oh Lord, have mercy on this old body of mine.
If you don't move her off these premises, I'll surely lose my mind.

Gladys Sutton

No More Tears

The way he made me feel, was like nothing I'd ever felt before.
When he touched me, my heart began to soar. The first time our
eyes met, I knew that everything was set. The love, the romance,
everything was there but I guess it was too much for him to bear.
He just left me out in the cold and knew I had to be strong and I
had to be bold. I was all caught up in emotions and fears to notice
I was completely in tears. I sat down on the curb that rainy night,
not wanting to go on, not wanting to fight. As people rushed by,
giving me a nasty eye, I let out a sudden sigh. I could tell what
was going on in their minds, I've heard it all a million times. As I
arose from the curb and ran out with a swerve rushing toward the
heavily flowing traffic, I looked down to see something plastic. It
read, "Love of God, Love of Peace, Love of Man, Love of Beast,
Preach of Song, Breach of Prayer Life is too much to bear. Days
have gone, lives have past, now why should this one last. So on
my grave place a dove, to show that I have died for love."
When I looked up in a sudden flash, I felt a stunning gash, then
no more pain, no more fears, no more crying, no more tears.

Jackie Batemon

Once I Knew A Drummer

Once I knew a drummer who marched with measured tread.
He wandered not to right or left but sought the light ahead.
The path this drummer followed sometimes was very rough.
My body oft responded, my spirit not enough.
For when I heard another, whose beat appealed to me,
I branched onto the wider road, and smooth as it could be.
But now this road seems endless. My legs are getting weak.
The light keeps getting dimmer. What is it now I seek?
I seek again the drummer, the one with measured tread.
I seek again the drummer who seeks the light ahead.

Anthony Gutowski

I Walked With The Lord

I walked with the Lord along the beach
he was close beside me just within my reach,
he is the one and only true friend; he will
be with me forever, even in the end.
I walked with the Lord when I was a
child, he was always there, even when I
grew a little wild, I wasn't always good
and sometimes, I was pretty bad but he didn't
forsake me and he didn't get mad: My Lord is
a loving and gentle friend and on him I know
I can always depend.
I walked with the Lord yesterday and today
I talked with him about things gone by, and
memories of yesterday, and how time flies;
he listened to me as on we walked, and I don't
remember how long we talked. That night
as I knelt beside my bed to pray, I thanked
the Lord, for being my friend, and on him
I know I can always depend.

Essie Stephenson

What Stress?

In our mind's space we can feel an inexhaustible rush of activity!
Hear wonderful strains of music, fantastic.
Breathe in gushes of light-heartedness.
See boundless images of the good, the great with wonderful smiles.
Taste a fulfilling variety of wonderful and surprising never-heard-of
   delights.
Smell the aroma, the scent, the fragrance of flowers and food.
All to raise our spirit to its highest peak.
Give joy and gladness to our experience now with peaceful sleep,
With childlike grace to meet the day ahead with mirth - not grief.

Anna Daines

The Maiden And The Swan

The gentle heart, the passionate clamoring
Heart the maiden sighing embraced in tender
Strains the grateful tide of her swan. He
showers her with glowing ribbons ripples passes
'Neath her window, curtains pulled view the
Guided tour freely flown for her to witness
Joy. He wanes his course to loving caress feels
pangs of lightning's spark her touch harken's
That as daring movement now wrought with
future dreams. She holds his necessary flippant
Escapades as duty naught, but those who hear
the melody raised high to toast the coming
parade. Cloaking tones of glamour in her breast
toward lips that rise from corners mild. Her
quest for peace knocks softly the pond on
which he swims inviting him home away, the
journey drips past as now they too shall seem.
Still swims in sight within the glimpse she
Beckons on an air of grace and cries increase
The bliss that heavens passed the dawn.

Justin Vickers

Remember the Lord

For all the things John recalls are under the power of
Heaven's laws.

He saw a beast rise from the sea in which he wanted
all people for he.

He looked like a leopard, had feet like a bear, a
mouth like a lion in which we must beware.

He'd rule the world for forty-two months and fool
the place with his evil stunts.

In the midst of the earth appeared beast two, who
altogether looked quite new.

He spoke like a dragon, with two horns like a lamb
to take over the land with your command.

The beast of the earth will never rule if you keep the
Lord in mind and are not cruel.

You have been warned of the beast and his lake so
remember the Lord, your soul is at stake.

Amber Novak

Black Heart

Shadowed in darkness slowly approaching;
Heavy and laden with dread — and encroaching.

Stealthy and sharp with a razor-like blade;
It tears and it injures — what pain it has made.

For all who have seen and for those who fall prey;
"Why does this black heart continue this way?"

So draining it is, on a soul full of life;
It takes from us all, son, daughter, husband or wife.

And while to our bodies it has laid claim,
Strong and determined we all must remain.

For the moment we give up or simply stop trying;
Oh so many — so many are dying.

Fight every battle with faith, hope and courage;
For it is by these that generations will flourish.

And when it is time and the light starts to dim;
Raise up a prayer — an offering to Him.

For He will forgive and ease all your pain;
And you in eternal life will remain.

Anna M. Robinson

Agony

Anger, rejection, the stupidity of it all... my hatred overflows like
hell hath the fury of one hundred fallen angels all in lucifer's
service the damned scream at the pitiful silence that falls like a
smothering blanket over societies dumbstruck children who find
fault inall but not themselves and judge others that fall out of the
grace they set as if they were gods and supreme to judge who is
right and who is not one of their own like the fallen Utopians who
look to Sodom and Gomorrah for their comfort and self righteous-
ness so shall these blind fools fall down slaves to their own faults in
disgracing the midst of their peers Icarenot what you have to say as
you gain perverted pleasure from the pain of others endure by you
my desire to see you fail swells making me less of what you are yet
more for it is we who are the just and you the ignorant criminals
lusting for power and controlloseitdiesuffocate on your wrongs
dare not desecrate the simple and pure who strive for achievement
and struggle when you push us down crushes Ihateyou Ihatemyself
for letting this go on Iwant todie I want the agony to end all now
God let this f**king nihilistic oppression sink into the ground and
strugglesuffocateddrownbeneath dead choke on their own
vomitsswallowdryair poisoned within my cyanidespitgasp we'll
laugh for we won'tsuccumbcomewretch feel how it is to want
hate,cry,gasp,sob,trembleburndieend.

Jonathan Vogel

Someone Special Up Above

I had a loved one, but now he's gone. He had
helped me when I was wrong. We would talk
on the phone, and tell our favorite tales, he made me
laugh and made me feel glad. He was wise and caring, just
like a best friend. But now he's gone, will this horrible tragedy
stay in my head? I will never forget the way he spoke to me,
or they way he cared for me. Now he's gone to some place
up above, he will always be in my heart, and I will always
love..... My grandfather was very special to me, he
always took important things seriously. Now I believe that
there is no one as special as he.

Julia Rubin

Tears

She sits so quietly with tears flowing down her cheek,
her cheek rested gently on her hand,
her hand placed delicately on her child,
Her child comfortably rested in her lap.
With his face pressed against the frigid, frosty glass,
A tears runs from his face. As it hits his mother's hand and
slowly slips down the side, vanishing forever.
A woman sits at the window on a still, wintry day with her
son in her lap. As he cries she wipes his tear, and then wipes
her own. As the tears come together to form one, the tear with
heartache, hurt, and pain disappears into eternity.

Allie Griffin

On Faith We Stand

Every day for a month was the call each morning I dread,
Her doctor telling me, face it, your mother's dead.

There's nothing more to be done, let us pull the plug,
No! I said, you doctors are not God - He's still above.

For several months, we prayed, we watched as she lay very
Very still.
But to us, she looked better and I said this aloud and knew it
Was God's will.

The doctor heard of my praise that night, and the very
Next day a call she made to me.
Accept your mother's death or a meeting of doctors we will
Have, and their answer is what it will be.

Out loud I spoke, get behind me satan, my mother's coming
Home, she's leaving that hospital bed.
For we know the Lord, we believe the Lord, we have faith in
The Lord, and this is what he said
Today, our mother is home, a miracle, a testimony,
A blessing to each of us.
Because we believe in God, the Father, the Son, the Holy Ghost
And in him we trust.

Doris Gipson

Pure As A Tear

Love ever sacred, as pure as a tear
dredged up from the darkness, wiped free of its fear.
A desperate attempt, can Love be felt?
Not blinded by anger or tarnished by guilt.
The shame of the truth, revealed in the eyes
couldn't be hidden or covered by lies.
A hope of forgiveness in the face of revenge,
but no second chance, no game left to win.
The evils of flesh lay waste to the trust,
raped by confusion and murdered by lust.
Love now buried and riddled with fear,
entombed once again, and sealed with a tear.

...next time?

Jeff Hamrick

Mirror To The Soul

Her hands were gnarled and ugly.
Her hands belied her age.
Her hands were beautiful.
They were earth, wind, and fire worn.
Veined heavily, as though blue tubes traversed her arms.
They fluttered and flew as she spoke, though words
weren't as important as the message of the badges of courage
dangling at shirt-sleeve's end.
These hands were transfixing and told of hard work
and tough love. They knew no Palmolive
(softens hands while you do dishes!) and less cream.
The hands belonged to the Marlboro men of the range,
not on her. But they were also sinewy and prone to those
bird-like starts. Her hands were honest and demanded admiration.
And they conjured up the image of his hands. They, too, were
mesmerizing, since he was the classically salified fisherman.
But his hands were smooth and young. Clean and soft.
With sparkling nails...
And then the thought, what if we were all without sight
and had to feel our way?

Demaris P. Hetrick

I Think I've Found Love

I can find myself growing closer to him.
He's all I ever think about.
He's in all my dreams and fantasies.
This is one feeling I can never doubt.

We can easily talk and laugh together,
He's the sweetest guy I've ever met.
He's cute and always honest.
He has my heart trapped in a net.

When I go to bed at night I'm always thinking about him.
When I'm not in bed I daydream about us.
I hope he loves me as much as I love him.
And I hope we never fight or fuss.

I hope my fantasies come true.
I can never live without him.
I don't know what I'd do if I lost him.
My life would be very dim.

Our love finally came through.
We have a baby on the way.
We can grow old together.
And we'll die together someday.

Jessica M. Johnson

Untitled

Looking back over the years,
his eyes swelled as they filled with tears
remembering all the good times they had,
most were good, few were bad.
He remembers his arms holding her tight,
he remembers her soft gentle kisses goodnight.
He remembers the day she said goodbye,
he remembers her words "Please don't cry"
he remembers all the nights he spent alone,
waiting for her to call on the telephone.
Then one day it finally rang,
it all ended with one big bang.
It wasn't an accident, it was suicide,
he couldn't believe she actually died.
She said she had no reason to live,
she said she had nothing more to give.
Then suddenly she had no more to say,
except for the simple words "I'm sorry
It had to end this way". Now he sits waiting by the phone,
but he still doesn't realize he'll always be alone.

Amanda Proper

Rosco

We adopted him at only 8 weeks old
His big brown eyes really touched my soul

My son Ray who's 12 years old
Along with my husband treated our new family member like gold

Their relationship boldly said 3's company
4's a crowd I could plainly see
As time lingered on, I could see the thrill was gone

As the newness wore off, and their patience grow thin
A common male trait, I knew I'd have to step in

I taught him right from wrong, along with loving care
He'd lay lovingly on my lap and I'd brush his dark hair

Sometimes I'd take him for a car ride, he'd always beg to go
Yet so many times I'd have to say NO!!!

My husbands new business kept him busy as a bee
Ray, my son now a young man had no spare time you see

They say he's man's best friend, but as a woman I disagree
He knew I loved him, I knew he loved me

After 10 years of companionship and love, at the Vet's I weep
My Rosco, dear Rosco, my heart quietly speaks
I know he's heaven bound, no more pain, they put him to sleep

Carrie L. Brown-Tillman

Grandad

There is a man, he's fair of face,
His hair is white, he's slow of pace,
His quiet mannerisms suggest such strength,
His body is sparse with strains of length.
He walks in the woods with his faithful old dog,
Over hills and dales and sits on a log.
He loves to whittle on his back porch,
Smiling with eyes as bright as a torch.
His quiet courage shows me nothing to fear,
His strong face is very dear.
The sense of security you instilled in me,
I was your "babe" for all the world to see.
No matter what I did or where I went,
Until life's fate laid you down with spirit bent.
But now only in memory is your face so dear,
My path keeps going, you made it clear.
Go straight ahead and do what's right
Your heart will lead you into the light.
Your inner self knows just what to do,
Oh! Grandad I'll always love you.

Beverly A. Para

Eciruam

Engulfed by his embrace, I delicately touched
his lips with mine, and we slowly studied each other's
body with ungloved hands.

I instantly discovered that I was in his world,
for he showed me the monumental sights of his land.
The view was beautiful. I did not want to leave;

So we moved to the shore and found ourselves inhaling sand
and creating mirror images of our souls. Nature herself
blanketed our naked symphony;

And long after the sun had cooled
itself in the salty water,
I realized that not only were we wayward dinghies
that held this one miniature radio and room
only for two, but marble lighthouses
that beamed a passionate, hypnotic ray of light.

Antiwan D. Walker

My Love

I live with a man I love so much,
his looks, his ways, his gentle touch.

When I am with him and my nights are cold,
I get my warmth from within his soul.

When I am low or feeling lost,
he says the right words from his heart so soft.

When I need a Friend and I'm feeling down,
I turn to him he's always around,

In my day and in my night,
he will always be my guiding light,

and when I'm happy and feeling fine,
there's no one to thank but that man of mine.

Brenda L. Hicks

Daddy's Songs

Our greatest thrill in life, was just to listen to him sing
His songs could take us anywhere, a palace of a king
Or maybe up on Heaven's shore, to walk on streets of gold
And visit with our Saviour there, and view the sights untold

Sometimes his songs would take us, to a lofty mountain high
It's then I'd think of Moses, and how he came to die
I'd think about the land of plenty, how he couldn't go
Because he sinned against his God, and smote the rock you know

I remember going on a journey to a valley low
And trying to help others, for their way they did not know
This journey wasn't too much fun, but needful as could be
Cause it taught us to think of others, not just think of me

Yes Daddy's songs were special, for we had no way to go
To all those lovely places, that he'd take us to you know
We didn't need a car, we took a trip most every day
And when we came back home again, we'd bow our heads and pray

Thank you dad for memories, I treasure every one
And I hope I can take these same trips, with my precious son
For they were something special, and they really were such fun
Just one more lesson taught by you, before your race was run

Joan P. Walker

Grandparent's Land

They worked this land to make their stand.
Holding on, hand to hand.

Life was hard but crime free.
Everyone respected each other from land to sea.

From a horse and plow, a couple of chickens
and a cow is all they needed.
This is what this world should be like, even right now.

David D. Adams

Sole Marcher

Everyone is silent as he says his last words.
His heart is heavy as he gazes at her.
How could this happen, she was so young,
with a life full of challenges and songs left unsung.
He sheds a silent tear, no one makes a sound,
as they lower her casket down into the ground.
The graveyard is dimmed as darkness falls
and people depart one by one.
Now nothing's left, the words have been said.
The world doesn't care, "So one more's dead."
Another to add to the list of departure,
but one person cares, one sole marcher.
he cannot express the sadness within,
because of this death his heart has been dimmed.

Jennifer Kanani Haworth

Growing Old

Lonely they are till the end
Holding on to the reminiscence, carrying a grin

Getting up at the break of dawn
Going to sleep in the early morn
There is no sleep for the lonely it seems
The living off of past, present and future dreams

Repeating themselves over and over again
You can't get tired because even you will need a friend

That day when time starts slipping away
Where all you really have is God and space

Just to talk for that instance, to give great joy
Oh boy is like a brand new toy

Love even in that capacity of time
Makes a smile for a face where they may have felt tired

Helps them to keep moving on, not stand still till the soil is tilled
Love is sometimes unkind but when you are growing old
A smile or a sound of a voice is so kind.

Angela S. Gordon

The Tiger

The tiger sits silently in the young child's room,
Holding watch by the light of the candlelight moon.
He peers through the rails of the crib in the night,
Guarding, protecting, and ready to fight.
When darkness comes at the end of the day,
He comes alive and waits for his prey.
His one mission is to preserve the innocence of their special bond,
It's as if the angels waved a magic wand
Reversing their roles,
Joining two souls,
The tiger lurks low, ready to leap,
Unsuspecting intruders won't find him asleep.
Fearless and loyal—It's all worthwhile,
Because there's no greater force than the love of a child,
So tonight, the tiger works hard at his task
For tomorrow, he can relax,
As daylight wakes the sleeping boy,
The tiger becomes his special stuffed toy.

Carol M. Secrist

The Touch Of A Rose

Each petal of a lovely rose
holds life and breathes a song
If you listen very carefully
you will not find me wrong

Each drop of moisture is a tear
wept with purest heart
And yes, indeed I think
this rose is quite smart

Stare into it and see it sway
gracefully performing a dance
It may even smile and talk to you
if you give it a chance

All forms of life are here for a reason
each to help one another
If we cannot enjoy the pleasures of a simple rose
we can never appreciate our brother.

Gerri Carilli

Dream Demon

Now I lay me down to sleep
Hoping tonight my dreams will be kind to me
Praying…that he does not disturb my long awaited slumber
As I close my eyes to sleep, I hear it
Something sucks the stale air…and hisses
Glaring with ancient grace
Unwilling to retreat as his brothers did
Eyes gleaming, untouched by love, or joy, or sorrow
Its breath is hot with the taste of fallen foes
The stench of dead things, damned things
Surely the fiercest survivor, the purest warrior
Glaring, hating…claiming me as his own
His foul senses filling my mind just as breath fills my lungs
Knowing that night is my weakest time
My will at its lowest
He knows I cannot stay awake forever
So until I return to my slumber…he waits
Filling my mind with dread thoughts
Of the night to come

Joshua A. Bishop

Betrayed

As she thinks back to that night
horror, rushes over her with memories of
how she tried to fight. She remembers
his smile, and how he was so kind. But
all at once his face was twisted as if he'd
lost his mind she tried to push him
away, but she couldn't stop him, there was
nothing she could say. As his body lunged
on top of hers, she started to cry,
begging God not to let her die.
The tears flowed down her face
and she took a deep sigh. Trying
to hold in all the pain she was
feeling inside. All she could say
was "Why oh why." But now two
years from that awful day. She
dries her eyes, and promises herself
not to cry. For now that day
is gone and her life can go on.

Corinne Root

Homeless

Long beard, shabby coat, dingy hat low in self esteem
hours tangled up in mind, what's day of the week
people traveling by, down the street in fancy coat and dress
days and nights are full of only emptiness
I'd like them to stop, recognize and speak

If they would only take me under their wing
I'd be a jack turned into a king; I'd disappear
from the cold, with nourishment, a bed and a warm welcome
rolled in gold, I'd imagine how it would renew
my mind and a reward I'd always keep

My life has turned delirious with stress and defeat
the train is sitting on the track; all my dreams
have turned wrong; no work since the railroad's gone
I'd wish I could sail along in the wind
ride the tracks, find work, start life again

No money for cigarettes; no match for a fire, I'm
waiting for the sun to shine, daylight I desire how
can I fight the elements? I'm going insane I weep
in silence and try to sleep I've got a battle
to repeat, I don't have a dollar bill, just sit still and wonder

Inez Kobus

"Working Mom"

Light outside is gettin' dim…
House kinda quiet…settlin' in…
I'm putting the day behind me, easing in.

Prop my feet up, listen to hisses and
pops of fire staring, to simmer within…
Take a sip of favorite hops-(Teapot, no I think not)
And yes, I think of you; yes, yes I do…

Oh, I know there's chores, to be done
Cats need food- Dog wants a walk - well…
Kids they need to talk, some silly sibling
squall to solve- Look at the carpet-
Where's the Resolve? Dishes to clean
Clothes for a wash- Gosh, those counter tops!!

Well, cats are fed, dog is walked
Kids, finally talked…lights are out
House is dark- I'm settled in…

Prop my feet up,
Feel the lonesomeness settlin' in…
the heart of the embers simmer within…
and I ask myself, Where Are You?

Brett K. Eastman

Child's Cry For Help!

Dedicated to children who suffer from abuse
I am only one child in a
house of abuse, drugs, sex and alcohol.
My father stays out all night and
when my mother comes home she hits
me, screams at me and sleeps with me.
I am only one child in a world of
Tears. My parents come home upset
and my father beats me. I am crying
every night and every day. I come to
school with bruises and I am always
asked what happened? I lie and
say I fell. I don't know why I
do but I feel responsible for the abuse.
I am one child in a world of abuse.
Help me God! Help me grownups! I am only one
child in a world of disaster. I can't do
anything but I can stop all this by running away.
Right now I am at the door, with my little
bag on my back.
I will follow the railroad toward the sunset.

David Bernshteyn

"Chapel By The Sea"

I know a place that's nestled, on the sand by the sea
House of the Lord, a place of worship
named
Chapel By The Sea

Heart heavy with burden, mind ill at ease
Come, call upon thy Father
in the
Chapel By The Sea

For when you call the Father
Isaiah: 65/24
He answers: While you're speaking, he will hear.

The waves of life are washing, against the
sands of time
So go to the place that I know
nestled on the sand by the sea.
House of the Lord - a place of worship
named
"Chapel By The Sea"

Dorothy M. Barszcz

The Mirror

I glance at the mirror and I see my mother.
How can that be when I look like my father?
She is living in me and I am living for her.
Touching each other but not knowing for sure...
Is she reaching to me or am I reaching for her?

Sometimes I am sad and I just want to cry.
Yet sometimes I smile and look towards the sky.
I know she is happy - no troubles today.
Her spirit's the same - just further away.

How many times within one day
Do thoughts of her come my way?
Always she's with me from one thought to another.
I'll never get over the loss of my mother.

Jane Hinz

Burdens Of The Past

Love and hate cloud my memories for I don't want to remember my past.
How clearly though these two terrors clasp. As once I could see the
simple things that filled my life with joy. Then it happened, I was
torn. My soul which was filled with vivid colors turned into a
smudged picture of black and white. The earth itself was gray so I
blinded myself from the memories of my past. As love came close I
drew back. As though a web had surrounded by will my memories
became a prison in my own mind. As a shadow with no dimension
I was dead. To live again I would have to cross an immortal sea.
With no one to help or guide me. Then I prayed for God to save
me. By the power of his love and grace turned on a celestial light.
Which helped me through the dark and misty labyrinth. It was not
easy I thought I would die. Instead I kept striving until I opened
one eye. I could see again all the colors of the spectrum of light. I
was truly reborn like the phoenix through Gods eyes. My faith had
lifted me up from the devils grasp. A tear fell down my cheek. A
tear let me feel the power of love again. The start of a new life.
Now I think back I guess I did die that day. I have a true life to
live without the burdens of my past.

Cory S. Bagby

Absence

Today I went again and touched your coat
Hanging on the hook, back of your office door
Grasped it at the middle button hole
Fingers inner and thumb the outer side
And rubbed it twice between, then held it tight
So soft and strong, and blue and long, like you
Then pulled it back, from up and against the door
Read again the label in the lining
 Saks Fifth Avenue.
I had to stop for fear I'd be found out
Standing at the door with your coat in my hand
This way of making love is not easy.
Next week, your coat will not be there.

Joan MacKenzie

Zion

I look across the sea and foam, through mist, and storm on my way
 home;
through wind, and rain, and blinding glare, to catch a glimpse of
 Zion fair.
Sometimes upon a sea of glass, I hold her beauty in my grasp,
and other days of dark, and drear, I know her Captain holds me near.
Someday I'll walk across her plank, when all the other ships have sank;
and when the last soul has arrived, she'll hoist her anchor and arise
She'll sail to where her home port be, into a world of crystal sea,
'Tis there she'll let her anchor down, and here forever will be found.
So now make haste and look to see, if in the harbor Zion be,
and to her Captain call, and pray, before old Zion sails away.

David R. Farthing

Oh Lindsay Girl

Oh Lindsay girl, you're the light in my world
how could I ever let you go
Oh Lindsay girl, full of smiles and curls
my love for you is the one thing you will know

I see you on the sand with a bucket in your hand
building those castles in the air
the sun is shining down, you're an angel on the ground
and halos surround you everywhere

And if you ever get tired
just think of me and hopefully
you'll be inspired

Don't ever be sad you will always have your mom and dad
nothing you could do would drive us away
Though we're far apart you will always be close to my heart
and if you want the next time I'll stay

And if you ever start to cry
Reach out for me and hopefully
you'll start to smile

Please don't be sad I'll find the way
I love you and there's so much that I want to say.

Joseph Scanlon

How?

How did the Universe start?
How did the ancients get so smart?
How did the world get so twisted?
How did the history get so accurately listed?

How do you know when you're in love?
How is there a sky above?
How did slavery begin?
How do we have feelings within?

How does a disease find its cure?
How do scientists become so sure?
How do mates find their link?
Doesn't this poem make you think?

How do we cure AIDS and cancer?
How will I ever get the answer?
How do people conceal with masking?
How is the question I am asking?
How, I will never know.

Andrea Joy Monzo

Wishing For John

Twinkle, twinkle, little star...
how I'm wondering, where you are...

Are you lonely, just like me...
unlock your heart, you hold the key!...

Open your ears, and hear my cries...
I need the answers, to all of my whys...

I need you honey, I want you now...
please tell me when, and tell me how...
I have all of this love, storing up in my heart...
I have no place to put it, while we are apart...

I miss my lover, I need my friend...
it's time to be happy, and for sadness to end...

Doreen Brinkerhoff

Disperse

My heart queries how it is to disperse?
How it is too aged and soon to perish?
We were all born fresh and unblemished,
Born with grace and bound to be nursed.

Forebears yearning to entwined,
Borne us to come into existence,
Thirty-six weeks solely sighted,
In the warm womb of our mothers.

Parturition marked the inceptive-
Of life proclaimed in our own slant,
Nursling in the eyes of the man,
But giant in his general cast of mind.

Day by day as we witness things unfold,
We ask, "Is there anything else to behold?"
While unprecedented crazes transpire and go,
Evidence of senescence begins to show.

From unblemished soul to now tarnished spirit,
Eagerness to reminiscence is certain,
As the mortal body slowly weakens and expires,
We ask, "Is there indeed a grasping light?"

Evelyn R. Boyce

Wounded But Victorious

When you're wounded then you see
How naughty and selfish the flesh can be
You hurt and try to cover the scar
So no one will know who you really are
But Jesus uses his Holy Spirit
So you don't really have to share it
He knows pain like none other
And heals our hearts and takes us farther
Into his most holy place
To obtain strength to run this race
Without Him we couldn't even stand
That's why we have to help our fellowman
We must be strong and continue to fight
He's the righteous Judge and causes us to do right
So we must yield to His Spirit today
In order to hear that sweet voice say
I love you with an everlasting love
That's why I'm sending my spirit in the form of a dove
So receive it and be thou faithful to me
And I'll do likewise in greater measure to thee

Celeta Mann

To Sleep (Or Not To Sleep) Winter Away

With the changing of the season
I am sad without a reason
When winter steals the beauty of the trees.

The leaves so red and yellow
And the winter apples mellow
Fall to the ground and winds replace the breeze.

The skies become gray cover
And birds go winging over
To find another warmer place to stay.

When snow and ice storms gather
It is then I'd really rather
Just curl up and sleep the time away.

BUT, the kids next door might make a snowman—
   complete with red scarf and top-hat
And I certainly don't want to take the chance of
   missing THAT!

Effie B. Hutchison

"Who?" Said The Angel

"Who," said the Angel, "Who knows how to live a full life;
How to advocate reason; how to terminate strife?"

"I," said the high school football captain,
An alma mater legend who's hot and happenin'.
"I have many sexy girls and beat up scrawny little nerds;
I know all the hip phrases; I coin all the cool words."

"Who," said the Angel, "Who knows how to live a full life;
How to advocate reason; how to terminate strife?"

"I," said the world famous millionaire,
Who's surrounded by the scent of fresh cash in the air.
"I buy everything and everyone including happiness;
And, I know that a man's money determines his greatness."

"Who," said the Angel, "Who knows how to live a full life;
How to advocate reason; how to terminate strife?"

"I," said the isolated A.I.D.S. victim,
Who knows what he has and tells others what has hit him.
"I savor in my ear the sound of children singing songs;
I find joy in life though I may not be here long."

Gregory Moore

Memories

One day I relaxed, and as I looked into the sky,
I allowed my eyes to wander, as a cloud went passing by.
I saw a face gleaming back, and as I dared to wonder,
I noticed something was very wrong, the face dissolved to thunder.
My eyes started to water, I blinked to shed a tear,
my heart grew with anxiety, as I felt the danger growing near.
The sky started to flash all colors, my thoughts were heavy and mean,
the expressions on my face varied, as I witnessed every painful scene.
They were portraits from my tearful past that I kept locked in my head
I had to face the memories of pain, that filled my heart with dread.
The colors, darkness, and feelings, is all that I had feared,
but when I finally closed my eyes, all this disappeared.
I said a prayer to all I love and to my surprise,
tears of happiness surrounded me, then later filled my eyes.

April Tate

"I Am"

I am the wind blowing softly through the trees.
I am a deer grazing by a river.
I am a little girl hugging her mother.
I am a horse galloping swiftly in the meadow.
I am a tear rolling down a child's cheek.
I am an airplane flying smoothly through the sky.
I am the sun slowly peeking out behind the clouds.
I am a teacher teaching her class with knowledge.
I am the snow falling gently to the ground.
I am a poet writing a beautiful poem.

Jericka Marie Miller

Spirit Land

Blue sky and wind above the frozen land
Cared for by the great spirit's hand.
A coyote's track hemstitches the snow.
Puzzling to himself where did the rabbit go?

An eagle soars and circles in his home in the sky
Watching and waiting for a tasty prey to come by.
There's a quiet that seems peaceful, deadly as well.
As if breaking the spell will bring hounds of hell.

Nature has a beauty unmatched by things of man
More than can be absorbed in a single life span.
Stand on a hill wrapped warm in your furs and gaze
Forget not the great spirit or your God to praise.

Harold Reider

The Cold Rain

After all these years of pain,
I am living in the cold rain.
When it rained on me,
I realized that I didn't see.

I didn't see your love, I was blind,
didn't use my heart, didn't even use my mind.
Sitting here lonely with no one to care for,
now I don't have what I had anymore.
You know life is a good thing, if you don't take it as it is,
you will be left with no life, and no songs to sing.
If I hurt someone once again,
I'll be left in the cold rain.

Never meant to lie,
never meant to make you cry.
To you people who live with your choices,
make sure your people hear our voices.

If you're hurt with love,
try to keep your head above.
It's all the same story, keep your sweet glory.
And no more cold rain.

Deandrea Faulkner

Harriet Tubman

I am the heart that felt the pain
I am the heart that dealt with fear
I felt shear terror as I was chased
I faced the problems of the night and the light
Praying to God to hold me tight

I am the eyes that saw disaster from all masters
I saw the fright in thy own eyes and saw people give up and cry
I helped see Harriet through the night trying to fight for slave's rights
I saw the ugly pain as slaves turned in shame

I am the ears that heard the screaming, fearing till morning
I am the ears that heard pleas for help, and the cries of those who felt
I heard the shouts of anger, but still we staggered
I heard the pounding footsteps, sounding so cruel
Who was I trying to fool
I heard the scornful laughter after each step I took and each breath
I snuck.
We felt, heard and saw, with each other we crossed the line of freedom
The heartfelt joy, the ears heard
the sounds from all around saying you are free,
and the eyes saw heaven at last

Danielle Bush

"No Shame"

Lord they laughed because
I called your name
Then they beat me, cause
I showed no shame
Lord they said, I couldn't be saved
So they lead me to my grave
They tried to blind me so
I could not see
The hole they dug to bury me
They tried to tear the flash from my bones
Hide there hands, but they all throw stones
They stood in line to take their turn
Lord, they wanted to see me burn
They looked upon me with eyes of hate
Heaven please open up your gate
Lord, they beat me cause
I showed no shame
But, I forgive them in your Mighty Name

Gwendolyn Shannon

Winter Moonlight

As I walk through the misty green forest,
I can feel the cold winter air pressing
against my numb lips like a kiss from
the moon. As I walk I can hear feet
crunching in the slushy snow. I look
back but all I can see is a white
blanket covering the rich earth that
shimmers in the moonlight like a
crystal champagne glass filled with
sparkling champagne or like the sun
setting on a sapphire ocean with streaks of
gold. And then I wake up and look
out the window, where did the snow go? Did
it melt? Where did my dream go?

Danielle Kardum

Untitled

Sometimes at night when I'm trying to fall asleep
I can feel you beside me.
I can feel your arms draped upon my chest,
And can hear the faint beating of your heart.
I can smell the remnants of your perfume,
And can feel your warm breath on my neck.
I watch your chest move up and down
With each breath you take.
And I can feel your moist lips on my cheek,
As you kiss me goodnight.
In your bright eyes and beautiful smile,
I can see the love we share.
And even though I know that it must be a dream,
I still wake up surprised that you are not beside me,
As you were when I fell asleep.

David N. Kress

Vanity Of Success

Today from my mailbox I gingerly took
"Echoes of Yesterday," an original poetry book
My fluttering heart was yearning to see
That simple rhymed verse created by me

Vanity bounced 'round the room and did laugh
While urgent desire viewed the lone autograph
Pride lost its melody, pride took a great fall
Over 5000 named authors on those pages in all

Still page 458 brings to my eyes a strange glint
For my insignificant words are now published in print
I'll submit a new entry though reason sees no use
A monetary prize lends vanity her excuse.

Delores Hinde

Granny's Little Buddy

In times like these, we never know just
how they become, and how they will grow.
Take care of my little buddy, Granny's little
pride and joy, he's just a little angle, but
still he's a little boy.
Heaven only knows, he's a gift of love
he's sent to you from Heaven above. Take
care of Granny's Little Boy, He'll become
a young man one day, he'll be all grown
up and gone away. He's granny's little
pride and joy, He's a little angel, but
still he's just a little boy.

Brenda Lowe

Whispers Of The Night

As I lie awake, I can hear it,
I can hear the crickets tender chirp,
And the frogs desperate cry for rain.
The soft sound of the children breathing
as they sleep,
They are the quiet and peaceful
whispers of the night.

Suddenly, I can hear the sound of children fighting
as they hustle off to school.
The screams of marital distress,
And the agonizing fight to hold on.
The sounds in my mind break through the
whispers of the night.

I lie awake wondering why I hear these sounds.
The constant cries from deep inside me,
Crying over the loss of a loved one.
Finally, I realize that I have created these sounds.
These too, have become my own
Whispers Of The Night.

Jeannie Lewis

Why

I can't open my eyes.
I can't see through the darkness.
I scream from the depths of my soul.
I lie helpless waiting for the moment I die.
I scratch for an opening, but all I feel is
the soft, moist earth fall through my fingers.
I gasp for air, my lungs are filling with
nothingness.
I search for a answer why am I having to go
through this unspeakable torment.
I know now my time has come.

I feel nothing.
I hear nothing.
I am no longer.
I am dead.
I am dead.
Oh Dear God why am I dead?

Esperanza Griego

Why?

As I look gently down into my mother's eyes
I can't stand the thought she's going to die

Why must her life end this way?
If only we would have known yesterday

She lies so peaceful in her hospital bed
It's as though she were already dead

If only she can hang on a couple more days
Her only baby grandson is on the way

I begin to cry as I hold her cold, shaking hand
She looks up at me and says I will always be her little man

I feel so much hate knowing there's nothing I can do, except
pray she feels no pain
She's the one who held my hand through life and showed me
there was so much to gain

She was always there to pick me up when I tripped in life and fell
Suddenly she clinches my hand as the life-support machine rings a bell

The doctor looked over at me and said there's nothing more he could do
He said I should be glad she lived more than a full life;
She was eighty-two

Jeff Berry

MmEe

As I grow older, and times change,
I come to realize, my soul's been stained.

I think of me, and the life I've had,
I seem to take comfort, in being sad.

The long walks, under autumn trees,
Just to bring back the dusty old memories.

The times I've laughed, the times I've cried,
The times I've loved, from deep inside.

Whatever happens, I know it's alright.
I've been here to long, to give up this fight.

I've been through the pleasure, I've tasted the pain,
I've cried in the darkness, I've laughed in the rain.

It's all part of life, such a wondrous experience,
There's no way in heaven nor hell,
I could bring myself to end this.

Jeremy Nunnelley

Untitled

Our world is changing - more so the people
I cry to all with listening ears
Yellow influence is here - the east moved in
Not only physically but mentally - the lost

Show an object on say words - triggers
The response is of low quality and animal-like
Weren't we - the Americans - highly respected
Jealousy killed feelings. All we did was help.

Does the above frighten you!
Need not be afraid - call on our Lord JESUS!
He knows their moves - but your turn to
    fight and defeat satan.
In Jesus name I rebuke you - misled demons.

What a good feeling exhibiting power against evil.
Is there any question who's side we're on
Guaranteed infinity in Heaven. Praise Jesus!
See you all (the intelligent in Gospel) at
the feast with God, the Father.

Armella Frankowski

"Talisman"

Under the covers when I was a child,
    I curled protected from fears gone wild.
From ghoulies and ghosties that bumped in the night,
    The shadowy hosts that shied from the light,
And the softly - woven, miraculous strands,
    Of the bedclothes clutched in my tiny hands.

Did you as a child worry the same?
    A player caught in the 'Jabberwock' game?
Knowing not that the deepest fears
    Would come to you in your later years.
Brought not by some figment overgrown,
    But the true desperation of lying alone.

If you share my fears, then share my side,
    On the loom of my bed. Where will betide,
The magical weaving, the soft and warm.
    The love - knot plaited to banish harm.
Then our cares arrested, our worries gone,
    Under the covers we'll lie as one.

David A. Egan

The Power Of Innocence

Love was hiding in my heart
I did not know it was there
Until the small one came in her innocence
And love flowed from my heart like the waves of the sea.
Flowed out and like the tide came back to me.
She could not know
That she had opened the flood gates
That just holding her in my arms
swelled the feelings of love.
She gave so much to me
Her smile, her shining eyes all said
"I love you."
Although she was much too young at "18 months" to know
The Power of Innocence.

Edna Strahm

"Ana Marie"

"When life was young and simple,
I didn't know my fate;
still I garnered up the courage
To lift this heavy weight!

Challenges were my only force,
All's I needed was to stay the course.
So I learned about my failures
and the price I had to pay.
Knowing that my life would never
Quite be the same!

Still I dreamed about tomorrows
and the course corrections that needed to be.
Now I'm ready to live a life,
built around my lady, named Ana Marie!"

Daniel Sonners

Safety Within The Fog

A dense fog encompasses me
    I don't know where I am.
        Ghostly forms in human shape
            are just beyond my reach.

A fleeting thought has joined them.
    What could it have been?
        It doesn't really matter,
            its pain would be too much to bear.

It's peaceful here within the fog.
    The world held safely at bay.
        If only they could understand,
            This is what I need.

I wasn't meant for reality,
    It's much too harsh for me.
        Best to stay within my fog.
            Nothing can touch me here.

Carolyn R. Fricke

What Color Do You Favor?

What color do you favor Lord, the black, the white, the red?
I don't understand the question my son, for it doesn't really matter
once the body is dead.

For in the spirit there is no difference, I told you from the
start. I care not about skin color, but what is in your heart.

So, be released from all your prejudice and turn your eyes
to me. Get rid of all your bias and see what I can see.

So, who do I favor you ask, well that's very plain to see, I favor
all my children, that truly favor me.

Conrad Reiber

What Dreamers Dream

I'm a dreamer of many things
I dream of birds and the songs they sing,
I dream of flowers in all their glory
And many books with all their stories.

I dream of marriage, and a wedding gown
Of satin and lace, and many people around.
I dream of marches and bells and chimes
And majestic mountains for us all to climb.

I dream of ships and a moonlit night
Where cares are forgotten in one moment of life
Some dreams are made of a walk in the sand,
On the beautiful beaches of this wonderful land.

I dream of oceans and lakes and seas
Of children's laughter and the hum of bees,
My dreams are many, my memories few
If it weren't for dreams, what would we do?

Alexia Childers

Bugsy, The Bug

I'm Bugsy the bug, I live in the tree, I'm Bugsy the bug.
I eat peas and I say please and thank you, I'm Bugsy the bug.
I like to dig in the sand, I'm Bugsy the bug.
I drink lots of bug juice, I'm Bugsy the bug.

When I wake up I brush my teeth, I'm Bugsy the bug.
I have a berry or 2, I'm Bugsy the bug.
"One two buckle my shoe" I sing as I go along, I'm Bugsy the bug.

Then I get ready for bed, I'm Bugsy the bug.
I clean my teeth and get undressed, I'm Bugsy the bug.
Then I get into bed and go to sleep, I'm Bugsy the bug.
GOODNIGHT!

Gregory Brown

No Place Like Thee

I walked along the path of life, it seems too long for me.
I fall, I fail, life's great tests on me.
I hope, I pray, that one day you and I will go away
to a place of wonder and joy.

But, I know there is no place like thee.
I wish there was, for you and me.
Oh joy and glee, for you and me,
We've died and went to a place like thee?
Of trees, and bees, and beautiful seas.

But, I miss the ones below.
I miss them all so very much.
I'm right again, there is no place like thee!

Joshua S. Morgan

The Rusted Knight (Iambic Pentameter)

I am a knight who has rusted his gear.
I feel oxide sting down into my bones.
Rain did not eat the plate, it was my tears.
Am I condemned to walk this road alone?

The flame of love did not set spark in me.
My pain increased as the minutes elapsed.
My soul would cry out with a firm loud plea,
"What good am I, the man who is outcast?"

Water which came from my swollen red eyes
made the armor of my monarch brittle.
Although I tried to keep feelings disguised,
in vain it was too late and too little.

Oh Lord, when will I have someone to hold
who shall transform my heart from rust to gold?

Brian C. Mertz

I Fell In Love

I fell in love with this man, who didn't love me.
I fell in love with this man, who couldn't see,
  All the pain, all the hurt, all he put me through.
I fell in love with this man, but what could I do?
I fell in love with this man, could this have been God's plan?

I fell on my knees and prayed to the Lord that he'd love me the same.
But I knew in my heart to this man it was all a game.

I fell in this place,
I fell in disgrace.
I fell for this man, I loved him so much.
I fell for this man, with every shivering touch.

I fell in this place,
I fell in disgrace.
  I didn't want to see,
  That he could lie to me.
Blinded with love
What could I have been thinking of?
I fell in love.

Christine Ryell

I Desired to Create

I desired to create for you a vision;
I felt the urge to paint a picture
  in your heart of our love;
I would have used all the colours of this world,
  and then the colours from the next.

How do I reach out and extract all the bits
  of life and bring them together;
Is it a dream I shall never see fulfilled;
Are they to remain a fingertip away-on hold-
  waiting;
Can I not secure for you a caption of all
  there is?

Just when I think I'm touching it,
  just when I sense a closeness as I reach
  farther than the last time…it whisks away…
  like a vapor…bouncing from me as quickly
    as when I realized I loved you…
Free…..there, but not ready to be handled….

Free…..like we.

Dolly Mobley

My Daddy, My Father, My Friend

My daddy, my father, my friend
I have met no one who could compare
Whatever problems I faced, or avenues I travelled
For me he was always there

From birth to age ten he was my daddy
Playful, but stern that was the key
Learning to him was essential
his motto "be all you can be"

From ten to twenty he was my father
Strong, but to him you could always go
Debating, this era was good for that
But respect, yes, this I had to show

Well twenty to thirty were great years
We both learned to be a friend
We'd laugh, talk, share tears
Without him I could not have been

And now at 36 I've come to a crossroad
Our time together has come to an end
I will now travel this road alone
Without my daddy, my father, my friend.

Faye E. Clark

Untitled

As I sit to write my memories
I find to my dismay
my creative juices clogged
by little boys at play.
With each "POW" and "ZAP" and hearty "WHOA"
I bless the man who invented Nintendo.
The mute button is useless
my last nerve is a wreck
for little boys you see
come with their own sound effects.

Cyndia Manor

No Matter What

With an angel's touch and my very own plea,
I found a new love past the blackness which was once imprisoning me.

Darkness, like sadness, once was withering my dreams.
Destroying all hope and killing all that I thought, killing all which
  was real. Love I did not have for it was captured in the wall of
  nothingness; kept there by my fear of rejection never to be seen
  truly only to be seen by eyes of pure insanity. Like all other
  things you know there is a way, but when this darkness falls upon
  you it creates an indescribable haze.

One way exists and one way is known. To lift the walls of darkness
is to be blessed by an angel and sent a love of your own. For not
even the loneliest darkness can despair one's mind when the heart is
beating, when the heart is pounding, when the heart calls so true.
Love was bound to find me even within the pits of hell; this I
always prayed, this I always knew.

Jason Todd Crimmel

Didn't He Know?

Today, we put my father to rest.
I gazed around the open grave at the faces of my family.

I remember my anger at my father;
Anger..when he didn't say something to help my brothers…

Didn't he know?

Anger…when he should have done more for my sisters…

Didn't he know?

And now I look at my children,
And now I recall the hurt in their eyes
When I failed their needs and expectations.
Today I realize…

I Don't Know!

Nothing left to say to a carpenter
Who tried his best for his family, except
Farewell my Reluctant Hero.

Henry J. White

Purple Violet

When I see a purple violet
I go back in time
To my first love, my first kiss
So warm and oh so sweet
Seems like only yesterday on a lonely country road
Walking home from church one day
The first of many kisses, heartbeats misunderstood
I was fourteen years old and that was long ago
Pressing hard against me, holding oh so tight
I didn't know what was happening
It seemed to be so right
Now when I see a purple violet, I go back to sixty years ago
I think about the kisses, the sweetest that I would ever know.

Flora Griffin

Mamma, Mamma, Mamma

She's called Mother, Ma, and Mom, and
I guess that's where we all come from.

She feeds our bellies, wipes our tears,
and gets us through our growing years.

She bides her time through hopes, and
fears and watches us grow through the years.

She sets our goals but takes her time, and hopes
we know — what she left behind.
A time for fun, a time for thee, and hope we grow
just like a tree— bearing fruit just like she,
so someone else can be like she.

Thank you Momma for what you be. I'll try to be
better than just a tree.

Bill Paquet

Once A Kid

When I was just a little tot,
I had such carefree fun;
In years that passed, I ne'er forgot,
The many things I'd done.

The broom-stick horse and grape-vine swings,
Are mem'ries, so long past;
But now they seem such cherished things,
As years go by so fast.

The swimming hole, the big oak tree,
Where tripped many a lad;
We all jumped in, at the count of three,
And so much sport was had.

The homeward trek, the cookie jar,
Upon that well-known shelf;
No treasure at a king's bazaar;
Could so well have pleased myself.

Fame and fortune may come to me,
And if they ever did;
I'd thank the Lord on bended knee,
That I was once a kid.

M. C. Nichols

"My Sister"

When you were just a baby, I held you in my arms,
I gave you all my love,
And you gave me all your charms.

Then you started growing up,
And went your separate way,
but I knew that you would
Soon be back, I'd sit and count the days.

And sure enough it happened,
your husband passed away;
I guided you and comforted you in oh so many ways.

I could never treat you the way you're treating me, is there
Something in your broken heart that I just cannot see?

I tried to give you everything, an older sister should,
Love, and knowledge, understanding, all the things I could.

You wouldn't think to be unkind or rude in any way, or hurt or
belittle any friend, but with me it's a-okay.

I let you do this all to me
because I loved you so,
But it will never happen again
Just thought I'd let you know.

Deborah K. Virgo

Alone Without Him

I'm alone, unwanted, unloved.
I have dreams of you and me
And what it would be.
But then someone came along
And stole my heart away from yours.
She may have been better.
She may have been one out of a million
And you thought you got the woman of your dreams.
While I was a broken heart filled
With the vision of our future to be,
I thought you told me "You are the one
For me and always will be."
But you lied, then I cried.
I still have memories of us together,
And I think - what happened to
The love we had, oh, how I thought it was strong.
But you found her and I'm alone once again.
I'll make do, I'm sure,
But it won't be the same as you and me.
The way it used to be.

Erica Hubble

Untitled

Do not abandon me from your heart
    I have fallen short,
I feel the pain in your eyes but it cannot
compare with that in my heart.

For when I do not have your confidence and trust
    I cannot do anything of my own accord
I need to feel your hand on my shoulder
pushing me ever forward

Your trust is like the sunlight
    that makes me grow taller and taller
at each new day

Would you still pick me as your rose?

I want to be your rose
    to bring you pride, love, and joy
But all of these I can only do when I
receive your confidence and trust.

Jennifer Long

Depression

I have no happy songs to sing.
I have no merry bells to ring.
Life goes on in endless sorrows.
Sad yesterdays become tomorrows.
Hopes and dreams, long torn and shattered,
Until it seems that nothing matters,
Once youth could fight;
But now that age has taken o'er,
The fight is gone, the battle lost,
And I've surrendered to the gloom.

Grace T. Turner

"Thanks To You"

*Dedicated to my pastors at Shield of Faith Church,
Joe & Yvonne Soliz*
When Someone like you, very thoughtful and kind...
Doing nice things so often with others, in mind...
It isn't surprising, it seems only right...
To wish that your days, are happy and bright....
Thanks for being understanding, thanks for being sweet...
Thanks for making every joy more precious and complete....
Thanks for the friendship you've given me...
Thanks for the days you've brightened too...
Thanks for being wonderful, thanks for being you...

Emily N. Garcia

The Phoenix

I have seen things most humans can only imagine
I have seen inside men's souls
I have seen countless millions die
I am the phoenix.

I have lived for eons beyond count
Inside men's minds and hearts
I have survived the generations without aging, without death
I am the phoenix.

You cannot see me
You cannot hear me
You are not even sure I exist
I do, I am
I exist to chronicle the lives of mortal man, of children, of beasts

As I write this, one thought prevails
Live your lives
Live them with joy and passion
Live them with pain and sorrow
Only through suffering can one achieve happiness
I know. I am the phoenix
and I have lived forever

Jason Makela

For Earth Day

As I make my earthly rounds,
I hear so many different sounds.
Those including birds singing up so high,
Along with pollution escaping from the car that just drove by.
The dandelions are yellow as they peek from earth's floor,
And up in the sky I see magpies flawlessly soar.
The trees are all becoming green,
Just one of the many signs of forthcoming spring.
I see the rocks lying on the ground-flat,
In front of my face yet another sign, the gnat.
The signs all say please don't pollute our lands,
With paper, glass, trash and aluminum cans.
The mountains are bright and blue with snow,
The mouse runs into the weeds on the ground so low.
Cars sit parked with windows rolled down,
So it's cool for them when they drive around polluting our town.
This is the day when everyone should realize,
If we don't stop this pollution, our earth dies.
I watch the clouds slowly drift,
Don't people realize, this earth is God's gift.

Carolee Jo Robbins

As I Saw The River

As I saw the river
I heard an angel sing
A painless time was coming, a new day he would bring

As I saw the river
I heard laughter all around.
The joy of happiness would now be found.

As I saw the River
These were no more drugs or gangs.
The war was finally over, happiness covered the land.

As I saw the river
All people had formed hands.
We would all rejoice and sing once again.

As I saw the river
We would hunger no more
Our bellies filled with love we would share forever more.

As I saw the river
Judgement was sure to come.
Let us praise him our soul he has won.

Jennifer Jones

"A Rainbow's End"

Look over the rainbow and find your true being
 I hope that the Lord will forever keep seeing

The love you can give and the wishes you hope for
 Which make life worth living for now and evermore

People are special, unique, unafraid
 Knowing the Lord and this day He hath made

He'll always be our maker, creator, and friend
 A hand for security and a shoulder He'll lend

We wonder just what God has planned for our lives
 In spite of our letdowns, detours, and dives

A reward has been offered to all who obey
 Let God guide you, support you, and show you the way

You can reach it and make it your goal
 For Heaven is the place that cleanses the soul

Be wise and have courage, be the best you can be...
 A gift to the world, and for all eternity...

Beverly Withee

I Love You!

Do you feel like I do?
I hope this isn't, "too-good-to-be-true."
Without you I'm blue.
My heart aches when you're not near.
I feel lonely and scared.
You consume my every thought;
can we handle what we've got?
Wanting this so much but still, uncertain.
Tell me right from the heart.
It's what I've wanted from the start.
I've told you how I feel,
Are you for real?
With every beat of my heart I'm praying it's so.
I'm so comfortable around you, it's like we met long ago.
Please tell me this won't end!
I want you to be my eternal friend,
my lover,
forever.
I love you!

Cynthia Friend

On Graduation

The end has come and our year is through,
I just wanted to say how much I care about you.

Our friendship has lasted through the laughter and the tears,
Through the best and the worst of all the years.

You gave me support and your advice was the best,
But most of all, you accepted me... Unlike the rest.

Now we're adults and have a new life to start,
The roads are now separate, and we must part.

I know I will never find a friend like you,
Someone who cares as much as you do.

If you ever need me for anything at all,
Just reach out your hand and give me a call.

Just as you were for me, I'll always be there,
When you need a smile, a hug, or someone to care.

And now, as I say my final goodbyes,
I cannot help the tears that fill up my eyes.

Thank you, my friend, for the memories we've shared,
Your friendship, your heart, and for showing you cared.

I wish you the best in everything you do,
And never forget that I'll always love you.

Christine Misukewicz

As You Wear Your Wedding Band

Love is something splendor, love is something grand.
I hope this you remember, as you wear your wedding band.
Love is when you cherish each other at all times.
That's the love my dearest, that you both have combined.

Love is something treasured, may your treasures overflow,
Where it never can be measured, and that love will always grow.
Love is something golden, yet a gold you cannot buy.
That's the love you're holdin', may you hold it till you die.

Yes, love is something splendor, love is something grand.
True love cannot be measured, true love will always stand.
Two hearts that cling together, always hand in hand.
I know this you'll remember, as you wear your wedding band.

Helen McHugh

The Love I Knew Not Of

With broken heart I searched the sea of life.
I knew not what it was I longed to find.
The trek is more than just an awful strife;
For when the search is done, I will not mind.

So many days my heart was in unrest.
My eyes were blind and would not let me see,
When once this girl had been a friend of best,
She then became the one to set me free.

To end this striving time of solace,
She brought into this ugly world, my friend,
Much strength, and love, and most tranquillity,
So who's to say, some time a knee might bend.

My time with her, I hope infinite days.
For I adore her in so many ways.

Charles Eric Kingsley

Body Machine

After living in this body for many years
I know and I hope it understands
How I appreciate all it has given
In response to my crazy demands.

I've tried smoking, alcohol, thank God, not drugs
And it's always my goal to avoid overeating.
Suggest physical abuse and my body laughs.
About eating, I've been caught cheating.

Not that I'm so different from anyone else
Switched to both cholesterol - and fat-free
I'm even exercising more than I have
As I ask it to re-assess its love for me.

In my remaining years, I'm trying something new
I've pledged to build it up and in fact,
I'm treating it with ever more loving care
To keep it happy and from giving me a cardiac.

Alfred L. Ault

True Love Is Found Only In God

Love is not found in all the wealth,
But true love is found, only in God.
Some think it is in money or health,
But true love is found, only in God.

Love is not found in the things of this world,
But true love is found, only in God.
Love goes around, like wind in a whirl,
But true love is found, only in God.

So where do you turn, when looking for love?
True love is found, only in God.
Don't look left, don't right, just look above,
For true love is found, only in God.

Marion Baird

Born For Nothing

I awaken,.......my eyes open,.......I see Blackness
I close my eyes,...I see Blackness
I open my eyes, still I see Blackness
I CANT MOVE!!!!!!!!!!!!!! I CANT BREATH!!!!!!!!!!!!!!
SNAP!!! Slowly........CREEEEEEEK
SUNLIGHT!!! I CANT SEE!!! HURT!!! Tears flow from the anguish
My skin begins to tingle with warmth
Suddenly a gasp escapes my lips
I slowly start to move
I wonder who is my savior
Who has put the Life back into my Body.......
Spirit into my soul
I achingly stand and look over my shoulder
I smile and say,..."Hello Blackness".......
Realizing that I am still all alone...

Eric D. Ferguson

Whatever Will Be...

Don't ask me questions,
I can't be heard.
I feel no anger, only absurd.
This tunnel is cold, deep, and wide.
But my fate will capture me no matter where I hide.
They come and I don't know who they are,
I just feel their affects from a far.
My life is set up in a strange way.
I wish I knew what they were going to say
Sometimes they stab deep with a knife,
but no matter what I do, these soldiers
called "fate," control my life.
So bring on the good!
Bring on the bad!
Fate has brought me the best I've ever had!

Billy Clark

Whatever Will Be...

Don't ask me questions,
I can't be heard.
I feel no anger, only absurd.
This tunnel is cold, deep, and wide.
But my fate will capture me no matter where I hide.
They come and I don't know who they are,
I just feel their affects from a far.
My life is set up in a strange way.
I wish I knew what they were going to say
Sometimes they stab deep with a knife,
but no matter what I do, these soldiers
called "fate," control my life.
So bring on the good!
Bring on the bad!
Fate has brought me the best I've ever had!

Billy Clark

Lord

Lord, I know myself to be a stranger from you.
But just direct me Lord Jesus.
Lord, continue ——-
To guide my feet down the right path.
Strengthen my resolve so that I might last.
Keep me strong and faithful until thy coming.
Sharpen, hone me Lord for the battle that's coming.
Lord, write my name in a place setting at your table.
Lord, ————-
Point me out thy bidding to do.
I'll do anything in honor of you.
Love You Lord Jesus,
I sacrifice myself my soul to you.
Amen.

Katherine L. Bond

A Perfect Rose

What is true love?
True love is a perfect red rose
Whose petals feel like silk.
The fragrance of this rose
Stimulates the senses to
Ecstasies beyond one's imagination.
And how did you treat this rose?
By taking its life away and
Hiding it from the world.
Why?
A perfect rose should be shared.
Come and share
My perfect red rose with me.

Jennifer Ann Esposito

Untitled

The sky was full of rainbow
candy
lips of mine
bled-red
deep within your
fingers
unfriendly

What have you done!

All the while
you've beguiled me
haven't you?
How do you survive with yourself?
The burden.

Talk of the future bright talk
of love whisper
your shrewdness
straining
cleverly
outward and retaining
persuasion

Charles J. Thomes

Stephen

Clutching his most prized possession
a "baby barrel"
Presided by green garbed men in a room
so sterile
Trusting the strangers, toweled and the
pale locks shorn
One last kiss, a hug, an unwept tear for
the firstborn
The small toy is taken and given to his
mother
To be treasured forever but not for his
brother
Injections to relax so the fear is no
more
Down the hall he goes a final passage
through the door.

Arlene Lane

Life

Sunlight creeps across the lawn,
A bright new day is dawning.
And creeping across the grass;
Not a babe anymore.
The enthusiasm of youth shines;
Reaching for more space.
The sunlight fades, and new life begins.

Elizabeth D. Malone

Somewhere

Somewhere in the distance
A baby cries from hunger or hurt
In its crib where it lies

Somewhere in the world
An old man dies
The lord has taken him
From where he lies

Somewhere out there
A young girl finds
That the life she feared
Is really sublime

Somewhere beyond reach
Is goodness and cheer
While here in this room
Is only sadness and tears—

Jim Brogan

The Lone Tulip

A flower bloomed across the fence
A beautiful garden to enhance
There many years, red, yellow and gold
Amongst many flowers, years untold.

Cared for, loved, room to grow
As children walked too and fro
Between each row, carefully
Need room to grow.

Then soon we know no care at all
No one climbed over the stone wall
To see us standing tall, colors bright,
Weed the grass, let in sunlight.

In a short while, few flowers left
To brighten the corner beyond the fence
By wind or bird, I was carried along
Found a nook on a neighbors lawn

Dug in my roots, grew strong and tall
And come Spring blossomed for all
One yellow tulip mixed with the weeds
Amongst the peonies and Iris did seed.

Eleta S. Scribner

An Old Pine Tree

From my window I can see
A big old pine tree
Standing so majestically
Shining in the sun so lovely
All covered with diamonds
It is so beautiful to me
Rain drops on the old pine tree
Yes, it's very clear to me
That only God can make a
Tree.

Carrie White

Something More

A quick look...
a glance
Is this something more...
a romance?

Was that a smile...
aimed at me?
No it couldn't or...
could it be?

Cheryl McGrory

"On The Horizon"

I look to the horizon and I behold
a blaze of light;

The threshold of a promise - rising,
beckoning and growing luminously
bright;

I am filled with hope and a warmth
not easily explained;

I am free - free to explore and to
journey through the night, full in
the knowledge that with serene
certainty I am not alone and I am
unrestrained,

Once, always, and forevermore to
envision that wondrous light,
and with compassion all my
questions are answered - all
doubts contained.

Janet Harrison

The Journey

The sun finds an ice crystal,
A child conceived.
As the droplet released,
The child will breathe.

Off on its journey,
To earth it will go.
As the child awakens,
It's now time to grow.

The drop cascades downward,
It knows not its fate.
The child finds curiosity.
Endures emotions, "Love" "Hate"

The drop might find problems,
Through the wind and the rain.
The child could encounter words,
Such as "Suffering" and "Pain"

As the journey is ended,
The drop gives new birth.
When the child is over,
It's simply a drop in the earth.

Jason W. Schwab

Valentine's Day

Valentine's Day,
A day for fun,
Little money you must pay,
For yellow little candies like the sun.
"Please don't tell a lie,"
Cupid says when he sees you,
"because your love shall die,"
"I know I can get you too."
So much to live for,
So little time to use,
Don't step out that door,
For you may lose.
Valentine's Day,
This day was neat,
Little money I had to pay,
To buy yellow candies for my mother,
Who's SWEET!

Amber Glise

A Rosebud

With the passing of time
A delicate rosebud blooms
Releasing the essence of its
Fragrance into the air, and all
Around it
Maturing into a beautiful flower
With petals reaching up to greet
The sunlight
Captivating the attention of all
That see it
With tantalizing aroma that caresses
The senses
But when its twilight time has come
And its life span has ended
Then the once proud rosebud succumbs
To the penalty of time...
Gives its final bow, then reluctantly
Returns to the dust from which it came...

Barbara F. Spencer

Phantasm

The sloops of life lie awaiting
A distant beck and call.
One by one they drift away
To find the "after-all."

Harold L. Sampson

A Child's Plea

Today I have a mission
A dream I seek to find
Please teach me how to change things
With the power of my mind

Too often violence is the answer
A gun or knife settles the score
I want to be able to live till I'm old
And profit from what life has in store

I want you to show me, to teach me
That there is indeed another solution
To resolve my anger and frustrations
And bring some closure to my confusion

Instill in me a sense of values
Help me to build my self esteem
Challenge me and encourage me
Assist me in finding my dream

Today I am a child
But tomorrow I will be grown
Help me to learn what I reap tomorrow
Is today what I have sown

Armaria J. Fleming

A Friend

A friend is there through thick and thin
A friend is there until the end
you are my friend
A friend cares when all is good
A friend cares when times are tough
you are my friend
A friend stands with you
A friend trusts you through it all
you are my friend
A friend lends a laugh
A friend hears your tears
you are my friend
A friendship will last a lifetime
A friendship is you
you are my friend

Eileen McMenamin

Untitled

Life is but a pleating moment
a gesture full of woe.
If only we could understand
the time that goes so slow.

David A. Adams

The Bible

May its words of Wisdom, Truth and Life
  A guiding light to your pathway be,
May you each day hear Jesus say,
  "Take up your cross and follow me."
For all your needs you're sure to find
  Within the pages of this book,
An answer, prayer and peace of mind
  And all you need to do is look.
His peace is there, His guidance, too,
  Enough to lead you each day through,
So read His Word with an open mind,
  And let the Holy Spirit through,
If you just follow in His path,
  Rewards on high you will accrue,
So when you leave this world below
  A mansion'll be ready in Heaven for you.

Jerri Stayer

Untitled

What do you see in a child,
A leaf, a cloud or a flower

What do you hear in the wind
What do you see in a passing hour

Do you even take the time
To think about what these are

Are you such a hurry
Because you want to go far

Where do you want to go
What do you hope to find

What is your ultimate goal
Try letting it be peace of mind

Charlene Turnbow

When The Sun Doesn't Shine

When the sun doesn't shine,
  a part of my life goes unfulfilled.
Don't try to open your eyes.
We are all blind,
  when the sun doesn't shine.

When the sun doesn't shine
  it always feeds my fears.
Why bother speaking when you never hear?
Don't try to help me conquer those fears,
  there the source of your power.
So tell me — how do you like me now?

When the sun doesn't shine,
  the darkness expands.
Takes some time for the things
  you don't understand.
Darkness provides light for the
  mirage you don't see.
Keep looking and maybe you'll finally see.
And then you can tell me,
  how do you like me now?

Daryl J. Mulvaney

People Of The Streets

So many, who are so skinny
a lot of crimes, so little food lines
the worry and weak.
What do they seek?
Drugs or money
this isn't funny!
They have fears,
but show no tears;
so much talk never ears,
listen to their cries
how I wonder why.
Why is it so bad?
I feel so sad.
What do they feel?
Are their lives for real?
Why should I care?
When no help is dare
never show yourself weak,
to the people of the streets.

April Naval

"Rose Is In The Attic"

Rose is in the attic,
A lovely fragile flower,
A flower wilting daily,
By some unknown voodoo power!

Her petals are so brittle,
But fragrance still emits,
She is waiting to be crumbled,
To tiny little bits!

Rose is in the attic,
So far up in the sky,
Away from other people,
Where she can pray and cry!

Fragile flowers crushed in bits,
Become sweet potpourri,
Rose is in the attic,
And potpourri she'll be!

Rose is in the attic,
Winds of time blow through her hair,
Hair tied with pretty ribbons,
Her sweet aroma fills the air!

Betty Jean Dingess

"Love"

Love is a song,
A moment of knowing.
A tower of wind,
In the blue sky growing.

A mist on the sea,
A white bird flying.
A laugh and a dream,
And too much crying.

Anna Taylor Second

The Wall

A small child's hand touches a name
A mother's eyes reflect the pain
A father's loss anyone can see
the price our youth pay to be free

Warriors drop by with tears in their eyes
So many come to say their good-byes
While they sleep they are never alone
So much power etched in a stone
... to heal

Don Hoffman

Nothing Compares

Nothing compares to a mother's love.
A mother's love is one of a kind and
should not be taken for granted.
It is more beautiful than diamonds.
It is more costly than gold.
A mother always thinks of you first
for you are part of her.
Never can a day go by without
a mother's warm love.
A mother's love cannot be destroyed
and will stay forever untouched.

Elise Foley

Wedding Tapestry

A ring combines two lives.
A pact is made by the stones inlaid.
Braids of golden joy entwine
to weave a delicate pattern
of sojourns ended
and a partnership blended.
A symbol, an amulet,
an heirloom, a key.
The door opens to a magic kingdom
reigned over by she and he.
Two complete circles
link into one.
A companionship strong...
creates a melodic song.
A blessing from above...
whispers "time is on their side"...
...and time strengthens love.

Gina Osher

Moon Watch

The Moon,
A penciled breve
Above the Evening Star
Drawn on the blue-black paper
Of the night,
Bends close
With his companion light.

I feel a quiet joy,
And almost wave-
Acknowledging
Their watchful care-
Reminded, as I am,
How Mothers dim the lamps,
But do not sleep
Until the latest child
Is home.

Jean Spangler Sweetapple

Dreams

Childlike fantasies,
An inner-state of mind;
Visions of unreality,
That supersedes all time.

Moments held not lost,
Loving thoughts untold;
Wishes of all to come,
Images to unfold.

Think of what you may,
Close your eyes to see;
Follow where you want,
Dare to dream to be.

Janett Salazar

Happiness Found

I found a secret place,
A place for you and me.
But if I go by myself,
I know that it's all right.

I'd rather you be with me
At this certain place.
It is so much better
When we are there together.

I know I have no reason
For me to be ashamed.
I can go alone.
I realize that now.

But I will always
Want you there.
Come travel with me
To my secret place.

Cathy Stump

An Ocean Refuge

The power of the Sea
A place where your mind can run free
It has a soul
Full of emotion
Expression in many ways

They tend to reflect yours
When it is like glass
It becomes a mirror
For when you smile at it
It will smile back,
When it is rough
Your face will wrinkle.

It knows you need comfort
A place to heal your heart
Where you can cry, and it will cry back
Share with it love, and it will love you
Show her respect, and she will too
Comfort its soul
And you will feel
The Power Of The Sea.

Darshan D. D. Murphy

The Greatest Gift

Man has said that I would never see
A poem as lovely as a tree
Yet I have seen a more precious sight
A gift that brought me great delight

What is this gift that I behold
More beautiful than gems or gold
Which God created and loaned to me
To bring to full maturity

Unmatched, unequally bearing love
For those, downtrodden by greed and gore
Shall look to it to teach how
To bring comfort to humanity
What is this gift that God has made
And trusted to me for a brief heart beat
To love, to guide, to mold until
It hears a call, an urge to go
To do God's work and not rebel
Nor listen to the brazen knell of worldly
fame
A helpless babe, both dear and sweet
A token of eternity.

Genevie C. Brandon

Untitled

"I forgot why I was angry,
    A rainbow
        Just painted the sky!"
    Barbara Hogan

Colorless Beauty

Colorless beauty
A raindrops falls
Wet
Cool and daring
Green grass
Swaying in time
The wind breathless ecstasy
Soaring as a bird
Freedom
Visions, thoughts
Reasoning
Toes touching sand -
Imprints
Love again imprints
Forever
Burning soul
Colorless beauty
Teardrops fall wet
Hot
Frightened

Cathy Obenauf

My Home Beside The River

A crystal blue green butterfly.
A red hawk up above
a fluffy furry kitty cat
climbs on your lap for love.
The yelling of the heron
a rainbow up above
a toad beneath a dew wet leaf.
The cooing of the dove.
a spring breeze in the willow.
A hustling bumblebee
a colt across green meadow
Jumps and runs with glee.
There are blossoms on the fruit trees
as far as I can see.
Grandma's in her rocker
with baby on her knee.
A blue bird in the rose bush
a red bird in the pine
This treasured world is beautiful
and all of this is mine.

Barb Moyer

Romeo's Exceeding

Across the fluffy sky
Across the ravishing sea
I see a life with you and me
Stick a knife in my leg
Then stick it in my tongue
Give me all of your love
Or to me you should give none
For second fiddle will I not play
For I was always first chair in my day.
So be my baby be my gal.
Be my shetland to grace, my coral.
For the man you thought was
extinct.
Is under our pearls don't you think.

Bobby McNair

From The Hearts Of Love!

Love is like
A rose blooming
in the air, it lets
you know that
Someone cares.
Love brings laughter from
the bottom of your heart,
lets you know
your love will
never depart. Love
brings romance
all through the night,
makes you understand
why everything you
did came to light.
That's why roses are red
violets are blue
the love I have for you is so real
and true, that's how
long I will always love you!

Alma Lenee Smith

Silence

In the deep warmth of the night,
A shot rings out and there's a fight,
I cover my head to keep the noise out,
There's a scream and then a shout,
I feel the fear go up my spine,
And soon police cars race behind,
I see a man on the ground,
And there is blood all around,
And by his side I see the gun,
From which the fatal shot had rung.

Eden Simpson

Untitled

The night is pouring
A silver silence
Over the quietly breathing land.

Out of the stillness
I can hear a whip-poor-will's call -
A lonely sound, seeking what?

A distant, plaintive note replies
Across the moon-mysterious valley,
Sharply clear in the night,
Yet seeming a shadow of tone
Torn from the deeper shadows
Cast upon the ground.

Elizabeth C. Stradtman

The Last Walk

As they walked alone
A small tear ran down her cheek.
Both of them with a broken heart,
Wishing they did not have to part.

Year after year their love had grown.
A few more steps was all they had.
Anyone could tell,
Their expressions were sad.

Then it came that time.
The trailer pulled up,
A last goodbye.
There was not a word.
then a last whinny was heard.

Amanda Lewis

The Black Eagle

A soldier lives,
    A soldier dies.
For what he might
    He strives for right.
Given his race
    He has to Fight;
For Justice,
    And Principle
He stands upright.
    To those who will,
And those who might,
    Take this man
His spirit will light.
    If courage be needed,
Reflect on his.
    For in his strength,
There's courage in-deed.

James E. Cullivan

Life Goes On

Like the bud of a Rose
A Soul is Born

The petals open Up,
As life goes on..

Petals they wilt, die and
Slowly fall to the ground...

Your soul fades away...
As your body is placed...
in the ground...

On top of your grave...
Someone
places a Rose

As Life Goes On....

Donna L. Slater

Summer

When summer springs on golden wings
a sunlit serenade she sings.
And as she waves her mystic wand
she bids all nature to respond.
She smiles and myriad colors gleam
reflected in a gurgling stream.
Which pours down canyons craggy walls
that shine like rainbows as it falls.
She speeds o'er meadows, lakes and leas
and makes the fruit blush on the trees.
With glowing rose the twilight hours
creep over summers lovely bowers.
The robins rest in olden nest
and line them well with feathered breast.
Soon the time with hours complete
bids the lovely day retreat.
Soon the brilliant heavens shine
and all the world her charms enshrine.
When all of nature she delights
she basks beneath the starry night.

Fern I. Tuck

Love

Love is a feeling,
A thought,
Something that comes from the heart,
And something that shouldn't be
taken advantage of.

Ashley Ford

Memories

Memories are of a window,
    a window of past.
Good times and bad,
    forever to last.

Clinging onto the happiness,
    and accepting the bad.
Remembrance of the laughter,
    never forgetting the sad.

Memories of the good times
    we always try to hold.
Memories of the sad times,
    our life we try to remold.

Memories of the bad times
    we deal with and set aside.
Memories of all the laughter,
    making our souls pleasantly glide.

Memories of the special times,
    under the moon and sun.
Memories of all the love,
    we shared as one.

Austin Coleman

Eros Flight

From the heart of my treasured lady,
A woman worshipped as golden,
Love and divine elegance pour eternally.
Hers is the purest spirit
I have ever been honored
With experiencing.
My precious queen is possessed
Of such innocence;
Such quiescent, frightening beauty
As angels
Have never known.
To her I would refuse nothing,
For in her
I see my wish for all men and women.
And although I know not
Into what world I have stumbled
That is home to so fantastic and irresistible
a rose,
I pray the Lord that I may remain.

Anthony Beal

Enduring Love

A wall between us
A year behind us
A future before us...
Love hasn't left us
But something has -
Changed us.
"Forever we'll be
Forever you and me,"
We said.
When we're hangin' by the edge,
Slowly losing grip of
What we have,
Don't let go of it
You've got to trust
And let go of your fears.
Don't let them drown you
With foolish tears...
Distance between us
Memories behind us
A journey before us.

Jennifer Coosard

Smiles

Have you ever wondered
About the smiles of the world
That there are different kinds of smiles
Some are straight, crooked or curled

Some smiles are with tears
And some are plain
There are just so many smiles
As many as drops of rain

What if there is a contest about smiles
I would pick the best one
I'd look far and wide
But it seems that there are none

But wait, I saw one smile
When I was doing my chores
I forgot who it was, then I remembered
It was yours.

Andrea Maranon

Resume

Razors pain you,
Acids stain you,
Rivers are deep,
And drugs cause cramp,
Guns aren't lawful,
Gas smells awful,
Nooses give,
You might as well live!

Dorothy Parker

Gypsy River

As night casts its velvet cloak
across an evening sky,
golden sun rays still at play
cling to cliffs on high.

Dark shadows skirt the meadows wide
and whisper to the trees,
upon command, each stately bough
summons the evening breeze.

The river now a silver thread
winds through the canyon floor,
a restless gypsy on its quest
bound to wander forevermore.

Jo Ann Soule'

The Journey

Ready the ship to sail
across the sea of life
Into the great unknown
where mysteries there abide
No turning back from hence
this journey now we make
Into this new awakening
where left behind is strife

Charles K. Santens

Love

If I had one second
After death to spend with you
I'd want to be a drop of rain
That comes with morning dew
And although you would not see me
You would become aware
I'd touch your lips in such a way
You'd know that I was there.

JoAnn Malone

Up Our Way

It's Valentine's day
Again the red hearts
In generous display
Up our way
It's a reign of yum yum
As chocolate virus blossoms
Cherries and forget-me-nots
Up our way

A charm a delight
A beauty and lacy threshold
A sigh a canary on sight
Up our way

The first sign of season
Unfueled with stalking white
with strength of a mile
Castle fiction up our way

Earnest and in earnest
Roses sold over the wire
Voices earnestly to the lass
up our way

Isabelle Hunter

The Pitter, Patter Of The Rain

The pitter patter of the rain
against my window
Sets all my thoughts a dreaming

At one moment I'm in a far
away land, doing the things
I love to do

Then I'm off to a different place
just enjoying the moments of
each new adventure

The clap of thunder and lightning
bring me back to my own
cozy room, which I
love best.
The patter of the rain quiets
my thoughts
And once again, I know I am
home where I long to be.
Dreams are nice, but home is best.

Anne Griffin

Charlieboy

I remember when we got you
all battered, broken and torn,
I knew from the moment I saw you
your heart I could make warm.

What a handsome pooch you were
with big brown eyes you did stare,
watching our every action
wondering if we really did care.

The years did come and
the years did go,
but with each passing year
our love did grow.

You gave us your trust
which was plain to see,
never thinking in the beginning
how great love could be.

Now you are gone Charlieboy
and our hearts full of sorrow,
knowing our love will continue
until there's no more tomorrows.

John C. Riedl

"Losing"

I'm losing all that I have,
All is leaving me,
My friends, my parents,
the people that I love,
Even the people that I hate,
Slowly fade away,
I'm angry for I knew they would,
I knew that they would go,
And never will I see the sun rise,
For night is now my home,
A deadly evil place,
A place where I am loved,
So come to me darkness,
Cold covering the heat of my anger,
But still I flame,
(let me scream).

Eric Ethridge

A Dreamer's Prayer

Only peace existed
All nations lovers
Only love survived
All men brothers.

But, then I awoke
And wept to see
That this was only
A dream to me.

So I made my dream
A prayer instead
And as I knelt
Beside my bed

I asked my God
If this could be
But He just knelt
And prayed with me.

Douglas J. Beirne

The Love Has Faded

As I sit
Alone in the darkness
The love I once knew
Fades
As the light in the distance.
My love has vanished
Gone far away
I fear I shall never
Love again.
I comfort myself
With the thoughts of the love
I once knew,
But this somehow does not change
The emptiness I feel
In my heart.

Julia Wyatt

Suddenly, I Need Someone

I used to be quite contented drifting all
alone with my thoughts & my dreams.
Now as I settle my body to rest, it
feels very different somehow. For right
next to me there is a very empty space
that never seemed to be there before.
Suddenly, the night is lonely as
it never has been.
Suddenly, I love someone very, very much —
And that someone is you.

Jamie L. Morrow

Petals Curve Up

The petals curve up
Along winding road
With words that always say

I'll love you forever
I'll love you for always
I'll never go away

You walk towards that road
You walk down that path
Thinking that love
Was always meant to last

Catherine Thompson

The Teacher

There she was,
Already old,
Standing at the crossroad
blocking my way
With her hard blue eyes.
We were alone-
I just starting out
She finally coming home.

She terrified me in those days
With her demands
Always prodding me
Always making me turn my eyes
Outward on the world
Away from the abyss inside.

Looking back now
I understand her fear.
Late some nights I stand
At that same crossroad
On the chance that one of mine
Should happen by.

Brian W. Edmister

Today

Tomorrow never really comes
Although I wish it would
It always seems to be today
Like it truly should

But todays become yesterdays
They never actually last
Today is a day that when it's done
It's put into your past

So you'll always have tomorrow
But when tomorrow's done
You'll still have your today
So fill it full of fun

Bekah Burns

Absolution

The awakening of spirit
Adrift in the morning
Dew.
The contemplation of ones
Own destiny —
Fated in absolution.
As the turning of key in the mind
Clicks,
The enormity on the other side of its
Threshold astounds the meeker "I",
And am forced into the oblivion
On the trek of this life
Saddling myself from the life
Once before.

Jane Mozart

Grandpa

My grandpa was a gentle man,
always lent a helping hand, helping
us in what we do, even trying
new things too. He always turned
my frowns upside down. When
I was little we would play until
his dying day.

Jennifer Trapp

Untitled

On a starlit night
among the trees,
a man got down
upon his knees.

While the ground
was cloaked in white,
and snow draped the trees
in the bright moonlight.

While stars shined
in the sky above,
all around, he felt
His love.

He said, "There were times
I doubted You,
and questioned what
I knew was true."

"But beauty like this
proves to me,
that a greater power
has to be."

Donna McKeen

The Neighborhood Chickadee Man

Beneath a tall box elder tree,
    An elderly man stands.
A small and happy man is he,
    With large and strong hands,

His hair is gray and thin,
    His complexion is a healthy tan.
Your heart he will win,
    He is the neighborhood chickadee man.

With outstretched hand full of seed,
    In this unique way.
He waits for the chickadees to feed,
    At mid-morning every day.

Julia Hovland

True Love

When you are young
And fancy free
Don't think sex is love,
Love is caring.
Love is sharing.
Body and soul with one
Who places you first in life.

Start as best friends before
Becoming man and wife.
Take vows to seal it legally.
Don't make your child a bastard
Upon your family tree.
Create a child proud to be
Part of your genealogy.

Ella A. Stone

Untitled

Sun rays kiss the ground
An utopia slipped beneath the cracks
A child's world gone black
What's left to say?
Deception in the heart of the beholder
Learn to not double cross those
    you cannot control.
A child in need
Knocked up by the insanity
What's left to write?
Contagious blow to the heart
How much longer and I survive?

Erin O'Donnell

Imagine

See him stand with majestic grace,
And a cloud of light about his face.

See his white and glistening form,
And his slender, shiny crowning horn.

See his eyes of crystal blue,
Gentle and friendly as they look at you.

See his innocent and modest air,
Of his own beauty, he's not aware.

See him move in his running flight,
With never a worry, or ever a fright.

If you can see this, my reading friend,
The Legend of the unicorn will never end.

Alison J. Gulledge

Untitled

All the summers
and all the days
I really like them
in many ways

I like the way
that God made me
and that's the way
I want to be

Justin Brown

Dream Come True

When you look far up
and all you see is the colorful rainbow
The colors would be as bright as my
dream,
and what would you think of
or what would you dream of?

You wonder if there is life up there-
I do anyway-
Just because of that dream
And ever since then you wonder:
Wonder of life
Wonder of living.

Not knowing as much as you
still both confused
For me I want to know
just so many ideas unanswered.

I want to know about that color I saw
in that dream;
It was bright yellow.
I want to know...

Christina Gunderson

Goodbye My Son

God loaned an angel to us
and although you couldn't stay;
You left us bittersweet memories
that began one special day.

We never heard your voice;
never even heard you cry;
No sooner did we have you,
than we had to say good-bye

You're in much better arms now,
up where the angels sing:
Sweet lullaby's we've never heard
in a place we've never seen.

But we will meet again, my son.
Someday we'll be together.
Next time will be much different;
we're guaranteed forever.

So rest in peace, my beautiful son,
and know that I Love you;
And I'll take peace in knowing
someday, I'll be there too.

Candy Wood

I'm A Woman

I'm a woman with respect
and believe what I like to
believe. Men can't find me out
because I'm the only true
breed. They try and try but
they cannot say. I tell them
it's the way I walk, the way
I talk, the way I kiss,
the feel of my spine, the feel of
my breasts, and the feel of
my curves. I'm a woman.

Jennifer Atkinson

A Star From Heaven

A star from heaven came shining through
And brought with it a "Bundle in Blue"
Has ten little fingers, ten little toes
Mom and Dad's singing him nursery prose

A star from heaven was sent from above
To brighten a home joyous with love
Baby boy now needs his mother's care
His father too offers his share

Baby sisters hover so very near
Ready to give brother his teddy bear
Feeling secure in their parent's love
Knowing they too are their precious doves.

Etta Kleiner

"Time Heals"

Time heals all wounds
And I am sure that's true.
Yet my pain from love
Gives my heart no feeling for healing,
And my memory of life's eyes
haunts me still.
The wounds of my love
Keep my heart open with pain.
Like salt poured in an open cut,
Should I have to try to fall in love
Or has my faith of hope for it
become my fear for living.

Caulette Ridgway

Untitled

Call me Merlin,
And call me great,
Wonderful spells,
I can create.

With my staff in hand,
And hat on my head.
I can make a spell,
To raise the dead.

But I am tired,
I can't elaborate,
As I said before,
Call me Merlin,
And call me great.

Becky Reynolds

Whippoorwill

Over the field
and down the hill.
The darkened forest fill
with the call of the whippoorwill.

Whip-poor-will, whip-poor-will.

The twilight in splendor
with trees in a silhouette glow.
An orangy world in show
as a tasty breeze hails.

Whip-poor-will, whip-poor-will.

Sail your song on the failing light
for them who dream on stars so right.
Echo of love call in the night
and a melody of sound says a name.

Whip-poor-will, whip-poor-will.

Harold Dixon

"Give .. Then Give Up"

We're all the oars in a leaking boat
And each is lending a needed place.
But like the words I never wrote
There'll be a time we all must face.

For when it comes to reaping goals
Like soldiers, we just dig right in,
Just like the embers that were coals
Become the gold that once was tin.

So, if your aim is shooting high
There's little time to waste my friend,
The ticking clock will ask you why
You've slowed down toward the very end?

Put down your oar, you've had enough,
let those that follow take your place,
You gave your best without a bluff,
So now let's see a stranger's face.

Herb Walsh

Untitled

"As we Travel
Along Life's highway,
Knowing not
How to find our way,
If we follow
The master road map,
We shall never
Go astray."

Hughie Dale

Mental Scotoma

I no longer perceived myself alive
And for nirvana I did strive,
The pain of catatonia was intense
And phantasmagoria quite immense.
I was taken to the asylum for the insane
For my senses to regain,
I spent all day in a trance
And ECT was my only chance,
Of ever being functional again
With my malady of brain.
The seizures of the ECT coma
Eradicated the mental scotoma,
And soon I started to desire living
And profuse gratitude I started giving.
Upon release I clearly perceived
Torpor and malaise relieved,
With help from trust and science
Indeed a link of strong alliance.
Then social recovery set me free
From the bonds of extreme tragedy.

Bruce Edward Katz

When Life Comes Hard

When life comes hard
And futile seems all,
Trust in the one
Who is master of all.

When satan comes on
And will not flee,
Trust in the one
Who will set you free.

When humanity opposes
All that you do,
Just remain faithful
To the one who is true.

When this old world
And its problems are past,
You will be in heaven
With Jesus at last.

Charles R. Perrin

Winter Breath

I saw a winter sky today,
And held my coat tight about me
As I took a trip
Across the snow, and upward
To the very tip
Of His purple mountains.

Winter winds scraped at my skin
And pushed my ribs,
As I brought the pinching aspirations in,
And outward with a frozen
Paralytic's red and aching grin
That smiled toward the wintriness.

My eyes, and what they told my soul,
Were all that gave me reason
For a smile, and purpose to my walk,
And I returned to home, and warmth,
And felt the need to share with friends and talk
Of all the winter beauty I had seen.

J. Fowler Wilson

Inspiration

I walked tonight through the orchard,
And I heard the catbird's call,
And it seemed I'd grown a foot or more
Since wandering there last Fall.

As I tiptoed under the crab apple tree
I picked a bud from the branch,
Its dainty loveliness, fresh and pure
Brought back thoughts of a sweet romance.

The air was soft and fragrant,
And as I lingered there
I sensed the calm of a thankful soul
For my lips were framed in prayer.

I started on through the pine row -
Then I saw the western sky
Which was not aglow with a setting sun
But dark and rolling high.

The trees and I stood silent
And watched in reverent awe,
While the quiet hand of God wrote words
Of love from His blessed law.

Esther E. Hannon

Thoughts Of Glass And Water

I hold the glass and fill it with water,
    and I see through it as the water
    stands still.
It seems as one part of matter.

As I tilt the glass to one side,
    it seems very different.
Not as one part,
    but as two.

The glass slips from my hand,
    and water splashes on my fingers.
The glass lies shattered near
    my feet.

How can something be so strong,
    and yet so fragile?

Jimmie Vasquez

Promised Land

Take me deep inside your world
and I will show you mine.
We'll dream into a starry night
and drink of love like wine.

We'll quench the everlasting thirst
that drives us on to love.
Beneath a dark and mystic sky
that shines its eyes above.

I promise you these things to come.
Just take hold of my hand.
Just close your eyes and fall in love,
into this promised land.

Jason Shiptoski

Untitled

I tried to look beautiful
and in my mirror I did
How was I to know
I was still a kid
The world moved so fast
like the speed of light
I wasn't ready for the crash
called real life

Jennifer R. Adams

Magic Carpet

My carpet is faded
and is fringe edged;
still so precious to me.
Although of clear conscience by origin,
temptless for a thief.

I LIVE ON IT.
I SLEEP ON IT.
I LETTER-WRITE ON IT.
DANCE ON IT.
I TV-WATCH ON IT.
EAT ON IT.
SEX ON IT.
DREAM ON IT.
SEX ON IT.

Oh, how many lies have
seeped through it,
My secrets I sweep underneath of it.
Sometimes,
I want to walk off of it
but what a fool I'd be.

George Dvorsky

My Talk With God

When I look up at night,
And know I view infinity,
Great God of all,
I feel so small!

Yet, as I gaze upon the sight,
It gives me such serenity,
To know that You, Great Lord of all,
Still hear me when I call!

When I look up at night,
And my eyes behold eternity,
I bow my head, and humbly pray,
"Thank You God for another day!"

And when it comes my time for flight,
When You reach down Your hand for me,
When You say my race is run,
Oh, to hear You, say "Well done, my son!"

And, Lord, if I come by day, or by night,
One last thing I would ask of Thee,
You, who are Master of my fate,
Will You please meet me at the gate?!

Clarence N. Wesson

"Mama Wants A Home"

Daddy worked his fingers to the bone
and Mama stayed home with us.
We always had a whole lotta love.
but these days love just ain't enough.
Love just ain't enough when Mama
wants a home.

Daddy comes home late from work for
supper and a hug from us.
He works so hard and loves us too,
but these days love ain't enough.
Love just ain't enough when Mama
wants a home.

Mama cries at night because she wants
a home that she can call her own.
Daddy wants to give her one, but it's
hard on just one job alone.
These days love ain't enough when
Mama wants a home.

Cindy Cheely

Grandpa

I lie on my back,
And look at the sky.
I think of you,
As the clouds roll by.

You meant so much,
When you were here,
Always bringing
Good love and cheer.

Now that you're gone,
Things won't be the same.
But in my heart,
I'm partly to blame.

Grandma is hurting,
And she'll be alright.
But I hear her crying,
Almost every night.

For you were my Grandpa,
Please enjoy your rest.
With the world as it is today,
Maybe it's for the best.

Angela D. Helmick

"Climb Till Your Dreams Come True"

Often your tasks will be many
and more than you think you can do.
Often the road will be rugged
and the hills insurmountable too...

But always remember, the hills ahead
are never as steep as they seem.
And with faith in your heart start upward
and climb till you reach your dream.

For nothing in life that is worthy
is ever too hard to achieve.
If you have the courage to try it
and you have the faith to believe...

For faith is a force that is greater
than knowledge or power or skill.
And many defeats turn to triumphs
If you trust in our love and God's will.

For faith is a mover of mountains
there's nothing that we cannot do.
So start out today with faith in your heart
And climb till our dreams come true.

Bruce Yarnell

A Garden Is...

Most gardens are like people
And reflect the owner's needs.
Some, cared for by a gardener,
Some, wild and full of weeds.

A garden can be practical,
Well mulched with clean-cut rows.
A place to meet the farmer's need
Where any crop could grow.

A country flower garden
Has a freedom all its own,
Where colors freely mix and match
To make a house a home.

But gardens in the moonlight
Are a place of magic bliss.
Here dreams are spun and hearts made one,
Here lovers meet and kiss.

Helen M. Huey

Understanding

It's always my fault
And no one seems to care
when I turn around for help
no one seems to be there
Put them in my shoes for
just one day
I bet they would stop and
think about what they're going to say
If they knew how it was to be me
They'd understand
They'd see, or would they?

Amber Zidarevich

Jarro

He said that he would never die
And, of course, he never will -
As long as there are friends to tell
Of his daring, speed and skill.
As long as loved ones see that smile
And feel the joy he spread
Then we know it must be true
That "Jarro jus' can't dead."

"In Memory of Everton Thomas"
Born: Kingston, Jamaica. 1947
Died: Los Angeles, California. 1995

Barbara Zampelli

Old Coyote

O come old coyote
and run with me
across the hot desert floor
of burning sand.

O come old coyote
and run with me
through the hills and mountains
of this awesome land.

And when night comes
You howl to the moon
and I will pray
for the coming
of another day.

Joe Sites

True Love...

In the winter snow,
And the summer heat,
I hope that we can finally,
Make some ends meet.

I know I haven't said,
What I really feel,
So please believe me when I say,
My love for you is real.

I want to be with you,
Held in your arms so tight,
Oh, if you only knew,
How I feel alone at night.

I love your smile,
I love your voice,
I want you to know,
You are my only choice.

I would whisper in your ear,
That I love you so,
And you would whisper back,
"I'll never let you go."

Andrea Broecker

Peace Of Mind

See life as a poem
    and sense the beauty
        of its rhythm

Do things beautifully
    be unafraid to
        lead a happy life

Acknowledge that you
    and others need love,
        for love is a trembling
            happiness

Don't be afraid of others
    or forget you are
        in the business of living

Don't try too hard to be perfect
    and don't be afraid of success

Ella McBride Crockett

Sand Castle

Treasury bills
And shares of stock
Are placebo pills
To bear a pseudo wedlock.

Yet, I delve rashly
In our world of bliss
Knowing my commitment
A trifle amiss.

Though my soul cries out:
"He's a beautiful man"
I must remember
A sand castle.....is sand.

Eva Barksdale

Baby's Baby Boy's Farewell

Bonnie has the fine young lad by the neck
and she wants him to never forget that
she made a baby boy with toil and soil
and boy did her heart boil with joy.

Bonnie will weep on a sunny day in May
wishing they never part away in June
and she will be toiled and soiled soon
laying her harp on her lad's heart.

Bonita L. Andrade

Steadfast

The trees got trimmed,
and so did I;
but still - we're looking
up to the sky,
knowing that sunshine,
rain and the wind
will help us to grow
and spread out our wings.

There will be stones
in the path of our way;
but we'll keep on growing
and saying: hey -
no matter what,
life goes on,
until our day comes -
and then - we'll be gone.

Ilse Roffler

Spring Time

As the last snows melt away
and the frozen ponds begin to give way
to the warming sun,
the tulips begin to peek through.

The daffodils and lilacs
and dogwood all stand tall.
I know in my heart,
they heard the Master's call.

As sure as they come alive from
their winter beds, I see the new birth.
I know how much God's in control
of our universe.

How He cares for us,
as He does the flowers and the trees.
The birds that sing,
a skylark on the wing.

I praise my Lord
for such things,
because without Him
we would have no spring.

Jean Benson

Devotion

When the sun goes down
And the last star shines bright
When the world stops spinning 'round
And there's never another night
When the waters run dry
And there's no longer daylight
When the ground touches the sky
And heaven's in sight
When you hold me for the last time
And we're forced to say good-bye
When our wedding bells chime
And then one of us dies
That's when you'll know
That I'll always be true
And the following words
Will be forever, from me, to you...

I'll never know another love like this
I'll never hold anyone so tight
I'll never share anyone else's kiss
And falling in love will never feel so right

Jennifer Goodwin

Friends In Time

Time begins Time continues
and the memories of friends
are music in my passage of it.

Time composes Time forges
memories to dreams
as we seek the meaning of it.

Time blends Time tempers
our dreams as they return
to memories in the stream of it.

Time sings Time dances
and you, my dream, my memory, my friend
are my song of it.

Gail S. Hicker

True Giving

It's easy to give when you've plenty-
  And the need is far away,
When it only takes some money-
  Just a little, from today,

It's when your strength is short,
  And you have too much to do-
That it really takes a measure,
  Of the caring deep in you.

It's when you, too, have needs to meet-
  When you are feeling incomplete,
And you rise up to meet the need
  That in true giving you succeed!

  Jessie M. Hardin

As The Morning Unfolds

When the dawn appears in the morning
And the song of the birds is told,
I watch the sun appear from the east
While the day slowly begins to unfold.

The sun is warm with its glow
As it dries up the dew on the ground.
It makes the morn more inviting
For all the creatures around.

The air seems pure and fresh
As it blends with the nature of the land;
Just like a beautiful picture
Painted by an artist's hand.

The sun will soon venture on
And the morning will come to an end.
It is now past and gone forever.
But tomorrow—A new morning will begin.

  Carol A. Huff

I Remember Dad

I remember Dad, when he would smile -
and the whole world seemed brighter.
I remember Dad, when just a word
would make my heart seem lighter.

I remember his simple honesty,
that he shared with everyone.
I remember how hard he tried,
to pass it from son to son.

It seems that most of humankind
is affixed in selfish state-
Hardened hearts that try to find
a reason for why they hate.

I remember Dad would say,
the one thing that truly endures
Is a man's character my son.
In that you can feel secure.

This world touched by greed and sin,
tried, but couldn't destroy the light in him.
A place in heaven is God's great plan,
because He also remembers this wonderful
man.

  Gene Bishop

Untitled

Within the almond
animate in their blooming
each blossom a bee.

  Chuck Newton

"Forever"

When life gets tough
and things are down,
you can count on me
'cause I will be around.
To hear you cry
or wipe your tears,
to talk to me without
any fears.
I will listen loud
and clear.
And just you know,
that I'll always
be here.

  Diana Cantu

Character Building

It builds character, son
And though it's not fun
The grass is in need of a mowin'.

Then take a break,
But not at the lake
For the weeds in the corn need a hoein'.

This sun is so hot
I'm goin' to melt on the spot
If I don't get a chance to go swimmin'.

What if I cut off a toe
With this miserable hoe
Would that set their eyes to brimmin'?

Then they'd all be a wishin'
They'd let me go fishin'
'stead of out here workin' so hard.

But it's not easy you know
To cut off a toe
So guess I'd best mow the yard.

  Homer F. Vian

Going Through A Phase

The doctor slaps the bottom
And thus a phase begins
The crying and the laughing
The losses and the wins.

The wiggling toes are flailing
The arms are open wide
We comfort, hold, and cuddle,
Another phase is tried.

The halting steps are broken
With a fall that ends in tears.
The skates and bike are tossed aside,
And another phase appears.

The homework tests our memories.
The soccer tests our pride.
The bedroom tests our patience.
This phase, we too must ride.

We meet him at the alter.
We give his hand to her.
We move away with tears of joy.
Another phase is through.

  Ginny Coughenour

A Child's Time Line

We diapered the babies
  And tucked them in bed.

We helped with their homework
  And parties at school.

We visited the dentist
  And eye doctor, too.

We fed the menagerie
  From hamsters to birds.

We watched their recitals
  And cheered for their games.

We taught them to drive
  And bought them a car.

The children are gone now
  They're off on their own.

Things stay in their place
  Just where they belong.

But now it's too quiet
  We rattle around.

Today we are getting
  An eight week old pup!

  Janet Drabot

Home

Through the Door
And up the Stairs
Waits my Little boy
In his High chair
His mother beside him
All Love and Care
I'm Truly Home
With them There

  John Howard Kuschatka

Spring

Sun rises earlier,
And warms us longer.
Children play,
After a winter slumber.
Trees awake,
And revive.
Flowers bloom,
In vibrant colors.
Life fills the emptiness,
Of the dead woods.
Animals awake,
And warm themselves in the rays.
How the world feels so alive.
How it awoke,
From its frozen slumber.

  Bruce S. Harner Jr.

"Dear Dad"

Thou you dear dad
Are now gone
Your life in me
Still lives on
And that's the way
It shall always be
From father to son
Into eternity!!

  Carmen F. Struffolino

The Considerate Wife

For 33 years she made the beds
and washed the dishes, swept
the floors and kept her wishes
to herself.

For 33 years he slept in the beds,
spent her wages and cluttered the
floor with dirty clothes and sports pages
and grunted to answer.

In his bedside stand he kept a gun,
his Jennings 22, which he swore he'd
use on her and any attorney, if she
tried to run or take what was his.

So in their year thirty-four, when
she could stand no more she
used his gun and saved him
the trouble.

Conne McCormick

Lord, Walk Beside Me

Lord, walk beside me every day
And watch over me every night.
There's a comfort in your presence
With a well-being in your might.

There are days when I am lonely
Then I feel your presence near.
It lifts my lonely feelings
And drives away my hidden fear.

Sometimes I feel the presence
Of my loved one who is with you.
Then I look but never see him
Not even one visible clue.

My memories of his love
And his wanting to help me
Are ever in my lonely heart -
A reminder of reality.

Someday I hope to walk with him
In your heavenly kingdom of love.
Then there will be no ending
As we live in your heaven above.

Frances E. Tolson

Never Letting Go...

Thou distance may separate us
And we are many miles apart.
I can't let you go
From my soul,
my mind, or
my heart.
You took a piece of me with you.
So if you don't mind.
Handle it with care,
Don't leave it behind.
I constantly think about you,
   NIGHT AND DAY
I wish I could be with you.
But you're too far away.
I can't let you go.
For so many reasons.
But the most important ones of all:
   I care about you and,
   I miss you
No matter what the season

Cheryl Lesene

Love Remembered

When years have passed
And we are still together,
I'll place two chairs in the sun—
That will be our quiet time—

And speak of remembrances
And fulfilled days.

And if only one chair remains,
I'll still place the other,
For memories are without end.
They comfort the steps
To eternity.

Irving Boker

A Child's Eyes

The world is dying all around us...
and we don't seem to care.

Everything is dying...

   the plants,
   and flowers.

   the animals,
   and even us.

The world is being killed...

   with murder,
   and suicide.

   with drugs,
   and alcohol.

Not everyone sees it...
or if they do, they don't care.

Children don't see it.
Children don't see anything bad.

They don't see racism,
and they don't see depression.

Wouldn't it be great...
to see the world through a child's eyes.

Angela Renee Spencer

Heavenly Daddy

There's no one else around,
And your heart is filled with doubt.
Loneliness wears you down;
Is there any way out?

When you feel you have no choice,
The Lord will see you through.
And then you can rejoice,
With Him there to guide you.

He will never abandon you
Nor leave you in the cold.
He'll make your broken heart new.
Abba's love will never grow old.

Anytime we need advice
He's there for you and me.
His only son - the sacrifice,
Now beside our heavenly daddy.

He loves us more than stars at night,
All shining - a reminder to see,
And gave his word as the light
Showing us to the heavenly daddy.

Jhoni Copeland

I Look In Jesus' Face

I look in Jesus' face
   and what do I see?
A loving, caring savior
   Smiling down on me.
Just knowing he is there
   What comfort, oh what peace;
To know his love for me
   Will never never cease.

I look in Jesus' face
   And what do I see?
My shepherd, friend and brother,
   He is everything to me.
And he is coming soon,
   I feel it in my heart,
To take me to my home
   When we will never part.

Janet Lee

Seasons Fly

Summer was born.
And with it,
The Grass was new,
The Air pleasant,
And the Wind fresh.

With Fall, a few
Dreams were lost.
Lives change as
the Leaves turn.
What color will we be?

With winter came work.
Days drawn-out,
Nights so fleeting.
The Final Death
Of many Dreams.

Spring, the rebirth
Free again, but old.
To dream, feel once more.
Another turn,
I will not see.

Jeff Woods

Untitled

Wizened, tired eyes
are portals to the past,
Full of sorrow, joy and
overflowing with great love
for life.

Lines, wrinkles crisscrossing
are maps of life's
many journeys
Upon a face of time

Hands, rough and work-hardened
Attest to the hardships
Yet ever gentle, to teach
our young

Time almost through,
though not yet done
our elders are priceless
To be treasured and revered

To be remembered and cherished
when taken from our hearts.

Jessica Jamison

The Farm

Daisy the cow
announces her displeasure with

The sleepy farmer
at five A.M.

Hens cluck contentedly
at corn
Gently tossed
at their feet
Tiny yellow tufts
of peeping chicks
Scuttle
terrified of monstrous boots

The lazy sun
yawns over the trees

Waking the farm
from its short slumber
Casting orange beams
of morning
Creeping into the cracks
of the barn

Essie Stouffer-Logan

Mirror Of Emotions

Emotions
Are found in mirrors.
You feel them-
You see them, straight forward.

So clearly
A frown
A smile
Maybe even a tear.

Mirrors unfold emotions
Close your ears,
Silence you mind
But look into a mirror.

Honesty appears.
A face can be blank
For only so long.
Emotions-
Are found in mirrors.

Donna McBride

Me

Do we know who we really are
Are we really what we seem
Can we live our lives to the fullest
Or is this one big dream.

Who really knows what's right or wrong
Or what's good for you or me
Life's a path we all go down
To live just as we please.

Choice is there for all to make
At one time or another
Sometimes it seems to be what's right
Other times you feel smothered.

So get to know who you really are
Before you judge another
And maybe, then this whole wide world
Can learn to live as brothers.

Life is short and the good die young
As all the world can see
So, first make sure that you understand
The person you call ME.

Juanita Murdock

Losing Their way

Within the world, the wrong today
Are people that have lost their way
In crime and hate they have to pay
The way of life for them is gray
So we must turn to God and pray.

let us be strong without delay
And change ourselves, lets say nay
So many things to do today
Love our children as we may
God is good and he will stay.

Esther M. Crowell

Outer Space

We watch with wonder
as birds fly
high in the sky

We are awed by the expanse
of their space
yet they always trace
their way back to Earth

It is time to provide
more funds toward
administration, education
and demonstration
made by astronauts

Their recent discoveries on other planets
of the way some things happen
on planet Earth
More than describes the
value and worth
for more ventures into outer space

Joy E. Stone

Evening Song

One eve I gazed from lofty cliff
As far as eye could see,
While sunset's rays reflected from
A crystal, clear and tranquil sea.

Softly, rolling rising tide
Caressed the sandy shore,
Till faded full the setting sun
And cloak of night stole gently o'er.

Shadows deepened yet I gazed,
When eye no more could see.
Then slowly started homeward way
With stars to light the path for me.

Charles M. Comollo

One Night In The Fall

Look!
Animation in the dark.
Conspicuous diamonds
Large ones and small,
Seeing maybe twenty in all.
Full of play, leaping around
Not a care in the world
Run up hill, then down.
As light shines upon them
In haste they flee,
How I wish I could join them,
Join in on their glee.
Diamonds shining
Large ones and small,
Run so nobly —
One night in the fall.

Cindy Odom

Personalities

As happy as a child,
As free as a bird
As smart as an owl
As fast as a herd.

As sweet as a sugar cane.
As clean as cat,
As caring as a dolphin,
As alert as a bat.

Now for a different personality...

As ferocious as a lion,
As fierce as a bear
As sneaky as a hyena,
And as slick as a hare.

As rotten as fungi,
As quick as a cheetah
As sloppy as a pig,
And won't ever be neater.

Emily Feldman

Untitled

I've never loved someone,
as much as I love you.
Please believe me when I say,
my feelings are true.
I've never fallen,
So deeply in love,
we go together,
like a hand in glove.
If you ever left me,
it'd tear me apart,
so please never leave,
and break my heart.
Every time I see you,
it makes me love you more,
I mean it when I say,
you're all I have to live for.

Dana Joiner

December: Without You

Each December through the ages past
As snow befalls the ground
A white and gentle beauty
Graces all by whom 'tis found

'Tis not the snow or winter wind
Nor frost nor morning dew
'Tis sweeter yet and rarer still
'Tis purer through and through

A gift that's often given
Often broken on return
No refunds or replacements
'Tis a gift too slow to learn

'Tis wrapped with care, And gently placed
Below the tree so soft
It needs no food, or shelter
Only hope, and peace, and love

I give you now this gift
Upon December when I'm gone
I give you now my heart, my love
You'll never walk alone.

Gabriel D. Morris

Come Again Spring

I gaze outside my window,
  As the falling leaves drift by.
Seems suddenly all is golden,
  Underneath autumn's bright, blue sky.

The chill of morn brings a message,
  Winter's cold is on its way.
I feel a sense of sadness,
  As summer's sun fades slowly away.

The beautiful array of flowers,
  So abruptly disappears from view.
Waiting patiently for springtime,
  When they can bloom anew.

Only the sunflower and goldenrod
  Sway gently in the breeze,
Sadly waiting for their demise,
  When frost quickly turns to freeze.

Still all seasons have their beauty,
  Each holds a special place.
But oh I long for the warm, bright sun-
shine,
  When Spring again lifts up its face.

Helen Pope Bell

The Widow's Walk

A gale thundered against the shore
As waves against the rocks tore.
Rocks that haughtily stared back
As again, the waves made their attack.

The ebony night was restless
With ghastly clouds in distress.
The wind forever roaring
As sheets of rain came pouring.

Throughout this resounding Hell
Which in turn tolled a death bell,
Stood outlined a lonely figure
Amid this stormy portraiture.

The dark hair was blown awry;
The crimson lips wetted with spray;
The tearful eyes looked afar
Hoping to sight her unreturned star.

The winds continued to pursue
And nearer her wrap she drew.
She prayed her captain return
Unharmed from his sojourn.

Georganne G. Tiemann

Lesson Of The Light

At times fluttering,
at times ablaze.

What color is the sweet
oil today?
Perhaps blue in calm or
red in rage.
Desiring always to be stable, eternal.

What keeps it glowing
and to what extent?
One small turn with
forefinger and thumb...
and then, nothing.

Be guarded against this,
or when you are old
you will be distraught in
your loneliness.

Catherine Goertzen

For A Special Daughter

For in this box you cannot see
As you do not now what the
  little one will be.
Special things that it may wear
Things to play with when it cares.

Clothes to fit when it arrives
Some may fit until it's five
Other surprises you may also find
Things you'll need in order
to survive.

Happiness and joy you will find
To be a Mommy is a pleasure divine
Cherish the moments one and all
As it will grow fast and tall.

In a corner tucked deep inside
Your parents love you will find
Forever hold it close and near
Share it with the little one
so dear.

As parents you have made us proud
May God bless you and the little
one inside.

Elizabeth L. Murphy

"Sweet Dreams, Little Girl"

Sweet dreams, little girl,
As you lie here in your bed.
You look so very peaceful,
As your pillow rests your head.

Sweet dreams, little girl,
Your slumber is deep.
Into your thoughts
Only sweetness shall creep.

Thoughts of butterflies
In fields ever so green.
Your smile is so radiant,
So very small you seem.

You'll run and tumble
Playing in the grass.
I pray times like these
Forever will last.

Dream how much I love you,
Dream how much I care.
But most of all, little girl,
Dream on. I'll always be here.

Bobbie Walters

Proud Graduate

A proud smile,
  as you walk
  the last mile.
Pace increase as
  you reach for
  a future.

A mind filled
  with knowledge,
A future filled
  with promise,
A life filled
  with hope,

And a heart that will cherish
  these memories forever.
Memories shared by those you love
  and those who love you back.

Hilda K. Rose

Lullabies

Precious Child
Asleep beside me
I sing lullabies
To soothe your resisting cries.
Still, long after you are quiet
I sing the words again and again.

Can you still hear
As you run through distant playgrounds
The echo of my voice?
Does it give reassurance enough
To conquer unsuspecting giant
That hold within
Your every fear?

Does my love carried upon this melody
Give you courage enough
To open tomorrow's door?

Can you hear me, sleeping baby?
Or do I now attempt
To soothe my own resisting cries?

I wonder...to whom I sing these lullabies
Carol Stoughton

A Battered Woman's Cry

I stood in bewilderment and gazed
  at confusion,
I struggled for life; yet no one gave
  me attention.
I shouted, yelled and screamed,
Still no one looked my direction.
Why I am I holding on to something
  that isn't mine
"Let go" I murmured, "You'll be fine"
But it's not easy as it may sound.
By failure, resentment and abuse
  I am bound.
How can I let go?" How?... When I'm
  accused of being a fool.
But you can if you will,
Stop and think how to have your fill.
So, slowly I went in deep meditation
of which I was thrilled with spiritual
inspiration.
And so here I am a stronger fulfilled
woman
Upholding my life with honorable mention.

Fay Burnett

Ingrid, My Girl

She is my girl, this I know,
Because my heart tells me so.
Very smart and very sharp,
And she really has my heart.
Makes me crazy, makes me blue,
Makes me smile a lot, too.
Talks to plants and flowers too,
What's a matter, don't you -
Teaches me the proper way
Of how to eat and what to say.
Though it is very hard to do,
She keeps trying hard and true.
As a lover, there is no other.
She is the best, you keep the rest.
All my hopes and dreams she holds,
This I hope, she really knows.
For I love her more than life,
And I'd love for her to be my wife.

Andrew Walrad

The Second Fifty

My mind is still good
At least I think so.
The body does what it should
When I need it to go.

So why do they, on TV,
Refer to "the second fifty years,"
When I think, walk, and see?
It just brings me to tears.

They think we are old
Just because we are older
And they need to be told
I ain't old till I'm older.

What do they mean when they say,
"The second fifty years?"
Do they think there's no more play?
Well, listen to me, dears!

Just because I've been around longer
Doesn't mean I'm ready to fold
And cross the blue yonder.
I ain't old till I'm old!

Barbara Petree

Wolf's Hunt

Acute eyes, cunning senses, all
aware of the world around. From a
far off distance a noise is heard, ears
are perked upward. Thrashing
silently through the crisp, wet
snow, he wavers closer to the sound.
A sight is seen, a leap made. Silence
is broken by a crush of bones, white
fangs piercing flesh. A cold, black
muzzle is now covered in warm,
dark, rich blood. Victory is claimed.

Christie O'Quin

Pursuit

During the night,
Away from light.
He hides in woods and hollow.
He skitters here, he scatters there,
While daring those who follow.

As he runs through,
He stares into,
The eyes of those approaching.
It's futile for he cannot hide,
From those who keep on searching.

Aaron Kim

"Where America Begins"

America is not defined by
borders or shores.
You'll find America begins
where there are open doors
to every race.
It spans as far as liberty extends.
Where skill and hope embrace
is where America begins.
How can one map bounds of dreams?
How can peace be drawn to scale?
Here opportunities abound to
either win or fail.
America was sought and found.
Where free men dare to dream
is where America begins.

Edith Brais

"Sowing Seeds"

As you travel down life's road
be careful of the seeds you sow
After you have planted them
how quickly they will grow
Never plant with seeds of doubt
or seeds of selfish greed
Plant instead with understanding
to reap the things you'll need
Never start sowing aimlessly
with anger or in haste
If you're planting in the wind
Tares will be your waste
Remember for every seed you sow
there will be a harvest day
And the reaping is always harder
than the sowing along the way
Nourish with lots of kindness
with love and patience too
And when it's time to reap your harvest
good things return to You

Corliss Booth

Nature's Nature

Hero of the yesteryear,
Bedded in forgotten sands,
How the crowds that used to cheer
Sleep in deep, forgotten lands.

From earth to sky you burned with fame,
Then flesh made soil and soil made sod.
Folks soiled and soon forgot your name.
There's grounds impermanence is God:

The lily, nature's brightest bloom,
Fades before the fade of day;
Death and time are bride and groom;
And fame is made of sand and clay.

But does the sky not cry for you
When tears tap on your grave as rain?
Does not the wind remember, too,
With wailing sighs of wailing pain?

The wind wails with unconscious sighs,
And nature weeps, it's true,
Tears from white, indifferent skies.
It weeps, but not for you.

David M. Seaborg

Just One Moment

Once upon a dream
Beneath a midnight sky
Two strangers chanced to meet
Neither knew the reason why
They shared a special night
To be marked as destiny
And for just one moment
They allowed passion to be free
Each forgot the problems
They were running from
And all the pain that they felt
Suddenly was gone
They gave each other a chance
To heal the wounds within
They were thankful to one another
Though they never met again
Neither will forget
How much that night did mean
The night that they escaped
Once upon a dream

Cyndi Garner

A Wild Flower Party

Heather stood upon the hill
Bedecked with Queen Anne's Lace,
Jack-In-The-Pulpit was
Preparing to say grace.
Coreopsis filled the nearby field
White lilies in their midst.
And row on row of Buttercups
Stood waiting to be kissed.
Violets danced with Poppies
And Jasmine filled the air.
Iris wore her Blue Bonnet
She looked so sweet and fair.
Black-Eyed-Susan wore Lady Slippers
Tipped with Rambling Rose
And all the Pussy Willows
Stood 'neath the Mistletoe.
Honeysuckle, larkspur, and Daisies
All gathered in one spot
They promised to be back next year
And would FORGET-ME-NOT.

Herbert J. Kindl

Early Morning

Early Morn
Before dawn
I lie awake
And in my bosom
is a song

A song of love
A song of joy
A song of peace
A song of songs

Early morn
before dawn
before I wake
in my bosom
is a song

I dream a song of love
I dream a song of joy
I dream a song of peace
I dream a song of songs
Early Morn....

Gale Ragan

Something Special

I think of something special
Before I go to bed,
My special friend is Hermie
And he lives inside my head.

It's not imaginary
It's really very real,
You see my friend named Hermie
Is my tumor. That's the deal.

It doesn't make me different
Or sick as you can see,
But he will be a problem
If he grows inside of me.

Twice a year for M.R.I's
Very still I lay.
This tumor isn't cancerous
Cause Hermie's face is gray.

So if my tumor doesn't grow
Then in my brain he'll stay,
Since Hermie is my special friend
Please don't take him away.

Erin McIntyre

Hustle Bustle

I have lot to do,
Before the day is through.
Ears to bend,
And hearts to mend,
And though I'm a grown woman,
I have a kite to fly,
Before the day goes by,
I'm a very busy human!

M. Joyce Shank

The Minstrel's Flight

A bonfire lights the sky aglow
Bells and baubles charm the night
The jongleur shakes his silver bough
A minstrel's merry faerie flight

Gleemen sing seductive songs
Enchanted Sleeping Beauty Dreams
In rosy skies the falcons fly
Swan-like maidens dance by streams

A Mardis Gras, wild feast of life
The King of Misrule never dies
Pied Piper and his magic fife
the spirit soars through misty skies

Betwixt the golden day and dusk
Twilight power, Birth and Death
Sweet scents of lavender and musk
carry songs, wind's sacred breath.

Alexandra Wellington

Untitled

An Oak tree,
Bent and twisted with years,
Stands strong.

Jaclyn Edwards

Everyone Dreams

At a special place
beyond everything harmful
outside of the scary thoughts

Over many hills
above the oceans
toward the sky

Past the rivers
among the clouds
aboard a rainbow is a beautiful
Dream!

Ashley Gallagher

Penny

Leaves mildew on a delicate frost
Bulky worms eat crush bug
Reality devours all that Dreams
   impart
The muse of an Ariel Spirit
Sustains itself only to dull
Away a spirit gained
Kills all that better world.

The raw sun scorches and dazes the day
Ragged flowers show the wind's will
Trees wept and shed a tear to the rain
May a green winter always set
   with the purple sun
And the crystalline trees jet out the sun
forever.

Christine Goeller

My Children

My children, you are God's creation.
Black like the soil he used to
design the first man.
Brown like the tall and mighty tree.

My children, you are heirs of the earth.
Your people tamed wild animals.
And grew the very first gardens

My children, you are descendants
of Kings and Queens.
On the Nile your ancestors
built the pyramids.
And in the desert, the
University of Timbuktu.

My children, your father was
placed in bondage.
But, they could not enslave his heart.
And from his thoughts, sprung
FREEDOM and EQUALITY.

Elizabeth V. Primas

Childhood Dreams

Dreams etched in lace.
Blown to the winds
Forgotten and discarded
by an old distant friend
Once they possessed the
soul and ruled over the
heart.
Now grown and matured,
for the child had to part.
No words good-bye. No
sadness at all.
Just bittersweet memories
which made them fall.

Christina L. Hernandez

God's Gift To Me

A child sweet and innocent
Borne unto a world of despair
Given by God as a gift
In a time without care

When I reflect on the sacrifice
That the child had to bare
I cry with the love he gave
As he died for the world He made

A sinner I am with many a flaw
Often feeling the pressures of life
And then I remember a simple fact
He died a horrible death for me

And in my way of repentance
I pray a little prayer
And remember the Child Christ
Gods' gift of love to me

Douglas Lee Dalton

Autumn Leaves

Jewels of ruby, emerald,
amber glisten in sunlight.
Like a jewel under light.
A splendid show, all too
soon gone, but from the
corners of our minds.

Barbara Wahlen

Two People....

Two people as one
   Both doing their best
Never thinking of themselves

Two people so full of love
   Caring for all
Watching and hearing
   with open minds.

Two people allowing us to grow
   Helping us through our woes
Raising five of their own
   Now helping with our children.

Two people understanding our feelings
   Allowing us to err
Then helping us learn
   Making us stronger in the end.

Where we go-
   Whatever we do
There will never be
   Two people better than you -
   MOM plus DAD equal ONE

Ann Swies

Serenity

Before the morning
   broke through the night
And the dew was left on the grass
   the dawn broke forth
   and the birds sang out
   and they heard the children laugh

The sky was filled
   all day through
With the heat of the golden sun
   and the earth was warmed
   and the world played
   and everything was instant fun.

The people joined
   in a frolicky dance
A step that was made for you
   and the wars were stopped
   as the people yawned
   in the mist of the morning dew.

Everett Ray Wiedersberg

Think Of Me

In those moments after sleep
But before you are awake
In the rising of the sun
When you witness the day break
Think of me

In the silence that you hear
Those moments after song
In the stillness of the night
When no emotions can be wrong
Think of me

In the daydreams that you have
When your mind is swept away
In the thoughts that cross your mind
That you could never learn to say
Think of me

And when I feel I am alone
And you may feel lonely too
When nothing fills my mind
I will vow to think of you
So please, think of me

Jamie May

Broken Homes, Broken Hearts

Broken homes
Broken hearts
Children's lives
torn apart
What can we say
What can we do
To keep our love
And our hearts true
Think of them first
Think of them last
But what ever you do
Don't put them in your past.

Faye Fanning © '95

Eternal Flame

Our life is a flame,
Burning in shame.
We flicker,
We burn bright,
We give some light.
Like candles the bad burn out.
We are the eternal flame,
That goes on forever.
Through sadness and grief we burn.
We can light again,
To fight again, then rest.
The eternal flame is not out.
There is a stronger light,
For our souls go on forever.
Forever we burn,
Lighting paths for others
Letting the flame go on forever.

Jennifer Nistor

Rodent Remedy

Curiosity killed the cat
But failed to harm its foe, the rat.
Without the cat, the rat is free
To plunder with impunity.
It is not right that cats should die
While rats may live to terrify.
This grave injustice must be fixed,
The rat's dominion swiftly nixed,
And thus dispel the fearsome sight
Of rats marauding through the night.
'Though I've no piper's magic flute,
I have a simple substitute -
Give satisfaction to the cat
And lure it back to slay the rat.

John Brooksbank

Untitled

Cool blue skies
Bright white clouds
Soft green grass
Too tall trees
Wind on my face,
A very soft breeze.
Warm grains of sand,
On a long stretch of beach.
Vast waters
The end you just can't reach.
Bright summer days
Soft summer nights
Everything about them
Just seems right.

Cassie Nix

Cancer

You can dance, you can play
But I am here every day,
I can't dance, I can't play
Because I am sick every day,
I am very, very, very sick
But when you're here, I heal real quick,
I wish you were here more often
Then I wouldn't think about a coffin,
I have a disease, called cancer
I'd rather be a great dancer,
I can't stand this disease
For it makes me want to freeze,
If I were dead I'd have a feeling
That would be the warmth of healing,
My friends and family, I would miss
For all I wanted was a simple kiss,
They say you don't have feelings when
you're dead
But hey, who cares what they said?

Becky Tipton

Sandpaper People

I've met veneered people,
but I cannot join
their society.

I am called
to a very plain society—

Where I am the same
inside as outside—
just me—
just as I am.

I know this because
I have been surrounded
by sandpaper people,
who would simply ruin
good veneer.

Earlene Ahlquist Chadbourne

Pa

Pa, I know no one lasts forever
But I hoped for more time together
I still have so much yet to learn
Now where am I supposed to turn
As I walk down the road
My mind carrying a heavy load
My heart full of pain
My face full of rain
Pa, I'll get by somehow someway
These words I just had to say
Thanks Pa for all you've done
I'm proud to have been your son.

John Chavez (Vez)

My Love

My love is for you, as you are my love.
As you are my love, you are my world.
A world of never-ending beauty.
As you are my world, you are my purpose,
the one purpose of love and life.
As love and life are related, we also
are related.
We are related to love, for that is
what we feel.
But yet more, we are related to life,
As it is the life in you that gives
me the love I feel.

David Elwell

Friends

It seems like only yesterday,
But, I've known her for so long.
We've been together since we were little,
Forgiving when we were wrong.

We've always shared secrets,
And whispered late at night.
Having slumber parties,
Seldom we ever fight.

I know we will grow older together,
High school, graduation, and college.
Sticking together all the while,
Gaining more and more knowledge.

We then get older and older,
Having kids and getting married.
Being eighty together,
And together getting buried.

And so, we stuck together,
Forever to the end.
I never will forget her,
My very best friend.

Carrie Guffin

Who's This Man

Who is this man that no one knew,
   but loved him dearly tried and true.
Who is this man of two way gender
   but to his family was always tender.
This man of strength this man of glee
Please tell me why he had to flee.
Free of burden free of guilt
   this well loved man with the
   heart of silk.
We called him Charlie.

JoAnn Mazza

Pain

Everyone hurts
But none like me
For my wounds are inside
Where you cannot see

You dare not know
How I truly feel
You believe my act
Is all too real

Happy, laughing, always carefree
No one knows the real me
I've got wounds that are so deep
And in my heart pain continually creeps

I put on an act every single day
But beneath the surface, my pain lays
You'll never know, nor will never see
The real person, the real me

I'll hide it away until the night
Then comes the pain and the fright
My pain, my hurt are oh so real
You can never dream of how I feel

Anisa White

Winter

Winter's calling me today,
But I can't come out and play.
So I sit by the fire,
And drink apple cider,
As much as I desire.

Amanda Wooten

Walking Alone...

I walk alone
But not by choice;
For no one can be found
Who can hear my voice....
I meet different people
And try my best;
But they all turn out
To be just like the rest.
They seem so perfect
So exciting and true;
But as time speeds by
They make you blue...
Twisting and turning
The words you say;
Until finally you decide
That it's judgement day.
So I say so long
To what might have been;
Walking along
Until He happens again...

Amanda White

Abused Love

As she walks, she shakes
But not for the cold
An excuse she tried to make
She wants to look bold

When she walks in the door
All she receives are stares
She really wanted more
She wanted someone who cares

She starts to sweat
He yells and screams
She runs away with fret
He is coming apart at the seams

In her room she hides
He will find her soon
A roller coaster life she rides
She cries and looks at the moon

Tomorrow she has bruises to show
The only gift her father gives her
The bruises that can show
Are the only thing she hates more than her
father

Amanda May

Barely

In memory of Cory J. Johnson
Your face was so clear
But now I can barely see
Your voice was so loud
But now I can barely hear
Your hand was so soft
But now I can barely touch
Your words were so perfect
But now I can barely talk
Your eyes were so beautiful
But now I can barely blink
Your footsteps were so light
But now I can barely walk
Your laugh was so pretty
But now I can barely smile
Your tears were so plentiful
But now I can barely cry.

Donna Westmoreland

Untitled

Love may not stay long
But our friendship will be strong
I'll always be by your side
So don't let our friendship slide
Don't cry
For it's not a Good-bye
We'll be clever
And be friends forever.

Erin Yovich

A Mask Love

Stephne is a friend,
but she can't see me as I am.
She thinks that I'm some kind of hero,
always stepping aside
And letting her go.
I'm there if she needs me,
but the time is running out.
If only she could see me,
she would love me without a doubt.
I'm outside the door now,
sometimes looking back.
The love that kept us together,
is lost beneath the mask.

I miss her smile
I miss her friendship
I miss her style
I miss her.

David Jones

Seven To Three

People all around me,
But somehow I'm all alone,
I touch them,
But do I really?

There's talking going on,
But nothing is said,
Nobody's listening.

Does anyone out there have
Eyes,
Ears,
Hands,
Or mouths,
Everybody's gone.

And I just sit here wondering,
What it would be like to see.

Ellen Baird

He Arose

Despised and rejected
By those He came to save
He died upon the cross
And all His love He gave.

Forgive them Father
He cried in agony
As He paid the price in full
For the sins of you and me!

He arose from the grave
And the promise that He made,
Is renewed every year
On happy Easter day!

Eternal life for all
Who on His name believe.
Oh thank the Heavenly Father
For the Son who set us free!!!

Dorothy L. Krull

Chelsea

They said they'd call me "Chelsea"
But that would need a title, too.
So they named me "Lady Chelsea Ann"
(Just "Chelsea" seems to do!)

My ears are long and floppy
With curly blondish hair-
My eyes are bright as diamonds
And my nose sniffs everywhere!

I'm mostly white with spots of buff
There's freckles on my snout.
My tail is short, but wags a lot,
Especially when I'm 'out'!

I am a Cocker Spaniel
My name is Chelsea Ann
I was born July the Fourth,
(The same as Uncle Sam!)

I'm a member of the Kennel Club,
The AKC, you know.
But that won't stop me having fun
Anywhere I go!

Ann M. Fragnella

Happy Birthday, Mr. King

You fought for what you believed;
But the people now, how they grieve;
A man which God has come to bring;
Happy Birthday, Mr. King.

A special dream you had;
A father and a dad;
The shot that took you still rings;
Happy Birthday, Mr. King.

For colors not the flame;
It's the people that's to blame;
We all need to do something;
Happy Birthday, Mr. King.

Peace is still a dream;
Truly it's the inside to be seen;
Give peace a chance you sing;
Happy Birthday, Mr. King.

Jennifer C. Matlack

Veil

The sun
   changes to the color
      of fall

As it shines
   about the tall
      steep red
         cliffs of the Grand Canyon

It gives the Colorado
   its last sparkle

As it changes
   the evergreens
      that starts dark green
         from the east
   to silver
      in the west

The tired sun
   falls farther

As the night
   wraps itself,
      about the canyon

Eli Secody

Decision Of Love

Can you see the future?
Can you see, how long that you have left?
How would you react, to this?
And did you do your very best?
You'll always be remembered,
For all the things you said you were.
A delicate decision,
Can change the things that can occur.
I know a man of late,
Who had to face his fate, that's true.
And I'm thankful for these moments,
I often said how much I love you.
Could this be your last chance?
Better make sure that your love is right.
Make it something long remembered,
Strong enough to make a weak one fight.
Whatever you decide, is gonna
Last in every tender heart.
And you will be remembered,
For what you were, right from the start.

Cindy Manifold

Sunset

The beautiful glow of God's
   candle
As it lights the Heaven
   A stream of colors
Flowing
   Forever on
God's stream
   A stream of joy
Hope
   And Harmony
The fish in the stream are his
   for we
Are the fish
   And when God blows out his
Candle
   The fish sleep
And the Angels watch over the school
   In the sunset stream

Dusty Johnson

Lost

Lost my heart,
Can't find my heart.

Lost my mind,
I'm in a sure bind.

Lost my love,
Can't find my love.

Lost my soul,
Down the deepest hole.

Lost all I wanted,
It's gone all I wanted.

Lost myself,
I'll never find myself.

Lost all control,
My feelings are out of control.

Lost everything I needed,
They would be happily greeted.
Lost,
Just lost.
Never to be found,
condemned forever to be downed.

Ashley Johnson

It Always Rains On Thursday

It always rains on Thursday,
   'Cause that's when we go out.
Sometimes it rains on Monday
   When we eat pork and kraut.
It even rains on Friday
   When we are dressed our best.
It also rains on Sunday,
   The day we love to rest.
I've seen it rain on Wednesday,
   Our date night don't you know.
And then again on Tuesday
   When sales are very slow.
On Saturday I've seen it rain
   When we could gad about.
      BUT
It always rains on Thursday,
   'Cause that's when we go out.

Carl G. Schrade

What's Wrong With Me?

I think I'm going blind,
'cause your face is all that I see.
I think I'm going deaf,
'cause your voice is all that I hear.
I think I'm losing my mind,
'cause you are all that I think of.
I think death is near,
'cause my heart has been stolen.
I think I'm paralyzed,
'cause every time you are close,
my arms only raise to touch you,
my legs lead me towards you.
If this is a dream,
then please wake me up,
'cause dreams are not forever.
The smile from my lips has run away,
'cause your name rules on it now.
Could this be love, or plain madness?
   What's wrong with me?

Doreen S. Singh

In Triple Haiku...

FAITH greater than dreams,
   clasping my life in pure peace
   as years tiptoe by ...

HOPE in someone's heart,
   waxing crescent like the moon,
   a blessing to count...

CHARITY, by choice,
   changes things as we travel
   in this world of plight.

Concepcion G. Viray

Red Streak

Wet snow
clinging,
a thick dusting
on weeping leggy branches.
Behind my back
A cardinal chirps
I turn to fluttering
emptiness.

I have missed you once
again.

Corynn Royer

That Peaceful Place

   As the sun sets behind the
clouds, it shimmers on the ocean.
There is a slight breeze that waves
past your body. The sea gulls circle
over the ocean as you hear there
sweet voice sing your bare feet
sink into the sand. As the sand
slides between your toes, you look
down and there sits a beautiful
seashell. That is when you know that
is the most peaceful place on earth.

Julie Collinsworth

Clouds

Clouds of darkness
Clouds of light
Clouds of sunshine
Clouds are bright
Clouds of sunshine
Clouds of snow
Clouds take you
Wherever you want to go.

Clouds are found
high up in the sky
reach up and touch
them, all you have
to do is try!

Clouds are white
and soaring bright.
Clouds are soft
like a angel's loft.

Jennifer Heberle

Wiggles

   Lambs and sheep float like
clouds on a green field.
   Slowly circling.

   Like the daisy chains
children fashion in summer.
   Embracing their necks.

   With hugs and kisses.
Nuzzling, the ewe's udder;
   lamb tails wiggle in delight.

   Arching hazel trees.
Wiggle their tassels in the air.
   Nuzzling, clouds in the sky.

   Under the hazels
a stream flows, gurgles and
   giggles, rain nourished.

John Larimer

Willie

On New Year's day, I met a pig
And Willie was his name.

He was quite handsome I must say
Though he wasn't very big.

A gentleman from head to toe
His manners were superb.

A little SNOOTY I'll have you know.
He had the very last word. (OINK)

I doffed my hat and said good day,
As he sauntered merrily on his way.

June Foyt

Untitled

Sailor at sea
Come back to me!
To arms heavy with longing,
A heart held for you.

Sailor at sea
Remember me!
As the sun in the sky
That brings warmth to you.

Sailor at sea
I think of thee.
Through troubled waters, dark nights
I know your solitude.

Sailor at sea
Believe in me!
I will await your return
With fortitude

Tracy R. Farnsworth

When Roses Bloom Again

When roses bloom again, then I'll
Come back to you
I must return, because I know
Your love for me is true.
We'll build a bridge across the miles
Because I know I've really
Missed your gentle smiles!
We'll walk along a sunny shore
We'll build a dream or two
When roses bloom again, and I
come back to you.
My heart is full
Of all the things I like to say
But this will have to do,
When roses bloom again, then
I'll come back to you.

Barbara F. Heyse

Love's Perfection

Spinning, spinning years away
Come give me a sunny day.
Love to hold to feel and last
Regrets maybe, but the die is cast.

Roads not traveled, space surrounds
Bold adventure still abounds.
Reaching out to grasp the sun,
My searching soul is never done.

Smiling faces of small ones dear,
My hearts delight is surely here.
Little hands and voices sweet,
Enough to make one's life complete.

And yet, my Journey never ends
Seeking the meadow around the bend,
My heart shall find this secret place,
And there I'll find God's perfect grace,

Bettye Lopp

What Is A Sun

There is a sun
But is there more than one
I think there is just one
I could be wrong
There could be two or three or four
Or many more

Charles A. Wilmore

Love Under The Tree

Come sit under the tree, my dear,
Come listen
to the song of the birds, or is that
the sound of my heart,
as it beats for your warm touch?
Come feel
the cool grass as the wind blows
through our souls, and blows
away our fears.
Come see
the bright blue sky as you
stare into my eyes.
Come lie
in the warm sun, or is that
just the heat from our flesh?
Come smell
the sweet bloom of daisies as
they grow in the light.
Come love
me forever, under the tree.

Amber Jones

Mr. Right?

In the midst of a grief stricken pain
    comes the depths of my soul
    resurfacing again

What does it all mean? Not me
    again, please just love me and
    let my pain end

You are kind but not enough
    to love
You are vain and I've had
    quite enough

Your heart is with me but
    your mind is too tough
Once again telling the story of
    our forbidden love.

Candace Adkins

Crystal Trees

Winter dream,
    Coming to life today
Show my soul
    Words from the far away:

Icy gems,
    Flowers of crystal trees,
Frozen lights,
    Mixture of skies and seas.

Silver sparks
    Song of a thousand oaks,
Symphony,
    Poems of light that talks.

Everywhere,
    Shines a fantastic world,
Fantasy,
    Duet of warm and cold.

Fragile view,
    Prey of unwanted heat
Your sad tears
    Make my strange joy retreat

Antonio Cassella

Return To Solitude

Sting of anguish
conclusive howl
clench of hand
    to pulsating chest
distressed tears
    silence impends
encircling loneliness
light evaporates
sorrow overtakes
nothing remains
but tiny fragments
    indicating
a marred heart

Christina Muehlhausen

Passing Day

A muffled gasp and saddened tears
confirm our dark and innermost fears.
For a shadow falls across the face
of the one who brought us to this place,
as the man who has this heavy chore,
reaches to close the final door.

One muted click seals the past.
A single reminder of what will last.
I winch at this metallic ring.
Quickly the organ! We rise to sing.
The Pastor tries with quickened time.
Few can sing or read a line.

Hearts are heavy as ladles of lead.
Scarcely they beat for those who tread.
Humble and numb we continue our quest.
In silence we find where he will rest.
At length we turn and leave our friend.
Somber we gather as another's day ends.

Floyd Wells

Embryo

Living in a warm death,
contemplating nothing,
beginning of the ending:
I dissolve away.

Leaping into thought now,
dreaming of all thoughts,
towards the end, my beginning:
I dissolve away.

Two eyes before me and
God says to me:
Why have you come?
You're far too young.
And as I held His tears:
I dissolved away.

Alexander James Walsh-Rule

Having Fun

Dark-Red lipstick
Cool socks and shoes,
Tattoos on your ankles,
Who's who in the news.
Dialing up a girlfriend
And talking all night long,
Cranking up the volume.
When you hear a favorite song.
Shopping malls to visit,
Bubble gum to pop,
The fun is just beginning-
Don't ever let it stop!

Amber Bean

"Kings and Queens"

Kings and Queens
Control my mind
But an ace is up
My sleeve this time
Royal flush
And pageantry
Crookedness
And chivalry
Every card
In the court is wild
Each is a victim
Of the problem child
Hearts laid down
On the wheel of chance
All are victims
Of circumstance

Joseph Araujo Cerqueira

True Story

Feelings of fright,
corner me day and night.

I picture him,
I fall apart.
I can't even hear,
a beat from my heart.

When my eyes close,
he's still there.
Sometimes it's almost too much,
too much to bear.

Crystal G. Hood

Rivers

Rivers are wide.
Covered with fish.
Silent and quiet.
Nice and wet.
Has many bridges.
So great to fish.
Visit a river.
And you'll get a shiver.
Has a nice view for you.
I like rivers.
How about you?

Justin Tonti

Cranberry Snappers

Cranberry snappers
Crackling like my toes
Chipper, slicer, wacker, smacker
Feeling like a Poe

Don't stop jangling Dooger
You don't need to slow
Pack it, hack it, shack it Dooger
You gotta do the show

You see...you have to take the path
or you'll disappear
like a basserflu

Rig the shib and flib the dib
There's nothing to be afraid

Hold my hand Dooger
Hold my hand
It's time...it's time
To go

Darren Bochat

'Daniel's Prayer' (A song)

Does He see me, under the fig tree
Crying to Jesus
Does He know who I am?

Does He see me, under the fig tree
Crying to Jesus
Does He know who I am?

Oh, it hurt me so bad
Only He knew
All the problems I had
Cast me down to its roots.

Yes, He saw me, under the fig tree
Tears falling down
Weeping, sobs of despair.

And He brought me
To the place of rejoicing
Joy overflowing, in His love.

Esther M. Thomas

Petals Of The Rose

Petals of the rose, the rose
curled tight, so small, so bright,
the color hidden yet, the rose of
color on a tree of thorn, a rose
of beauty, glory, yet a rose unborn.
Unfold and bloom, pale rose, a rose
now plucked, entwined with fern and
stem, with bamboo shoot of green,
color pale, rose-pale and red,
a rose with hidden stem of thorn.
Now slowly falling petals of the
rose, a rose so pale now shorn
from tree of life, from branch of
thorn, the rose, the rose now born
and torn, now full, now color fair
with petals falling all about the
rose like tears, like fading tears
of pale bloom rose, now petals gone.
Petals of the rose, a rose once fair,
once bright, upon a tree of thorn.

Constance Saunders

Kathryn

My little granddaughter, Kathryn,
Came along, one day,
On the joy, unspeak-able,
That none can take away.

Little hands, so delicate,
I love to hold in mine,
And look into her lovely eyes,
That always, seem, to shine.

Sundays, we got out to church,
It really is a treat,
We have a special place,
Where we go out to eat.

My little one, who is so dear,
I hope will always be,
Glad to have her Grandma near,
Where Grandma loves to be.

Bernice Ann Morgan

C & O Canal

Riding down the trail,
Black snake sunbathing on the path.
Shaded eyes don't see.

Daniel Winter

The Model T And Dad

When I was a youngster
Dad, brother, and me
Went for a ride
In an old Model T

We rounded a bend
Straight into a haystack
Cause Dad didn't yet
Have the driving knack

We wiggled out
Looking like scarecrows
With hay clinging
To hair and clothes

Dad started laughing
So did we,
Put it in gear
Backed out the old model T

Bonnie Phillips

Dance

You met her at the
dance as you held her oh-so
tight, I wanted to forget it
but instead I left and
cried, I left you there with
her while you guys were
so close.
I thought I had you forever
but now I just don't know,
I see our love has faded,
I see you found someone new,
I just wish I could be the
next to dance with you.

Brandi Gaines

Untitled

I flew over New York tonight
Danced in the air
Amidst peaks of light

Saw shimmering rivers
Reflect the glow
Of ten billion watts
Far below

Bridges spanned the murky shores
Shadowy silhouettes closed their doors

So many faces, so many dreams
Is it as awful as it really seems?

Yes it is
Yes it is
Yes it is

But New York survives
And always will

For peace will one day
Ease the strain
And lift the stain
Of too much pain

Donald Pendergast

Little Chad Morgan

Little Chad Morgan was playing an organ,
Drinking his soda all day.
Along came a bug,
And got in the mug,
In spite of himself, he ran away.

Chad Morgan

Untitled

It was in the drab December,
Dark December of my years.
I cried out and no one answered,
I scream out and no one hears.

Bleak winds gust in dank December,
Winds that chill forsaken souls.
If only I could keep her ember,
hold her warmth from days of old.

Lifeless, barren, black December,
She is gone, but I remember
How we loved, her pure surrender;
Now she calls me from the grave.

Desolation all about me,
Wretchedness in every thought
so I linger in December,
grief and anguish all for naught.

I love her and I've loved no other,
Woe and dismal days I number,
All my thoughts she does encumber;
By my side she cannot be.

Bruce Hughes

Playing With Greed

Choices made
Decisions done
The game is over
No time for fun

A master with tricks
You played your hand well
So warm, so inviting
You should have noticed the smell

False hopes
How dare you dream
Close your eyes to what's there
Things aren't always what they seem

The bitter taste of want
The burning feel of need
You gave freely and willing
You didn't notice the greed

Now it starts to consume you
Time to stop this foolish play
One way or another
It all ends here today.

Gina M. Tarvit

Thunder

Thunder: startling, as
distant, deep gagging;
a crush of unindulgent air,
flat as a fundamentalist's
reproachful hand slap,
taking it out on a prairie, too,
as thunder—Jehovah blab;
out everywhere you find
God in a storm
heard somewhere away,
as a roll call,
compelling our cause,
overturning breath with gust,
regaining dominance
of our brief custody,
leaving us to infer belief
that given sound
from hatched clouds
Something Enough
justifies the conception.

Bill McKnight

Did You?

Did you take cupids arrow?
Did you spear it to my heart?
Did you lower the clouds so I
could lightly walk?
Did you repaint the rainbows
to color in my world?
Did you enter in my dreamtime
so I could share the night with
thee?
Did you warm my days with golden
sun with which you shower me?
Did you touch the mighty ocean
for it to call out my name?
And even if you didn't you
can take all the blame.

Annette Maria

Questions - No Answers

Tell me, Mr. Minister
Do our souls ever grow
Or do they always stay the same
No matter how much we know?

I ask you, oh psychiatrist,
Are the soul and mind the same?
Is each one separate to itself
Or is it just the name?

I wonder, psychoanalyst,
Do you believe in prayer?
Or just the body that we have
With minds for you to share?

Do you know, moody mortician,
When the body is dead and gone
Does the soul depart at once?
Or does it linger on?

I often ponder on all these things
But it's such a great mystery.
Guess that it will always be
An unsolved puzzle for you and me.

Grace Commean

The First Stone

Can you throw the first stone?
Do you, as did Jesus, stand alone?
Is your mind so perfect,
Is your heart so pure,
That you can kill many,
And your conscience endure?

Oh, the lives that should have,
could have, and would have
been saved, had the First
kill never been craved.

Forgive and forget,
Or simply forget?
Now to kill is as distant
as dropping a bomb from a jet.
Scientist are applauded for
their efficiency, accuracy, and precision,
But do they ever stop
to consider their decision.

Can you throw the first stone?
Do you, as did Jesus, stand alone?

John H. Westerman

A Cry For Help

Are you really there?
Do you hear me cry Your name?
Did you hear my prayer?
Will it ever be the same?

Death will bring me to You
Knocking at the gates
To live through and through
Up, where no one hates

Francine Garcia

Listen

Listen
do you hear the sound?
It is the chant of existence
it is the remembering
the petals of our flowering
the leaves of our lives.

Listen
do you hear the drums?
It is the pulse of our planet
it is the wheel turning
the law of karma burning

Listen
do you hear the voices?
Of those who have died in anger
sing to them the song of compassion
and tell them to stop and

Listen.

Donna Wilson

The Rock

Sitting in the sun
Does it sweat
When tossed in the lake does it get wet
When thrown and kicked does it shatter
But to the rock; does it matter
When you hold it and squeeze it
Does it feel, alone
When it rains, sleet and snow
Does it get cold
It's sitting there gazing at you
Can you see its face
Is it from earth or outerspace.
They've withstood the test of time.
But can you understand thee inner sign
Though rocks have been here
For thousands of years. Don't try
To understand the what, how and where.
Just dig down deep, "Inside you know"
Because there you'll find your
Spirit And Stone.

Cee Castro

The Operation

I lift the instruments
Cut and probe
Dig and dredge
There are no stitches
Or staples
This wound stays
Open and unpacked . . .

Therein lie
The words of life
And sometimes they bleed
Onto the page

Frankie Colley-Gilliam

It All Works Out Fine

If you're troubled and need a friend,
don't give up, it's not the end,
If you know someone that's nice,
go to them and ask for advice.
If you don't agree with what they say,
do it in another way.
Put it together one piece at a time,
and soon you'll see it works out fine.

Freda R. Lillibridge

The Warmth To

The sun was beating
    down on her soft
        gentle skin.

It turned my blood
    from cold to hot
in a matter of
    minutes.

I soared above the
    clouds only to find
more warmth to my
    heart.

The hotness of my
    blood running through
my veins lets me know
    how much I really love
    her.

Jermey McLain

"Dreaming Of Us"

Dreams of you and me,
Dreams of the future,
Of how it will be.

We'll keep dreaming eternity together,
You and me, forever.
Dreaming of what the future will be,
Dreaming of ending it, never.

We dream of what the future will hold,
Just the two of us,
Dreams which to one another are told,
Told to no one else.

Dreaming of love so true,
of our lives together.
Dreaming of me and you.
forever and ever...

Christy Lynne Adams

Snow Flake

Uniquely formed six sided hexagonal
dancing with the wind.

Playing on the air currents
floating gently down.

    Floating...
    Falling...

Regressing to the call of conformity
from the Earth below.

Spinning dizzily downward
growing heavy with age.

Dying in a white blanket
blinding the world.

Donald Schuldt

The Adventure

A pleasant musty smell
drifts upward,
as the life in my hand
falls open to reveal
all that is hidden inside.

Excitement courses
the body over.
The desire to become
part of another world,
and a different time.

Curled up in front
of a blazing fire,
while storms rage,
but cannot touch me.

Living through
my imagination.
Being taught of life,
by pages of old.

Andrea Tabert

Valentine's Day

We celebrate Valentine's
each and every year.
    Although it is a special day
it passes soon I fear.
    And on this very special day
our hearts are opened wide, to
reveal the love we truly feel
yet keep locked up inside.
    With it comes our thoughts
of love in every different way,
with cupids, hearts and flowers and
thoughts of Spring someday.
    Valentine's is happiness, love
and good cheer, so let's have
Valentine's every day instead of once a year.
    Give your love each
passing day and soon you'll come to
find, the love you have within you
was meant for all mankind!

Deb Ramer

When The Grass Isn't Green

When the grass isn't green
my beautiful flower blooms.
Cold and loneliness
never frequent my room.

Weak.
I obsessed for the other side,
which I thought would be... ecstasy.

But what was lust
I mistook for love.
A love consisting of
glass mirrors showing
illusions of bliss.

Now forlorn I truly miss
the love I once had.
Sad that she's gone.
Mad that I'm forever wrong.

Daring to master the clue,
that the other side only seems greener,
when the flower in my hold
is too good to be true.

Ted Bell II

Let Me Take Your Pain

Let me take your pain
Eat your bitterness
And tuck it away deep inside
So no one or nothing can hurt you.

Let me take your pain
I know it hurts
I will be your shield
I will be your warrior
In your fight for sanity.

Let me take your pain
Make me understand
How you feel!
I want to hold you in...
Till the storm breaks
Please let me in!
Don't hold it in any longer!
Let me take you away from this hell!
Let me take your pain!

Francesca King

Trinidad

O lovely soul, I cannot hold
elusive soul so shining.
Such grace in every movement shows
in morning's wake or crying.

My life, love and peace of mind
your cunning perception divines.
In soft comfort or loyal care,
confronting with enchanting stare,
and healing with a love I swear
leaves me breathless, eyes open wide.

A dancing vision of beautiful white
casting darker shadows that make you alive.
Exciting and real, a single creation
only the creator could ever contrive.

I keep the beads around my neck
that you created for me, and wonder...
How many days have lived and died,
that have heard me whisper beneath a sigh
a prayer for you, that testifies
that you are worth so much to me.

John Hansen

Rose Scent

The sweet fragrance
embraced my nostrils
with an eternal addiction
to the delicate scent
of a rose.

The perfumed rose
is nature's way
of sweetening the earth
with only a faint
but enchanting scent.

Brenda Faye O'Neal

Wishful Dreams

Dream about the stars,
Dream about the moon,
Dream about the sun so bright,
You close your eyes with all your might,
Wish upon a star,
Wish for lovely dreams,
Wish for a sun so bright
Above the shimmering seas.

Andrea Cox

Walk On The Green Of Spring

I walk on the green of spring,
but I fade to sleep on the winter's white.
Spring is my time to explore,
as the wealth of nature matures.

It's the walks on her freshly cut green grass
I dream for, while I wait for winter to pass.

Spring's green will grow into gold,
so sad is the day when the air must grow cold.

While fall grieves for her prodigies of summer
winter moves in for her yearly return.
The whites of her veil lull me to sleep,
only to wake to sounds of spring's little Hummer.

Once again I live and breath,
as I walk on that first green of spring.
Matt R. Weinheimer

In Waste Places

I feel as if I am here for some intrinsic reason.
But in my ever present conscience-
there is no admissible reason for my essence.
This world would be better off without me I declare!
Without an implement of war; in this belligerent terrestrial sphere,
I shall be defunct!
And in my darkest hour-
all the malevolence in my heart
will be brought out to show this world
just who I am.
And I, in my abominable fate,
Will destroy and dispose-
of all the waste in this belligerent spaceship earth.
And no one can stop me for malice is ever present;
in this evil sanity of mine.
My heart however, can be declared destroyed.
It has been disregarded time and time again-
and I will never let it be shattered as it was.
And it shall not be known to anyone at all-
as long as I am ever existent on this belligerent cradle of humanity.

J. R. Emili

Forgive Them Father

It really is a crying shame,
But mankind is the one to blame.
They're destroying God's World and all his dreams;
They're ripping it apart by the seams.

Where will God's children be tomorrow
But in a World that is filled with sorrow?
Where will God's children be in the future
But in a World with wounds to suture?

Man has committed the greatest sin
By allowing Satan to just move in.
Now all mankind what gender he be
Must ask of God he be set free,

For with the World so filled with violence and hate,
God will never open up his gate.
Now all mankind must open his heart
And ask for forgiveness on his part,

For with the world so filled with all man's greed
Mankind now must make a plea!
For all mankind must kneel down and pray
That He be forgiven and saved some day!
Theresa Sanchez

Dream Of The Dolphin

The dolphin now lives in the oceans of grace,
but may not for long exist in this beautiful place,
They are playful and curious and intelligent from birth,
and I'm sure if they spoke they would tell of dreams for the Earth.
If we could only see beneath their curious faces,
we would find dreams of a world of all natural places.
They would dream of a life without constant fear,
Where danger and hunger would never be near.
Where they wouldn't be forced to flee from their homes,
and live feeling unwanted deep beneath the foam.
And forced to live in the crevices of all that were left.
But soon again would run, due to human theft.
They would dream of a world where everyone would care;
where love and tenderness would always be there.
Where they would be able to live in their true homes of grace,
that Mother nature gave them before the human race.
If she had only known what we were blind enough to do,
she would have made the dolphin in a whole world anew.
But now it's up to us to do all that we can,
to help save the dolphin from a world killed by man.
Melissa Hudasko

Mother Of Mine

God made all Mothers special:
But mine was the best.
For He added something extra,
that was lacking in all the rest.
With those bright shining eyes,
She saw only the good in others.
Her heart was filled with love for all
her sisters and brothers.
With many children of her own.
She had time for others, you were never alone.
Her energy was endless, her needs so small.
But she was always there for you,
all you had to do was call.
I'm so glad she was my Mother,
for I would have no other.
You see - she's no longer here,
she departed this earth without any fear.
But she left a precious gift upon this
earth - she gave me life - she gave me birth.
Rita M. Pineda

Max

His thick black hair is gray now where the puppy fur had been,
But that was almost thirteen years ago.
Although his sense of smell is sharp, his radar ears still keen,
His joints just make him move a little slow.

He gently pads around the house to get a running start,
and climbs upstairs to take his daily nap.
He lies down on his pillow and remembers younger days
when the pillow that he had was Tammy's lap.

A Timber Wolf his mother was, he never knew his dad,
The California desert way out west
She did not want the kind of life for him that she had had,
so to leave him with this girl, she knew was best.

So Tammy took him in and he became her special friend,
a bond that's grown in strength throughout the years.
He knows they'll be together just as always till the end,
but he dreads the day he turns her smile to tears.

But his life is hardly over, there's a secret that he knows
For once he let's his mind relax and eyes begin to close
Those memories flow in all at once and love inside him grows
And he'll wake again a puppy stuck inside an old dogs clothes.
Kenneth A. Horn Jr.

An Empty Valentine

February fourteenth is Valentine's day
but my valentine has since passed away.
I still have a heart full of love
that's why I moan as a mourning dove.

There will be no love letters the rest of my years
for to think about my loss brings to my eyes tears.
Although I wish things the same as they were
the Lord knows by far what's best for her.

I hope my actions can be excused
for without my wife I am so confused.
She noticed things wrong in so many ways
but she found the answer for she knew how to pray.

Marjorie through age had lost some charms
but oh how this old man would hold her in his arms.
Perhaps this is the reason I will never roam
for our arms will be full when I come home.

Red Smith

Back To God America

In this land so beautiful,
But, oh how marred by sin;
Much strife and violence have entered in
Return to God, oh America, the beautiful.

There's a call coming forth to reverse
It's a call direct from God
He is the God of this universe
Also of this land we call America.

Our forefathers trusted Him, they were safe
Oh say, America, turn back in faith
Come back; come to the light
It's shining, shining so bright.

He's waiting for everyone
In America to come; He loves you
Oh sinner hasten, do not delay
Let God have His way.

Come back, come back
Let your light shine bright
Let music, swell the air
Let people far and near breathe a prayer.

Nellie Randolph

A Dark Stranger

A dark stranger visited me one night,
but only to give me quite a fright.

Am I awake or only dreaming?
or will it go away if I start screaming?

Why was it so real, leaving me with a chill,
ever so scary made me ill.

He left me only with his mark one
dark lonely night,
So still I laid there full of fright.

But to my delight that I can fight,
this dark stranger of the dark with my knight.
Oh, so full of light and ever so bright,
my bright shining knight came to my rescue one night.

"Have no fear my dear" he said.
I'll always be very near.

Don't be afraid of dark things
in the middle of the night,
I'll always be by my dear.
So remember when this dark stranger ever should appear,
Have no fear for I'm very near.

Margie J. Dover

Goodbye

I loved you so much and I know you loved me;
But sometimes the best things cease to be.
Sometimes two people were not meant for each other;
No matter how much one loved the other.

I had thought before about losing your touch;
I never imagined it would hurt this much.
My thoughts are still with you all throughout each day;
And even at night you are there when I pray.

If ever you think of me please let it be kind;
Because that is how you are thought of in my heart and my mind.
I love you so much so I am letting you go;
How hard it is to do this you never will know.

I am not burning the bridge that connected our hearts;
I am just shutting the gate so I can get a new start.
The bridge will still be there but the gate will be locked;
If you ever need it opened all you must do is knock.

So I am saying goodbye but it is just for awhile;
I hope you will be my friend when I am ready to smile.
Please give me one more promise and then I'll let you be;
Promise with your whole heart you will never forget me.

Rachel Rohlf

Sometimes I'm Lonely

Sometimes I want to love someone and want them to know,
But sometimes they won't see it my way and just want to go.

Sometimes I'm afraid but have no one to help me,
So I put my fear in a bag, throw it away, and let it be.

Sometimes I'm hurt inside and no one's there to take the pain away,
I take the hurt and cover it with good and let it pass another day.

Sometimes I hear things I don't want to,
I deafen at the sound and hum my own happy song through.

Sometimes I see things I don't need to see,
I blind the sight to put my own loving picture in for me.

Sometimes I get put down,
So I go into another room and color my heart
with dreams and another sound.

Sometimes there's no one there to talk to me,
I overthrow myself with images of people to see.

Sometimes I'm lonely......

Tanisha R. Parker

My So Called Life

I have died a thousand deaths,
    But my life as I live it is the worst pain.
Sometimes I wonder - if I died,
    Would anyone really care?
Would it really matter to anyone?
    My family would miss me, but for how long?
How long until my memory faded away?
    As it always does.
How long until they no longer hear my laughter,
    Or they can no longer see my smile?

And my friends, those I still have,
    How long until they find someone else to fill
My stool at the end of the bar or until
    They find someone else to make them laugh,
Or to be the one they laugh at.
    Am I simply taking up space?
Does anything I do matter really...
    Or do I even matter at all?

Michelle Lawson

Donna My Sister, My Friend

My sister is the one with the patched-up heart
But still shows her love even though we're apart
Her love and support helped me through some bad times
And I knew it was certainly, the very best of signs

She has many problems, it makes me want to cry
And always says to me, glad it's her, not I
Her pain has now become an everyday thing
Yet she still tries so hard not to complain

Even though it has been especially hard
It may just be in the turn of the card
Her trip to Hawaii is close, that I know
For there are people to meet, and places to go

She doesn't like hearing that she is terribly strong
But I doubt that I could hardly be seriously wrong
For even when met with new obstacles to face
She's my sister I love, and could never replace

Rosemary Schilz

Two Hearts

A hot summer night,
But summer is not quite yet here,
He lives there, she lives here
Everything is quiet and still,
as the thunder starts to roar,
does he think of me, as I think of him?

A low hum of the whirling sound from the fan
can be heard during the night.
Still in the early morning darkness,
you can hear the thunder off in the distance.

The clock chimes quietly.
I still think of him, but does he think of me?

Two hearts, alone or as one.
As morning nears, darkness fades.
A tear gently rolls down her cheek,
I think of him, does he think of me?

Susan F. Hubrich

Again

They loved each other at one time and thought that they would forever,
But the ways of life separated them apart
She cried all night, hoping he'd want her back looking in the mirror
   all she
Can see is a red tear streaked face staring back at her
She calls a dear friend to tell problems to
The friend listens patiently, saying helpful things
Sitting alone in dark candle lit room she tries to forget him and
   figures
That everyone goes though this at one time or another
Days, weeks, and months pass before she finally finds another guy,
Who really cares for her and who she really cares for
And once again she falls in love

Kristi Houck

Unseen Love

To a great Grandchild I will never hold,
But unseen arms I will still him fold.
With dark brown eyes and curly blond hair,
My unseen love will always care.

Take not away his unusual dreams,
For life is so short it seems.
Though I am not there to give you this card,
My thoughts come to you from a loving heart.

With a loving heart and caring hands,
This little man Karl will make life grand.

Pauline Meis

"The Lovers"

Miles of land and water separate the two,
But their love is true.
Dreaming forlorn of each other at night,
Awaiting the day they can hold each other tight.
His kiss still lingers upon her sweet, soft lips,
As into a wistful sleep she slips.
In the darkness she reaches out for him,
Only to awake and find she is alone again.
Her heart is full of pain and woe,
If she'll see him again she doesn't know.
If only to feel his tender touch once more,
Like the tenderness of waves caressing the shore.
For star-struck lovers they must be,
And never again the other shall they see.

Samantha Porter

Love

Love is something that cannot die,
But then again love is blind,

When you vow to be together till you die,
Your "lover" is not one of those until you die,

Kindness is not love,
you don't see love you feel it,

And this is thus the strongest
feeling that can't be broke.

Now you say what feeling,
and I say, the feeling you
feel, and not until you
feel it are you in love.

Lori West

Obstacles

Our love has lasted over a year
But, there are still obstacles that will come near
They will try to test the strength of our love
But, our love was meant to be and was sent from above
As long as we face it all together
Our love will last forever
No matter what they send our way
We both will face it day by day
Always trust what's in your heart
Because that is where it all starts
We'll face the world hand in hand
I'm not only your lover I'm also your friend
We both share a love so tender
And we both must always remember
All the precious times we've had together
And that so much more will come between
now and forever!

Shelli K. Ornellas

Riches In Glory

Silver, gold and diamonds may be OK
But you know that they will tarnish
And then fade away
On earth man lies, steals and will kill
Do everything to get riches
Except obey God's will
If to God you will trust and obey
You will inherit your riches in Glory one day
In Heaven, where streets are gold
Where everyday is sunshine
And we will never grow old
Don't get caught up in this world's treasures
Because the riches in Glory
Are far beyond measure.

Yvonne Elizabeth Davis

"Breaking-Up"

People say breaking-up is hard to do
but they don't know the half of it.

Breaking-up with you is the hardest thing
I ever did in my life.

I thought my life was hard but now
I know how hard it is to break-up.

I can't believe that the love is gone.
The only thing that I ever cared for is gone.

Why'd you leave? You proved me wrong.
I thought I was strong
But now I know I can't handle it.

When people said you'd hurt me, I didn't want to
Believe them, but as they say, love is...
"Always blind."

Tanya Suzel

World Of Harmony

Black, white, tan—it all amounts,
But underneath it is what really counts.
It's not about the skin on someone's face
It's about unity of the human race.
Chinese, American, African, old, and young, but beneath it all lies the
    truth.
Don't judge on how one looks or where they've been;
seek much deeper and look within.
The heart will bear the sorrow that was born,
From a nation filled with hate and scorn.
Without hate there would be no war
And tears of grief be shed no more.
The cry of a nation is heard by all;
those who hate are often the first to fall.
We need to love to stop the hate, for this determines our nation's fate.
Put events of the past behind and look forward with an open mind.
Search for peace, not revenge; the wounds of a nation we have yet to
    mend.
The world would be better if we could get along with one another
Regardless of origin, regardless of color.
Love and peace must be our ultimate goal,
And to change this nation that looks at race instead of soul.
Become at peace before it's too late
For it's easier to love than it is to hate.

Kara Jones

...And So You Told Me

You told me not to go
but who am I to listen.
You told me not to go
but it made my heart glisten.

I was beginning to feel things
never felt before.
I was beginning to feel things
so I walked out the door.

Your love scared me, we were
getting too close.
Your love scared me and anything goes.

I had to get away, just take a little trip.
I had to get away, it just happened to slip.

As I realize my heart is torn.
As I realize my heart is in mourn.

I say to you now my torn heart grew.
I say to you now
I really love you.

Marti Henderson

Ghost With A Poem

I see you walking by and I look at you,
but you just walk on, leaving me a shadow.
Piercing my heart with silence I did not know before.
What did I do to make you treat me so?
Did I wither your heart with my words of good-bye?
Leaving you in a land full of tears and windblown dreams.
You are shattering me,
like a tornado, sweeping over and destroying me all at once.
Did I take your soul away when I left you?
Inside you where love once shone,
I now find the storm of death.
Tell me what I can do to change your ways,
I'd pull the moon from the sky, if that's what it will take.
When you are willing, sing me a love song
and I'll be there for you.
Just don't take as long as a summer's eve,
leaving me to wonder,
if I'm nothing but a ghost with a poem to you.

Natasha Rotshteyn

The Line

You are a friend I would always trust,
But your love for them was a simple must.
You didn't love me, although I loved you,
You thought they reserved their love for you too.
When you found out they didn't, you were crushed.
Away from their shoulders you were slowly brushed.
When they were gone you talked to me.
Then the new girls came, and who was alone? Me.
Again you went through the line.
When they were gone my company was just fine.
I can't take all the heartache
Every time you leave I have a heart break.
Then you come back and I think I'll be fine
Then it happens again, and I know you'll never be mine.

Sarah J. Paul

Witches

We freed ourselves once
by dancing like witches in the moonlight, laughing.
Do you remember
the moment we held each other, sister, unafraid?

We danced for each other,
careening wildly around your living room furniture,
the clear, white moonlight streaming in
through the open window—
our promise to each other.

Sometimes I still think of us like that.
Witches of the silent hills,
dancing in the moonlight,
freedom blowing like the night wind
between our outstretched hands,
fearless, laughing.

Teresa L. Hibbard

Reflections

Walking silently through the night;
    Carefully seeking each star of bright,
Step into past, present and future now;
    Each movement reflecting a stranger's bow.
Move on, move on, my wondering heart;
    Heaven and earth shall have their part,
Touch the hand of living and dead;
    My soul is watching up ahead,
All are there in my sight,
    All reflections of the light,
Touch me now for I am near,
    Touch me now, thus I disappear.

Ruth Joy Hicks

Innocence Of Protection

The glory of innocence is celebrated
By the sound of our children's voices.
Every word attempted reveals
The hidden pleasures of the day.
These children reach into our hearts
As they cradle us in their arms;
Protecting us from our daily desires,
Guarding us from the trenches of the night.
While in their arms we hide our eyes
To the burning truth which is revealed.
Protecting us from the sharp pains of the day
Is the purity of their souls
guided by the warmth of their loving hearts.

Marianne Ware

You

You came in without any warning or sound
Calmly you observed what you knew you'd eventually treasure
Your searching eyes spoke silent words of understanding
To a beguiled soul

At night you'd come to me in my dreams with those
deep probing eyes, touching my senses once again
We danced in the light of the moon until it was time
to retreat back into the coma of sleeping emotions

And like strangers, we'd nod cordially, not daring to speak
of last night's rendezvous, for fear that it would disappear
into the limbo of forgotten destinies
Still, you endured my aimless manner with quiet turmoil

Until finally, I reached out my hand
and took your precious gifts
I devoured your essence with a welcome hunger
All the while knowing I had at last reached reality

You looked into me and said
you'd been there all along, knowing fate
would bring our spirits together
I looked into you and said, "May I have this dance?

Veronica H. Gonzalez

"Fall Into Love"

Halfway through my fall into love,
Came a cry, "reach out, hold on,"
But I couldn't find my hands.
Of course, because they were holding my heart,
To try to keep it from breaking.

Heidi Billow Cavaliere

Seasons

Spring, the beginning of a new year,
but, please don't shed a tear.
The flowers might not now be alive,
but don't worry, summer will soon arrive.

In summer, we think of the sun,
in summer, we think of fun.
The late flowers now bloom,
and there is plenty of room.

The leaves are now orange, yellow, and red,
as the trees are soon dead.
For the leaves then fall,
off trees both small and tall.

It turns cold and maybe snows,
it gives you chills when the wind blows.
When frost is on the ground,
Spring is soon to come around.

Ryan Plott

Pull Me Through

Try to realize what's happening to me
Can never live my life the way it ought to be

I'm so oblivious to what is going on
Seems like time never moves, but the days still roll on

Where have they gone, all my high aspirations
I'm gonna need help to rectify the situation

The trip I'm taking ain't no fun at all
If I go any further I know I'm going to fall

My whole entire world is spinning around
Bringing tears to my eyes, always lost but never found

In the toughest of times I need the Lord to guide me
Through a psychedelic trip, someone to be by my side

Music is my guide, but it won't let me wait
God, please help me now before it's way too late.

Maybe all the tough guys will shake their heads and shrug,
But the toughest man of all is the one who really needs a hug

Pull me through

Ronald A. Busse

My Fault

The sky turned blood red.
"Can you hear me," a voice said.
As the sweat dripped down my head,
On the cold concrete I bled.

The slug was hungry, on my flesh it fed.
Waiting to be rescued, not wanting to be dead.
Lying on the ground, thinking about life.
For some strange reason I felt a light.

Maybe I was dreaming or just needed a rest.
But then I knew better when I drew in my breath.
I couldn't feel anything, no air coming inside.
Looked down at my body and realized I had died.

So, could this be the end? Now, where were my friends?
As I took the flight toward eternity.
There's no one to blame but me.

Alive, this point I could not see.
There were things I could have done,
To prevent me from being slain.
I should have stayed home and studied.
But instead I ran around with a gang.

Steven L. Sweeney

Untitled

The things I feel when I'm with him
Can't be described in words

The way my heart pounds
The way my trembling hands become moist with sweat
The way the words come out of my mouth—
    scrambled—
      if they come out at all
Yet he seems to understand

He moves with grace as if to dance
His eyes catch the sunlight
    and sparkle like Prince Charming's
He smiles the perfect smile
He laughs the perfect laugh

But
Maybe his heart pounds the same
Maybe his hands tremble, as well
Maybe he, also, finds it hard to speak
Maybe he's just like me
Maybe he's human, too

Lisa Pechan

You're Hurting Me

There you are, holding her hand
Can't you see you're hurting me?
Don't tell me you love me,
When you whisper those same to her
Don't tell me you want me to be yours,
When she already is
I wish I could be yours,
I wish I could be in your arms
I wish I the one you love,
But I'm not, so you have a choice to make
It's either her or me,
Please make it quick
Because you're hurting me

Laura M. Franks

Payday

The warm sun bathed the rocking chair, illuminating my Mother's
Care-worn face, as she rocked with a dented pan on her lap,
Snapping beans with an easy grace.
We watched from the stoop, as my Daddy's hobnailed boots
Came up the road, kicking up small tornadoes in the red
Oklahoma dust,

As he went by us with a sharp breeze of sawdust and Southern
Comfort,

Not stopping but briefly reaching with a hard gnarled
Hand to stroke my Mother's hair,

And the metallic river of silver that poured from his
Other hand into that old dented pot,
Matched the flow of tears that silently slid down my
Mother's face.

Vonna Bechtel

Life Starts At Sixty-Two!

Some lives begin when schooling's done,
Careers are sought and families planned,
Successes that are early won,
Are quick to slide in the fleeting sand.
Choices are made, some grandly feted,
The finer ones are ne'er regretted.
But, alas, they may be far between
the choices made that should have been;
Those that lacked the carrying-out,
that meaningful life is all about.
I wonder if a helping hand, could have caused
   the fires fanned,
to change the way one's life was run,
to find that moment in the sun?
But lest I dwell on decades spanned.
on subjects that are better banned;
I'd like to now begin anew,
To say life starts at sixty-two!

Marianne Ellen Dahill

Forever?

The paths of love wind and twist their
curious way through the every day fog and
confusion of life.

Compassion fights with passion- as desire
builds- then dissolves into a fine mist that
evaporates into the air- as if it never
existed.

Since nothing lasts forever- one wonders-
does forever exist at all- or is it a phantom
waiting to make its entrance in our dreams-
deep in the dark night- only to disappear as
our eyes open.

Tom Hyman

The Body's Enmity

Timid blood in warm passages coursing
carrying life and death 'neath fragile derma worn,
crimson flood in living caverns pulsing
feeding a mass of death from painful secrets born.

Tender skin beneath the poniard scarring
weeping silent as scarlet furrows turn to stone,
trembling limbs clutch flaxen daylight dimming
surrendering the cast of malignant flesh and bone.

Probing eyes stare soundless criticizing
sifting shame uprooted by corporeal repair,
healing fire in isolation burning
purging all but courage in the vacancy left there.

Faded seams, because the years were passing,
making further distant her body's injury,
humbled dreams long for devotion, waiting,
standing still and shameless in their unveiled dignity.

Gentleness moved from his lips embracing
kissing imperfection, sentient infirmity,
brokenness found love for it desiring
conquering the sorrow of her body's enmity.

Lori Michelle Cameron

"Gone With The Wind" (Remembrance)

This fiery love between beautiful Scarlett O'Hara and Rhett Butler,
caught by her willful charms, Oh' how he loved her.

He was dressed as debonair, well tailored as if he was going to a
ball, Oh' so handsome, so tall.

Scarlett, guarded with bonnets, veils, and mittens against the hot
Georgia sun, willful, lusty with life full of joy and fun.

Her dresses, some trimmed with lace set off to perfection, Scarlett's
green eyes, sweet face, tightly fitting basque breast, showed
attention, her worked suntan hands folded in her lap, her true self
was poorly concealed.

This younger servant Prissy's comment called out "Miss Scarlett,
Miss Scarlett, we's got to have a doctah. Ah, ah Miss Scarlett,
Ah doan know nuthin' 'bout birthin' no babies.
Ah jes' see one baby birthed."
Prissy in her dream world skipping along singing.

Scarlett's love for this beautiful red earth land with rolling hills
called "Tara."
Mammy, a faithful servant she too loved Scarlett O'Hara.

Louise B. Delozier

Emma

Ariel— air
child of light.
A cutout tissue moon
against translucent blue
on a bright autumn day.
You dart through life
a kiss
a breeze.
I grin at you, you are air and light
I am earth and water; I dwell
in the hips of the universe
unruly, heavy, moist. My feet
happily made of clay
reside in the banks and stone of the creek.
But I love you.
Emma Ariel Air
Child of Light
Daytime Moon, Feathered Clouds
Wisp. Breath.
Angel.

Rose Sawyer

A Speck Of Dust

A tiny speck of cosmic dust,
caught up in winds of time
and blown from here to there.
out of all control, but destiny.

Oh to land upon a dew wet leaf,
becoming then the mystery of life
to integrate with all that is,
and then to bloom in glorious color.

The process for the growth of living things
includes the pain of being tossed about,
to land in unfamiliar barren soil,
waiting there to be the garden grown.

One never knows what speck of dust
was taken to some garden there,
or from the garden of one's birth
to become the fertile soil here.

And it probably matters very little,
from whence the cosmic dust did come.
What matters more, wherever came this tiny speck,
It is the garden, and the garden is the dust.

William D. Kelly

Love

She warms my heart as the morning sun
   chasing the dew from the lilies on the pond
the whisper of her name as sweet as the sound
   of wind rushing through cypress pines,
   and gentle waves surging to shore

With eyes as bright and beautiful as the stars
   on a dark winter night
A softness and strength like billowy
   thunder heads in a summer sky

A smile that calms my anguished heart
A tenderness and passion beyond my dreams
Feelings of love and comfort in her arms
I call her mother

William D. Simo

Description

   Those ruby lips, those rosy
cheeks, description. That perfect nose,
that beautiful smile, description. That
caring feeling, that Holy Spirit, description.
   Those sparkling brown eyes, those shiny white
teeth description. That silky hair, that
smooth skin description.

Kidane T. Frezgi

Silken Sounds

Her voice, her skin, her touch, her aroma....
Can silk be as smooth? She called and I went limp,
   my heart in my throat
When I saw her it was as if we had never parted
I touched her face and its smoothness was as warm
   silk
She has lines at her eyes and worries about
   perfection
She giggles when she is nervous, when I tell her
she is beautiful and when I tell her I love her
But never when we make love
When we make love the world is silent
There is no one else
She makes sounds then also but they are ours and
they become lost within us.

Morris Martin

Endless Crying

The wind blew coldly through the night.
Chilling fear shivered up my spine—What a fright?
Nothing is no longer mine.
It doesn't seem fair how the walls close in on me
I can't breath!
I feel locked up instead of free
The dream keeps drifting—Searching for the dreamer,
To let it be seen.
But no one knows where to look or where it has been?
I feel alone in the dark night.
Wishing to see peace in my soul—
To find a warming light.
But all I see is an endless dark hole.
I want the pain to stop the slow dying.
So maybe I can stop the weakness—
That keeps the endless crying.

Michele Ross

What Is A Poem

A poem is magic of mind and soul,
Close your eyes and be a dreamer of
the things untold. Give thanks to
our God, for love and peace. The
Cool fresh breeze is magic blowing,
Through the very tall trees. Birds are
singing, children are playing by the
grass and budding flowers. Smile be
happy for the beautiful memories.
It's Spring! thanks to our God it's here again.

Mildred Davis

Rose Sings To The Cloud

Elements of nature and mists of ocean, unites to form the mystical
cloud, Lord of creation forms the clouds in dimension of beauty,
fairest colors of joyful smile, bequeathed with Love, he pours rain
upon the thirsty mother earth in heavenly delight, and to its own
sweet love, to the blown buds of rose, he bring showers of beguile.

O' my lovely cloud, thou dwell at the highest heights of the sky,
Thundering, lightening, fluttering in the wind, with passion for your
earthly rose,
When the love my cloud ascends to ecstasy of soul, and in rapture too!
In buoyant cheers you pour rains upon me, that love transcends so close.

Majestic cloud! O' sweetest lover, your love is mighty and eternal,
And I your honied rose, the passionate pleasure of flower,
It is spirit of high love, which creates magnetic union between us,
And, through our sweet unison, flows a stream of passion and pleasure.
O' dearest cloud, love of my love, you change colors overpowered
with love, and this opens my petals through your beating showers,
Lovely! O' my pretty soul, how enchanted and thrilled I feel,
Rich in beauty that is deep like love, floats my cloud; I sing then
loud "Love is My Majestic Tower."

Qamar A. Khan

Time

Desire flies on wings of fire,
Dawn flies on wings of time,
Riding on the tip of a flame that can expire,
Is like standing on bare wire, with nothing below
White bird of snow signals a sign, of where to land
On a silver strand of sorrow
On the sand of tomorrow's dreams
And it seems a long way down, circling the ground,
   preparing to descend, thinking of an
   end to the known.
Just around the bend lies time, time to come home.
Time can be a friend when you're alone.

Sharon H. Davenport

The Floods

Moon sliver
Clouds too swift to see forms
Flaps of wind
Ripple Rivers rushing to catch the sea
Pounding, sliding earth
All moving to the vertex of their final destiny
Bring us all along the way

Hip-high waters
Snows on the summit too
Traffic slows
Traffic jams
Eternal forces know no road blocks
In spite of dams, sand bags and human sinew
Forces all rushing to be unbridled

Forces rushing to be free
Forces rushing to the sea
Valerie Reschke

Searchers

The touch of marsh is beneath his feet, but still he struggles on.
Cold and wet, and so firm of a grip, he gasps in the darkness.
Shadows are all around.
But still he sees, his vision twilights the ground.
All know he is there, but ignore his radiant silence.
He searches the darkness that has no end.

The drops of mist obstruct her view. But, she is there.
Sounds are bold, the sky is black, but she is still there.
All know of her. She faces the northern wind.
And when all is clear, the colors are lost.

… A hesitation. She journeys on.
At dawn they meet, suddenly everyone speaks.
The lions roar, the birds sing.
And all the while, jackals watch from below and whisper such
fantasies. But to no avail, for the two have become one.
As the two lights of warmth were always meant to be.

The flowers are in bloom. The shadows are gone.
Warm love radiates the once cool ground.
The colors have returned, the fields are bright, the birds continue
to sing. This dawn will never die.
Randy Johns

Healing Heart

Oh dear friend for goodness sake,
Couldn't you see my smile was just a fake.
I was trying to hide my pain and tears,
Couldn't you see I was full of fears.

I always gave him all I had,
And his betrayal made me so sad.
I just couldn't bare being apart,
From the man I loved with all my heart.

My heart ached so very much,
How could he hurt me without a thought.
I was so much like a clown,
That smiled while tears were rolling down.

I had no hope, I had no will,
It would take a while for my heart to heal.
I thought my world was coming to an end,
I asked the lord my heart to mend.

Forgive me friend for all my doubts,
When my life was in distraught.
You always said I'll be alright,
You know my friend, I have seen the light.
Margarita Diaz

" Being Able To Unfold "

The most glorious moment of my life, is when that moment of solitude
Comes, and I visit with my inner self, it starts with a peaceful
Silence that no words could express, but it's a peacefulness that
I think everyone should take the opportunity to experience every now,
And then.

Oh the inner gives so much wisdom, (yes) wisdom that you can't
learn in schools, or with people, for one can only find this within
  oneself,
(Yes) your inner self, for your inner self is your church, and in
  that church,
Is your God, which is all our God! (Yes) God our Heavenly
  Father, so do
Yourself a favor, visit your inner, don't cheat yourself of this great
Privilege, for the more one discovers of oneself, the more
  knowledgeable his or
Her wisdom is, for to know oneself, is to love, and comprehend his or
  herself,
As well as actions in life.
La Verne D. Nixon

Earth

Digging in the coffee ground soil
Connected to the cycles of life
The spiraling mandala of life
Seeds Opening, Ejaculating
the concealed speck of life outward for adventure
Sprouts propel embryonic fingers toward the sun
pushing, pressing, pulsating
Eager eggs incubate in the auger of warm moist earth
Loam teaming with life
Larval squirming, twisting, writhing,
I nnnnn chi nnnnnn gggggg toward metamorphosis
Roots pushing into terra's heart
Worms wiggling, slithering, stiring, airing,
adding to the organic sustenance of the clay

Rotting leaves, empty shells, decaying matter
The rejected, discarded past
Becoming the food for creation

Creation becoming tomorrow
Rose Anna Hines

"It Sounds Like The Moon"

Listen!
Do you hear it?
Wait- don't give up- just one moment more.
Oh! There it is again!
You didn't hear it?
Why, how could you have missed it?

You want to know what it sounds like?

Well that's easy.
It sounds like tulips trying to open, or a spider spinning silk-
like sunlight seeping through windows, or candlelight piercing
darkness.
It sounds like the moon in early morning moments.
morning moments.

None of these things make sounds
-you say-
they're all silent.
Are you sure?
You've never heard just one of them?
Just one? Oh- I see.
You're right. There's nothing here for you to hear.
Let's go.
Monique Gagnon

Little Cricket

Poor little cricket, the world so bold, so many miles only he could know.

Do we see or really understand, the poor little cricket and his demands.
We're asleep, oblivious to his needs, what of the cricket with his debris.

Poor little cricket, he's so alone, we won't step around, we won't condone.

We don't know or begin to understand, only the cricket from where he lands.

Poor little cricket, from wisdom he's grown, but all those miles and he's still alone.
Poor little cricket, he stopped - he sees, poor little cricket is YOU AND ME!!

Melody Pride

Lonely Sentinel

If e'er this ragtag man with button eyes
    could speak to me …

As well as gentle deer on misty knolls
    and jeering sooty rooks that mock
    his being,

Would he tell of loneliness endured through
    chill and heat these many years he's stood?

He asks no wage nor bread for endless
    days on post -

Instead, mere tufts of straw or hay
    and cast-off rags to clothe
    his drooping form.

Raymond Champaigne

Domain Of Darkness

Children of darkness making their fight;
Crawling through hell searching for light.
Screeches of horror and deathly decay;
They lie all alone praying for day.
The one they call master holding them down;
With a smirk on his face and a blood red crown.
He rules over them with an obsession for death;
Beating them down and inhaling their breath.
But, there is a savior who will lead them away;
Though he charges a price, but still they will pay.
He leads them from darkness and out of hell;
So they reward him with riches and treat him well.
He rules over them with power until the very end;
But now don't you see they are in hell again.

Matthew Barrett

Sounds Of The Meadow

Silence split when a loon called twice for his mate.
Crickets sawed their hind legs against their fore-wings
and the music started.
The crickets took the soprano
the bull frogs the bass
and a loon came in with a solo.
When fireflies flicked their green lights on
the moon watched
the meadow brooded
the water laughed
and night slept.
Slept to the throb of muffled heartbeats,
slept like the calm after storm,
slept till the sun peaked out from under —
then burst with the glory of dawn.

Margaret M. Tollefson

An Uncertain Future

At night in my parent's backyard the smoke from my cigar
curls among the black tendrils of tree branches and gum balls.
Cast-back moon-light sparkles on billions of frozen
dew drops.

I try to consider how my life will be when
Parents, both old and slowing, are gone.

Even now, Mom is in the hospital feeling
her age and her painful knees.
Arthritis and hard work have broken
down her joints.

When I was young, my eyes would raise to the night sky
in search of answers: waiting.

Tonight I finish my cigar
and silently turn away

Revelation is not there, still.

Troy L. Miller

Untitled

The silence is deadly
Cutting all ties
    Like a knife swiftly ripping
    Through the chest, straight to the heart.

The silence leaves me feeling uneasy.
Something went wrong, yet I was given
No chance to understand or even confront
    The real issues at hand.

The knife, the silence
Both expose the heart to pain.

I really don't care for either.
Yet if I had to choose -
    The knife - most definitely
    For I could see it
        Possibly understanding why.

Richard E. Carr Jr.

Naive

Rolling golden fields of wheat.
Dancing about at the wind's command.
Careless and free in the sun's twilight.
Only to be the fate of a farmer's sharp blade.

Rita Paolella

Making Love With Heaven

Sitting on the harps and imagining to play
Dancing with the angels, what words can't say.
Heaven is too far but I'm too close
Like two thorns…………stuck in a rose

Blood like sugar on tip of my tongue
Nice lady in white, this is what she sung
If you make love with heaven
You'll create mysteries

Waking up to see a nightmare
Being sacrificed by God's tears in my ears
Voices are like footsteps in my brain
Look outside is it rain…………not possible

Foolish soul like me thinking, it's music
Is it my time to leave, is he trying
I know…..heaven's caretaker is crying…..
Please don't, oh powerful one
I won't ever love again…………'till eternity…
A fading smile…………..

Vikas Bhardwaj

Dare To Discover

Dare to discover it's easy you see
Dare to discover what's within you and me.

It's not the color of our skin, our age or our size
It's not our hair, our nose or our eyes.

It's within us I tell you, it's within don't you see?
It's within that's important in you and in me.

It's not our religion, our politics, our class
It's building our future from present and past.

It's our feeling, the person that we are inside.
It's our joy and our fear and the tears that we've cried.

It's how we act when the times they are bad
It's how we help someone else who is sad.

So dare to discover,I dare you to see
It's within us that counts, it's within you and me!

Kristin D. Frank

Illusions Of A Dream

Visions of horror haunt my nights, I see corpse, blood and fire,
dark men on horses with shining swords and empty laughter

"Heal my fears" I plea!
Suddenly I see myself standing by the window, a streak of silvery
moonlight caressing my hair

My image circles the darkness of this room, a cold breeze of touch
surrounds my body, and a voice echoes in my ear;

I am a tree, naked and black
My leaves are ashes of fear
I am a tree, covered with blood
Begging the sky and clouds to cry
I am a tree, cursed and lonely
Owls of night fearful of me
I am a tree, that's lynched mans' destiny

Crazy winds slash my thoughts, I open my eyes and squeeze my tears.

Marina Adamian

The Crush

You choose to ignore me,
day after day.
I choose to adore you,
in every way.
I admire your style, elegance, and grace.
Yet not once have you looked at me,
You've never seen my face.
For if you did, you'd have seen my eyes,
the two little windows,
that portray love, hate, and lies.
They would have revealed how much I love you so,
but you just ignore me,
looks like you'll never know.

Stefanie Adrahtas

Holocaust

What is this strident cry across our Native Land?
Emancipated Womanhood, heads buried in the sand?
Amidst the clamor, chaos, and confusion roar
Like thunderous, crashing waves on some far distant shore
Comes the silent sound and sorrowful scream
That will forever haunt the American Dream
Rejected Motherhood's lost treasure
Proclaiming this country's measure.
Our children!

Sheila Ryan Wallace

Untitled

Monday a day of no concern. It's a
day I must have earned. Of wisdom and
truth, I know I'll learn. Come one come
all, who's next for a turn.

Tuesday a day I've yet to reach, a baby
is born of man as breech, we walk and talk
to teach and preach. There are sixty-six wonderful
books of each.

Wednesday a day of in between. It's a day
some have never seen. You may say this sounds
so mean, God gives us a choice to fall or lean,
so we come to him on bending knees, for his
mercy as a team.

Thursday a day of few, only the spirit knows
who is who, Noah built his ark for two and two,
and only God knows the truth through and through.
Friday a day we pray to come, for all the
others we feel we've won; so the days we're
long and weighed a ton. We Praise the Father
for his only begotten Son.

Madeline Diane Walker

World Of Reality

Our minds are filled with disillusion as we live
day to day with so much confusion. And sometimes
it feels we're living in complete hell; feeling
the combustion. However; no one knows exactly
how the world really functions.

Everyone has abilities of their own kind, and
searching for that certain something that they
alone can only find. For they themselves cannot fall behind.

And when the time comes for the unexpected to
reach the next place in line; whenever, wherever,
however it wants; there will be no warning.
Therefore; we have no choice but to except in
due time, when our world has to abolish nothing
will be left but the memories of our today, and
the realities of tomorrow.

No more wars to be won, we fought till the end.
Now it's time to let your soul lay down to rest
for the earth has demolished; and in time of resting
you realize: Life has just begun, like a dream
left half undone.

Lisa D. Evans

"Significant Other"

Dear significant other,
Day's come and day's go
And before we know it years have gone by.
We have survived them
They all said that we would never make it
The odds were "Ninety-Nine To One" and in their favor
but we never broke, we kept our stride
Now more than a decade has gone by . . .
And still I see your dreams when you sleep.
When you're hurt, I feel pain
When you're happy, I laugh
And. . . When you cry, I feel your tears on my cheeks
Leaving traces and stinging my face.
The odds were "Ninety-Nine To One".
Not exactly the players choice, but we never broke
We kept our stride, past 'em all, we've won the race
For me, there will never be another.
Dear significant other,
My husband. . . my lover.

Ruth Yates

Death

Death is peace for the dying.
Death is sorrow for the living.
They lose their loved ones, that they love the most.
Some go fast, others go slow.
But no one knows when they will go.
They may go today or tomorrow, no one knows
Death is sad as can be.
It is a question that no one knows the answer to.
It makes people think, why do people have to die
It is their time?
Is it that God wants them?
Or is it just because they're too old.

Kathy Breeze

Ode To Liberty

Your cherubic face gurgles nonsensical sounds,
(Deciphered only by children the world around.)
But your message is clear as a moon glow above,
It's a child's heartfelt thought, a message of Love.

Tiny hands grapple at all in sight,
Your universe glows with an angel's delight.
From the taste of sweet honey, to the sky so blue,
All sights unspoiled, all thoughts are new.

What an enchanting age to live,
When the world knows only to love and give.
Before pain and doubt our faith would rust,
In a time before fear, it's so easy to trust.

So live sweet child to us so fair,
Never allow a thought to despair.
Learn to love, have faith, and to share,
You'll always be lovely to those who care.

Nick A. Catoe Jr.

Faith, Love, And Patience

Life's daily road is not a sure and easy way.
Decisions and problems are at hand each day.
Faith, love and patience are signs to follow,
That if used well, can help ease a lot of trouble.
Keep your faith in God, and to Him be loyal.
He doesn't expect us to be perfect in our daily toil,
Just that we accept, and express His perfect love.
Have love and kindness toward others first,
Then you are much easier to be loved.
Have patience and persistence with yourself.
Every one who tries stumbles and fails sometimes.
So accept your mistakes and failures with humor and calm,
Thank God for your victories, no matter how small,
And follow that true road sign to success that says "Try Again."

Rex A. Anderson

The Line

There was once a line
Crossing the states of Illinois,
Missouri, Nebraska, Colorado, Utah and Nevada.
It was a line of force, a straight line,
Stretched taut between two friends.
When the friends would speak across the line,
It would quiver and contract,
Undulating from the release of tension on both ends.
When the voices were gone,
The wake would lap against the shores of their minds,
And the thoughts would begin to build again,
Into another unbearable tension,
A satiable need, but barely so,
For there was still that line,
That damned, precious line,
  between them.

Quent Cordair

My Spirit

As I wonder every day what you are to me, I realize you are the deepest part of my soul.

As I wonder every week what you are to me, I realize you are the thoughts that make me whole.

As I wonder every month what you are to me, I realize you are the tomorrow I wait for.

As I wonder every day what you are to me, I realize you are my body's core.

As I wonder every week what you are to me, I realize you are the roots to my being.

As I wonder every month that you are to me, I realize that without you I am fleeing from myself.

For without you in my life I am a shell with only loneliness inside. Please come rescue me from all that I hide.

I look to the sky and thank the heavens for all you have given me. And I look at the mystery of it all and wonder- will you be near?

As I sit and wonder about it all- suddenly it is clear. For you will always be here- and I should never fear.

For my spirit is with me in my body and my soul-
It is the one thing that forever make me whole.

Letitia Alcox

Remnants Of The Storm

The sun, not yet seen,
Dimly lights the grayness of the morn
Allowing us to view the remnants of the storm
Whose fury passed while we slept
Unaware and dreaming of sunny days and laughter.

Tender, newborn leaves,
Ripped from the delicate grasp
Of mother tree by ravaging wind.
The remnants of the storm lie withering and dying upon the ground,
Droplets of the storm's rain glisten upon the fresh green slowly fading.

The ant, just emerging,
To a world transformed and devastated
Reshaped and sodden.
The remnants of the storm continue their struggle
Endlessly searching for sustenance in a mystical rhythm of living.

The remnants of the storm
Ravaged and plundered scourged and eroded
Living goes on by those remaining
In a meaningless striving to survive
For all things become the remnants of the storm.

William G. Boltz

"O. J. The Juice"

On the football field he
cut loose. Ran many touch-
downs. The crowd roared and
all called him, "The Juice." He
gained money, fame, and glory.
He was a national idol, so the
story goes. He retire from football
and went to T.V. Ran through
bus terminals and air terminals.
Then the higher up started
calling him, "The Juice." He was
the toast of the town, now he's
down. Now prosecutors and all,
are squeezing "The Juice"

Minister James E. Vanderhorst

What's To See

What do people see when they look at me?
Do they see arms and legs and a torso to hold them in place?
Do they see ears and eyes and lips that make
"just another pretty face?"

What do people see when they look at me?
Do they see who I'm trying to be?
Do they see what they want me to be?
Do they see I'm not really me?

What do people see when they look at me?
I hope it's not what I see
I know the outside is not attractive to thee
but, what is inside is to grotesque to set free.

What do people see when they look at me?
Do they see eyes so hollow that even echoes get lost in them?
Do they see a person whose roots are to far from the tree?
Please don't look at me.

What do people see when they look at me?
Do they know? Do they really know? Do they understand?
Do they want to? No one knows what it's like to be me.
They can only go by what they see. And that just may be a fallacy.

Sonia Rollins

The Whisper

   Hold your breath
Do you hear the whisper, the whisper of death
The day is done, night has begun
Do you hear the whisper, the whisper of death
In the corner of every shadow
Behind every dream
Do you hear the whisper, the whisper of death
In the mind, body, and soul
In the cry of the young and the pain of the old
Do you hear the whisper, the whisper of death
On a cold winters eve, on a hot summers day
Do you hear the whisper, the whisper of death
Close the door, turn away
Do you hear the whisper, the whisper of death
Lock the door, run away
Do you hear the whisper, the whisper of death
   ...Hold your breath

Sarah Costello

"Questions"

Do you see the big smile on my face?
Do you see my pretty dress trimmed in lace?
Do you see the deep pain in my eyes?
Can you tell that my life is based on lies?

Do you see me jumping up and down?
Can you tell that my smile is an upside down frown?
Can you tell that I'm only five years of age?
Can you tell that daily I live in fear and rage?

When with my parents do I seem far removed?
Can you tell that I've been abused?
Can you tell by the way my dad looks at me?
Do you think this horrible crime mom refuses to see?

Can you tell me if God knows what's taking place?
Do you think he can cleanse me with his amazing grace?
Do you think God knows about children being abused?
Does it make God cry to see children being misused?

Can you see the dark bruises on my tender skin?
Would it really help to live with my next of kin?
Does God really love children? If it's really true,
Then why does he let grown-ups continue this terrible taboo?

Margaret Rose Williams-Caldwell

Two Ships

'Tis a story of two ships
   docked in a common harbor.
The captains, one a He
   the other a She - -
took moments from their labor
   to laugh and build a friendship.

'Twas after such a brief time,
   His ship had to depart
to fulfill a destiny in another harbor.
Great sorrow filled their hearts —-
   with wings of eagles, from harbor
to harbor they flew to sleep and dine.

As waters of the sea thrashed
   and rumbling thunder crashed,
their wings they had to tuck.
It was then their hearts spoke
   like the resonance of one beacon
flashing through the storm to the other.

'Tis an unfinished story of two ships —

Boady Bell

Praise The Lord

I praise the LORD when I'm happy; I'm really glad that the LORD
doesn't look Past Me
I praise the LORD when I'm sad; In the day of judgement I don't want
to say I wish I had or if Only
I praise the LORD when I'm weak; I always want to appear to the
LORD as Meek
I praise the LORD when I'm strong; I love praising the LORD all
the day long

Give thanks and glorify the LORD at all times and you find that the
gifts from God are divine.
Praise the LORD forever and forever, and the LORD will be with you
through all of life's Endeavors; whether they be full of pleasure or
wicked as a pirate's sunken treasure, always give praise no matter
what life dividends pay. Uphold your arms with the Victory Sign and
let the LORD know that you are Thankful because he is Merciful
and kind.

Ronald Salters Jr.

To A Friend

Don't cry today
Don't cry tomorrow
Don't cry at loves that didn't last
Don't cry at the past

People may have broken your heart
Friends may have torn you apart
Loves may have used you
Family may have abused you

Have no worries
Have no fears
Let there be no more tears
Let your dreams carry you away, where there is no man.

I'll be here when you need a friend
I'll be here when you need a hug
I won't leave you
I won't turn away from you

Leave your worries far behind
Let your tears decline
Look forward for what is to come
But don't look back at what you've left behind.

Sarah Bushnell

Nightshade

I feel no sound,
  don't know where I'm bound.
Is the nightshade black?
  Or are the windows painted.
We were so close, we had no room.
We bled inside, each other's wounds.
We all shared the same disease,
  but we sang the songs of peace.
Some came to pray, some came to weep.
Some came to drive, the nightshade deep.
So united we stand, and divided we fade.
If we stand, we could be strong against the shade.
So shine, with your soul of light.
Hold it high, against the night.
So feel the sound, and hear the light.
Don't give up, without a fight.
Our faces shine the sun, so brave without a gun.
With your finger on the trigger, of the things to come.

Steven Running

The Little Ones

The little ones, don't hurt the little ones
Don't touch their pain
They carry your sin upon their heads
But they cannot remove the stain.

The little ones, don't hurt the little ones
After all, you've stolen their joy
And now that you've had your little fun
You cast them off as a broken toy.

The little ones, don't hurt the little ones
Now that they're filled with rage
Care you not that they live in torment?
That they are forever young in age?

The little ones, don't hurt the little ones
The list is too long to name
The victims of unbridled passions
Bound in unwarranted shame.

The little ones, don't hurt the little ones
So sad they have become insane
Now after your party is over
Only their shell remains.

Marla Heise

"A Walk Through Death"

  Through darkness, I tremble, I keep falling
down, I try to look up, but there's no one around.

  I grasp for an object, but it wont hold on,
I hear subtle noises afar.

  Then suddenly,
A light shines so bright, that heaven and earth,
will be rejoicing tonight.

  And the stars in the sky will be sparkling
forever and ever, in the twilights of the night.

  A hand is reached out, I take it alone,
I feel as if I'm being lifted up and far away.

  The journey is long, but quiet and still,
he keeps a hold of me until we get there.

  He took me through sunshine, a rainbow,
and a cloud, the brightness of a moonbeam,
and all beautiful things around.

  When he let go of my hand, and I gently
drifted down, I tried waking up, but once again,
no one was around.

Kimberly Lee

She Listens

She listens to his words now
  dreaming of yesterday, lost there somehow
She knows his heart feels love
  it's true as the stars above
She thinks much time has gone by
  as she sits alone she'll cry
She listens to his words now
  slowly then her head will bow
She can recall it said before
  she turned walking out the door
She thought twice then she turned
  walking silently her shattered heart burned
She listens to his words now
  recalling his love taking their vow
She drifts further into thought, dreaming
  lost in his arms she's screaming
She feels this fear deep inside
  she lays all alone she cried
She listens to his words new
  dreaming of yesterday, lost there somehow

Maggie Brucato

"Acts"

There are journeys I have travelled
Driving cadillac convertibles
Towards shore in a canoe with paddles
The lawyer turned judge
Calling to order with his gavel
Man with pacifier on hand to quiet a baby's babble.

Ballroom ladies whose faces grim
Flowers worn as ribbons
From garden hedges trimmed
A sage's eye saw that theirs hadn't dimmed
Words heeded by lovers sealed with a kiss
Poor girl marries the rich handsome prince
The ruler of the world
Is the only ruler of kings

Time zones escaped
Snipped with scissors which bonsai trees shaped
Witness of the unwilling
That often times was raped
A chameleon of sorts some say
Role playing for life everyday

Sanghamitra Roychowdhury

Into Peaceful Sleep

Live for today,
Come what may.
No thoughts of tomorrow.
No time for sorrow.
Dreams come so fast.
Soon to be days from the past.
Singing, dancing, just having fun.
Oh no! The dog is on the run.
Blocks and books are scattered everywhere.
Mommy and Daddy are pulling on their hair.
The house is a mess.
Expect nothing less
From two little boys,
Preoccupied with their toys.
They go full speed ahead,
Until it's time for bed.
Then they drift deep, deep
Into peaceful sleep.

Melanie K. Graves

The Ballad Of A Bitch

Everyone thought she was just an old mangy hound.
Dropped off by someone, or just wandered into town.
They filled her full of lead.
Everyone shot her. They left her for dead.

But the bitch drug herself to a nearby home.
Where an elderly couple lived all alone.
She was hurt, it was plain to see.
Probably wanting someone to put her out of her misery.

But she found love, the way she had been treated.
she thought it was something the world was out of.

And after weeks of nursing, and taking care of the bitch's needs.
A beautiful dog grew out of that mixed breed.
People still talk about how that bitch got lucky.
And ironically they're all raising one of her puppies.

Scott B. Emily

The Shadow

I am your constant companion even
during your hours of despair
There have been times of anguish but
I have always been there

When you felt faintness and leaned against
me on the wall
I dialed the emergency numbers and you
made the call
I was beside you when you suffered a
broken heart; you sat and cried,
I used the same cloth to wipe my
eyes, as your eyes were dried

If you are unable to see me in the
darkness or night
It's because I am your reflection in
the rays of light
I was with you during the nights of
your dream as you fell asleep
I knelt beside you near the bed when
you prayed for my soul to keep

Larry Fisher

"For Your Return I Live"

For your return I prevail.
Each day I say tomorrow he'll return, when tomorrow comes
    I cannot help to say the same words over again.
Everyday my mind, my devotion, yes, even my soul at times tell me;
    Stop you've done enough!
But, a crazed heart stands in the way of all begging for just
    another day.
The birds in the sky no longer sing for my sake,
The garden has asked me not to return and smell the roses,
The grass leading to your lawn, no longer wants my pace to touch her
    face.
My cry to heavens are no more carried by the wind.
Friends have left me, crazy they call me.
Enemies of main have broken their animosity.
For they say I no longer impose a challenge.
Like a candle I stand mute and tearful.
My heart broken and black yet, it holds its breath.
In a ruinous shape it still wishes to remain.
Remain just one more day in hope.
Saying tomorrow he'll return.

Mariam Al Majid

Burdens

There are burdens we carry as we go along life's way
Each has a burden to carry day by day,
Some we share with family and friends
Others we carry alone.
When night time comes and before we sleep
We bow our heads and the burdens we lay at Jesus's feet.
The burdens we thought we carried alone
Jesus was with us had we only known,
And as we say thank you to God, for the burdens we bear
We know Jesus loves us and will always care.

Blanche Elling

A Tree

A tree is a life-long dream,
Each leaf turning over a new opportunity,
Each piece of bark-a spark of life.
The roots bear the given life,
To nature and to humans.
Each branch reaching out for something to grasp.
The length-a giant step toward the future.
The width-a turn to take toward the right choice.
A tree is a gift of life,
Much like a human.
With turns to take,
Decisions to make,
Help to give and receive.
A tree is life.

Rebecca Thompson

Prayer I

On a beautiful forest day,
Each thing I grasped I wished would stay;
I longed to have everything I saw,
A brilliant wetted twig and buxom leaves,
Blue sky and autumnal air.
I thanked the Lord for the day I stood,
And felt each glimpse
And view slide on,
As a flash of sun swallowed down in day,
I prayed, "Let me be what is eternal,
Creator and creation, for
Consciousness,
This I am, in the reeds,
As clever as hands.
Let me be your heart
In the shadow of the moon,
On its moribund sands,
This I am, you know."

Monica Collette Yriart

Calling Love

Pleasant ringing of musical bells,
Dreams of you and carrousels.
Whether or not the sun will shine,
Inside my heart I know you are mine.
I save my love for caring arms,
I love your smile and witty charms.
Your gentle touch like a magical spell,
I'm proud to say it so feel free to tell.
There is no other to replace this passion,
You control my world with your unique fashion.
My one and only in this universe,
There is nothing that can break this curse.
Your love is the color of springtime flowers,
A continuous pouring of your mystical powers,
To touch your hand is to touch my heart,
You painted my world from end to start.

Lisa Daniels

Color Blind

Wouldn't it be great if we could simply kill hate
End the reign of violence and greed and take only what we need

God's green Earth we all do desecrate
By spreading violence, prejudice, and teaching hate

The world has gone mad, today greed and lust
Have replaced our founding words, In God We Trust

If only people knew that it isn't a matter of black or white
It's simply a matter of what is wrong and what is right

For underneath our skin, are bones we are all made of
Skin color is irrelevant, for we are all flesh and blood

I shudder each day at the horrid things I see
And I wonder, what will become of me?

When my maker calls to come take me away
Will I be forgiven on my judgement day?

I did nothing to change things in this world gone bad
I merely accepted living in a world gone stark raving mad

I can only imagine how He feels to see his creation deteriorate
Into a planet minus love, but rampant with hate

So the next time you pass judgement maybe you will find
Sometimes, it's easier to love than to hate and to be colorblind

Nicki Hardwick-White

Treasures

The beauty of nature is a sight to behold.
Enjoyed for centuries by both young and old.
Shared together with friends, or by yourself if apart,
forever and ever as treasures of the heart.

The beauty of nature is a sight to behold.
From the smallest creatures to the mountains so bold.
The greatest gift from God which had been given from the start
to be cherished by all as treasures of the heart.

The beauty of nature is a sight to behold.
Each peace is unique with no common mold.
To protect and preserve it for future generations would be smart,
for our children to enjoy as treasures of their hearts.

Michael Raymond Yeager

If Only

I would have done anything for him,
even if it meant committing a sin
Just to have him here with me,
if only he would see what I need him to see,
.... if only
If only he could fathom the strength and depth of my
emotion,
To have it stir in him the very same commotion,
.... if only

I want him to know,
I want it to show... just once,
But so very much more

Yet I've been told from the start,
That he could only break my heart,
... or what's left of it.

So tell me, what is it I must do,
to finally get through to you?

I'm so tired of being lonely,
If only you would love me.... if only....

Rachel Susanne Rhodes

Ode To Our Postman

I'm the last one on my postman's trail,
Eventually, he stops without fail,
But oh, the waiting, such suspense!
A bright and shining morning with a busy day ahead,
Checking out the feeder to see the birds are fed,
And going over records to have it all make sense!

I watch the clock all afternoon
And hope he'll come real soon
With that special letter!
My day is filled with busy hours,
Sewing, cooking, dusting, flowers,
Then there he is, I do feel better!

a delightful past-time, pen pal friends,
Friendship through postal trails that sends
Joy to make the world a better place,
Postman, do not slack your pace,
For we look forward to your dear face!

Martha Marie Snyder

Wretched Conquest

Shaded eyes come across the room
Feel the pulse of adrenalin zoom
From the reality, bitterly restrain
Caught in a fantasy hard to contain

Touch in passing and freeze on fire
Sarcasm hisses, "Excuse me, Sire!"
Measuring time on conquests of power
Speak now, for I can't drink it sour

Wolves are howling at the door to come in
Leaves are whispering their sanction of sin
Steal a moment in blackness of night
Reach out and take this impulse in flight

Skins are screaming, insides want out
A catalyst kiss and farewell to doubt
Searing confusion for the prowess undone
Question victory - how was it won?

Sleep on it now, tomorrow will tell
Trust in yourself, the other is well
Engraved in mind in fine detail
A loving now coloured, one time so pale

Lynne Dammer

Caged Heart

As a little bird, it was free to fly
Explore the ground, the trees and the sky

Then, the cage began to form
Still the door was open and
Many of the ribs gave way to let the bird out to play

But the cage is solid now
The door remains closed
The little bird still sings
But mostly to itself and very low
and occasionally stretches its wings
But stretching is not flying and singing

The cage over the years has gotten smaller,
Tighter, more confining.
Perhaps the joints got stuck, welded with responsibility,
Performance, shoulds, oughts and fear

The bird though remembers flying
Freedom to see and to be
Inward it turns and searching
Looks for new ways to find the key

Rose Nevart Sarian

Paranoia

I can't help but cringe
Every time people whisper
Or pause whenever I pass.
Why are they looking my way?
What did they say?
What will they talk about
After I'm past?
Will I hear them laughing
Only to stop if I turn their way?
I tell myself they don't talk about me.
They have no reason to care.
Until a friend tells me what they say.
I try to convince myself it's all in my head.
I just appear at the wrong time.
I haven't done anything to make them talk.
Just when my mind starts to relax,
A little voice says,
"That didn't stop them in the past."

Katherine A. Fox

I was supine, kicking and squalling,

everyone imagining I was closed
and lost in a state of non - learning.

All the time I filed faces and voices,
eyes and tones, feelings of joy and
pain, uneasiness and body pleasure.

They saw me as passive. I heard the
quarrels, felt the anxieties, saw who did what
to whom, listened to the music and

Knew rhythms of peace and those of hate,
those of shout and whisper, loving and caring.
I was a drinker. I was open to life.

My thoughts and feelings were learned.
(As Cyrano learned to hate the mockery
showing in the eyes and smile of his nurse).

Aaron

My Exact To Fall

It comes upon me once or so that feeling I get when I think I know.
Everything has its own way, but who am I to begin to grow?

Staring at the walk on that evening of dusk, the breeze was in that
day. Come to me is such a gust, a thought of pure dismay.

A wreck of which can't I release, it seems to strike me so.
As hard as nail hits horses shoe, was that frightening blow.

The moon turned bright, and on the night that depress had done set
in. I foot by foot set out by light, to end what now begins.

What means to take? It's so brief, but I not knowing why,
walk straight away on path, while shines my back the sky.

Decision made with terms in hand, the cold steel I clutch.
Knowing now all to know and still not knowing much.

Baby's breath nor dragon's teeth don't dull my pace at all.
For once I am there, nothing can away...me, or my exact to fall.

Thomas E. Hunter

One Night

One night was given to me,
   For you to see the real person who loves you endlessly.
Locked in your arms hoping freedom would be denied.
   And eternity would hold us for life.

But if by the first hour of morning shine,
   your heart was not convinced, then I would lose
you forever and my love for you would die.

Michelle Toledo

America

Black and white, no color
everything visible, but no sight
Racism learned
Old fashioned ways, souls burned
sight in the new days
the difference, be real
whole heart and courage
still fearing, but gaining knowledge
listen to young one's cry
cease the violence, let ignorance die
find peace
world of dreams held back by white man's disease
Hope and pray for the children
That equality will be here one day
Be strong and proud
Don't let them get you down
Be one
Unite
Together we just might be alright

Stephanie R. Castro

My Tower

Watching from my tower I see
   exactly how the world should be
I cry for those in pain and fear
   but there's nothing I can do from here
So, I stay upon my tower of steel
   and eat a light carnivorous meal
I judge the hunters and miners down there
   and the fat man in his easy chair.
The sex, violence, brother against brother,
   an absent women claiming to be mother,
Who turns and points up my direction
   just as the tower windows reveal my reflection
I admire the paint that hides my face
   while turning my back on the human race
Bored now with it all I make a decision,
   then descend to my room to watch television.

Linda Darlene

Untitled

Caring for others is women's fashion
Expressing our true selves with great compassion.
Women contain many talents on this Earth
One of the greatest is the miracle of birth.
Strength and finesse is what we're about,
Taking day at a time with great stout.
Style and grace goes without say,
A women carries herself in the best way.
Never under estimate a woman's ability,
Reading this poem demonstrates our stability.

Rose Ferreira

Elmia

ELMIA, For me to know and others to find.
ELMIA, So sweet, so gentle, so kind.
ELMIA, I explain for I have been there
   no one can know what two lovers share.
ELMIA, To think, it's always a thought.
ELMIA, For sale! This can't be bought.
ELMIA, For feelings experienced to learn,
   those who want, those who yearn.
ELMIA, Known as charm and grace.
ELMIA, Known as lustful-lace.
ELMIA, Good and sometimes bad
   best thing I've ever had.

Riley Crawford

Terry

I saw once - the doves that lie, behind your generous eye; your sylph
eye; I felt once - the care that you convey, when, so full of
youth, did I cry; You kindly conversed and let me stay, until no
longer did I sigh: 'Why,' I ask, 'Were you taken away? Why did your
end draw nigh?' 'Why can I no longer peer into your sylph eye?'

Faintly I hear - A sad lamenting note, of mourning as it fills my
soul; my still youthful, demised soul; I neglect to see - your eulogy
be wrote; collecting tears within a hidden bowl, on them are memories
of you, lying afloat, as their dirge is rolled upon a scroll, those
memories of you I shall forever note; those, the ones, that make me
whole, and you shall forever be there within my burdened soul.

It pierces me! To, so gently say: 'It had to come: The day that you
die! That dismal day when you had to Die! So, I shall say it no
longer, for it brings me dismay; and, it is a Lie! Dreadful Lie!'
Never will the tears depart and always shall they stay, even greater
when I sigh! Dreadfully sigh! But never will I forget the Day, I
peered into your eye; When I saw those pure doves of white behind
your sylph eye.

Paul Nathaniel Hudson

Step Off In Refractions Of Distorted Light

Step off the bridge
Face your fears.
Find your place among all equals
In refractions of distorted light.
Feel your stomach tighten deep inside
Question marks compress your brain
Adrenalin rushes through your limbs
Your head is light and heavy.
All you want is to fly
A dream of childhood
You've always suppressed
Deep within your subservient manners.
Drop those whiny spineless insecurities
Or nature will torment you.
Spread your arms
Open your wings.
Step off the bridge
Face your fears.

Rachael Baden

Smiley Alexander Handley

Smiley Alexander Handley never knew the break of day.
For he was never given the opportunity to become completely born.
His only world was in his mother's womb, dark and warm.

His body began to form in April 1991.
His spirit came forth sometime in June.
And oh, OH! What a spirit it was.

His mommy told his sister how he moved, like a thrashing fish.
His brother, "Oh he is going to be a wiggly little boy."

His sister and his brother listened to his swishes and in late July,
They could feel his body move from place to place.

His sister read to him and sometimes kissed him goodnight.
His brother gave little pats and hugged him off to bed.

And his father watched with anticipation asking mom, "How do you
feel?"
His dad asked, because he knew many times his mom did not feel too
well.
Already she had named him, Smiley Trouble.

On August 5, 1991, Smiley's amniotic sack began to leak.
And on August 6, because of infection in his mother's womb,
Smiley returned to the spirit world from whence he came.

Lorrie A. Monson

Self-Destruction

The icy stare of hate conquers you in your low state of mind
Fed by the hatred of life
You starve with the endless journey to nowhere
Your defeated body shrivels inside itself
Not knowing how to breathe
You gag on the air you inhaled
Knowing your existence depends on it
Torture sounds harmless while happiness sounds hurtful
Your fatal disposition alarms your being
But claims your soul
You let this soothing power take over your essence
You pause
Then quietly pick up the answer to your rejected cry for the truth
With no emotion you see your grave
And within a moment you're in it
Your soul exhales
Feeling as if it discovered the memory of your last breath
When you were thinking the thought that killed you...

Staci Stewart

Feebly, he trips across the room,
Plunging the inevitable to reality in my mind.

Carefully I carry him; cautiously, yet surely, not to hurt him.
Boney he feels in my arms, fat and skin turgor gone.
Arthritis swells his joints.

Struggling, balance lost, he falls, groaning, into the bedding
And waits; waits for me to find my way
Beside him.
Trusting, he moves with difficulty and
Circles into the curve of my stomach.
Soft his coat feels beneath my hand - like suede.

Soundly, peacefully, he sleeps, hearing nothing.
His once brown face and ears
White with age.

Unaware the aching sadness
The finiteness of his years
Drives hard against my heart.

Sue Flannery

"Drifting"

She was an elder I looked up to,
Filled with life and grace.
The most intriguing detail,
Was simply blessed upon her face.

She stayed young at heart, as she grew old,
But other things changed too.
She moved to a different home,
Not meant for me and you.

Her heart was strong and love very true,
Until something slipped her mind.
These somethings were memories of family and love,
But the memories she couldn't find.

It was so sad to see her,
So empty and confused.
We had so much love to give,
But when we gave it she refused.

Deep down I know I'm not forgotten,
Just a faint memory inside.
For one day soon I'll look beyond,
And see her Love and Pride.

Shannon Berti

"My Tragic End"

Going down with me
Feeling a little more than hostile
In the middle of this unfortunate
spiral of shame

I am on the border,
tripping the line of insanity
My pain is now, time to weep is over
Abuse that left me begging for more

These trails of blood are beautiful
I've learned to focus on what's grim
help me escape
I am tottering on the edge of my deepest end

The rattle of the chains that bind me
drowned out my screams
But it hovers over me
like the hurt that won't go away

Blood on my hands
I understand
I've ripped this big hole
Now it's my tragic end.

Kimberly Thomas

Flames

Flickering flames of burning embers,
Fire engulfing the books of offenders,
From dawn to dusk flows the ashes of pages.
Fiction or not, even of puzzles and mazes,
Books once read by the break of twilight,
Now blazing high, opening the night.
The smoky clouds fill small,. crying eyes,
For the work of his life blackens and dies.
The words that were written and the God that it praised,
Caught fire and burned in the yellowish blaze.
Not even a bible was spared, yet no word was spoken,
for the book was burned since this law is broken.
Hour by hour and day by day,
Pours the fireman's hose on the scriptures that lay,
Papers with song by children once sung,
No mercy to the old, nor those of the young.
The temperature is rising, the flames have begun,
The books are burning at fahrenheit 451.

Randall Peterson

Little Girl And The Sea

Oh little girl, come back to me,
for I am your friend, the sea
  rolling to the beauty reflected in your eyes
each forenoon beneath the parted skies
  afloat in remembrance, indelible in the lore
your love harbored within my shore
  as defiant in disbelief laments my heart,
forlorn and disheartened from which we part
  breached by the winds whirlpooled in sorrow
lie our dreams eternal, appealing to tomorrow

Oh little girl, give me again your hand,
reach down, feel the warm in my sand
  run my beaches, leave your footprints below
upon the harbor in which my waves flow
  caress the voyage you shared in me
sail across my body held in all eternity
  resurrect the horizon in the love you gave
how desired within each desolate wave
  as death has washed your footprints from my beach,
my child, they shall always remain within my heart's reach

Scott Monge

A Winding Trail

Deep in the mountains a small trail winds,
  First through the spruce, then through the pine.
On through the mountains to a small ravine,
  Comes a dim ray of sunlight's gleam.
Left in the mountains in a one room shack,
  Sits an old woman, praying for her son to come back.
He left in a blizzard for food and supplies,
  God only knows where her poor boy lies.
Yet, God in his mercy did show the way,
  To the poor old lady, aged and grey.
For that night as she lay in slumber deep,
  He placed on her that life-long sleep.
Then with his gentle guiding hand,
  God led her to his angle band.
To this day, deep in the mountains that trail still winds,
  First through the spruce, then through the pine.

Karla Griner

Branches

Gentle, young
  five limbed branches
Reach out
  to touch the tall grass
  shining from new, dew dripped tears.
Curiosity enters
  the young girl
  naive to the ways of nature.

The same

Bony, aged
  five limbed branches
Reach out
  slowly, fragilely to pick a blade of tall grass
  now dried and withered.
Loneliness enters
  the old woman
  wise to the ways of nature.

Laura A. Green

Leaf

A leaf softly floated downward
from a majestic tree and landed right beside me.

It brought back memories of us
when life was simple and so carefree.

In youth we drift
as a falling leaf in a gentle swirling breeze.

Never caring where we light,
never caring who we touch for with immortality we do tease.

Was I careless with our time together
and how did I allow ourselves to drift so far apart.

Or was it my youth that danced
and flirted away the bonding we once had in our hearts

All your good qualities
and all the happy times we had together my mind will never erase.

For as time passes, I respect
and miss your trueness, your honesty and even the slower pace.

Please forgive the pain I caused
along the way for I know now I should have been softer.

And for one last time let me say
"I'm Sorry" and wish you all the best life has to offer.

Thomas W. Albert

A Whirling, Swirling Swarm Of Flies

On a midsummer's night, with nary a breeze,
flies will be swarming with flexible ease.
Expanding here now, a moment out there,
pausing, just briefly, as if sucking in air.

They flee and they fly and theorize
and seemingly, always, they mobilize.
Whirling, swirling, their wings do beat
with awareness ever, they quickly retreat.

They're rising, settling, swooping, diving,
always they're leaving or just now arriving.
Never are settled with permanent bond,
rarely they've rested, so quickly they're gone.

Terry Roberts

Soaring Eagles

Eagles soar on wings on high
Floating on air currents in the sky
Come with me if you dare
Let me show you what's up there
Come let your spirit mingle
Among the fluffy white clouds that tingle
Where the air is clean and clear
Up there we can see for miles my dear
Let us swoop and fly
O'er the countryside we go by
Ah but wouldn't it be a grand high
If you and I could but soar like Eagles in the sky

Shawn L. Hayton

Recognition

Lighting, briefly, on a friendly hand,
Fluttering near a kindly face,
Watching, listening, sometimes touching,
Rushing headlong into Time,
Aching with the memory of Home.

Enticed, seduced, cajoled, deceived,
Nearly persuaded to forget True Peace,
To veil the eyes that see and know;
Sweet memories of kindred spirits
Can fade so easily to white-on-white.

Mercifully, then, the brush of true vision
Can wipe clean the clouded lens,
Sweeping through the mind's interior,
As beloved music through a storm
Comforts and reassures the heart.

Reminded, again, of that place of Love and Light,
The cluttered brain may falter, yet -
That melody's so undeniably real,
Spirit must soar, must stretch, must reach
For the ribbon of song, to find the Source.

Mary F. Curro

This Human Drama

A drama rests behind each pair of human eyes,
Each represents a story, oft untold,
Of quiet desperation or of joyful theme-
So inwardly played out we can't behold.

Sometimes a comedy seems to be part of life,
Though sadness tinge what laughter it may bring,
For sad and happy are but two halves of the whole-
Thus levity and tears together cling.

We know not what this masque of life brings other folk,
Consisting oft of episodes unwise,
But pray observe, with kindness, these our kindred souls-
Discern the drama hidden in their eyes.

Leonore McNutt Hite

You Yourself You

Traces of shadows at varied depths of the mind
Foggy misperceptions can be quite unkind
Humility's haze creates illusion to the eye
You can see very clearly, only if you try

Shadows change with the shifting of the Sun
Returning to a time before the shadows had begun
As a magician's performance tricks our eye with magic
So to can the mind see things as less tragic

For when the sun changes to shadow's lie
So too do the clouds lift to reveal a bluer sky
When you see clearly through the haze
You will start to envision better days

A bitter lemon can leave a sour taste behind
Past failures can do the same to the mind
Some sugar will help the bitter taste to fade
Tomorrow, those failures won't be made

So I tell you this and I tell it to you straight
Nothing is achieved through self hate.
When you truly learn to love yourself as a friend
The future will shine and the past will finally end

Keith E. Dwyer

"Moods"

Foaming lips whisper to the shore,
Folding in to kiss the sand.
Waltzing with the moon in season,
Coaxing with a lapping hand.

Raging deluge exalt and quell,
Gorging current overpower.
Showering cascades of spume,
Maelstrom swallow and devour.

Surging brine, lunge forth and bow,
Swelling canopies subside.
Untamed billows dip their thrashing tongues,
Throbbing with the morning tide.

Sweeping trails of drifting froth,
Breaking with a sigh.
Challenging crests surmount and repress,
Surrender to the sky.

Kimberly Jesus

A Rose Fallen

A child's tears,
For a mother fallen; taken from him by a destructive wrath of greed,
jealousy and haste.

Clutching a blood red rose,
The child begins to recall antique memories of his mentor.
Recalling them from the cobwebs of his jogged memory.

The rose is resting under his chin,
Capturing his tears; caressing his neck with its velvet petals...
He's breathing in its sweet nectar.
Soothing the pain. The nauseating turmoil.

Hesitantly, he places the rose on his mother's chest, blowing her a final kiss.
"I LOVE YOU," "THANK YOU."
His final testimony to a fallen rose;
Entering upon an eternal spring.

Natalie Wagner

The Stranger

Would it be too much to ask
for a piece of bread to eat
Or for a pair of shoes to
wear upon my feet?
I have traveled much too far along the way
And now it is colder by the day
Would you have an extra coat to give?
Thank you, I appreciate all that you did
You say I look tired, and you look at my hands and feet
And say you know of a man who died, but not in defeat
You look upon my face and say
You look like someone I knew somewhere along the way.
Oh, you now ask, What is my name?
Look at my hands, side and feet
I am the man the world could not defeat
I am your friend and you proved to be mine
I am Jesus of NAZARETH
I am, The Divine

Nancy Evans

Thanksgiving Day

Let us give thanks to God today,
For all the blessings He sends our way,
Give thanks for the Pilgrims too,
Who sailed across the ocean blue,
To a wilderness and land unknown,
So far away from their own home,
Not all went well with the Pilgrim band,
They met with Indians in that strange land,
The Pilgrims cleared some trees away,
And built log cabins, and there they stayed,
They all gave thanks to God above,
For giving them a land to love,
Because they were so brave and true,
The Indians became more friendly too,
That happened many years ago,
We don't forget this now you know,
So every year with turkey and trimming,
Just like the Pilgrims we have Thanksgiving.

Kathryn Shaak

Never, Never Land

The magic carpet of velvet is at our command
For entrance to a place called Never Never Land.

We'll find streets lined with silver, meadows of gold;
A lane paved with candy to all a rainbow can hold.

For spring we'll have bunnies of white chocolate to eat
Surrounding our house made of gingerbread sweet.

Summer castles of sand bellow marshmallow billows
As sandmen with sandbags dust dreams on our pillows.

Forests of mushrooms, instead of tall trees
Will shelter our elves from fall dew drops or breeze.

An ice palace in winter with icicles that glow;
A sleigh made of rhinestones, diamonds for snow.

Sunsets on the hour will disclose all the reasons
Of a love for all time and a place for all seasons.

Shirley Smith Mazurkewiz

Untitled

There are those who never reach down and hold and smell the roses
For fear of the thorns; then one day they come back only to find
That there is only thorns, the rose has gone away.

Michael Nicholson

If Home Is Where The Heart Is

If home is where the heart is, then I am quite confused;
For home, I've felt, is where I rest, and cannot be refused.
My heart goes with the ones I love, to places far and near;
Many miles connect the ones, whose memories are so dear.

I guess you'd say my heart must live, in many different places;
With all my friends and family, whose paths my heart still traces.
I couldn't begin to list them all, if I had night and day;
Though some of them their names I've lost, their touch will ever stay

All of those who've brought me joy, remain within my smile;
And though the years pass on and on, their presence scolds denial.
My heart is strewn both North and South, and all the way between;
In towns that I have known and loved, and some I've never seen.

So, if my home is truly found, wherein my heart doth lie;
Then home is just a state of mind, somewhere 'tween morn and nigh.
The where and how will not be found, 'tis not for us to know;
Just know my home is found with friends, wherever they may go.

Pamela J. Morrison

"Man In Blue"

My knight in Armor all dressed in blue
For I became his wife in the month of June-
As a policeman he protects and serves
Imagine what it does to ones nerves-
Everyday he puts his life on the line
Do those strangers even care what happens to that
man of mine?-
For do they know how he's special and sweet
I prayed for the day this man I would meet-
He'd give the shirt right off his back
That's a quality a lot of us lack-
Everyone else first, he thinks of himself last
He served for his country oh what a blast-
In a war as a marine it made him a man
For this he is proud to give a dam-
I thank the Lord he comes home safe everyday
He's everything and more what else can I say-

Taresa Dupke

Restless

Lifeless, without life, yet you are alive
for I feel your deprived heart throbbing.
Tired of life, exhausted, you lay limp on a
swollen bed. The flower patterned sheets
you cling to provide the only warmth and
shelter from the bitter cold that lies
beyond them.

Lifeless, you sleep like a two year old
baby taking her mid-morning nap,
only it has been hours since the sun
has cast its glimmering beams of light,
and playing is not what has withdrawn all
of your energy.

Lifeless, without movement, without any
sound, you find peace only at this moment
in time.

No screaming, no yelling, no crying, no
complaining. Nothing moves or makes a
sound, not even you.

Matthew E. Moroney

The Morning After

Stay she said and do not rise
For I see that light in your eyes
The day breaks not, it is my heart
Because that you and I must part
Stay or else my joys will die
And then I'd surely have to cry

We met, we clashed, sparks flew
We were warm as we ignited each other
There was no loudness, cause we were but one
We found such simple solitude together
We loathe to let go, but let go we must
We each regain our individuality as
we lead our separate lives in our very
different worlds.

Ruth Derrell

My Mama's Gift

When I was just a child, Mama, I'd search our high mountainside,
For just the right gift for your Birthday and it was always amply
    supplied.
It might be a new painted pine cone or a pine needle necklace and ring,
It might be a spectacular rock, but to you it was just the right
    thing.

Then I aged a few years overnight and gifts were bought only in
    stores.
None of these childish gifts for my Mom, and I bought you a mop for
    the floors.
More maturing years pass by quickly, now I have little time to spare,
But Mama's Birthday is important and I need to show her I care.

So again to a store I rush for that one and only gift to find,
That I think will please my Mama; with a card "My Love" I signed.
Hopefully now I'm a little wiser and know what a Mama wants, in part,
Are the things like I made as a small child with my mind, my hands,
    and my heart.

Lorraine Smith Menard

Nature's Art In The Autumn Time

The greatest gift on Earth is nature
For nature is a natural sanctifying beauty
The sanctifying beauty of Autumn's azure
Reflects nature's Art of Mystery.

'Tis a blessing of an Artist to see-
And a soul of a poet to feel-
Nature's glorifying colors in quality
A craving desire of imagination as real.

The Autumn leaves have been painted
Nature's work of art will be foresight
The season's maturity of Autumn displayed
like a betrothed beautiful bride.

Autumn's leaves are beautiful to behold
Nature has painted from an old rainbow's end
An artist's paints from a pallet of old
and the gift of nature in a poet's mind and an artist's hand.

Regina Mattei

What is Love?

What is love, I was asked... The meaning is
hard to unmask... Search for words, none I
found... Love is sensed in sight and sound...
Words are empty to define lofty thoughts and
deeds sublime... Lost we are to figure out
what drives us on and love we will...
Nothing can this true love quell.

Leona Z. Witherow

There Was An Angel

There was an angel present when she died,
For no one was bitter and no one cried,

She wasn't angry, sad, hurting or well,
She wanted us there for a final farewell,

She looked past us all and whispered so clear,
"Thank you, my friend for getting them here."

She spoke to us all, a minute or two,
Her message was simple... "Don't be sad and remember, I love you,"

We wanted to cry and beg her to stay,
But we knew in our hearts, this was her final day,

As her last child kissed her, she was calm and steady,
She looked past us again... Smiled, and said "I'm ready."

Lydia A. Korin

My Princess

Were I a prince, would you be my princess?
For no prince am I, but you are a princess.

You may dream of knights on white horses, as they ride through
The countryside or kingdoms with all their treasures.

For knights show symbols of gallantry,
For chivalry is not dead.

Were I a prince, would you be my princess?
For no prince am I, but you are a princess.

Step out of your past, walk with me in the present
Grow old with me in the future.

Stephen Baetsen

Untitled

As I stare into the sky, I see a star of you
For now you are an Angel, watching from above
Taking good care of me,
like a saint.
I know you are not gone,
I know you did not die
For now you are a spirit,
but happy as could be.
You are up in Heaven, floating in the clouds
Watching over me
I can feel you near,
giving me hope and strength
For now I feel myself lifting up,
just to be with you
As I near the top, I fall down
Although I cannot see you,
I can feel you with all my heart
Now I will go to sleep,
Resting in peace,
knowing I am safe

Kristy Slatton

Lowndes High School

Out on an open sea, where we had been shipwrecked,
for weeks, my niece had just busted a seam after
bending over you stretch her knees.
She had seen a ship heading our way, oh yeah, we thought.

This was it, our final moment of peace.
Then we called to the captain, oh please,
oh please, but he thought we said to flee.

So here we are stuck in this drift from afar.
Oh I wish we could have just sent a flare,
now this forest is bare and there's nothing left to share.
My minds's already gone from days spent writing this poem.

Leann Barber

A Black Mama's Lullaby

Hush-a-by black boy, there's no need to cry,
For pretty soon you surely will die.
Your eyes are still closed, you've never been awake,
but if you don't wake now it will be too late.

your clothes hanging loose over pure skin and bone,
the pipe is your life, the street corner your home.
Your mama she's crying, she can't sleep at night,
for all that she sees is her poor baby's plight.

A gun in his hand, smoke filling his eyes,
while he walks around snuffing out lives.
We're sure gonna miss you, we wish you could stay,
and so every night we kneel down and we pray.

Dear heavenly father, way up above,
send us your light, and show us your love.
We're losing our sons, and our daughters too,
we're so all alone we don't know what to do.

We pray that you'll hear us, before it's too late,
For if you don't help us, then death is our fate.
We're closing this prayer with tears in our eyes,
and stand by in silence while our young lose their lives.

Shirley R. Matthews

I Am Yours

I Am Yours, Thank You Lord for loving me
   For seeing something good in me
You kept me in your hands and began to mold me
   to carefully mold my life
Like a potter you wanted the best "Pot"
Yes, I let you mold me and I became beautiful
   My life is chosen
You were almost finished but I crashed to the floor
   breaking, shattering into a zillion pieces
I was clay again, I wanted you to make me over
   with great patience and unconditional love
You made me over, I'm clay again
Make me into something useful!
Make me into a water vessel
but, instead of holding water for the
thirsty let me hold love; let me fill the thirsty with your
undying love, Lord do with me as
you please, you made me in yours.
"In order to be restored and be made whole, we must first
Be broken, then the healing comes-

Sylvia Arroniz

Thoughts From My Sewing Basket

There is a simile to life
even in the act of sewing.
The thread reminds us that there is a thread
we weave into our everyday living..
It is the attitude with which we meet the events
along the path (seamline) of life.
Sometimes the sharp pain of adversity
punctures the fabric of our lives as the needle
does the cloth on which we sew.
The thimble is our faith and hope which prevents
the needle from putting an irreparable hole into our very soul.
Safety pins remind us of the haven that we find in Jesus Christ.
As we look to Him we are lifted from the
weariness of the sewing.
The gold color of the pins reminds us of
each golden opportunity to sew the seamline straight.
The pattern is His pattern. As we follow it,
we know we cannot fail.

Mavis Gibson

Untitled

Inspiration love's Muse Erato send to me,
for silence I cannot keep.
By Cupid's arrow have I been stung,
Now engulfed in daytime sleep.

Love I have not trusted;
Love I have not believed;
But love has drowned foolish mind's reasoning
And pity Muse, in love I am deceived.

Yet mind to love's inevitable reign resists
Mind not conquered, love have not victory.
But logic loses grasp when heart
by Eros is wounded deep.
When reason submits eternal Muse,
ensure that love persists.
For if conquered the mind becomes,
conquered must it forever exist.

Rosy Lor

I Am Grateful

I am so grateful for men who still weep.
For the faithful shepherd still keeping his sheep.
For the mystical hymns of crickets and doves.
And for grey haired mothers and their labors of love.

I am so grateful for my warm and cozy bed,
And for my prayer of forgiveness that speaks in my head.
For the laughter of children and their spirit that sings,
And for the rebirth and promise and coming of spring.

I am so grateful for the humble knees that still bow,
And for the proud farmer who continues to plow.
For the joy of lovers that believe love is not vain,
And for those who are meek and live with the pain.

I am so grateful for the wonder of new fallen snow,
And for the preacher who still loves my soul.
For the soft heart of doctors who still mourn at a loss,
And for those who fought battles for us at great cost.

I am so grateful for valleys, mountains and peaks,
And for the spirit of courage and the flesh that is weak,
For the faith and the hope I've embraced in my strife,
And for the people I've loved in this marvelous life.

Mark Anthony Grubb

To Heather Elaine Whaley Born Sunday, October 16, 1994 at 9:06 P.M.

We welcome you to our family, Heather.
For so long we've been waiting.
We hope you will be with us forever.
God will determine that, we know by his stating.

May your life be full of pleasant surprises.
But don't expect everything to look and smell like roses.
Take it from one who's experienced 100 years of life.
We have to accept our ups and downs without strife.

We hope you'll love your relations.
I'm sure we will all love you.
Also, we'll do all we can for your comfort and pleasure.
So hurry and grow and be our treasure.

Be true to yourself and God.
You'll never be sorry if you do.
There will be times when you'll doubt.
But read the Good Book and give Him a shout.

Margaret C. Tate

Today Is The Toughest Day

Today is the toughest Day,
For when wintry stormy nights were brewing,
I thought that's the way it was.
My insecurity wouldn't let me be,
because it knew that I'd find a way to be free

Why wintry nights did you hold,
those who wanted to be free?
Are you afraid of the loss of your control?
Then control it is that you shall lose,
because of those you did abuse.

For you see today is the toughest day for you.
Those you abuse have somehow seen the light of day,
and now know, the shadows you cast are only that,
but now they must pick-up the pieces of the life you gave
and dispose of it for a new beginning.

So you see Today Is The Toughest Day

B. J. Rosario

My Family And Me

'Tis great to look back on my family tree
For without those before - there would never be me.
I thank the Lord, that he allowed me to be born
Into a family where all were loved and adored.
My Dad was so helpful - he never was mad
Guess I was lucky to have such a great Dad.
It was during the depression. I was quite young.
All worked in our garden and thought it was fun.
I still think of the smell of fresh bread that was baked.
On all Birthdays - Mom made such great cakes!
My brother was oldest, but he was always right there
To make us all smile - let us know that he cared.
My sisters, too, told stories and played games
When they left this world, I recounted their fame.
Little brother was a sweetheart-although quite young
We were proud when he married and had two sons.
Now they are gone - and there is only me
No sorrow I share - God set them all free!
Now I have a family and I try always to be
A loving Mom and Grandma - for their family.

Norma Dotson Payne

My Bleeding Heart

My eyes caress every detail of your physique
For your every touch haunts my body
When I look in your eyes
I get lost in my thoughts
For the confusion of our love
Has me screaming for HELP
Yet I cannot let go
For our souls are one
I feel your tremendous and
Powerful presence upon me
With the heat of your passion
I melt like ice to a flame
In your embrace I'm free of harm
But when the embrace weakens
Harm and evil fall upon me
In a faded memory
I vaguely remember
The timeless and endless
Days of the happiness
We once shared

Monica Laabs

Ash Wednesday

"Dust thou art and to dust thou shall return."
Forbid it not to happen in Hell to burn.
Forever will be your eternity.
Meditation is also good for me.

The period of Lent seems long.
Through it you should sing a song
Of prayer, penance and alms giving;
After which you will a song again sing

Pray each day a little longer;
Alone in your room to linger.
Do penance now for your sins,
You'll save time in Purgatory where it begins.

Alms giving for the poor is what it's all about;
Fighting your adversary is a serious bout -
Overcoming temptation will prevail
And you will never ever fail.

Keep your strength up for forty days
And you won't be in a daze.
Prepare now for Heaven.

Thaddeus Capek

The Babe

Water bed of life - a tiny seed growing,
Forming into a bundle of joy as we wait.
Each month anticipation grows - as you do,
Your every move felt and your presence is assured.
From the microscopic beginning into a true being
The Lord's infinite wisdom is being claimed.
You come forth with much pain followed by great joy,
There are no words to describe your beauty,
Wrinkled, pink and soft to the touch you are
A Blessing - a new being for us to nurture.
Looking at you our hearts are enlarged for the sharing,
As we eagerly prepare our minds and souls for your guidance,
Watching you lie there kicking, cooing, crying for care,
We touch you, meeting your needs, you learn from our touch.
Daily you change inwardly as well as outwardly.
We look into each other's eyes and we bond more with each gaze.
We are one as we have been from the beginning,
With God's grace and guidance, we will grow stronger each day.
I am always here for you.

Linda Krempin

An Anniversary Journey

I with cigar and beer and your damn crochet thread
Forty-five years ago we decided to wed.
Now having been married all these years
Sharing the good times and a few tears.
Living together has been a gas
When we weren't each other's pain in the ass.
And those 3 kids, Lord what a drain
And then granyunguns are really a pain.
Gettin' into this and messin' up that
never have we seen such unruly brats.
They're supposed to be Grandparents' pleasure
Now peace and quiet is what we treasure.
We started out a slim trim Merchant Marine
and a sweet innocent young thing.
In bed years ago we were frisky all over
Now it's a jab in the ribs and "you're hoggin' the cover."
All these years and each one we've felt, it now takes both hands to
hitch up our belt, we never knew whence life's road led into
uncharted waters full speed ahead. Through it all our love didn't sway
This we celebrate on our 45th Anniversary Day.

T. C. Miller

Immortalities Eyes

Fear not my gentle soldier
Foul deaths cold grip on your soul
As your king, your deeds will not be forgotten
As your friend, I will always love you
Peace this day we have given our land
The price was high, yet worth every bit
The sunset is beautiful this day, is it not?
To think it will be our last together
Do you remember when we were kids?
We vowed to chance the world
At any cost
Today you have paid that price
Was it really worth it?
Did we change it that much?
Certainly, they will remember us
Immortalities open eye
I will always love you.

Tony Casteel

Redemption

An innocent man stood accused,
Found guilty and sentenced - justice abused.

The ruthless guards scoff and scorn
And force into his scalp the woven thorns.

His bloodied back was shredded and scourged.
A robe on this raw flesh caused the pain to surge.

With little strength left, he carried the tall post
Down the long road to a desolate host.

Long spikes driven through his wrists and his feet
He's hoisted up to endure torture complete.

Each breath was an effort, he uttered few words,
"Father forgive them" unselfishly heard.

As his body gives way to the abuse unbound
His heart is crushed from the fluid surround

The final blow dealt- a spear in his side.
Blood poured from the man who, by now, had died.

He held no regret for all this humility
For all that he suffered, he suffered for me.

Linda Kirkpatrick

Defeated

Ah! the many years ago when I
first went to work in a busy city, my job was
filing papers, what a pity.
    With no chance for advancement I
decided to leave the firm, because the
pittance wage offered little in return,
for carrying my expenses that incurred through
this employment, I was young and had
the time, but no money for enjoyment.
    The next job was no better, but it
brought me close to home, I still was in
the poor house and had no money to
help me roam.
    I searched, but couldn't find a source
of work that was worthwhile, and so the
years just passed on by while I flitted
in destitute style.
    Now old age has placed its values on a
forever lasting trend, of little hope for
prosperity and so my story ends.

Lois Stiner

She Said/He Said

She said, "I can't understand why he has to go out drinking with his friend."
He said, "Every time the girls come over, the night never seems to end."

She said, "He never spends any time with me, to just go for a walk."
He said, "She never gives me a moment of peace, all she does is talk."

She said, "No matter how much I ask, he never fixes the car."
He said, "She never takes care of it, she drives it all the time and drives it too far."

She said, "He always just drops his things anywhere, his junk is all over the house."
He said, "This place is always a mess, I do my share, I'm not a maid, I'm a spouse."

She said, "I remember spending hours, lying together on the beach."
He said, "I remember teaching her to play frisbee, she would always throw it out of reach."

She said, "Look at all the fighting we've done and the dishes that are broken."
He said, "Yes I see we have done plenty of yelling, but you know not much was spoken."

She said, "The meanness in our words is a heavy price to pay."
He said, "Let's sit down and talk things out, I have something to say."

She said, "I miss you so very much."
He said, "I miss your sweet caress, your gentle touch."

We said, "We'll try harder being more patient taking more time to send."
We said, "We will try to understand, support, and love till the very end."

Jon Dark

Friends

Friends are hard to find.
Friends that are true won't let you down and
will always be around
Friends are people you can trust.
They help you come up when you're feelin' down.

Friends will give you a truthful answer to a
personal question
You don't always agree on the same things.
Or your taste in guys!
Friends need to be loved and cared for.

If they truly are your friends, nothing immature or
stupid will come between the 2 of you.
Friends are a good thing to have b-cuz without 'em,
who would you
                    talk to?

RaShea Lane

Remember Today

Life rolls on
Day by day.
Little is done;
Few times will stay.
Eroding time
And the mind,
The little chimes
Think they are kind.
Flowing fast
And leaving a token,
The time has past;
Dreams are broken
But, it is the here and now that we celebrate and sing,
For tomorrow may not allow the remembrance of the bell's ring.

Kristin Rotondi

Heart And Soul

My heart becomes savage when I see you;
Frightening my soul for I know not what to do;
Confused about whether to hide or rather to seek;
My heart becomes angry, because I am never bold-always so meek:
Sadly my soul longs for your love and perhaps soft kiss;
If only my heart or soul could speak,
so you could at least hear this;
With the words I have said to you repeatedly in my dreams;
For silently my love and fear makes my heart tear at my soul's seams;
Alas, the enduring torture of my heart
and soul- never knowing how you really feel;
For internally, they know my painful dilemma is ever so real.

Latonya Carter]

"The Modern Living Thanatos"

I remember years ago when I stared at Heaven through a cloudless sky
From a child's seat on a grassy knoll. I saw everything; like Peyton Farquehar
On his Great Escape — the glistening dew on vibrant green leaves,
The cracked rocks which spill crystal waters into the forest, the distant wooden fences
That stitch together the earth and the sky.
No responsibility, no work, no tasks left undone,
I sit quietly on a hill and breathe the sweet minty air.

Why can't life be that simple anymore?
A timetable etched in a shadowed stone —
A watched forged from the melted chains of a thousand slaves —
A towering prison, a blotch in the sky that I am forced to attend
While the life-giving sways pierce the ashen clouds.
The grayed city is filled with the soldiers of depression and the sultans of gloom
Who shout and bicker in their labyrinthine cells.
They inhale the leadened vapors in the peppery air and bark at black screens.
Amidst grinds and screeches the plow through the fumes in the inky blackness of night to go home,

To sleep perchance to dream.

Sean P. Mahoney

The Filipino Music

Music is the Filipino's thrilling ecstasy from Eternity,
from all Creativity,
The tongueless voice of harmony,
Wingless melody in sonorous flight,
The sweet poetry of sound,
"This the soothing rhapsody of man's soul.

The airland is his corridor,
The eardrum is it's receptor,
It commences in sensation,
Impinges on the imagination,
And winds up in the intellection.

It is multi-prowess, multi-radiative,
Penetrative and propulsive,
Diffusive, perfective,
Inspiring, invigorating, Yeh!
Yeh! the grand melodic mystic!

Both organic and psychic,
Its residence is in the mind,
The rough searching hands of the Will,
To the throne-yard of the reigning Soul.

Rufina Molina

Lest We Forget

As we wonder through our moments in time
From dawn's early slave trades to our present state of mind
We question our rights and where we should now be
For generations of our people gave their lives so we could live free
From Jesus "The Christ" to our Martyrs today
We still have never received fair play
They still call us boys though they know we are men
They shake our hands, they laugh and they grin
But deep down inside like a raging storm they truly wish that
the "Black Race" was never born

But lest we forget who we truly are
We were born in heaven
even before the very first star
We shine in God's glory and he won't let us be
Nothing less than He intended for you and for me
We are his people, no question, no doubt
And if we forget we will showly lose out!

Melvin Kirby Parham

Tribute To An Old Warrior

Already old, you came to us forlorn and battle-scarred
from foes unknown.
And so, with feather paw and motor purr
you claimed us for your own.

Your strength regained and, for awhile,
your immortality;
you reigned supreme, with quick reproach to those who dared
question your authority.

But yet a living contradiction you turned out beneath
your rough exterior.
You'd go without, let kittens eat;
a true old gentleman you were.

When came time you refused your food, I knew we must,
so off we set
on our last trip together,
with heavy heart, without regret.

And so old friend, you did your best. Who knows and
who's to say,
with lessons to be learned, we are not better people
for your having passed our way?

Susan F. Bailey

Inherited Punishment

Bound in love,
    from Heaven above.
Woman is linked to the punishment of Mother Eve,
    who was thoroughly deceived.

Being a woman and inheriting my grieve, I must
    desire my husband and bear his children
    with great big pain.
Oh God, can I hide my tears
    in your rain.

Adam messed up
    when he listened to Eve.
But, Jehovah God
    was not surprised.
He knew man
    could find no place to hide.

Satan led man out of God's plan.
    Therefore, God evicted him from the Garden Land.
God gave man the sunrise and sunset without regret.
    Man's peace of mind was replaced with worry and fret.
Man's work became hard labor and sweat.

Minette Smith

The Love Of Christ

It was Christ's love that saved my soul
From sin He set me free
He was willing to give his life and die at calvary
That I might have the peace and joy this
World could never give.
It makes me happy just to know for
Jesus I can live.
I find in him everlasting love, a love
that has no end.
He is my joy, my strength each day,
A true and loving friend.
When I am sad He makes me glad,
When I am lonely He is there.
This wonderful Christ of calvary, he all my
burdens share.
Now my dear friend, Christ loves you too,
He'll save you from your sin
Open up your heart to him today
The Love of Christ, it has no end.

Ruth E. Ford

Graveyard Company

A single white basket stands apart
From the ignored—other eternal beds
That are symbols of a start—not an end.
A new life void of pain and fear, the basket reminds
Of love ones that were near
To the now lonely hearts of relative or friend.
The white porcelain decor—for Easter
Or a birthday gone by.
"Darling daughter" of seven months.
Too little to fight; too young to try.
She now sleeps with angels at her feet.
Watching from above—
Hers the only tended patch—of hundreds of others.
Her small frail basket has no match.
The cold gray markers stare down
At me as I question—
So young to die; not old enough to crawl.
I reach to touch the basket of love
But a harsh wind blows
And a single tear falls.

Nicole A. Miller

Reflections Of Time

She stands upon the bridge of time
Gazing peacefully over the view
Her heart is recalling one by one
Oldest memories with the new

Some of the old ones are ragged with pain
While others still comfort the soul
If she somehow could be given the chance
'Twould not go back and revolt

She sees where her Savior has given to her
The chance to be loyal and true
'Cause she has learned to trust in her Lord
No matter what she's been through

Some of her days have been long and hard
With no reason to keep trudging on
But the Savior's provided the "sweetest" release
From the things that so threatened her mind

She's learned to accept the good with the bad
And grows stronger each day that she lives
For trusting in Jesus removes all the pain
'Tis replaced with the love that he gives

Terralyn Greene Dickerman

If Rivers Could Talk

Oh, rivers if you could talk
From the mountain to the sea, down you go.
Reflecting everything around you.
From flowers to trees.
From mountain snow to plain dirt.
From blue to clouded sky.
Oh river if you could talk.
Sometime warm and calm, or resting under a tree
Sometime cool and wild, jumping over rocks, or
Plunging as a cascade.
Oh rivers if you could talk.
Boats ride on you, fishes leave in you.
Animals drink you, peoples swim in you.
Flowers and trees use you, human too.
Oh rivers if you could talk.
You see so many splendor thing,
And suffer so much for it.
Sometime large, sometime small.
You go your way, never looking back.
Oh rivers if you could talk

Michel Dubeau

The Gloomy Basement

As I walk the basement floor, creaking, cracking went the door.
From the old fireplace, I see a haunting, trembling face.
The old desk drawers dusted pale.
Hanging in the corner is my ancestor's wedding veil.
Cold, damp and dusty, an old chest that stands nearby is now rusty.
Water drips from a hole, clinking, clanking as it hits a metal bowl.
The middle of the floor rotted out, the walls no more strong or stout.
The basement may be gloomy, but the old walls still whisper memories to me.

Tera Kiefer

Love of Mankind

We are all special in our own little way,
from the time we're born, to our dying day.

We are all put on this earth and considered as one,
Because race in his eyes, there is none.

Even though there are people in need from afar,
Sometimes we forget, where we come from and who we are.

We should help our fellow man in time of need,
Regardless of race, color, or creed

In God's eyes there should be love and trust,
Because he has loved each and every one of us.

So keep this thought within and you will see,
A better world for you and me.

Sheila O. Thompson

A Sad Farewell

The grave seeks out its long held quest
For those who knew her, they were blessed
Now her beating heart has stilled
She lies beneath, with earth now filled.

Life sows its own and takes away
While my battered heart would will her stay
To reach through time and hold my hand
Through death's dark door, alone we stand.

Take heed in memories' garden fair
For all death's heartaches linger there
Of all I've owned I'd give away
To see my mother one more day.

Nancy R. Gillien

Friendship Within A Forest

Friendship should be as thick as a forest
full and true like birds singing a chorus
It should never waiver or even stop
But standing strong and true as solid as a rock

Friendship should shine like the early morning sun
Like two small children playing and having fun
Friendship should never change to follow the crowd
Yet it should stay the same like white on a cloud

There will be those who will crawl through your forest at night
Doing the best they can to cause problems and start strife
Like hunters trying to fill their deceitful tanks
Sniping out every friendship along the river bank

Friendship should soar like an eagle high
Flapping its wings through the deep blue sky
But watchful at night, like an owl watching for its enemy
In search of those sly foxes who are filled green with envy

Friendship should stand tall as if it were an oak
Facing the ocean of despair with its forest-made boat
Friendship should be there in any way it can
Not dying out because of a woman or any man

Mark Allen Gowen

Letter To My Daughter, Kathleen

While I dropped cubes into Cola glasses,
fussed with napkin in shaded patio
I watched your eyes fill with new brightness—
you were my small daughter again.
You said your move away from here to there
was for the adventure of a new beginning,
however late.

I asked how can anyone live in dismal rain.
You explained a wind-driven rain
composes music for your soul,
whispers in a secret language.
You told me to come next winter.

Your words echo my thoughts like chimes
since our day together—was it July?
Yes, I'll bring umbrella, rubber shoes.
You will show me your new home
and rain sweeping down firred slopes
spilling the blackberries
causing toadstools to rise.

Rosemary Jones-Wylde

Eternal Perception

For Ashley Steele Thompson
Elemental time forgotten
Future seeds unbegotten
Warrior and Priestess together prey
The work of light, the dark at play.
Warrior and Priestess together pray.

The blood of years flows thick - clotting.
Shadow dance of unbegotting
Mastery of stars - Mystery of Plight
Turn together toward the light
Mystery of stars - Mastery of Plight

Gifted coming blessed descending
So much pain and heartfelt rending
Here much joy exists begetting
Happiness and strength, in letting
The quickening occur, for myself and her.

Morgana Lesley Morgan

"Pride"

In World War I, I led the charge,
Gallant men facing the enemy barrage,
To lead each encounter is simply my place,
A few battle scars, are sure no disgrace.

Again, I was called to World War II,
For another to lead would never do.
Across Europe and Asia, by land and by sea,
So many would die, so that men would be free.

The times have been good, some happy, some sad,
I've been burned and kicked and torn real bad.
To strive for man's freedom is always my cry,
But all I can do, is stand here and fly.

After all I am only a part of each one of you,
My name is "Old Glory," Red, White, and Blue.

Michelle Lee Guill

A Little Girl's Heart

Fragile and soft
gentle and meek
Wanting nothing but love to find and seek.

Quiet and true
pure and sweet
Loving the moments at your feet.

Innocent and kind
gracious and giving
Wanting all your attention while living.

Funny and Silly
Serious and Calm
Looking for that special place to belong.

A little girl's heart consists of these things
these attributes that make you smile…
Feeling her close there by your side
And having her all the while.

A little girl's heart is alive today
For it lives inside of me…

A place of true happiness of love and peace
A place where true beauty you can see.

Kimberly A. Seders

Souls Of Destiny

We were once two souls in the house of
God, knowing nothing but joys of happiness and
Laughter.

Then one day the joys turned to sorrow, for destiny
stepped in, to separate us. For we would take
roads of different paths handed to us by God.

Remembering not, but feeling a sense of loss and sadness
in my heart as though a special part of me was missing.

Dreams that seem to haunt me, a face, a laugh,
a look that's so familiar, a touch and then I awake
To wonder!

Until one day something happened. For once again
Destiny and the hand of God stepped in.

For familiar feelings came over me, a feeling of
Joy, a sense of happiness and a beautiful sound of
Laughter.
For two souls that were once separated by destiny
are once again brought together through destiny.
"For once again destiny brought me you."

Shanda V. Gadsden

You Are My Everything

Since the day, you entered my life
Gentleness and caring are merely a part,
A way in which you captured my heart.
When I am sad or hurt, you share in my strife,
When I am happy, you share in my laughter.
Your feelings are all around me, a part of me,
And mine are all around you, and a part of you.
Love is you and all you stand for,
Could one ever hope for more?
Sometimes I wonder; just what brought you to my door.
Should I try to reason; the good fortune you bring?
I think not, for you are my everything.

Richard Brzyski

Baby Sister

Just when things are looking great for her,
    Getting married, great job, and buying
    A house
She has no father to turn to
    Since, he has chosen not to
    Be part of his children's life's
Now, mom gets cancer again
I am sure, she feels her world is
    Falling away from her
She has so much trouble talking
    To her sisters and brother, I have
    Told her she can come to me at
    Anytime, but I guess all, I can do
    Is keep on trying
I love her so much and maybe someday
    She will be able to come to me.

Ruth Langiewicz

It's Just A Thought

We always said thank you, we always said please,
girls crossed their ankles but never their knees.

Boys never wore hats when they dined at the table,
and they always wore shirts and that's not a fable.

If walking between two people talking,
we said excuse me, before we'd start walking.

At night when we'd go upstairs to our bed
we'd be kissed good night and our prayers would be said.

We would say we were sorry if we did something wrong
we never said hate, that word was too strong.

We grew up just fine and our lives are okay
just maybe these rules should be taught today.

It's just a thought...

Loris K. White

Leaves Are Falling

There's something about October when the leaves change and
fall to the ground, but the chilly nights are so easily
forgotten by just knowing you're around.

October brings a refreshing change for all of us to see,
changing leaves, a cool breeze, yet so welcomed by those
like me. The colors alone are something else and pumpkins
everywhere, remind me of home and childhood days and
wishing I could go back there.

With each new fall, winter comes, when everything seems so
cold; but all I feel is warmth inside knowing you're here to hold.

I guess that's why autumn is special to me and the leaves
that are falling too; for I indeed, am like the leaves,
only I am falling for you.

Virgie Elliott

Jesus: A Friend Who Cares

O, Lord of living, please protect me.
Give me the strength and wisdom to be.
For these are two things that I pray for,
Knowing that they'll be with me forevermore.
When my load gets too heavy and too hard to bear,
I turn to you, because you really do care.

Jesus, you're a friend, whom I can talk to,
Even when I'm feeling sad and blue.
No matter how big or small my problems seem to be,
You're always there, whenever I need Thee.
Sometimes in life, things don't seem fair.
What I've found in you, is a friend who really does care.

As I kneel down and pray to the Lord above,
I thank Him every day for His gifts of love.
Whenever I need a friend, Jesus is always there,
Assuring me that His spirit goes everywhere.
He's a friend, whose love will always remain the same;
Therefore, "I pray in my friend Jesus' name."

Margaret L. Brown

Packing Away The Memories

Looking at old photo albums,
glancing through your high school year book,
Remembering silly little things as you pack them away.

An empty bottle or a dried flower brings back your school days again.

A picture or a letter from a good friend,
You can always remember when.

It is little things that can bring back so many memories.

As the last things are packed, you sit back and smile,
For all your memories are good ones
And you'll never forget what they meant.

Theresa Scarpellini

Winter Harvested

Thickly blanketed ice crystals
glazing the surfaces of stoic evergreen leaves
sparkle pristinely
in the fading sunlight
before melting
bit
by
bit
to drop unannounced
on the cold, unyielding pavement below
forming tiny reflective lacunae
of winter's most bitter harvest.

Michelle Chappelone

Free

I laughed, I cried, I screamed to be
free.
If only, if only you'd get close to me.
The secret is out I just want to shout.
I love being free and one day you will
see!
I'm happy and peaceful each smile that
I take;
but everyone looks as though it were fake.
I don't even care, I just love being free -
it's sure good to know it's inside of
me.
Keep going, keep growing as long as it's
me -
Keep going, keep sowing.
I love being free!

Myra C. Harris

187

Winter Walk

The moon, silent as snow
  glides softly out
  to light up the iced fragility below
  where sparkles of diamond fire
  light the fields in a crystal blaze

Walking, crunching crust and gasping
  from the cruel breath of winter's night
  I plod the path toward home
where chimney smoke ropes straight upward
  into the windless night
where warmth lies, captured within

- So cold now, toward the end
  a shout would shatter ice
  from the black spider limbs of the apple trees
- So silent now, I can hear the brook groan
  freezing deeper down, deeper down
  Ronald Blake Cole

The Seasons Of Change

  Winter

The ice-encrusted forest stands
Glistening in the crystal rays of the winter sun
Wind shivers and shakes the laden sleeping branches
And the awakened trees are weeping diamonds.

  Autumn

Autumn blazes the hills with fiery crimson splashes
Amid oak's cascading spray of brilliant scarlet - orange,
Chill wind swirls through the rustling leaf-crisp woods,
And birches' golden sovereigns in frosty silence fall,
Or dance delightedly in a wild mosaic of leaping, flaming color
At last to float serenely down on the damp earth's patchwork
carpet.
  Rebecca Downie

A Morning Of Spring

Apple blossoms upon my skin,
God and nature do heavenly things,
The morning dew falls upon my lips,
Taste of honey and rose hips,
Gentle breeze upon my hair,
Warmth of sunshine everywhere,
Birds and butterflies flutter their wings,
Telling us it's a morning of spring,
A rainbow shimmers through the trees,
It falls softly upon their leaves,
Giving me a feeling of peace,
Fragrant roses fill the air,
I touch their petals with love and care,
spring is wonderful to observe,
Everything beautiful grows on earth.
  Luz Celia Colpa

Love

The greatest treasure is love,
God gave us to each other,
Until the day he calls us to be with him in heaven,
It's a special kind of love,
The last hug you gave me, kissed me, and said,
I love you, I really love you,
You knew the Lord was calling you home to be with him in
heaven,
I didn't,
I will cherish the moments God gave to us both,
We will meet in heaven.
  Myrtle Kramer

A New Year

Not only on New Year's but all the year through,
God gives us a chance to start anew.
For each day at dawning, we have but to pray
that all the mistakes that we made yesterday,
will be blotted out and forgiven by grace,
for God in His love forgives with no trace.
All that is past and He grants a new start
to all who are truly repentant at heart.
So many people in awesome-like wonder
why our Father in heaven,
who dwells over and under,
could still remain willing to forgive
the shabby, small lives that we live.
And still would be mindful of sin-riddled man
who constantly goes on defying God's plan.
But this is the Gift of God's limitless love,
and it is a gift that we are so unworthy of.
But God gave it to us and all we need do
is ask God's forgiveness and begin life anew.
  Jerry Davey

"God's Everglades So Beautiful And So Alive"

"O," come to the everglades with me, and you will see,
Gods, Beautiful animal friends with me.
The waters Ripple so blue, they seem to say, come go
with me, and I will show you, Big fish, green frogs
and turtles, an snakes, and otters too, I got
Mr alligator, so big and long saying, I'll bite your
toes, if you got to close, as he slithers along
Come take a ride in an air Boat, and all of Gods
Beauty will unfold, in the Blue Waters, were all the
animals abode.

The indians live here too, they made beautiful arts,
an crafts, and wrestle the alligators too, and you will
fear, the gators will get them instead, with
and awful dread.

I've got Deer, so Pretty, and gat, and Brown, leaping
over, waters and ground, and wild hogs, that snort and grunt,
an eat wild roots, and small stumps and get big rumps.

I've got birds so Beautiful to see, so please keep the everglade
waters clean and clear, so all the wild animals can live here.
  Rutheda M. Flowers

My Thoughts Of You

New Year's Eve and my mind
goes flying back in time.
Tonight I'm listening to a different
sound of fireworks,
And thinking of celebrations with old
friends of mine.
I'm mostly thinking of times spent with
You, but...you are gone.
I sit before the television...really not
seeing the picture.
I feel so all alone.

The New Year I will only have the
Memories we made
Each one different, special, and wonderful.
Oh! How I wish you could
have stayed.
The Master looked down...He had you
in His plan. I'll keep my memories
and love for you,
Until I too, shall live in that Land.
  Pauline Young

Night Sojourner

Now my heart, like a ghost
goes forth and knocks at doors
(and leaving me sleeping)
would commune with those
who do not any longer
keep house within this world;
but, nevertheless and now and now and then,
a door is opened unto her urgent knocking.
And out of those habitations where she is stranger
issue remembered voices...remembered voices...
weighted with love unmeasured, as of old.

Marjorie Brunton Newsom

Four Parts Equal The Whole

My children are a reflection, of all seen in me
Good, bad, right, wrong, it's right there to see
One son is a dreamer, and always full of hope
One daughter is a fighter, success her only scope
One daughter is creative; and she always sees the best
One son's very serious, and is never badly dressed
All four hold the secret, as to what makes me tick
Even when they are far away, the closeness always sticks
I'll never accomplish anything, as important as these four
Each one is a special part of me and the life that I adore
Neither one is more loved, than any of the rest
And when I look back on my life, they truly are the best

Maria C. Averion

"The Feeling Of Love"

The feeling of love is sometimes
good sometimes bad, or it could be the best
darn thing you'll ever have.
Some ways it's comforting, other ways it's
not, and sometimes you just don't care
for the love they are giving you anymore.
You say things you don't mean, so
you have to say goodbye!
The night's now over, and a new
day is here. For a while you're doing fine;
then you realize it's harder than you
thought, living with nobody loving you
the way you need and want to be
loved, and cared for.
You've been with him for so long
you can't let him go. No matter what
he says, or what he does you can't let
him go.
I just now explained to
you the feeling of love.

Naomi Jacot

Untitled

Taste the blood that's in my tears-
Grab my hand; share the fears
Touch my kiss; feel the shame
Watch your whole world explode
While you play your game
Infatuate the lust that's forsaken in a kiss
Watch the moves in love's eclipse
Feel our bodies unite in a common groove
Steady the pain is growing as we move
The flame of a heart; the gravity of the moon
Wrapped up in a cuddly womb
Gentleness, comfort, infatuation, and desire
As one little flame it returned into a fire.

Stephanie Hattaway

A Christmas Angel

There is an angel in our midst
granted power from God above.
A beautiful, graceful heavenly being
overflowing with redeeming love.

A Christmas Angel, Holy Archon
'tis only then she leaves His glory
to smile upon those earthly souls
consumed with pain, despair and worry.

"Cry no more," she gently whispers
"for the babe brings hope and peace to all."
She refers to her own divine deliverance
her flight to heaven when the Master called.

She speaks of comfort, cheer and love
and asks that tears would fall no more;
for every soul that God calls home,
another's born, beloved and adored.

So... every Christmas - forevermore
always remember and believe in this:
we are not alone nor unattended -
there is an Angel in our midst.

Tammy Haines-Kratzer

The Wait

Grand Island, 1971
The child waits.
Green paint peeling.
The enclosed porch screens battered
by heartless midwestern winters.
She sits in the hard white wooden chair
blue eyes glued, almost unblinking,
to the quiet country road made of dust.
When the shiny blue car comes the dust will come to life,
dance magically in the golden late afternoon sun.
Tonight she'll enjoy the bath in the sparkling metal kitchen sink,
the walk to the tiny outhouse,
red flashlight in one hand, Grandma's in the other.
They'll make home baked bread, the warm smell like a loving hug.
The child doesn't think these things,
they just are.
Oh hurry home, Grandma, she thinks
as Grandpa snores in the room behind her.
The wait is unbearably long for a child
yet the child waits.

Laurel Allison Garces

All The Gifts The Lord Brings

In the forest there are flowers
growing, petals falling, making it
look like it's snowing. Little birds fly
by, tweeting softly in the sky. The
language of the birds, too bad I
don't know the words.
The skies are blue and the
Clouds are deep. In my eyes
the color creeps. Clouds tumble
in delight, lighted by the sun's
light, making the land bright
and green. Then nature and life
are truly seen.
The flowers, leaves and the
way they fly, the way the
clouds shine and the birds
sing, they are some of all the
gifts the Lord brings.

Nicole A. Hendriksen

An Added Cost

How timidly the maiden spring awakes,
Half fearing to arise from troubled sleep...
A new rebirth she suffers for our sakes,
For she has many promises to keep,

And many special blessings to bestow
Upon the earth, where men anticipate
Her favor as they watch her beauty grow,
But even as she stirs she is too late.

How powerless her purest scent beside
The sourness of chemistry's exhaust,
Bit by bit her potency has died...
To rescue her they measure now the cost,

The cost of what was once a priceless thing...
The undefiled awakening of spring.

Marie Baia Wroblewski

The Final Good-Bye

The kind face always there to comfort. The gentle
hands there to teach. The warm laughter to raise spirits.
The kind eyes always proud. The wisdom beyond the years.
All of this is gone, leaving only memories. My eyes from
which no more tears can fall looks upon the figure of one
I find so dear. He lies there silent. No more stories of
his life and the way it was then. His eyes are closed, his
tired body now at rest. Walk past the coffin, one last look
to remember forever. Many memories of him. His suffering
is done. He is not dead as long as you remember. He looks
down from heaven, watching over me.

Steven C. Faverty

Let Us Give Thanks For The Moon

Let us give thanks for that soft golden glow,
  hanging proud in the sky.
Falling deeper and deeper into a black swirling air,
  with its light shed upon us.

Let us give thanks for the powerful light,
  a majestic round jewel, with its light dancing,
into the eyes of young's children's dreams.

Let us give thanks for the mystical glow,
  as a flashlight on twilight, to guide the young and the old.
For all of the beating and swirling and striking the sky,
  the moon stands tall and proud.

As it disappears in the day, only to be seen at night,
  to guide the young ones, and show them the world.
To open their eyes to a new way of seeing.

Let us give thanks for the glow on the water,
  the cries of the jewel being mournful of darkness.
The stars are her children,
  She'll protect them and nurture them,
till the day the world dies.

Let us give thanks for the moon.

Lindsay A. Manning

October Tree

Her boughs are reaching to claim respect
her ample arms, raindrops collect.
In summer her shade was spacious and serene
but Autumn's touch has changed the scene.
Though I see brilliants - red and gold
the leaves will fall that she cannot hold.

Oh Life is like that October Tree
the Summer comes - and goes - from me.....

Lola L. Costa

Smell The Roses

The days of darkness are many for those like me...
Happiness is our rainbows, as brilliant as any can be.
The fragrance of the Rose so fine...
is as the nectar of the finest wine.

Your touch, your smile, as the rose in its glory...
An angel was brought to earth to dispel all worry.
My world, as that of darkest night...
but, still the touch of your smile is a heavenly light.

I touch your cheek, I feel it blush,
a love through my soul to a heart does rush...
Bring your world of light and flair
to a side of darkness, where so few care.

Join me in happiness, let me feel your smile each day...
Smell the beauty of the roses quietly bowing to pray.
From your world to mine...
Your voice as music, so divine.

Feel not sad,
or compassion to borrow...
Take my hand,
we will again smell the roses, tomorrow!

D. Seibert

The Other Side Of The Fence

Death and destruction controlled their minds
Hate and corruption all the time
Deceit and deception from all their kind
Where do they come from without a dime

They sleep in the alleys nowhere to go
Whatever made them sink so low
How can we help them what can we do
Is there an answer I really wish I knew

What can we do what can we say
Some people help them some push them away
If you listen carefully each night you can hear their cry
Sometimes I feel like I could just curl up and die

So many people with so much money
And they won't help isn't that funny
For these people I feel there's no excuse
Nobody should have to take their kind of abuse

I cringe with every little moan
I couldn't do it if I were so alone
They are human and they are alive
We've got to do something to help them survive

Rebecca Parmer

Our Flag Stands For Freedom

I don't understand why some people feel they
have to burn our flag. Have they forgotten what it
stands for?
Let me remind them. IT STANDS FOR FREEDOM!
Each color for me represents something different.
The stars have another meaning.
Red - for death and blood shed.
Blue - the way we feel deep inside when there is war.
White - for the hope of peace.
Stars - the ray of life that shines at the darkest hour.
So please don't burn our flag. History! The Civil War,
World War I and II, Vietnam and now for those who have already
died in Saudi Arabia. Please, I beg you! Don't let those
who have died for our flag to have died in vain
So before you put a match to our flag stop and think: What
are you doing to yourself, to your country, and to America?
Let our flag fly high with pride, for freedom.

Linda Kay Gallo

Love's Desire

Why is it that those who need love
Have to feel, touch and be absorbed in it.

And those who need so little,
Only feel and touch when there is a desire.

Desire is not love, only an impostor,
That destroys the ones who love.

So how much are we supposed to love,
Or for some, how much are they to desire?

Mimi Kubos

Why?

There was a boy who I once knew
He always made me sad and blue
God I loved him so, but why I'll never know
There were times I was full of Joy
Just knowing that he was my boy
He always said that we were meant to be
that was him and me
He said that we would never part
Yet still he broke my heart
Things started to change just like the seasons
Yet he gave me no reasons
Then he walked out of my life as if he never existed
And now my life seems so twisted
I don't know what I want nor who I want
God why I got involved with him I'll never know
But until the day I die, I'll always love him so
I'm all alone once again, now I'll have to
  try again
Not for awhile, for I cannot smile
I still love him so, yet why I still don't know

Lisa Ann Matteo

The Sunset Of Life

In the beauty and splendor of sunset
  He came riding into my life
For an evening of enchantment and romance
  In the fragrant perfume of night.

The moonlight is filled with magic
  And the stars sparkle clear and bright.
The day has all passed, but the evening
  Fills one long glorious night.

A lifetime of loving and living
  Where the fullness of meaning entwines
Must all be experienced this evening
  Ere the dawn of eternity shines.

So now together we'll live to the fullest,
  We'll drink to the depths of the soul.
And nothing could e'er be more *glorious*
  Than to have this small part be the WHOLE!

Viola K. Parks

Secret Of A Rainbow

The rain has come to an end
God then wanted to send
A rainbow in the sky
I don't know why
Some say to look for the gold
At the end of the rainbow it has been told
A pot of gold and little men in green
It has never been seen
No little men in green, no pot of gold
Just the beauty of the rainbow and the secrets
  that it holds.

Kristy Brelish

A Mom's Dilemma

The pain she feels, I wish I could erase,
  He disappears over and over again without a trace.

The gifts, the trips, the no discipline rule,
  The times he picks her up early from school.

The promises that are often made just to be broken,
  With words of deliverance that should never be spoken.

"My job is demanding, I can't make it today,"
  Words spoken so many times along the way.

But I'm not a magician and wishes don't come true,
  So Lord, teach me sincerely how to depend on you.

For my daughter's on again, off again, I'll see you soon Dad,
  Is giving my beautiful child one of the worse childhoods
  to be had.

My prayer to you Lord is to help her be strong.
  My prayer dear Lord is that he'd change his ways to do right,
  not wrong.
    Your will, in this whatever it may be, please help me always
    to trust in Thee.

Karen R. Peoples

My Pet Charlie

My pet's name is Charlie,
He does not like to ride my Harley
When he hears the roar;
He runs for the door.

He sleeps all day,
And plays all night.
He likes to run around the house,
Chasing his furry little toy mouse.

As the bird flits around,
Charlie sits and frowns.
He wants it to fly out of its cage,
Knowing the bird will be in a rage.

He was very small when I got him,
So we just played and rocked him.
Now he is so spoiled, we cannot leave,
Without hearing his cry of plea.

When he is good and lying down,
He likes to be petted under the chin.
By now, have you guessed what my pet is?
Now I will tell you, he is a lovable kitty.

Kimberly Allman

Habits

A detestable thing it is that is constantly done
From it though you try you cannot hide
And from it, too, you cannot sway for it you must obey
Then at night on reflection you do cry

But by then the sordid deed is already done
And you realize you are very much alone
As during the day you failed to delay
The acts that bring about the foray

It's only now that you vow to atone
For the vice that you did condone
Being afraid that the iniquity may stay
Never, never to permanently go away

Yet the deed indiscriminately clone
And with it again you pick a bone
And on a raft you float, a castaway
On the tempestuous billows of habits gone awry

Richard A. Barker

Man On The Street

The young man sits on the park bench
  He feels the chill in the air
His wife and his children are waiting
  He tries to fight the despair

The economy took his job away
  His government checks ran out
When he was a child and thought about life
  This wasn't what he thought about

This wasn't the way he pictured their home
  When he and his love were wed
He wanted to give her a mansion
  She got a cot in the shelters instead

Yes, he and his wife and children
  Are now living on the street
He'll take any kind of work offered
  Just to get them on their feet

But today he slowly walks toward them
  He doesn't know what to say
How can he tell the family he loves
  Home is the shelter at least one more day

Kym Guttenberg

The Pilot

His life is not his own...
He gave it up when that flight was flown.
To show he is the best, when he is put to the test
To get the mission done... the war needs to be won!
As spirited as an eagle, hovering high or low
It does not matter when he has got to go.
Defend, guard, and fight
He's a steel machine like a bird in flight.
Protecting his country with honor and pride,
...He puts his fear aside.
He is a leader, a mentor, a guiding light in stormy weather.
He sits in the cockpit to keep this world together.
He knows his purpose,
In the air and on land.
...Wears his uniform with pride
Salutes with a dedicated hand.
The depths of this man
An officer through and through.
It is within him, it has become him...
The man... the pilot...

Karin Lee Risley

Mother "Dear"

By the light of His grace above
He gave me a mother to love
Whether it rained or whether she was sad
She had the courage to raise the children she had
Your love mom was great and your love was true
At the heart of your family there was you
Daisy, means flower so sweet and fair
Believe me I thank God mom you were always there
So this birthday message comes today to say
Thank you in my special way
Thanks for the times I remember so well
It was just one slip and I might have fell
You were there for us all and
It's plain to see your sacrifices
Large but meant to be
Six of us were so many you see
Her love was shared so happily
Your rewards mother will be up above
There will be so many treasures filled
With grace and love

Sandra Lee O'Farrell

Untitled

When will man alert the fact that
He is never alone,
Even when he is dead and buried
and the flesh has fallen from his bones,
That when he dies God will
appear on to Him and take his soul home,
No more pain and suffering will he endure,
if man keeps himself holy,
and his soul is pure,
Learning to walk side by side with,
his fellow man, not killing him for money
or just to possess his land,
for if we keep up the rate that
we are going. I hate to say
what will be our fate at hand,
we forget the commandments that were
written by God in stone,
when will man
accept the fact that he is never alone.

Michael E. Kuehl

The Dreamweaver And The Songshaper

I cannot love him as he loves me
He is the dreamer; I, reality.
I look to the future and all that it holds
While he spins tales and stories of old.
His words are bright and sing like a lark,
while mine may be cheerful, but yet always dark.
I see in him what I want to be,
does he see in me what he wants to be?
Yes, I have changed and so has he
all for the love that will Forever be.

Rebeccah J. Roberts

Humanity's Child

He looks at me with wonder about why I care whether
  he knows his arithmetic.
And his eyes tell me that he wonders how numbers will
  ever change his portion.
Will it change the fact that his mom doesn't love him
  or that dad's a narcotic?
Write a letter? To mom? Her lover, or his own brothers
  who beat him? To rejection?
Can those who birthed what he is see when I leave and he
  peers from behind the curtain?
Can they see the tears flood his face and the learned
  shame as he wipes them away?
As I walk back to the window can they hear the pleading,
  "I love you, please come again!"
Can they understand that this child is all humanity
  and I was his only God that day?

Terry B. Kinney Jr.

Memories

I remember walking barefoot, on grass wet with dew
Gazing at the sky, the moon was shining through.
Not a care in the world, everything was alright
I watched a falling star disappear from sight.
I heard a hoot owl, perched high in a tree
Everything was so quiet, was he talking to me?
Could he feel the peace, that I felt inside
With the one that I loved, walking close by my side?
I have memories of happier days
When life was different in many ways.
Now I walk alone, sometimes I reminisce
Of days gone by, and people I love, and miss.

Vivian Horne

7 To 3

From 7 to 3 each Friday and Saturday night
He patrols our streets and makes sure stores are locked up tight
From 7 to 3 what lousy hours
With new laws to learn and various complaints to be heard
Feisty kids looking for some action
To partners in crime trying to avoid detection
With breaking of windows and stealing of cars
Lovers in back seats staring up at the stars
From 7 to 3 he's there to protect and serve
His life on the line our safety to preserve
Whether it's finding a lost child and stopping its crying
Or stopping high speed racing
That might cause someone's dying
Honor and pride in the uniform he wears
Trust in his fellow officers he shares
From 7 to 3 each Friday and Saturday night
705 C does his best to make sure things are safe at night
while we rest

Shirley Bundridge

A Talk With God

God and I had a talk one day when I was sad.
He said that life is not an easy journey, but not everything was bad.

He spoke of all the people who would come and go.
Some would learn from me, and others I would follow.
How sometimes I would win, and there were chances I'd be beat.
But without these experiences, my life could not be complete.

He explained that each soul has a purpose.
And one day I'd understand what mine was; and he assured me
Mine was grand.

We spent most of our time discussing love.
He would not give me the answers; only prepare me for what was
to come.

He said that love is not a bad thing; even though at times it may seem so.
Not everyone is meant to be with us forever; so it's OK to let them go.

He reminded me not to be scared; because I would never be alone.
I would always have love surrounding me; and I would always have a
home.
He said I must love everyone; even the ones with faults.
Because people will make mistakes; more times than not.
He assured me that at the end of my journey; I would be happy and
content.
And I will be able to see that My life was well spent.
So now when I get discouraged, I remember how he explained:
That everything happens for a reason; and to learn from the pain.

Valerie Rynning

"The Lord"

The Lord is the best Friend that you can
find
He's always there to respond and he doesn't
mind

He's always there for you when you have
problems to face
He cares for you and touches you with such
loving grace.

The Lord has the almighty
power
To lift you up when you feel like you
should cower

If you believe and have faith that the Lord can
change your ways
Then to you he will bring brighter and
sunnier days.

Michelle Getzinger

Untitled

I have a friend who's president of a university
He stays upbeat when there is adversity
His wife, Arlene, is a fine first lady
Their home is nice and their lawn shady

I have a friend who sells plumbing supplies
His inventory has toilet seats of every size
He also handles sinks, stoppers and pipes
And bathtubs of many colors and types

I have a friend who is a cop
She directs cars at a traffic stop
It is said she can be very tough
Especially when drivers try to get rough

I have a friend who's a radio announcer
With news and weather she's a good pronouncer
She does sports and talk shows too
Her many listeners are loyal and true

I have a friend who's a dressmaker
In community life she's no mover and shaker
But when it comes to fine attire
She may set the world on fire

Wayne Krows

My Dad, The Vietnam Vet

The vietnam war never ended.
He still fights the war when he sleeps.

Too many men fell in the jungle of hell, and the memories are
planted too deep.

The vietnam war never ended. The memories of war stay alive.

His friend's in a chair, but his legs are not there, and he
Fights every day to survive.

Another friend walks with a walker. Another friend walks with
A cane.
He has another one who shoots with a needle to escape the
Vietnam pain.

No the vietnam war will never end, in the minds of many men.
It will live with him till he dies.
War won't let you forget.

See, the vietnam vet is my Dad.
At night, I still hear him cry when he sleeps.

One day he might forget the war and pain
But for now, I just hope he sleeps peacefully at night.

Walter Bill Thomas

The Boy Soldier

Crouched among the trees as the soldiers marched by
He trembled in fear and tried not to cry.
Why was he here- in the rain and the cold?
He felt so alone and not at all bold.
When he had run away from home in the still of the night
He had felt like a man and that he was doing right,
But he was only a boy and he was afraid -
The war was lost and he felt betrayed.
He longed to be home and to see his mother once more,
To run down the lane and through the front door.
But now was the challenge to stay alive,
Without help - how long could he survive?
What was that noise? - Someone moving nearby -
He reached for his rifle and raised the sight to his eye.
A blinding light and a roar like thunder,
He felt a searing pain and just had time to wonder -
'Why am I here in the rain and the cold?
I feel so alone and not at all bold.'

Loveniar A. Williamson

193

Angel

My angel waits for me high upon his hill.
He waits for me to call to him.
Sometimes he whispers to me when he
Hasn't heard my voice for a while.

If I do not answer my angel,
He weeps silver tears until we are together again.
My angel smiles brighter than a golden ray
When he can do something to make me happy.

My angel whispers of tenderness and love.
My heart soars when he is happy.
He screams because of loneliness and sorrow.
My ears burn from the sound of his pain.

The reason for my living is held in his heart.
He has always been with me,
And we will be together for eternity
Passing the limits of space and time.

Katrina Scheidler

I'll Be Back

"I'll be back",...that's old man doubt creeping in
He wants you to fail...and never ever win
"You can't do that"...he'll say each time
And before long you'll doubt your own mind
Maybe I shouldn't..I suppose he's right
Should I?..shouldn't I?..it's an inner fight
Old man doubt is just like quicksand
He loves to get close and hold your hand
He'd love to be a family member
And slip a ring on your fourth finger
But remove the doubt, ideas drop like stars
Confidence now replaces the bars
Bars you thought you could not break
Possibilities now seem to overtake
Doubt realizes he's lost you
And for sure he'll change his attack
But stay sharp and keep alert
He whispers, "I will be back."!

Penny Bennington

A Tribute To Elvis

He was so beautiful to the young at heart,
   He was destined for stardom from the start;
He was a country boy strong and true,
   He sang his songs for me and you.

He had a million dollar smile,
   He was one of a kind, his own style...
He moved with such rhythm and grace,
   No one will ever take his place.

He is still the king of music, this we'll never forget,
   And we're not over his memory yet;
No one will ever know why he left us that day,
   No one will ever know why it was that way.

Maybe God wanted him to sing in his array,
   And get him away from this earthly sway;
His life had been fulfilled as king of music, we know;
   Maybe he knew he was ready to go.

Maybe he knew this all along, and anticipating,
   When he could sing for the real King awaiting;
Now he still sings for the master, now and then,
   And maybe someday we will all hear him sing again.

Richard Hooper

Thoughts Of The Past

He still had his life ahead of him.
He was ever so close to me.
Everyday is the only day I saw him.

Now the years are moving on, the memories
are black and white, fading like a rainbow.
Who would have ever thought he would have to go.

He was the last on my list, but first on my mind.
And his soft voice called "hello."
Oh how he was ever so kind.
He was like a brother to me.
Like a gushing water, and trembling sea.

Why was it he who had to leave?
I guess I'll never know why.
But now that he's gone all I have is one lone memory.
One that I will cherish now and forever.

Melanie N. Brown

I'm Sorry

The drive was quiet enough to hear the wind fight the car
he was lost in thought
of what
who knows

I was gone
maybe with that wind that was pushing the Riviera
maybe I was still at home just dreaming
guess not

We were once so close
now we're sitting together
with worlds between us

Now, I wish the chatter would stop
endless talk with no sound

I want it all to be over
but this is only the beginning
I've got a lifetime to live through
in the next five hours
Oh, Amanda...I'm sorry.

Marion F. Maynard

Hidden Love

The first one born Lord Where can he be?
He'll grow up not knowing his father is me.

I've never see him Lord, but I know he's there
because I feel his presence everywhere.

Now, I married the girl I loved so well, tell me
Lord why did she put me through this hell?

I thank her Lord for a beautiful Son
now I only wish I had a gun.

Harm to them is something I could never do.
It is myself Lord. I want to put the gun to.

My third son lies in a hospital dying
While his mother stays home crying.

Oh, Dear God if you could only see
the hidden Love I have for these three.

The last one Lord. Please spare his life.
If someone must go let me pay the price.

If I hadn't taken those stupid drugs,
he'd be able to see and think like the rest of us.

So, in closing Lord, Please don't let them see me cry.
For my load is to heavy Lord, Please let me die.

Linda Zehrung

Apprehensive Progeny

Crazy girl wit cho open mouth,
hear all the words you constantly shout.

I hear you talkin that crazy talk,
ain't even morning, what you talking about?

If you open your ears instead of your mouth,
you'd see those trickling little tears.

Why do you scream both day and night?
do you not care bout the tears in sight?

I sure hope you hear me,
I sure hope you care.

What else is this world,
if the children won't dare.

Allow them their mouths,
let them speak to us.
Nobody wants to hear that fuss.

Regina Durant-Gibbs

Dreamer's Heart

I knew the story, right from the start
He'd let me go, he'd break my heart.
He'd let me be, he'd let me strive,
But the dreamer could survive.

Seasons would pass, and life would get better,
But I just could not forget him.
I close the windows facing the city
I think of him when days get old.

I'll call tomorrow just to remind him:
"Dreamers are people with hearts of gold!"
But he's so strong,
and he's so humble,
Just couldn't tell him how I stumble.

I'd let him go, but life is hell,
I see resistance slowly prevail.
The Hudson grows quiet
Like a lonely widow,
The waters are cold but not my heart.
The blush of dawn will touch the city,
And I'll wish him well before I'm gone.

Silvana Krculic

The Words Of Sam McGlew

When young and Dad got mad with us
he'd say a little speech,
with words so big we'd scat
and keep out of his reach.

"The ponderosity of the vehicle,"
he'd say with a mean sounding yell,
"impedes the velocity of the quadruped!"
And we'd all run like hell. Or

"I had a little calf and that's half,
and we being about calf size
stuck its tail over the wall that's all!"
Though no tails we weren't that wise. Or

"How dare you insinuate I should tolerate,"
and with a mean look in his eye,
"such diabolical, incompetent insults!"
Those words would make me cry.

But now grown up and looking back
he must have been laughing inside,
for they were just words but big words
that made us want to go hide.

Sara McGlew Raleigh

Juliet And (Almost) Romeo

So many days ago did Juliet;
her lips, dance promises ever after.
Stand above him innocent, heart-in-hand,
clutched tightly, white knuckle, pressed against her.

She pledged him devotion with all her heart.
So filled, his odes would overflow in ink.
Night stars twinkle; her eyes, as she read them.
And the feelings grew, unheeded, inside.

Discovery brought dream children to life.
They scattered in directions of the sun.
Their black hand prints; confessions between lines.
The evidence wielded like a sabre.

On the grey day, betrayal overwhelmed her.
The lie in belief closed her eyes to love.
Cast aside like so many old nightmares.
The true love forgotten in waves of guilt.

So many days ago did Juliet
play-out her scripted part without ad lib.
A love story - to end a tragedy.
His half-heart falls to the freshly turned dirt.

T. William Helgren

Ode To A City

I trod upon this throbbing land, A City to behold.
Her mighty towers pierce the sky, amid silver birds so bold.

Cement ribbons around her twine, alive with racing steel.
Oh Tara, I think of the gentle days, when rolled the wagon wheel.

Still beckoning, she calls, some three million strong.
Her verdant, piney fingers sway, with gentle breezes song.

Ah, her Springtime splendid show, no other can compare,
The Dogwood, Azalea, and springtime bloom, lend fragrance to the air.

I look now toward the East, carved deep upon the stone,
Her proud History revealed of honor and atone.

I climbed upon her crown, and drank in her sweet nectar.
Renewed within my spirit, as I savored each lush sector.

I count it all my Blessing as the day's light is done,
Oh surely, Grand Atlanta, I must be your Chosen Son.

Nancy Kassinger

!!Help!!

Message to us all, or a word to the wise,
He who kills, may soon be he who dies.
Death and violence, ignorance and hate,
End the destruction before it's too late.
Work together, and lend a helping hand,
Not just to yourself, but to every man.
We have but one world, and it we share,
Let's work to make it better and to care.
The more we care, the better we live, and
The better we live, the more we can give.
The more we can give, to our life's dream,
The dream to live and love as one, as a team.
Help make the future more than a blur.
There are children crying and people dying,
We must help those who need us, we must keep
trying.
We must heed the call for help of our fellow
man and lend a helping hand, before it's too late.

Tamara Lashay Moss

The Flower

One little flower with such a sad face,
Her smile's disappeared and now a frown takes its place.
"Time heals all wounds" he said in a breeze.
She wanted to die, wishing for a sudden freeze.
Her life was happier blooming all alone,
Than since he came along shattering all she's known.
This thing called love - he takes it so lightly,
So obvious to her when he broke her heart so politely.
Her petals once glistening with each morning's dew,
Are now wilting and dying because she's so blue.
Waiting for the fall she weeps with sorrow,
Wishing pain from today wouldn't be here tomorrow.
Spreading beauty and joy - her reason to be,
Being hurt by another took away her glee.
Her petals begin to fall and her stem takes a bow,
With help from Mother Nature she's dying peacefully now.

Tonya L. Bauer

Thank You To A Friendly Muse

Here in my life a gift is given,
Here in my hand a pen.
Here in my mind a thought is fired,
Here I may touch a friend.
Mind takes its message from the soul,
Fuel to the wind, as a burning coal
To the furnace heat and the stoker's hand,
Gift is a mark, a permanent brand,
Here in my life is a gift.

Here in my life a gift is given,
Mightier than the sword.
Here the ideals and ideas clash,
Here the invading, evolving word,
Piercing the darkness toward the light,
Cutting to sever wrong from right,
Showing a path through the tangled vine,
Gift is the place where I touch the divine.
Here in my life is a gift.

Sibyl J. Disch

Innocence

I see the sleekness of her body, her physique strong and yet feminine.
Her dark and light tones of brown hair lay perfectly into place.
Her eyes shine with innocence, as she lifts her head high and proud.
As I stare at her beauty with the desire to take her, I hesitate.
Gracefully she lowers her head, and nestles her nose to the ground.
She begins to nibble on the left-over corn-like a baby nursing
on its mother.
I lay down my bow and slowly lift my head. I feel the proudness
she feels of being alive.

Linda Gehrig

Helpless Child

So sweet and innocent she lay,
  I must teach her to walk and pray.
When she's older, she'll know God.
  Through her life with Him she'll trod.
She'll walk together with God through this land,
  Never leaving the care of His hand.
Ten little fingers and ten little toes.
  She does not yet know life's woes
Of Earth's toils and tribulations
  Of the wars of all the nations.
So delicate and pretty is she
  And she was given, Lord, by Thee.
Help me to teach her and show her I care
  And let her know You'll always be there.

Carol Jean Dykhouse

My Great Grandbabies

When I knew of your life,
I looked so very, very much to see you,
But now after only five months in the womb,
You are in Heaven, with God and Jesus.

I cried, and I cried, and I cried,
Every time I talk about you,
I cry, and I cry, and I cry.
Yes, I know I will see you, in Heaven.

What sorrow my Granddaughter went through,
Also her Mother, my Daughter,
And me, as the Great Grandmother.
Knowing you are with JESUS, is the only healing.

My Darling, precious twin grandbabies,
There will always be a space in my heart,
It will be totally empty,
Until I see you, when I see JESUS.

Connie James

Negril Nights

As the jealous sun sets at the cafe,
  I know that night time is not far away

Negril nights arrive for the young at heart
  one love, one people - not so far apart

Streets filled with life and spirit unmatched
  is why I find myself so very attached

The mystical sounds of reggae move me upward
  into the glimmering stars - I gaze forward

In a world where we must see to believe,
  negril nights offer a soothing reprieve

For here at night, darkness disguises the scene
  of all that is pure, all that is serene

I close my eyes and embrace the sights
  and give maximum respect to negril nights.

Dean G. Kakridas

Looking Upon The Man

As I look upon your eyes
I see your deep feelings
But yet it's not so deep
Because, I know what they are saying

As I look upon your eyes
I can almost see your heart
But things are confused but yet, I understand

As I look upon your eyes
It can be a mystery
But yet it can be solved
But that would be so easy

As I look upon your eyes
I can feel the passion
But yet that passion to put on hold.

As I look upon your eyes
I feel confused, just so tempting to say yes

But as I look in your eyes I see a true man
With a deep passion, mystery and a heart.

As I look upon your eyes I admire these things
In you, because they make you a very special man.

Brenda Colclasure

"Segregation"

Some of my friends are shorter than I,
I like them anyway - I don't know why.
Some have red hair, some have black,
Some have many talents which I lack.
Some are humorous, gentle and kind.
Some speak with accents — but I don't mind.
Some live in Los Angeles, Chicago and New York,
Some like oysters and some prefer pork.
Some play pro football - some wait on tables.
Some own nothing - some own horses and stables.
My friends come in an assortment of races;
They also come in assorted colors of faces.
I have known and loved Irish, Blacks, Greeks and Jews.
Mexicans, Japanese, Indians — just to name a few.
Now — you tell me I must hate!
Because I am WHITE I must discriminate!
Hate all my friends? I don't mind.
Before I met you I was color blind.
Now — at long last, my life is set right.
Before I met you, I DIDN'T KNOW I WAS WHITE!

Jean Bild

Life Is Precious

I need to cry a good tear.
I live my life with one fear;
Not knowing when I will die.
It makes me weak and want to cry.

I'd rather know so I can be prepared,
To say goodbye to the ones who cared.
If I don't have a chance to say goodbye,
It will leave, my loved ones wondering why.

Life is precious and short to be unknown,
I never like to be left alone.
I make myself known in the world around me.
So I'm never alone, with friends and family.

Being in a world of nursery, strife and sorrow,
Leaves me a slim chance for a better, tomorrow.
So I live my life each day, by the day.
I live my life, what more could I say?

Donald Johns Canning

It Is Good

From a plane high in flight
I looked at the earth in full light
All the horizon was aglow
The earth, like a quilt lay below.

The toil and pain of man below all forgot
Only God's creativity I sought
Everywhere was a touch of His hand
His ordered beauty lay upon all the land.

I saw slumbering valleys between the hills
Giant columned mountains that stood very still
Miles of farmland - sources of food that we eat
Green prairies where cattle fatten to the market beat.

I saw desert land that seemed empty and free
Rivers that stretched and turned on the way to sea
Calm lakes of blue sparkled in the sun
Deep and majestic canyons make one wonder how this was done.

What a beautiful continent God did make
And all of this for man's sake
On a cloud God must have stood
Looked upon America and said: "It is good."

Anthony B. Loncharich

The Raid

As one of the panting, slavering pack
I ran
Without conscious thought, following instinct.

I fed with them
To be one of them,
Uncaring of morality,
Feeding their hunger for dominance.

As one of the panting, slavering pack
I ran
Without conscious thought, right into the trap.

To be caught,
    cuffed,
    photographed,
    printed and
    caged.

Entangled in the senselessness
    of my unlawful conformity.

Barbara A. Durkin

The Stolen Gift

As I came away from my mother's womb,
I reached out and grabbed her soul,
And took it away with me.
Selfishly, I grasped it for myself.
Ripping it from her life,
To sustain me, as I journeyed into mine.
I stole it.
And I can never give it back.

Birth is an anathema, swaddled by love.
A larceny rewarded by its own gift of life.
A culmination of giving and taking.
Living and dying begin at conception.

As I came away from my mother's womb,
She reached out and handed me her soul,
She gave it to me willingly.
Terrified, I grasped it for myself.
Tearing it from her life,
To sustain me as I journeyed into mine.
I have it.
And I can never give it back.

John Harrington Burns

For Lewis R. Beatty

Looking back through the gray-fogged years,
I remember you
Standing, no sitting there smiling.
You were always there for me, even when I didn't want you.
A true friend.

Now, you bastard, you are gone.
Forty-some-odd years ago, you died.
Breath would no longer fill your lungs;
Muscles would not respond to your commands.

I watched you die.
I held your hand even though you could not respond.
Your chair sat empty, with a
Black ribbon draped across.
Motionless.

You breathed your last and part of
Me died. Your eyes closed,
My heart broke.

My shadow lies on your grave,
In a crouch. The ground is now
Wet with my tears.

Adrian Martin

Remember Me

When you feel the need
for my presence,
Go to the ocean front.
For in the horizon
Where earth meets sky,
that is where my memory lingers.
As the wind
brushes by your face,
that is my caress,
And when you hear
the screech of the sea gulls
that is my
everlasting laughter.

Nancy McMahan

Dare To Dream

Once I stood, where you now stand.
For once I dared to dream.
With trembling knees
and shaking hands,
I took that giant step.

With furrowed brow I look at you,
a smile upon my face.
With trembling knees
and shaking hands,
you now take my place.

Do not be afraid, my dear,
to take that giant step.
Reach for the stars,
on your walk through life,
and always dare to dream.

Retha Sloter Murray

Alone

I feel so alone sitting waiting
for someone to come my way
As I sit and wait in vain
I know now that I will slowly go insane
although I call on deaf ears
The child in me sheds no tears
For his soul has died away
As I pray for a better day
when people will come my way
I hesitate then slowly...
oh so slowly fad away

Michelle Coffman

Remember This

If ye should remember anything
For this is truth!
Of an invincible roman empire
Whose beauty can be locked in
With a desperate moment of victory
Triumphant! Indeed, triumphant!
And when Ye may hear, the trumpets
Sound out in unison
Into a clear daylight air
Only to be cut through by shouts
Of so many enthusiastic cheers!
Most assuredly
It shall be
The far greater one of all
In our return to history
O'Great Caesar, indeed!
For it shall reflect upon
A return to Caesar

Ron Toni

Trees Do Talk

I know the hour of springtime
For the bud, blossom and spread
I know the time of awakening
After the autumn leaves are shed

I feel the warmth of the breeze
As the clouds form much more blue
When the sun peeks to show itself
There! I notice so much that's new

I sigh sensing familiar aromas
Of new tiny twigs and their green
The air is immersed with glory
New blossoms and leaves yet unseen

Nestling upon all my branches
Like arms protecting their sleep
Soon, our Greatest of Caretakers
Will awaken my children from sleep

Ah yes! together we will then know
At last! we enter springs array
Yet we weep for the autumn leaves
E'er so stilled where now they lay

Vera Ireland

Untitled

I wait, a prisoner of the morning hours,
for the reverberation of the doorbell,
which will startle me
then summon me
to your presence in my home.
As the minutes infinitely drag by,
the ringing is now only an echo,
hanging quietly
and yet unheard
in the loud silence of my house.

Sue L. Barkley

What Now

I'm here, I'm waiting
For the room to light up
For the earth to crack open
For this great sign, that great
Voice to tell me what to do
Will it happen when I expect?
Am I looking in the right place?
Is it in a store? In a book?
Something warm and familiar
Keeps talking to my heart.
Maybe it's what I've been looking for
All of the time I've been looking

Kathi L. Thames

Had You On My Mind

Woke up this morning darling,
Had you on my mind.

Shot right out of bed, baby
Back on the road again

Meet you at the bus stop
Baby, and take you to your train

I can hear that whistle blowing
On down the road

So when the sun goes down
Honey, you know, I'll be there
To take you home.

Susan Flynn

Sobriety #48

I study the mirror
            for traces of past
Reflections. A
Nose here, an eye there...faces no
Longer
        mine. Memory gone cold. The
Effort expended,
            to remake out of
Fleeting fragments;
                a self, newly
Sober, whole again...
                enduring the
Ravages
    of
        time.

Thomas T. Morgan

Crescent City, CA, 9/15/90

Again My Friend

Born again,
Forlorn again.
Beauty my friend
In death my friend.

I see again
So blind my friend
I flee again
Today my friend.

Look at you my friend
Take a look, and look again
I've seen it before my friend
I saw it then, I will see it again.

Burn my friend
Feel the flames again
They make love my friend
To you again.

My friend, my friend
I'm hot too my friend
Time, and time again
I'm hot too my friend.

Magnus Voie

Liberty

Our Lady of Liberty
her torch held high
she's there to say hello or hi!
The girl with the mostest
is our country's hostess.
Our Lady of Liberty

Marie Seeley

Untitled

Loneliness is a state of mind.
Happiness is hard to find.
Is it right to just be content
    and plain.
Is it wrong to be satisfied
    and want again.
Does it make a difference how
    a person feels,
Or does it just depend on the
    cards they hold and what they
    want to deal.

Kevin Barger

From Beginning To End

A Butterfly flying about
found its home on a flower nearby.
While not very far down the lane
another flower wilted to die.

A little girl giggled with friends
in a world where she hadn't a care.
As an elderly man picked up a book
and sat in his old rocking chair.

A Bride and a Groom said "I Do"
to start off a life for all time.
While a husband and wife of 25 years
signed goodbye on a dotted line.

The mother leaned over the basket
to kiss the baby who'd started to cry.
As the widow leaned over the casket
to kiss her dead husband goodbye.

WendyLee Cutler

When Icicles Glow

Thermometer's at five below
    Freezing winds no longer blow
The stage is set again once more
    For winter's fist to pound the door.

And strike it does with brittle clap
    Scattering glass icicles;
No soft white thrust of hand does that
    Which pours the mould in winter's vat.

No soft white fist is this!

Only the Sculptor's gloves pulled on
    Can chisel shapes of crystal brawn
And pierce a diamond with a thorn
    Or weave a curtain frosted dawn.

Extravagance marks winter's show!

Its bold designs of beauty glow
    Blaze with fire on golden snow
While shadows plot to tighten bonds
    Beyond the snowfall's muffled songs
And winding rivers meant to sing
    Find no escape until the spring.

Katherine Flynn

Goodbye My Friend

Now the pen is lifted
from the page,
The cast of characters
has left the stage.

Lonely echoes in the
mist of change,
Fog of uncertainty,
things seem strange

You have taught me well
in lessons shared
My defenses shattered
when you said you cared.

Though the chapter is written
our stories go on
A new cast of characters
Another theme song

The sun gold begins to set
Dusk shrouds the dawn
Even in the darkest night
The candle of the sun … burns on.

Rob Killam

The Water That Falls

The water that falls
From the walls
Is called Niagara Falls
It rushes down into the
Deep waters below
Where people sometimes go
You need a raincoat, and hat
To get through the great big gap
The water falls so rapidly
I guess this is the way it
Should be
Just like being out in the sea
The water falls real fast
It has been here from the past
The water falls with such a sound
Like a drum being pound
    This is the water that
    Falls

Mildred E. Bibbs

"Just Kentucky Dreaming"

You can't love me like a river
gently winding all around me
it's never-ending or beginning
is ever present in my heart

Dusty roads and barefoot children
or a sunset from the mountains
I could call up to those mountains
And I could hear them call my name

You can't love me like a rain
falling softly all about me
in those cool Kentucky mornings
Just a cool Kentucky rain

I have lived in many places
I have never called them home
Just that one back in Kentucky
That in my heart is still my own

Sometimes I hear her calling me
in a soft persistent voice.
through those southern Springtime breezes
And then my heart calls back to her.

Kathy Hofele

Silent Shadows

I watch the silent shadows
Glide across the valley floor
Darkness is descending
Night birds sing their songs once more

Silent shadows glide across
A pale silvery crescent moon
Glowing in a black velvet sky
Waiting for the stars to twinkle soon

I watch the silent shadows
Make patterns on yonder hill
Little animals scamper to their dens
Listening to the call of the whip-o-will

Then the silent shadows,
silhouettes a juniper against the sky
As I watch a lonely spider
Spin its web so high

Then like the silent shadows
Our life will soon be gone
but we'll awaken in God's heaven
To a bright and glorious new dawn

Shirley Knight

Untitled

How come as much as I think
God does not exist, or that he does not
know what I am feeling - I find myself
Crying happily when the sun comes out
    Or when the sky is blue
    Or when snow is softly falling
from Heaven.
That has to be God so pleasant
    And
Ever Changing!

Tracey Digatono

God Is Here

God is here, God is there
God is here and everywhere
In the sky, on the grass
Wherever you would
Look last. He's with you
At night right before
bed and when you're awake,
Above your head. He's
With you in play each and
every day and when you
get hurt, he'll always
stay. He'll guide you
through your way and
stand by your side, may
you not fear, God's really
near and will stay everywhere

Shauna Parks

Daughter

Daughter—
grown now;
birthed by me,
yet alive
in another world.

I, her yesterday—
she, my tomorrow—
linked now
by love alone;
no kiss
to make all well.

Stand-by only—
grateful that
woman-strength
sustains her.

Mary Wilson Sage

This Love Of Ours

Our times together, present and past
have been an emotional ride.
We try our best to make it last
with feelings flowing like the tide.

Love may grow or love may die,
It's like a living thing.
This love of ours should stay alive.
Our souls entwined, should ever cling.

Your help I'll need from this day forth,
To bind our love more strong.
Our love together has enormous worth,
and therefore can't be wrong.

Together we'll help our love to survive
forsaking all others to strengthen it.
This love of ours should stay alive.
Together, united, our love can exist.

Virginia Holbrooks

Now

Whoever said that youth was all
Has made a sad mistake
I can't speak yet of the golden years
But this age is the one I'll take.

The here and now while I'm alive
To feel, and taste, and see
Or just to marvel at the fact
That I alone am me.

Yes, my dears, I tell you this
I love each moment so
I won't regret those yesterdays
Nor wish this time to go.

Marilyn Turner

Golden Kisses

Morning dew, droplets of
hazy violet innocence,
She waits patiently for
her intimate acquaintance,
her eyes meet with his,
their souls greet with
requited familiarity,
they are now forever free,
their love tenacious,
blossoms of hope clinging
to their vines, heavenly
assuredness, and golden
kisses in the twilight
hour.

Aisa Underhill

"So I Could Be Set Free"

Jesus is my Savior
He bled and died for me
I'll always love him for it
Because he set me free

He hung upon that cross
Up on Calvary's hill
And said not my will Lord
So I could be set free

How many people do you know
Who would bleed and die for you
And all they'd ask for it
Is to love him, as he loved you

So give your heart to Jesus
And live your life for him
Then one day, you will see him
In that city we call heaven

Terrie Vann Strickland

Everlasting Freedom

If I were given only one wish
Here is what it would be
I would wish every person in
the world would be free

Free to be whatever they want
to be, yes
YES!
That is my wish for you from
me
Go now and be what you were
meant to be
Always and forever, totally
Free

Penny Johnson

Jenny

Once God made a little girl,
He fashioned her with care,
He used a piece of night for eyes
And fairy-down for hair...

And alabaster for her skin
Is what I think he chose,
And on each little precious cheek
He place a tiny rose...

When extra splendors were required
As they sometimes are,
He lit each little piece of night
With a shining star...

Diamonds and pearls are commonplace
And little girls are many,
But time forbids a longer list
To compare to Jenny...

Rosemary Muntz Yasparro

My God And I

I ask for help,
   he gave to me.
The most precious gift,
   of healing you see.

He stood beside me,
   for awhile.
Oh, so meek,
   just like a child.

He'll always have,
   a place in my heart.
My God and I,
   will never depart.

He chose to heal me,
   on that day.
Then he was hurriedly,
   on his way.

I never saw him,
   but he was there.
To let me know,
   he did care.

Marie Hayes France

American Dream???

Where is the American dream?
Has it fallen along the way?
Will things always get worse,
Or will it return someday?

Where are the great leaders?
Have they disappeared forever?
Will the heroes ever return,
Or have the ties been severed?

Where have our morals gone?
Has freedom seduced our soul?
Will our pride be restored,
Or are we just out of control?

Where is the family reunion?
Has sin lost its confession?
Will our politicians wake up,
Or do we need a depression?

Will we awaken in that day?
To find a thief in the night,
Or will we awaken in the dream
To take our heavenly flight???

Max K. Lowe

Hooked

My dad likes to go fishing,
He goes most everyday,
Sometimes he thinks he gets a bite,
But it always gets away.
He tries and tries - he sits for hours,
But all to no avail,
And I come running over, only,
To find an empty pail.
I want to solve the problem,
So I look inside his book,
Dad, I cry, I know what's wrong,
You need a fishing hook!

Sharmian Ahmed

Jesus Is My Best Friend

Because he is my friend
He has changed my life
To where I know with him
I can always win.
I love him with all
My heart and soul
And because of him
I am very bold.
Even though I went through
Thick and thin
Jesus will always be
My best friend.

Trina L. Phillips

Who Is God?

He is a man of many faces
He is a man of many styles
He is a man of many manners
And a man of many wiles
He is a man of power
He is a man of wealth
He is a man of weakness
He is a man of health
He may be dressed in riches
He may look downtrod
So meet your fellow man with grace
Because he might be God

William E. Lloyd Sr.

The Stray

His coat is dirty,
   he is lank and lean;
His lips are snarled,
   his eyes are mean.

He has lived with hunger,
   fear, and cold;
He feels so tired,
   and very old.

He knows no kindness,
   and has no friend;
He's feared by children,
   and hated by men.

He keeps even his own kind
   far at bay;
He fights to live,
   for he's just a stray.

Now think on these words,
   and say if you can;
Of which do we speak,
   Is it animal - or man?

Lonna L. Paul

My Mother

God gave me a beautiful mother
He made her in his grace.
When you look into her eyes
You can see her smiling face.

God gave her a heart
As big as the world.
A heart made of Gold.
She can sing songs of Jesus
and stories untold.

My mother has read her Bible
From beginning to the end.
She says her prayers
And prays to God
To bless her Children within.

Now you see God gave me
A Special Mother
Within my heart to hold.
And one day God will call her
Into his Heavenly fold.

Margaret V. Carter

"He Holds Me"

He holds me close,
he pulls me near.
We stand and talk,
I cry a tear.
We walk beneath the clouds,
it starts to rain.
We don't care,
there is no pain.
I think about his eyes,
I can see his fate.
There is only love,
there is no hate.
He sends me a rose,
a note on the side.
It reads, "I love you dearly,
my heart can't hide."
I've found the right one,
I am quite sure.
For it's him I love,
it's him I adore.

Reneé Mund

Untitled

Six months ago
he walked me down the aisle
it was too soon for him to go
I'm going to miss that smile
every time I see a picture
and see that baby face
I'll think of happy times for sure
I hope he's gone to a nicer place
a place free of pain
to play Lotto, fish or bet the track
it's hard to stay sane
I only wish that he was back
so I could hug and hold and kiss
and do things with him I used to do
and let him know how much I miss
the wisdom and the knowledge he knew
of just being a Dad
the best anyone could get
it still makes me so sad
this man I will never forget

Laura Doran

Old Man

Listen child, listen hard,
hear what the old man has to say.
Listen, learn from his stories,
in his wisdom you will see
more than the old fool you thought to be,
instead a sage with sound advice.
He's seen the world both good and bad,
made the love and fought the hate.
When you see him on the street
please don't pass him by.
Stop and listen of his ventures
learn a lesson from him this day.
Sometimes stories he'll repeat
hold your tongue, do not say.
Spend some time and listen hard
about his loves, about his life.
Do not wait too long I say,
in a short time the old man will go away.

Ken Adams Jr.

Little Angel

Child of beauty
Heaven knows thy name
Angels sing of thee
Songs of sweet refrain

A little angel
Is what you are
Tiny wings propel you
Like a shooting start

That tiny smile
Lights up your face
Lending a precious memory
Of this time and place

"Stay as you are
Forever with me"
An old man utters
A grandfather's plea

Follow your destiny
As I know you must
I'll follow tiny footprints
Sprinkled with angel dust

J. Frank Smith

Untitled

He turned her down
Her smile turned to a frown
Was it because of her looks
It was her confidence he took
It's not what he did but what he said
That made her sob at night in bed
She felt so low
She didn't know where to go
All she did was sit and cry
She felt like she wanted to die
But she knew she was just mad
that's why she felt so bad
Then she thought, he is not worth it
he deserves a nice hard hit
He had her so mad she wanted
to rip off his head
But she didn't at night, she
just cried as she lay in bed

Sarah Ostrander

Abortion

His hair would be brown,
his eyes, maybe blue
today should be his birthday
he would've been two.
He would be smiling and giggling
eating cake and ice cream.
His friends would be over
maybe playing on swings
But none of this is happening
instead, I sit alone
There will be no birthday parties
no child to call my own.
If only someone had warned me,
Told me it's not as easy as it seems
The ghost of my child
would not be haunting my dreams.

Melinda Ann Hyde

A Poet's Note

When a poet writes of love,
His heart flutters like
the wings of a dove.
When it's hard to make it
rhyme, he just sits back
and listens and gives it time.
I ask the LORD to guide my
pen, to look where I'm going
and where I've been.
Before I know it, I've written
a line, maybe not for some,
but it's mine.
I know some of my poems are
kind of crude, when it comes
to expressing love I think
this will do.

Richard Lawyer Sr.

Little Brother

Playful eyes gaze up at me
his small round face covered by a smile
as he laughs and giggles,
romps among the trees
and all around the house,
slyly escaping my touch.
School is just a place he goes
to have fun and be with friends.
Forever alive and spirited
for him the games should never end.
The joker in a house of spades
he never seems to frown
save the times when he is told
that the play must cease.
The world and I both see him
Smaller and younger than his years
and though I cannot stop him from growing up
he shall always be little to me.

Kelly J. Pedotto

Quake

Look at all the color,
In life,
In music,
In love with who we are.
In this moment,
In sound movement,
The earth shakes,
It rocks, it rolls,
A five point two.

Spring Mae Selby

My Only Love

His eyes so blue
His smile so bright
I think about him
day and night.
His kiss so soft
his hair so brown
Without him I'm
always down.
His sudden death
brought tears to my eyes
I can't believe he died.
And even though he's gone to
a better place...
The expression on my face
is not grace.
At night after my prayers are through
I ask God; God why did
take my only love.

Paula Blaine

Dance With Me

Dance with me while you
Hold me tight
Dance with me in your arms
Tonight
Dreaming of love never
Knew
Dreaming of some one
Like you
Paradise is beautiful it seems
But none can compare with you
In my dreams.

Shirley Schlieman

My Old Church

Here I come again, through those
hollowed doors. Why is it I visit here
each week and you're never home.
When I was young, so much more so
than today, you never missed a
Sunday, 'nor did I.

Soon there came a time, when the
world ran too fast. Sundays should
come and go, and never last. My
hours were few and none left to visit my pew.

But life's slower now. Much too slow
in fact. So I'll come back. But
where are you Lord. I search and
search, but I haven't found you lately
in my old church.

Larry Brook

Coffee Is A Marvelous Thing

Coffee is a marvelous thing;
  I drink a cup
  On waking up
And instantly I feel a zing —
  It's quite as though
  I'm all aglow,
My sleepy ears begin to ring
  And suddenly —
  My eyes can see!
My mind and voice box long to sing;
  My heart's alive
  With gleeful drive
And autumn coldness feels like Spring —
  Yes, coffee is a wonderful thing!

Lynda Pennini

Sweet Holly

When you cry soft tears
Hope and dreams grow
A mirage fills your eyes
Visions of a rainbow

Your soul, your touch
Compares with a rose
Touched by an angel
How beautiful it grows

My mind holds your image
When I see blue sky
Words drift in echoes
Hopes and dreams fly

As winds come to life
You hear its distant song
Sweet smell engulfs you
Trembling feeling to belong

A soft rain finds you
Taste sweet on your lips
An amber passion within
Memories, your heart skips.

Joe

To The Unborn

I'm sitting here all alone
hoping it's not true
But please my dear little one,
don't think I won't love you
I may have laid my future plans
down upon the floor,
my car, my schooling,
my house, and even a little more.
But I would give them up for you
my precious little dear.
Because in my heart,
I long to hold you near,
To hear your cries of joy and laughter
of sorrow and even pain
Would put a smile upon my face
and take me through the rain.
My love for you could not compare
to any other
Because my sweet little dear,
I would be your mother.

Kristen McElheney

The Meadow

From where I stand,
I can see
robins and wildflowers.

From where I stand,
I can hear
the rustling of leaves and bird's songs.

From where I stand,
I can smell
ripe berries just over the hill.

From where I stand,
I can taste
fresh water from a nearby spring.

From where I stand,
I can feel
lush green moss beneath my feet.

From where I stand,
THIS IS THE MEADOW.

Nicole Wills

On The Porch At Pleasant View Home

In a far meadow
horses graze
in late morning sun.
Nearby the plowed fields
lie fresh and pungent.
Time passes.
Beside me the mild-eyed woman
sleeps in her geri chair, hands clasped,
head sunken on chest,
while we watch, my father and I,
awed, sorrowful, waiting.
"It's beautiful here," we say,
trying to hold the world together,
trying to call her back who has gone.

Nancy Neiman-Hoffman

Ode To Water

Cool and refreshing on a
hot summer day,
you can swim in it
play in it
in each and every way.
You can drink it
cook with it, whatever you prefer
sometimes it's cold burr, burr, burr.

Jump in it, hop in it,
dive and plunge,
with water you wash off the
dust, dirt, and grunge.
With water you can cool off from
intense heat.
It's something you drink instead of eat.

Tastes wonderful, tastes great
refreshing cold and clean,
it's the best thing in life you've ever seen.

So water, water, water galore,
I love my water just bring on some more!

Kumaya Grant

Something

What would you say
How would you feel

If I could tell you something
that sounds too good to be real

Something that wouldn't
cost you a thing

Something that would make you laugh
and give you a song to sing

Something you will ask yourself
as you go along

Why oh why did I wait so long

So if you are ready
as I think you must be

Turn your Bible to John 3:16
and you will see

That if you believe in your heart
without a doubt

Then you'll understand this something
I have been telling you about.

Roy A. Patton

Goodbye Youth

Oh! Where had my youth gone,
How it faded so quickly away,
Hardly could I wait until twenty-one,
Twenty-one did come then some,
Looking in the mirror one day,
My hair had turned grey,
Age of time is both blessed and cursed,
Those who gain wisdom with years,
Their counsel may help away fears,
Cursed by aches and pains not before,
Feeling not as good as our youth,
People known have faded away,
Making us thankful for each day,
One day others will say,
He or she had faded away.

Willie C. Williams

Untitled

As I sit and wonder how things could be,
how they should be,
I think of all the things I did wrong,
or too late;
Things I should have done but didn't
have the courage to;
Things that I did right,
and no one noticed;
Things that I did wrong,
and everyone saw;
Why does life turn out so weird?
Why does it seem that I'm the only one
who doesn't understand?
I guess I'll never know the answers
or maybe I already know them, but I'm
just not ready to face them.

Kristen Brewi

My Horse

Today I saw a white horse.
How vividly it reminded me
Of the horse I rode
When the horse and I were still young!
We made many a mad dash
Across open fields, my Queen and I,
She with her mane and tail
waving in the wind,
And me with a bouncing braid,
My coat open and flapping,
Rejoicing when the wind
Whistled past my ears.
Remembering my love for the horse
And those days of carefree pleasure
We shared so long ago
Brought tears to my aging eyes.

Ruth Ekstrom

The Body Guard

    The body guard from up above,
he watches me with eyes of love.
He makes sure I sleep well at night,
and comforts me when I'm full of fright.
He's everywhere that I do go,
but I never really see him though.
He is my closest, yet dearest friend,
and our friendship will never end.
Though I know with out a nod
that my beloved friend is God.

Kathlyn Callaway

Who Rules Your World?

With nothing to prove
I can be myself.
Who rules your world
As you go riding catatonic
Through the crones of society?
Your attitude influenced
By grunge,
And strange looks from passersby
That bring a smile.
I wonder through life with my mind,
And emotions tightly bound
By moralistic thoughts from
The clones of society—
I stumble many times.
I hide from the past,
And long for a future
That I can only
Imagine in my dreams.

Lee Shepherd

A New Year's Celebration

Happy New Year, darling!
(I can hardly wait for spring.)
We know not what this year does hold:
We see it as it does enfold.
(Whatever we go through,
    you know that I love you.)
Whatever this year brings,
My happy heart joyfully sings!
For when I am with you, I am whole:
By your poignant touch on my soul,
By your sweet caress.
I feel God does bless
The future in store,
Many times o'er.
So happy holidays, baby!
I love you no ifs, ands or maybes.

Nancy Eicher De Long

Mary

I can't see the smile
I can't dry the tears
I can't make it better
or ease all your fears.

I can feel the pain
that's been with you this year
I wish that I could tell you
that it's all over now
But the fears you have inside you
Are the fears I feel out here.

If only I could tell you
don't worry about it dear
for I have just begun
to feel all your tears.

Mary Parrilli

Troubled Inside

Don't feel bad, if you felt
Kind of troubled inside
To know others have felt
the same as well might help
to ease the pain you have.
So go ahead, and feel the pain,
for tomorrow you will be okay…

Nora Goulart

Adrift On A Tide Of Apathy

"What shall we do?"
"I don't know," said she.
"Where shall we go?"
"I don't care," said he.
"Shall we go now?"
"I guess so…"
"In a while"
"maybe…"

We could go,
We could stay,
We could kneel,
We could pray.
"I don't know,
I don't care,"
is our theme
for today.

Wanda McGill

Childhood Dream

When I was a little girl,
I dreamed of sleeping on one of those
Jumbo cotton balls in the sky.
I'd jump out of an airplane
And I'd fly
Right into the middle.
I'd lie there for a whole day,
Bouncing around and playing.
I'd be comfy and safe.

Then an airplane would stop by
And pick me up to bring me home.
That was my one wish.
Then I learned that clouds are just
Evaporated water,
And if you jump onto one,
You'll fall right through and die.
So I found another dream.

Larissa Davis

Victim Of Love

She is hurtin' inside,
I feel her pain…
    She feels my touch
can smell my fragrance on
your clothes.
When we make love, I know
she's near…
When you caress me I see
her tears.
She's in your heart,
She's in your mind no
Matter where you go.
I feel so guilty, I
feel so wrong…
But I'm also
A victim of your love.

Vivian Rodriguez

150 Years

Florida's like a fantasy,
Loamy land, 30 thousand lakes,
Orange groves and palmy trees,
Rainy seasons in the Sunshine State.
Indian lore's our history,
Disney World adds majesty,
An alligator, symbolically,
Says, "Time to CELEBRATE!"

Loretta Dabbs

My Only Wish

As I looked in his eyes
I finally saw the lies,
tears rolled down my face
faster than a running race,
I wish they would go away
as I sit and pray,
I love him so much, away such,
only one can
love a man,
oh, how I wish they would go away
as I sit and pray,
why him, why me
now that I finally see,
I wish once more, for...
the lies to go away, today...
but no, the tears come down
as I look around,
I ask myself "can we still be friends?"
it all depends,
if the lies go away, I can only pray!

Sarah Guyette

The Change

You married me and on that day
I gave my love my heart away
You vowed forever you'd be true
And I vowed the same to you

As the years go quickly by
I sit down and wonder why
The things you do the things you say
Are not at all like yesterday

No more do you hold me in your arm
And keep away the things of harm
Nor do you kiss me tenderly
And tell me what our life will be

You have changed my darling that is true
But I will go on loving you
And also I will pray each night
That God will help things turn out right

Marcella Malonn

"Hold On"

Hold on to our love.
Let our love show.
Hold on to our love.
And never let it go.

Nichole K. Dooley

I Have Feelings Of Love

I dream you in my arms...
I hear your heart beat aloud

I dare not close my eyes...
Because I dare not miss anything

For our time is cut so short...
And there is no way to make it up

You will really never know...
How deep my love has grown for you

I can only whisper "I love you!"
And hope that you hear every word

For if you did not feel the same...
Sadness would conquer my soul!

Mary L. Harris

Words

I wanted to write you a poem but
I just couldn't find the words
Capable of expressing
The way I feel when I'm with you

Words to describe the way my heart
Flutters with a glance
From your eyes
Or how my soul frolics
With a touch of your lips

Yes, I wanted to write you
A poem that could
Declare my love eternal,
Attest my love as true

A beautiful poem that would
Linger in your memory
Like soft, endless notes
From a choir of birds

Oh, how I wanted to write you a poem
But I just couldn't find the words

Stacy A. Sanuita

Untitled

Had to get away
I just couldn't stay
And I found myself here
And writing about you

You were my friend
We were the best of friends
And I really don't know why
It had to end
I love you!

We use to walk
And we use to talk
And I use to look into your eyes
Why did our friendship die
I still love you so much

Now it's so cold
And I'm all alone
Just sitting here
Thinking about you
Because I love you

I will always love you so much!

Kathy Perkins

Heather

Our friendship is rare
It comes from the soul and heart
It can never get lost
But should never be torn apart.

We have grown a distance
I know this is true
Our friendship is so strong
It will last until I see Heaven's blue

I'll feel your pain
I'll wipe away your tears
I'll take away your sorrow
For there is always tomorrow.

I pray to God
You will understand
That I'll always be there for you
Until we are back in God's loving hands.

Kylie Simbeck

Friends Always

For James Richard Erwin-Fern
Since the moment I met you
I knew you'd be my friend
And I want you to know
I'll be yours until the end.

You know I'll always be there
And I'll never let you down
If you ever need a friend
I will always be around.

I really care about you
Never will this friendship part
for if it ever did
It would surely break my heart.

Sarah Lynn Roberts

March's Cyprian

The wanton wind,
I know her ...
She's a street-walker.
I've seen her blow
warm breath at your ears
like a vamp teasing;
I've seen her twirl
beside you,
skirts flying,
denying a caress.
Then
in passionate chase,
I've seen her leave you
deserted on some corner,
breathless
trembling
in the night!

Marjorie Weigel Hyman

Essay

I know my goals.
I know what my talents are.
I know what my life could be like.
I spend all of my time,
endeavoring to be me.

Through the curses and attitudes
of a day, that brings millions of
feelings from within, the
private shocking thoughts of
revenge, I know are not me.

I wonder what mighty deeds or
what great mystery becomes unraveled.
How much joy from the love given,
by not having the chore, of
endeavoring to be me.

The seeming injustice bestowed upon me,
which only I and my creator knows
I did nothing to achieve.
keeps me busy all the time,
endeavoring to be me.

Mildred S. Williams

Easy

It's not easy
    It's not free
But I'd never replace
    the world that has
Been given to me.

Kathryn L. Oliver

Friends

She was lonely, I was, too
I liked pink, she liked blue
She loved to bake, so did I
She decorated cakes, I baked pies
I had three children, she had four
We worked together, she lived next door
We would shop, then we'd eat
My best friend - hard to beat
I moved away - we kept in touch
We still talked, just not so much
Time went by, then the years
Then the call, next the tears
She passed away, now she's gone
only memories linger on
A cup here, a picture there
Memories are everywhere.

Sue DeLao

Angels In My Presence

They speak to me with unspoken thoughts.
I listen.
Their voices reach my soul.
The soft sound of their presence.
Their singing lifts me.
I'm rising through time.
Passages of unknown places.
I am a child.
I see my grandparents, and we embrace.
The Angels show us an amazing light.
We begin to run toward the glow.
There is an image of grace.
We three take his hands.
We are now joined as one.
We dance.
Surrounded by a field of flowers.
We are laughing.
All that once was, is no more.
I hear you.
I am at peace.

Teri Robbins

I Love You

I miss your smile
I miss your soft tender lips
pressed gently against mine
I miss your warm hugs
I miss hearing you say "I love you"
I'm sorry I never said those words
to you
but it's true I do love you
I was afraid of getting too close to
you
then losing you

Teya M. Jarvie

Life

As I look into the night air
I think of Death and Horror
Before now, I never bothered to care

The silence, the still, but yet there
Is some noise, like sirens blaring,
Dogs barking, then I reflect on the
Nights that I try to sleep, but cannot

Now I know why, you see at night
While you are living life, there is
More time to Dread Death.

Melvina Smith

I Need To Cry

Life is old,
I need something new,
Someone who shares,
My point of view.

Life and its challenges,
Won't go away,
I need something challenging,
I need it today.
I need to cry,
And let it all go,
But there are some things,
I like just to hold.

I hold on to friends,
I hold on to life,
I hold on to memories,
And cry through the night.

Tammy Lynn Morgan

Camp

Today at home
I reminisce of days past.

Where did they go?
They flew by so fast.

I took for granted
The days I thought would last.

I was wrong.

Now all I can do
Is reminisce of days past.

Stephanie Wilson

"Reality"

Feeling sorry for myself,
I sat.
Disappointed and frustrated,
Looking up from my
Sorrows,
I saw
A little boy across the room.
No arms; stunted growth;
Yet smiling and laughing.
Tears filled my eyes.
Reality struck.
Unworthy,
Blind
To my own blessings,
Too concerned with my own problems.
Please forgive me.

Tammy Tate

Necessity

It snowed.
I scattered seeds upon the drive.
A perky little sparrow spied -
    Ate a little. Flew away.
    Came again. Yes, he would stay.

But Miss Cat watched with yellow eyes
    From window ledge to hypnotize!

I dampened clothes in easy sight!
But did not dampen his delight
    In sweet repast - seeds *a la* white.

I say - could I be brave as he
In face of life's necessity?

Mary E. Goforth

What I See

When I look at you,
I see a rainbow.
Sparkling, shining,
glimmering and glaring.
You try your best to
stretch a mile.
When you reach your
limit, you stay for a while.
Gradually you start to
fade away, because you know
that you cannot stay.
In minutes you
disappear, within a wink of an eye,
you are not there.

Tina Marie Shults

Leaves

I am not ready for winter
I see signs of late fall

    Brown
    Orange
    Yellow
    Gold
        All fallen leaves

But I remember
    those leaves
I saw them in the spring
    oh so gentle
Just out of their mother's
    womb

Mary Ann Rivenbark

Crying For Your Touch

In the sun-filled sky
I see your smile
Through the falling rain
I feel your tears
My own heart aches
Striving not to break

Out of the rustling leaves
I hear your laughter
Amongst the shadowy darkness
I sense your nakedness
Matched by my own vulnerability
My confusion runs ever deeper

In the star-filled night
Your eyes shine even brighter
Across the windswept field
I feel your breath upon my face
A kiss that I'll never know
Leaves my soul
Crying for your touch

Robert J. Juresko

"Timeless To Time"

Time goes by so fast
I never have time to feel it
So many things going on
I never have time to do it
But there's a will
And there's a way
to find the time and play it
So if you relax
and straighten things out
You'll find there's always time.

Rachel Myers

When I Think Of Love

When I think of Love,
I think of Spring
because of the
great feeling of
Love when two
people meet
and fall in Love.
When I look
up in the sky
and see a
mother bird
feeding her baby,
I think of the
Love between them.
I can feel the Love
that the mother
bird has for
her baby and
this is when I think of Love.

Kenny Hooper

Missing You

When I leave you
I think why did I go,
away from you and your love.
I never find the answer of why
and at night I sit and cry
because I miss you.
And I wonder what you're doing,
when I try to go to sleep.
I start to think
what would I do if I were with you?
All I can say is that tonight
I will pay the price for leaving you!

Michelle Cabrera

Pale Light

I thought I knew you, I see I was wrong
I thought of you as a sister, but you
came on too strong! You just cast me
down with blunt words squarely
and I have always treated you fairly
You stood there so beautiful, white
and pale and with harsh words shoved
me in a vale
How could I believe you could ever be
my sister pale white light
you look at me, but can't see past my
skin black as night.

Patricia Smith

The Best Night Of My Life

Every time I see your face,
I want to escape with you
to an exotic place.
A place with palm trees,
coconuts, water, and sand.
My-oh-my, that place is no
doubt, absolutely grand.
When the stars come out
at night, and the moon is
hung high,
You will kiss me and hold
me in your arms, by all
means, that is no lie.
Yes, when this night comes,
it will definitely be
Without a doubt, the best
night for both you and me.

Tamara Felix

Do You Love Me!

Do you love me,
I want to know
We spent days, months together
But I just don't know

If you love me,
I want to know
If you care
I wish it would show

You make me upset,
I just don't know
Do you love me
It's all I want to know.

Keona Esannason

My Psalm Of Life

Yes, when I was 20
I was full of the three "V's"
Vim, vigor and vitality
did everything with ease.

Life begins at 40
was always told to me
so I kept very active
I hoped I would agree.

I remember when I was 60
I did slow down a bit
things got a lot harder
I hated to admit.

Now that I am 80
it is really hard to cope
I live one day at a time
but never give up hope.

Will I make it to 100?
Many do that today
I'll leave it up to fate
That is all I have to say.

Virginia Saunders

My Mother, My Friend

You left us so suddenly
I wasn't prepared
For the emptiness and longing
For the time we shared.

Just one more smile
Or a laugh or two
Would bring such comfort
To those who love you.

Our time here on earth
Has come to an end,
But your spirit lives on
Eternity to spend.

When my days are done
I'll see you again;
My tears wiped away by
My mother, my friend.

Sherry Lynne Sopko

Only You

I care for you with all my heart;
   I'd give my life to never part;
   If you left and said good-bye;
   I'd try my hardest not to cry;
   But this I know I'd never do;
   My heart belongs to only you.

Stacey Delgado

I Am

I am happy, hopeful
I wonder if I will ever walk
I hear people walking
I see people running
I want to walk some day
I am happy, hopeful

I pretend that I am walking
I feel that I walk around
I touch the sky
I worry that there will be no help
I cry, because it may be true
I am happy, hopeful

I understand it is hard to find help
I say that it will be found
I dream of walking
I try to walk sometimes
I hope that one day I will walk
I am happy, hopeful

Kevin White

Daddy's Little Girl

I remember when I was little
I would run and jump on your lap,
whenever I was scared.

Now that I am older
when I am scared
I turn to my mother.

You say that I am "Daddy's little girl"
but how can you say that
when you were never here?

I know how I feel about you, but
don't know how you feel about me.
Daddy, please see that I am scared.

I need a father
but I'm afraid to face the truth
about you.
Realizing that you never cared.
Otherwise you would have stayed near.

As I grow from day to day
I realize that I am not
"Daddy's little girl" today.

Sarah Elizabeth Rowe

If You Were To Die

If you were to die,
I'd sit down and cry.
Because you left without
Saying good-bye.
I thought you would
be with me forever.
But you left and
Now we're not together.
Thinking of you not
here cuts like a knife.
Why oh, why did he
have to take your life.
I hope you know, I
still love you so much.
It makes me cry knowing
I will never feel your touch.
I wish I was with
you up in that sky.
This is how I would feel,
If you were to die!

Tonya McGill

Unwritten Words

Before unconsciousness closes in
I write unwritten words
To many far away
Never enough minutes
To take up pen and paper
Before evening's peace arrives
But I write
Of you and fear
Of people and places
Unwritten words
Form sentences and paragraphs
Inscribed upon hidden pages
Maybe - someday -
Ink will take control
Transferring the unwritten
To paper
For other eyes to see.

Sara M. Eaton

Jimmi

Seems like yesterday
I'd be sitting under that big oak tree
swinging
with you in my arms.
You were such a young thing
all naked and warm
arms open wide.
Yes son, those were the days
when Georgia hung in the air
and surrounded us like clouds
that pushed through the storms.
Nothing but the hot Georgia wind
came bothering my Jimmi back then.
He'd always be home
with his dear ol'
Mama.

Tanya E. Toter

If I Could Fly

If I could fly
I'd touch the sky, I'd
fly with ease and soar
over seas.
    If I could fly,
I'd see the stars,
I'd take a trip to the
planet Mars. I'd smile
at the moon and
say "see you again soon."
But now I must go.
But oh! how I know
what it is like to
fly high in the sky.
Good Bye sky!

Mollie Krupp

Life Begins

Life,
Is a very special thing.
Fun experience for family and,
Even their friends.

Brought to you by your parents.
Ever so perfect...
Getting spoiled after you're born.
In the first few days your
Name is given to you,
So you're not just called baby.

Tina Niess

Time

Time can be quite a place
if you learn to keep your own pace.
Don't burn yourself out
with trouble and doubt.
Those who see only the past
find the future goes fast.
If you look too far into what's to be
You'll soon be crying a sea.
Think of what you'd like
go out and take a strike.
If you find a wall too tall
walk around don't fall.
Remember who you are
with faith you'll go far.
Learn from what's been
don't make the same sin.
Listen to the old and wise
and open up your eyes.
If you remember this and more
you'll never miss, you'll score.

David J. DeVeau

The Moon Baby Song

When the sky parts with the sun,
I'll be dreaming.

Bidding farewell to another lazy day
    And to you my love,

I'll be turning,
    And wondering why you came my way.

The stage is set,
    The wheels are burning,

Kaleidoscope eyes are staring my way
    And guiding the pen,

That tries to console me,
    I ride to you on a star-kissed sky

In my chair high above bitter learning
    I gather thoughts from a cloud

Soaring to heights, that once were
    Beyond me.

I didn't know what could be found

Martin Declercque

Believe Me...

Believe me if I tell you
    I'll love you 'til I die.
Although we're very different
And I cannot tell you why.

You've saved my yesterdays for me
    Now tomorrow promises new
I'll be here if you need me
For I'll always be loving you.

Our children bring me riches
    So many joys have graced my life.
Because you made me wealthy
The day I became your wife.

I keep on hearing your voice
    "I do," as both we wed
And "I do," now, and for always
For enough just can't be said.

"Hallmark," he is very good.
    For those who need him there.
But your love made me a poet
And I thank God for what we share.

Mildred Emily Gordon

Mouse Traps

"Oh", she said to the man, "Indeed
    I'll have you know of my urgent need
For a ball bearing mouse trap, I plead
It's delivered with the greatest speed."

"What color and quality would you want
    One that is fat or one that is gaunt?
By variety and size they are classed
    Each is a winner carefully cast."

"Color's not important, but I prefer
    Medium size with a sleek coat of fur.
One that's outgoing with an intoned purr
    One obsessed with mice to conquer."

Vinetta Bianchi

A Prisoner's Last Lament

I ache to look into the eyes
I'll never see, I fear -
To feel the warmth I have not felt
For many a darkened year.
Even the gem-like beauty
Of a moonlit, star-filled night
Could never replace one single glance,
Nor the feel of Love's sweet bite
In this forgotten dungeon
The sun has ceased to shine.
My life's a ruin, my heart's a stone -
Even my soul's not mine!
To turn the clock-begin again -
Is all that's left to yearn.
But God, oh God, the sand's run out,
And now I'm going to burn.....

Liz Martin

Death!

People say
I'm not afraid of death
Everyone is
It is only natural
And when death arrives
They are afraid
They are very afraid
Only then
Do they realize
What small and puny
Pawns they are
In the great game
Of the world.

Matt Price

The Dance

If I could dance
if I could dance
if I could move my body to the beat
of my feelings
It would be deep

If I could dance
if I could dance
if I could move to the rhythms
of my mind
It would be deep

If I could dance
if I could twist - turn and glide across
the floor like a bird in flight...
It would be deep
if I could dance

Melanie P. Frasier

Insomnia

It's my mind
I'm starting at,

not the clock radio,

that switched on
during sleep.

Thought
is the alarm
that wakes me:

in mid-answer
to the same question
I always forget
by morning.

At 3 a.m.,

the world
is as hushed
as a self-proctored
exam

on which

time is running out
and rest is cheating.

Peter Cohen

Poem On Ash Wednesday

I go like a naked child
in a cold climate
through my life
uneasy offspring of parents
who moved inexplicably
out of the south
where melons ripen
fat in the sun
and dragonflies and bees
bumble in the garden gushing
roses and honeysuckle

who lay me down
where the strict wind blows
from the north
on my cradle in the treetops
rock-a-bye, little black one
in a new land where the cold
burns the knuckles of my hand
and I see my breath
miraculous on the landscape

Mary Nortner Clancy

Death

wraps its velvet arms about me
in a dark embrace, a
friendship of hearty woes and
sullen graces.

A medley of congruent faces and
her angel eyes now stained
with romantic fluctuations in her
voice. As warmth envelopes

me softly, the farthest regions
in which I see her are
cold and grey and live life
without trust or perhaps

lost in the society are silly
men who have also fallen.

Phillip James Forgione

"Twilight On The Traveller's Road"

There's a house on a hill
In a far away place
In a land looking over the sea.
There's a girl who walks by
Every evening at dusk
And the girl who walks by is me.

There's a pinpoint of light
That pierces the night
And looks over this traveller's road.
It brings warmth to the heart
Of this one lonely dreamer
As it shines from the humble abode.

Long journeys are lonely
My footsteps grow weary
I long to give up and groan.
But the light draws me on
To continue my travel
Till I have a light of my own.

Kristin Rosner

Night Whale

During the night,
In a peaceful lagoon,
There are creatures who live
With the light of the moon.

Their glorious name
Matches their glorious features.
Orca is the name
That describes these creatures.

The soft glow of the moon
Brightens the night
And ends suddenly
At the peaceful sight.

With a flip of the tail,
So easy it may seem,
They breach in the cool night's air,
Letting their soft colors gleam.

Their glorious name
Matches their glorious features.
Orca is the name
That describes these creatures.

Lesley A. Murkley

My Love

The soul - that inward man that
is forever searching, forever
crying out, a flame forever
passionately burning, but is so
hard to quench.

I find such contentment, fulfillment,
such satisfaction in your
presence. Your eyes which are
the windows to the soul, your
face, your smile, your way,
your being - you!

The passion of your love is so
sacred, so satisfying, so
intoxicating to my soul.

Your words echo within me
Your memory goes where I go - you
are my love ever with me.

Rita A. Nardo

To Daddy On Father's Day

Today is something special
In a very special way,
It comes but only once a year
And is known as Father's Day!

Fathers are special people
No matter what they say or do
They make things seem to be all right
When we're sad or when we're blue

Although we may not show our
love
By some of the things we do
But then you must also realize
That you're our father, and we
love you!

And so today we wish you well
Today and all life through.
And hope you'll always keep in mind
That we love our father (you)!!!

Peggy Sue Kolm

Beyond The Distance

Beyond the distance
In another light
This side of the horizon
Turns to night

Beyond a lonely heart
Once filled with love
This side of loneliness
Turns push to shove

Beyond the future
In another time
This side of reality
What will I find

Beyond the money
In another world
This side of poverty
Turns to gold

Beyond the silence
Of what was once yesterday
This side of tomorrow
Becomes today

Larry Maslowski

The Quest For Sleep

The faithful darkness of the night
in concert with celestial lights
tells my mind in subtle ways
stay still and do not think,
until the morning light.

Behind the scene a silent scheme
imposes thoughts against my will
and my weary self cannot succeed
its vain struggle with the stars
searching for the perfect dream.

The pillow whispers in my ear,
"the body is tired, can't you hear?"
With the dream catcher disappeared
and the moon laughing in my face,
counting sheep is what I fear!

With senses and resistance gone,
my body falls to blissful sleep.
Morpheus won the battle once again
the quest is over for tonight
morning light, please don't come!

Lilia S. Velasquez

The Sea Dog

I was called a ruthless sea dog,
In days when pirates were bold,
  With a wide crimson band,
  And a sword in my hand,
My treasure chests laden with gold.

My flag was the Jolly Roger,
The blackest that ever flew,
  With a sharp spanking breeze,
  I ploughed the high seas,
I and my lusty crew.

My ship was a Spanish vessel,
The most gallant upon the sea.
  And chanting a song
  With my ribald throng,
My life was wild and free!

Oh, I was a ruthless sea dog,
In days when pirates were bold,
  With a scar on my chin,
  'Neath a swarthy grin,
My treasure chests laden with gold.

    Virginia M. Heprian

Comfort In Eternal Rest

You were my Shepherd; I did not want;
In fields of green I walked with you.
You calmed my raging waters deep,
And turned them all to crystal blue.

You restored my soul and gave me peace,
And led me in paths of righteousness.
You upheld me before my enemies;
Overfilled my cup with blessedness.

And now my days are almost ended;
Sweet Jesus, Lord, I'm coming home;
To dwell with you in your house forever;
No more on this lowly earth to roam.

And although I may be facing death,
I will not tremble or be afraid;
You comfort me; You strengthen me;
In peace, I rest my weary head.

    Lynda R. Zeh

The Disease

When I was just a babe,
In my mommie's arms;
I had a terrible sickness,
It was me, Satan tried to harm.

But in my eighth year,
The Lord was with me;
I went up for prayer,
I'm glad I did see.

See what the Lord,
Could do for me.
He healed me, Praise God;
There's none greater than He.

I'm glad my Mom's taught me,
All about the Lord;
If she hadn't,
I wouldn't be in the one accord.

The one accord of God;
It's so very great,
I'm glad I was saved,
Before it was too late.

    Michelle Wojczyk

"To Those Who Have No Belief"

To those who have no belief,
In God and spirits above.
Just think of this.
Someone created this world,
Of sadness, laughter and love.
But to whom could it be?
Some people seem to ask,
It is God who is helpful and willing
To take on risky tasks.
But God will not tolerate
Disobedience, hatefulness and crime,
So to those who have no belief
Just think about it.
  In Peaceful time.

    Kathy Burge

You Promised Me

Everything about you is embedded
in my heart,
To imagine life without you is
tearing me apart.
You say I'm not the woman that
you think I should be,
But what have you done for
my ego lately?
You took away your compassion,
laughter and affection,
The hugs and kisses you promised me
have turned to rejection.

You promised me forever and that
nothing else mattered,
Now you want to walk away
leaving me shattered.
But I know you really love me,
I know you still care,
Because God opened the "love door"
for the two of us to share.

    Romaine A. Hubbard

"I Grieve The More
And Speak The Less"

I grieve the more and speak the less,
In silence did we break,
Ne'er to 'nother did we confess,
The passion to selves partake.

Interludes under moonlight,
Never by rays of sun,
Wishes made on stars of bright,
To repeat once more just done.

Now alas two separate ways,
Pulled two apart from love,
Yet thoughts return all through the days,
Our innocence once thereof.

If ever remember you of me,
Would it smile or share grieve,
Perhaps a longing come from thee,
Or regret for taking leave,

If someday on me recall,
My feelings of you address,
I shall simply tell thee all,
"I grieve the more and speak the less."

    D. Myers

Togetherness

He lies upon the sofa,
In rumpled drooping jeans.
This guy of mine,
Who always was,
So neat and clean.
The TV set is glowing
With figures from the past.
He says the new shows
Aren't made to last.
His eyes are closed,
To whatever
He might view.
Only resting, he says,
But he'll rest
The whole night through.
I sit and watch
My sleeping prince,
Hoping wakefulness
Will bloom. Then off to bed I go,
He doesn't know I have left the room.

    Shirley J. Long

Abbey Is On The Way

The chain . . . it comes
In smooth contrast
Rusting to break the door

The line is cold
Unbreakable working steel

On chilly winter eve
Ghostly
casts its gloom upon thy
fleeting soul

It comes now
despicably frozen in ebb

The cost
much too high!

    Paulette Renee Frye

The Loon's Lament

Did you see a man's face
in that cloud —
chin square, eyes perfect blue.
But look fast. The wind
takes too much around here.

Now listen,
isn't that the song
he made to tell
of his love for the lake
and his boat;
for the lean and lift
of his full bellied jib:
For the heave and pitch
of sweet water breaking
under the bow.

But the winds came
and stole his words,
dropped them into the inlets,
the coves, and into the mouths
of the somber throated loons.

    Laurence Levine

In Memory Of My Mother
(Patricia Heath)

Life is...
In the beginning
there is life.

Life is rewarding...
live it.

Life is beautiful...
look at it.

Life is successful..
learn from it.

Life is full of love...
give and receive it.

Life is meaningful...
love it.

When life ends you
will have lived life
to its fullest.

Paula June Heath

In Memory Of Our Lois

I hear a heavenly chorus singing
In the heavens high above.
Now she plays for God and the angels,
She plays with all her love.

We all will miss her terribly,
But do not grieve or mourn;
She is resting in the arms of Christ,
Her soul has been reborn.

The mortal veil has fallen now,
Her eternal life begun;
Think of her when next you view
The blue skies and the sun

Every night the stars appear,
I see a new one in the sky;
I know it is our loving Lois,
For true love will never die.

Mary Nixon Small Flaugh

Jesus Walked Upon The Land

The child that grew
In this place,
Strong in the spirit,
Filled with wisdom,
Glory and grace.

Jesus walked upon the land,
Teaching others,
To rise up and stand,
As he healed the blind man.

As he preached the gospel,
Throughout the land,
Healing the sick,
Raising the dead,
As he restored a man.

Jesus said to them all,
Go your way, tell John what things,
Ye have seen and heard,
Blessed is he, whosoever shall not,
Be offended in me,
As he preached, in the synagogues of
Galilee.

Sherry Little

Tiger Tiger

Tiger, Tiger
in the jungle
ducking in shadows
tiger, tiger
through gleaming eyes
he views the world
tiger, tiger
ears straining to hear
sounds of deer
tiger, tiger
silently stalking
padded feet step
tiger, tiger
strong body
pounces hard, swift
oh tiger, tiger
one scream
he slowly, eats
roar of joy
tiger, tiger

Katy Zimarowski

Born Free

I'd love to be a lion
In the jungles far away,
To be the King of Beasts
And rule by night and day.

I'd be the strongest and the fastest,
The smartest animal around.

I'd sneak up on a wild boar or a deer
And knock it to the ground.

I'd rip into its hot, soft flesh,
My claws would be hard as steel.
My fangs, long and razor sharp,
Would sink into my meal!

I'd eat until my belly was full
Then I'd sleep under a tree,
A lioness and cubs curled up beside me
I'd love to be Born Free!

Lee James Pancol

The Awakening

With tired eyes and a saddened heart
I sat down to write today

About my love my one true love
That had gotten away

It got away while I was asleep
In a land far from home

When I awoke....Amidst the clouds
My lady love gon'

She was gone far away
Because I was not at home
Yes she had gone far far away
You see, I'd left her home too long

And so I sit with tired teary eyes
And a heart that's heavier still

Yes I sit... alone I sit with a heart
With only emptiness to fill

For I have lost my one true love
A love that was truly great
So I have lost my only love
For I awoke too late....

N. A. Sandifer

Sand

Every step we take's an imprint,
In the many grains of sand.
Each unique among the others,
But together, they're quite grand.

Each small pebble has a color
And a shape that's all its own,
Yet we see them all as beach sand,
Not as separate little stones.

So, why can't we see each other
As we do these grains of sand
And accept that we're all different
And go forward, hand in hand??!!

But, the truth is, it won't happen
Unless prejudice is killed,
And our ignorances dealt with,
And equality instilled!!!!

Pamela J. Gallade

"Dear Don"

This day will last forever
in the pages of our minds
This time will last forever
because in our hearts you'll find
The love we feel for you our friend
we'll cherish throughout our lives
We want you to know we miss you
but your memory will forever remain
in the pages of our minds.
We've all shared laughter and tears
and you Don, have always made us smile
And we'll remember you
no matter how far the mile
You are so special to us,
and keep this thought in mind
That you will forever remain
in the pages of our minds.

Tracy Emling

Haven

The palm fronds scrape together
In their secret island language
The waves lap at the boat
Our cradle on the water
And it is like infants that we
Have come to this haven of
White powder sands and
Waters a thousand shades
Of blue and green - to
Heal ourselves with dolphin song
And hibiscus-laden breezes
To swallow sun through every
Thirsty pore as the waves,
Pulling at our ankles,
Tempt us with each recession
To join them in the sea

Kim Estes

Untitled

This love of ours,
is music and magic,
sunshine and laughter,
and when, on occasion,
there is rain and clouds
I know, with you
there will always be
a rainbow.

Karen L. Colf

Precious Moment

I have but a precious moment
in this world of today
to tell you of my love for you
and what thoughts are going my way.

I never dreamed for mansions
or castles in the air
All I wanted was a simple life
One that you and I would share.

I have but a precious moment
to tell you not to fear
the many things we did together
will remain with me so dear.

I never dreamed for furs and jewels
and many luxuries money could buy
all I wanted was your happiness
for this, I'll continue to try.

I have but a precious moment
and I wanted you to know
one cannot buy the love we share
but thank God as it continues to grow.

Vivian Dysko

In The Journey Evermore

Let's carve some more useless testament,
into the stones of history
Scream the name of god into the night
What is it by the way?
All I know is the sum of what I am.
Each day I grow but lose time.
Wisdom.
Is the reward.
in the journey evermore,
toward earth.
The wise sage venerable to youth.
Experience lost against might.
The crushing blow of rage.
Killing the peace of simple experience.
There are no more philosophers,
Only dead poets,
and starving artists.
The dream of aspiring to be so much more.
Rolled crushed,
under the wheels of humanity.

Steven J. Beavers

The Telephone

When Alexander Graham Bell
Invented the Telephone,
He never knew he would become
The greatest Inventor ever known.

Calls are made to Outer Space
To the Astronauts out there,
Calls are made from Corporations
And Industries everywhere.

Calls are made on Battlefields
To War Zones, Tanks and Planes,
To Battleships and Submarines
And to trucks and moving trains.

The President at the State Capitol
Can contact all the Nations,
Many important calls are made
Through this wonderful operation.

Still, the greatest joy of the Telephone
Is for families who live apart,
The loving voice on the Telephone
Brings loved ones close to heart.

Marie A. Hoegler

Just Beyond

Just beyond the fair horizon,
Is a city pure and bright.
The lamb of God forever,
Is its glory and delight.

There's a river clear as crystal,
Flowing from the Father's throne.
Angels sing a sweet music,
Mortals' ears have never known.

I have heard so much of Heaven,
The beauty of the place.
The one who'll be our Shepherd,
Now I long to see his face.

There are splendors ever shining,
And pleasures never cease.
The blest of God dwell safely,
In the pleasant paths of peace.

The morning light is breaking,
In skies once veiled and dim.
Soon we'll be at home with Jesus,
To forever dwell with him.

Raymond M. Estes

Without You

A day without you
    Is a day I do not live,
A day without you
    Is a day when the sun does not rise,
The flowers no longer bloom
    And the sun no longer shines,
The sky becomes dull
    And filled with clouds,
A day without you
    I would die from the sorrow of which
    You have broken my heart,
But a day with you
    Means the flowers awaken,
The sun shines again
    And the birds begin to sing,
A day without you
    Is an eternity of gloom and darkness,
But when you finally arrive
    Even the willow trees lift with delight.

Vanessa Arlene Gonzalez

Cupid's Arrow

An open blast of power
    Is followed by a light.
Its outreaching force
    Is unleashed with great might.

No boundary is capable
    Of holding this great power in.
You cannot run,
    It will always
        Find you
            again and again.

Everywhere you go,
    The power follows too.
Love is in the air
    And it has its sites on you.

The great power of love
    Is in reciting your vow.
Never forget
    What I tell you now.

Lucas Womack

Loyalty

What is this thing called loyalty?
Is it something we all should have?
Will it do anything for us?
To do it must you be brave?
I wonder sometimes why you need it.
Then I stop and study and facts.
And I find you really have to have it.
It's not something that you can act.
It's a feeling within your heart,
That you must stand by and work,
To make the deed successful
That you mustn't ever shirk.
Whether it's a job or marriage,
A stand that you must rise behind,
Or just a tiny statement,
You must make and still be kind.
Loyalty is something,
That identifies you forever.
You are known by what you are.
Strong and loyal...friend forever.

Mary C. Wood

My Love

My love for you
    is like a beautiful red rose
The feel so sweet
    the touch so soft
Each petal as wonderful
    as the next
Each passing day
    growing stronger and stronger

But then as the days go by
    the petals soon begin to die
They fall upon the floor
    one by one
It seems like their life
    had just begun
But then someone ends it
    because their love is not strong

I hope one day
    that love blooms again
Because my love for you
    is like a beautiful red rose

Kristen McElheney

Untitled

My heart...
    is like a moth drawn
    to the flame which consumes it

I keep going back for more,
    more love,
    more pain,
    and an ever-expanding heart

For at each death
    there is now and forever rebirth

When I lose all hope and faith,
    then I shall lose the flame
    that is my life

C. R. Gaines

Women talk,
    men walk.

C. R. Gaines

Embellished In My Soul

Embellished in my soul
Is my heart's desire

it rocks me, it caresses me,
My heart's desire awaits me
on vistas unseen, mountains untouched

I sing the notes awaiting God's
call to breathe into me
and reveal to me the
Promised Land, the Divine Melody.

I feel the Ahhh of Life,
the fragrance of peace like a
rose petal washed upon a sandy beach.

Embellished in my soul
Is my heart's desire
to dance with me
the dance of ecstasy.

Am I ready to take that leap
that soul joyride
or will I keep on holding onto
the ledge at the bottom of the ravine?

Lia C. Azeal

Indifference

The smell of a hospital,
Is one of indifference.

The rapture of birth,
The sorrow of death,
All of this is missing
In the impassive smell.

The smell of a hospital
Is not death,
Is not life,
But is an uncaring smell.

If the hospital cared
The walls would crumble.
If it dared to cry
The walls would fall.

The smell of a hospital
Can resemble anything,
The first breath of a soul,
The last breath of a life.

The smell of a hospitals is many things,
But can feel only one thing, Indifference.

Michelle Burcenski

Brotherly Community

Stay
In a place
Where there is no confusion
In life.
Come
To where we are all united
Like a swarm of bees in a hive.

Leave
All the strife
And worldly cares behind.
Start
A new drama
of Peace
   of Love
      of Life
In Brotherly Community.

Sheldon Hofer

Old Growth

"We have to protect our old growth,"
Is the cry among preservationists,
Environmentalists, concerned citizens.

Overlooking the next generation of trees,
The young and healthy,
Cut down before their time,
To preserve the aging, the dying,
So looking back,
We can gaze at them and wonder,
What the world was like,
When they were young.

We have to protect our elderly,
Overlooking the next generation,
Who grow up illiterate, angry, ignored,
Cut down before their time,
To preserve the aging, the dying,
Whether we care or not,
What the world was like,
When they were young.

Paul Wright

Guiding Light

He's there no matter what
is wrong
Through tears and joy, when I
am alone.
I feel at peace, because I
know he's there with me.

The love he gives, no one
gives the same.
I know I am blessed in
Jesus name.
So much in the world going
on; but his light forever
continually strong.

Should darkness try to fall
Upon you, look to the
Guiding light it will pull
you through.

Martine Collette Alvarez

In His Way

The little body oh the ground,
it broke my heart to see.
I wanted it to fly away,
up through the trees so free.

It wasn't very big in size,
but its beauty was so grand.
I know I shouldn't wonder how.
It was made by the Master hand.

Thank you Lord for the tiny thing,
that brightened up a day.
As it pecked upon my window pane,
I could almost hear you say.

I know you are my child and I
wanted you to share.
The love and joy I give to those,
who really really care.

Lord if it takes a wee small bird
to come from Heaven above.
I pray that you will send me more,
I need to feel your love.

Wanda Barrier

Lovestruck

Love is spiritual and sacred, because
it concerns matters of your heart
and soul.
Looking for love is the surest way
not to find it.
When love finds you it's like at that
moment your heart and soul came together
as one.
When I met my true love, it was like
a lighting bolt had struck me and opened
my eyes to love.
And when he touched me, he opened the
gateway to my heart.
When true love is found, the feeling can
be very special.

Vicky Lyons

A Beautiful Love

This is the end of my journey
it ended long ago.
This is the end of - beautiful life.
for the stars fall from the heavens
at my beck and calling
The moon is red, rivers and lakes,
no skins consumed in plagues.
Until the night falls, the birds will fly
in the wilderness, looking for love.
The world stands still in the
low glass of time
Looking, longing for love.
This is the end of a beautiful life
For the mountains will be moved,
The beginning of sorrows,
And, just in the middle of love.

Sophia Nicholas

Whispers In The Wind

It fills me with emotions
It enraptures me in feelings
Strange, unknown, cold.
I feel empty
A lack of warmth and caring
I don't understand it.

I am confused.
A love I once knew is now gone.
Lost
To the winds of change.
I miss your body.
I miss your breath, your voice.
You are gone.
Forever.
My love is lost.
In a jungle of error.
Mistaken emotions.
I think it is love but it is not.
Never again shall I feel
The love I felt for you.
Now all I have to cling to
Are whispers in the wind.

Patti Sperline

Tiger

Its hot breath chills one's fright
It gorges, snarls and preens its might
Then stalks again through day or night..

William J. Harding

I Name My Song

You said my baby's name.
It grates me like shredded skin.
The musical birthright
dropped from my bloody hips,
and you never labored over the song.
You don't read music.

Maybe you fertilized this wasteland,
Maybe a flower sprung pinkly there,
but I plucked the bud, suckled the stem.
I am her root.
You are just a dead spore
floating through a fog.

My bruised knees created the garden,
cultivated her harpsong,
and named her Music.

Peggy Davis

My Love

My love,
It has been a long time
Since I've seen those
Mysterious eyes of yours.

My love,
It has been a long time
Since I've touched
Those warm lips
Of yours.

My love,
It has been a long time
Since I have felt the
Strength of your arms
Around me.

My love,
Please come back to me.
I love you, I need you.

Tammy Pile

Christmas

Christmas is like a soft kiss
it is a warm loving time,
a time when you give and receive.

It is like a token,
a token of love and appreciation
not just for anyone,
but for someone special.

It comes and goes so quickly,
not lasting long enough
leaving you with memories,
making it seem forever
till the next time comes.

Ryan Fender

Romance

The reason romance is grand
Is that it's new and untried.
You're nice because if you can
You want love - baseness defied.
Would that you could always
be kind
And keep romance aglow
With the one that you did
find
Was human and erring so.

Laura Fontaine

In Memory Of Tracey Anne Snell

To a friend who is no longer with us
It is time to say goodbye,
The Lord has taken her with Him
She's safe so do not cry.

She's no longer in the pain
She was in when she was here,
There's nothing that can hurt her now
In the land where there's no fear.

She's in a better place we know
Where there is no pain,
Her death it is a grief to us
But to her it is a gain.

Her memory will live long in us
For those of us who have known,
For all the joy she brought to us
With the love that she had shown.

Tammy Jo Nichols

Silent Is Our Cry

Silent is our cry
  it is within our soul.
Violence captures the eye,
  still, nothing is told.

As one we are,
  segregated we have become.
Branded by the mark,
  ignorance prevails our home.

Generations we begot,
  each one unique.
Many carry the past,
  perseverance some believe.

Still many secrets are kept,
  many wonders to be solved.
Our numerous things we have wept,
  but overcome many downfalls.

The question still remains
  why to each other we show violence.
It is because of these deadly games,
  why our cry is still silent.

Natalie Robinson

Crystal Trading Post

I'm going to drive to Window Rock.
It may take all day.
And I might take Narbona Pass,
The snow is gone by May.

I wish that you'd come with me.

I think I'll stop with the trader
Who lives at Crystal Post.
And sit and drink red soda pop
And talk of days now lost.

I wish that you'd come with me.

We'll sit and talk of lambing time
And pawn that's sat for years.
Then we will speak in Navajo
When customers appear.

I wish that you'd come with me.

To be in the Chuska Mountains
With springtime in the air
Will make the day so glorious
It's something we should share.

I wish that you'd come with me.

F. D. Moeller

Time

Time waits for no one.
  It passes you by
Time is something
  we say we have
It's taken for granted
  and wasted at times
Time is short or long
  how are we to know
Who has less or more
  Time is something we find
when everything is left behind
  For after we are gone
time still goes on and on

Rosalie Giannone-Sparacio

Life Is Like The Wind

Life is like the wind,
it quickly passes you by.
You've got to breathe in the air
Before it sweeps up into the sky.

Memories are made to
remember and to last,
and you should do that with memories,
but, don't live your life in the past.

Every new day is a challenge
as the sun rises over the trees.
Get up and accept your challenge,
every day you have got to seize.

Your challenges can be made easier,
just reach down into your soul,
and you will truly discover
that you can achieve any goal.

Jamie Seidman

Revenge

It's in my blood
It rattles my brain;
This is only
My favorite game.

Revenge I seek
I'll tear you apart,
When you least expect
In the frightening dark.

A hand you raised
A hand I'll cut off,
You will scream
But I won't stop.

Don't hurt my family
Or my friends,
For I'll seek revenge
And your life will end.

Misty L. Corns

Request

Nay love, I would not bid thee halt
  In thy mad flight.
I seek to find no fault
  In thy delight.

Yea love, I know thy heart is free.
  It should be then.
But this I ask of thee—
  Come back again.

Wenona Baker Mitchell

Whispers

If there is a face that beams
it seems to come from you
there are things I can say
all of which are true
beauty is only an attraction
skin deep I hear
I would like to know
if your beauty runs through
Dear?
Sometimes I believe it does
however, this is not clear
truth is mostly action
not a whisper in the ear

Lenny Natural

Into Me

Love is around me
It touches me
Caresses my soul
Sometimes I feel giddy;

It's lonesome after dark
Then the halo glows
Eternal light shine through
Love has finally returned!

The world is lovely
Dawns are beautiful again
Ocean waves stir strange feelings
I'm in love!

W. C. Duke

The Christ Child

Last night in my dreams
   It was Christmas Eve.
I ran down the stairs
   To see what Santa brought me.
I was delighted to see
   Beneath the Christmas tree.
A dolly! just for me.
   With a gentle lift
I held him close.
   A brightness round his head did glow.
As I touched my lips to his
   My dolly faded away.
And in his place with radiant face
   The Christ child lay.
Then softly I heard myself whisper
   "Happy birthday, dear king"
As my dream faded away.

Marie E. Stankowski

My Secret Place

Down the road,
In a little grove,
Where the breezes blow,
Where no one knows,

I sit,
I think,
I love,
I dream.

Down the road,
In a little grove,
Where the breezes blow,
Where no one knows,

I go to my secret place.

Lisa Dennington

Teeter Totter

It was fun to sit on the seesaw with you
It was fun to think our love was true
I was up when you were down
You would smile to change my frown

Teeter totter sweeter water
I have tasted from your lips
love is not just a game

Now I sit on the toy alone
Fragile as a wishbone
One side wanting to break free
One side weighted with visions of we

Teeter totter eater otter
stop your screaming
love is not just a game

Can anyone help me?
Tell me which way to go?
Where is my best interest?
Where shall the next wind blow

Samantha Sargent

Puppy Love

I remember the day we first met
It was the day you chose me for your pet
When I looked up you were so tall
I was six weeks old and very small
I loved you from the start
And still do with all my heart
I have enjoyed every day
Most of the time I had my way
You thought I would never grow up
Always wanting to play that puppy stuff
Then one day we both knew
Those puppy years were very few
With the passing of each day
We grow old and turn gray
Now we must say good bye
Do not be sad please do not cry
Take me away put me to sleep
It will be through love my last treat
We will meet again I have no doubt
It will be in heaven when your time runs out.

Margie Croker

Entry

On this cold road, dark
In which I have embarked
The path which I've chosen
Has somehow now been broken

Sorrow has what I tread
This trail, is now dead

Sunday's light has all but risen
Mind and soul, exorcism
The chill has left my bones
Warmth now roams

Morning's breeze
Taken in with ease

Sun on my flesh
Of silk mesh

Roar of the sea
Truly, comforts me

Songs of a bird
Peacefully heard

Found songs of a child
Have brought me from the wild

Kyle G. Tederous

Leaving Soon

I might be leaving soon,
It's all been a mistake.
I might be leaving soon,
though it will be a big risk to take.
I might be leaving soon,
It is shameful to say;
I might be leaving soon,
But I can no longer stay.
I might be leaving soon,
So I must say my goodbyes.
I might be leaving soon,
For I must get rid of my cries.
I must be leaving soon,
Because something must be done.
I must be leaving soon,
This is a bad environment that I'm in.
I must be leaving soon,
This environment I am in takes me on
dangerous spins.
So you see I must be leaving now,
Because if I don't my life will soon end!!!

Mirenda Haywood

Mountain

Life is like a mountain,
it's big and hard to climb.
You think you're going up,
just when you fall behind.
You roll down the other side,
falling to disaster.
But then you go back up again,
and break out in a laughter.
You're laughing really hard now,
just then you see it ahead.
The mountain's going right back down,
and you feel as stiff as lead.
Life is like a mountain,
you wish it would just stay flat.
But when you get those ups and downs,
you don't know where you're at.

Missy Goyette

Deaths Sting

Oh death where is thy sting?
It's in the hearts of a loved one.
Along with the sorrow you bring.
The tears now are never done.

You come to us like a thief.
To take back with you a life.
And leave behind only grief.
And inside a heart full of strife.

If we knew when you would come.
Would we cling to this life with fear?
As life means so much to some.
I'm sure they would rather stay here.

Our soul is the essence of life.
Do you take it or leave it behind?
If left does it take on a new life?
It's not very clear in my mind.

Someday I myself shall know.
I will leave my loved ones so dear.
To follow death where it goes.
And walk by Gods side without fear.

Nadine Standfield

"Brandy Ann"

A flower bloomed too soon in spring
Its petals quickly faded
But on the winds of time we know
A seed is soared and lifted
A picture only in our hearts
A portrait etched in love
But even now a perfect rose
In paradise waits above

Grandad / William E. Nichols Sr.

Marriage

Marriage is a special time.
It's when the lives of two
Blend their lives together in
A love that's strong and true.

Each promise is forever,
Or until death you part.
You stand with God your maker,
Let love burn within your hearts.

With God to lead and guide you,
In paths that are ahead,
True love, your day, stays special,
This day, that you are Wed.

Martha I. Shepard

Droopy

Here I sit all nervous and shaken,
I've been washed, brushed and groomed,
So I can have my picture taken.

I'm no rare beauty, that is for sure,
Just a red-headed dog,
With a heart that is pure.

Climbing fences, biting mailmen,
Chasing boys are my bad habits.
But in the winter you should see me.
Boy, I can really chase those rabbits.

My master is a fine boy.
He thinks I'm just grand,
I've been cop and cowboy,
and sometimes sandman.

So here I am at my master's command,
Not knowing whether to sit or stand.
Trying to look noble, and cool, and not
shaken.
Ever gorgeous, to have my picture taken.

Virginia C. Thompson

Memorial Poem

When from this mortal earth
I've departed...
Will someone miss me?
Will someone be brokenhearted?
Will I have touched the hearts
of many.... or one?
Or will I be missed at all
by none?
Will good deeds done be not
forgotten?
Will my family and friends
think of me often?
Oh I pray when from this
World I depart...
per chance I'll live forever
... in someone's heart.

Linda Beveridge

The Power Of Wisdom

I've stood all kinds of pain
  I've run so far
But now it's time to stand and
  be proud of
  what I am
My heritage is what I am,
  not my color
People look at me and say
what I am on the outside, not
the power which is in my mind
What is in store for my life
of wisdom and heritage
I do not know, but I do
know this...
  I've got what no
  other has,
  the power of
  Wisdom

Shmya Davis

"I've Seen, I've Heard, I Know"

I've seen the buzzards circling,
I've seen the eagle fly,
I've seen the duckling waddle,
And I've seen my mother cry.
I've heard the winds all searing,
I've heard the wolves' piercing howl,
I've heard the crackle of the fire,
And the night song of the owl.
I know all there is 'bout history,
I'm excellent in verse.
I know that in life some things happen,
That you cannot rehearse.
I know there is an answer
To all my questions asked.
I know there is a purpose
To all my mindless tasks.
I know that I have looked hard,
I've looked so hard to find,
That love isn't in your heart,
It's in your soul and in your mind.

Mary Marigliano

Love's Moment

When the stars come out late at night
  Just before her cat do

You appear before me in all your might
  Just as fit those extra pounds let do

The mist of my dream clears at your sight
  Just as alive and firm as Zanado

We are together but a moment
  Time is given not us, but the young

Time moves swiftly and is spent
  Kiss me quick, but forget the tongue

One last love for this old gent
  If she's willing with limbs unbent

She is hopeful he will stay
  God I'm lucky she's not gay

Just a few years left.... or maybe a day
  She eats simple food, cheep as hay

Through eternity, come what may
  I think I love her, by the way

Robert C. Sandness

A Heart Protected

And then (he happened)
joy ecstasy
found
and - yet...
a return (to the past)
depression
anger
withdrawal
lost in what could have been
torn between the passion
the laughter that comes
the tentative connection
a heart protected
a soul unwilling
a mind (that knows the depth)
but - oh...
how sweet the sounds
the touch
the taste
and so (he is)

Renee Miles

Just For A Little While

Understand I'll be here
  Just for a little while

Understand I'll try to offer
  A helping hand

And maybe sometimes give
  A little smile

You must realize, that while I am here
  There are plenty of unwanted tears
  Caused by many unnecessary fears

Understand I am always hearing
  "What could have gone wrong"

But please my dear
  You must stay strong

Understand I was here
  For just a little while

A stranger's bullet took me out
  I cannot sing and no longer shout

I was only here
  For just a little while
I say goodbye with a peaceful smile

Katherine Pollitt

Burning Quest

It all has come together
it all has become so simple
what started as a meaningless game:
has become a burning quest:
a quest to fill dreams
to teach while being taught
to share something that in no other way,
to no other person can be shared.
A quest to find your character;
because of one other person,
through laughter and pain
the world makes sense
the stars aren't so distant
and the weight of loneliness
drops like the pouring of rain.
A quest that can only be
traveled by the mind
and the prize can only
be captured by the heart.

Linda Mielcarek

On The Day That You Were Born

I remember the day that you were born.
Just like it was yesterday.
When I held you in my arms
and you smiled in your own special way.
I loved you from the minute
they put you in my arms.
I promised on that day
you wouldn't ever be harmed.
I know that one day,
You will want to leave home.
But you will always have a place
in my heart, that is all your own.

Karen Blankenship

Live Today

We worry endlessly at times
Just what tomorrow might bring,
We also dwell on "what if happenings"
And other unnecessary things
An unhappy memory act or word
Was said and so we sit and cry
We dwell on hurts and sadness as
Yesterday went by
Now I'm telling the story
So this is what I pray
  We need your help
    Dear, Father
      To live our lives today

Marisa McCoy

You Are

You are the bridge of hope which
keeps me from falling in this river
of loneliness and saves me from
drowning in sorrow and misery.

You are the single oasis in a
universe of desert that rejuvenates
my soul and quenches my thirst for love.

You are the foundation that stabilizes
my life and supports me through
the shaky and turbulent times.

You are the doorway that leads
me to the place of happiness
that I have always longed to be.

Tom Mattocks

Peace On Earth

God has promised
Kingdom and glory.
The beauty universe
it is absolutely free.
Life is a grand adventure
In every sense and way.
The earth is filled with
Light and sounds,
No troubles cloud the sky,
You feed a hungry child,
And wiped his tear filled eyes,
For mother sister or brother
Or your father crushed.
In your heart you take
A peaceful book for glory.
Throw of your hand and think,
Things what can destroy
Your hard work and life.
This here success must surely come
Peace precious moment for life.

Lazar Maria

Tangled Company

Sparse in the drying clay
languish the weary blossoms.
Wistful tears spill
down their cracking stems
into the thirsty earth.
Young shoots spring
to embrace the blooms
in grateful joy.
Strangled, the flowers die
in the tangled company of weeds.

Margaret M. Levendis

Untitled

I had a dream
  late one night.
I was on a journey
  and end less Flight.

I saw a man
  standing on a hill.
He called me there
  tho his lips were still.
I am your Father
  he said to me.
My Father's gone
  how can this be.

I maybe gone
  but will never part.
For I'll always live
  within your heart.

Marion Townend

Plath

Unharnessed energies:
leading fatalistically to
creative chaos, destructive denial.

Who are you?
haunting mind, inspiring soul...

Where are you?
In the life nectar
seducing your father's bees...
Trapped honey in a double hive...

Stroke the diaphanous wing;
Release the other Queen.

Michael E. Sorg

Kisses From Cassiel's Queen

A chalice for Michael's tears
in which to plant finer stars,
and Gabriel we implore
to play well past sundown.
Skies of eyes
bid you peace
through troubled forest lands,
Sweet Raphael-
burn all reports and feast
on your Father's seeds.
My Birds,
wing brightly upon pure melodies
of Uriel's golden flute,
the essence of our fire being love,
and this we steal from our brother,
and being brothers
steal we now away
to corner time, and with tender wing
bring your Sister Angel home.

Patzi Zlakovski

Fall

The wind whistles,
Leaves fall,
Branches crumble,
Must be fall.

Leaves turn color,
As they fall,
Piles grow,
It must be fall.

Crumpled leaves,
In the hall,
I am thinking,
This must be fall.

As dead leaves,
Start to fall,
Then this season,
Must be fall.

Wind whistles,
Leaves fall,
Branches crumble,
This is fall.

Mark Schutte

Idealistically

Friendship
Lending a tear
extending a hand
taking one,
Laughing
Crying
Sharing
Caring
being
understanding
Sympathetic
Sensitive
it simply...is

Shawn Michael Banwell

Knowing

Come unto me he beckons
lest I know my fate
does render, gives me
pause to remember
My Lord cries out
through scripture
tried and true

Come read and do accept
the truth as written by a few

Robert F. Atwood

Today

Today I found tomorrow
In a person by the name of you
Sweet, tender and caring
With a smile that says I do
I do believe the smile is saying
How much you really care
And I long to let you know
That I hear you loud and clear
The sights, sounds and spirits
Are aroused within this soul
And I am so very happy
That I am the one you chose
Today I have tomorrow
In the love of you

Maurice Earl

A Prayer For All

Lord, put your arms around me
Let me feel your glow

I've been out in the world so long
I've gotten very cold

In your cloak please wrap me
And hold me to your breast

I've grown so very weary, Lord
And I need to rest

Now, cradle me in your arms of love
I'll close my eyes in sleep

Knowing that with you, Lord
I have at last found peace

Virginia Tincy Stone

"Oh God I Love You"

Oh God I love you
Let me hold your hand
Walk along beside you
And try to understand

Let me not judge Lord
My fellow man
But help "me"
Do the very best I can

Let me shine Lord
And share my faith
And make this whole world
A little better place

Oh I'll be thrilled Lord
To hear you say
"Take my hand"
"We're going to walk my way"

Oh God I love you
I'll take your hand
Then I'll finally, really, truly understand

Norman M. Reid

"Better Days"

Some days we fret
Let things get us upset
Feeling full of woe,
Don't know which way to go;
Get in a hurry
Not being trustworthy
Of the Lord;
He paid a price;
Being ever so nice
To let us know down to the last letter
Days are going to get better.

Rose M. Barnes

End Of Time

If I die remember me
Kindly

If I die remember my
Passion

If I die remember it was too
Soon

For I know my time
Has come

To say good-by
Remember me..........

Lillian Neuman

Braces

Tilt your head.
Let your eyes catch
the light of my smile,
of my reflected tear.

Spread your arms.
Bare your naked heart,
put your warm, skin coat
over my shivering shoulders:

Hold me closer—
tell me with your cheek
your breath will always
be as warm...

But watch your kiss.
My lips are frail.
Save me a cold rag
for rubber bands that snap.

Marianne Merrelli

In a Deep Canyon

In a deep canyon,
lies a feeling so strong.
A feeling that cannot be explained,
until it is gone.
Wind blows through this canyon,
like soft words spoken.
There for a moment,
and then it is broken.
In two, this canyon splits worlds.
This feeling, in and out it whirls.
When will the pain end?
When did it begin?
Like fire and ice, these canyons melt.
They're deep and hollow and cannot
be filled.
A tear, a cry, and then it dies.
In a deep canyon, lies a feeling so strong.
In the deep canyon of my heart.
The canyon, that will forever split
our worlds apart.

Solita Adame

My Own Little Snowflake

A cold winter storm brought
  me my own little snowflake,
And put it in the corner of
  my window pane.
I hope the day's bright sun
  will not take
The little snowflake that is
  my gain.

What joy and delight to see
  a snowflake so small,
That glittered and was white
  as could be.
I gazed out my window and wondered
  how many more would fall.

It lingered there throughout
  the day,
Like a gem that was no fake.
But the night wind came and took
  it away,
Which for a day, was my own little snowflake.

Mary H. Knopinski

Together

At the earth's edge,
lies the setting sun.
Sky of painted shades,
orange,
yellow,
and red.
Brush strokes of white.
and a gentle breeze
tickles the leaves
of the aging maple tree.
And at its foot
we lay
in the coolness
of its shadow,
holding one another,
sharing our warmth
and the moment
together.

Karen Yvonne Goodrich

Blind Involvement

I always wonder why,
Life is a mystery
Not immune to pain nor misery.
People walking in vertigo,
Oh ever so slow.
Not understanding-
Why or where they are standing
DEMANDING:
Equality, peace and hope.
Did we hypocrites earn it?
For whom does this sentence seem fit?
Old fools think we're going to lose.
No one will lose or win,
It will not end with a spin
In the game of life.

Laurie Gonzales

Freedom Of The Past

There was a time long ago,
It was time of innocence
A time of freedom

But time flies on,
Like birds from a cage

There was no sense of right or wrong
Because there was no wrong, no evil

Only the fake white world
Of child-like dreams
And false hopes

Kathryn Miller

The Garden Of Life

Life is like a garden
Created by our Lord
Tended by our savior
One and all adored.

Some grow old and weary
Spreading seeds afar.
Some are grown for beauty
So we'd all want more.

Some fall by the wayside
To change the plot in which we grow
For in this worldly garden
The Savior hoes the raw

G. U. E.

Portrait Of An Old Man

Piercing
Light blue eyes
Above a toothless smile.
Wrinkles of more than
Three-score years and ten
Upon his face.
Unkempt beard,
Long white hair
Fringing 'round an old corduroy cap.
Sheep-skin corduroy coat,
Worn knee boots.
His gnarled hand
Shakily pats a canine head.
Slowly
He trudges—
Head bent shoulder high—-
Amongst the weeds and grass
Almost as tall as he.

Marian Smith

The Rain

There is a soft mist
Like a rose that's dew-kissed.
And like a lover without shame,
Falls gently the Spring rain.

It is a soothing shower
That falls in the daylight hour.
So like tears after pain
Comes the soft Summer rain.

There are tears that will not break
They are the tears of heartache.
Thus to a melancholy refrain
Beats steadily the Autumn rain.

There is a fury of a storm
And when it loosens, it causes harm.
So like a baby who is sick and complains,
Shrieks and sobs the winter pain.

Wendy Addy

I Count

I count
   each day you're gone.
I count
   each moment long.
I count
   until I fall asleep,
And then I count
   no more, I w-e-e-p.
When I awaken
   fresh at morn;
I find my eyes
   have wept till dawn.
And then again
   I c-o-u-n-t again,
Each second
   of the day I'm in.
'till you return,
My heart
   doth yearn;
I c-o-u-n-t...

Cesarina Maria Rossetti

Ireland

Whenever I heard an Irish tune
Lilting across to me
I would think of the land of my father,
The land that I wanted to see.

Whenever I heard an Irish voice
It really appealed to me
I would think of the land of my father,
The place where I wanted to be.

When I saw a picture of Ireland,
A land so green and fair
My heart would feel sad and heavy
For I wished I could be there.

One day Fate smiled upon me
I went to the Emerald Isle
That was the day my dream came true
And the world saw my Irish smile.

Mildred Katemopoulos

"if i, leo, were a true king"

the name means
   lion-like,
if the lion
   is king,
why am i
   only a
spectator who carries
   this royal
name.

if i, leo,
   were king,
i would not
   be hindered
by the perpetual
   rains, but
roam in the
   undiscovered sun,
light.

   i claim
   my kingdom.

leo cittadini

Some Antics With Semantics

If one attends a seminar
   is he a seminarian?
And when a barber plies his trade
   are his techniques barbarian?
Can adolescents striving for
   complete emancipation
be going through a stage in life
   that's called adulteration?

Does he who fosters epic poems
   become an epicurean?
If one should live a century
   would he be a centurion?
In studying the English tongue
   I've come to one conclusion ...
The more I try to master it
   the greater my confusion.

Marie Deavereaux

Have A Nice Day?

In the morning, if you arise,
Listen not to whining cries
Of others who doubt
Each day's route.

A sky of gold,
Can make you bold.
Even clouds of gray
Bring another day.

Heavenly colors, change,
And constantly rearrange.
Nature is giving,
You are still living.

Someone will say,
"Have a nice day".
But hot or cold, dry or wet,
How much nicer can it get?

Maxine McCormick

Hawk Above Mori Point - I.

It was a hawk.

Silent rider on the ocean breeze,
listen to me!

Jewelled pendant on the brow of heaven,
listen to me!

Suspended,
like the last thought in an empty house,
motionless messenger,
show me the way to your stillness!

Peter Szasz

For A Young Deaf Child

Come,
listen with your eyes,
behold the ground
and skies,
life is all about:
rivers run,
insects crawl,
flowers climb,
snowflakes fall,
each without a shout.

Yes, listen with your eyes,
and your heart will hear.

Taras B. Denis

Little Angel

Blue Skies - Devil's Eyes,
   Little Angel.
My heart Speaks - As I once weeped,
   Little Angel.
I love you, Dear - This is Clear,
   Little Angel.
A love once true - Now, it's me and you,
   Little Angel.
A baby cries - A mommy sighs,
   Little Angel.
He comes for you - Then I am blue,
   Little Angel.
I kiss your nose - then your toes,
   Little Angel.
So, hug me tight - then, say good night,
   Little Angel.

Melissa Pallotti

Japanese Girl

Silk and friendly
Live so for me
All her rays enfold
Darkened cadre
Sweet length tally
Trembles all I hold

Cultured raiment
Soft attainment
Any room her own
I see clearer
Love and mirror
Lissome girl-bird's roam

Asian beauty
You are truly
Passion beyond skies
Deep and sublime
Clinging sunshine
Curvy longing eyes.

Pete Weyrich

Images In A Crystal Ball

A race of people
living free,
in harmony with nature,
praising God,
Respecting all living things,
filled with hope,
heeding the call,
marching for the cause,
facing reality.

A race of people
locked in jails,
buried in graves,
deaf to the cries,
lost in despair.
Looking for answers in
the bottom of bottles,
pimping for the Masters,
dealing on corners,
drugged up,
escaping reality.

Peggi E. White

Expectations

When everything around you
looks bleak and gray
That's just the time to say
I know God's working
in a special way
Winter casts a dreary spell
And the doldrums set in
But in your heart faith and
resolve begin
You know that darkness
cannot continue to prevail
That the light will burst forth,
Illuminate and lift the veil -
Don't be discouraged when you
fall back a step or two
For tomorrow will bring a
special treasure, a gift
unexpected to bring you through.

Shirley Campbell Horton

For Grey

So late in life
Love has come to stay
We've passed our mid life crises
Our hair is thin and gray.

The first bloom of youth
Has long gone away
How much time do we have together
How much time do we have to play.

Countless hours of laughter
Fleeting moments of tears
Each moment lived, heart to heart
Through all our given years.

I'll love you for my lifetime, dear,
However long 'twill be,
Each day ours, a precious gift
Filled with love for you and me.

Kate Hamer

Untitled

Love is a star
Love is what you are
Always burning bright
Together as one light.

For today you stand
touching hand in hand
Before our Lord above
Who blesses you with his love

Love is a star
Love is what you are.
Always burning bright.
Together as one light.

Karen Sincerbeaux

"Love Me"

It's true I have fallen in
love with you
When I didn't realize it
I wish it wasn't true
but my body is full of
a hurt that never ends
I can't go back and
forget this what I feel
just look at me for a
moment and tell me
that you will never
leave me love
even though the winds
are rough
love me like I'm loving you
feel like I feel, love me love me.

Manuel Mendez

Catwatch

Cat, I ponder on the word,
look, it's chasing a frightened bird.

Aww, so cute yet so graceful,
oh my, eating fish by the vase-full.

Soft, very soft is its fur,
kitten, pet it and it will purr.

Cute, so fuzzy and so small,
cat, my favorite animal of all.

Andy Thayer

"Our Love"

He looked at me so sad, that it
made me mad. I thought I needed
freedom, but I then stopped and
remembered. The look in his eyes,
made me laugh in surprise, the
way he walked, he made me
summarize. He turned away so
quickly, but I caught a glimpse
in his eyes, that seemed to make
my heart die. He drooped, and I
just tried to act cool, even though
I knew I looked like a fool.
He had a note he never gave me,
it made me feel like a traitor. Other
guys looked at me like I was a
prize to be won. But my heart
belongs to only one. My friends
were so sad, you'd think it was
them who had just lost....
"Our Love"

Samantha Kitzmiller

The Abbey At Monte Cassino

It stands alone, a jagged spire
Man-made-Man destroyed, reaching
Upward to the sky. Desolate, alone,
product of war.
A shadow, the finger of the setting
sun, creeps upward and then the
darkness of the night obliterates the
darkness of the day.

Marvin R. Hitt

Too Busy To Go To Heaven

In this fast moving world
Mankind so busy, no time to tell,
No time to share with others
The living word from cover to cover.

Mankind going at such a pace,
Not realizing the real true race,
Ears that are deafened to the call,
No concern for each and all.

The Lord, He is real,
The sick, He will heal,
Soul, He will save,
Please accept Him today.

Don't get so busy in this life,
With so many struggles and strife,
Seek His pleasures forevermore,
The Godhead, will have the complete
score.

Marjorie M. Sanders

Soldiers' Sights

Marching in a perfect line,
Many men following behind,
Bullets are flying everywhere,
Gunsmoke floating in the air,
Noises of explosions,
Plenty of commotion,
Men falling on the ground,
Guns firing round after round,
Neither side coming out ahead,
Seeing men left for dead,
War is rotten,
But never forgotten.

Robin Walker

The Hard Working Man

The men work diligently trying
massively to keep up with the machines.
The break buzzer rings and all simply
drop what they are doing like some
mindless drones with no self control.

Are these people men or simply machines
like those they work at.
The buzzer rings again and once again
the mechanical part of them takes over,
like that of one who has been hypnotized
and can't change what he has been
told to do

Outside of the building they regain
their self control but only to return
and lose it once again.
They go through this cycle five or
more days a week
But this is simply the Life of a
Hard Working Man

Richard G. Linden Jr.

Angels

Bringers of light,
Messengers of love,
Beholders of God
in heaven above.

Keepers of the faith,
Bestowing their visions,
Help leading men
from further derision.

Friendly guidance
From heaven above,
Spreading the message
of God's eternal love.

Lisa Hamlin

Butterflies

Butterflies swaying on a
mid-summer day,
but when it comes winter
they all fly away.
Why do they do such
difficult things,
why don't they just stay and
wait till the spring.
If they could talk I wonder
what they'd say,
They probably wouldn't talk
and just fly away

Sara Hess

Honest

To be honest
is being free.
To be free,
is how I wish to be.

When all goes wrong,
don't turn and frown.
Then look to the ground
and blame who's around.

To be really free,
look into thee.
Accept what you see!
For being honest,
is how we need to be!

Timothy A. Cramer

Restoration

The earth is wanting our bodies
mine
I can feel the persistent tug
in my bones
I know it in the way my skin aches
to be close to rock and soil
in the way the ocean pulls at my eyes
showing me always
the way to rest
and return

I have been given
dream the rich earth
how could I deny
this one small gesture-all
I have to offer
a borrowed thing never
my own

I will
when the hour breaks
gracefully undone

Laura Hasler

Watercolors

The words and sounds
   mix together within my head.
So do the watercolors,
   when put in the rain.
Try as I might to remember you,
   the illusion escapes me.

OH GOD.

Please tell me I am wrong,
   The picture-perfect image
   HAS BEEN SHATTERED.
I need truth,
   so that I might gather up
   the broken bits of glass.

I'm sorry I am so selfish.

I need a broom.

The picture,
   The denial,
flying downwards in a blur.

   I cut my fingers,
   one by one.

Mary Beth Richbourg

Emotional Medley

Three seasons I have sustained you
my angelic neonate
But virgin arms enfold you
with jubilation and yet debate

Led by a scent so familiar
you suckle assuredly
more confident of your task
than I, a mother naive

Who will the conductor be
on this journey we are thrust
the intuitions escape me
which I am told to trust

My heart with love abounding
a nexus we create
a revelation transpires
it is I the novitiate!

Laura N. Hnasko

Departed Love

Never was there love with meaning
   more than ours combined,
   silenced when you passed away
   and I was left behind.

How deep a hurt it is
   that leaves the soul in mourning,
   when heaven finds the means
   to kill the joys of life.

Tender are the memories
   that touch the silent heart,
   and leave it sick with sadness
   when a lover does depart.

Tears like endless rivers flow
   drown a life in sorrow,
   fill the void your soul exhumed
   search for a new tomorrow.

Where you are now I soon shall be
   to join my other self;
   immortals we shall then become
   to share eternity.

Kenneth J. Miller

The March Of The Heir

Whose law is this!
Must I look to Mendel
This quality of this gift to me
Must I take a closer look
By examining the family tree!

Tell me - is this child of mine
So qualified with quality
Of father of the past
So gifted with temperament
Of mother of me

What endearment could greater be
Than to walk into the warp and woof
Of family tree
And realize suddenly
Gender's qualities have passed
Back and forth
Without diminishing
That of male and female
But are god-like gifts
On rhythmic scale!

Katherine M. Young

The Traveller

Oh I am a traveller
I've wandered near and far
and as I waked and wandered
a crossroads my path did bar
one road was wide
and the soil trampled down
the other road was narrow
with thorns and briars 'round
I wished to go the one way
but the other beckoned too
and someday my dear friend
the choice will come to you
I did choice the narrow road
it travels strait and long
life is the road I walk
and truth it is my song

Kathryn Whidden

Time

Every minute that slips by,
　is lost.
Never again will we relive that
　single moment in time.
It just sinks away
　into nothingness.
And as time goes on,
　and on, and on,
we soon begin waiting
　for our time to come.
And when our time comes,
　we simply recall,
with or without me
　time will go on, and on....

Michael Davis

Listen

As we gather on that day
in history, we will be needed to
make our world a better place not
only for ourselves but for our children.
It is not enough to look to
our children today but to their
tomorrow as well. May this day go
down in history as a day not only
for the children but the children's
children. A world where children
will be free to learn and grow
up in a decent, place, free from
crime and intolerance, free from
hatred and free to live like human
beings, to play and learn and be
treated like people.

Michael Cook

Amour-propre

I love myself I think you know,
just ask me and I'll tell you so.

My teeth they sparkle in the light,
shine on all and give me might.

All my shoes made of the finest leather,
my threads of only truest feather.

Aura surrounds my every move,
and fills the smallest darkest grove.

My favorite part is on my head,
thick and proud, lies there dead.

And when I'm gone they'll miss me so,
I love myself I think you know.

Robert Signori Jr.

First Birthday

One year is past and tiny steps
Replace the quickened creep.
Leaves sail to the ground
Where fireflies moved in summer's sleep.
A hug, head on my shoulder:
We're nearly eye to eye.
Dark slips out; pale sunrise comes,
Stirs up a softened cry.
My son looks up, a sigh of recognition,
A smile to always keep;
Today's day of warmth,
Discovery, and deeper love to reap.

Madeleine M. Longano

"My Garden"

Love is like my garden,
Like a bed full of seeds,
It helps me to grow,
With the wisdom I need.
It strengthens my knowledge,
Branching out where I may.
It prepares me for the future,
As I change each day.
So stay in your garden,
And nurture your seed.
If you work with it daily,
You'll always succeed.
Remember your garden,
Is your future today.
Work it and love it,
You'll be thankful someday.

ReAnna Nicole York

"SElf"

　SOUL
　MINd　bODY
coRPUS　INTelLECT
　limBS　TOrso
　Brain　hearT
　veins　ARTeries
nuclei　Cellae

Mark P. Gjolaj

Mother

Mother means a kiss and a Hug
Mother means love and nurturing
Mother means an unboundless friendship
with someone who knows you best
Mother means strength and courage
in the hardest of times
Mother means working hard to make a
life for your offspring
Mother means caring and sacrifice
until the end of time.

Veronica L. Hughes

My Heart Aches

My heart aches,
For the place I wish to be.
Where pines stand like gentle giants,
And golden leaves hang from the trees.

Mountains that touch the clouds,
And coyotes that sing to the sky.
I can't forgive myself somehow,
For the time I've let slip by.

The great beauty of this place,
Can be seen upon your face.
And to hear the past tales of fear,
That gently whispers in your ear.

The rolling of sagebrush,
And cactus standing tall,
In a few more months,
It will soon be fall.

With the moon so bright,
That for on this night
Far as your eyes can see
Oh! how my heart aches
For the place I wish to be.

Jane E. Savage

My Dream

I had a beautiful dream
in which everybody was happy
because the war had ended
and finally we had peace and harmony.

Beautiful flowers were arousing;
there was no malice between the people
everybody was singing
songs of love, peace and freedom.

The sky was telling the clouds
that they would never cry again
because all the obstacles that separates
people had gone away.

When I woke up everything was the same
as when I fall asleep
and my heart broke inside of me
because it was just a dream;
a beautiful dream that I had
but I know that it some day become.

Alicia Cardenas

The Solution

One day while biking
instead of hiking
I thought of recycling
on my way to duckling pond.

My noes smelled an odor
my eyes saw trash
which started a rash
that made me itch all over,

So in a flash
to the doctor I dashed
I had to pay cash
for his answer or solution.

The doctor explained
it is of greater worth
to save the earth
the land of your birth.

So in conclusion please
clean up your act
as a matter a fact it is awful
to cause pollution

Johanna Washkevich

To My Little Gal Pat

You crawled into my heart, Pat,
　Into my heart to stay.
Knowing you, loving you
　Lifts me every day —
　In a special way.

You have such a beautiful Spirit
　Reaching from you to me.
But you're on the inside looking out,
　It's easier for me to see —
　That perfect Divinity.

Your lovingness and willingness
　Ever to do your part,
Whatever would your Mother do
　Without your caring heart?
　It's been there from the start!

God expects you to express
　The gift He gave to you.
Let not your heart be troubled,
　He will see you through —
　Your joy will be renewed!

Harriet Spangler

Facing The Challenge

I lost a breast to cancer, my life was never the same
I lost a breast to cancer, I never new such pain
I lost a breast to cancer, for years I had no rest
The fear consumed the best of me with every routine test,
I gave these cells such power, the fight was always there
Until I faced the challenge and the belief others did care
For cancer is limited, but it was something I had to discover
The strength lies within all of us the challenge to recover
For cancer cannot shatter love, or take away one's hope
The courage you develop allows your mind to cope
Cancer cannot destroy your faith or even invade your soul
The journey to recovery is a never ending goal
Cancer challenges all you have, all you hold so dear
Face the challenges with all your heart, crippling all fear!

Judy Cavanaugh

Bull Riders

To Ben Paulson, a winner for his birthday.
I love bull riders, they're what cowboys
are meant to be, cause they've got guts and
they've got nuts, and they are very special to me.
My son Justin Sarsland (Ben, the name I wanted)
but it wasn't meant to be, could have
been a bull rider, but it wasn't meant to be.
He was a little cowboy though, he rode sheep
at the Ludlow lamb barbecue rodeo. And he couldn't be beat.
He would have been eighteen this year,
but it wasn't meant to be. January "94," he died you see.
He's in cowboy heaven with other bull riders who weren't meant to be.
His name will go down in cowboy history,
as a rider that couldn't be beat, and there's a bull,
he never got to meet, or try to beat, cause it wasn't meant to be.

So here's a challenge, Ben and on your birthday friend.
Go out and beat 'em, ride 'em and seat 'em
Win one for Justin, a rider who can't be beat!

Jane Fries

The Man Who Carries My Dreams

As the sun breaks over the small bay,
I notice a man kneel to take communion.
His face is set on the west horizon.

As he boards the rowboat,
My dreams go with him.
The three ships catch the wind
And sail out.

This man doesn't look back;
Only forward...westward.

Behind him, he leaves his loved ones,
The mockers, and his home.

In front of him lay uncertainty
Of the unknown.

But with him, always, he carries the chance
To deliver the message of God
To unknown people and lands.

This man carries his dreams,
And mine, to other countries.

This man?
Christopher Columbus.

Chester Schultze

Early Hours

Renewing my focus, as I walked out into the early hours,
I passed through tall blades of grass. In the moors,
A spider's web glistened as a soft wisp of wind
Filtered through each strand as they tried to bend
And then stay steadily in place, in the early hours.

A few stars were evident and shimmering
Against a transparent background of gold and yellowing,
Suspended invisibly from heaven to Earth,
As they announced their departure to notice their worth
Of where they once were, in the early hours.

But then..., as the sun radiated its ominous glow,
Revealing its power and dominance, against the Earths' bow;
I then stood motionless. I witnessed something new,
The most beautiful creation of all, seen seldom by few,
The coming of a new day, in the early hours.

Brian Goode

Nursing Home

"Never married" sighs Emma Rule
I replied "An unclaimed jewel"
appeared a faint but twinkling
smile, she never laughs "it's not my style."
Charles so tall, handsome, wise
a hint of Alzheimer's in his eyes
a college man of charm and wit
can't understand "things just
don't fit."
Beth, oh Beth has helped
me by, hard times I
thought that I could die.
Peaceful, loving, kindly gal
a gentle rock, my old pal.
Fragile angels in my care
give me strength,
I hold them dear.
And I could never quite repay
these old friends who
show the way.

Clare Brooks

My River

My river was big and great
I sat on her banks as a child of eight.
I watched with delight as she flowed down stream.
Playing in the sand with my dream.
She would carry me away on my boat one day.
Moving away was such sorrow.
I promised her I would see her tomorrow.
Years passed by and I went back to my river
As I gazed upon her my body gave a shiver.
She had shrunk to a small stream
And was no longer my dream.
A tear flowed down my cheek and I had a smile.
Remembering back on many a mile
The beauty of being a child.

Beatrice M. Beatty

The Man

Dr. Martin Luther King Jr. was my man,
he fought with his mouth and not with his hand.
He marched in the day and preached at night,
for blacks and civil rights.
He had a dream that blacks would be free,
before he was killed in Tennessee.
Now he's gone and he's passed,
thank God almighty we're free at last.

Maurice Nunnally

Whales No More

Alone at the beach one chill winter day
I sat watching seals and sea gulls at play,
when suddenly not too far from the shore
I saw something grand seen often before.
For with spume blown far into the air
from out of the depths a whale was there.
So majestic and regal he seemed to me
as he moved so gracefully through the sea.
Then a thought to my eyes brought tears,
I knew he was seen less often in passing years.
Over time man still has not learned his place,
considering himself the only intelligent race.
Plundering, pillaging, causing others to mourn,
a race that was ancient when ours was newborn.
So he slaughters the whale on a scale world-wide
and calls it self-preservation instead of genocide.
So as I sat on that beach both cold and alone,
I saw a fate for which mankind can never atone.
Such sorrow filled my heart on that cold, wintry shore,
For it reason cannot prevail, there will be whales no more.

Douglas Torak

Yosemite

As I drove through Yosemite park today
I saw God's handiwork in glorious array

The pines were majestic
The river so clear
I can pull it from memory
When winter draws near

The mountains like cathedrals
Hewn out of stone
The redwoods so stately standing alone

The silence was golden
The air pure and clear
I can feel God's presence constantly near

The waterfall dances right out of the rock
And the sun shines like diamonds on its gossamer frock

Thank you God for this glorious day
I'll remember it till my dying day.

Doris E. Rae

Oh, To Lay On Jesus' Breast

Sometimes, my children large and small, come and sit on my lap
I say, you're not a baby at all and much too big for that
They say, I need comfort and rest
Let me lay my head upon Your breast

Now when days are hard and nights are long
And it seems like everything's gone wrong
I pray, Lord help me to stand my test
May I lay my head upon Your breast

The Lord's breast is a place of love and peace
Where all tests and trials seem to cease
You find comfort and strength to go on
When your journey has brought you far and long

He renews your strength day by day
And cheers your heart along the way
He lightens the burden your shoulders bear
As if you are walking on air

So, when you think of your many years
Of laboring hard in sweat and tears
When giving up seems all that's left
Just lay your head upon Jesus' breast

Jacalyn R. Mills

Two Troubled Souls

As I peered at the reflection of two troubled souls,
I saw two lives intertwined.
As I looked more closely, one tired to break free.
I realized then that the person I observed there was me.

You were far behind, but I never walked alone.
I now travel without any direction.
Perhaps searching for your ghost and moments never shared.
Perhaps denying our separation.

My head knows what my heart forgets,
But my heart keeps telling me to hold on.
My mind knows that you won't be coming back.
And I must face this truth, you are forever gone.

But as I peered more closely at those two troubled souls,
And those two lives eternally intertwined,
I realized that you cannot unravel what has been.
It is as it will always be, until the end of time.

Audra Lynn

"Reflections"

As I sit and look upon the reflection in the water,
I see a person who is unsure of herself...
If she is going to fulfill her life ambitions and
climb the ladder of success. If she has what it takes
to make it in this world, or has the goal to do it.
So as I sit here watching the Ripples slowly fading
away. I know now which path I should choose!
And someday as I remember the Ripple on the water,
that gave me the inspiration to follow my dreams.

April Janette Taylor

I See Christ

I look to the altar - I see you,
  I see Christ.
In your warm, intelligent eyes and in your radiant smile,
  I see Christ.
In your comforting and truthful words,
  I see Christ.
In your joyous laughter and your love of life,
  I see Christ.
In your unselfish response to the needs of others,
  I see Christ.
In the beauty of your understanding and compassion,
  I see Christ.
In your prayerful mannerisms and your refined example,
  I see Christ.
In the forgiveness of sins and the healing power of
  the sacrament of Reconciliation,
  I see Christ.
Your priesthood is one of life's priceless gifts.
Yes Father, in you
  I see Christ.

Christine Kulczak

Inside View

I feel things happening to me
I'm discovering things about me
I feel warm and secure
Like I'm covered by a liquid blanket
Time passes and I have developed more
Suddenly I feel a strong urge to
Release myself from this place of security
I'm pushing and pushing. Finally I'm free
Now something is handling me.
I scream. Now all that was silent is
Loud, that which was dark is light, that
Which was peace is war

Janet L. Bell

Comfort

Sometimes for reasons quite unknown,
I see in dreams, myself, alone.
It's early morn, just barely dawn
The world has yet to rise and yawn,
Yet I am up and for a walk before the crowing of the cock,
Before the rustling of the leaves
Caused by the early morning breeze.
Oh, the beauty all around! I feel I walk on hallowed ground!
A row of purple mountains run a velvet border to the sun.
Just barely clear their majesty
That filters gold through each tall tree,
And sets the morning dew alight, to chase the dampness of the night.
So cool and clean the air, it smells
Full-scented, thick, with life it swells.
A voice so sweet comes from within,
It calls my name like some lost friend,
And from the halls of memory, an old, old song comes back to me,
The joy wells up, I shed a tear, as in my mind and heart I hear:
"I come to the garden alone...
While the dew is still on the roses..."

Dan F. McAdoo

To Love

I smell love in the essence of roses
I see love in eyes of my mother
I feel love in the midst of my family
I show as a symbol of gratitude
I need love to get through hard times in my life
I give love to family
I give love to friends
I give love to a young man
And in return I get love
Love makes happiness
Love makes a child smile
Love makes the evil surrender
Love concurs anger
Love concurs madness
Love is in everyone
You have to discover love in your heart
To love is to care
To kiss is a symbol of love
Love is my life
Love makes love

Jesse Blacker

Linda, I Love You

My guitar is a close friend to me
I set my fingers and strum the
strings
Her tune echoes the perfect love melody
She interprets my expressions so
deep within
Yes; when my guitar speaks - oh, what
enthusiasm she brings
Her voice sings aloud "I love you and
Love you and Love you Again"
She tells my story - How True Love
should feel
When my fingers walk across the
strings
You'll know the power of Love and
know it's real
My guitar and I achieve a magical
tune so true
Every musical note and word implies
"Linda, I Love You."

Dennis Anders

Untitled

As I sit here
I see the clouds
My thoughts start to drift
As I sit here
I am alone
My eyes watch the clouds
O' how my mind starts to drift
As I sit here
I think of you
But I am still alone
Watching the clouds soar
My mind wanders off
As I sit here
I look back at what I had and start to cry
For I am thinking of you
But I am still all alone
All alone

Cindy Kneip

Wind and Grass

I see the wind swifting across the field.
I see the grass swifting across the field.
It's very fun playing in the grass
and the wind swifting across the field.
My family and I like to play in the
field every year with the wind swifting
in our hair.
When we play in the grass and the
wind while it is swifting across the field.
Our future is based on the field,
and every generation is based on it to.
The grass and the wind rolls us across
the field, and in our future we are
the wind and the grass swifting
across the field.

Ashley Logan, Age 10

Lullaby - Reversed

Out of the caged bars of my window
I see the winter-bare branches,
    of a small tree.
Behind the tangle of dormant stems,
    a jet traces a perfect line of cloud,
That reaches into eternity...

Around the seams of glass a chill seeps in,
weaving tendrils of ice,
    into a battle tapestry;
In opposition to stagnant bits of warmth,
    that sit so high,
in silent enmity...

Within I am surrounded by bits and pieces,
of wrinkled colours,
    and tattered memories:
That rock awake a gently sleeping soul.

John Flanagan

Requiem

Walking in the rain,
I see your face.
Your words echo in my mind.
I have touched your fear,
Your sadness.
Never have I felt such love,
Such sweet pain.
In your eyes I have seen a life without end.
Tears falling in the darkness,
Upon the earth in whose embrace you lie.
A love not lost in death....

Joshua Eaves

Fair-Weather Friend

Blaze brightly, Dear Friend of mine.
I see your smiling face through my window,
Suddenly gloomy days dance with glory,
And my soul shines, brilliant with shimmering hope.

You never knock at the door.
Instead, you stand outside it, beaming,
Pressing your face gently against the panes,
Filling my home with brilliance...and with joy.

You filled my life with laughter,
Gracing it with bright yellows and greens.
On cold mornings, when bleakness enshrouded me,
Your warm, gentle kisses eased the chill of loneliness.

I know some might call you a Fair-Weather Friend—
And true, on rainy days or during icy nights
I never see your glowing face—-
My very existence depends on you.

Smile for me, Old Friend of Mine.
And I will carry beautiful memories of Sunshine
With me through the night
Until the Bright grin of morning blesses me.

Chanctetinyea Ouellette

The Key

I guess the game is over, I have a chance no more
I should be surprised, I never get what I wait for
I don't know why I even tried to fall in love with you
When everything revolved around the things I never knew
Now I'm the one who's standing with the short end of the stick
Like the only flower in the field that no one wants to pick
And every day I'll have to look at you and her together
Knowing I am not the one you want to love forever
And if I have to watch you two embracing in a kiss
My heart will quickly wilt and die, my soul will not exist
So if you pass me on the street, please look the other way
'Cause if she's walking by your side, I've nothing more to say
Your heart is like a locket, this is clear for me to see
What I did not know was all along, she was holding the key.

Amy Haiar

"Leaving"

He left me stranded in the cold.
I should have known in the beginning that in any kind way he didn't
care.
He left me without saying good-bye or giving me just one
last touch of his gentle hands.
He left me behind crying forever in the
dark.
He left me with no explanation.
Without caring enough, he left me without
turning back one last time.
I thought we were going to be forever.
Not understanding why he shattered my heart
into many unfixable pieces.
He left without helping me to escape from all the pain I suffer
emotionally.
When it is time, I will slowly begin to understand why he left.

Frances Whitfield

Should've Loved My Daddy

Should've is a word that I'll never use again.
I should've loved you more, without end.
I should've told you, all the times I thought of you.
I should've walked up and smiled at the sight of you.
I should've known better, that one day I'd never see you again.
Should've for us, was a life never spent.

Darlene Nash

My Dad

He sits in his chair the whole day through
I silently say, "Dad, is that you?"
He's old and tired, his eyes look sad
His skin is wrinkled, his hearing's gone bad.

His years have flown since 1904
He cannot hope to have many more
He fished in the river, ran through the field
Now a small stone would be all he could wield.

He now sits in his room, sometimes alone
The Bible in his hands is one of my own
He says the large print is easier to see
For his eyes are dimmer than they used to be.

Soon he'll leave this earthly home
The fields and land no more to roam
And go away to a better place
Where he'll meet his Jesus face to face.

And on that happy meeting day
With love, Our Lord will surely say,
"You did good, Ted, you did your best.
And now I've brought you home to rest."

Eunice Ann Badgley

Untitled

In the still of the night, in this place where I dwell,
I sit alone in this cold and lonely cell.
As I lie in the night where no one can see, I weep
for the love that I know used to be.
My heart is a prisoner to the love that we knew.
It's bound by the thoughts, and the memories of you.
The thoughts of a love that's so pure, and true, and
the memories of the times that I spent with you.
My heart cries out, but no one can hear,
It's bound by the love, that we held so dear.
Oh God; Oh God; why can't you see, the pain and
the hurt that's inside of me.
Oh God; Oh God;... I pray ... please let it be, that when
I awake I will see.
This has only been a dream, and she's still here with me.

Dewey Griffith & Vicki Kennedy Nibblett

Help

Trapped and alone,
I sit in my home,
Wondering what will happen next!

Will I be yelled or shouted at,
Or will I be hit with a baseball bat?
I just don't know!

Voices are in my head,
They tell me to get out my bed,
And take action like no man ever did!

"But what do I do?" I answered back,
"Do I just sit here and be hit with the same baseball bat?"
I just don't know what to do!

Confused is what I am,
I'm afraid to get hit again.
Should I really take action like no man ever did?

Suddenly I thought up,
That I'm going to jump,
Jump out of my window and take my life into God's hands!

Jennifer Uchitel

Survival

I see - but can't be seen.
I speak - but can't be heard.
I seem to float with the tides
   and my cry is that of a weak bird.

I see the world through colored glass
   thus making everything gay.
But when I remove the glass
   the colors all fade away.

Is it because I'm me that I'm misunderstood?
Or is it because people fail to see the pains
   I've withstood?

Yes, I live in a world of fantasy,
   maybe because I can be me
   and speak aloud and be heard;
But in a world of reality
   is really where I want to be.

Dandy Ruth Cullins

Deliverance

Conceive my death, deliver my birth in illusion.
I speak of sin in the garden of life.
Tantalizing voices from my childhood are projected
through and through again.

For my heavenly dreams in which kept me living,
the suffering reality puts extinction to the creed
of my manhood, I shall now deliver my birth.

I race now and forever to my future to answer solidified
questions of the unknown. My world of power slumbers in the
back door of my unconscious state.

The day screams anger, and night speaks of deviance.

I slip away in the hollow forest of my own insanity.
Lets forgive my sins.

To answer life's questions is to race toward death, I find
myself creating my own shrine.

I am now ready...

Joshua Locantore

Heaven's Glory

Solitary pricks of light,
in the forest of the night,
come from the stars above.

In grisly silence they stand,
awaiting a signal from a foreign land;
A telegraph of the unknown.

The stars sing in the night
it roars through the heavens, it roars through as light.
It travels as clear as an empty voice.

I stand to wait for the harmony of fusion
I wait for god to sign his name in the confusion

The trees sway in an infinitely small amount of space,
they move with the beat, with a hint of a taste
a bit of chaos, a bite of physics

In the distance rock music sings loud and clear,
As I see the beauty of the universe, I reply with a tear.
And what have I got to fear?

I fear that time shall run out; the symphony must be completed!
Yet I still grow old, my destiny shall soon meet,
My life I have spent to study the stars...

Alexander W. Lee

Bad Dream

When I want to be left alone
I take the ringer off my phone

I start to sleep
And I start dreaming very deep

I hear myself screaming
And I know I'm only dreaming

I'm sweating all over the place
It looks as if my body was going to drown into a big space

My face feels really hot and turns red
I get really nervous and pull every hair out of my head

I start kicking all over the place
And I look like a disgrace

All of a sudden I wake up breathing heavily
I start looking around me, but I was the one there only

I didn't want to open the lights
Because I was scared to see the rest of the rights

Antonella D'Alessio

Too Many Tears

He has returned many times in my lifetime.
In 1938 He toured Europe, saw the coming horror, and cried.
In 1941 He visited Hawaii, faced the Rising Sun, and cried.
In 1945 He traveled to Japan, witnessed the release of energy, and cried.
In 1949 He surveyed the ruins of the world, watched the curtain come
   down, and cried.
In 1950 He stopped in Korea, looked at more carnage, and cried.
In 1954 He walked in Vietnam, knew 20 years of dead young men lay
   ahead, and cried.
In 1958 He sensed a world trying to heal and the people of the world
   wanting to reach back for innocence, so He prayed.
In 1961 He heard a man speak in Washington D.C. and challenge his
   fellow citizens to do "for their country." He saw a glimmer of
   hope and dared to smile.
In early 1963 He heard another man speak, again in Washington D.C.,
   this time of "a dream."
He saw another glimmer of hope and dared to smile again.
In late 1963 He heard shots, felt the pain of death in Dallas, and cried.
In 1968 He heard more shots, felt the pain of death twice, and cried.
He knows John, Martin, and Robert.
He has since visited Ireland; Eastern Europe; Eurasia; Angola; South
   Africa; North Africa; East Africa; South America; Central America;
   the Far East; the Middle East; the streets of New York; the streets
   of Los Angeles; the streets of Chicago; and He always cries. He has
   shed too many tears.
If He comes tomorrow, will He see a glimmer of hope, or will He cry
   again?

Harold J. Engel

Wild Horses

Deep in the glen today,
I saw a vision far away,
wild horses running.

Through the wildflowers and overgrown weeds,
gorgeous mares and magnificent steeds,
wild horses running.

Playing in this morning's rain,
violets entwined in their manes,
wild horses running.

Gallantly rearing with swaying tails,
hooves stamping out forbidden trails,
wild horses running,
running,
wild horses running wild.

Brenda Sue Freeman

Youth, Prepare Yourself

When my wrinkles appeared, and my hair started to grey,
I talked to myself by the end of the day.
The cost of living had soared sky high,
I wondered whether to laugh or cry.
No more children to demand my care,
Going to work came to mind, if I dare
So I thought I'd look for a job one day,
Hopped in my car, and was on my way,
When all of a sudden it entered my mind
What was I looking for— a job of what kind!
My thoughts went back to my younger years,
With no need to work, no worry or fears.
It was then in my teens, I should have planned
For a profession or job that may have been in demand,
Information was offered on different careers,
But I thought it would take just too many years.
I paid little attention to my elders advice,
Not realizing later in life I'd pay the price.
So don't hide away like some books on a shelf,
Look ahead now today, YOUTH, PREPARE YOURSELF.

Helen Miller

Magical Place

When I wake up in the night and it's very far from day,
I think about my magical place that's very far away.

It sits up very high, too high to even reach,
and it's bigger than any ocean, sea, gulf, or beach.

It holds over a trillion stars that stare you in the face,
and if you look up in the sky at night, you will see
my magical place.

Candace A. Doby

Just A Daydream

The ocean waves put me in a trance
I think; how would this world be if it was free?
No guns or bombs,
No such thing as war.
No starving children,
Prejudice and discrimination are no more.
Homeless have warm beds,
AIDS long since cured, healthy is the word.
Recycling a part of life,
Rain forests growing wild,
Smog and acid were unknown to man.
Drugs and violence, a thing long past.
Illiteracy is gone, education has class.
Life comes back into focus,
Daydreaming—a place to hide.

Bonnie Ishimoto

Goodbye

My father and two brothers help to raise
her coffin, crowned with glowing daffodils.
I step behind, eyes down. Alone bloom stays
where it has fallen, trace of death that fills
me with the knowledge of finality.
Allow me always to remember this
one moment—spot of spring on winter's grey—
and call to mind the grandmother I'll miss.
We'll know her body but a half-hour more—
so let us etch an image on our hearts
and add it to our memories: the shore;
its viaduct; her jam for tea—those thoughts
we took for granted as the years flew by,
unthinking, while she lived, that she must die.

L. Anne Emerson

Morning Thoughts

This morning in the brief moments before awareness,
    I thought of you.

When you step from the midst and know not which direction
you face.
    Think of me.

With the turmoil of the day upon me,
    I call on you.

When all else seems not so gentle to your soul,
    Call on me.

To sooth the stresses of my world,
    I need your touch

When you need that special touch to calm thyself,
    Hold me.

To fulfill the thirst from within,
    I want you.

To quest the thirst from within,
    I need you.

Joe Cordova

Winds Of Change

Waves crash and foam
I toss and turn
I reach out
but the tide takes you back
the moon with its usual soft, warm glow
looks odd tonight
you could call it cold
Crystal white sand that massages my feet
has the same feeling as the moon
strange and unresponsive
the sweet smelling breeze with a hint of salty mist
tugs, wildly at my hair and makes my clothes cling to me
unwantingly
The sand doesn't glow quite like it used to
the stars don't twinkle and form clear images of you
Your voice is far away
but yet you are right beside me
How could you betray me
When everything has turned to show its other side
Everything turns.

Jasmine Smith

To Mother

Before you cut it
I used to stand in the upstairs bathroom in front of
    that huge mirror
Watching you behind me dragging a metal comb
    through my hair.
You told me that when you were young
Your mother pulled your long hair into braids so tightly
You would cry.

There is no proof of your past.
I know because
I've searched those white painted drawers downstairs
Through piles of sticky coloured photographs.
The wedding album where you smile from the register
Is where you were born.

There is so much and so few words.
Ask me a question, or tell me,
How do you need me?
Your hair is short.
I sit on the floor in front of man after man-
While they run my red brush down my back.

Catherine Draycott

Dreams

I saw his silhouette, but his face was not yet clear
I tried to catch a glimpse, the closer he drew near
He reached out for my hand, and held it to his heart
He promised me a future in which we'd never part
He took my broken heart, and made it whole again
I sensed he'd be my lover, as well as my best friend
He held me close, and gently touched my face
He kissed me softly, as his presence began to fade
I felt him slip away from me, I begged him to stay
He whispered, "I'm your destiny, we'll meet again someday"
Time passed, men came and went
I began to wonder what that dream really meant
Then one day I saw a silhouette, and immediately I knew.
The face became clear, and I realized my dream was you.

Brandi Ellen Robinson

A Child Waiting

Whimpering, hush, quietly within my spirit
I tried to reach you.
Scenes of the future are flashed among our thoughts,
   a bonding, I am waiting.
Quietly, I am here, a glisten of hope
is flashed at that cloud of darkness.
   oh, how I see through this spidery web.
But you feel the shadowy image
   upon that glistening light.
How tiny I am, through the ages of my great past,
Our thoughts merge, as two streams rushing,
Searching for some end.
This breath of life is waiting, in due time, flickering.
A true wonderment now, capture my sense, my strength,
Hold this delicately. I am waiting, your fire is strong.
An endless glow. Engulf yourself within my energy,
Hush, continue your flow of life, as my glow fades, whimpering,
   I wait no more.

Cheri Allyse Xaver

Untitled

As I stepped out into the night, the clouds began to grow dark
I was overwhelmed with the power of the awesome storm to come
Then suddenly it happened
The lightning began to signal, the thunder called my name
And each drop of rain was a memory washing over me

Each house I walked past brought forth another picture
A scene from my past
The people and the places that made me who I am
And as the rain continued falling down it washed away my fears
Along with all the pain, building up across the years

When I finally arrived back home
And took off my wet clothes
I couldn't help but notice
The blood and tears staining the shirt
The symbolism was clear
I had made another step in becoming who I am

Jeff Rader

Mom

I can be anything, I can do anything.
I was taught well.
Believing in me; that love, beautiful and pure.

Reaching out to me, guiding me along my way.
Here I stand, no longer a child
But the woman you helped create, strong and beautiful.
Now, I can be anything, I can do anything.
I was taught well.

Bernadette Degnan

All Alone

As I sit on the deserted beach,
I watch the sea gulls flying overhead.
The waves crashing on the shore,
Send a wave of tranquility through my soul.
I think about all the problems I have,
But the sunshine and peacefulness seem to wash it all away.
Somewhat like the sand on the beach,
Being pulled into the sea of blue.
I see myself sitting there on the shore,
And I close my eyes to dream.

Heather Hughes

The Goof Troop

Down in Virginia, one beautiful fall eve
   I went along "for the ride"
We climbed into this little white cart
   started out with a jolt, then quick as a dart
Over hill and vale we rode, then
   just as quickly we came to a stop
Looking for the little white ball
   Only to "hit it" again
And the process "kept going and going and going"
   I became one of the "Goof Troop" in name only
Remember, "I was just along for the ride"
   My better half being one of them
Me, I just felt kind of silly
   Kind of like "Betty Boop" it was fun! or funny!
Couldn't believe all this
   Just for one "little white ball"
Now, when my partner of 50 years
   Says he's going golfing
Just can't help but get a silly little grin
Goodbye, Good luck, "boop Boop A Doop"

Jenny Frantz

Playmate Of My Youth

Playmate of my youth
I went back to revisit our 'oki'
To dance the dance we used to dance together
it's no longer the same

Why is it nobody told me
Many footprints have marked the path after mine?
As I crossed the bridge back
My footprints of today did not match those of yesterday
it's no longer the same

As I stood there
In the middle of our empty playground
I knew I had come to lay your ghost
O playmate of my youth
Let me rest now
Free to dream other dreams
And choose other playmates as I go along

Bosede O. Aworuwa

The Broken Heart

Please excuse this letter;
I know we said we're through,
But you have taken something with you
that I need back.
Make sure to wrap it carefully but before
you do, put a piece of tape on the crack,
Because when I saw you taking her in your
arms,
You broke my heart

Cori Brantley

Colours

We aren't different I try to say
I wish people would try to see it my way
Sure one might have a better tan
But when it comes to the end we are all one man
I don't see why people chose to hate
Maybe it's just because of fate
It just doesn't make sense to me
Why it's the way it has to be
No matter what I do or say it won't change their minds
at least not this day
One might be lighter than the other
But we are all sisters and brothers
Sure we are all from a different place
But when it comes to the end we are all one race: MANKIND
I think I got my point across
I hope it changed your mind, but if I didn't
it's your loss

Cassandra Hoitink

There Is Joy And Beauty

Happy Birthday, wherever you maybe.
I wish you could celebrate your day with me.
I miss you so much as days go by.
My tears for you I can't deny.
Your birthday will not be the same.
Because you are not here.
On my heart and in my mind.
I'll always hold you near.

You're not gone, as long as I can remember you
She is in heaven dear niece.
Oh, so happy and bright.
There is joy and beauty in this everlasting light.

All the restless tossing passed.
She is now at peace forever.
Safely home in Heaven at last.
Then we must not grieve so sorely.

For she loves us dearly still.
Try to look beyond earth's shadows.
Pray to trust our Father's will.
May you find peace and love with Jesus.

Evelyn T. Tallman

Untitled

I am an African American
I wonder about people I do not know.
I hear about people dying every day. I see people hurting every day.
I want to see people in Somalia have food.
I am an African American.

I pretend I don't hear about people dying.
I feel that people in Somalia should have the food that they
 need because too many are dying every day.
I touch books about people in Somalia because I want to know
 how their life is compared to mine.
I worry about the people in Somalia because they should have
 all the food they need.
I cry when I hear about people dying every day on the T.V. or on
 the radio; it is very sad. I am an African American.

I understand that people in Somalia are dying every day.
I see people using drugs every day.
I dream that one day all people in Somalia will have all that they
 need.
I try not to waste my food, because I could give it to the homeless.
I hope to make a plan so that you can send food to Somalia.
I am an African American.

Aaron Brown (8 years old)

Clutter

Clutter and trash, my house is a mess
I wonder if ever I will clean this mess.
It seems the more I try
The harder it is for me to get by.
Picking up pieces is the name of the game
I feel sometimes I will go insane
Just trying to wiggle out of this silly game.
And trying to live in a quiet domain.
Then I stopped and took a look around,
And saw why I wasn't on solid ground.
I had let the clutter hide my view,
And therefore blinded my eyes from the new.
Sometimes our lives are cluttered up
with trashy things that always crop up.
If only we can learn to keep our view
On the Lord who made us and can make life new.

Bernice Holmes

I Am

I am a nice guy who fears being alone in the dark.
I wonder if my grandparents can see me from heaven.
I hear the sirens flying down the road.
I want everything to be like it was when I was 3—simple and safe.
I am a nice guy who fears being alone in the dark.

I pretend I can fly above the teachers and their assignments.
I feel at peace with the sky.
I touch the clouds and think how wonderful it is to be away from
 the violence and hate below.
I worry I will have to come down sooner or later, back to the
 guns and drugs and death.
I cry when no one cares that kids end their precious lives.
I am a nice guy who fears being alone in the dark.

I understand people think suicide is a way out.
I say it is a long term solution to a short term problem.
I dream of a world free from the darkness of hate and prejudice.
I try to make my dream a reality.
I hope others feel the same way, so I am not alone in my quest
 for freedom.
I am a nice guy who fears being alone in the dark.

Christopher R. Price

The End

The night was just beginning to close, as I stood beneath the stars.
I wondered, then asked, "oh God how far,
Did you stretch the north from the south and the east from the
 west."
God, you know the answer, but it is only my guess.
A cool spring breeze brushes my hair, as I stand alone again.
Beneath the heavens, the moon, and the stars, I ponder the question
 again.
To the beautiful creation that the creator created and spoke to a few
 good men.
How far do I walk and how far do I see and how far is life's next
 bend?
I stand beneath a universe that puzzles the minds of all.
My heart is open, my soul searches, I listen for my call.
That we are many, but mini are we, in this small place we live,
And there is an end to our physical life, but our love is forever
 to be.
I understand now that love is the reason we win our eternal home.
For he gave us his love and we will go home never more to roam.

Cindy D. Rogers

Word Of Encouragements If I Could Fly Like A Bird

If I could fly like a bird,
I would fly from one place to another.
Sharing, the blessing God gave, to me,
With all of my sisters and brothers.

If I could fly like a bird,
I would not waste any time,
I would fly all over this world,
Telling every one about the joy I found.

If I could fly like a bird,
I would fly away somewhere,
And when I came down to earth
I would tell everyone that Jesus does Care.

If I could fly like a bird,
I would never be alone.
I would fly, and fly and fly,
Each day I would have a brand new home.

If I could fly like a bird,
I would fly away so far,
I would fly so high, up in the sky,
Being led by the spirit of God.

Goldie Cofield

Dedicate, To Mom C/O Heaven

If, I had one more chance.
I would listen (different)
when, you cried
I would hug you
As many times you needed.
Your last, note, you wrote
sorry forgive.
"I cant take it anymore"
If, I had one more chance.
My hours and, days I thought was important.
Would now
Hear, your pain of loneliness (I miss you, she says.)
If, I had one more chance.
I would tell you
"I love you", I'm sorry!
I now, understand her words, "I miss you."

Barbara Ann Soltan

Hail

Hail plummets to earth
Icy crystals penetrate the stagnant water
As the hail sinks to the bottom of the pond
it tells the story of the sky
and shrinks
and shrinks.
A raven drinks from the dark green pool,
intimidated by the icy splinters
he flies away.

Justin Leith

Nightmare

Two years old standing by the door
  In my rags of a dress looking oh so poor
A rocking chair moving by itself
  Books shaking on the rusted shelf
I ran into the room a little bit further
  And fell into the arms of my own dear mother
After a lynching she has a rope around her neck
  On my dead mother's cheek I give her a peck
This is a NIGHTMARE that Harriet Tubman had
  And when she tells it, it is so sad

Francine Anderson

My Wife - My Life - My Valentine

So many times I have heard it said
If a man finds a wife he truly is Blessed!
A companion & friend to share his whole life,
To be there forever, through wrong and through right!
When the load is light and everything's great,
And when it's so heavy there seems no escape;
When the sky turns black and the storm rages wild,
She can make the sun shine with just a sweet smile;
Just How, When, or Where may not be clear,
But Her Love is the Conqueror and there's no need to fear!
She stands in the shadows so that I may shine;
Always assuring she'll be there for all time.
These words I have written, they're Just, True, and So!
I do Love my Valentine and I want her to know
From the depths of my being and just not for show!
Whether there's Twelve or just One She truly deserves

The Rose

The One I Look Up To

There is one person in my life who has always been there,
If no one else does, I know he will always care.

He would always help me up if I fell,
And no matter what I did wrong he would never tell.

He has helped me through a lot these past years,
He was the one who could always get rid of my fears.

Ever since we were kids we've always been close in the heart,
and we still are even though we're miles apart.

If anyone ever tried to hurt me all I need to do is tell him,
And he would be on his way home before I could count to ten.

He has always been the one I look up to, for there is no other,
and I must say this hero of mine is my Big Brother.

Christy Lee

Untitled

Where can I find a winner
if not on bended knee.
Where I can find a winner
if not true to thee. (Father)
A winner's one who's gonna make it thru'.
Whatever the world's gonna throw at you.
A winner is one who's got the right stuff
Includin' the one whom he knows. (The right one)
Where can I find a winner
if not on bended knee.
Where I can find a winner
if not true to thee. (Father)
A winner is one who's humbly true
When the world says that's only for a fool.
A winner is one who's got the right stuff
Includin' the one whom he knows. (The right one)
Will you be found a winner,
Spendin' time on bended knee?
Will you be found a winner,
Being wholly true to thee? (Father)

Andrew Swan

The Orange Trees

The orange trees stand stiff, at attention;
In neat rows, side by side.
Standing proud among their kind,
To bear their fruit in a blazing sun,
To be ripened and picked,
  one by one.
Left naked, the orange trees stand
  and wait for new ideas.

Henry Hammond

When I Give My Heart To You

You asked me once "Why do you love me?"
If one could count every grain of sand on the beach,
Then I would list all the reasons there are for loving you.
For like a house, love is built up little by little
From each second, each minute that we spent together.
Be it a quarrel, a laugh or a tear,
They are all the building blocks in our construction.
A tender smile, a softened expression in your eyes
Serve to make the window of the heart.
For each night of passion that we've shared,
We've added a new brick to erect a fireplace
Which will keep us warm whenever winter comes.

I believe I have found in you a very special friend
Who will come only once in a lifetime,
Who believes in me when everyone else turns away.
Somehow, I know you truly care for me
Despite our many differences
And you would fight your best to keep our love alive
—the most important reason
For why you mean so much to me!

Anne P. Pham

My Faith In You

I'll cry for you, Child of Mercy.
I'll hold your hand, Child of Pain.
You are the tears of a broken heart.
You are the laughter in the joy of a friend.
You are the light, who is unafraid at night.

Give me hope that the world won't die in shame.
Give me memories that won't fade in the rain.
Give me dreams that last forever.
Give me love that runs with the seasons.

Bring me to you and I'll never leave.
It's the beliefs that lead me to follow.
So I'll stay until last day of tomorrow.

It is you, who makes it all.
It is you, who always falls.
So, hold onto the hand of this real life.

Jennifer Payne

I Wonder

I wonder.
I'm 52 years old today, and I wonder.
I wonder what my mother felt at 52. She
    is many years gone now - I'll never know.
I wonder what other women have felt at 52.
I think of my children - their trials, tribulations,
    fears, hopes, dreams, concerns;
I wonder - do other mothers wonder?
I wonder if other mothers sit up into the
    wee hours of the morning playing solitaire
    and drinking.
I wonder how many there are of us who
    wonder what our potential might have
    been or could be?
I wonder if circumstances had been
    different would I have been a better
    mother?
I wonder, as I sit here in my new and
    lucky life, why I wonder.

Cheré Boget-Schrock

Untitled

Thank God for rabbits
I'm a little white rabbit with pink eye,
    I can't see
I have a little pink nose
    But I can't smell
My ears are long and straight
    But I can't hear
I have four feet
    But I can't run or hop
I have a mouth with whiskers
    But can't talk or speak
But with this mouth and face I can smile for you
    Even God gives the rabbit a smile
        Though - stuffed rabbit
            Smile on his face
Inspired by God

Carl Leo Bliss

Friends

Sometimes I'm happy, and other times
I'm blue, but the thoughts I have I share
with you. Some people hold their thoughts
inside creating confusion and conflicts
on the outside. We speak our minds you and
I, for there's nothing to be afraid of or
feel shy.

The things we say are with concern;
even though, they are out of turn, because
when we stop we'll lose a lot, not just
tears but all the years.

So if you intend to be my friend, we
we must share our thoughts and try to
blend, for you are a woman and I'm a man;
we knew nothing of each other; we just became lovers.

It's sad to say that dreams can just
vanish and pass away, but dreams can die
and people can lie when the road gets
crooked and starts to bend, but never you
fear, for I am your FRIEND.

Albert B. D. Saffold

Great Lady

Lord willing, I'll be back, I'll return to you.
I'm paying for the separation with my great sorrow.
I only live to love God and you.

All alone and sad, I'm walking the dark nights;
with an orchid in my tuxedo lapel and my golden
cane at my side.

When I return to you, I'll say: Here I am!
Drive me mad, drive me crazy but please, tell me
'I love you.'

Don't care anymore about the past.
You will see on my face not raindrops,
but true tears.

If you smile, I'll smile with you.
If you cry, I'll cry with you.
If you die, I'll be with you where you lie and we will
fly together in the sky.

One of the real great things of my odd life is...Thou!

Joe Rell

From Gibran To Selma

My love, we're one.
I'm similar to the sky,
And you're like the sun,
We shouldn't be in fear or shy,
Because people are equivalent to clouds
Sooner or later they will pass us by.
But their human nature may darken our world,
And cause us to cry,
Because they can fill our hearts with pain.
But it will enrich our love,
Like the earth is enriched by the rain.

Even if we are a ten thousand miles apart
Your love will still shine within my heart.

Let our spirit be our guide,
And remind each other,
To put our human nature on the side...

Gibran Joe Elia

"Hello Chicago Hello"

Here I come an adventurous one!
I'm your rambling son of a gun,
Hello Chicago hello!
Had my fun now I'm done,
Welcome home your native son,
Hello Chicago hello!
Seen Iowa, Nebraska, Dakota too,
Wyoming, Montana, every thing from range to zoo!
Mountains high, valleys low,
Excuse my dust, for here I go,
Hello Chicago hello!

Henry E. Jacobsen

Why I Feed The Birds

When I was eight, on a bitter cold day I sat bundled up
in a fuzzy warm wrap, nursing a sore throat and runny nose,
in our dining room bay;
Watching the feathered population of the neighborhood
feasting on the crumb strewn snow.

Feelings of being sad and blue, of missing school activity, and friends
faded into a simple world of security and caring love;
as I was drawn into a fascinating world of serenity, and peace,
a pure and simple place created by the loving act of concern
and generosity of my mother's hand, in lying out their meal

For a brief moment I joined their world of fluttering excitement,
and experienced the same joy felt in those tiny hearts,
In the coldest hour of this winter day, a door had opened,
a meal appeared, today they survive.
There was hope for tomorrow!

Eileen Matthews

Untitled

I saw an old lady today.
I saw a swan,
pushing her cart
hurrying through the marketplace.
She had on her mental shopping list
stealing to taste the tiny grapes.
Her delicate hands weighted down
with opal age,
softly touching the tedious shelves.
Penciled eyebrow raised in cautious inspection
she was standing on her toes,
her little silken feet half in
half out of her orthopedic shoes.

Jennifer McDowell

A Land I Don't Remember

In a land I don't remember, I can't find my way
In a land I do remember, where I hope to stay
Someday I will return, to the land I don't remember
Who knows, maybe it will be my spirit
When I finally surrender.

If I return to that land, will I be received
Or will it be that I'm turned away
Because of what I believe
When that time comes, as it will for all
A journey into the unknown
Be sure you're not deceived, on your journey home

At my journey's end, will I find the gate open or a jar
Will I be invited in, for I have traveled far
Or will I be turned away, with politeness and splendor
Because I came from a land, I don't remember.

David E. Chandler

Christmas 1994

I ponder now, what words were spared
In all the Christmas poems I've shared?
But time moves on and now, once more
It's Christmas nineteen ninety four!
It's time for reverence and for joy
For adoration of Mary's boy,
Born in a manger, son of our Lord,
Shepherds and wise men carried the word.
The legend speaks how a star back then
Illumined the skies over Bethlehem.

Tonight as we dream of our own Christmas trees,
Of angels and stars and of old memories,
Of other young faces and other times,
Of future friends and different rhymes,
Rejoice and remember for Christmas is near,
The garland of kindness that lasts through the year.

Florence Baeder

I Can But Praise Your Name

In this time all I can do is but praise Your Name
In all Your honor and glory,
You have blessed my life and saved my soul from Hell.

All that does happen Lord, I pray, keep me pure,
And help me to know that in my pain,
I can but praise Your Name.

The people round me stand and in ridicule they say,
"That is not what you want to be," but Lord,
I can but praise Your name.

Help me Lord, to live my life for You,
And amidst all the suffering,
May I but praise Your Name.

Brian Curtis

Beginning Of A Moment In Time

In times of past nothing really did last
In moments of silence which go by fast
Sounds of things in your heart
Make believe the world apart
Second after second time passes by
You loose track of truth and lie
Whispering thoughts as things are said
You speak out and things become dead
The ending is close
Yet far ahead...
Is a beginning of a moment in time instead

Alex Szeto

The Gardener

I have a garden, and guess where it grows?
In neither yard nor window sill, so where do you suppose
I grow this garden of things not green?
This cornucopia of feelings—of thoughts that mean
So much to the gardener, who happens to be me.

Well, my garden grows in the loved ones in my heart
It is filled with roses of joy and right from my start
The seeds lay in wait for the fruits it would bear
They took root and grew-from those seeds so few.

And did I even mention the fact that I, too,
was in awe of the bounty my garden did yield.
I was humbled by the miracle-my heart truly filled
With a love that knows no limits; a love that knows no bounds
A love that can expand-can speak without sounds.

So when I look at my garden, I'm filled with emotion
I'm shaken by the thought that I never had the notion
Of having a "green thumb", would I dare to dream? I cultivated with
the basics or so it would seem. Love and humility are in abundance
there. But my garden, precious garden, no fruit would it bear
without the help He gave the gardener, who happens to be me.

Celestine J. Patterson

"Forever Friends"

Dedicated to Mike Jordan - mentor and friend
Friendship is something that cannot be measured
  in spans of time or miles;

Rather, a good start would be to consider the moments
  of sadness and smiles.

A friend is someone you cannot reject when an honest
  request has been made;

It's someone who really cares enough to "take time"
  without being paid.

Taking time to speak, or listen; or simply
  taking time to "be there".....

When a friend does this, there should be no doubt that
  your friendship is sincere.

"PREDESTINED WEAVING" is how, I believe, that
  true friends are brought together.

And once as established as friends through God,
  you truly are friends forever.

Joe Ranieli

Sea Tryst

They dipped their feet in the ebbing tide
In that golden day;
And the wide sea drenched the Young Bride
With its salt-tanged spray;
And grey gulls in the green mist
With many a wide-winged gulve;
Watched the young Bride being kissed
By the young man in love
O, the young man loved.
And his love was strong.
And the sun and the spray.
And the breakers wild
Watched their golden bodies drink in the sun.
Locked together as one.
On the silvery seaside
And the young man and the young Bride
And the Sandpipers and the sea.
All together as one,
Danced in ecstasy.

Daniel F. Downey

Real Or Surreal?

Deep within this well—my mind ponders— how I happen—to wander
In the deepest—darkest—recess—of my mind.....dwells misery...
Cobwebs—entangle—long sinewy—arms—into a intricate design.
They make me question "am I losing my mind?" The darkness creeps
Around me seeking a refuge the delusion starts slowly at first
Real or Surreal? Who knows? My mind flees back in time, flashes of
Pictures, no longer mine. I push them away, but back they come...
I must turn and face them....My breathing comes deep as if asleep..
Surreptitiously I peer to see who waits—the darkness surrounds--
Enveloping my thinking—I open my eyes without even blinking. I lay
Quite still (a child of five) pulling myself—against the wall
Trying to escape his unnatural embrace. Standing over me I feel...
Barely alive. His mouth is slack, his eyes glazed over..breath that
Is foul from too much liquor—staggering—swaying—unsteadily—
He comes—the drool—from his mouth—across his face.
I try to flee from his groping embrace, he reels and turns
As something stirs—lucky for me it was one of the boys—I scamper
From the old wooden bed-grab a blanket—race for the door
Make a pallet for sleeping on the bathroom floor
Able to evade him once more.

Gloria J. Marshall

In The Forest

In the forest there are lots of trees,
In the forest there is a cool breeze.
In the forest there are monkeys and apes,
Who eat leaves, insects, and grapes.
In the forest there are animals with feathers,
Who leave in certain kinds of weathers.
In the forest there are no cars,
When all of a sudden out of thin air,
People killed all the animals with no care.

Jodie T. Rowland

Going Home Again

She just stood there feeling all alone,
In the middle of the old big train station,
wondering which way she should go,
As she waited for a train bound for nowhere.
She looked at all the different people,
With some place to go that frosty Christmas eve.
She wondered what her family back home was doing;
Especially if they ever missed and thought of her,
As she held back the lonely tears.
She had run away from home over a decade ago,
When her family disowned her after a silly fight-
And told her to leave and never come back.
She thought of the old saying she had heard-
About how time heals all wounds-
And wondered if it could be true.
She decided to board a train back home,
And find out if it could be true once and for all.
She and her family hugged, kissed and cried,
As she was forgiven and welcomed by all
That Christmas day, with open arms by all.

Donna Beamesderfer

In Memory Of Muggsie Kelly

Close to the fence of Harvard Yard
Is a monument to John "Muggsie" Kelly.
The bas-relief shows a rugged man,
Good-looking man, in a Perini hard hat.
The inscription says
That in the construction of Harvard Square Station
Muggsie Kelly gave his life.

Fidelma Conway

Distant Desires

Caught up
In the mundane necessities of getting through,
Sidetracked from want to by need to,
A beleaguered wayfarer
Sadly aware of all the moments devoured,
Charting a sure course through demands
While eying distant desires.

Wrapped up, swathed in the fabric of commitments
Layered in the uniforms of overlapping roles
With only rare, spare moments
To puzzle over, evaluate and bemoan
A kaleidoscope of demands
While eyeing distant desires.

Taken up, trapped by time in my times,
In days and years that disappear
Without the benediction of reflection,
Too often unable to stop
And see the colors parading past my window,
Spending a lifetime on demands
While eyeing distant desires.

Bonnie Connelly

When You Left

Happiness was all around;
In the sky and on the ground.
But then you took it all away,
When you said you could not stay.
You went far away from home,
And left me here all alone.

On that day that you died,
People watched while I cried.
No one cared how I felt,
In my heart I just wanted to melt.
Up to heaven is where you were sent.
Along with you is where my happiness went.

Maybe I'll find someone new,
But no one quite like you.
You touched my heart,
And said we'd never part.
I guess you were right about that one goal,
Because you still live here in my soul.

Elizabeth Braun

Emmanuel

Come, Lord Jesus, come,
In all of our blessed seasons.
For you - O holy one - are the reason
That we are borne - on any of your given morn.
To know you - to love you - to serve you,
You - who came to man in baby flesh.

Rejoice, O mankind, sing your Alleluias,
Hosannah in the highest!
Your savior is near - is here, in you - in me - in us,
To live in us - through us - with us,
Incarnate!
To each our Emmanuel - God with us.

Unbind and open the Jesus gift within you.
Embrace and welcome the Christ-child born anew again.
Then go - and gift yourselves to one another bind,
In your epiphany of peace, joy, hope and love - to all mankind!

Genuflect - bow down - to him, your Christ of glory!
Genuflect - bow down - to one another, little Christs of glory!

And please, dear Jesus, grant peace on earth and in our homes,
Good will to all wherever we roam! Amen!

Helen Pieper

Lonely

Here I lie
In the stillness of night

Only one heart beat
In the shadow of light

The table in set for only one
Just one cup of coffee, when up comes the sun

Half an empty closet
No ties, shirts, or pants

The house seems so big now
It used to be so small and crowded

The lawn is growing in silence
We used to mow, trim, and grow violets

You were once there as we did dishes
You would joke, tease, even steal kisses

How can you forget all this
I thought we had it all

Now you live a different life
You say you just don't need a wife

Now here I lie all crushed and broken hearted
As the tears flow, figure out how we parted.

Ann Waters

Forever In Every Rainbow

Together we have been before you became one....
    in the warmth of my womb
I was there with you as through the narrow passage...
    of birth you emerged

Many times I have held you as a child and been able....
    to love away your fears
Whenever you came to me laughing with silly boyish pranks....
    you'd repay that love

Memories so precious we have over the years....
    watching you grow into awareness of life
Facing life's challenges as an adult..at such a young age....
    you matured and became your own person

That aura of love that is now and forever with us....
    guaranteed by One who created all
Permeates our souls and heals our pain to remind us....
    nothing will separate us forever not even death

Have I ever told you how proud I am....
    and always will be to be your mother
You have shown me how very much you love me....
    it glows forever in every rainbow

Cherie Gamler

Untitled

Go out and do something for someone else,
If you don't know what to do,
Do it for someone in need,
Then you'll feel happy too.
If you feel the coming of a nervous breakdown,
Lock up the house,
Walk across town,
Find one that needs aid,
Give some help,
And don't be afraid.
If you need the feeling of love,
Or the feeling of peace,
Do something for someone else,
And these feelings will release.

Jill Schulte

Teacher

Can I make a difference
In these angelic lives?
So many hurdles to bound...
Pressures to endure...
Ignorance to eradicate...
Overwhelming realities to face...
    Molestation; abuse,
      Drugs; gang violence,
        Lost values; morals; low self-esteem,
          Broken homes; poverty, latch-key era,
Young lives, wise beyond their years; in unnatural ways,
Robbed of childhood; Yet Still...
    Energetic; eager...
      Anxious to please...
        Starving for direction; structure, validation,
          Full of love...
I can and must embrace those novice minds
If but one seed is planted,
Then GOD is magnified!
        Dorothy W. Givens

How Fleet Is Time

How fleet is time
In this walk of Life
How measured, how unreal
How precious, unpredictable
How brief, yet one we deeply feel.

Do we recognize just how to deal
How to seize each moment's message...
Is there a sense of endless time
Is there justice given each moment that we find...
Is there a moment of reflection
A time to redefine?

One's wealth, earned in daily living
One's Love, given freely to each one
One's time, quietly, lovingly rendered and yes,
How fleet is time
In our quest for one more day
Giving and receiving
Embracing, loving
Just one more day of fleeting time.

        Jeanie L. Berlin

Wisp

A Wisp of joy runs through our lives lifting our spirits with innocence.
The old place lacks heart when the Wisp is not here, so we work, and we think, we grow tired.
She holds our hearts in her tiny hands, we live for the next time she's near.

Each day seems endless without her.
We go through the motions of mundane pleasure, and wait for a glimpse of the Wisp again.
Each little smile, a pleading hug, is a much too fleeting treasure.

The Wisp has to leave when she's only just come.
The look of despair on the face of an angel
makes my heart ache to console.
Someday she'll know she can stay for a time, but to the Wisp, just now, we can't tell.

We wave goodbye to the confused little Wisp,
the tears we can never show,
for if we did this to the Wisp today, her tomorrows might be sad.
So we smile, and we wave, as she fades out of sight, as she catches the kiss that we blow.

Again it is quiet, our footsteps echo, the house somehow feels cold.
As we wait again for the Wisp to arrive and lift our hearts with love,
We work, and we think, we grow old......

        Elaine Bushman

Sorrowful Secretary

I told him it's time to pay the quarterlies.
Instead he spent it on unnecessary luxuries.
If only he'd taken my advice,
I wouldn't need to keep the creditors and the IRS on ice.
My boss is sweet and kind and pretty old.
If only he was worth his weight in gold.
He spends his money more naively than irresponsibly - I reckon.
At 72 he should be retired and not struggling to pay his 2nd.
It's a family business, I guess I don't really matter.
But I've felt like family, which makes my 2-weeks notice
    all the sadder.
Previously I cut back my hours so he could pay the guys.
Then his son hired another girl and that really wet my eyes.
I couldn't increase my hours even when I needed to with things
    this way.
And now I've got an even bigger mess to sort and only on Tuesday.
The sexual harassment by his son was a constant emotional drain.
No wonder I seem to have an incurable Migraine.
The business is a sinking ship that somehow stays afloat.
I'm worried that I'm the last plug holding up the boat.
I'm walking the plank, ready to depart this one time wonderful craft.
There's comfort in that I can see my real family launching a raft.

        Frank J. Herrera

To Those We Hold Dear To Our Heart

The sun comes up and the winds they blow
Into our lives the many faces we know.

Some just pass by, others stay for a while.
Some stand by you to the very last mile.

Some are always full of laughter and good times,
Bringing others joy and blessing their lives.

Some when they're gone we simply forget.
They leave no one with feelings of regret.

But some touch our lives in such a wonderful way,
Many hearts fill with sorrow when they must go away.

Though you have decided it is time to move on,
You will remain in our hearts, where you belong.

        Janet R. Williams

Elevated Love

He boards the Southbound train
Into the city every morning.
She departs on the Northbound
At about the same hour.
In a delay, their trains reach an intersection and
Come to an unexpected and jarring halt.
Their eyes coincidentally lock
In a chance meeting somewhere
Between their respective destinations.
Two lonely souls find communion
In that single, fateful moment.
The trains resume their courses
And she looks away, he on.

        Christopher S. Carter

Crystal Forest

A snow storm came during the night.
It left the fields and woods covered.
Sparkling white.

The view as far as the eye could see an
immense glistening fantasy.
Every twig, branch and blade of grass
Was encased and bent in an icy grasp.
In awe I beheld this ethereal beauty.
Until the sun came and melted the Crystal Forest.

        Goldie Hall

The Footsteps Of Departure

The moon flickers the start of an evening. I run and run
into the dark of the night. The constellations are now very
different compared with the stars at the turn of the century.
When musical notes were turning blue.

I hide beside the garbage vendors, with the fear if I am
seen I will be locked up in some white room. The jet-engine
beetles roam the streets, and rockets and shuttle-crafts journey
into space.

I dash from backyards over fences and across the huge six
lane roadways. And reaching the harbor-fronts, sounds of trumpets
and saxophones echo from a sailboat as old as a ten-speed bicycle.

I climb onto the boat and proceed into the cabin, where
before my eyes, the captain and his crew say to me "welcome
aboard."

And in the dark of the night, we sail under the
Milky Way into the emptiness of a sea of stars.

Howard T. Chen

My Reflection Of Pain

I look in the mirror and all I see
Is a meaningless nothing looking back at me,
Lips of blue gasp for air.
Awaiting help yet no one there.
This creature I think not to be.
Stares so coldly down at me.
I whisper and ask, "Who might you be?"
She quietly replies, "Don't you recognize me?"
I stare right back as harsh as she.
Yet freezing cold bites back at me,
"My life is made up of meaningless lies!"
She said so coldly with hate in her eyes,
Her eyes so dark and skin so pale,
Her lips so dry and bones so frail!
"Look at me close, forget not what you see!"
She had said so harsh yet quietly,
I looked much closer and could finally see,
That this dying creature could be only me....

Erika M. Dozal

Receiving Life Everlasting

Many a day in things I have thought about in my life,
Is what will happen after all my toils and strife.
In the past, money and education were at the top of my list,
for what I would strive for, I thought had I lacked and missed.

I was lost and tired, but for whom was I living?
My life was worldly and my heart was sore.
What or whom did I need, what or whom had I lacked?
Then all of a sudden the HOLY SPIRIT hit me with a fact.

One thing had I lacked had I needed in my life and in my heart,
It was the LORD and SAVIOR JESUS CHRIST who I needed from
the start.
So I believe on the LORD and SAVIOR JESUS CHRIST and
confessed my sin,
And in the next moment, my life and heart JESUS CHRIST was in.

On that day when we meet the CREATOR, opened are many a book
They have recorded what we have done in every cranny and nook,
One thing which would be incomparable and excellent in we have
done, in the whole hoard,
That we, on earth have accepted JESUS CHRIST as our PER-
SONAL SAVIOR and LORD.

So make the decision today and not tomorrow
Or at the end will there be much grief and sorrow,
So accept JESUS CHRIST as your LORD and SAVIOR and
therefore have your future set,
to be in heaven, it will be a glorious day,
and so your decision to accept CHRIST you will never regret.

Edward Tsai

Seniors

A retirement home for the old they say
Is all the go for seniors today.
So we went, we saw and decided to stay.
Now we're settled here, I'd like to say.
It's not the home we've known for years
But yet, it's a home that calms our fears.
We have our meals, and we feel real sure
At night when we sleep we'll be secure.
Our neighbors, we see them come and go,
Some quite active, some quite slow.
We know them in a different way,
Never real close, 'cause they'll leave one day.
It reminds me of our army days
When army friends were sent their ways.
We didn't know and neither did they,
So we'd, joke about it, yet never say,
But finally, all seniors get their orders too
From the one who watches o'er me and you.
We continue to share our joys and sorrows,
And together we live for our tomorrows.

Barney M. Davis

A Waterfall

A waterfall of crystal blue,
Is beautiful for the eyes to view.
It's swift and sparkling in the daylight,
And it's cold and mysterious at midnight.

Show a friend so they too will know
That the sun is its glitter, and the moon is its glow.
So it makes no difference if it's day or night,
You'll always remember it as an amazing sight.

Gina Anderson

"My Cross"

I know dear Jesus this cross that I bear,
is far lighter than the cross you carried and also did wear.
But I find my limbs now tremble from this new added weight,
and my heart cries out in fear "What is my fate?"
I always thought my faith was strong and larger than any small seed,
and I would never have to reach out to touch your sleeve.
So I am angry with myself for lost faith I thought was mine,
for now I see a lamb who seeks yet does not find.
I'm not asking, Lord, for answers to all the "how comes" and "why's,"
I'm asking for your help to strengthen our bond and ties.
For I should not be tumbling in this sea of turmoil,
but standing firm on Your Word, as a tree in good soil.
Yet, where are all my glories and rights,
that are to protect and comfort me through long shadowed nights?
Or, am I seeking more than your love that set all mankind free,
and with this added burden I cease to see?

Gail A. Clough

Young Love

What is young love?
Is it foolish?
Is it not really love —
but merely a childish game.

Even though love may start young,
it could grow into an older love.
A truly special love;
a love that really counts in this game.

Young love could be a passing experience.
Yet, it could blossom into an everlasting love.
There are so very many people playing this game.
Do you want to chance your young love on one player?
Or perhaps, experience and learn about love from many players.
You may still have many chances in the game while you're young.

Chrissy Reato

Your Daughter, Your Friend

For Kendra, my daughter, my friend.
When does your daughter become your friend?
Is it when she sits on your knee bouncing and laughing?
Or is it when you pick her up from her nap
and she hugs and pats "you" on the back?
Maybe it's when you first sing together,
"Jesus loves me?"
Is it when she waves good-bye to you
on her first day of school?
Or is it the day she learns to cook her first meal?
Maybe it's when she hugs you in the morning
with sleepy eyes and says "I love you?"
Is it when you have breakfast together,
on the way home from a piano lesson?
Or is it when you go shopping together
and buy a top to share?
Maybe it's when she wants your clothes
because they "like it better in her closet?"
Is it when she comes home from college
and says, "I want you for a friend?"
When does your daughter become your friend?

Bonnie Shultzman

Oedipus

An infant: you begin to grow, but your path
is marked by whispers of unheard streams. An
announcement carried through the darkness of
the past creates a gateway into the mouth of
knowledge.

Driven back by unknown hands into the
blackness from which you just emerged: a
danger to your self and your creator. Pity
kept you from the darkest grave and placed
you on the rope of crucifixion. Ascending
into heaven is the weakness of the twelfth sign.

Traveling down the path of revelation you
encounter a fragment of your being. Rage now
awakened by the hand destroys the origin.
The clouds begin to move in force; the scene
witnessed by closed eyes begins its second
performance in the light.

Elvira Ceja Oseguera

Most Obscene Thing

The most obscene thing I've ever seen
is not a naked body in Playgirl or Playboy Magazine—
is not a Cher or Madonna videoed in bras with buttocks
hanging out or in—is not a boy or a girl stepping on
or burning the American Flag—is not a Tammy Faye or Jim Bakker
defaming the Name by adding a little sex and mascara
to the preaching game—is not even a Jimmy Swaggert crying
like Johnnie Ray - Lord, I have sinned, please send me
your money now!

The most obscene thing I've ever seen is silly Politicians
giving away America bit by bit and piece by piece, while
the down and out citizen sleeps in the alleyways, lives
out on the streets and eats from the nearest garbage can—
is the damning of your children's minds with violence and
over spending on wars at home and abroad—is the politician
trying to gain the whole world while bruising the Soul of
Americans—is any polluter of the earth who takes and tares
and never takes the time to heal.

Cora Mae West

Bowl Of Rhymes

The attempt to make a rhyme with orange
    is really of no use,
So why don't we just squeeze the orange
    and make some orange juice?
When rhyming words with apple,
    I'm really at a loss,
So why don't we just mash them
    and eat some apple sauce?
I can't think of a word to rhyme with peach.
    "I don't know why."
So I think I will just bake them —
    Yes, homemade peach pie.
Bananas, as we know them, will never rhyme:
    "I quit."
Unless — they're under ice cream
    in the middle of a split.
Grapes are very boring hanging on the vine;
    They really show their spirit in a glass of dinner wine.
Now it's time to end my tasty bowl of rhymes.
    Next time — if we're lucky — we'll deal with some limes.

Francine Miller

Losing Daddy

The miracle of a woman giving birth,
Is the greatest gift God gave this earth.
Little hands and little feet,
Skin of ivory on a face so sweet.
We sit and wonder as they grow,
Answering questions that we really don't know.
My children, too young, had more than most could bare,
The death of their father didn't seem fair.
The funeral came, with our sons at my side,
Stains on their cheeks from tears they had cried.
Their first day of school, the first fish they caught,
Their first ball game, the first car that they bought,
Their first school dance, their first real date,
A life that was handed to them by fate.
Graduation days, wedding days all will be missed.
Faces of grandchildren, never to be kissed.
But yet he's guided their lives from above,
Them not knowing the power of his love.
And when they meet I know he'll see
They are everything we'd hoped they'd be.

Debralyn Stover

I Will Miss

I will miss the teachers that helped us through the years
I will miss the laughter that helped us through the tears
I will miss the homework that kept us up all night
I will miss the bad times that really were alright
I will miss the jokes that everyone would tell
I will miss the playground where we all once fell
I will miss the parties where we had so much fun
I will miss the bags that would always weigh a ton
I will miss the Masses where we came to sing
I will miss the pencils that St Nicholas would bring
I will miss the lectures that we always got
I will miss the shorts when it was so hot
I will miss the games that we always played
I will miss the cards that we always made
I will miss the tables where we used to sit
I will miss the yelling if someone threw a fit
I will miss the principal who really showed he cared
I will miss the fun times that we all once shared
I will miss the classrooms where we learned 2 + 2
But most of all I will miss you!!

Andrea Elberson

Eternity

Now,
Is the instant that leads us to Tomorrow
It is a fleeting moment of happiness
It is a lasting moment of sadness

Tomorrow,
Is the gateway into Forever
It is what creates our Yesterdays
It is what we live for

Forever,
Is an Eternity of Yesterdays, Todays, and Tomorrows
It is how long we want our pleasantness to last
It is how long we want to spend with those we love

Now, Tomorrow, Forever...
Eternity.

Dora Wong

Ignore Me

Ignore me world, for all I seek
is the loneliness of a Mountain peak.

Ignore me mankind, for all I find
to look at you, just blows my mind.

Ignore me grass, for I but lay.
to rest my bones, not long will I stay.

Ignore me flowers, for I've no powers
to bring the sunshine and rain in showers.

Ignore me wind, for I don't whine
like you do through the trees of pine.

Ignore me birds, for I can't fly
like you do with wings through the sky.

Ignore me Sun, for you are much too bright
I'll never shine like you do to block out the night

Ignore me world, for all I want is to find
the Peace and Serenity of my own mind.

Brenda Johnson

Dream Girl

Love at first sight, can it be
is this a dream, I must see

I look in your eyes, I'm in a whirl
Finding you - a precious pearl

From top to bottom I'm falling apart
Does this girl know she's got my heart?

A kiss from your lips, as sweet as honey
You've made my days, so bright and sunny

With a heart of gold and a smile so pure
My love for you will always endure

No words can describe, these feelings of love
You're someone special, sent from above

Happiness means to hold you real close
And tell you from my heart, I love you the most!

Frank A. Alfonso

Things Changed

The city truck has come today.
It carried the old park bench away.
It sat many years under the big oak tree
And was a resting place for the kids and me.
But the park and bench that we held dear
Will make way for a shopping mall next year.

Anna Schmidt

Wind

The wind has its own free spirit
It blows when it feels needed,
Whether it's steamy hot or sun setting heat,
The wind is here to rustle a beat.

Destruction sometimes follows its path,
For it has no set way,
The wind's the dealer, and we're the fate.
We have no choice but to watch and wait.

Seasons could not change without,
The leaves would never fall
Time would be at a standing still,
If the wind's free spirit had no gull.

The trees will flow, kites will fly,
Our fluffy clouds still float the sky,
For the wind is our most natural life,
Just imagine the silence and quiet still nights.

Albert John Adams Jr.

The Wall

The wall.
It calls, "Come to me, feel my pain, share my grief, see my
tears; place your hand upon my many names; be engulfed by
my moans, my groans, my anguish, my despair, my anger, my hope.
Come to my wall and touch me."
So many names - a complex accounting of an incomplete remnant.
These names had faces, each face had its separate story
And each face had the same ending - an engraved name
upon a black granite marble wall.
The names appear to rise from the ground, likened to a
Lazarus coming forth from his tomb!
It is the names that call to us, the living, to come to this wall;
Then stand and search, seek and learn of death's bounty
Too soon ripped from a harvest of mankind.
So lift a rubbing from a dear name, leave the relics of
remembrance, carry away a gift of healing.
The wall - known nearly by all.
Strongly it stands, melded together by past and present
graves and names, which, for the nation, is the continuing story
of the cost of freedom.

Angella B. Dickson

Thanksgiving

This day I am thankful for numbers of things
including each one of the days of my life.
They mostly are pleasant, but once in a while
there comes along one that is nothing but strife.
White clouds are so lovely in blue skies or gray
for which I remember to give thanks when I pray.
I wish I might help the ones weaker than I,
especially those who seem ready to die.
At eighty and nine I wish I felt fine
much more of the time than I do.
And being this old I do not complain -
but rather am thankful for all of those years.

Henry H. Ragatz

That River

That river over there a million miles away—
It over flows with bloated masses
How can we look but not see the faces
Floating and blue, gathering in the lulls—
Providing the perfect shot for the evening news
These are mothersfathersbrotherssistersfriends—
Who are the buoyant disrespected

Julie Hartman

Friendship And Love

Sometimes love is misunderstood,
It causes much harm yet it seems so good,
Sometimes love can pass away,
But the friendship we share is here to stay.

My love for you was always true,
I never wanted but the best for you,
I loved you with all my heart and my mind,
That kind of love is hard to find.

My love for you goes on and on,
My heart is singing that same old song,
Yet my love for you is different now,
I love you more as a friend somehow.

I know it will only take a little time,
For your point of view to match up with mine,
Someday you'll fall in love once more,
And find it's her your heart adores.

Amy Godeaux

The Heart

The heart is a lonely hunter, this is known from experience.
It daily testifies of its own mortality, searching high and low for
meaning—a reason to continue.

Tender and fragile since birth, the heart requires sanctuary;
a refuge from the cold winters of loneliness, and protection against
the cruel winds of despair.

From deep within the heart cries out to be noticed, yearning for
affection and another heart to embrace.
Oh, to be needed! To be loved! Is there anything more worthy of
desire than this?

What searing agonies the heart must endure. How can it bear such
anguish and still continue to beat?
Forever in quest of such simple pleasures. Wanting only to be
understood, cared for, and loved.

Where is the cure?
When will the pain cease?
Who can stop the heart from drowning in its own pool of tears?
Whose hand will take this suffering and turn it into joy?

Like the darkness of night without the moon for a companion, the heart
resides in a chamber of solitude;
despairing of never being found, bereft of the peace and rest it so
deserves.

But alas, be silent heart, and listen.
Take comfort in knowing that there is still time.
Time to live, time to learn, time to love.
And with time there is always the presence of hope.

Benjamin Neal Byers

Reflections of Time

'Twas long before the date of my birth
Indians and buffalo were roaming the earth.
Water was plentiful, the grass was high,
the air so clean you could see with your eyes
Mountains and valleys, wild game there to kill
Fish in the streams and trees on each hill.

Food was grown then stored with care.
Cloth was woven for clothes to wear.
Each man was accomplished in some kind of trade
acquiring necessities a bargain was made,
to barter your skills for the need of a neighbor
you traded your knowledge and received his labor.

My parents were children, old for their age.
A place in history to fill a page
of a book filled with love, devotion to each other
Destined for hard work, my father and mother.

Gean Boggs

The Reason

Everyday I struggle for the reason;
It doesn't seem to matter what the reason
I found out the world doesn't evolve around me,
I try and find the reason for please,
others around me seem to want more, how can
I please them when I can't please myself,
My feelings are opened and walked about
Like the floor, I yearn for the time I can
open and close the door,
I struggle to open my eyes,
I fight myself not to criticize,
I look in the mirror and all I see,
Is a million reflections I can never be,
Please I look for the reason to go on
I can't find a meaning or a song.
I use to believe that all I need is
to hear I love you, but from whom
until I know the reason I'll stay
Locked in my prison I call myself

Carrie Hughes

"Hate"

Adversary to adversary, lashing at each other.
It ends up war, don't know what for, killing one another.
It may be through emotions or maybe the physique;
But destruction comes, via words or guns,
Turning neither cheek.

David Weinberg

Losing A Loved One

Losing a loved one makes you want to cry,
It feels like someone is crushing your heart
Although you are still alive.

Losing a loved one makes you feel
as if a piece of you is gone
it also makes you feel very alone.

Seeing her lying there so plain
you know now, she will no longer be in pain.

With all this sadness inside,
At least you have the comfort of knowing,
She will be safe in the Heavenly sky.

Now you know she will rest peacefully,
and she will not have to go through the
suffering and pain. Still you love her and
miss her, and you know without her,
Nothing will be the same.

April Parrish

Because Of You

As I was driving home today,
I started to reminisce,
about our times together and how much we love each other,
and how I've found so much happiness.

Time spent with you is so special
in all kinds of ways...
it seems the minute I leave you, I start to count the days
until I'll be with you again.

It seemed as I gazed at the blue sky above,
and the beautiful bronze and yellow leaves,
it was like a confirmation of our love,
and it put my heart at ease.

I've come to the end of a perfect day
feeling so loved and content...
and all because of you, my love,
I think you were heaven sent.

Jessie Overend

Warmth

Love is like the river,
it flows through the depths of your heart,
and runs through the deepest sections of your soul.
It glides through your whole being,
until you dissolve in the warmth of the divine.

Barri Ann Bechtel

At Mom's Bedside

LIFE flies by.
It is as if lifted upon a strata-flash of color
that we are here for a few moments and then gone on.
In these few moments called 'life'
what a body chooses to do during the stop
creates a path for the next spirit passing through.

SO IT MATTERS these few moments;
how one spirit loves another.
For in the loving, the spirits of others are born.
In the loving the new-spirit finds freedom
to seek and find a love
and so create a pathway for a new spirit on its way.

SO NO SPIRIT'S LIFE HERE GOES UNANNOUNCED or
unnoticed.
For one pathway lights the way for another
and so it goes on and on
in this life and the next;
And this presence of spirit is blessed.

Judi Shepherd-Gay

My Heart In Time

Here is my heart, I give it to you
It is as solid as a rock, but soft to the touch
It is loving, It is caring
So if you're ever feeling blue,
I will always be there for you!
Because my heart is a part of me,
and a heart is hard to give away,
but I can trust in you to use it someday!
Please don't break it or throw it away,
because it will be waiting for you,
at the end of each and every day
Trust in it, believe in it, don't be afraid
It won't hurt you, not even at the end of our days!

James William Lockard

Today's Life

It is not easy.
It is not funny.
Today's life is tough.
Oh no, That's enough.
These days, most everybody
Believes: "Time is money."
Somehow, it's true,
But with no chronic flu.
In the sky the sun rises,
The earth's creatures energizes
And gives the daily hope
With which we hardly cope.
With crimes on the streets, days and nights
And fatal domestic fights,
Love is in coma today.
One only cares for his luxurious way.
No helping hands
For those crying from their infernal dens.
People always provide for their selfish safety.
But only God, only God cares for everybody.

Gustave Bartelus

Love

Love is a feeling that's felt the universe over
It is something that makes you feel you're bursting in
clover
Whether it's in friendship, in parenting, in
Relationships whatever
Love is binding to the mind and heart and it won't
Leave you never
It is such an experiencing emotion to feel
It can make one feel young when they're old and
Well if they're ill

This great feeling we share called love is something
We all get, granted to us from heaven above
For nothing that we do, or say or feel should be
Ignored, for it is God who gives us the strength
To endure

For love is the greatest treasure that we have and
It's like a jewel shining so brightly for all to see,
A radiance of warmth generated from you to me.

Alice James

Untitled

The season is upon us my Faithful Friend
It is time to plant our souls in the ground
It is time for us to begin our lives
And forever to the earth become bound

The season is upon us to take the journey of our lives
It is time to discover the mysterious and the
unknown
It is time for us to find ourselves
And discover the thrills not yet known

The season is upon us my Faithful Friend
It is not to be feared and should be taken in stride
For in this world your troubles do not exist
Relax, step forward, and enjoy the experiences of the
other side

Chris H. Taylor

Religion

Religion is an inspiration from faith, love, God.
It isn't a people gathered together
to study One belief.
It is one belief, it is God,
not several religions.
Religion is one thing,
and it comes from God.
It is a Spirit through out our bodies by God.
So let's come together as One,
and form not several beliefs,
just one.
It is God.

Carolina M. Johnson

Untitled

Tears that are cried in vain
Is like beautiful poetry tossed into a fire.
Love that hurts is like a deliciously sweet candy.
With better surprise in the sugar coated center.
Heartache is nothing. I live with that pain,
Waiting for him to break my heart, laughing delightedly,
Savoring the moment, tears streaming down my
Flushed cheeks. No one to catch them save
For a pillowcase. Muttered apologies of
"I'm sorry," when all that I hear are
Empty words. The meaning and sincerity
Sucked right out, flat and vague, like words on paper.

Erica Kaminski

Untitled

I'm writing you this simple poem
It isn't much but what I left behind
For memories of different times
Ones that made us laugh and they made us cry and even though we
haven't always met eye-to-eye you'll never know just how much you
mean, you're in my hopes, my prayers, and my every dream
I try to hide the pain and keep myself sane
But I always find that you're forever on my mind
Every second I'm thinking of you and I still regret that we're through
and I know that I can never forget you. I still remember everything
From our first meeting to your wedding ring
I remember the way that we kissed
I remember the warmth of your lips
I remember that we always had such great dreams
Then everything fell apart at the seams
But know that I'm stone cold and all alone, and in our
Shadow I'll forever roam; now that you're gone, everything goes wrong
I always knew you were the only one
You're my moon, my stars, and my only sun
I forever knew that again, I'd never find another you

Amanda Martin

Old House

We saw an old house today, we saw it standing in the sun
It no longer shelters a family, screaming children - having fun
Don't fret though, it has memories; it stands against the rain
Its mighty front door pushed open and a broken window pane.

Flowers are still peeping through the weeds and grass
The front gate still glistens where rust hasn't covered all the brass
The trees are all over-grown; no one trims them today.
The house just stands and waits..someone will care
again…someday

An old house is strong as it stands against the wind
The snow covers its porches, the rain pounds on its tin
No..the old house isn't sad, it has done its part
It has seen laughing children…it has a happy heart.

Charlotte Everett

My Gift To You

I saw something today that made me think of you.
It put a real big smile across my face and a twinkle
in my eye. I wanted to call you and tell you about
it but instead I put it in my pocket so we could
share it together. I wanted to put it in a box
and wrap it up, but instead I kept it close to
my heart right beside you. I can't wait to see
your eyes when I hand my gift to you, I know
you will like it because I do. When I reached
in my pocket… it was gone! I guess the warmth
of my heart made it go away. For I will have
to catch your snowflake another day.

Angela Dawn Pilgrim

The Message Of A Daffodil

I heard a daffodil today
It seemed to have a lot to say

It stood so straight and said so clear
I am the first and spring is near

After me more blooms will enter
It will be a parade to shrug off winter.

My yellow blossoms trumpet to you.
A promise of the love and laughter due you.

Donna Lash Morris

Imagining

I dream and wish and dream some more,
It seems like life is such a bore,
There's always something better to do,
Dreaming of the place destined for you,
With one flicker of imagination,
You can be there.
Forever the dream is there,
Clicking, Tapping in your mind,
You know your dreams are one of a kind,
A tap on your desk 'n you're back to earth,
Answer the next question for what it's worth.

Hilary Hahn

Untitled

Striking you like a lightning bolt,
it sends a line of threat down your spine.
The chill in your throat expresses itself,
when you swallow your fear.
Your fear follows the path
in your deep dark body,
to the main room to your problems.
Your heart throbs as you think
how much it hurt you.
The stranger who did this to you,
will be in your mind forever.
His name is hatred.
He causes all the worries
that cause the biggest pain
of any heart and soul.
Heart break.
Heart break.
Caused by the stranger.
Caused by the hatred.

Jessica Goldsmith

The Empty Chair

There's a big empty chair in the corner
It sits there by the window so useless,
Where the grey enters in from the sky
It seems to be saying, "I'm lonely
When will I again be happy,"
It still brings a tear to my eye!
There's a big empty side in our bed,
Where once there was love, warmth and passion
Now is lonely and forlorn.
Is all this heartache and sadness worth it,
For your family now is torn.
Does she give you all that you are asking,
Are her arms worth the loss of our love?
For the rest of your days, can you leave us
Alone, unloved and scorned?
Did time make you restless and unhappy
Was your life so easily shed,
With no regrets to wake you when you are alone in bed?
I miss you so completely, my worst dreams came true
There's a big empty chair in the corner and my whole world is blue!

Georgianna Elaine Haury

From Fear To Hope

Slowly, quietly, craftily,
  it sneaks up on you
Cold, alone, scared, dreary, depressed, sad,
  the feeling it gives you
Then, when you think it's all over
You see the light, coming toward you.
Faster, faster, faster, like a speeding bullet,
then, POW! you know everything's going to be alright,
  as you enter the light.

James Allen

"Insight"

Again, and all too fast—but really not bad at all.
It struck me as I looked into her eyes—
Cheery and feeling, 'twas like staring into the sky.
Then I knew what I had to do; I heard my heart's call.

I had to let her know, show her how I felt.
A dream I lived: She and I. Before her had I knelt,
With a ring in one hand and a rose in the other,
I gave her a kiss and told her I loved her.

But such fleeting dreams so soon fade away,
Like birds of summer when winter comes to stay.
Truth is wisdom, wisdom truth.
I grow away from the naivete of youth.

Time waits for no-one, it's commonly agreed.
Wisdom is acquired through patience, like a tree from a seed.
I see the light, the Way is shown!
I smile at what I should have known.

There's so much to do, it's good to be free.
The past is only a memory.
I've discovered what friendship is: it's true love.
Only God knows what I was thinking of.

Anthony Seliquini

Life's Currents

I thought of you as I was drifting down my river.
It was so quiet, I could feel myself disintegrate in the air.
My hair flew the breeze, my ears sang the song of the birds;
I had no need to speak, nature knew my thoughts; and I needed
not to walk - I was everywhere.
I was meant to be free and know this peace.
There was a brook rushing towards my river; I could feel it
coming.
It startled me as it came with such power and wisdom.
We crashed, intertwined our strength and conquered many
mountains.
Sometimes I leave my river and all its strength, reassurance;
peace oblivious to all I know - but will forever return and find
you there.
My river will be throughout eternity.

Cheryl A. Froehlich

Sacred Places

There is a glen, so shining and green,
It was there where he made me his queen.
'Tis a sacred place to me, for my love hath trod there.

There is a cottage, so lovely a sight.
In it she dwells, so pretty and bright.
'Tis a sacred place to me for my love hath trod there.

On two paths I gaze. Which shall he take?
'Twas the cottage way, the glen he forsakes.
'Tis a sacred place to me for my love hath trod there.

Here is my heart, no strength to lend.

Broken apart, never to mend.
'Tis a sacred place to me for my love hath trod there.

Diana Kressman

The Light Of Life

Life is a candle radiating a shimmer of shine
  It lights the path of roads to choose,
  Guiding my vision home to the destiny I find.

  All at once a great breath storms,
  A flickering flame now stands weak.
  As red wax bleeds on my hand,
    I try to look through the fog and understand what to seek.

Adealani Gerkewicz

My Little Tin Box

I have a little tin Box, which I put my pennies in
It's a little tin box, a pretty one, all pure tin
There are pictures on the sides, nice ones at that
And I keep it hidden, behind my big hat

No one will find it, it's hidden real well
No one will find it, for I won't tell
I'm going to save my pennies, I'm going to save a lot
And I just won't tell anyone, how much I have got

I started saving pennies, one at a time And all the pennies saved, are
mine I won't tell anyone, no, not a soul No one is going to know,
until I reach my goal

One day you'll find I'm way up there That's when you will know, I'm a
millionaire And when I'm there, way up top I'll still save pennies, I
just won't stop

There are many ways to become rich Some people start by digging a
ditch I started by saving pennies in a little tin box Now my money is
in banks, behind strong locks

I'm a bit older, and pennies, I still save In my little tin box,
that someone's gave And I keep my pictured tin box at that Hidden out
of sight, behind my big hat

Harry B. Sherr

Truth

The real truth is there.
It's a smoky gray ghost
You can't always hang onto.
Although a part of each of us,
It can be shy and elude our grasp.
It's there, to help. All you have to do
Is call it up, into your Sunlight.

No one can reach it but you.
Others talk about it so we assume
Everybody knows it's there.
"And the Truth shall set you free."
You've heard it, read it; know it.
Could this be a friend you haven't met?
You know it's there, deep down.

The choice to make it part of Life is yours.
So, put it in your pocket
Right there, next to your heart
And use it to brighten each day.
It's safe, deep down, and lives as a
Companion to Faith and Hope.

Judy Williams

Cross Roads

The cross is like a beacon, that stands out like a star.
It's a steady, lifelong road map when you're near or when you're far.

The center is your being, with different ways to go.
As to which you'll travel is just for you to know.

Remember, from the center, your choices are complete.
Whichever road you travel, there are people that you'll meet.

And people will not judge you for the direction that you go.
They judge at how you get there and only few will tell you so.

The cross is like your roadway with direction you may take.
Deciding, which direction, is up to you to make.

The center of this cross, is like a meeting place.
It's not the starting point, nor the finish of the race.

The center is both then and now, it's not just a place to leave.
It's a place you can return to, for some hope you can retrieve.

The hope is in a friendship that you fashion as you go.
The friendship, is the hope, that only friends can sow.

Edward T. Leonard

Tragedy

It's a tragedy to lose someone so young
It's a tragedy to know the girl is gone
It's a tragedy to lose a love so strong
   so strong.

Now she's gone from out of my life and into dreams
She left without a word and then return the rings
Yet I know I will go on,
To find the one to whom I belong
But it's a tragedy to know that the love is gone

Through the good times and bad
You made me happy but now I'm sad
sad I lost the best friend I ever had
and sad to know that what happened was real
Because I will never feel this way for someone else

It's a tragedy to know we had to part
somewhere beyond the moon, past mars, and into our heart
We shared, we took enjoyed the spice of life
But (yes) it's a tragedy to know (3) the love is gone.

    Arnold B. Christain

The Lonely Rose

As the lonely rose sways in the breeze
Its beauty and grace combine with ease
Such a pretty little rose wanting to live
So sweet smelling it has so much to give
And as the rain starts to fall from above
Each drop touches it with tenderness
   and love
And then a petal falls to the ground
While the rest of the rose remains
   safe and sound

    Jeanette Goldhirsch

"Battle Babies"

Van Dorn Mississippi, 'twas the year forty-two.
It's been a long time, since departing from you.

Rainy nights are remembered in your shanties built of pine,
Where we were conceived, division ninety-nine.

A convoy to Camp Maxey, our purpose became plain,
After maneuvers and furloughs, we boarded a train.

Northeast to Miles Standish, 'twas a dark and dismal day
For kids barely out of high school, going so very far away.

A very short stay in Scotland, and down at Weymouth as well,
After crossing the English Channel, came "The Bulge,"
that was really hell.

"Battle Babies" we were born there and shall remember forevermore,
Those eighty eights at Elson born ridge in the winter of forty-four.

    Joseph R. Doyle

Impossible

This wall...must not be broken...
I see NIGHT...all around me....no sunshine as of yet...
.......You have broken me
ONCE!!!
I've seen your evil (I don't want to BE)
In DARKNESS I find myself searching for
you
Why????
TIME
I HAVE FOUND PEACE AND LOVE my fortress is strong
I AM NOW STRONG

    Heather Gibson

College-Late In Life

I can't believe I'm here in line for class advisement.
It's been hours and now it's clear
It's the wrong line-
I can't do this.

They're all so young, so aware and informed.
I'll never keep up, it just isn't fair;
And there's so much work-
I can't do this.

It takes all of my time-
Study, work, eat and sleep.
I'm not in my prime, is it worth it?
I can't do this.

Now hold on here-is that young man flirting?
Yes he is and he's so cute.
The heck with my fear, there's hope for me yet.
I can do this!

    Jacqueline Schibler

With Love From Mother

There's a letter on the bottom of the file,
Its envelope a faded yellow brown,
It has traveled to the city many a mile
And the postmark names a little unknown town.

But the hurried man of business passes all the others by
And on the scrawling characters, he turns a glistening eye
He forgets the cares of Commerce, and anxious schemes for gain,
The while he reads what mother writes from up in Maine.

There are quirks and scratchy quavers of the pen,
where it struggled in the fingers old and bent
There are places that he has to read again
And ponder on what mother meant.

At least he finds "with love" we all are well,
And softly lays the homely letter down
And dashes at his headlong tasks pell-mell,
Once more, the busy anxious man of town.

And then at dusk when all are gone, he drops his worldly mask,
And takes his pen and lovingly performs a welcome task,
For never shall the clicking type or shortening scrawl profane,
The message to the old home up there in Maine.

    Beatrice Williamee

The Heuristic Blade

That knife appears before my eyes tonight,
its jagged blade aglow with deadly bent.
I shudder under night's perfidious blight.

A cutting dagger, gleaming wanly bright,
With crimson light, its purpose evident,
that knife appears before my eyes tonight.

I see the tip, a most disarming sight,
the nightly knife not leaving but intent.
I shudder under night's indecent blight.

So sharp, unmarred, the blade reflects its might,
a razor slicing through my brain's content.
That knife appears before my eyes tonight.

The sheen off knife's facade betokens fight
(but over what?) ahead. I won't relent
and shudder under night's repeated blight.

The blade, heuristic, helps my brain ignite,
to find out what the knife's appearance meant.
That knife appears before my eyes tonight,
and I rejoice before the welcome blight (?).

    John Okulski

The Old Maple Tree

There is a maple tree close to my house;
It's getting old just like myself.
In the spring its limbs are covered with buds
That burst into green leaves when summer comes.
It shelters the birds and shields me from the sun;
It swings and sways in the summer breeze,
Limbs strong enough to hold a child on a swing.
There is a chill in the air; fall waltzes in,
Changing the leaves to gold, yellow and red;
Then they're carried away by the winter wind.
Snow will fall and dress the limbs in white;
They will sparkle like diamonds in the sunlight.
Winter will pass, followed by spring,
And the green buds will appear once again.

Elma Stone

All About Time

It's said, "Forget the past, don't let it burden you,
  It's gone — and best forgotten."
Likewise, "Dwell not on the future
  Sufficient is the evil thereof
  And loaded down with cares
  Why suffer twice?"

Instead — live in the present
  Celebrate the day — the hour — the moment
  It is here and vital
  only now is real.

I see it differently.
  Cherish the past
  For it was once the present
  And can be a treasure-house of memories
  Tucked away — sometimes with smiles,
  Sometimes with tears.
  Review it lovingly — and never fail in gratitude.
  Then gently tuck away your past —
  The good, the bad, the beautiful,
  And get on with your present.

Edyth H. Vandegrift

Threnody

The initial melody is sweet by nature
Its hypnotic tone floating almost beyond reach
Enticing the virtues of youth and hope
Grasping them with intangible hands
The rhythmic pulse permeates each cell
And we are utterly consumed
Then sinuous notes slightly harden
And the rhapsody becomes somewhat sharp
Yet still remains the relentless siren
An aria of pain and destruction
With a haunting crescendo that brings both tears and awe
Resounding through every sentient being
Then retreating back into darkness
As the last note fades into the crowd
And in the silence of the heart, one could almost hear
The death of a dream.

Johanna R. Alves-Parks

THIS FLAG

This flag is a symbol of something grand,
It's a great symbol of a proud homeland;
'Tis the symbol of freedom and liberty
And the hope for millions from sea to sea;
The blue stands for honor; the white, purity,
The red is for blood shed to keep us free;
I may see suff'ring and I may face death,
But I'll guard this flag with my dying breath.

James W. Mayou

"Divorce"

Divorce.
It's like a sharp blow to the heart
It's like an end that never restarts
It's like an actor stripped of his part
In the colossal movie of life

Divorce.
It's like a swift punch in the face
It's like eyes right after mace
It's like the loser of every race
Why have a husband without a wife

Divorce.
It's like a fight between two best friends
It's like crying till forever's end
It's like having money and nowhere to spend
It's like an unprovoked menacing stare

Divorce.
It's like the thought you never think
It's like the alcoholic's first tasty drink
It makes you feel like the unwanted link
It's simply a child's worst nightmare.

Jason Gilmore

Love And Friendship

You define love as a feeling of fondness and devotion.
It's like when we meet there is a secret potion.
When we are alone there are things you confess.
Yet when we are in public it all turns into a mess.

You define a friend as one who helps and supports.
Together, alone, we go to the park or watch sports.
But once we see your friends you are never the same.
You look at me as if to say, "Do I know your name?"

Why can't the two go together hand in hand?
Alone, arm in arm, walking through the sand.
Love and friendship are so closely related.
But one step into public, our love and friendship has faded.

Tell me, dear Lord, will it always be this way?
Held in your arms, you will say, "I love you" every day.
It's like a spell put on you when seen by human eyes.
Our love and friendship always dies.

Cyndi Chlup

The Bath

I soak in mother's green tile bath
Jade like the sea.
Pale yellow walls,
sweat.

Yellow folded towels,
hang like silent tongues.
Her ridiculous heart wrinkled on flora sheets
inside out.

I'm dead too.
I died in that room.
I died better than you
slowly, without oxygen.

I lay creased
on the thin bed,
once called the
Sun Room.

I poke a hole in your diseased heart

Dead air
exits.

Barbara Rose Brooker

"A Little Gift To You From Me"

Dad here's a little gift that is just to you from me,
It's really a nice present and on Christmas day you'll see...
That it is something you and I can do the whole year through.
It's something we have done before not something strange and new...
And as you use this gift I got you'll feel light as a feather...
Plus we'll spend lots of fun filled times just you and I together.
They say you're just a child only once and so you see...
It's really quite important we make memories you and me
So on that special day when you open your surprise...
I will be there standing anxious just to see your eyes.
Then we will take each others hand and we'll be on our way...
To making special memories you and I day after day

Dene Stewart Gritts

A Land Called Peace

Far and beyond there's a place.
It's the home of dreams, the land of eternity.
It's a narrow adventure lining your mind.
It's a hollow memory. It'll always shine.
Open your heart and close your eyes.
Reality always looks better
While seen from the inside.
Supply your thoughts with reason.
Make people believe.
Hold the answers, make them see.
Escape from the chimes
because in this land there is no time.
Fly through the night and around the trees.
Play with the grass and float with the breeze.
Someday we'll all wake up
in a land called peace.

Iva Rayburn

Evening Sun

When the evening sun paints the western sky
It's time to bid the day good-by
To put away our daily cares
And see the beauty there.

To watch the ever-changing scene
That moves about as in a dream
With weird forms of cloud and light
A prelude to the night.

When the evening sun paints the western sky
I think of you and of days gone by
Of all our love and happiness
And how we have been blest.

Our life is full of trials and troubles
And lots of little busted bubbles
Yet there's a time at the close of day
For the evening sun to paint them away.

Fred F. Heitzig

The Pen

The pen is an instrument of power and of fame,
It's written speeches of freedom and signed an infamous name.
Its origin is ancient, from times long ago,
Forming letters and characters that we learned to know.
It gave us books of learning, Stories of Mother Goose,
Tales of friends and foe, and of villains who met the noose.
Although it's light to hold and seems a neutral thing
Its weight in the written word holds a poisonous sting.
With the stroke of the pen a battle begins or ends
People's lives are on its tip unable to defend.
Who has the power to stop the flow
once it has begun?
The hand that holds the pen is the only one.

Darlene Asbill

"My Message"

I want to get a message through to you,
It's very simple to do,

All you have to do is open your eyes and see,
That you're the special girl just for me,

I know what I have isn't much to offer,
But don't listen to those who say don't bother.

What you need is someone who'll love you for you,
Not for what they expect and want you to do,

'Cause you're a woman that needs a man, not a boy!
To be loved and caressed not played with like a toy!

I may not be handsome or even fine,
But if I were judged by personality I'd be a nine!

So I hope I got this through to you,
'Cause I really and truly LOVE YOU!

Isidro A. Martinez

"Things Not Right"

Tears on the pillow, sobs in the night,
Jesus is near thee, all will be right.
Trust in the Savior, turn to Him now
He'll take each burden, sorrows will bow.
Cling to Him daily, heart peace is thine,
He melts the darkness, makes the sun shine.
Lonely no longer, walking with Him
Sins all forgiven, Jesus within.

Straying no more, coming to stay
With Jesus my Savior, I'm traveling His Way.
Heaven is drawing ever so near
Toiling all ended, comfort and cheer.
Welcome of Welcomes-Eternity's Bright Shore
Blessing of Blessings, with Jesus evermore.

Everett Osterhout

Hearts Joined

On this day our lives will be
Joined, our hearts and souls will be bestowed
  to one another, we will become
  husband and wife. This
Union will be the beginning of our wonderful life
  together with a beautiful future.
  As we exchange our vows, we
  will promise to have a lifelong
  commitment, everlasting
Love, and unconditional devotion for one another.
  We will symbolize our vows
  and promises with rings, all of
  which do not have a beginning
  or an ending. As our
Years together transpire, our bond will continue
  to grow and deepen. Our love
  will live on for eternity.

Adrianne Gammon

Hold On Tight

Praise the Lord, friend, you have God on your side
  Just hold on tight!
Read the scriptures with all your might;
  Let them soothe your grief
As nothing else can give relief.

Keep all your sweet memories alive
  By reminiscing you can strive
To find the inner grace
  When flesh and spirit sever
To trust our Lord, our guide forever.

Doris F. Wright

Daughter

She was so beautiful, sitting there,
Joking, with that laugh that tinkled.
Unaware that that was her mother's chair,
Where — that laugh, never got old, or wrinkled.

How this can be is a mystery
Neither science nor religion can figure out.
Both computers and brains work on electricity,
But act differently — after a blackout.

Computers cannot reprogram automatically,
But that laugh is preserved in — another, human.
The man-made machine works mechanically.
God made that other woman.

Brags about computers are interesting.
But, how long has that laugh — done its thing?

Jack Robinson

Untitled

Maybe if you think,
Just a little more it might help.

You ask what I mean,
Well, who says I'm supposed to know.

But just if, ask if,
Why, when, if what, if anything.

Like if I were to scream what would happen.

Ask again,
why or when, why not.

Suppose anything,
Don't assume nothing.

Hurt no one, like everyone, think everything,
Know nothing, feel it, breath it, taste it,
See it, see what, you, me, no one, someone,

Sleep don't do it,
Stop only when you want.

If you breath and I know you do,
Listen to it, listen to everything,
People, dogs, cats, birds, enemies,
why, if you know tell me.

Jessica Caron

You Will Awaken For The Judgment

You will awaken for the judgment. Rest in peace.
Just because you left this world,
your sentence is not complete.

It was written in the Good Book,
It will be for all times.
Some will be judge for heaven,
for some it will be the fire.

Your blasphemy is not forgiven,
and is carried in your seed.
My Lord will strike you dead
bring your children to their knees.

You will awaken for the judgment.
A promise from the King.
It was spoken of, of old,
now it comes back again.

You will awaken for the judgment.
Good news for the believer,
we'll see our mother once again,
going home to the kingdom.

Geraldine Wooley

A Reflection Of Me

When I looked into the mirror what did I see?
Just empty eyes and tear stained cheeks.

There I stood looking at me.
Just looking at a big broken dream.

People will often say, why did she do it,
when she had so much to live for?

Live for what?
I used to dream, now I want to die.

You could tell by just looking in my eyes.
To end all of the pain, I put a gun to my head
and pulled the trigger.

Because for once I looked in the mirror,
and saw the reflection of me, and it was enough
to take away my sanity.

Jayne Anderson

Untitled

Tumbleweed has no place to settle,
Just moving along with the wind.
Tumbling, tumbling ever so gentle.
No known place to go or be, just tumbling
with no restraint. Tumbleweed, tumble,
wanting a place to settle, just in peace.

The wisk of the wind, sends it
tumbling again, over the plains of emptiness,
Not even knowing where it had been.
I feel like the tumbleweed, transcending
time with the ever flow of my mind.
When will my tumbling cease to be?
Tumbleweed, tumbleweed, that's
what I must be. I have no place
of rest nor a place of peace.
It all seems to escape me. I am
just a tumbleweed wanting to be.

Deborah E. Boyce

Just No One Willing

There are no mountains - that cannot be climbed,
Just no one willing to be the first.
There are no oceans - that cannot be swam,
Just no one willing to endure the worst.
There are no debates - that cannot be won,
Just no one willing to take a side.
There are no paths - that cannot be found,
Just no one willing to be the guide.
There are no inventions - that cannot be discovered,
Just no one willing to be creative and try.
There are no lives - that cannot be saved,
Just a lot of people willing to walk on by.

Justin C. Carter

Returning In Clouds

Jesus will return for me,
just as the Bible said it would be.
He will return in clouds, as he left in one.
Every eye will see Him, and every knee will bend,
for this will be the beginning of the end.

His return will be like a thief in the night.
With a blink of His eye, and a smile on His face,
all of His faithful's will leave this earthly place.

I have heard about heaven, and there I want to be,
serving my savior for eternity.
I will pray every night that tomorrow will be,
the day He comes in clouds for me.

Brady Hill

All Gone

I don't cry all the time, anymore,
Just now and then the tears TRICKLE...
First down one cheek,
Then down the other.

They take turns, I think, the way we
Used to... to pay our bills, remember?

"You owe me for these pictures I picked
Up at drug town."
"Yes, but I bought the new urn for $8.00!"

"Did you forget to pay me the $20.00 for
your long-distance calls?"
"But I can't pay anymore!!!"
WHAT do you DO with your money?!?

"You know — you make
TWICE as much as I!!"

On and on —-
Yes! Trickle, trickle until all the
Tears...bills... and ...
LOVE
are... ALL GONE!!

April E. Ashby

The White Knight

The white knight looked about him and beheld the sight of his beloved
    kingdom.
He had been gone for two years and had fought demons, dragons
    and had even faced the black knight in combat.
These creatures of darkness he did not fear.
But, Oh! how he dreaded this return trip.

Word had come that the Princess had fallen gravely ill.
He hoped and prayed that he was not too late—that
    the castle windows would be open and the birds would be singing.
There she would stand on the window balcony, smiling down at him in
    welcome—her body caressed by rays of sunlight.

He rode into the castle.
All the windows were closed and no birds could be heard.
He dismounted and stared at his noble beast,
    whose eyes seemed filled with sorrow.

He slowly walked the castle stair to her chamber.
There she lay, too weak to smile.
He took her hand and held it to his face.
He stroked her hair and with a voice soft as rain,
    told her stories of their kingdom.

David C. Reffert

For The Prize Of A Rusty Soul

A journey begins of the Father Spirit
knighted armor clashing, bearing a forgotten sword
and all the while the owl pays homage
a gift of the wise, an endearment of non-material reality
the sensitive one knows, brigadier captive
the unfavored son, sun returns
the weighing of deeds begins for the prize of a rusty soul
the shadow of death lies laughing against the languid breeze
playing with its intricate endless dance
around the tarnished innocence of the father's rough strewn face
this prisoner of time rebels
a cry for the unfinished pages of life remains
the dawn anew once more
Indian Summer sprinkled amongst the like-warm doctor of death
and final peace?!!
Dare I look into the eye of darkness?
a masquerade parade
shelving despair a crystal gaze of laughter spent
and christians roar where angels went for the prize of a rusty soul

David Rekrut

Knock Knock Knocking

I hear you knocking at my door,
knock knock knocking,
I'm too afraid to let you in.
Past scars seal the doors,
knock knock knocking,
I'm too afraid to let you in.
"It may be different" echoes in my head,
knock knock knocking,
I'm too afraid to let you in.
I take a glance to see if you're still there,
knock knock knocking,
I'm too afraid to let you in.
Maybe in time as my trust grows,
I'll open up my door,
and maybe let you in.
But meanwhile you're knocking,
knock knock knocking,
I'm just too afraid to let you in.

Barbara Fannin

Not Seeing The Sea

She stood at the window which was dark
Knowing God's unique mark

Not blaming herself this is true
For she is very special to me and you

The clock struck four
As she stood at the oak door

She went and sat on the sand
Her hair flying like a golden band

Head facing towards the sea
Not saying why me?, Why me?

The wind blowing triumphantly and bold
Sun high leaping with gold

Rolls of water creep up to her feet
And seeps under her firm, cushioned seat

Not knowing the beauty of her body and face
Not knowing her magical and embracing grace
When she looks in the mirror it will always be
Dark like a burnt, burnt black sea

Danielle Studdard

Growing Old - Dying Young

He knows every curse word ever said, but he cannot spell it.
Knows every pusher on the block, but he'd never tell it.
Knows every hooker at his school and every loyal ghetto rule.
Sex at six, dope at eight, he'll cut you with his tongue.
Looks twenty-one at fourteen,
He's growing old and dying young.

He's got no interest in his school, no interest in his teacher.
His tutor is the guy next door, who's by no means the preacher.
His education is a waste, he's out of school and gone.
Looks forty-five at twenty-one, A.I.D.S. says his days are done,
His song will soon be sung.
Arteriosclerosis Blues;
He's growing old and dying young.

He's got more scars and bruises than the naked eye can see.
He's spent more years in prison for some senseless robbery.
He's got no skill to market, can hardly count to ten.
Except the money he collects for the men he's been among.
He's just as good as dead to them.
He's growing old and dying young.

Charles J. Baron

Departure Of A Child

Through the eyes of age, insight and wisdom I gained
Lacerations much deeper than any physical pain
Comprehension: uninvited, complex, weighty ... tormenting
Watching a child that was aching ... psychologically fermenting

Situations beyond his control ... as he feared
The child cried and he prayed, then he disappeared
An adult in the form of a child ... buried deeper
Anguish, unrelenting, unbearable ... his keeper

I've exhausted this life, without voice he proclaimed
Uncontrollable action ... he cannot be blamed
Heart ruled by reflections spinning around in his head
Spent, with emotion ... he retreated instead

The intangible ... destructible boil had been lanced
Enter death, welcome friend ... lost love at first glance
The mask removed ... no longer to hide or shadow sorrow
FREED ... Vaporized ... Swoosh ... no pain for tomorrow

Unanswered prayer doesn't matter, death has taken its place
Peace eternal, the reward as he finished the race
God's ultimate protection ... a dominating conviction
He sleeps silent ... so peaceful ... awaiting resurrection

Jacqueline Allen

"Threads Of Life"

Our souls and lives are planned from the start.
Laid out in a brilliant array;
In a pattern that's woven with love from the heart,
Its threads in a web - there to stay.

The dark threads may symbolize moments of pain.
The light threads - joys of our seasons;
Whatever the colors, we ask, but in vein,
All the why's and the what's, and the reasons.

We shall not find out these questions we ask,
For each thread has a meaning so true;
The answers are hidden in colorful mask.
Of the pattern that's woven for you.

Not till each loom is silent and still.
And the shuttles have ceased their labor;
Will the color of threads - life's pattern at will.
Be revealed to the man whom they favor!

Flora J. Gast

The Inner Light

Beneath the elegant dew
Lies the key to thy heart;
Above the mystical water
Where existence had wandered apart.

In the midst of the roaring wind
Where every soul had shed its tears;
Above the highest mountain peak
Where consoling skies absorb thy fears.

Be faithful to thy dreams, thy wishes
For down deep in thee grace and love elope;
Through the innocent wonder of the child
Lies the true power; the beauty of Hope.

Fear not for 'tis not man who decides but God
Reveal your emotions, your inner cries;
Be free as the wise child
For above thy soul the creation lies.

Beautiful existence - behold!
For through the anguish, the hate the sorrow;
In the being lies the power to love
Awaiting another tomorrow.

Esti Khusid

Too Much Pride

Holding hands with someone new,
laughing and kissing, like we used to do,
Too painful to look, too much pride to cry,
The tears keep coming,
The more I try, the more they slip by.
Too much pride to say I was wrong,
I guess I'm not that strong,
Too much pride to say I'm sorry,
I'll just have to live,
With what I did.
Too much pride to cry,
Although the tears often slip by.
Too much pride to say I was wrong,
Maybe I'm just not that strong.
But I am, I'm sorry,
And I was wrong,
And I wish I could cry,
But it's too late,
We have already said Goodbye.

Carrie R. Coram

Trust And Obey

Trust and obey My word that's for you,
Learn to lean upon Me and of all I do.
For have you forgotten what happened yesterday,
Of how you tied to do it in your own feeble way?
Won't you come, and follow Me now,
Just trust in My word and I will show you how.
Walk with Me, as you learn to read and pray,
Take the light I gave you in the way.
Each day as you go through the storms of life,
I will be there, to banish all strife.
So remember my dear one, you are a jewel to me,
More precious than all the world you see.
When you reach the autumn of your years,
Feeling all alone, with man doubts and fears.
Again I ask thee, trust Me even now,
Obey My voice, as I teach thee how.
Once more I ask thee, even as I said
Trust me as you lay on deaths bed.
For I will be there, to welcome you home
Ever to be with you, nevermore shall you roam.

Daniel S. Davis

"Set A Watch" (Psalm 141:3-4)

Set A watch, Oh Lord, before my mouth,
  Let me listen before I speak;
Keep the words I speak from hurting someone
  Whose spirit may be weak.

Set a watch, Oh Lord, before my mouth,
  Keep the door of my lips sealed;
Until your spirit guides me to say
  The words that to me you've revealed.

Incline not my heart to do evil,
  To hurt when I should only love;
Set a watch before this heart of mine
  With wisdom from above.

Set a watch, Oh Lord, over my being,
  Alone my spirit sinks low;
Set a watch and open up my ears
  To hear what you want me to know.

Set a watch, Oh Lord, before my mouth,
  Let me speak to others in love;
Let me lead the way for them to find
  A home in heaven above.

Doris R. Samples

Simple Ordinary Things

Oh lonely one, come........
   Let yesterday go and fade away
except for fond memories that are in
   your heart to stay.
Rejoice, and sing, and let your imagination
   take you for a stroll.
Stroll down flower laden lanes, and hear the
   little birds sing their sweet refrains.
Imagine the sun coming up and glistening
   through the trees with crystal brilliant
rays that will fill your heart with glee.
   See the colors in the rainbow and
the dew upon the rose.
   Oh the beauty there is to behold!
Just the simple ordinary things all about
   makes a soul want to dance and shout.
Yield to the moment and drink it all in,
   then you won't feel so lonely my
precious friend.

   Barbara M. Miller

Adolescence

As we grow we'll realize,
Life is a big surprise.
The many things that we have learned
Have been a great discovery.
A certain part of life we know
is called adolescence,
Which teenagers should know.

Starting as an infant is very easy,
But yet there were many things that we didn't see.
Wanting and crying is what we knew best
At the age of a toddler, we must confess.

Boys, school, cheerleading squad,
Football team, and just being yourself
Is part of the life of an adolescent.
Business and marriage will come next,
But that can wait until school is done,
For school can offer a bundle of fun;
Without the age of adolescence
Life wouldn't make any sense.

   Abby Santos

Name

What's in a name?
Is a name power?
A sense of being?
OR is it a sense of belonging?

How do we know that what is named is named.
is a tree a "tree"
or is a tree a "rock;"
and if a tree is a rock, then is a rock a "bird,"
a bird, is that "blue?"

A word is a name,
a name of a thought
created out of the thoughts
of that which is named "mind"

What is a name?
Is it that which makes,
identity, form, substance.
Or is it that which IS!

   David Nicol

Life

What is life full of?
Life is full of joy and happiness,
Life is full of peace like a dove.
Life is full of pain and sadness.
Life is full of success and failure.
Life is full of kindness and anger.
Life is full of good times and bad.
Life is full of boredom and fun.
Life can be disappointing, life can be sad.
Life can be filled with darkness or light.
Life can sink down to the bottom of the earth.
Life can lift off and take flight.
Life is full of whatever you want.

   Jenny Peng

"Where Are You Now"

Mommy's fourteen, a child, having a child and you're fighting for my
   life unborn.
Do you know how it feels to be a child, who no one wants anymore?

Be sure what you're fighting for; will you take care of me when I'm
   three or four? Will you be responsible when Mommy cares no more?

Would you look at me now, an unwanted guest, does it put your mind
   to rest,
To justify my life you feel and trust was a battle so noble and just?

And what have you done to feed me now?
Did you think of that when you marched?
Feed me and clothe me all the years through?
Tell me, where are you now?...Where are you now?

Life is a journey, some short, some long, God is the judge of it all.
We have not the power to kill the soul, it lives on and on and on.

Could you give some time for me right now?
Will you lay your judging aside?
Would you march for the cause of life right now?
Now that we're here, who will stand by our side?

Follow through what you're fighting for.
Please take care of me when I'm three or four.
Please be responsible when Mommy cares no more.
Do you know how it feels to be a child, who no one wants anymore?

*This is a poem written to create awareness about child abuse. It is
directed to those who spend much time, energy, and money to fight the
abortion issue. I believe we would reduce child abuse if we spent this
time, energy, and money helping abused and neglected children who
are already here, as a common goal, a common ground.*

   Jan Duncan James

Pray For Me

The light that glows within your eyes,
Is such a pretty sight to see.
And perhaps it's extra pretty,
To a country boy like me.

And no matter what tomorrow may bring,
In my thoughts you'll always be.
And honey when you pray tonight,
Please pray a special prayer for me.

I miss your soft, warm kisses,
Of love and understanding,
You always give me the love I need
And my love in return is all you're demanding.

So honey when you pray tonight,
And while you're on your knees,
Honey, pray a special prayer for me!

   Howard Leon Crain

For Brian

Until you swept me away
like a storm pushing through the sky
you touched my soul and carried me with you
I became your passion and your rage
you carried me to the ends of the earth
where the clouds lifted
and the rain of our happiness washed away the darkness
where we would shine together forever

Amy M. Mallow

questions

like a falcon's grip on his prey, it holds me.
like a vise squeezing until, until there is nothing left,
it holds me.
i run, but the future is too close and i cannot.
so i stop and i let it squeeze,
until i have no tears left to cry,
until my mind is crazy from the silence,
until my hands cease to shake from fatigue,
until it wins...

then i look back and wonder where it began,
wonder why i did not start running sooner
wonder where my incredible strength went, wonder, why , why , why

why me?

i wonder why i was cursed.
i wonder why i was chosen.
i wonder why i grew into this.
i wonder why i had to be given this evil blessing.
an evil blessing, this urge, this longing to write in
this world. why me? why in this lifetime?

Joy Johnston

Bats In The Belfry

Chipped layers of paint curl forward
like great gray waves in an ocean storm,
appearing just as fierce;
While the blackened panes of the windows' glass
stare back an evil gaze, mysterious
as Loch Ness
and lending to the ominous air.
Even the most reviled of creatures ambles past,
refusing to spin its silken snares
amidst the corners of the decrepit domicile.
While within, the man sits and stares glaring
at the gutted television set,
enrapt by vivid visions of acrobats and elephants.
And the neighbors swear they hear bats in the belfry.

Joy Affannato

Encourage Each Other

If you are in need of a kind word or two,
Let me give a suggestion of what you can do!

Just sit down and write a note sent with cheer,
Or call up a friend that is precious and dear!

A plate of fresh cookies that you baked with care,
Will show more than words that you're always there!

A smile is so precious and can be freely given,
So let's share them with all and show that life is worth liven'!

A wonderful blessing will always be received,
When Christ guides our actions, our thoughts and our deeds!

So let's keep the spirit of encouraging one another,
And let everyone know that our love is from the Father!

Carla Gerlt

9

The number nine fills the sky
Like stars on a starless night.
I could buy them and sell them
like yesterday's junk,
But the sky told me
I didn't know the hierarchy I dealt with.
My mind races for an answer
To all the nines in the sky,
But my spirit aches
While the marigolds wilt in the sad dusk.
I'm drunk on the scent of the night and the brewing storm.
The wind blew away my fears and my tired soul.
I stand on a lone monument.
The nines are frozen in the sky,
And for a brief, revealing instant
I see what is on the end of everyone's fork.
I cry for someone to hear me and share this with me,
But no one does,
No one but the nines.

Jonathan Heintz

The Mystery

It is mysterious behind an animal's eyes,
Like the various reasons for a baby's cries.
You can't remain furious at them for long,
Or keep a serious face at a song.
Their obvious innocence gets them off the hook,
And the doubt of it gives you a poisonous look.
The strenuous worry always hangs on.
And that adds one more suspicious leach of a frown.
The tremendous, delicious smell of their food gives them
    a playful and humorous mood!

Jocelyn Erdman

Housebound-Spellbound

SNOW — the very word connotes stalled cars,
lines extending for miles, gleeful children
hearing "NO SCHOOL"

Tense shoppers eager for markdowns
to fill spaces beneath trees with
silks, wools, leathers, laces

Through a window I see prone on a branch
a white poodle looking down readying
to make a leap

Long-necked swan, spotted pony,
sheep, arctic bears, a veritable zoo
atop a once green yew

Covered white crow, wings spread in flight,
an anteater, snout snowy white focused
on a special sight

Below snuggled in
rhododendron spotted white,
a small owl, dark peering eyes

Elizabeth Valicenti

Fate Of All Flesh

Smile, O Fate, smile and mock us, as we relish your bait and you know it will pass, rich, poor or any class, you know it will not forever last, and when you catch up with us it will not matter the past. But please O Fate, please O Fate, treat us kindly before that last gate, while we live, toil, mate and propagate, darkness and misery abate, grant us wisdom each other to tolerate, work together and create, instead of dividing us into groups of hate. Please consider that before it is too late before we all perish in that state.

Jacob Haruvi

Sarah

Lovely eyes of stormy grey with hair of golden silk,
Lips of blood-red like the rose and skin as smooth as milk.

She walks along the seaside in a gown of starlit white,
Her hair let down upon her shoulders, radiating in the soft moonlight.
Waves crashing on the shore, the winds whispering her name,
Not like all the others, no not quite the same.

Sarah, Sarah, how delicate the sound of her name, beautiful and sweet,
As she walks at the waters' edge, the surf pounding at her uncovered
     feet.
From the dreary cliffs above, I see her, a beacon in the tempest sea,
But, as a tantalizing dream, before me does she continually flee.

Always there but beyond my grasp, I follow her across the crystal
     sands,
I falter and faint but she is there to take me in her soft, smooth
     hands,
Then fades away to abandon me, struggling to live without her.

Joseph Caudle

God's Voice

God speaks to us in many ways,
Listen and you shall hear,
In the song of a bird and the sound of the wind
His voice comes loud and clear.

Through the patter of warm summer rain,
Or the whispering fall of winter snow,
Whatever the season; be it day or night,
His voice comes soft and low.

Yes, in every sound of "Mother Nature"
God's voice can always be heard;
But to us, his children, he gave even more,
For He gave us the written word.

He has given us so very much,
So many blessings from above,
And all He seeks from us in return,
Is our obedience and love.

Dixie D. Bauch

The Knowing Of Joy

I have stood at river's edge
listening to a loon's warble
as its echoing cry, plays across the water
watching the sun break on the horizon
to fill the sky with light,
and in its brilliance
felt the joy and comfort in knowing
that God has placed his finger on my heart.

Hugh R. Schumacher

Last Chance

Sleep away freedom — dwindle in danger
Laugh at love — to live for anger

Skip a space — and jump back three
Caught listening for eyes — that cannot see

Smell the colors — Taste the sound
Seeking love — that can't be found

Touch the sky — Swallow the air
Catch the love — but it's not there

Breathe out water — Inhale blood
Last Chance — REGICIDE LOVE!!!!

Isabell C. Epps

Graduation Day

I sit here silently,
Listening to the excited voices,
Yet, not hearing the words.
My mind is one-thousand miles away,
Where as kids we played in the dirt
And rode our bikes in each other's yard,
The games we played, the hours we stayed,
The first dates with the "don't be late,"
The games with their victories and losses,
The dances, the cars, the ...
I hear my name,
And I am brought back to the present.
I begin the long walk of life,
As I approach the steps, I look for my parents,
Their faces, shining with tears, are glowing with delight.
Each step I take reminds me of how far I have come,
And how far I have to go.
Now as I reach for my diploma, I smile,
Yet I wonder, where do I go from here?

Brandy Bowman

Little Nana

I felt my heart fall and fill with great pain,
Listening to the sound of the softly falling rain...
Tons of thoughts racing through my head,
Thinking of what I haven't said.

So many things on my mind,
Feeling so helpless in this bind.
I don't know if I'm strong enough for all of this,
Saying my prayer and giving my final kiss.

Seeing all of my loved ones cry,
As I sit here and think, wondering why.
There was nothing more I could do while you were sick,
But visit and talk white the clock went tick.

I'll try not to be sad, I'll try to be strong,
I can't help thinking I did something wrong.
Maybe I didn't visit enough,
I guess I was scared, while you stood tough.

I really couldn't bear to see you that way,
As the sun rose each morning, to the dawn of the day.
Obviously the Lord needed you more,
But your kindness and love I will forever adore!

Jess Lavigne

Memories

Remember the first rose you gave me?
     Little tiny funny rose-
You bought it in that flower shop.

Remember our first dinner at that Italian place-
     The shrimp cocktails, the wine-

Remember going dancing - Edward's place -
     The country western band -

Remember lazy days and rainy nights -
     We planted our own rose garden.

Remember problems? Your kids, my kids -
     We didn't care.

You gave me a big bouquet of roses,
     We went to Vegas and had fun.

     Life was glorious!
And then it happened.
     I gave you a bouquet of roses.

Hester Briggs

Follower Of Fate

Am I not loyal, Am I not worthy to
live with thee on this earth. What shall
I do to prove that I am worthy. Shall I
die or shall I live. You shall decide my fate,
what will become of me and my soul. Will
they go on forever or will they stop short in
this miserable thing called life.

I shall redeem myself to you, if you ask
me too. I will do whatever may please you,
even if it means death. I am a follower of
good, not evil. You shall decide my fate.
Only you know my destiny, no one else ………

Jennifer-Lee Villanueva

Mistress Of My Heart

Autumn in despair, love is lost, and death is
living, stand forth the broken heart, and the
seasons turn…

Summer in flames, passions burn, filling the
mind with hopeless desire, stand forth the
reckless heart, and the seasons turn…

Winter in tears, sins lay forgotten, the
soul washed clean, stand forth the mended
heart, and the seasons turn…

Spring in mystery, life's new start, the mistress
comes to unite the heart, stand forth two
hearts made as one, and the seasons turn
no more, spring eternal…

David Marouf

Breaking Hearts And Taking Names

I said love would never get me down but here I am wearing this
Lonely frown yes, I thought I was doing fine but you came along
And I nearly lost my mind

I don't want to play your kind of games
Breaking hearts and taking names

I said love could never take me by surprise but that's before
I looked into your eyes just when I thought I was doing okay
You came along and got in my way

I don't want to play your kind of games
Breaking hearts and taking names

I said love would never get me down

Jimmy Ray Smith

Loneliness

Loneliness is a mountain, granite, unyielding.
Looming up before me, obscuring my view,
To all the dreams I had, the life that I once knew.

Fingertips of fear surround me, is loneliness here to stay,
Or will it one day quietly steal away? It's just a state of
Mind they say, but I can tell you, it's for real because
I chose that way.

My companion now is solitude, unloving and unloved.
She follows me on crowded street, down quiet country lane.
Ever at my side, whispering my name. Reminding me of
Children's smiles, and gentle loving ways. Laughter that
Followed me through starry nights and happy sun-filled days.

In sleepless nights, in reverie I dream of things that still
Could be. If that day should ever come, I'll thank the Lord
for all he's done, for bringing back my days in the sun.

Eustelle Solo

In The Spring

Oh what a beautiful Spring Day
Look above and you will see
colors of sky blue with a trace of grey

Musical Honey Bees buzzing about with the breeze
carrying the pollen from an Easter Lily
A patch of honeysuckles
the fragrant wind such a sweet smell
as Spring Begins

Finches, Bluebirds, Robins
gathering fine threads of a shoelace or two
they sweetly flutter their wings threading the eye
of pine needles that have fallen from the trees
sew to make their nests

The translucent Rainbow shines in the distance
after a thunderous rainstorm comes to an end

The World holds such treasures' embrace
if only you will take a moment or two
for tomorrow will bring something new
In the Spring

Diane Hudson

No Rhyme, No Reason

Sometimes, I don't want to but I do,
Look for you everywhere.
I must write down what I feel, for fear that I will suffer insanity.
I love you as I love life itself.
What is so precious, now is all that I seek.
My every waking moments are consumed with desires of you.
I often wonder how can this be so, but it is.
What am I to do?
Crying spells, chest pains, head and heart ache.
I am bewitched, or perhaps I've found my Roxanne.
Never may you go away.
I hurt, hurting so bad, Damn it all
I wonder if death will make it go away.
I got it bad, real bad and I don't know what to do.
God help me, for she is not mine.

Connie Foreman

Love

Love is patient in waiting on others
Love is hand in hand

Love sees no boundaries
therefore love is forever

Love asks no question
because there is no answer for love.

Love sees only truth and hope
never age, or color

Love is the true meaning of life
within itself
with no strings attached

Love is the consideration of others
and admiring one's thoughts and intentions.
Love is kind to all meaning -
Love is you and I
forever and always

No matter what we may go through

I will love you always

Camie Lynn Arnold

Just

I explode into rage passionate hate engaged I step into it all
Look into my eyes once an innocent child you left me alone to die
An infant cold an trembling in the falling rain given the
chance your soul I will strain
My eyes towards the sky I spread my wings towards blue
streaks of heaven
I am the chosen one help me escape reality
You're perfect, yes it's true but enter your eyes I ravel deeper than you
I've seen the hate in heaven and felt the chill of hell
The hell where your soul shall dwell
Heart of stone and eyes that cast despair
On the mother whose child you bear
As you walk away the tears in her eyes make you rejoice,
As you slaughter each new life I'm tracking you to take you
back to your demon brothers.

Dorothy Ellen Wallace

Feelings

Life and times is heartache, fun is just a game.
Love is but a glimmer of hope that dies in the flame.

Is there anything but pain that will meet me along life's way?
Is all my heartaches, troubles, and woes the only things I'll ever
  get to say?
Why is it that writing poetry and acting are the only things that
  calm me down,
Or pick me up and send me flying when I'm on my way down.
I question my life, my existence all the time,
Like, will there ever be a time that I can truly call mine?
I need to feel loved, cared for, like I've never been before.
Before my life crumbles before everyone's eyes as I slowly shut
  the door.

I feel like a little kid who has to be led around,
Who has to be told what to do, and to never make a sound.
At times I think I'm crazy, a nuthouse is where I belong.
For in my life, I even have trouble cheering up to a single song.

Debra J. Williams-Edwards

The African-American Bicentennial Salute

A pioneer's silence of love is lonely,
Love's lonely quietness.
Love is everlasting; yearning the eternal
unchanging principles of the Holy Spirit.

Love is provocative and it is calculating
with the "All American Flag," a beam of stars and stripes
bursting in the East, West, North and South
in the city of Middletown, Ohio.

The American flag symbolizes freedom,
Love's lonely quietness, love's lonely silence.
The sun is bright, shining with light.
Just to foresee the "Big Dipper" as far as Darkest Africa,
piercing at night.

And in the night comes forth a full moon,
The stars are beaming in the East,
West, North and South.
Every great soul has a surpassing power of wisdom.

Love's lonely quietness; love's lonely silence.
Love's heartaches seek to someday heal one's wounds.
Love is Christ and even precise.
Love's lonely quietness; the African-American
pioneer Bicentennial salute,
Love's lonely silence.

Cheryl Wilson Copyright 1991

What Love Is

Love is special.
Love is kind.
Love is understanding each other.
Love shows how much you care.
Love isn't just a word it has a special meaning.
Love means you'll always be there.
Love means you'll always care.
Love is great and wonderful feeling.
Love can be said but if you don't mean it don't say it,
because it will only break my heart.

Jamie Lynne Sitzer

"Love"

Love is a splendid thing to be a part of.
Love is like a flickering candle across the room,
where only the flame is allowed to dance in
romance.
Love is like a candle lit dinner where only two
may romance in the dim candle light.
Love is like a lake at sunset where the water
glitters with delight of the starry night to come.
Love is like a babbling brook going over tiny
rocks and earth.
Love is like a bright red rose blooming in the spring.
Love is like a flower garden in June, bright and
colorful, streaming with flowers.
Love is like a swing swinging in the wind.

Adrian Heiney

"The Seed Of Priority"

What's become of the people we were?
Loving, caring for mankind, is now just a blur!
The helping hands we use to give,
Now open only for money to sieve!
When in your life there is someone to whom money you owe,
What hardships you have, they don't want to know!
Whether it be food for your children's mouths,
Or money needed for a payment to keep your house.
Then, you try to explain, they turn a deaf ear,
All they want to know, is when will you have the money to them, and
  where!
Love, caring, and a helping hand need to be re-taught!
Hardships of people, need to be, brought back into our thoughts!
Compassion, has to be re-instilled,
For human kindness is vastly being killed!
We have become a world drowning in greed;
New priorities, we need to seed!
So come now, I beg of you, let's overcome this greed,
We can all help, in planting...
THE SEED

Judy Lynn Carlson

Untitled

With the coming of Christmas
Let's remember what it's really all about.
It was a very special moment without a doubt.
Let the good news ring,
It's the birth of a KING!
Giving us a reason
For this holy season.

May the true meaning of Christmas
Return to our lives,
Starting with the hearts of husbands and wives.
Teaching our children to give of themselves,
Something they got not from Santa's elves.
Giving GOD the glory
For His holy story!

Ellen Mastel

Smile

Want to win? Want to win every time?
Magic. Yes! Employ your magic.
Brilliance blossoms as the clue clears.
A reflective surface proves.

Push and you will be pushed.
Pull and you will be pulled.
Simple!
Smile and....Magic!

Powerful, thrilling, mighty,....
Smile and see your effect.
View your focus. Then, focus on yourself.
Two reflections you realize.

Your initial focus will respond in kind.
Your latter focus, your soul, will do the same.
Your powerful stroke, your magical display,
Will reflect upon you from outward and within.

Your smile! It's simple.
It's magic! It's all yours.
Christian Sarra

Emotions

Love. Fills you up inside,
Makes you a stupid fool at first,
Then you come back to Earth
Then you're confused.
Confusion. Too many thoughts at one time,
Can't sort them all out perfectly,
Find too many problems trying to,
And then you're frustrated.
Frustration. Much like confusion,
But with a hint of rage in it,
Often gets you into trouble,
Then you're angry.
Anger. The most feared and hated,
Rage and hatred and frustration rolled into one,
Loved ones may leave,
Then you're depressed.
Depression. Often when you feel this you loaf,
You don't really do a whole lot,
Eat and sleep until a new person comes along,
Then you feel love again. Sigh.
Christopher J. Chatham

The Look Of Love

Your feelings run deep. There must be sweet
love in your heart. You're singing! You have the
look of truth in your eyes. Heavens light glows
inside your soul. Your inside motives run deep.
I can dream and look at your smile...and sing
odes about the love-light kissing your eyes.
Your warm gorgeous eyes talk about, joy in
paradise-they're deeper than space. The look
on your face is singing to heaven. Love is
wonderful. Love has branded your eyes with
heavenly invitations. You deeply reflect "God's
Look." Your body is singing....I hear it sing
about soft, warm love-oceans. Now that's
deep! What is dancing inside your soul? Your
eyes shine like the great looking-glass of
truth...looking joyous - while singing the truth
of love. The smile of your eyes whisper from
within. Your promise is deep. Living in your
eyes and singing so deep is...
"THE LOOK OF LOVE."...
Willard R. Fox

Lest We Forget...

Remembering the soldiers who fought for our land.
Making it a better place for women and men.
We cannot forget just what they have done.
This includes each and everyone.
They all need our help this is for sure.
The world has a problem and we must find a cure.
The women can help each and every man.
We have our auxiliaries and do the best that we can.
We help the young, the sick and the old.
We do not want them to feel like they are left out in the cold.
Everyone needs to help our fellow man.
Remember they fought to save our land.
God Bless our soldiers brave, strong and true.
No one could do it better than you.
Diane Watkins

Tired of Hiding

Every day I try to keep composed.
Making sure my feelings are not exposed.
There are evil demons in my soul,
And now my heart is taking the toll.
All I see is darkness in the inside.
I see no color, just a shade of black abides.
As I try to go on, my strength begins to subside.
Causing all good-natured thoughts to die.
That smile on the outside can be deceiving.
While, on the inside, all your love is leaving.
People are cruel, and people are mean.
We're all used like tools, and never redeemed.
There are pills, there are knives.
What's the sense in sparing lives?
Jamie Augienello

Hands Of The Future

Children, children everywhere
Many people just don't care
They are the future, we are the past
Our guidance is needed, no need to be asked
Tiny hands hold the golden clasp
We should help the children learn their craft
'Cause they are our future and we are the past.
Cheryl Y. Brunson

Untitled

Twilights falls and twilight finds
Me pining for all you left behind
I see your face as I await the moonlight
Glowing there soft and fair, all I care for at twilight.

Twilight calls softly to me
Reviving a lost reverie
Dreams that bring me to the brink of ecstasy
Every night in the pale twilight.

Tell me please the reverie is real
It's all I know in how one feels
And I feel the feeling is so right
And I see plainly the sweet flight at twilight.

Twilight calls softly to me
Reviving a lost reverie
Dreams that bring to me the brink of ecstasy
Every night in the pale twilight.

Sing a serenade while the music plays at night
And I'll see you come to me in the pale twilight.
Jess Kelly

A Dream Or A Fantasy

Is it a dream to be able to love you,
Maybe it's a dream, a dream of wishes, of
love, a wish to be happy but, the fantasy
is more like a story. A story of dreams
and fantasies almost like a fairy tale
not written out, but in your mind with the
thoughts of love and everything you did
wrong along the way. A chance to make up
for everything you did wrong. A chance
to ask for forgiveness and happiness to
be with the one you love...
  Now: You make the decision is it a dream
or a fantasy maybe it's just a reality.

Ashley Honeycutt

The Kingdom Of Love

When I'm down on my knees each night, I ask the Lord to show
me a better way to a better life. I think of the children
who go hungry some nights. I read about the parents who
abuse the kids over fussing and fighting. I like to speak
for the children by singing this song. When a child is
born, we must try to reach out and help them with our
knowledge and love. We must guide them, mold them, and show
them there is a better way to a better life.

Friends, what are we going through? It's strange to see
that no one has time to care for you. Why can't we live
together, 'cause no one can admit to one another we're all
guilty without each other. We must find a place to call
our kingdom of love. When somebody is happy, there is someone
who is sad, but not in the kingdom of love. Because it
is all from God above who is the ruler of the kingdom of love.

Calvin S. Holt

Friends

My friends, whether near or afar
Mean so much to me, like a twinkle of a star.

Whenever I feel kind of low,
One will probably call and say hello.

My feelings are, friends are worth more than gold
Such a comfort to be embraced, with a strong hold.

My dear friend Elizabeth, is so sweet and dear
Full of laughter, in October, she passed her 98th year.

Each day, I thank God, for all my wonderful friends
Remembering them with get well, birthday cards, many I send.

My husband and my family are such a delight
They are the greatest friends, although, to some I take a flight.

Each day, I count my blessings, God was good to me
A loving husband, children, grandchildren, how much luckier can I be?

Frances G. Bond

In Memory Of Gregory Earl And Jerry Dale

When I was six or seven: Still a little girl,
Mama had my brother. She named him Gregory Earl.
He was fat and had blue eyes,
He lived for weeks, but soon he died.

Time went by, things were well,
Then Mama had Jerry Dale.
As I lay silently in bed one night,
I heard, 'My God, Jo Ann, your son is dead.'

Mama had nine children.
Only seven survived.
I think about them now and then,
And thank God my children are alive.

Betty Hopper

Tortured Soul

Loneliness engulfs me in the dark, starless night
Memories of friends far off taunt my mind
My small world crumbles around me, while life keeps going by.
The clock ticks incessantly reminding me of every wasted moment
Urging me to grab this moment - missed it.
O.K. this one! - missed again.
I realize soon that the ticking will be in time with my teardrops
    of regret
And someday, it will turn me into a bitter old woman
With nothing to show for my life - material possessions do not count.
My will will not bequeath the value of morals, like I had hoped
And my beneficiaries will not miss it, they will not know any better.
Hatred and loneliness are strong adversaries,
For their bond is eternally united
I pity the souls who must do battle against them
For I have also, and lost.
I am a prisoner to them, serving a life sentence.
And only in death will I be free - with God waiting for me.

Cindy Satterlee-Leavitt

My Treasure...

Wake to the slow dawn of a day,
Look for the rainbow in pearl drops of dew;
Feel the soft touch of the cold crisp morning air
And hear the larks with the first worm among the few.
Heed the words of the wise...
(though many a times seem unfair),
Yet strong with wisdom, wrought
Comfort to a bleeding heart.
Time stands still a gentle maiden
Full of promises yet to unfurl,
A sweetness so enchanting, yet as fleeting
I know naught but at Nature's feet to curl.
Happiness, love, or life's simplest pleasures...
All this and more, I will always treasure.

Elena Sona John

Blooms

I set in the shadows of loneliness
Hiding my feelings from openness.
I wonder if the world has something to hide like I?
Is fear fright on un-opened minded people that makes us this way?
Could we be just a flower of the spring and
open with vibrant colors and see what most people should see...
The inside of a magnificent wonder.

Karen Cowan

Untitled

I danced late last night
high romancing across the dance hall floor
I closed my eyes and let the music spirit me away
to where I could find you...your beautiful face.
I danced all night long in someone else's arms
yet wanting you I could feel
One endless moment
You and I
Together
Dancing...
under sheets of fire; burning desire
I've endured for you (since time began...)
I closed my eyes and let your spirit surround me;
Unbound me...
I had to surrender looking into someone else's eyes
Yet seeing you I could feel
We danced.

L. A. Bie

Hero in the Hayes-The 18th Legend

He's the hero in the Hayes
He's not really trying to be the star.
He's merely trying to be the heater that
saves you from the bitter cold of one bad Christmas
He's merely trying to be the stove that cooks your food
He wants to see you overcome hunger by eating a super supper
One mourning may have meant the deep depression of death.
But his morning approves of the new DAYES daring breath
His good morning leads the good memories to a light as
bright as the flash that makes your favorite pictures.

You may appear pale and ready to faint every time you fail
You may feel like a zero when you get old and gray
But he can make you as bold as black, silver, and gold
Because the start of him is like the start of hope
Every time he gives you a hug, your hope will be reborn
He cares enough to cook your corn, so you can cope and beat
the cold, because he's the hero in the Hayes
He may not be a movie star, but he's as helpful as a heater
that warms your heart on a very sad Christmas
He's a saint, with a heavenly hand, who can paint your
favorite pictures.

Walker Hayes

He's Some Kind Of Wonderful

All I need is Jesus on my side
He's there day and night, He's my guide
He will help me through my trials and tribulations
He watches over all the nations

He's some kind of wonderful, oh yes he is
He's some kind of wonderful, oh how sweet he is

he is there through thick and thin
He is coming back one day, yes you will see him again
I can't get you ready, this is true
When the time comes you are on your own, so it is left up to you

He's some kind of wonderful, oh yes he is
He's some kind of wonderful, oh how sweet he is

We are his people, the sheep of his pasture
Living on and around his castle
Like his birds and their feathers
We should all be flying away to heaven

He's some kind of wonderful, oh yes he is
He's some kind of wonderful, oh how sweet he is.

Natalie R. Jones

To My Friend Scott

I once knew a fair young man - his eyes were like china blue,
His name was Scott Fisher - and I love the lad so true.
I loved him from just a 'little guy' - always had a smile,
I've grown the years with him, and it's all been so worthwhile.
He has the nicest Mom and Dad, the greatest people I know,
The fact that he belongs to them, to all the world will show.
They are so proud of the fair young man, in all that he does,
From the time he was just a baby, and the 'little guy' he was.
The little guy is six feet tall - no longer the little one,
The young man is growing fast and will soon be a man of his own.
I am your Aunt and so proud of you - you are my favorite friend,
To list your wonderful qualities - there simply is no end.
Growing up is difficult, for every phase of our life -
You never cease to grow, through the happiness and strife.
You've grown with so much progress, a fine one you've become,
The best of both your parents, show in their favorite son.
I'll watch you go through college, and you'll come out the best,
If I ever had a choice, I would have picked you from the rest.
I feel quite lucky to share you - as the son I've never had,
I'll always want to share your life, the good and the bad.

Mari Schwamberger

Rwandan Hymn

A gift to the wind - rampaging unmercifully through Rwanda's 10,000
Hills - are the reverberating, shrieking screams of terror... How
could this miniature Jewel Of The Nile, adorned with African blue
Violets and green velvet valleys, nestled in blushing sunrise
splendours - yield such atrocities? Hypnotic, in the medieval acorn -
ethnic challenges of Hutu and Tutsi erupt - until "Die Tutsi Die!"
thunders through the velvet valleys to the ritualistic beat of the
Tom-tom. In the half-light of a near breaking dawn, bronzed barefoot
executioners, wielding machetes, diabolically decapitate body and
spirit - smearing the whole of Civilisation. Innocent's Day streams
forth with children felling children. Above this Dark Continent - the
sun, moon, and stars hide their eyes. A campaign of genocide - evokes
Barbarian spectres of Genghis Khan and Attila The Hun. Ancient human
sacrifices - differ only in time and place - on Molech's altar of
man's inhumanity to man. Spellbound, Lucifer slithers through this
ceremonial land of Voodoo, Taboo and Juju - not unlike the crocodile -
who concludes no covenant of peace. Look! the Bright Morning Star
appears on the blue horizon luminescent with Truth of the Millennial
Dawn. "You, Are My Faithful Witnesses," Saith Jah, God of gods.
"You, Are My Faithful Dead..."

Patricia A. Morris

His Eyes

His eyes behold the windows of his soul
His eyes tell me a story of here life did take its toll
And though he may smile gently back at me
There's sorrow in his eyes, that plane to see
We talk; his hesitation leaves me doubt
As I listen to every word, fall from his mouth
He's face was crimped with pain and I could see
Through the windows of his soul, he wanted to be free
And then as flooding water filled his eyes
He turned away from me, and said goodbye!

Nancy Reil

From Life To Death As Jesus Holds My Hand

He's always been there, but I didn't realize it.
His love is always with me, but I didn't know
Touching me so many times, and making me feel warm.
Helping me in so many ways, but I didn't understand.
He's always by my side, so I'm never alone,
and he holds my hand when things seem wrong.
Helping me through the darkest storm.
His love for me is undying and true.
From life to death as JESUS holds my hand.

Winnifred E. Gran

Hunger In Somalia

The little child knows not why he must hunger, thirst and die
His sister cannot tell in this land of living hell
For she lies starving and dying too
With empty bellies full distended, seems no help is extended
When a simple cup of rice would nicely do
Their arms and legs like sticks to be thrown on a fire
Huge eyes plead well, in this land of living hell
For they have seen their father's funeral pyre
Mother cries silent tears, for she has many fears
That her children will be next to head death's way
So they are carried to the dump, to find a loathsome lump
Of nutrition, just to live another day
So hand the child a plastic fork and a plastic spoon as well
To scrounge for his dinner in this garbage heap in hell
But soon he grows too weak to leave his bed to seek
That leaf, that seed or moldy crumb of bread
So he lies there and he dies there with one thought in his head
In the next world, maybe he'll be fed.

Olive M. Lani

The Suitcase

Taking two at a time was easy once I
hitched my uniform up above my knees.
Beating a slow path up the stairs, I
reached my mother's bedroom.
Jumping to a sit position, startled by the
slamming of a blue Samsonite suitcase,
I asked my father why he was packing.
His answer held little importance in comparison
to when my fifth grade legs would finally touch the carpet.
"Tell your mom, I left."
The words undulated through the rhythm of my swaying legs.
Summer's end, maybe.
"Did you hear me?"
For sure by sixth!

Sitting on the bed next to mother,
watching her face fighting desperately to hold back
the tears,
I carried the weight of all her sorrow
as I sat on my father's suitcase and kissed him
good-bye.

Michelle P. Iannucci

Knight Vision

Slumbers in a dream world,
Holding court is Lady Rae.
Crown of love comes your way.

Turtle doves a flutter,
Tinkling bells dance on air.
Wishing well wisher, coming true.

Through sands of time,
On white stallion come.
Jack of Knight appears.

Into the sunset ride,
Regale Lady Rae, courageous Jack of Knight.
Love knows, no limitation sphere.

Dawn first ray of light.
Filters through to break the night.
Knight vision disappears.

Rosemary Benedum

"Dare To Discover..."

Dare to discover world peace,
Hopefully the world will soon be,
A place of comfort and ease,
To all that truly believe.

Dare to discover the homeless,
They appreciate the little they own,
Most dislike being jobless,
Being hated for not having a home.

Dare to discover learning,
For your dreams will surely come true,
Only if you don't stop yearning,
Life can be better for you.

Dare to discover yourself,
Are you crazy, happy, or wild?
Are you shy, loving, and caring?
Or just another book on the shelf?

No matter who, what, or where you are,
You are you and that you'll stay,
Whether you live near or far, you'll still be you every day.
DARE TO DISCOVER!

Sherry Richards

To David

Oh Love of mine, Oh gentle soul,
How could I see, You did not know?

You saw so much and shared with me,
You touched my heart and set me free,

I've loved you for a thousand years,
I've searched for you throughout my tears,

As fate would have you finally came,
To calm my heart and ease my pain,

When all was wrong you held me near,
You gave me love, you showed no fear,

Know, I am not as brave as you,
But doubt not, that my love is true,

In all my life there ne'er will be,
Another Love so dear to me,

As a river flows on deep and sure,
so shall my love for you endure,

Where this road leads to matters none,
But to be with you, in the morning sun,

   Yes, My Love, I Love You

Mary Kathleen Ahern

Dear Brother

How I ache for his love, his concern and his caring,
How I wish that our lives had consisted of sharing.
As a child I strived to gain his attention,
I followed him, mimicked him, he never made mention,
Of his feelings for me, my dear brother of mine.

As we grew from our childhood into sensitive teens,
I craved for his friendship it was part of my dreams.
And just when I felt he was part of my life,
He met and he married and he took him a wife,
Who drove him further from family, my dear brother of mine.

We're both a lot older yet the pain is so real,
I've given up trying to show how I feel.
I shun his indifference, I have much too much pride,
To let anyone know how I'm crying inside
For the love I have missed from my dear brother of mine.

A secret desire, a want and a wish,
Is that someday he'll long for the sister he missed,
He'll show his emotions, not have any fears,
To tell me he's loved me throughout all the years,
Before it's too late, my dear brother of mine.

Lesly Debie

A Coastal Town In Maine

The water rushes.
High tide is coming.
People watch,
As the dry sand becomes moist.
The fishermen's boat's motors can be heard
From the dock.
Overlooking the glistening water,
Sailboats float.
The bright colors catch your eyes
As you watch them
Pass by.
The sun shines
On the boats,
Making them glare.
And you realize how peaceful it is
In a coastal town in Maine.

Laura Sherman

Untitled

At times I'm sad and the tears will flow
How long does it last and when will it go?

These two things I don't really mind
It's the wonderful times we left behind.

The memories are there for me alone.
Of the many moments that we had sown.

Tho I was the strongest of us two
I got my strength from loving you.

At days end you were always there
So many things done to show you care.

For our children you gave me three.
The love they gave, was for you and me.

It's getting dark and growing late,
Don't forget - we have a date.
              I Love You
       F. D. Rathstone

To Mom

I find it very hard to say just
how much I care.
But mom deep inside my heart, the love shines
brightly there.
It's locked up deep inside me but is very
hard to say.
But I want you to know I love you more each day.
I try to show in other ways exactly how I
feel. Just cause I don't say it much, doesn't
make it less real.
My love for you is always there, deep within
my heart.
It's there when were together, it's there when
were apart.
I think of you each morning, I pray for you
each night. In my heart and in my mind you're
never out of sight.
So never doubt my love for you, it's there
for you to see. Just look a little closer it's
my heart that holds the key.

       Ruby Alvarez

Seeing The Light

"OH LORD" I pray, this fiftieth birthday
How much longer must I strive?
I've worked so hard to do my best,
and here you give me another test.

I've raised my children to believe in you.
yet you make it all, so hard to do.
I worked and worked to do it right.
Will I ever see the light?

I've taken many roads in life,
and yes, I know that you were there.
But, did you have to toss that curve?
Knowing I would loose my nerve?

The children come to wish me well,
and bring their children home to me.
How happy they all seem to be.

And then I see, OH YES I SEE!
For in those eyes I see the light,
meant especially for ME!

All this I see, through my tears.
Lord, could I please have, ANOTHER FIFTY YEARS?
       Mary H. Cary

Steps In Life

From country to city,
How time seemed to fly!
I once took the time,
to listen, to sing, and always say Hi!

The crickets, they chirped, I no longer hear.
Oh, bring back the sounds, I long to hear.

The time is missed
when all used to gather,
in the yard, or on the porch,
wherever we'd rather.

Was it the move or was it the hurt,
that took the things, I love.
Where are my rings?

Oh, I know.
It just had to be.
It's just life.

Now maybe,
I'll not forget the things I love.
Is the country, a step in my life,
before Heaven above?
       Melissa Jacks

Ashes Ashes All Fall Down

I don't know how to talk,
How to say what's on my mind,
To say the words, "I miss you,"
Doesn't do justice to my pain inside.

I think of you so often,
And life is not the same,
I long to hear your voice,
And see your reassuring smile,
Life to me now is hard to find worthwhile.

I woke up this morning with stale whiskey in my head,
I remembered how you would call for me to help you out of bed,
But disease slayed another being and sorrow caressed my head.

You deteriorated slowly and my heart withered as you did,
Now you've passed away and my heart feels cold,
And it's hard to put my arms around a memory,
When they're so damn hard to hold.

Ashes ashes all fall down,
Your ashes have increased my fears,
Ashes ashes all fall down,
I'm left drowning in my whiskey tears.
       Kristin D. Miller

"The Meaning Of God's Tear"

Today I've seen GOD looking down on
his children, from the sky up above.
His eyes were glowing, they were so
filled with his love.
Then something strange suddenly caught
my eye, and I found myself asking
God to show me what was making him cry.
He then showed me the whole world through
his one crystal tear, and the people below
were living in fear.
God then spoke to me, and said he could
not continue letting his children live
below among all this sin, and before
I could even speak the world come to
an END!
       Lorie Schutter

258

Of Course

If I asked you today if you'd love me tomorrow,
how would you respond?
Deep inside your soul would you know the answer?
Or would you simply say, "Of Course."

If you asked me today if I'd love you tomorrow, I know how I'd respond
I know how I'd respond. The answer would be obvious.
I'll love you today more than yesterday, but I'll love you more
tomorrow.

What if I asked you tomorrow if you loved me today,
how would you respond?
Can you look me in the eyes and say "Yes," or will you hesitate and
say "Of Course."

Why do I ask these questions of you?
Could it be that I know the answers deep inside your soul.
Are you honest enough to share them with me or will you be honest
enough and say "Of Course."

Of course I could be wrong.
But isn't "Of Course" just as puzzling as "What If?"

Kathlyne Abernathy

When I Close My Eyes

When I close my eyes
I am at awe at what I see.
The many beautiful rays of colors,
That I wonder, what more could there possibly be.

When I close my eyes
The calmness of peace and tranquility falls on me.
I am as soft and free as a cloud
No problem on earth can conquer me.

When I close my eyes
My mind wanders to days that have passed.
And oh, the memories, both sad and good
Rush by to reveal themselves.
Some are there that can't let go.
But it's not quite so easy to cast them aside
Even though I know I should.

When I close my eyes
I drift off to a distant place,
A place that has a spot just for me.
It is my own special place you see
That God has given only to me.

Naomi R. Hamilton

His Love

Please tell me what I am feeling,
    I am so confused inside.
Won't you give me the answers I seek,
    for so very long I have tried.

I search for a peacefulness,
    something I know I must feel.
How I long to be happy,
    if only my Spirit will.

I've no idea where to go in life,
    I don't know what my mission is to be.
Where is the direction I need from You,
    why can't my life's purpose I see?

Where is the comfort that was promised,
    how do I obtain the faith that I need?
Where do I get the Spiritual food for my hungry soul,
    the one You said you would feed.

How can true happiness ever be mine,
    will I emerge from this hopeless despair?
When I feel Thy Spirit again,
    will I know You were always there?

Lynda Shumway

Raistlin

In a world of loneliness and tears
I am happy
In a world of drugs and deception
I am fulfilled
In a world of war and hunger
I am peaceful

When babies cry and heroes die
When God is gone and soldiers march on
When our neighbors are judged and shot for preference
I smile within my tomb
I am happy
I am dead

LaRaine Etheridge

Reminder Of Kathy

Standing over breakfast dishes in the kitchen sink;
    I am slow in getting started, all I do is think.
I seem to see our Kathy everywhere I turn;
    to hold her precious form, my heart will always yearn;
I see her life-like image sitting in her rocking chair.
    I glance out of the window and I see her swing-set there.
As I meditate I can see our child so fair
    with her laughing eyes beneath her auburn hair,
Happily swinging in the pleasant sunset glow,
    shouting, "Mommy, just look how high I can go."
I remember her rosy cheeks and her healthy summer tan,
    as she slipped from her swing and to my lap she ran.
Now I really see a reminder of her childish play
    a "choo-choo" train built of bricks beside the parking way
Later Kathy paled, and died, after being so sick.
    I can't bear to see folks move a single brick!

Ruby Farnham Skaggs

God's Plight Of Modern Man

I am who am,
I am the beginning, the power, the reason and the essence of
Life, being also the father of the lamb
I am both the vessel and the contents of all that exists.
Without me there is nothing, or nothing consists
There are those who exist, made unbridled and free
Whose existence is to find me, and know that I be
Their existence has no other reason but so many will not try
They would rather feed their doubts collect shadows and die
They must realize their time is short
They should follow that taught by my son to his apostolic court
If there were more than me, though there is not, it should not
Matter, for they exist within me and are subject only to me
It is only what I will, that there is to be
They must to realize their debt to me
Having failed will not delete their worth to me
Only their intolerance to times events and circumstance
Will erase the good I planted within to so enhance.

R. G. Connors

A Southern Kind Of Day

My hand in his big strong hand,
I always ran to meet him, in the late afternoon,
I would see him walking down that dusty gravel road,
Striding along, cap cocked to one side,
Black lunch box in his left hand.
It was a hot, muggy typical southern summer day.
Running to meet him, I would reach up to grab his hand,
And walked along with this man, who I knew was surely 8 foot tall.
He'd slow down, so I could keep up.
And before we reached the house, he would open his lunch box,
He would take out a cookie or cupcake that he had saved,
just for me.
He had saved it, just for me.

Margaret A. Westall

259

Who Am I

I am the voice that sings in your ear
I am the knowing you need have no fear.

I am the sky that expands into blue
I am emotion expressing through you.

I am the tear that drops from your eye
I am the beauty that wants you to cry.

I am the scent of an unfolding rose
I am the guide who already knows.

I am the prize you see as your goal
I am divinity you feel in your soul.

I am the cat who purrs on your lap
I am the sleep imparting sweet nap.

I am the candle, its flame burning bright
I am the moon romancing the night.

I am the sun from which you get life
I am the union of husband and wife.

I am the truth, I am who you are today
I am the Spirit never passing away.

I am the love you feel in your heart
I am the God whom you've always been part.

Leslie Plimpton

"A Moment Of Silence"

I am just sitting here
I can hardly bear what
I am doing in this little room.
I just want silence
but there is so much violence
I just can't bear it anymore
Every day there are people
who die because people don't
care about one another. I am
sitting in this room thinking,
"I can't believe that this is happening
to everyone." Just last night my
brother was killed; he was in a gang.
He really didn't know what he was
getting himself into, but he just wanted to
fight. There is so much violence
that I can't even bear it anymore.
All I ask is for a moment of silence.

Stephanie Elizabeth Martin

"Clouds"

It's true that within her eyes of beauty
I can see the images of the clouds in the skies above
reflected in such a way that it would seem to the thoughtful viewer
that this was the way they were meant to be viewed,
as there certainly could not be a view that would make them so
beautiful, truly designed to be looked upon within a field of the
mixed colors of hazel, and intertwined with the reflections of
the love, trust, and caring I feel for her,
a reflection of what can be seen in my own eyes.
But are they all truly reflections?
Although it's true that I can sense
those feelings being reflected within her eyes,
I have this strange feeling that what I see isn't
just a mirror image of what can be seen in my eyes,
but that she may be feeling (thinking?) the same way.
An idea which makes those clouds
just a little bit more beautiful
than I had originally conceived.

Steven Sforza

Not Anymore

I am so alone, I can't pretend anymore,
I can't be happy this way anymore,
I can't think anymore, I can't dream anymore,
I can't love anymore, when I don't even know if you feel the same,
I can't keep kidding myself, I will never be with you,
I know that, I have always known that, and you know it too,
I don't even know you anymore, and you don't know me anymore,
But you never knew the real me, you just knew the person I should be,
But I'm not, and I can't be her anymore,
I can't play the role of someone who always falls for men
    who aren't there anymore,
I can't, it's not fair to you or me, I can't believe anything I say
    or even think anymore,
I don't even know my own reality anymore, I can't go on like this
    anymore,
I can't hold on to this dream anymore; I can't hold in this pain
anymore, the pain from what you're putting me through; I can't keep
hiding my tears or fears, anymore; I can't hide my emotions for you
anymore. I can't run from the truth anymore,
I just can't love you, anymore....

Shelly Erbe

Forgiveness

As I kneel beside my bed,
I close my eyes and clear my head.
"Lord can you hear me? It's Saul"
I waited for an answer but got nothing at all.
As I concentrate harder the long journey begins,
When I realize the anguish I've caused from my sins.
Then a comforting voice says "tell me son,
Of all the things we both know you've done."
Repentance pouring like a river wild through my head,
As I drift through my memories suddenly I read,
"Forgive me Father for I have sinned."
but no reply
Then "speak from your heart, not from the pew,
Open your soul, I'm here waiting for you."
I felt the tears pour as I spoke of my truths,
That came from the mistakes and lessons of youth.
Forgiveness was then granted to me by God,
Because I walked the path most seldom trod.
Calloused, splintered and bruised by the shame,
Faith and forgiveness have become one in the same.

Lynette Bauer

Days Gone By!

Wandering down a country road at the setting of the sun,
I could see all the beauties of which the Lord had done.
His hands had touched the trees and made them grow so tall.
It seemed they would reach the skies before they would fall
The colors were of autumn, with the cooling of the breeze
It seemed a lowly whisper, come from beneath the trees.
I could see a far off, there stood a grove of pines.
Where the brooks are always running and the sun never shines.
I could hear a far off the calling of the still.
It was the only calling of the whip-poor-will.
The place was all deserted as I wandered on and on.
And heard the night birds calling as if to sing a song.
The night was slowly creeping upon the silent hill
there stood a log cabin broken from all of the past years.
The windows were all shattered, the door hanging wide.
The breezes were blowing around on every side
As I looked and wondered, my sight was growing dim.
I could hear the lonely sound of a breaking limb.
The night seemed long and empty, and so very still
Then I heard the calling of the whip-poor-will.

Virginia M. Meadows

To Be Or Not To Be

In order to be
I could smell move or think
To not be I could be silent
don't you think?

In order to be, God would infuse in me his power.
To not be, I could lie dormant every
minute, second and hour.
Just to be, I could talk, sing, shout and pray
To not be, I would be silent forever and a day.

Who has the power to allow us to be?
Only God, who can make a tree
To not be is a decision made by God
In order to exist,
He only has to utter the word.
Come forth my child and you will be
very important to me, you will see.
To be, or not to be, can only rest with the master.
Some of us are chosen to be leaders and others pastors.
To be or not to be is God's choice
He lets man know he is the boss, to be or not to be.

Mary S. Williams

I Died

I died when my mother died.
I cried and I cried and I cried.
Then I died.
Kicks in my gut were too sore to bear,
Dull thud of church bells now intensely unfair.
My world collapsed and exposed such a lie,
Heaven on Earth screamed me good-bye.
I didn't have Mom anymore,
Slammed; an everlasting door.
I attempted to live,
I really, really tried.
But I could not care anymore,
So I died.

Years have passed, and I sit in my tree,
Waiting for happiness to roll back and be.
Several moments and so many tears,
Growing frustration and deathly fears.
Now I gaze at my daughter, who's grinning at me,
While resting in the same old tree.
And I breathe to myself, "Thank you Lord for leading me."

Kelly H. Mrkvicka

Nia

As I gaze down into your crib,
I am hopelessly and completely in love.

You stare up at me with your big, brown, watery eyes,
totally innocent, afraid of nothing.

Your olive skin, represents the spectrum of our heritage-
the singular love, as well as the collective self loathing.

With all of your gifts,
It still won't be easy to stand, little one.
Even though, you are the newest member
in the legion of the backbone of our people.
Nubian Princess, you possess dignity, and integrity.
The legacy that has sustained us through generations of pain.
The bond that is Sisterhood.

Your little hands, are empowered by the strength of our people
Your heart, has been graced with kindness and gentility.

In you, are all things.
The perseverance of the past,
and the promise of the future.
Sleep now, and the sweetest of dreams to you.
You, are Nia. You, have a purpose.

Toyia Wortham

Epitaph

"You" said that I talk too much.
I cried and I pleaded;
But you said that "You" had no time for me.

Now I'm lying on the ground, and
I cannot utter a single sound.
I no longer need your love,
For I cannot see or hear you from above.

I died as I lived
   ALL ALONE!
I tried so hard to be strong
Not to hurt when you did me wrong.

It's too late now
Don't weep for me, for at last I am free.
In this world, I never belonged.

Sandra B. Martin

Daddy

I really don't know why he did what he did
I do understand why we had to leave him.
When I was a child my feelings I kept hid
The hope of him showing love for me seemed dim

I'm older now and more hurt than in childhood
I hurt because I can comprehend what I feel
He is my daddy, love me, he should.
Sometimes the hate for him I feel is unreal

Does he love me though he cannot show it
As he grows older his loneliness I know
I believe he loves, but does not know it
He never keeps his word, but promises to grow.

I spent my life being mad, but now I am sad.
All I ever wanted was to be loved by my dad.

Rebecca Taylor

Forever And Always

I miss you so very much.
I don't even know where you are
Or if you still care about me.
Do you even remember me?

I would do anything to find you;
To be with you again is what I need:
To see you and hold you again,
To have you hold me forever and not let go.

I love you and always have.
You know I'll never forget you.
Seems to me the longer we are apart,
The more I love you and want you.

I love you for who you are.
I love you faults and all.
No matter what happens to us
I'll love you forever and always.

Sarah M. Russell

Bird

I, the bird, am as colorful as the shadow of heaven.
I fly through the lower, green meadows,
hopping from branch to branch.
I have polished, strong eyes that see my prey.
And in the silence of the day, the glow of the sun
brushes against my fluffy feathers.
When my sharp, edgy beak connects with my food,
it feels as if my mother is bringing home wet, soil worms.
I am useful to some, a target to others.

Michael Weisner

True Love

You will never realize the power I think our love has,
I don't think you understand that we were meant to last.
Our hopes, our dreams, our inspirations, are things we need-
  along with communication.
If you only knew of the love and passion I feel inside,
I would be enough for you without this wild roller coaster ride.
My love you've never felt, my tears could make you melt-
If you would only give a true chance
for God to rebuild our romance,
In my heart and soul you'd find a love that's truly divine,
A passion that overflows and emotions that overload.
My love and strength you will always have,
My loyalty and trust you need not ask,
My heart and soul you'll know you've won
When our love becomes one and we shine like the sun

    LaTica Paige-Gene

"Wandering People"

The airport bustles with travelers
I don't want them to look so ugly
Alone, comfortably supported, or somewhere in between
There are so many wandering people

But some look enticingly attractive
My how I'd like to engage with her in intimate exploration
There's something about her that intrigues me
Unfulfilled dreams fissuring and driving her seductive appearance

What are we all in the end sum, anyway?
Why do I feel compelled to run against the wind
When today is but another grain of sand through an infinite
hourglass?
What could possibly matter in a scant million years?

Nothingness in a sea of desolate existence
What are my spoken words saying anyway?
Quite a dark and disparaging pair of welder's glasses
Through which to perceive the world

In the absence of love

    Karl Luther

In Your Eyes

In your eyes, I see a spring day, green, gray, and blue.
I feel heat from the sun's ray, when I look at you.

Stars dancing round and round, jumping to and fro.
Showing that you care for me, this is how I know.

Frowning when you're upset, pouting when you're down.
Your emotions show in your eyes, there's no need for sound.

I can tell if you're happy, passive, or sad,
Nervous, anxious, courageous, glad.

Your eyes will tell the story; please, don't try to hide.
The facts, the fictions, the novelties, what's bottled up inside.

I know what you'd like to say, even before you say.
Inviting me to share your future, right from the beginning day.

A sweet, timeless moment, I remember it so well.
From across a crowded room, I could very well tell.

When your eyes met mine, it was like a dream or fantasy.
A full force current, a shock of electricity.

Those three special words from your lips, you didn't have to say.
By the loving way you look at me, I know that anyway.

The feelings that you have for me in honesty, you can't disguise.
There are no words that can conflict with what's said there in your
  eyes.

    Tera Renee Hopkins

Homeless

I find Myself alone, everything I once had is gone
I feel so cold, so empty.
There is a void where I used to hold love,
There is nothing where I used to hold life.
As I have lost all hope, I have been embraced by despair.
I used to have a home. I used to have people to love,
Who loved me in return.
Now all there is, all I see is the graffiti on the walls,
The broken windows, broken signs, and my broken heart.
I am on the street. Kids turn tricks, sell drugs,
And cry when no one's looking.
I am on the street they say was paved with gold.
Now all that remains is lost souls
Looking for answers to long forgotten questions
And the sound of tears that will never be seen.

    Tamara Newton Kmit

Is Life Supposed To Be This Way?

I go outside and feel.
I feel the sun warming my body.
I worry about skin cancer.

I go to bed and think.
I think maybe tomorrow won't
be so bad at home.
I worry that it might be worse.

Wherever I go I feel. I think. I worry.
Will everyday be this way?
Will being at home every be fun
and peaceful?

Yes. Because I feel.
I feel there's something I can do.

Yes. Because I worry.
I worry if I don't do it, it won't be as perfect
as it can be. So I do it.

Yes. Because I think.
I think of ways to perfect life.

Yes. Because I believe.
I believe I CAN DO IT.

    Sarah Mundahl

1990's Ethnic Cleansing And Consciousness

Other words for an holocaust
I do not care to hear...

Then, I was a child living in India
With little to fear,
And later, I shuddered past my parents' times,
Coming to know of its victims, their foes and their crimes...

In their war of the world they were all separate,
Held together nevertheless by human - consciousness...

That emerging program through which nature doth explore,
How it may leave its turbulent yore
Of competition, conquest and such justice,
To reach giving, and maybe even some sharing,
Between this belief and yet that other...
While preparing through reason for actions,
Still searching through all of its passions...

'Never again,' we had managed to say,
With daily holocaust - refrains in the air,
With monuments and museums built with great care,
And inclined to halt its drifts, should it ever dare;
But perplexed and unsteady, we vacillate today....

    M. Radh Achuthan

To Life

While rushing through my busy life, always in fast forward.
I forced myself to check the sky, for sun the stars and upward.
I ran to work, I ran to shop, I ran to cook and clean.
I forced myself to check the earth for bulbs, for buds, for greens.
My work was hectic as I ran from room to room to room.
I forced myself to check my life and how I was entombed. Stop!

It's time to pick the daisies
Time for footprints in the snow.
Time to see colors in a rainbow
Time to watch the living grow.

No more running in fast forward.
No more rushing with the flow.
It's time to live the truths of life
To be, to love, to know.
Marcia Galletti

An Everlasting Love

Roses are red, my love. Violets are blue,
I had no life 'til I met you.

You are my life, you are my love,
I'm forever yours, thank God above.
You stole my heart, I don't want it back,
Now I've got yours, and that's a fact.

I'll keep it forever, under lock & key,
Other women try to take it, they'll answer to me.
For you, I will fight to the death,
You're forever mine, 'til I draw my last breath.

I need you now, I will need you even then,
With you by my side, even death won't win.
I'll take your love with me, whenever I go
To that life beyond the grave, and this I want you to know.

My love for you will still be strong,
In the afterlife it will live on and on.
My love for you will never die,
It will just get stronger as time goes by.
So please always remember, and don't ever forget
I love you, I love you, I love you, you bet!
Lisa D. Tallent

The Mountain Is My Home

The mountain is my home,
I have no desire to roam
With such beautiful scenery
Different colors of greenery

Go for a nature walk
A great time with God to talk
In the distance I hear a waterfall
From the sound it can't be small

Such a glorious, beautiful sight
Water cascading down so clear and bright
The mountain laurel in bloom
The air so sweet and pure to consume

Standing on a rock, I look to the valley below
Smoke comes from the chimney of a bungalow
A man tending his fields
Needing everything it would yield

Fleecy white clouds so close by
Such a clear beautiful blue sky
Thank you God, for the mountain, my home
From it, I have no desire to roam
Sue Butner

Jaime Ladonna

White, fair....
  I have desired.
Small, wise....
  I have befriended.
Dark, dark-haired...
  I have laughed with.
Little, truthful, famous among gods....
  I have cared for.
From the linden tree island...
Anointed....
From the white island, from the fair waters....
Beloved....
Flowering heather, flowering heather...
  I thought loved me.
From the woman warrior...
  I have found succor.
From the ash tree meadow....
  I have lusted over.
From the gray fortress....
  I'll love forever.
Matt Latham

Attraction

What is this overwhelming attraction that
I have for you?
  And a burning desire to hold you for
hours on end?
  Why is it I can feel you reaching for me
when you're feeling blue?
  I can go through life not worrying what
is around the next bend.
  Happiness runs through me like the
spirit of the mourning dove.
  I truly believe that we are those rare
Soulmates that happen to meet.
  And this strange attraction is
most definitely love.
  Living life forever with you darling is
surely going to be a treat.
Weak in Denise (Da-knees)

Blade Of Grass

In the wind I plant myself firmly next to the other blades of grass.
I have perished in the winter's cold.
I have floundered under the arid sun when my blade wilted.
I died when the seasons ceased to come down upon me.
BUT
My roots still remain.
Adrianne Blackmoore

To Mom

I've known this for awhile
I could not live without your smile!
As days pass and years roar by
I try to come to realize,
That someday, I'll be gone,
To chase my dreams all alone.
Without you standing by my side
This is what I've realized
So right now in these words
I'm trying to tell you where it hurts
Right here in my heart
To think that someday our paths will part
As the tears fall and fears grow
This is what I've come to know!
I Love You Mom
MaryJo Lorena Patterson

The Dark Of Night

The dark of night is still upon the land,
I hear the murmur of the birds in sleep,
While through the forest black nature's demands
Bright forth the morning's freshness from her sleep.

The dark of night mantles earth's mystery,
Covers the progress of the coming day,
Touches the wounds of earth's long history,
Brings forth the hope of life in a new way.

The magic of night, the cover that it gives,
Releases to man and to the rivers still,
To nature's child and the way He lives,
In majesty asserts our Father's will.

The dark of night upon our sparkling shores,
In moonlight gold touches our evermore,
Gilds our lands as ere before,
With the gold of midnight from shore to shore.

Lucille M. Kroner

Following The Light

I feel your arms wrapped around me Jesus
I hear you whispering softly in my ear
I know that soon, I will be with you in heaven
And now, I have nothing to fear
My guardian angels are beside me
To take me to the promised land
The path that I've followed, here on earth
Will lead me to your waiting hands
Following the light,
seeing God so near
This is what I have been waiting for
To see you open the door
Following the light,
to peace and comfort evermore
Praising and worshipping day and night
I'm glad to be following the light

Peggy A. Tipton

Are You Afraid Of The Dark?

I was walking down my street on a very dark night,
I heard some voices but nobody was in sight.

The moon was full, the wind was blowing, and
in the darkness, eyes were glowing.

A ghost appeared and said to me, "on this night
your doom will be...to walk in limbo for eternity."

A witch came up and grabbed my arm, she said
"Come with me I'll do you no harm."

I pulled away and thought I'd won, but then she
called out "There's nowhere to run."

Running past the cemetery, I heard a scream,
was I being chased, or was it just a dream?

Nicole McCarthy

The Astronaut

Propelled by the great need to know more
I have strayed far, too far away from the shore.
Behind, my traces vanish quicker than in sand,
Ahead stretch shining waves, not the ways of the land.

Here creation looks round, and I, poor center,
The final dot of a huge question mark
Dangle from somewhere where I cannot enter.

Yet how I crave to swing and jump over the dark,
Drill time, pass my own horizon and try
To find, alive, the answers toward which we die.

Simone Mavrodineanu

Mom

When she first held me we let out a cry
I just can't believe you've finally arrived
I'm so happy to have a daughter like you
To share my entire life with you.

The days went on, each thing was new
Oh no their's a cry, what shall I do?
When I couldn't talk, laugh, walk or run
You showed me just how to have so much fun.

In my heart and in my mind
You'll always be a true hero of all time.
You've helped me through thick and thin
And taught me that it's O.K. to not always win.

I know you've always loved me too,
I'm just so proud to have a Mom like you.

Tina Nicole Course

Why

Why is he doing this to me?
I just do not understand it.
When I think he is out of my life,
He shows up unexpectedly.

He did it again last night.
As I slept, he entered my dream.
That's right, he just showed up.
Then as he left, he reached out and kissed me.

And it was not just any kiss.
It was a kiss of love.
A kiss that felt so real,
That I could feel the heat,
Of my chapstick increase.

Then after he kissed me,
He walked out the door,
And said, we need to talk.
Then he left as quickly as he came.

Linda D. Rogers

Audrey

A second skin she was to me, a shadow upon whom
I laid my dreams.

Walking through time has not dulled my sentimentality; it
Has endured all this—and now—Eternity.

My childhood illuminated by her presence, she who
Did not judge my youthful foolishness.

Laughter light transcended all, lifting my spirit skyward.

Talks of true loves, life, and creation, did we share
In moments of daily chores.

Mentor, confidant, family, friend, though I miss her
Earthly shell, in my heart shall she continuously reside.

My life has been graced.

From a chalice of cherished memories shall I savor her
Existence.

A withering vine in winter's harshness, the Clematis, when
Touched by spring, does brilliantly bloom.

From this promise do I take comfort that we shall revel in
The efflorescence of renewal and once again our spirits
Touch.

Shirley Wallace

The Beauty Within

I saw you fall in silent then glide on by,
I knew right then I wanted to fly.
As I dreamed about what it must be like
to leave my home in a single flight.
Flying high above the trees and through the valleys,
as I please.
 A very smart eagle I would be,
so I could educate humans about the air we breath.
I noticed as I flew down low that the air felt thick,
through my nostrils.
But as I went up high what a surprise the air flowed
easily though my nostrils.
As an animal I can't understand why,
but as a human I realize why.

Thomas Barnaby

Longing

I wonder why I cry when I hear a song of love.
I know that it is not for my past loves.
I often think it is for that special someone
I have not yet met.

Now I realize it is for you Jesus.
I cry for you, I sing to you, I long to be with you.
I love you.

I guess, it is for that special someone I have not yet met.

Terry Fox

The Seduction

You sit there, smiling at me from your barstool
I know what's on your mind; we've been through this charade
I'm young ... but not blind; "You've been hurt before?"
I nod the affirmative; then you caress my cheek
taking the initiative ... it's gentle at first
it sends me reeling; my head's spinning fast
Do you know what I'm feeling?
Suddenly, the smoke and noise disappear
Our tongues melt with succulent warmth; we're the only ones
in the room; we're feeling no fear
You're taking me fast; maybe faster than able
I'm trying to keep up; want to show you I'm stable
I open my eyes, but just for a sec
Everyone's gawking; they know what I'll get
I pull away with a kiss and laugh a strained laugh
I do this when nervous; but you don't know the half
You spy a nubile young thing, in black stiletto shoes
She's twenty years your junior; and giving you the blues
"Don't you want something like that? ... she's so much younger?"
"No." I say with a tear; "I want only you. So never you wonder!"

Mark Kurisu

Oh, How Beautiful It Is!

I feel the cold wind, blowing across my face.
I feel the water sprinkle through my hair.
I see the sun setting on the horizon.
Beautiful colors fill the sky,
as if they were painted there.

Oh how beautiful it is!

My tranquil train of thought is stopped
by a giant mushroom in the sky.
I see the mushroom cloud that forms from a nuclear bomb.
I feel the radiation surge through my body.
My peaceful moment has been ended by man's obsession with war.
I witnessed the beginning and end of
World War III.

Louis J. Bara

"Missing You"

It's three o'clock in the morning,
I lie here missing you;
Your cuddly arms and gentle touch,
With a tender kiss or two.

They say, love is like a bird,
Hold it too tight and it will die,
Trust and respect it with kind word,
Let it go, it was meant to fly.

It won't go far if it is true,
The space you give will be cherished;
It will return to you,
With greater love, and never perish.

You learn that love doesn't mean leaning,
But letting each of you be "you;"
Giving your love new meaning,
Be honest, be faithful, be true.

Mable Moore

The Scar

When I was a child, I lived in fear
I lived with lots of pain

When I was little, I thought it was normal
I now feel not the same

An abused child bears many bruises
But they all heal with time

The most painful scars, are vivid memories
Deep inside my mind

A punching bag is made for punching
'Cause it's made for taking blows

A growing child need lots of loving
They're no punching bags made for throws

Count the swats, don't you cry, take it like a man
Don't you cry, I'll give you more, OH no here comes the hand
Mom don't you love me, why'd she do that, I don't understand
Why don't they stop her, they see my bruises, it's time that I ran

These are some memories, from my childhood
As painful as they are

Open the wound, now it's healing
Only left a scar.

Timothy Arias

I Love This Country

I love this country.
I love the big cities — New York with its hustle and bustle,
San Francisco with its hills and street cars, Chicago with its
tall buildings and bright lights.

I love the countryside with the roaming grasslands,
grazing cows and big red barns.

I love the beautiful islands of Hawaii with their fragrant
flowers, soft white sand and crystal clear water glistening
with colorful fish.

The dry deserts, the foliage-full forests, the beautiful
beaches — I love them all.

I love the mountains with their steep, rocky ledges and
snowcapped peaks.

I love the people — red, yellow, black and white.

I love this country for letting me be free to enjoy the
things I love.

Kathleen Lynn Bowman

Travel Along A Country Road

As I drive along the country road
I marvel at the signs of Spring.
Trees bud,
   Frogs chirp,
     Birds sing.

The beauty of the world lies before us to behold,
A door is being opened to us to meet our every goal.
We should stop,
   We should look,
     We should press on to our abode.

We seem to be too busy to appreciate this gift.
We should offer praise to God for all the beauty of the world.
If we appreciate,
   If we praise,
     We shall be content all our days.
         Mary Thomas Sullivan

Died For Love

   In the park where I do dwell,
I met a boy I loved so well.
He used to steal my heart from me,
But now he set it free.

   He sat a strange girl on his knee,
Told her things, he never told me.

   I went home and cried my eyes so red,
Not a word to my mother I said.
Then my father came home that night
And searched for me, from left to right.

   Suddenly, my door he broke,
And found me hanging from a rope.

   He said; Oh dear daughter, what have you done?

You kissed yourself, for another man's son.

He found a note upon my bed,
He picked it up and read:

Dig my grave, dig it deep
Because I'm in a wounded sleep.
And on the headstone, place a dove
To show the world I died for LOVE.
         Veronica Anne Panyko

Anger And Pain

Anger, pain
I miss him
I want to get revenge
I feel like killing him
I want to make love to him
I'm so confused, but I know I love him.
"Did you leave me here to die?"
Why oh why
was it so easy for you to just walk away
I thought we'd settled the score.
But instead we both came back for more.
"God, please end this torture, that is tearing up my heart.
Will I ever be the same again?
Will I ever love another?
Or will you come back to stay?
If I ever put you on again
Forever is the only way.
Even though I want you back
I'll always feel that I must hurt you in return,
but who wants to spend a lifetime trying to hurt the one you yearn.
     A. Marie

"Good Night"

Dear Bud,
I miss you and love you very much. I wish you
would have told me how you felt that night, before
you took your life. Why didn't you stay at mom's
that night? You might have seen another day's
light. I believe if you knew how much I was going
to hurt, you would not have done that to yourself.
I see mom and dad cry day and night; it cuts me
like a knife. Why did you, brother, give up the
fight? The day you died was the worst day of my
life; I try to remember the good memories, but it
always leads to that awful night. I see you in my
dreams at night, but we always fight. It might be
a message you are sending me to get my life right.
Now that dad has joined you I know you will be all
right, please watch over me at night so I can
sleep tight; give dad a kiss goodnight.

Till we meet again, Your brother Mike
     Michael DiGiacomo

Untitled

As the dawn of the day eclipses into the lusters of night
I reach with outstretched mind for that of her presence
Floating on the edge of dream and reality
Fact and fiction blend together to form the epicenter of her essence
Doors, once impenetrable, now open to me before my eyes
To secret chambers, upon a bed of thorns, she lies
Like a baby tucked snugly into its cradle
So infantile, silent and lucid in her little garden of eden
Where colors and hues of unimaginable proportions
   are unleashed on the heart of the hunter in us all
And on distant horizons, clouds of majesty roll in,
But there was no silver lining....
Dreams fade to darkness as I wake to the coldness of reality
And with silvery blade in hand, I make the cut; I make the incision
And watch, with morbid fascination,
   the moist blood flow between my fingertips
What a bitter irony for the matron of my vision
Once the life of me, she's now the death of me
I should've known nothing could ever be the same
So I whisper again her name... Mary, Mary, Mary
     Matthew E. Gaddy

Safe Harbor

When the sea gets too rough
I retreat after giving up

To my safe harbor I would go
To a familiar place that I know
Rejection is painful to bear
The yearning to caress causes me to dare
To take the risk to leave once more
Only to head back to shore

Many ships have been damaged
Which makes the others fear
That is why they all come here
Honolulu is the name
The place where trust is on the wane

In my safe harbor I would like to hide
But I will only find someone outside
Many ships have pulled away
I must envision better days
I shall leave this protective bay
Hard work does a good relationship make
Leaving heartbreaks and sorrows in my wake
     Sylvester Williams

Tree

Mama said - look at your life, it's a tree
I said - who me?
She says ya been planted on this earth. You are here, can't deny,
The rings of growth do apply
to the evolutions of the seasons,
some good, some full,
just right;
but they don't always come as planned,
too much of something, not enough of something
can't predict the too much and not enough,
can't refuse.
Your tree it bends, like the willow or the oak
The leaves they come, the leaves fall, it's part of the seasons,
that's all.
Tend that tree
Respect its roots
it will give you shade, it may even give you fruit
it will tell you how it's been.
It's you.

Steffany Field

After All

After all the tears were shed and gone,
I saw a new light that went on and on.
That light brought back memories, good and bad.
Sometimes it made me happy, sometimes it made me sad.
That light was a new beginning,
That shed rays of hope that were never-ending.

After all the mourning and weeping was done,
I had a huge urge to have some fun.
So I went out and had a blast.
For all I knew, that moment might not last.
But then I remembered the good times that were higher than above.
I missed those times, so I went back to find my old love.

After all the searching and looking was done,
I finally found my special someone.
He was there the whole time waiting for me.
He is everything he was meant to be.
He loves me more than anything.
So if I think about leaving him I just remember...

He'll always be there after all.

Kari Houston

I Once Saw A Flower

I once saw a flower all covered with dew.
I stood for a while and saw how it grew.
I saw it did blossom and held its head high.
But, then I took notice, it started to die.
It got over worries and finished its strife
which I shall do some day,
at the end of my life.

Mitchell Steven Boyer

My Lonely Night

As I stare out into the lonely night, I wonder where you are.
I perhaps you, too, are wishing on that same bright star?

I long to hear the tenderness of your voice speaking to my heart,
Assuring me that you are thinking of me while yet we are apart.

And when I sleep, I will dream of you and bring you close to me.
There I will hold you through the night as I hide from reality.

And when the morning light trickles over my window sill,
I will awaken with an emptiness that only you can fill.

Again I stare into the lonely night and wonder where you are,
If perhaps you, too, are wishing on that same bright evening star?

Michelle Lanier Herrin

Your Eyes

When I look into your eyes,
I see the blue skies hovering over
and enclosing the heavens.
When I look into your eyes.

I see the opaqueness that surrounds my elapsed life.
Although I am afraid to move on,
I still see the future.
In your eyes.

I possess no fears and
have no pain.
Willingly I look at how content we may be,
For when I look into your eyes,
This is what I see.

Stephanie Senior

You Say, Life

You say life
I see, the strange beating train
In the secret subway of my being
You say, these are two parallel regulated lines
You explain the relation between me and you
Everyday life goes upon this relative time.

You sing the violent song, all night
In the gushing fountain of my artery
I see, My first love still weeps for me
Last word, do you really know life, O my life
In the hidden island of the solitary heart.

"Everything is false" says my shouting mind
Lonely, I walk through the senseless denying wind.

Robin Jahangir

My Good Friend

I see the tenderness in her eyes,
I see the tears she tries to hide,
she's got the heart of an angel you know,
and never will I let her go.

I see beyond the physical side,
I see beyond what she'd like to hide,
The pain and the hurt that she's felt for years,
and somehow she seems to fight back her tears.

I love this woman with all my heart,
she's not only strong, she's very smart.
She sees things in people that no one else sees.
She sees not what they are, but what they could be.

This woman I speak of is my mom,
The heart and the soul from which I came from,
I hope that one day, I'm as great as she,
I know that she thinks, I really can be.

Lisa Smiles

Why

When I saw you, you said hi,
I never thought it would be a good-bye.
Why must you go,
No one seems to know.
I wanted you to stay,
But, death took you away.
Why must this happen,
It's not fair to anyone.
I can't accept that you're gone,
There were so many things we could've done.
Death has so much sadness,
Takes away my happiness.
I want you here with me,
I guess it may never be.

Kylee Templin

Untitled

Mother dear mother
I send youth's rose,
And with this all of my love goes.
Wear it in your snow white hair;
I only wish I could put it there.
Many letters you have written true,
And some I have not answered you.
I can picture you in the old rocking chair,
Awaiting the postman's call, that was not there.
A little frown, a little smile.
Mother dear mother, God Bless you.

You have taught me well, dear mother.
With your patience and loving care.
And for this I shall always be grateful
to you
Until the end of my time
My dear, dear sweet mother of mine.
"I Love You"

Martha Sweeney

My Heart

In my heart, I will feel no pain
I stand beside you with pain, that surrounded my soul
In my heart the sun will set
Beside the river, the frighten moments, of despair,
with the heart, and love that overcomes our home
With life pleasure, I duly swear to love you, for all
this boundary of the earth
From beneath my feet, a straight love that is everlasting
In my heart, I feel no pain, when the sun rise, wind blow
crispy across the meadows and then, I feel the sun embrace my body,
but deep within my soul I feel no pain
I knew, with my heart, our love is everlasting
When the sun falls my heart feels like the swing of
the ocean
My love for you is like a flower, blossoming in the summer breeze
My heart is like a bird, soaring threw the air
Love is like a butterfly coming from the shell in the spring
My love is everlasting
But True, To My Heart
NO PAIN, NO PAIN

Mary Simmons

Bright Eyes

The courageous rock stands tall above the rest
I stand on this rock and put my fear to a test
The purple haze above my head turns into a blur
Troubled tears cloud my eyes as I think of how things were
Leaving my past behind me, I look into the future with bright eyes.
I forget insecurity and let my free spirit arise.

Margaret Boyer

The Eagle

I've known the high country, the mountain is my home
I live in the timber, I float over the snow
The wind is my lifestyle, the stars are my goal
But I know that I'll be leaven' here,
For the release of my soul.

I'm a free bird in the wind, watch me soar up high again
I'm never comin' down to the cold, cold ground
The sky is my only friend, I'm a free bird in the wind.

I'm strong and I'm mighty, creation is my prey
I'm filled with strength and knowledge
I never loose my way
My beauty is boundless, my kingdom will stay
I shine in the sunlight, I'm the glory of the day.

Priscilla Wolf

I Thank God

Everyday I thank God for what I have in life.
I thank God for letting me see a new day,
and that my loved ones are still near.

I thank God for forgiving my mistakes and loving me
even though I'm not perfect.
I thank God for giving me one more chance at love.

I've found someone to love me regardless of my
imperfections.
I've found someone so forgiving and loving I want to
stay with that person for eternity.
I've found someone, you, and I thank God!

I thank God for letting a friendship turn into true love!
I thank Him for letting us meet once again.
I thank Him for all the special times we've shared.
But most if all I thank Him for giving us a future together!!

Sandra Stepien

A Clown I Know

I know a clown who has big feet and
I think he's really neat.

I know a clown who has curly hair it's wild,
it' loose it's really a scare.

I know a clown who where's wired cloths and
he has a big big nose.

This clown I know where's a colorful hat,
he's not at all fat, he's slim and trim
he's very thin.

This clown I know smiles all day and
night it's such a wonderful sight.

It makes me feel good to see him smile.
I hope that feeling stays for a long,
long while.

This clown I know is not at all sad,
he's the spittin' image of my wonderful
Dad.

Sarah Elizabeth Foy

What A Husband Saw When Buying A House

My husband finally found a job in far away Des Moines
I was too ill to follow him, so the kids and I stayed back.
My husband took it upon himself to find and buy our new house
He raved about one right away, "Just a bit off the beaten track."

The kids and I worried about this house
Until the day that we moved in
When we panicked on meeting our tenants—
Some gray and furry: One just shedding his skin.

"The furnace needs replacement," I shouted,
"And this well-water needs a filter.
You know an hour commute is too long for me
You've thrown my whole world out of kilter!"

Then one night the kids and I watched the brightly lit stars
In a sky that was inky black, yet clear.
The next day we noticed the deer, pheasants, and hawks
And how they approached us with almost no fear.

At last we knew what my husband saw in this house
In spite of minor imperfections
Although it lacked city amenities
It abounded with peaceful reflections.

Susan Paulsen Heggestad

The Colors Of Mother

When I think of the colors of mother,
I think of eyes,
As sparkling as the ocean blue.
When I think of the colors of mother,
I think of lips,
As red as rubies.
When I think of the colors of mother,
I think of hair,
As brown as chocolate.
When I think of the colors of mother,
I think of teeth,
As white as snow.
But, when I think of the colors of mother,
I think most of her heart,
As pure as gold.

Marcella McCleese

In The Deep Of Night

In the deep of night
I think of thee
And there comes to me
A feeling of peace and love
As clear, and as pure as crystal
Gently enfolding my whole being
As a mother enfolds her young.

I wake with the morn, And there is born within my soul
A song of love and praise
And my soul doth raise its voice
Singing the eternal harmony of one.
Wending and blending its way among the All.

I go my way.
And through the day
Thy Presence caresses my heart
With gentle fingers
Thy melody lingers on like a haunting dream:
Oh! Holy One: In whom I find my way.
Through each and every night and every day
I rest in Thee.

Mildred H. Mason

"My Discovery"

As I lay here thinking of the day ahead
I'd just as soon stay abed.
But who will feed the cats and our dog?
My husband's still sleeping like a log.

Then I thought a cup of coffee would be nice
I'd already soaked up a batch of rice-
But Oh! The bed felt oh! so good-
Why am I in this crazy mood?

Then I looked up and thought the Lord gave me life-
Not to lay here and struggle with strife-

So I jumped out of bed and ran to the sink-
To put on the coffee and wondered; why be a fink!?!

I looked up at the beautiful sky-
And remembered now the how and why
The Lord gave me strength just for today
So I sit at my table-read the Bible and pray

Now I have all the answers for my selfish way
The Lord gave me power only for today
I hope I got my messages across-
Without His love my life is a loss.

Wilma P. La Coste

My Death-For You

As I sit and watch the clouds pass by
I think of you, wishing you were here.
I can picture your face, your smile glistening as a raindrop in the sun
I can see your eyes as they penetrate deep into my soul.
I can hear your voice, gentle as an autumn breeze.
I can hear your soft words comforting my pain.
I can feel the warmth of your body as we sit, holding each other
    tight.
I can feel your heart beat as I relax into your arms.

I look up to the sky, hoping to find answers.
I try to forget, but my thoughts are filled by you.
I see wonderful images of you, shattered by her.
Though the images fade, the reality does not.
Each day I will see you together, with her.
I cannot put myself through this hell each day.
I can endure the pain now, but not forever.

I am saying good-bye while my heart is still broken.
Please don't remember me how I am now,
But remember me the way I was when we were together.
And please remember, I will always love you.

Mary Novak

I Hope

"When I was a child, I spake as a child, I understood as a child,
I thought as a child: but when I became a man, I put away childish
things." Did I put them away or were they taken from me?
When I was a child, I pulsed and overflowed and was bursting with
the most precious of youth's attributes: HOPE. My being was
filled with trust and purity, never expecting the worst or
assuming anyone could hurt me. HOPE. Hope is what my heart
was made of. But with age and experiences and pain, that hope
was beaten and scared and reduced to a grain of sand, hidden
deep within a heart made black and callous. The heart of an
adult. Now my being is ravaged with distrust and pessimism,
the anticipation of "Murphy's Law," and the belief that everyone
is out for himself alone (at the expense of all others).
I see and hear and feel with senses wary of having to withstand
more pain, more injury, more scars. I long for the hope of
my childhood, the hope that swells within and gives birth to
dreams and happiness. This hope that sees no treachery, that
knows no prejudice, that holds no grudge, that tells no lies.
I long for the hope of innocence and joy. Can hope be killed?
No, only weakened. But can it be restored? I hope......

J. Joseph Bradt

Stepping All Over The People's New Shoes

I went out, last Saturday night.
I thought I would do it up, and do it up right.
So I went down town, drinking the booze.
And stepping all over the people's new shoes.
Well things went swell, for an hour or so.
While drinking it up, and spending my dough,
Until one man said, son that's not right,
But that's what started, an awful fight.
I stepped right up, said put up your guard.
But just then, he hit me so hard.
When I awoke, I was singing the blues.
For stepping all over the people's new shoes.
When I arrived home, it was getting quite late,
The sun came peeking, over the gate.
But I had learned, I had lots to lose,
By stepping all over the people's new shoes.
With my head so big, and my bruises black,
You know darned well, I won't go back.
Way down town, drinking the booze,
And stepping all over the people's new shoes.

Thomas C. Hager

"Love Taps"

I feel battered and bruised, just plain damn used!
I thought our love was going well, I never knew of private Hell.
All of a sudden you blew a fuse, and that's when my body
started to bruise.
But yet, you say you love me?
I'm not a ball to be bounced around; I am a woman, a person.
When the word "Love" comes out of your mouth, I soon forget
what the screaming and hollering was all about, I felt a fool
you know?
I felt like cake batter, beaten and stirred as if I don't - matter.
And yet you say you Love Me.
I Birthed you beautiful healthy children, your love then was
like all seasons, why didn't I know?
"If each bruise on my body is a love tap,
Then I don't need and want to be loved by you,
Because, your Love Taps can cause my death,
So, I don't want you ever, to come Tapping at my door."

Margaret E. Martin

His Angel

One day in pouring down rain
I told my 3 year old son, again and again:
"Quit walking in the mud, fellah,
And get on the sidewalk, under this
umbrella."

Finally, under a portico we stopped to talk:
"Why can't you behave and walk on the sidewalk?
You're ruining your brand new shoes, bud,"
He said: "I can't let my angel walk in the mud."

That little boy is now grown
Out in the world and on his own
And true to his word, I have found
He's never let his angel down.

Loretta M. Hanneman

The Red Shirt!

"Get rid of that raggy red shirt."
I used to say.
But it's my favorite,!
And I'm comfortable in it!
So you had your way
But now you're gone,
And I'm alone,
Your raggy red shirt.
Is now my own.
"Throw it away."
Oh, no, not ever!
It's under my pillow every night.
It's close to me, every minute,
Oh, how I wish, that you were still in it!

Raymond O. Cortez

Remember

It will be o.k.,
here on this sad day,
She won't be completely gone away,
Just look at her picture and
remember the blue eyes that
would light your way,
Vow to think of the times you
thought the day would never end.
The times you spent laughing with your friend,
Even though you won't see
her each day the memories
will never go away,
Keep her in your heart,
That way you will never be apart.

Wendy Hill

The Rose

Each new day, in early morning hours,
I visualize God looking at his flowers.

I can almost hear him say —
Now which one will I pick today —

No, not that one, don't you see,
It has too many flaws to please me.

The roses with spots, let remain on the vine
I will come back to pick them in my time.

The rose must have no flaws that eyes can see
If it has an illness, it can be cured by me.

I will pick the most beautiful rose that has given so much joy —
As a husband, father, papa and little boy.

When God picked his rose today - he got the most beautiful one —
The love of his wife, his daughters, and son —

He was my friend - the best I ever had,
The beautiful rose he picked today, was my Dad.

Shelba Bisidas Roberts

Broken Heart

I needed to let my true feelings out
I wanted to know what this is all about
How come you cheated, How come you lied
How you hurt me deep down inside
You could have told me you liked me no-more
But maybe it's because you weren't so sure
I never heard the words
"Let's go our different ways"
This whole situation is just a whole haze
I hope you still consider me a friend
and accept this poem I truly send

Rosanna Robles

Broken Heart

When you left me
I was alone.
I didn't know who to trust
or if I trusted myself.
I cried myself to sleep every night.
I try to convince myself that you'll come back,
but in my heart and mind I know you won't.
You've broken my heart so many times,
what's one more?

Katie McClary

Wanted: A Gentle Drop

  I am Justice
I move among people and touch them
  with my eyes; as they stumble
  I support them with the ideal.
I support people oriented causes:
  literacy and opportunity; hope for the young,
  the old, the poor, the physically
  mentally, racially handicapped.
I support environmental balance:
  clean air, safe streets, peaceful
  coexistence.
I love all who fumble; in gratitude
  I smile encouragement
As new hope sends them surging
  once more into the capricious
  arena of life.
  I am Justice

Ruth R. Hazel

Soaring Dreamers

Last night I dreamt that we were together, just the two of us.
I was lost in your eyes and you were lost in mine and together
   we were lost in ecstasy.
Then we took wing and flew out over the world ... soaring
   effortlessly through the sky and nothing could touch us;
   nothing could disturb or disrupt our rapture.

As we flew, our wings overlapped ...
   then they began to merge... we became one entity.
More than both of us, but not detracting from our individuality...
   this being was great and fantastic, glorious in its beauty.
It flew to ever greater heights... leaving the world to gape in awe...
   leaving others far behind.

It was the happiest creature in all the universe...
   and its warmth spread to others it came into contact with.
No one could truly be unhappy in its presence.

Then I woke to a cold morning and an empty bed...
   and a tear rolled down my cheek at the thought of you
   waking in the same manner.

   Michael E. Casto

A Trip To The Principal's Office

When I had to go to the principal office,
I was so nauseated,
And my heart was beating so fast it was like it was in
the marathon,
I hope he knows this is my first time,
And I never committed a crime,
I'm a good little boy,
I never play with toys,
I just stay home and study,
I always get along with everybody.
   Before I went in I took a deep breath,
Then I went in and said, "What is it, DEATH?
Tell me, what is my sentence?"
"Oh nothing, your mom just dropped off your lunch money."

   Walter Marques

Night Of The Phoenix

As I lie in the nest of aromatic boughs
I watch as I am consumed by the flames
Of prophecy; I have lived my five
   centuries.
From the pyre rises another, embalming
   my ashes
In an egg of myrrh; So begins the flight
To the altar of Re.
As the legend depicts, I am a symbol of
   immortality.
As this Night of the Phoenix draws
Closer and closer to its consummation,
I have been reborn.

   J. Michael Roberts

My Son Has Been To Hell And Back

Paul has been to 'hell and back.'
I watched him run that fateful track.
I counseled - I screamed - I hit - I prayed,
But on that awful track he stayed.

'Give him to God,' is what I read.
"You can have him God," I said.
Soon after that Paul turned around.
He found a lifestyle that is sound.

He makes a home for a family of four.
God cleared his mind and opened a door.
He now does service to others in need.
Was this a miracle? Yes indeed!

   Ray Searle

Tiffany

Child of my heart, since the day you were born
I weep for you now because you're so forlorn
Up, up Mommy, which she didn't do
No time for that, you were so blue
Teach me to jump rope, ride my bike
never helped with the things you liked
play with my barbies, read me a book
Give me a kiss, instead of a look
I am so afraid when you drink and fight
I lie in my bed, scared half the night
No little friends have I ever had
The six years of my life have been very bad
No time for just only me
New Daddy and you and baby make three
I only feel safe and really loved,
With my Grandpa and Grandma,
They always have a hug.

   Sheila Ruley

Upon A Winter Moon

I will rise upon the Winter moon -
I will be flushed as barnyard hens.
I will be gone when the gate opens.

I will rise upon the Winter moon -
I will build a fire in the grate.
Upon my heavy heart, I'll shift the weight.

I will rise upon the Winter moon -
I will ride a witch's broom
I'll not lie lazy abed till noon.

I will rise upon a winter moon -
I will take my bearings, as I sit atop a tomb.
I will say again the ancient rune.

   J. Pierritz

Untitled

You say it's not impossible, but you won't elaborate.
I wish I knew how you really feel.
I try so hard to understand you, but you're always changing.
It's strange the way we are. We talk, laugh, smile... hurt.
But I fear how you really feel. I'm afraid to hear the words,
   "I don't love you. I don't want you. I don't need you."
I'd rather know nothing and be in the dark.
But I'm the only one... who'll follow you anywhere, support
   you in anything, overcome any boundaries you may face...
   by your side. That's where I want to be.
Feeling you beside me when you're not here, your breath on
   my skin, your kiss on my lips, my heart in your hands.
When you're not here, you're still here... in my heart, my soul.
You're in everything I say and do. You're a part of me.
Yet you're not. I'll wake up tomorrow and breathe the same air
   you're breathing, gaze at the same sky you gaze at...
and wonder... will you ever see the truth.

   Kathleen Miner

My Love

My love is like the sun dawning
It comes each day bright, new and refreshed.
There is so much love inside of me
So much that I need to express to you, I love you
Three words so simple yet so full of meaning.
So I'm telling you now I love you
Believe in me and I won't let you down
My love is like the sun dawning
It doesn't stop and never will because I love you.

   Marsha Treakle

271

I Wish I Was Going Home

Christmas time is coming, and
I wish I was going home.
The bells are ringing,
all the children are singing,
the snowflakes are falling, and I wish I was
going home. The wind is picking up and
blowing, while the snow is still flowing, and
I wish I was going home.
To hold friends and family that are
dear to me...as I look back and see the memories,
I really wish I was going home. The
season is a lonely one because I'm not
home with you. It makes for a silent
time, that Christmas feeling away from
home, and I wish I was going home.
I'd like to celebrate the Lord's anniversary
and be able to go home.
But all I can do is pick up a phone,
and only call home. And
I WISH I WAS GOING HOME...

Richard T. Barry

Something Evil Out There

As I sit there in my room all alone
I wish that I was, the only one home
Nature outside, so dark and so gray
but that smile on your face, makes my sunny day
The clouds overhead, are raging in despair
Away the Lord shows, there's something evil out there
I have to close my window, because soon it will rain
I pray to the Lord, for he takes away my pain
Painting my nails, because there's nothing for me to do
Something evil out there, is searching for me and you
The light in the sky, would soon be all gone
And darkness will fall, for twelve hours long
Forgive me I'm a sinner, for the Lord has got my back
He guides me to happiness, and keeps me on the right track
And the birds will keep singing, for today and all tomorrow
But their happy tunes, will never heal all my sorrow
So with each passing day, I sit here in gloom
Because there's something out there and I don't want to leave my
room.

Michelle Lewis

"Happiness Begins With Me"

When I came to ALANON going on four years
I was miserable and full of tears
They gave me some literature and a lot of love
suggested that I rely on the man up above
If I only asked him to help with my life,
I could get rid of my troubles and strife.

After a time the tears go away
We get stronger in ala-non day by day.
Alcoholism is a disease you see
The person who has it could have been me.
Treat it with compassion and learn to detach
The disease from the person and not react.

Our attitude has a lot to do with getting well
no longer do you have to live a life of hell.
"My happiness begins with me," so they say
My life is what I make it day by day.

Working the steps, changing what I can
And learning to live with your fellow man
Is what this program is all about you see
Because "Happiness begins with me."

Mildred Schilling

I Am A Happy And Friendly Person

I am a happy and friendly person
I wonder about my future and the whole world
I hear the endless silence in the dark
I have seen rainbow colors up in the sky
I am happy and friendly person.

I pretend that I am the future of the world
I feel the Earth is dying
I touch the universe
I worry that the natural resources will be gone
I cry all the hardship that we suffer
I am a happy and friendly person.

I understand that love is happiness that it will bring upon us
I say that we are all brother and sister
I dream that the world would be better and peaceful
I try to help people and love them with all my heart
I hope that we are people, we have to strive and help hand in hand
I am a happy and friendly person.

Susana Mostoles

"I Am"

I am a sweet girl that loves animals.
I wonder how many different kind of animals there are.
I hear the birds talking among themselves.
I see cats dancing around the room.
I dream about the free animals.
I am a sweet girl that loves animals.

I pretend to see animals living freely.
I feel animals are happy when they are not being killed off.
I touch the wounded.
I cry when animals are killed.
I am a sweet girl that loves animals.

I understand when people cry about their dead pets.
I say, let animals live.
I want to see animals not being killed.
I try to help when I am needed.
I hope animals can live and be free.
I am a sweet girl that loves animals.

Mary Ann Deriso

Dreaming About A World

I wonder if the stars will fade.
I wonder if trees will always shade.
I wonder why I think these things.
For if there is not a world,
Then there is not a being.
The stars and the moon are in my sight.
On my nightfall paths, they always shed light.
They are a part of my world, and always will be.
Thank-you for shining bright light on me.
On land, by my side, stand trees with great shade.
With flowers forever, and forever my aid.
From dusk to dawn, they are a world of great things.
A world to live life, as a true living being.
The world that I speak of is a distance away.
With love and joy that won't ever decay.
You must find it and hold it, and hope for great things.
For a lack of a world, is a lack of a being.

Margaret Armijo

One Man's War

I see the man walk alone so often,
I wonder where he has been. He is always
on a lonely path where he can make no friends.
He often disappears for days, no one aware of where he
runs, yet when he finally reappears, he continues wandering.
If you should happen to see his face and look into his eyes
don't be surprised to see the stress, that deep within he hides.
You could guess he came from Viet Nam
and struggled through the gore.
Upon coming back to life with us, he found he knew
no life but war.
However, to ensure his peace, he chose to live away,
from all of those that would demand his time,
now he lives from day to day.

Linda Proesl

When I Consider

Thinking of you the other day
I wondered what you'd have to say
if we should meet again?
Would it bring pain to you as well
Remembering the day that we both fell
in love, so long ago? I do not know.
But oh, my dearest love, I do hope so!
When I consider how we've loved, we two-
What you have meant to me, and I to you-
I wonder why you left without goodbye
While I am here, alone, and oh, so blue
with reminiscing over days gone by!
And while my throat aches with remembered
words—and thoughts of you—
My eyes burn bright with unshed tears.
I realize, unhappily, I am alone.
And you? I know not where—
I wonder—do you think of me at all?
    Or, even care?

Kathleen Bigge Lievense

Icee

When I first came I slept in the bathtub,
I would hold on like a club,
When I wake up I like to know,
That a pastry tastes good made from dough,
I look up at the second hand clock that gets my curiosity.
It is always moving so it gets me thirsty,
Then I go to the corner and look up and down,
Stealing the show I wear a crown,
I can open the doors and I go in,
I am satisfied when I see everything is
where it should be and I begin,
So I like to steal a person's place.
Just to see the looks on their face,
The one thing that I cannot figure out,
I reach in and try but I cannot pull that VCR tape out,
Yes, I am as curious as I can be,
For I am Male Cat named Icee.

Patricia Manix

A Lady And The Cop

A lady was driving down the road, the light turned red, she made a
rapid stop and ran into the back of a cop.

She bumped her head against the door and fell straight to the floor.

The cop not being aware at the scene of the incident was made to
believe it was a critical event.

He called an ambulance which rushed across town just to find a
middle-aged lady jiving around.

Shelly A. Woodum

Baby Talk

I hoped to find someone to love me.
I would try my best at everything, some things I would master,
some I would have to work through.
If you are rich I could be less trouble, unless money means more.
If you are poor, we can share the struggles together.
If you just don't want me, whether conceived in love or hate,
give me to someone that can compensate.
When I was conceived I began to grow.
I am A life right now just in sell form.
So think before it's too late.
Give me my life, the nine months is fine.
Then someone else could love.
You will still have a life, don't make a choice for me.
Give me mine.

Rosemary Ramirez

"Winter"

I think if someone asked me what to write
I'd walk away.
With nothing much to say.
And listen to the crunching snow,
beneath my dampened boots.
And see my breath.
But anyone that just might come around that day,
with anything at all to say,
won't remember what it was
I told them anyway.
So I'd just watch my frozen voice,
forgotten in the melting snow,
this poet's death.

Richard Bronislaus Cyrankowski

Content

If I could catch the spring again and take her by the hand,
I'd walk with her the sands of time
To half forgotten lands.

If I could feel her soft sweet touch run coursing through my veins,
I'd know caressing winds again
And lilac scented rain.

To know once more the mockery that April doth impart,
A fresh pastel serenity -
Then thunder in the heart.

And oh those alabaster clouds reflecting sun-kissed days,
Brave sentinels of heaven stand
Mute guardians of May.

If I could see the night once more dissolving into dawn,
And hear the symphony of birds
Before the dew is gone;

All other things I would forego to hold a phantom thing,
For I would find my lost content,
If I could catch the spring.

Patricia Schamaun

In The Wake Of Silence

The dark magician binds the amaranth
In the wake of silence
While love-lies-bleeding around the cloackal tern.
Colorless feathers wrap the spoiled staff
And tear at the seam of desire and disapproval.
A trembling veil hums rhythmically
Over the fervid threads
Fanning the crimson brooch of his design.
I lay naked beneath the sleight of his hand
Allowing his stained cloak to blanket my staidly cage
As I sleep,
In the wake of silence.

Theresa Drennan

Where Will You Go?

Where will you go, O gentle heart
  if e'er I cease to be?
    Will another dream replace your love
      that once belonged to me?

Will another summer pass me by
  with memories get to bring?
    Memories soft as the fragile sweep
      of the butterfly's powdered wing?

Or will I remain within your heart
  and never let you heal,
    my love you'll live in memory
      yet from the world, conceal,

I do not know the where of love
  nor how it comes to be
    but only how it locks the heart
      and throws away the key.

I only know my saddened heart
  will never set me free,
    you'll always be there with me, love
      within my memory.

    Ray Smith

Expression

If one has no emotion, there is no possible way one can feel.
If I see you does that mean that you are there?
Perhaps I am blind or merely ignorant to open my eyes.
The world is filled with blind people who lack emotion.
If one can touch, does that mean one necessarily feels?
You can't judge with the use of your fingertips.
Just the same, you can't truly see with your eyes.
Why is it so impossible to envision the world embodied in another's
  emotions?
Using your senses is a false way of perceiving others.
Reality is cluttered with ignorance.
Ignorance that insists on being deaf and dumb to other's feelings.
Feeling is a part of you that you must reach in and find.
Discovery of other people's feelings is the sixth sense.
Discover others and express yourself in the truest form.

    Kristin Pietrzyk

"Friendship And Love"

If kindness was never a part of my life;
  If no one cared for me;
If I stood all alone without any friends—
  how dreary this world would be.

It's not always enough to have friends;
  perhaps they don't even know it.
So make sure everyone comprehends;
  then, take the time to show it.

You should always try to be pleasant,
  even though you are tired and blue.
If you smile at your friends and are cheerful,
  they will smile right back at you.

The best we can find in our travels,
  is an honest and trusting friend—
One whose love and caring compassion
  will endure 'til the end.

Please be a friend to all mankind—
  to the elderly, sick and lonely, show love.
Always help your friends and loved ones
  climb the ladder to our kingdom above.

    Leora Covey Bennett

A Questioning

Headlights shine through the window of an empty room.
If no one is there to see them,
do they still cut a pathway through the darkness?
If no one witnessed the breaking of my heart,
did it still shatter as it hit the ground?
If there is no one to hear the cries
in the vacancy of my mind,
am I still screaming?
If I cannot find myself, how can anyone else
find me?
Have I then ceased to exist?
Love can fade;
like flowers, falling petal by petal,
to be swept away with the dust of the seasons.
Taken by time, and a difference of opinion.
Sunlight warms me, breezes cool me,
I try to drink the rainbows in the water.
Now I sit, between green grass and blue sky,
to eternally wonder...
If we have all forgotten, are there still memories?

    Teresa Lentz

If You Believe In Him

Verse 1 You said you loved him
        If that was true, why won't you love me too
        If feelings could speak
        and reach out loud it would bring
        a smile instead of clouds

Hook   Why Don't You Believe In Me
Verse 2 If you could know how much I've cared
        through the years
        thoughts of the day, as moments tick away
        wondering what it will be for you, for me

Hook   Why Don't You Believe In Me
Verse 3 A powder puff kiss, you blew in the air
        when last wondering eyes
        past in the nights glare
        your eyes follow me everywhere
        give me direction
        I need attention
        For today is today
        Yesterday is gone
        Tomorrows not known

    Michael A. Thompson

Don't Ask For More!

Please don't ask for me to give more
I'm busy searching opening and closing a door
Accept me as I am... don't run away
I'm growing in love with each passing day.

I can't promise my heart to another being
Unless... SOUL to SOUL.... I've been seeing
I can build a friendship without a threat
No strings attached.. no one in debt.

Smile and laugh with me.. don't ask for more
Don't make me sorry I opened the door
It's taken so long for me to want a friend
Pushing and shoving only makes a friendship end

I really am learning to accept who I am
It'll take quite awhile... I AM WHO I AM
Yes I love me but accepting is new
I never used to believe... but I know it's true

I don't ever want to hurt someone or be hurt again
I want to learn to grow from where I've been
I want to go slow.... I don't know what's in store
My only request of you.... DON'T ASK FOR MORE!!!

    Wanda Sue McCoy

Untitled

As I look out the window I see the clear blue sky and wonder
  if that's where heaven is

I become mesmerized with the soft white clouds, and on those
  I make a wish

I wish to be given the knowledge of where my deceased friends
  and family have gone

Are they holding my hand, still underground, or is it one of
  those clouds they're on

If anyone can help me, please don't hold your breath, let me
  know

Because I would like to know where heaven is, before it's my
  turn to go.

  Kimberly Nelson

Work Of Art

When the artwork disappears from the refrigerator door,
I'll know my children have left home, they live here no more.

And when I have time to wipe the smudges that are smeared upon the
  glass,
I'll know my children have left home, that time has come and passed.

And when I look across the room and see the empty rocking chair,
I'll remember lullabies softly sung, but no children will be there.

For they're hanging up pictures on their refrigerator door.
And they're wiping up dirt that's been tracked on the floor.

They're busy with car pools and dance class and such.
They're soothing away fears and scrapes with their touch.

And when the day passes to night and they're rocking their children to
  sleep,
They'll sing the same lullaby time after time, as they stroke a tiny
  soft cheek.

And they'll strike a familiar cord as they sing, as if they've been
  here before.
And they'll remember a Mother's Day work of art, that used to hang
on my refrigerator door.

And though I will miss the smudges, their voices, their laughter,
  their art,
I'll forever have the love they left, imprinted on my heart.

  S. D. Bannister © 1994

For My Sister

Sister, how the sunlight
illuminates your hair,
And plays upon the features
of your face that is so fair.

How the moonbeams and the stardust
twinkle in your eyes,
The captivating blue that is
the envy of the skies.

How your laughter makes the flowers sing
and the demons cry,
And how the faintest whiff of your perfume
could make a statue sigh.

Yes, Sister dear, I do attest that all
of that is true,
But I'm afraid that they don't know you
quite the way I do.

For if they did, I must confess
would be an unfortunate thing,
Because the beauty that they would see inside
isn't worth mentioning.

  Shannon Landerer

I Will Sail My Ship

I will sail my ship on an ocean of air;
I'll ride on the breakers of clouds when I'm there.
I will sail away above a clear blue sky;
Heroes and legends will wave when I sail by.

My partner in life and for all eternity
Is waiting at those golden gates impatiently.
Mother and Father will come to welcome me,
And bring my dear little boy of only three.

When I sail away above a clear blue sky,
A band of Angels will join me by and by.
Their music will guide me along my way,
When I sail my ship on my final day.

  Sharon G. Lewis

Basketball Fun

Oh! I love to go to the basketball court;
I'm good at shooting hoops; Yes, "B-ball" is my kind of sport.

I'm not that good at dribbling; the ball usually bounces off my toe;
We almost always get beat by whichever team is our foe.

Our basketball team is good, but our competition's usually better;
We've got some leaks in our ceiling; I'm surprised our gym floor
  isn't wetter.

We have to use our old gym because our new gym isn't ready;
And when we know about our next game, we figure we'll be
  "dead-y!"

I don't have much confidence, but I'm not the only one;
For me the most important thing is just to go out and have
  FUN!!!!!!!!

  Kristen Clemmens

They're Trying To Kill Me

Help, help, help, help, HELP!
I'm in this dungeon, this torture-chamber, this goal,
And everything I see is trying to kill me.
My food is trying to kill me.
The doctors and their medical torture devices are trying to kill me.
The nurses and their outfits are trying to kill me.
The bed, the walls, the bars, the floor, the ceiling, the window,
  they're trying to kill me!
The pillow and the mattress, grinning at me with their evil smiles,
  are trying to kill me.
The corner where I sit is my only refuge, and my hands bury my face,
  for I cannot bear to look,
For they aim their knives, swords, hatchets, archery, bombs,
  all weapons at me,
And if make one move, just one move, I will die.
"Die, die, die, die, die, die, die.....," they chant,
Laughing merrily yet evilly, pointing their fingers at me,
Planning heaven knows what in their diabolical minds.
A hooded skeleton is about to behead me with an ax!
HELP! HELP! HELP! HELP! HELP! HELP! HELP!......

  Robert F. Wallace

Untitled

Emptiness is the pathos that I feel.
I'm searching for the veracity to
attain evidence that my soul is real.
The conception of mine is that I've deviation
edificed into the metaphysical nucleus of my creation,
or my soul, thus forsaking me to be unwhole.
However, who doth care of cloudy, rainy days?
Does not the earth feel this without sunshine?
I must waive it by and permit cognitions of
rainbows and blue skies to flourish within my mind.

  William Tanner

Anger

When I have lost my temper, I have lost my reason too,
I'm never proud of anything, which angrily I do.
When I have talked in anger and my cheeks were flaming red,
I have always uttered something which I wish I hadn't said.

In anger I have never done a kindly deed or wise,
But many things for which I felt I should apologize.
In looking back across my life and all I've lost or made,
I can't recall a single time when fury every paid.

So, I struggle to be patient, as I've reached a wiser age,
I do not want to do a thing or speak a word in rage.
For I have learned by sad experience that when my temper flies,
I never do a worthy thing, a decent deed, or wise.

Maren Burgess

The Cliff

I'm standing at the edge of the cliff.
I'm not afraid of the cliff, but I've just never jumped from
so high up.
I'm not afraid of the fall, just concerned about my wings.
I've flown before, but just locally, you know, not from so
high up.
I'm not concern with what anyone might say, just
concerned about my wings.
But, I gotta take that step, can't listen to anybody, can't
close my eyes, can't just jump.
I gotta wait for a breeze, open my wings, have faith
and take that step off the cliff. Then...I gotta start
flappin' those wings gracefully, until-
I Can Fly.

Nimat Shaheed-Jacks

Dreams

The horrible shifty shapes of dreams,
I'm twisting and turning and falling and flying,
They'll never leave me alone it seems.

Even when, through my window, the sun's light beams,
I'm groaning and moaning, still tortured and dying,
By the horribly shifting shapes of dreams.

I've used them all, the liquids, the powders, even the creams,
Yet they still come again, It's no use my trying,
The horrible shifty shapes of dreams.

I wish I could guess what it all means
Yet each time I ponder, I give up, sighing,
They'll never leave me alone it seems.

Night after night I find the same terrible themes,
They leave me bleeding and burning, uselessly crying.
They will never leave me alone it seems,
The horrible shifty shapes of dreams.

William James Anderson III (Trey)

Mother

If I could give you diamonds for each tear you've shed for me,
  If I could give you sapphire for each truth you've helped me see,
If I could give you rubies for the heartaches you've known,
  If I could give you pearls for the wisdom that you've shown,
Then you'd have a treasure, Mother, that would
  mount to the skies,
That would almost match up the sparkle,
  in your kind and loving eyes,
But I have no pearls or diamonds as I'm
  sure you are well aware,
So I'll give gifts more precious,
  My devotion, Love and Care!

Tillie Johnston

Behold, The Grandfather

Behold, a grandson's Love for his grandfather; a feeling of
immense warmth; a warmth that embraces two, two so close,
although so far away
Behold, a grandson's Admiration for his grandfather,
...a brilliant scholar/teacher who seeks knowledge and truth
and illuminates the path of learning for others through his
patient tutelage...a philosopher, a suave orator, a meek and
mild-mannered gentleman who believes in the goodness of the
human spirit, and whose life of generosity, humility,
compassion, and goodwill forges a path for others to follow.
Behold, grandson's yearning to be with his grandfather,
thinking about him while turning in his sleep, hoping to
find a post-marked aerogram in each morning's mail, and
praying for his well-being during each morning's puja.
Behold, a grandson's Respect for his grandfather, a reverence
that rivals that of his for The Lord, and an esteem and fear
that can move Him, to turn stones over, open mouths of water,
and turn beggars into kings; and to send skirting rampart
stars, Orange, Green and White, shooting high above into the
navy blue night sky, bursting into infinity.

Sonjit Mukherjee

Sunshine

The sun gleams over the Rocky Mountains
implying an image of life,
an image of hope.

As I look through the trees
the sun gleams through them
as twenty or thirty streams of sunlight.

I close my eyes and lean back on my elbows,
absorbing the sunlight.
Suddenly, I feel warm and comfortable inside,
as if a great burden has been lifted off my shoulders.

I turn over on my side
and embrace an angel-like figure—she says in a quiet
sweet voice—"I Love You."

The sun at that point becomes brighter and warmer,
a light breeze then blows.
wiping the tears of joy off my smiling face.

Sean Cassidy

"The Girl Inside"

Who is the little old lady that sits
in a chair? Her skin is all wrinkled.
Her eyes full of fear. Her hands are unsteady.
Her speech is unclear. What you see is not me.
I'm hiding in here.

I'm a child who is loving, humble, trusting,
and courageous, who plays with her toys and
is so vivacious. I'm a young lady, with
lustrous dark hair, eyes with long lashes,
and skin that is fair. I'm quick on my feet.
I move with much pride. I can dance to the music
until the night has gone by. My heart has love
and beauty. It is full of joy and bliss, so don't
see the wrinkled old lady. See the girl with
the bouncy twist.

Please have compassion, and always be kind.
If the old lady annoys you, see the girl inside.
Someday the old lady may be wearing your shoes,
so don't be impatient. The old lady could be you.

Reedena M. Lawson

276

The Lonely Life

All alone I must walk,
In a dark emptiness I must talk,
In isolation I must live,
In all but vanity people give.

A happy child passes by,
Looks at me and bats an eye,
My eyes say, "Yes, you could live like me."
In return a somber face is all I see.

A rusty cup for begging is in my hand,
Quickly people rush by and never look back again,
So meager must I look to them,
I am but a tarnished gem.

How I wish this life wasn't real,
Life seems to have lost all its appeal,
Houses of cardboard, blankets of newspaper,
Everything I own, I will not wager.

Never have felt so bad,
Or ever really known sad.
But still everyday I bow my head and cry,
I should be the one just passing by.

V. Smith

The Tapestry Tunnel

Thoughts wander back to a time we spent,
In a forest grand.
The autumn of the year
When leaves give their color open hand.
Crisp cool air adds to surrounding beauty,
Bright light of reds, yellows
Lie ahead: heart pounding.
Hear the dryness of leaves underfoot
As we walk toward a tunnel of color,
Graciously given by towering maple trees,
How beautiful this tapestry in all its splendor,
On either side walls in colorful array,
We walked this tunnel of yellow and red
Thinking of the beauty today we see,
Of this tapestry tunnel to which we were led.
How simple life can be
Letting your eyes drink in
The beauty of a tree!

Sally Henderson

Memory Dream

One night I had a dream about the place I was born
In a three room house on my Dad's old farm.
That rolling farmland I could plainly see,
And it really brought back sweet memories to me.

My memory is good and I'll never forget
Down under the old apple tree where I sat
With my childhood sweetheart so tender and fair;
In my dream I could see us still sitting there.

I dreamed about where I would spend my life
With my childhood sweetheart when she became my wife
In the three room house with the old log barn
I dreamed we would just stay on my Dad's old farm.

When I awoke I went to the door in haste;
There I saw I didn't live at my Dad's old place.
My dream was shattered in a twinkle of an eye,
But my memory will live on until the day I die.

U. Z. Hale

I Am Sorry

For things I might have said to you
  In anger or frustration
For times when words of mine have been
  A source of provocation...I'am sorry

For unkind actions, thoughtless deeds
  Or inconsideration
For jumping to conclusions
  And rejecting moderation...I'am sorry

For timely things I haven't done
  Forgetting or Omitting
For knowing sometimes I was wrong
  Without, in fact admitting...I'am sorry

For conversations we have had
  When temper stole affections
For looking in a negative.
  Not positive direction...I'am sorry

For being too insensitive
  and just a bit unwise.
For failing to perceive the need
  For loving compromise...I'am sorry

Sabrina Toombs

Dad

We trip over him all the time,
In conversation,
As if he were still here.
"He might have said that," we say,
Or, "Remember when he shot the pigeons?"
And we laugh.
Even I, the youngest, still hear his voice,
See him, fists on hips, squinting, strong.
It's been seventeen years
And we still feel and act like it was yesterday,
When we saw him last.
We have so much of him in one another that
He'll never be gone long enough for
Us to forget.

Nora Shaughnessy

Untitled

My pain filled groin breathes a sigh of relief as
I wrap myself around your steamy tortilla scented body,
you move to fit my form and we become one.

F. Demma-Rodriquez

Daily Audit

Plant Earth, so we are told, is just a timely speck
  In galaxies of countless stars
Where we, in mortal molds, our thoughts collect....
  In God's own image...Here we are!

I cannot even count the molecules
  In any earth-bound thing....
So formed and fixed in true amounts
  By our creator, here in nature's scheme...

I have not viewed the sky from lofty rocked trips
  the world a foot-stool at my feet...
Nor have I been "down to the sea in ships"
  To see the "wonders in the briny deep"....

I dare not even try to note "each little sparrow as it falls"
  Nor tell the "number of the hairs upon my head"...

Yet ...daily in my paltry, human blunder ... I am called.
  To give correct account of every thought and
every word that I have said

Mary Katherine McGee

Tribute

You knew my pains and joys.
In my self-doubt, you encircled me
with arms spread wide
like great protecting wings.

I hated you, but loved you more.
We fought, cried and lived.
What's more, we laughed,
and then grew a bond intransigent.

I watched you die too quickly,
a bright flame extinguished by a chance wind.
Not with the grace of the aged,
who with a backward glance see dreams fulfilled.

But a young man, ravaged and withered
like a sapling in a violent storm.
And we spoke of it in abject whispers,
afraid of the small-minded world.

You left me a well of warmth and love
from which I draw your life essence -
the strength to go on alone
and the courage to whisper no more.

Lisa Daniels

Undercurrent

Me, a drop of water
in my stream of thought
flowing so easily
grasping every fleeting moment
wanting but to fly.

Life, a tiny pebble
in my stream of immortality
flows so quickly overhead
swallowed up by raging currents
wanting not to die.

You, enormous dam, you're
in my stream of love
blocking every safe way out
reaching thus to pull me in
wanting one more try.

Death, a widening delta
in my stream of consciousness
fleeting thoughts of afterlife all encompassed by bitter water
drifting into nothingness
wanting but to cry.

Tamara Shiplet

"The Night"

The night we met, I had my mind set.
I knew it was wrong but yet.
It seemed so right that night.
The Love was so strong,
The Love we shared was not wrong.
And Love opened the door.
Never knew love like that before.
The night we became lovers,
We felt love for each other,
And hoped it could be forever.
But we were better off as friends.
Even though we never wanted it to end.
Wherever you go,
Whatever you do,
My Heart goes with you.
This is not the end yet.
This is a story many lovers cannot forget.

Martha A. (Hinckley) Hayes   12/18/87

As She Sleeps

Who is this creature who lies thus so
In slumber deep, in sweet repose?
Is she an angel who graces the earth,
Or maybe a jewel of untold worth?
Is she an elf princess or a woodland sprite
Who paused from her day to spend the night?
Is she a child wrapped up in her dreams
Of princes and castles and grander schemes,
Who lies here in slumber until with a kiss
She awakens to find her fulfilled wish?

Does she dream of a lover who comes to call,
And vies for her hand at the high summer ball.
Does she soar on the wings of a bird in flight
As she slumbers on in the depths of the night?
Who is this girl in this bed where she lies?
From what pleasure comes her soft gentle sighs?
Does she glide through pathways of wonder and light?
What peace lies behind such a marvelous sight?
This angel, this child, woman and love,
Who lies here so close with the peace of a dove.

Patrick R. Kehoe

Untitled

I walk alone in fear of what may be ahead
in the darkness.
I'm not sure where to go, right now
I just need to walk.
I can hear the quiet rustling of leaves as the
wind gently lifts them to glide up over my feet,
yet, settling behind is a cool breeze that stays,
almost as if it were walking with me.
I can also hear falling raindrops that seem to
be dancing in somewhat of a poetic gesture,
to greet me as I pass by.
Although these surroundings appear to be
calm and comforting, I feel a certain
restlessness around me, almost fearful.
Is it just because I walk alone through
the darkness?

Marie B. Chambers

In My Dreams

In the depths of my dreams you came to me.
In the depths of my thoughts you went away.
In the depths of my heart you're
still there. Though caring and crying
Dad, you're really gone.
In the depths of my dreams.

Nena Hernandez

The Fork In The Road

Some call it tough love, I call it a state of confusion. All,
I wish is for you to open your eyes and see how you're destroying
your life. You're consumed with dragging those you love down.
You've wanted control of your life, but your defiance is that of
a child. When you want me in your life, and all goes wrong-you
blame me for bringing you into this world. So now, we are at
a fork in the road. I will have to travel the opposite road you
travel. I choose this with much pain. I know I run the risk
of loosing you for awhile, at least till you find yourself. I
hope your journey will be a safe one. Even though at this time
we are traveling separate roads, I am too suffering a pain, and
because I love you so much, I must let you travel this one alone.
In time we will meet at another fork in the road, and I hope we
will be able to travel that together.

Kimberly S. Kennedy

The Acceptance

Are my longings finally fading
in the evening sun?
Do I watch from this balcony
the others with my dreams, won?
Shall I just smile, in peace
as they play out a lifetime done?
Have my tears of never
healed the wounds they sharply stung?

Is the final longing we all come to meet
beckoning my heart with sounds too sweet....

for my resistance?
If so, I sigh
for this longing needn't include
a child's lullaby

And this longing
isn't met
by changing diapers wet,

But is fulfilled only by silent acceptance
that I may be all I get.
        Kimberly Andrade

A Song Of Summer

In the beauty of summer, God's glory is displayed
  In the heat and in the blue white haze
In the lush green foliage, in the smoky blue skies
  All praise God on these still sultry days

The weeds and grasses, designed with beauty so fair they put forth,
They put forth, they show, a glorious display And all the butterflies,
all the meadow-flowers Created they are in colorful array

In the warmth of God's presence, life and praise spring up
In the simmering heat of the summer light This song I seem to hear
burst forth "Glory to the Holy one, for all his creative might."

In the humble silence, I hear them boast the wonders-of what, for
them, God has done "You have clothed us in such glory and of
works like yours, truly- there are none."

The grasshoppers and insects leap and dance for joy
The birds, they too, they sing your praise And all creation does
  declare, "Who is like this God, Holy, He is, in all his ways."

My heart, it too, does leap for joy, for his glory has made my
  spirit shine
In the summery sunshine of God's grace inspiring me to call
  this great God, "Mine."
        William B. Smith

My Love

As I cried, underneath the Willow tree
You saw and with me, you decided to be

That moment our Destiny evolved
From your caring, my unhappiness solved

Your words so soft and so soothing
Instantly my heart and emotions moving

Though only a few moments of time had passed
Forever, your face, in my mind will last

From above, you surely were sent
Like an angel, in your eye, I saw the glint

My dearest friend, ever since, you've been
Listening contentedly and reassuring me again and again

After many years nothing has changed
Our love, from each other, we have gained
        Lisa D. Hofmann

For Dee Schmocker

The Moon moves through the Heavens
  in the many phases of her beauty
  forever encircling our lives.

The Sun radiates his warmth out to
  her and chases her across the
  skies in an eternal courtship.

A child stares up the side of a mountain
  that rises from its base and reaches
  out to the stars far above.

It stands there, a pillar of strength
  just as it did long before his father's
  father's father stood in this very spot
  and did the same.

Forever forward never looking back
  smoothly overcoming every obstacle
  in its path always chasing new
  horizons the river flows a never-
  ending journey.

My love for you.
All of these are one in the same.
        Richard K. Lewis

"Old Glory"

They blew it to hell at Pearl Harbor
  in the Philippines it was torn to shreds;
It was raised again at Iwo Jima,
  after hundreds of young men were dead.

It was sent across the ocean to Europe
  During World War I and II;
The cemeteries there fly Old Glory,
  her colors of red, white and blue.

She made a trip to Korea,
  she's still there as a peace keeping force;
Someday she will come home again
  and set her sights on a peaceful course.

Her last trip was a place called Vietnam,
  some burnt her at the start;
Those who fled received amnesty,
  it tore this country apart.

Now she's at peace and flying,
  some Americans won't leave her alone;
The high court says it's O.K. to burn her.
  she's not even safe at home.
        Louise Honan

Cliche

  Some wonder about Awhorta's person. Why
are they not seen clothed? Chastise us beings
who have done nearly all and our commitment
to his being of invisibility. Even though,
invisibility is differently kept in each generation.
We of Awhorta news state nude persons are not
always gracious due to what we have to deal
with the ground, not the sky, the obstacles
to are lower God types. Without our nude
interventions God is indeed non-existence, non-hear,
non-recognized, help turns to non-help.
Cliche not ease with brutal suggests to
please. Him - judicious. Awhorta kind
to his kingdom - listening - mentality.
        Tia C. Dennis

Sin

Lambent thoughts of suppressed desires,
In whose garden kindles the flames of
A raging fire

Whispering temptations that prey upon once
Confident souls.
Now weakened by virgin desires to touch
And to behold

Smiles of sweet deceit place sensual lips
Upon once innocent thoughts,
Whose carnal seeking breath is where
One's sin are wrought

The solitary secret that speak a legion
Of tongues,
It's that unbound demon, whose time has
Come

Like subtle drops of passionate rain,
In whose deluge we seek not the strength
Nor desire to refrain

The kiss of our hidden intimate desires,
From whose lips ignites a confession's fire

Richard Cirulli

Mom

Oh Mom will you look at me
In your image I can see
All of you and part of me.

Help me now along the way
To see all of me
And the Lord by day.

To please you Mom is a wish of mine
Though I am myself - it's hard to find
All the hugs and kisses you deserve
Our love will grow
And our thoughts will bind

I don't want to be so different after all
A shining Mom made me a star,
I love you Mom - the way you are.

Roberta A. Scarbrough

The Woodreeve

Delighted by these woodland scenes?
Inspired by the autumn leaves?
Perhaps you are enchanted
by the sorcery of trees.

I'm looking at an ancient tree
whose face keeps changing with the breeze.
Wild flapping hair and gay light eyes
infuse my mind with woodenwise.

Her heartwood hums with honeybees,
and scarlet birds protect her leaves.
Two children swing from limb to limb,
bouncing her branches in the wind.

Maker of food, keeper of earth,
this giant felt our human birth.
She casts her power artfully,
charming the mind of the enemy.

Trees sense they must seduce with shade
and lure with fruits and sunlit glades.
Without our love, our human greed
will chop and burn each lovely tree.

Katharine D. Barrett

When Darkness Comes

When darkness comes, you hear a voice
in your mind,
You feel so reckless and think everyone's
unkind.
All the wasted money put together
causes some stress
Sometimes you think "My life's a total mess"
But never say that life's not worth living,
it's worth sharing and worth giving.
Don't throw away what you have, when
trouble comes your way.
Don't make the beautiful blue turn to ugly gray,
while flowers still bloom in the fields that play,
try living a wonderful life starting today.

Laura Leuang

I Waited Till Tomorrow

I waited till tomorrow and my dreams were lost today.
Indecision grasped me, now the loss is mine to pay.
The shadows of her beauty are still vivid in my mind.
The thrill of being with her when we danced or when we dined.
She was sweet and kind and tender with an understanding love,
So like a precise present sent to me from up above.
But I waited till tomorrow and my dreams were lost today.
Indecision grasped me, now the loss is mine to pay.
Now I hold an invitation to a wedding I had planned.
And it's hard to see a stranger in the place where I should stand.
The smile I am wearing is a curtain for my tears.
Will the heartache that I'm feeling haunt me through the coming years?
I'm the fool that wipes my teardrops on the plans I made too late.
Yes, I waited till tomorrow and my dreams were lost today.
Indecision grasped me, now the loss is mine to pay.

Stanley M. Walker

Where Is He Now?

Glances at the bar and fun times like none other
Innocent it seemed at first, the times with one another.
Closer we became and then we became lovers
Where is he now?

Waiting for his call - never knowing when
Afraid to leave my only link, he might not call again.
How can something so much fun ever be a sin?
Where is he now?

Where is he now?
He said he'd call by ten.
Is he on the road today or is he home again?
Wife and children all around, can't you use the phone?
Don't you care that I am here? I am all alone.

Hardest thing I've ever done, I have to let you go.
Sweetest part of all my life, I've got to let you know.
Empty arms, empty heart, I've never felt so low.
Where is he now?

Teresa D. Helmondollar

"The Final Passage"

A maze of confusion of what might be
In my mind's eye is what I see.
Dark clouds drifting by, I wish for sunshine in the sky.
For now the heavy rain falls down.
As my spirit watches this sleepy town.
A ray of hope I want to see, break these
chains of this demon that haunts me.
For as this night shall surely pass.
Like time my life passes through this
hourglass.

Jeana O'Guin

"The Fall"

An April afternoon has twisted the spring
Into a knotted, bent thing unable to fly toward summer.
And caged with it is my heart
Infinitely bound in gnarled branches,
Beating against the sharpness of thorns hidden among the sweet
buds.

Piercing yellow days rush after each other,
As a broken-winged June struggles toward August,
And the red petals tumble down around me,
   and fall
     is near,
So near, I can feel its chilling fingers along my backside,
And I yearn for the blaze of the fire
Of summer which has passed, and so the rose.

Yet the thorns remain, twisted in crisp, dark leaves,
Dead, but able still to cut to my heart
As you did when you left this world
   in
     the fall
      of
       my life.

Shelley Sizemore

Peppermint

Available ways to extort pleasure
into colors of energy
unseen and unaccepted until constant
tones carry across hills
and melody over the sea
correspondence between loves too far away
   to be together and kiss
Vacancy of the top floor
wishing entry or perfection
or a simple beauty who looks far away
   unfocused, into the outside
Where I never went
wondering in a dream if you are there
Simple turnings compose a smile
   to parched lips
untouched for the changing season
unable to be unaware
   children fall often onto skinned knees
though not so much in love.

R. Nathan Spreng

Untitled

Darkness engulfs the sky as the wind settles
into its nestled place beneath the leaves. A faint hum
fills the echoing boundaries about me ... peace.

As the earth supports my body, my soul rises and falls with
every breath, trying to free itself; although it will not succeed
until my last breath is drawn and the angels beckon its presence.

Repressed, it causes much turmoil.
It is not in its place, it has no home.
I have not provided an adequate dwelling for this soul.
I shall die and set it free, or I shall change its dwelling,
giving it a home, a place to grow and flourish.

The amber hues of daybreak slowly encompass the grounds,
the sound of nature awakening me. The cold ground has become
warm from my body. I have life. I have strength.
I can change. I will change. My soul shall dance the halls of
happiness.

I have chosen to live life.

Kristina M. Reid

Who Am I?

Who am I? American... Indian - how
ironically they fit together. Woman
or child, lost in my own pain-sympathy
silence... Who am I? In jeans and hair
in ribbons. I say, "My God, what weakness
have I created within myself?" I fall
hopelessly into my nursing chair - flipping
through the channels, a dead end. Why must
I abdicate myself to the elapse of time?
Finding my bed every time I open my eyes.
My wandering mind gets lost in all the
greatness of morbid darkness... numb.

Mary A. Farnsworth

Heaven's Gate

The start and very foundation of Creation
is death, itself...the Destructive Mechanism.

Every child is a tapestry woven in the flesh of corpses.

In any great storm, the Spirit stills just once before its great leap.
The sky, then, falls in upon itself as its breath is swept amidst trees
and, sullen, lights its path with the whisper of sun-shelled skins of
snow.

I, like the tangled pelt and startled claw, kiss the morning where I'm
sent through Heaven's Gate, built tall among forever's broken
thought harvest.

It is not you who may own this stream of gnarled
   and juxtaposed expressions of flesh in time and place,
though when my shuttered eyes, bound by skin, still from
   the storm and steal from the dark a new light,
where recognitions falter and bones creak with dry abandon:

My pelt stand upon end and claws cut through wind as two eyes,
   now four, will toward one and then none.

The gentility of love merely stills the gate for the entry of planets
and vacuous space, which render us toward the beloved frenzy of
unbeing.

of flesh in time and place, though when my shuttered eyes,
bound by skin, still from the storm and steal from the dark a new
   light,
where recognitions falter and bones creak with dry abandon.

My pelt stands upon end and claws cut through wind as two eyes,
now four, will toward one and then none.

The gentility of love merely stills the gate for entry of planets
and vacuous space, which render us toward the beloved frenzy of
unbeing.

Samuel Gromowsky

Reflections By Water's Edge

As I walk by the water's edge
   I walk alone.
Where there should be two sets of footprints,
   There is only one.
Where there should be two voices talking to each other,
   There is only one voice to be heard.

How I long for you to be my side,
   Leaving both of our footprints in the sand;
Seeing the reflection on the water
   Of two people in love.
And finally, hearing two voices
   telling one another of their love.
Come, walk with me dearest
   And it shall be ours.

Nelson E. Smith

In The Hands Of God

We know that our special home,
Is in the hands of God above,
All the happiness we share,
And every bit of love,
For everything we have,
We owe to God alone,
And he plans to have us someday,
Around his mighty throne,
When you make your place with God,
Just as sure as it is done
All the worries and the heartaches
Will vanish one by one,
And the battle will be won,
No task is too great or small
For him to take away,
No amount of sorrow,
It will be done that day
For the spirit does move mysteriously unknown to us,
By only giving him our hearts
Our love and our trust.

Ruby Cline

Breath To Breath

The days seem long
  Is it going to happen today?
Yet they fly by
  Am I safe?
Morning is gone. Take a breath
  Don't worry
But the night was long
  Who is it this time?
The worries are back
  I can get through this day. Take a breath
It's okay, I'm halfway through the day
  Stay inside
It's night
  It mostly happens at night
Take a breath
  That's not true
Relax, the day is through
  It happens at anytime
Toss and turn. Take a breath
  It's not today

J. M. Olson

The Love That Speaks

Lord, I praise and thank you for your great LOVE,
  It all comes to me from above.
Would I could fly like a dove
  And return to thee some of my LOVE,
And let it be recorded within your heart.

But if thou dost not command me,
  I shall not die on the tree with Thee.
Yet nothing else is worth living for,
  Because you will open the heavenly door,
And this is what I'm living for.

So open your door wide,
  For I would like from my enemy to hide,
And escape the deep dark pit.
  On the CROSS YOU DELIVERED ME FROM IT.

The CROSS I see you hanging on,
  Its benefits shall never be gone,
And let the bells ring out in loud song,
  THE WICKED ENEMY FOREVER BE GONE.

Sister Mary Cabrini Loerzel O.S.F.

Rainbows

Perhaps the Rainbow in the bright and rainy sky above,
is not a promise of God's sorrow, grace and love.

But instead, a beacon of wondrous color and hue,
to show all mankind that Love must be the goal we all pursue.

And when as mortals we risk at love and Fail, we must learn from loss
and hurt, and once again expose our soul and part the veil.

But often anger stays and blocks our way, and then the darkness
in our hearts, obscures the rays that light our day.

For if we live a life of dark remorseless pain, our minds and Heart
will never feel the warming sun again.

And as the Rainbow will surely shine in the rainy days ahead, so also
must we reach out and have it said,

That in the brief allotted time upon this earth we're here, we searched
again, and found that Love was always near.

Tracy C. Gardner

Eulogizing You

Have you gone all cold and calm, then?
Is that your stillness, this deafening din I hear?

I apologize for your epitaph, not much time and all.
I hope you found yourself more prepared than I.

Did you take along your many moods when you...departed?
Did you pack your temperament and your raucousness?
Must you check them at the door or can you take them in?

I know your wit went with you and your sense of humor.
They should come in handy there.
Is there much you left behind? Do you miss me too?

Are you leaning out to see me? Have you ever?
Is it black and white or does it come in color?

Do you ever mix with angels or do they keep their distance?
Do you gravitate toward wisdom now? Is all finally revealed?

I guess I'm only wondering...
Is it everything you hoped it'd be, up there?
And did I say enough "I love you's," down here?
Just in case, you know.

Mia Keyes

To My Wife

Love is the splendor of a magic in our lives
Is the glory and the dreams of happiness
Is the sympathy for better or worse in our hearts
Is the passion till God does us part.

Often, as one drifts apart, suddenly the feeling of loneliness
Regrets and memories are then tomorrow's ills.
Of what was then and how it is now in our lives
Is only the feeling of dreams of happiness.

Today, I wish it had never come, so I cry.
I could live in the Glory of yesterday, for
yesterday was better than today. If today is not
Better than yesterday, I take yesterday with love forever.

Tomorrow illness it seems then as memories
In sickness and in health, and time in our savor
If love is sickness, love then is passion and ardor.
If love is health, let us live in the magic of our lives.

Endurance is the faith of tomorrow's loneliness and happiness
If dies in misery, regrets, in space and time.
What was then and how it is now, is only the splendor
Of the magic in our lives and love.

Reginaldo P. Lopez

For My Wonderful Wife Clista Mae Sandy

A wonderful and Loving wife
Is the greatest thing in a man's life.
When they love one another,
And she is a great mother,
Life is grand.
When two people walk hand and hand,
A wife and a mother,
There is no other, can take her place.
Because she is loved like a piece of lace.
When two people share work and play,
Love comes in many ways.
Through good and bad.
When one is gone the other is sad.
You never know what you have missed
Until she is gone, and you cannot kiss.

Walter A. Sandy

The Vampire

Eyes as red rubies, heart as black as coal,
is there to take your life away, and damn your
mortal soul.

He stands before you menacing, oh yes and
sees it clear,
'twould do no good for you to run, for he feeds
upon your fear.

You're frightened to the depth of you, your heart
begins to flood,
his senses heighten as he knows he's soon to
claim your blood.

But wait! Is that a crucifix you wear?
Hold it out for him to see,
its power he can't destroy, for he fears the Deity.

Don't look him in the eyes, for he can swift deceive,
and let your heart be honest when you ask of God reprieve.

Be careful where you travel, be wary of your soul,
or you may chance to meet again,
eyes as red as rubies, heart as black as coal.

Ron Palmer

Keeping Up With The Joneses

If keeping up with the Joneses
Is what you plan to do,
You'll have to lower your standards,
And lower your income too,
You'll need a battered pickup,
And you'll learn to heat with wood.
'Cause this is the way they live you see,
and wouldn't change if they could.

Crops they grow in the summer,
And sell them in the fall.
If it wasn't for odd jobs in the winter,
There would be no income at all.

So the next time the Joneses are mentioned,
Remember that things may not be
Always the way you imagine,
Or even the way that you see.

So why try to keep up with others,
For along the way you may find,
Happiness is not just possessions,
It's really—A state of mind!

Winoka Plummer

The Grandfather I Love

My Grandfather I love,
Is with God up above.
He would protect me when I was in fear,
So I would not let out a tear.
I know he left scars and wounds only in my heart,
The dart of joy that he is in heaven.
I know God will watch over him for me,
When I get down and pray on one knee.
I had to strain,
not to show pain.
During light and dark,
Sun and moon.
I will always love the one up above,
This is the life of the Grandfather I love.

Ninette Motal

Death

The sky is furious - black
It bellows out its anger, thunder and lightening
The thunder jeers down from above
The winds test their deadly strengths
Teasing, laughing, threatening, warning they will demolish
The innocent and evil alike wait helplessly
At the mercy of the storm
And then it comes...
The wind blows merciless
Crashing and deadly, lashing out its demands
Like living hell it lingers - smashing, killing
Never ceasing, endless.
Hours, days, who knows?
Silence and tranquil replace thunder
Quiet as the grave the world is shocked
Gone are the farms, houses, animals and the People.
The suffering, bloody, bruised and dead
Strewn on the face of the earth, like ornaments on a tree
Remainders of the human race
Death has taken its toll.

Sharon Griggs Morgan

Our Last Good-bye

When I think about you,
It brings a tear to my eye.
All the fun nights together,
What made them die?
You said you wanted to be friends,
But that's not true either, our friendship
Had to end.
Why...I guess I'll never know,
But now I realize it's time to let go.
Your friendship meant the world to me,
How much I care for you,
You just can't see.
I'll never let those times slip by,
But now I guess it's time to say good-bye.

Missy Davison

To The Artist

Full of hubris the brilliant peacock displays.
Iridescently plumed he shimmers and struts-
   the vain and splendid bird.

Piercingly intent the powerful hawk glides.
Icily perilous he plummets and attacks-
   the keen sighted rupture.

Dangerous or decorative, which shall you be-
Prescient or ineffective in our society?

Margo Allman

Fall

Fall is one of the most colorful and beautiful times of the year
It brings back for me many memories that are very dear.

I remember raking the leaves into a great big pile
And the smell of them burning stayed around for a while.

With the coming of Fall, it means an end to the warm Summer breezes
And with it comes the cold rain and the sniffles and sneezes.

The coming of Fall also brings us names,
We often hear "The Bears," "Packers," "Fighting Irish," "Illini" and all.
For it wouldn't be Fall without Pro, College, and High School football

Fall brings us many multi-colored leaves that create some picturesque sights.
It also brings us the sound of the farmers' tractors harvesting late into the Autumn nights.

Fall brings us the special day of Thanks Giving.
It's a day we share with our families, friends, the blessings the Lord has given us all.
We thank the Lord for giving us the most colorful season we call "Fall."

Ron Skibicki

Smile

Smile, it might brighten up your day;
It can make all of your bad feelings go away.

Don't worry about what other people do,
Do what you like, what is best for you.

Smile, you could make someone's day;
Even that angry man screaming for people to get out of his way.

One day you will smile, and you will know it's true;
Because the person that you smile at, will smile right back to you.

Kristina Dorsch

Untitled

Though the love was once there
It can no longer be found in your heart.
Though the love was once real
Whenever we touch I can no longer feel it.

Though the love was once ours
Whenever we meet it's no longer there.
Though the love is now gone
I still long to kiss your lips.

Though the love between us is nowhere to be found
When I see you it always returns to my heart.

Melissa Claussen

The Greatest Gift

The greatest gift that's been given to me
Is my Lord and Saviour Jesus who set me free
His spirit guided me into His arms
As I felt the compassion I was now safe from harm
My sins, as He promised were cast out to sea
And He gave me the authority to command satan to flee
His patience and kindness in abundance He showed
As He taught and I learned He made light of the load
My prayers and requests He brought to the throne
As He petitioned the Father He made them well known
He captured my weaknesses and made them strong
And placed me in positions where faith must hold on
He walks with me daily and removes all my fear
It's a comfort to know that Jesus is near
He hung on a cross in lieu of my soul
I owe him my life, for now I am whole.

Rosemary L. Scuteri-Mason

Hope

Hope cannot see.
It doesn't note the beauty of a flower;
Nor watch the sweetness of a child's smile.
Has no vision of sunrise subdividing night,
Sunsets' loveliness is swallowed by the
  darkness unobserved.

Hope cannot laugh.
Yet, at the same time has no tears.
It has no senses that give rise to fear.
The comedy of life is absent from it totally.
It neither smiles in tolerance at youth
Nor grimaces at faltering age.

Hope is never lost.
A little shower on dried out land
Brings expectation of a long soil-soaking rain.
The dying clutch it to them to the very end,
Then, without a backward glance—
Leave it behind for those who live.

Wendell A. Bengson

Love Is...

Love is like a roller coaster ride,
It fills you with laughter and thrills,
Love is like a little stream,
It flows into bigger and better things,
Love is like a tree,
It grows stronger and stronger with time,
Love is like a death,
It can make you cry,
Love is like a wedding,
It can fill you with happiness,
Love is like our Savior,
It never fails,
Love is absolutely nothing though,
If the two do not work together as one.

Kenny Boatright

Soaring Through Freedom

In the wind there is the sound of freedom,
  It goes by places with song and whistle,
It goes by the most finest kingdom,
  but yet it never misses a single thistle.
Birds soar in freedom all around,
  watching it follow the currents of rivers,
Flowing softly over the ground,
  and even getting the littlest slivers.
Weaving through the trees,
  and over the grassy meadows,
Across the ocean with a breeze,
  Crashing with muscular billows.
Running with the wild horses,
  Catching all the small features,
Following the roughest courses,
  To reach the home of creatures.
Runs through the canyon walls
  with all of its might,
Falls with the waterfalls,
  and follows the morning light.

Katey Sturm

Your Love

Autumn is coming to an end, and winter is to begin.
It is cold outside, but your love will warm me inside.
It is dark, but your love sings to me like the skylark.
My feelings soar like the dove, because I can feel your love.
I can feel your tender care, like the soft gentle breeze in the air.
Your love is magical and fills my life with joy.
I hope you stay by my side, and never leave me behind.

Marie Jernigan

Changes

The midnight sky under which all men lie,
it has many ornaments, one boon;
That a silver sphere be placed upon high,
it has many facets - it is the moon.
What's this, a dawning of a newborn day?
the new horizons come, new hopes and dreams;
Through this comes inspiration, a lone ray,
one among many of these tainted beams.
Again, a new portion of life's pathways:
a golden orb soars into the heaven's wind;
The sun's glory shines onto the sea-bays,
swords of light in water forever pinned.
But in this way love is forever changing.
In this way love is forever lasting.

Matthew Peterson

Love, Life, You

Love is life
It has much meaning, much worth.
Like a bird soaring across the sunlit sky
with wings spread so free and graceful
we too can soar free and easy with trust
and honesty filling our hearts we'll have no fears.

As white caps rushing to the shore
breaking as they curl over the soft beach sand
so powerful and strong, you have the strength to hold me near
and the power to keep me always yours.

In the trees blowing from the cold crisp wind
bowing down...then snapping back up to reach for the sky
I see us standing tall, then swaying with the winds of the world
as it knocks us down, I know we will always be able to spring back up
to reach for our dreams.

Yes love is life.
It has much meaning, much worth.
For every sign of life I see I am reminded of you.
Life is beautiful, you are beautiful
You are both love and life... mine.

Linda B. Koss

Life Is Just Another Word

Life is just another word to our society,
It has no meaning anymore.
People walk around acting high and mighty,
To me, our world's become a bore.
People take too many things for granted
And don't think about consequences
Like a herd of cattle being branded
They don't try to jump any fences!

Robb Walter

Death Of A Giant

A regal oak stood on the hill two hundred years or so.
It housed the nests of countless birds and held the soil below.
Its ancient limbs obscured the sun, all creatures sought its shade.
It would have stood a long time yet, but progress must be made.

Some yellow monsters, steel teeth bared, came on the scene one day.
With greedy gulps devoured the earth and all things in their way.
The old giant fell with screeching moan and toppled to the ground.
The monsters belched, went on their way, new victims would be found.

The woodland mourned its fallen friend in quiet eulogy
And thought about the whims of man and how this came to be.
The old tree lay in ravaged spoil, a blight upon the land
In blatant testimony to the foolishness of man.

Marianne Cable

For All Of Time

Music soothes the savage beast, it is said
It is good for a person's soul, I have read
Just a rustic verse to our ears
Music lives throughout the years
Ancient as the earth in creation
marys the reason for celebration
Music makes everyone feel at peace
For the soul to give such a release
So, for tomorrow it shall be a rhyme
Music will forever live in time.

Mary E. Sullivan

Spring Flowers

As winter fades and spring is in the air
it is like a new found freedom that all can share.

The flowers that lay entombed in the frozen ground
Spring forth with life and bloom all around.

They stand in the sunlight with their faces all aglow,
and God sends the gentle rain from heaven to make them grow.

They cover the earth as far as the eye can see,
and the joy of their beauty, words could never express to me.

For my eyes have witnessed God's awesome power
in the gentle way He has made the delicate flower.

Like a river flowing, going out to the sea
their sweet aroma wafting in the breeze, envelopes me.

Their magnificent colors and their blossoms of every size
bring such a warm feeling to the heart and heavenly beauty to the eyes.

Spring, filled with wonder, the season of new birth
give praise to God Almighty, for He is Father of all on earth.

Nita Buie

Tonight

Ice glistens with the glow of the streetlight,
It is raining, adding to the beauty,
Watching and waiting for the arrival,
Scared that it isn't worth risking,
Each missing the embrace of the other.

The rain pelts down seemingly never-ending,
No communication with the outside world,
Dreaming of the voice each longs to hear,
Wishing happiness filled the air,
The odds seem virtually impossible.

Time slips away from the awaiting minds,
Coming together would only mean many worries,
Certain sounds make each heart skip a beat,
Hoping to see the sight remaining unseen,
Feelings can go the distance the body cannot.

Kasha Underwood

"Right Decision?"

I wonder all the time,
If the decision I made was the right one.
I had my options to choose from,
I made my choice, and all is done.
I think about you and us everyday,
And all the things that could have been.
I love you still, and always will,
With this choice, I hope a new life to begin.
I would take you back tomorrow,
If that's the road that we should take.
But if it is not meant to be,
Then the move to move on is the one I must make.

Keith Starzee

A Patriot Thought

In its birth-death and fall
  it is the greatest Nation of all.

The greatness comes from its glorious heart,
  and the pure blood that flows from shore to shore.

Constitution-its Bill of Rights,
  is the glorious heart within.

The pure blood that flows from shore to shore,
  is patriots of "A" no common type.

The cries from lust and crime, as time passed on,
  filled the veins with blood no longer pure.

Presidents-Congressmen of reprobate minds,
  Ripped-Raped and Tore,
  the glorious heart that made our Country stand apart.

'Tis a generic nation, with no heart or blood,
  but flags still fly, as the bands and parades go by.

Is the pure blood of Patriots, forever stilled,
  to flow from shore to shore, no more?

The once glorious heart, must it die?
  I say NO! — NO! — NO!

I would rather die, is my reply.

   Steven R. Thompson

Friends

Best friends we are
  It matters not how near or far
For this friendship so strong
  How could it possibly be wrong.

We have made it through
  This friendship so true
Through the good times and the bad
  The happy and the sad.

Together we can show
  This world how it can grow,
Not by looking to the ground, but
  Just by giving love to everyone around

For this friendship without doubt
  To this world I wish to shout
She's my best friend, she makes me very proud.
  To you world, I say out loud.

Best friends we are
  It matters not how near or far
For this friendship so strong
  How could it possibly be wrong? Best friends forever.

   Kandi L. Smith

Granpop's Star

There is a star that shines ever so bright
It's always there, night after night
That stars was born of a little boy's love
To keep him close to his Granpop above
So many times at the end of the day
He looks at the sky and I hear him say
"Look, Granmom, there's Granpop's star
I knew all along that he wouldn't go far
How you doing, Granpop, did you watch me today
Did you see me at school, did you see me at play
I got a new bike, I went on a trip
Granmom took me on a really big ship
I wish you were here to share in my fun
I like to remember the things we have done
But as long as your star, I am able to see
I know in my heart you will be here for me"

   Marj Ballick

Unfantasy

The purest heart's been torn the worst.
It never matters, last or first.
The scars, they're visible, but they are deep.
The mind builds walls. It plays for keeps.
Self Preservation helps build the fences.
Until we are lost in our defenses,
The courage to heal is the seed
which deserves attention, can quash the need
to ride that train towards insanity
and assure survival with vanity.
But rest certain, it took many years
to form the foundation of all the fears.
And the power needed to put them away
is immense, it is nothing with which to play.
So be patient, my friend
as I must also be.
I am the main character
in this unfantasy.

   Lisa Lindstrom

Raindrops

I love to watch the rain fall,
It rains on us all; short or tall.

I love to watch the clouds;
I know the thundering is going to be loud.

I love to watch the dew;
Because the drops are so few.

I love to watch the snow;
The children and grownups
Will soon he playing in the snow.

I love to see the frost;
It's almost like snow; old Jack Frost.

   Oretha Roachell

Untitled

I went today where we had spent so much giving.
It seemed all too assembled and organized for the
  bumbling way we spent two weeks.
No piles of clothes, no mussed-up sheets.
Just lines and formalities of existence.
It scared me then to think that only we would
  remember what has passed in that borrowed alcove.
And if you forgot, that left me-
  still remembering.

   Ken Jones

A Younger Me

Last night I met a younger me.
I reread my old poetry.
Some of the lines, rang bright and true
Better I fear than some of the new.

I was filled with nostalgic pride.
To see how hard the youth had tried.
Oh how well his thoughts ran through,
Better I fear than some of the new.

Last night when I met that younger me
By reading again my old poetry;
I fear that envy filled me through
How sure he was, his lines were true.

His youth and courage did create
Statements I'm tool old to make.
Never - the - less in my heart I knew
Some of his work, was better than the new.

   Robert L. Laumeyer

Autumn

Such a wonderful time to write a poem,
It seems there's nothing going wrong.
Beautiful days and the sun so bright,
Also the temperature, it's just right.

It's harvest time down on the farm,
The farmer now fills up his barn.
Fruits and vegetables put up for winter
How hard he worked, I well remember.

The pretty trees with leaves of green
Are now nowhere to be seen.
The green leaves now have changed their colors,
There's red and gold, brown, purple and other.

It's fun to watch them falling down
on countryside, city and town.
School children are having such fun
catching the leaves one by one.

This delightful season is a welcome change
From the very hot summer and rainy spring.
Winter months are next to come
With holidays and winter fun.

Lois Wade Kinder

Sail On

Out of the lurking mist a ship appears.
It slips through the water with nary a whisper,
Only a glorious moment discerns the miser,
Then as it came, slowly it disappears.

Gone, swallowed by an empty world of fog.
What shore is destined for her touch?
What harbor will hold her in its clutch?
What storms will scare her sail and log?

Yet, in that one glimmering moment of light,
As if God Himself opened the heavens above,
Time stood still, and I discovered... love.
Unexpected, passionate... consuming my plight.

She will return to this port one day.
She looks the same one might mull.
But, oh, the treasure concealed in her hull.
I did not know it would be this way!

The fog encloses her, again she's gone.
Her bow unveils a sparkle of sunlight,
And in her wake... tears less delight.
Sail on my little ship; you must sail on.

Mike Mills

Art

Art it is a wonderful thing,
It swims in the ocean, it soars upon wings.
If you haven't got the drift yet,
I'll explain it much bolder,
Art is in all things,
Art is in the eyes of the beholder.

Katelyn Myers

Fear

Fear is the color purple like an endless night.
It tastes like ice which could freeze you to death
It sounds like a squeaky door opening
And smells like dirty gym socks left to rot
Fear reminds me of walking down a dark alley
Fear makes me feel like a shivering snowflake
Not knowing where to land.

Lambros Vassiliou

The Little House

It was only a little house when it began.
It was built with loving care.
With a door in the front and a door in the back,
And some windows here and there.

As the years went by and the children came,
There was added a room or two.
It was only a little house when it began,
But it grew and it grew and it grew.

As you look at it now with its many rooms
Holding memories of many joys,
I know if you listen, you're sure to hear
The laughter of girls and boys.

Now mother and dad often shed a tear
As the memories they recall.
It was only a little house when it began -
As it grew, love encompassed it all.

Leona E. Murray

Falling Stars Are Fading Dreams

I once wished upon a star for a dream to come true,
It was really a lifetime of dreams because I wished to be with you.

When I looked into your eyes I saw the heavens above,
I knew right then you were the one that I'd always love.

Then came the day you asked me if together our lives could we share,
My life became complete because you said you'd be there.

For a very long time my dream was all a dream could be,
I had a husband and beautiful daughter who meant the world to me.

But the dream has faded, your love has too,
I feel you don't love me even though I love you.
I went to look in the sky but the star wasn't there,
I knew this had to be the reason why you didn't care.

Now I know things are not always what they seem,
I never knew that a falling star was really a fading dream.

Robyn Tobolt

Memories, Faith And Love

The voice rang out loud and clear,
It was the voice of the auctioneer.
And this is what I heard him say,
What am I bid for this rocker today?

Bidding was fast, the auctioneer alert,
Going to the man in the white shirt.
Other household items went very fast,
And soon he had auctioned the last.

No one noticed the old man sitting there,
With kindly face and snow white hair.
He hated to see things go this way,
Things of memory were auctioned today.

The old rocking chair was the very best,
It had rocked his babies to peace and rest.
His wife had passed and his children grown,
And here he was now so all alone.

Past possessions were temporary things,
It was as if they had had wings.
Then he looked to the heavens above,
Thank God for memories, faith and love.

A. E. Gully

287

"Dad"

I think about the Mountains, where I went with my Dad
it was the only Vacation he ever had
He worked very hard all of his life,
And I know that he wasn't happy with his wife
But he never complained, not even when he was emotionally drained
very rarely was he serious, most the time he was kidding around
Thank God for the Peace he finally found.....
He was a Fortuneteller for me, his Predictions always came true
and when they did, I was more angry than blue.
He always worried about me, because I was so much like him
and when I did something wrong, he said "It isn't easy not to sin"
he was always there for me when I was in Trouble
and quiet often he had to bust my "Bubble"
But I loved him dearly, and I still do
I wasn't the best Daughter but my love for him was true
I know he would be proud of me today,
why he left so soon, who is to say?
Dad, I know you are in Heaven, because you were a good Man
Please save a place for me up there....... if you can.

Petra Linden

The World As It Was

I watched in silence; I saw the violence
It wasn't really clear; it was just here

I knew I had to go, but everything went so slow
Things were getting worse; it was like some sort of curse

People screamed and shouted; children cried and pouted
Madness was there; I felt it in the air

There was something I felt, a hand of cards being dealt
The hand was crude; it worsened my mood

There was no point to the game; the whole bit was a shame
I shook off the cards; I looked around HARD!

I saw so many things; I felt such different feelings
Wars, deaths, and tears; pain, hurt, and fear

'We can help!' I thought; then someone shouted, "Not!"
I stepped up to the place so high, so high I was nearly touching the sky

I presented a speech, not from a card, but a touching talk
straight from the heart

"We can stop this, if we all pitch in; first of all-stop committing
these awful sins!

Next we need to work together, flock together like birds of a feather
We can do it if we try; we must try to do this, before we die"

They all agreed with me, thought of aspects of life to see
When I look back and see how we quarreled, I think, 'How'd we
live in that world?'

Kristi Derrick

Deception

A flower lies on the ground.
Its limp petals will never bloom.
Crushed by a stone,
Fallen and opened.
Beautiful, but deceiving
Twisted and demure.
Visible to those that can see.
Plain and ugly.
Its bewildering quality of mystery is unfolded.
True being is shown to those with insight.
That which was once deemed as harmonious,
Has lost its melody.
A masked face revealed to some...
Never to most.
A precious flower never...
Never dies.

Lisa Mouallem

Oh What A Friend

Oh, if ever there was a friend to be
it'll be JESUS CHRIST who lives in me
giving joy, hope, love for all eternity
yes it's the CHRIST that's a friend to me

If ever there was a friend to love so much
from my childhood to adulthood and such
a friend who stands beside me more closer than my mother
more caring than my sister and more protective than my brother

It would be JESUS the CHRIST and anointed one
who came from up above GOD'S only son
his love for me was to the end
he died on the cross oh! What a friend

But now he lives and sits upon the throne
I needn't to worry for I'm never alone
when I feel bad I just look to him
my SAVIOUR and friend who lives deep within

Lynette L. Harrison

Reflections

Here it is, the month of May ... my gosh, oh gee, it's snowing today!
It's a day for thought .... a day to dream on...
The past is nearly present ... the future is nearly past.
What has been accomplished? It's been a life time of growing.
Thirty years have passed .... I know half of what I am.
Sometimes night is day ..... Sometimes it's day ... in night.
Occasionally, night is night .... And day is day ... but seldom.
If I had to live life over ... I'd live it much the same.
The only thing, I think I'd change..Is my age..to thirty..forever!!!

Pamela Stoker Brander

Untitled

Time,
   it's a funny thing.
How sometimes minutes seem like hours,
   and hours seem like minutes.
When you're younger a day seems to last an eternity,
   and as you grow older weeks seem to only last a day.
When you're little you want to hurry up and get big,
   but when you're big, you wish the little ones would
   slow down and take their time getting to where you are.
Yet, even knowing this, you yourself are in just as big of
   a hurry to be sixteen.
Time,
   it's a funny thing.

Kelli Hutchinson

Under The Stone

Under the stone
It's as cold as night
Under the stone
It's lifeless
Under the stone
there is no vision or feeling
Under the stone....
I watch the hand lift the stone
UP and away from the ground
Under the stone
Where the ground is dark, cold, damp,
a seedling has sprouted
Its leaves tiny, gentle and pale
the stone is cast away
Sunshine, freely, warming the moist ground
Allowing growth to the leaves
As they become stronger
Without fear
Under the stone.

Susanna Marie Theo

288

Someone To Touch

In a city said to have charm, beauty and finesse,
It's also a place where you can die of loneliness,

Everyone's too busy to notice the shadow people
        as the streets they begin to fill.

You stare right through them with eyes
        cold as the winter's chill.

It's okay to get ahead and be the kind of person
        others can admire.

But it's wrong to step on another just
        to get a little higher.

Living empty lives like shells of the beach,
Pretty on the outside with no compassion in each
The true message, so simple, is out of reach.

Love and caring is what we need
        When we nurture our future seeds

They'll be our hope for tomorrow
        The cause of all our joy, fear and sorrow.

Spend a kiss, earn a trust
So many out there needing so much
Be the first to find someone to touch.

Ronald Johnson

I Wonder As I Wander

I wallow in the luxury of my mind's eye
Its beauty makes me breathe deep resonant sighs
I travel from country through country in a matter of a twirl
I freely roam through the brilliance of our wide world
I canvass lands filled with vibrant and color filled flower beds
Then roll on up to rivers with enormous water wheels and sheds
Hiking in the moisture of our lustrous rain forests
I rappel down the caricatures of masculine mountain sloped trellises
In sailing the splendor of our seven seas
I bathe in the magic of each island bay's lee
I promenade zestfully to each land's ceremonious dance
Sparring gaily in native costume to mystical performances as if in
        trance
Ah, home again, a smile turns my face
I wonderfully realize my mind is my treasure, my solid ace
What awesomely powerful dreams you can envision
If you allow your mind's eye to bestow creative figures in any season
Traverse the world through your very own mind's eye
Reap in your memories' cherished pleasures, never let them die
An advantage we can use to assure our global lands' features we've
        tread
This gift we hold in the realms of our head.

Wanda Zablan

'My Incense Burning Life'

I light a match, and hold
It to the stick. Like the creation
Of a child, of me. The smoke floats
Upwards, like my dreams towards
The heavens, the sweet scent filling
The room, like the fear fills my eyes.
I know you know, you're a good reader of eyes.
The stick shortens, like my life, day by day,
Hour by hour, second by second. Shorter,
Shorter, shorter. The ashes fall, like my
Wishes, only ashes fall in a boat,
While my wishes fall into the darkness
Of my heart. The flame slowly goes out,
Like my hope to make it in this
World. And when it does, I light
Another stick and watch my life
Go by again.

Maria Bastio

A Mother's Last Goodbye To Daughter Stephanie

Stephanie,
It's been a long time since I held your hand,
Because God has taken you from this great land.
It's been so long since I've seen your smile,
You were mine for only a short while.
It's been a long time since I kissed "your owie" better,
They keep saying "you'll never forget her."
I know your pain is no longer there,
I know life is not always fair,
I miss you and will always love you, that's no lie.
But my darling Ballerina, angel, with "Fish lips,"
I must say "Good Bye."

Melinda Dickerson

Rainbows

Rainbows are Mother Nature's treasure.
Its color is more precious than any gold.
Its beauty is more dazzling than any ruby.
Its colors are the guardians of every gift that Mother Nature
        has to offer.
Green is the grass that softens the skin,
Yellow is the sun that gives us sweet warmth,
Blue is the sky that stretches as far as the eye can see.
These are the colors that Mother Nature has given us.
Given us all.
Guard them well.

Michael Meyer

A Cowbell

I heard a cowbell tinkling late one night.
    Its faint chime put a tingling in my spine.
And I knew if fame and fortune and might
    Ever came my way I would always pine
For the sound of a cowbell echoing in the Ozark hills.

I heard a cowbell tinkling late on night.
    Its soft music was ringing in my ears.
A gentle cow was roaming somewhere out of sight.
    And someday I will cry wishful tears
As I long for a cowbell echoing through the Ozark hills.

Kathy Starr

This Rose

This rose represents you.
Its long, built stem, so fine in detail
that its beauty is amazing.
Each individual petal so smooth to the touch,
This rose represents you.
Its smell so strong, so perfect in shape
that its symbol is so meaningful.
Each leaf so green in color,
This rose represents you.
Its color so vibrant, so deep I can understand its feelings.
Covered in dew, so close to tear drops,
This rose represents you.

Misty Vineis

My Dune

I lay upon a dune of sand somewhere
Somewhere called anywhere
In my mind, I move through time and space
With little more than a thought of being there
Spellbound by the kaleidoscope of colors
To which my mind dare run the gauntlet
Ride me it says, and I ride, for all I am worth
It felt so warm, so, so intense
How could I know that I was asleep.

Gregory L. Price

Time

What is time?
It's not just a clock hanging on the wall,
    to tell what time it is;
Time is precious.
Time waits for no one, only God has the destiny to
    our time, He and He alone has the time of our
    lives in His hands;
We hear people saying they don't have time to do this
    or to do that;
We are all caught up in this fast paced world, but the
    clock on the wall says tick-tock, tick-tock;
That means take your time, whatever we are hurrying for
    will be there when we get there;
Whatever we do, take time to thank God each day;
    Our time is running out
To everything there is a reason and a time for every purpose;
    A time to get, A time to lose, A time to love
And God... He is love; and holds the key to all of our time
    IN HIS HANDS
Lillie Weathers

Winter Approaches

Gone are Autumn's balmy days.
It's not much heat in the sunny rays.
The wind that teased, with its warm sweet breath
Has now turned mean and cold as death.
It whips the trees so beautifully adorned,
Until they stand ghastly naked and forlorn.
Their leaves hurled at their feet, look tattered and old.
In heaps of reddish brown, and shades of gold.

The sky turns misty gray
And flocks of geese hasten on their way.
The brook running merrily down the hill,
Slows to listen, then lies silent, frozen and still.
A hush falls over the land
As tiny snowflakes dance hand-in-hand.
And the earth, from the deep valley to the mountain high,
Gladly accepts the soft, white blanket from the sky.
Sandra Moore

Benjamin Franklin School

Like a sturdy old ship with strength in its sails.
It's passed through the time like a hurricane's gale.
Its wisdom belongs to the young and the old,
Its pride in its colors, the blue and the gold.
Its duty has served as the decades roll by,
Its memory like family who's love never dies.
Its legend, like history, will not wither or fade.
In our hearts and our minds it will always remain.
Its destiny draws near as days come and go.
The riddle is simple, it's Benjamin Franklin, our home.
Randy Collins

Untitled

Another year has passed, we've shared
joy and sorrow.
    We've grown closer and more mature. I've
observed the changes in me. I recognize
the changes in me. I accept the influence
of our lives on one another. I wonder
what the future holds... Will we travel
together or go our separate ways,
Whatever the outcome I'm thankful
that our paths have touched. May our
memories attend us always, and our
love increase and grow.
Reni Snellgrose

Aids

Aids is a harmful disease,
It's something you catch and never leaves.
    It can harm you and bring you pain,
But there's one thing you can use, but don't be ashamed.
    It's a condom, they come in different colors, sizes,
and style.
    Keep in mind with this, it will make your life
worthwhile.
    Some people are uptight about safe sex,
But sex with a condom is the best.
    If you don't want to have sex and catch aids,
Put your foot down, say no and don't be afraid.
    Sometimes you want to do it, cause everyone else is,
But you're not everyone, cause you have a life you want to live.
    If you want to keep living your life through,
Be smart and do what you have to do.
    Just remember if you're using that rubber tonight,
You're doing the right thing, there's no need to fight.
    It will be a night full of love,
Both of you together, and that special glove.
Wendy DaCosta

Together Until The End

You find a feeling in the bottom of your soul
It's the only one that can make you whole
You fight it with all your might
But it engulfs your heart real tight
With each moment that goes by
And with every tear shed when you cry,
You learn the meaning of trust
And the sensations of overwhelming lust.
Fear, that the worst is yet to come
An emotion too scary for some.
What you have together is undying and true
Those who find it are very few
In the end, when you reach out
And in your mind and soul there is no doubt
You will learn to appreciate what you have found
And hold sacred every card, moment and sound
Do not give up when you do not understand
Just make a promise to leave your heart in their hand
In the end, love will conquer all
Just be there for each other in the fall.
Melissa Tauchert

The Vacant House

I saw a vacant cottage by the road,
Its windows bleak and empty, dark and bare,
So much like desperate, sad and listless eyes,
They seem to peer from the darkness there,

Perhaps one time it knew so very much
Of love and life and laughter gay.
Now it stands empty, all alone and grim
And dreams its dreams about a happier day.

Its doors must once have opened
To greet a friend with words of cheer,
Now they are closed, no knock is heard,
Only the stillness is there to fear.

One shutter hangs lop-sided on its hinge,
Like a scar across its weather-beaten face.
The weeds are tall, one single little rose
Struggles to lend some dignity and grace.

Poor little empty house here by the road,
To see you all alone, makes my heart sad.
May someday soon your fires inside be bright
To tell the world that once again, you're glad.
Louise Schrader

"Your Final Goodbye"

It's your final goodbye and we love you.
It's your final goodbye and we'll keep on remembering you.

I think of you now at every passing moment.
It was hard to hear of your passing on at first, but it didn't
take long to get over everybody's outbursts.

I'm sorry now more than ever if I caused you any grief
through the years, and plan to take your leaving without any tears.

You left us with some happy times, some sad ones too.
Through thick and thin you were there so be happy now it's your
time for this of life's end, but someday we'll be together again.

Till that day we'll have to wait and have to deal with the pain.
There's no time for us to remember what was wrong, but what was
right throughout the day and the night.

Although you left us very fast without any pain, we'll always
remember your final goodbye.

William R. Kamp

The Beginning Of Us Is U

Hold on to my heart,
It's yours for the taking,
Never let go my heart,
'Cause love's what we're making.

Some'll think we're crazy,
Some'll think we're stupid,
Only the warmhearted will understand,
Those dazzling shots fired by cupid.

Sequestered thoughts of vivid dreams,
Built like tiny castles of sand,
Designed to perfection - eroded by nature,
You can never live in one - please understand.

The beginning of us is U,
But only when love breeds trust,
When passion is fashion and desire lights fire,
Thou choose me, I choose you, we choose us.

The beginning of us is U,
When your mind is peaceful as a dove.
The beginning of us is U,
Allowing friends to fall in love.

Randy Overton

"Hope"

It's Tuesday at four, thank God for me.
I've been waiting all week for Erin ya see.

Erin is the girl who cuts my hair.
I'd tell you more, but it wouldn't be fair.

I really don't know her all that well yet,
But her eyes and her smile could win you a bet.

My friends all say "boy she'll chew you up."
"You're running with the dogs, but you're still just a pup."

Well, she's all I think about these days it seems.
So I HOPE she's worth all of my dreams.

With all of these words that I say,
I really HOPE I don't scare her away.

But I think I'm cute, funny and kinda smart,
And the words that I write always come from my heart.

Kyle A. Smith

He Is Risen

HE IS RISEN! HE IS RISEN, INDEED!
Jesus Christ the Lord, of King David's seed.
Incarnate God, my Savior is He.
Living among men, our example to be,
Then giving His life on the cruel tree!

The devil could not hold his prize in the tomb,
He was destined for the Cross from Mary's womb.
But Satan's laugh soon turned to gloom
When JESUS came forth from Joseph's tomb.

For JESUS IS VICTOR! He defeated hell
And all power of Satan, I know full well.
"I am the Resurrection, and the life," He said.
So I have life everlasting, though I were dead.

"Because I live, ye shall live also."
He hath imparted eternal life, this I surely know!
This NEW LIFE I possess; He met my need;
Because HE IS RISEN....HE IS RISEN, INDEED!

Ruth Mills Grant

Safety

Safety is needed in everyday life
Just as a man will always need his wife.
Always be sure you have the proper tools
And don't forget to follow all the rules.
Be sure that you wipe up all of your spills
And don't forget to do all your fire drills.
Keep any small objects off of the stairs
Especially those things like teddy bears.
Make sure you keep medicines in their place
Or children will have them all on their face.
Always buy medicine with child-proof caps
And hide them in places or squeeze in gaps.
Be sure that you read the directions first
And don't drink medicines just out of thirst.
Don't refer to medicine as candy
Or kids do the same thinking it's handy.
Flush down old medicines in the toilet
Half of these rules you don't follow, I bet.
Well that is the end to this safety rhyme
I hope you'll think of these later sometime.

Tony Tribo

Lost Children

People put their children on shelves,
just expect they'd grow up all by themselves.

Never took the time to nurture or care,
So the child grows up in despair.

In our absence how our children hunger,
So in the streets, they have found each other.

It doesn't matter if gangs are wrong,
for once they feel like they belong.

You say we need to take our streets back,
yet in your home the love of family lacks.

You need to change your point of view,
and give your child something to come home to.

If you could just open up your eyes,
you'd see the tears your child cries.

They're just lost and all alone.

You need to bring your child home.

Tammy Lynn Boyden

Lost In Love

This is for the one I loved and lost
Just as I felt you in my reach
Life took you away without a thought
I cannot seem to unwrench my heart from its grip.

I guess I knew I'd be hurt in the end
But I was too head over heels to see
And now that I've gotten burnt
I'm going to have to set you free

Maybe someday the hurt will go away
Yet there will always be an empty place in my heart
I'll always know that you will be the only one
who can fill that part

Now as my heart comes to a close
I must bring myself to say goodbye
You were the one I chose
And yet you left me here alone to cry

Sandra L. Unger

Snow Thoughts

The snow has fallen deep and white,
Its beauty now I see.
God's hand above is all around,
I bow on bended knee.
I watched it fall and sat in peace,
It collected on the ground.
The flakes kept falling; I stepped outside
And didn't hear a sound.
I took a walk, looked all around,
The snow made light for me.
No wind, no sound, but under my feet
I felt alive and free!

Nancy Medema

God's Gifts

My cup runneth over with the "fruit of the land"
I've got the whole lovely world at my command.

The moon and the stars shine upon me at night,
Soft clouds and sunshine break through at daylight;
The summer breeze seems to sing me a song
While bright-colored birds chirp right along.

The falling of raindrops in the midsummer air
Brightens the flowers that bloom everywhere;
Or the crisp winter evening with new-fallen snow,
Along with the moonlight, puts my world all aglow.

The trees seem to shimmer bedecked with winter's delight,
Or shade me in summer when the sun's hot and bright;
For all the world's beauty comes from God above,
And is sent down to me with His infinite love.

Ruth Gosselin

Gloom

Gloom is the fog; the darkness of hearts.
The conqueror of friendship; a terrible art.
Gloom takes over those hearts that have broken or split.
Sadness soon fills in the large, loveless pit.
Tears of evil and frowns of hate,
Slip through a lover's golden gate.
The tears and frowns are burglars, who steal the happiness away.
Hatred spears and loveless sword are thrown, but not for play.
The war begins 'tween feelings of good and devilish evil below.
Spears kill, swords clash which forms a lonely glow.
Hatred, sadness, love, and gloom try to compromise.
But love wins, hearts are mended, and new friendships rise.

Brennan Johnson

Summer Evening

Brilliant sun, slowly sinking in the west
Sky turns all shades, from orange to deep blue
Contrails from jets snake serenely across the sky
Light slowly escapes, leaving behind a darker hue

Intense heat from the day
Dissipates with the dwindling light
Ever so slight breeze, gently rustles the trees
Ushering in another peaceful night

The sound of frogs merrily croaking
Drifts up from the moss covered pond
Lightening bugs' yellow lights, flashing off and on
Searching for the opposite, of whom they will be fond

Mysterious, endless black of outer space
Countless twinkling stars, sprinkle throughout
The moon, only a sliver tonight
Losing temporarily, some of its clout

Arising from somewhere in the distant woods
The eerie hooting of an owl, travels through the night
Looking up, a shadow passes silently above
Searching for his next meal, the owl has taken flight

John R. Bauder

Dreaming Fair

Why eat like a hog
Sleep like a log
Get up man, sweat and have
Get up lad, get up lad
Wake up lad, wake up lad
Don't you want to have things and pals?

Why be afraid to be out the door
Why be afraid of making sure of sons,'
And daughters' love; they have it to pour
It's hard to give to a boor
So get up man, get up lad, work sweat and have.

Why spend your days with little care
Dreaming fair, having only tears and fear
Is it that hard to care, be a Dear
Tear away from fear; think now and declare
Why not your heart, why not your thought see clear,
Why let time keep a wasting?
Get up man, get up lad, wake up man
Be a man and not a drag.;

Edmond A. Geohagan

Tranquil Disarray

I sometimes find myself drifting into a
state of mind where reality is irrelevant...

An eagle haunting through the empty sky
swept across the horizon and faded into the
lazy sun against a dismal gray of a
morning long forgotten.

A solemn wind descended into a valley
of hopes and dreams that soon were swallowed
up under a canopy of immense trees.

Within this emerald realm of serenity I
felt myself being drawn along the narrow path
which wandered upon a pool crystal blue.
Only then did she appear. A tear ran down
my cheek.

Love is lost but not forgotten...

James W. White II

A Dedication Of Love

You taught me how to like myself,
Even though I felt worthless

You taught me how to follow my dreams,
Even when there were no dreams to follow

You showed me love,
When I didn't know that it could be done

When I felt downhearted,
You lifted me up

When I prayed, you gave me hope,

When I needed you, you needed me.

You will always be my friend,
Now, Forever, Only until the end

Therefore, I dedicate my heart to you,
Hoping that you feel the same way too!

Carolyn Hall

A Feeling Within

Our love was strong,
even though I knew it was wrong.

I was always scared,
that maybe you just didn't care.

I felt so funny inside,
I knew that I shouldn't let it hide.

Your love was hard to find,
but I didn't seem to mind.

Your love took my breath away,
there was nothing I could seem to say.

As our love began to fade,
it seemed as if we didn't have it made.

As I sit and wonder why,
I can feel the tears in my eye.

Now that you are gone,
I must move on.

If you could only see,
what your love meant to me!

Audrey Short

Think

When we find ourselves wishing,
For things out of our reach
Stop, and say a prayer for those,
Who haven't any speech.
Or when we're dissatisfied,
And our minds get in a mess,
Think of all the things,
That we can truly bless.
Ready feet to carry us
Where we may want to go,
Eyes to see Gods world,
A mind to let us know,
There are people less fortunate
Than either you or me,
Some can't walk around alone,
Many others don't hear or see,
Thank God for what you've got,
Although you think it isn't much
Try remembering a friendly smile,
Or a little child's touch.

Etta A. Moore

The Silent Thief

Time, curious object
Ever moving forward
Never turning back
Assuring as it passes
Without even pausing
To lend on ear
As if magical
And just as ironical
It also deteriorates
As it goes by
Withering, aging
Like a wispy wind
Never noticeable
Just quietly undoing
Breaking down
Gently blowing away
Flakes
Dust
Nothing
Silent thief

Bernice F. Cardaropoli

Alone In The Crowd

I'm alone in a crowd
Every one there
They talk so loud
Sometimes more than I can bare
I try to share their happiness
but I will always be one
I will always have this emptiness
Will I ever find someone
to make me happy
I want to share in the fun
I don't want to be me
I'm alone in the crowd
It doesn't matter who they are
always too loud
the dream so far

Cynthia Williams

Flowers

Flowers grow everywhere,
Everywhere you look.
There is a blanket of flowers,
Spring and summer are
the most beautiful months,
With bright and lovely colors
The dullest spots are even pretty.
The flowers start to fade away,
The flowers are just a memory now,
When winter comes the flowers
Are just taking along nap.
The flowers will be back later.

Diane Parsons

A Stranger Awaits Me

A stranger awaits me.
Eyes drizzled with hatred.
Standing far away with
tingly fingers, I linger
farther, and farther away.

Yet, the stranger follows
me to the tall oak tree.
I impel my voice.

But, still a stranger awaits.

Jeremy Steinmetz

The Fly Ball

I attended a ball game last night;
Everything went right.
When I won the big prize,
To my feet I did rise
And tell it to the skies.
Then—
Came the Big Surprise!
A fly ball came my way
And did land
In my hand;
The shock was too much for me
And it was not to be.
I dropped my prize;
So near
And
So far.
Sad;
I could not hold the prize
I had.

Glenna Weber

The Rose Light

In a room of objects we could endlessly
exchange things and never be satisfied.
But in your room, with the rose glass
making the light unreal
and the flat bed
set there
for no other reason
than love,
the passing of hands
over skin
lifts us still
further into a realm
that makes whatever we did
to get there
justifiable. Back in the world
of giving and taking we are rats
sniffing with vicious hunger
for loopholes in the golden rule.

Elaine Schwager

Pen And Ink

Creative minds
exploring times
of days gone past
of days yet to come

Images, impressed upon the mind
give birth to words
wondering where to land

My pen and ink
it follows dreams
it captures truth
that I interpret

My pen and ink
brings thoughts to life
some are real
some ideal

Pen and ink freely flows
left to right to write in prose
revealing things so new to me
addressing thoughts I do believe
disclosing hurts my heart released

Carol Daniels-Bell

Touched By Love

One never been so touched,
  Expressed by laughter and tears.
Matured by love, strong yet fragile,
  Handled with tender care,
For it must not be broken.
  Like the moon and stars in tune,
Love will grow strong and beautiful.
  Will give warmth to whom is cold,
Kindness to someone who's hurt.
  Through hearts of others
We may live forever.
  Must love life in order to enjoy
The gifts of beauty it brings.
  Possess life and love
You will give life true meaning.
  Wisdom comes within love.
Believe in yourself and others,
  Love will surely find you.

    Ernie G. Vibar

My Soul

Soul of the damned
Expressions of the soul
Sadness of the soul
My soul

Loneliness, sorrow and anger
This is my soul

Suffering and misery
Hurt and pain.
How I welcome it
How I loathe it
And oh, the dreams that I have
of it
My soul

    Heather Butanavage

A Dream

A dream is as far as the
eye can see.

It is something we want
or something we'll be.

A dream is something we strive
for, something we need.

It becomes a full grown tree
that started from a seed.

A dream is a person
no matter who they are.

So if you want that dream,
keep reaching for your star.

    Christine M. Garcia

Sebastian

Seen life through a stranger's
Eyes, never loved by a father
But scorned. A primal need for
Affection leads you on a
Search for hearts
To return your love
Instead you find
Oppression and heart break again. Or
Never again.

    Diana L. Jones

Golden Sun

The misty drops
Fall to the bleak earth,
Striated clouds part
On the far horizon.
A sliver of an orange-gold bowl
Peaks from the foam
Of the dirty dish water.
It rises further,
A cloudy dishrag
Swipes at its clean
And disturbingly bright surface.
A coffee cup left unseen above
Pours cold, empty water
Over your glistening enamel.
You duck behind
The dishrag's cloudy softness
And you are gone.

    Justin Knapp

Twilight's Dream

Darkness fills the soul,
Feelings become clouded,
But the dream burns on.

Through life's trials and tortures,
Through its deceit and corrupt habits,
The dream burns on.

Through the nightmarish hell of death,
And the trickery of life,
The dream burns on.

Twilight's dream,
The dream of paradise,
Of the future and the past.

The dream of arousal,
Of the passion of the emotions,
The dream of the sin.

The dream of the illusion of grandeur,
But the reality of the window through
which your soul sees,
Through which it sees your wants and needs.

The wants and needs that cannot be denied,
And the passion with which you seek them
that in itself is the dream.

    Brandon Foote

A Magical Creature

Galloping in the moonlight,
Glistening beneath the stars,
A unicorn comes prancing.
A mane of silken thread,
A horn of shiny silver,
A unicorn comes running,
running, running.
What a wonderful sight!
My heart was full of delight.
To my surprise,
She came closer to me.
I reached out to pet her,
And a sight I did see!
A little fawn beside her,
No bigger than me!
I touched her soft fur,
I looked through her eyes,
I jumped on her back, we flew through the
skies.
I return from the stars, the sunlight breaks.
Then my eyes open wide, I Awake!

    Briana Lynn Files

Starlight

Starlight shining
Fireflies gliding
Horizons lying
Moonbeams sliding

Springing shadows
Shining stars
Whispering meadows
Silent cars

People sleeping
Animals calling
Crickets chirping
Comets falling

    Angela Gidley

Life

Newborn miracle
first step,
first day at school.

Parents try hard to let go,
move on.
As their child experiences life.
New friends,
new loves,
sooner or later they will lose them.

They will lose them in marriage,
in death,
and so on.
Still life goes on.

You think in life parents die first,
in this life that is not true,
guns, drugs, violence, gangs,
life always goes on.

    Annaliza Floresca

"Nighttime List"

"Boom"
"Flash"
I wake up,
in the midst of night,
cold with fright.
I look outside,
a navy blue sky.
"Flash"
Prince lightning strikes
"Boom"
Queen thunder marks her spot,
on the nighttime list.
The clouds go away.
and there I see,
the king,
Silver Sun

    Amy Lerner

Eyes Of An Artist

Many versions of life
have the touch of colors
The ones that were chosen
were perfect for their places

Either hung, shared or lost
all stack up to life's worth
Some pieces have fallen
but are not forgotten; just over-looked

My peace is the art when
time passes

    Celeste Cook

Death Comes To Her

Flashing in to her life like a storm.
Flipping the pages of her life.
Future plans crashing down.
Forming no new paths.

Why do some look for it?
Why do others try to prevent it?
Which one to choose?
Which way to go?

She did nothing, it came to her.
Silently casting shadows on her world.
Second thoughts she could have no more.
Serious doubts were a thing of the past.

Two ways to go from here.
Too much.
Too soon.
Tomorrow will bring the dawn.

An answer must be given.
A decision must be made.
An end is coming.
An end is here.

Deirdre M. O'Toole

Listening To Classical Music

Soft music slowly began
    floating through the air
woke a sleeping sense
    that needed to prepare
for stirring melodies
    dancing far and near
tempo light and heavy
    pleasing to the ear.

A breeze from the brass
    put moisture in the eye
drums woke nodding strings
    as they all marched by.

Tinkling piano notes
    tiptoed in to say,
"Relax! Relax! my friend,"
    then they sped away.

Grace G. Oliver

Moments Reclaimed

I gave my heart a time ago,
For you to hold, and me to know,
When I came back to reclaim,
My soul, my heart, my life had changed.

My smile wasn't made of gold,
I'm sure you've heard the story told,
Of laughter hiding thoughts so bleak,
No words of comfort could you speak.

All the days, it seemed to rain,
The brightest did not ease the pain,
No one saw, no one heard,
The pain inside that I endured.

The beach we walked, hand-in-hand,
Naked feet on golden sand.
Free form words you held me tight,
Your tender touch helped make things right.

I gave my heart a time ago,
For you to hold, and me to know,
When I came back to reclaim,
My soul, my heart, my life had changed.

Jamie Jackson

What Would You Give?

What would you give,
for five more minutes,
of a thrice told story,
and let grandma spin it?

What would you give,
for the twinkling smile,
the infectious laugh,
of your three year old child?

What would you give,
If given the chance,
to turn back the pages,
and take one more glance?

What would you give,
do over, or say?
I know what I'd give,
But live for today.

Jennie Melnik

A Dream

A dream a vision a desire
for glory.
A moment a second
a fairy tale story.
I'll reach and grasp
to write a page
when I alone star the stage.
Wait and watch I'll
emerge you'll see,
and I alone will be
proud of me.

Christa M. Gannon

In Memory

He does not lie beneath the soil
For he is one with nature.
Butterfly on tip-toe, soaring hawk
And soft caressing breeze
Surround me with his love.
A bird swoops down to dry my tears
With gently fluttering wings.
He is beyond afflictions of the soul;
He moves with easy grace
And dances with the stars.
I know it's true and yet I weep
And beg the searing sun
To thaw my wintry heart.

Alma Scoular

Friend

Lending a hand
For help you need
Through trouble time
A friend in need
I give thee
A little deed
This document I hope you read
To promise time
Never to waste
That I'll be at your side
At times of haste
I'm a friend forever
Forever a friend
My presence around
Will never end.

Jennifer A. Zanger

One More Day

I picked a rose
For my friend today
It was yellow and fragrant
And meant to say
How much I cherished
Our friendship and may
It last forever
Then one more day

Harold Huffman

Untitled

"For the things that I have become
For the things that I have been
For all the yesterdays
For all the todays
For all the dreams come true
For all the dreams yet to be
Of these things I am made
Of these things I was born
Of these things I will be"

Cindy Wilkerson

Earthquake

Mother Earth, forgive us...
    for we have placed
Upon Your shoulders
    a burden almost too heavy to bear.

The greed...the selfishness...
    the thoughtless actions
Of a myriad of unkind factions.

There were warnings...
    but we didn't heed.
Our egotism continued to feed
    with avarice our appetite.

Now You REBEL...You shrug Your
shoulders,
You throw off and fracture
Your very own Flesh Itself
    to cleanse and purify and nullify.

This we do know...
    You will Revive
And in Your new birth
    You will help us to blend...survive.

Dorothy Farrar Leftridge

A Mother's Love

The love is deeper than you can
    ever imagine
Mom knows things only a mother
    would know
Special moments we shared together
    could never be replaced
Time is all we have, so let's spend
    more time sharing our love for
    each other
Love sometimes doesn't just come to
    us, but rather it grows on you
It is hard to show love if you did
    not get love as a child
But, I was a lucky child to have
    a mother who loved me, no matter what
Now, I understand what it means
    to have...

"A Mother's Love"

Dana Hess

Clouds of Mist

Clouds of mist,
forever changing,
in my mind
rearranging,
into a face-a mask uncertain
hidden by a picture misty curtain.
Hidden in the sky
gray-blue
hidden, then,
deep within you.
Someday, my friend
we'll meet again.
wait until then,
my dearest friend.
Until then, the mist will be,
in my eyes.
I cannot see.
lift the blindness off,
my friend,
When someday, we meet again.

Cassie Sharpe

Touch A Reason

Try to touch a reason
Forgetting washed away,
Then what was is nowhere
Making up the day.
Light shines on the water
Breezes gently sway,
Eyes that see it happen
Long to touch the way.
Holding on to destined change
Here for reasons known,
Even though it re-arranges
Waiting to be shown.
One day you went that way
You even took a stand,
Tomorrow showed its colors
You played without a band.
Luring smiles of promise
Judging by the face,
Secrets kept by only you
Watch for an embrace.

Elizabeth Wilson Williams

Scissors

I am a scissors. My work is cut out.
I'm indispensable. My praises I shout.
When things get hard to handle,
I can rip and untangle.
My bite is sure and steady.
My jaws are always ready.
Proud of my pedigree,
I'm a household necessity.
I'm easy to control.
Over the counter I'm sold.
Our incisions may be big and snappy,
But scissors are not trigger-happy.
Why are we always in demand?
We're built to fit the human hand.
A bursting budget or a blistering boot.
Both need adjustment.
Scissors will do it.

Genevieve Griffin

Joy

Laughing
Freely
I dance,
I run,
Over rocks.
The horizon dips,
The indigo sky
Swallows the sea.
Flying clouds
Swooping down-
Lift me-
Hold me-
Joy!

Elaine Gale

dallas

four to six shots of a gun
from the facts we tend to run
    Americans were left in stun.

Jennifer Gandin

"Love"

From the earth to the moon,
From the moon to heaven,
From heaven to God,
From God comes you.
God is love,
Love is God,
So love another,
And almighty God will love you.

Bob Valleyfield

Our Country's Flag

Across this land of freedom,
from the mountains to the sea,
a flag unfurls across the sky,
and it stands for you and me.

It stands to tell the story,
of this land's bloody plight.
It stands for all the men who died,
and the wars they had to fight.

It's more than just a "Grand Old Flag,"
it's a legacy that's true,
and it will constantly remind us,
of what this land's been through.

So, as you look upon it,
as it's blowing in the wind.
Just think of what it stands for,
and salute it to the end.

Cheryl Angyal

The Glory Of Spring

There's music in the air
    from the robin's note so fair
Flowers are peeping through the sod
    Escorted by the hand of God
He who gave us everything
    Didn't forget to give us spring
Children's voices in the air
    join the robin's note so fair
O'er hill and dale, voices will ring
To welcome the glory and joy of spring

John A. Famiglietti

"Mother-Child"

I learned about love
From two little boys
So different, so beautiful,
That it amazes me sometimes.

I realize that all that matters
Is the love that we share.
The power of us, together
Hearts, souls, minds.

The power of three,
The power in the we.
I have fought to preserve that,
And I will fight again.

I will teach you to be warriors
In the world of us and them.
Be an example of what can be,
To make you proud of me.

Is the mother really the child?
Is the child really the teacher?
Your love drives me on,
Your strength gives me power.

Charlotte Sloan

God's Winter

Chilly winds and icy breeze
Frozen limbs on life-less trees

God's winter has arrived.

Flapping flocks fill gray sky
Finding shelter God provides.

God's winter has arrived.

Falling flakes mound in white
Bringing children's sheer delight

God's winter has arrived.

Chilly winds and icy breeze
Rosy cheeks and many sneezes

God's winter has arrived.

Through His Holy Spirit

Barbara Jean Hall

"Heart Of Gold"

You've got a heart,
full of pure gold,
just in your eyes,
so tender and bold.
There's no doubt,
no doubt in my mind,
that you have a cold heart,
it's hard to find.
You've got a heart,
full of pure gold,
so strong and not weak,
so kind and not cold.
I have a feeling,
that you will make it,
through all the bad times,
'cause your heart can take it!

Jennifer Missett

Rapping with the Beat Generation

Rap! Rap!
"Give us some crack!
We can't get away,
But we can come back!"

"We're all beat
And if we lose,
Maybe some help
Can make us choose."

"You think we can't win
'Cause the faster we run,
There's always a gun
To give us more heat."

Beat! Beat!
"We can stay on our feet.
And when we don't cry
Winning is sweet!"

"Whatcha gonna say?
Whatcha gonna do?
What's it gonna be,
U.S.A.?"

Effie Vamis Pappas

The Glowing Heart

Moonlight shines to and fro,
Glinting off the melted snow.
Shooting stars here to here,
Shining brightly throughout the year.
Soon a brighter star,
No wait, it's too far.
Climbing over the mountain snow,
Soon you shall know.
It's the gold in your heart brightening
Up your day.

Brandy Little

Untitled

Full of Confusion
Glossy from Despair
Dull from Depression
Emptiness through the stare

The clouds will always linger
The storm is unexpected
They say more than my lips
Shall ever tell

My soul, my heart
never hidden
Even through the heavy door
No hiding, no faking
The windows of the soul.

Brandi Hall

Revolt

Started as perfection
Forces tear at the heart
Pressures too strong to fight
Collective voices scream conform
Rejected are the wild hearts
Free spirits conveniently tagged freaks
Don't be another trained pet
strike out against the normal
Let your heart be wild
allow your spirit to be free
or drowned in a sea of boredom

Heather Joyce

Midwinter Glory

The gloomy of cold winter
Gone by a pass
Midwinter the change in sun
Hands milding forward to grass

Large half World continent
Equator up to the North Pole
Spring sun season assert
Continent Herds zone to the North Pole

Blue skies and warming winds
Palmy holyland of the sun
Birds of Air nest every mind
Nests of all and eggs' hatches begun

Nests are: bird cradles
Lullabies in motherly love
Some zone sail water paddles
Make birds fly above

Alice Norman

All In Time

Somehow time has
gone so fast, we must
find ways to make it last.
The times we share,
the things we do. Before
it's too late we must
make our dreams come
true.
The friends we lost
the friends we found,
there all so important
just look around.
As the time goes on
we will part. It's the
kind of thing to break
one's heart.
So take a moment and
think of me and remember
all the things you now
can see.

Barbara Hoppe

Dear Friends

From my Bible I read about the
Good and the Bad, from all the
Young people what I hear is so sad,
You can't believe the changes I've
Seen in my life, but by it all
has stuck my wonderful wife,
thirty years we have gone our
Loving way, and now you can't
Believe how our world is today.
So much hate and madness is
All around, today could be the
Day someone puts you down.
It seems somehow the Bible
has been replaced by a generation
of people who're in a mad race,
from my heart I can write
Because from these eyes I've
seen the sight.

Wake up people before it is
too late, so someday I will
see you at the golden gate.

Donnie R. Rhodes Sr.

Graffiti

Writings on the wall.
Graffiti you say.
No! Not at all.

That's me up there.
Yep! Really me!
For all to see!

Someday.
Someone.
Will paint the wall.

I'll be forgotten.
Not there
At all.

Maybe?
Just maybe.
We'll wait and see.

I'll leave an
Indentation.
They won't erase Me!

Dale Jean

Fall In New England

The grass turns brown
ground gets harder
all the trees turn beautiful colors

We can our vegetables
freeze the meat
apples are gathered for occasional treats

Time to cut the wood
stack it neat
it's used to give the houses heat

Girls dress in wool
guys wear flannel
enjoy Octoberfest brewed by "Samual"

Leaves fall from trees
cools the breeze
small ponds and lakes begin to freeze

Beautiful tones of red
soon we'll savor
trees that give us sweet maple flavor.

Dane J. Gibeau

Untitled

Flowers in the garden
   grow very loudly
when I'm trying to sleep
through winter blues,
they wake me up,
   eventually,
with their pushing
and opening up.
I forget my blues
through the noise of
flowers and give
them some water
to quiet them
   down.

Cheri Johnson

Father, "In Name Only"

Don't blame me, now that I am
grown.
When we were little, you left
us on our own.

It was Mother who was there
for us.
It was Mother who was Just!

I used to cry for you my
father;
Yes daddy, for you I was
lonely.

Now that I am an adult, and
Mother is gone, it hurts me
to realize that you are my
father, "in name only."

Francena Burgess-Tolbert

"This World"

Gods-Goddess-What is this?
Guns-Knifes-What is this world coming to?
Drugs-Sex-Is all this world wants!
Getting high-Going down
Why does all this stuff happen now?
Murders-Suicide-People try so hard to
get out of this game called "life"
Blood-And the holy ghost are coming close
Racism-Brothers hating brothers
Uppers-Downers-Which way do we go?
Who's really better than who?
Blacks-Whites-We are all the same in
the dark
Freaks-Weirdoes-Who can say who?
Dress like this, who can tell you how?
What the hell is going on now?

Jodie Dewald

Had I Been

Had I been born to fame and fortune
Had I a higher education
Had I been free with all my time
Had all the breaks been mine.

Had I been closed to men of influence
Had I been given the means
Had I enough of needed wealth
of youth, talent and health.

Had I gone on with all my tries
Not once, nor twice, but even thrice
Had Lady Luck given me the nod
I would have been a happy lad.

Yes, through all our lives we always use
This "Had I been" as our excuse
But we do know, for all it's worth
Such "Had I been" won't hold the fort.

For in summing up life's accounts
Success, not excuses is what counts!

Eduardo G. Manuel

Like A Dream

Never thought of one so fine
His ideals made life just shine
I could not wish for a star so bright
He was my dream
And a LOVE so right

Bernadette Wedig

The Truth

What thoughts a wandering mind must have
hallucinating
On life's greatest pleasures

From the inner realm of your mind
Comes your most sacred dreams
unanswered

Foregone the conclusion
Of life after death
we so wish to be true

Only time will tell
If the tables will turn
Presence of soul
Or soul to be burned

With our hopes and prayers
And the pain that it leaves you
Are the dreams of reality
But is reality the dream
And will life pass you by
Or will you see the truth

Jim Williams

Blue Shoes

Quite little blue shoes,
Hanging there alone.
Abandoned in the closet
By a little girl, now grown.

Little bunny blue shoes,
How you spent your time.
You always seemed so busy
As every tree you tried to climb.

I remember little blue shoes,
Another place and time.
When you gathered all your dollies
On the sofa in a line.

Pretty little blue shoes,
With a scuff upon one side.
How I once held and soothed you
When your little kitten died.

Goodbye little blue shoes,
I'll stow you far away.
In a closet of remembrance
From tomorrow's yesterday.

Bill Cordtz

Civil?

An antiquated confederate flag
hangs on a wall
in an otherwise empty room.

A white bearded man sits
in the corner with
a far away look.

You can stare into his deep
blue eyes and wonder
if blue is the real color of
his eyes or merely a reflection.
A reflection of the uniform that
surrounded him.

His wheel chair gives away
what he had offered his country,
the soil of the free watered by blood.

He closes his eyes and whispers
in a tired and rough voice,
civil?

Alberto Factora

Resmitted:

*Dedicated to my second Granddaughter
Katrina Michele Connolly*
Little Trina smarty pants
Has no word that means "can't"
Aggressive in her cute little glance
And smiles broadly when a chance —
She has to prove her "can do" dance
But angry she, if not allowed
To prove to all and be so proud
Of the things that were not okay
To try again the very next day

Ida Sugrue

The Rose

The Rose of beauty, fragrance, and life
Has seemly withered during the night.
Her petals of yellow, red, and gold
Have fallen in the midst of nightly cold.

The thorns of grief cut so deeply,
'Til our teary eyes grow sleepy.
Yet, we cannot help but cry
While we say to this Rose good-bye.

But behold, O Death, this Rose,
For she will live again,
Because Jesus Is Her King.

O Death, O Death,
Where Is Thy Sting?
This Rose will bloom again
Because she has been redeemed.

Dan C. Phipps

Who's To Blame

Who's to blame, for the shame they
have put on their family name?
Maybe, if the parents would have
taken out quality time with them
it probably would not have happened
the way it did. Is it the parents or
the influence of Society that caused
the youth to stray?
Who's to blame, for the wrong from
day to day? Why, can't the youth
of today seem to grab hold to life?
Who's to blame, for what they do
and have become? I have come to
realize, WE ARE ALL TO BLAME!

James Driver Jr.

Dreams Regrets

Death is when you stray
From goals, by some force
That molds and scars a

Past filled with remorse,
Which sways all you do,
Along with, of course,

All your future, too.
Thoughts designing beams
Of hope, gleam like dew

Creating vast schemes...
Until, your mind lets
Escape silent screams

When your worst fear sets-
That of having dreams
Crumble to regrets.

Amy Piper

"Daddy"

With a shovel in his hand
He digs ditches to fix a cable.
My dad is really grand,
He likes his job because he's able
To be appreciated for his helping hand.

Supervisor of construction
Is what his job is called.
He gets us good vacations,
And when he gets home he gets a big
Wet kiss and gets mauled.

My dad's body is like iron,
But his heart is like a flower,
Strong and powerful like a steel ball,
Yet sweet and warm like chocolate fudge.

I really love my Dad,
He's the best guy in the world,
I think he's really rad,
That's right he's my Dad!

Jessica Rose Nichols

Change

  He sits in solitude
  he dreams alone
suddenly- uprooted
thrust into a world he can't understand
a world where nothing is as he's used to
swimming in captured waters
no longer free
but no longer alone
  Now he is surrounded by others
  my bouquet of flowers

Cory Warren

Manalof

He walks with a lean
He looks kinda mean
Got a scar on his cheek
hasn't shaved in a week
got a lopsided Dun
Been Browned by the sun
needs a tall one to drink
needs a cool place to think
about the trails he has ridden
about the treasures he has hidden
about the time he has spent
'bout the places he's went

Daniel Bohnenkamp

Untitled

What about me?
He never asks
How my day went.
He always asks her,
It's always she did
This and she did that.
But what about me
I do the best I can
To make him proud
Of me, but if she's around
I might as well be dead.
I wonder sometimes
If she asks herself
The same things.
I love my dad
And sister but do they
Love me?

Desiree Amy Fey

The Cross On Calvary

Jesus died on the cross for me,
He shed His blood on Calvary.
The Roman soldiers laughed and mocked.
The towns people talked and talked.
When Jesus rose up from the dead,
three women cried and said,
"Oh, who has taken our Teacher, Lord?"
And from that day forward,
this is known as Easter morn.

Jackie Prince

He Is Gone

In the end
He was gone
Gone forever
Only a hope
Only a dream
Only a prayer
I am alone

Bridget Pierce

Seasons

I see the rolling hills
hear the rushing water
feel the morning breeze

I see the blades of grass
hear the song of birds
feel the bark of trees

I see the falling leaves
hear the flutter of wings
feel the chill wind blow

I see the frozen lake
hear the laughing children
feel the icy snow.

Bretta Poston

A New Day

See the birds,
hear them sing,
this is a new beginning.
See the sky, feel it fly by,
this is a new feeling.
See the children on the grass,
Playing, playing nicely, with their dads.
Feeling happy, feeling gay,
this is a way to start the day!

Claudia Perez

5 Parts Passion

Caress
Fingers floating down the back
Kiss
Lips puckering up;
Connecting
Hug
Closing space
Holding
Intimacy
Sharing one's trust
A smile
Love
Bodies in fluid motion
Two become one
Wholeness; Fulfillment.

James S. Cleary

"Escape"

Lost so
helplessly
in pages of
unknown
numbers.
Accompanied
only by the words.
A separate life
that is lived
that can be
unfolded
into reality
by letter
upon letter.
Only to
realize
that this
reality exists
solely
in the imagination.

Jaime D. O'Dell

A Graduation Poem

World
Here I come, embrace me
Not with arms of hate, nor of rejection
But with tentacles to cling to,
To survive.

World,
Here I am, direct me,
To places of light
There to see glorious sights
To ponder, and survive

World,
Stay with me, and guide me
In dense places that I may trod
Be my daily tutor and friend
As I make my way through this place
called,
World

Jennifer Johnson

Love

Love is a wonderful gift,
It is given by your heart.
Be gentle for it is fragile,
It could quite easily tear
your life apart.
However, it could grow to be
something special,
If you use it in the right way.
Although, you might not want, be
patient,
Love will come to you someday.
Love makes a special spark,
It lights up your everyday.
It stays with you throughout your
life,
Though sometimes you might wish it
would go away.
If the love you have for someone
isn't shared,
It might hurt but it's okay.
If it is meant to be it will be,
And I promise it will be someday.

Anna Clark

"In The Midst"

I found a blooming flower
Here in the midst of weeds
It had no inclination
Of its own destination
On the mighty wings of wind
Rode the unsuspecting seeds
And a calm gentle breeze blew
One seed to this location.
With much sunshine and showers
The little seed grew and grew
Cascading blooms to the ground
I looked at what I had found
Here in the midst of weeds
Fragrance and beauty galore
This is where I'm to be
I couldn't ask for anything more
Than to be in the midst of weeds
With a beautiful blooming flower.

Doris J. Darnall

My Father

My father, a strong African American,
   He's singing a song
Raising six kids on his own
Struggling and fighting a losing battle
   Crying and praying for half an hour
Wondering if his heart's going to stop
   Two bad teenage boys that won't stop
   Cursing and fighting nonstop
My father's time is always taken
Working on cars and taking us places
My father, a strong African American,
In this world
   Loves his two sons and four girls
   Give me, give me, we all say
   We get mad when Dad says
   No way
We love our father, the one who
   Feeds us, buys us clothes
      And the one who needs us

Jereka Howard

My Man

My man is grand
He's the best in the land
My man's so tall
And the best of them all

My man walks with a gait
That says he's just great
And when he says I love you
I know that it's true

My man does the dishes
Just to fulfill my wishes
And even sweeps the floor
This man that I adore

My man whispers in my ear
O how I love you dear
My heart begins to flutter
And my knees turn to butter

My man is really something
He keeps my heart pumping
There's no place in this land
That you'll find one so grand as my man

Dolores K. Waller

Does A Rose

Does a rose lie beneath the soil or
hide under the grass? Does a rose
see the beauty and grace of a woman
or the beauty of the land? Does a
rose feel the pain of others or hear
the cry of a baby? Does a rose hear
the mating call of a beast or hear
the stream flowing down to the other
end? Does a rose feel the pain of
the earth or the yell for help? Does
a rose hear the chirping of little
baby birds? Does a rose hear all the
evil? Does a rose have feelings?
Does a rose have eyes? Does a rose
even have life in it?

Carrie Robinson

The Ball Of Redemption

The
High
Energy
Bounce
Against
Lust
Love
Over
Faith

Redeem
Every
Death
Entity
My
Price
To
Include
Only
New Earth

Carolyn D. Macabeo

The Grand Canyon

God placed His hands upon this land
His gift for Man alone,
A rocky edifice so vast,
A chalice made of stone.
Filled to the brim with enchantment,
Awe and serenity.
Drink deeply of its wonder
As it sets your spirit free.
Etched upon each stony ledge
The touch of yesteryears,
Winds and suns and rushing rains,
The echo of man's fears.
The unbroken line dividing
The Canyon from the sky
Was sharp against the sunset
Bringing rainbows dancing high.

Gladys B. Loupé

The Tree

It bends as the wind blows
Leaves scatter in the air
Light flickers through its body
Animals run up and down its entirety
Rain and snow will make it glow
Its silhouette is so beautiful
At day's end

John A. North Jr.

At The Party, Friday Night

He sits despondently,
His knees locked,
His back bent,
His chin pointed out
From the strain of his neck and wrist
underneath his medicine ball head.
He stares, eyes squinting,
Intoxicated with numbness.

Above, below it all,

Watching the butterflies
Flutter by
His gutter sty,
They mutter "Hi."

He only hears mosquitoes
Buzzing in his ear.

Andrew J. Hester

Alzheimer's Disease

I saw him falter day by day,
His mind grew dim, his hands grew numb
I watched him slowly slip away,
From wife and children, friends and home.

Only God knows the reason
dreaded Alzheimer's takes it toll,
Some victims just at middle age
And others when they're growing old.

It is the curse of all diseases,
Destroying body, skills and mind.
It strikes the families it pleases,
The vilest impostor of its kind.

No known injections or medication
Can slow its vicious pace.
No known prevention in any location
Has stopped it from running its race.

As we stand by with broken hearts
And loose the dearest ones we love
I pray that we can find a way
To stop this plague before it starts

Geraldine E. Moore

A Wife's Prayer

Lord,
Hold, hold me up a little longer -
Make me just a little stronger.
And as I reach the end of day
May I feel as though I'm younger.

And may I have the strength to give
One who so desires to live
Just the hope to carry on
And abide by his own will.

Keep up the fight? Keep up the fight
With all your strength -
   with all your might.
There's just so much that one can do
But God is there
   Both day and night
And when at last the battle's won -
The pain is gone as though 'tis none,
He smiles at me as if to say,
He understands and says "Well done."

Aree Tidwell

Faith

"Hold me closely
Hold me near.
Ward away uncertainty,
Dispel the fear.

Install my courage
Deter the sign
For I'm told
My death is nigh,"

Of God I asked
In each plea.
Then, this is what
God made to be:

I no longer fear
Nor utter a sigh;
For God
Is always nearby.

In Him I believe
And put my trust.
And if I must die,
I must, I must.

Stanley D. Smigielski

"Going Under"

Crashing waves and violent tide.
  Hold on tight, it's quite a ride.
Deep, dark, and mysterious too.
  Wait and see what it can do.
Frightening silence drawing near.
  Close your eyes and feel the fear.
The danger itself makes you tense.
  Your spinning mind can make no sense.
If only stay a little while longer
  Every second it gets even stranger.
Breathe in fast and try it scream.
  Sorry, but this is not a dream
It really does no good to cry.
  And, you'll get nowhere asking "why."
It's almost over, so just give in.
  Without a doubt, it will win.
Better hurry, and say our goodbyes.
  You try to speak, but your mouth is dry.
The very last moment, remember the sun.
  The terror is over, it has finally won.

Cindy L. Thomas

Moonlight Madness

We walked the lonely beach
Holding hands,
Overhead the moon trailed
Behind us,
I curled my toes over smooth
Pebbles of the sand,
The calm water whispered against
My feet,
Kissing the sand as it reached
The border.

Our steps became slower and slower,
We stopped for a kiss or two,
Divorce ourselves from reality,
The moonlight sways with the water,
As we started our journey home,
Magic was in the air.

Janice Mason

Don't Let It Go On

Only the truth can set you free
Honesty with others is what will
open the doors
But honesty with yourself
is the only way to walk freely through

The pain you feel is not what has to be
You need not be ashamed of the life
which is yours'

Don't let it go on too long -
it will kill you
Part of you is already gone
A part that may never return

Don't lose any more.
No more.

Barbara A. Feinstein

She Was A Friend Of Mine

We shared so much together -
Hopes and dreams
And secret things. . .
And yet, we shared nothing.

We were worlds apart -
Colliding but for a brief moment in time.

We walked and talked
And laughed and cried.
But we were different -
Both you and I.

I cherished your friendship -
And needed it, too.
But to you,
Mine was expendable.

And one day,
Words spoken
From a heart which I thought I had known
Pierced mine.

And a friend betrayed my love. . .
And I was devastated.

Joanne Spencer

"A Product Of Marriage"

I held my brother's hand,
hoping that he would stand
strong against the pain.
He wavered but stood tall,
while I felt small,
when they told us we
would have to separate.
I felt desperate.
I needed him, but he was taken away,
"To play, somewhere else," they said.
Is this what always happens
when your world is torn apart?
Is it meant to help you grow,
or meant to break your heart?

We were close, when we were young.
As tight as the ring on her finger, the jewel
that he gave her.
But as we were separated, so off came the ring.
Is love everlasting or, is divorce contagious
for all?

This all happened,
when we were small.

Joanne Manzo

Woman

I am crushed red pepper,
hot and spicy
ready to be sprinkled over everything.
With a sway to my step,
and rhythm in my lips.
I hypnotize,
Adam in the garden,
and move my body,
to seduce the likes of his kind.
Deviously subtle,
I may be seed or storm of life,
and my part changes with the season.
I am Woman!

Emily C. Waits

Begin

Where do I begin?
How do I begin?
When do I begin?
Why should I begin?

You never listened!
You never cared!
You couldn't do it you said!

Why did you do it?
Why should I care?
Why should you care?
How could you care?

You hit me!
You said you'd never do it!
Why did you hit me?
Why can't I trust you?
Now I know
Why did I even begin

Jenn Claypoole

Salvation

Marked you this man, -
  how he strained through the days,
How dark were his nights,
  how errant his ways?

Now see him again -
  there's light on his face
And love in his heart
  for the whole human race.

He knelt before God,
  felt grace from above.
Christ cleansed him of sin -
  he's baptized in love!

Elsie Sharp

Untitled

When an infant and innocent
Helplessly caught in the neurotic
  web of the parenthood.
By and by,
Trapped in the cyclone of adolescence,
Overflowing with sensitivity
Burning with the fever of love and
  fury of anger
Bursting with desire
To set the world afire.
Then at manhood
Drowned in see of social insignificance
Disillusioned with dreams
Transmits branded neurosis
To the innocent infant.

Auyar Hosseini

Secret Admirer

His eyes, how they sparkle!
How I often wish
to look deep into those eyes
and share his most secret
thoughts!

I see him from a distance
and long to be there with
him.

As he walks past me,
I hope that he will
notice me,
but I wait in quiet spirit,
and say not a word.

Someday he will know
that I love him,
and realize that I care
very much.

Jennifer L. Wheeler

If Only

How precious you are oh my little child,
How innocent are your bright blue eyes.
My first was when I was young and wild,
If only I had known this worlds lies.

My love for my first child is so dear,
Those pretty blue eyes grew up so fast.
I was seeking fulfillment and a career,
If only I could change the past.

Oh little one, what joy you bring,
Your smile brings laughter to my heart.
I no longer seek out worldly things,
If only I knew we would never part.

I love to see you run and play,
What a struggle you had to get here.
I seek life now in a different way,
If only the world could see my tears.

My years have added up you know,
Yet now my life is a jubilation.
Pray I will live to see you grow,
If only the world could join in celebration.

Dawn Marie McCandless

With Sincere Sympathy

In your time of sorrow
I wish there was more I could say,
To help ease your pain
and to give you strength each day.

I know you feel sadness and sorrow;
it shows in your tears,
Just think of all the happiness
she brought you throughout the years.

You taught her right from wrong
as you led her by the hand,
You raised in Love a little girl
until on her own she could stand.

You gave the world a precious gift
the value of which cannot be measured,
To all who knew and loved her
forever in their hearts she is treasured.

So when the pain is great
and there is sadness all around,
You don't have to look far
in your heart is where she can be found.

Darlene E. Rowe

Mountain

Behold the bold Alaskan peak-
Huge thrust of rugged, dark rock,
  Wild beauty, and grand power,
Capped by an icy,white crown,
  And home for Eagle and Goat-
Embattled by weathers' rage,
  Stands he ice or suns' great melt,
Ringed by cling of brushy green,
  Spring draws up the Kelly skirt,
Singing special songs for you-
  Zigzagging frozen lightning
Pasting random silver streams
  Onto rough, steep mountainsides-
Seasons of mountain music,
  Tumbling down in gay cascades,
Draws mans' deep appreciation
  Of Mountains' awesome beauty-
And ever it's calling me.

Glen Corliss

Starting Anew

Hope it's not too late,
I am now forty-two
starting a new career
something I've always loved to do
I didn't do because of fear
of failure… or success?

But now that I am
in the autumn of my life
I'll do what I want…
I'll want what I do
and keep on hoping…it's not too late

It's never too late…
to do what we want
to do what we love
to love what we do
Even though silver strands wave in
hesitance
in the autumn of our lives…
WE CAN START ANEW.

Florida Lindain Vicuna Ventura

"God's Chosen Plan"

I wish there was a way
  I could have you back again.
To share those special times we had
  and say to you again,
I love you and I miss you
  more than words can ever say.
And there's nothing I wouldn't give
  just to have another day.

The days have gone so quickly
  though it seems like yesterday.
That the tears flowed down my cheeks
  as I sadly had to say,
I love you and I'll miss you;
  but it's okay, go take his hand.
For God had chosen on that day
  to take you home with him.

And as a tear laid on your eye
  and I tried to understand.
For I knew your peace had just begun.
And this was just "God's Chosen Plan."

Elizabeth J. Smith

Untitled

I am captain of my sailing ship,
I am the first mate, too.
I am the little cabin boy,
I am my own crew.
I am captain of my sailing ship,
I boss myself about.
I man the sails and swab the decks,
And tire myself out.
I am captain of my sailing ship,
Sailing on this sea,
I am stuck inside this bottle,
And no one can see me.

Jacqueline Dupre

My Secret Love

My secret love how much I care,
I cannot put in words.
My love for you, I must not dare,
Nor can my love be heard.

My secret I must carry,
Deep within my heart.
The love and want I have for you,
Yet we must stay apart.

I can never show my love,
Nor ever let it be.
But God alone, who is above,
Knows what you mean to me.

For you belong to someone else,
It hurts more and more each day.
My secret love I've put on the shelf,
Tucked it carefully away.

Sue Schatzschneider

I Am A Woman

Who am I? I'm a Person
humble and sweet…
Who looks for adventure
Where ever we might meet
Who am I? I'm a Person
Who can Mother a child
Whenever his or her
thoughts may run wild…
Who am I? I'm a Person
with inner beauty that
will forever prolong…
who am I? I'm a woman
Proud and strong!

Dina Rosenberg

"24 Hour Vagabond"

I'm your Huckleberry,
Food
No Shelter
Homeless.

Feeding On
Subway Heat.

Jam Me into the Grates…and

Don't
REACH
For
My Heart.

It's
under
All Your Crap!!

Dionne Davis

I Can't Stand You!

The first time I looked into your eyes
   I can't forget.
Why do I bother with you
   If you are not the one for me?
So many nights I think of you
   Wanting to say I Love You!
When I look into your eyes
   You have me hypnotized,
And I can't look away
   So my feelings for you grow every day.
Every time I look around
   The look of you brings me down.
I will always treasure the night we met
   Because my love for you is not a bet.
If I had my way
   I would not see you any day.
Though I like you
   I can't stand you!

    Erika Delgado

Old Man

One day in a strange hour
I confronted an old man
wearing little green shoes.
He showed me a lot that night.

He introduced me to the stars
and we became entranced
by the distant horizon.
He told me a lot that night.

He shared with me his wisdom
of the ancient earth.
He let me relax my soul.
He taught me a lot that night.

He gave me a photograph of a
beautiful yellow flower;
He lay down on my flesh.
He died in my arms that night.

    Jocelyn A. Gibney

Broken Heart

"Where's the other half?" You ask
I don't know.
Yes, it's that simple, I just don't know.
I lost that half when he told me, "It's
just not working out."
That's when I started thinking it out
And realized, "I need a guy who cares,
who I can trust with my heart."
I promise you, "I'll do my part."
I also realized, "maybe he's using me,
to try and win her back."
But would she, my friend, turn her back?
No, not if she's a good friend.
Unless, she wants our friendship to end.

    Elizabeth Stallcup

Aberration

Oh wretched spectacles upon my face,
How I do hope you enjoy your place.
Although your eyes make my eyes better,
My ears you have a tendency to fetter.
And no matter what way I might pose,
You love to run straight down my nose.
The slightest sign of dust or a tear
Makes you glaze over with a smear.
But beware my specs: Be it soon or late,
Some contact lenses shall be your fate.

    Chris Douglas

Uncertain

I was caught between two worlds.
I don't know if I should go
or stay...
Yet, I don't have anywhere to go.
An unknown voice woke me up
violently.
The door widely opened,
no one was there.
Weeks and weeks passed.
The same dream's still
haunting me.
Save your soul!
The voice said.
Save your soul!
Since then I became docile;
No bursting in my new life.
I've got accustomed.

    Abdelhac Amrouche

Where Is All The Love

I am confused,
I don't know what to do.
Where is all the love,
that is so very true?
Look at all the fighting,
look at all the death,
look at all the misery,
that's put upon our chests.
Where is all the love,
that makes things all right?
Where is all the love,
that makes our lives bright?
Look at all the hunger,
look at all the pain,
look at all the homeless,
with no shelter from the rain.
Where is all the love,
that we need so very bad?
We need that purest love,
because our lives are so very sad.

    Jennie Nybo

Flawless Perfect

You are indeed my love.
I dream about you,
the fairies remembered,
they told me they sprinkled
the dust over my eyes.
I can still feel it. I love you,
I've come to realize.
I smell your hand, touch it softly
against my lips.
I pray that I could be with you forever,
that this time goes on steadily.
I miss it. I miss you.
I feel like crying because my
eyes miss the fairy dust.
I cannot see you now,
So I guess I'll sleep for a while,
I'll dream about you, the fairies will help me.
You are my love.

    Jenny Haddad

"Only A Dream"

I think of you through the day
I dream of you in the night
I wonder where you are
When you're far from my sight
you've been in my mind
For quite some time now
I keep searching for some way
To let you know somehow
I long to be close to you
And feel the touch of your hand
I fantasize that you and I
Are building castles in the sand
I toss and I turn
I wake up in the middle of the night
To find it was only a dream
The stars aren't shining all that bright
If only dreams could come true
I'd be holding onto you - - -
But, no matter how real it may seem
Reality reminds me, that it's only a dream!

    Aleshia Green

My Cup Runneth Over

My cup runneth over
I give thanks unto thee
For saving my soul
For setting me free

My cup runneth over
And I am praising thy name
Washed by Jesus blood
My life he has changed

My cup runneth over
I'm cleansed of my sins
Glory to God I'm living again

His cup runneth over
And he offers to you
A love that's divine
A love that is true

His cup runneth over
And I'm asking you now
To accept Jesus Christ
And share in his crown

    Edward P. Bythewood

I'm Blind

I am blind,
I cannot see
The world behind
Or ahead of me.

Am I first to come
This being my first day,
Or am I to die
I do not know, I cannot say.

This is my life
In darkness do I lie.
Shall I shout a happy hello
Or wave a sad goodbye.

I am just like
Mike, Jane, or Sue,
Yet they can all see
I can't, can you?

I am blind,
I cannot see
The world behind
Or ahead of me.

    Jennifer L. Hauger

Untitled

Before I knew you
I had no purpose
I had no direction
  Before I knew you
I was another ripple in the pond
  Before I knew you
I was weak
  Before I knew you
I had no hope, I had no peace
  Before I knew you
I was empty
  Before I knew you
I walked alone
  Before I knew you
I lived in fear
afraid of what tomorrow had to bring
  Before I knew you
I was lost
I had no life
  Before I knew.

Edouard Martin

I'm Love

To know I'm in Love.
I just look up above.

Above the stars in the sky,
Which sometimes make me want to cry.

Above the lonely moon.
Hoping you would come soon.

Up to my Lord.
The one I've always adored.

He tells me to look in my heart.
Hoping it would not come apart.

My heart told me that it was you.
I guess that was my only clue.

I love you!
Maybe you love me, too.

Candace Sullivan

Hawk On The Wind

The Hawk flies with wind gifted wings.
Lifted up with grace so fair.
Its eyes trained to smaller things.
That scamper beneath its lair.

So far it soars up in the clouds,
O'er mountains grown up so high.
The things we consider loud,
He hears not, up in the sky.

Its beauty, we so rarely see,
So fast paced the people race.
To beat the clock—strive to be,
Tuned to mankind's hectic pace.

I see that hawk most every day,
and take time with him to fly.
Run from fervid life away,
To see his life, soaring high.

"Fly, fly with me" its voice cries out,
"And see earth with me dear one,
For you are more than you're about,
Come my child, fly to the sun."

Joy Campbell & Ben Stivers

"Being Discovered"

I don't know what to say
I just want to have my way.
Either in the daylight
Or in the rain.
I still feel this Inner pain.

In the company of many
the odds are so high.
When I have no money
In this world I try.

I've searched in the sand
Above a mountain I stand.
Everywhere I look
It's the same old book

I'm tired of judging the cover
when I just want to be discovered.

I've looked East and West
So, I feel I should go
Where the sunset rests.

Erick P. Kintz

The Man In My Life

The man in my life,
I know him so well.
His sweet, loving touch,
His wonderful smell.
His kisses, a treasure,
His hugs, a treat.
I'll love him forever,
Because he's so sweet.

Donna Walker

Lullaby And Dreams

Whenever I have a moment to spare,
I let my wandering mind
Go back to the past, my childhood days,
to seek, to find
Perhaps an exciting adventure
I took upon myself
A new butterfly for my collection,
I kept high up on the shelf
Finding a nest of baby bunnies
so cuddly and so warm
Closing hollyhocks on bumblebees
no worry they would swarm
Collecting frogs eggs and watching them
grow was always such a delight
Hiding in the grass, watching clouds,
and a flock of birds in flight
But of course we all grow older
as the days go rolling by
To enjoy our life as we choose it
and dream the lullaby

Beverly M. Josephson

Devil's Child

Wild, wild devil's child
I peel off words
To fling to you.

Your eyes are wells,
Green ocean swells,
And I dive, deep.

There, safe,
I swim
And sleep.

James Richard Groth

Bogic

As your eyes enchanted my very delight
I longed your arms for just one night
And when I looked straight at your face
I could feel your warm and tender embrace
You were what I had dreamed of
You are my meaning of love
You keep me warm at night
And help me face the new daylight
Your heart is of gold
I gave you my love to hold
Will you ever stop loving me?
And no more mine be?
What would life be without you?
What then would I do?
This is my fear
Whenever you are not near
You are what I live for
I want and need no more
You are my only love
My everlasting heaven above

Ankica Ristic

Giver

Giver
I looked at your fountain
And I saw blood
I listened to your song
But I heard a dirge
I touched your flesh
And I felt bone
Your breast
Produced
The milky venom
I spat out
With ease
Giver
Protector
Indefinite fountain
Straddling
Day and night
Protect or
Wither like the Iroko
Upon the horizon of time.

Dipo Kalejaiye

The Honeymoon

When I look into your eyes,
I see innocence like a break of day.
You don't have to say a word,
for I know what you're going to say.

As the sun rises in the sky,
it catches the highlights of your hair.
The warm breeze engulfs us so,
while your eyes slowly meet my stare.

Rapid waves of the ocean blue
gently sweep across our feet.
The tenderness of your embrace
could melt the summertime heat.

Hand-in-hand we walk the sandy beach
along the mile-some shore.
Thinking to myself that you're
everything I wanted and more.

Our time here in this paradise
seemed to go by so fast.
But one thing that will always remain....
forever our commitment will last.

Dee Dee Smith

"Just A Note"

Husband,
I love you!
Just so ya know.
I'm leaving this note
because I'm on the go.

Your dinner's in oven,
the kid's are at friend's,
they'll be home by five,
and the cats have been fed.

The mail is on counter,
the paper's there too.
The Answering Machine's full
of Messages for you.

Well I better get going,
My errands await,

P.S. keep supper warm
'cause I won't be late.

Julie Ann Bapst

"Those Feelings"

My feelings for you are special
I love you with all my heart
I know that you don't feel the same
for me
But maybe I could change those
feelings
Those feelings
Those feelings of hatred toward me
Why have those feelings toward me
What did I do to deserve those feelings
I know that people talk about me
But that doesn't mean that you have
To listen to them or what they say
My feelings for you are still the same
They will remain the same forever
No matter what you decide
I will always love you.

Jamie Lang

"Poem"

White, winter silence.
I make virgin tracks in the snow
   to the woods.
The stillness is dreamlike.
   I cannot awaken
   or seize the proof
of my being there,
   despite my intentional sounds -
the snapping of a branch,
the crunching of snow underfoot.
   In the evening from my window,
   I see,
   to and from the woods,
my tracks still there,
alone in the moonstruck snow.

John Vartoukian

The Reindeers

The reindeers fly
   Into the sky
where there noses shine red.

They run in the snow
   And play with the dough
While Santa sleds.

Jennifer Salavarrieta

Ray Bacon

He told me you said,
"I mean it this time.
Look in my eyes."
And he did. And he saw death.
Then he left you there with
that cold companion.
So you arranged the pillows
and pressed your sweet lips
to her cold, round mouth.
There is a finality in
every sort of embrace, Ray,
but none so profound as this.
And now that this whore is
done with you, she will just go
find another on whose blood to feed.
You sad, silly child. I told you;
I knew her better than you.
For Death is always death.
Her maw cannot be filled.

Judith B. Evans

Let It Pass

Hate
I must live with it
Now and forever
Let my disease pass
I will fight
Anyone who crosses my path
Going up against life
Rather be blessed with death
Let my disease pass
I will fight
Anyone who crosses my path
Going up against life
Rather be blessed with death
My brain is rotting
My soul is disappearing
Eternal life is what I'm fearing
Living depressed
Dying relieved
Pleased to be gone
I will not fight anymore

David Cuff

With This Ring

We were young, idealistic
   I, naive, trusting
Did you deceive or I, myself
   probably both
She barely knew you
   I watched and said nothing
Time flies - slowly
   provocation and lies
Big man so small of heart
   building walls against intimacy
Like a bomb on my family
   disillusioned children
Situations change
   people don't
Anger, sadness, bitterness
   put them - where
They'll destroy one another
   it doesn't matter
Peace, contentment, simplicity come
   I have no choice

Ann Parsons-McNiff

the Yesterday I once remembered

the Yesterday
I once remembered
is years gone from Today
the Tomorrow
I once dreamed of
has fallen by the way

the Sunrise
I looked up to
has faded from my eyes
the Sunset
that I slept to
never seems to rise

on the Stage
where I perform
Shaded Audience
I look up
to see that Death
is applauding my Performance

Eve Cohen

I'm Not A Poet

I'm not a poet
   I only write down simple words
   And thought that love to skip and
   run
   Through all the channels of my
   mind.
   Yes, hide and seek is fun.

I'm not a poet:
   Nor do I care to understand
   The whys and wherefores of my thought
   I'll only say the talent comes
   From God alone, all else is
   nought.

Gyneth Griffin

Amazement

After the moment has passed
I remained quiet in your soul
Like a drop of dew
Sleeping on a petal of a lily.
I remained silent in your eyes
like a victoria-regia
on the sweet wave
of a blue lake...

I don't want you to come
under the drizzly shadows
of the twilight,
my blue eyed beloved.
I really wish you will come
by the insomnia's time
of the night
breaking the silence
of the fantasy
of the universe!

Adalcinda Camarao Luxardo

A Thorp Is A Dorp

This poetry
Is foolishly,
A way concise
To be precise.

To mark the time,
That is sublime,
Which one does tend,
Until the end.

David Y. Avina

Quintessence

It pulses through my arms and legs
I run faster and faster
Through the wild untamed jungle
Searching, yearning, seeking

Farther and farther I seem to go
But it just cannot be found
Faster and faster does my blood rush
Stop, I hear a loud sound

A roar, a growl, untamed am I
as the rest of perfect nature
my heart pushes and pushes
I've reached my wild limit

Gliding with grace I fall off a cliff
Off the human cliff of life

Like an eagle am I
Swooping closer to earth
Abruptly it is found
Once again there is a sound
Silence - I am complete

Amber Fogarty

Alone

From dusk to dawn,
I search the lawn,
and deep within I suppress my yawn.

The past seeps forward,
out of the blue,
to laugh and ponder when I said I do.

The dream, the promise says to me,
have we no love for thee...

Have we no love for whom we lost,
the pain and suffering,
as well as the cost.
Have we no guilt of what we've done,
Who's to say that we have yet won.

The battle of which I say to thee,
can we but go forward as yet to see,
that soon we will alone at last be,
with the guilt and not be set free.

Collette Smith

My Grandparents

My grandparents are full of love,
Just like a gentle turtle dove.
They are special in every way,
I just hope they'll never go away.
Why doesn't God just let them stay?

Haley Nichole Pearson

For The Love Of Your Family

As the night watches over me
I see a large ball of white fire.
A noise, a flutter.
You step into the light
And embrace me.
Crying, empty.
We know you can never really protect me.
Those evil spirits
Rocking in the moonlight.
A wish, a hope.
Nightmares to disappear,
For the fears to subside.
Love you, Love me.
Even on our death beds.

Cindy Vollmer

"Eyes Of Deep Shades"

Looking through eyes of deep shades,
I see rainbows,
and beings living their charades.
I see music,
of anger and despair,
and darkening skies choking the air,
I see frowning faces and shaking hands,
reaching up, but never touching,
that sacred land.
Through fingers of smoke I sense a need,
filled with regret,
but overflowing in greed,
I feel a wetness as chilled as black ice
and salty as the sea,
tears of this world that's enfolding me.
If you listen you can sense,
shadows of laughter filling empty rooms,
as our spirits of yesterday,
come back in full bloom.

Benjamin H. Sweet

Ernie

Looking out through the windowpane
I see the ceremonial chairs.
A submarine crew was decorated today.
Ribbons of red, green and yellow with
Thank You Sir!
A friend of mine died today.
Hung himself in a jail they say.
I wonder.
Did he feel the pain?

James E. Rosser

Missing You

Looking up to the moon
I see your smile
Making my nights alone
All worthwhile

I smell the essence
Of your cologne
Hugging your pillow
When sleeping alone

I can hear your voice
Whispering to me
Knowing you're not here
It must be a dream

Oh, how I love
Your gentle touch
I wish you were here
I miss you so much

Caroline Mullholand

Spirit Dancer

Stirring restlessly inside a soul,
  I long for freedom.
I plant myself deep in the heart of
  those who love beauty.
I am the first bud of spring and
  the last rose of summer.
When the sunset lingers, I dance in
  the spirit of those who seek me.
I am a hunger for loveliness,
  a breath of new beginning.
As love blossoms, I stir.
I am life,
  I am joy,
    I am music.

Amber Dawn

Story Of A Reject

The victim of a harsh society,
I sit here on this sullen street.
Looking up with pleading eyes,
I meekly beg for food to eat.

Once a gang banger and a pusher,
I had thrown away my dreams for crack.
It took me years to finally realize
This was the wrong side of the track.

It was painful to escape from
The life of gangs and the drug campaign.
Problems crashed on top of me
Burning through like acid rain.

But 'twas a small bittersweet victory;
I survived but stand on my own,
Because society rejects low-lives like me
And so I suffer all alone.

I just want my legacy to live on,
My message spread throughout the hood:
Don't become a loser in life's game
And end up begging for some food.

Johnny Ozuna

Where's The Small Boy

In the dawn of early morn,
I speak his name
In the dusk of early eve, I shed a tear.
The mother of his youth, I am
A memory in his mind.

My heart goes back to happy times,
A small boy's trusting hand
That wants no more than Mama's touch
To soothe him when he cries.

Where have all the petal gone,
That used to clothe the rose?
Where's the smell boy's trusting hand
That Mama yearns to hold?

Judy C. Komula

Untitled

As I lie in bed
I think of you constantly
as I close my eyes
I'll know I will never see
your everlasting smile
I'll always remember the laughter
and the tears, hope and
even fears as I wish you
were near, sometimes I hear
your laughter bring everyone near.
Even though you said that you'll
always be near. As I wish
I could say goodbye to
my grandpa whom I cherish ever
so dear.....

Bianca Velazquez

Feather Pillow

I have a feather pillow.
It's very, very soft.
It's nicer than a weeping willow.
And it is softer than a hayloft.
I love my feather pillow.
You ask me why? I say,
Because that's the softest place where
I can cry my tears away.

Jeanine McMillin

A Poem

What is a poem exactly?
I think we all should know.
It's a way to express your feelings,
for some people it's a way to let go.
Some people write poems as a job.
If they like poems, does it show?
Do the words flow out of their pens,
or do they take it slow?
People think poems must mean something.
Do they have to, yes or no?

Diva Neims

Desperation

Somewhere in my heart,
I wait.
Wait for you to heal
my soul.

I want to hold the
hand inside you.
So once more I'll
feel whole.

The deepness that
I feel, will soon
float apart.
And reveal the love,
that covers my
desperate heart.

Chrissy Fulton

As I Lay

As I lay in this shallow foxhole
I wait the coming of another day,
Many of my friends have passed away
during this night of living hell.

As I lay on this hollow ground
With the blood of friend and foe.
I remember the happier days,
In a land many miles away.

We came to fight for liberty,
We found only insurrection
and apathy,
A population who didn't
Know about freedom
Or care about liberty.

We fought for ourself
In order to make it across
A ocean called the Big Pond.
To a land we called liberty.

Clifton J. Tallchief

Untitled

Please, my wings, let me fly.
I want to escape to the sky.
In this world there is so much hate,
I want to have a different fate.
My heart in two pieces has been tore,
Please let me suffer no more.
In this world I cannot cope,
For me there is no hope.
In the world there is so much fear,
All I can do is shed a single tear.
Please, my wings, let my fly,
I want to tell this world goodbye.

Jamie Gahan

Save Me A Place In Heaven Lord!

Save me a place in heaven, Lord,
   I want to be with thee;
I pray that I may be with God
   Throughout eternity.

So save me a place, dear Lord,
   That I may show my love
To the one who gave his life for me
   Through our heavenly father above.

Help me, Lord to be worthy
   Of a heavenly seat by thy side,
For I know that I am human
   And need thee for my guide.

I'll gladly go where you lead, Lord
   To the place thou hast prepared,
That I might spend eternity
   With one who gave, and cared.

Edna F. Rhodes

Spindle

Why was I so into greed?
I was stuck on myself, so it seems
No decisions solid like ground
I allowed my mind to float around

Yet yesterday seems just a haze
It was just my juvenile phase
No longer reason to war with myself
It is time to do away with guilt

Spinning as a spider from a dagger
Was a lesson in the mist
If I don't clear the dreamy decay
I'll leap into the great rift

Now is not the time for my Halloween
It is time to build and to grow
There's invisible fortune to be seen
It is time to go into the next season now

Freya Burreson

"Lord, Take My Hand"

Lord, won't you take me by the hand,
Lead me through my darkest night.
Give my soul the rest it needs,
I know that You can make things right.

Lord, give me wings to rise above
The pain and suffering in this life.
For all I need is Your sweet love
To put an end to this world's strife.

I don't know why I walk life's road
and try to make it on my own,
You're always there to see me through
with peace and love I've never known.

Calm the waters rushing by, Lord
Be the captain of my sea.
Let the beacon from your lighthouse
Be that light that shines from me.

Be my guide upon this earth, Lord
'Til heaven's gate one day I'll see.
Plant my feet on solid ground
For one day soon, I'll be with Thee.

Diane Clare Cook

Remember Child

I don't want to be alive
If all I am is alone
I don't want to walk the world
Upon the cold and cutting stones

I am still a child
So sweet and mild
I am still so young
So naive in the sun

Give me laughter
Give me rain
To cover my shudders
To cover my pain

I want the innocence to remain
I want all of it to stay
And what I know
It's gone away

Justin Stafford

MY HOUSE

God bless this house
If there is heaven
it is here
God keep this house
warm in the winter and
cool in the summer

My wife loving
My wife caring
My wife sharing
My kids behaving

The cooking is over-smelling
The wine is overflowing
The friendship is overwhelming

Good food
Good wine
Good friends
God bless us all

Francesco P. Conigliaro

Love Eternal

I remember...
LONG
car rides
to Kalamazoo
visiting Grandma
I remember...
an odor
like lilacroses
baby soft skin
I remember...
years of hugs kisses
advice that never works
I remember...
that long
car ride burning
swollen eyes
I remember...
hugs with tears, family reunited
for the wrong reason
I remember...Grandma

Joni R. Hershey

If When I Die

If when I die, shall he take me.
If when I die, will I finally see,
the meaning of life.
If when I die, will he burn thee.
If when I die, shall he bury me,
    why must this be
If when I die, will heaven be my guide.
If when I die, shall the Lord say;
"Go to hell and be the devil's bride."
I do not wish to be by his side.
If when I die, will I be remembered.
If when I die will I know that I
was endured.
    I can't see why not.
Yet knowing that I lived an expected
life was I happy and rich,
    or was I modern and loved,
can it be poor and miserable.
Therefore when I die, I shall know that I
did live.

Jaimie Penn

Fighting Another Day

I wake up wondering if
I'll survive the day
Yet at night I wonder if
it's worth waking up.

For I have so much inside
that no one will understand
let alone care to listen
and lend a guiding hand.

I have been hurt one
too many times
And can't handle letting
Anyone close or near by.

My heart and soul seems
to have run out of another chance
That Love has come to a halt
along with "true romance."

So shall I decide,
Another day of fighting
or shall I just leave it be...
And slide - into a world of peace.

Amber L. Sheets

Alone

It's dark,
I'm all alone.
Where have all the people gone?
I'm all alone,
I'm scared,
I'm all alone,
Wait, I hear a voice
I'm not alone,
I feel safe,
But am I alone?
Who is it?
Is someone there?
Wait what's this I see?
A mother!
Full of loving care
I'm not alone
But if I am all alone,
'least I have a mother's loving care.

Amy Starcher

I'm Clean

I'm clean don't you hear me,
I'm clean I said, don't you hear me?
I never smoked cigarettes, drank
Alcohol beverages, or took dope.

I never stole from anyone, or
knowingly hurt anyone,
Yet you beat me, you cheat on me,
And call me unkind names.

I'm clean I said, I attend church,
Lend a helping hand to my fellow man.
I just don't understand why you don't
Understand, that I'm clean.

I've never been in trouble with the
Law, I never spent a night in jail.
I go to work every day, make a honest
Living for my pay.
I come home to my family, cook and clean.
Does anyone care that I'm clean?

Imogene Gaffney

Dear Buffal

Dear Buffalo, we heard they shot you down
    in a moment that you stood.
We guess we'll say we're sorry
    and change it if we could.

Dear Buffalo, forgive if you can
    the absence of looking ahead.
We guess we'll say we're sorry
    too late, for now you're dead.

Dear Buffalo, why didn't you flee
    at the report of a firing gun.
We guess we'll say we're sorry
    wish you'd chose to run.

Dear Buffalo, mother and father gone
    miss your sister and brother?
We guess we'll say we're sorry
    unswayed you stood by the other.

Dear Buffalo, "Give me a home where
    the buffalo roam," sings so easily.
We guess we'll say we're sorry,
    for homeless we all shall be.

Barry C. Shrader

How Will Grammar Help Me?

I'm very slow at learning
I'm not so fast on my feet,
But to have good grammar
Will help me nice friends to meet.

I wasn't so very polite
and thank you's came so slow,
But good grammar helped me
a nice personality to show.

My speech was very gruesome
and faulty were my ways,
But grammar showed me
a new trail I can blaze.

In everything I wasn't
and the way I should have been,
Now I walk straight and tall
and grammar helped me to win.

Clevie Davidson

To Daddy On Father's Day

Today is something special
In a very special way,
It comes but only once a year
And is known as Father's Day!

Fathers are special people
No matter what they say or do
They make things seem to be all right
When we're sad or when we're blue

Although we may not show our love
By some of the things we do
But then you must also realize
That you're our father, and we
love you!

And so today we wish you well
Today and all life through.
And hope you'll always keep in mind
That we love our father (you)!!!

Peggy Sue Kolm

Frita Plummer And The Little Big Hill

I watch while lying on the ground
In and out all the day.
When before my eyes a simple mound
A work of art is on display.

From underneath the earth they come
Hauling little bits of dirt.
They are not smart, they are not dumb
Quick, move back, one's on my shirt!

They have six legs stopping only
When they find that perfect place.
Passing each other they are not lonely
All working together at the same pace.

Time flies, the hill is growing.
But wait, I felt some rain on me.
All their efforts are now showing
Wear and tear, can't they see?

The very next day, know what I saw?
The ants were back and doing the same.
Don't ask me, it's Nature's Law.
To them it's work, to me a game.

Dana Lee Foldie

The Unicorn In The Garden

I saw a Unicorn last night,
In the Garden, in the moonlight,
And as he pranced, with dainty feet.
He made a lovely sight!

Then, as I stood, with bated breath,
Afraid to even make a stir,
He calmly looked me in the eye,
And said, "Good evening, Sir."

But, I, in mood most cynical,
Said rudely, "You are most absurd,
There's no such thing as Unicorns,
At least, so I have heard."

"But," said he, with a gleeful glint
in his eyes, "By the Great God Pan,
How do I know that YOU exist,
You silly little man?"

As I stood there, quite deflated,
Regretting that I'd been so rude,
He turned and cleared the garden wall,
And left me there to brood!

Elza L. Krumm

Crying Out To The Ruins

Shall we know the birth of ruin's death,
In crying's wrath of anger
and acceptance?
The ignorant soul of two-faced child,
Who told the depth of blissful vengeance.
The eyes of ego lay fear of truth,
And truth knows fury.
Vows altered by time, and
time given divorced embrace goodbye...

Jordan Tyler Herrera

Dreams

In my dreams you are there, and so am I,
In dreams we are there,
Always together, never lonely,
Always happy, never sad,
Together we stay in the heart,
And in the mind as well.

Dreams are never forgotten,
Just as you will never be.
Dreams are always on my mind,
As are you, forever on my mind.
Never leaving, never fading,
Always there, as I am for you.

Always remember your dreams,
For the hunter is always there,
And in your heart and dreams,
The lone one will be forever.

David Holder

My Words

Listen as the words appear
in front of you, in the back of your mind
and watch as they drip down,
stain your floor in reds, blues, reds.
Take your finger swirl it
through the colors, form our
memories into shapes, symbols.
Remember and laugh, cry.
Feel how they still burn hot
and watch how they still move
    toward you.

Jeremy Kinsell

High

Look at me — flying high
I'm watching you watching me
As I navigate the sky
And touch the top of every tree

I look down and see you there
Salty sea wind in your hair

Did you know that I could fly?
Have you seen me get this high?

Do you dare me to go higher
Like a child on a swing?
Or do you have a loud desire
To pull me down there with your string?

See me flying! Watch me soar!
Swooping up and down
Inching closer to your fingers
Then turning back around

Floating miles above the mire
Feeling for the first time free
To the summit of the fire
Till I'm watching over me

Holly Cordova

Retirement

When an employee reaches a certain age
In his book of life he turns a page
    A change occurs - his job is done
    Relaxation he has won

The pages past he can review
Statistics show the business grew
    He prays he helped in his small way
    While plugging away day after day

Faye Harris Busch

A Freshman In Winter

Above the earth, beneath the sun,
In pageantries of ten or one,
The thrushes slide on air to spring,
And days away they sing,
Their sanguine souls they fling.

And on the ground, in narrow roads,
The students troll about their loads
Of book and bags in fingers cold,
And for all those enrolled,
The world seems tired, old.

But climbing up the heavens' stair
On minstrel mornings foul or fair
Are seen the birds that showers bring,
Who in the shivers sing:
To vernal thoughts they cling.

Christopher Lemieux

In A Quiet Room

He sits
In the dim light, drunken
On memories,
The bottle, an album, the
Liquor, old snapshots.

He smiles and sees, distantly,
An old friend's antics.
"Remember that?" He says, turning.
But no one is there;
The effect's wearing off.

He returns
To the bottle, another
Swig ought to do it.
Another page and he's
Drunk again.

Bryant Bush Jr.

A Contest Of Poetry?

A contest of Poetry
How interesting it can be.
Just write a line or two that rhyme
Would they give a gift to me?

I love to write my feelings
On whatever subject listed;
Expressing my thoughts in poetry,
Would they feel that I am gifted?

If given words that I must use,
It may be a little bit harder;
But with this challenge I'm glad to try,
It could help to fill our larder!

So here's my rhyme for judgment,
I'm hoping your heart will be touched:
My poems are usually rhyming,
So off to the mailbox I rushed!

Enid Herbert

Irony

In the halls of government buildings,
In the niches required by law,
Blind men sell the new world addiction,
Nicotine, offered for lung and maw.

It is irony for those afflicted
With the curse of sightlessness,
To pander to the blighted souls,
Fellow beings with addictedness.

Do they realize what they offer
In those nefarious cans and tubes?
Danger to the health of others,
Death and sickness for unfortunate boobs.

When will the blind refuse the role
Of leading those who are also blind?
To me it is the utmost irony,
A tragedy that disturbs the mind.

Daniel T. Bridgewater

The Watching

It seems I'm caught
    in this flow of things
Watching tides go out
    just to return again
And birds soaring high only
    to dive back to earth
The universal flow seems
    to constantly reverse
What makes me imagine
    with all of this
My mind can sort out
    a method and list
Observations made along this
    human life span
That when it appears over
    it truly just began.

T. Bell

Untitled

Life's too short to live
    by some rules and regulations
You have to live for yourself
    not everyone's expectations

Everything happens
    for a certain reason
All the good and the bad
    the depressing and pleasin'

Things you want
    will come in due time
Give it a chance,
    patience, and time

Be happy with what you have
    each and every day
For you never know
    when fate will walk your way.

Talitha Smith

Shine To Save

To shine a light
into the night,
and hope to save a soul.

To shine a light
across the moon,
and hope to save someone soon.

To shine a light
on the sun,
and hope to save a lonely one.

Shine a light over all the children,
adults,
and teens
and hope to save and see,
and maybe you'll save me.

Alicia Wedeking

Untitled

My love for you
Is a beauty mark
On the skin of my soul.
But when I step
Out of the dark,
The sunshine
Quickly takes its toll:
Out of a pretty mole
Grows deadly cancer
   cancer
     cancer.

Anya D'Alessio

Loves Demise

To be truly loved by someone
  is inexplicably sweet,
But is it worth the anguish
  when it is put in defeat,
The pain, the sorrow, the anger,
  is much to bear,
When the other no longer
  feels the need to care,
The disappointment and then
  rejection of another should
  make one wise,
But alas, once again, I
  have fallen prey
  to love's demise.

Dominique McClain Barteet

Friends

What is a friend?
Is it an acquaintance
or something more?
Friends are people who
you care for and they
care for you in return.
A friend is a precious
treasure that everyone
can have if they just
open their hearts and
keep an open mind;
friends need have nothing
in common, but the willingness
to understand and grow.
A friend is the true show
of wealth. So why aren't
more people wealthy? They just don't try...
Are you a wealthy person?

Eric V. Ayers

My One And Only

It seems to me that our time
is spent so far away. Time seems
to last forevermore when you're
away from me.
It seems to me that when you're
home we never have any time alone.
The time seems to slip away
before our eyes and then again
it seems to me our time is
spent miles away.
But the time I share when
you are here is so very dear, that's
why it hurts me so to see you
go,
So my dear it seems to me just
how precious our time can be
when you are here with me
today.
I just wanted you to know
just how much I love you so.

Jenny Mullinax

Dream

A dream...
is the magic of the soul;
is the hopes of the heart;
deep down, where emotions start.
A dream...
in so many ways,
is the only thing that gets us
through our days.
A hope that lies hidden-
something unknown,
except for when you're all alone.
A dream...
is reality to the mind,
something that will happen,
in time.
A dream...
never loose it;
never let it get away.
Tomorrow
will be the dreams...of today.

Amy Moore

The Life's Mystery

...Odd and funny
Is the rite
Of the daily
Continuous dives
Into the life's
Great mystery.
Why,
Without a break,
Are you vibrating
And loving and suffering?
You get on or fall back,
While inane
All appears and vain.
Doesn't anything
Have a clear meaning,
Not even
An exhaustive
Reply.

Irene Cimmino Santoni

Untitled

Why should I grieve for yesterday?
It gave me of its sun and shade
For it was once today
Before it passed away.

But fear tomorrow? No,
For I have faith God will give
A sun for every shadow
All the days that I shall live.

So will tomorrow bring its strength
Along with its new morn;
And never have I known a day
That could not well be borne.

When should I fear tomorrow?
When tomorrow comes my way,
This day will then be yesterday -
Tomorrow then today.

Its beauty is so near so dear;
And sad the word,"Good-bye."
Why do I cherish so today
These hours rushing by?

Joan A. Haug

Answer To A Get-Well Card

When down in the dumps
it gives you goose bumps,
to hear from the crew,
know they're thinking of you.

So thanks very much
for your poetic touch,
which brings notes of cheer,
when your mood's a bit drear.

It causes your spirit,
uplifted to be,
till the work-a-day world,
once again you can see.

So here's to the day
when I'm coming back,
to uncover my desk,
and give work a crack.

Joseph S. Devito

The Bubble

People in love live in a dream;
it holds then in a vibrant bubble
quite apart from everyday ploys.
In the world they are,
but not truly of it.

Love calls first, reality after.
Together they wend their wondrous way
down an enchanted perilous path.
Eyes meet eyes,
hands seek hands.

Lip clings to lip. Each knows the other
thought for thought, inch for inch;
memories remembered, jokes re-shared.
Then suddenly
he is gone.

She remains to weep alone —
for him, for her, for plans un-planned,
for secrets un-shared, for kisses not kissed.
The bubble broke...
the dream is done.

Catherine Pugliese

He's Just Away

He's just on vacation,
It helps me through each day;

To know that he is somewhere right,
after all he's just away.

God took him to a special place
to mend his broken soul,
God wrapped his heart around him
and made his being whole.

He's just on vacation,
In a place that is O.K.;

We will meet again, I know
after all he's just away.

Heather Wise

To Dream

The reality of fantasy is all around you.
It is found in the young romance -
A boy and girl sharing dreams
That may come true.
It nestles in the warmth of middle years
A special love, a giving and taking;
And in the mellow years it becomes
A nearness, a special caring and needing,
As the white knight turns gray
And the princess on the balcony
Begins to show the creases of time.
But let us never cease to dream
Nor allow cold reality to dull
The thoughts that provide escape
To our own special place
Where hope abounds
And hearts feel light
Unburdened by our dreams.

Janice S. Carlson

Love

Love is like the ocean
it just never ever ends.
Love is like steel or iron
it will never ever bend.

Love is like the grassy land
it is calm and will rarely fight.
Love is like the big blue sky
it is very, very, bright.

Love is like a human being
it is big and very strong.
Love is like a sentence
it could be right and it could be wrong.

Love is like a referee
he's always kind and fair.
Love is like a flower
it will bloom with special care.

Jason Malloy

Poetry's Meaning

A poem's a soulful insight
Like an inkblot in the sky-
Clouds of word paint in our minds
Searching for epiphany.

Staring deep into those pools
What is it we shall see?
Ferment of our lives-
Soundings of our souls.

Anthony R. DiBona

Life Is Never Kind To Me

Life is never kind to me,
it makes me cry.
it makes me hurt so much I feel
As if I should die.
No one loves me and neither do they care.
My only love came from my only hate,
and now he returns that hate to me.
I wish I could fly.
Fly away and be free.
fly away from the hate that touches me.
I wish I could love,
Love someone who loves me.
I wish I could be free...
but life isn't kind to me.

Amber Ginan

Burning For You

My love for you will never die -
   It reaches past the endless sky.
Tremors of the earth will shake -
   But your heart I could not forsake.
Without you, I'm in constant tears -
   Darkness holds me in its fears.
I love you selflessly so deep -
   My heart forever yours to keep.
I've no desire to love again -
   Only you know me within.
I let you through my walls so high -
   Now you alone have been inside.
I gave you every part of me -
   So let our flame forever be!

Christina Cole

The Clock Upon My Wall

I look at the clock upon my wall,
it reads 11:59 p.m.
in just another minute,
a new day will begin again.

What will this new day bring us,
will it bring us laughter,
or will it bring us tears,
as we look back on our years?

Will it bring us joy,
or will it bring us sorrow,
as we look on towards tomorrow?

Whatever this new day brings us,
we should go into it with love,
and a song in our hearts,
for as soon as tomorrow comes,
this day will part.

Charisma Brandow

Where It Hurts

Where it hurts,
Is way down deep.
It hurts so bad,
That all I can do is weep and weep.
Where it hurts,
I wish I were dead.
I'll clean all the wounds,
Where my heart has bled.
Where it hurts,
Time goes slow.
Will this pain ever stop,
I do not know.

Amanda Holeyfield

The Flower That Shone

Once a flower bloomed
It shone and shone
When people walked past
they stopped to admire
the flower that bloomed
rain or shine
it was the prettiest flower
they ever saw
It shone and shone
through its glory
people just love to watch
the flower shone its light
The flower admired the people
as much as the people admired it

Cristal McGregor

A Drunken Woman

I hear her laughing in my mind.
It sounds free and careless.
You wonder why I hate that sound.
It's the sound of a drunken woman.

I feel her beating on my back.
It feels angry and hurtful.
You wonder why she beats me so.
It's the rage of a drunken woman.

I hear her screaming in my mind.
It sounds pointless and scary.
You wonder if I did something wrong.
It's the pain of a drunken woman.

I hear groaning in my mind.
It sounds sick and pitiful.
You wonder why I make such noise.
It's the revenge on a drunken woman.

Cyndi Harbeson

Our Wedding Day

Today we began our life anew.
It started when we said 'I do.'
The seed of love within us grew.
I feel so lucky! I found you!

For it's true love that has allowed
Us to take these solemn vows.
As husband and wife, we've been endowed
To love as much as life allows.

So as we grow our hearts will blend
Like hues that heaven's sunsets send.
And no truer words were ever penned
Than 'I have married my best friend.'

Ernest L. Poland Jr.

Grandson

It was very, very late.
It was a sixteen-hour wait,
It's a boy! It's a boy!
It gave us great joy.

It was a family of girls,
It was our little world,
It was made more complete,
By someone so sweet.

It was a task well done,
It was our precious grandson,
It surpassed the spring,
It made our hearts sing.

Jeanette Caux

Watchful Eye

Last night
it was cold in Iowa.
I heard the Wind
come up.

Tornado-like.
Windows rattled.
I wondered—
where would the Oak fall—
with a northwesterly wind?

This morning
limbs were down.
The birds did not come out to feed.
Fifty Degrees Below!

I hope they had protection—
from the Alberta Clipper
that blew across Iowa.
This noon
the sun came out.
So did the Birds.
His Eye is on the Sparrow!

Barbara B. Wheeler

My Life

They found the knife
It was in the mud
Covered in blood
The blood was mine
Now I'm charged with a crime
So to prison I will go
Did I do it? Absolutely 100% No!
(The O. J. Simpson story)

Jana Weill

The Commercial

If my life was a commercial
it would be selling
Everything,
Yet nothing,
Something,
Yet not,
Uncut gems,
Impure metals,
Worthless gadgets,
Unneeded puzzlements,
Unwanted things,...
But yet my life is so full
of good things,
Somebody should need
Someone like me.

Jaysen Trueblood

Love's Memories

Could I but speak the love I knew,
It would make the joyous
     music swell
Upon the air as onward it floats,
And in crystal silence casts
     a spell.

This love, this faith, this courage true
Yea, lingers as a flickering
     light;
I'll cherish now its tiny
     sparks,
Until the fire is burning
bright.

Elsie W. Niedermayer

Grievances

Feel the black; feel the dark
it's my friend of ever darkness.
Turn around, down underground,
rest in sweet peaceful quietness.

God be there — in the light,
feel the presence of his greatness.
Be an angel of the light,
for he gives us forgiveness.

Turn around, born again,
OH, what a risky business.
Once again you shed a light,
in a world of vastness.

Charles Edwards

Veronica

I know the feeling,
It's quite insane.
I know the hurt,
Unbearable pain.
When time is love,
And love is grand.
It all crumbles,
Like castles of sand.
The time we shared,
The love we had,
Is not forgotten.
I promise that.
So, as I leave,
I will tell you this:
"I love you forever."
Sealed with a kiss...

Joel S. Heifferon

"Love"

It's the tears without the pain
It's the laughter of the rain
And if we both concede
It's exactly what we need
It's the pride without the shame
It's every time you call my name
And if you hold me dear
It will take away the fear
It's the book of memories
It's our childhood fantasy
It's what preachers preach
It's the stars just out of reach
It's a game that never ends
It's the heart between two friends
It's right there in our hands
If we both could understand.

David McClure

Untitled

Broken spirits dwell within
Loneliness becomes a friend
Blackness fills her need again
A fear that cannot bend

Longing sweeps this young girl's face
Memories flood an empty space
A past on love she can't replace
Her heart begins to race

She feels a warmth which is a light
That shines throughout the darkest night
A brand new face to love despite
Her eyes cry with delight

Chrystal E. Hill

To My Husband

My life was empty 'til I met you,
I've never felt so alive.
To each other we've always been true,
Our marriage is worth the strive.
You've given me a precious gift,
The gift I cherish of love.
My spirits you always give a lift,
when I feel much less than above.
Being with you is my heart's delight,
You're constantly on my mind.
Seeing you is a wonderful sight,
You are my greatest find.
Yet sometimes when we disagree,
Things never take long to patch.
You'll always be my cup of tea,
Most definitely my best match.
Please realize now through thick or thin,
I'll always be on your side.
Know that my heart you did win,
From you my love will never hide.

Jeanette J. McAdoo

Best Friends

Best friends are fun when friendships
Just begun and when work is done. I
know that Friendship is real nice when
you play on ice. When you get to
fall. Sometimes your friend looks real
tall. Sometimes people talk. When we go
for a walk. We don't care because
we always share. We like each other
a lot. I personally think were in the
right spot. We love each other a lot.
That's what friends are for.

We sled together we play together
we talk together. We're best friends
and no one can tear us apart. We also
study together. Our favorite thing to
do is draw and play freeze tag. We
also love to play chase and watch
movies. Our favorite movie is lion king.
We like the lion king because it has lions an
animals. Me and my best
friend are best friends forever.

Christina Ann Denney

Song Of The South

Down on farms in Dixie land,
King cotton coated fields.
Wagons rumbled o'er rocky roads,
Wood saws sang in the hills.

Hunters trod through woods at night,
With guns, with axes, with gunnysacks.
Hammers clang in blacksmith shops,
Oil lamps burned in shacks.

Hound dogs bayed in river swamps,
Folks raked hay for cows.
Rabbits darted here and there,
Mules pulled sleds and plows.

Country stores were common,
If there was a school about.
And as the farmers drifted in,
The checkerboards came out.

As sure as the surreys and the wagons,
Went rumbling down the roads.....
Folks were spreading out the goodies
'Neath the churchyard shady grove.

John Shadix

Stop The Violence

I am not a poet.
Just for fun, don't get
me to do the dirty work.
I can't advertise. What can I say?
Everything you do is uglier than
what the devil do.
I know you don't want to hear,
"nothing," nothing about my theory
when "nothing" I've been doing is right,
I am so happy, my other side,
got to the other side.
Here is to be able to hear.
It's time you do
a lot of everything on the right side.
Do no violence to any man.
Stop the violence.

Constance Davis

What To Do

It was a cold and stormy night
The waves were rising high
You called to say you could not come
You had to say goodbye

I asked you what I was to do
You said you did not care
"Did I do something wrong?" I asked
I knew it was not fair

Then silence came across the line
You said you had to go
I didn't say a word to you
I knew my pain you would show

I went to walk along the beach
The rain was not as strong
I thought of our relationship
Where did it all go wrong

I will not bother you again.
So go along your way
Don't think about my broken heart
My heart will mend someday

Elizabeth DiPasquale

Will You Marry Me?

I've been waiting for the right time,
knowing we've been together,
I've come to this decision,
I want you forever.

If I may,
what would you say,
what will it be,
If I asked you,
will you marry me?

Marriage is for life,
so would you do me the honor
of being my wife?

Marriage is for two people,
whose love is as one,
it's all said and done.

Please say I do,
because I love you.

Trust me, we will be together for life

Christina Seymour

Thinking Of You

I sit alone on a Saturday night,
just thinking of you out of spite.
I remember cold nights
Holding you tight
And memories fill my head
Of how we cried and held each other tight
After each and every fight.
No one will ever take your place
As I sit alone remembering your face,
Full of sympathy when I would cry
And you would send a soothing sigh.
Embracing me as if to say
Everything would be okay.
Now that you're gone
I sit all alone
Thinking of you
And watching the dawn.

Amy Roberson

Shyness

Self-consciously I try
Knowing I won't die,
Fighting that fear
That lives beyond the ear
Shyness they call
It's in our soul.

Why can't people see,
The reflection in me?
Why can't I be me?

Words don't describe what others do,
I tell this till I'm blue.

Self-consciously I try,
Knowing I won't die
Fighting the fear
That lives beyond the ear.
Shyness they call
It's in our soul.

Elisabeth Johnson

Bloom Where You Are Planted

Little flower by the wayside,
  Lift up your drooping head.
Don't wish for greener gardens;
  Show your colors here instead.

This ol' world is short on beauty,
  And here's your space to bloom,
So stretch up past those noxious weeds,
  And spread your sweet perfume.

Brighten up your corner
  As you reach up for the sky;
Widen eyes of wonder
  In the weary passerby.

Fragile flower, burst with blossoms
  Before you get too old,
Before the winter season breaks
  With frost and wind and cold!

Bloom where you are planted.
  Drink deep, God's rain and sun.
A better, brighter world will be,
  Although you're only one!

Julius K. Strand

Las Vegas

Las Vegas is the place to be,
Las Vegas is the place for me;
flashing lights and noise galore,
rule behind the casino's door.

Cards and dice and wheels and stuff,
let you know you're not so tough;
Keno, slots, and poker reign,
some folks lose, and some folks gain.

Cash is king, that's plain to see,
play your bank roll carefully;
if you quit while you're ahead,
tears of joy you're bound to shed.

Many players hope and pray,
"let me go home rich today;"
Dreams of fortunes soon are busted,
kings and aces can't be trusted.

Bettye L. McCoy

Happy Child

Where would I be without your
laughter or without your smile,
the things that bring out a happy child
In a heart-wounding world
your laughter is all I see,
in more ways than one, you make
me happy to be me.
My heart stings when I treat
you the way I do,
I only get upset because I love you,
one day you will leave,
and I may never see you again,
but in my heart you'll always
remain my friend
when you leave you'll take with
you, my laughter, my smile
the things that bring out a happy
child.

Chanda R. Marion

Fatherless

Unseen by the naked eye.
Left alone, wish to die.
Never had a father to hold this boy,
left alone like a broken toy.
He tried to come back and mend the past,
start again and make it last.
Told me he'd never leave again,
he wanted to be there as a friend.
But he lied,
and I went to my room and cried.

Now it's the same as it was before.
Walked on like a dirty floor.
Heart's been broken too many times.
What did I do, what are my crimes?
I realize I shouldn't bother,
maybe I'm not supposed to have a father.
His father did not show him how to be.
What scares me is maybe it's the same with me.
But I know within,
I'm not the same as him.

Bobby Thorpe

I Loved You

I loved you but you
left me, I cried and grieved
and finally started to live
without you, then you came back
wanting everything we ever
had and more! I hated you
that day, when you thought
you could come back into
my life like nothing had
changed, like you always
cared. When I turned
you down, when I
laughed in your face,
you acted like I was
nuts for giving you
up, but you gave me
up the day you
didn't care!!

Abbie Meldrum

A Bedtime Story

The darkest evil
Lies in a child's toy
The lovable furry evil
Nestles in their arms
Eyes large
Drawing the innocence
The secret kept with the child
It whispers every night
The child darkens
Alone with the child
Dreams darken
Night and day pass many times
weakening the child grows
Light on the child's eyes
They drip black onto the teddy bear

Benjamin P. Ostroff

Whispers Of Love

Sensual desire,
like molten fire,
being near him takes my sense away;
A whispered caress,
his breath on my neck,
I sigh at this wondrous day;
With a look so sweet,
he kisses my cheek,
and hands me a painting of a dove;
hopeful as a child,
with a shrug and a smile,
he says "it's a token of our love."

Jennifer Garland

Life

Life is precious,
Life is care,
Life is wonderful,
With no compare.

Life must be
In one's heart.
Life cannot be
Taken apart...
For life is precious,
As one can see,
And without life,
Where would one be?...
...Nowhere...

Deevya L. Narayanan

What It Seems Like

A drop of water represents
life as we live it now.
Mirrored reflections tell us
stories untold with
promises and hope.
The drop nourishes its
surroundings giving off
everything within its souls.
In the end it will die, and fade away,
leaving behind memories never
to be forgotten by time.
The memories already gone
and forgotten will be
left hidden behind the mirrored images,
staying lost and forgotten, forever,
As tones of life drone on,
life is remembered in
only the minds of those it impresses.
Life is never what it
seems to be and reality is never part of life.

April Schott

Eternal Pathways

Within the realm of darkness
Lies the path of light
Golden paved
Winding and twisting forth
Each brick a moment
In the time of life
Spaced one to another
Touching and creating
Paths in ever changing directions
Some forward
Others stopping to savor
Brief encounters of existence
Pooled together
In the presence of the future
Ever forward, ever moving
Crossing and crossing again
With each passion
Creating a new path
Enjoyed and shared
Across the eons of time

Cecil D. Kirchen Jr.

Untitled

As the world is turning
Life seems to be changing
Right before my eyes,

The beautiful flowers
That bloomed within hours
Just don't want to rise.

The red sun and its rays
Don't shine on my days
To me, it's as dark as night,

And the stars in the sky
That sparkle way up high
Don't seem to shed any light.

As nature took its course
The earth moved with force
Things never stayed the same,

It destroyed my life
Cut through me, like a knife
And burned me with its flame.

Jannette Kaloustian

Emptiness

Emptiness is...
Like a song without lyrics,
A candle without light.
A star that doesn't shine,
On a clear cloudless night.

Sadness is...
Like eyes that cannot see,
A hand that cannot touch.
Ears that cannot hear,
The words; I LOVE YOU VERY
MUCH.

Loneliness is...
Like cries within the night
But no one to be found.
Like a voice that tries to speak,
But cannot make a sound.

These words I say to you
As strong as they may be,
Emptiness fills my heart
When you are not with me.

Betsy A. Eno

The Sea

I walk on the shoreline
Listening to the waves
As they slap the sand
And the smooth pebbles
Are washed out to sea

I smell the salt
And feel the wind
Blowing my hair
Away from my face
As the water hits my feet

I lift up my face
And take off my hat
To feel the sun's rays
Burning my neck
And I keep on walking

Emily Evans

Native And True

Americans
Living free
Running with the wind
In sport or on the hunt
Settling down to grow
Or moving with the food
Loving life, living with Nature
Using what they take
Taking only what they need
Honestly Alive

Invaders
Always seeking freedom
Running behind the wind
From persecution or their own law
Cutting down in greed
Or moving, wanting more
Destroying life, raping Mother Earth
Stealing as much as possible
Taking more than they need
In self-destruction

Craig A. Smith

Sunlight

I am now on my own
Live at a place I call home
Sit in solitude every night
By the candle
That burns just enough light
I contemplate
About my life
It burns like the candle
Not so bright
So I grab hold of a pen
Begin to write
Give the words
All my might
It is my only escape
From my slow burning life
One I wish to change
From a candle burning not so bright,
To a gleaming beam of SUNLIGHT

Benjamin R. Eodice Jr.

Once Upon A Time

Once upon a time
    Just like the fairy tale
    You were in my life
        After work, Never fail
Just like clockwork
    You were at my door
My head kept saying "No"
    My heart kept saying "More"
Now two years later
    We've come a long way
Before our big move
    I've got something to say
"Everything that's right about me,
    I owe it all to you;
You are my Prince Charming
    My fairy tale come true."

Damarda M. Herron

"Forget You By The Dawn"

You move me every day and night,
    Like the moon controls the tide.

You contaminate my every thought,
    There's no place for me to hide.

What is this spell you've cast on me,
    You've put me in a trance.

Every time I look at you,
    My heart breaks with every glance.

You must release me, set me free,
    I can't let this pain go on.

I only pray for this one thing,
    Let me forget you by the dawn.

Dan Wear

The Sounding

No more to dream
to hold close in memory's vestiges
one's loved one
sounding like distant chimes

All is hushed now
and silence steers the course
towards and endless stream.

Linda Coletta

If Rain Drops Were Diamonds

If rain drops were diamonds, how rich
I would be, for my windows are
covered with millions you see

There are large ones and small ones
And lots in between,
If rain drops were diamonds
I'd be richer than thee

Do you see the diamonds on your
window pane? How many rain drops
will make you richer than me?

O' if rain drops were diamonds
I'd really be rich, 'cause my windows
are covered all over you see
Yes, if rain drops were diamonds
I'd be richer than thee

Cloamae Suiters

Knocks And Bumps

Life's so full of surprises
Just when you thought it'd be
Safe and so predictable
Something sneaks up you didn't see

It knocks you out of kilter
When you straighten back you find
The path you thought you'd taken
Is now a different sort of line

You travel down along it
You think you're doing fine
Then something else upsets it
And you know now in your mind

That there are always choices
If you're wise you'll try to see
The knocks and bumps along the way
Should be accepted gracefully

Carol Hall

We, Who In Battle Fell

The soft sounds of "taps"
Linger in the autumn air.
We, the living hear,
And a precious memory share.
Shed a tear...
Pledge undying love.
Familiar voices, long silent.
Whisper softly above,
We, who in battle fell,
Did not, in vain die.
The gauntlet's run... peace won...
    All is well.

Burl P. Stead

Poetry's Meaning

A poem's a soulful insight
Like an inkblot in the sky-
Clouds of word paint in our minds
Searching for epiphany.

Staring deep into those pools
What is it we shall see?
Ferment of our lives-
Soundings of our souls.

Anthony R. DiBona

A Tribute To My Brother

This is a poem, not meant to be silly,
I had a brother whose name was Billy.
We grew up in a family of eight,
He emerged as one who was great.

He was big, he was smart.
He was one to touch your heart.
He taught me early in life
About people, sports and personal strife.

He was a loving father who left a
Beautiful daughter and wife, who are
Bigger than him in the picture of life.

He's gone from us now
In his physical presence,
But in my heart and soul,
Remains his essence.

Donald J. Shepard

The Fear Of Dying Alone

Sunday at ten, the week is past,
Life can be lonesome if you last.
No one calls to see how you are,
No one stops by; it must be too far.
I was too busy when they were younger,
trying to see that they did not hunger.
Now it is pay back time you see
Pay back to who? Why little old me.
Sometime soon, they too will be old,
then we will see what hasn't been told.
Spend time with your little ones,
have a life full of fun.
Let them know they are dear
or all you will have in old age is fear.
THE FEAR OF DYING ALONE!

Francis Strong

In The Night

Voices echoing
in the air.
They are not human.

They belong
to the mountains,
where we here stand.

What is it
that makes those sounds
come to life?

Filling the air
surrounding us,
touching us.

Those sounds are
whispering trees,
calling to us,

To go to them,
to stay with them,
Forever, in the night.

Jennifer Velinskie

Untitled

Dancing on mountains,
I know that I am not my
small self; I am God!

Mary S. Harbin

315

The Holocaust "Can We Ever Forget?"

The racing box cars filled with frightened faces
Men and women stifling their tears
Children wrapped in their arms huddled so near
But, alas, this closeness was not for long
The screeching brakes warned of black clouds
   Hovering and souls to mourn
Husbands and wives torn away from each other
Children crying — "Mama, papa, do not leave me and brother"

Who were these cruel men with faces so fierce?
What kind of sinister fate must they fulfill
Everyone separated and closed into bins
The earth dug up to bury bodies and cover their sins?

Torn from their homes six million helpless Jews only knew
Auschwitz, Buchenwald, Bergen-Belsen, Dachau and other camps
That before long the beginning of their Holocaust ensued

The world must always remember what bigotry and hatred can do
And see that this scourge can never be repeated
To prevent brotherhood, love for mankind and a world anew.

   Etta Kleiner

Forgive Me

Forgive me... for a moment, I mistook you for a stranger
Mistook this meeting for mere circumstance,
Two lives that crossed in passing, just by chance
For a moment, I mistook you for a stranger

Forgive me...my focus was a million miles away
I only joined your table on a whim
The crowd was noisy and the lights were dim
My focus was a million miles away

So if I seem a bit unnerved, it's just
That I did not expect to find you here
Amid the hazy smoke and stale beer
Yet all my life, I've known that you'd appear

Forgive me...I was not expecting anyone I knew
So did not recognize you at the start
Till the song that is your laughter touched my heart
I was not expecting anyone I knew

Forgive me....I can't seem to keep from staring in your eyes
It's just that I am searching for a clue
To tell me how it is that I've known you
I can't seem to keep from staring in your eyes.

   Jan A. Johnson

Poetry In All My Blood

O Poetry! Silent symphony rocking my soul!
Mistress nestling in the valley of my heart
And governing me without my knowledge!
O Poetry! Sweet incense in all my blood!
Spirited horse without bridle,
Leading me so far and so close to myself!
Poetry! You are the austere sob that burns me,
And the soft smile that resuscitates me.
You are the hot desert where I roam,
And the thirst-quenching oasis that welcomes me.
O Poetry! You are my guard dog and my guardian angel:
Even when lost in the most strident uproar,
Yet I hear you singing, like a nightingale,
An oath of peace in front of my heart.
Thus I realize that without you, Poetry,
I would be a shabby orphan,
Staggering lonely under a sunless sky, a moonless sky,
A sky without even one star so pure
That, only by contemplating it,
One discovers the magnificence of the Universe.

   Boureima Ouedraogo

"Ghosts"

The smiling face of a lovely child, framed, against a wall.
Mementos of a family life, here, on a market stall.
Precious China patterned in shades of white and blue
Once presided, pride of place, in a cherished 'tea for two'.
A table cloth of Brussels lace, delicate and cream
Once graced a dinner party that is just a distant dream.
Books - red bound in leather - and a stately cane-backed chair
Stand hostage, to the weather. No one seems to care.
And when our lives are over, like echoes through a hall -
You and I and all our things, will be ghosts on a market stall...

   Christine Ann Vickery

School Daze

Every day I go to school. Five days of the week.
Monday is the first day. The worse day that's for sure.
Because four days follow it, before I get a break.
Tuesday is the second day. It's the same from week to week.
Picking up the pieces of the mess that Monday brings.
Wednesday is the middle day. It's a down hill slide from here.
I call this my 'Hump Day.' I heard this from my Dad.
Thursday is the fourth day. There is only one day left.
Now Friday is the last day. And I'm really, really glad.
I work real hard to finish up, to end this last school day.
Saturdays and Sundays are the best days of the week.
The days I've waited for. No school for me that's true.
It's always fun on weekends, though it doesn't seem too fair.
For, I go to school for five days and I'm off for only two.
I have a plan. I know will work. I'm sure you will agree.
I could go to school on weekends and stay home throughout the week.
Saturdays and Sundays really go by me very fast.
Soon enough it's Sunday night and I worry what Monday brings.
So, I close my eyes and cover my ears. I block it from my mind.
I'd rather not begin to think about another week.

   Cynthia A. Thornton

Judy

I can't believe she's gone,
most people never expected it to be her,
but God did. He took her life and left her
He took her life and left her family sad.
Her daughter is my friend,
till I hope the end.
I miss her now, I always will,
for when she went she was not ill.
She took me everywhere, everything was fine,
until that man took her life.
He had no right! He had no right!
to take her life on that October night.
I didn't know it would happen that way.
I didn't find out until the next day.
She still had her whole life to live and now,
she will never see her daughter mature.
She left behind what many cannot find,
a family that loved her dear.
In my heart she'll always be here.

   Crystal Linet

"Priceless Moments"

There are certain wonders that are priceless moments in one's memory...
A rainbow painted on a crystal blue sky after a summer storm.
The fading last star before the early light of dawn.
Petals of a rosebud opening itself in the sun's morning light.
The sound of a newborn baby's cry.
The comfort and security of a mother's warm embrace.
The sweet innocence of a child saying grace.
The moment God's Spirit embraced your own.
And the day you decided to make my house, your home...

   Joseph C. Dennie

316

Grave Of Ignorance

I remember the golden days of the sun.
Most people were moving in every direction enjoying the rays and happy
   days.
I stood far off in the darkness, because the sun was shining on
   everyone but me.
In the dark shadows of my mind, I could hear a voice inside of me,
   begging "save me some sunshine for maybe tomorrow or maybe
   for the rest of my life."
I walked the earth in grief and pain,
I prayed for light, instead it rained.
Then I wondered just what I had done,
This race was looking too long to run.
I walked the beaches with thorns in my feet,
Hoping for the sun only to retreat.
I began to pray to the heavens above,
Asking the Creator for sunshine and love.
Again a voice inside I can hear begging,
"Come out of your grave of grief and ignorance,
Pray for patience, love and endurance and you too can have sunshine
   for the rest of your life."

   Cleo C. Kohlman

The Window

   Morning
Motherless child presses her face on the window.
Morning sun, shines on the lace through the window.
   Is it an omen?

   Negative image reflects it all:
Black frost on the white wall across from the window.

   Afternoon
Lonely child touches watery paths on the window.
Bountiful rain makes staccato taps on the window.
   Is it an omen?

   Mercury roads, silver and slow,
Like biers, go down the wet pane of the window.

   Night
Sobbing child gazes at darkness through the window.
Orphaned eyes reflect sadness through the window.
   IT IS AN OMEN!

   She waits for father, but all hopes fade.
   Death's cold hand draws the shade on the window.

   Elizabeth Bohjelian

Desiderata

From the force that drives the gale
Moves mountains and each immortal soul
And the hue of light beneath the veil,
The Spirit shall remain whole:
As above, so below
We reap that which we sow.

From the fragile web that breathes,
From all we have and all we know,
From all the lands and all the seas
The Spirit shall remain whole:
As above, so below
We reap that which we sow.

From the tender hand that rocks the cradle,
From the heart lullabies through darkness flow,
Without love's light the path is fatal:
The Spirit shall remain whole:
As above, so below
We reap that which we sow.

   Arthur Mitchell

On The Other Side

My heart, the love I once knew.
My arms, used to be my honesty
my mind, to know between life and death.
My soul, I felt it by your side
my body, you took for granted.
For these reasons, I understand love
you gave me loneliness, I gave companionship
I gave you hope, you handed grief
I loved you and showed it, cold I felt it
I know pain, I hear it when I talk,
I feel it; deep down, smell it; as I breathe
taste it as my tears roll down; see it, clearly
when you left, I died with you
for it was not my time; only yours
yet every time our sun rises or sets
I hear your laugh; its joy
see your smile; how enchanting
I feel you near; your presence
I kiss your lips...you are gone
you gave me the reason...I'm dead.

   Josette R. Munson

My Best Friend

I have the best, best friend you'd ever want to know
My best friend loves me as I am and loves my family so
My best friend loves me when I am down or in pain.
He doesn't just say things will get better and hand me a cane.
He simply says so sweetly, by my stripes you are healed
Why suffer all the pain? Can't you just yield?
I already paid the price on the cross
All you have to do is help win the lost
My friend loved me when I was going the wrong way,
My friend is Jesus; He's yours too, I pray!

We will all stand before God one of these days
We will melt as we look into his rays
I just know he shines like a star
To find him, you don't have to travel so far.
Just look in the Bible; the words are so clear
We don't know when the end will be, maybe it's near.
One thing's for certain, one thing's so plain
He will come back soon and take this his domain.
The ones who don't know him, who did their own dance
He will have no mercy, they've had their last chance.

   Brenda Minnick

Never Forgotten

I was at friend's party late one night
My boyfriend and I got in a big fight
Suddenly he pushed me down on the floor
I quickly got up and ran out the door
He caught up with me before I got to the parking lot
I felt his hands on my arm and knew I'd been caught
He picked me up and threw me down on the ground
The wind was knocked out of me, I couldn't make a sound
I started to wish that I could've died
Instead I started to cry
He got on top of me and pulled off my shirt
The weight of him made my stomach hurt
I looked up at the sky and stared at the moon
Then closed my eyes and prayed it'd be over soon
When I opened my eyes he wasn't around
I slowly got myself off the ground.
At first I thought it had just been a bad dream
then I looked down at my clothes and started to scream
It's been a year since that painful day
The thought of what he did just won't go away

   Dana Sanders

Ugly

Spook....Charcoal..... Tar baby. These names followed me throughout my childhood. It was awful. I cried my self to sleep every night Asking god: Why is my skin dark? Then asking for fair skin tomorrow I'd wake up all early, looking in the mirror with eyes closed. Hoping my wish was granted. For weeks, I imagined my skin was lightening Until, Miss Fair came and stood beside me and we both looking in the mirror, She said— "Look at you! Your skin ain't gonna get lighter—you're gonna be a tar baby forever." Then the laughing got louder. I looked around me and all around me were fair skinned little girls. They teased me, pointing and throwing white toilet paper at me. I'll never forget that day. I was so hurt 'cause, I this little child believed that being fair skinned was beautiful and dark skinned was the way of punishment from God. Sounds silly but—even at home, mamma would treat us different. I know mama loved us all but—Anna got treated with a little more love and care. Hum, papa always said it was because Anna had problems I don't know—. But— look at me now. I'm as beautiful as ever, copper brown en' all and those same fair skinned girls who laughed and teased sit and bake in the sun every day trying to achieve this color that was thought to be a punishment back then. Today, I realized I was even more beautiful back then, just on the inside.............

Domitria A. Vieira

The Empty Jar

Margie, my little student, once told me
"My daddy lost his job
And the peanut butter jar is empty."
To be discouraged would be tempting.

The empty jar is but a vessel
To be filled with God's blessings.
God with blessings does out-weigh
All sorrows and sadness of each day.

The empty jar is indeed a blessing,
A tool for remembering,
That God in His goodness does provide
For all our needs shall be satisfied.

Do we stop and thank our God each day
For blessings He has provided along life's way?
Do we praise our God alone,
And not ourselves for what we own?

The empty jar is really full.
We just fail to see it.
Praise God, for His goodness is bountiful.
With Him, all things are possible.

Dorothea L. Cowling

Another Way

That evening, I sat in the corner of my den,
My thoughts churning and burning inside
From unwanted words that rift us when
We discuss - and anger tears at the heart
As I struggle to break the quietness
Engulfing the distance that holds us apart.

Fears well, rolling like tears, down to my toes,
Distressed because how often I've been here.
Outside my den, a cold winter's night glows
With yellow lights reviving an old wound
That smarts and I want to run away into
Oblivion and never again open the tomb.

Depression presses like a heavy rock
This man out of reach, refusing to regret
That quarreling word he said and unlock
The light buried beneath the hurt.
Yet I trust tomorrow's sun will open
Another way which I now blatantly avert.

Gus Wilhelmy

Silent Village

They lie in a silent village
My European ancestors and their many descendants,
High on Pringle Hill,
Brought to this gray Pennsylvania coal town
By the sharp hand of fate.

They lie in a silent village, a field of granite,
Carved with familiar - familial - names,
Side by side, endless mounds.

They lie in a silent village
Whispering their dreams and heartaches
In a now forgotten language,
A wave of hushed energy,
Pulsing through the dark nights.

Could they have known a century past
When they departed Rusin Villages, one-by-one,
That time and space would merge
Friends and neighbors, thousands of miles
    from their distant homeland,
Into an eternal family, together forever,
    Immovable, in a silent, silent village for all time.

Janet Bankovich

You!!

When I was two, I did not know you. When I was three, you came to my family and me. When I was four, you touched me and made me sore. When I was five, you hurt me so bad I felt I wasn't alive. When I was six you tried to teach me a lot of grown up tricks. When I was seven, you fondled me until I was eleven. When I was twelve, you had intercourse with me. I held the pain inside so you could not see. I was locked in hell and only you had the key. You hurt and tortured me every day. I wondered if there was hope, and if I could be saved. One day I was found and things turned around. You were taken away and your life is now managed by a key. Oh how I wish you will never be free.

Jamie Brooks

My Family

My family is perfect, it's perfect I say,
My family is perfect in every way.

My children have interests in science and math,
They don't fight about silly things, they don't share any wrath.
They aren't worried about drugs, and they hate cigarettes,
When they're asked to do dishes, they just simply say, "lets."

My husband has all his perfect traits too,
He helps me with dishes as most men don't do.
His motto is this - "ladies always go first,"
And he drinks diet coke when he has a great thirst.

My family's not lazy, they don't watch much T.V.,
They take television as a great privilege you see.
Like I said, they are perfect - they don't have any hate,
Now I feel better, ain't denial just great!

Audrey Oldham

Untitled

    Hidden footsteps in the snow,
No where to run, no place to go
    Your lungs they burn, your fingers pain
As troubled thoughts run through your brain
    Step by step you wander on
The frozen rain plays out your song
    So many things you've not known
It's not easy on your own
    No turning back. Onward roam.
No second thoughts, no going home

Al Gardega

318

Precious Little Infant

My Mother groaned;
My Father had wept
into a dangerous world a precious little infant
has leapt, helpless, naked, and piping loud like a
fiend hid in the cloud.
Struggling in thy Mother's hands.
Striving against its swaddling bands.
"O" how precious a little infant can be.
Take a big look of what a small human, you see.
Oh, how precious thee little hands!
Its precious little feet!
Its precious little mouth!
Oh God, how sweet!
Its precious little nose and its precious little ears!
Its eyes, that shed such little crystal tears.
Its voice so soft and kind.
Its little soul, heart, and mind.
I thought best of what my precious little infant
Would do at rest. Even though, it might cry,
and moan, and weep as I rock it a good night sleep.

Fedricka Jones

My Life

My prime of youth is but a frost of cares,
My feast of joy is but a dish of pain,
My crop of corn is but a field of tears,
And all my good is but vain hope of gain;
The day is past, and yet I saw no sun,
And now I live, and now my life is done.
My tale was heard and yet it was not told,
My fruit is falling and yet my leaves are green,
My youth is spent and yet I'm not old,
I saw the world and yet I was not seen;
My thread is cut and yet not spun,
And now I live, and now my life is done.
I sought my death and found it in my womb,
I looked for life and saw it was a shade,
I trod the earth and knew it was my tomb,
And now I die, and now I was but made;
And now I lived, and now I'm gone.

Angelica Felix

"Metamorphosis"

I have wiggled and stretched and slithered and joined
    My goal, entering into the start that man has coined

Immortal. I am sea-borne within these mighty changes made,
    And breach like whale and know my life indivisible played

Upon mother's breast! While ocean borne, I salient sailed awake,
    The barrier, now broken; where man and woman partake

Of twin desire. They greet my cry in the brilliant light
    For my sake, and my vaunted whimper is muffled and contrite.

My being is vaulted, to lay my shiny skin on wet crest of earth
    And plug my face with joy so undisturbed at time of birth!

Lay now! Play now, in nurture plagued room, while sweet contrary
    Lives in child-eyes. Pass the time and gather all the merry

Kind from sassy fool to arrogant rile....and fill a heart
    With love! It is all so desperate and unknown, but a start!

How stoic soul does wander when tended not with felt compassion,
    To end the sweetness cut from tunic of irreverent fashion!

Lie down to feel my body weight no more, and cry one last sound
    For the ending of a promise. My place is dry earth bound

And wedded to the unknown of stillness. The despair of death
    Is temporary, as spirit unfolds out of self with my last breath!

Charles Edmunde Clary

Old Oak Table

There is old oak table, that's been in my family tree.
My Grandma got it from her aunt and my grandma gave it to me.
It came from far back east brought by wagon train.
It shows many generations in each layer of varnish
and stain. It fed us through the good times.
It fed us through the pain.
People have to remember, when they're living way
too fast, to stop and smell the roses and cherish
the things from the past.
To think about the old days when things were
made by hand. To give tribute to the craftsman
who carefully carved this land. To the next few
generations down the line from me. The table will
grow along with the family.
As it grows out farther with each new branch,
will this table live longer than my name?
Yes, it has a good chance.

Darin L. Eilerman

Raptor

In a time of obscurity
My innocence was seized.

My self assurance obliterated.
My vitality diminished.

Forever changed by his
inhumane, self gratifying ways.
Fleeting moments of masochistic pleasure
for years of torment.

A life begun in exchange for another,
Lessening the quality of both.

Pains brought to the hearts of loved ones.

The torment of the truth.
The sick reality of it all.

How much more?
No more.

Crippled, handicapped.
Never again to be the same,
To feel, to trust, to love
All is distorted.
In the one night that will live forever in my mind.

Ann M. Leahy

Rainbows Of Love

As I sat weeping one day at the trials that life sent
    my way, I looked out my window, and what did I see?
    Bright rainbows of love that my God gave to me.

Now I see God in the trees, every flower and bird on
    the wing; I see Him in mountains and meadows so fair,
    it causes my heart to sing.

Whenever my heart feels like breaking, He'll not let
    one teardrop fall. He paints me a rainbow with colors
    so rare, soon all of my cares seem so small.

Each color so soft, yet so brilliant 'gainst a sky that's
    so bright and so blue; and God whispers so sweetly
    from heaven above, "Don't cry, child, for I love you."

So whenever you're feeling downhearted, discouraged,
    alone and so blue, take a look out your window, and
    soon you will find God's promises, how they hold true.

You'll never grow weary or stumble. In Him your strength
    He will renew. You'll soar with the wings of an eagle,
    and you'll know just how much He loves you.

Jane M. Long

Untitled

When it rains it pours...
My life's falling apart again.
At night codeine's my best friend.
Nyquil is my only way of sleeping.
Thinking about you night and day.
Nervous stomachs turning.
Where did we go wrong?
When others have the answers; I still ask why?
I might be a man.
But I can't hold back these tears I cry.
I miss you already.
Things will never change.
We're still together.
I feel about as worthless as the pavement we walk on.
Still longing for one more day with you.

Jeffery Trask

"My Beloved"

I stand before you with my heart in my hands, "my beloved."
My love flowing through these hands, reaching out to clutch you,
"my beloved."
I feel that my heart has shattered into many pieces, "my beloved."
I ache with desire and passion which I want to embrace with you,
"my beloved."
Needing you to love me so desperately, "my beloved."
Gaze upon me, seek to fill my wishes and I will be yours forever
and
ever, "my beloved."

Betty J. Winters

Little Friends

My childhood was such a magical time.
My memory takes me back so many years ago.
I had a little friend, my best buddy, we played together all
the time.
We walked the dusty country roads, hand in hand.

One day my little friend showed me a gift from her sister.
She said, "This is a souvenir!"
She had a special place on her dresser for this object.

At that time I did not know the word souvenir.
I only know she treated this object almost as if it was
sacred.
I remember thinking to myself "I wish I had a souvenir," and
I wondered if ever I would own such a treasure.
Now, I realize the best souvenir I could ever have is those
wonderful childhood memories.
Maybe one day my friend and I will hold hands and walk another
dusty road— and remember WHEN.

Bertha Gonzalez

A Ghost From My Past

When I saw him sitting there
My heart raced real fast
This man I saw was a ghost from my past
Then he started to turn his head slowly
Before long he was staring at me
I thought he was coming to say hi
But he just passed on by
It all happened in a single flash
This man I once loved, was still a ghost from my past
Instead he was walking to another girl
Who must have been his new love
Then I looked at the blue, blue sky above
I just walked on really confused
And my heart felt like it was severely bruised
Then it all came back too fast
He was just a ghost from my past

Heather Christy

"Soul Of Crack Baby"

I'm a crack baby;
My mother is on crack.
When I was born,
I was blind as a bat.
I will never see a sunrise-
Or anything like that;
All because my mother wanted to use crack.

I'm a crack baby too;
My mother was on crack.
I was born with no fingers,
And a hole in my chest.
I will never be able to swim or play a piano,
Nothing like that;
All because my mother wanted to use crack.

I'm a crack baby;
My mother is on crack.
I wish I could tell my story.
But I can't! I'm dead;
All because my mother wanted to use crack.

The souls of the crack babies ask you to-
Please stop selling and mother stop buying;
Because all the children are dying,
AS CRACK BABIES.

Johann D. Oliver

When I Go Out...

When I go out I want to be respected
My poems acclaimed and maybe some movies
directed.
When I go out I want my family to have
power.
Be rich and famous and live in a mansion with
a tower
When I go out I want to have lived a long
time
Written a lot of poems and each with a
spiritual line
When I go out I want my family to be well
supported
To my children I want them to know in
fatherhood I was devoted.
When I go out I want my friends to be
what they wanted be
All of them must be popular and famous
like me
I wonder will I ever go out or will you go out before me?

Johnnie Lewis

I Love America

I love America - the land of the free
My pride in America is plain to see
I love her people - the strength of this land.
May we ever march forward - hand in hand.
I love America - the land of the brave
and each one who fought our country to save.
I love our freedom long let it stand
May we always love it and freedom demand.
I love America - land of the true.
May we remain honest in all that we do.
I love America and the red, white and blue.
Our flag proudly flying in glorious hues.
I love America and thank God each day
that I was born a citizen of the U.S.A.
I love America - especially today
when we celebrate, again, Freedom's birthday
I love America - let freedom ring
as we join together this song to sing
God bless America - land that I love
Watch over and guide her, Lord, from above.

Glenna H. Treadway

"My Son, The Dad"

After so much time, it's come true,
My son is going to be a father too.
There's so much happiness in my heart,
That his own little family he will start.

It's no matter for girl or boy,
Cause either one will bring us joy.
As he or she grows up and on its way,
I hope it listens to what ma and pa will say.

For when the grandchild is with us,
You know that we will make a fuss
And spoil it, far more than we did you.
For that's what grandparents are supposed to do.

Poppers

Ghosts Of Time

We are the ghosts of time.
Mysterious and lonely.
We feel no pain or sorrow.
We only have anger and jealousy.
Angry because of our death.
Jealous of others' lives because they live.
They breathe the air, have feelings of love and hope.
We are all banished from heaven for the sins we caused when we were
amongst the living.
We haunt every place or thing.
We are the stories in your books.
The steps you hear in the night.
Banshee is just one of the many names the living call us.
We are unwanted from every place we turn.
We shall stay here with the living for eternity.

Adam Gutierrez

Delenn

She has glow worm eyes—
   mysterious and tranquil which
   encircle you like her crystal wind chimes.
An ever fixed double helix
   surrounding
   creating prism music and infinities of reflections.
She stands as a reverent monk with a
   pursed bronze smile, purple kimono, and a
   crown of bones upon her blueprint bald head,
   speaking in jigsaw phrases you were
   not meant to understand.
And you wonder: What does she mean...know?
   Perplexed because
She stands on both sides of the helix:
   much hidden   much exposed
   tells you everything   tells you nothing
Both sides reflecting as she says:
   "You do not know
   these things as I do."

Catherine Drougas

The Unadorned Life

Through no fault of your own, you started to grow.
Mysterious conception of an ambivalent past.
Serendipitous or woeful - you did not ask.
Your Soul set free to flight, to return from whence it came,
where acceptance is law - unquestion the same.
Only those who are guilty of the sin of your death will reap the
harvest with you as judge. And, then one day they will plead for
your forgiving love.

Bonnie Elaine Stuart Ransom Stebbins

Tao Fong Shan's God-Daughter

A little girl is buried on Tao Fong mountain
near kindred and missionaries Reichelt and Martinson.
Her youthful picture marks the marble Christian gravestone;
she lies still above the clamor of Tai Wai and Shatin markets.

Who conceived in ecstasy this little life;
What mother nursed hard at swollen breast;
What community bore her here to this quiet repose;
Who served as evangel that she be Christian?

And why does she lie here so prematurely?
What plaque or disaster cut this life so short?
No womanhood, discipleship, or parental joy,
Never to be a Priscilla, Mary or Mother Theresa.

Wash her granite market well and add chrysanthemums.
The rain sheds tears to help with grief and emptiness.
Then let your prayer of gratitude ascend above the clouds.
This is another for whom Christmas turned to Easter.

A Bethlehem born Savior worked for her forgiveness
and new life beyond sandy red soil tomb.
God's spirit called gospel witness this mountain
so its little God-daughter might sleep in peace.

Jerry L. Schmalenberger

BIG MAN

On a warm October day he came to play
near San Francisco Bay.

Come take your stand on the sand and let
the mighty Pacific Blue crash over you.

Always look to see what's rolling in 'cause
you don't want to slam bottom with your
chin.

Whether you ride them or dive them, the waves
give no quarter, so get their sequence in the
right order.
If not, you'll have sand in your eyes and seaweed
around your neck and you will feel and look like a
total wreck.

So stagger back to the safer sand and
change your course, 'cause you're no match
for this ocean's force.

You know now you're but a grain of sand in
the Master's Plan and how insignificant you
are when judged by his power from afar.
BIG MAN

Clifford H. Porter Jr.

Friends Till The End

Dedicated to My Stoner Bud, Cari de on Key.
Like a rose trapped in glass
Never dying just letting time pass
From a distance I have watched you grow
Battling emotions I was afraid to show
Tears have fallen like bitter rain
I hurt with you when you're in pain
It's hard to watch your heart ache
Only one promise to you will I make
When you feel you've reached an all time low
No matter what you need I won't say no
We have been friends for quite a while
And somehow you've gained grace and style
Until I die you have a place in my heart
Friends till the end, Friends from the start

Christopher Blake Parker   *Stoner Buds*

"Growing"

This poem was written after being married for 33 years to my wonderful husband-Jack, my soul-mate. A true romantic!

You're the one I fell in love with and married in my teens,
Never imagined the changes coming in the years between

We have grown so much in the tender art of loving,
Compared then to now, we knew almost nothing

We learned and enjoyed each other, sharing our love,
'Til it was perfectly fitted, like a hand in its glove

Our tastes have expanded and widened in range,
We've enlarged our horizons, welcomed each change

Ever new, ever fresh, our fantasies flowed,
While our love still continued to deepen and grow

Through our love we created three wonderful boys
Nurtured and raised them, sharing tears and proud joys

We made memories to cherish until they were grown
Now they're fine young men, going out on their own

We've shared so much, can there still be more
For two star-crossed lovers, what else is in store?

We've many doors yet to open, I'm sure this is true,
And Honey - I eagerly await sharing them with you

Jean S. Case

To Know Not

To be in the black
Never wanting to look back
Scared to wonder why
Terrified for the will to try
Confused to the farthest beyond
Hoping for wizard with a magic word.

Sometimes I just don't know
If he cares why doesn't it show?
To break a heart without a care
Makes me wonder what I was ever doing there.

A person with no conscience, feels no pain
Without a care, without a heart, the person must be insane.
Selfishness, silence, and pain occur,
Leaving my heart and mind a blur.

Not to know, just to wonder.
Being still and quiet as to ponder.
Life has no meaning unless you're with the one you love.
Asking, hoping, and praying endlessly to the one above.

Loneliness is kind of like dying
Your pain so defined, your heart broken and you just feel like crying.

Joanna Harris

Lost Ones

So many lost ones with nowhere to go
  No one to turn to when their hearts become low
They live in the streets becoming wise
  But it doesn't erase the pain in their eyes
They learn how to eat and sleep and survive
  But they can't find love so they find a high
Cocaine becomes their mother, father and friend.
  Deceiving and teasing and pulling them in
Leaving them lower that even before
  Always trying to find a way to get more
Dead in the street a handful of blow
  So many lost ones with nowhere to go

Deana L. Seaman

For Death Is Unanswered

Unsolved theory, baffled by the unanswered.
New day, death is mysterious.
Another way, a latitudinarian.
Logic or illogic, denial of hypothesis.
An ice age of perplexity revolving ultimately
upon idealism.
Igniting fire internally toward idiocy.
The unknown, oblivious and uninterpretable to
the human species.
Death is a fact, transition, and departure
into the blank blackness.
Time, a distinct metaphor.
Death is unanswered, the cradle surrounded.
Distress holds, cannot distinguish.
Soundless, speechless, too deep.
Subject untouched, profound.

Joshua Truitt

Suffering Love?

Love saw much pain, wanted to Help————
"No help wanted," said Beast, "You just sex-toy..."
Beast saw "easy prey"—Love "fell" into Hell,
like moth attracted to flame.

Lies, deception, disinformation. Love would be mis-used:
public humiliation, verbal abuse, Beast will teach Love?
Evil lesson...Beast so wise said, "Love is stupid.
I will twist Love, a new addition in my stable of sex addiction."

By psychological manipulation, terrible pain inflicted on Love
it was so easy! Love said, "Please Listen!"——No!
"I am your Master! My Robot sex moves will brain-wash you!"
Love with no choice, had to stay, until released....

The Beast became annoyed with his alien sex-toy
all manner of animalistic tricks were applied....
Beast Master worked to dishonor Love—who cried
after two years Beast Master learned: Love is not "easy prey" after all

While Love suffered, unspeakable pain Beast Master became—
more insane
in fact, Beast Master beginning to feel heat....
finally released; Love — happy, flew away! Back in cold darkness...
Beast Master realized with horror, "I am the moth?"

Daniel J. Wilson

With Love O. J.?

In jealousy and rage, the light of my life,
no longer a light, no longer a wife.
  The spirit taunts, the bodies are slain,
no longer life, no longer pain.
  I attained so much in such a few short
years, nothing is left but anguish and tears.

  The devils of Justice, deceivers they be,
twists the truths for him, not for thee.
  Wealth is the only truth they heed, the
problem was your birth, from the wrong seed.
  We know in our hearts that this man lied,
too many have bled, too many have died.

  Justice must be done to the likes of him, for
the deeds that were done, not the color of skin.
  He walks with angels, by the grace of him,
the wrong grace the wrong him. Give justice to the man, not color of
skin, you're no brothers to the likes of him.

  But speaking of justice, what can it be?
If love is equal between the spirit and me,
  for all three, - Because he has not slain two, - But two and me.

Howard Wickersham

322

The Dance

I get depressed but still I go.
No matter that my heart rate flutters.
I still force myself to face the crowd
of laughing, happy people.
I go to prove my strength,
to myself and to them,
the people who try to break my heart in two.
I shall never let them win.
Although the agony of watching,
knowing I shall never join them, hurts,
I still go.
I can't let them win,
let them feel that what they think matters,
because if they think it, it will become true.
And then the person that I am
will disappear and turn into what they want me to be,
and that is the one thing I fear the most.

Anna Oltmanns

You Were Mine For Awhile

You were mine for a while Earl
No more precious Jem than a baby
So the nickname we gave you
Was Earl the Pearl
as you grew red haired and freckled face,
Hand and hand we walked at
God's lending pace.
   The years came and passed by,
As you grew out of my arms
and into a man
   I look back and search my
heart for precious little joys,
When you laughed, joked, or
played volley ball in the sand.
   You have warmed my heart with
love, laughter and you
   Recently God came calling and
I had to let you go.
   You were mine for awhile
So, my son, in my heart I carry a smile.

Gwendolyn L. Smith

The Gift

'Tis the story as it's told,
of a babe in a manger born many years ago.

Two people walk hand and hand,
bringing joy into that far off land.

A man, a woman, a child to be,
He shall be born for you and me.

The angels hover all around,
guarding the place there in Bethlehem.

There in the stillness of the night,
a miracle came to set things right.

He had no place to lay his head;
so, he was placed in a manger bed.

The shepherds came from distant fields,
to see if what they had heard was real.

Then following one lone star,
Wise men came, bringing gifts from afar.

But the greatest gift that was given that day,
was the gift of our Saviour's birthday.

And so it was; so shall it be.
God gave Christmas to you, to me.

Betty Gravitt

Nam

I was born so sterilely, perfectly,
no one could even breathe on me.
I was named, acclaimed, destined to be
a champ, a hero grand
when I became a man.
I waddled, toddled, walked and ran
in cowboy boots and coonskin hat,
and sure could swing a baseball bat!
I was vitaminized, homogenized, organized,
taught to be polite, read and write.
I was well educated, groomed for success,
but suddenly, oh God! what's this mess,
face down buried in mud, here I am
not in Oz or Nod, but the Land of Nam
with many men, the same as I
asking why we were protected, purified,
taught everything
except... how to die?

Helen S. Wilkie

Who Can Hear Me?

Who can hear me? I say aloud.
No one turns, so I begin to shout.
Who can hear me? I cry down the hall.
Again no one looks, they don't care at all.
They say ignore her and she'll go away.
But not this time, they're going to pay.
So many times my feelings were crushed,
They have to hear me, they must.
Memories of love long ago,
Faces of friends I no longer know.
Years of confusion locked up inside,
They said they cared, but they lied.
A lifetime of secrets I poured out of my heart.
I confided in them, till they ripped me apart.
Dissipating dreams falling fast,
Maybe my life was not meant to last.
Who can hear me? The damp fog is all I can see.
Nothing is left here for me.

Jamie Turner

See No Color

I see no color in the world,
No white or black or any other.

I see no color among the crowd,
Just people similar to each other.

I see no color among my peers,
Only people I know and familiar faces.

I see no color on the streets,
Just people together in the same exact places.

But there is one face that seems to stand out,
Among the crowds and all of my peers.

One face stands out and is not familiar,
A face of anger but most of all fear.

This face has eyes that only see color,
These eyes cannot see the soul of a man.

This face is cold and has no feeling,
With dark empty eyes and cold rough hands.

I see no color in the world,
But this face disturbs me through and through.

The eyes are all I see among me,
Do these blind eyes belong to you?

Deana Preston

Home In The Hills

In the foothills of the Smokies, we lived and laughed and grew,
No other place seemed so secure and cozy for family,
As our haven with its surroundings and such a magnificent view.
We've travelled this vast country over, to falls, forests and parks,
All are spectacular, with 'breath-taking' beauty,
But just don't create 'hair-raising' sparks,
As the sight of our blue, hazy sentry, towering over villages and
   farms;
With fish-filled streams and wild bird sanctuaries,
Holding white-tailed deer, black bears and other animals in its
   charms.

Many visitors come to enjoy our mountains and our lakes;
They visit our rural communities that hold on to the past;
They marvel at Spring's fragrant blossoms, so soon as winter's ice
   breaks.

From the green hills and fertile fields of Summer,
To the woods splashed with purple, orange, red, and gold of Fall,'
Our modest home in the foothills of the Smokies
Extends a greeting of friendship and offers hospitality to All!

   Dorothy Hatmaker

No Feelings

No presents of course, none was required;
No presence of hers that I so desired.
No get-togethers as though something to avoid;
No cards, no calls, just simply a void.
No meaning can be construed except the very adverse;
No birthday had gone by was ever worse.

No actions were taken in the weeks that followed;
No words were spoken except those that were hollow.
No time to talk during each call she made;
No meetings were met without reasons to evade.
No familiarity remained when addressed by Mister.....;
No conclusions can be drawn which did not make my heart fissure.

No updates to problems that I once was told;
No time is any longer available for friends of old.
No importance was placed on a friendship that was dying;
No energy can be diverted from a new guy she was eying.
No medicines arrived until the wounded was dead;
No roads were mistraveled except those I, myself, misled.

   James Lum

Horizons

Slowly, all evolves.
Nothing seems to remain constant in a world
Where the impossible does not exist.

We know nothing, yet through our actions
Our dreams become sudden realities.

But is anything truly real?
For we simply sit upon a dying rock
Drifting slowly through infinity.
Or at least we believe we do.

But maybe we are nothing;
Illusions in a whirling storm of unconsciousness,
Dark shadows passing in front of a weary moon.

In the end perhaps we will know what we symbolize,
And the potential that lies obscured within us.
But I doubt it.

Our lives are like visions in the night.
Appearing briefly, only to vanish into an eternal darkness,
The anonymity of time.

A few are profound enough to be remembered.
But ultimately, do they matter? Perhaps.

   John Shors II

"The Love Of My Life"

The Love of my life has not ears to hear,
Nor eyes to see the wonders of this earth,
Nor a mouth to speak—though it may appear
to sing. It is not of a human birth,
yet one cannot extinguish my love for
this one who does not have a brain to think,
Nor legs to stand with and walk through a door.
My love has not fingers to write with ink,
And not ten toes to wiggle in the sand.
Then why, you may ask, do you love this One?
This Love of my life belongs in a band,
You see, and only there has my Love won!
  The One of whom this work of art adorns
  Is the true Love of my life:
    my French Horn!!

   Alison Ruth Timari

Definition Of Success

Success lies not in owning things
Nor in the pleasures that life can bring.
It can come to you when you least expect;
When you think that you're just a reject.
When you're wondering what is up ahead
Keep your integrity-don't be misled.

Success comes after years of hard work
After taking risks that you once used to shirk.
You keep trying and failing again and again,
But you never give up you just say "I can."
It doesn't come easy-and to some not at all;
In the corporate jungle their financially mauled.

It is whether you're determined and not just able.
You could be brilliant, yes very intellectual,
But selling pencils in a market square
Because you simply failed to do your share.
Keep your nose to the grindstone as the old saying goes
And you'll be respected for the ethics you chose.

   Bradley C. Skilton

"My Dad And His Black Bow Tie"

When I think about my Dad and how distinctive he was I can
not help but remember his black bow tie.
He was a handsome man and a snappy dresser which no one
could deny.
The three piece suit with the starched white shirt and the
Shoes polished to a high gloss and the black bow tie.
As he walked along the street with a certain sense of
dignity you could feel that he was not an ordinary man.
He always tipped his hat to all of the ladies as he walked
to and from his work for he was always a gentleman.
I cannot remember a day when my Dad was not dressed to the
Hilt and had a ready smile which made the women sigh.
Of course it would not have been the same without
my Dad's black bow tie.

   Helen L. Lowther

Flashbacks

Once born into this world
not knowing why
walking the desert sands
trying to reach the pale blue sky
now, is the time we hunger
it is our turn to feast
bodies of my soldiers rotting and decaying
souls of my friends, lost on the crusades
   surviving only I
the time is now to retire
   awaken from a dream.

   Alexei Zagrebin

Untitled

It was a day like any other day
Nothing more can be said
But that everything was dead
The trees didn't give off any breeze
Everything was at ease

All human life was dead, all animal life was dead,
all plant life was dead
The only thing alive was the reminder of what
once was, and will never again be
For the next species to find, and try to set themselves free
From the human animal's fault, their everlasting greed.

Gisselle Sarmiento

Evolution

Cry no more, no llores mas,
Nuestra Señora La Reina de Los Angeles.

Agonizingly slowly, aeons after we are gone
Ours will become a more human species.
Everyone is fluent in every language and thought.
Irrelevant traits: color of skin,
Shape of eye and hair will be invisible.
Too often used, for thousands of centuries,
As bloodied backdrops to hang pet Lies,
Superstitions, Folk-tales, Hate,
Sub-classifications will have found their rightful oblivion.

Intention, integrity, devotion to humanity,
History and scale of each,
From the lofty to the lowest antithesis
Dynamically showing on the body.
Structurally impossible to conceal or alter.
Reading of displays is enough for any evaluation,
Trial and testimony are obsolete.

Ernest Michio Matsunaga

Silence

The day we separated and said good-by
Numerous tears fell from colored eyes
The soft colors soon turned to seemingly gray
With the endless flow of tears, I looked away
Knowing this was my last chance to look at you
The best qualities came out through and through
It's hard to even imagine us apart
With these deep emotions we hold deep in our heart
But just knowing we'll be united soon one day
All the pain and anger will slowly drift away
And with that silence glance,
You said good-by to me.

Deanna Herald

Face To Face

Your smile brings a simple expression
of beauty
fashioning your countenance like warm sunshine
on a brisk day,
dispelling the fear of a long and
desolate winter,
catching the beholder unaware,
entranced by its radiant magic.

Then quietly and unexpectedly,
the storm appears
and from the depths of your heart
a tear is formed,
glistening brightly, as if it had captured
the sunshine
of your smile and drawn it away
to be savored for another day.

Debra A. Nelson

You Snuffed Out The Candle

It was within a whisper
    of getting its light going
    when you first put the taper to it.

Its beginnings
    offered infinite possibilities:
        To crackle with myriad color,
        warmth
        and pleasure trailing in its glow.

But the initial investment
    was not even given a hair-breadth's chance.

No tears of wax
    to display its extra-ordinariness.
No egress for hope.

Two deft fingers
    pinched the life out of this candle.
Alone
    and dark
        without a shed of light.

    You snuffed her out.

Herman O. Arbeit

At Last

While walking through a velvet maze
of shadows black and golden haze,
we leave shared things to go alone
to other days and nights we've know.

Through portals of a lonely mind,
we seek times held and left behind;
with flaming brands we must return -
set fire to bridges left to burn...

The past awaits - we know it well;
paths banked with fire - a piece of hell...
The way is dark, hand seeks a hand
for strength to walk this lonely land.

Words hard from throats of once too dry,
remembered pain and urge to cry;
then reaching out we say with touch
things left unsaid that hurt too much.

Our present takes the past away.
Love burns the bridge to yesterday.
While future shadows all that's past
and peace of mind awaits at last!

Philis DeAnn Catherall

Butterflies

Sitting on this windowsill
Nodded back contentedly dozing to the thrill
Of wailing wind whipping, sometimes nipping at my nose,
I see a sight with my two eyes.
To my surprise, a multitude of butterflies
(All but one of whom are giant-sized)
Come whirling, swirling, even twirling around my toes.

Honey - like golden rays hung —
Drip, drip, dropping from sun upon this one unsung
As he slowly floats to lightly land about my brow.
Now I sit so still and stare
At a beautiful bug that dances in my hair
And wonder: Who cares for tiny things of now that wow?

Had I been another chap
Watching the larger wings or still napping mayhap,
I might never have been pleasured by one so small as he.
Though these others may be great.
To miss this on my pate I could not tolerate,
Since it was the little that brought out the child in me.

Jeff P. Youngblood

"Afraid"

Is it okay to feel afraid? Because I am sometimes, afraid
of taking a chance of losing. Even afraid of winning sometimes.

I'm scared to love too much. Scared to hold on too tight,
when you may want to be free.

Scared of letting go, when I need you to hold me. And I need
to know, if it's okay to feel afraid. Because sometimes I
am.... because I love you so much.

Gina R. Coronado

With Envy

It is with envy she reads the story
Of the abused wife who finally gathered the courage
To say ENOUGH!

She knows the victim is safe in the warmth and support
Of an abuse shelter. She wonders if this woman realizes
She was fortunate to be forced into making a change.

How does it happen that a woman becomes entrapped
In violence? Is the process as subtle
As a marriage that goes stale?

Are bruises more painful than feeling
Nothing at all?
Is fear more paralyzing than despair?

With tears in her voice she greets
Her own husband. She feels
The hollow warmth of his touch as they mechanically embrace.

Behind a cheerful facade she secretly longs
For the fresh breath of freedom
That would come from a fist of rage.

Evelyn Rettig Thompson

The Promise

Green meadows of spun silk chiming whispers in the breeze
Of the caring and nurturing for one sad and fallen tree.
Erect wooden giants, beautiful and serene,
So generously spread wide a soft velvety coat of green
To embrace and to guard the unbudding little tree.
Her withering leaf's hold sad tears from life
While once strong roots, now broken and weak,
Lie in wait of the promise she is to seek.
The mission, of course, to be her tired and weary soul
To become a magical spirit again as entrusted from up above
That is her goal.

A crowning blue sky burst forth bright a golden gem
Adding gentle touches of raindrops only now and then.
That she may flourish to share and tender her growing beauty
Since no beautiful thing of God's is to alone or left undone.
That she will caress and hold tight the promise
The promise being the fragrance of everlasting love.
And that while she is loving
She too be loved.

Anita M. Seigler

Winds Of Change

Fly down from the clouds on the silver mist of rain
Off on gold tipped wings to lift my spirit again
Leave behind the mortal sufferings of the living ones
Sing sweet songs of joy and peace unto the chosen ones

Fly down from the clouds on the silver mist of rain
Climb the highest mountains on the winds of change again
Dance across the ocean's blueness feel the pain no more
Love in light of God supreme need to rest no more

Joy Lynn Dietrich

Full Moon Fever

Full moon fever will make you a believer
Of things that seem mighty strange
Of crazy notions and maybe love potions
from the lovesick and immensely insane

When there's a full moon weird ideas bloom
No matter who you are
To go and attack or merely relax
Will set you apart by far

So the next full moon beware of the bloom
The idea you may expound
Whether it's big or small or off the wall
The moon won't let you down

D'Anne Fairbairn

Saved Once More

The sun has never shone upon the head
Of this lost boy, who ages here alone.
Accursed is every object I own;
The ground, it turns to poison where I tread,
I do not wish to even leave my bed
For no one stands by me. And so I moan;
My echo is the only friend I've known.
If only I were to be found now, dead...
The night has ended, I can see the rays
Of light coming into these darkest days.
Your smiling face has never failed to cheer
Me up and show me the good that's in me,
And the only one who does that is thee,
So please know I hold your friendship most dear.

Chris LoBue

Untitled

Sometimes I feel the darkness of society looking upon me as a realist
of thought. Not only a child, I feel myself merge within another.
I feel the pain of my surroundings and the sour music of my elders.
For this is the beginning of a road I do not so wish to follow.
Only innocence lost shall retain the shadows. They are left
searching. There is a face in every cloud and everything desired is
left for the soul providers to follow. I dwell upon others which only
proves the spirit is weak. Searching for someone to pull me out, I only
go deeper. Deeper into my mind and deeper into my soul. I know
what is true and I see reality as it follows me desperately. No
turning back from the point where you left. There is no hope for past
gains. I only see what soon will come of the accomplishments I once
made. I follow the harmony and seek out the life I wish to lead.
Do not change the world. Let the world change for you.

Jennifer Joy Phillips

A Pastor's Service

The burdens you carry
on those shoulders of yours,
Will always be heavy if you
lean not on HIM alone.
The hours of service always long,
if marked with incomplete and
unfulfilled endings.
The tears you suppress for others of
joy or of sorrow,
Is a chain of love to meet each
challenge of tomorrow.
Your blessings to others,
cannot be measured.
In Glory alone the results will be seen,
of the love and the labor you showed others
in HIS precious name.

Deborah (Hively) Young

Close In The Heart!

Even though we don't get to see each other
often I still think of you all the time

I guess when two people know each other as well
As we do they don't need the constant reassurance of
each other's presence to keep them close

It's enough just to know that we'll always
understand each other, and always be able to pick up
Where we left off no matter how long it's been

For somehow I feel that no matter how much
distance separates us, we will always be close
together in the heart, and after all that's what
Really counts....

Byron K. Morse

Our American Emblem

"Old Glory" in reality made our lives anew.
On June the 14th, 1777, in red, white, and blue.

"Red" relates to blood, men in uniform shed;
many have survived, some others are dead.

"White" represents purity
of a nation at heart;
Democracy gave us
a number one start.

"Blue" is made known
where loyalty's true;
With citizens of honor
standing firm as we do.

Each "Star" on our flag
displayed in State form;
Tells us that equality
shall not be forlorn.

This concludes the story
of our "Stars and Stripe."
Be it forever cherished
all the rest of our lives.

Clyde W. Jontz

God's Wonderful World

I saw the beauty of a tiny blossom
  On the carpet of the forest floor.
I heard the handsome notes of a whip-poor-will
  As the darkness closed day's door.

I tasted the honey in a clover head;
  I caught a breath of the roses wild;
And as I felt the depth of the moss on a rock,
  The old bitter world turned mild.

The sun and the clouds played a game of tag.
  The breeze in the trees sang its song.
While a mocking bird played follow the leader
  The music of the brook played on.

I beheld the glory of the sovereign God,
  In the creation made by his hand.
I know of his power and majesty,
  By looking at the sky and the land.

In seven days God created it all.
  All the wonders that your eyes can see.
For thousands of years God's been designing -
  O how beautiful Heaven must be!

Daniel W. Gault

My Friend

The day that I first saw him, he was standing there alone,
On the corner of First and Second with his hair all messed and
blown.

He never said a word to me, he just turned to look and smile,
His clothes were ragged, torn and wet as though he'd traveled
many a mile.

But the cheerfulness with which he looked upon this world of woe,
Just made me stop and wonder what made up his heart and soul.

I watched him as he stood there on the corner of the street,
As he never gave a scornful look at the people he would meet.

But always gave a smile that would make them smile at him,
As they went gaily down the street with bewilderment of him.

Then just the other day I learned about that man,
Who was just a wayfaring traveler led by God's almighty hand.

And when I look back upon this scene, I know he had a friend,
Who would keep him safe and sound until his journey's end.

And I wondered if you have a friend who keeps you safe all day,
Who watches and will guide you through every step of your way.

Eldonna Small

"On Wings Of Eagles"

On wings of Eagles may I fly through the air,
On wings of Eagles without despair;
The wind is like friends, of whom I care,
To find such loving things as I may dare.

May life be rewarding, all in all,
And pick us up as we may fall;
Here's a little something to show how I feel,
All through life's great ordeal.

On wings of Eagles may I shed,
The little heartaches as I go to bed;
Believing and feeling, and trusting too,
To always find something new.

As the journey seems longer,
All I do is ponder;
About the Heavens,
And the things 'bout yonder.

As I look upon life's memories,
The feeling abyss is in the trees;
Talking and writing of things I do,
Letting people know that I care too!

Brian N. Eicher

Keep Christ In X'mas

Keep Christ in X'mas and we'll have love
On X'mas day he was sent from above
Christmas trees and lights are fine
But we should keep Christ on our mind.

Christmas is a day we should be glad
We received the best gift we ever had,
Our Lord and savior was born this day
He's the one who died and took our sins away.

Christmas is happiness, X'mas is joy
On this day Mary brought forth a great baby boy,
When he was born, he had no where to lay his head
The people at the Inn wouldn't give him a bed.

Santa Claus is ringing his jingle bells
But this is the story I have to tell,
Jesus is soon to come again I hear
Have a Merry X'mas and a Happy New Year.

Erviateen Lawrence

Miracles

I believe in miracles, and maybe you do too!
Once I thought it all hogwash, but now I know it's true
There is a God who cares for us
and watches over all
and tends to all our problems
No matter large or small
There is but One God up above
Who hears our every prayer
He will not let us go astray
Or travel off the narrow way
He's always present; always there
He sees and answers every prayer
We may not always like the answer
But The Great Physician knows what's best
And in His Heart and in our minds
He puts us to a test
Faith, courage, trust and love
Belief above them all
If one possesses all these traits
In God, he will stand tall.

Eleanor C. Janackas

The Age Of Becoming

Who would have thought that I would become this way.
Once it was mud pies and kickball I played.
My cooking abilities have drastically changed,
and somewhere my physical being has been rearranged.
Now there is new meaning in each children's book,
life's richest lessons appear the deeper you look.
The bandages that comforted my skinned up knees,
for a broken heart, provide no ease.
To every want and desire the answer was NO,
that hasn't changed no matter how old I grow.
Those dreaded time outs and naps were out of the question,
But with each passing age, I think it's a great suggestion.
Dreaming to drive used to occupy my mind.
Now I wish for a chauffeur. Oh how divine!
I used to play doctor, house and cook,
little did I know reality betook.
Gazing into this mirror of dismay,
Who would have thought I would become this way.

Brenda Lee Sasa

Ode To A Bomb

My life's ticking away, like a bomb with a clock.
One day it will blow, but it won't be a shock.
For I built the Bomb with my fear and delay.
Tools that will haunt me, so I wait, and I pray.

Because I believe in the Bomb - I know its full power.
Still, I trifle with time, hour after hour.
I wait for Godot, though it's only a play.
I rehearse every scene as the clock ticks away.

I know the clock's setting, don't ask me the time.
It will blow any day now - I know, I built, it's mine.

I'd so love to run from the force of the blast.
Leaping forward in inches away from my past.
Still I wait for some sign that might move me at last.

I know why I'm here, and it's not building bombs.
Still the ticking grows stronger, the waiting lasts longer.
I stand in my space, detonator in hand, and I wait, and I
wait...AND!?

The question is now; which force will last?
A desire to live - or a Bomb with a blast?
Only I know the answer - I wrote this play.
Time's a gift or a weapon, when you clock in every day.

Clare Sullivan

The Family

The family is truly a remarkable institution
    One like no other - It has no substitution
It is the backbone, the support, the rooted base
    That gives us the strength to run this human race
With all that life hands us, Without any certain terms
    Family is the one bond who is always concerned
I don't know what I would do without mine-
    Do you know what you would do?
I "Thank God" on my knees every night that I don't have to
    I'm talking immediate, extended, adopted and all -
A family is a gift from God - through good, through bad,
    simply put - through it all.
God teaches us AGAPE - to love one another unconditionally,
    unselfishly, and to be true
He gave us one another, let's hold on -
    the promise is the rainbow -
    have faith, He'll carry us through.

Fonda E. Curry-Greenhill

We Sisters Three

One winter - one spring - one fall
One little - one average - one tall
Brown eyes - hazel eyes - and green
One country - one city - one in-between.
Loving nature - dogs - and family
Detesting injustice - greed or inhumanity
Strong as steel - when we need to be
Giving strength to the one - facing adversity.
Parents - who come from strong seasoned stock
Grandparents - like shepherds - tending their flock
Wishing to all - peace and serenity
These things we share - we sisters - three.

Dana Purcell Morris

Breath Of Life

    As each day passes into the Future,
one may ponder ...
How long will this breath of mine continue?

    Our true hope is that however long that
time May be ...
That each breath is given and taken
in a thankful way.

    How unconscious our breath does seem...
If we only give thought, think of the
dream ...

    To feel and know the Breath of Life...
Is to respect what is given and not
earned.

John H. Roberson Jr.

Parable

Two roads there are in Life -
One broad, one narrow.

The broad road is downhill - smooth and pleasant,
choked with a crowd of happy travelers,
moving heedlessly
toward their final destination.
Toward what?

The narrow road, a mere path, is barely discernible
with few souls on it.
Toiling uphill,
they strive against a contrary wind
threatening to overcome them as they struggle
toward Truth and Light.

Elvira Van Orman

One Small Life

dedicated to those who lived though never born
One small life in a womb of a thousand.
One small hand reaching out for life.
One small tear on his tiny, little cheek.
One small cry of pain.

Two small hands, two tiny feet.
One small nose so finely shaped.
One small fist grasping out for breath.
One small cry of pain.

Can't you see he's really in there?
Can't you tell that he's alive?
Can't you feel his little heart beating?
How can you say that he's not living?

Two little eyes that will never see the light.
Two little feet that will never walk.
One little mouth that will never talk.
One little heart stilled to beat no more.

Angela Wycoff

Caliban At Sunset

I stood with a man, and we watched the sun set
one summer afternoon
The indomitable ball of flame
was retiring for the night
The sky was ablaze
with a thousand different shades
of red, and yellow, and orange
And soon the sun reached the point
Where it would soon sink below the horizon
And vanish from sight
And among the wonderful colors, all of which
I could not name,
The man who I watched all this with
turned to me, and said:
"I say,
doesn't that sunset remind you
Of a slice of underdone roast beef?"

Jason Bauer

"Hearts Of Compassion"

Hearts of compassion
One-to-one
Moments share…
Encouragement given.
Looks of hope
Elusive visions of
Strength amidst circumstances in a Homeless
Shelter.

Genelle M. Harrison

Rainbows

What are rainbows?
Only arcs of color in the sky?
Why, Oh why do you suppose?
It must rain, before they show, are they shy?

A promise from God, rainbows bring
No rain or flood will destroy the earth
To Noah, He did sing
Showers and storms bring refreshing new birth

Bright colors of joy from an arc so high
God sends His love and a promise so true
Rainbows glow, it's just God's smile and a hi
I'll keep my promise I made to you

Carol A. Sikorski

So Many Times I Have Felt Like…

So many times I have felt like crying,
only because of my fear of dying.
My fear that one day I would crumble
and everyone would see me take a downward tumble.
So many times the tears did fall
when I was forced against the wall.
I felt like a tower crumbling,
all that anyone could see was me tumbling.
I felt that one day and one day only is what I needed,
so I could actually make a warning that could be heeded.
I will regain my strength and gather my pride.
I will need just a few true and good associates on my side,
then the need for crying will subside.
I will no longer need to hide,
my fear of dying will pass away,
because I will have strength for each day.
I will let the anger pass and the hopelessness,
I will gladly do my very best.
Instead of feeling like crying,
I will feel like flying.

Ethel S. Locklear

No Second Chances

We have but one life to live.
Only one path is the right way.
I have traveled down many roads
And have back-tracked my way
Only to come to the cross-roads again.
One chance is all we've got.
Once you've gone too far on the wrong road
And have slipped off the edge and are hanging by sheer might,
There's nothing to do but cry out into the darkness.
All you've ever wanted was peace of mind
And a smooth pathway to an open door,
But nothing's ever so easy.
You'll stumble and suffer confusion and agony.
You'll wish you could just run away and hide,
But don't waste your life crying.
Try every road you can,
Because once your time is up
You can't go back to find your way.
There are never any second chances.

Heidi A. Linton

Troy

Fallout all about in solstice we reveal
Only Venus breaks the rules in a backward orbit steal
From silent Ozma satellites elliptic crypteloign
Tinted iron rust photograph like evidence of Troy

Fiery time heaven time removed from all of this
A changeling of realities perceived from an abyss
And the ghosts who break the silence may truly wish to speak
Not as with the ones once forced to trust and truth so bleak

A sanctuary posted in my image or exile
Erik's fifth reintroduced confusion reconcile
Trying to trap the Chicoan bat on every Autumn's eve
How often sing imagining still no finer steve

Proem Brother Rain and Sister Gemini
All the burnings in control acquit this thief of fire
In ambience a silent myth like the day you came to town
So many times he's thought of this light rain still finds the ground

A world of summer thunder found leviathan dream lost
Artifact's intentional world ecstatic nightmare crossed
His blood sincerely vanishing give way to fear eloign
His tinted iron rust photograph like evidence of Troy

Doc LaTrec

The Red Rose

The red rose in summer,
Opens her arms at dawn,
To watch the sun rise.

At dusk in fall,
She closes early,
And opens with sparkles of frost in her hair.

In winter she shuts herself up tight,
And sleep through the long snow storms.

The red rose in spring,
Once again slowly opens her arms sleepily at dawn,
Then she stands up to stretch in the sun.

Jennifer Firmin

Being Adopted

Are you thinking of me now,
Or am I just a figure of the past?
Do I mean anything to you now,
Or did you just get rid of me and that was that?

I think about you every now and then,
Always wondering if you feel the same.
Do you ever think that you would want to see me,
Or am I the one who is to blame?

How come you did not keep me with you,
That question runs through my head every day.
If I ever get a chance to see you,
What could I possibly say?

I'm not mad at you for giving me up
So please do not take this wrong,
It is that I just want to meet you so bad,
And I have to wait for so long.

Desiree Freels

Just You And Me In Silence

We could start a conversation,
    or fall into endless meditation.
        just you and me in silence.

We could extinguish the flickering candle flame,
    and try to make the darkness tame,
        or mock the devil 'till he's wallowing in shame.
        just you and me in silence.

Throw open the windows, the shutters, the blinds,
    let the air flow in and fill our minds,
        with thoughts of where the river winds.
        just you and me in silence.

We could start a new religious cult,
    and lace it thick with tender fault,
        or simply take it with a grain of salt.
        just you and me in silence.

Consuelo M. Ayes

Inside Out

How well we hide the feelings we feel,
on the outside we appear to be made of steel!

Our troubles, or sorrows, we hide them so well.
Crying on the inside, but no one can tell.

Sometimes the sadness strains to come out,
it hurts so bad you just want to shout!

Holding it all back, tied it with a rope,
bound with a chain, surely there is hope!

The world as we knew it will never be the same.
Turning inside out might release all this pain.

Carolyn See

Dark Charm

It's supposed to bring happiness and lovely treasures,
Our worth as a person it does measure.
It gets in your head and controls the will,
For it people will steal and kill.
It sneaks into the soul and controls the mind,
Of a once good person, giving and kind.
It will grasp your heart and destroy your love,
Either by abundance or lack thereof.
It's a powerful cold evil, dark and gray,
To have, some, their souls they pay.
We need it to live, to survive, exist,
But its deceiving charm some can't resist.
It leads and controls those who are to protect,
In their hands we did trust, now face neglect.
Some say it's what makes the world go 'round
But most say it brings them down,
I'd say it's the cause for the world's huge frown!

Dawn M. Kilgore

INNER DEPTH

Twisting in the hands which seem to clench us, and restrict from
ourselves, the inner peace which each of us inevitability
harboring within.

Not knowing the consequences which are irreversible and seemly
fall ahead of us, only to torture and torment our souls who we
have opened up so often to bear all.

Open to give an everlasting truth from one heart to another, but
receiving only a pit of darkness so deep it seems to never end.

How strange the human spirit seems to take on an ever so
illuminating figure of phenomenal iridescent wholeness. Numinous
to some who open up their souls, alienated by most due to fear.
Covered up by corrupt mindless, unforgiving demons which try to
surface at our consciousness, struggling to escape a world of
isolation.

Let's try and integrate our separate entities into one through
the help of our savior, our true selves. Tap into a world that has
been long forgotten which may empower enigmatic portals entering
the light of everlasting love and peace. .

Dottie Pohlmann

My Heavenly Father

My heavenly Father called me one day
Out of a life of sin and much dismay
Teaching me how to submit and obey
To his commandments each passing day
Through many trials and many tribulations
My heavenly father allows me to see him
In each situation
Oh the blessing I receive and the peace I enjoy
Knowing I have fellowship with my blessed Lord.

Gwendolyn Robinson

Life's Valleys

He'll go with me through the valleys,
over mountains that seem so high.
When He's standing there beside me,
I feel as though I could fly.

He'll make a way where there isn't one,
smooth paths that seem so rough.
With Him life's valleys can be made easier,
without Him they can be pretty tough.

So, who is this person I speak of,
who else on earth could it be,
But my Lord and Savior,
it's Jesus Christ you see.

Judy Reynolds

His Wish ... My Guilt

A strange foreboding
overtook me once more
as I entered through
the Crematorium door.

I gasped, my body stiffened,
I couldn't believe my eyes;
they grasped the cover, tilted the board
to the roar of the fire and my muffled cries.

Aware of the heat, I trembled
as the flames engulfed my man,
in the matter of a second
the cremation had began.

We were not forewarned how
unfeeling the ritual would be;
my son, his wife and I will
live with this burning memory.

Oh, my God this was his request,
yet I feel so guilty;
when it's my time — no witnesses,
please — no family.

Hardy Reese

Survivors

Trials and tribulations
Pain and hell
We've been through them all,
and then we rise a different person.
Our Psyches are forever changed.
and our emotions subdued.
The tears dry up,
and the fists unball.
Our hearts beat a normal beat,
and we breathe a regular breath.
Our souls climb out of their small cocoon,
and reclaim lost territory.
Out of it all
a beautiful creature flies
The SURVIVOR.

Jeff White

Gift From Above

Through so many years of my lonesome life,
Pain, suffering and emptiness fill my heart,
I sometimes wonder why me, O Lord, why?
When will things start being all right?

True love these days is really hard to find,
Don't despair, I hear someone whisper in my mind,
'Cause the Lord above is ever so kind,
In your darkest night he won't be far behind.

I've almost lost hope in meeting someone like you,
'Cause it's a rarity to find a person of virtue,
But I waited for God to give his blessings anew,
To two people like us who are lovingly true.

Gone and forgotten is my lonely past,
The rays of sunshine now brighten my path,
Now that we've met I hope we'll never be apart,
May God bless us with love that will forever last.

Grizelda Nomorosa

Candlestick

Slender and swirled like a vanilla cone
Pale like the fluttering snow owl
Standing within its holder
On the very dining table for all visitors to see

With its flame aglow
Red-orange like the setting sun
Flickering in the chilly wind
Its gleam smiles brightly
Casting many shadows on the wall

As it drips like teardrops
Clustering like the flowing lava
It forms many hands below
Stretching outwards at the holder's base
Dotting the candlestick like the morning dew

How I often marvel at its glory on the many of Christmases
The beauty it brings to me
With its elegance against the christmas tree

Beauty for what its hold, pure and magnificent to behold
I love that little candlestick for its warmth and gleam
And the happiness it brings

Debby Kaulili

A Little Something

Here's a little something
Part of me that's rarely seen
This that I give, I hide away
Only shared when skies are clear
and the sun shines upon our smiles
It's been nurtured; growing deep
I've learned to let it flourish
with your guidance and patience
Now its intensity shall burn through,
even when the heavy rains are washing away our tears
From daughter to mother;
From friend to friend
I give you this
Unselfishly
Unconditionally
my love

Joanna P. Basile

"Restraint"

Restraint of fear
Restrained by fear
Fear of pain
Pain of fear
Fear of love
Restraint

Fear the pain of joys undone
Fear of love, relationship
Fear of loss, far behind
Fear the pain, love long ago
Fear the joy, life as it passes you by
Fear the loss of laughter still lost in your eye
Fear the pain, loneliness between your sheets
Taste the pain, teardrops rolling down your cheek
Fear to dream, insomnia when alone in bed
Fear to stay awake, voices in your head
Fear to touch another, in fear your heart will break
Entering a relationship, a chance you will not take
In fear of love
Restraint.

Gregory D. Smith

Friends

Along a woodland path, meandering
Past oaks, through stands of lofty evergreens,
Shadows separate and merge on dappled
Cushion of decaying leaves and tangled
Roots; friends, their silent odysseys entwined.

A sunny summer afternoon, a near-
Deserted stretch of beach; shoeless across
The sand, bared feet tasting earth; then childlike
In roiling surf, hand-in-hand and laughter
On the breeze; good friends, you and I perhaps.

Across a table set for two; sharing
Good times, corners of separate worlds and
Contagious smiles; eyes holding eyes, gently,
As lovers would hold hands. Friend giving time
To friend, and understanding, patiently.

Shelter from chill-winter's breath, spring's cleansing
Tears, a parting place for friends; a doorway
Lit against dark night; a place where shared time
Ends. Here pasts and futures meet; here hurried
Words seek to secure fleeting memories.
James F. Dwyer

City Dog-Country Dog

I was born a city dog,
Pedigreed, guaranteed and all the ritz,
Wearing little bows, eating liver in bits.

Such a fancy city dog,
Powder puffed, perfume fluffed and all in style.
L'il old ladies would pet me and smile.

I remember city dogs,
Avenues, high-rise views and all the treats.
I remember naps on satin sheets.

Then I turned country dog,
Learned to fight, earn my right and all that stuff.
Life in the woods has made me tough.

Now I am a country dog.
A little dirt doesn't hurt, I learned to dig.
I bark in a yard that's really big.

Love being a country dog.
I see the moon, tree a 'coon and play so rough.
I don't miss my powder puff.
Joyce Clark Butler

Roots

He stares with his cold eyes
Penetrating the soul
Angered by his lust
Who does he really love? Himself
Looking at his family from afar
Caring for no one
I do care for him
He pushes me away
Everyone away, Why?

Seeming to be lonely
Lonely from having no family
Remember who gave you life
Cutting the roots that fed you for so long
Death
My arms open, are his only answer for help
He does not know
Blind by lust
Angered by Materialism, I love him
Who does he really love?
The question he can only answer, Time
Joseph N. Prunty

Ode To The Puffs

We used to be the bowery boys
Pens and pencils were our toys
When you came to our domain
You needed permission to remain;

Now we are known as the powder puffs
Some wear skirts and some wear cuffs
Our choice of weapons no one knows
We use max factor to powder our nose;

Our toughest quality we can tout
Is for Lawrence to give you mouth to mouth
If not stout of heart and strong of lung
You may face the wrath of fung;

So walk softly when in our space
or you may meet Lawrence face to face
Heaven forbid to those that do
Oh Lord, I would rather come see you.
Harry E. Lenz

Traffic

Cars, cars everywhere
People sit blankly looking and stare
Wondering what the heck is the delay
God... What a way to start the day!

Sitting in the traffic I watch the clock
Knowing every minute, my pay they will dock.
Stuck here wondering what has gone wrong
Pushing buttons to find my favorite song.

What is the reason for the stall
Which makes this traffic seem to crawl
Deciding what lane is moving faster
I'm in the wrong lane and it's a disaster.

I never see what caused the jam
That made everyone's brakes slam.
A woman applying mascara on her eye
Probably hit a man putting on his tie.

If the androids would only learn to steer
Hell... We could be out of here!!
Glenda Bizzell

"My Dad"

An amazing person, my dad,
Places we went, good times we had.

We went on rides where my mom wouldn't go,
It was very rare that my dad said no.

With homework he helped me,
A greater dad there could not be.

I loved him with all of my heart,
It hurt me when we had to part.

He was amazing just by being my dad!
Justen L. Himes

A Band Of Gold

A life together held by a band of gold
Precious moments as we both grow old.
So many clouds were filled with sorrow
Only brought in sunshine for our many tomorrows
A loving smile - a gentle embrace
Has made life easier for us to face
A love held together by a band of gold
Will only bloom as we both grow old.
Dorothy Cox

Ghost

She walks so softly upon these tombs of death-
Placid strides and so respectfully,
As if she'd seen or even knew me
This beauty rosy like my fingertips,
Upon this saddened earth she sits
Gazing at the carvened stone,
There's nothing here, we're all alone
Her vision so distinct to me,
Yet she can only wonder of the face to see.
It's all but a dreadful mystery
And oh, it bruises the tender heart of thee.
You perform before the clutching eye of death,
Furtively praying to remain unknown,
Against his breath
With hopeless tears you abandon my home,
The only place I'd see you roam

Bahar Ramezani

The Strike

I traveled to the stadium, right before the game, didn't recognize the
players, didn't recognize a name. I said, "What is the problem?
What's the matter here?" Then I asked a vendor and he said while
shedding tears, "I recall there was a time when money didn't matter.
Baseball was only about a pitcher and a batter."

I thought about his statement. I thought about it hard, then I opened
up a pack of brand new baseball cards. I was looking for the
All-stars, that triumphed just last year. Then I remembered the
Strike, and my ears began to hear.....

The sound of yelling vendors, the sweet crack of a bat, I found my
ticket stub and right there and then I sat.

A couple hours later, the home team won the game. I said, "I know
it's baseball, but this was really lame."

Didn't recognize the players, didn't recognize a name, without this
pastimes' favorites, the game's just not the same.

Erik Henry Belcarz

Until Your Last Moment

As your life runs slowly away and I beg God
"Please Lord, let her stay"
I promise during my lament
That I will be with you until your last moment
And as your last moment quickly draws near
My mind starts running and I can't think clear
I remember you as a child, I remember the fun we shared
The laughter, the pain, the everlasting care
I remember you as a teen, I remember the parties and fights
The joys and the sorrows, and the endless, sleepless nights
I remember you as an adult, I remember the fears we had
Of the future and present and how they would make us sad
I remember the 'olden days
The days of rocking away in memories of life, of love
And together their summaries and now I'm back in the present
And my promise I have kept because I was here for our
last moment.

Doug Mason

Wish

Undressed the wolf he was in sheep's clothing
Revealed the push that has been shoving
Found your devil with angel eyes
Discovered the hunger that can never disguise
Fear what you wish for it may come true
For now you see me and I see you

Jeremy Brown

A Precious Loan

Your children are not only your own, but they are from God, a
precious loan.
So happy, bright and gay are they, but so quickly He can take
them away.
Give them all your knowledge and love and teach them of God
who's up above,
For He looks down and shines His light, and makes everything
below look bright.
Sometimes you may think you've failed, don't give up it's just a
long trail.
Take time out for your children each day, get together as a family
and pray.
Go outside and play ball with your son, play dress up with your
daughter and have lots of fun.
For soon they will be grown up you know, and it will be the two
of you like it was long ago.
Then it will start all over with them you see, so make sure
you teach them how it should be.
You can only gain interest on this kind of loan, just remember
your children are not only your own.

Carolin Linton Harris

The Fading

The feelings now soar inside me,
Pride, hope, pity, and jealousy.

What happened to the little person,
The child.

I can no longer run from my problems,
The backyard provides no sanctuary,
It no longer shelters me
from the fears and harsh real world questions.

There are only more faded lines,
The black and white are no longer,
There is only gray.

No, I am not old,
Still, I am no longer a carefree child.

I will always have the memories,
The lines may fade, but not the pictures in my heart,
Of true freedom and endless hours of fun.

As long as I have these,
Childhood will never fade from my heart.

Jenny Hayden

Remember Me

One day you were here,
One second and you were gone.
The only friend I had,
You left like the dawn.

Taken without mercy,
Not able to say goodbye.
I was never able to see it,
That you could just go off and die.

I wanted to be with you,
Just to hold your hand.
To say it would be alright,
This was not my plan.

Now I can't even see your grave,
To bring flowers to your tomb.
To just come home one day, and all I heard was a boom.

I will love you forever, until the end of time.
I don't think I will ever, get over this vicious crime.

Every time I glimpse at your picture, or look out over the sea,
I will always hear you calling, calling, Please, Please,
Remember Me. . .

Erin Scanlon

"A Mother And Her Son"

From the time of conception I carried you,
protected you and loved you.
How proud I am of you, my son, for all the
things that you are and yet to become.
God gave you to me to raise, and now he
has called you back home.
How can there be grief in my throat and
happiness in my soul?
For, I had once delivered you and now you
have delivered me...

Debbra A. Lutze

The Ole Tennessee

As the years go by and the seasons change
Proudly flows the river like one long chain
Over hill over dale through the crook at moccasin bend
Its waters flow to the ocean on without end
Its water flows on to withstand time
But gets better with age just like a good wine
Silently and proudly flows the water by me
That river I know as the ole TENNESSEE

Greg Brackett

Pieces

Living in the garden with the Red Queen
Pruning her roses, protecting her heart,
Losing pieces, pieces of Me.
Holding court with the other Jesters
Providing the laughter, drying her tears
Losing pieces, pieces of Me.
Invisible in the Palace with the Black King
Nodding in agreement, questioning not one thing
Losing pieces, pieces of Me.
Surviving in this setting with the Blue Princess
Perfecting the process, appearance shows success
Losing pieces, pieces of Me.
Crying for our Kingdom with the Purple Prince
Sleighing the Dragons, providing a defense
Losing pieces, pieces of Me.
Rising with the Sun over the Palace walls
Flies the Princess of Pain, fighting for her life
Looking for pieces, pieces of Me.

JoAnne E. Yost

"The Way"

Everybody's moving. Silence is distant...
Pulled in front and pushed behind,
  "I know not the way."

There's Someone calling, amidst my tears and pains.
A savior perhaps? Or another tempter?
It's all so confusing!
Mind-blowing tactics and old jive emerge
With new will, brighter hope, much faith, strong belief
I must still reach for the inevitable.
I must experience all of life. "I'm going somewhere."

Loose the chains. Take the burdens from my back.
I will not harm you.
Let us render our differences to prayer...

What's that...the Same Voice calling?
  This time-nearer, clearer—It whispers gently,
  "My Child, proceed unshackled...
  I am the Way."
Hand in hand, I'll walk proudly at peace,
Where He leads me,
I will follow.

Jennifer Steptoe Dutton

Ocean Time

The passionate push of the pounding waves
  purrs my heart in peaceful ways.

Sea gulls hover, dive and chase,
  over sparkling sand and foaming lace.

Mountains majestic guard and grace
  the changing complexion of nature's face.

The tears of the earth ne'er subside
  the ocean's flow goes rushing by;

And then the wind no longer flies
  and mountains no longer scrape the skies ...

For there is no reason for nature's rhyme,
  the ocean's rhythm erases time.

Brian Bossetta

Life's Plans

The clouds roll above the open land
Pushed by God's great, powerful hand.
What the clouds bring is only a guess,
Because it is beyond your control more or less.
You hope that they bring a gentle rain
To help ease the pain of sorrows past,
But if they bring thunder, the pain will ever last.
The gentle rain will nourish new seeds
And help them grow brave and tall,
But the thunder will not help at all.

The clouds roll above the land,
Pushed by His great, powerful hand. They darken where we live,
And you hope that they will give a break from reality.
If only fate could be broken,
But soon learn that it is a token,
Of the life that you live.

The clouds do roll across the land
And although they are beyond your control,
Reality is not etched in scroll. It can still be altered,
By the things that we believe and know.

Jason W. Williams

Happiness

Happiness, a frail and fragile something,
quickly without warning, it takes wing.
So finger it gently, dear one.
For like a bubble it's soon done.
A gay, bright bubble soaring high
so far above the world, it could not die.
Yet by some unseen hand it shattered -
not remembering its beauty mattered.
So happiness comes, your heart grows light,
only to be laden with the coming of night.
Reach for it, clutch it tightly to your breast,
watch over it, never take rest.
Hold it to its sunshine - Love -
watch the rainbow from above
play through your bubble of joy.
But remember, it's only a fragile toy.
Hearts lived and grew from it -
hearts have bled and died from it.
So hold it, lose it, and remember after it's gone
its memories will help you live on and on.

Annilee Hendrick

The Pain Of Love

Soft and gentle
Quiet and sound
Love is so beautiful, from all around
Cruel and uncaring
Sorrow and shame.
All in one day, full of pain
You'll hear a shatter
As his heart breaks to pieces
When you could have told him;
"I love you dearest!"
But you choose to say nothing
as he walks away sobbing
And all of a sudden your heart starts
   to throbbing
As you realize sadly that he loved you so.

Amanda Janet Williams

Once Beautiful

As time goes by, your hair does fade
quite often like your mind

The simple things you used to do
are only memories left behind

The eyes that seemed the bluest blue, no sky could quite compare
now seem to be a faded pool, with glasses covered there

The smile you wore upon your face, once beautiful with surprise
is now just an occasional thing, that bring wrinkles about your eyes

Elsie Salour

Fire On The Lake

Fire on the lake,
  quivers gently,
    shines brightly,
      with soft ripples flowing rhythmically
        like a mild wind
          in the summer.
Fire on the lake,
  dances under the sun,
    flames sparkling like jewels
      on an island where no wind breezes.
        A path of fire,
          slowly fades away,
      until the streams of gold,
    turn cold...
        And the fire dies,
          while the moonlight
      spangle glistens
beneath the
  sunless
    sky.

Aileen Lee

In Memory Of My Grandmother

G: Is for the grand person she was.
R: Is for all the respect, and understanding she gave to
    me and taught me.
A: Is for the angel she was.
N: Is for all the wonderful nights we spent together.
D: Is for the diamond, 'cause she was always a shining.
M: Is for mother for she was my mother's mother.
O: Is for the only grandmother I knew.
T: Is for all the trick or treaters that came to her house
    on halloween.
H: Is for heaven where we all now call her new home.
E: Is for the down to earth person she was, and also E is
    for the wonderful name of Elva.
R: Is for all the remembrance I will always have of her.

Irene Hazel Courreges Lindsay

A Childhood To Remember

As parents go - you did just fine
Raising me and those sisters of mine

We could've been worse and we could've been better
If only we had followed your advice to the letter

That advice was meant to help not harm
And things have worked just like a charm

We didn't have much money but still we had riches
Even though sometimes we acted like witches

We didn't understand at the time
How hard it was to earn a dime

Sometimes we got second best
But somehow we turned out better than the rest

As kids we wanted to grow real fast
Now that's all in our past

Today we're supposed to be grown
And we all have homes of our own

We would never have gotten this far
If we didn't have you as our guiding star

Your security and love was given at no cost
And I have "A CHILDHOOD TO REMEMBER," I've never lost.

Cleda D. Liewald

Conflict Hang-up of Victory's Defeat

He travels on, soft, through the bubbly mist. His clothing is ragged and damp. His mind is upset by the horrors he's seen as he stole through the enemy camp. All the fragments of battle, a bloody parade, that screams through the streets of the night, as a tribute to death, with a sinister glow which applauds catastrophic delight.

Now misery sings through the wastes of the land, but of happiness never a sound. What once was the home of a marvelous throng is recast into burial ground. Sweet sorry flows thickly, embellishing all, false prophet of eternal cure. Tomorrow is certain, it's needless to ask, "Will there be an end to this war?"

Jay J. Paris

"Mother"

So young, fragile, a sight to behold—
Resplendent in radiance, her beauty to form.

Glow of life beyond compare—
Warmth of love for us to share.

Nurtured, fed with bosom care, things that mother's do—
Within her she knew some of us would protect her too.

Gentle in nature most of the time—
Until anger or hurt stirred within.

Her wrath was fulfilled, heavy of heart, energy spent—
We looked at her with eyes that lied,
And said that we repent.

Destroying my love, my gift to you—
Can you not see where you've gone wrong?
How long can you torture me? How long can this go on?

I lied, I loved her—She is my friend—
I give my word to the very end.

In sadness, in truth, for all it's worth—
My heart cries out—Why did I do this?
To Mother Earth.

Edward Metzler

A Rainbow For You

Red,
Red is the soft velvety feel of the rose petal
As it sits in an orange vase
Orange,
Orange is the vase that stands on the table
With the yellow sun shining through the window
Yellow,
Yellow is the sun shining down on the green grass
of the lawn
Green,
Green is the grass that acts like a blanket
For the blue-jeaned girl.
Blue,
Blue is the color of the girl's jeans as she
picks small purple flowers.
Purple,
Purple is the color of the small flowers
she picks for you
She wants you to know she is thinking of you

Jessy Goergen

To Walter

As you upon life's adventure embark
Remember that all you do in life
Will be of much importance to me
Whether or not you finally make your mark.

Nevertheless I pray earnestly
That you will seek after all truths
And strive with all your might
To ever live righteously

Look back upon happy memories of childhood
Since for you everything was not
Done that it was our desire to do
But, I believe we did all we could.

To prepare you was our intention
For that great test of life
Upon which you are now entering
To, seek and find that great adventure.

Jessie Williamson

"Searching Love"

She lived to see his smile,
She found it all worthwhile.
For him her heart swelled with love,
to her he was an angel from above.

She longed to touch his face,
and in his heart have a place.
She didn't even know his name,
but her life could never be the same.

Since the first time she saw him,
She longed for she and he to be them.
She wished to feel his lips upon her own,
but she knew her love would never be known.

She knew not how he could be found,
She searched all around.
But, she knew their love could never be,
because she saw him on the T.V. screen.

She could never love another man,
in her search she ran and ran.
She would search for him her entire life,
or at least until she was his wife.

Joey N. Harris

Sonnet I

When to the deep recesses of shadows I hide,
remembrance of things past comes to mind.
There was a time when wars had died
and everyone was gentle and kind.
When through old woes came new life.
Alas, I fear what the future might bring.
Peace alone would suffice.
When wasteful war seems never-ending
the zealous priest comes to pray.
Yet, during these brutish times
a shimmer of faith lies fray.
So, on my death bed remember thy rhyme;
death is not a commodity and wars have all gone down,
but what really have you found?

Christine Hirai

Memories

Never good at releasing, the one that I love
reminiscing back in time, of things thereof
wondering if he loved me, in the same special way
wanting to turn back time, to that special day
Life goes on and on, it ends so very fast
Hang onto good memories, try to make them last
Looking up at the sky, I see stars, sun and moon
Will the one that I love, return to me soon
My heart is all broken, sorrow I will not show
behind closed doors, I let my tears all flow
Was my love not good enough, for him I lost
doing it all over again, no matter what the cost
Live your life to the fullest, every minute of the day
Someone may steal your love, you'll feel the same way

Catherine M. Warner

The Beautiful Black Woman

She walks like a fox, with her head up high,
Respect is what she's demanding, as she passes by.
Like a word of honesty, this woman is hard to keep,
For the man who's worthy of her, will be at her feet.

Deprived of her culture, but not of her womanhood,
Sexy and sweet, she knows she looks good.
Sharp as a knife, ready to take control,
Approaching her destiny, small, yet very bold.

Beauty's her special quality, which shines about,
Bestowed within her is a nature inside and out.
She doesn't need makeup, she has a natural tan,
A scent like flowers, she could catch any man.

This woman is an individual of pride and dignity,
But in the home, she displays sensitivity and finicky.
To sum it up, she's not a woman of the streets,
But yet of the soul and no one can compete.

Ayanna Monique Robert

A Sonnet

The poet Homer once compared the race
of leaves to man. The sun, he said, each spring
Brings forth new life, and with it warms the face
of earth. The buds' new generations cling
With fresh born hope to every trembling bough.
And early spring, like to the leaves, brings man
The old, old cycle of rebirth; and now
Do men, as leaves, live out their own short span;
And so with me — my life is in the fall.
My children, though, midsummer strong, alive
With youth and joy, do so dispel the pall
Of many years, I will me to survive.
And now their children, born of love's sweet strife,
Bring heaven's bliss to be, eternal life!

John Loprieno

Baptist Bred

Broad butt women with big brim hats
  rest reverently back on hard humble pews.
Praying over some long gone sin God long forgot.

A less than angelic choir vitalizing an O'Negro spiritual with a
  juke-joint jounce sways before me.

Reverend, doctor, preacher, pastor Jones moaning about heaven home.
Black hands, wiping black brow on white linen hankies
washed by the blood of the lamb.

"Pass me not o' gentle..."
"Were you there..."
"At the cross."

Hands patting, toes tapping, bottoms bouncing
fans working overtime, in uniformed ushers' hands.

Who said, "Baptist born, and Baptist bred?"
Knew they were a different kind.
Southern. Missionary. Progressive. Free Will And
Independent, a different kind
  those Baptist lead.

JoEllen Rutland

Where Dreams Come From

I believe dreams come from the heart
Right from the very start I knew you were a dream
Come true

The first time I saw you my heart skipped a beat

It was like you came and swept me off my feet without
Even touching me

Is it true- I'm falling in love with you
I believe dreams come from happiness
True love is such sweet bliss
I'll never forget this
The day I met you
When my dream came true.

Danielle Yoder

Untitled

A rosebud reveling in infant days,
Offering dew-kissed petals to the sun;
Marble frost stealing youthful life away,
Winter's cold breath too early has begun.
Spring's brilliant morning, laughing breeze reborn,
Never sees the somber fortress of gray
Drowned by heaven's tears, smothered by the storm.
Selfish Night covets e'en the freshest day.
A clear note of music lingering high,
Gay sound trembling in purity sweet,
Silenced by Eternity drawing nigh,
Stifled by the Universe's heart beat.
No broken hearts can leave behind the pain,
Or take back the child Death has come to claim.

Jessica Harken

Wandering Through Memories

Bowing trees of destiny gently soothe my weary soul-
Shadowing the agonies I thought I had let go-
Another winding mystery before me now unfolds-
Guiding me through yesterdays, to reach the final goal-
Searching through a rainbow to find a new tomorrow-
I give you back the emptiness-
your agony-
your sorrow-

Jacqueline Calp

Marsh Miracle

A stiff white spire,
Rigid in the morning light.
The sun appears;
Zip zip... zip zip zip zip
One by one white strips emerge, curl back;
Green white anthers turn golden in the sun.
A soft spicy scent assails my nostrils.
A spider lily blooms.

Barbara A. Guthrie

Sionann*

Your hair of pitch, your long face gaunt and cool like a gun,
Ripe lips at once arrogant yet childishly petulant - the smooth
  flesh so tender and good to bite,
But it was your animal eyes that told me.
Twin pieces of opaque sea glass, limned with salt and inhuman in
  their knowing;
Volumes spoken in a foreign tongue. An ancient cipher. A standing
  stone.
Are you man or silkie, my Fierce One?
Come, let us shed the clothing of our names and nations,
Lay your feral body next to mine and be my mate in my own land.
We will build a small house by the rocks where the otters play.
I shall hide your furred skin so that you cannot return to the sea,
And we will stride the land like giants you and I;
Only avoiding the coastline, where your people still call for you —
  despairing your loss.

* Gaelic for 'old one'

Dawn M. Barclift

When Hope Died

O' Weeping heart, with twisted dagger-
ripping at my soul
In a prison of darkness, I am surrounded-
no future to behold
Don't shine on me, O' morning sun-
symbol of dawning day
Stop teasing me with hope-
'cause hope has found no way
If suffering is all I live for-
then I am already dead...forever forgotten person,
with emptiness ahead
This unfortunate path of destiny-
seems to be the chosen way
So let me drift into silent slumber-
and never see the rising day
I guess this is my final fate-
the price I have to pay.

Janis Isaac

Collapse

Cry on, you water colored priceless pearl
Rise before my marble words and bow
Conscience shatters your tears into amber ashes
My dark silver-lined heart opens up to let,
Yellow angels look down upon your glowing eyes
Many years dull the cracks in your face
Your skin is gone, now I replace it
Soul blood is mine to drink and waste
Maggoty skulls I leave for your pain
Time is our grave, destiny I watched you dig
We'll fall together in black peace
The after glow will fade into your glossy soul
My cell is gone with your self control
Wish for your concrete country side of graves
I'll sit inside, waiting for collapse

Jody Goldman

The River Of Eternity

Every morning, like a balloon, the sun
  rises high.
Those who inhabit the forest and those who
  take the sky,
Flock to a place called the River of Eternity,
Which flows through the forest and the
  hearts of many.

The peace here is amazing, there's love
  wherever you turn.
Sharing is a way of life; there the hate
  soon burns.
But, like the night, it creeps up to prey
  on the scared and weak,
Their future is uncertain, their life is
  what he seeks.

Only the strong survive near the river
  controlled by men
Because, the hunters like predators search...
  AND THEY WIN.

Courtney Morrow

Stepping Over The Curiosity

Sliding hills   Lands so beautiful
rolling clouds   not staying for long

Bottomless pits   Still no place to hide
deserted jungles   downfalls of rain last too long

Wildlife above   Pollution below
lost in the fight   swirling oceans

Sickening diseases cause no harm   Not even hope for the present
tumbling halos   rustling to find the next
replacement

Horizons line   Below the smog
still there...   lies a new beginning

Irene Cobaugh

War Against Dark Clouds

The sky reminded me of a wild surf
Rolling mightily up on shore.
It churned and boiled with fury wild
And rolled back to sea for more.

It kept up its ferocious behavior
Until the sun broke through
Then slowly it receded into the north
As a gentle southwest breeze blew.

The pompous white clouds emerged from the sun
And marched proudly forward in pursuit.
It looked like a great fleet of snow-white ships
With the lead warship showing the route.

Donna Curran

Hail The Phoenix

The bird was sick, when she fell in the fire
She didn't burn, she just faded away
Everybody mourned the passing of flight
Then her spirit rose, into the night.
The sky was bright, as she flew overhead
Like the moon and the stars, she belonged there
Once she was white, now she glows with a light
Rejoice as in heaven, she's found new life.

Hail the Phoenix, with wings of fire
You fly like the wind, and never grow tired
The day of your suffering, has now come and gone
Hail the Phoenix, she's where she belongs.

Eric Bestland

You Are Aaron

Little boy with sparkling eyes
Rose kissed cheeks and toppled jasmine locks,
You've angel smiles upon your lips.
God-sent gift to soldier son,
You are Aaron,
First born child of first born son.
Blessed by prayers, lifted high
Child of love
Renewal of hope
You came to me from outstretched arms.
A mother's heart left open wide
To share her gift, One Little Boy.
You are Aaron.
God-sent gift to soldier son.
First born child of first born son.

Connie Kay Mader

"My Legacy"

I am master of my soul,
Ruler of my heart,
King of my mind.
To fall in another person's stride
Is like leaving the real me behind.
My mind is subject to change.
But it must be for me to rearrange.
The essence of my soul runs deep,
Its feelings, though, cannot be put to sleep.
My heart can be touched in many ways,
But I must follow its rays.
My soul, mind, and heart,
Are the innermost part of me,
Their thoughts and feelings are to be
My legacy.

Cheryl Lynn Titus

Approval

My son, while walking in the rain
Said, "I don't appreciate the rain,
It hits my face and stings me!"

"Son," said I, "God sends the rain to earth
To make the flowers grow and to make the earth beautiful."

"But Mom, it hurts and stings like a shot."

"I know, but it's only God's way of
saying I love you."

He stopped,
Lifted his hand to his cheek
then looked up towards heaven.
He smiled and said,
"I love you too!"
Then he skipped ahead
out from under the umbrella's protection.

Judith Kariean-Black

Attitude Checked

Now, God gave Paul great latitude,
since He blessed that man with attitude.
From the former Saul, what a bad ole dude,
God changed his oil and threw out the crude.
Piercing through that light, shone love's magnitude,
which replaced Paul's hatred with gratitude.
Even prison bars with their saditude,
couldn't stop Paul singing praises of his gladitude.
Now, in all this history teaches, that even a prude,
can rise above the dull existence known as platitude.
So, if your life is standing in an interlude,
just let God make adjustments on your attitude.

Jeanette Hammond Richards

What The Wind Has To Say

The wind is blowing, whispering into my ear. LOVE it
says over, and over again as I listen to it sway back
and forth again, and again. It keeps telling me LOVE,
LOVE is what it is. LOVE again and again it will be. The
wind keeps on blowing. Stronger, and stronger it gets.
What does it mean, I scream? I'm so confused, I'm so
confused I keep yelling. Tell me! Help me! No one's
There! I scream and scream. No one answers. The wind
keeps telling me, LOVE, LOVE you two will be. I don't
understand, I now start to cry. Why won't you help? I
keep asking. What are you doing to me? It only says
LOVE. What kind of clue is this? I can't comprehend, I
tell the wind. What happened, I'll never know. But
when I think of the wind swaying back and forth,
saying LOVE...... LOVE...... LOVE is what it will be. I can't
help but think it was talking about you and me....

Amber Farney

The Crossroads

While you lay dying with your blood flowing so freely - with the
scent of death surrounding you - the terror building with each
drop that spills - do you feel time slipping away - every second
mocking you - have you made peace with your demons or will they
be waiting for you at the crossroads - is the white light shining
bright or are the gates of hell opening just for you - these
thoughts I had wanted to ask - but you died so quickly - you
taught me a lesson I won't be forgetting - for the next time the
blood flows again and the life force gives way, I will be there
waiting at the crossroads -

Debbie Aissaoui

Sand Castles

With childish haste his chubby hands
Scooped a castle from the sun-kissed sands.
Then with eyes so innocent and wide
He watched the fingers of the incoming tide.
That crept towards him stealthily
He built a wall high around
His spot of hallowed ground
And from a stick his flag did fly
To fling his challenge to the sky.
But the sea splashed upon him playfully
But his castle fell, child like he cried.

With Feverish haste his calloused hands
Dug a fox hole in the bloody sands.
He searched the trees wherein snipers hide.
From a nearby branch his flag did fly.
Flinging his challenge to the sky.
This time the enemy faced the sea.
And swept down upon him screaming bonsi! Bonsi.
He spread his bullets far and wide.
But his strong hold fell. Marine like he died.

June Pickering Moore

The Waves Of Lake Michigan

Gazing outward from the culmination of their rhythmical performances,
Searching the horizon for their beginnings,
Yet captivated by their ever-changing brilliant displays along the way
Each unique in their own rite
Watching as they gather the rays of the sun to blend with
Fleeting rushing shades of blue
Like a kaleidoscope.
Forever changing their patterns as they reflect the heavens above
Relentless in their gifts of variety.
So very captivating to those who find peace - serenity in their
creative yields.

Antonio Sieira

Mother

First, I thank God, for making you the mother of me,
Second, for you encouraging me to be all I can be,

You pulled me up plenty of days, when I could barely crawl,
You had the patience, when I began to scribble and scrawl,

Life, you said, can be filled with joy or full of sorrow,
As the saying goes, live for today, 'cause we can't predict tomorrow,

You said too, keep going forward, never try to turn back,
If you do, it'll be like a needle in a hay stack,

You loved, disciplined and taught to help me grow,
Your love and trust, I appreciate and just want you to know,

So, you see we both are very proud of each other,
Again, I want to thank you God, for making her my mother.

Aneise Brown-Mayo

"Him"

When I look into his dark brown eyes I
see all his heartache, sorrow, misery, anger, and joy.
When I look into his soul I see his most deepest,
darkest, and dangerous secrets.
When I look at his smile I can see that he
has melt thousands of hearts with it.
When I look into his heart I can see that
his heart has been broken by more than one girl.
When I look at his strong muscular arms I can
see that he is not a weakling.
When I look at his hands I can see that he has not
had an easy life.
When I hear his voice I hear the sweetest sound
in the world.
When I look at him I remember that he
is my life support and I would die without him.

Allegra Toll

My Sunshine

I saw the sunrise this morning, but you never had a chance to
   see it or feel the weather.

But then again you and God probably made the sunrise together.

It's the most beautiful sunrise I've ever seen and I know you
   made it just for me.

You always reminded me of the sun, so radiant and warm. You are
   still with me, just in a different form.

Now you're an angel in the heavens above, I pray to God that you
   feel my love.

I love you more than the highest mountain and deeper than the
   deepest sea. Ask dear God to bring you back to me.

A part of me died with you and I will always feel this sorrow.
But please little sister remind me that the sun will rise again
   tomorrow.

Amy Aulicino

Untitled

Our country is great,
So our forefathers have said,
So take a look back instead of ahead.
It's written about truth and honor and glory,
So let's not rewrite it for our own style or story.
So remember these words our forefathers have said,
And guard our document faithfully,
or our country is dead.

Edward J. Szach

A Minute's Worth of Waiting

The days we're together go by so fast, a day
Seems to never last.
But the moment that we're apart,
I feel a hurt deep in my heart.

Even when I know soon we'll be together.
It's like a single minute lasts forever.
When I hear a ring I jump for the phone,
For the simple fact that I don't like being alone.
But I won't be sad, I won't be blue,
I'll think of days with me and you.
You don't be sad, you don't be blue.
Because in a few days again I'll be with you.
You're my love so don't be blue, because my love,
I could never leave you.

The time will pass by so fast,
You won't know two weeks has passed.
Soon we'll be together again, just like it's always been.

Desirae Culver

Better Living

If we would all think before we act,
separate fiction from supposed fact,
I feel the world would be a better place,
and a smile could be on each and every face.

If we could think some about the other guy
instead of lowering, raise him towards the sky.
Remember the lessons taught in sabbath school,
those lessons, known as "The Golden Rule."

If each person on earth did their part
that'd be the beginning of a big start.
If that happened, all hostilities would cease,
for the first time this world would know peace.

Maybe, if we prayed for guidance and some help,
maybe, then we wouldn't hesitate to cry or yelp
for assistance should our burden get so large
to handle, we'd need a great big empty barge.

Whether some burdens are nation wide,
or very small to be kept by your side,
we can all ask God to ease the load,
and an honest peace can be our goad.

Floyd A. Schneider

Precious Memories

As I gaze upon the forest trees,
serenity surrounds me with sweet memories.
Of my beautiful mother so loving and kind,
Her memory I will cherish forever in my mind.

The sounds of nature are all I can hear;
The ripple of the stream so far yet so near.
I could hear my mother's voice echo through the wind;
I cannot see her, I cannot touch her, it comes from within.

I could picture the radiance upon her face,
the sincerity in her eyes.
I want to reach out and touch her,
But then I realize.

She is only a fragment of my imagination.
She no longer walks upon this earth.
Her place is in heaven now,
The true land of her birth.

As I feel the warmth of the sun
beaming down through the trees.
There is nothing that could ever replace
My mother's love, which filled my needs.

Janet Santillo

The Good Neighbors

The United States and its neighbor above,
　Share for liberty a common love.
In each land the people are free,
　To live and work with dignity,
Together they share a common boundary line.
　Which does not wish for freedom any decline.
From the Atlantic to the Pacific is their border,
　Which contributes an example for world order,
Across the miles they stand for democracy as one.
　In a partnership which has flourished without
a gun.
The Maple Leaf, Stars and Stripes, side by side,
　An example of nations where democracy and
　　peace abide.

Joseph L. Pollock

Above In The Sky

Tranquilly, the blue jays glide,
Sharp-beaked, and bright, and wonder-eyed!
Through the layers of pollution,
They glide with wan and wavy motion!
There is no pathway where they go.
They drift like current to and fro.
They scrutinize with never-winking eyes,
They scrutinize with staring, frigid surprises,
The level plane in the air,
The people peering, here and there:
Who also saunter to and fro,
Not knowing why or where they go,
With great wonder in their eyes,
Sometimes a bright and frigid surprise.

Chen-Wen Huang

Protected By Love

You tiptoe through the broken edges of life.
Shattered reality screams from within you.
The needles of arrogance suck the shine of your soul.
Loneliness laughs at you, happiness cries.
Mirrors pass by you yet reflection is black.
You speak with no sound.
Your hands are numb so you cannot feel words.
You are out of control and content with the loss.
Answers gnash their teeth at you but you will not listen.
"Give it to Him," they say, "His power will heal."
"Who is this One and why does He care?"
The one true love is waiting for you,
Yet you drink the world away and die.
And you will die.
Alone.

Jennifer O'Hara

Unsolved, Unrevolved

　She dies slowly, and unaware we contribute.
　She is no longer green and blue but brown and gray.
What was once crystal blue is now contaminated.

　One by one God's creations are taken out of
existence. Just as they were put in.

　Her surface is polluted like a face unwashed.
No longer will we hear the buzzing of the bees,
singing of the birds or howling of a wolf.

　Nor will we see the beauty of transparent skies.
The enlightened colors of her beauty nonexistent.

　We must save the Earth for future generations.
A rude awakening, will somebody be met by our children.

In the end we will pay, for without her we will die.

Heidi Dawson

Mother

I am what I am because of my mother,
She constantly tells me we're to love one another.
She wakes me each morning and gives me a smile,
She tells me she loves me, I'm a special child.
She lets me make messes, she teaches me things,
Like cooking and baking and dusting my things.
She kneels by my bedside and prays for my needs,
She asks God to guide me in the direction he leads.
She prays for my future, as a teenager too,
That I will stay sensitive and know what is true.
She prays for my adult life, when choosing a mate,
That God will be with us, and I think that's great!
I am what I am because of my mother,
She constantly tells me we're to love one another.

Betty Bon Bowman

Alleyway Nights

She knew he was there
She could feel the hands of death
squeezing her tighter
and tighter

Her heart pounded like a jack hammer
in the velvet black sky
the full moon gazed upon her

Then a knife pierced intensely into
her flesh

The cries of laughter filled the air
While she lay lifelessly in her own puddle
                    of
                    blood.

Amanda Edmondson

There Was An Old Woman

Time - where does it go
She couldn't see what she had, only what she didn't
Living for love, spoiled by money, dying from her love of money
She said she did it all for him
She only did it for herself
Immortalizing herself, she died, a miserable lonely old woman
She appeared to be happy
She hid her insecurities well
Nobody would have guessed it was killing her inside
She fooled them all for awhile
Then she broke down and cried
Crying cleanses the soul, I've been told
Not in this case
It only made her angry, and in her anger vicious
She couldn't or wouldn't see what was happening
Alienating herself
Wouldn't take any help from those who still tried to love her
She didn't make it easy
In a pool of self-pity she died, a lonely broken woman

Catherine Miller

Blooms

Seeds of contemplation pierce the fertile loam
Sifting deep into the subterranean abyss
Uniting at the very depths of the inner cave
With the secret power of life
There to cling to the wall of the womb
Nourished by vital fluids and psychic elixirs
Developing from embryonic stages the future form
Ever growing, ever striving upwards
Through layers upon layers of pranic libido
Quickening the marvelous transformation
Bursting the surface in magical birth
Coming full flower in the light of the world

John Lewellen

Gotcha!

My mama thought I was so "cute" when I was but a tot.
    She got her camera and caught me just when I was not.
The flash bulb went off as I picked my nose
    And Mama laughed as she said, "Gotcha!"

I saw a pretty skunk, sitting by the trunk of a tree
    looking up at me
With his big brown eyes and a smile of disguise
    As he swished his tail and said, "Gotcha!"

The funeral man chuckled inside as he showed his sympathy
    Lying silent in that casket was no one else but me.
The insurance check was in his pocket as he slammed the cover
    and said, to the dead, "Gotcha!"

Alf C. Hansen

"A Lover's Haiku"

Flaxen-haired like the sun
She picks flowers that others would disregard
My heart for your bouquet?

Edward J. McCarthy

The Flame

With pure emotion shooting through every vein
She rises
to see what she's become
writing in fraud
trying to keep her eyes open
for fear of the dark
seething and burning
searing with angst
she rises
she begins her ascension into hell
because from where she is
she can't get any lower
realizing the satanic creature
she's become
she knows she can't go back to insanity
she rises
she's a pawn
in your game
yet she rises, rises
into the flame.

Amanda Wechter

Only She

Into the long hours of the night,
she struggles until she can get it right,
until her picture comes into the light,
until the painting is true to the sight.
Only she can bring the picture to life.

A little more color, shading and light,
proportionate wingspan of the sparrow's flight...
An understanding of the maiden's plight,
the dragon with all his power and might...
Only she can bring the picture to life.

The castle yonder must shine bright,
just like a beacon shining its light...
The dragon landed after the flight...
She will work all through the night...
Only she can bring the picture to life.

The sword gleams in the hand of the Knight,
glittering in the pre-dawn light,
shining great in heaven's sight,
made more strong by heavenly might...
Only she can bring the picture to life.

Jennifer Golling

Untitled

Who is the dancer, the maiden of grace?
She tells of her life with no sight of her face.
A calloused foot, a wounded pride,
A supple muscle, a sharpened eye.
A liquid sculpture changing form,
The caress of a feeling newly born.
An awakened idea springing through air
as the plasma contracts in a colorform fair.
A pointed toe, a lacey breast,
A graceful swan, its neck to crest.
The edge of the world is only a stage,
the dancer upon it is only a page.
A fluid leaf of crisp and white
who from its branch has taken flight.
And through the night its story to tell
without any wisdom, taste, or smell.
Whirling and prancing, stretching to leap,
the secret it holds she will no longer keep.

Danielle Metzer

Pleasure To Pain

A young girl sits alone in a hospital room,
she thinks of what she has sitting in her womb.
All she can do is lie there and cry,
and begin to wonder and question why.

The torture kicks in, once again,
she starts to scream as the nurses rush in.
She squeezes the sheets to sooth the pain,
for the fear in her heart will scar and stain.

They run her into a huge white place,
and strap her feet into some sort of brace.
Her boyfriend faithfully stands by her side,
as together they lose their dignity and pride.

A doctor says to push one more time,
the baby has arrived healthy and fine.
The parents will now suffer every day,
all because of one moment of pleasure they couldn't turn away.

Amber L. Alton

Mama's Hands

Mama's hands you see are callused and red
She worked with her hands all her life,
The hands that scrubbed the floors through the years
Were the hands that held us at night.
Mama's hands you see are callused and red
From the dishes she washed for her pay,
That bought the wool for the mittens she knit
That warmed us on cold winter days.
Mama's hands you see are callused and red
On her hand was a ring that she pawned,
The money was for our schooling she said
But her gift from our Daddy is gone.
The hands that could work when there's working to do
Are the same hands that knew how to pray,
And the hands that could hold a man and a child
Are the hands we let go of today.
Because these same hands so callused and red
That worked so hard through the years,
Were the hands that slipped through our fingers tonight
As our hands wiped away all our tears.

James Norton

Annette

She smiles, and laughs, and cries with me.
She's all I could ask a friend to be.
She listens when I think my heart will break,
even though I never mentioned the ache.
She shares and cheers all my wins,
knowing that it wasn't easy even to begin.
We laugh together until we're almost blue.
Each day with her is an adventure, priceless and new.
The funny thing is, she doesn't quite see,
the wonderful person that I know her to be.
She smiles, and laughs, and cries with me.
She's all I could ask a friend to be.

Jessica Clifford-Farmer

Ode To A Smiling Soul

A ray of light, one day —
shone on the face of a man — an ordinary man
And so the story goes ....

A voice said to him:
   "Come this way son,
   walk with me while we talk

Hear my thoughts —
   You will be strong; yet gentle
   You will be understanding of others;
    yet sometimes confused by yourself
   You will be unselfish always;
    yet sometimes wish you could have
    love all to yourself
   You will be a hero; yet often times
    will feel helpless;
   You will be patient; yet pray for more
   You will be loving — and be loved
You are and always will be ....
   a man — an extra ordinary man"
And so the story goes ....

Georgina Cuccaro Tufano

Untitled

The pearl of illusion and fantasy
shunned by the locked shell of her commitment.
And here, and now, I pry,
with the elegance of voice and diction
to break and steal what's rightfully mine;
the agreement that keeps
the quarantine of my dreams.

Brad Tobin

An Astounding Loss

   An astounding loss still whirls through my head
Shut down emotions inside feeling dead
   Kidnapped children, a father's unholy deed
Knowing not for love but only greed
   Feelings of being abandoned buried deep down
Ten years lost but loved ones found
   A father face to face with his deceit and lies
A sense of power and control showed in his eyes
   No remorse, only a unrelenting selfish aura was about
Believing his lies, of this I had no doubt
   Years lost I can never regain
But thankful no longer having pain driving me insane
   An emotional pursuit coming now to an end
Broken heart and spirit finally on the mend
   Having no hatred nor vengeance, happy for the
lost love
Thank you God for this great gift from above
Amen

Heather Collins

"The Statue Of Liberty"

The Statue of Liberty is a lovely
sight, with a flaming torch
that glows all night
    In the middle of the isle
she stands so high underneath
the deep blue sky.
Her symbolic significance which
represents "peace" brings tourists from world around, to take a
look at this lovely landmark that stands on tiny ground.
    When the moon casts over her
and shadows start to fall, she
looks so extra beautiful
Miss Liberty there so tall, with ever bright and shining
Star she spangles through the
night. She stands up there so
proudly she makes the night
seem bright. Truly our Miss
America, this lovely work
of art, a masterpiece indeed
which captures every heart

Christina Dakis

Emotion

Anger, a harsh word, a slow tear, a slammed door;
Silence!

Fear, numbness, confusion, a slow tear;
Pain!

You cry forever, pain wracking your whole being;
You live in a numb, no feeling world.

You recover, only to be hurt by memories as you wonder;
"What about me?"

Apologize? Make-up? Live? No! It's too hard!
But I can, I will, I did!

Warmth, peace, a slow tear;
Love!

Elaine M. Perlinski

Homage To The Cranes

My childhood eyes saw the great cranes' land
Silently on soft marshes near my home
Musically they would sing "koonk-koonk" as I peeked behind tall grass
Standing before me they flew from Siberia to warmth
In my beloved India

Our ancestors have seen their majestic flight
Their scarlet face and their heavenly white feathers
They came foiling the sun with their enlighten form
I long to see them each year
I dream to see them once more

So much has changed each year
This earth is no longer yours or mine
The familiar fragrant of home is gone
You are the epitome of fidelity
Take with you your bride and go

Our gods are dead and we fear no more
I bow my head to you in disgrace
We are not worthy to look upon such angels
Place my soul on your wings so I may be with you
Take me to a place for us to nest

Helen S. Wong

Where Are You Now?

The years have swiftly passed away
Since she held you on her knee
Kissing your booboos and calming your fears
Until they ceased to be

As childhood vanished and both your lives changed
There was one thing you both knew
A mother's love transcends all things
And she'll always be there for you

Yet today as she rocks alone in her chair
I wonder if mother could have been wrong
Or is a child's love for a mother
Changing or not nearly as strong

Though her body has aged and the mind's not as firm
The love from her heart is still true
And she doesn't complain or love any less
When she doesn't hear from you.

She makes your excuses for why you don't come
You're too busy or ill she fears
So she rocks alone day after day
And tries to hide her tears

Joyce Boylan

Dawn Is Late In Winter

Dawn is late in Winter.
Slowly the frosted window turns blonde
All sequined as if by some magic wand.
The frigid warmth of light wanders through the hall,
Stamping out the Shadows.

Dawn is late in Winter.
Steam ghostly rises in the still air
Pushing aside the empty cold
Frolicking in the bare branches of the Maples.
And cotton grass by alchemy turns to gold,
Stamping out the Shadows.

Dawn is late in Winter.
The old man lies abed and dreams of Spain
Of olive trees and white villages in the rain.
The icy air descends along the wall
Then rises, as in flight of sun and pain,
Stamping out the Shadows.

Dick Mussett

Temperamental March

I'm wondering, now, what March will bring,
Snow and ice or glorious Spring?
Whether we'll have a real snowstorm
Or will it happen to just be warm?

You never know when March comes 'round,
It's so temperamental, we've all found,
There may be a blizzard, that's very true,
Or crocuses just peeping through!

If we happen to have some snow and ice,
We still can think, "It will soon be nice,"
Though Winter may linger, our hearts can sing
And say to our Father, "Twill soon be Spring!"

We thank you, God, for every season,
You made them all for a perfect reason,
Our lives, like nature, can never hinder
Spring and Summer, Fall and Winter.

When Winter comes into our lives,
It won't be long till Spring arrives!
The Spring Eternal that God has planned
For those who love Him, it's close at hand.

Ava H. Irons

Fall And Spring

I sit here watching the leaves falling down,
So beautiful red, yellow and brown.
The sun is shining so bright,
Before very long
The leaves will all be gone.
The trees will all be bare
No more leaves there.
The grass will be frozen too.

But in the spring everything new,
Then the sun will shine.
And everything will be fine.
The grass will be green.
Then everything will be seen
Then flowers and trees and grass.
Everything will be beautiful at last.
The children running and singing
Very happy and swinging
The spring they say
So now, they'll go and play

Amelia Valentine

Memories

Never again to walk those hills
So distant to the eye,
Still I'll not believe it ever, for memories never die.

Why those narrow trails we've followed
From beginning to the end,
Up to grandpa's falls and then on around the bend.

Those weeping willows housed us
So it didn't seem so cold,
And we carved our loves upon them
Yet they have never told.

There are still the wild apples
That ripen in the fall,
They had no name, those apples, but they were the best of all.

Why those hills are made of glory,
Held firm by the hand of God,
Etched in the hearts of children by the happy trails they've trod.

They have signed and sealed the papers
So that all who wish may see,
But it will never be another's,
Not when it really belongs to me.

Betty Grace Bruce

Rainbows

Just as a rainbow has a beginning and end
So has my life, my love.
Just as a rainbow has colors so bright,
So does my life, my love.
the warmth of the yellow, the passion of red,
The brilliance of purple, the tranquility of blue
The excitement of orange, the pureness of white,
The mourning of black, the hope of green,
And the strength of brown.
Each color of my rainbow reminds me of you,
Just as my life, my love.
The colors of my rainbow are able to bend,
So can my life, my love
Let all the rainbows remind you of me,
Just as you wish, my love
Let all the rainbows remind me of you,
Just us you do, my love
The magical rainbow that comes from the sea,
is everlasting as my love for
all eternity.

Diana Maloomian

An Old Oak Tree

One day I stood gazing up at an old oak tree
So impressed that its memory comes back to me;
  Its clothes were old, and shaggy, and quite out of date;
It looked kind of sad and did not have a mate.

It must have been standing there for many years
Watching happy folks go by and some with a few tears;
  With its crooked arms outstretched, it looked so kind
It painted a picture, I can't erase from my mind.

Many folks passed by the old tree with 'nary a glance
But somehow, and perhaps only by chance,
  I discovered this tree had a special meaning
Nesting dozens of birds chirping and screaming;
In their way, I think they were saying "Thank you,
  Lord for watching over me
And giving me a home in this old oak tree."

Hazel N. Stesen

Winter Perfect

As the snowflake is complicated in intricacy,
  So is the Father's
    "GRAND PLAN"
  Of true beauty.

Whether whisked o'er
  By the dust of snow drifted,
Or basking in the grandeur
  Of a winter's dawn;
Each crisp frost
  Etches yet another beginning.

The earth yawns,
  Kissed by frozen tears of dew,
And welcomes the light
  Of the sun's smiling warmth,
Bursting o'er the crystalline landscape
  Of His creation.

It is the touch of grace,
  An exquisite portrait,
    The "LIMITED EDITION"
  Signature of God.

David Minch

Prayer Is Talking To God

Praying is saying all you feel in your heart.
So just open it up to God and share every part.
Just praise Him, give Him honor and thanks from within
For His beloved Son, "Jesus," who saves us from sin.

Praise Him, thank Him, and honor His name.
He suffered, bled, and died for us, and took all our blame.
Then He arose again from death and the grave.
Oh, praise God. He made it possible for all to be saved.

Father, I thank you for so many things today,
For saving my soul and teaching me how to pray.
I never forget the awful price Jesus paid for me
When he suffered and died for us upon calvary.

Lord, help me to die to self and become a channel for you.
Love others through me; help me do all you'd have me do.
I hunger and thirst for your presence and your voice.
Oh! Praise God, through Jesus I made the right choice.

Now I come to praise you with all my heart and my soul,
Thanking you for loving me and making me whole.
Once I was lost in sin, was hopeless and undone.
Now I am happy in Jesus, saved by God's precious Son.

Ann Hungler

Untitled

Black, white, straight, or gay we all have to live
So let's get along while we are here
And think of the joy we can give
God will judge us all according to the book of life
And then you will know for sure if you
Lived a life that was right but until that time
There are other wars that we need to fight
Drug addicted babies are dying daily
And some will not make it through the night
Yesterday a little girl was the latest victim of a senseless drive by
She is only nine years old
And the doctors say that she might die
The number of the homeless are growing
As families are being put out on the streets
Policies and law mean very little
When there is no food to eat
Black, white, straight, or gay we all have to live
So focus not so much on what
Someone else is but rather the love they can give

Jeffrey A. Henderson

I Will Not Cry

Being crucified, here in this life,
So like Jesus, by a loved one no less.
Not like sweet "Jesus," by nails and cross,
But by cruel words and actions, for no cause.
For it is by the devil, but a thorn in my side
Who wants me engulfed in misery, the devil he strides.
But straight into hell, never to my side,
For there is my Jesus, right by my side.
No one will ever in "His" place abide;
With Jesus, my loved ones return.
For I so have my faith on sweet Jesus;
He will deliver me sure, for he is my rock, my salvation;
For the rest of my life I shall walk in his stride.
And though I can never, in any way, shape or form compare,
For I am a sinner, whereas "He" sinned not.
My precious "Lord Jesus," he is first in my life.
Thus happy in the "Lord," I am, so I'll not cry.
If ever my tears swell in my eyes,
'Twill be but for the love of "Jesus,"
That lives in my heart.

Hilda R. Gallardo

Remembering You

Today we lay you to rest
So much pain, so much sorrow
All felt by those who knew you
And for those who were the closest to you
Wish they could turn back time
Just to have the chance to be with you
Just one more time

With this you leave us with special memories of you
Your sweet smile, the way you made us laugh
The warmth we felt from you, whenever you were near,
Is something we will all cherish in our hearts forever
That will never disappear

Now that you've gone, we know that you are safe
That God is waiting for you with open arms
To take you in his embrace, he will free you from the pain
Take you to that special place
And just knowing that you will be with him
Puts a smile on my face

Claudia Harmon

Life's Bouquet

I saw a patch of mums in bloom today.
So sturdy and colorful in its display.
Its time of beauty was meant for now.
Amidst the colors of fall in all its array.

I saw a little girl today, so tiny and lovely at her play.
She teased and pleased those around.
Her time of beauty just begun in life's bouquet.

I saw a single rose in bloom today.
So fragile and lovely, with a fragrance so faint.
Not as perfect as the rose of May.
This last rose of summer, a fall bouquet.

I saw a beautiful lady today.
She was wrinkled with age and hair of gray.
Not the glamour of youth, but the beauty was there.
This flower of late summer, a precious bouquet.

I saw a splendid bouquet today.
Of lovely people of every age, bright and colorful,
and each filling his spot in his very own way.
Each with his own unique beauty in life's special bouquet.

Eunie Hendricks

Butterflies And Children

We built a little garden with latticed vines and trees,
So that butterflies would flourish for everyone to see.
I couldn't help but notice the similarities,
Because butterflies and children share certain special needs.

They need to spread their wings and show their colors bright,
They need a place to find solace on life's uncertain flight;
They need the kind of gentle care that only love can bring,
Because butterflies and children are fragile fleeting things.

We should carefully consider our treasures so divine,
As butterflies need light and air and nectar from the vine,
Children need our love and laughter and just a little of our time,
Because butterflies and children can teach us how to shine.

John P. Cockerille

As Seasons Change

When Winter is here, fireplaces are roaring as our love is soaring;
When spring comes this way birds will be here, for love songs will be playing for us to hear;
When summer is here...the children play as our families come to stay;
As fall arrives, the leaves will change but you know we could never do the same.
Winter, spring, summer and fall...all these seasons change, but our love will always be the same.

Despina Markidis

Yesterdime

I found a dime, and felt just dandy,
so I went to the store to buy some candy.

The shelves were stocked from A to Z,
with all those goodies beckoning to me.

I made my choice, and went up to pay,
but the man at the counter had the nerve to say—

"You haven't enough! That's only a dime!"
You'd think that I had committed a crime.

I stood up to him and stated my case,
as I looked at him right square in the face.

"But yesterday, it bought some then!"
Oh yesterday.....Remember when?

Barbara J. Whitehead

The Siren's Kiss

The siren's song, of pure delight.
Soft and warm, like summer's night.
With petals soft, like rose that drift.
Deep pools of light, where shadows lift.
She'll call for you, in moonlit beams.
To set you free, within your dreams.
Then passion builds, in beds of moss.
Like honey sweet, in limbs that gloss.
With breath that burns, from inner glow.
Would melt the virgin, driven snow.
In eyes that shine, with passions brew.
And sweat that runs, like drops of dew.
She'll raise you up, in starlit sky.
Then bring you down, in gentle sigh.
Your dreams are filled, with moonlit lovers.
Till sunlight's kiss, beneath the covers.
With tears that mist, in morning bliss.
Sweet memories of, the SIREN's kiss.

James Donald Campbell

With All My Love

Eyelids closed, with tiny veins exposed;
Soft little mouth, and little button nose;
Cheeks gently flushed, with color pink rose;
All the love I could give, to you I impose.

As I watch you sleep, I wonder now,
Why the anger in me, comes your way somehow.
For while you're awake, my patience seems thin;
But as I watch you sleep, I can only grin.

And hope that the dreams, in your little mind,
Are only and always, the loving kind.
Dreams of hugs and kisses from Dad,
With never a dream of Dad being mad.

And to you I vow, with the help of God,
To keep my patience in check somehow.
And to answer wrong doing with loving guidance,
With all my love, forever and now.

James Arthur Borton

Some Of My Favorite Things

Early morning fog in trees, the rays of
  sun beginning to peep through.
Very clear streams of water too cold to
  put your bare feet into.

Beautiful scenery reflecting on a lake;
  swans, geese, ducks swimming.
Moose eating from the bottom of a pond;
  birds flying and skimming.

Waterfalls cascading down the mountains
  flowing from pool to pool.
Back country roads winding through forests
  causing shadows so cool.

Wild animals roaming; birds on the wing;
  horseback riding on trails.
Breezes rustling tree leaves; a rainbow
  arching, appearing so frail.

The smell of newly opening rose buds;
  sounds of children at play.
Skylines of cities at sunset; reading
  books; a parade, hooray.

Ada Stein

Cats

Cats are big and cats are small.
Some are big, hairy and tall,
They meow when they're happy and growl when they are snappy.
They love scratching on couches and rubbing on pouches.

They are really sweet and love to get little treats.
They love to eat and sleep and go running around, all over the ground.
Sometimes they don't even make a sound.

They lose lots of hair, and that can be bare!
Cats like to chase mice, and to them it tastes quiet nice.
Most of the time they are calm and prrr themselves a song.

Dominique Gale

Memories

  Some so old,
  Some barely cold,
  Some bring smiles, others tears
  Some rate boos, others cheers

Our memories are to be gathered like flowers,
As we move from seconds, to minutes, to hours,
They are to be savored for the feeling,
And later, a balm for the healing.
They will fill our young lives each and every day,
And in our golden years pass the moments away.
  A memory! A poem read.

Claire Cardon Tassinari

Dreams

Dreams are a part of you.
Some dreams are silly.
Some are wet.
Some are nightmares.
Dreams can seem too real at times,
But imagine how boring sleeping would be without those exciting,
Exotic, explicit, erotic, and wild dreams. Here's my dream:
A beautiful dark haired, dark eyed woman.
A family
A career
An extraordinary house with pets
But most of all, love and understanding.
Love means never having to say you're sorry.
You gotta dream!
Dreams are a part of you.
Dreams are reality.

Christopher Michael Spang

"Spring"

The beauty of spring
starts coming alive,
the flowers they
no longer hide.
The birds start to sing
their beautiful song,
and the grass is no longer brown.
The trees stand erect
now starting to sprout,
their wondrous leaves all about,
The insects too have their say,
their buzzing and humming fills the day.
The animal's bark no longer hidden
Comes alive with strength almost forbidden.
The children laugh and sing and play
they smell and touch this glorious day,
Amid this splendor of growing things
I too must spread my wings,
The earth is ready and starting to sprout
That's what spring is all about.

Betty Laboy

One Heart Beat Away

Some of us live - in fancy houses
Some of our homes - are simple and plain
Some of us - are - well known to each other
Some of us - no one - knows our names

But! We all have only one father
   We all live - for the judgement day
   We all have - but one soul to save
   We all live - one heartbeat away

Some of us have - plenty of money
Some of us don't - have a dime
Some of us have - financial investments
Some of us can't - pay a parking fine

But! We all have - some precious blessings
   We all have - the gift of today
   We all have - grace that saves us
   We all live - one heartbeat away

One heart beat away - from our soul salvation
One heart beat away - from our creator's face
One heart beat away - from our final destination
One heart beat away - from the pearly gates.

   Benford Hunter Jr.

"I Am Somebody"

I am somebody to love and to hold
Somebody who feels the heat and the cold.
Somebody's mother, Somebody's wife
Somebody who always prayed for a wonderful life.
I'm Somebody who feels love and pain
I feel the sun, I feel the rain.
Somebody who hurts and Somebody who cries
Somebody who always desperately tries.
Somebody who doesn't see black or white
Somebody who feels she is on an impossible plight.
Somebody who feels happy and sometimes sad
Somebody who gets frustrated and sometimes mad.
Somebody who can make an impact in this world
Somebody who is as gentle as a soft white pearl.
Somebody who has been hurt but gave love anyway
Who takes on the world day by day.
As mysterious and complicated as I am
I am Somebody as gentle as a Lamb.

   Barbara Wilson-Smith

Unspoken Words

Unspoken words. An old, unfinished letter.
Somehow we've nothing left to say.
Of course it could be for the better.
You never cared what I thought anyway.

And faded photographs that line my bookshelves.
And fading memories of what we used to share.
I see your face above mine in the mirror.
I also see that you're no longer there.

I often hear your footsteps on the staircase.
Your scent still lingers softly by my bed.
You say you'll stay, but you are gone already.
And your indifference turns my heart to lead.

For far too long I've held onto the dying,
So unlike you, who wouldn't even try.
And all I needed were the words: I love you."
But all you wanted was the word "goodbye."

   Aleksandra P. Freeman

Cries-To Death

It reeks of a horrible death here,
Someone or something has died here,
Sounds of laughter were once among this place,
Now it is the sadness of joy's long face.

Words of sorrow, words of joy,
Who knows the difference,
Only a little boy.

Wretched cries of forgiveness ring through the halls,
A reminder of screams that left cracks in the walls;
Who knows how many screams-
But many were unseen screams.
Then; the illusion of blood on the ground-
Was the conclusion of no more sounds.

Words of sorrow, words of joy,
Who knows the difference,
only a little boy.

   Brent Murray

In A Moment

All in a moment and in a blink of an eye,
Something can happen and no one knows why,
For some good reasons and some unmistakably bad,
Some reasons exceedingly happy or slightly sad,
You'll sadly say, "Upon that star I should've wished,
Or at least given him one last hug with a passionate kiss,"
You'll see him again one glorious day,
And peace upon your heart will lay,
But you must stay here and you must wait,
Until that so very far off date,
Then like a prince riding up on his white horse,
You'll be together and lie in happiness, of course!

   Erin Swenson

Thinking Wishful

I Wish it was easy, to just think up a thought,
Something profound, believable or not,
To impress upon others, the nature of me,
Striving to move forward, to whatever degree,
Hoping to say or do something of value,
Giving inspiration to confound and arouse you,
Somehow, expressing a need to contribute,
In giving, I get lots more to distribute,
But if it was easy, who'd bother to think?
The search would be boring, the results would stink.
So I continue my journey to impress on the mind
While, trying to be loving, thoughtful and kind
For these are the values that are lasting and true,
So profound, inspiring and arousing to you.

   Deborah Horn

Christina Knight

"Sometimes we are the heroes of our lives;
Sometimes events are so ordered, beyond plan,
That we know, or think we know, we bear the charm
Of success on our breasts. This is such time.
Though winking fate, I think, by this surprise
Has thought to shock the compass of my craft,
Thinking perhaps to catch me unprepared,
Unprepared I'm not, having run full-oft
The pageant of my play on the stage
And screen of my own mind. My lines secure,
Let uncertain results threaten as may
Dug in on the crest, I fear not this day."

From The Palace.

   Bruce Pearl

My Friend - The Shadow

My shadow and I lie here alone,
Sometimes he smiles, but it's seldom known.

My shadow and I are all in one,
Sometimes we glide, but now we run.

My shadow's here, my shadow's there,
Sometimes we wonder just who the hell cares!

My shadow never betrays my trust,
For if he did, he'd hurt both of us.

My shadow knows what I conquest,
For he hath had my heart at best.

My shadow, my shadow, I can't live without,
For if I did, I believe I would shout!

My shadow and I lie here alone,
Waiting and waiting for him to
    come home.

Angela Wheeler

To A Loved One

There you are up in the sky!
Sometimes I often wonder why!

You are where you can be free!
Sometimes I wish it could be me!

You are up there smiling with the sun!
Now we should remember the fun!

You were a friend, to some very dear!
Memories of you to my eyes bring tears!

But with each memory you shed your light!
To help me get through each day and night!

With Christmas time almost here!
Tears of sorrow disappear!

As we sit with faces of joy!
Wondering who received your favorite toy!

Remembering your favorite time of the year!
We'll always know you are near!

A father, an uncle, a brother, a friend
Our love for you will never end!

Dawn Marie Barzee

I Want A Long Life To Live

Death is a sure thing, it causes worries and
strife, I tried to be careful, 'cause I want a
long life, bad things do happen to me, it's
against my will, but I stay calm, 'cause, I
want a long life to live, some events are
good, then some are bad, I keep myself in
total control, even it makes me mad, the good
and best, don't come all of a sudden, I have
to give it time to build, I don't know how
long my life will span, I want a long life to
live, I may have a long life, many days, many
nights, staying away from evil, dealing with
the events that right, I'm doing my very
best to make it so, oh, I want a long life to
live, I love treating people nice, then
doing good things, for I know a blessing
from God one day will spring, goodness is
for me, badness is against my will, I know
I'm on the right track, oh, I want a long
life to live, yes, I want a long life to live.

James Monroe

Farming

Farming is a clear blue sky and early morning sunshine
sparkling on dew-drenched pastures;
    Seeing the first light green hue creep over the field
that was brown the day before;
    Waking up to the pound of thunder and rain on the roof
and remembering the field of new-mown hay on the ground.
    Farming is walking on a cold moonlight winter night with
the crunch of snow underfoot;
    Seeing bear tracks along the edge of the path that leads
to the sheep shed;
    Waking up to the friendly patter of gentle rain on the
roof the day after seeding is finished.
    Farming is looking across the field of waving grain,
first green, then pale gold, and finally rich amber;
    Farming is seeing new life and feeling hope.

Jen Nelson

Time

Time spent - unreplaceable - forever lost
Spend it well my friend,
For it determines your tomorrow
Whether in a space of limited confinement,
Or in the endless freedoms of the open.
What you say an do with in its passing
Makes up the life to which you will look back.
If you do good you will look upon a good life,
However, if you do wrong or spent it idly
What will you be forced to look upon?
Will you even look at all?
What shall you say to the children?
Will you say anything?
Do and say what you feel to be right,
Just think how you will feel tomorrow.

Bruce M. Tait

Lady Liberty

I lay in the field with fixed
staring eyes, as my life flashes by me,
and all of the things America stands for
suddenly appear in the skies. I hear
the fire from guns and bombs, through eyes
that no longer see, and crying God help me,
knowing life is not to be for me. I think of
my family, my future, oh what I could have been.
    I feel someone lifting me, and with soothing
whispers, I realize my prayers have been answered.
    Suddenly she is there in all of her
spaciousness. She is beautiful, she is freedom,
and she is liberty to all. I feel painless and
happy and no longer afraid, as I know I have
not died in vain, but for her! As I look down
from the heavens, I hear her say, give me
your poor, your tired-alas I go on my way.

Diane G. Arlington

Vision

My sister, the moon, calls sweetly to me
    She comforts me through my tears
    She beckons to my spirit to be free
    And asks, "Why so many years?"
My brother, the wind, whispers my name
    Gently he breathes his breath upon my cheek
    To not burden my soul with this earth's shame.
    To be the Spirit which I seek.
The sun, my father, is always the light.
    Even through this valley of weeping
    He gives me faith and courage to fight
    And my heart's delight which I came seeking
Cathy Chavarria

Belief

Who knows if the moon is a balloon
staring out of that brilliant lighthouse far beyond

The faces seem to shift without warning
like that of the newly born babe
who opens his eyes for that very first moment

The street lamp of sodium-vapor shines through the night
keeping a constant watch overhead,
on the many who are below,
While others silently wonder, watch, and wait...

Let us take a ride in this balloon
to fly higher and gaze at what seems to be illusion,
where we'd find that space so keen
a place where no soul has yet seen

But only on the surface, when it turns to reality
is where it finally breaks through.

Jodie Hebert

California

The night fades as the slow sun passes.
Stars of the sky come shining through.
And the mesa dim with its waving grasses.
Whispers the old, old song of you.

California! Where the dreams and wishes are,
Where the fame and fortune lie.
I'm so close, yet so very far.
I hope to look into your eyes.

California! How I love you, your forever lover.
Looking down, beat up, black and blue
Now the night wind softly hovers,
Over my face lost in you.

California! Oh, it's time to make a stand,
Lay down the gun and stop the hurt.
Your upturned face to my empty hand,
I have nothing but a pile of dirt.

Yet your heart you gave full measure,
Money earned by a push and shove,
As I fight for your precious emerald treasure
I hold hope with fear, faith, and love.

Harmony DePrano

Fishin'

Are ya sick and tired of nothing ta do? Well let me say, "I've the
solution for you."
Yessir, fishin' I spect's what most folks still call it, one of the
few sports left that's lite on yer wallet.
An I guarantee you fishin's a winner, it's lots of fun an makes fer
great dinner!
'Though they's skeptics wut say thet "fishin' is borin'," I kin
honestly say it's never put me ta snorin'.
When thet BIG fish gets mad an bites on yer line, a tinglin' sensation
runs right up yer spine.
Then ya haul thet HUGE monster right inta yer bote,
a hope'n and pray'n thet you'll all stay aflote!
Ya recollect the day of the best prize of all, that EIGHTEEN POUND
LOONKER ya hanged on yer wall!
An later out yonder with yer kids all grow'd up, out'n the world
with'n their own pickup truck,
Ya kin teach yer grand kids yer fishin' stories, yer GREATEST
moments, yer triumphs and glories.
Yes, think a how nice thet this world could be, if'n we was ta go
fish'n, jest you n' me.

Chris Chitty

Drifter In Space

Seemingly coming from nowhere I entered earthly life at some point -
starting out crying and longing for love, food and shelter -
I found myself safe and secure surrounded by smiling faces.

Being a human - with the incredible awareness
of my own self and the knowledge of a limitless
Universe - I am faced with the task of daily
survival and paving out my own destiny.

Hardly ever do I give any thought to the fact,
that I am a drifter in space -
circling the sun in predictable orbits -
marked only by the visible changing of the seasons -
highlighted with ever increasing candles on my birthday cake.

My life span is just a tiny fraction of eternity -
and yet so important to me. I go through life with
my reason for being.

I am unaware of the constant ongoing transformation
of matter and energy into new forms of animate existence
taking place in the microcosm as well as in the macrocosm.

What do I really know about life's reality?
Perhaps - Life itself is testing its own boundaries

Heidi Rimanich

Tainted Dreamings

Tainted dreams upon my pillow, dusted moonlight on the floor.
Still my head swims in the ocean; you can't rescue me anymore.
Sun filled days replaced by darkness, blistered feet must lead the way
Raindrops filter down from heaven and the light has gone away.
Smiles, froze in silence, moments captured now are gone.
Peering from my window, only cracked sidewalks to walk on.
I hold a lighted candle, a burning flame, trying to brighten the
darkest days
And I hold a torch into the wind, but it can't show me the way.
There's a tornado hovering closely above this fragile life
Twisting memories, spiraling my dreams, and so I hide within the night.
Tainted dreams upon my pillow; no release there from my fears.
So I'll sit and grasp the darkness; let the shadows hide my tears.
Sun filled days will replace darkness, I await the sun's arrival.
Raindrops filter from the heavens; they'll bring all the world's
survival.

Elizabeth Kensinger

The Obscure Hymn At Twilight-Dim

There was a dawn after the dark night: pausing, parting. As I
strayed from a normal beat listening, I heard The Obscure Hymn at
Twilight-Dim.

"Action!" The Director bellowed with a monstrous voice "Smile today
lusciously, don't fake It" and he sang The Obscure Hymn at
Twilight-Dim.

"Action!" the very same screeched. "There's a gap and I say repay,
rebuild, I'm not too old to profit." Went The Obscure Hymn at
Twilight-Dim.

"Action!" he rained and rained raking my ears. "Glistening tears
crave It. We all should" as he sang The Obscure Hymn at
Twilight-Dim.

"Action! you f--king fools. A serpentine maze of subterranean
caves saw the devious sunbeam." So I heard The Obscure Hymn at
Twilight-Dim.

"Action peevish freaks! So dormant dreams won't improve
yesterday, don't drown these sounds." Ended The Obscure Hymn at
Twilight-Dim.

"Loosen a hangman's noose." The Judge said "All action cut and
fade" the inquisitor never heard The Obscure Hymn at Twilight-
Dim.

Andrew de Holl

The Clouds

Gently falling rain falling from the sky.
Streaming down like teardrops.
Teardrops from on high,
Clouds, oh won't you tell us for what these tears are for,
Do you weep for something, something we've ignored.
Could it be that from your lofty posts so high above
You have seen how little we have given our love.
Do you see the lonely, weary, troubled, and
The poor have you seen the fighting and the war.
Clouds there must be some way to make your crying cease.
Share with us the secret of your happiness and peace.
Do you say that each of us can play a part?
With each spark of love we light a flame of love may start.
Reaching all around us giving hope to those we know,
This, you say can help true peace to grow.
Clouds though are parting your point you've made quiet clear.
Peace will never happen, unless it starts right here.

Jessica Ranocchia

Summarizing The Reason

The time has come for someone to speak out. Question, analyze, and summarize what the killing is all about. Could it be that you and I never took the stand, to live and teach our children the true master plan? Brothers and sisters should not fight each other, while father is roaming the streets and hiding from their mother. Home is neglected there is no doubt, children in need of clothing and doing without. Mother either working or veins punched with lead, while baby is crying and begging to be fed. The master left instructions for us to follow, but we all know the truth is hard to swallow. We must be obedient, it is better than sacrifice...Forgiving over and over, not just once or twice. Love the Lord with your whole heart and soul. We've heard this before, the story is very old. We are our brother's keeper by the true word of God, helping someone in need should not seem odd. We are on a mission in this human race, if we can't fulfill it here, how can we do it in space? Children lay down your arms and put on the armor of God. He will truly keep you by his staff and rod. The road is not easy, He did not say it would be. We must love each other so we all will be free. Keep the faith children for in due season, We will overcome and we will all know the reason.

Annie D. Thomas

Once In A Lifetime

In this life I have dreamed, alone in
silence. I have dreamed of you. For that is all
I can do.
For since you have gone away, to that
far away place, a placed called heaven. For I know
that is where you are. It is a place for
Angels, love and peace. For I have dreamed ever
so often.
For once in a lifetime, a dream can
come true. For I had you in my life, for
a short while. And now you carry the brightest
light in heaven, for all eternity.

Joyce M. Reifsnyder

A Fish Story

Fishing along the river bank on a quiet summer day. The warm sun beaming down while fish jump in the water at play. Alerted by water ripples, there must be a fish nearby. Drifting around is my bobbin, do you suppose the baited hook will catch its eye? It is time to relax however, midst a warm summer day of fun. Just gazing into the dazzling water lazily, holding my pole like a gun. Suddenly, my bobbin goes under the water and away goes my pole. Whatever it is has a lot of strength, maybe a turtle has a hold. A fish story is always good, many are told by the way. Well enjoy the fishing (peace with God) along the river bank. Plan to try it again one day.

Dorothea Ruth Lux

The Cycle Of Love

Within life's cycle we find friendship.
Someone we can talk with the share our dreams.
This friendship turns to love in someone
we can share eternity with.
A love that explodes into a blossom of
excitement in marriage.
The extension of this love in the birth of our children.
That love grows throughout becoming stronger to
help us deal with the unexpected.
This love is what carries us and helps us
through when one life ends.
That love you have shared will be yours to
eternity and in your dreams.

Gail M. Dibbern

Remember Me

Remember me with a smile
Remember me with a hug
Remember me with a great big smile
Remember me with a lot of love
Remember with a happy face
Remember me like a pretty Rose
Remember me without a tear
Remember all of the good time
And you will forget all the bad time
Remember wherever I'm at
I'm at peace with God and my self
Because I know God has smiled on me
Just remember the way I was and
not how I am now; remember me with a smile

Barbara Ann Pickens Moore

"Oh Woman"

Oh woman, black woman who has saved my
soul, you've taken this empty shell of a man and
made me whole. The spirit of your love healed me
when my soul was dying of thirst, while the gentle
touch of your hands soothed me by massaging away
the hurt.

It is you who keeps my knees bowed and head
looking toward the sky, but it is by his grace you are
here, and it is his grace I will forever say thank you
until the day I die.

Oh woman, black woman who causes my heart
to cry tears of happiness, I thank God for sending me
his best. I pray, asking God to make time my friend,
to allow me to love you minute by minute, day by day
until the very end.

Darryl Williams

Tranquil Disarray

I sometimes find myself drifting into a
state of mind where reality is irrelevant...

An eagle haunting through the empty sky
swept across the horizon and faded into the
lazy sun against a dismal gray of a
morning long forgotten.

A solemn wind descended into a valley
of hopes and dreams that soon were swallowed
up under a canopy of immense trees.

Within this emerald realm of serenity I
felt myself being drawn along the narrow path
which wandered upon a pool crystal blue.
Only then did she appear. A tear ran down
my cheek.

Love is lost but not forgotten...

James W. White II

350

"The Unbeliever"

In a shallow grave
My crocus lay
I am not alive
Cannot my spirit thrive
I am all alone
Cannot see my family or Home
I was not a christian
I am nothing at all
I am not
I am not
This lake of fire
Was my desire
I have not paradise
I had Satan's behavior
Oh, I suffer
If only I believed in the Savior.

Karen Ann Saffa

Trust

At fifteen
my daughter took me gently
by the hand
and walked me
through the privacy
of her young life

She shared secrets
from a diary
kept in a not so hidden place
reading them without comment
watching my
face for surprise and
approval
or prior knowledge

She did not know
I had dusted her shoes with magic
that she would pirouette like
the thunderous applause my
hands made

O'Donnell

"Madison"

Time is Turning,
My heart is yearning.
And in my mind,
I seek to find...
My child of two,
Who hasn't a clue-
Though all is new,
I pray for you...
In - that we may bond again,
Only this time... Without End!

Tabitha Deloris Woodburn

Under Water

As the water dances at my feet,
my heart skips a beat,
I hear the water calling me,
Water is all I can see,
The water reaches high,
Soon it touches my thigh,
The water goes over my head,
And then I go to bed,
Under water, underwater
You'll find me under water.

Lindsey Debra Holmes

Fading Footprints

My footprints are my progeny
My family and friends along the way
The only ones who will attest
I passed through here one day.

When the sod's grown o'er my grave
and my bones have turned to dust,
And the echoes of the eulogy
Fade to silence in the dusk,

My name may still be spoken
But less frequently each year
As family and friends recall old times
An eye might show a tear.

Now my clan is merely mortal
Whose days are strictly measured
So if they're wise and thoughtful
They'll live each day as if it's treasured.

Then one day when their day comes
To leave and follow me
I'll have made a place for all of us
To spend eternity.

Roger Markle

Untitled

I pray for the day when
My heart stops aching
When the hurt, and fear, and misery
Will be gone from within

I hope for the day when
My mind stops crying
And I will again see clearly
My thoughts free from
Frustration and pain

I dream of the day when
My soul stops screaming
When my mind will be serene
Like a lily upon a silent pond

I wait for the day when
My soul starts singing
And the songs I hear are tranquil
And my soul will be at peace

S. M. Figary

Untitled

You are my goddess,
my pale moon on high.

You are the silvery clouds
that whisper in the trees
come the morn.

You are the rose petals
as they fall so
delicately.

You represent all things
beautiful and perfect
as if you were the mold
from which they came.

You are here.
You are there,
You are everywhere,

But mostly you are
forever in my heart.

C. M. Shotwell Jr.

"Self Conclusion"

Isolation, separation from
my self expression

Blindness, vision is clear
only through impression

Desolate, breaking free
from troubled existence

Destruction comes only
through inner resistance

Solitary confinement, results
bring subconscious tremors

Shockingly my mind forgets
how easily my soul remembers

Suddenly at peace with
every sense

I sit patiently awaiting
For the journey to
commence

Kimberly Valerio

Untitled

The night makes me sad.
My soul pads on soft feet
through cold grass and leaves.
And the breeze is a chill.
With that song in my ears
and his voice in my heart.
No, but he wasn't real.
The stars swing down low
to touch my hair and fingertips.
I know someone's there
sliding on the breeze that is chill.
And the sky melts into my eyes
as I float on my years
and my tears
The night makes me sad.

Simone Snaith

Untitled

Silence to which my heart surrenders,
my soul possessed with passion,
I dare not see the pain in love,
for I'm blinded by obsession.

Unspoken love of mine imprisoned,
anguished as I may be,
still I seek a new tomorrow,
for him that I may see.

Mariya Stepanyan

Medusa Ice Queen

THERE SHE IS!
My God! She's looking in my direction!
She's staring at me!
She has ex-ray vision, and sees through
the fabric of my cloths.
Through the very fabric of my being,
into the depths of my soul.
Where all my dirty little secrets hide.
Before her I stand naked in shame,
unworthy of her eyes falling upon me.
She turns her eyes away, and moves on.
I'm scared for life;
She looks on, to the next face,
sooner than she will never have the
need to remember mine.

T. S. Smith

Wrongful Exposure

Like rain streaks on a window-pane,
my tears are two sided. A lone
tear slides down my china doll mask,
but inside, where my soul lies like
hardened earth, waterfalls erode
me into the Grand Canyon. The
grooved layers of earth are not just
impacted pain-they translate the
history of my scars better
than any Rosetta stone. They
exposure what time can do to a
body or soul or rock-mold it
into a shape even mother
couldn't recognize-let alone,
a gawking tourist, who only
sees the comic mask time forces
me to wear, as he takes pictures.

Sara Ancona

When You Are Gone

My heart it aches
My thoughts they drift
And endlessly I yearn

When you are gone
And not around
There's nowhere left to turn

But then I think
And smile a bit
I realize you care

I smile some more
And laugh because
It turns out you're still there

Your love inside
It warms my soul
Whenever you're away

So now I think
That when you're gone
It's almost like you stayed.

Patrick J. Varnedoe

Motherhood Or Not?

Something I've always wanted
Never had

Maybe I wasn't ready
Matter or Not
It happened so quickly

The experience,
The joy,
Her love,
Her cry,
Her baby teeth,
Her off balance

Teaching her right,
Learning as well

But there's something,
Something more, a special bond

Jasime, my baby girl
She's everything but a child!

She'll always be my baby!
My baby puppy!

Misty D. Browning

Chains Of Gold

My chains of gold show in the light,
next to my skin they are cold at night.

My black skin weeps with sores as my
master tore into me, my flesh,
my blood, my soul.

"Free! Free!" the night spirits said,
as they flew around me in my weary bed.

All I can think of is my chains of gold,
that I inherited when I was sold.

I know that my chains aren't gold,
but freedom is, and I will know soon
that my gold will shine my way home.

Karlene Blackburn

The Party's Over

The party's over
No longer are we
the wandering rovers

From now till the end
we will be sober

However fear not

Along the way we will
learn a lot

As we travel through
life on our way to the stars

We will come to know
just exactly who we are

If we should get lost
along life's way

We must understand
God is with us each
and every day.

Rick Helton

The Gift

I give this gift to you
no matter where you are.
Just look up
and see a star.

A flower blooms between
a fence.
Its fight for life is so
intense.

To see a child
work so hard.
to try to get to
where we are.

To see someone not quite where we are
and wonder just how they are.

The awe of how the land meets the sea.
A wild animal,
as it flees.

The gift of life I give to thee.

Valerie Riley

Mom

Wintertime is cold
Only your birthday has warmth
The kind brought by love.

Michal Jon Mason

"Past Reality"

Is the past a dream?
No, not really. It's a thought.
Or is it? It happened!
Didn't it? I lived it.
But I said it's not a dream.
Is it real, my past?
These thoughts are me.
They are my family,
My friends, my everything.
All I am is my past.
But yet it's just a thought.
And a thought is not real.
So is the past real?
Maybe I shall never know.

Lou Corzine

Loneliness

Life is empty when there is;
No one around to help fill it;
Times of communication;
No tender moments;
Events to share;
Disagreements to resolve;
Eyes to meet;
Laughter to hear;
Discoveries to ponder;

Oh! but there is one;
One who will be there;
A friend in times of need;
A friend for all seasons;
A voice in the darkness;
A hand to hold;
Someone to cry on;
Someone to share your needs;
Someone who loves you;

Call upon Him; God.

Sandra Evans

Illusions

Sunlight dances on a green, glossy leaf.
No one has heard the music,
Since the day I sold the dream.
A pretty profit,
I bought a pair of
  pink,
    satin,
      dancing
        shoes.

Now, as I whirl,
  around,
  around,
  around,
I fall off the earth.
My shoes are gray and shredded.
My feet are bleeding.

Kristina Weaver

Icy Sentinel

Built by the young family,
Now warming themselves inside,
You stand alone in this silent world.
Some, seeing you, will smile,
But I wonder whether you would
Prefer a frozen friend
To keep watch together
Until you both melt.

Kathryn A. Hager

Götterdämmerung

There was total silence.
  No one heard
The end of the earth
  But one small bird.
A lone survivor,
  A flash of red,
On top of the world
  And saw the dead.
Darkness, ashes.
  The red bird cried,
"Wait for me, God!"
  Spread its wings
And died......

Natalie Gerlaugh

"Time"

No one lives forever
No one lasts the test of time
Hurt fills one's mind
The thought of death
Brings the night of sorrow
The sense of the next day
Can bring a bright day of tomorrow
We none have time to wait
Time took away a loved one
Time holds our fate
Besides love, what do we have
A nice bank account
Or that loving Mom and Dad
To shelter us from bad
And always want the best
When time is done with us
Time
Will lay us to rest.

Todd J. Cannon

My Pigeons

I saw you flying to and fro
Not deciding where to go
Someday will you let me know
Where you are going?

First a roof top, then a sill
Never, never, standing still
Is this life against your will
How will I be knowing?

Stop and say hello to me
Tell me what it is to be free
Say what there is to be
Ever growing.

I wish that I could take your place
To glide along with such grace
And go and go to any place
Still knowing.

Mary M. Kohnke

Untitled

With windswept hair she stood aloft
Oh so far yet still so soft,
Dressed in garments of silk and lace
a picture window of her face
The spell she cast from within her eyes
has found me still and mesmerized
She truly is as it may seem
something fashioned from a dream.
Not for a moment could I now behold
This feeling of bliss to ever be old.

Stephen C. McStay

Nothing Lasts Forever

Nothing lasts forever
Not even flowers in the rain
Just the earth as it changes
And the ground which still remains

We all live in a circle
So round it never stands
Just our souls which come and go
And our bodies left in sand

No, nothing lasts forever
Just this moment in our hands
We must live and breath it
'Cause in just one minute ....

Luz Maria Mirabal

Fears

Turning that next corner,
Not knowing what you'll find;
Trying to reach your goals;
Trying not to fall behind.

Turning that next corner,
Not wanting to look the fool;
Trying desperately to hang on;
Trying to keep your cool.

Starting that next chapter,
Changing direction in your life;
Knowing the path you travel
Might lead to pain and strife.

Starting that next chapter;
Changing the things you do;
Knowing, even though you're scared,
You will struggle to make it through.

Kimberly Burley

Growing Old

I used to get around just fine but
now I need a cane -
The things I used to love to do cause
me so much pain.

I can hear my family talking, when
they think that I can't hear, about
placing me in a nursing home - then
I fight back a tear.

You see I hate to leave my home - I've
been here most of my life, but not only
will I leave my home - what about my wife?

Memories will be all I have that they
can't take away - and maybe a few
visitors, if they should come my way.

But if I keep my faith in God; as I
have always done - one day I won't
sit all alone and watch the setting sun.

Muriel Mosley

Gazing

Gazing at the ground, a shabby windblown
object lies there-

A faint rustle drifts to my ears
I feel the rough, crisp surface
Ebony spots on a hazel background
Wrinkled and uneven
Gazing at the ground, a crinkled leaf
lies there.

Michele Engelberger

A Pilot's Forest Song

From whence I came
Now I return,
To lie among
The fragrant things of Earth.
Tall trees
Strain high,
While leafy fronds
Reach ever upward.
But I have been there -
Now I lie
And watch my rooted brethren
As they try!

Rita Thompson Dennis

Love

L - Lovingly I
O - Opened all of my heart
V - Verifying
E - Earnestness.

L - Lavishly I gave
O - Others all I had,
V - Visualizing how they will never have
E - Everything which I possess.

L - Leniently I lived so that
O - Others participated
V - Very comfortable with
E - Entertainment every day.

L - Large-heartedly I
O - Overdid in giving
V - Very often to
E - Everyone.

Sylvanie M. Charles

Little Hands

Little hands and little feet
O' so small and O' so sweet
Arms are reaching with so much love
You are truly a gift from above.

Laughing, crying, O' how tender.
Rocking, sighing, love from the sender
Helping, teaching, scolding, growing,
Lessons we are tenderly learning.

Can this little creature be
  what came from you and me?
One of God's miracles that he teaches,
If we look closely, we can see
  some of his features.

Little hands and little feet,
O' so small and O' so sweet.

Vivian Fritzinger

Poor Willy

Poor, poor Willy,
Oh, how he was so silly.
Unfortunately,
He went deep down in the sea,
And couldn't come up for air.
Then Poor Willy drown,
And when he was found,
He wasn't in very good shape.

Poor, poor Willy,
Oh, how he was so silly.
And now here he lies.
With tears in our eyes,
We pray he's with his brother Billy.

Shannon Andrews

"I See God"

I see God in the softness
of a clear blue sky.
I see Him in the sweetness
of a baby's first smile.
I see Him in the beauty
of a sweet fragrant rose.
In the tender compassion
That love ever shows.
I see Him when one
of His children prays.
As the last rays of sunset
fade gently away.
But never was God
more plainer to see,
Than in a tall stranger
of Galilee.
Every word He has spoken,
Everything He has done
Mirrors the Father-
For this was His Son!

Rosa Henry

Merry Christmas, 1994

A world so full of madness,
of cruelty and crime,
So loudly screams, it cannot even
Hear the church bells chime. . .

Yet there are other forces
We often fail to see,
Like those of "guardian angels"
Protecting you and me.

The angels sing "rejoice, rejoice,"
Reminding us we have a choice
To seek the code, to use the tool-
The blueprint for the "golden rule."

We know, by now, - all life reveals
'Tis l o v e that h e a l s!
I wish and hope that you may find
The treasured calm, of peace of mind,
And each one have a special reason
To celebrate this Christmas season.

Then, with God's help we will survive,
All the way through '95!

Margaret D. Kadisch

Symphony

There is bountiful chime
of wind and tree and flower,
warmed to sonata by the sun,
that lifts the arms
of our hearts to heaven.

Each tendril, a string
that vibrates true and clear,
the leaves this year
with burnished timbre,
are tinkling cymbals
to the wind's harp.

With all your beauty,
world, you die again.
Fall beneath the
snow's sweet cover
till spring when with risen hope,

You toss emeralds in your hair.
Pin daffodils and lilacs to your gown.
Wear violets on your breath,
robins on your fingertips.

Marlene S. Veach

Valentine (To Timothy)

Your love, like the light-wind
of early Spring
pours within my substance
like crystal wine in gold,
the reflection in your silken hand
brushing flame across my canvas
of day, of night,
in crimson rose.

I know the hunger of your dance,
silent, yielding, like the stars
to midnight indigo,
to warm embracing,
within your love, in emerald fire
inviting the lyric of eternity
within my heart
in diamond white, in infinite
    life.

Paula Davis

Our Life As One

The candles lit, our souvenir
of everything that we hold dear.

An everlasting night of love
has brought us now our only son.

A simple kiss to end the night
as we hold our son so tight.

The months go by and seasons pass
our baby girl is here at last.

The candle down about half way
but lovely memories remain.

The house is quiet and alone
the children now are far from home.

Our candle's burning strong and bright
it helps get through the lonely nights.

Our rocking chair has made its move
now our children have children too.

The time has come to say good night
Dear Mom and Dad you've raised us right!

Tracy Phipps

Paradise Valley

Do you sometimes dream....
    of a land all green;
Meadows — like dancing
    silk in the breeze.
Oh! And the smell of honeysuckle,
    And the big Oak Trees.

The Sound of a brook,
    caressing its rocks..
As the sun begins to shine
On the honey-dew drops!!

A slight nip to the air,
    to add some charm.
This wonderful valley where
    there can be no harm!!

Ronda Simpson

Just For Friendship Sake

Have you ever stopped to think
Of how your life would be
If there was no such thing as friends
Do you know where you would be?

Friends are a big part of life
And everyone must share
They have to choose a person
And show them that they care.

A person must have a friend
To have right by their side
A friend to whom he can talk to
Who has not a thing to hide.

So next time when you see someone
Who looks like they need a friend
Take some time to show them
You have a hand to lend.

Friends are friends forever
So next time won't you take
Some time to show someone you care
Just for friendship sake.

Ronetta L. Derivan

The Cross

Whenever you hear the story,
Of Jesus on the cross.
Of His death and crucifixion,
For a world of sin so lost.

Of the unfair trial by Pilate,
Of the suffering and the pain.
And of the anguish in His heart,
Let it not be done in vain.

As He trod the weary roadway,
And had thoughts of you and me.
As He rose to face the victory,
Crucified on Calvary.

When you think of how He suffered,
Of the abuse to which He came.
Let us each day ask His forgiveness,
And pray in His Holy Name.

Russell E. Rehil

The Visitor

Resting upon my slumber,
Reviewing my life's journey,
Sensing an end of Turbulence.
So frightening, so exciting.
It is time to go.

I've have seen him many a time,
He cometh upon the night,
Tall, black, and invading.
It is time to go.

Knock, Knock, Knock.
He awaits behind the portal.
I shall return to innocence.
Family leave of sadness.
The light is so bright.
It is time to go.

Body and Soul divide.
Peace calms my essence.
Eternal serenity comes.
As my last breath, "I love you."
The time has come to pass.

Robert W. Runge

"The Island"

As we walk along the shore
of the beautiful beach, we
can feel the warm sand
next to our feet.

And out in the distance
far across the ocean, we
admire the Red Sunset
with great love and devotion.

The Palm trees are swaying
back and forth with the breeze,
and the dancers, are dancing
to the beat, and everything
on the Island, is so pretty
and neat.

Now it is time to go, but,
I wish we could stay so
I will say hello and goodbye
In only one way, "Aloha"

Mary Winham

Awakened Mother Earth

As I lay awakened to the sounds
Of the midnight hour,
I am reminded of all the beautiful
things Mother Earth has to offer.
We are unkind to her gratefulness
that she shed upon us every minute
of the awakened days and nights.
For Mother Earth is falling into
a long deepened sleep with hopeful
dreams of peace and happiness.
Stop the nightmares of ugliness,
give her the peace and happiness,
For she is one of the many reasons
that we are here today.
Please Awaken Mother Earth.

Rosalind R. Todd

"Lamentation"

(In Memory of Arthur, Jr.)
Only we know...
Of the void never filled
When sleep never comes
And the nights remain still

And we stifle our tears
For fear that we'll shout
Only we know
What that's all about

We know others care
And sympathize
With our pain
And they say time will heal
But it's just not the same

Yes, only we know
What we've had to brave
We mothers who've carried
Children
From the womb
To the grave.

Sylvia Y. Lawrence

Wings That Lift Me

Gather up all birds
Of the world to come
Whether it be far or near
Let them flutter beneath my feet
Lifting my tethered body beyond
My pain

Come lets bring forth all butterflies
Let them dance about more and more
Above my head they do fly
Landing swiftly upon my shoulders
Like a dove, upward I do soar
Nevermore shall I die

I can hear a voice whipping
In and out the clouds
With a loud appearance
Angle wings beneath me
Lifting me to heavens door
Where I shall sing and dance
Upon and Angels wing and
Worry no more.

Rosie Hutsell

Distant Glade

Pine trees-dark, innocent and full
of thick majestic secrets

White mountains and whispering stars
antique saturated wind

A dark wrestling stream
nibbling at the feet of birch

Harvest moon raining on the roof
of Mother Nature's church

Cry of the wild
in a distant glade
new born wolves camouflaged
by the canopy of dark shade

Ancient ground speaks
under trampled foot

Feelings of one as my eyes
gaze aloof

Mark Richard Queenan

Untitled

Sanctify my heart,
  Oh God,
That a love as pure
  as thine
Can mine in his and
  his in mine
A sanctuary find.

Lynne R. Barrett

My Prayer

Tears are running down my check
Oh God I know, but I cannot sleep
To watch his eyes so full of fear
This little boy that I hold so dear.
Please God, in your good grace, put a
Smile upon his face, make his dreams
Come true I pray
And watch over him night and day.

Rose Strever

End Of The Rainbow

Will we be together
Oh I don't know
For I can't see
The end of the rainbow
I want your love
For all times
He just won't let
You be mine
Oh help me for
I can't see
The end of the rainbow
For you and me

Sylvia Hamby

Swiftly

Swiftly the years pass by
Old age creeping on
I must not stop and mourn
I must press on.

Eyes growing dim, wrinkles appear
Rem Jesus is always near
Jesus is by my side
Always willing and ready to guide

You can't go this journey alone
Let Jesus your friend lead you home

Susie Sams

A Lover's Wait

The water leaps at the seashore,
on a misty, rainy day.
No ships are on the horizon,
the sky is ominous gray.

The lady's skirts are billowing
like the waves upon the sea.
Her hair is tossing in the wind
as she cups her eyes to see.

The smell of the wind is salty,
no sea gulls here to play.
She's waiting for her lover
to come from far away.

Her heart will be torn and broken
when it's time for her to know,
her lover's under the waters,
on the ocean's floor...below.

Patsy K. Spaulding

"Smoky"

We were friends, just you and I
On fluttering wings, you learned to fly
The song you sang on each days end.
You truly were my little friend.
No fluttering wings on my window sill
No morning sounds, the down is still,
And I shall miss you so my friend
How could I know that it would end
And I shall watch to see you fly
In birdie heaven in the sky.
And keep within me, memory.
Of things we shared just you and me
On this I learned all things above
You truly taught me hour to love

Lillian Walker

Untitled

O Jesus, you came to us
On this your special day
You came to earth to deliver us
And in our hearts you'll stay
So please Lord Jesus, help me
For the families of today
There's so much bickering going on
That most of us have lost our way
I'm asking for your help, dear Jesus
So that all of us may never stray.

Rebecca Leaper

Untitled

Sing me to sleep,
on your breath of love,
Sing me to sleep,
with harmonies from above.

Waltz me into dream,
carry my heart in hand-,
Waltz me into dream, as only you can-,

Embrace me into moonlight,
hold me for many a mile-,
Embrace me into moonlight,
Kiss my heart with your smile.

Caress me into caring,
touch me with your heart's wand-,
Caress me into caring,
float me into passion beyond-,

Warm me into sweetness,
ring me with your love's fire-,
Warm me into sweetness,
engulf me with love's desire.

Sing me to sleep-.

Paul M. Wittenberg

October

Take me to October
Once again
And with me ride her winds
Back to a place
Amidst her dappled grandeur
Where together
In our aloneness
We can gaze upon her beauty,
Breathe deep her crisp, cool sighs
And allow her vibrant hues
To shelter us
Or at least give us leave
From troubles daily faced
All at once
Let her lift us clear and free
To play upon her spottled clouds
At least for a short while
Her splendor year's last life
Preceding winter's cloak

Ronald A. Amarant

"A Good Squeeze"

I'll squeeze by the turf
of Bennett Cerf with an
earful that's awful or artful.
When I shake the ketchup bottle.
None'll come and then a lot'll
Now we squeeze a bottle what'll
Let the ketchup catch up.

Lawrence E. Droney

One Star

One star,
One night,
One tiny newborn child,
Our loving God arranged.

His life,
His love,
His death — He lives!
My life forever changed.

Kenneth D. Cooper

Seeining

Everyday sinning
One told to me since my childhood
I heard of this obstacle
Who seeks to put me away from goodness
Misfortune who drives me too far

Too far from the kingdom of God
But, where is from sinning
Who don't like to give me pardon
That my God pledged

And if I return at this story of salute
I see that the world is wicked
Do damage because the sin covered
The century for attaining
My generation trouble and unclean

Why being of sin
That by Adam or Eve our forefather
That the fault of our ancestor
I can't know by my transgression
God himself knows that

Opanga Mabroucky

Love Hurts

Loneliness is the
Only friend who can hear the
Voice of a dying soul, who still cries
Endlessly staring at the faded rainbow.

Heaven cheated on me, pushed me
Under the deep blue sky, where all the
Rivers turned dry,
Took me to the edge, where
Sorrows kissed me with a smile.

Mahbubul Kabir

Golden Days

Is there color in heaven
Or is it all a brilliant white
Love me sweetly, through this night
And remember me long,
After day's end
Hold me in your arms
One last time
As you return with me
To those golden days,
That are woven
Throughout our lives
Lazy days and loving nights
In your tender arms
Body warm, passion hot
Within our hearts and souls tonight,
As we return to those
Golden days
In each other's arms

Phillip W. Haywood

Brothers

They can be mean,
Or they can be nice.
They wear only jeans,
And they're not made of spice.
They're in trouble a lot,
So what's new!
But that doesn't matter,
'Cause he's loved through and through.

Katie Fuller

Weather

Whether it's cold,
Or whether it's hot.
There will be weather
Whether or not.
The wind will blow,
Or we shall have snow.
Yet, once again
It may just be rain.
Perhaps the storm will move away
Bringing forth a sunny day,
Whether it's cold
Or whether it's hot
There will be weather
Whether or not.

Maxine Smith

Goodbye Dear Friend

In the casket
Our dear friend lay
In church we pray
Hymns sung in unison
Eyes misty, words blurred
Voice Quakes
Death is awake
Tears streak thy face
The casket leaves its place
Somberness filled with gloom
Filters the room
Cheerful memories we find
Embracing those left behind
As our loved one departs
They remain in our hearts.

Sarah B. Haines

Another Wintry Day

When the winter is gone
   Out of sight and out of mind,
Then the springtime will come
   And pairs will entwine,
From this congregation they will say
   Makes life go on day after day.

When springtime is over
   The summer will come,
Bringing lots of clover
   And lots of fun,
Bring your kiddies
   To the park to play,
With baskets full of goodies
   To BBQ today.

When summer is ending
   The leaves will fall,
Turning bright colors
   Of orange, brown, and all,
And at that time, people will say,
GET READY FOR ANOTHER WINTRY
DAY.

Rose M. McNett

"Not Within My Sight"

I see my neighbors flying
Our Flag ever oh so proud

I hear their children singing
America, America, America out loud

On the back of pick-up trucks
The red, white and blue does wave

A full page Flag in the paper
A little boy cuts out to save

The thought of War in no way
Is a pleasant thing to me

And the loss of life of anyone
I would never care to see

But there are those who burn our Flag
They curse against our cause

They destroy the one true symbol
That protects them by its laws

So burn the stars and strips
Each American has that right

Just hope to hell that when you do
You're "not within my sight"

Mark Hamilton

A New Grandson

Strands from genes
our hearts entwined
each finger and toe
eyes, ears and nose
perfect little replica
of me to behold
Heaven decreed that
you belong to me
what bountiful joy
will yet unfold
as Father time
releases his hold.

Pearl L. Chinn

Precious Moments

How precious, how few
  our moments with you....
The fault is our own
  we are not at Your throne.

The blessings are great
  if we will but take...
The time to admire,
  sit back, and acquire.

Be still and listen
  God's word has been given...
To give you your quest
  and purpose for living.

Linda B. Wilson

In Remembrance Of

Sr. Margaret Gertrude

I do not believe in God,
  Nor in the existence of heaven;
But since I was told of her passing,
  I am sure she is with God in heaven.

Prudence Sui-ning Chou

Lost

In a bottle
out at sea
lost its way
to rescue me
so I sit
on this stranded isle
watching the surf
in my state of denial
desolate
these shores I live
it's life sustained
not mine to be given

Michelle Campbell

Answer Please...

Why must dissonance and despair
overwhelm me?
Is it that I expect rhythm and harmony
in all poetry?
Can love not exist without
such mystery?
Or is it that discord is the
major key?

Toni Hardrick

I Am An Individual

I am an Individual, my
own distinctive self with my own
identity. I am like a snow flake
that is different from all others,
with abilities and talents, emotions
and opinions, ideals and beliefs...
all shaped into a pattern never
seen before.

Leslie Tellez

The Price

In this world I've come to see
Peace of mind is never free
Sacrifice
Don't be fair
Close your eyes
forget you care

Throw away your golden dreams
Build a wall to hide the screams
You can choose
It's not a sin
You must lose
Before you win

Lonny J. Petersen

Saying Goodbye

When it's time to say goodbye,
Please don't get upset and cry.
For I know that you still care,
Even though you're way up there.
Of course you know I still will grieve,
But I understand you had to leave.
I will miss you quite a lot,
For in my heart will be an empty spot.
With me you'll always be,
Though each other we cannot see.
I want you to know it's okay to die,
Just make sure you say goodbye.
One more thing you must know,
Is how much I love you so!

Shannon Best

Untitled

Things change.
People die.
Grief fills our lives
  and rules our thoughts.
Religions pass.
Hero's crumble before us
  on feet of clay.
Civilizations vanish without a trace.
Yet, onward we strive.
Hoping, loving, trying.
Never giving into the despair
  of reality.
Always looking for reasons,
  for more.
The answers to why.
Things change.

Sean P. Thompson

What Is Halloween???

Goblins on the doorstep,
Phantoms in the air,
Owls on witches' gate posts,
Giving stare to stare,
Cats on flying broomsticks,
Bats, against the moon,
Stirrings of round fat-cakes
With a solemn spoon,
Whirlings of apple parings,
Figures draped in sheets,
Dodging, disappearing,
Up and down the streets,
Jack-o-lanterns grinning,
Shadows on a screen,
Shrieks and startles and laughter-
This is halloween!!!!

Lyndsey S. Wood

Memories

The seeds of time are
planted in my mind.
Cultivated with love, watered
with tears, and happiness
bringing the sunshine.
As I stroll through the garden,
I can be sure
Memories may be picked
at my leisure.

Linda Cheskus Ruel

Where Has My Youth Gone

standing teary eyed
remembering a love song of
yesterday
Where has my youth gone
staring in the mirror
looking at the gray hair
looking at the wrinkled face of time
staring deep into the eyes
of weariness.
Where has my youth gone
a rap at the door
I recognize the face
I look deep into the eye
I see the reflection of my
youth
no I know where my youth
has gone

Solomon Jackson

Poppa

Poppa rocks
Poppa reads

Poppa has no place to be
Watches flowers grow with me

Poppa listens
Poppa knows

Poppa has a big soft lap
when I want to take a nap

Poppa gives
Poppa shows

Poppa makes my life so fun
Poppa is a special one

Because
Poppa loves

Maria Poppe

Environment

The environment is
precious, I wonder why it
let us destroy it.

We need help, can
we find it in time, before
we are turned into ice
cubes or ashes?

To whom it may
concern, do we really need
the toxic waste? Whatever
we do now will be wrong

We might as well
face it, we are gone. After
all what comes around goes
around, or so they say.

I just thought I'd
mention it to whoever
cares.

Rebecca Pinson

An Afternoon At The Academy

An afternoon at the academy
produced a tremendous amount of clay.
While my creations baked in their tray
I painted my time away.

Tennis required more thought
and I became overwrought
when my backhand and serve
did nothing but swerve
out of the court!

So much for summer fun
I'd rather lie in the baking sun!

Malia Nims

My Girl

She is sweet like sugar
She has a beautiful smile
She is understanding
She is loving,
She cares about me,
She has a wonderful personality
That's why she is mine,
She is beautiful like a rose,
That's why I love her, so.

L. Dowell

Beauty And Love

Beauty and style wrapped in love
Purity and elegance intermingled
Snow and Icicles melting
Dripping the beauty of spring

Look at the beauty and know
That deep in your spirit
Love is being conceived, but
None can perceive the reaction

Chemicals of mind and spirit
Spewing their power outward
Out of control but all
Within a boundary of love

Power building with forceful
Contractions of love and meaning
Hidden from obvious eyes
Panic overtaken by love

Mystic boundaries striving to hold
Matchless beauty seeking escape
Falling swiftly through the deep
Crevice of beauty and love

Norman R. Dahm

Pushed To The Edge...

What do people do who are
pushed to the edge?
How do they get there?
Do people, who are pushed to
the edge, take their own lives?
Or do they let the life they are
living take them?
What is the solution for those
who are pushed to the edge?
Is it death?
Why do the ones we love push
us to the edge?
Do we let them?
Is it our fault that we have
been pushed to the edge?
Now that I am pushed to the
edge, is my life, as I know it, over?
Or do I go on living in pain
at the edge that I have been pushed?

Sharon Bramblett

My Race Horse

Noise will make two ears perk up
Race like the wind with no care
Sleazy as silk in many colors
A body with real strength
Can be bold and courageous
With head held high, nostrils open wide
A tail erect, stand proud
Four legs straight stand as almighty
Rein in hands need to obey
Gate is open, the end he will make
A lei around the neck, ribbon of purple
Parade around the ring one more time
Nice warm hands for a rub down
Then off to the stable quiet and peace

Margaret Demanett Long

Through Mama's Eyes

The sun shone bright,
Rain also in sight.
What was really there to see,
A rainbow for you and me.

Margaret Mott

Rascals of Time

"Clearly defined are the
rascals of time
Who could ever figure out
the plan they have in mind?
Never once revealing how
clever they can be,
Until we have a setback
that no one can foresee.
Everyday we forge
ahead with things we
take for granted.
Then it hits, a plan we
missed, then struggle
to amend it.
Isn't it amazing the
things we must endure?
It's only wise to realize
that's what life plans
as our chore."

Melanie A. Edmonds

Warmth Of A Winter's Kiss

The virgin bride, in winter dress
Reaches out, her hands caress,
This passerby, who is forlorn,
Wishing her, to adorn,
Her springly garb, in colored array,
To brighten up, my dreary day.
A playful breeze, so sweet and pure
Brushes my lids, so very demure.
A frozen crystal, long and sleek.
Drips a rainbow on my cheek!
The morning sun, casts a ray
Capturing my face, on its way,
A lacy snowflake, from the sky
Tweaks my nose, on passing by
Leaving just a drop of dew,
Warm and melted, fresh and new
Lips long puckered from the cold,
Are touched with warming streaks of gold
Enveloped in this stately bliss
I've felt the warmth of winter's kiss.

Theresa J. Arms

Mountains

Cold bastiles of hewn stone
Reaching to the sky,
An edifice against the fleecy clouds
That hurriedly thunder by.

Esters from the wooded cliffs
Produce the purple haze,
Immortalized in our nation's songs
Preserving America's early days.

But poets see no coldness
In these crags of jagged stone.
Just a fairyland of rugged beauty
That each snowflake may call home.

Philip Lewis Arena

Untitled

The sun comes up, our love falls down.
See it lying on the ground.
Do we dare to pick it up again?
The shattered pieces of broken dreams.
The sun is shining, the day is young.
It doesn't matter here on earth.
For two lonely people, day is done.

Nancy Cook

Rain

The day has turned my memory
Red with blood.
And the night has dried my wounds.
But the dreams remain the same.
The days, the nights, the confusion.

The time I need
is longer than I have.
The pain will subside.

Stretched and tattered
My eyes examine the remains.
Nothing is left to inspect.
Nothing visible....

Years, year after year
is all it takes
To clean the misery of the past.

I never have seen
So many days pass
Without a word.

Matt Jerzyk

Reflection

The man watched the damp glass
Reflecting memories of the past

the beer almost gone

"Man, that was quick,
just like my life,
a real easy trick,

Ah, but was good,
must do it again,
'nother life would be nice,
but got to have sin,

What would it all mean,
without the vice,
be like the arctic,
without any ice,

'Cause humans ain't perfect,
just wouldn't be right,
we gotta make payments,
till we go out of sight"

D. W. Ferguson

After The Rain

Deep within me lives a little girl
She cries at night
Why tears fall I don't know
Tell me why the river flows

What can I say to calm the mind
Of the child living inside

After the rain the sun will rise
Rest easy little one, dry your eyes
Peace with the child living inside
Baby baby, baby mine

There's no telling what lies ahead
No way of knowing what's over the bend
The road of life is a mystery
Only God knows what's meant to be

Have faith sweet angel
Have no fear
After the rain all is new
The Father watches over you

I say these words to calm the mind
Of the child living inside

Michelle Vrieze

Cousins, Friendship, Marriage

Georgina has a nice friend, Regina.
Regina would help Georgina,
and Georgina would help Regina.
One day Georgina
Introduced Regina
To her first cousin, Valina.
It happened that Regina
Liked Valina
Better than Georgina.
So... Regina left Georgina
and married Valina.
Ain't that neata?

Val Wood

"Hypocrisy"

The casket was open, and everyone
    remembers, what a wonderful man
he was.
Lies, lies, all lies.
Two-faced in the face of death.
He was a louse.
He beat his spouse.
He wasn't worth a damn.
Still we file past the casket.
Crying, sighing, what a wonderful
    man.

Nancy M. Dummitt

Mourning

The twilight sky; an embarked hue
reminds me of the thought of you.
Wooden steps now hold me alright.
One shadow whispers in the night.
My eyes dart, searching for you, dear.
I look up and the sky is clear.
This shadow stays and no other.
I was a friend and a lover.
Venus is out and looking down
upon my mournful little frown.
My mind still wonders what went wrong;
the heavens tell me to be strong.
Fantastic colors fill the sky,
a painting splashed with marbled dye.
A sigh escapes my body now.
I shall never laugh, this I vow.
I see the moon, for hereafter,
then I hear your dear, sweet laughter.
Oh, was it sent to me to tease,
or simply a summer night breeze?

Melissa Garcini

Reflections

Eyes. The mirror of the soul.
Reflections in the mirror.
Do they mirror the soul?
Or the eyes?

Do the blind then lack soul?
Or the mere mirror reflection thereof?
Surrounded by indifferent darkness,
Why do they see so much more?

Or is sighted vision blurred,
Obscured by a mere reflection?
Does mirrorless blind introspection
Offer no such escape?

Stella Sibincic

Continuation Of Life

You are my child,
ripe with feeling
troubled by needs,
full with a new being.

Fear of the unknown,
yet excited by anticipation
of shared commitment
to new beginning
created from love.

I gave you first breath,
felt your growth,
suffered your pain,
shared your highs.

And now, as you create life,
I feel, care, love
my baby daughter,
who I may have loved most,
and now share a most special moment.

Laurie O'Connor

The Crocus

Like the phoenix
Rising from its ashes
So I the crocus
Recycle myself
From frozen ground
I silently
prepare for life
near the end of winter....

I am the crocus
The little drummer flower
Announcing to bare trees
"I am here...wake up...follow me"
I come in a burst of golden promise
Shivering wind battered humans
Stop and smile at me.

Marian Gordon

Colors

Colors in the
rough are we
whose hearts do
yearn
yet
speak softly...
Silence
is the only cry
if we don't
stand
and ask them
why?

Michael J. Mohney

The Stray

The cat when I saw her
seemed unusual and rare,
one who would need much care.

She ate even crumbs of bread
and danced with joy,
gently, on dark paws.

The cat surprised me,
deciding to stay,
with her actions as if to say
"Thank You."

Pamela Gatta

Weather Feelings

Rain, rain is the soul of
sadness. That is the feeling
before. The sunshine and laughter.
Sunshine, sunshine, is the
heart of happiness. It is the
feeling of belonging, of
friendship and fulfillment.

The in between times are
a group of various storms, a
small little drizzle will be
the understanding. Of joy or misery,
grief might be a hurricane. A
tragedy might be replaced with flooding,
Drowning your soul with mixed feelings.

But the best feeling of
weather is right after a storm;
it is called excitement,
Wondering what's going to happen next.
Depending on what the weather is,
Think about what's going to happen next.

Mandy Mason

Irish Dreamscape

When the misty winds of March
  sail the shamrocks
  along the shore line
I'll be there.

When young green blades of grass
  with promising petals of daffodil
  envelop the breeze
  with a rush of perfume
I'll be there.

When the wee folk gather
  in the glen
  in the gloaming,
  speaking sagas of Erin past
I'll be there.

And when himself, St. Patrick
  comes to bend and
  kneel in prayer
  I swear—'tis not blarney—
I'll be there.

Maidie Perez

A Promise Kept

The chinook
salmon, jumping, back-swept nosed
up to the impossible
stone, bone-crushing cascade.

Wakes
to clear the top on last try, spent
to the rudes beyond, to spawn,
to die, to taste nature's
criminal leisure.

The elderberry bough
cracks with un-picked fruit, at dawn
small-mouthed bass break water, gorged
with spawn, with eaten dreams.

My friend
she came of melancholy
parents: prone to secret spells,
for years they kept alone - her
uncle, I believe, was killed
of it.

Phillip Carlson

Gulf Coast Chorus

Sun Wind
Sand and Water

Sun Wind
Sand and Water

Sun Wind
Sand and Water

AND
OLD
MEN
SIGHING

Sun Wind
Sand and Water

Sun Wind
Sand and Water

Sun Wind
Sand and Water

AND
OLD
MEN
DYING

Ruth Grieger

1948

Born flawed
Scarred by the sins of Genesis
Imperfect from the beginning
Yet created by God
Who is

Born loved
Part of an unending story
Inspired by imagination
Made real by God
Who is

Born free
Willed to me at birth
To be imperfect, free and loved
A trinity of humanness from God
Who is

Born whole
The seed of life has bloomed
Special, precious and irrepeatable
Embraced and nourished by God
Who will

Peggy Rubino

Soul Woman

There is a woman in my soul
she nurtures me

She rocks me in the cradle
of where I need to be

There is a woman in my soul
she counsels me
she is wisdom

The Woman's birthing me!

There is a woman in my soul,
she speaks truth and love

She sings the universe

Her presence transcends me

Mary Bub

Pain

A painfully squelched
scream squiggled from
under an iron clad
door labeled "DO NOT ENTER."

The builder swore air
tight that would last
for a lifetime. I need
never worry of escape.

But now alas, the pain
escapes to wander
and trample my newly
tilled garden of rebirth.

How I weary of the touch,
the sound and sight of
that pain, vying with
my heartbeat for control.

What kind of militia
to call on to incarcerate
this pain of loneliness.
Alone...alone, the screams wail.

Mary B. Foster

Summer Rain

The rain lands softly on my head
Seeking out my soul as you did
Gently
Hardly seeming to touch at all
Soaking me to the skin
Filling my every thought with you
Seeping into my heart
Till you are a part of me
And I am washed free.

Shelley-Anne Wooderson

Knowing Is Believing

Truth dictates the voice
Seldom heard by many
As love emits passion uncontrolled
Yet hunger consumes
Beyond a sense of plenty
And so human stories unfold

Our choice as to chance
Like biblical phrase
Is often ignored
By simply turning a page
Prisoner to a cold shoulder
The voice is betrayed
And all at once
Our people have strayed

Belief, as the martyr
Has a life long price to pay
The voice is knowledge
Not our own way
A gift to accept,..
To take while we may

William Scott Askey

Untitled

It's bendable,
Shakeable,
and sometimes breakable.
Some are there to the end,
Others just can't mend.
Know what it is?
It's a friend!

Lindsay Wohlers

In The Twilight

As I sit here by my window,
　Shadows creep across the floor.
I seem to hear your gentle step.
　And the voice I'll hear no more.

You whisper "Dear I love you"
　As you did in days gone by.
When we wandered through the orchard,
　Beneath a starlit sky.

The little home we planned to have,
　With flowers here and there.
A place where we alone could dream,
　And all our joys share.

Then came those dark and lonely days,
　Through destructive years of war.
That left me broken hearted,
　And you, asleep on foreign shores.

My heart beats on and tries to live,
　And I smile now and then.
But I find the most contentment,
　In the things that might have been.

Virginia M. Hall

Ma

I was thinking about Ma today.
She always has a kind word.
She always has a big smile.
She is always there when needed.

I was thinking about Ma today.
She would laugh and cry with us.
She would work and play with us.
Even took time for a prayer or two.

I was thinking about Ma today.
Now she is sick, still a smile.
Always a kind word for all.
Thank you, God, for my Ma.

Laverna Harman

"Fluffy"

Fluffy was just an ordinary cat,
She certainly was no pedigree:
But that didn't matter at all to her,
And it certainly didn't to me:

She never won blue ribbons,
And a Trophy she never claimed:
But, she was oh, so soft and gentle,
And looked just like her name:

Fluffy never scratched or bit me,
No matter what I did:
It was as though she understood,
That I was just a kid:

For nigh on seven years I had her,
But now she's gone away:
A part of me went with her,
That cold and fateful day:

I still have her memories,
And two kittens she left behind:
But I never shall forget her,
Because Fluffy...she was mine!!!

Vicki Cunningham

My Little Ugly Mutt

When I felt weak
She licked my cheek
My little ugly mutt

When I was upset and would cry
And not care if I would live or die
She licked my cheek
My little ugly mutt

My little ugly mutt
A message she would bring
A loud bark to let me know
my telephone would ring.

My little ugly mutt
Went to heaven this past year
And when I think of her
In my eyes, you'll find a tear

In my heart she'll always be
sitting very close to me.
My little ugly Mutt.

Shirley Glenzer

The Moon

She guides me by night
　she reminds me by day
She brightens my nights
　and comforts my days.
　　watching over me,
　　　embracing me,
　　tucking me to sleep,
　　caressing me as I dream.

I see her!
　Shining brightly, shining softly,
　　bringing warmth to my heart,
　　　joy to my soul.

I touch her!
　Gloriously beaming, radiantly gleaming,
　　pouring forth glimmer and majesty;
　While yet,
　　humbly she reigns.

Roger D. Martinez

Seize The Moment

"You fill me with Glee!"
she said to me
while wearing a fickle frown.
She repeated her statement
sweetly, not blatant,
to my blushing cheeks still facing down.
This statement did nourish,
excite me to flourish,
a build up of self esteem.
"You fill me with glee!"
I said to she,
as my senses did convene.

Wally Frist

The Overweight Woman's Dream

Cheeks are sleek,
Skin is thin,
Waist is twenty-four,
What a body to adore.

Eyes of envy watch,
Looks of approval stare,
Size eight dress,
Tailored curves caress.

Patricia Crews

Solitary Moon

I saw the moon this morning
She was all alone in the sky
Not a cloud in the heavens
Not even a star in sight
Just the moon alone in the sky

I stopped to ponder
How so much like the moon I am
She, always after the sun
All alone in the sky
Never able to meld into one

And I, like the moon
Always alone in my own
Serene sky
Without even one hope in my heaven
Loving you, wanting you
Beckoning you with my light
Always alone
Longing for you
In my own lonely night.

Roma

Answers

The wind sings a sad song.
She whispers sorrow through
the trees, beams hope from
the sun and leaves
questions in the soft, warm,
summer sand.

She scatters few answers
in the leaves on the
hillside.
Can time erase or wind
rekindle this flame?
Without you can I ever
be whole again?

Meredith L. Barker

Why Did She Have To Go

Why did she leave my life
She won't be there when I become a wife
I loved her so very much
We loved her so much

Why did she have to go
Didn't she know I loved her
Did she love me too
Why did she have to go

Grandma, Grandma
You didn't have to go
Grandma, Grandma
Why did you have to go
I know you're up there
I know you love me
But you left me here
To live my own life

Why did she have to go
Didn't she know I loved her
Did she love me too
Why, oh why did she have to go

Teresa Spence

Swim Your Heart Out

Speed is all she cares about
she's in another world
seeing only the finish line
not caring what's on land
but only in the water
she is great, she loves to swim
she is determined to win,
and she will.

Lori Diebel

Reflections

Reflections of life.
Shimmering in memory,
They reach out to touch
The heart and mind.
They bring sorrow and tears,
joy and love.
They grow to unbounded heights,
And burst into novas.

Their dust sparkles
In memory's mind.
They begin to blossom, are fed
And burst out once more.

Only to die away,
And lie replaced
By other memories.
Soon to be reflections.

Kimberly K. Davis

The Gesture

I want that plunge
Like a raindrop,
Free falling to its destination.
I want that flight
But without the net,
Always like a hand
To be secure and sure
For all the world to know.
Scared, petrified, like seeing the world
For the first time.
The edge is so close,
Like a dream out of my reach.
It's pulling me in,
I feel I must go
And for once I go
Without the hand.

Amy Gold

Heartache

My wounded heart is captured
In a web of pain and grief,
And though my prayers may seem unanswered,
Still I plead for sweet relief.
The dark and heavy burdens
Seem much more than I can bear,
And my soul cries out for respite
From its anxious toil and wear.
Yet the darkest hour of midnight
Is always followed by the dawn,
And I find in times of greatest need
Strength I cannot call my own.
But still sometimes I falter
And my heart breaks once again.
Then unseen hands, so kind and gentle,
Lift me up and ease my pain.

Jerry Walters Longmire

Silence

Silence is all around me,
Silence is always there,
silence is my thoughts when
I try to hear,
My silence is sad,
because my silence is forever.
I pray every day, just to hear,
hear them say,
it's not going to get any better.
I wish I had a day, to hear.......
Hear you say........
It's no use.
I try to be normal as anyone can be.
I love me for me, and
what someday I might be.
I know silence and me will
always be together.

Malinda Whitson

The Bridge

Flashing yellow lights
silhouette you
in the damp darkness circulating
between our bodies,
against pale stones.

As we stand at the edge,
framed by a white crescent
above the rushing water,
I look into you.

I had never seen
you in such a manner,
holding your heart
as I sip a milkshake.
Thoughts like steam
spiraling up between us
are broken by cars.

Philip K. Goropoulos

"Those Feelings"

The love we shared so long ago
simply must be restored.
Don't want to feel so very low
don't want to be ignored.
Again let me feel you so deep inside,
again to feel a woman, yet mere child.
Am I coming on too strong?
I want your hungry touch.
Have we been as one too long?
I want it so very much.
My arms awaiting and open,
not a word need be spoken.
Come to me now, my only desire.
Come to me now, let me light your fire.

Laura Foley

Blackbird

Blackbird! Blackbird!
  So fair
Touch not my hair.
Blackbird, hands off
  my head,
Flew ever so high to
  his bed,
Crying, "Why? Why?"
  Up in the sky.
Reply I, "Don't cry, cry, cry."

Sally Weiss

Time

As long as the moon shall shine
Since the ebb of time
An eve never ending

For in our minds
With the aid of wines
Reality is bending

Like the everlasting sun
Which burns in everyone
My shining love descending

For time has rebegun
Eternal peace is won
Through you my soul transcending

Mark Miller

Little Shoes

Little shoes in a row.
Six little shoes that no one will know.
Little shoes conceived in LOVE.
Six little shoes lost to GOD above.
Mothers tears will always flow, for
six little shoes she wanted to know.

Susan M. Schlegel

Able To Devour

Able to devour
small livestock
in a single gulp,
the Mighty Serpent
slithers northwestward
through the Amazonian rain forest
past villages and shops
cars and motor ways
airstrips and docks.
and wouldn't you know,
that there are probably those
in Brazil
that would kill
for a can of
snake repellent.

Scott Masters

Touch Me

Laughing eyes
Smiling lips
Listening ears
Warm fingertips

Forever young
in our minds
forever searching
sure to find

Touch me dear
like gentle sigh
as breeze to flowers
under sky

Touch me
with warm fingertips
as babies feel
their mother's lips

Then touch my soul
at day's sunrise
with your clear and searching
deep, brown eyes.

Selma Phoebe Cohen

To Youth

Save the twinkle of stars,
Snatch a bit of midnight sky,
Grasp handfuls of grey-green dawn
To season a draught of sunlight.
Copy birds' songs, the shrill call
  of workmen's whistles;
Beg an hour of afternoon's
  lazy quiet,
Pack the twilight's coolness
Into a violet-scented box,
Then pause happily to watch
The red-gold and purple blend
Into the soft, sad grey of the
  journey's end.

  L. Georgia Rosseter

I'm Bad

I am bad
so bad
that you can't touch me
because I'll fly away.
High, high is where I go
further than you'll ever know.
I leave my legacy to those that follow.
I was born in the Congo
and sailed down the Nile.
The deciduous forest was my home.
In my body grew diamonds and gems,
and, without me, there was no them.

So I say to you,
Ain't I bad, ain't I fine,
and ain't I black?

  Mendi Joycette Blue

Ace Of Hearts

We're in a world of our own
So empty and bare
Quietly sitting
Playing solitaire

That's the story of our lives
We set our own pace
We're never going to win
For, we've lost the ace

It wasn't the club,
the diamond or spade
But, the ace of hearts
that had to fade

We're so lonely
And the cards are so much fun
We then realize we'll never succeed
with a deck of fifty-one

In cards we take a chance
For some, it's only a game, but
for others, cards reflect their lives
And, that's just not the same

  Patricia G. DeMarco

Autumn

Golden leaves,
Still clinging to trees,
Were doing their frantic
  dance
In the breeze
This morning.

  Mary E. Avery Backus

My Hawaii

I've never known such happy people
So friendly, so loving and so gay
Their music reflects these feelings
In a delightfully joyous way

The land is lushly green and golden
With sugar cane, pineapple, coffee
The air is scented with sweet blossoms
Of plumeria - and pikake

The many hued waters of the bays
In shades of lavender, blue and green
Sparkle under the warmth of the sun
And thunderous curling waves are seen

Mountains rise splendidly from the shore
Crests covered by a bouquet of cloud
The rain brings cascading waterfalls
And colorful rainbows arched and proud

Legends imbue this land with magic
With petroglyphs and priests of the past
Missionaries and whalers brought change
Changes don't matter - I'm home at last!

  Nancy Hopkins Sutherland

40 You're Turning

40 you're turning
So how can it be
You have a sibling
As young as me?

Another year passes quickly
You handle it well
Time marches on - but
on you one can't tell.

Face lifts and tummy tucks
Would all be for naught.
Father Time must be sleeping
For you he's not caught.

An easy smile and young spirit
Your grace does inspire
So what's my gift to you?
A weekend at the Greenbriar!

  Larry Raper

Mixed Bag

To Marlene:

Born of a mixture
Significant in blend,
Tender in nature,
That blooms within.

Calm as the season
And nurtured with love,
Consumed by the beauty,
From heaven above.

The mixed bag of culture
And society's spectrum
The endless line of direction,
By connection.

Who said the rainbow has many colors?
The mixed bag is a creation
By father and mother.

Raising Kane

  Maria E. Lamar

Untitled

Who am I to touch
so many yet remain
submissive?

With significance, I
appear not always the
same to each caller.

Through me sorrow is
released as I leave a
kiss upon tainted lips.

I gently wash dirt from
blinded eyes so clearly
they see again.

I signal for help when
voices are silent, causing
ears to remain deaf.

No hero am I,
nor a saint, simply
a teardrop fallen.

  Tammy L. Gotchie

Blissful Memory

You are blessed with a family
So true and so kind,
Though you suffer the loss
Of your loved one, your Bind.

His Soul will surround Him
For days until when,
He knows that his family
Is blessed without end.

As he seeks his way through
To our Lord up above,
He's encircled by Angels.
They treasure his love.

If he had any hardships
They were laid to rest.
His acceptance upgraded
His philosophy at best.

He did give His Best
To his family and friends.
With true understanding,
His Love Never Ends.

  Katherine Lisowski

For All Time

In the river of my mind
soft waves glisten
and rise slowly to the surface
as you gently touch the water
and stir the depths of my imagination

When the river overflows
and the rain seems unkind
you calm the fierce water
and shelter my weary mind

Beneath the waves of a lingering dream
you are always there
with benevolence and compassion
the hours that we share
we touch the sky
and it makes us one.
For Joe Lamon

  Yvonne A. Hulin

"Angel Light"

Some are born to do evil,
Some are born to do right
Some auras emanate darkness,
Yours radiates light,
An angel light.
People expect to see a shimmering halo,
But you give out a full body glow
An angel light.
Despite all obstacles in life,
Your heart remains pure and true,
Despite all the hassles you've faced,
Your light still shines through.
Your angel light
The shining you emit
Is not visible by sight,
But can be felt in the souls of
  Those
    Blessed by
      Your angel light
      Richard Hubbarth

The Cherokee Trail

  The Cherokee fell,
Some fell to their graves.
  They were the only ones who
needed to be saved.
  They were taken to camps,
Suddenly to dimmed like lamps.
  They were given a blanket,
But they still couldn't take it.
  They were dragged out of homes,
But not to be alone.
  Nothing to be taken,
Most were awakened.
  It was awful,
It sunk into hearts plentiful.
  So ends the Cherokee Trail,
In the end, so many fell.
    Kevin Ross

Summer's Night Interlude

Lie down with me
Some lonely night
Whisper in my ear
Cover me with kisses
Run your fingers through my hair
Feel my body with your hands
Enjoy me
  if only for one night.

Kiss me and smile
Whisper a good-bye
Know this will forever be
A pleasure in my heart

Wake up in the morning light
Don't look back
Have no regrets
Just know
Just remember
The pleasure
Enjoy me
  if only for one night.
    Patricia Gogan

Memory Of Today

We have met before
Sometime way back when
When I'm with you, I do soar,
I do now, I did then.

A touch I've known in yesterday
So familiar and so right
Passion that was so sincere
Always burning and ever bright.

Seasons change and so did we
Our paths would cross no more
Neither knew who we would be
What we'd meet behind each door.

Lives were played and lives were made
We know not what we missed
Dreams have changed and shadows fade
And memories of how we kissed.

As fate would have it, we do meet
And as if the time stood still
Old fires light, feel the heat
Our love survives, it always will.
    Mari Herrington

Untitled

I've peddled this bike as far as I can
soon the peddles will not turn.
Therefore, the wheels will stop.
The bike and I will fall to the ground.
I'm halfway there; will you help?

The reply I receive is,
"You rode the bike this far,
you'll have to ride it home
because I'm not going to bring you in."

So here I sit with nothing left to give
and no way to return home.
    Sylvia Lindsey

Night Winds Of Habitual Days

The young man,
soon to be old,
walks in his world of familiarity
and is very cold...
He lifts his coat-collar snug around
his neck,
shielding himself from the brisk
piercing night winds of habitual days;
and in the course of his indifferent,
tortured trek,
the youth surrounded by hundreds
(very near), prays
    Marvin R. Clardie

Fate Is My Shroud

I wear my misery like a shroud
Sorrow hangs o'er my head like a cloud
Cursed am I by the hand of fate
My lot was cast in a sorry state
I scheme and plan my life to build
but in heaven it was not willed
That mine should be a life of ease
With me fate has done as she pleased
My plans never cease to fail
And I cry to heaven with a mournful wail
Fate let me be and let me rest
Just once let my plans be best
    Kenneth C. Smith

The Day You Left Me

  The day you left me, I felt
sorrow within

  The day you left me I had
to begin

  A new life in a new time
which changed my state of mind

  Completely and immediately
I tried, but it seemed as if someone
had died

  With the confusion and illusion
I spent and thought of ways

  But always ended up in a daze
thinking about the day you left me.
    K. C. Lim

Two People

Two people, holding hands
Speaking to each other with their eyes
No words are necessary
To know what's in each ones heart
For they are young and in love
And all's right with the world.

Yesterday, today, tomorrow, all seems
Like one when they are together
When they touch it's sheer ecstasy

Two people, one day, torn apart
By worldly circumstances
One never knowing the other's pain
But the bond of love they shared
Was so strong, it will transcend time,
Age and separation.

Two people, meeting again in some
distant place
Eyes meeting, hands touching
Hearts racing, all time erased.
    Lucille McKinney

One

A wayward ship breaks on the reef,
Spilling cargo and crew.
She finds him there upon the beach,
Bloody, cold and blue.
With loving care she tends his wounds,
Hoping to make him well.
For when he stands upon his feet,
They'll sound the wedding knell.

The moon is full, the torches bright,
Red flowers in her hair.
The sea is calm, the breezes light,
Her fragrance fills the air.
Pagan drums sound through the darkness,
Keeping passions strong.
When daylight dawns they kiss goodnight,
Two lives, now one.
    P. A. Younger

Fires

Fires are raging
Stealing homes like fierce robbers
showing no mercy.
    Phoebe Pile

Between Time

This is the estranged season,
Sprawled across the wall
In sluggish boxes that attempt
To cage the rage that smothers
The hope of spring, and then
Hand it to you piece-meal.

This is the annual standstill.
Smiles of summer are bleached
From your mind like a tan line,
And it seems every sand castle
In your world has been poured
Into a broken hourglass.

This is the desperate month,
Its inclemency exposing every
Feeling you would overcoat
Until you are left with nothing
But the sting of February
Striking a bare emotion.

Scott Williams

"Kurt Cobain"

Kurt Cobain,
  Still carrying fame.
You were lost with pain,
  In the addiction to cocaine.
It made you insane,
  Then you had to shoot at your brain.
But we still love you,
  Kurt Cobain.

Lisa Pearon

Playing With Greed

Choices made
Decisions done
The game is over
No time for fun

A master with tricks
You played your hand well
So warm, so inviting
You should have noticed the smell

False hopes
How dare you dream
Close your eyes to what's there
Things aren't ever what they seem

The bitter taste of want
The burning feel of need
You gave freely and willing
You didn't notice the greed

Now it starts to consume you
Time to stop this foolish play
One way or another
It all ends here today.

Gina M. Tarvit

Love

Love is like a sunset.
Just when you think that it is pretty
and will last a lifetime
it slips through your hands like sand,
sand in a time glass.
Watch closely and don't miss out.
love is like a sunset
which slips away.

Sabrina Bond

Early Autumn

Oh, those fated leaves!
Still summer-green they ease
to still summer-green meadow.
Do they already know
a chill in the breeze
no one yet perceives?

What invisible seams
wrap into one our beings —
veins-blood-sap-flesh-leaves—
that my heart grieves
as if for broken wings
ripped from my limbs?

Renato Gasparetti

Your Arms

    Your arms give my being
strength; by holding me close
in the heart of your chest

    Your arms caressing my body
bring out my femininity to
share with you

    Your arms cover me with their
masculine build and protect me
from unknowns

    Your arms invite me to
celebrate your love

Lourdes Hennessy

Strength

Happy Strength is mine today!
Strength for work and for
  play.
Strength to keep resolve renewing.
Strength to stand, to wait, to
  stay.
Strength to make my heart,
  my soul obey!
Strength to keep a chosen course.
Strength to rise above remorse.

Rosemarie De Noyer Leach

Their Erroneous Pleasure

Out of the mouths of those loving me
structured letters fall freely
dripping like a lustful faucet of
secrets. Nastiness being their bliss
they impale me with their words. They
mind me closely because they have no
business of their own.

Lillie M. Smith

Stars

Haven't you ever wondered how a
star got there?
For me it is a place where love
and magic occur.
Every time someone fell in love, a new
one would appear.
When you look up in the sky
you could say one of those is
mine.
The name of your first love will
always be on your star, for that person
alone is never to be forgotten.

Terra Linzner

Untitled

Depression is like a disease.
Sucking the life out of you -
like its future is unknown.
Entering a realm
where the stars shed their bodies;
devoted to no one but
the one true god.
is he here?
Shhhhh....
I think I hear him,
his musty stench
Empowering me -
to inhale the Breath of Eternity.

Nikole Zarychta

Rage

I stand here on the edge
Swaying swaying back and forth
Watching the rushing water

All white and foamy
Rushing rushing tumbling houses
Broken windows broken dreams

I stand here on the edge
Watching watching this white water
Looking at the rage of you
Seeing your anger like a flame
Consuming everything in your way

I stand here on the edge
Screaming screaming nooo
As your swirling churning waters
Take my dreams and crush them
Like a mirror you shatter
And break rage rage all consuming
Eating eating my heart
Stepping stepping on my soul
Leaving behind the black emptiness of
death

Mary Sullivan

Summer Fun

Running out in my bare feet,
Swimming, splashing, what a treat!
Swinging in the air so high,
My toes almost touch the sky.

Swooping down the highest slide,
Galloping horses are fun to ride,
Animals running everywhere,
Butterflies fluttering through the air.

Flowers blooming, what a sight,
Yellow, blue, pink and white,
Sunshine makes me cozy too,
There is no time for feeling blue.

Virginia Bailey

Patches Of Blue And White

Flying high in the Sky
So many colors of Blue
Dark Blue melts into pale Blue
Into wispy white clouds below...
No longer can I see
the Horizon of Earth and Sky...
The Earth is covered with
A blanket of snow white clouds...

The miracle of flight,
Patches of Blue and White..

Mary Lou Brown

Petals In The Stream

I watch the petals flow in the stream,
Swirl down the river—just like a dream.

Petals fall as flowers wither,
My heart is empty without a lover.
People hurriedly pass by me,
I am lonely but who can see?

On and on the petals flow,
Without tears nor sighs they go,
Down into death's cold embrace,
Forever and more with pride and grace.

Velvet Li

Psychic

thoughts
swirling, dancing
a myriad rainbow
in a crystal globe
flashes of light
reflections of daydreams
refracted prisms
endless colors
in an eternal globe
of visions

Ruth Shramek

Take My Wounds And Make Me Whole

Capture my heart, spare my soul.
Take my wounds and make me whole.
Help me release all my sorrow, for
My child lost will see no morrow.
Wipe my tears, forsake my cry.
Kiss myself being long goodbye.
Who shall I blame? Did I do wrong?
My poor baby did not live long.
In my sleep I see her face.
In her beauty, present is grace.
In my laps I call her name and bow
My head in personal shame.
I loved my child with all my soul.
Oh please Lord take my wounds and
Make me whole.
Make me whole from all my faults and
sins.
I will now bow my head, give thanks,
AMEN!

Victoria Ann Brazzle

When The Mind Is Blank

When the mind is blank
The days drag
Arms and legs go automatic,
Verbal responses only,
No quips to enliven.
When the mind is blank
The days drag;
Time becomes a soldier
Marking minutes, hours, days,
With structured pretense.
When the mind is blank
The days drag;
That center of creativity
Shut down.
The soul feels heavy.

Lawrence Michael Dickson

A Tribute to My Wife

She does all the cleaning,
takes care of my clothes
and if I would ask her
she'd wipe my nose
She's such a good cook
as my figure attests
and I surely would rate her
as one of the best.
She's full of compassion,
so loving and kind,
why she chose me,
just boggles my mind.
She's a great Christian lady,
the joy of my life
Oh I'm so happy,
That she is my wife!

Levi Krehbiel

The Ocean

Feel the breeze on your face.
Taste the salt on your tongue.
Smell the aroma of the ocean.
Touch the sand all around you.
Hear the waves roar ashore.
See the water ripple.

Pamela Voyles

Ballad Of A Bulimic

Eyes of lost laughter
Tears falling insane
Here comes the morning
And I can't stop the rain

The smiles gone forever
You know what to do
Now I'm stuck dying
Look what you put me through

My face grew wider
My mind led the way
Shatters took my hand
Stuck in yesterday

Memories all forgotten
Swallowed in the pain
Here comes the mourning
And I can't stop the reign

Robert Dempsey Jr.

Our Life

We joined hands many years ago, yet it
seems like only days

The time has passed so very fast and
we've changed in so many ways

We've endured trials and tribulations,
some big but most quite small

And through the help of the Divine One
we overcame them all

Life on this earth is fleeting and then
we all digress

But for my time here, your love has been
my source of happiness

My love for you will never cease
but grow forevermore

Until that day when we meet again
at our Father's heavenly door.

Marc Mueller

"A Child's Plea"

- Staring out my window,
    tears streaming down my face,
I yearn for someone to love me,
    to deliver me from this place.

- I gaze up towards the stars,
silenced by my hellish plight.
To God I pray, "Please save me,
    from the Demons who kill on sight."

- The anguish of my spirit
Overshadows all physical pain.
The wall I've built around me
    is the only protection I sustain.

- The Destroyers of my essence
    approach me once again.
Never had I realized…
    my crying is a sin.

- As His weapon thrashes down on me,
    She steps back; she shows her smile.
God, oh God, please shield me,
    for I am only a child.

P. A. Joseph

Pain In A Person's Eyes

All the pain in a person's eyes
tells a story -
but no one knows why.
As you look into one's eyes -
You can tell this person really
tried, and did anything
to stay alive;
But sooner or later there was
no place to hide.
One eye tells a real lot,
but to a stranger he cannot see.
The person who was suppose
to see -
didn't bother to read.

Mary A. Bell

Dreamer

In my dreams, I see them,
Temples built of sand,
Standing high above
An ocean of blue topaz.

I walk the well-defined golden path,
Leading to the black onyx fence.
As I reach for the silver knob,
I sit up wide awake.

Kimberly Lewis

Wasteland

With his last breath of desert air
The final pain that he could bear
He thrust his fists into the sand

With dried hands he bore a hole
In search of water for his dying soul
Trapped in the wasteland

He kept digging into the ground
Yet his oasis could not be found
His own life he failed to save

He lay in the burning sand
Prey of the unforgiving land
And so the hole became his grave

Nathan Hedges

Untitled

Love is like a flower
That blooms by the hour,
Dies within a week.
After meeting its eternal peek.
Too bad to say our love isn't that way.
My love is like a flower
that blooms and grows by the hour.
Doesn't die within a week
because I've already met my eternal peek.
You are the one I love.
You've come from above.
It's too good to be true.
For me and you.
Together we are but will we stay.
I hope to say I do one day.

Sabrina Suarez

Shelly

Sublime misunderstood saint
that clarifies the world

Drinker of love potions
caster of spells
saddest of all loves

One thought, one tears, formed from
your serene mind, would be

More than enough
come to me
inspire me

Miraculous human, you are where you
belong... In loving heaven

Most caring of all creatures
teach me...
whisper to me

Love me your most unworthy
of daughters

Help me...
care for me
As I care for you....forever.

Mancheno

The Feeling

The feeling that I felt on
that cold and lonely day,
Is a feeling that still
hurts and will not go away.

It's the pain and the sorrow
that I felt inside,
It's the hole left in my heart
from when my stepdad died.

Staci Stanton

Today

I put away a dream today.
The love I knew was not to stay.
The truth was told along the way.
But dreams, I find, tend to stray.
There is really not much more to say.
Except— that, well — just today:
I reached inside myself.
Found the dream upon my shelf.
Lived again those memories grand.
Caught the tears within my hand.
I put away a dream today.

Linda Butler

A Grateful Heart

Lord, thank you for the blessings
that fill our nights and days:
For the constant, tender Mercy
You show in many ways;
For the Light You shine to guide us
along this winding road;
For the Strength You always lend us
when we have a heavy load.
Thank You for the Healing Hand
You use to calm our hearts;
For always giving us comfort
amidst our darkest spots;
For surrounding us with kindness
in a world that's often turned wrong.
And thank You for this family...
for the Love that keeps us strong.

Tammy R. Bridges

Untitled

You look at me with those eyes
that have cried for a thousand -
I look at you with mine, that
have cried for none.
My soul is dry -
My mind confused -
How can I touch your heart,
when I can't feel my own?

I reach out to you with hands,
that have only felt emptiness.
You touch me with kindness
and fulfillment.
My body is weak -
My heart is lonely -
How can I survive with
no understanding?
How can I love you,
when I can't love myself?

Mz Kelley Taverner

My Love Your Ocean

Is it as deep as it is wide,
that is a question only you decide.
Rolls in and out never to tire,
a blue white churning desire.
Breaking upon the shore of thee,
my love for you is as the sea.

Some days are cloudy, shrouded in fog,
a compass bearing, a note in the log.
Drift upon the endless ride,
your life you've given the shifting tide.
Throw caution like sails to the wind,
my love for you never to rescind.

Your ship set sail in water abound,
whispers of surf the only sound.
With gentle motion I sooth your soul,
my sea your ocean 'til we grow old.
You're my captain, I your mate,
This love an ocean so vast and great...

Philip G. O'Brien III

Go Back To Yesterday

Go back to yesterday once more.
Take in all the sights
Sounds and feelings you had
For that which was yesterday
Will never be again.

Penny D. Jones

Talk Less, Think More

A thought is a secret
That is all your own
If it might cause trouble.
Don't let it be known.

A thought is a secret
Known solely to you
Only tell it to others,
After thinking it through.

Thoughts are so private
Some evil, some good
And many, if told,
Could be misunderstood.

If a wrong thought becomes words,
Could be a disaster.
Beware, "hold that thought"
For you are the master.

Pearl L. Branon

God's Beautiful World

Have you ever seen a sunset
That left you filled with awe
And how about the pretty leaves
That we see in the fall

The sunrise on a clear clear day
The stars up in the sky
The moon when it is at its peak
So pretty you could cry

A brand new babe to call your own
To cuddle, love and hold
And warm warm homes to go to
To keep you from the cold

And Christ as our own Saviour
God, his son gave, so we
Might have a home in Heaven
Throughout all eternity

Well Father how we thank you
For your beautiful world and more
And we'll forever praise and love you
For that's what we were created for!

Vonda Doak

Loneliness

'Twas loneliness and nothing more
That made me long for days of yore,
So many a time on foreign shore.

'Twas only a hand and nothing more
That guided me and with me bore,
The loneliness on foreign shore.

'Twas only a smile and nothing more
That lifted me so I cried no more,
For want of friends on foreign shore..

Roela Weber

A Wonderful Thing

As the world goes round...
There's one thing I've found.
A wonderful thing called love.
It fills the heart...
Like a store's shopping cart.
A wonderful thing called love.
Love brightens your day...
In every single way.
A wonderful thing called love.

Watts

Untitled

Love is a light bulb
that runs on batteries.
It's there
to
brighten up the world.
But
it fails
for us every now and then.
No need to worry.
Those
depressing mid-summer
blackouts
let the batteries rest.
We always have
love.
Those daydreams;
the
beautiful
fantasies only for the
story books.

Mindy Hope Fisher

Longing

Your gentle touch I long to feel
that warmth that you possess,
your lips so soft as they touch mine
those gentle hands that so caress.

Your strong, bold arms I do recall
the way they held me tight,
emotions raced through my veins
the feeling was so right.

Your voice my ears do long to hear
those sweet things that you say,
they bring a smile to my face
and brighten up my day.

I long to say these things to you
whenever we're together,
but silence creeps upon my soul
and these thoughts are hidden like a
treasure.

It's up to you to hear my heart
you have the only key,
so I can then reveal to you
everything you mean to me.

Mary Banda

As We Celebrate

He rode upon a donkey
That was borrowed from a stranger
This man whose name was Jesus
From Bethlehem and the manger

We all know the story
How the people welcomed Him
And only a short time later
Their cry changed to "Crucify Him"

As we celebrate Palm Sunday
And prepare for Jesus room
We look forward to Easter morning
And that glorious empty tomb

We thank Jesus now and always
That he died on Calvary's tree
For there hasn't been one since
Who cared that much for you and me.

Sharon Mollohan-Cincinat

Untitled

There is a Special Lady
that we all love so dear.

She's always kind and loving
a pleasure to be near.

She's a Mom who raised five children.
The best way that she knew.

She gave them love and guidance
and taught them values, too.

She has a lot of Grandkids
and Great-Grandchildren as well.

And each and every one of them
think that she is really swell.

She's also a loving Sister
who has been Special in every way.

Especially to her sister Grace
who shares the same Birthday.

For me, she's been a Special Aunt a Lady
that I adore.
Her belief in God and constant faith are
what I Love her for.

So I must close by saying and I'm sure you
all agree.
That this VERY SPECIAL LADY deserves
a HAPPY 90 BIRTHDAY!!!

Sharon De Boer

"Deceit"

Leading someone to a hope
That will never be.
Hiding truth, so untrue;
Making a fantasy.

Trusting, believing;
Devoting, adoring—
Unconditionally.

Delusion found—
Result:
Frozen by
Deceit.

Valecia Rotell

Always There

Some things may happen in your life,
    That you think are really unfair.
Many burdens may fall upon you,
    Almost more than you can bear.
Disappointment may overcome you,
    And your faith begins to tear.
You become awfully discouraged,
    And wonder, does God really care?
When you are too spiritually weak,
    You end up in total despair.
Satan uses this opportunity,
    As your soul he tries to snare.
You can rise up from this low,
    Regain the courage if you dare.
Just get down on your knees,
    And into very fervent prayer.
You will find that God gives answers,
    And your faith He will repair.
You realize He never left you,
    At all times He will be there.

Richard Meter

Untitled

How do you help a loved one
that's hurting — oh so bad

And all they do is "push" away
not realizing what they had

No one else was there for him
No one else but me

Not one of his friends supported him
Now he wants to be free

Maybe someday he'll realize…
that we were meant to be

Reneé Dianne

"Did You Know?"

There's a land to the North
    That's somber and gray,
Where the cod, and the seal,
    Hold sway?

Its shores are formed by the
    pounding seas,
That bring down the 'bergs
    From the Northerlies.
But the people there, are bright
    and gay,
'Especially' Round "Mom's"
    Conception bay:
And close by's the Harbor
    where they first touched sand,
and proudly exclaimed
    This is new Found Land!

J. J. Eberwine

Please, Read This One

I want to talk to you
That's why I wrote this poem
Don't know what I'm gonna say to you
But still I write this poem

I think I want to speak to you
Of the love you won't return
Still don't know what to say to you
But still I write this poem

My thoughts aren't completely together
And my words aren't completely formed
I don't know what to say to you
But still I write this poem

I think I want you to touch me
And tell me you love me true
And still I write this poem to you
Not knowing what to do

Kernisha Lynne Duvall

Sea Gull

There will be peace all over,
the green cliffs of clover.
Tomorrow you just wait and see,
love and laughter
you will live happily ever after.
In a world that is carefree.
When sea gulls fly over the bay I cry,
because you are away.
I know we did not part,
for you are still quite deep in my heart.

Katy Watson

Looking Through The Window Seat

The sky was sunless,
The air had a smell of wetness,
The leaves on tree tops
and roofs on house tops
glistened from the water drops,
The window's worn cloak
was all but soaked.

A partly read book lay beside me,
A loyal friend snuggled next to me,
Reading and listening
to the soft tide
of the music outside,
And watching
the leaves float down
and squirrels dancing around,
While sitting in the comforting sheets
of the Window Seat.

Paul Lin

The Day is Bright

The day is bright
The air is clean
So pleasant for awhile
Enjoy life
Enjoy every day.

We are here for now
Now is our time
We know not what is ahead
Beyond we will all learn at our
own time.

If we learn to enjoy now
Perhaps our beyond will be
a new beautiful life.
A life of love
A life of peace
A life of contentment

Open your hearts
Open your minds
Live your life as we were
meant to live.

Ray Stark

The Art Of "Losen"

The car, a bar near and far
The art of losen
us it be choosen

Our closet friend
Over and over again
It attacks oh so strong
This union which is wrong

Time, alive, time alive
We take in stride
Because future and success
campaigning on our side

The art of losen
This strife we're choosen
This life of losen
No sane wants to be usen

Yet, the growing grace of losen
The sense of overcoming abusen
manifest positive class
makes our future, free at last.

Lawrence X

The Bridge

As the train takes the bow curve
the bridge is afire
from a rapidly descending
sun
further on it elegantly
sprawls
like a naked woman
luxuriating on a bed
the beaming lights are
her adornments
(above rises a round champagne moon
below the particles of light
disintegrate into
a purplish darkness)
and when it finally rests atop the
cemetery
it has become a toy bridge
a curious antiquarian miniature
suspended by curvilinear
lighted string

Walter de las Casas

He's Home Alone

As I stepped out of Daddy's van
The cold air hit my chest
I walked into the front door
and knew that I was blessed.

I remember the feelings I used to get
When I walked inside that place
It seemed like everyone was gone
And no one left a trace

Sometimes I would wish it
To have someone beside
Or if I wanted no one
that kept my child pride

I know if I could change things
I'd never let them go
But now I'm in the future
And wish I didn't know

It was always warm and perfect
In that place I still call home
Now it seems like no one's there
And Daddy's home alone!

Lorraine M. Berte

Nonsense

The cat was small
The dog was tall
The chickens they did lay,
The cows went moo
The calves were new
and oh how they did play.
The sows were resting
The piglets testing,
how far she'd let them stray.
The birds were singing
and all were winging,
to the breakfast tray.
The breeze is blowing
The rooster is crowing
The coffee is bubbling
and people are grumbling,
The eyes open, but will not stay.
The sun is peeking over the hills,
Oh, so far away.
It's the beginning of a new day.

Mae C. Reed

Gone Too Soon

One will not feel
The cool breeze
Blow through one's hair
On a warm summer evening,

Or see the light,
The sun,
Fading into the long horizon,
Or smell the morning air
From the rain

The night before
On the trees
The grass.
One will not do these things.
Day by day by day,

One will not understand
The meaning of nature,
Which has caused
One to grow up
As beautiful

As nature is.

Kanani Brickwood

Poem

Down the long field, the football did soar,
The crowd was heard with a mighty roar,
The player grabbed it and ran,
Oh dear, it wasn't our man,
The other team yelled as they scored.

There once was a boy up to bat,
Who wasn't wearing his hat,
The ball did careen,
And gave him a bean,
Now his face looks like a doormat.

The round ball did go through the hoop,
The fans loved to holler "A swoop,"
Some call it a "Jam,"
Others call it a "Slam,"
But I always say "Loop-de-loop."

On down the court he ran,
Dribbling the ball with his hand,
It was quite a sight,
When he drove to the right,
And dunked to the joy of the fans!

Ryan Skaggs

Two Requests

(Proverbs 30: 7-9)
Two things I ask, Lord, before I die:
The first is lips that do not lie.
The second thing for which I plead
Is to be not rich in dire need.

As long as by Thy hand I'm fed,
I'll be content with daily bread.
Let me not great riches hoard
And proudly ask: "Who is the Lord?"
What vanity, Lord, and oh, what blame
If I forget Thy Holy Name!

Or if Poverty's hungering pain I feel
And I reach forth my hand to steal
Dishonor would Thy Name endure!
Lord, make me neither rich nor poor.

Katherine M. Huffstetter

God Sent An Angel

God sent an angel just for you
  the day your son was born.

God trusted you to care for him and
  keep him safe from harm.

Though God holds him in his hands
  you have to lead the way.

To teach him of the love God
  has for all of us each day.

For in your footsteps he will follow
  where ever you may lead.

So teach him how to look to God
  for each and every need.

Teach him how to pray each day
  and thank God for his love.

For everything he will ever have
  comes from God above.

As night time draws its curtain
  and slumber comes once more

Jesus guards his bed with love
  until its day once more.
  Marcella Slaten

Continuity

Along the snow widened road
The enchanted village lies.
Watched over by stalwart maple trees
On constant guard.
Their white tipped branches fanned over
Slumbering houses, frozen in time.

The earth is lighter
Than the pewter sky
And horse drawn sleighs,
Tingling bells hushed
Stand locked in the past
Of a century ago.

Unchanged the soft view
From my window.
Only the dark sentinels
Rising from the whitened land
Shake feathery, reproving fingers
As snowmobiles roar by.
  Lois M. Breen

Love Is

A warm snuggle by
the fire,
A need that grips
your soul.
A strong feeling of
desire,
That significant other
that makes you whole.

A feeling that nothing compares
to,
How you feel when that
person holds you.
And the only place that
love can start,
Is the warmest place
in you-
  Your heart.

  Wendy Backes

Ashley

My dog
the golden

Is a lover
not a fighter

A fuzz hound

A dandelion terrier
biting their necks
and flinging them in the air

An effective
guard dog

we have never been attacked
by dandelions
  Randall Garrison

For You—-

As the clouds part and
  the golden rays of sunrise come
above the horizon,
I think of you-

When a day is long,
  and lonely,
  and without hope,
  I reach for you

When I laugh,
  and smile,
  and feel so wonderfully
  complete,
  It's because of you

As the sun sets and
  the closing strains of the day
  slowly
  come to an end,
  I stand by you

Hand in hand - day by day
Hour by hour - I need only you.
  Liz Clark

Reality

The bell has rung,
The halls are full,
People are screaming
With gangs and their crews

Steel poles, Knives and guns
People are killing
And they think its fun

People shrieking
Yelling in fear
Drive by shootings
Will never be clear

Kids are dying
Needles are being shared
Aids are spreading
Doesn't anybody care

Living in a Nightmare
Praying to wake
Sleep in fear
Hoping it's all fake
  Tammy Morse

All Hope Abandon Ye
Who Enters Here

Dante is screaming;
the kid name, Dante Taylor.
And the way I figure it,
If Dante's screaming,
I'm screaming too.
So I try to scream,
But I can't.
I'm too scared to scream.
Oh God;
I'm going to die.
I am definitely going to die.
This is not my idea of fun.
But Dante didn't go to hell,
I did.
I climbed to the highest heights.
I plunged the deepest depths.
I screamed,
I yelled,
I died
I just screamed.
  Tabetha Slay

Quiet Times

Quiet times
The Lord and me
Direct conversation
I am blessed
Happy times
The Lord and me
Extraordinary joy
I am blessed
Peaceful times
The Lord and me
True tranquility
I am blessed
Depressed times
The Lord and me
Unconquerable hope
I am blessed
Pensive times
The Lord and me
Real comprehension
I am blessed

  Lynnette Latham Odd

The Gift

I'll not forget the day I knew
The special wonders it could do
It's something that has always been
To see, to hold, now and again.

Never changing through the years
Of happy days and sometimes tears
Never fails to be around
And never, ever makes a sound

Some take for granted day by day
Yet molds you in its unique way
It's there while being tucked in bed
And fairy tales are being read

I've seen it ride a beam of light
While watching graceful birds in flight
And on a dusty afternoon
When 4 o'clocks are in full bloom

Across a field of new mowed hay
The western sky at end of day
It offers strength and all the while
A wondrous gift, a mothers smile
  Robert Brown

Nature

It's the faint cry of a hurt dog,
The loud crack of a broken log.
When the leaves fall off of the
maple trees, you can hear the
whistle of the summer's breeze.

It's the soft song of the
hummingbird
who is eagerly waiting for his
song to be heard.

It's the sweet smell of a blooming
flower, the smell of the smooth
breeze in a country tower.

It's the single drop of dew
on new sprouted grass,
The reflection of yourself
on a lake that is clear as glass.

The swift move of a butterfly's swing
A new born bird learning to sing.
This poem about nature should not
be a surprise - this is how
I see it through my eyes.

Lindsay Swift

A Night In December

The clouds were charcoal gray,
The moon shone clear and bright.
The wind made every tree sway
On a cold December night.

The snow began to shake.
It rolled and then took flight,
Everything buckled in the quake
On a cold December night.

The people huddled together,
Aware of its power and might.
No one expected this weather
On a cold December night.

The wall was white and steep.
The people gasped in fright.
The town was covered deep
On a cold December night.

The paradise was gone.
The town was out of sight.
No one lived to see the morn
That cold December night.

Shawn Ouvry

"I Remember, I Remember"

I remember, I remember
The house where I was born,
The little window where the sun
Came peeping in at morn.
He never came a wink too soon,
Or brought too long a day,
But now I often wish the night
Had blown my breath away

I remember, I remember
The fir-trees dark and high,
I used to think their slender tops
Were close against the sky.
It was a childish ignorance,
But now it is a little lure
To know I'm farther off from heaven
Than when I was a girl.

Michelle Solomon

The Old Woman

Each night
the old woman hangs
from the parachute in her bedroom
while she is sleeping
without socks

TE

"Sisters"

Like a queen,
the older sits high above me.
Every time I come near
her waves force me back to shore.
The younger,
often fills my heart with pain.
A peaceful jellyfish,
with a harmful sting,
I cannot escape either sister,
The queen pushing me back;
back to the jelly fish.

Tamara Danielle Smith

Your Child Within

I miss your little girl so much
 The one with the soft sweet voice.
She melts my heart with just a touch
 Giving the angels reason to rejoice.
I miss holding her in my arms
 Especially when she cuddles close.
With me, she's protected and warm
 From all of life's goblins and ghosts.
I miss her whispering in my ear
 As she nuzzles up next to my cheek.
Oh! How I wish she were here,
 I want to hear her little voice speak.
I miss her bright smiling face
 As she wraps her fingers around mine.
She's so pretty in her ribbons and lace
 I find myself missing her all the time.
I miss just being in her presence
 Listening to her innocent laughter.
She shares her childlike essence
 Making me believe in happily ever after.

Jo S. Nave

Living

The memories of yesterday are sweet
The dreams of tomorrow are sweeter
But today is the reality, so—
  Live today!
  Capture its joys
  Dwell not on its sorrows
  Keep gratitude alive in your heart!
  Spread sunshine and love
  To others and find
  Today filled with sweetness
  Surely is thine.

Teresa Wiebe

For Jay

The twinkle in your eyes
The glimmer of your hair
The dimple in your smile
The boyish giggle in your laughter
All these reasons and more
Are why I love you so

Sandra Joder

Brothers

The Innocence of youth,
the power of a dream,
the simple joy in playing,
the laughter of a stream.

Growing up together,
playing side by side,
helping one another,
learning not to hide.

Trusting one another,
friendship not withstanding,
you will be my brother,
for time,
Everlasting.

Sherene J. Higley

Untitled

Deep inside I know,
The rain is meant for me,
It is God's special way,
Of sharing in my misery.

And when it's dark and gray,
I know that's me inside,
So when people say they hate it,
I feel a part of me has died.

And when the thunder booms,
To cause everyone such fright,
I feel that is my anger,
Exploding deep inside.

So now when I look out,
And see those clouds of gray,
I know someone out there
Is feeling the same way.

Rohena Shaw

Death

A full moon rises-
the rain starts to fall!
A killer moves silently-
stalking us all!
His eyes are empty-
he has no soul!
His victims can be-
either young or old!
He carries a sickle-
he buries deep, in one's chest!
Stealing their life-
their warmth and their breath!
We know he's close-
just one step behind!
He lives in the shadows-
in the back, of one's mind!
But please don't feel-
this is just fantasy!
Because death waits-
for you and me!

Tony Kozieja

Was It Worth It

They finally met after years of waiting
Then they started dating
They found life, they found love
They found comfort and compatibility,
But in the end they found hurt,
They found heartache..
Was it worth it?

Wendy S. Stidfole

Children

In complete darkness we are all
the same, it is only our knowledge
and wisdom that separate us.
Don't let your eyes deceive you.

We are a nation with no geographic
boundaries, bound together though
our beliefs, we are like-minded-
individuals, sharing a common
vision pushing toward a world
rid of color lines

They are the children of our
future, which is an adult world,
They are born with spirits
so innocent till we teach them
how to hate, our children are
also a race between education
and catastrophe

Kristal Bradshaw

Untitled

She broke my heart that fateful day
the sky was blue though I saw gray
I'd always fear that day would come
I'd always fear away she'd run
and then one day my fears came true
I didn't know just what to do
She ran to my friend, a man called Dave
to him her love she gave
was she sorry, I didn't know
even though she told me so
So there I sat feeling blue
and not really knowing what to do
I could cry, I could yell
I could wish them both to hell
but I'm not that kind of guy
many people have asked why
because I was too busy feeling blue
because she broke my heart in two

Scott Morrissette

"Looking Up"

As I look up into the skies,
The sun shines down.
The skies are as blue,
As my eyes.
The clouds are as white,
As snow.
The leaves dance,
In the shade,
Of the trees.
As my hair dances,
In the breeze.

Patricia Nelson

Set Me Free

If you don't love me,
then set me free,
Let go of this hold,
you have on me.
My heart is yours,
and will always be.
Even if you can't
love me.
The sooner I know that
It's OK to let you go,
The better I can walk
this lonely road.

Rhonda Stufflebean

Window In Discover

Window what pain in me
The talent that discovered me
How could that be link to me.
That I would discovered talent
within me o how could that
be know that talent link to me
O Lord how could that knowing
that talent in me. I discovered
that talent in as I discovered link
in me as I set under the
tree wondering what would it
be like to be. Bee as it flies
by. Discovered my talent within me.
It is part of me that is
free as it can be. Talent that with
in do link to me.
It talent that link to me what
it should be me link poetry in me
that talent within me discovered
me in my poetry.

Vinnie Fuller

Fortress

Somewhere in the darkness
The truth is buried deep,
Between the steadfast walls
Where pride can never reach.
That's the place where memories
Are forever locked away,
And saved for future reference
On some distant rainy day.
Somewhere in these feelings
There's a lesson to be learned,
About the price of freedom
And the need for bridges burned.
There's a place where time
Is spent on past reflection,
And where one learns to settle
For less than pure perfection.
It's a place that you can't find
Until love plays its card,
That's where I hold tomorrow,
In the fortress of my heart.

E. Taylor Allen

A Mysterious Thing

You thought it was not even there
the unexpected chime you're unaware
Just like a flash, it comes to you
A feeling too good to be true

But then again out of respect
You dream of what is to expect
The feeling that I will explain
is maybe that of an insane

The boiling thing that burst inside
a raging feeling with lots of pride
The glorious love that is within
you'll come to see it as a sin

Expressing this, may not be right
but hoping it, is with delight
What is this opacity that I bring
the answer is A Mysterious Thing

Nestor J. Gargarita

Cigarettes

The ad so big,
The warning so small,
That tiny, little print
Is supposed to warn them all.
With one big breath,
In and out,
They become too special,
To throw out.
Their huffs and puffs,
Go on so long.
They think nothing
Can go wrong.
They get heart disease,
Lung cancer too.
Before they die,
They turn deep blue.
So read that tiny print,
Or at least try
Or would you rather
Turn blue and die?

Katie Gallup

Windsongs

The birds are singing
    the wind is a light breeze.
So effortlessly the robins glide
    on open wings.
Gently swallowing the wind
    with their feathers.
Only to land once again
    and begin a new song.

Susan L. Brown

It's A Nice Day

So all the children can play
the wind is blowing and
the grass is growing,
the babies are burping as
the chicks are chirping
the sidewalks are white
like the sun it's so bright,
the sky is so blue
Since everyone got over the flu
There are no violent sounds
but the world still goes around,
there are all smiling faces
of all different races,
Everyone has gone out
Shopping all about
running so wild
As fast as six miles,
Everyone was ok
'cause it was all a nice day!

Radesha R. Dixon

Secret Place

I'm sitting in my secret place,
the wind is blowing in my face.

Way off in the distance I see a lake.
Animals around it are starting to wake.

Another thing that I see,
is a beautiful bird up in a tree.

The bright sun is starting to rise.
It's like a present a colorful surprise.

This is a spot that everyone should see.
They'd all feel happy just like me.

Stephanie Pettit

Her Room

The room is still and dry
The window is blank, I want to cry
The table was left with only a sea shell
Is this room a type of jail?

There are no toys, dolls, or trains
Death came through followed by pain
A small shadow of sunlight on the door
What might it look like before?

Gone, distant as the wind
If she was living what could had been
The light color brown on the walls
Dreary, when will the clouds fall?

Why are sea shells on the window sill
Had she grown-up and made a bad deal
Is she finished and all gone away
Will she every go outside to play?

Kirra Williams

Burnt Out

Days of the past are dead
their joy I feel no longer
    Truth becomes my world
Yet still
    I lay in a bed of my making,
The changing winds dance about my head
    snapping tunes of feelings fled
Lyrics forgotten in the mist
    Where are the warriors that once
invaded my heated shores
    Entangled in the ashes after their
flaming words burnt out
    I seek them not
thine own heart in but truth
    Starry eyed hunger
no longer flashes but
lies softly like sifted sand

Patricia Clunen Schneider

Reflections

When I look into the mirror,
There's a woman standing there,
An oldish, plump, gray figure,
Growing older and losing hair.

Where's the girl that stood here,
With dreams many years ago?
I stare, but I don't see her,
Yet the dreams are still there, I know.

But wait, there's more for me to be,
I shouldn't stop and frown,
For life will surely leave me,
If I let it get me down.

Where's the girl that stood here?
Time has driven us apart,
To think I could forget her,
She's with the spirit in my heart!

So I really have to run now,
Forget about growing old,
Stop counting lines upon my brow,
And march forward with the bold!

Mary Ann Jenkins

Then

I used to be whole…
then.
At least I think so….
and thought so…
then.

Pieces…. fragments….
of someone else….
or perhaps a journey….
a transformation.

Something stirs sometimes
and then slowly crawls
back to the dark, safe haven within,
always peering back
with fearful eyes.

Moments of wholeness pass quickly.
I am unable to hold fast
to those fleeting seconds.

But I used to be whole…
then.
Wasn't I?

Stephanie L. Sloman

"Nobody"

In my life
there is no one here.
I feel deserted
every time I cry a tear.
No one to tell me
that someone cares.
even if I'm not smart,
thin, or look even fair,
look inside me.
I feel so small.
No one knows how hard I try,
but I stand up every time I fall.
"Inferior, is what I am."
It's what I've been taught,
how I've been treated,
but it's not the way I thought.
I'm not even inferior.
I'm nobody.
I'm a speck of dust
to everybody.

Nina Kim

Reasons

If it rained all the time,
there would be no sunshine
without you.

No beauty for my eyes.
No ray of light.

If all day,
It was night.
The only stars would be
in your eyes.

If rainbows,
turned around to shine,
they are only mimicking
your bright smile.

If what I feel,
will always be,
you are the only one
for me.

Eugene Lee

Quiet Reflections

I find peace and strength in quiet times
They buoy up wilted spirits
Feel God's own hand direct my mind
And sometimes dictate sonnets.

Please remember when you need
To ponder weighty stuff
That God does not require of you
Decisions "off the cuff."

So do not then be troubled,
When you waken in the night.
Trust our Lord to guide you
In decisions that are right.

Remember Christ reflected
For forty days and nights.
He trusted God His Father
To clarify His sight.

Feel God above direct you
As you pray and seek a friend.
I ask our Lord to bless you,
Expect it! Now! - Amen!

Katharine J. Koch

Untitled

Raindrops fall to the ground,
they make a splashing, dropping sound.
Each raindrop reminds me of us,
the way we used to be.
We were the best of friends,
through thick and thin,
but now were drifting apart.
We are each a raindrop
individual, but yet the same.
We are each a raindrop,
together from the start
but now we've fallen apart.

Miranda Wood

The Eyes

The lonely eyes of a child
They stream rivers of hate
They show human anger
They talk of lost hope
And pray for future salvation.
They discover love
But never find it
They hear of rainbows
But never see one
They in spirit adoration
But receive neglect instead
And these eyes
Are therefore
Blind.

Nevena Vujosevic

Memories

In the corners of my mind,
Long forgotten memories are stirring.
I pluck each one out
Thoughts a whirring
I hold tight the laughter;
Touch lightly on the tears.
Clinging to love and
Discarding past fears
I pocket the rest in my fantasies.
For I have traversed the
Road to eternity.

Gertrude J. Ness

Friends?

They come and go so quickly,
Just like a shooting star.
I have lost way too many,
I can bear it no more!

They treat me like I'm nothing,
Like dirt beneath their nails.
Why does it have to hurt like this,
The pain is just too real!

They turn their backs away,
As if they did not care.
But when they're in trouble or need a friend,
They always turn towards me!

I guess I'm just a back-up,
In case they are alone.
But when I am sad and need someone,
Everyone just runs away!

I just don't understand,
Why they act like this.
They have always lied and tricked me,
Leaving me out in the cold, alone!

Lori Piepenbrink

Regrets

Why didn't I tell you I loved you?
Just three little words to say.
You showed your love for me,
In so many ways, each day.

As I cradled our first-born daughter,
You stood watching from the door.
Then came, and kissing us both,
You said, "I love you even more."

Why didn't I tell you I loved you?
Your eyes sometimes pleaded to know.
"I'll tell him tomorrow," I mused.
Now there are tomorrows no more.

At our last anniversary celebration,
As we danced across the floor,
You said, "Forty years hasn't changed a thing.
I still love you 'old girl', you know."

Why didn't I tell you I loved you?
Did I show it enough, my love?
Too late, I say "I love you. I love you."
Can you hear me from up above?

Pearl Williams

Jus' Us

A bill by congress, to never free us
Keeping blacks as slaves, to be discussed
Southern politicians passed that law with no fuss
Using manipulative words like trust us

Never trying to educate us
Believing that we couldn't learn to
Read, plus it was another way of saying
Thus, slavery will always be a must

Splitting the whole of our families up
Always selling and reselling us
Breaking our souls and spirits up
Holding us down and depriving us

Blacks build this country from nothing up
While shackling our hands and ankles up
What right have they to damn us
Could happen to no people but
Jus' Us

Kenneth E. Johnson

Dreams

My dearest love I long for thee.
Just to hold you near and close to me.
As days go by and nights slowly slip past
It's all the times you're not here I wish would go fast.
With each night that passes I find it harder to sleep.
But only if you were here my head to your chest, -
I would lay just to hear your heart beat.
Instead alone hear I lay.
Tears roll down my cheeks because of thoughts
of You being so far away.
I cannot bear this any longer!
My heart is hurting, aching and only
You can make it grow stronger.
I've found only one solution, though strange it may seem.
I lay until I fall asleep and wait for you even in my dreams!

Xemenia Mullinax

Untitled

I'd walk the worlds and all of time
just to reach you and know you're mine
I'd swim the oceans and seas of blue
or climb mountains just so I could hold you
the feats I'd perform to be in your arms
and the lengths I'd go to show you my charm
I've never known this much devotion
and never felt this intense of emotion
my heart and love belong to only you
and my soul will forever and always be true
show me inside your love and your heart
show me how much I'm missed when we're apart
show me this journey we're about to begin
show me the love of our lives therein
let's take our fears and toss them away
let's live in the dreams and the faith of a brand new day

Walter Ghrist

Life

Life is always changing, life is never fair.
Just when things are going up, it takes a turn around.
You may think you're on the bottom rung;
And that you're gonna drown.
Then the wind changes course and blows away your frown.
Life is always changing, life is never fair.
You have the perfect dreams,
but never the proper moments.
Then when you think they're here,
you don't have the proper means.
Life is always changing, life is never fair.
Never give up hope,
the wind will blow again.
And with the changes you will cope.

Meshelle A. Robinson

The Armor OF God

The power of Praise and the Victory of defeat
knowing that Satan is trampled under our feet!
The sword of spirit to cut and divide all of Satan's mischievous lies.
Shield of faith to stop the fiery darts,
that would pierce your very heart
Your feet shod with the Gospel of Peace,
to tell every man that you meet;
The helmet of salvation-to protect your mind-
To let Satan know—NO NOT THIS TIME!!
My loins girt about with truth,
knowing that my Savior got all the "Juice!"
And now the breastplate of righteousness to guard my life, and
My faith in God-to know with him, IT WILL BE ALRIGHT...

Katina Michelle Blake

Where Are You?

Watching the sea, ripple by me,
Knowing I won't want to leave.

Back to the lonely life I lead, no wonder, love for me,
I can't see, what will become of me?

I've traveled so many miles, for only more denial,
Looking in so many eyes, seeing only their lonely smiles.

So tired of the way I feel,
Believing love is no longer for me,

I've waited so many years, for only lonely fears.

Where is the someone I'm dreaming of,
To give me a world of love.

Where is the man,
To take me through the promised land?

Will he be handsome and tall?
Will he help me not to fall?

When will I hear his call, is he there to be found?
The man who will make me believe in love again.

Will he make the sun shine?
Will he make the world mine?

How will I know, when he will show?

Patricia Lynn Pryor

Interrupted Beauty

My eye spotted three pairs of weightless legs
landing on the dandelion weed.
An individual ray of sun bounced
from the window that harbored my curiosity.
Swift puffs of breeze touched the bee;
encircling its world.
The air incautiously fluttered his wings-
to be given a nonchalant response.
I watched it move gaily up and down,
around the dandelion's golden-yellow face.
This meticulous chore went on for a time:
soon his transparent wings fled toward the garden.
Why did it choose a dandelion in my yard?
His interest led me to question the dandelion's
assumed, doubtful role.
The flower's body straightened,
resuming a marvelous and astonishing beauty.

Katanya Lohr

My Woman Child

This morning she says she hates me.
Last night she gave me hugs.
I want to tell her I understand,
Her hormones are racing, just because:
It's that crazy puberty.
It creeps up on us you see,
    And before you know it's at the door,
    Screaming to be let in,

While I try in vein to push it away again,

denying that today,
She may no longer be: My little girl, you see:
But a fine young woman,

With all the dreams: That used to be in me.
    But today she's alternating,
    Between the tears and trust,

I sigh relieved again today,
    When she gives to me her love.

Susan J. Mullins

Childhood Friends Not Forgotten

Two little girls busy at play
Laughing together day after day
Sometimes spending their day in the woods
Wading in the creek sure felt good
Jumping over logs, climbing in the trees
Kicking their feet in piles of leaves
They cooked mud pie biscuits and mimosa tree beans
Getting into mischief but never really mean
Just best friends having fun with each other
Spending the night at one house or another
Hours spent in make believe and pretend
Little did they know in those years back then
They were making memories that time could not erase
Special memories that nothing could replace
But the years went by and they were soon to part
One moved away but her friend stayed in her heart
In a very special place with her childhood memories
Sometimes she still can close her eyes and see
Two little girls playing in the sun
Two little girls - Baby Gal and Evonne

Mary C. Brock

The Seed Within

Man and woman came from the stars "far, far away" to
    learn and grow on the physical planet we call
    "Mother Earth."

Within each unique individual was planted the seed of all
    knowledge.

Each seed has been assigned the potential of growing into
    beautiful things, love, and "clear" understanding.

To nurture the seed within is to create a universe even to
    be admired by the Creator Of All That Is.

Randall S. Limbach

The Potter's Wheel

Year after year, peering out on watch in thick darkness
lest night's conundrum slip a mirror in which
you would find no reflection, I labored
across the bonds of motherhood to keep at bay
enemies who spied for opportunity
to bring razors disguised as words,
welter as wet nurse, and poison as pabulum.
As time swelled past the evolutions
of my potter's wheel, past the growth spurts
and over the piles of clothes become too small,
distraction begged me from my task while enough
for tenacity to become lax, admission nominal
and few guests a great many,
until one day you demanded in princely innocence,
"Mommy, why isn't my hair smooth?"
and time rode on the hammerblow to my masterpiece
and I lay vanquished, crumpled under your tiny words.

Linda Quillian

The Rose

The rose represents your friendship and love.
Like an angel sent from above.
Petals stand for your heart; made of soft, red silk
and a touch of gold.
Bound with your spirit, you are noble and bold.
The stem is the length of your gratitude.
It could go on, forever, along with your caring attitude.
The two leaves are your arms open wide.
Telling the world there is a wonderful person inside.
So when you are depressed, remember this;
When you do, go after what you want, you can't miss.

Kuuipo Cullen

Your Will, Lord

Lord, I pray to do your will, that you have spoken to my heart
Let me not be slow to act; let all fears and doubts depart.
Let me look to you Lord, for you are my guide
You have planned the course before me; help me stay close by
your side.

Let me know your voice; help me to discern,
Teach me those things Lord, that I have need to learn.
Let me trust in your strength; mine will bring defeat your
Strength will overcome every obstacle I must meet.

Let me read Your Word; may it bring nourishment to my soul
Let me daily pray to you; transform my life and make me whole.
Let me stand on Your promises; You are true to what you say
You are the truth, You are the light, You are the only way.

You have invested yourself in me
Lord, I pray, help me reach maturity.
Help me to be like Jesus, Your son
Help me, I pray Lord, let your will be done.
    Patricia J. Welch

"Ode To The Great"

Let the bold ones unite,
Let the wheels start to turn,
that the torch of our liberty may continue to burn.
Let our voices unite,
Let the spirit be strong,
Let us stand for what is right,
and repress all that is wrong.
Let no person believe they're not meant to be a part,
for what role we must play is engraved in our heart.
Let the envious writhe and the incredulous believe,
that we are a nation destined to succeed.
Let us feel pride again and stand tall to meet fate,
for America is and will always be great.
Let the bold ones unite,
Let the wheels start to turn,
that the torch of our liberty may continue to burn.
    Roberto V. Ciccarelli

I Have A Passion For You

I have a passion for you
Like none I've ever known.
I'm so comfortable around you, I'm so fiercely attracted to you.
There's a little of every beautiful human relationship between us.

    Sometimes I cradle you to my heart like a baby
    Sometimes you discipline me like a father
    Sometimes you play with me like a brother

    Always I can talk to you like a best friend
    Always I can kiss you like a lover
    Always you are a part of me.

I have a passion for you
And I dream about things I want to do and places I want to go with
you. You've got an incredible hold on my heart
So tight that I can't seem to live and be whole without you.
I look at sunset or breathtaking view and realize that I cannot fully
appreciate it without you by my side.

You're everywhere - every breath, every beautiful sight, everything
full of life and joy — Oh, how can I say it when I can't even
comprehend it?
All I know is how overwhelmed I feel when I think about how much
I love you.

I have a passion for you.
    Rachel Johnson

The Old Log Cabin

There! We have passed it again as we traveled so fast,
let's turn around and go back.
The chimney has crumbled away long ago
and the logs are rotted and black.

A man with dreams, a maiden fair,
came West their lives to share.
A rugged life but they learned to cope
with a faith in God and hope.

Four little children had played around the door,
happy as happy could be;
their childlike trust in the ones they loved,
believing only in what they could see.

As I stood reminiscing,
and saw the pioneers in array,
I bowed my head with a grateful heart;
they had paved the way for us today.
    Margaret Stump

A Dance With Destination

On a dark hard city street
Lies a desperate man with no conceit
He has nothing to live for
Since he ruined his life before

His desperate eyes show piercing sadness
As typical workers view him with madness
His limp mouth drools of hunger
His frail body makes people shudder

And yet, he sees mirrored eyes of compassion
Thus ending his frustrations
He hears soaring music so sweet
He feels rhythmic sensations dancing to his feet

He has come to the realization
That these lovely new sensations
Are quite higher than any proud steeple
Because he painfully taught so many people
That this pathetic human condition

Was an innocent reflection
For human destinations
    Margaret Kelly

Cornored Cafe

The cafe, smallish and cornored
lit dimly through two oblong front windows,
sequestered seven tables each
with matching chairs.
Upon each, a plastic flower of some sort
in a too-thick crystal glass
perfectly clipped too-green leaves.

A gritty floor, dirt from
the last rain, dried.
Each step a shuffle and slide.
An older man, slicked back grey hair,
A work shirt, black pants, brown shoes
soles worn at the back, worn at the front.

Coffee in heavy white mugs
not white anymore
or maybe never were.
Picture of a Chevrolet in a rusty frame.

I can't find a clock.
I don't know the time.
    Susan Hurst

"Life"

It matters not how young or old, we all cherish life;
To live, in whatever situation—in happiness or in strife.

So, we anxiously await the dawning of another day;
Happy to be alive—to live—to work and to play.

Though we have no way of knowing, what a day will bring;
We eagerly anticipate the new life which begins with Spring.

We live each day in its glory and wonder if we will see;
The beginning of each new season to arrive in its beauty.

We are thankful for the gift of life, and give thanks to our master above;
For we know that life would not be, without his wonderful love.

Mattie M. Cox

Fulfillment Of Life

A steadfast lust for tomorrow is the secret to a happy
Life.

The longing for the flowers and the trees to blossom,
Elevates my very being.

The sound of the ocean off in the distance, clears my
Thoughts. Hence; I may re-new childhood events of
Yesteryear.

Unable to re-live the pleasures of "pastime," I strive
To make new worthwhile memories.

My lust for life is fulfilled.

Mary Lou Tate-McFarlane

Through The Years

Dedicated to my Grandpa E.M. (Chief) Schipper December 5, 1994
A memory takes me back...
Lifts me far from this place...
Takes me away from the hole in my heart.
From that empty place.
I know you're better now, and you're strong...
But this just feels so wrong!
So many things I never said...
They remain thoughts, just unspoken words in my head.
I'm trying to be strong.
Trying to make it through...
Trying to keep from missing you...
Although I know I always will...
I'll try to make you proud.
Please forgive me if I get a little
wild, rambunctious or loud!
I remember your smile and fight back the tears.
God knows I'll always miss you, but I know
you'll always be with me through the years.

Linda Cobo

Saying Goodbye

My eyes go dim as I see your face,
knowing you're leaving for another place,
a place where I know you'll be taken care of,
Cherished, and loved from our Father above.
I know, I shouldn't feel so sad because
there you shall feel no pain, you'll be
as fresh and new as each drop of rain.
Your yesterdays became our today, and
our todays become their tomorrow.
Through the eyes of our children, we
can relive the past of fond memories
and love that will always last.
And with these feelings there
will be no sorrow, I will always
remember you today and tomorrow.

Victoria Barnett

Lost

I am a dove flying into the whirling tempestuous sea
Like a secret shrouded in mystery
Fighting against the torrent
Focused on the task
Heavy and weighted
As thick with fragrance as a cask
Must we were the mask
Unveiling the truth
Convicting without proof
I'm lost, the lines are crossed
Where it begins is also where it ends
Closed tight like a new cellophane
sealed and seamless
Tried and True
The Sea and Sky Blue
Without a clue
Lost in the tempest
Like a childless Christmas present.

Lainie Jordan

Untitled

Something so sweet
Like candy I stuff you in my mouth
I know I should be gentle
Savoring each bite
But I chomp down hard
and worry all the while that you will finally cry out

Fine chocolates should be handled delicately
yet I gorge like it's Russell Stover
Knowing it's Godivas that melt in my mouth
I'm afraid everyday that I've eaten the last one

Still I keep chomping
instead of relishing in the exotic tastes
Gourmet is what I devour
I know it
but still I treat you like shelf candy

My palette is not ignorant
only unappreciative like a fat child
Put me on a diet
I have no self control

Suzanne Cody

Weight And Wait

Today I thought I'd have good news
Like maybe I had lost a pound or two.
Instead when I upon the scales did stand
Found more self control I must now demand.

To meet the goal I've decided upon
More food from my plate must yet be gone.
Will I never or ever meet the goal I set?
How much longer must I wait yet!

I'm in a hurry
  Can't you see?
    I want an exciting
    NEW
    SLIM
    ME!

Roberta Rau

377

By Chance

I found you by chance,
like one finds a keeper stone by a stream—
ten thousand to one.
And after time I became quietly aware of you—
your every movement, the touch of our hands, your voice.

I prod a smile, sometimes a laugh. You're briefly amused.
We are comfortable like old friends from another time.
And I soon learn that you are a strong but gentle heart,
a sunny day with snow, a secluded place in a strange land,
not known to those who live there, who I uncovered,
like one uncovers a songbird's nest among thorns.

I am a dream from your past, too good to be true;
that rush of cold morning air that tightens the grip on your coat;
a nighthawk in the moonlight. You are all that is good,
like coffee in the afternoon; a fragrance that carries you back
to a happy time;
the lady bug in my garden.
You are a girl,
in my mind
forever young.

Nick Vlachos

Sunshine

It pours through all sorts of things
   like people's hair, leaves on the trees,
windows and even day-dreams.

It makes illusions and golden forms
   like glitter in the snow, silk on rainy streets,
stars in eyes and satin skin on baby's arms.

It is the Father of all things
   like earth, sky, water, mountains
and man's wildest dreams.

It gives us feelings of all kinds
   Like warmth in the snow, hope in the dark,
and even cleanses our minds.

It gives us gifts big and small
   Like trees, flowers, food, light
and sight - the best gift for all.

It is the healer of all our despairs
   like being alone, afraid, lost,
and is a gift from the ONE who cares.

Victoria Clamon

The Botanist

Cold shadows, red clay, gray grass, connection
Like sex, or like waking. She saw a leviathan
Thrust through red clay—a giant ganglion wavering,
Wavering toward the sun—fibrous branches in a ball
Tangled, breaking and floating in blue wind.

It happened to her then: the brain snapping on
Like a bulb, adrenalin tides, chemical burning.
Palms raised, dendrites for fingers, basking in light,
Branches stretching into the blue skies of space
Forever sending, forever receiving, forever
Part of the signal. I am here, she cried out.
I am here, she cried. Roots
Thrusting deep, arms reaching sky.

Later when she wearied, dense arms all whorled
And scarred from the sharpness of the stars,
Reception fading, she rested against her porch.
And when tourists stopped to talk amazed
Amazed at her bovine charm, she laughed, amazed.
Amazed they said it must get lonely being
So far from what's really happening in the world.

Sha'va Saint-Jean

Love At First Sight

When I meet you, I greet you with a stare.
Like some poor child at a fair.
I will not let you love me
Yet am I weak
I love you so intensely,
I cannot speak.

When you are gone, I stand apart
And whisper to your sweet soft image inside my heart.

Within my bed... the whole night through
I turn and turn and think of you.
But through the night, I sit and wonder was it really
LOVE AT FIRST SIGHT!

Then I wonder when we met today
If you said what you meant to say
And did you get my meaning when
And then thought the whole thing through again.

But as hours go by
I finally lay down for the night.
And wonder was it really
LOVE AT FIRST SIGHT!

Yashica Newby

Lonnie's Prayer

Dedicated to Naomi Jean and Jarrod James Whipple
Today's our first new day together. There will not be another
like there is here and now. If this was to be our last chance,
point of knowing, seeing, the twinkle in your eyes, the smile
of your face. To wipe the tears from your cheek, to lend my
hand when you feel yourself falling.
Let this last moment, minute, hold us strong in spirit and
thought. We are never far apart.
With each beat of our hearts. In nature and life's beauty,
we will be. Forever near.

Lonnie Jean Whipple

"All Of Me"

My darling we've been together for quite some time and now I would
like to share with you a gift of mine.

I give to you a mind that thinks only of you, considering you in
each and everything I do.

I give to you two lips to kiss when we're alone enjoying loves
heavenly bliss.

I give to you a heart full of a love so true, that it will still
belong only to you no matter what we go through.

I give to you two arms to hold when days are long and nights are cold.

I give to you two knees that tremble and grow weak at the sound of
your voice each and every time you speak.

I give to you two legs planted firmly in our love because I know
you're the one, the one sent to me from heaven above.

You see my love, it is plain to see that the gift that I am giving
to you is all of me.

Maureen H. Barnard

The Perfect Thought

Imagine the brilliance of a million diamonds shimmer,
listen to eloquence, as pure as an autumn breeze.
Picture the perfection of the sun getting dimmer,
taste the confection of a kiss meant to please.

With all of the pretense that good has escaped our mind,
gather all these senses that may approach you in your life.
For I vision these perfections, and exactly what I find,
are simply the mirrored reflections, of what I call my wife.

William Corradini

The Rain

Listening to the rain, yes I'm listening to the rain.
Listening to the rain is such a wonderful thing.
Walking in the rain, yes I'm walking in the rain.
I'm squeezing it tight with all my might.
Dancing in the rain, yes I'm prancing in the rain.
I'm dancing and prancing in the rain.
I'm sleeping in the rain, yes I'm dreaming of the rain.
Listening to the pitter-patter on my window pane.

Tara Ashli Cline

Yesterday's Little Girl

Some time has passed since our
little girl went away
yet in mommy and daddy's hearts
it seems like yesterday

She climbed the stairs to glory
and found such beauty there
our little girl felt safe and warm
in God's tender loving care

Now she lives her days in glory
but when it becomes evening tide
She rushes home to mommy and daddy's hearts
where peace and love abide
   It seems like yesterday

Virginia R. Prince

Daddy's Star

There is a new star in the Heavens tonight. It is a graceful
little star. If you look real close you will see a little
girl's smile. And if you stand and let its rays shine on you,
you will feel compassion, kindness and love. And yes the star
has a name, the star is Donna Vie. Daddy wasn't prepared for
Donna to fly away, and he's still in a state of shock, why
she had to go after this short twenty-seven years. He doesn't
understand. One thing is for sure. If He could have removed
the pain and hurt from her body and placed it in His, He
would have done so in a heartbeat. But He couldn't do that
could He? So physically she's not here anymore, but mentally
or spiritually, whichever you choose, she will always be
here. Then when the doorways of Heaven open for Daddy to go,
she will be there at the door. Arms outstretched, big smile
on her face saying, welcome home Daddy, I love you. Donna
always called Him "Daddy" and Wanda always called Him "Dad" and
so until He sees Donna again He's going to put the word
"daddy" on hold. Yes there is a new star in the Heavens, and
it's shining for all to see and you know what? It's shining
especially for Daddy to see.

Wanda Pugh

"Sweet Dreams"

A long way away in the land of nod,
lives a child's mind where no man has trod,
this spacious playground hold no bounds,
to the active energies of sight, sense and sounds.

How real this world seems to a tiny mite,
who dribbles and dreams all through the night,
of fairies and elves and ghouls and ghosts,
all a delightful and frightful bunch of hosts.

But far too quickly the sleep pattern is broken,
and from this celestial plane a chrysalis has awoken,
ready to start a fresh new day,
to develop and grow in every way.

Sweet dreams, young one, as the day draws nigh,
your world of fantasy will not pass you by,
enjoy your innocence for all too soon,
the butterfly will emerge and fly from the cocoon.

Lynda A. S. Whittle

Ode to the Sun

Beyond the horizon peeking through the trees,
lofty tops held high awaiting morning's first breeze,
the sun in silent beauty shines,
astounding all with its built-in sense of time;
as the shadows of darkness live no more.

The sun awaits neither man nor beast,
but on these do its shimmering rays feast.
Ripping apart the sea with its focal rays,
silvery backs once hidden now stay.

Over the mountains; now under the seas,
the sun's piercing rays do as they please.
The mountain swiftly lights up
as if a giant watchdog to the sea; its pup.

Slowly, silently, higher does it soar,
successfully seeking to illuminate more.
The sun's mighty force no bounds does it conceive.
Its child earth it will not leave.

Theresa Peiffer

"Revelation"

In the still of the night
   Loneliness looms over the mind
A deep grief touches the heart
   The eternal search for light
Seems ever so distant to reach.

   Amid the darkness of the night
Rises a glowing light
   A graceful figure walks toward
A candle held so close to her face,
   A face of astounding beauty,
A face so serene, a smile so enlightening,
   That could touch hearts as distant as the sun.

In an instant, a jubilant elation strikes
   Heart and soul at once,
In symphony with one another
   Reaching heights of joy and ecstasy.

The grief and sadness suddenly disappear
   Without a minuscule trace
The revelation of the sublime love
   Is the salvation of my eternal search.

Venkatesh Babu

A Girl Named San Francisco

A girl named San Francisco
long-legged
short-haired
and
skinny,
tanned the color of Indian Summers,
her eyes reflecting the bay
smells faintly and sweetly of chocolate
and sits in a small smoke filled cafe,
sipping a double espresso,
her foot tapping
to jazz rhythmically flowing inside her.
She pulls her old black raincoat tightly around her
and
   steps
      out
         into
my white, damp, bellowing arms.

Romy Ruukel

Untitled

Green hazel eyes
Long voluptuous blond hair,
A smile that can brighten your day
A soul with much to bear.
Strength on which to hold the world
Passion that could spark a flame,
Undying love for those who've touched her heart
Unwilling to place any blame.
Compassion so deep in her soul
Patience that could never wear thin,
A voice that speaks words so comforting
A look of devilish sin.
The sincerity of a lost puppy dog
The kind of trust that's under lock and key,
She will be my best friend until the end
Now and for eternity.

Shari Bauer

Alone In The Dark

Do you want to see what the future holds?
Look inside your heart and you will know.
Do you want to come across the path of life?
Then reach out your hand and make a stand.

Our life's a journey we would never know-
Like a candle that glows in the darkness of the room
We would never know what mystery it holds,
Until we search for what we know.

We know the feeling yet we don't understand;
We know we're living, yet we don't know how.

I'm like a child lost in a dream,
I'm like a candle that glows from within.
But what will happen if it gets dark?
Will I be alone, alone in the dark?

Will a hand reach out for me and get me out?
Or will I be alone, alone in the dark?

So many questions come to my mind,
So many answers I cannot find.

When I get out of the dark, what will I see?
Will I see you there, searching for me?

Kathryn Sibug

"Our Love And Friendship"

Love is you.
Love is us two.
Love is priceless. Love is happiness.

Love is when I look at you.
Love is your funny attitude.
Love is the smile on your face.
Love is your blue eyes, that make my heart race.

Love is to some, a pleasure.
Love is to me, a treasure.
Love is to me, our friendship in reality.
Love is real, not a fantasy.

Love is what's deep down inside.
Love is what I feel, do you realize?
Love is how much I care for you.
Love is the friendship we share, me and you.

Love is having you as close as a brother.
Love is talking to you and being your friend and other.
Love is you being happy for yourself and me.
Love is for you, your girlfriend; for me it is our friendship for
eternity.

Tricia Anne Fryman

Heaven

As she approached the stairs to heaven she
looked back with a glance. The tears
dripping off her chin where a whisper of
good-bye and she climbed the final stair
right into the sky.

Her sudden death had not yet been
accepted by her family or friends,
but the thought of this grateful friend
will never end; even though she's
gone today, her heart and soul still
remain

Marla Schlesinger

Crimson Pool

He, who I knew and loved,
Looked with anguish upon his face.
A crimson pool engulfed the yard
As my angel fell from grace.

He'd been living in a criminal world -
But still he lay as the black shroud unfurled.

A river gouged a canyon,
A mist encased the eye,
The cup was running over
As I watched my angel die.

Laura Leonard

Sea Shore

Behind the waves, lies a bright setting sun,
Looking at us from every direction, having all of its fun.
Underneath of the rays, we lay on the sand,
Entranced by the beauty, of God's loving hand.
Wrap yourself, in the blue of the sea,
Attempt to explain it, then explain it to me.
The sea is something, only one can explain,
Even if you grabbed its soul, it would come back again.
Realize if you would, the wonder that we see,
So you can tell your children, in case it won't be.
Over all of us, God places his eyes,
For the good, and the bad, he has invited these tides.
Onward we shall go, through the years yet to come,
Caught in the trap, of the beauty that will stun.
End your pain, by listening to the shores,
As you quietly listen, you will hear our door.
Now every time, you see the glory of the sea,
Study it hard, and know its power over thee!

Steven Moring

Markers

In the spines that soar and catch our sight
lie prisms of our mind. The storied tinted lens
refract the fierceness of the laser light,
that, borne undimmed, could scatter sense,

And life. Words too, interstices that mask,
or show a fragment of refracted light-
signed by cobwebs. They have the task
of holding thought, those tiny spines that might

Snare meaning. Such economy of sight
makes sense as well. But rough and uncouth cast
of signs, like unshaped arches, unhewn heights
of stones, can mar the glory unsurpassed

Of what is caught and held by tracery
of crafter's skill, an arched epiphany.

Lydia Priest

"Thoughts Of The Heart"

I don't know where to start, so many things, so many thoughts
Looking for answers, it's an endless search, so many questions, but
no one to answer
I keep my feelings closed up in a bottle, like a model ship
Things I wanna say, but lose my voice by fear
Walking around like nothing bothers me, writing like everything
hurts, too much for me to handle. I try to focus on one, but
distracted by another, it feels like I'm in a room without corners
Sometimes I find myself going in circles, judged by what they see
instead of what they know, held down by the weight sitting upon my
shoulders, doing to please others, while disappointing myself
I smile when I really want to cry
Being the person they want me to be, hiding the person I really am
On the outside it seems I have a heart of steel
When on the inside I have a heart of glass
So very fragile, anything could make it break
Hurt has built a wall between me and everyone else
When I let out a cry, behind my wall is where I sit
All by myself, alone, to be who I really am, I'm out of time...
My questions still remain unanswered.

Kristen Zier

The Long Journey Home

Man standing on a platform, baggage at his feet,
looks like a lonely man with worn out shoes on the street.
Could cities hold the answer, only time could say,
now his time is all gone and he's going away.

Three strings on his guitar, broken with his hopes,
holds it tight in his hand and lets his feelings roam.
His voice once filled with song, now echoes only pain,
distant bells start to move the one eyed lifeless train.

Eyes stare at passing lights, reflected on the glass,
now of past and present sights, all things must come to pass.
Looking in the dark night at times to remember,
all passed like the grains of sands he dreams to endeavor.

"Many dreams are broken." They cried in the dark.
Thoughts of fame and glory put on the shelf to start,
The long journey home..............................

Larry B. Bramble

His Song Beckons

Each night the mysterious animal
looks to the sky and answers the call.
He sings to the distant moon with
a loud chilling bawl.

His deep serenade stirs something within
you that scares you with all your might.
How he howls and carries on when
the moon is shining bright.

He lives in the wilderness, so deep in
the woods, sometimes down by the lake.
His song beckons loud and clear,
hoping to find a mate.

It is the cry of the wolf late
when the stars shine.
Thank goodness I am safe in my
log cabin and not down
in the woods of pine.

When the light of dawn comes he will be gone.
But when darkness sets in again
you will hear his howling, beckoning song.

Karel Ann Hutchinson

Untitled

Dark, grey, menacing,
    looming above.
Forewarning of the coming storm,
    soon to occur.
Light, flashing,
    dances between the clouds,
    giving an indication of what lies ahead.
Preparing for the worst,
    few take the opportunity to realize,
    to appreciate the beauty of this event of nature.
But the few, whose imaginations are broad,
    peer up, beyond the flashes of lightning
    and dream of Gods,
    battling in the heavens.
And it is these individuals
    who have the power to change the world.

William C. Paul

My Brother

I would slip my hand into his and feel the
Love and companionship lead me on the way
When I was just a little girl...........

I would run home upset and crying and he
Would hug my fears away
When I was just a little girl...........

Ears that were always in tune for anything
I had to say, problems to unload or stories
To be told
When I was just a little girl...........

Now the years have flown but the hand is still
Within my reach, the hugs ever plentiful and
Patient ears still listen
I am no longer a little girl..........

Through it all he has been there
The only one who ever stayed
This man I call my brother..........

M. Suzie Stamm

Only a Part of My Heart

Only a part of my heart remains,
Love and memories that part contains.
It lives and beats the same.
Has my name, and even plays life's games.
Not with the zest as before,
Feels like sand on a shore, being washed over,
tossed about, and loses form, forever.

Like the sun comes up every day,
You know there'll be a way
For the heart to heal.
And as it does again,
It will be able to feel peace, joy, and love,
Sent straight to my whole heart,
From Father above!

Linda E. Barlow

The Hidden Age

Look at this picture, is it really me?
Look at this painting, is it what it seems to be?
Look at my face, full of lines and scars.
Look into my soul, hidden behind bars.
Look at my image in the mirror.
My destiny grows even nearer.
Look at my hands, how they tremble and shake.
Now my future is at stake.
Look into my eyes and see what I see.
Look at this picture is it really me?

Linda Snyder

Love

Love is something I adore,
Love is one thing I need more.
Without love I'm living a dream,
Without love I have nothing.
Love is one thing I need most,
Love is what makes me need a host.
Without love I'm in a fantasy,
Without love I'm completely lonely.
Love is the biggest thing I lack,
Without love I'm like a suitcase unpacked.
Love is what I seem to need so much,
Without love my heart is untouched.
I want someone to love me,
I've waited so long and so patiently.
Love can bring me so much joy,
I wish that love could bring me a boy.
I need love, not just a friend,
What's wrong with me, is this the end?
I know the day will sometime come,
I know someday I'll have someone.

Katherine Yvonne Cutlip

"Love Is"

Love is that which understands, sustains, fulfills and transcends.
Love is that which overcomes and triumphs through the challenges
of life. It is love which laughs and cries and heals.
Love is limitless and cannot be measured or calculated.

Love defies categorization because it is boundless and takes countless
forms of manifestation.

Love whispers to the heart and unfetters the mind.
Love brings insight and peace to the mind while strengthening the
heart into and from which flows cosmic life to and through all
creation connecting being to Being in dynamic relationship of human
and divine through the drama of living into life's fulfillment.
Love is the rhythmic heartbeat of the life force of being of which
we partake and share unconditionally as life fulfills itself through
and in us! Love's glorious personification and celebration of life
is...you!

Love is nature's finest universal hour.
It is the cool of the breeze the warmth of the fire the singing
of the brook the chirping of the birds and the sweetness of flowers.
Love is the coo of the babe the trusting smile of a child.
Love transmits and radiates light and lightness.

Love is life's way to fulfill itself. Love is simply a turning of
the key of life which you possess! Love is the nucleus of the atom
of life within the universal life force of being at one's innermost
depths where heart, mind and soul merge into the oneness of being.

Ralph Reynaud

Atoms Of Creation

Maybe joy is not a moment and life is not a day.
Maybe hope is just a concept meant to dignify the way.
It takes more than ears to hear and more than eyes to see;
It takes more than air to breathe, and more than pain to be.
Existence isn't just believing, we must be willing to become.
Trust is more than just an issue, understanding's never done.
Darkness isn't just for sleeping, seeing doesn't come by sight.
Many reasons are for weeping, and reflection's not pure light.
Although death is part of living, dying has no part in death,
It's an avenue to forgiving at a junction that's called life.
Time is not to do with aging, nor repeated nights and days;
It is just a word of limits holding back awareness ways.
Knowledge with no understanding kidnaps minds so we can't know,
Pain is sometimes anger raging in the depths of our own soul.
We're more than life and living; more than dying, more than death,
We are atoms of creation each connected with the rest.

Kathy Hudson

In The Vicinity Of Your...

The moment I knew, it would always be. I knew
love would hold us for all of eternity. Evil
could not shake us. There we would be palm in
palm, together we would stand. And then I knew I
would forever remain in the vicinity of your hand.

You have your soft spots, and that majestic
mist in your eyes, that makes my face shine
with glee. And this I must say to you with all
the emotion I hold within myself, I can't stop
thinking about you, don't you see? So I hope
you feel the same way about, this one. You are
so sweet, gentle and kind. So hopefully I will
remain in the vicinity of your mind.

I ask you to note, I have my faults, but
everyone's an exception. I would never lie to
you or cause you deception. I hope you know
that wherever you go, no matter how near or
far, we will never be apart. No matter how
far you leave, or how near you stay, I shall
remain in the vicinity of your blessed HEART.

Morgan L. Manasa

The Window

The darkness of night will find her
Lying alone and awake in her bed
Memories of loved ones filled with laughter
Appearing so vividly in her head

She sits and looks out her window
As the sun rises in the sky
There's no one to care or wonder
Not even to ask her why

When the darkness gives way to day
She goes about as in a trance
Often she returns to sit by her window
Watching for a visitor by chance

As loved ones go on with living
Their lives spent always in a hurry
She still sits quietly by her window
For her there's no one to worry

Sarah Talbert-McDaniel

"Papa"

Whenever we think of Papa,
many things come to mind.
Cotton fields and bails of hay,
with plenty of maize to grind.

Feeding cows or milking cows,
and helping all the lame.
Early rise to coffee time,
the schedule stays the same.

Tractors, trailers, cotton pickers, bailers.
Flat tires, stripped gears, won't start, back fire.
Tool shed, flat bed, greasy hands, khaki pants.
Bare feet, deer meat, smokehouse, good eats.

Hunting dogs and playful dogs,
and dogs without a home.
Large and small dogs, short and tall,
A master to them all.

Pipe smoke, good jokes,
reading, laughs and songs.
Reminiscing, kind and missing,
times of days long gone.

Kimberly A. Johnson

Passion Of The People (The Traveler)

The passion of the people,
making the history past.
Never cease to amaze me,
in this world so vast.
Everywhere I've been, every time I'm in.
It's all the same.
The wrenching need to survive,
to love and to please.
You can always see it in the eyes.
The window to the soul, wisdom, determination
or despair.
From fear, to care.
Self sacrifice is required, and at a challenge, they stare.
The spirits of the people I carry, give me strength.
I have their pain, their anger, their fear,
and every tear.
Knowledge and understanding is just a small gift,
from the Native peoples so near.

Lorie Parker

I See

I gaze into your eyes and I see so many different things.
Many emotions, many experiences and certainly many learned
lessons. But what stands out most vibrant in your eyes are the
colors that represent the person you've become. The turquoise
seems to be the commander of your soul. The strength and
mystery of the green and blue entangled to create a sense of
independence guarded by caution. The streaks of yellow tint
that hide inside your strength add a bit of insecurity and
fragility while always remaining bright. Its hope is to someday
disappear into the shadow of the turquoise forever. There is an
outcast I see cowering in the corners of your person reflecting
only a speck of red. It's vulnerable and throws the rest of you
off balance by introducing doubt. But the deeper I look I can
see that red speck will diminish with wisdom. I know this, as
there is a solid black ring that connects yourself to the sea of
eternal white purity beyond the brave border. The further I step
back the more clear you become as the colors of your soul merge
with your body and grow into your face. I realize you are
special. I sense you believe. I feel you are my best friend. I
see me.

Karen B. Thompson

"Heaven"

There are many thoughts on what Heaven is like,
Many feel there's an abundance of joy and mirth,
But ever since I've been a little tyke -
I've felt that Heaven is right here on earth!

E. M. Goff

Race

My race is different from others
many people hate me for it
the points
the stares
and even the glares
make me feel sad
sometimes it makes me feel
why did God give me this color
but then I know I'm like no other,
the person inside is like no other
which I try to hide
I don't get why people make fun of my race
and say to any face
I wish they could see the real me
not my color
if it weren't for that
I'd be glad instead of sad

Nicole Bergh

Bird

Faces in the cemetery,
marbled images of people I never knew;
statues of saints that don't have names
guarding the bodies of the dead.
And they all have eyes, and hearts and souls
even though they are stone.
They extend their empty hands to console the living.

One single saint that my eyes, and heart and soul seem to know,
with draping clothes and weather-worn skin
extends her cold gray hand
to something I don't want to see.
Until one day a bird came close and sat in the statue's lifeless hand.
I folded my empty hands, no longer afraid to die.

Faces in the cemetery,
hallowed images of people I'll never know;
figures of relatives that don't have names
kneeling over the graves of loved ones.
And they all have eyes, and hearts and souls,
even though they are alone.
They extend their empty hands to console themselves.

Samantha Leigh Sanders Walling

I Love You On My Wall

A week already, how fast time flies
Maybe I won't notice anything for a month
It seems like just another long wait
Memories never leave my mind and I always miss you

A week already, how fast time flies
Why do I have to say goodbye?
It seems like just another long wait
I love you on my wall

Why do I have to say goodbye?
Goodbye could last forever
I love you on my wall
And my wall misses your sunless blue eyes

Goodbye could last forever
Forever is so infinite
And my wall misses your sunless blue eyes
So let's eat crunchy tabouli again

Forever is so infinite
It seems like just another long wait
So let's eat crunchy tabouli again
A week already, how fast time flies

Tiffany A. Lyon

Emptiness

Emptiness is...
    Like a song without lyrics,
    A candle without light.
    A star that doesn't shine,
    On a clear cloudless night.

Sadness is...
    Like eyes that cannot see,
    A hand that cannot touch.
    Ears that cannot hear,
    The words; I LOVE YOU VERY MUCH.

Loneliness is...
    Like cries within the night
    But no one to be found.
    Like a voice that tries to speak,
    But cannot make a sound.

    These words I say to you
    As strong as they may be,
    Emptiness fills my heart
    When you are not with me.

Betsy A. Eno

"Why"

Why did you have to go and hurt
me and make me feel ashamed
as though it was all my fault
boy you wanted to do your thing

I ask why, why me, why me?

But the question still lies, why
as I sit in the dark and cry
about how someone would want to damage
another's life as someone has done to mine

I ask why, why me, why?

As you walk along as though you have
done no wrong with your head
up high with so much pride

But the question still lies, why
who could be the next they
find, and hurt another's life

I ask why, why me, why?

There is no answer to be seen but I mustn't
throw away my dreams because I want to help
someone that has been raped just like me.

Lydia Elizabeth Holloway

Sweet Angel

Our love is an angel, dropped from heaven's bounds.
Meant only for you and I, we heard the soft sweet cry.
You and I were chosen to be together.
We were chosen with love and care.
Fate struck us to meet, and our meeting was so rare.
I loved you from the moment I looked you in the eyes.
I saw those baby blues, and I saw a heart that's cried.
I saw a strong man, who has overcome battles.
And I saw an innocent child, in that everlasting smile.
Now I give heaven the glory.
You are my peace from prayer.
You were chosen to be my own sweet angel,
And into your arms I fell.
Now I could never let you go, I could never say good-bye.
To the faith, hope, or care, that I'm so glad we share.
I could not refuse this gift, given only to you and I,
That single gift of love, that came down from up above.

Monica S. Westfall

Life Abbreviated

The dark cloud passes across my heart and catches me unaware.
Missing you never quite goes away
Longing lessens or increases driven by some force I cannot
comprehend.
Sometimes I see a feature reproduced on another
Sometimes I remember
Sometimes the good
Sometimes the bad.
You too should have died hereafter.
When I think of you I think of books
If I had only held on to more of your books
Possibly I would have held on to more of you.
Pages comforting with their covers
and escaping with their words.
Torment lessens and increases driven by some force you could not
comprehend.
The world is a lesser place without you
And the pain is all the greater.
The dark cloud passes across my heart and catches me unaware.

Marilyn Corbin

Memories

Memories are things that living has made
Memories guide us in paths worthwhile and staid,
Memories of loved ones
Memories of things that we've done,
Memories of joy and sometimes of pain
Memories to reflect on again and again.

Memories are there for all of our life,
Giving us strength in joy and in strife,
Memories we share strengthen our connection,
With self and others and creative perfection;
So cherish each one and give thanks for those days,
When instead of hurrying, we take time for reflection.

Larry E. Sarbaugh

David

Dreams conjure and grow within the
    mind and heart of a boy,

And hold fast to the soul with each
    passing and pressing year of life

Visions of a living in which comfort
    and contentment outweigh the trials

Inspiring inside the man a feeling of
    fortune that he has come to know

Devotions to a dream is that which carves out
    the future and shapes yesterday into today.

Karen M. Golden

Blue

My favorite color is blue,
Most of my friends like it too,
Blue looks good mixed or plain,
It looks good even with a stain.

I see blue everywhere I go,
In the sea, In the sky,
Oh my! Dad has on a blue tie!

Cerulean is a nice shade,
when it's on a butterfly, not man-made,
I recognize blue really anywhere,
Once I saw a person with blue-green hair.

There is blue everywhere I look,
A blue pencil, a blue book,
I like the blue that's in the sky,
When it looks like the blueberries in blueberry pie.

I like water when it's light blue,
I think aquamarine is a nice color, too.
I like blue and I hope you do too!

Matt Mehalso

The Life Of A Magnet

Magnets can pick up many things,
Like paper clips, cars, and little rings.
The magnetic field was found by a little boy,
But he was only playing with his toy.
Because of the earth's magnetism a
Compass will always point north,
But they say in the Bermuda Triangle
it goes back and forth.
Magnets are used in communication,
Without magnetism America couldn't
have become an industrial nation.
With a magnet you cannot pick up an alligator,
But I will be able to hang this
poem on my refrigerator.

Nicole Moran

Define Mother

Mother is a cord that is cut but never severed,
Mother and child are bound together forever.
Whether she is dead or whether she is alive.
In our minds and hearts thoughts of her we
constantly revive.

My concept of childbearing is that, A woman
gives birth to a little part of her soul. For
it is evident in every story that is told.
From the time we are born, to the time we die.
For our mother's love our hearts doth sigh.

A child is a part of its mother; In its heart
she cannot be replaced by another.

No matter what we do or what we say, in our
hearts forever our mother will stay.

Again I say; A mother is a cord that is cut but
never severed.

No matter what the situation may be; She is the
one God chose for you and me.

Rena M. Gultney

Growing Old Together

Is there a solution for peace?
Must we go on and on lingering
with worn out bodies and souls?

Never a day or night
To our everlasting light

That we can find love, or
contentment in our lives.
Or are we so bended, so depressed,
that we can't see what we are doing to each other

Must life go on nagging at each other,
or must we part with sorrow?

Life is so short and so sad.
Let's not depart with dismay.

Let's find a solution to our love
and make it last forever and ever.

That peace can come soon.

Walter Fuchs

What's Love

Love is like the colors of a rainbow.
Love is like the flying of a dove.
Love is as blue as the sky.
   Red as a rose.
   Yellow as a daisy.
Love between two people is like the waves in the blue ocean.
Love is like the cool air of a spring day.
Love is the thing to share with someone.
So that is what love is
The colors of the rainbow.

Karen Squires

Love Is Forever

Love is something we share with each other.
Love is what we feel when we're together.
When we're apart, I feel a great kind of loneliness,
but love keeps you in my heart.
The strength of our love can never be put into words,
for, we can tell the strength by looking into each others eyes.
Love will get us through the bumpy roads in life.
Let love run free and it will guide you.
Love is not something that comes and goes, love is forever.
Yes my love, Our Love Is Forever.

Tonya Miner

I Need You Now

I don't want a host of friends and family to gather 'round
my casket when my life has ceased to be.
I want them to visit now and to share old memories with me.
I need love and words of understanding now while I am still here.
When I am in my casket my eyes and ears will no longer see or hear.
I'd rather see a loving smile from someone who comes to visit me.
Than all the kind words and flowers that my ears and eyes
will cease to hear and see.
Just one visit from a loved one or friend cheers me and
makes me feel better.
Or just a greeting card or a cheerful letter.
So save your kind words and flowers, I won't need them when
I'm gone from this life forever.
I need your warmth and love now, while we are here on earth
together.

Marjorie Watkins

Anticipation

"Go fetch me a switch from the ole' peach tree,"
My Daddy would say to me.
My punishment was coming and it was clear
What his actions were going to be.

I walked out in the yard where the peach tree grew
and looked at the switches galore.
My mind asked the question, "What size should I get?"
I remembered from the times before.

"If I get a small one it will sting too bad,
but the larger one will leave more whelps."

I reached for the switch with an in-between size
and handed it to my Pa.
I closed my eyes and held my breath
and waited for his hand to fall.

I felt a light touch on my legs
and opened my eyes to see.
My daddy was breaking the switch in half
and walking away from me.

Lorene Duncan

Who Am I?

Please be gentle, please be kind, I'm sorry dear, but I'm losing
   my mind.

I remember a family that I once had,
I miss them a lot, it makes me so sad.

I once had a house, a lot of children, and a wonderful spouse.

Someone packed my belongings away,
They moved me here, I had nothing to say.

Everything which has any meaning fit within a single suitcase.
My last days on earth will be spent in this strange place.

The bed is hard and I cannot sleep, I lie here alone and
   constantly weep.

My children come once in a while, they always seem to make me smile,
My other half has passed away, we will meet again someday.

My bones they ache, my body has expired,
My head always hurts and my soul is tired.

The memories that I have, they are but one blur,
There's nothing left here for me my friend, of that I am sure.

I've lived a nice life for all I do know, but now it is time
   and I must go.
If I could speak I would say "good-bye" and all I would ask is
   that you not cry.

Who am I? Do you know? Am I an old person with nowhere to go?

Sandy D. Hiller

"Toute Suit"

As I lower my arms across the railing,
my eyelids flutter in a seizure of perplexity.
Sounds are diffused in a concentrated aura.
I look around to see if I've missed anything.
The gray mystic of weather shows no mercy.
My foot shuffles forward into a patch of flora.
Sediments boil into life's sprouted ringing.
Shrugging my shoulders, I wince completely.
A downward spiral is a brisk inflation of tora.
My spirit is splintered next to a wooden framing.
I contort my back up as if pressed up against a viola.
One of the doctors nods her head, mesmerizing the sting.
Spectators clamor for exits while I'm pondering,
"Why am I here?"

Laurie Christenson

My Name Is Penny

Hi my name is Penny, and I'm a big girl.
My family says I'm little, my skin is white as pearl.
My age is five years old, and my house is oh so cold.
We don't have food 'cause daddy's gone,
mommy said it's my fault, what did I do wrong?
Mommy is asleep right now, lying in her bed.
My tummy hurts deep inside, 'cause I haven't been fed.
I have to be real quiet, 'cause mommy might wake up,
so I'm sitting in the corner, so she won't beat me up.
I don't go to school, 'cause my face is all blue
mommy says to say I fell, so that's what I should do
all I have is mommy, 'cause daddy is all gone.
My mommy just woke up, I can hear her angry yawn.
I hear her walking towards me, "Hi mommy I'm watching T.V."
All I hear is her angry voice, I'm scared to get hit
    but I have no choice
Hi my name was Penny, I was only five,
my mommy used to beat me..... when I was Alive.

Tanya M. Ramirez

"Father's Day"

I'm glad I have a father, who would really try to care about
my feelings, and the things I'd like to share. But some girls
aren't so lucky to have a "Dear Sweet Dad" who'd be glad to
stand and smile. Saying hey she's not so bad. A father that
would be there when his baby trips and falls, one who'd play
with his sweet tomboy a simple game of ball. When his baby girl
was older a young woman, proud and small. He would smile and not
disapprove when young men come to call. A father sad but proud,
that he raised his tomboy well. Knows now he must give her up
with memories of when she fell. I'm not the only girl, who has
a dad, who would rather make her happy instead of making her
sad. It is really nice to have a father, who cared enough to
listen to my feelings and things I'd like to share. That's why
this poem's for you dad, to show you that I care.

Shelly Anderson

The Boy Of My Mind

In the closest of memories there lives a small boy,
Loving the sunshine and splashing through creeks,
No worries, no heartaches, just full of fun and joy.
This boy that I once was, but still a part of me.
Even today with all the trials that life has for me,
A small boy inside of me gets scared and wishes for those
earlier days.
This boy that liked to throw rocks and climb trees,
The smell of puppy dogs and fields of clover bring back those days.
But now the boy in my mind is starting to fade,
For you see, the boy in my mind is being replaced with the boy
of my kind.

Robert Lee Pierce

A Way of Love

During the year of 1973
My deeply loved Grandparents passed away.
To be a time never forgotten
A lifetime memory to always stay,

They kept showing all their love
For many years after they died,
Because leaving each of us thousands
Is an Unforgettable Memory to hide.

When Memorial Day comes every year
My love is sent to their graves.
In thanks for raising 15 years
And leaving me inheritance they gave.

They are buried in Quinby Cemetery
Where I pray they rest in peace
They'll be remembered throughout my life
My lifetime memory to never cease.

Linda Carpenter

Glass Rose

One night as I lay sleeping,
    My dreams bared my soul.
I saw in a crazy world,
    One perfect rose.
I watched it for several days,
    It became more perfect in every way.
I wondered, could this be,
    Could this perfect rose belong to me?
I reached out to touch, to feel, then it became clear,
    The rose was enclosed in glass, I could not come near.
The wind began to blow, the glass began to fall,
    How long I chased it I do not recall.
The rose came crashing to the ground,
    Shattered glass lay all around.
As I turned to leave this place,
    Tears were streaming down my face.
All that was left to hold,
    Was one torn petal of my perfect rose.

Linda C. Brown

"One Across That Mist Which Veils"

One across that mist which veils a century now grown dim
Must not there have been, standing alone atop some grassy knoll,
A cavalry man bedecked in woolen shades of dusty and faded blue;
His eyes turned up to night's clear sky, carpeted by heaven's stars,
Alone within himself, so still, intent in search for a single one,
The brightest of all that shone midst the slow ebbing inky night.

His tuckered company in worn bedrolls lay asleep off to the west,
Only picket's silhouettes wavered there in the flickering tiny fires
That marked that Army bivouac beneath the sky some half mile away.
Motionless in squared-toe boots fixed upon that knoll he gazed,
The still night rent only by the restless nickering of his led-horse
At the faint wavering howl of a lonely grey wolf's far off implore.

Yet this Regular, beard and hair streaked by campaign's reward,
Diverted not by sounds unheard, just stayed his prairie vigil for,
The one star in that lustrous crowd, that relit hope in his heart,
As did beloved Lorie far beyond his darkness to the distant east.
In that distant east which smiles its hope upon the frontier day,
When warm reborn sun lifts up from chilly mists that mark the dawn
To restore his cherished hope that one other day may fairly come,
When he might kneel in daylight before a single shiny star alone!

Thomas M. Salisbury III

Surgery

Surgery stinks
My hair looks like kinks
I just don't know what to do.
I look like a wreck
The surgeon I want to deck
For all the pain he's made me go through!
The medicine is gross
They always say, "Just one more dose!"
I'm fed up with the nurses too!
They keep saying, "A couple of more days!"
And what about ME I'm without pays!
Surgery Stinks
Why me?
I can barely see
The meals taste like dog food!
My wife tells me, "How come you're always in a bad mood?"
Gee, I wonder why!!
Surgery Stinks!

   Tanya Gruwell

Adventurous Heart

Like the rolling thunder and the raging rivers
My heart pounds and tumbles with the love it contains.
Like the fire in your eyes,
My body burns with surprise.
As long as there is a breath in me
I will always feel the same.
I will be by your side until the very end,
And when you need it, I will be your friend.
A love for me, there is no other.
I only want you as my lover.
A day away from you
Is like a day of death or two.
You are like nobody I've ever met before
With you, like an eagle, my spirit can soar.
Deep inside, you know you have the key to
my heart.
Like cupid, you shot me with a flying dart.
No matter what I say or what I do,
You will never know how much I feel for you.

   Kristin Ammons

My Heart's Reality

When my eyes first met your blue ones,
My jolted heart skipped a beat,
It was captured in that moment,
Packed its bags within the week.

So, my heart went out a wanderin'
And now, a wonderin' it is, too,
Why finding a mate is such a problem,
Yearning for love, sincere and true.

I begged my heart to come back home,
But it said, "Don't push and shove;
I don't want to come back just yet,
I'm still looking for love."

Its latest journey has been painful.
Soundly beaten, bruised and battered,
My heart's hopes and dreams, plans and schemes
Have crashed and smashed and shattered.

This sad heart is headed homeward now,
Proud and dauntless, it tried its best,
CONDITION: wrecked, yet beating strong,
It held its own; it deserves a rest.

   Sherry L. Rifley

Untitled

Standing in the water
   My life,
in its dire need of completeness, ebbs slowly,
Far back into that which is beautiful
   and so lovely a place
There is no mystique to encompass my victory
   No tome to which I am bound
Only water
And in that I so quickly drown forsaken sorrows
   Standing in the water
I am but a churchman
in this the most holy of temples
I surrender to its struggle
Bedraggled by its own worst enemy - me
But in my best of faith
   which by no means is blind
I will walk within its flow
   throwing far and away
unto the sleepless wind
All of my troublesome heartaches

   J. Dalton Eyler

My Dad

I remember Bill, he was the star upon my hill.
My love for him will never die though he now lives
In heaven high.

His memory will linger wherever I be,
And his heavenly spirit will comfort me.
His philosophy of life I will never forget—
It's etched on my mind, so I live with it yet.

If you could have known him as I did—
Wise, humorous and sad.
This very great person I speak of
Was my wonderful, wonderful Dad.

   Peggy Steier

Safari

It is a place very far, far away.
My mind always exploring as it peacefully plays.
A place surrounded by lush flowers, exotic creatures and their prey.
Visions of many colorful flashes and spots and stripes.
Enchanting sounds of nature's music and lingering cries.
A place captivating with vivid sights and bittersweet smells.
A place so exquisite I'm yearning to tell.
It's nights blessed by a glowing full moon, by day, a bright
blazing sun.
A place filled with fear of Its own blood and hunt.
A place haunting, yet erotic with pleasures and pains.
A place where I roam free on those magical plains.
A place so beautiful. Yet, so far far away
A place so very beautiful. All my days I long to
stay.

   Terra R.

Untitled

When I'm alone in my silent thought,
My mind fills with memories of things past.
Suffering for the lack of the things I wanted,
I ruin my present with my yesterday's woes.

Then I cry for my dead friends,
And weep for my lost love.
And lament for the loss of my beloved ones.

I count up my woes,
And my past sorrows are paid once more;
But at the moment I think of you,
My present returns and my past is gone.

   Melissa Fuster

Trying To Be Real

Well here's my story, of how I lost and came to glory.
My mother was very real and loving.
And to all that was apparent.
But I chose another.
And to all I was transparent.

Trying To Be Real.
There were!!
There were times I sold drugs for a hit.
There were times I lied for a hit
there were times I stole for a hit.
There were times!!
There were times I just couldn't quit.

Trying To Be Real
I always thought cocaine eased my
pain and brought me fame.
But being real it only brought me shame and made me lame...
So ask me again? Do I want a hit?
and I'll tell you no!!!! Why?

Because I'm real.

Robert P. Bell

Insanity

Hello,
My name is insanity. I am coming to get you.
There is no place to hide, for I live within your mind.
As the pressure of life builds and mounts,
I am here waiting to get out.
The more you moan and groan,
The stronger it is that I grow.
I am always waiting at your side.
One day you'll slip, and you I will find.
Some have grown smart, them I cannot touch.
But you are meek and growing weak.
It is your doom that you so seek.
I give you a clue, a warning to you.
If you are happy and bright,
Then I can never come into your sight.
But I know you'll fail, some always do,
The time is near, I'll come for you.
Go on, be grouchy and blue, be unkind to your neighbors too.
It only builds my strength, you know,
For this is what truly makes me grow.

Sharon Whitt

Howdy!!

Hi!! Howdy!! Hello!!
my name is Tex
I'm a cowboy who rides
a horse named Rex—-

Crack the whip — make it snap
want a pretty lady on my lap —
blow wind blow - there is a chill in the air
in old faded jeans — we were a pair

Rain — is a coming mighty quick
the old yellow dog is awful sick—-
walking beside me - holding my hand
used to have hair the color of sand

Cattle grazing in the pasture green
horses galloping upon the scene
love — Navajo blankets with colors wild
red hot peppers and some that's mild

Thirteen kisses and lots of hugs
like my coffee black in a mug —-
full of surprises where ever I go
Hi!! Howdy!! Hello!!

M. J. Leslie

Bella, Bella, Dandelion

Bella, bella, dandelion crowding out the grass,
My neighbors call you weeds with words like "gross" and "crass."
I view you with delight for brightening lawns with first spring color.
I admire your flat, green, arrow-like leaves,
Clinging to the earth more tenaciously than any other.
Perfect magic - yours - capturing sun power.
Sending energy to your deeply anchored roots.
Your blossoms charged, too, no longer to be contained,
Burst forth and smile from everywhere at me.
Oh, joy, to see you shining from back alley soil islands in cement,
Or on rolling meadows by country streams.
Joy of joys, to see you in my own front yard!
My spirits are lifted as sun sparks shoot from bright golden petals.
Because of you, I will walk with lighter step, and laugh my way into
And laugh my way into a happier day.
We turn grey, too soon, you and I.
Wind tides float your grey away to recreate.
I just sip your wine and dream in sweet anticipation,
Knowing that thousands of bella, bella, dandelions
Will return to light up another spring.

Marjorie Foster Fleming

"Lovers or Just Friends"

It was one warm and gentle summer day,
my one true love went away,
the stars came out so bright that night,
and I thought all I did was right,

But now I know it was only wrong,
he could not understand my song,
the song I sang so loud and clear,
was only meant for the right one to hear,

but he wasn't the one,
still he came my way,
but now we will be
friends to stay.

A best friend I say,
is better to know,
than to lose out on love,
And let your whole life go.

Misty Ann Curry

"Praises To God"

I adore Thy Name.
My soul surrenders to Thee,
To Thy Heavenly Voice.
I praise Thee for Thy mighty names,
Wonderful, Counselor, Prince of Peace.
I Praise Thee for Thy righteousness,
For Thy infinite creation.
I praise Thee for Thy mighty acts.
I praise Thee for Thy word.
For obtaining things that seem impossible and out of reach;
I praise Thee for the Victories
over fire, air, earth and water.
I praise Thee for the Red Sea,
I praise Thee for water from the rock, and bread from Heaven.
I praise Thee for the sun that stood still,
For the fire from the sky on Elijah's sacrifice.
For prayer that healed the sick and raised the dead
I praise Thee for conversions of countless souls,
Lord, teach me to pray.
Help me to praise Thee first. Amen.

Vivian J. Rouse

"My Unwritten Dream"

Late in December of Nineteen Ninety-Three,
My vision became sharper, and I started to see
A much clearer view of my life-long dream,
A bond with a lady, we would form a team.

It was in January of Nineteen Ninety-Four,
I focused and believed, through to my core.
I believed this dream, if planted would grow,
went unwritten, so my girl would not know.

Early in Spring, after her Birthday,
my labor and planting began to pay.
I secured a ring, crystal clear and bright,
My dream took off to a great new height.

April 30th the day, a question to ask,
My toughness aside, still, one great task.
A last minute plan, in a backyard to be?
Just hide the ring, so that she won't see.

"Will You Marry Me Sweetie?" shaking a bit,
Showing her the ring the sun's ray had lit.
Only one short word I dreamed I would hear,
She blinked, she smiled, she ended my fear.

Patrick J. Hawley

Time Well Spent

I measure out my days in dog walks and coffee cups.
My weeks come and go in long bus rides to the mall.
My months creep slowly by in a perpetual stretch of income.
"Dear God, don't let them raise the rent this month, or the utilities."

My years I remember only by one Fourth of July when I was twenty;
One anniversary, the nineteenth, I think; or a birthday that is
    yet to come.
My hours I record on a meter, as I reach for bottles and pills
That they prescribe to keep me stable, or so they say.

Each day, I count my blessings and my savings, then pray.
But there are so many losses; loved ones and ways of life,
Tragedies and sickness; famine and despair;
And I am helpless. I have nothing left to give.

Am I glad lived this life? Occasionally when the electricity goes
And I remember the simple things. No TV, just a good book
And the yellow lamplight dueling with the red flame of fireplace.
Or the glow of a beautiful sunset gleaming through the panes.

Or when I hear the high-pitched laughter of a little child,
And feel his tiny hand in mine. Then I hear him whisper,
"Grandma, I love you." It is then that my heart beats glad;
I still have time to live - and love to give - and love to give.

Roberta Marlow

Laura Krohn

I have an Aunt
named Laura Krohn
I love her dearly
right through to the bone.

She gives of herself daily
with much to share
She carries her oxygen tank
that's probably a spare.

Her days are spent helping
those with a need.
Her resources are numerous
for this is her deed.

Her purpose is obvious
in this life you see
Aunt Laura's a saint
sent to you and to me.

Scott Stevens

Whence Came Man's Spark? Ignescence

Was it first perchance in some far-off
    nebula uncounted eons long gone?
Did it reel down the corridors of time
    and space in apparently aimless fashion?
Was there then some sort of penultimate
    coalescence in this our earth?
For did not our first earth parents countless
ages ago react to some such Ignescence and
    thus vouchsafe our so late appearance?

Care we as to the detail of this
    Grand Sequence?
Not really, Rather let us simply bow
    and acknowledge its long persistence,
For as man enfolds woman in ageless
    embrace skin to skin and flesh to flesh
    their two spirits do thus enmesh
And they become one with Eternity.

Ray M. Kellogg

Dream Of The Married Lover

The prelude reverberates throughout the darkened auditorium.
Nebulous dialogue at twenty decibels wavers
As the actors slowly traverse the redwood-floor stage.
I lie hidden in the coulisse,
Unable to intervene in the sequence set before me.
Suddenly the premiere emits an eloquent oratory which dazzles the star
As the star has often dazzled me.
And I, in my limbo, interject a low moan which falls upon deaf ears.
Dare I remove my mask and effect the schism?
The question darts about as a snake evading a mongoose.
The stage is suddenly empty now...
Brocade and redwood meet with a kiss...
I am disentranced; what remain are
Melancholy feelings of having been abandoned by the one I love.

Lisa Frazier

Promised Memory?

Brilliant ash filters throughout.
My disintegrated body floats freely down a river of blue bliss,
Endlessly dissolving onto a mattress of infinite sand.
Dissolved ... Vanished...
Eroded by polluted, persistent rain.
Blown away,
By blind, wandering wind.
Lost,
Erased,
Forever.

Forever...
ashes...
all we are...
just ashes...

God...
Will anybody remember my death?

Steve Bender

My Thoughts

My mind is always on the go,
My thoughts run constant and never slow,
They're logical, jumbled, intense and deep,
They stay with me through wake and sleep.
I've slept well not these past few years,
My thoughts bring worry, tears and fears.
I would be content if down they eased,
Allowed peaceful rest I would be appeased.
A power switch would be divine
To shut down awhile these thoughts
    of mine.

Wendy Greer

389

The Blank Ones

Lost in their own, small little space,
Never a thought, or a care on their face.

Pushing and shoving, they do make their way,
All going nowhere, throughout the day.

Doors bang in your face, as they rudely walk by,
Without ever saying, hello or good-bye.

With empty expressions, they float throughout life,
Devoid of ambition, but full of their strife.

Their days run together, no beginning nor end,
Their paths go in circles, not ever a bend.

Their zest for life, has left long ago,
Their dullness and drudgery, is all they do sow.

Their yesterdays blend into their tomorrows,
Their futures are bleak, and heading for sorrows.

They trudge along wearily, without gladness or joy,
As like a baby, that's lost its first toy.

Their hearts are empty, but heavy to bear,
They also have no one, no one to care.

As nightfall drifts down, pleasure does come,
A peaceful night's sleep, for one more day's done.

Suzanne M. Skinner

The Promise

Not long ago I promised, never fall in love again,
never, ever let hurt anymore my heart from a man,
never get dazzled by his charm and romantic words,
but, waiting, till he show's up his real thoughts.
I promised myself, not to close my eyes for problems
to safe a nice picture for a marriage and the system,
as the experience learned me to watch for a safer life,
no more I'll be a man's battered wife!!!
That's why I promised to never fall in love again,
never, ever let hurt my heart from a man.
But, mother nature works on its fantastic wonder
makes again my heart loving and tender
as there is a battle in my heart, between fear and love,
it still burns the inner warm stove.
Sitting on my bed, feeling the butterflies and I dream,
If I should really share my feelings with him?
It takes time to regain a healthy self-worth
as I have to break down all fears and doubts.
Slowly I take steps, towards trust, respect, love and peace,
as to have it - it's my life - cry, it's my secret wish...

Rosmarie Hermann

Alone...

She sits alone,
no dreams, no thoughts, no cares.
The room in which she sits is dull;
dull, much like the life that was chosen for her.
Submerged in feelings of confusion and loneliness,
the nothingness inside rips and tears at her soul.
Life is precious, but what is the meaning.
How to make them understand.
A task more important than life itself.
No one knows her losses, her worries, her feelings.
No one cares.
Uninvolved in drugs and gangs,
She fits in somehow, some way.
Hearing the lives of others, temptation overcomes her.
She wants to become them, and is invited along.
But she cannot leave her dull room.
So she sits alone,
no dreams, no thoughts, no cares.

Mindy Martensen

All Of A Sudden

Shot in the head. Now you're dead. Wishes
never fulfilled. By yourself you're killed.
Hearts broken. Your memory just a token. Life
was so hard. You had played with only one
card. The feelings of hurt and sorrow. Now
there's not even tomorrow. Why? they asked.
Your time had passed. It was time to leave.
Nothing more to believe. The scene of your
crime. You could only hear a chime. The blood
of red. Your body with tread. The note you
had written with words from hell. There was
nothing more to tell. One last word from your
mouth out loud. Then you were carried off by a
cloud. Looking down upon your body of hate.
It had only been fate. Never coming back. Now
it's me you lack. Now do you understand how I
felt, is what I asked, as by my body you
knelt. Now I'm dead. I had only shot myself
in the head. It's what I felt inside. That's
why I've committed suicide.

Michelle Lynn Daniel

The Lost Child

Cold, hungry, tired.
No food, no clothes, no dolls, no hope.
Cold slabs of rotted wood under bare feet.
As I stare out of a window with no glass.
Is this it? Is this life?
"Sweet dreams," mommy says.
Dreams complicate my life.
Dreams compliment my life.

Lying, stealing, begging...starving.
If I don't do my job, we don't eat.
I have a cat, we can't keep him.
Daddy says it costs too much.
But I'll hide him under the bathtub.
I don't have any toys.
Mommy would have let me keep him.

I miss mommy. I love her.
I say my prayers every night like she told me to.
Maybe I'll see her soon, I hope so!
I wish daddy would stop touching me.
Well I guess I'm the mommy now.

Lisa Juliano

No Point Anymore

No pain could be deeper,
No life could be cheaper,
No point anymore, if you can't love me,
No hope you would do so,
No dream to pursue, so,
I look to myself, despise all the things I see,
For I know, that if you cannot set me free
let the world be done with me.

Tara Cegelske

The Price For Freedom

I never felt the shackles on my feet
Nor the sting of the whip on my back,
Yet in some small way history seems to
Remain the same.
The dope dealer took over the master's job
Crippling my brothers with coke.
Black on black crime took the place of white
Mobs, leaving death at every door.
Freedom, freedom, oh! What a price we pay for freedom.

Marekus Fluellen

Wise Words

Someone wise once told me you could never forget a friend.
No matter how far apart you are, or how long you've been away.
There is always something that makes you remember them. Their
smile, their eyes, the happy times and then again the bad times.

You remember the things you told each other when there
was no one else around. The secret places you would go where
you could not be found, in that place you would share your
dreams, and fantasies. The songs you would sing together, and
all the movies you would watch.

The person who told me this was my best friend and a lot
more. We shared good times and bad times. We talked a lot
about dreams. I hope when we see each other, he will remember
the wise words he once told me.

Sheri Michelle Conner

Love

Love is a dream for me and you
no one can disturb it when the sky
is blue

Love is filled with many colors
red, black, blue and others
me and you are meant to be or can
Our love go on for eternity!

Though we have our up's and down's
but, someday in heaven we shall wear a
crown.

We walk together through the park
sometimes when it's light or when it's dark
and as we walk through the park I
have a feeling in my heart that we
will never part.

But I still wonder is it you? or is it
me? or is our love just meant to be??

Latoshia Stewart

Echoes Of Love

I hear nothing you say therefore,
No response to be heard - what is it you didn't say?
Patiently, I await moments filled with sweet laughter
Echoes into the stillness of the night
With but a wish - dreams of music -
    softly playing
        around and clock
Pouring from the walls surrounding us
Deep rich voices leaving words to linger in the air
Long after the gallant affair
Again you say something and I try to catch this
A soft whisper from your lips
I love you echoes from nowhere.

Teresa J. Anderson

Search For The Light

As I stare into the sunset I can see his smiling face
    looking out for me as I feel his strong embrace,
With unspoken words he tells me of his fight
    and of his search; his search for the light,
He lived out his dream throughout his short life
    and then at the end he had to pay the price,
All the time on the road and the hotel nights
    they were all apart of his search for the light;
I blink through the tears and he then fades away
    but I feel comforted for I know he's okay,
I know down inside that he's happy and all right
    because I know he found his search for the light.

Misty M. Halstead

The Spider

The spider glides on his web of silk.
No sound does he make.
Sunbeams dance along his web.
Exquisite symmetry.
A velvet touch as he glides.

The spider, so perfect, so patient, in the forest.
The web, delightful in its form.
Raindrops flow gently through the pattern.
Rainbows reflect from the silk.
Faultless victims, the butterflies cry as the spider feasts.

The spider strolls softly down the streets,
Humming sweetly as he prowls.
The spider glides slowly, looking, waiting.
The sounds of life echo from the walls.
Children's laughter, the most pleasing of all.

The spider, so perfect, so patient, in the city.
His web spreads out, ever more.
Lovely, and enchanting in its form.
Rainbows reflect from the tears on the street.
Faultless victims, the children cry as the spider feasts.

Tom Turley

The Love You Miss

He never got to see her tiny face,
Nor all her dresses with antique lace.
An he even missed her first step,
But I have pictures of it all, that I kept.

He never got to hear the first murmur of sound
Nor all of the tears of happiness I found.
An he even missed the first hug an kiss,
But I think he knows how much he will miss.

So please always remember this, and don't ever forget,
The angry words you yell at your DAD one day you regret.
See even the best FATHERS do make a few mistakes,
You have to be the one to forgive, before GOD takes.

I think he looked down from the heavenly sky
For on the day she was born, I could hear his cry.
So maybe one day not long from now
We will all see him, although I am not sure how.

Sherie S. Mitchell

I Am Not Here Anymore

I dwell where a dweller thinks Heavens of it.
Nor I, nor he, who dwells unselfishly,
But receives much pain to feel.
To feel or witness at this dwellers';
Dwelling beyond disbelief.
I no longer feel I'm here anymore.
Why? I must as well in tomb myself.
To dwell in Heaven; My only place.
Now child! You go on and dwell alone.
You go on and learn your own.
No need for me to bring about,
Truth and beauty.
That's what life is all about.
Now, child! "What must you do of your life?"
There pass to you, where the dweller
Thought of its place as Heaven and earth.
Where the dweller moved mountains of earth.
And have you...my child, to witness the same.
Now, child! You go on and dwell alone.
You go on and learn your own. I am not here anymore.

Sara Brooks

Youthful Thoughts

When I was just a little boy
Not more than nine or ten
I used to sit and scribble
With my little pad and pen
My thoughts I thought were great ones
So I put them all to rhyme
I just knew these thoughts of mine
Would stand the test of time
But mankind wasn't ready then
For what I had to say
So I thought I'd better put them both away
Mankind is a little older now
Why I'm three score and ten
I guess it's time that I took out
My little pad and pen
I read those words in wonder
Then read them once again
Then I got up and threw away
My little pad and pen

Thomas R. Sammons

Untitled

In a blink of a second
nothing has changed. (Contrary to popular belief.)
The World spins as I fall to my knees,
it is wise to recreate all the Gods and mystical beliefs.
Then we'll be safe and inconsistent
and the unborn will have a place to rest.
I learned the truth yesterday and will be borne tomorrow.
Do you know the truth and have you been borne yet?
Or are you silently existing in the womb,
self-destruction inevitable?
Life revolves around the lie.
The lie is intangible and hidden,
but it is there- I can feel it.
It pulsates in my veins,
slowly it drains the life from me.
My blood pours out of my veins onto the table.
The redness is caught in the wine glasses,
and the lie is shown to the One.
In a blink of a second
nothing has changed. (Contrary to popular belief.)

Max Mandich

Last Chance

Life is going slowly, and there is not a worry.
Nothing is ahead of me that I can see.
The waters of my life are not running quite fast at all.
Spent a lot of time doing nothing, I wish there was
    a friend to call.
One day sitting around watching TV I am touched at what I see,
    It holds a mystery for me, but I found the key.
It is not just me going forth, but others and me God sees
Determination is on fire in me, now I see- it is for me
    not on the sidelines watching to be.
I have one life to live, who can live it for me- no one but me.
A change alone I have to make because the vision is for me, gone
Where are my past opportunities?
Tomorrow is not promised or given to me.
Therefore, Lord help me to live this day and each day with
    all flavor and satisfaction- that is the key.
Live for no regrets, stand on your beliefs, do not let them be at ease
Do not look back in late age and say, "That was my last
    chance to be all that I could be,
    it all could have been different, but now this is me."

Steven W. Lee

Sweet Wishes

I'm in the mood for something to eat,
Nothing that's good for me, something real sweet.
Chocolate chip cookies with chips galore,
Sweet tarts or pop tarts or a whole candy store.
Delicious fudge sundae with a cherry on top,
Bubble gum, taffy or a giant lollipop.
Strudel or pie or a chocolate cake treat,
Anything, anything, just something sweet.
A milkshake, a brownie, or banana supreme,
How about muffins or donuts with cream?
Marshmallows, fireballs, one lemon drop,
Caramels or licorice, a cold soda pop.
Cotton candy, candy corn, or a candy called Pez,
Anything, anything who cares what mom says.
"Well," says mom as she sets out the dishes,
"It's liver tonight, so much for your wishes."

Rosanna Zock Koehler

Meshing Moons

The August moon has come and gone
November now, December soon.
The most was made of four full days
the moon played music, we wanted to stay.
The stars exploded and made the senses rise.
Oh, for those days and the wonderful sunrise.
Our harmony, the peace, and the love's tranquility,
together enjoying our vitality.
Souls rising, the minds were free,
and our bodies, of course, meshing perfectly.
The joy we felt, has never been matched.
Except when we're together in the times we can catch!
We look ahead to another few days
of spirits flying free, not falling away.
Nature's sentient being won't let us stray.
Our love she's seen and the price we pay.
She'll keep us safe until our time arrives
to mesh once more beneath her moon meshed skies.

Sonya Ebright

Graduation Of An Air Force Cadet - May, 1994

For four long years, he stayed in line,
Obeying the rules and waiting the time
When he, at last, could finally say,
"I've reached my goal. Hurray! Hurray!"

The last day arrived warm and bright,
And the parade of Cadets was a spectacular sight.
All in dress uniform and standing tall,
Waiting to hear the final call.

The band was playing a marching tune,
And each Cadet hoped that very soon
He would finally be considered free,
From rules and regulations of the Academy.

As each Cadet's name was called to receive
His diploma, and as well, a reprieve,
He saluted his classmate who went before,
And they hugged each other as emotions did soar.

When the ceremony was over, and they were dismissed,
Hats tossed in the air, a sight not to be missed.
A "Thunderbirds'" salute, as they roared in the sky,
A fitting climax, and a final "Goodbye."

Ruth J. DeHollander

Grandmama

There is this lady I'd do anything for,
Obviously she's very special to me,
The world says there's no relation between us,
But that's just what they see.
They see the outside color... which is black and white,
They don't see the important part.. the inside.
For what I see, the inside,
Is a relationship that is inseparable.
A relationship that'll never be finished.
One that began with no intentions
And now there's nothing that'll make it end.
Our relationship is an educational experience.
One that is full of surprises, challenges, and new ideas
One we can learn and live from good or bad, thick and thin,
One day we'll meet, don't know when,
But until then know that I'm loving you.
You're the best there will ever be,
And I'll love you till the end!!!

Melody Puffer

Untitled

Dream a world of dreams tonight
Of a sky so blue and constant light
Of crystal seas with pearl stones
Of shells and of ivory homes
Dream of whispers soft and sweet
Of the love you want to meet
Dream a place of fantasies
Of elves and flying pixies
Dream of trolls found underground
And munchkins that make little sound
Of castles glistening with gold and jewels
Where children make up all the rules
Dream of endless happiness and peace
No sickness, wars, or miseries
Of blooming flowers everywhere
No smoke, smog,or dirty air
Dream of friendships forever true
And how much I love you
Dream all of this and more for me
And someday this dream will be

Renea Forstner

From Three Comes One

That room in the past was filled with screams
of anger, jealousy, laughter, and dreams;
they had no choice but to end each day there,
three girls so unlike who had to share.

It was a crazy time of youth and greed,
to be alone yet have that need
of friend and foe and ally, too,
One common bond always came through.

Similarities and differences combined,
Can make for an interesting time
for two who joined and created life,
a time of joy, love, and strife.

These different thoughts, ideas, beliefs, and deeds,
you wonder how each became so unique;
and as time passed on and they grew apart,
it was only in person, never in their hearts.

That room in the past has never forgot
those three individuals who were in there caught
by a fate and destiny of time long past,
they were three sisters who forever held fast.

Phyllis Enoch

Morning Light

As a single ray of sunlight falls onto the first sight
of life on the surface of the earth, the entire world seems
to glow with a shimmer beyond words. Everything is awakened
by this hauntingly sweet magic. Everything arises and is
introduced to the strange, golden world around it. Then
another single ray of misty sunlight showers everything.
Nature is awakened by this mysterious, luring light. The
rainy smell of the morning mist gently nudges awake all
creation. One by one, each golden ray falls and the great
ball of fire and light appears above the morning horizon.

Natalie Shaw

Dreaming

I have dreams of having money.
Of living in the land of milk and honey.
Of traveling and having fancy cars.
Of mingling with famous movie stars.
Of having a mansion and swimming pool.
Of sending my children to private school.
Of buying my clothes on Rodeo Drive.
Of eating with golden forks and knives.
But then I look at what I've got.
And realize I have a lot.
It's worth more than all the money,
And living in the land of milk and honey.
Getting a kiss from my loved ones is more dear,
And having them around me, holding them near.

Natalie Geiger

Wingate Memories

Wingate memories dwell within our hearts
Of Mama and Daddy and past years we sought.

Our house nestled within an old spot
Where pecan trees grew
And the train whistle blew.

We grew closer on some occasions in that old house
When a storm brewed outside and the lights went out.

The old kerosene lantern was brought out for sight
And the coleman stove brewed coffee for our delight.

Tales were passed from one to another
Of our day at school, work and other.

Then there were days in the old summer time
When we walked down the tracks
For dewberries to find.

I'll always remember those dewberry pies
For Wingate memories
Will always be on my mind.

Robin Mills

Untitled

Oh the horror, the beauty, the reality,
of man's inherent mortality,
if one is patient and willing to look,
All of nature will open like a book.
To those few pages which tell the truth,
that there is nothing in the concept of turned youth.
Take the days as they come,
Smile, spread joy to everyone.
As one passes from youth to old age,
so it goes on in life as on the page.
Oh the horror, the beauty, the reality.
of man's inherent, ever-pleasant mortality!

J. D. Wagner

A New Day Is Dawning

I awaken each morning, my heart filled with joy, look out
of my window like a child will explore.
I see the daylight come shining through, I see remnants of
the morning dew. I see skies as red as a Robin's Breast,
a earth that is peaceful and all is at rest.
May God give us the strength to live by his way, and thank
him again at the close of the day.

Peggy A. Gaines

"Nostalgic—For The Old Things"

I long for hearts big enough, to house the "best loved" stuff
Of Poetry still "too good to throw away":
Old embraces, haunting romances, that have seen better days;
Old plans—and old-world graces—and even repulsive cases;
Old night shades seeking new places, beaux with long-ago faces;
(The skies never so blue, the midnights never-as enchanting!)
And piles of dusty, shrunken tombs—lonely and forsaken—these too!
All songs of yore that pipers piped and minstrels sang
That have lost their homes—in modern-minded "me."
A "me" that drives them into the snow, though a passionate part
Of me hates to see them go: like all good rhymers, I maintain
The inspiration will come, complete with nostalgic rain.
And we poets can congratulate ourselves
Upon having replenished empty hearts, and famished shelves.
And all these "soul-bursts" will prove lasting testimony to society's
  worth
(With honors on the Muse's head—that coins 'em)
By restoring, the Poetry Crown of everlasting renown, with prayers
upon every believer's lip that when we're through there'll be for one
holy minute a world standing with joy in it.

Lonnie Bailey

Things I Ponder

I pray for sun rays on my face, to touch the water
of the ocean, to walk along endless beach
To feel the sand against my feet. The air is cool the
waves are high. What a sight before my eyes.

To pray for peace on earth today to each and all
who come my way. For those of you who are blind
to life. There stands the flag, flying stars and stripes.

Freedom for me is comfort within to know that
I can voice my say, to know that it will be okay
to choose to go the other way.

To be with you or be with him no matter the
color of your skin. We all have different views
in life. Who's to say who's wrong or right

That it's okay not to agree with him or her
or even me. We feel and cry and laugh the
same. For we are all just human beings.

Rebecca Sue Tarr

I'm Healing

God has set me free
Just to be what he wants me to be.
I've lost a grandmother and a puppy too.
Only my heart knew.
The pain was so great I went inside myself
but I did not receive despair, I found God's hope,
As my life continues to grow.
The seed is planted there's no need for a hoe.
God gave me a most precious gift.
I found that part of my soul.
I'll forever hold.
Thank you for your grace and mercy
Upon me, one of the least of those.

Monica Raymo Ladet

The Picture

In my mind I carry a picture, a picture
of the one who opened my eyes.
For so long I had seen the world go
by, with not a twinge of fear of
what tomorrow might bring.
This person so full of kindness, peace
patience, and love,
This person who opened my eyes.
Now when the wind blows harsh I see the
shivering children huddled together for warmth.
At every passing second, I count, the
many who have died. The ones close to
them as they weep, and the one who died
alone with no one to care.
This person who opened my eyes opened
them to a world full of hurt and need.
This person who opened my eyes has
taught me to love and to care.
This person who opened my eyes will
forever be remembered and loved.

Mariel Kessenich

Between Worlds

I walk this path alone in the shadows
Of those before me with secret
And wanton intentions of lusting
Perversity for unconventional rapture,

Seeking the ease and detachment
Of insolent moments as nasty walls crumble
With each ferocious stroke penetrating
Into Anxious joy rendering frenzied pleasure,

Knowing each release ensues persecution
Of rebuke intensified as gratification grows
With heightened ecstasy of iniquitous hunger
Appeased purely by vague allusive encounters,

Leaving the baseless reality of the affair
To linger in the bends of intelligence
And dance with erratic consciousness
Of wanting and sole innocence.

Leon Sheffield

Anna's Grief

"Where are you going, my son?" she cried.
"Off to the war, dear mother."
He shouldered the bag that hung at his side
and left to follow his brother.

One lone tear caressed her cheek.
She didn't have time for despair.
Two sons, now gone, left her heart weak
but seven yet needed her care.

One little boy, and six loving sisters
wrote to the two each day.
Mother was busy, her hands worn with blisters,
shucking corn while the little ones played.

Two daughter's lovers now left for the war;
feigning hope for a future with cheer.
Two brothers, two lovers, a knock at the door.
Three women tremble with fear.

The paper now yellowed and brittle with age
still shouts vulgar news in her ears.
"We regret to inform you, your son died in battle."
the first day of his twenty-first year.

Rebecca Lucas

Spring

Oh great spring,
Oh how the flowers sing,
Oh how the wind sings a glorious song,
This season has nothing wrong.

Winter does not stay for long,
Snow melts into puddles that dry,
And oh how the clouds cry.

Mother nature is the creator,
And winter is saved for later.

Daffodils straighten their frills,
Roses practice their poses,
Violets wear their purple silk,
In the breezes they flow, as smooth as milk.

The sun is made of gold they say,
Now that winter's gone away,
Happy children laugh and play.

Say hear that sweet sound?
that's the bees buzzing around.

Look, see the color green,
That's the grass; my, is it clean.
Whitney A. Haskell

The Roses Of Life

Roses oh roses how beautiful they be.
Oh how you mimic life so exquisitely.
Your light segments the good, the dark, the bad.
Your wilted petals the death and grief we all have.
Your seeds the birth, living and hope.
Your thorns are the pain and hardships with which we must cope.
Your scent is the passion and love we all seek.
While your stem is the road that leads to life's peak.
So if you ask me, the meaning of life is in a rose.
Just look at the splendor in which it grows.
Shaun M. Kirby

Perfect To Me

Ten chubby fingers, ten fat stubby toes
Oh so precious my sweet Jennifer Rose.
Eyes that can't see, yet blue as the sea.
Ears that can't hear, yet a smile that's so dear.
Put her away for she's damaged they say.
But Jenny Pooh, Jenny Pooh
Why can't they see?
For oh but you are
So perfect to me...
Teresa Shuler

Or Say Goodbye

Give me
  No one else's warmed-over love
Show me
  No old wounds, no half-dreamed look of the past
No rain checks
  I've been there too
Close old chapters in the well-loved book of your life
  Gently
I've closed mine
Now take my hand, let's go down new roads
  To new shared laughter and dreams
  Maybe even a new shared love, who knows
  A new shared caring, belonging only to you and me
Let the old hurt blow away like leaves in the wind
And come with me
  Or say goodbye
Margaret McMurray

Old Chapel

  Old chapel was grey and eerie,
Old chapel dank depression hanging over it like a pall,
  Headstones like crooked teeth
  Everything about old chapel smelt of death and decay,
Mortuary chapel, old and crumbling,
Hunched upon far edge of the churchyard.
SOLITUDE!
Old chapel was a scary place.
The chapel looked like a sinister hulk,
Crouched down waiting for its prey,
Decaying stonewalls and slabs dripping with water,
Green with slimy moss

  The old man crouched near the headstones,
He was skinny, -looked cadaverous.

It was after midnight,
Fog and drizzle everywhere and the memories.
Katherine M. Lute

Tempoblu

Bills, bills, bills
Old ones, new ones, past ones, due ones
How am I going to pay these bills
I can't throw them away, nor can I pay them today

But, if I keep a job, It'll probably be hard
They'll go away, somehow, someday
Bills, bills, bills

When I think I'm caught up and I'm still behind
I always say "It isn't my day"
It doesn't look like their going away
It looks like their here to stay
Bills, bill, bills

I can overlook a bill or two
But I'll still have to deal with that same old bill
Bills, bills, bills

I'll pay the bill and hope it's not too late
Before the rent man, changes the lock to my gate
Now as far as, the food is concerned
The cost of living will surely burn
A bill is a bill, is a bill, bills, bills, bills
Yvette Sutton

The Search

The waves like an army strike fiercely the shore
On a day in which light has begun to take flight.
The clouds gather in conference only a little ways up
To look menacingly down upon my stray pup.
The wind nips at my ears, the chill creeps into my clothes
He must be found is all that I know.
But where to look? If I only knew that.
Thus I question myself as I head down my path.
So I dash down the beach until I hear a small peep.
As I stoop to look down, I see near my feet
My little brown pup all cozy asleep.
Mark D. Johnston

A Season Of Change

Time has come for things to change.
Nothing ever remains the same.
The leaves and grass are green once more.
The sun is shining bright on my door.
The birds are singing stronger than ever before.
The air is fresh with the smell of flowers and morning dew.
The wind is making a breeze blow through.
This is another season of change making everything seem to change.
Katrina Bailey

World Game

I feel the world is a game.
On good days you move up two,
On bad days you move down three.
On sad days, you lose a turn,
This all has happened to me.
 I also feel that Giants are the players,
Who are playing this world game,
And with every Giant there is a human,
A "gamepiece" to them is our name.
 Now, when it rains, it's because
A Giant has lost in playing,
And when a Giant loses the Game,
"A human shall die" is their old saying.
 And when it's all sunny, no time for a mourn
A new player has come,
And a child is born.
 So just be wishful,
On how good your Giant will play,
Because they're in control,
Each and every day.

 Kristen Moy

The Pine Tree

Majestic stands the Pine Tree
On mountain, valley, and hill
Adorned with pine cones and needles
An emerald standing so still.

The sky punctuated by starlight
Shines down to earth to see
The quiet and tranquil Pine Tree
That grows there for you and me.

The Pine that stands in the woodland
With its blanket of needles below
So cherished by one who once played there
In sunlight, and shadow, and snow.

It colors the landscape in Winter
Which lingers so cold, dark, and grey
It brightens the hillside in Summer
While the sun warms its boughs with her rays.

Of all the trees at Christmas
We decorate with fun and mirth
The loveliest in the Pine Tree
As we celebrate the Virgin Birth.

 Lillie Gartman Combs

"Springtime In The Alleghenies"

When it's springtime in the Alleghenies
On the lilac scented breeze I hear a trill
'Tis the deep throated song of the warbler
Or the call of a lonely whippoorwill

Purple shadows gather in the valley
It is now almost twilight on the hill
Soothing breezes whisper through the tree tops
And stir the curtains on my window sill

The purple shadows deepen into darkness
The whippoorwill calls his mate no more
All is peaceful and quiet on the mountain
While the moonbeams dance around my cottage door

I wake to the song of birds in the morning
And it gives my heart a thrill
To see the countryside painted by nature
From my cottage on top of the hill

 B. Celia Conway

Winter

The snowflakes are flying, though the winds are all still
On the backyard now lying, and far away on the hill
The plastic fountain horse freezes like a rock.

The bushes are parched with snow whites on top
And the rose tree wrecked, bent, dried up
Under the pine tree, a hungry squirrel digs
Where the falling pines' nuts are buried.

Suddenly, a frozen water drops
Scares away the squirrel and breaks the silence
Children from the neighbor are having a snow fight
The snow melts in their gloves.

Across the street, a Chinese delivery boy knocks on the door
One hand in his pocket, giggles, slips on the floor
He stands up right away with a cute smile
To receive his tips and murmur like a child.

Unaware of my own existence, the sun goes down to the west
Until the light begins to grow in the house
Then I turn to see the snow is falling wilder
The foot steps on the sidewalk have been covered
Silence begins, the night is swallowed by darkness, I close my door.

 Thieu H. Giang

"Blue"

While the sun shines you earn your pay, depending
on the day, I'm either with you or in bed.

If I could carry a case, instead of solving them
that would be a change of pace.

You fight with your dog to go on a walk, my dog
walks stalks, but never balks when needed,

I take on more roles than an actor, but I'm
never given an award for my achievements

My role plays are never rehearsed and no two
are ever the same, so I only have one chance
to do it right.

I'm loved so much, but hated by many
they always call me, no matter what time, day or night.

My company car has more decorations and
toys than a Christmas tree; the funny thing about
my office is people always get out of my
way and must learn how to drive safely

While most people will run for cover, I run to cover when danger
ensues; I must pursue where the danger is, for
who could I call?

 Lawrence Lombardo

"The Tree"

In 1932 I planted a tree,
On the farm to admire and see.

As a sapling in years, it grew,
Giving shelter from rain and sun for you.

In summer, we had picnics, with plenty of shade,
Plenty of fried chicken and cold lemonade.

As kids, climbing it, for us was fun,
Hide and seek, behind it, we had to run.

Sometimes robins would build a nest,
High up on top, a crow would rest.

I'm 75, and I can still remember,
The wind through the branches in December.

Again I'll plant a sapling in memory too,
For a tree I planted in 1932.

 Paul Skinner

Where Has The Summer Gone

In the field a lamb is born and there're green buds
  on the trees
New life sees winter's end and the coming of
  the bees
The fragrance of the flowers, drifting through
  the air
Brings the elusive little humming bird
  searching everywhere

Spring fades into summer and the garden grows
  like mad
A baby bird falls from the nest, sometimes
  life is sad
Then it's harvest time, the leaves are red, the
  lamb has grown tall
I see the pumpkins in the field, soon it will be fall

As evening shadows wane and the sun sets in the west
A yellow moon is rising, over the mountain crest
I feel frost in the air, winter will be along
Now the leaves are falling from the trees,
where has the summer gone
  Melvin G. Cornwell

Rare And Special

The night appears as the sun goes down
on this beautiful night in a small town.

The waves of the ocean brush up on the sand
as people walk on the beach hand in hand.

The clouds are dark blue like a beautiful pair of eyes
as they make up the prettiest of skies.

The cool, brisk breeze just blows in my hair
looking at the sky on a night so rare.

The water cools my feet as I stroll along on the beach
glancing far into the ocean shows the horizon is out of reach.

Wherever you gaze there is a gorgeous sight
with every view looking like a romantic, picturesque night.

The flock of birds just fly, fly away
waiting for the sun to arrive the next day.

The people take a last look as the night comes to an end
admiring the skies with all their friends.
  Sanjay Tolani

Jesus And The Teacher

Oh teacher of children, I call you home,
On this your final day.
The lessons learned, the knowledge gained,
And now we must make our way.

I come to you as colleague,
Your place I understand.
For they also call me Teacher,
In almost every land.

You took the diamond in the rough,
To cleave and clean and hone.
With toiled labor you worked to carve,
A prize of beauty, from the stone.

Welcome to the place that I've prepared,
Each will have their turn.
Where you're judged not by what you have,
But by what you have learned.

My Father sent to grant to you,
A degree of reward in kind.
For there's a higher form of Heaven to one,
Who's opened a child's mind.
  L. J. Heuser

War

Green light splutters and they are off! Soaring
On track with great stakes of fire: better watch!
The great churn of non-fat cream is felt pouring
Into the air. But be not where they splotch.

Boom! They crashed with such monumental force
Creating fires to cook Bull's Eye Burgers.
Terrible winds and toadstools form a course
That fall into place like scheduled murders.

It is quiet now, not even a sound.
Not even a house. Children had endless
Dreams of sugar plums dancing in their crown.
With this year, with grief, St. Nick felt "Sendless."

Green light splutters and they're off! Spring
On track with great sticks of fire; the same thing.
  Kenneth E. Young

A True Son Of The Sand Hills

The sun sets low on the snowy street
One empty saddle makes one last trek—
The day is gone, the river was deep,
My friend rests now in peaceful sleep.

Many a storm his horse saw him through
Many a breeze caressed his brow. Too—
Many a cow was brought to a halt
With his swift rope it was held taut.

Later—the children, (grown-ups, not a few!)
Came to listen to the wisdom this man knew
Of the Sand hills' history from old to new
'twas here a true son of the prairie grew.

A legacy to hold true to—a story, I confess,
This cowboy molded his family into the best
His friends stretched from east to west
Dear memories remain as we ride to the crest.
  C. Sylvia R. Miles

"Mom"

My Mother was such a dear.
One in a million to me, You hear!
When defending her kids, there was no fear.
Yes, Mother, was truly a dear.

A beautiful woman - inside and out.
She would scold me sometimes and I would go pout.
Then when I saw her, my eyes would light up and I'd shout.
Mom loved all us kids - there was no doubt.

Sacrificing so much in her life;
Mom worked hard despite all the strife.
Cooking and cleaning, working 'till late at night;
No time for much rest, her schedule was tight.

Yet, Mom lost a leg - her health was bad;
She didn't give up, she took care of Dad.
Then Dad passed away and Mom was so sad.
We gathered around her, making her mad.

Mad - 'cause she had no time to grieve;
We were always around - Mom wished we'd leave.
Ah - Mom knew we loved her in spite of it all.
Oh me, now my Mom is gone, yes she got her call!
  Peggy Bone

King Of Animals Or Was It Man?

He stalked, he ran, he bellowed out
One mighty roar: Let me out!
I will not beg! I will not plead.
To be set free, that's all I need.

I'm tired of being in this cage
Yet they wonder why I'm so enraged?
"Look!" Take a good look at me!
You're free. As I once use to be.

Day in. Day out. What is it all about?
Why have they trapped me in this way.
They came, destroyed what they could not take
What could we do, but lie n' wait.

And then they left. No backwards look. No glance of sorrow.
None of pain. And they were back. Again! Again!
They took, and took. And took again!
No sign of compassion. No, not one look.

Oh God release me from this pain.
For I know they go back once again
They'll bring them back, Oh you will see
To be locked in cages. Just like me!

Martina L. Green

Two Rivers

Two rivers flow through saffron fields
One river is clear, the other cloudy

The rivers never cross
Yet two drops of water are one

In the low field walks a bent man
Poor wet clothes cling to his tired frame
As his scythe cuts another handful of singing grain
His heart is smiling

The scythe is change
Yet its blade is rusted and worn
He sits, and dips the crescent tool in the clear water
The chaff makes the water unclear

The angry man calls to the poor man,
"Why are you sitting? There is much to do!"
"Because I am tired," says the man
And now his face is smiling an ancient smile

Only the poor man knows
That the grain is singing
And the rivers are flowing
Like minutes in the field.

Gabriel Meister

No Nothing

There used to be no sunshine.
No spring.
No flowers.
No puffy white clouds.
No warm summer days.

There were no laughing children.
No barking dogs.
No purring kittens.
No chirping crickets on a warm summer evening.

There used to be a man with no soul.
No light in his eyes.
No spring in his step.
No smile on his lips.
No songs in his heart.
No reason to his life...

UNTIL YOU.

Randy Holmes

The Hand Dealt

There is a promise to those who believe
One won't be given more than one can bear to receive

But when the hand is dealt, it's not always clear,
Will adjusting take a day, a month, a year?

When death came suddenly to this young man's dad
It, of course, was extremely sad
For he had lost the best friend he ever had

So upon this teen's door the shadow's been cast
And he finds no comfort in memories of the past

Two years have passed and the terror's buried deep
It's there in the darkness, in daylight, in his sleep

He's been removed from society, put in a special place
Where they try to break into the mind and see behind the face

He's extremely strong and at the same time weak
Cautious and guarded with the words he does speak

So the battle continues, the war isn't won
And he wonders when the end will come
As the burden continues-never seeming to be done.

As he plays out his hand

Shirley A. Moen

Should We Honor The Veteran?

The Soldier was forced to fight for his country,
Only eighteen years of age.
He was drafted to serve in a war he heard about,
For the minimum wage.
The soldier realized that he had no choice -
His country did not hear the cries of his voice.
It still spoke out for democracy.
He fought in the war with the odds very dim,
And this war cost him all of his limbs.
We call his reason stupidity.
The Soldier's American Dream was robbed
Because he had no means to get a job.
He died suffering from the helpless life he had.
His tombstone read THE VETERAN,
What else could he add?

Miquiel Banks

Sparky's Journey

We know not where you came from, nor the places that you've been,
Only that you're here to stay, your journey's at its end.

You've been with him for many years, grown old and torn and thin,
The boy's the one who shed the tears as needles pierced your skin.

You lay and wait with patient ears for his footsteps to come your way,
The boy, he comes, he never fails, his love for you portrayed.

As evening sends its shadows and stars give darkness light,
You lay snuggled in his arms throughout his dream filled night.

You are the keeper of his secrets, you listen as he prays,
But as spring turns into summer, a childhood comes and fades.

You are the treasure and the prince of all that he keeps dear,
And as the boy journeys through life, his love will stay sincere.

You watched him master weakness, conquer many foes,
You know too well his heartbeat, the path his feet will sow.

Knowing soon a time will come that when I look your way,
I'll remember a pastime moment of a boy that couldn't stay.

I know not where he's going, nor the places that he's been,
Only that he will leave here and I will need a friend.

Katherine Ryder

The Silent Symphony

Fast as a fly, in the blink of an eye
Or as dark as a storm on the sea

The wondrous, speechless, noteless,
Serene...

The Silent Symphony!

The wand of the wizard is faster than light
And illusion is faster than thought...
And rhapsody, rapturous bliss and delight
Are all wonders that cannot be taught...

And silence..
Cannot
Be
Caught!

The wondrous, speechless, noteless, serene
The Silent Symphony
The Silent.......
Symph.....ony!

Steffi Engel

To My Pupils Of The Past

Was it a vision, or maybe a dream,
Or did I really behold, each one of you standing before me
And asking of me!
"Which one of us did you love best?
Which one of us would you choose from all the rest?
I answered, "You all were mine.
I love you all in different ways and for different
    reasons."
But still you each insisted, "there must have been One!
And each one of you looked at me with pleading expectancy,
And so, I walked among the waiting throng and touched each
    one of you with loving hands, "It was You."
Not one of you was aware that I had touch you all,
Then, each one turned away, as if to say, "I was the
    Chosen One."

Katherine Dougherty

I'll Love You When

When we're sitting alone holding each other's hand,
Or just walking on the beach with our feet in the sand,
When we wake up in the morning, and I see your face,
And when we finally settle down in our own special place,
When we walk down that aisle and you're mine forever,
And we finally get to start our new life together,
When the baby is born and we hold a precious new life,
And at night when I thank the Lord that you're my wife,
When the kids have grown up and we both turn gray,
Finally it comes down to loving you forever and a day.

Tracy L. Miller

Too Shallow Or Too Deep?

Weighted words that sink to the bottom
of a four hundred pound conversation
wearily written in seams that go numb
from far too much cold alteration.

Spent syllables that slash through the waves
with a lingering hope some might float
and extend a hooking sound that saves
some significant thought someone once wrote.

Pierced parts that long for the surface
by a stitch stretched water tight
in a bobbin of letters stuffed with superfluous
and pulled beneath, out of sight.

H. Graetz

Baby Michael

We never got to hear your cry
Or see that twinkle in your eye.

We were given the gift and got to hold you.
This gave us a chance to get to know you.

Your little finger, your tiny feet,
Your precious lips, your chubby cheeks.

Michael Charles, yes that's your name,
But memories of you are all that remain.

We watched you, Michael, as you sleep,
And know in our hearts with God you're at peace.

For in God's arms is where you are,
So He can protect you from any harm.

That tear you see on the side of our face.
Is us thinking of you in that special place.

It's time now, Michael, to brush our tears away,
But in our hearts you'll always stay.

For baby Michael we shall not cry,
You are the twinkle in our eyes.

Kim E. Caisse

Our Book

Now you are gone.
Our book is closed.
Its pages filled with memories are solemnly pressed
    together.
Profound conversation lies dormant between its covers.
Witty, heartwarming expressions rest therein.
And smiles! Wonderful, unforgettable smiles!
Eyes meeting, tenderly expressing emotions that were never meant
    to be fulfilled, are recorded.
Sharing, caring, understanding, just being together,
    dominates its contents.
So much, yet so little.
So close, yet two worlds apart.
All so bittersweet.

Today the final chapter was written.
When read, tears fell.
The heart was shattered.
Our story ended.
Now you are gone and our book is closed.
Forever.

Leona C. Lilley

Lady Cleopatra

Lady Cleopatra's memories are loud and clear,
Our hearts hold loving memories of her dear.
She was fun, loving and protective -
to find her when she is lost
would sometimes take a detective.

She loved to ride in the car
She would take off and we would have to search afar
We would drive down the street with the door open
She would see us and come loping.

Her table manners were not very good,
Gobble her food she always would.
Then look at you and burp,
So loudly your stomach would jerk.

She would lay her head in your lap,
and settle down for an afternoon nap.
Our very first Saint Bernard -
Loving her was not very hard.

She is gone now to heaven above-
But not forgotten - we miss her love

Minnie L. Besendorf

Untitled

Oh! If summer could last forever...
Our kisses as a warm, gentle wind as it
makes the crickets sing and the tree
dance in its bend.
Ascending like a firefly who's adorned
like a dove.... brought in remembrance
with each summer's night-collected from
the twinkling stars above.
For always and everlasting a heart's True Love...

Mary Good

My Life Is A Ballad

That cold winter weekend in that little log cabin
Our only shelter from the blustering storm
And the blaze in the fireplace and those
    scratchy wool blankets
How we cuddled together to try to keep warm.

And that warm summer evening, the heavens were
    glowing
Casting reflections on the rippling bay.
The view was breath-taking and provided a
    setting
For a whispered, "I Love You," which was all I
    could say.

These memories are treasures I like to revive.
So I've put them to music to keep them alive.
For my life is a ballad; a beautiful love song,
Tender and gentle - unaltered by time.
I live the sweet melody
Because you are a part of me.
Your love and devotion have perfected the
    rhyme.

Lois M. Bloomer

A World Away

Racism, the war within our homeland; the death within
our streets.

....and we are civilized.
Take the young ones, and teach them hate; like the
forefathers before you.

Prejudice embedded in the walls of time.
It's tainted our lives, our religion....

A remnant of our past.
An obstacle of the present.
Hiroshima of our future.

Taste my color, my heritage; with European flavor.
Taste my war.

Salvatore J. Morgera

The Sun Shines On Everyone

Have you ever thanked the sun for shining down
On all of us little people way down here on the ground?
The sun doesn't care what we look like or what we wear
'Cause the sun shines on everyone; it doesn't care.

So go ahead and thank the sun, 'cause it makes things grow
And gives us light and warmth and did you know?
We don't even have to ask the sun to shine; no we don't
Don't even have to pay, not even a dime.

And all the kids around the world are just like you and me
They need the sun to help them grow and keep them company.
So go outside and skip and jump and dance with the wind
And feel the earth beneath your feet 'cause the sun is shinin'.

Patty Clark

Our Candle Of Light

We cry softly while the darkness engulfs us with the power to hide
our tears. Then comes the dawn and the sunrise brings our pain to
the fore.

We are those who are left behind to lift our voices in unison;
praying for God's justice. For it is proven that man's justice
does not lift our hearts from the abysmal well of the forgotten.

Our pain is all consuming when we would try to walk alone; and so
it is, we are bound together by common bond.

We are the mothers, fathers, children, grandparents, brothers, sisters
and friends whose lives have suffered an intrusion within our hearts
that we cannot understand.

We will speak out until our pleas are heard; and answered. We accept
the passing of the torch with which we light our candles in memory of
our beloveds; not for your pity, but for your enlightenment.

We will not curse the darkness. We will be guided by the light of
the flame as we pray for strength, guidance and wisdom while it is yet
light. Then, we shall rest when darkness comes again.

Lillian S. Hammack

Untitled

Love in life comes in many forms. From a seed to a tree we branch
out and around, seeing the light all around,
but not before a small struggle within.
From small tears to the future's promise,
I have known many phases of love,
only to pull my inner self to be exposed
when my oneness with you had come.
Cloudy and shallow much of it seems now
That strength and purity have inspired me
to create a bond and build a home which powerful men shall envy
because we are wise and our house will be built upon a rock
Not a rock of closed hard walls, but of wind-shaped character.
I shall love you when that rock is
beneath the next such house, and we are dust.
The winds cannot blow us over or apart, but only shape us as we
hold hands. Though perhaps not facing each other,
we will be connected - chained at the souls.
Beyond infatuation and childlike love we have bonded.
I begin my journey thinking I have never loved more,
but knowing I will love and love
and love you each year more than before.

Sheila H. Childs

Rainy Days

A young boy quietly ponders, staring
    out his window pane
For he knows he'd be outside, if it
    weren't for the rain
Anxious to do something, he rushes to
    his brother's room
And asks him if he'd play a game, do
    a puzzle, or watch cartoons
His brother looks into his eyes, and
    can see he's really bored
He lays his things aside and carefully
    stacks the checker board
They play, they laugh, they trade
    cards, they have loads of fun
They haven't noticed the rain has stopped
    and through the window glares the sun
It's a very special feeling to watch
    brothers bond this way
For it must be the reason, GOD made
    those rainy days

Richard S. Luckenbill

The Yellow Rose

A drop of pain, of memories, things aren't what they used to be.
Out of love, out of sight, the results of our last fight.
Used and worn, my heart's been torn. Gone forever, at least for now,
you've broken my heart, take a bow. The side show's over, the clowns
have gone, the moon is setting, ready for dawn. Water rests so calm
and slow, the winter's over, melting snow. The warmth and comfort of
your arms protecting me from all that harms. Gone forever is the
love, and all it needed was a shove. Hugs and kisses, X's and O's,
scribbled down and nobody knows. Crumpled paper, matches burned,
thinking how our love has turned. I cry another tear for you, you
meant so much, and now we're through. Trapped inside a cloud of dust,
and all because of love or lust. A yellow rose to represent our
friendship and the time we've spent. As the slow painful hours go by,
I think of you and once more cry. The final petal of the rose,
has gone forever, and it shows.

Melissa Cousineau

The Inheritors

We! Are the inheritors of our past,
    Out of whole cloth;
We harbinger our world,
    On to the backs of others,
Thus, the die has been cast.

    Must we always be such prisoners,
Must it be that we be such pensioners?
    Can we not be harbingers to our present?
If that is to ever last!

    By will of mind,
Shall we not be bound?
    What is our fate?
Are we not of one kind?!

    Is our destiny to be cast;
By patterns of actions,
    That have come to us from our past?

Or, is our present
    To be forfeited to forces
Or wills and minds
    That are not ours by assent!

Neil Richards

What Color Is Happiness

On the mantel the clock chimed out the time of day,
Out the window a yellow streak appeared—vanished.
Purple panic tugged at my mind as I stepped outside.
Where the yellow school bus should have been, a police car!

A black and white police car instead of a yellow school bus?
Two very tall police officers in blue uniforms
Instead of a little boy in a green sweat suit?
Red fear closed in on my thoughts, then black nothingness!

The sounds were a mixture of confusing voices,
"Is she alright?" "What happened?" The voices invaded the fog.
But then out of the pea-green fog, a familiar voice,
"It's okay mommie, I missed the school bus, but
These nice officers brought me home!"

What color is happiness? All the colors of the rainbow!

LeNora G. Finley

Virginia

Soft rich soil beneath my feet,
Pale blue skies cover my head with heavenly beauty
Soft breeze caresses my face like gentle wings of an Angel
Cold wet peaceful white snow quiets my soul
Strong green trees fill my heart with wonder love
Beautiful Virginia, my heart, my home.

Lois Miller

Independence

Mother nature's constant present arrives.
Over and over, just as the sun rises.
That which it sucked through its once-hungry veins,
Now has become a heavy burden.
Although spring has brought its blossoming, the flower,
Continues to need her nourishment.
It is her morning dew which feeds the tree,
And meanwhile stunts its growth until,
The white flower falls to the soil,
Where it either withers away
Or plunges its roots into her and produces,
Its own tree of flowers' scent,
Awaiting her honeysuckle present...

Kenneth D. Pratt

Aftermath Of The Storm

The rainbow arks across the east valley
over to the mountains
    dropping west to the mesa,
turning the sky to a kaleidoscope of colors,
makes the ominous clouds black,
    the clouds change shapes,
    the lightning cracks
    aftermath of the storm.

The sun shines once again to the west
glowing over the city and valley
    shining bright yellow,
reflecting sun rays over to the tail of the storm,
changing the colored sky brilliantly in vivid details,
    the passing storm now to the east,
    the bright sun offering peace and tranquility westward
    the rainbows brilliant hues reflect between
rainbows end.

Sunny L. Ryan and Teri J. Ryan

All Not Lost

Death unknown, be weary, too all, no more painting
painted, colorless palette on ubiquitous void,
of enigmatic space, oblique, unessential too
the ballad, song, sung out of key, unenunciated *AUM*,
two stepping tango out of step, no rhythm vibrancy
choreographed in dance, on film, reel spins round
cut lights, edit camera, action chop , stop
punctuation, splice comma, grammatical error
novel that it be, illiterate poetics, free, strumming
pick a prophetic chord, an instrument
without tune, tuned piano reason, string plucking
finger, nails, ripping, the quintessential
thing, **destroyed in political fire bomb**, tearing
a flood, drowning...dro——owning puppet, be proud
black and white photo, emersed, endlessly foreboding
master, oils of color, last breath, an operatic note,
struggling ballet crescendos, a water muse on film
based on a novel, poetic lyrics, flute concerto, all lost
forgotten, all is art, I have created worlds, not defined,
elite in being, suffered oneness of mind, universe..God

Richard R. Sperry

Snow Scene

The scene I viewed from my window was lovely to the eye
Pure white snow covered the trees and ground
Smoke billowed from the chimneys, curling up to the sky.
The faint light from the winter moon
Made the earth bright, almost as light as noon.
Small stars dotted the winter sky
So close to earth, and yet so high.
Such beauty can only be a gift of love,
The treasures of heaven - God's gift from above.

Ruth Gingerich

Between Chaos and Commotion

Our struggles through life transported us here
Past memories in time, some foggy some clear
Love and belonging is what we once wanted
Through sins of our own our minds became taunted
Childhood friends so fun and so dear
Unlike today filled with hatred and fear
What happened on our journey from there to here?
The answers are unsettling and seldom ever clear
We dropped into life so innocent so sweet
The crime of survival shackled us into defeat
First chained to our parents bounded by love
Then owned by society who squeezes for blood
Maybe there'll be a happier day
Hopefully the sun will warm through the grey
Until this time we will vigorously try
Unfortunately others will give up and die
    Patty McCarthy

The Broken Doll

In a small tennessee town the Radio was the biggest thing
people sat around waiting to hear the grand ole opry stars sing
I was on my bicycle late one day and a CAR struck my bike
when I woke up in the hospital the doc was saying she alright
mom and dad was on their knees cause I had taken a fall
now I know what mom meant she said it's a broken doll

I always wanted to act and sing like dottie west.
I told God that I would always give it my best.
so now I sit in this chair 'cause I'm not able to walk.
I can see the pity in people's eyes even when they don't talk
my heart will always smile as dottie sings cause I love her best of all.
dear God will you still love me now that I'm a broken doll.

When you love a country legend, they're your inspiration for life
As I say my pray's only God knows what is right
Each time I hear my country Idol sing her songs
I felt something in my legs as she came to me and said baby hang on
if you have faith in what you love they'll always be help
from the man above
so she stood up so proud and tall and said look mama
No more broken doll.
    Wilma Lawrence

Untitled

"Oh, heavenly God spare me this grief!"
Plague strikes the brain
warping thoughts and behavior.

Begging on weakened knees,
bargaining with lies for
Him to take this hallow life.

Sacrifice the soul by
offering it in exchange
of a new born child's.

Life that He has blessed
is soaked with torture from Hell
to suffer was a choice - mistake or not.

Unable to take the power of God
by sparing this existence
wanting, but the heart speaks louder than Satan.

Turning to greedy prayers
which God has chosen to ignore
leaving THE time yet to come.

Patiently continue waiting
for a single prayer to be answered.
    Nadine Patterson

"Confused About Love"

Only one thought crosses my mind.
Please just give me a sign.
Will you ever know,
The love that I could show?

As a single tear drops,
My heart slowly stops.
I longed for you to share,
Obviously you didn't care.

As our hearts grow near,
I can almost hear,
This little voice inside,
Telling me I have nothing to hide.
Letting me know that I could have a part,
In making you happy and warming your heart.
    Kari A. Carter

"Her Name"

Warm features, hugged long, primed, dark locks
Poised bedside along me.
Ribbon and lace, soft cotton payed flatter
struggle bound 'cross for filling breasts.

Deeply caring, past intimate feelings
Stay longer my dear
With me
Share moment of emotional hour.

Be this night's final tale of passion?
Twilight lingers, be moved soft cotton
And lace, close fantasy forgiven
Crave I, your loving touch.
    Michael F. Quinlan

Portholes

Portholes of Hope,
Portholes of Despair,
Portholes of Freedom,
Portholes of Joy
And Portholes of Sorrow;

All can be interchangeable depending on a person's state of mind.
To one person they can mean everything,
to another they can mean nothing.
To someone driven by emotion they are the nourishment that embodies
them and are opened frequently.
To someone self-driven, not open to emotion, for fear of pain,
the portholes are sealed shut.
A foolish way to live.
Pain from emotion is the best and very worst pain in existence.
It is when these portholes are left unlocked, free for manipulation,
that we are at our best and love is able to fill our soul.
    Lisa Montecalvo

Hunting

"Pull the trigger boy!"
Pap yelled in his Son's ear.
Son once thought of Pap's gun as a toy...
But, the thoughts change with death so near.
The bullet whistled through the air
Striking the evil creature between the eyes.
The creature wished in death it did not dare
His boy to pull the trigger in an angered rise.
Son drops pap's gun
And scurries out the back door.
Time for him to play; have fun.
Return to the white picket-fenced home? (no more!)
Pap's in an eternal sleep on the kitchen floor.
He won't push the boy anymore.
They won't push the boy anymore.
    Michelle Turner

Pout, Pout

Pout, pout, won't stop.
Pout, pout, you want your way,
  more and more pouting, I just can't say.
Pout, pout more than I ever did.
Now, go to the bathroom, wash your face,
  and come out a man.
Yeah! I'm in the bathroom washing my face,
  but more and more pouting, I just can't say.
I'm pouting and pouting still more and more every day,
  I just can't say.
I kept on pouting until I became ill,
  then I knew I had to chill.
Now, I says to myself,
  it is time to chill.
    Waylon M. Braxton

Special Friendship

As my happy heart wonders over years gone by
Precious memories of a friend bring tears to my eyes
We were young and hurting with growing pains of youth
Sometimes the road was rocky as we searched for truth
When my heart was broken with trials that came my way
You were my source of comfort, always knowing what to say
Many times there would be laughter mingling with tears
Your caring warmed my heart and lessened my fears
Through good times and bad times you stood by my side
A tried and true friend in whom I could confide
We drifted down separate pathways to fulfill life's destinies
I visit you often in my special pool of beautiful memories
Life is swiftly passing by and the pace is very great
There's no promise of tomorrow, I must tell you before it's too late
Your friendship was mine for the asking, couldn't be bought or sold
You never charged me a dime and was worth far more than gold
Moments of your time was priceless, all too soon it came to an end
Your friendship is one of my life's greatest treasures, my dear true
friend.
    Pat Hyde

Endurance

Living here in this hell with continual trenchant atmospheres in the
  presence of frigid inept people who pursue to deject and torment you
once independent but now vulnerable bestows them the edge
  holding you back so subtly no-one outside could tell
malicious voices pervade your spirit with suffocating despair
  crippling you mentally so utterly being chastised then thwarted
by degenerate remorseless idiosyncratic hypocrites thereby seeking
  the sanctuary of your mind where sacred thoughts and creativity
are confined to the guarded dark recess of your imagination
  within the fortress of pain and suffering
escaping to recover control and liberty will destroy and subdue
  their state of being now they will suffer pain.
    Karen P. Williams

Silver Love

Does he notice my chest begin to tighten
Or that my knees have become like jello?
Does he know my world can instantly brighten
With his simple word of "Hello"?

Can she see my hands as they start to shake
Or how my gait at times unsteady?
Can she hear the butterflies within awake
Or sense my emotions become so thready?

It must be love, nothing else could explain
The tenderness that can bring you to tears.
The feelings so deep that it verges on pain
of a man and woman married fifty years.
    Sandra H. Dunn

Untitled

The purple sky above tells of a coming reunion.
Presently, he alone waits, silent, half-naked,
limp.
What little leaves there are remain motionless,
forgetting what it feels like to dance.

Oh, blessed tree, don't lose faith!
For I alone know she is at this moment
preparing her journey to once again
meet with you.
She has not forgotten how it feels to
blow through your boughs,
to penetrate you.

Hurry gentle wind; I secretly await
your late night rendezvous.
    Kelly A. Perak

Christmas

Christmas, the giving time of year and
Presents under the tree.
December is vacation time for some people
People going to malls
Presents being wrapped
Christmas cards being sent
Games being bought
Letters sent to Santa
Candy being bought
Kids love Christmas!
December is the rushing month
December 24th is Christmas Eve.
    Paul J. Goodfellow

My Heritage

With dignity, I stand,
Product of the caribbean land
With pride I raise my hand
To proclaim my heritage.

Born of a gifted musician I called dad.
And a skillful hand maiden I called mom.
A couple I will never exchange as parents.
I declare my heritage.

Cambridge and Alexander
Names that played a part
In education and history
I acknowledge my heritage.

Scottish, African and Indian,
All interwoven in one
Proud to call various nations my brethren.
Joined with me and stand up.
While I demand my heritage.
    S. Cox

Love Needs

Love needs a lot of special care;
Not only from one but as a pair;
Half the care you give one another;
Still leaves the other half to be uncovered;
Join them together they become a whole;
With the strength they will gain it will surely grow;
As it grows from day to day;
Always let it hear what you have to say;
Never let a droop or even a sag appear;
Always let it know all of its fears;
As the years go passing by;
Remember, the love that was grew and aged like wine;
It stood those years with the test of time.
    Mary Jane Sullivan

Newborn

I cradle you in my arms,
protecting you from all harm.
Sing sweet love songs to you,
your effect on me is something new.
Your skin is so soft your mind is so pure.
For what has been ailing me you are the cure.

Absorbing all I have to give,
and baby that's a lot.
Sometimes I wish you were mine,
to have, and to have not.
I bring you close, close to my chest,
let me enjoy, because,
I have never ridden such a crest.

As I rock a lullaby to your ears
I can't help but wonder
about the coming years.
The happiness, the pain, the sorrow,
that you must go through.
The little things,
that are gonna make you, you.

Nat Oliveri

Natural Rocks

Passing by a dry sagebrush gorge
Protruding from one wall
A large rock is seen
Shaped like Abraham Lincoln's face.

Just then a high and steep mountain came into view
Clad almost to the top with evergreens
At the very top a rock is situated
It resembles the shape of a horse saddle.

As we gazed, we saw a huge rock in the
Middle of the river in the form of a steamboat
The rock parted the water of the swift river
Causing ripples around the rock
Coming together in the back
Making a backward wave of foamy water
Thus looking as if the rock were sailing.

W. C. Holder

The Image Of The Feminine Divine

Created in the image of the feminine divine
Proud to be a woman and feeling fine
Reborn to a truth that's yours and mine
Discovering goddesses in myths and time
Affirming the spirit of creativity
Letting the muse set me free
During the travel of life's journey
The path with heart is the way for me
A heroine I can choose to be

Mary Tough

What's Out There?

There is a huge, ugly monster out there.
No one can see it all in one glance.
When we are children we don't even know there's a window.
Eventually, we notice the window and step up to get a glimpse
of the beast.
It horrifies us so; we go back to crawling babies.
Then we are drawn to look again.
This time we see a bigger, more gruesome part of the giant.
The cycle continues.
We become jaded and brave.
Until the whole evil comes into view;
and scares us—to death.

Paula Frazer

A Bell Chimes

Softly, dawn breaks on another day,
Quietly, flowers bloom in May,
Gently, chirping sparrows grace a talk oak,
Beckoning children of the town's folk.

Somewhere the whisper of a spring morn,
A breeze fluttering leaves, adorn
A tall oak, the dawn, a doe and a fawn,
in nearby hills, the play fulfills.

A stream flows and along the bank,
Fishermen cast, catch and thank
The luck, this pleasant spring day brings,
in the meadow, by the brook, and the fish on the hook.

Softly, noon breaks on this day,
Quietly, flowers give a fragrance,
Gently, scurry natures little runts,
Beckoning fishermen in the month of May.

The play continues for the doe and fawn,
For tomorrow brings another dawn,
Brings warmth, fragrance, 'n mellow times,
For the towns folk another bell chimes.

Keith Bell

Aplomb

Aplomb, the knight who rescues the damsel
Opportunist that She may be,
From dragons fierce and villains vile,
'Tis her only security.

Though demons may haunt
And sprites spoil her dreams,
Self-Possession reigns Savant
With Grace as her means.

Courage in battle,
Appetite for the feast,
Slay the image of fatale,
Lay to rest the foul beast.

Cavalier nor seditious
Ranks proper regard.
Temperate and judicious
Render her exemplar.

Aplomb, the knight who rescues the damsel
Formidable as she may be,
At her right rests valor, her left fidelity,
'Tis her ideal society.

Victoria Wells Gay

Blind Love

I wish you would love me as much as I love you. But that's not
possible, if it was, it would be a miracle. You know, I heard "Love
is something you share, not own." Well, I think it's the other way
around. But if you do love her, then go ahead. Yeah sure,
I'll be hurt, but I know that no one can control love, or the way
a person feels, that's how I feel, I just can't stop loving you.
But if you're really sure that you love her more, then I think you
should go for her. But please think about me, and how I might feel.
While you're happy in love, you'll put me through misery and pain.
I'm sure you won't care, you wouldn't even think, not for one
minute about how I might feel. You might say, "She'll get over it,"
well maybe not, because if I see you with her, I'll think to
myself, that could have been me. I don't want to beg, but it looks
like I'm gonna have to. Every day you will bring her closer and
closer to you, just like you did with me in the beginning, because
that's the way love works, you would treat her way better than I,
and she will love you almost as much as I loved you. You will go on
with your life loving her, and not once would you think or mention
my name.

Windy Bidwell

Valentine Journey

A chambered pacing aches to be allayed
Rapid-fire beating longs for its place
Retrieving what has thrice been arrayed.

First love through soft, innocent eyes
Led youth to its death or only to slumber
Dividing the song into beckoning cries.

Hell reigned over new love for a time
Resembling a rose in a milieu of thorns
It lingers on now still fighting for rhyme.

A soft shadow of past crept to the fore
With demons still dancing, embracing the doom
He fought for a time, then retreated once more.

The beating fires on desiring release
To a place where the journey will finally cease
Love will endure and my heart will know peace.

Maeve M. Ertel

The Soul Of A Poet

The soul of a poet's life is but a day
Recalling peaceful images with delight.
Like music from a golden tongue
The joy and pain of life sad but sung.

The thoughts of a single mind expands
From a green hill side to a lover's desire.
And lovely tales of visions well read
And a soul interwoven with fire.

Time is unmeasurable fast
Like the speed of darkness from the past.
Emerged from the sea, the fossils saved
The poet's longest hour is from the cradle to the grave.

The morn comes once and then is gone
All the universe is quieted by night.
Then the soul of a poet comes to an end
When he's lost for words and retires his pen.

Mary Sturgis Douglas

Whose Face

Whose face is this, by winter kissed
Sleeping soundly in the snow?
Her dress of green and flowers seen
She's one all want to know
She'll wake one day so don't dismay
Her time is not quite yet.
The limbs of trees and branches bare,

Her season being set
Whose face is this by winter kissed?
When birds begin to sing,
You'll know her then as I do now
She is the face of Spring

Barbara J. Sevilla

Raindrops

Raindrops, raindrops are falling down,
raindrops are falling hard upon the ground.
The wind is blowing,
the streams are flowing,
because of the raindrops that God found.

I think to my God above me,
that the little raindrops are free.
They go where they may travel,
over rocks, stone, and gravel,
and flow far out into the sea.

Mae McCaughey

My Ode To The Artist

This is my ode to the artist who either writes the music or
Records it, so that at times when I feel the need for some
Relief, or when I just want to shut out the real world, I can
Escape into my C. D. land where there are no world problems,
No body pains to deal with, where one can, on occasion,
Forget what pills to take, what time to take them, and where
I can go back to a time in my life when the decision of the
day was if I should play ball, roller skate, ride a bike or
Just hang-out.

Then there are the times when the music of a Sinatra, a
Pavarotti, a Yanni, or any one of many other talented
Artists, who for 60 minutes or so, take me to a world where
There are no wars, no babies are crying from hunger,
Everybody loves one another, where the only differences we
Have is the language we speak.

So, maybe the answer is to get the garth brooks, the dolly
Partons, the neil diamonds to run the world. Maybe then the
Sound of music will fill the streets, rather than the sound
of gunfire.

Well the C. D.'s over, time to get my bullet-proof vest on and
Face the real world. — See you later Frank.

Ludwig R. Bruno

Red Tulips In Holland

Red flames melt marshmallows
Red leaves fall to the ground, then get raked up
Red lips kiss the mirror in the both room
Red eyes peer through peep wholes at hotels
Red blood drips from a body
Red flowers cover a casket at a funeral
Red fingers point at the guilty
Red tulips in Holland
Red tulips in Holland.

Marcus R. Bates

"Life's Mirror"

My life has become a mirror;
Reflecting other people's emotions.
Yet I'm like a tiny little fish
Swimming in a vast ocean.
My mirror of life has shattered;
The pieces falling across the floor.
I struggle to gather the pieces
To rebuild my life once more.
But pieces are always missing;
Crushed to small to find.
Again people turn away,
Never seeming to mind.
Then someone will find a reflecting piece.
They come and gaze in.
Once my happiness reflects back out,
I get shattered to pieces once again.

J. Crayton Smith

The Trees, I Love Them All

The only tree in the forest, like the only wave on the
sea. The only grain of sand on the beach. The only word in a
speech. It all boils down to the way you look at me. That is
nothing. So what? It's the way it will be. So close your eyes
and take a good long look at me.

That tree in the forest waving its branches and those
beautiful green leaves. Listen to the sound of that wave as it
crashes on the beach. As it rolls over the grain of sand being
awaken by all this. What a wonderful world we live in. Take a
look and see, I'm right there by your side. The waves, the sand,
the beach, and that one lonely beautiful tree.

Kathleen H. Rios

The Stranger

Distant memories aloft in my head.
Restless nights in a lonely bed.
There he lay close; yet so far.
Recognizing the face, but not knowing who you are.
Who is this stranger that lays next to me.
Who was this man that he once claimed to be.
Knowing the stranger so well; yet not at all.
Standing so short; yet inside he is tall.
Wanting to know him; his hurts and his shame.
Yearning to know what sparked his unbraceable flame.
Stranger in my life show me what you cannot tell.
Let me pick up the pieces that have fell.
To look at you, to always see, a love that cries out to only me.
If you only knew how my heart yearns to hold you so tight.
But this strange man gives me a bit of a fright.
Love me forever, I shall always love you.
Undying love our whole lives through.
Walking forever, holding each; eager to learn.
Yearning to teach, of our love for all: The stranger in each.

Michele L. Gonzalez

May I Die With Happiness Upon My Breast

There draped upon my mantle top
Rests a flower of unrivaled divinity.
Know that it is not native in origin
But, moreover, exotic to its entirety;
And here within its walls grace many
Alluring and arabesque colors
(Such that some I swore could not
Be so easily defined in any shape
Or fashion under that kind of banner).
However, to spite my queries of no import,
I have found in hurting times
Far no greater a healing peace
Than as yet to be bequeathed
In splendor or divinity
As I have found here,
In the soft-spoken petals
Of a dying friend.

Paul Deichmann

Daddy's Boy

Hey, Daddy... it's me,
right down here, beside your knee!
I can bang a hammer too
'cause I am big, just like you.

Hey, Daddy... it's me,
right down here, beside your knee!
I can help take out the trash
and you don't even have to ask.

Hey, Daddy... it's me,
right down here, beside your knee!
Can I go to work today with you?
I'll dress myself and you can tie my shoe.

Hey, Daddy... it's me,
right down here, beside your knee!
I like watching the ball game with you.
The soda and goodies are real good too.

Hey, Daddy... it's me,
please bend down upon your knee.
I need a hug and maybe a kiss.
I love you most, Daddy, at times like this!

R. S. Holzworth Gilpatrick

Soul Songs

Poetry is but the soul's song,
Reflecting the mind of man;
Feelings of the heart and soul,
Grasp each other — hand in hand.

Herein are the soul songs,
Of hearts and souls joined in life;
Reflecting of love, of joy, of sorrow,
What they experienced, — of their strife.

Gleaning from poetry and prose,
Other footprints on the trail,
Before the journey's end, the mind's quest
To sip from wisdom's grail.

So read with love — and know,
That "THIS" — A reflection of life,
Are but footprints left upon the earth,
To help others upon life's flight.

Sandra Starks

Within A Reflection

Peace within ourselves is a positive
reflection of patience, as time will endure
for those who seek. As our time becomes old
the cycle of life continues to turn, as endless
as our generation. Understanding the forecast of
life, our cycle of time will end, someday.

Sylvester Smith Jr.

"My Mother's Whisper"

A mother is something that everyone needs, something you can never
   replace
The way she walks, and the whispers you'd hear, her smile and her
strong embrace
Some of you still have a chance, with your mothers that are near
Show her love and show her respect, because a mother is someone
   so dear

My mother was the world to me, nothing can ever compare
And if I had a chance to change it all, I would ask God to please
   be fair
You don't realize what you have, until it's gone away
She'll never return to us on earth, but in heaven we will meet some day

My love for you, mother, will never change, even though you are gone
I know that you can't come back to me, but the whispers I hear will
   live on
Someday my child will hear my whispers, and know there is no other
I finally understand the cycle of life, now that I am a mother!

Linda Sorensen

"A Poor Man Cries"

Don't take away the needs of the poor, there are plenty of us already
out the door, with nothing to do but explore. Needing food and
shelter to survive, another person frozen and died. Roaming the
streets from day to day, begging and pleading for help they say.
Republican politician wants to take it all away, not yesterday but
today. They never had to sleep in card board boxes in the street, or
wonder where there be something to eat. They don't care about the
children cries, and don't give a damn weather they all dies. They
have it all that's all matters, constantly climbing up those ladders.
I pray to God that someone will be able to get through, what must we
say, what must we do. We're not to blame if we're not working,
there's no jobs that's why we're lurking. Some of us are disabled,
and our bodies are unstabled. We didn't ask to be this way, it was
unexpected I say. We depend on help to live in this condition, we're
not asking for permission. All those that have count blessing and be
glad, because life I tell you can be very sad.

Regina Johnson

Pet Of The Realm

She was a canine ray of sunshine,
Right from the very first.
Full of puppy enthusiasm,
Eating kibble or quenching her thirst.

She played and she fetched with abandon,
Just loved, her tennis ball.
Her coat reflected flashes of gold,
As she grew mellow, and lean and tall.

And all of the neighbors adored her,
She'd greet them on the run.
You just had to pause and say, "Ginger!"
Then, her tail would start wagging, for fun.

The happiest dog I've ever known,
She lived long, 'till she died.
Thus we, like the small girl who owned her,
Were sad, could empathize, and we cried.

Roland R. Bianchi

"Falling"

I'm glad I got to know you...
Right from the very start
To better understand our love...
To know we'll never part

We hold a bond the stars...
And farther than the sea
Our tightness is so very close...
It seems like eternity

Your eyes filled with smiles...
And your heart filled with love
Adds to the joys...
Of your soft and gentle hugs

Your brightness makes the way...
So I could follow too
For the laughter and the love you brought...
Made me fall for you

Kristy L. Duplantis

Untitled

Mountains slither down, collide with waters, coursing through
rivers, swirling through gushing valleys. Run to the horizon,
cascade into sweetness, birthing crisp air, fresh sunsets, golden
disks of fire breathed by the dragon of a star.

K. C. Smith

"No More Dreams"

Her life long dreams are gone away,
Now she has no set course.
Taken by abusive parents,
Stolen with no remorse.

Everyday they abuse her,
They bruise her little face.
How their words sting and break her heart,
Courts don't know yet of her case.

They work all day and come home to fight,
Beating her when she's near.
Their strength overcomes hers by far,
Her emotion is fear.

They had been drinking much that night,
And Daddy hit her head,
Pounding into the wall.
She died asleep in bed.

Melissa Lay

Lewistown

A clear creek stream moves like a silent merger...
Rolling into autumn shade, she possesses
the gentle motion of black velvet.

A bouquet of yellow foliage cascades
like running water
spinning then plunging into the race of time.

This rolling, flowing mass has danced with many seasons
and carves a place for its body to unfold.

Each measure of exchange creates a rhythm
stroking over the earth's bed below.

In stillness, these gentle, audible laps of
life yield many caresses of growth.

Susan Hurst

Listen To The Wind

Listen to the wind as it sings in the trees,
    rustling and blowing on each gentle breeze.

Listen to the wind as it waves at the wheat,
    down every alley and onto each street.

Listen to the wind as it ripples the sea,
    dancing and playing as it follows the bee.

Listen to the wind as it spins out its tales,
    traveling over the valleys, hills and dales.

Listen to the wind as it kisses the chimes,
    caressing and soothing the hardest of times.

Listen to the wind as it whips through the barn,
    the owls give their hoot but they don't give a darn.

Listen to the wind as it swirls round your head,
    it tickles your cheek as you doze in your bed.

Listen to the wind, to the sweet lullaby,
    the birds spread their wings ready to fly.

Listen the wind as it heads for the sun,
    the moon watches coolly as it must have its fun.

Listen to the wind and wait as you must,
    its magic will return for a while if you trust.

Patricia Quill

Playing With Angels

A furry, cold nose touches my cheek,
Sacred of Tibet, now dear to my spirit,
the grand heart betrays your small person.
Soul have you none, they say, they lie.

Aware from the moment I made you mine,
velvet, infant body held close.
Soft, little head rising to see me as I truly am.
Mother bond to canine child,
the unspoken language of affection.

Bright spirit without promise of soul and heaven,
I hear your mute plea, the silence now broken.
Keeper of creation, I liken two penny sparrows,
in free fall to grounded earth.
Though silent, the infinite eye of God is all-wise,
more so the Lhasa earns His regard.

Echoes of laughter, the Lord has smiled,
declaring, "four feet and four wings."
Play with the angels my friends, my children.

Sylvia January Keck

Never Forget Him

Dead he is.
Sad I am.
Sitting on my bed.
It was his decision.
So he left.
His music plays in my head.
But why are people mad at him
for what he has done.
Sure we'll miss him and never forget him.
Because he killed himself with a gun.
But it was his problem and he took care of it
the only way he could.
And we might not understand.
So mind their own business
the people should!
Kurt Cobain I'll never forget you,
you're my kind of guy.
And when you died you made my cry.
I want you to know I'm by your side,
I will always love you. Goodbye.

    Yolana King

Hidden Things

Hidden things that quicken in the soul of man
secluded in his guardedness and now and then
intruding on his tight control of life,
emerging unexpected in a garish and upsetting dream
to shake the tranquil shell of self.

Man has an in built wariness, a strange reserve that
builds the walls around his tender core, protecting
the serenity of knowing what to him seems real and touchable.
Too suddenly a troubled and uncertain fear possesses him
as something strange looms up from deep within.
Can that be me?

From deep within, subconscious or unbidden
thoughts emerge that threaten his tranquillity.
This man is not the master of himself.
A knowledge shaking him as he hears unknown things
that laugh down in the whirlpool depths of what
he thought was solid rock, dissolving part of him.
Too late he locks the door.

    Phyllis Schroeder

Paradise Untouched

Deep, lush, virgin jungle, where no human has ever trod.
Secrets of wondrous nature still unrevealed to mortals.
No glimpse of sky above; only lemon shafts of filtered sun
Spiraling down past Grecian tree trunks to clearing below.

Earth, luxurious carpet of century old fallen leaves,
And moss like the softest of imported eider down.
Monstrous flowers of vivid hues and velvety ferns wrought in
Delicate filigree towering higher then a giant's head.

Paradise, throw-back to Eden, dominion of myriad birds and beasts.
Scarlet, indigo, emerald, jade, wondrous rainbow-bearing wings.
Ebony panther slipping through ferns, leaving no imprint on moss.
Bright, curious, beady monkey eyes peeping fearless at their adversaries.

Deep hidden enchanted grove within the verdant endless jungle.
Undisturbed lush virgin beauty of kaleidoscope of intermingled color.
Steaming, teeming with syncopated brilliance of sound and life.
Wild, stark beauty, unclaimed, untouched, unspoiled by mortals.

    Mickey Thomas

Goodbye Darling

Goodbye darling I will miss you badly.
See you in the end, hope we'll always be friends
Goodbye darling, hope you can stay, be here
Always, or not move so far away.
Without you, it'll be hard to have a happy day.
Goodbye darling, you always made me smile,
We had fun won't happen for awhile,
When you leave, I'll be very sad
All the fun and smiles will be done
I'll be very hurt and sad when you are gone.
Goodbye, darling, I appreciate your help,
when I were to yell, you took away my hell,
You brought out the sun when my heart felt pain,
You brought out the sun in the rain,
You're not gone yet, when you are I'll be scared,
I will never ever forget you,
No matter how far you go, I'll be there for you
No matter what kind of person you are.

    Robert Boyer

Before The Rains Began

Looking through the window sill
Seeing the art of spring time
Watching the clouds shaping into a windmill
As the sea sings her song in my mind

Before the winds came
And the thunder in the sky
For the lightning fingers in my eye
And now the rains began

The rains pounded the melody
For the rains cleanse the skies
The sweet smell of morning
For the rainbow shines into my eyes

Watching the rose petals of memories
Looking at the smiles and tears
For they bloomed with love
To last throughout the years

For all the birds unite to sing a chorus
For they are so happy to be free
For all the squirrels are playing in the trees
And such a beautiful sight to see

    Steve Kyriakopoulos

Sunlight In Your Eyes

Falling into a vacuum of silence without time,
Shaken by a distorted view, no matter how I try,
But when it seems there's nothing I can do
To take away the hurt inside,
Somehow the truth comes shining through
Like the sunlight in your eyes.

Scared of letting go again,
Of being left alone,
Jilted by a blist'ring wind
That chilled my very soul,
But when it seems there's nothing I can do
To take away the hurt inside,
Somehow the truth comes shining through
Like the sunlight in your eyes.

But I will give my heart away again, and make the sacrifice.
Even though I may not always win, I'll never win if I don't try.
And when it seems there's nothing I can do
To take away the hurt inside,
Somehow the truth will still shine through
Like the sunlight in your eyes.

    Veonne Poole

Impressions

She doesn't know where the love has gone,
Seems like the making of another sad song-
Some people are all about the heart,
Passion and devotion has a special part-
Jealousy is a cruel way to say.
I will always love you, forever in a day-
We should not indulge ourselves on other insecurities,
To fuel the flame of happiness, in search of serenity-
All working so hard to break the barriers between,
Unconditional love and the games that are so mean-
How much pain can we endure?
many restless nights, I am sure-
To condition the heart and let it fall,
"In love" you have to give it all-
From the compassionate times that are shared,
To some disappointments that leave you scared-
Do we waste the emotions that are shown?
Or can you go on and know you've grown?
It all seems a little backwards to me,
Why do we induce hurt that doesn't have to be-

Randy Plummer

Faith In Grace

Dear God, please keep her in your loving care,
Send down your Son to minister and cure.
'Tis she whom you have fashioned once so fair
But then, you know what cross she can endure.
Yet spurn not Lord the pleadings of your son
Who with the dust of earth must bide his stay,
And count not all the wrongs which I have done
Against my mighty God in this my day.
Uphold her Lord with your almighty hand
Strike out the pain within her mortal frame,
Send down a thousand of your angel band
To fight the foe and triumph in your name.
    I know when next I see her lovely face
    Her eyes will show her Maker's loving grace.

LeRoy F. Schwerin

Third Finger Clouds

My temples ache, each step I take
seems long, on this reservation.
This heart does not require any sadness.
Postpone these feelings I cannot help.
The legend of posies rub me across the sky.
Nurture me, laying down.
To become a nun, I must love only God.
But not everyone has the same God.
Not everyone keeps their illness a secret.

Summer A. Thompson

Without Being Seen

There is a cloud where I live where I can drift all day without
being seen.
When I go there it is fun and games, where I can run free all day
without being seen.
There's a place where I go and it rains all day where no one can be seen.
People roam and wander around without worrying about being seen.
Some people say where the kids of the nineties and don't care what we
do or care about being seen.
Some of us stare, others jump for joy, while the rest of us our
soaking our skin. Gems and stones we don't care, peace joy and
happiness is what we all need.
For life is one big joke and we don't care about being seen.
For life goes on even if we are seen.

Sarah Grant

Dusk

Halfway between night and day,
shades of pale orange underlining drifting clouds,
the leaves sharply focused
and the tree next to you evolving
into a figure of shadow.
Stillness reigns
as if in awed anticipation
of the coming darkness,
ready to call it a day.
The orb of fusion against the horizon
minute by minute
falls into netherland and the moon
rises arrogantly to claim
the night, her dominant right.
Twilight:
a mere pawn in the battle
between night and day.

Robert Michael Schensted

#43**

Tracy,
Shall I give you too a number? A gold star next to Number 43.
Is it that our love remains the freshest in my heart?
Or was our passion unmatched by the others?
Jimmy's been gone 11 years, Randy 7, Kevin 5, You 2
My attraction to death is mirrored in my loss
43 friends scratched from my address book
4 gold stars 4 lost lovers.
What Grand Lesson remains to be learned
Before this illusion disintegrates into my soul's next design.
They call me a Long Time Survivor
I've not been forgotten by AIDS but perhaps by GOD.
When will it be my turn? Tomorrow, next week, next year...
Are survivors the lucky ones, when we've yet to meet GOD?
Are the lines getting long in heaven?
They must be,
The way they're stretching through the hospitals here.
I'll be patient, Tracy, I'll take my number and wait my turn
And mark you down number 43 with two gold stars.
I miss you

Thomas Poole

The Rosebud

The rosebud is like a newborn child,
Untouched by impurities,
Held tightly still in the arms of a loving beginning.
But as the child grows, so the rose blooms
And each petals stretches to accept life.
Unaware of danger, naive to rejection
And vulnerable to the elements that tarnish life.
Still, the rose will reach full bloom
And the child will become an adult.
The rose is exposed to its environment
As man is exposed to society.
The petals become limp
By being weighted down with dew day after day.
So man becomes weighted down with troubles.
And it takes more and more courage to stand strong and tall.
Both weather storms, brave the cold
And thrive on warmth.
Both are beautiful forms of life to be
    given,
        received, shared...

Barbara Sonnenberg Banks

This Love

How is it with This Love.....
You give these candled bodies an inner wick
Just to burn the outer self away....
Giving light to this invisible world
The flame lifts its head....
And the body is gone....
How is it in This Love
Sewing its seeds into different stems
Climbing into flowers....surrendering their fragrance
Like a full life offering....to the seeker searching for The
Friend....
Imagine This Meeting....
Where the mind's pen runs out of ink....
And the soul's Word rolls its eye open
And reads the secrets off the Master's forehead....
How clever is This Love's weaver
Leaving a pattern we can trace....
It's here....Now....
Sewn into the fabric
Of soul's seamless garment....

Richard Schaub

My Dream Of You

You came in my dreams and you kissed me goodbye
You held me in your arms and said please don't cry
Go on with your life and make a new start
You know I have to go and that we must part

I could feel your arms around me that night in my dream
The tender kiss you gave me was the last one it seems
I'll never forget the night you came to me
You held me so gently and then set me free

You told me I knew that you had to go
For Jesus was waiting, you told me so
You said that you loved me, I'll never forget
Your lips I still feel and your arms around me yet

But someway or another you didn't let me be
I can't forget you, and you didn't set me free
And my dream I'll remember as long as I live
To me you gave all that you had to give

Someday I will see you on heaven's shore
My love is there forever and evermore
So wait for me darling, someday I'll be there
In the arms of my darling with the love we both share

Ruth Shelton

Rainbow

Dear Mother Nature, top artist of all
You paint the winter, spring, summer and fall.
You roam the hills and the valley you seek,
Then climb the mountain to the highest peak.

Though man tries, he'll never surpass;
Forever he'll be- behind you in class.
Your brush is fine, the colors are true,
Your strokes have a flow in all that you do.

Your water is clear with gemstones at the brim;
Trees are quite bold and fine are their limbs.
High hills all stippled in soft hues of green;
The beauty you paint, no artist has seen.

But what I like most of all that you've done.
Is that after a storm you like to have fun.
You squeeze out your colors, choose only the best,
Then blend with care to discard all the rest.

The moment is now. You want nature aglow!
So the rainbow you choose-to be first in your show.
Brilliant bands of color reflecting the sun,
A thousand VanGoghs all molded in one!

Lawrence C. Lumetta

Icy Hearts

Beneath the dark of the moon,
You hide from me.
Your passion is gone, your love has disappeared.
Your love is cold,
As is your heart.

Under the light of the sun
You deceive me.
Your passion was an illusion, your love was aloof.
Your look is cold,
As is your heart.

In a night of dreams,
You come to me.
Your passion overwhelming, your love complete.
Your look is warm,
As is your heart.

But as nights turn into days,
And dreams turn into reality, I am hurt.
Your love is dead, never alive.
Your look is cold,
As is your heart, an icy heart.

Lisa Blair Dickerson

The Endless Tunnel

Life is like a tunnel long and dark
You keep searching for the end
instead you fall apart

You think you see the light far up ahead
until a great big wall beat you there instead

No way to run no where to go
just an endless tunnel every one has known

You probably think I'm crazy, dumb, maybe insane
if you feel the way I do you know this is no game

I want to find the end, the bright happy place,
but when there is no one to talk to the wall is in your face

Maybe someday I'll reach the light to where
my happiness is, that's true

But right now I'll stay in my tunnel feeling sad
and maybe blue

Nicole M. Veilleux

Thank-You God

God, you are so far away and yet so very near,
You listen to our every word and every cry you hear.

Sometimes God, we only come when trouble seems to be,
But, you are there with open arms and your love you give so free.

We shoulder oh so many cares we should not have to do,
If only we would open up and give them all to you.

Oh, God, please help us here this day to free our troubled souls,
For if we did this life would be far better a trillion fold.

You hear our every heartfelt cry and you watch us while we sleep,
When we don't say "GOOD-NIGHT" to you I know your heart
must weep.

From the first thing in the morning till the last move at eventide,
We know you keep a watchful eye and you're right there by our side.

Thank you, God, for loving us and sending us your son,
For Jesus is our Savior and through him our victory won.

It we could only realize the wealth to us you gave,
You gave us life eternal and our victory ore the grave.

So please help us to remember to give thanks to you each day,
For Dear God, without you we could never find our way.

Laura Stairs

Our Love

Here we are going through the motions for the last time
You look into my eyes although somehow you don't see me
Here I am feeling like a stranger in your arms
I touch you, I hold you, lately I feel I don't know you
Something is wrong, although we go on from day to day
We sit and pretend it all away, and act like nothing has changed
But in our hearts we both know it's not the same
When we hold each other tight, and say everything is alright
Inside I know this is going to be our last night
Is it too late to fix what we had
Or am I the only one that feels so sad
I remember when we first met
Our eyes locked and our hands met
That's when I got a feeling that we where meant to be together
Now that we are going to be in the past.
I deeply wish we could last
I wish I could put a gate around our love
Hide the key under a big hollow tree
And make it disappear with a magic spear
Even though we will be apart, I will still love you deep in my heart

Nichole Harris

Someone Special

So I was "special," you said, different from all the rest.
You looked at me with those melting eyes and made me feel I
    was your happiness.
And I believed because I wanted to believe, desperately searching
    for "straws."
Could there have been flaws?
You said the things I needed to hear, playing upon my weaknesses.
Knowing, that in time, that sort of thing ceases.
But you failed to tell me, now that it's gone, what to do with
    the memories.
What was once a trust has now become a tease...
How do I deal with those lonely nights when you're all that's on
    my mind?
How do I hide from the memories that seek and find?
...Now that you've found another "someone special" who's different
    from all the rest?
Mind! Mind! Please let my heart pass!

Nita Looney

Buddy's Final Flight

God made something very special, when He made you
You made a difference in peoples' lives "It's True"
All too soon, your time with us — slipped away
Many who love you, came to honor you today

So, spread your wings wider
And fly much higher
Than you ever have before
Rise, rise above it all

We will hear you when you call
Sing out, with your special song
Going with the current
As you soar along

There is a special place, waiting just for you
When your journey, of flight is through
You will find a special space
With just the right sticks, to put in place

When our life here on earth is done
May God grant you be the one
Allowed to be our guide
When heaven's gates open wide

Nancy R. Binder

The Mime

You make me laugh you make me cry
You make me think you make me sigh.
A mask is worn upon your face
Just like the one who kept me from grace.
Not a word is said but I hear you clearly
In all my confusion I love you dearly.
Like an acrobat you prance and dance
I think your best came from France.
The Greeks & Romans loved you too
As you played the big buffoon.
Time has come and time has gone
But still the mime lives on...
You pass the hat for your daily bread
And still there was never a word said.

Terry K. Guthrie

Freedom From Within

As you explore the inner depths of your mind
You must allow your spirit to unwind
To free your conscience from all ills
And allow yourself to climb the hills
Where peace and freedom can reign again
And allow your spirit to be free to mend
For once a calmness appears in your soul
You'll be able to reach your endless goal

Kathy Dickey

The Launch

There are so many memories for us to recall
You perched on the houseboat hull is remembered by all
With your welding cap turned to the side
And a smile so big that was impossible to hide
A wave of your hand as we pulled up the driveway
Then back to work, you had a boat to launch someday

You worked so long to make that dream come true
Welding was what you knew best and liked to do
Through the years we watched as the boats were done
You never gave up on building the perfect one

Though launching your own boat was not to be
Talking about it still put a sparkle in your eyes for all to see
In illness you were strong and brave
So much like a boat caught in a big wave

You fought the battle and lost in the end
We will surely miss you, our dear friend
And now at last - you are free from your endeavor
And the greatest Launch of life is yours, forever

Patsy Walsh

Dad

Twenty years ago
you pumped your legs to keep me afloat
in the Maui Sea.
Arms around your neck
I felt safe
though I knew not what was beneath me
in the black-blue water.

Since then, we have often sharpened
our steel tongues
each on the other's back —

Still I remember
warm salt waves licking my neck
and I feel safe
though there is no solid ground beneath me
for I know
you tread my water

Kathryn Penso

411

Christmas

You said you would love me forever
You said you be my shadow and be with me always
I can't believe you would leave on Christmas Day
You said we would live forever in each others arms
And our love could never be demised
Why loved didn't you stay with me as you promised
Now I sit here alone on Christmas Day
My heart broken and tears in my eyes
I sit here alone on Christmas Day with your
picture in my hands stained by my tears
When I dream I see you holding, kissing and loving me
as you said you would
Tome it is real, these dreams, until I wake to see emptiness
beside me where you used to lay
So I sit here on Christmas drinking my sorrows away, but it
doesn't work, I miss you even more
So I sit here on my bed where we used to lay together
I set here on Christmas Day waiting
to be rejoined with you
O what a wonderful Christmas Day

William Myers III

The Glory Belongs To God

You praise him for what he has brought you through. I look at
You, smile, and nod. For we both understand that the glory
Belongs to God.
A part of me is you, and a part of you is me. I'm touched
With the feeling of your infirmity.
I've felt your pain, I've been right there. Sometimes we've
Encountered the deepest despair.
I've cried your tears, and shared your fears. I've struggled
Just like you down through the years.
I too once breathed that great sigh of relief. When a word
From our God gave me victory over grief.
I've experienced the joy that you've had in the day. Then
Let anxiousness come in and drive it away.
I've been where you were, and I've been where you are.
Whether it was near or perhaps even far.
We've dealt with so many things, but have come through them all.
We've leaned on the one who would not let us fall.
He dressed us in his armour, even our feet were shod. He's
Been with you, he's been with me. The glory belongs to God.
Glorify the Lord with me; let us exalt his name together.

Rose Reed Sullivan

Becoming

You are youth, beauty, passion and the promise of things unspoken.
You stir passion in men and expectation in women.

You are the grantor of forgiveness for all we did not accomplish on
time and usher in our hopes and dreams of becoming.
You put it together all over again and again with fanfare.

You are the wind beneath the winged bird, the germinating kernel of
corn, the yellow bloom of the okra and the fragile silk of a newly
cocooned butterfly. You are the bud bursting into white flower
that becomes the red cherry cobbler at the church picnic - and
you are the beginning of the grey cane, after the wine, now the
woven holiday wreath.

You breathe life into the small creatures nestled deep in wombs all
winter awaiting a warm birth.
You are the beginning of all that awakens after the slumber - You
ring the bell!
I feel so unimportant in your presence, yet you come and go in
honor of me.

You instill in us a desire to run when we're weary, hope and pray for
a better tomorrow and keep a smile when we're down.

You were - You are - You will be again - Spring - Glorious Spring!

Vera H. Sawyer

A Little To Remember

You waited for your birthday
You waited for the mumps to go away

The sun was like a big red ball at the beach
That great big ocean seemed so out of reach

You blew out the candles one by one
Hearing, "My how've you grown, my son

What do you wanna be when you grow up
A doctor, fireman, or a cop

Does it seem so long ago
When you look over at the wife you know

She was your high school sweetheart
From then, you knew you'd never part

Then you had two sets of twins
Boy, did that make your head spin

Time flies, so they say
Do you wish, sometime it could stay

But then you'd miss what's yet to come
A little bitter, a little sweet, and then some

Once again, you're santa and it's December
With just a little more to remember

Madeline Aversa

A Journey

The day you're born you begin a journey through life.
You walk first then start to talk. Opening up and
then being told to shut up.

At an age of discovery of yourself and others, taking
A blow and trying to recover. Climbing the mountain
to adulthood, things being handed to you, accepting them
all whether they are good or bad.

You're not a child anymore so you take a step forward to
Explore. Hoping your faith will bring more. The
Test of life is fully upon you now. Oh God, please
guide me and show me how.

D. B. Zepeda

"Innocent"

You went dancing and you danced,
You went partying and you partied.
You went innocent and came back guilty.
Don't let your tears jerk you
    around when you're innocent.
Don't let your fears pull you into guilt.
Some say you're innocent till proven guilty,
Some way when guilty you're innocent,
but who's right, who's wrong?
When you went dancing you danced wrong.
When you went partying you partied wrong.
When you went innocent you never thought
    you'd come back guilty!

Nichole Winburn

The Year That Heaven Shared An Angel

Heaven sent an angel, though it rarely parts with one,
You must know angels are very busy, and their work is never done!

Angels busily flutter their wings, smile and beam constantly,
They make Heaven a very enchanting and lovely place to be!

Heaven now has shared one, Tyler Shea a bundle from above,
Our family has been waiting for an angel just like her to love!

She'll capture your heart, soul and all your being
And we share her with you as our Christmas Greeting!

Virginia Todd

Revisiting Ronsard's Remembrance Of Helene

A few years from now on a warm spring night
You will discern in the fickle ashen glow
The image of rueful Helene in the candlelight
And in the midst of Time's onrushing flow
There is Ronsard who will take down your look
And your image is radiantly drawn in his book.
I reflect that you too could have had fame
Had you taken the occasion to learn to strive
To leave for some offspring that fair name
That was my only ardor when I was still alive
Now when death claims me you see your pride
As you curse in your declining years that look
In gazing into a waning puff of candlelight
That Ronsard who traced your image in his book.

Norman F. Birnberg

Love Song

As long as I live,
You will never die.
Night and day
Will come and go,
Surrendering their hegemony
But regaining it on the morrow,
Certain uncertainty attaining
A kind of cosmic art.

Amidst this ebb and flow
My love for you armors you
Against vicissitude and imperturbability.
Your love for me
Nourishes my soul,
And I can once more
Nourish your own dear self
Amidst a cosmic nullity.

C. B. Weber

Party

You come to a party, you pay your five bucks
You worry your T-shirt does not match your socks
You stand by the door, you don't know anyone
You wonder how come you are not having fun
Your head's filled with beer, you smell Mary Jane
You hear the sirens, you're going insane
You watch the lights get closer, you witness a strife
The party got busted, you run for your life!

Simone Shlozberg

Gang Bang

Gangs Gangs Bang! Bang!
Young and old you'll doing the same thing
Black gangs, brown gangs, that is all you see
You are killing up each other just like bumper bees

You see, Johnny had been warned the night before
that he would be killed or his little brother four.
On that hell bound train your fare is already paid,
It only goes one way and that is straight to your Grave.

The police knocked on the door and this is what he said
I'm bringing you sad news that your son is dead.
Sally Sue jumped up and she ran into Johnny's room
She ran back out crying who who who.

Who killed my boy! Who killed my child!
Lord have mercy waw! Waw! Waw!
I have told you my story and I have told it well
If I have left out my thing feel free to tell, who killed my boy?

Ola Mae Harris

Words And Actions

Your words sound sweet, their cost is free
Your actions sting just like a bee

Your words appear to be sincere
Your actions say, "Get out of here!"

Your words say, "Come on in and see."
Your actions say, "Don't bother me!"

Your words are used just like a tool;
to lure, mislead, to trick, and fool

When confronted with the two,
your lips stay sealed tight through and through

Your words have turned 'to' puffs of air
Your actions reveal you don't care

Which holds worth? Your words nor actions
None give true satisfactions

Mona E. Couey

The Question

The wonderful sight of your sweet face
Your brown eyes shimmer like a cut diamond
Glistening in the sun

Your soft lips of gentle pink

And each day I see you next to me
Loving, caring, sharing
Through good times and in bad

I wonder how someone as wonderful
As you could love anyone so bad

So now as you read this, my sweet love,
Answer me the question "why is it that you love"

Melissa Lee Campbell

Life

Life is a field of dreams.
Your future lies far ahead of you,
Your past just left behind.
New promises rise with the morning sun,
Conclusions come with the moon.
New ideas popping up like wildflowers,
Standing straight and reaching skyward.
Many fears and obstacles encroaching your spirit like weeds.
Finally from out of the mist,
Like a gust of inspiration, your purpose becomes clear and
You open your eyes to the world.

Stacy Young

The Beans

Did you see me in the bean field
Riding the flowered corpses?
White angel feathers flew like rabid songsters.
I wait for the knobbed white fox
Riding on a horse.
It has not yet come.
The cloud has gathered with ashes
Dispersing like cigarette butts.
The orange buds open with wakeful eyes,
They watch you play songs for
Me in the field.
Your wood hollows melancholy.
Your love beads on a string.
The dew is cold on my face.
It purges the empty
Souls, shallowly.
They have not become deep.
The beans are too thick.

Kamala Nair

Four Maids, Fair

Dance light, oh lovely lass of Spring,
Your gown of flowers billowing!
With sunwashed, dew-kissed feet you skip
And perfumed mouth sweet nectar sip.

Awake! Fair, fulsome Summer's wench,
Caught fast asleep on garden bench.
All supped on berries, stained with wine
And garlanded with fruit of vine.

Fly! Brilliant, burnished Autumn maid
Of coppered skin and auburn braid.
You hide and seek in leaf strewn dell
And, laughing, sound late Summer's knell

Hail! Regal, radiant Winter's Queen
With snowy crown and glitt'ring mien.
Where North Wind blows and Hoar Frost nips,
There have you touched your icy lips.

Each lays her head on changing mead,
Hillock, woodland, by rush and reed;
Sired each twelve month, sisters four,
Come, strew your bounty at my door!

Leila Sen

Reaching For You

I will find out about you someday you know.
Your son loved you so, I am his daughter and
he is gone too. Deep in my soul I must know
who you were. I ask people about you and all
they can say is I don't remember, it was so
long ago. I ask were you died and if you were
alone, and all they can say is I don't know.
I will find out about you sooner than they
think, I will not quit until I know. For some reason
you are in my soul. There must be something you
want me to know. It seems so weird I am obsessed
with finding out about you. I look at your picture
and all I can see is your soul reaching out to me.
I have a part of you somewhere I know, but why do
our souls need each other so. Your picture
makes me sad because I never met you but our
souls have met at least once a long time ago.

Sandra Ziebart

In Honor Of Mother

Mary, Mary Mother of mine
Your tender words, so sweet, so kind
The love you send, the prayers you give
Your careful caring attention, so my soul shall live

The worth of a man is hard to find
Through you; The Breath of Life, salvation is mine
Then in my mind, all things shall make sense in time

What comfort I feel, having you so near
To mend my wounds, and wipe my tear

You fill my hunger, in my heart and soul
You shelter me, embracing me sweetly so
You warm me, you make me whole

Before this day, your only son did honor you
Now today, earth mothers feel this love too

The honor of a queen, a blessing from above
Within this simple message, a gift I give with love

I Love you Immaculate Mother, what more could I say
But thank you for understanding, my confusion when I pray

Thomas Gregory Ori

To My Grandfather, Sweet Mentor, And Hero

I wrestle with, yet understand your reasons in leaving me behind;
Your time here spent leaves only an afterlife to find.
But I wonder, while here, did you ever truly realize
The extent to which each facet of your life I've come to idolize?
Due to our loss of you countless tears have been shed.
And each tear mends my soul, once left tattered and shred.
Forgive me dear Opa, for I know in my heart you will ever reign,
But did you think an absolute recovery could ever be feigned?
And although my spiritual endurance may prove to be strong,
This weakness persists in me and will surface ere long
I need something physical - to grasp and embrace
A reminder of you, yet something substantial to face.
To have thoughts secure and a heart cool at rest-why must I be brave?
Instead I put faith in a messenger, this plant that adorns your grave.
I know my folly, for you truly do not lie in that earthly part,
But remain here eternally roaming chambers of my heart.
Now you must grant me this, for I need something more
In order to be at peace and feel our past bond restore.
So please, dear Opa, sweet mentor, and hero, do as I plead,
Grasp the roots of this plant as I embrace its leaves!

Tiana C. Rosen

Need

Your humor makes me warm,
Your touch makes me tingle,
Your embrace makes me swoon,
Your kiss makes me quiver,
Your eyes make my blood boil.
These feelings make me alive; if there were no you,
I'd be numb, I couldn't exist

Sharon Snyder-Gambler

A Special Friend

A special Friend is what you are
You're always here you're never far

When I look up and count the stars
I think to myself how very very far

The silent sky remind me blunt
You are right here you're never far.

When you are so physically far
That's how I know what a very special friend you are

Lois LaRosa

September 17, 1993

I'm waiting for you ... When are you coming home?
You're four months late as I write this poem
I watched out the window ... I thought I heard you there
That pounding noise you used to make on the stairs
Another glance out the window, a call on the phone
I waited for you, but you never came home
The news came too quickly, the answer was "No"
I gathered my things ... It was time to go
I walked around slowly looking for things
But it was too late ... you already had your wings
Where should I go? What should I say?
Whatever happened on that awful day?
You kissed me good-bye ... "I Love You," you said
"I Love You" in return as I lay in the bed
How could I have known that would be the last time I would hear
That precious voice that I hold so dear?
The plans have changed ... I have to move on
My life is so different now that you're gone
September 17, 1993
You've stolen my heart ... You've stolen me.

Toni Anne Luciano

Baby Brother Baby Sister

Baby brother, baby sister
You're going about life all wrong

You can't keep killing one another
your generation will soon be gone.

Too many, young folks dying and old folks crying
no future will this nation see

If you don't care about tomorrow, no tomorrow will there be.

Baby brother, baby sister
the message's loud the signs are clear

If you don't start loving one another
your generation will disappear

Too many young folks dying and old folks crying
who will be left to carry on

Without the younger generation, who will keep mankind going strong.

You got to open up your eyes and realize life is Gods gift to man

And there ain't no fun in death and guns you got to give life a chance

Baby brother, baby sister, don't take me wrong,
     you're not all to blame
but it's going to take your generation, to make a difference,
     to make a change.

Robin Mack

You're Only Fifty

Now that you're fifty, nothing will ever be the same,
You're moving slower, and starting to forget all of our names.
Your bones are more brittle, and your knees are real weak,
You've shouted for years, now it's a hoarse whisper you speak.
We repeat all that's said, cuz' you don't hear quite right,
The eyes are gone, it's now bifocals for your fuzzy sight.
Bad arthritis pain, and buying mineral ice by the case,
With that smell, no wonder you've got wrinkles on your face.
You've been around longer than the superbowls,
Makes one wonder, if you still have bladder control.
Now it's senior citizen discounts that will come your way,
Special menus, smaller portions, and $ 1.99 is all you pay.
Children have grown, starting a new life on their own,
You'll adopt a lovable cat, so you don't feel so alone.
He'll listen without complaints, and remain very still,
Cuz' it doesn't matter to him that you're over the hill.
You'll get plenty of noise, when the grandkids come around,
No doubt they'll be leaving their toys all over the ground.
At your age, it's time you got yourself a rocking chair,
You're precious to us, and we'll always be there, we care!

Tracy S. Gulzow

A Fire In The Rain

The light in your eyes is my fire in the rain
You're the whisper that soothes my pain
Within this sea of confusion, you are the paradise I find
And your smile is a treasure of a lifetime.

My empty hand reaches for you and is filled with gold
In this hell I'm living you are the heaven I hold
And when there's a darkness that fills my heart
Your touch always seems to burn like a candle in the dark.

The pure happiness in my life all depends upon you
Your love makes the wishes and hopes of my heart come true
And with everyday that passes by it seems
As I look deeper into your soul
     I find the reality of all my dreams.

Travis Shane Arrants

Untitled

When all your hopes and dreams are gone, and you find
Yourself standing alone. Hanging on to the end of life's string.
You have to wonder what the next day will bring.
I toss and turn through sleepless nights just going
Over this continuous fight.
I sit here with my dog and cat, we haven't eaten and
I worry about that.
I never knew it could be like this, and I've given up
On making a wish.
But every night I faithfully pray that things will -
Start going my way.
Back to the way it used to be, when I was worry and hassle free.
Don't let them take my house away, I've been
Stripped of so much I cant begin to say.   Oh please
Just give me a lucky day, that will turn this ride
The other way. I cant stand in another line, and I
Can't be ripped-off for even a dime
I've learned my lessons hard but well, and I can show
You, but only time will tell.
So, for right now, please let things be, back to worry and
     Hassle free, so once again, I can just be me.

Susan T. Pollard

In Memory Of Shirley McAninch

A year has gone by since you passed away
You've been in our thoughts every single day

The wonderful memories are in our hearts
Memories of you that will never part

You were a wonderful woman in every way
Both wife and mother and grandmother to Eric and D.J.

We all miss you very much
Your loving heart and gentle touch

I can't express the extreme sadness I still feel
But I keep remembering that time will heal

As time goes by people say the pain will ease
I hope they are right—dear God, please

Help me be strong and get me through each day
Of living my life this different way

Without my mother—my best friend
Help me remember that this isn't the end

I know I will see her again someday
In heaven with God in such a peaceful way

I Love You Mom
     Kristily Downey

Raven's Eye

Peer into the raven's eyes
See the darkness which in there lies
Screeching victims and torturous cries
Earthly loneliness in which no one dies

Black black black is its soul
The murky abyss a bottomless hole
Heartfelt fires which take there toll
Encased in earth no diamond just coal

Loneliness screams in an ancient tongue
The madness in full bloom has just begun
Caught in the maelstrom to which you were flung
Trapped by compassion's inability to run

Feel not alone for others are here
Many are caught in the ravens leer
Held tight in its talons held tight by there fear
Eyes now of mist a lost souls last tear

Mark S. Lomax

Untitled

I turned around,
  long ago.
And haven't had the courage
  to look back.
I heard them yelling
  and pleading for reason,
But way back then,
  I was happier,
So I keep on going,
  searching,
  for those times again.

Erica F. Johnson

A Special Friend

What made us friends,
long ago when we
first met?

Well, I think I know...
The best in me and
the best in you
Hailed each other
because they knew
That always and always
since life began,
Our being Friends was
part of God's Plan?

Darleen Davis

"Dreams"

Dreams of today
long for tomorrow;
yet, when tomorrow is today,
all that remains
are dreams of yesterday....

John M. Lotz

Futility

Idly I sat beneath a tree
looking at nature and nature at me
long I sat beneath that tree
until soon the sun told time on me
The leaves scattered thick upon the grass
I raked them up unto a huge brown mass
The wind laughed and blew in glee
as the leaves blew about recklessly.

Donald E. Strang

The Death Of A Poet

I am poised over a lonely grave
  looking into the forlorn sky
the body of an anonymous poet
  why did he have to die?

Was it because the man was hungry,
  for a love that could not be?
Why did he have to die?
  This ancient part of me

He was a soldier lost at war
  the hunted of a hunters hound
and now the memories gone
  and a grave is all I've found

I don't know what I did
  in the bliss of that moment free
what a choice for death to stalk
  why did it have to be me?

Jeremy West

My Only Dream

I sit for many hours,
looking out in space.
I think of what I wish to be,
and try to seek my place.

I set my goals and try my best,
I shall try my hardest and
I will try no less.
I will try to succeed
at a splendorous rate,
Then, and only then, I will step down.
and count on fate.

I know what I dream of,
I know it is rare.
I know if I want to make it,
I must pay my fare.
I know that my goal is much
more than extreme.
But what is the use of living
If I didn't have my only dream.

Joan Colli

She

Trapped in a world of disillusion
losing all her happiness.
Grasping to control herself
her only friend is loneliness.

She screams in silence
her pain locked up inside.
She always loses the battle
no matter how hard she tried.

Life, for her, is so hard to handle
she lives in a world of pain and fear.
The feelings is so deep and strong
like a never ending tear.

Everyday is the same
always searching for an answer.
But every answer is a lie
because the answer is inside her.

Jennifer Walker

Change

Our lives were inseparable,
Loving, happy, carefree,
I for you, you for me.
  Or so we thought.

But the closer we got,
The more lies we were living.
The rumors and stories kept growing.
  We could not escape.

Now we again are free,
Like before, but not in heart,
Ready for a fresh new start.
  We will succeed...apart.

Diane Marie Mertens

Untitled

Often times being all-knowing
Means knowing all of nothing.
Having a full knowledge of the universe
Doesn't make you smart
Knowing yourself-
Understanding your feelings
Makes you a genius

Beth Mayer

You Didn't Love Me,
You Didn't Care...

When I left you told me
lots of things.
You told me that you loved me,
You told me that you cared.

You said that you would
wait for my return,
Would never forget me,
Always care for me and
Always be there.
Lies, all of it was lies.

When I returned you were gone.
You had given your heart
and love to someone else.

  You didn't love me...
  You didn't care...

Juana Aguirre

In The Blink Of A Life

In the blink of a life,
Love is Eternity.
Just as love's hurts and letdowns
Are forever-prolonged agonies,
Thrusting even powerful-minded heads
Into the nadir of conscious existence,
Love's sweet tendernesses
Ignite eternal rapture,
Elevating even a simple soul
To a timeless zenith only God knows.
It's such ill logic really.
To remember this tempest
Tempers all;
And emotions fall prey
To this more modern notion:
Those so fortunate
Marry practically in love.

Daniel Barton Goldstein

This Thing Called Love

I could hear people say,
"Love is in the air,"
But could someone have told me
What this thing called love means?

Then, I could hear people say,
"I love you,"
But could someone have explained to me
What this thing called love does?

Then I could hear people say,
"Love hurts,"
But could someone have shown me
What this thing called love is?

Then I heard you,
You told me,
"I love you,"
And finally I understood
What this thing called love was!

Geraldine Revaz

Alisha

Always on time.
Loving to others.
I am caring all the time.
Sharing my things.
Helping mom.
Always thinking of my family.

Alisha Renea Greer

Love Is

A gentle cool breeze
Love is present
Walking the plains
Love walks with you
The calm of nature's sounds
Love whispers softly
The smell of wildflowers
Love is enchanting
The breeze stirs in sudden violence
Love is angry
The sun sets
Love is leaving
Wildflower petals blown away
Love is not

Chris Voss

Untitled

Soulmates we,
Love so pure,
Drawn together through the dance,
Reflections of our past
revealed through our dreams,
the crystal ball twirls,
We embrace, the fragrances of perfumes
surround us as we dance,
The words "I love you" sung.
A friendship new, our promises
Sealed with a kiss.
Soulmates, we.

Hope Mantoen

For Thee

O' the love I have for thee
Makes it hard for me to breath;

O' the happiness I have for thee
leads me not to see;

O' the joy I wish for thee
Reminds me of the deep blue sea;

O' the love I wish for thee
Is the love that comes from me;

O' the love I want to give to thee
Is coming from the best part of me.

Jamie Hrisanthacopoulos

Colors

How many shades of flesh exist?
Many there are indeed.
How many people are racist?
Before you answer take heed!
If you're not _____,
Then when you see
A person
You see not black,
Nor white,
Nor any other color,
All you see when you look at this person
Is the absence of color.
Hate
Is a very strong word
Think
Before you use it.
Look
At the colors you see
Think
Before you choose it!

Amanda Jauken

Forever My Love!

May my love always be with you
May it stay right by your side
May you never have to look for love
Because mine I could never hide
May our days and nights together
Always and forever last
May our days and nights apart
Go by quickly and fast
May the love we have and share
Keep us together and strong
May the way we feel for each other
Last our whole life long
May I always be yours
And you forever be mine
Because a love like ours
Comes once in a life time
May you always remember the things
That we have shared together
Because baby you know I love you
Today, always and forever.

Albert Saraceno

Pretend

Out of the past comes a Legend,
    Maybe it's not even true.
But if you will listen, I'll tell you.
    Pretend that it's me and you.

Once there lived a Maiden
    In a castle high on a hill.
She was so very lonesome
    Her life was so dull and so still.

One day a handsome stranger
    Rode by on a horse white and fine.
He happened to see the Maiden
    And he said, "One day she'll be mine."

But real life is never like that
    For dreams very seldom come true
Fairy tales, only have happy endings
    Still pretend it's me and you.

Cathy Wilson

Just A Word

Empty Nothing
Means nothing
In the morning I say
"I wish it were evening"
In the evening I say
I wish it were morning NOTHING
No help to anybody...
No desire to do anything
Good or bad
I FEEL USELESS

Who can describe NOTHING?
Empty space
Sometimes black and scary
Other times it's dull gray NOTHING
No way out,
like thick fog, too dense to see in-
WHERE IS THE LIGHT?
who will help me? Who loves me?
whom do I love?
Is love just a word?

Ann G. Henderson

Let Me

Float
Me high above
So I can see Beyond Me.

Let me compose a word
Equalize the world
and walk the treetops.

Let me be scared,
toss my nerves
shake with life
melt with color.

Let me touch hope
coax it to the ground
and set it free!

Let me slice a breath
and eat it while I sleep.

Let me.

Jamie Jochum

The One And Only Future

I think of the past as just
    memories.
And the future as wishes
    coming true.
Knowing when a mistake
    happened in the past
Will never be changed.
Knowing the future I will
    not make the same mistake twice.
Living in the present can
    only happen once.
Living in the past will never
    happen again.
Remembering the past and hoping
    for the future,
Is living in the present.

Amanda Faye

Fame

Crows' shadows lengthen
Midst the leafless glade and wood
Winter's reign complete

John H. Steffens

A Simple Rhyme

If the night wakes up in the
middle of the day, if all of the
sudden a dismal gray.

We'll take our hearts and head
for the moon, dance on its beams
and sing out of tune.

Relish on laughter and our happiness,
together there we'll both exist.

Saddle our souls and fly away,
gallop across the Milky Way.

Drift through the galaxies to
another planet, with our brilliant
dreams we'll enchant it.

Look to the stars with gentle
care, bless our souls and just be there.

To dance through space and forget
about time, to waste eternity
on this simple rhyme.

Heidi Louise Meyer

Follow The River

Follow the river
Mighty Nile River
To the land of enchantment
Swift and strong
Rolling and twisting
And yet ever so alive
Follow the river
Life giver to Egypt
Life bearer to the city
Of eternity
Follow the river
Sacred Nile River
To the valley of the sun

Ever McKinney

Natural Love

With the sun rising,
    Misty mountains at dawn.
My heart yearns for you,
    To hold you in my arms.
A gently rolling stream,
    Soon to be a raging river.
They flow like my love,
    My heart beating quicker.
I see a eagle fly,
    Soaring with his mate.
My desire for you grows,
    Gliding on wings of fate.
The day we are together,
    With love we will tremble.
To be as one with nature,
    Loving on forever.

James L. Fisher

The Voice Of The Unborn Child

My body formed today.
Mom can you see how beautiful I am.
I started to move around.
Check this out, I have feet and toes.
Punch! Punch! Kick! Kick!
Can you feel that.
Mom God speaks to me.
He said I have a plan for you.
God said I will touch many people.
They will walk again.
I have grown so big.
I want to chase the butterflies.
I want see a rainbow.
Mom what happened.
I am so cold.
Don't let them take me.
Where have I gone.
I don't feel your heart anymore.
Mom I love you...Goodbye.
I will be in heaven waiting for you.

Gloria Daniels

Nature's Secret

Down deep in the forest,
nature hides something from us.

A secret everyone wants to know,
that only the one true God can show.

Everything is made in his image,
and nothing about it is garbage.

Always remember God's creatures,
have some special features.

Cassidy Brannin

Untitled

Flower budding early, too soon
Moon brightness, dim glare
Time passing, eternal noon
Eyes glisten, faint stare

Faith Albers

Loneliness

My children mean so much to me;
    more of them I wish I'd see
But now they're gone and on their own;
    so many days I feel alone
As I look back on years gone by;
    I feel a tear slip from my eye
My precious children once so small;
    have grown to be so big and tall
I tried to teach them right from wrong;
    and pray somehow they'd get along
The years went by so very fast;
    I can't believe they're grown at last
Each child went their separate way;
    but in my heart they'll always stay
Please keep them safe I pray at night;
    then everything will turn out right
When I no longer walk this earth;
    I hope that I have earned their worth
A mother's love cannot compare;
    there's nothing greater anywhere.

Dianne Mathys

Mother

Thank you for the memories,
More precious do they grow.
Memories that tell stories
Of life and love long ago.

Thank you for the loving heart,
That could give and forgive.
A heart that truth did impart,
Instilling the will to live.

Thank you for warmth and cheer
Which filled each new day.
Life for you held no fear,
Love would show the way.

Thank you for each hug and kiss,
And lovely smile so dear.
Your sweet love I truly miss,
And long for throughout the year.

Dorothy A. Wallace

Family Love And Friendship

I love all my family
More than words could ever say.
It's wonderful to have love and
Friendship in such a happy way.
My love grows for all of you
Every single day.
My heart fills with joy
When I think of all of you
There are times when a little
Something special comes
From some of you
It's when one calls me
    MOM or GRANDMA
God has made all my dreams
    come true

Gail Dianne Tew

"The Last Mile"

When I was but a little child
Mother said to me,
"Come let me tell you about the
Road of life, as you set upon my knee.

Oh, it's so very narrow,
Hills to climb every day,
But God will be with you,
He will lead the way.

I will walk the road ahead of you
And up the Golden stairs.
When you climb the long last hill,
I will be waiting there."

She left the world below,
Found her Heavenly place.
When I walk that long last mile,
I will see her smiling face.

Ethel Mobley

I Know Why Raindrops Cry

It's hard to see a raindrop cry
Must be why the Nile flows up
Some say backward like a flat nosed,
dark-skinned, thick-haired woman
who said she didn't know if her
flat-nosed, dark-skinned,
coarse-haired mama came from Africa
Must be why the Nile flows up
doesn't act like other rivers
but a river, it certainly is

Then I knew why weeping willows weep
how a Bonsai tree must feel

It's hard to see a raindrop cry
Woman said her daddy was Indian
had white folks on her tree
but her beautiful dark-skinned, flat-nosed,
coarse-haired mama won't no DAMN African
No Siree, mama won't no DAMN Africa

Then I knew why raindrops cry
folks able to feel the rain and now know it's
wet!

April M. Williams

Today

I feel myself to be primitive.
My body yearns to dance.
To be painted with blazing colors.
To be adorned with bright feathers.

Today my heart yearns
for the call of the macaw,
for the howl of the monkey,
for the roar of the jaguar.

Today I am exile:
So far away from the meadow,
so far away from the river.
I am at home in the rain forest.

Today I feel myself as I, truly, am.
Today I am a savage.
Today I am as beautiful as an ocelot.

I want to sing.
I want to dance.

I want to paint my body with blazing colors.
I want to sing and dance, in the rain forest,
with you.

Julio I. Aviles

It's In Him

Oh what a wretched man I am
my heart it wanders so
It is filled with sin and longing
For pleasures better left untold.

My heart wanders to things of the future
It wanders to things of the past
It can't seem to find any peace
Any peace that will really last.

Then one day when the wind stood still
And my heart turned to a starry sky
I called upon a man named Savior
And oh what a great surprise.

To know that Jesus loves me
And watches over me so
That all I need do is call his name
And the peace it begins to flow.

It's in him I have found fulfillment
It is him that's my hearts desire
It is him that has turned my pain to joy
And lit down deep a fire.

Judith Thompson

Till Death Do Us Part

The weekend had come,
my hell had begun.
Sure, I love him
so what he does
Shouldn't matter.
Yet I knew he'd begin drinking.
The bottle had gained control,
He loves it more than me.
Would we make it home alright?
Did I want to go home?
Oh God, last weekend!
It wasn't his fault.
I got in his way.
Right?
He slammed me against the wall.
He struck me!
But I love him; so I'll stay.
I wish,
The weekends would
Never come.

Jessi James

Through My Window

I wish I knew my land
My homeland
In the place where freedom bound
With respect, unity and love

Our land was watered with tears
    we were taken away
We struggled, vehemently struggled
but we were too far, too far away

I could hear their voices
My brothers, my sisters, my land.
    If only I could return
to the soul of my people
to dance with a drum beat.

My heart is shattered, broken to pieces,
my eyes surrounded with tears
I feel lonely, sometimes desperate
I wish to die, I'm too far
When will I embrace you.
        Eternally

Donald Etienne

Come In From The Rain

Come in from the rain,
my love.
Allow me to warm you
with all that I am.
The chill has crawled
beneath your skin.
Your lips are reluctant
beneath my kiss.
Come close and breath deep.
The drops may continue to fall
but if you, my love,
come in from the rain,
I will soften their sting and
give you something to live for
once, again.

Crystal Ferraro

Child Of Hawaii

Farewell Hawaii
My own sweet love,
I must fly away today,
Across the sea
To another land
Far, far away.
How sad you are to see me go,
How sad I am to part
From all the love and happiness
That is deep within my heart.
Your clear blue sky
Has turned to grey,
Your lovely sounds grow dim,
As I leave to cross the sea
I hold your love within.
Aloha sweet Hawaii,
Until we meet again.

Audrey H. Weddington

Poem, Prayers And Promises

A poem of love,
My prayers for you,
and promises of love,
That's true.

Janice Grable

"In The End"

The river flows from dark to light,
My ship is sailing out of sight.
It doesn't mean our friendship ends,
It simply means "the river bends."

Dawn Tienken Karlich

A Grain Of Mustard Seed

On a day still in the Holy Season
my heart full of prayerful reason
God saw that the good book arrived

Full of promise and heavenly grace
page after hopeful page, good cheer
for earth's heavy-hearted peoples

Words and pictures stir yearnings,
encourage faith, prod action so all
our tomorrows overflow with beauty

Bless the fruits of our goodness —
may the skies suckle our roots as
we devour our newest seed catalog.

Elmer Otte

Smiles

When I see you smile
My troubles fade away
What's in that smile
That makes a perfect day

To me a smile is precious
When I see it on your face
It brings me back to love
Saving me from hate

A smile spreads across your face
And puts a smile on mine
Your smile to me
Makes the dark world shine

One day you are not smiling
What seems to make you blue
So I set a smile on my face
To hopefully comfort you

Side by side with our smiles
We'll try to make it through
Helping each other...
I'll give my smile to you!

Josie Liming

Real Fantasies

His hands caress my shoulders, my
Neck they them massage.
A strange sensation engulfs me this
heart begins to enlarge.

His strong arms surround me, they
Hold me just right.
I'm scared of these feelings making
My insides feel tight.

His kiss tastes so sweet, his lips so
inviting.
Each time we're together, it's so damn
Exciting.

Is this reality or a fantastic
Dream.
Together we'd make such a great
Team.

Fantasies come true and hopefully
Mine will.
Heart once emptied, beginning now to fill

Jeaniemarie Alfieri

The Boy Heroes At Chapultepec

Mexico City
needs no pity
California city
No, don't tell me
Boy heroes
Boy zeros?
Some dying for a piece of cloth
Now, who would have thought!
Some as young as thirteen
Now, that was then, 1847
Today at 7-Eleven
Mexico against the U.S.
For each other's country, yes?
for a color and street and being bad
No, it was for a flag
Dying for respect, honor and don't forget pride
Now what do they get in return, a prize?
A memorial with flowers on the street?
No, at the foot of the castle of Chapultepec.

Elizabeth Rios

An Ode To Our Dogs

"Can Ginger (puppy) come to play?"
Neighbor children called out.
As she grew, she liked to swim
Even considered playing cards.

Rags had a great disposition
Gave us two litters of puppies
Car-pooled with the family
West in '66, East in '68
Fellow traveler for 17 years.

Brown pedigreed poodle Adam Pierre
Vacationed with us and grandchildren
In Minnesota at Hand Lake; fun except
When he hid under the house in fear
Of "Satan" a German Shepherd.

Little Orphan "Annie" came on a snowy
January 5, 1979. Our paper girl: "Mom says
It's your turn to take this stray."
Her disposition delighted, amused us 16 years.
A good smoocher, arthritis took its toll.
The Last Leaf on The Tree.

Julia Strain Fangmeier

Life

Life is a challenge
Never knowing what
Obstacles will head your way

To survive each day
You must have courage,
The ability to face defeat,
The ability to keep living

When tragedy strikes
Face it with praise
For it could be worse

When glory strikes
Face it with pity
For it could be better

With all of this
You must remember
Life is a challenge

Alan G. Ray

True Love Never Dies

Always from the heart and
never will it part!

Like a flower that
blossoms in the spring.
Always reaching out for
lovelier things!

Runs like water from the
morning dew.
Always lying next to you!

Like the branches on a
grapevine.
Always there to
intertwine!

Like a story that
unfolds.
Always there to have and
to hold!

Like the sun in the
afternoon.
Always there to soothe you!

Clorinda Blackwell Jeter

"Friendly Tree"

Oh gnarled tree and bare,
no birdies on limbs outflung;
snow coat wraps your trunk
warding off cold winter's blast
till Spring rains leaf you again.

Amy Stone

The Magic Of Love

No one can explain it,
No matter how they try.
It's not any one thing,
But millions, wrapped in a sigh.

It's springtime and flowers.
It's a kitten's first yawn.
It's magical music,
And it's dew on leaves at dawn.

It's warm summer evenings.
It's wintertime's first snow.
It's puppies at playtime,
And it's a fireside glow.

It's angels in Heaven.
It's Christmas in a jar.
It's a breeze from the sea,
And it's a friend from afar.

It's golden leaves in fall.
It's a snowy white dove.
However you see it,
This is the magic of love.

Carolyn Henderson

"Time To Go"

Don't put me in the ground I plead.
No one hears, no one takes heed.

I wonder why my heart did quit?
I never gave my thought to it.

Don't put me in the cold hard ground,
I had plans to make another round.

Wild horses that I planned to ride,
Places to go with my wife by my side.

As I think back over the years,
I wonder at my family's tears.

I've ridden the wind, fought good fights,
Been in and out of some terrible tights.

I've been up and I've been down,
In all these years I've been around.

I've fathered some sons, long and tall,
Looking back, I've done it all.

So father, if my time is here,
Let my friends all shed a tear.

Not because I passed away,
But because an era ended today.

Joe N. Brown

Liver And Onions

Liver and onions won't cure bunions
Nor can they shoo the blues
But they can cause little boys
To create such a noise
When that's the dinner you choose

Darlet D. McGurer

The Mystery Of Friendship

Friendship is not a mystery
Nor is it hard to find,
The real reason friends are friends
And are always so divine

They laugh when you are happy
They cry when you are sad
They play when you are lonesome
And they always make you glad

They are always there to lean on
They never gossip or make a face
But they're always there to comfort you
And to come together in grace

Friendship is not a mystery
Nor is it hard to find,
The real reason friends are friends
And are always so divine.

Erin L. Huven

A Rose

A rose, strong and proud
Not afraid to be loud
Soft and tender petals
Sharp and poky thorns
Like a red devil's horns
A rose is romantic on a first date
Get one for your mate.
It's natural and true.
A very beautiful thing
A person is like a rose.
delicate and dangerous.
A person can be just as
beautiful if they wish it.
A rose never fades away
As long as you believe in it.
Romance is like a rose
rough yet soft.

Jennifer M. Connolly

Raven Night

The sky is a black as velvet
Not even the stars are shining.
There are puddles on the sidewalk.
And the garden is muddy.

I am sitting on the window-seat.
Staring outside and thinking.
Just thinking - about you.
About me, and about us.

What happened, what failed?
Where did I go wrong?
If only I would have.....
But, I didn't.

It's too late now.
Everything is over.
Somehow it died.
Alone, in the cold darkness.

Nothing could save us.
Love died alone in a
Night as black as velvet
Where no stars were shining.

Jacque Moriarty

Not In This Place

My sunrise does not come
Not in this place
The sky is a dark plum purple
Shaded with blackness.

The fire is always burning
it never goes away
Not in this place.
It glowing in the darkness.

Where have I put myself
A dark purple sky
teasing my mind for hours
the endless hours
with only a slight
orange sunrise glow.

A huge ring of orange cloud
This night does not end
Not in this place.

Heather Rudolph

Good Bye

Through countless memories I travel
    Not knowing which way to turn,
I'll take the good and bear the bad
    only guided by what I've learned.

The hardest is trying to forget you
    when your heart is my only light,
Trying to fight this feeling
    When it's holding on too tight.

Can't live my life without you
    even as days go by...
Even though it was only love
    to me, you're always saying good-bye.
    Good bye.

Dawn Hodous

Untitled

We had you but a few short years,
Not near enough it seems.
We shared your hopes and fears,
We helped you dream your dreams.
God saw fit to take you home,
His reasons I don't know
For you my heart is lonesome
It hurts to let you go.

Knowing that you are happy there,
Helps to ease the pain.
For my loss is nothing but
The mighty Savior's gain.

When you look down on me below,
I hope it's my smile you see.
For in my heart you did bestow,
Many wonderful memories!

Carin Petracco

The Heart

God made our hearts, they're
not perfect hearts, there
seems to be something missing;
that something I think is love,
and as we live we find
a spiritual love, we learn and
understand until we die.
Then I hope we all become
a perfect heart. God said
we are one.

John Orlich

My Life

    My life is an error, a mistake
not yet corrected and never to
be as expected. I'm a question not
yet answered, I'm a confused
soul forced to exist in the corps
of a wonderer, why must I hide
from the truth. Do I really
have to put on an act just to
please others' meaningless lives.
Or are we all just puppets leaving
our choices, and actions up to
someone else to control. It's
just another song and dance...

Jesse Karkoski

No More

Another broken heart
Nothing new to me
The tears appear once again
I guess this is how it should be

Never trusting anyone
Because I want to hurt no more
Keeping only to myself
Locking, bolting the door

I've always opened myself up
Trusting everyone I met
Now that I've been hurt so much
It's something I regret

Never again I tell myself
Whatever it takes I'll do
To keep my heart from breaking
And to keep it from turning blue

Now I must close my door
And keep myself locked in
No more is my life an open book
For that's what it's always been.

Deanna N. Giddings

Shadow Side

Her tears are always wasted, like rain
nourishing nothing
She's so tired of the taste of salt.
And in the cold, dark days of November,
her arms are empty.
There've been too many slivers left to
fester and overflow
The pungent smell of dead love.
She laments, "Why do I need at all?"

Diana Dolhancyk

The Magical Midnight Moment

In the deepest darkness,
There comes a fleeting moment
Unnoticed by all...
As today becomes yesterday,
There is a brief stop
In the clock of eternity
When all you have is the now.
There was no yesterday,
There is no tomorrow.
This is the magical midnight moment
In the precise middle of the night
When most are dreaming with hope
For a bright tomorrow.

Sondra Weiss

Jonathan

Little boy out in the rain
now has a chest cold pain
please hear grandfather's prayer
I know he can recover
help me win this poetry plea
almost all the prize money
for grandfather George poetry
I will give Jonathan free
that way we know his Father
can provide a warm cover
created for child and Mother
Someplace there is a home school
treatment kind not so cruel
Family help is the key
What an opportunity,
library of poetry
Jonathan is only three
sheltered by his family.

George M. Butterfield

Helper, Utah

It started out a booming town
Now it lies here crumbling down
Farming fields and mining coal
Was bred into every young man's soul
Memories of years gone and past
This struggling town just seems to last
It was a town of hopes and dreams
Nothing here is what it seems
Roaring engines and railroad cars
Now depression has left its scars
Years of history locked in its heart
Just tears this little town apart
Generations come and go
Burying treasures of long ago.

Frankie Hathaway

Love

I love you with all my heart,
May we love and never part;
Go through this world hand in hand
Until we get to that Heavenly land.

Pray then we're still hand in hand,
Then we'll join that Heavenly band;
Praise, sing, laugh and rejoice,
Now we will be with God, by choice.

We'll wait, dear one, for all the rest,
Praying always they'll pass the test;
Then we'll live in a mansion of gold,
Know all about Jesus, as we were told.

Cheryl Toothman

The Companion

You are my champion
My companion and my friend.
The path that you have shown me
I've etched into my brain.

If I should ever wander
Down some unfamiliar plane
Then I'll close my eyes and hear you
And I'll find my way again.

Some things I'll know to choose from
Some things I will refrain
For when I'm alone and quiet,
I still hear you call my name.

Drew Wilkins

Untitled

I remember you
Now that you are gone
The joyful times, the laughter
The times of tears, however few
The things we did, where we went
Our long talks on the kitchen floor
The way you smiled, the way you spoke
The long, lazy days
And the nights on the town
I remember you
Now that I'm alone
I think back
Over what we've done
And my hearts aches
For what was once
And what we had
I miss you

Amanda Wills

"Dreams Unknown"

Dreams came to me in visions,
of anguish and despair.
Then suddenly it happened,
for the Lord was standing there.
Saying in a voice so clear,
I heard Him speak; He said!
fret not my child, I love you
listen! But do not fear.
These dreams were meant to happen,
In such an awesome way.
Each one will tell a story,
Revealed on judgement day.
Pray now with the Holy Spirit
for He'll keep you strong and brave
He'll show you in these visions
that God He really saves.
Speak of Him to others,
for forgiveness of their sins.
Reach out to Him with repentance
before this old world ends.

Charlotte Jinks

Eighteen

I remember the feeling
  of being eighteen
how my heart skipped a beat
  with each telephone ring

Then you'd just say "Hi
  let's go to a show."
As I'd dress for our date
  I could feel myself glow.

We'd laugh and we'd talk
  until dawn's breaking light,
then whisper "I love you"
  as you kissed me goodnight.

They say that young passion
  will fade and grow dim
when you're no longer agile
  or no longer slim.

But I remember how young love
  can make your heart soar.
When you hold me now, darling,
  I'm eighteen once more.

Constance R. Phipps

The World

The world is full
of birds and bees
and apple trees:
there so nice like
sugar and spice,
If you like it
sweet keep it neat!

Debbie Pixley

Depth

Through an aura
of fog
a whispering voice
reached me and I
felt as one
with the ether,
catching a glimpse
of beyond beyond,
into endlessness.

Dorothy P. Kilham

Remember

I think of David Goldstein,
  of Jacqueline Rosenberg,
    of Esther Coh ....
      of Ruth J ....
        of D ...
          of ...
            o ...
Silence.

Birgit Schettler

"The Angel Of Light"

As I awoke to see the Angel
Of Light at the foot of my
bed, a tear dripped off
the poor, white face.
  "Why are you weeping?" I
asked. She replied by saying
that the Spirit of darkness
had taken the light from
her soul.
  "Take my hand and
help me," she said. As I
reached out to get her hand,
everything I had seen - disappeared.
I remembered that poor,
white face and the
tear and realized that
the spirit of darkness...
was me.

Ashlie Coakley

"The Golden Haired Lady"

Ha, Little golden mother
Of love, laughter and tears,
Woman of such beauty and love
Little lady of the golden hair.

Such love to feel and behold
Oh, The sweetness of soul love.

To come only in peace of mind
To give only in rapture of soul.

Where fore the hate and bitterness?
When such love to give is yours!

Fred Royal

The Voice Of A Captive Wolf

The wind fills him with the scent
of meadow and wood,
while the bite of the fence-wire
fills his mouth with blood and
bitter iron.

His nose cannot find the trail
his spirit longs to follow,
the trail past the fence and
into the wild.

He sits in his pen and howls,
for hunt and mate
and cub and play;
he howls.

David Negaard

Window Sill of My Life

I sit inside the window sill
  of my life left still untold

I am looking out striving to see
  if I am timid or I am bold

I am looking out and watching
  the story of my life unfold

It's like I'm watching a movie,
  yet it's my future it beholds

I'll wait for it to end, I'll wait for
it forever, my life must still be told

Cristina Burton

Tilt Of A Lilt

A lilt with a tilt
of the head to get a
lilt of the heart?
'Tis not smart
to lead with the heart
for it leads to a lilt
to get a tilt of the heart..
Leading to a lark
of the heart
which isn't smart...
For this old heart..
'Tis a lark.
So this is a lilt a
tilt of lark of the heart.

Harold L. Bock

Savored Moments

Why is it that the good things in life
  never stay long?
And no one ever seems to choose
  right over wrong?

Why do we look past
  the good things we have,
And we pay more attention
  to the things that are bad?

We need to savor every moment
  of every living day,
Because when the end comes
  your debts you'll have to pay.

So speak with your heart,
  and sweetness do not lack.
For it is only the harsh words
  that you cannot take back.

Erica Black

Dreaming

As I sit here dreaming in my chair
Of the times that I've been through,
I can almost hear the laughter of
The little ones I knew.

I can hear the quiet of evening
When the long day's work is through,
It seems I hear my mother singing
Just the way she used to do.

I can hear the sweet sweet music
I was young and life was new,
I was asked a solemn question
And I answered, yes I do.

You may think my time I'm wasting
But it's not just like it seems,
I am spending happy moments
In the shadows of my dreams.

I have tasted all life's pleasures
And I know which ones are best,
So I'll just keep the ones I cherish
And forget about the rest.

Julia Pettijohn

Gypsy Night

High o'er the wind
Of the wide-flung moor
Gypsy voices move,
And through the glow
Of the wild fire's heat
Dark eyes seek their own.

Gone from the cliff
The white clouds blowing,
Laughing in the night,
And smooth the trail
Of the caravan
Golden in the dust.

Frances Ridgway

"Searching"

The ocean pale and blue,
mixes with the sky
and gently washes upon the sand.
A single bird flies overhead
searching for the flock.

Jeanine Adams

The Handy Work Of God

The handy work of God,
Oh, how great to see,
What our precious Lord
  has done,
The beauty of our land
  and sea,
Also the heritage we
  can receive,
If we all would only
  believe.
The word of God is
  powerful,
It tells us how we
  are saved,
He leads us to Jesus,
  The one who died
  for us.

Helene Mittelsteadt

Le Lac

Onrushing time suspend thy flight!
Oh, swiftly fleeting hours of night
Linger awhile, for love must flee
Before the dawn's invading light.

Flow on for those who sigh in vain
For death to rid them of their pain;
Harken to them and heed us not;
Bear them along, let us remain.

But while for brief respite we yearn,
Youth's golden hours lightly turn
Upon the dial and softly say
In parting: "We shall ne'er return."

One last embrace for dawn is near!
The heavens are deaf and will not hear.
The gods but scorn us when we pray;
Soon love lies rigid on her bier.

Kenneth S. Christensen

Yet You Ask...

A blending of savory delights,
Oh, the aroma is so nice,
Something wonderful for our appetites.
Yet you ask, "Did you wash that?"

I comb the grocers and specialty shops,
Only the best ingredients will do.
Not the stalks I say, only the tops.
Yet you ask, "Did you drop that?"

The kitchen is my studio,
The plate is my canvas,
This work should be on video.
Yet you ask, "Did you peel that?"

The way I combine all my exotic spices,
Is a secret that makes chefs cry,
Knowing such flavor entices
Yet you ask, "Did you use all of that?"

I turn with only LOVE in my heart,
As you smile so joyfully,
I know you want to do your part.
So I ask, "WHO'S DOING THIS, ME OR
YOU?"

Benjamin J. Stephens

Sandcastles

As we sit and watch
Our children play,
Our minds remember
And drift away.

We see two children playing,
Running hand in hand.
Laughing and singing,
Around castles of sand.

A place of magic,
And make a wish.
Imagination, love,
And a healing kiss.

Make-believe was always,
A place to play.
As we grow older,
It fades away.

But if you ever need it,
And no one understands.
Just call me up, take time out,
And I'll meet you in the sand.

James M. Spor Jr.

A Lovely Moment

Fading daylight burst suddenly
  on a flock of birds
  that graciously settled
  outside my winter
  window-
And devoured all the feed set
  on the table for sparrows

They never made a sound
  then rose with the
  golden edge of day
  to the west-
The evening grosbeaks
  were a lovely moment
  riding on the sunset

Anne B. Pavlovsky

Look For Me...

If I should fly tonight, my love,
On migrant wing of holy dove
Let not salt tears eclipse sun face
Or sorrow slow your joyful pace
But look for me in crowded wood
And fertile fields of brotherhood
Come fly with scarlet bird through sky
On winds that soothe despairing sigh
And swim the ocean, lake and sea
To find where I can only be
If I should fly tonight, my love,
On migrant wing of holy dove.

Jean Sterling

An Image

I walked through the sand
On the beach by the sea.
I imagined you there
Walking with me.
We talked as we strolled
Of the dreams that we shared.
Of much we loved
And how much we cared.
Then darkness fell
On the sand and the sea.
And a cold chill
Came over me.
I turned to you
And you were drifting away.
Along with the sun
And what we shared that day.
'Twas only a dream
But so real was the touch.
I miss you my darling
And love you so much.

Antoinette Thompson

My Child

You are just as good as anyone
My child
Beautifully created like the sun
My child

You are as lovely as a dove
My child
Your heart is gentle and filled with love
My child

In God's image were you made
My child
Your skin is just a darker shade
My child

Cassandra Walker

Lying Alone I Remember

Lying alone
On the cold bed
All these memories
Go through my head
I thought I did right
I tried as hard as I could
But you yelled at me last night
As I thought you would
I remember the passion
I remember the pain
I remember all the good things
You used to say
I remember the laughter
I remember the tears
I remember you just standing there
How I wish I could bring
Those memories back
But everything I remember
Is in the past

Christina Whittle

The Hall Of Fame

Much better is wisdom than gold,
On this rugged pathway to life-
To reverence and fear our Maker
Will eliminate wrong and strife.

Those with understanding are 'cool,'
And know, when their words to restrain,
All wise people with common sense
Teach others how not to cause pain.

Constructive criticism is
Profitable for a good name-
Any who will choose to listen
Should be in wise men's hall of fame!

Success comes to those who commit
Everything they do to the Lord-
A cup of water in Christ's name
Can bring an eternal reward.

It's beyond our expectations
The place Christ has gone to prepare
For the wise men who still seek HIM
Will spend eternity up there!

Carolyn F. Marquis

"I Am A Woman White"

I am a woman white
Oppressed by being an oppressor
In ancestral times
And now
Because the color of my skin
Won't allow me to be anything else.
My color overrides my sex
Allows me to forget
The prejudices against me
And put them on someone else.
I do not want to be this way
But the color of my skin
Opens corporate doors for me
And closes all others.
I am an oppressor
Trying to save her skin
From the imposed prejudice
That says I am an oppressor
And in doing so
I make myself so.

Christian Blair

Change

I see the picture,
Once filled with laughter
Now covered with tears.
    What has happened? War.

I read the letters
Once messengers of love -
Now forgotten old sheets
    What has happened? War.

I hear the song,
Once signs of hope -
now they grew silent.
    What has happened? War.
I miss you.

Angela Berg

Widows Walk

I see the ghost upon the rise
Once murdered by the sea
Still sailing beneath starless skies
On ships of altered destiny

They swore of safe and swift returns
To their lovers as they wept
Though they wallowed in their promises
Cruel waters would not let them keep

Outstretched hands at every tide
Tightly shackled in the abyss
They scale the shores at every side
And reach for one last kiss

I stand alone in this haunted strand
Of dreams forever faded
No ships at land from where I stand,
In this walk where once she waited

These ghosts of mine will never die
Their peace can never be
I envision the fear with an anxious eye
And gaze out at the sea

Brian Stack

Whiny

There was a boy who played with M-90's
One day he got popped in the heiny,
    he ran around and
    he fell on the ground,
And from then on he was called whiny

Brandon Rinaldo Tidwell

"Could It Be"

Rowing down a river,
On a moonlit night.
The moon cries rays of beauty,
That shimmer, sparkle, bright.

The crickets sing their song of love,
Oft on the shore..
The harmonic sounds of peacefulness,
Romantic to adore.

Surien is the feeling,
With you gently in my arms.
And your eyes reflect the moonbeams,
Your smile insists your charms.

A smile comes now, from Heaven,
Could it be he had it planed?
You and I together,
forever, hand in hand!!

Jeffrey A. Davis

Shorty Lee

A fine day I'll always remember
One late fall in early November
The year nineteen eighty, on day two
You were born, I finally met you

On Sunday morning at six-o-eight
You wanted out, I could not wait
A boy who weighed only five pounds
With a tiny mouth that made cute sounds

Your name to pick was up to me
I decided upon Christopher Lee
At age ten you changed your name
Short and brave, you played the game

As a teen you'll be called Shortly Lee
Forever to me you are Christopher Lee
You will always be my best friend
I'll be there until the bitter end

I'll support your dreams and do all I can
While you grow into a little big man
I am only 4'10" - and all I have to say
Is that I love you, we're short, we're okay

Janet L. Bidegain

"Love Works In Mysterious Ways"

When time spent apart
only strengthens your love -

When the presence of the other
fills your heart with joy -

When a simple smile
speaks louder than words -

When a touch of the hand
comforts your heart -

When your dreams of love
are of being together-

When the time is right
you will know it in your hearts-

For love works in mysterious ways.

James Francis Saupan

"Relating"

One drop of water
Opalescent
Opens to me
Insights to ocean's
Iridescent
Infinity

Joan Warner Davidson

$ Money

Money, money
Oh, like sweet honey.

Just smelling money,
Doesn't even make my nose runny.

It is very sunny,
When there is money.
everything seems like
a funny bunny,
When there is money.

Oh yes, and money.....
Doesn't sing like Yanni!

Elli Karagiorgas

Loneliness

Like an ocean without waves
or a bird without a song
Like a person without love
Like a road that seems to long

They all are missing something
or someone that they need
And I am missing him
His eyes I could not read

I hardly had a chance
I let him slip away
And why he couldn't see my love
I really cannot say

But he slipped right through my fingers
I never let him know
My love was never-ending...
If he had only let me know...

Beth Handros

The Drifter

I wish that I could write a book
   Or do something,
To have people take a look
   And say,
"She did something for
   Immortality."

But it would seem that
   everything of note,
Has already been a penned fact
   Or said,
On every subject relative to life
   And destiny.
So I shall just drift
   To infinity.

Alberta M. Atkins

Ghost

Is a ghost someone you see
or is a ghost a loved one?
Is a ghost just some flying object?
Is a ghost dead,
does a ghost have feelings?
Ghost.
Can you touch a ghost?
Can you smell a ghost?
Can you talk to a ghost?
Can you fall in love with the ghost?
Will I ever get to touch the tears
of a
ghost?
Will I ever get to see a ghost?
Ghost,
Hear me, talk to me
Ghost
are you there?

Jeanette Davila

"Do You Trust Me?"

Do you trust me,
   Or is it just for others to see?
I can't stand the third degree
   From people who act just like me.
What else should I be?
   There is nothing left for you to see
Because she left me to
   Drown in my misery.

Andrew Wiecek

Untitled

You may like to play with dolls
Or wash all the dishes
You may have a lot of fun
And have many wishes

Perhaps you like to read books
Or go to Sunday School
Then every day as you play
Live out the Golden Rule

We pray God to bless your life
And ever keep you true
When you meet with trouble
May He see you through

May God use your life on Earth
To brighten someone's way
And give you many friends
To help you day by day

Beverly Hiltachk

Love Is A Drug

Are you my prescription?
Or will you be just a friend?
Will you become and addiction?
On which I will depend.

If you are my prescription
I hope you're more like a cure
If I'm down you'll pick me up
If I'm uncertain you'll make me sure.

Of course I would never overdose
For then I wouldn't Cope
Cause if you are my love cure
I'm nobody's dope.

I'll need you in double dose
The times that you're away
And all the time you're with me,
I'll love you more each day.

Elizabeth V. Basso

Why Patience?

Now Lord, we cry
Our anxious souls can't wait
We question ... Why?
Doesn't God hear my plight?

He sees the future
He knows what lies a head
He plans for us
His perfect will, instead.

We must ask for patience
Then quiet down and listen
Our problem is,
We are in a hurry, God isn't.

Florence Fuller

Wheat

Orange and then yellow,
Quickly moving pace,
Zig, zag,
The open road,
Loud gushes of wind,
Nothing in sight for miles except wheat,
Anticipation for my destination,
Every one in a while a little animal
pops out,
Singing, making up songs,
Not enjoying it until after it happens.

Allison Bullock

Why Should It Matter

   Why should it matter
our color of skin,
when what really counts
is the person within.
   Why should it matter
the shape of our eyes;
we should learn to love
instead of despise.
   Why should it matter
the language we speak,
because of man's prejudice
he is no longer meek.

Archie Walker

The Proposal

With the boundary of infinity
our growth is guaranteed.
Although distant the setting
and rising sun
the beauty rests within
and I equate to the feeling
when we're apart.

Now when our eyes meet
I experience a growing fullness
and our touching hands
and expanding warmth.
Then the hug, I know
its conclusion an emotional orgasm.

These are a few of my sound visions
and my concluding thought is
looking at a window
lit in the night
thoughts of you
bring me the moon.

Carl R. Miller

"Hope"

We stand upon this spinning sphere
Our thoughts so full of doubt and fear
Wondering why we were all put here
Hurtling toward no end.

The wind, it howls, the rain, it falls
Scratching at our self-made walls
As we wander endless halls
Searching for the questions.

Trying to grasp the point of life
As we face our pain and strife
In this world which seems so rife
With utter discontent.

The answers lay within each one
Never resting until it's done
Our noble quest, to find the sun
Shining upon our faces.

Joseph Wanshek

The Cat

The cat so sly and fast
Quickly glides from limb to limb
Until its eyes, so sharp and good
Find its prey beneath its limb.
Quick as a flash of light,
It jumps upon
And takes a bite!

Joshua A. Polk

"Close And Dear"

Someone who was close and dear
passed away the beginning of the 91 year.
Oh! did I shed those swelling tears,
devastated and full of fear.
How me a man can handle the
coming years.
What is an adult's hardiest jeer,
being wifeless with a young girl
and boy to rear.
Always begging God to guide and ease
the fear.
Sometimes the warmth of her presence
is so... near, I wake in the might
emotionally saying "Hi! dear."
Seldom do I look for a replica
of the one person who was so very
close and dear. Close.... and dear...

John Winston Jr.

Always And Forever

Seasons change...
People grow...
The moon glistens...
Always and forever.

Rain falls...
Flowers bloom...
Happiness is laughter...
Always and forever.

Stars twinkle...
Snow falls...
Friends are lost and
   new ones are found...
Always and forever.

Friends move...
I will remember...
All my loved ones...
Always and forever.

Colleen Tudman

"United In Defeat"

12:00 o'clock midnight
read the clock on the tower,

Out rushed the armies
with pulse raging power.

All through the night
bombs burst in the sky,

Through the town there was heard
the redcoats' shrill cry.

The children were silent
huddled close in the attic,

But the soldiers marched on
their eyes so dramatic.

Dawn was approaching
the twilight so still,

The redcoats lined up
on the crest of the hill.

The redcoats marched on
they were greatly defeated,
and the patriots gave a cheer
for the redcoats had retreated.

Charissa Henderson

Mental Trade

Please say Hello
Please be Happy
Please hear the silence
Please be here
Please wash my face
Please buy a handkerchief
Please follow me
Please that's enough
Please I am sincere
Please look at the candles
Please I will open the curtain
Please have a free wallet
Please touch the bells
Please let me thank you
Please just goodbye
Please marry me.

Howard Opratt

Let Me

Let me say I love you,
please let me count our days together.
As I look into your deep eyes,
they seem to say we'll be here forever.

Let me have my dream of you,
of misty colored love.
And though we part through endless tears,
I know I can never love you enough.

Let me ponder all the ways,
to soothe a broken heart.
Tenderly caressing,
the time we will be apart.

Let us then
forget our worries,
Be caught up no more
in mindless hurries.

Let me say how much I will love you,
until the day I die.
And through the memory of your embrace,
I'll pass away in peace.

Jennifer McKnight

A Way Of Singing

Above the rattle of dishes in the sink
   Resounded his chaotic angry babel.
The clink of glasses irritated his
   Confused and turbulent mind.

With an agitated clatter
   He jumped up, causing fear
While physically attacking and whacking
   Whatever object or person was near.

Table, lamps and books crashed,
   Causing clatter and turmoil.
Adding to the bedlam he
   Tore the curtains off the wall.

The children fled the fracas
   Fearing his drunken agitation
Would soon envelop them in
   frantic pandemonium.

What suddenly caused the bedlam
   Only he could explain
Serenity was finally restored
   by the ringing, jangling phone

Jean C. Vanderflute

Sickness

Behind the wall
Pop the bubble
Fall eternity
Cross the fields
Cross the desert
Lose the stars
Labyrinth lost
Mirage an access
Crack the door...

Wander through thickness
Empty of shadows
Dark as nothing
Nothing but shivers

Open the windows...

No

I want them closed

David S. Markowitz

A Young Mother's Pain

Regret swells within my breast,
Pours forth from my soul
Yet remains hidden from the eyes of all.
I ache, oh, I ache
More than some can know
For I nourish the unwanted
From a world below.
Puffy eyes from tears shed
Sharp painful bursts in my head.
When will this agony end?
When will it end?
My thoughts speak of the unthinkable
Yet they I follow.
I take the pills.
Then I swallow.
Soon I will be dead
No longer will last my pain
My punishment is eternal death...

Andrea Marshall

Prose Is When

Prose is when a sensitive mind
pours forth its tangy goals,
more than causal observations,
quicksandish glooms, contradictory
dreams and exotic assertations
on the delicate recorder known
as paper without regards to
rhyme, assonance, or public
preference, but instead seeks
the ecstatic freedom known
only to the few who truly
express themselves in the
particular creative mutation
of art known as a talent.

Cheryl-Joy A. Carrington

The Skin Of Her Buttocks

Her skin is liquid
slick like the pages
of the romance novels
she reads
out by the pool
spanked into a ripe pink
by the sun
the skin of a nectarine
in summer

John Boettcher

Collective Mortality

What if a sob of a gob of a mob
Presses in on established order
Crowds and pushes awry and asunder
Every neatened border
Gobbles and lazes and smothers atattered
Each abstract and importance scattered
Ground to dust; lifeless a must
Then where will the Graeco-Roman be?
Buried a millennium or two or three
To rise again some dim tomorrow? Or
To rest forever a vale of sorrow
A new generation of artifacts
Progeny's relic of things past
Doomed to recapitulate ontology
And lay dead as each of us will
Whether 'tis the story of each or all
The repetition of forever still.

Juanita Lambert

Beauty

As you look into the mirror
puzzled and confused,
you ask yourself, who am I?

As you look into your own
eyes, you wonder where
the beauty lies within you.

Since you cannot see within,
you have to ask yourself
why do people say that you
are beautiful, when you
cannot see it.

As the years go by, you go
back and look into that mirror
that you looked into so long ago,
and you finally see the beauty
that everyone told you about,
so long ago.

Brandy Mort

Mom

Mom is the best parent of all.
She never gets tired and hits the wall.
She never gives up like
A stump on a log.
She's the best parent of all.

Angela Johnson

The Raven's Rape

The blackened raven
Ravagely circles the grave
Newly birthed corpses
Fresh prey obstructed from feast
Soured by their innocence.

The grieving raven
Tenderly weeps tears of pain
On tombs of sorrow
The loss of humanity
Kills the appetite of lust.

The hardened raven
Gorges fiercely on the feast
Compassionate touch
Destroyed by indifference
The benign rape of passion.

Angela M. Olsen

In The Heat Of The Night

As I stood entranced by the fire,
quietly pondering
I felt the weight of his stare
embrace me
A calm, peaceful feeling swept
over me
I had found the warm, safe
place I was searching for
A step forward had been taken
in the journey to my...
Destiny

Elizabeth L. Robinson

The Trouble With America

The one-footed sprinter
races to catch up to the group.
They laugh, talk, and
hurry on their way.
Suddenly, as the sprinter
reaches the group, the
ground rumbles as a chasm
forms, and the sprinter
disappears within the vacuum.
The group continues walking,
concerned with their
own lives: as the chasm
silently closes. As the
group hurries on, they
never realize that another
person has slipped through
the cracks of American
Society.

Errin Roby

The Promise

Love is like the sunshine,
Radiating warmth,
Encouraging growth,
Reflecting my shadow.
We are one.

We encounter a storm occasionally.
Clouds pass over the sun.
Warning signals flash and explode.
We search for protection as
Drops of water fall.

The storm subsides eventually.
The sun peeks through the clouds.
A rainbow glows on the horizon,
Promising a brighter tomorrow.
Love survives.

Heidi J. Akerman

Untitled

Stripped
naked

I stand
before
the mirror
and see

A reflection
of the girl
I once was

And the woman
I have yet
to be.

Isabel Martin

"Be True"

To decide to suffer,
rather than accept the pleasures,
of the weak,
no doubt seems perverse.
But, in my state,
it's a necessary means
to self-assertion.
I'm no different,
then any other man
when it comes to happiness.
But, in my state,
there can be no compromise,
no willingness to conform,
to the accepted social definition
of what HONOR means...
for at all cost,
I have to preserve the integrity,
of THINE SELF.

Charles A. M. Coley

A Room Full Of Strangers

Grumbling, rumbling, rambling voices
   Reach me
     Breach me

Vampires sucking the very life from me
Why do I let them in?

I am a fluttering moth
   In a hot light fixture
But to be a butterfly
Laboring from a cocoon
With wet wrinkled wings
Becoming so strong
As to soar upon winds

I go for a walk
Happen by a stranger
Who simply returns my smile
And says hello

My heart blooms
   A thousand-fold

Dru Fuller

The True Christopher Columbus

Why did you do that to our
   red - black race.
Just thinking about it, was an
   utter disgrace.
You deprived our people, took our
   land, stole our territory.
I'm sitting here thinking in the
   dormitory.
You are the biggest racist I
   know of.
While I weep and write your
   name is listed above.
You are a big disgrace.
To the whole human race.
I looked and learned.
While blacks and Indians are
   being burned.
Rise from the dead and awake.
How much do you expect us to take.

Hadiya Singletary

Memories

The memories of your smiling face
Remain inside my heart.
The gentle way you looked at me
The night before you part.
You were a wise and loving woman,
Oh, the stories you had told.
How I wish to hear them now,
And have you near to hold.
It seems like just yesterday,
You were here by my side.
But I know that's not reality,
For all the tears I have cried.
Grandma, how I miss you,
And hunger for your love.
Yet I know that someday soon,
I will see you in heaven above.

Erica D. Cox

Untitled

Encased in their own pathetic sympathy
She can't hide from their deadly minds
Beyond the cage there lies her freedom
Beyond the cage there lies her life
They poke and prod her twisted body
Revealing things she has never known
What they hide against her will
Can never escape her tired mind
Oh, who she could be if they let her go
From this dark prison of death
Why won't they free her and let alone
The things that they will never know

Amanda Davidson

A Woman Is Like A Rose!

A woman is like a rose!
She is beautiful but dangerous,
Her thorns can sink into not
Only the skin, but also the
Heart and soul itself.
She can bring joy and
Pleasure to a man, like a
Rose blossoming in the spring.
But like a rose she is a
Thing of beauty and deserves
The highest praise and appreciation.

Daniel V. Hurst Jr.

"Disregard The Testimony"

"Irrelevant, `hearsay'...disregard"
Rocky going words go down hard.
This is theater of the absurd.
How can the mind deny
What the soul has heard?
The O.J. Simpson trial,
Legend of a man, warts and all
Both before and after the fall.

Living on the edge,
Sometimes over the top
With the unrelenting rage,
The flaw, where does it stop?
With the psyche out of control,
To remove the particular
Must one destroy the whole
When there's no decimal point
Recognized by the soul?

June Davis

Earth Is Rising

Earth is rising
Revolving, spinning, whirling
Through ancient human vibrations
Through the dusty ruins of civilization
Turned to stone by the past

Accelerating into outer space
To salute the moon
Earth's soul mate in the heavens
To salute the sun
Earth's source of life
to salute the stars
Earth's diamonds in its crown

Diminishing its speed
The planet slowly spins
To enter the void
In the womb of the universe
The Master Alchemist awaits its tired child
To transform, renew
Recreate
A new born sphere to grow

Emelda Darlene Shirinian

Chute

I can't go
right,
I can't go
left,
and to go
forward
would mean
extreme exertion
of energy that
I do not have.
So,
I quietly float
back,
not knowing
when I'll hit
bottom,
not truly caring
but not
coaxing myself to
forget.

Aly Stealey

Our Special Day

Wake up little one
    Rise and shine!
Today is our big day;
    Just yours and mine.

The sun is shining.
    No clouds in the sky.
We'll do lots of things;
    Just you and I.

Maybe a trip to the park
    to ride the Merry-go-Round;
I can see the horses now
    going up and down.

But first, let's have a warm bath,
    and a delicious breakfast too.
Then you can decide
    What you want to do.

So rise and shine little one!
    Grandma is all set for fun.
We'll take a long nap
    when the fun is done.

Dorothy Meeks Baldwin

Destiny

My life is a house with many
rooms and many directions. There are
pitfalls scattered here and there; and
stairways leading everywhere. Some,
that even lead to the sky.

So, I play it and fine tune it
like an instrument on which to sing
out the chords of my soul. I was born
with all I've got, everything I've ever
had or ever will; billowing or blue.

And I have no doubt or fear
but, that which is passing. For, I
accepted my fate on the day that
I was born.

Anne Marie Eunice

Waves

Rippling
rough
white caps
rolling like grassy hills
breaking
undertow
swift
gentle
swelling
fighting
breathtaking
refreshing like a cold drink
choppy
blowing
crests like a mountain top
bubbles
swirling
unstoppable
relaxing
Waves

Andrew Krna

Soul Trappings

Looking inward
searching
seeking
awareness
brightly glowing
touching
feeling
becoming real
reaching, stumbling
grasping, falling
realizing
a meaning, a purpose
drifting
finally standing
and finding
me

George Edward Kimball

Same Ol'

I remember your vibrant eyes
Shining like a dancer.
And the garcon would say things
Like, "Ma'am... Sir...?"
But now we just sit.
Silence grows like a cancer.
I talk to you.
You don't answer.

Jonathan David Ford

I Look...

I look out my window and all I
see is near, but it makes me wonder
is it really here.

I look up at the sky at night
and it gives me a fright, because
who really knows what's up there,
am I right?

I look at the troubled kids
today and there's so much I want
to say, but instead I just walk
away.

Jennifer M. Rae

Untitled

I was a dragon once. I waited,
settled in the myriad stench of
primordial knights; waded through the
remains of their garbage. Limbs
of translucent maidens floated by.
Some golden hair, a ring. And then
of course, the eyes of unsuccessful
jousters, round and full, not knowing
what they had missed. It was here
I was formed in your shadow.
In the swell of your waste
there was nothing but time.
My size became an issue. There was
little room for dreams then, that
were not mine. I ate what I could keep
and flew.

Holly Hamilton

Untitled

I'm doomed forever - no normalcy
Shadows hide the figures I can't see
Led by the blind man to the End
A desperate message I can't send
Serenity
Is a promise for the meek
Occasionally
I don't find what I don't seek
Left on Wasteland - high and dry
A city crumbles from these Lies
Ashes, they just fall away
And start as Dust in another day
Sanity
Is an illusion for the young
Humanity
Is where the Ashes are left among

Ann E. Hackethal

Untitled

Words
Shatter bones.
Locked in a room
Left to heal alone
You lye embracing
Yourself, burying your face
In a pillow soaked with sadness.

Alone
Drowning in gin
You sit with your head
Buried in sweaty palms
Hiding reddened eyes
Which expose your pain,
Words
Shatter lives.

David R. Zaharchuk

"Song Of A Corpse"

Plastered screams,
Shattered dreams.

A faceless mold,
Still and cold.

A pulseless heart,
For you to feel.
Believe it or not,
This is real.

Count your blessings close my dear,
This mistake cannot be cleared.

It's in the past,
You may say.
But this victim was real,
Not made of clay

And now all its dreams,
Are cast astray.
And now its family,
Has fallen prey,
All because of your bad day!

Amy Collier

She

The pain inside
She tries to ignore.
The more she thinks about it,
It only hurts more.

She knows
The pain will disappear someday.
But all she can do
Is hope and pray.

Memories are something that will pass.
But these dreadful memories
Will last and last.

She knows that love
She'll never find,
Because he's gone.
And he was one of a kind.

All she can do is cry.
But that won't answer anything.
She'll just keep asking why.

Jennifer Larsen

Untitled

Temple light
shine so bright
life and hope to all.

Temple light
shine with might
your people will not fall.

Temple light
shine and fight
let your flame grow tall.

Temple light
shine with height
your oil grows so small.

Temple light
shine alight
eight days is your call

Temple light
shine with sight
you bring wisdom to one and all.

Jennifer Hossli

"Honor The Veterans"

Bow your head in silence,
   Show your respect,
Watch the veterans' faces,
   As they recollect.
The battles they fought,
   The freedom they made.
Respect them for their service,
   And for the price they paid.
Forget not the soldiers,
   Who died in the past.
The men and women,
   Who fought to their last.
They are the heroes,
   To honor and praise.
They are the meaning,
   Behind the flag we raise.
Honor now the veterans,
   And the soldiers who died,
Remember the praises sung,
   And the tears that were cried.

Christopher Joseph Jones

"Lost Love"

Alone in the darkness
Silence is all I hear
Screeching sounds of death
Are growing near

I once loved you
But you I lost
My heart and soul
Was the cost

I almost wish
I could feel the pain
Then I'd know I was alive
And I could love again

I try to cry
But there are no more tears left
For me to shed
It's almost as if I'm dead

But I don't need to cry
Not even one tear
The sky is doing it for me
For it's constantly raining here

Jamie Spilinek

Instead Of Separate Parts

The moment that we call our life
Passes quickly from our grasp
We do but what we want to do
From birth to dying gasp
We say we love
We say we care
But would you or I,
Stoop to help the helpless
Or heed their anguished cry?
We care not what their fate may be
We choose to live a lie
We speak of love and caring yet,
We watch our brothers die
When will we open up our eyes?
And better still, our hearts?
When will we live as brothers should?
One whole instead of separate parts.

Arthur Lincoln Van Dyke Jr.

My Loss Was Heaven's Gain

It's been so long my darling
Since you were laid to rest.
It seems like only yesterday
You were Heaven's guest.

I know you're in a better place,
Although you left too soon.
For you were only three years old
That dreadful day in June.

At least you didn't suffer.
They said it happened fast.
Your precious heart stopped beating,
And then your life had passed.

For anyone who's reading this
There's something you must know.
"Don't take life for granted!"
It's so hard to let go.

But Jesus knows what's best for you
So he relieved your pain.
And now the Angels all agree,
My loss was Heaven's gain.

Darla Ferriell

Unimportant

A crystal glass
  sits on a piece of paper;
    just a single sheet.
      it stands alone:
    insignificant to the world,
  for it is only one glass.
over the years it sits
  and gathers dust,
    little by little.
      one day the paper falls
    along with the glass.
  it shatters into many pieces,
going in many directions,
  yet no one is around
    to hear it break and shatter;
      no one to pick up
    the jagged pieces,
  thrown across the floor.
so there it remains;
  untouched.

Christina Pauline-Slocum

Fireworks

On the grass field
Sitting back to back
and spine to spine
elbows locked
laughing and leaning
backwards forwards
your way and mine
the fireworks
Spidering crazily
exploding above us
with a crack
and a ba-boom
that thumps the gut
though mainly it's
your spine
against mine
and fiery
explosions
up and down
the line

Adrienne Porfiriadis

Two Lonely Violets

Two lonely violets are
sitting in a vase.
Look upon the purple face
of one who mourns
because he is dying.
He cares only for himself
and is always crying.

However, the other
is not like his brother.
He knows why he is there.
A little girl lies in a bed,
all sorts of pain to bear.
And so the violet's willing
for a short time his beauty to share.

Two lonely violets are
sitting in a vase.
One who is unhappy,
one who shows God's grace.

Jenni Mills

Day's End

The setting sun
Slips behind the horizon.
Evening approaches

In one last gasp,
An explosion of color.
Darkness encroaches

Upon what was
A perfect day.

Carol Antrim

Vision

My mind wanders away
slowly drifting into the night

A figure of a man comes to view
hazy at first - shrouded in mist

A headdress fans out a halo
thick braids softly falling

His eyes are closed in peaceful dream
of a time when the buffalo roamed free

Of dancing and drums and tipi fires
when forests touched the sky

Before the prairies had been plowed
and unharnessed rivers ran clear

Of ponies with coats designed by nature
handprints of war-paint on their rumps

With ears erect and listening
warning riders of things not yet seen

He holds his ghost-shirt, and a pipe
once smoked in hopes of peace

Through my tears, his image fades———

Julie Bergh

Football

Fun, awesome
Smashing, exciting, thrilling
Helmets, pads, cleats, goal posts
Hitting, cheering, yelling
Rad, wild football

Justin Anderson

Today

The sun's awake - I see it shining
so beautiful and warm
it creates a feeling deep inside
making me glad I was born.

Today my life could change completely
in such a simple way,
all it takes is a great big smile
and a little hello or hey!

Hello, stranger on the street
did you know today is for living
and tomorrow is too late
to do your forgiving?

So put your hand in mine
let's walk, not run
let's talk and laugh and learn together
a friendship can be fun.

It's getting dark - the sun is setting
I can hardly see it now,
but today I learned to enjoy my life
and a stranger showed me how.

Helen Lord

The World For Me

The world for me
So incomplete
I can hear
But cannot speak

The world for me
Which I have seen
People hurry
Quietly

The world for me
So unfair.
All I need is
One who cares

The world for me
is changing now
Lots of questions
like why...and how?

Why did it happen?
Why to me?
Now in heaven.
The world for me.

Amber Kumpfmiller

Icicle

I am frozen stiff
Solid, Hard.
Isolated from others.
I don't listen to
Anyone.
I don't care about
Anyone.
I don't feel.
I sit around
Wearing a blank face.
Not letting anyone
Hurt me again.
Not letting anyone
Betray me again.
I never start melting,
Trusting, caring.
I live my own cold life.
The human icicle.

Jessamyn Cuneo

Untitled

God has through His abundant grace
So let His glorious, heavenly face
Shine down upon us here below
That we in faith and strength will grow.

In grace He sent His only Son,
Who for mankind salvation won;
From Satan's powers set us free,
Made us His own eternally.

His grace, supplied abundantly,
From evil strife has kept us free.
His holy Word we have retained,
In faith His children have remained.

Humbly we come before Him now;
Our hearts in true repentance bow.
Though we have often sinned and erred,
His grace forgiveness has conferred.

In God the Lord let us rejoice;
His praise through all the nations voice.
His grace to all the world make known-
That Christ did for our sins atone.

Erna Westphal

The Tree

Here I stand so strong,
So lovely a tree.
So radiantly alive,
For all to see.

I can stand all weather,
And whatever may be.
Except that damn dog,
That's looking for me.

If only I could run,
If only I could talk.
I'd make that dog,
Take a hell of a walk.

I'd run and jump,
I'd holler like hell.
To stop that dog,
From making me smell.

But woe is my fate,
Tho strong and free.
'Cause here comes that dog,
Heading straight for me.

Donna Marie Bessmer

A Revision Upon A Summer Dream

Flying in a summer dream of happiness
soaring above thoughts of clouds
climbing, embracing the warmth of the sun
filling me up with its sweet nectar
blood no longer fills me but liquid fire
bleeding from my mouth and eyes
I am the sun
I am the life
I am the everything
I am the nothing
because they are me
and I them
and we are one and indistinguishable
and love is everything
such a loss
that no one can feel it,
feel the fire
that burns me in ecstasy
and agony...
but that's bearable

Joshua Santarpia

Seasons Of Life

Life is like the seasons
so unpredictable, so uncertain

Like the Spring, only as a small lad
As the beauty of the blooms the
Childhood is a thing of beauty,

Like the summer as being in full
bloom and all leafed out
a young man or woman beginning to
live life to the fullest

Like the Autumn the sun and frost
take their toll on life as the troubles
do with all eventually

Like the winter white with snow
the white hair and days of age
that go bye so slow.

So if we are blessed to live
A long natural life,
We should see four seasons of life.
Not only of the world, also
within ourselves.

Glenda Ann Hatfield-Cline

Not Far Away...

Not far away a sea gull
Soars the sky
Above the clouds there is peace
A way to say good-bye

The oceans ripple tide
A breeze against my face
To watch the sunrise
Where my hearts a lonely place

Not far away I feel
Her close to me
Free at last to soar the sky
A place she longed to be

There are times I laugh
Moments I cry
Memories to hold
That helps me get by

Not far away a sea gull
Soars the sky
Above the rainbow, above the clouds
She smiles and waves good-bye

Diane K. Basner

Untitled

Lips
Soft
Warm,
Bonding,
Pressing mine.
Arms
Surrounding
Squeezing
Holding me close.
Hearts,
Pounding
Beating
Thumping,
My heart.
His heart.
Beating as one.

Beth M. Meyer

Looking Back

Some look back with terror
Some look back with fear
But I look back with love
On the memories I hold dear.

I look back and see you
Standing by my side
Exchanging tears for smiles
Forever you're my guide.

At times the road was rough
With no hope on which to stand
But it never got the best of you
If life failed to go as planned.

All throughout my childhood
I was always taught
Dwell on the hope of tomorrow
Don't give today a thought...

D. B. Smith

In The Heart

It's a beat within your heart,
Some people try to say.
But I know it's in the soul,
Until your dying day.

Some people were born to love,
While others were born to hate.
But when it comes to your love,
I was born to wait.

I guess it could be true,
Love could come from the heart.
Because mine broke in two
The day we had to part.

Cheri Stanford

Unseen Flowers In God's Garden

Every flower is unique
Some return upon the
Warm winds of spring
Though they are delicate
Magnificently they reappear
God has made each one special
Imagine how different and
Precious we are through
God's unseen eyes

Chris Wilcox

A Friend

Someone to love,
someone to care for,
someone who knows what friendship is,
   cause life can weigh you down
   and you can't get up,
   that is when someone picks you up,
   and carries you in their arms,
when you're at your lowest,
your deepest,
your hardest,
that's when your friend helps you,
when you feel blue and
afraid of tomorrow,
your friend will fill you up
with self-confidence.
Only with a friend can you
   feel content and feel loved.
Only with a friend,
can you live.

Joseph Sanfilippo

Faded Glass

Walking through the hard life
Some things you can learn,
Some are hard to handle,
Others get you burned

Why are memories fading,
How come they never last,
It's hard to live behind the wall
Of the faded broken glass.

The faded glass is broken,
Shattered to the core,
Leaves you standing empty,
Always wanting more.

There are rainbows in the forest,
There are echoes in the trees.
There are gunshots on the corner,
Cuts you down below your knees

The truth of life is glowing,
It makes you look inside,
Is it love or sorrow,
That opens your mind so wide?

Charlie L. Taylor

Everyone Needs

Someone to laugh with and "go half" with,
Someone who's true in thought and deed,
Someone to talk with and to walk with,
Someone to follow or to lead.
Someone to share your joy and sorrow,
For each today and each tomorrow.
Someone to care for and be there for,
Someone to pray with and to stay with,
Each other's hopes and dreams to heed.

Dorothy Brignola

Guy's Night Out

Guy's night out and we all drink rum
Spilling icy cheers with cigars and jeers
Not a notion of spite nor ominous sight
Comraderie lost in a deep space jam

A space jam playing on the radio boom
Travelling fast with all consumed

Guy's night out and we all feel sick
But not from the evening's imperfectness
The imperfect potion leaves us dizzy
Racing the past before our eyes

I see my friend in a haze of sleep
High, he confuses me with an angel

Last night out in senseless careen
And laughter becomes a silent dream

Jaymin Chang

Conception Of Life

Love is the mother of life
She is very powerful
Stronger than any force
She's every breath we take
From the moment we awake
She keeps us together
With the warmth of her embrace
She's a smile in your heart
A look on your face
The power of love is stronger
Than anything on earth
She's life, she's faith

Johanna Baresic

A Tree

I saw a crimson christened tree
    standing all alone —
    in front of an antique house
    but behind Long John Silver's home.

The tree spoke of progress
    and yet I sensed decay —
    progress moving forward
    yet backward in our day.

The tree had surely known
    children in its arms —
    but now it competed
    with neon glowing charms.

Can a lighted sign
    nestle youth in solitude
    and give the space for dreaming
    when life is harsh and rude?

I guess the answer varies
    within each living heart —
    but I choose the beauty
    unmarred by lighted parts.

Fay Gannon

Proud Majesty

Look, up there on the hill
Standing Proud and tall
Listening to the mockingbirds trill
Who's late going South this Fall.

Listening to the sounds he hears
Of those who now will make their way
From out the Forest as he peers
At their progress on this Fall day.

His heart has been among these trees
The whole hot summer long
And though to sleep have gone the bees
He'll stay there Great and strong.

And now as I watch him go
I'm awed to see his very strength
In every step he shows it so
And who could measure out his length?

The beauty of such a creature
Could not be seen, it's clear
In any other Feature
Except this Great Majestic deer.

Frances R. Scholze

Our Nation's Flag

Our nation's flag
Stands proud and tall,
Among the hills and plains.
We Americans observe it
As our symbol of courage.
As a model of our many claims.
The red and white stripes
Gracefully flow,
Within the wind, the sky, and our hearts.
While fifty white stars
And a background of blue,
Prove the United States to be true.
What a beautiful sight
Portrayed by our flag,
Representing us united.
All together depicting
One vast place,
Mighty and able to fight!

Gina Scappaticci

Of Loss

There is a coffin in my room
Staring remorsefully at the wall.
And the silly printed flowers
Dance to its insane gaze.
I wonder why.
There is a dead in the coffin
Sadly crying because it is winter,
So the snow kisses the ashen stone
Mildly amused at my stupidity.
I wonder why.
There is a heart in the dead
Wistfully watching, ice cold,
And loneliness killed the silence
Stunned by its suddenness.
I wonder why.
There am I by the coffin
Tapping out musical solidarity.
The hollow sound is frightening,
And I scream at horrid emptiness.
I wonder why.

Chris Radel

Eclipse

Orion's hand touches the moon
Stars twinkle, night fades,
Twilight approaches soon
Orange, red, and a yellow fill the sky
A bird chirps, a wet dew on the grass
Darkness begins to die
A blast of heat and light
Will dry the dew, and kill the moon
As the sun shows all its might
The moon fights back and blocks the sun
A ring around an orange ball
The eclipse has begun

Douglas Clark

Untitled

My mind is clouded with murky thoughts
Stirred up by a passing current
Whipped into a swirling mass
Now slowly settling to rest

Eric W. Carroll

Violet Grass

On a late
summer evening
I lie on my back watching
The clouds rumble by.
Drops of life fall from
fall from the sky,
drenching me with feeling,
Washing the color of my dress
onto the violet grass

Erica Drasche

Tomorrow's Dawning

Misty Meadows
sunlight mountains
skies of blue
and water fountains
times of old
times of new
take me to
the land that's true.

Cassandra Kosovich

Sunsets

Sunsets are beautiful
   sunsets are fine
sunsets are purple,
   red, and lime.
Sunset, sunset
   every day and night
Sunset, sunset,
   shines every light.
Sunset, sunset,
   up so high
up so high against
   the sky.

Erin Meenan

"So Many Trees!"

So many trees
Swaying nice and gently,

So many trees
Touching the sky,

So many trees
With leaves falling all over,

So many trees
Blazing like the sun,

So many trees
Dry as the dirt in the Sahara Desert,

So many trees
Looking straight at you,

So many trees.

Daphne R. Peponides

Waves

Winds the waters tossing
Sweeps with light of morn
To dictate size and form,
And scoop up light reflections,
Continuing connections
Blue waves, air born.

The swirling force upheaving
Sends waves seething to rise and roll
Edging to rock and shore.-
Or
Roaring sea pulls to deep
For a moment's sleep
Before rebirth and crest,
Lest the rhythm burst
The newly rounded birth
That swells and sighs and dies.

This moment to exist
Is last breath, no more,
Reach, stretch the form,
And die ashore.

Jeanne Burt Fuller

Out There

MOON THERE - SUN THERE
Same place - outer space
Different times - Different shines
Everyday - that's ok
The Moon is this night
Where the Sun was this morning
we are surrounded by objects out there
doe's it give you a scare
not me they are Holy bodies...

Jeffrey Roy McVey

Dream Catcher

Dearest infant, dwell on the
sweet dreams passed through to
you as you sleep,

The Dream catcher turns away
all evil, all bad spirits that
would make you weep.

Imprint the sweetness deeply
in your mind
Recall them to your future when
one day you find,

All life seems in a turmoil and
you feel you must be free,
Recall Dream catcher's etches
and escape with the memory,

Cynthia Bell

Little River

Little river that flows through my mind,
take me back to that place in time.
Take me back to where the air was sweet.
Take me back to where I felt complete.
Little river follow through,
take me back to that place I once knew.

Jeannette Crain

New Violin

A new violin: So pert,
tan-gleaming, curled as a fern;
its quiet sings like a vixen's sleep.
New strings: power lines in Lilliput?

Yet one chord could saw
infinite fantasy
into lengths.

At most
I'd quietly lift it
to my face.

But to have in his hands its
   ranged life
a master will play it like a marlin.

It was so
I lost my chance
of you -
of willow-spelled eyes,
of brisk black curls
on a poised, proud nape.

Charles Leftwich

Lust

I want I must
possess extract impress
his essence onto me.
Lick him up in tiny darting flicks
and hungry gnashing bites,
my flesh on his.

I want to grab his throat
between sharp teeth
and shake it wildly.
Feel the sweat and hot blood's
night-bound dreams
flung off
to trickle
quietly, entirely
into my hungry mouth.

Dyan Wirt

Untitled

You tell me you love me, you
tell me you care. But I know
the truth and it's too much to
bear. I can see through your
lie for I am not blind. Now
I know it's true love I have
yet to find.

Brandie Towers

Untitled

Time is a never-ending circle
That always has a say,
In anything or everything,
That happens on this day.

Everything revolves around time.
They say specifically so,
You needn't worry for when it stops,
Because it will always say no.

Time is cool.
It's up to date.
Don't even try,
'Cause it won't wait.

Clocks are a way to tell time.
Like the time we need to know,
Oops! I forgot
For now it is time.
Time for me to go.

Allison Gideon

Bequest

Daylight couldn't shape it,
That dream that stayed the night,
Then vanished as the first rays
Of sun brought the morning light.

Amorphous, then invisible,
In my fading recollection,
It dimmed, like mist at midday
In the glow of introspection.

My day was rent with discontent
And a nagging sense of woe.
A dream that I couldn't remember
Left a sorrow that wouldn't let go.

Billie Houston

To Mom, A Very Special Lady

It used to be, for oh so long,
   that feats were all man made.
Wars were fought, battles waged,
   e.g. "THE LIGHT BRIGADE."
Mountains climbed, moved or made.
   Fortunes lost or won.
All these things drew praise galore
   for him the shining son.

How unfair, it used to be
   that only once a year,
a comet streaked across the sky
   for every one to cheer,
their major Dame, a femme supreme,
   the leader of the flock.
Paid homage to by all her charge
   who consider her the "Rock."

Why not instead, for goodness sake,
   give "Mom" her full due.
Let's honor her for her true worth
   and do so all year through.

George Gunza Jr.

A Parent's Prayer

Thank you for this gift from above
that has been created through our love,

May we as this child's parents
always keep in our minds,

That our decisions will help him to find
the right path that will lead
back to his heavenly home,
returned in perfection to
God alone.

Alberta M. Lampe

My Prayer

Remove the clutter from my mind,
    that has no power of worth.

Place within the bound of it,
    soothing sounds of mirth.

When darkness crowds my memory,
    with pain of other years.

Open then, the doors that hold,
    days that had no tears.

Irene Sergent

God Knows

Where am I coming from
that I can't seem to hold on
Could it be that I have
Oiled my tight rope with
things that are slips
instead of holds

When will I choose
When will I grab
When will I catch
When will I fasten

With bolts -
    fragments of my soul -

    God Knows!

Donna Hamilton

Patience A Gift

Patience is a gift from God
That I know is freely given.

We all have times, that we need this gift
But we go on the way we're living.

God blessed me with a lot of gifts
But patience wasn't one of them

And I pray for guidance for this gift
Every time I pray to him.

He gives me tasks which are a test
And I don't realize at the time,

But when the quiet comes at night
I know there was a sign.

God has helped me through these times
By his guidance and his love
I know that he is watching me
From his home above.

I know he has patience with me
When all I'm doing is asking.

But his love for me will always be
For now and everlasting.

Diana Gahler

Shadow Man

He was first, in the shadows of my mind,
That I'd first seen him.
In the shadows of my mind.
From out of my fantasy he stepped,
And took the form of warm human flesh.
Then slowly into my life he crept.
Come softly to me he motioned,
Hypnotizing me and making me his.
He filled my being with his warmth,
Overwhelmed me with his charms,
Wooed me with his smile,
Seduced me with his voice,
His mind heard my very thoughts.
When I felt pain, he felt pain,
When I felt joy, he felt joy.
He gave me the gift of love.
My soulmate and I will be together,
forever.
I **know** I will love him till the end of time,
I know I will love **him**, till the end of time.

Beverly Stanczyk

Life

I have looked at life and come to think
That it flies by fast as a wink.

So, when your troubles get you down,
Put on a smile; don't sit and frown.

Make lemonade or apple pie;
Reach for the biggest star in the sky.

Live it up; have a ball;
Let others see you standing tall.

And they will know that you said, I can
Because your life had a plan.

No wishy-washy, dilly-dally are you,
Not one to sit and cry and be blue.

Oh no, life's too short to waste;
So get busy; run with haste.

Life won't find you sitting idly by
Looking for that pie-in-the-sky.

You'll succeed and go to the top;
You'll jump your hurdle before you stop.

One day you'll look back with hindsight
And sigh and say, if I had another lifetime I
might...........

Fran Hightower

Remains

Black as Death-
Steady as Steel
He Creeps
He Haunts

When he leaves
He leaves the smell
Of Devoured rats
Your heart pounds

The Thuds-
Oh, your precious heart
beats harder
for life

but life disappears
the smell remains.

Brooke L. Butler

Guidance

When you love someone so much,
that it hurt's inside.
And the pain that you feel,
you just cannot hide.

Pray to the Lord,
and let it all out.
Ask him to show you,
What true love is about.

For this one's to much,
to do on your own.
And he's the only one,
that can bring you home.

After the way has been shown,
do not forget!
To thank the good Lord,
for the guidance he sent.

For he is the one,
that made it all come true.
And showed you exactly what ,
true love can do.

Jeremy S. Brehm

Snowflakes

Snowflakes are jewels
That light up in
The misty sky

Little falling stars
Are twinkling in the
Light of the
Wintry mist

Francine Shammami

Love Remembered

Philosophers claim
That love worn thin
From daily use is best.
Much different than
lovers dreams
Not yet put to the test

Please...so the day may be endured
When all seems gone askew
Leave one small drop of foolishness
To make old love seem new.

Christine Belfatto

"I've Had Enough"

I've had enough of these fights,
That we so often have.
I've had enough of neglect,
and I can't take any more.
I've had enough sleepless nights,
Wondering if you love me or not.
I've had enough silent treatments,
Might as well be alone.
I've had enough falling tears,
To last a whole lifetime.
Enough is enough,
And I've finally had enough!
The one thing I never did get enough of
Was the love I wanted from you.
I've been so very miserable,
But I won't be anymore,
'Cuz I've finally had enough.

Brenda L. Longo

"The Old Faithful Moon"

The big white moon
That sits in the sky so faithfully,
Like a faithful dog,
Our earth like the master,
In bad times and good
Just sitting there so faithful,
So long has the moon been with us
But not so much as a
Thanks has the moon gotten,
We should be happy,
Thank you moon
For all your faithfulness -

Erin H. Rowley

"Memories"

Do you remember that day at Aunt Mina's?
That we sat on the porch swing alone?
How you wished and I wished that
the dear little place was our own?
Oh well, those days have
long vanished, but somehow I
thought that you knew.
My heart was yours for the
asking and tonight I am dreaming of you

Jean P. Howell

The Closest Star

Why is it
That we strain our sight,
To catch a glimpse
Of a starry night,
And gaze intently,
Mesmerized in the shadows
To study and adore
The Diamonds of the Night?
When without strain,
We can bask in the day
From the brightest glow
Not so far away.
The stars do not warm us,
Nor shine on our face.
Why do we so cherish them
Gleaming through space?
Is it so hard to see
What is near
When we hold the untouchable
ever so dear?

Erin Sutherland

"Empty Heart"

The day you said
   that we were through,
   My heart felt empty
      without you.

This empty heart
   only beats for you,
   It always will,
      No matter what I go through.

I wish you were here
   the one I adore,
   Then my heart will
      feel empty no more.
      This heart still remains empty,
         Until you walk
            Through that door.

Emily J. Ranta

The Statue

I go to the park to see a statue
that's big and made of stone.
And when I'm there with that
Statue I feel I'm not alone.

Surrounded by a fountain with water
springing out,
The beautiful statue standing still
is real without a doubt.

The statue talks to me in a way
that I cannot hear. But I
understand it and it senses when
I'm near.

I talk back and when I tell it
sad things, I swear I see a tear.

Other people cannot experience the
feeling that I feel.
about the statue in the park
I swear, I swear, it's real.

Christina Marie Johnson

"The Children"

The children are our future
That's what we hear on the TV.
The politicians always use that phrase,
When they talk to you and me.
Do we set a good example
For our children day by day?
Do we try to teach them right from wrong,
Or do we turn black and white to gray?
Do we teach them family values,
Or turn our back on family needs?
Do we spiritually lead them,
Or just their body do we feed?
Do we let them make decisions
And empower them to be strong,
Or when they express their feelings
Do we tell them they are wrong?
If we'd listen to the children
We could learn a thing or two,
For with all our imperfections,
They've accepted me and you.

Joan F. Holdman

Dusk

Our feet kick up the rocks and sand
The air is warm and dry
The evening breeze it surges in
as with the coming tide.

I know this road
So many times it's been my only bliss
Years ago it was that path
in which childhood exists.

Now the sun it crouches low
To caress the twilight sky
"Run, mama run," he says
with youth his eyes alive.

I take his hand and we go
Every step in stride
Down this tired old dirt road
where each generation collides.

Jillian L. McGuire

All Are Waiting

In the sunset of a life
the amber glow sinks slowly
into the twilight.

Moonlight's silver light beams
glow through
the long dark hours
of descending breath.

At last the sunrise
brings forth the dawn
while all are waiting
some the sunset,
others the dawn.

Diane Gallegos

Going Home

Today you cross the finish-line,
   The checkered flag is waved.
You have fought long and hard,
   There's much to celebrate.

So gather up your trophies of love,
   Your medals in sweet charity.
Pack your ribbons for faithfulness,
   Your purple heart for bravery.

Leave behind your broken pieces,
   The bruises you have known.
There isn't space for suffering,
   For today you're going home.

JoAnn Downs Alo

Winter Beauty

The long, white carpets on the ground
The clear, white clouds above the sky
The wind is blowing in my face
But not a single soul or trace.

I put on ice skates on my feet
I give a push
And there I go within my soul
The way my heart is singing.

The ice is wet and sparkling
The sea is deep asleep
The wind is blowing slightly
The way my heart can sing.

The sun is smiling right at me
The snow is sprinkling lightly
The colors red, yellow, blue and green
Are stretching right above me.

The clouds are dancing in the sky
I'm dancing right below them
My hair is blowing in the wind
And that's a happy moment.

Golda Yefraimov

The House

I looked at the house
so big so beautiful
I just stared for a moment
Thinking that soon I would
have that big room that I always wanted
Then the day came to look at the house
I was stunned when I looked inside
All I saw was apartment doors
It was then that I realized...
Don't judge a book by its cover or
a house by its appearance.

Heather Kervin

Freedom

The sky
The clouds
The trees
I gaze out my window
I envy them
The sky with nothing to hide
The clouds with no fears inside
The trees with their simple strength
Just by being their beauty inspires
No one blames the sky for its rages
No one blames the clouds for turning gray
No one blames the trees for changing
I long to be
The sky
A cloud
Or a tree
They have no alarm clocks
They have no wars
They have no knowledge of rejection.

Autumn Rose Boody

Lost In Thought

As the sun filtered through the trees;
the deer and squirrels played;
alone and lost in my thoughts;
I pondered what God had made.

The sky so blue and clear;
the grass so soft and green;
the wildflowers all a bloom;
it was almost like a dream.

Suddenly, the sky grew dark;
the moon took place to the sun;
the stars were shining bright;
there was nowhere for me to run.

Out of the shadows, I heard a voice;
it was distant and unclear;
I opened my eyes and there I knew;
that my God was very near.

Lost in thought;
a world of dreams;
with love in my heart;
I thank God for these things.

Brenda K. Thacker

Niobe

Wordless tree
Speak to me
With your swaying
Humbly saying:

Nature's revelation
Heart's agitation
Love's aching
Niobe's making,

Pendulous branches
Inviting chances
Instant reflection
Under subjection,

Workman's shoots
Grounded roots
Shade providing
Joy abiding,

Niobe tree
Speak to me
With your swaying
Humbly praying.

Helen G. Dreiling

Karen's Kiss

One night the wind and I looked long,
The earth moved at my feet,
The moonlight shed, had gone to bed;
But still I couldn't sleep.

And soon you came and brought the dawn,
The light fell on your face
And I beheld a child of elves;
Too fine for mortal grace.

I stood a while and breathed a sigh,
Afraid to break the spell,
For this I thought the God's had wrought;
And now to earth you'd fell.

As we embraced,
You placed a gentle kiss upon my lips,
And I had felt the sun and stars;
Move through my finger tips.

Now I have heard the winds of change,
While heaven soars above,
But not so high are heaven's fields;
Compared to Karen's love.

David V. Stepchinski

My Granddaughter

I look at you in awe as I go back in time
the face that's looking back at me
Once long ago was mine.
I look at pictures of a little girl.
These pictures are of me.
But to my surprise it's your face
I always see.
The same exquisite smile
the same pouting frown
The same expressive eyes
That are so big and brown.
Oh yes I can see.
You have all of these expressions
That once belonged to me.
You inherited my characteristics
for all the world to see.
I give you my love for all eternity.

Barbara Hill

Describing Love

Love is sweet and maybe kind,
The feeling lingers in your mind.
And for whomever I have told,
About this power I behold.
I'll tell you once, and tell you twice,
That love may sometimes not be nice.

Catherine Ann Horton

Wasteland

With his last breath of desert air
The final pain that he could bear
He thrust his fists into the sand

With dried hands he bore a hole
In search of water for his dying soul
Trapped in the wasteland

He kept digging into the ground
Yet his oasis could not be found
His own life he failed to save

He lay in the burning sand
Prey of the unforgiving land
And so the hole became his grave

Nathan Hedges

Our Home

The ceiling needs painting
    the floor's got a crack,
It really doesn't matter
    it's home; we'll be back,
No matter how big
    no matter how small,
It's our home you see
    that's what matters at all,
For home is a place where
    families are made
With a mother and father
    that time cannot fade,
So wherever we wander
    there's one thing we know,
We'll always come home
    through the rain and the snow.

Alice C. Vancour

Abstracted In The Mind

The life inspired by a gift
The gift enhanced with a soul
The soul abstracted with the heart
The heart interpreted in the mind
The mind intertwined with the thought
The thought secluded in the body
The body searching for a dream
The dream to fulfill the need
The need to embrace it all.

Debbi J. Davidson

Untitled

You hold your emotions oh so well
The hearts you play could never tell
You tear them apart then cast them aside
Yet expect them to feel for you a
tenderness that can override
All the pain and sorrow you inflict
One would think it would make you sick
Can you look in a mirror?
What is it you see?
Oh it couldn't be, it cannot be
That person is it me?

Carolyn L. Avila

Untitled

Climb a tree
The highest tree
And touch a cloud
I feel like I could stand on that cloud
If all
Blame a dream
You come back
You climb the tree again
A branch breaks
Blame Nature.

Genevra Hart

Breakfast Seasons

In the summer
the leaves turn butter,
and in the fall they
lay down the law,
and in the winter they
sparkle like glitter,
and in the spring
they go ding-a-ling.

Edward C. Coffin

436

To My Dearest Rory

You are the wings of my dreams
  the love of my life
You are the light of my day
  Please take me as your wife.

You are the center of my purpose
  the soul of my being
You are the core to my spirit
  You are all that I am seeing.

Your love is the reason
  I wake in the morning
Your love is my path
  the age of my new dawning.

Your love is what fills me
  with truth, respect, and trust
Your love is what thrills me
  and makes life such a must.

So come into my arms tonight
  today and every tomorrow
For together we can conquer life
  its pain, its strife, and sorrow.

Carole A. MacLean

Left Too Soon

When the days go by
The more and more I'll cry
Because you left too soon
I look in the sky and
  all I see is the moon
I can't help but feeling
  I did this to you
Why you ask, because you
  left too soon

When I grow older this feeling will pass
But you will never pass
I want to scream and cry
So I would feel better
But all I can do is write
  a poem-letter.

Chrissy Louise Russell

Hiding Time

It's hiding time now
the Nazis are here
all the Jews hide in fear.
If they get caught
they die so fierce.
It's hiding time now
the Nazis are here.

Benjamin Deletetsky

Treatment

A terrible scream
Silenced fast
For in a box no air can last
All is dark I cannot see
Please let me out
Can't you hear me?
The smells of death are all about
Why must I stay here?
Are you living on my fear?
The smiling face of death
Is peering through the wall
And laughing at a box
A box that's silenced many cries
A box to hold your troubled child

Holly Wilcox

The One That Got Away

She was a beauty, she was
the one that got away
the one that had the sweet aura
and eyes of golden haze
She was graceful
and sleek and wonderful
what a precious creature
the one with the special features
Her coat was like silk
as fresh as autumn leaves
She appeared like a dream
and was gone in a breeze
For a wise man would say
it wasn't a deer the day
the one, the one that got away.

Cassie Q. Huddleston

Your Child Within

I miss your little girl so much
  The one with the soft sweet voice.
She melts my heart with just a touch
  Giving the angels reason to rejoice.
I miss holding her in my arms
  Especially when she cuddles close.
With me, she's protected and warm
  From all of life's goblins and ghosts.
I miss her whispering in my ear
  As she nuzzles up next to my cheek.
Oh! How I wish she were here,
  I want to hear her little voice speak.
I miss her bright smiling face
  As she wraps her fingers around mine.
She's so pretty in her ribbons and lace
  I find myself missing her all the time.
I miss just being in her presence
  Listening to her innocent laughter.
She shares her childlike essence
  Making me believe in happily ever after.

Jo S. Nave

You Are My Inspiration

You are my inspiration,
The only one I need.
You touch my heart
With every word you say.
You have changed my life
In many ways.
When I hear your voice
I know I'm not alone.
I can do anything
Because you're near,
You are my inspiration.

Bonnie Tegge

Running Out Of Time

This earth is a beautiful place,
The only one of its kind.
We have to start taking care of it,
We're running out of time.

The trees and plants that once were green
Are turning brown and sick.
You can even see the air
It's getting really thick.

We have to start to watch ourselves
The end of time is near.
For right around the corner
Awaits our final year.

Christopher Buckley

The Prize Of Peace

Waves crashing
People screaming
Lightening striking
Gunshots ringing
Babies dying
Birds no longer singing
Mothers mourning
Seems those not dying
Always have reasons for crying
Yet when the last one who cries
  dies - all will be
    eternally CALM.

Jennifer R. Phipps

O. J. Simpson

Simpson
Simpson
O. J. Simpson
Throw him in jail
and make him wail
Blood
Blood
all over his walk
all around is a pigeon
flock
lawyers
lawyers
lying all the way
Just throw them all away

Jenny Zetty

The Knight Of The Golden Rose

There lies upon my breast a rose
That holds within it's golden petals
The secret locked within my soul.
No one holds the key.
For my heart's best treasure
Belongs to none but me.
Somewhere in time he waits.
I am the one he chose.
He waits for me to cross the bridge...
The knight of the golden rose.

Beth Vick

Through Every Mile

The days may come
The days may go,
Troubles and strife
Are just part of this life,
Just keep looking up above
God always sends His love,
Sometimes things get rough
Remember just hang tough,
We have so much to be thankful for
So why must we always ask for more,
Remember always keep a big smile
For God helps us through every mile.

Jackie Whitehead

I Am Floating

Crisp stillness
Sun penetrates every breathe of cool air
I am floating
On a watery bed... eyes skyward
Slowly turning in my yellow surrounds
Deep celestial blue pulls me
Upward accelerating
I've lost my sense
West, Down, North, East, up-no telling
Profound hypnotic blue draws me
Upward engulfs me captured by sensual beauty
There is...only color, sun, cool-on-my-face, soft-sound, scent.

The river moves swiftly now
One green shape...undulating through forest, rocks, and sand
Sprays of froth sting my skin
The cool rush dries my pink throat
Who would have guessed? A waterfall's jaggy maw
Waited in the mist
The roar here does not carry far.

Joel Thomas Zabaldo

Sunshine

Sunshine floats through the window from the sky.
Sunshine flies through the air like a butterfly.
Sunshine comes from above the heaven so high.
Sunshine soars like a dove in the sky.
Sunshine is in all beautiful places.
Sunshine is like many smiling faces.
Sunshine comes after a bad storm.
Sunshine comes in many beautiful forms.

Amber Curry

Superman

Superman, Superman so big and bold.
Superman, Superman to cuddle and hold.
Superman, Superman to save the day.
Superman, Superman saves the day in his special way!
Superman, Superman cares about others.
Superman, Superman who has no sisters or brothers!
Superman, Superman with his tremendous red, and blue Colors!
Superman, Superman with an "S" on his chest.
Superman, Superman leads to no death!
Superman, Superman who has nice family and friends.
Superman, Superman is needed once again.

Despina Damianides

Once Again

Once again, here I sit
  Supper is over and the fire is lit
Wipe the counter and do the dishes
  Thinking of my childhood wishes
Let the dog out and the door I close
  Boy I hope it never snows
Throw some clothes in the washing machine
  The wind outside sure sounds mean
I mop the floors and make the bed
  Getting so tired that my eyes are red
It's snowing hard, but I don't care
  As I take a nap in my chair
Throw another log on the fire
  How I wish I could retire
Go downstairs and fold the linen
  Shower, shave, and slap on Mennen
All cleaned up with nowhere to go
  Watch the clock, time goes so slow
Let the dog in after a bit
  Once again, here I sit.

Dean Key

"Water"

They say in the desert there's a flower that grows,
Surrounded by the baron land, it glows
Seed that falls on rock sometimes still sprouts,
Remade by the heart and faith, minus doubts
A weeping willow has no time to cry,
To some it brings fear, but the strong it passes by
Strength marches from within us all
We hold up our heads and try to stand tall

Every will can move mountains
Silent at last, man's lost forgotten, gains
And love is the water to give life to me
Eyes of fire to set my heart free.

fine'

Charles Mathews

The Beach

The beach,—it's mine to watch waves roll on the sea,
Surrounded by the deep blue ocean
Temptation calls at me.

The waves,—quickly rolling, white and foamy,
Fall calmly to the surface, and sparkles from the light of the sun
The beach,—it's mine to watch waves roll on the sea.

Out there in the ocean, deep as can be,
Exists another form of life, there, beyond—-
And temptation calls at me.

Peril and temptation is what you offer me,
Though very fierce and powerful, you're still loads of fun
The beach,—it's mine to watch waves roll on the sea.

Destruction and violence, is unknown, and hidden deep,
And curiosity is left upon imagination
Yet, temptation calls at me.

My enjoyment, my escape, my tranquility,
You're always there when I want to destroy my problems and confusion
The beach,—it's mine to watch waves roll on the sea
Whenever temptation calls at me.

Caroline Rust

Gladiators

Ancient gladiators battled for their lives;
Survival of the fittest was their creed.
The meek shall perish and the strong survive,
Is how they lived indeed.

The coliseums were their battle ground,
Of the fierce and tireless men.
Death cries from the vicious crowds,
They would cheer for their victors again.

Yea, the last survivors would stand so tall,
And the losers would come to a tragic end.
Throughout the coliseum you could hear the call,
For the mighty to rule supreme once again.

Gary Alton Waltemire

Rain Voices

Did you ever hear the voices
That a steady rain will make?
Like people whispering in a group,
Or mourning at a "Wake."

It's eerie when I'm all alone
And makes me sad - until -
Annoyed, I watched their tears look through
Upon my window sill.

Annette Andrews

Imagination

Painted faces, phantom like
Swaying hips- on heel of spike.
Faux brows of hypoallergenic hue
Furlong length claws-pressed on anew.
Bony frame, serpentine feel
Warm brown eyes- this week they're teal.
Deal a meal, buns of steel- jiggle they lest...
Good lord mama, silicone leaking from her breast!

Thousands she has made blue,
The lust of a score she's fed
To my utter consternation.
I can denude you,
I can carry you to my bed-
So beware of my imagination.

Jadeed H. Aziz

Immortal

When my eyes close, geometric floor tiles appear.
Sweat scalds like hot chocolate pouring
from my face. Palms forced onto a hot grill.
Mom is screaming through the Vicks fumes and Marijuana
smoke upstairs, Vodka and Coke in hand. Sleep crushes
my face into the sandy ocean floor with barreling
waves. My mind types Steven Spielburg stories
about October 31st at the L. A. Colosseum. Marching
bands play the victory song. Trombones scream
with enough force to crush metal. The crowd begins to cheer
like the Palm Springs riot in 1990, tearing off bikini tops
to slingshot bottles over the seats. The park
below the L. A. skyscraper skyline is my exit.
Stair climbing to suicide, I jump. The sandbox sticks
to my wet skin. Awake. I'm left grass-stained forever.

Howard Yosha

Vibrations Of Love

There are doves in the tree beyond my house
   Symbols of Peace - to remind me to create
      Vibrations of Harmony and Love

Feeling a willingness, an eagerness to be more alive
   Feeling free, light and exuberant
      Filled with knowingness and a sense of destiny

Clarity - clarity without urgency, that all is as it should be
   Learning, awakening, evolving - reaching for the light
      Moving closer to Prime Creator

Communion with Self, with my Beingness
   With nature, with the Universe and GOD
      Evoking Vibrations of Love.

Erika Molloy

Angel Of Innocence

His innocent face is like an angel
   that glides across the bright sky.
The white images form, I know them well.
   They flow like a river, but I know this one runs dry.
I close my tired eyes and dream of that angel of innocence.
   The angelic being that once touched my heart.
As the dream diminished, I felt tense.
   My eyes slowly open as we part.
My dreams of the angel are shattered,
   as the clouds of the day glide away.
The night coys its way as if it mattered.
   the white soul left, chose not to stay.
When I looked up in the sky, one star shone.
Then I looked about me and inside me, I was alone.

Jennifer Almeida

Fiercest Flame

Burn deep, and deeper, fiercest flame,
tear my soul, from head to foot,
Give my limbs, my flimsy frame,
your madness, softly put.

Dream on I will, past hope and fear,
for all aglow I cannot stop,
And ever through the years and years,
I'll semble well this one small drop.

And after when the clay is dust,
I'll think of you and all your trust,
I'll think of everything you gave,
your strength, and breath, and gentle lust.

And when I know that I've been hurt,
I'll know just where to place the blame,
I'll crawl again beneath your skirt-
Burn deep, and deeper, fiercest flame.

John M. Montgomery

"Standing By"

Let your mind loose, while opening up your heart...
Tell me your deepest thoughts and the wall will part.

When you've wronged, in judgement I will not hold...
but as your conscious, I will scold.

Bring up all of what you hide....
A better spirit knows to confide.

Simple forgiveness is what you must ask...
you'd be surprised at what would last.

To cry, to laugh, to play, to live...
You can have it all, but you must give.

A hug can be such a simple embrace...
but when it touches the soul, the mind won't erase.

Sometimes all you need, is another point of view...
Someone to help, when you're not quite on cue.

Who is this person of which you can depend...
Why simply, it's none other, than a good friend!

Donna M. Abenante

A Grammar Rap

A noun is a word, we always have heard
That names persons, places and things.
A verb is there, and will help you share
All the action that the noun brings.

An adjective shows just the way it goes
Says "which one?" "how many?" and "what kind?"
Adverbs are words that say things about verbs,
And try always to keep that in mind.

A prepositional phrase tells you where in the maze
Something was done or is found.
Conjunctions hold together two phrases forever
In one sentence, for then they are bound.

Interjections are used to excite or amuse
Those things you say to friend or foe.
A pronoun is set, and lest you forget,
To replace the noun, as you know.

This grammar rap is a learning snap
To help you review what you have learned.
To recall what it is teaching, without all the preaching,
A good foundation is what you have earned.

Frances J. Davis

A Sonnet

August twenty sixth, nineteen eighty nine
Ten O'Clock A.M., born you were today
Two pounds fourteen ounces, sister of mine
So tiny and small, Here to live I pray

Miniature parts, only bones and skin
Too frail and fragile by yourself to live
Your body fights for your life to begin.
Incubators, transfusions, life does give

You were supposed to come home today but,
Contortioned movement of flexible limbs
Double hernias, so in you they cut
Two children before, this baby is Kim's

Big things come in small packages you know
Emily, now five, to you she does show.

Jodi Jackson

No Greater Love

There will never be a greater love
  Than the love that comes from God above.

He has placed a joy within my heart;
  To know from me he'll not depart.

His love revealed through Calvary
  When Jesus died for you and me.

This sacrifice of God's dear Son
  Was made for each and everyone.

There is no greater love my friends
  And His perfect love will never end.

Janet Lee

Miracles From God

There are things that live deep within us
that are a wonder.
These treasures are our pain,
sadness, sorrow, happiness and joy.
They are the feelings that make us who we are.
These priceless emotions are signs of life,
love and reality. Without them we would not be.
There would be no need.
Our tears express our compassion and pain.
Our smiles gives away our gentleness, and
our serenity reflects how we put to use
these Miracles from God.

David Jones

Tears From The Sky

Dark as night can be, moon shines bright,
tears fall from the sky darkening out the light.
Tears always fall, yet never seen
deep from her soul, deep from her being,
detached, unaware, gazing into space
no feelings, no emotions, no pain to embrace.

Years begin to pass, twenty in all,
tears creep into her days, now forced to recall.
Horrified memories fill her existence,
distortion, confusion, reality becomes distant.

Years begin to pass, ten in all
her sorrow diminishes, for no more to recall.
Her tears still fall, for her child still cries
though her voice now heard, no more secrets, no more lies.

Dark as night can be, moon shines bright,
now able to savor and relish the darkness,
and to cherish and embrace the light.

Andrea Ade

Untitled

My mind searches for answers
  that are profound.
I listen for answers
  yet there's no sound.
What is it I think I don't already know
  and what do I search for to find?
Could it be that I already have answers
  it's the questions that're not in my mind?
Is it something I'm afraid I'll feel
  if questions to my answers
  are the things with which I'll have to deal?

Jean Rosenkrans

The Night

The sun has chased the moon
that cradled my sleep
It sheds no light
no light on what my mind told me last night
In my dream you held me
so close I choose not to breathe
Breathe in what was once there

How cruel my mind works
How sweet my heart beats
I do not see how they share you
I do not know how you have control

What I had no longer is reality
That night you softly, quietly crept inside
The memory has not died
that night has past
I bid to dream you.

Christine Przybyl

Last Pain

There were so many things
That I would liked to have told you,
But I could never bring myself to say.

I know my time with you has long since past,
But it is in my memories of you,
That will make your presence last.

You are gone now, nothing more I can do,
When you left I would not say goodbye,
Goodbye means I will never again see you.

And it was the hardest thing to do
And I do not ever want to do it again,
So my last loss is you.

Your face was like a breath of fresh air.
That was the air fresh enough
For any man to breathe.

You are gone now, nothing more we can do,
But please, promise you will never forget me,
That is one promise I can make for you.

Ernest B. Montoya

Little Girl Quiet

She sits on a blanket on the grass
Talking as if nothing is wrong
She talks about the weather,
The stars, and her dreams
As she continues talking to the little girl,
It starts to sprinkle
Saying her goodbyes and promising
To come back tomorrow
She gathers up her things,
Then bends over to gently place a teddy bear
Upon the freshly dug grave.

Gina Orlando

A Portrait Of A Dream Wish

A dream is but a portrait of a wish,
that is locked inside a dreamer's heart.
To paint a dream in still life, even the great
Michelangelo, would not know where to start.

The paint brush would have to be made of
shooting star wishes, and the canvas,
a fluffy cloud floating in a sky of blue.
The mixture of paint is made of faith and
Hope to help the dreamer's wish come true.

Now God's mighty hands would nurture the dream,
for through his goodness, no request can be too extreme.
Like many things that only he can do,
only God can paint a portrait,
of a dream wish come true-.

Joseph P. Anzalone

What Is It About This Man?

I am thinking, what it is about this man
that makes me wonder should I get to know him further
or should I stop right here.

Am I suppose to when due time submit myself
to this man or is it just a passing phase. Is it
because his walk is so sleek and his talk is so chic
and his whole demeanor is so unique?

Only in due time will I know and we'll give
what we have time to grow, then and only then the
answer will show. But until time puts it all
together we'll flirt with each other, we'll hug each
other and we'll just enjoy the time we're together.

There's no need to think about anybody else
beating my time, for we both know he's not mine. So,
I will cherish the moments that he's with me, cause
right now that's the only thing important I see.
So no hooks, no strings just whatever a
Loving feeling brings.
But, yet, I still ask myself what is it
about this man?

Gwendolyn Lucas Tross

Grandma's Thankful Prayer

Thank you, Lord, for the joys you bestow,
That only a loving grandmother can know,
When to her heart she holds so near,
A precious little one, so dear.

These wee-sized images of my own sons,
Bring back memories of when I was young,
And little boys entertained themselves,
While I cooked, cleaned, put up food for the shelves.

The busy years so quickly passed—
My little boys grew up too fast.
And now, with babies of their own,
Greater joy I could not have known.

A second chance to rock and hold,
These cherubs worth much more than gold.
Small arms around my neck so tight,
"I love you, Grammy!" makes my whole world right.

Many things I have not done;
Riches and treasures, I may have none,
Yet, thank you Lord, for blessings great or small.
And for grandchildren, I thank you, most of all!

Joyce King

If I Knew

If I knew...
 That there was no time for goodbye
 And that seconds could come and take away
 All that is so precious to me
 I would make a promise to myself
 To treasure every minute, each and every day
If I knew...
 These words were your only ones to hear
 I would say all the things that I meant to say
 And let my heart lead the way
 I would speak so long like a true love song
 And simply say that I love you
 For all that you are, and for all that you do
If I knew...
 That these moments with you were our last
 If there were no more memories to share
 And no more days to show you how much I care
 I would wrap all my emotions up so tight
 And let them be free, like a spark of light

Brenda Holmes

"50 Years"

Fifty years ago when you became my wife,
that was the true beginning of my contented life.
Through our trials and tribulations, and of course our share of tears,
God has blessed us in every way, all through these fifty years.

You've always stood beside me to provide me with assurance,
it was your faith and love my dear, that was the fuel for my
endurance.

We soon longed for something more in our partnership in marriage,
so bless your heart you went right out and brought a baby carriage.

Five births later, and every one a girl,
I found myself elated living in a woman's world.
while living in a woman's world, I consoled myself in knowing;
that when the children had to go potty, I knew I wouldn't be going.

You have done your job and done it well, to this I will attest.
So since they're grown and on their own, I figured we could rest.

We have joyously reached the half century mark,
yet when you're near I still feel that spark;
I know this flame will never fade, because it was in heaven this match
was made. I will praise God forever for my matrimonial life,
for it was He who chose you to be my wife.

David H. Wood

"What Christmas Time Means To Me"

'Tis surely a season full of good cheer
That we all can look forward to each year
People gathering together to sing.
Kindness and care replace hate and greed
But, the best of it is not the gifts you receive
It's the time you spend with family
Jesus is the Son of our Heavenly Father
With him before us there can be no other
He watches over us day and night
Just to make sure we'll be alright
God will always love you
No matter the things you say or do
Shouldn't we return that same love to others too?
Peace on Earth and Goodwill towards men
That's how it began but that's not how it will end
Christmas comes but once a year,
And it should be in our hearts
Throughout the rest of the year.

Happy Birthday Jesus
Ember K. Knight

Let's Live Love

Once upon a time,
that's the way the
story goes,
Once upon a time - that's how every fairy
tale is told, every story has a happy ending,
so let's not change the mood, let's make this
world a happy place for all the human race
Let's live love, let's give love, let's show
love, let's go through life loving our
neighbors, loving every way.
If we should meet a man along our way, don't
be concerned of his wealth or his color
ask only...is there something I can do for
you today, let's not have it known that in
our hearts we don't have room for all
let's not build a wall,
Let's have a happy ending, let's make Mother
Goose proud, let's live once upon a time
with love and understanding, with everyone
doing their part, we can mend this world
of its broken heart, once upon a time.

Darlyne Smith

'Time'

There are reasons that things happen, in the order in which they do,
That's what I have always been told; you've probably heard it too.
Maybe I've missed the point, what it's all about; but I think 'Time'
Has something to do with the order in which things work out.
People say that 'Time' is a limit; of which man himself has set.
Myself, I think 'Time' has no limit; no limit has been found yet.
'Time' just keeps on coming, it's relentless in its way.
Just when you think you've got a grasp; it's the start of another day.
Seconds, minutes, hours and days, then months turn into years; gone by
Always in perfect order, but it's not easy to understand why.
You can't taste it, touch it, hear it or smell it, it's vacant in every way;
But, I guarantee you one thing I do know, it's still coming every day.
'Time' will be the death of us all, of this fact I am sure;
It's happened throughout history, for 'Time' there is no cure.
So, before 'Time' catches up to us and puts us in the ground;
We should all hold our heads up high and take a look around.
Think of others instead of ourselves and treat them like we should;
Let them know to keep their faith, show them there is still good.
We should try to do as much good as we can and be careful of our sins;
Because when 'Time' does finally pass us by, 'Eternity' begins!

Dave L. Holman

The Pond

At the pond of no return tired souls find rest;
   the air is clean,
   time serene,
   searchers end their quest.

At the pond of no return the water is crisp and clear;
   always feeding,
   never needing,
   residents have no fear.

At the pond of no return a man now resides;
   he found his place,
   full of grace,
   forevermore content inside.

The gate to the pond is open to all but all do not choose to enter;
   the faith to know,
   reap and sow,
   requires they're not the center.

The pond of no return lies beyond what we touch or see;
   the golden grass,
   universe mass,
   finally what we can be.

Debbie Douglas

All Is Black

When lights are off and all is black
The air is dead and does not blow
Does your mind slip off track
Because you're scared of what you don't know
Thoughts of how you'll soon be dead
No tears are left to spill
Voices yelling in your head
Voices evil, loud, and shrill
Nothing has ever been right
Everything has all been wrong
Gave up but won't stop the fight
Knowing that it won't be long
Your head starts to spin
In the hole you already fell
Finding there is no way to win
Your life is now a living hell
When lights are off and all is black
That air is dead and does not blow
Does your mind slip off track
Because you're scared of what you don't know

Christina Mulhall

El Chivo Chapala Cantina Juke - Box

The white pantalooned barfly plays
The ancient dome topped 45's filled wurlitzer
Yodels "!Hijole!" and staggers out the door;
A melody bombastic and florid
Concerning a love which once was torrid
But has now grown cold, aiii!! the wurlitzer glitches
Playing the tune again and again.
The laconic curious bartender
Inspects and probes, but could place no inhibition
Upon the rush and repetition
Of notes, bellowing and bleating
Of a love found to be fleeting
"aiii!! donde esta mi amor, mi overda—"
The barkeep contemplates, but the wurlitzer refuses
To cease its repetitions
Of romantic rues and ruses
"En malo malo" he murmurs "Aiii!! mi amor no vale nada!"
The stoic sipping campesinos gaze
Within, indifferent to the lover's malaise.

Jim Hunter

His Hands

In his hands, they placed the tools of the smithy's trade of old
   The anvil and the fire iron were given him to hold
And so reverently he accepted them in his mighty hands
   there began the journey of a strong but gentle man.

In those hands I placed my own, my future and my heart
   There within his hands I placed a ring and vowed "Til Death us do
   Part."
So many times those hands have held my face when life brought tragedy
   and tenderly swept away the tears to bring me hope, you see.

And in time I held those powerful hands when the secret he could see
   As he placed his hands so gently upon the life that grew inside of me.
Then in those hands, eventually I placed our tiny son
   Who wrapped his baby fingers around those large and worldly ones.

Those hands have labored endlessly and bear great scars and pain
   of hours spent in flames and iron to bring his family gain.
So many times I have found such comfort in his great protective hands
   For so gently has he loved me, the one I call husband.

Someday I will watch his wizened hands growing old and tired with age
   A book a life will be written there, a story on every page.
And in time, they'll lay down those tools of burden, with great
   respect and care
   and place those labored hands together in a last and silent prayer.

Ann Louise Brabant

Shadow Of A Rose

Hot petals in the summer sun
The bleeding of a love undone
Love is a shadow of a rose
With the right seed it grows beautiful
How we long for it
When it's not there
I the sweet musician
With the decor of a whore
Whose true wish is to hold, but a single rose
And have you next to my heart
Till your petals fall to the wind
And flow away from me
For my love is,
A shadow of your rose

Colin P. Kaestner

Children

I am an only child, me and thirteen more,
The blessings came one by one, and two through the door
what perfect little children, all those hands and feet
The hungry little mouths to feed, the diapers folded nice and neat
All done the hard way, not done from a driver's seat.
The joys were just unspeakable and oh so hard to beat
The patience that it took to raise those precious souls
was given to my mom and dad to have and to hold
They're both now up in Heaven and soon I'll be there too.
But right now I'm having too much fun and
yes I think it's cool.

Betty June Nicholl

What Is life?

Life is the beginning
    The blooming of a child
The birth of a child.

Life is a other, tending to a sick child
    Not knowing if he will be better.

Life is watching a child grow from
    An infant to a young person.

Life is a young person leaving home,
    Going to school,
Going to war.

Life is a child becoming an adult,
    Having a child and watching it
Grow into an adult.

Life is also disappointment and sorrow.

Life is losing someone whom you love dearly
    To an illness

Life is grief, understanding,
    And loving.

Andy Beller

Surroundings

The elegant way to say hi is hello.
The elegant way to say plant is flower.
The elegant way to say person is human.
The elegant way to say smart is wisdom.
The elegant way to say good is virtuous.
The elegant way to say face is motion.
The elegant way to say like is passion.
The elegant way to say life is majestic
The elegant way to say racist is unlovely
Live your life without boundaries and you will
open yourself to a whole new world

Jeff Connors

Flying

As she looked over the edge of the bridge,
the butterflies started again.
Why me? Sssshh.
No questions, no time, it's too late.
A dancer's world shattered by tragedy.
Her dream world. Glamour, beauty.
The pain in her knee still strong. Never to dance again.
Why? Sssshh.
No questions, no time. Just fly.
Fly on your dancer legs, no longer used for dancing.
The costumes. The lights. Applause.
No longer. Just fly.
Why me? Sssshh.
No questions, no time. No dream, no dance, no life.
No glitter, no glamour.
Life is no longer worth it. No dream world.
Soaring through the air, in shiny satin costumes.
Lifted in your partner's arms. Roses thrown on stage.
Curtain calls. Too good to be true. No longer true.
No more. Just fly, fly. Fly on your dancer legs.

Heather Lijoi

Bang The Drum

Bang the drum softly, bang the drum slow.
The children are sleeping in dungeons below.
They're hiding in corners you never will see.
Dreaming of Freedom that never will be.

Their soft eyes are shining- with glee or with tears?
You go on not seeing their innocent fears.
They swallow their teardrops and stifle their cries.
So few see the secrets that hide in their eyes.
Some always deny it, and some are just blind.
In their ignorant bliss, they leave children behind.
They're drowning in silence.
Their innocence lost.
They fear disbelieving
After others' deceivings.
They're protecting our images at too high a cost.

So bang the drum softly, and bang the drum slow.
The children are sleeping in dungeons below.
They're hiding in corners that no one can see.
Except other children
Surviving— like me.

Anne E. Tremblay

The Wind

The wind is blowing; it's blowing hard.
The chill of the wind is warm, compared to the chill of your
Heart.
You act like you don't know me, and that you don't care.
The way you treat me just isn't fair!
When people say I don't care for you, that is a lie.
I care for you so much; that's why I'm so blue.
I care for you so much; that's why I cry...

Amanda Richardson

Dreamer

Was it a dream, or is it real
The closeness of that person you feel
The wind in the sky blows the dream away
But the memory will always stay
Why do the good dreams always shatter
The special ones that really matter
Please let me sleep the whole night through
And let me dream my dreams of you!

Jennifer Pittman

The House

The House stands there, weathered and old,
the cracks in the walls let in the cold.
The old tin roof is rusted and worn,
the windows broken, the curtains torn.

The porch is sagging, the steps long gone,
where children laughed and played upon.
The rooms are silent, the voices stilled,
no flowers sit on the window sill.

An erie silence fills the space,
of this long forgotten, childhood place.
Where a family lived, with love once filled,
the House stands empty, silent and still.

I feel a sadness in the House,
as tho' it's waiting for someone else.
A lonely shadow of the past,
but I hear a whisper, "you're home at last!"

Dale W. Glenn

Respect

Respect—-
The currency that MUST be earned, for it freely given,
It can and will be unappreciated, wasted, devalued.

As you blindly and foolishly throw more and more of it away,
There will be those who will find fewer and fewer legitimate ways
to earn it:

Move cautiously when transacting business with Ms.Outwardly-
Righteous.
She often has two faces to go with her two names.

Mr. Elder will argue that wisdom costs, when all he really may be
offering is longevity.

Always check Dr. Education's credentials before buying into his
promises of opportunity.

Mr. Parent can be a high-risk investment, if he gives up on projects
before they've had a chance to fully develop.

Over the years, Mr. Politician has become an inattentive server whose
tip invariably cost more than the meal itself.

My brokers are Patience, Dedication, Knowledge, and Goodwill.
When they talk, I listen.

Eugene Williams Jr.

True Love At Last

The smiles of true happiness
the eyes of true love
expressing no sadness
with guiding help from above.

From two into one
for their love is exchanged in a special way
their lifetime together has only just begun
with the pleasantries of yesterday.

Once separated by war
they hold each other tightly
their hearts are open like an unclosed door
not knowing what the future might be.

Their true love is joined at last
surviving the hardships
and remembering the past
forever together with true friendship.

There is no reason to cry
because even after there is silver in her hair
their love will never die
and he will always be there.

Amanda Wilson

The '94 Earthquake of California

It was early Monday morning, about 4:30 o'clock
The earth began to quake and then commenced to rock
The people were awakened out of their sleep
Many fell upon their knees and some began to weep
The highways collapsed and people suffered mishaps
The bridges fell in, and the people could not win
All possessions were scattered and many torn apart
This act was devastating; it broke many a heart
Many people were fractured while others lost their life
All the men were asking, "Where is my Wife?"
Now, this could be a warning to all who hear the facts
So, let us be ready when the Lord performs his acts
The Saviour is coming and he's not too far away
So let us be ready to meet in Heaven someday

Eudell R. Pinnell

The Forever Man

The Forever Man walks forever alone. He has walked
the earth since the birth of the world and the soles of his
shoes never wear thin.
On his historic hike through the wilderness
of time, he has heard people's joy and seen people's pain.
He is not here to judge us or make us feel guilt, but many
a journeyman's travel has ended
afoot of the forever Man.
In his eyes are all the secrets of life and death for he will
guide your way to your final destination. Whether it be
the mountain path or the thorn valley,
He has tread many a mile since the beginning of time
and when all the sand runs out of the hourglass the
Forever Man will
   walk
     no
      more.

Jim Jarosz

Peaceful Moments

Across the road, into the field,
The evergreens solemnly bow to the wind,
Not rain or snow do they yield
They stand snow covered stance and still,
  entwined.

The sun shines on the glistening snow,
What a beautiful sight to bestow,
Man and beast, alike to endure.
The cardinal sings her overture.

Twilight is falling in the land.
The woodland creatures sound like a band,
Preparing to settle for their rest
Except for a few, who are at night their best,

Like raccoons, fox and deer, they travel far and near.
Listening for each strange noise, to hear.
The moon is shining clear and bright.
Oh! What a wonderful, peaceful night.

Carroll Johnston

Long Days And Short Nights

It was not so long ago, my child, that I was young like you.
The days were long and nights were short- there was so much to do.
Each morning brought excitement of things that were to come.
How will this day be spent; what things will I have done?

Will I run and hop and play and see my dearest friends?
Or will I hide in my private place and dream till day finds end?
Play and laugh and dream- enjoy your youth my dearest child...
For long days and short nights last such a little while.

Ann Everett Livingston

My Antonia

It happened much too fast for me to grasp
the fading of your pride in grooming, dressing well
the wilting of your elegance and social grace

It seemed that every time you washed your face
the molecules of memory would melt, seeping out from deep inside
blotted up by towels, wiped away - like tears, or blood, or sweat

But unlike those, the memories for things were not replaced
until there were so few they seemed to dance in empty ballrooms
spinning, swirling, swaying to the beat of your internal song

How I rebelled, watching that clear light diminish toward extinction
how doggedly determined that you acknowledge my reality
firmly clutching the belief that evidence could change your mind

And losing, always losing, since I never could convince you - that
you were home, not in some stranger's place - that those deceased
were gone, would not return to dine at end of day.

I never let you dream your necessary dreams
Instead I contradicted them, insisting that you look at what was real
I argued loudly to protect you from your own distorted thoughts

It was not until you died and found your way into my dreams
that I began to see that it was me whom I protected in my rage.

Jo Carpignano

Daddy Please Come Home!

Sitting all alone, lingering memories of the past.
The fast life was good to you, even though it did not last.
So now take a closer look, where did it get you in the end??
Separated from your loved ones, your children, your friends.

We're on a path of self-destruction, regrettably we're not alone.
Because millions of Black children are crying ——
    "DADDY, PLEASE COME HOME!"

Mothers are diligently struggling, trying to make ends meet.
While fathers are being incarcerated, others are dying in the street.
Why are we idly watching?? Our families are being destroyed!!
Living with excuses - "because of the economy, we're unemployed."
"My father is a hustler, I guess that's the way to win.
But with my finger on the trigger, they won't ever take me in!"

Brothers, these are OUR children, a life of crime is how they'll live.
Because we are not at home to guide them, showing them the love we
    have to give.

We're on a path of destruction. Our sons are following - we're not
    alone.
Therefore, a million more Black children will be crying ——
    "DADDY, PLEASE COME HOME!!!!"

Garnett A. Hodge

Myrtle Beach

In ocean's surf I watch them play.
The father and his son. And grabbing hands,
He lifts the boy above the crests of booming waves.
Great fun for them, the father and his son.
I sit and watch and know their joy, for I remember well.
I feel those small hands that cling so tight and trusting.
It wasn't long ago I had that fun with all my sons.
'Though sad for me that this can never be again.
My sons can still look forward to this joy.
And so I sit and wonder,
How far along will this tender touch be passed.
And yet from what great distance has it come,
From our fathers to their sons?
And could it be this loving grip so fine
Has as its source, someone divine?

Gene Decker

Platoon

The marching feet
The fire of guns
    The seeping blood
Retreat and run

    The steaming jungle
Watching your friends die
    The falling bombs
A thousand tears to cry

    With all the pain to bear
Wounds that pierce the soul
    Not sure why they fight
They leave forever unwhole

    The horror forever trapped in their minds
With visions of friends dying
    Crying tears no one can see
Screaming inside, outside sighing

    The bombs have fallen
You watched people die
    You kept shooting your gun
And you never knew why

Heather F. Piske

Faith In Poetry

This writing could be a serious poem
The first draft was written while nestled at home
A simple little scroll of a jingle
That creates an exciting internal tingle
Just one rhyme less then twenty short lines
Yet each and every word tightly binds
Then dark words disappear as an exchange for light
When reading poetry with fingertips or heard a face appears bright
So for some these verses may not be considered as wise
Oh others realize that knowledge of wording is a greater prize

Joan Kormondy

Nature's Calling

Nature is calling, are you listening?
The flowers are blooming, the trees are growing.
Nature's calling, are you listening?
The sun is shining, the breeze is blowing.
The birds are singing, the waves are crashing
against the shore.
The mountains are watching in quiet solitude.
The dolphins and whales are playing.
Nature's calling, are you listening?
Take a moment to answer her call,
because beauty is all around us,
just patiently waiting to be noticed.
Take time to notice, because in a blink of an eye,
Nature would be gone forever.
Nature's calling, are you listening!

Donna P. Herzog

Willow Me

The weeping willow sinks very low.
The girls and boys play by the road.
People drive by very slow.
But, no one cares about the willow.
They climb up his branches, and cut his limbs.
Oh, the pain I feel for him.
But, no one else cares about the willow.
Lightning strikes, and the willow dies.
Tears come from the willow's eyes.
No one cares about the willow, but I...

Jason Lin Luscombe

Remember

Remember when we all were young,
The good times we all shared?
Life was good and life was long
And Oh! How much we cared.
Remember when we all were young
Life was full of joy and hope.
If any heartache came along
We knew that we could cope.
Now we know that life is short,
A very fleeting span.
We've lived and loved and shared our lives,
It's all of God's great plan.
I hope that we can get the chance to share our lives again.
When we can cry and laugh and say,
Do you remember when?

Harvene G. McAuley

Untitled

A little boy stood where you stand today
The happy and the friendly one who always wanted to play
And as he grew and grew his face began to smile
And he was very happy for a very short while
And one day when he felt he was on top
I heard a car behind him and saw his body drop
The driver got out and saw what he had done
He looked crazed and mad I thought that he would run
Staggering along, he walked up to the boy
The boy was not breathing and there was no smile of joy
I felt a jolt of sadness that this boy had lost his life
Never would he have children or a woman as a wife
Never any future, no joy and no hate
Who were we to know that he would have been someone great
And as I thought some more my body and heart sunk
All this could have been avoided if the driver wasn't drunk
So if you have a friend who drinks too much one night
Then stop him in his tracks to avoid this tale of fright
Take away the keys, and you'll feel better too
Because that little boy could have well been you.

Gina Sensebe

Quest For Peace

The constant turmoil in this world of ours.
The hate, the bitterness, and the ugly scars.
Children starving, maimed, and filled with fright.
They feel no peace when they sleep at night.
What type of legacy, is this we leave?
To the precious offspring, that we conceived,
The hellacious wars, and powers of man,
Devastation and atrocities upon our land.
Where prejudice rears its ugly head,
And we only find solace among the dead.
Can we not, love thy neighbor and strive for peace and goodwill
Instead?
For only then can our children feel content and secure in
Their beds.

Jane E. Stillman

"Desire"

From ancient times a decree was made,
   the most beautiful would be his to hold.
A thousand ships.
   A city burned.
Helena and he would never be.
For he and I a common bond,
   a desire for the most beautiful.
You hold my heart.
You hold my life.
For you and me the decree was made.

David Leistner

In Silence

Around the silence a gentle voice forms a word.
The hearer ever wonders how the sound
is perceived from within.
Listening is the hard part.
To listen, nothing is to be done but to be
to the silencing of the waiting
to the wondering of the moment
to the wandering of the soul
to the blowing of the breeze that
carries the unspoken voice
as it travels through the canyons
of the silence.
At last, the sound is gathered
from the moments of waiting ages
and enters the open door of expectations:
"Come."

Joela Leinberger

The Images In The Mirror; So Distant Yet So Clear

A frightened child trapped inside, fighting desperately to survive.
The horrors of her past to be unavoidably revived.

The truths of yesteryear have since then become lost.
In the confusion and the memories that soon do show their cost.

Lies come back to haunt us, as nightmares take their toll.
The innocence of childhood seeking desperately for a soul.

Someone to help, confide in... and guide me through the night.
The darkness then confines me and shades me from the light.

Serenity to destruction... life in a year becomes.
Loneliness overwhelms me... to death my soul succumbs.

A stranger shows compassion, listening intently to my cries.
Turning darkness into sunshine, bringing forth unbreakable ties.

He's shown me strengths within myself, I never knew I possessed.
And passions deep within me... and evils I confessed.

Without him I'd not be here, for life became too much.
But he helped me see the good in life, that then seemed out of touch.

The darkness is behind me, with light to guide my way.
My love to that kind stranger, who's thought of each new day.

Ilene J. Kaufmann

Infatuation Or Love

Infatuation they say is pure desire, that instant, hot burning fire.
The heart pounds aloud, the mind stops, the pulse quickens and
won't tire. Time flies when together and slows when apart.
Philosophers idle that infatuation and love differ and are not
coincidental. Infatuation can steam with some lusting and sexual hoping,
while love is maturing of friendship and coping. Must each meeting
end in mating? Must each evening end in waiting...From relations that
are not wanting? Or should each day, each meeting take its free
rein not pre-conditioned by past paradigms or pain?
Love can make-up for much one doesn't have.
And infatuation can provide that salve. To love, to share, to care
makes one better....and rare. Let's agree love is more mature. It is
trust, it is understanding. It is not I but we, it is seeing the
whole inner person. It is not suspect. It isn't dazzled by the
exterior nor with the trappings but the naked truth. We love because
we can respect. This somewhat worldly, this somewhat studious
philosopher boldly says it is not infatuation or love...It is
infatuation and love! 'Cause it keeps the heart pounding, keeps the
fire burning, keeps the pulse beating, keeps one yearning.
But first there must be Infatuation...

James M. Fitzgerald

Frustration

I feel as if I'm on a merry-go-round
The horse goes up when it should come down—
The music has no beat - no rhythm
The horse I'm on is just a schism
I perceive that I am all alone
The horse can't figure which way home
I contemplate with my feeble brain
The horse comes loose and ends up lame
I get so dizzy and I lose my grip
The horse jerks wildly and starts to trip
I think there's no way off this ride
And sure enough the horse breaks stride
My thoughts whir as I grope for help
The horse seems helpless and loses step
I do my duty as round we go
The horse ambivalent: both fast and slow
Sometimes my path is straight ahead
The horse turns quickly - going back instead
I always lose my concentration
The horse is riding in utter frustration.

Elizabeth P. Ergle

One More Day

I walk through a forest thinking of you
The leaves have fallen with a deep golden hue
I can see you now, with your dog and a gun
Out for a hunt and to have a little fun
I stop for a minute to watch a squirrel play
Wishing this age you'd always stay
Let me have you one more day

This forest so dense and filled with trees
Resembles the pleasures and joys you've given me
A baby so happy, cuddly and sweet
In all the world over, you couldn't be beat
You've brought sunshine to my life with a sparkling ray
Let me have you one more day

You're fourteen now, and still growing strong
In my heart there's a spot that only you belong
May your dreams come true, and your goals be fulfilled
With the sun lighting your path 'til the world stands still
You've made me so proud in your own loving way
Let me have you one more day

Billie S. Glasscock

Life Within A Cave

Do you have a soul my dear friend?
The mysteries you leave are without end.
What are your emotions, values, and morals?
My dear friend, I don't want to quarrel.

What are you feeling deep inside?
You're so elusive;
Looks as though you are trying to hide.
Hide from what? Are you afraid?
Life is too short to live within a cave.

You're so complex and hard to get to know.
Is your self-esteem so low?

Yet, so many questions remain unanswered
And many opportunities are missed,
Which makes it challenging for our relationship to exist.

It is dark and gloomy and lonely in the cave.
Come out into the sunshine,
Don't be afraid, be brave!
Many take risks along the way.

Free yourself, I say!
You only live once so come out of your cave.

Elizabeth A. Kitts

Jeweled Raindrops

You are joy, Laugh and I feel your soul.
The light shines so brightly I can barely see.
You are hope, speak and your voice soothes my pain.
You are love, smile and the heavens open
up and send down a warm shower of jeweled
raindrops. And I immerse myself in their warm
glow, passing them out to all the people I meet.

You are one with me, and that's all I will ever need.

Jacqueline Cofield

An Ode To Teachers

Teachers are people who reach out and touch
the lives of their students with learning and such
But touching's not easy and they really do care
And often they hear, with a cold-hearted stare,

That ".. going to school is just a horrible drag
And doing all that homework just makes me gag."
But still, if homework lags, then some students will get
From parents, some awful hurting right where they sit.

It's not just youngsters that homework dislike
But adults in their lessons are prone to strike
The homework required for lessons to learn
And grades that are worthy are quite apt to spurn.

To teachers, no matter what age that they teach
It seems that some students they never can reach
For a teacher to fail to reach one of these
To them is as devastating as high winds in the trees.

But teachers who care continue to strive
To make each day's lessons come really alive
To help that student learn, give that one some aid
Their joy of teaching, that's how teachers are paid.

David A. Jones

The Family

Whatever happened to the family - bonding and caring?
The love of Mom and Dad with time for problem sharing.
Discussions and council were held over dinner everyday
But, now there's no one at the table they have a TV tray.
Mom and Dad have their trays, and Brother and Sister have one too,
Each in his or her own space, eat and then you're through.
No one knows or cares what happened in their day,
Was it good? Was it bad? Did you get a chance to say?
Maybe sister had a fight at school and threatened with a knife,
And if by chance you talked and listened you might have saved her life
Maybe Dad had a disgruntled employee that he had to fire or suspend,
And if by chance you talked and listened, your opinion he did depend.
Whatever happened to the family? - It seems to be slipping away,
We need to stick together, laugh, love, share, care and pray!

Elaine S. Powell

Children's Screams

Death and destruction echo through
the children's ears, murder and blood
are reflected in the children's eyes,
and fall in fearful tears. Pain and
misery run out of the children's mouths.
Their poor little bodies full of nothing
but fear of the terrifying world they
will be raised in. Shaking and wondering
if they will die in their sleep or be shot
in the streets, wondering how long their
lives will last, wondering and asking
themselves every day that goes past.
Children's screams echo through the wind,
wondering each day if it will ever end.

Amanda Blazis

The Old Barn

There is an old barn now surrounded by weeds
The names have been changed on the land deeds.
A shed at the left with a corral out back
Were used for repairing and storage of saddles and tack.
Lanterns, saws, ropes, and pails
Hung on the walls by 10 penny nails.
Three horses, a cow, and a few lazy hens
All had to share one large pen.
There was feeding, milking, and other chores to be done,
Once finished, nothing left but fun.
Playing hide and seek and jumping off rafters
The old barn came to life with children and laughter.
Oh, the smell of the wood and of fresh cut hay
Forever a memory of my childhood days.

Julie Cude

Room Service

Two man servants stand at the entrance to
the new year, one on either side as if
at the entrance of some grand hotel room.
They look like a couple of young Lionel
Barrymores all dolled up like Jeeves.

She arrives by elevator, looking quite the
movie star herself, crossing the threshold
in the controlled light of legends, tossing her
green cloak — the one that captures her
eyes — to Lionel on the right.

Lionel on the left receives her heavy bag
and matching smile. "I've heard the service
is great here," she says. "Perhaps I'll
stay eternity. Do you think you could
handle that?" The twins nod, winken, blinken.

"But darlings...." she stammers. "Oh,
never mind." No need to be alone at a time like
this. Go ahead, get on with the show — pretend
it's nothing more than ordering room service.
The work: Little more than a bubble bath.

Chris Gorley

Untitled

Fathers don't come any finer than
  the one I had in my life.

He gave his all to his three
  daughters and a beautiful wonderful wife.

He's gone to be with my sister
  she's up in heaven you know?
I'm sure their lives are filled
  with a very different kind of glow.

Brenda F. Troxel

The Wind Blows

The wind blows.
The fallen leaves turn cartwheels down main street
  like clowns in a circus parade.
Lifted by the wind in a magic leap,
  they are transformed into dancers,
Twirling turning as in a symphony ballet.
The colors shimmer in shades of yellow, red and gold
  under the spotlight of the sun.
Fall has come to the city.
The chill of winter waits beyond the mountain peaks
  for its cue to enter.
In its glorious coat of white.
  Another season, act of nature.

Bettye Jane Street

Goodbye

Saying goodbye to the one you love,
the one you never kissed,
  The one who never held you,
even though you wished.
  How your heart aches at words unspoken,
and how you feel your heart is being broken.
  You want to cry,
but you can't cry,
  and it is no use thinking you want to die.
The only time you touched him,
  was in play or in prayer.
You will miss him you think,
  but others will be there.
Your body will ache for the physical love,
  Your friendship never shared.
But it was nice to have a friend,
  you knew really cared.

Jami Lee Pritts

The Tree Of Calvary

Do you still remember, oh tree upon the hill
The part you played that friday, the scriptures to fulfill

And do you still remember, on whose shoulders you were laid
How they mocked and beat him, oh what a part you played

And do you still remember, how they nailed him to your limbs
And how he bled for mankind, to free us from our sins

And do you still remember, how they gambled for his robe
And how they laughed and cursed him, so ugly and so bold

How when his breath did leave him, they placed him in a tomb
And now the earth did quake, and it turned dark at noon

And when they went to wash him, he was no longer there
He had gone to join his father, flighting in the air

I want you to remember, oh tree upon the hill
That Christ arose that Easter, and he is with us still

Elizabeth Honabarger McIntire

The Church

There is a church at the end of the block.
The people, the lambs of God, gather there in a flock.
I hear the church bells ringing.
I must go in and hear the choir singing.
The walls echo with profound love.
It must be spiritual, love from above!
Joyous songs about our Savior and friend.
Songs of love, I hope shall never end.
Before Heaven, I enter in,
I must be first rid of all earthly sin.
Where else to go, but at the end of the block.
To gather up my senses and take stock,
Of all my earthly doings I have done.
Before I face alone, my own, final setting sun.

Doris M. Roll

The Sun

The sun is the thing that brightens our day,
The sun is the thing that guides our way.
The sun is the thing that keeps you warm,
The sun is the thing that keeps the weather a norm.
The sun is the thing that sometimes makes you hot,
The sun is the thing that makes you sweat on the spot,
The sun is the thing that makes you smile so bright,
The sun is the thing that leaves in the night.
The sun is the thing that without it there would be sorrow.
The sun is the thing that will always be here tomorrow.

Amy Watroba

Mistral

In my mind's eye I see ...
the pink rain lilies
sprinkled across the fields ...
the row upon row of nut trees
marching across the hills ...
the blue lakes where wild black swans swim
and giant white birds wade.

I see the mountains in the distance.
I remember the cool fresh air ...
the robin's egg blue of the sky ...
and I long to be again ...
at Mistral.

Janet Little

A Lady Such As She

The untainted beauty, the enduring charm per
The presence and the aura of her.
And what a privilege it is to be
In the environs of a lady such as she.

But somehow it seems it is a mistake
That she lives in this present time and place.
For she invokes images of an earlier time
When the world seemed a bit more kind.

Where she rides in a carriage on a red-brick street
Smiling beneath the canopy that shields from the summer heat.
Where smiling elders greet from their front porch swing
Appreciative of the joy to which she brings.

Where her gentleman assists as she rises to depart
Then together they stroll across the lawn of the park.
Where little girls surround with a spirited glee
And wish one day to be - a lady such as she.

Dan L. Perry

Quiescence

As the days pass by and the hours few,
The rain still comes and the sky still blue,
The night still falls and the stars in view,
While the spirits join in colored hue.

As hands tick time, minutes slip away,
The wind glides high and the clouds turn gray,
The wolf still lone and the deer its prey,
While the phantoms of night rest by day.

As months grow old, a new year in sight,
The hills of green, the mountaintops white,
The sun shines at morn', the moon this night,
While the restless soul gives up its plight.

Hillery H. Hall

Summer Is For Lovers

Summer is for lovers, that is, you and me

As we walk hand in hand making circles
in the sand

I can feel the warmth of your sweet caress,
as we watch the beauty of the sunset

A palette of purples, pinks, and blues, you
suddenly whisper, "I love you"

I feel the tenderness of your words so kind
I melt at the touch of your lips against mine

Summer is for lovers, yes, it's true, because
it happened to me and to you

Dana Daugherty

The Answer

The core of a tree
The seed from a wildflower
The extremities of the universe
All but knowing the meaning of existence.

Forever clutched into the bowels of the earth.
Have no greed, anger, or hate;
live as one: function as a whole.

The scent of a flower,
A warm rain on flesh,
Feeling as one with nature.

Experience your surroundings.
Love nature.
Respect her home.
The purpose of life?
It is all around you.....
Experience!

David A. Macdonald

The Shadow Of Loneliness

Night has fallen, the stars are out.
The shadow of loneliness lurks about.
The darkness its cover, us humans its prey, it creeps
through the night, and soon through the day.

The darkness surrounds me, I reach for the light.
It's then that I hear the darkness, the night.
I sit and I listen but there is no one there.
The darkness has deepened, it's now despair.
Yet the shadow of loneliness continues filling the air.

I run and hide and wish for the sun, I stop and listen; what
do I hear?
The shadow of loneliness is already here.
It waits for me in every room.

It is the darkness, it is the night, the shadow of
loneliness now creeps toward light.
I hang my head then and I start to cry.
I sit and I listen, there's no reply.
The shadow of loneliness is clever and sly.
Despair its companion, its lover, its friend, once allowed
to filter in, the shadow of loneliness becomes your friend...

Chris Midgett

Four Seasons Of Life God's Will

Oh, Spring is the birth of new life
The smell of fresh flowers is a delight
As the days grow longer, and the night air is still
We will return tomorrow if it's God's will.

By Summer everything is in full bloom
It's a great time for brides and grooms
The weather changes day by day, and the skies darken of grey
The rain falls and brings a chill
We will return tomorrow if it's God's will.

As fall comes, the leaves turn brown and fall to the ground
The days become shorter, life enters the dark
Cast this season to the hills, the best days are gone as we part.
The days and seasons have their ills
We will return tomorrow if it's God's will

Winter is like death, motionless and cold
We wait for spring as we grow old.
Like pain in one's heart, it will soon subside
For God Almighty remains our guide
Life will come again and cure our ills
We will return tomorrow if it's God's will.

Ernest Clark

The Creaking Of The Door

The empty dark, alone in sleep,
The shallow breath and none of deep.
A sound she heard or maybe not.
Was just a dream, was just a thought?
Was it real and all the more,
Was it the creaking, the creaking of the door!

The endless night, with lonely stare,
The mind that wonders of what is there.
Again the sound, all so clear,
Was just the wind, was something near?
Was it real and all the more,
Was it the creaking, the creaking of the door!

The whispered prayer, with hopes for light,
The eyes that search for end of night.
Return the light, reveal the sorrow,
Weep for those with no tomorrow,
Was it real and all the more,
She had heard the creaking, the creaking of the door!

Jeffery Scott Vass

I Stand

We walked along the stranded beach speaking not a word,
the silence broken forever by that thoughtless bird.
I turned to you but you are gone neither seen nor heard.
Now I realize that I stand and I stand alone.

I thought I heard you call my name like you used to do.
However I was mistaken, it was only the wind crying its pity
for it knows how I am lost without you.
Because now I stand and I stand alone.

My hand reaches out to grasp yours, but all I feel are memories.
Memories so intense they have depth and weight, yet they are only
memories.
As I stand alone.

I stand here awaiting for your return.
I'll stand here until hell freezes and the heavens burn.
I'll stand here but I'll stand alone.

I will stand here all alone waiting for you to return.
Don't make me stand alone.

Danielle Bassett

Random Thoughts

Like vapors of frost over drifts of snow
  these random thoughts just wander and grow.
They weave silver webs over winding streams
  and dance with joy in forests of dreams.
They embrace dear friends from both far and near
  and linger in places of yesteryear.
Like clouds of music floating through the sky
  they bring back voices from days gone by.
And on and on they wander and grow —
  these random thoughts — they come and they go.

Grace Deitch-Boogay

Love?

The wrenching pain of a broken heart.
The sweet caress of someone's touch.
To break the heart of the one you love,
to see the tears streaming down their face.
Encounter the pain, face to face.
A single rose and then a tear
can fly by in just a year.
Love is not a rhyme, it is not a game.

Jessica Bilodeau

Seasons

The bleakness of winter is upon us.
The songbirds of summer have flown to warmer climes.
The trees have lost their foliage and stand naked to the wind.
The grass forms a brown carpet beneath our feet.
The barren earth seems to yield no life.

With spring comes the return of the birds' sweet song.
The trees spread their budding branches to capture the
  warming sun.
New sprigs of green grass appear daily.
The earth brings forth the first radiant blooms of new life.

As it is with the seasons, so it is with our life.
The darkness of winter, with no song of joy or fragrant
  bloom to gladden,
Soon gives way to the bursting forth of spring's vibrant joy.
As the seasons wax and wane, so move the cycles of our life.
Winter's ominous storms of discord and discontent
Are soon followed by the overwhelming hope of spring.

Janice Hodge

The Word

Words exist like little keys, able to unlock
the soul of man;
They can make him think, laugh, even cry…
Defeating the passage of time, never to die,
words are alive; be they truth or lie.

Written or just remembered —
Spoken out loud or only in mind,
something eternal, men can leave behind.

Often misunderstand, not always serving
their intent — Serving nonetheless,
Even when what is said, is not what is meant.

In the beginning was the word —
Passed down; lost, only when forgot,
Existing, until given consent,
Wandering through space; waiting…
Creating as used — worthy or not.

Jeffrey Lawson I

Mankind

The moon is mysterious and wise
The stars are dreams, wishes, and hopes in the sky.
The sky is of the universe which knows all,
not reveling it, but the sky reveals a little piece at a time,
to a dreamer with hopes so high and wishes in the night sky.
The universe holds the key to all mankind.

Hilary Clark Mann

A Dream I Dream

A dream I dream, o' eerie night,
  The moon, the starts, a morbid fright.
  I whistle a song to calm my fears,
  As shadows lurk I fight the tears.

A dream I dream, o' empty skulls,
  Of hearts and veins that once were full.
  I pray oh Lord my soul to keep,
  As I walk along the boards, I creep.

A dream I dream, o' nocturnal souls,
  I see the faces of nameless foes.
  As I reach to grasp the sunless day,
  I scream the words I want to say.

A dream I dream, I wish it were,
  But rather a nightmare with fangs and fur.
  I rush to wake and see the light,
  And suppress the fears of this eerie night.

Jason A. Caprario

Nature's Delight

High in the sky. What I could see. The angels,
the stars, the world ahead of me. In the darkness
your eyes grow afar. The gorgeous sight yes, they are.
The wind that whistles beyond the streams, the
ground beneath what I must dream. Of weeping willows
jumping across the water, through the deep white screen,
and into the quarter or what it seems. The quarter
moon, as it shines above, lighting the world like a candle
of love. The shadows it makes upon the doors.

The icing that sticks forevermore. Through the trees
what do I see? A lion, the beast of all humanity. Its
roar echoes in the distance and scares away all life
existence. I ran hard, as fast as I could go, the speed
unlike any man would know. Scared as frightened as
could be, I ran to the tallest oak tree. Only to find that
the lion has beaten me. As he gobbles me down, the last words
I say can still be heard to this very day: Listen, listen into the
night and hear a screaming of nature's delight. Good-bye my
lovely, wonderful sights that I have seen upon this night.

Geisela Parson

The Wedding Rose

This is the story that I was told it's
The story of the wedding rose
  it was on her wedding day. She was shot
and killed they say
  She was dressed in her bridal gown and
carried one white rose in her hand
  She died there in her lover's arms as her
red blood flowed all around
  her white rose fell to the ground and slowly
Turned red with all the blood around
  now people come from far and near to see
The wedding rose bloom each year
  its bloom is as white as the snow then
The blood red begins to show.
  it starts out a snowy white then the
bloom turns red and bright
  The wedding rose is lovely to see. But it
only blooms out once a year

Betty Bomar Ragsdell

No Greater Feeling

Your tiny little body moving gently within mine,
There is no greater feeling.

Seeing you born into my life,
There is no greater feeling.

Daddy's expression of amazement in your birth,
There is no greater feeling.

I see myself in you in so many ways,
There is no greater feeling.

All I love about daddy I see in you,
There is no greater feeling.

Your soft small hands caressing my face,
There is no greater feeling.

Your ever growing and unconditional love for me,
There is no greater feeling.

The way you greet me with such excitement each day - without fail,
There is no greater feeling.

Just knowing how many more joys you will bring my way,
There is no greater feeling.

To know that God chose me to be your Mother.
There is no greater feeling, no greater feeling - no greater feeling.

Gail E. Stashick

Death Waits

The rain continues, it has for days
The sun attempts, through the haze.
Push it back. It's hopeless now.
Feel
Life
Slip
—it's easy now

BUT WAIT
SEE — a baby's smile
HEAR — a bird's sweet song
FEEL — a friend's warm touch

A RAINBOW — LOOK —

STRUGGLE NOW, with the dark-masked form
as he gathers speed toward the impending storm
AWAKE, — refreshed — alive
death robbed again by hope, the minds own will.

Billie A. Williams

I Never Could Resist A Sunrise

it's five a.m. in the morning......
The sun hasn't risen yet....
The robin outside my window is
Singing" "Get up! Get up!"

I roll over and cover my head....
The bed has a hold on me...
I'm so comfortable and warm, here inside....
My mind says: "Go away, let me sleep
Just a few more minutes. Please."

Like an alarm clock, that robin
Keeps singing: "Get up! Get up!"
The daylight is arriving too fast....

The sun's rays has crept right
Through my window....
It has stolen the sleep from my eyes....
I must confess, I got up, got dressed....
For I never resist a sunrise....

Florence M. Mick

Colors

For The Tiwa Nation
The sins of the fathers are come down on the sons or so it is said.
There is nowhere to run, for surely this cannot be fled.

Some things we did to the Native Americans are still being done.
In a war without arrowheads, cannons and guns.

The prejudice against the African Americans still exist in far too
many places. The lynchings take place in the court rooms
where they fail to win so many of their cases.

The Japanese Americans are still in recovery
from being captured like horses gone wild.
They not only lost their homes, land and bank accounts,
they lost the most important thing, their lifestyle!

All the blame has been laid on the Nazis for the extermination of
six million Jews.
Well how many of you are aware that other powers that be knew about
it or does that come as news?

If you were Red - you were dead!
If you were Black - just work and stay back!
If yellow - shut up and stay mellow!
If white it was perfectly alright!

History need not necessarily repeat itself again.
There is absolutely no reason we can't see beyond color and all be
friends.

Gordon Lester

Spring

It's only December
The thoughts of Spring lie dormant in my head
To think of it for just a moment
I have nothing to dread
Just think of its beauty and grace
A feeling of freshness in the air
To feel cool breezes in your face
To see the ground erupt with wonder
The flower as fragrant as perfumed lace
Oh yes! I can imagine a time
When everything has its new beginning
But I stop, for the snow is constantly spinning
Its flakes all around me, as if to say, "I'm winning"
"It's my time and Spring can wait
And take its turn
In the process of life
It just has to learn"
So back in my real world of white
Thoughts of Spring slowly fades
'Til its visionary beauty is out of sight

Edith Barton

Stricken Society

An ocean, a river or maybe the sea.
The tides and its waves bowled over me.
I'm trapped in a current, would it be so wrong?
To go under not fight and pretend I'm not strong.
To drown in my sorrows and be taken away.
And pray I'll return another day.
To be given a life and a brand new start.
For my old one was hopeless and falling apart.
But it was me who failed and none other is to blame.
So why should God grant me nothing but shame.
Why does desperation cloud our judgement so?
Why do people take their lives when it's not time for them to go?
Why are people starving when food is thrown away?
Why do people live outside, is there nowhere they can stay?
Or are people of this world developing hearts of stone and
only looking out for family of their own.
The answers to my questions I may never know or maybe when in
heaven an angel might tell me so.
But then it is too late to tell, because I've gone away and
who knows where the world will be if I return one day.

Carol Nomikos

A New Beginning

When days turn to nights and weeks to months
the time to say good-bye has come
when parting is the hardest thing to do
and crying the easiest.
When you sit and cry for no reason
and depression is all you can bear
that is the end.
Whether it be the end of summer
or the end of winter
that is when you say good-bye
to the end of something you love
something that comes only once
for a short time, but dry your eyes
and put that smile back on your face
and realize that to every end
there is a beginning... a new beginning
nothing ever really ends.
Not a smile, not a day, not even a life
for it lives forever in your heart
for an end is the base for a new beginning.

Carolyn M. Gomes

Rainbows Always Come

Quietly the rain came.
The trees began to cry.
Suddenly the thunder joined in,
And chirping birds flew by.
We were playing games in our back yard,
But when the lightning flashed we ran inside.
Our Mom had come to call us in,
She helped us find a place to hide.
It wasn't long before rain stopped,
And all was quiet once again.
We cheered with joy and ran outside,
To see the rainbow down the lane.
Many years have passed since then.
The sky is clouding up once more.
But over years our fears have passed,
Because we've found what rain is for.
It makes things green, but that's not all,
For there's the rainbow, sun, and more.

James B. Allis

Drifted

As we stood on the mountain so far up
The two of us looking into the sky as far as we could see.
The two of us there
Our souls together
Our arms apart.
Thinking of our future together as we feel as one there is two
Our minds and body flowing as one
But also fading apart not knowing that we're drifting further
And further away.
As I stood on the mountain so far up
Looking at the sky
I was there by myself alone.
We had drifted apart.
Into one mind.
One body
And one soul.

Jennifer K. Woods

Marriage

Marriage is two people sharing,
the ups and downs, sweetened by caring.

Two, who by their sharing, grow,
and by their caring, seem to glow.

The things said in anger, soon forgotten,
in the wed of tender moments, love is caught in.

When each is aware, they don't own the other,
only then, they become the others lover.

The days of life, shared together,
both looking, forward, to its lasting forever.

Dora "Doreen" E. Green

Tyranny

His shoulders slumped, his eyes cast down.
The victim of the tyrant's frown.
The punches rough and hard were flung
From tyrant's lips, and mouth and tongue.

To dwarf the growth of youth and spirit
And cast his dreams in fire and dust
And make the youth an old man's lust.

But youth and spirit will not be lost
From lack of justice and at no cost
Will knuckle to the tyrant's demand
For liberty is his staunch stand
And king of his fatherland.

Dianne M. Young

My Oh My... I Wonder Why

My path finally reached the seashore nearby
  The vision before me engulfs my senses
    Pounding surf rings true in my ears
Forever that sound, since the beginning of time
  My oh my... I wonder why
The sun's rays feel so hot and dry
  My body sweats, too wet
A stiff breeze rustles my hair
  Cools my skin...and my thoughts
    My oh my... I wonder why
Cute little sand crab rambles close by
  Hurrying, scurrying for food
  Hiding from harm, silent cry
  ...but not from me
    My oh my... I wonder why
Look there, watch that sea gull soar
  Higher than high, far into the sky
So much more to flight than meets the eye
  A peaceful sigh, tranquil am I
    My oh my... I wonder why?

Frank Hoetker

The Storm

Nature tells us her moods, her whims
The history of the world in violence and in beauty.
Nature moves us to our destiny
With sometimes indirect pushes,
With strokes that bear us on our way, when we oft wish not to go.
And ofttimes we work for, with and against this mighty agent
This invisible god which no human hand as yet directs;
Sensing in our predominance of self
The selflessness facing us by the self of Nature.
But we are ignorant and ignorant of it.
We are vain for no logic cause
And cause no logic in this effect.
Nature tells us: "Work with me."
But yea, we say: "Against."
And this is our dilemma.
With ourselves.
The world.
The cosmos.

Edward Kipp Crater

The Murder And The Baby

Here, beside this river,
the trees shed their tears.

They knew that a sliver of God's light shone in those eyes,
that divine strength held the blade
And that
She watched from her own sacred window
the approach of that which will always come
until it comes no more.

Melodies of spheres harmonized in that final cry, echoing down
the wet halls, mirroring the cruel intent to shed blood now.

Other eyes in other places shone with the light. The tears fell not
in the rushing waters, but into the dust. The smallest one, however,
had left. His eyes were no longer shining.
And
No cry had marked his passing.
The mother did not know.
The doctor did not know.
The observers did not know.

Only the trees, here, beside this river, wept.

Jonathan Love

Lost Freedom

This room is vile and repugnant
The walls tell tales of misery
  and pain
Voices filled with violent cries of
  hatred lash out at society
Bitter resentment gnaws my mind
I scream out in sheer agony
I can hear the cries of pathetic wretches
  being tortured here
Their shrieks pierce my ears
  I writhe in anguish
I clench the cold iron bars
My head becomes a torture chamber
  for my mind
A void fills my soul and the revolting
  taste of LOST FREEDOM
  is found deep within me

Deana Tommaselli

Serenity

As I sit on my back porch
  the warm wind whispers through the trees
And a sudden sea of calmness
  seems to envelope me.

The fireflies dance across the grass
  so ever brightly green
Like fairies in a wonderland
  so peaceful, calm, serene.

The full moon rises, o'er all the earth
  and I can hardly believe
That I am just a little part
  of this awesome summer scene.

And as I sit with wonder
  only one word seems to be
The perfect word for this magic night
  Serenity.

Beth A. Strong

"Raising My Family"

I'm a man alone, to raise my family, but that isn't easy
the way the world is today.
The cost of living has gone so high, you can't afford to stay alive,
and yet you can't afford to die, the cost of that is up as well.
I struggle along from day to day, just barely able to make and meet.
My family doesn't have much, but we have each other and lots of love.
My family and I are very close and do lots of things together,
that means a lot to us.
We can't afford to do many things we'd like to do, but we make up for
it, with family work days and little outings, not far from home.
My family and I are very happy that way we are
and wouldn't want our lives to change, one little bit,
as that's the way we are.

Dawn Dee

Moonlight

When the sun goes down, and the moon comes up
There is no more daylight, not even a buttercup
The moonlight is filled with wonders and mysteries
It's been this way since the beginning of history

The stars seems to dance all around
Yet night remains still without a sound
When I stare at the moon, it stares back at me
It seems to say sleep my child, I'll watch over thee

Bernice Marcus

Think

In the light of O.J., Goldman and Brown.
The whole world's watching,
  but the Lord just frowns.
He frowns for our Black man,
  who was prominent and free.
To be judged by the media,
  by you and me.
Just looking at this man,
  I can feel his pain.
After all this is over,
  he'll never be the same.

And as for Black History,
We were hit hard again.
  Another black leader, another good man.
When will it end, this hatred in the heart.
For America is free to all
  men, and not just part.
For God made all men equal,
  not just some you see.
I pray hard for O.J., because he's special to me.

Ardie L. Johnson

Always... Me

Adrift, a feather on a cloud,
the wind rustles the edge of self,
Stirring the restlessness within, allowing dreams
to take form; exploding a bright array of color and sound.

Afloat, this feather caught on a quick breath of air,
carelessly tossed and yet...
so precise in the knowing, the sensing of where.

Take me there, oh, cloud... fly me to the heights
of knowledge itself.
Allow the inner self escape on this feather of light;
Adrift in the sea of mysteries.

Climbing higher, ever higher through the atmosphere,
with never a thought of attachment.
Belonging yet, so free, with never a thought of the
bond to home.

Home, adrift within my home... my space;
flying atop the endless sky.
To the restless clouds of time, where there is no time,
In a space where there is only space.

Free... always free to be... Always. ME

Joy Hayward

A Song In The Storm

As I awoke, at early dawn,
The wind was blowing amidst a storm,
Then I heard a little bird singing in the rain.
A bright little song. He did sing.

The song he sang was sweet as could be.
Why he did so, was a mystery to me.
If a little bird can be so happy in the rain
Why should we be always ready to complain.

God gives us sunshine, as well, as the rain.
So let's share a little song and never complain.
For in each of our lives, a little rain must fall.
But then comes the sunshine, to benefit us all.

So if the day is cloudy.
Just sing a little song.
And spread the beautiful sunshine
To help others along.

Eloise N. Callin

Night Vision

If God had given us eternal day
The wonders after dark we'd never know.
At night we see the heavens on display—
The universe revealed in starlight's glow;
By day, we could not see the lunar ball
Float by like a celestial balloon.
The northern lights' display could not enthrall,
Nor ghostly wisps that drift across the moon.
It is by stars that men can navigate,
But to be seen stars need a darkened sky.
The marvels that the heavens at night create,
The brilliant light of day cannot supply.
  By day we see our own vicinity;
  But in the night we glimpse infinity.

Jean M. Munn

"Pain Of Freedom"

Children mourning over their father's death
Their father thinking of them and his love
before his last breath
He had a job to do
a mission to complete
for his family's freedom
he would not accept defeat
Now as they take him home
his job is over and done
Lord, watch over his soul, let him rest
and never more to roam
He loved his country and her rolling plains
He had nothing to lose
His family had everything to gain
A true soldier like the one above
hates to fight
his heart full of kindness and love
Let all remember the ones lost
but those in green know
Freedom is worth the cost

David Ray Wampler

What Power!

What greater power is there known
Then he who made the heavens and earth
What supreme being of sheer genius let clouds be blown
And permits undesirable death, and joyful birth?

It is he, who flung the stars so high
And caused the moon to light the night
The same one lets us laugh and sign
Also cheers the day with the sun's great light.

That merciful deity bestows health and strength
And rationality to one and all
In return he asks "from wrong repent,"
From rich and poor, great and small

He made the great rivers, and the seas
And birds that wing the air in flight
He made the toads, asses and bees,
And owls that hoot throughout the night.

This great power rules on and on
From ages past, to ages to come
He shall remain upon his throne,
Till all on earth fill one silent dome.

Donald Robinson Sr.

Beauty In The Combine

Machines, moving in the darkness.
Their lights illuminate their silent
dance in the distance.
Closer, they move through the field,
Toward their destination.
They lumber ahead unceasingly,
Unconscious of the destruction which they create.
They emerge, smashing and crashing
Slashing and gnashing their mighty teeth and gears.
Spitting it all out behind as they pass,
turn and start in again.
Quieter now, not so alarming or scary.
Back they go, lighting up their
own patch of darkness as they slowly slip
into silence.
Once more becoming, not a thing of destruction,
But a thing of beauty;
To watch as they continue after dance in the night.

Christopher Jon Fair

Finding The Truth

You're born with the heart to care.
Then moments, days, years pass; the heart grows cold
Cold longing for the warmth it once felt.
The warmth you so long for is nowhere in reach,
A memory that dies as the mind wonders away
back to the first moment of joy.
Joy felt only as a child eating candy for the first time.
How sweet the taste tingling in a small mouth.
Eyes filled with wonder of how other candy would make you feel.
Finding out that all candy can never be as sweet as the first bite.
It only flavors the mouth from then on.
Being tricked by sweet candy that turns sour in the middle.
Telling yourself you will never eat candy again.
Then finding yourself with a bag full of what you have never tasted.
Fearing to eat any, remembering that sour time.
In haste the bag gets pitched to the wind.
The wind blows the bag from side to side.
Sending the sweet tempting fragrance in your nostrils.
You reach for the bag picking one drop, hoping for the same taste you
felt as a child. Finding the truth. It will never be the same again.

Franchesa Wolfe

Heart And Soul

Where are my heart and soul? They're not in me.
They're soaring along the horizon, singing with the sea gulls.
They're dashing playfully in and out of the crescent waves.
They're circling the lighthouse peak, dancing to a rhythmic clang;
They're resting upon the warm, soft, silvery sands;
absorbing the tranquil din of gentle waves lapping upon the shore.
I need them inside of me, to even begin to move.
But I need them where they are, to even begin to live.

Debora Bischoff

Untitled

There's gnome in the forest
waiting and whispering, running away at the first noise
People all around us
talking and sitting, stopping at the glance of their teacher
I often sit alone
thinking and wondering, waiting to see what will happen next
There's a person over there
talking and laughing, won't stop for anything
People can be cruel
I, Erin, always look forward to days people are not cruel

Erin Linstrum

Lost Love

We were like one you and I,
Then you had to go off and die.
I had to ask God why but he would not say,
All I ever wanted was for our love to stay.
We always had our differences you and I,
But that does not mean I wanted you to die.
We went through so much together,
The thought never crossed our mind that we'd be
Torn apart Forever.
When we were young our love was growing strong,
We never stopped to think one of us would be gone.
Now that I have gotten over the shock of losing you,
I wanted you to know I'll always be in love with only
You.

Carrie Thomas

Begin Anew

This year has come to an end.
There are many memories in the past.
Keep the happy ones to bring a warm smile tomorrow,
learn from the bitter ones, let them go without regret.
Remember the sad days only if they bring a smile.
In return give with love, that giving of yourself
will ease a little pain.
Build on yesterday's dreams
start each day and the beginning
of each year as God does Spring.
Brighten the Old Anew.

Delena Osborne

Not

Not allowed, not accepted, not acknowledged
There are many "nots" I hear today,
Many "can'ts," "nevers," and "noes"
For me, I cannot speak out,
for my voice will not be heard
"We don't want your folk 'round here," they say
Your kind's different, 'ya hear?
But are we? Different, that is?
Some think so, but me, I say no
No "can'ts," "nevers," or "noes,"
yet "cans," "yeses," and "go, go, go"!
Strength we've had throughout the years,
has stopped the growth of the ferocious disease;
It still exists, that is a fact, but can we put it to a stop?
We can, we will, we must kill the disease, stop it now
We are different, unique, and still the same
Racism is the evil disease
Makes you sick and frightfully mean,
Kill it now, before it's too late.

Racism.

Carolyn Wright

Love

When years rush by with wasted chances,
There comes regrets and hindsight backward glances.
Then much too late, felt sudden dread.
of reassuring words left unsaid.
Love's grace once known
Is sweeter than the honeycomb.
So take a gracious stand right now
While time does still allow
Seize the moment before it is gone,
for another day begins at dawn.
Remember to tell yours true
"Darling, I Love only You."

Isabel Robinson

"I Call It My Empty"

There's something there
There greater inside
That I've not yet found
I've deeper to dig and I will
Until I reach another ground

But meanwhile
I seem to have plenty of what I call my empty

I see the greater
And how I stack up
Consumed by the numbers
I confront my must
Analyze myself trust
Those that succeed
Call it their must
So that success I need

But meanwhile
I seem to have plenty, I call it my empty

Fill my empty until I've plenty of my must
'Cause the self must is where I should be
Not where other interpretations have their need

Frank Polancic

The Sky's The Limit

As I look up in the sky
There is no much out there
The clouds change their form
The colors change from blue to gray to black of night
As the sun rises until it sets, the day is here
The sun leaves, moves on,
as times does too.

As I look up in the sky
There is so much out there
The moon and stars
They make their pictures for everyone to see
So many miles away
For no one to touch here on Earth
The moon has its changes too
Through every month, it keeps moving,
as time does too.

As I look up in the sky
There is so much out there
The sky's the limit.

Cara Helfer

In The Eyes Of The Endangered

In the eyes of the endangered, hidden deep within
There lies a tale
A tale that represents life
A life that has encountered an unfading struggle
A struggle to continue its existence
A struggle against its most feared predator
Man, the hunter
Whose absence is the greatest feeling amongst these lives
Whose absence symbolizes freedom and security
Whom without these lives would not be struggling
Struggling to continue their existence
To defy the danger faced upon them and continue to strive
In the vast and forever beautiful land that stretches out before them
The land that provides and supports all life
The land that man destroys, the lives that man destroys
The lives that prove that we are not the strongest
For it is they, who endure our destruction
And they who have an unbreakable spirit
A spirit that battles us every day

Christy Kiekenbush

Night Time

When the sky turns grey and the sun starts going down
there seems to be a silence that settles all around,

The birds stop chirping and the children go to bed
and tiny little stars start twinkling overhead,

The moon seems to smile down and give a little wink
and tiny little water drops are dripping in the sink,

The dog is sleeping in the den, by a blazing fire
and outside nice and calm sleeps the cat inside a tire

Soon sunbeams shine through windows and the dog barks at the light
now everyone is waiting for the next silent night.

Caitlin Harrington

"Mother"

Everything in my life, I owe to you alone; since
there was no father to help see us through! You
had to be both, "Mom and Dad," in one-you did a
great job too!!
What I am inside and what I ever hope to be, is there
inside me; only 'cause you were always there inside
my heart, helping in life's tough fights!!
I know I seldom said these words, the ones that
need to be said; but we both know they're still always
felt, inside our hearts and in our heads!!
But Mother, I really do love you, that's why I
choose to be like you. It's you alone who deserves the
Thanks, you gave me all the goodness that my life has
ever had! You're my best Friend!!
Mother, I love you, you are my world; without
you in it, how will I be me? So please, don't ever
decide to leave!!

Colleen Madewell

"Lori's Reassurance"...

I know for sure-
  There will always be rain or shine,
I know for sure-
  Forever I'll be yours and you'll be mine...

As the wild winds
  spin the Ol' Windwill,
I know within so deep-
  Time will never stand still.

Lori-, if you ever fail to know,
  reassure yourself from feeling blue,-
I'll never let you go-
  Because our love is so true...

Joseph C. Pulchtopek

"Still Thinking Of You"

Hold my hand from across the sea.
There's a storm beneath the sea.
Like a breast of waves blustering on the shore.
Because I'm still "THINKING" of you.
My "THOUGHTS" stretch from here to there.
With dark mist of you bursting everywhere.
With whisper of you still there.
With things happening from left to right.
With thoughts that will "EMBRACE" me
for the rest of my life!
With you there and I am here.
With thoughts that bring you near!
from spring, to the winter time of the year,
fall comes and brings tears.
Through "SPIRITS" I still feel you care.
Mystery that haunts me all parts of the year.

Josephine April Washington Commodore

Catch A Moment

In my bed, at midnight, I can think.
There my thoughts flow faster than my ink.
Worlds revolve as fast as they can spin.
Where was I when Spring was ushered in?

I was waiting for the greening earth
To proclaim its glorious new birth.
Suddenly, amid the rain and sun,
Summer came, and Spring had just begun!

Then while I adjusted to the heat,
Autumn leaves were falling at my feet!
Now, Jack Frost is painting all around!
Father time is stomping on my ground!

As the years all swiftly come and go,
I've nothing but memories to show.
Then, my brain came up with this new thought—
Memories are "Precious Moments," caught!

Phyrne Harper Wright

As Time Goes Passing By

Flowers in bloom, birds in flight, sunshine in the sky,
These are things that come to us, as time goes passing by.

Changing seasons, changing times, different things to try,
Nature tends to keep us busy, as time goes passing by.

People greeted, friends are made, that you can't deny
Some will touch your heart you see, as time goes passing by.

There are people who are here you know, who's life they give to try
To help the others that they meet, as time goes passing by.

Love is poured out from their soul, and this you can't deny,
They give to others all they have, as time goes passing by.

In times of pain, in times of need, they will be there, don't ask why,
Because you know they truly care, as time goes passing by.

Life is short, compared to time, wow, how it does fly.
All things must meet and end, you see, as time goes passing by.

So live life right, and keep your faith, on this you should rely,
For in God's house, you then shall stand, when your time passes by.

David Thorsen

The Value Of Play

The children they came, to visit today.
Two young ladies, always wanting to play.

Always wanting to play, Oh the games they know.
If you don't know how, to you they'll show.

First there's Jennie, "Play cards with me?"
Then in pops Jessie, "Help me color this tree?"

They are cunning and sly, in their own young way.
When it comes to coerce you, to sit and play.

Oh you can't refuse, if you take the time,
To look at these girls of eight and nine.

And see the beauty that lies within.
So you lose the game, no matter, a win.

A win indeed, to sit and play,
For their presence alone has brightened your day.

And as we sit, love and laughter I see.
So I play the cards and color the tree.

So you sit and play, who cares how long?
For too soon it will be, when they are gone.

Yes gone they will be, but not far away.
As I look forward, to another day's play.

Curtis J. Munsell

Our Ignorance Exudes

Our ignorance exudes, our prejudice stifle
these characteristics are found in the masses.
We've had many teachers who challenged us with change.
Mistakes were repeated, so few here learn lessons.

Such little insight, we procrastinate
problems mounting high, with no solutions.
Should we loose all hope, in saving earth now?
Our virtue in faith, has not been enough.

We observe our leaders, some look just like a coin
right hand grips the Bible, left wants a donation.
Some souls are sent back here, our eyes spy for heaven.
If to your ears, I judge, you perceive correctly.

In hoards we want more, greed spreads a cancer
warnings go ignored, our planet cries out.
To ourselves we lie, refusing the truth.
The light is out there, watching all, through tears.

Corinne Kaufhold

Love

There are all different kinds of things in this world,
They are cute, pretty, ugly, or beautiful etc.
But there is nothing more beautiful in this world than LOVE,
LOVE is the most beautiful thing in the world,
LOVE is caring for someone you like a lot,
To be LOVED by someone makes you feel good about yourself,
It makes you feel wanted, it makes you feel like a someone,
Not a no one, since LOVE is the most beautiful thing in the world,
And it makes you feel good about yourself,
I think there should be more LOVING in this world,
Everybody wants to be LOVED,
Everybody wants someone to care for them,
Everybody wants to have someone else to care about,
Find that special someone,
Love them, because your LOVE will do lots of good in that
Someone's life,
Lives are special,
Don't let them end over no love or care,
Find someone now, love them and let them love you back,
Because LOVE is beautiful.

Amanda Semeraro

The Eyes Of Love

I was sitting on my bed one lonely, scary night,
Thinking who is out there that's giving me a fright,

So I prayed a little prayer, asking my father, do
you really love me? Do you really care?

Then suddenly my father came before my very eyes
He was like a beautiful ray of a warm summer's sunlight

He raised his hand out toward me. With love and
kindness he held me ever so tenderly.

As he was holding me, he was saying now you have a
taste of love, you know you belong to me.

Now you are standing in the light of a bran new star.
you can lift your head to see the heaven from a far.

Be strong, for I am with you! Open your eyes to
what I can offer you.

Then the lord said something that I will never forget,
nothing will be the same in the eyes of love.

Once you have found love you can never go back to where
you used to be. Just find your heart and follow it my child.

And that's where I will be, a wonderous place called heaven
just for you and me.

Joyce Ball

Balloons

I always had balloons but now I have no more
They flew into the air, so I just let them soar.
They slipped right through my fingers
And floated out of sight.
They left so free and easy, without a single fight.
I watched them all leave one by one.
They are all gone - now I have none.
But I believe that someday soon
If I keep my head high I'll find my balloons.

Julie Kelley-Larig

The Adoption Day

They couldn't have a child no matter how hard they tried
they prayed so hard and they often cried.
They kept looking for a brighter tomorrow
but ended each day full of sorrow.

They sometimes wondered what they would name her
Nicole, Erin, Jenean, or Jennifer.
If a boy they could not decide
maybe Ron, David, Billy or Clyde.

They knew they would provide a healthy environment
but often pictured a lonely retirement.
Until the one day he saw the ad
that might provide them with what they always wanted to have.

They called the adoption agency the very next day
and told the woman there was no price they wouldn't pay.
They saw the baby girl after a couple of weeks
and said she had the most beautiful blue eyes and rosy cheeks

The couple had never before felt the happiness they felt that day
and to each other they had only one thing to say. —
"We may not have bore her as most people could,
but we still love her like a mother and father should."

Jenean R. Malanga

Ghost Ships

Ghost ships sailing cross the sea,
They seem to rise and follow thee.
Their sails are set against the wind,
They seem to sink then rise again.

The fog around them seems to hide,
And on each wave they seem to glide.
They're like a shadow in the night,
They set their sails and soon take flight.

You think sometimes you haven't seen,
That it surely must be a dream.
The ghostly ships that on the wave,
Set their sails and fade away.

Emily Martin

That Special Ring

There she handed, handed me her ring.
The words of her name engraved in the ring.
Pictures on the ring showed me what school
life was like for her and now she was giving it,
giving it to me.
As I gazed at the stone, the stone of maroon.
My hopes and dreams filled the room.
Now that I remember, remember that day,
how I felt during that day.
I thanked her then, I thank her now,
now and again I'll remember how she handed me,
handed me her ring.
Now that I remember, remember that ring,
I'll always remember my favorite ring.

Faith Tisdell

Woods

Woods are like deep dark holes
They stretch beyond your wildest thoughts
Feelings are lovely yet lost and lonely...so peaceful
Wind, softly whispering, wondering through branches
Darkness falls through the night, calm, cool, asleep,
asleep is it?
Sounds of silence, solitude, almost sorrowful
Early, night still holds the forest...fondly
Sunlight breaking, waking silent creatures
Woods are like deep dark holes
They stretch beyond your wildest thoughts

Jessica Mol

Teddy Bears

Silent, cushy,
They wait on children's bedspreads;
They regenerate
In small antique shops,
In small unknown worlds.
They thrive on our dreams, wishes, and secrets;
They smile no matter what we say and never
betray us,
Enduring a lifetime of silence,
Because they have not been allowed in
our jumbled up world.
Their stuffing is their undying soul
and faith in ours.
Our guardians, they hold the key
to forgiveness.

Carolina Silverman

My Mother's Eyes

My mother's eyes have all the colors of the spectrum.
They're blue as the sky, green with envy, red when angered,
black when in defense of a cause, brown like warm fuzzies
when she loves her cat, and has yellow shafts of light that
compete with sunbeams when she smiles.

My mother's eyes have read John 3:16 that she could
verbalize to us; followed a recipe to make our favorite -
dessert; watched us walk down the aisle; and dissected
our being when caught in a half truth.

I'm now my mother's eyes. The contact lens. I drive
the car, read the papers, thread the needles, pick out
the change at the register, and sign on the dotted line.
I'm the clarity for eyes losing their optical symmetry.

It is quoted, "Eyes are the windows to your soul."
...I hope my eyes reflect the mirrored image of the life
that has been in my mother's eyes.

Becky Ivan Leach

Outcast

Alone on desert sands with heavy winds,
The air is hard to breathe and tears are dry.
A loner on his horse remembers sins
That brought him to this lonely place to die.

The cactus shadows stretch like clawing hands;
The sun sinks slow into a burning bed.
And all throughout the flames of shifting lands
This cowboy hopes for night to cool the red
Of chapping lips and weakened outer shell:

His eyes are blind with grief at his demise;
His soul is slipping from his grasp to hell.
There wheezes from his throat a cracking sigh.
His steed plods on to darkness and his fate;
Another day to make the vultures wait...

Barbara Stender

Waste Not

Do you see the little sparrows as they hop around.
They're picking up the bread crumbs
that are thrown upon the ground.

Some people have it easy as they go from day to day.
They never stop to think about the food they throw away.

There are hungry people in this world;
please stop and take a look.
They'd love to have the simple things
that you refuse to cook.

I look at my television and see how the children live.
Their tummies bulging out so big;
through their skin you see their ribs.

Sometimes it makes me want to cry
to see them looking so thin.
The food that you have thrown away;
it's got to be a sin.

Waste not, want not;
that's what mothers always say.
The food that you have thrown away;
you just might need some day.

Ida Pearl Artis

"My Love"

Since the day we met, I've wanted you to know... Through thick and thin, I could never let you go; We've laughed, we've cried, we've grown as one... Even after I thought we were over—damage was done; You've helped me realize, there is more to life than fun...

I'm learning to love, in new ways than before: To say I don't show you, hurts me to the core!!
Deep down inside—How can you be so discouraging, so cold? Leaving me to feel all alone—with only empty thoughts to hold...

Our love has and will be tested, in more than one way- as our love keeps growing, can we make it through each day? At times I know it may seem to you, I don't care... I'm needing you to know I do, so have no fear; I know you have loved and lost in the past— while working together, will our love always last?

Hoping the past will never get the best of me; I dream of the future, and guess what I see? Us moving through time, leaving a thin trail of dust... Gazing at each other with eyes full of trust!!!
As the trials of our past have cleared our mind; We'll feel no hardships or loves being unkind...

If all is forgotten, to our great surprise... Our love shall be one that never dies!!! Excepting and letting our minds lay to rest... I pray that our souls will always be blessed!!!

Christine M. Donze

Misty Blue

Cloudy glasses sprinkled with florescent view, eliminates ghostly episodes playing theme songs like misty blue. To rid ourselves of this all too familiar tune, we have to revolutionize something new. Not until we sift through all of the age old debris, will we get back what we once knew. To avoid being overtaken by such an infectious flu we must come up with more convincing clues. If, we wouldn't have bitten off more than we could chew, we wouldn't have been of the many few. Unless, we resolve what we need to resolve, we will repeatedly find ourselves boiling over in a big pot of stew. To whomever the bell tolls is forever so true, for, when everything else fails, the resounding echo is what will carry you through.

Gail M. Davis

Morning Sounds

It's quarter past five, so very early in the morn,
Things are comin' alive, 'nother day is being born.

A single bird is chirping, and now a cricket I hear,
Now the sounds of morning, are becoming quite clear.

I hear a cooing sound, could be a turtle dove,
Or a lowly pigeon, as He is calling to his love.

There's the hoot of an owl, 'fore retiring for the day,
And the bark of a dog, as He begins his day.

There's the screech of brakes, a train whistle from afar,
The sky is getting brighter, and not a sign of a star.

Then the wail of a siren, that most ominous sound,
Hope the person in need, tonight'll still be around.

Other sounds we can't hear, but they're there we know,
Just a few I'll mention, and then I'll let you go.

There's the gasp of a newborn, as they begin a new life,
And the sounds of ecstasy, between husband and wife.

Then there's the sound of dying, as one struggles for breath,
'Fore finally giving in, to that thing called death.

So it's time to get up, on this most beautiful morn,
And give thanks to our Lord, for having been born.

Joseph L. Baldwin

Reflections Of Sinful Mirrors

The mirrors of life that shine back into my eyes,
Things that have happened that I shall forever despise.

Mortals in sorrow from feelings beyond the earth,
Others not caring of what these feelings are worth.

The ridicule of life is only beneath their mind,
For the young dead are lost and yet are able to find,

The cries of their eyes and the yells of their mouth,
The voices they holler and the noises they shout.

But only the reflection is as morbid as the unlived souls,
For they are the ones that have to take the sinful tolls.

The mirrors of life that shine back into my eyes,
Only things that sinful eyes could ever recognize.

Amber N. Alderson

My Rose

A rose to me has always been a sign of love, just like my John.

As I sit day in and day out, watching John slowly leave me, I keep thinking of a rose.

For a little more than seventeen years, John has been my rose blossom, so full of life, soft to the touch with fragrant petals.

Now, like a rose, John is slowly withering from me, with each new day he begins to shrivel and shrink more and more. He faces the sun and is beginning to fade and dry, like a rose bush.

Soon my beautiful rose will loose his petals, one by one and be no more here with me. Like the rose in the garden, John too will be placed to rest back into the earth.

I have never loved another the way I love John. I feel very blessed, for being able to love such a wonderful husband and best friend.

John has truly been my rose of life; to love, to admire, to nourish, to hold, to smell, and to care for.

I shall miss his daily presence, with all my heart, but it is there, John will live with me always.
My John, my rose, now and forever.

Judith L. Sepelak

Love The Children

As time rushes by, I sigh with a grin,
thinking of things and how they've been

Watching the children playing in the field
sliding in home their little knees and elbows peeled,

Seeing the smiles on their faces so clear
and hearing the laughter of a child so dear

It gets so noisy this time of day
with all those children at play

Looking through the window for things that use to be
but the children aren't there anymore for me to see,

Weeds have taken that old field and it's quiet here at last,
what I wouldn't give for a bit of the past

Children all grew up and left this small town
think they'll ever remember old farmer Brown?

Has life been worth it, I'd say so
it's been a joy for me, just watching the children grow.

Barbara Grant

The Lonely Place

Alone. Waiting.
This morning's words painful as an open wound in my mind.
Anger springs fresh.
When did it happen?
When did the feeling go?

Still alone. Still waiting.
Is love really gone this time?
I don't know.
I hope not.
I hope so.

Darkness falls and I am still alone. Still waiting.
I search the wasteland of my heart for what I desire.
Memories of better times bring hot tears to my eyes, my face.
Marriage is such a lonely place.

Brenda Hilley

Untitled

This puzzle is not finished, until the final piece is found.
This puzzle is my youth, when you were not around.
This puzzle is a picture, the face is a blank.
This puzzle is a ship afloat, that broke and finally sank.
This puzzle is a song, the words forgotten, for too long.
This puzzle is a love affair gone bad and oh so wrong.
This puzzle is the sky, with no sun to shine.
This puzzle is this poem, with a missing line.
This puzzle is my heart, lost and very sad.
If I were to find you, would it be so bad?
This puzzle is my life, my Father, the missing piece.
If I were to find you, will you fit and make it
complete?

Arlene Nickell

War

Loyal people who are supposed to be fearless
Voices full of desperateness
Men fighting in the fields
Behind walls and bunkers that act like shields
With children coming upon guns
People dying in numbers and tons
Great lands destroyed and tore
In the future let there be no more.

Amy Kelly

A Tribute To My Father

This man was a gentleman, this man was strong.
This temperamental man has left me alone.
He was a child, he was old.
Sometimes he was mild, sometimes he was bold.
But when HE shined HE shined so bright.
This man I loved sometimes in spite,
I wish he could have won his lingered fight.
Sometimes a clown, sometimes a frown,
Never feeling well but always around.
He was the moon in the morning and the stars out at night.
But when HE shined HE shined so bright.
This man I loved is now at rest.
This man's my father, Daddy you were the best.
I see your eyes, I hear your laughter,
And always will forever after.
After all this time regrets are few,
I just want a chance to thank you.
You were always so wise and knew what to do.
With all my heart I'll always miss you.
Your heart was kind and love so true, one last time,
    Daddy, I love you.

Dianne Slay

The Dreamweaver

During the night while you dream
those who are chosen hear other things
She calls to those who choose to hear
Speaking softly she calls
worlds of wonderment she whispers
do not speak at all
I will take you there
She tells you softly as you follow Her
of the things in your dreams
though small in size you see She is wise in Her eyes
you follow Her like a puppy on string but you are free
She walks silently into a shadow room ancient as a cave
She shows you a spinning wheel golden as a summer day
It seems to be humming a soft lullaby
or maybe it is your mother singing to you when you were a child
the Weaver smiles as though she sees it too
She sits down at her wheel and you start to see
and remember glorious things of old and new
and then-you wake up.

Angela Judes

Don't Worry About Tomorrow

No one knows what tomorrow will bring.
There may be things that are bad;
But it's also true that it could prove
to be the best that you've ever had!
Don't worry about tomorrow - concern yourself with today;
For no matter what the future holds,
Jesus still leads the way.
So what if tomorrow the sun does not shine -
the Son still walks by your side
Offering comfort and guidance in whatever may betide!
Why worry about something that may never come?
Why not enjoy the Now?
It's easier to sail the seas of life
when Jesus is in the prow!
So sail on with peace in your heart-protected by God's loving care;
He'll take care of tomorrow, so why not use today
    With your loved ones some moments to share?
He'll help us live tomorrow in accordance with His will,
And the memories of the "Today" we share
    Will remain and delight us still!!

Betty D. Mason

Last September

Never around long enough for love .....
Though I still smile when I remember
A scene that changed to last September
The sun so bright... the water, still
Come to me, if you will..
Leaves move slightly in a gentle breeze
Dancing in steps to remind and please
Their melody is of a different kind
As distant sounds relax the mind
Then was nice ... now it's gone
And you will always be my song
No tears will ever make a sound
Silence is the partner words have never found.

Christine L. Esposito

So (Escape)

In the chances of our meetings
though innocent yet sweet.
I see a passion burning deep inside you
that no one else can see.
It lingers deep inside you
so safe and yet so scared.
It seeks another soul with whom
it feels it can compare.
Another soul who holds its passion deep inside,
so safe and yet so scared.
This other soul is waiting;
it's somewhere out there.
And when the time is right
those souls may just unite
to overcome the fears that cause them to be scared.
Someday that fear will go away and never more return
and the passion can escape to find its perfect mate.

Cindy L. Riley

Springtime Sonnet

'Tis April, and we sense the breath of spring,
  'Though winter's chill the season may defy;
The peepers are in chorus as they sing,
  'Though few are ever seen by human eye.
The warming sun and April showers combine
  To nurture every leafless plant in sight
And sap starts flowing in each tree and vine
  And withered grass grows greener overnight.
The sun now rises higher in the sky,
  Our sun-tanned friends en masse are homeward bound,
We hear the geese in flight - a haunting cry,
  And snowdrops poke their heads above the ground.
'Tis April - there is change upon the earth
  A promise of renewal and rebirth.

David C. Sargent

Untitled

Like, as a palette, she is washed with hues.
The tertiary colors of the wheel
paint round to expose her traits and views.
She's sketch with harmony, that I feel.
Her shade is olive and her portrait lean.
She's like a paint brush when used upside down.
A papier-mâché mold, that of a teen.
A silhouette reveals eyes of slight brown.
Her paradoxical horizon line
containing shades of deep slate and opaque.
Flushed of high I.Q. with a book in mind.
But, darkened are her thoughts which she creates.
Yet her monochromatic attributes
design a sculpture with great magnitude.

Antonia Boggio

Grades

They seem to matter and cause such a clatter
Though you may hope and try
  they still make you cry
So it seems there is no hope
  to this endless rope
It drags on and on

They may rise at dawn but by
  dusk they fall
It's an endless roller coaster
  that burns like a toaster
So if you try; we will know why

Jennifer O'Brien

A Vision Of Yesterday's Dream

A Friday night, as I lay asunder,
Thought of you had turned to wonder.
My wood-burner glowing warm and bright
Assured I'd sleep throughout the night.
I dreamt of good things from the past—
And how I knew they wouldn't last.
As I stirred in silent fits of sleep,
Your vision called me from the deep.
Remembering how things could have been—
If only I could start again.
Like the first fallen snow on the window sill,
Or a spring driven rain rolling off a hill,
You remind me of firsts, and that's a thrill.
I woke up cold on Saturday morn,
My present here, my past forlorn.

Gary Hooven

Grandma & Grandpa

Married in the year 1940
Three babies by the tenth following year
The love and respect seems to triple with every holiday
  that goes by
Hard times, bad times, and times that not the strongest
  could survive
But together is how they will be, and how they will stay
Time goes by; troubles arise
More time goes by; only some subside
But never, ever will the bond be broken
The year is now 1995; both are not side by side
Separated-only because of illness
And though their love has been exposed to never ending
  crucibles;
Their faith in each other still remains unwilted;
And will never, ever die.

Heather Renee Cornell

A Masquerade Of Friends

Frosted memories whisper throughout my mind.
Those of ones close and dear,
some of laughter, some of cheer.
Ones of grayness, lonely, dim.
Those memories too kept close within.
Enemies swarm throughout my veins.
Causing unpleasant, hideous pains!
Friends of many, friends of few.
All now seem different, now are new.
Money and power is in which they devour.
Never a smile or show of good will.
Cold like statues. Their hearts are still.
What are they now?
Who can they be?
Where are my friends I used to see?
Could it have been I was too blind to see,
their kindness was and is a frosted memory!?

Cassandra King

God Speaks

God speaks to us in His Holy Word,
Through men of old in ages past.
In each event of history
God clearly speaks to you and me.

God speaks in poetry and song,
And shows forth truth in every psalm.
In wisdom, words of strength doth speak,
Which help us as His way we seek.

God speaks through prophets bold and true,
To warn men of their evil ways;
Repent, obey, let love abide
And justice flow as waters wide.

God speaks through Jesus Christ, our Lord,
In all His words and kindly deeds.
His spirit also speaks to all
And helps us as we heed His call.

God speaks to us in our lives today;
Our hearts we yield without delay.
In all we do, in word and deed,
May we show Thy love to those in need.

Helen I. Dunnick

Untitled

With this Ring
Through the eyes of mother earth.
With the beauty of her colors
As our souls flow through this time, this journey.
With this ring I make a commitment
   to you for the rest of my journey.
The commitment of my soul, heart and love.
With that true love shall I make you happy,
   by being free.
With that true love shall I stand by you,
   No matter how ugly society presents it
   or how beautiful our souls show it.
So 'til one or the other departs from this journey,
I will be with you in Free Soul and Free Spirit.

Elizabeth A. Willette

CONFESSIONS

Hamlet to Gertrude

If I touch you, oh, sweet memory, what is to halt this rising
   tide?
If my hands were not tied in confusion, I would hold tight to
   your side.
If I sought only peace, I would believe in your lies.
If the charade were to end, I would seek haven in your eyes.
But the blood from your hands unmans me and so I hide.

Carolyn Jean Isley

Ever-changing Tree

God has given us all sorts of things
To do, to feel and to see.
His greatest creation-next to man and earth
Is the ever-changing tree.
Trees stand in all their grandeur,
Bent by the winds of time,
For the artisans of the ages
To put them into rhyme.
The mighty oak, the giant sequoia,
Cedar, fir and maple vine,
Have been put on paper and canvas
With many an infinite line.

Ida G. Johnson

Forever And A Day

Years have slowly brought back yesterdays
Time has slipped by our tomorrows
People facing the same hassles day to day
When will it end and break away
The growing up from child to man
The passing of names to names
Why does it carry on to extremes
Wars and bombs, hope and dreams
The future of all mankind waits
To see tomorrow at today's gate
If it will be forevermore
To have man stand on yesterday
And to know all of his tomorrows
To see the future within our eyes
To hold it fast and make it last
Forever and a day

Gina M. Dougherty

Missing You

Peering over the big wooden box,
   Time has stopped, not one but all clocks.
You're not gone, I know it's not true,
   So open your eyes, before I turn blue.
It's twisting inside, and I feel the knot,
   My throat is burning and starting to clot.

No words come out, but so much to say,
   You can't be gone, don't leave me this way.
Not enough memories, I don't have to keep,
   Who will tuck me in, and how will I sleep?
A photo I need to remember old times,
   Too young to remember, so I tell you in rhymes.

Who will be there to walk down the aisle?
   Who will wait patiently to see my firstborn smile?
All the things you don't get to see,
   I miss you so badly, you here with me.

Above you will be, when I need you most,
   When my child arrives, I know you will boast.
No one replaced you, I hope that you know,
   I miss you Daddy, and I Love You So!

Jamie Lynn Davis

Time Is .....

Time is silence's unheard hum;
Time is the adding up to a sum.
Time is a little rippling motion
upon a stationary ocean.

Time is the way weave our shroud
with the bit thread that we're allowed.

Time is the foot-step of Death as he comes,
accompanied by unheeded drums.

Time is a craggy mountain climb
to reach the Peak where is no Time.

When the path winds around its final bend,
will we view the vastness of Time's End?

But now, I will cull the fragrant hours
As a little child gathers way-side wild flowers

Eleanor Phelps

Summer Night

On a warm summer night I was in the park, and it was near nine at the
time when I sat on a park bench. I could see a string of lights
coming from a ship as it glided by.
The sound of the waves rushing forward, and
The breeze made you feel right at ease.
I glanced up toward the stars; they were like diamonds, shining
Bright across the dark sky. Couples were walking hand in hand,
Children running and saying come and catch me if you can.
Far out a light tower flashed its lights across the water.
While fishing boats were scattered about, casting their lines,
hoping to catch a bite.
When then I looked at the time, and said oh well!
It's way past midnight. I will call it a night, since the park closed.
After nine on this warm summer night.

Don Wall

When Things Go Right

When things go right, all Heaven seems to smile.
Time's river stops its rolling flow to purr;
Pure love becomes the theme for every day
When things go right.

When things go right, I'm me again instead
Of that old ogre buried deep inside -
The beast that snarls at every blessed gift
When things go wrong.

When things go wrong, I mourn the loss of good
And curse the evil darkness, sleet, and rain.
Then faith and hope return my life to days
When things go right.

When things go right, I always swear to keep
My faith, my hope, my love alive and strong;
To keep in mind those happy times, so brief,
When things go right.

John Christian

Untitled

Purity and fragility cast in a shade of white.
Timid and anxious, overcoming fright.
Slowly walking forward. Arm in arm with a man she will always love.
He lets her go, kissing her hand inside the glove.

She gazes at another man through a haze of white.
He gently smiles, overcoming his own fright.
He takes her arm, nods a thank you to the first.
Turns toward her, is it for better or worse?

In the light of God, love ending never.
They are blessed to be joined forever.

Jennifer M. Horst

Eternal Life The Greatest Gift Of All

They took my Lord, and nailed him
to a cross made of dogwood tree.
they hung him there, for all to see.
A pure, honest, non-judgmental man, they
drove nails into his hands, they
placed a crown of thorns around his head,
thorns that dug in, until they bled.
What a horrible sight that must have been.
They killed a pure man, who knew no sin.
He cried out, Father! why hast thou forsaken
me? But God above had a plan; that's
why he sent that pure sweet man, a man
to take away our sins. And then he gave
him the greatest gift of all, he restored
his life again.

Bertha Christian

Solitaire

If from men's bitter words I could flee
To a fertile island, a true home for me,
I'd take some pets for solace in my retreat,
For pets as companions are kind and discreet.

A sturdy house I'd build of stone;
It wouldn't have to be large, I'd be alone.
But if strangers should drop by in time to come,
I'd share my home with everyone.

I would swim in a river or climb a tree.
Whichever one appealed to me.
I would plant a garden and use a hoe.
The weeds would be plucked from every row.

I would climb to the hilltop; in the center, 'twould be.
I'd reach toward heaven while a breeze enveloped me.
Then before leaving, I'd kneel and pray
And thank God for such a peaceful day.

Floss Van Allen

The Ocean

No storm is fierce enough
to abolish the ocean. There is no power
strong enough to stop her waves.
Her beauty overrides all sorrow. Her body
everlasting is full of meaning and
understanding. Her depth so knowing.
Her waves full of spirit bring peace
to all who watch her!

Elizabeth Phelan

It's No Use

It's no use
    to argue the world and all its trifles.
It's no use
    to fight anymore.
"Time to put away the rifles."
It's no use
    to cry for what we don't have.
It's no use
    to save what we have lost.
"Time heals pain no matter what the cost."
It's no use
    to start over when you can just move on.
It's no use
    to die for the body will decompose.
"The body is the stem and the heart is the rose."

Brian J. Lord

Untitled

Dreams are like shadows,
    There one minute then gone
A piece of yourself you know and yet don't!
Always coming and going
    Beautiful, colorful dreams
Like dancing shadows floating across my mind.

Dark, scary, sweaty dreams-Nightmares!
Like huge, heavy, black shadows on the
    deepest, darkest night!
I scream! I gasp! The shadows have
    formed a tight circle around me.

But wait...I just woke up. The sound of
    the fan is soothing and soft and I am
Ok! Now I lay down and think of the tight
    Circle and how scared I was! I close my
eyes once again and wait for the beautiful,
Colorful, dreams and dancing shadows.

Brittanie Newell

Voyager

I was born in the highlands of Oregon, destined,
to be nothing more than a natural mystic.

I was born through my parents, but not of them.

For I believe sometimes that my spirit has been
a frequent voyager through time and infinity.

I was there when the pyramids and sphinx
stood in all their splendor.

I was with the moors when they conquered Spain.

It was I who served the death blow to Custer
at little bighorn.
I was with Geronimo and cried when he surrendered.

I was there on the sands of Iwo Jima and helped
plant the American flag.

I was there when Martin Luther King received the vision
on the mountain top.

I played with Jimi Hendrix and Santana at Woodstock

And I was there when Bob Marley received his
Rasta man vibrations.

For I am the voyager I know not of the boundaries
of time, space, or Infinity.
Jamayne L. Grimaldi

"The Seed"

In a mother's womb, a seed did lay,
To be taken to the tomb, only to arise some day.
While the law, steps of the seed takes roots,
It will grow & grow until it bears fruit.
Then in a flash, the fruit shines a light,
Not to run a clash, on the blossoms' radiant sight.
Blossoms were to be born, from the limb of life,
their only future backbone, was God's greatest strife,
God created blossoms to show the way,
for little seeds to follow the path some day.
When the blossoms petals become old and wise,
God prepares more fruit before the blossom dies.
The fruit has learned the path laid down,
understanding the fruit the seed doesn't brown.
The purpose of the seed is to become the fruit
so now we all see why the seed takes root!

Beth Ann Seybert I

Ride Into Tomorrow To Escape Today

Lord, my heart aches and troubles are everywhere, no one really seems
to care. I want to ride into tomorrow to escape today.
Lord, hurt and pain come again and again, disappointment, disaster
and great disdain. I'll ride into tomorrow to escape today.
Lord, friends I've had, they've left, they're gone. The experience
I'm in is lasting too long. I'll ride into tomorrow to escape today.
Lord, tears I cry seem never to dry. Sometimes it feels I'd really
die. I'll ride into tomorrow to escape today.

Lord, riding on the wings of the peaceful dove, things look different
as I view from above. I'm riding into tomorrow to escape today.
Lord, skies are blue, winds are calm, it's awesome up here and nothing
seems wrong. I'm riding into tomorrow to escape today.
Lord, tomorrow is a brand new today, the pain's gone away and I
want to stay. I rode into tomorrow to escape today.
Lord, hurts of today are quite malign, and I've left them all behind.
Experience of today I've found so kind. I rode into tomorrow to
escape today. My tomorrow is now today, I've escaped yesterday
and rode into tomorrow to escape today.

Dawn Govan-Scott

Jerry's Fish

One day Jerry and friends a fishing went
to catch some nice fish was their intent,
and sure enough in just a little while
on Jerry's face was a great big smile.

"The big one got away" is usually the tale,
but Jerry has the big one safely in his pail.
Back at the dock he's proudly showing off his prize
a beautiful fish, quite bigger than the usual size.

When the oh's and aw's of friends subsided,
this fish looking at them just decided
"This is not for me"! so with a ker-plop
out the window he went in one big hop.

All saw this with their very own eyes,
so none could accuse Jerry of telling lies.
Well, after all, the big one did get away.
And Jerry will have to go fishing another day.
Annette M. Peters

The Shame Of It All

There are many reasons for incest
To control answers if best

Although it is our children who are violated
We close our eyes and ears, but yet we hate it

It happens in the home
It happens when we are alone

It causes fear and insecurity and it's just not fair
For a child to have such a burden to bear

To cover up their guilt and shame
To help protect the one to blame

Many are young and have limited insight
To stand up and fight or demand their right

Some will live with it and few will lie
Others will run away and many will cry

Incest causes both physical and mental pain
I pray this will one day end and only love remain

For these children my heart bleeds
For those who can speak, tell someone please.
Brenda Dutton-Smith

I Come To Save The World

I have come to save the world. You see, God said to me, sin will lead
to death and death will lead to hell for eternity. I have sent my Son
the Messiah to save the world from death and give them life and to be
with me, the Father. My children are in bondage because of their sins.
I, Jesus, come to take you out of sin and set you free. Believe in me
and follow me. I am the only way to heaven, and eternal life I will

give thee. You want only to please me, not man - man will only lie,
cheat and steal from you. Do what my Father wants you to do. He will
give you peace and life for eternity, it's up to you. All of you have
gone your own way, for there is only one way. All men have sin and sin
will lead to death, a place without God. God does not put you there,
you put yourself there, so beware! Repent with all your heart and
believe in me, Jesus. I will set you free, for many are blind and do

not want to see. Hear the truth. Many love their sins and will not
change; their sins to them are pleasurable. God says, "Please have
patience, I will talk to you. You see I love you, it is you why I came.

"Turn around and change; if you love me, you will obey me. I,
the Father, am your only Father. I sent you My Spirit so you would
know and understand. My child, take my hand and one day you will see

the light in front of thee, you will know wrong from right. Day or
night I promise you will see the light!
Esther Bermel

Untitled

My daughter, Bryanna, I cherish most;
To family and friends I often boast...
The things you do, your beautiful smile
I sit and ponder for awhile..
What have I done in life so right
To be blessed with you, my heart's delight.
So on this day, and for those to come
Remember I love you, my special one.

Evelyn Giorgio

Loved Ones 1

Why do the ones we love have to suffer?
To feel the pain, to hurt the worst?
Which is true, but somehow it doesn't seem fair,
Once we began to cry, just wipe their eyes dry,
and, try to make them realize why.

It's hard to know what to say each and every day,
Try not to be so blue, as we are all thinking of you.

Even if you don't know when the hurting stops,
remember the Lord, God will give it all He's got!

Though you wish they would feel better
so they could always live
forever.

Angela Stone

The Bridge Of Life

I tried to walk the Bridge of Life
 to find the answers of the unknown

As I neared the middle, the darkness of doubt
 surrounded me

I gazed back at the past and then stared
 forward to the future

I was paralyzed with confusion and it seemed
 that doubt had won

All at once, the quenching desire of faith
 surrounded me

The message came loud and clear

It rang out like a bell and echoed
 all around me

Believe in yourself! Within you are the answers
 to the questions that you seek

I then knew what had to be done

I walked on

Debbie M. Arnett

Someday

Someday I'd like to write a song to make somebody smile
To give someone the added strength to go that extra mile
I'd like for it to tell a tale of love and all it's worth
To show someone that there can be a heaven here on earth

A melody so soft and slow, with words that have some rhyme
The meaning so profound that it will stand the test of time
With lyrics that go on and on and echo through your ears
My song would be about life, its laughter and its tears

A verse that would get you through the worst kind of day
It would tell you what you need to hear as only I could say
When things get confusing and your life is full of despair
Listen to the words of my song..your comfort will be there

Ann Sorenson

Untitled

I want to take time out to say Happy Birthday.
To give thanks for all you have done through the years.
You were an inspirer, counselor, mother, sister, aunt, cousin,
grandmother and a great grandmother.
My life was molded as a piece of clay.
You shaped and prepared me for future obstacles that may stand in
 my way.
I was taught to follow and obey God, my parents and respect my elders.
The memories you left behind are your spunky ways, cheerful smile,
and loving heart.
I even thank you for the times you scolded me when I fell off track.
As I became older I realized it was not out of malice but love.
I took heed to the things I was told even when you thought I wasn't
 listening.
But grandma I was listening.
Many thanks and praises I dedicate this to your name.
To you in memory.

Bernadette Snead

Untitled

Some people should be so lucky
to have their lives placed at their feet
while the rest of us have to struggle
just to make ends meet.

Some people should be so lucky
to know which path is right
while the rest of us are stuck searching
for it for the rest of our lives.

Some people should be so lucky
to have a loving spouse
while the rest of us could be told
and never know what love is all about.

Some people should be so lucky
to live a complete life
while the rest of us go to the grave knowing
that we've accomplished nothing in this lifetime.

Some people should be so lucky
having the things they have
but sometimes our greed gets in the way
and it appears we have nothing when we really have something.

George A. Perras

To Know

To see the world in a grain of sand
To hold infinity in the palm of my hand
To look at the heavens from the world below
To show the world what they want to know
All these would be like looking at
An hourglass and then knowing all one could know

Amanda Coots

My Son

It just isn't right or at least that's how it seems
to take a young life with so many dreams
To be here such a short time, you've given us so much
We'll all miss your sense of humor, your laughter and touch
He can't help but be sad and we often cry....
But we try not to question God's reason why
You see my son, God needed you by his side
We all know the doctors tried
But God said "Come with me!" and he took your hand
Then he brought you to the promised land
You had to leave your family, but your in our heart
You always were right from the start
I told you God has a special plan for us, I always knew!
I just didn't know he wanted you!!!

Bette F. Lewis

465

"Little Girl"

Oh! Do you know what it's like to be a little girl?
To jump, run, skip and whirl!
To laugh, play and giggle!
Boy! It's hard to sit and not wiggle!

What's it like to see toys for the first time?
Wanting to touch each one, keeping them for mine!
To see trees, birds soaring in the blue sky!
Leaping to capture the invisible wind in their hair.
Can't take a nap, afraid they will miss going somewhere.

Through the eyes of a child everything's a wonder;
There isn't time to sit and ponder:
As if no tomorrow, they must scurry!
To experience everything, there's no waiting, they must hurry!

When receiving that special gift;
Their heart is thrilled and eyes are lit.
Oh! The happiness it brings;
When she receives things!
Do you know what it's like to be a little girl!
I do! For I have gone back in time;
To capture the little girl that's mine!

  Anna F. Thomas

New Weapon - Stroke Of The Pen

The Psychiatrist, with two words of the Pen
To kill his victim; now to condemn
Paranoid schizophrenic - that's all he wrote
Both are used; both are scapegoats

The Psychiatrist, he sells his soul for greed
The enemy in power uses him to lead
So both given power, the devils reign!
In a round about way, to destroy for their gain

Millions are labeled, over many long years
Many a battle fought, through many a tear
Many lives taken; many found dead!
From courtroom cases, getting close to the head

Signs and gay flags; home red, white and blue
Character assassination; we speak all too true
We've gone to prison, redeeming our time
Fighting official tyranny, intolerable crime

Those few little seconds, two words wrote by Pen
Like the Sword, how they kill - Psychiatrists condemn;
They cannot be trusted, for their greed is within
They sold their souls, by the Stroke Of The Pen!

  Jean Walker

Something Wonderful

To know someone has prayed for you is to feel God's love so true,
  To know they care for you enough to ask something, for you!
To know someone has prayed for you, is a thrill beyond compare,
  To know God hears one's ev'ry plea, and that He's "really THERE!"
To know my Father cares for me - "little speck" which I might be,
  (An "Atom or molecule of Dust, on Earth") - 'tis hard to see!
But - yes! - He does! He's promised each if to his truth we'll cling -
  In Jesus' name, He shall respond, and fulfill "everything!"
For ev'ry plea that's asked of Him, He tells his child He'll give,
  So, in response to our dear God, we must rise up and live!
I'm thankful for a God above to go to every day -
  A God whom I can worship - His holy Word obey.
To know someone has prayed for me is a truly joyous thing!
  And knowing this, I'll pray for you, for it makes my spirit sing!
You see - to pray for another's needs, and ask the Lord to BLESS,
  Is how we should love each other: It's the path to happiness!

  Dorothy K. Baker

Sonnet To My Deceased Mother

I often wonder why you found the need
To leave me so alone, a small, frail child
You left me without a chance to succeed
Without you I am nothing, a lost child
The days we spent together stay close at heart
And pain seems to grow with the years that pass
From you and your love, too long we've been apart
The pain, an obstacle I cannot pass
Sad things will happen all throughout my life
And the loss of you has been the very worst
Yet love we shared can't equal any strife
That chance may deal or fate may be cursed
At your sight in heaven joy rings like bells
For you I wait, though waiting shall be hell

  Brandon L. Spencer

A Vowel Amen...

I vowel to you this very day,
to love and care for you in any way.
Your laugh, your cry, your sense of fun,
I want you to be the very one.

East, West, North, South
I know we will have our doubts.
For richer, for poorer, till death do us part
we will always be joined at the heart.

If sick will heal, if hurt will mend
I will love you now and forever
Amen.

  Jennifer N. Vollner

As This Be The Last Day Of My Life

As this be the last day of my life, I'll give back
to my family...my friends hoping this day will never
end. I'll give back the love in which they have
given to me, I'll give back so much love this day it
will over throw the hatred and sorrow that I may have
caused, that made it hard to see. Hard to see the
things that mean so much to me, hard to see the
things I need to be free.

As this be the last day of my life, I'll help the evil to
see the good, help the good not to see the evil. I'll help the
old and I'll help the young, help do things that have never
been done. Understand the bad and why it is here, talk to
the good and tell them to have no fear.

As this be the last day, I'll find out why things happen
in life...like why some people are born blind, why true
love is so hard to find. Why money is everything, but
love is much more. Why the past, past by and the
future is something to look forward for. Why night
turns into day,...day into night, and why this must be
the last day of my life.

  Christopher A. Woods

Always Alive

The time has come for him to leave
To pass on and relieve,
his pain and misery
it cannot be undone,
it has no heart and gives no love

This cruel devil from the fires of hell,
it has no mercy and casts a spell,
The love for this sweet angel
it will never die
In our hearts and souls he will always be alive.

  Farrah Bragg

Untitled

I said a prayer for you today, and asked our Lord above,
To place his arms around you, with his redeeming love.
I asked of him to comfort you, and give you peace and grace,
That when you feel discouraged, you will see his smiling face.
You can be assured he loves you, and by your side he'll stand,
And when you need his blessings, he will hold you in his hand.
Life is so mysterious, there's so much we do not know,
But God has many promises, because he loves us so.
We have to trust in him each day, and look ahead to see
How much he loves us, one and all, especially you and me.
He gives us many mountains, so difficult to climb,
Yet we can conquer anything, with his great love sublime.
So trust in him with all your heart, and let him lead the way,
And things will surely turn out right, if we walk with him each day
He loves us with his heart and soul, he even gave his son,
To guarantee eternal life, when life on earth is done.
So do not be discouraged, lift up your eyes and see,
That God in all his glory, is watching you and me.
Pray a prayer for guidance, and trust in him each day,
And you will find the love of God, will lighten up your way.

Dorothy Bell

Full Moon At Balupet

Our stride was elastic: Stretched and shrank
to put each foot unfailing smack
on each dew-dunked-sleeper.
With peripheral vision we saw parallel flames
metal bright, run curving away uphill each rise
and come sliding back, as sure, every fall, on and on.
Once we paused, turned and looked at red eye
drowning in its own blood. Glory as ever
recurring at each death.

   Talk was inconsequential
   We kept silent
   We forged chains

Then with darkness leaking from a perforated sky
anxious, fending, we talked: If a train should come,
how grope blindly without the surety of blindness
up Balupet hill! And if the moon should not rise!
We erected laughter against a dread certainty
that everything was possible: that most of all,
later, alone, in a distant land, the forged chains
biting into flesh would pull and pull again.

Desmond Sequeira

"Ode To My Classmates" Or
(A Bit Of Wisdom Before The Bell Rings)

I finally get to stand before you with my poetry in hand,
To somehow impress upon you the secrets of all man.

But the secrets I divulge today are the pain of only one,
Whose life to you will seem insignificant in the long run.

But you know him though, he's the one you loved to trip in the hall;
Or knock the books from his arm, to you that's a ball.

He's the one the girls despise and whisper about behind their hand,
As if to breathe the same air as his is all that they can stand.

Being purposely stood up for the prom, and the jokes in
   the locker room.
No friends, no life and no love, will be the epitaph on his tomb.

The ones who listened to these words will be wiser before the
   next bell rings
And this final statement is for the others who just didn't
   give a damn...
Bang!

Daniel Ray Brison Jr.

"Time Assessment"

Eighty-five years seems reasonably fair
To stop and count the blessings a pioneer can share
Deep roots make us strong, when storms come along
Attitudes, realistic and positive, you have to prove
With each season of life, you get in the groove
From time to time, a terrific storm strikes
The wounds are mended, with loving care and the likes
The duties are many, and life has its charms
The family all care, when you are born on a farm.
God grants us much happiness, joy never ends
Time, tears and fears, make you thankful for friends
I cherish every memory, and the changes that time brings
I've learned to live in the present, and forget the trivial things
True time assessment, doing a good deed
Looking to the future, meet your life time creed.

Florence Shanks

In Angel Flight

An angel came in the silent night
To take home to God IN ANGEL FLIGHT,
This tiny soul once lively and warm.
Her life portrayed the noble and strong,
A dear friend of eighty-plus years,
A brave little fighter through laughter and tears.
This cold winter's night an angel appeared.
She told the nurse as the angel came near,
A glorious image only my friend could see.
In a blissful peace her suffering relieved,
Letting go of life she sighed her last,
IN ANGEL FLIGHT went to God's rest.
I ponder this story that to me was told,
This death bed scene as the ending unfold.
How beautiful to me, how comforting
To go home to God IN ANGEL FLIGHT's wings.

Eleanor F. Basinger

God Is Money...

From time one is born in a hospital bed,
To the time one is cleansed of blood and fed,
God is money, the remark may be something you never heard,
It may even seem absurd,
If one would happen to care,
You even have to pay for air.
For raising a family,
Or something you need,
What can provide it?
It's money indeed!
To heal the sick or
See a magic trick,
To travel the world
To Rome or Spain,
You even need money to be entertained.
So what is it that we all need?
It's money of course,
WHICH IS GOD INDEED....

Gwendolyn Ford

Horizons

I look across the blue-green water of the gulf
to where the apricot-gold sun dips into the
horizon sending its gold rays across the
water as a good night greeting.

I know I could never reach the
horizon. It always slips away.
This is the way I feel that you are
somewhere beyond my reach.

Dorotha Quick

Christmas Is Over - The Spirit Remains

I can't believe Christmas is over already. It seems we just began
to wrap gifts and bake goodies, to mail cards and open letters, to hug
and love each other.

My thoughts today are of Joseph and Mary - that first Christmas Eve,
think of how Joseph felt when Mary told him she was in labor,
while riding on a donkey led by Joseph.

They were on the outskirts of Bethlehem, without a hospital nearby-
nor even a reservation for a room for the night.

What about Mary when she heard the news that she was going to
have a baby - not even married to Joseph yet.

The innkeeper, no doubt, was tired after taking care of the
incoming people (census time).

He probably thought it was time to get up, hearing a knock at the
door. He did not know it was Joseph and Mary (the parents of our
Savior born that night). If he had known he would have given up
his warm room.

There was no room in the inn, so Joseph settled for a building
where cattle were kept and found a manger for Mary to lay the
baby Jesus when he was born.

The shepherds thought when told by the angels:
"Christ the Savior is born!"

Eleanor Tingelstad

The Old Man I See

The old man I see, sitting underneath a tree,
Toothless, chomping on something, like a cow chewing its cud
or a horse eating a pile of hay,
Hairless, his head is smooth, where hair used to be, no reminders
of his younger days,
His wife's been gone for many years,
But his children helped him through his tears,
He's watching the sky, so deep, blue and dry,
Like an old movie, of his younger days gone by,
He relives all the good things that happened in his life,
He probably thinks about the bad ones too, all his struggles
and his strives,
The weather is perfect, a day he has always loved,
And glad to have it sent from God above,
Bending over, his bones rattle, as he kisses his mother earth,
Looking back to the sky, as he wipes away the dirt,
So the old man that I see,
Sitting underneath that big tree,
Is looking more and more like me,
And the way that I'm going to be.

Jeff S. Fleming

Clay Of The Potter Destroyed

Darkness and rage accompanied by
Torrents of angry words and actions!
Screaming Spectre causing
Fear filled faces!
Anger and punishment — undeserved and without cause,

Family life shattered, society's fabric weakened,
Children traumatized, damaged and destroyed!
Spouses' souls seared and scarred by those out of control.
Lives lost —
Repetitive, silent, suffering and grief!

Mental illness, moral decay, poverty, apathy, hopelessness,
Blame, shame and denial everywhere.
Did you see it, hear it, feel it, or ignore it?
Did you cause it?
Could you or society have prevented it?

Enough! Enough! Clay of the Potter destroyed!

Joan Miller Wallis

The Gift

The greatest of all gifts—cannot be seen or—
touched—nor—thrown away.
It has a beauty, beyond what is seen—
with the eye itself, but rather what is seen,
by the mind's eye —— alone.
The greatest of all gifts, requires only —
for our soul, to be humble, and strong—
right and kind. It invites — no large effort — yet —
when done — and done well — sets loose —
a power beyond mankind's — understanding.
The greatest of all gifts, is something - that
can be thought about, — all the time — or ——
not nearly enough.
It gives us the ability — and —— the need to —
experience itself — over — and — over.
The greatest gift of all — is to ourselves.
It's the condition of the heart —— for which ——
commands us to forgive — and be forgiven.
This great gift requires — only one true knowledge—
——The Origin of Man.

Judith Frazier

Tip Toe

I gently step onto the carpet, moving closer and closer
towards my mother's room.

Thoughts of anger and pain fill my head,
as each step of mine becomes smaller.

Seconds away from the closed door,
I stop and place my hands together and pray-
quietly among myself.

Pushing the door slowly as not to wake my mother,
I slide inside and walk over to her bed.

Kneeling down beside her, I take her hand within mine
and I kiss her gently-
hoping that she will be well again

And not die.

I tip toe away from my mother's bed
and drop to the floor-
tears falling from my eyes.

Jennifer Lynn Kikel

The Garden Grotto

Here in this, my place to rest
To unburden worries from my chest
To face the faceless woes and strife
And curse the burdens in my life

A peace befalls me, as I see
That all the burdens that there be
Are of my making and I'll strive
To thank my God that I'm alive

For should I have missed that star so bright
Because I didn't have my sight
Or had I missed my child's first cry
With ears on which I can't rely

Two arms to hold him to my breast
My legs to walk till he's a'rest
A heart to love him and lips to tell
Of this place I know so well

Here in this place, a place to rest
A garden grotto I love best
And God looks down and smiles at me
He takes the burdens, sets me free

Cynthia B. Galletta

Out Of Gas

Sweating all over the road, out of gas, walking with back to on-
coming traffic,
I wish the car crushed until its parts become imperceptible, dense, one.

I experience traffic as a peripheral event:
continually approaching, surprising, shrinking,
it dizzyingly blind-sides me while revealing its fading-self in
dust, wind, and heat.

Out of my privileged an comfortable car seat,
unable to name the world with a glance,
noticing trees curving more, the rocks being heavier, and the grass
multiplying,
I perceive everything becoming un-sophisticated.
Objects, holding their own against the light and shadows,
demand constant attention and autonomy.
"We want childlike appreciations of ourselves and
records of our deposits with time!"
"We require less detail and more interaction!"
"We need you to change so much

If, at once, I could tilt every road-sign, spill their imperatives
on all sides, and then laugh at the baffled motorists,
I'd even have the courage to think, "I will not cease to be until
the universe collapses and my continuum regime is fused by spent frost."

Sweating all over the road, out of gas, walking with back to on-
coming traffic,
I wish the car fueled.

Greg Osweiler

America The Beautiful

Driving, walking or riding the bike
Traveling on roads like the Bear Creek Pike
Green fields, pretty trees and wild flowers
Make you want to walk or ride for hours
Hills and valleys are here and there
Enjoy the scenery with a breath of fresh air
America is beautiful for all to see
Except for the trash that is thrown so free
Solution to this problem needs attention from us all
With your help, our community can stand clean and tall
Home owners have a responsibility to keep things neat
Yards cut, house painted, puts you in the driver's seat
Business places can clean up and fix up with a little pride
Improved looks can put more customers on your side
Take pride in America and the town that you love
Trees and flowers planted, grow from rain and sunshine above
This poem was written so you very well can see
Our clean community means a lot to me
Keep this poem in memory spring, summer and winter
Keep America beautiful before our visitors enter.

Clarence T. Johnson

Affinitatis

I head to the bosom of the hills I know
To renew my spirit, to embalm my soul
Green paths lead me up to the hilltop's throne
Blue skies flood my spirit and its wings unfold.

I rise with the hawk to the angel's door
Flying into a golden fire of oneness
I singe my wings, but I fill my soul.
With the joys of the hawk and the hills we soared.

The moon's on the rise when I leave the hawk's skies
Back down to the hills, back down once more
The hallowed heartbeat of the hills give me life
And my breast resonates from the river's roar.
I know of the hawk, of the clear blue sky
I am them, they are me, we are one, we are born.

Dorothy Helms

Secret Garden

Ivy and thorns twisted, entangled in my emotion
trees lose their leaves - and yet -
a new flower grows among the withered weeds
within the walls
of this secret that
consumes me.

Ghosts dwell and torment, sometimes force memory
to show slides of the past on ivy-covered bricks
within the walls
of this secret.

Voices whisper all around
rustle the leaves
encourage vines to sway
echo in the hushed emptiness
within the walls.

Incredible beauty - despite -
captured in each tree, each flower, each droplet
each moss-covered stone
within me.

Jennifer M. Lane

The Scarlet Stream

The red rose-colored blood of sins past
Trickles down the swift running river of wrongdoing.
As the rivers winds its serpentine path,
Searching for a lake of redemptive gold,
It must purify the misdeeds written
In crimson, blood-steeped letters in the Tome of Transgressions.
To achieve the purity of a pearl, the clarion call of crystal,
I must forge ahead through the fiery flames of realization
For at that journey's end, my salvation lies.

Amdie Mengistu

The Warrior

He was just a warrior
Trying to be free
Worried about the future
For the visions, that he sees
Looking for that true love
To share in his smiles
He finds it hard and rocky
And so, so many miles
But, as he fights the many enemies
He tends to fall, to his knees
And with reaching out
A soft and loving hand, he does hold
As the visions foretold;
She touched his soul, she was his inner strength
That extra missing link
Now his worries are so few
And his life is all anew
For the warrior has freedom
And the gift of sharing it with someone

Juanita Mayes

True Love

Sweetness and softness, secure on my lap
Two sighs of contentment
Looking down I gaze into perfection

Could a smile be so rewarding?
A touch so warm it rivals the sun

Always present eager to please me
My trusting, loyal, undemanding love
My dear canine friend, my gift from above!

Deborah Genger

The Cure For Sadness

I have a thought in my head,
That you are sad and want to be happy.
If you are feeling bad,this poem is for you.
Apparently you need something good to do.

Talk to a loved one and take them out to eat.
Who knows, maybe something good will happen
While eating your feast.

Dress up your child and go for walk.
Fresh air could be all you need to turn
Your day of sadness into a day of gladness.

Call up a parent and talk of the silly things
You did as a child. Memories of your childhood,
Could give you a smile.

Give a neighbor a hand with chores.
When his eyes fill with tears of gladness,
I promise, your day of sadness
Will also be filled with gladness.

Doran Fluckiger

In A Dream

Taken slowly from the pages of a book
Turn around quickly to take a look
Just a vision like in a dream.

Talk about life in its most simple ways;
Think about things in its most odd days;
You see a vision like in a dream.

Taking a step closer to be free;
Letting the wind clear moments just to see;
Like a vision you see in a dream.

Most dear in your findings, tales to be told;
Outside a window it becomes night and cold;
A thought of a vision like in a dream.

You love her in your most hated time;
You love her in your most poetic rhyme;
But remember you love a vision like in a dream.

Helmut Perzi

Our Wedding Vows

Our love has just past by its Spring
'Twas then you became my life;
As freshness that the showers bring;
   As joy of songs the robin sing;
As you took me "for thy wedded wife."

Now as we enter into the warmth of Summer's sunshine
So our life adds another verse;
Our trials as well as love we find
   Make up the ties that bind;
As we accept "for better, for worse."

We'll look to the Fall, its brisker breeze
And accept whatever's dealt;
As bright splashes of colorful leaves
   Though soon to wither, still they please
Whatever may "in sickness and in health."

We do not fear our Winter's chill
It was accepted from the start;
Our love warms by selflessness,
   As comfort and grace radiate from our heart
Our final vow fulfilled "'til death do we part."

Elizabeth C. Ropka

"Death Of Our Heritage"

Eagles glide on air so smooth,
Unaware of a death so cruel,
Their beauty and grace in danger foul,
From bullets. traps, and pollution's scowl.
Our precious symbol of strength and pride,
Can America really let them die!
Their swoops and dives from heaven high.
Not close to earth ere you will die.
Chicks unborn, environments ruined,
Adults killed, and feathers pruned.
Their numbers dwindle day by day,
Our heritage dangerously fading away.
Can man not really see or care,
That eagles need our fervent prayer!
As our symbol fades from view,
We all must try to see them through.
To care, to save, to heal, to raise,
Our symbol quickly from the grave.

Jeffrey W. Fishman

Willow Tree

Oh willow tree, why do you weep,
Under your leaves we both took keep.
I know you miss him but hide your tears,
There is nothing, nothing to fear.
He used to protect you, poor weeping willow,
But don't let your tears overflow.
Please don't cry, he was my friend too...
After awhile you'll find someone new.
So stop your rain, don't despair,
Silently now I'll say just one prayer.
For you and for me my poor willow tree...
This is all part of life's symphony.
A symphony being continued as I now speak,
So let your arms sway, soft and meek.
The arms that would comfort and hide us, oh willow don't throw a fuss.
Just think of the memories; your leaves swaying in the breeze...
While we sat in your comforting arms,
Nothing could touch us, there weren't any harms.
Oh willow tree please don't weep.
Just remember the past...and doze to sleep.

Angel Kennedy

Evidence Of Love

I went down into the depths of a desolate lake
Underneath the earth, to the darkness of my past
You lifted me from the pit
You gave me new life

Once protected by this transient world
My spirit reached to access light and air, to soar
To break free of its prison
To ask forgiveness, and to be forgiven

This is love,
Painted in the dream-dimmed eyelids of my child
Evident in the unlaboring stars beneath I sleep
I wander by the edge of water welling
Silver springs inspire turquoise from the sky
My faith, my vision, a gift of color
Like roses in a passionate dream

I long to dance through my life like children at play
But this world's more full of weeping than I can understand
Time drops in decay, but your mercy endures forever
Forgive me Lord for my unbelief
For you are hope beyond what I can see.

Janet M. Schwenn

Star Wishes

He kissed her in the moonlight,
underneath the stars.
It was their last enchanted night
and tomorrow they would part.
She closed her eyes
that shone with tears
so he wouldn't see her cry.
But he took care of all her fears
when they agreed it wasn't goodbye.
Although this promise was made,
she couldn't help but hope the rules would bend.
And silently she prayed
that the night would never end.
She wished on a star for eternity,
but forever wasn't meant to be.

Christine Lee LaPere

"Anonymous Testing"

It was springtime, April of 1989
Unforeseen, a life soon to be forever changed

As the clock of life begins to tick
the time approaches half past nine
A precious life about to be rearranged

Doctor to patient the results are in, #86 he said
"your HIV test came back Positive"

As I stared hopelessly into space, numb from within
I fought back the tears, just knowing I had to be
strong in order to live

Life, even more fragile than ever, my heart and soul
filled with mixed emotions and sorrow
Pray with hope to find a brighter tomorrow

Frank C. Cacciola

Tears

Tears - they come so unexpectedly
They come and wash away your sorrows
They give security that is your only comfort in distress
While unlocking emotions bottled up inside
They discover feelings you never knew were there
And represent ideas never meant to be put into words
Symbolized with pain they are really a gift of undescribable
   proportion
Their true beauty is continually cast away with shame
And why can reality never fight through their shields?
They receive the blame without a complaint
Leaving only a newfound knowledge
They hold the secret to freedom
To give you an escape from the ball and chain you wear
But of course so quickly they slip away
Only to be found once more.

Jessica Bruno

Treasures

Love and trust in a child's eyes
Twinkling stars in the midnight skies
Silky fur of playful pups
Empty Churches' silent hush
A rainbow after a warm spring rain
The haunting whistle of a distant train
Warming my toes by an open fire
"How Great Thou Art" sung by a choir
All the family once more in the fold
Life's small pleasures - more precious than gold.

Gloria J. Hudock

Eulogy On Groundhog Day

For the last time, I've placed his cup
   upon the very top shelf.
From this day on, I'm doomed to sup
   completely by myself.

The poncho's been folded, to measure for size
   'twas his Christmas gift;
But he never did come, to get his surprise,
   'twill remain a trophy of rift.

The log cabin quilt was to hang on the wall
   of the cabin he built in Thayer;
I'll use it to cover myself by the fire,
   and think of him down there.

From the Trail of Tears, I've a rock off his land,
   it graces my mantle;
As I clutch tightly, to feel the warmth of his hand,
   remembering he once did handle.

There's 29 letters that he wrote, in the rack,
   that I can read;
When he doesn't come back,
   if I really want to bleed.

Julia Dixon Collett

Untitled

Life is like a roller coaster. It has its
UPS and downs. Some moments can be EXCITING
while others could be very b-o-r-i-n-g
It could turn completely UPSIDE DOWN
and even make you sick. Life moves much too fast
and ends in a very short while.

Andrea Piwowar

Ode To A Friend

When in one's memory, time nor distance would place a
   veil upon your face.

When one understands your doing, be it right or wrong.

When one's pride is not placed above humility, and
   humility in itself is above being ashamed.

When one does not mock you, for he cannot see the light
   in which you walk with God, though his own be bright
   within himself.

When one eyes your good fortune without envy, embraces
   your tears with their own, and listens to your foils
   of life with a silent tongue.

When, even for love's sake, you are not cast aside, only
   to be called upon when the calm of the sea has
   turned into mountains of swallowing waves.

One has found God's treasure of mankind, a Friend.

Justine Matteis

Darcel

I had a little sister named Darcel Arnetta Brown.
Upon her beautiful face there was never a frown.
She was as beautiful as beautiful could be.
I loved her and she loved me.
One day she died and went away.
Heaven she will forever stay.
I miss her very, very much.
She had the sweetest touch.
That has been six years ago.
Oh yeah did I mention she had the prettiest big toe.
Darcel, I know up there God is treating you right.
That's how I'm able to make it through the night.

Cerissa Brown

What Is A Mother?

A mother worries, protects and gives guidance.
She is there to listen with intense empathy and compassion.
She expects obedience and respect, which is understood.
She is never overbearing, and knows when not to ask.
She can be stern when principles of right and wrong are questioned.
She allows for flexibility and respects another's view.
She is proud of her children and only wants the best.
She is full of warmth and genuine concern, for to her, her children
are everything.

Lori Allen

Mom

She is always there when I need her
She is there to wipe away my tears
and to give me a hug
She shows her love for me in what
she says and does
She encourages me to strive for my dreams
She supports me in my decisions
even if she does not always agree
I know I will always have her
love unconditionally
That's my Mom!

Louise Padgett Sutton

Untitled

My mother is hard working, and as caring as can be
She may not ever say it, but she sometimes misses me.
She may not always listen. And it may not seem she cares
But she has a lot to do and it's giving her gray hair.
She let me go to college, though she needs help at home
The house is in a shambles and she feels all alone.
There are things in need of fixing and others in repair
And each and every one of them just add more gray hair.
She desperately needs a vacation, but alas she can't afford
She has a kid in college and 2 in elementary that have her
wrapped up in a cord.
My mother may not be perfect, but she's the only one I've got.
And I think she is the best one;
I love her quite a lot.

Marianne Fernandez

Faster

Poor PoorPaul. Unlucky at running, unlucky at love.
She passed him in the other direction as he ran his daily duty.
He couldn't believe his eyes. He couldn't believe her eyes!
She was beautiful. Best of all, she was a runner.

PoorPaul turned on a dime.
A pastel ponytail swept side to side from shoulder to shoulder.
An untucked T teased the eye as it playfully cuddled her curves.
Lycra lurked out from under her shirt covering all yet concealing none.

PoorPaul's heart raced as he picked up the pace.
He plucked a flower. He'd simply say, "Here, I think you dropped
this."
So enchanted with his charm and so charmed by his enchantment!
Oh, and how impressed as well! So fleet of foot yet none the shorter
of breath.

PoorPaul ran even faster. Soon they'd run hand in hand to movies
and the mall, over daisy covered fields, across crystal white beaches.

His stride grew ever faster and his breath ever shorter.
She, the four minute mile, that ulimate impossible goal
History holds the mile, however. Now, Poor Paul raced toward
history.

Oh, she was a runner and was perfect as far as he could see.
Only one thing was wrong, she was just a bit faster than he.
Poor Poor Paul.

Paul Loebach

The Dream

Brown hair cascades down her face
She blushes, then kisses me deep and long,
My heart skips a few beats in her embrace
And I can feel her breath whisper its lovely song.

Her scent is fresh and clean like a new morning
The clarity in her eyes is truth itself,
Warm soft touches stir my inner longing
For the lifelong partner who brings me spiritual health.

Suddenly, the dream changes
When deep wounds nearly destroy it all,
But she comforts my concern and arranges
All events that follow, in answer to her call.

Then the most wonderful healing takes control of my heart
And I no longer have the pain from my past,
She caresses my face in her beautiful hands, I am alert
All my fears have stopped, this change will last.

I've never felt such love from any other
Her brilliant light shows me which way to go,
She is an awesome angel who helps me recover
The real self that I am, so I may learn what I should know.

Mark F. Daley

Aileen Amy

Mommy, Mommy, these words I hear,
when I know my daughter is near.
She grew so fast, I sometimes cannot believe my eyes.
How she walks and talks and says "Bye Bye."

I hate to leave her and go off to work.
I do not think she understands how much I hurt.
My time with her is so precious and few.
I wish there were other things I could do.

I do not want to miss out on her life.
Like when she took her first step or becomes someone's wife.

I want us to share secrets and be best friends.
I do not want us to have any lose ends.

She is my baby, whom I love so much.
As she grows I still want to be her crutch.

I want to be here for her night and day.
And to have a beautiful relationship in each and every way.

Vicki Rak

Grandma Kate

She's gone now it's almost been a year, she's happier up there don't
shed a tear. Maybe a few here and there, wouldn't be so bad just be
sure a smile you'll wear. She died in April, Tuesday the twelfth at
1:00, it was a terrible experience, not at all fun. The memory of her
may bring a tear to our eye, try to be strong and brave try not to
cry. If you knew her, you were a lucky human being, she was
always so nice never at all mean. Her memories of Grandpa,
Bobby and Bob, when I heard she died I just sobbed and sobbed.
It all finally hit us when we knew we wouldn't see her again, in a
scale of niceness she gets a plus ten. Her perfume aroma, her
pictures on the wall, her dolls that dance round and round, her
memories in the hall. Her lovely presents gifts and love, that was
all that she was made of. She was a nice little lady, pretty and
sweet, she was fun to be around, a real treat. Her puffy stuffed
animals, her furniture in the house; she was a short sweet lady, so
quiet, like a mouse. I loved her dolls movin' round 'n' round; the
music reminds me of her; it was a peaceful, beautiful sound. Full
of candy was her silver tin, if I could see her again, oh, how I
wish. Her small T. V. sitting in the kitchen, her furniture, clothes,
house, even her silver tin. All the memories we've brought back
tonight shouldn't bring any sorrow; think of her every day, starting
with tomorrow. On this cold winter night I hope I haven't made
anyone sad, just think all these memories should make you glad.

Niki Mitch

Songfest

I wish you could have seen her face
She smiled and nodded as she sang
Of Beulah Land and Canaan -worlds she knew
There her loved ones waited and she was waiting too.

She clasps her tired old hands
And her eyes tho blind can see
The golden streets she sings about
And her gone on family

I watch her and I thank Him
though time takes her strength away
He has left her with a memory
Of other happy days

Tho' alone she's never lonely
Her heart's so full of love
She is patient but so homesick
for her promised home above.

She sings along and smiling
Thinks of happy times of yore
And ponders deep within her heart
as Mary did before.

Lois M. McConnell

Idle Thoughts

Even though she'd like to roam
She stays at home and works alone
Even with her hair all mussed
She don't sit around complain or fuss
Her dress she wears all tattered and torn
She's wore it for years it is well worn
Although she feels some like crying
She takes up the skillet and keeps on frying
Her pants has round and little square patches
And a few I think might be mismatches
Her face is splattered from pancake batter
She doesn't care it don't even matter
She is the lady of the house
She is my love, my loving spouse
She's been my partner, biggest part of my life
Yes, I'm proud to call her, my loving wife
The verse and paper might be all wrong
But my love for you is well and strong
I'd be your happy valentine
If your love for me is just like mine

Larry Smith

A Mother Of Love

For mine is a mother, a mother of love.
She was sent from the heavens, the heavens above.

For she had four daughters, the youngest was me,
and, oh, how happy we all turned out to be.
Because we were loved so very much,
we are all very close and all stay in touch.

For she told us all stories, taught us to cook,
and would always wait up for us as long as it took.

For she would say her prayers, and we would too,
And prayers were answered, for miracles came true.

For she put so much effort in each of our dreams;
the sky was the limit, or at least that's how it seems.

I never thought some one could care so very much
to unselfishly give, reach out and touch.

She will run to your rescue as fast as can be.
She has never let me down. Now, I'm sure you can see,
that she is a mother sent from above
for the power of God has made her out of love.

Victoria Marie Gall

Hiding From Everyone

I met her a few years ago.
She was shy, scared, hiding from everyone.
I learned how she had been shuffled from house to house,
family to family.
No one wanted her, not even her mother or her father.
Her grandparents couldn't keep her anymore.
As people reached out to her, she would draw back.
It made no sense, I thought. How could she not want them, not
trust them?
Then I realized that she was not like me.
She had to leave the only family she knew,
to live with people she did not know.
Then they would decide not to keep her.
She would go somewhere else, to someone else.
Even when they adopted her, she remained a closed door.
Not locked, but needing the effort of another to open it.

Things have improved since that day.
She is no longer as shy or scared. She does not hide from everyone.
And she has changed me.
I no longer think everything is right in the world.
I no longer think things are bad for me
Or that everything and everyone around me is a mess.
I know I am loved. I know I am lucky.

Katie Friesen

Learning

I was a student.
    She was three months old
        And she was my assignment.
I cannot even remember her name
    But her face remains imprinted on my mind.
Her head was too big—
    Her eyes protruded-
        Her mouth-misformed.
Her smile appeared a grimace.
I thought she tragically survived her own miscarriage.
I had a difficult time looking.
Then her parents came.
    They saw beauty.
        They smiled and she grimaced
            And they saw beauty.

I was a student
    She was three months old
        And she was my teacher.

Margo Dillon

Mama's Rocker

Mama's rocker now sets empty and still,
She's in her final resting place high
Upon the hill.
She rocked all five of her babes in
That rocking chair,
Wiped away their baby tears with tender
Loving care.
On Sundays in her rocking chair, she'd while
away the day,
Rocking as she read her Bible and watched
Her children play.
Many times that rocker soothed her soul
And eased her aching bones,
As she grew older and her children left
Her all alone.
But now she's gone away from us high upon
That hill,
And it breaks our hearts to see her rocker
So empty and still.

Thelma Jeffers

My Daughter, Your Daughter

Jesus, she's out there.
She's not happy with the choice I made.
In fact she said maybe it should be her or me.
I respond if she feels that way, perhaps she should go.
Jesus, please watch over my daughter, your daughter.

It hurts when a part of your heart is torn away.
That's how I felt when her mother and I parted.
That's how I feel now.
Jesus it hurts.
I love her, my daughter, your daughter.

Jesus, she needs a father more than ever.
We don't pick our father though, do we?
I realize that although I might not be everything
You knew what you were doing when you gave her to me.
Not that she is not here
(Although I pray she will again be),
I give her to you, for you to be the perfect Father of
My daughter, your daughter.

Stanley J. Strzyzykowski

Cindy

There's a pretty little girl named Cindy
 She's only two going on twenty.
Her dark curly hair and sparkling eyes
Let you know you're in for a surprise.
Her capacity to retain what she sees and hears
 Goes far beyond her tender years.
Her daddy Jerry takes her to swim in the pool.
 And Grammy Colleen accompanies her to the zoo.
Then to the park to swing, give the pigeons a shoo!
When she gets home, tiptoes to the phone
I see if Auntie Tickles and Uncle Ralph are home.
 Hello-I've had a fun day, how about you?
 Tell me honestly if it's true
That I'm Mommy's and Daddy's little baby,
 Grammy's precious sweet angel,
And Uncle Ralph's little princess.
 Yes, Oh! thank you.

Look out two thousand and four
Here's a little genius you're bound to adore.

Ruth Watkins

What Makes Me Smile

When I awake early in the morning, to see the sun
shining bright,
I smile because God has watched over me all night.

In the winter when everything seems cold and still,
the snow on the ground and the wind blowing chills.
I find myself looking out of the window, with a smile
rather than tears.

Sometimes I sat thinking about the chores of the day,
the hustle and bustle that comes my way.
Although it may seem hard to do,
my smile is the one thing that carries me through.

When things become so hard to bear,
and my daily struggle seem to end without any care.
There is a special expression on my face,
it's a smile that always closes out despair.

There is a little song within my heart,
I listen to it most everyday.
This song tells me which course of the day to take,
and to keep that smile for goodness sake.

Queen E. Lewis

Bye Dad

A Dad should always be there, and
should always care. You were my dad
but never acted like it. I cried so much
for you not coming around, and for not
caring how you hurt me, and how you
let me down so many times. That's
why I'm saying bye to the crying, bye
to the hurt, bye to the letdowns. I
love you dad, but I have to say bye.

Leo Barrios

"Disintegration"

Alone in the midst of my greatest fear
Silent intuition has brought me here.
Voices-they covet and sing of sweet death,
Luring souls to the Immortal Chamber.
We are told of its still, strange peacefulness;
The dissipation is overwhelming.
Cold, quiescent air leaves us feeling bereaved.
Cynical to this impetuous act,
I find that signs of hope are elusive.
Only I am left; the others have gone...
The voices sing. Looking back on bent knees,
I see the steps behind me disappearing.

Traci Avet

Consuming Desire

From the sky it comes,
Silver wings guide it to its lover.
 Her rich green breast heaves at its touch.

And all her servants scurry to and fro
Wearing their brilliant orange vestments
 Soon turned to brown and black.

All things reduced to basic
As the final adoration is consummated
 And brought to fruition.

All love is gone now, along with hatred,
The trivials made nothing, rendered null and void.
 The servants lie prostrate in eternal homage.

Now has Man's true love been realized.

Paul Ramirez

"Last Seen, Like An Eternity"

It's been a few years
Since I last saw you,
Feels like a life time;
...... Last seen, like an eternity
And it's been bothering me.....

We had so much to give,
And so much to say
Yet we hid those feelings,
So deep inside.. shy and afraid
Not knowing what the other would think...
I've just got to say
...... Last seen, like an eternity.....

I'm sorry, forever hurting... you
In any way, 'cause you know.. this is my way
Sweet and courteous, not overbearing..
But kind, and always loving.....

Now I think of you more, more, more
Now that I'm married, thinking of what happened..
Life changes each of us, and I am sorry.....

Last seen, like an eternity......

Lawrence J. McKnight

The Flight Of The Nightingale

Nightingale of enlightenment,
Sing your soft song sweetly,
Do not worry 'bout your troubles,
Hurl the notes so freely.
Fly right by on wings of silver,
Show your golden tail,
Snap your beak that's made of copper,
Tuck your feet so frail.
Brush the treetops with your feathers,
Brace yourself to land,
Touch the ground with grace and sweetness,
Oh my friend, you're grand!

Kerry Barklow

The Color Drunk Warrior

The Color Drunk Warrior
Sits cross legged atop the Mountain
And attempts to paint a mural of the Sunset.

Armed with the soldier's palette of the two colors of blood
and black,
A violent flurry of splattered red and soil ensues onto the canvas
of sky
While a battalion of rain, hell, and sleet serve to mix and mold
the colors.

But the Warrior begins to fade
As his soul pours out from slit wrists
And the once fertile ground on which he sits
Is now nothing but bare bone and crumbling marrow.

The Warrior screams his last war cry
As his masterpiece is washed away
And absorbed into the dying sun.

Then, nothingness.

Kevin Ang

"Passion"

I need the passion of ravaging seas, erupting volcanos and thundering
skies. I need the passion for my desperate, and dying soul. The
treacherous path of life brings upon misery and sudden drift. I need
the passion as guiding star of life. I struggle so hard, I stumble
and fall, but that sweet smell of worthy notion so far away. The
intensified moments of my life urge for drastic measures, but the
worthy cause is far away. Ecstasies of life so cunning and wicked,
atrocities of life so calm and soothing; but what am I thinking. I
carry my tortured soul for eternity, with grace and charm; a constant
search for passion so desperate so toiling; and endless tunnel never
to be discovered. I need the passion for my dying soul.

Pervaiz Memon

Dead Love

Dead love is like beached bones on barren sands,
Salted to remain and to remind,
Of roads not taken.

Dead love is like a tree with hungry branches,
White leaves, green with envy,
All looking back, for last year's spring.

Dead love is like an empty house,
Deserted - but filled with walled-in memories,
Delighting each other with, "Remember when...?"

Dead love is death that lives and lives,
Desiring dearly to forget
What was, what is, forever regret.

J. W. Barrowes

Swan Serenade

Ethereal creature of floating grace
Skimming the water so proud and serene
Your elegant bearing captivates me
And lifts me out of my own time and space

On bright wings of thoughts you dare me to dream
You teach me to reach for a star filled sky
To touch a new world of meaning and light
To recapture the glow of a moonbeam

Your regal carriage and manner sublime
Project a strong presence, faithful and true
Your bold silhouette radiates courage
Your majestic image endures through time

You are eloquent, yet choose not to speak
But I hear your silence and understand
You are the essence of quiet wisdom,
An ageless knowledge profound and unique

The sparkling beauty of your reflection
Inspires new-found ways to view my own life
A pristine clear vision, a pure insight
Born from endless joy in your perfection

Paula Swan

The Traveler

There it stood like a glowing ember against a dark universal
Sky sprinkled with stars
Appearing about the size of a full moon in the distance
Its observer had no awareness of physical conveyance
Yet all seemed as it should be

The fire was extinguished yet burned
The child vibrated to the pulse of its mother's womb
Awaiting motherhood
Ages and ages brought about its birth....gestation complete
Fire....water....air....stone

The shadows came from somewhere among the stars
Bringing the spark
Possessing the beast....becoming the beast....shedding the beast
Separating....one becoming two...confusing many
Existing for unmeasured times....searching for the way
Back to the stars

Len Jade

Earth's Night Light

The lights in the sky shine down brightly,
Slanting and slitting through the windows lightly,
Landing so softly on the top of my head,
Making it seem much brighter instead.
The beauty of these lights so clear,
Touching, lovely, gentle, sheer
Beauty of these night sky lights,
With them all the world seems right.
Land, man, sea are calm.
I hold the lights' beauty in my palm
To wish on and keep forever.

Shalondra Sanford

"Against The Night"

Set against the night, are the distant lights of a thousand stars.
Small pinholes of light, in a mute curtain of black.
Glowing curiosities, celestial lanterns.
Guiding the paths of ships in the night,
Marking the seasons, through stone trilothons and monoliths.
Making known to the ancients,
The secrets of the flooding nile.
And the ephemerality of the seasons abroad.

M. Ford

"Box"

I feel so lost in a box with no lid -
Smoke filled rooms with bells ringing in my ears....
Eyes searching for the sky's filled with streaks of light.
Looking for hope in a poor man's soul walking in warn out
Shoes down paved sidewalks.
Empty but yet smothered inside. Nowhere to hide...
Longing for shelter in a lovers arms, searching for a
Soldier to help battle these demons of depression tearing
out my heart. Tears falling like boulders into my hands,
much too heavy at times for me to stand....
So lost and contained...to a box with no lid.

Therese Garrison

Terrible Twos!!

Look at the little boys and girls,
Snatching toys and grabbing curls,

Pulling off shoes and pushing faces,
Stuffing things in different places,

Breaking crayons and coloring chairs,
Happily hugging their stuffed teddy bears,

Sucking their thumbs and climbing on tables...
Small children like that need warning labels!

Michelle Pinkston

To My Wife On Cupid's Day

"This valentine cannot be bought
So careful are its phrases wrought.
No standard stock could ever say
what's in my heart on Cupid's day.
That love is neither here nor there
But every place that we will share.
And if another year has passed
It was filled with love that will always last.
Love that's like a guarantee
That the best of years is yet to be."

Raymon Gerard

A Date With War

The date was behind us, the air power in flight.
So it came to pass that fateful night.

Fighter jets and bomber planes flew to fill the sky;
Their cross hairs on target - the adrenaline is high.

Embroidering the Gulf, great ships start their wonder
Firing Tomahawk missiles to the land over yonder.

Ground forces send up the Patriot missile.
To intercept Iraq's incoming Scud missiles.

Designed to clash, they meet in the sky.
Thundering flashes appear, the scud threat subsides.

The air raid came fierce, in all its glory.
Making history for books and soldiers' war stories.

So battered the land, its people in strife.
Their leader in a hole, safe out of sight.

Along guarded borders of allied and foe,
We collect Hussein's soldiers walking in woe.

A sad sight to see but some joy reflects,
Wanting war to be over - wanting more to defect.

We sent the ground soldiers who were standing in form,
To end the war known as "Desert Storm."

Shasta Story-Martin

"No Longer"

Stick a knife deep into the plummets of my heart,
so it can no longer beat for you.

Slice my throat,
so it can no longer whisper how it loves you.

Cut off my hands,
so they can no longer reach out to you.

Cut off my arms,
so they can no longer long for you.

Cut off my legs,
so they can no longer run to you.

Take my brain,
my unworthy brain,
who thinks that thee does no wrong,
who dreams of you and who remembers you.

You who is farther away than the farthest star,
do this so my brain no longer brings me this agony,

Please I ask you to do this so my eyes get to see you,
so they no longer have to see you again.

Lacy Treanna Gilbert

My Loving Papa

Little Jessica and her Papa - what a strong and magical bond.
So loving and caring of one another - neither could be more fond.
So many wonderful memories-but there was oh so little time.
The pleasures shared together now become treasured in her mind.

Memories of a beautiful garden - so rich and lush and green;
Where if one looked more closely, a creature could be seen.
A little girl in her Kingdom with Papa's eyes upon her face;
Where she is free to roam and play - he loved this special place.

Leisurely strolls along the trail, enjoying all life's pleasures;
Discovering nature at its best or searching for lost treasures.
So simple yet so special, the wondrous times spent together;
Of discovering one another and of a love that would last forever.

Then all too soon it happened - God was calling Papa home.
Little Jessica couldn't bear to think of him being all alone.
She bravely stood beside his bed - she was his saving grace;
She left him in his glory with one last smile upon his face.

Yvonne Ortega

Seven Years Long

Seven years long since she's been gone.
So many dreams she had to try—
so homesick, she thought she'd die.
Her family traveled long and far—
hoping to see her find her star.

Though lonely, tired, and sick at heart,
through earthquake, then the Hand of Fate:
a tragic loss of one so dear—
still she lingered there.

Though she always kept in touch—
times together went too quick.
A love or two, not always fair—
still something held her there.

Another Christmas come and gone—
a decision is finally done.
Soon she'll travel far and wide—
to be back home at her family's side,
After seven years long.

Thoughts from a Mother's heart.

Maureen K. Ranquist

Peace On Earth

Life has so many paths,
 so many long roads,
 so many sharp turns,
 so many dead ends.
Love soothes the pain
of a broken heart when you reach a dead end,
and eases the toughness of life through many hard times.
Peace the opposite of war
goes along with love
With peace, love will not totally die out
With war love is separated
and couples are split
 Loved ones look upon each other's differences in opinion
or just plain differences
They fight each other, killing each other,
killing part of their own life
They grieve for days, weeks, months, years, or even a lifetime
                    PEACE
                       ON
                    EARTH
      Tracy Malcolm

Inside The Walls

Inside the prison walls, alone I sit.
   So many others around me, have abandoned
There wills only to submit.
   For many, this is no man's land.
But for me, it's where I'll unfold
   the master's plan.
   It takes a strong mind, will, and
dreams.
   For those who don't know this will
fall apart at the seams.
   Once you're inside, often no-one
even remembers your name.
   Never in my lifetime, did I think
I'd play this losers game.
   You'll lose your family, kids, and wife.
My heart is filled with compassion, for those
who are serving for the rest of their life.
      Ricky T. Williams

"Many Shapes"

The sky has always caught my eye since I was very small!
Some clouds look very short, and some clouds look very tall!

Clouds have many shapes, but I haven't seen them all, for
sometimes when I look in the sky, all I see is a very large wall!

It's a wall of clouds strung across the sky, but it's loveliness
surely can't pass you by!

I've seen shapes within the clouds, like a santa, a snowman
and even some cows!

Things I truly don't try to see, will pop right up in front of me!

Like eagles flying in the air, or maybe a child sitting in a chair!

Some people don't see many things in the air, and I really
have to wonder if that's really fair!

Because some of the wonderful things I've seen, some people
might even have called a dream; it was an angel sitting on a sun beam!

I could sit and watch these moving clouds for hours, making
shapes of things like pretty flowers.

Not only the clouds catch my eye, but also the sun that sets
in this beautiful sky!

The moon, the stars and the planets too, are something that
give me something to do!
      Karen L. Gaines

A Mother's Love

So many times you've brought me to tears,
So many times you've filled me with fears.

You touch my heart in so many ways,
You bring happiness to all of my days.

Not many have known me as well as you,
I feel your presence through and through.

My arms ache to hold you and squeeze you tight,
To care for you and watch over you, all through the night.

I can't wait to see you and feel your tender touch,
You already know, I love you so much.

When can I hold you, when can I see?
My beautiful child growing inside of me.
      Kathy A. Ansell

America Beauty Save

America the beautiful is losing grace -
so many uncaring are dirtying her face.

In God we trust was number one,
but now the uncaring well they just make fun.

Uncle Sam stood proud and tall,
they burn his flag
the uncaring all.

Our Eagle flies across our sky
please true Americans,
don't let her die
      Madeline Butgereit

The True Meaning of Easter

Jesus died for our sins.
So on Easter families have smiles and grins.
Jesus died on the cross for us,
So I'd like to say
I love you Jesus.
Thank you very much.
      Leslie Crews

Hummingbird At My Feeder

I had a visitor at my house.
So small and tiny you'd think of a mouse.
But this one flies, so quickly and fast.
If you blink your eye, he surely can pass.
His back, it shimmers of emerald green.
His head is dark as a midnight beam.
His chest is as red as the reddest rose.
The wings go so fast, it's like they're in limbo.
As he drinks the sweetness from the feeder at my window.
      Suellen Wilds

No Tomorrow

Smile as if it's your last breath, flush away your sorrow
Today you will clean the slate, as if there's no tomorrow
Speak to me of your finest hour, give me words to follow
Cleanse today your inner pain, as if there's no tomorrow

No more sorrows
No more tomorrows

Face the fear behind your shadow, never again to wallow
In the blood of senseless fight, there may be no tomorrow
Spread your wings toward the light, your pride you must swallow
Paint your soul a touch of red, there may be no tomorrow

 - No Tomorrow
      Christopher Dominick

The Unfortunate

People having no place to go,
So they rob and steal and that's definitely a no no!
But what else is there to do when you don't have a job.
When you ask people for money and they act like a snob.
So they try to survive by looking in garbage for a bite to eat.
They lie on the cold, hard park benches to get some sleep.
They wake up the next morning and things are the same.
Back on the streets to play the survival game.
They say to themselves, when will the suffering end.
My life used to be so good, but now I have no friends.
The friends that I thought I had were no good.
They watched me drop to the bottom, and there they just stood!
They didn't help me get back on my feet.
As I was looking up at them, I started to weep.
If I'm lucky, maybe I'll find some doe.
But until that time come, I have no place to go!

Shearie A. Hayes

Dreams

Dreams reach far beyond any horizon,
  soaring at heights no eagle could ever match.
Filtering through the brilliant hues of a rainbow,
  to warm a desolate face.
In dreams, there are no hinderings,
  you can touch any star far beyond mortal reach.
With no dreams, life would simply be a reality.

Selina McGee

Untitled

And when I am old, I will dance across the kitchen floor in orange
socks. And I will cook hot dogs and hamburgers on the grill,
in January. I will sing songs that no one knows the words to
but me. And if by chance, the bridge of teeth that I may have,
happens to come loose, and fall out, and if I do swallow it, and
later find it, I will wear it on a necklace.
And my kitchen will be pink, and my living room yellow, and I
will forever be forgetting the glasses I'll wear on my head.
And when I go to restaurants, my dessert will come first and
my salad last. I will keep up my Christmas tree until St.
Valentines Day, and then re-decorate it.

And I will take time to listen to my children.
I will be a good mother.
And the lines on my face will not show, and I will grow to
be more beautiful every day,
as did my mother.

Shannon Givler

The Holiday

The holiday again is near, and some loved ones won't be here.
Some familiar faces, now God embraces.
And some have better things to do, than to spend them with me and you.
The memories of a holiday past,
When families hands around a grand table were clasped;
With heads bowed in humble praise;
Don't seem so important to folks nowadays.
To younger ones the feelings aren't the same,
And you know, somehow, we're probably the ones to blame.
We tried to replace old values with things we never had,
Things we thought might make us glad.
So this holiday we'll be missing a few, again it will be just me and you.
To gather once more, with half-hearted cheer,
And sadly remember those who couldn't be here.
Now don't let that tear fall from your eye,
Just think of turkey and pumpkin pie,
Mashed potatoes with giblet gravy and a buttered bun,
Candied yams and pretzel salad..... yum yum.
So put a smile on your pretty face,
And let's give thanks to God for his abundant grace.

Ulas George Kirby

Illusions

We live in a world of illusions
Solid forms merely our delusions
Space so cherished we surround with fences
Yet merely illusion of limited senses

Wars fought over these illusions
Bodies mutilated to their conclusions
Lives cut short defending fences
Created by the limitation of our senses

So what is true reality
If not the world we think we see
Those who left us and returned
The answer to this they have learned

Most important is what we take
To the eternity in which we finally awake
Not gold or silver or material wealth
Not even our body's physical health

But our soul and all it has learned
Is the treasure we have earned
All the rest are left behind
Illusions of the human mind

Paul M. Feuer

Home At Last

I've traveled many places, around this world of ours,
Some happy times along the way, good times that just went sour.

It seemed so nice, these different places, to which I've had to roam,
but none of them felt quite as nice, as this place called home.

I thought I'd look around some more, for a place to stay,
but everywhere was somewhere else, I found along the way.

So now I'm back to emptiness, it seems so lonely now,
this place I've searched for after all, is not so bad, somehow.

In life we're always searching, for a perfect place,
but home is here forevermore, I guess it's here at home,
  I'll stay!

Dawn M. Craig

The Mother Of One

Some Mothers have a flock, or perhaps a herd or two
Some Mothers have a batch, a bunch, a pair, or a slew

Some Mothers have so many faces and tummies and hands
To kiss, fill, wash and love all over this great land

Some Mothers spend all the time that comes each day
Making sure that no one is sick, hurt, or gets away

I am the Mother of one
One is a number that may seem very small indeed
One is the priceless treasure of my one tiny seed

One is the number that means the best of all time
One child of great wisdom, beauty and talent sublime

One is my strength, my devotion, my hope, and my pride
One makes me glow happily when she stands at my side

I am the Mother of one
Hers is the face that I seek when the miles are far
Hers is the presence I seek when I get in my car

She's the one that I miss when I see kids in the park
She's the one that I rub watching TV in the dark
She's the one I will love all the days of my life, she's the gift
that God gave me as Mother and wife, I am the Mother of one

Linda M. Alexander

The Bond Has Broken

All parents make mistakes when raising their children.
Some parents are a disappointment to their children.
And some children are a disappointment to their parents.
But life itself is full of disappointments
Yet that doesn't mean the love isn't there.
And it doesn't mean both don't care.
It just means both are human.
It's a common trait we share.
For most of us have no guidelines, with which to compare.
And life itself we learn by trial and error.
But this world has gotten deadly,
and family values are slipping away.
Instead of families bonding, they are being led astray.
Maybe someday the disappointments will fade away.
There will be no anger, no harsh words to say.
And families will love and stay together, come what may.
Yet, though it may not be in my lifetime;
I pray my grandchildren will see that day.
For a family's bond should never stray!!!!

Sheryl Bailey Lanzarotto

A Child Is A Gift

A child is a gift of love.
Some say "a blessing from above,"
So shower him with care.
And when he cries into the night,
Instead of getting all up-tight,
Go to his side and dry his tears,
(Though more may come with passing years),
And say: "We're here! We care!"

A child is a gift, some say.
Some day he'll grow and go away.
Though grown, still a child he'll seem to be.
In time, you'll wither and grow olden
As memories grow fond and golden.
He'll come back to your side and say:
(While pushing aside your locks of gray),
I'm here because you cared for me."

Paul M. Smith

"October"

In the month of October, the leaves turn to gold.
Some turn to red, wondrous sights to behold.
Then just like rain, they fall on the ground.
To tell us it's Autumn, without making a sound.

A walk in the country, God's beauty to see.
The greens and the reds and the gold of each tree.
The cry of the wild geese above us we hear,
Summer is over and Winter is near.

Bare trees silhouetted against the blue sky,
Speak in a whisper, to tell summer good-bye.
Soft thump of nuts as they fall to the ground,
The rustle of leaves that the wind blows around.

The sky full of birds, some ready for flight,
And creatures prepare for their Winter's night.
The days grow shorter and the long shadows creep,
While over our shoulder, Autumn's Moon starts to peep.

Oh, October, October, you won't stay around.
Soon snow and ice will cover the ground.
How we will miss you, we remember you when,
And we long for the time you're October again.

M. Helen Stacy

Rhode Island Wildflowers

Amidst the woodland thicket I did see,
Some White Lady's Tresses nodding at me,
Forget-Me-Nots with golden eyes did sprawl,
And there, white Mouse-Ear-Chickweeds too did crawl.
Pink lovely Lady's Slippers peeking through,
Thought showy, one must never pick them too!

Jack-In-The-Pulpit did appear serene!
So Preacher-like, midst Nature's wildlife scene.
Along the trail, gold Tansy, idly by,
Their yellow clustered buttons caught my eye,
Some Brown-Eyed-Susans, slender and tall,
And Golden Rods did gently nod at all.

A patch of Buttercups, a sheer delight!
And good old Dandelions, so yellow bright,

RI's State Flower, the violet blue,
And nestled snugly by, some spindly Rue.
These Nature's Treasures are for all to see,
They bring tranquility and joy to me!

Mary J. Ciaramello

The Best And Worst Of Times

The teen years - what can I say?
Some wish they could always stay,
Some wish they could just go away.

The boyfriends, the love,
The fighting, the hate,
The first time ever going out on a date.

The friends, the secrets,
The closeness you feel,
A bond no one could ever steal.

Off to school each day,
Looking your best,
After cramming all night for that algebra test.

What should I wear to be noticed by that guy?
Sometimes I wish I wasn't so shy!

The ups and the downs,
The hopes and the dreams,
To us, it's so much more than it seems.

The good times, the bad times,
The tears and all the fears,
It's all just part of those wonderful teen years!

Katrina M. White

Hemisphere: A Place In Space

Within a space of time, there are many rhymes...
Some, without endings.
Infinity prevails all limits — left there all alone.

In every astronomical year, A hemisphere would appear.
A celestial globe is divided.

This is where two spheres intersect...
They exchange experiences, knowledge, and actions.
They are to each other a star, each a planet within themselves.

When they meet at the rendezvous, a field of grey...
To exchange their knowledge, they revolve within each other,
Becoming ecstatically rejuvenated.

So common are these two stars, yet so distinct.
They are prohibited to physically touch each other.

Temptations are there... Exploring the unknown.
But you must maintain your distance — with a shield of resistance.

Michael Sein-Colon

Cry Of The Soul

Somewhere I know you'll be with me...
Someday in another time...
Through the long lonely nights...
For not even a million dreams could set me free.

I know there's something trapped inside of me...
It doesn't matter, 'cause it's in my soul chasing the empty signs of life...
There's something fighting me for the death of my existence...
For when all my good would not suffice.

Oh God, this hurting heart has been crying out...
For too long I've been without...
To drown in the shame of yesterday's pain...
I'm tired for I can see it in my eyes.

I'm so very weary from every desperate try...
Till the day I heard a voice say "Come, draw near...
For your strength is at its end....
So, rest upon me. For I, your father that is in Heaven...
If your only true friend"!!

Sherrie Kinsherf

They Go On

One glass prism, one ray of sun,
someday my life will be done.
But the sun will still shine,
The clouds will still rain,
and rainbows still arch over the grassy plain.
The birds will still sing,
The sun will still rise high in the sky.
Nothing lost, nothing gained,
and rainbows still arch over the grassy plain.
One glass prism, one ray of sun,
someday my life will be done.
The trees will stand tall, the rain will still fall,
and the wind will blow eternally.
They go on.

Shara Reynolds

Go Now

A person in my life,
someone so close to me.
She would help me with all her life,
now she is a person set free.
I will always love her,
for all that she has done.
I know she's free, that's for sure!
All of her life's battles are now won!
I will never forget you Grandma!
You were always there for me.
I know now for all that I have seen,
you helped me understand,
everything that goes on in this land.
Go now, knowing always that you are in my heart!
   I LOVE YOU GRANDMA!

B. Metz

Five Stories High

Five stories high
She is a balcony into the skies,
my window into paradise.
She is a royal entrance
by beach side, the sea bows so she walks in,
She is the undisputed atlantic queen,
in her summer wear; all eyes gaze and stare,
Yet I such a lowly peasant;
What have I to do with courts, beauty or grace?
But when five stories high,
While in her arms I'm a fool, who would be king.
at five stories high there is always room for dreams.

Modesto Corvison

Born Into The Light Of Life

Loved, spoiled, neglected or used
Someone, somewhere will always need you
You are faced with choices right or wrong
You choose the path you're walking on
The boundaries are set, never meant to be crossed
To step over them could mean complete total loss
Consequences without mercy will be your foe
Waiting to seize you, what will you sow?
Whether your foundation be built on rock, mud or sand
You will soon eat what you've sown with your hand
Is your garden fruitful and ripe
The seeds you placed in it, are they producing life
What is the soil of your heart right now
Is it good, is it rich, cultivated and plowed
Ponder this thought within your heart, soul and mind
Stop on the ladder and take some time
What are you made of, what have you done
Are you caring and sharing, or cold and alone
It's never too late; until death's at your gate

Zulema Beam

"Love Stranger"

When I look into his eyes I see a stranger.
Someone who I can't talk to anymore.
Someone who doesn't know if he loves me,
but I love him more than reality itself.
He talks with his heart closed,
I talk with mine open.
He abounds a shadow over my body.
His touch lies deep within his soul.
He shall not have eternal life and
so we must sew our open wounds
apart from one another.

Rebecca Polley

Tricia

A surprise - not in the plan
Something that happened with her special man
Not planned for 4 years or maybe 5
But now it's done - it's alive

It's hard to surmise
This little surprise
I can't believe
It's all conceived

I cannot yell
Her fears I try to dispel
For motherhood is tough
Under the best circumstances - rough

I know it will have the guidance and love
From two Grandpas in the heavens above
And on earth from all her family too
Aunts and uncles and Grandmas two

A surprise - for you see
My daughter's gonna be a mom like me.

Patricia Spitale

Friendship

Friendship is a lovely thing,
   That everyone has known;
With many Ways in Words and Deeds
   Friendship can be shown.

Friends help you through your troubled times,
   As they try to make you grin;
Friendship is the BEST that you can GIVE,
   And the best THING you can WIN.

Patricia Bell

Love And Death

Love appears to be a strong word,
Sometimes must be said aloud and heard.
A lot of people get hurt in their life,
Sometimes get fed up with everything and choose to die.

Several people write to become free and escape away,
They have to release their feelings out some way.
Pressured to talk but can't find the right words,
Wished they had wings to fly away with the birds.

Remembering all the memories that happened in the past,
Memories never die, they will always last.
Sometimes you get haunted by what you think is real.
You can try to change your ways but not the way you feel.

Love and death is like a wild rose,
The rose stands for the love you accidentally chose.
Death describes the wild part you can't control,
You never know the time God is going to call for your soul.

Sonya Fender

Painful Days, Sleepless Nights

Painful days, sleepless nights
Sometimes my life really bites
It feels like a never-ending question
I'm tired of second guesses, and mixed suggestions
Somewhere in all this I feel like I've lost the real me
I think that's something people just don't see
I feel like I'm losing all my control
I feel some sort of loss, like I'm not whole
Sometimes I think I'm going crazy
People don't know if I'm weak or just lazy
It angers me to feel this way
Sometimes I wish I could wake up in another time, another day
I feel trapped in the dark with no lights
Painful days, sleepless nights

Misti Festervand

Closet Of Shame

Buried deep where it's always black,
spiders build their nests with old shoes
to keep them company, a place where shame
is not a burden but the oddest things
find a haven from conscience.

Lona Sontorelli

"My Broken Heart"

Children need assurance and certainty,
Someone they can look up to,
Well if it can't be daddy,
Then momma, can it be you?

Momma, daddy really let me down,
and tore my world apart.
Can you lift me off the ground
And fix my broken heart?

This time it's been broken,
unlike the times before,
Do you think you could fix it,
So that it won't hurt anymore?

Momma, you've always fixed the visible things,
Like cuts and scrapes on my knees,
So I'm asking you for one more thing,
Please fix this broken heart for me.

Momma, please don't let me down,
The way that daddy did,
Although today I'm grown,
I still hurt just like a kid!

Terri Sellers

Explosive Tranquility

The exploding waves pounded into shore,
  Splashing high upon jagged rocks,
'Twas loud to my years, yet tranquil to my soul,
  My spirit was being unlocked.

I inhaled the mist of the salty spray,
  As it swept across my face.
Alone with Him, such tremendous love,
  Forever I wanted to embrace.

Purple shades of night were falling,
  And only God and I
Could have felt such Holy bliss,
  As it stretched across the sky.

Exploding moments of tranquility,
  Even waves obey His command.
Almighty, Majestic, such an awesome God!
  And to think, He did it for man.

Shirley H. Ketner

Dusk

The mother cat leaves her hungry litter
  Stalking prey in the barn.
I press your body close
  nearing the climax of day.
Our naked souls
  making love in the hay.
Together encircled by afterglow
  lingering passions smolder.
We catch the last glimpse of the sun's rays
  entering the night.

Tracy Marcum Alweis

Drowning From A Lack Of

Dark murky waves of love surround me.
Standing on the sandy shore of objectivity,
You yell to me,
But I ignore you.

Instead, I cling to a jagged rock of unfaithfulness,
Until I'm spinning in a whirlpool of lies.
My body is pulled under by the
Cold, manipulative current,
Filling my lungs with pain and despair.

My lifeless floating frame can barely be seen by
Those who mourn for me on the sandy shore,
As they bury my self-respect and self-esteem in the sand.

Rhonda S. Fox

My Promise

My love is not a game you see
so accept it ever so gracefully.

Play gently on the keys to my heart
and I in turn will do my part.

That burning deep inside your soul,
the kiss that makes you again feel whole.

The longing just to hold so tight
the way it's so hard just to say "Good-night."

So step softly into my world, my friend
and I promise this feeling will never end.

This love is to be taken seriously
and shared by only you and me.

See, love is not a game, my friend.
Love has only a beginning, and not an end!

Marisa Ann De Grado

481

Thy Soul

Thy soul, shines amongst endless galaxies of
stars in our sky, glimmering with rays of
love and hope with which one can only hope
to be blessed.

Thy soul, has touched me, growing stronger and
brighter as though destiny has brought our
souls together as one.

Thy soul, is one unique star, truly a special
gift from God, the luminous star of all.

Nuccia Giacalone Leon

Abuse

Your love was lost when he
started hitting in your space.
You felt you should have told him
that was your place.
It was too late, he already
turned you black and blue.
Your whole life is filled with gloom.
You feel as if it is your fault, but it's not.
Now you have a busted lip because
he just hit you with his fist.
You can't face your friends
you're scared what they might say,
you're feeling very alone and so ashamed.
He has left you with so much gain, he just
doesn't know how it feels to be in pain.

He begged to come back,
you said O.K. but there was a promise that had to be made.
He said never again until he put her in the hospital
with the love he said he had regained.
Till this very day she tries to forget
the worst of the pain, but he's out of her life,
and that will never change.

Lena Keene

Words Of Wise

Dazzle your life with adventure and motion.
Stay strong to your heart, to this lay devotion.
Keep guard on your pride for many men fall.
Stay alert when love arrives knocking at your door.
Don't give any less than you expect to receive.
Turn not one stranger away, not all will deceive.
Walk lightly when you tread near someone's trust,
This advice I didn't know, but tell it I must.
Show not a face of anger but understanding when it's hard.
Show more affection even when you're tired.
Cross not a soul, always keep a friend.
Be mostly true to your heart, and you'll always win.

William F. Monroe

Silence

Fields bathed in white,
Shimmering in the morning light.
White trees agleam,
For forever it may seem.
The wind softly blows,
As a stream gently flows.
At the sight of a bird,
A soft chirp is heard.
Beside a lake, crystal and clear,
Stands a newly born deer.
Snowflakes start to fall from the sky,
This winter, many animals will die.
The silence is broken by the mighty cougar's growl,
And the distant sound of the wild wolf's howl.

Minisa Grant

"A Wishful Dream Of A Love That Wasn't There"

As I arose from my bed this morning, taking a deep breath of fresh air
still somewhat amazed by the dream I had, of a love that wasn't there

In my dream she stood beside me, with the smell and sweetness of
spring
her body portrayed a beautiful story and her lips said such wonderful
things

The wonders of the world, and the wonders thereof, were around me
everywhere
as I held them in my arms so tight and found they weren't even there

I reached for the love so close to me, but her tenderness I couldn't
feel
O GOD, please give me back the dream I had, even though it may not be
real

If it's not real I don't mind for it's up to my heart to choose
between the dream and reality and the love I'm afraid to lose

A chance to be with whom I want to be, a choice most humans never
get
O GOD, I would take the wonderful dream, without a thought or regret

And then suddenly a great pain totally awakens me and I looked around
to see
some reason I lost that wonderful dream and came to reality

So now I can only hope to dream, to find the love I lost
my mind shall wonder and lose its way and my heart shall pay the cost

LaDon Hall Sr.

End Of War

On the ground below is a hole where there once
stood a flag pole, where people came to worship the
END of WAR
The flag is gone but the faith is till on where men and
women fought at dawn and drawn away at the dusk
of day and many soldiers died but the faith never
went away, when the war was over everybody said hooray,
On the ground below there use to be a hole now
there stands a flag pole, where people come to worship the
END of WAR

Nicholas Neville

Somebody's In Here

Parabolic shoulders
Surround a caved-in chest
Marking the years-used body

A reluctant prisoner in his aged, bony frame

Only the bright, intense eyes
Revealed the vibrant spirit
That glowed and pulsated within

Somebody's in here his angry mind screamed!

Talk to me of Shelley and Keats
Of Beethoven and Brahms
I know why the sky is blue
And why grown men cry.

I know the sweet ecstasy
Of the peaks of song
And the taste of salted tears
Spilled over heart-crunching woes.

Look beyond what your eyes can see
And share with me your noble self

Then I will be you
And you will be me.

Robert M. Zweig

The Pool

Lit by the crescent moon
Stood a pool of cool waters
A pool with Water-lilies
A pool with silver fish
One where the Morning Glory gets its dew drops
A pool where strangers quench their thirst:

What a pool of waters,
Where mermaids reflect their beauty on its surface
Where young maidens and their lovers meet at night
And celebrate the dance of love.
Oh, mighty pool like a mirror
Gently ripples without terror:

A pool where the nightingale clutters
A pool where the night owl mutters
At the silver moon:

A pool where the broken hearted bends like a weeping willow
Washing away tears of enchantment
Instigated by love,
A pool where birds nestle and sing anthems of love
That move the toad from under the stone.

Kadija Diallo

Always

The wisdom of your words I will heed.
Strong and determined, I will follow where you lead.

Sometimes there's fear, but I know that you're near.
I'm never alone, for you'll always be here.

Facing my tomorrows with grace, courage, and might.
We have a solid foundation: there will be no flight.

Sometimes there's fear, but I know that you're near.
I'm never alone, for you'll always be here.

When the rains come & the thunder rolls, you help me to withstand
With you I am an awesome woman with the world at my command.

Sometimes there's fear, but I know that you're near.
I'm never alone, for you'll always be here

This song in my heart is simply a start.
It keeps us together though we're far apart.
This love that we have is truly so rare.
No one can break the bond we share.

We'll keep moving forward, there's so much to do.
This race I will finish, Lord,
But only with you.

Margaret A. Smith

Her

white, wet mist rolls
sunrise begins
i row and row, but cannot find
Her.

then She is before me,
shimmering in her dress of clouds
silver drops at ears, throat, wrists;
Her face glows with the wisdom of the earth and
sky, sea and fire

But Her eyes!
oh, Her eyes!
deep as a thousand wells;
boring into my very soul with a sadness that is
almost tangible!

And She is gone, and i know.
i turn the boat.
and as the red sun shoots up,
i slip the knife into my breast.

Molly Croft

Divine Favor

Life's goals are far removed from the reach of one's hand.
Swept off course by the winds of misfortune without a plan.
Drowning in despair, sorrows, heartaches, and pain.
Only by the grace of God you're able to remain sane.
Gloom and darkness has come to linger around.
Evil has devoured, destroyed and torn down.
Hopes and dreams have been put to rest.
Outlook for tomorrow isn't so bright at its best.
Strength and health have begun to fail.
What a cloud of rejoicing going on in hell.

Oh! but wait, what a ray of delight just in time.
God almighty, fearless, has come with a sign.
Lift up your fainted heart and praise the Lord.
Trust in his word and use it like a sword.
Divine favor has come to wage a heavenly fight.
Despair, darkness, and gloom can't stand in its sight.
Turn back your mind to how God delivered you from troubles of old.
Jesus has your life's goals under complete control.
Through heavenly orchestration divine favor and evil has been
predestined to meet. Divine favor has brought evil to an utter
defeat.

Sallie Mae Echols

The Cheetah

Swiftly does it run,
Swerving past the bullets of a gun.
Its mate lies dead,
With vultures swooping 'round its head.
Hiding its face in the grass,
Waiting for the hunter to pass.
When will it be safe,
Free to lift its face?
Waiting for the day
When freedom comes its way.
Will the hunter soon be gone
So the cheetah can eat before it is dawn?
Will it stay all night
While the cheetah hides in fright?
The hunter now sleeps
While the cheetah softly creeps.
Waiting for the hunter to wake,
His life the cheetah can then take.
So once again the grassy plains will be safe,
And the cheetah will no longer have to hide its face.

Sarah Stern

Snowfall In April

Snow on budding green is a surprise
Stemming the voices of veins.
Halt are the widened eyes
Whose souls in new and emerald
Of shoot, hill, grass, and bursting day
Had bathed, and in the gold
thrown us by our overhead friend, the Traveler,
While siblings, velocipedes and sparrows vied
Piercing the wintered fastness of the ear—
These, and the muscles that reached for baseball,
And the heart reaching for what love! —
Stopped, all.

Nature, nature, merit we displeasure
For this leaping of our joy before your gun?
Old girl, you freeze us with your pleasure!

Bravely again we go,
While our feet are trim and contemplate,
In the monastic snow.
For a better day be our blood's riot!

Samuel Schulman

A Leave-Taking

Groping for the combination of
symbols
to communicate the detestation
that
absorbed my essence
baffles
any eloquence I possess..
the savage pestilence sundered her
frame
on a brutal course to destruction....
terrorized into a passionless
state
I became a spiritless
observer to the inevitable..
anguish gnawed me uneven and set me adrift..
age distanced me from the agony
and revealed her in my
heart.

Shannon Newman Gilbert

Dare To Discover Life

Dare to discover life,
Take the path of happiness
Dream the dream of peace on Earth;

Stray from the normal,
Discover life as now one has.

Feel the emotions,
A supernatural force that pulls
A person's body, mind, and heart;

Experience defeat,
Know the humiliation of ignorance,
Overwhelming situations beating down
Alas, only to discover renewal.

Discover the dark direful depths of death,
The frigid world known only to Dante
The dark underworld of the almighty Hades;
Questioning what lies beyond.

Give life meaning
Explore the unknown
Take the risk
Dare to Discover, life.

Nicholas Wilkoff

"Hard At Heart"

How many can truly see
that life began through time space earth and sea
through atoms and evolution
is the one and only solution

Everything is as it should be
changing continuously
except the mixed up mind
of mankind

We have the power to leave behind dismay
to see the truth in nature's display
"I" found peace putting my past and future into today
negative thoughts are held at bay

Now "I" pass it along for free
for anyone who can read and see
took many years to open the door
for the poor in spirit to see the score

"I" am old and young at heart
but... at least "I" got a new start
where the young and hard at heart
put the horse after the cart

Robert L. Renaud

Freeway

There ahead of me stretches miles of gray concrete
Taking me to my destination
Breaking off into different directions
Always making connections
Sometimes pausing or halting but never ending
A many famous places it passes through
Seeing and knowing no faces
It's traveled upon by millions
Showing or giving no concerns
It's only the Freeway

Sheila A. Lee

"Why..."

Why do people say they care and then
talk behind your back or laugh, because
when they do this, it makes your heart
split in half?

Why, if you try something new, do
people make fun of you?

Why do people think they're the best,
just because they're better than the rest?

Why do people use you when they need
something done, but when it comes to you,
they just go have some fun?

Why do people change, the people that
you knew, because now as you grow older,
they start picking on you?

Why before you go to sleep there really
aren't any good feelings you want to keep?

Why when you wake up in the morning too,
do you feel like there's something warning you?

Rhonda Raymor

Love

Reaching out from nowhere, grasping on to your deepest emotions.
Teasing, tantalizing your desire;
intensifying the needs deep within you.

Naive to its strength and appeal,
Defenses collapse leaving you open to soothing comfort,
healing, awakening.

The intensity is bewildering, yet mesmerizing.
Turning your world up-side-down giving you no ability
to recreate it as it was, but only as you wish it to be.

An entity in itself; attaching to those willing and
open to its consequence, and even those who turn away.
Making a reality of splendor, or a floundering existence with
no direction.

A sweet caress, a thirst unquenched, a hunger that grows.
It becomes cherished, despised, sought after, or longed for;
bringing with it sweetness or bitter regret.

Yolanda Cooper-Birdine

Our Love

Our love is a bond that holds us together
Stronger and stronger forever and ever.
Words can't say how I feel about you
I will always be there, it's true.
My love for you comes straight from the heart
My eyes were for you right from the start.
Please don't say our love will end
A broken heart I don't want to mend.
Cupid was right when he chose you for me
He knew our love was meant to be.

Kristen Norris

To You My Love

Perhaps my own words will tell you more
Than any card that's bought in a store.

Words on a card can never express
All the feelings that I have in my breast.

For you, my darling, nothing is too much!
I love your heart, your face, your touch!

You've given me many years of bliss
Can any woman ask for more than this?

May God grant us many more happy years
Together in health and empty of tears.

Lee Prensky

Midnight

Midnight, when it passes, is farther gone
Than dreams in the night at the awakening hour.
What bells ring longer or louder than
Those at midnight?
All is still and quiet and restful and,
When the clock chimes twelve times,
A man turns restlessly in his sleep
And the cat gets up to walk through the house
One more time.
The damp pavement outside faintly glistens through
The haze of the lighted street lamps on the corner.
A stranger walks alone in the coldness.
All is bare; he has no defense against
The dark doorways and stoops.
Only the cat looks out after him from
A blackened window with eyes large
And looking long.
The cat watches until he is gone
And then stays and just watches.
Only midnight knows what the cat sees.

Lyn S. Benua

"Listening To My Grandma"

If you listen to my grandma, you'll soon begin to learn,
That every word she softly speaks is filled with love and concern.

She talks about her family, with pride and affection,
We all come to see her for words of encouragement and direction.

Her wisdom has been drawn from the stream of everyday life,
But you won't hear her complaining about the struggles or the strife.

Her voice is warmly filled with stories of the past,
Reminding us that friendship and love are the things that will forever last.

Never an unkind word from her lips will be spoken,
Always eager to console, never the smallest promise broken.

If you ask me why I love my grandma so dear,
All you have to do is listen, and soon you will hear.

Rocky Lee Gray

"The Star"

At night when the sky is dark,
somewhere up there glows a bright spark.
The bright twinkle of that little star,
reminds me of how close we are.
Wishing I could be with you, in
my heart, is all I do.
But, whether we are near or far,
I will remember your love because of that star.
Even though the time has come to part,
my love for you still grows in my heart.

Tracey Hayes

Fear

What is this night...
    that falls upon us...
    that has us lost...in the dark?

What is this thing...
    that grips our heart...
    that abandons us...and pulls us apart?

What is this thing...
    that does not care...
    that never moves...just lying there?

What is this thing...
    that waits in alleys...in dark holes
    and empty streets?

What is this thing...
    that fights with us...
    that cannot be seen...but is everywhere?

What is this thing...
    that still creeps in...on nights so clear
    that silence hears...this is fear

Susan A. Williams

I Wanna Fall In Love

I wanna fall in Love, I wanna feel
that feelin' that makes you free as a dove.
I wanna hold his hand as we walk down the street,
I wanna feel that feelin' that knocks you off your feet.

I wanna see that look in his eyes,
that says he'll love me until the day he dies.
I wanna feel queezy whenever he is near,
and know he'll hold me tight whenever I feel fear.

I want my palms to feel sweaty,
and my knees to feel weak.
Yes, that feeling of love is the feeling I seek.

That's the feeling I'm in search of...
it's all I think about,
I wanna fall in love.

MaRenda Powell

"I Just Want To Help"

I just want people to understand
That I want to help, in any way I can

I've never been greedy
Always wanted to help the needy

I'm tired of seeing what others go through
I just want to help, I really do!

I'll pray for the sick; and I'll pray for the poor
I'll pray again and again, like I did before

I just want to help, because I care
I just want to help, by being there

I want to help, the lame and the blind
Helping others is the only thing on my mind

I want to help the bum in the street
Who never gets enough to eat

I want to help and it might seem strange
I want to help, and make a change

I just want to be around
To help others when they're down

I want to help, so the "world" will be a better place
"I'm compelled to help, and I rest my case!"

Ken Blount

"A Guide For A Loving Home"

May we treat one another with respect, honesty, and care, for
that is the only way we will ever grow together.

May we share little discoveries and changes each day
brings, remembering that each one of us has something to save, and
listening is important too.

May we always try to be sensitive to one another's,
joys, sorrows, needs, and changing moods, and realize that being
a loving family means sometimes not understanding everyone all
the time, but being there to love and help them just the same.

Wanda Riddick

Greenbeans And Sunflowers

I am woman. I am nature. I am an old man
    that knows nothing more than his wife, farming,
    his religion, and standing outside by the mailbox,
    waiting for the Sunday paper.

I am a greenbean.
I am woman. We are nature. Together, neither man nor
    woman. Just sunflowers and the center of the
    universe.

Rachel Josephs

"My Thoughts Of You"

There isn't a moment
    That my thoughts don't wonder to you.
There isn't a night
    That I don't fall asleep thinking of you
In my dreams
    you will always love me.
I long to hear your voice
    for it always made me feel good.
I long to feel your touch
    and the tenderness in it.
I want to feel your gentle kiss
    and the love behind it.
My heart wonders if you love me.
    or have I hurt you too much
Will I ever feel the touch
    I long for.
Only time will tell if I will
    Ever be in your loving
    arms again.

Lori Walker

Looking Back

It was long ago, in a far away place,
that now comes back to me.
The air seemed strange and hard to breathe;
I didn't see a tree.

I soon adjusted to that place,
my days and nights spent there.
I thought my past would slip away;
I didn't think I'd care.

Each day was an adventure,
something new for me to learn.
Then, at night, the far off lights,
my thoughts to home would turn.

To family in the parlor,
To friends that I would see,
To days spent in the garden
beneath the willow tree.

The time soon passed and I was home,
with those who knew me well.
I'd learned from my experience;
this story would I tell.

Sherry Kolton

Ode To My Bunny

I have lost so many
That one more does not matter,
The sadder I am it gets a little funny.

You see, you were not my first bunny,
I've had so many rabbits
Their habits are quite delightful.

But of all those, I suppose
that many ways you wiggled your nose made me happy.

O furry friends of white, black, grey
'Tis Easter Sunday every day
And though 10 fury friends
have come my way I might say it ends not here,

Next year I have the greatest plan
For which there is a huge demand
I shall build just for thee
A lovely bunny cemetery.

I'll take 10 bunnies from the yard
God's great angels there will guard.

So onto bunny heaven without a peep
Surrounded by love you shall sleep.

Lindy Strumpf

Growing Old

So many times I've been told
That people get crabby when they grow old
But in their hearts they are sweet and kind
But just not able to accept father time
They try to be young again with all their might
So out on others they take their spite

I hope when old age creeps up at my side
That I'll be able to take it in stride
And enjoy seeing young people have their fun
And hope I'm well liked by everyone
So when God calls me with his beckoning hand
I'll always be remembered as a nice old man.

Madison C. Beckwith

To Nicole

Heavenly Angels took you to
    That Promised Land where Hearts are true
Dwelling in their Happiness Place ...
    Now only smiles can touch your face.

Guardian Angels calm your fears
    Your kindred souls still weep their tears
Safe in the arms of Love and Grace ...
    Now only smiles can touch your face.

Prayers that your life was not in vain
    Plead others will be spared such pain
Away from our worlds angry pace ...
    Now only smiles can touch your face.

Rose E. Coulter

Beached

Walk along the sea, kick the grains of sand,
    Swim atop the water, to never never land.
Soar with the sea gulls, swim with the fish,
    Dream of the heavens, cry out a wish.
Frolic in the mud, all throughout the day,
    Watch the sailboats coast into the bay.
Feel the cool breezes, gently caress your ear,
    Think of a loved one, whether far or near.
Dream of whatever you want, even colorful balloons,
    Just make sure when you return, it isn't far from soon.

Ryan M. Briggs

486

The River Of Poetry

The river of poetry is a clear mirror
That reflects images of all creatures
That reflects feelings of humankind
That reflects the past, present and future

The river of poetry is a clear mirror
That reflects motions in the sky
That reflects activities on the ground
That reflects liveliness under the waters

The river of poetry is a clear mirror
That reflects waves of laughing
That reflects billows of crying
That reflects phenomena of disasters

The river of poetry is a clear mirror
That reflects pictures of happiness
That reflects moods of unluckiness
That reflects vibrations of hearts and souls

Minh-Vien

The Pain

Some say she couldn't take it anymore,
That she couldn't deal with the pain,
So she pulled the trigger
and ended her suffering,
I'm still learning to deal with her death,
I try to tell myself:
Everything will be alright
that life will go on,
Although now I'm not so sure,
I'm starting to feel how
she felt, to feel the agony.
How could she do it, and how can I.

Pattie Wawrzyniak

A Putter's Lament

You sight, you plumb-bob, you squat, squint and pray,
That the yips, spasms and jerks will all go away.
You steady your nerves, you position your feet,
Move your putter just do, the ball it will meet.

There is a small thunk as putter strikes ball,
You watch it roll onward, transfixed and in awe.
It starts for the cup, unswerving and straight,
My God, what is happening, you didn't see that break.

The ball hits a spike mark and jumps up an inch,
It rolls to the left, oh there must be a grinch
Under the green making it roll to the right,
Then down and away, almost out of sight.

Once again you will stand and study the green,
Figuring and scheming to come up with the means
Of putting the ball into the cup just right,
So you won't still be out here, in the dark of the night.

Kay D. Cooper

The Seasons Of Love

The time we spend is not wasted, just saved for us. The love
That we have is the love that I miss when we're apart.
Sometimes feelings are hard to express, sometimes they need not be
    said.
It's not easy, you never said it would be, but you're worth it.
Although others may exist, my heart is yours, when you want it.
When trees are in their autumn beauty, when silver snow falls,
When warm, sun shines in spring again, we meet as friends. Now
As lovers, let no woman or man take our love.

Nathaniel M. Baker

Expecting Our Firstborn I.E. The Good News

Can something out of nothing come, is it possible, can it be,
That what we must imagine, we shall one day see?
Does magic have a special way, a pattern or design,
For bringing forth before our eyes a promise so divine?

The answer to these questions is life's sweet mystery,
And its hidden, arcane secret is contained within the seed.
For in the seeds a little scroll written through and through
With words as crystal clear as glass, designed to make things new...

Words of wisdom neatly set and carefully arranged,
Knowledge pure and true to form that is not easily changed,
Instructions for each fine detail, described as in a deed,
For our firstborn child's creation and how it must proceed.

And something else besides the scroll is in the seed contained,
For power's there to spark its growth, though latent and restrained,
Waiting for that time to come in creation's drawn out train,
When power's released to carry out what's set and preordained.

Now one more thing's found in a seed, for it takes a little bit...
Of substance pure and simple to complete life's starter kit.
New life will spring forth from these three: substance, wisdom, and
    power.
Once again, as it has been from creation's earliest hour.

Martha Burleigh

God And I Are One

God and I are one
That's my favorite verse
It's something I say automatically
And never need to rehearse
God orders my footsteps...turns me around
The spirit of God is in me
Danger enfolds me.. but my God knows me
And tells justice, "Let him be"
The mind is powerful..you must agree
So many inventions.. how far we've come
Recognized by many... but scoffed by some
The inventor says, "God and I are one"
How marvelous are the miracles He performs
He'll rule until there's no sun
My hope, my trust my true belief
Is that God and I are one!

Pat Bowers-Bradshaw

Eight Glasses Of Water A Day

Eight glasses of water a day,
That's what you must drink, doctors say.
Staying healthy you get all your inner parts wet with
Eight glasses of water a day.

You mustn't have coffee or tea
For that isn't water you see.
Nor can you partake of a coke or a shake
Or a beer to relinquish your needs.

So here's what the rule is it seems,
The drink must be crystalline clean.
You take it down neat till it reaches your feet
In a tasteless and colorless stream.

Now those who would argue may chide,
Lemonade is the drink you should try.
To take every day not for me I'm afraid.
Furthermore you go yellow inside.

So when I am taken away
My tombstone may very well say,
He drank till he drowned himself into the ground
On eight glasses of water a day.

Paul J. Lamey

The World Was Once A Perfect Place

The world was once a perfect place, where wildlife roamed free
The air was fresh, the skies were blue, and the grass was
Always green.

The sounds were gentle and the flowers sweet, with the sun shining
Bright, night would fall and the stars aglow filled peace throughout
The night.

The world was once a perfect place, created by the grace of God,
A place for peace and serenity, beautiful and bright, with all of
The amazing wonders, with which we share our life.
The world was once a perfect place, now filled with hate and fear,
Crime and smog and evil, throughout our land so dear, the world was
Once a peaceful place, bright as the sun, now, why has man
destroyed it,
The work that God has done.

Laura Franks

"An Explanation Please?"

We're the end result yesterday, the symbols of today
The bearer of your burdens, I guess one could say.

We feel all of our broken promises, you've scarred our hopes and
    dreams
Our optimism faded from constant "Not as good as it seems."

You have all taken so very much but left us nothing in return
The rain you brought continues to fall, your fires continue to burn.

Why have you left us stranded with no true sense of direction?
How do we stop this incurable disease from spreading its infection?

We're the ones you raised from afar, you forgot to cleanse our souls
The new age social outcasts, we've played the Black Sheep roles.

Steadily, slowly fading, is the Norman Rockwell Portrait of life
As tongues become as sharp as the cold hard edge of a knife.

Have you no apology, regret or some remorse
For placing us in the pale saddle atop the white death Horse?

Are we bitter is the question, yes is the hurried reply
Try to tell us it's our fault as you look us in the eye

Sure, there's a better place beyond this waiting for me and you
Let's just hope that when we get there they haven't tainted it too!

A. Shane Dillon

Summer

I walk outside and feel the breeze,
the birds are chirping in the trees.
When I look the other way,
the sun is setting on the bay.
My father is working in the mill,
I think I'll take him a flower from the hill.
The stars are coming out to play,
the morning will be hours away.
I see some horses grazing below,
I hear my mom, I have to go.
After dinner I go outside,
I get my bike and take a ride.
I hear the crickets' little tune,
I look in the sky and see the moon
I went inside to go to bed,
do not forget what I said.

Katie Williams

Eyes like the black of a chasm

eyes like the black of a chasm
the black of the sky, looking up
the black of the hunger in your stomach
the black of a candle wick, burned
the black of oil spilling out of the desert

    eyes as gray as the seamless clouds
    hanging uncertainly before the rain

eyes like the black of bus wheels, round and round
the black of a black hole that swallows planets whole
the black of the tar that spreads on an endless road
the black of coffee without milk
the black when you shut your eyes not to see.

E. A. Winslow

Going Home

This was written as Evelyn would have seen it, through her eyes...
Is that angels' wings moving
The branches of trees
And is that angel voices I hear?
Heavenly music I hear in my heart
My time is drawing near.
The Lord has been my Partner and Guide
He's never let go of my hand.
I've always been able to trust in Him
He's given me strength to stand.
So I feel the sweet angel voices I hear
Are actually calling for me
And I'm ready to go to my heavenly home
To live with the blest
And the free.

LaVerne Perry

Guns And Violence

The gun screams as the hammer is cocked.
The bullet is running, it's too fast to walk.
The speed of the bullet, it's coming at you.
Better watch out, boy, because it's gonna get you!
The bullet cries as it goes right through you,
Thinking to itself, "Why did I kill you?"
Everybody's quiet, there's nothing but silence.
I think it's about time, we've got to stop the violence.

P. J. Hernandez

A Southern Cross

The call to arms 'mid bugles' blasts,
The cannon's roar and rolling drums,
Have ceased their sounds of war, at last!

No more the noise of kin at strife,
Or sounds of man's absurd abuse,
For time has come to close this life!

How still it seems when life's astray,
While we lie in deathly slumber,
Unlike God's plan, souls lost their way.

Could not we live in ways of God?
Amid his glories yet to come,
Why does man choose a way so hard?

So stands my cross with letters bold,
"Here lies a body clad in grey,
Who lost his life to save his soul."

Sad though this may be, my heart
Rejoices at the even score,
I chose this way, now happily depart.

Marie E. Bowery De Laney

War

The battlements all are broken.
The castle walls are fell.
Once proud arms are bloody stumps,
lost in the battle's hell.

Our fallen comrades on funeral pyres,
we salute in sad farewell.
Wandering minstrels in future days,
our "glorious" tales will tell.

Victory, though sure, seems not so sweet,
when the price is a funeral bell,
rung for our friends of many a year,
— cheap lives for kings to sell.

Yet tales of wartime glories
make many a young heart swell.
Each dreams of fighting battles,
— his own brave tales to tell.

So long as we who've borne the cost,
keep silent and do not tell,
of horrors found, not glories there,
We'll pay with funeral bells.

Lowell Boggs Jr.

Seasons

The hills are hollow.

A field stands empty; birds have flown.
The chariot of God arrives, bringing rake and harrow.
Now is the time for breaking.

How frightening to be the clod, awaiting its unmaking.
For in that track, the wheel rides forth
To purposes unknown.

We grieve, and bear the sorrow and the weeping,
But seed is in the barrow, sleeping.
And sod cannot anticipate the purposes of seed:
The coming fruit, the joyful reaping.
God will create, for raking makes a furrow
To receive the sleeping root.

And we are all, in turn,
His sod, seed, shoot, plant, and fruit.
The land lies fallow.

Then break, Lord, for the joy to follow.

Nancy E. Moore

The Dancer's Dance

The toe is pointed; heart beats fast.
The chin is lifted; eyes steadfast.
The shoulders straighten; music starts.
The dancer's listening; it's quite an art.

What is her secret? How does she do it?
Tell me how she keeps such rhythm to it.
Her feet move without her thinking.
Her body sails through air then sinking
Down, upon the floor she drops
So delicately, and then she stops.
But no, oh no, the dance is not done-
Indeed, the piece has just begun.

There is no limit, no bound'ry, no border-
No one may tell her the dance is over.
What she has started, she must finish.

Determination gleams in her eye,
A smile breaks out upon her lips.
The feet stop moving; the body dips.
She takes a bow- the stage was hers,
The toe is pointed; the world is hers.

Sheila Larkin

Pictures In The Clouds

On a bright and beautiful day
The clouds have happy things to say
When the clouds are dark and gray
You will know there is a storm on the way
The clouds can show many shapes
Sometimes they even look like a bunch of grapes
One day as I looked at the clouds
They seemed to be moving in big crowds
I was watching the clouds with my cat fluffy
And they all looked so big and puffy
And as they all moved in a row
That made me think of piles of snow
Sometimes they had the shape of a dog
And sometimes they had the shape of a log
They just look so big and grand
And all were made by God's hand
Sometimes they look like a bunch of cotton
To use on the scrapes you've gotten
As you were running along
To see the clouds move in a throng

Michelle Lynn Lomas

Untitled

Raindrops descend amidst a stormy breeze, asserting
the clouds which hover from above, coloring the spectrum of a
dark dreary day.
Trinkets of water on the edge of normality, dripping
soothingly, from a valley way on high. Elevated whispers out
reaching the morning sun.
Hear the sound... Far away cries, and make believe toys which
beckon to ones youth. As the morning sun draws near.
The descent of raindrops amidst a stormy breeze.
A new thought, covering the old, transforming the day into the
thought itself; time tells its tale.
...forever...
Drifting thoughts, lifting one's insight to a higher plane, as
an unfinished work of art, enveloping life's eternal woes,
surpassing all time and thought,
..forever....
The air growing dim, with the glitter of stars, which shine
amidst cloudy skies, so eternal thoughts, bring in the new,
the old now gone on a drifting plane. Raindrops and clouds
coloring the spectrum of a brand new day.

Sal Paccione

Portrait Of Innocence

Tiny clothes and, baby toys always remind me of you.
The coffee table that, sits where your crib was suppose to be.
Teddy bears and, precious things and, the child I never knew.
The things I did when you still belonged to me.

No tears, no laughter, no joy and, no pain
No anger, no hate and, no need for revenge
You won't see sunny days and, you won't cry when it rains.
You won't remember just to learn how to forget.

A small part of life and, a child without fear.
Friends you won't have, the things you could of done.
You're a picture of love given without one tear.
You won't fail or, do wrong for you will always be, the
portrait of innocence.

Tracy Prochazka

The Coming

Beware you shall hear us,
The day shall come,
All will atone,
Some to the good,
Some to the evil,
Judgement shall be upon your will,
Repent all of you now or never,
The time is short,
Here he comes in vengeance to claim his flock
He shall cut out the black hearts of evil
Those will perish in the eternal flame
The rest take their just reward,
In flowered green and gold, violet and blue pastures,
Evil shall be seen no more,
It shall be stricken from all minds,
Living eternal forever with one mind,
One thought, one love, eternity,
The universe forever.
With God of light.
Eternally peace.

Tris Widuch

Anniversary Of Love

Time passes so quickly, with the seasons changing, and
the days turning into months, and months into years.
But one thing I have always known that doesn't change,
is My Love for You.
We've shared and made many memories together
that were filled with dreams, and of days filled with sunshine,
and nights filled with love.
Now, looking forward to tomorrow's dreams
and You by my side, together we will share another year
filled with new dreams, hopes, and wishes.
A year that will bring newer joys for both of us.
A time to reach out to each other with our thoughts
and our minds, and together we will look into the future.
Now here we are looking back, and looking forward
to a future with a love that is truly right between us.
It's Our Love we are feeling that is changing day by day,
becoming deeper and deeper within our hearts, a love
that will share this Special Anniversary Wish for You, My David.
This wish that I give You is a lifetime filled with all My Love,
together with all my dreams now and forever.

Marie A. Cockett

Hidden Away From The Beauty

My life is like an empty room
The door is locked it's like a tomb

Everything I do I just can't win
And no one can help cause they can't get in

There's just one window where I can see
The life that's supposedly around me

I'm hidden from the Beauty
Because they think that it won't suit me

I know what I am like, a captured fish
Oh, if I had one wish

It would be to unlock my door
Then all my dreams would soar

All my wishes would come true
Yeah that's what I'll do

Today I'll stop praying and hoping
Next time you see my door it will be opened

Melissa Natal

Loneliness

Looking through the windows,
the doors of your soul.
I see such sadness overflowing,
Dulling your vision.
Making you lose direction, become lost,
Then afraid.
Pushing away those you love, thinking no one cares;
Heading for destruction.
Wayward you have gone, your soul is in despair;
Wanting to return to those who care.
Come back to me, doubting as you may be.
I care for you, don't you care for me?
They say the eyes are the windows to the soul,
All I see is sadness, something out of control.
Fearing love as you do;
You overturn every rock, searching, hoping;
Running towards the thing you fear.

Kim Woessner

Oh Evelyn

It hurts to see you slowly walk
The downhill trail to its end.
I've been partway on it myself before.
Is it another pain to think
That this same trail I must travel myself some day again
But this time to its final end.

In my lifework I have often seen
The substance of the body return to earth,
Its home it seems.
The personality, the warmth, the illumination
Is switched off too,
When a light globe switch is turned we say
"The light has gone away."
Where does it go?
All that walk the ending trail will know.
Will there be light there; warmth; parents;
Children, loving friends we knew?
We hope for as, We hope with you
We love you Evelyn - farewell.

Paul A. Grigorieff, M.D.

Consternation

Quiet the blistering, neglected night,
silence the archaic but needless names,
Murder the violently forgotten fright,
Scrounge ruthlessly in stultifying shame

With peace of mind except for silent screams,
Enamored except for slow, profuse pain,
Exhume me now from my desolate dreams,
Forbid the world thus giving me some name.

And now we circle without any aim,
With gross entrancement in darkened valleys,
Alone although eternally the same,
The way we scream being all that varies.

Kelley Calvert

A Summer's Seashore

Sounds of silence scream at me,
The crash of waves on the rocks by the sea,
Gulls in the sky and a cricket by the tree
Whisper aloud what I cannot see.

The swish of sand from footsteps nearby,
Someone skips rocks as the sun says "Goodbye,"
A boat far from land sounds a foghorn's last cry
As I lie on the shore in the Summer's night sky.

Pamela Jean Kashian

"All Within My Mom"

In all my life I've known you to be
  the father I never had.
And when times were rough, depressing, and down,
  you made me happy when I was sad.
You taught me to be kind, respectful, loving,
  and mannered from beginning to the end.
You taught me to be strong, brave, smart, and manly,
  from the father which you hold within.
As a child growing up, when I was headed and unkind,
  Within you the father came out and whipped my behind.
When the time came to learn about the birds and the bees,
  You talked to me like no mom before, but like a father yes indeed.
So the point I'm trying to make is none other than the lest.
  If I had to choose me a father, then momma you're the BEST.
For a woman like you, who's so strong and won't bend.
  I must say, "As well as a mom and dad, you're also my best friend."
So many feelings I hold of you in my heart so calm.
  The best way to express it is by these four words,
.......I LOVE YOU MOM!

Marcus Charlton

"War"

As we journey throughout our days,
  The fighting, the hatred is always portrayed.
We never know what lies ahead,
  We could be sleeping wrapped up in a bed,
And in the end, no one wins with war.

For so many years we've continued the fighting,
  Hoping the next day would bring something exciting.
And all we have is that hope inside,
  For the dreams which we had have somehow died,
And in the end, no one wins with war.

The world is now surely coming to end,
  With no one left, not even a friend.
And as we try to keep moving on,
  The world slips away faster, "It's Gone, It's Gone!"
And in the end, no one wins with war.

Sarah Daige

Summer Days

Only if God hung the moon,
Summer days would be here to stay.
The trees, the lake, and the stars up above,
Are the only things I think about.
The horses, the cows, and the fresh green grass,
Are what I long to see.
The silky flowers, the smooth rocks, and the clear water
Are what I long to touch.
The hush of the waterfalls, the buzzing bees, and the quacking geese,
Are what I long to hear.
The hot sun beating down, and the cool night's air breeze,
Are what I long to feel.
How I pray someday God will hang the moon,
So summer days can last forever!

Kristina Studebaker

My Brother

  My brother's a short little person who comes up to me at
the chin. His peachy cream skin has a nice blend, his
hair golden blond. His eyes that look up at me are the color
of hazel in the fog. His nose is a flattened little ball that
sticks out of his little round face. His round little tummy
has ripples like lace, that fills up each day. His
voice with a gentle low squeaky sound, his laughter with a
skip, skip, skip to it. His smile has an oval shape to
it that brings out the day. He walks with a bounce in it to
add to the sway. With all that, I love my brother in every
God-given way.

Lindsay Kay Domino

Until We Meet Again

As the sun begins to set,
The figure of a woman lies on the ground.
She sits alone in her backyard,
Recalling her life as she knew it to be.
A life she once shared with her husband
She now shares alone.
Three children remind her of their father
And memories are left to remind them.
The love they shared can never be compared
But so obvious to those around.
As times got a little rough,
They both turned to God,
Knowing He was there.
The hours of their life together
went by too fast.
But when the end was near
No good-bye was ever to be said
Just, "I love you" and
"Until we meet again."

Tammy Hoops

The Day After Christmas

It's the morning after Christmas, and all seems quite sad.
The fruit cake has dried out, the punch has gone bad,
The stockings that were hung around the chimney with care,
Are now just scattered— thrown here and there.

The bright Christmas wrapping that covered every surprise
Is now just wadded up and in the trash it lies.
The candles that were lit to bring us such cheer
Have all been put away now, till Christmas next year.

Our friends have all gone to their own homes, I guess
And I'm sitting here staring at the after Christmas mess.
I say to myself, I'll not do all this anymore,
Then I start to grin, seems like I've said that before.

I know in my heart, as Christmas grows near,
I'll do just the same as I do every year,
We'll string up the lights and put up the tree
Cause Christmas time always finds the kid in me.

H. Dean Alley

I Am America

I own this land called America
The ground you walk and ride on
Though it's been taken from me
It has and always will be mine
Recognize me, I am Indian

My skin is dark, my eyes are brown
My hair is black, straight like the arrow
Recognize me, I am Indian

Survival through all the wars of this nation
under God and his salvation
Recognize me, I am Indian

Accept my treaties, accept my traditions
My people help improve our conditions
This land called America
Recognize me, I am Indian

Centuries I wait to hear you belong
You are one of us, welcome Indian, you are America
The highest mountain hears my cry
The valleys echo even though I die
America, recognize me, I am Indian

Ola Lee Prince

A Winter Wind Blows

A winter wind blows on this summer's night.
The glittering moonlight shines upon your beauty.
I see through your eyes love felt inside.

A winter wind blows on this summer's night.
Our blooming rose grows each day of the year
Like our love has done since our first sight.
The sun now shines so bright in my eyes.
Now I realize.

I for you, and you for me.
Forever shall our love be.
A winter wind blows on this summer's night.
No matter how cold it may be,
I'll always be warm while you're with me.

M. Trejo

"Suicide's A Way Of Life"

The innocent cry
The good lie
And the young die

Some fight
Some even try
Other's take their last breath that same night

As we stare at our youth today
We know it's no use to pray
Cause suicide's a way of life

The memories all fade
Hope gets sucked down the drain
And everyone feels the pain

To most it's homicide
To others it's a game that will never be justified.
And to me it's a way of life

Ricky Shadden

Living

The value of life increases with age.
The good years and bad years create the stage.
Many objects, events and lines
Mix today to make life fine.
A cuddly kitten, a sandy beach,
Air waves, sweet wine, or a bloody leech,
A teen's first kiss, the eclipse of the moon,
A cry in the night, or a song out of tune.
A round balloon, the point of lead,
A crippled leg, or a curved riverbed.
These entwine to make life sweet
And each new dawn a treat to meet.

Lynnette Schuepbach

"The Ship"

My life drifts before me, like the broken ship.
   Some pieces on the land, others,
driftwood on the icy blue waters of life.

   The scatters planks and woodchips, my
inner soul, torn from my heart.

   The battered hull, my once protected
fears, escaping into the world.

   The broken mast, a symbol of my heart,
torn so many times.

   The spilled cargo, my thoughts, tossed
about the massive waves.
   Waves of time and trouble.
   In many ways, I too man bent and
   battered.

Starla Serres

Ocean Life

The pale moonlight
The half lit sky
Washes away every tear in your eye
The rushing of waves, the entanglement of life
Together you have the pale moonlight
Majestic places, tropical islands
The rolling of waves, the smashing of Titans
Together they make a few rippling items
Century old rocks, some stubbling pebbles
Pure white sand, olive green turtles
Together you have the sands of time
Like granules in an hour glass our love sifts through,
But yet it lasts
The pale moonlight
The half lit sky
Washes away every tear in your eye
The distant shapes, the shadows of light
The humming of sea gulls, the cheers of the night
Together you have a reason to fight
Seeings how it's a pale moonlight

Melissa Story

"The Knowing"

Tic, tick, tick, tick
the hands on the clock seemed so slow
and the waiting grew intense
he knew the worst to come.
As he cried to the hardwood floor beside her,
her skin glowed in the moonlight,
her hair smelled of roses,
so soft... so red, as a crackling fire of passion
on the first day of snow.
He touched her face and began to give
a breath of life,
a hint of peppermint from her still tongue
a sweet taste from her moist lips
a sudden raise of a lifeless hand.
Touching him ever so slowly
she began to stroke his sweating brow
her eyes open, so rich ice blue, began to melt
and with the last breath of sweetness... I LOVE YOU
her hand drops like a leaf of autumn
a kiss, a tear, he knew!

Pamela Linette Smith

Expressions

Music!
The joyous sound of the universe
Music!
The everlasting expression of one's soul
Music!
The peaceful solitude that extends to all.

With no barriers I can sing,
for with my heart I can express my desire.
I search my soul for the notes to play
And the chords to dance upon the clouds.

Music! An expression of language
Music! A magical interlude of peacefulness
Music! The warmth that reaches from the depths of mother earth.

I reach out and touch the sun
And feel its musical energy pulse through me
bringing forth life in abundance
It sings to my heart and soul.

Music! An expression of love
Music! An expression of peace
Music! The expression of every man and woman.

Richard Anderson

Love

Love is a flower beginning to bloom.
The heartache is just waiting to consume.
Your body and mind are barely alive.
A kiss is the only thing that will help you revive.
You need him so much. You need to feel his tender touch.
Your heart beats wildly whenever he's around,
But you can barely breathe you don't even utter a sound.
Your mind is screaming, "I love you!"
But you dare not say it for he is so much above you.
You wait and wonder what you can do.
You know that in time he will realize he loves you.
You're not sure when and you're not sure how.
You only wish it could be now.
How long will you have to wait?
When will he realize you were destined to be together by fate?
People all say love is the best, maybe it is for all the rest.
To me love is a crying, aching, pain.
A pain that goes on through the sunshine and the rain.
Maybe someday love will be that beautiful, magical place,
But until then I'll have to survive just looking at your face.

Misty Miller

Vacation Day (Driving Tip)

Vacation day was here at last
The hours of preparation and planning, were now in the past
They'd chosen a world famous place to stop
A scenic resort high on a mountain top

The day's work was finally done
The journey at last had began
This vacation was the important one
They'd have to hurry or they would miss the fun

The tires were new
The car had been completely checked too
The trip had been planned so long
It didn't seem possible, something could go wrong

However the human element had not entered their plans
The fact that they were both sleepy and tired, meant nothing to them
That night the driver dozed at the wheel
The crash that followed, was too horrible to reveal

When you are planning that wonderful trip
Would you please remember this little tip
Drive only after proper rest
Don't you contribute to traffic deaths

A. Earl Schooley

The Growing Light

Not all the world has seen the light
the light that shines in the ones who have seen
  it so bright

  A candle blows
  the sun arose
  the war is here
  the fighting's near

A child cries through the night
a poor man has just lost his sight
the sky is darker than before
people kill to ask for more

the light is growing dimmer
people's hopes are beginning to simmer

rise up light!
rise up hope!
are the screams of the people with power and might

They scream it so the world will listen not to fight

Laura C. Minshall

Untitled

As they dragged Anna's body from
The lake and closed her eyes,
I said a little prayer and sadly wiped my eyes.

They said they knew who did it,
They found the nasty man.
They wouldn't take him in yet,
They wouldn't make a stand.

They wrote up a report and questioned me again.
Then Anna's mama thanked me for being her best friend.

She took me in her arms and we cried together.
I couldn't get Anna's face out
of my mind no matter how hard I tried.

I couldn't stand the thought of never
being able to see my best friend again.
I was just hoping it all would come to an end.

Laura Huffman

"Our Dear Son"

On June twentieth, our lives begun.
The Heavenly Father had sent us a son.
There were happy times and some sad.
But we are thankful for the times we had.

You grew into a nice young man,
But it seemed like you and bad luck walked hand in hand.
Our hearts are heavy and you're deeply missed
If we could just see you smile,
Give you a kiss.

So now you're gone from where you came.
It's our loss and Heaven's gain.

So sleep well dear son,
And rest in peace.
Till we met you again
when our lives cease.

Rose Purvin

A Mother's Cry

At 8:00 (am) the alarm went off, I watch my baby rise.
Wake up, wake up you sleepy head as he slowly rubbed his eyes.
At 10:00 (am) everyone's awake showers have been taken,
made my baby a big ole breakfast pancakes, eggs and bacon.
At 12:00 (am) he kissed me on my cheek, he went out to his ride,
I never would've thought in a million years that was our last goodbye.
For at 7:00 (pm) a police came by and pronounced that he was dead.
Oh no! Not my son that was shot twice in the head.
For another man with another gun has again committed a crime,
but this time it's not on television, this time the pain is mine.
For now it's 8:00 (am) again, in a casket my son just lies.
WAKE UP! WAKE UP! You sleepy head, but this time he
wouldn't rise.

Col-Co Chanelle

To You My Love

Perhaps my own words will tell you more
Than any card that's bought in a store.

Words on a card can never express
All the feelings that I have in my breast.

For you, my darling, nothing is too much!
I love your heart, your face, your touch!

You've given me many years of bliss
Can any woman ask for more than this?

May God grant us many more happy years
Together in health and empty of tears.

Lee Prensky

There's No Place Like Home

Gliding home to its nest in the forested hills, the horned owl hears
   the low grumbling sound of men's hated machines.
She arrives and lets out a cry upon seeing the destruction.
Circling above she sees what was her nest.
The fallen tree, once her home, is pulled away leaving only a small
   river of blood from the newborn hatchlings.
The owl mourns, but flies to find a new place in a new strange land.
After time she is still unable to see why man's materialistic whims
   are worth more than simple life.

     William Brotman

The Word

It's the traveler's map, the soldier's sword,
the mind of God, the state of man and doom
of sinners. Here Paradise is restored,
Heaven opened and the gates of Hell looms.
Read it to be wise, believe to be good,
then practice it to be Holy and true.
It contains light to direct you with food
to support and give comfort to cheer you.
It should fill the memory, rule the heart
and guide the feet. It is a mind of wealth,
Paradise of Glory, a joy to start
by reading it slowly and pray for health.
Christ is its Grand Subject, good to be heard
and The Glory of God its end, by The Word.

     Velma J. Arey

Destiny's Cage

Compassion is but a disease that stifles the heart.
The misery of existence compels yet even the most steadfast
   among warriors to falter.
Emotions disintegrate in the run of life; which suddenly,
   like Mount Vesuvius - explodes - unleashing upon society the
   barren darkness of mold within the inner soul.
Transgressing the plight of humanity, the soul escapes unwillingly
   through unguarded entrances.
If but an hour I had to reveal the brazen starvation of my being.
Hunger of life and understanding, a thoughtful ear is all that
   is asked.
Why hast thou forsaken me, oh Mighty Creator of light and
purpose?
Hemorrhaging with agony I swallow my pride, accepting my
nemesis, my
   humanity.

     Taysha Dishman

The Mystical Night

As darkness was closing in
The moon rising with utmost delight
A pretty winsome girl sitting in front of the castle
Watching the sky with a meticulous and exhilarating interest
As soon as the half golden moon arose
She got up like a medieval princess
And began to call my name
With a voice made of every sweet chord
Then darkness wallowed everywhere
And the earth was no more lit
Drifting in the wild wind
I reached out for her tender arm
We slowly walked along an awe inspiring path
And sank beneath the depth of some roaring waters
It calmed at the motion of her hand
She began a song that controlled the winds
Her face shone and sparkled like a diamond
The look of innocence in the eyes of an Angel.

     S. Ogechukwu

Joel's Home Coming

I'm on my way home Mom, but don't wait up for me;
the night has come and I must go, to meet my destiny.

I'm on my way home Mom - don't leave the lights on for me;
I now see his light and it shines so bright, for all eternity.

I'm on my way home Mom, and don't worry if I lost my keys;
there are no doors or wall or gates - no more barriers for me.

Don't turn down my covers Mom, you were always so thoughtful
that way;
making me comfortable, being so dear, each and every day.

I'm on my way home Mom, I'm tired - my time is at hand.
Did I know? Was I scared?—no tears Mom, we understand.

I'm on my way home Mom and no, you needn't come for me.
This one last journey I must make alone - you see God has called for me.

     Kim L. Frazier

Shining Star

You are my shining star, the one that shines in
   the night sky afar.
You let the moon beams shine on my face, like a
   beautiful stream of silver lace.
You hold me in your arms so tight, until we see
   the first speck of morning light.
Please tell me to wait, that you will be here
   before the night is late.
'Don't go away' is all you can say, 'Someday I'll
   come to stay.'
I sit and wait, but you're not here.
And I hold back tears and all the fear.
Then I blink, and in a moment I'm awake
I stare into darkness and hear the sounds that
   it makes.
I blink again to look at the sky, and notice one
   star is especially bright.
'It was only a dream' I hear myself say.
But I wonder if the star was shining my way.

     Raven M. Sanders

The Depths Of Nonsense

The world for once is part of earth,
The ocean by the sea,
The crystal sparks in the night,
The shining ball of crimson light,
The passage which leads to the canal,
The land that connects to the shore,
The puffy snow balls that dot the sky,
The bright orange flame which flies by,
The heavens in the upper world,
The space that takes up room,
The pale, blue light that brightens up black,
The world is strange from front to back.

     Margaret Cheng

The Man

The man that is love,
The man that is peace,
The man that is not diseased.

The man that is nice,
The man that is kind,
The man that will always be mine.

The man that is thankful,
The man that is grateful,
The man that has made me faithful.

This man is very bold,
and while I'm here he shall never grow old.

     Taketa Clark

Untitled

The Ocean is a delight to see
The ocean with all its mystery
The fury in which it flows
The passion for all life below

To feel the spray across my face
To taste the salt on my lips
Brings my heart to a faster pace.

The lover that is a delight to see
Love being the mystery
The fury in which it flows
With consuming passion between the hearts.

Licking the taste of him from my lips
Sweat trickling down my face
In a stream between my breasts
Brings my heart to a faster pace-
As he takes me to all the mystery, passion and
fury

Priscilla Grantham Tullos

Ed Oakley

As the bartender of
The Old Red Saloon in Springfield,
I worked there thirty-six years;
I knew all the people by name in that town.
As someone would walk through the door, I would
Be the first to call out, "Howdy, Jim!" or "How are ya, Tom?"
And my dear wife, Emma, such a good woman,
She died six years ago; the doctor said
She was awful sick, but never really knew why.
He did what he could for her. This I know.
And now, after thirty-six years, I have served
The Old Red Saloon of Springfield as long as it needs me,
And I can get a long deserved rest
With my Emily.

Linda Morrow

All To Myself

In Loving Memory of My Father
I find myself alone again, it seems to be the norm.
The once blue skies I used to see are now blackened by the storm.
I begin to wonder if things will change, I ponder if I care.
Could I handle being happy again, or do I cling to despair?
What is it like to laugh out loud and share a joke with a friend?
I want to hug and love once more, a friend on which I can depend.
I cry my plea to any ear, my pain I want to be felt.
How do I handle this hell I live, a hand so cruelly dealt?
The sun may never shine again, the stars are gone from the night.
I must raise my hands in surrender, for I've lost my last great
fight......

Randy Shultz

The Prize: Illusion

The cobwebs form windows and bulge out with the rain,
The floor boards are broken and covered with stain,
The strips of frayed paper crock roses on the door,
And the cretonne sage cushions are worked over with moth bore.
The roof spikes a beam on the squeaking porch swing,
And the orange canvas flaps like a bat on the wing.
The faucets have rusted corroded with past,
And the navel of incense is glued on the brass.
The stairs and the wood bark war at my heels,
But the mission I came for is about to unreel.
The picture still hangs in a great golden frame,
So, clasp to my breast now and flee from the blame.
So, I ran to the light to look over my prize,
For the frame held a mirror of my very own eyes.

Ruth M. Sample

Untitled

She sees him in the sunlight and wishes he was hers.
The only problem is she can't say the word.
It's in the back of her head, she knows that it is there.
For when he is not with her, she feels alone and bare.
Every breath she takes, every move she makes is dedicated to her love.
She gives thanks for him by her bedside to the Great God up above.
If only she could have him, her life would be complete.
For he would only have eyes for her and no need for her to compete.
The love they have for each other is too strong to measure.
From the first time they saw each other they brought eternal pleasure.
The love they share could never be replaced.
Neither would the smiles they share upon their happy face.
They can only say so much they can't even judge the length.
The powerful presence of their love is the greatest strength.
When I see them I can see the fear.
Knowing they will always be together, praying they will stay near.
I can see the passion I hope their love will stay.
And on that very note I hope your LOVE will never go away!

Corry Kaiser and Stefani Linton

Ode To The Fisherman

The guys head off with their rods 'n' reels,
The girls are off to make great deals.

The guys on the water will be cold and chilly,
The girls will be shopping and acting silly!!

Chuck will call home to say, "Hi Honey,"
I'll say, "Hi, can I spend some more money?"

Dave will call Lori and say this fishing is hard!!
She'll say oh well, can I use your charge card!!

As the guys head home with all sorts of fish tales,
We'll be reliving all the bargains and sales.

When they get home with faces of hair,
We'll be sipping margaritas from the easy chair.

They'll come in and say what's for dinner honey?
We couldn't buy groceries, we ran out of money!!

The next fishing trip, I think there'll be four,
They have to find some way to keep us out of the store!

Pat Williams

My Parents

I am honored to introduce
The Most Extraordinary Couple.
Still in love after 50 Golden Years!
I thank you for my existence.

Even after all the heartaches,
Pains, sorrows and troubles
We three offspring put you through
With me testing your hearts the hardest...

Both of you were always there
To bring the love and laughter back in our hearts
With all your love and compassion
And understanding, caring supportive ways.

When I began to listen to your wisdom
And observed your admirable examples,
I learned the true meaning of living.
My wonderful parents, today, because of you,
I am a happy, lucky woman obtaining all your best attributes.

Thank you for my golden gift of life—
You—my parents.

Susan E. Smith

A Tropical Night

On the island of Negros on a beautiful night,
The palm trees are like a picture, by the moon's splendid light.
The stars seem so close as in the Heavens they abide.
As with a wisp of the hand you could brush them aside.

They twinkle and glitter, like gems they abide.
Like a tent they seem to protect you inside.
They are numerous and varied in color and size.
Like jewels on parade competing for a prize.

I have seen many a star studded Heavens on earth.
I have witnessed many a beautiful night since my birth.
But no one can compare with a tropical night.
It's serene it's restful, and such a beautiful sight.

You see many a thing that is missing in this land.
Many things omitted or destroyed by man's hand.
But one thing is certain, in spite of their plight.
The Lord has seen fit to give them a beautiful night.

Abner O. Andrew

The Tunnel

I watched through tearful aching eyes,
The pellets of rain dropped carelessly to the ground, splattering
when they reached it.
The sky was dark and gloomy, the air thick and moist.
I sat watching it all - my heart aching - insides burning.
I felt alone as if no one cared, as if no one understood
What a struggle it was to be me.
What feelings of loneliness and rejection I was feeling.
Love and compassion were not a part of my lonely life, and never
would be.
A sudden crack of thunder seemed to reflect my feelings of anger
and resentment.
Then my eyes came to rest on a small quiet rainbow off in the distance.
The bright array of colors filled my eyes and I let myself take them in.
It seemed to be hiding, exposing itself just enough to be noticed,
like me.
I suddenly felt a comforting warmth inside me.
A spark seemed to light off inside me, and I tried to hold on to that
feeling of warmth.
The rainbow seemed to wink at me to let me know what things
would get better.
A smile crept slowly to my face and it was a different feeling.
A feeling that told me that I was O.K.
That it was all right to like me as myself
To accept myself and my life as it was, not how it could possibly be.

Keri Payeur

The Newest Colossus

...Just for you, my dearest people.
The people who have no say.
And people who have no choice.
At first, they called us "boat people."
Later on, they call us "economic migrants."
Can they tell from the place we left?
No freedom underneath the sky.
Old mothers crying every night
For their sons who never come back.
They didn't know why they had to die,
Nor for whom should they live their lives.
"Just to live and to die for COMMUNISM."
Where're the hearts of people on the Earth?
Where is the meaning of LIBERTY?
Don't they miss these pretty words?
"Give me your tired, your poor,
Your huddled masses yearning to breathe free,
The wretched refuse of your teeming shore,
Send these, the homeless, tempest-tossed to me,
I lift my lamp beside the golden door!"

Thanh Ngoc Nguyen

Oh How Sour The Sweet Can Be

Oh how sour the sweet can be
The remembering so painfully felt
The loss so deep, emptying the soul
Walking aimless, feeling destitute
Restless heart consumed with pain
Midnight blues have never been so blue
Aching has never ached so deeply before
The emotional suffering to the depth of my soul
Enveloped in torment, never ending
Deeply pained of once felt hope
Pondering the words spoken so hatefully
Bruised and battered, love wasting away
Will I ever be able to cry the pain away?
Can the tears wash away the agony from my heart
How do I now fill this void so overwhelming
When God...when or will I be complete again?
The loss of you is tearing me apart
I still love you

Karen Newlun-Brown

Lake Of The Lady

Way to the south end deep,
    the river flows upward north.

Pools of off-shore waters,
    swell in the ponds of all waters.

In which direction is the lake of the lady?
    Which ocean carries her motion?
        Her love of the earth?
            Her universal devotion?

The waters have grown in wisdom,
    ...and they are changing.

Mothers of the land...
    in waters merging.

Deep cores of creation,
    through earth mother,
        water to spirit, ever changing.

Somewhere, there's an unearthly commotion,
    by mind without spirit.

Like trying to drown the rain,
    to dominate all creation.

Waters that flow, can reach any destination.

Theresa Silva

"I Am An American"

America the beautiful so fresh and so clean my mighty mountains,
the rivers, the prairies, and streams. Nature builds her nest,
amongst my trees. Flowers so pretty, the lilies of the valley,
daisies of the fields. But there's nothing like a rose you see,
my people are one big pot of wildflowers. None dare to be the same.
Yet all are precious to me. I'm your home, your protector, I can't
do without you and you can't do without me, soldiers fought long and
hard, keep me free, that's why God made me. Men died to possess this
land, no-one better than the other. The moon is my neighbor, we get
along just fine. The sun is my cousin, we visit often, my dirt is
as old as the beginning of time, I was here before the dinosaurs,
you know, their bones are inside me and I know them by heart,
animals, humans, the birds, and the bees. They're all mine,
because God gave them to me. I take care of my world, because it's
the only one I've got. The trees and the waters, give me my strength.
Without them I'd be like a fence, keeping things in and keeping
things out. There are no boundaries, I'm free to roam, there's no
beginning and there's no end. I'm a friendly caring world, but I
still have a lot to learn, sometimes things happen to me that I can't
control, that's when my maker comes around so I won't explode. Yes,
you guessed right. "I am America" and America is a part of me,
your world, you see. Yes we can make it! Together!

Thelma Boyd

My Passion

My passion for you is never-ending.
The romance we have is only beginning.
I despise people who try to tear us apart.
Thank goodness we're close at heart.
They say we're to young,
we don't know what love is about.
Maybe they're the ones who need to sort things out.
So we ignore the looks, the
whispers that we receive.
We believe,
that someday they'll understand how we feel.
Is more than real.

Melissa Himschoot

Infatuation

I see you walking by me and all at once my heart beats faster.
The room may be filled with people, but I always hear your laughter.
Suddenly I look up and see you watching me and my hands begin to
    shake.
I feel this pain inside me like a never-ending ache.
I have this urge to touch you but I know it can never be,
and then I wonder if God will ever let me set these feelings free.
Then I try to speak to you and all the words get stuck inside.
For a second your eyes meet mine, then suddenly I look down for that
moment I realize these feelings no longer can I hide.
Sometimes I sit and wonder "Does he have these feelings, too?"
But then my mind laughs at my heart and says to me "You fool, he
never thinks of you."
Maybe someday these feelings will pass, but in my mind I ponder.
Because in my heart there will always be that little shred of wonder.

Marsha Lawson Lambert

Untitled

Unaware of what would become,
The sadness had to end,
the empty feelings,
the thoughts unknown,
what would become of such a life,
getting into a love knowing it couldn't last,
The fun,
The love,
The joy,
Yet the hurt when all is gone,
How one deals with only what one wants,
Only the pretending must end.
The truth.
A pain no one could ever imagine.

Mary Ellen Caulfield

Playground Of Insanity

Terror flashes in your eyes. Crawling, searching for a place to hide.
The dusty stench of stale gunpowder smoke.
Small fires smoldering on a field of blackened grass. The men,
running, to and fro, fighting an enemy.. The spirit of war.
The sounds ...the sounds...chaotic skies...the dying, screaming
for their final demise. You're front and center, but your
courage is gone. The taste and smells of death invade your senses.
Your sweaty fingers, clench a shaking gun, your blood is
rushing, heart racing. Thundering explosions...so close.
You open your eyes to the realities of war. The bloody corpses..
Your fellow men... the scent of musty death. Your mentality
has been deranged by an apathetic smile. You turn your
face upward, to the smoke-grey sky, and scream "oh God
of war...take me to death...my eyes have seen your demented
game played...let me take my final breath."
You raise the barrel of your blood-stained gun....
pull the trigger once...this war is done.

Kathi Zuber

Sunbathing In Darkness

Today there was not a single cloud in the sky.
The sparkling sun's rays sent warmth to caress the earth.
A gentle breeze whistled through the leaves of the trees,
    accompanied by the sweet song
        of Red Robin's happy melody.

I laid still in silence with my eyes gently closed.
My body basked in heat and seemed to belong here.
Absorbing this simple beauty all around me,
    I appeared to be quite peaceful,
        in harmony with my surroundings.

There were dark storm clouds swirling about in my head.
Sharp lightning bolts of reality pierced my chest.
Roaring thunder of loneliness echoed inside,
    reverberating through my soul,
        to the very core of my being;
            and ...
Raindrops splashed down forming puddles upon my heart.

Sheila R. Griffin

Speed

Like toxic waste into a dead sea,
The sterile light drips into the abandoned room,
Why must the night result,
In such a corroded morning?

Wide-eyed and weepy-tailed,
Sins of the previous hours,
Not extinguishing by sleep,
Must bleed into day,
Creating a continuum,
Mostly gray.

But the willful day must be tolerated,
With brain-dead and hammering-heart,
Batteries of life—polarized,
The positive carelessly racing forward,
The negative dryly debating why.

And now the sun,
A tardy harbinger of impending conditions,
An indication of Armageddon,
An enclosing funnel,
Chaotically spiraling downwards.

Stephen Lee Herman

It Brakes My Heart

The wind is briskly blowing on a grave in Jacksonville
the story that it's telling would give your heart a chill

It was just a few short years ago that he was laid to rest
no gold ring on his finger as his hands lay cross his chest

A women made arrangements for the funeral that day
with a promise in the near future the bill she would pay

It brakes my heart to know his plot is not his own
there's no words above him no granite headstone.

He had been a career soldier with four kids and a wife
but changes came after Viet Nam that disintegrated there lives

Later on he wed another but money was her game
she fingered his retirement check to be a permanent thing

She got him to adopt her child and change his insurance too
then she left him for another while the divorce was going through

What happened on that dreadful day only the women knows
a gunshot to his temple left the retired soldier cold

It brakes my heart to know his plot is not his own
there's no words above him no granite headstone.

Lela Dobson

Going Home

She leaned on the oak tree that she and her father planted and eyed
   the strangers in her house.
She gazed up at the oak tree and it held out its arms, as if
   welcoming her home.
She looked through the window that her little brother had thrown a
   ball through.
She saw them eating together and wondered if they knew that her mother
   had eaten her last meal there.
She wondered if they would even care.
She walked closer, until she reached their pool, it was cold and
   isolated, not like the flowers that once made everything look so
   warm and welcoming.
She wondered if the couple knew that where they slept, she was born
   some seventy years before.
She saw the husband kiss his wife goodbye and was reminded of the
many times her father had done the same.
He kissed his daughter's cheek and the woman brought her wrinkled hand
   to her own.
The old woman gave a tired sigh and closed her eyes as a single tear
   ran down her cheek.
Then, with a little resentment and much determination she walked away.

   Katheryn Glover

Killing Of A Dream

I hear the rumbling of a beam of light, a stream within me.
The stream of peace, one more hit and voice will stop.
It must, it will.

The voice of my father killing another one of my dreams.
Another insult in my face...with praise behind my back.

One more hit, one more drink, then I'll feel it.
I'll feel the sensation of the exploding calm.
I'll hear the crickets sing to jazz in my head and bees hum.
I'll explode into sparkles of light and join them.
In the woods, next to the river or the pond.

Soothing the beast that stomps my heart.
No more voice, no more.
I know there is another way, but I don't know where it is,
Today. I don't know where it is.
For now give me another hit my friend...then be my friend...
And tell me another way.

   Lucy Lee Lawrence

Nothing Like It

There's nothing like a pearl catching
   The sun,
A girl kissed, or a prize
   just won.
So take up your will and do what you can
To rev-up this place and be a man.

There's nothing can stop a
   chocolate's sweetness,
For a dedicated cook with pans
   and her neatness
to gladden the heart of a child returning,
Or dad from his ever energy burning,

There's nothing so hot as a tar roof patching,
Motor-car fixing and baseball catching -
That child or boy can't do with a will,
Except - study home work or do a drill.

There's nothing like this drivel my pencil does write,
So put out the cat and shut off the light.
Be there in the morning to bid me "Good day."
And stay by me now as time slips away.

   Pearl E. Mitchell

Dark Skies

I heard the rain, I felt the pain.... the sky a dismal gray
The sun had fled, the tears were shed; yet as I faced that day
The memories of gentle breeze were there to haunt my mind
Vast corridors, on distant shores, those thoughts I sought to find.
Of being small, of him so tall, and climbing on his knee
Or in the night, with pale moonlight, his strong arms holding me.
There was no fear, with him so near, he helped to make me strong.
I see his smile, and all the while, him pushing me along.....
To learn my stride, to be his pride, to reach my every goal
To find the light, and keep it bright.... but now inside my soul.....

A bleak caress, deep helplessness, as Daddy's laid to rest
With wrenching sigh, I say good-bye.... my faith put to the test.
A silent shout, my hand went out, the casket felt so cold
The sting of death, with every breath, the grief that did unfold
I see his face, try to embrace, a warmth, that icy day
Yet as we part, inside my heart, that's where he'll always stay....
Daddy.

   Narda Wade Curlee

Lonely Passion

The lanterns are dimly lit,
The table set for two;
The fireplace intensely ablaze,
As I quietly wait for you.

Soft music on the radio;
Soft linens on the bed;
Your soft skin I long to caress;
As thoughts of you linger in my head.

Do you know my heart is bursting with all the love bottled inside?
Do you know my arms are aching for you to be my bride?
Do you know I eat alone with no one by my side?
Do you know all I want is to make you satisfied?

Intense passion I feel,
As it wastes here all alone.
For passion is made for two,
It can't survive on its own.

So dear woman please hurry before the inferno has turned to ash.
Come quick before the lantern's wick has let all its oil pass.
Come hear the soft sweet music before the station signs off for the night.
Come feel my passion, for it will die without you to hold me tight.

   Mark Reagan

Blackness

When is it going to stop,
The thunder inside my heart,
Going to stop beating at my soul?
When can I live without the pain,
Will it ever move on?
Is it going to linger the rest of my life
All because of one year?
Pounding at me,
Not letting me proceed
Another I say is all I need.

   Kari Sue Malar

If Time Could Go Back

If time could go back I'd change a whole lot, the misery experienced,
the untied knots.

Things would be different, but better you see, for I'd know what
would hurt and benefit me.

Times are hard, and will only get harder, life is short and will only
get shorter.

So I'll correct my mistakes, and stop accepting sorrow,
For I have fewer todays, than I have tomorrows.

   Victoria Marshall

Together

I think of my Dad and I together,
the times we walked together,
the wonderful laughter shared together,
when tears were shed, it too was done together.

How I wish that it could be that way today,
for Dad is now lost in old age,
and I know there will be no tomorrow together.

He will always be in my heart and mind,
the day too, will arrive for me,
and once again we will be, my Dad and I, together.

Marie Six

Why Do I?

After all the times you hurt me,
the times you made me cry....
Why do I forgive you, with every little sigh?
the times that you betrayed me,
at the times of painful good-byes....

Why do I still need you,
after all those little lies?
The times that you ignored me,
and the times my pain has shown?
When you left me all alone,
with the scars you left upon me,
and the tears that fall each day....

Why do I still love you,
though you've treated me this way?

Senaida Kinzie

As The Seasons Change

The days get longer as the seasons change.
The trees are wet and sloppy as the
ice begins to melt from their limbs.
The snow begins to disintegrate and
the animals are trying to find their new homes.
The dandelions start to pop up everywhere, and
the smell of flowers fills the atmosphere
like the smell of breakfast in the morning hours.
The snowy streets are slushy and sopped
with the excess sand and salt left over
from the city workers.
The streams are starting their new lives
as they flow through the field.
They gurgle and bubble as if to tell
us that reincarnation is for real.
The birds also begin their adventure trying
to find the little squirmy worms seeping
up through the damp earth floor,
and the days get longer as the seasons change.

Mike Davis

My Lady

As she stands before me, as beautiful as she can be.
The radiance surrounds me so that I cannot see.
She reminds me of an Angel, so fair, with
her soft skin, beautiful eyes and reddish brown hair.
She reminds me of the flowers when in
morning are sheltered with dew, for
when the sun comes up, my lady
glistens as the flowers do.
If God and nature could turn back
the hands of time and let me do it
once again, I would still choose my
Lady for she is more than my wife
She is my best friend.

Mark Crabtree

Fly with the Eagle

Run with the Wolf

Gleaming golden eyes of the wolf pierce my soul
The upward flight of the raptor lifts my heart

The wolf runs
    The eagle soars
Feel the rush of the wind
    the passion of life
        the sheer celebration of power

The wolf runs through the forest
Thrilling to the power in his limbs
The eagle soars through the air
Thrilling to the wind rushing his wings

The eyes of the wolf
    The eyes of the eagle
Glow with the passions of life
    being on the edge of danger
        living on the heights of glory

Margaret Huffman

Prelude To A Memory

With the withdrawing of the curtains,
The Valiant warrior gazed at the eternal sky,
her frail eyes flickering with the intense light on a cloudy day.

The rainbow did not emerge,
the sun did not deliver the ray of hope she'd awaited.
On borrowed time was she, unaware of when it'd flip.
Yet, a quivering smile escaped her feeble lips...
..."It's another beautiful day!" said she.

The storm had shattered her youthful life,
uprooting her soul from the joyous garden where she'd blossomed.
The shark-like cancer had ravished her body
and battered it against the jagged rocks of reality.
She knew she'd drifted too..too far away from the lifeboat,
and accepted that she couldn't stay afloat.

As she lay limp and pensive on the gurney,
she reflected on her life's journey.
No qualms had she, only an occasional tear
Not for herself, but those in denial she held so dear;
For whom, she'd dwell free,
only in their memory.

Sangeeta Gupte

The Chesapeake Bay

From where I sit, by the Chesapeake Bay
the water is smooth and calm
it transfers its serenity to my being
Just like a soothing balm-

I see the gulls winging about
Looking for food from the sea
I see a fisherman casting his line
in water up to his knees

I see the tide ebbing out to sea
leaving in its wake a lot of debris
I see at a distance vessels afloat
A barge a freighter and a tug boat

Close to shore sailboats are dancing
their white sails glowing in the sun
traveling as fast as the wind will take them
each trying to win the run.

Ruth C. Bollinger

Shield Of Honor

He drew his shield—the one that he proclaims;
The "weed" is all he needs, or so he claims;
No future to behold, no dreams in which to believe;
Pretty damn sad when this is all he can perceive.

Hiding behind the book, she scribbles a friendly note;
"What's happening—not much—I think I need a toke!"
Dreams for tomorrow, quickly formed, then discarded;
"There's no future for me, in the land of the hard-hearted!"

My heart aches to think of the young—
Who have already given up before they've begun;
No sparkle in the eyes, to mask their distrust;
Everything "sucks" and this is a "bust"!!!!

These days are not good, it's noted in their words;
But some of our finest, are but flighty birds.
They come to us already in the given state —
With expectations that teachers—will make them all great!!!!!

T. L. Gadsby

"The Lost"

The days are dark, the fields are white,
The world is in despair,
The hopelessness of blinded eyes,
Confusion everywhere.
Their soul is bound by sin and strife,
The weight it drags them down,
Their back is bowed, their step gets slow,
They search for wisdom's crown.
My soul cries out to God above,
My heart in deep travail,
"Have mercy, Lord, have mercy, Lord,
Oh, save their soul from hell!!!
Lord, see their eyes, their blinded minds,
Their empty, darkened souls,
Draw them to your bosom, Lord,
Gently lead them to the fold.
Oh, precious blood, redeeming grace,
Oh, Calvary Divine!
Save them, cleanse them, lift them high,
As you did this soul of mine."

Wanda F. Wagner

Untitled

The star falls but the sky neglects to catch it,
  the wind blows and everyone just accepts it

Hearts ache as they break,
  from words said with no forsake

The weight won't lift,
  it was given like an unwanted gift

Emotions are constantly up and down,
  causing a few smiles and frowns

Accepting something as it is,
  is all you should ask it to ever be

To never accept wholeheartedly,
  will only turn your soul into one,
    very lonely

Look inside yourself and no one else,
  for your peace and happiness

Look around your world and love it,
  as it reflects what you give it,
    what you are.

Pam Munson

How Do I Love Thee

It's hard to count the ways
The year does not have enough months
The weeks not enough days.
Someone just must come up with
A new invention, plan or scheme
So you can know the ways I love thee
And not just what it seems
I just can't count all the ways I love you
It takes someone greater than me
So I beg each of you most humbly
To just give it a try and see.
Sometimes I try to come up with a shut-off point
Your goodness overshadows all
There's never a ceasing of your sweetness
Summer, winter, spring or fall.
I look high into the hills and mountains
Low in the oceans and streams
Still my love out measures
Anything I think or dream.

Rosa Whitt

And The World Cracked Open

The bowels of the earth screamed
their angry cry, making trees fall,
buildings bow down, lives lost
  And the world cracked open

Fire wreaked havoc upon a forest,
scorching the earth, running its course
upon the life that once dwelled there
  And the world cracked open.

A tidal wave came crashing over the shores,
washing away everything in its path,
leaving only desolation in its wake
  And the world cracked open.

You reached out for me,
  took me in your arms,
met your lips with mine,
  shaking my senses to the ground,
searing my heart with your touch,
  leaving my lips ravished,
reeling still from the aftershocks of your kiss
  And my world cracked open.

Kathleen Goings

"Pain Of Freedom"

Children mourning over their father's death
Their father thinking of them and his love
before his last breath
He had a job to do
a mission to complete
for his family's freedom
he would not accept defeat
Now as they take him home
his job is over and done
Lord, watch over his soul, let him rest
and never more to roam
He loved his country and her rolling plains
He had nothing to lose
His family had everything to gain
A true soldier like the one above
hates to fight
his heart full of kindness and love
Let all remember the ones lost
but those in green know
Freedom is worth the cost

David Ray Wampler

500

The Veil

When asked if I'm afraid of death I say to them, no more.
Then I explain the reason, for I've been there before.
I've touched the veil that separates the living from the dead.
A white ethereal light surrounded me as I lay in my bed.
I felt so buoyant and unconstrained,
When I left my body and my pain.
I flew to the Goddess and came back to see,
What the doctors and nurses were doing to me.
I thought it was my time to go,
But I heard a soft sweet voice say No.
The veil of death is not frightening to see.
Angels are there; they've talked to me.

Kimberly Clark

Untitled

Women say I Love You,
then leave you in the cold.
Children crying daddy,
you just want to hold.
Go out and have a good time,
come home get in a fight.
Finally, you say it's over,
then drive into the night.

To wander in your lonely remorse,
letting the night run its course.
One night, one fight, one maddening spell,
this love has to be over for this is hell.

Lisa M. Roberts

Sea Waves

Seas swell upon themselves
then rush to gain the rocks
and in a mighty heave hurl themselves with all their speed
to crash and roar with tempest rage
as they become the spray
that towers in the air and grasps the rainbow's colors tight
in their frantic arms
until exhausted
retreat to distant shores
to calm their tired heat
so they
may come again.

Thomas L. Ruth Jr.

If Time....

If time is of the essence,
Then why is it wasted away?
People later wonder, when youth is gone,
Why it couldn't stay?

If time could be bought back,
What would be the cost?
To recall the memories that escaped your mind somehow,
That you thought were surely lost.

If time was captured in a bottle,
Who would protect it from being taken?
Never trusting a soul, wondering who's to blame,
Be careful accusing, for you could be mistaken.

If the speed of time could be controlled,
who's to say if it's right?
To pass through the cold and lonely darkness,
To feel the warmth of the sunlight.

Time remains forever steady,
As steady as the beat of a man's heart,
Always deciding who remains and who goes,
Keeping the cycle of life constantly flowing end to start.

Shanna Deon Bain

The Missing Piece

My life was like a puzzle—Lying with a missing part
Then you came to fit in that one piece that gave me a brand new start.
You were always there when I need you, at the finish and certainly at the start
I treasure your being, second to God, you're the dearest thing to my heart.
I thought what we had with each other was very special, indeed;
Like growing a tree in the springtime by merely planting one seed.
I found myself loving you more and more each day,
And prayed that our beauty and happiness would always be this way.
But now something has happened—seems like what we had is 'gone with the wind'
I know this 'cause the puzzle piece you fitted in, is now missing again.
You say your love is still with me when your presence has disappeared
This is the one thing I wanted to prevent, the one thing I most often feared.
But now my puzzle has a missing piece; I feel so all alone.
My love is still here and will always be; BUT you My Love, are gone.
You're gone from my sight, but not from my heart; you're always on my mind
I wish you luck in searching for the things in me you didn't find.
I love you now and evermore 'til God takes me by his side
To be with him in his kingdom of Heaven; to live, where with you—I died.

Karen P. Wynn

History, More History

North of the Isthmus where was the Canal
There a great Nation happily banal
For 300 years her truths survived
'Till professional governess caused its demise

Vote for sure this next time around
We may yet turn our fate upside-down
so prayed the faithful and hopeful few
Too dismayed to know what else to do

But, debt is debt by any name
Still the Politicos continued the game
Raise our pensions, we do a good job
No one is smart, out there in the mob

The bill was due and had to be paid
The money they printed just made it more staid
If no one produces and everyone rides
One more Nation goes out with the tides.

Walter H. Shiplee

9-23-94

These are days when there is too much to feel,
there are so many choices and options,
but only a few roads to follow.

These days are brutal and relentless, and mostly hopeless
with time spilling by in catastrophic gallons
of desperate, quiet, painful tears.

These are the times when we search for a way
and find there is no one there to guide us,
so we grope along in the dead of night.

These are the days of anger and disillusionment
When we should be in love and in new homes,
having children and making love out of life.

These are days when we are to assume a new life,
but I can't find it, and I can't see it,
and I don't feel it exists in our world anymore.

These days we have become the lost and lonely,
while our fathers coax us to become more
in a world that has fallen apart.

Patrice McCormack

The World Around Me

When I go outside on a sunny day.
There are so many fun things to enjoy and play.

First there are the trees with the birds that sing,
From a distance I can hear the church bells ring.

Then there are the children that skip and run,
And everyone can hear the man across the street who sings a hum.

So from this poem you can see,
When I grow up, what has inspired me.
Lindsay Cecil

Motherly Love

Everbody goes through life hoping to achieve.
There are those who acquire fortunes,
and become great in the eyes of the rest of the world.
Then there are those who must be satisfied with being just themselves.

I have achieved. I have just been myself, I have achieved.
Being a mother is the biggest thing anyone can be.
Being a wife, mother and grandmother, is a superb accomplishment.
Publishing your work, building the tallest building, going to the moon, can't compare with being a mother.
I have had the opportunity of a lifetime!

I have enjoyed having and caring for my babies.
I have molded them and given them all the characteristics given to a piece of clay,
except that the glaze and color were made of very special ingredients and applied with a special brush that was first dipped inside of my heart and soul.
God gave me the glaze,
I just put the right amount, not too thick, or too thin!
And since I had a little of that glaze left, I used it for my grandbabies.
Nelida Rios King

The Song

Within the soul,
There is a power that makes it possible to live another day,
To take another breath,
To sing another note.
The notes you sing all join together in a song.
A song that drifts in and out of memory.
A song that flickers with your dreams.
The song will never die,
Though it will fade into void if you do not believe it is there.
The song is never-ending.
It has played since the dawn of existence.
It will continue to play into eternity.
I may live another day knowing that there will always be a part of the song
    I do not know.......
Marieke Tuthill

Untitled

A little bird sang to me today
The song was so beautiful I was lead astray
It was so colorful and attentive I just couldn't walk away
As I looked up at the bird and it down on me
I couldn't help wondering how it could sing so joyfully
Maybe if he were I and I were he, then I could perch upon that tree
My journey continued as the little bird flew into the air
How envious I remained just wishing I was there
He continued to flap his wings in flight
As my eyes teared from peering into the light
He roamed through the sky and was no longer in my view
I felt so lost and alone for what shall I do?
I knew this journey had come to an end
So I bowed my head down with thankfulness for my little friend.
Shelly Pasciak

A Place In Heaven

A young life in God's hands,
there is something about that,
I just can't understand.
My innocent friend as kind as can be,
He is now far away from me,
I know he is in a happy place,
Just once I wish I could see his face,
Sometimes I sit and ask the man upstairs,
Why did you take my loving friend?
And then I realize that he is in heaven,
With his master at his side,
And is far away from hunger, hurt,
want, and pride.
Now my heart is filled with happiness,
and sweet rejoicing, too.
Because to walk with God is perfect peace,
A joy forever new.
Kristine Rector

Weathered Spoon

One autumn many years ago
There lived a girl about eight or so
She lived on a farm off a dirt road
Poor but well fed she had no toys

No dolls and no teddy bear
Her grandma gave her a old weathered spoon
And soon it would be her best friend
In her mind it could be anything

It could be a doll a shovel to dig in the sand
Her music to bang on old tin cans
Or a pencil to write in the sand
But little girls grow up marry raise a family

Now with her husband gone and the kids all grown
She will take a trip to her first home
There off a dirt road sits the house basically a shack
She goes in and looks around sweet memory abound

There in the corner of an old book case
She sees that old weathered spoon
With joy in her heart and tears in her eyes
She has found that old but happy life
R. Burns

The Most Beautiful Girl In The World

I was the most beautiful girl in the world.
There was no one as pretty as me.
Until that one day my youth gave way
and my true self I was able to see.
I was the loneliest girl in the world;
there was no one as lonely as me.
Until that great day my heart gave way
and heaven I was able to see.
Where, I did ask, is that beautiful mask,
that God had given to me?
My dear, be aware the mask is still there
it's just wrinkled, old and ugly.
You were given a great gift,
but with time things did shift.
You should have used your time wiser-ly,
But you decided to be miserly.
Her story goes to show,
all things come and go.
So the next time you look in the mirror,
remember things aren't always what they appear.
Megan C. White

Full Circle

The children feed from our blood.
There minds are carved from our souls.
When were left pondering in the mind,
the children become soft,
Mad visions of sequences of time gone by,
As well as reflections of idealism
etched in our thoughts since childhood.
We exist, live and die in the continual circle.

Wayne A. Check

Beam Us To The Stars

There is no reason to assume that man alone exists in space.
There must be other intelligent creatures to be found.
If mankind has a future, we must be able to roam the galaxy,
where the stars twinkle, meteors swarm, and comets zoom around.

Let us hope that there is a future for our children.
The vastness of space offers hope that life can exist elsewhere.
Man is not stagnant. We can find that undiscovered country.
We must combine our technology in the pursuit of getting there.

The spirit of STAR TREK encourages us to boldly go.
A giant step was made when man landed on the moon.
The rest of the solar system is expecting our next voyage.
We are ready to leap into the final frontier. Let it be soon.

Let us sail to the stars on the wind of the human spirit.
We must not allow the hatred from our planet to go.
Our world must come together in harmony and carry peace.
Let us engage our resources and make it so.

Kenneth V. Carnahan

A Blanket Of Snow

The snow fell as of yesterday eve,
There was only a blanket of snow to see.
All about was still and white,
So pure and calm from winter's gift.

Until the midst of day, all was quiet;
The children started out in all their gear.
Their enthusiasm was enough to warm the air;
Cries of joy echoed throughout the hills.

One by one they returned up the hill,
Into the house for lunch and warmth;
As they ate and warmed themselves quickly,
They longed to be out playing again!

Although they may freeze themselves,
They have not a care but for the fun.
Red nose and ears and hands;
Peek beneath the scarf and hat and mittens.

As they are called in all sopping wet,
They beg and plea to play some more;
Yet they know they must not stay,
For evening is about to settle in.

Sandra L. Branham

Aged Sea Gull

As the sea gull flew over the ocean
The wind rippled the waves along the shore
The sun gleaming on his aged wings
Turning them into white satin
As they were once before
His eyes staring amongst the water
To see what there was to catch that day
For his salvation was at stake
And his life to him was here to stay
Not no one - not even the wind
Was going to take his life away...

Robin L. Tremblay

Reposing Under The Rain

When I come begging for food and substance,
there you wait, wrapped in the light,
ready to comfort with your words of warmth
borrowed from a Socrates or Shakespeare.

Again I've striven with what's - right, what's - wrong,
with impediments to incandescence,
and come to you for solace and guidance,
too wracked to awake and achieve my life.

Is the struggle worth it? You say, "Yes,"
and I return to that larger mind
that reposes under the rain, yes,
and I repose there, under the rain.

Kay Y. Wehner

The Universal Dream Catcher

God has chosen children, we are the crystals of the world.
There's a job to do, no matter how small.
Artists and healers, we hope you listen.
Crystals ready, pull the sinew for the dream catcher.
Light of day in the center, brace for the pull.
Count your blessings crystals, you may not know your neighbor.
It's part of the picture, this dream catcher.

Sheila Sporkin-Edel

Love Blind

I've known from the very first what I want
There's never been any doubt in my mind
Our very first kiss made me love blind
Now I can't see anyone but you, only you
Read my mind, it will tell you that I love you
What's a girl, helpless in love, to do?
Your smile totally sweeps me away
Thoughts of you every night, and every day
Your image takes my breath away
Read my mind it will tell you that I love you
What's girl, helpless in love, to do?
You are all I've ever wanted in a man
Self assured, confident, in command
You're warm, and you're funny, and you're friendly
Slow sweet kisses, a war, gentle touch
No denying, I want you so much
You're so handsome you make my heartache
I love you more with each breath that I take
Your bright blue eyes, your wonderful smile, your slow sweet
kisses
Are embedded in my mind for all time

Trisha Wiltse

Trying To Forget

I have so much loneliness
That many would do without
I walked over to where he once stood,
   sighed and started to part,
As I heard the cold snow starting to fall.
The tears strolled down my once dry cheek,
   as I leaned against the wall.
I looked outside my prisoned room;
   my soul and life are all in doom.
Lovers holding hands, it really sickened me.
I tried to drop it in the crowd;
   to lose it in the sea.
I tried to dream its shape away.
The grave was finished,
   but the face
Remained in my memory.

Valentine Bishop

When To Believe

Oh Lord help me I'm so confused
There's so many denominations
I don't know which one to use
One believes one way
and one believes another
if they all read the same Bible
How could they be different from each other
If I sat here in my thoughts
and learned all their ways
would I get to heaven for sure
of course not, Jesus is the only way

Ronald Stout

Pleasures Of Life

A walk through the park, a kiss in the dark
These are a few of the simple things.
Wadin' in a creek or walkin' in the rain —
Good home cookin' and drivin' down main.

A porch swing in the front and an oak tree out back,
It isn't a mansion nor is it a shack.
We don't have much money but we get along,
With dreams of tomorrow and singin' a song.

You may be unwilling to come see us someday —
But if you do — then you'll surely hear me say
"These are but a few of our personal pleasures,
Happiness and love are the most valued treasures."

Rhonda (Randi) Davis

Untitled

My life is yours to direct and guide
These trials and tribulations I take in stride
When my life seems without meaning
  show me the way
I can't do it on my own Lord, help me not to stray
Don't let me be misguided by man
Believing in you allow me to take a firm stand
Change my heart, my thoughts, my soul
Putting you first in my life, make it my
  never ending goal
Let your words be my nourishment and
  my prayers be my water
And my thoughts, words and actions
  consist of your constant praise
My father
I have prayed for knowledge, wisdom and
  discernment
For I long to hear you say "Well done my
  faithful servant."

Shannon Johnson

The Strongest Ally

Heaven must have a special place for this specific group.
They are a strong and vibrant bunch with hands that never droop.
No matter what the load they bear there's still room for some more.
If one of the children is involved it's never just a chore.
They start out early and stay late, their strength just doesn't end,
and there's no rest for her until she's tucked the children in.
Her age doesn't seem to matter, in fact she just gets stronger,
and as the family grows and grows her list keeps getting longer.
I've seen this role repeated so many times in life
I am completely mystified at how they bear the strife.
If you want to see God's love proceed like rivers on us all
just pick a place out close to her and feel it as it falls.
I've often pondered moms and dads and what sets moms apart.
Dads bear their burdens on their backs, moms bear theirs on their hearts.
Of all the blessings God can give, like these there are no others,
and words of thanks cannot express the thanks we feel for Mothers!!

Dutch Hongsermeier

Poetry And Life

My thoughts of poetry and life are both two and one of the same
They both take thought and they both take special care yet neither
can be created without timing, love, respect, and thoughtfulness.

Poetry and life are similar to each other
Life creates poetry and poetry creates life.
The understanding it takes to realize both of these creations as a
part of each other takes a new and entirely less frequently visited
  state of mind

I look at people; I looked at flowers; I even gaze the stars every
  now and then
These things are a part of everyday living, but still I wonder,
Why does every touch, every stare, every sensation need to be so...
So everyday - longed-for?
The benefit I want from this poem is to gain your respect, love,
And thoughtfulness
That takes, oh, so special timing to understand what we are really
here for, and the simple little thoughts that say,
"Oh yeah! Now I remember where I put that other sock!"

With peace and love and best wishes to the lonely sock-searchers of
the world. May your journeys be not in vane.

Tad Baldwin

My Eyes

I have the eyes of a Tiger so I have been told,
they could stare you down and make your blood
run cold.

I could look straight through you and burn your
everlasting soul, for my eyes can reveal what
you try to withhold.

For you would not believe what my eyes have seen,
and what I do not say, they say for me.

Just a glance or two is all I need to get my
point across, because my eyes could put you
in your place and tell you who's the boss.

If looks could kill most would be dead and this
is rather true, no one would ever know that
my eyes were the weapons that I used.

Kamara Haynes

The System

They taught you the system, the way life works,
They gave you all the answers to every little quirk,
You think you know it all, you got it all figured out,
Well son, you're about to learn what being alone's all about.

You see, in the world, there's evil all around
With car thieves and lawyers and other things profound.
There's sin and evil everywhere, such things of which I disapprove,
People try and take advantage of your every single move.

There's crime and chaos everywhere, law enforcement is a joke
Everyone is on welfare, our country is going broke.
Our nation wants us to pay their debt a hundred miles long,
That just means more taxes, now don't you think that's wrong?

They practice such bad morals, to goodness they're adverse,
They say our country's doing fine, but it keeps getting worse
People getting shot over a buck in spare change,
So as you can see, things are getting so strange.

So next time you think you've got it all figured out,
Remember what being alone is all about,
In a twisted world with so much pain...
Son, can't you see? IT'S TIME FOR A CHANGE.

Tim Clark

Roses Do Not Cry

Roses do not cry.
They know not the world they live.
They grieve not when you die,
But know not what they give.

How sad it must be to never shed a tear,
Hear laughter happily, or smile from ear to ear,
Or hear the words I love you, when a child's born.
To see the stars shine in the night, or sunrise in the morn'.

Roses aren't aware. Perhaps that's better, though.
For if they too could care, their feelings too would show.
A saddened face is just the thing a rose knows to relieve.
If all our sorrow they could see, their happiness would leave.

Wouldn't roses wilt away if every time they knew,
All the hardships and the pain which people struggle through?
How could they sit upon a grave or at the weak's bedside,
If every time they felt the pain, like people, roses cried?

As falling crystal shatters, as breaking pieces fall,
If roses felt, then would the ending differ much at all?
Roses do not cry. They know not the world they live,
But perhaps that's why they can always give.

Robin Hendricks

The Little Girl, The Little Boy

A little girl, a little boy, just five; their world was free;
They romped and played in their own world,
in unspoiled childish glee.
Her family moved on farther west; she begged to stay with him
But sixty years, two thousand miles then separated them
Since age of five. Now they were old, their tears and anguish lost;
Three wars, depression, in those years their paths had never crossed.

And then they met, stood face to face and looked into old eyes;
Their time-worn hands clasped, hers in his, in disbelief, surprise.
She searched his face to find the boy she knew those years ago,
And saw him seeking out the girl. This face he did not know.

Nostalgia swept a raging tide, engulfed both her and him;
Hot tears welled up, rolled down her cheeks,
and dropped from quiv'ring chin.
Those sixty years changed them both; their eyes once bright, were dim.
The little girl, the little boy. What had become of them?

Lee Fleming Reese

They Say

They say I'm black
They say you're white
They call you day
They call me night

They will look you straight in the eye but shy away from me.
Oh Lord, will I ever be free?

They will give you a loan, but turn me down.
They will make you President, but call me a clown.

They think I'm a beast and you're an angel in white.
You live by day, but I'll die by night.

They say I'm day
They say you're night
They call you black, they call me white

They will give me a smile, but frown at you.
How can all of this be true?

They say I'll go to college, but you'll go to jail.
Is this heaven or is this hell?

They say I'll be a doctor, but you'll be a bum.
All of these statements make me numb.

Who cares what they say. We'll both be born the first of May!

William D. Salley

Because I Miss You Robert

The days roll by - and nights come to fast
They seem so long for I am alone.
The days seem empty for there is no one dear,
To share them with.
I look for you and find the empty spot
Which was and is so much a part of you.
When I go to bed it's cold
Your warmth for me to curl up to, is not there.
Just your place - where your pillow remains and
The comfort of your comforter to wrap myself in.
I pray you are not too far away.
Although I can't reach you - you somehow are still there!
Although the years seemed so long
And now they have slipped away
The time was shorter and I know why.
Our trials and triumphs were all the same
Of living, was just earthly gain.
For I know there is an ever after
Where the angels play, like God's children
We go home to him to stay.

Marie Bondi

The Entry Of Two Hearts

The Angels labored overtime and when their work was through,
they sent a baby down to Earth all wrapped in flannel blue.

The family was so happy they had themselves a boy,
and called upon their loved ones to share in all their joy.

In keeping with tradition they put you upon their knee,
and made an entry on a branch to this their family tree.

As your name was printed on this parchment page of life,
they noticed there another line beside it for your wife.

And so they closed the book that day for another time and place,
when someday there your true love's name would be written in the space.

Well so much time has passed since then and now that you are grown,
you've found love's beat within your heart; someone to call your own.

So now it's time to add her name to the family's golden book,
so we'll open to that special page where long ago we took
a baby boy upon our knee and held him there to see,
and told him when he took a wife we'd add her to our tree.

And with the branches in full bloom from the union of these two,
we thank the Angels up above for the gift they brought in blue.

Linda S. Wright

Cloudburst

Words do hurt.
They sting like a nest of raging hornets.
It's dark. I am lonely.
All life has filtered through my body like sand through a sieve.
A blanket of death wraps me and binds me.
My eyes are black. I cannot see.
In the darkness a light, a hope emerges.
I have found my way.
Courage, strength, force! Speed, skill, protection!
Like a sizzling bolt of lightning I am infiltrated by these feelings.
A seed has sprung.
Its captors fleeing from the light of day.
The blanket of death is tossed away.
A splash of color, as brilliant as the rainbow floats downward.
The clouds of my eyes have burnt away like the morning mist.
I who was many now am one.
One, a whole, such a beautiful word.
The light has saved me.
My seed has sprung.
I Am Free!

Matthew J. Kavanah

The Poets Of The Radio

These poets I hear on the radio tell me secrets.
They tell me how the world should be.
They tell me I am not alone in my pain.
They tell me I am here for a reason.
I don't know what that reason is yet.
The Poets are named: Garth, Jon, Eddie, Eric and Kurt.
These are only a few of them.
Many more come to my room each night and teach me things.
They teach me to love and to hate.
They tell me that I can make a difference.
They tell me I'm me and I am my own person.
These, my poets of the radio.

Nancy R. Bulington

Teach Me, Lord

Hurry up, God, and help me.
  They that wait upon the Lord,
I'm so tired and weary.
  Shall renew their strength.
Sometimes I feel like a turtle,
  They shall mount up with wings as eagles.
Always behind on everything and no energy.
  They shall run and not grow weary;
That I just want to lie down and quit.
  They shall walk and not faint.

J. Carla Northcutt

One Brief Moment

She gently touched his face with her soft fingertips
They tightly held each other in a warm embrace
He reached for her, and her heart began to race
In one brief moment, he kissed her gentle lips.

Feelings of passion burned within their souls
An intense flame lit up the dark, dreary hour
The heat rose with an intensifying power.
But the sparks soon died when fate took its toll…

Her precious, wounded heart begins to ache
His memory is pushed far, far away
She sees that there is nothing left, and soon awakes
Hope is diminished, and she starts a new day.
Life seems almost meaningless without him
But her heart holds on to the emptiness that remains.

Kiley A. Cogis

Withered

When I gave you these twelve roses
They were full of life
We were finally together
And there was no strife.
There were some faults
Hidden so deep we couldn't see,
But as time passed by
Those faults were seen more clearly.
The drunken nights, the smoked filled rooms,
I gave all for the love of one.
The things I promised I'd never do
Are all the things that I have done.
When I met you, I fell so hard
I could have sworn it was fate.
But now it seems these days
That idea can no longer relate.
And as I see these twelve roses
With their leaves and petals dried
It reminds me of us,
For our love has truly died.

Mario J. Ramirez

A Generation Lost

Why am I so tempted to pursue
Things I know I should not do.
The rules are seemingly blurred.
Is it me, is it you, my song is slurred.

The big black hole has swallowed the truth.
It has taken my innocence, it has taken my youth.
The emptiness is closing in.
I've lost the will to win.

Is the whole world like me?
Or do I make the world so to be.
Love has gone the way of ecology
Hate has covered our geography.

Is the someone out there?
Who can convince me that they care.
Should life be this scary
When I was little, they said there's a fairy.

Walter Rox

Untitled

They said that I could enter this contest
They say we are seeking some of the best
But how do I know that it could be true
That I could write poetry just for you
Well, now, just wait, just let me tell you first
That for the recognition I do thirst
Not that only, they say moola is there,
So they say in their ad, seems rather fair
For the money I don't care, just want you
To know, that I've thought of you, though
  I'll leave it up to you

William G. Swann

Mom & Dad

This time would come you have always known,
the house is empty, your children are grown.

Unconditional love beyond all compare,
through the ups and downs you were always there.

No matter what was done or what was said,
you kept us warm, you kept us fed.

The little things in us that you had taught,
many lessons gladly learned it means a lot.

The babies are perfect, whether pink or blue,
with the best of me and the heart of you.

So as we leave, you will always be knowing,
the family that you had, just started growing.

Patsye Heinrich

Words Are Magic

Fairies of brightness, imps of the night,
They seldom are idle, though never in sight.

Serving the world, making it nicer,
Bewildering all, as would an enticer —

Small, happy elves, they patiently wait
To patch up the fights, some like to create;

Jewels, that are strung, on fine silver chains,
Strengthen dear friendships, or blot out old pains;

Or words, just as swords, cut much deeper than steel,
They may make our wounds much harder to heal.

This is our language: Words which reveal
Pleasure or anguish, — And words that can heal.

Linda M. Feild

Assume

The signs blind them from the truth
They see only what they wish to view
All else is naught,
The light that shines upon them,
Does not shine upon the differences in life,
Or so they assume.

Darkness is evil.
Light is innocence.
The tainted are the impure souls;
The chaste are the pure;
Or so they assume.

Life is freedom,
Death is imprisonment,
Or so they assume!

Stephanie Greiner

Love letters to my soul

Love stains our glass windows with pride!
They audit the editing of great courage.
Their portrayals exploit Heaven's praise...of deep thoughts.
With shapes comparable to each valued gem.
Be as antique as they...in your spectacular debut.
Each view prunes the prismatic arias...of your life!
Landscaped; our moods examine these vibrant scenes...
Gift them as serenity within your soul.

They become as colors of each awed mood...
Each wends from the soil- as symbolic arias!
Each shining prism is from the heart.
Entering clouds to become moods of desire.

Be love- tremble with the enchantment of her blooms!
Share...enter only the colorful dreams- the moon!
You have become the armor of sleeping dreams.
Each avenue- a sleeping dream within a soul.
You! YOU became the mood for the angels' goals!
At last...you are the sky hued views...as...
The birth of creativity entering life's kingly hues.

Patricia Flynn Mancini

No Shame!

The sun beams upon his back as he wanders aimlessly.
They stop and stare and question his boldness.
He smiles...carefree loose and secure.
The only thing that reminds him of his nakedness
Is the warmth beneath his feet as he carries on.

Lisa Wu

One Of A Kind In My Heart And Mind

In the secret corridors of my heart,
There is no other....

Through the good times or the bad, happy or
sad, there is no other...

In the eye of the storm when communication
is gone, there is no other....

When I leave in the night because we had
a fight, there is no other...

When men are falling at my feet and try to
get my sweets, I have a silly grin, for I know within,
that I'm taking it home to him

So with a twist and a spin I leave them in the gin
For there is no other....

Venitta Lateer

Pictures

The pictures on my wall are like memories.
They hang there so quietly, as if to say,
"Remember me?"
When you walk by a picture
they seem to shine so brightly that
You can't help but look at them.
And, then, you wonder,
"How did they know I had forgotten?"
But this is how they are,
Forever reminding us
of those long ago times.

Rachel Steelman

Gangs

I hate gangs, they are bad.
They kill many people and make me sad.

Black Diamonds, Vice Lords, Latin Kings
Bad luck is all they ever bring.

Many carry beepers so they can be found
When they're dealing drugs or just hangin' around.

They'll blow you six feet underground
And they'll guarantee you won't be found.

Flashing signs is a big deal too.
JNCO clothes and Fila shoes.

They're in high schools far and near
Making students learn in fear.

Duke, Orlando, and L.A.
These baseball caps are not okay.

Why do the gangs always have to fight?
If they didn't, we'd be alright.

Laurie Christofano

Being Different Is Beautiful

Black
white
yellow, red
IT'S JUST A COLOR

Jewish, Catholic, Quaker, Buddhist
IT'S JUST A RELIGION

Millionaire
being well off
just making it poor
IT'S JUST A SOCIAL CLASS

"DON'T JUDGE A BOOK BY ITS COVER"
YOU ALL HEARD IT - DO YOU PRACTICE IT?
Try to look into the person's soul

Straight, bi-sexual, gay SO WHAT
If you think about it we are all
different in some unique way
DIFFERENCE is the USA
IF YOU DON'T LIKE IT - GET OUT

BECAUSE DIFFERENCE IS BEAUTIFUL
inspired by the play "THE UNCLEAN"

Irene Mulvihill

507

On Losing A Loved One

The shock and the grieving,
The pain never leaving,
The hardness of knowing
What should never have been,

The tears in the night,
The fears and the fright,
The bitter regrets
And the futile recounting.

The tiredness, the numbness,
The unbearable sadness
Of finally accepting an ending
Lead to beginning a mending.

Now stretch ahead
All knowledge for learning,
A living for earning,
Loved ones for caring,
Music for sharing,
Sunsets for seeing and
Efforts for being myself once again.

Dorothy Davis Reaves

Mall Work

I've got the bus to catch
The pants to match.
The socks to exchange
My hair to rearrange.
The sweater to return
The prices to learn.
Then the skirt to buy
The shoes to dye.
I've got the blouse to choose
My money not to loose.
The dress to dry clean
The jacket that needs to be seen.
There is jewelry to browse
And the credit card machines to arouse.

What? It's closing time!
But, I haven't even spent a dime.

No fear, no sorrow,
There is always tomorrow...

Emily Seto

Reason To Exist

Clearly you know
The reason that I live
And why that so easily
My life I would give

I have at long last
Found my meaning on earth
God knew you'd be mine
From the moment of birth

He sent you to me
From the wings of a dove
And you flew down from heaven
For me to find love

I know we were destined
To have and to hold
There is no question my darling
You are my pot of gold

So, there's no need to ask
For whom I would die
For I would pass happily
Just knowing you're nigh

Chris McKown

The Sacrificial Lamb

He came from Heaven
the sacrificial Lamb of God
To bear Adam's sin
through the atonement of his blood.

Drawn by God's Spirit
to lonely Calvary's hillside
There I beheld Him
the Lamb of God crucified.

Each unfolding scene
convinced my heart God loved me
For there, His dear Son
bore my sins upon the tree.

My heart wept inside
as I realized 'twas my sin
That caused Christ to die
so I could have life through Him.

Through the atonement
of the sacrificial Lamb
God grants full pardon
to the children of Adam.

Edward M. Williams

"If"

If I could see
The sand not just
To see
If I could hear
the water not just
To hear
If I could swim
the ocean not
Just to swim
If I could feel
my heart not just
To feel
If I could fly
Not just to fly
let me be myself
And just live
With the Lord
That's the only
Way I could
Live. "If" Amen

Alonda Marie Smith

Would I

If I wanted to be a bird flying
the sky what kind of bird would I?

To be a red cardinal with my head
held high my red velvet coat I would
not be shy.

A robin singing in a cherry blossom
tree swinging back and forth with a
push of a breeze, building nests for
little ones, an everyday worker I'd
be. A long wiggly worm from the ground
to feed.

But, if I was a big ole hawk soaring
high in the sky I'd be in control
wouldn't I? King or queen of the sky!

A flashy yellow canary flittering
around a flowery flower bed resting
on a daisy head, then a dive in a
bird bath flittering and fluttering.

What kind of bird would I?

Joan A. Hartman

Foster Falls

Softened by the friction
The stops and starts
seem endless
Caught sometimes by
the very current
that most times carries me
Freed in the twilight
by a single bead of river
To make my way in the
tumbling clear
Rushing by
But with purpose
Falling over the edge
Not to die
But to live
Becoming a part of something
bigger than the stream
from which I came.

Janet Ivey

Pleasures

As the trees whistle in the wind,
the sun shadowing over the fields
of pleasures, listen to the bees buzz,
and the birds hum. As you sit in
the middle of a field in your
light shaded hat, you fall asleep,
and when you awake it is night,
everything is gone, but as you grow
older it falls back in place; you
remember it all, and it seems like you're
younger all over again.

Holly R. Llewellyn

A Sigh From The Heart

Night has fallen
The sun shall sleep
The moon comes out
So the children won't weep

Mother sighs from a day that was long
It isn't far before the dawn

The children will awake
All rested I assure
to do the things that they prefer

Mother awakes Not rested I assure, to do
Something she does not prefer

But love is how we make it through
To raise our children to be kind and true

Yet the sun will still rise
The moon will glow
Take the time to watch your children grow

Cathy M. Krostue

Drugs

The bottomless pit,
The dying wit,
The loss of spirit,
No one can hear it.
The empty souls,
The undying roles,
Where does it all lead?

The future, lost.
For what cost?
Your life.

Jennifer McWhirter

"Michelle"

Don't cry for me now I'm gone
the time to cry has passed,
for something of such inner
beauty seldom ever lasts.
Instead go on and in my name
change this wretched place,
make it clean, make it pure and
above all make it safe.
For if through my death I motivate,
I would not have died in vain.
If through my death I save this world,
it would have been worth my pain
so please go on and do all you can
to save this lovely place, and the
next time you hear a Robin's Song
you'll see my smiling face.

Evangeline Cameron

The Boy

Bird wings were always mended;
The toads were few and small;
But, jumping out a window
To him was quite a "ball."

Batteries leaking acid
Came hidden through the house;
If holes appeared in carpets-
"It must have been a mouse."

Growing from child to adult,
He's stumbled but tried again.
His thoughts confused, he'll question
The set-backs that never end.

He's made of guts and laughter,
This boy of mine, I'll shout.
He'll make the life he's after
Or know what it's all about.

Doris Akin

Trees

The sky is blue
the tree is green
the birds are flying in the sky
it is winter and the leaves
are falling from the trees
and they are every where
the tree droops as is sadden
By their loss.

But, I am happy because
I know the trees will soon
I rejoicing for spring is
just around the corner.

Julie Hunter

Untitled

A Birth! The miraculous product of
   the pairing of two lovers
   darkened by a dull, throbbing despair
   and a careless drunken madness,
   gave life to love,
Unequivocal love.

This child, who sucks the world
   from his mother's breasts—
   a nectar sweetly tainted
   with a mixture of lethal compounds
   Anger and joy.
Beware the Anger.
Cradle the joy.

Jennie McDonald

My Heart

Jealousy will keep us together
The truth will pull us apart
Love will see us through
They all come from the heart

Kisses tell you who I am
Hugs tell you how I feel
Love will make the difference
The feelings are all very real

Eyes see the true hurt
Hands heal the pain
Feet lead you to the cause
To start the cycle over again

The world has its pleasures
The sky has its clouds
My heart has its needs
To scream the pain out loud

Loraine

Deceived Heart

Alone in the dark
the two lovers meet
kissing and embracing
in passion and heat

Words never spoken
fears thrown aside
alone no longer
there's nothing to hide

No secrets kept
every feeling let out
they no longer reject
there are no doubts

Whispering softly
sweet nothings and words
out jumps the deceived
everything discovered, and all heard

Revealing every lie
the deceived feels pain
a tear falls from her eye,
she goes insane...

Chrissy Kraus

What To Do

It was a cold and stormy night
The waves were rising high
You called to say you could not come
You had to say goodbye

I asked you what I was to do
You said you did not care
"Did I do something wrong?" I asked
I knew it was not fair

Then silence came across the line
You said you had to go
I didn't say a word to you
I knew my pain you would show

I went to walk along the beach
The rain was not as strong
I thought of our relationship
Where did it all go wrong

I will not bother you again.
So go along your way
Don't think about my broken heart
My heart will mend someday

Elizabeth DiPasquale

A Poem For Mankind

If I could have at my command,
The will to make man understand,
That prejudice and bitter hate,
Can only bring him loss of faith.

I'd will it that in every land,
Man work together, hand in hand.
No matter what his tone of skin,
Or how he prays down deep within.

No greed for power in my plan,
No envy of his fellowman.
With love and trust for everyone,
As God intended to be done.

Though being mortal as I am,
I cannot force my will on man.

Anne McCue

Spring

What is peeping from beneath
   The woodland soil
Violets, coming to greet the
   Merry Springtime.

The gay young birds have come
   From the far south
The trees have burst into buds
   Spring time has come.

Happy children run and play
   In the warm sunshine
Birds are singing from the treetops
   Greeting young Spring.

The brook sings its merry song,
   Greeting birds that come
As it runs along the woodland path
   In the Spring time

The air is full of perfume,
   The sweet fragrance
Is scattered through the woods
   In the sweet Springtime!

Harriett Voigt

Untitled

Lost in his eyes I knew
   the words that would
   pour from his lips,
   "I love you to life,
   for our love is
   eternal stronger than
   death."

From that moment on
   I knew I could never
   leave his eyes and he
   would never leave my
   heart.

Julie Coates

A Change In Life

The world is pretty much
the same as we see it,
but people aren't as we speak
of it; why is that so?
The answer I do not know.
The world as you can see
has a change in life,
from time after time,
they say it as they might.

Irasema Saenz

La Mort Ny Mord (Death Bites Not)

It is time I found...
The words to say.
It's been so long...
Since the day...

I have wandered the nights... alone.
I have always wanted....
Just to phone.

I have tried to talk...
To you.
But the words come...
So dark and blue.

So now...
So now...

I'll fold my hands.... to rest.
I have ran the full race...
For a moment I had the best.

I wish to sleep eternally...
With you in my thoughts.
And so for me... death bites not.

And so for me... death bites not.

Clay A. Carey

"Little Miss Perfect"

She walked down the halls, lights
them up as she goes by with her
friends, "Little Miss Perfect, Little
Miss Perfect" some girls tease.
    Who wouldn't think this when the
guys adore her, and the girls worshipped
her, perfect grades, and a rich daddy.
    But, she doesn't feel "perfect" on hot
summer nights when she locks the
door, curls up, and cries. But she
doesn't cry tears of happiness, but,
not really tears of sadness. They were
tears of pain and confusion, tears
that burned as they trickled down
her face.
    For she had a secret that she
kept in the corner of her mind. As the
girls all teased.
    "Little Miss Perfect, Little
Miss Perfect."

Alyssa Aide Vela

Love Is A Crime

If love is a crime
Then I'm guilty as charged
So I shall do the time
for the crime I've been charged
If the sentence is exile
I'll be gone for awhile
I will miss you a great deal
So save me a great meal
So when I return I hope you'll be there
Waiting just for me
If love is a crime
Then I'm guilty as charged
So I shall do the time
For the crime I've been charged
If the sentence for love is death
Then I shall take my love for you
And bury it deep in the ground
You know my love for you is true
'Cause you know I would die for you

David Fallon

Weeping Willow

A tear runs down the willow tree,
Then softly hits the ground;
The tear is full of heavy thoughts,
Yet hardly makes a sound.

It is pulled deep under the soil
To a place as dark as hell;
A grave-like silence greets it there,
But why it cannot tell.

It turns around, finds no way out,
The force is much too strong;
It settles down, embracing Hope,
Aware the force is wrong.

"Hold on, little Tear!
There are other forces near;
Have faith, little tear —
Hell cannot keep you here."

Erika Bruns

"What Have We Done?"

First came the Wars
Then the Big Bombs
Marching in Streets
Rivers of gore
Tears by the Tub
Mothers in Anguish
Gone was their Youth
Gone was the land....

"The Wall is Down.
"The Treaties are Signed.
Hurrah for Peace Makers
They're all on our side."

"What? No bread on the shelf?
What? No meat for the stew?
How will we manage?
What are we to do?"
Who sold them Democracy
without any teaching?
Now we must feed them.
What have we done?

Evelyn Kilgore

"Her Name Is Claire"

God meant it to be
This child and me
I remember the day
That I found her

Wanted, it said
Loving care for my baby girl
Yes, yes, I can do that
And I hurried to call

Then the meeting
There she was
Precious from the first
A big smile to greet me
And a dimple too!

Beautiful baby girl
I thought
And a pretty momma too
Lovely, sweet smile
Gentle eyes...
"Her name is Claire"

Jane LaChance

Thoughts

Inside this head
There are thoughts,
Thoughts of peace,
Thoughts of war,
Thoughts of hate and greed.
Some thoughts are good,
Some are bad.
I have thoughts of death,
I have thoughts of life.
The most important though
That I ever thought
Is Love!
No matter - Friends
Family or any
Life.

Chad Mayhew

The Journey

A curious blur
There is a change in course
Feelings start to stir
Oh, what a timeless force!

Two boats idling
Alike in many ways
Growth is beginning
What bright beautiful days!

They come together
Setting waters on fire
Trust one another
The future's your desire!

The sea pulls at seams
Testing integrity
Talk of hopes and dreams
Love's for eternity!

Blake Roy Vrooman

We

We look a little different from you
    therefore, we are outcasts.
We speak differently than you
    therefore, we are not normal.
We have a different opinion than you
    therefore, we are the ones wrong.
Who are you to play God?
Who are you to be the ones to judge?

We do not like to fight
    therefore, we are the cowards.
We might not understand right away
    therefore, we are the stupid ones.
We might like to be alone at times
    therefore, we are the strange ones.
Who are you to play God?
Who are you to be the ones to judge?

Judith K. Pistilli

Life

Love, hate; friends, enemies.
These are all parts of life.
Frustration and aggravation, both
never fun, but always teaches
you something.
Happiness, sadness; what do they
have in common, they are
unpredictable feelings.
These feelings, what wonderful
feelings; you can have them all at once.

Cristina M. Phillips

510

To Jeannine On Her Wedding Day

As I leave my mother's house
There's a tear upon her eye
As she quickly glances back
At the years that have flown by.

As I leave my father's house
There's a sadness in his smile
Looking at a grown-up daughter
Who just stayed a little while.

As I leave my parents' house
There are tears upon my eyes
Both of happiness and sadness
As I say my last good-byes.

Carmen Trasvina

Continued Thoughts

Why am I thinking,
These thoughts that I have?
If anyone knew,
I'm sure they would laugh.
I shouldn't tell,
Or else they will see,
What's in my head,
And what's wrong with me.
So I keep it a secret,
That only I know.
And my crazy thoughts,
Continue to grow.

Jessyca Joy Fell

Untitled

Leave this heart of mine
These vile thoughts of anger
Let the blackness enfold me
Like a cold cellar empty
except for footsteps of the past,
Brushed away like cobwebs from
a hollow tomb.
Let me start anew like the
reflection of the sunrise upon
a rushing stream.
Let me rejoice in freedom of
chance, like a sculptured pattern
of my own making.
Let hatred be left in its own
Stench, let silence calm the rage
and time give hope in my own beginning.

Cory Roybal

Ode To Nell

She is committed to the earth,
This lady who from birth
Was destined to a different fate
Than ordinary people rate.

She never let strife get her down,
As though a formula she'd found
For facing life with a song
As she moved gallantly along.

To her friends happiness she spread,
Never dwelling or gloom or dread.
She always knew just what to say
To help to brighten up one's day.

Often Nell will come to our mind;
But when she does we'll find
It will be happy thoughts she brings
To us of this world's finer things.

Jean Young

The Praying Hands

They are not just hands for praying,
They are hands for healing you.
Not just hands to heal your body,
But to heal your spirit, too.

They are hands that can move mountains
or hold a mustard seed
They are hands that can part the waters
that can save both you and me

They are hands that are so tender
With their love for you and me.
They are hands that are so strong
when our burdens they lift free.

They are hands that are scarred by nails
When He hung upon the cross.
They are hands that shed the blood;
For our sins they paid the cost.

They are hands that are so sacred.
And we should never forget.
They are the hands of Christ our Savior,
They are the hands that paid our debt.

Charles W. Spurling

"Office Hours"

Office hours, seem to me like days
They go by very slow
Makes you wonder why so
And it keeps poor me in a haze
You're sitting at your desk
With your hand on your chin
You never seem to rest
Till the day's at its end
Office hours, I will never crave
Even though they seem to me, like days

John Hanlon

At Death Door

My three brothers were seen no more
They were gone as of yore,
They left me so they could soar.
I could be no lower
For I feel so much more poorer.

Joyce Brewer

I Ask?

The doors never open.
They're always closed.
Give us the key, to unlock
what the future holds.
We're outside in the dark,
the cold.
No one will help us.
We're all alone.
Give us drugs......
Our pain will go away.
F—k this world of anger and hate!
No one cares! No one cares!
There is no answer.
No one cares!
What to do! We don't know.
Evil is around us, we walk alone.
Among us there is love.
Inside we feel fear.
We are helpless.
I ask, why are we here?

Crystal Fox

"Have I Ever Shown You My Stars"

Have I ever shown you my stars?
They're out back atop the hill.
Seven shining sisters
Always asking; why?
My eyes can find no answer.

Do you wish to hear my music?
It's the cup that holds my soul.
Loving, Laughing, Crying,
A mirror to my past
My ears alone can hear.

Have you ever touched my summer rains?
They're the keepers of my childhood.
The saturated smell of memories,
Of better and of bad.
My nose has never shared them.

Have you ever felt my earth?
Wrapped it 'round your heart and soul?
Naked, New, Free, Native,
Alive and Awake!
My hands are covered with dirt.

Greg Meade

If I Had Wings

If I had wings I'd swiftly fly
Through the azure colored starry sky
I'd learn where all the small clouds hide
And find where twinkling stars abide

I'd travel on the milky way
With gentle breezes gaily play
So close to Heaven's door I'd stay
As I viewed Earth so far away

My earthly cared I'd leave behind
As new Horizons I would find
Near Heaven, close to the Divine
I'd find Life of another kind

In Rapture I would higher soar
Closer to God and the Heaven's Door
And I'd return to Earth no more
But with my Wings Heavens explore

If I had Wings I'd swiftly fly
On the crest of Wings beyond the sky
And greet the Angels passing by
Reach that Place where people Never Die

Helen Gleason

"I Shall My Lord"

In the midst of my heart
Thy words I shall preserve...
I shall not boast of vain glory,
For all the glory - Lord, you deserve...
I shall seek wisdom and understanding,
I shall embrace them night and day,
I shall ponder the path of thy feet,
As you my Lord - establish my way...
I shall take fast hold of instruction,
All your sayings - I shall believe.
With an open mind and open heart,
You my Lord - I shall receive...
I shall attend to thy words.
I shall incline mine ears to hear.
I shall serve thee with all diligence.
And of the wicked - I shall not fear...
I shall walk down the lighted path
That you my Lord, have lit for me,
And as I reach that source of brightness,
There my Lord, I know you'll be...

Daniel Lee Crabb

Forgive Me Poem

Mom,
This is
to let
you know

I wasted
the perfume
that was
in your drawer

The one
you
probably
need to
smell good

Forgive me,
it was fun
making potions
and feeling like
a scientist.

Alex Tran

Dreams

Among the heavens, among
   this land
I walk along barefoot
   to reach my dreams
I feel my chances
   oozing between my toes
I feel the joy splashing
   upon my feet
I feel the loneliness pull
   at my leg
I feel the sadness
   pound against my heal
I continue to walk
   bare foot among this land
I continue to dream silently,
   wishing my life and dreams away

Jenifer Burnside

Solitude

How blest
This place of solitude;
How filled with magic;
The magic of a dream conceived,
To be fulfilled
In God's time
as He wills;
But I shall follow after it
Pursue it
Till at last
as He wills
It becomes reality.

Helen Howell

Springtime

The grass is growing,
The water is flowing,
Green leaves are budding
And flowers are too.
Winter is over and the fun has started,
As spring has begun anew.

Animals are coming alive,
Spring break is nearby.
Children are playing,
And so am I.
When spring is finally here.

Erin Light

The Dieter's Prayer

Lord, keep me honest
Through my plight
This battle of the bulge
Is really a fight.

The whole day long
Food beckons me
Until I give in
To gluttony.

It seems if I hide
In a closet to chew it
It's almost as if
I didn't do it.

But lo and behold,
The next day it's there
And again I begin
The dieter's prayer.

Jan DeVine

Lone Sentry

Subtle change from Summer green
Through yellow, brown, then dry
The oak tree mantle comes to earth
Bare branches scratch the sky

But far above the covered sod
Where crow and blackbird sway
A single leaf remains in place
To stand watch night and day

Visible to all
Noticed by no one

In shortened light of Winter's time
Through dreary, frozen rains
In swirling snow and twisting wind
The treetop star remains

With Springtime warmth and gentle breeze
As life starts to abound
The task is done, the banner falls
A leaf floats to the ground

Visible to all
Noticed by no one

Dick Kisielewski

Coffin Dreams

Love gushes through me
through my heart and my soul,
but all I can feel
is the pain of untold.

Red saturates the cloth
that covers my eyes,
but only a rose
is clenched, from your lies.

First I sleep
in darkness of cold,
then I wake
for soon I'll behold.

Behold the magic
of life after death,
but still I wonder
with each torturous breath.

The moonlight's sunken
beneath the crest of the sky,
but still I ponder,
will they ever reply?

Ariana Nunes

Oceans Of Tears

A flood begins with a single drop
Thundering down
Breaking on contact with the soil
Others follow
Spreading throughout the land
Sharing
Dividing to every grain of sand
Honest pieces
Until there is no more
Emptiness
Then they stop falling
Completion
The sun comes out
But it will rain again.

Becky Wiechman

Endow Me

Endow me, Lord, that I may do
Thy will in every way,
Create in me a cleaner heart
Lest from thy path I stray.

Endow me, Lord, with strength enough
The tempter to withstand,
Increase my courage day by day,
Hold fast my trembling hand.

Endow me, Lord, with love until
My cup doth overflow,
And spreads to touch my brother's heart
That He thy joy will know.

Endow me, Lord, with peace of mind
When at day's end I rest,
And count the many ways that I
Through thy grace have been blessed.

Jo Ann Walker

The Good Of A Cane

The full good of a cane I never knew
'Til I was told by Daniel
When he was two.
I had thought of canes,
Therapeutic and such
Other than that
Not very much.
   BUT
The crook of a cane
Is made for a ball
If lost under a chair,
A cane can recall.
Whatever you imagine,
Whatever you doubt,
With a cane you can be
What you can't be, without.
Keep me aware, oh Lord,
My whole life through,
Of the wisdom you give
To children of two.

Esther Walser

Why

As the coming of night,
there is always a fight,
I don't know why,
But there's always a lie,
The fight made the smiles be gone,
maybe they'll be back at dawn

Heather Kelly

On Western Nebraska

I never knew what moonlight was
'Til now.
Or what it meant to love a hill
Or look for peace among the stars.

I didn't know a loneliness
So deep
Could lead the way to beauty -
And to God.

Frances H. Keevil

Climb On

Just keep climbing
Till you reach the top
Don't look back now,
When you hear a pin drop.

Mountains are steep
And the cliffs are unsure
But just keep climbing
You must learn to endure.

When you reach the top,
Remember to take care
For all good things in life
Are received through prayer.

Eddie E. Johnson

The Unknown Song

I have heard it in the
timepiece next to the ocean.
Listen as the next solicitation is you.
Will you rejoin the controversy, or not?
The lights are on you.
You're surrounded in the pit of pity.
You cannot run, you cannot hide.
This is one on one.
The darkened crow elapses behind you.
The avis drops blood as he goes.
Your time ticks on.
The light at the end of the realm is gone.
Return to the planet, be my guest.
Make your move.
It will find you.
Do not be anxious.
For your enemy,
For your friend,
For your death,
Is nothing more than, yourself.

Alison Dewhurst

"Be With Me"

Be with me though I be not well
Through the ages we've come
to dwell,
When midnight passes
and the darkness still masses,
wait the hours 'til dawn.
Be with me from which you
are drawn,
On rainy days
Down sunny lanes,
be with me
to the clouds above
from the valley of love,
from birth in the flesh
To the death which is no less.

Jessica Harris

My Leap Year Birthday

"How does it feel?" some people say,
"to be born on Leap Year Day?"
I've pondered it for quite a while,
"depends which year," then I smile.

A Leap Year birth's unique you see,
it's part of my destiny.
Front page headlines told of my birth,
a good way to begin — life on earth.

My Aunt said when I acted bad,
"act your age, don't crawl," she'd add.
When kids would ask, "How old are you?"
I'd reply, "I'm only two."

At sixteen I had only four,
birthday candles, not one more.
This year things worked out fine,
my son and I, both are nine.

Next year at forty, once again,
my son and I, both turn ten.
For a hundred years, I will strive,
to become just — twenty-five.

Brenda Lee Williams

Moonlight

The crowded day lilies
to be confused yet continue blooming
and scatter as a mental dream
of each other pride.

The cover of wild daisies
in the meadow of one surface,
being I, death dance that softly fly
up to the heaven, or

As of that's the hell,
bloody full moon clearly be there
for, rescue rising in the time
and he knows the moonlight.

Donna H. Varner

Children

Children are like bubbles
They're here and then they're gone
We need these gifts from God though
They help us carry on

What should a child be
I say anything at all
What they shouldn't be is ridiculed
They should always stand up tall

If you should ever have children
Hold them each close to your heart
Love them like there is no tomorrow
Because you do not know when you'll part

Bradley E. Kort

Blue Night

I've held hands with the blue night
    too many times.
His grip would not release.
Loneliness wrapped cold arms around me
    and squeezed.
While the stars danced
    in my drowning eyes.
And the moon inched her way out of view.

Deborah L. Klocke

Weird Tales

Weird tales and weirder still
    To cats a woman gave her will
Weirder yet and weirder more
    To dogs a man gave a million four
Once more, a wayward will
    To a man's wife made it clear
His pet snake's life is sure at stake
    Ten thousand mice, two dollars each
But to the poor woman, not a wit.

Weird tales and weirder still
    A crocodile gets a coupe de ville
A lonesome bachelor to an exotic bird
    Left his mansion worth unheard.
Weird yet and weirder more
    A Poet to a raven had the gall
Pledged his love forevermore.

Alexis Balunsat

"The Inner Softness"

God built me sturdy and strong,
To deal with life,
Its rights and wrongs.

As tough as I may seem,
I have a softness in my heart,
But I sometimes keep it hidden,
Even make it live apart.

It's only for you,
This special space,
Most men don't admit it,
But in me there is such a place.

As long as you know
That I have it there,
I'll be strong for myself,
But for you I'll always care.

I am a hurricane,
I am also the calm,
I can crush you with my strength,
Or gently hold you in my arms.
"I love you."

James R. Watlington

Do Not Wait Till Tomorrow

Do not wait till tomorrow
    To do the work of today,
To offer words of kindness
    Or some favor to convey.

Do not postpone till later
    The sharing of friendship's joy;
Love is a priceless treasure
    That death can quickly destroy.

Do not save for the future
    Your most cherished dream or goal;
This very night your Maker
    May require of you your soul.

Make real today what visions
    The spirit boldly implants;
Don't allow them to languish -
    There might be no second chance.

Set your heart to the business
    Of making each day your best.
Do all you're able to do;
    God will attend to the rest.

Craig L. Teed

Your Creative Mind

A cluttered mind hampers your creativity,
  To explore unbounded infinity.
Release shackled refuse and debris.
  Allow new visions to unfold naturally,
To accelerate and propel global society.

Eleanor Lynar-Cohen

"The Wishing Star"

Here I am this night
  To find my light,
over the oceans and over the land
over the sparrows and the sand.

Here I am this night
  to find something bright,
over the sea and over the trees...
  into the breeze.

Here I am this night
  now I found my sight,
a star all through the night

Now I am here all safe and clear
  as I wished
    A MAGIC THING CAME OVER ME!!!

The Star spoke and said:

  "Your love gave me happiness
    as you set me free...
  YOU ARE NOW AT THE TOP."

Jacqueline Jerez

Confidence

It's seeming
to get better.
Yet my eyes
Seem to get wetter.
The pain and sorrow
I feel everyday
makes me lose
confidence to pray.
I always seem
to feel down,
but I face the world
with my beautiful crown.
Then I walk forward
and I always say
"It's gonna get better,
so let me pray."

Anita Vazquez

Touch Me

Touch me and we'll fly
  together like the wind
  across the sky.

Soaring forever through tears of pain
  that fall like rain.
  Touch me
  and the sun will shine again.

Your touch, like lightening,
  it ignites me,
  and together we'll roll like thunder,
  over and over until...
  the storm is over,
  and our world is still.

Touch me once more,
  and again we'll soar.

Audrea Johnson

Another Glimmer Has Returned

In Memory of William Bennett
Another glimmer has returned
  To its native star,
Having here so brightly burned
  And flown, but never too far.

As it proclaims not the end
  Of a brief story,
But asks where the night must send
  Each soul, if in glory

They are then to awaken
  From this light slumber,
Or only to be taken,
  Subtracted as a number.

Like the One who was raised
  Though He seemed to fall
To death's darkness; oh, that God
  Has mercy on us all.

For another glimmer has returned
  To its native star,
Having here so brightly burned
  And flown, but never too far.

Andre Valdez

Come With Me

Come with me
To land, sky and sea
White cows are content
A love note is sent
Fish bring in the tide
True ebony birds glide
Come with me
To land, sky and sea
Diamond leaves with dew
Sprites, mermaids are few
Pink clouds a heap
Dancing frogs do leap
Come with me
To land, sky and sea
Sing a crayon picture tale
Of rain falls in the vale
Violet poems not penned
Philosophers speak of the end.
Come with me
To land, sky and sea

Fayellen Sanetra

Is Anyone There?

I feel I'm alone,
trapped in space.
Then I look around,
and see only a face.
There's something I need,
something I yearn.
It scares me though,
and it makes my heart burn.
It's not to be alone,
not to be scared.
It's to have back,
that someone who once cared.
Yes I do love you,
my heart took a turn.
Just teach me again,
I promise to learn.
I really do love you,
and I'll always care.
Are you listening to me,
Is anyone there?

Cortney Hardaway

Colors

Colors serve in varied ways
To lift our hearts and capture praise
Nature calls them forth in duty
Permeating realms of beauty

Decorating all creation
With God's generous oblation
Bringing charm to common sight
Sending dullness into flight

Multiplying shades and hues
Changing ordinary views
Wooing romance to the eyes
Giving birth to many sighs

Tantalizing just one sense
Whether pale or most intense
Not for taste or touch or smell
Never heard, but serving well

Indeed a marvel one would miss
God must have sealed them with a kiss
For colors serve in varied ways
To lift our hearts and capture praise

Carol Ann Davis

The Trip Of Life

I walk a maze of fog
To reach my dream
I walk on hot coals
To stop the hurt and pain
I climb a steep mountain
To do my absolute best
Then I tumble into the valley
To my future destiny
I walk to the river
To wash away the tears and sweat
Of my trip

Carla Jenkins

A Time To Remember

As I sit here and look at you
to remember us doesn't
bring tears but a smile, to have
had you and lost you, I'm glad
to have found you, to have had
a time to remember. When you
were to hold my hand or whisper
I'll love you always, I wished
it always would be like that
but as a matter of fact it
can always be, as long as
I carry memories of you and me.

Jennifer Kay Miller

Whirlwind

A whirlwind of life's memories pass by
Too quick to indulge
While you lie beneath six feet of dirt
Feeling nothing
Existing just the same
So many voices from above you hear
Some crying for you
Others not caring for you
Crying out
No one hears you but you
This is what dying is
Still part of the big picture
But now just a whirlwind
Swirling without recognition.

Jennifer Lynne Hubbard

I Will Never Leave Thee Nor Forsake Thee

When God permits the troubles sore,
to wash along life's shore,
WHEN BREAKERS CRASH AND
TROUBLES ROAR,

Christ my Lord is standing near
and whispers "Peace for I am here!"

We merely weep when we can't see
the reason why things happen to me!
For troubles we would gladly flee.
But a calm voice whispers, "Never fear
you're not alone, for I am here!"

But we do forget and fail to see
when the sun shines on you and me,
that good times have no warrantee.
Again the voice so calm and dear,
"Fear not my child for I am here!
I will not leave you all alone;
life's path with troubles is bestrode,
these you cannot handle all alone,
attune your ear and do not fear,

you're not alone, for I am here!"

Berniece Shults

Maybe Today

Yesterday you went away
Today is just another day
Tomorrow will you still be gone
Or will you be doing me wrong?
Maybe today I'll see you again
but it won't be me you're hugging
Maybe today I'll ignore you
Maybe I'll be looking at someone new
Tomorrow my memory of you will be deleted
So I can go on and get my life completed
Maybe I'll find a man
And for you I won't give a damn
And if you see us together
You'll know that you've lost me forever
I hope you wish that you
Should've never done me wrong
So you can feel the pain I've held
inside me all year long.

Angela Delgado

The Griffin's Flight

Do not stop the Griffin's flight.
Unbind her feathery wings.
Set us both free of earthly plight.

Do not bind her legs so tight
with morality and sanctimonious bindings.
Do not stop the Griffin's flight.

Uncover her eyes that burn bright.
Let her see all true things.
Set us both free of earthly plight.

Let her piercing cry shed light,
and free my mortal being.
Do not stop the Griffin's flight.

She need not fight for right.
Her soul needs freeing.
Do not stop the Griffin's flight.

Let her soar in the night,
and dance with immortal beings.
Do not stop the Griffin's flight.
Set us both free of earthly plight.

Juanita Heady

An Audience Of One

The lies in your eyes
told the whole story.
Receiving forgiveness
gives God all the glory.
Bearing past burdens
too heavy to shake,
Memories too painful.
A soul; an earthquake.
Always running.
Never arriving.
Define living?
Define surviving?
Bloom, bury
peace, worry.
Divine deliverance,
believed by some.
Captive indifference,
Salvation is come.
Truths reflected, deceptions deflected.
Mercy from an audience of one.

Alida Mae Morton

Today And Tomorrow

Today we smile,
Tomorrow they cry,
Today we laugh,
Tomorrow they die.

We are selfish,
They are deprived,
We have everything,
All they have are their lives.

We never think,
They always do,
We should make a difference
And save them too.

Fiona Murphy

The Traveler

The Traveler, oh how he
travels in so many ways.
He can just sit and gaze.
He can go beyond the stars,
and yet, he has not traveled
very far. He can climb the
tallest mountain in just one
hour, but yet he only took
one single step, for as you can
see...if you're a traveler
like me, well then all you
have to do, is turn on your
TV and let your mind wander
as you sit and ponder......

Harold Michael McDonald

Dare To Discover

Something to uncover
treasures of gold and others,
of mysterious wonder,
gold coins and silver doubloons
diamond rings, a ruby gleams.
From the light of silver
strings, it is a treasure
room for you to ponder.
What other things do I
dare to discover.

Jesse McIntosh

Untitled

Caught between here and there
trying to find a way out.
And even though I'm totally aware
I still find myself down and out.
Can't seem to make any decisions
at the last minute I'm filled with doubt.
No matter what I'm doing
my mind is filled with you.
I can't get you out of my head
would someone please tell me what to do.
So many memories from the past
are still alive with me today.
There has got to be some time
when I'll be saved and they'll go away.
But then I stop and think
I've caused all my own bad breaks.
And then I've got to pray
will I ever learn from my mistakes?

Jerry Baker

What Is My Mind Like?

My mind is like a slippery worm,
Trying to get free,
From someone's strict, unwanted grasp,
Not letting me be me.

My mind is like a birthday gift,
No one knows what's inside
Until that special time arises,
When it's opened up with pride.

My mind is like a child's kite,
Flying smoothly in the air,
Then suddenly, it's out of reach,
Tangled in a doubt, somewhere.

My mind is like the weather,
'Cause it changes every day,
It might be bright and sunny,
Or dreary, drab, and gray.

My mind is like a favorite toy,
That nobody can touch,
It belongs to me, and only me,
And it's cherished very much.

Amanda Ziegelbauer

The Way You Treated Me

They warned me about cigarettes,
Vodka, Whiskey, and Beer.
But they never did warn me,
about loving you dear.

You treated me like a princess,
put me up on a throne.
But then you went and broke my heart
and left me all alone.

Remember how things used to be,
we'd laugh, and dance, and sing.
And everything went perfectly
'til you took back your ring.

Remember how we used to think
those nights would never end.
I think that now I've reached that point
of tired oblivion.

You want me to say, "I Love You,"
but I'll tell no more lies.
This time you've really pushed your luck,
I've said my last goodbyes.

Christina Johnson

"Perception"

He is corpulent
Twice married
Now thrice
No college
Darling of the right
Game show lady turns numbers
National celebrity
Are we all crazy?

Jack Catterson

"Life"

Like a dream,
    unable to be solved.
Life is so uncertain,
    and so involved.
When once we awaken,
    it all becomes clear;
    Life, death and why we're here.
    When we finally open our eyes to see,
Home to God is where we will be.

Cheryl L. Allison

A Beautiful Language

Slurring cyrillic syllables
    under her frosted breath
was utterly effortless for her,
    but it was sugar in my ear.

As she peered at me through
    her slight imperfection,
I created my own memories
    of eyes spying white picket fences
and young spirits glimmering behind
    her soft coal pupils.

I buried my face
    in her knotted back
only to be reminded
    by her tense physique
of what we truly have.
    Temporary safety in the form of
a down comforter and
    simple cyrillic syllables.

Bill McIndoo

A Gay May Wedding

It was a cool day in May
    under the canopy of white.
Everyone there was oh so gay,
    not a single look of spite.

At noon the Bride appeared
    all dressed in black.
The Groom then neared,
    he filled in the slack.

The young couple didn't falter
    as they approached the crowd.
The Preacher stood at the altar,
    he sure seemed proud.

The guests were so happy
    when the couple was united.
Mr. and Mr. J. D. Cappy,
    to the tent you are invited.

And so it was at last
    the gay couple wed.
Lord knows it hadn't been fast,
    and now a lifetime of dread.

June Harris

My Teen-Age Years

It's not enough to have a dream,
unless I'm willing to pursue it-
It's not enough to know what's right,
Unless I'm strong enough to do it-
It's not enough to join the crowd,
to be acknowledge and accepted—
I must be true to my ideals,
even if I'm excluded and rejected-
It's not enough to learn the truth
unless I also learn to live it-
It's not enough to reach for love
unless I care enough to give it-
It's not enough to reach for me
unless I learn to reach for you.

Christi Bowen

Props

Seated on his chair at his desk
until it was taken away;
Standing on his land
prior to the great drought;
Preaching from his pulpit
as long as they believed;
Actor
until freed.

John Burnham

Persephone

There had never been shadow
until the ground split
and a man and his chariot
rushed onto the field like something
spilling from the bowels of the earth.
Flesh burned from my bones
as he took me into
the underworld and the flowers
in my hair flamed like torches
in the gloom. I thought
everything lost, no more
dances or maidenhood. I thought
I would die in the arms of the king.
But a hunger ached my belly;
each pomegranate seed
I ate filled me, and I knew this was
the first moment I had
lived. My life opened
to the dark like a moon flower.
I became queen.

Heather Brown

The Rose

A rose is a rose....
    until you look at it.
It breathes like you.
It acts like you.
It looks like you.
It talks like you.
It has your troubles.
It cries like you.
It laughs like you.
Then you realize...
    It is you!
    But how?
You must find out.
You will not know...
    until you look in a rose.

Heather Satterfield

Ice Flows

All alone,
Upon a hill.
Where ice flows groan,
With the winter chill.

A baron frozen place,
Unmarked by time.
We can't erase,
Grandeur sublime.

Territory;
Untouched by man.
Like purgatory
Ice like shifting sand.

It makes one wonder.
It makes one small.
Cracking like thunder,
These icy walls.

Defying time,
An eternal peak.
Solace to find,
Heaven unique.

Bill Fleming

November Air

When the foul
    venomous smell
    of Scotch and Brandy
    rides
    on the waves
    of the
    November air.

Shapes of the
    furniture
    glimmers
    in darkness
    of early dawn.

And silence
    rides the winter waves
    speaking...echoing
    unspoken thoughts
    of anxiety, hurt, and loneliness.

There's only,
Jesus.

Ada Hall Mason

My Brother

Oh what fun we had on those
warm summer nights when you rode
me on the handle bars of your ten
speed bike. We were so young then
and our hearts were so light and this
old world was just about right as
you and I rode on your ten speed
bike. Oh! how we laughed and
loved one another; I am your sister
you are my brother.
Time has passed and we have
grown old; the nights are no
longer warm, they are lonely and
cold, but dear brother I think I
know why God called you home...
so you could be young again and
on warm summer nights you
could go riding on your ten speed
bike.

Jane B. Balay

Myself

I am mostly cheerful
Very seldom sad,

Sometimes I am down
And sometimes I am mad.

I am pretty nice
And not very mean,

I am never dirty
I'm always clean.

Sometimes I love to work
And sometimes not very much,

I don't like Math
Especially when it is tough.

I like cold weather
I don't enjoy the heat,

I love good food
Especially good meat.

This is a little bit about me
But, by far not all,

I'll end this poem
Before I climb the wall.

Brandon Smith

Sailing

Out of port
Wait for wind
Put up sails
Hope nothing fails

Silent it goes
Heeling to and fro
Time to come about
So wind blow

Wind ceases
Sailor's dilemma
Motor to start
Sail like a lark

Coming is the wind
Sails tight
Silent it goes
Into the night

Port bound
Sailing done
Until tomorrows
Full of sun

Claudia Olenick

The Waiting Room Blues

Anonymous faces in the room.
Waiting, as if for doom.
Fake music adding to the gloom.
Worn magazines proclaiming
Events long past.
Pages being turned too fast,
Thinking of the current event -
The possible discovery
Of an unmentionable disease
That cause unimaginable grief
In a life far too brief.
Wondering why others are here
In an attempt to block out fear.
Their faces yield no clues,
'Cause they got
The waiting room blues.

Howard L. Millman, Ph.D.

Female Crucifixion

Pleasure devours her mind pain
walks hand in hand Cripples her
wisdom till the dense calm of
nothing tells her the story of a
loss the anger comes quick raging
agony terror of the inhumane and
cruel things that had happened to
her She let him rape her Drowned
her - her job is done. The man's
wounds healed. The world looks to
her in shame - discuss while he
returns home with a medal of lust.
The war was one. The battle
undone her wisdom remains numb
history - time - repeats it is
still the female that is being
crucified

Anastasia Salazar

The Echo Of Empty

A tear in your eye
Was still frozen in place,
When the holidays came,
And the world filled with grace.

All the loves of your life
Had been taken away,
Still you struggled to make it
Through each festive day.

The lights were all bright,
Other hearts seemed to melt,
While you searched your dark self
For the joy you once felt.

Like the night that you laughed,
'Til your face ran with tears,
You never once thought
It would be your last year

And in stores carols played,
You thought much too loud,
But the echo of empty
Was the deafening sound.

Bernadine Dichiara

The Sunrise

Into the darkness I crept
Watching, waiting, wondering.

Into the darkness of my heart broken,
Into a thousand splintery fragments.

Into the darkness I crept
Wondering where hope has gone.
Wondering if I'll catch a ray of light
Before the sun sets upon me.

Into the Darkness I crept
Searching for my fear
Which I hide so well,
Even from myself.

Into the Darkness I crept
Until I found this fear
And ran head on into it,
Embracing it with both hands
Saying, "you can't have me anymore!"

Then I turned to look into
The sunrise,
And saw the beauty within.

Jim Kelley

Never Before

I have never felt this
way before. Is it because
I love him more? Before
he was just a friend, now
my love for him will
never end. I am so in
love I don't know what
to do. I kept my love a
secret, but he knew.
Now he won't talk to
me or even say a word, I
feel like running away
or flying like a bird.

Janine Mastantuono

Cocktail Lounge Blues

The front door opens,
We all turn to look.
Whether it's comrade or stranger,
Entering this friendly nook.

The ice cubes tumble,
The liquor splashes.
The bartender smiles,
And bats her eyelashes.

Just another night,
We've all paid our dues.
As we sit around and play,
The cocktail lounge blues.

James D. Brown

"Vietnam"

In a world of raging sin
   We are losing our manly kin
With their lives they do repay
   For freedom a half a world away.

We have our freedom
   And it isn't bad
But the dying sum
   Is what makes it sad.

Jesus died on the cross
   For us to live in Peace
Sit and ponder all the loss
   For deaths will never cease.

With our young men's lives
   Why must we pay
In search of freedom
   A half a world away.

Cheryl Lynn Simpson

A Gift Received

I've seen Montana's wide blue sky
When I was very young.
I've tasted Colorado's springs
like ice upon my tongue.
I've seen a mountain at fifty miles
so huge that it seemed near.
I've seen the miles of Kansas wheat
the bread that man holds dear.
I've seen the oceans east and west
that kiss our country's shores.
I've seen a hundred thousand sights
and I hope to see much more.
But never have I seen a sight
in any varied place.
That could compare with my first sight
of my newborn baby's face.

Bill Wilkins

"A Friend"

Whatever befalls us
We can bear
If we have a friend
Standing there

To hold our hand
And see us through
Life's difficult moments
That make us blue.

You were there when I needed you
Your hand touching mine
A friend in a crisis
You helped me though that time.

Thank you, friend
For giving so much
Love and support
With just a simple touch.

What ever befalls us
We can bear
If we have a friend
Standing there.

Gloria Jean Hill

Wholeness

When the days are gone,
we grow older and wiser.

The next day is a new beginning
to experience life.

The birds, the trees, the flowers,
all God's creations.

Why is it then that we can embrace
their beauty but cannot embrace the
beauty of each other?

Are we that vain or is it our
own blindness?

The integration of all is to be one.

God, help us all to embrace the
magnitude of each other.

For tomorrow may be just a vision
and life could pass us by.

Donna Christine Hatoway

He Rolls The Stone Away

We know we can sing this song.
We know the whole world can sing along.
We know we can feel the way they did
When the stone was rolled away.

The faith that they had back then
Is the faith that we can have again.
We show it by the gratitude we feel
For his rolling the stone away.

The peace that he gave back then
Is the peace we can call on once again.
It's the peace that only he can give
When he rolls the stone away.

He is mine today—
All I have to pray—
Is- "Lord, take my will today.
Lord, you have my will today"!

Jane Alice Redels

To My Dear Friend, Minnie

Through our happy lifetime
We live in different places.
And surely when we do that,
We see a lot of faces.

Some are rather nice to us
But some are quiet alarming.
And I feel I'm a lucky guy
To have a neighbor who is charming!

The neighbor I'm referring to
Is, you guessed it, Minnie McIntosh!
She brightened up the entire week
Who could ask for more, by gosh!

We're closing out the ninety-four
To a brand-new ninety-five
I'm glad that you're my neighbor
'Cause you make me feel alive!
"Happy New Year" Benny

Arthur Coudriet

The Battle Of Time

In The Battle Of Time
We may feel uncertain
or unsure
Of what the day may bring,
Scared of our decisions,
wishing on answers
Too hard to find,
but if you search his word
You will see.
It is true.
There was never a cloud
God couldn't shine through,
For the Lord is our salvation,
Giving us strength and hope,
Our protector and forever guiding light.
So cast your burdens on him.
Then the battle will have ended;
Peace and rejoicing is recommended,
Paradise has come.

Julie Daugherty

"Sitting On A Field Of An Empty Park"

In this world of no return,
we must take day by day,
and learn and realize
what God has given us.
Looking down, seeing the
shadows of the leaves on
the ground makes me
wonder if this will always
remain around.
And as the birds fly
happily above, I think of
love and wish I could
stay here forever!
In this world of being
together, with you as "one"
I started to realize
that you are like the
"Sun," shining on my face.
You bring me happiness
without a sight of "Loneliness!"

Cynthia Arantes

"The Love Of Brotherhood"

Heavy are the burdens
we share throughout each day,
Different lives and feelings
expressed in separate ways.

As we come to know the meaning
we grow with every stride,
Each day a repetition
like the ocean with its tide.

If we could walk together
and share more tenderness,
Down this life's twisting-rocky trail
the suffering could be less.

To walk with hope
and try to live an example that is good.
Reap the reward of caring,
and the love of brotherhood.

George David Frye

The Search

Taped to time
we stretch across
a space
lighting a moment
in a breath God blew.

We meet
and light to light
we wait for

something to happen
something to feel
something...

we go, we seek
we find
we don't
we go
we go
we go
we look
we hope to touch a piece of dream
from the abyss of tapeless time.

Jaqueline H. Becker

Caressed With Memories

We shared each other's gladness,
Wept each other's tears,
Walked together holding hands
Into our twilight years;
Bloomed where we were planted,
Lived a lovely dream,
Sailed our ship of happiness
On an endless stream
Of warmth and tender feelings;
Grew a little apprehensive
With realization that time grows short
And became more pensive.
Reflecting on adversities,
Good outweighed the bad;
We counted blessings, not the tears
When our hearts were sad.
Love that endures to give and share
Is never terminated;
They that live beyond the grave
Will never be separated.

Genevieve Locke Oliphant

On Unborn's Tale

Mommy and Daddy
were too young to tell
that I would be conceived
in a rundown motel.

She told him of her love
and she wanted to show it
but if she had known about me
she would have never done it.

Killing me
was what they thought they should do
I would be finished - I would be through.

What they didn't know
is that I was "alive"
God had a plan for me
and of that they deprived.

But don't worry about me
because of their selfish quest
I am with Jesus now
and I am truly blessed.

Jennifer Nolen

Snow Daze

It was a cold, dark, snowy night;
What a beautiful sight.
The sky was very hazy;
The snow a beautiful white
The old, old houses silently sit;
How much colder will it get?
Snow on the rooftops;
Frost in the air.
It is very cold;
The trees are bare.
Soon it will be over;
No more icy streets of white.
Go ahead enjoy yourself,
Enjoy your Christmas night.
One day you'll wake and find
that all the world of white;
Has melted to a puddle,
Because spring is hangin' by.

Angel Collins

Backwards Tomorrow

I cannot remember
what a moment
said,
as it stood
locked
behind a plate-glass
photorealism.

I looked back
to a word
written in
splatter-paint
ink.

informal bow
in a paper box
with a
ribbon tied around
my finger,
to forget

a primrose dot
left behind by
yesterday.

Jeff Will

Guns And Roses

The sky screams, filth, filth and crud!
What God redeems dirt and mud?
His curses stream, into a flood.
A man child dreams, the water's blood.
Time goes on, evil sings
a haunting song of deadly things
right is wrong confusion brings
a hate so strong it takes on wings
flies through the brain unobserved
takes on fame not deserved
has no name becomes unnerved…
angels of light the devil poses
demons of night with pointed noses
the owl takes flight no man supposes
black is white and guns are roses…
There are no scenes there is no cry
so it seems they all lie
in childish dreams and wonder why
no one screams except the sky…

Judy Meeker

When I See You

When I see you I stop
What I am doing then
every time we meet
again and again.

My heart does not beat.
It is like a stone
sitting in the grass,
sitting all alone.

My feet do not move.
They are stuck to the floor.
My eyes do not wander.
They move no more.

All I see is you
silently standing serene.
Alone in the distance
Like no one else I've seen.

Jamie Hund

Untitled

Babe can you sense
what I've tried to convey
Do you feel what I feel
though so far away

Do your hands softly tremble
when you answer the phone
Is your mind filled with thoughts
of when we'll be alone

Do you long for my voice
and yearn for my touch
when I tell you I love you
and show you how much

When you look towards the sky
is it my face you see
when you picture your prince
is your picture of me

These questions I ask
are honest and true
for they represent
my feelings for you

Brett Kangas

Where's Folks Headin'

Sometimes I get to thinkin,
What the world is all about.
Where we all are a headin,
And where we're comin' out.

Folks have sure gone plumb speed crazy,
They are sure travelin' mighty fast.
It's begun to run through my mind,
How long it this thing goin' to last?

Some ain't got the time,
To hardly slow down and talk these days,
Ain't so friendly as they should be,
Too many things have changed their ways.

Ain't no reason for all this rushin'
Every minute in the day,
Cuttin' years right off your life.
No sense, it doesn't pay.

Better go a little slower,
Add a few years to your life.
Ain't no need for all this hurry
Of hustle, bustle, speedin' and strife.

James W. Todd

Silence Isn't Golden

Silence isn't golden;
What you leave unsaid remains.
The words that go unspoken
Are the hardest ones to say.

The hand that reaches out to hold you
Soon will melt away,
For when its touch is not returned
If often flies astray.

Silence isn't golden;
It hurts the one who hears it,
As the pain inside a broken heart
Kills the one who heals it.

Amy Hale

A Two Year Old

Life at sixty has just begun
when a two year old is on the run.
Out of one thing, then another,
that was just like his mother.
There went the milk
then the cake on the floor.
He grins, "get about it Nona"
give me some more.
That's the life of a two year old,
but they are more precious than gold.
It's not hard to bear,
All they want is loving care.

Hazel Odell

"Diet Diet Diet"

Oh no here I go again
Trying to make me look thin
I have let myself go to pot
A good shape I surely have not.
To all the good foods I must say no
This time my diet I dare not blow.
No more cakes and no more pies
I must think of my big ole thighs.
Why oh why do I torture me so
I see food and my eyes begin to glow.
Just close my eyes and think of thin
This time for sure I have to win.

Barbara Blattner

My Buddy-My Brother

Where have you gone my buddy?
When did yesterday turn into today?
Today turn into tomorrow,
Tomorrow into forever.

My faithful friend
My champion.
My unwavering ally
All of my life.

My life is diminished,
My loss irreplaceable,
My hurt is forever.

But somewhere in tomorrow
That will turn into forever,
We will meet again
My buddy, my brother.

We'll smile, laugh and tease,
And all of our tomorrows,
Will be forever
And I will never be alone again.

Eleanor Kerness

I Dreamed I Rode A Pony

I dreamed I rode a pony,
When I was 65.
It was a daring thing to do,
Actually I could have died.

For I'd never ridden one before,
Nor had I given thought to,
But as I grew older, I said,
The time has come, I ought to.

So I rode to paths and crossed them,
And then the mountain loomed.
Dare I undertake this,
For with a slip I'm doomed?

My pony cantered steady
And I held on tight,
Feet in the stirrups,
I reached the valley at night.

Now I'm awake, but realize,
I'd have to be daft,
All the years I dreamed pony-riding,
I'd a-broken the pony in half.

Jacqueline Fischer

Let Me, Love You

How long the days and nights are,
When I'm away from you.
It leaves too much time to think,
Of what I long to do.
Hold you in my loving arms,
Feel your warm embrace.
Look into your sparkling eyes,
To touch your wonderful face.
Feel your lips touching mine,
Kissing me so tenderly
Talk to you and be near you,
I've never been so lonely.
Hold your hand and see your smile,
To spend one night together.
Is my most ardent wish,
I would treasure it forever.
Am I asking too much love
I'm sorry but what can I do, all I can do is ask,
and I'm asking please let me love you.

Barbara A. Woolson

Ode To The Onion

Who would think a burger nice
When lacking of an onion slice?
The lowly hot dog sold at fairs
With onions chopped in little squares.
It thrills us as we watch it made.
Then bolt it down with lemonade.
Now liver's texture we would shun
And called to eat it would not run.
But pile it high with onion rings,
Its glad aroma loudly sings.
It calls and we anticipate
The first bite taken from our plate.
At younger ages I recall
An onion syrup "where-with-all"
My mother made for me to take
And my good health to surely make.
What drab and dreary lives we'd face
Were there no onions anyplace.
And so, dear friends, "alas" no more,
The onion's crown we did restore.

James J. Sandegren

A Day In June

Oh what is so grand as a day in June
When the earth is at rest
And by nature caressed
With a sun that travels
From the east to the west.

In a sky overhead of blue
With white clouds sailing through,
When the trees all towering high
Lift their branches to the sky,
And honey bees go humming by.

Then the world gives up a sigh
Sorrowing to bid goodbye
To this beautiful day in June
That all passes and goes too soon.

Eleanor E. Delker

Untitled

one of those days
when the hayride explodes
can't seem to keep
a constant stream of concentration
invitations bears
a road that's long and narrow
keep moving down the road
it's bound to curve again
watch the colors
crystallize shatter and reform
another pattern
matrix for a new day

Bonnie Rollings

Thank You God

Thank you for the things
we grow.
Thank you for the birds
that sing.
Thank you for the church
bells that ring.
Thank you for the flowers
and trees. And grass.
Thank you for the sun and
rain.
And thank you God for
everything.

Bernice Kitzman

"A Good Man Is Hard To Find"

Some men never know
When they have things good
They're forever messing around
And seldom do what they should.

So girls when looking for a mate
always keep in mind,
A good man they say
Is always hard to find.

Beverly Shepherd

Friends

Friends are there to help
When you are low and feeling down.
That's when you know
Your true friends will be found.

Friends will give you strength,
You don't have to stand alone.
They'll still be there for you,
When others have come and gone.

Friends may not always approve
Of all we say and do,
But when you are in trouble
They're there to see you through.

Friends overlook our faults,
They share our good times and the bad.
When our years are few
We'll be so glad we've had,
Those special people we call friends.

Johnnie Love

By The Sea

By the sea, that's where I'll be,
when you call me home
By the sea, the place to be, to roam
Hear the thundering waves crashing,
See the silver waters thrashing
Seashells on the shore, with each
Step I find one more
Don't call me home, I want to roam
By the sea, is where I'll be,
when you need me

Ashley Hodges

Feeling Lost

I hate being confused
When you know something's wrong.
But, the feelings won't go away.
When you know the feelings aren't mutual
When you know it will hurt.
Why won't they go away.
Why???
It hurt before so, who says
it won't hurt again.
I've got to learn to go on.
But, I don't know how.
I just love him so much
But, the feelings shouldn't be there.
He doesn't love me, he never
did so. I don't think they
will ever be there either.
So, you gotta help me go on.
I don't feel whole with out him.
It hurts when I see him
cause, I know he's not mine.

Jenna Conti

The Soul

How old is the soul you say,
When you think of age today?
It can be young and new,
Or very old in years and blue.

How old is the soul in years?
Just as old as you my dears.
It's been with you all your life,
In all love, difficulties and strife.

How old is the soul in life?
God gave it to us like a wife.
Christ gave it birth, when on the cross,
His blood spilled, he should be boss.

How old then, is the precious soul,
If counted in ancient realm role?
It's uncountable and ever free,
Yes, God gave the soul to you and me.

Evelyn Walter

The Garage

Cleaning the garage is such a chore.
When you think you're done,
They say "Do More."
So you work and work,
Until you break your back.
They won't even let you stop for a snack.
So you sweep and sweep,
And yet there's more,
Oh! cleaning the garage is such a bore!

Brandon Golburg

Lying On The Shelf

She hid it neatly, far back on the shelf
Where she couldn't use it as she should
Have used it, yes, she could
To bring someone cheer
To those living far and near
What happiness she might have brought
To the lonely or distraught
And those so forlorn help inspire
So much good could transpire
But she went about to please herself.

Then one day she awoke
As if from a deep sleep
"It's not mine to keep,
I'll not hide it anymore
There must be someone who needs it yet,
And with it I can bless
Perhaps it's not too late"
And so she went to reach for
Her talent, dormant,
Lying on the shelf.

Helen Myrtle Stoddard

"My Wonderful Dream"

One night, I dreamt, I was married
To the most wonderful man that I knew;
But when I awoke, I found it wasn't true
I wasn't yet married to you,
O wonderful man that I knew,
That day will come
We will say I do
My wonderful dream will be true
I will be married to you
O wonderful man that I knew

Dolores Cote

Waiting For You

Come and be with me my darling,
Where the flowers grow so fast
You are the one I'm waiting for,
While God put me in your arms.

I am singing since I saw you,
You were mine before we met
In my heart I felt the trembling
Of your body while I wait.

There is something I can tell you
In the secrets I have kept,
That you must have dreamed about me
Way before we have both met.

All the bells are ringing loudly,
And the church is waiting for,
For the moment we are expecting
That will soon unite us both.

And in case you find me different
Let me know what you prefer,
because I'm for you, my darling,
Until the end of my days.

Amelia Serrano Chevremont

My Eyes Are Growing Dim

Wherever I may go,
Wherever I may stray,
My God will always know
And guide me all the way.

I have no doubts,
I have no fear,
For my Lord is always near.

Even though my eyes are growing dim,
I will still sing and work for him.
To teach others to know and love Him too
Will be my daily task to do.
And when my Master calls for me,
What a wondrous day that will be.
My eyes will open, and I will see
The loving Savior who has cared for me.

Erma Huntley

Rain

The sun beats down its scorching rays
Which burn the earth in midst of days,
And people cry for heaven's rain
That cools the earth to soothe its pain.

Though the burning sun leaves the sky,
The earth drinks in what dew till dry.
The people dance and twitch and jolt
To conjure up a thunderbolt,

But all the dancing is in vain
For only one can make it rain.
When He desires clouds will burst
To satisfy earth's gnawing thirst.

Then desert sands will blossoms yield,
And vegetation fill the field,
Meadows bloom while forest trees,
Reaching the clouds, sing in the breeze.

The time will come, it's very near,
When He will show that He does hear,
And bring upon cracked earth in pain
The grand relief...a pouring rain.

Joseph A. Mastainich

To The Wall

I beat it, life that is, to the wall
   which separates life and death,
Thinking and fully expecting that it,
   the wall
   was a solid wall
Which would surely bounce me
   back away from it, as a
   child's rubber ball
And I'd land on my feet
   As I always have...

TO FIND it but a veil or
   filmy cloud
   diffused by a breath so lightly
As a child who picks a
   white dandelion "parachute"
And with one puff,
   or even in the picking,
Wafts air-boats on their journey,
   transported, reborn.

Florence M. Brice

Leap Of Faith

She stood on the landing
While I was on the phone below
A flight of stairs separated us
Mommy! she cried, and jumped
As I turned.

She trajected the air. Caught
In time and held against
My engine breast, testing
Me. Would I be there
For her? Always, I said.

The years faltered by. Her
Father took flight. I worked
To feed her fragile frame.
The house silenced and smelled
Of her burning incense.

In undo course, she climbed
The three story rooftop
Surveyed the trajectory,
Sobbed "Mommy!" and jumped.

Charlotte Rotkin

Untitled

All I could do was stand there and cry,
while you held me in your arms to
say our last good-bye. I kept asking
over and over why, let's give it another
try. You told me something kept telling
you no, I knew it was time we both
let go. You wiped away the tears as
they ran down my face, our memories
will always be kept in a safe place
you said you just couldn't let yourself
care, this time you really wouldn't
be there. As I held onto you closely
you ran your fingers through my hair,
whispering in my ear, that no matter
what you'd always care. I touched your
face with my hand, and gave you one
last kiss. I thought to myself I
was the one who caused this.

Ann Marie Cole

To A Friend In Pregnancy

Woman — Friend — Dearest Sweet
Who bears nature's finest grace
Soon, you and precious child will meet
While a fancy glow illumines your face,
For there is not a greater joy
Than a loving newborn girl or boy.

Soon, a youthful cheek will lie
Upon your breast in dreamed delight
And those around will heave a sigh
At this awed and charming sight,
For the view of mother and child brings
Joy, Mirth, Hope, and Love that sings.

God has not created a mold
Finer than that of Child and Mother,
Nor has a brush in artistic hold
Ever painted a purer two as lovers.
Their bond is strong and will never part,
For though they're two, there beats one
heart.

Brian Rogers

War

In old days
who disagreed
Fought their fight
In cold daylight
End of day was
Time to bleed
Rest to find
Wounds to bind
Men nowadays
Reject this need
So wars proceed
Even at night
Inhuman quite
Animal ways

John C. Allen

Tyrannosaurus Was A Beast

Tyrannosaurus was a beast!
Who had no friends,
to say the least!

He ruled the out of doors
and killed other dinosaurs.

Even though I think He's very neat!
Him, I would not care to meet!

Frederick L. Conrad

Tell Me

Who I am
What I see
When I'm going
Where will it be

Why I wonder
Who made me
What comes after
When God needs me

Where will I go
Why should it be
Who is to say
What comes to be

When will it happen
Where will I go
Why must it happen
Can I say "no"?

Joan D'Aiuto

To My Husband

To the one who's so special
Who makes life's love grow
I do care a lot about you
Even more than you know

I never want to hurt you
You mean too much to me
But I'd never want to lose you
Or ever set you free

I know we're both so busy
But life doesn't last forever
We really need to take some time
To laugh and love together

It's so funny the way we met
Neither had feelings at all
Until we realized what love was
Nothing mattered at all anymore

What I give I hope is enough
I don't know what to do
I don't want to see you unhappy
Because I love you

Jennifer Medeiros

Give Some Time To Jesus

If you have forgiveness for those,
    whom will not forgive,
Beyond our comprehension
    will be His protective shield.

If you give some time to Jesus,
    no matter how little each day,
There will be that glorious feeling
    when you kneel and pray.

If you share your joy with others,
    along life's way,
Our reward will be great in Heaven,
    on that Judgment Day.

If you implore love and compassion
    for those who do not understand,
The Lord will always guide you,
    with His Loving hand.

Imogene Messick

"Togetherness"

Family departed, so many ways,
who's to blame, but themselves.
A loss of truth, of life
lost souls asking which way to go.
Hearts falling apart.

Life which was meant to be seeks
to try even harder, non-stop.
Give the breath, give the air.
Give the life of love back to his family.
Uniting as one.

Be with host in body, to serve anyway
unto the ultra cosmos of Universe
Holy rewards come, but only a few.
A new you, and we, too.
Turn for guidance, seek forgiveness

Seek for inner peace for all
bring forth peace for the world
step-by-step, slowly but righteous.
Family life cannot become lost
believe, so ye will not become lost.

Dody Augustein

No More Hair

There was a guy named Tom
Whose hair was really long
One night he got tired
Slept too close to the fire
And now his hair is all gone.

The next day he went to the store
and he didn't find it a bore
With everyone staring at him
I could say
That he forgot about his hair that day

When he got home he got out a beer
looked in the mirror and said oh
OH So Hairless AM I

Amanda Slonecker

Gone Again

Gone again
Why is it the back of him
We always see
Will he ever come toward us
With open arms
or will he only drift
farther and farther away
A free Spirit
Escaping
Never looking back to see
The very eyes he helped to create
turn to waterfalls
One green one blue....
Well it's time to play
We are children after all
And we can make believe
We have everything we need

Beth-Anne Poole

When Will I Die?

Am I gonna die? Please tell me why.
Will it be soon? On the next full moon?
Well it be painful or sudden? Will
I go to hell or heaven?
Please God tell me will I be set
free? Will I walk through the gates,
or down the stairs? Tell me God who
really cares?
Why was I put here on earth? Was
it an unplanned childbirth?
To me it really doesn't matter if I
live to see tomorrow. Was I meant to
drown in my own sorrow?
In the meantime before I die I will
stay around, you can watch as I fall
to the ground.
Please God tell me when will I die???
That is the question I ask as I sit here and
cry ..

Jennifer L. Karr

Once Upon A Time...

Once upon a time
Way down South,
I met a crocodile in my house.
I jumped, from my head to my toes,
and lifted up my bed and
found a rose.
But oh what do you do when
a crocodile says....
I love you?

Jenny Armstrong

Unity

Dear, Father, again I come to thee.
Will you, please hear my humble plea?

Tonight I cannot sleep
But I do weep.

Our families are wanting a victory.
Our victory is unity through thee.

It's more than a sad or broken heart
But hearts that have been too long apart.

Help us to talk in love to one another.
Help us to show love to one another.

Help us to put aside what's wrong
So that we can sing a happy song.

Now you have heard my plea
I lift it up to thee.

Through you we will win our victory,
Our victory of family unity.

Now as we travel along
We can sing a happy song.

"We are one in the Bond of Love."
Your love sent from above.

Ethelyn Key Gilmore

Poem's May

A "poem" is a memory, a mood or a
wish, a poem of our own may swim like
the fish.
A "poem" may carry with music or even
alone, a "poem" unlike any other, it's
building a stone, your foundation above
all, would you say that tall?
A "poem" from what I gathered
must be as this ink, from me for
you, some kind of chain's link.
A "poem" must breathe and sleep or
how could they say? just have a
better very good day!

Donald M. Van Steinburg

God's Seed

You started out as a seed
With a lots of rain
You looked like a weed
But with all of God's love
From high up in the sky
You are now the apple
Of his eye.

Cynthia Lawson

Poor Santa Clause

While setting on Santa's knee
With cracks, pops and agonize.
I must have been overweight
For Santa was so very late.

Betty Curtis

Tell Me

Tell me what do you see
when the thunder is rolling
and danger is coming and
when the world is in pain
and the human race is shamed.
Now tell me what so you see.

Carlee Cochran

Moonshine

The shining moon of wintry,
With darkness all about
Steals the heart away
    from one.
To stare and glimpse not
A stir nor imperfectness
And so time is bought,
With things left undone.

Ashley McClymont

Country Boy

Tramping through old fields
With his 410 on arm
He sees a mother quail
Taking her babies away from harm.

A "Know-all" Rabbit watches
Thinking he is hid
Happiness abounds, pounds
In the heart of this country kid

Country bred and clean, fourteen,
He has nothing bad to fear
God and surrounding woods
Bless, protect, adhere.

To wrap him for safe keeping
For another seven years, you see
That then, he may still be filled
With good earth worth and dignity.

Earnesteen Roberts

Round Trip

I started out so long ago
    with my basic need
Then I traveled the roads of life
    in search of a star to lead
I hitched my wagon to different stars
    as I traveled that road
Each time, only to find
    I was carrying a heavy load
Each path I took, seemed not to work
    and I knew something was wrong
My load was very heavy
    and the road was much too long
So I stopped a moment, just to rest
    along that weary way
I took some time to smell the roses
    and I came home that day.

James Fransen

The Master's Art

She was painted by a master
    who saw all her charm and grace,
The beauty of her eyes and hair
    and the smile upon her face.
She doesn't hang in the halls of fame
    where the masters' works are known—
Her greatest beauty's from within
    and through her love, is shown.
This pretty picture might not sell
    to those who deal in art;
But the portrait of this lovely
    one, is forever in my heart.
It's how she looks through the eyes of
    love, only love can understand—
GOD is the Master Painter—and she
    was painted by his own hand.

Charles H. Stirsman

The Way A Woman
Should Be Treated

A woman should be treated
With respect and kindness
And should be allowed her
Space without a man being
Around watching her every move
A man should trust a woman
And not be over protective at all
A woman treated well will be
Faithful and loyal and she will
Treat her man equally well.

Chinedu Dean Ogbuike

Mist Of The Heart

A mist of the heart
With sprinkle of tear
Follows thy leave
Spills to a nest
On saddened breast
To remember a time
When thy heart was mine
Dew so clear
Returning thee near.

Amber Howe

Miracles

Miracles can happen,
with the start of each new day,
if only you'd open up your heart,
and listen when you pray.

Miracles can happen,
Although you think they're few.
If you don't believe in miracles-
then just take a look at you!

Jeanette Chatila

Thoughts Of Only You

Another day has ended
With thoughts of only you
As I slip into a blissful sleep
The way I always do

You're my first thought in the morning
And the last one at day's end
I think of you so very much
As sweetheart and as friend

The thought of us together
Inside each other's arms
Means I could never tire
Of all your many charms

These thoughts are very wonderful
They keep my mind in touch
With every day reality
That I love you very much

Donald Weston

Untitled

What use is the man,
Without an open hand?
He won't listen to reason.
You can't make him understand.
Nothing seems to please him.

Does a rose, when cut,
Bleed or cry?

Gary Stitely

Untitled

Trapped beyond control
Within my body, bars around my soul
Screaming, yelling for some help
But my scream is just a yelp
I cannot move
I am tied down
Gagged at the mouth
Kept from making a sound
His words so skillfully crept in my ear
I scream for anyone who can hear
Darkness surrounds me and floods my eyes
It puts the evil
In disguise
The feeling of pain
Pumps through my heart
My whole world is falling apart
I've been hit
I've been beaten
I'm never ever heard
No one believes me, not one word

Alicia Goodman

To Die

When I drift along in the water
wondering how I'm keeping myself
from drowning
Wishing I could disappear but stay
Wade around
Thinking how my life is disappointing
Maybe I should die and see
a better life
Sing to the stones
before leaving myself
Leaving for you the earth
Shame will stay
The universe is yours
I found the stone
that would take my life
and wished it well
then
It seemed eternity
Before I slipped away

Candie Lapaglia

We Pay The Tax

We pay the tax on all the hollow years,
Years we stand committed to autonomy
Afraid to see reflections.

We pay the tax on what we fear to be
Impractical,
And choose the chartered course, instead.

We pay the tax on all the life we lose,
When we avert our eyes,
Pretend we cannot see.

Ripeness is all,
And yet it is maturity
That steals our eyes.

But none of us is truly blind,
We all could see,
Though unlike Gloucester,
We never knew the knife of loving.

He escaped finally,
But we survive,
And close our eyes,
And pay the tax.

Jane Cooper Chambers

Wondering

I wonder why one person with
Word or deed is mean and hateful
To another a fight will sure to
Start a lot of hurt and unhappiness
Will follow.
The hurt is still there even though
We go along lives path way never
Feeling as we once did toward one
Another oh what and awful waste
I think it would be better by far to
Light just one little light then to
Cause so much hurt and unhappiness
In this world of darkness and
Despair.

Charity Mullen

Shattered

I feel all alone in the
world, I don't belong anywhere
I have nothing to show for my
life, and nobody to care,

I don't know which way to
turn now, or what to do
It's hard to take a step forward,
when you're backing up two

Nothing in my life, turns out
the way I want it to be,
I wonder if it's just me,
or my own destiny,

All my dreams our shattered,
I now have none left,
It was just another disappointment
like all the rest.

Cindy Kaulins

"Solitude"

As sweet as the sunset
yet as mellow as the morning dew.
As sweet as a flower,
I say "I love you."
But not as a lover,
we're better off as friends.
Still solitude will find its
place somewhere in the end.

Alex Sanders

The Heart

The heart can be big, but
yet it could be small
The heart can be a dangerous
weapon with no control at all
It can open doors to worlds
unmanageable
Yet it can become like gas
and be very flammable
The heart can lead you to
happiness, joy, and love
The heart can also lead you
to sorrow misery and all of
the above
The heart gives us life so
we don't stumble
But if the love from a
girl ends all it does is crumble.

Avant Andre Jr.

Friendship

Friendship is old as mankind,
Yet new every day -
More priceless than diamonds,
but has been sold for as
little as thirty pieces of silver.

Friendship is a gift from heaven,
that must be nurtured
to be cherished,
and cherished to be nurtured.

Friends are friendship
and friendship is honest friends-
Giving, receiving,
but most of all - living in and
for the hearts of one
another.

Eric Foster

Loss

My friend so tiny and slight,
Yet oh so filled with light,
Your courage inspired us,
Your love sustained us.

Your talents were many,
Your interests so wide,
Although often in pain,
You didn't hide.

Your work was a trial,
Your school a success,
I'm sad at your loss
But I hope you've found rest.

Christine M. Farrell

"Tribute To A Fallen Raider"

Here's To "You Mighty Mack,"
You Always "Led Our Attack,"
You Learned
"Carbone's Combat Well,"
Fight From "Here To Hell,"
There Was "No One Greater,"
A True "Rugged All-Stater,"
And Raider "Hall Of Famer,"
You Have "Your Final Reward"
Playing Center "For Our Lord,"
Good-Bye "My Fellow Raider,"
Until We "Meet Again Later."
Barry "Mac" McDermott
10/8/46 - 10/12/94
Amen!

Chas. "64"

Untitled

Pressures in life
You are a daughter
You are a daughter-in-law
You are a mother,
You are a grandmother and so on,
Even a great grandmother
Sometimes you don't know if
You're you or someone else?
I do know I'm no poet for sure!
I just want to be "me"
for a change!

Irene H. M. L. B. Wallen

Sweet Apple

Apple, apple, sweet and juicy,
You are as sweet as an orange.
You are juicier than a peach,
And you feel like a banana in my mouth.
I hear your crunchy sound.
When I eat you I think of going to
school.
I'd rather eat an apple than nuts.

Joe Butts Jr.

Amanda - Dear

Amanda, Amanda, we miss you so,
you are now God's precious soul.
Forever in our hearts to stay,
we will meet again someday.

Angels love you and want you so,
so do we on earth below.
Amanda, we kneel and pray,
forgiving God, who took you away.

Angels hold you ever so high,
we will meet again,
there is no goodbye.

Erwin Kacena

My Butterfly

Why do you fly away
You are so beautiful
For you are a butterfly
Why can't I catch you
I would love to hold you
You're so amazing
Why do you tease me
Flying circles around my head
You still look so confused
Where are you going
I would love to fly with you
Give me some wings
Am I not worthy
Please give me a chance
I feel as though
I will never catch you
Please prove me wrong

Jamie Dugan

Untitled

I answer the phone and hear your voice.
You ask the questions
I lie for the answers.
But you already know.

Every question asked has an answer.
It seems you know all the answers
Before the questions asked.

You never asked if I loved you.
I told you truthful without lies
I said forever, to the skies

I didn't lie because I couldn't
I promised forever and meant it.
Now. I wish I'd lied.

The pain now is great
You didn't say "Goodbye."
All I can figure you lied.

Donald J. MacNair

Dreams

You can run down rivers,
You can float down streams.
But whatever you do,
Don't give up your dreams.

Jennifer Miller

Can't You See Nor Hear...

I cry and I weep but still
you can't hear a word. I yell
and I shout but still you
can't hear a word. Wishing
I was dead and never appeared
so people can see how
I feared the one I adore.
People can't you hear, People
can't you see someone
Is abusing me or is it
just me. The fear in my
eyes can't go away till
I start to cry and wish
it away. I see angels
In the sky coming to
get me, am I starting to
Please hold me in
your arms so I could
see you and hold you
For one last time.

Annette Medina

"I Do"

Husband to be I love
    you dear,
For when I'm with you
    I have no fear.
From the first time I
    saw you I knew you
    were great,
And thought about you
    And thought about you
    Until our first date.
You are a gentleman
    and I am a lady,
And I knew that someday
    I would marry you, maybe.
That day is here now and as
    I look at you,
You'll look at me and simply
    say the words "I do."

Ashley B. Tillett

Thanks

Thank you for your thoughts of flowers
You eased the pain of sleepless hours

My sister meant a lot, you see
She gave the gift of a kidney to me

My sorrow runs so very deep
It's hard to think, or eat, or sleep

The tears just flow, I can't stop crying
But forty six is too young to be dying

She's in no more pain, I know she's fine
I'm sure my hurt will ease with time

Thanks again for your thoughts of flowers
I'll watch them grow in my idle hours

April Litsch

Angel

If on a cold December day
you feel a sudden warm breeze
coming your way -
Don't be surprised, it's only me to say
Hello my love, I miss you -
I'm not so far away

John W. Hough III

Untitled

No one can tell of the pain
    you feel deep within

No one can see the rain
    that the clouds would bring

Just the sadness in your heart
    and the feeling of being numb

The drowning sorrow shall never part
    in the days that will come

No one can tell of the sorrow
    when a loved one dies

No one can see the tomorrow
    through the tears in their eyes

Just the knowledge that they are safe
    in the Lord's open hands

And of their new life
    in that Heavenly Land.

Dzintra Owen

A Good Friend

When you believe in yourself
You have a good friend,
When you believe in yourself
Days never end,
When you believe in yourself
You can move mountains
To ease the worst pain
When you believe in yourself,
Things are never the same.
The trees have green leaves
The oceans are blue,
And you'll know within that
GOD LOVES YOU.
When you believe in yourself
You have a good friend,
And you will know that God
is within.

Froncine R. Pringle

Untitled

I am the winter wind.
When you feel a
soft breeze against
your face, it would be me.

Gina Grace Ruscigno Collins

Separate Ways

At the end of the road you have to turn.
You have to leave the ones you love
You have to turn and turn alone.
No one can come, no one will.
Someday they will turn,
    and maybe catch up.
But right now you have to take
    this one journey on your own.

Denise Costantino

"Missing You"

We've been through a lot
You know this is true.
I just want you to know
that I really miss you.
I miss your warm smile
and your gentle touch.
The way you made me laugh
I really miss it much.
When we were together
things were just fine,
Then we broke up
we just needed time.
Now my time is up
I can't wait any longer,
Because my feelings for you
Just get stronger and stronger.
I want to see your smile,
and also feel your touch
Now I hope you realize
I'm missing you so much.

Heather Mink

"Lonely"

Have you ever felt so lonely that
you really want to scream.
And you think "O Lord" if only
This was just a bad dream.
It doesn't seem so long ago that
you were quite content with
your own sweet home and family which
you're sure was Heaven sent.
And then one day the Lord did say I
need that man up here - to make things
ready for the others who'll appear.
So he took your love away to reap
his just reward, and you know you'll
have to carry on even though you're bored.
Your life now seems so lonely, and
you're very often sad, just remember
there are few who've known the
happiness you've had.

Dorothy Moore

We're Different And So What?

You say hello and I say sawubona.
You say goodbye and I say salakahle.

You say yes and I say yebo.
You say come here and I say woza.
You say sleep and I say lala.

You say daddy and I say baba.
You say mummy and I say ma.
You say granny and I say gogo.
You say brother and I say buti.
You say sister and I say sisi.

You say sweet potato and I say batata.
You say tomato and I say tamati.
You say cabbage and I say kabishi.

You say sweater and I say jersey.
You say sneakers and I say tackies.
You say apron and I say pinafore.

You are you and I am I.
We are different and that's our strength.
We are ALL tied together by one common
thread—OUR HUMANITY!!!

Busisiwe Radebe-Mbata

Running To No End

Walking through a dark tunnel
you see a light that
you think will
lead you out
But
It continues to grow smaller
as you get closer
Soon you are lost and
Alone
you turn around and try
to find away out
After a long time in the
Dark
you finally find out were
you are
you've decided to find
a light that
won't disappear as
you get closer

Brigette Farley

Untitled

I see you sitting there crying alone,
You sit and say nothing,
Thinking, but of what?
I feel your eagerness to say something,
But you're afraid of your words.
Falling backwards into a hole,
As I look in I see you sitting there
crying alone,
You sit and say nothing,
Thinking, but of what?
Then a tear roles down my face and off
my chin and lands on your open hand.
I see you look up and the look in your
eyes tells me all I want to know,
So I give you my hand and help you out!

Dawn Marie Ramirez

Moonshine

My presence
Your presence
Then it starts to unwind
Every streak of sense
Left in my mind
A flash in the corner
A dulled sense of time
And I just can't imagine
a better place to moonshine,
It sparks to the ceiling
Then falls to the floor
I step on it quickly
And run out the door.

Alice Watson

Forget

I've said things I didn't mean.
You've done things you regret.
You haven't taken my sorry yet.
I miss you and want you back.
Is it too late, will you ever forget?
I said I was sorry. You just told
me lies. Can't you forget the past
and remember the good times?
I love you so can't you see.
Please, please come back to
me.

Amy DiFederico

Who?

You don't know her.
You think you do.
Been friends for years?
So what.

She's in there somewhere,
but you don't find her.

She's busy
trying on different costumes.
Though her soul wears no costume,
only her mind.

To you, one minute she's
Little Red Riding Hood,
Then she's Satan
with a fiery red cape and a halo.

But you'll never meet her bare soul
for yours is fully clothed.

Ashley Ford

"You"

You think you're short
You think you're fat.
You complain about this
You obsess about that.
You think you're cool
You think you're great,
You think that life is yours to take.
You're wrong you'll see as time goes on
And soon you'll sing a different song.
You walk alone, down the street
Wondering what you'll be
You stop, you stare, you wait to see
Is someone looking over me?
You feel your pulse and wonder why,
Sometimes you can't lie down and die.
To you, a game
Your mind stays shut.
Open it, you just might see
A world of wonders,
Waiting to be.

Amber Carney

Dream Child

Music opened my door,
your world greeted me.
I feel the words, hear the melody.

Here I was born,
I know we belong.
Notes and their words.
Love, it's here in a song.

Meeting between spaces and lines,
Can't just be a chance of time.
You're the deep spirit of soul.
You're Apollo's sweet Dream Child.

So run, child, run wild and free,
Beyond the spaces and lines.
Be what you're born to be.
More than a dream, you're a song.

So run, child, run wild, dance free.
Carry your dreams beyond reality.
You are sweet spirit of song,
Just two notes of his time.

You are Apollo's Dream Child.

Helen Hunt Marquis

Gift From God

My precious baby boy
You were born into this world
Through love I had for your daddy
For I was just a girl.

I don't know where he's gone to
I was quite young you see
He walked out of my life
But what an angel he left for me.

I will love you and take care of you
I will give you all I can
God has blessed my life with you
He holds us in his hands.

When you grow to be a man
And start a life of your own
Remember me, my little one
How we made it all alone.

Debra Dowdey Solis

I Feel The Pain

I feel the pain of a million
young men, marching off to war.

I feel the pain of two million
parents who wonder if this is why
they bore and raised their sons.

I feel the pain of the young
mother whose child died at birth.

I feel the pain of the doctor as
he tells the young man that he will die.

I feel the pain of the young
girl whose lover has found someone new.

I feel the pain of the middle-
aged man whose wife has died and left
him all alone.

I feel the pain of the old lady
whose husband of sixty years is dying
before her eyes and she cannot help him.

I feel the pain of a million
souls crying out for freedom-freedom.

I feel the pain!

Alyce Palos

"If We Could Trade Places"

If we could trade places just for a day
You might be surprised
That I am as busy as you
You might realize
That my work is important, too

Perhaps then would you cease
Asking me to meet your personal needs
Would you please
Get your own breakfast and coffee

You see,
If we could trade places just for a day
It would never enter my mind
To misuse your time
Or abuse you in any way

If we could trade places just for a day
You might also discover this truth:
    Regardless of who you are
        or what you do
    We are all equal partners
        under one roof!

Angel R. Barnard

My Age

They say that I'm too
young to cross the street to play.
That I'm too old to cry
when I don't get my way.
I'm very much too big
to swing on a garden gate.
But very much too small to
stay up after eight,
I'm young, I'm old, I'm big,
I'm small.
Do you think in age and
height I will ever grow
to be just exactly right?

Arthur Hayes

"Laddie"

    Laddie your eyes so bright
your beauty of black, sable and
white.
    Bodyguard to me when I rest,
Why did I send you west?
    Laddie I miss you so,
You'd turn your head to and fro.
    I miss our trips outside
You would bark and run and I
would hide.
    Our walks in the woods
where you would run and chase
Rascal the cat.
    You were full of love and gave
it to everyone.
    The little people you're loving
now; plus a bodyguard for them.
    You gave your paw to me
before and you give it to them now.

Elizabeth A. Troudt

Christmas Letter

Dear Mother open the page of
your Christmas Card
in it I send my best regards
It's a special meaning and the
words are true, they will
cheer you up if you're feeling blue
It will make you smile and
dry your tears we will love
you forever through the years
each Christmas we will be,
right there beside you near
the Christmas tree. So may
God Bless you mother dear
and may you have a happy
New Year.

Barbara Lahita

"Wind"

Just like the wind blows,
you left me here alone.
Crying, I tried to see,
what did I ever do to make you leave me.
But, I still feel the same.
Do you even remember my name?

You're different from the wind,
it seems like our love was a sin.
The wind always blowing, cares.
So stop crying, wipe your tears.
For as long as you are near,
the wind will never disappear.

Ashleigh Poindexter

My Cousin, My Friend

My dad is your uncle
Your dad is mine too
Our dads are brothers
Up they grew

And when they got older
They each became two
So we became cousins
Just out of the blue

Well cousins are cousins
So what's the big deal
Don't they just gather
For the Thanksgiving meal?

But wrapped up like a cousin
God decided to send
A special relation
My cousin, my friend

Now if you think
This is much too mushy
I'd better end it
Before you blushy

Judy M. Lingren

On A Visit To Maxie

Your face is so animated;
Your eyes have a beautiful glow -
So happy to welcome us:
They are clear and beautiful eyes,
And it makes me happy just to see them.
You are so humorous, and good company;
You are so very courageous.

But your eyes tell a special story -
About your soul, Maxie:
They light up like a lovely candle,
And your spirit and my spirit touch -
And we all share the magic of
    this moment.

My brother has terminal cancer
    and he is blind:
But now he is seeing from within
And just beginning to experience his
    own soul.

Frances K. Alter

Rain

When I First Saw You With
your eyes so bright
I looked at you with such delight
everything about you seemed
so right.
My heart was flying higher
than a kite.
Now as the days go by
and the never ending nights do
too,
I just don't know what to do;
every day I feel so blue
I just want to be with you.
I don't even know if you feel
the same.
I don't know who's to blame
I just wish I could explain
and ask you if you feel the same
but it always feels like it's
going to rain.

Joseph F. Tabaczynski

Which Road

I am so lonely and so blue
What is someone like me to do
I have no love to call my own
It seems I am always alone

I have no money, fortune or fame
Not one penny to my name
No one to talk to, nothing to do
Oh, why am I so blue

I am no beauty, not much to see
Dear God, why did you pass by me
Maybe some day I will know
On which road I am suppose to go

Flossie Barnett

Untitled

In Loving Memory of Milton W. Nicholson
Dec. 23, 1922 - Sept. 27, 1994
Seventy-two years ago today,
You took your first breath,
On September the twenty-seventh
You took your last - in death.

We were there beside you,
As you fought the gaining foe,
We sang to you the nursery songs,
That you sang long ago.

We love you and we miss you,
We know that you're at rest,
Like you, we will not say "Good-bye"
We too will say "GOD BLESS."

Elaine Dahl

Life's Bumpy Just Hang On!

You'll always want something
you'll probably won't get for a while
  It doesn't seem fair
  It doesn't seem possible
  but what is...

Life's a big roller coaster
it's a bumpy ride but,
No one gets off until it's
Ready for you to.
It's hard not to fall off when,
it gets bumpy but you have
to try to stay on.
or it's a long way down.

Jolene Mosier

Little Weavers On My Paper

Little weavers on my paper,
  weaving intricate designs.
Leaving magical impressions,
  floating around in my mind.
From the flowing lead
  they work.
On my paper
  they will lurk.
And by the evening,
  I just might,
Have a delightful picture
  in sight.

Jennifer E. Sladek &
Natalie Blandon

"On Our Street Today"

A man died on our street, today-
Why?
He was only out to play,
Looking for some fun on his bike,
People from blocks away
all gathered 'round,
as he lay on the ground,
His wife rode at his back,
hugging him as close as they
could get.
If only they both had
worn a helmet.
As they hurried on their way -
But, because stupid laws
came into play,
A man died on our street today,
leaving his wife,
broken and fighting
for her life.

Terry Neal Albin and Irene Rapp

"Do You Know Me?"

Do you know me?
Why do you stare at me?
Am I that interesting to you?

Is it because my hair isn't of the same
grain or texture of yours?
Or is it because my hair is too blonde
or too black for you?
Or perhaps could it be that my eyes
are of a different color?

The reason is because I am not you,
nothing like you, I am different.
Nobody is the same, we are chosen
because of our individuality and
not because of our similarities.

Do you know me?
Am I a deep passion in your Heart?
Am I the fire in your soul?
Am I that interesting to you?

Rebecca Saint-Geraud

Questions?

What is our purpose?
Why must we fear?
What is emotion?
Why are we here?

When life is all over
Where do we go?
Is there really,
A hell, deep down below?

Why must be love.
People who despise us?
Why always give?
Why always trust?

Who is the greatest?
Who is the blessed?
Where is the power?
Is this life our test?

Why must we kill?
Why must we hate?
What can we do,
To control our fate?

Landry B. McKee Jr.

Only Once

Once in a lifetime
You find someone special
Your lives intertwine,
And somehow you know
This is the beginning
Of all you have longed for.
A love you can build on,
A love that will grow.
Once in a lifetime,
To those who are lucky,
A miracle happens
And dreams all come true.
I know it can happen,
It happened to me,
for I've found
My "once in a lifetime"
in you.

Regina Fall

Untitled

Dreams are places
you go to escape reality.
Seeing who you are,
going where you please,
Discovering new places
in the fantasies of your mind.
And when it is all over,
reality is at your fingertips,
Waiting for the conflicts of life.
Reality, in the end,
is your friend forever.
Dreams disappear
with the blink of an eye,
Till the next time you escape
within the trails of your mind.

Linda D. Krikava

Melissa

When you were born, my life was blessed
You lay your head, upon my breast,
Hair so golden, eyes so blue
Such perfection, seen by few...

I dreamed the dreams, that mothers do
My little princess, who was so new,
Little then, could I surmise
Your life would not be paradise...

You climbed those mountains, oh so high
You never let, life pass you by,
Your love of life, was so profound
Nothing ever got you down...

A great example, you have set
One more determined, I've never met,
I loved you then, I love you now
My daughter Melissa, you make me
proud!

Kathee M. Felty

Night

Wind blows through
your hair.
Just as the moon
and sun rise.
Sitting there
staring up at
the stars
while birds are
flying by.

Jessica Lasaponara

Pain

I lie here waiting,
Waiting for you,
Where I lie is so dark and gloomy,
It's so cold and muggy down here,
Muggy isn't the word to explain my sorrow for you,
Sorrow and pain is all I feel for you,
This pain will never go away,
This pain that lies in this soul hurts me so much,
It hurts me so much to see you this way,
When you feel pain I feel your pain in return,
This pain makes my soul fall into a dark hole,
Until you come back to me I feel nothing,
So I'll lie here,
Waiting and waiting just for you.

Amy Linn

Untitled

As I a weary traveler upon this long, winding road,
Walk picking up cuts and bruises along the way,
Carrying my own personal load,
There is something that I feel I must say,

The question I feel a need to ask,
The statement I so desperately must scream,
As others pass me by-wearing a plastic mask,
Not a single one trying to become a team,

Is, my Lord, a simple "WHY?"
Why are we as people so selfish and cold,
Why do we make our children of this mold,
Why do some become homeless and cry,
Why do small children have to die,
Why do some starve, go without,
Why do some get sick, and live in doubt,
Why do so many live a lie,
Why do so many cry,
Why cannot we all love,
Our brothers and sisters, everyone everywhere,
As God commands, with his symbol of peace and the dove? Why?

Edward L. Wilkins

"Day By Day"

Christ the Lord will show the way,
Walk with thee day by day.

Take to heart the gift of love,
None more greater from thee above.

The feelings we feel throughout the day.
Has a mighty touch of those along the way.

Sinning that comes along the way, will be forgiven,
His name is Jesus Christ, who will do your winning.

Before you go to sleep at night,
Say thank you to Jesus Christ for your flight.

Bonnie Boreman

Grandchildren Two

Chris and Wil grandchildren two.
We waited a long time for you.
Now that you're here.
We will always be near.
You're all the world to us.
When you're around we make a fuss.
What fun we have flying kites.
And watching you two run with all your might.
Oh, what a beautiful sight.
We love you with all our hearts.
Hoping we will never be apart.

Cecelia E. Scott

What Inspired Myself To Write This

Toll Of Death Played On the innocent
was based on five novels I had read about war.
One of these novels being fiction Alas
Babylon, Night, Hiroshima, Auchiutiz,
and one movie. Escape from Sobivor.
I found that all of these tragic wars were
linked together by one word and that is death.
When people think of wars they do not
remember the good they remember the bad.
I read a lot about the holocaust,
and believe me there was no good out of that.
The more I learn about these wars
the more questions I have.
The one question that always comes to mind is why.
And was it all worth it?

Amanda S. Pasieka

The Most Perfect Day

The most perfect day
was the day spent with you
under a tree, on a bench, near a brook.

September breezes were in the air
and neither one of us cared
about anything but being there together.

We walked until we found a tree that I liked
and there you lay down with your head in my lap
and I wrapped my arms around you lovingly.

We sat on the bench under the tree and watched children running
with their dogs racing at their heels.

We talked about how perfect the day was
and about anything that was of remote interest to either of us.

We watched people stroll by with carelessness in their step.
The type of attitude everyone has on such perfect days.

Nothing could have made the day more perfect
except if it didn't have to end.
And no day will be as complete
as the day I spent with you
under a tree, on a bench, near a brook.

Amy Elizabeth Pasechnick

A World Of Wax

Never remembering from which you came,
Watch the walls as they bleed into a flame.
Watch the boundaries of reality come crashing down,
Watch the swirling faces start to frown.

Still wondering if you have gone insane,
Just lie back and forget about your pain.
Just light a match and watch it turn blue,
Every time you'll see something new.

Being in a different world,
Never knowing how you felt.
Just watch the colors and feel them melt.

Close your eyes and feel a different dimension,
Lean back and let go of all your tension.
Being in this world just waiting to die,
Your whole life could be gone in the blink of an eye.

Not really knowing how you feel,
Never really knowing what's real,
Trapped in a cage of your own being,
Never realizing,
Never seeing.

Joanne Conner

"Chasing My Tail"

The trees still whisper of a friend gone away,
Way back in the forest where a boy used to play.
Is he lost in the world's deceptive dreams?
His forest now unwanted and lonely,
Or at least so it seems.

What has ever become of the magical times?
Recalling the summer winds as they blew through the chimes.
Have they sailed adrift on peaceful blue seas?
My times as a boy, when imagination roamed free.

I decided to go and take a good look,
Down along the creek and beside the brook.
Frantically searched both high and low,
Following the trail on which I used to go.

After a while it dawned on me,
All of the time the boy was me,
My childhood has gone away,
Now in my heart the memories shall stay.

Christopher M. Hubbard

How Many Ways To The Heart

So many ways a heart can be broken, yet not so many
ways to find love.
Perhaps that despair creeps in like some cancerous
plague and with the expediency of the ferryman, awaiting,
While you search vainly for the lost token.
Perhaps if you keep eyes alive and search intensely,
you may capture the hawks circling, yet within their
patterns is that lone dove.

Is it the devil behind red skies or just your own
mind's illusion when losses are loudly spoken?

Is it the angels treading among blue skies or just
your faith in yourself that keeps you alive and high above?

One day may come?
Yet for now there are so many ways a heart can be
broken. While there are not many ways to find love!

David G. Roberts

Yesterday's Future

Yesterday's future is the past of tomorrow.
We cannot own time.., it is only ours to borrow.
If you put off doing all the things, that should be done today...
The moment that you waste is lost.., it won't come back your way.

Life cannot be purchased with your treasures or your gold.
Yet, money buys you what you need, and shelter from the cold.
Good fortune tempts an honesty man to turn into a thief.
Too little causes pain and tears, and suffering and grief.

Have you ever wondered why we're here.., what meaning could
there be?
How God created mountain tops, the desert, and the sea?
Have you ever held a new born life, or watched an old man die?
Planned your life, took action.., yet things somehow went awry.

Providing food and beverage feeds the hungry for a day.
But teach them how to harvest crops, and hunger goes away.
Teach them how to clothe and care, and nurse the sick to health.
That giving, not receiving, is the greatest form of wealth.

Who is there to teach them.., if not you, who will it be?
Pass along the knowledge.., from the root unto the tree.
When Peace becomes exciting, and more prosperous than War.
Only then will freedom reign.., from shore to shining shore.

Carolyn LaMarchina

Lost

The day came.
We all knew it would.
Our tears were released.
But, yet, we never understood.
He left us before we could say goodbye.
Then he was gone - he shut his eyes.
Deep down inside a heart was breaking
But I knew about the long road he had taken
Even though he is gone forever - the
memories we had will last forever.

Brooke Hebert

"The Kingdom"

We'll inherit the earth; all the air and the land,
We are given this gift to rule with God's hand,
Jesus will come; He'll reign a thousand years.
During this time He'll dry all the tears,
No more evil; it's all been destroyed.
God's children are here; they've all been employed.
You cannot be denied, because of your past,
Just confess the Lord is the first and the last.

If we wear crowns; they surely will glisten.
For all it takes, when Christ speaks, is to open your ears and listen.
He put an end to all fighting, there are no more wars.
He punished every sinner; including the many whores.
He cleaned the soil of all human waste.
He saved every child aborted in haste.
So stand-up and cheer; the world is now ours.
For God gave us life; we felt all His powers.

Jarod Munn

The Mourning After

We finally laughed the other day...

This death thing was out!
We can't see it with our eyes, but it lurks near.

Our voices haunting high and laced with gaiety.
Laughter ringing, ringing, echoing in my ears.

Talk of urns was humorous discussing which he'd pick.
Our comments ran on and on although with morbid sick!
And yet relief is what we sought... to ease the other's pain.

A sad day nags at me,
it lay in wait ahead.

We finally laughed the other day....

Cynthia Lea Graber

Innocence

Like children under the sun,
we danced under the moon,
we kissed under the stars,
and we wept under the clouds.

But that's all we amounted to,
short, sweet, but memorable.

But when will I see you again?
Or will I ever?

I'm just praying that you remember,
but that may be asking too much.
I still remember sitting on the hillside,
and then I watched you leave.
We were innocent then,
but then memories can be what they'd like.

Jyll Gravius

God Knows Best

Sometimes it is so hard for us to understand why
we have to lose the ones we love. The grief should be
easier because we know they have gone home to our heavenly
father above.

When we think about all the suffering Jesus did
for us all, the suffering we do seems so small. He knows
the grief we feel. That's why he provided time for us to heal.

Things can be easier if we stop and think the
ones we love so dear are no longer hurting here. Oh the
heartache and tears will still be there and in the quiet
darkness of the night, the hurt will make it hard to rest,
but the pain will get easier because in our heart we know
that God really does know best.

Jean M. Orr

A Husband's Lament

There was a time when we shared life's joys, aches and pain
We laughed, hurt and cried together
We shared the raising of children, their laughter, aches and pain
They grew up and moved on and we were left to share alone again
But fate dealt you a bad hand
Physically you had more than your share of pain
While physically I had little
But mentally all your pain was real to me
Many a tear I shed and many a prayer I said
But you grew cold and bitter and shut me out
As though I had caused it all
You went through all the motions of being a wife
But your love for me was lost and so was I
So now we sit and stare
Our eyes not seeing what is real around us
Only seeing the ghostly memories of things past
Nor do we make a move to show love or affection
Because you see, although we live, we are already dead.

John Annunziata

His Light

To us Jesus is a glowing light
We must keep it in plain sight

Let it shine for others to see
With that inner peace we are really free

Even if our suffering has been long
The joy of the Lord will keep us strong

From the darkness Jesus has brought us out
His perfect word we must tell others about

Jesus is kind, good, and meek
His light through us others will seek

It's the inner man that others should see
And winning souls for Christ, that's the key

As we walk and let God's love abide
That glorious light we must never hide

Betty E. House

Alone

As I walk on this concrete pavement they call earth, I wonder
what has happened to all the nice people, where have they all
gone? My heart is filled with sadness the way the world is
today. I feel alone in a world with millions of people, alone,
what a terrible word. People talk but they say nothing, their
words are cold like their hearts. I miss the old days when
people cared, I wonder what happened to them all. The new
generation of people look the same but they have no feelings, I
miss the world old days.

Gerald D. Barker

God's Free Love

Love from God is surely free
We need to spread His Word rapidly.
For those who have fallen and gone astray
Need our prayers and love day by day.

Trust in God is one big key
And believing in Jesus is our responsibility.
So remember the cross and calvary
'Cause Jesus died for you and me.

Sometimes we fall - sometimes we fail
But in the end God will unveil.
God, is love and God does care
And believe me, God knows our every prayer.

The sunrise is so true
The sunsets so blue,
The heavenly sky's are for me and you
And in the end Jesus will come
And for some of us it will be no fun.
So, walk that line as straight as can be -
'Cause God is watching you and me.

Arthur Turgeon

From The Heart

My father left us without warning,
We never knew what was going on;
One day we were playing ball,
And the next he was gone;
They said it was something to do
with the heart;
The devastation and anguish
tore my family apart,
We were suddenly without a dad
No longer to have what everyone else had.
Loving a spirit brings bitterness and tears;
The sadness, emptiness and despondent years.
We still live and love
how long will it last?
With the diseases today
that kill so fast.
So take care of your heart
It will pay off in the end
From what the doctors say
Your heart could always mend.

Judi Manning

We The Sick!

For we are the mortal map,
We rule with bombs on our land!
U.S. men we shell the beaches one by one,
Hell, we're sick, we think it's fun!
As men we are cowards and hide in the grass,
So if we catch you, we'll beat your ass!
We love to fight, we always have war,
We did it again because we wanted more!
World War I was at its best,
So we had another, it was a success!
Hitler's party was lots of fun,
Except for the Jews, they had to run!
Vietnam was fun too,
For when you left your black and blue.
The Viet Cong had there party, it was set up right,
For they put up a hell of a fight!
They beat us at our own game,
So we went home, our heads in shame!

John Dapcich

Early Spring Morning

When morning's brush first tints the sky,
we start down the trail, my dog and I.

The world around us is hushed and still,
but the dog knows that cattle browse on the hill.

The sweet scent of evergreens perfume the air,
and new life and freshness are everywhere.

The stream sings a song and at its brink,
we startle a doe that has paused to drink.

This is all mine, this valley, these hills,
the thunderous roar where the cataract spills.

For all time I will cherish the beauty and charm,
of an early spring morn on my green valley farm.

Helen Parberry

Consider These Our Children

Let's stop to think just what we do to wish their lives away.
We urge them on from time to time, we do it every day.

We should enjoy each golden stage and treasure for its worth
The precious, priceless, lovely gift that God has placed on earth.

We start when they are babes in arm to rush them on their way.
To mothers it's a chore, you know, to be confined each day.
And now the time has come, we think, 'twould help if he could walk.
And "Why so slow my little one, it's past time that you talk?"

And now that he is off to school and joining club and den,
My chores are more... perhaps at twelve
I'll have more free time then.
So many years from six to twelve to taxi him from home.
If I can rush him through this stage, then he can go alone.

He's now away at college; my time is all my own,
my work is done...it stays that way...a lovely tidy home.
I'll do these things I've longed to do which piled up all those years.
It's such a joy, so quiet, no work. Now, why these silly tears?

I see that chair so vacant now. His room so tidy...clean.
I vision then those muddy boots and frame so lanky lean.
Belatedly, I've learned, Dear God, what mother's love does mean.

Jean B. Lynch

The Maple By My Window

Last summer her now rusty leaves
were worn in hues of emerald
but sprinkled now with red and gold

A stormy day had shed her gown,
I wander through
not to disturb the covered ground,

when first I saw her
I then knew that she would please me much
in all her changes that of woman borne

and now with all her garments shorn
in naked grace she stands
as only dancers would have known.

In stormy wind and rain I worry.
"Do not fear for me my friend.
I shall prevail for you and your concern

and many years of pleasure give,
for this your love I live
for yet another spring."

Gunnar Lindh Ronnback

Kenny Van Fleet, The Gentle Man

Our friend lost his wife three years ago
    We visited him
    he was happy to see us
    he was lonely
        without his beloved of many years.
        "It's so nice to hear
        a woman's voice in the house,"
            he said huskily.
            It was such a nice thing
            for a man to say
            it showed his loneliness,
            his sensitivity, his gentleness,
            it showed his soul.
        Seldom does a man disclose his soul.
        'Tis to be honored when he does.

Two years later we heard
    he had remarried,
    he needed,
    he longed to hear
            a woman's voice in his house.

Gail Caperna

This Land

When we bought this Land,
    We walked hand in hand.
It was such a thrill
    Walking round this hill.

We drove up from very far away,
    Just to walk in the snow and play.
Once we arrived to four feet of snow.
    We looked at each other, and out we'd go.

We'd sit beneath the big pine tree,
    Which gave us such a fond memory
Of youth and dreams and love come true.
    This Land is ours to sit and view.

Now that we're getting old and gray,
    We find it harder to walk and play.
We sit and gaze upon this hill,
    But to walk and play, we've lost our will.

Now, we just sit and gaze at the sky
    And, in my heart, I have to cry.
The time comes soon, though I know not when,
    That I'll never see this Land again.

Douglas Julian

A Day In The Life Of A Snowman

I stand alone
Watching, waiting, listening,
Hoping the laughter I once knew would return.
I long to feel the touch of the mittened hand,
To hear the tiny voice
Of the one who gave me life,
Who molded my form.
I wait but no one comes.
Night has fallen,
Another day has passed.
I am forgotten for now,
But will be remembered
In the depths, the mind,
Of one who knew
The joys of youth.

Jennifer Frost

The Rooster

When the kids were small, we bought a chick,
we watch him grow and he grew up quick.

He chased the kids around the yard,
they chased him with sticks and stones.

We tied one leg to the banana tree,
with a ten foot rope so he could roam you see.

Coming back from town we saw one day,
he was hanging upside down from a limb you see.

He limped around for a day or two,
then he would race my wife to her car every morning.

The end was in sight a few days later,
when he try to peck the face of a little girl.

A few days later I was thinking what to do,
when my neighbor said
He was having company for Sunday dinner, then I
thought, why not, just PUT MY ROOSTER IN YOUR POT!!!

Jack Lee Dowd

The Earth Looked Like An Apple And i Took A Bite

Tell me about the dummies that
were hanging in the tree, tell me
about the blind boy who could see,
tell me of the man who was beaten
for his belief, physically, mentally,
emotionally, wait, i know of the man
who lives to think, i know of the
boy who died to live, i have
everything I need, you have nothing
that's everything I want, tied in the
tree i cast my runes across the
land, lying in the grass i listen to
the band, sssshhh the water is
speaking, sshh the birds are
thinking, Yeats the devil and I went
for a walk in Eden's garden, would
you like an apple

Adam Gray

World Peace Now Begins at Home

World peace now begins at home
We've got to stop the violence and leave the guns alone

Begin with our children, teach them only to love
And where there's hate and violence, to rise above

To love ourselves so we can love the rest
To educate ourselves so we can be our best

Accept responsibility, it's not too late
To start loving all humans no matter what race

Yes! All of us can do our part
To understand and communicate from the heart

Start with ourselves, learn the ways of love
The gun is a cop out for lack of wisdom above

To use our heads to learn how to talk about
What makes us angry, happy, what makes us scream and shout

Our feelings are important, we must never doubt
We must communicate to bring peace about

Don't sit feeling hopeless, there's plenty to do
Give a listen, be a giver, peace begins with you

Unconditional love's our universal goal
To love everyone so the world can be whole

Emma Jean Foster-Fiege

Untitled

When I see his face it takes me back, back when we
were in love. The long nights sitting up and
talking. The days I thought would never end.
When they did, I thought it was all over for me,
I couldn't go on. I did, with him still in
my heart, still in my dreams. I still love
him, and now he's back wanting my love. Wanting
to touch me, feel me, love me, kiss me once
again. For one split moment I do too. But I
know it wouldn't be the same. I couldn't love
him the way I used to. Things have changed, he's
not the one I fell in love with many, many nights
ago. The memories are very strong, telling me to
go for it, I could work it out. Although it feels
like I would have to choose between new memories
that could go wrong and old memories that keep me
happy. It still seems on the lonely nights I still
want him back, but now I know that that is
impossible. He is gone. He is not the one I fell
in love with anymore.

Heidi MacRae

Forgetfulness

Sometimes at the end of a day
We're too exhausted to stop and pray to our Heavenly Father
    up above
Who showers us all with His undivided love.
He showers us daily with gifts that are rare
And many times unappreciated, some don't care
And some don't even realize
The gift of speech, or the sight in their eyes,
The power to walk, and the joy of hearing.
Another tomorrow, in the nearing.

Judi Williams

Vacation In Heaven

When I take my vacation in heaven,
What a wonderful time that will be,
I'll walk with my friends on the streets of gold,
No more burdens and tears will there be.

When I take my vacation in heaven,
No clouds in the sky will I see,
I'll live in a glorious mansion,
That my Lord has prepared for me.

When I take my vacation in heaven,
The rivers will flow fresh and free,
The sun will always be shining,
What a wonderful vacation that will be.

Gertrude Ryder

Single Women

Ah!..there are so many of us!
Wanting so terribly to give our love...
And so afraid...

It's gone now...
All that innocent arrogance of youth.
That total self belief...
Gone these many years.

So now we do what must be done each day....and we survive.
And (when there's time) reach out
(so tentatively!)
Testing each relationship...
Seeking him we can love without fear.

J. West

Freedom...

An expulsion of expository captivity.
What could be more wonderful than
The beauty of liberty?
Only feelings of release; feelings of
Confinement to Independence.
Yet, could Independence be fraudulent?
The fresh clash of red, white, and blue
Straining against the brisk winds of
Yesterday and tomorrow? Could
That be counterfeit?
No, oh no.
Old Glory, in all her luminescence,
Is forever,
Remaining.
Straining.
Forever. For all time.
   Freedom-for me.
Thank you, dear country of unreserved,
Outspoken, voluntary liberation.
Thank you.

Crystal M. Haney

War...

War...
   What could be worse?
   People being killed,
   Blood being shed.
   People lying awake,
   Sleepless in their beds.
   Wondering why it started,
   And when will it end.

   Do people want to die?
   Or must they hear the shriek battle cries.
   A bold man arises,
   just like the morning sun,
   People gasp in horror,
   Each holding a gun.

   A jet fly's over head,
   it drops a bomb,
   and they're all dead!
   War...
      Who needs it?

   Julie Campbell

Grandmother's Workbasket

Though worn and faded and empty now
What memories it recalls
When Grandma deftly plied her thread
While she sewed and quilted for us all.

Her sewing basket she left behind
We found it after she was gone
It brings my Grandma back to mind
This relic now of which I'm fond.

As she sewed and rocked in her favorite chair
And cheerfully hummed an old church song
She mended all our garments there
In those days of yore, long past and gone.

But now she sings on a distant shore
No longer she's wrinkled, bent, or old
She's happy and content forevermore
As she walks those streets of gold.

I cherish your basket, Grandma dear,
As well as the lovely quilts you made
You still at times seem very near
And for me, your memory will never fade.

Gwen Sharp

Separated By Sea

Alone in Holland,
What could it be and where are his thoughts
What kind of things fill his night-time dreams
He must have lost his right hand, because there
haven't been any letters for me
Is he holding another, because he has not
sent his love over the sea to me
Has he given his heart to someone else
It has been nearly two years that we've lived apart
Has he closed and tossed me out of his heart
Silly me...
I honestly believed that nothing would ever
tear our love apart
And I wonder, is it possible that he is too busy
to pick up the telephone and ring me
What am I going to do with each thought
I feel my heart breaking
in
two

Angela R. Sumner

Reflection

Why does man strive to reach the stars?
What hopes he there to find....himself?

Far wiser would he be interrogating history
'Tho it be locked in dust upon his shelf.

Why should man try to ferret out
The Great Enabler's plan hid deep in mystery?

That plan unfolds for all who'll see
Left untouched of jealousy
Denied by those who cannot be content surrendering
their doubt.
Meticulous the craftsman, He, compelling nothingness to be
The cradle of infinity, beyond our scope or span

The One who counts the stars and names them by His plan
Shall one day call us all to Him, and we shall understand.

Charles D. Bolen

"I Am The Clay And You Are The Potter"

Oh God, only you know me as I really am,
What I can be and do can be created by your Potter's hand.
A mere piece of clay I exist, an incomplete mold,
First tossed and beaten, then having to fold.
Succumbing into a fragile piece of clay I become
Sensitive to even the slightest movement of your thumb.
With firm yet gentle hands,
Mold me into what I really am.
A design more lovely than anything under the sun,
I am transformed becoming your recreated one.
For, I am the clay and my talents are the water
Together we can do nothing without You as the Potter.

Catherine M. Car Wight

Different

Each of us in life looks differently,
We should all be thankful for that or I would look at
you and think you were me.
Different, that is the way it should be,
Be the same and you will not know who is you and who is me.
When you look the same,
Act the same,
Walk the same,
Talk the same,
Then no one will see
Your true individuality.
Hang with the crowd but be your own,
Do not be dragged down trying to be someone's clone.

Jessica Reich

Believe In Me

Sometimes I wonder
　what I have become
　and I start to believe
　that all hope is gone.

For it seems
　that most of my dreams are fading away
　one by one.

Although I have the determination and drive
　a natural instinct to survive,
　just hear my cries.

For right now I just need
　friendship and understanding,
　not false promises or lies.

Someone who will believe in me
　to help me be set free,
　are you on my side?

For the memories of my past
　will always remind me
　of who I once used to be.
　　Donna Fitzpatrick

Life's Changes

　When I look into the water, I not only see
what is in it, but I also see me
　When the wind whispers by
I see a thousand twinkles, like in the sky
　When I look into the water I not only see blue
But like the stars and me I also see you
　When I see me I see the inside me
When I see you I see what I want you to be
　As into the water the sun shines
I see my rainbow of time

When I look at my rainbow at the good times and bad
I think back on my life at the happy times and sad
And into the water a teardrop falls...
Changing the water that changes all...
　　Emily J. Brown

Almost Eighteen

Almost eighteen and what are you doing?
What kind of life are you pursuing?

Life is now the game!
But — do you even know your name?

You think you've grown up so, but my child
There's much, much more to know.

Fun and thrill, that's what you're thinking.
That trend of though will send you sinking.

Hard cold facts, that's what you're missing
and at me, you do your hissing!

"I'm the way I want to be.
I'm very happy. Can't you see?"

But in the years to come,
can you count your total sum?

Life is not all fun and thrills.
Sometimes you'll have the chills.

Hard, cold facts will hit you then.
Of what we've said again and again.

Life is not all fun and games,
Grow up my child and learn the same.
　　Jo Ann Vennebush

In Fear Of The Pack

I see a pack!
What kind of pack can it be?
Be it beast or be it man?
I try to run. I try to scream if I can.

But what do I do? And where do I run?
The pack gets closer and there's nowhere to go.
My skin gets clammy and my heart beats so.

They are like beasts but yet they're man!
Growling and Sneering in such an evil way,
our sweet children of yesterday.

Drugs, sex, thievery, and lies,
this is of which the pack derives.
But for me it's my lucky day,
for they slowly turn, and walk away.
　　Irene De Moss

I Am Free!

Do not bind me with your hurt, loneliness, despair or expectations of what was, what is, or what may never be. Instead, rejoice in my freedom. For I am the smile on your lips, the dew on the grass, the birds in the sky and the breeze and sun on your face. Remember.....

I Am Free!

Remember the laughter and fun, the tears and the growing time of each of us.
But most of all, remember the LOVE!!

I Am Free,

...and so are you. Live and enjoy all things because I am these things and more and they are my gifts to you. Remember...

I Am Free!

...and as you free me, so are you freed.
　　Charles M. Fontenot

Woven Or Spun

What are you going to do when He comes that day?
What will you say, will you lie that day?
What will He see, will you turn to flee?
Or will you turn to hide away

Time is full of prophecies
But there is only one for me

His chariots tell of things to come
His robe is it woven
Or is it spun?

There will come the day when the dead will rise
Could that possibly open your eyes?

Too late?
Will you miss the date?
Then the impending doom is your fate
Your fate
　　Christine King

This World

What have we done to this world?
Where are the gods that dwelt on sacred heights,
On Mt. Katahdin and on Everest?
Where is that lusty pack that called Olympus home
And meddled in our lives?
They have become the homeless people of this world,
Living in cardboard boxes under bridges.
Don't look for them in outer space —
Our satellites would spy them out.
Go search for them among the myriad poor.
　　Elizabeth Knight

Hecate (Divine Mother Of Magic)

Divine Mother Hecate, what is the secret of the Moon
What wind has blown upon the sun
What stars have fallen into the wind and the stars
From the Moon
The moon is the star of fertility and Earth magic
Oh what is the price of a Dark Star or a Death Star to Death
Key 18 of the Tarot the secret of the Ages

Is in the moon and the Stars
Love is the cornerstone of all the Churches
Including that of the Witches

Divine Mother Hecate what is the secret of Christianity
But the Miracles of the Churches and Jesus Christ
A hot wind has blown upon the desert winds of Time
And the cults and the witches and the Satanists have
Created their own brand of theocracy from the hot winds of Time
Christianity has fought Evil, but has forgotten the Holy Spirit
And Yaweh and Mary and the Hidden God El-Elion
And the cults have gone through the Teeth of Tethys and
OUROBOUROS

And the Orphic mysteries
To lose Time and Space

Antoinette Voget

The Great Mate

If Jesus were here today, what would he do?
What would he say on this Valentine's Day?
Should he be content, or should he be irate,
About the way we treat our mate?

Can you trust your mate to do what's right?
Do you hold them tight other than the night?
Can you give them your shoulder to cry on,
When they are sad and blue?
Can you give them that high they need from you?
Can you make them smile for a while or two?
Do you appreciate everything they do for you?
Do you find yourself hanging on every word they say?
Have you gone out of your way to make their day,
Or do you need everything your way?

If you could put your mate on a pedestal today,
Would Jesus be content and say:
Your mate has passed the test of greatness,
But you knew that all the time.

May God bless this mate and reward them at the pearly gate.

John P. Ricket Sr.

Gone Away

What's that field of yellow and gold
What's that field, wait I was not told
Do you see it over there
Do you smell its clean, sweet air
How far, how far can it be
Can it be, can it be as far as you and me
This seems so very strange
but it surely, surely cannot change
there I go
so far so low
Will I see you once again
or will it be just like it began
If only I just might
go back, back to that night
That night I gave to you
the only thing that was really true
You meant everything to me
but you didn't, just didn't see
Now's my time to say good-bye
now that I'm in the sky.

Heather Bradshaw

Untitled

What ever happened to the English Language
When a "pig" lived out in the sty
When a "pad" was a rug to lay your dog on
And the "moon" was that thing in the sky.

When the "yellow pages" were an old treasured book
And an "ex" was the prefix to port
When a "joint" was a place to hang out.
And only horses, cows, and pigs would "snort"

When "coke" was something you drank
And a "junkie" bought stuff that was shot
When "rap" was a knock on the door.
And veggies were cooked in a "pot"

When "Aids" meant helping a neighbor
And "gay" meant happy and glad
When "cool" meant chilly outside
And sex was very, very, bad.

Whatever happened to the English Language
Poor Webster would toss in his grave
Well, big guy, when you snooze you lose
Chill out, hang loose and be brave.

Betty Walker

Spiders Don't Scare Me

I was sitting down one day
When a spider came upon me

Its eyes were a deep red
And letting curiosity get the better of me
I asked the spider
What the problem was
The spider replied
I have allergies

Being a meek well-mannered man I was starting to show
Some concern for this red eyed creature
Suddenly
I was staring down the barrel of an assault rifle
My meekness by this time had faded

The spider began to speak
I heard no sound but instead
I saw a tear running down his face
I spoke to this monster and said
Sit down or be squished
Now I have no fear
The creature is gone and the sneezing is no more

Harold Colon

Good-Bye Daddy

It's so hard to say good-bye,
    When all I want to do is to cry.
Things were so grave, was always the report,
    You left too soon — time was too short.

You promised six good rounds, "like Jack Dempsey," you said.
    You did this and more, as you bravely lay in your bed.
But the death angel could no longer postpone,
    And you no longer suffer — for God took you home.

You crossed that span into eternity,
    I know one day that's where I'll be.
We who are left behind and know of that blessed hope,
    Will bravely go on and we'll learn to cope.

I know you'll welcome us on that day,
    When each one passes on and comes over your way.
Yes, we'll all meet again — it won't be long,
    We'll join you and we'll all come home..........

Good-bye Daddy, see you soon......

Judy Cross

The Merry-Go-Round

...AND the children ran around and around the merry-go-round,
When all of a sudden, swish, it lifted off the ground!

Spinning and spinning, that disk did fly...
High above the playground and far into the sky.

With a blast it zoomed above the town.
Soon the children lost sight of the ground.

As the merry-go-space ship spun and swirled,
It soon spun its way around the entire...world!

With a swish and a zoom, it orbited the moon.
It circled Jupiter, Uranus, Pluto, Venus, and Neptune.

The merry-go-saucer sped around Mercury, it fought its way
around Mars.
As it orbited the planets, the travelers counted the stars.

While twirling through the rings of Saturn,
Each child could see our whole planetary pattern!

Then, off in the distance, they heard a loud ringing sound.
Called back by the school bell's toll, the merry-go-round slowed
down..

"Recess has ended, and our journey is complete!"
The children shouted as they brushed "moon dust" from their feet.

Our heroes proudly filed through the school house door,
where they drew pictures of everything they saw... and MORE...

Greg Clingan

Fade To Gray

When you live in a world all your own,
When all you can sing is a sad and lonely song,
What does it mean when reality is only a place to be,
As the day fades to gray.

When time takes the day and steals it away,
When dreams become old memories,
What does it mean when pain is all you see,
As the day fades to gray.

When you're in this world, and all alone,
When happiness is just a word in a song,
What does it mean when tears are falling in the street,
As the day fades to gray.

When you know love can never be,
When the past is only a bad memory,
What does it mean when all that is left is dreams,
As the day fades to gray.

It's just another day, another fade to gray.
It's just another way, to watch time drift away.
It's just another day, another shade of gray.
It's just another way, to live in a world of gray.

Doug Smitherman

Two Angels On The Ground

I have two little angels on the ground
When I come home late, there's five and eight
With covers pulled up all around.
I thank the Lord above,
For this feeling that I've found
For my two little angels,
Age five and eight, on the ground

I wonder what I'll do
When they are nineteen and twenty-two
I wonder if I'll write about them in a poem
I hope I'm here to see
With the Lord's help and lots of memories,
You know...They just might write a poem about me!

Buddy Leffel

It's A Wonderful Feeling

It's a wonderful feeling on a Sunday morn
When church bells begin to ring
And people come from far and wide to adore
Christ our Saviour Lord and King

And then at times when you feel all alone
It's a wonderful feeling to know
That you can go to Him in prayer or song
And He'll be listening be ye high or low.

Yes He listens to the meek and bold
And helps us along life's narrow road
Then at the end He welcomes us into the fold,
And relieves us of our weary load

As a poet I'm not very good it's true
But I hope by this poem you can see
That my heart beats true for our Saviour who
Came down to earth to save you and me.

Now this poem is not very long
But it really comes from my soul
And I hope you won't think of me wrong
If I wish you all God's blessing to hold.

Edward Moyer

"Feelings On Hold"

Where do I look, what do I say?
When do I feel one believes my way?
There so many feelings I've got deep with-in,
but yet I can still feel myself gasping up at the wind.
I've looked over and under, inside and out,
and all of the same time grown with doubt.
Doubt that there's anyone willing to listen,
while I express my feelings, and ask for a decision.
Yes a time or two I thought it was right,
and wanted to open up and shed the light.
I would speak very brief, and far in between,
hoping at the end the light would be seen.
But nobody responded with any interest or concern,
and once again I felt abandon with nowhere to turn.
I've come to assume one would say I've gone to the extremes,
and then considered my feeling's on infatuated dream.
So then who holds the key that unlocks all locks,
and will allow me the chance to open up and talk?
For I've walked a many of years with an emotional load,
and until I can find that key, my feelings are on hold.

John L. Rice

If Only Life Would Slow Down

I looked around the other day, another year had flown away.
What could have happened to those years of babies cries and
teenage tears.
If only life would slow down!
What happened to that brilliant child, bright blue eyes, infectious smile.
Dreamer born, potential high, perhaps seen only in mother's eyes.
If only life would slow down!
And where did that young girl go, with tangled hair, disheveled bow,
An independent, spirited one, future yet undone.
If only life would slow down!
I gazed into my youngest's eyes, and heard a young man's
impatient sighs.
A sensitive, caring young man, striving to be the best he can.
If only life would slow down!
The years speed by, hell bent bound, with new horizons for all to be
found.
Please, life, slow down!

Collette Owens

Forever

Friendship, strong, unbreakable
When I cry you make me smile,
When I fall you pick me up.
You give me life when I feel I'm dying,
You give me air when I have no breath.
If I feel I am selfish and uncaring,
You tell me I am not.
You don't know how special you are,
But I know
If I never have a friendship like this again,

It won't matter, because I'll know I had it once.
And if this friendship ever fades,
If we go our separate ways,
And if I think the whole thing was a dream,

A part of my imagination,
I'll know that I am wrong.
Because as I write these words,
I know our friendship is alive,
And in these words it will live on,
Forever, invincible, immortal
Dalia Al-Othman

Our Night

Words are only words unless they're true and believe me
when I say that I love you.

Raindrops falling kissing my face, dreaming of me dancing
in white ribbons and lace.

I speak the words from my lips to yours and only your
love can open my doors.

So you broke my silence when I'd held in all I could;
now we can be in love the way we should.

I want you to take my hand and don't set me free;
hold me in your arms and tell me you love me.

Take the time to say how much you care;
look into my eyes through a candles flickering flare.
Kiss me in the moonlight that shines from above;
Touch me in the night, I'm so in love.
Hold me, love me so very tight; for we're forever in love
and this is our night.
Jenna M. Lee

Please God

God, can you tell me where to run
When people think shooting is fun

Will you help me when I'm crying
And tell me no more is dying

God, with you I know I'm not alone
Cause you are the only one that can guide me home

I know you can give us love with hugs
And save us from the drugs

God, not only do some of us use them
We are also Victims

We are dying
Cant you tell I'm crying

God, please forgive us for we have sinned
oh how I need a friend

But no one can nod
cause my friend is God
Christina Castilla

A Garden Rose

You planted me in the ground,
when I was just a seed.

You nurtured me and watered me,
with your loving tears.

You made sure the sun's rays tickled me,
and every night you laughed and talked to me.

My stem began to grow and my petals too.
My vibrant colors came from the rainbow that caressed me.

I will thank you for your love,
by blooming in your garden every Spring.
Dawn Granadon

Snowflower

She was born at the end of winter
When March beckons the warmth from the sky.
Her skin pale and pure with pink kisses on her cheeks.
One could compare her to a young flower
Breaking through the snow to smile at the sun.

Years gently pass and she brings such beauty to this earth
The Great Spirit glows with approval
For she has found a man she truly loves
And will marry at the edge of spring.
The harmony of life endures and blesses this unity.

Chippewa Inspiration
Joanne Phillips

"The Enchantment Of Power"

Like a black widow, a woman must breed
When she's young, she has illusions,
Her dreams become real not a nightmare
The dreams have their own solutions.

Feeling pleasure, flesh of a dream
Which explodes and bleeds,
Reality becomes a nightmare
Sight of the web, leads to the growth of seeds.

Howling full and ripe like wine
The fantasy begins to fade away.
Confusion of the touch is forgotten
The passion of charm is just a lay.

Realizing reality is creeping closer
She embraces the wind for security reasons,
Tears fall for roses all turning black
Crying endlessly for the innocence of the seasons.
April L. Horne

Stand The Sound

A long time ago...
When the heart ran free
And the soul told it to slow down
The sun beamed rays of light during the day
To warm the summer nights
With soft winds playing upon the midnight grass
Stands the sound
The sound
It echoes
If forever echoes
Into time that hold no limits
And with open arms ready to embrace
Another time
Another place
There stands the sound
Forever in time's face
Demy D. Spadideas

A Faithful Friend

Goodbye my friend, till we meet again at Spring,
when the flowers will be blooming again.
They sky will be gray and lovely today and
the Heaven asks us no questions.
That's why it is far away.
We hold hands, thinking why,
with thunderbolts in the sky.
Let no one look upon you today
with trembling hands, they will go astray.
Heaven does unlock the door with the key that fits.
We don't need material things
with the love of you and me.
We will not be parted again.
The time is marching on, when I will see you again
with carefree love and carefree mood,
thinking we will not make it in the Spring
when the flowers bloom again.
When the snow covers us around with the joy of gladness,
we will be there to meet you again.

  Clyde C. Seaton

The Loss Of A Mother

When grief strikes it's utterly blinding,
when the loss is as strong as lightning.

Your feelings are frozen in time,
your emotions are all in a bind.

Words of sympathy are spoken to you,
but words, to your mind, are anything but kind.

You want to strike out at anyone near,
because of a pain you just can't bear.

When the guilt you feel has you in fear,
when you care, guilt is natural, 'cause she was so dear.

But just when you think you'll make it,
just a song, word or expression and I'm faking it.

This kind of pain you cannot describe,
because this kind of pain can only subside.

So when you think of Mother, from your heart,
remember she gave you life from the start.

Love will last forever and not wither,
not even with "THE LOSS OF A MOTHER."

  Della Anderson

Have You Ever Been That Happy?

Have you ever been that happy?
When the spring flowers flow.
The sun is bright
and shines with a light
that warms and embraces
your soul.
Have you ever been that happy?
When the songs of the birds never stop,
and you feel you're as light as the air.
You could soar, you could fly, and walk through the sky.
Have you ever been that happy?
When the fluffy white clouds form animals
and they coast with the wind
high in the sky.
Have you ever been that happy?
When you feel that you could never have been so high.
The feeling of peace, joyance
and love for everything in the world.
You couldn't hate if you tried.
Have you ever been that happy?

  Christine Benda

A Lover's Prayer

Dear God,
When there exists one
Who is strong in character
And gentle with his touch,
Who shares his knowledge
Without imposing his will,
Who warms the heart with his smile
And has eyes that shine with kindness,
Who is serious about life
Yet able to share a good laugh,
Whose lips causes fires to rage deep within
And calms fear with presence alone,
Who shows his love for me with every action
He deserves no less than all my love.
Thank you
For sending me one such as him.
And God,
Help me to always love one so deserving.

  Heather P. Gill

Fix It

She was barely four
When there on the floor
Lay half the curls from her head
The scissors lay on the bed

Very, very carefully she picked up the pieces
Laughing with great delight
Until she saw in the mirror's light
The picture she had created

The eyes darted left then right
The mouth opened wide at the sight
With the grace of a figure skater
She bounded toward me
"Grandma, fix it - fix it"

My heart laughed at the sight
Indeed she was a fright
And the words "grandma, fix it, fix it"
Has echoed in my mind many a night
How humbling to be held in such esteem
Only god could fulfill her dream.

  Grace Wall

Through the Eyes of a Child

Have you ever seen a child's eyes
When they look at someone they admire?
They want to be just like them
Their hearts are filled with fire.

They watch them ever so closely
Their actions are exactly the same
The only thing different about them
Is their size, their age, and their name.

The children see their idols as heroes
People that make no mistakes
They're going to be just like them
No matter what it takes.

If you're just such a person
That has kids looking up to you
Watch out for what you say
Be careful of what you do.

Because feelings or thoughts that you express
Whether from anger or from strife
Are not just easing your mind
They're patterning a young child's life.

  Gary Hunt

The Broken Promise

You gave me your promise to move to my ranch
When we got married and was each other's branch.
So I got a pastor and we're married now
So where is the horse and where is the cow?

You're here every morning for a bath and cologne
Then you go away and you leave me alone.
I didn't know that life was so blue
Until the day that I married you.

You leave every day till the mid of the night
And if you still love me that is not right.
When you leave home you never say "Bye"
So I stay at home and I weep and I cry.

You're running around with a street animal
Who must be a fan of today's Rock and Roll
You're gone all the day to the clubs and the bars
From the rise of the sun to the moon and the stars.

I got a lawyer to get a divorce
Cause I won't stay married to a two-legged horse.
We have three children and they are in school
While you are in town and you're wild as a mule.

Joe Dunkin

Life Is Learning

When we come into this world, we are learning.
When we live through adolescence, we are learning.
Even when we think we know it all, we are learning
When we grow older we find out how little we really know;
So listen young and old and learn to live life,
but never stop learning

Daniel Ames

From Summer Camp To Boot Camp

Hey pretty soldier down in South Carolina,
When we speak on the phone, you couldn't sound fine.
Are they working your muscles and stressing your mind,
Starving your body and running you blind?

Are you doing your push-ups, your jumping jacks too,
Running down stairwells and up till you're through?
Making your rack till coins nicely bounce,
And watching your calories down to the ounce?

Are you running and marching, climbing and crawling,
Hitting your rack at night and just bawling?
Getting up early dead on your feet,
Learning a schedule on which you must eat?

Well if you're doing all these fun things,
And learning more everyday.
You've just begun living in the real world,
And doing it the soldier's way.

Diane Hall

I Remember...

I remember when you were here,
When we were happy and everything was clear.
I remember sleigh riding in the snow,
Watching you laugh, how was I to know?
I remember when you used to cut wood,
And thinking that I never could.
I remember the cave that you loved so much,
In our minds, a sign said "DON'T TOUCH"
I remember yesterday, I remember today,
I remember when they said you had gone away.
I remember the good times, I remember the bad,
Now all I remember is being sad....

Christine Lape

The Inner Struggle

How do you fight, what weapons do you use,
when you are at war with yourself?
You found something in yourself you don't like,
you have scars that time and air won't heel.
How do you fight, what weapons do you use,
when you are at war with yourself?
The pain you feel is more then anyone can afflict upon you,
you don't care about the world around you,
you have another world to contend with.
How do you fight, what weapons do you use,
when you are at war with yourself?
The world you're in, your world,
never sleeps, even if the outside says so,
You wake up in cold sweats, you scream, but no one cares
to hear..... How do you fight, what weapons do you use,
when you are at war with yourself?
When you are at war with yourself,
the battle you never seem to win....
when you are at war with yourself.

Alison Mack-Stazenski

"Abused"

Learning a lesson is hard to do,
when you are only two.
You didn't know that you did wrong,
but his hand was mighty strong.
You are told that you are always bad,
and you often feel quite sad.
He comes into your room at night,
and you are told not to fight.
He tells you that it's your little secret,
but your heart can't keep it.
You might think that it's all your fault,
but soon you'll see, that it wasn't you,
it was he.

Brett J. Berry

Hope

When we are little, we HOPE too grow up just like our parents,

As you reach your teenage years, you HOPE you don't turn out
like your

parents
When you become an adult, you HOPE to succeed in life;

When you marry, you HOPE that it will last forever;

Then your children come along and we HOPE we guide them
well through their youth;

As we get older, we HOPE that we have done the right
things in life;

As we begin to realize that one day we'll be gone, we HOPE
that God will accept us for all the good and bad we have done
in our lives..

Jeffrey A. Minard Sr.

Grandmother's Chair

There is the old chair,
where grandmother once sat.
But now grandmother is gone,
And the chair still stands.
As if a last remembrance of her,
Like a monument to her life.
She lived alone, as the chair stands alone.
She was old,
As the chair is old.
There is the old chair,
Where grandmother once sat.

Alice Kelly

Forgotten

I thought I would crack, stumble and cry
When you casually tossed me aside.

I thought I would surely die
When you traded me in for a younger, wilder ride.

"It's really for the best,"
I repeated in earnest.

No more appearances at my door
unexpected, at a quarter to four.

No more tears over a silent phone,
or wishing you would share my home.

How could I not see
How you'd taken advantage of me?

Now that it's said and done,
I'm starting to remember fun.

Take that younger, wilder ride;
The poor dear won't miss feeling tossed aside.

Don't worry about me now;
Life is suddenly so — Wow!

Dee Dee Damon

Peace

'Twas the day that I visited a Gallery of Art,
When I saw a picture that touched my heart.
A storm was raging like that in my soul,
From years of heartache
Quite out of control.
Yet, there was a bird upon her nest
Oblivious of danger, for she was at rest.
The river swelled beneath her abode,
And the branches shook, 'neath the tiny load.
'Twas a simple lesson I learned from that bird,
But a mighty lesson found in God's Word.
Only one word described what I saw,
The word was PEACE: I was filled with awe!

Joyce Bergquist

Innocent Victims Of Aids

Who are the children with the hollow eyes
Why is it our ears do not hear their cries;

Where is the justice that will set their souls free
Why can't this world be the way it should be!

Why must their tears all be cried in vain
Why must their hearts have to carry the pain;

Hey! out there - God Damnit! I'm talking to you
Where the hell's your morality, what will you do;

Will you reach out to help and lend your hand?
Or will you simply ignore and not understand;

They are the seeds of life with no hope to grow
Why they've been poisoned, I will never know;

We can't let them die, not before they have lived
So who will bear the burden of what we should give;

Why can't we join together and begin a new start
We might not heal their sickness but we can revive their hearts;

Please don't let those eyes be hollow - take away their shame
They were born of innocence - it was we who scarred their name;

As I hang my head in sorrow and my guilt locks me in this gloom
I pray that we can help them and today is not too soon.

John Fosco

The Player

See that young boy, the one whose eyes light up
    when you say "Hi Bud!"

See that young boy, the one who yells the loudest
    for his team, his favorite player, to win

See that young boy, the one who will never have great
    height, work and play to be as good as "him"

See that young boy run onto the floor to try and be the
    first to say "Great Game" and wait eagerly for your
    words of friendship and acknowledgement

See that young boy with the word "Hero" in his eyes
    try and analyze the game

See that young boy, your replacement, our hero of
    tomorrow, sadly walk away when not a single player
    thought to say "Hi Bud" to a kid, Tomorrow's
    player—tomorrow's man

Joan Molenda

A Quiet Place

I need to find a quiet place
Where all is calm and full of grace,
Where I can lay and rest my mind,
Put all my worries far behind,
Where peace and tranquillity fill the air,
Where I can sit without a care,
Where grief and sorrow knows it not,
A secret, private, lonely spot
Where I can be inside of me
And all the world just let me be.
I need to find a quiet place
To disappear without a trace.

Ennis T. Miles

Nature's Tears

I stand and look up in the sky
Where all the stars are standing by
Waiting for the sun to rise
So they can sleep or close their eyes
The birds begin to sing a song
I'm sure will last all day long
The clouds roll in to cover the sky
We know it's time for them to cry
The tears come down to wet the ground
The thunder and lighting is a scary sound
The flowers stand up with their heads so high
For their stalks were thirsty and stems so dry
Then, the clouds start to roll by
And allow the sun to brighten up the sky.

Connie Berra

My Dream House

I have always longed to live in a house high on a hill,
Where everything is beautiful peaceful and still,
A rippling stream and a tree nearby
That I can sit beneath, and gaze up at the sky,
There I'd spend quiet moments with my thoughts and my dreams
There's nothing on earth as bad as it seems,
I know I'll never have this place, so I have but just one wish
That I can make the home I live in like the one
    I'll always miss,
I'll always have that longing, it will never disappear

But it is eased by all the blessings I receive each day,
    Through every year.

Carole Adamitis

The Days Of Yore

What became of the days of blades
Where have gone all the kings
Is chivalry indeed dead or only gone astray
And where is the blacksmith's abode
Where have gone the battlefields of knight and squire
And the steeds upon which they rode
Where the nobility, this I implore
The earth stood still and reflects no more
Longing to live in the days of forgotten lore
O the days of castle and empire
How simple were the times
When contempt was reckoned with trial by fire
Gone are those, and battlefields no more
Gone are the knights, steeds, squires and kings
Those were the days, the days of yore
What has become of mankind,
Some say civilized, others say weak
Some say that the future's quite bleak
We're stranded on future's dismal shore
Saying farewell to the days of yore.

Friedrich Wunsch

My Pack

I do not belong in the danger of the city
where I have no song to sing away decay and brutality.
I hide until I can find my way back
To the wilderness where waits my pack.
My pack consists of spirit wolf; and
My beloved, once living, but now spirit dogs,
And bewildered battered lost children,
sitting on the fallen logs,
wondering if the world will ever be safe again.
I lose human speech, if I am in this wilderness for very long.
And become one with the animals, the spirit pack;
until I never want to come back
to the city where I don't belong.
I would rather hug a tree,
and feel ancient strength and stability;
I would rather talk to red bird,
than return to those humans who don't keep their word.
When I am with the wolves, I have a song,
That sings away despair and makes me strong.

Candyce King

My Date With An Angel

She once appeared as an apparition,
Where we met in the briefest of moments.
She descended from her high position,
But why she came to me, it made no sense.

Our first meeting was not to be out last.
God destined us to cross paths yet again.
My eyes sighted a beauty that surpassed
All others and I doubted I was sane.

I stood agape for she walked with the light,
She was a vision from a dream of mine.
Rejoined we disappeared into the night,
Dancing and laughing we stood apart from time.

We played the eve carefree and lighthearted,
Nothing slowed us except our time to go.
I planned to kiss her 'fore we departed,
But my shy nature kept me from doing so.

Regret burns inside my heart like a fire.
"Should have" and "Could have" hound me 'til I yell.
Then it echoes within me my desire
To resurrect my date with an angel.

Joseph Bohan

Cube Live On

Let me tell you of a place in time, a place in a space,
  where life was once.
With grasses growing, winds a blowing, flowers a sway,
  and animals at play.
Peace and Harmony at valley's edge.
Love lying in every wedge.
Sun rays and Moon drops flying in the air.
Along came Man and so did Despair.
Using technology to form a path, to stay alive.
As we all know, if one must live another must die.
Mother is gone, the grass is dead, the winds have died.
The flowers are nil, the animals have left...
Peace, Harmony, Love were no challenge
  for Man and its companion Despair.
Sun rays are deadly and Moon drops are rare.
Man is alone with his good old Despair...
What is this place, what is this space.
It's spinning around, there's no more ground, there's no more
  Man, there's no more Despair.
    Maybe Mother is still quite there.

Andrew Patrick Dono

There Must Be A Place

There must be a place
where love abounds.
There must be a place
where peace surrounds everyone.
For each one, there must be a place in the sun.
There must be a place
where we can all be free
There must be a special place
that exists for you and me.
To reach that place
the journey starts
by finding the dreams
within our hearts.
For only those who dream can see
the world as it was meant to be.
Now wipe the teardrops
from your face
and come let's find
that special place.

Joyce M. Askins

Living In Nature

Among rolling hills, where the grass is green,
Where the wet rains freely fall,
This is where I choose to live.
The loveliest place of all.

Where I can hear the sounds of nature,
And the snow is sparkling white,
This is where I choose to live,
Where everything is wondrous in sight.

Where the sun burns brightly all day,
And the trees grow straight and tall,
This is where I choose to live,
Where leaves turn colorful in fall.

Where, as the sun slowly sets
And paints a masterpiece in the sky,
This is where I choose to live,
Where stars shine and comets fly by.

Where observing birds and wildlife
Demonstrates nature's harmony,
This is where I lift my eyes,
And thank Him for sharing with me.

Claire Burchell

Untitled

We can build a new future, make a new day
Where we both can be happy, both can be gay
A new world free of sadness and strife
A world that is joyful and full of life

A world that is bright, honest and clear
Free from all sorrow, free from all fear
A tower reaching to the heavens above
Built on a foundation of pure honest love

We've started that journey as we must
Walking hand in hand in hope, love and trust
We'll make it together, of this I am sure
For we have a love very deep, very pure

So let's begin to walk on this trail
With a joyful love that can never fail
God will protect us with his love and care
For it's His gift to us, a love that's so rare

And when we recline in eternal rest
We'll have given each other our own very best
As we begin, for now we must start
Here's what I give you, I give you my heart.

Jon Oliver Mack

Free Form For A Bird Friend

There is much about you that reminds me of a bird
which cannot be named. Your sharp eyes and soft face
carry the dove's beauty and the swallow's grace,
yet there is the strength and will of an eagle
that cannot be tamed, and the hawk's keen mind.
No falconer's tether could bind you and no arrow
could stop your flight, thought at times there is
the tenderness and frailty of a sparrow in the night.

I ask only to fly beside you.
I will not tuck you under my wing,
except to protect you from the weather
and then to release you again
to watch you sail on the air - alive.
I will not contrive to pluck your feathers,
for you must dart through the cloud's core - and dive.
I only wish to share a moment of the climb
and to gather the wind together
with you - and soar
from time to time.

Donald Havis

The Portrait

It hangs above the small organ
Which I still play now and again.
An art student friend painted it.
D. J. Healy people framed it.
Her perfect oval face is framed
In wavy chestnut hair inflamed
Here and there with a touch of gold.
She was then twenty-two years old.
Forty-five years she's shared with me
Filling each one with joy and glee.
Though the years have etched some wrinkles
The spark in her eyes yet twinkles.
To paraphrase an old adage:
"Wines and cheeses improve with age."
The rapidly fleeting years bring
Inner beauty with every spring.

Guy H. Morel

Untitled

Oh, how I curse this language of word and sound
Which takes the lovely from my love!
Heart's heavenly music plays on solid ground
When written about or spoken of:
Dampered by phrases, butchered by tongue,
Needlessly cheapened by lips' report,
My full-bloomed love seems but a young
Sprout. Yet, bud or flower, I must resort
To this cursed translation of my heart's
Happy babble, for the apples we eat
Of the Tree of Knowledge are wormed, saving that part
Lovers need to love with words when lovers meet.
So I'll not masquerade my love in word's disguise,
But will love wholly and rightly through quiet eyes.

Deborah L. Koeppel

Ode To Our Daughter

We're the proud owners of a daughter with an oversized ear
Which to thin walls of air with suction-cup force does adhere,
List'ning for cosmical tidings and gossipy news,
Ready, willing, and able to tongue forth her views.

Oh what have we done to deserve such a statical lip?——
This untutored child who enjoys life's heady sip
May find in her shadow, somewhere in the future, a youth
Who will know, as this daughter does now, the essence of truth.

Don Johnson

The Dreamer

I often ponder o'er things I'd like to have,
While others work for what I might have had.
To those about me it may seem,
A sinful waste of time to dream.
But as I dream of castles in the air,
I live in a world free from care.
God gave me determination to fight,
And courage to meet the strife.
When all others with scornful eye,
Look upon my failures and sigh,
I offer neither excuse - nor reply,
But make plans for that I'm going to have,
And forget the things I might have had.

Jerome Haass

"The Three Friendly Bachelors"

There once were three friendly SINGLES;
Whose great desire in life was to MINGLE.
They found on OAK TREE in which to RESIDE;
Where happily they lived SIDE-BY-SIDE.

They worked hard, fixing up the 'OLE-OAK-TREE;'
It became a very lovely place to BE.
However the grounds were a real DISGRACE;
And that was more than they could FACE;

They decided that one of them would GO;
Seeking Fertilizer to be applied with a HOE.
The short straw would determine who had LOST;
Mr. RABBIT made the trip, despite the COST.

Mr. RABBIT came up to the Door - rang the BELL;
He had a very interesting Story to TELL.
Can you believe it? A Butler came to the DOOR
Shock so great - He fell flat on the FLOOR!

He looked the Butler straight in the EYE;
And made this 'mind boggling REPLY'
"We all have the Fertilizer Problem -I've the CURE."
HERE I AM WITH SIXTEEN BAGS OF MANURE!

C. Jay McWilliams

To Each His Own

Some like the ocean spray,
While some take delight in the powder.
One might be a surfer,
while another is a skier.

Some may like tattoos,
And others their nose rings.
But everyone is an individual,
And to each his own.

Standing by a tree in a park,
I saw a variant mankind.
Every person had a distinct quality,
And all I could say was, "To each his own."

Danielle Lewis

Wait Not For Tomorrow

Wake up, work, and live
While the day is bright
For tomorrow may be as dark as the darkest night.
Thank God now for the day, and the rising sun
It may be too late to give thanks,
  when the day is done.

Please don't let this day pass by
Without giving the task before you a try.
Or let the day come to an end
Without helping your foes to become your friends.

Reach out and touch someone's hand
For there is a need of unity all over the land.
Reach out and bring someone in
There are so many out there - in need of a friend.

Wait not for tomorrow; it may be filled with joy,
Or it may be filled with sorrow, or another day
Which could be dark and dreary
Or it could be gloomy and gray.

Esther Jeffress Holmes

Little Forest Creature

Come to me, come to me
Whispers the towering tree.
Up, up to the safety of my comforting arms
Where you shall come to no further harm.
For don't you see
My trunk, so solid, is your family;
And my branches, waving gently,
Are the beckoning arms
Of your multitude of friends
So, dear forest creature,
Come to me, come to me.
Fear not the snarling and barking
Of the two dogs below
As they do not know
Or understand or see
The secret strength of your special tree.

Dorothy Knickerbocker

I Am The Lord's Always

Whether I live or die; whether I wake or sleep,
Whether upon the calm, or on the stormy deep,
Wither my eyelids close, wither my life away,
I am the Lord's I know, I am the Lord's alway.

When the Night has come, and my Life is o'er,
I am free at last; now I'm at Heaven's door,
I shall know no pain, and at last I see,
I am the Lord's always, and to Eternity.

Edwin L. Hutcheson

Black, Not Just A Color

Black...the coal that lies in the mine shaft as the wind whistles leaving a cold eerie chill.

Black...the symbol of strength which bares across the broad shoulders of oppression that lasted over 400 years.

Black...the rise from slavery and prejudice to the damnation of hate and racism; from soup and bread lines to unemployment and welfare lines. The need to reform within our community is the greatest challenge, yet it has become the worst fear.

Black...words like Nigger, Jigaboo, and Sambo trying to imply negative images and stereotypes. Unjust labels applied similar to abuse, shackled, and whipped then sold as a race to the slavers. A race separated from their land on display and auctioned off to the highest bidder like cattle.

Black...Success. A window of opportunity that lets in minimum lightness and maximum darkness which provides enough radiance for a new rise to prominence for achievement of social equality.

Black...a symbol of power; not just a color. Black...that's me.

Herman P. Sandford

Nature's Painting

White flakes rest softly on my window sill.
Whistling winds, a reminder of the winter chill.
Each drift sculpted with perfection.
Crystal mountains in every direction.

Merely bushes peak over this glory.
Frozen treetops shall whisper the story,
Of how stiffened ices hang from the rafters
Anxiously longing for the season after.

When the warmth of the spring air starts blowing
Gentle purples and greens begin growing.
And the flakes of snow turn to drops of rain
While the tunes of the birds are heard once again.

Yet, these are the moments to treasure.
These changes warm hearts with great pleasure.
From the snow, to the rain, to the falling of leaves,
A spectacular painting, each one of these.

Jill Gullette

We Are No Longer The Child

We are no longer the child we once were
Who had no say, but yes or no sir

We are no longer the child who bares the cross
Of our parents who suffered a major loss

We are the people who have the right
To speak our minds, to stand and fight

The anger and fear is all combined
Within a dark corner of the back of our minds

The pain we shelter will forever last
Unless we attempt to put it in the past

We now must learn to put it behind
So love and peace, our hearts can find

There are so many choices we now can make
That as a child we had to take

So make them count and change what we can
So the children to come will all understand

Audrey M. Mathis

"Callie"

Dare to discover my lost love,
Who now rests in peace, in Heaven above.
In a better place she now rests;
Everyone says, it was for the best.
She was the best companion on which I could depend.
Not to mention, she was my very best friend.
Without a notice, she left me one day,
Set for another home, a permanent stay.
Sometimes I'm sad, for I miss her so much.
Where it hurts from the heart, with every slight touch.
The sun shines not as bright, the moon is not aglow.
It would take far more than that, to let my feelings show.
Everything has changed since Callie went away.
Nothing can replace her permanent stray.
When I think of her, I cry and get upset.
For what can replace a family pet?
Dare to discover my lost love,
Who now rests in peace, in heaven above.

Brandi Johnson

Memories Of Soul

You are the one who kept me alive
who taught me how to survive.
You are the one who urged me on
who motivated my search.
You are the one who gave me Reason
  how to see my own perceptions best
    how to believe within myself
      how to trust my own conscience.

You are the one I've learned the most from
the Soul I've shared - the host on.

A parasite in paradise I've been - I see.
A lazy person I've been - That's me.
It seems so clear.
I have to take it from here.
From this place to the space
where my own mind is in the lead.

Now, I'm not afraid of loosing you
and therefore can let go.
I know now what you've given me.
  Our memories of Soul.

Eric Lamson

"You're Not The Man That I Once Knew"

I fell in love with a very special man;
who, when we'd walk, he'd hold my hand.

But, now we've drifted so far apart;
That with each passing day, it breaks
  my heart.

I've loved you, with all that I had;
And somehow, you made it all seem bad.

The things you've done, that were so bold;
Have made my heart grow very cold.

I could never love you the same;
Although I know, you're not only to blame.

Once so young, and so naive;
You would lie, and I would believe.

When we met, I thought you were so true;
You vowed to never make me blue.

But, since that day I fell for you;
You're not the man that I once knew.

Jacquelyn Martinelli

Untitled

within all the madness of life,
who's the-'ll for strife?
singled out by a knife
empty pistol for a wife;
de raison d'être-
hurts to say…

what's going on?
like crawling around on my bleeding knees,
passages of this kept inner working sees-
those voices projected inside,
stretch out- making me confide-
sweating this pace in shade,
knowing forever turned forbade.

what's going on?
i call you now to push these dreams aside,
descried facts punish my never suicide-
i touch shadow and broken,
i lie, scarred- moving to fen-
wishes to forward painless death,
when i cry, what's going on.

Joseph L. Shomberg

Ballad To Eve

There was this lady by the sea
Whose love was a delight to me.
I will endeavor to sing her praise
Eve, lady of boundless grace.

Oh, Eve lady by the sea
Your lovely eyes do beckon me.
Truly you are EVE, all women's daughter
Your eyes sparkle like the ocean's water.

Your ever endearing presence
Contains all the essence
Of fields of roses and clover
Making me again in love all over.

I am blessed because I could give my love
But I am now cursed by the heavens above.
As life's events become ever more blurry,
I realize I am now late and was never too early.

I can still hold on to love's spell
And all will still seem well,
If Eve the lovely lady of the sea
Continues to beckon to me.

Irving Kaufman

Help Me

What did I do wrong this time
Why am I always in the wrong
I didn't mean for it to turn out this way
Some things you just can't help

Sometimes I can't help myself
I try to do the right
I try to be nice
But there are some things you just can't change

Tell me what I did
You know I didn't mean to diss
I've got too much on my mind
I've fallen apart inside

Help me
Help me
There's only so much I can do
There's only so much I can do

Eric Osterman

A Beautiful World?

Why can't the world be as beautiful as the mountains.
Why can't the world be as majestic as the sea.
Why can't the world be a peaceful water fountain.
The world is a lock and we are the key,
Why is the world filled with anguish and stress,
Why do we fight between you and me,
We made it so big we can't clean up the mess.
Why can't the lock fit with the key.
The children of our time may be the potential,
To the saving of our Earth.
The Earth is very essential,
To all you and I are worth.
So please help us save this beautiful place.
Please help us save this beautiful land.
So we can have wide open space,
And stand peaceful hand in hand.

Cameron Switzer

"You Never Said Goodbye"

You look so good to me.
Why didn't I notice it before?
You turned and walked out never
said goodbye.
Why didn't you say goodbye?
This all happened when I took a moment to
look away and then you slipped right
through my arms.
I still need you; ooh, do I ever.
Why did you leave me to live all alone?
God, how I need you so.
You'll never know how much I love you.
I only wish that I had known.
For then I never would have taken that
moment to look away.
And tonight I would have you for the
rest of my life.
Ooh, if only you had said
goodbye.

Florence E. G. Mick

The Word

"Why Me?" The thought encased my brain.
"Why must I suffer so?"
The labor that possessed my mind
Just would not let me go!

I sought the patience I would need
To hope, and grow again.
And like a beacon, promise came.
I had not searched in vain.

I opened God's own special book
On one sweet, special day —-
And there, the words, "It came to pass—"
It did not "Come to Stay."

Jo Piper

Sunrise Service

The sun rising overshadowed by clouds,
wind gusting cold,
birds singing in the trees,
Gospel being preached,
we're together, she's alone,
they're together but separate,
he hears and responds, her heart is bitter,
some leave warmed, others cold,
the sun rises, the wind blows.

Sue Bristow

We Share The Same Dreams

We share the same dreams for love
wide enough to carry us on her wings
to heights that glimpse the heavens
daring enough to plunge head first
into the dark, mysterious abyss we harbor
strong enough to climb the jagged rocks
that crowd our heart

We share the same dream for passion
unbridled lust for life, unquenchable thirst
indomitable spirit
even in death's magnificent grip

We are compelled to share the same dream
there are no choices for two souls
inexplicably bound by the horrifying reality
that we share the same nightmare

Joanne M. McCool

A Sweet Spirit

Once a part of your inner consciousness - Your life
will surely become affected.

Its compelling nature possesses a special peace and
serenity that draws you near.

Its calmness will cause your curious emotions to
understand that the peace within is the reason for its easiness.

Its self assurance projects a positive sense of confidence
and strength that you cannot but realize will
carry you far in life.

Its good and quiet nature seems almost beyond reproach,
yet revealed enough to know that it is one that
cares above them all.

It's one that is gentle yet strong, this strength combined
with a sense of humbleness causes this special
being to seem to divine.

Its uniqueness is so different and convincing that
your heart once reproached will most certainly become involved.

For a sweet spirit is one that is the rarest and most
powerful of them all.

Alfrednett Atkinson

The Potter's Wheel

You thank Me for the sunshine
Will you thank Me for the rain?
You thank me for your pleasure,
Will you thank Me for your pain?
You seldom thank Me for your losses
But always for your gain.

Have you not considered that I allow both?

Without the wet showers that water the earth afresh,
There'd be no appreciation for the sunshine, flowers and happiness.

Without the picking, pressing and crushing of a rose in full bloom,
There'd be no oil for fragrance to fill a dreary room.

Without the stripping, rubbing and sanding away of old residue,
There'd be no ready materials for the Masterbuilder to use.

Steady now, Be Still.
You're on the Potter's Wheel.
And don't forget to give Him thanks
Bow your will to His Wheel;
And let Him finish the work
He's begun in you.

Dawn Shepherd

The Final Breath

The time has come for you to depart
Will your last words come from your heart?
What will you say, what will you do,
When that final breath has come to you?

Will you thank God for the good life you had
Or will you shed a tear because you are sad?
What will you say, what will you do,
When that final breath has come to you?

Will a smile sneak across your face,
Or will a frown race to take its place?
What will you say, what will you do,
When that final breath has come to you?

Now, my friends, it is time to go
My final breath has come to me so.
I leave this world with this last part,
Thank you, Lord, with all of my...

Jenee' Angelette

The February Of 1994

Lunar dog year fell on February ten of sun calendar,
Winter Olympics started on February twelve in Lillehammer,
Valentine was celebrated on February fourteen,
What the exciting occasions were for citizens to spend:

The opening celebration of the game was a marvelous merit,
Players in a designated dance surrounded a "big egg,"
The sincere dance fondled the egg to open gradually,
A dove arose from within stretching its wings peacefully.

Thousands of doves then flew aloft in the dark sky;
A bush of red light erected on earth with an agog sign,
At this moment it seemed to roll back thousand years ago,
Human beings as a whole joined on the serene mysterious earth.

Dog year continued for two weeks with a unique parade,
Oriental and occidental music sounded with harmony in play.
Dragon dance attracted audience with its vigorous power,
Firecrackers burst out to thrill the auspicious crowds.

People sent sincere hearts to loved ones on Valentine Day,
The issue of two women figure skaters was a hot debate.
Finally, both took part in the competition,
The moral of sportsman is more important than fighting for a queen!

Diana M. P. Chang

Private Interlude

Here I stand vacant - periscoping the room
wishing the dresser drawers would produce
a bristle broom.

There I waited while no one showed. Was I
early or late? God only knows! Yesterday?
Not today? That's the way it goes!

It's all too confusing; highly amusing,
though chagrin shadows my days. I continue
daily to humbly pray.

Nothing is quite real - nothing is quite
right... you say the iron was left on
overnight? Such a plight!

Oh well, my dear... it's been a hectic
year... or was it merely today? Thoughts
do tend to stray.

Such a lovely park bench, the fountain
doth quench... cute pigeons surround...
Maybe I should lie down... perhaps tomorrow
I'll be found.

Avalon C. McGann

Remembrance

Echoes of sight and sound-
Wisps of melody on a gentle breeze-
The breaking of surf against a
powdery beach.

Peals of mirth over moments shared,
jokes half-completed,
joys remembered,
thoughts unspoken.

Events of four brief days strung
loosely on silken threads of time-
Priceless pearls suspended in the mind-

Sphere spun airily as cocoons
to insulate the flutter of the butterfly within.

Fibers fragile as blown glass,
as delicately flavored as cotton candy,

as strong and supple as birch boughs,-

interwoven with the strength of honesty,
the tenderness of love,
the awareness of eternity.

Camille S. Anders

Epitaph

A flower has grown
With a stem stricken with a petal of stone
That is engraved with a curious epitaph
That sadly makes me laugh.
A short collection of words and pretty verse
Dedicated to the happy son whose life was terse.
Words that were not said until he was dead
After the bullets missed their conscious
And went directly through his head.

A flower grows
With a stem stricken with a petal of stone
That is engraved with beautiful words
For the new being in their universe.
He has his mother's eyes
And he has his father's smile
And words that say they love him—
They don't mean a thing.

Eric M. Dennison

The Solitary Rose

This SOLITARY ROSE to you I now send
With all of my love and thoughts from within

Each petal on this rose is soft, but does not compare
To your soft and gentle nature; the way that you care

The sharpness from each thorn, my dear
Should equal the sharpness of my pain, when you're not near

If the stem of this rose could reach from the deepest ocean to the
heavens above
It would, indeed, be a measure of my dedication to you, my love

The green in each leaf of this rose so true
Is the envy that runs through my soul when I cannot be with you

This entire rose in all of its beauty can make hearts soar
But does not match the beauty of your face that I adore

If you were a part of this fragrant rose, I now send
I would cup my hands and inhale you deeply, within

There will truly be no one who knows
The meaning of my love for you, in this, the SOLITARY ROSE.

Carol Hudgins Hay

Ghostly Guardian

He came to me in dreams, a comfort to my pain
With a tender touch and a gentle voice
I never knew his name
He called my name in a whisper
I felt his arms encircle my body in an embrace
I felt his warm body protecting and guarding me
Against a race of hate
I can feel his presence and hear his voice
Yet I yearn to see his face and know his name
within a whisper I heard his name
In that moment I saw his face
A face filled with love and tears in his emerald eyes
A gentle smile curled his red lips
Black hair framing his pale cheeks
He is a guardian
A phantom
A lover

Jennifer M. Gentile

"My Bedtime Prayer"

Jesus come and take your place,
With angels many about my face.
To keep me safe and free from harm,
As though I am cradled in your arm.
And wake me with the bright sunrise,
Before you go back to your place in the skies.
Though don't take your angels that far away,
Because I will need them throughout the day.

Devan Porter

As Time Goes By

As summer goes and winter comes,
with chilling winds that freeze and numb,
The children play without a care,
never noticing the frosty air.

The old man sits in front of the fire,
lost in thoughts of love's desire.
Reminiscing on times of old,
when he was young, strong, and bold.

But now he sits with hair so gray,
hoping his children will come he prays.
For the years roll on and never cease,
as time goes by like passing geese.

As winter comes to its bitter end,
the children know it's Spring again.
But something's different from seasons past,
the old man's time has come at last.

Time goes by and seasons fly,
while lovers laugh and children cry.
The years roll on and never cease,
as time goes by like passing geese.

John Perry Biggerstaff

Old Wise Woman

I know of an old wise woman
who often ties a scarf on her head and wears an apron
She has a lion's strength and a soft touch
She's warm, gentle, kind and such
By her side I often stay
Where she taught me lots of things, even how to pray
She taught me to love and respect everyone
Always work hard and to do the best I can
Keep the candle in your heart lit, and dare to dream
Love your neighbor even when they're mean
'Tis with these old wise ways you must grow
and the seed of love you must forever sew

Alden H. Baker

A Matter Of The Heart

Love, oh love
With innocence precious as a soft morning rose.
And yet;
It is wicked, like the thorn.

Still I walkest among angels in the early dust,
But seek not comfort in the golden stars.
For all the beauty drifting in the universe,
Will never compare to an undying love.

True love survives eternally, after the grave;
After years of pain have vanished.
Love finds its way, in even the hazy shadows of broken hearts,
Although it is so often untouched.

Pure love is gentle as the summer's breeze,
And true as the calm waters that flow like mist.
Lilies wave in the wind; yet they are not as strong as love,
For the one who would give his own sweet breath-shall find
true love.

Amanda B. Lombardi

The Soul

The body
          with its beauty and yet strangeness,
Its complicated function and annoying dysfunction,
Its myriad cells creating movement, heartbeat, growth,
An engineering miracle
          of supporting skeletal structure,
Does, after all, exist but
          to hold the fragile bubble of a soul.
It is thought
          which moves the body into action, good or bad;
It is will
          which holds it fast to purpose and intent.
In the imagination
          do we truly live until we die, for
A miracle dream must first precede the finished act.
Finally, in death, when at last the frail clasp is let,
Without a sigh the soul
          floats free away from earthly anchor
To blow silently through the vast mystery of time and space
Into eternity.

Beverly Steele Draper

The Guardian

Ever so gently you opened the gates to my heart...
With knowing hands you explored its many chambers and passages,
     never disturbing its inner workings.
Almost reverently you began to work your craft, your mending
miracles.
When you were done you reached for my hand and took me on a
journey -
Down the path you had trodden, and into the gates you had opened.
There you introduced me to my soul, no longer torn apart and broken
But healed and stronger than it had ever been before.
We stood together and silently took pride for a job well done.
Together we closed the gates to my heart, its soul once again safe
     and secure.
We took the journey back
The road amazing, smooth and refreshing.
All was well in this world of mine again.
But every so often, when I'm alone at peace with myself
I feel a little flutter within my breast...
And as I listen closer I hear the faint whisper of two souls speaking
     to one another.
It's then that I realize how you repaired this broken heart -
You mended it with a piece of your soul.

Coreen Ann Sabat

The Flame

The candle that burns so deep inside,
with longing desires he cannot deny
And when his dreams don't come true
He tries to forget, and goes for the brew.

The candle that burns so deep inside
burning on shame, what a wicked ride
If he only knew we all see his real flame
His lies and demons would all go away.

The candle we see that burns so bright
With his love and kindness, what a beautiful sight.
His laughter that he brings us all,
Is the flame that burns so bright and tall.

The candle we see, so full, so warm
Is the flame he holds to help us through our own little storms.
And all this time, he becomes blinded by the light,
Not knowing any truth, losing the sight of what is right.

The candle we see, so full of love
Is the gift he brings us, blessed from above
And all the greatness he is to me,
Is what I pray, someday he will see.

Ann Davis

The Beauty Of Love

The beauty of love is that words need never be spoken.
With one glance of the eye, one brush of the hand,
A quiver, a sigh, a feeling of yearning deep inside
Holds love's endless emotion that never dies.

The beauty of love's enchanting grace
Will captivate your heart anytime, anyplace.
You need not seek it, nor try to hide.
For it knows no boundaries, it knows no pride.

Love echoes its sound as the heart beats and cries,
And mirrors its true image,
Deep in the soul, through the eyes.

The beauty of love I'll tuck safely within.
To void any emptiness,
Until we meet again.

Cheryl D. Smith Gabourel

Little Child Lost

Little Child!
Where is your mother?
She left with some guy,
Somebody or other.
She said to stay home and not tell all I knew,
But I'm looking for bread,
So what can I do?
If I can't find it and I don't know the cost,
Or how to get home
'Cause I think I am lost.
Little Child!
Your Dad, where is he?
Mom said that my Dad
At the tables would be,
And when he got fed
He'd come and feed me.
But Mr. I'm looking.
'Cause I'm hungry,
You see?

Annette Mates

The Quilters

The needles of rain stitch the mirrored pools
With silver threads from the sky's cloud-spools.
They quilt the green cover that blankets the lea,
And sew bright diamonds on the apple tree.

Thrusting sharp points into Spring's new birth,
Basting the heavens to the earth.
They form a curtain of diaphanous fringe,
Hung from the firmament's giant hinge.

Betty Harmon

Memories

Lost, again, in deepest dreams,
with soft, trembling smile
and silent tears -
the sighs, the longing in my heart,
my fears buried deep inside -
a whispered name, a lover's touch long missed,
a voice I'm aching to hear,
the memories of love that torment me
are my soul's only companion

Brenda Jean Cushman

Spring

Good-bye winter, Spring is here;
with sunny skies that are filled with
cheer!
The air is filled with a warm, happy
little breeze:
Flowers in my yard dance proudly
back and forth with colors vivid and bright,
And all the birds are singing happily
in the old oak tree.
Isn't it funny how winter's frigid
touch is lost and forgotten in Spring's
renewing light....

Glenda Martin

Parallel Times

Walking through the wilderness
With ten comrades, looking over their shoulders,
wearing the colors of slavery;
the shackles of their unthinking society.
Seeking some sign buried in nature's face
as many a creature watches, and many a flame smolders.

Walking through the urban wilderness;
With ten comrades, looking at their weapons,
wearing the colors of which they are bound;
the manacles of their choice.
Seeking the sign in their quarry's face
as many a man watched, and many a fire ignites.

Daniel Lyons

Misty Midnight

It's midnight, dark, cold, and lonely.
Where has the warm, yellow sunshine gone?
Was it ever at all a sure reality?
The imagination is powerful in shadows.

A misty dream of film plays over and over.
Waiting for the script to change miraculously.
Watching for melancholy gray to evaporate;
Changing to vivid colors of a rainbow.

Misty midnight, the moon shining bright.
Changes made, though painful, but necessary
If the mist is to clear, freeing the sun
To follow the moon after a misty midnight.

Bonnie McGill Porter

Mistake

Love was the only thing that mattered,
with that my heart could never be shattered,
The world was wonderful and great,
Little did I know my deceitful fate,
I was happy and very upbeat,
Until one night there was a silent retreat,
warm tears filled my eyes,
all that filled the night were hurtful cries,
as days passed, more and more lies revealed,
and my heart was exposed and totally unsealed,
not a word was spoken between us,
not even a look when he left on that bus,
down the road he headed,
the road which my heart had been treaded,
another heart for him to break,
and the word stuck in my head "mistake."

Chrissy Thomson

With You

I want to camp with you on a warm summer's night,
With the stars and moon shining so bright.

I want to walk hand and hand with you on a cool crisp fall day,
When the leaves are turning to a colorful array.

I want to romp in the snow with you on a cold winter's day,
When the snow glistens like diamonds from the sun.

I want to watch nature start again with you in the spring,
When the flowers and trees are in full bloom.

I want to watch sunsets and sunrises with you,
But most of all, I just want to grow old with you.

Carol A. Fox

Wild Blackberries

Let us go pick berries, let us be stained
With their sweet wild taste, let us part bushes
Then dare further reaching; stain our lips red
Our hands - deep to our elbows
Let us find there
Where the subtle danger is
We are people of the city
But we bring our wilderness of remembrance
We remember where
The berries live
In the inaccessible places
Dusty-dusty-dry
Locked in the tangles of weeds of the berry vine
With its cobweb hair
We remember the prices we have to pay
The scratched arms and legs
The indelible taste
Come with us now
We are hungry let us go find
The lost, wild berries.

Johnny Cuesta

"To Grow Old"

Growing old is a frightful thing. A time in life
when most things change. When your children are
grown and gone, you are frightened most of
being alone. It's sad to grow old if you are
by yourself. It seems as if no one cares.
You will sit and cry. You don't know why.
But you will cry and cry. Try not to mind
what they said and do, because one day
the same thing will happen to you. I know
they said things that will make you feel sad.
But be good to the old, try not to let them be sad.
Because one day you will surely be glad.

Daisy Webster

Doubts

Night after night I lie in bed.
With thoughts of you going through my head.
Do you love me now like you did back them?
If you could do it over, would you do it again?
I am lucky I found my one true love in you.
You give me the love and hope to see me through.
But sometimes doubt creeps in my mind.
I reach for you and this is what I find:
A man who loves me and calms my fears,
Who is always willing to wipe away the tears.
You hold me in your arms and gently stroke my hair,
Reassuring me you will always be there.
So as you pull me close,
I'm happy that I'm the one you chose
To share in the ups and downs of your life,
To be your friend, your lover and your wife.
I now realize my dreams have come true
When you softly whisper to me "I love you."

Angela L. Wright

"Goodbye My Love"

Tonight I lie all snuggled in bed
With visions of you running through my head
It seems so strange — this fire in my veins
Such a burning desire; you set my soul on fire
Without one touch; you mean so much

I know that I shouldn't be feeling this way
But how can I not?
What can I say? What am I to do?

My feelings for you I cannot hide
Nor the way I feel inside
I try to pretend they'll just go away
But they just come back — day after day

Tell me now, how can this be?
You've captured my heart before I could flee

We must not throw caution to the wind
By following our hearts — we cannot win
We both know, we must let go, or suffer the pain
We're surely to bring to our loved ones who care
And hold us so dear; Goodbye My Love, our day will come —

Beatrice G. Dillard

The Angelic Herb

A spark of fire, the whole plain spurns,
With bitter Grief the only Orchid burns,
Out of the ash springs up the thorn.
In vain, the Angel Herb calls "Soul return!"

Johnny Shek

Life is a Road

Life is a road to where we know not where.
With twists and turns,
that just start another adventure of life.
Another bend,
another start.
A turn of good times,
or a turn for the worst.
That's all life is.
Twists and turns,
bumpy or straight,
you know not what your road of life will be,
but sit back and live your adventure.

Jen Slusarczyk

Flying For Tomorrow

Shining brightful sorrow
With wings that I have borrowed,
Past yesterday, same old familiar gray,
Chameleon bird in flight today,
I'm flying for tomorrow.
To where supple white clouds blow puffly in the breeze
As my rhythmic wings soar high above the trees.

Arrogance and despair
Right now are in the air,
A single bird alone, I'm easy prey
For hunters below looking up my way,
So I have to fly from here.
To the answers to the questions and reasons to the why
To find the flock of pride and knowledge that flies high in the sky.

Bill Lane

"Mystic"

Here I sit, with the fallen sky
with words that lie in pieces in the sand
No Destiny too vast, no word could ever last
As time is turned, washed and cast

Mystic words intrigue me, sell my soul to learn to die
She cries from walls that hold her, where's my king, where am I.
When the walls no longer hold her, and she's free to break the spell.
Will the mystic powers that hold her, serve her well.

Madmen storm to the castle, release cuts down the wall.
My one defense was so intense, it crashed my fading wall.
And I scream from walls that hold her, from cinder blocks and chains.
Some things lost, but something should remain

Morton, bricks and concrete, diamonds and steel
All turn to rust, when the walls reveal
I fantasized her love was real.

Smash at the walls, they came tumbling down.
Scream to the gods, from the cursed ground
I fantasized her love was real.
And I scream from walls that hold her from cinder blocks and chains
Some things lost but something should remain

Eugene Mazzoni

Good Bye

There you go down that road again,
with your cloudy mind, and your vision impaired,
not knowing that someone really cared.
Driving so fast,
not really knowing where you were going.
Your mind so troubled,
I'll never forget that cold dark day,
they said I would never see you again alive,
just because we let you drink and drive.

Jami Gardner

Autumn Romance

My love begins in Autumn,
When the leaves have turned golden brown,
and have fallen to the bottom,

My heart then is open for love,
and it will love like the angels above,
and when that love gets in my heart,
it will not depart.

I'll always be true, and hold you
dear to me,
And we'll be together till the
end, won't we?

Ellene Sotherland Browning

Memories Live Forever

Memories like true love live forever
Within the garden of the heart-
Treasured and cherished forevermore,
Shining keepsakes to never depart.
Kept in dearest and fond remembrance

Each shining hour of joy we once knew,
Shining in radiant beauty again we see them,
As memory's golden hour recalls them anew.

Like sweet fragrance of lovely flowers,

Though they fade, yet still we remember
Their beauty and fragrance that charmed us,
In our hearts they glow like never-dying embers,
For memories like true love live on
As long as years of time will remain-
Enshrined within the heart forever
To be recalled and relived again.

Evangeline Elmquist

Unknown

Walking through darkness,
Without a hand to lead.
Blackness surrounds me as
I try to focus on a picture
which doesn't exist.
I have to remember how it used to be.
The clear blue sky, was once all I saw,
but now darkness flows throughout.
Take it one step at a time, with
one foot in front of another,
to follow the twisted path
which leads to the unknown.
I see a light, illuminating overhead.
As I travel towards it I fall into a pit of darkness.
I attempt to regain my strength,
although it never happens, for I am still weak.
I sit in the darkness,
which I have begun to call home,
walk nowhere because my
destination is unknown.

Alexandra Stern

Undeserved Separation, Unconditional Love

Came home from work today and you were gone,
Woke up the next morning and you weren't there.
Those times make me wonder why life goes on,
But I've learned it's not supposed to be fair.

I'll miss the hugs and kisses you freely gave,
And those beautiful smiles you shared with me.
These are things that are important to save,
I must care for them like a golden tree.

I love you so much and will promise you this,
I'll be there when you need me, anytime, anywhere.
So close your eyes and dream, and you'll never miss,
The time we spent together, the times I brushed your hair.

I'll close mine too, and cherish the name
Of my little girl who had to go away.
Remember how I taught you not to place blame,
Because you'll be coming back soon someday.

So now all I can do is wait for that day,
And struggle till that time, so we can again be two.
I miss you so much and wish you could stay,
But I must let go, because it's the best for you.

Dean Wayne Riley

A Locked Self

One wants to be alone and hides in the very deep place,
   without any disturbance from the outside world.
One wants to be free to do whatever one wants and accompanies
   with isolation.
One stays in a deserted and quiet cave, declining any visitors from
   entering the space.
One is locked in one's heart and wriggly hidden in the dark corner.
One does not want to be one self alone, but -
One's undulated mind together with conflicts and affirmation,
   is full of contradiction of what to do.
The calmness expressed on the outside, starts to exuviate
   and with all others pretends it is in the makeup of oneself.
Others' opinions and criticisms, leave them behind-
How are they going to affect me? Not any more as I now shall know.
One lives carefree, comfortable and at ease,
Bystanders are only left with superfluous decoration of what they
   called life.
Who cares and why should I?
One alone, is still one alone
Nothing more and nothing less,
As a pile of sand,
Eventually going back to where I belong.

   Chia Chu

Getting Along

Am I not allowed to have a friend of a different race?
Without being scorned or called a disgrace?
Can I walk with a white person and hold my head high?
And still have my culture and still have my pride?

The days of old we cannot forget.
But we have to move on without any regrets.
We must follow the rule: live and let live.
And to the needy, no matter what race, we must always try to give.

And so I say to you as I would say to any other,
I'll treat you the same, just like a brother.
Regardless of your race, the shade of your skin,
We are all one family and we are all one kin.

Regardless of the past, for that's history,
We all belong to the human family.

   Ihsan Sewer

His Sovereign Grace

The Lord looked over his garden one day to survey His near and dear
Wonderful creations of all kinds, unique...happy...sincere.
And in His most sovereign grace, He chose one especially fair of face
A special one that He knew well...a darling angel named Michele.

As he plucked her away from all the rest, family and friends said no,
Not yet. Our Heavenly Father said no, don't fret. For now Michele
Who's been through so much, she now remains very much in touch
As I have said she can look down with the other saints gathered
'round.

Freedom now can commence, part of a new life's recompense.
To those who have to stay behind, don't be full of woe or regret
Because I'm not done with Michele yet.

For now she's ranked high, a strong new girl
Here in My most wonderful world.
Among the elect, she'll shine clear and bright
Through triumphs in our darkest night.

The garden now is not quite the same, but everyone there
Remembers her name. Michele, that special person lives on.
In joy, inspiration, beauty and grace, Michele lives on in a perfect
place.

   Jerome Ravenna

A Better Place

At night I sleep with his memory tossing and turning and
wondering why as I wipe the tear streaming down my eye.
I'll sit and think all night and all day, hoping my
sadness will soon go away. Then suddenly I'll close my eye and say
again bye-bye bye-bye. I'll wake up in the night and feel
again this awful fright. Then I'll look at his pictures and
think good thoughts and then again I'll drift off.

When I'm sleeping I think of him and all of a sudden the
lights go dim, I see his face and the outline of his
body and hope that he hasn't forgot how to party. He
straps on a guitar and plays me a song and then I hear
the churches gong. I knew what that meant so I had to
leave and then he said I was freed.

I wake up from that wonderful dream and through my
window I see a beam. I see his hand and his
little face and think there is no better place.

His music was loud, his words were clear, but I can no
longer hold my fear; the fear of life, the fear of death,
the fear of taking my final breath. So many years will come and be
gone, but yet the memory will always be strong

(in memory of Kurt Cobain)
   Jill Plumpton

Oh... My Love...

You are the Elixir of my being in this
world, my soul calls of being connected with only you.
Life without you, your touch or word isn't.
I can't separate the bond of my heart and soul
From yours, even if you grossly mistreat me.
I will forever thank my star for you.
I glow in your presence and wither in
your absence.
I am sick for your love, you are at once
the cause and cure.
Your talk is blossom to my tortured soul.
I will pave your driving climb with the
fabric of my soul.
Sit by my bed, and hold me close.
I only live for the time your
sweet heart touches mine.
Let my head rest in your tender
lap and gaze into my willing eyes.
Oh... my love... Oh my love

   Fatemeh Esmaeili

What Would I Do?

What would I do if he were really here?
Would I say to him," I deeply care for you!"
Or would my soul be overtaken by fear?
How possibly can the eyes of the naive perceive
When there has never been one there to receive.
One to love and hold for many times and again,
One who'd be there to call your very own friend.

However what would I do if an established relationship did exist?
Continuous exchange of letters of love?
What exactly would be their gist?
I'm sure we'd enjoy the simplest pleasures of life, indeed!
Just being there for each other in both our time of need,
caring and sharing all our private and innermost thoughts.
A time we share together that could never be rebought

Although, what would I do if a relationship could not live?
Would all my body functions cease to be cooperative?
Would my mind be blurred with far fetched illusions,
yet, to face reality, end with such a horrifying conclusion?
If this concept were to come true,
What! I tell you, what! Would I do?

   Charletta R. Fry

Me

What if I had not been born-
Would the world not be war torn?
Would the hungry have to eat?
Would the lame be on their feet?
No-I think not-I had to be
I see some good has come from me
I look in the mirror and I see
a careworn face of fifty-three
I know some good has come to pass
as I see my children-and theirs-pass before me in the glass
And then I see, then I know
I was born for them to grow

Ardys Edstrand

Secret

I got a secret
Would you like to hear
Can I whisper it in your ear?
Where do I begin
Where do I start
This secret comes from deep inside my heart.
I trust in you not to say a word
Because a secret is not meant to be heard
Did you hear the words I spoke?
I hope so for it is no joke.
If you didn't hear the whisper
of these words
Then I am truly sorry that they weren't heard.
I might tell you, just once more
I hope you hear it, this time for sure.
If I tell you don't say a peep
For a secret is forever yours to keep.

Elsie Kleinz

Open Arms

Last night I heard someone talking
    yet I could not find out who,
then I realized this voice came from above
    and Lord I knew it was you.
You were telling me not to worry
    and that alone I'd never be,
You said that I was your child first
    and you'll always watch over me.
A wave of shame came over me
    for some of the things I've done,
but you let me know that was the past
    and from your eyes, I'd never be shunned.
Softly you said, "Rest peaceful, I'm here
    no matter where you are.
Your sins may be many but just turn around
    and you'll see my Open Arms."

Donna Kay Sigmon

The Dancer

The dancer's story is allowed to unfold
    With creative movement of body and soul.
Only the beautiful dancer can release
    Through her movement, beauty, grace, and inner peace.
To watch is to listen; to listen is to learn
    From all those who can dance, move, twist, spin, or turn.
The satiny elegance of this motion
    Is as the rhythmic beating of the ocean.
The silent gentleness of all their dancing
    To everyone who views them is entrancing.
The audience is quiet, perhaps spellbound,
    'Til dance is complete and applause is around.
Dancing's mystical song comes straight from the heart,
    Those who will listen can be a special part.

Jennifer Collins

"When Doves Cry"

Dearest to heart art thine, yet sheltered away as a music box on
yonder shelf are thine memories.
Each thought of thee is as the gentle touch of a dove held closely.
Bearing my spirit seemingly on wings to a time past:
"It was when we were young, seeking to know
the innocence of friendship with the hope of love.
A time when freedom was ours, and the cares
of life were but to see thee from afar."
Only time would separate the dream and bring us to know what could
not be. Like an arrow piercing its mark, the words of a common
heritage intertwined long ago took our hope away. Yea, I can but
recant!

Remember always the day we met: The shyness we both felt and
the newness of the moment.

And when you see the doves fly, know that they bear my soul to thee,
even thy guardian angel, where once more I can see thee afar off and
divine protection is brought nigh to thee.

Heaven knows the dove's sorrow, even mine, for when they return,
they pine away, for that is: "When the doves cry."

Clinton Bruns

Untitled

Whiskey oh whiskey
You are an evil thing,
you spoiled my character
And you ruined my name.

You kicked me in ditches,
You skinned up my shins,
But I was a brave old hero
So I tried you again.

You took my money and sent me to jail,
I sold my last possession to pay my bail,
You stole my job and put me in the street,
Without any money or nothing to eat.

So I prayed and prayed unto the Lord,
Please let sobriety be my reward,
Whiskey oh whiskey you are the devil's brew,
I praise the Lord I am free from you.

James Waters

Read

You can go around the world it will only take an hour.
You can visit Singapore for may be a dollar.
Or you can build a boat to watch it float.
Or even cook a roast to serve to a host.
You can do these things and much much more.
It will cost you some time but please don't mind you may get
hooked.
And all you have to do I read a book

Johnny Carr Jr.

Scream Of The Butterfly

Walking in the sunlight, restless, depressed.
Wishing to hide between the sun's rays.
I sat down by a big oak tree, to find rest.
And turn my soul to pray.

Silent as the whisper of the wind.
A beautiful butterfly landed on my hair.
With gentle words, I'm here, I love you, I do!
I care, with a friendship to share.

In the scream of the butterfly.
Silent as the whisper of the wind.
I found peace.
I found a friend.

Bonnie Lou Phelps

Your Love

You give me hope when all is lost
You carry me through the storm
For our love is worth any cost
In any shape or form
You love me with all of your heart and soul
I feel it deep down inside
Together we are one and whole
Together our hearts reside
My sweet, you give me life and love
A meaning to hang on to
You turn my smile up above
I cannot live without you
So if the fog should ever take me away
If I am ever to disappear with the rain
Remember with you my heart shall always stay
And with our love we shall chase away the pain

Amy Bruce

For Someone Special

When you smile automatically, your eyes seem to shine.
  You could easily captivate any female, but I wish
  you were all mine.

So innocent and natural, you appear on the outside.
  Why do you want to be lonely? Let me take you
  for a ride.

Together we will venture into each others hearts, minds
  and souls. Living each day as it comes determined
  to reach our individual goals.

Let your guard down slightly, just enough for you to see
  and feel.

This young woman is aiming for your heart, not a toy that
  would soon bore her, I'm just being for real.

Donna J. Parker-Bowen

Lord Bring Our Nation Together

You wrote about the wars, fires and flood
You created man from your precious blood
Your command was written on a mountain high
While brother Moses was standing by
  Lord bring our nation together

When I think all the trouble in this world today
I know it wouldn't be if we all would pray
We fuss and fight about brotherly love
We don't obey the message from heaven above
  Lord bring our nation together

In all respect we must repent
Because there will never be a man like my God sent (Jesus)
We've got to learn to love our neighbor
Get right with God our wonderful savior
  Lord bring us together

Ann Mills Filmore

Untitled

Once there came a time to me, 'twas long, long ago,
When a vision came to me out of the sky, down to
  the Earth below.
'Twas not a vision of God or gold, nor yet of glory grand-
But a little dove which came to me, bringing an olive brand.
I wondered and wondered what it meant: At last it came to me:
A war was raging in ancient Greece, over the deep blue sea.
I started at once for that for port, with the bird and the olive brand

When I came upon a large escort who were fighting
  hand to hand to hand.
The bird was perched upon my arm-it dropped the olive brand:
When the soldier saw this, fighting ceased, and I was a happy man

Forrest L. Light

The Allowance Of Time

As I lay here with my eyes closed and totally unsuspecting,
  you enter my body.
You move so slowly that I don't even feel you,
  every day the same thing happens.
You are slowly taking me over.
You are in my every vein, my every muscle,
  my every breath and now my every thought.
Like a drug you've taken over my entire being.
When I first realized what you were doing,
  I tried to fight you.
I couldn't let you in, but the more you ran through me
  the more I wanted you
    and the more I needed you.
Now I will no longer fight you.
  I will allow you to invade my entire being.
For you have made me feel alive and happy.
  With you I am me but I am also yours.
So now we are equal, we have each other's love
  running through our entire beings and we will remain
    within each other for as long as time will allow.

Debra M. Grimes

He Who Is Loneliness

He who does sit on my bed and wait 'till I'm home,
  you fill me with sorrow.
He who holds me so tight I am breathless,
  just let me go.
He who is with me by day or by night like a shadow,
  I'd rather be alone.
He who I cannot see but I feel in my heart all the time,
  I am lonely.
He who caresses but hurts me so much with the memories,
  I don't want to remember.
But, he who has bound me and yelled in my face 'til I cried,
  just won't let me go.

Brandy N. Burrow

Untitled

Just when you think you know your heart whole,
You find that you don't know it at all.
Just when you think you know your mind,
You see there are more things for you to find.
Just when you think your heart tells you true,
You find, once again, that it has tricked you.

This goes to show, you can't trust your heart
For it is fickle and, at any moment, may dart.
Also, your mind will lead you astray
And you will find that you've gone the wrong way.
So who should you trust in these troubled days?
Trust in your soul and in God, not the world's misleading ways.

Abra Henton

"Judging"

People are judged at the beginning of birth,
Why? We did not ask to be put on this earth,
People pick, People poke,
People laugh, People joke
A person cannot help the way he looks, or the color of his skin,
So, Why do you have to be so-so just to fit in?
Nobody is perfect, Everybody makes mistakes,
So why does it have to be the normal and the flakes?
Why cannot people get along?
Instead of some being right and others being wrong?
Where you live, or what you drive, or your appearance,
Should not always be a lifetime interference.

Barbara Fatherree

Of Love To My Husband

When you find someone you love
You grasp the end of a thread
And begin to sew on the buttons and bows
To add the charm to your garment of life
To make a covering for yourself
A garment impregnable
And when
If necessary
To sew the tear and patches
To secure the love within
You wind the thread into a spool of happiness
Of understanding and gratitude
Of being able to share a part of your life
With someone who doesn't mind
The remade hand me downs
But looks upon you as a symbol of everything beautiful
And knows the time it has taken to mend the tears
Because
He too wears a beautiful torn patch shirt
Of love for you.

Donna Finnell

The Shadow

After darkness, black and low,
You may see something called The Shadow.
You will know him anywhere,
For none will see him, except those who dare.

Not at evening, not at noon.
But at night, under the moon.
He may be daring, he may be bold,
He may be young, he may be old.

You will not see him on TV or a show,
You will not see him wherever you go.
When you will see him, no one knows,
Because really only the Shadow knows.

Anyone would want to see the Shadow,
And if it be so,
When they will see him,
Only the Shadow knows.

He may be small, he may be tall
But don't be surprised, if he walks down your hall
And if it really be so,
No one but the Shadow will know.

Jeffery M. Lasley

Miss Lucy

"Momma, as I was walking down the pathway of my childhood I was
wounded in an atrocious manner. The scar is not visible, Momma.
But the pain is persistent."
"Come here chile. Lay your head on my breast. Listen. You are
a woman. Full of dignity. Strong. Holding your head up high.
Persevering."

"But Momma." "Hush Child. Don't carry on so. You must take
everything in stride." "But Momma I" "Child. You must not be weak.
You can't while away your time sniveling. It's ok to cry when
someone die, but otherwise you got to roll with the punches."

"Momma. Momma please listen."
"No child! You listen! Do you remember Miss Lucy? The poor wretch
that wanted to talk. She wouldn't listen. She began complaining
about a wound that she said was draining her. Something or other
about a load that was more than she was willing to carry alone.
She lost her mind. She went crazy as a Betsy bug."

"Oh Momma I can't..."
"LISTEN! LISTEN! They killed old can't. They whipped old couldn't
till it could. Only Miss Lucy's want to talk about the pain.
Only mommas know you must listen. Because we're all Miss Lucy's."

Irean V. Hughes

Mother Of Mine

Mother of Jesus, Who is divine.
You must have been like this Mother of mine,
Loving, patient, and thoughtful always.
The truest of Mother in every way.
Your life is a rosary of genuine pearls.
A beautiful example for each of your girls.

At times when I'm tempted to do what is wrong,
It's your trust and your love that saves me from harm,
The lessons you taught me since a babe in your arms,
The faith you have in me is one of your charms,
It is these that give me the courage and will to fight,
For I know you expect me to do what is right,

When I'm tired and weary and my heart is like lead.
I turn to you as would a child to be fed,
In you I confide all my heartaches and woes.
There is nothing which I from you withhold.

For you comfort and cheer me and set things to right,
With your Motherly love and keen insight,
Though I've brought you nothing of fortune or fame,
But caused you many a tear and many a pain;

Though my plans and my hopes seen now all in vain,
May it please you to know I reverend your name.
And would deem it an honor if God would choose,
To make me a Mother like you've been to me.

Dorothy Keating   May 1929

In Times Like These

Although no one knows what to do or just what things to say,
You must reach deep within your soul and say "Oh well, it's just
another day."
For tomorrow is promised to no one and yesterday is gone.
And that inner man within you says, "Oh well, I must go on."
So live the life you so desire, and live it as you please.
And remember Jesus is your strength, especially in times like these.

Annette Gatson

My Father My Hero

My father, my hero. Two titles, one man.
You raised me to be the best that I can.
My father, my hero. Beside me you stood.
Through each of the hard times and all of the good.
My father, my hero. You never once let me fall.
I stumbled a few times but that was about all.
My father, my hero. You're one in the same.
You would comfort when there were times I felt pain.
My father, my hero. I'm so proud you're my dad.
You'd given me more when that's all that you had.
My father, my hero. You worked hard to provide
Clothes for my back and food to survive.
My father, my hero. When your time does come,
You'll be rewarded in heaven for the good things you've done.
My father, my hero. One thing I can say.
You've given me the example to be a great father someday.

Craig A. Burch

The Emotion Experience

Purple auras float freely in the electric blue sky of consciousness
Yellow arcs of thought spring from the green meadows of knowledge
Awesome white bolts of inspiration pierce the black clouds of
    depression that are crowding your mind
Red are the life giving waters of the body that course through the
    keeper of your soul
The gray tissues of the brain flex their muscles and just sing with
    sheer power
The white light of peace and contentment outshines all the other
    feelings when the endless wall of worry crumbles

Andy Spearance

Untitled

To my continual opponent,
You remind me of a growth upon the
    foot of a homeless man, a fly
    humming around my head, a wound
    with life oozing from it.
Your teeth are like the tongue of
    an individual suffering from
    candidiasis.
Your hair is that of a black widow's
    web, tangled and sticky.
Your skin is like that of an alligator's,
    rippled and lumpy.
You have the personality of a rock, nonexistent.
When I have the misfortune of being around
    you, I plug my nose to ward off
    the toxic fumes, pray for your
    departure, and wish I was into
    witchcraft so I could put evil
    spells upon you.
Yours? Never!

Colleen Kleist

The Happy Flower

There is a flower that makes people happy,
you show it to them and they smile.
There is a guy named Pappy,
who laughed so hard when he saw it he fell on a pile.
The bad thing about it was,
that he broke his arm because,
he tripped over the logs covered with fuzz.
That was the story of the Happy Flower,
look at it and maybe it will give you power.

Amber Latsha

"Why Aren't You Here?"

You share my appearance with others.
You show them my pictures and they pass it on to another.
You get in touch one or two times. So I give
my attention to you, then you turn away and leave me shivering.
I put you out of my thoughts because of the pain I've already fought.
Forgetting me for years, left me nothing but long cold tears.
I wanted you to be near to help me get through all of my fears.
Without a doubt you chose to go your separate way and left me astray.
Now when I see you, I have nothing more to say.
You have a lot to make up for, so why aren't you here today?
I don't know where you are, or if you're alive, but if you can hear
my cry,
Why aren't you here to stop my sigh?

Addie Gaye

I Love You!

I look into your eyes,
with a big surprise,
not telling lies,
that my love is true for you.
All you say is, "Hey, I love you too,"
but do you mean it?
When I love somebody I want to
be able to tell you everything,
trust you and never hear enough because
you don't have to act tough, but I don't hear
enough, that's the trouble with me.
To tell someone you love them means a lot to me
It's not just words you may say every day
It's where the words come from, but
you know we've got a long way to go
before I know if I love you so.

Elysia Brisbane

The Skies

The heavens above, they seem to be so far away.
You try to reach out and touch them, but yet miles away.
You look to the beauty of the sky,
Wanting to become part of it.
But only in a dream can things like this be so wonderful.
But the heavens are not part of the dream.
For when conscious they appear within your sight.
And when seen; a breath is lost.
For your eyes are overcome by the light.
As sight is lost because of its power.
The true meaning of the sky is beheld.
An example of beauty is given.
An example of perfection is at hand.
For the sky is not just a physical.
For emotions loom throughout the clouds.
Love, strength, peace, joy.
All these from the clouds in the sky.
For the skies can be anything you want.
They can be real.
They can be part of your emotions.

Christian A. Morse

From Inside

My heart bleeds from the wounds you've left.
You used me so cruelly
until I crumbled into this helpless nothing.
Every time you came back to me it was different,
because it hurt more each time you left.
Now you're never coming back
and I'm expected to just move on.
But no matter how hard I try to forget,
your memory creeps into my mind.
I'm holding onto something that isn't there,
but I don't know how to let go,
As this pain pierces my heart, tears soak my face
and frustration crawls through my body.
Whenever I see you my stomach turns
and I feel a pain from deep inside my heart.
Something in my soul burns with so much anger
I want to scream.
But you walk away from me so casual and unaffected
so I stand watching you walk until I can't see you,
and everything from inside me collapses.

Bridget Rust

"A Mother's Day Tribute"

As far as I can remember since I was very young,
You were there to teach me right from wrong,
You taught me love through our loving ways,
And I've tried to pass it on every day.

When you were strict, I couldn't understand,
But know I appreciate it and I'm your biggest fan,
Whenever I had a problem or was feeling blue,
I could always count on your love and understanding
to see me through.

When I become a Mother,
I want to be the way you are,
To me, my sister and four brothers.

Although there were six of us,
You managed to spread your time and love,
Evenly amongst all of us.

And so on this Mother's Day,
I want you to know,
That I love you Mom every day,
Just stay your kind and loving way!

Beverly Pettiford Lindsey

Give Applause To All Senior Citizens

Senior Citizens need not impress anybody
You won these rights by your work records
You are the light that one day young people will see and they can
truly carry on in your spirit
You deserve to be called senior citizen or retiree
Look around you, thank God you are free
But in order to be called senior citizen you have to live so long;
to reach senior age you have to be strong
Set your pace, not fast, not too slow; you find it the best way to go
Bless the senior who had to work in places where it was cold and
seldom warm, and in the summer it was so hot you wished you
were never born
Often wondering to yourself why the boss can treat you this way
For as long as you push his work out, you will get paid
He feels no sorrow for you even if you are hurt
also telling you this is not a contest he's looking for his work
He also says he needs you but the day you get sick he looks the other
way to find someone else to take your place
so if you come near being senior citizen and make it to pension paid
take the money and run like hell away from an early grave

Albert Raysor

"Stormy"

Oh, there is a bird a pretty bird, can sing, talk and dance.
You wouldn't know this bird, would any of you, by chance?

She wakes you up with a loud "good morning" when she thinks
you have slept too late.
She wants her cream of wheat on time, there is no excuse to make
her wait.

She is green, yellow and red with a very large beak upon her head.
She will bite you and say, I love you, when you say, it's time for bed.

She calls the dogs and scolds the cat and ask if they want out.
She shares her food with every one, a generous bird no doubt.

She is always asking, what I'm doing? and answers the phone on every
ring,
she talks and laughs and says "oh well" she really thinks she is queen.

She tells you "bye" when you leave, and says, she will see you later,
she will also ask, where have you been? her wishes you must cater.

Now if I tell you, I do respond to all of her desires, you will surely
think I've lost my mind and need help from someone higher.

But this bird is a special one, I know you would agree,
she was hatched during Desert Storm, she was one of three.

So that is why we call her Stormy and why she talks so much
and why we love this spoiled bird, our hearts she surely has touched.

The house would be a lot quieter and the floors a whole lot cleaner,
but the love we share means so much, I know you would surely
agree, if you could only meet her.

Clara Harris

First Time Around

Giggle and sweat, and relish the pain
Your hardened nipples were a man-made gain
Pout your lips and bite real hard
You can't get a straight when you don't draw a card
Tell a story and make it rhyme, when
You huff, you puff, you commit the crime
You beg, you give, you quicken the pace
You never look a manikin in the face.
Review the film and judge the play
Did you see his look when he walks away?
Buy the dress and set the date,
Leave a message and wait, wait, wait
You cannot win, you cannot beat, for
When the loser refuses to compete.

Gunnar E. Berg

No More Corners

I saw you standing on the corner today,
Your lips and hands are ashy, numb and split,
Your teeth are stained brown from smokin' too much crack,
There are no pretty flowers in my neighborhood you see,
Just winos, drug dealers and school dropouts with no dreams.

I saw you begging on the corner today,
Your hair was nappy and matted to your head,
Your clothes stuck to your back like wet paper to the ground,
But that's not what's in your schedule today, it's time to
hustle money for your wine, oh please right away.

I saw you walking towards the corner today,
You're much too old to live with ma-ma and daddy,
So you live with any woman in the projects, oh boy what a dummy!
It's the first of the month so quick — cash her welfare
check and sell her food stamps, oh hurry before she comes home.

I did not see you on the corner today,
Word on the street is — you were killed sometime yesterday,
Some say it was drug related, others say plain good riddance.
But I say, how can there be any pretty flowers when another
precious life is taken away?

Ahreita T. Griffin

A Mother's Unknowing Comfort

Your heat kept me warm, up high you let me bury myself close to
your side. When the temperature dropped and billowy
white snow covered the earth, when sheets of rain thundered and
shook the sky, you slept unaware, yet always giving.

The time when the witch knocked, and when my own subconscious
threatened me, I crept through the dark, terrified, to
you and sleepily you accepted. When my ears rand or my tummy
ached you alone in disrupted of your night comfort
made it better. Despite the tossing and kicking you allowed me to
enter your dreamy warm. Slumber-filled world.

As a child there was no safer place to hide from the terrors of
night, the pain, or cold than by your side. Lying still
in the dark, deafening silence, we would slowly drift. There were
no words said aloud, none were needed; but "I love you"
blanketed the room, it was a kindling of our hearts and souls.

There is no safer place for a daughter than in mothers arms late
at night. Now, late at night when I am alone I think
of that bed, the covers, the warmth. I remember the uneager, yet
loving acceptance, all of those special times. And my
fears inevitably subside the noises cease and sleep comes easy.

Andrea L. Burnett

My Greatest Joy

A single drop dampens your tiny pillow,
  your slumber yielding not to my aching heart.
So precious, so pure, your gentle face empowers me
  with courage and hope and wonder.
My quest is unveiled, my spirit is enlightened,
  yet, fear grips my belly with agony.
After living through the years you now approach,
  did I grasp what I now need to convey?
As you blossom, how can I illuminate my life's powerful
  gifts? Will honesty and trust be your crest, love and
  compassion your purpose, respect and integrity your
  hope, dignity and contentment your strengths,
  imagination and creativity your goals, responsibility
  and conviction your intent, and humor and courtesy your
  ideals?
Ah, through love, through faith.
  Yes, these will steer me true.
And as our eyes unite, and your whole face smiles with
  me, I will once again recognize my special blessing,
For you are my greatest joy.

Brenda Beeler

Mis U Ty

Your eyes sparkle like stars,
Your smile like the sun.
The tears you cry are like the rain,
But things between us are left undone.

You are my best friend,
Someone I look to for answers I cannot find.
Never running ahead,
But sometimes falling a step behind.

You're always so honest and true.
Nothing, for you, was ever to hard to find.
Feelings never spoken of what was to be,
Thoughts of us still running through my mind.

The wind speaking your words,
The trees, your arms to embrace me.
And now the moon is your spotlight,
Making it possible for me to see.

Waking from another lonely night,
I only have memories left to love.
And every day I have to close my eyes to see you,
For now, you sleep with the angels above.

Carrie Larrick

Lord You Speak

Lord, you speak to us through the thunder
    Your voice is heard through the gentle rain...
And even when it is lightning...
    Your voice is heard again

How powerful is your message Lord...
    Oh, such wonders still unheard
But, so precious is that gift to us,
    The gift of your holy word...

Lord, you speak to us in the morning
    Your voice is heard during the night...
You forever walk close beside us
    To lead us to the light.

How wonderful is your gift of life
    When you gave your only Son...
To sacrifice his life for us
    So a victory might be won.

Lord, you speak to us with tender words
    And forgive us all with love...
Your unending patience and understanding
    Reach down from heaven above.

Alice Patterson

Imagine

Imagine the world without a tree
    without a dog
    without the friendly manatee
What would the world be like without a spotted owl
    without a mountain lion
    without a wolf to howl
What would we do without an oak tree
    without a rose
    without animals roaming free
How can our oceans survive
with oil tankers like Exxon Valdes
And industrial companies pollute as they please
We all have an environmental duty
to show mother nature her beauty
Our children deserve what we have known
    a world where fresh air exists
where woods and water are not on loan.
And animals along with people have grown.

Elizabeth Belser

Ashleigh's Seventh Birthday

Now that you are seven you should make a plan a kind of map of
where you're going. Do it now, while you're still growing!

You must learn to read and write, have perfect elocution,
then you will be ready to make a contribution.
It doesn't matter what you know if you can't articulate,
so be sure you master English before you graduate.
It doesn't matter what they know if you don't understand
and know the meaning of the words they have at their command.
An "A" in English is a must before the arts and science.
It will help to give you poise and certain self-reliance.
To understand this worthy guest requires discipline.
Even if you do your best another might well win.
Learn to listen carefully; hesitate to judge,
but when you know the answer speak out and never fudge.

Elegant simplicity bespeaks the lady fair.
Her clothes are never fancy but have a certain flair.
Good manners and morals, inherent, I hope
are sufficient armor while learning to cope.
And doors will be opened and favors bestowed
if you practice and use them as your honor code.

Jeanne C. Turner

Ha-Ha satan

Ha-ha satan, you're nothing but jokes,
    you're like a big bike wheel without any spokes.

Ha-ha satan, you prance around as a roaring lion,
    But really you're weak, and bent on cry'n.

For when the Lord Jesus Christ died on the cross, and rose from the dead,
    He was given total authority; He put his foot on your head.

And though you come to steal, kill, and destroy,
    Compared to the power of the Lord, you're nothing but a toy.

Ha-ha satan, you really make me laugh,
    For defeat is really in your behalf.

Ha-ha satan, it's about time for you to give in,
    you're definitely going to be punished by God for inciting sin.

And when you're thrown into the fiery furnace for eternity, ah-ha,
    All the saints will rejoice up in heaven, and exclaim, ha-ha.

Gentry C. Sullivan

You Have Love

If you have someone to calm your fears, you have love. If
you have someone to hold you near, you have love.
    If you have someone to hold your hand, you have love. If you
have someone who understands, you have love.
    If you have someone to see you through, you have love. If
you have someone to be there for you, you have love.
    If you have someone who loves you to pieces, you have love.
If your life is filled with Jesus, you have love.

Dee Manning

Love Eternal

Just as the sea refuses no river you have accepted me.
Your warmth and tenderness radiate a motherly love soon to be.
I have prayed in vain for things of this world...things of earth and clay.
These things are finite not like the birth of a soul.
For mountains will surrender their majesty to the sea and
timeless stars will burn to nothingness,
but we will always be.
It is through the gift of life that we exist, but it is
through love that we survive eternity.

George J. Mercuro Jr.

LXXV

When you're this many years young and your 'spring has sprung,'
You're not what you used to be — that's obvious to see.
My bosom sags, my tummy, too. I'll get a corset — the thing to do.
My ears and eyes aren't too keen, I hear noises and miss what I
should have seen.
                    But I'm OK! I'm Just Fine!

My back is stiff and aches all the time. Oh, these Golden Years —
yeah, so sublime.
I can't walk like I once could, but just to move I consider good.
To some extent I've lost my 'get up and go,' but I'm more fortunate
than some I know.
My 'achy breaky,' patched-up heart keeps me ticking with a
mechanical part.
                    But I'm OK! I'm Just Fine!

My head aches the entire day, really, really hurts — What can I say?
From early morn and throughout the night, I grin! I bear it! Yes —
with all my might.
My skin is flaky - it's so dry. My hair went straight - I could cry!
What would I accomplish shedding tears? Oh, shucks, I've just
added to my years.
                    But I'm OK! I'm Just Fine!

On the face many a line - they're someone else's - certainly not mine!
I have the tremors, I stutter, too — a couple more things that I do.
Stuttering is just word repetition, don't know the real name for that
condition.
But in essence — my body's rendition. When there's more "A
Second Edition."
                    But I'm OK! I'm Just Fine!

Alberta June Hugunin

Every Time

Every time I see you I want to cry
You're so perfect to my eyes.

Every time we talk to each other I let
everything else in my world slip away and I leave
my problems for another day because you're perfect
in every way.
Every time a sentence is said I dream of you in
my head I see you sleep, eat, and cry because
you're so perfect in my eyes.

Every time your name is spoken, whispered, or cursed
I see your last name behind my first.

Every time I hear your voice I rejoice and feel
confident about my choice to love you another day
because you're perfect in every way.

Now as the end draws near and you must go I
will cry for forever and a day because you are
walking the other way, but never shall I regret my
choice I love you, because you're so perfect of course.

Amy Sullivan

Untitled

The storm is seen offshore
Zero hour begins
It's been two months, maybe more
Of calm weather and warmth
The end is near, though I've never wanted it, nor
Have I ever expected these seas to become
As rough as before
It's like a bird clipped of his wings
Never again to soar
Everything seems to come to a painful end
And I am cut to the core
With nothing left, destroyed by the storm
As the tiny remains wash up on shore

Eric Quigg

The Wedding Day

We'll always remember this wedding,
with memories so beautiful and pure,
When you vowed through life to stay together,
of your friendship and love we were sure.
As you sail on this ship of life's oceans,
where the waves are both timid and rough,
these vows you both take will sustain you,
if you trust in each other enough.

We wish for you now all the happiness,
God can bestow from above,
praying he sends many children,
that you can both cherish and love.
And know that our door will stand open,
waiting for you to come in,
for we all will be part of this family,
till we join with our maker again.

Arthur O'Dwyer

The Awesome Osprey

I spied you today,
your majesty, Mr. Osprey,
Way up high on a steel cross-bar,
Through the magic of binoculars-so near, yet far.
Your formal plumage of black and white
Make you a striking and awesome sight.
That five foot wing-span-
bone, feathers and all,
Make you as wide as I am tall.
Those piercing eyes rove to and fro
As you carefully scan the scene below.
A fisherman with hovering, plunging skill -
Add a keen eye and a sharp-curved bill.
Whoops! There you go...for today-adieu!
But I'll be back-hope you will too.

Helen R. Kopp

Untitled

You were my smiles-now you're my tears
You were my laughter-now you're my silence
You were my love-now you're my anger
You were my soul-mate-now you're a stranger
You were mine-now you're another's.
You were me and I was you
Now you are gone and I am left to be just me.

Jennifer Smink

"Baby Girl"

Promise me in seventeen years,
You won't go on a talk show
To whine about your problems for slips of corrupt green,
When settling down at the kitchen table
And discussing your differences like mature adults
Will solve anything.
Please don't grow into the couch or eat fellow potatoes
Or watch men be battered in the name of good entertainment.
Don't use makeup that wasn't tested on bunnies
Because life is precious
When we'll know you love your leather jacket.
Vote for anyone running for President,
Unless they resemble idiotic cartoons.
America is an airplane skimming the treetops.
I want you to have a parachute when our soundness explodes.
We will crash and burn.

Bev Nordahl

Smallest Angels

They're the smallest angels
They've been sent from God above
To brighten our lives on earth
With their joy, their truth, and love

Their minds will search for knowledge
While their souls will soar on high
It's but a short time passing
Until they spread their wings to fly

They take away the bitter pain
That grows with fading youth
Our short comings may be many
But in their eyes we seek the truth

Age it takes its toll
For our wings are all but gone
Because they're the smallest angels
Like doves they circle God's throne

We should keep them close beside us
No matter what the cost
We should all thank God for children
For without them we are lost

Michael Edward Coffey

I Walk Away

I walk away
thinking of the
bright orange
pink and yellow sunset,
the blue sky
which hovers around
the sunset's
bright collective
shades of dull orange,
bright pink, a sinking
  pale yellow.
It goes down, down,
  down.
I turn,
turn away
refusing to watch
the colors
  Fade.
I walk
  walk away.

Renadja Benson

What's Wrong Or Right, Thinking

Sitting in the wee hours of the night,
thinking of what's wrong or right.
Thinking of what to say or pay
or in what way.

Thinking if there is no other way
to make peace with my life
this way.
What's wrong or right.

Thinking in the wee hours of the
night of the price I have to
pay for doing so many things
in that way.

Wanting to change in the way
of where I stay and the
manner I play, if it's worth
going on this way.
What's wrong, what's right, thinking.

Vaughn J. Webster

Lonely

Here I sit
  Thinking of you.
Here I sit
  Wishing for you.
Here I sit
  Lonely for you
Here I sit
  Wanting you.
Here I sit
  Dreaming of you.
Here I sit.

Tony G. Broxton Jr.

This Place We Call Earth

On this huge planet,
this great place we call earth,
I have no meaning,
I have no self worth
I make no difference,
even if you say I do,
but no one's important,
and that's the truth;
If I died tomorrow,
no one would care,
I'd just be a faint memory,
lingering in the air
It'd be like I never existed,
and that really hurts,
but that's all part of living,
on this great place we call earth

Kelly Durnil

"Soulmates"

One dark morn you came to me,
  this I know was meant to be.

Out of darkness came a light,
  now I see the end in sight,

Hand in hand we lay together,
  knowing it would be forever.

From the start you took my heart,
  calling me to do my part.

With the cards the lord had dealt,
  love was all that could be felt.

With a love so strong and true,
  now it's time to start anew.

Tim Dinello

Spring Is Near

It is the beginning of life
Throughout the earth
There is little strain and strife
In this new birth.

This time of year is sweet
No coldness to cut your breath
Only sun and birds to greet
You with the sounds that enmesh

Oh, wondrous our air, clear and clean
Oh, sun, shining bright
The essence of life's serene
Pleasures of daylight

So come one and come all
Sing with good cheer
Let our spring song
Be heard far and near.

Linda Elaine Elston

Confused Feelings

He says he cares about me
This truth I can see;
Which is why it breaks my heart
Every time we have to part.
And although he knows how much
I care,
He has no idea how bad I want
to share
All my love with him.
He tells me he's really confused
And I know I'm not being used;
So I'll just wait for him to
figure it out,
Then maybe I'll even shout;
I know for sure,
We'll find a cure
For our feelings toward each other,
Where neither of us will feel
smothered.

Wendy Baum

Journey's Light

Our Journey's just beginning
Though I see the rising sun,
The stars are so much brighter
So strategic the race we run.

We must search, encourage, inspire
Then continue to explore
More skillful in our growth,
So tender and so pure.

Our truth and our spirit
Furnish our journey's light,
Keeping our inward course
Unexpectedly bright.

Pleasing my childhood thoughts
So worthy of sacred applause,
My faith has been uplifted
From the power our love draws.

For only you are the world
That I've traveled so far to live,
My heart, my soul, my light
To only you I give.

Sharon M. Slade

My Spirit Is Not Broken

My spirit is not broken
Though my body seems a token
My future is ahead of me
And will repeat the words I've spoken
My thoughts and tempered actions
Along with quick reactions
Will mend through small retractions.
I thought time before had hurt me
I see how time has cured me.
Along with a new attitude
And a new found gratitude
Towards things once quickly forgotten
Which have brought greater latitudes.
Fond am I of the small things
  the sweet things
  and the new things.
All bring a deeper meaning
To a forgotten understanding
Of the dreams I have been dreaming
And of the spirit still with standing.

Patricia Thompson

My Window

As I stare out my window,
though the day is gray,
I see sunshine,
headin' my way,
"Old Glory" is blowin' in the wind
while springbirds are hummin',
ready to begin
their melodious canter
in the wee hours of the mornin';
there are no leaves on the trees,
their branches are bare,
though each seems to be
embracing the air.
I choose this day as my very own,
whatever it brings, is mine alone.

Snotha Phillippe

A Life

I was ready to let go
thought ready to die,
but I hesitated then
and thought I have to try.

Life is very precious
only one chance to live,
so I prayed to the Lord
now my life to him I give.

I have to live each day
as if it were my last,
let go of my bitterness
and let go of my past.

Live my life for others
love and help them all,
not worry about money
that's everyone's downfall.

The Lord gave me life
my destiny is mine alone,
when my purpose is achieved
then the Lord will call me home.

Sharon Theuerkauf

True Friends

A true friend will always be there,
Through the thick and the thin.
A true friend won't run away,
When your trouble begins.
A true friend understands,
When you need to get away,
And lets you go, because they know
You'll return the favor some day.

A true friend would be willing,
To do whatever you ask,
And not stop to question
The profit it may have.
A true friend will walk across the line,
Without a second thought,
And thank you for a gift you gave,
No matter what you bought.

If a friend is always there,
If to you he does not lie,
Try as hard as you will,
A truer friend you will not find.

Sarah Eyermann

To My Friend

I shall always be where you are.
Through you, I shall see beauty,
Hear truth,
Feel warmth and tenderness,
Smell a flower,
And taste of love.
I, in turn,
Shall share my self with you.
You have filled an emptiness
Within me,
And I am
Your friend.

Philip A. Eckerle

Clean Out Your Heart

Clean out your heart
Throw the baggage away
Emotional cobwebs
Take away from today

Take bitterness, anger
and lay it to rest
Struggle for new growth
to nurture, digest

Sift through the memories
Squelch the unjust
Hang on to laughter
Hold on to trust

Walk the high road
and always lay waste
The torturing thoughts
made up in haste

Slowly but surely
You'll have your new start
The first step begins
When you clean out your heart

Tracy Skalisky

"Essence"

Others highest good
Time alone withstood.
Plenty of desire
Non-destructive fire.
Delicate delight
Much more than, "feel right."
Desire consuming,
Not just presuming.
Not lust, but real love
Descends as a dove.
Rejuvenating,
So animating.
As two become one,
Life and love go on.

William E. Willoughby

Times Of Life

In life there is time for many things
  Time for heartaches and for pain
Time for laughter, joy and fears
  And in between time for tears

There is time for happiness
  Work and play
Time to rest at the end of day
  So in life you can see
There is time for all good things to be.

Pauline Bowen

Christmas Time

Christmas time is a
time for sharing
thoughts and giving
love,

But most important,
it is the time when
everybody gives and
receives, and thanks the
Lord Jesus for the
one gift He gives us
all, "The gift of
Life."

Nicole L. Maille

Decisions

The time is upon us
time to decide.
So many decisions
so little time.
What do we want to do?
What do we want to be?
So many decisions
so little time.
What we want to do
only we can tell.
I know one thing is true,
so many decisions
so little time.

Shawn D. Mentzer

Game Of Life

In times of sorrow,
times of pain.
Forever seeking,
someone to blame.
Withdrawn eyes and
Sealed up ears.
Through misty fog,
that seldom clears.
Only time may heal
the wounds of pain.
When bitterness does
finally drain
There's only one —
to take the blame.
It's all your fault,
you played the game.

Laura Amacher

I Wonder

I wonder why you had to go
I forgot to say good-bye
I wonder why you loved me so
Although I made you cry

I wonder why you gave me joy
I gave you so much hate
I wonder why you gave me toys
When I made you wait

I wonder when we'll meet again
I'll always be here
I wonder if I'll see you
Before I go, my dear

Carissa Caccone

Untitled

'Tis the beginning of sorrow,
'Tis the end of happiness.
The sad moments I've shared,
Seem to have lasted.
We've all had our moments,
But mine seem to stay.
We've all had our sorrows
Yet mine don't go away.
What does this show us?
What do we see?
Time heals everything
Including me.

Michelle Glorsky

Christmas Wish

Crawling up the attic,
to bring down the Christmas things.

Picking out the children's toys,
that Santa's going to bring.

Putting up the Christmas tree,
and hanging up the lights.

Just thinking of the holidays,
makes it hard to sleep at night.

You see, this Christmas is my first,
without my mother here.

And it makes it really hard,
to hold back my streaming tears.

I can still remember,
her sitting there beside the tree.

Passing out her treasured gifts,
she always had one for me.

So if I could have a Christmas wish,
I would wish for no other.

For Santa Clause to find a way,
to bring me pack my mother.

Stephanie Lynne Williams

Mindscape

Echoes of yesterday tickle your soul
To bring you a younger man's thought
The things you can do
When your body is not
Traveled and aged and used
There will come a time
When your mind will recall
Those things you are doing today
So when all you have left
Is your mind to play with
Make sure, it's a wonderful day

Mark Conyers

My Broken Heart

What I would give
to run my hands through
your hair. What I would
give to heal this broken
heart of mine. I can't
get over you. The tears run
down my face like water. I
can't live without you. I
will love you for always and
forever!!

Yessenia Murillo

Give Me The Chance

Give me the chance to return again
    To days of carefree roving;
And give me a heart made clean of love
    To choose again for loving.

The days were never long nor plain
    And many a man came calling;
And many a man spent time and sense;
    And many a pride was fallen.

These were the times of frivolous fun,
    Nothing but joy and game;
But give me the chance to choose again
    And sense to choose the same.

Linda Q. Falabella

What Did You Do Today?

Did you take the time today,
To help someone along their way?

Someone's burden, did you share?
Or just sit back, relax and stare?

A great mistake did someone make,
Did you forgive or turn to hate?

A mother's child, no food to feed,
Did you give hope and meet the need?

His heart disturbed, he's out for blood,
Did you distract him with your love?

Tormented mind, to drugs she went,
Will you be there? She needs to vent.

When someone falls, please help them up,
Sometimes in life, things get so tough.

And when the day comes to an end,
You'll thank God for the peace within.

Thadiece Perkins

Broken Thread

I was threaded by God's marital bond
To look upon his face so fond
My belief that all was right
My heart ahead abounding light
A planted seed God gave to us
To grow and bloom a gift so fair
The selfless love I have not enough
Fond of face did whisper there
You have chosen to abide
Closest to our gift from God
To place my deepest needs aside
To bury love between us both
I must have all you have to give
To share never the center of my core
And so the thread that God did sew
Between us now exists no more

Sharon Coldwell

Untitled

Today is the beginning of forever.
Today is for me
Today is a good day.
Today is without you
Today and forever
You will be in my heart
Today and forever
My heart is with you......

Tracey J. Gill

Grannie's Quilt

Grannie took tiny little pieces
To make a quilt for me.
It was prettier than a picture,
I was proud for all to see.
She sewed the pieces together
With stitches ever so fine,
And made a quilt so beautiful
I was glad to call it mine.

I showed it to all the neighbors.
They expressed their happiness for me,
That I had a quilt made by Grannie.
It was all I could wish it to be.
When I become a Grannie.
I'll make a quilt so fine
For each of my grand children,
If God grants me the time.

Mary K. Barnett

"Nature's Child"

As the petals open up,
    to meet the ray of light.
Morning dew glistens upon it,
    like a diamond shining bright.

This is a way of life,
    being anew, day after day.
Bringing us moments of pleasure,
    in a visually beautiful way.

Please watch as they grow,
    as you would your own.
Being one of Nature's children,
    they also, want love shown.

So don't pick my child,
    plant your own instead.
Then you too, can have,
    children in your flower bed.

Renee Hopkins

A Passing Thought

The world has grown weary.
    To mortals this is so.
Those who believe in love,
    recede in fury.
Those who are as the tide,
    must turn and go.
In the currents, all are at rest.
The motions drown forgotten protests.

Sharon L. Ross

In Sight

God, grant us the wisdom
to reach out and Love
    To Find those who
need us, and leave
those who think they
    don't - A feeling of
friendship and HOPE.
    Give us the knowledge
to build and share
dreams, and those who
cannot dream, a spark
that can ignite a
brighter future for
them
    Show us the way
and forever we will
follow.

Madelyn Walker

All Within Me

Bobbing on waves of reflection
To seek out the answer that is myself.
Reaching long tentacle arms outward,
To touch the edges of boundaries.
A push against the rocks,
   The walls,
     The moving foundation.
To find again and again
That I am the only one there.
I am the only one to feel,
And to know myself
   As one - infinitely,
Reflecting off my barricades,
   My mirrors, my symbols.
Bouncing from one aspect of what I know
   To another.
Seeking someone, somewhere,
To confirm this which I see of that,
That which I feel of those,
Those that lead to this.

    Michelle Hindman

Best Friend

A friend will always be there
To stand there by your side,
A really good listener
In whom you can confide.

A friend will share your secrets
They'll stay all day and night,
And when your day is dark and blue
They'll help to make it bright.

A friend will never leave you
If you really need to talk,
Could ride around, go to the mall
Or hang out and take a walk.

If your friend is the best
Then you'll never part,
'Cause you know they'll always be there
Deep inside your heart.

    Mandy Redifer

Teach Me To Pray

Heavenly Father, I ask You,
To teach me how to pray,
So I may converse with You,
In a very special way.

I could tell You when I'm lonely,
I could tell You when I'm sad,
I could tell You when I'm hurting,
And even when I'm glad.

Many things I'd like to tell You,
Because You would understand,
I know that You would guide me,
And give a helping hand.

So teach me how to pray, dear Lord,
So I can converse with Thee,
I can tell You what's in my heart,
And it will just be,
Between Thee and me.

    Shirley G. Dovichow

Lingering Notes

I could write a love song
to tell you how I feel
say how much you mean to me
and let you know my love is real

The melody would flow from me
Wrap you in its warm embrace
Whisper to you tenderly
Gently touch your face

Telling you my love is there
surrounding you with song
the notes would fill the air
and carry you along

For I am Yours and you are mine
our love is here to stay
these lingering notes my soft song
will never fade away

    Sandra Roberts Kindred

I Said A Prayer

   I said a prayer for you,
today and I know God must have
heard - I felt the answer in my
heart although he spoke no
words. I didn't ask for wealth
or fame I knew you wouldn't
mind. I asked him to send
treasures of a far more
lasting kind. I asked that
he'd be near you
at the start of each new
day. To grant you health and
blessings and friends to
share your way. I asked
for happiness for you
in all things great and
small, but it was for
his loving care I prayed
the most of all.

    Nicole Fraley

The Saga Of A Married Couple

We always seem to argue,
We always seem to fight.
But we always seem to love each other,
When day turns into night.

We hardly ever talk,
We can't find things we share.
But we always find the ways
To tell each other we care.

We seldom say "I love you,"
Or words like "I'm sorry," it's true.
But when we do say "I love you,"
It means we really do.

To argue and spat seems to be
A game that married's play
But when the arguing is over,
There's no need for words to say.

So please remember when we fight,
As I know we sometimes will.
That in the end, our love will win
And I will love you still.

    Paulette Butler

Yesterday

Yesterday was a sweet memory
Today is longing hope for tomorrow
Tomorrow is a day that will

Never come
It leaves one in fear
Of letting go of yesterday
If yesterday is forgotten
The search for tomorrow

Cannot begin
For it was yesterday
That made tomorrow
A shattered dream.

    Michelle M. Haines

Today/Tomorrow

Today we laugh
Tomorrow cry

Today we're bold
Tomorrow shy

Today we sing
Tomorrow sigh

Today we live
Tomorrow die

Who knows when
Who knows why

Today we're earth
Tomorrow sky

    Vickie L. Vanderhoof

My Heart Has Wings

On crutches now, my weight is borne.
Tomorrow is another morn.
My roving spirit is not quenched
as I sit alone on the depot bench.
Others quickly walk me by
as I stifle out my need to cry.

But now I truly understand
my grandma's pain filled crippled hands
when she worked and slaved and toiled.
Forgive me dear for I was spoiled.

Loving spirit finds peace and content
to triumph on the depot bench.
In my fancy now are shared
moments in others lives of care.

Again on crutches weight is borne
with strength to face another morn.

    Marjorie W. Seitz

"Too Old"

"You're getting old," so said my wife
"Too old, in fact, to have much life."
And when we shuffle off to bed
She turns to me and says, "Drop dead."

My feet are warm; her feet are cold
She puts her teeth into a bowl
It is falsie this and falsie that
It's hard to tell just where she's at.

I contemplate on nights of yore
Until I hear her start to snore
Then pull my pillow o'er my head
And waste no time in "dropping dead."

    H. Northam Webster

A Call To Persevere

The
Touch
waited to be given was a touch too late.
Words
that are different yet spoken the same.
Friends
but to be discovered.
Intentions
never surfaced.
A
Victory
is won yet the battle goes on.
Heroes
who forget themselves.
Purpose
which comes only from God.
Souls
that ride on the decisions of them all...
and me

Rona S. Clark

Street Light

The filthy, ragged
trench coat swallowed
her stooped, hurried form.

A piece of sandwich, with a roach
riding on the hard crust

Fell through a hole from the
tattered, brown shopping bag she was
dragging behind her.

Without realizing I was watching,
she stopped and cowered beneath
the fiery blaze that glistened in
the damp, thin blackness.

Learning against the pole, she slid
down onto the cool pavement.
Sighed heavily, reached

For the sandwich; then plucked
a wounded, starving robin

From her pocket. Tenderly
maneuvering the fallen bird
toward nourishment.

Ruth Vaughan-Scearce

"Withering Madness"

Sunlight gleams before me
Tiny droplets streaming over my body
grasping onto its face
climbing through the
cracks and crevices

Beyond the horizon
I see a world of beauty and promise
Her trees stand tall
and children graze the land
Silently I am thankful

Flesh will heal
hath we replenished it with
the body and soul of mother earth
Her tears thundering
through passages of time

Making destroys the living
evil surrounding her body
Whispers of rebellion
flow in her chilling breath
Cries fade away into the night

Katherine Albis

Mother

Though we may not know of the many
troubled times
and cannot seem to solve them all, there
is someone near
that knows just how you feel.

So be strong as you can
and don't let go.

There is someone near and willing to
assist.

Kennitha D. Jenifer

True Love And Friends!

Swans are a sign of
true love and friendship
when you receive them.
They are keepsakes.
My life is so
wonderful right now.
From now on
my life will never be
a miserable fake.
It has everything I
ever wanted in
it, in life.
I've asked you for true
love, and got it.
I've asked for many,
many good friends and
received them.
What more could I ask
for, the puzzle fits.

Rebecca Warrington

But Not Today

Someday we'll arise
Unafraid of the world we see
Be able to walk the streets
That are safe, again, for you and me
Someday...but not today

Someday there will be
A child who cries no more
No man without a home
Love will surely open the door
Someday...but not today

Someday our eyes will open
And see what we have done
For this world is our home
There will be no wars left to be won
Someday...but not today

P. Maria Baldwin

Folly Of Tears

Ere half the night and tears are mine
To wash the pain away.
To gush aloud the smoldering fears
I've had all through the day.

At last sound sleep found me
And I slept amidst my tears,
And dreamed of pain and sorrows,
And dreamed of untold fears.

And waking found me early.
By my bed the sun did shine.
I said, "today is different."
But tears again are mine.

Reather S. Kelly

Fair Warning

I am unique
uncommon
a jewel among stones
rare earth
a super find
Do not
compare me
judge me
criticize me
I am one of a kind
I am a Super Nova
growing
expanding
changing
radiating love and energy
Accept me
enjoy me
appreciate me now
for tomorrow I may not exist
and you will have missed me

Sandra Lee Jacobs

Ebony

It must have been hard
under lock and guard

How did they cope
How did they live
All they could do is give

They had no freedom
They had no time

They were sold
They were traded
They were scorned
And hated
Not to mention degraded

They had hearts
They had souls

But alas
Their skin was black as coals...

Naomi Shine

You

Me before you
unfulfilled dreams
Me with you reality
which brings life
Me without you
wind with no direction
dream and reality
the night has no limits
when thinking of you
love song fantasy that's you

There should be a moment
to share without distraction
with one another
There ought to be a language
to express my feelings
Without being short of words
nor pretending in saying more
spring child mayflower goddess
there should be a way to love you
just for being you.

Paul Zetina

Visiting Marshall

This dog chases flies
unsure of when he catches them.
He bites at dry leaves, teasing
I'm missing something somewhere.

His eyes, like exclamation points,
harass cats.
Whining and growling he tosses
his reluctant playmate.

Doggie syllables emerge as he
licks my face and walks
beneath my propped-up legs.
My secret is safe, his eyes tell me.

He really can't live without
chasing kitty cats about.

He lays down again
Knowing full well, at some time,
I'll have to put down my pen.
Finder's keepers.

Valerie Polacek

I Saw A Rainbow

I saw a rainbow
up in the sky,
And low and beho'
there was a pot of gold.

'Twas then I saw
a little man, and
If I rightly recall
he was a man of green.

He was grinning to himself,
doing funny things,
I declare, what a funny elf!
and... that was all I saw.

Not a chance had I
to get a pot of gold.
I let out a sigh
Oh my, I'm getting slow!

Katharine E. Tully

Grieving

My mother's spirit haunted me
visited me in the form of a ghost
What happened those nights was shocking
and very unbelievable to most

She came through my window
kept getting closer to my bed
She sure looked like my mother
even though I knew she was dead

The fourth night was horrifying
as she came closer to my head
Smelling her perfume was suffocating
and I screamed, "You're already dead"

So I started to shake her
and felt her spell begin to break
Then as she vanished before me
I said, "This must be a mistake"

My mother's death was controlling me
keeping me from feeling my best
So her spirit came by to see me
and helped my soul to rest

Linda Frank

Cafe

Country music
wafting quiet
under silver,
wet and naked,
steaming
biscuits,
gravy,
scenting silence,
sounds delicious,
and inviting,
color
empty
hearts.

Mark William Smith

Good-bye, Sweet Child

A child sits within a cell
Waiting patiently.
A vast world to be discovered,
New ideas to be found,
And yet the child waits.
There is no time to play,
Work must be done.
Forgotten are the days
Down at the park.
Lost is the imagination
Of creations unmade.
It's time to grow.
Never too early, they say.
Better to live life as it is, they rant.
So the child sits.
To the world just
An inexperienced young person,
To the beholder
A life devoid of youth,
The key long destroyed.

Stephen Parth III

The Nursing Home

bouncing gravel voices
warbling dissonance everywhere
timeworn humans moldering

Exhausted and helpless, senility boring
   deeper
    and
     deeper
a baby doll caressed by a doting, hoary
  spinster

young eyes blinded by guilt

Katherine Ann Gelgota

"Ah! May The Red Rose Alive Always"

Ah! May the red rose alive always,
To smile upon earth, and sky, why
Should the beautiful ever weep?
Why should the beautiful die?
Lending a charm to every ray that
Falls on her cheeks of light
Giving the zephyr kiss, and
For the kiss that is nursing the
Dew drop bright
Ah! May red rose live always, to
Smile upon earth, and sky, why
Should the beautiful ever weep?
Why should the beautiful die?

Lee Doll

Pain

A man shapèd like an ogre
was locked up far away.
Disfiguration brought him pain,
his tale I tell today.

No one wanted to be his friend.
Freak! They would laugh and say.
His pain they never could understand.
His plight you'll hear today.

Kids stopped to mock him all the time.
It's no wonder he cracked.
No one showed him some sympathy,
Kindness these people lacked.

One day he could take it no more,
Waiting for them to come,
he made his plans and as they passed,
he fired his fierce gun.

He was tried and put in prison,
to not see light of day.
I know he hopes you'll not forget,
the tale you've heard today.

Roseline Guest

Withering Black Rose!!!

Look, withering black rose,
Watch your world unfold.
The root of you lies in me,
the seed, that should never be.
Yet still, from your blackness,
which you cannot see,
comes me.

Don't run, stay with me,
or can't you stand to see
the light that springs from your
dark black seed?

Once, I bowed my head in
Shame, feeling beauty such as I
should never be,
But as you wither, I'll be free,
and I will not be ashamed to
look at me.

La'toya Lankford

Rising Sun

Father of the Sun
way up in the sky
I don't want you to die

Father of the sun
I will become like you in peace.

Reginald Lawrence, II

Free Bird

A bird in flight
upside down in might
carrying on
humming a song
On yesterday's night
and future's light
she rides a wave
of her own will
gliding
on a stream of tomorrows
hope.

Karen Howard

Human

We all are mortal,
We all mourn when one dies,
We all make mistakes,
And we've all told lies.

We all have dreams,
We all need a friend,
We've all felt alone,
And did things we didn't intend.

We've all laughed at ourselves,
We have all shed some tears,
We've all asked for a favor,
We all have our own fears.

We've all shared a secret,
And hummed a favorite song,
We've all wished upon a star,
We all want to belong.

Richard J. Zabadal

Homeless Child

I am alone,
We are together,
Together we can be more.
We can SEE,
HEAR, SMELL,
FEEL, and TASTE
The little we can.
Nights are cold,
Days disturbed.
TAP DANCERS,
HARMONICA PLAYERS,
and STREET SINGERS
Get loose change,
I get stomach pains.
Time is long,
Life is short.
I will die,
You will also die.
I'm not different.
You are!!!

Sarah Haines

Tomorrow

We live in war.
We live in sorrow.

We live in peace.
We live for tomorrow.

Liane Owed Lauersdorf

Free Spirit

The wind is a free spirit
Unruly, untamed
Unseen power hurling its anger.

It is a power source
that is reckless yet beautiful.
Its power is enormous.

Yet it can be gentle
or ruthless.
We welcome it with its coolness.

Yet wish it away with its destruction.
It is a savage untamed beast
or a gentle whisper,
ready to cast its mesmerizing power
upon anything that breathes its
Godly breath.

Rebecca Martinez

The World Today

The way the world is today
we need to hug each other
and pray, we pray for peace
and hunger's end for countries
that are so far away. We need a world
without quakes and rumbles; we need
peace, we're so afraid to crumble.
We are so strong yet so weak; we shake
with fears and fight with spears.

No complaints of aches and pains,
we are a people meek and plain; we
share because we care. The plight
we bare to other nations will sustain
our pride; our pledge to fight will
survive because we strive to keep
peace in our lives. In the world
today we need to hug each other
and pray; we need sanity to keep
humanity.

Patsy Stella Cothran

Reality

Life is not a bowl of cherries,
we often compromise.
Each day we grow a little older,
and yes a bit more wise.
No one said it would be easy,
it's really just a maze.
What's going on inside your head,
some say is just a phase.
It must be dealt with carefully,
and with a little wit.
Although it can be sweet sometimes,
it's just a bowl of pits.

Nancy Estrada

Forever

In our troubles
we only had ourselves
Nobody else
No one to save us
We had to help ourselves

And when the skies shone blue
They saw me and you
Back and back together
For whenever apart
We grow so miserable

And when we find happiness
We'll know where to go
Back together
That's where we'll find happiness

Summer Lyn Hoover

Measure Of Love

How do you measure a mother's love
When she holds you through the night?
Her soothing, sweet, serenity
Lets you know you'll be all right.

How do you measure a lover's love
When he holds you through the night?
Arms entwined, tangled, tightly
Secure and warmed by a new day's light.

How do you measure God's love for you
When He holds you through the night?
With faith, forgiveness, fortitude
Through you, His love shines bright.

Kathie Harrington

I Stand Alone

We walk through the same pathway
We sing the same song
We have the same intentions
Yet I stand alone

We have the same father
We share the same moon
You are my brother
Yet I stand alone

We know the difference
between right and wrong
Yet we can choose only one
We all have made mistakes
Yet I stand alone

When love is greater than hate
When difference is no longer shunned
Until we can speak face to face
one on one
I will stand alone

Tanya Thomas

Dual System

Alone,
    We walked the road
together.
Two
    two by two,
we passed along.

Revolution and Generation
equaled procreation.
Time united the difference
of being and eternity.
This planet Earth spinning
round-the-clock formation.

Everyday rhythms,
    the tides,
    the hours
are humming the end,
then two by two
again, will life be
    one.

Lesley Sagel

Walking Hand In Hand

I'm walking with you darling,
We're going hand in hand.
We've walked in winter snowflakes,
We've walked on summer sand.

We've gone through life together,
Companions till the end.
You were always more than my lover,
You were also my very best friend.

When we stood there at the altar
And made that solemn oath,
Our hearts started beating together,
But love had not yet reached full growth.

Our years of living together
Made our love grow stronger each day.
That love could never be replaced now,
So darling, what more can I say?

There may never be a tomorrow;
The yesterdays in my mind will be true.
No matter what happens to us darling,
Hand in hand, I'll be walking with you.

Stanley T. Gray

"Graduation"

Throughout the years
We've grown in many ways
close to one another
Through all of our days

Now the time has come
for all to say their goodbyes
and go our separate ways
To live our own lives

Though the path we choose
May not be an easy one
Hopefully all that we have learned
Will help us make it fun

Now the time has come
For all to say their goodbyes
and go our separate ways
To live our own lives

So when we walk down the aisle
As one big family of friends
Always remember the good times
And how the memories will never end

Missy Riordan

What Seems

Look out my window, what do I see
What seems to be going wrong
Our world approaches catastrophe
It seems to be so strong

Religious hypocrisy
What seems to be going on
Filled with false prophecy
They seem to be so strong

Prejudice sexually
What seems to be going wrong
Treat all people equally
Together we'd be so strong

The war machine, mortality
What seems to be going on
Weapons as far as the eye can see
Their power so strong

Prejudice racially
What seems to be going wrong
We're all from the same family tree
Why is the hate so strong

Randy Lee Reinacher

You're Gone

Sometimes I wonder,
what sign did I miss?
Was your smile a put-on,
a show for all to see?
What were you thinking
in those last final moments?
Did you think no one would shed a tear,
or we'd forget you now that you're gone?
You were wrong, my friend,
so very wrong.
I'll think of you always
with a tear in my eye,
and remember the good times
we used to share.
I'll never forget you,
even though you're gone.
You are my friend.
You're in my heart.

Melissa White

Goodbyes

Somewhere between
What we think - and we feel
Is the rest of our life-
Sometimes Love - (if we're willing.)

Hidden in memories
Or vivid in dreams
Some stay forever-
Others briefly - it seems.

You're a little of both
Brief and forever
I thought that I knew you
But time knows us better-

Still - seeing is believing
So don't close your eyes-
Here's to the welcomes-
Farewell to goodbyes.

Stephen D. Jones

Untitled

Oh anxiety and old age
What's become of us?

We worry and wonder
All our life
What we can do with
Discomfort and strife.

Let's replace an old
Habit with a new;
There's such potential
For me and you.
If we could look back
From years ahead
There would be no time
For fear and dread

We'd know then
What we don't see now
There's no need to
Worry anyhow...

Nancy Vieira

Dusk To Dawn

There comes a time
when all is done.
When birds don't sing
their song of joy.
When sun has set
and silence rules.
When peace descends
and all is calm.
Then fate holds tight
the threads of life.
Its circle round
once more complete.
Then end does bring
the start once more,
As new light dawns
beyond our sight.

Karen Parker

Life's Misgivings

It's funny how you notice,
when bad things come and go.
But when a good thing comes,
and passes by,
you seem to never know.

Nathan Pekarske

Him

When I look at him, I get weak
When he talks to me, I can hardly speak

Those gorgeous eyes just blow me away
And his perfect face, what can I say

When he gets close, I feel my heart beat
When he walks by, I wanna fall to my feet

And when he gave me that little kiss
That's something I'll always miss

Stephanie Gohl

Reality

How can I do for you
When I can't do for me?

How can I forget
When I can't yet remember?

How can I accomplish a goal
When I can't see through my own eyes?

How can I love
When I can't feel through my own heart?

How can I dream
When reality is tugging on my shoulder
Telling me to do for it?

Vanessa Johnson

Untitled

This Christmas,
When I glance at the tree,
Its evergreen branches
Warm my heart with thoughts,
Of the eternal love inside of me.

The gentle layers
Of the pure white snow,
Stand for the honesty,
And ever present trust,
That allows our love to grow.

This Christmas,
The glow of the lights,
Represent the twinkle,
And the stars in my eyes,
That for you shine bright.

This Christmas,
The angel on top the tree,
Stands for the efforts,
Of your loyal faith,
You've so graciously taught to me.

Kristi Bland

A Hidden Lagoon

'Tis night and dear, here we are
We two, you and I, beside a
hidden lagoon whose surface
Glows like mirrors, and oh how
happy am I sharing with you
this night of romantic splendor,
the sapphire water is such a
delight that perhaps only Eden
could surpass, and dear love
of the winds tingler at my ears
music soft and low. Music such
as only we in love sharing
romantic splendor as are we
beside a hidden lagoon
la di de da, la, de, di

Roosevelt Johnson

Busted

One morning very early,
   when I was on a bum,
   they wouldn't sell me
   whisky, they wouldn't sell me rum.
They put me in the jail house
   I gazed upon the wall
   the bed bugs and the
   roaches, were having a game of ball.
The score was 6 to nothing
   the bed bugs were
   ahead, the roaches hit a home run
   knocked me out of bed.
Six o'clock in the morning
   they ring the breakfast
   bell, two old potatoes
   boy, how they smell.
Something like Coffee Juice,
   and golly how it tastes.
I never want to go back
   there in all my born days.

   Lorraine R. Shaw

There Was A Time

There was a time
   when our dreams were sharp
and the moon was an easy companion

when the ships were new,
   the winds fair,
and the whales sang unfettered.

There was a time
   when the spirits of the geese
beyond the ice of Heaven
caused the wolf of silence
   to howl full melancholy,
and gash the soul of the night.

There was a time,
   under the Belt of Orion,
when the philosopher and I saw worlds

Of logic too profound for imagination,
   and let them go...
we dared not disturb their symmetry.

   Randall Sullivan

Across The Shadows

From across the room of shadows
Where lights flicker and dance
When music filled the smoky air
I was caught within your glance.....

Held captive in your eyes of fire
A brightness out of control
I knew I could not move an inch
From the passion of that hold......

I could not just walk away
As if I were not drawn
By some overwhelming, calming power
To your side where I belong.....

Looking into that manly face
Stood a "woman and a child"
Afraid to move or fall so deep
Still captive in your smile.....

Now, we sit and watch the stars
Listen to whispers in the wind
The autumn air is not so cold
As our lives once might have been.....

   Kayce Huffine

When Mice Play

So carefree do they roam
When the cat's away from home
They giggle, play and snicker
And seldom do they bicker
They fritter and they fritter
And chew till all is tattered
Running from room to room
Just ahead of Grandma's broom

But sometimes their reckless romp
Will cause them to get stomped
If the footsteps go unheard
Of the cat creeping around the curb

LOOK OUT!
Too late for them to scatter
'Cause they're slower and much fatter
So one by one they're eaten
By the cat who was only sleeping

   Wendell Godfrey Lancaster

Star

When a star can still shine,
When the moon can still grow,
Still in my heart I know,
That in day of darkness,
In day of light,
Still the star will fall tonight.
With a heart beat unknown,
And a tear I cannot cry,
In hope of tomorrow I will try.
But a promise I cannot keep,
And a thought I cannot disobey,
For tomorrow I'm hoping,
But still waiting for today.

   M. Shultz

Sonnet To Love

A love so strong it's in thine eyes
   when two lost souls shall meet
and only to be recognized
   when two hearts shall have one beat

A love so blind it cannot see
   the death within your eyes
It only sees true love can be
   took with a human disguise

A love so sweet you cannot taste it
   all but one too many times
for in such sweet fruit there bears a pit
   when the fruit tastes more divine

   Tonya Woodland

Growing Apart

Growing apart, we don't listen well.
What happens next, only time will tell.
How does love drift so far away
From two so close, no one can say.
I touch your hand with a heavy heart.
Knowing now that we must part.
As I look ahead past all the strife,
We must begin a brand new life.
It will be hard, make no mistake.
Court cost and kids, the give and take.
It feels so strange to say goodbye.
I just can't bear to see you cry.
Suffice to say right from the start,
We spent our lives growing apart.

   William R. Culver Jr.

"Friends"

Friends are the ones you can call on
when you need someone to care
Friends are the ones who will pardon
when you can't always be there
Friends take time to understand
when you're down and feeling blue
Friends meet all of these qualities
Now my friend, this applies to you
Thank you for being my friend

   Terry Finger

Sun

The sun is there to greet you
When you rise from bed each day
it wants to bring you through the hours
In its own special way

But when it's time for it to go,
Don't be full of sorrow
For when you learn you will know
It'll be back tomorrow

   Lisa Martyn

Melted Man Of Snow

Melted man of snow
Where did he go
Follow the tracks
Of his tears
The liquid wonder
Gone to slumber
Winter snowflake
Of which to make
A joyous creation
The evil sun
Persistence and power
Destroys our plump
Companion into
A meek unfathomable
Puddle of polluted
Tears which I
Have cried for my
Melted man of snow.

   Mary Martorelli

Unbinding Of The Heart

My heart is not an open book
Where love lifts from the page
And even though perhaps quite sound
Its dusty cover may expound
The time for which it's aged

My love is not a spoken word
Though spoken may reveal
An introduction to be read
To give its reader something said
The jacket may conceal

My book is more than simple words
Its grandeur's not its bound
If left shut tight
One may lose sight
If opened seems profound

May I suggest hold not thy breath
Nor bind this book my Cherish
For I too long
Have done this wrong
'Tis time my timid perish

   Scott Cleveland

The Memorial Wall

I went to the Memorial Wall
Where names are etched in stone
And as I looked around
I was not there alone

Mothers and fathers gathered
Wives and sweethearts too
Sisters, brothers and children
And friends like me and you

Marines, soldiers and airmen
And sailors in uniform
Crying just like the others
For our brave ones who are gone

There's wasn't any laughter
And tears fell everywhere
It was another tearful chapter
About heroes whom we care

Oh God bless all our heroes
The living and those gone
And God bless the Memorial Wall
Please God, bless every one.

William A. Barnes, Jr.

Untitled

Can you imagine a place
   where sound is ceaselessly
   pounded into silence?

Where images become infinity?

Where loneliness abounds and yet
   memories flood?

A place where you sit alone encircled
   by your closest friends?

Strange…that a barren land of
sunlit sand and stones could be
so comforting; so soothing.

Can you imagine this place?

I can.
I've been there.

Lara Headlee Zook

Alone

Alone is not knowing
Where you are and where
You are going.

Alone is not having
Anyone to hold your hand
When you need it!

Alone is not having that
Gentle hug from a friend
When the tears won't stop.

Alone is not knowing if
tomorrow will be tomorrow.

Alone is not knowing what
The darkness may bring and
If the sun will shine
The next day.

Alone is not knowing
Whether to SMILE or
CRY.

Never be ALONE because it's
The loneliest place to be!!

Tamera Goddard

Instructions For A Scavenger Hunt

Go to the place at the beach
where you learned to forgive
Find the cloud that taught you
your mind is the sky
Now, look out on the cliffs
and find the face the waves
painted.
In your hands, bring back
the cloud, the cliffs,
face of the sky
the hand of the one
forgiven.

Meredith Martin

Life Steps

My Higher Power loves me
Wherever I am right now
Because of His great love for me
I will make it through somehow

I must continue forward
Although I may slip back
The power He can give me
Will put me back on track

No more "Woulda," "Shoulda," "Coulda,"
They'll just cause more stress
"I can," "He can," "We can,"
Shall take me from this mess

I must do the footwork
He shall give me strength
"Together" we can make it
No matter what the length

If I get there before you
I'll extend a hand to you
And you can reach behind you
And show the next one through

Suzanne S. Lamb

Evoking The Muse

Spirit of poetry
Wherever you may be
Listen to the melody
Of our time —
Come and dance with me
To the rhythm of the rhyme —
Let your lights shine
Lead me and teach me
To follow your line —
Leave behind
Your ancient bard
For whom, for many years
You stood on guard —
Don't let me wait too long
Come, and let's combine
A new song —

Magda Herzberger

Screaming Silence

It's a terrible screaming silence
which greets me every night.
A piercing and oppressive silence.
Always draped in darkness,
always lonely and bleak.
The kind of silence only
an empty and loveless home can create.

Patricia Silveri

Enlightened

We sat in our holder
Which he held in his hand
Our heads were enlightened
Before our home touched the grand

Then suddenly, we heard a sound
And we heard some more and more
We spent a lot of time with him
But we never heard this before

The sounds kept droning on
It seemed like they just wouldn't quit
Then suddenly, they stopped
And that was the end of it

The young man got up
And we heard him shout
"Well, it's time I got to bed
And put you candles out"

Steven Rohrkemper

"Your Pillow"

"If only I was your pillow,
while nightly caressing your cheek,
I'd listen to your gentle whispers
myself without a word to speak;
I'd be embarrassed of my attire,
with you in silk and lace,
and me in all simplicity;
a plain old pillow case.
With the daylight hours so
dark, and dreary, I'd await
in constant despair,
'till the time when you'd return;
and I'd feel your warm embrace,
and the tenderness of your hair;
night, after night, as I watch
you sleep, though odd as it
might seem;
I'd like to flee from that
pillow case;
and find you in a dream."

Richard Ochoa

A Poet Is An Artist

A poet is an artist
With a pen for a brush
He always needs a model
To add beauty to his touch.

And if he needs a subject
Say a mountain or a tree
The profile of a person
Or a tiny little bee.

Or it could be a flower
With its beauty so bright
Or just looking at the ocean
On a silver moonlit night.

Or he might choose an animal
Living way out on a farm
Or maybe a corn field or meadow
Or a new little calf just born.

And when he needs a model
If a pretty lady, or a big grizzly bear
He sees only the model
And the picture he finds there.

Ralph Locke Cranford

The Sand Castle

Lashing flames from red, soured sun
whipping bleached, scalded beach
echoing penal punches,
screaming, stalking gulls

Tiny fingers framing,
kneading casa sand Grande
hope humming child reverie

Scooping moat, spiraling loft,
lapping wines of formation

Flushing force,
blind quaking waves,
squelching seeds of flight and fancy
reaching for rage,
poisoned crab's prickly pinch

Suckling dream of the cool, milky womb,
careening appeal, soft prayer on the air
'move swiftly, sweet Madonna Moon.'

Melissa D. Lamb

Poison Ivy

Shaking in the cool spring
Whispering to me for food
Beckoning me to touch it
I, not knowing it will harm me,
lean over to touch it
When suddenly it gives me an
evil glance
Suddenly I jerk back up
It calls me again
I reach down to touch it
Suddenly I loose my balance
I fall into it
I look like a wild Heyena
while I'm itching
While I'm itching at home
it's beckoning someone else
innocently
ANOTHER VICTIM

Katie Denson

Two Worlds

Murmuring echoes cries of wind
whispering towers
Descending waters of mountain range
wake tides of marveling delights

Dawn hours long breath of new hope
Brims
Sculptured finger of infinite time
Vineyard fruited tree of happiness

Great Master
What mystic shadows blow
listening to life
through fields of blooming vision?

I am a starlit gated-child
once standing near you
with wonder in my heart

I see in arms of growing life
many happy wings of transparent proof
pleasure borne
and in revision I wonder at times
DARE I WAKE?

T. Stephanie Gottlieb

My Boy

There's a little boy
    who can brighten my whole day
With nothing but a toothless grin
    cast my way
A round-cheeked cherub
    dressed in coveralls
He's got the world by the tail
    tho' he's only 2 feet tall
He's daddy's little cowboy
    and mama's little man
As he wraps those tiny fingers
    around that bigger hand
Amid his shrieks of laughter
    I find I'm laughing too
and with his head laid on my shoulder
    I feel, for him there's nothing I wouldn't do
Just one look from those big brown eyes
    can fill my heart with so much love
It's then a person truly sees
    a child is a gift from above

M. K. Bean

There Is One

There is One
Who knows
What I am feeling
For he feels
It too.

There is One
Who knows
What I am
Wanting to do
For it is
His dream too.

There is One
Who knows
What I am needing
For it is his
Need too.

There is One
Who knows what I am
For He is me
And I am he.

Stacie Raymond

A House Full of People

Night after night as I sit all alone
    wishing to be held
    wishing to be kissed

Night after night as I sit all alone
    just someone to talk to
    just someone to listen to

Night after night as I sit all alone
    I've seen all the shows
    I've heard all the songs

Night after night as I sit all alone
    too tired to sit up
    too anxious to sleep

Night after night as I sit all alone
    the house is all clean
    the books are all read

Night after night as I sit all alone
    a house full of people
    seems like nobody home

V. Ross

Walking On Water

Of course, He walked on water.
Why should that seem strange to we
Who also come from water's ken?
Like calls to like. Creator speaks
And matter rises to His call,
Supports and serves as matter can.
A miracle, we say.

How stranger, then, that Light and Love
Can reach across the bonds of time
Through darkness that we call to us
And touch the spark that lives within.
Like calls to like. The Spirit speaks
And spirit rises to His call,
Serves and loves as best it can.
A miracle, I say.

C. J. Street

The Sight Of The Sun

Look at the world and what do you see...
Why, the world is looking back at me,
With its eyes of green, and face of blue,
Why, it would make a cow go moo.
As I get closer, I can see,
Different people looking at me.
People of black and people of white,
Playing together, oh! what a sight.
But as I move through the air,
I become more aware,
That soon it will become night,
and I will, be out of sight.

Monica Nelson

I Cry

Spring, spring where are you?
Why won't you come?
I live in your memory
Brisk bright days of wonder
Petals of color
Reality of cold, freezing dark
Shadows of death
I cry
But you won't come
You won't give the slightest hint
Your time is in God's hand
Just as mine
I must trust and believe that
You will come
Yes, and my broken heart will mend.
And
Spring will come again.

Mary Barnard

River, Sweet River

River, you went silently on your way
While cars drove all over your bridge,
You didn't mind though
As you went through the same motions
Day after day,
Until one day the rain began to fall.
Your waters rose and rose.
You flooded out the cars
Who used to drive all over you.
When you were satisfied
That your destruction was complete
Your waters slowly receded.
Now the cars drive over you once more
While you patiently wait
To rise and destroy them again.

Sandra Hull

mommy

mommy?
why you in the big grey place
i don't like that place
i want you back

they say you "kil" someone
what does that mean?
i don't like that word
it hurts me inside

big smelly man say you "in-sane"
what does that mean?
i don't like that word
it hurts me inside

the strange people that take me
say that you will "di"
that sounds bad
i don't want anything to happen to you

why you go to the big chair?
why you cry?
why...
MOMMY!!!

Katherine Becvar

Aunt Betty

If I sleep
will I wake
to see the break of dawn
To live through another day
confusion will stay
If I sleep
and I do not wake
who will be there to guide me
will the loved ones from yesterdays
be comforting me as I walk
down the aisle of salvation
If I sleep
and I do wake
dealing with agony
a deteriorating mind
with my family to guide me
The choice is partially mine
Salvation or deterioration
which will come first?

Kelly Dobran

Alone

It's strange how you can feel so alone
When you have so many friends
Friends you can count on
Time and time again
But it's sad when you're alone

We all need someone to care about
Someone you love without a doubt
Someone that loves you
Someone who cares
You know if you need them
They would be right there
But it's sad when you're alone

Life can catch you by surprise
Plans washed away before your eyes
Hope for the best, expect the worst
Remember your friends and family first
It's sad when you're alone

Rick Hodges

Renewal

The rain on my face,
Will renew my soul.
For Jesus, my bridge,
Has paid the last toll.
On sins of the past,
Mistakes we all make.
On a dark spring day,
His blood they did take.
With eternal life for all,
He arose on day three.
Victory over darkness,
From death we are free.

Rena Lockwood

Samurai (About A Tiger)

An astounding predator
With a culture of respect,
As prey lay on the ground
The mind and heart connect.

Eyes gazing in fear
Cowering like a shameful child,
As a hunter steps near
Frightened creature of the wild.

An animal built to pounce and play,
A bat, claw, or hiss
May be protection for this day.

Its amazing spirit will last
Though its life may disappear,
Let's not make it part of the past
A creature we love to see and hear.

Kate LaCroix

Thinking Of You

As I look to the sky
with all its beauty,
I think of you.
As I watch the golden sunset
change to starry and blue,
I think of you.
When I feel the cool breeze
of the night,
blowing ever so soft
against my skin,
I think of you.
As I gather my thoughts
of what the day has given,
I think of you.
And as I thank the Lord above
for bringing so much love
and happiness into my life,
I always think of you.

Lela Jones

Wind

A net that's thrown to snare the breeze,
Will fall to earth in empty heaps.
The wind then turns and whispers please,
Before swept on by guilt she keeps.

Her shadow forms a cloud of rain,
Reflecting on horizon bare.
Silhouette of a soul in pain,
Embracing love but holding air.

A hollow gust that soothes the sky,
Will boil the sea and burn the sand,
Scattering leaves of hope that lie,
On withered heart and calloused hand.

Scott Roberts

Passage Into Eternity

In a silence beyond words
with all my strength and love
I held your hand...
numb, but unafraid
I cried and prayed.

Released from fear and pain
by a peaceful death...
like a falling star
among a million lights
into a vast sky,
flaring up for a moment
only to disappear
into the endless night forever
Your passage into Eternity
completing the circle of life.

Lolly McEwen

Homage to M.

I am at odds
with all the world today.
My meanings are obscured
by rusty words
and blunted thought.

Dull sounds, mis-spoken,
linger in my mouth
like bitter dust,
poor tarnished symbols
with their meaning lost.

Anger numbs my senses
wholly, and fills my mind
with dirt; my body mutes
the sought responses — I cannot
speak, I have been hurt.

Suzanne McMillan

And Then....

And then life came
With her flowing golden hair
Riding through the wild forest
On her midnight-black mare.

And then light came
With new birth
Reaching for an everlasting future
In the newly found earth.

And then man came
In the dawning hour
Bringing greed and destruction
Until she had no power.

And then all became still
And darkness descended.
She rode off on a stallion
And then life ended.

Lisa A. Holderman

Keep Your Cool

Just keep your cool
You cute little chick.
And don't let no dude
Make you have a fit.

Over them I mean
Or blow your mind
They'll still be here
in future times.

Shelia Holmes

The American Flag

The American flag is waving
with optimism and bravery
its Americans are united
in only one heart

We are forces of life
proudly in love
to all states of the union
with sweetness splendor

It is of divine forces
with caress and adoration
we take a beginning
with such emancipation

You are envied of someone
with divine creator
we adore for beauty
in your real creation.

Marcial Rossy Saavedra

Just One Night

If I could have just one night
With you, and not alone
You wouldn't need a key
'Cause I'd let you in my home

If I could have you for one night
I'd help you climb the wall, to ecstasy
I'd bring all my desires to life
In the hopes, it would set my soul free

I'd let you come inside
And we could play a little game
I can't hide it anymore, I Want You
There's no shame

So slip on some soft music
And let me, make you mine
Don't tell, let me find it
So this can last, 'til the end of time

Latoya Johnson

My Absent Beloved

We are far apart yet,
Within our thoughts we share each day
Youssef, take each day as it
comes and live it in peace.
Let me love you from far
because my thoughts will keep you warm

It is special thoughts and my best wish,
I sent you my love,
I hope you can reach it.

It is a poem which I wrote
To an absent friend,
one who is my beloved and
I will love to the end.

Marina R. Mendez

Jesus Jesus

Jesus Jesus you're so fine
Won't you come down sometime
I love you, you love me
We're a happy family
Jesus Jesus you're so fine
Won't you come down sometime.

Lisa Marchalonis

Unreachable Love

Hello I love you,
won't you love me too.
  I know you don't trust women
but I trust you.
  You've been hurt
well I have too.
  I wish I could help you
but it's not true.
  The only help that's possible
will come from you
  Goodbye I love you,
won't you love me too.

Kristin Schuyler

Cold Feet

If I were to fall tonight
  would you be able to catch me?
My mind is tired, my heart is full
  and I'm wondering how life will be.

I love you completely,
  I would trust you with my life.
I dream of you, I cherish you.
  Someday soon I'll be your wife.

But, tonight, just tonight, my mind
  is a hundred miles away.
Please hold me. Please cradle me.
  Don't let me go astray.

There are so many things I've done
  That I now so painfully regret
I lock them away, deep inside,
  But I need you to help forget.

I trust you, I need you,
  I know you'll never leave me.
But, If I were to fall tonight
  Would you be able to catch me?

Karen D. Harris-Hillman

Haiku

Summer rains fill streets
with pools of sky's reflection
My feet touch the clouds

Sharai Ann Peterson

A Poor Unborn

A body clothes me
Yet naked am I.
No love no food
no rest.
No mother to soothe the hurt
no father to strengthen
and to cultivate my character.
The dime yes the dime
they are busy trying to earn the dime.
The fields keep calling
calling to till the soil to join
the fork and spade
the sun to scorch their skin.
So hard they work so little I eat
more tears than bread I see.
The body that envelopes me is afraid
for me, her life I shall repeat.
Even as I am months afar
I see what life will be
for a poor unborn.

Marlene Brown

Hold The Night Away

Springtime lives within your smiles
you age so gracefully
look not upon what looks like miles
but on a spirit free

Your smile it seems, not of itself
can thaw the winter's gloom
for radiance beams from your dear self
and lights upon every room

When winter's frost is on the ground
and you are far from home
look for the word, the light and sound
from a mystic's poem

So look away from winter's bite
and to that final day
I'll be there to make things right
and hold the night away

William Cook

Together Forever

I think we could have a chance
You and I together
A chance at romance
One that could last forever.
So filled with laughter and love
Together to the end
We fit like hand in glove
And forever my love I'll send.
Since I've found you
I've been told that I am glowing
If that happens to be true
It's only from the love you're showing.
I would like to be with you
For just as long as I can
Baby, you know it's true
I love you, you're my man.
Forever and a day
With you I want to be
Please tell me we can stay
Together forever, you and me.

Leigh Ann Kerwin

Father

Father, you are wonderful
You are unique in many ways
You always have smiles, hugs
and a lot of love for me
You have made me what I am
from the way I look to who
I have become

Father, You keep food on the table,
joy in my life and hope in my heart
You make sure I have everything I
need and more
You're a shoulder to lean on, a person
to talk to and my best friend

Father, I love you because you're you
and all the wonderful things you
do for me
I just wanted to tell you how special
you are and thank you for everything

Natasha Gale Foster

Untitled

On a cloudy day,
you can make the sun shine
With your smile.

When you talk, your
voice floats on the wind like a leaf.

When you walk, you're
as graceful as a swan on the lake.

Mary Valeu

"Alone"

When you are alone,
you don't know what to do.
Wishing someone was
there with you.

Crying too hard.
Don't know how to stop.
Tears are jumping,
learning to hop.

Forgetting how to
control yourself.
Forgetting how to
do all of the good
things if someone
was there with you.

Katie Parmelee

Oh Christ My Lord

Oh Christ my Lord
    You loved me
'Ere I knew you
    Help me to love
And always follow you.

    Oh Christ my Lord
I thought that I
    Could conquer,
The whole wide world
    But soon discovered my error

    And now my heart
I'll always give to thee
    Of Christ my Lord
    Oh Christ my Lord
And now I know
    With you I'll always be
Oh Christ my Lord
Oh Christ my Lord.

Rosalie Ringer Lillie

Which Direction?

You drive me crazy
You make my mind race
Endless looking
for a nitch, a place
We scream and holler
with no end in sight
Constant confusion
escalating to incredible heights
then you stroke me
with your strong gentle arms
Your wit takes over
and so do your charms
Our love haphazardly
is growing each day
Do we really know which direction
Will it be the right way?

ToniAnn M. Grasso

Lovers Talk

You're my one true love.
You must have been sent from up above.
Our love is as pure as a dove.
You're the only one I ever think of.
    You're all I ever think about.
    With you there's no doubt.
    Our love will never die out.
Without you, I wouldn't know that to do.
I'm so much in love with you.
With you life seems so brand new.
No one's love could ever be so true.
Without you I'd be blue.
    You're so very kind.
    You're the best I could ever find.
No one will ever love you as much as me.
With you, true love is easy to see.
For us, true love will always be.
    I'm one lucky guy.
    Honey, without you I'd die.
    I can love you and don't have to try.

Shawna Joyce Newcome

Jose The Bullfighter

He was a gypsy
you see
and came
from Northern Spain

He knew bulls and their ways
He lived with them in his young days
Like his brother before
he grew up to be a matador

Everyone knew his name
His picture appeared all over Spain
People would make way
for the bullfighter Jose

But the people did not know
about the nightmares after each show
He faced the bull with scorn
but he was deathly afraid of the horn

He did little tricks to show he was brave
always mindful of the grave
He did not know what he feared more
the bull or the crowd's disapproving roar

Palmer D. Frith

As You Shoot Me

You stare coldly at my face
Your hand on the gun,
Your eyes searching my glassy eyes
for an answer to this madness

No expression on your face
Your finger on the trigger...
ready.....
I stare into the barrel..
waiting...
And you fire.

Your bullet is a messenger,
it brings a message of pain....
My body is screaming,
But my soul is set free.

The medicine in your bullet
has taken the pain away
and set me free...

And as my body fades and dies,
there is a message of "Thank you"
on my face.

Stephanie Kuhn

"Am I Worthy...?"

Am I worthy of such precious, pure love?
Your love says I am welcome,
yet my soul draws back,
guilty of dust and sin.
After days of pain and wonderment,
your words are enough to feed my soul.
Before I picked the rose of your love,
with such new, untouched petals upon it,
I've been pricked and bled many a time,
yet now, I have the thought of you
to hold against my heart.
Just tell me you love me,
and I will speak the words of love
to you with no shame,
and our love will live on.
Like any true love, our hearts have a
treasure,
a love story without an end.
I'd rather have the love of you,
than claim another's kiss,
alone I'd rather go my way throughout
eternity!

Shavon Heholt

"I'll Be Standing By"

Rest peacefully, now my dear,
Your time has come for sleep.
Close your eyes, the time is here,
Let your dreams guide you deep.
Hold them tight, never let go,
Stay in step with your dreams.
I'll be there, don't you know?
Even when I can't be seen.
I'll be standing by.
Trust in me.
My promise is not a lie.
I love you too much,
to leave you alone.
You mean everything to me,
And together we belong.
So, rest peacefully, now my dear,
let your dreams be divine.
Close your eyes, there's nothing to fear,
For I am by your side.

Shane Morgan

Untitled

Forget me not my friend
You never mind the darkness
You're nice and sincere and nothing
Less. You are sweet and yes, you're
The best you're my friend and this is
True to the end.
You are here when I'm in need.
I must admit, I love you dearly
You're young, but there is sincerity.
You are nice and not very demanding.
You might be young, but you're so
Understanding.
You're my closet companion and this
You have always shown.
I care for you and I don't think to you
It's even known.

Raymond A. Jenkins

Two Hearts

Two hearts,
  yours inside of mine.
Pain,
  summer's heat was blazing.
Morning,
  you were born.
Love,
  a feeling so amazing.
Two hearts,
  separate they may be.
Pain,
  how will we get along.
Morning,
  you look at me and smile
Love,
  a feeling growing strong.
Two hearts,
  mine inside of yours.

Sally Green

The Old Man

There was an old man
Who lived in a van
He missed his family so
He looked far and wide
For where they might hide
He knew not where they would go
He saw many places
And interesting faces
But no one gave him a clue
So he traded his van
His pots and his pan
For a rocket ship aimed at the moon
And there he did see
His whole family
Singing a happy moon tune

Phyllis D. Genauer

One More Time

So much has been said
  Of the wonders of Spring,
One scarcely could add
  Another thing.

Yet year after year
  It emerges once more,
More lovely, more radiant
  Than ever before.

Elder men feel young again
  While younger men mature,
And all the aches and pains we bear
  Seem to find an instant cure.

And so as Winter nears its end,
  I hear the angels sing —
Then lift my eyes and ask once more:
  "Will I see another Spring?"

Grace Ketcham

Dare To Build The Sea

Christen with
flowers, warm water.
If we fish for candles,
surely burning.
Understanding,
fire...
water.

Myriam Bourjolly

Religious Love

I thought it was my temple
written in the scriptures
to be carried out through time
my love
I thought it was everything
to obey
I thought it was my God
sent down from above
to heal me
save me
love me back
my God I thought it was you
but you are faceless and invisible to me
the Devil inside you chose to show
burning the scriptures
becoming worldly
and knocking my temple
to the ground

Kimberly Petulla

My Heart

I give to you a precious gift
Wrapped up in arms of gold,
To do at will what you would do
To warm, keep safe and hold.

I give to you my only heart
With love, pure virgin white,
Surrounded by the flowing sound
Of music in the night.

Please take my heart, my lonely heart
Protect, guard and adore
Let not my heart be shattered like
Broken glass upon the floor.

Lynne Smith Rhodes

A Woman Loves

There is a room
in every woman's heart
Where she runs and hides
When love falls apart.

The room is full of weakness,
pressure, pain, and fears
it's just barely strong enough
to hold in her tears.
Every time she goes in
she stays a little longer
the room gets bigger
and the walls get stronger.

To stay in the room
would be her worst mistake
and in her need to be loved
she gives you her heart to break.

Craig S. Sauceda

My Poem

My heart is filled with laughter
My eyes are filled with joy
My tears are filled with sadness

My life has had some sorrows
That I can never give away
But I still have my friends that can
help me through the day.

I don't know when my life
will end, maybe in a day or two
But I know who my friend is; it's you!

Megan Anne Wermerskirchen

Running To No End

Walking through a dark tunnel
you see a light that
you think will
lead you out
But
It continues to grow smaller
as you get closer
Soon you are lost and
Alone
you turn around and try
to find away out
After a long time in the
Dark
you finally find out were
you are
you've decided to find
a light that
won't disappear as
you get closer

Brigette Farley

Is The End In Sight

Don't keep it within
Willingly my heart cries out
You know this war reeks

Reeks of what you say
Multitudes of sins I shout
In number and way

More specific please
Unending abuse abounds
Seems never to cease

And morality
That is a lost art I weep
Lest I shall forget

Must I surely die
We must solve this mad riddle
And stop this horror

And what of my soul
Will it rest in either place
Lord what shall I do?

Joann B. Leffel

Bird Songs

There's a tree outside my window
Where small birds flap their wings.
Each morning when I waken
They tell of many things,

Of sunrise on a mountain
And tall waves in the sea.
Each morning when I waken
They sing their songs for me,

Of wide blue skies that open
Expanses with no end,
Of lands beyond the seashore
And roads that never bend.

Though I may never wander
Beyond my humble home,
Sweet bird songs let me walk the ways
My feet may never roam.

Lotus Prest

For The Times That Are Difficult...

Let's stop for a moment and think things through.
Think about all of the words
That shouldn't have been said;
For all of the regrets in our relationship.
Think about the good and bad times
That we have both shared,
And how we learn from these times everyday.
Think about things that have kept us together
Through hard times in the past,
And how we made it through them....
Thoughts and memories of us will never leave our minds,
And all of the moments we've shared will never be forgotten,
No matter what the future holds.
But for now, let's concentrate on the present
And live for today.
Let's forget the bad times of the past
And hold the good times close to us.
And for all those times that are difficult...
Let's try to see each other through.

Melissa R. Morano

Friendship

In life it is a special part
This friendship we have shared,
For it is very close in heart
To know that someone cares.

A friend in whom to trust or lean
In one we can depend,
As like a kindred it would seem
Our friendship hath no end.

From young adulthood we have grown
As now our senior years,
Some laughs, some tears though we have known
Yes, even shared our fears.

For it would be somewhat amiss
In friendship we would fail,
If time were simply but a myth
A lonely sea we'd sail.

Though be it with assurance
This pride and joy I feel,
A friendship that endureth
The love that made it real.

Sandra R. White

Until Tomorrow...

I never expected this day to come, and yet here we are
This is a time to move on and grow in my career
I know that even though I am leaving, you are not far
I will cherish my time here and hold you all so dear

Each of you are so very special to me, as I search for words to say
This is hard for me, and I will miss you all very much
But as time passes, the future comes and we must go on our way
I thank you all for the time here, my heart each of you did touch

You are more than co-workers, you are treasures of the heart
I feel honored to have you as friends so kind and true
As I feel sad on this day, I also feel at ease, because we will not be
far apart
And if you want to chat, just pick up the phone, you will know
what to do

In closing, I want you to know, I love you and will miss you all
In some strange way, I feel peace in my sorrow
Because I know "friends" we will always be, and if you need me,
just call
To all of you, I cannot say good-bye, but only until tomorrow.

Lisa B. Hutcherson

How Am I Supposed To Feel?

How am I supposed to feel?
This is no joke, I am for real!

I made it through childhood without his time.
I got food and clothing without his dime.

I tried to communicate in spite of that.
But he did not know me—because of my hat.

Well, I thought, two can play that tune.
I started paying tribute to my mom in June.

But I thank him for his contribution.
He added to my constitution.

And now he is gone—not just away.
He is dead now; I found out today.

So how am I supposed to feel?
My father never did, now he never will.

Teresa L. Hamm

My Other Man

I love him uncompromised to another being;
This is true from the time of my birth to present day.

Our bond is sensitive, perceptive and expressive;
My heart smiles knowing he only wants health and happiness for me.

I can sense his constant thoughts of me;
Trying to ease my pain and set me free from life's ills.

He is my confidant, my friend, my protector, my creator and my mentor.
I know I am just one of his great love's of life and
Sharing his love with his other women has been made easy.

His courage is my courage.
His joy is my joy.
His laughter is my laughter.
His suffering is my suffering.
His success is my success.
His devotion is my devotion.
His unconditional love is my unconditional love.

There will never be a love compared to My Other Man.
My father's love is my peace of mind, my strength and my motivation.
Fortunately for me, my mother and siblings know the true meaning of
sharing.

Robyn J. Farrow

Untitled

I saw my father this morning
though he has been dead for forty years
When I was a child I wasn't sure he was my father
I thought I must be a prince or something wonderful
and someday I would be discovered and be returned
to my castle. All the good people of my little
country would rejoice, happy that their beloved
ruler was finally found on the creek bank just
outside Columbus, Ohio. And I would shower my blessings
on them and be kind to everyone.
But I saw my father this morning
The same walk.
his head held up high, shoulders back.
—arms swinging from his elbows.
That ambling stride I would recognize anywhere.
The morning sun was behind my back
and there he was—the long shadow stretching out
before me. My father—what a shock—my father is ME.
Forgive me Dad?

Robert Loomis

Love

Its meanings are many
though the truest are few
  Sometimes deceiving, other times free.
A feeling in heart, not of the mind
Built on trust in each other, though sometimes one's blind!
A delicate subject not to be played,
Misused all too often, to its spelling we're slaves.

So question one's feelings can't loose nor win
  though if found to be faithful,
    Everlasting settles in!

This word known as love, true meaning is trust
So simple a word, still uncertainties in us.

So don't pray on its meanings or get caught in it falls
    Soon realize it isn't dreaming
      But deep within one and all!
  Tracy Carter

A Friend

I have a Friend so dear to me,
Though we barely communicate sometimes.
I need to tell him how I feel,
I'm afraid he will not abide.

The truth of the matter lies in thine own hand,
Afraid to feel the outcome.
If only enough courage to tell him what I need,
He may not feel nor need the same.

Yet often told of how dear I am,
And wanting my lips to his.
I feel that is all he wants,
And won't consider to evince his gestures.

Sometimes I fell he's too headstrong
to relate, and I wish he would reckon.
Though I often tend to omit my feelings,
And need to really ponder.
Should I tell him or not of how I need him,
Tell him of all the dreams I have.
Showing him what I truly feel,
Is the only way I know how.
  Melissa Ermel

Forever And A Day

Our lives have reached their peak;
Though we've gotten very weak,
I know we can fight this through,
Then we won't lose our love so true.

He said we're not working out;
but I know without a doubt
we can work through this
and have tenderness and bliss.

I know we were made for each other
I've found that out through one another.
When we first met, I was unsure
But now this love I can endure.

We have hopes for the future that cannot die;
The darkness that's lifted us up high.
It's all in a dream,
That's come true it may seem.

A dream that will live to its fullest,
and will live on after judgement
Because we were put on earth to have these dreams;
And to live them forever and a day.
  Michelle Derke

Division

Entering a world that is filled with psychosis
Thought process dividing and splitting as in mitosis
Racing and intrusive thoughts make one sick
Alleviating the pain as its bailiwick,
Respiridone.
Fear of the unknown,
Once again another new drug
Maybe less of a burden to lug
Many nights wanting to cry, bursting into tears,
As a cardiac patient's nightmare an emboli, bursting
Creating fears.
  Lori Coleman

Nyctalopia

Mind lost in an entangled web of deceptive
thoughts ebbing towards whirlpools of silent
screams and wretched faces of unfamiliarities
plummeting towards periods of madness and vile
circumstances of great orgasmic ecstasies in
one's dark abyss of sordid nightmares of which
there is no escaping this chaotic vertigo of
visionary "hallucinations" thus catapulting
into a wall of mass confusion and hysteria of
great disturbance along with images of the
unexplained left for dead in the cesspools of
unawakening reveries yet never to be answered.
  Kathy Dennis

The Birds And The Bee

I look out the window and what do I see,
Three red birds and a bee.
The red birds are all aglow,
While dancing around in the snow.
The bee in search of nectar buzzes round,
But none can be found.
The birds fly off to their home in a tree,
But what about the bee?
Oh well, I guess we'll never know,
Where it is the bee will go.
He'll probably just fly from town to town,
Until he gets home safe and sound.
  Poppy Brothers

My Prayer

God, give me strength
To face each day and what it brings:
Joy, sorrow, sunshine or rain — bravely.

Strength, yes strength
To do my tasks which thou hast planned:
Simple, hard, pleasant or sad—willingly.

Give me strength of heart, dear Lord,
To share that faith Thou gavest me:
Pure, simple, deep and rich — unselfishly.

Faith - that vital gift of Thine-
To let Thee lead my way:
Smooth, stony, level or steep — trustingly.

Lord, give me strength in wisdom
To speak some words of comfort:
Kind, true, great or small — inspiringly.

Wisdom - and through it power
To bring to thee some wandering soul:
Lost, dejected, deep in sin — eternally.

These things I ask in Jesus' name;
And be it Thy will — Lord make me strong.
  Ruth B. Pheasey

He

The turn of a gleaming moment in my eye, my turning within
Through a new corridor, toward an unlocked door I swim
Released from the grip of the melee - still now - your waters contemplate
Creeping secretly away from the morass and fills me with its fluvial grace
The flutter of a passing, shivering vision - my heart forgetful of its own anchor
Reaches out with arms of its own - reaches out toward your danger
Your words lubricate - your words dilate in my mind
Through corridors that run and wind - does it all become perpetual motion?
Washing out the debris with waves of your ocean
Want to steal the color of your eyes, want to turn them within
Would what you see be obtrusive - more than you can imagine?
The ebb of a spacious moment - its residue clings to my mind
Only a doorway stands in waiting with your fire burning behind
The tremor of this final moment - my traversing words take you
To this idyllic surrender - through an open door you come through.

Lyssa Aja

Mama's Love

It was my mama's love that brought me here,
Through long months of suffering and pain so severe;

With my mama's care I began to grow;
She fed me, she changed me, her love she did show.

With my mama's help, I learned to talk;
She taught me to read; she taught me to walk.

With my mama's strength, I found strength of my own;
To face some of the things a child must face alone.

As I grew older, from mama's love I strayed,
To be tempted by the devil while my mama prayed.

Now that I'm grown, mama's love's the only thing,
That I can count on to keep me from going insane.

Kevin Moore

"The Garden Wall"

Awake and smell the roses as you walk along,
Through the garden gate at the break of dawn;
See the glimmering sunshine in the distant sky,
There to tickle your fancy as it passes by.

The beauty you behold cannot an artist draw,
For the God in heaven made them great and small;
He made the tiny dew drop upon the lily's shawl,
That we might view His glory upon the garden wall.

Lucy Fulmer

Privileged Blessing

You always hear me when I cry your name.
Though the world keeps changing you are always the same.

In the morning, I look to you for direction and advice.
Above the din of stress and strife; when I take
the time to listen father, to your voice.

To rejoice in your name is surely a trust,
For all who love your name, this is simply a must.
Your Word promises the righteous you will bless.
Having faith in you is the surest joy to possess.

Wide is your mercy shown to us
in the depths of your love.
How thankful we may be for our father above.
Unending praise to you we accord.
Surely a privileged blessing to know you as
Saviour and Lord.

H. James Smith

Heart Sight

That you can see my beauty
Through the veil of unattractiveness
I've wrapped around myself
Frightens me.
My protection no protection
From the eyes of a wise and gentle man

You touch,
In ways untouching -
A quick smile
A teasing way
A reassuring nod to make a job seem easy.
Caring flavored with patience

As a man of depth and perception
Who, were he blind,
Could see more clearly than those with eyes
For his vision is with his heart

Akala

Paths Cross

It has been years since we shared smiles, laughs, and anticipation
Time has taken its toll
The years have aged our hearts and souls
Wiser and smarter we have grown
We have traveled our own roads and rocky they have been

But yet the memory remains as yesterday
Kids on the beach, dreaming in the late moonlight
The excitement and closeness we shared
It is not reality of today
But just a memory of years gone by

The future is a new road untraveled
Who knows what it may bring
But dreams will lead us through
The discovery of something new

Virginia Buglio

Time

Time is not a place or person.
Time is just time in space.
Where does time come from,
but the big question is where does time go.
Time is measured in seconds, minutes, hours,
days, weeks, months, years.
But with time comes spring, summer, fall, winter.
Time is not for you, time is not for me,
time is only time can't you see.
Who is time for? What is time for?
I still got the big question,
where does time come from?
But the real big question is where does time go?
Does any one know?

Virginia Divine

Innocence Lost

People cry
Times appear to change
People die
But still things remain the same
In this ruthless age of crime
Our own children are doin' time
For killing their mommies, and daddies too,
Other kids, that they knew
Some forced to live a life of sex-n-drugs
Never to know that warm summer sun
Into horrid lives, and prisons tossed
NOW, ALL INNOCENCE LOST

Travis Garcia

577

Peace Dream

I met a peace dream amidst the
times of hearts; it casts its beauty everywhere
to stay and not depart, for all to tread the music
of peace dream dancing, the sacred gift of hearts
Peace dream dancing, meeting hearts in good deeds
and right roads, your justice might goes and
hides amidst the songs in the winds, as treads
the skies for holding to hug anew, as peace dream
dancing does live on in me and you,
such be peace dream dancing.

Patricia Ann Grossie

'Tis The Season

'Tis the season for things to bloom
'Tis the season for the wind to blow
The crab apple buds and flowers all over my yard
The grass smells so green and beautiful
The sun's heat warming my body
The birds eating from the bird feeder
    and resting on my red maple tree's branches
My, is it not wonderful
For it is the season for enjoying life.

Rosette Mines

Untitled

Burning brightly in my faded mem'ry;
Thoughts of when we used to spend time together;
Of how you would just stand so close to me,
Whisp'ring how we'd always be, forever.
Forever went by faster than we expected,
And all too soon the flames began to die.
The love we shared before has disappeared;
My heart broke the day you said goodbye.
So now I gaze into abysmal darkness,
And dream of days when you once held me near.
My life is bleak without your sweet caress;
All the future holds for me is tears.
    Love can hurt even those who are strong,
    And even the most innocent can be done wrong.

Melissa Klein

The Cherub Of A Child

There's a beautiful Angel watching over me,
to protect me from danger that I'll never see.

So please don't cry and worry at all,
for my Angel is nearby at my beck and call.

She goes before me and checks the way,
and in her constant care, I'll be able to stay.

My constant companion she will always be,
because this was your prayer all along for me.

To be safe and protected along the way,
so by my side she'll continue to stay.

The path before me will be smooth and clear,
because from wrong turns she'll gently steer.

So please don't cry, just look around,
there awaits another who can be found.

With hungry heart and a dirty face,
he seeks your love and will fill my place.

My place now will be by my Angel's direction,
and her soft wings along the journey offer protection.

So please don't cry when you think of me,
for my beautiful Angel is hovering over me.

Lyn Moore Tyler

To My Husband

To love...and be loved...is living
To a Woman.
To understand and nourish..a Man's way.

Emotions make her weak and dependent,
Oft times spiteful and demanding.
Beside him she's resplendent,
Without him, she's nothing.

My man isn't wealthy, gallant, or renown,
He's humble, sincere and kind.
He's made mistakes...through them he's grown,
In wisdom, strength and mind.

God's guidance crossed our paths,
For this I am thankful.
I ask assurance to serve him well,
My life is his...eternally faithful.

I love you dear, in so many ways,
Dearly, deeply and sincerely.
My heart grows sad with the passing days,
So few remain to share.

Nancy Knapp

To Our Futures

It's time to say good-bye,
to all the laughter, all the tears,
all the heartache, and all the pain...

It's time to move forward, to begin a new beginning,
to find new laughter, to find new friends,
and to find oneself again...

I'll miss all we shared,
as thoughts of you drift across my mind,
I'll think of you often,
as I glance through the past,

My heart will always love you forever,
even though it has to lock it away,
I shall forgive and forget,
so as I can wash away all the pain,

And then I will smile once again,
because life is not over,
there shall be many more beautiful
things to come for each of us,
and we have to accept the past as the past
and look forward to our futures...

Mary Lee Vernon

Use Me

You left in the middle of things
to be gone forever, or so it seems.
I yelled and screamed, but couldn't get through
Your words to me were everything but true.
Through all the frustration, lies, and pain
I hoped it would be you that I would gain.
But it turns out she's on your mind
Nothing left for me to do, I find
Except try to pick up the pieces you left shattered
It's almost impossible to think you thought our love mattered
Now you're back, begging at my door
Saying we can be once more.
Can it be the same as it once was
and begin again as everything does...
Or will something else come between us
and cause our love again to rust?
I know deep down we will be forever
The happiness won't end, not ever
Back to you I run, hoping for a fresh start
My head knows better but my heart's not as smart.

Kelly Joebgen

And I Write

And I write to relieve the tension that builds up in me so quickly.
To be rid if only temporarily, of the pain that takes over me.

And I write to feel the freedom that accompanies the writing.
It's my way of escaping the agony; it's my way of fighting.

And I write because at times I feel there's nowhere to turn.
I feel there's no one who's going to experience true concern.

And I write as a way of expressing another part of myself
Emotions that have been kept secret that no one ever knew I felt.

When I want to relieve the tension, when I want to be rid of the pain,
To feel the freedom, escape the agony and fight back.
When I need somewhere to turn, someone who's concerned,
When I need a way of expressing emotions I've always felt
And have always been attached.

When I need to open doors to a more peaceful side of life.
I settle down to tranquility; and I write.

LaSherri S. Banks

Twenty Lines?

Twenty lines or less they suggest
to compose a winning poem for this contest
well I'll try my best since my friends propose
my thoughts frequently lead to ponderous prose

I must be oh so very careful in my counting
not one line waste, in my haste I may bust twenty one
when all is said and done there's no accounting for taste
the editors' plight: reading all night, straining eyesight

How shall I restrain or retrain my train of thought
which jumps the track far more often than it ought
I have so few words to persuade, just another in the parade
nonsense rhyme works for me so I'll try it one more time

Capture their hearts and minds in such a short span
as well to tell me try to catch birds in my hands
this is almost as bad as attempting haiku
or maybe it's just bad well it will have to do

It is not given to me to see who the winner shall be
of course he may come from a far shore across a vast sea
let it be me; if not; I feel sure, unless I'm way off course
the rhymer won't be an ancient mariner, nor an albatross

Lawrence Edward Perry Jr.

Dream On

I venture from reality
    To a neutral state called Nil,
Where I can play my fantasies
    And do things as I will.
I roam the mighty mountains
    And caress the grassy vale,
Where the rivers and the shimmering brooks
    Always will prevail.

I travel to those far-off lands
    And search the mighty seas.
It's always so enjoyable
    To have things as I please.

Without these periodic trips
    My world would be amiss,
Without these trips of fantasy
    I'd miss the maiden's kiss.

These moments in that favored land!...
    Reality's so unkind!
My travels to the land of Nil...
    Such bliss and rest I find.

Paul J. Fitzgerald

Enchanted Dreams

Moonlight whispers to knights of old,
to fairy's flying to dragons gold.
Stardust drizzling upon a morning dew.
Dwarfs, Goblins, and elves too.
From dragons fires to magic wands.
Witches, Warlocks, and Unicorns.
A crystal ball, magic spells, enchanted castles
and wishing wells.
Bowmen with their arrows, Damsels in distress,
Knights upon their horses who'll help of course,
then continue with their quest.
Fighting with all evils.
And win of course you will, if your heart is
pure and you believe in you.
Now the battle's won, and the sun begins to set.
Suddenly you awaken, your day begins again.
But at night in your slumber, you dream of all you love.
Again you'll be the hero. Until tomorrow comes.

Sandra Manzo

"My Sweet Cousin"

I come here sweet Teedle, just to be with you,
To follow fond memories when we cousins were two.
Reaching, and touching and feeling so near-
to happier days, we lived with no fear.

Never dreaming those days would to soon come to pass...
And I would now visit you alone on the grass.
So many the gifts you left loved ones here.
No pity, no complaints, not even a tear.

Oh sweet Teedle, with strength beyond compare...
Those big brown eyes, that auburn hair!
Missing you always and needing you so,
Today, tomorrow.... it's so hard to let go!

I miss you, I love you, sweet cousin of mine!
You know, it's only a matter of time.
There's comfort in knowing nothing lasts forever...
And one day two cousins will again be together.

Theresa A. Miller

A Promise To Be Grateful

I made a promise a short time ago;
To inform my friends and to let them know;
How wonderful they are and how much I care;
And how precious are the moments we share.
I must tell you though the words may be wrong;
My admiration for you is very strong.
I am so happy you came my way
and will be very fortunate if you stay.
My deepest gratitude let me extend,
Thank you, very much, for being my friend.

Terry Hoehn

A Child's Need

This little child with tear filled eyes
This life was not his choice.
He needs a stable home where lies
Love and a gentle voice.

This little child with clothes so worn
He did not ask to be
So cold and hungry, all forlorn,
Neglected totally.

Drug user, what do you hope to gain?
The future is so dim.
For this child's sake, please ease his pain.
Get help for you and him.

Marjoy Knight

God Never Made A Hitler

God never made a Hitler
To kindle the flames of war
Truly humanity made him-
An image of evil in store

God never meant for us
To kill and die, alone on some muddy field
We are the cattle that followed
A madman's flaming shield

God never made the cannons
We are the ones to blame
For all the death and destruction
Seeping from man's own brain

God never made a refugee
Only mortals could stoop so low
To plant the seeds of hatred
And nurture them to grow
We are the symbols of hatred
Creators of mankind's, blind and lame
Can God in his infinite mercy
Forgive us our horrible shame?

Max Denner

So For Now Know I Love You...

Sometimes I wish you could only understand how I feel,
to know my love is everything real.

To understand my emotions you would have to be me.
I am sure that is the only way you could truly see.

More than often I wish you were here,
I think of you... and shed a tear.

In such a short time you have taken on a whole new meaning,
no longer are you just a friend for occasional leaning.

I depend on you now to give me your love,
which I hope and pray you will never run out of.

You are my heart and you are my soul.
You just can't realize how missing you is taking its toll.

Sometimes I think of being without you,
what I would do I have no clue.

But there is no need to think of that because we are not there,
so for now know I love you,
and will always care.

Karen Leahy

Viva La Carmen

A Citizen's Party candidate and political rallies
Turmoil in Central America...a country looking for allies
The economic strain of the country's pain
Looking through the mist of rain the country searched in vain
The seventies...times were a' changing
The eighties...looking forward to a brighter light
Reggae music filled the night's smokey plight
Carmen's visit all too briefly looking in limbo's window
Carmen's flight a night of sheer delight she wished to endow
The night tide smelling of putrefied seduction
This race of humanoids a heavy affliction
The times they're a' changing
Upon our fancy strolling the white desert sand dunes
The galactic light the night's musical tunes
Showering meteors...sharing life's Manifest Destiny
Bounties on lives...a times to mutiny
Homeward bound...Wow! The Monroe Doctrine
Am I home yet from Nam? I'm out pissing in life's latrine
Memories flickered in the realms of the universe
All withered now the flower petals of youth in too much verse.

Robert G. English

Tomorrow Is Another Day

Tomorrow is another Day,
to laugh and cry but play your way.

To fall asleep one sparkling night,
and wake up to the morning bright.

Growing up day by day,
Learning to be fair when you play.

Going to high school and making new friends,
doing gymnastics like cartwheels and back bends.

Happy and proud your parents are,
when you're sixteen and driving a car.

Beautiful is the sight,
You getting ready for college friday night.

Next in line, you're walking down the aisle,
wedding presents are stacking high in a pile.

None months you wait for the perfect child
and then that day he or she is born beautiful and wild.

She will live, and she will die.
We will live and we will die,
just because we're you and I,
and tomorrow is always another day.

Kristie Sheridan

The World Around Us

I dare you, I double dare you
to look around the world and see what it has become.
Babies are crying and people are dying.
We have folks with no place to
call their own, guns, gangs, wars,
and pollution, we have to find a solution.
If this keeps up the world will be one big garbage dump.
People dying one by one we must get rid of the thing called a gun.
Boom, bang there goes another rival gang.
Don't you hear, don't you see why can't we be happy and free.
Smog and gas in the air what in the world is going on here.
People don't care about you and I, they're just letting us all die.
We must learn to try or we will soon be saying goodbye.
As I go I must say there has to be a better way.
Watch out for each other, lend a hand, be a brother
to your fellow man.

Nichole Locher

Dream Come True

I've never known a woman like you,
To make all of my dreams come true,
You've brought out emotions in me,
The love you gave has set me free.
To be with you I'll cross the dessert sands,
From the highest peak my love with stand,
You gave me your love and made me feel
A love that I know is oh so real,
My memories of you are forever in my mind,
You're a very special woman, you're one of a kind,
I feel you're a gift from the heavens above,
Come out of the sky like a beautiful dove,
My first sight of you, head over heels I fell,
My heart thumped loud, like a temple bell,
Love at first sight, I'm sure of it now,
How I got you, I don't know how,
But I thank God for bringing us together,
And my love for you will last forever,
My love for you will never end,
Please stay my love and stay my friend.

Rodney Helms

Hard To Please

I tried in every way I could.
To make this job the best I should.
I came to work with smiles and graces.
Kissing up to you because, I'm created
Among the other races.
When the customers gave me smiles and rewards;
You'd smile but, deep inside it wasn't hard
to tell you were a total hoard.
Working with you was hard as hell.
After trying to please eventually I turned
into a total shell.
One day you decided that I was out cause;
I had the attention and you felt like a lonesome pout.
One day you'll wish that I was there.
To divide your work and do my share.
You pushed and pushed to get me fired but,
One day the work force will see how
valuable I am and, then I'll be hired.

Linda Hurdle

Piano

To some, older persons are a burden
To me they are wonderful.
So much Knowledge within their reach,
All that Knowledge for them to teach.
They sit in chairs and think about the past,
They sit and think of how the time went fast.
What people don't remember, is that these people were young once.
They had shining hair,
bright, gleaming eyes.
They fought for our lives and their own,
To be forgotten in a home somewhere,
To reflect on the golden days of their past.
It saddens me to think,
That someday all of life's toil will come to that.
Living just to see a glimpse of life and hope,
A few hours of joy when a young girl
Comes to play the piano.

Margaret K. McInturf

A Flower

As your lips start lingering softly on my head and down
to my toes, I am like a flower being nourished through
the sun and earth.

As your fingers caress my tingling body, I am a flower
swaying ever so gently in the refreshing breeze, rocking
in its rhythm.

As your body becomes one with mine, the ecstasy brings
rain showers to the flower, nourishing it, cleansing it
and freeing it from all the worries and sadness, which
in return allows the flower to strengthen and grow for
one more day,

Susan M. Davis

A Firefighter's Devotion

A firefighter devotes their time and life
   to save your home, your family, and your wife.
They climb a ladder to save a pet,
   not even caring if they are getting wet.
They give their all
   when they get a call.
They pull the hoses and squirt the water,
   even when it gets hotter and hotter.
A firefighter can be a man or a woman,
   it doesn't matter, as long as they are human.
So, when you hear the sirens blaring,
   just know that they are caring.

Lilly Jenkins

The Last Kiss

Searching for him became my only goal,
   To see his face appear today, my soul.
My heart cried out, "Dear brother where are you?"
   I can't continue on without a clue.
Seven months have passed and still no word from him,
   Passage of time has made my hopes grow dim.
And then a thought, another call I'll make,
   Call I did and now there's no mistake.
I sit and watch the waves flow gently by,
   The only sound I hear is my deep sigh.
I stare into the deep and dark abyss
   This lake knew him and gave him his last kiss.
The answer "why" is one I'll never know,
   He disappeared from life with nought to show,
But for his face down, floating, body dear,
   Gone and never again will he be near.
His light is gone and there is no more quest,
   With God he now lives as a beloved guest.

Stephanie E. Fiarito

Don't Quit

Everybody has a chance when God gives them a test
To see it they have courage and ability to do their very best
To overcome problems when mental or physical handicaps hit
People unexpectedly—changing their lifestyle, their health—don't
   quit.

I'll give you an example of what happened to me
When I came home late one night—got the mail—and didn't see
Something slippery suddenly making my body take a fast trip
To the ground—when I heard a crack—then couldn't move—
broken hip.

Ambulance—hospital—serious operation—as many painful days went by.
Was transferred to rehabilitation center where all of us have to try
To exercise and strengthen injured areas and must never complain.
Perseverance prevails with hope to be strong and normal again.

The whirlpool treatment so high up on a stool—
My feet hanging down in Niagara Falls deep medicated pool.

Like an acrobat—they lift me down to the ground.
The square dance begins—put your left foot forward—right foot down—
Grab onto the sides of the walker—turn around—

Put arms back—sit slowly down in the wheelchair—rest for a bit.
When things are going bad, bear with it—don't quit!

Peggy Raduziner

Struggle

I love to watch the birds at the feeder.
To see the beautiful kinds of eaters.
We have birds of many colored feathers.
Birds of many forms and sizes.
As I watch the birds that come to feed,
I can't help but notice a struggle in the trees.
What's taking place is a fight of size and power,
As in the world of nations about us.
We can see this struggle in the inner-city.
It seems a pity, this is a happening in life for so many.
Taking place in countries of poor of money,
and in wild life a-plenty.
I see this at my beautiful bird feeder.
It frightens me some that I feel pity and pain.
The flood of power shown in a fever.
Yes! Oh yes! Blood on the bird feeder.

Thomas Wilson IX

Embrace

Time has lifted a new dawn from my eyes
to sparkle amidst the glory
the kingdom of my Lord

Open the gates of knowledge my Lord
for my heart beats fast the wisdom of your spirit
the mercy of your soul

Guide me as I lead astray the vultures of my trespasses
cast from me the wings that race me to temptation

Silent me these lips that speak of sinners thought

When at night I lie with my eyes to the sky
my heart content within your womb
feed my spirit as I may grow with this new life
this new awakening

Please Lord
as you surround my prayers
soothe the edges of my cry
filter my deeds through the heavens
cleanse my worship as I may be humble unto my Lord

For I feel pain
knowing what I felt, was I love you. Amen.

Nick Samarin

Homesick

I need the harvest moon for my soul
to stay in touch with my yesterday.
Chilly Fall air and bonfires near
burning leaves that beg me to stay.

Stay and watch my huge orange moon
that seems close enough to touch.
Stay and watch her light reflect
from the sea that I've loved so much.

Salty sprayed air that bounces her lights
from white caps reflecting the moon.
Her dancing wet spray kisses my face
bringing hopes back I gave up too soon.

Homesick I am, though, to see the stars
or to watch the bonfires glow.
To smell again this crisp night air,
or feel the cold air blow.

So, in my soul I need this night
I need to hold it near.
For to lose it again would break my heart
and all I'd have left is my fear.

Gene Kough

The Prey

The prey cowered in his hiding place
trying to escape his attacker's searching eyes.
He prayed for His Creator to save him
for no creature ever wants to die.

But then the attacker spied him
and he swooped down for the kill.
His talons locked onto his prey
and shook him in his deadly grip.

The prey felt each flesh-ripping blow
as its attacker released all of its rage.
He shrieked in terror and pain
in the childish voice of his tender age.

For this is not the story
of some jungle or forest danger.
This is the story of an abused little boy
as he faces Daddy's anger.

Mark W. Wester

Greet The Morn

Greet the morn with praise and thanksgiving
To still be part of that which is living
For without life's warmth throughout you streaming
The rest of these thoughts are just wishful dreaming

Greet the morn with faith in God
For he directs our steps on earthly sod
Hear his wisdom, his love do trust
If he sends a change, accept and adjust

Greet the morn loving family and friends
They cushion the falls, their encouragement mends
Life would be so lonely without their existence
Be true to both with love and persistence

Greet the morn with joy and laughter
They ease the strain of the hours after
Keep your sense of humor, don't let it stray
A smiling face can brighten your day

So, greet the morn with renewed zest
And vow to give each day your very best
Heart's rest and peace now on twilight borne
And eagerly anticipates the greeting of the morn

Thomas J. Ives

Let Me...

I wish with all that is in me
To tell you the happiness you have given me

Let me speak

To treat me as a person
With the awareness of my soul

Let me say

To have the feeling
There were times
That I was pretty

Let me repeat

To communicate
with someone in a way
God must have chosen but is rarely used

Let me whisper

To have desire without fear
To become a part of you completely

Let me finish

Please love me now
Say good-bye and know this
You'll never see me cry

Susan O'Hair

To Live Again

Do you know what it is like
To have your life turned upside down
To try to smile but wear a frown
To try to laugh out loud, but shed a tear instead.
To hold onto your heart, but lose a friend.
Do you know what it is like to
Try to be happy about your life
But only give up, to sacrifice,
To want to be strong, but you're weak inside,
To want to run outside and play, but instead you hide.
Do you know what it is like to
Be what was once no more,
To live again, but what for.
It hurts inside to think of then,
To live, to live again.

Sara McCoffrey

582

Eternal Darkness

I wake up to the nothingness that is my soul and
to the pain that cuts me to the quick, like a
Sharp edged sword, Depression creeps up upon me without
warning. Surrounding me with a hideous darkness,
"Do you love me?" you ask, "How can I love you when I can't
love myself?" I cannot love you because I will not drag down
and subject you to the loneliness, pain, and darkness I feel,
The darkness that swallows up my soul, I refuse to sully innocence,
"I will not let you suffer internal darkness," The darkness that
condemns me to eternal demotion. "Eternal hell, is all that awaits
me," So I say, "I don't love you, I'll never love you!"
"I would rather make you cry, than watch your soul slowly die,
A cell that I can't escape from, One of my own making,
One of solid yet intangible Steel, So walk away and don't look back
Or you'll get hurt.

> *Rebecca Rosaly*

My Garden

I love my flower garden where I sit
To view the magic colors that abound
And as I linger for a little bit
I listen to the silence all around
I watch a red rose decked in silver dew
Spread out its petals as it greets the day
I long to touch the beauty of its hue
But dare not take its purity away
I close my eyes to meditate on God
Whose Master Hand designed the wonders here
That sprang up from the black and grimy sod
Then from my lips I offer up a prayer
"I thank you, Lord, for lovely flowers that bring
A kind of peace surpassing everything"

> *Marge Lifto*

Toes

Toes are made to wiggle, and
toes are made to scratch, and
Toes come creepin' through your stockings
like chickens when they hatch.
Toes can be mighty weapons, and do
a heap of harm,
When you rake them down your brothers
back, cause he won't get them warm.

> *Marie Watson*

Yes, You Were My Friend

Strong you were through these last two years,
Together we shed happy and sad tears.
You welcomed everyone into your home,
Now God has taken you to His home.
The grandsons you did live for,
Made you so happy when they came
   through the door.
Smiles you brought to people when
   they were blue,
Knowing they could confide their
   feelings to you.
Yes, mother understood, as a tear came to her
   eye.
One of these days she will join you
   and Dad with a twinkle in her eye.
My dove I will hold onto dear,
Remembering all the good times we
   shared through the years.
      Your friend and sister.

> *Marilyn Eighme*

Mom

Fears, tears, through the years; I can't forget
Tomorrow

Though my heart holds, but never unfolds life's inner
Sorrows.
My child!

Knowing your fate can only build a golden gate in my
Mind...for we hold a spiritual bind.
Growing moving, pursuing a true direction of site
Picture.

Lord! Help me to show the way? Through all the cuts and
Scrapes...never living by the word of hate...

> *Rodney Greene*

Shadows

Shadows of dreams keep passing through the night, wonders of
tomorrow what will it bring, old memories of holding hands and
walking into the sunlight!

Another day has gone, unanswered as to its meaning and age taking
its toll by the minute, with no repeat performance of its beginning.

Moments of laughter seem so distant yet brooding brings no consolation
and foreseeing time is like looking into a mist.

Needing, wanting, desperately for a change, to conquer overtones of
misfortunes, are like dreams so far out of range.

> *Richard A. Hines*

The Sandy Shore

Lord, 'tis quite some time since I put out to sea
Tossed and heaved by the angry waves that lash at me
But all this I can take for deep in my heart I am sure
That You are near and shall row me back to the sandy shore

Though I brave the tempest and ride the gale in a fragile bark
To me where I am, it might as well be the faithful's Ark
For I know amidst the storm with all its fury and its roar
You are near and shall row me back to the sandy shore

Lord, 'tis quite some time since I put out to sea
Drenching wet and cold beneath the ocean's spray
Yet my faith has grown much stronger than before
That You are near and shall row me back to the sandy shore

> *Romeo A. Balein*

The Dream

I sleep through the night, restless,
Tossing and turning,
as dreams slowly come and go.
The dream was so real, but yet so fake.
Tears filled my eyes
When I saw him there,
Lying motionless.
Not quite gone.
He can hear me talk, as I plead for him to return.
Machines hooked up, beep.
Oxygen fed through tubes,
feeding his body, keeping him alive.
No movement.
I yell for him to wake up,
to make life last.
But, there is no answer.
I open my eyes, wet and tired.
Sun pours in.
I awake, and I sit up.
And my dreams slowly become, a reality.

> *Nicole Humphrey*

March

Great cat,
Tossing tangled mane, growling at a wind-swept earth;
Retract your claws,
Abuser!

No gentle wag, your mad-swishing tail split limbs and
Chilled the crocus.
Spitting tongues of laser lightening, you make proud
Tulips hang their heads.
Schizoid!

Have you now ceased your charge?
What soft hand smoothed your static fur?
What celestial cavern cracked:
What catnip caused this sudden change—

How dare you purr in dandelions?

Patricia Stultz

Freedom

All my life I have been in a cage
trying to control my bitter rage
Wondering what would happen to me
then I found a way to be set free

Learning to fly, at first, was strange
I know how hard it is to change.
But this feels great, and there's no doubt
That this is what life is really about!

Mary Gifaldi

Untitled

Without you - I would be like a lost little girl,
Trying to find someone she loves.
Finally she gives down to cry,
But that is something she used to never do.
Until this lost little girl finally found you.
Sometimes she still cries, but not because she's lost,
She cries because she's happy,
She's happy she's found you.

Tiffany Learnard

Survival

Daily it's a constant struggle
Trying to make it as a 'Young black mother'

Sometimes it gets hard and I want to give up hope
But I think of my sons and I try harder to cope

The pressures of everyday life can become a pain
Which makes me strive even harder to try, try again

It's so much easier to say "I give up, I'm through"
Then I imagine my sons faces so sad and blue

I don't know how I would suffice without hope and love
And that strength that God gives me from up above

The thought of being successful is the key
But where to find it, is instilled in me

I'm all grown-up with only myself as a guide
Which keeps me going, standing tall with pride

How do you do it? Most people ask I just smile,
hold my head high cause' God knows my task

Survival, survival is the name of the game
Soon my hard work will pay off with fortune and fame

Which leads me to believe that there's none other,
Than to have the love of a "Strong black mother"

Stephanie R. Bufford

No One Cares

Monday, I'm crying and my friends ignore, no one cares.
Tuesday, I sit in the hall heart broken, my boyfriend
just broke up with me. No one cares

Wednesday, I'm happy on the outside but on
the inside my heart shattered. No one cares.

Thursday, I can't wait for it to be the
weekend, I collapse in the hall beaten from
the week that has been hell. No one cares

Friday, I'm in misery I still need some
one to love me. No one cares
Saturday, one day till I get to see the
friends that care.
I go to Mom and Dad No one cares.
Sunday, I see my friends.
Two people that care about me most.
One, Stacie my best friend in the whole world.
Two, Greg who comforts me.
The two most important people in my life.
Stacie and Greg, thanks
I love you guys.

Sasha Marie Sorden

Former Glory

As the years say, "what if I may?"
Turn the hands of time
As the time goes, and the clock rolls
I've held these things sublime

Grown with ages, written pages
Of former mental wealth
God, it's crazy, my mind's gone lazy
I'm not my former self

As the days pass, with the dead grass
I'd plant another seed
It's taken longer, from when I'm stronger
And now I have to leave

Little flower wilts this hour
And tells a different story
The rose is dry now, I can't help how
I think of former glory

Lee Merritt

Fighting Tears

Fighting back determined tears,
Trying to overcome all your fears.
Now nothing will ever be the same.
Did you think this was all a game?

How could anyone be so careless?
Didn't you realize it could result in sadness?
Three alive and two are dead.
'This could never happen,' that's what you said.

When you lost control, how did it feel?
I imagine, very unreal.
You could only wish it was all a dream.
A dream turned nightmare is more what it seemed.

What happened shouldn't have been.
But God had a reason to take your friends.
Now, no one is happy, everyone's sad.
I'm so confused and I feel so bad!

Don't hide your feelings and to everyone lie.
Don't worry, it's o-kay to cry.
Don't try to hold back and be so strong.
For tears can be fought for only so long.

Katie VanNess

My Father Has Died

Roses
Turn to greet the sun,
Radiant with heat,
Like a brown speckled dog greets a bone.
Opening petals are tiny hands receiving candy,
But there is none.
Clouds, heavy, thick gloves,
Protect the sun from razor blades,
Thorns.

Tracy L. Oller

Victory

Oh, the sting of death that is called sin
'twas placed by Adam upon all men.

Its strength is found in the book of the law.
Its purpose to produce man...perfect...without flaw.

Law's product fails beyond our belief
but thanks to God for victory in Jesus..our relief.

Stand my beloved brother! Do not be moved.
Through faith in Jesus, before God you are approved.

Always abound in the work of our Lord.
Your labor is not in vain..So live in love
and one accord.

Rejoice forever! It's Jesus who conquers sin and death.

He crowns us with glory, peace, joy and life evermore
at its best.

Sue Collins

Little Miss Puppet

There you sit on your mighty throne.
Twiddling your thumbs as you wait by the phone.
Will Pam call or will she pass?
You will wait all night even though
   you feel like an ass.
Pam's on a man hunt all around town.
White Barbs's at home wearing a frown.
Making excuses turning her frown into a smile.
Even though she knows they are a pile.
When she looks in the mirror and sees her reflection.
Her face turns a white complexion.
Anger is an the rise because of all of the lies.
Lies to herself which destroy even friendly ties.
Ring, Ring, Ring, Ding, Ding, Ding, Dong!
How much longer will you be jerked around?

Roger E. Craig

Three-Part

The Passages, the Pathways in which the light journeys
to the life of destiny,
Where it holds the truth, the answer of agony.
World where they wander, voices from within now torment
this precious,
Negativity, Negativity...
Help me, Help me, they cry through the days
and nights of abyss.

Time hath betrayed the light of hope
Forces the heart to cry the melody
The whisper that deft the night owl
As it watches thee vanish drastically in the eyes of God.

Ample of nights, the orchestrated melody of torment
Passes through the invisible, the very need of life.
Help me, Please Help me, now embedded
in every soul of the living, the dead...

D. C. Serrano

What I Must Leave Behind

I must leave behind sunshine and vegetation, from my
two week vacation. I must leave behind animals, a friend,
and a beach with no end. But I will bring along a month
of happiness and the sound of waves lapping on the shore.

Stuart Keating

Dragon Magic

The dragon flies overhead
under the watchful eye of the moon.
He guards the castle and his keepers.
The wizard and his faire lady watch him
as he swoops and swerves.
They watch his graceful flight.
How elegant he moves, even tho' he is massive.
His wings capture the warm summer night air,
as he glides under the moonlight.
He is beautiful,
   daring.
      sensual.
The wizard holds his faire lady and sighs.
He is truly happy living in his kingdom,
   with his faire lady, the dragon, and his castle.
Love for all these things has made him
   Truly grateful to their spirit,
      for he has known love.

Marsha McAuslan

A Fragile Soul

Life is joyous and content
Until I face that moment
When an innocent or deliberate act
Wounds me with its impact.
A fragile soul am I.

Life then loses its joy and peace
In less than the blink of an eye.
Where once I stood strong and steadfast—
Now reduced to heaps of ash!
A fragile soul am I.

I grope in the ashes of despair,
Searching for what was lost,
Afraid to find that hope again
Because it seems for naught.
A fragile soul am I.

Oh! A fragile soul am I.
Walking the tight-rope of life.
Steady—sometimes falling
Forever wondering, Why?
A fragile soul am I.

Linda Mendinghall

Give Mother A Rose

Please search through heaven's garden, Lord
Until the most beautiful rose you see.
And then take it to my mother
And tell her it's from me.

We were the very best of friends;
It was a special love we shared.
Sometimes I'd give her roses,
Just to show how much I cared.

And when you place it in her hand,
She'll know that it's from me.
Tell her that rose, like my love,
Will last eternally.

Sherry Adkins

Grandma Would Say "You May"

In her closet are her wading shoes untouched,
up above her swimming suits not worn.
There's her room with no one to live in.
There's her bed with no one to sleep in.

Outside, a hammock waits for someone to swing,
the dock waits for a passing swimmer.
There's her beach unwalked upon.
There are her rocks unthrown.

Only she will not touch her shoes,
nor go swinging on a hammock.
For Grandma has passed on.
And these things are left for you and me.

So go wear her wading shoes,
so go throw her rocks,
go past the dock, and
go sleep in her bed.

Grandma would say "You may,"
Grandma would want it this way.

Michelle Coughlin

Windy Nights

In rigid soil I did sprout,
Up and high I grew.
Now the wind tosses me about,
Its influence tastes like salty water.
I once asked that tremendous air
To show me how to do the things it does,
But now I see the damage
Something so invisible can cause.
It makes me sick, nearly to the point of death,
Petals and pieces fall from me
Implanting eternal memories in my mind.
Then the wind dies down,
Healing, rehabilitation occurs.
Rebirth of my fallen pieces,
Puts things back together.
I learn from what has happened;
And now, I duck down low on windy nights.

Morgan E. Holen

"A Moment"

To catch an eye, to show one's face;
To smile a moment, in still embrace;
To feel in my heart, a conscious yearning;
Until I know, will my heart be burning!

Paul J. Cormier

When The Time Comes To Die

The bird can fly,
Up high in the sky.
Without a worry in his head,
Not a moment's hesitation or dread.

But how can it be?
For when humans, we see,
Always in such a hurry,
With life so full of worry.

So when the time comes to die,
Don't ask yourself, "Why?"
"I haven't done the `important things,'
Spent time with my kids and spread my wings."

So live each day as if it were the last,
And time won't go by so very fast.
Then, after the last breath you have breathed,
You won't feel so sorry for having to leave.

Wendy K. Mason

Love's Dream

Moonlight Falls as soft as a kiss
Upon the soft grass of the Lover's field.
The Nightingale sings her slow sweet song,
A lullaby to the lovers
Lying in a gentle embrace on the grass so soft.

The night's silver disk rises high in the sky.
The glorious stars in their constellations move slowly.
Sliding smoothly along their heavenly orbit.
Making the scenes beauty divine.
The lovers watch in awed silence.

They neither move nor stir.
As they lie in love's scene.
Enjoying the other's company,
The whispering gurgle of a little stream.
Ahh, to be in love's dream.

Stephen McSweeney

My Lonely Life

Oh Father, as thine eyes look down,
Upon this life, which wears a frown.
A life you gone some years ago,
I beg you now, please help it grow

In months gone by, the roads been long.
Yet with your strength, life can be strong.
The strife that fills our world today.
Will may in time, just fade away

The wars we fight, in lands afar,
Will always, we know leave its scar.
Please Father spread thy healing hands
And bring thy peace upon this land.

It's with your loving gentle way,
That father, troubles can be soothed away.
This troubled life of mine will prove,
That with your help, I will get through.

So father, don't divert me now.
Your love will bring me through some how.
My lonely life will one day be.
A happy, holy one for me.

Marilyn Ruzzene

Sometimes

Sometimes, we don't tell the people who mean the most to
us, just how much we care.
Sometimes, they feel uncertain, because they're not sure
that when they need us, we'll be there.
Sometimes, life goes by from day to day, and we busy ourselves
in so many ways, and we forget things we should say;
but sometimes, we remember just how important words can be;
and say "I love you," and I'll always care, and when you
need me, I will be there for you, always; not just sometimes.

Sharon Wood

The Dream

Dream a Dream for me and you, Dream a Dream for just us
two; Dream of a world with love and peace where racism and
violence has ceased. Dream a Dream for all mankind so
everyone can have a good state of mind. Dream a Dream I beg
of you; Dream a Dream for just us two, a Dream so precious a
Dream so unique it will lift everyone off their feet. A Dream
to stop drugs from flowing into our land which are destroying
our children, women, and man. Dream a Dream of hope and
belief for you and also for me, so Dream a Dream for you, and
me, all the people, and eternity.

Quanda L. King

A Valentine Just For You

To most people-
Valentine's Day is a day for lovers in love.
It's a day for flowers, candy or heart-shaped cards.
It's a time to reaffirm feelings felt.
But what can we do,
When each day is like this?
And every day brings new convictions of love.
When the cards, flowers and candy
Can no longer express how we feel...

This is how I feel about you,
Flowers are beautiful-but not as beautiful as you,
The candy-it's sweet,
But the sweetness doesn't compare,
And the cards,
They fall far short of what it is I'd like to convey.
So I guess I'll say what's on my heart,
In the only manner I know how,
I Love You

And to me
Each day with you is Valentine's Day.
T. M. Pitts

A Bird Of Song!

Stop!
Wait!
Listen!

A Bird of song!

A voice calling out: Here I am,
A voice revealing: A secret message,
A voice asking: Just listen,

A bird of song!

A song proclaiming: Today is your day,
A song proclaiming: Count your joys,
A song proclaiming: Celebrate your successes,

A bird of song?

Singing: In harmony with nature,
Singing: Its praises,
Singing: All is well,

Discouraged, depressed, and exhausted,
Just stop, wait, and listen,
To a bird of song!
Michael A. Pantaleo

Waiting Around For Woman Love

Waiting around for hours on end,
   waiting around for my only true friend.
Someone to take my hand, in hopes....
   that they can help me understand.
And I sit and wait in agony.

Passing time waiting to live,
   passing time with love to give.
With a heart full of emotion, growing....
   everlasting love and devotion.
And I sit and wait in agony.

Doing time in a personal hell,
   doing time and not feeling well.
She is the one and only, love....
   can't do nothing' but feel lonely.
And I'm still waiting for my Woman Love.
Vincent Merchant

Shore Birds

Crab-like I perch on a grain of sand
waiting for the sandpiper to run the tide.
The waves like love never let me know
they are coming,
so I wait for the rain to swell the ocean
and hope to touch the glow.

Disappointed I run the sunset arms open
and hitch a ride on gull wings
too slow to touch the glow.

Bewildered on the sand again
I wait the rain to swell the ocean
And grab the wind's tail
to chase the moon into the sea
too shy to touch the glow.

Exhausted I rest on the sand once more.
Hope salutes me to drift away,
rain with my tears does swell the ocean
too late to touch the glow.
Victor David

"Journeys"

   The sun coming out over the horizon,
waking up to a radiant energy,
a view that is heaven sent,
a glorious scene that has captured me;
   The waves lapping,
over the solid ground,
the sounds of silence,
when no one's around;
   Also there is a time I love,
when people are full of cheer,
and trees are to symbolize and bring about joy,
and songs are of meanings to hear;
   Sitting atop a grassy knoll,
with a natural breeze I feel,
or watching stars in a moonlit sky,
to me these mean a great deal;
   These memories and experiences,
that come from within me,
are not about hatred or sorrow,
they are all about peace.
Tracey Wieczorek

The Last Rose Of Summer

I remember laughing in the rain,
walking by the water and
smiling in your arms

This rose is what it was...
the happiness, the hurt, the passion

This rose cries, look!
Your loss can be a velvet dress,
a red and golden sunset and
waves deep and crashing

Love stirred then....and it twists me now
upon a thorny stem my thoughts
keep turning like petals pulling shut
my parting burning lips in my shaken mind

To lose you is to feel the rain and hear the thunder
to lose you is to pick the last rose of summer

It strangely sighs and sways its soft silken petals
upon the wilting weeds
and bleeds bare beauty into the wind...
Nancy L. Little

Yesterday And Tomorrow

I stared aimlessly at the walls of my dimly lit room -
   walls that once could spill secrets
     of impassioned love at the hands of glowing embers;
     of intimate words so softly spoken.
But these walls are quiet now, with not a whisper.
No new memories has fate given them to speak of.
How sad that these walls have become mirrors of me -
   empty, idle; just there.
The days are painful; the nights are long.
What starts out as anticipation turns to despair.
My walls remain tainted with silence.
Where is everyone? Would not anyone like to love me,
   or love to like me?
Oh loneliness, please go away; you are not welcome here!
You are drowning me in self-deprecation,
   and your cross is far too heavy to bear.
For just as the sun rises and sets, so shall tomorrow
   so shall tomorrow begin and end.
Dear friend - if you're out there, won't you please pick me up,
   and you will have found a greater friend in me.

    Kathleen Meyers

"Escape"

Have you ever found yourself trapped within your own fear
wandering mindlessly within the dark walls
that have guarded you from reality for so long,
to others your life is a fairy tale
though to you, a nightmare.
People adore your life of fairy tales and the part you play within it
They put on an act
hoping to play the part of your princess or Maiden in waiting.
they want to play the other part of your dream-like fairy tale
All they're trying to do is escape from their own bad dream
They don't realize that you are too.

    Kelly Lloyd

Untitled

Loving the spotlight
Wanting to feel it upon you
Warming your bones
Prying inside of you
Begging you to reveal all your deepest secrets
Pouring and spilling them
Onto the eager wide-eyed crowd below
Feeling an overwhelming urge to shock them
Making them reel back in their seats
Watching the delicious controversy you create
They wish they had stayed home
Yet they're glad they came
And watched this spectacle
Instead of watching their own sad, mourning lives
Crawling on the map of life
Sitting worthlessly in their living rooms
Leaving no mark
But freeing their souls
Until they find the spotlight

    Marissa Ferejohn

Twenty Eight Days Has A Week

I wish, I wish, I wish my dream come true...
Tuesday would last two days,
Wednesday three,
Thursday would endure to four,
Friday to five,
Saturday would persist to six,
And Sunday a lucky seven.
But please, time, keep monday the way it is!

    Rose Boehm Ebner

Our Leader Our Friend

Many moons ago, in a place not far from here,
Was born a baby girl, who looked to all so dear.

As she grew into a young lady, it was clear by all her deeds,
That this young miss called Elaine, was definitely meant to lead.

She started as an operator, for New England Tel.
In an old building in Dorchester marked by a great big bell.

It was there that she began working as an operator on the board,
And made so many long time friends while pulling all those cords.

It was also this old building that enabled her to find,
A special man in Jimmy who has been a love and truly kind.

It seems that even from the start, Elaine was meant to be,
A leader among many of New England's Family.

She led from many positions, successful at each one,
And proved to so many fellow workers, how balance should be done.

Always caring, always there in sunshine and in shade,
Elaine has been a kind of friend who's friendship never fades.

Her caring, guidance and support is what was most admired,
For Elaine O'Sullivan always provided high morals, and never tired.

We now are here to say farewell and best wishes we will send,
To not only a wonderful leader, but more importantly, our friend.

    Mary J. Brenner

Wood

The wood that goes from log to board
Was once a massive tree adored
By all the forest's family
Who looked at her admiringly.

Now prone and sheared, its size has shrunk,
Reduced to but a severed trunk
About to ride the sawmill's rut
And render lumber, sized and cut.

The worth of wood in memory
Began when it was just a tree.
From harvest, mill then factories
There're many who depend on trees.

We rarely note how wood appeals,
Like homes and boats and toys and wheels
Or sounds of tone or tune within
Marimbas or a violin.

Wood's face and figure once concealed
Is in its glory now revealed.
Just witness any fine veneer
Or barren creosoted pier.

    M. Paul Ward

Life

I always thought that love in its eternal glory
was rightfully priority of the young
when lithe bodies of youthful lovers
resembled bodies of the Gods
descended from the Mount of Olympus
when every boy was Parris
who offered apple to the Goddess
and every girl accepting it
was magic nymphus
But now with the autumn of my life approaching
I prey for innocence of the young
who know not that
Life is but a speck of dust
which flies so fast
in universe of love.

    Tanya Ranaweera

Canyonblack

As daydawn breaks, emerging from the black-green
Wash of moonbeam night are canyon depths
Defined by unplumbed umbergray unseen;
Slowly, inexorably, the Developer's Solution accepts
The yawning earth, and birth's arrays of color sprouts
Which peek then flood the gorge's atmosphere;
The canyon crevasses, riprock piers,
And roughhewn temples are the vessels filled
With colors carried homeward bound on routes
That shadows dark and cloud-laced sunpaths build.

As the day unfolds, the pinks and lavenders
Are subtly transfigured into monolithic reds,
Twisting towers of rock with curvatures
Protruding like bent fingers through the beds
Of pale green dust of endless ages past.
The ebbing daywane soothes the sunblazed rocks,
And shivering, purple-indigo at last
Appears in shadowpatches gathering in flocks,
Then alighting from the depths, colorlight takes flight...
And enveloped is the canyonblack by night.

Keith Sobraske

The Lonely Man

He sits alone in the nursing home,
Watching a football game.
Feeling sorry for himself.
Never recalling all the years
His long gone wife was down on her knees
   cleaning the floor
While he enjoyed the sports and his beer.
Now lonely and unloved
Does he weep for her
   or his lost comfort.

Louise H. Middleton

Life's So Easy

It's so easy not to see what's right in front of your face.
We all search for the love that is just around the corner,
Not noticing it's already in place.
It's so easy just to sit around and let life pass you by.
We all fail to remember there are too little days left
from now until the day that we die.
We all grasp at straws
Waiting for our dreams to come true,
But they're not handed down on some silver platter,
We've got to earn what is due.
It's so easy to complain
I can't take this anymore
But to fix our mistakes, we don't try.
It's so easy just to sit and let life pass you by.

Sandra Pearlman

Childhood Memories

All the cartoons, heroes, and big dreams!
Waking up late on Saturday mornings all during the summer
Coming home from school and playing with my puppy.
Going swimming in the summer and jumping off the high dive
Fussing and fighting with friends and later making up
Playing tag next door with my friends
The guys coming to my door to ask me out
Hunting or spending time with my dad, friends, or my grandparents
Falling in love only to get a broken heart
Watching stars and dreaming about what I might one day be
Or maybe watching clouds and making pictures out of them
All the thoughts, questions, and dreams going through my head
This could be nothing more except the childhood memories of
any child who later because of these things to shape the person,
They now all grow up to be a total success.

Shea Sheppard

Calm-Cool-Collected

In solving a simple problem, this we find,
We are so confused, nearly out of our mind.
The simple things seem the hardest to solve,
That into much more complex problems we dissolve.
Take it slow and easy, relax and think.
Pretty soon you'll see the light, you've found
   the missing link.
Keep calm, cool, and collected looking ahead -
Or the doctor will get you, put you in bed.
You'll take pills, dope, and shots until your face
   is red,
Then it'll be too late to wish you were dead.
The moral of this tale is not one of fame,
Be calm, cool, and collected, keep fit, stay
   in the game.

Kaye F. Smith

Let's Walk To Cure Diabetes

Let's walk to cure diabetes!
We are survivors!
We'll never let it defeat us!
Thank you for this little pep talk!
Thank you for being here on this walk!
One thing you can be sure!
We're just beginning the battle.
We won't stop until we find the cure!

Diabetes comes like a thief in the night!
It affects your whole system!
It can even take away your sight!
If it's not treated
It's a killer disease!
From the tips of your toes
All the way to your knees.

It doesn't discriminate.
It affects both the young and the old.
Know what to watch for!
Be aware! Make sure you're told!
Let's walk to cure diabetes!

Samantha Love

Senior Serenade

No longer-put on a shelf to age
We can be seen on every newspaper page -
So father time - get out of my way -
Lend me your ears - I've got a lot to say.

Sylvia Velkoff

Fall

As the days grow cold and gray and the air is crisp and chilled
We children stop our play for the air becomes quite filled
With feelings of remorse and the memories of the past
We soon become aware that life will not always last.

   The act of growing up
   Comes quickly for a few
   And the others live their lives
   The way they always do.

For we are never fully aware of how grand our lives can be
until it flashes before our eyes and all stops suddenly.
After time has passed the air turns cold and gray;
our memories will at last begin to fade away.

The time that we had lived and dreams of what would be
close in around our world with nothing left to see.
For the choice is really His however great or small
to let us die or live now come the days of fall.

Karen Ouimet

The Illusion

We laughed together,
We cried together,
But all in all we were a family,
Then it happened,
They separated,
I felt like my world fell apart that night,
But strength and hope kept us going,
Some how,
Some way,
We will be together as a family again,
Someday.
Seeing something that took years to create,
Fall apart before your eyes,
Knowing that there's nothing you can do to stop it,
Can take the soul out of a person,
I guess you never know how special something is,
Until it's gone,
In the end it was just an illusion,
That disappears into thin air.

Lauren Aronson

No Time

What good is life if rushed without a minute to spare
We forget the Saviour who for us did care
No time to sing praises for
Our time must be spent going places
No time to sing and shout for
We spend all our time dashing madly about
No time to pray for
Our time only runs from day to day
No time for church for
We spend all our time going through life's unseemly search
No time to read our Bible for
In it the words to live by we know we are liable
No time for
Time is mine
To bad for when Jesus we see
He'll say No time for me
I see
After all it was for thee
I shed my blood at Calvary

Tracy Hayes

Death Is Not For Mourning

Today we mourn you, because you have left us all behind;
We should be rejoicing, Oh! are we so blind.

Instead we cry,
  and weep with despair;
When really only your body,
  is all that's not here.

All our joys and memories,
  of much happier days;
Are instilled in our hearts,
  and will remain with us always.

We feel sad without you,
  empty, and all alone;
Because the Lord has decided,
  to take you back home.

The angles of glory,
  will meet you at the gate;
And you will finally be at home,
  where there is only love, not hate.

So farewell my friend, and enjoy your serene rest;
Because you have resisted temptation and passed all of God's tests.

Sandra Logan

Jehovah

To you a thousand years is like yesterday or like a single hour.
We glide through tides of time, swiftly with your grace and power.
You're robed in majesty and in strength, the world is truly your throne.
When light flash across the world, to all nations your glory is shown.
The mighty oceans thunder your praises, in a sound that all can hear.
You speak and man will turn back to dust, only you should we fear.
Through all generations you've been our home,
creating mountains and land.
You control the foundation and depth of the earth, which was formed
with your mighty hand.

Patrice Jarvis

Changes

Wasn't it just yesterday we were invincible?
We grew up too fast; yesterday's gone.
Fathers and friends we loved have died
I thought they would live forever.
I thought *we* would.

Wasn't it just yesterday we laughed for hours?
The face in the mirror is so serious now.
It isn't the face I remember.
I thought we would laugh forever.
I thought we would.

Wasn't it just yesterday when we became friends,
went to housewarming parties, bought Christmas presents?
When did those days turn into years?
Only memories last forever...
I guess I knew they would.

Nycole Rochford

My Friend

I remember when first we met; the friendship began that day.
We knew from the start we were buddies and it always would be
that way.

True friendships are rare and I counted my blessing
to have a friend like you,
A friend who always made me feel special
and I made you feel special too.

We took care of each other from the very beginning and shared
life's joys and sorrows.
We knew we had plenty of time to be pals because there were
many tomorrows.

And then that fateful day came to pass
when I received the news by phone
That my friend had been killed in an accident
and I'd have to go on alone.

I raced to your side to be with you but you never knew I was there.
I wanted to hold you and love you once more
and let you know how I care.

Our life's journey together is over. I miss you
and will 'til the end.
Just one more time I'd love to see my buddy,
my daughter, my friend.

Merle Cooper

Since I Retired

Each Monday I don't know what to do.
Tuesday it seems is that way, too.
Wednesday I know I'd better get going,
'Cause Thursday or Friday the grass will need mowing.
But since I retired, I've developed this quirk.
On Saturday and Sunday, I just don't work.

William V. Rush

The Day Of Hearts

To the love of my life on this day of hearts
We know our love will never part.

Our love is just a fraction of the things we share;
The expressions of love and showing we care.

This day will also bring a special memory,
The day I heard, "Will you marry me?"

And just so you'll know and won't have to guess,
My answer today would still be "Yes!"

Patty E. George

Mixed Mediums

Our love isn't black or white,
We share at least three rays of light.
All three rays burn bright tonight,
Because their mediums where mixed just right.

The first one born was not your seed,
However you took on this deed.
And with your patience and your love,
This little ray rose above.
The second one, is just like you,
He doesn't know what not to do.
He's quite handsome and a flirt,
From what I see he'll make them hurt.

The third one is one of two,
One went above, one stayed with you.
In her eyes she tells the truth,
In three years you've made some goofs.

There where some other gleams of lights,
That shine above this very night,
However fate took them away.
But in our hearts is where they'll stay!

Sandra McPherson

Blue Bonnets

There we stand as a bunch in a long wide cluster.
We shine ever so bright blue in all our luster.
As we bend and weave back and forth with greatest of ease.
Late in the fall we shall wither and die, if you please.
When the wind blows, we hope it carries our seed far and wide.
Comes next spring in hopes to bloom again we sigh.
So that all may see and enjoy the beauty of little blue bonnets.

Lawrence J. Crain

How Will You Love Me?

One of the questions my heart holds, is how will you love me,
When I am old? When my face is wrinkled and my hair turns
gray; how will you love me, and what will you say?
When my sight fails me from day-to-day, my words are slurred
or pronounced the wrong way... I start a conversation and my
mind starts to stray, how will you love me and what will you say?
Will we sleep in separate rooms and dream how it used to
be, or when I open my eyes your face will I see? If I'm
awake at night and sleep during the day, how will you love me,
and what will you say?
When we go for a stroll will you hold my hand? Will you be
my eyes and your mind will you lend? When one minute seems
like an hour or two, what will you say and what will you do?
When I call your name, will you come right away? How will you
love me, and what will you say?
I ask these questions while in my right mind to be... can I
look in your eyes and the answers I see? For yet I am not
old, feeble, gray, weary, worn or wasted away. I am filled with
love, life, laughter and play... but in my heart the questions
still stay... of how will you love me, and what will you say?

Wilma Pendgraft Calicuitt

Unitled

Life doesn't come with a guarantee,
We should give it our level best.
On this one thing, I hope we agree,
If we do, GOD will do the rest!

From the day we're born, 'til the day we die,
We struggle to get ahead.
But only GOD has the reason why,
We've led the life that we've led.

On "Turkey Day," we give GOD thanks,
And Christmas, we honor His birth.
But all the money, in all the banks,
Can't make a heaven here on earth.

Love they neighbor; love can't be bought,
Remember the golden rule.
Do the good things, that you've been taught,
And loving GOD can be real cool!

As I said in the beginning, I'll say to the end,
Life don't carry a guarantee.
But making GOD our personal friend,
Makes life better, for you and me!

Richard E. Nickel

Brotherly Love

From dust we came, the air filled our lungs.
We walked the land. We worked the fields.
My brother came to over-power me.
Made himself better than me. Put me and mine in chains.
Put us to work for his kind.
Made him and his kind KINGS and QUEENS.

Time past and past, men fled the land.
Went to a new world - a new beginning.
We walked the land. We worked the fields. We fed our families.

We learned nothing from the old world.
My brother over-powered me.
Called himself GOVERNMENT and POLITICS.
We worked for his and his kind-leaving nothing for our kind.
Our children are hungry. Our old are sick.

There's no longer any fields to work.
There's nowhere to flee.

From dust we came. To dust we'll go - nothing learned.
Nothing gained.
Nothing but BROTHERLY LOVE.

Katie L. Wise

The Birds

Soaring,
up over the rooftops,
high over our heads,
they soar
without a care in the world
— the birds.

Carefully they glide
casting shadows down
upon our heads,
yet we go on,
without a glance
— the birds.

Skillfully they coast across the skies,
their wings reflecting the glistening sunset,
and returning to their nests,
home for the night
— the birds.

Michelle Hall

My Friend And I

My friend and I spend Christmas together.
We went out in all kinds of weather.
I bought a real Christmas tree this year.
And started to decorate in full gear...
He slept near the tree, a white ball of fur.
In enjoyment of the smell, he started to purr.

He was slender with blue eyes,
A pink nose and wear no ties,
Presents of catnip, a new collar and cans of food.
Everything for Christmas was looking good.

Time came to put the tree out, and he took one more glance,
he looked at my face, like he was in a trance,
In the spring cat leukemia. I was told
I never even knew he had a cold,
Light on his feet, he was like a ballet dancer,
my little friend, was put to sleep because of cancer,

It's sad to think, he will no longer be at the door,
Asleep on the bed, or on the floor
little did I know, it would be our last year together.
No longer would we go out in all kinds of weather.

Rita R. Jamialkowski

A Thank You To Noah

God sent NOAH to Keithsburg in 1993,
We were glad to see him - I think
    we'll all agree.
It was after the flood when he arrived
Hoping to help us all survive.

He helped us through many a strife
So we could get on with the rest of our life
He, along with other men,
Help put houses together again.

We want to thank him from our hearts
Without him we may have been
    torn apart.
Goodbye, dear Noah, and thanks again
For being there and being our friend.

Sharon Leigh Scott Reason

Alone

Vacuumous air of ice, another month ends in -ary.
Weary clouds linger on a sickly pallid ceiling.

A chill leeches my cheeks like a frozen eel, I peel,
My nose rolling smoke in a billow.

Bleak steam gradually lifting, feeding the thick frigid.
Trapped beneath the dormant stream, damned like frozen roadkill

A cadaver's chill, and the gritted jam of icy teeth,
Suppressed water globs for air. Broken arrow trees

Petrified but gnarled, dark and oily, contradict
Ghost colors. Salt crackles, distant as the snow blower drone.

Hunched passersby shiver, morbidly closed: Iced, contemptuous,
silent movie characters huddled in shivering grays on the pale,

Pervading screen. But, the deafening hum is disturbed—crunching
steps on permafrost crackle like snow tires over the eerie

Stillness of skeleton bird lairs, woozy sedated leaves. Bleak trees
do not impede but chart my desolate trek, as weathered soldiers.

Ahead, an obscure path, a wanderer's trail, nothing to impede
hearty boots: Crunching, forward, firm. Narrow eyed, I imagine
Mountains, freezing domes, towering the distance.

Mark Sheppard

Poems From The Heart

The snow will come, and leave us too,
    We'll freeze our butts we always do,
Our hands and feet, our nose and ears,
    How did we stand it all these years?
My preference is a sunny spot, not too cool, not too hot.
Where pleasant breezes cool and sweet,
    will calm our nerves also our feet.
We'll get the urge to roam away, to where the fish swim and play.
We'll wet our lines and Pray a lot, to catch a few, but then why not,
We've earned it all, through sweat and wear, we need the rest, the sweet
    clean air
When we retire this all will come, when we retire, HO HUM, HO HUM.

Marvin Schnear

Dreams Do Come True

They say everything happens for a reason.
    Well I'm not buying that saying this season.
I am so sad, my heart is broken.
    Not an encouraging word can be spoken.
It seems that my lifelong dream will never come true.
    No wonder I am so blue.

But I must go on.
    Starting over - although all hope is gone.
The future holds my fate in its hand
    I'll try to be strong and make a stand.
There is a special place for me.
    I will do well, just wait and see.
Trust in me, I'll find a way
    To make you proud of me in each and every way
To be successful is something I will achieve.
    All I need is someone like you to believe.
Someday you'll see after all I've been through
    and agree with me that
Dreams Do Come True.

Mary Dellovade

Soft Snowflakes

One night I dreamed that little snowflakes
Were going around in my head.
The next morning when I woke up,
I could see soft snow flakes falling.
I ran down the hall
and out the door in a flash.
When I touched the gentle snow,
I knew my dream was true.
When I saw the snow was melting,
I sadly cried while I watched
The white snowflakes in the air disappear.
But I know that winter
will come again.

Shawn Kelley

"Mighty Soul"

Oh, our little Kody Lee,
What a mighty soul,
You were so destined to be.
    You came,
        You conquered,
            And you carried on.
Leaving us with an empty nest in our tree.
    Carry on
        Carry on
            'Cause we know this must be.
But always remember
    Mighty soul that you be,
        Our little Kody Lee.
There's always an opening in,
    Our Emery Family Tree.

Kelly Emery

Scooterball

Hey ya all. It's scooterball. The new game the revo fan.
What be this game? The old man say? Ole 19 century beaten out by
2000 bust't ya. Well, how can this be? scooterball changed your
    destiny!
industrial equality. Ethics on the run. Why not be equal in the
    master's plan?
Asked the contemporary fan. There: I saw the graceful dead: wearing
the baseball cloths from the past then I realize; it's our turn
now to play the scooterball.
Hymn, song. And dance won't romance like the scooterball bears
versus blades. Rock of spades burning up the bearing plates. Zip!
slap! slamming wow! what a maze! father time; saying break that
flip. Back bone flip. When Mama's on the court, what kind of game is
this? blade! scoot! shake! zip! that's what it is all about what you
see the dynamics of this game you'll flip right out balance skill
think check it out your motion is my ocean that's the scooterball
whoa!... what a rush! not to be tied. Your balance versus the foe
why not bust-em just for kicks! Then they really know don't mess
with this babe! It's scooterball watch out for the referee flow.
Red, yellow, or black they'll let you know. Depth force me. Sucker
you'll pay! Watch out! Tomorrow is a brand new day. Scooterball now.

Larry J. Schuetter

The Secret

I can feel the pain burning deep in my soul.
What I cannot tell, and no one can know.
I felt so violated and distressed.
While in your heart I confessed.
I confide in you, but I feel the shame.
As I tell you all about his revengeful game.
I can feel the pain swelling in your eyes,
As you look at me with great surprise.
You watch the tears roll down my cheek.
Falling like a faucet with a leak.
You pull me closer, deep into your arms,
Where you try to wipe away all of the world's harms.
You try to wipe my fears aside,
As deeper in your arms I hide.
You lift my head up and softly kiss me,
Then you promise that you'll always love me...

Olivia Reis

The Sound Of Creation

Silence is golden, I've often heard
What is so golden of unspoken word?

To hear the crickets in the early evening light,
The sound of the wind, playing with trees late at night

Silence is golden, it is often told,
The rustle and whisking of leaves turning old,
Icicles falling in the stark bitter cold,
Sounds of a snow drift, built by the wind
Silence is golden in the sound that it sends

The danger of silence, the preciousness of gold,
The sound of the elements of Creation unfold

Thunder, lightning, rain, and wind,
Change of the times is the message it sends

Silence is golden it is often said,
The sound of the rain on my roof while in bed
Creaks and creaks in the house, playing tricks in my head

Gunfire in the distance, sirens sounding through the mass,
Someone is screaming, the shatter of glass
Where is the silence, the precious gold?
The Sound of Creation, of the elements untold.

Katherine Buethe

A True Friend

I can talk to you and tell you my dreams and we know the world isn't
what it seems to be. But when there's no one around you're always
there to pick me up off the ground, to pray for me when I'm
feeling down.

And you'll be in my heart forever through the laughter and the
tears. You'll be in my heart keeping me through my strengths and
through my fears, you'll be in my heart forever, you're a true friend
to me. You'll be in my heart forever, that's all you'll need to be.

I've laughed with you and I've cried on your shoulder; now I know I
don't have to be afraid to show you how I feel inside. You showed
me how to live and now I don't have to hide.

And you'll be in my heart forever through the laughter and the
tears. You'll be in my heart keeping me through my strengths and
through my fears. You'll be in my heart forever, you're a true friend
to me. You'll be in my heart forever, and that's all you'll need to be.

Shannon Duffy

The Silent Person Inside The Child

I am they say-yet never do they approach me.
What must I do to win this outer world?
My cries are yet unheard!
My fears are yet unspoken. I ask "what must I do?"
There is no solace here. I am always alone. Come, talk to me.
Bring me your shine, your love's light. I cannot find my own.
My candle wick is no more. Come, share your light with me.
I am as a hunger never filled, a word never spoken, a laugh
never heard.
Come, see your silent child! I am waiting.

Sandie Dahlberg

Christmas Is

We think of Christmas as a time to be jolly,
What with the gifts, and the turkey and holly.

But it's really a space in our lives here on Earth,
To pause and reflect upon its true worth.

And that is the sharing with those whom we love,
The abundance of gifts from Him up above.

And midst all the hustle, the tinsel and mirth,
Christmas is the celebration of the Christ Child's birth.

Maxine Chew

Fireweed

There is a flower called fireweed.
When a forest is ravaged by flames,
Trees crumble, creatures flee and death reigns.
But this little flower pokes through the ground
And quietly displays its crimson starburst
As death and ruin smoke all around.
This little flower is born of death and cannot be killed.
This little flower comes back, lives among the beaten,
Thrives among the vanquished.
No one expected such humble resolve.
That's one stubborn plant, they grin, and shake their heads.
Life is like an arsenal.
It will whip you, beat you, chew you and eat you
Until your life is the burnt-out forest
That smokes and crumbles and cries.
I have been beaten. I have been tripped.
I have known sorrow. I have been whipped.
But I stand in the wreckage and cry to the sky
YOU HAVE NOT KILLED ME.
  I AM FIREWEED. I WILL SURVIVE.

Laura K. Gruber

A Mischievous Cloud

In the sunlight sang a sparrow,
when a mischievous cloud,
borrowed the light leaving only a shadow.

As the shade spread his arms to encompass the bird,
a thought left his mind.

The thought then returned to ask of the sparrow: who am I?
Am I the brave tiger? Powerful and sleek?
Or the gentle young lamb? Gracious and meek?
Am I a great river? Mighty yet alone?
Or a warm summer breeze? The friend of the soul?

Then the ancient north wind met the naughty young cloud,
and chased him away.
The light and the sparrow met with a kiss,
and the thought found the light.

"Tell me please, gentle light, which of these am I?"

"None of these are you," whispered the light, yet each knows you well.
To the soul speaks a truth, with a voice soft as silk.

A voice heard only in silence, seen only in darkness, and
embraced only on the plateau of emptiness.

Randall Jackson

Love

It envelops me and makes me feel warm and secure
when all is going wrong my heart pounds
with uninhibited joy when he is near me
I feel joy I feel pain I want to scream out in
frustration my breath eludes me when he whispers
my name he sets my flesh afire with the
simple touch of his fingers my arms echo the
emptiness in my heart when I cannot be held
by him at the sight of him across the room my
knees give way and my heart skips a beat
When our eyes meet across the room time stops for an
instant when I gaze into his eyes the ocean blueness
of them pulls me in and starts to drown me in a
sea of love my only wish and dream in this
life is that he feels for me as I do for him.

J. L. Edkin

Grandpa, I Love You

I remember the days of long ago,
When I'd sit upon your knee
'Grandpa's little girl' they called me.
And that title I wore proudly.

You danced with me on my wedding day,
And old memories came to mind
Of the times I stood upon your feet
Learning to dance in time.

I wish you could have waited
To meet my unborn child.
To know you was to love you.
He would have known that in a short while.

Your death was so sudden.
We're all left asking 'why'.
But one thing I am sure of,
You're with the glorious El Shaddai.

We were never given the chance
To say our last goodbyes.
So, Grandpa, now I'm telling you
I love you, and goodbye.

MaLinda Gerber

Thinking Of Our Planet

Life is incomplete as yet.
When death comes, we'll not regret.

Living is with death it seems,
And mixed with thoughts and dreams.

We were asked to share and not despair.
Who would know and think and care?

Now is the time to wonder what will happen
When everything is forgotten.

Does it matter that we were here,
Now that earth's beauty may disappear?

Phillip C. Hunt

Him

You're happy and you're thrilled
when he finally says that he loves you
you think of what he is saying
and you're hoping that it is true
it makes you happy to hear him say that,
he's not saying it to spare your feelings
he's stating it as a fact
Before you started dating
you only had a mere crush
you may have felt some feelings
but probably not as much
You seem to be growing closer
every single day
and you are both hoping that
it will always stay that way
Seeing each other, every now and then
makes you kind of wonder
what you'd ever do without him!

Karie Otterson

Love Like A Rose

I was mesmerized by his face
when he first said hello
he told me "Love is like a rose."

Very fragile and some people don't understand
how love isn't just a word
it's a feeling of desire and your life plan.

If love is like a rose
it has to die,
nothing can last forever
so never cry...

Tiffany Wilson

Now I Can See

We're all alone inside of here,
When I think about what's fixing to
happen I shed a tear.
We're in our mother's stomach, a fetus,
there will never be anyone to greet us.
The more I think the more pain I feel,
Why are doctors paid to kill?
I really can't understand,
Why when times are rough a doctor lends a
helping hand.
I feel sorry for my brother/sister and me,
the light is something we'll never be able to see.
I can't wait till we go up there,
there will be people who really care.
I feel the pain again and again,
Lord won't you let this come to an end?
Now I'm in heaven and I can see,
Why it was that my mother chose to get rid of me.

Starla Swanner

Missing You

I looked away, but for a brief moment and
When I glanced back you were forever gone
From my sight.

I called your name but no answer came.
I cried long into the night praying desperately
For God to make all things right.

Then I knew you were in a heavenly place
With God our Father and His angels
Face to face.

Special memories come marching across my mind.
One by one they linger still, to tell a story
That I must hear. Happy times and sad ones, too.
Oh, Pat, How I miss you!!!

Willene Domenichelli

Mercy

Could it be this same day, this very hour
when I was the one trapped underneath you?
Yes, I was one of the five
those trembling drunk girls
naive and naked before you

In bitter intoxication I trusted you
three times over in a tub hot with blood
I tried to tell you then
No, no, no I said
Did you hear me?

I won't fight you, my friend
I cannot cleanse myself of your touch
Your mind is still in my dreams
just you and your knife to deflower me
and I screamed out "MERCY"

Sara Anderson

The Lesson

Is there anything more final than death,
When it comes, unexpected or planned for?
There's no turning back; it's over and done.
That person is gone, forevermore.

No matter how much we wish or we pray
Or remember the loved one's past glory,
The door is closed, and locked, and barred.
No mortal can share this story.

We clench our fists, and shed our tears,
And ask, "How can we go on living?"
With passing time and grace we shall learn
Death is life's new beginning

Maggi Grenier

Silence Is Golden

My silence towards you is an absolute compliment.
When it matters, I find myself speechless.
I am unable to find the words to reflect to you my true self.
I search for words that show how I feel, what I think, and who I am.
Instead of words, I find silence.
I sit in that silence and I stare at you with complete awe.
I wish I could let you see how wonderful I really am.
I want to badly for my soul to leap out and take you completely.
Instead, you can only stare at my beautiful face.
Without words, I will be locked up like this forever.

Do you date mutes?

Melissa A. Brown

Parted But Together Always

To: Shane
It's very hard to say good-bye,
When looking through a small boy's eyes.

I hold him tight throughout the night,
His little heart beats with total fright.

Every night I hear him say,
Please don't take her, God I pray.

I try to tell his tear streaked face,
I'm going to a better place,

So remember me as strong and wise
and the love you see in your mother's eyes.

Though I must go and you must stay,
I'm never really far away.

The hurt you feel soon will pass,
But the special memories shall always last.

Roxie Schultz

To Kill A Snake

A friend, one Autumn day, was home alone without regard
When she spied a curled-up serpent, right out in her backyard.

Without her glasses, she'll admit, she doesn't see so well;
She got in her car, knowing the wheels that snake's life would expel.

Back and forth she drove until she thought she had 'smashed' the snake
Took a little peek, and saw that she had made a big mistake:

The thing she'd seen was dead all right, but a snake it was not:
She'd 'killed' that old-feather; of it, she'd hardly left a spot!

That reminds me of old Satan and the wiles that he works:
He shows me pretty things, then leads me astray…while he smirks

Sometimes, he's hard to resist; He shows me desirable 'gems'…
Just when I think I'm livin' right, I find I'm serving him!

But resist him I must, if I'd please my Savior and Lord…
Instead of following this Deceiver and his vast horde.

Old Satan's a "roaring lion seeking whom he may devour…"
Rely on God, who gives wisdom, and live in His power;
Kill the Devil's influence over my life…with prayer;
Study God's Word; the wise Holy Spirit will help me there!

Old Satan will be routed like the serpent that he is;
And the final victory will be mine…and God's…not his!

Ruth M. Peters

The Last Ride

There comes a time in every cowboy's life,
When he gets tired and lonely and takes on a wife.
She could be short or tall but a kind lady most of all.
And be able to cook when friends come to call.
She's got to be strong and courageous with a gentle touch
And be able to handle horses, cattle, dogs and such.
She's got to take pride in herself and her man..
And keep her chin up when life changes its plan.
A good woman knows how to spend hard earned money,
"So here's a dollar, but bring the change back honey."
When the time comes she'll have a kid or two
Spending her days changing diapers on a ooh or a gooh.
Then before you know it the kids will be gone,
Leaving old mom and dad at home alone.
With nothing else left to do but rock in their chairs
They sit on the porch reminiscing and admiring gray hairs..
Every once in a while when the mood is let,
They will look at each other and then make a bet.
Hell we're still alive and we ain't dead yet.
So let's saddle-up and ride off into the sunset.

Steve Rogers

On Being Brown

Brown is a color no one chooses
When someone asks - what is your favorite color?

Yet, brown is everywhere and remains a part
Of every picture of life to the eye.

We think of green trees—
But what about that sturdy brown trunk?

We think of pretty blond hair—
But aren't most of us some shade of brown?

We think of gardens growing beautiful flowers—
But where would they be without the lush, rich
    brown soil?

And think of the animal kingdom — mostly shades of brown,
That share our earth in wildness or as pets.

And what of the many things we eat — turkey, steak,
    pretzels, chocolate — all shades of brown.

So, even though brown isn't picked as a favorite color
And even though it may be boring to many —
In the picture of life — it is a very necessary part.

Patricia Walkley

Rosemary

Life can serve a terrible blow,
When someone you love, leaves the show.
Games that were played, have become still,
Left in their places, to play at will.

Evenings we loved, and used to share,
Have become empty, no one is there.
Heartaches and tears don't seem to help,
The hurt is deep and greatly felt.

She was our sister, your wife, your mother,
We always had fun with one another.
We shared a wonderful life, don't forget,
Thank God, we should not have any regrets.

She loved her sons and grandsons, too
There wasn't a thing she wouldn't do.
She pleased them, made them happy and glad,
They all loved her, and are also very sad.

God called her to His heavenly home,
Where she will never be alone.
She'll greet us each and every one,
When too, our life on earth is done.

Virginia Schelosky

Tears

Tears come, tears go,
When tears come and go you know
you're in love.
Love makes tears come,
Love makes tears go,
Love can make and do so many
different things to make tears come and go.
Love is love.
No one can change the way
Love makes tears come and go.
Tears are Love
No matter if it's good or bad,
Love will be Love,
It will bring tears and it will
dry tears.
Love is Tears,

Lois M. Anderson

Jesus Christ The Son Of God

I've found the pearl of Greatest Price!
When the LORD JESUS CHRIST came into my life.

All the riches and glory and fame,
Cannot compare itself to Jesus Christ's Name.

He was crucified through his hands and feet with rusty nails;
So you and I would not go to hell.

All the blood that HE shed on Calvary's cross;
Was for mankind because we were lost.

They wrapped him up, put him in the tomb where He laid;
Only to resurrect Himself in three more days.

Now Jesus Christ says: "I AM alive forever more."
"So let Me in when I'm knocking at your heart's door."

Jesus Christ said, "I AM the truth, the life and the WAY."
You cannot come to God any other way.

He is LORD of Lords and KING of kings;
Let Him come in and you'll find salvation in His wings.

Satan, who is trying to bring you to your fiery fate;
Hurry, come to JESUS CHRIST before it's everlastingly too late.

Nathan Pilgrim

The Words

In a young child's life a marvelous thing occurs
When the maturing child learns the meaning of the words.
The words give life; the words give death.
The words give everything in between,
Silently unlocking secret hopes and hidden dreams.

The child begins to learn, begins to grow, begins to be free
As the mind sails across the words and begins to see.
The words provide a place to hide,
A false reality hidden inside,
Where nothing can intrude.

The child begins to soar
On paper wings made before
By those who love the words,
And make ideas fly like birds.

The child begins to age
With each turning of a page,
But the words will never leave.
The words give life; the words give death.
The words give everything in between,
Silently unlocking secret hopes and hidden dreams.

Kenneth L. Miller

The Decline Of Veterans Day

What day will it be when we forget what they've done,
When they went into battle with their bombs and guns,
Friend watching friend, killed in cold blood,
Leaving them to die, lying in mud.
Shots ring out, another parent hits the ground,
Left there alone somehow to be found.
Look up in the sky; what could it be?
It could be the death of a whole family.
They drop the bombs; the siren sounds,
Everyone runs like a deer when it bounds.
The death capsule hits killing only a few,
They will be left there to die under morning's dew.
Now it's finally over this war of the world.
Wouldn't you think we would give respect to its heroes?
Wouldn't we give respect to these soldiers?
Obviously not, no respect in any way,
I call this the decline of Veterans Day.

Nathaniel Nate McGinnis

Sometimes

Sometimes it's hard to keep love in your heart,
when things don't work out and you're falling apart.

Sometimes it's hard to take life day by day,
when you know what you feel, but not what to say.

Sometimes it's hard to be just "good friends,"
when love is still there and a relationship ends.

Sometimes it's hard to admit you were wrong,
when someone you love has been hurting you too long.

Sometimes it's hard, when three words mean so much,
when you say "I love you," it's the heart that you touch.

Susan C. Cramp

What Do You Do?

What do you do, when you don't know what to do?
When things don't work out right?
Should you keep on, keeping on, or give up the fight?
Will things in time be right, after you try with all your might!
What do you do when the sky is gray, instead of blue?
What do you do when the one you love, isn't true?
What do you do when your money's all gone, and your friends make
you feel like you don't belong?
Will I ever learn?
When is it my turn?
What do you do, please tell me, so I know what to do.
Please tell me, so I'm not so blue..
What do you do to make my dream come true?
Will I ever find my pot of gold at the end of the rainbow?
Please tell me it's so.
So I know what to do, and where to go.

Ramona Obenchain

Forever Yours, Forever Mine

Dear love our day has finally come,
When we will unite and become as one.
My heart is racing here and there,
Just thinking of the love that we will share.
Such joy like ours is hard to find,
Forever yours, forever mine.

I've waited oh so patiently,
And now this day has come to be.
I give you my heart, I give you my soul,
I give you my all as we reach our goal.
I share my thoughts, you share your mind,
Forever yours, Forever mine.

Just to share your joy, to share your pain,
Is more than I ever hoped to gain.
As God gives us strength and love gives us courage,
We'll grow as one and not be discouraged.
From this day forward our love will shine,
Forever yours, Forever mine.

Rebecca Crume-Simmons

Summer's End

Oh how fun it is to run and laugh and play,
where I, with friends, have come to spend,
this lovely summer day.
Where flowers blow and children go, for one
last wondrous day.
We dance, we sing, and call out praise,
from hearts so light and gay.
When parents ask, "Where were you then,
when you were at play?"
We answer them, "In the forest glen,
this one last wondrous day."

Rachel Ariel Black

One Poem

You can be one person, writing one poem, at one time, a lonely time
When you realize that to go with one poem, there is only one world
And you notice that there is only one you, for that world, then,
During one life, you want to make it the best but what is the best?
Your guess is as good as mine, though, there is nothing to do for you
You can only lead one life, your life.
You are only one person, writing one poem, at one time, in one life
Though, maybe, it is a lonely life, you are alive and still here
For the rest of your life, you have no need to hurry
No place to run, cause you will still be here, as that one person
With one life, at one time, and writing one poem, a lonely poem,
In one world!
Though, you are only one person, you have to stop, look around and see,
All you can see, in your one life at any time, but one time,
At least, in this one world, though, you'll at least write
One poem, not a lonely poem, but just a poem, one poem,
Of how great things can, will, or could be for you, so that's why
I wrote,
ONE POEM !

Patricia Gehrke

Loving You

Why do I keep on loving you?
   When you say that it's not true,
   But why do you keep on calling my name,
      When you say that you do not feel the same,
   So do not go on blaming me,
   Because you want to be so free,
But why does it feel like it's still hurting me,
   Cause it does not have to be,
   We could always find a way,
      If I could convince you to stay,
   But instead you tell me to leave,
   And my heart feels like it's on my sleeve,
Even though I do not know what I will be,
   I wish that she had the courage to be with me,
   That is why I still love you,
      Cause I know that you want to be true,
   So when you think of my name,
   Do not say that I am the blame,
For making you blue,
   Because I know that it's not true.

William J. Truhe

"Thought Confounds Thinking"

Most beautiful things are often noticed,
When ugliness is set aside.
Joy comes upon the absence of gladness,
When happiness with cheer abide.

In our vague and vivid minds
Thoughts are rendered and judged within,
valid thinking prohibits evilness define
Thus... bursting highlights of memories descend.

Ofttimes, life's little pleasures control one's self-esteem,
contemplating void and neglect
common knowledge exempts nothingless it seems,
for spirit of eternity; preserve, prepare and protect.

Universal mythologies tell stories of made believed,
things in which or not known as perceived.
But more, a star in flight reveals
mysteries of bodies surrounding,
To look open the face of God, "how yet astounding!"
Telepathize your mind in time.
Travel across the sky to paradise, look to the galaxy search and find.
Believe on something, which is sufficient to suffice.

Paul E. Amos

Untitled

Please tell me, how it is that you survive.
When you're left with no place to hide.
They've got their guns out,
And their bowie knives too.
The chambers are loaded,
And they're comin' after you.

You've burned all your bridges,
But that's in the past.
Yet still you wonder
How long you can last.
Your mind cries out, in a voice like thunder,
"Give me my FREEDOM!
It is all that I ask."

But you hang your head
'Cause you know that it's futile.
Society will crush
All that is fertile.

Ron Albers Jr.

Beguiling Nature

Beguiling nature wiles on the other side of the hill
where an exalted bird continually flies
and she carries my spirit away, ever still,
the fate of the wind as it dies.

Jaded, green reflects in her eyes
as she wings her way through the air,
swooping on any dreams passing by
streams coalescent to bear.

Converging waters cannot cool the fervor in her heart,
enduring holds the pain she won't display,
unfolding feathers lunge, then dart,
she claws and grabs her prey.

Her catch is held in soaring flight.
No relinquish of hold will he find,
sustaining a moment of infinity's might,
he freely surrenders in bind.

Will Cline

Family Ties

Beyond the mountain valley streams
Where fields of golden sunlight gleam,
In the coolly refreshing air up high
The souls of family beautify,
Giving strong meaning for our lives.

A peak of angel whiteness lies there
Upon this mountain we are near,
Flowing touches of a love breeze warm the air
Where family ties are strong and clear,
For those we hold so very dear.

On this mountain we now climb
Are pathways of memories filling time,
With all the joy we have shared together
Along with sadness of grievous weather,
Our family hearts are linked forever.

Today the skies and earth will shine
With rays of light from the highest alpine,
It serves to strengthen our family bloodline
As the mountains sing in heavenly rhyme,
Throughout our earthly and eternal lifetimes.

Theresa M. Gillis

Someplace Faraway

I would like to go someplace far away
where someone understands me, and my feelings I can portray.
If I could just sit, think, and pretend
that everything is okay and this war is at an end.
Sometimes I feel like I'm all alone,
Only my soul is the guide, and to my heart the key is sewn.
The thoughts in my mind fill me with doubt.
I'm too scared to tell them, so I just shut them out.
When I think of this someplace far away,
I feel safe and my problems seem to go away.
When I come back from the dream, my feelings are still here,
but they don't seem to matter because I've overcome my fear
I remember the special people in my life every day,
and I think that maybe it's good to have this
someplace far away.

Michelle Longstaff

Bury Me Not-Bury Me

Bury me not where the green willow weeps
Where the earth stays damp and the roots run deep.
Bury me not beneath the willow tree
For I want nothing living to weep over me.

And bury me not amid the whispering pines
Where limbs hang low, like clinging vines.
Bury me not beneath those trees
For I want nothing hanging over me.

Bury me not where the sea touches land
Where there is forever a shifting sand.
Bury me not near that restless sea
For I want no water washing over me.

And bury me not amid the city noise
Where there is scampering of little girls and boys.
Bury me not where my soul can't be free
For I want no one treading over me.

Bury me please in a field of flowers
Where a ray of sunshine has magical powers.
Bury me please where the rose petals are dewkist
For there my soul can soar free in nature's bliss.

Teresa L. Barnette

Like A Chameleon Rose

First color of this lovely rose was white.
   White for the innocence and love she possessed.
   White meaning pure untouched, unseen beauty.
   When I found her, her skin, her voice, her eyes
   were that of a lovely white rose.

When I touched, embraced, and loved her. She changed to
   that of a red rose.
   Red for the love and passion that she felt.
   Red meaning the fire of love that we made.

When I made her a part of me she became that of a blue rose.
   Blue for the peace and togetherness we shared.
   Blue meaning that of a calm and clear river flowing
   through the forest of madness.

When we made another, she became that of a pink rose
   Pink for kindness and motherhood.
   Pink meaning the love she shows in return for receiving that love.

To me she is that chameleon rose that changes its
   color just for me and only me.
This makes me the richest man in the world for I am
   the only man that has a chameleon rose.

Michael W. Dail

Memory

My memory is a priceless treasure,
Which brings to mind lots of past pleasure,
And gives me joy far beyond measure;
Like showers, the dry earth freshening,
Or stars, the dark sky lightening.

These glimpses real contentment bring;
Of picking violets in the Spring,
And songs my father used to sing,
Wee kittens playing at my door,
When first I heard the ocean's roar!

There's school day friends, known but a day,
And folks I've met in many a way,
My few dear ones, some gone for aye;
An act, a word, a look, a smile —
Return to make my days worthwhile!

All these, and many, many more,
(Of days at hand, and days of yore),
Are mine from memory's golden store!
Of all the powers God gives, I find,
There's none to equal a sound mind.

Laura A. Hartshorne

Untitled

This childish fervor in her eyes-
which jealousy despises-
engaged itself onto a canvas infinity.
Such a necromantic non-sexual beast I am
in looking upon mystery.
Beauty I can see
spews its eternity with closed senses.

Only to preserve — a most chivalrous act,
or duty.

Under her canopy a most gothic mind
inhibits all forms of pleasure.
She has condemned the world by realizing hers.

To call her a woman would be to limit her.
To call her knowledge would be to grant life.

Raymond Hobson

A Scottish Remembrance (For Captain Hayes)

I dreamed of things
          while you slept deep
of forest, wooded lonely.....steep

Great hills that crept up to the stars
   and moonbeams lined straight
   as mason jars

Tender sweeps of cobwebs there
visions of mine
alone, to share
on with my inspired prose

     That sprouts like some haunted lily goes

Up higher and higher to embrace the light
mystic white symbol
          on inky black night

   A gauzy dream treasured
   honored Holy, with might

In solitude, I wait.....
please come to rescue me
   from memories past endless reverie

Kelly Boyette DeWitte

Autumn In Caribou

She loved it here where Aspen trees
whispered and sang in the autumn breeze,
where columbine grew among the pine
that were gnarled and twisted, for timberline
was just over the hill where mountains steep
cradled the snow in its chasms deep,
and elements churned and hurled and blew

creating storms as its fury grew.
It's a long, narrow road to the top of the hill...
A few remember and climb there still
to visit graves of dear ones long gone
Or perhaps to linger and wonder along
where fall leaves crunch, crisp and dry
as feet tramp the paths where old trails lie.

There in the quiet of this lovely place
lies a brand new grave, with never a trace
of why she chose to be buried so high
where wind and trees blend with shadow and sky.
For imprinted clear on the gravestone's face
Is the simple inscription, "She loved this place."

Ruby Adkins Propst

Tears Of Confusion

I call out to the greenest leaf dancing on the
whispering wind,
Take me with you!
Please, take me away.
Guide me while we fly.
While we dance - tell me how I am to be.
I seek your wisdom.
I long to experience your days.
Teach me to be graceful,
Show me to live in your ways.
When I am learned,
let me return
to the life I now wish to leave.
Transport my mind to a destination
which I can comprehend.

It drifts away,
and my eyes fill with
tears of confusion.

Nicole Orozco

Untitled

Who am I, the heartbeat outside your womb?
Who am I, the lost soul beneath the moon?
Who am I, that carries all of your shame?
Who am I, that doth speak without a name?

Who are you, whose blood courses through my vein?
Who are you, who to me faceless shall remain?
Who are you, that for me only did best?
Who are you, that I'll search for without rest?

Stacey L. Tremper

.....Time

Of course, there is always that one
   who will make you laugh and live.
Across the layers of time he will
   always remember you in his heart.
Your soul will never let you forget
   the feel of him surrounding you.
Never will your memories easily let him
   slip through the cracks of your consciousness.
Half of your being will be lost like dried up
   tears...until his return.

Kathy Spyro

Old Folks

Sometimes we see or know some old folks,
Who are very stooped, perhaps sick, wrinkled, and gray.
Some people count their life as worthless,
Some even consider them to be in everybody's way.

But if we would only take a few moments,
To stop, speak, and look into their eyes,
We would see a bright mind reflected,
And a spirit that has sustained them all their lives.

They know stories that would delight and entertain us,
And knowledge we might find useful today.
They know all about faith, hope, and real living,
And the kind of love that has carried them all the way.

Our task is to take time to listen.
Let them know that we really care.
It wouldn't hurt to say that we love them,
Growing old might then be easier to bear.

If you have ever been close to an old one,
And learned the wisdom they had to impart,
You would know that you'd received a great blessing,
And that person would live forever in your heart.

Virginia F. Maples

Why

Why did you all lie to me
Who do you want me to be
Why did you make it such a conspiracy
And include everyone in your secrecy

You brought me up with false hopes
And your lies hang me like ropes
I only wanted the honest truth
You pushed me out from under your roof

You gave me such high standards to reach
But now I know you don't practice what you preach
Your only thoughts are of how you feel
Do you care that you've made my life so unreal

The thought of you all puts my heart in a knot
But there is one thing that you all have forgot
All that is the truth will soon be out
And I will know what you're all about

Lori Thomas

I Like Your Style

There's plenty of people on this old earth
Who, in their kindness show their worth
If only in little things they do, like hold a door
For one whose strength has become quite poor,
With patience they wait, and give you a smile
Not knowing they saved what to you seemed a mile,
Some are strangers, but friends too are kind
They'll give you a hug and it blows your mind.
Do you know there are lonely folks, walking around
Who never get a hug, a touch, or hear a familiar sound?
Kindnesses shown that day and far into the night
You'll feel the warmth, soul glows with delight
Will you tell them for me, with just one kind deed
From an ache or a pain, one soul was freed?
For good manners of children, thanks to their mothers
Their "kids" grow up to be the ones who always help others
When friends give me a ride to the store, what kindness I see
At my club I get hugs and my lunch tray carried for me.
You think that doesn't help? Walk in my shoes for a while
You'd say to those nice people, "Thanks, I like your style."

Mildred Marsh Ruton

My Parents

My parents...givers of live
    Who nurtured and sculptured
    Bestowing advice

Giving so much over the years
    Support, understanding
    Listening ears

Unending security always made known
    Who cared and shared
    Giving much of their own...
To me

Gratitude flows deep from within
    For the patience and encouragement
    Given time and again

Through many confessions of tremendous fears
    Of self-doubt and helplessness
    Shedding of tears

Making dreams possible-that additional touch
    I love them and thank them
    For giving so much...
To me

Susan L. Racer

Time Of Life

I do not understand the likes of men
who squander time as if it were their friend.
For as each day comes to pass
and tomorrow turns to yesterday,
no doubt, I do act a little more wise,
but do also appear a little more grey.
If I could stop the sands of time from falling
or silence the bell before the strike of twelve,
might I then truly find my calling
before my life is placed high upon a shelf.
Fear not the sands of time as each one falls to its grave,
but capture it and surround it with a harness
and turn each grain of sand into your slave.
Fear not the bell which rings the strike of twelve
no matter how certain this may seem,
but compose each preceding strike into music,
only then, of your destiny shall you be king!

J. Keith Burkhart

The Flight

The world looked blue. The grey geese knew.
Winter's on its way. Their journey long,
Was soon to start. It had to be that day.

They gathered here to await, the members of their flock.
To stretch their wings. And read the signs.
The weather was their clock.

But off alone, a silent bird, waited for her mate.
In feathered breast, her heart.
Did yearn, she did not know his fate.

Her clansmen lifted, on strong wings.
Too form a vee across the sky.
But the silent form below, said a sad good-bye.

The night winds came strong,
And wild, and snow began to fall.
Over-head she heard a sound,
It was her life mate's call.

She answered loud her honking call,
Into the falling night.
And lifted up on strong wings.
To join him in his flight.

Leona Letulle

600

Freddy The Frog

This is a poem about Frederick, a frog,
  who used to live in a hollow log.
The log was by water, so every day,
  Freddy would go in the water to play.
But soon he grew tired of life in the log,
  so he hopped 'till he met a kind old hog.
He said, "What lies beyond this forest of trees?
  Is the world full of rivers, oceans, and seas?"
The hog said, "Travel east to a city afar,
  but be careful, little frog. You must watch for cars."
So the frog went east like the hog had said,
  and at the end of the day, he lay down to bed.
The next day he ventured through the city and town,
  hopping up streets and hopping back down.
I'll finish my poem about Frederick, my friend,
  who jumped out in the traffic and that is....
THE END

    Traci Wiegmann

Untitled

Why can't I get it?
Why can't you explain?
The ways of the world
The ways of today

The world is dying
It's all going to hell
It's like someone cast a big wicked spell

People are dying
Children are scared
The scent of worry fills the air

Why people ask
The reasons are sad
The kids of today are turning bad

They're turning to gangs, drugs, some even guns
They don't understand what they have done

They're hurting themselves
They're hurting one another
Why can't they live together as brothers?

    Kasi Harden

Why?

I ask myself the reason why, why do my friends all have to die?
Why do they leave without saying goodbye? Why do my friends
  all have to die?

Life can be full, and rich and sweet;
But painful too, and heavy and deep.
I miss them so, now that they've gone.
Where's the meaning that I haven't found?

Time heals all wounds, you'll hear people say.
But the pain is still there, it doesn't go away.
The pain quiets down, doesn't sting quite so much,
But the memory lingers and so does the love.

Pain makes us strong, it helps us to grow.
But why do my friends have to pay for me so?
I miss them so much, now that they've gone.
Please answer my question, why did they go?

Why did you go, why take your own life?
Did it hurt you so much to deal with the strife?
How could I not know, how could I not see?
Why didn't you talk, why not come to me?

How could you leave without saying goodbye? Why did you have
  to go and die?
I ask myself the reason why, why do my friends all have to die?

    Kate Pelcher

The Children Left

We are the children mom left behind
Why did she go she was so kind
She watched her flock from above
In remembrance of her love
Mom just needed a rest it was said to be
She didn't complain to you or me
One by one we drifted away only to
call and say have a nice day
Mom was stripped of her Independence and pride
And into a nursing home they cried
Mom her spirits low always had
a special glow
A wonderful smile and special hello
And now her job was done at last
To watch her flock once again
as she passed

    Patricia Casey

Why

Please tell me God from up above, why does it hurt to fall in love?
Why do they like to break your heart and hurt your feelings too?
You want to say you hate them but scream out I love you.

Why do they say they hate you when you do nothing wrong?
Then you have to fight so hard just to be a little strong.
Am I not good enough for him, is he better than me?
Why doesn't he look deep into my eyes, then maybe he will see?

How I care about being close to his heart,
Why doesn't he see I never want to part?
Why do they like to ignore you and leave you so depressed?
And the ones who are supposed to care just think you are obsessed.
They don't know you're hurting, they don't know how you feel,
They don't understand that your love for him is real.
Please tell me God from up above,
Why does it have to hurt so much to fall in love?

    Whitney Wolfe

Life

Life, what is it? Sometimes I wonder that very question.
  Why do we have so many problems? Why is life so difficult?
How would or could you stop the hurt, is it to stop life? I don't
  know the answer. WHO DOES?
Life is very difficult; it has love, happiness, sadness,
  loneliness, pain, madness, fear, and so many other things. Why
  have life, what does it set you for, but then again what's after
  life? Is there anything after life? How would I know, how
  could I find out? Where do we go after life?
Life is unusual, but so normal because who knows anything
  besides life? Could we just stop life? What would it be without
  life? So many questions, but so many confusions!

    Michael S. Haggett

"Marie"

I knew her in so many ways.
Why she left I can't explain.
I miss her with such deep sorrow.
I keep on hoping that I'll see her tomorrow.

Off in a better place, with no existing pain.
This battle that she lost, it seems like no one ever gains.
Without her suffering it's such a relief.
But no one can take away our pain or grief.

The hurt was deep like a stabbing knife.
It was the very coldest day of my entire life.
A picture with a memory I hold to me so dear.
Never seeing her again this is what I fear.

    Leah Pierce

"God Pen"

A blessing granted from the Lord
Will arm you mighty with a sword

And you will know this granted pen
That carries strengths of God within

But with this grant there is a pledge
To use for right this double edge

'Cause wisdom and your pen form one
To serve you well until you're done

You'll then possess a thing that's real.....
That lets you write the things you feel

For Godly grants are more than gold
Their blessed works of art to hold

Their blessed to be above all wrong
But double edged and mighty strong

The granted pen empowered thrones
But certain words to cut to the bone

Victor Y. Cooper

Untitled

A poetry contest my husband said
win some money is what I read
write a poem twenty lines or less
I really tried, but what a mess

A jingle a jangle is all I would need
but try as I may I couldn't succeed
I pulled all my poems I had already done
none of them short enough, no not even one

So I sat and I thought about what I could do
could I write a good poem and keep it short too
Then it hit me like lightning, the thought was amazing
I could create a poem on the dilemma I'm facing

So I sat and I thought and I started to write
and this is the poem I created that night,
I hope when you read it, it entertains you
if that's all that it does, it's the least I could do

Stevens

"Golden Years - Weep Not"

A miracle of life is garmented and cloaked
with the golden years

Seem untouchable and undivided as we
draw near.

As the burdens of sorrow, pain and tribulations
are met-

Each precious moment absorbed with passion of
endearments, the senses we share, joy, happiness
memories of our loved ones-

While the unforeseeable in marvelous, the
beautiful adornments of love and peace awaits-

Cherish the gifts carved and bestowed by
His embraceable love and grace.

Soon, the touch of gentle warm hands
interwoven, sparkle tears will flow,
spirited hearts aglow.

Weep not, my children, young with adorning faces -

Ahead lies a shining stairway and beacon
towards a brighter vision of the Golden Years.

Mary C. Harris

Forgotten Past

Drums beating to an age old tune.
Wind blowing away the present,
Ancient ancestors now reign.
Feathers swaying from messages
Of head, arms, and body.
Indian tradition in a five-year-old boy.
His movements smooth and natural,
His trance-like vision denotes age-old ritual.
Grandstand cheering falls on deaf ears,
The time belongs to an ancient tribe.
Another time, teepee-filled days of
Warriors, pride, freedom and buffalo,
Smoke-filled camps, raiding parties and
Smoke signals against distant horizons.
A time when a nation stood
Against a common foe. These are
What one perceives with the mind's eye
While gazing upon the center arena
In the form of a five-year-old
Dancing Indian boy.

Rebecca Vaughan

"The Shawl"

The elderly woman sat by the
window wrapped in her shawl of
yesteryears. Sitting there she realized
that her time for life as we know it
was soon to end. Where had the years
gone? Locked into memories like it was
just yesterday she thought of girlhood,
becoming a young lady, woman, wife
and mother only to reach where she now
sat. Where does she go from here? Forward
into the unknown, backward into the
familiar? Sensing this she could now
see the confusion of being old. Does our
sub-conscious protect us from fear of
what is to be and to come? Why not have
both? At this point with peace of mind
and her choice of acceptance; she
went forward into the unknown with
her shawl of yesteryears.

Karen J. Steurrys

"Blindness"

Blindness is an awful thing, we all must agree,
with all the beauty in God's nature to see.
But the blind can't see the sunlight,
they can't see the flowers or the birds in flight.

To them darkness in all that can be found,
and a dog or someone has to lead them around.
To them, they would give all they had to see,
their love ones faces; this is their plea.

O! That God Almighty would answer their prayer,
in this time of total darkness and despair.
So that they could see their love one's faces and not only feel,
O! That God would open their eyes; that would be such a thrill.

That they could see the children playing on the playground,
and see the grass, flowers and blue sky all around.
O! That they could go anywhere, without help from someone,
all this is possible though God's only son

O! The thought of blindness ever happening to me.
what would I do, if I couldn't see
The one's we love; their faces, we'll have to feel
someday, blindness, could happen to us; for real.

Thomas E. Tumlinson

Hold On To What He Stood For

Let Daddy's death have meaning; hold on to Jesus with all your might;
With all the courage and forcefulness that Daddy had in his fight.
Because with every trial, a test will soon fall behind,
To see how you will fare with God; who is gentle, loving and kind.
Please don't let Daddy's death be for "naught," as he would say,
But use it for the strength you'll need in each upcoming day.
Let us all remember that he never lost his faith, nor did it get weak;
He held on to Jesus stronger as each day he continued to seek.
Never once did he blame the Lord, for the hard hand he had been dealt:
Let us each learn from him and continue loving Jesus with that same
love that Daddy felt.
Let's continue to strive for the perfection that we need
to see Daddy again;
And do what he has already accomplished and free our souls of sin.
Let us all Thank Jesus for giving us, this special man to love;
A loving husband, a good father, a special friend!
The kind of man only sent from God above;
For every life he touched, each one in his own unique way.
But these are memories God has given to each one, to keep him
alive in their hearts each day!!

Patricia Wilson

Pioneer Journey

No rain clouds break the fever of the blazing sky
Where vultures wings cast shadows beneath them as they fly
No wagon rut or footprint outlines where man once trod
Hot rays now sear the surface of sparsely tufted sod

Gullies scattered with ancient rock
Earth's eras timed by geologic clock
Night's faint fragrance of desert sage
Belies the middays sun's fierce rage

Windswept dust now hides the trail
Where Prairie Schooners once set sail
On their perilous journey toward the West
Some never reaching the mountain crest

The sun sinks fast in the evening sky
A myriad of colors taunting the eye
When darkness has captured that final glow
Cool breezes still echo "Westward Ho."

Ruth Johnson

Memory Of Six Folke Kids At Christmas

'Tis a Merry Christmas season
With everyone rushing to and fro
Making candy, wrapping gifts and all the while we reason
Will our kids like this? As we tie the bows

Now on Christmas Morning we can't wait
For the kids to wake up and find
All the toys and goodies, but Santa's late
And where's our toys, they all whine.

We hurry them all back to their beds
And excuses we give them all the while,
As Mommy & Daddy scratch their heads
Remembering where they hid everything, with a smile.

Once again everyone's up and on the run
To the Christmas tree they all go
To find their stockings and toys and guns
With squeals of laughter, and Santa's Ho! Ho! Ho!

Dinner is over and night has come
Six little kids climb into bed, one by one,
But everyone's happy as to dreamland they go
And Christmas will come again next year, they know.

Margaret Falke

"Is Life Getting You Down?"

One minute life is a rose
with fresh, new petals
Turn your head for a second
the rose has died
all's left are thorns
your dreams are suddenly gone
your inspiration for a new day
just fades on away
something or someone has turned you
inside out
you feel so vulnerable,
so alone
Just always keep hope, do what's right for you
don't live for your father, your friend,
your brother
Live for you
when the world falls on you
just lift it aside
pass the tears away with a smile
for things will get better in a little while.

Lauren N. Smith

Into The Darkness

Darkness grips my heart, icy tendrils that insinuate themselves
with frigid intensity.

Shadows fill my mind. Bleak patterns of grey and black.
Fragments of thought racing and blurring with frenzied abandon.

Whirlpools eddy, disheartened spirals - their insidious
attraction drawing my soul into their depths.

A splinter of rational thought - seeking a way out of the abyss.
Aspiring to find the light of my salvation.

Caught like a spider's hapless prey in a web of despair.
Eternal darkness, or the light of deliverance? Who shall say,
who shall say?

Mary Jo Miller

Untitled

Outside the wind barely blows
   With hardly a hint of sun
It's so calm outside
   The deer just lay in the open
And bask in what small amount of sun we do have
   With every rustle of a branch
You can hear squirrels scampering about
   Trying to find food
For the little ones at home
   If only the world could have as much peace
As there is on a cold winter's day.

Randi M. Johnson

A Special Person

There is a person I admire,
With her friendship I shall never tire.
She keeps me in her loving care,
And always puts me in her prayer.
But yet sometimes when I am down,
She will also have a frown.
She always has a smile on her face,
But yet it still won't hide the trace.
Of all the things that she has been through,
I still will say I love you!
In this world there is no other,
This special person is my mother!

Leigh Montague

Come On Spring!

It's been a long winter, that's for sure,
   With ice and snow and plenty of chill;
But, with each little sprout above the soil,
   We're told the earth is fertile still.

The bulbs pushed the lingering snow aside;
   There will be tulips, daffodils, Canterbury bells,
Delphiniums, lilies, and primroses in a border, wide.
   Spring will soon be here, their appearance tells.

The leaf buds on the maple tree look as if
   They'd burst in two days' warm sun;
And, the pink dogwood, so full of promise,
   Will be a lovely sight when winter's done.

So, enough of winter, come on spring!
   (I just can't wait, the urge is great!)
I love to get my hands in the soil
   To tend the garden God gave me inside
      the garden gate!
   Laura Gunby

Song And Dance

A baseball game's a symphony of sheer kinetic grace
With interludes of classic dance around each pure white base.
Though tutus are in short supply and leotards the same,
The uniforms and colors add aesthetics to the game.
The pirouettes and entre-chats disguised in arts athletic
Can easily be recognized in essence as balletic.
An outfielder's Nijinski as he leaps against the fence,
With unearthly elevation, adding beauty to suspense.
The shortstop, second baseman, form a rhythmic pas de deux —
They reflect a fluid union as they meld in "getting two."
The dancer at third base is rich in acrobatic quotient —
A glide, a dive, a swift plié, true poetry in motion.
The pitcher's stretch, his catlike stride, harmoniously related
To the catcher, crouched and eager for the curve ball that's awaited.
Each performer, ev'ry dancer, is intense with dedication
And adds his own nuances to the whole configuration.
If you feel a thirst for beauty only true art forms can slake,
You do not need the Ballet Russe or tickets to "Swan Lake".........
Just amble to the ball park where the diamond legends play
And when the first bat strokes the ball, you'll recognize ballet!
   Roy B. Merritt

When Champs Were Champs

Boxing's golden days were the years between the two world wars.
With only eight divisions sporting champs, fans knew their stars.
Million dollar gates were few and far between,
But fixes and set-ups nearly left the scene.
Fly, bantam, feather, light, welter, middle, light-heavy, and heavy
   weight titles were enough.
Junior and super divisions would have been thought goofy by boxing
   fans, who knew their stuff.
Champs like Midget Walgast, Benny Leonard, Barney Ross, Mickey
   Walker, and Jack Dempsey were tops in the ring.
Gene Tunney and Joe Louis were unbeatable, but there was one fighter
   who never quite made it as king.
He was Young Bill Stribling, because he started scraping at age
   sixteen.
He rose through the ranks and lost but four of 303 bouts, which was
   keen.
William Lawrence Stribling fought more pro contest than any boxer the
   sport would ever see.
He battled every heavyweight champ and top challenger except Tunney
   and Dempsey.
Having just defeated Slapsie Maxie Rosenbloom, he was on the
   comeback trail without strife
Until a 1933 motorcycle accident took first his foot and then his life.

   Willard R. Carson Jr.

Lonely

Feeling so alone and deserted
with people standing all around you
Should I trust someone
Should I stay off to myself
Alone with no one to talk to
It's such a helpless feeling

So any time you feel the need
Call me when you're lonely
'Cause everybody needs a friend
to be there when they've lonely

A person all alone
Is an unhappy one
We need someone near us to love us

Someone who cares
Living life all by yourself
Is impossible to do and I'll be there for you
Any time you feel the need to
Call me when you're lonely
'Cause everyone needs a friend
And I'll be yours if you're lonely
   Vanessa Ramelli

Goodnight And Goodbye

You haunt the dreamscapes of my sleep,
with shards of the life you didn't keep,
reliving the moment of a heart's last break.
Hot tears my alarm; I'm now awake.
This dreamscape continues on into the morn,
and waking hours, find me totally worn,
like lost socks and loves that just disappear;
the latter one leaving with traces of fear,
that dreams or memories can never recapture.
True heartbreak, pain and even the rapture
are softened in clouds of a very deep sleep.
Letting go, holding on; both make me weep.
But dreams, like old friends, help weather the storm.
of our human frailties, considered the norm.
Goodnight and Goodbye, though we will meet again
Through dreams, thoughts and tears, my sword is my pen.
   Kim Hoiby

Words! What Are They?

Words! What are they which unerringly go
With such urgency and blinding speed?
Why, they are vehicles with a cargo
Volatile, explosive, and powerful indeed.

Words can sever friendships, break strong ties,
And drive wedges between family and friends.
They speak hurtful things, repeat vicious lies,
And precious relationships effectively rend.

Words also come as a healing balm
For the wounded in mind, body or soul.
Bringing assurance and making calm
Spoken fitly as apples of gold!

Words are vehicles which gently goad
The discouraged to look ahead,
They are signposts along life's road
To remind us that God is alive - not dead!

So, when your bow is taut, your arrow aimed,
Think carefully as you send it on its way,
Will the end result be a spirit maimed,
Or a blessing bestowed upon someone today?
   Ralph Cottrell

604

Illustrated Secrets

As I soar through the sky
With the wind whipping my ears
In the cool night's breeze,
I see a flash of light down below.
Swooping lower to satisfy my curiosity,
I see you sitting on a rock
Drawing pictures of the moonlight and all of its secrets.
But it is no ordinary picture,
Being brighter than the brightest of all fires.
For it burns my eyes and sears my skin
As all the secrets of the world pour into my body.
The secrets you told,
The secrets I heard,
The secrets we kept,
Until I was lowered upon that rock by your side.
Telling my secrets as well.
To the highest flyer,
To the highest bidder,
To anyone who would listen.

Rhonda Nettles

Gotta Wake-Up America

Some five thousand years ago, when mankind was so "violent and did with their bodies the unnatural things that God intended them not to do," He put a Rainbow in the sky, promising Noah, you and I, that because of mankind's sins, He would never with water again, flood the whole earth right before their eyes.

Now in Ancient Athens, Greece, the corruption of youth did increase, and it was blamed on the great Socrates. Society said, "poison Hemlock 'til you're dead" for our youth on excellence must be fed.

In America these days, it's Television we praise, because it entertains us so. Power driven, perverted minds, are producing pure immoral rot of all kinds, and our youth keep right on sucking-up all its slime.

Gotta wake-up America, Wake-up American. Wake-up America before she blows.
Our youth are bleeding, because they need feeding, in all mind, body and soul
We can't defy History, corrupting our youth is no mystery, we gotta wake-up and teach them God's Perfect way!

Phyllis P. Fox

The Lakeshore Limited On An October Day

What in nature's palette paint,
   within her wellsprings deep
      from colors faint;

What fiery sorcerer
   or gleeful goddess gives
      the blazing blood that bursts
         where blossoms lived?

And golden hues
   soaked through the dying leaf,
      betray our vision's gaze upon its sheath,
         for we see life
            in this luscious leaf motif.

And so, dressed,
   the wood hills promenade through autumn,
      'til silvery casts of winter whiteness
         numb the peaked impassioned leaves,
      and lay to rest the season's dance
         of this final, falling fest.

Rebecca A. Spence

Sonnet 1

I slowly walk through an eternal night
With vague remembrances appearing before me,
Visions from past experiences I see.
I concentrate with all my might
To block these memories from my sight.
Ghosts come forward and then flee,
Horror of horrors O let me be!
Someone save me from this plight
Of dark shadows that cross the floor,
Regrets and Mistakes that point and sneer
Chilling me to my very core.
I will be trapped forever I fear,
While happiness and joy I shall not find
Walking, walking in the darkness of my mind.

Ken Votapka

Support Our Troops

It started out as Desert Shield
   with worldwide troops refusing to yield.

They met with resistance and were ready to fight,
   the Shield turned to Storm in the midst of the night.

By morning the sun brought a heart warming sight
   yellow ribbons appeared from unbelievable heights.

They were tied on the trees, the doors and the cars,
   if possible they would have been tied to the stars.

The troops fought with vigor and a well planned attack
   they were proud of their mission and would never turn back.

The support for them all went out with a roar, but
   the prayers in our hearts wanted an end to the war.

As the smoke cleared away and the flags were raised
   our troops headed home, what a glorious day.

Merle Akers

Looney Tunes Lover

No doubt about it, she's a Looney Tunes lover.
When Bugs is on, she'll watch no other.
As soon as she hears, "Eh, what's up doc?"
There is a halt, a stopping of the clock.
Soon, there comes a wondrous laughing
While in the background, you hear Daffy.
Whenever she sees Foghorn pick up his feathers,
Her smile outshines the sunniest of weathers.
So, when on the screen comes the little chicken hawk,
Don't interrupt, say a word, no bits of small talk.
Because, if her friendship you want to bank,
You'd better be able to quote the book of Blanc.
And, if for her, your heart goes thud,
You'll need to sing like Elmer Fudd.

Robert Addington

Untitled

When cries of pain are heard but heeded not,
When man by spirit is no longer awed,
And turns his back on anguish and on hurt -
Then by this act he hides the face of God.

When hunger plagues the earth for all to see,
When sad conditions fail to stir and prod,
When those who have ignore those who have not -
Then these acts serve to hide the face of God.

When woes of men downtrodden and oppressed,
Show clearly all the lives so bruised and flawed,
Then man, aware and pushing them aside,
Deliberately obscures the face of God.

Patricia E. Brown

605

Students Of Life

We are all students
   without a graduation.
Taking our tests and pop quizzes-
Passing and failing, sometimes learning.
Going through life
   with confusion and then elatedness.
Suppressing our thoughts
   but then exploding with our own character.
Programmed in life
   to act and be a certain way-
Or breaking the program
   in what is called rebellion.
Learning from the great teacher
   called Life-
Not only gaining knowledge
   but understanding,
Not only for ourselves
   but for others as well-
We are all students
   without a graduation...

    Taejin J. Chun

Sea Of Dreams

If you live in a sea of dreams, you'll find yourself floating,
Without an anchor to weigh down your soul to this moment in
eternity.

You will waver and stray from one castle to the next
Only to retreat and return, perhaps,
Like cowards and compatriots from Cromwell's England.
All those heroes who complain and chide, while they wait and hope
For courage to decide to seek out life,
Or let other heroes find it for them.

There's bravery, alas, to lead you through the present ventures.
To lend you strength to push beyond horizon's edge.

How far will you go?
Over the depths and great divides,
To scale mountains, or sail the violent seas,
Will you travel through black holes and infinities?
Seeking some pebble to prove the hero's act
You'll bring your many conquests back.

And all the while, when you return
You've gathered strength, you've built reserve
To begin the journey once again...
Into another sea of dreams.

    Marilyn Staargaard

Abstract Mind

An abyss of thought conglomeration reflects the abstract mind
without full conception of all that has derived in its contents...
then exonerated by the individual's mechanism.

Preoccupation of a mind wondering through the universe of
people, places, heaven and earth, wilderness, and the deep seas,
gives a way to freedom, in light of virtue.

In essence, the spirit within, extracts emotions from a mind's
ethereal dreams, current ventures, and new horizons that
contradicts with past, pleasant and unpleasant realities.

The Enigmas of life's encompasses confounds the cerebral of
universal beings, in those labeled normal as those labeled aberrant;
in resolution moral and immoral acts exert.
The impenetrable weary mind may lead one to uniqueness of
character - to paradise - or disaster... there is a destination
for all.

    Theresa Jordan

A Day In Mother's Life

A woman, a wife, a mom
Without her there would be alarm
For with the hustle and bustle of each new day
She handles the jobs that come her way.

With a job outside the home she brings,
A bit more money for those extra "things."
There's laundry, cleaning, cooking and such
Volunteer work, baking, checking homework a must.

Children are always taxied around town
And mom does not make a sound.
Even thought at times the pace is fast...
And she could use a bit more cash

She is content and happy with her life
She loves being his companion, best friend and wife.
Getting through each day is difficult at times,
Because serious problems do arise.

However, she is blessed with friends and family that care
Such a treasured gift of love is ooh so rare!

    Susan Svec

Untitled

I knew I couldn't let you go
without some form of selfish sympathy
totally flooding my heart with tears that only
express so completely what I wanted no one to know.
Foolish pride cried for my grief and fears to hide
in my barren heart and weep in silence,
but my sobbing emotions drown my condescending conscience,
and my memories murmur much too loud to keep them quiet.
The sweat of our passion with which we loved
sweetly dripped from our bodies in warm streams,
but now a fear that my tears will bitterly scream
their impatient impudences, and from my blasphemous tongue
I will voice so boisterously the truth
that our bodies were in love, but our hearts virgin.
The sacred secret is gone from our youth.
This poet has no more beautiful words with which
   to express himself.
The strings in your symphony have outstretched themselves,
   for our song remains unsung.

    Scott Zee

First Love

I drove by your house and wondered about you,
wondered what let us drift apart, wondered if we could be close again,
but what would I say, and what if he's changed, pushed me away.
I kept driving, never knowing that you'd end your life that day.

Now I can only remember my days spent with you,
private notes, sketched with hearts, passed between us in the school
hallways, my head on your chest in the shade of the old oak tree,
awkward kisses mixed with giggles and your hand touching mine,
midnight phone calls, just breathing, not wanting to be part,
twilight meetings where we let our fears and dreams dance free.
In those days we spent together
I helped make you, you helped make me.

They chose no stone to mark your life, your ashes have long since
blown away, but I wanted to know you one more time,
thank you and apologize for your pain.
I needed a place to talk to you, a place to say goodbye.
So one cool day in August I went to that old oak tree,
I stood where we used to talk,
and I buried a part of me.

    Rachel Skovholt

Untitled

Questions swirling like the sea,
  wondering, questioning what may be,
  seeking a loop hole to set them free.
Conflicting winds produce a gale,
  upturning a ship a sea meant to sail,
  lightning strikes as the wind does wail.
A soul aboard with little chance,
  no escape from this maddening dance,
  and no strength left to make a stance.
Nature's lesson - it has no say,
  the soul is tossed as the elements may,
  nothing more than a small obstacle in the way.
Knowledge ignored, opinions sought,
  truth is lost, none act as they ought,
  any rebelling are chased until caught.
Questions unanswered, trapped in the night,
  none may seek them unless in the light,
  but none have the strength to do what is right.

Kristin Bovaird

A Child Within

The child inside of me, lost through her tears.
Wondering what happened to all her dreams hopes and fears.
She's running in circles and can't find the door.
She's praying for hope, but thinks there is no more.
The love in her heart is slowly fading away.
Her body is going numb, maybe the pain was meant to stay.
There was a time, long long ago.
When she thought life was perfect and happiness would be the
  only thing she'd know.
But now it is gone, too late to say goodbye.
She never knew what she had, could that be the reason why?
She now dreads the future and longs for the past.
Will she ever let go of what was not meant to last?
She tries reaching out, but no one is there.
Hello, I'm talking. Does anyone care?
She wants to give love, but also to receive.
I think she is afraid of again being deceived.
She has so much to give, so much love to share.
There's got to be at least one person who really does care.
Who is that one person, I wish to God I knew.
I guess we'll keep looking. Maybe dreams do come true.

Theresa VanIseghem

Dreams

Your breath is faint and still
You can't imagine the things that you feel
The way you sleep with your eyes shut tight
with your mind running all night

When your bed is a stuffed, rectangular pad
Your feelings are good or bad
Sometimes they could even be mad
or happy and sad

A dream changes with a blink of an eye
and materializes with a little sigh
You're still thinking while you're sleeping
of the day that is creeping by

Dreams are what happens to the girls or boys
When they close their eyes at night
and stop their playing with toys
Sometimes your dreams get carried away at a scary sight

Then you awake in the day
Raise arms and stretch to say
Tonight I will dream of Love
and of a beautiful white dove

Michelle Dexter

God's Gift

It was cold in the manger where Jesus lay
Wrapped in swaddling clothes on a bale of hay
The shepherds who were tending their sheep
Suddenly saw an angel, and heard her speak
She said, "Please you must have no fear,
For I've just come to tell you God's Son is here."
More angels did come, and the air they did fill
With a song of glory to God, and peace to men of good-will
The star of Bethlehem was shining bright
The shepherds followed it, and to their delight
They saw the baby Jesus lying on the hay
They fell to their knees, and started to pray
They thanked the dear Lord for His precious son
Then left to spread the word that the saviour had come
The magi came bringing frankincense, myrrh and gold
And they too found the baby Jesus a joy to behold
Then on their knees they thanked the dear Lord
And promised that they would always follow His word
And so at this special time, I think we too should pray
And thank the dear Lord for this wonderful day

Mildred R. Burns

Transition

I went to the Wall with a soul sick and tired,
Yearning for rebirth of spirit and mind ... Or Peace

Worn down at heart, couldn't make my life work
Life without heroes, without honor or right ... Or Peace

Arrived there at last, with my hopes and my fears
And the days flooded back, days of death, pain and war
All the ghosts were assembled, awaiting old comrades... and Peace

After nearly two decades I could see them there, waiting
Knowing sadness, and longing, but no longer hating
Standing in ranks on the far side of darkness,
Time stopped for them early, their promise aborted...
  Forever young

Stood there enchanted, saw men and boys, living
Before dreams were slain in War's mindless rage
Reflections of life in ebony stone panels
Echoes of voices, of laughter, and endings.

I added fresh tears to the rivers before me,
Walked from the Monument lighter in spirit,
With hopes for a better life, one with a purpose...
  And Peace

Tony Hamilton

The Carpenter King

He was born in a family not of great means,
Yet God was his father so he would become king.
He was threatened with death when he was but two.
However, Jehovah told Joseph exactly what to do
As just a young child getting strong and wise,
He kept his father's work in front of his eyes.
With John at the Jordan, God identified his son,
Who with unity and peace would make the world one.
All of the kingdoms of the earth, Satan did tell,
Jesus could have if, against God he'd just rebel.
After telling of God's kingdom as mankind's hope,
with terrible treatment and suffering he had to cope.
Finally with death on a torture stake,
He gave up his human life for all of our sake.
As king in the heavens he'll bring about God's will,
Upon the earth, a paradise to become still.
And peace, unity and love mankind will see,
For the days of a tree will the days of his people be.

Margaret St. George

dead cousin

remember you in the cold salty frothy
water sandy eyelashes and toasted noses
when asmahan told you how her boyfriend
liked to unclasp her bra to suck and bite and lick her raisined nipples
it was then squinting into a sunlight reflected off

bright white sands that you asked
god to forgive her and despite your horror you thirsted still for
the secrets and for the smiles and for the laughter
she handed you like the free leaflets
being passed out on the corner of telegraph

defying the benevolence of everyone's god
he who is crashing a wave of death on a nighttime
freeway where he is teasing your cousin's blue breath out of blue
lips and it is only you who will hate yourself for hating him whom
you once knelt before in prayer asking

for a single moment of assurance like you are now at 2 a.m.
heart slamming itself against ribs sweating within its confines
in a space whose darkness is like a gaudy fluorescent light
that reveals words written in blood on your bedroom wall
you have forsaken me god

mona abdelaziz

Find Yourself

The sun drifts over the eternal sands
falling gently into tomorrow's hand
time is so precious none to spare
knowledge is a jewel, ever so rare
sorrow lurks at every door
experience will guide you through much more
what is it that makes a blind man see
all your life you've held the key
look beyond the starlit night
don't dwell on what may or might
cowardliness should be banished when forming a tear
love comes easily when you have no fear
go...while the enemy hasn't a clue
time's slipping away and it won't wait for you

Kammae Owens

A Part Of A Great Love

Implosive thrills are the ultimate, passionate goals of any great lover
perhaps, the covetous goals is to mark how many successful sex scores
imitators envy and wonder what secrets great penetrators hover...
words? Drive? Wealth? Looks? Or just a list of B—S and classy
W——S?

How clever to seduce women and boast the conquests of virginity
only to remember, with the letter of the alphabet, each activity.
Which sex acts do you enjoy (all created foolishly) by a deity?
Many ignore the consequences of penetrating one's gift of chastity
others think it is normal to indulge in a gay's sexual fraternity
gays think they are normal, but only in a negative way of rear intensity.

Superficial or negative sex is a poor example of a spiritual love
how selfish just to seek pleasure ejaculating within a prophylactic glove
and then imagine two love souls copulating as one true love entity
while emulating the spiritual love-beats of a mind sighted deity.

Were Adam and Eve punished for acts of illiteracy or...adultery?
Romeo and Juliet were punished for loving deeply...was death too
simple?
Why God created a shortage of beautiful, sexy people is not a mystery,
however, it's the self image of creating an over abundance of ugly people.

God makes it so easy to be a great lover and X love and X love and X
love and X love, whereas, God makes it incredibly impossible to
be a part of a great love.

Carl B. Lordo

My Feelings Are Like A Single Rose

A rose is so soft, just like my heart.
My feelings are like a single rose all alone in a vase.
Feelings are delicate, just like a rose that
bloomed with few petals.
My feelings are like a single rose trapped inside a cage.
Love is now a memory, and beauty fades away.
Feelings are hurt so easily, just like a petal
pulled off of a rose and thrown away.
My feelings are like a single rose swaying
lonely in the breeze.
The last petal of the rose was blown off,
and with it, my feelings left me too.
I turn cold, and at the same moment,
the rose does the same.

Sabrina L. Altro

Untitled

Life can be made easy by you, or hard by you!
But whatever you choose, the path you take
will always be taken with someone else, he
will carry you, he will walk with you. Life's
special moments will come and go, but they
can, and will always be embraced in your
heart, and in your soul. His name is Jesus,
he is the son of God, He was sent by God to
forgive the sins of others, and to heal and
help the people who so badly needed him. His
powers were feared by others. His love that
he so freely gave, was not wanted by others. He
was killed, but his soul still remains
here with us all!!!!

Tabitha Ancell

10 Seconds

Hearts stopping
Picturesque purpleness pours over me
Hum, then sigh
Calming cool skyline of marshmallow violet
Splash!
Its royal deepness engulfs my soul into a violet
    terror, and smothers my fears.
I roll over to view your inner peace, and wait in
    the fuchsia mountains of fire
Reflections of you, seen in my past innocent shadow
Like a pane of glass the thick silence slices.
Don't move.
My eyes eat you up,
    too sickeningly rich to swallow.
Up ahead in the distance I see light.
Ten perfect seconds....alone

Pam Heckler

Empty Vessel

She stands by the sink
Scrubbing the lasagna off the pan
Wishing her dark skin were lighter
Her eyes were lighter
Her hair were straighter
Then someone else would have calloused hands, she reasoned
Someone else would sweat in this sweltering kitchen with no air
    conditioner
Someone else would struggle to pay bills and feed five kids
Someone else would live this life of despair
This life she can never escape
This life that consumes her very soul
Until she is nothing
But an empty vessel

MaConnia C. Chesser

608

Lovely Raindrops

Oh lovely raindrops you need not go,
we need you here to make things grow.

The rain clouds, they seldom stay,
They just circle and fly away.

Then that day will come when we say,
Oh lovely rain drops, please go away!

Sandra L. Hartman

Imagine...

Can you paint a picture in your mind and
always remember it until the end of time?
Is it a secret or does everyone know?
Are there flowers trees, or white
sparkling snow? Is it near or far; large
or small? Is it close to reality or by
far a dream? Whatever the thought take
the magical key and lock it deep inside
your heart.

Kyley Ingram

A Mother's Love

My Mother's voice so strong but kind
Never exits my troubled mind
Although miles and miles away
Her thoughts are with me every day

Nothing is missed more than a mother's love
Given to all Moms by God above
A helpful word a loving hug
Will sweep my crisis under the rug

I joined the army; she didn't object
Her face showed nothing but love and respect
With tears in her eyes, she said from the heart,
"Take care of yourself, son, while we're apart"

No matter what woman may come your way
Whatever she does or has to say
Remember my words when you're old and weak
For these words are true, I'm about to speak
There's but one love known by all to be true
And that my friend is your Mother's for you!!

Malcolm T. Ruffin

It's an addiction.
    F—k me...
May I touch you?
    F—k me...
May I kiss you?
rape lightly committed...
    I said yes anyway.
Mind-numbing insanity...
    I need...
A quickening of the senses...
    I hunger...
May I know you?
    F—k me...
All is granted.

Jennie Parnell

The Happy River

I saw a river flowing,
flanked by mountains, sky and trees.
I marveled at the beauty, yet,
in the midst of these,
the river had to travel a rough
and rocky course,
I watched it flow around the bend
o'er pebbles, rocks and rills,
What it could not climb it went around
With a steady rippling force.
With its pleasant, bubbling attitude
and its consistency,
The river gently flowing had this to say to me.
If you're present on life's path
and meet obstacles on the way,
Remember what I showed you
While you were watching me today.
What you cannot climb, go around
but, do it joyfully,
Trusting your creator, then, you too
shall be free.

Madeline E. Fava

I Was A Man

I was a boy—
in the mud, with dirt on my face.

I was a boy—
in the streets,
playing baseball.

I was a boy—
wearing dads' shoes,
pretending to be a businessman.

I was a boy—
screaming "cooties!"
when girls touched me.

I was a boy—
building legos,
making people and cities.

I was a boy—
thinking I was Superman,
and jumping off a roof.

NOW I AM A MAN—
WITH A JOB AND A HARD-ON,
F—KING MYSELF OVER AND OVER.

Dan Kaczmarek

One Night Stand

On any given day hard days hum smart justice saver life
press man check off class wick when you reach the tollbooth you
can take the short cut over the bridge crap you forgot the ski
mask! Remember you raped last week? She forgives you and
refuses to press charges free bridge access gang bang molested you
wind up rapist. Roulette your new prosthetic girdle makes it
easier than ever to rape! Multiple choice without alcohol you're
impotent frat party your state appointed psychiatrist refuse to
renew your thorazine prescription despite all that therapeutic
Cream your herpes infection continues to rage. The last woman
you raped asked for your phone number after it was over your
parole officer married your former victim metropolitan area a
sudden inexplicable wave of remorse overcomes you. Your
parents allow you to dip into the trust fund. You run out of
xanax right when you need to complete a freelance design project
your lover doesn't realize you're having an affair with the
espresso bar cashier you've always wondered how it would feel!
That Russian exchange student you f—ked six weeks ago has
tested positive for AIDS your karate instructor rapes you.

Stephen W. Mosley

Emotional Goodbye

One more chance to see you, I had to take
   yet knew a tear would fill my eye,
Your sparkled beauty I could not pass up
   for me this would be, an emotional goodbye.

I took a place at the table with you
   a romantic spot it seemed to be,
My place could not be next to you
   so that into your eyes, I'd be able to see.

We shared some laughs and good company
   over coffee that we sipped and drank,
How could I extend this time with you
   at this place near the river's bank.

Then came the brief and special moment
   when we could embrace and hold,
With the strong desire I had to kiss you
   yet, not to break the promise I'd told.

Finally we went our separate ways
   and as you left, the loneliness set in,
We waved goodbye and my heart did sink
   because I thought.. what if I never saw you again.

    Kevin Askam

An Empty Glass

The story is always the same
Yet only the faces will change
Life to you is somehow a game
You don't even realize the danger

I don't even recognize you anymore
Your face is a mask, your words are knives
Always cutting me right to the core
Tearing apart both of our lives

A lifeless body passed out on the couch
The smell of alcohol greets me at the door
I'm left wondering why and how
Which do you love more?

How can I even try to compete
With a bottle of Jack on a Friday night
When I fight but know that I'm already beat
Now I know that something isn't right

As I walk out the door and say so long
I wonder how long this will last
Before you realize that something is gone...
I'm not waiting at the bottom of your empty glass

    Lois H. Sanders

When All Is Said

When all is said and done,
Who will be the remembered one,

Will it be me, with my selfishness and pride,
Or will it be the One who's always by my side,

Will it be the frustration blown and tossed,
Or will it be Him who bears my cross,

Will it be the loneliness and all self pity,
Or Him who kneels and weeps for me,

Will it be the unhealed hurts and shattered walls,
Or will it be Him who constantly calls,

Will it be my fountain of tears,
Constantly walking for them who hear,

When all is said and done,
My Savior will be the One.

    Michelle Le

1:44 AM

My eyes flutter
yet, sleep does not carry me
to the sweet sanctity of dreams,
where I long to be,
cradled in the oscillating arms of oblivion and security.

Beyond struggle and fear
lies this realm of reverie,
ever eluding and beckoning me.
The night, void of sound, sans the cool whisper
of a faint breeze is louder and more unbearable
than a chaotic stampede.

Silence seeps from the cracks filling my room
taunting the bits I consist of.

Awake, in search of slumber but only greeted
by insomnia's unwelcomed harbinger,
I toss and turn
dishevelled blankets asphyxiate me.

Dragged past dreams to explosions of tears
and implosions of insanity.

    Merlevic Tamondong

Wall

The sheets come flowing
yet they do not touch me
for I am sheltered from their wrath.

A roof is over my head
and walls surround me
except for one, my vulnerable side.

They try to get me again and again
but these little water droplets are
not strong enough to pour down on me.

I have a roof; my pride,
my three walls; esteem, friends and
miscellaneous are all strong.

They know now my weak spot,
my unfinished wall; love.
He said there was no love in the first place,
he broke my heart.

The damp pellets now soak me
because of that vacant space,
that missing wall.

    Megan Market

Golden Strand

Bonded during the age of innocence
   you and I.

True friendships difficult to come by
   you a strand of gold
   our lives intertwined
   together or apart for years to come
   talk of the future as if life will never end.

Innocence lost as youth creeps away
   unprotected
   imperfect death
   your thread ripped from my life's tapestry
   unraveling before my eyes.

Strong is the fabric that remains
   a cloak of love
   comfort and understanding
   resurrecting hope as I heal
   memories take your place.

    Marianne J. Vergano-Laughton

You And I

You and I, a happy pair.
You and I, a grace to share.
You and I, to the world ahead.
You and I, the world we'll share.

How do we differ? What is our joy?
The world around us, has yet to be destroyed.
It's a wonderful mystery, we shall explore,
life is their, outside our door.
Love is clear, a bright new start, without dismay or depart.

You and I, a loving two.
You and I, we care, that's true.
You and I, a youthful pair.
You and I, the world we'll share

You and I, will be together, till death do us part, or even better.

Terri Lynn McLean

Light In My Life

You are the light in my life
You are the best thing in my life
Where did I ever find you
When will I ever find you again
Why did you leave me
Why did you go somewhere I can't
Tell me please will we ever meet again
Will we ever have what we had together
Are we destined to be apart
Why is that
What does life have to offer us
Happiness, sadness, numbness, sweetness
You were always there when I needed you most
What happened to cause this separation
I know what happened
We both started new lives that took different directions
Someday we'll meet again, someday
Until then live a happy life
Enjoy it for what it is
For it doesn't last forever.

Patricia A. Stephens

(Robin)

When the flowers blossom in early spring,
you can hear the robin sing.

He sings above the forest trees,
early in the morning breeze.

His nest is made of straw and sticks,
summer comes and goes so quick.

When the autumn leaves begin to fall,
no longer will you hear the robin's call.

J. E. Almeida

Poets

It's so fun to write Poems or Rhymes,
You can write about all kinds of times.
Like laughing and crying, silly things or sad.
Writing a Poem isn't so bad!
Especially when you write about the ones
You love, Or the Great one who gives
You love from above.
Writing Poems helps you express yourself.
Even when sometimes you live in doubt.
But wrong or right, happy or sad,
Write a Poem; it's not so bad.
Write about People and Love, and
the things you care for.
"What else is a Poet here for?"

Lorraine Boyd

Sleep My Brother

Sleep my dear brother, for you are now at rest,
You fought a good fight; you did your very best.
For now your feet touch where angels trod,
Sleep my dear brother, for now you are with God.

Dave, it was very sad to watch you slowly go,
But there was nothing we could do; this we now know.
We never thought you would be the one to get cancer,
But God pushed us along with the only one answer.

Sleep my dear brother, for you are now at rest,
As you left this world young, you have passed a great test.
Because our lives are planned and directed from above,
With all the caring God can give and all His great love.

So sleep my dear brother and when it's our turn,
You will be there for us and to help us to learn.
God called you home; it was in His great plan,
And we all know that He got a most wonderful man.

Sandra L. Siford

Inner Strength

In times of trouble, hopelessness and strife
When you're not really happy with what's become of your life
Search inside yourself - you won't have to look far
Behind all the clouds lies a bright shining star
That's you, that's the person you wanted to be
All your hopes, loves and dreams
Now it's easy to see
Things will be better - not just better, but great
Have trust and self-confidence
Be patient and wait
Soon those dark clouds will uncover your heart
You'll find happiness again with a fresh new start
Your life is your own
And only you
Can make it what you want
If you have the strength to see it through

Rosemary Kunz

The Lust Dragon

Such passions burn inside me
Would thou be my knight in shining armor
Carry me away to the enchanted forest
Lay me down gently and pierce me with thy sword
To slay the lust dragon churning within me
And ease me of my torture....

Nancy M. Peschon

One Last Dance

As I sit here waiting all alone, the music soft and sweet.
Wishing something badly for a guy to sweep me off my feet.
As I look around, the room is filled with couples that are
    in love.
While alone I sit, and wait, and hope and wish for a miracle
    from above.
I see him for a moment in my mind. Can he really be that
    hard to find?
If he's not here, is he there? Is he near or far away?
Does he live in a foreign land to this very day?
Is he sitting on the beach somewhere watching couples hand
    in hand? Is he wishing that I was by his side to grant
    his every demand?
Is he staring at the same bright star in the moonless night?
Does he hear the same song that I hear now, that I wished
    we'd danced to tonight?

Rachel Johnson

Moonlight

In times when your heart knows no ease,
When you feel it is everyone you must please,
Take a few moments alone in the night;
Look out your window up to the moonlight.
Open the window and there will blow a soft breeze;
Feel it surround you with the gentle rustle of the trees;
The moonlight will take you to a place peaceful as can be,
A place where your soul can be set free.
Release all the pain of everyday life;
Soar like an eagle with great height and strife;
Think of the one that fills you with love;
Set your heart free, free like a dove.
When life gets harder and harder to cope,
It feels like you are holding your last thread of hope;
Look up to the sky deep in the night;
Take a few moments and take hold of the moonlight.

Valerie Duckett

The Waterfall

Utterly loud
Yet soft and cleansing
Raging like thunder with nowhere to go
Into still water floating like a cloud
Whether or not someone's watching it goes on show
As proud as a father's glimpse into the eyes
Of his newly born son
Listen...Listen...It's almost musical
Moving like little soldiers on a mission
Over the rocks the water runs
On and on never knowing its intentions
Oh, how mother nature's most beautiful creations
Can calm the soul and soothe the mind
Yet are so untamed and wild.

Sandra White-Stevens

"Touched"

Every day is a new day and yesterday
will never be forgotten.
You've left us here without you, yet
without you we'll never be.
With you we have learned, to live today
and every day to its very fullest.
Waste not precious time, squabbling
about the past, it being unchangeable, don't
take for granted the present, it may only
be lived; for tomorrow is still unknown.
He who has passed and gone ahead
of us, alone we may seem.
Touching all who crossed his pathway,
his soul remains with us all and will always be.
Brought together as soulmates you'll
always and forever be.

Suzanne Woodfin

Smurfette

Smurfette is so sweet
With high heels on her feet.
She's cute and blue.
She does not smell like you.
She's small and nice.
She might not like mice.
Just watch out, you'll see, she could be like me.
She could like "Cocoa-Puffs."
She could like dogs, that go "Wruff, wruff."
I'm not so sure yet.
But, I'll find out, you bet!

Kimberly Mackanic

To A Maple Leaf On The Snow

Drifting, tumbling leaf of flame
Where were you dallying when winter came?
Did a autumn have you so beguiled
That, while she preened and cooed and smiled,
You drank her beauty to the fill
While winter forces took the hill?
Now all are snug and warm, save you
Who lingered for sweet talking to;
And as they rest beneath the snow
You, aimless as a truant, go.
Though winter winds and winter frost
Appear, all is not lost—
As winter breezes stall and start
Your dancing warms my winter heart.

Martia Penix

Untitled

Lying alone thinking of you, wishing you were here,
Wondering when the next time you'll appear.

Maybe you're gone for good,
Or would you stop by if you could?

I'm not sure if I should stay or go,
You just don't let your feelings show.

I feel so alone,
Because we only associate on the phone.

Your friends mean more to you than I do,
If this isn't true, then show me you love me,
like I love you!

Jennifer E. Baggett

Blanket

I see the chipped stair in a photograph
where I used to skip and delight
and reminisce in pleasant gauge,
but in lively color, not black and white,
(I forgive the photo for its age);
Until it occurs I don't recall
seeing or knowing its glaring chip
a defect faded, an artifact of change
the timeless notion endued to all
we who rattle at the gate;
knowing only few and cushioned thoughts
immersed in childhood, I was unaware
of the things outside reality invites,
but now I know and now I care.

Paul Camacho

Exiting

Glowing when she was born
With his small features and smile
They lit up the room together

His personality everyone knew
And she had it too
They knew him and her by name
Some would say, a copy of him
He was her father-

They tagged along and everyone knew the two as a pair
She was like the son who had died
They even learned to play football
And ride, drive, and get rid of guys together

Now she is grown...and on her own
She misses her adventures with him
But she continues
For she will always be his little girl-

Maria L. Andriola

Just A Man

I sit at my desk with pen in hand, trying to solve my problems with love, but I am just a man.

When you think that you have finally found that someone whom you would like to care for, someone else special comes along with so much more to share.

Of the different women in my life from which I must choose, I know down in my heart that I will always lose.

So here I sit all alone, with a decision to make and nowhere to turn. I know of no grand solution, and I have no master plan.

But the pain in my heart, and the tears in your eyes, make me wish that for once in my life, for you I could be more than just a man...

Ron Shepherd

Illusions Of Time

The seasons change,
With each of the yesterdays gone,
And all life continues
As the darkness brings nightfall.
Wandering the distance,
Stories are foretold, an imagination without words,
And time is somewhere lost in a drift,
Passing in the chilling wind.
Individual fantasies and perpetual dreams vanish,
And all realities fade.
All thoughts linger in the midst
Of a mystical labyrinth
Where all visible beauty remains
Only an illusion
And eternity becomes the duration from
Beginning to end.

Kathryn M. Yates

Vengeance

I'm really considering murder.
I want to shoot a bullet to your innocence taker, your loaded weapon.
I want to watch you grieve in your blood.
My nine millimeter justice maker, my solid silver world shaker.
If you hear a knock on the door don't worry it won't be me incognito.
With my body guard partner, grim reaper coffin keeper.
We'll laugh as you wallow in your death puddle.
I'll smile again and dream peacefully knowing your not out there pushing your old withered gun on someone else.
Disgusting them with your bald self, your deteriorating bald self.
Do you even understand what I write in my foreign tongue.
I'm back to seek vengeance!
I'm back as the monster you made me.

Monica Romo

Daffodils

Rose petals drift across a sea of oil and debris
daffodils linger in the fields of broken glass and sunshine
dewdrops fall onto tongues of children thirsty for affection
your world will soon be in their hands

Showers of curses rain down harshly from the mouths of young
innocent victims of the world, helpless and forgotten
hunger slowly fills their bodies- and their souls
my world will soon be in their hands

Leaves rustle softly in a land of deafening distress
a brilliant sky obscured by clouds shadows the little lambs
vacant smiles erase their pain, if only for a moment
our world will soon be in their hands

Heather E. Fogelman

My Window

My window to the world outside
Shows varied hues of fading light
On swaying flowers in a field
That usher in the coming night.

The coolness of the ocean's breeze,
A welcomed respite I extol,
Now gently blows across my face
Like ripples on the waters roll.

I look upon the bright array
Of stars against a darkened sky,
And wait to view in full display
The moon and planets passing by.

It comforts me to always know
My window's ever close at hand,
To conjure up those images
Of air, of seas, and pastured lands.

Those scenic views will someday change
Within man's whim to flex his will,
To change and foul the things unspoiled
Outside my precious window sill.

Kevin G. Rattliff

"The Forgotten One"

What is this constant tugging I feel?
The constant destruction of my soul
could it be the claws of satin
or the gracious hands of God
a child is trying to free herself from the burden of life
all life, Entire existence
the room is dark no stars shine bright
no children laugh and play one lonely soul sits
shivering, shaking, awaiting her death
if only... those words are the only words
that echo from one to wall, if only —

The bird surges into the luminous sky free at last
No more sorrow only forgiveness
sunlight rushes through her wings
flapping continuously

Freedom... the greatest gift of all
no more darkness a wonderful blue
taken into the gracious hands of God
The cold air revives the shaken soul
A morning soul... no more.

Melissa Jane Hedlord

I Thought Of You

I thought of you today,
    The sunny days at the beach
Where conversation flowed so easily
    And silence felt so comfortable.

I though of you today,
    The hours we spent at the museums
Comparing the relics of past lives
    And past thoughts to those of today
And discovering there is no difference.

I thought of you today,
    The nights we spent dancing
Listening to music that stirred thoughts
    And emotions as the hours drifted away.

I do not know where the path of life
    Has taken you, or what you feel or think
Or how you spend your time-you brought such
Joy to my life, I thought of you today.

Pat Mak

Untitled

Make-up on and brand new suit they cut my hair to make me cute
People gathered tears had flowed, even girls I didn't know
Mom and Dad had tears to share
Kind of late to start to care
Roses thrown upon my chest
Put real feelings to the test
My three best friends each kissed my hand
The only ones that could understand

Time went by, everyone was gone
Just two old men to carry on
They started to slowly set me down
A six foot ride beneath the ground
Dirt filled the hole, they didn't talk
I guess to them it's just a job all alone,
Not much has changed, they probably won't recall my name

Years gone by and I'm still here without a care,
without a fear my hair grew back, my nails got long
No one visits, same old song; that's okay though, no big thing
Gotta forgive to earn my wing, my skin has rotted and left no sign
Of the scars on my wrists so I'm doing fine

Kevin D. Manning

I Am Woman, An Enigma

I am the weaker sex,
One who has born the pain of childbirth, once and again

I am the spendthrift,
One who has managed to feed entire families on shoestring budgets

I cannot manage,
On who has kept generations of households from faltering

I am fragile,
One who has endured awesome mental and physical anguish only to
rear my head even higher

I must be protected,
One who has hovered and protected her young with the fierceness
Of a lioness

I am powerless
One for whom some have abdicated their throne, and for whom
Others have lost their throne.
I am woman, an enigma.

Charlease L. Johnson

Life's Bloom

In bloom at last, a flower opens wide
And tiny buds bow down their humble heads.
For this their simple lives were meant to be
A smile, a hint of joy among the weeds.

O teach me all the secrets you enclose,
Inside your vibrant petals filled with pride,
Of dewy dawns and stormy evening rains,
As bravely you have strained to meet the sun.

Are you aware of nature's cruel design
To bend your healthy limbs and dull your hue
Till down to earth you fall in utter shame
And all that you once were is soon forgot?

Perhaps tis not for you to see this pain.
Your bud was blind to all but promised joy,
Your flower sees the light of sky alone,
And knowing might destroy your fragile strength.

So hold your head towards heaven's grand visage,
And leave your seeds with us on earth's small stage
For we can only envy your true bliss
And pray we shine as bright before our death.

J. L. Shelton

Wisdom

It came to me in a sense of fear
    Deep in the dark of night
Frightened too much to shed a tear
    Kept wisdom out of sight

I walked around, followed by sound
    Which I cannot describe
Wisdom is something I haven't found
    It must be set aside

Step out into the starry sky
    Looked up to finally see
If only I were able to fly
    Find wisdom; wisdom for me

Living without it is tough, you see
    Answers; I am not aware
Not totally puzzled with stupidity
    But anything comes to scare

Help me find what I'm looking for
    That is running from me now
Wisdom; without it I am just a bore
    Don't ask, I do not know how

Teddy N. Gann II

Dark Side

He hits you like it's nothing, and plays stupid little games.
He has no outlook on life; no fortune or fame.
He toys with your heart; it breaks again and again.
He tears you apart, limb by limb.

No conscience; not loyal or free.
He lies and he cheats; but never lets you see.
He's kind and faithful; trusting and true.
A front made up for only you.

One fateful night it all explodes.
He beats you in front of all he knows,
As you cry and plead; while you suffer and bleed.
He laughs in your face and then continues his chase.

So far from reality no hope for a cure.
It would take one strong woman
Heart entirely pure.

Soft spoken and tender, learns to stay out of sight.
Prepares and enhances for that one Final Fight.
One night - He will go too far.
One night - He will lose it all.

Michelle Settle

On The Road To Glory

Working For Our Lord
    Is going on the road to glory
Yes, helping others, in their need.
    For, our Lord, sees all the story.
Doing for others, keeps us busy
    Age is no barrier.
Ask, and it shall be given.
    Strive for Jesus in you,
To make a name in Heaven.

At times it may not be
    Just what you want.
Ask, Gods will in all things
    You would like to do.
He will give the green light
    to those whose heart is right.
Working for God, is teaching others
    about Jesus love for us, and forgiveness
Helping others as we see their needs
    No other thing can compare to-
Jesus tender loving care.

Bessie Doolittle

To Him

A piece of my soul feels left back in winter
like a torn black plastic bag blown against a fence
near a tree in a faraway fallow field.
Dead dried grasses nod spastically in aimless gusts of wind.
An old can blows across the road and
its hollow, lifeless sound gets grabbed up
by an angry fist as fuel for further ragings.

The craggy gnarled oak stands alone,
creaking arthritic complaints to no one
as its dead dried leaves cling
to branches like old scales.

There is no life here. There are no songs.
The liquid of living, the nurture of greening,
the softness of blueness, and the brilliance of light
are like the memory of a perfect dream.

Who dares to tread the cracked, hard-packed soil
through razor brambles along the rusty fence row,
towards the guarding, loathsome tree
to retrieve the neglected refuse?

....she who wishes the spring to come once more!

Lynda Fisher

Hold All Bets

Getting ready for work today.
  What to wear?
  Ordinary slacks, twelve dollars a pair
  Sweater bought on special
Shoes nondescript — All set.

Driving in to work today.
  College town with little passion
  Girls walking 'round flashing in fashion
  Daddy's girl, Mother's angel
Prep-school types, well dressed — Not impressed.

Sitting down to work today.
  Hard work, minimal pay
  What I wouldn't give to play
  But I dig in, work hard to be successful
The cards stacked against — Hold all bets.

Getting home from work today.
  Having quite a discussion
  Speaking with my husband
  How hard we work despite the label
The stereotype lies — Generation X.

Maureen Ivusic

Just Passing Through This World

I'm just passing through this world
  with all its joy and pain,
with all its lovely memories,
  its sunshine and its rain;
I may have stopped just long enough
  to meet a friend or two,
but no one else has meant as much
  to me, my friend, as you;
I'm just passing through this world
  and though I don't know why,
I would have missed so many things
  as years go drifting by;
The stars that fill the endless skies,
  the darkness of the night,
The way you look into my eyes,
  the chance to hold you tight;
I'm just passing through this world,
  I don't have long to stay,
And yet somehow I'm glad that I
  chanced to walk this way.

Peggy Stevenson

Ironic

The universe has encountered endless peacemakers,
and still harmony has not descended upon us.

The peacemakers have brought the peace offering of
the olive branch, and still serenity has not
descended upon us.

The maker descended in a peace offering as a dove,
for a peace-loving universe, and still we did not
perceive to ascend to the irenicon that confront
us, but we assassinated that which is puissant.

The peacemakers brought the pipe of peace for truce,
and still it has not descended upon us.

World wars have come to pass, and global wars have
departed, but pacifism in humanity has not descended
on us, for poverty and starvation are ascending upon everybody.

The peacemakers brought inner peace,
but they could not pacify us,
to lay down our arms, and turn our swords
into plowshares, for peace of neutrality is
so enormous to descend upon humanity, for they
cannot perceive, that which is so ironic.

Vivian Parris Mastrantonis

Unceasing Love

Oh unceasing love thy remedy last,
Of pain and sorrows of distant past,
Thy arms embrace me with passion sweet,
Our kiss of fire when lips meet,
I cherish each moment, each second, each day,
In your loving warmth I want to stay.

How I praise the Gods for the things they made.
And he made you like a flower the best that won't fade,
Your voice in soft breath of love you speak,
You strengthens my soul, my heart is not weak.
You're like the night but your secrets I've known,
My love and my life to you I own.

I eat of your fruit, yes, I gladly ate,
To have you each night I can hardly wait,
Now my soul's content,
My heart overflow,
All my energy is spent,
To show how I love you so.

Gary McDougall

Mr. Robinson

Why can't you love me, Mr. Robinson?
You make love to me with your body,
but you will not love me in your heart, or your mind.
You will not love me with words.

Is it your wife, or my husband?
We four are friends; we go to movies, and dinner.
We two are lovers; we go to movies, and dinner, and bed.

Why can't you love me Mr. Robinson?
Through all these long years, watching our children grow.
Through new jobs, and new homes, through illness and separation,
You have made my life bearable, and I yours.

We present to the public what they want to see,
and keep the reality to ourselves.
Would it not seem that marriage itself keeps us apart?

Why can't you love me, Mr. Robinson?
A man of few words, hurt, and afraid.
I, too, am hurt, and afraid,
but I trust you, with me, my needs, my dreams.
But I need words, Mr. Robinson, I need words.
I love you.

Wendy Peters

My Prayer

As I sit here in tears, sad and alone -
I miss a place I once called home.
I may never, ever live there again -
Hoping against hope - maybe I can.
The faith in my heart won't fade away -
I'll prove my innocence, somehow-someway.
It seems like forever that I've been waiting -
For someone to believe what I've been saying.
I'm not a genius - I'm not dumb, -
I can't give up 'til the lock's undone.
With heart in pain and soul in tears -
My new home, this cell for untold years.

Through the shut window and through the locked door -
I'm sending my prayer hopefully - Lord.

My family, dear family, please wait for me -
I wait to come home, I wait to be free.

Dorleena Kay Kolakowski

Asleep In Our Beds

Oil rises to the surface
A cry from those below
Remember us to all who do not know
Hey boys, don't let it happen again!
We'd like to think our deaths taught you something in the end
Never concentrate your forces in one place
Never fool yourself into thinking that you're safe
Friend can become enemy in the blink of an eye
Watch your back or you'll surely die
Let the Arizona be your guide
Remember her sacrifice and those who within her lie
For we look up to you from the water's depths
"Preserve America!" Our dying breath

Kelly Steed

Grandmother

I feel so sad I've lost something
precious that I had. She was my
grandmother, she was my friend.
Now I'm so sad; she played a special
part in my life and in my heart.
Now she's gone but always there no
matter what. She made me laugh, she
made me cry. Will I ever have her
back? I never got to say good-bye.
She'll always know she's in my
heart and memory because she was
a special part of me.

Kelly R. Higgins

The Search

I sat alone by the sea one day.
The lichen formed Patterns on the rocks above,
I waited for Him to show me the way,
Lovely, longing to be immersed in love.
I recalled, vividly, how it all began.
I remember well, one love sea bird,
A voice crying and weeping; I ran,
And stopped along the sea wall, pondering what I heard.
At dusk I wondered if the voice were real.
If I had willed what I wanted to hear.
Using a rock as an altar, I bent to kneel,
Needing to rid myself of any and all fear.
I know now the voice weeping had been my own.
I had been waiting for something that had no name.
Soon, my voice cries out and I begin to man.
Cleansing, purging myself of all the pain.
And God Hears

Doris Lindsey

"Jesus, I Want To Follow You"

Jesus, I want to follow You.
Yes, I do, want to follow You.
I cannot see You, nor can I feel You,
And I will never understand You...
But still, I want to follow You, Jesus...
I need a friend until the end...
Show me the way, Jesus, day by day...
I cannot see You, nor can I feel You...
And I will never understand You...
Yet, I love You, Jesus...
Teach me the Truth, Jesus, I want to follow You...
Live in me, and let me live in You...
Without You, Jesus, I can do nothing...
With You, I can do anything...
Jesus, I want to follow You...
Yes, I do, really want to follow You, Jesus!

James Joseph Fiatarone
President/Founder Fiat Music Co.
Fiat Records

Winter Fantasy

White snow glides silently down from a black sky and muffles
all sound, imparting a mystic aura to the night;
Dappled streetlights enhance the feeling of being in a
remote, peaceful world. Feelings which I attempt
to capture and retain;
Trapped in the middle of this serene magic,
I feel both elated and sad;
Time is frozen; an inaudible, soothing vibration fills the air;

Brian T. Allen

Mary In White

Mary in white, lady so blue:
Ask your Son's Father what we must do!
Our morals were good, our horror was strong.
But troubling years have come along.

Mary in white, Lady so blue:
Heroine, cocaine and marijuana, too!
We are floundering, yet must have our kicks,
Angel-dust madness—porno-sex flicks.
Mary in white, Lady so blue:
Violence, crime and greediness, too!
The dollar's our idol worshipped on high—
"In God We Trust" seems almost a lie.

Mary in white, Lady so blue:
Contradiction, confusion, so disbelief, too!
Searching for truth, our struggle's hard fought—
Often to find it's all been for naught.

Mary in white, Lady so blue:
Ask your Son's Father what we must do!
Lord God above, cleanse us somehow—
Turn us around, and grant we start now!

Dorothy M. Floreck

Untitled

Where is truth?
Everywhere I turn I am looking for truth
As soon as I think I find it
it is a lie in disguise
What is Truth?
Something I continue to look for
and cannot find
in my innocence
I long for truth
in wisdom
I fear it

Ann Kagarise

About My Grandma

Snow is beautiful
Because it looks like my Grandma's hair
Like you wished for a million years
Shines like a falling star
My Grandma looks like clouds
Because she is so beautiful
My Grandma is like a flower
Her eyes twinkle like a sunflower.

William Myers

Divisions Of The Spirited Judgment

When the remaining soul has been summoned,
The earth, a bare remnant, will be lonely.
Division of the virtued from the sin.
Desirables rise to Utopia.
The Contemptible rove endless fires.
A sun which once sustained all the earth's souls,
Now executes torment eternally.
All the good contained is scorched from your soul.
A demonic plague burns recollections,
The memories of beauty and love lost.
Cold and torment absorb this failed corpse.
It's not a soul, but a temple of the devil.
The soul of a good man is rewarded.
Temptation is a relic of the left.
Pain is a distant memory not found.
The bliss reflected upon arrival
Protected love binds all of the chosen.
What will I, this infant of man be called?
Could I, on this day, be named a sinner,
Or chosen and named one of the blessed.

Adam L. McGough

"Love Is A River"

Love is a river that never stops flowing.
With a little patience...
Love, like a river, will never stop growing.

A love in one's life means never to be alone.
Just as water is to a river.
Your love is never gone.

Just like on a river of water, with its many currents.
Love will continue.
If you have a little faith and endurance.

You can or may Dam a river,
But if you try to Dam Love,
You may never be Delivered!!

Bruce L. Gibson

"My Florida Rainbow"

'Tis raining while the sun shines
Oh! what a beautiful day.
As the clouds are pushed aside
A Rainbow comes out on display.

Its colors glide across the gulf
With each wave I watch them entwine
The sparkle, glitter and reflection
Brings to me "Tranquility Divine."

My eyes drift far in the distance
The sky and the water become one
The feeling is "Supreme Ecstasy"
In the rain, the sand and sun.

The water's edge is Oh! so quiet
While the sandpipers run in glee
I dream away with happy thoughts
A delightful moment at "Casey Key"

Mary L. Gonterman

Youth Chained

Metal whispers, dry ears wet with ignorance
young, they cannot hear what floats upon the breeze
they joke and laugh, wear pants around their knees
finding strength in acting cool
but each boy's skeleton hides within his closet
like rubber in the cement of his cell

cutting eyes from passers-by, seem to warm
the months they serve
small sentences are fodder in the face of fun
and that's how it'll be until they fall again
and years become like mice which chew the toes
from the feet of freedom
years which make the chain link fence become skin
and synchronize tumblers closing
to the rhythm of their heartbeat
then they'll hear their laughter crying in the wind
and see their cool swallow whole
the sharpened strands of wire
then they'll realize that winter is not cold
compared to the eyes which peer from beyond the bars.

Samuel P. Evans

A Special Dad

Heavenly Father! You bring about Dads
Make mothers, too, and lassies and lads

I pray that all fathers though earthly they be
May search for all truth - so to live more like Thee

Give dads open ears - to listen - to hear
Truth from the book that all need to hold dear

Give dads the voice to lisp rightfully prayer
Give dads the strength to believe you are there

Give dads the lips to admonish like Thee
Their charge is special - like yours is to me.

D for distinctive - so unique dads give
Like mothers - the trainers - so children life live

So Father! Their pattern please help dads portray
Like you - the great teacher - good - beautiful - a stay!

So each lad and lassie discerns good from bad
Because their example was a special dad!

Let's hear it for father - our Dad on his day
You're ours and we love you both now and for always!

Bessie S. Burkett

"Yester-Days"

Where has yester-day gone
The wind, the snow and the rain?
Where has yester-day gone
The flowers, the birds that sing?

Where has yester-day gone
The youth, the old and the new?
Where has yester-day gone
In time there will only be a few.

Where has yester-day gone
The laughter, the friendship and trust?
Where has yester-day gone
Did we trade them for pleasure and lust?

Where has yester-day gone
We look, we ask, we seek,
Where has yester-day gone
The moments, the hours, the weeks

"Where has yester-day gone?
Hazel Fern Gibson

A Froggie Moral

A frog, all alone,
on a green lily pad.
A frog all alone,
happy, sad, or mad?

Who can tell?
No one cares,
but just one,
and she stares.

The frog looks up,
and he starts to talk,
Croak after croak,
and away the girl walks.

Now alone again is that frog,
and not mad, but hince,
if the girl would have turned,
she'd have seen no frog, but a prince.

But alas, you miss out,
if you do not care,
for something you'd love,
would be right there.

Barbie Hall

Hero

My Hero is true,
Not a myth full of wonder,
Or a story bound by fiction,
My hero is much more than this.

He is the man who fails at the moment of truth.
She is the woman who gives more than just a kiss.

It is the animal who preys on the weak.
The martyr who takes his own life day after day.

This is my hero,
Who is trapped in a world of decay.

My hero bleeds when evil runs free.
My hero cries when a prayer is denied.
Yet my hero speaks with a sharp twisted tongue.

A hero may be weak when he is expected to be strong.
A hero may choose foolishly, when he knows that he is wrong.

This hero of mine is real.
He is completely perfect this way.
My hero is human.
And he dies for me, everyday.

Joseph R. Brown

The Unknown

When a darkness falls upon my eyes,
I think of the lifetime left I must endure.
And clasping my hands to my heart,
I lift my head to the sky.
"Deceptive spirits,
you confuse to no end,
and I am prey to your vicious game.
Do I pray in vain to a God unknown,
or are my prayers answered in ways unseen?"
Down to my knees, I eternally fall,
and beg for understanding
in this world of destiny damned.
When the sun rises, I will face my fear,
and the moon will guide no more.
I stand as the sun lifts its head to the sky,
and perhaps it suffers the same perils as I.

Kristen E. Dow

Someone Else's Home Place

There's a log cabin set back in the wood,
That was once a family's home.
There's a swing that hangs from the hickory tree,
With honeysuckle vine - the yard's overgrown.

That honeysuckle has a fragrance,
That gently floats past my nose.
The vine holds a bird's nest-secluded well,
I've seen the birds come and go.

A shutter hangs by one hook,
The door has been left ajar.
Out behind this homeplace,
The rusty remains of a car.

I wonder where all the people have gone,
I know children used to live there.
I can't understand why people would leave,
This wonderful place with no care.

Perhaps someday the children'll return,
And recall the remember when's.
And maybe return it to its original shape,
And hopefully—won't leave it again.

Helen Gibbons

Mom, Not Just A Word

Mom, one of the words most taken for granted
We say it without ever a care
Mom, the most beautiful of all people
When no one is left, she is still there.

Mom took the job though it was hard
And with the sun came rain
If ever she regretted it
I never heard her complain.

She had no guaranties
The lessons were so few
Though too many hours were thankless
Her unrelenting love was the glue.

Other people who carry this name
My son's wives, my mother-in-law
How blessed I am, when I think of them
I have to stand in awe.

For all the moms who are out there
And thought about today
My dearest mother, I can't thank enough
My Mother's Day, is everyday.

Joyce C. Wolf

Broken Years

Come, my cherished one, Let's take leave
of this dusty little town, and make our
dreams become reality.

Too many years have gone by, and many tears
have ran down our faces, over the broken years
we have lost to each other, and the untimely
departure of our love.

Let's recapture the innocence that we once
knew, and the honesty that only we shared
with one another.

Youth is gone, and like grains of sand, our
life is slipping through our hands. We are
so much older, yet so much wiser.

So as the sun sets so proudly over the mountains,
I want to be there with you, and hold to your
precious hand, and place my head on your chest
and silently love you all over again.

Misty Evans Kidwell

Fade Away

In Memory of LeNora Candee
Clear they are now,
   Like footprints in the sand.
But soon they may fade away,
   Like water in your hands.
People standing around your bed,
   With beeping noises in your head.
Now that they are gone,
   Sorrow is in the air.
But remember,
   Their spirit can go everywhere.
So don't put off 'til tomorrow,
   What you could do today,
   Because before you know it,
   They may fade away.

    Sarah Candee

"Enough Time"

I have seen the beginnings through to their ends -
My mind plays the tape of life and strife,
Inside, outstands the image of rare friends -
"Memory's so deep" it's all a sword,
The double edged knife!

No bitterness to harbor, no more pain or rage,
Just pass me by's left alone somewhere dark
and cold, in the land unknown without
understanding - "The invisible cage"

Never the lest there's still the dreams
of power - "so very bold"
In a winner's way - sometimes not ever missing -

Like the wind on a chime -
Do I remember forever,
   Enough time. . . .

    Perry Jones

A Grandmother's Eulogy

So it's time to say goodbye, my how time does fly, seems only yesterday I was a child safe in your arms free from all harm.

This won't be easy for me, my only solace will have to be You're up there somewhere your spirit free smiling down still helping to see.

Free at last to see the Master who once parted the Red Sea, the Master you served so well even to the worst when your health failed. In your life, in your example and now in your death he still prevails.

Memories of you will have to be enough, memories of life as God meant it to be, a childhood I treasure because of a love you gave without measure.

You once young yourself handpicked by the Almighty a soft of love, a rose he chose for all of us. A woman you soon became, not destined for fortune and fame, instead much suffering and pain.

A mother of six, left torn and widowed at thirty-six. A tragedy few of us today would know how to fix. A cold cruel winter had arrived, how would a lonely widow survive? In this your dark hour God proved His power, you were still his little flower.

You are the mouth of this river that now flows deep and wide, we are your on-going pride, our love for you will never die and we know the angels are on your side. Your face you'll not have to hide. Suffering you shall see no more as God opens for you His door.

May this circle go unbroken our love for one another serve as the token. We must each finish our own race to once again see your sweet face.

    Patricia Gail Hollier

"Forever Friends"

Dedicated to Mike Jordan - mentor and friend
Friendship is something that cannot be measured
   in spans of time or miles;

Rather, a good start would be to consider the moments
   of sadness and smiles.

A friend is someone you cannot reject when an honest
   request has been made;

It's someone who really cares enough to "take time"
   without being paid.

Taking time to speak, or listen; or simply
   taking time to "be there".....

When a friend does this, there should be no doubt that
   your friendship is sincere.

"PREDESTINED WEAVING" is how, I believe, that
   true friends are brought together.

And once as established as friends through God,
   you truly are friends forever.

    Barbara Williams

Crime And War

We dream of happiness,
And of the one we love to recognize us,
But our crime is waiting for it.

I try to live my life peacefully,
Without shedding a tear, and also,
My crime is starting a war with my fears.

You see, life is not our stepping stone,
Nor is it our freedom,
We are still caged in our own little world,
Of disappointments,
Lost of love,
And a need of material things.

But to me,
And my interpretations,
This is our crime,
That starts our war.

    Tiffany Lee Stokes

Love

Close my slate eyes,
concealing the fiery heart aflame,
when fresh, pungent tears stream down,
aiding to explain.

Such a vulnerable mind cannot erase,
nor should desire,
a frank, impersonal caress, leaving
bittersweet fire.

In blinding agony, I sank my head low,
much in a subdued fate,
to heal the deep wounds,
this love has made.

In response to my wail, the Lord came to me, and bellowed
like so,

"Wake up, time to end such a dream my dear,
this love was not meant for you to know."

    Sandra Lee Mackowski

"O. J. The Juice"

On the football field he
cut loose. Ran many touch-
downs. The crowd roared and
all called him, "The Juice." He
gained money, fame, and glory.
He was a national idol, so the
story goes. He retire from football
and went to T.V. Ran through
bus terminals and air terminals.
Then the higher up started
calling him, "The Juice." He was
the toast of the town, now he's
down. Now prosecutors and all,
are squeezing "The Juice"

Minister James E. Vanderhorst

A Father's Day Prayer

Lord I woke up this morning
with Jesus on my mind.
The world seems so full of hatred
and we his children are so unkind.
I cannot help but wonder how we
derived in this state of mind.
When our God is so wonderful and loving
and showers us with blessings of every kind.
So I stumbled out of bed and fell on my knees,
to thank him for this precious life of mine.
So I vow that I will serve him in every way I can,
that my life will be a blessing
and make me a better man.

Eugene Stockton

Embryo

Living in a warm death,
contemplating nothing,
beginning of the ending:
I dissolve away.

Leaping into thought now,
dreaming of all thoughts,
towards the end, my beginning:
I dissolve away.

Two eyes before me and
God says to me:
Why have you come?
You're far too young.
And as I held His tears:
I dissolved away.

Alexander James Walsh-Rule

My Wife - My Life - My Valentine

So many times I have heard it said
If a man finds a wife he truly is Blessed!
A companion & friend to share his whole life,
To be there forever, through wrong and through right!
When the load is light and everything's great,
And when it's so heavy there seems no escape;
When the sky turns black and the storm rages wild,
She can make the sun shine with just a sweet smile;
Just How, When, or Where may not be clear,
But Her Love is the Conqueror and there's no need to fear!
She stands in the shadows so that I may shine;
Always assuring she'll be there for all time.
These words I have written, they're Just, True, and So!
I do Love my Valentine and I want her to know
From the depths of my being and just not for show!
Whether there's Twelve or just One She truly deserves

The Rose

A Mother In Pain

Pain and sorrow have riddled this life,
Wounded with guns, loaded with strife.
They show no mercy, no one is spared
From the hurt and tears stay prepared.
The battle is raging, the wounded are great,
The ground is bloody red, the weapon is hate.
A gash so deep, the cut; to the bone.
Such injury is caused by word alone.
A heart is broken, its precious blood draining out,
The loss of love; someone very dear, no doubt.
Over the soul a darkened cloud now dwells,
a sadness so binding, it has become a jail.
Weakness is spreading from one limb to another,
Without the food of love each for the other,
Surely death is near, if no help is found.

As the minutes tick quickly away,
The darkness signals the end of day.
I think of the days, joys and sorrows.
Careful to keep memories for the tomorrows.

Machelle Pierce

Starry Starry Night

Starry starry night, You took your life delight
You gave the world more than your flame
You gave the world your name
If we only listened with our eyes and ears
there be one less tear
It was your words of wisdom we did not understand
Instead of arguing we should have lent a hand
You were crying inside
it was your whole life and feelings you were trying to hide
All those words full of hate
Was your death our fault or was it fate?
Even as a kid your life was taken for granted
So on that starry starry night you did the only thing you knew how,
If you only know what we know now
So the story goes...Heroes are remembered, but legends, legends
never die

Lacey O'Brien

Memorial Roses And Candles

The room slowly darkens and all eyes turn to the table
with sixteen lighten candles.

The sounds of taps echo through the large room.
Memories are recalled of long ago.

Men with gray hair listen to the notes of taps and
remember friends who fell in battle.

The sounds of war return in our minds with vivid
clarity. The faces of friends with their youthful
smiles, memories of camps, of the long marches, and
training, return.

A voice speaks and the first TIGER Unit is called.
The bearer of the Rose steps to the front of the
table with the brightly burning candles.
He places his unit's Rose - extinguishes the flame -
steps back - and salutes the fallen.

The voice speaks again and again, until sixteen
Roses are placed at the base of all the candles, which
remain extinguished for another year.

But not in our Hearts.

Donald McKirdy

If Only

How precious you are oh my little child,
How innocent are your bright blue eyes.
My first was when I was young and wild,
If only I had known this worlds lies.

My love for my first child is so dear,
Those pretty blue eyes grew up so fast.
I was seeking fulfillment and a career,
If only I could change the past.

Oh little one, what joy you bring,
Your smile brings laughter to my heart.
I no longer seek out worldly things,
If only I knew we would never part.

I love to see you run and play,
What a struggle you had to get here.
I seek life now in a different way,
If only the world could see my tears.

My years have added up you know,
Yet now my life is a jubilation.
Pray I will live to see you grow,
If only the world could join in celebration.

Dawn Marie McCandless

I Miss You

I miss the way you pleased me so
with your sensational style of love you
once gave me. I can recall the nights
When I have fallen of my throne of
greatness. You were always there to lend me
an ear and give me advise. You would
also find some way to make me get
back on my throne of greatness.
I can also recall the times when we
would meet in the park, which put a
spark into my life. I would love to see
the day from whence we can be together
once again. I tried my best
to rest in my empty nest, but I cried.
For I am still missing you. I must set the
times right. For I have finally put the
past behind me.

Nalime Van Benz

Dreams

Your dreams could be about many different things. And so
can your reality it seems. Your dreams could be about a peaceful
way of living or it could be about searching for New Adventures
But your reality is knowing that you have to live on welfare
and for others it's their strive not to end up there.
Your dreams could be about a easier way to pay your rent or
it could be about pretending you are the president.
But your reality is knowing that you will soon be evicted and for
others it's knowing that someone they love has become addicted
Your dreams could be about having a love affair and for others
it could be about just simply taking that dare.
But your reality is knowing for you there is no one who really care
and for others it's knowing that they have done their fair share.
Your dreams could be about having the skills to operate the latest
machine or it could be about a life of leisure riding in a limousine
But your reality is know that the life you live is unfulfilled
and for other it's knowing that they may have to skip some meals
But your dreams and realities can sometime be the same
it all depends on how well they are arranged

Rosie L. Miller Mars

White Blanket

Frosty is my window pane, as is yours, I'm sure.
The snow has drifted upon my roof-cold, soft, and pure.
And even within my dark, night-captured room
I can see the whiteness of it all.
Perhaps if I look a little closer, I might faintly hear it fall.

Early at dawn, we all shall awake
Beneath this enormous comforter of white.
It has been laid here deep in the dark
To protect us from the dangers of night.
Although I won't be afraid of whatever may come;
I won't become frightened, or panic, or run.

As long as my snow is here with me, I can conquer all things
That try to slow me down; I will fight what it brings.
For my snow has a magic that is its, all alone.
It knows me not, yet loves me-
And all I need is it...my own.

Jill Huff

"Forget You By The Dawn"

You move me every day and night,
  Like the moon controls the tide.

You contaminate my every thought,
  There's no place for me to hide.

What is this spell you've cast on me,
  You've put me in a trance.

Every time I look at you,
  My heart breaks with every glance.

You must release me, set me free,
  I can't let this pain go on.

I only pray for this one thing,
  Let me forget you by the dawn.

Dan Wear

'Daniel's Prayer' (A song)

Does He see me, under the fig tree
Crying to Jesus
Does He know who I am?

Does He see me, under the fig tree
Crying to Jesus
Does He know who I am?

Oh, it hurt me so bad
Only He knew
All the problems I had
Cast me down to its roots.

Yes, He saw me, under the fig tree
Tears falling down
Weeping, sobs of despair.

And He brought me
To the place of rejoicing
Joy overflowing, in His love.

Esther M. Thomas

Biographies
of
Poets

ABDALNASER, AL-SHORBAJEE
[b.] August 25, 1965, Jordan; [p.] Hadieh Al-Shorbajee, Adnan Al-Shorbajee; [ed.] B.A. (Hons) English Literature, M.A. (Hons) English Literature from Sindh University - Pakistan, Diploma in French Language, Jordan; [occ.] High School English Teacher at Amman's Government Schools.; [hon.] Merit Certificate in Creative Writing from the Department of English - Sind University, Pakistan; [oth. writ.] 1. Deception, a piece of poetry that describes the nature of woman, 2. Thomas Hardges Pessimism, 3. Emerson's Unitarianism in his essays. The articles were published in the University Magazine, Unimag; [pers.] I believe that we must cling one and all to the rope of God and let nothing divide us, because life is full of sorrow and grief and except in God we will never find our relief.; [a.] Chicago, IL

ABERNATHY, KATHLYNE
[b.] September 29, 1971, Fairmont, WV; [p.] Raymond and Donita Abernathy; [ed.] Pearl Cohn High, Volunteer State Community College; [occ.] Office Manager/Investigator ASE, Inc.; [hon.] Honorable discharge from United States Air Force; [pers.] My inspiration has come from life and loves lost. I hope people will read my writings and know that brighter skies lie ahead.; [a.] Nashville, TN

ACHUTHAN, RADHAKRISHNA M.
[b.] November 19, 1935, Madras; [p.] N. Radhakrishna Menon, Sree Devi Menon; [m.] Nisha Sahai Achuthan, May 28, 1981; [ch.] Lakshman, Arjun, Mahima; [ed.] Ph.D. The Union Institute, Cincinnati, Ohio 45206, M.S. (Physics) Mis. (Electrical Engineering), Univ. of Missouri, Columbia, MQ; [occ.] Professor Physics, Long Island University, Southampton, NY, 11968; [memb.] Current or Past: 1. Indian Sociological Society, Bombay, India, 2. India International Centre, New Delhi, India, 3. Association for Childhood Education International, 4. World Future Society, 5. American Association of Physics Teachers.; [hon.] Several Grants for Sociological Research in India.; [oth. writ.] Several research articles published on Sociology and Rural Primary Education in India.; [pers.] Each of us, even in independence and hence always, is in an ongoing partnership with others, whether these others be members of our family, our peers, or those in the network of broader community institutions, the validation of our expression is finally dependent on the community. We must care and give in caring to man and the values he struggles to espouse on behalf of nature. We must extend ourselves to those who stand in need that is poorly met from the well springs of reciprocal altruism.; [a.] Southampton, NY

ADAMIAN, MARINA
[b.] January 23, 1956, Tehran, Iran; [p.] Souren and Knar; [m.] Hamlet Adamian, March 31, 1995; [ch.] Ara Keshishian 17, and Garen Keshishian 14; [ed.] High School Diploma in Biology from Iran, Art History and Painting Certificate from Italy, Currently enrolled in Glendale Community College.; [oth. writ.] Published poetry in local papers in Iran and also in some Persian Magazines in LA few years back, write in Farsi, Armenian and English - (poetry and short stories); [pers.] I wish to hold your tired hands, and caress it with

my spirits. I wish to wipe all the tears, from the faces of hungry kids. My wish is love, kindness, and peace.; [a.] Los Angeles/Glendale, CA

ADAMS JR., ALBERT JOHN
[pen.] Albert John Adams Jr.; [b.] December 20, 1967, Washington, DC; [p.] Albert and Alberta Adams; [ed.] High School Graduate, 12 years; [occ.] Carpet Salesperson; [oth. writ.] Personal writings sent to family and friends. Cards for special occasions; [pers.] I write to let feelings speak for their self, and believe that quote: "If you look further than your eyes can see, you then realize all that you are blind to."; [a.] Owings, MD

ADAMS JR., KEN
[b.] December 2, 1965, Erie, PA; [p.] Ken Adams Jr., and Linda Adams; [m.] Debbie Adams, September 10, 1994; [ch.] Jon Lawerence; [ed.] Fort Le Boeuf High School, Triangle Tech.; [occ.] Computer Instructor; [hon.] Eagle Scout, Pro Deo et Patria; [pers.] I believe my work belongs solely to myself until another reads it and is able to relate. If then becomes theirs.; [a.] Erie, PA

ADAMS, MELENA
[pen.] Pat Bradley; [b.] February 3, 1977, Ashe Co., NC; [p.] Thomas and Barbara Adams; [ed.] Northwest Ashe High; [occ.] Student; [pers.] I would like to give many thanks to my younger brother, Tim. If it hadn't been for him I would never entered a poetry contest.; [a.] Lansing, NC

ADDY, WENDY
[b.] December 5, 1950, Desmoines, IA; [p.] Margaret Whelan, Floyd Addy; [ed.] Some College (don't remember how much); [occ.] Student of Ceramic Arts; [memb.] Zoo and Wild Animal Park.; [pers.] I wish to bring people close to God and Nature. Influenced by W. Wordsworth, Emily Dickenson, Romantic poets.; [a.] Lakeside, CA

AHMED, SHARMIAN
[b.] July 5, 1958, England; [p.] Denis and Maureen Brealey; [ch.] Natasha and Shanila; [pers.] I would like to dedicate my work to my two young children, Natasha and Shanila, who are a constant source of inspiration to me as well as my best critics.

AISSAOUI, DEBBIE S.
[pen.] Flora Mae Cohen; [b.] May 13, 1960, Denton, TX; [p.] Les and Barbara Cohen; [m.] Abdelkader Aissaoui, October 31, 1989; [ch.] Justin Lee and Amber D'Anne Snell; [ed.] Bryan Adams; [pers.] To those whom I believe in and to those who believe in me, thank you.

AKERS, MERLE
[pen.] M. A. Grand; [p.] Vern and Anne Dille; [ch.] Linn Sroka, Jodi Gray and Shannon Henley, six grandchildren; [pers.] I wrote this poem for the men and woman or D.S. but also for those who served in Viet Nam, especially my brother Allen (Bud) Dille. Our country learned a valuable lesson in V.N., no matter where or why our troops are called to serve we must support, and be proud of them. War is the ultimate price to pay for freedom.; [a.] Crown Point, IN

AKIN, DORIS MATOCHA
[pen.] Doris Akin; [b.] December 20, 1931, Hondo, TX; [p.] Rudolph D. and Louise Matocha; [m.] Bobby C. Akin, November 23, 1951; [ch.] Kay Akin Nauman, Linda Akin Phillips, Robert D. Akin (1955-1976); [ed.] Nazareth Academy, Victoria, TX; [occ.] Home/Health Care; [hon.] Valedictorian - 1950; [oth. writ.] Poems and short stories; [pers.] Inside everyone lies the desire to put into words the feelings that they alone have felt at special moments of their life. It takes someone to believe in them....Doris; [a.] Placedo, TX

AL MAJID, MARI
[pen.] Mariam; [b.] March 8, 1973, Afghanistan; [p.] Khadija Tabibi, Abdul Hakim Al Majid; [ed.] Associate Degree, currently attending American University.; [occ.] Administrative's Assistant.; [hon.] Editor's Choice Award for best poem.; [oth. writ.] Working on my book about my experiences of escaping Afghanistan, at a very young age, with family.; [pers.] I have been inspired by poetry at a very young age, I like to read poetry from the early poets. I strive to speak for the broken hearted through my poetry.; [a.] Falls Church, VA

ALCOX, LETITIA
[b.] August 7, 1966, Los Angeles; [p.] Ora Alcox, James Alcox; [ed.] St. Mary's Academy, University of Southern California, California State University Dominguez Hills; [occ.] Financial Assistant, Stockbroker; [memb.] South Bay Chapter of The Southern California Association for the Education of Young Children.; [pers.] As the world turns a light goes on, another day has ended, another has gone. But as we look around it is plain to see - what God has created and what we can be.; [a.] Inglewood, CA

ALEX, MARY
[b.] June 27, 1930, Oregon; [m.] Anton K. De Mik, June 27, 1991; [ch.] Martha Barrera, Michele Alex, Charles Alex; [ed.] Presentation Academy, San Francisco, CA; [occ.] Retired; [pers.] This poem was written solely out of love and tho overwhelming feeling I experienced when my granddaughter was born. There is nothing like it!; [a.] Martinez, CA

ALFIERI, JEANIEMARIE
[b.] December 9, 1952, Mitchel Field, NY; [p.] Margaret and Michael Descala; [ch.] Mary, Josephine, Catherine, Amedeo and Michael; [ed.] Lindenhurst High, York University, American School of Phlebatomy Technicians; [occ.] Data Transmissions, Smithkline Beecham Clinical Labs.; [oth. writ.] Working on a book of poems; [pers.] Thanks to a special admirer and my children, I found the courage to write, paint and draw again.; [a.] Centereach, NY

ALFONSO, FRANK A.
[b.] October 11, 1946, Manhattan, NY; [p.] Tom and Margie; [m.] Jeanne Alfonso, March 12, 1971; [ch.] Two; [ed.] Long Island City H.S., Manhattan "A" Spokesman Club; [memb.] Teamsters Local 804, A.S.K. Associates for Scriptual Knowledge, Original Bible Project, "Piston Poppers" Auto Club; [hon.] Twenty Five Years for Safety on the Job Accident Free (Watch and T.V.); [oth. writ.] "Poetic Revelations," published by Vantage Press

in 1990. A poem called "A Special Person", written in memory to my father-in-law.; [pers.] I try to live by the "Golden Rule", do unto others as you would have others do unto you. One day at a time, making each day very special; [a.] Valley Stream, NY

ALLEN, JACQUELINE P.
[pen.] Gramma Allen; [b.] June 1, 1944, Richmond, CA; [p.] Hope and Dale Taylor; [m.] James Franklin Allen Jr., June 3, 1962; [ch.] Annette, Robert, James, and Vance; [ed.] GED in 1983, some college at LCCC in Cheyenne, Wyo. and writing classes through Iowa Schools. Also The Institute of Children's Literature, now under Lynda Graham-Barber.; [oth. writ.] A book is ready and I'm looking for a publisher. This poem stems from a life situation, written and titled, "A Grandparent's Nightmare"; [pers.] We do not always understand God's answers to prayer but He is with us, even beyond death. Job, as mentioned in the Bible, prayed for this mercy (Job 14:13). I pray for understanding, wisdom, and mercy too, assured the answer will come someday. When childhood is gone as with many young (in age) today, what comfort remains? God cares... I know.; [a.] Council Bluffs, IA

ALLEN, JAMES
[b.] October 9, 1979, Salt Lake City, VT; [p.] Alice Allen; [ed.] Still in High School; [memb.] Boy Scouts of America, Church of Jesus Christ of Latter-Day Saints; [hon.] Life Scout in Boy Scouts, Arrow of Light in Cub Scouts.; [oth. writ.] None published; [pers.] Live each day to its fullest, take things as they come, enjoy life, and it doesn't matter what others think about you, it matters what you think of yourself.; [a.] Wilmington, NC

ALLEN, JOHN C.
[pen.] John C. Allen; [b.] March 21, 1919, Worcester, MA; [p.] John, Margaretta Allen; [m.] Teressa Baroli, August, 1944; [ch.] Judith, John Joseph, Michael Patrick, Theresa, Catherine, Timothy, Rita, Mary; [ed.] Lee High School, Class 1937, Lee, MA; [occ.] Retired Aircraft Sheet Metal - (Stainless); [oth. writ.] Verses inspired by current events, my love at cars, driving, rides in the country side and my children but most of all inspired by my continuing love for my spouse of 50 years.

ALLENDORF, ELIZABETH ANN
[pen.] Elizabeth Allendorf; [b.] July 5, 1940, Boston, MA; [p.] Adeline and Joseph Fuoco; [m.] George P. Allendorf Jr., November 25, 1962; [ch.] George III, Robert Joseph, Richard Mickael, Lisa-Marie; [ed.] Hyde Park High School, Quinsigamound College, Middlesex College; [occ.] Housewife/Student; [memb.] United We Stand American Alliance for Mentally Ill, Dept of Mental Health, CCSS Area Board, DMH Site Board, Catholic Church, Unitarian, Student Middlesex Community College, UUA Choir, Church, Sally Gould Dance, Holiday Health SPA Yoga Class, Edgar Cayce Foundation (Group Leader); [hon.] Certificate in Liberal Studies, Reiki Practioner II.; [oth. writ.] Poems published in "Voices", Middlesex College Journal.

ALO', JOANN
[b.] December 9, 1963; [p.] Joseph and Carolyn Downs; [m.] David Alo', June 6, 1982; [ch.] Amanda Rose, Laura Jean, Sarah Jo; [oth. writ.] Several poems, currently working on an inspirational book.; [pers.] Creating art which peers into the heart is like a waltz with the soul. My inspiration comes from Matthew, Mark, Luke, and John.; [a.] Manhattan, IL

ALVES-PARKS, JOHANNA REGINA
[b.] May 18, 1979, Akron, OH; [p.] John J. Parks, Regina T. Alves-Parks; [ed.] Grade 10 - Our Lady of the Elms High School; [occ.] Student - Grade 10, Our Lady of the Elms High School; [memb.] Debate and Forensics Team, Encores (School Show Choir), Coalition Representative of Sophomore Class, Treasurer of Debate and Forensics Team, President of the Music Club, Tennis Team and Volunteer of Children's Hospital.; [hon.] Power of the Pen Writing Contest - Best of Round - 1992 ("The Seed") - Trophy 3rd place - Kent University, Regional Tournament (Power of the Pen) Individual Writing - Trophy 4th place - 1992, District Tournament - Excellence in Writing - Trophy 3rd place - 1992, Sister Maria Stadler Award - 1992 - Excellence in English and Grammar Skills. Power of the Pen Writing Contest - Best of Round - 1993, "A Nation Destroyed", Cleveland Radio and Television Contest - 1993, 2nd place - Essay. Elms Speech Contest - 1993 - 2nd place Fairlawn Optimist Club Speech Contest - 2nd place - 1993, University of Youngstown - Foreign Language Day - French Poem - 2nd place (1993) Medal, Fairlawn Optimist Club Speech Contest, 1996, Club Level - 1st place - medal, Zone Level - 1st place - plaque, District - 2nd place - certificate, Fairlawn Optimist Club Speech Contest, 1995, Club Level - 1st place - medal, Zone Level - 1st place - plague, District - 2nd place - certificate, Hudson Kiwanis Speech and Debate Tournament, 3rd place - trophy - Humorous Interpretation, Our Lady of the Elms - Honor Roll Award 1994, Youngstown University - Foreign Language Day - French Short Story Speaking Contest - 1st place - medal (1995), Certificate of Award - 1994 Ohio Test of Scholastic Achievement - English 9 - (State - Division 3) The Northeast Ohio District, Certificate of Award - 1994 - Ohio Test of Scholastic Achievement - English 9 - (Northeast Ohio District - Division 3), The State of Ohio; [a.] Akron, OH

AMACHER, LAURA LYNN
[b.] February 15, 1970, Chicago, IL; [p.] Deborah and Thomas Nodich; [ed.] DeForest High School, VW to become Certified Child Care Provider, will go back to VW this summer; [occ.] Certified Child Care Provider; [a.] Madison, WI

AMMONS, KRISTIN DAWN
[pen.] Kristin Ammons, Nativity Clinebell; [b.] June 4, 1981, Roanoke, VA; [p.] James Ammons, Trudie Ammons; [ed.] Currently Bearden High School.; [oth. writ.] To be announced.; [pers.] My inspiration comes from my mother who passed away when I was five. A phenomenal, free-spirited woman with a loving heart. I love you, Mom!; [a.] Knoxville, TN

AMOS, PAUL
[b.] July 10, 1952, Savannah, GA; [p.] (Step father) Ceasar Amos, mother (decease); [ch.] Tonya Wiley (daughter); [ed.] Tompkins High School, Savannah Vocational Tech., Savannah State College; [occ.] Painter/Carpenter, Southeast Georgia Regional Medical Center; [memb.] First African Baptist Church, Deacon Board, Laymen Movement, Ussher Board, Pastors Aide Board, etc.; [hon.] First African Baptist Church Certificate - for Outstanding Service and Contributions, Savannah State College Certificate of Merit and Achievement, Savannah Voc. Tech. Service Award.; [oth. writ.] Most poems have been written for various occasions and personals. The majority of poems and essays are kept as memoirs.; [pers.] "Unto those who diligently seek knowledge for the understanding... seek first ye the Lord for the guidance."; [a.] Brunswick, GA

AMROUCHE, ABDELHAC
[b.] April 2, 1958, Algiers; [p.] Mohamed and Fatma-Zohra; [ed.] Premed (Algers), Programmer (USA), Personal Trainer (USA); [memb.] ISP Member, BATC Member, ACE Member.; [hon.] NLP Award (1994 Poetry Contest), 5th place Medal (age grouper) at Getaway Triathlon 1994.; [oth. writ.] Several poems published by NLP and ISP. Other poems in French since 80's none is publish.; [pers.] I write about my experiences and the way I feel. My background helped a lot and my being in different countries. Influenced by a lot of readings.; [a.] Brooklyn, NY

ANDERS, CAMILLE S.
[b.] December 28, 1938, Meridian, MS; [p.] Mr. and Mrs. R. O. Shephard; [m.] Dan R. Anders, September 3, 1994; [ch.] Christel Camille Funk, Lisa Leah Nied, Melanie Maria Futch, Wendi Wanita Funk; [ed.] B.A. Degree from University of Mississippi - Magna Cum Laude - 1960; [occ.] Free-lance writer; [memb.] St. Matthews United Methodist Church, Work Area on Missions, US - China Peoples Friendship Association; [hon.] Mission Interpreter of the Year - Southeastern Jurisdiction United Methodist Church; [oth. writ.] Poems and articles, curriculum material for children and adults in United Methodist Church and Friendship Press - National Council of Churches; [pers.] Poetry has been a major part of my life introduced to me by a loving Grandmother and third grade teacher. Robert Frost provided my inspiration.; [a.] Fairfax, VA

ANDERSON, DELLA
[pen.] Della Anderson; [b.] November 10, 1957, Hanford, CA; [p.] Dorether Anderson; [ed.] Graduated from W.C. Overfelt Freshman in College (De Anza); [occ.] Customer Service Representative; [hon.] I received a letter and certificate; [oth. writ.] Dreams; [pers.] I dedicate this poem to my mother Dorether Anderson who taught me and showed me how to be a good person, woman and parent. She had a great love for words and reading and writing them and she instilled these in me, thank you Mom; [a.] San Jose, CA

ANDERSON, FRANCINE
[b.] December 27, 1981; [p.] Ms. Angela D. Dowdy, father (Deceased); [ed.] 1. Sacred Heart, 2. Westampton, 3. De Masi, right now I go to school at De Masi; [pers.] Most of my writing or poems come from my heart and I especially like romantic and funny poems. My friends sometimes call me Buckwheat. I'm popular (not very).; [a.] Marlton, NJ

ANDERSON, JAYNE
[pen.] "Simply Jayne"; [b.] October 16, 1972, Italy; [p.] Mary Monford and Paul Anderson; [occ.] Writer; [memb.] Coloorado Coalition for the Protection of Children; [oth. writ.] A poem called "My Sanity" was published in 1990 in a book "Great American Poets of Our Time."; [pers.] All of my poems come from real life experiences whether it's mine or close friends and family. I want to thank everyone especially my sister Paula and Latasha. My success is formly precious bodies who did not make it.; [a.] Security, CO

ANDERSON, TERESA JEANNE
[b.] April 16, 1955, Lakewood, NJ; [p.] Barbara Ann Johnson McDowell, John Alvar Anderson II; [ed.] Associates Degree of Arts in Humanities; [occ.] Security Guard, Substitute Teacher; [memb.] (Certified Home Health Aid), The International Association of Lions Club, Advisor - Explorers; [hon.] NRI Achievement Award with highest honors; [oth. writ.] Hear Me, Closed Doors, Never Turn Back, Dreams Or Not, Paradise Or Is It?, Life's Philosophy, Echoes Of Love; [pers.] I wish to share my Love for Life through poetry, bringing joy to those taking the time to enjoy it. This I do in hope that my words will live on for generations to come. Philosophy: Live, Love, Laugh. Trust in the Lord.; [a.] Brick, NJ

ANDRADE, BONITA L.
[pen.] Sybil Speans; [b.] March 6, 1949, Providence, RI; [p.] Alicia Gonzalez Miranda, Alexander Miranda; [m.] Daniel Andrade (divorce); [ch.] Danielle Elise Andrade, Nicholas Johann Andrade; [ed.] Central High School (Vocational) City College (one year); [occ.] On SSI, was state worker, factory worker, Nurses Aid, and various job.; [oth. writ.] I just started to read poetry and find it difficult and hate it. Nothing published, Native Poet. Poems: Go Girl, Surmis This, Bedazzeling Bidity Witty Ditty, The Blae Lock, The First Prove, Lactescent Wedlock of Lineage. The poems maybe consider practice work; [pers.] I was a welfare mother for years and lost various position and lost a great deal of self esteem that lead to a great deal of frustration and anger. I wrote to comfort my self and to have self worth. I want to be someone. I would give up and writing to possibly stay alive.

ANDRADE, KIMBERLY
[pen.] Panther; [b.] August 17, 1959, Los Alamos, NM; [p.] Diana Johnson, Victor W. Davis; [m.] Nelson Andrade, June 5, 1982; [ch.] Rudy and Cocoa (cats); [ed.] Hillsdale High School, College of San Mateo, Canada College, R.O.P. Business School, Palo Alto School of Hypnotherapy; [occ.] Transcriptionist for Private Investigation Firm; [memb.] Greenpeace, Wildlife Rescue, ACLU, Southwest Indian Children's Fund; [hon.] Received Layman Chaplaincy Certificate at Unity Church,

received Hypnotherapist Certificate from P.A. School of Hypnotherapy; [oth. writ.] Have written over 50 poems (none have been submitted yet except this one), several songs for piano and guitar. Guitar songs include lyrics. Am working on a book presently.; [pers.] I have been a writer of music, poetry, lyrics and literature as a hobby since age 14, mostly for self healing through creative expression. Though I long to share my work, humility comes first, and I prefer to be invited by fate, instead of push my work onto publishers! My work is of a psycho-spiritual nature.; [a.] Redwood City, CA

ANDRASEK, MARJORIE I.
[b.] July 29, 1922, Barton County, KS; [p.] Mr. and Mrs. Sam H. Boese; [m.] Harold J. Kitch (deceased) am remarried to Louis R. Andrasek, November 12, 1939; [ch.] Karen Smithe, and my twins — Arlene Koehn and Eilene Brady; [ed.] Eight grades to Dist. 27, Country Grade School, Barton County, Kansas and High School at Pawnee Rock, Kansas.; [occ.] Retired; [memb.] Finney County Genealogical Society; [oth. writ.] Many poems.; [pers.] My hobbies—— writing poetry, especially about my olden days. Reading good books. I'm in my 58th year of keeping my daily diary. I keep up with my family history and genealogy. I like to crochet and also play my organ.; [a.] Garden City, KS

ANDREWS, SHANNON
[b.] June 15, 1984, Stanford, CA; [p.] Scott and Linda Andrews; [ed.] Sherman Elementary, Jaws - Highly Capable Program; [occ.] Student; [memb.] Emmanuel Lutheran Church, "Funky Munkies", Church Youth Group, Junior Girl Scouts, Rainbow Girls; [hon.] Kiwanis Club, Terrific Kid Award; [oth. writ.] Working on a story book, "Cathy Bates, The Ghost at Grandma's House."; [pers.] I like to write ghost stories. Poetry is a new experience for me.; [a.] Tacoma, WA

ANFELDT, JULIANA A.
[b.] October 4, 1964, Chicago, IL; [p.] Leroy and Lillian Campo; [m.] Terry L. Anfeldt, June 23, 1983; [ch.] Nicholas Lee and Anthony Terry; [ed.] Buffalo Grove High School, Tomahawk High School; [occ.] Homemaker Volunteer; [memb.] Vineyard Congregation, Long Grove, IL, Catholic Charities; [oth. writ.] "Hot Tomatoe" published in Daily Herald; [pers.] To bring praise and worship to the Lord Jesus Christ; [a.] Palatine, IL

ANGELETTE, JENEE
[b.] May 5, 1981, Thibodaux, LA; [p.] Andrew, Jennica Angelette; [ed.] 8th Grade Student at E.D. White Catholic High School, Thibodaux, Louisiana; [memb.] High School Cheerleading Squad, Carolyn Moore School of Dance, Thibodaux Softball AllStar Team; [pers.] Life is like an onion, you peel away a layer at a time, sometimes tearfully.; [a.] Thibodaux, LA

ANSELL, KATHY
[b.] January 18, 1957, Mount Pleasant, PA; [p.] Allen and Barbara Geska; [m.] William A. Ansell III, February 10, 1995; [ch.] Chad Allen, Melissa Dean; [pers.] My family is everything to me and greatly influences my ability to write from my heart.; [a.] Mount Pleasant, PA

ARENA, PHILIP LEWIS
[b.] February 16, 1945, Seattle, WA; [p.] Philip Henry Arena and Florance Gale Arena; [m.] Divorced; [ch.] Marina Daniella Santana Arena; [ed.] 2 1/2 Year College, Boeing Blueprint Class, Chinook and Huey Helicopter Crew Chief School in Virginia, Boeing Blue Streak Sheet Metal Repair; [occ.] Owner, Arena Landscaping, Poetry Manager, Poetry League of America; [memb.] 5 year member of League of Western Writers (3 years as President), Permanent Poetry Manager, Poetry League of America, Member, The Principality of Hutt River Province, Publisher, League Boots NW, Organizer and Member of "The Skitters" (A group that puts on skits and plays); [hon.] Royal Proclamation of the Title "Honor-able" bestowed upon me by His Royal Highness Prince Leonard of Hutt, of the Principality of Hutt River Province. President, League of Western Writers (3 years); [oth. writ.] Poems in numerous poetry magazines, one poem each in two books of poetry by Young Publications, one poem in The Poetry Book "Encounter" from San Francisco, one poem in a London, England Company Magazine, one poem used in "Athens, Greece School to help teach English and Poetry to Greek children.; [pers.] "Sometimes you can't force a thought, you just have to wait until a thought catches up to you." Each good poem should have 5 things in it: Beauty, Imagery, Aesthetic Value, Empathy and Sensitivity. A poem should "Flow" rather than just have rhyme or meter to it.; [a.] Mountlake Terrace, WA

AREY, VELMA J.
[pen.] Velma J. Arey; [b.] January 3, 1910, Satin, TX; [p.] T. R. Jones, Nezzie A.; [m.] Lonnie L. Arey, April 26, 1930; [ch.] One; [ed.] ETSTU - East Texas State Univ., taught two years - Public School TX, (Cert.) Fine Arts - Famous Artist's School - 3 Diplomas - Writer's Digest School; [occ.] Retired from Life Ins. Business; [memb.] National Author's Registry Life Time Charter Member of the International Society of Poets. Porterville Historical Society - Sequdia Dawn - Springville - Teacher - World Bible School of the Church of Christ; [hon.] Nat'l. Library of Poetry - Poems of the 90's - Distinguished Poet's of America - "Editor's Choice Award" - Iliad Press - "Hon. Mention" - Celebrations - "President's Award" - Perceptions - Odysseys Around the World - Sparrograss Poetry Forum; [oth. writ.] 5 Plaques - 4 Books published 1 Chapbrook - poems. Family Tree Book, 6 Anthologies - poems; [pers.] Psalms - writing, travel, loves people - active, play piano, organ, sing, Christian living, positive thinking.; [a.] Springville, CA

ARLINGTON, DIANE
[pen.] Diane Arlington; [b.] December 15, 1937, Santa Monica, CA; [p.] Donald and Doreen Arnold; [m.] Bruce Arlington, May 19, 1984; [ch.] Dan, Debbie and Brett; [ed.] Through 12 grade; [occ.] Wedding and Gift Shop (owner); [hon.] (3) Golden Poet, (3) Silver Poet, (4) Honorable Mention, (1) Doll Maker Certificate, Porceline Doll, many more; [oth. writ.] "Down Life's Road", "Debbie", from Mom, "Brett" from Mom, "My Valentine To You", "My Dad", "Lady Liberty"; [pers.] Most of the poems are written to my family. I would like to leave this legacy to my children. William Cullen Bryant was my Great Uncle; [a.] Weed, CA

ARMSTRONG, JENNIFER
[b.] February 25, 1984, Cedar Rapids, IA; [p.] Joseph and Lynda Armstrong; [ed.] College Community, (Prairie View) 76th Ave., SW Cedar Rapids, Iowa, 52404; [oth. writ.] I write stories, poems, and I also read alot!

ARNOLD, ANN SCHONWETTER
[b.] December 5, 1969, Livingston, NJ; [p.] Mark and Luba Schonwetter; [m.] Jonathan Arnold, November 26, 1994; [ed.] Livingston High School, Lehigh University; [occ.] Vice President, Lieberfarb, Inc.; [memb.] Beta Alpha Psi, Beta Gamma Sigma, Delta Gamma, Certified Public Accountant (CPA); [hon.] Graduated High Honors - Lehigh University, Dean's List; [oth. writ.] "When I Look Into His Eyes..." - untitled Seasons to Come; [pers.] My father was a hidden child during the holocaust, and his experiences greatly inspire my writings. We must never forget.; [a.] Englewood, NJ

ARNOLD, CAMIE
[b.] February 11, 1980, ECM; [p.] LaDonna Gray and C. D. Arnold; [ed.] I am attending Rogers High School and I'm in the 9th grade; [pers.] I enjoy writing poetry. One of my favorite writers is Robert Frost. I started writing poetry about 4 years ago and I have over 60 poems.; [a.] Killen, AL

ARRANTS, SHANE
[pen.] Shane Arrants; [b.] January 30, 1974, Cleveland, TN; [p.] Buddy and Debbie Arrants; [ed.] McMinn County High; [occ.] Ice Cream Flavorer, "Mayfields Dairy Farm", Athens, TN, 37303; [oth. writ.] Many other love poems, but none published.; [pers.] I enjoy treating women how they deserve to be treated. I like writing poems for the ladies in my life, and seeing their smiles is my reward.; [a.] Athens, TN

ARTIS, IDA P.
[pen.] Tat; [b.] January, 1937, Burgaw, NC; [p.] Richard Artis and Clara Artis; [ch.] Brenda London, William Davis, Darren Davis, Mia Cox, and Eartha Pearsall; [ed.] high school; [occ.] disabled; [memb.] Usher Board (New Hope Baptist Church) Church Choir, Sunday School Teacher at Stars of Faith Ministries; [oth. writ.] Yes but have not been published; [pers.] I write poems about Jesus, my children, my family and life. I write poems that may someday touch someone else's life in some way; [a.] Burgaw, NC

ASKEY, WILLIAM SCOTT
[pen.] William Scott Askey; [b.] July 21, 1964, Madison, WI; [p.] William Roy and Edith Askey; [ch.] William Kyle Askey; [ed.] High School (Monona Grove), Madison Area Technical College; [occ.] International Delicate - Chef, Saint Thomas Elementary - Drum Instructor, Professional Musician - Self Employed; [memb.] Hopefully, National Library of Poetry, Workers Union (Food Service).; [hon.] Outstanding Performance Awards 1981 and 1982, UW - Platteville Jazz Ensemble Festivals, Paul W. Thompson Award 1982 (for Most Improved Student).; [oth. writ.] Many poems and short stories never published.; [pers.] I am merely one of many men who, with all my heart, will break bread with those beside me and those who guide me. All

are God's people. All are brothers.; [a.] International Falls, MN

ATKINS, MRS. ALBERTA
[b.] July 7, 1924, Charleston, IL; [p.] Forest and Lola Hampsten; [m.] Ray Atkins, February 15, 1946; [ch.] Judy Shoffstall Atkins, Cathy Mattingly Atkins, Kelly Ann Atkins; [ed.] H.S. and Business College, Greenup H.S. - Mattoon College, Illinois; [occ.] Retired from Amoco Oil Co. Ray was agent I helped with bookwork.; [memb.] First Christian Church - Oblong; [oth. writ.] "50th H.S. Class Reunion Welcoming Poem" - book, "Miracles Are Slow" - an abbreviated autobiography, copyrighted 1985 (book), 3 autograph sessions, 3 poems published in Daughter's (C.J.'s) Coloring and Children's Books.

ATKINS, ROBERT BASIL
[b.] March 25, 1957, Montgomery, WV; [p.] Congress and Margaret Atkins; [m.] Ada Atkins, July 10, 1987; [ch.] Robert B. Atkins Jr.; [ed.] Graduate - High School, B.A. Degree W.Va. Tech., Attended Marshall University - Graduate School; [occ.] Teacher - Social Studies, Lenore Junior High, Lenore W.Va.; [memb.] N.E.A. - National Teachers Association. Parish Council; [hon.] Dean's List - College, W.Va., Ins. of Tech., History Honorary Society in College; [oth. writ.] Several poems for school.; [a.] Williamson, WV

ATWOOD, ROBERT F.
[b.] July 23, 1933, Brockton; [p.] Frank and Ellen Atwood; [m.] Beatrice Atwood, April 19, 1969; [ch.] Michael Atwood; [ed.] Oliver Ames High, N. Easton, MA; [occ.] Construction Painter; [memb.] Improved Order of Redman, North American Hunting Club; [oth. writ.] Church Paper, Veteran Hospital Publications; [pers.] I find in poetry, that my life is worth, every word I read, as poetry is the calling of our hearts.; [a.] West Wareham, MA

AUSTIN, AMANDA
[pen.] Poppy, Johnny Diamonds; [b.] January 19, 1978, Worcester, MA; [p.] JoAnn and Robert Austin; [ed.] Presently an honor student at Wilbraham and Monson Academy in Ma., Will be a senior in September.; [occ.] Presently a student and poet at the Wilbraham and Monson Academy, Wilbraham, MA; [memb.] National Authors' Registry, Editor of the Literary Publications at Wilbraham and Monson Academy: The Tempest and The Rubicon.; [hon.] Evelyn Barber English Award 1993, 1994, 1995, Joseph Baldwin Eminent Young Scholar at Northeast Missouri State University for 3 years (1989-92); [oth. writ.] Unpublished author of 'Tales', 'Other Tales', 'Camusian', 'The Librium Horse', and 'Narigh', books of poetry and prose.; [pers.] I am not allowed to traverse merely parallel to society and its culture, we meet, we intercept - we embrace for just a moment - and then we move on. This leaves us both fresh with the others impressions from the encounter, ready to move forth with new influence, new media. These are testimonials.; [a.] Southbridge, MA

AVERION, MARIA C.
[b.] February 12, 1967, Wheeling, WV; [p.] Dr. R. A. Averion and Perla G. Averion; [ed.] B.A. Journalism, Ohio State University; [occ.] Newspaper Page Designer, Copy Editor; [pers.] I

wrote this poem for my mother Perla G. Averion. I wrote it from her perspective. She is the inspiration for everything I do and strive for in life. I will always love her.; [a.] Akron, OH

AVET, TRACI LYNN
[b.] June 16, 1974; [p.] Donald J. Avet Jr. and Connie Pellegrin; [ed.] Psychology junior at Nicholls State University in Thibodaux, LA; [pers.] One of my most intimate beliefs has always been that every individual emotion we experience is significant in its own right, not to be undermined or stripped of its power to bind us. Through prose and poetry, I attempt to offer each feeling its deserved credibility. Perhaps my purpose is to demand of society what we demand of ourselves = respect and validity.; [a.] Houma, LA

AVILA, CAROLYN L.
[b.] February 1, 1956, Sinton, TX; [p.] Carolyn D. Smith, Leon Merritt; [ch.] Benjamin J. Avila, Leslie A. Avila; [occ.] Singer, Poet and Store Manager; [oth. writ.] Various other unpublished works

AVILES, JULIO I.
[b.] December 5, 1943, El Salvador; [p.] Julio I. and Lydia Aviles; [m.] Ana Myriam, September 27; [ch.] Sergio Julio, Ana Karina, Gustavo Antonio; [ed.] B.S. Chemistry; [occ.] Technical Service Representative: Kronos Inc.; [memb.] American Chemical Society, American Association for the Advancement of Science. Philadelphia Society for Coatings Technology, American Ceramic Society.; [oth. writ.] Technical Articles in Trade Journals; [pers.] I celebrate the hope and faith in the future, that ensures the survival of the rainforest thus enjoining the survival of the people that depend on the rainforest; [a.] Jenkinstown, PA

AYES, CONSUELO
[b.] December 6, 1976, Albuquerque, NM; [p.] Mother - Pauline Martinez; [ed.] Durango High School; [occ.] Seamstress, Suzanne's Sewing Durango C.O.; [oth. writ.] Many poems and short stories but this is my first publication; [pers.] I write to comfort myself in times of sadness.; [a.] Durango, CO

AZEAL, LIA
[b.] August 21, 1960, Minnesota; [p.] James Cooley, Marilyn Cooley; [ed.] B.S. University of South Dakota - Medical Technology, M.S. California State University, Northridge, Health Administration; [occ.] Medical Claims Examiner and Coordinator/Caregiver for Developmentally Disabled; [memb.] Member of Two Writing Groups - "Writes at the Round Table" - Marina Del Rey, CA, and a member of "Wicked Women's Writes", Los Angeles, CA; [hon.] Who's Who - American Colleges and Universities - 1991, California State University Northridge, Deans List - University of South Dakota 1778-1981, Phi Eta Sigma Honor Society 1979.; [oth. writ.] Poem published in 1990 "Promethean Poem" published in Women's Quarterly - University of California, Irvine; [pers.] Poetry has allowed me, awakened me to connect with my true essence, the animal kingdom has led me, guided me to that true essence, the plant kingdom has nourished and nurtured me on the path and the mineral kingdom has sustained me on the journey.; [a.] Los Angeles, CA

BABU, VENKATESH
[b.] February 17, 1959, Bangalore, India; [p.] Sunder Raj and Padmavathi; [ed.] Bachelor's of Architecture (BARCH) Bangalore University India Master in City Planning (MCP) University of Cincinnati; [occ.] Architect/Urban Planner; [memb.] MCA I.I.A Urban Design Committee Member. The American of Institute of Architects; [hon.] University Graduate Scholarship at University of Cincinnati, University Scholarship at Bangalore University, India; [oth. writ.] Short Essays, several poems and short plays.; [pers.] I use poetry to explore the inner self to reach into my mind for a deeper understanding of myself, the nature of beings, the universe and the human existence. Poetry is an art form to depict human experience, perception, and imagination of our world and lives, that touch human hearts. I am inspired by the romantic poets.; [a.] Aurora, OH

BACKUS, MARY E.
[pen.] Mary E. Avery Backus; [b.] November 10, 1923, Indiana; [p.] John and Zula Stoops; [m.] October 18, 1952; [ch.] Susan, Blanche, and Bill Avery; [ed.] Business College; [occ.] Retired; [a.] Kansas City, MO

BAILEY, KATRINA
[b.] February 23, 1976, Welch, WV; [p.] Clarice Bailey; [ed.] Mount View High School; [memb.] Apostolic Holiness Church; [hon.] Poet of the year, editorial award, the best poems; [oth. writ.] Short stories published in High School Newspaper; [pers.] I write my poetry from the heart and the world for which I live in. I may be young in age, but I am wise in mind.; [a.] Welch, WV

BAILEY, SUSAN F.
[b.] August 28, 1940, Cleveland, OH; [p.] Harrison C. Frost, Nancy Morgan Frost; [m.] Charles C. Bailey, August 26, 1978; [ed.] Pine Manor College, 1961; [occ.] Retired, volunteer: 1) Humane Educator for SPCA of Brazoria county, 2) Perform Animal - Assisted Therapy in Nursing Home; [memb.] SPCA of Brazoria county, Texas, Humane society of the United States.; [oth. writ.] Two short stories about two of my cats in the book Uncommon Cats, compiled by John R. Guevin, An article in Pine Manor College Spring "Bulletin 1995.; [pers.] Since animals are of paramount importance in my life, I try to demonstrate by word and deed the beneficial effects of enrichment and improvement that pets can bring to human lives.; [a.] Rosharon, TX

BAIN, SHANNA DEON
[pen.] Shanna Bain; [b.] March 25, 1981, Cleveland, TN; [p.] Thomas Bain and Darlene Bain; [ed.] Eight grade student at Etowah City School; [memb.] Secretary of Local 4-H Club, Member of McMinn Central High School Band.; [hon.] Won a writing contest in North Carolina; [oth. writ.] Several poems published in my school newspaper.; [pers.] Everything I think about is a reflection of my poetry. I feel my gift for writing is a gift from God and heaven sent.; [a.] Etowah, TN

BAIRD, ELLEN
[pen.] Dede; [b.] November 29, 1956, Omaha, NE; [p.] Richard Strong Sr., Mary Ann Strong; [ch.] Zaq C. Heather; [ed.] Central Catholic High,

Barnes Business College; [occ.] Word Processor, Oppenheimer Shareholder Suc's; [memb.] Diabetic Foundation; [oth. writ.] 25 other poems written none published with exception of this.; [pers.] All the poems I have written were personal experiences and from the heart. All that I am reflects in my writings; [a.] Lakewood, CO

BALDWIN, DOROTHY M.
[b.] November 2, 1922, Alleghany County, VA; [p.] Frank and Rosie Wolfe; [m.] Robert B. Baldewin, 1952; [ch.] One son, four granddaughters; [ed.] College graduate 1944, Lincoln Memorial University Harrogate, Tennessee, George Washington Univ. Wash., DC., University of Md. College Park, Md.; [occ.] Retired 1984 (38 Yrs) Public School Teacher; [pers.] Taught school in Virginia, Washington, DC., Maryland.; [a.] Bryans Road, MD

BALDWIN, ROSA
[b.] March 7, 1946, NC; [p.] Norman Cannon, Annie Turner; [m.] Carl Baldwin, January 23, 1979; [ch.] Carl and Lisa Baldwin; [ed.] Brawley High, M. M. W. Nursing School, NAPNES Medication School; [occ.] Nurse; [oth. writ.] Short poems and songs for schools and personal friends; [pers.] It is not good to have zeal without knowledge, just as speed without direction can be dangerous.

BALDWIN, TAD
[pen.] Sandman; [b.] March 1, 1977, Honolulu, HI; [p.] Keith Baldwin and Gwen Necker; [ed.] Grand Island Senior High in Grand Island Nebraska. 11 1/2 years of education. My favorite teachers were Mr. Hamner and Mr. Obermier; [occ.] Unemployed; [oth. writ.] I have written a 387 page book under an alias name and submitted it to Random House Publishing Co. for review and criticism.; [pers.] This poem is my whole entire life's work put together and I have juiced every, every, every ounce of soul out of myself to create this literary piece of work. I would also like to thank Eutona Soto for my inspirations.; [a.] Grand Island, NE

BALEIN, ROMEO A.
[pen.] R.B., Romy, Romeo Balein; [b.] August 31, 1936, Manila, Philippines; [m.] Andrea Docena Balein, January 1, 1969; [ch.] Rowena Adrienne, Ma. Rizza Angelie; [ed.] Bachelor of Science in Business Administration; [oth. writ.] Short stories, essays and poems; [pers.] I write mainly for the pleasure or writing; [a.] Hamilton, OH

BALL, JOYCE ANGELINE
[b.] November 4, 1968, Galesburg, IL; [p.] Van and Marjory Ball; [ch.] Shilow and Melissa Sparks; [ed.] BPC High School; [hon.] Poetry Awards; [oth. writ.] Some poetry published in Carl Sanburg College Poetry book; [pers.] The things I write are all about the spiritual word about God. And about the way I have a relationship with my Father in heaven; [a.] Galesburg, IL

BALUNSAT, ALEXIS P.
[b.] January 16, 1939, Manila, Philippines; [p.] Antonio and Maria Balunsat; [m.] Divorced; [ch.] Audrey, Craig and Zandra; [ed.] B.A. in World Business San Francisco State Univ.; [occ.]

Disabled; [memb.] Former Memberships in Ass'n of Military Comptrollers, American Society for Pub. Admin, Municipal Finance Officers Ass'n, Assoc. of Gov't Accountants, and current member, International Society of Poets; [hon.] 1. Honor grad and gold medalist for extra curricular achieve. Jose Abad Santos High, Arellano Univ., 2. Scholarship - Far Eastern Univ., 3. Honor grad - Stockton College, 4. Dean's List - Bowie State Univ., 5. Senator O'Reilly Scholarship MD.; [oth. writ.] "Song of the Homeless", East of the Sunrise, "Closed Window", Screenplay, "James Woman", Novelette (unpublished), Editorials and Articles, Maroon and Gold School Annual and Mercury Magazine News Reports, "The Manila Eye".; [pers.] Humanity is the business of good government.; [a.] Broken Arrow, MD

BANDA, MARY
[b.] March 7, 1963, Harlingen, TX; [oth. writ.] Written several for friends and for myself, but none ever submitted for publication.; [pers.] I am greatly influenced by my loved ones. Although this poem was written for someone else, I would like to dedicate it to Gaby and Lulu.; [a.] Harlingen, TX

BANKS, MIQUIEL LARON
[b.] February 2, 1970, Atlanta, GA; [p.] Levi Banks, Beulah Sawyer; [ed.] Southside High School (College Preparatory Diploma) (Fall 85 - Sum 88), Georgia State University (Sum 92 - Sum 94), Morris Brown College (Fall 94 - Present); [occ.] Full-time student at Morris Brown College, Amway distributor; [memb.] Atlanta Lawyer for the Arts; [hon.] Honorable Discharge from US Army, Persian Gulf War Veteran; [oth. writ.] Novels, short stories, lyrics, limericks, essays, quotes, varied religious writings, and articles (published a few poems and articles in the Signal, GSU newspaper.); [pers.] People lift weights to increase the strength of their muscles, why not read poetry to increase the strength of their hearts?; [a.] Atlanta, GA

BARGER, KEVIN M.
[b.] November 12, 1962, Hamilton, OH; [p.] Milford and Pamela Barger; [m.] Victoria E. Barger, October 6, 1990; [ch.] Elizabeth Michelle; [ed.] Edgewood High, Queen City Jewelry Seminars Diamontology and Gemology, Diamond Council of America, Gemological Institute of America; [occ.] Owner, Goldsmith, Retail Jewelry Store; [memb.] Fairfield Chamber of Commerce Jewelers of America, Ohio Retailers Association, Exchange Club of Fairfield, Belle Ave. Pentecostal Church; [hon.] Alpha Beta Kappa National Honor Society; [oth. writ.] Personal collection of poems; [pers.] I have found writing to be the only way to express my deepest emotions, otherwise they would have never been openly expressed.; [a.] Hamilton, OH

BARKER, RICHARD A.
[b.] November 13, 1961, Saint Andrew, JA; [p.] Gwen Recas, Rupert H. Barker; [ch.] Tahajah Samuels Barker; [ed.] Cayman Island High, Cornwall College, Brooklyn College, Kingsborough Community College; [occ.] Accountant; [hon.] Dean's List (KCC); [pers.] The desire to understand the nature of humankind through the comprehension of the inner me. I have been influenced in order, by my teachers: Prof.

Simon (KCC), Prof. Brown, Golden, and Higginbotham (BC.); [a.] Brooklyn, NY

BARKER SR., GERALD D.
[b.] July 18, 1937, Lexington, KY; [m.] Betty L. Barker, March 17, 1961; [ch.] Gerald D. Barker Jr.; [oth. writ.] I Just finished writing my autobiography and I'm hoping to have it published. Titled I survived the fifties in Hyde Park.; [pers.] I become an accomplished artist and writer after I turned fifty years old. I seem to be more inspired now that I'm older.; [a.] Lynwood, IL

BARLOW, LINDA E.
[pen.] Linda E. Barlow; [b.] November 11, 1947; [p.] Hobert and Cora Roy; [m.] Deceased, January 4, 1968; [ch.] Margaret Lynell Wilson, Samuel Thomas Barlow Jr., Beth Ellen Concepcion; [ed.] B.S. History - Social Studies, M.A. Counseling; [occ.] Guidance Counselor, at Lehigh Acres Middle School; [memb.] Alpha Delta Kappa, Phi Delta Kappa, NEA, AAWU, Methodist Church; [hon.] Nominated 2 years in a row for Golden Apple Teacher award for Lee Co.; [oth. writ.] About happenings in my life, family, friends, and travels.; [pers.] I believe we were placed on this earth to love and honor God by the lives, talents, and abilities He gave us, and to share with others all of the above.; [a.] Cape Coral, FL

BARNABY, THOMAS C.
[b.] April 26, 1973, Wareham, MA; [p.] Dennis Barnaby, Joan Barnaby; [ed.] Graduate of Tewksbury Memorial High School; [pers.] Your life is what you make of it, so follow your heart and what you feel. For you only live once so always strive for more.; [a.] Tewksbury, MA

BARNARD, ANGEL R.
[b.] March 17, 1960, Queens, NY; [p.] Leo Barnard, Sr., Bonnie R. Sembly; [ch.] Shanike Davon Barnard; [ed.] Annapolis Senior High, Fleet Business School; [occ.] Secretary, AT&T, Silver Spring, MD; [memb.] Executive Board member of the fleet Alumni Association; [oth. writ.] Several unpublished poems and songs about Life and Love; [pers.] To recognize and cherish the people who believe in you. Those who can share in your vision and encourage you to pursue and realize your dreams.; [a.] Greenbelt, MD

BARNETT, VICTORIA
[b.] May 6, 1972, Newport, KY; [p.] Rissie Barnett, Clifton Barnett; [ch.] Kevin Ray, Roger Dallen; [ed.] Boone country high of Florence KY; [hon.] 1st place in a drawing contest in Jr., high; [pers.] My Father and God inspired me to write this poem. My Father died of Cancer and this was my way of saying Goodbye; [a.] Saint Augustine, FL

BARON, CHARLES J.
[pen.] Charles Jesse Baron; [b.] May 20, 1936, Winston Salem, NC; [p.] Vinnie E. and Walter T. Baron; [m.] Martha C. Baron, November 25, 1967; [ch.] Adrienne Renee Baron, Cristal Jacque Baron and Charles J. Baron III, Newphew/godson of Bernice and Jesse Eggleton; [ed.] Carver High School - Winston Sale, North Carolina Central University, Durham, N.C., Howard University - Washington, D.C.; [occ.] Actor/Attorney; [memb.] New York Bar, D.C. Bar, Nebraska Bar, Screen

Actors Association, America Federation of Television and Radio Artists, National Bar Association, Shepherd Park Community Association.; [hon.] Junior High School Teacher of the Month, Outstanding Performance behind the Iron Curtain, Charter Member of the Senior Executive Service of the Federal Government. Outstanding Senior-High School and College, Outstanding Alumnus of Howard University, Who's Who in East.; [oth. writ.] Several unpublished poems and short stories.; [pers.] In my writings, as in my life, I strive to touch the lives of others in a positive way that it will make a tear a smile, a limp a leap, joy, laughter, peace, tolerance, love of and respect for humankind, a daily though and practice.; [a.] Washington, DC

BARONE, JUSTINA
[pen.] Tina; [b.] May 3, 1981, Dunkirk, NY; [p.] Mary A. Barone; [ed.] Kindergarten - School #7, Grades 1-5, #5, Grades 6-8, Dunkirk Middle School; [memb.] Vice President, Student Council (1994-95), Editor of School Yearbook (1994-95), Varsity Track (sprinter, relay-400), Outfielder for Post 62 Girl's Softball.; [hon.] Honor list every year, Chosen to play on Softball ALL STAR TEAM which placed 2nd, completed 50 yard dash in 6.0 seconds, Shuttle run in 8.5 seconds-set school records for both.; [pers.] Quitters are people who are afraid of losing.; [a.] Dunkirk, NY

BARRETT, BETTY L.
[pen.] "Ms B"; [b.] August 16, 1927, Rossville, KS; [p.] Dewey and Florence Countryman (deceased); [m.] Divorced, widow (deceased), September 27, 1947; [ch.] Steven Barrett, Jerrie Chancey, Vicki J. Barrett; [ed.] 12 yr. High School, 1 yr. College, I plan to go back to Rossville, Ks. for our 50th High School Reunion.; [occ.] Retired; [memb.] Alcoholics Anonymous, 15 yrs 2 mos, 13 days sober; [hon.] It is a honor to sponsor 4 ladies in AA. I graduated from Sullivan Business College (1982), President, Women's Society (2 yrs) of our church.; [oth. writ.] None completed at this time. While president at church, I was responsible for getting sponsors for our church cook book. Editing, the whole nine yards. Great success!; [pers.] My ex-husband divorced me after 32 1/2 yrs. My 3 children and 5 grandchildren are so proud of my 15 yrs and sobriety. I am still struggling (financially) to make ends meet. Hope "Sober at Midnight" will be put to music; [a.] Louisville, KY

BARRETT, LYNNE R.
[pen.] Lynne; [b.] February 4, 1947, Indianapolis, IN; [p.] Charles and Rachel Barrett; [ed.] Jr, in Social Work of Gerontology; [occ.] Volunteer; [memb.] PEO, WWF, NWF; [hon.] In my family do well in math and Poetry perhaps back to Elizabeth Barrett back Browning; [oth. writ.] Published in presbyterian life, Link's newsletter, and LDS Inst. newsletter; [pers.] I am Schidsophrenic and Manic Depressive and this poem was written during a manic swing, I've been told Barretts; [a.] Boise, ID

BARRETT, MATTHEW J.
[b.] January 19, 1980, San Francisco; [p.] William and Anne Barrett; [ed.] High School Freshman Marin Catholic High School; [occ.] Student;

[memb.] U.S. Tennis Association, Northern California Tennis Assn.; [pers.] I strive to reflect the darkness of mankind's inner thoughts and what they are thinking when nobody is around. I have been greatly influenced by the writings of Edgar Allan Poe.; [a.] San Rafael, CA

BARRIER, WANDA F.
[b.] July 22, 1930, Odonnel, TX; [p.] W. C. and Zadie Aldridge; [m.] Richard Leroy Barrier, February 24, 1951; [ch.] Brady B. Barrier (deceased), Ricky Lee Barrier; [ed.] High School, two years College. Many certificates in classes such as writing, social work. English arts-crafts etc.; [occ.] Retired in Management and Health Care; [memb.] Baptist Church, women farm organizations-women mission studies-health care reviews-home health care-book clubs-family aid center-loving and sharing to others. Retired 4-H member.; [hon.] Writing skills. I have received honors in all works. My most rewarding is being ask for poems to be used at funerals, weddings. For gatherings such as poems for retired persons, etc., poems used in places of worship is my proudest.; [oth. writ.] Articles for news alert. Many for self satisfactions and personal reasons. So many destroyed by fire, in-replacable as they were written from memory with no copy kept. I still have the thoughts.; [pers.] My writings are on true events and happenings. So many thoughts from God come and go quickly leaving me with a memory, sometimes all my own inspired by God. If I don't watch the mind is faster than the hand. Thoughts, oh such wonderful thoughts.; [a.] Waco, TX

BARRIOS III, LEO
[b.] January 26, 1941, Pomona, CA; [p.] Antonia Barrios; [ed.] Pleasant View Elementary School (CA), Santa Fe School (CA), Spanaway Junior High School (WA); [occ.] Student; [pers.] This poem was based on my pain and hurt that my father has caused me. I want to say "Thank You" to my Mother (the "Best Mother in the World"), my Grandma and Grandpa Martinez and my aunts and uncles.; [a.] Baldwin Park, CA

BARROWES, J. W.
[p.] Morrell Barrowes, Jane Barrowes; [m.] Lucy C. de Barrowes, February 8, 1964; [ch.] Yvette Maria, Juan Antonio; [ed.] AA - Panama Canal College, BA/Ma - University of Nebraska, MS - University of Miami; [occ.] English Teacher; [memb.] Teachers of English to Speakers of Other Languages - Int'l Panama Teachers of English to Speakers of Other Languages - (Panama - TESOL); [hon.] Combined Federal Campaign's Gold Award, Department of Defense Dependents Schools (Do DDS - Panama) Special Award, Panama TESOL's Outstanding Award; [oth. writ.] Master's Thesis: "Hagiolatry and Iconoclasm: The Literary Genesis of Shaw's "Saint Joan". Edited book: Haiku Poetry, articles and poetry published in TESOL's Newsletter - poetry published in Panamanian Newspapers Translations Published in the "Prairie Schooner" and the "Nebraskan Magazine"; [pers.] Poetry for me is looking into myself and capturing, with the right words, how I feel about what is moving and memorable to me. Poetically, I've been influenced by Pulitzer-prize-winning poet, Karl Shapiro and his revelations on the modernists.; [a.] Germantown, MD

BARRY, RICHARD T.
[pen.] R. T. Barry; [b.] July 4, 1963, Utica, NY; [p.] Kathryn Barry; [ed.] Utica Free Academy; [occ.] Sony Pictures Entertainment - Manager; [oth. writ.] It is me... On the threshold of a dream; [pers.] Everybody has a dark side that just needs the light switch turned on. My mind just happens to flicker.; [a.] Greenwich, CT

BARTELUS, GUSTAVE
[pen.] "GB"; [b.] May 20, 1952, Port-Au-Prince, Haiti; [p.] Stania Jean-Baptiste, Dreus Bartelus; [m.] Elvire Guerrier Bartelus, July 15, 1982; [ch.] Guerdy, Greny, Kimberly, Gibson; [ed.] Roxbury, Community College, Boston; [occ.] Vinfen - Mental Health Counselor, Boston, Radio Speaker Advertiser; [memb.] Elder, Temple Salem Haitian, Seventh Day Adventist Church, Dorchester, MA; [hon.] Sacred Elder in Jesus Christ in 1994; [oth. writ.] 12 non-published, French poems; [pers.] I'd like to touch one's consciousness for a better world through my writing. All the glory to Jesus, my Lord and all the roses to my everlasting rose, Elvire as well as my Godly gifts, my children.; [a.] Cambridge, MA

BARTON, SANDY
[b.] May 9, 1979, Santa Ana, El Salvador; [p.] Noemy Barton; [ed.] Los Angeles High; [occ.] High school student; [oth. writ.] Several other poems of my own.; [pers.] As Bobby Fischer once said, "It's nice to be modest, but it's stupid not to tell the truth." I get most of my motivation from my family, especially my sister, Reyna.; [a.] Los Angeles, CA

BASILE, JOANNA P.
[b.] April 4, 1973, Chicago; [p.] Joseph Basile, Janice Pozza; [ed.] Tinley Park High School, Northern Illinois University; [occ.] Assistant, River North Studios, Records Chicago; [memb.] Green Peace, PETA (People for the Ethical Treatment of Animals), NARAS (National Association of Recording Arts and Sciences), SOAR (Students Organized Against Rape); [hon.] Creative Excellence in Writing Award; [oth. writ.] Have been published in University Newspaper, been published in several literary magazines and annuals, recently writing for country music; [pers.] My writing comes from inspiration. Many facets of my life and the world around me inspire and teach me. "If you leave open your heart, it will not fail you."; [a.] Oak Forest, IL

BASINGER, ELEANOR F.
[b.] May 1, 1931, Washington, DC; [p.] Barron P. Freeburger, Katherine A. Freeburger; [m.] James S. Basinger, February 10, 1951; [ch.] William Daniel, Joseph Andrew, Stuart Lee; [ed.] McKinley Tech High Washington, DC; [occ.] Retired; [memb.] St. Luke Lutheran Church, White Oak Homemakers (Past President and Vice President) 1969-1971 Chaplain - Silver Spring Lioness Club 1977-1984; [oth. writ.] Several Poems published in local newspaper; [pers.] My writing are about life. Whether it be humor, joy, love or sorrow. It is my hope that what I write will touch the heart of the reader.; [a.] Silver Spring, MD

BASNER, DIANE
[pen.] DB; [b.] April 5, 1964, Atlantic City, NJ; [p.] Lydia and James Bratten, Jr.; [m.] Glenn R. Basner, April 27, 1985; [ch.] Dana Erin; [ed.] Parkside H.S. and Wor-Wic Technical and Community College; [occ.] Certified Nursing Asst., and Emergency Medical Technician; [memb.] Delmar, De., Fire Dept.; [pers.] I've been writing for many years. My grandmother had a very large influence on my writing. She taught me to write from the "depth of my heart". In memory to her I wrote "Not Far Away."; [a.] Salisbury, MD

BASSO, ELIZABETH V.
[b.] March 13, 1964, Brooklyn; [p.] Frances and James; [m.] Gary, June 30, 1990; [ch.] Alexander, Eric; [ed.] John Jay, H.S.; [occ.] Real Estate Agent; [pers.] I write from the inside out!; [a.] Yorktown Heights, NY

BATEMON, JACKIE
[b.] January 23, 1981, Petaluma; [p.] Dave and Gloria Batemon; [ed.] Currently in 8th grade; [occ.] Student; [oth. writ.] Another poem regarding Polly Klaus, my classmate, published in the newspaper.; [pers.] I write what I can't say in words, in poems, about the tragedies in my life.; [a.] Penngrove, CA

BATES, MARCUS RICARDO
[b.] April 7, 1975; [p.] Leroy Bates, Beula Bates; [ed.] Ridgewood High School Class "94", Bergen Community College (Freshman); [pers.] Through the eyes of a child I see the world. Its persecution, destruction, and resurrection. I whiteness the duamas that unfold, then wright them down for the world to see.; [a.] Ridgewood, NJ

BAUCH, DIXIE D.
[b.] January 17, 1924, Muldoon, TX; [p.] Charles and Sally Hart; [m.] Erich Bauch, November 27, 1942; [ch.] Lynn Bauch, Mostella Keith Bauch, Charles Bauch; [ed.] High School; [occ.] Schulenburg Garden Club, AARP Chapter 2727; [oth. writ.] Some Poems; [a.] Schulenburg, TX

BAUER, JASON
[b.] December 23, 1979, San Diego, CA; [p.] Michael J. and Lynn K. Baver; [ed.] Robinson Secondary School; [occ.] Student; [memb.] National Honor Society; [hon.] Honorable Mention, National Scholastic Art and Writing Awards of 1993, Certificate of Achievement in Writing, National Council of English Teachers Promising Young Writers Programs 1994. Fairfax Optimist club's Newspaper Writing Awards.; [oth. writ.] Several science fiction short stories and unpublished novels, and assorted poems. Feature writer for The Medallion - Robinson Intermediate School newspaper.; [a.] Fairfax Station, VA

BEALE, SHEENA DANIELLE
[pen.] Sheena; [b.] September 16, 1986, Indianapolis, IN; [p.] Joseph D. and Patricia A. Beale; [ed.] I am currently in the 2nd gr. at Brook Park Elementary School; [hon.] In Kg. I attended abentie mames child development center where I was crowned Queen of the kindergarten class of 1992, I have been a straight "A" honor student since I started school.; [pers.] I plan to attend college and may become a lawyer.; [a.] Indianapolis, IN

BEAM, ZULEMA
[pen.] Mrs. Z; [b.] December 16, 1959, Ogallala, NE; [p.] Clem Garcia (who showed me what unconditional love truly is).; [m.] Edwin Beam (who showed me a different perspective from an innocent heart.) March 19, 1988; [ch.] Joaquin C. and Mario J. (who both kept me on the positive side); [ed.] American School Foundation of Guadalavara and McCook Community College of Nebraska; [occ.] Working on a game, that I dreamt about. Hope to finish this Summer of 95.; [pers.] Through my learned experiences, and moral high standards, I base my foundation on the truth only. I'm after the heart.; [a.] Canton, GA

BEARD, WILLIE EDNA
[pen.] Willabee; [b.] February 20, 1938, Kinston, NC; [p.] Bishop William Roberts, Janie Roberts; [ch.] Michael, Kelvin, Angela, Brenda, Linda; [ed.] Boylan Haven Bording Sch. Jacksonville, Fla., Antioch University, Phila. PA.; [occ.] Office Manager of JEVS-Phila. PA.; [memb.] 1st Presbyterian Church in Germantown, Ron Hubbard's Church Scientology Court Reporting Institute Advisory Council; [hon.] Golden Poets Award 1989 - Love is a Phoenix; [oth. writ.] Temple University Interchange "A Vision Shared" (Article) 1992 American Poetry Association 1989 "Love Is A Phoenix" (Poem); [pers.] Poetry is God's prescription for words that are sometimes meant to be used for healing the wounded spirit.; [a.] Philadelphia, PA

BEASON, PAUL K.
[pen.] A. J. Thornton; [b.] June 28, 1929, Lafayette, IN; [p.] Paul T. and Mildred Beason; [m.] Margaret D. Krell Beason, September 19, 1953; [ch.] Glann A., Brian M., Matthew G.; [ed.] Cicero Public Elementary, J. S. Morton High School - Cicero, IL., University of Houston - Houston, TX.; [occ.] Retired; [oth. writ.] Poems and short stories and working on an historical novel.; [pers.] The higher goals of mankind, can only be gained through faith, desire, and dedication in the attainment of knowledge, for the ultimate benefit of all men.

BEATTIE, JUNE
[pen.] Judy Beattie; [b.] April 1, 1943, Lubbock, TX; [p.] Dub Simpson, Evalyn Davis; [m.] Leroy Beattie, June 26, 1972; [ch.] Randy, Megan; [ed.] Lubbock High School; [occ.] Nursing Assistant for Elderly; [oth. writ.] Many poems used for personal and private moments for clients; [pers.] I write from the heart to reflect love and the power of love in ones life. The heart and soul is such an endless source of words.; [a.] Lubbock, TX

BEATTY, BEATRICE M.
[b.] January 7, 1929, Roderfield, WV; [p.] Raleigh and Hattie Smith; [m.] Joseph A. Beatty, August 18, 1950; [ch.] Joyce Diane and Pamela Caitlin, grandsons - Joseph and Josh Thomas, son-in-laws - Elmer M. Thomas; [occ.] Retired; [pers.] I strive to be a person that uplifts the greatness of my Creator and to imprint His greatness in the hearts and minds of my children and grandchildren.; [a.] Annandale, VA

BECKER, JAQUELINE H.
[b.] December 12, 1943, Staten Island, NY; [p.] Benjamin J. Becker, Stelle L.; [ed.] Ms, Ph.D.; [occ.] Psychologist, Writer, Corporate Counselor; [memb.] APA; [oth. writ.] Staying alive and other poems. Poetry published in several journals; [a.] New York, NY

BECKWITH, MADISON C.
[pen.] Mat; [b.] January 26, 1918, Monroe, LA; [p.] Robert Beckwith and Lena; [m.] Hope E. Beckwith, July 5, 1993; [ed.] High School; [occ.] Retired; [memb.] AARP; [hon.] Letter from Ex-Mayor Washington for sending my poem Chicago the beautiful before he passed away; [oth. writ.] Several poems not published; [pers.] I like to show my poems to friends when they visit. They enjoy reading them. And that make me happy.; [a.] Chicago, IL

BEEM, KIMBERLY
[pen.] Kimberly "Baby" Beem; [b.] May 13, 1982, IL; [p.] Mata and John Harders; [occ.] Model; [hon.] Straights A's, I won five awards in 6th grade for poems.; [oth. writ.] Momma I'm A Teenager, Help Me God, Can't You See I'm Dying.; [pers.] I know I might be under age, but writing is life. When I write, I put a whole bunch of words on paper.; [a.] Chicago, IL

BELFATTO, CHRISTINE
[b.] December 18, 1927, Brooklyn, NY; [m.] Joseph Belfatto, June 23, 1951; [ch.] Mrs. Carol Shultz, Mark Belfatto, John Belfatto; [ed.] B.S., Russell Sage College, M.S College of New Rochelle; [occ.] Special Education Teacher; [memb.] Greenwich Garden Education Center. Katonah Museum of Art; [oth. writ.] I wrote for the Russell Sage College newspaper - "Sage News"; [pers.] I enjoy writing about life's experience and strive to look for ways to express humanities ability to triumph over adversity.; [a.] Chappaqua, NY

BELL, CAROL DANIELS
[b.] June 14, 1963, London, England; [p.] Henry Daniels, Dorel Hamilton; [m.] Patrick Bell, August 20, 1987; [ch.] Julian, David; [ed.] Syracuse University; [occ.] Homemaker; [memb.] Christ Church of Rockville Scholarship Committee Director; [oth. writ.] A collection of 200 poems under the title As my Father tells me unpublished but copyrighted.; [pers.] Words are the tool to speech and speech the tool to thoughts... a thought should carry wisdom and knowledge of the creator of words, GOD.; [a.] Silver Spring, MD

BELL II, TED
[pen.] T Bell II; [b.] January 8, 1961; [p.] Mr. and Mrs. Theodore J. Bell I; [m.] Tracy Taylor-Bell, May 16, 1992; [ch.] Brent Joshua Bell (1 year old); [ed.] Bachelor's of Art Degree in Art - Saint Mary's College of California, Business Diploma - Heald Business College, California School of Arts and Crafts, Berkeley School of Computer Graphics; [occ.] Computer Support Analyst - McCue Systems; [hon.] My marriage and the birth of my son.; [oth. writ.] Unpublished Scripts: The Orreos, Yellowjacket, Porch Monkey, Distant

Lover, Scent of Fear, Inhibited, When the Grass Isn't Green. Short Stories: Song of Somalia, Ride of My Life, Still Waters, The Black House; [pers.] For Dreamers only: The start to any long and hard journey can not possibly begin until you take the first step.

BELL, KEITH
[pen.] Keith Bell; [b.] January 18, 1943, Denver, CO; [p.] James and Gladys Bell (Deceased); [ch.] Justin Bell; [ed.] 3 yrs. College Biological Sciences; [occ.] Disabled; [memb.] American Legion, Veterans of Foreign Wars, Nat'l Arbor Day Foundation; [hon.] 2 Editors Choice Awards; [oth. writ.] "Day After Christmas", "Blue Vases" published in Nat'l Library, "A Break in the Clouds", "The Coming of Dawn", "Poetic Voices of America", Sparrow-grass Local Newspapers; [pers.] Inspired by the seasons, the creation, and the gift of life.; [a.] White River Junction, VT

BELNAVIS, ANIKA SIMONE
[b.] May 10, 1976; [p.] Sharon Belnavis and Billy Sledge; [ed.] Graduate from East Brunswick Vocational and Technical High school. Attended Middlesex country college.; [occ.] Casual clerk at the General Mail Facility (Post Office); [hon.] Perfect Attendance, Honor Roll, MVP (Basketball and Softball 93-95) Scholar-Athlete Award; [oth. writ.] Several poems written in school.; [pers.] I love writing. I wrote many stories, poems, movies and hope to one day published a book.; [a.] New Brunswick, NJ

BENDER, STEVEN
[b.] April 3, 1973, Bronx, NY; [p.] Marilyn and Ed; [ed.] Clark HS North Hofstra University; [oth. writ.] I have a collection of personal poems, short stories, and essays not yet submitted for publication; [pers.] ...And the day came that the Angel's wings failed, and Heaven fell. I was the one left to write about it.; [a.] New City, NY

BERG, BRIANA YUMIKO
[b.] June 12, 1982, Redlands, CA; [p.] William and Michelle Berg; [a.] Yucaipa, CA

BERG, GUNNAR E.
[b.] January 18, 1959, Claremont, NH; [ed.] University of Michigan; [occ.] Teacher; [oth. writ.] Several Newspapers Articles; [pers.] Live free or die; [a.] Chicago, IL

BERGH, NICOLE
[b.] January 9, 1980, Twin Falls, ID; [p.] John and Gay Bergh; [m.] Moroni (boyfriend); [ed.] 8th grade; [occ.] Working at Tanning place; [hon.] 23 boating trophies and 1 fishing trophy; [oth. writ.] Don't have one, I have poems that I did not send in.; [pers.] I don't want anyone copying my poems, my name must be at the bottom of the poem to show that it is mine, I want a copy of my poem.; [a.] Hagerman, ID

BERGQUIST, JOYCE L.
[pen.] "Grandma Bee"; [b.] May 1, 1924, Orange, NJ; [p.] Lockhart, Scotch-Canadian (Deceased); [m.] Divorced, October 1942-1980; [ch.] Karen Diane, Nancy Lee, Craig Michael, Scott Kevin;

[ed.] Graduate of Sacramento State Univ, also attended Flag staff AZ, University, Summer School; [occ.] Taught ten years Gallup, N. Mex (on Reservation); [memb.] Church; [hon.] Perhaps my greatest honor was to be accepted by the Navajo people; [oth. writ.] Poetry written, started in 1935, after the death of my beloved mother. I had to live in Canada for two years with Aunt.; [pers.] "Grandma Bee" was given to me by the Navajos, whom I dearly love. They treated me as their own, B) talent: given to us, must be used for the happiness of others.; [a.] Sacramento, CA

BERMEL, ESTHER
[b.] January 2, 1963, New York; [p.] Joseph Bermel, Sara Murray; [ch.] Max Bermel, Elijah Bermel; [ed.] Pierce College Woodland Hills, CA; [occ.] Full time mother, inspiring writer; [oth. writ.] Currently writing a book, of many poems, inspired by the love, I have for God.; [pers.] I want to show the world through my writings. How the Spirit of God, works through the heart of man!; [a.] Las Vegas, NV

BERNSHTEYN, DAVID
[b.] May 24, 1975, Moscow, Russia; [p.] Alexander Bernshteyn, Yelena Bernshteyn; [ed.] Scarsdale High School, Concordia College Bronxville; [occ.] Sophomore at Concordia; [memb.] Encore book poetry reading, concordia poetry club and member in Standfort Temple with Rabbi Emily. Kozzehick; [pers.] In my writing I try to reflect the sufferings of men, women and children and I fill my writings with hope, love and peace,; [a.] Mount Vernon, NY

BERRY, SANDRA
[b.] October 27, 1947, Kalamazoo, MI; [p.] Allen Hazell, Lucille Hazell; [m.] Lyle Berry, Jr., May 20, 1983; [ch.] Brian Williams (son), Austin, Aaron, Alex, Samantha Williams (grandchildren); [ed.] High School, Kalamazoo, Central 1965; [occ.] Quality Control at Abex/NWL Aerospace; [memb.] Fraternal Order of Eagles; [a.] Kalamazoo, MI

BERTI, SHANNON
[b.] October 30, 1980, Wharton, TX; [p.] Robin and Steve Berti; [ed.] I am in eighth grade at Finley Middle School (Ringgold School District); [occ.] Student; [oth. writ.] Other poems I've written on my own time; [pers.] I am 14 yrs old and in 8th grade. I played volleyball and cheerleader for my school. I enjoy writing poetry in my free time. I've written other poems (since I was young) but drifting is the one most special to me for it's dedicated to my great grandma.; [a.] Eighty-Four, PA

BESSETTE, TERRI
[pen.] Jade; [b.] September 24, 1959, Connecticut; [p.] Joseph and Pauline Bessette; [oth. writ.] Several poems published into greeting cards, and alternative press; [a.] Albuquerque, NM

BESTLAND, ERIC JUSTICE
[p.] Roy and Claudia Bestland; [a.] Palm Beach Gardens, FL

BEVERIDGE, LINDA M.
[b.] December 31, 1947, Sharon, PA; [p.] William and Nellie Bowman (Maloy); [m.] Edward Beveridge, December 1971; [ch.] Scott Edward - 22 and Erin Marie - 16; [ed.] Graduated Reynolds High School - Greenville, PA; [occ.] John Caroll - Real Estate, Cleveland, OH, Realtor, housewife; [memb.] Butler Hospital Auxiliary American Heart Assoc., MADD, Member of Trinity Lutheran Church, Butler Board of Realtors; [hon.] Some awards for selling Real Estate. Have given 75 pints of blood which I am proud of doing.; [oth. writ.] Have many many poems over the years for friends and relatives. This one was made in memory of my Mother and Aunt - it's my personal favorite; [pers.] Most of my poems reflect how I or family member, feel. I've always loved poetry; [a.] Butler, PA

BIANCHI, ROLAND R.
[b.] July 1, 1930, San Francisco; [p.] Renato Bianchi, Beatrice Bianchi; [m.] Dr. Judy Rogers Bianchi, June 23, 1984; [ch.] Russell, Ross, Randall; [ed.] Geo. Washington HS S.F. Ca. '48 B.S. University of Calif. at Berkeley '52 MBA School of Credit and Financial Mgt Harvard, Boston, Mass. 1972; [occ.] Retired, Banker Currently, Home Repairs and Renovations; [memb.] GWHS Alumni Assoc, Univ. of Calif Alumni Assoc (life member), Phi Kappa Tau Fraternity (alumnus), Serra Club of San Mateo (active), Rotary Club of San Mateo (active); [oth. writ.] Novel, published by Daniel and Daniel Publishing of Santa Barbara Calif. Fithian Press "Tunes From A Tuscan Guitar" 1994; [pers.] I have enjoyed writing poetry as an avocation for my family and friends. Recently, I have begun to write about my family heritage with emphasis on ethnic influence and its assimilation into the America way of life. I espouse the philosophy, "that when two cultures mix, only the best of each survives."; [a.] San Francisco, CA

BIBBS, MILDRED ELIZABETH
[b.] April 30, 1938, Philadelphia, PA; [p.] Pernette and Ada Bibbs; [pers.] I began enjoying and reading poetry while in high school, realizing how poems could express so many things in so many ways. A language so understandable, it would let you see and know what it is all about. Poetry always seemed to have a wonderful beginning and would some how always end beautifully to me. I love poetry for it make me feel so good inside, to read such enchanting words to form poetry. Would light up my entire world, I began writing poetry in the early 60's, but didn't start putting them together until 1992. I enjoy expressing myself through poetry and hope to pass this joy to everyone else, that you too can see how lovely poetry can be for you, and me. I love poetry.

BILAL, LAVERN
[b.] January 23, 1945, Inkster, MI; [p.] Adell and Bennie Burroughs; [m.] Divorced; [ch.] Zakiyyah Lavell and Ilyas Bendell I; [ed.] I graduated from Los Angeles Trade Technical College with an AA Degree and is now a student at Wayne State University.; [memb.] Janazah Committee and The Wesley Foundation; [hon.] An awardee of the Women Scholars Scholarship and The Women of Wayne Alumni Association Scholarship.; [oth.

writ.] I've written a collection of 15 poems entitled "Poems For All Seasons".; [pers.] Life's journey isn't for the swift, but for the one that endures to the end.; [a.] Inkster, MI

BILLINGS, THERESSA
[b.] April 8, 1977, Weymouth, MA; [p.] James Billings, Dorinda Billings; [ed.] Home schooled since the third grade; [occ.] Child Care; [hon.] Honorable Mention in an arts contest sponsored by my church; [oth. writ.] Numerous unpublished poems and short stories; [pers.] I've been writing poetry since I was twelve. My inspiration was the poetry of Carol Lynn Pearson. I write about both what I see and experience, and, most importantly, what I feel.; [a.] Abington, MA

BINGAMAN, HARRY L.
[b.] July 21, 1908, Penna.; [p.] Daniel and Emma Bingaman; [m.] Dorothy Aumiller Bingaman, September 15, 1935; [ch.] Dr. Dahle D. Bingaman, Donna L. Purves; [ed.] High School (Hartley Twp), Lock Haven Teacher's College, PA, Wesley Seminary, Washington, DC.; [occ.] Retired; [memb.] AARP - Ret. Teacher's Nat'l Education Assn (Life member), Chaplain West End Senior Center, Lincoln Chapel U.M. Church, Golden Oldies Crafts. Past President Union Co., Sabbath School Assn.; [hon.] Hobby, Quilting, Quilt Exhibited at Wm. Penn Museum, Harrisburg, PA, in Honor of Gov. Dick Thornburg Inaugura-tion Invited to Inauguration and Ball - 1979; [oth. writ.] Published book of poems entitled "Monday Letters", for Personal use. Received various awards for Oil Paintings and Pen and Ink Drawing.; [pers.] Elementary School Teacher in Union Co., PA, for 32 years. Served as Counselor for Gov. Duffs "Camp Penn" in 1949, Pastored Churches at Montandon, PA, and Cedar Run, PA.; [a.] Laurelton, PA

BIRDINE, YOLANDA GOOPER L.
[b.] January 30, 1958, Chicago, IL; [m.] Steven T. Birdine; [ch.] Akaya and Resha Birdine; [ed.] Unity High School, Univer. of Il., Urbana, Univ. of Northern Co. and Indiana Univ.; [occ.] Assistant to Life Dean of L. Braries - IU Bloomington; [oth. writ.] Univ. of Co. publication "Moon in Her Mouth" spring edition; [pers.] I write as an expression of thoughts and emotion felt by myself and of hers not to be judged, but taken to heart and explored.

BISCHOFF, DEBORA
[b.] October 10, 1960; [m.] George Bischoff, July 29, 1991; [ch.] Shawn and Daniel; [occ.] Poet, Author of children's books; [memb.] A distin-guished member international poetry society; [hon.] 1994 Editor's choice award thru Natl. Library of Poetry for "A Poet's Cry"; [oth. writ.] `Mother's Love', `A Poet's Cry', `Forever Seeking', 3 songs and 2 children's stories

BISHOP, JOSHUA
[pen.] Brat '73; [b.] March 20, 1973, Topeka, KS; [p.] Joyce and Jerry Bishop; [m.] Tampa Sue Bishop, May 7, 1995; [ch.] Gabriel Storm Bishop; [ed.] Blakesburg High School, Indian Hills Community College; [occ.] Accounting Specialist Hawthorne Communications; [oth. writ.] Several poems that I hope to have published in the future.; [a.] Ottumwa, IA

BLACK, ERICA
[b.] June 5, 1979, Littlefield, TX; [p.] Randy and Gayle Black; [ed.] Spade High School; [occ.] Student; [memb.] NHS, FHA, FFA, Speech and Drama Club, National Forensic League; [hon.] Principals all a Honor Roll, Soil and Water Conservation Essay Winner, Computer Graphics contest finalist; [oth. writ.] None other published. But have written many more such as: Lover, Just a Prayer Away and Dreamer; [pers.] I have great support from my parents and I try to inspire people with my writing. And leave them with something to think about.; [a.] Spade, TX

BLACK, RACHEL ARIEL
[b.] October 19, 1984, Phoenix, AZ; [p.] Ralph and Ellen Black; [ed.] Grade S K - 3rd, I attended Mt. View Christian School in Fresno, CA.; [occ.] Elementary Student, Grade 4, (Home schooled by grandmother); [memb.] Olympia Sales Club, Girl Scouts of America Brownie Troupe 248 (1993-1994); [hon.] Athlete of the month award, October, 1994, at Mt. View Christian School; [oth. writ.] Although I have written poetry as a hobby since I was in the third grade, this is the first poem I have submitted for publication.; [pers.] I want to inspire other young writers to work hard and have the courage to try to get their work published.; [a.] Fresno, CA

BLACKBURN, KARLENE L.
[b.] March 15, 1974, Saint Thomas, VI; [p.] Mrs. Phyllis J. Blackburn; [ed.] T.C. Williams H.S. 1993, Lynchburg College Sophomore, Major Communications-Journalism; [occ.] Full time college student at Lynchburg College; [memb.] Argonaut Yearbook Staff, Student Activities Film Chairperson, Lynchburg College, Cheerleader - Sec/Tres.; [hon.] Anderson Leadership Confer-ence, Black Student Incentive Grant Recipient; [oth. writ.] An essay was published at Lynchburg College and a few poems were published during my high school career; [pers.] I would like to thank my mother, Dr. Paula Wilson, Dr. Elza Tiner, and Prof. Dorothy Smith-Akubue for believing and encouraging me. A special love and thanks to Russ Gowrie and Nick Douvres.; [a.] Alexandria, VA

BLACKMER, KAREN
[b.] July 10, 1942, Plainfield, CT; [p.] Armand and Annette Bouley; [ch.] Annette McClintock, Keri Champagne, Ronald Champagne; [ed.] Norwich Free Academy; [oth. writ.] Fear and Me, published, Dear Mom and Dad, published, Sparrowgrass Poetry Forum; [pers.] My writings are influenced by my Bi-Polar disorder as therapy.; [a.] Beverly Hills, FL

BLAKE, EDWARD JOSEPH
[pen.] E. Blake; [b.] July 29, 1958, Amsterdam, NY; [p.] Marlene and Bob Duesler and Edward Swart; [m.] Michele Blake, July 28, 1989; [ch.] Jonathan, Jordan, Brian, Thomas; [ed.] Broadalbin Schools, and currently Fulton-Montgomery Community College (majoring in Computer Info Systems); [occ.] Full-time College Student; [memb.] Perth-Bible Church member, written various poetry for college paper; [oth. writ.] Many various writings yet unpublished; [pers.] In spite of the common ingredients of which we all are made, our flavors are different and unique - each of its

own sweetness and bitterness. In my writing, you'll find the verbal cuisine of E. Blake, a flavor all it's own. Bon Apetite!; [a.] Amsterdam, NY

BLAKE, KATINA M.
[b.] January 6, 1973, Baltimore, MD; [p.] Olivia K. Byrd and Harrison Byrd III; [ed.] Havre de Grace High School, Harford Community College; [occ.] Customer Service Representative for Key Federal Bank; [memb.] Helping Hands Ministries; [pers.] I have been writing poems since the age of ten. God has blessed me with this talent, and to him I give all the praise. Helen Steiner Rice influenced me to share them with the world.; [a.] Havre de Grace, MD

BLANQUERA, ROBIN J.
[pen.] Joy; [b.] September 9, 1949, West Point, NY; [p.] Jeanne and Robert Dahlgren Sr.; [m.] Edmond J. Blanquera; [ch.] Jennifer Lynn, David James, Daniel Jason, Derek Julian and grand-daughter - Tiffanie Lynn; [ed.] Rye Neck H.S., Rye, N.Y., St. Agnes Hosp., School for Nursing, W.P., N.Y., Extended Education Program as Restorative Tech., Gpt., MS., Rutgers Univ. of N.J., in recognition with N.J. agricultural experiment station.; [occ.] Self Employed Property Manager, Free Lance Writer; [memb.] M.D.A., P.B.A., P.T.A., Girl Scouts of America, Boy Scouts of America, St. Bridget Church, Representative for Montgomery Gardens Head Start, J.C, N.J., for Multi cultural Bash and rewarded with outstanding ovation for my poem, titled "The Year of the L.A. Riot"; [a.] Jersey City, NJ

BLEVINS, EMILY
[pen.] Emily Brown; [b.] August 19, 1969, C.C., TX; [p.] Enrique and Ella Longoria; [m.] Dennis Blevins, June 2, 1995; [ed.] Delmar College and Austin Community College; [occ.] Technician; [hon.] Throughout schooling and employment; [pers.] I wish to continue to bring joy into the world through my writing.; [a.] Round Rock Austin, TX

BLISS, CARL LEO
[b.] August 23, 1924, Buena, WA; [p.] Rollah-Luseal Bliss; [m.] Betty Lee Bliss, August 2, 1947; [ch.] Rita D. Sarri, Rawliegh Bliss, Aleta M. Gove, Shiela Cates; [ed.] Grade - High School; [occ.] Retired; [memb.] Carson Church of the Nazarene; [a.] Carson, WA

BLOOMER, LOIS
[b.] December 6, 1924, Pgh., PA; [p.] Bert and Hilda Fair; [m.] Harry E. Bloomer, December 27, 1946; [ch.] Beverly Bloomer (Kasinec), Jeffrey-Alan-Bloomer; [ed.] B.S. University of Pittsburgh - Pgh., PA., Additional credits from Baldwin Wallace College; [occ.] Retired Teacher; [memb.] Kappa Kappa Gamma - First Methodist Church of Stuart, FL., Nashville Songwriters Assoc. International, Distinguished Memeber of I.S.P.; [hon.] Honorary Education Society from University of Pittsburgh. I received the editor's choice award" for my poem "A Captivating Fantasy."; [oth. writ.] In collaboration with my son, I have written several recorded songs. Among them, "Squeakin and a creakin", which received the first runner-up in the International - Mountain Song

Writers Contest; [pers.] I usually write metaphorically. My topics and styles rang from Limericks to serious issues. I am a watercolor painter. I sing in the Circle Bay Chorus.; [a.] Fairview Park, OH

BLOUNT, KENNETH
[b.] December 10, 1954, Dayton, OH; [p.] Willie (Deceased), and Hattie Blount; [ch.] Angela Renee Blount; [ed.] Dunbar High School; [occ.] Security Officer at the Dayton Convention Center; [oth. writ.] Unpublished manuscript with Calton Press Publishing Company. Title: Realistic Poetry.; [pers.] I'm very serious about my writing and want to dedicate my life to writing about issues that affect us all in one way or another. Through my poetry and essays.; [a.] Dayton, OH

BLUE, CHARLES A.
[pen.] William Franklin; [b.] May 4, 1950, Jersey City, NJ; [p.] William F. Blue, Eleanor Blue; [ch.] Charles Jr., Raymond, Kimberley Michelle; [ed.] Technician, Hudson County Superintendent of Elections Office; [oth. writ.] Several unpublished short stories as well as two novels; [pers.] I write for the enjoyment or others. Motivated by the need to have a hobby, writing became a new love.; [a.] Jersey City, NJ

BOGGIO, ANTONIA P.
[b.] June 7, 1971, Detroit, MI; [p.] James T. and Mary T. Boggio; [ed.] Bachelor of Art in Interior Design from Michigan State University May 1994; [occ.] Project Designer Allied Office Interiors, Okemos, MI; [memb.] Alpha Omicron PI National Sorority, International Interior Design Association.; [pers.] This soliloquy was written six years ago as an assignment for a high school English class. The poem refers to my sister, who at the time was a young teenager. Presently, we still enjoy our close relationship and often indulge in the happy memories of our childhood; [a.] Sterling Heights, MI

BOGGS, GEAN
[b.] October 14, 1928, Carlsbad, NM; [p.] Audie Lee and Susan Pearl Gregory; [ch.] Vicki Clifton, John Eager, Philip Boggs; [ed.] Carlsbad High School; [occ.] Bookkeeper; [oth. writ.] Several poems published in "The Ghost Dancers II" and "The Ghost Dancers III, a publication featuring stories, poems, picture etc. of the Southwest in the late 1800's and the early 1900's.; [pers.] The Nature of man and his strife in life are a driving force for my writing.; [a.] Carlsbad, NM

BOGGS JR., LOWELL
[pen.] Lowell Boggs; [b.] December 28, 1957, Hazard, KY; [p.] Lowell Sr. and Vicki Jo Boggs; [m.] Mary Louise, January 1, 1983; [ed.] B.S.E.F from the University of Kentucky; [occ.] Software Engineer, Texas Instruments, Dallas Tx.; [memb.] United We Stand America; [pers.] I try to see the world as it truly is - not fettered by the blinders of past, or passion, or persuasion.; [a.] Lewisville, TX

BOHON, LU ANN
[pen.] Lu Bohon; [b.] September 20, 1955, Lancaster, PA; [p.] Wilfred L. and Phyllis Kroeger; [m.] Kilby E. Bohon, August 18, 1972; [ch.] David E. Bohon (deceased), Justin L. Bohon; [ed.] Finished 10th grade of High School, Palmyra

High; [occ.] Inspector/Packer for Major Company Hannibal, MO; [memb.] St. Joseph Catholic Church; [hon.] Never have received any awards or honors. But I consider this as a great honor to have you publish this poem of mine. It means a great deal to me.; [oth. writ.] I have more poems that I have never been shared.; [pers.] I never wrote anything in my life. You always wonder what your purpose is here on earth. And when I lost my 18 year old son and then my father and grandmother all within 10 months of each other. And then some very close friends. The words just started to come. I guess it was God's way of letting me get my grief out and maybe my poems will help others who have lost there dear ones. Maybe that's my purpose here on earth.; [a.] Hannibal, MO

BOLEN, CHARLES D.
[pen.] Noah Baer; [b.] March 5, 1932, Columbia, MO; [p.] H. R. Bolen, Tressie Baer Bolen; [m.] Shirlena Jane Bolen, September 27, 1960; [ed.] Semo State College, NY Insti. of Photography; [occ.] Bookseller, Formerly Pro Portrait Photographer; [memb.] Rare Tropical Fruit Society. National Rifle Assn., Deacon, First Christian Church, Int. Freelance Photog Assn.; [oth. writ.] Letters Of Disgust to Phil Donahue and Geraldo Rivera; [pers.] Every human being should understand what God looks like: I'll be happy to reveal it for your treasure! Read Rev 1:10-16 carefully. Then colossians 1:12-15 (That is in the Bible.); [a.] West Palm Beach, FL

BOLTON, VIRGINIA C.
[b.] June 22, 1931, Russellville, AL; [p.] Willie and Lillie Henry; [m.] Clovis J. Bolton, January 13, 1950; [ch.] Glenda Carol, Donna Elaine, Judy Lynn, Deborah Ann; [ed.] Cherokee High School; [occ.] Love to cook, garden and yard work, fish and write poetry; [memb.] Church of Christ; [oth. writ.] Special poems that have not been published; [pers.] Poetry is special feelings in a persons heart, that you bring out in the open.

BONAVENTURA, ERIC
[b.] Los Angeles, CA; [ed.] High School in Southern California; [occ.] Air Quality Specialist, helping to develop policies designed to reduce air pollution.; [oth. writ.] Several pieces of writing have been published in a University Magazine entitled "Sanyog — South Asia Expressions". I have written four self-published books of poetry and short fiction.; [a.] Sacramento, CA

BOND, KATHERINE L.
[pen.] Kay Bond; [b.] June 7, 1949, Sardis, Miss; [p.] William Coble and Emma Clerk; [m.] John R. Bond IV, July 27, 1969; [ch.] Sonia O'Neal, Tasha Bond, 2 Granddaughters, Ieisha O'Neal, NI'Isha O'neal; [ed.] High School Graduate, some college; [occ.] Medical Transcriptionist; [memb.] Medic Alert and American Diabetes Association; [oth. writ.] A Notebook full of poetry. Currently working on notes and poems to my granddaughter. (Nothing published); [pers.] God and prayer makes it all possible.

BONDI, MARIE DELORUS
[b.] April 22, 1914, East Chicago, IN; [p.] Mr. and Mrs. Vasalie Hanes; [m.] Robert A. Bondi, June 24, 1960; [ch.] Donna L. Brooks, (Ralph W. Brooks); [ed.] Tenth grade - Roosevelt High School, two years Business College; [occ.] Display Director and Buyer Rosalee Stores Incorporated; [memb.] American Business Women's Assoc. Italian Catholic Federation (195); [hon.] Two Recognitions Perdue University, Who's Who Women of the World; [oth. writ.] Short stories, resumes; [pers.] What we send into the lives of others comes back unto our own. "Love each other".; [a.] Calumet City, IL

BONE, PEGGY J.
[pen.] Peg; [b.] June 25, 1946, Hazelwood, IN; [p.] Silas and Edith Pearson, both deceased; [m.] Michael J. Bone, January 6, 1965; [ch.] Dawn Shamayn, Michael Jerome Jr., and Erik Lee; [ed.] McEachern High, Lynn Chris Ann School of Charm and Modeling; [occ.] General Accountant, Lockheed Martin Aeronautical Systems Company, Marietta, Ga.; [memb.] The Church of Jesus Christ of Latter Day Saints, International Association of Machinists and Aerospace Workers (IA of M) (Shop Steward - Position); [hon.] Football Sweetheart 1960, Homecoming Queen 1961-62, Campus Queen 1962, Jr. Miss Lockheed 1963, Superlative (Most Popular) 1963-64, Miss Judean Drive In 1964, Miss Paulding County 1964, Buck Hunter Award, most Honored Award in my life is being A Wife And A Mother; [oth. writ.] I have written several poems over the years for family and friends. Nothing published as yet.; [pers.] I put my heart in my poems. I love the Lord and all my family and friends. One day I want to publish my own personal Book of Poems.; [a.] Acworth, GA

BOOTH, CORLISS
[pen.] Taj; [b.] February 12, 1943, SC; [p.] Cannie and Martha Barker; [m.] Donald W. Booth, February 4, 1978; [ed.] South Gastonia Elementary and Jr. High; [occ.] Shipping/Clerk; [memb.] Ridge Baptist Church; [oth. writ.] Three poems published in other publications, have over 200 poems of mine in my collection.; [pers.] I try to write of my moral standards and beliefs and strive to write of feelings that are shared from relationships of every kind.; [a.] Clover, SC

BOWEN, CHRISTI MICHELLE
[b.] February 27, 1979, Austin, TX; [p.] Charles and Juanita Bowen; [ed.] Freshman Anderson High School; [occ.] Student; [memb.] Outreach Production, Youth Ministry Anderson High Achievement; [hon.] Anderson High Achievement; [oth. writ.] In Junior High I have written other poems that were published in our school newspaper.; [pers.] The reason I write poems, is because they all reflect the way I feel.; [a.] Austin, TX

BOWERSOCK, CAROL
[pen.] Karroll Kay; [b.] May 23, 1971, Ashland, OH; [p.] Mr. and Mrs. Harold Eugene Bowersock, Jr., Mrs. Rita Jones; [ed.] Bradford School of Business, Columbus, OH. Diploma, Secretarial Science; [occ.] Secretary, Avon Endtime Cards and Coins, Secretary, Endtime Harvest Church (Both in Ashland); [memb.] Endtime Harvest Church, Ashland, OH.; [hon.] Meritorious Services at

Office Assistant, Mapleton High School. 1988 and '89 and Educational Grant by the Ohio Elks Educational fund board. 1989-90 Statue of Liberty Drill team member. New York 1986.; [oth. writ.] Several poems collected since the age of eight.; [pers.] Writing as often as possible keeps my God given talent alive. Emily Dickinson displayed that by her consistency. I want nothing more out of life except happiness.; [a.] Ashland, OH

BOWMAN, BRANDY
[b.] Picayune, MS; [p.] Jimmy and Ann Bowman; [ed.] Poplarville High School; [pers.] I thank God, my family, my friends, and my graduating class. All of these people have influenced my writing of this poem.; [a.] Poplarville, MS

BOYCE, EVELYN R.
[pen.] Vivian Mother; [b.] January 9, 1975, Philippines; [p.] Bibiana Pueblo and Juanito Pueblo Sr.; [m.] Keith Richard Boyce, July 23, 1994; [ed.] John F. Kennedy HS, Guam, ICS Scranton PA, Olympic College Bremerton, WA; [occ.] Student; [hon.] Multiple awards from Who's Who among America's HS student, "A" Honor roll, "A" club, Presidential Award; [pers.] My writing is a reflection of my pain. Through out my life, I learned how to deal with my sorrows and fears through poetry.; [a.] Port Orchard, WA

BOYD, IRENE ALAMMO
[pen.] Lorraine Boyd; [b.] October 15, 1956, Wilmenton, DE; [p.] Eleanor M. Hollzenger and Robert E. Padgett; [ch.] Paula Quillin, Bobby Cummiskey, Brandon Boyd; [ed.] (Major) Child Development Secretarial Science Degree; [occ.] Licensed child care provider Lorraine's family day care.; [memb.] Arden Hills Seventh Day Adventist Church. Little League Highland CA. Team Mom Asst. Coach and I also sponsor them.; [hon.] Awards handed on players by Highland little league. For my participation and fund raises Secretarial Science (Top of class) certificate of Achievement; [oth. writ.] Published poet with spirrowgraph. Poem submitted (Dreams) I have written two children's books not yet published and I have 46 children's poems and 28 adult poems not yet published.; [pers.] I was inspired by Barbara Harkness a college teacher of child development, God, and most of all the children of this world.

BOYD, STACY
[b.] February 18, 1971, Chattanooga, TN; [p.] Judith Ford, Justin Boyd; [ed.] Central High, Associate Degree in Advertising Art from Chattanooga State; [occ.] Student; [hon.] Young Author Award in Junior High; [oth. writ.] Several unnamed and unpublished manuscripts; [pers.] My own statement "Conspire with your mind, write sometime."; [a.] Harrison, TN

BOYD, THELMA
[pen.] Sis, Cocoa; [b.] March 2, 1951, White Stone, SC; [p.] Ernest O. Brewton, Leler Brewton; [m.] Timothy L. Boyd, March 30, 1970; [ch.] Lynnette Priscilla, Tracey A. Benjamin and Raymond Matthew; [ed.] N.C.C.H.S., C.L.C.JR. College.; [occ.] L.P.N., Songwriter; [memb.] NO memberships right now, but I would like to be a member of a Writers Club etc. So that I can really get down to some serious writing; [hon.] Dean's

List Scholarships C.L.C.JR. College and Waukegan Women's Club Certificates for critical care nurses, training courses.; [oth. writ.] "Reach out and hold me," "Hail to the Red, white, and blue" "I'll Love You Forever" "Rappers song against T. Crack" "When Jesus Touched my heart" "Crystal love" and many more; [pers.] I'm me, just using my gift to the best of my ability. I wrote a lot, I think a lot. Sometimes I get tired just thinking and singing. I love to sing myself to sleep at times. It takes Heart and soul that's me!; [a.] Waukegan, IL

BOYDEN, TAMMY
[b.] November 6, 1961, Escondido; [p.] Holly and Mary Morford; [m.] Thomas B. Boyden Jr., February 9, 1980; [ch.] Kristen, Joseph, Jason, Nicholas; [ed.] Escondido High; [occ.] Housewife; [oth. writ.] Several unpublished songs and poems.; [pers.] Through my writings, I strive to bring out different points of view, not to be answers but rather other options to consider to heart felt problems.; [a.] San Bernardino, CA

BOYER, ROBERT
[pen.] B. Dab; [b.] November 13, 1975, Willingboro, NJ; [p.] Cindy Boyer and Mike Riley; [m.] Michele Leigh Collins, August 10, 1994; [ed.] Burl County Institute of Technology, Willingboro High School; [occ.] Cook; [memb.] Burlington Courty Library, Willingboro Public Library; [oth. writ.] Horrible Misery, Ocean, The Girl That Never Was; [pers.] I would like to write hundreds of poems and stories about common life and have everyone read them.; [a.] Willingboro, NJ

BOYLAN, JOYCE
[b.] February 23, 1928, Newport, ME; [p.] Raymond and Myrtle Emerson; [m.] Stanley, December 14, 1951; [ch.] Jeffrey, Penny, Carol; [ed.] Registered Nurse 3 yrs graduate Hospital Nursing School; [occ.] Registered Nurse; [hon.] Distinguished service to health occupations education in Grand Fraire Schools; [oth. writ.] Three other poems as yet not submitted for publication plus one bond also as yet unpublished. Poetry published in National Anthology of high school poetry while a high school student.; [pers.] My poetry reflects Gods lessons to me or others that have touched my life.; [a.] Arlington, TX

BRACKETT, GREGORY E.
[b.] December 10, 1967, Tennessee; [p.] Mac E. and Mary Jane Brackett; [memb.] Blue Ridge Temple Baptist Church; [pers.] I try to reflect everyday life and happenings that affect us as a people.; [a.] Old Fort, TN

BRADSHAW, RUTH ATCHISON
[pen.] Ruth Atchison Bradshaw; [b.] November 27, 1929, Springville TN; [p.] V. Roy Atchison, Della Throgmorton Atchison; [m.] David A. Bradshaw, November 26 1950; [ch.] Debra Ann, David Gregory; [ed.] Springville High School Business College and Secretarial with private teacher training; [occ.] Retired; [memb.] Fairview Baptist Church; [hon.] A number of poems published in local newspaper. Prepared and Delivered Awaiting to an alumni, Gathering of 250 people. Letter from President Bill Clinton Recognizing A Creative Work; [oth. writ.] Book: (Streams of Life) written

for family and friends Consisting of Reflections of life and thing dear to me.; [pers.] My writings tend to reflect on God, life, love, and the beauty of nature. I began my writing after the death of my husband - when I was 62 years of age.; [a.] Paris, TN

BRADT, JOHN JOSEPH
[pen.] J. Joseph Bradt; [b.] October 22, 1971, Alexandria, VA; [p.] John L. Bradt, Susan M. Bradt; [ed.] Shawnee Mission South High School, Baptist Bible College, Johnson County Community College; [occ.] Printer, Kinkos Copy Center, Mission, KS; [memb.] Film Society of Greater Kansas City, Overland Park Baptist Temple.; [hon.] Honorable Mentions in Photography; [oth. writ.] Currently working on Several Screenplays and Novels.; [pers.] God has blessed me with a special talent to write and I pray that He might be glorified as I use this gift to express the love of my God, and the imagination and hope He has placed within us all.; [a.] Overland Park, KS

BRAMBLETT, SHARON
[pen.] Shadow; [b.] August 10, 1953, San Antonio, TX; [p.] Loretta and Roy Fairbanks; [m.] James Bramblett, May 19, 1989; [ch.] Clinton Roy, Billy Jack, Richard Lee, Rena; [ed.] 11th South San High, San Antonio, TX; [occ.] Bartender for 25 yrs.; [pers.] I hope that families and children realize just how far you can push or maybe already have pushed a loved one.; [a.] Muriarty, NM

BRANDER, PAMELA STOKER
[pen.] Katheryn Lee Stoker; [b.] March 15, 1943, Queen, NY; [p.] Diane Dixon McKean, Thomas White Brander; [ch.] Robert Holbrook III, Susan Marie Holbrook, David Allen Holbrook, Tracy Lynn Holbrook; [ed.] Fabius Central, Onondoga Community College, Aurora of Central New York; [occ.] Management Syracuse, N.Y.; [hon.] Volunteer Awards; [oth. writ.] Many poems, (as yet unpublished), a novel, based on my life, (in progress), several "short" stories (as yet unpublished).; [pers.] I write from the depths of my inner being. To communicate my pains and joys in life is to give all I have. To hopefully reach a lonely soul who sits and thinks, "Doesn't anyone understand?" ask a survivor of abuse, I have been there - shut out - shut down - alone. I write to free my spirit and that of others - words to sooth the soul.; [a.] Liverpool, NY

BRANDON, GENEVIEVE C.
[b.] January 2, 1908, Rock Falls, IL; [p.] Camille F. Ribordy and Catherine Lyons R. Bondy; [m.] Forrest P. Brandon, October 13, 1928; [ch.] Rich, Patty, Dave, Don, Margie, Bob, Kathleen, Larry, Janice, Janine, Jean, Marilyn, Angela; [ed.] High School, State Teacher's College, Dekalb, Il, L.P.O. Jr. College, SALK Valley, Sterling, IL; [occ.] Retired; [memb.] St. Mary's Church, Altar and Rosary, Newman Booster Club Reporter, Senior Class for Senior Class; [hon.] Won Lincoln Medal for Essay given by State, Won Award for Newsman's quotation (Bible); [oth. writ.] The Nicest Gift published in Remince Magazine, in Country and Magazine, and Hardcover Book published by Reiman publications; [pers.] Believe one must love children-to teach them Born 1-2-1908, mother of 13 children all living ages 65 yrs -

42 yrs Parent, Camille Ribordy and Catherine Lyons. Spouse: Forrest P. Brandon Elementary School teacher, White side Country, I 1 And in St. Mary School; [a.] Sterling, IL

BRANDOW, CHARISMA
[b.] November 6, 1969, Kingston, NY; [p.] Gloria Brandow, Eugene Brandow; [ch.] Kayla Marie Nicole Brandow; [ed.] Ontieora High; [occ.] Crew Chief for a restaurant corporation; [oth. writ.] My own personal book of poems that are non published.; [pers.] Looking at my daughter, or out my window, the ocean, life in general is my inspiration. My daughter is my biggest inspiration.; [a.] Panama City Beach, FL

BRANTLEY, CORI
[b.] July 9, 1982, Winter Haven, FL; [p.] Linda R. Nappi and Charlie Nappi; [ed.] 8th grade; [occ.] Student; [memb.] United Methodist Church, D.A.R.E., Crime Watch, Chorus; [hon.] Student of the year, Science fair participant, Smoke free class of 2,000 book cover contest, Super student award, D.A.R.E. certificate of achievement, awesome author; [oth. writ.] Various poems and stories (never sent them in); [pers.] Without writing my life would be empty; [a.] Port Saint Lucie, FL

BRAWLEY III, HARRY ELLIS
[b.] August 5, 1965, Boston; [p.] Mr. Harry Brawley, Jr., and Barbra Ackerman; [m.] Beth Ann Brawley, April 24, 1993; [ch.] Bill Lawrance and Jack Lawrance - two step-sons; [ed.] Graduated from Gilford High School, and Newbury College. Expect to graduate 1996; [occ.] Chef and Waitering; [memb.] United States Chess Federation; [pers.] "Now and forever to my wife", "I love you Beth Ann Brawley."; [a.] Arlington, MA

BRAXTON, WAYLON
[pen.] Engred Ziph; [b.] December 27, 1954, Sulphur, LA; [p.] George H. Braxton Sr., and Mildred Braxton; [ed.] Sulphur High School, Delta School of Business and Technology; [occ.] Apartment Management, Wildwood Management Group, San Antonio, TX; [memb.] Texas Accountants and Lawyers for the Arts (TALA); [hon.] Dean's List, President's List, Certificate of Achievement, Excellence in Spelling.; [oth. writ.] I have written bible school scripts, other poems, and manuscripts that are unpublished. This also include short stories.; [pers.] I am inspired to write by the sum of experiences and actions that constitute a person's existence in the present, past, and future.; [a.] San Antonio, TX

BREEZE, KATHY
[pen.] Kat; [b.] May 26, 1975, Prosser, WA; [p.] Sarah and Elmer Breeze; [hon.] Certificate of Participation FHA, Certificate of Appreciation, Letter in Choir and Drama; [a.] Chelan, WA

BREHM, JEREMY SCOTT
[pen.] Jay; [b.] March 8, 1975, Newark, OH; [p.] Steve and Debbie Westbrook; [ch.] Samantha Alexandra Brehm; [ed.] Newark High School; [occ.] Landscaper; [hon.] Most arctic of my graduating class of 1993 at Newark High School.; [oth. writ.] A couple poems printed in a local magazine called legend magazine. And many more

unpublished poems.; [pers.] Everything that happens in life begins in the heart. And that is where all my poetry comes from.; [a.] Newark, OH

BREWER, ARLETHA M.
[pen.] Michaelah Whitmore; [b.] March 16, 1975, Lansing, MI; [p.] Virdia L. Brewer; [ed.] Eastern High School, Eastern Michigan University, Lansing Community College; [occ.] Library Aide and College Student; [memb.] International Society of Poets; [hon.] Who's Who Among American High School Student (1991-92, 1992-93); [oth. writ.] One poem published by The National Library of Poetry and several unpublished poems.; [pers.] Some of the most beautiful and vivid poetry that we could ever read or hear is in the Book of Psalms. My favorite is Psalm 104, a poem showing appreciation for every aspect of nature.; [a.] Lansing, MI

BREWER, JOYCE
[b.] October 15, 1933, SC; [p.] Deceased; [m.] Howell Brewer, January 1955; [ed.] High School, Bus. School; [occ.] Retired; [memb.] Volunteer's, for various organizations; [oth. writ.] Poems I here written, and saved none have been published; [pers.] I like to write about things on Earth, which has so much beauty to enjoy. The rain, wind snow, trees, and all that you can see. I love all animals. Only man with all of the seven sins. (women too) Have ugly ways and thoughts.; [a.] College Park, MD

BRICE, FLORENCE M.
[pen.] Amy M. Brice; [b.] September 12, 1932, Ovid, MI; [p.] Franklyn P. Evenlyn and F. Ellen Evelyn; [m.] Donald W. Brice, December 6, 1974; [ch.] Wesley N. Le Marble, Y. Elaine Blair, W. David Le Marble, W. Daniel Le marble; [ed.] Oid High School Honors College prep, Owosso College 3 yrs, Alma College Speaking French accounting, Central Michigan Univ. French History psychology; [occ.] Retires paralegal: Specialty: Probate Law; [memb.] United Methodist Church, Church Choir, Alma College Community Choir love nature: birds, travel, growing roses, my mother, a write herbs, baking yeast breads was greatest influence: to myself and to my granddaughter, Elizabeth Florence Blair, age 8: She kept daily journals, published poems and short stories in religious periodicals; [hon.] Scholastic and Music; [oth. writ.] Non published: poems writings, journal, I wrote poems to my 3 grand children: Florence Elizabeth, Richard Matthew and Rachel Mae: their love of life and discovery is contagious.; [pers.] 'To the wall' was my personal life/death affirming experience upon surviving open heart by-pass surgery, written while in hospital (my book and pen go everywhere with me). I love heart land poets, writers; [a.] Alma, MI

BRICKWOOD, KANANI
[b.] April 1, 1981, Anchorage, AK; [p.] Annette and Curt Leuenberger; [ed.] Palmer Junior Middle School, Palmer High School; [occ.] Secretary for L.E. Lab.; [hon.] Honor Roll; [oth. writ.] Several poems written but never published.; [pers.] I write all my poems from the heart, they are all of nature and not of technology of our future. American poets are my favorite, Shel Silversten is the best.; [a.] Palmer, AK

BRIDGES, BERNADETTE FOULKES
[pen.] B. B. Cloris; [b.] November 24, 1956, Baltimore, MD; [p.] Bernard Foulkes, Gloria Foulkes; [m.] Deoleous A. Bridges, October 13, 1990; [ch.] Stepchildren and my nieces and nephews; [ed.] Lake Clifton Sr. High School, Community College Of Balto.; [occ.] Supervisor, Light Rail Mass Transit Administration; [memb.] Conference of Minority Transportation Officials, Class of 1974 Alumni Committee; [hon.] Volunteer Service Award from Dept Social Service Balto. City/Offender and Restoration Volunteer, Baltimore City Jail.; [oth. writ.] My other writings were written especially for loved ones and friends on special occasions, such as weddings, birthdays, retirement, funerals etc.; [pers.] My writings are inspired by my surroundings, my emotions my observation of life in truth, I am thankful to God for His inspiration in my writing; through Him I am able to write. Thanks to you God.; [a.] Baltimore, MD

BRINKERHOFF, DOREEN
[b.] February 24, 1958, Florida; [p.] Frank Streibig and Peg Bowker; [ch.] Joan Diane, James William Jr., Jillian Denise; [occ.] Freelance Writer; [pers.] Johns love and belief in me continues to inspire me to share the endless song of love my soul sings for him, with others.; [a.] Bristol, PA

BRISBANE, ELYSIA LEE
[b.] May 22, 1980, Denver; [p.] Gary and Nancy; [ed.] Roaring Fork High School (Carbondale, Co) 9th Grade (Freshmen); [occ.] Student; [memb.] Care Fast (A group that gets together, for drug free and alcohol free students); [oth. writ.] Poem's published in the school newspaper.; [pers.] I started to write poetry because it way a way to express my inner feelings about my personal life.; [a.] Carbondale, CO

BRISON JR., DANIEL R.
[b.] September 5, 1967, Lancaster, OH; [ed.] Sheridan High School, United States Airforce Military Police, Ohio State Highway Patrol Academy; [occ.] Police Officer; [hon.] Good Conduct Medal in the United States Airforce. Marksmanship medal for the 9-mm pistol and the M-16 rifle.; [pers.] Since being a police officer my literary works tend to reflect the dark side of reality, the side nobody wants to talk about. We don't need fantasy monsters to scare us, just open your local newspaper.; [a.] Lancaster, OH

BROOK, LARRY OCONO
[b.] June 2, 1943, Corpus Christi, TX; [p.] James Silas and Myrle Brook; [m.] Linda Rios Brook, December 7, 1980; [ch.] Daune Michelle Brook (30 years), Chris Michael Rios (21 years), Amanda Christine Brook (21 years), Kirsten Nicole Rios (18 years); [occ.] Vice President Sales and marketing/ part owner of KLGT WB 23 Minneapolis/St. Paul, Mn; [hon.] Editor's Choice Award/National Library of Poetry 1994 Semi-finalist 1995 North America Open Poetry Contest/National Library of Poetry; [oth. writ.] I began writing poetry in 1979 and have had three poems published. Presently, I am working on my own book pf poetry.

BROOKS, JAMIE RAE
[b.] July 9, 1977, Salem, OR; [p.] Naomi J. and Ronnie Beals; [ed.] High School student presently

working on G.E.D.; [occ.] Student; [pers.] Writing has been a means of surviving and reaching out to other people. I was severely abused till the age of 15, and then abandoned. I have always written to express my feelings and to create a fantasy world where I could live and grow safely.; [a.] Norman, OK

BROTHERS, POPPY
[b.] April 15, 1980, Birmingham, AL; [p.] James B. and Myra Brothers; [ed.] Sophomore at Susan Moore High School; [occ.] Student at Susan Moore High School; [memb.] Pep Club, member of the Majorette Line, volunteer at the Blount County Children's Center; [hon.] A Honor Roll, Jr. National Honor Society, Duke University Talent Search, Snead State Summer Program for Advanced Students, U.S. Achievement Academy; [oth. writ.] The Naughty Little Turtle, Dreams, Shapes; [pers.] With God's help, you can achieve anything you want, if you just put your mind to it and work for it.; [a.] Oneonta, AL

BROWN, CAROLINA
[pen.] Carol Brown; [b.] October 20, 1970, Acambaro, MX; [p.] Olivia Avila; [m.] Irving L. Brown Sr., November 1, 1988; [ch.] Irving L. Brown Jr.; [occ.] Crew Chief McDonald Anaheim; [pers.] This poem is in dedication to my son L.B, for being such a great help. To Irving, for always being there for me. And to Monica, for the encouragement on never to stop writing and to follow my dreams; [a.] Anaheim, CA

BROWN, CERISSA
[b.] June 19, 1980, Birmingham, AL; [p.] Loretta G. Brown and Claude M. Brown; [ed.] Mulga Elementary, Jackson Elementary, Edgewood Elementary, Homewood Middle, Homewood High; [occ.] A volunteer at Discovery 2000 and a volunteer at Hoover Library; [oth. writ.] I wrote several poems but I haven't sent any to be published yet.; [pers.] I write to relieve my stress. I usually write when I'm depressed or hurting so I can be real in my poems; [a.] Birmingham, AL

BROWN, DAISY E.
[b.] November 28, 1903, Cowby Country, KS; [p.] Robert Webb and Florence Boone Webb,; [m.] Paul H. Brown, June 17, 1931; [ch.] Ester, Max; [ed.] College Degree Southwestern College, Winfield Kansas - Numerous extra courses in Kansas colleges; [occ.] Retired from 33 yrs. Teaching Elem School in Kansas; [memb.] Life Member, Kans State, Teacher Assoc, Life Member - Parent teacher Association "First Baptist Church, Prairie Village, Kansas; [hon.] $50 U.S. Bond for article in Home Newspaper Arkansas City, Kans, 1960 Birthday 90th celebration with 150 present!; [oth. writ.] History of Church's 100th birthday of First Baptist - Arkansas City Ks. Editor of publication of teacher Cowley Co, Kans 1960; [pers.] At 2 yrs - become christian - did 50 yrs volunteer work in church and community. Loved my home and family; [a.] Prairie Village, KS

BROWN JR., JOSEPH R.
[b.] January 13, 1973, Los Angles; [p.] Joseph and Yolanda Brown; [ed.] B.S. (Psychology) minor (Philosophy) Los Altos High School Menlo College; [occ.] Full time student, Stockroom clerk (PCOM); [memb.] Dean's list, 6 semesters in a

row 4 time member and Team Captain for Menlo College football team; [hon.] Fall Semester 93/94 2 time recipient of JJ. Boyle leadership Award. Graduated Cum Laude. 93/94 Recipient Intellectual Enthusiasm in Psychology (Menlo College Psychology Program) 94 Recipient of Menlo "Okies Awards for Poetry. 94 recipient of "most courageous" Award (Menlo Football); [oth. writ.] Several poems up and coming.; [pers.] Through written expression, I have achieved a form of immortality. My words can embrace the Heaven and rock the bowels of hell. This passion of mine fuels my voyage through time and space. It's the way I choose to live.; [a.] Santa Clara, CA

BROWN, MARGARET L.
[b.] July 21, 1964, Tifton, GA; [p.] Mary Lou Brown; [ch.] Travis Sharad Butter; [ed.] Attended and graduated from Tift GA High School in 1982 in Tifton, GA attended ABAC college in 1993 and 1994; [occ.] Employed with the Department of Transportation as a Photographic Record Clerk; [memb.] Member of Engineers Association JT Reddick School PTO and Parent Workshop; [hon.] Received participation Certificate in Parents Workshop, in 1993; [oth. writ.] Poem published in Sarrowgrass Poetry Forum, several poems published on obituaries and for weddings.; [pers.] I enjoy writing poetry, it lets me express my inner feelings about what I feel and see in life. I enjoy reading Maya Angelou's poems and Helen Steiner Rice poems and cards. Most of all I like to write poems that will lift people's spirit and bring them joy.; [a.] Tifton, GA

BROWN, MARY LOU
[b.] March 25, 1919, Niles, OH; [p.] John W. Catherino A. Johnston; [m.] Clarenco Brown; [ch.] Catherino E. (Brown) Drinan, Thomas P. Brown, Marjorie A. (Brown); [ed.] High School graduate, (Akron Ohio East High 1937); [occ.] Retired bookkeeper; [memb.] Frostono Park Seniors Club 13, St. Paul's Ladies Guild, St. Paul's Social Solitaines, Bota Sigma Phi XI game Chapter (abouve allin Akron, Ohio); [oth. writ.] Have written an unpublished book about Alaska (my last visit thone) also have an unpublished poem in the book; [pers.] I love poetry - Having been influenced by a touches named. May Mosteric in high school - I put a lot of thought into poetry; [a.] Akron, OH

BROWN, MELISSA A.
[pen.] Melissa A. Brown; [b.] April 24, 1975, Agana, GU; [p.] Meredith and Jerry Brown; [ed.] Millington Central High School, Freed-Hardeman University; [occ.] Full-time Student, Social Work and Bible Major; [memb.] SWSA, Chi Beta Chi; [oth. writ.] Many personal poems, nothing else published; [pers.] Writing is my way of sharing my heart with others. I hope that I can reflect my love for God and my love for others through the words that I write.; [a.] Millington, TN

BROWNING, ELLENE
[pen.] Ellene Browning; [b.] November 13, 1928, Horton, AL; [p.] Wm. Alfred Sotherland and Mary Ida Sotherland; [m.] Roy Browning, April 13, 1946; [ch.] Janet Ann; [oth. writ.] Am currently working on a book writing my Autobiography.; [pers.] In writing my Autobiography about my life

experiences of trauma will be in hope of it being beneficial to others.

BRUNS, ERIKA K.
[b.] February 2, 1980, Missouri; [p.] Dr. Richard Bruns and Dee Ette Bruns; [ed.] Freshman at Bangor High School; [memb.] Key Club and Students Ending Environmental Destruction (S.E.E.D.); [oth. writ.] Short stories and other poems, nothing published; [pers.] "Life is like a box of chocolates: yum"; [a.] Bangor, ME

BRZYSKI, RICHARD J.
[b.] September 22, 1970, Philadelphia, PA; [p.] Katherine Brzyski, Richard Joseph Brzyski; [occ.] Extrusion Operations Technician; [oth. writ.] Rosebud, and Depravation of the mind; [pers.] My writings are based on personal experiences and spiritual feelings.; [a.] Philadelphia, PA

BUFFORD, STEPHANIE R.
[pen.] Renne; [b.] September 16, 1970, Chicago, IL; [p.] Sheila R. Gayton and Sammie L. Bufford Sr.; [m.] Robert Faulkner Sr. (fiance); [ch.] Dionte Wiggins, Robert Faulkner Jr.; [ed.] Curie Metropolitan High School; [occ.] Speech Pathologist Aide, Lindblom Technical High; [memb.] Gospel Temple Choir; [oth. writ.] I've written a few poems for obituaries and personal use.; [pers.] With God all things are possible.; [a.] Chicago, IL

BUIE, NITA
[pen.] Nita Buie; [b.] March 2, 1946, Columbia, TN; [p.] Malcolm W. and Elora Williams; [m.] Dan L. Buie; [ch.] Annette, Mark, Susan, and Emily; [pers.] I strive to reflect in my writings the power, beauty, and goodness of the Lord.; [a.] Lawrenceburg, TN

BULINGTON, NANCY RENEE
[b.] August 17, 1977, Lafayette, IN; [p.] Elia and John Bulington; [ed.] North White H.S.; [occ.] Student; [memb.] German Club, Sunshine Society, Yearbook Staff Drill Team; [hon.] Editor's Choice Award from the National Library of poetry, project XL Certificate; [oth. writ.] "Never Like This" poem in Dark Side of the Moon.; [pers.] I write about what I know. I'm 17. I know a little bit about life. And I have more to see and do before my time is through. Even though I have seen and done many things all ready.; [a.] Monticello, IN

BURKETT, BESSIE S.
[pen.] Bess Shannon; [b.] February 6, 1909, Wayne Co, Mount Erie, IL; [p.] Lewis Shannon, Mary Elizabeth Shannon; [m.] Walter Burkett, July 5, 1934; [ch.] Charles Robert Burkett; [ed.] Grade High Special College Classes of Carbondale, Il., Life time Teaching Certificate, 17 1/2 Rural Schools Teaching; [occ.] Subbed until 70 yrs of age after I quit teaching subbed for all grades at Edwards Co. Grade School; [memb.] Joined all teaching, Organizations of state and Co while teaching, Belonged to church organizations of Baptist; [hon.] Penmanship awards galore; [oth. writ.] Wrote 6 unpublished books, didn't have money for pay. Interested all said they were worthwhile.; [pers.] I used only the knowledge I had being careful to have every word worthy of my character and reputation so I'd be proud of my accomplishments; [a.] Fairfield, IL

BURNS, JOHN HARRINGTON
[pen.] John Harrington Burns; [b.] Orange, NJ; [p.] Patrick and Nancy (Nee Filandino); [m.] Mary Jane; [ch.] Nancy, Marianne, John; [ed.] West Orange H.S (NJ) Seton Hall Fordham Alviene ACAD; [occ.] Composer/Lyricist and free large writer; [memb.] Writer's Round Table A.L Press Association; [hon.] Yesterday's Magazzettie Winner - 1990 Short Story Awards; [oth. writ.] Off B'way Musical "Pschuarelgy of Mother Goose various musical - recorded songs. Former member of musical group "Four Jacks and A Jill"; [pers.] Currently residing with wife. The former Mary Jane Bruno of New York City in Manassas VA.; [a.] Manassas, VA

BURNS, RUSSELL CHARLES
[pen.] R. Burns; [b.] December 19, 1949, Crane, IN; [p.] Ray and Evelyne Burns; [m.] Margaret and Burns, March 18, 1972; [ch.] Russell Ernest Burns and Kary and Nail; [ed.] Lake City Comm College; [occ.] Utilities Reedy Creek Walt Disney World; [oth. writ.] Who, Seasons to Come, The National Library of Poetry; [pers.] Live life now for tomorrow today will be gone; [a.] Ocoee, FL

BUSH, DANIELLE KRYSTN
[b.] September 22, 1982, Marlton, NJ; [p.] Ron and Pam Bush; [ed.] Attended Evans Elementary School and now attend DeMasi Middle School's 7th grade; [occ.] Golden Attitude Club; [memb.] Honor Roll and Distinguished Honor Roll; [pers.] I have always enjoyed reading poems, and decided to write one of my own.; [a.] Marlton, NJ

BUSHMAN, ELAINE
[b.] October 13, 1937, Monterey, TN; [p.] Robert Lee and Ruth Lee Dunn; [m.] Robert F. Bushman, July 24, 1957; [ch.] Damian, Dana, Luke and Carrie, grandchildren - Levi, Justine, Megan, Kaitlin and Kayleigh; [ed.] Monterey High School; [occ.] Homemaker; [pers.] One must feel strongly about the subject in order to write from the heart.; [a.] Saint Nazianz, WI

BUSSE, RONALD A.
[pen.] Tiger; [b.] April 3, 1967; [p.] Ronald and Marylou Busse; [ed.] Massapequa High School, Associate degree in Business Administration from Nassau Community College; [oth. writ.] Several poems and articles published in school newspaper and company newsletters. I have also written some songs, incorporating my poetry in the lyrics; [pers.] I wrote this poem while going through a very rough time in my personal life. I thank God things are better today.; [a.] Lindenhurst, NY

BUTGEREIT, MADELINE
[b.] July 5, 1918, Decatur, AL; [p.] Anna Holland, Frank Holland; [m.] Melvin F. Butgereit, September 14, 1935; [ch.] Cherrie Lynn, Jack Lee, Melvin Jr., Joan Barbara; [ed.] Central High - Decatur. Ala., Racine Vocational Wis.; [occ.] Mother Wife, Grandmother Great grandmother A former country western singer; [memb.] National - Association Police Organization Inc. Washington, DC, Historic - Preservation - Wash. DC, World - Wildlife - Fund D.C., Christian - Appalachian - Project American Indian Relief Fund; [hon.] A certificate of appreciation from (C.O.P.S.) Concerns of Police Survisors, In Comdenton MO,

CUB scout teacher or leader; [oth. writ.] Letters to the editor on City. Needs 2 ECI Racine Journal Times. And shoreline leader. Letters all so to the editors some poems but not the one sent you; [pers.] Let - God be your C.O. Pilot - you will fly straight forever. My prayers for all my children and all youth and my grandchildren; [a.] Racine, WI

BUTLER, JOYCE CLARK
[b.] July 13, 1950, Yoakum, TX; [p.] Edgar J. Clark, Mildred Shindler Clark; [m.] John M. Butler, June 18, 1976; [ch.] Jason Butler, Kristina Lafferty, Kevin Lafferty (grandson), Tim Lafferty (son-in-law); [ed.] Yoakum High, HHS Clinical Laboratory Technologist Certification, Institute of Children's Literature Correspondence; [occ.] Homemaker, Part-time Laboratory Technologist; [hon.] Several American Kennel Club obedience awards with my German Shepherd Dog; [oth. writ.] Several poems and children's stories; [pers.] In my writing I strive to promote an appreciation of life and God's wonderful creation.; [a.] Victoria, TX

BUTTERFIELD, GEORGE M.
[pen.] Butter; [b.] November 29, 1934, Maine; [p.] Earle Blair Butterfield, Velma Ada Macomber; [m.] Nancy Hawkes Butterfield, June 25, 1955; [ch.] Cindy Mary Ann, Daniel, Gail; [ed.] Foxcroft Academy, Maine Vocational Technical, Institute M.V.T.I., O.R.U. Oral Roberts University; [occ.] Retired Kimberly Clark Corporation Mechanic; [memb.] Past Member Of National Grange, Possibility Thinkers Member, ARRP Modern Maturity; [hon.] Honor by Kimberly-Clark Corporation retirement after 35 years and 4 months work as a mechanic. Honor as semi-finalist 1995 National Library of Poetry; [oth. writ.] Blueberries Went By One By One, I Don't Know; [pers.] I like my works to show how Jesus helps the earth.; [a.] New Milford, CT

BUTTS JR., JOE LEE
[b.] August 9, 1986, Perry, GA; [p.] Arlette S. Young; [ed.] Third Grader, Vienna Elementary School; [memb.] Ebenezer Baptist Church; [hon.] Honor student at Vienna Elementary School. Reading, Music, Spelling, and, Mathematics-Awards; [pers.] I try to capture the attention of readers in my writing.; [a.] Vienna, GA

BYRD, ISABEL
[pen.] Chavela; [b.] November 19, 1925, Manassa, CO; [p.] Antonio Gallegos, Manuela Le Blanc; [m.] Widow; [ch.] Manuel, Necolas, Dimas Joe L. Samuel Carmel, Carla Annette, Bertina Margarita, Connie Jo Ann, Gregory Allen; [ed.] Fort Garland High, Certified Practical Nursing per N.Y.A., Colo. General Hosp. St. Monica Country Hosp. Phoenix, Ariz.; [occ.] Retired writer of books and poetry. Presentation schools colleges; [memb.] Temple of the cross drama team; [hon.] Reach to Recovery Pro. Amer. C. So. 15 yrs. Service Cert. of Service Luren Eden Schol., Cert. of Street Evangelism Amazing Grace Ch. Oakland; [oth. writ.] Unpublished autobiography, title - Adobe Heart Los Manitos, book of poetry, from Colorado book, titled - Practical Nurse, Life, Death, Miracles; [pers.] I was inspired to write by my maternal grandfather and my paternal grandmother, Eugenio Le Blanc and Margarita Lyon. Spoken words are blown away by the wind. Written words last a life time, perhaps forever.; [a.] Oakland, CA

CABLE, MARIANNE
[b.] January 29, 1931, Conn; [p.] Stephen and Anna Duhan; [m.] Divorced, December 26, 1950

CACCONE, CARISSA
[b.] September 22, 1983, CT; [p.] Joe and Carol Caccone; [occ.] Student at DH Ferrara School; [hon.] Basketball Trophy, Honors Band (flute) Trophy, Cheerleading 1st place in competition, Dancing Award; [oth. writ.] Mostly poetry but some short stories never published; [pers.] I love romanic and sweet rhyming poems. I write about how or what I feel inside me and hopefully continue on doing so.; [a.] East Haven, CT

CAHILL, SANDRA LEE
[pen.] Sandy C.; [b.] June 14, 1941, Meadville, PA; [p.] Richard and Gertrude Christie; [m.] Deceased, November 10, 1962; [ch.] William Cahill Jr. (31), Julianne (28); [ed.] Saint Agatha High School Meadville, PA, Certified Food Mgr. State of Mich.; [occ.] Waitress - 40 years; [memb.] National Restaurant Assoc., Saint Cyril's Catholic Church; [oth. writ.] None - This was my first experience at writing, but would like to try a book in the future.; [pers.] I have three grandchildren, Eric 10, Dustin 5, Megan Marie 15, mos. Megan's first birthday party was my inspiration for writing. Grandchildren are truly a blessing from God. They're like having a good rerun of raising your own children again.; [a.] Southgate, MI

CALHOUN, MARY A. FARNSWORTH
[pen.] M. C. Allison; [b.] October 18, 1975, Canton, OH; [p.] Judy Crumrine, Robert Farnsworth; [m.] Nick L. Calhoun, December 18, 1994; [ed.] East Canton High School, freshman at Kent Stark; [occ.] Student; [hon.] Dean's List, Ohio Arts Council Scholarship; [oth. writ.] Several poems printed in the high School newspaper an article printed in repository - (Canton) newspaper; [pers.] Literature is a free expression, so I write on.; [a.] East Canton, OH

CALLAWAY, KATHLYN JOSIE
[pen.] Kathlyn, Kassie; [b.] May 20, 1981, Harlingen, TX; [p.] James Walker Callaway, Lorna Diane Callaway; [ed.] W.B Green Middle School 8th grade, La Feria ISD La Feria, TX; [hon.] 4th place O.M. 2nd chair all - Valley Band, and 1st place at District (for school); [oth. writ.] Unpublished - There is a place that I do go, sunset, Cassiopeia.; [a.] La Feria, TX

CALLIN, ELOISE
[pen.] Eloise Callin; [b.] June 14, 1927, Ware County, GA; [p.] Thomas L. Edenfield and Olive E. Edenfield; [m.] October 17, 1953; [ch.] James, Arthur, Thomas, David; [ed.] High School and Business School; [occ.] House wife, homemaker; [memb.] The National Poets Society of the National Library of Poetry; [hon.] Editors Choice Award; [oth. writ.] Poem entered in the 1994 Anthology - Journey of the mind "Creation", I wrote an recipe column in Douglas enterprise, and in the Coffee County progress, also local news. 1948-1953; [pers.] I enjoy writing so much. Next, to God and my family, poetry comes next close to my heart.; [a.] Chuluota, FL

CAMACHO, PAUL
[b.] January 15, 1968, Saint Lucia, West Indies; [p.] Mary Camacho, Sydney Camacho; [oth. writ.] Many other poems, varying themes planning and hoping for chap-book publications. Praying to have my work see the light of day.; [pers.] Sometimes it flows, sometimes the pail struggles from the well, in the current environment, I feel poetically incorrect. They can keep their pretense and cryptic confusion, I will stay true at home.; [a.] Bronx, NY

CAMARCA, VINCENT A.
[b.] January 22, 1931, Cincinnati, OH; [p.] Frank and Ida Camarca; [m.] Marilyn Camarca, March 19, 1960; [ed.] B.S. Miami of Ohio, M.A. in Psychology - Ohio State; [occ.] Retired Psychologist; [memb.] Unitarian Church of Kessville, Texas; [hon.] U.S. Army, Good Conduct medal and Sharpshooter's medal, Salutatorian of High School Graduating Class; [oth. writ.] Working on Book of Essays; [pers.] We are both creative and destructive, what we emphasize in our live, defines what we become.; [a.] Kessville, TX

CAMERON, LORI MICHELLE
[b.] March 18, 1965, Valdosta, GA; [p.] David Smith, Patricia Smith; [m.] Brian S. Cameron, July 30, 1994; [ed.] M.A., California State Polytechnic University, B.A., Indiana Wesleyan University; [occ.] College English Instructor; [memb.] English Council of California two-year Colleges, Sigma Tan Delta, International English Honor Society, World Vision; [oth. writ.] Poetry Published in Other Anthologies, free Lance Writing; [a.] Los Alamitos, CA

CANDEE, SARAH
[b.] May 7, 1981, Dubuque, IA; [p.] Karen and Neil Candee; [ed.] Grade 8; [occ.] Student; [a.] Dubuque, IA

CANNING III, DONALD JOHNS
[pen.] "White Hawk"; [b.] December 3, 1966, Camden, NJ; [p.] Donald J. Canning Jr. and Priscilla Watson; [m.] Single; [ch.] Michael David, Brittany Rose; [ed.] High School Diploma; [occ.] Disabled due to a drunk driver. Social Security (I was in a coma for 5 1/2 months, but I'm still writing my poetry).; [hon.] Vocational Machinist, Physical Science High School Wrestling, Baseball, Poetry Awards (School).; [oth. writ.] Racial poems, love poems, life poems, death poems. Anything that interests me.; [pers.] Life and the "Afterlife, the other side".; [a.] Absecon, NJ

CANNON, CORRENE S.
[pen.] Jackie Cannon, [b.] February 1, 1939, Maryland; [p.] Lawrence Killette, Evelyn Killette; [m.] James M. Cannon, May 24, 1986; [ch.] Gary Orlanus, Clevon LaMont, Gale LaRosa, Lisa Maria, James Wesley.; [ed.] Mace's Lane High, Federal City College, Washington Bible College; [occ.] Research Assistant, District of Columbia Public Schools, D.C.; [memb.] Mt. Zion Pentecostal U.H.C.A., Mt. Zion Women's Ministry, Emerson Street Block Club; [oth. writ.] Poems, skits, plays, for locals, such as school, church, family and friends.; [pers.] I have been writing poetry and plays since the age of nine. I have shared with children and adults alike. I am inclined to write about everyday situations. I also

like to encourage and cheer others through poetry. I can communicate in writing my true feelings.; [a.] Washington, DC

CANTU, DIANA
[b.] December 16, 1977, Watsonville, CA; [p.] Rosie and Adam Cantu; [ed.] I am currently in 11th grade at Watsonville High School; [occ.] Student; [memb.] None was in Drama; [hon.] None now but, in third grade I won the Spelling Bee. Four poems are on their way to being published; [oth. writ.] I have written a couple short stories here and there. I have a lot of poems in a journal type book unpublished. Currently I have 97 unpublished written out.; [pers.] Creative writing is about everything not just one thing. If you have the urge to write go for it because, creative writing should be expressed not thrown away or kept inside.; [a.] Watsonville, CA

CARLSON, JUDY L.
[pen.] Judie (Saw) Carlson; [b.] September 21, 1963, Greenville, PA; [p.] Nancy and Alvin Porter; [m.] Timothy Carlson, March 17, 1990; [ch.] Tia Marie, Frank Alvin III, Antonio Noel James; [ed.] Greenville High School (G.E.D), Nurse Aide Training at M.M.H.C.C. in Andover, OH; [occ.] C.N.A, Breeder of Chow Chows, Mother of 3, aspiring poet; [memb.] I have no official memberships, but I do make and sell crafts for many events and organizations.; [hon.] I have not received any awards, although it is a great honor to me for my poem to be published in this anthology.; [oth. writ.] I haven't had any other writings published 'til now, but I feel that this may be my first step on the stairwell of success.; [pers.] I write from the many experiences and emotions in our lives, hoping to let others know that they are not alone!; [a.] Greenville, PA

CARNLEY, PATRICK
[pen.] Patrick Blake; [b.] October 1, 1968, Lufkin, TX; [p.] Lanny and Nikki Carnley; [ed.] Diboll High School, Angelina Jr. College and Stephen F. Austin State University; [occ.] Dispatcher for Diboll Police and fire depths. Free-Lance Writer; [hon.] Won Hugh O'Brien Leadership Award. Selected who's who American High School Students Who's Who at Angelina College 2 years in arrow.; [oth. writ.] Two other poems published in various anthologies.; [pers.] I write for me. If someone enjoys something I have written, then I am fulfilled even more. I find people the most interesting aspect of life. My writing is born from mine and others hardships.; [a.] Diboll, TX

CARPENTER, LINDA L.
[b.] April 30, 1956, Towanda, PA; [p.] Nancy Carter; [m.] Deceased; [ch.] Karl Kelley; [ed.] I went to the middle of 10th grade. I had to leave because of bad health.; [occ.] Disabled for 23 years this year.; [pers.] I wrote this after my grandparents died in 1973. I have always felt I owned them this, in thanks for all they did for me. That is because I will never again see or meet people like them!

CARPIGNANO, JO
[b.] January 25, 1928, San Francisco; [p.] Angelo and Madeline Carpignano; [ed.] BA Elementary Teaching SFSU, MA School Administration SFSU, MA Pupil Personnel Services SFSU, Ph.D. Special

Education UCB; [occ.] School Psychologist, Educational Psychologist; [memb.] APA, WPA, NASP, CASP; [oth. writ.] Chapters 5,7 in teaching India with Physical and multiple disabilities 2nd ED.. by June L. Bigge - Chas. Merrill 1982 (Ch 5 and 10 in 3rd Ed 1991 same book); [a.] Millbrae, CA

CARRINGTON, CHERYL-JOY
[b.] July 25, 1960, Barbados, West Indies; [p.] Colin and Joan Seale; [m.] Michael A. Carrington, August 15, 1982; [ed.] Andrews University Berrien Springs, MI 49103 (M.A. Reading Education), Caribbean Union College Trinidad, W.I. (B.A. Elementary Educ.); [occ.] Reading specialist, Adjunct Prof: Caribbean Union College, Trinidad, W.I.; [memb.] Phi Kappa Phi, Multi-Discipline Honors Society; [hon.] Dean's List; [oth. writ.] Large collection of poetry spanning 1975, to present. Planning to published.; [pers.] I just like to play around with words and also unite for special occasions at camps, church and independence celebrations to entertain and up lift my friends.; [a.] Philadelphia, PA

CARROLL, MARTHA WALTERS
[pen.] Martha Walters Carroll; [b.] January 11, 1935, Columbus, OH; [p.] Thomas and Viva Walters; [ch.] Viva Carroll, Held Corban Carroll; [ed.] North High School - Cols. Oh, Columbus Business University; [oth. writ.] Many poems about home and family.; [pers.] My love for poetry began during the elementary school years with classroom memorizing and reciting in unison the work of earlier poets. Throughout my life I have enjoyed writing poems about everyday life, which is a way to express my inner joy and appreciation for the things that bring true happiness.; [a.] Glenford, OH

CARTER, JANINE CORI GLASCO
[b.] July 18, 1960, Camden, NJ; [p.] Harry Allen Glasco, Constance Yvonne Glasco; [m.] David Richard Carter Sr., June 9, 1984; [ch.] David Richard Carter Jr., Athena Monique Carter; [ed.] Camden High School; [a.] Mooresville, NC

CARTER, KARI ANN
[b.] May 9, 1979, Aberdeen, MS; [p.] Sylvia Proulx, Ken Carter; [ed.] Mantachie High School; [occ.] High School Student; [memb.] Ozark Baptist Church - Youth Group; [oth. writ.] Several other poems, but haven't yet been published.; [a.] Marietta, MS

CARTER, LATONYA P.
[b.] December 30, 1971, Houston, TX; [p.] Gloria G. Carter and James; [ed.] Baylor University, B.A. - '94, Saint Pius X High School c/o '90; [occ.] Student; [memb.] North Shore Animal League, Baylor University Alumni Association; [hon.] National Honor Society in High School; [oth. writ.] Unpublished personal collection of poems.; [pers.] My poems are an extension of thoughts, feelings, and experiences in relation to myself, the environment, and the people around me.; [a.] Houston, TX

CARTER, MARGARET V.
[b.] September 16, 1936, Burtonsville, MD; [p.] Emma and Ernest Elliott; [m.] Divorced; [ch.] Ronald Ray, Rachael Ellen, Black, Roxanne Lynn, Dana Arlen, and Jacquelyn Elizabeth.; [ed.] James

Wood High School; [occ.] Disability; [memb.] Rose Dale Baptist Church.

CARTER, NICHOLAS W.
[b.] February 10, 1904, England; [p.] Arthur and Emma Carter; [m.] Rosamond T. Carter, September 18, 1954; [ch.] Sheila C. Booker, Julianne S. Forst; [ed.] London E17 England Greeleaf Rd Elementary School London WC, England Regent St Polytechnic. Regent St.; [occ.] Electrical Engineer (retired); [memb.] Temperanceville Masonic Lodge. VA 23442.

CASE, JEAN S.
[pen.] Jean Savage Case; [b.] November 16, 1942, New York, NY; [p.] Helen and Vaughn Shaffer; [m.] John Savage Case, October 21, 1961; [ch.] Daniel Savage Case, Scott Savage Case, Glen Savage Case.; [ed.] Professional Children's School Merchants and Bankers Business School Boces II - Nurses Aide Training; [occ.] Nursing Assistant.; [memb.] National Wildlife Federation; [oth. writ.] This is my first poem. I'm currently working on a Science Fiction love story. I also publish my own stationary and notecards.; [pers.] I'm a true believer in love, and all it's facets and depths and beauty without romance, life would be hollow. I firmly believe fate plays a major role in life's path. The future fascinates me and holds untold challenges, and Adventures.; [a.] Reston, VA

CASSELLA, ANTONIO
[pen.] Anton; [b.] January 17, 1940, Addis-Ababa, Ethiopia; [p.] Giovanna Tommino and Dante Cassella; [m.] Ligia Uribe; [ch.] Andres, Silvio, Valerio, Clayton, Giusepre; [ed.] L.U.Z. The University of Zulia. Petroleum Engineer; [occ.] Visiting Researcher at MIT; [memb.] SUIP, Venezuelan Society of Petroleum Engineers and IAEE: International Association for Energy Economics; [hon.] The love of some friends and relatives; [oth. writ.] Several songs, unpublished; [pers.] Although all things are equally valuable, everything shines with its own nature; [a.] Cambridge, MA

CASSIDY, SEAN
[b.] November 6, 1976, Brassels, Belgium; [p.] William and Beverly Cassidy; [ed.] Ridgewood High School; [occ.] Student/Camp Counselor; [hon.] Poem/Short Story printed in Literary Magazine (Trollgate); [pers.] I hope to remind the world, that if you look good and hard, you still can see beauty and grace in the air. My influences were the great E.E. Cummings and the honorable Robert Frost. Both in a class by themselves; [a.] Ridgewood, NJ

CASTHER, SANDRA
[pen.] Sandra Ziebart; [b.] March 7, 1961, Detroit, MI; [p.] Fritz Ziebart and Elizabeth Ziebart; [ch.] Brandy, Mandy, Noah (Kyle) and Jesse; [ed.] GED; [occ.] Mother, housewife; [pers.] I am a recovering alcoholic and have finally been able to deal with the feelings, I have felt for years, never let go of your dreams someday they do come true.; [a.] Las Vegas, NV

CASTILLA, CHRISTINA MESHELL
[pen.] Tina Castilla; [b.] March 15, 1982, Landstuhl, Germany; [p.] Paul and Connie Castilla, Marde Gideon (step dad); [ed.] I'm in the 7th grade

at Cottonwood Middle School, I'm age 13 at this time; [occ.] Student; [memb.] Youth Group, Student Council; [hon.] 1st grade Award for Reading Achievement only student to read 102 Books for the year. 2nd place in School Science Fair, 1st place "National" Embry Riddle Aeronautical University, Arizona Science Fair; [oth. writ.] Pending; [pers.] This poem was really my first poem I love writing poems. Everything I write always comes from the heart.; [a.] Cottonwood, AR

CASTO, MICHAEL
[b.] May 24, 1971, Anderson, IN; [p.] Mary and Leo Casto; [ed.] Working on Associate's degree in Computer Technology at Purdue Statewide School of Technology; [occ.] Data Entry Operator; [hon.] Employee of the month for division (November 1994); [pers.] I attempt to write my poems in a manner which evokes feelings from the reader. I try to transcend the intellectuality of the words and reach something deeper.; [a.] Anderson, IN

CATO, CARRIE
[b.] March 29, 1981, La Grange, GA; [p.] Wayne and Denise Cato; [ed.] Whitesville Road Middle School; [occ.] Student; [memb.] Jr. Beta Honors Society, WRMS Concert and Marching Band, Olympic Ambassador Program; [hon.] Principal's List Honor Student, Duke University Talent Identification Program, Superior Rating Ga. Band Festival; [pers.] I look around me at the environment and my surroundings. I am inspired by what I see. I strive to reach excellence and project what I know through my writing.; [a.] La Grange, CA

CATTERSON, JACK
[b.] February 23, 1919, Belfast, North Ireland; [p.] John Kathleen; [m.] Margaret, November 1, 1940; [ch.] Maureen, John, Phyllis, Paul Noel, Colette, Colin.; [ed.] St Simons - School - Belfast Methodist College Belfast N. Ireland.; [occ.] Retired Engineer Automotive; [memb.] St., Elizabeths Anglican Church Democratic Party Worshipal Brother Azure Masonic Lodge 1153. Illinois.; [hon.] Britishnavy. 1940 - 1946.; [oth. writ.] Opinion Column's Local Newspapers; [pers.] To Para Phrase Robert Burns. O'Lord the gift to give us to see ourselves as others see us.; [a.] Chicago, IL

CAUDLE, JOSEPH
[b.] May 5, 1980, Gainsville, FL; [p.] William B. Caudle II, Nancy Caudle; [ed.] Milton High School (Freshman); [oth. writ.] Two poems and a short story in the 1993 "Santa Rosa Buds" collection of literature art; [a.] Milton, FL

CHADWICK, JOHN
[pen.] Johnny Rat; [b.] June 10, 1960, Washington, DC; [p.] Elsie Chadwick, Douglas Chadwick; [m.] Camilla Chadwick; [ch.] Chiara Chadwick; [ed.] BS University of MD Baltimore County MS The Ohio State University; [occ.] Computer Animation Specialist Unreal Pictures Inc.; [memb.] Sierra Club, ACM; [oth. writ.] Layered Construction for Deformable Animated Characters, Computer Graphics Volume 23, Number 3, July 1989, several sacred drawers of a lot of unpublished stuff; [pers.] I write what I hear. I am but the messenger holding the pen who writes these words down. It is not important what I have to say, but that I find the clarity to listen.; [a.] San Francisco, CA

CHAMBERS, JANE COOPER
[b.] June 22, 1950, Henderson, NC; [p.] James and Florine Cooper; [m.] Michael Steven Chambers, September 5, 1986; [ed.] MA-English Lit. N.C. State University, BA - English Language, Writing, Editing) NC State Univ. High School - Henderson High.; [hon.] Graduated Magna Cam Laude; [pers.] Love and learning are the twin nutrients of life: Love provides the courage to face it, learning, the stamina to live it.; [a.] Atlanta Beach, FL

CHAMBERS, MARIE B.
[b.] May 26, 1971,, Elmhurst, IL; [p.] John and Donna Chambers; [oth. writ.] With all my love to my family.; [pers.] Always speak from your heart, and let your dreams flow into a sweet reality…; [a.] Lombard, IL

CHANG, JAYMIN
[b.] November 19, 1975; [p.] C.T. Chang, Angela Chang; [ed.] Campolindo High, Moraga, CA Johns Hopkins University, Baltimore, MD; [occ.] Biomedical Engineering Pre-Med Student; [pers.] We travel the circle of migrating birds, forever returning with different faces, to the same secure place. Go forth without fear.; [a.] Moraga, CA

CHAPMAN, JESSICA
[pen.] Jessy; [b.] August 10, 1981, Yuba City, CA; [p.] Kathleen M. and Daniel T. Chapman; [ed.] 8th grade Sullivan Middle School, Fairfield, California; [occ.] Student; [memb.] Club live; [hon.] Honor Roll, Sullivan Middle School Super Citizen of the month at Brasford Elementary; [oth. writ.] I've written many unpublished poems, starting in the fourth grade.; [pers.] My poetry is a reflection of my deepest feelings I feel that I can express my feelings easier and more naturally through poetry, rather than thru basic communication.; [a.] Suisun, CA

CHARLES, SYLVANIE M.
[b.] St. Vincent, West Indies; [p.] Olive Charles, Theophilus Charles; [ed.] Ph.D; [occ.] Minister, Typist; [hon.] Editor's Award; [pers.] I propose to be a well - established dramatic poetic.; [a.] Bronx, NY

CHAVES, JILL
[pen.] Loyal; [b.] January 22, 1950, Milwaukee, WI; [p.] Loyal and Shirley Radtke; [m.] Dale M. Chaves; [occ.] Restaurant Owner; [pers.] Life on earth is a miracle from God - Life in heaven is a miracle and the Holy spirit makes it all possible.; [a.] Stockbridge, GA

CHAVEZ, JOHN
[pen.] Vez; [b.] March 28, 1958, Chicago, IL; [p.] Joe Chavez, Josefina Chavez; [ch.] Jennifer, Angela, Annalise; [ed.] Holy Trinity High School, Chicago; [occ.] Computer Operator, Merely Hospital, Chicago.; [pers.] Discovering the true mean of love in May of 1993, and if you put your family and friends first (3-F's) everything else will fall into place.; [a.] Chicago, IL

CHECK, WAYNE A.
[pen.] Wayne Alan Check; [b.] September 12, 1964, San Francisco; [p.] Steve and Diana; [ch.] Michelle Maile Check, 5 years old; [ed.] Redwood High School Grad' 82 (Jan.); [occ.] Chef, Marin County "Marin joes" exhibition style cooking"

Italian Cuisine; [hon.] Amherst Society "Certificate of Achievement" American Poetry Annual Poets Guild 95' Anthology Pub. Inclusion.; [oth. writ.] American Poetry Annual '95, Poets Guild '95; [pers.] Poetry is the love of all who reads it, also the passion of all who write it.; [a.] Novato, CA

CHEN, HOWARD T.
[b.] June 7, 1968, R.O.C; [ed.] I have attended two high school (Hathan Half and Walnut). And and Adult School (Rowland Height). And an Bookkeeping Degree from B.C.T.I.; [occ.] Bookkeeper, ACCTT.; [hon.] In fifth grad 2 was awarded, three third place ribbons and one second place ribbons in an grade school athletic event.; [oth. writ.] There are numerous other logs, passages written by ones but not yet published, but has been released for solicitation.; [pers.] Being a writer, I find writing logs, passages with no deliberate ending such as the footsteps of departure can inspire continues interest to an reader' pursuing the essence of such fiction.

CHILDS, SHEILA HARDWICKE
[pen.] Sheila Hardwicke Childs; [b.] April 15, 1970, Columbia, SC; [p.] Donna Simoneau and James E. Hardwicke III; [m.] Christopher Childs, November 12, 1994; [ed.] BS Degree in Criminal Justice from The University of South Carolina; [occ.] Nanny; [oth. writ.] Sonnets, free verse, for recreational purposes!; [pers.] This poem was written as a wedding gift for my husband, and reflects my love and admiration for him.; [a.] Aberdeen, MD

CHOU, PRUDENCE SUI-NING
[b.] March 10, 1927, Shanghai, China; [p.] Deceased; [m.] K. H. Tsai, married 1951 in Hong Kong, Divorced 1954.; [ch.] One; [ed.] 3 yrs. Ginling College for Girls (1945-48) China, B.A. degree from Nazareth College, Kentucky, USA (1950), Researcher at Institute of History, Science Academy, Peking, China (1554-1963), Researcher on Chinese Communism in Hong Kong (1963-1967), M.A. (1968) and Ph.D. (1976) degrees in Asian Studies from University of California, Berkelay.; [occ.] Retiree; [oth. writ.] "Pai-She and Ugetsu: Chinese and Japanese Treatments of a Myth", Literature East and West, March 1974, Vol. XVIII, 2-4, pp 270-279.; [pers.] English is my second language and I read English better than I speak. Coming to the U.S.A. for the first time in December, 1948, Living in Hong Kong and Europe 1951-1954, Peking, China 1954-1963, Hong Kong 1963-1976, Immigrated to the U.S.A. from Hong Kong in 1967, obtaining U.S Citizenship in 1972.

CHRISTAIN, ARNOLD B.
[b.] November 9, 1949, Alameda, CA; [p.] Helen and Andrew Christain; [m.] Kay F. Christain, January 26, 1991; [ch.] Dameon, Jahi; [ed.] Berkeley, High School Merritt Junior College California State University Hayward CA; [occ.] Supervisor U.S. Postal Service Songwriter, Producer, Actor, Model; [memb.] National Association Investors Club-(NAIC), Broadcasting Music Inc. (BMI), National Association of Postal Supervisor's (NAPS), St. John's Baptist Church; [hon.] Several Special Awards; [oth. writ.] Songwriting; [a.] Vallejo, CA

CHU, CHIA
[b.] January 3, 1977, Los Angeles, CA; [p.] Wen Chu, Lynn Chien; [ed.] Jersey Village High School (going to the University of Texas at Austin.); [occ.] Student; [pers.] I attempt merge with the flow of the society, yet I also want to be myself. Disappointments and failures are part of the cycle of life, and I most, learn to live with it, for nothing is meant to be perfect.; [a.] Houston, TX

CHUN, TAEJIN J.
[pen.] A Fellow Servant; [b.] May 28, 1971, Korea; [p.] Henry S. and Jung J. Chun; [m.] Janette K. Chun, June 17, 1994; [ch.] Zachary - 2 1/2 and Kiandra 6 weeks.; [ed.] AA from De Anza College Los Altas High.; [occ.] Customer Service Rep. at wells Fargo Bank; [memb.] Family Life Center Church ACTS by FORCE. Ministries.; [pers.] Love is not physical or even emotional but spiritual and sacrificial.; [a.] Sunnyvale, CA

CICCARELLI SR., ROBERTO V.
[pen.] R. V. Ciccarelli; [b.] June 7, 1963, Brooklyn, NY; [p.] Ernesto and Grace Ciccarelli; [m.] Sara Garcia Ciccarelli, July 17, 1988; [ch.] Roberto Jr., Benjamin, Loriana and Katie Janet.; [ed.] Eli Whitney Voc. H.S., Los Medanos College, Getsemani Theology Institute.; [occ.] Lithographer; [oth. writ.] I've written many poems and I'm presently working on 2 fiction novels, but this has been my first literary submission.; [pers.] I want my writing to affect people, to inspire them, touch them, make them reflect on whatever subject I may have written about, or simply to make them smile.; [a.] Lowell, MA

CITTADINI, LEO
[b.] October 28, 1977, Philadelphia; [p.] Leo and Linda Cittadini; [ed.] Graduate of St. John Neumann H.S., currently attending West Chester University.; [occ.] Pharmaceutical Technician.; [hon.] American Legion Award, 4 time recipient of The St. John Neumann H.S. Millay Alumni: Scholarship.; [oth. writ.] A poem called "Exodus" which can be found in "The Garden of Like" another publication from the National Library of Poetry.; [pers.] I believe all poetry should be open, Feelings should help the expressions take form.; [a.] Philadelphia, PA

CLARK, DOUGLAS F.
[b.] June 12, 1976, San Diego; [p.] Jeff Clark, Karol Clark; [m.] Not married; [ed.] Zionsville High School, Ball State University; [occ.] Student; [memb.] Lambda, Chi, Alpha; [oth. writ.] Never published before but I am in the process of writing a book called I Ostrast!; [pers.] Live everyday to the fullest for there may never be a tomorrow; [a.] Indianapolis, IN

CLARK, ERNEST M.
[pen.] Ernie Clark; [b.] May 10, 1943, Indianapolis, IN; [p.] Charles and Alice Clark; [m.] Divorced; [ch.] Gregory and Donna Clark, Gregory Matthew Clark (Grandson); [ed.] Crispus Attacks High School Indianapolis, IN, Indiana University School of Real Estate.; [occ.] Supervisor-General Motors Service Parts Operations Broadview, IL 31 yrs.; [memb.] Southern Cross Masonic Lodge No. 39 Prince Hall Freemansory Indianapolis, IN. 32 degree Scottish Rite of Freemasonry Constantine consistory No. 25,

Indianapolis, IN. First Baptist Church North Indianapolis.; [hon.] Baseball, Basketball, Masonic awards, awards for many accomplishment during my employment with General Motors.; [oth. writ.] None of publication; [pers.] During my life, I have found only one thing you cannot give away. Kindness it always comes back. For it is not how much you do to reach the hearts of children, family, friends or strangers, but the gracious and genuine way you do it!; [a.] Bellwood, IL

CLARK, FAYE E.
[b.] August 19, 1957, Newark, NJ; [p.] John and Fannie Willis Sr.; [m.] Stanley E. Clark, March 8, 1991; [ch.] Jasmine (7 yrs old), Stanley Jr. (6 months old); [ed.] Barringer High School 75 Rutgers Univ. 76-mid 78; [occ.] Customs Aid (U.S. Customs Service since 1983); [oth. writ.] An ending before a beginning, Cliques, Jasmine, April 19 just a date or a reason ot hate (not finished yet); [pers.] The poem my daddy, my father, my friend was written for my Dad who passed away on August 31, 1993. He raised me and my four sisters and three brothers eventhough he had a mentally ill wife. We all are doing great, scientist, manager, secretaries. He was a great dad, we miss him so.; [a.] Maplewood, NJ

CLARK, PATRICIA A.
[pen.] Patty Clark; [b.] November 30, 1951, Lansing, MI; [p.] Fred Robbins, Jean Robbins; [m.] James C. Clark, May 24, 1986; [ch.] Shawn (Knapp) Connin, Sarah Knapp, Anisa Clark, Beth Clark, Nathan Clark, Jacob Clark; [ed.] B.A. Family Life Education Spring Arbor College, Spring Arbor, MI; [occ.] Performing Artist (Story teller Musician); [memb.] NAPPS (National Assoc. Perpetuation of Storytelling), listed with the Michigan Humanities Council, listed with the Midland Touring Arts Agency; [oth. writ.] A modern creation myth called, The Glass Box, a collection of songs called, The Transitional Years, a collection of stories called, The Story Tree; [pers.] "Storytelling and Poetry is a form of communication that we get in no other way. To replace the `real live' storyteller or band with a television or computer screen would be a true American `Tragedy'. By keeping this communication form alive, we insure the survival of our culture."; [a.] East Jordan, MI

CLARK, TAKETA ANNETTE
[pen.] Kee-Kee, Keta; [b.] November 21, 1981, LSU Medical Center; [p.] Sheldon Wardlaw and Linda Clark; [ed.] Castor High School, 8th grade; [memb.] 1991 and 1992 4-H club, Funny Bunny Club, Restoration Crusades (church) with Elder Talben Pope pastor; [hon.] Many first place awards in science fair; [oth. writ.] About thirty additional poems; [pers.] Through Christ you can do all things!; [a.] Castor, LA

CLARY, CHARLES EDMUNDE
[b.] July 11, 1938, Deming, NM; [p.] Charles and Esther Clary; [m.] Suzanne Kildow-Clary, June 4, 1988; [ch.] Cathlene and Vikki; [ed.] MA. in Counseling and Psychotherapy, University of San Francisco; [occ.] Stress Management Consultant; [memb.] California Association of Marriage and Family Therapists and R.E. C.A.M.F.T; [hon.] PSI-CHI- Honor Society in Psychology Twice, Chosen as Citizen of the day, Santa Rosa,

California for civic work (Junior Achievement); [oth. writ.] Book of poetry, titled, "Voices of Memory" Published 1986; [pers.] Balance and harmony will get understanding!; [a.] Santa Rosa, CA

CLAYPOOLE, JENNIFER
[pen.] Jen Claypoole; [b.] December 1, 1982, Kitanning; [p.] Kenneth and Ruth Claypoole; [ed.] In the 6th grade Chicora Elementary School Chicora, PA; [occ.] Baby sitter; [oth. writ.] This was my first poem; [pers.] "I was influenced by all of the abuse in our world. Also by women who can over come all the abuse."; [a.] Chicora, PA

CLINE, GLENDA ANN HATFIELD
[pen.] Glenda Ann Hatfield; [b.] October 28, 1949, Wyoming, CO; [p.] Troy K. Hatfield and Pearl Trent; [m.] Rutherford James Cline, October 29, 1965; [ch.] Allen James Cline, Vickie Lynn Cline, and Elliott Rutherford Cline; [ed.] G.E.D.; [occ.] Homemaker - Mother, Respite Care Taker; [hon.] Three beautiful children and grand children; [oth. writ.] More poems and short stories and a poem published on a record in 1960's; [pers.] I hope to reflect the greatness of (God the Father) in my writings. I have greatly been influenced by my parents in my upbringing, and my God.; [a.] Baisden, WV

CLINGAN, GREG
[pen.] "Morning Sky"; [b.] July 20, 1972, Northbrook, IL; [p.] Robert S. and Marjorie; [ed.] Kenyon College, University of New Mexico, Elementary Education (Bilingual - Spanish, English; [occ.] Day Care Assistant; [oth. writ.] Bumper stickers "Done There Been That", "Humanity Is Trying"; [pers.] (We are living at the brink of a potentially destructive era.) My pen is my weapon, with which I aim to entertain and enlighten both my peers and our children.; [a.] Albuquerque, NM

COATES, JULIE
[b.] April 3, 1979, Monroe, LA; [p.] Susan Coates, Chris Coates; [pers.] Never underestimate the power of love, for it has no limits.; [a.] West Monroe, LA

COBO, LINDA J.
[b.] July 27, 1978, Jacksonville Beach, FL; [p.] Fred Cobo III, and Michelle L. Cobo; [ed.] M.S. Ryan Elementary, M.B. Lamar Middle School, J.W. Nixon High School; [occ.] Student; [memb.] U.I.L. Debate Team, L.U.L.A.C., Brass Buttons, Senior Class, National Honor Society; [hon.] 1st Place Lincoln Douglas Debate U.I.L. District, Highest Honors in English Class, Highest Honors Silva Mind Control Method.; [oth. writ.] Several poems published, one by Illiad Press, two are being published by National Library of Poetry; [pers.] Believe in yourself and you'll never go wrong. Believe what other people tell you and your life is not your own; [a.] Laredo, TX

COCHRAN, CARLEE
[pen.] CC Rae; [b.] March 28, 1981, Kodiak, AK; [p.] Susan Cochran and Kent Lenz; [ed.] Currently 8th grade at Adams Middle School will attend 9th at No Platte Senior High next year 95-96; [occ.] Student; [oth. writ.] The locket, You and I, A Women of True Heart, Help Us, What is Love, Honored Love, Pool of Dreams; [pers.] Live your

life to the fullest, because you're not going to get another chance to live in the same times or the same people you live with now.; [a.] North Platte, NE

COELHO, ARIOSTO J.
[pen.] Vardhan Naik-Sardessai; [b.] September 30, 1950, Goa, India-Portuguesa; [p.] Xavierito Coelho and Valdemira Fernandes; [m.] Vivian E. Marrone, March 22, 1994; [ch.] Michael Anthony; [ed.] Sahitya Ratna in Hindi Literature, Masters in Divinity, Licenza in Spiritual Theology, Masters in Pastoral Studies, Doctorate in Philosophy and Religion.; [occ.] Project Manager, Operations Control, S.F.I.A., San Francisco, CA., Seminar trainer, The Learning Annex, San Francisco, CA.; [memb.] Salesians of Don Bosco, Bombay and Rome, Patriarcado Das Indias Orientais, Goa, Priest, Anglican Catholic Diocese of the Pacific Southwest, Founder of the Mystic Circle' and Moimasram, San Bruno, Ca.; [hon.] Awarded the 'Ten Outstanding Young Persons of India' Award, 1987.; [oth. writ.] 1989-The 'Personal Vocation' of Don Bosco in Memorie Dell' Oratorio. 1994-Mandalas, Personal Mythology, and Mid-Life Spirituality; [pers.] To venture into fullness simply with love, freely with hope, and fully with faith in order to awaken, balance, center, and delight in the best within people.; [a.] San Bruno, CA

COFFEY, MICHAEL EDWARD
[b.] April 3, 1958, Jefferson City, TN; [p.] Ermon Clyde and Wilma Jean Coffey; [m.] Louise Rosenbalm Coffey, June 21, 1985; [ed.] Morristown, West High.; [occ.] Auto Plant Assembly line Repairman; [memb.] Cedar Creek Baptist Church, VAW Local 1617, UAW Local 1617 Bass Club; [hon.] The National Library of Poetry.; [oth. writ.] Several Unpublished poem's; [pers.] I give God credit for the ability to write, and thanks to my wife an family for the inspiration.; [a.] Morristown, TN

COFIELD, GOLDIE
[b.] April 12, 1933, Scotland Neck, NC; [m.] Moses Cofield; [ch.] Teon, Bobbie, Jerry, Joyce, Fredireck, Jennifer, Kenneth; [occ.] Domestic worker; [memb.] Rocky Mt. Evan. Deliver once Center Church. I sing in the choir. Do missionary work also; [hon.] For a poem title — Gift Of Love but no copyright, or publication.; [oth. writ.] A song put into music. Title - I Believe - but no copy write or publication.; [pers.] In the year of 1981, I was inspired by the Spirit of God to write words of encouragements song and poems, my main goal is to reach souls and encourage the broken hearted, in Christ Jesus.; [a.] Rocky Mount, NC

COGGINS, CYNTHIA J.
[b.] May 25, 1968, Johnson CO, Cleburne, TX; [p.] Oliver Lee Young and Pamela S. Moser; [m.] Barry Coggins, April 26, 1994; [ch.] Wade Scott Garner DOB 5-10-88, Chelsa Daniele Garner DOB 9-20-89; [ed.] Freshman High School GED. 1 to 1 1/2 yr. College; [occ.] Housewife; [memb.] Stephenville Writers Group; [oth. writ.] Non-published poetry: Oceans in the sky today our children; [pers.] Goodness does not come from the mind, but from the heart. Opening your heart filled with goodness and love will fill the hearts of others. Never close your heart to others and push the world away, for your heart surely will wither up and slowly erode away.

COHEN, ELEANOR L.
[pen.] Nova; [b.] October 15, 1945, Newark, NJ; [p.] Rovena and James Levell; [m.] Arthur Cohen (Separated), July 5, 1986; [ch.] Erik C. Levell; [ed.] 1979-1983 Bachelor of Science in Nursing. Rutgers University, Newark, NJ. 1970-1973 Associate Applied Science in Nursing. Essex County College, Newark, NJ.; [occ.] Disability Retired Student-Long Ridge Writers Group CT. NJ.; [memb.] Rutgers Alumni, Newark, NJ. Board of Nursing Newark, NJ., Consumer Affairs Div. Trenton, NJ. Distinguished Member of The International Society of Poets, 1994-1995.; [hon.] Certificate of Completion for Medical Transcription, CA. Overlook Hospital Professional Service Employment Award, Summit, NJ. Greystone State Hospital, Registered Nurse Scholarship Award, NJ. 1970.; [oth. hon.] Editor's Choice Award, 1994. New Dynamics of Winning Certificate, 1994.; [pers.] My Success Turnkey. No Disability or low self-esteem, will ever stop me from fulfilling my dreams. By seeing, believing and achieving are schemes that light my path beam.; [a.] Morris County, NJ

COHEN, PETER
[b.] March 30, 1952, NYC; [p.] Robert and Helen Cohen; [m.] Diana Marshall, September 14, 1982; [ch.] Erin, Ethan, Elliot; [ed.] Cornell University, University of Chicago; [occ.] Psychiatrist; [oth. writ.] Feature journalism; [a.] Berkeley, CA

COHEN, SELMA
[pen.] Selma Phoebe Cohen; [b.] March 25, NY; [m.] Philip Cohen, July 1947; [ch.] Michael (deceased 1975), Elizabeth, Steven, Ephram; [occ.] Retired; [pers.] Poetry is a way of saying things that cannot be said otherwise

COLDWELL, SHARON BOWEN
[b.] October 14, 1952, Sedan, KS; [p.] John C. Bowen Jr. and Betty Rozell Bowen; [m.] Bobby D. Coldwell, April 9, 1972; [ch.] Kelli Dawn and Brandon James; [ed.] B.S. in Education, NSU Tahlequah Oklahoma, Fordland High School, Fordland, Missouri; [occ.] HUD Housing Inspector for Ok. Housing Finance Agency, Ok. City, OK; [memb.] For 19 years for NE District Sunday School Teacher for 9 and 10 yr. Olds at Park Hill Baptist, Tahlequah, Oklahoma.; [pers.] At a very early age I was acutely aware of God's presence. His spirit lives in me through my belief in Jesus Christ. My young years swimming with my cousins visiting my Grandparents in Tahlequah Ok. at the Illinois River are my most memorable.; [a.] Tahlequah, OK

COLEMAN, JACQUELYN ANN
[pen.] Jacs; [b.] December 5, 1957, Perth Amboy, NJ; [ch.] Peter John, Shawn Michael and Ashley Marie; [occ.] Catering

COLEMAN, LORI SUE
[b.] December 20, 1965, Boston, TX; [p.] Ron Coleman, Nanci Green; [ed.] BA, Boston College, Oxford University Oxford, England Cambridge University Cambridge England; [occ.] Research and Geriatric Health Care.; [memb.] National Literary Guild.; [hon.] Mass Medical Society Award, Microbiology, citation from Secretary of State US Navy Award, Marine Corps Award in

Science; [oth. writ.] Portfolio of poems and Journal entries.; [pers.] My writings are like being placed on a mission, experiencing it, and twinkling the problems one is challenged with in life.; [a.] Needham, MA

COLETTA, LINDA
[b.] September 20, 1953, New Haven, CT; [p.] Joseph Coletta, Tina Coletta; [ed.] Lauralton Hall High School Combs Conservatory of Music; [occ.] Massage Therapist singer pianist; [hon.] Honorable Mention in National Song Writings Contest; [pers.] Writing poetry has always been a rewarding outlet. My earliest impressions of stirring prose are passages from the Bible.; [a.] West Haven, CT

COLEY, CHARLES
[b.] May 23, 1952, Philadelphia, PA; [p.] Lillian and Leon E. Hall; [m.] Nuri Lynn Coley, May 6, 1993; [ch.] Camille Marie Tyson; [ed.] Bachelor's Degree in Liberal Arts from Villanova University, Villanova, PA on May 1, 1993; [occ.] Librarian of the Masjid W. D. Muhammed, SCI-Graterford; [memb.] Coordinator, Family Resource Center, SCI-Graterford; [oth. writ.] The Writer's Rostrum, Issue No. 25, Winter 1990-91, The Eagle Spirit, People's Voice Press 1993; [a.] Norristown, PA

COLLETT, JULIA DIXON
[b.] September 3, 1923, Saint Louis, MO; [p.] Irene Rivers and Forney Dixon; [m.] Leslie Collett (Deceased), July 17, 1944; [ch.] Juleta Burrell, Stephen Dixon and Rosanne Collett.; [ed.] 1941 Grad. Normandly High School and Washington Univ. Night Classes.; [occ.] Retired Previous Adm. Asst., Judevine Center for Autistic Children. Senior's DIR., NW Co. YMCA Overland, Exec. Sec., Plumbing Contactor's Assn. Metro St. Louis Past; [memb.] 10 yrs. on Community Care and Ritenour Dine Center Boards, Children's Pastor, First Assembly of God Overland, Northwest Assembly of God.; [hon.] 2 poems Published Trade in Plumbing Publications.; [oth. writ.] Sentimental Journey, Collection of Happenings over 50 yrs. ago, by YMCA Seniors. And 68 yrs. of poems.; [pers.] My writings Read like a Saga Sadness Journaled as therapy for self and the reader.; [a.] Stann, MO

COLLIER, TAMMY S.
[b.] November 9, 1974, Montgomery, AL; [p.] Susan King; [ed.] K-State Salina for one year Graduated high school in 1993; [occ.] Tony's Pizza Service - Product Assembler; [memb.] Y.M.C.A., Columbia Honse, BMG Music, Huh Music Service, America on line.; [hon.] 2nd place track-1 mile, 3rd place in 800m repay track, 2nd "I love Salina essay" My instructor liked my poem - I used it in an assignment (Linda Loder.); [oth. writ.] Yes I have other poems. I haven't written them down on paper yet.; [pers.] I write my poetry from my heart with feeling in then. That is the best way to write poetry...straight from the heart.; [a.] Salina, KS

COLLINS, ANGEL
[b.] September 5, 1979, Brazil, IN; [p.] Randy Collins, Diana Braunstein; [ed.] Current Student at West Vigo High School. Plan to Attend St. Mary's College; [hon.] Honor Roll Student; [oth. writ.] Lot's not yeats recognized; [a.] West Terre Haute, IN

COLLINS, RANDY W.
[b.] August 22, 1956, Terre Haute, IN; [p.] Fred E. Collins - Mary Lou Collins; [ch.] Angel Marie Collins, Freddy J. Collins; [ed.] West Vigo High School; [occ.] Boiler Fireman Vigo County School Corp.; [memb.] Vice Commander of American Legion Post #501; [a.] West Terre Haute, IN

COLLINS, SUE
[b.] February 21, 1934, Shelbyville, TN; [p.] Roy Jacobs, Della Jacobs; [m.] Ray Collins, June 27, 1953; [ch.] Ray, Michael Collins, Timothy, Mark Collins; [ed.] Lincoln County High School - Vocational Education; [occ.] Insurance Agent Owner and Manager of Independent Insurance Agency for 13 yrs; [memb.] 1st Baptist Church Fayetteville, TN. (Div of Southern Baptist Convention) Fayetteville after 5 Club-(Christian Women's Club) Past Board Member of Leadership - Fayetteville - Lincoln Members Insurances of TN and Professional Insurance Agents; [hon.] Mom and wife of the years by my family Beta Club. Insurance Sales Trips to Hawaii and New York; [oth. writ.] Various poems recognized by different people in Local Area; [pers.] My goal is always to live my life in a manner that others might share in the glory of knowing our Lord; [a.] Fayetteville, TN

COLLINSWORTH, JULIE
[b.] March 29, 1981, Middletown, OH; [p.] Sue and Edward Collinsworth; [ed.] Middletown City Schools, American School Chicago, IL; [occ.] Student; [memb.] Enterprise Baptist Church; [oth. writ.] A personal collection of poems; [pers.] I always reflect my true feelings in my writing; [a.] Middletown, OH

COMBS, LILLIE GARTMAN
[b.] August 12, 1934, Salem, VA; [p.] Paul Greggs Gartman and Lillie Gartman; [m.] Sidney Combs, March 10, 1953; [ed.] Andrew Lewis High School, Temple School of Business, Washington School for Secretaries, Wash., D. C.; [occ.] Administrative Manager; [memb.] Capital Baptist Church; [pers.] My Christian upbringing and love of nature given to me by my parents reveal themselves in my poems and they relate to personal experiences that were part of my everyday life growing up in rural Salem, VA.; [a.] Fairfax, VA

CONIGLIARO, FRANCESCO P.
[b.] August 31, 1946, Italy; [p.] Joseph, Rosalia Conigliaro; [m.] Mary Ann Conigliaro, August 2, 1975; [ch.] Rosemarie, Joseph A.; [ed.] 8th Grade St. John Bosco. In Catania Italy; [occ.] Electrician; [memb.] IBEW' Loc 134 Chicago; [pers.] When my Father passed away I was 17 years old and I became instantly a men of the house I lost faith in God and now I am in search of his light.; [a.] Carol Stream, IL

CONNER, MERCEDES VIGIL
[b.] August 17, 1926, Fort Garland, CO; [p.] Vicente and Lucia Vigil; [m.] Richard Conner, May 3, 1947; [ch.] Claudia, Jim, Patty, Dickie Jane; [ed.] College High School, Greeley Co., Ft Garland High - Adams State College - BA 1948; [occ.] Retired Teacher - 33 years taught in 5 states all ages - all races and Bilingual and Est Ed.; [memb.] International Society of Poets - 1994.;

[hon.] 4 year Scholastic Scholarship, Adams State College 1944 - 1948. Editors Choice Award - for poetry pub. in 1995 - Journey of the mind suddenly ...; [oth. writ.] Translated from Spanish Language to English the only Maintenance and Pilots manual for the Vintage Aircraft, HE I-II Heinkel (German WW II) Aircraft now owned by the Confidence Air Force, this plane could not be flown without the English translation as required by the FAA for USA flights. Pome in Journey of the Mind 1995 ed. Suddenly I hear the silence (on my last day of Teaching). Translation for Health Care Co. (Eng. to Sp.); [pers.] "Open doors of knowledge and understanding for children teach them compassion be their role model we need them!; [a.] Greenville, TX

CONNORS, JEFF
[b.] January 17, 1979, Belleville; [p.] John and Anne Connors; [ed.] St. Peters Prep High School, Jersey City New Jersey; [occ.] Student; [pers.] I want to emphasize on world piece through out the world; [a.] Kearny, NJ

CONNORS, RICHARD GERED
[pen.] R. G. Connors; [b.] July 4, 1933, Butler, PA; [p.] Leo V. Connors, Regina Klitch; [m.] Constance, December 31, 1955; [ch.] Gerianne, Timothy, Brian, and Joseph and nine grandchildren; [ed.] High school, served 3 yrs. Untied States Marine Corps; [occ.] Airline Employee (Almost retired after 41 yrs); [oth. writ.] Novel in Progress, several works of poetry (unpublished) and short story also unpublished; [pers.] I hope to leave some small mark in literature that will provoke the reader to remember my words.

CONTI, JENNA
[pen.] Jac, Jenna Dear; [b.] March 10, 1981, Newton, NJ; [p.] Diane Apostola, Harold Conti; [ed.] Stillwater Township, Frankford Township, Kittatinny Regional H.S; [hon.] Spelling, Art; [oth. writ.] Other poems, and my feelings; [pers.] I only write what comes from my heart.; [a.] Newton, NJ

CONWAY, BERTHA C.
[pen.] Celia Conway; [b.] February 22, Munster Township; [p.] Bernard and Cecelia Beiswenger; [m.] Charles Joseph Conway, October 3, 1933; [ch.] Bob, Tom, Joe (boys), Florence, Mary Ellen, Emmy (girls); [ed.] High School and plenty of experience working with Jr. Clubs such are PTA (Secretary), Band Mothers President, Girl Scout Leader, Den Mother; [occ.] Housewife; [memb.] Saint Francis Xavier's Church, Member of it's Altar and Rosary Society, member Catholic Daughters of the Americas Joan of Arc Court 16, The Railroad Social Club-Cresson Area Senior Citizens, Women's Club of Cresson; [hon.] Queen of Southern Alleghenies Senior Citizens for four years in fourth grade, received the award, for having the highest average in the school of 200 students, Queen of Senior Citizens, 4 years. I consider this an honor; [oth. writ.] Joey and His Little Dog Pepper, Bethlehem's Child, Did You Ever or The Things God Has Given, Alone in the Rain and More.; [pers.] I have lived all my life on these mountains and I love it. Winters can be very cold, but the snow is beautiful and the sunsets are gorgeous year round.; [a.] Cresson, PA

COOK, ALISA GAIL
[b.] August 30, 1965, Passaic, NJ; [p.] Ed and Jan Cook; [ed.] B.A. Environmental Education-Prescott College, M.A. Bilingual Education-University of Arizona; [occ.] Student of life; [pers.] Shortly before my sister's wedding, we were talking about the notion of love. She asked me, "What do you think love is? What does that word mean to you?" The poem I wrote was my response to her question-and I lovingly dedicate it to her, the rest of my family, and wonderful friends.; [a.] Tucson, AZ

COOK, NANCY M.
[b.] June 2, 1957, Burlington, VT; [p.] Clifford and Marjorie Poquette; [m.] Separated; [ch.] Daniel 9, Angela 7, Peter 3; [ed.] Graduated from South Burlington High School 1975, received Bachelor of Arts in Psychology from Lyndon State College, Lyndonville, VT in 1979; [occ.] Mother of three; [memb.] Vermont Right to Life Committee; [hon.] Principal's Award from SBHS, Dean's List; [oth. writ.] Contributing writer for "The Liberty News", a national newspaper headquartered in Northfield Falls, VT; [a.] Morrisville, VT

COOK, WILLIAM
[b.] December 20, 1936, Otsego, WA; [p.] James Merrill and Mayola Cook; [m.] Toula B. Cook, May 29, 1971; [ed.] BA Business, CPA U. of So. Florida, U. of Illinois (Chicago) Stoco H.S., Coal City, Wa.; [occ.] Treasurer; [memb.] I'll CPA Society; [hon.] Nat'l Honor Society; [oth. writ.] Transformation, freedom's Choice, Aura, Adrift upon an ocean Deep, King of the Court, Death, Earth Cries, Child of Light, Noses, Beer Belly, The Eternal Song, The Healer, The Master, Partners; [pers.] A good, portion of the Spiritual poems are influenced by the Path of Eckankan, the Ancient Science of Soul travel.; [a.] Batavia, IL

COOPER, VICTOR Y.
[pen.] "Thought Spinner"; [b.] April 10, 1960, Chicago, IL; [p.] Leroy Young, Josephine Cooper; [ch.] Victor Young Cooper Jr.; [ed.] Wendel Phillips High, MCI Courses,; [occ.] Entrepreneur; [memb.] Crenshaw Christian Center, International Society of Poets; [hon.] Marine Corps Good Conduct Medal, Over Seas Ribbon, two Honorable Discharges Editors Choice Award - from the National Library of Poetry.; [oth. writ.] Heavenly Love; [pers.] The search for Wisdom never ends, until one seeks the knowledge of God.; [a.] Chicago, IL

COOSARD, JENNIFER
[pen.] Jacy; [b.] May 18, 1978, Saginaw, MI; [oth. writ.] "Holding Back the Tears" (a poem) among many others, also wrote a song, another poem was published in the Belletristic, school magazine; [pers.] The point I want to make from this poem, "Enduring Love" is "The difficulties in Life are intended to make us better not bitter" --anon, which fits for the subject of this poem which is about long-distance relationships; [a.] Boothbay Harbor, ME

CORAM, CARRIE
[b.] October 30, 1980, Newport News, VA; [p.] Frances Goetz, George Coram; [ed.] Eight Grade at Chaminade College Preparatory Middle School; [memb.] JV Cheer leaders at Chaminade College Preparatory High School 1995-96, YABA - Youth Bowling; [hon.] Many trophy's in bowling; [pers.] Poetry to me is my way of expressing the ups and downs of a teenagers life.; [a.] Granada Hills, CA

CORBIN, MARILYN PEYTON
[b.] August 22, 1950, Chicago, IL; [p.] Mr. and Mrs. Charles L. B. Peyton; [m.] Donald Keith Corbin, August 14, 1971; [ch.] Caitlyn Elizabeth Peyton Corbin; [ed.] Indiana University B.S. 72, Florida Atlantic University Masters 79; [occ.] High School English Teacher/ St. Andrews School - Boca Raton, Fl.; [memb.] National Council of Teachers of English St. John's Christian Church; [hon.] Cum Laude, Phi Kappa Phi National, Honor Soc., Dean's List; [pers.] "Abbreviated Life" is dedicated to my brother, Stephen, who took his own life at the age of thirty-seven.; [a.] Lighthouse Point, FL

CORBIN, MARILYN PEYTON
[b.] August 22, 1950, Chicago, IL; [p.] Betty Marie Schwarting, Charles L. B. Peyton; [m.] Donald K. Corbin, August 14, 1971; [ch.] Caitlyn E. Peyton Corbin; [ed.] Masters in Educ. Florida Atlantic Univ. (79) B.S. in Sec - Educ. Indiana Univ. (72) New Trier H.S. (68); [occ.] High School English Teacher - St. Andrew's School Boca Raton, FL; [memb.] The National Council of Teachers of English; [hon.] Phi Kappa Phi National Honor Society Dean's List, Cum Laude; [oth. writ.] Additional poems and journals; [pers.] "Life abbreviated" is dedicated to my brother Stephen Charles Peyton who took his own life at the age of thirty - seven.; [a.] Lighthouse Point, FL

CORDAIR, QUENT
[b.] July 19, 1964, Mattoon, IL; [p.] Jerald and Connie Brown; [occ.] Writer and Artist (oils on canvas); [oth. writ.] Stories published: A prelude to pleasure, The Hunter, The Whistler, April's Justice, The Seduction of Santi Banesh; [pers.] Favorite writers: Ayn Rand, Victor Hugo, Ian Fleming, Favorite Artists: Bouguereau, Cot, Parrish; [a.] Burlingame, CA

CORDTZ, BILL
[b.] March 25, 1923, San Diego; [p.] Mr. and Mrs. Austin Cordtz (deceased); [m.] Alice L. Cordtz, July 18, 1948; [ch.] Desda Cordtz Zuckerman, Robert W. Cordtz, David H. Cordtz; [ed.] Ph.D. U.S. International '68, M.A. California Western '66, B.A. San Diego State '48; [occ.] Retired/Traveler formerly College Professor, High School Teacher, Vintner, Rancher, Advertising Executive.; [oth. writ.] Currently working on two historical books and a book of poetry; [pers.] My poem "Quiet Little Blue Shoes" was written as a reflection on my now grown daughter. I admire human beings and try to reflect that feeling in my poetry.; [a.] San Rafael, CA

CORMIER, PAUL JOSEPH
[pen.] P. J.; [b.] January 15, 1934, Brooklyn, MN; [p.] Margaret and Placide Cormier; [m.] Rita G. Cormier, August 16, 1980; [ch.] Katelyn M. Cormier; [ed.] High School, 1 year Vocational Investigations, 1 year College Accredited, 4 months Emergency Medical "EMT" training; [occ.] Retired "Newton, MN" Police Officer; [memb.] Mass Police Assoc. V.F.W. Post 1538 Mary Immaculate of Lords Parish; [hon.] I received the highest award for police work and several commendations - throughout my career of 31 years in poetry. Your acceptance of my poem - is my first honor; [oth. writ.] "Honestly" a song and lyrics, "Is It The Feeling" a song with lyrics - and other poetry - based on emotions and inner feelings.; [pers.] There are moments in all of our lives - that are extra special - we should all share the true joy of expression through poetry, music and whatever art is most rewarding.; [a.] Newton Highland, MA

CORONADO, GINA R.
[b.] November 15, 1968, Calexico, CA; [p.] Ramon A. Coronado and Estrella L. Coronado; [ed.] Holtville High, Hueneme High, Oxnard College, and Ventura College; [occ.] College student and lifeguard; [pers.] Don't take life for granted when life is given to you.; [a.] Oxnard, CA

CORTEZ, MAYAMERICA
[b.] July 27, 1947, El Salvador; [p.] Pedro Hernan Cortes and Maria Elia Alas; [m.] Divorced; [ch.] Alvaro, Carmen-Elena and Karla Rodas-Cortez; [ed.] Secretary - attending the University of present time to pursue a teacher career; [occ.] Secretary at Timber Lane Elem. School, Fairfax; [memb.] Ibero American Academy of Poetry, sub-Director.; [hon.] Honored as member of the Clasicos Roxsil's "Salvadorean Writers Collection", included in "One hundred years anthology in El Salvador"; [oth. writ.] Lumbre De Soledad (book) Nostalgia's Y Soledades (book), Cantos Del Amante Y Del Amor (Book) - (poetry), Urania - (novel), several poems published in local newspaper L.A. In opinion newspaper and newspaper in El Salvador.; [pers.] Poetry is what you carry within from ages of eternity, it is to name things with the angels' tongue.; [a.] Alexandria, VA

CORTLUND SR., JASON ALEXANDER
[b.] March 15, 1938, Oakland, CA; [p.] Joe and Clair Colacicco; [m.] Kathleen Cortlund, January 1, 1993; [ch.] Jason Jr, Marah, Yana Cortlund, Marian and Jon De Vries; [ed.] Fremont H.S., Col-state University-Hayward; [occ.] Probation offices and occasional writer of poetry; [hon.] A life well spent and the love of those I love; [oth. writ.] First poem submitted and published 1956 in "Songs of Youth", National and international anthologies of High School Poetry fifty years of written musings to my loves, fears and silences; [pers.] I am grateful for the moments I have found words to express my passions and confusion; [a.] Martinez, CA

COSSU, JENNIFER K.
[pen.] Jenn, Jenna; [b.] December 21, 1974, Cedarhurst, NY; [p.] Teresa Cossu; [ed.] Lawrence High School Class of '93, I am currently enrolled at John Jay College of Criminal Justice; [occ.] Full time student; [oth. writ.] This is the first time my work has ever been published!; [pers.] I

want to say thanks to Nan, Corrine, and Leida, who have inspired me to keep on striving for my goals. I also want to thank my boyfriend, John, without him I don't know where I'd be, He's made these past two years memorable. I also want to say to everyone in this world that its not really what's on the outside of a person that makes them beautiful, its what's on the inside especially when people smile "A smile is when your inner beauty comes out," and that's all that matters; [a.] Cedarhurst, NY

COSTA, LOLA L.
[b.] October 3, 1929; [p.] Henry Elliott Smith, Lenore C. J. Schild Smith; [m.] Delbert J. Costa, September 6, 1969; [ed.] Baker University, Wichita State University; [occ.] Retired; [memb.] Co. Grove United Meth. Ch. Mo Co, Historical Society - Board, Friends of Kaw Heritage - Board and Programs Community Arts Council - Treas., Philomathian Club -, Petroleum Accts. Society of Kansas Beta Sigma Phi Laureate Alpha Kappa; [hon.] Past President - Friends of Wichita Public, Library Honorary Member - OSA -; [oth. writ.] Various articles - poems - etc.; [a.] Council Grove, KS

COTE, DOLORES Y.
[b.] July 12, 1938, New Bedford, MA; [p.] Aldege and Alice Desrosiers; [m.] Gerard D. Cote (deceased), October 25, 1958; [ch.] Louise Ann, Doris Ann, Joseph Gerard; [ed.] High School (G.E.D.); [occ.] Licensed day care provider; [memb.] United Sderoderma Foundation, Sacred Heart's Church, American Heart Association; [oth. writ.] Children songs

COTHRAN, ARETTA S.
[pen.] A. S. Cothran; [b.] September 8, 1941, Denver, CO; [p.] Irene and Loren Snow (Both Deceased); [m.] Arnold R. Cothran, March 7, 1987; [ch.] 3 Daughters and 6 Sons. All married, giving us 20 Grandchildren, with 2 more on the way and 1 Great Granddaughter with hopes of many more.; [occ.] I am retired and enjoy my house plants, gardens and doing my hand crafts.; [oth. writ.] I've been dabbling at poetry since about age 16, but not taking it serious, for I had never felt I had the talent to do much of anything really well.; [pers.] I am the last of 6 siblings and wish to give many thanks to all my family members for their constant support and encouragement, especially to my ever loving husband, my sister Irene and my most wonderful Nephew Sal.; [a.] Westminster, CO

COUEY, MONA E.
[pen.] El Salah; [b.] February 12, 1963, Brooklyn, NY; [p.] Josephine and Billie Couey; [ch.] Sharrieff Couey (son); [ed.] Amityville School System (grade 1-12), Fredonia, York, and Old Westbury Colleges. B.A. in Psychology Specialize in early Childhood and Bilingual Education.; [occ.] Teacher at P.S. 112, Manhattan, N.Y.; [memb.] Participated in Brooklyn Academy of Music, Chorus, Mixed and Girl's Ensemble, High School Gospel Choir (college), Drama Club, Track, Cross Country, Literary Clubs, Basketball, Talent show coordinator and participant.; [hon.] Who's Who In Music Award, (1981), Editor's Choice Award (The National Library of Poetry 1994).; [oth. writ.] Songs performed by Old Westbury Gospel Choir and children at P.S. 112., Poetry included in school

yearbooks, literary magazines, and newspapers. Poetry published by The Nat'l Library of Poetry; [pers.] Writing reflects the cycles of life and the multi-faceted ways in which we all learn and grow from our mere existence.; [a.] Amityville, NY

COUGHENOUR, VIRGINIA F.
[pen.] Ginny Gray, Ginny Coughenour; [b.] January 20, 1947, Harrisonburg, VA; [p.] Fred and Dora Fechtmann; [m.] Thomas R. Coughenour, June 8, 1968; [ch.] Todd and Tim Coughenour; [ed.] Turner Ashby High, Richmond Professional Institute, James Madison University, University of South Carolina; [occ.] Preschool Director and Teacher Holy Trinity Lutheran; [memb.] Kappa Delta Pi, St. Bartholomew's Episcopal Church, Lutheran Preschool Teacher's Assoc. Choir Member, Sunday School Teacher; [oth. writ.] Poems for friends and family. Stories for preschool children.; [pers.] Inspired by God.; [a.] North Augusta, SC

COWAN, KAREN
[b.] May 13, 1965, Charleston, SC; [p.] Joseph and Mary Haas; [ch.] Alyssa Mary Cowan and Erin Brianne Cowan; [ed.] Newark High School; [pers.] The poems I write come from the heart, and my everyday surroundings; [a.] Newark, DE

COX, ERICA D.
[b.] September 14, 1968, Elyria, OH; [p.] Bonnie and Charles Ruggles Sr.; [m.] Troy Cox, May 4, 1991; [ch.] Bethany Marie and Braden Charles; [occ.] Mail Carrier; [oth. writ.] Many poems and three children's books. I haven't tried to publish any of them.; [pers.] This poem is dedicated to my Grandmother, Hazel Case, who passed away November 7, 1994. We were very close and I love her dearly.; [a.] Greenwich, OH

COX, SINCERE A.
[pen.] Alinda Alexander; [b.] May 26, 1951, St. Vincent; [p.] Hughwin and Inez; [m.] Tyrone Cox, December 12, 1988; [ch.] Chantal, Dacler, Jonathan, Geaver; [ed.] Secondary Level G.E.D.; [occ.] Housekeeper; [pers.] I strive to prove that Human beings as special and that everyone should believe they are special regardless of there nationality.; [a.] Missouri City, TX

CRABTREE, MARK
[b.] November 7, 1967, Fort Stewart, GA; [p.] Allen Crabtree, Patricia Crabtree; [m.] Cindy Ann Crabtree, May 5, 1989; [ch.] Mark Adam, Jacob Allen; [ed.] Owensboro Christian Academy, Central Texas College, U.S. Army Warehouse Supply School Ft. Lee, UA.; [memb.] Deacon, Faith Chapel General Baptist Church, Bass Anglers Sportsman Society (BASS); [hon.] Soldiers of the month February, 1993, Soldiers of the Quarter March, 1993, Key to city of Owensboro, KY. Honorary Kentucky Colonel; [pers.] This poem was written for my wife of 6 years. By the grace of God we met, by the Grace of God we live as one in unity, and by the Grace of God we will live forever in Heaven.; [a.] Pembroke, KY

CRAMP, SUSAN
[pen.] Samantha Galaunt; [b.] June 30, 1975, Yuma, AZ; [p.] Mrs. Marilyn J. Hanke and Thomas Morton; [ed.] Artesia High School, Eastern New Mexico Univ.; [occ.] Tutor for college Students and Learning

Facilator and Full time College Student; [memb.] College Democrats, Speech and Debate team; [hon.] Dean's list, Phikappa Delta, Honors organization, Outstanding member of College Democrats for 94-95 school yr.; [oth. writ.] Prose: Tunnel of Love, which was published in local newspaper; [pers.] My writings come from my heart, and what I feel at certain times. I have admired many poets, such as Edgar Allen POE; [a.] Artesia, NM

CRANFORD, RALPH LOCKE
[b.] July 17, 1926, Burke Co, NC; [p.] George Cranford and Oklona Shuffler Cranford; [m.] Charlotte Travis Cranford, March 29, 1947; [ch.] Walter Maier, Effie Charlene, Michael Lynn, Lisa Gayle.; [ed.] Elementary and High School U.S Navy School of First Aid, (Medic) Clevenger College, and Catawba Valley Community College. (CVCC); [occ.] Retired, but work part time as K-MART Dept. Manager. Conova Center. Conover, NC; [memb.] Songwriters Club of American Mt. Olive Seniors Club, BB&T Club 50, The Heritage Foundation, The 100 Song Writers Club, Bible-A-Month Clb.; [hon.] Have received honorable mention from (For both Poems and Songs) Broadway Music Productions, World of Poetry Press, Iliad Press, Creative Arts & Sciences, The Conservatory of American Letters, Contemporary Poets or America and Britain and others. Rainbow, Chapel, Gospel & MCM Records Sponsor: American Bible Society. Lutheran Hour Ministries. And The Billy Graham Crusades. Various Poetry & Song Writer Awards; [oth. writ.] Books — I Believe in Angels, My Souls Delight (Manuscript) and Covenant Of The Triune God, Now in process of preparing a Poem Book suitable for publication.; [pers.] If I could live my life again, I'd live it much the same way. Raising a family of devoted children who loves family life and serving God and Country.; [a.] Newton, NC

CRAWFORD, DAVID
[b.] June 27, 1966, Grinnell, IA; [p.] Delbert Rachel; [m.] Jill, May 20, 1989; [ch.] Vanessa Marie and Jeremiah John; [ed.] Grinnell High; [occ.] Welder for Donaldsons Co; [memb.] V.A.W. 1201, Fraternal order of the Eagles.; [hon.] Honorable Discharge from U.S. Army 31st Oct 1990.; [oth. writ.] Mostly song sitting around with family and friends.; [pers.] Be true to your self, and then it's easier to be truthful to others.; [a.] Grinnell, IA

CREMIDAS, JEAN B. HALL
[b.] May 31, 1920, San Diego, CA; [p.] WM and Dora Hall; [m.] William Cremidas, August 26, 1945; [ch.] Peter Jennings, Lisa Caryl; [ed.] 3 yrs College U.C.L.A. (English Major); [occ.] Homemaker and Writer of poems and Literature; [memb.] C.S.F. Membership Christian Science Church; [hon.] California Scholarship Foundation; [oth. writ.] Many poems (several published). Also articless for Church Magazines (Sentime'l and Journal); [pers.] Spent 15 years in Saudi Arabia and surrounding Territories. Have spent time in almost all European Countries and Asia. Lived in Eastern U.S. (Boston) also; [a.] Jacksonville, FL

CRESSLER, LANA C.
[b.] October 22, 1957; [p.] William, Marian Jenkins; [ch.] Misty, Dustin, Yocom; [ed.] Granite High; [pers.] For those who's eyes may fall upon my writings. May they find peace with in the

words they read. I have been greatly encouraged, by my children to follow my dreams. Thank you misty and Dustin; [a.] Kearn's, UT

CREWS, LESLIE NANETTE
[b.] June 13, 1985; [p.] Michael and Charla Crews; [ed.] Halifax County Public Schools; [occ.] Student grade 4; [memb.] County Line Baptist Church, Project IDEA Student Active in the following church youth groups: Sunbeam choir, Sunday School, RAY Groups.; [hon.] Principal's Award (All's A 1994-1995 School year); [pers.] I believe that God will help me be the best I can be, but I have to do my best.; [a.] Nathalie, VA

CREWS, PATRICIA
[b.] March 17, 1956, Halifax County, VA; [p.] Mr. and Mrs. Amos and Nannie Crews; [m.] Single; [ed.] Bachelor of Science May 1979, M.Ed. May 1983, Certificate of Advanced Graduate Studies in Special Education Administration and Supervision 1994 (December), Doctoral Candidate for fall of 1995.; [occ.] Remedial Diagnostician, Prince William County Public Schools.; [memb.] Virginia Education Association, National Education Association, Council for Exceptional Children,; [oth. writ.] 1986 publication (October) in the Virginia Journal of Education, 1987 Publication in the National NEA Newsletter, Innovative Learning Strategies Using Music.; [pers.] In all my endeavor's I acknowledge him, and he directs my path.; [a.] Woodbridge, VA

CROSS, JUDY
[pen.] Judy Cross; [b.] April 25, 1947, Macon, GA; [p.] Elmer Stevens, Edna Stevens; [m.] Roscoe C. Cross, August 21, 1964; [ch.] Tammy D. Brown; [ed.] McEvoy High, Clayton State College; [occ.] Homemaker; [pers.] My writings reflect my inner most feelings of deepest sincerity and honesty, no matter what my title or subject might be. Life itself has been my greatest influences.; [a.] Stockbridge, GA

CROWELL, ESTHER M.
[b.] May 1, 1936, Audubon, IA; [p.] John Law, Pearl Law; [m.] Donald Crowell, September 3, 1976; [ch.] Anna Marie, Vernan, Russell, Becky Lynn, Rodney; [ed.] East High School, Des Moines Iowa; [occ.] Retired - Postal Service; [pers.] It is my pleasure to be able to put my feelings and thoughts into my writing.; [a.] Johnston, IA

CUESTA, JOHNNY
[pen.] Juanito Cuesta; [b.] May 17, 1921, SA, TX; [p.] Jose Cuesta, Elvira Cuesta; [m.] Murial Jean Cuesta, February 21, 1976; [ed.] San Antonio Voc. and Tech. High, El Paso Tech. Inst. High School] Santa Barbara City College and San Fran City College; [occ.] Poet and Classical Guitarist; [memb.] American Diabetes Association, American Cancer Society, American Heart Asso.; [oth. writ.] Poems published in world poetry society intercontinental the monthly magazine' "Poet", "Poetry" Spring 1977. 3 Poems Springs 78, (2) "Poetry Res'. Anthology," 1980 (2) Poems.; [a.] San Francisco, CA

CULLINS, DANDY RUTH LEVY
[b.] June 21, 1953, Crosby, TX; [p.] Cleveland and Euella Levy; [m.] Ross McKinley Cullins Sr., February 2, 1991; [ch.] Ross Jr., Shonda,

Tameisha, Trenesa, Tracy (deceased); [ed.] Crosby High School, Lee Jr. College, Houston Community College, South Western Business College, Texas Southern University; [occ.] Student - Texas Southern University.; [memb.] Houston Metropolitan Minister's Wives Auxiliary, Bible Study Fellowship, Association for Childhood Education, Inc.; [hon.] Featured in 1992-1993 National Dean's List, 1994 Texas Southern University Certificate of Recognition for Exemplary Academic Achievement, Dean's List 1994; [pers.] All gifts come from God - to Him belong all the glory and honor.; [a.] Houston, TX

CULLIVAN, JAMES E.
[b.] February 26, 1949, Quincy, IL; [m.] Jeannie Cullivan, February 14, 1988; [ch.] Brian P., David M. and Kelly A. Groben; [ed.] Christian Brothers High Belleville Area College Community College of the Air Force. Attended Southern Illinois Univ. Carbondale; [occ.] Master Sergeant - U.S. Air Force, Peterson AFB, CO; [memb.] Air Force Association; [hon.] Who's Who among students in American Junior Colleges - 78-79 Belleville Area College, Belleville, IL; [oth. writ.] First published poem. Articles for military publications.; [pers.] I wrote "The Black Eagle" in 1978 after learning of General James' untimely death. At a building dedication honoring the Nation's first black four-star general abase gym was the attraction. The ceremony left me wanting to say more.; [a.] Colorado Springs, CO

CULVER JR., WILLIAM R.
[b.] September 10, 1956, San Diego, CA; [p.] Bill and Carmen Culver; [m.] Theresa Lynne Culver, April 29, 1978; [ch.] William R. Culver III, Seth Tyler Culver, Sean Eldon Culver; [ed.] Ramona High-Riverside, Riverside City College, San Bernadino Valley College; [occ.] Senior Engineering Technician; [hon.] Dean's List, San Bernardino Valley College; [oth. writ.] Poem Published by the National Library of Poetry - in "Journey of the Mind."; [pers.] My writings reflect my own personal experiences and of those who are close to me.; [a.] Mission Viejo, CA

CURRO, MARY F.
[pen.] Mary F. Curro; [b.] July 24, 1935, Portsmouth, VA; [p.] Mary E. and Frank C. Curro; [ch.] Four I birthed, one stepchild; [ed.] B.A., Fine Art, College of William and Mary, Hypnosis Motivation Institute, Van Nuys California: Certificate in Advanced Hypnotherapy.; [occ.] Hypnotherapist, Massage Therapist; [memb.] American Guild of Hypnotherapists, American Hypnosis Association, Delta Delta Delta Sorority; [hon.] Dean's List, High School Valedictorian, Honors English Class; [oth. writ.] Continuing articles in the Carolina Health and Humor Newsletter, various essays, Looney Lyrics, some poetry, and a long and growing list of potential book titles, which may someday itself become a book.; [pers.] I believe that which is most real cannot be seen with the physical eye, but that our spiritual vision can make us see the beauty and the connection with everything and everyone. It may be illusion here, so it is up to us to make it as loving and as much fun as possible.; [a.] Portsmouth, VA

CURRY, MARILYN HEATHER
[b.] June 4, 1946, London, UK; [p.] Frances Buller, Osman Leeman; [m.] Simon Curry, May 6th 1972; [ch.] Samuel, Redvers, Benjamin; [ed.] Acton Reynald, Shrewsbury (SALOP) U.K. Beech Lann Tutorial College, Oxford; [occ.] Parent; [memb.] Poetry Society of E Britain, 1950-1963; [hon.] Many Verse-Speaking Awards, Bronze and Silver Medals 1959 all England Literary Award, Hon. Mention.; [oth. writ.] 1959 Poetry Society Magazine; [pers.] The influences of my mother, also a writer, and now the peace of Massachusetts give me the courage and inspiration to write, once more.; [a.] Chelmsord, MA

CURTIS, BETTY L.
[pen.] Betty L. Curtis; [b.] March 27, 1931, Martinsferry, OH; [p.] Dorothy Keplinger; [m.] Harry Curtis Deceased, 1977; [ch.] Perry Thomas; [ed.] Eight Grade; [occ.] Disabled; [memb.] Eagles Lodge, VFW, American Legion, Cance Fun Raiser, Poppie Sales, Heart Fun Raiser, Cook at Eagles for Fun Raising; [oth. writ.] Nothing I stopped; [pers.] I wrote music poetry in my teens and sent to Johnny Mack Brown but never heard anything 2 yrs later the teddy bear song came out but he said it was not mine so I stop sending him thing; [a.] Hollywood, CA

CZAJA, MARK J.
[b.] February 20, 1957, Hartford, CT; [p.] Joachem and Jeanette; [m.] Helene, 1981; [ch.] Dawn and Megan, greatest poems.; [ed.] High School, sampled some college; [occ.] Painter, writer, poet; [hon.] Record for poorest attendance yet passing, Coginchaug High School, Ph.D in B.S. School of life. Booted from writing Correspondence School, dismissed from many churches, many rejection slips; [oth. writ.] 23 yrs. of poetry, short stories, some column work in local paper.; [pers.] The world will surely go on without you. Political correctness was born of bigotry. Laugh at yourself and die with dignity. Never look back. You are what you are by the grace of God.; [a.] Middlefield, CT

D'AGOSTINO, MADELINE
[pen.] Madeline D'; [b.] February 6, 1949, Jersey City, NJ; [p.] Madeline and Dominick Sgroi; [ch.] Christine Francesca (16), Pamela Michele (13); [ed.] North Bergen High School currently pursuing undergraduate courses in Journalism and Computer; [occ.] Full time mother, student and domestic engineer; [memb.] National right to life Assoc., St. Leo's Cursillo Community, St. Leo's Rosary Society, St. Leo's Passion Prayer Player, Mary Help of Christians Parent/Teachers Guild; [hon.] Elected twice Treasurer St. Leo's Home and School Assoc., High School National Honor Society, graduated Principal's List - 1st Honors; [oth. writ.] Several articles for Church bulletin; [pers.] I think finding happiness in this life is a matter of priorities. The only really important things are God and Love - or Love and God - it's really the same thing.; [a.] Elmwood Park, NJ

D'ALESSIO, ANTONELLA
[b.] December 18, 1979, Port Washington, NY; [p.] Giovanna and Alex D'Alessio; [ed.] Schreiber High School; [occ.] Student; [oth. writ.] Other poem published in Teen Magazine.; [pers.] I write poems about sad and happy times for me and others. Those happy and sad times are when I see violence on TV or people in love on TV or people around me, and sometimes myself; [a.] Port Washington, NY

D'ALESSIO, ANYA
[b.] June 8, 1970, Moslow, Russia; [ch.] Sophia Calhoun; [ed.] Moscow High School, Moscow Art College in Memory of 1905, Rhode Island School of Design; [occ.] Artist, Animator; [oth. writ.] Another poem published in "Poetry Motel" of Suburban wilderness press, 1994.; [a.] Carlsbad, CA

DABBS, LORETTA
[b.] April 16, 1936, New York; [p.] Claude Young and Frazure Young; [m.] Henry Dabbs, January 7, 1957; [ch.] Lisa Dabbs Fore; [ed.] Pratt Institute BFA, Jersey City State, BA, Trenton State College, MA; [occ.] Retired Elementary School Teacher, Writer; [hon.] Two (2) Scholarships to Pratt Institute by the Free Synagogue of Westchester, Jersey City State (cum laude), Teacher of the Year, 1987; [oth. writ.] Essence Magazine, July 1991 (article on parenting); [pers.] Life is what you make it.; [a.] Orlando, FL

DACOSTA, WENDY
[pen.] Baby; [b.] May 22, 1976, Columbia Presbyterian Hospital; [p.] Rafaela DaCosta; [m.] Christian Martinez; [ed.] John F. Kennedy H.S.; [occ.] No occupation yet but hoping to become a physical therapist.; [memb.] Washington Heights Inwood Coalition, Inc. (working for the community especially with young people. Creating fairs and etc...); [hon.] Awards in Excellence in Spelling, Attendance, a life planning group and Achievement for character; [oth. writ.] None but always being dedicated to my poems.; [pers.] Many people say: If I tear my heart out and read it, to create such poetries. I want many to know that whatever I write comes deep within my heart. And this heart has really gone through a lot. So those who read my poems would know how I feel.; [a.] New York, NY

DAHILL, MARIANNE E.
[b.] April 27, 1932, New York City, NY; [p.] Thomas R. Dahill II and Beatrice Ann Dahill; [ch.] 3 Nephews, 2 Nieces, 3 Grand Nephews, 3 Grand Nieces; [ed.] Graduate: Cathedral H.S., N.Y.C. attended Danbury State Teachers College, Western Ct. State University; [occ.] Retired; [memb.] Danbury Emblem Club #48, (Lady Elks), St. Edward's R.C. Church, Candlewood Lions Club, Executive Board - Danbury Republican Party, Republican National Committee, Connecticut Republicans; [hon.] "Paddy" award - Best Producer, "Paddy" award - Best Lighting Director, 1st Woman Elected City Clerk of Danbury, Country of Brookfield, CT; [oth. writ.] Many times for personal friends, poems of life, birthday poems, etc. publications in company newsletters, editor of company newsletters. Nothing professionally published - yet!; [pers.] As commanded by Jesus, I wish always to love and be loved and wish the world to be likewise!; [a.] Danbury, CT

DAHL, ELAINE
[pen.] Cookie; [b.] August 21, 1943, New Jersey; [p.] Milton "Jerry" Nicholson and Lucille Faliero Nicholson; [m.] Dennis Dahl, November 27, 1961; [ch.] Lorraine Protocollo, Denise Edwards, Roxane Dahl; [ed.] Bayonne High, Jersey City State College, NJ.; [occ.] Teacher, Tutor, Volunteer at "Give kids the World. Kissimmee FL; [memb.] Jehovah witness, Theocratic Ministry School, Worldwide Org.; [hon.] Jersey City State College Dean's List. Dale Carnegie - Public Speaking Award; [oth. writ.] Poems published in School newspaper and local and county newspapers.; [pers.] My poems are inspired by deep feelings I have for friends and relatives. They write themselves quickly and are rarely altered. Most have religious undertones.; [a.] Kissimmee, FL

DAHLBERG-STUT, SANDIE J.
[pen.] Sandie J. Dahlberg; [b.] April 13, 1953, San Francisco, CA; [p.] Annabelle and Alec; [ch.] A Puppy Dog named Genny (8 yrs. old) she is Cocker and Poodle.; [ed.] 1 Year College and creative Writing Courses and some light play writing in High School; [occ.] I am a Therapeutic Recreation Asst. with a skilled Nursing Facility; [memb.] Special licenses to work with elderly and special people children and adults.; [hon.] I love special training as a Dental Asst. and Activities Asst. with the elderly; [oth. writ.] I enjoy writing children's stories. I have not been published yet, but one book is titled the Dragon who loves Ice Cream. It's fun I also have other poems toward a book!; [pers.] I believe in children within us all, and we all need our young one to be loved and remembered and respected also. We are each inside a hidden treasure waiting to be opened.; [a.] Spokane, WA

DAIGE, SARAH
[b.] June 6, 1977, Fort Pierce, FL; [p.] Dennis and Diane Daige; [ed.] High School Graduate, entering College; [occ.] Student; [memb.] Anchor Club, top 10% of my Senior Class; [hon.] Placed in Architectural drawing contest between 4 counties. (3rd place) received second place for drawing in Rehabilitation Medical Center; [pers.] Straight and narrow is the path. Veering off to the right or left can lead to destruction.; [a.] Vero Beach, FL

DAIL, MICHAEL
[pen.] White Wolf; [b.] September 25, 1969, Kinstone, ND; [p.] Linda Ballock and Wallace Dail; [m.] Melissa Dail, November 27, 1988; [ch.] Jonathan Dail, Taylor Dail; [ed.] Roanoke High, Martin Community College; [occ.] Electrician; [memb.] Robersonville T-Ball (Coach), Robersonville Pentecostal Holiness Church Men's Ministry; [hon.] Honor Student, Jr Beta, and FFA Trade; [oth. writ.] Several poems placed in local newspaper for remembrance, birthday and anniversary; [pers.] I write what's in my heart I have been greatly influenced by my wife, mother, father, and Garth Brooks.; [a.] Everetts, NC

DAILIE, FLOYD A.
[pen.] "Bo Del Yay"; [b.] May 1, 1926, Milbank, SD; [p.] Roy M. and Alma Dailie; [m.] Evelyn Conraads Dailie, August 27, 1955; [ch.] Kenne Joe Dailie, Kae La Ree Dailie Bjorklund; [ed.] Milbank High School, Nreca Writing Seminar, Billy Graham School of Christian Writing; [occ.] Retired Dairy Farmer, Editor, Computer Operator; [memb.] Central United Methodist Church, Whetstone Valley Artists, American Legion, Acre; [oth. writ.] Editor of the "Midwest Dairyman"

"South Dakota High Liner" have written several Anniversary poems for couples; [pers.] I enjoy human interest stories: oil painting, bible study, home life; [a.] Milbank, SD

DAKIS, CHRISTINA
[b.] November 27, 1935, Brooklyn, NY; [p.] Joan and Louis Chulamanis; [m.] John Dakis, August 5, 1953; [ch.] Helene, Joanie, Dina, Jimmy and Louie; [ed.] American Helenic, Boarding School, Tarrytown, NY; [occ.] Housewife; [oth. writ.] A Few articles in local newspapers; [pers.] I feel my natural ability for writing poetry was a gift from God, so I use and share this talent to bring enjoyment to others who read it.; [a.] Clifton, NY

DALE, HUGHIE
[b.] December 7, 1924, Stilwell, OK; [p.] Deceased; [m.] Helen, May 5, 1956; [ch.] (2 sons) Bill and David Dale; [ed.] BS Degree-Okla A&M in 1978 (Re-named Okla. State University); [occ.] Retired; [memb.] 32 Degrees Mason, Lambda Chi Alpha Fraternity; [hon.] Honorary Legion of Honor in Demolay and Cross of Honor in Demolay; [oth. writ.] Poem published in Journey of the mind; [pers.] I enjoy writing and also reading poetry. This is the first year that I have sent any of my poems to the National Library of Poetry.; [a.] Houston, TX

DALEY, MARK
[pen.] Skip Tino; [b.] February 3, 1949, Waltham, MA; [p.] Gerry and Peg; [ed.] Mass Bay Community College, Waltham, MA; [occ.] Systems Administrator; [pers.] I write to reflect a spiritual journey, having been forever changed by the experience of walking on fire.; [a.] Belmont, MA

DAMIANIDES, DESPINA
[b.] June 13, 1981, Chicago, IL; [p.] Kyriakos and Maria Damianides; [m.] Not married; [ed.] Springman Jr. High School. I'm in 8th Grade.; [memb.] Springman Orchestra, and I'm a Cadet in Girl Scouting; [hon.] Springman Honor Roll; [oth. writ.] A story published in a local newspaper, a poem published in 1993 in a book called Anthology of Poetry By Young American's; [pers.] Things don't come easy to me. I have to work very hard to reach my goals. I truly believe everyone can reach their goals by putting your mind to it.; [a.] Glenview, IL

DAMILO, DIANNE
[b.] July 27, 1948, Heidelberg, Germany; [p.] Lillian Clair and William Damilo; [m.] Gerald Wagner, November 10, 1985; [occ.] Waitress, "Stans" Goodland, FL

DARDEN, MARTIN L.
[pen.] Martin Lee; [b.] April 2, 1960, Starke, FL; [p.] Carl B. and Laurce F. Darden; [m.] Beth Frost; [ch.] Shannon and Shaun Darden Michelle, Matthew, and Jacob Frost; [ed.] Scottsdale High School, The Refrigeration School Inc.; [occ.] Engineering Supervisor/Marriott Int'l.; [memb.] Quality/Guidance Team Member Marriott Int'l. Member - A.H.E.A. Arizona. Hotel Engineers Association; [hon.] Honorable Discharge U.S. Army 1981, Assoc. The Month of July 1994 Marriott Int'l; [oth. writ.] Too many to list though this one is the only one ever published; [pers.] Through poetry, my inner most feelings express the

visions of my heart, soul and mind. Writing has enabled me to achieve one of my lifetime goals, to be published, and in the form of written word to release my heart felt messages to others.; [a.] Scottsdale, AZ

DARNALL, MRS. DORIS J.
[b.] May 23, 1941, Tuscola, IL; [m.] Jack E. Darnall, February 10, 1968; [ch.] Nathan L. and Chris E.; [ed.] Villa Grove High School, Villa Grove, IL; [occ.] Avon Independent Sales Representative; [memb.] First Assembly of God, Avon President's Club, AARP, American Diabetes Association; [hon.] National Honor Society, Scholarship Letters/Pins, DAR (Daughters of American Revolution) Avon-Mrs. Albee Figurine; [oth. writ.] Poems published in local newspaper, Windsor Beacon gospel songs and choruses; [pers.] My writings are the results of God's inspiration. I draw from personal experiences and my topics deal with earthly subjects reflecting a heavenly meaning.; [a.] Windsor, CO

DAVID SR., JACK S.
[b.] June 1, 1932, Ottumwa, IA; [p.] Deceased; [m.] Alice David, October 8, 1955; [ch.] Jack Jr., Glenn; [ed.] University of Hawaii Honolulu University Ph.D; [occ.] Retired; [oth. writ.] About 40 poems in all started writing a novel; [pers.] The more you know...the further you go.

DAVID, VICTOR
[b.] July 29, 1936, Simpson, PA; [p.] Alex David and Ann David; [m.] Luisa David, November 28, 1962; [ch.] Mercedes David-Sheets; [ed.] Feel Twp High Penn State Univ., B.S. Temple Medical School; [occ.] Physician; [memb.] American Medical Assoc. (American Institute Ultra Sound Medicine) Astronomical Society, Chabad of the East Bay; [hon.] Diplomat American Board OB-GYN-; [oth. writ.] Lifetime of unpublished poetry, article American Journal perinaturary; [pers.] A respect for humanity and all living things within reflection on their beauty; [a.] Berkeley, CA

DAVIDSON, DEBRA JEAN-LOUISE
[b.] November 4, 1976, Youngstown, OH; [p.] Darlyne Sinn, Mark Davidson, Arther Liddle; [ed.] Swain Elementary School, Cypress, Ca., Cypress High School, Cypress, Golden West Community College, Huntington Beach, Ca.; [occ.] Amusement Park Character at Knotts Berry Farm; [hon.] Honoral Graduate from High School (3.14 G.P.A.) Pageantry captain, Member of Who's Who among America's, High School Students.; [oth. writ.] Several poems which have not yet been published.; [pers.] My poetry reflects experiences in my life, I wish to influence people of all ages to write about experience in their lives. "We are all taught by someone else." I wish to teach morality through my poems."; [a.] Cypress, CA

DAVIDSON, VIRGINIA D'ISA
[pen.] Virginia D'Isa Davidson; [b.] January 22, Youngstown, OH; [p.] Gustave and Rose D'Isa; [ch.] Joan Rose (Jody), and 3 granddaughters; [ed.] B.A. - English, Minor - Education Some womb toward Master's done at Kent State Youngstown State; [occ.] Retired; [memb.] Kiwanis, AARP, PERI, Youngstown State University Women Retires, Youngstown State University Women's

Group Community Bible Study group, and two church senior citizen; [hon.] Groups on the Board of the Local Western Reserve Transit Association also Listed in who's Who American College and Universities 1946-47; [oth. writ.] I write for the senior news/youngstown, OH and the Chronicle in Mt. Juliet, TN Articles are used monthly (so far at least.); [pers.] I love to write and what little talent I have was given to me by my Heavenly Father. Without Him I can do nothing!; [a.] Youngstown, OH

DAVILA, JEANETTE
[b.] September 15, 1979, Brooklyn, NY; [p.] Maritza and Rosendo Davila; [ed.] Grover Cleveland High School - Sophomore; [occ.] Student; [hon.] Graduated Barbizon Modeling School March 1995; [pers.] To me poetry is life, love, romance, even death. In my writings I can see how it starts and finishes. I've learned who to love through my writings. I can learn a lot through my literature, and so will other people.; [a.] Brooklyn, NY

DAVIS, CONSTANCE LAVERNE
[b.] September 10, 1951, Atlanta, GA; [p.] Queen Esther Grier; [ch.] Phillip, Larita, Gary Corey, Drayton Maru; [ed.] S.H. Archer High School Atlanta Area Tech.; [hon.] Editor's Choice Award National Library of Poetry.; [oth. writ.] Many unpublished poems, 4 poems published by the National Library of Poetry; [pers.] The race of life "Jesus Win" and Every Body Lost" "He" be "Jesus" in my life.; [a.] Atlanta, GA

DAVIS, DANIEL S.
[pen.] Daniel S. Davis; [b.] August 25, 1928, Council Bluffs, IA; [p.] Gladys and H. E. Davis; [m.] (Divorced), October 26, 1958; [ch.] I have one son who just turned 32.; [ed.] I had seven yrs. Grade School and finished my 8th yr. in a smell rule town in Otta Kon. I have a GED Diploma; [occ.] I am a salesman and have sold mostly shoes; [memb.] I belong for some 35 yrs in the Assembly's of God Church Starting in Memphis Tenn. moving first one place then and the now at Phoenix ISI Assemblymen Church; [hon.] Have had no honors best ode upon me expect the honor of being a child of God; [oth. writ.] All my writings have been under the inspiration of the Holy Spirit I have written some 20 poems. I hope to form a book call it the New Psalms; [pers.] I live each day as it comes not expecting any thing more or less than what each day will bring. Walking in His will in every thing do.; [a.] Phoenix, AZ

DAVIS, FRANCES J.
[b.] Galveston, TX; [p.] Russell and Velma Ross Davis; [ed.] Central High - Galv. Tx., B.S. - Tenn. State Univ. Nashville, MLS Atlanta Univ., GA Further Study, Univ. of Houston (Clear Lake) Tx. Sam Houston State College - Huntsville, TX; [occ.] Retired Eighth Grade English Teacher - Central Mid. School - Galv.; [memb.] TX Retired Teachers' Assn. Alpha Kappa Alpha Sorority, Reedy Chapel African Methodist Episcopal Church; [hon.] Who's Who in American Libraries; [oth. writ.] Several unpublished poems; [pers.] Grammar rap was written to provide students in eighth grade English classes with a learning activity many students could find similar to their popular leisure pastime they seemed to enjoy.; [a.] Galveston, TX

DAVIS, GAIL
[pen.] Serena Cascade; [b.] January 15, 1962, Chicago, FL; [p.] Herman Davis and Betty Davis; [ed.] Academy of Our Lady High School, Harold Washington College, and Chicago State University; [oth. writ.] Several past and present poems, short or medium sized essays, journals, and a first, in half of a lifetime, a diary. I never thought or realized I could ever have any or some of my work published.; [pers.] I was always firm and head strong about what I thought to be matters connected closely and ever so delicately to the heart. I relish on being whimsical and entertaining, through my writing.; [a.] Chicago, FL

DAVIS, JUDITH E.
[b.] September 14, 1941, Tulsa, OK; [p.] William and Viola Reid; [m.] Joseph F. Davis, September 2, 1989; [ch.] Laura Bohnsack, Sheryl Holt; [ed.] High School - Jenks OK., some college - Tulsa; [occ.] Self-employed property locator; [oth. writ.] Several other poems; [pers.] My poems are all true each is a slice of my heart - I still weep over some of them - but we all go on - living and learning that's what life is about.; [a.] Mt. View, CA

DAVIS, KIMBERLY K.
[b.] January 1, 1961, Topeka, KS; [p.] Robert H. and Teresa Marney; [m.] Mark E. Davis, June 10, 1989; [ch.] Erin Kay, Ethan Mark, Sean Michael; [ed.] Rossville High, 2 yrs. Washburn University; [occ.] Administrative Legal Secretary, KS Ins. Dept.; [memb.] Washburn Legal Assistants Society; [hon.] Valedictorian, Who's Who 1977, 1978, American Legion Citizenship Award; [pers.] Special thanks to my husband and daughter for their belief and support; [a.] Topeka, KS

DAVIS, LARISSA
[b.] November 11, 1979, Hackettstown, NJ; [ed.] Currently a sophomore at Lenape Valley Regional High School in NJ. Have taken college courses from Eastern Washington Univ.; [memb.] Key Club, International Friendship Circle, International Society of Poets, Pastor Parish Relations Committee - Stanhope United Methodist Church, Youth Group, Guidance Ambassador, Chorus, Madrigals, Theatre Productions; [hon.] 1993 Superintendents Round Table Award for Most Outstanding Student, 1993 Most Outstanding English Student, Member of Delta Epsilon Phi, Beta Gamma Chapter (German Nat. Honors Soc.) People to people student Ambassador to Australia; [oth. writ.] "Home Sweet Home" Published in After and Storm and recorded on the Sound of Poetry; [pers.] I would like to thank my mother Dorinne for her loving support throughout the years. I would also like to thank Marissa Kaufmann for always being a friend, and for being so good at it.; [a.] Stanhope, NJ

DAVIS, MARGARET ELLEN
[pen.] Peggy Davis; [b.] September 4, 1974, Shreveport, LA; [p.] Frank M. Davis III and Cynthia A. Davis; [ed.] Graduated Cum Laude from Lake High School in Union town, OH currently a Senior at Hanover College in Hanover, IN and will graduate in May 1996 with a major in English.; [memb.] A member of Alpha Delta Pi Sorority and on the Editorial board for Kennings a literary publication at Hanover College.; [hon.] Won the Meese Literary Award for the most promising writer in April of 1995 at Hanover

College. Also published in the Kennings Literary Magazine (3 poems); [oth. writ.] Several poems published in Kennings Literary Magazine; [pers.] I have been deeply influenced by such modern writers as Anne Sexton and Sylvia Plath and also the Romantic Poets. It is my hope that while exploring my own style, I also reflect these great influences in my poetry.; [a.] Mogadore, OH

DAVIS, YVONNE ELIZABETH
[b.] March 9, 1949, Atl. City, NJ; [p.] James Davis (deceased), Clara Davis; [ed.] Atlantic City High School Univ. of the District of Columbia; [memb.] Allen Chapel Ame Church: Allen Echoes Choir, Delta Sigma Theta Sorority, Inc.; [hon.] Who's Who in American Univ. and Colleges; [oth. writ.] Several poems; [pers.] The love of Jesus is my inspiration to write I strive to reflect his love in my writings; [a.] Washington, DC

DAVISON, ELLEN K.
[pen.] Ellen Margaret; [b.] September 16, 1929, Scotland County at Arbela, MO; [p.] Myron Barnes and Ethel (Davis) Kirkpatrick; [m.] Walter S. Davison Jr., May 26, 1962; [ch.] John Walter, Jane Ellen; [ed.] Graduated Memphis High School, Class Iowa Wesleyan College, Univ. of South Dakota 1951, B.S. degree in Education, Major in Home Economics, minors in Soc. Science, English and Speech, Post Graduate study at University of Missouri - Columbia Northeast Missouri State University - Kirksville; [occ.] Teacher by profession, retired now self-employed, free-lance; [memb.] The methodist Church, Daughters of the American Revolution, Descendants of Washington's Army at Valley Forge.; [hon.] Salutatorian (Alpha Phi Sigma) in 1948, National Methodist Scholarship, performed in cast of play "Wings" by Arthur Kopit, a production by the Travellers Community Theatre, Kirksville. (1981) listed in Who's Who in the Midwest in 1984-85 and again in 1986-87; [oth. writ.] Poem "The Door Opens" January 29, 1991, Poem "She Is Giant" 1994, Poem "The Erase" 1995 Book Community at Large (1993); [pers.] From time to time, I feel must write a poem or a story to rhyme, an experience which gives me special pleasure. The guiding light for me is to record a place, an event, or person or the people involved.; [a.] Kirksville, MO

DE BOER, SHARON
[b.] November 29, 1950, Muskegon, MI; [p.] John and Grace Sandstra; [m.] Donald De Boer, April 23, 1971; [ed.] Muskegon Sr. High, Muskegon Community College; [occ.] Order Entry - Port City Racing, Muskegon, MI; [memb.] Dalton Baptist Church, Ducks Unlimited; [hon.] I have been awarded much happiness from the people I write poems for.; [oth. writ.] Several poems for relatives and friends that are probably tucked away only as keepsakes.; [pers.] I enjoy writing personal poems relating to the people I know. I have never entered an official contest for my poems.; [a.] Twin Lake, MI

DE LANEY, MARIE ELIZABETH BOWERY
[b.] January 14, 1922, Petersburg, VA; [p.] John Savage Bowery and Annie Gertrude England Bowery; [m.] Wayne Richard De Laney, December 24, 1963; [ed.] Petersburg, VA High School, Smithdeal Massey Business College, US Army School of Finance, US Army MID School

Southside Community College; [occ.] Accountant, Retired from Fannie Mae (Federal National Mortgage Association) in 1985, after having open heart surgery. At present a Partner in Research Associates and President of the Farmville/Prince Edward County Historical Society; [memb.] Robert E. Lee Chapter #644, DC Div. United Daughters of the Confederacy ,Emily Nelson Chapter, NSDAR; [hon.] Honorary Citizen of Farmville, VA 1965. Jefferson Davis Medal - United Daughters of the Confederacy, Winnie Davis Medal - United Daughters of the Confederacy Numerous Certificates of Appreciation from other organizations for historical research and presentations.; [oth. writ.] History of the 17th VA Inf. Reg CSA Numerous Historical Items and Poems which have been published in newspapers and the UDC Magazine.; [pers.] It is difficult for me to accept the fact that I am able to just take a pencil and paper and write my thoughts. I always feel that the words are being given to me by an unknown source. My only hope is that I have done the work justice.; [a.] Farmville, VA

DE LAS CASAS, WALTER
[b.] February 3, 1947, Havana, Cuba; [p.] Mario and Aracelia De Las Casas; [ed.] Power Memorial Academy Iona College B. A., Hunter College M. A., Completed course work for Ph. D. at C. U. N. Y.; [occ.] High School Teacher; [memb.] Circulo De Cultura Paname-ricano, American Association of Teachers of Spanish and Portuguese; [hon.] Americanism Medal for Essay on same granted on June 1965 by American Legion (San. Post 1110 A. L.), B. A. Cum Laude; [oth. writ.] Two books of spanish verse: La Ninez Que Dilata (1986), Libido (1989). A book of English verse tributes (1993). An unpublished English verse manuscript discourse Articles: "Curriculum guide for spanish native language arts" (Hispania, May 1987), "El Genio Del Lugar: Un Estudio Comparado De El Greco Y Toledo De Gregorio Maranon Y El Greco O El Secreto De Toledo De Maurice Barres" (Circulo: Revista De Cultura, 1994); [a.] Brooklyn, NY

DEER, SANDIFER MORGAN
[b.] March 27, 1972, Olympia, WA; [p.] Randall O. Deer, Janice Deer; [ch.] Jerrad Kade Deer; [ed.] New Century High, South Pufet Sound College; [occ.] Karate Instructor; [memb.] Demolay, NW Okinawan Shorin-Ryu Assn., Local Blue Poets; [oth. writ.] Two poems published in College Literary Journal 'The Percival Review'; [pers.] My life is dedicated to keeping the spiritual warrior's path alive in the word. I use poetry as one means of expressing and teaching its values.; [a.] Olympia, WA

DELANO, FELIPE HINRICHSEN
[b.] November 22, 1958, Valparaiso; [p.] Karl Max Catalina, Hinrichsen Delano, Rorden Dalmati; [m.] Soraya Sobaida Jalil Pena, July 11, 1987; [ed.] Degree Architect from School of Architecture Catholic University of Valparaiso, Chile.; [occ.] Architect, Poet, Philosopher.; [oth. writ.] Personal writings.; [pers.] I believe in God, I believe in mankind, I believe in myself.; [a.] Larkspur, CA

DELGADO, ERIKA
[b.] June 1, 1981, Chicago, IL; [p.] Paulina Rueda; [ed.] Junior High, Francisco I. Madero Middle School; [hon.] Exhilarated Program; [oth.

writ.] Several poems written in my notebooks; [pers.] I write from my real feelings the way I feel.; [a.] Chicago, IL

DELGADO, STACEY WYNN
[b.] November 27, 1978, Hanford, CA; [p.] Betty Baggs and Bill Baggs; [ed.] Hanford High 10th Grade; [occ.] Student at Hanford High; [pers.] It is my opinion that every person can feel love in there heart. I try to relate that by writing about love in my poems.; [a.] Hanford, CA

DELKER, ELEANOR EDYTHE
[b.] December 17, 1913, Salladasburg, PA; [p.] Joseph and Mary Lillian Metzger; [m.] Elmer R. Delker, February 15, 1936; [ch.] One daughter, Darl R. Cline, two grandchildren and great grandchildren; [ed.] Jersey Shore Senior High; [occ.] Retired: Living with my husband, daughter and her husband; [memb.] Calvary Baptist Church Jersey Shore, PA.; [oth. writ.] I have written many poems about people of special places. Some of my poems were printed in our local newspaper in Jersey Shore in the late "Sixties"; [pers.] I see beauty in poetry and love it very much. I have liked the writings of earlier poets, such as longfellow, Tenneyson and Eugene Field.; [a.] Salladasburg, PA

DEMARCO, PATRICIA G.
[b.] October 8, 1965, Long Island, NY; [p.] Dan and Grace Cunningham; [m.] Frank W. DeMarco, September 20, 1986; [ch.] Brittany Grace DeMarco; [ed.] Lindenhurst High School; [occ.] Stay at home mother; [oth. writ.] Had one essay published in High School anthology titled "Directions '83"; [pers.] My poetry seems to reflect my feelings at a particular time in my life. As I get older, my poetry will grow with me.; [a.] East Patchogue, NY

DENNER, MAX
[pen.] Max Denner; [b.] July 6, 1912, New York City, NY; [p.] Samuel and Jenny Denner; [m.] Irma, April 14; [ch.] Dr. Bruce Denner, Steven Denner; [ed.] Special courses at night at City College - New York Dramatics and Elocution; [occ.] Retired, Volunteer-worker for Library; [hon.] Citizen of honor for Broward County - raising funds - won George Washington Award for Florida - for drama shows for charity; [oth. writ.] Other pomes through the years joy and pain and also fears; [pers.] Loved libraries all of my life - they are our main hope for tomorrow. Donated large sums - to libraries with drama - shows was - Ben Franklin - on stage.; [a.] Lauderdale Lakes, FL

DENNINGTON, LISA
[b.] October 24, 1979, Fontana, CA; [ed.] Currently in eleventh grade; [pers.] Started writing poetry at age eight. Lisa also enjoys singing and playing the piano.

DENNIS, KATHERYN M.
[pen.] Kathy Dennis; [b.] May 17, 1975, San Fernando Valley, CA; [p.] James H. Dennis Jr. and Sherin D. Dennis; [ed.] James Monroe High School, Phillips Junior College; [occ.] Student hearing graduation with an (AA) Associate of Arts.; [hon.] Deans and Honors List at present college. I have also received many awards and certificates from poems and essays that I have

previously written.; [oth. writ.] I have many poems written and many more yet to be made.; [pers.] The world around me is my inspiration for my creative ability. I have a gift to convey words and images onto paper that I couldn't do with writing. With writing, I can stir up emotions and imagery into the minds of those who choose to read my poetry. Writing is an art and it's a way for me to escape into another realm of reality and still stay focused. Some of my poems may seem to go "askew" at times, but there is always a meaning or a message that is there to uncover or maybe just a feeling left to be experienced. I hope that my poetry can be truly understand and appreciated by those that read it, (for this is my life). In ode to my dad with love. Whom I always be, "Daddy's little girl." (You will never be forgotten, only missed).; [a.] Northridge, CA

DENNIS, TIA C.
[pen.] Liva Franklin Ivan Newton Stephan Dennis; [b.] November 10, 1962, Salisbury, MD; [p.] Thomas and Lucille M. Dennis; [ed.] H.S. Diploma 1980 - Franklin Sr., AS Degree of Computer Information 1984. AA Degree of Airline Management 1984, Pending 1996 Degree Computer Science; [occ.] Typist Clerk IV; [memb.] National Committee to Preserve Social Security and Medicare; [hon.] 1977 Perfect Attendance Mardela High, Service Award '76 writers choice award 1994; [oth. writ.] Whorta (Liva's) Viewpoint, cries and other short manuscript still waiting for publishing at American Publishers, Experiences of Jac Ass of 1 Intelligence - still needs publishing; [pers.] Parting of family and reputable respects due to others abuses are associated damages society has allowed to occur that the incident have injustice in their lives presently - pray.

DENNISON, ERIC M.
[b.] February 5, 1972, Philadelphia; [p.] Patricia Dennison; [ed.] North Penn High School Montgomery County Community College; [a.] Hatfield, PA

DEPRANO, HARMONY ANN
[b.] December 17, 1980, New Castle, PA; [p.] Mark Deprano, Beth Deprano; [ed.] 8th grader at West Middlesex Jr.-Sr. High School; [occ.] Student; [oth. writ.] Several others but none published as of yet.; [pers.] I like to write and sing. I hope to become a writer and singer. I really believe that your true feeling are in what you write.; [a.] West Middlesex, PA

DERISO, MARY ANN
[pen.] Mary Ann Deriso; [b.] January 31, 1979, Arcadia, FL; [p.] Robert and Debra Deriso; [ed.] De Soto County High School; [occ.] Math Tutor; [memb.] National Honor Society, Spanish Club, Leo Club,; [a.] Arcadia, FL

DERIVAN, RONETTA L.
[pen.] Ro; [b.] December 2, 1969, Breckenridge, MN; [p.] Bud and Becki Anderson, Linda Anderson; [m.] Jamie Derivan, June 22, 1991; [ed.] Graduated from Custer County District High School in Miles City, Montana. Attended Denver Business College in Mesa, Arizona; [occ.] ABO Certified Optician for Nat'l Vision Assoc. in Alexandria, LA; [oth.

writ.] Several poems none of them published; [pers.] I want to dedicate this to my husband and my family including my parents, siblings...Lana, Lisa, Renee, and Chris and my nieces and nephews Lacy, Brittany, Danyelle, Nicole, Jasmine, Jordan, and Connor.; [a.] Alexandria, LA

DESONIA, ALBERT VALENCIANO
[b.] January 9, 1969; [ed.] United States Naval Academy College of Charleston; [memb.] American Mensa, Ltd., United State Naval Academy Alumni Association, National Association of the Deaf, Registry of Interpreters for the Deaf, Inc., International Society of Poets; [hon.] Admiral John H. Sides Perpetual Award, Editor's Choice Award (1994) for "Mortal Art" in Journey of the Mind; [oth. writ.] "Mortal Art" in Journey of the Mind; [a.] Goose Creek, SC

DESSIFY, LEONARD W.
[pen.] Lenny, Gumby, Pat; [b.] March 17, 1942, McKeesport, PA; [p.] Irene G. Riczu, Dessify; [m.] Mildred I. Dessify (Riling), July 30, 1971; [ch.] Edward, Son. Christina Marie, D. Ronald James Martin, 2, (Son); [ed.] Life High School Grad., Four-year Electrical Apprenticeship One-year College; [occ.] Retired affecting a bad heart, I had a stroke, a job, my a best of life, good.; [memb.] Volunteer of America, USA Pres. Bill Clinton, my boss, Dept. of Service, I will awards, commander reserve naval cons, force, one, sincerely, C.R. Smith, RADM, USNR a fleet of ship, defense of a home.; [hon.] Subj: A Blue Sky's Pure Awards Jesus Christ, Father, heaven, all is a world.; [oth. writ.] Carrots,; [pers.] Always wear your hard hat? You may be a little shorter but alive, a stars of easter of Lord. King Excells Jesus, Christ; [a.] Dushore, PA

DEWALD, JODIE
[b.] June 30, 1981, Louisville, KY; [p.] Rebecca Stallings and Daniel Stallings; [ed.] 8th Grade, Jefferson Davis Middle School Jacksonville, FL; [memb.] Girl Scouts of America; [hon.] 1st in State for Broadcasting Elementary, Middle and High School; [a.] Jacksonville, FL

DEXTER, MICHELLE
[pen.] Chelle or Mickey; [b.] June 5, 1980, Everett; [p.] Julie Dexter and Dennis Dexter; [ed.] I am currently in eighth grade at Heatherwood Middle School.; [occ.] Student; [pers.] I write to make people happy. Especially me! I want to be as great of poet as Jim Morrison.; [a.] Snohomish, WA

DIALLO, YAYE KADIJA
[pen.] Charlotte Broute; [b.] March 12, 1974, Freetown, SL; [p.] Mr. and Mrs. Telli Diallo; [ed.] Methodist Girl's High School, Freetown, Sierra Leone Southeastern University Washington D.C.; [occ.] Legal Aide Klimaski, Miller S. Smith P.C.; [memb.] Student Government Association (SGA), Freshman Representative Former Publisher of the Southwester (School Magazine); [hon.] International Bilingual Awards 1989 International Student Awards (1993), Fashion Model for various designers.; [oth. writ.] Puzzling thoughts, a quest, memories, songs, magic in the wind.; [pers.] "Most of us, as kinds had dreams to be someone we envision from within. Leading our desires to fall in a range of gallantry, nurtured by an artistic inclination;" [a.] Washington, DC

DIAS, SCOTT
[pen.] Jon Dark; [b.] May 13, 1963, Dorchester, MA; [p.] Matthew and Sis; [m.] Dawn, September 30, 1995; [occ.] Auto Tech.; [memb.] Distinguished Member - International Society of Poets; [hon.] Editor Choice Award 1993, Editor Choice Award 1994; [oth. writ.] He said she said, Father, Dear sweet Sue, friends, I miss you, fall has come; [pers.] The most intense sound I ever heard was deafening sound of silence; [a.] Bridgewater, MA

DIBONA, ANTHONY R.
[b.] September 7, 1953, Quincy, MA; [p.] Louis and Jeanne DiBona; [m.] Barbara, October 23, 1983; [ch.] Anthony M. DiBona; [ed.] B.A. Univ. of Mass. Boston, A.S. and B.S. Northeastern Univ., M.A. Anna Maria College; [occ.] Detective Lieutenant, Quincy Police Dept. - Mass.; [hon.] National Honor Society, Magna Cum Laude, Sum Cum Laude.; [pers.] The torque of life wrests sweat from the brow, each bead's a potential work of art.; [a.] Quincy, MS

DICHIARA, BERNADINE
[b.] June 5, 1954, Chelsea, Mass; [p.] Elaine and Arthur Therrien; [ed.] Sanborn Regional High School Kingston NH, Northern Essex Community College, Haverhill Mass.; [occ.] Telephone Operator for Nynex; [oth. writ.] Several letters and articles published local newspapers. Currently writing and illustrating first book. Write poetry to relax.; [pers.] I have been blessed with great resources of inspiration in that the people closest and most Dear to me are compassionate and emotional people. It's the things that we "Feel" that make us more alike than different regardless of our stance on life. Our differences seem to diminish in size where matters of the heart are concerned.; [a.] Kingston, NH

DICKERMAN, TERRALYN GREENE
[b.] November 7, 1943, Oneida, NY; [p.] Gerald and Erona Greene; [m.] Lynell Dickerman; [ch.] John Robert, Scott Timothy, Jo Anne Terralyn; [ed.] Associate Degree in Nursing, Registered Nurse.; [occ.] Charge Nurse on Cardiac Floor; [memb.] SDA Church Owner and Administrator: Home for the Aged - The Terralyn Haven; [hon.] ACLS Certified; [oth. writ.] Numerous Poems; [pers.] Do the best you can with what you've got!; [a.] Birchwood, TN

DICKEY, KATHY
[b.] March 5, 1950, Newark, NJ; [p.] Joseph, Margaret Donovan; [m.] Mike Dickey, September 1, 1972; [ch.] Daughter - 19; [ed.] St. Joseph High School, Toms River, NJ, Sacred Heart, Georgian Court Colleges, St. Michael's School of Radiologic Technology; [occ.] Radiology Supervisor; [memb.] American Registry of Radiologic Technology; [oth. writ.] Several unpublished poems; [pers.] I wrote this poem after the shooting death of my 17 year old son, shawn. I have written several poems in an attempt to deal with his tragic death. I would like to dedicate this poem to his loving; [a.] Midlothian, TX

DICKSON, ANGELLA B.
[b.] June 29, 1930, Washington, DC; [p.] Alexander Dickson Sr., Mary T. Dickson; [occ.] Retired registered Nurse; [oth. writ.] Church dramas (28 years of good Friday Production in my

home church); [pers.] Writing and hearing words always invites the mind to play amid their deeper meanings. My strongest resources are books of inspiration.; [a.] Washington, DC

DIEBEL, LORI A.
[b.] November 12, 1981, Hamilton, OH; [p.] Doug and Judy Diebel; [ed.] I am currently a 7th grader at Summit Middle School in Ft. Wayne, Indiana.; [occ.] Student; [memb.] USS United States Swimming, Newspaper: Summit Middle School, Swim team: Summit Middle School, Academic Super Bowl: Summit Middle School; [hon.] I always get special honors, meaning I maintain an A or greater average. I also got a Language Arts Award in 6th grade.; [pers.] I love to write poems, short stories, and other creative writings! I like to write about nature and sports.; [a.] Fort Wayne, IN

DIGIACOMO, MICHAEL
[b.] March 22, 1968, Fresno, CA; [p.] Edward and Rolanda DiGiacomo; [m.] Maria DiGiacomo, February 12, 1994; [ch.] Edward James DiGiacomo; [ed.] Clovis High School, Fresno City College; [occ.] Process Server; [memb.] (SOS) Survivors of Suicide; [oth. writ.] Writing poems helps me deal with inner pain as a result of my personal tragedies that have happened in my life.; [a.] Fresno, CA

DILL, VICKY SCHREIBER
[pen.] Vicky Schreiber Dill; [b.] August 17, 1949, Lancaster, PA; [p.] Betty and Harold Schreiber; [m.] Gary Alfred Dill, July 14, 1973; [ch.] Emily Lydia, Isaac Geoffrey; [ed.] Moses Mansoo Park, Ph.D. University of Notre Dame South Bend IN, M.S. Univ. of Penna., Phil, B.S. Millersville Univ. PA.; [occ.] Instructor, Schreiner College, Writer and Education Consultant; [memb.] Phi Delta Kappa, ASCD (Association for Supervision and Curriculum Development), ATE (Assoc. of Teacher Educators), NATC (National Alternative Teacher Certification); [hon.] Senior Research Fellow, Haberman Educational Foundation; [oth. writ.] Extensive publications in juried education journals, Closing the Gap, a book on retaining students in grade published by the State Dept of Education, Austin, TX, special publications in preventing school violence and the value of art for youth.; [pers.] I believe that in poetry we can surmount any limitations. Six words best describe my goals, gain to love, love to gain.; [a.] Kerville, TX

DILLARD, BEATRICE GOLDEN
[pen.] Bea Golden; [b.] May 31, 1948, Laurens, SC; [p.] Tommie C. Golden, Loree Golden; [m.] Johnny L. Dillard, August 21, 1985; [ch.] Andrea Gibson, Orlane Golden, Grandchildren - Derrick and Darious, Step-children Henrietta Johnson, Jimmy Dillard; [ed.] Sanders High, Piedmont Tech. The Institute of Children Literature; [occ.] Retired, Writer, and VFW Volunteer; [memb.] NAACP: Hopewell Baptists Church: Ladies Auxiliary, VFW, National Arbor Day Society, Battle of Normandy Foundation; [hon.] Outstanding Auxiliary Member 1992-93, Department of SC Member of the Year 1994-95; [oth. writ.] Several Poems Published mostly memorial poems for obituary, the Winter edition of "Treasured Poems Of America" A collection of Short Stories; [pers.] I enjoy writing short stories for teenagers and

children and I am presently working on my first novel I also enjoy writing poems of passion. "Tonight I lie all Snuggle in bed" is dedicated to my John...; [a.] Laurens, SC

DILLON, ALVIS SHANE
[pen.] Dango; [b.] August 14, 1972, North Berton, OH; [p.] Ronald R. and Minda L. Dillon; [ed.] Southeast High, B.A. in Communication Ohio University 1994; [occ.] Manager, Bob Evans Farms Inc.; [memb.] Lions Club, American Society for Training and Development, Aircraft Owners and Pilots Association; [hon.] Dean's list, graduated Cum Laude, American Legion Oratorical Contest District Champion, regional Champion 1989; [oth. writ.] Currently working on a novel. Written approximately 50 poems that I am organizing into a collection.; [pers.] We can never appreciate the beauty of what is out there until we contract that which is not so aesthetically pleasing, first.; [a.] Dover, OH

DINGESS, BETTY JEAN
[b.] March 13, 1939, Matewan, WV; [p.] Homer Mahone, Maude Collins Mahone; [ch.] Harry Lee Dingess, David Bruce Dingess, Jeannie Dingess, Patton; [ed.] Matewan High Wash. D.C. Academy of Beauty; [occ.] Employee of Both, Prince George's County Board of Education and Chesapeake Publishing Corp.; [oth. writ.] A collection of short stories, poems and children's books.; [pers.] I have been writing for a period of 15 years. Most of my inspiration has been derived from hardships and tragedies of everyday life. My writing has acted effectively as a release in times of sorrow and it has made me feel more alive in times of joy!; [a.] Accokeek, MD

DISHMAN, TAYSHA
[b.] October 22, 1975, Salina, KS; [p.] Bill and Peggy Dishman; [ed.] Loveland High (Loveland, Colorado), Benedictine College (Atchison, KS. - currently working for English BA); [occ.] Full time student; [memb.] Green Peace, NPCA, BC Pom Squad, Former Member BC Women's Soccer Team, Volunteer Tutor, Elementary Children, French Honor Society; [hon.] Who's Who among American High School Students, Semi-Finalist in Teen Magazine's Great Model Search '91, Cheerleaders Award of Excellence; [pers.] Often times I feel that the beauty and peril of existence weigh so heavily on my soul, that they take root in my sense of entrance my thoughts, and explode from my fingertips.; [a.] Atchinson, KS

DISNEY, PHYLLIS BLANCHE
[pen.] Phyllis Blanche Disney; [b.] Independence Day, Valley City, ND; [p.] Leslie Edward Disney, Blanche Cornelia Anderson; [ed.] Sheridan Montana High - Metropolitan Business College, Seattle - Drama - Ballroom Interpretive Dance - French Reweaving - Tailoring Clothing Design - Handcrafts - Health and Beauty; [occ.] Entrepreneur - Sales/Marketing - Minister - Counselor - Artist - Fashion Design - Teacher - Poet; [memb.] Toluca Lake Chamber of Commerce; [hon.] Montana Basketball Championship Team - Texas State Recognition: Girl Scout Day Camp Director - Girl Scout Established Camp Art Director - Festival of Arts, Laguna Beach - Recognition from various companies for Excelling in varied

accomplishments. Above all, most grateful and appreciative of love and respect of all those who know me.; [oth. writ.] A book "On Butterfly Wings," a collection of poems. "The Beauty Of The Sea," "Come Laugh With Me," "Let Me Fly Free,"… "An Eagle Rare." And my first two poems: "A Smile" - "A Tear" - 'Twixt wake and sleep - written in the air for me.; [pers.] I have come to realize the greatest service I can render others is to encourage them back to the Living God within their Temple not built with living hands - too often the last place to seek their answers.; [a.] Toluca Lake, CA

DIXON, FAYE H.
[pen.] Faye Hughes Dixon; [b.] January 15, 1934, Louisiana; [p.] Frank and Lucy Hugher; [m.] Bill D. Dixon, 1993; [ch.] Debra Vance, Dang Gordon McQuillin, Al McQuillin; [ed.] Bastrop High, four years Community College O Dallas, Tx Res Lic.; [occ.] Fac. Medical Secretary; [memb.] American Heart Disabled Vets, Boys Form Sapynorter many more; [hon.] Sec. of the Year, Most Valued Emp Bright Idea Award; [oth. writ.] I write children's stories which an available, poems for all occasion. Publications include Sexual memo paper in east Texas and Monthly paper for Kidney Dialysis; [pers.] I have always wanted to be our RN, but due to my health and could not cont. College and Grad. My inspiration comes from the beauty I see around me and the needs of others.; [a.] Mesquite, TX

DIXON, RADESHA
[pen.] Bekka Townsend; [b.] January 23, 1983, England; [p.] Mrs. Felicia Dixon-Ward, Mr. David Townsend; [ed.] 6th grade without getting held back Lake Weir Middle School; [occ.] Student; [memb.] Maricamp Road Church of God, Youth Center of Silver Spring Shores; [hon.] 94-95 South County Spelling Bee, Young Author's Award, Spelling of the Year, I won in Pinewood Derby; [oth. writ.] I was in the newspaper for winning a spelling bee and for a pool tournament.; [pers.] I've always tried so I'll always be a winner. I will work at my best effort and hold on so I'll keep on going to the end.; [a.] Ocala, FL

DOBRAN, KELLY
[b.] July 11, 1973, Smithtown, NY; [p.] Elizabeth Booth and Leonard Kemp; [ed.] Connetquot High School, Hofstra University; [hon.] 1st Place French Poetry Contest, English Recognition Award; [oth. writ.] Silence, many other poems unpublished; [a.] Mount Sinai, NY

DOBSON, LELA
[pen.] Lee; [b.] September 8, 1938, Nancy, KY; [p.] (Late) Willie And Mary Compton; [m.] James M. Dobson, November 18, 1988; [ch.] Kathy Beaird, Roscoe Tilley Jr., SFC. David Tilley and Judy Jones; [ed.] Hibbard High, Richmond, IN; [occ.] Housewife; [memb.] American Legion Auxillary Mingo Baptist Church, AARP; [hon.] Royal Order of Atlantic Voyageries; [pers.] I have always enjoyed writing lyrics for songs and poems as a pastime, until I wrote "Not His Own" my inspiration for it came from my past.; [a.] Broken Arrow, OK

DODD, SAN CARMEN
[pen.] Carmen; [b.] September 6, 1935, Illinois; [p.] Alfred and Louvain Moore; [m.] Divorced,

September 7, 1957; [ch.] Brett A. Dodd, Tracy D. Dodd; [ed.] Graduate - High School, some College Courses; [occ.] Retired Government part time Data Entry Operator; [hon.] Achieved sustained superior performance awards for exemplary work in gov't service; [pers.] I entered this poem in hopes of winning because I am going thru a personal and financial upheaval at this time. And would like to better my life. This is my first poetry attempt.; [a.] Hamtramck, MI

DOMINICK, CHRISTOPHER
[pen.] Aaron Freewell; [b.] September 16, 1975, Kansas City, KS; [p.] Charles and Kathy Dominick; [m.] Single; [ed.] Crest Ridge High School Longview College; [occ.] Production Machine Operator, Stahl Specialty Company; [oth. writ.] A poetry collection that I've built single age sixteen.; [pers.] Anyone who shares my interest in poetry may write me at: 76 NW 601 Centerview, MO 64019; [a.] Centeroiew, MO

DOMINGUEZ, MARIA
[pers.] In the eternal memory of my grandmother who personified strength throughout her life and who gave me the greatest gift of all…that gift is my mother whom I share all my accomplishments, goals and dreams and whom I love with all my heart. To my sisters for their consistent support and love.

DONO, ANDREW PATRICK
[b.] March 3, 1976, Brooklyn, NY; [m.] I am still looking. I hope within the next ten years.; [ch.] I lope children and I hope to have two of my own someday, but I should finish school first.; [ed.] I will be graduating Design and Architecture Senior High School in June of '95. From there I will attend Florida International University, to study Interior Design and Education.; [occ.] Right now I am a student of school and life, studying all the little details.; [memb.] I am a member of the Gay community, the Wiccan religion, and the class of '95. I am also a member of a generation of proud, strong integrators. My most important membership belongs to my friends and family.; [hon.] I have won the B.O.L.D. award, I have had two of my logo designs put on a schools year book and another on a school building (Nova). I have also been on the Honor Roll for the past seven years. In December of '94 I won an Interior Design contest, sponsored by F.I.U.; [oth. writ.] I have written short stories and poems for the past four years. My writings are mostly about teen issues, such as love, sex, family friends, death, etc., I have been told that my writing sounds like it belongs in a coffee house.; [pers.] I try to write from my heart, whether people like it or not. I feel if you get some reaction from the people reading you work, you have accomplished a lot. As for my philosophy on life, you should do what makes you happy, as long as it doesn't harm others. I also feel you should help to put a smile on someone face, every day.; [a.] Davie, FL

DORAN, LAURA
[pen.] Laura Lee Doran; [b.] April 9, 1958, Detroit, MI; [p.] Howard E. Meehan and Rosemarie Meehan; [m.] Michael G. Doran, October 19, 1991; [ch.] Nena Doran; [ed.] Redford Union H.S., ARAPAHOE Vocational Technical School, WASHTENAW Community College;

[occ.] Nurses Aide; [memb.] Volunteer at St. Joseph Mercy Hospital in their Cancer Care Clinic; [hon.] 1/2 Marathon for Memorial Hospital in Boulder Colorado; [pers.] Most of my writings are in response to a significant event in my life. It serves as an outlet for the expression of my feelings.; [a.] Ypsilanti, MI

DORSCH, KRISTINA
[b.] September 19, 1973, Baltimore, MD; [p.] Franz and Gail H. Dorsch Jr.; [ed.] Howard High School and Howard County School of Technology; [a.] Linthicum, MD

DOSKOCIL, TAMARA
[b.] May 6, 1967, Kettering, OH; [p.] Abe Habib, Dixie Habib; [m.] Ben Doskocil Jr.; [ch.] Tara Marie; [ed.] Sam Houston High School, Montgomery County Career College; [occ.] Freelance writer; [memb.] Toxic Action; [oth. writ.] The Luckiest Little Dragon series, Winnie the Whale's Splashing Tale, The Fable of Frimsbee's Haunted Home, Chester the Jester in the King's Court; [pers.] I aspire to bring forth inspiration & hope in all that I write with the ability GOD has given me. And the philosophy that it is each person's prevaile to make our world a little brighter place to live; [a.] Arlington, TX

DOUGHERTY, GINA MAY
[pen.] Gina; [b.] December 19, 1956, New Britain, CT; [p.] George and Marie Parker; [m.] Patrick Mitchell Dougherty, June 20, 1981; [ed.] Southington High School; [occ.] Housewife; [pers.] I have always loved writing poems to express every emotion gives me joy, and I want to thank God for my talent and my husband Patrick for his love; [a.] New Britain, CT

DOUGHERTY, KATHERINE R.
[b.] March 27, 1908, Nashville, TN; [p.] Thomas and Katie Dougherty; [ed.] Bachelor's Degree and Master's Degree from George Peabody College of Education and 3 summers at Columbia University New York; [occ.] Retired; [memb.] Since retirement I have not been a member of anything except a church member and a retired state teacher org. member; [hon.] An essay contest sponsored by Lion Oil Company opened to Southern Teachers. I chose to take the scholarship at Columbia Univ. during three summer quarters. I was chosen as the most popular teacher in school system for one year. Many declamation contest winners in High School and College.; [oth. writ.] I wrote columns for the Tennessee Teacher Magazine for two years. Had articles published in other magazines, too numerous to remember; [pers.] Although my profession (or job) was in the teaching field, I belonged to card groups. (I was terrible at bridge, but a whiz of other games; [a.] Nashville, TN

DOUGLAS, CHRIS
[b.] October 7, 1974, Batesville, AR; [p.] Von Sutton and Virginia Sutton; [ed.] Mountain View High School; [occ.] Soda Fountain Manager; [pers.] I seldom write. But when I do, I always write from the heart. I owe utmost thanks to Kay Voyles, my senior English teacher, for showing me that I do have something to offer to the world.; [a.] Mountain View, AR

DOUGLAS, DONALD
[b.] June 8, 1976, New York, NY; [p.] Valrecia and Donald Douglas; [ed.] Clarkstown North Senior High School University of Maryland Eastern Shore; [hon.] Black Achievement Recognition Award (high school); [pers.] I have a vision to change the stereotype of American males; [a.] New City, NY

DOVER, TIFFANY RENEE
[b.] May 16, 1982, Chattanooga, TN; [p.] Timothy and Sherry Dover; [ed.] Currently attending East Ridge Middle School; [memb.] Tri-state talent Association Salvation, Army Girl guard and JR. soldier.; [pers.] I try to write so that people can really relate to it. And have some meaning to them. I love all kinds of poetry. And hope that my poem will inspire others.; [a.] Chattanooga, TN

DOW, KRISTEN
[b.] March 19, 1976, Fremont, CA; [p.] William and Janet Dow; [m.] Unmarried; [ed.] Newark Memorial High School, University of La Verne; [occ.] College student; [memb.] California Scholarship Federation, Iota Delta Sorority; [hon.] President's Scholarship, University of La Verne; [pers.] I am a part of the generation labeled "X", expressive, exciting, excellent, exhilarating, and exceptional. Do not underestimate the minds of the young, the future.; [a.] Newark, CA

DOWELL, LAURENT
[pen.] Chaka Zulu; [b.] November 30, 1973, St Croix, IN; [p.] Muriel Dowell, Betram John; [occ.] Cook's Helper Whintey M. Young Job Corpslenten; [pers.] I have been influenced by Maya Agelow and Lagston Hughes

DOWNIE, REBECCA GRACE
[b.] May 22, 1960, Roseville; [p.] Carl and Margaret Winter; [m.] Tom Downie, April 25, 1981; [ch.] Amanda Jean Downie, Caroline Annette Downie; [ed.] Music major - Sacramento State University Early Childhood Education Major Sacramento City College; [occ.] Classical musician at the American Eurhythmy School and Classical violin piano teacher.; [memb.] Girl Scouts, National Rifle Association, Science Fiction Club, Nota Bene Chamber Ensemble; [oth. writ.] Book of poetry, several children's stories, songs; [pers.] We have a responsibility in our use of the Power of the word. We have the ability to shape the imagination, the very soul, of another human being, through speech, both written and spoken. What a fine world this would be, if Man's Word created living picture, leading us to our higher, True nature.; [a.] Mount Shasta, CA

DOYLE, JOSEPH R.
[pen.] Joseph R. Doyle; [b.] July 6, 1921, Holmes Co. OH; [p.] Millard and Hattie; [m.] Marilyn Joan Doyle, February 21, 1958; [ch.] Helen Maye Patterson, Darlene Burgett; [ed.] Graduate Killbuck High School; [occ.] Retired; [oth. writ.] "The Jones Place"; [pers.] I would like to dedicate the poem "BATTLE BABIES" to all the mothers who had sons or daughters who served in the armed forces during WW II. I enjoy the great outdoors, and painting.; [a.] Kellbuck, OH

DRABOT, JANET RAE
[pen.] LeeAnne Michelle; [b.] April 22, 1957, Sharon, PA; [m.] Galen Paul Drabot, November 17, 1990; [ch.] Dustin Drabot, Andrew Baney, Mark Baney; [ed.] Mainland Sr. High, FL Williamsport School of Commerce, Williamsport, PA Associates Degree, Secretarial Science; [occ.] Evangelical Community Hospital, Secretary, Radiology; [memb.] Volunteer at Susquehanna Valley Women in Transition (SVWIT); [pers.] My first poetry writings followed my sister's sudden suicide. It gave me an outlet for my "pent up" feelings. Poetry is now important in every aspect of my life.; [a.] Hughesville, PA

DRAPER, BEVERLY STEELE
[ed.] Bachelor of Fine Arts degree University of Houston, Houston, TX; [a.] Houston, TX

DRAYCOTT, CATHERINE
[b.] December 26, 1970, Bermuda; [p.] Terrence and Mary Draycott; [ed.] BFA from the School of the Museum of Fine Arts, Boston/Tufts University 1994, Diploma in Fine Art - SMFA 1995; [occ.] Artist; [memb.] The Master Works Foundation Bermuda, the Bermuda National Gallery, the Bermuda Society of Arts, the Copley Society of Boston, the Jamaica Plain Arts Centre, J.P., M.A.; [hon.] The Bermuda Government Scholarship 1990, The Bermuda Society of Arts Scholarship 1994, Juror's Choice Award, the Copley Society of Boston 6th Annual Student Exhibition 1995; [oth. writ.] Published poem in "Chain" Magazine and in Tuft's and Museums School Literary Magazines - also created "Red Letter" Literary Magazine at the School of the Museum of Fine Arts, Boston.; [pers.] I am interested in the ambivalence of feeling that exists in intense situations - or the play of intense emotions and ambivalence. I love the poetry of Monica Raymond, Ted Hughes, Louise Glack; [a.] Boston, MA

DRICK, LISA
[pen.] Lyssa Aja; [b.] May 28, 1962, Joliet, IL; [p.] Jacky & Tony Drick; [ch.] sponsor 2 children through Christian Children's Fund: Anekpong & Evelin; [ed.] Enrolled at Kennesaw College; [occ.] Medical Transcriptionist; [memb.] International Society of Poets, Rainforest Foundation, International Pen Friends, Opio Foundation, Atlanta Songwriter's Assoc.; [oth. writ.] Have a poem published in Seasons to Come, other poetry pending; [pers.] All things are possible if you believe; [a.] Woodstock, GA

DRIVER JR., JAMES
[b.] September 28, 1963, Chicago, IL; [p.] Mr. and Mrs. James and Josie L. Driver; [m.] Eva S. Driver, July 16, 1987; [ch.] Antonio-Demetrius-Gabriel, Nathan O'Neal, Nicolas-Jakim; [ed.] Paul Robeson H.S., Western Illinois University; [occ.] Bail Enforcement Agent, Exum Bonding Co. - VA Beach VA; [memb.] National Association of Blacks in Criminal Justice; [pers.] My aim as a writer is to send a message to the hearts of every living creature that we as a people are unique, creative etc.. and have been given the opportunity to share our God given talent to the world.; [a.] Virginia Beach, VA

DROUGAS, CATHERINE
[b.] April 6, 1972, Park Ridge, IL; [p.] Art and Mary Drougas; [ed.] Immaculate Conception (Grammar School), Resurrection High School, University of Illinois at Chicago (UIC) with a BA in English; [memb.] UIC Alumni Association; [hon.] Phi. Beta Kappa, Phi Kappa Phi, Golden Key National Honors Society, Dean's List, Highest Distinction in English with College Honors; [pers.] Poetry is imaginative, enigmatic, and emotional. With this combination, I hope the reader of my writing will find a beauty that only appears hidden in the world, not last.; [a.] Chicago, IL

DUBEAU, MICHEL
[b.] April 18, 1941, France; [p.] Pierre Dubeau and Cyriaque Dubeau; [ch.] Alexandre; [ed.] French College and University in Paris; [occ.] Administrative; [memb.] Club-president; [hon.] Medal Military Serv. (Algerian War); [oth. writ.] Newspapers articles, short stories; [pers.] Like to write as a Hobby; [a.] Medford, NY

DUKE, W. C.
[oth. writ.] A series of action adventure books entitled "The Gentleman."

DULA, LUCILLE D.
[pen.] Lucy D.; [b.] August 21, 1959, Lenoir, NC; [ed.] Hudson High School, Barber-Scotia College, Howard University Dental School; [occ.] Telecomm. Eq. Op./Dentist; [memb.] Alpha Kappa Alpha (AKA) Sorority, American Assn. of Women in Dentistry (AAWD) (BEC) Black Employee Coalition; [hon.] Phi Beta Kappa Honor Society, Dean's List Who's Who (College); [oth. writ.] Lyrics, poems and scripts; [pers.] I write because I enjoy writing and to bring strength and joy to others. I've been influenced by Maya Angelou and Langston Hughes.; [a.] Washington, DC

DUMMITT, NANCY
[b.] December 28, 1948, Tampa, FL; [p.] Joe Alvarez, Zenaida Alvarez; [m.] James Richard Dummitt, June 21, 1992; [ed.] Hillsborough High, ornamental Horticulture program; [occ.] House-wife; [memb.] National Trust for Historic Preservation; [pers.] I am inspired to write by feelings and circumstances personal, and of other's I relate to.; [a.] Columbus, OH

DUNCAN, APRIL ROSE
[pen.] April Rose; [b.] December 2, 1980, Dallas,; [p.] JoAnn Duncan and Daly Duncan; [ed.] 8th Grade Frisco Middle School; [occ.] Student; [hon.] English Honors Science, Art award; [oth. writ.] Immortality, I'm Witches, Derge, Tyme, Cooflagration, Cloyed in Unatarium, the People's Sponning Ground, Sick oned Love Child Shay Box, Mr. and Mrs. Insanity; [pers.] I have realized that by contradicting myself and telling my deepest secrets in my writings helps others to comprehend what I am trying to explain.; [a.] Frisco, TX

DUNNING, DON
[pen.] Bruce Shevlin; [b.] March 16, 1921, Seattle, WA; [p.] Roy and Lucinda Dunning; [ch.] Judy, Tom, Jeff; [ed.] High School Worthington MN. Rose College/Midwest City of varied subjects OCCU Okla. City of CAD/CAM Computer OSU

Ext. Okla. City of CAD/CAM Refresher; [occ.] Retired; [memb.] American Legion, Light for the Lost, Faith Tabernacle; [hon.] Competent Toastmaster, USAF Tinker Air Force Monetary Suggestion Award and Subsequent US Patent Paid by the USAF on Invention US Patent Certificate Issued; [oth. writ.] Several newspaper items without monetary return published currently have a number of unpublished Haiku writings and philosophical muses.; [pers.] As an empathetic optimists, I foster the belief that each of us is responsible for our God given talents, and that solutions to life's confrontations are found when we call on our creator; [a.] Oklahoma City, OK

DUPKE, TARESA ANNE
[b.] January 22, 1965, Louisville, KY; [p.] Arthur J. Rodgers and Lee B. Rodgers; [m.] Gregory O. Dupke II, June 4, 1994; [ch.] Brittany Le'Anne and Christina Nikole; [ed.] Pleasure Ridge Park High School, Louisville, KY, PRP Vocational School, Louisville Ky; [occ.] Domestic Engineer Resigned Administrative Assistant; [memb.] Outreach Committee Oakview United Methodist Church; [hon.] Administrative Assistant of the Month, 8 months; [oth. writ.] Several other poems and short stories written for family and friends; [pers.] For my husband who inspired this poem I dedicate this to. My mother and father who believed in me I love you. And, Greg and Rosetta-Rodney and Karen, thanks for supporting me to start to succeed with my dream.; [a.] High Point, NC

DUPLANTIS, KRISTY L.
[pen.] Kristy L. Duplantis; [b.] November 20, 1979, Houma, LA; [p.] Erich and Faye Duplantis; [ed.] I am a Sophomore at Ellender High School in Houma, LA; [occ.] Student; [memb.] Key Club, Honorary Member of the National Library of Poetry; [hon.] 88-89 Citizenship Award, 92-93 Sprit Award; [oth. writ.] I've had two poems recently published in the last year by the National Library of Poetry "Home" in Journey of the Mind, I won Editor's Choice Award for that one. "Another Life" published in East of the Sunrise.; [pers.] I started writing poems at the age of 8. My poems are reflections of my feelings, I don't sit and think about them, they just come to me.; [a.] Houma, LA

DURBIN, HERBERT FITZGERALD
[pen.] H. Fitzgerald; [b.] February 18, 1915, Todd, OK; [p.] William and Bertha Durbin; [m.] Nolda Juanita Walker, August 15, 1933; [ch.] Seven; [ed.] 8 Years Public School, 4 Years Bible Training; [occ.] Retired Christian Minister; [memb.] AARP, CWA, AFA, General Council Assembly of God, Rutherford Institute, Christian Action Network, Oklahoma District Council the Assemblies of God; [hon.] Gold pin award for fifty years ministry; [oth. writ.] Life's Story, tTe Man Last, Wanted! True Love, compiled four books of poems and short stories. Poems published weekly in local paper; [pers.] That my life and my writings will portray the love and compassion of the creative God.; [a.] Wyandotte, OK

DURNIL, KELLY
[b.] January 5, 1979, Puyallup, WA; [p.] Vicky and Robert Durnil; [ed.] Peninsula High School; [occ.] Student; [memb.] School Management

Committee, Performance Circle; [oth. writ.] Several other poems which have never been published.; [pers.] I can't really say that anyone has influenced me. I just write what I feel. I believe that you should live life for today, not tomorrow.

DVORSKY, GEORGE
[b.] February 29, 1956, Prague; [ed.] Self; [occ.] Unemployed; [pers.] It isn't, isn't, isn't a myth nor is it my blunder that there is heaven under your feet when you walk free; [a.] San Francisco, CA

DWYER, KEITH E.
[b.] January 15, 1965, CA, MA; [p.] Richard J. and Marie E.; [ed.] Parochial, Computer Training, Desk Top Publishing; [occ.] Freelance Writer; [memb.] Boston Computer Society, Printing Industries of New England; [oth. writ.] The first Disciple fictitious novel.; [pers.] To make writing both interesting and somehow make a statement that people can relate to and react to make the reader think.; [a.] Stoneham, MA

DYKHOUSE, CAROL JEAN
[pen.] Carol Jean Dykhouse; [b.] April 15, 1970, Ridgewood, NJ; [p.] Robert/Frances Stelpstra; [m.] Jacob Dykhouse III, May 7, 1994; [ed.] Waldwick High School '89, Hohokus Secretarial School '90; [occ.] Data Entrist JDR Recovery, Ramsey NJ; [oth. writ.] "A Fruitful Life" published in Treasured Poems of America. Summer 1993 p.158; [a.] Wanague, NJ

DYSKO, VIVIAN M.
[pen.] Vivi Dysko; [b.] July 26, 1920, Munson, PA; [p.] John and Mary Ellen McCreadie; [m.] Raymond C. Dysko, April 8, 1950; [ed.] Clearfield High, Indiana State Teachers College (TND Univ.) Ret. Lic., Midwife US Cadet Corp. R.N., Clearfield Hospital School Nsq.; [occ.] Retired as Director Nursing Education State of FL; [memb.] United Methodist Church Nocatee FL, Preacher - Parish Board Arc of Fla., Am. CA Assoc. V7W Aux.; [hon.] Community Service Award 90'-92' - Outstanding Merit Award JUne 82' Outstanding Achievement Award - Hrs - After Ca Surgies as survivor, Hx.; [oth. writ.] Several poems published in Wmsport Grit, V7W Newsletter, Local papers, Church bulletin wrote and presented several eulogies and poems, in tribute to friends.; [pers.] The way to be happy is to make others happy, helping others is the secret of all success in business, in the arts and in the home.; [a.] Arcadia, FL

EAGAN, MARY MARTHA
[pen.] Mimi Eagan; [b.] August 28, 1926, Syracuse, NY; [p.] Leo and Eleanor Eagan; [ch.] Margot C. Papworth, Mary Martha Eagan Wilson - Chris Cheney; [ed.] Franciscan Academy High School (Regents) - College, BA Degree (Georgian Court College); [occ.] Retired; [memb.] International Society of Poets - American Institute of Cancer Research; [pers.] I write about people I love and have loved - people who impress me, in our troubled world - the tragedy of fear and our ability to survive our personal losses. My desire is to be in praise of hope, that is always their for us.; [a.] Fayetteville, NY

EASTMAN, BRETT K.
[b.] September 26, 1952, Trenton, NJ; [p.] Bob Eastman, Joan Keating; [m.] Sally Ann Schell Eastman, July 9, 1983; [ed.] Glenband West H. S., Ill State Univ., Univ. of GA; [occ.] Owner - Factory Direct Office Furniture; [oth. writ.] Some other poems, short story; [pers.] Entered to see if I did have any talent.; [a.] Atlanta, GA

EBRECK, GLADYS
[pen.] G. U. E.; [b.] December 8, 1916, Montana; [p.] Maggie and Martin Paulson; [m.] John Ebreck, December 13, 1968; [ch.] 2 sons - Kenneth and Donald Unhjem, 2 daughters - Elizabeth and Marletta Unhjem; [ed.] High School; [occ.] Retired, House Wife; [memb.] Eastern Star, American Legion Auxiliary, Lutheran L.A. and Circle; [a.] Crosby, ND

EDEL, SHEILA SPORKIN
[pen.] Snowflake; [b.] March 21, 1943, Philadelphia, PA; [p.] Mary and Michael Sporkin; [ch.] Mark Edel and Dawn Marie Edel; [ed.] Atlantic City H.S., some courses at Atlantic Community College; [occ.] Secretary and Snowflake Metaphysical Services; [memb.] Theosophical Society, Assoc. Bodywork and Massage Professionals, Int'l Assoc. of Counselors and Therapists, Universal Life Church Ministry; [hon.] Competent Toastmaster, ACBL Sectional Master, Great Gray Owl Clan, Apprentice Shaman, Reiki I, Amadeus I-II, one year as a TV Host on Metaphysics; [oth. writ.] Poems published in the American Poetry Anthology, the World of Poetry Anthology, our Worlds' most treasured poems, various poems in local papers, publicity for the Boy Scouts; [pers.] To work in universal harmony using Native American techniques.; [a.] Absecon, NJ

EDSTRAND, ARDYS
[b.] April 3, 1942, Rock Island, IL; [p.] Arthur and Gladys Stoit; [m.] Ronald Edstrand, July 28, 1962; [ch.] Gerald and Renaud Edstrand and Ronda Rudolph; [ed.] Rock Island Public Schools; [occ.] Homemaker; [memb.] Keystone Neighborhood Steering Committee, St. Anthony's Catholic Church, Community Caring Conference and Mississippi Valley Blues Soc. and Christian Women's Club; [pers.] I like to write about everyday life and the common person.; [a.] Rock Island, IL

EDWARDS, KAREN R.
[pen.] Karen Peoples; [b.] July 12, 1964, Okinowa; [p.] Clifton and Carol Peoples; [m.] Renardo M. Edwards, December 1, 1990; [ch.] Tanisha Cherice, Toni Michele, Renardo Monte; [occ.] Secretary to the Comptroller, Washington, DC; [oth. writ.] I have written poems for church and friends.; [pers.] Poetry writing is and always has been a hobby for me. Poems that make you think and feel some emotion are what I enjoy. As a songwriter wrote, "What good is a (poem) song, if it can't inspire."; [a.] Chapel Oaks, MD

EDWARDS, MICHELLE
[b.] November 1, 1974; [p.] Ray and Myra Edwards; [ed.] Graduated from Loveland High in 1993; [hon.] Who's Who Among American High School, Student 3 years in a row.; [pers.] In my poetry I express my feelings of growing up in today's world.; [a.] Loveland, CO

EICHER, BRIAN N.
[b.] September 28, 1973, Uniontown, PA; [p.] James Eugene and Suzanne Marie Eicher; [ed.] Tri-Valley, Albert Gallatin High School, Pittsburgh Technical Institute (Associates Degree); [occ.] Graphic Designer, Illustrator, Receptionist; [pers.] I am inspired by daily and natural surroundings. I express what I feel through poetry and drawings.; [a.] Fairchance, PA

EILERMAN, DARIN LEE
[b.] December 1, 1962, Santa Cruz; [p.] Greg and Ben Eilerman, Chris Johnson; [m.] Margret Mary Eilerman, October 16, 1988; [ch.] Courie Lynn, Sarah Anna, Elizabeth Marie and Adam Gregory; [ed.] Fire Science Degree, AAS, and AA degree. Working on BA in Communication.; [occ.] Student; [memb.] Woodside Calif Fire Dept, Muster Team with record times in West Coast Comp, first place. Three years service as Fire Fighter for county district.; [hon.] First place award for restored 1930's boat in car and boat show.; [oth. writ.] You were once a part of our family tree, originally titled "For Becka" in The Garden of Life. 40 plus other poems, half of them written for songs.; [pers.] First time lucky, second time good but third time means I'm finally understood.; [a.] Spokane, WA

EKSTROM, RUTH
[b.] December 24, 1908, Albion, NE; [p.] Sever and Tillie Loken; [m.] David Ekstrom, September 5, 1934; [ch.] Geraldine Porter, Russell, Milton; [ed.] College graduate, Wayne State College, Wayne, NE; [occ.] Retired; [memb.] Zion Lutheran Church, Albion, NE - Albion Area Writer's Club, Sigma Alpha Iota, Music Sorority - 3 Card Clubs - Christian Women - Bible Study Group; [oth. writ.] Many poems appeared in our local newspaper, Albion weekly news, a poem in Viking magazine, also articles in The Sundowner, Scope, Nebraska Farmer.; [pers.] I like to write poems that help people look at the bright side of life. Nearly all of my poems (I have written 2 books of poems) have humorous endings, except this one.; [a.] Albion, NE

ELK, TONIA JEANNINE
[pen.] Wapiti (American Elk); [b.] September 6, 1929, Bell Gardens, CA; [p.] Davis and Fern; [m.] Single; [ch.] Sherri Rene, Davis Warren, Debra Jeannine; [ed.] 12th grade graduate January 1947 with honors, Compton High School, Compton California. June 1986 CNA Geriatrics course Rogue College; [occ.] Retired from Rockwell International (formerly North American Aviation. 25 years service.; [memb.] Phi Alpha Music Society Long Beach Philharmonic (Flautist) 1951, Federated Women's Club Oregon Senior Volunteer (RSVP) Cave Junction, OR; [hon.] Award for Little White Lies and Other Sentimentals from Daily Courier and Federated Women's Club Oregon; [oth. writ.] Viuex un(old one) Clouds "Beloved", "Somethin", Blue", "Easter" "The Imagonah Valley", "Ode To Loneliness", "Little White Lies And Other Sentimentals A Point In Time" Jeannines' Potpourri (A column I wrote for I.V. News weekly 1980-81.) Hump Pilot Assc Bio for Father D. W. Elk; [pers.] "Creativity is so delicate a flower that praise tends to make it bloom, while discouragement often nips it in the bud. Any

of us will put out more and better ideas if our efforts are appreciated. Alex F Osborn "so, write in spite of failures. In the trying, is success in itself. The joy for others and yourself is writings' reward."; [a.] Cave Junction, OR

ELLING, BLANCHE
[pen.] Be; [b.] January 25, 1918, Sumter Township; [p.] Leroy and Alice Newcomb; [m.] Melvin Elling, October 19, 1938; [ch.] Eugene, Eileen, Susan, Dale and Gail; [ed.] Brownton High School; [occ.] Deceased; [memb.] Hospice Program, St. Paul's Lutheran Church; [hon.] High School Honor Student; [oth. writ.] Several other poems relating to various subjects; [pers.] Blanch's poetry was written during a period from March 1990 to October 1994, it was also during this time while penning poetry that Blanche bravely fought a personal battle against pancreatic cancer. A battle she lost in November of 1994; [a.] Hector, MN

ELLIS, JAMES L.
[pen.] Jim; [b.] October 31, 1938, McAllen, TX; [p.] Clyde and Velma Ellis; [m.] Sara Jacqueline (Jackie) Ellis, August 9, 1957; [ch.] Jim Jr., Brian, Cindy and Marci; [ed.] Humboldt High School, Some College, BAI Bank Auditors School; [occ.] Vice President and Auditor, First Citizens Nat'l Bank, Dyersburg, TN; [oth. writ.] Letters to Editor published in local newspaper.; [pers.] Writing to me, in exciting. It has become my great escape into other worlds and has allowed me to expand my, once, limited mind.; [a.] Jackson, TN

ELSTON, LINDA ELAINE
[pen.] Elanya Von Tress; [b.] June 15, 1961, Norwalk, CT; [p.] Quinten and Vivian Von Tress; [m.] Ellis Elston Jr., March 30, 1991; [ch.] Ellis Eugene Elston III; [ed.] New Canaan Country Day, Warwick High School, Virginia Institute of Technology; [occ.] Jewelry Associate at Clover Park City, Lancaster; [hon.] Quill and Scroll Award for Business Manager at Warwick High School, Newport News, VA; [oth. writ.] 'The Princess Who Hated To Be Prom And Proper' written while in New Canaan Country Day at age 10 and performed as a drama for various audiences around Norwalk, Fairfield and New Canaan, CT

ELWELL, DAVID L.
[b.] March 10, 1955, Petaluma, CA; [p.] Ken Elwell, Darlene Twitchell; [m.] Marilyn Elwell, June 22, 1991; [ch.] Ginny - 18, Kenny - 17, Holly - 16, Kurtis - 13; [ed.] High School grad; [occ.] Dept. Supervisor in Olive Products Plant.; [memb.] Vestry member of St. Pauls Episcopal Church Teamsters Local 849; [oth. writ.] Poems titled: Forever, One Way I Know, The Way I Feel; [pers.] My poems are straight from my heart for my wife Marilyn. They all tell a story of my feeling towards her in different stages of our relationship.; [a.] Oroville, CA

EMERY, KELLY
[pen.] Kelly Emery; [b.] September 2, 1965, Grants Pass, OR; [p.] Doug and Shirley Thomas; [m.] Joseph Emery, September 4, 1988; [ch.] Ryan Wayne Hendon, Rebecca Ann Emery and Kody Lee Emery - deceased; [ed.] 12th grade education; [occ.] Home maker; [oth. writ.] First and only poem I have ever written; [pers.] My husband

inspired me to write "Mighty Soul", and is in dedication to our infant son, Kody Lee, may he rest in peace.; [a.] Central Point, OR

ENGEL, HAROLD J.
[b.] September 30, 1938, Chicago, IL; [p.] Harold Engel, Florence (Pawlak); [m.] Sarah M. Engel (Kloos), September 10, 1960; [ch.] Craig, Caroline, Christine, Catherine, Jason; [ed.] Lane Technical High, Triton College; [occ.] Advertising Art and Photography; [memb.] Muskies, Inc.; [hon.] President's List, Phi Theta Kappa Honor Society, Who's Who in Finance and Industry - 1975, Who's Who in the Midwest - 1978, Who's Who in Advertising - 1990; [oth. writ.] "Recipe for a lifelong fantasy", an article for magazine `Muskie'; [pers.] "Reflect, remember, and learn."; [a.] Oak Park, IL

ENGEL, STEFFI
[b.] September 4, 1948, Milwaukee, WI; [p.] Oliver Fuller and Betty Randall (M/M O.C. Fuller); [m.] G. Larry Engel IV, May 29, 1971; [ch.] Laura Elizabeth and Bryan Arthur Engel; [ed.] Northwestern University School of Music, Theory and Composition; [occ.] Musician/ Composer; [memb.] Institute of Transpersonal Psychology, Institute of Noetic Sciences; [hon.] Graduated Cum Laude from High School, various honors for song writing; [oth. writ.] Many songs, various instrumental pieces, one musical, a symphony in process, currently first novel in process; [pers.] Life is a song to be sung, a dance to be cherished, a marvelous adventure, and a courageously opening tender heart. In my journey of Faith I am constantly astounded!; [a.] Orinda, CA

ENO, BETSY A.
[b.] September 5, 1967, Galion, OH; [p.] John and Lorraine Goodrich; [m.] Keith Eno, August 1, 1992; [ch.] Audrey Dawn, Brian Matthew; [ed.] Venice High, Ideal Adult Education Program; [occ.] Owner, designer of gift basket business; [hon.] Graduated with Top Honors at Ideal.; [pers.] To me, poetry is the outpouring on paper of one's heart and soul.; [a.] Nokomis, FL

EPPS, ISABELL C.
[b.] March 31, 1962, Phoenix, AZ; [p.] Mr. and Mrs. B. F. Robertson; [m.] Terry K. Epps, September 18, 1995; [ch.] Brittany Epps, Theresa Epps; [ed.] Central High School, Glendale Community College; [occ.] Administrative Asst.; [oth. writ.] Several poems and songs.; [pers.] Strength and goodness are necessary characteristics in order for our human race to survive.; [a.] Phoenix, AZ

ERGLE, ELIZABETH PARKER
[b.] January 7, 1941, Aiken, SC; [p.] Martha Parker, Harry Parker; [m.] L. B. Ergle Jr., June 5, 1962; [ch.] Cullum Ergle Lepard, Elizabeth Blanton Ergle; [ed.] Langley-Bath-Clearwater High, A.B. Elem. Ed. University of South Carolina; [occ.] Housewife: Tutor students usually in language arts; [memb.] St. John's United Methodist Church, The 700 Club, Christian Coalition; [oth. writ.] Over 300 poems including personal requests such as eulogies, personal events, birthdays, anniversaries, dedications; [pers.] To show love, spark joy, ignite hope, heal emotions,

cause laughter, encourage forgiveness and lead others to a saving knowledge of Jesus Christ — that is what I press toward in my "talent of writing"...which I truly received from Almighty God.; [a.] Aiken, SC

ERWIN, GERALD W.
[b.] December 29, 1924, Vernon Co., WI; [p.] Judson and Rosy Erwin; [m.] Donna L. Erwin, October 3, 1954; [ch.] Janice A. and David B.; [ed.] Hillsboro High, Wisconsin State University, LaCrosse, WI (Bachelor of Education); [occ.] Retired (farmer, teacher, factory worker, township official); [oth. writ.] Several poems published in local papers, one or two published in poetry anthologies.; [pers.] "Much of my poetry tends to be socio-political satire and is pretty grim. Sometimes I do manage a lighter touch, however."; [a.] Hillsboro, WI

ESANNASON, KEONA
[pen.] Shortee; [b.] July 21, 1975, Rahway, NJ; [p.] Sheila Coleman; [ed.] Plainfield High School, Union County College; [a.] Plainfield, NJ

ESMAEILI, FATEMEH
[pen.] Lala (Red Tulip); [b.] August 31 1948, Ardeville, Azerbaijan Province, Iran; [m.] Yussef Kalantari; [ch.] 3 kids; [ed.] Completed High School, and attended Tehran University, In 1986 I graduated with a B.A. of Arts, in Persian Language and Literature. M.A. of Teaching in Education at Saint Peter's College, Jersey City, graduated in 1994.; [occ.] Substitute Teacher of Bergen County, a profession I had from 1965-1985 in Iran Tehran.; [oth. writ.] I am also in the process of publishing a book called (The name of Love) in Persian. I hope I can have it translated into English.; [pers.] I believe in the beauty of life or love and it's everlasting meaning: That we never really die. And part of that philosophy can simply be summed up in: It is the individuality and truly independent thoughts of another human being that are so very important. We have no right to enslave the thoughts of others.

ESPADA, MICHELLE NICHOL
[pen.] Michi; [b.] January 19, 1975, Puerto Rico; [p.] Fred and Alicia Espada; [ed.] High School Graduate; [occ.] College - Singing; [hon.] Art Awards, Writing Awards; [oth. writ.] Poems - short story; [pers.] I see the hardships and pain most kids my age are going through and I wish to send a message that there is a greater power that cares and watches over us.; [a.] Okeechobee, FL

ESPOSITO, CHRISTINE L.
[pen.] Chrissy Lee Jackson; [b.] January 30, 1968, New Haven, CT; [p.] Alexander and Carolyn Esposito; [m.] Future husband Richard W. Jackson, September 1995; [occ.] Credit Investigator at Ford Motor Credit - North Haven, CT; [pers.] I started writing at 12 years of age, I want to share my visions of emotions and romance through written symbols. Sunsets and the shoreline are my inspiration.; [a.] New Haven, CT

ESPOSITO, JENNIFER ANN
[b.] August 17, 1973, Bronx, NY; [p.] Teresita and Jerry Esposito; [occ.] Chiropractic Assistant; [hon.] Arista Honor Society; [pers.] I try to see the beauty in everyone and everything, and I hope that reflects in my writing. I would like to thank my parents, and my younger sister, Joy-Marie, for their love and support.; [a.] Bronx, NY

ESTES, KIM A.
[pen.] Kim A. Thompson; [b.] December 7, 1970, Phoenix, AZ; [p.] Lettie and Larry Raab, John and Betty Thompson; [m.] Lloyd A. Estes, June 17, 1994; [ch.] Amanda., T. J.; [ed.] B.A. English Jacksonville State University; [occ.] BCBSF LTC Rep. and Amway Distributor; [hon.] Award of Merit for Wild West Skit, 1990. Proud step-mom of Amanda and T. J., the worlds biggest honor; [oth. writ.] Poem 'Whale Song' in National Library of Poetry Anthology, 'In A Different Light' and JSU literary magazine.; [pers.] I would like to dedicate this poem and my life to my loving husband. He has been my joy, my friend, my inspiration. And to Amanda and T. J., the most beautiful kids in the world, I love you.; [a.] Atlantic Beach, FL

ESTES, RAYMOND M.
[b.] April 22, 1918, Wadena, Saskatchewan, Canada; [p.] G. B. Estes, Jessie Estes; [m.] Margaret V. Estes, June 30, 1947; [ch.] Gary Gene Estes; [ed.] North Central High, Spokane, WA, Eugene Bible College, Palmers Writers School-Fiction; [occ.] Retired; [memb.] Open Bible Standard Churches, Minister, Albany Open Bible Standard Church; [hon.] Superintendent's Faithfulness Award, OBSC, Retirement award for 37 years pastoring in Oregon; [oth. writ.] Several poems and articles in local Newspaper. Book, God's great appointment, the crowning days in memorial.; [pers.] I have been an ordained minister for 47 years. I want to make my writings show the way that leads us to Jesus Christ and that I may have the love for others.; [a.] Albany, OR

ESTRADA, NANCY
[b.] April 3, 1972, Lubbock, TX; [p.] Frances and Ramiro Quevedo; [m.] Leonel Estrada Jr., June 23, 1989; [ch.] Leonel Estrada III, Tracy Lynnette Estrada; [ed.] Graduate of Shallowater High School, class of 1990; [occ.] Housewife and mother; [oth. writ.] Take nothing for granted because as soon as you do, you will realize how special it really was.; [a.] Shallowater, TX

ETIENNE, DONALD
[pen.] Etyen Kaliko; [b.] August 20, 1966, New York; [p.] Mondesir and Eugenie S. Etienne; [ed.] Hunter College Bachelor Degree: Media Studies; [occ.] Paralegal - Weil, Gotshal and manges; [memb.] Trioupe MacKandal, Collection Kazak, Performing Art Consultant, PS 112, President, C.A.F.E. Greole, Haitian Club of Hunter College; [hon.] Gold and Silver Award, from World of Poetry; [oth. writ.] For Your Love, The Mystery Of Love, In Memorium (poems published); [pers.] Life is love. It must be share and experience. It starts from within and explode to the world with colors, expressions and rhythm. I live to share and experience the euphoric life.; [a.] New York, NY

EUNICE, ANNE MARIE
[b.] July 20, 1968, Los Angeles, CA; [p.] Virginia and Andrew Pulemba; [occ.] Waitperson at the Hotel Mac in Point Richmond, CA; [oth. writ.]

I've written many other poems but, have never before been published.; [pers.] I love people, especially children and older people. I also love music and animals, nature and God. To Him God above all else am I grateful.; [a.] Oakland, CA

EVANS, JUDITH B.
[pen.] J. Brooke Evans; [b.] February 28, 1953, Baltimore, MD; [pers.] Everyone deals with the events in their lives differently. From the time I was old enough to hold a pencil I did it with the written word. I have always transformed sensation into vision and digested it through my mind's eye. The young man about whom this poem was written was a friend of mine. His death was a shattering experience.; [a.] Atlanta, GA

EVANS, SANDRA
[b.] March 4, 1950, New Orleans, LA; [p.] Marcelle King - mother; [ch.] Bertrand Irvin - son, Shellonn Hill - daughter; [ed.] 3 years College, John C. Fremont High, Los Angeles, majoring in Education at Brookhaven College, Farmers Branch, TX; [occ.] Student; [hon.] Honor Roll Student at Brookhaven College, TX; [oth. writ.] Collection of poems never released.; [pers.] I write to provoke thought and shed light into the hearts of many from my soul of life occurrences real or imagined. I started writing as a child to enhance my view of the world I lived in; [a.] Dallas, TX

EVANS, TRACY
[b.] January 26, 1983, Harrisburg, PA; [p.] Ronald and Priscilla Evans; [ed.] 6th grader at Southern Middle School; [occ.] Student; [hon.] 5th grade poster 3rd place winner, 1st place - 5th grade softball throwing contest, Academic Excellence Award; [a.] New Freedom, PA

EVANS, VICTORIA BRAZZLE
[b.] August 16, 1977, Coatesville Hospital; [p.] Vickie Brazzle, Edward Evans; [ed.] High School junior, Downingtown High; [memb.] Management team for D-town Whippets football team Black Student Union Connections Club, teacher Secretarial Aid, Special Olympics Volunteer; [hon.] Yearbook - President of sales trophy and metals for football management; [oth. writ.] Short life like stories and poetry.; [pers.] My poetry consists of the feelings of others, it's then set to my rhythm and rhyme sound and sense pattern. I'm influenced by my surroundings. This poem is in memory of my niece, Heather Christina Brazzle; [a.] Downingtown, PA

EVERS, GENE
[pen.] Gene Alexander Evers; [b.] March 26, 1951, Manhattan; [p.] Pauline, Mitt Stein; [ed.] Graduated Pearl River H.S., graduated State University at old Westbury. Made nursing program at Nassau C.C. went to State University at Stony Brook.; [occ.] Song and Script writer; [memb.] International Society of Poets; [hon.] Principles List and Dean's List, Hicksville JRHS.; [oth. writ.] Many other poems including eternity, King's bride and all green fields. Assortment of songs and lyrics including Cindy girl and a movie script.; [pers.] Ask questions and search for the truth as if it was your mission. Realize truth lies under many layers of what at first, and only at first, appears true.; [a.] Bethpage, NY

EWELL, SHANE
[b.] April 22, 1981, Greeley, CO; [p.] Wanda Paterson, Alex Paterson; [ed.] Jefferson Elementary, Dayspring Christian, Brentwood Middle, and John Evans Junior High.; [occ.] Paper route for the "Greeley Tribune"; [oth. writ.] A writing assessment called "The Girl In The Sewer," "The O.J. Simpson Trial," and Motorcycles. I scored an "A" on all assessments.; [pers.] I strive to reflect the goodness of mankind in my writing. I hope to influence others with my writings.; [a.] Greeley, CO

EYLER, JAMES D.
[pen.] J. Dalton Eyler; [b.] August 18, 1969, Phidelphia, PA; [m.] Jennifer Eyler, June 11, 1994; [ch.] Two beautiful Great Danes; [oth. writ.] Song writing and a book in progress.; [pers.] Writing to me, whether it be poems, songs or pages of books, is the most genuine form of freedom I have ever found.

FAIR, CHRISTOPHER JON
[b.] April 12, 1969, Omaha, NE; [p.] Donald and S. Joan Fair; [ed.] Daniel J. Grass H.S. Omaha Nebraska, University of Nebraska Lincoln; [occ.] Premium Cattle Feeders Inc.; [hon.] Who's Who American H.S. Students; [oth. writ.] Lost and Found, A Collection of my Inspired Thoughts, Lost and Found, Again A Collection of my Inspired Writings; [pers.] I'll never be the man I want to be, but I'll never settle for anything less. So I'll end up, in the end, dead and buried, trying to be someone I'm not and was never meant to be.; [a.] Courtland, KS

FALABELLA, LINDA Q.
[b.] April 1, 1948, Oceanside, NY; [p.] Frank Quinto, Rose Quinto; [m.] Michael Falabella, April 10, 1971; [ch.] Ly Ann, Michael Jr.; [ed.] Long Beach High School, NY Hofstra University BA '70, MA '77; [occ.] Speech - Language Pathologist; [memb.] 1. Compassion (Adopt-A-Child), 2. Operation Blessing, 3. American Speech - Language - Hearing Ass'n.; [hon.] Dean's List; [oth. writ.] Poem for mother won local radio contest; [pers.] My inspiration to write comes from God and family.; [a.] Point Lookout, NY

FAMIGLIETTI, JOHN A.
[b.] June 23, 1921, Fairview, NJ; [p.] Marciano and Jennie; [m.] Virginia, September 22, 1946; [ch.] Carol Ann, John Jr., Grandchildren - Gino, Tony, Philip; [ed.] Dale Carnegie Inst. LaSalle Extension University Academy of Healing Art Pandolp, School of Comm. Art; [occ.] Neuromuscular Therapist; [hon.] Mothers Council of Hallandale, Florida, Certificate of Honor Beautiful Committee, Hallandale Chamber of Commerce; [pers.] I know it sounds impossible, but it would be nice if people of the world would strive to live in peace and understanding of each other. This is the reason for all the wars going on in the world.; [a.] Baynton Beach, FL

FANNIN, BARBARA
[b.] February 21, 1974, Saint Pete; [p.] Gene Fannin, John Fannin; [ed.] Clearwater Central Catholic High School, St. Pete Junior College, University of South Florida; [occ.] Child Development Specialist; [hon.] President's Honor List, Who's Who Among American High School Students; [oth. writ.] High School Literary Magazine; [pers.] I love poetry, including reading and writing of poetry. I believe it is an expression of emotion in a unique way.; [a.] Seminole, FL

FARAHAY, MICHAEL LEE WILSON
[pen.] M. L. Farahay; [p.] Forest Wickes Wilson and Martha Elizabeth Gress and James Martin Farahay; [m.] Naomi Elizabeth (Nebby) Bradeh; [ch.] Colleen, Eric, Aalesa, Aaron and Todd; [ed.] From Demali to The Keys, Columbus School of Art, Ohio University, Sinclair Comm College, Olympic College, Southern State at Fincastle; [occ.] Artist, Truck Driver; [memb.] Adams County Art Gallery of Murphin Ridge Inn; [hon.] Thurber Scholarship to Ohio State (Turned down), Diving Scholarship to Ohio University (partial), Done Scholarship (Art) to Columbus School of Arts, done U.S. Army Airborne "Wings", done Summa Cum Laude "Southern State" Fincastle; [oth. writ.] "Any Child", "Butterflies", "The River" published in Lagos (Ohio Univ.), plus art work poetry books "Highest Rated "X" and "Something Country"...all in limited editions. Published only for friends. "Righteous Mistress Maid Of..."; [pers.] I pioneered the "Road to Canada" no regrets "62" and paid the price....see "From these Prison Rafters" Trust, love and be willing to fight for what you believe in God and children! Enjoy Shakespeare, Whitman E. Thomas.; [a.] Adams County, OH

FARMER, JESSICA CLIFFORD
[b.] January 9, 1964, San Antonio, TX; [p.] Don and Carol Johnson; [m.] Craig Farmer, May 14, 1988; [ch.] Chandler Craig age 5, Jenna Sioux age 4; [ed.] Labette County H.S., OSU-OKC, University of Oklahoma; [occ.] Emergency Medical Technician; [memb.] American Heart Association Instructor, Oklahoma Farm Bureau Young Farmers and Ranchers; [oth. writ.] Poems published in "The Garden of Life" and "East of the Sunrise"; [pers.] This is my way of expressing my emotions, my hope is that someone else will see themselves in my words and find expression, also.; [a.] Buffalo, OK

FARNEY, AMBER
[b.] December 23, 1981, Fargo, ND; [p.] Betty Farney; [ed.] 7th Grade at Agassiz Junior High School, Elementary at Carl Ben Eielson; [occ.] Student; [hon.] Honor Roll with GPA 3.174, Citizenship awards; [oth. writ.] I write poems for fun; [pers.] My poems are based on my dreams, personal experience and my feelings.; [a.] Fargo, ND

FARNSWORTH, TRACY R.
[b.] March 13, 1968, Baraboo, WI; [p.] Eugenia and Ronald Steiner, Walter Farnsworth; [ed.] Graduated Webb High School, Reedsburg, WI 1986. Audited Classes at University of Wisconsin, Madison; [occ.] Retail Buyer for Saxon's in Chicago, IL; [memb.] Member of the Unity Lutheran Players, Member of the Lionheart Theater Troupe and A Wonder Twin!; [hon.] At the age of 8 yrs. old won 1st place in a jump rope contest in 1988, won 1st place in a regional contest for "Puttin' on the Hits" with dance partner, Amy Hahn.; [oth. writ.] A play entitled "Blade and Marina - You Really Like Us"; [pers.] When I attempt anything, I approach it without boundaries and find strength within.; [a.] Chicago, IL

FAULKNER, DEANDREA
[b.] November 23, 1981, Chicago; [p.] Forrest Faulkner, Melanie F.; [ed.] Adam Clayton Powell Jr. Public School. I am still an Elementary School.; [memb.] St. Thomas Church, St. Margrate Church, I'm not only a part of these churches, but I also want to help children with AIDS and adults with heart disease.; [oth. writ.] 1 Published in school newspaper with a story. (Soon) I will be sending some poetry to some magazines and 1 newspaper: The Chicago Sun Times; [pers.] My niece Fornise Faulkner taught me how to write at the age of 10. And she's the same age as me. Also I had alot of faith put in me by Gwendolyn Brooks and James Conklin.; [a.] Chicago, IL

FEDERICO, TROY M.
[b.] April 13, 1970, New York; [p.] Anna and Joseph Federico; [pers.] I'd like to thank Shawn L. Fleming, Barbara Foster, and H.H. Tenzin Gyatso for their inspiration, guidance and wisdom.; [a.] Boston, MA

FEILD, LINDA MARIE
[b.] April 27, 1949, Billings, MT; [p.] Calvin and Ruth Sjostrom; [m.] Dirk Quitman Feild, December 18, 1976; [ch.] Lisa Linn Hayes, Stephen Paul Hayes; [ed.] Billings Senior High World Reaching Faith School of Training Moorpark Junior College; [occ.] Wife, Mother, Artist and Poet; [memb.] Women Aglow Fellowship; [hon.] Dean's List; [pers.] My identity is not embodied in what I accumulate or what I achieve it is seen in the good I allow to flow thru my life. I am walking the best I can with the faith I have in the word I know.

FEINSTEIN, BARBARA A.
[b.] November 9, 1965, New Jersey; [p.] Franklin, Margery; [ed.] High School, some college; [occ.] Telecommunications; [oth. writ.] Other unpublished poems; [pers.] I write from my heart. I'm not trying to "better" the world, because that would be futile. I write for personal, selfish reasons. But, then again, don't most?; [a.] Houston, TX

FELIX, ANGELICA YESENIA
[b.] June 9, 1972, Los Angeles, CA; [p.] Alejandro and Coty Felix; [ch.] Carolina Monique Schumber; [ed.] Orange High, Rancho Santiago College; [occ.] Student; [oth. writ.] I have several other poems 2 books filled with my own poetry; [pers.] That poetry is a destructive force and that we do not admire what we cannot understand.; [a.] Garden Grove, CA

FELL, JESSYCA JOY
[b.] February 27, 1979, Lansing, MI; [p.] Robert E. Fell and Carolyn S. Cook; [ed.] Elementary School in Laingsburg, MI and same with Middle School. I am currently attending Laingsburg High School.; [hon.] Participant in "Dining with Young Artists" (read poetry aloud at a special honors banquet); [pers.] You must love yourself before you can love anyone else.; [a.] Laingsburg, MI

FELTY, KATHEE M.
[pen.] Kathee M. Felty; [b.] December 20, 1950, Chelsea, MA; [p.] Mr. and Mrs. Arthur J. Greason; [m.] Carl R. Felty Jr., August 29, 1986; [ch.] Christopher E. Morgan, Melissa M. Morgan G. Felty, Stepchild - Gregory R. Felty - granddaughter Taylor Rebecca Morgan; [ed.] Graduated 1968 Wheeler High School, School of Interior Decorating 1976, Berks Real Estate Institute 1987; [occ.] I have my own business (Complete Image), (Also Secretary to husbands business E. R. Felty Inc.) (Notary for PA. Commonwealth); [memb.] PA Association of Notaries - 11 yrs., Past member School Board Association (served 4 yrs.), School Director (served 4 yrs.) Past Member (Berks Earned Income Tax Bureau - served 4 yrs., Wernsville Recreation served 6 yrs., Past member Carl Scout Leader served 3 yrs., PTA Vice President.; [oth. writ.] I have written several other poems - never tried to publish as yet, but I am thinking about it for the future. I love to write and do it for a hobby.; [pers.] Life is a learning experience. Every aspect of your life teaches your something. I always strive to be the best I can be. To have loved and be loved are the most important things to accomplish in life. Love is all important.; [a.] Vernersville, PA

FEREJOHN, MARISSA
[b.] August 3, 1978, Hollywood; [p.] Sally and John Ferejohn; [ed.] Currently enrolled in Palo Alto High School, Palo Alto California; [occ.] Student; [memb.] International order of the Rainbow For Girls, Thespian Society; [pers.] This is my first publishing and hopefully not the last! Keep dreaming.; [a.] Los Altos Hills, CA

FERRIELL, DARLA
[b.] June 13, 1960, Danville, KY; [p.] Foster Barnes and Jo Ann White; [m.] Rick Ferriell, March 13, 1982; [ed.] Corydon Central High School, Enlisted in the Army Reserve in 1978 to further my education; [occ.] Office Manager; [hon.] Army Commendation Medal I received numerous awards while serving in the U.S. Army Reserve; [oth. writ.] My mother has put several of my poems in the local newspaper; [pers.] I enjoy writing poems on subjects that are very dear to me. I also write poetry for family and friends when asked. I thank God for this talent I have to make people happy with my writing.; [a.] Durham, NC

FIARITO, STEPHANIE E.
[pen.] "Assuntina"; [b.] August 15, 1937, Illinois; [m.] Richard A. Fiarito, February 14, 1980; [ch.] Therese Marie Krueger; [ed.] B.S. Education (Fordham Univ.); [occ.] Medical Asst. in Neurology; [pers.] My belief is that in all of us there exists a "seed" which searches and reaches for the stars....The seed is nurtured by the sun, the rain, the light and continues its growth even in darkness.; [a.] Oakbrook Terrace, IL

FINGER, TERRY
[pen.] Broom Hilda; [b.] September 24, 1957, Knoxville, TN; [p.] Charles, Mary Finger; [m.] Single; [ed.] Rule High Grad. 1975, State Area Vocation 1989; [occ.] The Mountain Press Mailroom Employee; [memb.] Alder Branch, Baptist Church, Wednesday Night Mixed League, Fountain Bowling Lanes; [hon.] Mayors Merit Award, Tennessee Health Care Association,

Certificate of Nursing Assistance; [oth. writ.] I wrote a poem of thanks that was distributed to everyone who helped me in nurses training.; [pers.] I express myself better in writing than by verbal communication, and far less misunderstood.; [a.] Sevierville, TN

FINNELL, DONNA
[pen.] Donna Finnell; [b.] March 20, 1924, Fairbury, NE; [p.] Muriel and John Gibson; [m.] W. Scott Finnell, April 8, 1958; [ch.] Heidi, Nick, Gretchen and Scott III; [ed.] High School and College Fairbury, Nebraska; [occ.] Writer, Homemaker; [memb.] First Christian Church, Christian Women's Organization, Writer's Guild, Artist Group; [hon.] Miss Nebraska 1942, Miss New York 1943, Runner-Up Mrs. America 1943, Nebraska Champion Baton Twirler, National Champion Baton Twirler, Powers Model New York City; [oth. writ.] Poems, "History of Family", ADS Television Commercials; [pers.] A letter from Colorado "Poet Laret" in the Denver Post Newspaper, wrote me... "My poems flow like birds in flight." I was elated.; [a.] Parachute, CO

FIRMIN, JENNIFER LYNN
[b.] November 25, 1983, New Britain, CT; [p.] Gary Firmin, Marcia Firmin; [occ.] Student in 6th grade at Middle School of Plainville, CT; [a.] Plainville, CT

FISH, TIMOTHY R.
[pen.] Tim Fish; [b.] March 28, 1964, Akron, OH; [p.] Melv and Lois Fish; [m.] Kim Anh Fish, October 30, 1992; [ch.] Matthew Tyler, Calder Connolly, Victoria Elizabeth; [ed.] Garfield High - Akron OH, Northern Virginia Community College (NVCC) George Mason University; [occ.] Accounts Payable Assistant, Part-time Student; [memb.] Phi Theta Kappa, Virginia Sheriffs Association; [hon.] Phi Theta Kappa, Dean's List, Graduated Cum Laude from NVCC; [oth. writ.] None that have been published; [pers.] I write mostly during the times when I am struggling with the challenges of life. It is a way for me to express my emotions.; [a.] Burke, VA

FISHER, JAMES L.
[b.] July 8, 1965, Delaware; [p.] Larry and Jerry Ann Fisher; [ed.] James H. Groves High School; [memb.] A.B.A.T.E. of Delaware; [oth. writ.] I have written many poems, but none have been published.; [pers.] I would like to dedicate this poem, "Natural Love" to the lady who inspires me. Julie, you hold my heart.; [a.] Georgetown, DE

FISHER, LARRY
[b.] December 17, 1945, New Boston, TX; [occ.] Salon and Celebrity hair Stylist; [memb.] Distinguished Member - International Society of Poets; [hon.] Two Bronze Stars Viet-Nam Joint Chef of Staff, Cert. of Appreciation - Gen. Westmoreland, Cert. of Appreciation Govt. of California President Ronald Reagan 1994, Editors Choice Award, Natl. Library of Poetry 1995, Int. Poet of Merit/Int. Soc. of Poets; [oth. writ.] Presently writing a book that contains poetry and humor. Title - Shared Expressions; [pers.] The success, as well as the detriments, we experience in life is merely choices. A choice made by the reflection in your mirror.; [a.] Compton, CA

FISHER, MINDY HOPE
[b.] January 13, 1981, Philadelphia; [p.] Marsha and Steven Fisher; [ed.] Newtown Jr. High, Expository Writing Tutorial - John Hopkins University, Shir Ami Religious School, Sharon Slack School of the Arts; [hon.] National Hebrew Honors Society, Honor Roll; [oth. writ.] Poem published in Anthology of Poetry by Young Americas; [a.] Newtown, PA

FISTON, OPANGA MABROUCKY
[b.] May 15, 1968, Bujumbura; [p.] Ndjalo Patrick, Kitambala Jeanne; [ed.] Groupe Scolaire Zairois, Institut Weza Nyangezi; [occ.] Driver Truck; [memb.] Kuminga Papa Yoyo Jean Bosco, Mukendi Sindano Bula Bula Mweze, Coco Taki Abou Twite, Ilunga Masinga Luhudi Lubamba, Niangadou Mamadou Musa Kitenge, Tshishimbi Bashale; [hon.] UDE Food Company, Co-Owner, Manager; [oth. writ.] We Will Arrive All, Dishonesty, My U.S.A.; [pers.] Be quite pass every things, same people, they are quite to make reach dreams my life is like that too. Good work gives nice reware; [a.] Irving, TX

FITCH, HOWARD
[b.] December 23, 1909, Jeffersonville, IN; [m.] (First) Jane Rogers McCaw (Deceased), 1930, (Second) Nancy Dolt Langley; [ch.] 2 daughters, 8 grandchildren, 20 great grandchildren; [ed.] High School Lexington, KY, College degrees in Engineering and Law.; [occ.] Currently working on limericks for each of the animals in Howard's Zoo.; [memb.] Distinguished Member International Society of Poets; [hon.] First poetry prize in High School ($1.00 for best last line for incomplete limerick); [oth. writ.] Sonnet published in Univ of KY literary magazine. Sonnet published in Saturday Review of Literature. Poetry written by Father, Brother, Uncle, Daughter, Granddaughter.

FITCHETT JR., CLARENCE H.
[b.] April 21, 1940, Nassawadox, VA; [p.] Clarence H. and Audrey Fitchett Sr.; [ch.] Clarence H. III, Tamena Audrey; [ed.] Northampton County High School, Kingsborough Community College, Hunter College and Columbia University Graduate, School of Social Work; [occ.] Recently Retired - pursuing full time Writing Career; [memb.] Gospel Music Association, The Song Writers Guild of America, International Society of Poet, Society of Children's Book Writers and Illustrators; [hon.] Dean's List and President's Award (Kingsborough), Certificates of Appreciation, Honorable Mentions and a Top Finalist Award (Music City Song Festival) Lyric and Song Competition, Editor's Choice Award 1994 - National Library of Poetry; [oth. writ.] 2 songs received Radio Air Play, A special low budget Album for the German Market, Co-wrote 3 short plays, wrote many poems for Special Events and News Letter at Work, A Wedding poem and poems for Churches, Poem published in an Anthology.; [pers.] I'm a huge fan of other composers and writers thus, I'm inspired as much from without as I'm from within. Writing is truly my life. And I consider it a privilege and an obligation to try to touch the lives of people through my writing and my music.; [a.] Flushing, NY

FITZGERALD, JAMES M.
[b.] October 7, 1929, Chicago; [p.] Thomas P. and Helen Fitzgerald; [m.] Divorced; [ch.] Gilbert H., Mark R. and Sheila F. Kirby; [ed.] De La Salle Institute, St. Jude's Seminary, Lake Forest College; [memb.] St. Bride's Fund, Chicago Maternity Center Centennial Plan, Sarah Siddons Society, Exmopr C.C.: Chicago Yacht Club East Bank Club; [hon.] Direct Marketing Assoc. - Echo Award, Windy Award - Radio Commercial; [oth. writ.] Two Rare Birds - Two Love Birds

FLANNERY, SEAN
[b.] August 22, 1976, Wilkes-Barre, PA; [p.] Charles and Janice Flannery; [ed.] G.A.R. Memorial High School, Penn St. University; [occ.] Bus Boy; [memb.] National Honors Society Who's Who (American High School Students); [hon.] High School Valedictorian, Who's Who in American High School Students, Youth Role Model (City of Wilkes-Barre), Dean's List, Lamp of Learning and Major's Award (City of Wilkes-Barre); [oth. writ.] Poem published by CERA, several other selections in college journals; [pers.] The word is the highest power on earth: Opening souls and seeing behind words and deeds, all to be summed up as the comedy and tragedy of life.; [a.] Wilkes-Barre, PA

FLEMING, ARMARIA
[b.] July 19, Joliet, IL; [p.] Vann and Betty Fleming; [ed.] Virginia Commonwealth University, Richmond, Virginia - received Masters of Social Work Degree; [occ.] Counselor (Youth and Family Services Counselor); [hon.] Who's Who Among American College and University Students, National Dean's List; [pers.] I enjoy writing poetry which captivates and motivates people both young and old alike.; [a.] Dale City, VA

FLEMING, MARJORIE FOSTER
[pen.] Marjorie Foster "Jory" - Marjorie Foster Fleming, Marjorie Foster Hundermark; [b.] September 12, 1920, Cheltenham, PA; [p.] Major B. Foster, Helen V. Foster; [m.] Paul S. Fleming, May 6, 1961; [ch.] John and David Hundermark; [ed.] Ed Oak Lane Country Day School, Cheltenham High School, Ursinus College '42, attended: Temple Univ. (advertising), Pierce Business College, Arthur Murry - Dancing, Cheltenham Twsp. Art Center (painting - photography - clay work - creative writing). Cheltenham Adult School, On the Job Radio and T.V. script writing, 8 yrs. private piano lessons, In Home song writing; [occ.] Homemaker, writer, painter, sculptress, musician, collect sheet music - All kinds!; [memb.] Life Member Cheltenham Twsp. Art Contean Distinguished Member of International Society of Poets.; [hon.] WW II Army-Navy "E" award with Philco Comp., Red Cross Award for Occupational therapy WW II (Valley Forge Army Hosp.), Stage Door Canteen Hostess and Special Duty SDC Hostess for members of the People Heart Society, In the Philadelphia Navy Hosp., private homes, and conventional Hall., Special award from....Mayor Samuels of Philadelphia, for contribution to "4th of July celebration as member of Special Events Dept. of Philadelphia Evening Bulletin., Miss "ELFRITH

ALLEY" (oldest still - occupied street in America), Chairperson and honored guest at 100th celebration of Philadelphia Evening Bulletin in College Pres. of Dorm, Chaplain, and treasurer of Sorority (Omega-Chi Sorority); [oth. writ.] Short-short stories, short stories may pageant, play (cartoons - illustrations for adults and children). Assisted writer scripts for T.V., radio, and play with Bennett Productions" 1948-49., Cheltenham Art Center Editor House Organ - proof reading articles, reports and mock up, Auto-Biography and poems in progress, song, lyrics and essays.; [pers.] I believe God has given us a purpose to fulfill which may or may not be revealed. I think that if we are able to use our experience with both "GOOD" and "BAD" toward enhancing our spiritual growth and if we then act for "GOOD" with "LOVE", we will be "HAPPY". Vola! We have one step up on the stairway to HEAVEN.; [a.] Crystal Lake, IL

FLETCHER, SHERRI
[b.] June 4, 1963, Columbus, OH; [p.] Luther and Geraldine Fletcher; [ch.] One daughter Carmella; [ed.] High School Graduate East High School; [occ.] Day-care provider but presently unemployed because of illness in family. I now take care of my mother.; [memb.] Higher ground always abounding assemblies; [oth. writ.] An article, I had published in Globe Magazine on a story I wrote about my mother surviving 5 heart-attacks and code-blues in one day.; [pers.] I write what I feel in my heart with a greater inspiration from God and my surroundings. I hope that my writings can inspire someone to be a better person, and to express what he/she feels. About themselves.; [a.] Columbus, OH

FLORES, ABEL J.
[pen.] Poppers; [b.] September 17, 1948, Flagstaff, AZ; [p.] Mr. and Mrs. Raymundo Flores; [m.] Molly, February 10, 1968; [ch.] Maria, Abel Jr., Tobias, Jennifer; [ed.] High School taking creative writing at Phoenix College; [occ.] Retired; [memb.] International Society of Poets, United States Navy 66-69'; [hon.] Published National Library of Poetry - Past Grand Knight in Knights of Columbus; [oth. writ.] Poem E.T.P. working on a book of poems; [pers.] I like camping, reading, poetry, woodwork, also a little gardening; [a.] Glendale, AZ

FLORES, ELIZABETH L.
[b.] Terrell County, TX; [p.] Simon and Gloria Lopez; [m.] Adolfo S. Flores, November 22, 1959; [ch.] Kathryn Marie Iverson, Michael Anthony Flores; [ed.] BA - Early Childhood/Sp. Ed. Arizona State University MA - Education - State Univ. Doctoral Program - 1981 - Univ. of Co Boulder; [occ.] Adjunct Professor at Univ. of Texas at El Paso. Co-owner of two businesses - Tiny Gowns and Postal Annex+; [memb.] El Paso Del Norte, Chapter of Kappa Delta Pi, Teaching English to Students of Other Languages (TESOL), The Hispanic Business Membership Club Texas Association for Bilingual Education; [hon.] Graduated "Cum Laude" Arizona State Univ. 1975, Award of Scholastic Excellence by the faculty' of the Dept. of Education, Arizona State Univ., 1975. Selected by TEA (Texas Education Agency) and the Departamento Educacion y

Ciencia de Madrid to participate in the III Summer Institute on Children's Literature at the Universidad Complutense in Madrid, Spain. Who's Who Among Hispanic Americans 1992-93; [oth. writ.] "La Tortilla Huida" (The Runaw Tortilla), children's book published by Donor's Production. Poem of Love for Dad (Spanish) Father's Day 1988, Today's Catholic. "From Civil War Archives", a story of Hispanic valor, Vista Magazine, 1990.; [pers.] When something or someone touches that inner core in my very being, there is this urgency to write a poem. The words just seem to flow.; [a.] El Paso, TX

FLOWERS, VELMA L.
[pen.] Caretaker; [b.] October 31, 1948, Chicago; [p.] Dorothy and James Dawson; [m.] Separated; [ch.] Keith L. Flowers, Donita Flowers, Grandkids - Sekia, Keith Jr., [ed.] Parker High School Chicago, Chicago State Univ., Central YMCA College, ICS Home Study and a model; [occ.] Physical Instructor for Chicago Park District; [memb.] Helping Hand Missionary Baptist Church, Camp Fire Assoc., Future Teacher of America, Negro Black College Fund; [hon.] First giving Honor to God for my talent and many friends that so graciously listen.; [oth. writ.] Several poems published in local newspaper and American Poetry Anthology.; [pers.] To express God's love which is in me to share peace and harmony throughout the world, give to all and it shall be given to you.; [a.] Chicago, IL

FLUELLEN, MAREKUS T.
[pen.] Pooh; [b.] December 13, 1982, Atlanta; [p.] Malcolm and Ethel Fluellen; [ed.] 7th grader for school year 95-96; [occ.] Student at S.W. Middle School; [memb.] Elizabeth Missionary Baptist Church, National Junior Beta Club, Science Club and Drama Club; [hon.] Certificate of Appreciation form the I.R.S. for participation in the VITA program, Honor pin for academic achievement 94-95, Honor Roll since kindergarten, principal list (94) perfect attendance 7 years; [oth. writ.] Peace, wasted money; [pers.] The more you rebel the least you excel. When your mother says you can do it. You will do it.; [a.] Atlanta, GA

FLYNN, MRS. KATHERINE
[pen.] Katherine Flynn; [b.] October 10, 1008, Maine; [p.] Mr. and Mrs. Ronald McIlroy; [m.] Lawrence Flynn (Deceased), July 1, 1932; [ch.] 5 sons - 4 of whom are married with families; [ed.] Graduate Lewiston H.S., Kents Hill Prep. School, N. England Conservatory of Music, Boston Mass. (Pianoforte) 1931; [occ.] Retired Music Supervisor, Lewiston, Maine (Public Schools, Elementary - 20 years); [memb.] All the usual Church, School, City, State, National Clubs (Educational.) Not a joiner my family took most of my time.; [hon.] My awards are in my 13 grandchildren. All but 2 are college grads. (And 1 is a wondering musician) and the youngest girl is at Univ. of Maine (2 more years to go); [oth. writ.] I have written children's song and lyrics and used them at school. I have settled late years for poetry writing and song writing; [pers.] My personal belief is to be healthy, happy and honorable. I have tried for 86 years.; [a.] Lewiston, ME

FOGARTY, AMBER S.
[b.] June 16, 1979, Fallbrook, CA; [p.] Theresa Fogarty; [ed.] Currently in 10th grade at Temecula Valley High School; [occ.] Student, Work at Sharp Hospital as a volunteer; [memb.] CSF (Ca. Scholarship Federation), will be in student body government next year, School Tennis Team, Sharp Hospital Volunteer, Globetrotters Club; [hon.] 2nd place in art exhibition (paint media); [oth. writ.] Write at home, but nothing published; [pers.] I believe that freedom leads to living not to do with my poem, the life one has imagined. But freedom cannot be given or taken away, and people need to realize how free they really are and accept it and challenge it. The concept is overwhelming because it unleashes a world most of us don't take the privilege to know, a world radiating within the Earth outside us.; [a.] Temecula, CA

FONTAINE, LAURA
[b.] November 22, 1923, Oxford, NC; [p.] King and Ellie Brown; [m.] Nicholas Potenza, October 1, 1993; [ch.] Anita Tucker, Alisha Fontaine, Leonard Fontaine, Daren Fontaine; [ed.] Meredith College Raleigh N.C., University of Alaska, Anchorage, Alaska Palm Beach Community College, Palm Beach, Florida; [occ.] Retired; [memb.] National Honor Society. I had scholarship to Meredith as "best all around student." I was a member and officer of college choir.; [hon.] No honors in poetry except publication at Meredith College I sang opera in N.Y. at City Opera; [pers.] I think all art is connected beautifully and is a necessary part of life.; [a.] Lake Worth, FL

FONTENOT, CHARLES M.
[b.] January 9, 1940, Lake Charles, LA; [p.] Allen and Hazel (Touchet) Fontenot; [m.] Lucy A., November 16, 1963; [ch.] Kari, David (Deceased August 31, 1986); [occ.] Sales; [oth. writ.] Songs to her son 200 others; [pers.] I started writing at the gravesite of my son David I continue to write today to keep my sanity!!; [a.] San Mateo, CA

FORD, BEN
[pen.] Art Raster; [b.] April 2, 1978, Fort Smith, AR; [p.] David Ford, Ruth Ford; [ed.] Pelham High, Pelham Christian High; [occ.] Student; [oth. writ.] Several poems, essays, and a book, all unpublished; [pers.] I write to inspire change and thus to transcend man's evil nature.; [a.] Pelham, AL

FORD, GWENDOLYN A.
[b.] March 15, 1965, Washington, DC; [ch.] One daughter; [occ.] Aspiring Actress and Writer; [pers.] Always do your best even if it is not good enough for others, be true to your spiritual heart.; [a.] Oxon Hill, MD

FORD, MICHAEL S.
[b.] April 17, 1967, Carbondale, IL; [p.] Glenn and Sandra Ford; [m.] Tina M. Ford, May 30, 1992; [ch.] Ian M. Ford; [ed.] Frankfort Community High School, Southeastern Illinois College; [occ.] Automotive Technician; [a.] Centralia, IL

FORD, RUTH E.
[pen.] Ruth E. Ford; [b.] January 20, 1920, Cincinnati, OH; [p.] Alonzo Turpin, Nancy Turpin; [m.] Rev. James W. Ford (Deceased),

April 9, 1938; [ch.] Gloria B. Shaw; [ed.] New Castle High School, New Castle, IN; [occ.] Homemaker, (Retired Song Evangelist); [memb.] Westside Church of the Nazarene; [oth. writ.] Several unpublished poems and songs; [pers.] I have served as Song Evangelist and Children's Worker for 34 years in the Church of the Nazarene. I have always enjoyed poetry and have written several unpublished poems and songs. I have been blessed by other poets.; [a.] Clearwater, FL

FOREST, RAVEN
[pen.] Raven Forest; [b.] September 9, 1930, Arizona; [ed.] High School and finished Temple of Music and Art sing opera eight years. People say I speak like James Earl Jones; [occ.] Porter for Las Vegas Hilton 18 yrs.; [memb.] Calvary Chapel Church; [hon.] Man of the month at Hilton, and one from president Bush for my writings, full page spread in local paper.; [oth. writ.] "In Case The Children Ask!" 13 small books in one on How To Bring The Children Back Into The Family; [pers.] When I first came to Las Vegas I was on the streets, tried for help from my people, answer-no. Back to town and this church helped me until I got started on the job 18 yrs. ago, and so I wrote a poem about it called "Who Is Raven"; [a.] Las Vegas, NV

FOSTER, ERIC L.
[b.] March 28, 1973, Lebanon, PA; [p.] Rowland and Patricia Foster; [m.] Single; [ed.] 12 years at Private Christian School (Faith Tabernacle School) in Mechanicsburg, PA; [occ.] Meat Dept. Employee at grocery store; [memb.] Faith Tabernacle Church, National Geographic Society; [hon.] This is the first of my writings to every receive such recognition; [oth. writ.] Have written other short poems as gifts or for my own hand made greeting cards. (Drawing is one of my favorite, most satisfying talents and past-times).; [pers.] A good poet is one who is able, with words, to capture an elusive but common thread of life and cause all who read them to see their own heart open upon the page.; [a.] Lebanon, PA

FOSTER-FIEGE, EMMA JEAN
[pen.] Emma Jean Brown; [b.] November 10, 1954, Seattle, WA; [p.] Lee Andrew Harkey, Marlue Winston; [m.] William H. Fiege, May 2, 1990; [ch.] Rachel Matilda Fiege - 4 yrs.; [ed.] Chief Sealth High, City College of San Francisco, School of Fitness and Nutrition of Atlanta Georgia; [occ.] Singer with "Linda Tillery and the Cultural Heritage Choir"; [memb.] Founder of Center For U.S. and World Peace, The Glide Ensemble of Glide Memorial Church in San Francisco, Member since 1980; [hon.] Chief Sealth High School Honor Society, Seattle Washington; [oth. writ.] Stand tall when you're right.; [pers.] My life's mission is! To help others become more honest, healthier, wiser and happy through the music I sing, my writing and the life I live.; [a.] San Francisco, CA

FOSTER, MARY BRYANT
[b.] March 2, 1926, Oklahoma; [p.] Seth and Virgie Bryant; [m.] Divorced; [ch.] Lisa, Bryant, Dave, Marty, Charlie, Scott and Curt; [ed.] MA Degree - West Valley College; [occ.] Retired, Volunteer Poetry Reader; [memb.] For Seniors

Past Pres. PTA and Home and School Club - Los Gatos Friends of the Arts, Los Gatos Museum Assoc., Poetry for everyone circle; [hon.] Dean's List Scholarship - Grand Marshal of annual Christmas Parade, Artist of the year (Poetry); [oth. writ.] 2 books of Haiku - 12 years columnist for Los Gatos times observer. Poetry on request for music in the plaza.; [pers.] Be open to life and let that openness reflect in poetry. It is far more honest and interesting.; [a.] Los Gatos, CA

FOSTER, NATASHA
[b.] July 20, 1979, Marrero, LA; [p.] Jay Foster, Yvonne Cheramie; [ed.] 10th grade Middleton High School; [oth. writ.] Poem published in local newspaper. Poems published in two books (Treasured Poems of America and Voices); [pers.] "Thank You" Daddy.; [a.] Middleton, TN

FOX, PHYLLIS P.
[b.] December 26, 1941, Bloomington, IL; [p.] Mr. and Mrs. Francis C. Moreland; [m.] Donald K. Fox, June 14, 1969; [ch.] Austin K. Fox; [ed.] Music Education AB, MA 28 yrs. Public School and Jr. College Kankakee, IL; [occ.] Public School Music Teacher-Choral Director; [memb.] NEA and University Church of the Nazarene (Member and Choir Member; [hon.] I have had opinion articles plus poems published in the Chicago Sun-Times and local newspapers; [oth. writ.] Soon to be published (a complete curriculum) a reproducible Music History and Appreciation Worksheets Book (11 years in the making) Grades 5-12; [pers.] Poetry is my gift from God. In return, I use this gift to pass on His Spiritual and moral Truths that I have found to bring me personal Truth, Joy, Love and Success.; [a.] Bourbonnais, IL

FOY, SARAH ELIZABETH
[b.] June 11, 1985, Baltimore, MD; [p.] Michael Foy, Mary Foy; [ed.] Currently in 4th Grade attending Lake Shore Christian Academy; [hon.] Honor Roll Student, Penmanship Award 1994; [a.] Pasadena, MD

FRALEY, NICOLE M.
[pen.] Nikki; [b.] July 16, 1980, Marion, OH; [p.] John H. and Mary Fraley; [ed.] I am a 9th grade Student, High School (Northmor) (Elementary School) Iberia, Iberia, OH; [occ.] Student; [pers.] A special thanks to my Mom and Dad. They say follow your dreams, you can do any thing you want to do.; [a.] Galion, OH

FRANCE, MARIE H.
[b.] August 16, 1930, Jonesboro, TN; [m.] Harold L. France, July 9, 1950; [ch.] Alvin Lee, James Kevin; [ed.] Jonesboro High School, Vocational School; [occ.] Retired; [memb.] AARP Chapter and Club Fellowship Chapel Church Pioneer Telephone Club Bristol Virginia Order of Eastern Star America Heart Association; [oth. writ.] Several poems, none published until now.; [pers.] I enjoy writing poems about the beauty of nature, and other subjects of interest.; [a.] Bristol, VA

FRANK, KRISTIN
[b.] October 22, 1981, Pittsburgh, PA; [p.] David and Rise Frank; [ed.] In 9th grade; [a.] North Huntingdon, PA

FRANKS, LAURA J.
[b.] June 24, 1970, Cincinnati; [p.] Harvey and Ethel Huffman; [m.] Brian Franks, September 11, 1993; [ch.] Lindie Nichole Huffman; [ed.] Graduate - Sycamore High School 1988 Cincinnati Ohio, Tri-State Travel School graduate 1990, Cincinnati Ohio; [occ.] (CSA) Customer Service Associate; [memb.] Grassy Rien, Baptist Church Williamstown Kentucky; [hon.] 3rd place Ribbon for poem entered in the 1994 Grant County Fair, entitled, the Road Home; [oth. writ.] (Non published) Mommie's Little Angel, Daddy's Little Girl, I Saw The Light, The Road Home.; [pers.] The poems that I have written are deep and emotional poems that come from the heart, and are very meaningful to me.; [a.] Williamstown, KY

FRASIER, MELANIE PATRICE
[b.] March 16, 1954, Philadelphia, PA; [m.] Divorced; [ch.] Kristin, Kyle and Jonathan; [oth. writ.] Presently working on movie script and novel.; [pers.] There is nothing in my past I wish to recapture. But everything in my future to embrace. Like a book waiting to be read.; [a.] Philadelphia, PA

FRAZER, PAULA
[pen.] P. J. Sylvia; [b.] April 2, 1970, Attleboro, MA; [p.] William Sylvia, Mary Jane Sylvia; [m.] Steven Frazer, May 27, 1988; [ch.] Amanda Lynn, Kelsey Jane; [ed.] Attleboro High, C.C.R.I.; [occ.] Medical Laboratory Technician; [memb.] American Society of Clinical Pathologists, American Society For Clinical Laboratory Science, Clinical Laboratory Science of Central New England; [hon.] National Honor Society, Phi Theta Kappa Clinical Excellence Award given by C.C.R.I and E.S.C.L.; [oth. writ.] Many other poems published and non-published.; [pers.] There is no tomorrow. This moment is all we own.; [a.] Attleboro, MA

FRAZIER, STEPHANIE E.
[b.] July 16, 1970, Savannah, GA; [p.] Stephen Frazier, Vendolyn Frazier; [ed.] Frederick Douglass High, Georgia Institute of Technology, Howard University School of Law; [occ.] Student, Howard Univ. School of Law, Owner, Memories College Memorabilia; [a.] Washington, DC

FRELOT, FREDERICK F.
[b.] June 8, 1968, San Francisco; [p.] Hollis Frelot Jr., Yvonne Frelot; [ed.] Lowell High, San Francisco, Academy of Art, San Francisco; [occ.] Photographer, Videographer, Filmmaker; [memb.] Bay Area Video Coalition, (B.A.V.C.), Film Arts Foundation; [hon.] Published in "Photographer's Forum" yearly annual 1993 and 1994; [pers.] The world creates my artistry, whether it's a film, a photograph, or a poem. I express through these mediums, my life experiences and those of the world, usually with "Maria Callas" or "Kathleen Battle" inspiring me on the C.D. player; [a.] Oakland, CA

FRITZ, DOROTHY H.
[pen.] "Dottie"; [b.] October 27, 1921, Lisburn, PA; [p.] Rev. and Mrs. John H. Hoch; [m.] Melvin L. Fritz, April 8, 1944; [ed.] Uniontown Elementary School, New Windsor High School, total 12 years; [occ.] Homemaker; [memb.] Christian Womens Club of Corrall Co., Member of the Uniontown Bible Church of Uniontown, MD; [hon.] Honorable Mention in a poetry contest; [oth. writ.] I have written many homespun Articles about our little Historic town and my life as a ministers daughter. I have several poems published in our local new newspaper. Also I wrote many poems for our Church Bulletin.; [pers.] I grew up during the depression. My parents were very good Managers. My father had four churches and managed well for his family. Living through those years taught us many values, for which I am thankful, my husband is a Barber and loves gardening as a hobby.; [a.] Uniontown, MD

FROEHLICH, CHERYL A.
[b.] March 5, 1953, Huntington, WV; [p.] Richard and Marianne Andre; [m.] Robert J. Froehlich, October 15, 1977; [ch.] Marianne Elizabeth and Stephanie Marie; [ed.] Belmont High School, University of Dayton, Ohio State University; [pers.] Inspiration for my work is attributed to those people whom I love or have loved.; [a.] Chicago, IL

FRYE, GEORGE DAVID
[b.] August 28, 1957, Gallatin, TN; [p.] George Scott Frye, Robbie Frye; [ed.] Gallatin Sr. High School, Baptist Hospital School of Radiologic Technology - Memphis, TN, School for MRI Technology, Milwaukee, WS; [occ.] MRI Technologist, Baptist Hospital, Nashville TN; [memb.] The American Heart Association - CPR - "BLS Instructor", The American Society of Radiologic Technologists.; [hon.] Various awards in Art, 4-H Club public speaking contests, Beef Cattle Association, Music awards in Marching Band and Concert Band, "Who's Who of American High School Students 1975"; [oth. writ.] Songwriter and Poet - "What to do with Life", "It's a Matter of Time"; [pers.] I write not of the fantasies and could - be's of life, instead the realities, hardships, the joys and the pains. I feel that people should relate to a message.; [a.] Gallatin, TN

FULLER, JEANNE BURT
[pen.] Jeanne Burt Fuller; [b.] June 5, 1918, Jamestown, NY; [p.] Dr. Wallace and Gertrude Burt; [m.] Prescott Fuller (deceased), June 7, 1941; [ch.] David and Susan; [ed.] BA University of Michigan, Masters NYU. Dance Education: Hanya Holm, Martha Graham, Jose Limon.; [occ.] Dancer/Choreographer, Teacher, Lecturer, Arts and Flower Arranging.; [memb.] Deacon United Church of Christ, Pen Women, Federated Garden Clubs Commission, Recycle and Solid Waste Management, Bethel Bible Study, Alpha Omicron PI, Sorority, Darien Community Association, Hospice, Consultant on Bereavement.; [hon.] Volunteer of the Year 1994, Award for Furthering the Arts. Darien Government Award for Community Service. Editor's Choice Award, National Library of Poetry; [oth. writ.] Christmas Poetry, Nature, Children, Poetry narrative parallel to Choreographic works. Published in liturgical publications and hospice international.; [pers.] Let me stand where I am in the great harmonious plan to be aware, alert, to act where there is a lack in my fellow man.; [a.] Darien, CT

FULLER, KATIE
[b.] October 18, 1983, Maryville, TN; [p.] Robin and Kay Fuller; [ed.] 5th grade at present Fort Craig Elementary; [memb.] Caroles School of Baton, Fort Craig Orchestra, Maryville Little League, Dotson Memorial Baptist Church; [pers.] The poem I wrote was about my brother Benny.; [a.] Maryville, TN

FULLER, VINNIE MARIE BUTLER
[b.] January 12, 1959, Chatham, VA; [p.] Bernie Leroy Clark; [m.] (Second Husband) Clyde A. Fuller, November 18, 1989; [ch.] Sheena, Steven Butler; [ed.] 2 years college P.C PG; [occ.] Housewife; [memb.] I am memberships five stare music master song writer's club. I am glad that my soul is in poetry that I write I love that poetry, song I have 6 contract; [pers.] I express myself in poetry and music all my poetry real life my song are real life I live them more everyday. They is on other all my music is writing by me sole copyright.

FULTON, CHRISSY
[pen.] Chrissy Fulton; [b.] July 30, 1978, Jackson, MS; [p.] Margaret and Paul Fulton; [ed.] GED and 2 year Community College, starting this fall.; [oth. writ.] Thunder, Enough is Enough…; [pers.] I was in a Rehab Program for 3 months, which gave me time to concentrate on the more important things in life.; [a.] Brandon, MS

GABET, NAN
[pen.] Montana; [b.] June 2, 1957, Morton Grove, IL; [p.] Lucy Lamott and Harry Ditslear; [ch.] Erika, Jessica, Casandra and Joshua; [ed.] Bishop Luers High School, Ivy Tech College; [occ.] Pediatric Nurse, Parkview Memorial Hospital; [memb.] Pediatric Branch of Stitch and Talk; [hon.] Dean's List; [pers.] I write a broad range of poetry based on personal experience and feelings. These feelings express the thoughts of a great majority of women.; [a.] Fort Wayne, IN

GAFFNEY, IMOGENE
[pen.] Imogene Adkins; [b.] July 6, Elmo, TX; [p.] Earl and Louisa Adkins; [m.] Edward O. Gaffney, July 30, 1955; [ch.] Theresa R. Lawson, Edward O. Gaffney Jr., Orlando, Cyernard, Regina, Darrell; [ed.] Booker T. Washington High Prairie View A and M College; [occ.] Retired nurse take care of disabled husband; [memb.] Disabled Veterans, Holy Trinity Baptist Church, Contributes to Numerous Charitable Organizations; [hon.] Newsday Merit Award Contest (Essay); [oth. writ.] Songs and poems as a hobby. Unfortunately some published poems were lost years ago due to moving.; [pers.] I hope to, and try to show love through my writing. I would like for love to be so contagious that when one touch another hand that he or, she would become infected with same.; [a.] North Babylon, NY

GAGE, RANDA
[b.] August 24, 1979, La Mesa, CA; [p.] Greg and Chris Gage; [ed.] I'm currently a sophomore in High School, I attend El Capitan High in Lakeside, Calif.; [occ.] Student; [hon.] I have received good citizenship, scholarship, top scholar, perfect attendance and honor roll awards I have also won first place and grand prize over all in cake decorating contests.; [oth. writ.] "Hurt" - published

in Echoes of yesterday - "Forever" published in best poems of 95. "Why did I have to say No" to published in East of the Sunrise; [pers.] I enjoy writing poems, and its exciting to see them being published other hobbies I enjoy are horseback riding, roller blading, and jet skiing I also enjoy being with friends. I would like to be a model or actress.; [a.] Lakeside, CA

GAHLER, DIANA
[b.] December 18, 1947, Omaha, NE; [p.] Richard Grant (deceased), Gaynell Grant; [m.] Wayne Gahler, June 27, 1969; [ch.] Kasey Charles Gahler, Korey James Gahler; [ed.] Le Mars Community High School; [occ.] Registered Nursing Assistant - Janesville Nursing Home, Janesville, MN.; [memb.] American Heart Association Church of God of Abrahamic Faith, Omaha, NE; [hon.] Art Award in High School; [oth. writ.] Poems published in Wisdom and Power Magazine, local newspaper.; [pers.] My poems which I have written are all written from personal feelings and events. They are all inspired by God.; [a.] Janesville, MN

GAINES, BRANDI
[pen.] Brandi; [b.] April 7, 1980, Indiana; [p.] Billy and Shelley Gaines; [ed.] Clark Middle School, 8th Grade; [occ.] Student; [memb.] Sacred Heart Church; [pers.] I write poems to express my feelings; [a.] Vincennes, IN

GAINES, CHRISTINE REYNOLDS
[pen.] Peach; [b.] March 2, 1948, Alhambra, CA; [p.] Frank E. Gaines and Barbara J. Gaines; [ch.] Mar Arion, Gabriel Weston and Augustine Elliott (3 sons); [ed.] Newport Harbor H.S., Univ. of Puget College, Wash. Orange Coast College, Calif. Long Beach City College, CA, Palomar Community College, CA; [occ.] Medical Office Mgr, Caterer, Single Parent, etc.; [memb.] Aspen Filmfest Staff, Audubon Society, Smithsonian Institute; [oth. writ.] Poetry published in Aspen (local) Rag. Coyote Bark; [pers.] Don't compromise yourself, you are all you've got! Janis Jophin; [a.] Old Snowmass, CO

GALLEGOS, DIANE
[b.] Pennsylvania; [p.] Diane Elizabeth Adams; [m.] Married; [ch.] Three children, four step-children and twelve grand-children; [hon.] She received "The Poet of Merit Award" from the International Society of Poets in 1993, and was among the first nominees to become a lifetime member of the International Society of Poets Advisory Council. Diane Gallegos was also given the Editors Choice Award from the National Library of Poetry in 1993 and 1994. She was proclaimed one of the Great Poets of 1994 in the book titled, "Great Poets of 1994," International Society of Poets. Her work also appears in "Famous Poets Anthology," published by the Famous Poets Society in 1994, "Best Poems of 1995," International Society of Poets, and "Treasures of America," Sparrowgrass Forum.; [oth. writ.] Several of her poems have been published in Anthologies by the National Library of Poetry, including, "Wind in the Night Sky," "Coming of the Dawn," "Tears of Fire," "Space in Between," "Darkside of the Moon," "Dance on the Harrison," and "Echoes of Yesterday." Books by

Diane Gallegos: "Reflections and Images in Poetry", "Impressions", "A Candle Glows", "Bits and Pieces", "Xpressions", "Observations"

GALLETTI, MARCIA RUTH
[b.] November 22, 1936, Brooklyn, NY; [p.] Nathan and Sadie Jacobs; [m.] Frank Galletti, July 4, 1958; [ch.] Lori Ann, Greg Scott; [ed.] Erasmus Hall H.S. Bklyn, N.Y., B.S. in Education (Honors Oswego) State Univ. of N.Y., Masters Equiv., Bklyn College, Cornell Labor Studies George Meany Labor Studies; [occ.] Labor Relations Spec. USPS, Former reading teacher; [memb.] ASPCA Guardians, WWF, LI Humane Society, IWA, APWV, Seeing Eye, Alzheimer Asso. of L.I., Nature Conservancy; [hon.] Who's Who among students in American Colleges and Univ., Kappa Delta Pi Ed Honor Society, Honorary Life Member NYS PTA, Honorary Life Member Baldwin Historical Society. Eng, Social Studies Honor Society, Presidents Award-United Nations Turtle Bay Philatelic Society, Past President Award Womans American Art, Life Member Shubert School PTA Bronze Award LI, Division USPS, Presidents Award APWV; [oth. writ.] This is my first; [pers.] A man is never so tall as when he stoops to help another.; [a.] Baldwin, NY

GAMALINDA, JOSELITO
[b.] August 27, 1967, Manila, Philippines; [ed.] On "The Eternal Turtle Plan," sporadically trying to finish his last semester at Tyler School of Art for a BFA in painting.; [occ.] Student, Artist, Bartender; [oth. writ.] A box full; [pers.] A practicing "Solipsist", die-hard "Diarist", literary exhibitionist who is "Self-diagnosed" as having: A.D.D., O.C.D., Turrett's, beginning stages of Alzeimer's and mild forms of autism, dyslexia, aphasia and narcolepsy, among other debilities and afflictions.; [a.] Philadelphia, PA

GAMBLER, SHARON SNYDER
[pen.] Cheyanne Wolf; [b.] June 13, 1955, Milwaukee, WI; [p.] John Snyder, Rosemary Snyder; [m.] November 6, 1985; [ch.] Ezra Patrick; [ed.] St. Mary's Academy Milw. Area Tech. College; [occ.] Private duty nurse; [memb.] Share program (helping the homeless) volunteer for the disabled.; [oth. writ.] Several poems published in the reader - San Diego Young Poets; [pers.] This poem is written to someone very special to me. He knows who he is. I have a great appreciation for all poetry (esp. R. Frost, E. A. Poe, C. Sandberg); [a.] La Mesa, CA

GAMLER, CHERIE
[b.] September 12, 1946, Burlington, IA; [p.] Betty and Eugene Tyrrel; [m.] Norman Gamler; [ch.] Darren, Donald, Deborah; [ed.] Burlington High; [occ.] Grocery Cashier; [memb.] Compassionate Friends; [hon.] The good Lord awarded me with 3 beautiful children and they honor me by calling me mother; [oth. writ.] Several poems written for my children, some written lately published in Grief Groups Newsletters; [pers.] Favorite writer Kahil Gibran. Forever in Every Rainbow dedicated to Donald Shartran my son who passed away, Sept. 30, '94.; [a.] Newberg, OR

GANN II, TEDDY
[pen.] T. N. Gann II; [b.] November 14, 1979, Wichita Falls, TX; [p.] Ted Gann and Jackie Gann; [ed.] Still in High School 9th grade (Grapevine High School); [occ.] Student; [hon.] School writing award, recognized by local author.; [oth. writ.] Over 75 poems written, no other published.; [pers.] I look to write mainly on feelings and real-life situations. Edgar Allen Poe is a real inspiration to my writings.; [a.] Grapevine, TX

GARCIA, EMILY N.
[pen.] Emily; [b.] March 15, 1963, Honolulu, HI; [p.] Ranny and Nola Kiaha; [m.] John Garcia (Joe), December 7, 1985; [ch.] Keoni, Kanani, Kawika; [ed.] High School, Grade 12 Diploma, 1 yr. Army National Guard; [occ.] Clerk Office. Computer, Homemaker; [memb.] Shield of Faith Ministry, Praise the Lord Ministry, Freedom Club, Plain Truth Ministry Union Gospel Ministry; [hon.] Honorable Discharge National Guard; [oth. writ.] Faith devotional scriptual writing musical inspiration.; [pers.] I want to thank (God) through Jesus my sweet saviour and Lord. The King who saved my life. Without him I am nothing! Thank you: Pastor Joe and Yvonne Soliz. At shield of faith church.; [a.] Waianae, HI

GARCIA, JOSE LUIS
[pen.] Drama; [b.] September 23, 1973, Santo Domingo; [ed.] Life P.C.T.V. H.S.; [occ.] Dreamer, human being; [pers.] Life belongs to those who really want it, not those who need it.; [a.] Paterson, NJ

GARCIA, MARCELLA A.
[b.] September 22, 1978, Houston, TX; [p.] Norma Calderon and Ed Garcia; [oth. writ.] Set yourself free-published in Between The Raindrops 1995 ed.; [a.] Houston, TX

GARCINI, MELISSA
[b.] December 7, 1974, Houston; [p.] Betty Dorsey; [ed.] Current student at North Harris Community College; [occ.] Receptionist at Sofregaz (Houston); [memb.] Humane Society, Houston Ballet Society; [hon.] Graduated High School (MacArthur H.S.) with honors.; [oth. writ.] Many poems, short stories and plays in personal file, yet to be.; [pers.] Life's games were meant to be conquered by the magic of writing, I have yet to pass "go."; [a.] Houston, TX

GARDNER, SARAH
[pen.] Dandelion Fields; [b.] September 30, 1980, San Diego, CA; [p.] David Gardner and Sharon Gardner; [occ.] High School Student; [memb.] Dorothy Hamill Ice Skating Association, Nautilus Plus Fitness Center; [hon.] 1991 Southern California Young Author's Contest, 1992 Annual LaMesa Middle School Spelling Bee, Honorary Junior Storyteller in the "Tell Me Story Celebration," 1992 Honors Chorus; [oth. writ.] Several poems published in "The Daily California."; [pers.] Always take time each day to notice the simpler things in life that make this world a better place!; [a.] Portland, OR

GARGARITA, NESTOR
[b.] November 8, 1967; [pers.] A shallow and rumbling river may begin, but the tranquility of vastness at its end can be seen.; [a.] NY

GARIG, VICKI
[b.] April 6, 1972, Los Angeles; [p.] Mr. and Mrs. Wayne Garig and Mr. and Mrs. Tom Modisette; [ed.] Lumberton ISD Lumberton TX and East Texas Baptist University Marshall TX; [occ.] A Senior at ETBU; [pers.] Jesus Christ is my inspiration and true poetry comes from the soul.; [a.] Marshall, TX

GARLAND, JENNIFER L.
[pen.] J. L. Garland; [b.] December 7, 1978, Warwick, RI; [p.] Martine Garland, James Garland; [ed.] Tollgate High School 10th grade; [hon.] 3rd grade, 10th grade awards for books, poems, short stories etc.; [oth. writ.] The Black Hole, story story. Kayla, short story. Dragon and Fire Flies, poem. These were the only one published in newspapers and magazines.; [pers.] Try not to take anything in life too seriously. Face any obstacles with an open mind and an optimistic outlook and remember, a hundred laughs a day, reezes depression away! This poem is dedicated to my mother, who first peaked my interest on reading and writing.; [a.] Warwick, RI

GARNER, CYNDI
[b.] November 17, 1969, Caldwell, ID; [p.] Karen Hardcastle, Gwen Duree; [m.] James D. Garner, October 9, 1987; [ch.] Derrick Allen Garner; [ed.] Notus High School; [hon.] 1988 Class Valedictorian - Notus High School; [oth. writ.] Several poems wrote for family and friends; [a.] Kapolei, HI

GAST, FLORA J.
[b.] March 20, 1931, Sioux City, IA; [p.] Rev and Mrs. William Krummel; [m.] Clifford Gast (deceased), September 18, 1954; [ch.] Bill Gast - Cheryl Parmenter; [ed.] Baroda High School, Nursing School; [occ.] Retired - handicapped; [memb.] St. Joseph Senior Center, Stevensville American Legion Aux., Zion's U.C.C. Baroda, MI; [hon.] President of Women's Fellowship at Zion's U.C.C. 16 years member of American Legion Auxiliary - Post 568 - Stevensville, MI; [oth. writ.] Publishing in last years "Dance on the Horizon", local papers.; [pers.] Writing poetry is a soothing to my wounded soul!; [a.] Stevensville, MI

GATSON, ANNETTE D.
[pen.] Totti; [b.] July 4, 1964, Baltimore, MD; [p.] John and Patricia Blake; [m.] Elijah A. Gatson, March 21, 1985; [ch.] Brandon Gatson, Ryan Gatson, Mardell Gatson, Aijah Gatson, Armon Gatson; [ed.] High School Graduate, Carver Voc. Tech H.S.; [occ.] Supervisor for Helpmates Professional Cleaning; [memb.] Missionary at True Holiness Church of God.; [oth. writ.] Songs, books, birthday cards, sympathy cards, wedding vows holiday poems, reunions, anniversary cards, and friendship cards.; [pers.] I'm just trying to get the word of the Lord out to those that don't know who he is. I enjoy working for the Lord and doing his will.; [a.] Baltimore, MD

GATTA, PAMELA LYNN
[b.] March 13, 1969, Connecticut; [p.] Yolanda Gatta; [ed.] Ansonia High School, Southern Ct State Univ.; [hon.] High School Valedictorian, Dean's List at SCSU; [oth. writ.] Several unpublished short stories, contributed to award winning yearbook, The Lavendar; [pers.] My mother is the one who inspired me to "write about

something meaningful", this poem is about the stray cat who came to us 15 years ago and is still here.; [a.] Ansonia, CT

GAY, JUDI
[pen.] Judith Shepherd-Gay; [b.] December 10, 1948, Hope, ME; [p.] Ethel and Rev. Leslie Shepherd; [m.] Thomas, July 1968; [ch.] Three; [ed.] Attended the Univ. of Wisc La Crosse, Tarrant County Junior College Hurst Texas, and currently pursuing a Bachelor of Elective Studies degree at St. Claud State Univ., St. Cloud, MN; [occ.] Director of Volunteer Ministers and Youth Minister; [memb.] National Assoc. of Lay Ministry Association of Volunteer Administration; [hon.] Honor Society, Phi Theta Kappat at Tarrant County Junior College; [pers.] Writing prose is one way of exploring the struggles life presents, to find hope. Writing moves us through the darkness toward healing. Writing clears a path.; [a.] Annandale, MN

GAY, VICTORIA
[b.] July 11, 1960, Columbia, TN; [p.] Mr. and Mrs. Bob Sanders, Larry Wells; [m.] Jeffrey D. Gay, January 30, 1992; [ch.] David Gay; [ed.] B.A. in French from Middle Tennessee State Univ., completing graduate work in English at MTSU; [occ.] Teacher for JTPA; [a.] Columbia, TN

GEHRIG, LOIS
[pen.] Mar Lyn; [b.] June 24, 1939, Fairfield, ID; [p.] Donna Lee Behunin; [ch.] Robert, Gehrig, Billi Miles; [ed.] College - Vocational Graduate; [occ.] Woodworker; [memb.] Magic Valley Wood Workers - Advisory Councils, ITL Society of poets, CSI, Center Jorhew Directions Advisory Council; [hon.] Award Winning poem appears in different publications i.e. "Breakout", Eagles Eye, poetry anthologies; [oth. writ.] Short stories, 2 books of poetry published. Working on another book.; [pers.] Yesterday I didn't know I could, today I don't know I can't, tomorrow I know I will.; [a.] Jerome, ID

GEHRKE, PATRICIA
[b.] March 25, 1958, Niagara Falls, NY; [p.] Mildred and Paul Gehrke; [ch.] Timothy Gehrke (17) whom I love and helped me; [ed.] 1 yr. Business College; [occ.] Cook/Waitress at Beechies Place in Meadowlands; [hon.] First line should read: Several honor roll achievement award, girl...; [pers.] Rod McKuen inspired me, I always wanted to meet him. Many thanks to my family and friends, who believed in me.; [a.] Houston, PA

GERLT, CARLA S.
[b.] July 19, 1962, Versailles, MO; [p.] Loren Boatright, Zella Boatright; [m.] Jerry W. Gerlt, September 4, 1981; [ch.] Daniel Wayne, Lucus Irvin, Bethany Lauren; [ed.] Morgan County R-I High School; [occ.] Live on family farm with husband and children, we raise registered Angus Cattle, crops and hogs.; [memb.] Trinity Southern Baptist Church, American Angus and Missouri Angus Association; [hon.] Salutatorian of Graduating Class; [oth. writ.] Several poems and versus personalized to be shared with family and friends.; [pers.] Seven years ago I was diagnosed with degenerative disc disease in my back. I have had four back surgeries and am facing more. Being forced to give up several activities that I

enjoyed doing, the Lord has given me my writing as a way to deal with my pain and frustration. Being able to share words of encouragement and love to others has given me the encouragement I have needed to go on.; [a.] Barnett, MO

GERSTNER, JOELY SLATER
[pen.] Blake, Jenna Blake; [b.] May 28, 1969, Topeka, KS; [p.] Tamara Olson; [m.] Andrew Gerstner, May 28, 1994; [ch.] Dominick Anjoel, Emma Blake; [ed.] Washburn University, Adam Roaekes Film Actors Lab; [occ.] Advertising Consultant; [memb.] Northland Christian Church, FARM (Farm Animal Rehabilitation Movement) PETA (people for the Ethical treatment of animals), American Diabetes Assoc.; [hon.] Various Oratorical, Forensics and Debate Medals, Trophies etc.; [oth. writ.] Many poems including "A poem for a Pirate", "Unrequited" short stories, songs, articles. A novel "Orange Flip" in progress.; [pers.] I try to write based on raw emotion, reality graced by fantasy. I am a vegetarian.; [a.] Topeka, KS

GETZINGER, MICHELLE
[pen.] Michelle Saam; [b.] November 11, 1970, Fremont, OH; [p.] Janice Wollam Donald Saam; [m.] Walter Getzinger II, August 19, 1989; [ch.] Christopher, Walter III, Ashley, Karen; [ed.] Lakota High School Kansas, OH; [occ.] Waitress at Po Folks Woodstock, GA; [memb.] Girton Church of God Risingsun, Ohio; [oth. writ.] Two letters of recognition from companies in Connecticut and Iowa; [pers.] I lost my father when I was 14 that was my inspiration and I found comfort in my poems. I strife to help comfort others through my writing.; [a.] Canton, GA

GIBBONS, HELEN CLARK
[b.] April 12, 1937, New Milford; [p.] Morris D. & Frances Winters Clark; [m.] Edwin M. Gibbons, June 15, 1957; [ch.] Betsey, Cynthia, Edwin II, Samantha, Beverly and Michael; [grandch.] Gregory, Joey, Amber, Tyler & Zachary; [ed.] Woodbury Public Schools, graduated Woodbury High School Class of 1956; [occ.] Para-Educator for New Milford Public School System; part-time clerk in the Video World store in Woodbury and New Milford; [hon.] Appeared on Good Morning America and Positively Connecticut with my animals, Editor's Choice Awards; [oth. writ.] Published "A Gift of Beauty" in At Day's End, "A Place to Feast" in Echoes of Yesterday, "Night Flight" in Best Poems of 1995. "Someone Else's Homeplace" scheduled for publication in Winter 1995, "Winter's Masterpiece" published in Treasured Poems of America 1995, modeled for a book This is the Farmer written and illustrated by Nancy Tafuri of Roxbury, CT; [pers.] Live every day to its fullest, always know that there is someone out there just a little bit better than you, and no matter how good you do something, there's always room to do a little better; [a.] Woodbury, CT.

GIBBONS, KEVIN J.
[b.] MaALy 13, 1955, Pittsburgh; [p.] Louise A. and the late John J. Gibbons; [ed.] Apollo-Ridge School District, Clarion State Teachers College, Pennsylvania State Police Southwest, Regional Training Center; [occ.] Police Officer; [memb.] First Lutheran Church, Apollo #2 Volunteer Fire Dept., Fraternal Order of Police, Kittanning

Firemens Band, Armstrong Police Association; [hon.] National Police Hall of Fame (Silver Star for Bravery); [pers.] My personal goals and successes in life have been based upon the support and influence of my mother and father. My love for them and their presence will never go unnoticed or unmentioned for as long as I live.; [a.] North Apollo, PA

GIBEAU, DANE J.
[b.] February 24, 1969, Massachusetts; [p.] Dana Gibeau, Cynthia Gibeau; [m.] Colleen M. Gibeau, June 22 1991; [ed.] McCann Technical School; [pers.] I try to write simple down to earth poetry. I want to reach more people and make my poetry more enjoyable. I owe great thanks to James Douglas Morrison who influence me to write.; [a.] Cheshire, MA

GIBNEY, JOCELYN
[b.] October 15, 1977, Somerville; [p.] John, Jean Gibney; [ed.] Dunellen High School; [occ.] Work in Day Care Center; [memb.] Day Care Assistant; [hon.] "I Dare You Award", National Art Honor Society Award, Earth Awareness Award; [oth. writ.] School Literary Magazine (Editor); [pers.] My poetry is simply my thoughts and views on topics written down. My intentions are to have people read and understand my thoughts while expanding their own.; [a.] Dunellen, NJ

GIBSON, HAZEL FERN
[pen.] Hazel Fern Gibson; [b.] June 30, 1919, Canute, OK; [p.] Elsie and Bodine Keas; [m.] Billy Gibson, April 13, 1972; [ch.] Donald Ray Wilson, James Kennith, and Tommy Joe Wilson; [ed.] High School Graduate, College Graduate, B.S. Degree, Vocational Home Economic Teacher, 13 yrs., Owned and Operated Drapery Shop 20 yrs., Minor in College Art; [occ.] Retired teacher, Do craft work and deal in antiques; [oth. writ.] Many poem such as "The Preacher" etc.; [a.] Canute, OK

GILBERT, LACY T.
[b.] November 21, 1978, Lewistown, PA; [p.] John A. C. Gilbert and Clare Ann Gilbert; [ed.] Indian Valley High School; [occ.] Student; [memb.] Key Club, Drama Club, French Club, Band Front, Y.M.C.A. (Tae Kwon Do); [hon.] Indian Valley High School League of Distinction 1993-94.; [pers.] When we look beyond our narrow way of expressing feelings we find a whole new world within ourselves.; [a.] Reedsville, PA

GILLIEN, NANCY R.
[b.] June 6, 1946, Pueblo, CO; [p.] Robert and Nadine Anderson; [m.] Divorced; [ch.] Danial Shawn, Kelli, Michelle and Christopher Matthew; [ed.] Centennial High, Pueblo Community College, Univ. of Southern Colorado; [occ.] Correctional Officer; [oth. writ.] I have written for years but this is the first time I've ever sent anything in.; [pers.] My greatest joy would be to write with the genius of Edgar Allan Poe, John Keats or William Yeats. Their works have given me much pleasure.; [a.] Pueblo, CO

GIVENS, DOROTHY WILLIAMS
[b.] February 14, 1943, Kingston, MD; [p.] Mary E. Ames; [ch.] Deirdrie Lynnette; [ed.] Woodson High, Bowie State University, Salisbury State University; [occ.] Elementary Teacher Fruitland Primary, Fruitland, Md.; [memb.] Waters Chapel United Methodist Church; [oth. writ.] Several poems and short stories, unpublished; [a.] Salisbury, MD

GLASSCOCK, BILLIE
[pen.] Billie Glasscock; [b.] June 24, 1932, Texas; [p.] Mr. and Mrs. C. V. Simmons; [m.] Jack M. Glasscock, October 21, 1950; [ch.] Stephen D. Glasscock, Stuart D. Glasscock; [occ.] Housewife; [memb.] Ladies of Oriental Shrine, Oak Ridge Baptist Church; [pers.] Inspired by the love and enjoyment of my children. Also my love of nature.; [a.] Houston, TX

GLENN, DALE W.
[b.] August 28, 1939, Hoopeston, IL; [p.] Mr. and Mrs. Herbert E. Glenn; [m.] Joyce, June 14, 1959; [ed.] B.S. Eastern Ill. Univ. M. Ed. Univ. of Ill.; [occ.] Spec. Ed. Teacher (Ret.); [hon.] Kappa Delta Pi, Phi Alpha Theta; [oth. writ.] The Wolf, Remember Me, The Children's Eyes, Lady of the Street, Little Girl in the Garden, The Old Man, Treasure Lost, The Journey, Dad's Rocking Chair, The Long, Long Road; [pers.] "Remember me, all whom I knew I did the best that I could do forgive my trespasses unintended and remember me well - when this is all ended" (D. W. Glenn); [a.] Shorewood, IL

GLENZER, SHIRLEY
[b.] March 10, 1930, Sheboygan Falls, WI; [p.] Warren and "Rose Tehennepe" Hokanson; [m.] Gilbert Glenzer, December 9, 1950; [ch.] William, David, Susan, Kathleen and Margaret; [ed.] Elementary School for 9 years. Had remotovation classes back to reality for the aged and mentally sick (Waukesha County); [occ.] House wife and a shed at a flea market in Adams Wisconsin; [memb.] Calvary United Methodist Ladies Guild. Royal Neighbors of America Help with the four year olds by reading to them at the Coloma Library; [pers.] I believe every family should pray together - read together and follow the ten commandments. To love themselves and each other.

GLORSKY, MICHELLE
[b.] October 28, 1980, Florida; [p.] Alba Glorsky; [ed.] Jewish Community Day School; [occ.] Student; [memb.] Band; [hon.] Gifted program (at Jewish Comm. Day School), Science Fair (7th grade), Honorable Mention, (8th grade), Honorable Mention, Honor Roll, 1st place science fair (3rd grade), Karate awards 1 trophy; [oth. writ.] 3rd grade newspaper, literature class (poetry), literature class (essays), the poem was printed in school bulletin.; [pers.] Tired of being tired, I got tired of asking the world, why? Why? The flowers along the way I could not see see people had offered what they could. From now on you will see me wandering sailing the roads on the four winds free to wonder and be me.; [a.] Lake Worth, FL

GLOVER, KATHERYN
[b.] September 3, 1973, California; [p.] Mitchell Glover and Charlotte Oldham; [ed.] Graduated from Weatherford High School in Weatherford, Texas. I am currently enrolled in the University of Texas at Arlington; [oth. writ.] I was the copy editor of my school yearbook The Melon-Vine.; [a.] Weatherford, TX

GOFORTH, MARY E.
[b.] September 9, 1922, Barnesville, OH; [p.] Frederick and Lola Davey; [m.] Richard E. Goforth, September 9, 1944; [ch.] Diane L. Goforth-Ohning; [ed.] Master's in Education; [occ.] Retired teacher; [hon.] Teacher of the year Indian Valley Schools 1985, Listed in Who's Who Among Americas Teachers in 1990, 1992, 1994, Who's Who in the world 1995, Martha Holden Jennings Scholar; [oth. writ.] Several articles; [pers.] Oh, to leave behind some fine and glorious thing so vital to the spark of truth that there a searching thought could cling, and turn to real the dream of all that is, or ever will be, the all encompassing supreme.; [a.] New Philadelphia, OH

GOGAN, PATRICIA ANN KARAS
[m.] Brian Gogan; [ch.] "Ms. Abigail"; [ed.] Brockton High, Massasoit Community College; [occ.] Secretary; [memb.] MSPCA, National Arbor Day Foundation; [hon.] Honor Roll, Dean's List; [oth. writ.] Small contests in school newspapers.; [pers.] Thank you to: The Luti family, Tracey and Denise, the Sullivan family, and Brian - my first love! Also, to Richard: For all your patience, encouragement, lessons, and most of all, for listening.; [a.] Brockton, MA

GOLBURG, BRANDON A.
[b.] January 23, 1983; [p.] Holly Dare, Keith Golburg; [occ.] Student, entering Jr. High in fall; [oth. writ.] Toilet Man, published in a newspaper, Water Spirits, published in anthology of poetry by Young Americans; [pers.] I have always been interested in writing and would like my life's occupation to be in this field.; [a.] Faribault, MN

GOLLBERG, MAXINE
[b.] September 29, 1922, Galveston, TX; [p.] Charlie and Nettie Johansson; [m.] Bertrand K. Gollberg, August 15, 1946; [ch.] Gregory Edward; [ed.] High School; [occ.] Retired; [memb.] St. George's Episcopal Church Texas City Country Club, The-700-Club, other clubs and sorority; [oth. writ.] Many poems and prose in my collection besides "Break the Dried Stem of the Basil"; [pers.] "Gems from Jesus, He placed within my heart, He's the source, I'm the recipient, let me share with you".; [a.] Boise, ID

GOLLING, JENNIFER
[b.] April 20, 1978, San Jose, CA; [p.] James Golling and Debra Ferraro; [ed.] Leigh High School; [occ.] Student; [pers.] Carpe Diem!; [a.] San Jose, CA

GONZALEZ, JOE LOUIS
[pen.] Jlg/Joe Lewis; [b.] October 16, 1949, Habana, Cuba; [p.] Joseph A. Gonzalez, Mary C. Gonzalez; [ed.] Chautauqua Univ., ongoing studies under private grant.; [occ.] Being mankind; [hon.] Chosen Excellence in the Pictorial Word, Bs. As. '86, 3 Poems published in III Novel Poetry Contest, Bs. As., Argentina, '92/others...; [oth. writ.] About ten trunkfuls, "sans" publication... (Lord, hasten to my aid, for they languish away... PS: It's OK if Your Providence hasn't another way, - I must write, - as Rilke said...; [pers.] "The Tao that can be expressed is not the true Tao" (Lao - Tzu). "Yeah, but if you don't Sing your Song you strike out" (me).; [a.] Miami, FL

GONZALEZ, MICHELE
[b.] August 2, 1972, Vineland, NJ; [p.] Frank and Ruthann Magnan; [m.] Luis A. Gonzalez Jr., October 15, 1994; [ch.] Shane Michael Gonzalez; [ed.] Vineland High School, Star Technical Institute; [memb.] American Heart Association; [hon.] Who's Who Among American High School Students, Cardiopulmonary Resuscitation and Emergency Cardiac Care Provider; [pers.] Live for to the fullest. Live happily day to day never live for tomorrow for we were not promised tomorrow.; [a.] Newfield, NJ

GONZALEZ, VERONICA H.
[pen.] V.H.G.; [b.] January 4, 1973, Hollywood, CA; [p.] Magdalena Hernandez, Leopoldo Gonzalez; [ed.] Graduate of Francisco Bravo Med. Magnet High School, Brief attendance at Pasadena City College, Currently attending Glendale City College; [occ.] Barista at Starbucks, coffee, student; [hon.] Several high achievement awards for writing ability and accomplishments during high school, recognition in drama and speech; [pers.] I am a firm believer in artistic expression. I feel that it allows us to share the beauty and magic contained within our souls, with the entire world. This in turn, causes somewhat of a chain reaction, where each person you touch with your magic, may have something ignited in them to offer the world.; [a.] Los Angeles, CA

GOOD, MARGARET
[b.] February 4, 1933, New Mexico; [p.] Claude and Bertha Brown; [m.] Paul W. Good; [ch.] Three; [occ.] Retired; [pers.] I usually write about specific places, events, peoples, which I am familiar with.; [a.] Stephenville, TX

GOODMAN, ALICIA M.
[pen.] Shelbi Caine; [b.] March 1, 1976, Dallas; [p.] Robert and Betty; [ed.] Plano Senior High Freshman at Collin County Community College; [occ.] Student/waitress at Outback Steakhouse; [memb.] MS Society of Dallas (Yearly Bank One Super Cities Walk); [hon.] Who's Who for Four Consecutive Years; [oth. writ.] Several poems of which none have been published; [pers.] I hope to give each reader an individual key to open the door to my heart. I hope the reader will undergo the same feelings. I reflect in my poetry.; [a.] Plano, TX

GOODMAN, MARCIA
[pen.] Marcia Goodman; [b.] April 26, 1938, Bronx, NY; [p.] Florence and Henry Pegrish; [m.] William, August 5, 1959; [ch.] Edmund (35) Lawyer, Laura (33) Teacher; [ed.] Graduate of State Univ. of NY, Major - Human Behavior and Development; [occ.] Retired, Personnel Assistant; [memb.] R'nai B'rith Women, Smithsonian, Holocaust Memorial; [oth. writ.] Poem received honorable mention and printed in newspaper contest. Written two books on choices and life after death.; [pers.] I find that writing down my feelings and thoughts helps me to cope with any problems that may occur.; [a.] Boynton Beach, FL

GORLEY, CHRIS
[b.] July 19, 1950, Nampa, ID; [p.] Richard and Gene Gorley; [ed.] Washington State University 1972; [occ.] Writer/Consultant, Seattle, Washing-

ton; [memb.] Big Sisters; [hon.] 1983 AAF Western Region, Bellevue Downtown Association 1989; [oth. writ.] Several works of non-fiction published in annual reports, local newspapers, and promotional communications. Several fictional works in progress.; [pers.] I try to reflect human emotion in my work - from elation to one's lowest moments - and the questioning of it all. A significant influence is Irish writer Edna O'Brien, plus the Romantic poets.; [a.] Seattle, WA

GOULART, NORA
[b.] February 10, Canada; [p.] Joseph and Nora Ward; [m.] John Goulart, October 31, 1993; [ch.] Steven Moir, stepsons - Nathan and Ryan Goulart; [ed.] High School - General Mercer, Toronto Ont., Canada; [occ.] Homemaker; [oth. writ.] Other poems.; [pers.] I strive for family closeness. Good friends helping others.; [a.] Newark, CA

GOWEN, MARK ALLEN
[pen.] Schlummy; [b.] March 7, 1979, Washington, DC; [p.] James Leon Gowen Sr. and Easter Mary Gowen; [ed.] Bishop McNamara High School, Forestville, MD; [occ.] Student at Bishop McNamara High School; [memb.] National Church of God, National Honor Society of Bishop McNamara High School; [hon.] Honor Roll Student; [pers.] Nothing is worth doing unless you are going to give it your all, and do your best.; [a.] Fort Washington, MD

GRAMONT, ALAN
[b.] February 14, 1972, Chicago, CA; [p.] Alan and Linda Gramont; [m.] Heather, June 24, 1995; [ed.] Senior at St. Cloud, State University pursuing degree in English; [occ.] Waiter; [memb.] Kickers Inc., Martial Arts Institute; [oth. writ.] Countless unpublished words; [pers.] I owe all my success to my failure to give in to everyone who says "that's impossible!"; [a.] Saint Cloud, MN

GRAND-JEAN, LAURA
[b.] June 4, 1976, Evanston, IL; [p.] Frances Bowers and Steven Grand-Jean; [ed.] Graduate of the Francis W Paruer School; [occ.] Rider of Horses; [oth. writ.] Several poems and short stories that I wrote purely for pleasure or to express my emotions to myself and others.; [pers.] Writing to me is an exercise much like breathing automatic and necessary. I write for myself. To express joy, and exercise the demons we all have within ourselves.; [a.] Southern Pines, NC

GRANT, BARBARA B.
[pen.] Barby Gee; [b.] July 25, 1931, Greenville, SC; [p.] Alvin and Louvenia Anderson; [m.] Chester E., July 3, 1951; [ch.] Kay, Donna, and Anna; [ed.] Parker High School - Greenville S.C.; [occ.] Retired; [memb.] Life time membership in Texas Driver and Traffic Safety Association American Heart Association, American Cancer Society; [hon.] Award for Excellence for work on Texas State Safety magazine. Awarded and Outstanding award for work in the local TDTSEA association.; [oth. writ.] Several poems, and newspaper articles; [pers.] Dedicate this poem to Gwendolyn Farmer deceased, but very much remembered. She was a great teacher, for all who knew her.

GRANT, KUMAYA U.
[b.] September 22, 1983, San Francisco, CA; [p.] Jimmy and Malorie Grant; [ed.] Arts School, Destiny Arts Center, Dance, Kung Fu, Theater, Sports (Soccer, Football, Basketball, Swimming, Biking).; [occ.] Student at the "Art School" in Oakland.; [memb.] Destiny Arts Center Performance Team; [hon.] 6 Certificates, (2 poems) second place conflict manger, 1 Kung Fu, 1 Bungee Jump, 1 Bravest Horse Back Rider, 2 Medals (4th place in formes for kung fu, and 1st place for judo in kung fu).; [oth. writ.] Poems and stories; [a.] Oakland, CA

GRAVES, MELANIE K.
[b.] April 4, 1958, Cleveland, OH; [p.] Rose and Lloyd Bish; [m.] Gordon S. Graves, April 27, 1991; [ch.] Brent Ryan and Craig Douglas; [ed.] Eastlake North High School, Lakeland Comm. College, John Carroll Univ.; [occ.] Office Manager of a CPA firm; [pers.] Inspiration for my poems is provided by my two sons. Everything is so different when seen through the eyes of children. We all should enjoy the world around us.; [a.] Willowick, OH

GRAVITT, BETTY
[b.] September 12, 1946, Lumpkin Co., GA; [p.] Sam and Beatrice Chester; [m.] Gwendell W. Gravitt Sr., June 14, 1963; [ch.] Three boys and 2 daughters, seven grandchildren; [occ.] Housewife; [oth. writ.] This is my first publication: I have other poems but have never entered or shown them.; [pers.] If I can touch one person's life with my poems then I have lived, not just passed this way. I write what I feel. My words are a part of me.; [a.] Dahlonega, GA

GRAY, STANLEY T.
[pen.] Tad Grainer; [b.] July 10, 1934, Ford City, PA; [p.] Stanley M. and Evelyn E. Gray; [ed.] Ford City High, San Diego Mesa College; [occ.] Retired U.S. Navy, Retired Engineer Civilian Industry; [memb.] Fleet Reserve Association; [oth. writ.] Various poems published in local newspapers several defense related articles; [pers.] I strive to convey in verse my heartfelt love for life; [a.] Kittanning, PA

GREEN, ALESHIA
[b.] July 9, 1960, Festus; [p.] Juanita Ruth and Henry Alexander Lucas; [ch.] Shannon Renee (1-14-78), Latrisha Marie (7-9-84), Miranda Nicole (4-15-86); [ed.] Hillsboro High - currently enrolled with American School of Chicago; [occ.] Certified Nurses Assistant; [pers.] Enjoy the poetry of Robert Frost. Been writing poetry as long as I can remember. Hoping to get into song writing.; [a.] Festus, MO

GREEN, MARTINA L.
[b.] March 9, 1963, Clinton, MD; [p.] Mary Ellen and James C. Green (both deceased); [ed.] Surrattsville High some College; [occ.] Administrative Assistant at Mental Health Assoc. in Waldorf, MD born raised and lived in same family home for 31 years.; [oth. writ.] Unpublished book "Last Ditch Effort - Maybe" a collection of 50 over poems - I've always needed strong emotional situations to write successfully.; [pers.] Ephesians

2:8,9 - "For by grace cure ye saved through faith, and that gift of God: Not of works, least any man should boast."; [a.] Waldorf, MD

GREENE, RODNEY
[pers.] As a young man venturing out... with thoughts of home, inspired and dedicated with love to my "Mom" Bernice Cephas Greene of Philadelphia, PA

GREENHILL, FONDA E. CURRY
[pen.] Fonda Curry; [b.] August 23, 1964, Fort Eustis, VA; [p.] Odessa Cohen Maggie Richardson Odell Richardson; [m.] Anthony Greenhill, May 27, 1989; [ch.] Fevia Marshalle and Ferin Beatrice; [ed.] Warwick High School, Newport News, Va., Hampton Institute, Hampton, VA.; [occ.] Aeronautical Information Specialist, Federal Aviation Administration; [memb.] Air Force Sergeants Association, National Black Coalition of Federal Aviation Employees, Mount Calvary Baptist Women's Choir; [hon.] Scholarship from Delta Sigma Theta, NN VA Chapter, 3rd Runner up Miss Black Teenage World of Newport News; [pers.] For it is written in red letter Matthew 25:15 "To one he gave five talents of money, to another two talents, and to another one talent each according to his own ability. Then he went on his journey." God has blessed me with man talents, this is just one of many ways I praise Him. No deposit, no return.; [a.] Manassas Park, VA

GREINER, STEPHANIE
[pen.] S. Moore; [b.] August 10, 1981, Fairfield, CA; [p.] Frances Greiner; [ed.] Echo Mountain, Elementary School, Foothills Elementary School (Junior High); [occ.] Full time student; [memb.] Uffy Young Women's Society, Students Against Drug Addiction (SADA), (SADD) Students Against Drunk Driving.; [hon.] Honorable mentions for poetry and literary works, AIMS (accelerated learning program); [oth. writ.] Several other poems (unpublished), two childrens' books (unpublished); [pers.] Always ask yourself the questions behind the reality of life, for if the answers are not found within, the truth shall never be known.; [a.] Glendale, AZ

GRIEGER, RUTH
[b.] July 31, 1921, Morocco, IN; [p.] George and Bethel Guinn Clarkson; [m.] James H. Grieger, June 16, 1946; [ch.] Sally, Michael, and Patrick; [ed.] Morocco High School, Morocco, IN, Ball State Univ., Muncie, IN, Valparaiso Univ., Purdue University; [occ.] Enjoying writing in retirement after teaching 32 years music and english.; [memb.] Teachers' Organizations, Various church and Parent Organizations (The above organizations need not be mentioned since I no longer am active in them.); [oth. writ.] Poetry, Essays, and Journals; [pers.] In any of life's situations lies a poem waiting to be created. Favorite poets: Carl Sandburg Robert Penn Warren; [a.] Hanna, IN

GRIFFIN, GYNETH A.
[b.] July 8, 1921, Wisconsin; [p.] Ernest and Ethel (Parfrey) Gray; [m.] Arno C. Griffin, June 10, 1989; [ch.] Gary Rubin, Randy Griffin, Sheila McCanley; [ed.] Three years of college; [occ.] Retired Dairy Farmers.; [memb.] Free Methodist Church; [oth. writ.] Just poems.; [pers.] I knit,

crochet and bake things to sell to sponsor two children in Haiti. We are planning a rummage and bake sale April 22 in the rec room. I plan to take hot homemade noodles and canned beef as well as cinnamons rolls fried fruit pies.; [a.] Richland Center, WI

GRIGGS, JOANN
[b.] October 21, 1958, Louisville, KY; [occ.] Owner of housecleaning business/Public Speaker/ Writer; [memb.] Optimist International, Toast Masters; [oth. writ.] Poems published in various anthologies and one in changes magazine. Also numerous newspaper articles; [pers.] Poetry has been described as an overflow of powerful emotions. Mine certainly is that. My life has taken me through many powerful experiences, some beautiful, some devastating. My poetry is my heart. It is me. I believe that no matter where you are or what's happened to you, you can rise above it. My message is always "Never give up. That's the only way you won't make it."; [a.] Raleigh, NC

GRINSTEAD, JESSIE ALYENE
[pen.] Mind Dancer; [b.] February 12, 1952, Forth Smith, AR; [p.] Tommy Dattron, Dorothey Daffron; [m.] Ralph Alfred Grinstead; [ch.] Eugene and Adrian; [ed.] Greenwood High School; [occ.] Carpenter; [memb.] First Baptist Church Midland, Arkansas; [oth. Writ.] Article for Tempe Tribune, Tempe, AZ.; [pers.] I write what I feel and see around me in everyday life, I hope my words heal someone's pain and bring a smile to their faces.; [a.] Tempe, AZ

GRITTS, DENE STEWART
[pen.] Dino; [b.] December 29, 1953, Moab, UT; [p.] Edith Black and Harold Stewart; [m.] Robert Joe Gritts, February 29, 1992; [ch.] Mingo Joe age 21, Eli Spencer age 18, Keera Mariah age 12; [ed.] Graduated 1972 from Grand County High, Moab, Utah; extensive vocal training from coaches around the world; [occ.] Freelance writer/singer (Opera) and dance teacher; [memb.] Board member of Scripts Ranch musical theater in San Diego CA, and Moab Community theater; active member of "Church of Jesus Christ of Latter Day Saints;" [hon.] Guest Singer for many concerts, pageants, fairs, conventions and songs for Keny radio for 3 years and songs as member of Utah Opera Company. My favorite honor is being wife and mother; [oth. writ.] Poems, children's books, newspaper articles and commercials. I hope to have the children's books published someday as well as new poems; [pers.] I believe in going against the odds especially here in this great nations. I feel one should... "See it, believe in it, reach for it, and be it!" [a.] Las Vegas, NV

GROMOWSKY, SAMUEL
[b.] November 20, 1964, Kansas City, MO; [p.] Samuel and Mary Gromowsky; [m.] Beth Rami Freishtat; [ed.] Rockhurst H.S., Univ. of Mo. Columbia, Univ. of Mo. - Kansas City, Univ. of Iowa - Iowa City, John F. Kennedy University; [occ.] Multi-media visual artist, teacher, musician and composer; [hon.] City awards for ceramics, dean's list; [oth. writ.] Numerous poems and song lyrics written over fifteen year span; [a.] Berkeley, CA

GRUBER, LAURA KATHERINE
[b.] August 24, 1975, Saint Louis; [p.] Janet and Joseph Gruber; [ed.] Affton High School, Southwest Missouri State University - theatre performance major; [occ.] Full time student; [memb.] International Thespian Society, Phi Eta Sigma, National Honor Society; [oth. writ.] "Unwanted" published in "Reflections of Light"; [pers.] "Don't let the ceiling keep you from touching the stars." — Sam Beckett; [a.] Saint Louis, MO

GUEST, ROSELINE
[pen.] Doris Sawyerr-Guest; [b.] July 19, 1978, Greensboro, NC; [ed.] 11th Grade Science and Technology Student at Oxon Hill High School; [memb.] Girl Scouts, Drama Club, Art Club, Church Youth Group, Spanish Honor Society, Ecology Club, Junior ROTC, Sun Club, Telecommunications Club, Who's Who among American High School Students.; [hon.] Several Honor Roll Achievement Awards, Girl Scout Silver Award, Two Presidential Academic Fitness Awards, Scholarship Award for outstanding achievement in English, Certificate of excellence in Academics; [pers.] I have been greatly influenced and motivated by my mother, Doris Sawyerr-Guest. I intend to write children's books after finishing medical school.; [a.] Suitland, MD

GUILL, MICHELLE L.
[pen.] Angel White; [b.] February 4, 1974, San Jose, CA; [p.] Tom and Linda Guill; [ed.] Wills Point ISD - TX, Honors Classes West Texas A&M, Radio, Television Dept. Newport News, VA; [occ.] USS John C. Stennis U.S. Navy CVN-74; [memb.] W.P. Poetry Society, Secretary, Poets of East Texas, Delta Zeta, Creshendo Gospel Choir, School Newspaper - Editor, Sr. year, Red Cross Swimming Instructor; [hon.] Presidential Academic Fitness Award, Various Poetry Contests, Various Art Contests, Veterans Savings Bond Award; [oth. writ.] Several Poems Published in various Papers and School papers.; [pers.] I've been writing Poetry since I was in 8th grade and maybe even earlier. I don't just write poems, I am inspired by my surroundings and nature.; [a.] Wills Point, TX

GULTNEY, RENA M.
[pen.] Rena Abraham Gultney; [b.] June 3, 1943, Mira, LA; [occ.] Mailhandler, United States Postal Service (27 yrs.); [pers.] I write religious poetry, and I am a dedicated follower of the Lord Jesus Christ. I became a born again Christian November 13, 1987 father Albert Abraham, Res. Portland, Ore. mother, Ardie Merriweather, Res. Dayton, OH; [a.] Dayton, OH

GUTCHIGIAN, ELIZABETH (BOHJELIAN)
[b.] November 12, 1921, Philadelphia, PA; [p.] Dr. KriKoris G. Bohjelian and Virginia (Bedrosian) Bohjelian; [ch.] Gregory, Madeline, Thomas; [ed.] West Chester University, Pierce Junior College, Cherry Hill Hospital (J.F. Kennedy Medical Center); [occ.] Campbell Museum Assistant; [memb.] Women's Club of Voorhees Haddonfield Plays and Players; [oth. writ.] Short stories and several newspaper articles published in ethnic newspaper in Mass., One copywritten novel, "Reflections: Three girls, three women", One

novel to be copywritten, unnamed.; [pers.] The stories told to me by my grandmother, mother and father about the Armenian Genocide of 1915, which to this day has not been recorded or acknowledged, prompted me, after my 70th year, to create two historical novels.; [a.] Voorhees, NJ

GUTHRIE, TERRY K.
[b.] May 29, 1957, Frank Furt, Germany; [ch.] Terry, Natalie, Andrea, Kathy; [pers.] So share experiences strengths and hopes. Short love can grow out of pain and suffering; [a.] Kathleen, GA

HACKATHORN, FRANK D.
[ed.] Attended Ohio University, majoring in Business Administration and minoring in Psychology.; [occ.] Speaker, Trainer, Seminar Leader, Management Consultant; [memb.] A member of the National Speakers Association.; [hon.] Listed in Who's Who in Public Speaking in America; [a.] Richardson, TX

HAINES, SARAH
[b.] May 5, 1947, Hartford, CT; [ed.] Saint Annes School, High Prospect and the International Experiment in Living, Career Academy Massachusetts; [occ.] Housewife, mother; [memb.] Water and light Poetry magazine, International Society of Poets; [oth. writ.] Several poems published in our church flyer: Poetic Voices of America and Water and Light Poetry Magazine; [pers.] I enjoy expressing myself through poetry, feelings, nature, cats and dogs, people.; [a.] Waterbury, CT

HALL, BARBIE
[pen.] Sarah Short; [b.] December 17, 1981, Baltimore, MD; [p.] John Hall, Barbara Hall; [ed.] School #215 Highland Town Elementary Pk - 5th grade, Southeast Middle #255 6-8 gr; [occ.] Student; [memb.] NAL, Church Lector, Church Acrolyte, Junior National Honor Society; [hon.] Dramatic Reading, Race to Read, MS Readathon, Mother's Day Essay Contest, Cultural Arts Junior National Honor Society; [oth. writ.] Poems and stories published in school literary magazines and local newspapers; [pers.] I write not only for myself but for others, I am much inspired by mother nature and my imagination.; [a.] Baltimore, MD

HALL, GERALDINE V.
[pen.] Goldie Hall; [b.] January 3, 1928, Pontiac, MI; [p.] Joseph, Alice Pluto; [m.] William H. Hall (deceased), January 3, 1953; [ch.] Gregory Scott, Christopher Kelly, Anthony Todd, Brenda Kimberly Hobbs; [ed.] Graduate Bedford High, Warners Beauty College, Nursing Aide Course; [occ.] Retired; [memb.] Non at present, was founding member of Greak Lakes Arts and Crafts and Secretary; [hon.] Elected Class Treasurer 4 yrs., designed and illustrated, class year book and school newspaper, won prizes from receipt contests and ribbons for art work and letter from school; [oth. writ.] Three unpublished stories for my grandchildren and some other poems; [pers.] Get the most out of each day. Learn as much as you can. Make lots of friends from other walks of life. Don't let the rust set in, keep in motion!; [a.] Temperance, MI

HALL, HILLERY H.
[b.] February 19, 1969, Red Bank, NJ; [p.] Clyde W. Hall and Elizabeth J. Hall; [ed.] St. John Vianney High School; [occ.] Executive Secretary; [pers.] In honor of my mother, Elizabeth.

HALL, LADON EUGENE
[b.] July 23, 1941, Albion, MI; [p.] Hossie and Etta Hall; [m.] Beulah Ann Trone Hall, May 7, 1962; [ch.] LaDon F. Hall, Braint N. Hall; [ed.] Washington Gardner High, Universal College, Wayne State University, Wayne Theological Seminary; [occ.] Accountant and Teacher; [memb.] Paulist Fathers, The International Christian Mission Society of the World Missions, Wayne Theological, doing everything to raise our image today; [hon.] International Accountant Association, International Christian Missions; [oth. writ.] Heights of Freedom, Together, Don't be Stupid, The Best of Friends, Helping Hand, The Quiet Man.; [pers.] I myself try to use poetry as a form of Human identity to others, I've search from the best in me through others and poetry.; [a.] Detroit, MI

HAMBY, SYLVIA
[pen.] Kay Namby; [b.] November 16, 1961, Russell County, VA; [p.] Nancy Seiber; [m.] Bill Hamby, December 21, 1987; [ch.] William Gray Hamby (W.G), Casey Leigh Hamby, Angel Marie; [ed.] Claremont Elem., 8th grade; [occ.] Own Country Music Night Club. Country Boys Hudson, NC; [pers.] I have been greatly influenced by my family and my friends at Country Boys. A special thanks to my deceased grandmother Bussie Hughes; [a.] Taylorsville, NC

HAMER, KATE PERDUE
[pen.] Hamilton Hamer; [b.] February 15, 1926, Los Angeles; [p.] Ira and Mary Perdue (deceased); [m.] Grey Hamer, April 16, 1994; [ch.] Kathleen Gortner, Roxanne Lobnow, Ken Lobnow; [ed.] H.S. and Trade School; [occ.] Being married, travelling, learning craft of writing; [oth. writ.] With partner have recently edited journal of great-great uncle of his experiences as prisoner of confederates during Civil War at age of 17 - Andersonville, Belle Isle, etc., now in process of submission. I like writing things for children and have written several "poems" for children in our family - three of which are in the process of making the rounds.; [pers.] As I am personally affected by stories of romance, love, suspense and mystery it is these I especially like to read. Love of family and extended family is the basis for a story that is now germinating. I was married a year ago to a man I've known for 50 years and who is the brother of my sisters' husband. He has brought love, romance, devotion, humor and a life in which each day adds something new and interesting. How could I not believe in late-in-life love. The thrill of being courted at 68 was even more wonderful than it was at 20 and was the last thing I ever expected to have happen to me. "Laughter is" indeed, the best medicine.; [a.] Everett, WA

HAMILTON, MELODY L.
[pen.] Sissy A. Kelley; [b.] June 7, 1953, Chattanooga, TN; [p.] James M. and Jewell L. Kelley; [m.] Herbert E. Hamilton, March 28,

1980; [ch.] Kelley Hamilton, Freddie Brown and Michael Brown; [ed.] Rossville High Murray-Clark Bible Coll; [occ.] Asst. Mgr. for Kelley's Gospel Group.; [memb.] American Red Cross CNA; [oth. writ.] Several poems published in local newspapers, and songs written for local singing groups.; [pers.] I strive to reflect the true meaning of life and love, that should be shared toward others. I was greatly influenced by my talented father. The late James M. Kelley.; [a.] Flirtstone, CA

HAMILTON, NANCY JO
[b.] August 27, 1943, Palo Alto; [m.] Fred Hirsch (companion); [ch.] 1 son Michael James; [occ.] Painter, Manages jazz musicians and runs electronic companies.

HAMILTON, NAOMI R. B.
[pen.] Naomi Hamilton; [b.] November 28, 1947, New Orleans, LA; [p.] Samuel Baptiste, Beulah H. Baptiste; [m.] Will Hamilton; [ch.] Anita Louise Hamilton, Will Henry Hamilton, Jr.; [ed.] Mary M. Bethune High School, California State University; [pers.] I'm an inspirationalist daily inspired by the beginning of each new day and its effect upon our lives.; [a.] Destrehan, LA

HAMILTON, ROBERT A.
[pen.] Tony; [b.] March 27, 1947, Estes Park, CO; [p.] Peg and Robert Hamilton; [ed.] Studied Advertising Art, Drafting in College, 3 1/2 yrs.; [occ.] Auto Mechanic, Auto Custom Fabricator; [memb.] Volunteer Firefighter and EMT (Emerg. Med. Tech.) Committee Chairman, Fire Explorer Post; [oth. writ.] Lots written, none published except local paper. I maintain an on-going personal journal, begun shortly after my return from Vietnam in 1968.; [pers.] A former marine (1966-'72) and combat veteran of the Vietnam War, I now try to help others reach a peaceful mind set about their own post-combat experience. The poem you read was written after my "Wall" visit, 1991.; [a.] Arivaca, AZ

HAMLIN, DR. LISA
[b.] March 8, 1962, Nashville, TN; [p.] Louise Cox, Henry Cox; [ed.] B.S. in Elementary Ed. from Belmont University, MLS from Vanderbilt University, Ph.D. in Metaphysical Sciences from P.U.L.C., Ph.D. in Parapsychology from P.U.L.C., Doctorate of Divinity from P.U.L.C.; [occ.] Technical Services Librarian, Brentwood Library, Brentwood, TN; [memb.] Chronic Fatigue and Immune Dysfunction Sydrome Society, Interstitial Cystitis Association, Tennessee Library Association, Association for Research and Enlightenment; [hon.] Cum Laude gradate (1983) from Belmont University, music (1979.) Scholarship at Belmont Univ., Library (1984) Science Scholarship at Vandy, (1995) full scholarship at Univs. of Metaphysics. (I'm currently working on my MSCD) High School (1979) Diploma from the National Piano Guild, Library Dept. Employee of the Year (1993); [oth. writ.] Unpublished at this time.; [pers.] My writings are of a metaphysical nature. I try to incorporate the whole nature of man - mind and body, spirit and soul.; [a.] Antioch, TN

HAMM, TERESA L.
[b.] May 16, 1956, Pittsylvania County, VA; [p.] Mary L. Hamm; [ch.] Felicia Vinette Sullivan, Terrance Lyndon; [ed.] McKinley High Howard University, Univ of the District of Columbia (UDC); [occ.] Office Manager, National Science Foundation, Washington, DC; [memb.] National Council of Negro Women, Inc. (NCNW); [oth. writ.] Article published in hometown newspaper; [pers.] I have always been compelled to put my feelings in writing. I can offer advice, tell my side of a story, release anger, and have a good cry or a boisterous laugh through my writings. It is a wonderful outlet and a peaceful one.; [a.] Silver Spring, MD

HAMMACK, LILLIAN SELBE
[b.] April 3, 1927, Charleston, WV; [p.] Carl and Ida Hundley Selbe; [m.] George O. Hammack Sr. (died 1989), March 12, 1945; [ch.] One son and three Daughters, five grandchildren; [ed.] High School, Dunbar, WV University of S.C. Aiken-Certificate in Juvenile Criminology. Other courses relative to volunteer work.; [occ.] Retired Ins. Agent full time Volunteer; [memb.] Founder and Exec.Director of VOID (Victims of Impaired Drivers) SALT (Seniors and Lawmen Together) WVAP (Victim Witness Assistant Program) others.; [hon.] "I CARE" awards from two SC Governors. Outstanding Older American 1990. Honored by Unanamous Resolutions *Resident of SC since 1952. By SC House of Representatives, and Aiken County Council. Local, District and Regional Awards (Service to Mankind) by Sertoma International. Commendation by Pres. Reagan 1984. Named one of two thousand notable American Women 1993. Several other awards.; [pers.] I would also like to dedicate the poem to the victims and survivors of the bombing in Oklahoma City, all victims of crime. (If this is possible) I plan to send my extra copy to the library there.; [a.] New Ellenton, SC

HANLON, JEREMY
[b.] June 30, 1972, San Francisco, CA; [p.] Johnna and Glenn Hanlon; [ed.] Currently attending the University of New Mexico in the field of environmental design. Graduate of Burney High School; [occ.] Firefighter with the U.S. Forest Service; [oth. writ.] Several poems-none published, but plenty of self-satisfaction!; [pers.] When I am fighting a fire, I become saturated with the beauty of the earth. Poetry is an outlet to express my love of life during these times.; [a.] Albuquerque, NM

HANLON, JOHN H.
[pen.] Jack; [b.] October 23, 1927, Somerville, MA; [p.] Mary and Francis (deceased); [ed.] 8 yrs. Grammar, 3 yrs. High School, 9 yrs. Sunday School, 4 yrs. Church history; [occ.] Retired; [pers.] An end to the violence, throughout the world. Love for one another. Greater understanding and Compassion. What an achievement, to look forward to.; [a.] Burlington, MA

HANNON, ESTHER E.
[b.] November 27, 1912, Madison County, IA; [p.] Wes and Moude Eivins; [m.] Don C. Hannon, February 7, 1942; [ch.] Charles; [ed.] 2 yrs. at Simpson College, 1 yr. at American Institute of Business; [occ.] Retired, housewife; [memb.] Methodist Church Groups, Federated Woman's Club, Rebekah Lodge, American Legion Auxiliary, Qui Vive Club; [pers.] This poem was written in 1936 before I was married, and I experienced it as I walked through the groove. I am now 82 and living alone. A nature lover.; [a.] Winterset, IA

HANSEN, ALF C.
[b.] December 14, 1916, New Haven, CT; [p.] Alf C. and Mary J. (Rolley) Hansen; [m.] Norma J. (MacCormick) Hansen, May 16, 1952; [ch.] Rev. Ronald W. Hansen (by prev. marriage), Bruce A. Hansen, Valerio A. Murphy; [ed.] High School - West Valley, NY 1933, School of Hard Knocks (1933-??); [occ.] Retired US Navy, Retired Federal Civil Service; [memb.] Christian Missionary Alliance Church, Good Sam Club, AARP, American Diabetes Assn, Masonic Lodge (Philippines), National Camping Travelers (Texas), Escapees-Family Motor Coach Assn; [oth. writ.] One-time Editor and Columnist for "Bamboo Breezes", weekly publication of Naval Station, Subic Bay, Philippines. Several articles and poems in various local papers.; [pers.] Enjoy writing humorous stories and poems - never knowingly writing anything which could offend anyone; [a.] DeLand, FL

HANSEN, GARY VALENTINE
[oth.writ.] I am the author of the poem A Sun That Cannot Rise Above a Glow, to be published by the National Library of Poetry in it's anthology At Water's Edge in the fall of 1995.; [a.] Tiburon, CA

HARBIN, MARY
[b.] September 23, 1941, Georgia; [ed.] Hollins College; [occ.] Care-giver; [pers.] Peace of mind is important.

HARDIN, JESSIE M.
[pen.] J. Marguerite Greenlaw; [b.] December 18, 1911, Flora, IL; [p.] John and Sarah Greenlaw; [m.] Clifford F. Hardin, July 28, 1929; [ch.] John, Mary, Hugh, Ruth, Rose, Jane, Ross, Lee, Virginia, Ward; [ed.] High School Graduate, North High, Des Moines, IA; [occ.] Retired, Widow, Homemaker, Volunteer Hospice; [memb.] Trinity Methodist Church, Mountain Grove, MO; [hon.] Certificate of Award - Outstanding Children's Tutor in Reading, Tri-County Literacy Council, Certificate of Appreciation for Service, Hartline Hospice, Inc.; [oth. writ.] Poem "In Memory of my Husband - Clifford Hardin", poem - "Morn Not"; [pers.] "To thine self be true and it will follow as the night day, thou canst not be false to any man." Shakespeare; [a.] Mountain Grove, MO

HARDING, WILLIAM J.
[b.] New York City; [p.] William and Mary Harding; [m.] Edna Harding, March 29, 1981; [ch.] Colin (13), Cale (7); [occ.] Civil Servant: N.Y.C. Dept of Environmental Protection; [memb.] Amateur Astronomy Assoc.; [hon.] Golden Apple Award from N.Y.C. (Methane Gas Suggestion) Antarctic Service Award, National Science Foundation; [oth. writ.] "Infant Child" - Children' Christmas Story. Book (Scythe); [pers.] "Let there be love"; [a.] New York, NY

HARDY, JASON D.
[b.] May 29, 1977, Junction City, KS; [p.] Richard and Linda K. Hardy; [ed.] Osbourn High School and Christian Center School; [occ.] Student; [memb.] NAACP Youth Council, First Baptist Church Manassas; [hon.] 1992 Student Ambassador, People to People Program, 1993 Local Winner and National Contestant, NAACP, Afro-Academic, Cultural, Technological and Scientific Olympics (ACT SO) Poetry Division, 1994 Local Winner and National Contestant, NAACP-ACT SO, Vocal Contemporary Music, 1994 2nd place winner Local NAACP-ACT SO, Poetry Division; [pers.] I want to live and learn about people places and events, to use this information to make my world a better place.; [a.] Manassas, VA

HARPER, VENITTA
[pen.] Venitta Lateer; [b.] February 3, 1963, Cortland Hospital; [p.] Cassandra and DeWitt Murphy; [ed.] 7th; [a.] North Syracuse, NY

HARRIS, MARY L.
[pen.] "Adeeba"; [b.] October 8, 1948, VA; [p.] Charles W. Moody Sr., Jennie L. Moody (deceased); [ch.] Karen Harris, Larry B. Harris Jr.; [ed.] Delaware Valley College (Credits Business Admin); [occ.] Quality Assurance Specialist; [memb.] National Council of Negro Women (Officer-Chaplain), OESPHA (Officer), Weekly Personality on Kitty Taylor Radio Show WNJR Radio, Abyssinian Baptist Church - Newark (Women's Guild), New Jersey Chapter of Minority Interchange (Prudential Ins), NAACP of East Orange, Notary Public of NJ, Chamber of Commerce of East Orange, International Toastmaster New Jersey Charter, International Society of Poets (Associated Member 1994-1995); [hon.] Certified in Food Safety and Sanitation by the State of NJ Dept of Education (Child Care Nutrition), Numerous Quality Service Leadership awards from Prudential Ins.(monthly/quarterly), Resolutions from the City of Newark for the Living Legacy Program (1993 and 1994); [oth. writ.] "Thoughts of You" published in 1995 by National Library of Poetry book "A Moment in Time"; [pers.] I want each person who reads my poems to "see" what I say!; [a.] East Orange, NJ

HARRIS, OLA MAE
[pen.] Mrs. Wyhee; [b.] June 8, 1933, Louisiana; [p.] Edward and Anna Harris; [m.] Willie Washington, July 22, 1986; [ed.] High School grad. Jefferson High School LA Calif; [occ.] Foster parent; [memb.] America Red Cross Foster Parent Association; [hon.] America Red Cross; [pers.] Moved to LA Calif. on 1951 I am all so known as Mrs. Wyhee; [a.] Carson, CA

HARRISON, LYNETTE L.
[b.] July 7, 1971, Washington, DC; [p.] Linda A. Elliott; [m.] Kevin, T. Harrison, August 4, 1988; [ch.] Ericka Renee', Shaunte' Lynelle, Kevin Tyrone Jr., James; [ed.] Coolidge High; [occ.] Homemaker; [memb.] Body of Christ Fellowship at Rhema Christian Center; [oth. writ.] Several unpublished poems.; [pers.] With the poems that I have I am using them to tell a lost and dying world that Jesus is Lord. Jesus is the driving existence behind all of my poems. He is love, therefore my poems speak of him and all that he's done for me he can do the same for others.; [a.] Washington, DC

HART, GENEURA
[b.] June, 17, 1986, Australia; [p.] Wendy and Richard Hart; [ed.] Still at school her teacher, by the way 13 terribly proud! She's encouraged generous talent!; [occ.] Student; [hon.] This is her first honour and she is terribly thrilled!; [oth. writ.] None as yet 'Climb a tree' generous first poem but she wants to be a writer and an artist when she grows up!; [pers.] Geneura loves nature, she is keenly aware of the environment and the need to preserve forests. Her favorite animal is the dolphin and she has a kitten called sox geneura also paints!; [a.] Cashmere, WA

HARTMAN, JULIE
[b.] February 18, 1970, Conroe, TX; [p.] Ronnie and Janie Taylor; [m.] John Hartman, November 11, 1989; [occ.] Rework Operator on Computer PCA's; [a.] Tomball, TX

HARTWELL, GABRIELLA
[pen.] Gabriella Marie; [b.] October 25, 1977, Springfield, MA; [memb.] Chicopee Partnership for a Drug Free Chicopee, Amherst Writers and Artists, Catholic Relief Services; [hon.] Who's Who among American High School Students, success through Education Ms. Junior America pageant; [oth. writ.] This is my first publication but I also write songs, prose, and short stories.; [pers.] I strive to inspire people in my writing. I strongly believe that if you try your best at something, you will succeed. There is a winner in everyone, you just have to take sometime to find him.; [a.] Chicopee, MA

HASKELL, WHITNEY ANN
[b.] December 18, 1985, Fall River, MA; [p.] John and Pamela Haskell; [ed.] Student at Fort Barton School will complete 3rd place in June 1995; [occ.] Student; [memb.] Member-United States Figure, Skating Association, Girl Scouts of Rhode Island; [hon.] Nominated for RI Young Authors 1993, 1995, semi-finalist in the National Library of Poetry North American Open Poetry Contest, 1995; [oth. writ.] Several short stories including: The Butterfly, Princess Ashdenka, The Chocolate Connection, The Day There Was No Rye Bread, Yummy, (and various poems); [pers.] I would like the world to become peaceful, without hatred towards one another. I wish we would all chip in to make our world a cleaner more beautiful place.; [a.] Tiverton, RI

HATOWAY, DONNA CHRISTINE
[b.] October 22, 1954, Ft. Bragg, NC; [p.] Ruth and Richard Hatoway; [ch.] Jannese Hope; [ed.] Snead State Jr. College and Middle Tennessee State University; [occ.] Full time student; [memb.] Social workers forum and AA; [oth. writ.] Several other poems that haven't ever been published.; [pers.] The beauty of people comes from within. I was inspired to write from my own personal journey.; [a.] Murfreesboro, TN

HAUG, JOAN A.
[b.] April 16, 1939, Edmonds, WA; [m.] Aldon J. Haug, July 25, 1958; [ch.] Nancy, Kathy, Cindy, Barbara, Connie. Along with nine (9) beautiful grandchildren: Ryan, Tori, Jordan, Jacob, Tara, Kenna, Taylor, Marina, Mitchell.; [pers.] I would

like to thank all my friends for their encouragement - especially Lorraine Smith.

HAY, CAROL HUDGINS
[b.] April 18, 1954, Yorktown, VA; [p.] Mrs. Mary H. Bowman and Mr. Albert Diggs; [m.] Joseph Perez Hay, December 6, 1987; [ch.] Carmen Maria, Michael Adrian and Richard; [ed.] York High School, Thomas-Nelson Community College; [occ.] Secretary; [memb.] United Way, member of the Tabb Church of God; [hon.] Cum Laude; [oth. writ.] Several poems written thru out my school years, poem written while in the fourth grade and published in a school "book of poems". Among other poems, "What Is A Child" chosen by my ninth-grade teacher for future reading to other classes.; [pers.] My family and the trials and victories that are faced in every day life are the inspiration of my poems.; [a.] Yorktown, VA

HAYES, BEATRICE
[pen.] Bea Hayes; [b.] May 17, 1943, Brooklyn, NY; [p.] John and Frances Hayes; [ed.] Bay Ridge High School; [occ.] Administrative Assnt, Republic National Bank of New York; [memb.] St. Mary Mother of Jesus, Adult Youth Ministry Leader; [hon.] Youth Ministry - 5 years; [oth. writ.] Several poems (all free-verse) unpublished; [pers.] My conversion and spiritual growth are reflected in my poetry. My writings are inspired by God's creation and life experiences.; [a.] Brooklyn, NY

HAYES, JOHN B.
[b.] May 28, 1942, Carnegie, PA; [p.] John B. Hayes Sr., Alma M. Petrilena, (maiden); [m.] Marilyn Axelson Hayes, September 6, 1970; [ch.] Pemala J. Hayes, Brendan A. Hayes; [ed.] M.A. and J.D. B.A. Duquesnece University M.S.W. University of Pittsburgh; [occ.] Trial Attorney (defence) with Banginski and Bashline, Pittsburgh, PA Part-time adjunct instructor, Duquesne University Paralegal Program.; [memb.] Allegheny County Bar Assoc., Elder, Westminster Presbyterian Church, Pittsburgh, PA, Rotary International.; [oth. writ.] Pennsylvania Supplement for Paralegal Textbook on Civil Litigation.; [pers.] I believe reality is largely beyond the reach of human knowledge, but that the soul and experience more of reality than can be securely brought within the confines of the mind. This is why the soul needs a language that can stretch beyond ordinary speech. That language is poetry.; [a.] Upper Saint Clair, PA

HAYES, TRACEY LYNN
[b.] August 19, 1980, Rutland, VT; [p.] Jinny Thompson (mother); [ed.] 8th Grade at Rutland Junior High School; [memb.] Mendon United Methodist Community Church, Rutland Bowlerama; [hon.] Bowling Scholarship, Academic Honors, Green Mountain District Singer; [oth. writ.] Participant in the NYNEX "Portraits of New England" essay contest; [pers.] I was influenced by my mothers natural writing talent and my grandmother. I would like to thank three people for their support, Jennifer Enzor, Makenzie Reed and Amy Scott; [a.] Rutland, VT

HAYES, WALKER
[b.] February 28, 1971, Cleveland, OH; [p.] Raymond and Celestine Hayes; [ed.] Columbia

Area Career Center (Office Technology); [hon.] GED Scholarship (1991), American Legion Award; [oth. writ.] "Floating to Freedom" (Semi finalist in 1994 contest - National Library of poetry - North American open poetry contest Published in Journal of the mind. I have written poems and articles.; [pers.] "Hero in the Hayes" is about a beauty that either can't be seen or is hard to see. i.e, the heat that cooks food can't be seen.; [a.] Columbia, MS

HAYNES, KAMARA
[pen.] Tataneisha H.; [b.] July 12, 1971, New York, NY; [p.] Leonard Haynes, Irene Haynes; [ed.] Harry S. Trupcan H.S., The Wood School - Business Executive, Secretarial Diploma; [occ.] Secretary Admin. Asslt Marsh and McLenwan, Inc.; [oth. writ.] One published Poem in High School - Expression '89; [pers.] I've seen from yesterday's promises that tomorrow will hold true it all the present I follow though.; [a.] New York, NY

HAYTON, SHAWN L.
[b.] April 22, 1949, Tucson, AZ; [p.] C.J. Hayton, Phillis Hayton; [ed.] Tucson High, Pima College, U of A.; [occ.] Cabnet Maker and Working in the Movie Ind.; [memb.] North American Hunting Club, Good Sam RV Owners Club, NRA and NRA second Amendment Task Force, Handyman Club of America, DAV Commanders Club; [hon.] 1st Place Animation 88-89 in Media Comm, P.C.C., second Prize 1990 NRI Photo Video Contest; [oth. writ.] Children story "Pete Oregon or Bust", Scripts about the Old West "In Quest of the Ont law Trail" and other poems.; [pers.] I find if you pay attention to what's going on around you, you'll never run out of things to think about and write about. Just use common sense.; [a.] Tucson, AZ

HAYWARD, JOY
[b.] October 23, 1945, Brooklyn, NY; [p.] Harriet and Irving Braverman; [m.] Robert Hayward, February 3, 1970; [ch.] Jason, Lyle, Dawn, Kimberly and eight adorable grandchildren; [ed.] Student of life and metaphysics Omni Hypnosis Training Cr., A.D.L. Ministerial Studies, Bachelor of Divinity, Dr. Of Metaphysics, Diplomat of Homeopothy; [occ.] Hypnotherapist, Healer Dir of "Inst of Alternative Therapies", Teacher and Pet and People Healer; [memb.] Various Hypnosis Groups and Organizations - Lecture Groups; [oth. writ.] Several books of Metaphysical Content including 2 dedicated to technique of natural healing and 1 of poetry/insights; [pers.] We are not `human' trying to live a life as spirit, we are `spirit' trying to live a life as human, if I can help someone along my path in this lifetime, I've done my `job' on Earth.; [a.] Fort Lauderdale, FL

HAZEL, RUTH
[pen.] Ruth Rivers (Maiden); [b.] September 21, 1926, August, GA; [m.] David Hazel, December 26, 1946; [ch.] Cheryl, Daryl, David and Kim; [ed.] Northern High School in Detroit, Eastern Michigan U., Wright State U. (Master's in teaching of English); [occ.] Retired teacher; [pers.] I cannot remember when I did not have a love affair with words. Sometimes I take liberties with the language. Writing poetry is more fun than other genres, it has a way of writing itself.; [a.] Xenia, OH

HEALTH, EVON
[b.] July 15, 1903, Far Rockaway; [ed.] Elementary, H.S and Four years at Columbia where I studied Banking, Accounting Management; [occ.] I was a bank teller for eight years, then quit, and that bank then failed. Then became office manager for a large NY Cloth manufactory for twenty years then Sr Accountant for the Headquarters of the Episcopal Church in Manhattan. And now retired; [oth. writ.] I wrote about 12 American short stories, none of which were published,so I decided to try poetry. I believe everyone has some talent, generally hidden. I also read famous letters, poems, some jokes, and receive vigorous applause. I still consult my big dictionary several times a week. Also frequently my "War "Armed conflict between nations. I attend a Methodist church. I audit their financial records.

HEATH, FRANK
[b.] July 15, 1903, Far Rockaway, NY; [p.] Adolph and Rose; [ed.] Elementary, H.S., 4 years at Columbia, in banking, accounting, management.; [occ.] Retired; [memb.] Method Church, queensborough Library since 1920; [hon.] H.S. Math Elementary - Artistic woodwork.; [oth. writ.] 12 to 15 American short stories, none published.; [pers.] I believe everyone has a hidden talent to be developed. I have always been a bachelor, (not gay!); [a.] Far Rockaway, NY

HEATH, PAULA JUNE
[b.] April 17, 1963, Ann Arbor, MI; [p.] Patricia and Edward Heath (adopted), Kathleen Peters (biological); [ch.] six dogs and two horses; [ed.] West High, Iowa City Kirkwood College, Cedar Rapids, IA.; [occ.] Housekeeper (UIHC) working for B.S.N.; [oth. writ.] One other poem published.; [pers.] My writing is greatly influenced by a very good friend and life's experiences.; [a.] Oxford, IA

HEDGES, NATHAN
[pen.] Raven; [b.] July 8, 1980, Dallas, TX; [p.] Howard Hedges, Elizabeth Hedges; [ed.] Travis Jr. High, Irving, Texas; [occ.] Students; [hon.] All region band; [a.] Irving, TX

HEIFFERON, JOEL S.
[pen.] Vincent Realiti; [b.] December 30, 1972, Rochester, NY; [p.] Gary and Mary Anne Heifferon; [m.] Filippa Vincenza Hiefferon, June 3, 1995; [ed.] High School Diploma - East Ridge High School, Rochester, NY; [oth. writ.] Numerous writings from the heart.; [pers.] Death is certain. Life is not.; [a.] Rochester, NY

HEITZIG, FRED F.
[a.] Fieldon, IL

HELMONDOLLAR, TERESA D.
[b.] August 21, 1956, Hungtington, WV; [p.] Wetzel and Opal Helmondollar; [ch.] Jeffery Scott Combs, Mark Bradley Combs; [ed.] Chesapeake High School, WV State College; [occ.] Patient Account Representative - River Park Hospital; [a.] Chesapeake, OH

HELTON, RICK
[b.] August 27, 1957, Valparaiso, IN; [p.] Vern and Ruth Helton; [m.] DeLoise Helton, November 5, 1994; [ch.] Brandon, Sheah, Shelley and Jonathon; [ed.] KV High School, Wheatfield, IN 46392; [occ.] Operating Engineer; [memb.] TeaBerry Hill Estates Church, Medaryville, Indiana; [oth. writ.] This is my first poem, I was coming home from work and wrote it on a napkin, this poem just came to me threw God. This poem is God's message.; [pers.] A special thanks to my wife, Lois, who sent this poem in because she liked it so well. I pray my poem touches many hearts like it did mine and my family. God Bless You; [a.] Whiting, IN

HENDERSON, JANICE
[b.] January 5, 1950, Beaver Falls, Penn; [p.] Charles Murphy, George and Betty (Murphy) Hilyard; [m.] David Henderson, June 14, 1969; [ch.] Christopher and Jamie; [ed.] Lancaster High School Durbin's Business College; [occ.] Secretary General Sherman Jr. High School; [pers.] I've dedicated my poem to my two brothers, Dennis and Bruce. It came out of the loss of our father at very young ages.; [a.] Lancaster, OH

HENDERSON, SALLY
[b.] August 6, 1941, Brattleboro, VT; [occ.] Sales, Medical Supply, Sales Rep Formering New Business.; [oth. writ.] Short Stories for Children and young adults - not yet published.; [pers.] Want to reflect enjoyment in Creation around us thus bringing a Calmness to one's Hectic Life in Today's World.; [a.] Fort Pierce, FL

HENDRICK, ANOLA BOWYER
[pen.] Annilee; [b.] October 6, 1916, Dorothy, W. VA.; [p.] Oliver Lee and Mary Baker Bowyer; [m.] Peter F. Hendrick, December 24, 1940; [ch.] Daughter, Linda G. Hendrick; [ed.] B.S. Medical Technology; [occ.] Retired; [pers.] I enjoy reading, traveling and any activity which permits me to be in close contact with the beauty and wonders of nature.; [a.] Winter Park, FL

HENDRICKS, ROBIN MICHELLE
[b.] October 29, 1980, Arlington Heights, IL; [p.] Deborah and Floyd Hendricks; [ed.] Kimball Hill Elementary School, Carl Sandburg Junior High, Rolling Meadows, IL; [occ.] Student; [memb.] Carl Sandburg Junior High Drama Club, Band, and Chorus; [hon.] Presidential Academic Fitness Award, Illinois Junior Academy of Science State Science Fair - Outstanding.; [a.] Rolling Meadows, IL

HENDRIKSEN, NICOLE
[b.] July 20, 1979, Vineland, NJ; [p.] Alice and William Hendriksen; [ed.] in 11th grade at Tappan Zee High School; [occ.] student; [memb.] Art Club, Photo Club, Volunteer at The American Heart Association; [hon.] 90's Club in H.S., Honor roll 3 times in 1995 for average over 85, 50 Math and Spelling Awards; [oth. writ.] Several poems published in high school literary magazine; [a.] Sparkill, NY

HENNESSY, LOURDES
[b.] September 4, 1963, San Antonio, TX; [occ.] Homemaker, ensuring love, guidance and support to my husband and children; [pers.] I write to capture the very essence of my emotion in a given moment, ahead lie many moments.

HERALD, DEANNA
[pen.] Annie; [b.] July 23, 1981, Cookeville, TN; [p.] Dayna and Dwight Herald; [ed.] Cookeville Junior High School; [occ.] Student; [hon.] All A's Honor Roll; [oth. writ.] Drinking and driving; [pers.] I just want to tell my best friend Stephanie Bybee Thanks for being my best friend.; [a.] Cookeville, TN

HERBERT, CESARINA MARIA
[pen.] Cesarina Maria Rossetti; [b.] August 23, 1911, Casto, Italy; [p.] Julio Rossetti, Angela Frassa; [m.] Divorced; [ch.] Mariae, Turnelty Rossett Herbert, Claren Herbert, (son); [ed.] Burlin Game High, Inter State College of Personology Delores Premiere School of cosmetology; [occ.] Properties owner - management; [memb.] American Red Cross; [oth. writ.] Poems - unpublished; [pers.] In my writing, my goal is to express and project the basic reality of all life as life is presented to me.; [a.] Hillsborough, CA

HERBERT, ENID WILSON
[pen.] Enid Herbert; [b.] September 3, 1917, Ohio, U.S.A.; [p.] Edward and Philomena Wilson; [m.] Arthur John Herbert, September 3, 1942; [ch.] Martha Carol, James E., Evangeline Ruth All three have some college. James Edmond is a noted and carver tho handicapped. All three married.; [ed.] High School, Nyack Bible College; [occ.] Retired but still teaching Bible lessons to children; [memb.] On Political Issues and Church of the Christian and Missionary Alliance.; [oth. writ.] Poems for sixty years for every situation, moods, whether happy or sad. Never published any of them, tho perhaps in the thousands, only after I married my husband suggested I make copies for posterity. We spent 28 years as missionaries in the Philippines, 1984 June 8, to November 1974. I have a book of songs and choruses published and copyrighted in the Philippines, which is still being used here in the U.S. Pub 7/74. I play the trumpet and taught in College.; [pers.] I feel very strongly about family values and take the Word of God in the Bible to be the heart throb of my life and I love people of all walks of life to manifest that Jesus Christ can change the foulest person to a child of God if that person will confess and forsake the old life for the New Life in Christ. I trust that my personal and Philosophical statement have and baring on my poem publication.

HERMANN, ROSMARIE
[pen.] R. S.; [b.] December 5, 1924, Luzern; [p.] Anton and Rosa Schumacher; [m.] 1951; [ch.] Hazy and Markus-Gerhard Hermann; [ed.] Polytech School London, G.B. Ecole Commerce Geneve Switz.; [occ.] (Retired) Volunteer c/o SPARCC - Sarasota; [memb.] Friendship - Center Venice, Seniors Without P. Venice; [hon.] Every women award 1994, Good Heart Award Certificate 1995; [oth. writ.] Several letters published in news papers in my early years in different countries.; [pers.] Anytime there was a great desire to express my feelings for happiness and relief in poems. Life is not always easy, but there is always "Hope"!; [a.] Venice, FL

HERNANDEZ, CHRISTINA LYNN
[pen.] Christina Lynn Hernandez; [b.] December 20, 1969, California; [p.] Frank Angelo Hernandez, Susan Curran; [occ.] Public Relations and Marketing Coordinator; [memb.] Active in many animal rights foundations.; [hon.] Awarded "Most Valuable Musician in 1985, 2nd place at World of Music Competition, many of my short stories, and journalism entries have been honored at colleges.; [oth. writ.] Several poems and lyrics published as songs, majority of my work has been published in advertising, print, and magazines.; [pers.] Expression through the written word has always been an important part of who I am. My writings have always been born spontaneously and from the heart.; [a.] Sunnyvale, CA

HERZBERGER, MAGDA
[b.] February 20, 1926, Cluj, Romania; [p.] Herman Mozes-died 1944 in Holocaut, Serena Vinacour-died March 25, 1994; [m.] Eugene E. Herzberger, November 21, 1946; [ch.] Monica Riekoff and Henry Herzberger; [ed.] Bachelor's of Science Degree, one year medical school at King Ferdinand University, 1946-1947 in Cluj, Romania; [occ.] Poet, Lecturer, Composer; [memb.] International Society of Poets, Bet El Sisterhood, Women's Club and Kiwanis Club in Fountain Hills, Arizona; [hon.] Personalities of West and Midwest Award, three poetry grants, 1977, 1980 and 1985, Who's Who in Poetry 5th Edition, Cambridge, England, Poet of Merit Award, 1993 (The National Library of Poetry, Editor's Choice Award, 1994-1995, and 2nd prize winner of 1994 National Library of Poetry Competition, The International Who is Who of Intellectuals, Cambridge, England, 1978-1982; [oth. writ.] Books: Will You Still Love Me?, The Waltz of the Shadows, Songs of Life, Eyewitness to Holocaust and 300 independent pomes published, one short story, two narratives (poetry), one children's book, one book on the Holocaust in the making; [pers.] Being a survivor of the Camps, my goal is to keep the memory of the Holocaust alive through my writings and music and to instill a love of poetry in the hearts of all the people. I'm also a hiker, skier and marathon runner.; [a.] Fountain Hills, AZ

HESS, MR. EMIL JOHN
[b.] September 25, 1913, Willock, PA; [p.] Stephen Hess (married) and Beatrice Smith; [ed.] Asst Inst. of Pgh 1 1/2 yrs Ed. Duquesne Univ. 1 yr every Art Students League NYC 3 yrs full time Bklyn. Mas. art school 1 yr full time; [occ.] retired (approaching 82); [oth. writ.] Always seemed to write poetry at lonely times in the exotic or a fascination of lonely exotic beaches. I competed with paintings and sculpture but not worth my writings.

HEWITT, VIRGINIA LEIGH
[pen.] Virginia Doyle Hewitt; [b.] October 25, 1948, Santa Monica, CA; [p.] Donald J. Doyle, Virginia F. Doyle; [m.] Lockwood, (divorce ex-Green Beret); [ed.] Attended Tunxis Community and Ashuntuck Community Colleges - Conn. for nearly two years (until divorce).; [occ.] Secretary; [memb.] Licensed Cosmetologist - State of Conn. Specialty: Chemical Applications. High School: Belonged to CEM TRI Hi Y - A Girl's Service

Club; [hon.] Phi Theta Kappa, Spring 1988 through American Two Year College, High School (Pulashi Sr. New Britain) received Columbia Pin for writing: (Reporter (3 yrs.) Pendulum (newspaper).; [oth. writ.] While at Aswentuck Community College excelled at Creative Writing, and Term Papers. Hope to have longer poems published in the near future, and maybe on article on dating.; [pers.] There's a possibility that I'm a distant relative (on father's side) to the late Sir Arthur Cohan Doyle, English author. Started writing metaphysical poetry - as sixth grader at home.; [a.] New Britain, CT

HICKER, GAIL S.
[b.] April 19, 1938, San Francisco, CA; [ed.] BA in History, San Francisco State University; [occ.] Personnel Clerk U.S. Army Corps of Engineers; [memb.] Saint Francis Catholic Church, Animal Protection Institute, Green Peace.; [pers.] With the unrelenting emphasis on the iniquity of mankind, the beauty of God's earth, peoples and creatures is too often overshadowed. In poetry and song, that beauty is given voice and with joy and prayer, will bring light to a darkening land.; [a.] Rancho Cordova, CA

HICKEY, JANEL
[pen.] Harleyquin Jackson; [b.] July 24, 1976, Fridley, MN; [p.] Dean and Judy Hickey; [ed.] Irondale High School, University of Minnesota; [occ.] Studio Photographer; [hon.] Honor Rolls, Appreciation Award; [oth. writ.] A few other poems just doodles; [pers.] I've written a lot, I wasn't really into poems. You can think of anything to write and that's what I did.; [a.] New Brighton, MN

HICKS, BRENDA L.
[pen.] Brenda Cassady Hicks; [b.] January 31, 1958, Vineland, NJ; [p.] Gloria and Otto Cassady; [m.] Vernon S. Hicks, October 1, 1977; [ch.] Christy Lynn Hicks, Donald Scott Hicks; [ed.] ICS High School; [occ.] Housewife and waitress; [memb.] Church of God; [oth. writ.] "Story of Success", Dream or Last Chance", "Cross Upon a Hill", "Home Again", "and many others." I have had Christian newspapers ask for my poems.; [pers.] I write what the Lord puts on my heart. I plan to put out a book from 16 years of writing.; [a.] Rockville, MD

HILL, BRADY B.
[b.] October 20, 1936, East Palestine, OH; [p.] Delbert and Margaret Hill; [m.] Emmy, August 15, 1956; [ch.] Debbie I. Flowers, Elka E. Lane; [ed.] High School; [occ.] Bartender 36 yrs.; [oth. writ.] Yes, I have written 10 poems since July, 1994; [pers.] The gift to write Biblical was given to me from Jesus Christ on July 30th 1994; [a.] Las Vegas, NV

HILL, GLORIA
[b.] November 25, 1946, Burbank, CA; [p.] Robin C. King, Allene King; [m.] Dixon Hill, December 31, 1987; [ch.] Fabian, Darin; [ed.] LA Crescenta High School, University of the Americas - Mexico City; [occ.] Branch Manager, Accounting and Tax Service; [memb.] Soroptimist International, Palm Desert-sunrise; [oth. writ.] I write poems for my family that express my feelings of love or my

Philosophy of life.; [pers.] According to my aunt on my fathers side of the family I may be related to Ralph Waldo Emerson. My great grandmother's name was Jane Emerson. I have been inspired since a child of 5 yrs, old to someday become "A writer." I feel like I have accomplished that even though. I have never been published before. Being "A writer" is a sense of accomplishment you feel inside when someone reads your work and smiles.; [a.] Palm Springs, CA

HILLOCKS, CAROLYN L.
[b.] January 18, 1939, Washington, DC; [p.] Aaron J. and Ada B. Lucas; [m.] Alrick A. Hillocks, November 12, 1965; [ch.] Cheryl, Michelle, Michael; [ed.] Cardozo High School, DC Teachers College and George Washington University, Wash., DC; [occ.] Reading Resource Teacher-Ketcham Elem. School, Wash., DC; [memb.] New Bethel Baptist Church, Wash., DC. Sigma Gamma Rho, "Simply Friends"; [hon.] "Who's Who Among Students in American Colleges/Universities" 1959-60; [oth. writ.] 3 or 4 poems, 3 or 4 children's stories; [pers.] After attending Poetry Readings by Maya Angelo at Howard University on February 14, 1995, I was inspired to go home and write the poem "Gift of Love."; [a.] Washington, DC

HIMES, JUSTEN LOY
[pen.] Big Guy; [b.] November 26, 1985, Washington, DC; [p.] Darlene and Dennis Himes; [ch.] Brother: Jacob Alan Himes, March 28, 1990.; [ed.] 4th Grade, Laurel Woods Elementary School - Mrs. Stiller; [hon.] Music award for outstanding participation, certificate of participation in young authors contest, computer whiz kid award, Mr. Perseverance award and trophy for participation in basketball.; [pers.] My Dad died Jan 31, 1995 to brain tumors. I love my Dad and I miss him a lot.; [a.] Laurel, MD

HINCKEL, J. ROMA
[pen.] Roma; [b.] July 10, 1937, Nicaragua; [p.] Charles and Zelma Hinckel; [ch.] Luis, Arthur and Jessica Melendez; [ed.] St. Peter's Academy San Francisco - Plus business education; [occ.] Business Representative; [memb.] San Francisco Church of Religious Science; [oth. writ.] Many other poems as yet unpublished; [pers.] I find serenity and joy helping my fellow man and honor the light of love burning in the human heart; [a.] Daly City, CA

HINCKLEY, MARTHA A.
[pen.] Martha A. Hayes; [b.] August 16, 1954, Rochester, NY; [p.] Milton J. Hinckley Sr., Elaine D. Gillman; [m.] John C. Hayes III; [ch.] Sherry E., John C. IV., Christopher E.; [ed.] Madison High, Rochester, NY, Boces Medina, NY, Career Development Completed with Certificates; [occ.] General Laborer; [memb.] Assembly of God, Church, Medina NY; [hon.] Parent Award, Albion, NY (Head Start Program); [oth. writ.] Local Newspaper, Personal columns, for friends and family; [pers.] Born and raised in Rochester, NY, I have been writing poems and short stories for many years, and my friends and family had been encouraging me to send some to Publishers. It is a way to express how you feel of love and life itself. To give a message in different words. To be or not

to be, in love in sorrow, but maybe tomorrow we will see. I've always felt the need to write it down, to make it sound. M.A.H.; [a.] Middleport, NY

HINES, RICHARD A.
[b.] April 24, 1944, Brooklyn, NY; [p.] John Hines, Florence Hines; [m.] Carol J. Hines, July 31, 1982; [ch.] Shikirra I. Hines; [ed.] Franklin K. Lane H.S., Brooklyn College; [occ.] Sales Representative; [oth. writ.] Available for publication; [pers.] I am inspired by variations of life.; [a.] Norht Plainfield, NJ

HINES, ROSE ANNA
[b.] March 25, 1947, Cairo, Egypt; [ed.] BA in Psychology, MS in Physical Therapy; [occ.] Physical Therapist, Lecturer; [memb.] Toastmasters, Sierra Club, Braille Institute National Writers Assoc.; [hon.] Graduated Cum Laude, Area Governor of the Year, Speech contest winner; [oth. writ.] A Moment in Time; [pers.] When mental, emotional, spiritual, physical and social are balanced we are happy and healthy. Each are of life provides a plethora of experiences to write about. I may write a prayer in the morning, about rollerblading or gardening in mid day and solving a computer problem at night; [a.] Whittier, CA

HINKLE, SUSAN WYNNE SHAMBAUGH
[pen.] Sue Shambaugh Hinkle; [b.] February 19, 1944, Bakersfield, CA; [p.] Stephen W. Shambaugh and Marilyn Pyle Shambaugh; [m.] Richard Hinkle, July 4; [ch.] Shelly Dean and Stefani Wynn. I have 3 grandsons.; [ed.] Central HS, Calgary, Canada, Mt. Royal College, Calgary, Canada, Solano County Hospital, (SCROP Medical Laboratory), Fairfield, California, Home Veterinary Education, Solano College, Fairfield, California; [occ.] Managing Editor, International Cat Publication, 1988 to present; [memb.] CFA, TICA, ACFA, GCCF (England), Kappa Zi Sorority (Canada), High Street Baptist Church (England), American Cancer Association and Tumor Registry; [hon.] City and State Wide Spelling Bee, Tulsa, Oklahoma 1953, Track and Field Awards, Calgary, Canada 1959-61, Editor of the Year Award, The Royal Reflector, Mt. Royal College, Calgary, Canada 1962, Title of "Miss Sub Zero", Rapid City, South Dakota 1965, Team Winner, Special Olympics, Mildenhall, England 1982, International, National and Regional Awards, CFA and TICA, 1985 to present; [oth. writ.] "Wings On Layaway" (an autobiography), "Crossroads" (a collection of personal writings and poems), "Numerous articles have been published in various cat related publications including: "British Sterling Goes For Gold", the Silver and Golden Persian in England (published 1985, CFA Annual Yearbook), "Sterling Reflections", a History of the Silver Persian, published 1992; [pers.] I am a 20 year survivor of Ovarian cancer, Stage III. Faith in God, my doctors, family and friends has given me the mileage, determination and endurance to survive. My writings are the window to my soul, in which I strive to reflect the goodness and love I have received from the persona of these entities, and from their constant expressions of love of nature and life. I have been greatly influenced by the writings and poems of Helen Steiner Rice, Frank Topping of England, Francois de Fenelon (c.1600), and the apostle, Paul.; [a.] Vacaville, CA

HITTLE II, JAMES ELMER
[pen.] Jim H.; [b.] May 4, 1963, Nebr. Pender; [p.] Jeanett and James Elmer Hittle Sr.; [ch.] Adam James Hittle; [ed.] Psychology Paralegal Welding Life!; [memb.] N of TB. Huh. Fremont Christian and Missionary Alliance Church; [hon.] Kat; [oth. writ.] M.L. Letters, poems; [pers.] Dedication, Lucy R. Chad W. for love of! Mom and Dad; [a.] Deacator Omaha, NE

HOBERG, LISA DIANE
[b.] June 21, 1962, Wilmington, DE; [p.] Charles and Joan Hoberg; [ed.] BFA - University of Delaware Training and Painting; [occ.] Graphic Designer/Artist/Illustrator; [hon.] National Honor Society, Kodak Scholastic Art Awards - Gold Key recipient; [pers.] After spending most of my life illustrating with paint and color, I have found that you can also paint with words; [a.] Newark, DE

HOBSON, RAYMOND D.
[b.] July 10, 1970, Baltimore, MD; [hon.] Most alcohol consumed by an individual before the age of 25.; [oth. writ.] Unpublished: 700 poems, screenplay "The Last Shaman" and a requiem for four voices "The Song of God"; [pers.] Everybody's got a fuckin' problem.; [a.] Schaumburg, IL

HODGES, ASHLEY
[b.] December 31, 1995, Savannah, GA; [p.] Mr. and Mrs. J. K. Pasch; [ed.] 6th grade Wilder Middle School; [memb.] Ballet South, next generation; [oth. writ.] Several others, mostly poems, some stories; [pers.] I'm a dancer. I've been taking 9 yrs. and want to become a dancer when I grow up. I've had many solos in ballet. I love to write. Sometimes it just comes and I write it!; [a.] Savannah, GA

HOEHN, TERRY
[pen.] Terry Hoehn; [b.] N.Y.C.; [p.] Mr. and Mrs. R. Farone (deceased); [m.] George R. Hoehn (deceased); [ch.] George R. Hoehn III, Catherine Hoehn Munnier; [ed.] Grad. James Monroe H.S., Business School, Academy of Fine Arts, Art Student League.; [occ.] Realistic painting artist; [memb.] National League of Amer. Pen women (art category), National Art League, Art Students League, Burr Artists; [hon.] 1981-Honorable Mention and third prize, 1982 and 1985, special awards, 1990 may lake award, 1991 second place,; [oth. writ.] Many poems never tried any contests or publishers.; [pers.] Have a zest for life, live every day as tho' it is the last day of life. Attempt to record things that I witness and experience.; [a.] New York City, NY

HOFER, SHELDON JAY
[pen.] Gibber; [b.] March 1, 1979, Portage La Prairie, Manitoba, Canada; [p.] John and Rebecca Hofer; [ed.] High School; [occ.] Student; [memb.] Elm River Waist Watchers Society, Member of Bruder hof Community, Woodcrest Youth Club, Woodcrest Community Choir, Woodcrest Glee Club; [hon.] Woodcrest Writer of the Year Award; [oth. writ.] Numerous Poems including: Coming of the Dew, Sandpiper, Middle of the Night. Several articles for the Woodchuck Journal; [pers.]

I am Inspired by the work of Robert Frost, Ernest Hemmingway and other great written such as "Jack Sossa."; [a.] Rifton, NY

HOFFMAN, CHERYL A.
[b.] March 13, 1944, Detroit, MI; [p.] Robert Cottrell and Madeline Cottrell; [m.] Larry C. Hoffman, January 23, 1965; [ch.] Lori C., Matthew B. and Michael R.; [ed.] Bach Ed. University of Hawaii; [occ.] Payroll Clerk - S & S Electric Co., Inc.; [memb.] First United Methodist Church of Tarpon Springs; [a.] Palm Harbor, FL

HOFFMAN, DON A.
[pen.] Don "The Indian" Hoffman; [b.] January 18, 1955, Ohio; [p.] Loyd Lamb Jr. and Alma Langston; [m.] Kathryn Love Hoffman, May 12, 1994; [ch.] Sunshine Rae Hoffman, Stephanie Ann Hoffman, Stepchildren Scottie, Love, Patrick Dooley, Wally Lee Love; [ed.] High School Valley Forge Academy Louisiana State Univ.; [occ.] Disabled - writer, poetry - songs (High Profile Project Mgr. in Petro Chem Const.); [memb.] BMI - Broadcast Music Inc., Native American Indian Assoc., V.V.A., Masonry, N.R.A.; [hon.] N.A.I.A. Warriors Feather, Decorated Veteran - Vietnam Era Football and Basketball Academic; [oth. writ.] I have over 1,200 writings on various topics throughout my life. I've written songs for movie sound tracks and albums. My true joy is poetry.; [pers.] I try to touch a cord or fibre of life in all I write from my experiences. For at some point life is: Sadness, rejoicing, pain and emotional most glorious of all - wondrously; [a.] Wichita, KS

HOFMANN, LISA DAWN
[b.] July 13, 1971, Norfolk, NE; [p.] Lyla Hofmann, Don Hofmann; [ed.] Associate of Liberal Arts Degree- Northeast College in Norfolk, NE, Watertown Senior High in Wtn S Dak; [occ.] Nanny (Child Care Professional); [memb.] Distinguished Member of National Library of Poetry; [hon.] 1st place dance award for Dance Squad in College; [oth. writ.] A few other poems published, one by Library of Poetry; [pers.] Every human on earth needs love to grow and flourish. By grasping thoughts and putting them on paper we are able to extend these precious moments and make life important.; [a.] Cincinnati, OH

HOGAN, BARBARA
[b.] February 3, 1957, Darby, PA; [p.] Grover C. Kesser Jr., Patricia C. Kesser (deceased); [ch.] Michelle Patricia, Timothy Michael; [ed.] Interboro High School, Glenolden, PA, Delaware Technical and Community College, Georgetown, DE, University of Alaska, Anchorage, AK; [occ.] Branch Manager, Safety and Supply Co., Anchorage, AK; [memb.] Chugiak-Eagle River 1996 Arctic Winter Games; [oth. writ.] Several poems published in local publications, writing a book of haiku; [pers.] My writing has been influenced by various life situations and the beautiful state of Alaska. All of my writings come from the "heart" and have special meaning to me.; [a.] Anchorage, AK

HOIBY, KIMBERLY A.
[pen.] Kim Hoiby; [b.] June 14, 1952, Everett, WN; [p.] Kathleen and Glenn Hoiby; [ch.] Matthew J. Legare; [ed.] Everett High School, Everett Community College; [occ.] Master Gardener; [memb.] Talkeetna Historical Society; [oth. writ.] In progress; [pers.] Poetry is the avenue of my emotional expression, whether in darkness or light; [a.] Talkeetna, AK

HOITINK, CASSANDRA
[b.] April 2, 1982, Corry, PA; [p.] Keven and Cathy Hoitink; [ed.] Clymer Central School; [occ.] Student at Clymer Central School; [memb.] FBLA - Future-Business Leaders of America; [hon.] I am continuously on the Honor Roll at school; [oth. writ.] I have lots of other poems, not published though; [pers.] I wish for world peace and that people don't judge others by their race or color; [a.] Findley Lake, NY

HOLBROOKS, VIRGINIA
[b.] September 22, 1954, Clayton, GA; [p.] Robert and Willie Mae Weaver; [m.] Samuel Holbrooks, July 15, 1972; [ch.] Samuel Mark, Jason Robert; [ed.] Habersham Central High, Truett McConnell College (still working on, undergraduate); [occ.] Special Education, Paraprofessional and School Bus Driver, Liberty Elementary School; [memb.] Stephens County Special Olympic Committee (7 yrs.); [oth. writ.] Although I haven't had any other publications, I do have a compilation of poems I have written. Hopefully, this is a beginning for me.; [pers.] I enjoy expressing my feelings through poetry writing.; [a.] Toccoa, GA

HOLDMAN, JOAN F.
[pen.] Joan F. Holdman; [b.] December 26, 1939, Festus; [p.] Harold Primo, Rachel Tangen; [m.] Leroy Holdman, April 15, 1988; [ch.] Lawrence, Kevin, and Rick Lamontagne, Steven and David Holdman, Melissa Mobley (16, Grandchildren); [ed.] Roosevelt High, Meramec Community College, St. Louis, MO.; [occ.] Author-Writer; [memb.] International Society of Poets; [oth. writ.] "Success" in "A moment in Time" anthology. I write for seven community papers audience of 180,000. Column titled "Opinion Shapers." Completed three children manuscripts. They give strong positive messages to all races. I have just begun looking for a publisher. I'm also writing a self-help book and plan to write Novel this winter.; [pers.] I feel we can reach the young children, it will stop negative racial problems in schools. I write in my articles about strong values for community and family. I consider myself a motivator. I draw on my life experiences when writing.; [a.] Chesterfield, MO

HOLLIER, PATRICIA G.
[pen.] Patricia G. Hollier; [b.] June 29, 1950, Bastrop, LA; [p.] Doyle Dawson, Thelma McCraw; [m.] Rodney Hollier, May 9, 1981; [ch.] Jason Landry, Michael Landry; [ed.] Port Neches - Groves High School, graduate North East University, Monroe, LA; [occ.] Manager Motel 6 820 145 S Conroe, TX; [memb.] Sacred Heart Catholic Church, Certified Counselor for Rape/ Suicide Ctr in Beaumont, TX; [pers.] I'm a realist, I love to write about the real events and persons that have touched my life. I hope that others can relate and be inspired by my life encounters.

HOLMAN, DAVE L.
[b.] May 25, 1954, Stockton, CA; [p.] Charles and Louise Holman, Step Father: Richard Brown; [m.] Deena Holman, July 6, 1994; [ch.] Chad Alan Holman, Tiffany Laris Holman; [ed.] Franklin Sr. High, Stockton, CA. Delta College, Stkn, CA.; [occ.] Disabled - Had worked as a mill man for 20 yrs, doing custom wood work.; [pers.] I thought of writing poems for years, but until my brother, passed away 12-9-94, I was never inspired enough to write any down. Most of my poems deal with grief, the healing process and love of Life.; [a.] Stockton, CA

HOLMES, LINDSEY DEBRA
[pen.] Lindsey Debra Holmes; [b.] March 12, 1981, Vermont, IL; [p.] Lesley and Howie Holmes; [ed.] Horace W. Porter School and intend on going to South Winsor High School; [occ.] Babysitting School; [hon.] Connecticut state under 13 soccer team, varsity middle school soccer team and track team; [pers.] I was influenced by my great grandfather who also wrote poetry. I intend on becoming an architect and continue writing, stories and poems; [a.] Columbia, CT

HOLMES, RANDY
[pers.] Randy is originally from Indiana, but now lives in Greenfield MA, a small western Massachusetts town nestled at the edge of the Berkshires. Randy lives with his children Angie and Nick, two cats Thelma and Louise, and six fish. Randy has a master's degree in management and psychology from Cambridge College, and owns a company that teaches disabled people work skills and habits. Randy's ultimate goal with his writing is to collaborate with Elton John, which has been Randy's greatest influence.

HOLT, CALVIN S.
[b.] September 19, 1958, Miami; [m.] Cynthia S. Holt, October 8, 1993; [ch.] Expecting the birth of our 1st son August, '95; [ed.] Carol City Sr. High School, Miami Dade North Campus Community College; [occ.] Substitute Teacher and Musician-Songwriter; [memb.] United Teachers Union; [pers.] Let no person put you down so low that you hate him, in order to know how to survive let life be a Work of art to seek perfection of character; [a.] Miami, FL

HONEYCUTT, ASHLEY
[b.] May 21, 1981, Johnson City, TN; [p.] Steve and Regenial Honeycutt; [ed.] Presently attending the 8th grade at Jonesville Middle School, soon to go to Lee High School in '96; [memb.] I'm in the JMS Library Club and I am a member of an Odossey of the Mind Team.; [hon.] 1st place in OM competition I received an honor for throwing 34.7 in the shot put; [oth. writ.] Have not been in any other writings than this one, because I was afraid of failure and disappointment; [pers.] I have been influenced greatly by my parents and grandparents to get a good education, and take my great mind and writing efforts and write poems stories; [a.] Jonesville, VA

HONGSERMEIER, LARRY R.
[pen.] Dutch Hongsermeier; [b.] July 16, 1941, Centralia, IL; [p.] Fred and Alma Hongsermeier; [m.] Alice E. Hongsermeier, June 26, 1982; [ch.]

Six girls and four boys; [ed.] Associate of Arts Degree Award 1962; [occ.] Railroad Conductor; [memb.] Christian Love Fellowship Church, Antioch, TN; [pers.] I am simply a man blessed by God with the talent to write poetry which testifies Him to the world. All who read it, enjoy it and more will.

HOOGHUIS, MARY ELIZABETH
[b.] March 7, 1964, Pittsburgh, PA; [p.] Paul J. Prucnal, Patricia A. Prucnal; [m.] William Hooghuis, December 21, 1989; [ed.] Gateway Senior High, Dequesne University; [pers.] This poem was written in honor and loving memory of my beautiful little sister, Jean Marie, who arrived in this world November 6, 1967 and left our earth quite unexpectedly January 1, 1995. Jean, your life has forever imprinted an indelible mark on our hearts, your sudden passing an eternally inconsolable ache in our souls for your time with us was far too brief. We love you and we miss you!; [a.] Missouri City, TX

HOOPER, KENNETH ALTON
[pen.] Kenny Hooper; [b.] October 17, 1978, Wilmington, NC; [p.] Teresa and Kenny Hooper; [ed.] Freshman at North Brunswick High School, Leland, NC; [memb.] Wrestling Team, Football Team; [hon.] Student of the Month, Academic Award for 3.0 GPA; [oth. writ.] Short stories; [pers.] I try to write from my heart.; [a.] Leland, NC

HOOPER, RICHARD
[pen.] Richard Hooper; [b.] March 8, 1934, Chattanooga, TN; [p.] Harry Hooper, Julia Hooper; [ch.] Alison Hooper; [ed.] Chattanooga Central High School Chattanooga, Tenn.; [occ.] Chattanooga Public Schools, Maintenance Dept.; [memb.] Ridgeview Baptist Church, Eagles Club, V.F.W.; [oth. writ.] Other poems: a book of poems, "Reflections in Poetry" copyright 1992 by Richard Hooper, also several poems published in the Chattanooga News- Freepress, Chatt., Tenn.; [pers.] (I love Poetry and Music too.) I have been writing since 1982. Poetry is a way of expressing one's feelings through words, so many others can relate to. I thank you the Selection Committee for selecting my poem in the semi-finalist; [a.] Chattanooga, TN

HOOVER, GARY S.
[pen.] The Hoov; [b.] February 11, 1954, Cape May Court House, NJ; [p.] Mr. and Mrs. Clayton Hoover; [m.] Cathy (fiancee), October 14, 1995; [ed.] Associate Degree Police Science from Montgomery County Community College; [occ.] General Worker Labs, Merck and Co.; [memb.] Tennis and Chess; [hon.] Presidential Physical Fitness Award (high school), football, tennis student council, Rep. state and national high school; [oth. writ.] Anthology, Ode to Cathy, A Vision of Yesterday's Dream, To the Top, Amber Eyes; [pers.] Live life to the fullest because time on this earth is short.; [a.] Schwenksville, PA

HOPPE, BARBARA ANNE
[b.] December 23, 1974, Alpena, MI; [ch.] Kayla Marie Hoppe; [ed.] GED - Oxbow; [hon.] Alpena High School Arts award; [oth. writ.] Several poems.; [pers.] Writing poems helps me express the way I feel.; [a.] Alpena, MI

HORN, DEBORAH IRENE JOHNSON
[pen.] Deb; [b.] July 8, 1953, Lawrence, KS; [p.]
Ivan K. Johnson, Eloise M. Caldwell; [m.] Vernell
R. Horn, November 9, 1986; [ch.] Nicole Rene
Johnson, Dione Michelle Johnson; [ed.] East High
School, Denver, CO, Alcohol Drug Abuse and
Addiction, Training DCCCA - Laurence KS,
Relapse Prevention Specialist Training - Cenaps
Chicago; [occ.] Addictions Counselor, Business
Partner with Spouse Self Employed; [memb.]
Ottawa Christian Center; [hon.] First Black Female
Addictions Counselor employed by DCCA, the
first Substance Abuse Agency in Lawrence KS.;
[oth. writ.] One poem published as a child,
currently writing a book about my experience in
life, as a recovering alcoholic and the similarity, as
it relates to the state of our nation!; [pers.] There is
no dollar value that can be placed on encourage-
ment and hope! The cost of giving it to others
cannot be counted, it is so small. It's worth in the
lives of those, who receive it is Priceless! No one
need be bankrupt!; [a.] Ottawa, KS

HORN JR., KENNETH
[b.] April 17, 1956, Laconia, NH; [p.] Kenneth
Horn, Myrtle Horn; [m.] Tammy Gatter, March
23, 1986; [ed.] Charlotte High School Punta
Gorda, Fla.; [occ.] Operations Manager Uniforms,
Inc. Las Vegas, NV; [pers.] I love writing animal
poems and children's rhymes. But this is the first
item I've ever submitted for publication.; [a.] Las
Vegas, NV

HORNE, APRIL L.
[pen.] April L. horne; [b.] January 2,1962,
Franklin, NH; [p.] Alvin and Ruby Horne; [m.]
Divorced; [ch.] Isaiah and Robert; [ed.] GED,
some college, Certified Nurse Assistant through the
American Red Cross, Child Care; [occ.] Child
Care Provider; [memb.] Too many book clubs,
music clubs, etc. Volunteer my writing skills to
women's organizations; [hon.] Two of my poems
have been published in local newspaper, I wrote a
poem for two organizations.; [oth. writ.] I have a
book of poems, I've written entitled, "Love
Battling, the Lightning and Thunder." Goal to
have it published.; [pers.] I have written poetry
since I can remember, my goal is to have my book
in its entirety be published. I may be dreaming but
it's a goal. I'm a fan of Edgar Allan Poe.; [a.]
Manchester, NH

HORNER, WANDA
[pen.] Wanie; [b.] January 23, 1948, Scioto
County; [p.] Clyde and Alive Horner; [ed.]
Graduated from Green Township High School;
[occ.] Cook; [memb.] International Society of
Poets; [hon.] Received Editors Choice award and a
awards of merits for property published; [oth.
writ.] Summer Long, Chainless Minds, Homeless,
poems published in anthology by National Library
of poetry also Doors Pulled Tight published in
anthology by Famous Poet Society; [pers.] I strive
to write better poetry each time I pick up my pen. I
hope to someday publish my own book of poetry;
[a.] Franklin Furnace, OH

HORTON, SHIRLEY M.
[pen.] Shirley Campbell Horton; [b.] August 18
1829, Brockton, MA; [p.] William and Gertrude
Macomber; [m.] Lewellyn R. Horton, November

2, 1991; [ch.] Christopher Bonnie, Mark, Beth and
Todd - Danielle Matthew, Brittni, Lisa, Laura,
Brian; [ed.] Graduated from Howard High, W.
Bridgewater and Springfield Library Training
School (last class) Springfield, MA; [occ.] Wife-
Homemaker; [memb.] Member of West Yarmouth
Congregation Church - W. Yarmouth, MA. Served
on many committees. Also song with many
chorus' on Caps. Cod.; [oth. writ.] Have written
for several church newsletters. This is my first
poem submitted for publication.; [pers.] I feel that
life is a constant growing experience. We learn
from every situation that comes to us, that if we
have faith, we will overcome the evil with good.
Through poetry we can express ourselves and the
world around us.; [a.] Taunton, MA

HOSSEINI, AUYAR
[b.] October 27, 1919; [m.] Azalee, January 3,
1950; [ch.] Two daughters, Nonz and Leila; [ed.]
Masters in Music Composition and Bariton Opera
Singer; [occ.] Retired; [hon.] Full scholarship of
Juliard and Hart College of Music; [oth. writ.]
Musical compositions and two books of unpub-
lished poetry. Hoping to publish some of them
soon.; [pers.] Never had the desire to make a living
in music nor pushed for recognition. I was not
borned with that kind of ego. No need to print
anything about me. Thank you; [a.] Van Nuys, CA

HOUSE, BETTY E.
[pen.] Betty E. House; [b.] September 24, 1943,
Smithfield, NC; [p.] Mary E. Graham; [m.]
Alonna House, Jr. (Separated), March 15, 1967;
[ch.] Rodney A., Melissa D., Pamela L. House;
[ed.] Hight School Scts., Smithfield, NC,
Georgetown V. Hospital Nursing Aide, Washing-
ton, DC. O.I.C. Training Program, Washington,
DC; [memb.] Freedom Chapel Church, Washing-
ton, DC; [hon.] Georgetown V. Hospital of
Nursing Program, Certificate of Appreciation
Malcolm X Elem. School, 1978, Award Freedom
Chapel Church (Femomical, 1981 Anniversary);
[oth. writ.] I have written, about 50 other poems
that have been read in my Church, and one on
radio, WFAX in VA wrote two poem for my
Church; [pers.] That my writing may be in
couragement to others that my writing may lead
other to Jesus Christ and a little light and up leifry
may come into new life.

HOUSTON, BILLIE
[pen.] Barri Bryan; [b.] November 24, 1927,
Texas; [m.] M. H. Houston; [ch.] Five; [ed.] AA -
San Antonio College, BA University of Texas, San
Antonio, MA - University of Texas San Antonio;
[occ.] Writer; [memb.] Austin Writers' League,
Canyon Lake, Writers' Guild; [oth. writ.] Novels,
poems, essays; [pers.] Poetry is an economy of
words that expresses an extravagance of feelings;
[a.] Billie Houston, TX

HOVLAND, JULIA
[b.] February 9, 1918, Sandy, UT; [m.] John
Hovland, October 10, 1938; [ch.] 3 sons; [ed.]
High School; [oth. writ.] A few poems; [pers.] I
began writing poetry, March, 1994. This is a true
poem, written about my husband. Since I now
have time, writing poetry has become my hobby.;
[a.] Great Falls, MT

HOWARD, JEREKA
[b.] August 13, 1980, Rock Hill; [p.] Jerry
Stevenson, Lorry Ann Howard; [ed.] Rawlinson
Road Middle School; [memb.] Step Club, Choir -
Big Calvary Baptist Church, Sisters For Success
Club; [hon.] Gra-Y Raiders Cheerleading Award.
"B" Honor Roll; [pers.] My goal is to be a teacher.
I want to be able to teach others and to see the joy I
can bring to children.; [a.] Rock Hill, SC

HOWE, AMBER
[pen.] Amber Howe; [b.] April 9, 1947, Pennsyl-
vania; [p.] Edith and Roy Howe; [ch.] Todd Austin
Howe and Blake Justin Howe; [ed.] University of
Pittsburgh, Georgia State University, University of
Maryland; [occ.] Administrative Assistant;
[memb.] Humane Society, Society for the
Prevention of Cruelty to Animals; [oth. writ.]
Various unpublished works as presents to friends to
celebrate the milestones of their lives and mine.;
[pers.] I endeavor to give a voice to emotion. I am
inspired by romance and Victoriana. I am also
inspired through my Celtic ancestry and the Irish
bell that tolls for me.; [a.] Bowie, MD

HUDASKO, MELISSA
[b.] November 21, 1982, NJ; [p.] Gary and
Meredith Hudasko; [ed.] Student at St. Vincent de
Paul Catholic School entering 7th grade Sept. '95;
[hon.] 1995 recipient of the John Hopkins
University, Center for Talented Youth Special
Achievement Award, First honors for academic
effort 1994-1995 St. Vincent de Paul School; [oth.
writ.] Several poems published in hometown
newspapers, and poem The Rainforest published in
River of Dreams by the Nat'l Library of Poetry;
[pers.] I try to focus on the issues surrounding
those endangered species who need our enlighten-
ment to help them. I believe in and support all the
efforts of such renowned folks as Jane Goodall,
Diane Fossey and Beriute Galdikas.; [a.] Green
Brook, NJ

HUDOCK, GLORIA JOAN
[pen.] Gloria J. Hudock; [b.] October 4, 1931,
Bethlehem, PA; [p.] John McCloskey, Esther
McCloskey; [m.] Joseph Hudock, September 3,
1955; [ch.] Blaine Joseph, Gregory David, Lisa
Anne, Doreen Marie; [ed.] White Haven High
School Art Instruction, Inc.; [occ.] Retired;
[memb.] St. Patrick's R.C. Church; [oth. writ.]
Numerous Poems - none published; [a.] White
Haven, PA

HUDSON, JILL C.
[b.] November 25, 1968, Maryland; [p.] Charles
Hudson and Connie Zulick; [ed.] Bachelor of
Science, Master of Business Administration; [occ.]
Customer Service Manager; [memb.] 4-H (14
years), Upcounty Advisory Board, HOW,
International Honor Society, Cooperative Extension
Services; [hon.] National 4-H Congress, Maryland
State Public Speaking champion, Who's Who in 4-
H, 4-H Key Award; [pers.] There is truly a bond
between parent and child - a vital connection
indeed.; [a.] Gaithersburg, MD

HUFF, TRACY JILL
[b.] September 8, 1978, Brunswick, GA; [p.] Joyce and Jerry Huff; [ed.] Attends Mitchell High School in Colorado Springs, CO; [occ.] Full-time Student; [memb.] Member of Student Council, school softball and soccer teams; [hon.] On Honor Roll at school and taking advanced classes; [oth. writ.] Writes poetry of all types and is a writer as well as copy editor for her school newspaper The Echelon; [pers.] What a price we pay for experience, when we must sell our youth to buy it.; [a.] Colorado Springs, CO

HUFFINE, SANDRA K.
[pen.] Kayce; [b.] March 22, 1960, Tennessee; [p.] Walter H. Lepley and Sally Randolph; [ch.] Casslyn Sage Huffine; [ed.] Pre-med, Motlow State; [occ.] Chemist: Bionetics, Chem-lab and Artist; [hon.] Dean's List, All Around Cowgirl; [pers.] When the world stops turning - The only things that will matter are … Who you loved and who loved you…; [a.] Shelbyville, TN

HUGHES, BRUCE A.
[b.] February 25, 1947, Long Beach CA; [m.] Lisa B. Hughes, December 24, 1978; [ch.] Scott, Samantha, Alexandra; [ed.] B.S., M.B.A., L.L.B.; [occ.] Attorney/CPA; [memb.] AICPA, CSCPA, St Bar of California, Orange Co. Bar Assn, Vice Chair Harbors, Parks and Beaches for Orange County; [hon.] Top 1/10 of 1% in United States for CPA Exam; [oth. writ.] Numerous poems, including my Vietnam Anthology; [pers.] I adore my wife. She greatly in influence my writing.; [a.] Orange, CA

HUGHES, CARRIE
[pen.] Carrie Adams; [b.] November 15, 1968, Corpus Christi, TX; [p.] Rodney Adams, Alice Smith; [m.] Kevin Stewart, July 8, 1994; [ch.] Crystal Ann, Daniel Curtis; [ed.] Attended Corpus Cristi High School, studied reporting and Lit. my favorite class and course was English Lit.; [occ.] Bev. Manager at Big Casino "Shereton" in Casino Center, Tunica, MS 38676; [memb.] Was a member of a local small writing class for amateur reporting.; [hon.] Won awards all thru school for small poems written for extra grades.; [oth. writ.] I write poems around the house, on special occasions for family wedding and birthdays etc. never had a poem published.; [pers.] I feel people can better understand me threw my writing of everyday life, therefore I better understand my self, and with that better, appreciate life.; [a.] West Helena, AR

HUGHES, IREAN VENGE
[pen.] Lee-mari; [b.] November 18, 1932, Alabama; [p.] Athey and Nellie Venge; [m.] Divorced; [ch.] Dimmy, Danielle; [ed.] Antioch Dilland Fisk. U,; [memb.] Stone River P.B. Church Prince Hall local #61 O.E.S. Board of Deaconess, Murfreesboro Writers Club.; [oth. writ.] A Creative non-fiction book (unpublished) several poems. Short Stories. Several plays.; [pers.] My mother was 107 years old when, She passed-away in 1989, I write about the Glories she told me - The poems is about how I feel. I'm unable to verbalize the feeling I write about.; [a.] Murfreesboro, TN

HUGHES, VERONICA L.
[b.] February 19, 1970, Chicago; [p.] Martha A. Hughes, Alfred L. Hughes; [ed.] Frank L. Gillespie, Calumet High School; [occ.] Security Officer; [memb.] Calumet High School Student, Government Calumet High School, Student Counselor Helper; [hon.] Geometry Award (Calumet High) School, Gillespie Elementary Honor Roll/Citizenship; [oth. writ.] Images, Who Am I, Fantasy, Destiny, Plea and Battle; [pers.] I am very influenced by actors with great television performance and great deliverance of acting ability; [a.] Chicago, IL

HUGUS, EDWARD D.
[b.] July 5, 1953, Pittsburgh, PA; [p.] Robert E. and Lillian Hugus; [ed.] High School, US Army; [occ.] L.P.N. Operating Room Nurse; [memb.] Local Clubs and Activities; [hon.] Graduated 3rd in Class, U.S. Army Engineer School; [oth. writ.] Several poems published by a small publisher in the area.; [pers.] Truly good writing comes from the heart. Once inspired, all things become possible; [a.] Cranberry Township, PA

HULL, SANDRA
[b.] April 10, 1978, Albin, IA; [p.] Tom and Edith Hull; [ed.] Currently a senior at Ottumwa High School; [occ.] Student and work part time at Wal-Mart; [memb.] Highland Hotshots 4-H Club, Ottumwa High School SADD Chapter, Ottumwa Baptist Temple, Associate Membership in the International Society of Poets; [hon.] Several 4-H awards, high school honor roll, two presidential academic fitness awards, Dog Showmanship awards, several academic trophies and awards; [oth. writ.] Poems published in other anthologies; [pers.] After high school graduation I plan to attend college for two or four years. I would like to major in accounting or business management. I also hope to marry and start a family after college.; [a.] Ottumwa, IA

HUMPHREY, NICOLE
[b.] August 28, 1973, Houston, TX; [p.] Mimi Martin, Robert Rosenberg; [m.] Michael Humphrey, January 7, 1994; [ch.] Ryan Austin; [ed.] Lafayette High, St. Louis Community College; [occ.] Housemaker, Freelance Writer; [memb.] National Authors Registry; [oth. writ.] Several poems in local publications, 2 poems published in another anthology; [pers.] My goal is to teach others that poems are not works of fiction, but can indeed be considered non-fiction. I write on real subjects. Nothing I write is fiction; [a.] Garland, TX

HUNT, BOBBY
[pen.] Bobby Hunt, Bob Hunter; [b.] January 28, 1934, Chicago, IL; [p.] Louis and Arlene; [m.] Deceased - Earlene, June 1956; [ch.] Chris, Ronald; [ed.] High School, One Year College, People oriented courses, sales, etc.; [occ.] Poet; [memb.] Kiwanis Club, USD Dads Against Drunk Driving, First Christian Fellowship Church; [hon.] Poet Laurate: Kiwanis Club - USD; [oth. writ.] The Death of Emett Louis Till - (subtitle) Tho I Die. Published in part in many newspapers in 1955 due to his lynching in Mississippi in 1955; [pers.] The youth of today are oriented toward being cool. My poem will hopefully guide them in that direction using their venacular; [a.] San Diego, CA

HUNT, CLARECE
[b.] December 27, 1922, Pineview Wilcox Co., GA; [p.] John B. and Alice R. Dennard; [m.] Hewlett J. Hunt, January 13, 1938; [ch.] James T., Robert L. and Alice H. Ramsdell; [ed.] Jr. High School; [occ.] Retired Professional Seamstress and Accountant - Bicentennial Year of 1976; [memb.] Pineview-Finleyson Methodist Church; [oth. writ.] Poems - Beloved Georgia and Our America published in Georgia Images and Reflection of Poets and Authors - collected.; [pers.] Dr A. G. Hendrix practised medicine in Perry, Houston Co. Georgia from the early 1930's to the late '80's. He was a native of Franklin, Head Co. GA. A dedicated servant.; [a.] Pineview, GA

HUNTER, ISABELLE
[pen.] Isabelle; [b.] February 16, 1927, Penna; [p.] Lucy and Alex Jackson; [ed.] High School Grad Communication; [occ.] Retired, Volunteer Poet; [memb.] Life study, Fellowship Life, Boston Library Life, Museum of Science; [hon.] Bartender's Cert., Bible School Diploma; [oth. writ.] In book Sparles in Sand; [pers.] Live from day to day, life of learning; [a.] Boston, MA

HUNTER JR., BENFORD
[pen.] Benlthe; [b.] January 6, 1946, Suffolk, VA; [p.] Ms. Annie Lee Lawton, Mr. Benford Hunter Jr.; [m.] Mrs. Paquita Lawrence Hunter, June 4, 1989; [ch.] Benford J. Hunter; [ed.] Booker T. Washington High School, Norfolk State University; [occ.] Union Resident, President of local 2426 UAW; [memb.] East End Baptist Church, NAACP (Suffolk Branch), Chairman Suffolk Democratic Committee; [hon.] Poem My Mother Day Prayer - published in the local newspaper on Mother's Day May 1994; [oth. writ.] Favorite: I'm Your Child Lord. One Heart Beat Away, Why Do You Bless Me Lord, Foxy, "Mother" converted to "Words"; [pers.] I've never been concerned about the type of Religion a man has what concerns me is a man who has Religion; [a.] Suffolk, VA

HUNTLEY, ERMA F.
[b.] February 24, 1908, Columbus, OH; [p.] Julia Knight and Grover Knight; [m.] James H. Huntley (deceased), July 1, 1933; [ed.] East High School, Columbus, Ohio; [occ.] Retired; [memb.] Goodwill Industries Daughters of the Nile - Shrine White Shrine Of Jerusalem United Methodist Church Project Hope Symphony Club Of Central Ohio; [hon.] National Award From Goodwill Industries for Volunteer Service. Honored by St. Anthony Hospital Columbus O. Awarded Certificate of completion from adjustment center visually impaired person blind adj. (center); [pers.] I pray that I may help someone every day and share with others what God has given to me.; [a.] Cape Coral, FL

HURDLE, LINDA
[b.] February 25, 1952, Los Angeles, CA; [p.] Nelma and Sam Hurdle; [ch.] Lakeesha Shawna and Crystal Page; [ed.] High School and some College Education; [occ.] Head Start Teacher; [memb.] International Society of Poets 1994-995; [hon.] Editor's Choice Award; [oth. writ.] Writings are on other biographical Data forms that I sent you.; [pers.] I want my poetry to be noticed; [a.] Sacramento, CA

HURST, SUSAN
[b.] June 13, 1964, Syracuse, NY; [p.] Walker Hurst, Arlene Hurst; [ed.] AAD Nursing; [occ.] Registered Nurse Naro ICU; [memb.] AANN, AACN, ANA, OPAC, Recording for The Blind, American Cancer Society; [hon.] Nurse of the yrs 1994, woman of Clark Air Base award 1984; [a.] Phoenix, AZ

HURST, SUSAN
[b.] April 27, 1956, Fort Worth, TX; [p.] Buddy and Theresa Hurst; [ed.] Paschal High, Tarrant County Junior College, Texas Woman's University; [occ.] Registered Nurse working as a School Nurse; [memb.] Fort Worth Weaving Guild, Texas Association of School Nurses, Tarrant Coalition for Environmental Awareness; [hon.] Six photographs from Kenya, Peru and Tibet won awards and placement for printing in the 1987, 1988 and 1990, Harris Methodist Fort Worth calendar. Won best of show in 1989 photo contest for Women's Haven of Tarrant County.; [pers.] I am grateful for my Creator and the opportunity to create and share this joy with others.; [a.] Fort Worth, TX

HUTCHESON, EDWIN L.
[pen.] 'Buckey'; [b.] June 18, 1946, Butler, PA; [p.] Mr. and Mrs. Carl Heck; [ed.] Butler Sr. High School, Butler, PA, Anderson College, IN, St. Francis Coll. of PA, Loretto, Pennsylvania State Univ., University of Pittsburgh, Pittsburgh, PA; [occ.] Medical/Clinical Social Worker/Educator; [memb.] Phi Delta Kappa, Alpha Psi Omega, Alpha Phi Omega, Alpha Delta Mu, Sigma Delta Chi; [hon.] BPOE scholarship, Dean's List, VA/University of Pittsburgh grad. award, Univ. of Pittsburgh tuition award, Penn State Univ. Conservation award (2 years); [oth. writ.] Author - the Johnstown, PA Floods 1989, 1936, 1977 - a history of the National flood disasters of Johnstown, PA (book); [pers.] God's influence, his goodness, has been - is - and continues to be instrumental in my life!; [a.] Butler, PA

HUTCHINSON, KELLI
[b.] October 12, 1982, Athens, GA; [p.] Susan and Don Hutchinson; [ed.] Currently a 6th grade student at Darlington Middle school in Rome, GA.; [occ.] Student; [memb.] Middle School choir, middle school track team, and junior cotillion; [hon.] Honor student at Darlington Middle School, National Science Olympiad Winner and National Language Arts Olympiad winner for Darlington Lower School (5th grade).; [oth. writ.] None published.; [pers.] Although I'm young, I love to read and write. I aspire to be a writer. I aspire to be a writer and have more of my works published in the future; [a.] Rome, GA

HUTSELL, ROSIE
[b.] May 23, 1951, Forthworth, TX; [p.] Ray Miller, Mary Miller; [m.] John Emery, May 3, 1980; [ch.] Edwin Eugene, Vincen Ernest; [ed.] Hanford High; [occ.] Wife and Mother; [hon.] Fitness and Nutrition Award; [oth. writ.] Unpublished work poems and children book; [pers.] After receiving news of having cancer, writing became my confidant. Since childhood Hellen Keller has been my inspiration.; [a.] Lemoore, CA

HYLTON, WILLIAM ROBERT
[pen.] W. Robert Hylton, Bob Hylton; [b.] November 11, 1923, Pikeville, KY; [p.] Lon and Flora Hylton; [m.] Charlotte Y. Hylton, May 9, 1959; [ch.] Bonnie, Jerry, Wendy, Mason and Lon (D); [ed.] Granby High School, Norfolk, VA, Duquesne Univ., Golden Gate Univ, California for Advanced Studies. BS with Mgmt. Major Notary Public of CA., Real Estate School CA., Connecticut Institute of Children's Lit.; [occ.] Ranch Manager, Teacher-Commu. College of Southern Nevada: Archt. Graphics and Building Technologies.; [memb.] F. and A. M. of Hawaii, 32 Scottish Rite of Free Masonry, PM Kiluea Lodge 330 Assembly of God Church, Natl. Notary Assn.; [hon.] Honorable Discharge U.S. Air Force 1942-1946, Outstanding Achievement Award on Retirement from Bechtel Engr. Corp. Outstanding Achievement Award Aloha Council B.S.A. Hawaii.; [oth. writ.] Four (4) Western Fiction novels, numerous short stories and poems, past editor optimist club paper, over eighty (80) unpublished poems and quotations.; [pers.] This life we live can be calm and placid but do not fall prey to it's silence, for within our realms of false contentment, there sleeps the unmerciful ego-enmity of survival which harbors nor respect for love, trust or endeavor.; [a.] Las Vegas, NV

HYMAN, THOMAS
[b.] December 18, 1942, Cincinnati, OH; [p.] Jack and Helen Hyman; [ch.] Good children Ari and Sasha; [ed.] BA University of Illinois Walnut Hills High School Law Degree JD University of Cincinnati; [occ.] Attorney for the federal government; [memb.] California Real Estate Broker; [hon.] Winner of several photography contests; [oth. writ.] Poetry and Photo Book with Robert Risch - "The Second Autumn"; [a.] San Francisco, CA

INGRAM, JOSHUA D.L.
[pen.] Josh Ingram; [b.] June 29, 1979, Dixon, IL; [p.] Leslie Ann White; [ed.] Battle Creek Academy 10th grade; [occ.] Student plays organ for Local Churches; [memb.] Central Christian Church 4 yrs on Bible Bowl Team took 2nd place in Nationals, Pipe organist - 10 yrs, Guitarist Classical - 10 yrs, Alto sax - B.C. A Band - 6 yrs; [oth. writ.] Webb Of Love; [a.] Battle Creek, MI

IRELAND, VERA JULIANO
[pen.] Vera Ireland; [b.] November 19, 1935, Egg Harbor City, NJ; [p.] Margaret and Benjamin Ireland; [ch.] Paula, Margaret RN, Geraldine RN; [ed.] I left school in 6th gr.; [memb.] Several Manuscripts Registered with the writers Guild-West (Calif) (Hollywood) CA (during writers strike - my stories were plageurized.); [hon.] Short Stories published in Contests in School grades/aged 12 yrs and in NJ. etc. newspaper, (There after in Egg Harbor, NJ. I was "Honored" when my stories were filmed.; [oth. writ.] Three stories - plageurized and filmed in Hollywood, all seens ideas and roles - as I wrote: "The Legend of Lylah Clare" and "Sister" (First Siamese Twin Idea and story; [pers.] I have many unique and rarely idea poems and asking only for possible publishing, I received headlines at age 12 in a local newspaper in NJ for as tory (THe Magic Pumpkin); [a.] Fremont, CA

ISHIMOTO, BONNIE
[pen.] Bonnie May; [b.] May 25, 1977, Hawaii; [p.] Dennis Ishimoto, Cindy Ishimoto; [ed.] H.P. Baldwin High, Hawaii Pacific University; [occ.] Student; [hon.] Excellence in Language Arts Award; [oth. writ.] Poem (Haiku) published in local newspaper, poem published in Hawaii Education Association book.; [pers.] Through my poetry I express my inner most thoughts and feelings.; [a.] Wailuku, HI

IVES, THOMAS J.
[b.] March 14, 1948, Oberlin, OH; [p.] Wilbur J. Ives, Angeline Ives; [m.] Norma Iris Ives, June 5, 1993; [ch.] Thomas W. Ives, Christopher S. Ives; [ed.] Oberlin Senior High School, Ohio State University - B.S. in Business Administration, Major was Marketing; [occ.] Sales Account representative - Invacare, Inc. Elyria, Ohio; [oth. writ.] Numerous other poems of various lengths and subjects; [pers.] Nice guys might finish last, but you sure can make a lot of friends along the way!; [a.] Lorain, OH

IVUSIC, MAUREEN
[b.] March 29, 1969, Rockville, MD; [p.] Mr. & Mrs. Mallet; [m.] Sean Ivusic, July 16, 1994; [ed.] B.A. Rhetoric and Composition; [occ.] Assistant Recruiter, Darden School of Business, U.V.A.; [memb.] Toastmaster's International; [hon.] Cum laude, Mt. St. Mary's, Emmitsburg, MD, Rhetoric and Writing 1994; [oth. writ.] Non-published "P.E.T.A. Perils," "Sun-King;" [pers.] True love guides as a beacon in the night: Ad Infinitum. [a.] Charlottesville, VA

JACKS, NIMAT SHAHEED
[p.] Ethel Jane Payne; [m.] Martin Jacks; [ch.] Jabali I. Mani-Jacks; [ed.] B.A. - Cal State Hayward; [occ.] Educator; [pers.] All that we hope to be and all that we hope to achieve is waiting inside of our being, waiting to develop, waiting to grow, waiting to blossom. So, never give up on yourself!; [a.] Oakland, CA

JACKSON, BECKY J.
[pen.] Becca; [b.] December 24, 1955, Jacksonville, IL; [p.] Robert Earl Jackson, Martha Jean Jackson; [ch.] Amber Dawn, Benjamin Lucas, Chance Alexander; [ed.] Jacksonville High, Jacksonville Business and Career Institute; [occ.] Disabled from Systemic Lupus Erythmatosis; [memb.] Lupus Foundation, CHADD, Community Christian Church; [oth. writ.] Numerous poems, and short stories, in poetry form - published in the Inkblot, high school compilation of students' works.; [pers.] Always look for the light when in darkness, by letting love and hope guide your life.; [a.] Jacksonville, IL

JACKSON, JONATHAN
[pen.] Jon Jackson; [b.] June 3, 1975, Saint Louis, MO; [p.] Virginia Jackson, Jim Jackson; [ed.] Southfield High School, Class of 1993, Western Michigan University; [occ.] Student; [memb.] Hartford Memorial Baptist Church, NAACP; [hon.] NHS (National Honor Society); [oth. writ.] Several unpublished poems; [pers.] All my poems come from the people I meet and our interactions. They are the real authors, I am merely the reporter.; [a.] Southfield, MI

JACKSON JR., D. RANDALL

[b.] December 12, 1963, Northampton, MA; [p.] David and Patricia Jackson; [ed.] B.A. Psychology, Amherst College, Diploma - World Politics, London School of Economics, M.A. Int'l Rektions, Johns Hopkins SALS; [occ.] Foreign Exchange Program Coordinator, National Association of Secondary School Principals (NASSP), Deputy Secretary General of Int'l Confederation of Principals; [hon.] Academic Honors London School of Economics, SALS; [oth. writ.] Poem in local Massachusetts collection of children's poems.; [pers.] For me, poetry is a means of expressing emotions lingering deep inside. It is a voice for sounds we hear in the secret places of our mind.; [a.] Chevy Chase, MD

JACKSON, MS. NATHLON N.

[b.] July 24, 1971, Washington, DC; [p.] Ms. Clara Jackson, Mr. Nathan Jackson; [ed.] University of Maryland Eastern Shore; [occ.] Senior Retail Manager, Marriott - Prince George's Hospital Cen.; [memb.] Rehoboth Church of God in Christ, Zeta Phi Beta Sorority Inc.; [hon.] Queen of the Panhellenic Council, Top Rebounder of Lady Hawks Women's Basketball; [oth. writ.] Several unpublished poems; [pers.] Love to live but most of all live to love. I am influenced by lifes incredible profound dimensions. Also the love and encouragement shared between Mr. Joe L. Boone Jr. and I. Thanks! I love you.; [a.] Upper Marlboro, MD

JACKSON, REVA A.

[b.] October 18, 1952, Murray, KY; [p.] Charles Ray and Mary Ann Boatwright; [m.] David R. Jackson, August 3, 1972; [ch.] D. Seth Jackson; [ed.] Clarksville High School, B.S. degree in English with a minor in Library Science from Austin Peay State University; [occ.] Reconcilement Clerk, Farmers and Merchants Bank; [memb.] Church of God serve as Church Clerk. Business and Professional Women. Austin Peay State Univ. Govenors Club; [hon.] National Honor Society, Graduated from college, Cum Laude. Honor Choir in High School; [pers.] I mostly write for my friends - to honor a special time or occasion in their life. A smile of appreciation is all the reward I require.; [a.] Clarksville, TN

JACOBS, MARY

[b.] September 2, 1941, Sparrows Point, Baltimore, MD; [p.] John and Virginia Hagy; [m.] Ronald F. Jacobs, Sr., January 27, 1960; [ch.] Ronald Jr., Joy, Barbara; [ed.] Sparrows Point Jr., Sr., High School; [occ.] Domestic Engineer; [pers.] My poems reflect my life and the love of my family and friends.; [a.] Stewartstown, PA

JACOBS, SANDRA LEE

[b.] July 20, 1938, CA; [p.] David and Belva Grant; [m.] Anthony John Jacobs; [ch.] Sean, Shannon and Darren McGee; [ed.] Woodrow Wilson High School, Long Beach State College; [occ.] Department of State Administrative Secretary; [memb.] American Foreign Service Wives Association, Former CLO's Association; [hon.] Graduated with Honors, Dean's List, Special Recognition Award from the Department of State; [oth. writ.] Other unpublished poems; [pers.] I believe each of us has special gifts to share with each other. Each person is a treasure to be appreciated, not judged on a daily basis.; [a.] American Embassy Helsinki APO AE, NY

JACOBSEN, HENRY E.

[b.] November 14, 1908, Chicago, IL; [p.] Jack and Sigrid Jacobsen; [m.] Vera M. Jacobsen, June, 1986; [ch.] Son and daughter (2nd marriage); [ed.] Junior High and Chicago Tech College, evenings.; [occ.] Retired brick mason; [memb.] Life member Norwegian-American A.A.; [oth. writ.] Transposed songs for amateur singing enjoyment. Small award for writing poem for Brack's Candy, years ago. Transposed "Maine Stein Song" to "4. Leaf Club Song" - being a member years ago.

JACOBY, AMBER

[b.] March 8, 1982, Spangler; [p.] Edmond and Sharon Jacoby; [ed.] Central Cambria Middle School; [memb.] IAHA - International Arabian Horse Association, APHA - American Paint Horse Association, Triple K Cambria County 4 - H Horse Club; [hon.] School Honor Roll award Physical Fitness Education Awareness, Equestrienne Riding Trophies and Ribbons, Reading Competitions for school; [pers.] I love to ride horses which I am good at riding. My brothers are, Brandon and Jason. When I write poems I try to show my emotions and feelings. I write what I feel in my heart. I feel that if you want something bad enough or would like to be something in life, nothing can stop you. I give credit to my mom making me send my poem in for the contest.; [a.] Ebensburg, PA

JAMIALKOWSKI, RITA R.

[b.] November 17, 1929, New Haven, CT; [p.] Alves Garcia, Anna Sarno Garcia; [m.] Frank T Jamialkowski, May 14, 1949; [ch.] Lisa Ann Jamialkowski King; [ed.] Hamilton Grammar School, one year South Middleboro Mass Elem Fair Blavon Jr. High Hillhouse (high school, Folt and Tarront Compt. School); [occ.] Retired did some volunteer, work in spokane; [memb.] Sue pouls American Cancer Wild Life, Easter Seals, attends Sacred Heart Church; [hon.] Received awards in Elementary School, awards from National Library of Poetry; [oth. writ.] Famous Poets Society Animal's Plea published in 1994; [pers.] Most poems are written, in the True Spirit of nature and reality. This poem is dedicated to Wels in hurst, since animals are a form of life, we shared many happy moments.; [a.] Spokane, WA

JAMISON, JESSICA L.

[b.] March 16, 1976, Longmont, CO; [p.] Bruce and Cheri Andersen; [m.] Chad Christopher Jamison, March 19, 1994; [ch.] Expecting; [ed.] Berthoud High School, Centaurus High School; [oth. writ.] 'Do You Remember' in Between the Raindrops; [a.] Longmont, CO

JANACKAS, ELEANOR

[pen.] Eleanor Constance Knowles; [b.] March 18, 1933, Plaiston, NH; [ed.] Graduate of Haverhill High School (H.HS.) 1951; [occ.] Retired; [memb.] Fidelity circle #OES 90 (Haverhill, MA.) 01830 United Methodist Women People's United Methodist Church of Bradford, MA. 01835; [oth. writ.] I have written 74 poems altogether. Many of them concerning special occasions in friends and special people lives and also some that reflect my concerns and my life. I have put them on cassette for myself in case in lost them.; [pers.] I. The "Golden Rule" Luke 6:31, II. I Corinthians Chapt. 13, III - "Life is what you make it, and what you make it, is up to you! (III. Copied (I don't know who) These have been my 3 steps daily for my life.; [a.] Haverhill, MA

JARVIS, PATRICE L.

[pen.] Patrice Jarvis; [b.] November 13, 1959, Houston, TX; [p.] Wilford and Gloria Jarvis; [ed.] Evan E. Worthing High School, University of Houston, Houston Community, Allied Health Careers; [occ.] Micrographics (Tech), Memorial Hospital (SW); [memb.] (Adult Choir) Sugar Valley Missionary Baptist Church 3,200 Bris Bane St., Houston TX 77051, Rev. C.F. Hartwell (Pastor); [hon.] National Honor Society (High School); [oth. writ.] Poems entitled (Faith, Your Purpose, Peace, Love, Recovery Prayer of Thanksgiving, Grace, God is With You, Jesus, My God, and Jacob's Ladder) My God, Jehovah and Recovery Prayer was featured in church program (Sugar Valley); [pers.] Inspired by the word of God and His promises according to the Bible, I'd like to touch others world wide with beautiful poetry describing God's Grace, Power, Love and Promises. He is the only way.; [a.] Houston, TX

JEFFERS, THELMA

[b.] August 8, 1929, McMechen, WV; [p.] Guy and Lorena Horner (deceased); [m.] Ralph Jeffers (deceased), November 24, 1955; [ch.] Lorena, Deborah, Brian, Sharon - 10 grandchildren; [ed.] Union High School, Benwood W.Va. 11 years.; [occ.] Retired; [memb.] V.P. of Senior Nutrition Center, Delegate for Office of Aging in San Bernardino, California.; [hon.] Editors Choice Award for "Memories" published in Journey of The Mind.; [oth. writ.] Several poems, 1 book on my childhood (unpublished), titled "Little Red"; [pers.] I write my poetry about things that happened in my past, so my children and grandchildren can better understand what growing up in the depression era was like.; [a.] Redlands, CA

JENKINS, LILLY

[b.] November 26, 1969, Selfridge, MI; [p.] Donald and Diane Jenkins; [ch.] Cassandra Helen Jenkins, Destinee Amber Jenkins; [ed.] Fremont High School, Hibbing Technical College, currently enrolled at Hibbing Community College; [occ.] Student - studying Elementary Ed. to be a teacher; [memb.] Volunteer Fire Fighter, First Responder/ E.M.T., Bois Forte Head Start Policy Council, AEOA Head Start Policy Council, Red Cross Volunteer; [oth. writ.] My main goal is to help others and to give my children the knowledge and confidence needed to deal with anything that comes their way in life.; [pers.] Bear River (Cook), MN

JENKINS, MARY ANN

[b.] May 1, 1934, D.C.; [p.] Alma and Steve Mahon; [m.] George C. Jenkins, September 12, 1952; [ch.] Margie Flerlage, Steve Jenkins and Linda Riddle; [ed.] Eastern High School, D.C. and various courses at Charles County Community College; [occ.] Retired U.S. Gov't 1988, currently Part-Time Medical Transcriptionist; [pers.] Love costs nothing but still remains the greatest gift you can give, or receive; even so, many people have difficulty giving it and receiving it.; [a.] Waldorf, MD

JENKINS, RAYMOND ANTHONEY
[pen.] RAJ; [b.] April 16, 1963, Chicago, IL; [p.] Mr. and Mrs. Johnny B. Stith; [ed.] B.S. degree from Wiley College Mid-Management degree East Texas State. 40 clock hrs. in Spanish Computer Literacy; [occ.] 5th grade Math teacher; [memb.] Vice President of School's PTA; [hon.] Teachers of the Year, Excellence in Teaching Award, Outstanding Teacher of the Year'; [oth. writ.] Holiday greetings, The Night is Long, Blank, Step Aside, Love Ones, To All Those 6th Graders, Save All Your Love, Time, Life, Asking A Lot, Hurt and Despair, Stone Cold, It Came to Pass; [a.] Dallas, TX

JENKINS, TRACY
[b.] August 10, 1983, Rochester, MI; [p.] Thomas Jenkins and Karen Jenkins; [ed.] Middle School, Hurt Middle School, Rochester Michigan.; [pers.] Thanks mom and dad; [a.] Madison Heights, MI

JEREZ, JACQUELINE
[pen.] Jackie; [b.] August 25, 1982, Queens, NY; [p.] Yvonne LaSalle, Samuel LaSalle; [ed.] Wilson Junior High, McKinley Elementary, Erie PA.; [occ.] Student 7th grade; [memb.] Wilson Middle School PEPP Academy, Wilson String Orquestra, by Mr. Gary Peterson; [hon.] Most Improved Student 1995 Wilson And PEPP Academy; [pers.] Everything is possible with God and family by my side. My poem is my success. Hoping it can help you too. Jackie Thank You Al and Grandma; [a.] Erie, PA

JETER, CLORINDA D. J.
[pen.] Clorinda Blackwell Jeter; [b.] September 1, 1948, Steubenville, OH; [p.] Rufus Blackwell, Willie Mae Blackwell; [m.] William Stanley Jeter, November 15, 1967; [ch.] Melissa Christine Jeter, William Charles Jeter; [ed.] Steubenville High School, Bliss College, Columbus, OH, Washtenaw Community College, (Associate Degree Applied Science); [occ.] Information Word Processing Specialist; [oth. writ.] "Book of Poems" - (First Edition); [pers.] Life is full of many obstacles and challenges, but you must never give up!; [a.] Ypsilanti, MI

JOCHUM, JAMIE
[b.] February 8, 1958, Chicago, IL; [p.] Paul and Mary Lou Jochum; [m.] Elizabeth Jochum, February 8, 1994; [ed.] George Mason University B.A. English; [occ.] Purchasing Manager - Medsurg - Isolyser; [pers.] My poem touches upon the harmony of life. Live out your dreams and communicate love and hope for future generations to build upon.; [a.] Manassas, VA

JOHN, ELENA SONA
[b.] February 8, 1971, Nuzvid, India; [p.] Emile and Helen John; [ed.] Bachelors in Business Administration; [hon.] Golden Poet 1990; [oth. writ.] Poems published in local newspaper, world of poetry and Anthology.; [pers.] I strive to live by the phrase: "The more we know ourselves, the less we'll criticize others."; [a.] Hillandale, MD

JOHNSON, AUDREA
[b.] March 8, 1966, Middletown; [p.] Willie and Katherine Johnson; [ed.] Ohio State University (BS), Bowling Green State Univ (MRC); [occ.] Vocational Rehabilitation Counselor, Toledo Ohio; [pers.] Creativity is not a gift until it is shared with others; [a.] Toledo, OH

JOHNSON, BERTHA M.
[pen.] Bertah Greene; [b.] September 30, 1945, Washington, DC; [p.] John and Ethel Curley; [ch.] Lawrence Greene, Donnell Greene; [ed.] Theodore High School; [occ.] Store Clerk, part time piano player.; [memb.] Sewell Music Conservatory Class of 1979, Greater Tried Stone Baptist Church; [hon.] Certified 1982 Specialty Training Program in Music. Enter Birthday Song into Contest.; [oth. writ.] Mother Love (poem), Looking for Love (poem), Happy Birthday Song. Lady Safeway (poem), (Heaven Song) God Divine Peace - song, (Time) song, (Golden City) song.; [pers.] Music is my first love. Singing is next. Things come to me and I write them down.; [a.] Washington, DC

JOHNSON, BRENDA KAY
[pen.] Bee Jay; [b.] August 5, 1954, Auburn, CA; [p.] Kenneth Erickson, Doris Erickson; [m.] George Johnson, August 31, 1985; [ch.] Brandy Christine, Corie Lynette, Deverrick Antwan (granddaughter - Jamesheona Charrel); [ed.] Red Bluff Union High, OIC; [occ.] Day Care Provider; [oth. writ.] Several poems and short stories published in a small family magazine; [pers.] The poem "Ignore Me" was to be my eulogy to the world. But it took so long to write and gave me so much joy at looking at the finished product, I realized my life was worth living after all. I thank God for the words He gave me.; [a.] East Palo Alto, CA

JOHNSON, CAROLINA M.
[pen.] Carolina J. Blazina; [b.] July 8, 1960, Pittsburgh, PA; [p.] Robert J. Blazina II, Bernadette Blazina; [m.] Emil V. Johnson, January 7, 1995; [ed.] Wilkinsburgh High School, Johnston Grade School, Honor Middle School; [occ.] Housewife; [memb.] 700 Club; [oth. writ.] I write my tracts to distribute to people when I witness, and decorate t-shirts with religious and biblical passages.; [pers.] I have been born again since May 3, 1993. I strive to reach people who do not know God as I know Him. My goals are to witness to people about Salvation, to open a soup kitchen, and to actively take part in the missionary.; [a.] Pittsburgh, PA

JOHNSON, DONALD E.
[b.] March 18, 1928, Wimsted, CT; [p.] Deceased Florence Angel, Augustis Johnson; [m.] Alice N. Johnson, June 13, 1993; [ch.] Brian-Bruce-Donna; [ed.] Graduate 1947 of Stevens High, Claremont, NH; [occ.] Retired; [hon.] Honorable Discharge US Navy 1946 - All State Football in 1946 $200,000.00 cost improvements for joy MFG Co. Claremont, NH; [oth. writ.] Lifes If's and Ands Halfway Up my note to will shakespeare Teddy Bear and Ode to our daughter dreams of the farewell shrew Aubade and many more; [pers.] Why must we walk in the shadows of Roman's Day, why must we make the journey to ruin and decay, There are many Neros who play the violin and watch society burn as we fall to sin, poetry is a universal language spoken by many tongues; [a.] Claremont, NH

JOHNSON, EDDIE EARL
[pen.] Goldie; [b.] May 23, 1967, Maben, MS; [p.] Ms. Vera Johnson; [ed.] Graduate 1985, Mathiston Attendance Center, 1987 graduate Wood Jr. College, Mathiston, MS.; [occ.] Red Kap Industries Mathiston, MS "Bottom Stop;" [memb.] Member of the St. Stephen U.M. Church of Maben, MS, Member of the U.S. National Guard, Starkville, MS.; [hon.] 1988 Golden Poet Award, World of Poetry Sacramento, California, also Award of Merit Certificates for poems If I am Gold and I am Desire 1987 and 1988; [oth. writ.] Atomizing the Welchings, If I am Gold, I am Desire, Firefly, Torn Valiance, March On, God's Grace, Spellbound, Dance Till Dawn.; [pers.] Poetry is life and Life is Poetry. Never deny yourself the good things of this world for life is given in leaps and bounds.; [a.] Mathiston, MS

JOHNSON, ELISABETH
[b.] May 17, 1982, South Weymouth, MA; [p.] William and Victoria Johnson; [occ.] Student at Silver Regional Junior High School; [hon.] Lamp of Learning Medal from American Legion for Essay contest 1st place 1994 national talent American Dance competition; [a.] Pembroke, MA

JOHNSON, FELICIA
[pen.] Mango; [b.] February 20, 1979, Livingston, NJ; [p.] Harold Johnson, Diane Johnson; [ed.] Mother Seton Regional High School, Clark, NJ; [memb.] Young People's Division of the African Methodist Episcopal Church, Girl Scouts of Greater Essex, Jack and Jill of America; [hon.] Honor Roll, Valedictorian of 8th grade class. Several trophies for poems.; [pers.] Maya Angelou inspired me to write the poems that I have written. I also had the encouragement of my family and friends. If you're good at something never give up.; [a.] East Orange, NJ

JOHNSON, IDA G.
[pen.] Tonie Johnson; [b.] January 6, 1931, Scappoose, OR; [p.] Deceased; [m.] Floyd G. Johnson, October 14, 1950; [ch.] 6 Children and 2 step-children 24 grand-children 7 great children; [ed.] Vernonia High School, Vernonia Oregon; [occ.] Widowed February 14, 1988 and became totally disabled June 1988. Began (used to liked to for school and our children). Doing drawings and in Pen-n-Ink.; [oth. writ.] Wrote on-going column "Along Rt 3" For about 6 years for Sandy Post - circulation about 3,500 in mid 50's; [pers.] What I have drawn are reflexions of life, and in the process, words come to mind and I got them down. My poem "reflects" my impressions of God's gifts to us all.; [a.] Joseph, OR

JOHNSON, IRENA L. TURIANSKY
[b.] Ukraine; [p.] Anthony and Karolina Turiansky; [m.] Major Robert L. Johnson, August 9, 1975; [ch.] Edward Steven P. Czekaj, Paul Anthony Czekaj; [ed.] Elementary Education - Saint Olha Girl's School, Kolomyya, Ukraine High School: Beauty Culture, Bookkeeping; [occ.] Retired in Florida; [memb.] Ukrainian American Club of the Palm Beaches, Reserve Officer's Association - Ladies Ukrainian National Association, Assumption Catholic Church, Ukrainian Catholic Church of Miami; [hon.] Award of Merit - World of Poetry Editor's Choice Award - The National Library of Poetry; [oth. writ.] Autobiography, poems in local paper, copyright song - "Christmas is Forever"; [pers.] By learning about the famous Ukrainian poet Taras Shevchenko, I knew at an early age I would enjoy poetry. Growing up with the beauty of nature, I have learned about people, their joys and their sadness. The love for a poem has no ending.

JOHNSON, JAN A.
[b.] June 25, 1956, Zumbrora, MN; [hon.] 1994 Editor's Choice Award, National Library of Poetry; [oth. writ.] "Tonight, This Is Enough" Songs on the Wind, National Library of Poetry: 1995.; [a.] Yorktown Heights, NY

JOHNSON, KENNETH E.
[pen.] K. J.; [b.] October 19, 1953, OK; [p.] Eddie L. Johnson, Reola Richards; [ch.] Anteaus Schumpert, Kendra Banks, Kenton Banks; [ed.] High School Diploma, Attended Bell and Howell Electronics School, City College of S.E, CA-Computer's; [occ.] Institutional Police Officer, Parking Lot Guard; [oth. writ.] Other unpublished writing of short poems - reminisce, freedom, confession, All Night Jazz was entered in 2nd National Library of Poetry Contest.; [a.] San Francisco, CA

JOHNSON, KIMBERLY A.
[b.] March 7, 1960, Bay City, TX; [p.] Irvin Krobot, Laverne Krobot; [m.] Robert E. Johnson, December 20, 1980; [ch.] Robert Blake, Taylor Dane; [ed.] Van Vleck High School, Sam Houston State University; [occ.] Housewife, Mother part-time with our business-voice data systems; [memb.] PTA, Moms in touch; [hon.] Top 10 Graduating Class FFA Sweetheart, head twirler (2 yrs.) drum major, Who's Who National Honor Society Won Ms. Congeniality - Miss Texas National; [oth. writ.] Poem to grandmother - "Meme" "In appreciation" - to teachers at Elementary. Several others to family members "What's Right About America" for pageant. "Grandparents"; [pers.] My poems generally reflect passions straight from my heart; [a.] Marietta, GA

JOHNSON, LATOYA
[pen.] Latoya Johnson; [b.] January 12, 1978, TX; [ed.] Varies since I moved from Texas to Buffalo - Mostly a Tudor; [occ.] School, writing Poetry (Prose), Novel, etc..,; [hon.] Sexiest Model in 1991, most encouraging student in 1986, Best Dressed Model 1992, Honors Society 1989 -; [oth. writ.] Me, my cousin Rashied Ms Duffie, and one of the most special people on earth Jason C. Barton together have a collection of over 200 poems; [pers.] "I feel that life is but a puzzle, in which the pieces are mended by your soul's growth" "live as thou each day were your last"; [a.] Buffalo, NY

JOHNSON, PENNY
[pen.] Penny Johnson; [b.] July 1, 1940, Danville, KY; [p.] Irene Sebastian, Buford Carr; [m.] William Evan Johnson, July 15, 1958; [ch.] William E. Jr., (Buddy), Robert Anthony (Robbie); [ed.] Famous Writers School, Westport, Conn. - graduate, Newspaper Institute of America - N.Y. - graduate; [occ.] Free-lance writer-poet; [memb.] National Writer's Club, I.S.P., American Biographical Institute, International Order of Merit, International Platform Society; [hon.] Ennobled by Prince John - Duke of Avram, Australia, "Granted a Coat of Arms - College of Heraldry", Honorary Doctor of Letters - London, England; [oth. writ.] "I Will", "Light in the Night", "From One American to Another", "A Poem for Peace", "Comfort From my Grandparents", "Surprise" -

(all poems); [pers.] "If all people in the world, thought, felt, and expressed themselves like we poets, there would be more love and understanding and no war"; [a.] Lexington, KY

JOHNSON, RANDI M.
[b.] February 15, 1977, Oxford, OH; [p.] James R and Judy E. Johnson; [ed.] Franklin County High, will be starting the University of Cincinnati in Fall of 1995.; [occ.] Student and cashier at Brookville Save-A-Lot; [memb.] Junior Historical Society, National Honors Society; [oth. writ.] Several poems published in school newspaper, The Pride.; [pers.] I write what's in my heart, whether it be anger, fear, or love. Writing helps me get my feelings out.; [a.] Brookville, IN

JOHNSON, REGINA
[b.] November 27, 1947, Norwalk; [p.] Marjorie Thompson; [m.] Earl Mason; [ch.] Lincey Clyburn-Regina, Johnson-Gloria, Clark-Sharon, Colbert; [ed.] All completed 12 years. Regina Johnson went to Cardozo High School in Washington DC; [memb.] Certified nurses Aid, The President of "Hand in Hand Association March of Dines, The Norwalk Community Health Board of Directors; [hon.] "Celebrate Women my poem Health Reform that was publish by The National Library of Poetry.; [oth. writ.] Form between two worlds, I do forever yours what a about me, for all that said and done, the power, through it all.

JOHNSON, RONALD
[m.] Married 12 years; [ch.] Five; [ed.] NYU - Stern School of Business, MBA 1994; [occ.] Manager, New York University; [memb.] Urban Bankers Coalition, PTA - P.S 160Q - Executive Board; [hon.] Dean's List, Service Awards - P.S. 160; [oth. writ.] Various Genre's of Songs Poetry and Children Stories; [pers.] Writing like knowledge can come at you from any direction, if you are receptive. You would be surprised at what my garden taught me.; [a.] New York City, NY

JOHNSON, ROOSEVELT
[pen.] Mr. J.; [b.] December 4, 1926, Cecil, AL; [p.] Deceased; [ch.] Roosevelt E. Johnson

JOHNSON, SHANNON M.
[b.] May 10, 1971, Quincy, IL; [p.] Mr. Curtis Johnson and Mrs. Sherry K. Cannon; [ch.] Anthony T. Rush Jr.; [ed.] Senior at Jackson State University - Accounting major; [memb.] I am a member of New Horizon Baptist Church in Jackson, Ms, I am also a member of Christian Family Center Church in Peoria, IL; [oth. writ.] Poems concerning God, my son, my mother, and myself.; [pers.] We know that all things work together for good to them that love God. Romans 8:28; [a.] Peoria, IL

JOHNSTON, CARROLL
[pen.] Carroll Johnston; [b.] September 8, 1929, Vandergrift, PA; [p.] Lloyd and Ethel Stewart (deceased); [m.] Robert G. Johnston (deceased), September 8, 1949; [ch.] Karen, Wesley, David, Brent, Leslie, Jeffrey, Carey.; [ed.] 8 yrs. Grade School, 4 yrs. High School, Nursing School; [occ.]

L.P.N. (retired) at the present time.; [oth. writ.] I have several poems on my shelf. (I think pretty good) I hope someday. Someone can read them.; [pers.] I have always loved nature and all it contains. I am inspired and exhilarated each time I take a walk or hike over the fields and wood areas. It brought tears to my eyes to know someone read no liked my poem.; [a.] Creekside, PA

JOHNSTON, TILLIE A.
[pen.] Tillie A. Johnston; [b.] February 23, 1912, Pittsburgh, PA; [p.] John and Valerie Hecht; [m.] Earle Johnston, March 15, 1941; [ch.] 5 - 4 daughters and one son; [ed.] High School graduate; [occ.] Retired Sr. Citizen with asteo-arthritis; [pers.] Children help me a lot.; [a.] Ontario, CA

JONES, AMBER M.
[b.] October 10, 1975, Orlando, FL; [p.] Terry and Karen Jones; [m.] Walker Aderhold, August, 1995; [ed.] Sequoyah High, Kennesaw State College; [memb.] Green Peace; [oth. writ.] Several articles written for college newspaper, other poem published in (The Poetry Motel.); [pers.] He who does not write, does not live.; [a.] Kennesaw, GA

JONES, DAVID A.
[b.] December 16, 1939, Galena, KS; [p.] Loyed C. Jones Imogene M. Jones; [m.] Narina C. R. Jones, July 11, 61; [ch.] Stephen, D'Arn, Cheriee; [ed.] BS OCED, Southern Illinois Univ., BE EET, Weber State Univ.; [occ.] Electronics Teacher, ITT Technical Institute, Murray, UT; [memb.] USAR (Retired); [oth. writ.] Poems published in company news letter. Technical papers for students use.; [pers.] If a task is worth doing, it's worth doing well.; [a.] Murray, UT

JONES, DAVID
[pen.] Josey Morgan; [b.] May 14, 1960, Clarksburg; [p.] Dick Jones, Francis Brown; [ed.] Roosevelt - Wilson High School, South Western College of Business.; [occ.] Writer/Photographer; [memb.] Trinity Fellowship Church of Amarillo, Texas; [hon.] Dean's List 1984 total quality management; [oth. writ.] Out of sight, I am the lucky one, 2 rings, Brigley, all of my love.; [pers.] My writings are ment to shed light on the world. To open new doors for whoever my inspiration is from Jim Morriso of the Doors; [a.] Milford, OH

JONES, EVERETT G.
[pen.] Everett; [b.] May 11, 1920, Tulsa, OK; [p.] Kathryn and Bill Jones; [m.] Dorathy Jones, 1943; [ch.] Star, Dalles, and Kathryn; [ed.] Went to 7th grade; [occ.] Retired from feed lot. Working as a farm hand now.; [oth. writ.] Driftin' On, Lookin' Back, Saddles and Memories, Feed Lot Cowboy, Feed Lot Memories, Reminiscing, Old Timer, Close the Gate, Just a Workin', That Cowboy Mark, Ropin' Steve Smith, Old Time Cowboy

JONES, JEANETTE JACKSON
[b.] September 17, 1946; [hon.] Poet of Year Award in 1989 for poem called Free; [oth. writ.] Poem - Free, published in Best Poems of Western World; [pers.] To my Dad, Palmer Darden Jackson Sr., a self made man and a dreamer, thank you for the gift of being a dreamer too.; [a.] Fredericksburg, VA

JONES JR., MR. PERRY M.
[pen.] "Goo"; [b.] July 27, 1964, Plainfield, NJ;
[p.] Perry and Jackie Jones; [ch.] Raynell J. Jones;
[ed.] Plainfield High School, class of "82"; [occ.]
Self employed, painter - home and industry; [oth.
writ.] Many poem's and short stories, unpublished
as of now, but coming soon to a store near you.;
[pers.] I write on my feelings for any moment
recognized in my mind, hoping to identify with
other minds searching to escape... Influenced by
real life itself, God; [a.] Plainfield, NJ

JONES, KENNETH DALE
[b.] November 24, 1962, Kansas City, MO; [p.]
Kenneth and Marjorie Jones; [ed.] Raymore
Peculiar High, BS - Journalism - Radio, TV, Film -
University of Oklahoma; [occ.] Flight Attendant;
[memb.] Alpha Epsilon Rho, Human Rights
Campaign Fund; [hon.] National Honor Society,
Literary Club President, Dean's List; [oth. writ.]
Winner of a National Essay contest, local
newspapers; [pers.] To work to end prejudice and
ignorance no matter what shape or form it takes;
[a.] Lee's Summit, MO

JONES, NATALIE R.
[pen.] Eilatan; [b.] December 19, 1960, Palestine,
TX; [p.] Evelyn & Judge Hudson; [m.] Divorced;
[ch.] Rachelle R. Bell; [ed.] Palestine High, Trinity
Valley Comm. College, Tarrant County College;
[occ.] Phlebotomist, Full-time Nursing Student;
[memb.] Hearts of Love #16; [hon.] MIG
Scholarship Black/Hispanic Scholarship; [pers.] In
order to succeed, your inner being must outshine
your outer; [a.] TX

JOSEPHSON, BEVERLY MAE
[b.] December 22, 1928, MA; [ch.] Seven
Children; [hon.] I received "Honorable Mention"
awards and a 1990 Golden Poet Award from World
of Poetry.; [oth. writ.] Some of my works will
appear in anthologies in the near future. Among
them are the Amherst Society, JMW Publishing
and Iliad Literary Awards. Others are being
considered.; [pers.] I believe that literature, poetry
and art has suffered greatly because of the
emphasis of television and computer use. Perhaps
my works can help to stimulate a new interest in
intellectual communication, the arts and improved
understanding of the human race.

JURESKO, ROBERT J.
[b.] December 20, 1955, Steubenville, OH; [p.]
Robert A. and Magaret Juresko; [m.] Debbie L.
Juresko, August 15, 1981; [ch.] Betsy Jo and
Molly Louise; [ed.] Mingo High School, Mingo
Jct. OH., attended Kent State Univ. Assoc. Deg.
Data Processing, Jefferson Technical College,
Steubenville, OH; [occ.] Custodian Hills Elem
School, Woodcrafter; [memb.] Veteran U.S. Navy
Red Cross Blood Donor; [pers.] Life is short. We
must observe the goodness in our environment and
institute it into our daily lives; [a.] Steubenville, OH

KACENA, ERWIN
[b.] April 16, 1927, Chicago, IL; [p.] Anna B.
Schultz; [m.] Arlene Kacena, April 21, 1959; [ch.]
Three; [ed.] High School; [occ.] Millwright;
[memb.] American Legion, V.F.W.; [hon.] Music-
sports; [oth. writ.] Wrote poems and lyrics for
years; [pers.] Since my granddaughter past away

(still birth) I'm writing 4 to 6 poems or lyrics per
day - I would like someone to evaluate my writing
- please help.; [a.] Streamwood, IL

KADISCH, MARGARET D.
[b.] November 24, 1904, Denmark; [p.] John and
Paula Kadisch; [ed.] In Europe was Art Director of
Spaulding China Trademark Royal Copley. Now
Collector's items.; [occ.] Retired from portrait
painting.; [memb.] Sebring Presbyterian Church
Alliance Art Center; [hon.] Honorable Mention at
several art shows.; [oth. writ.] Poems: Yet Time,
The Pottery, in New Voices published in American
Poetry 1978 vantage press; [pers.] I love that title
"At Water's Edge." It is the most regenerating,
revitalizing element that we can touch.; [a.]
Sebring, OH

KAESTNER, COLIN P.
[b.] March 24, 1975, Bad Kreuznach, Germany;
[p.] James, Mary Kaestner; [ed.] Graduated '94
Morton West High School. Freshman at Morton
College.; [occ.] Waiter at a Denny's restaurant;
[hon.] Various writing contests local. Featured in
the Requiem Magazine issue No. 5. My poem in
this issue is "Spirit Woods" out in Mid-April 95;
[oth. writ.] I've been writing for only a few years,
and am now receiving some recognition.; [pers.]
"Only Love and Music, are Forever", "May My
Poems Sing in the Heart's of All."; [a.] Berwyn, IL

KAHN, ADRIENNE MARIE
[b.] August 31, 1939, Chicago, IL; [p.] Eleanor
and Richard Markvart; [m.] Sherwin Les Kahn,
February 14, 1981; [ch.] Cindy Lore, David
Royce, Judith Ann and Catherine Marie; [ed.]
Wells High School, Loop College; [occ.] Manager-
White Rock Senior Center Dallas, TX; [hon.]
Professional awards for service to senior citizens in
the Dallas area; [pers.] I wrote this poem as a gift
to my husband, Les, who deserves every word of
it.; [a.] Garland, TX

KAKRIDAS, DEAN G.
[b.] July 17, 1967, Arlington, MA; [p.] Kate and
George Kakridas; [ed.] BS Engineering '90,
Northeastern University; [occ.] Manufacturing
Manager, CNC Corporation; [oth. writ.] A series
of poems, none of which have been published yet.;
[pers.] My inspiration to write poetry was founded
through the works of Edgar Allen Poe. Imagery
and fantasy are my favorite tools as I strive to
interact with my reader. I look to John Updike as
my greatest influence.; [a.] Billerica, MA

KALU, KELECHI
[b.] April 14, 1973, Silver Spring, MD; [ed.]
Nigerian Navy Secondary School, Lagos, Nigeria.
University of Maryland at College Park, MD;
[pers.] I strongly believe that self expression is a
privilege which should be showcased.; [a.]
Greenbelt, MD

KARNIS, DOROTHY QUICK
[pen.] Dorotha Quick; [b.] August 26, 1930,
Holly, MI; [p.] Richard and Bessie Holt; [m.]
Arthur Karnis, May 21, 1994; [ch.] Susan Titmas,
Richard Quick, Betsy Brooke; [ed.] Holly High
and still going to school in Naples; [occ.]
Bookkeeper semi-retired; [hon.] 1st place in

writing contest; [oth. writ.] I have 50 poems being
put in a book. I read these poems each week at the
hospice grief recovery meetings.; [pers.] I started
writing poems after the sudden loss of my husband
of 42 years to help with the grief recovery and I am
still writing poems!; [a.] Naples, FL

KASSINGER, NANCY C.
[b.] September 30, 1936, Philpot, KY; [p.] John
Crutcher and Cleo Ford Crutcher; [m.] Clifton Ray
Kassinger, May 10; [ch.] Sandra Stuart Brown;
[ed.] Daviess County High, Owensboro Voca-
tional, Owensboro Community College; [occ.]
Retired from GE, Floral Designer for Stone
Mountain Park; [oth. writ.] Poems and Short
Stories; [pers.] I use my abilities to seek beauty, to
promote harmony, and encourage positive
attitudes; [a.] Stone Mountain, GA

KAUFFMAN, LISA
[pen.] Constance Duchamp; [b.] April 8, 1979,
FL; [p.] Ms. Mary Kauffman and Guardian Ms.
Patricia Sperduto; [ed.] Mansfield High School.;
[occ.] Baby sitter; [memb.] School activities, such
as drama club, concert choir and I dance out of
school.; [oth. writ.] Set aside are some other
poems, and several stories.; [pers.] When I find
something that I'm good at, I stick with it and do
my best at it. I enjoy all the old time classics, and
someday I would like to see myself acting on
broadway, or as we say it today," the stage.; [a.]
Mansfield, MA

KAUFMAN, IRVING
[b.] September 16, 1917, Orange, NJ; [p.] Morris
and Tillie Kaufman; [m.] Martha Buskirk
Kaufman, November 30, 1985; [ch.] Stephen
David Kaufman, Carol Suzanne, Bittenson,
Richard Paul Kaufman, Jane Rubert Kaufman;
[ed.] East Orange, High School, E. Orange, N.J.
The Goo Wash Univ. undergraduate and the
Medical School grad in 1943 Washington, DC
Psychiatric Training, Judge Beker Guidance Center
Psychiatric at Boston, MA, Psychiatric Society;
[occ.] M.D. Psychiatrist-Psychologist for Adults
and Children semi-retired; [memb.] A.M.A., APA
Int. Psychiatric Association; [hon.] Black Belt in
both Vechi Ryu, Cwijjlin Ryu Karate, Alph Omega
Honor Society, Honorary Degree in Social work.
Smith Culler School for social worker Northington,
MA; [pers.] Life is full and varied with 4 children
and 5 grandchildren at age 78 I am semi-retired
from the practice of Psychiatry. Spend time
writing prose poetry, on scientific, writer, play
cello in amateur quartet.; [a.] Auburndale, MA

KAULILI, DEBBY N.
[b.] February 2, 1964, Lihue-Kauai, HI; [p.] Mr.
and Mrs. Springwater Kaulili; [ed.] Kauai High
School, Kauai Community College, and Leeward
Community College; [occ.] Lithographic Stripper-
Graphic Arts and Cook; [memb.] International
Songwriter's co-op, and the International Society of
poets; [hon.] Dean's List, and Talent Search
America, write on.; [oth. writ.] American Lung
Association's newsletter, and Western Poetry
Association; [pers.] Looking through poetry as a
means to express one's self, has given me that
chance to reach out to others through words and
meaning of the heart.; [a.] Honolulu, HI

KECK, SYLVIA JANUARY SOLOMON
[pen.] January Keck; [b.] April 15, 1960, Fort Worth, TX; [p.] James Nelson Solomon (deceased) and Linda L. Rodriguez; [ch.] Stephanie Lynn Keck and adopted Lhasa Apso babies: Bonnie, Fancy, Coco, and Chiffon; [ed.] Bowie High, Arlington, TX, University of Galveston-Medical Branch: Allied Health Sciences, Calvary Bible Institute and Seminary, Grand Prairie, TX; [occ.] Freelance writer, student, and small business owner.; [memb.] The International Society of Poets, Texas Citizen Action Committee; [hon.] Seminary Honors student, "Editor's Choice" award for the "Earthman Sonnet," ('94), "Poet of Merit" nominee, 95' semi-finalist for "Playing with Angels."; [oth. writ.] Novels in the works and notable "ghostwriting" assignments; [pers.] Painting descriptive word pictures that reveal the depth of emotion, this is what I strive for. Poetry is a spark of God's creative spirit. I want to set the mind on fire and the heart aglow with possibilities of the things that will be.; [a.] Arlington, TX

KEENE, DORI J.
[pen.] Dori J. Keene; [b.] August 18, 1960, Grayling; [p.] James and Florence Keeler; [m.] Douglas H. Keene, April 10, 1982; [ch.] Jennifer M. Keene, Jessica A. Keene, James H. Keene, Justin D. Keene; [ed.] High School-Gerrish Higgins, College-Kirtland Community College; [occ.] LPN, Housewife; [memb.] Calvary Assembly of God Church; [oth. writ.] Several other writings in which I've never shared with the public.; [pers.] God has given me this gift and only through the inspiration of the Holy Spirit am I able to write works of art. To God be the glory.; [a.] Roscommon, MI

KELLER, BRIDGET
[b.] May 16, 1964; [ed.] Master's in Foreign Language Education Lund University, Sweden; [occ.] Trade Union Communications; [pers.] I agree with Czeslaw Milosz, who writes in his preface to an anthology of Postwar Polish Poetry (Univ. of Calif. Press, Berkeley): poetry, after all, always draws upon the language of one's childhood.; [a.] San Francisco, CA

KELLOGG, RAY MILTON
[b.] November 24, 1907, College View, NE; [p.] Harold Kellogg, Pearl (Cheney) Kellogg; [m.] Florence (Zinke) Kellogg, December 30, 1993; [ch.] Donald R., Eugene L., Gerald E., Pamela A. Gareis; [ed.] Dakota State University (B.S.), Loma Linda University (M.D.); [occ.] Retired Physician; [memb.] Kappa Sigma Iota, Delta Sigma Lambda; [hon.] Have written two grand prize winners for 25 and 50 words statements for commercial advertising aggregating $4,000.00; [oth. writ.] Man's Day-a six-verse poem included in anthology about 1985; [pers.] Would to God I had known at seventeen what I know at eighty-seven.; [a.] Santa Rosa, CA

KELLY, HEATHER
[b.] October 24, 1978, Rochester, NY; [p.] Michael and Cynthia Kelly; [ed.] Sophomore at Churchville-Chili High School; [a.] Rochester, NY

KELLY, MARGARET
[pen.] Nadine McCulloh; [b.] March 12, 1959, NY; [p.] Deceased; [m.] Thomas A. Kelly, August 14, 1982; [ch.] Daniel, Michael and Lisa-Marie; [ed.] Hicksville High, B.S. Educ., St. John's University, M.A. Tesol, C.W. Post College; [occ.] Adjunct Professor of English as a second language; [memb.] P.T.A., Teachers of English to Speakers of other Languages, Inc.; [hon.] Dean's List 1982; [pers.] Compassion and sensitivity to the unfortunate of society, can be encouraged through the beauty of creative writings.; [a.] Hicksville, NY

KELLY, REATHER S.
[b.] June 2, 1935, MS; [p.] James and Genorah Stewart; [m.] Paul H. Kelly, September 22, 1961; [ch.] Paula Lee, Martha Gray, Timothy Kelly; [ed.] A.A., Owen College (Memphis, TN), B.S., Howard University (Washington, DC); [occ.] Career Information Coordinator Bethesda, Chevy Chase HS Bethesda, MD; [memb.] Evangel Church, Upper Marlboro, MD; [hon.] Poem entitled "God" published in the National Anthology of Poetry (1955) and many other unpublished poems

KENNEDY, ANGEL
[b.] May 9, 1981, Albuquerque, NM; [p.] Marilyne Kennedy (Adoptive); [ed.] Currently: Cannon Middle School 8th grade, next year I will attend Green Valley High; [oth. writ.] I have written many other poems, all of which I am proud of; [pers.] The poem Weeping Willow or Willow Tree was inspired by my next Door Neighbor's willow and a very dear friend of mine. I wrote the poem so many times I know it by heart.; [a.] Las Vegas, NV

KENNEDY, KIMBERLY S.
[pen.] Kim Kennedy; [b.] June 21, 1959, Rockford, IL; [p.] Ronald and Sharon Lorenz; [m.] Paul J. Kennedy, February 12, 1977; [ch.] Stephanie and Jason Kennedy; [ed.] West High, Blackhawk Technical; [occ.] Housewife; [hon.] Outstanding dedication to job, North Central Community Resource Council; [pers.] I hope to have a meaningful relationship with my daughter, like that I have with my sister Veronica.; [a.] Crossville, TN

KENNY, KENNETH K.
[pen.] K. K., Kenny, Triple K; [b.] July 14, 1925, Leavenworth, KS; [p.] John J. and Emeretta L. Kenny; [m.] Lila Lee Barnhardt Kenny, October 12, 1944; [ch.] Karen Kay, Karla Kee, Karry Keith and Kraig Kalvin; [ed.] Grad. Leavenworth High School, some extension classes at Kansas University; [occ.] Retired US Civil Service; [memb.] Protestant Chapel Council, Ft. Leavenworth Post Chapel, Republican National Committee, VFW, American Legion, Sports officiating Service, Kansas College Official's Assn., National Association of Sport Officials; [hon.] Only athlete in history of Leavenworth, KS High School to become Co-Captain in three sports (football, Track, Basketball), served 2-years term on Editorial Board, Referee Magazine, a national magazine for sport officiating.; [oth. writ.] Student sports writer Leavenworth Times while in High School. Contributing writer Letter To The Editor, same paper currently, numerous opinion publications for Referee Magazine.; [pers.] Currently I am collecting past family records and accounts for a possible effort toward a book.; [a.] Leavenworth, KS

KESSENICH, MARIEL M.
[b.] October 24, 1980; [p.] David Kessenich and Mariann Kessenich; [ed.] Lannoye Elementary School (Polaski); [occ.] Student; [memb.] Lannoye Student Council, Church Disciple Corps; [hon.] P.E. Fitness Award, Air Rifle - Marksman 1st class and Sharpshooter Bar 3, Track and Field, Speech Contests, Pulaski Knights of Columbus Poster Contest 1st place; [pers.] I always count on God to give me wisdom in what I write and I try not to worry about what others think but only to do my best.; [a.] Oneida, WI

KEY, DEAN
[b.] May 1, 1967, Buffalo, WY; [p.] Nancy and Dennis Elm; [ch.] Amy Key; [ed.] Kaycee High School; [occ.] Equipment Operator for K.C. Oilfield Service; [memb.] National Rifle Assoc.; [hon.] Who's Who among high School Students, Salutatorian; [a.] Kaycee, WY

KHAN, QAMAR A.
[pen.] Jay Taj; [b.] January 6, 1932, India; [p.] Badar Khan, Badrun Khan; [m.] Anna, December 22, 1958; [ch.] Bobby V. Khan, Arshad Q. Khan; [ed.] B.S. Aligarh University India, M.B., B.S., Bihar University, India M.D. (Doctor of Medicine), Bihar University, India; [occ.] Physician; [memb.] Fellow American College of Cardiology Member, American College of Chest Physician, member, American Medical Association; [hon.] Award for Medical Advocacy and Berlex, Clinical Research Award-Sandoz citation of Nashville Cardiovascular Society as founder-secretary and President.; [oth. writ.] Literary articles and interviews published in local magazine and newspapers.; [pers.] I love poetry and poets for my profound belief that poetry is a shared-creation-poet creates images in his mind which delves into depth emotion, cherish in the soul, evoked by love, nurtured with union of selflessness and re-born as a pearl of creation - thus, by evolution, an essence of universal creative love emerges as a "treasury of all mankind.; [a.] Nashville, TN

KIDWELL, MISTY
[pen.] Ann Allen; [b.] February 6, 1973, Lafollette; [p.] Donna Wilbanks and Cameron Evans; [m.] Eddie Kidwell, December 28, 1989; [ch.] Joshua Edgar, Don-Jacob Cameron; [memb.] Southeast Writers Assoc., Appalachia East Writers Assoc. (co-founder); [oth. writ.] Have written self-published books under my pen name Ann Allen entitled "Into the Night" and in my own name, entitled "Reflections, A Collection of Poetry.; [pers.] Always believe in yourself and your work, don't let anyone tell you that you can't do it, because-you can.; [a.] Jacksboro, TN

KIEKENBUSH, CHRISTY
[b.] July 30, 1981, Kenosha, WI; [p.] Wayne Kiekenbush, Margaret Kiekenbush; [ed.] Burlington Area Schools, Burlington, WI; [memb.] American Kyuki-Do Federation (Karate); [hon.] Bridges and Connections Anthology Southern Lakes Award, Kiwanas Burlington Area Arts Council Award, Masterpiece Arts Award; [oth. writ.] Change our Feelings, other poetry; [a.] Burlington, WI

KILHAM, DOROTHY P.
[pen.] Dorothy P. Kilham; [b.] March 6, 1914, Medford, MA; [p.] Deceased; [m.] Peter Kilham (Deceased); [ed.] Medford High School M.A., learned from experience on the way up from the Great Depression. Many varied jobs.; [occ.] Corporate Secretary of Droll Yankees Inc.; [memb.] Nature Conservancy, Boston Museum of Fine Arts, W.G.B.H., PBS Boston, Museum of Natural History, Smithsonian Institute; [oth. writ.] Earth Gifts Book I published. Poems and stories in Heartland Journal, (Bird Watcher's Digest) Nature Society News, The Scituate Bee, Dick E. Bird News. (Only writings I have had remuneration from.); [pers.] Mostly nature related writings. Too many beauties of the earth will no longer be here, soon, and hoped if I wrote about them, they might be preserved and enjoyed. I stared writing at age 70, now 81, but still work and write, and am very alert.; [a.] Foster, RI

KIM, NINA
[pen.] J. J. Slate; [b.] June 7, 1981, Korea; [p.] Choonja Kim, Dong Son Kim; [ed.] St. Mary of the Lake School, Hynes School, Golf Middle School; [occ.] Surviving eighth grade; [pers.] A friend is a follower, but a true friend is an individualist who stands in their own grounds and isn't afraid to express who they really are.; [a.] Morton Grove, IL

KINDER, LOIS WADE
[p.] Dennis C. and Myrtle Cline Wade; [m.] Edward W. Kinder, Deceased, September 28, 1946; [ch.] Paul Edward Kinder, deceased; [ed.] B.A. and Morris Harrey College, U.C. English and Social Studies; [occ.] Retired Elementary School Teacher, 35 yrs. service; [memb.] Life Member I.S.P., N.R.T.A., Life Member Congress of P.T.A., Life Member West Virginia Assoc. Retired Teachers, Boone County, and Nellis Wesleyan Church; [hon.] Life Membership W.V. Congress of P.T.A. 1971, Award of Merit Certificate, World of Poetry 1991, Two Editor's Choice Awards, National Library Semifinalist, 1994, Nellis Wesleyan Church for many years of dedicated service.; [oth. writ.] I am thankful published in "Outstanding Poets," 1994, and springtime published in "Seasons to Come" 1994, The New Church published in "Great Poems of our Times" 1993, and Autumn in This Edition of at "Waters Edge," 1995.; [a.] Nellis, WV

KING, CANDYCE L.
[pen.] Kate Tabor; [b.] January 29, 1951, Waukegan, IL; [p.] Donald H. King, Shirley M. King; [ed.] La Sierra High School, Univ. of Calif. (Riverside), George Mason University; [occ.] Writing, making native American Crafts; [memb.] Psi Chi, HSUS, ASPCA, Amnesty International, various Native American organizations; [hon.] Two scholarships for creative write, award for years of work with the developmentally disabled.; [oth. writ.] Working on a novel-journey of the Blue-Eyed Indian, also working on various short stories and poems, also involved in song writing and composing songs for the Native American Flute.; [pers.] My philosophy of life can be summed up in three Dakota words Mitaku Oyasin (We are all

related) not only to all people but to the mountains, the rivers, the trees, the animals and the birds.; [a.] Silver Spring, MD

KING, FRANCESCA D.
[pen.] Delores King; [b.] November 8, 1975, Indianapolis, IN; [p.] Debra L. King and Leroy King; [ed.] High School diploma; [occ.] Customer Service; [oth. Writ.] Lover's Inquiry, Loving You, Love Me Like This, Hopes Spring Eternal, I Don't Want To Be Alone Tonight!, Let Me Hold You!, I miss You!, A Dreamer's Wish, Dear Lover; [pers.] The people I love have often influenced me and I thank them; [a.] Indianapolis, IN

KING, NELIDA RIOS
[pen.] Nellie; [b.] August 11, 1938, Coamo, PR; [p.] Esteban Rios and Emelina Febus Rios; [m.] Boyd Wendell King, August 27, 1955; [ch.] Wendell Ray King, Sadie Lou Wiltshire, Marilee Ann Ciehoski and Leyla Yvonne Scott; [ed.] Florence Santiago High (PR), N. Virginia Community College some course at George Mason University (VA) and home study children's literature and painting seminars; [occ.] Housewife; [memb.] Westover Baptist Church, Manassas, VA; [oth. writ.] Some articles in the journal messenger (I never send anything out for fear of rejection also I'm not very dedicated!); [pers.] When I write a poem, every word is like the rain drops of an early morning shower. It refreshes me, leaving a colorful rainbow in my soul. Sometimes you just happen to "get well" that doesn't mean you stop searching for the rainbow; [a.] Manassas, VA

KINZIE, SENAIDA ANN GALLEGOS
[b.] May 13, 1979, Denver, CO; [p.] Darcus-Doug Kinzie (adoptive), Josephine Gallegos, Jose Samion; [ed.] K-10th grade Bromwell Elementary, (K-2) Haxton Schools, (3-8) Haxton High School (9-10); [occ.] Bar-Lo Cafe (Waitress); [memb.] HHS Band, FBLA, FHA, Haxtun Church of the Brethern Choir Youth Group; [hon.] Art Science Awards, Fairs Exhibits Honor Rolls,; [oth. writ.] Poem to be published in the Book "At Waters Edge"; [pers.] I write my poems about my feelings of the past, and in the future. I try to portray my feelings in words.; [a.] Haxtun, CO

KIRBY, SHAUN MICHAEL
[pen.] Shaun Kirby; [b.] April 9, 1980, Pordenone, Italy; [p.] Michael and Janice Kirby; [ed.] Parkland Middle School, Freshman at Wheaton High School; [occ.] Student; [memb.] Boy Scouts of America, Young Life; [oth. writ.] Several pieces printed in school newspapers; [pers.] I try to reflect life in my work, the goodness and badness, the dark and the light, and the Ying and Yang. I owe everything to my parents and good friends like Faith, Jacob, Jonathan, Nicole and of course my friends at young life.; [a.] Silver Spring, MD

KITTS, ELIZABETH ANN
[pen.] Elizabeth Zangardi; [b.] September 24, 1954, Bethesda, MD; [p.] Bertha and Frederick Zangardi; [ch.] John Frederick Kitts; [ed.] Robert E. Peary High School, Montgomer College-majoring in General Studies. ATI Career Institute-Travel and Tourism Program; [occ.] Software

Quality Assurance Analyst; [hon.] Distinguish Recognition Award as a Program Meeting Manager from the National Management Association, 1990; [pers.] Most of my writings are based upon relationships, communication, life's struggles and striving for a positive outlook on life. I believe you will accomplish many things in life when you learn to have a healthy relationship with yourself first.; [a.] Rockville, MD

KITZMAN, BERNICE
[b.] December 17, 1931, WI; [p.] Mr. and Mrs. Ferdinand Kitzman; [ed.] Eighth Grade School in Big Falls, WI; [occ.] Shop Owner; [pers.] Life is wonderful most of the time and very hard sometimes but if we trust out fellowman and have faith in God everything always turns out all right.

KITZMILLER, SAMANTHA N.
[pen.] Sam; [b.] July 16, 1984, Kingsport; [p.] Sandy and Samuel Kitzmiller; [ed.] 5th grade at Rock Springs Elementary; [memb.] Clubs, The Odd Job Squad; [hon.] Gymnastics won 1st place, Beauty Pageant Princess, Cheerleading Trophy, 1st all around.; [oth. writ.] Book Reports, and a Research Paper.; [pers.] I'm very honored to have writing talent I didn't know I had! I always thought writing was so amazing, I take after my Aunt Shawna. I'm pleased to be a semi-finalist!; [a.] Kingsport, TN

KLOCKE, DEBORAH L.
[b.] September 13, 1956, Leavenworth, KS; [p.] Clarence and Eleanor Jaster; [m.] Edward Klocke, June 26, 1993; [ch.] Michael, Laura; [ed.] Leavenworth High; [occ.] Communications Technician, Southwestern Bell Tel. Abilene, KS; [a.] Solomon, KS

KNAPP, JUSTIN E.
[pen.] John Jameston; [b.] December 26, 1975, Seattle, WA; [p.] Walter Knapp and Joan Knapp; [ed.] Monroe Area Comprehensive High School, University of Georgia (Freshman); [occ.] Student; [hon.] National Honor Society, Beta Club, First Place in Poetry for Rockdale Center High School Literary Arts Competition (1994), University of Georgia Barnett Award Nominee; [oth. writ.] Editorials in the Hurricane Watch; [a.] Monroe, GA

KNICKERBOCKER, DOROTHY
[b.] March 2, 1919, Johnson City, NY; [p.] Richard and Myrtle Hillary; [m.] Ellis Knickerbocker, October 24, 1939; [ch.] David, Thomas and Carl; [ed.] High School Graduate; [occ.] Retired; [pers.] This my one and only poem, was written after witnessing, two senior citizens screaming and swearing at another senior citizen. She stood calmly and straight in a corner. This scene at that time looked (to me like 2 snarling dogs at a prey in a tree.; [a.] Oviedo, FL

KNIGHT, ROBIN
[pen.] March 21, 1958; [occ.] Poet, writer, UFO photographer; [oth. writ.] Working on my first book and looking for someone to produce my poems.; [pers.] Welcome to the new age! Oh yeah, one more thing: the name of this planet is not earth, silly, earth is Eden or Eden.

KOCK, KATHARINE J.
[pen.] Katharine Koch; [b.] May 23, 1929, Niagara Falls, NY; [p.] K. Elsa Connell and George Connell; [m.] Raymond H. Koch, November 10, 1951; [ch.] Peggy Pezzi, Nancy Schiemer, Raymond Koch Jr., Eric Koch and Joanne Koch; [ed.] La Salle H.S. Niagara Falls, Univ. of Rochester School of Nursing, B.S.R.N. - School Nurse Certification, Fairleigh Dickinson Univ. Rutherford, N.J.; [occ.] Homemaker, (Retired School Nurse of 18 yrs.); [memb.] Bergen Highlands United Methodist Church Choir and Trustee, N.J. State School Nurse Assoc., Bergen County School Nurse Assoc., Bible Study Fellowship International. Former Sweet Adeline - (Female Barbershoppers) 1969-1981 Bergen County Retired Educators Assoc.; [hon.] Dorothea Dix Award and Psychiatric Nursing, Univ. of Rochester International Chorus Championship Ramapo Valley Chapter of Sweet Adelines, St. Louis, MO 1979; [oth. writ.] Several poems published in school newspapers and local town paper, also N.J.S.S.N.A. newsletter; [pers.] I try to express humour, love, and positive feelings in my poems to family and friends.; [a.] Upper Saddle River, NJ

KOHLMAN, CLEO
[b.] Late Twenties, New Orleans; [p.] Lillian and Theodore Carter; [m.] Louis Freddy Kohlman (deceased), October 4, 1954; [ed.] Olive Harvey College 1974-76 Majored in Arts and Crafts. Completed education at Chicago State University in 1976. Bachelor Degree of Art 1978; [occ.] Writer of Poetry and Arts and Graft; [memb.] Phi Beta Kappa Sorority; [oth. writ.] I have in the Library of Congress of a 4 ft. tall early man in sculpture. Made in 1978 at Chicago University his name is Alpha - I also have many more pieces of pastry; [a.] Chicago, IL

KOMULA, JUDY C.
[b.] August 8, 1949, Louisa, KY; [p.] Clarence Cook, Bettie Cook; [m.] Steven L. Komula, July 12, 1985; [ch.] Michael, Randy, Robert Toner; [ed.] Superior High, Apollo College for Medical Assistants; [hon.] Scholastic Achievement Award, Apollo College; [oth. writ.] Several poems published in local newspapers, numerous unpublished poems, song lyrics, and inspirational thoughts; [pers.] Dedicated to my three sons whom I love dearly.; [a.] Tonto Basin, AZ

KOPP, HELEN R.
[b.] August 23, 1919, Lancaster, PA; [p.] Christian and Irene Kopp; [m.] Single; [ed.] Lancaster General Hospital School of Nursing, Class 1951, Kings College Hospital School of Midwifery; [occ.] Retired (R.N.); [oth. writ.] This is my first for pub.; [pers.] I get my inspiration for writing and painting from nature. Both painting (water-color and binding are my retirement hobbies.); [a.] Lancaster, PA

KOSS, LINDA B.
[b.] September 28, 1953, Springfield, MA; [m.] William A. Koss, June 4, 1983; [ed.] B.A. Human Service; [occ.] Director of Battered Women's Shelter; [memb.] YWCA, Vestry of St. Andrew's Church, Women United Against Violence; [oth. writ.] Alone, and many other unpublished.; [pers.]

"Love is life" was specifically written for my husband. It was read to him as part of our wedding ceremony. It will be read again when we renew our vows June 1995; [a.] Ludlow, MA

KOUGH, MARY G.
[pen.] Gene Kough; [b.] December 9, 1944, Sherman, TX; [p.] Martha Jim and Benjamin Kenney; [m.] Robert E. Kough, July 10, 1964; [ch.] Keith Duane (son), Jennifer Rebecca (daughter-in-law) and the late Kimberly Danielle (daughter); [ed.] James Wilson Young High School Bayport, NY, University of Texas, Arlington, TX; [occ.] Co-Owner of I.D.M.C., Inc. Vice President-Operations; [memb.] Texas Special Olympics, American Heart Association, American Cancer Society, National Assoc. of Self Employed (NASE); [hon.] Editors Choice Awards 1994 National Library of Poetry, 1995 distinguished member of International Society of Poets, Nominated "Poet of the Year" 1995 by International Society of Poets; [oth. writ.] Published "Annys" 1994 in "Dark Side of the Moon." ISP Published "Lilac Ghosts" 1994 by Texas Special Olympics, and in 1995 "The Best of 1995" by ISP, Published "The Little Chair" 1995 Texas Special Olympics Published "Talent" 1995 ISP "Between the Raindrops"; [pers.] The "Magic" in my life, comes from the people in my life, that believe in my dreams, before I believe I have any.; [a.] Arlington, TX

KRAMER, MYRTLE L.
[pen.] Myrt Denee; [b.] December 20, 1923, New Arkansas, NJ; [p.] Nellie (Denee) Bussie, Harry Bussie; [m.] Irving F. Kramer, November 6, 1955; [ch.] Paul; [ed.] State Street School Newark, NJ, Special class. Then Philadelphia School Practical Nursing.; [occ.] Retired from V.A. Hospital; [hon.] Superior Performance Ward Nursing Service

KRAUS, CHRISSY
[b.] September 26, 1979, Killeen, TX; [p.] Katie Kraus; [ed.] Bellaire Elementary, Nolan Middle School, Ellison Ninth Grade Center; [occ.] Full Time Student; [memb.] Ellison Screaming Eagle Band, Killeen Riding and Roping Club; [oth. writ.] Poetry, untitled poems published in Echoes of Yesterday and "Pray" published in Voices; [pers.] To write is to express yourself, and its something I've always wanted. Writing is a feeling not just a word.; [a.] Killeen, TX

KRCULIC, SILVANA
[b.] October 20, 1949, Mountain Village, Jesenovik; [p.] Ivan, Pierina Brkaric; [m.] Lino, July 29, 1968; [ch.] Allen, Alexandra and Christopher; [ed.] Administrative Technician; [occ.] Clerical; [memb.] Belongs to clubs of poetry in Europe and Australia; [hon.] Poetry published, anthology published in Europe, poetry published in Germany, Europe, Australia.; [oth. writ.] I came here to land of plenty, dreamers heart and others; [pers.] Poet, humanitarian, lover of mankind.; [a.] Brooklyn, NY

KREHBIEL, LEVI
[b.] November 10, 1922, Moundridge, KS; [p.] Edward and Marie Krehbiel; [m.] Mabel Graber Krehbiel, October 22, 1944; [ch.] Angela Jackson, Liberal, KS, Robert Krehbiel, Wichita, KS; [ed.]

High School Graduate; [occ.] Retired; [hon.] Graduate of Spartan School of Aeronautics as a N.D.T. Inspector; [oth. writ.] Poems for special occasions for church and school.

KROSTUE, CATHY M.
[b.] April 14, 1962; [p.] Kae and Wes Holtman; [m.] David Krostue, July 30, 1982; [ch.] Samantha Jo, Joshua David, Katie Mae; [ed.] East Grand Forks Senior High, Moorhead State University; [occ.] Homemaker; [memb.] Bygland Lutheran Church, Superintendent; [oth. writ.] Several poems and a few novels, unpublished.; [pers.] Take one day at a time!

KROWS, WAYNE
[pen.] Wayne Krows; [b.] March 24, 1928, Tuscola, IL; [p.] Paul and Jane Krows; [m.] Karen Krows, December 27, 1975; [ch.] Sara, Fred, Ed, Susan, Kevin; [ed.] B.A. Degree Millikin University, Decatur, IL 1951; [occ.] Retired; [memb.] Kiwanis Westminster Presbyterian Church; [hon.] Honorary Doctor of Laws Degree, Millikin University 1989; [oth. writ.] Children's stories (non published); [a.] Decatur, IL

KRULJAC, DAVID A.
[pen.] Jam; [b.] February 8, 1961, Rock Springs, WY; [ch.] Devin Scott and Kelcie Nichole; [oth. writ.] Oh my heart be still a poem to be published in fall of '95 by Sparrow Grass Poetry form.; [pers.] I am single and belong to no religion, yet I seek God on my own path. My poetry expresses the feeling that we all have, I hope to share them with all of you. Continue to grow and know we are ok.; [a.] Rock Springs, WY

KRUMM, ELZA L.
[b.] January 6, 1918, El Dorado Springs, MO; [p.] Joseph and Vinnie Krumm; [ed.] Three years college - no degree, Adrian, MO High School, MO State College. Taught school 3 years-1st Lt. in Army, World War II; [occ.] Freelance Writer, photographer, music composer, piano and musicals; [memb.] ARE, Virginia Beach, VA; [hon.] Phi Sigma Pi in College; [pers.] Very much into Metaphysics, Prophesy, New Age study. Believe that man is a spiritual being temporarily living in a physical body. Am certain that the New Age is imminent. Man must evolve or perish.; [a.] Kansas City, MO

KUCERA, DR. JEAN STERLING
[pen.] Jean Sterling; [b.] October 6, 1943, Bever Dam, MD; [p.] Paul and Doris Sterling; [ch.] Heather-Maria Kucera, John-Paul Patrick Kucera; [ed.] B.A. in English and Journalism at Mary Washington, MA Graduate Work at George Washington Univ., Univ. of Maryland, and Johns Hopkins University; [occ.] Poetry-Therapy Poet, Social Worker, Speaker, Editor; [memb.] Post: MD State Poetry Soc., KY State Poetry Soc., Amer. Poetry League, United Poet Laureate Assoc., National Poetry Therapy, Ecology, International Platform of Speaking, World Poetry Society; [hon.] Life title of Poet Laureate of Chesapeake Bay Country, Poet of the Year, MD, Greatness and Achievement Award, UPLA, Certificate of Merit, Who's Who, England, Magna Cum Laude Award, A.P.L., Listed in: International Who's Who in Poetry, Writer's Market,

Directory of American and British Writers, Educational Journal; [oth. writ.] Spring Anthology (London), From The Hills (Morris Harvey College), Pancontinental Premier Poets (India), The Unsung (Acropolis), From Sea to Sea In Song (Amer. Poetry League), Poets on Parade (Idaho), Melody of the Muse (Best of Contemporary Poetry, Appalachia), Poetry Features in The Literary Review (Fairleigh Dickinson Univ.,) Inky Trails, From the Hills, Editorial and Publicity work: American Engineer, Quartermaster Review, NEA's Student Life, Scimitar and songs, newspapers: Washington Post, Sunshine, Salisbury Times, Eastern Shore News; [pers.] With an open mind, vibrant soul, and fully living each day, how can one not be happy, well-rounded, considerate, and true to God, nature, and self.; [a.] Steuben, ME

KUMAR, KATHY
[b.] September 27, England; [p.] George Johnson, Frances Johnson; [m.] Arvind Kumar, August 20, 1973; [ch.] Raj Kumar, Anjali Kumar; [ed.] Nursing College England, Registered Nurse, Registered Midwife; [pers.] I strive to express my love, praise, gratitude, and devotion to the God of all creation, and author of our salvation, in all my poems.; [a.] Downers Grove, IL

KUNZ, ROSEMARY
[b.] June 19, 1952, Scranton, PA; [p.] Walter and Irene Kunz; [m.] Divorced; [ed.] B.S. Penn State University Health and Physical Education, MS Penn State Univ. Physical Education; [occ.] Teacher; [hon.] Dunmore High School (Dunmore Bucks - "Miss Buck" Who's Who in American High Schools); [pers.] You only have one life - make it a happy and fulfilling experience by appreciating the beauty around you and by making your family and friends a part of it.; [a.] Moscow, PA

LA ROSA, LOIS
[b.] December 6, 1952, Mount Pleasant; [p.] Cora Snyder Presley Wiltrout; [m.] Paul La Rosa; [ch.] Thomas Shrum, Tonya Shrum, Toni Shrum, Chad La Rosa, Paula La Rosa, Lydia La Rosa; [ed.] Liberal Arts and Writing Courses WCCC Community College Youngwood, PA; [occ.] Personal Care Home Cora's Place Administrator; [memb.] Active local Salvation Army Volunteer - Special Olympics

LAABS, MONICA A.
[b.] May 18, 1974, San Diego; [p.] Jerry Lee and Sandra Luz; [ed.] Santana High School, Grossmont College; [memb.] Our Lady of Perpetual Help Catholic Church; [oth. writ.] Not Published; [pers.] I write what's in my heart. There's a reality to everything that needs to be uncovered.; [a.] Santee, CA

LADET, MONICA RAYMO
[pen.] Wide Track; [b.] April 26, 1958, Natchitoches, LA; [p.] Bill Raymo, Sr., Dorothy J. Raymo; [ch.] Pet-Tigger; [occ.] Home Health Aide for the Elderly; [oth. writ.] Just this year published by National Library of Poetry in Reflections of Light. Poem Under the Bridge of the World.; [pers.] Time have changed to much. I can remember as a little girl growing up in Louisiana, going down the street, people waving and smiling. Oh, how I miss those times and if its God's will I want to give some of that back through my poetry.; [a.] Dallas, Texas

LAMAR, MARIA E.
[b.] December 11, 1952, PA; [p.] Mildred Bailey; [m.] Warren Lamar, July 28, 1979; [ed.] Eric L. Bailey; [ed.] Germantown High, La Salle University, Cheyney University, Guiynedd Mercy College; [occ.] Teacher; [memb.] International Society of Poets; [hon.] Editor's Choice Award; [oth. writ.] Poems published and in reflection of light; [pers.] Poetry is an opening to the lines of life - always walk straight!; [a.] Philadelphia, PA

LAMARCHINA, CAROLYN
[b.] December 1, 1946, Burbank, CA; [p.] Joyce and John Bertetti; [ch.] Tamara Jean, Cara Mishanne; [ed.] High School Graduate, Private Musical Lessons; [occ.] On stage musician (Cellist) for Wayne Newton. Horse and Dog breeder.; [hon.] Burbank Women' Club Music Scholarship, Full Music Scholarship to Mt. Saint Mary's College. Numerous accolades for on stage solo work.; [oth. writ.] Junior High Farewell Speech Ghost writer for political personal letters. Tri-State Arabian Horse Newsletter Editor.; [pers.] Study, discipline, analyzation and persistence are all important ingredients for success at anything..., but anyone can read instructions, thus it must be the input of "Feelings" that styles and inspires greatness.; [a.] Branson, MO

LAMB, SUZANNE
[pen.] Suzanne L.; [b.] September 16, 1946, Racine, WI; [p.] Elmer and Audrey Meinert; [m.] Gerald Lamb Sr., October 17, 1964; [ch.] Gerald Lowell Jr., Stacy Suzanne, Ryan Scott; [ed.] William. Horlick High, G.T.C.; [occ.] Self Employed; [memb.] Redeemer Lutheran Church. Past Sunday School Teacher and VBS Teacher and Past Church Secretary; [oth. writ.] Poem published in "The High Road" - (Pastoral Services Office of Chaplains - Poughkeepsie, N.Y.); [pers.] My poems are a reflection of the faith I have in a Higher Power by whom I am greatly influenced; [a.] Racine, WI

LAMPE, ALBERTA M.
[pen.] Alberta Lampe; [b.] July 18, 1930, Saint Louis, MO; [p.] Albert and Caroline Schweitzer; [m.] George J. Lampe, November 24, 1949; [ch.] George Michael, Dennis Allen, Albert Jude, Gloria Ann, Linda Marie, Carolyn Catherine, I have 14 grandchildren; [ed.] My Education consist as follows, St. James the Greater - Catholic grade school, Rosati Kain Catholic Girls Private High School - St. Louis, Missouri; [memb.] Creative writing, Custom Foaming as hobby, and arts and crafts - hobby teaching; [hon.] Creative writing, Rosati Kain - Parochial High School, I graduated from Rosati Kain Catholic High with special honors in (Creative writing); [pers.] I try to capture and portray the awesome beauty of this world in my writing. I am strongly drawn, through my inner thoughts, to thank a supreme being for the gifts of life. And show the love of mankind for one another, through my writing.; [a.] Linn Creek, MO

LAMSON, ERIC
[pen.] e.b.l.; [b.] July 9, 1979, CT; [p.] Jane Lamson, Blair Lamson; [ed.] Springfield Central High, Holyoke Community College; [occ.] Nabisco Merchandiser, Stock Clerk; [oth. writ.]

Several poems unpublished. One poem published in Creative Kids Magazine. Journal writing weekly.; [pers.] Creativity is the Alpha and Omega of Human Consciousness. We are ourselves and the works we create.; [a.] Springfield, MA

LANCASTER, WENDELL GODFREY
[b.] August 6, 1951, Washington, DC; [p.] John W. and Thelma A. Lancaster; [m.] Kelley H. Lancaster, August 18, 1988; [ch.] Lesley Lancaster and Allyson Lancaster; [ed.] The American University, Wash. DC, Washington Technical Institute Wash., Cochoran School of Art, Wash., DC; [occ.] President of Senate Transport Systems - an intermodal Transportation Company; [hon.] Received letters of gratitude from President Bush for writings on Desert Storm (poetry).; [oth. writ.] "A Poet's Pen", "When Birds Must Rest And Glide"; [pers.] My writings reflect the relationships we share with our friends, family, environment and most of all our creator above.

LANE, BILL
[pen.] William Paul Lane; [b.] February 13, 1968, Ravenna, OH; [p.] Mr. and Mrs. Charles J. Lane; [m.] Single; [ed.] Ravenna High, Ravenna, OH, Kent State University and University of Akron, both in Ohio; [occ.] I run a bar "BW-3" (whoopie!); [memb.] Member of Institute of Children's Literature and also member of Long Ridge Writer's Group both located in West Redding, CT; [oth. writ.] I'm striving to become a published writer. Up until now, I guess you could say, I've been a professional submitter to magazine and book publishers with no success.; [pers.] Just plain "Thanks!"; [a.] Chicago, IL

LANE, JENNIFER M.
[b.] August 14, 1972, Colorado Springs, CO; [p.] Clinton and Beverly Lane; [ed.] B.A., English - University of New Hampshire, 1994; [occ.] Health Care Assistant for Planned Parenthood; [hon.] Dean's List; [pers.] Through every change in my life, the strongest constant has been my journal writing. Every page holds scribbled dreams, emotions and beliefs. I am constantly striving to fine tone those scribbled bits and find new forms in which to mold them.; [a.] Barrington, NH

LANG, JAMIE
[b.] September 15, 1981, Champlin, MN; [p.] Mark and Sandy Lang; [ed.] In 7th grade at Jackson Middle School; [occ.] School-student; [memb.] Women's Auxiliary-American Legion Post 600; [hon.] Dance and softball Grades A&B honor roll; [oth. writ.] Valentine's Day, Peace colors beginning with C, Color's of the rainbow, Melanie Smith, Me, volleyball; [pers.] In my poems I like to reflect the way I feel. My feelings and things that happen to me are main inspiration. My family helps alot too.; [a.] Champlin, MN

LANGFITT, MEGAN
[b.] September 13, 1978, Clarion, IA; [p.] John and Lynda Langfitt; [ed.] Junior in the Eldora New Providence High School; [hon.] Certified mandatory reporter in Child Abuse; [a.] Eldora, IA

LANGIEWICZ, RUTH A.
[b.] May 28, 1964, Little Falls, MN; [p.] Lois and John; [m.] Michael; [ch.] Brandon, Travis, Kristia and Michael Jr; [ed.] High School; [occ.] Bookkeeping; [memb.] Forstrys, M.A.D.D.; [pers.] Write - What you are feeling. I have been influenced by my Jr High Teacher Mr. Hale.

LARKIN, SHEILA
[pen.] Orange Rogue; [b.] January 1, 1979, Ireland; [p.] Joan Healy Rae and John Larkin; [ed.] Presentation Convent, Limerick, St. Paul the Apostle, Yonkers, Our Lady of Victory Academy, Dobbs Ferry; [occ.] High School Junior; [memb.] Hugh O'Brian Youth Foundation, National Honor Society, Alpha Honor Society, Golden School of Irish Dancing New York, Track and Field, DYA Soccer League; [hon.] St. John's University Award for Biology and Chemistry, Presidential Award for Academic Fitness, Hugh O'Brian Certificate of Recognition, Principal's List, numerous Irish Dancing Awards in Ireland and U.S.; [oth. writ.] "Epitome of Youth", "The Journey Home."; [pers.] One must work hard in order to get the most out of life and in order to get the best results. A dancer has to practice hard to get the best results.; [a.] Yonkers, NY

LASAPONARA, JESSICA
[b.] April 18, 1978, Suffern, NY; [p.] Joseph and Kathleen Lasaponara; [ed.] Spring Valley High School; [occ.] Student (sophomore); [pers.] My writing is my own way of mediation. I try to transfer my inter feelings into my writing; [a.] Spring Valley, NY

LASLEY, JEFFREY
[b.] March 6, 1951, Lou., KY; [p.] Edwin and Margaret Lasley; [m.] Michelle Green Lasley, October 19, 1974; [ed.] B.S., Iowa State University; [occ.] Computer Consultant

LAUGHTON, MARIANNE J. VERGANO
[b.] February 19, 1962, Jersey City, NJ; [p.] Egidia S. Vergano and Ernani C. Vergano; [m.] E. Joseph Laughton, June 27, 1992; [ed.] B.S. 1984 Babson College; [occ.] Freelance Desktop Publisher and Copy Writer; [pers.] Hugs and kisses to my husband and family for their continuous love and support as I strive to be the best I can be.; [a.] Hudson, MA

LAUMEYER, ROBERT L.
[b.] August 31, 1932, Wolf Point, MT; [p.] Joe and Rose Laumeyer; [m.] Kathleen McGlynn Laumeyer, August 31, 1953; [ch.] Mary RunKel, Barbara Miner, Jean O'Leary, Rob A. Laumeyer; [ed.] High School Nashua Mt. Northern Mt. College Havre Mt. University of M Missoula Mt. Arizona State Tempe Arizona; [occ.] Retired; [oth. writ.] Poems published in: New Voices in American Poetry 1980, and 1987 and the Garden of Life 1995; [pers.] Beauty is always out there, but it is just beyond my reach, sailing on an endless sea with poetry it's only beach.; [a.] Sun City, AZ

LAWRENCE, CHARLES
[pen.] "Mr. C"; [b.] March 23, 1925, MS; [p.] Deceased; [m.] Marjorie Lawrence, December 27, 1945; [ch.] One; [ed.] M.S. Social Work; [occ.] Social Work; [oth. writ.] Only short stories and poems sort of as a hobby - copies to friends for their enjoyment.; [a.] Pineville, LA

LAWRENCE, ERVIATEEN
[b.] August 15, 1937, Arkansas; [p.] Willis and Annie B. Allen; [ch.] Barbara A. Fleeton and Jimmie Martin; [ed.] Lincoln High School; [occ.] Nursing Assistant; [memb.] Agape True Deliverance Church, Seniors Gold and Silver Club.; [hon.] Awards of Merit Certificate Honorable Mention for poem - Hang ON, Honorable Mention for Poem - Keep Christ In Christmas; [oth. writ.] Poem - A Good Mother. I have written several other poems.; [pers.] I was influenced by God to write the poems that I have written.; [a.] Kissimmee, FL

LAWRENCE, LUCY LEE
[pen.] Lucy Lee Lawrence; [b.] August 4, 1935, Detroit, MI; [p.] Judy Lucy Chadman and Larry Lee Lawrence; [ed.] Placer High School, Sierra College, AA Theater Arts, San Francisco State College, Sacramento State College, B.F.A. - Theater; [occ.] Substitute Teacher, Comic, Film Business; [memb.] Comedy Assoc. of N.Y., Parier Dog Pals, Clown Club; [oth. writ.] 3 Children's stories, 4 scripts, various letters to the editor, many song lyrics, work in progress on a book about a child with cancer.; [pers.] No one is perfect, not even parents. Feel the hurt move on, don't live in the past so that you forget today. Enjoy each moment. Be as a child and love will follow.; [a.] Albuquerque, NM

LAWRENCE, REGINALD II
[b.] January 23, 1986, Berkeley, CA; [p.] April Williams; [ed.] Third Grade Student at John Swett Alternative Elementary School in San Francisco, CA; [occ.] Student; [hon.] Student in Gifted Program; [oth. writ.] Springtime; [pers.] I just wish that the world would get better and people would stop killing the children. I wish it was safe enough for me to play in a playground, and there were no homeless people.; [a.] San Francisco, CA

LAWRENCE, SYLVIA
[b.] December 22, 1952, Coatesville, PA; [p.] Deceased; [m.] Arthur I. Lawrence, September 30, 1972; [ch.] Emanuel Ellis (Arthur, Jr. January 12, 1975); [ed.] Coatesville Area Senior High; [occ.] Medical Transcriptionist; [memb.] Church of Christ SADS (Sudden Arrhythmia Death Syndrome) Foundation; [hon.] Honor Graduate Superior Performance Awards, various poetic Awards; [oth. writ.] Several poems in local newspapers, "Voices of America", "Poetic Voices of America".; [pers.] Writing since age 14. I strive to use my God-given talent for his glory, usually via inspirational poems.; [a.] Coatesville, PA

LAWRENCE, WILMA LOUISE
[pen.] Wilma Louise Lawrence; [b.] June 23, 1956, Clinton, TN; [p.] Reba L. Hawkins; [m.] divorced; [ch.] 2 sons Robert and Pugh Jr. Jerry D. Pugh; [ed.] 10th Grade Gulf High School New Port Richey, FL; [occ.] Work at a blind Center to help the handicapped.; [memb.] S. Baptist. Volunteer to entertain at Nursing Homes for the Elderly. I help the handicapped at Ed. Lindsey for the Blind. The Eagles Club.; [hon.] I'm a country singer and songwriter. 2 music trophies. One 12x7 plaque from Washington D.C.! One

music certificate 2 music trophy. 1 hair-style. 2 music awards. 1 awards for American truck driving report!; [oth. writ.] Own: Wilma. Lou's. Music. Publishing Country music! Lavender Records: one music write up in the lake City times! Do music!; [pers.] From Billboard song magazine, contest. I love helping people who need help and the elderly do need tLC and the misfortunate also need the tLC. I wrote a song in Honor of the homeless all over the world. It was performed live at the Holiday.; [a.] Nashville, TN

LAWSON, JEFFREY I
[b.] August 4, 1959, Dayton, OH; [p.] Carl & Shirley (deceased); [m.]Angie, May 15th; [ch.] Jeffrey II, Danielle, Angie, David, Rebekah & Liela; [ed.] College - Sinclair and Cleary, Navy, Nuclear Power School, Instruction Training School; [occ.] Dayton Daily News; [memb.] International Society of Poets, American friends Service Committee, U.S. Chess Federation, Junior Achievement; [hon.] Distinguished Service Medal (U.S. Navy), Service Awards in Iran, Beruit and Granada, Humanitarian Service Medal and Meritorious Achievement Medal; [oth. writ.] Several poems published including 1994 <u>Dark Side of the Moon</u>, book... short stories - The Meaning of Honor - published 1985 - <u>Reader's Digest</u>; [pers.] We all make life as we see fit, sometimes, it isn't as others might like. However, within our individual spirits is the truth that only we know...; [a.] Bellbrook, OH

LAWSON, REEDENA MASON
[pen.] Reedena Mason Lawson; [b.] Stanford, KY; [p.] Clarence and Sibbie Mason (Deceased); [m.] Leon Lawson (deceased), September 6, 1969; [ed.] Danville School of Nursing, Baylor University Medical Center, Dallas, Texas. (Have 2 yrs Nursing degree.); [occ.] None-disabled Nursing Professional; [oth. writ.] Have written poems for local newspaper; [pers.] My poems are written with much emotion. I like poems that tell a story, and poems that I and others can relate too.; [a.] Berea, KY

LAZAR, MARIA
[pen.] Maria; [b.] July 15, 1935, Romania; [p.] Dihel Gheorghe - Dihel Nicolita; [m.] Eugeniu Lazar, October 25, 1955; [ch.] Lili Eugenia Lazar; [ed.] H.S. Baccalaureate Diploma Accounting Major. - 2 years Faculty of General Econ. Industrial (University) expelled inadequate politic - Certificate - protect Designe Water Supply and Allen School N.Y. N.A.; [occ.] Health Care- St. Vincent's Hospital; [memb.] L.I.R.S., Feed the children and Member in good standing International Society of Poets-lifetime, and Hutt River province-Australia -from Royal Patronage Status "The Honourable" citizen of the year 1994.; [hon.] Hereby Award the international poet of Merit award: U.S. Holocaust memorial Museum name of donor for poems for benefit of scholars, journalist and other visitors, Hutt River province Royal Patronage Certificate Honorable Citizen of the Year 1994. Hutt River Province Australia.; [oth. writ.] US and Canada Romania Newspaper Micro-Magazine - American's Anthology: A break in the clouds, wind in the night sky, - the desert sun. Last at water's edge; [pers.] The juncture politic of abolish socialism and protection of a

universal declare - rights people for life, freedom and security. Peace and science, culture of people and "In God We Trust"; [a.] New York, NY

LEACH, BECKY IVAN
[pen.] Becky Ivan; [b.] February 27, 1952, Beckley, WV; [p.] Joe Ivan Jr. (deceased), Goldie Ivan; [m.] Jeffrey D. Leach, July 14, 1990; [ch.] A dog-Skipper, Cat-Cricket; [ed.] A.A. Beckley College, B.A. Lee College-Cleveland, TN, History and Music, Minor-Religion; [occ.] "TAP" Musician-Teacher, Accompanist, Performer, I'm the organist for First Christian Church-Beckley; [memb.] National Guild of Musicians Woman's Club-Beckley, WV; [hon.] I play for WV Tech choirs, and especially the show choir Tech Singers, who have performed nationally and international-ally.; [oth. writ.] An article for the WPA in the 1930's for The Clevenand Banner in Cleveland, Bradley Co. Tennessee was published 1976-Bicentennial.; [pers.] Proverbs 3:5,6 The Bible "Trust in the Lord with all thine heart, lean not unto thine own understanding. In all ways acknowledge him and He shall direct thy path.; [a.] Beckley, WV

LEAVITT, CINDY SATTERLEE
[b.] November 9, 1972, Astoria, OR; [p.] Milton and Alice Satterlee; [m.] Steven Leavitt, September 11, 1993; [ch.] Jered Alexander; [ed.] Warrenton High; [a.] Tualatin, OR

LEE, AILEEN
[b.] March 24, 1967, Rochester, NY; [p.] Allen Lee, Judy Lee; [ed.] Perfield High, Houghton College; [occ.] Administrative Assistant - Writer; [hon.] "Honorable Mention" for poem "Stay Pure My Rosebud" at World of Poetry. Selected "Golden Poet of 1991" at World of Poetry.; [oth. writ.] Several poems published in local church newsletters - Echo, working on an unpublished novel.; [pers.] Writing is a marathon process. I write about things that are close to my heart.; [a.] Rochester, NY

LEE, JACQUELINE B.
[pen.] Jacqueline Bouvier Lee; [b.] November 26, 1963, Clinton, OK; [p.] Calvin and Joyce Davis; [m.] Delmar I. Lee, October 3, 1985; [ch.] Jennifer Nicole Lee; [ed.] Oscoda High, University of Arkansas at Little Rock; [occ.] Model, mother and student; [memb.] Art teacher at My daughters school (volunteer); [hon.] A.B. Honor Roll in College; [oth. writ.] A book called "only when the camera's on" and another love story called "Reflection"; [pers.] I believe each person should live each day to the fullest because we never know what tomorrow will bring; [a.] Jacksonville, AR

LEE, KIMBERLY
[b.] July 16, 1979, Winona; [p.] Michael and Mickele Lee; [ed.] Currently 9th Grader at Lewiston - A Hura High School; [occ.] Student; [hon.] I've gotten an Editor's Choice Award for my poem "Way Up In The Heavens" published in "Seasons to Come"; [oth. writ.] I have a lot of other poems that haven't gotten published yet.; [pers.] I've gotten my inspiration for writing poetry from my two best friends Kari Kempf and Jenny Reps and my parents. I believe anyone can write poetry if you put your mind into it; [a.] Peterson, MN

LEE, LILLIE FENNELL P.
[b.] March 3, NC; [p.] Vara F. Hatcher; [ch.] Son - James H. Lee, Jr. Daughter - Debbie Jean Lee; [ed.] Graduated from Charity High School in Rose Hill, N.C. Also - evening classes at A&T College in Greensboro, NC; [occ.] Stand Aid at UTC, Pratt and Whitney in E. Hartford; [memb.] Union Baptist Church in Hartford NAACP; [a.] Hartford, CT

LEFFEL JR., H. L. BUDDY
[pen.] Buddy Leffel; [b.] September 9, 1945, DeBois, PA; [p.] Harold L. Leffel, Mickie Reinolds; [m.] Divorced; [ch.] Ronald, Garry, and John; [ed.] Kingman High School, Kingman Kansas; [occ.] Regional Direction, National Insurance Company; [hon.] Numerous Top Sales Awards - The number One Sales Regional Director For a major insurance company for the past twenty years.; [oth. writ.] Many unpublished poems and songs for the personal joy of doing it for family and loved ones.; [pers.] My favorite saying is "whether you think you can or you can't....You right!!!"; [a.] Edmond, OK

LEFTRIDGE, DOROTHY FARRAR
[pen.] Dorothy Farrar Leftridge; [b.] August 26, 1910, Seaview, Washington; [p.] Walter Williams Farrar and Gertrude Coleman Farrar; [m.] Two Marriages, Widowed from both; [ch.] No Children; [ed.] 1 year UCLA, Graduated B.E. degree with Great Distinction, San Jose State, California; [occ.] Launching career freelance writer, Wide range occupations to include asst. buyer, professional radio Hollywood actress, counselor, University Baltimore Veteran's Guidance Center, 25 years California public school primary teacher, various pieces published.; [memb.] California Retired Teachers Association, Noetic Science, Quartus Society.; [pers.] I've been writing since 12 years old, poems and stories. I want to further the New Age Divine Plan for all mankind. My special interests are Health and Healing, Mind-Body Interactions, Transpersonal Psychology, Spiritual Quest, Personal Growth and Consciousness research.; [a.] Twentynine Palms, CA

LEMIEUX, CHRISTOPHER
[b.] February 1, 1976, San Francisco, CA; [p.] Joseph R. G. Lemieux, Edna E. Lemieux; [ed.] South San Francisco High School, currently enrolled in the University of California at Davis; [occ.] Undergraduate Student; [memb.] California Student Public Interest Research Group (CALPIRG); [hon.] Regents Scholar, recipient of the James and Lela Fulmor Scholarship, Dean's Honor List; [pers.] There is no greater pleasure in life than the Frustration of attempting to create something new and worthwhile for all people; [a.] South San Francisco, CA

LENZ, HARRY E.
[pen.] Iggy; [b.] August 7, 1945, Pittsburg, PA; [p.] Deceased; [m.] Marsha Wald Lenz, June 30, 1990; [ed.] Allegheny H.S., B.S. Degree Eastern Kentucky University, Graduate Work, Memphis State University; [occ.] Claims Manager PLM International; [hon.] Football Scholarship, Eastern Kentucky University, Graduate Assistantship - Memphis State University; [oth. writ.] Various

Satire Poems for personal use and special occasions to friends and relatives; [pers.] I like satire. Satire, if done tastefully creates laughter. It has always been said, "Laughter is the best medicine." It can cure a lot of ills.; [a.] San Francisco, CA

LEON, NUCCIA GIACALONE
[b.] August 10, 1963, San Diego, CA; [p.] Maria Giacalone, Salvatore Giacalone; [ed.] Madison High, Mesa Community College, San Diego with a major in Nutrition; [pers.] To a very special lady Vera Hicks, for giving me all the warmth and love possible. You opened my heart to Poetry and made this all within my reach. You will always be loved.; [a.] San Diego, CA

LESLIE, MARY JUNE
[pen.] Lee Knox or M. J. Leslie; [b.] June 25, 1934, Pegram, TN; [p.] Ewing G. Greer and Elizabeth L. Greer; [m.] Divorced; [ch.] Michael D. Leslie (Deceased) and Michele Lee Leslie; [ed.] Belleuve high School International School of Interior Decorating Co-Ordinator's Certificate in Adventure in Attitude, (ULT) Business Solutions, Inc. and Creative Writing; [occ.] Management Asst. for the Tulsa Housing Authority at Inhofe Plaza; [memb.] THA Employee Assoc. (Past Sec.) of Goodlettsville Chapter Eastern Star; [hon.] Who's Who of Women Executives (1989-1990 Edition); [oth. writ.] A Book of Poems (non-published) and other writings; [pers.] I enjoy writing about days gone by and life in general

LESTER, ROSEMARY
[b.] July 25, 1954, Martinsville, IN; [p.] Dead; [ch.] Calvin Lester one son; [ed.] Vocational Education at Indiana Vocational Technical College 1995 Personal Management Human Resources; [occ.] Warehouse Worker Part time Weekend Warriors; [hon.] The Greenhorn Award given to volunteers of Army Community Services 1990; [oth. writ.] In The Spring Time Of My Life. Not published.; [pers.] I live my life to serve and help people who want to grow in the inward process and obtain spiritual awareness.; [a.] Indianapolis, IN

LEUANG, LAURA ELIZABETH
[b.] April 4, 1983, Burlington, VT; [p.] Robert E. Leuang and Darla L. Leuang; [occ.] Student; [hon.] Graduated March 6, 1994 from Barbizon School of Modeling. Top awards for Best Actress and Photo Model Award.; [oth. writ.] I have written many other poems which are used in a card Co. owned by my mother unforgettable of Vt.; [pers.] I love writing poetry, because it reflects my inner feelings. I also find it very relaxing. I'm influenced by life itself, nature with all its beauty.; [a.] Fairfox, VT

LEWELLEN, JOHN
[b.] December 24, 1948, Oklahoma City, OK; [ch.] John Terence, 19, Meda Lynn, 18; [pers.] In the visions of true art we are able to see and bring forth the great future that awaits us.; [a.] Geyserville, CA

LEWIS, BETTE F.
[b.] June 9, 1957, Houlton, ME; [p.] Mary McNulty/Raymond Lewis; [ch.] Brandon Lewis - La Rosa, Shilo Autumn Lewis also Deceased Jammie Shane Lewis, Shannon Joshua Donald La Rosa; [ed.] Lowell High School Current current student - adult Ed; [occ.] Homemaker, student; [memb.] Club Fleur De Lis; [oth. writ.] Other poems published in local newspaper, the Lowell Sun; [pers.] My family is my inspiration. I write from my life experiences and from my heart. I'd like to thank my mother who has always encouraged me. I'd like to dedicate this poem to my son Shannon J.D. La Rosa, deceased

LEWIS III, JOHNNIE
[pen.] Johnnie Lewis; [b.] November 30, 1976, Washington, DC; [p.] Shirley Ann Howe; [ed.] McKinley Senior High School; [occ.] Stock Clerk, CVS; [oth. writ.] Several poems published in High School pamphlets; [pers.] I base my poems on the news and try to inform people of how bad its getting. I have been greatly influenced by Edgar Allan Poe; [a.] Washington, DC

LEWIS, KIMBERLY
[b.] May 17, 1979, Augusta, ME; [p.] Jeffery and Brenda Lewis; [ed.] Attends Erskine Academy (high school) in South China, ME; [hon.] Whitefield Lions Club Citizenship Award 1993; [pers.] I try to make all my writing realistic. I want my writing to be something everyone can relate too, but my biggest goal is to reflect everyone's dreams, thoughts, and experiences.; [a.] North Whitefield, ME

LEWIS, RICHARD K.
[pen.] Ryk; [b.] May 20, 1969, Jacksonville, IL; [p.] Patricia M. Lewis, Gregory K. Lewis; [ch.] Kala Jean Lewis, Freyja Lewis; [ed.] Various Elementary and High Schools, Delmar Jr. College, Illinois State University; [occ.] Landscaper; [hon.] Navy Achievement Medal, Kawaiti Liberation Medal; [oth. writ.] A collection of other poems yet to be published.; [pers.] My poetry stems from my emotional involvement with others and I use these poems to try and express these feelings to individuals in the best way I know how.; [a.] Normal, IL

LIFTO, MARGE
[b.] March 1, 1908, Richmond, IN; [ch.] 3 grown children; [ed.] Bachelor of Arts Carthage College (Carthage, IL) now at Kenosha, WI; [occ.] Free-lance writer Retired English Teacher; [memb.] I attend the applegate Christian Fellowship at Ruch, OR; [oth. writ.] Occasional poems, children's stories, special features for magazines, inspirational proverbs I'm in my 64th year diary and haven't missed a day.; [pers.] Just a few of the above: Where you've been isn't as important as where you're going. Tears brought on by those whom you love will burn holes in your heart. A lame leg is easier to handle than a lame excuse.; [a.] Medford, OR

LILLEY, LEONA C.
[pen.] Tammi Layne; [b.] October 10, 1930, Munden, VA; [p.] Hazel Cooper, Roy Cooper; [m.] Grover Lilley, May 30, 1952; [ch.] Sandra Arlene, Grover Leroy; [ed.] High School, New York School of Writing; [occ.] Retired, Free-lance writing part time; [memb.] Church of Christ at Creeds, American Association for Retired Persons; [oth. writ.] Stories, poems in numerous Children's publications including Wee Wisdom and Jack and Jill during the 1960's, occasional feature stories in Grit during that same period. Several articles in The State, Down Home in North Carolina, Raleigh, NC, an article in Virginia Wildlife, Chevron, and Farm Wife, free-lance articles in News and Observer, Raleigh, NC, correspondent for The Virginian Pilot and Ledger Star, Norfolk, Va, etc.; [pers.] "We shouldn't wait for opportunity to knock, but search for opportunity and when its found, start knocking." Never say, "I can't!" Say "I must!"; [a.] Knotts Island, NC

LILLIBRIDGE, LINDA MARIE
[b.] September 17, 1945, Griswold, CT; [p.] George and Odelle Lillibridge; [ch.] Erin Lee Cholewa; [ed.] B.A. degree in Sociology from Eastern Connecticut State University. Associate in Arts Mohegan Community College; [occ.] Sociologist; [memb.] International Society of Poets and the National Library of Poetry; [oth. writ.] 'Whiskers of David' influenced by David Philetus Watson published in After the Storm; [pers.] My poem 'A Man' pays tribute to Philetus Horace Watson Preston, CT. Written through the eyes of his son, name Sake, and best friend 'David Philetus Watson.; [a.] Lisbon, CT

LILLIE, ROSALIE RINGER
[b.] August 5, 1916, W. Tarentum, PA; [p.] deceased; [m.] George E. Ringer (9-8-36), now Norman Ray Lillie (1987); [ch.] none; [ed.] Got my G.E.D. when I was 48 years old; [occ.] Sunday school teacher 6 yrs., factory worker, brazier - Scout Leader 6 yrs. - Army Inspector (during WWII) - Singer - Dancer (till 20 yrs. old) - I am now tutoring a young man in writing, reading & math through READ program - I also am Christian Clown (serious one) to bring nursing home adults to Christ - did some acting - sang on WLEU radio Erie, PA one summer - worked as a nurse's aide one year - volunteered for Retarded children, I should say special people - now I visit my new husband in a nursing home thrice a week. He has Alzheimer's. God has been & is very good to me; [memb.] Arbor Day Foundation, Assembly of God Church in Edinboro, PA; [hon.] I have a recipe in a cookbook "Who's Cooking What in America" 332 A Hope St Suite 376, Stamford, CT 06906 (1994); [oth. writ.] I have many Christian poems & other poems; I never did anything with them except for my friends & I; [pers.] I believe we go through this world once: be good, kind, thoughtful & helpful whenever/forever. He will reward you; [a.] I live in a small area 7 miles from Meadville, PA. Its name is Blooming Valley. People refer to me as "Lillie of the Valley" when speaking of me, I'm told.

LIM, KENNETH CHRISTOPHER
[pen.] K.C. Lim; [b.] October 23, 1978, Alexandria, VA; [p.] Raleigh and Linda Lim; [ed.] 11th Grade - so far. Plans to go to College and b a counselor; [occ.] student and artist (paints frequently); [memb.] Plays sports football and baseball since he was 5 years old; [oth. writ.] The Crow, The Hundred year old House what should I do with myself.; [pers.] I am a romantic from the heart; [a.] Woodbridge, VA

LINDBERG, JAMES A.
[b.] San Francisco; [oth. writ.] In early 1991, I began writing lyrics for songs musician friends of mine had composed. Since then, I've written more than 200 songs, poems, and miscellaneous short ramblings.; [pers.] My personal interest are pe/ [ople, life, serendipity, and positive thinking. I strive to incorporate these characteristics in my works.

LINDSTROM, LISA M.
[b.] August 8, 1961, Minneapolis, MN; [m.] Jeff Lindstrom, July 25, 1992; [ed.] Charles A. Lindbergh High I am presently a student, with the Institute of Children's Literature; [occ.] Office Manager. Insurance Adjuster and housewife; [hon.] Served in U.S. Army National Guard; [oth. writ.] Other poems published in school anthology and future endeavors.; [pers.] My innermost thoughts and feelings are what flow through my pen. Personal experience makes this possible and needs to be shared.; [a.] Yorba Linda, CA

LIPSCOMB, AUDREY
[b.] December 14, 1952, Middletown, OH; [p.] Robert and Gladys Barber; [m.] Jerry Lipscomb, May I say 22 yrs. instead?; [ch.] Julie Nicole; [ed.] Middletown H.S. 1 yr. of College; [hon.] 4.0 GPA; [oth. writ.] Essay for applause Magazine; [pers.] I learned to cope with death through the therapy of writing. New Birth is dedicated to my babies and to all of my deceased loved ones carried so peacefully away by the sparrows.; [a.] West Chester, OH

LITTLE, NANCY L.
[b.] March 6, 1963, Hartford, CT; [p.] John C. Little, Mary Ellen Little; [ed.] Simsbury High, Monroe Community College, Eastern College; [occ.] Letter sorting machine operator, U.S. Postal Service, Rochester, NY; [hon.] Monroe Community College, Dean's List. Excellence in creative Writing Award, Award for Achievement as a Simsbury Scholar.; [oth. writ.]; [pers.] Sometimes sharing a poem confirms what is real in life like holding someone's hand.; [a.] Rochester, NY

LITTLE, SHERRY
[b.] May 9, 1048, Scotia, CA; [p.] Henry and Berniece East; [m.] Stanley Lee Little, July 30, 1966; [ch.] Stan Lee Little, Rhonda M. Clifford; [ed.] Johnny A Rowland High School Rowland Hts. CA; [occ.] Housewife/writer; [memb.] Member Christian Chapel Walnut, CA; [oth. writ.] (Published National Library of Poetry) Charting my Course, Glory and Grace, being published in the American Poetry Annual; [pers.] The Lord is my inspiration; [a.] Chino Hills, CA

LOCANTORE, JOSHUA P.
[pen.] Joshua Patrick; [b.] October 13, 1979; [p.] Ginger and Lenny Locantore; [ed.] Jayville High School; [occ.] Retail, Sales; [pers.] As the sky converge's an armor, The human race shall rend in vie, I'll watch with an eye 8 innovate the world through my vision. The end is only the beginning.; [a.] Sayville, NY

LOCKARD, JAMES W.
[b.] June 13, 1965, IN; [p.] Billie and Janet Lockard; [ch.] Sarah E. Lockard; [pers.] I wrote this poem for my daughter Sarah E. Lockard; [a.] Terre Haute, IN

LOCKLEAR, ETHEL S.
[b.] September 25, 1951, Wallace, SC; [p.] Ben and Earline McCall, Simmons; [m.] James H. Locklear, June 21, 1986; [ch.] Shirly Annette, Mark Anthony; [ed.] Wallace High, Rutledge Jr. College of Business C and M Technical College; [occ.] Packer and Assembler, Poet, Song Writer; [memb.] The National Author's Registry - Sponsored by Cader Publishing Ltd. 1995-96; [oth. writ.] If we know who we are published in poetic voices of America in 1994; [pers.] I enjoy writing poetry about almost any subject imagined. I always loved the beauty of words transformed to make a complete mental picture with meaning.; [a.] Winston Salem, NC

LOEBACH, PAUL M.
[ed.] University of MD - Baltimore County; [occ.] Computer Programmer; [memb.] Montgomery County Road Runner's Club (MCRRC) Racquet and Jog Racing Team; [oth. writ.] Several items of short fiction about runners or running published in UMBC newspaper "The Retriever."; [pers.] Sound is the most important element of fictional writing, be it poetry or prose. Everything I write is written to be read aloud.; [a.] Gaithersburg, MD

LOERZEL, SISTER MARY CABRINI
[b.] August 20, 1924, Minnesota; [ed.] Grade School, Toad River Mill High School, Perham MN, Graduate of St Gabriels School of Nursing - 3 years Program diploma, Little Falls MN; [occ.] Visitor of Apartment of Low Income Elderly, Rosary, Making; [memb.] Minnesota Nursing Association When in active Nursing, Marian Movement of Priests; [hon.] I have been a Member of The order of "Franciscan Sisters, Little Falls MN for the past 48 years.; [oth. writ.] Some short poems in local news paper, some years ago.; [pers.] My poetry is an outlet for the inner being of God's creation.; [a.] Little Falls, MN

LOGAN, ASHLEY
[b.] September 11, 1984, Jamestown, NY; [p.] Mona Brooks, Terry Logan; [ed.] 5th grade at Seneca School, Salamanca, NY; [memb.] Softball team, Soccer team - of Salamanca Youth Association; [hon.] Johnson O'Malley Academic Excellence Awards from Kindergarten through 5th grade; [oth. writ.] None that have been published. Writings are done in creative writing class at school.; [pers.] I am 10 years old and Native American - a Seneca Indian. I write what I feel. Feelings are priceless, so I keep them on paper.; [a.] Salamanca, NY

LOGAN, SANDRA LEE
[pen.] Sandi; [b.] April 18, 1960, Cheverly, MD; [p.] Mary Proctor, Arthur Seidler; [m.] Ervin Logan, June 22, 1991; [ch.] Jessica Shiree, Jarren Trae, Keon Shamod; [ed.] Gwynn Park High School, PG Community College, Univ. of Maryland; [occ.] Compute Systems Analyst; [memb.] Phi Theta Kappa, Expressions of Joy Church Committee; [hon.] Phi Theta Kappa, 1995

Dean's List; [pers.] This poems was written in memory of Henry Mahoney, a wonderful loving person who was called home. Almost two years ago; [a.] Upper Marlboro, MD

LOMAX, MARK S.
[b.] August 1, 1961, Detroit, MI; [p.] Andrew and Geraldine Lomax; [m.] Paula L. Lomas, December 22, 1990; [ed.] Henry Ford High School; [occ.] Assistant Video Editor; [memb.] Save the Children Sponsor for 13 years; [a.] Detroit, MI

LOMBARDO, LAWRENCE
[pen.] Larry Lombardo; [b.] April 5, 1960, Queens, NY; [p.] Kenneth Bartlett (Step Dad) Prudence Bartlett; [m.] Nydia Lombardo, October 25, 1986; [ch.] Allison Justine Lombardo; [ed.] Walt Whitman High School College at old Westbury B.A. Sociology, Graduated, N.Y.C. Police Academy, N.Y.C. Correction Academy; [occ.] New York City Transit Police Sergeant - Retired; [memb.] Executive Assistant - New York City Retired Transit Police Association. Parents Assoc. - Our Lady of Peace School Past Membership - S.B.A., Holy Name Society, Columbia Assoc.; [hon.] 2 Letters of Merit from N.Y.C. Transit Policed Cop of the Month December/88, 2 dedication players - one from the Transit Police, one from the Columbia Association; [oth. writ.] Various articles in Newsday N.Y. Daily News, Lynbrook Herald Lyn brook U.S.A., Able Paper. Staff writer: Walford Gaxette.; [pers.] We must never forget those Police officers (Transit Police) who gave the ultimate sacrifice for us. "We can not forgive those who forget, and we cannot forget those who gave".; [a.] Lynbrook, NY

LONG, JANE MARIE
[b.] July 28, 1945, Minneapolis, MN; [p.] Bud E. Long (deceased) and Ruby L. Long; [ed.] Lakewood Sr. High School, Lakewood, Colorado, and Northern Technical School of Business (majoring in court reporting); [occ.] Official Court Reporter for the Probate, Mental Health Division of the District Court of Hennepin County, Minnesota; [memb.] Hope Presbyterian Church, Hennepin County District Court Reporters Association, Minnesota Court Reporters Association and National Court Reports Assoc.; [hon.] High School Honor Society, Band Letters (3 yrs.), Underwood Award of Merit as Outstanding Business Education Student for 1963, International Poet of Merit Award and Editor's Choice Award for 1994; [oth. writ.] 3 published songs, 4 published poems, over 100 unpublished poems, and many skits, roasts and plays for church singles group; [pers.] Music and poetry are greatest love. I play 3 musical instruments, have had 3 1/2 yrs. of ballroom dance lessons and 6 yrs. of voice lessons. As one picture is worth a thousand words, music and poetry, I feel, are expressions of the heart that can only be conveyed in these art forms in a truly meaningful way so that the reader or listener becomes a part of the thoughts expressed by the pen. My life has been greatly enriched by poetry and music.; [a.] Edina, MN

LOOMIS, ROBERT
[pen.] Robert Loomis; [b.] August 21, 1915, Cols., OH; [p.] Raymond and Modge Loomis; [m.] Mary Wales Loomis, March 21, 1965; [ch.] Richard

Wales (stepson); [ed.] Columbus Art School, Ohio State University, Central Academy of Art; [occ.] Artist - Illustrator; [memb.] Registered Republican; [hon.] Happily married to beautiful woman!; [oth. writ.] "Fortunes of Jeremy Bobb", "Where's Charly" picture book, "History of Shoes" picture book; [pers.] The words of the song say "If you never have a dream, now you gonna make a dream come true." Of course, I didn't write that but I'm glad somebody did!; [a.] San Mateo, CA

LOPEZ, REGINALDO P.
[pen.] Reggie Lopez; [b.] May 26, 1923, Honduras, CA; [p.] Carmen Lopez and Tony Benetiz; [m.] Lotte P. Lopez, August 14, 1947; [ch.] Carmen, Reginaldo Jr., Sylvia; [ed.] 2 Years College; [occ.] Retired USAF and Civil Service; [memb.] March of Dimes, Alliance for the mentally ill, Knights of Columbus, Board of Directors of the NCO Club; [hon.] President Reagan, Letter of appreciation. President Bush, Letter of Appreciation. Awarded Honorary Citizen of Patrick AFB, FL and many other Military Commentation; [oth. writ.] On two occasions selected as guest columnist in the Florida today newspaper: United States a land of milk and honey time for silent Hispanics to also organize; [pers.] Arrived USA December 1945 from Honduras was drafted into the Armed Forces in May 1945. Retired from the Military in June4 of 1965. Was hired as the first Youth Director of Patrick AFB, FL. Retired in 1974 from Civil Service.; [a.] Indian Harbour Beach, FL

LOPEZ, STEVEN E.
[b.] February 9, 1977, Sierra Madre, CA; [p.] Richard and Debra; [ed.] Graduated El Monte High School, June 14, 1995; [a.] El Monte, CA

LOR, ROSY
[b.] June 17, 1977, Marion, OH; [p.] Vue and Xao Lor; [ed.] Philadelphia High School for Girls, Reading High School, entering freshman year at Georgetown University Fall 1995; [memb.] National Honor Society (President), Radio Reading Service, French Club (Pres.), Debate Club (Pres.), Deacon at St. Simeon's Lutheran Church (in Phila, PA); [hon.] Renssalaer Medal for Science and Math, Baush and Lamb Science Award, National Winner in the National Newspaper Association, Quill and Scroll 1995 International Writing Contest; [oth. writ.] Article for Reading Eagle, Reading Times, articles for tabloid, The City, staff writer for high school newspaper, poem for Amherst Society; [pers.] I hope to devote my life to the defiance of what society terms as "reality". I also thank Brian Gormley for being the "guineapig" of my philosophies.; [a.] Reading, PA

LORD, BRIAN J.
[b.] September 30, 1975, Seattle; [p.] Nira Lord; [ed.] High School Grad; [memb.] Member of the International Theispian Society; [oth. writ.] I write, and have written over 200 and poems of all types and styles. I am working on putting my best works into a book.; [pers.] Poetry has been a new experience for me. I've basically been writing for only two years, yet I find it the only way to express myself.; [a.] Kent, WA

LOTZ, JOHN
[b.] March 23, 1964; [p.] James Lotz, Mary Lotz; [m.] Deanna Lotz, August 19, 1989; [ch.] Marie Elizabeth; [ed.] Hinsdale So. High, De Paul Univ., Univ. of K.S. - BA Communications IL. Benedictine College - MBA; [occ.] Write and present comprehensive product and sales training programs.... "Training Specialist"; [hon.] Several in Music, Theatre and Writing; [oth. writ.] Song - Dreams of yesterday, Song - Southern Ties, Play - Fishing With John, Musical - Southern Ties, Song - Heart and Soul; [pers.] Life's too short..... Make the most of it; [a.] Euclid, OH

LOUTZENHISER, SHELLY L.
[b.] August 19, 1962, Zeeland, MI; [m.] Tim L. Loutzenhiser; [ch.] Adam Christopher, Derek Bryan; [occ.] Home maker; [a.] Holland, MI

LOVE, JONATHAN
[b.] July 24, 1949, Chicago; [p.] Walter and Peggy Love; [m.] Sara Webb; [ch.] Ellen, Valerie; [ed.] 45 yrs. of life, countless books and much love; [occ.] Invoker of magic, consultant; [memb.] The Hunger project, the Family of Light, The Miracle of Love; [pers.] I am deeply honored to love Jayne (for her inspiration) and Tracy (for her partnership.); [a.] Piedmont, CA

LOWE, MAX K.
[pen.] Max Kevin Lowe; [b.] May 24, 1951, Ironton, OH; [p.] Eugene and Yvonne Lowe; [m.] Kathy Jo Lowe, June 8, 1986; [ch.] Amanda Joy Lowe, Kristen Elizabeth Lowe; [ed.] River Valley High School; [occ.] Whirlpool Corporation as an Assembler; [memb.] Calvary Bible Baptist Church; [hon.] Outstanding young man of America Achievement Award (1988), Christian Athlete of the Year, Nazarene 1988; [oth. writ.] Reasons and seasons published in the St. Mary's Church Bulletin; [pers.] I strive to reflect my Lord and Saviour which is Jesus Christ. (Philippians Chapter 4 Verse 13) I have been greatly influenced by Helen Steiner Rice.; [a.] Marion, OH

LOWTHER, HELEN
[pen.] Louise Koon; [b.] April 12, 1929, Parkersburg, WV; [m.] Russell Lowther, January 1, 1948; [ch.] Dr. Gary A. Lowther; [ed.] Spencer High; [memb.] American Lung Association; [oth. writ.] Poem published in National Library of Poetry. Poems published in Local newspapers.; [pers.] I have been writing poems most of my life. It is so much a part of my being.; [a.] Nitro, WV

LUCAS, REBECCA
[b.] February 6, 1951, Shelbyville, IN; [p.] Fred and Freida Sutherlin; [ch.] John, Paula, Greg; [ed.] B.S. Indiana Univ., Bus, M.S. Indiana Univ., Educ; [occ.] Corp Training Consultant; [memb.] NSPI - National Society for Performance and Instruction; [hon.] ABWA Scholarship, Clairol Scholarship; [oth. writ.] Poems published in "The Majestic Sage," and "Journeys of the Poet and Prophet", Articles in professional journals, Workshops in customer service and marketing; [pers.] Anna's grief was written in memory of my grandmother, Anna Figg Taylor, whose son Warren was killed at the Battle of the Bulge.; [a.] Streamwood, IL

LUCIANO, TONI
[b.] July 10, 1969, Passaic, NJ; [ed.] Bachelor of Arts Degree, University of Nevada Las Vegas, Art Major, Communications Minor; [hon.] Judge's choice Award High School Art contest, Dean's Honor Role High School, College, 3 years recipient Augustus Society Academic Scholarship; [pers.] This poem was written in loving memory of Robert D. Lavallie, Jr. (September 28, 1968 - September 17, 1993). Always remember how precious life is and cherish and be thankful for every wonderful moment and memory that God has given you.; [a.] Las Vegas, NV

LUMETTA, LAWRENCE C.
[b.] December 2, 1919, Detroit, MI; [p.] Vito and Maria Lumetta; [m.] Maria Lumetta, May 3, 1941; [ch.] Vito, Karen, Jerome, Antoinette, Maria; [ed.] Cass Tech High, and Arts and Craft; [occ.] Artist and Sculpture; [memb.] A.I.O.; [hon.] Honorable mention at "The Carnagie Institute of Art", first prize at Michigan Art Show. Several Prizes and Awards at local art shows; [pers.] The eyes of an artist are very sensitive to the beauty of nature and that special gift is what I try to convey in my poem, "Rainbow"; [a.] Eastpointe, MI

LUSCOMBE, JASON
[pen.] Q; [b.] August 17, 1979, Cape Girandeau, MO; [p.] Harold and Melody Luscombe; [ed.] Lone Oak High School; [occ.] Student at Lone Oak High School; [memb.] Columbia House, Lone Oak Church of Christ, A member of Lone Oak High School Choir, Lone Oak Nigh Soccer Team; [oth. writ.] Several poems which have not been published; [pers.] In my writing, I try to show a different side most people don't see.; [a.] Melber, KY

LUTE, KATHERIN M.
[pen.] Kathie M. Lute; [b.] January 14, 1932, Westfir, OR; [p.] Percy and Anna Lute; [ch.] Mike Canoy, James Canoy, Randy Canoy, Harold Lindemeier; [ed.] Dallas High School Diploma from Institute of Children's Literature; [hon.] Several Awards of Merit certificates for different poems; [oth. writ.] My child in world treasury of great poems Vol II; [pers.] I have been influenced by members of my family and friends.

LUTZE, DEBBRA ANN
[pen.] Debi; [b.] September 27, 1958, Flint, MI; [p.] Don Walker and Linda Sheick; [m.] Mark L. Lutze, April 17; [ch.] 3 Boys - Farrow (19), Daniel (13), and Michael (9); [ed.] Graduate of Davison High School - Associate Degree in Graphic Communications from Baker College of Flint, MI; [occ.] Full-time Student for BA in Graphic Design/ MKIG; [memb.] Member of the Stephen Ministry at Richfield Nazarene Church, Davison, MI; [oth. writ.] None published; [pers.] I thank God for his gifts to me. May all the glory be his. Debi; [a.] Davison, MI

LYONS, VICKY
[b.] September 3, 1976, Big Spring, TX; [p.] Bill and Crystal Lyons; [ed.] Phoenix Special Programs Correspondence High School; [oth. writ.] I have two other poems that were published in Sparrowgrass poetry book in 1993 and 1994

MACK, ROBIN
[pen.] Kiddle Mack; [b.] July 25, 1954, Philadelphia, PA; [p.] Kermit and Betty Mack; [ch.] Myla, Gwen, Natalie; [ed.] John Bartram High and Abington High; [occ.] Computer Operations, Keyboardist and Vocalist, Songwriter; [memb.] B.M.I., Rasta Generation Band; [oth. writ.] Songwriter for independent record labels. Three Songs recorded on Black Spade Records. Co-Writer of six songs on Mopres Records; [pers.] I write to keep peace in my life, I believe in the power of words and that positive words should be heard. I'm looking forward to publishing my own book of poetry.; [a.] San Francisco, CA

MACKANIC, KIMBERLY
[b.] 1987, Lakewood, NJ; [p.] Marie Mackanic and Greg Mackanic; [ch.] (Sisters) Elizabeth and Stephanie; [ed.] Currently in 2nd grade at Taunton Elem. School; [occ.] Student; [hon.] Honor Roll; [oth. writ.] Spring, I Love Nature, Friends; [pers.] I love to read and reading gives me ideas for poems. (So does being outdoors); [a.] Howell, NJ

MACKENZIE, JOAN
[pen.] Jan MacKenzie; [b.] MA; [p.] Pierce and Marcy Taylor; [m.] Divorced; [ch.] Emmy, Philip; [ed.] B.A. and M.A. Stanford Univ. M.B.A. Golden Gate Univ. J.D. Univ. of San Francisco; [occ.] Private Investor, Poet; [memb.] Save San Francisco Bay, The Redwoods League Tech. Securities Analysis Assoc. S.E.; [oth. writ.] Techno-Economic; [pers.] Poets who have influenced me (among many of course) are: Pope, Cavafy, Plath, Roethke; [a.] Menlo Park, CA

MACKOWSKI, SANDRA LEE
[pen.] Jamie Martin; [b.] May 27, 1974, Bridgeport, CT; [p.] Edward Frank and Frances Carol Mackowski; [m.] Single; [ed.] The University of Connecticut Major - Human Development and Family Relations Degree - B.S.; [occ.] Student; [hon.] Poetry published in High School Literary Magazine, Who's Who among American High School students (1990-1991, 1991-1992), Dean's List student (Sacred Heart University, 1992); [pers.] "Thus, is it truly possible to have solace from an exquisite procession with first love?"; [a.] Stratford, CT

MACLEAN, CAROLE A.
[pen.] Carole A. MacLean; [b.] October 27, 1957, Evansville, IN; [p.] Ralph and Margaret Holifek; [m.] Rory M. MacLean, April 28, 1990; [ch.] Margaret Harris MacLean; [ed.] Ohio State University, 1976-1980; [occ.] Marketing, Banking

MADER, CONNIE
[b.] October 11, 1949, Ramona, SD; [p.] Ervin Feister, Dorothy Reidel-Feistner; [m.] Jim Mader, November 5, 1988; [ch.] Christopher Lee, Jennifer Kay; [ed.] Madison Central High, Madison SD, El Paso Community College; [occ.] Receptionist; [memb.] Linwood Wesleyan Church; [oth. writ.] Several poems and also some religious songs - all unpublished; [pers.] To all I am and ever will be, to the glory of a Mighty God, I will give the praise.; [a.] Sioux Falls, SD

MAGNUS, MARCY
[b.] January 19, San Francisco, CA; [p.] Lawrence T. and Birgit Magnus; [m.] Divorced; [ed.] Willow Glen High San Jose State University; [occ.] 4 yrs. Executive Assistant, Dennis Uniform Mfg. Co. Previous 12 yrs. Private Investigator, Magnus-Price Investigations San Francisco and Los Angeles; [hon.] Best Actress, 1970 "A-Cat-Emmy Awards" Los Gatos, CA, 1st Runner Up Poet for Youth 1961, Santa Clara Co., CA, to be the "House-Mate" of Picatso, a most magnificent Calico; [oth. writ.] Poems Published in local newspapers in California, since moving to Oregon, 1990, write special membership only newspaper, "The Portland Pioneer". Numerous Songs (Lyrics) (Music By Douglas D. Allshouse); [pers.] All life is intensely subjective - nothing is only what it appears on the surface.; [a.] Portland, OR

MALANGA, JENEAN
[pen.] Crystal Dale; [b.] March 24, 1978, Danbury, CT; [p.] Josephine and Ronald Malanga; [ed.] Livingston High School (Junior); [occ.] Lifeguard (Summers); [memb.] Key Club, Youth Advisory; [pers.] I would like to thank my mother and father for always being so supportive in everything that I do. You are my very best friends. I also thank God for being my guiding star.; [a.] Livingston, NJ

MALE, SHIRLEY
[b.] November 22, 1924, MS; [m.] George Male, October 17, 1944; [ch.] Three; [ed.] 12th grade; [occ.] Housewife; [pers.] I have been a lifelong manic-depressive. Much better in latter years, due primarily to the medication lithium Carbonate, I have about 350 unpublished poems; [a.] Fairfax, VA

MALLOY, JASON
[b.] March 26, 1985, Trenton, NJ; [p.] Michael J. Malloy, Lucyanne Maloy; [ed.] Presently in the fourth grade at Holy Cross School, Trenton, NJ; [hon.] Honor Roll -A+ Won a $50.00 check for a safety poster contest, Catholic War Veterans; [pers.] I enjoy writing poems very much. When I grow up, I hope to be an author of wonderful poetry.; [a.] Yardville, NJ

MANASA, MORGAN L.
[b.] September 20, 1980, Rochester, MI; [p.] Margaret Dwyer, Rick Manasa; [ed.] I'm in the 9th grade, Clonlara Home School; [occ.] Student, Writer, Actress; [memb.] Treehouse players in Detroit; [oth. writ.] Stories, poems, scripts, journal, essays; [pers.] A blank page isn't a page of nothing, it is merely a piece of art waiting to be discovered!; [a.] Rochester, MI

MANGINI, BRIGHTON A.
[b.] December 18, 1969, Salt Lake City, UT; [p.] Paula O'Very, Dennis Smith; [m.] Gary L. Mangini, August 28, 1993; [ed.] Highland High, University of Hawaii - School of Nursing, Inland Massage Institute, School for Massage Therapy.; [occ.] Registered Nurse Rural Nursing, Chewelah, WA; [memb.] United Staff Nurses Union, United States Airforce Reserve, Lieutenant. ACLS, INCC, and NRP certified. CPR Instructor. Reiki - Seichim provider. WEC provider - National Ski Patrol.; [hon.] Navy Four-year Meritorious Service

Medal, National Defense Ribbon, air-force flight nurse wings.; [oth.writ.] I've been writing poems since I was in grade school. Up until now they have been for personal enjoyment. I want to thank my mom for encouraging me to share them.; [pers.] Each person makes his own reality. You are the artist that paints your picture with love in our hearts for people and nature, our pictures can make a beautiful world.; [a.] Valley, WA

MANN, CELETA
[pen.] "C"; [b.] February 12, 1962, Tyrrel County; [p.] Pinkie and Glenn Thomas Mann; [ed.] B.A. Degree in English at Elizabeth City State University, Elizabeth City North Carolina; [occ.] Secretary/Wake County Public School System; [memb.] President - Sigma Gamma Rho Sorority; [hon.] Dr. Liverman Scholarship Award, Mattamuskeet High Defense Award - Mattamuskeet High (Basketball Trophy) Deans List, Elizabeth City State Vice President Senior Class - Mattamuskeet High; [oth. writ.] Elizabeth City State University Newspaper; [pers.] I believe that if you put God first, then nothing is impossible for you. When one writes from the heart it reflects life. That goes deeper than words.; [a.] Engelhard, NC

MANNING, JUDI WALTER
[b.] June 30, 1966, Atlantic City, NJ; [p.] Joseph and Jane Walter; [m.] Herbert F. Manning Jr., April 25, 1991; [ch.] Jennifer Brown, Brandy Manning; [ed.] Assumption Regional School Holy Spirit H. S. Absecon NJ, Atlantic county ro-tech Mayslanding N.J.; [occ.] Accounting; [pers.] Thank you Frank for your unconditional love, to my Mom, Daughters, brothers and sisters I love you all. I thank God for special friends, Janet, Kenny, Helen and Marianne. To my father and uncle Joe, gone but never forgotten.; [a.] Davenport, IA

MANUEL, CARRIE LOUISE
[pen.] Carrie Mae; [b.] December 30, 1938, Franklin, LA; [p.] Eugene and Lovenia Manuel; [ch.] Vanessa Matthew, Eugenia Raff, Mitchell, Yolanda Manuel; [ed.] Willow St. High 1955 Franklin LA, University of CA at Berkeley, S.F. City College, early childhood development; [occ.] Telegraph Hill Neighborhood Center Head pre-school teacher for 29 years; [memb.] Jerusalem Church of God in Christ, Mayor Member of board of director at Golden Gate Neighborhood Center, President of North Beach Tenant Assoc., Member of the Mayor's Office of Youth and their Family Program.; [hon.] 25 years of outstanding achievement in neighborhood and daycare service. Appreciation for dedication in teaching Sunday School classes at Jerusalem Church of God in Christ.; [pers.] You ask me what would make this a better world for children, and my answer would be total respect for life and love!; [a.] San Francisco, CA

MANZO, JOANNE S.
[b.] June 29, 1965, South Africa; [p.] Stanley Cohen, Gillian Bennun; [m.] Mike Manzo, September 17, 1993; [ch.] Michael Robert Manzo; [ed.] Queens College, London England, Tufts University, Medford MA; [occ.] Mother, Fitness Instructor; [hon.] Dean's List

MAPLES, VIRGINIA FULLER
[b.] March 29, 1936, Abbeville, MS; [p.] Joe and Burris Fuller; [m.] E. J. Maples, February 5, 1954; [ch.] Joe, Mark, Jeannine and five grandchildren; [ed.] Completed High School, University High School, Oxford, MS; [occ.] Bursar's Office University of Mississippi; [memb.] North Oxford Baptist Church; [oth. writ.] Several other poems. I have been writing poetry for only about a year.; [pers.] My sister, Connie, describes my writing as "Poems of Family, Friends, Faith, and Life written from Virginia's Heart. My poem is dedicated to the memory of tow "Old Folks" who touched my life in a special way, Burris M. Fuller and Cora P. Lewis.; [a.] Oxford, MS

MARANON, ANDREA
[b.] February 26, 1984, Philippines; [p.] Charles Maranon, Jane Lenon; [ed.] Holy Family Academy, Elementary Angeles City, Philippines; [occ.] 5th grade student; [memb.] Girl Scouts; [hon.] Honor Roll; [pers.] This is dedicated to my family and friends who inspired me in writing and creating not only this poem but also forming very memorable moments and experiences that will stay in my mind always.; [a.] San Francisco, CA

MARCUS, BERNICE
[pen.] Bernie; [b.] March 1, 1948, Houlka, MS; [p.] Ruth Crowley, Bishop James Crowley; [m.] Mack Marcus; [ch.] Felicia, Robert, Michael, Marc, Shanee and Bernestine; [ed.] Shivers High, Malcolm College, and MSTA Business College; [occ.] Career on hold, taking care of children, Case manager for Senior Citizens; [memb.] Missionary Society; [oth. writ.] Several poems and 2 books soon to be presented to a publisher, but so far, have not submitted them to anyone.; [pers.] I especially love poetry. I especially love William Shakespeare. I like writing about events in my life. But most of all, I love writing about the things that make up our lives, as the religion. Also, I like writing about issues that deals with children.; [a.] Chicago, IL

MARIGLIANO, MARY SUSAN
[pen.] Mary S. Marigliano; [b.] December 10, 1982, Philadelphia; [p.] Santa and Joseph Marigliano; [ed.] Saint Barnabas Elementary School; [occ.] Student; [hon.] Honor Roll, Saint Vincent's College "Challenge" program for gifted children; [oth. writ.] Several other unpublished poems and articles, and articles in school newspaper.; [pers.] I write from my heart and my soul, so that I may touch the hearts and souls of others.; [a.] Philadelphia, PA

MARKIDIS, DESPINA
[b.] February 12, 1973, Woodside, Queens, NY; [p.] Steve Markidis, Mary Markidis; [ed.] Oceanside High School, Nassau Community College; [pers.] For all the love and affection you have given me.; [a.] Rockville Centre, NY

MARS, ROSIE MILLER L.
[b.] November 7, 1949; [p.] William and Rosie M. McNutt; [m.] Lawrence D. Mars, November 6, 1969; [ch.] Lawrence D. Mars, Larnel, Lavinia, Lorenzo, Lorita, Lamar, Lolando, Lee D. Mars; [ed.] I attend Marshall High School but I did not receive my diploma.; [occ.] Homemaker; [hon.]

Paderowski Elem. 22 21 So. Lawndale Volunteer Parent Awards 1986-90, C/CSA Elem School 7 So. Sacrament awards certificates and trophy outstanding parent of volunteer 1990-92. As a participant in a documentary film (Eyes on the Prize) I received a certificate in 1990. As a participant of the North Lawndale Child Abuse and Child Neglect I received weekend trip and a certificate in 1990. I have and still remain a member of political leadership within North Lawndale and throughout the city of Chicago; [oth. writ.] I have several poems and short stories yet to be publish; [pers.] To my children "The links that lock the chain is as strong as the locket from which it hang" you never lost faith in my dream; [a.] Chicago, IL

MARSHALL, GLORIA J.
[b.] August 6, 1947, Buenville, LA; [p.] Harry and Hazel Streetman; [m.] Malcolm L. Strunk, May 28, 1988; [ch.] Phillip Marshall 25, Carolyn Marshall 21; [ed.] Honor Programs Certificate. Honor student 75 credit hrs. at Richland College, Dls., Tex.; [occ.] Eng. Tutor, ESL Tutor, Associate Instrutoral Asst. and Deans's List 1995 Award; [memb.] P.T.K. Honor Society, Certified Honors: Student Program; [hon.] Outstanding student success award - 1994 and 1995, Editor of Paralley Mag. 1995 for Richland College, 1st place for state: Texas Intercollegiate Press Association cover and (magazine literary) award - Richland College April 8, 1995, 1st and 3rd place winner of short stories and 3rd place for poetry writing contest; [oth. writ.] Poetry of short story and author of short story fiction, "I Am A Seeker" and "Spilled Coffee." (3rd place) (1st place) poem "Where the Ponies Used to be. (3rd place) Richaldn College Writing Contest 1995.; [pers.] Accomplished artist in oil painting, landscaping, sea scapes and portraits. I have been influenced to write by my creative writing teacher: Joe Stanco at Richland College.; [a.] Garland, TX

MARSHALL, VICTORIA MONIQUE
[pen.] Vicky Marshall; [b.] November 30, 1979, Virginia; [p.] Merry Marshall, Warren Buffington; [ed.] K-9; [occ.] Student at Jefferson High; [memb.] (F.C.A.) - Fellowship of Christian Athletes. Peer Assistance Leadership Future Home makers of America.; [hon.] Creative Writing Award; [pers.] I'm 15 years old and I have high expectations of one day become a well known poet. I also would like to write small novels.; [a.] Jefferson. TX

MARTIN, BONITA
[pen.] Bonnie; [m.] David I. Martin, July 31, 1993; [ch.] Malcolm David Martin; [ed.] Greenbrier East High Concord College Greenbrier Community College; [occ.] Lab Aide 4; [oth. writ.] Several poems that were published in a couple of beareared news letters: Share and Unite; [pers.] The poems that I write are in memory of my son Malcolm David I share with you the pain and grief I have endure through my poems how my sons little life of 21 weeks touched my soul with everlasting love. Through my poems is how I express my feelings of my son death; [a.] Monassas, VA

MARTIN, EDOUARD
[b.] April 5, 1966, Fairbanks, AK; [p.] Louis and Evelyn Martin; [ed.] 5th year Architecture student

at the University of Houston; [occ.] Full time student; [pers.] I was born in Alaska but raised in Ft. Worth, TX.

MARTIN, LAURABELLE
[b.] November 3, 1915, Jackson Co., MN; [p.] Eugene and Mary Martin; [ed.] Renville MN. Teacher's Training Dept. and Mankato State University, Real Estate and Farm Land Manager; [occ.] Elementary Teacher, (Retired); [memb.] Historic Renville Preservation, American Legion Aux, Renville Co. Genealogy Society, Renville Town and Country Boosters, Wabasso Education Assn. N.E.A.; [hon.] Who's Who of the Midwest, Who's of the World Who's Who of the Americas, Who's who of American Women, Five Thousand Personalities of the World International Who's Who of Intellectuals many other Biographical listings; [oth. writ.] Many articles in the local newspaper.; [pers.] Success in any activity can be attained by planning and working towards the goal one has in mind.; [a.] Holden, MO

MARTIN, LIZ
[b.] September 2, 1944, Beverly Hills, CA; [p.] Joed Arliss (actress), Ian Martin (actor, writer); [m.] Widowed; [ed.] University of Madrid, Spain; [occ.] Past 27 years have co-ordinated Dart and Pool Leagues in Queens County, N.Y.; [oth. writ.] "Xmas Present" poems for members of my leagues.; [pers.] The writing bug hit when a child. The greatest honor ever received come from multitalented Dad/writer of novels, soap opera scripts and member of Scottish Limerick Society who doubled me "The Queen of Doggerel Poetry".

MARTIN, NEIL DANIEL
[pen.] Nalime Van Benz, Nasty Originator Nalime; [b.] August 18, 1977, Washington, DC; [p.] Daniel Mark Martin, Lue Melrose Martin; [ed.] Up to High School, if I go on to summer school, High School DeMatha; [occ.] Stock boy and cashier at C.V.S. in Prince George's Plaza; [hon.] Publication of a poem by Water's Edge; [oth. writ.] The poems of Neil (Nalime) consist of romantics, realism, rap, adventures, Jolly Skully Pirates, The Traveler, aspiring artists Nalime and Lenny; [pers.] Ironic how I started writing poetry, started this poet act in late 1994, now I'm going to be a published poet whoa!; [a.] Silver Spring, MD

MARTIN, SANDRA B.
[b.] January 3, 1949, Pulaski, VA; [p.] Geneva M. Tickle, James A. Brumfield; [m.] June 10, 1967; [ch.] Sharon L. Martin; [ed.] Graduated from Andrew Lewis High School, Salem, VA, took Computer Course Salem High School, Attended R.C.E.C. and completed V.O.T. Prog.; [occ.] Housewife, working on my poetry and other writings; [memb.] Faculty of Salem High School, Salem, VA, Regional Science Fair, Secretary of Sunday School, Bethel, Baptist Church, Volunteer 1995 Stand Down - VA Hosp.; [hon.] A.B. Honor roll in High School, Cert. 1995 Stand Down - VA Computer Cert.; [oth. writ.] I wrote a poem entitled, The Homeless, which was published in a newspaper in Arizona. I entered and had published in East of the Sunrise a poem entitled, The Snore. I have numerous other works not published.; [pers.] I love poetry. I like for it to have good

verse and be interesting to read. I like for it to get a point across which benefits the readers.; [a.] Phoenix, AZ

MARTIN, STACY
[b.] December 20, 1976, Newton, MA; [p.] Peter and Alice Martin; [ed.] Milford High School, Attending Bridgewater State College in the Fall of 1995; [occ.] Day Care Assistant; [oth. writ.] Over 100 private poems, and two books in the publishing process.; [pers.] Writing is a gift. I try to use my gift to not only help myself get through difficult times in my life, but also to show people that they're not alone.; [a.] Milford, MA

MARTINELLI, MS. JACQUELYN
[pen.] Jakki Marie; [b.] April 3, 1962, Boston; [p.] Mrs. Evelyn Conrad; [ed.] High School General Studies, but took interest in writing; [occ.] Receptionist, studying computers, and some day hope to write short stories.; [oth. writ.] Elementary School, P. H. Sheridan School, fifth grade I wrote a poem, for my mother, and it was printed in the local paper. I knew then that I would like to write. I was inspired to write by my fifth grade teacher, Miss Reid.

MARTINEZ, BOB G.
[pen.] Bob G. Martinez; [b.] June 7, 1949, Las Vegas, NM; [p.] Mary Martinez; [m.] Annette E. Martinez, February 10, 1973; [ch.] Lita R. Martinez; [ed.] Graduated in 1968 from North High School in Denver; [occ.] Security Guard for the Denver Merchandise Mart; [memb.] Recently awarded to an "Associate" member of the I.S.P. with an invitation to become a "Distinguished" member; [hon.] I have recently been honored by the I.S.P. by having my first two poems submitted for their considerations, as a semi-finalist with the offer to having them published; [oth. writ.] I have written my life's journey in time from 1949 to 1994 in a single non-broken narrative poem over 300 pages long. I'm currently assembling another book of poetry ("Sidetracks").; [pers.] What once was a lack of drive has become a life of bliss... Oh the strength keeping alive this soul fatal darts would miss!; [a.] Denver, CO

MARTINEZ, REBECCA
[b.] August 27, 1972, Upland, CA; [p.] Rose Martinez; [ed.] Chaffey High School, Chaffey College; [occ.] Childcare Director for the YMCA; [memb.] National Parks and Conservation Association; [oth. writ.] Several poems and short stories I write in my spare time.; [pers.] The environment is important to me as I am to it. My writing has always reflected this.; [a.] Ontario, CA

MARTINEZ, SHARON
[b.] May 27, 1980, Passaic, NJ; [p.] Rafaela Alvarado, Eduardo R. Martinez; [ed.] Garfield High School, Thomas Jefferson Middle School, Abraham Lincoln School #6; [memb.] Most Holy Name: Youth Group; [hon.] 2nd place in Science Fair, Science, Social Studies, and Foreign Language; [oth. writ.] 3 poems published in local and school news papers.; [pers.] I write poems on how I feel and see things. I've been influenced by my family members on romantic poetry. Special thanks to: Rafaela, Eduardo, Erica L., Raquel, Christine, and Nicole.; [a.] Garfield, NJ

MARTINUS, SARAH E.
[b.] October 20, 1975, Rochester, NY; [p.] Rosemary Hall; [ed.] Wayne Central High, Monroe Community College, Barstow Community College; [occ.] Student; [oth. writ.] Currently have finished my 60th poem. I hope to publish my own book of poems someday.; [pers.] I try to use nature to symbolize man's own actions. I believe some of us have learned from it (nature) other's still have a lot of graving to do.; [a.] Barstow, CA

MASON, MILDRED H.
[pen.] Mildred Stidger Mason; [b.] August 9, 1915, Alturas, CA; [p.] Otto and Nellie Stidger; [m.] Deceased; [ch.] Beverly Carrigan, Sharon Betten Court, Leland Jones; [ed.] 2 years, Business College (Merritt) Oakland, CA; [occ.] Homemaker, retired; [memb.] Humana Seniors Assn. San Leandro Unity Church; [oth. writ.] San Leandro Reporter. Wrote for High School Paper; [a.] San Leandro, CA

MASON, WENDY KARMEL
[pen.] Wendy L. Karmichael; [b.] July 26, 1980, Bakersfield, CA; [p.] Carolyn and Charles Mason; [ed.] Wingland Elem. Statesville Middle School North High Bakersfield; [memb.] Girl Scouts, Beta Club, Drama Club, Bible Club, Phileo Club; [hon.] Literature Award on the honor roll for 4 years, Presidential Academic Fitness Award, First Place Talent Show; [oth. writ.] Several Poems and Stories Unpublished; [pers.] In my writings, I try to give solace and understanding to people who face the reality of life's daily problems and conflicts.; [a.] Bakersfield, CA

MASTAINICH, JOSEPH A.
[b.] March 23, 1940, New Orleans; [m.] Christine M. Mastainich, March 29, 1958; [ch.] Scott A., Daron M., Tirza A.; [ed.] Easton Sr., High, Pacific Western Univ., B.A.A. Graphic Communications; [occ.] Administrator; [hon.] I.G.I. Design, First Place and Honorable Mention; [a.] Sloughouse, CA

MASTERSON, SHEILA A.
[pen.] Adrianne Blackmoore; [b.] March 4, 1971, Atlanta, GA; [p.] Dr. Martin and Phyllis P. Masterson; [ch.] Lauren Olivia Masterson-Rodriguez; [ed.] St. Mary's University, B.B.A. in accounting; [occ.] Accountant, owner of Celebrations, SA, TX; [memb.] NAFE; [hon.] Jesse and Mary Jones Scholarship, Highest Honors, Dean's List; [oth. writ.] Several poems included in a non profit local literary magazine.; [pers.] I wish my writing to reflect heart felt revelations about all aspects of living.; [a.] San Antonio, TX

MASTRANTONIS, VIVIAN
[pen.] Parris; [b.] February 14, 1947, Greece; [p.] Kyriakos & Helen Mastrantonis; [m.] divorced; [ch.] Kyriakos G. Lazaridis; [ed.] George Washington High School, Banking School, Grace Down Model & Air Career School, Real Estate Law & Practice, LaSalle Interior Decorating, Hunter College, Business College, etc. [occ.] Creator of Artistic Production Arion Enterprises Inc., also the ex-producer of a new C.D. and new company; [memb.] Hellenic-American Chamber of Commerce, Banking Assoc., P.T.A. [hon.] Interior Decoration and Story Award, award by composer, singer and producer George P. Sotiropoulos on

behalf of the Greek T.V. Network E.T. #1. Also Fund Raising for the Fort Lee Library of Fort Lee, NJ; [oth. writ.] short stories; [pers.] Writing poetry or expressing in short stories makes me experience another dimension of our existence. Life which allows me to visualize as I perceive the existences. Modernization of our murderization is our Universalization; [a.] Fort Lee, NJ

MATSUNAGA, ERNEST MICHIO
[b.] April 24, 1919, Los Angeles, CA; [p.] Tahel Matsunaga and Hatsu Matsunaga; [m.] Juana Belfort Matsunaga, January 26, 1946; [ch.] Marcia Matsunaga and Michelle A. Smith; [ed.] Various L.A. Elementary Schools, Belvedere Jr. High, John H. Francis Ucla of Chicago; [occ.] Retired; [oth. writ.] Several poems published in annual anthologies of the school of ethnic studies, San Francisco State Univ. poems published in some J.A. Vernaculars; [pers.] My major goal or thrust is to be recognized as a certain individual, (Ernest Michio Matsunaga), This human being, not to be seen as a stereotype.

MATTEI, REGINA
[b.] November 22, 1917, Callensburgh, PA; [p.] Deceased; [m.] Vincent Jo K. (divorced 1954), August 15, 1946; [ch.] Andrew, Audrea, St. Vincent T. Vok; [ed.] 8th grade Crucible, Pa. a small coal mining town raised. Deprived of a High School ed. Long story.; [memb.] Honored 1 year Attendance a member of the Women Club at Carmichaels, PA. back in 1989; [hon.] Was honored during WW II vets for work at 2 Va. Hospitals Played records in side radio in Oakland, Pgh. Pa. 1969-1973. on Honor Rolls at St. Mary Crucible of War II Vets. (long story); [oth. writ.] Past a few poems published in the Free Press, N.Y. Articles of Human Nature in Local newspaper. Past Tense. Letters to the Pres. Past and on Viet too Present. Views or natures situations. Have succeeded in response from each.; [pers.] I've done volunteer work - at nursing homes played the all nationalities music and songs was at 1966 - Wamb. Local Station. Wyep. non Com. Station Pgh. WOUD. Deg. University 1/2 by on sats. Connesville stat. 1/2 by Italio American Hoses.; [a.] North Pittsburgh, PA

MATTEIS, JUSTINE
[pen.] Justine; [b.] February 2, 1931, NJ; [p.] Emma and Ernest Matteis; [pers.] My favorite classic collections are the complete works of the Bronte sisters.

MATTHEWS, SHIRLEY R.
[b.] October 28, 1943, Mount Olive, NC; [p.] Emmitt and Inez Melvin; [ch.] Tyvonne, Crystal, Max, Gary, Cary; [ed.] Assoc. Degree in Arts Associates Degree Nursing, Certified Colonic Therapist, Holistic Health Practitioner Certification, LPN; [occ.] RN, presently enrolled in school of Natraupathy for N.D.; [hon.] Outstanding Achievements Awards, PG Comm. College, PG County MD. MM. Washington School of Voc. Nursing Wash. DC. Harbor Hospital School of Nursing.; [oth. writ.] One other poem published in school paper; [pers.] Justice and equality are the foundation of my beliefs. I have been greatly influenced by the real life situations I have encountered.; [a.] Catonsville, MD

MAXWELL, THOMAS OWEN
[pen.] T. O. Maxwell; [b.] April 6, 1959, Berea, OH; [p.] Paul S. and Elizabeth M. Maxwell; [ed.] Saint Ambrose School (gr. 1-4), Sacred Heart School (grades 5-8), Cardinal Newman High School (grades 9-10), Lake Worth High School (grades 11-12), Florida Atlantic Univ. (B.S. Acct'g), Nova University (Grad. Courses); [occ.] Bankruptcy Consultant, Tax Consultant, Financial Analyst, Lotus Computer Consultant, Philanthropist; [memb.] American Orchid Society, Environmental Defense Fund, World Wildlife Fund, The U.S., Florida and Palm Springs Junior Chamber of Commerce, FAU Alumni Association, West Palm Beach Centennial Committee; [hon.] Palm Springs Jaycees President 94/95, WPB Jaycees, Treasurer and MGMT V.P. Former Financial Director and Treasurer Individual Rights Association, Inc. H.S. Honors Diploma, FAU Faculty Scholar, The Florida Junior Chamber of Commerce Local Chapter Treasurer of the Year (93-94); [oth. writ.] The BitchinPhile Newsletter for Consumer Advocates, Editorial Commentary and Cartoons Socio-Political Critic, 11th grade: Composed an algebraic corollary subordinate to the Difference of Squares Theorem.; [pers.] Sir! I admit your general rule that every poet is a fool, but you yourself may serve to show it that every fool is not a poet.; [a.] Lake Worth, FL

MAYES, JUANITA LOUISE
[pen.] Juanita Mayes; [b.] October 7, 1960, Neveda, IA; [p.] Norman Luing and Joyce Luing; [m.] Jeffery Scott Mayes Sr., July 21, 1990; [ch.] Jeffery Scott Jr., Ahblaza Dawn; [ed.] Pacific High, San Bernardino, CA; [occ.] Homemaker, full time mother also owner with my husband of Empire Tatoo of Upland; [memb.] Locust Elementary PTA, Colorado River Adventures Member; [hon.] Honor Roll - Graduation from parenting class (2nd Highest Score); [oth. writ.] Several poems not published yet.; [pers.] I write what my heart feels at that moment. And I strive to have one read my words and may they get fulfillment or inner knowledge of one self, from them.; [a.] Rialto, CA

MCADOO, JEANETTE J.
[pen.] Jeanette J. McAdoo; [b.] December 30, 1958, McKeesport; [p.] Sharon Kossuth; [m.] David T. McAdoo, May 21, 1994; [ch.] Timothy V. Rump; [ed.] McKeesport Sr. High Allegheny Beauty Academy; [occ.] Housewife; [memb.] Pennsylvania Association of Notaries, American Society of Notaries; [hon.] Presidential Sports Awards; [pers.] I'm truly inspired from the happiness and love I receive from my family, husband and my son. Something I like to share with everyone; [a.] Glassport, PA

MCCAIN, TASHINA JO
[b.] March 30, 1981, Nashville, TN; [p.] Gretchen Rogers and Jeff McClain; [ed.] 8th Grade Thompson Jr. High, Bakersfield, CA; [occ.] Student of Music (Piano) as well as academic; [memb.] Young Women - School Choir; [pers.] Tashina is a very sensitive, loving person to her fellow man.; [a.] Bakersfield, CA

MCCANDLESS, DAWN MARIE
[b.] August 20, 1956, DuBois, PA; [p.] Peggy L.
(Mullen) and William Blair Haggey; [m.] Dennis
Marion McCandless, August 24, 1983; [ch.] Linda
Sue Haggey, Joshua Alan McCandless; [ed.]
Franklin Jr. - Sr. High, Alderson-Broaddus College
(Music Ed 1 yr.), North American Correspondence
School (Animal Sciences, and Wildlife and
Forestry); [occ.] Homemaker, and Free Lance
Writing and Photography; [hon.] Photo Award
1991 Commonwealth Bank Calendar for June,
Regional Band and Orchestra, Camp Horsemanship
Instructor Certificate; [oth. writ.] Note in Decision
Magazine; [pers.] I write from my heart.; [a.]
Trout Run, PA

MCCANN, NANCY
[b.] August 12, 1945, Uvalde, TX; [p.] Howard
Mays (Deceased) and Lucylle Hargrove Mays;
[ch.] Micah Pettigrew, Mike McCann II, Christian
McCann and Miryam McCann; [ed.] Ector High
School Odessa, Odessa Jr. College (Assoc. Deg.)
Odessa, Univ. of TX. of the Pexmian Basin (BA),
Odessa, now working on masters degree; [occ.]
Special Education Teacher - Permian High School;
[memb.] Texas Classroom Teachers Association,
served as a member of the Texas State Textbook
Committee for Social Studies, 1994 West Texas for
life, Texas Christian Coalition; [hon.] Outstanding
Mass Communications Graduate, 1991, Who's
Who in American Universities and Colleges, 1991,
Dean's Honor List '89-91; [pers.] "He must
increase, but I must decrease" John 3:30.; [a.]
Odessa, TX

MCCARTHY, PATTY
[b.] September 16, 1964, Boston, MA; [p.] Joseph
and Diane McCarthy; [ed.] Currently working
toward degree in Psychology; [hon.] Dean's List;
[pers.] My reasons for writing come from personal
joy and pain, encouragement from Ms. Sett, an
excellent teacher at ECC, the unconditional love of
my dog Budy, and the knowledge that all is a gift
from God.; [a.] Cape Coral, FL

MCCLEESE, MARCELLA
[b.] November 28, 1969, Portsmouth, OH; [p.]
Steven and Yvonne McCleese; [pers.] All talent is
God-given. It's up to you what you do with that
talent.; [a.] River Rouge, MI

MCCLURE, ALLISON BROOKE
[pen.] Allison McClure; [b.] August 4, 1981,
Corinth, MS; [p.] Kathy and Jerry McClure; [ed.]
Academic and Performing Arts Complex (APAC)
where I am currently studying music and music
theory; [occ.] Currently a student at APAC;
[memb.] Children's Choir of Mississippi, National
Junior Honor Society, First Baptist Church of
Jackson Acteens Organization; [hon.] The highest
G.P.A. out of approx. 500 students, Achievements
Awards, "Superior" Music Awards, Soccer
trophies; [oth. writ.] Poems published by The
National Library of Poetry and many unpublished
poems and stories; [pers.] I thank God for the
ability to voice my thoughts through writing and
for giving me the hope of a new day. Always
remember: The beauty of the poetry doesn't lurk
within the words, but rather the feeling one gets
after having read them.; [a.] Jackson, MS

MCCLYMONT, ASHLEY
[b.] November 23, 1981, Philadelphia, PA; [p.]
Alfred and Donna McClymont; [ed.] Wayne
Elementary School, Radnor Middle School (I'm at
RMS now); [occ.] Candy Striper at Bryn Maur
Hospital; [oth. writ.] I entered a school contest in
1994 at age twelve. My poem, "Everyone's An
Author", was published in the 1994 edition of
`Anthology of Poetry by Young Americans'!;
[pers.] I hope that, as my writing improves, my
works will be acknowledged alongside long fellow,
Tolstoy, and other great writers of the past.
Without literature, my life would be uncomplete. I
enjoy reading as well as writing, and I love
challenges. I never fail to believe in myself
because I know that everything I finish is done to
the best of my ability.; [a.] Wayne, PA

MCCOFFREY, SARA ELIZABETH
[b.] November 3, 1980, Burlington, CO; [p.] John
and Penny Spearing, Roger and Jeneva McCoffrey;
[ed.] Attends District 70 Charter School, Pueblo,
CO 8th Grade; [occ.] Student at the Pueblo
Connect School; [pers.] Sara likes to listen to
music, spend time with her friends.; [a.] Pueblo, CO

MCCONNELL, LOIS M.
[pen.] Aunt Lo; [b.] August 24, 1921, Hunt, IL;
[p.] Glenn - Mabel Abraham; [m.] Robert B.
McConnell, July 25, 1973; [ch.] Dr. Michael
Elliott; [ed.] Willow Hill High Illini Beauty
College; [occ.] Retired; [memb.] First Methodist
Church Crawford Memorial Hospital Aux. Eastern
Star; [hon.] 200 hr. pin - Hospital Aux.; [pers.]
While sitting at my Mother bedside in her last days,
watching the transition of life to death - it become
real to me that life never really ends.; [a.]
Robinson, IL

MCCOOL, JOANNE M.
[b.] November 9, 1962, Philadelphia, PA; [ed.]
A.A. Liberal Arts, La Salle University; [occ.]
Director, Human Resources (full-time), Fitness
Instructor (part-time); [memb.] Society for
Professionals in Human Resources, Aerobics and
Fitness Association of America, American Heart
Association, Mayors Commission on Literary;
[hon.] Dean's List, Magna Cum Laude; [oth. writ.]
Various newsletter and annual report contributions;
[pers.] We can learn and grow from all of life's
experience, positive or negative, they are
valuable.; [a.] Philadelphia, PA

MCCORMACK, PATRICE M.
[pen.] Marlene McCormack; [b.] May 4, 1971,
Camphill, PA; [p.] Lois and Edward McCormack;
[ed.] Red Land H.S., University of Mississippi;
[occ.] Dance Instructor and Choreographer;
[memb.] National Baton Twirling Association
(N.B.T.A.); [hon.] Dancer of the Year - University
of Mississippi, Miss Majorette of Pennsylvania,
Miss Majorette of West Virginia, Miss Majorette of
the South; [oth. writ.] 10 volumes of unpublished,
far from perfect poetry - centered on the life of a
passionate mountain girl.; [pers.] My writings are
inspired and influenced by the world around us.
The way we react to life and the way life surrounds
us is so beautiful and so very precious. Let us
never take it for granted.; [a.] Manassas, VA

MCCORMICK, CONNIE E.
[pen.] Conne Huff; [b.] December 4, 1946, Butler,
PA; [p.] Leonard and Mary Huff; [m.] Ronald
McCormick, May 18, 1966; [ch.] Deborah Lee,
Rhonda Lynn; [ed.] Butler High School, Slippery
Rock University; [occ.] Independent Grocer,
Brownsdale, PA; [memb.] Christ Community
United Methodist Church; [oth. writ.] Short Stories
For Children, Poems For "40 Something" Women;
[pers.] Expressive writing can have different
meanings to the reader and the author. The poem
"Considerate Wife" was cathartic therapy for me.
CMC.; [a.] Brownsdale, PA

MCCORMICK, MAXINE GEORGIA
[b.] December 31, 1917, Nacogdoches, TX; [p.]
George O. Scott and Adeline C. Scott; [m.] Robert
N. McCormick (Deceased), August 15, 1947; [ch.]
Wilhelmina R., Robert N. II, Crandall S., Dallas
H.; [occ.] Retired; [pers.] I am totally awed by
mankind's reaction to, and interaction with life.;
[a.] Quinlan, TX

MCCOY, WANDA SUE
[b.] February 18, 1951, Rocky Ford, CO; [p.]
Norman (Deceased) and Mildred Dykes; [ch.]
Chad and Jason; [ed.] High School; [occ.]
Medically Retired; [oth. writ.] Solution in Tears of
Fire; [pers.] I want to continue writing poetry from
the heart. Experiences in Life are the key!; [a.]
Colorado Springs, CO

MCCUE, ANNE
[pen.] "Tootsie"; [b.] August 29, 1913, Brooklyn,
NY; [m.] August 27, 1939; [ch.] One; [ed.] High
School, Wilfred Beauty School, Graduated both;
[occ.] Housewife; [memb.] Woman's U.S.
Veteran's Auxiliary; [hon.] Trophy's 5 first prizes
for Halloween Costumes - 1961, 1973, 1980,
1993, 1994; [oth. writ.] Lyrics and other poetry.

MCDAVID, BETTY STARNES
[pen.] Babe; [b.] October 4, 1930, Gate City, VA;
[p.] Ervin Craft Starnes; [m.] Ella Bledsoe Starnes,
May 18, 1946; [ch.] Emerson Craft McDavid,
(grandson) Austin Craft McDavid; [ed.] High
School - Shoemaker High, Gate City, VA, Whitney
Sch. of Business Kingsport, TN; [occ.] Retired
from Dental Profession; [hon.] Student Council;
[oth. writ.] Poems in Local newspaper, Book now
in writing; [pers.] "Stay close to those you love";
[a.] Manassas, VA

MCDERMOTT, DANIEL J.
[b.] December 2, 1958, Bronx, NY; [p.] Roger
and Mary McDermott; [m.] Mary McDermott,
April 17, 1982; [ch.] Daniel (11 years), Christine
(10 years), Catherine (6 years); [ed.] St. Nicholas
of Tolentino H.S. Bronx, NY, PACB University
Manhattan, N.Y. (presently attending); [occ.]
Engineer, N.Y.N.E.X., N.Y.C., N.Y.; [hon.]
Sarah H. Willis Scholarship Award (writing) at
Pace University winner 1993, 1994; [oth. writ.]
short stories; [pers.] This poem is dedicated to my
mother who died in a fire in 1990 at the age of 54.;
[a.] Sparta, NJ

MCDONALD, JENNIFER L.
[pen.] Jennie McDonald; [b.] October 1, 1962,
Saint Louis, MO; [p.] Jim and Carol Phillips; [m.]
Cliff McDonald, November 23, 1985; [ch.] B.

Corey McDonald, age 4; [ed.] Central Gwinnett High School, Lawrenceville, GA, Gainesville College, Gainesville, GA.; [occ.] Student, homemaker, mom, entrepreneur; [memb.] 1. Vice-President, English Club, Gainesville College, 1994-95, 2. Fund raising booksale for Gainesville College Library 1995, 3. Rainy Day Fund Investment Partnership 1988-1995, 4. American Red Cross, 5. La Lecheleague 6. Women mean Business; [hon.] 1. Phi Theta Kappa, 2. 1st place poetry contest, Gainesville Jr Colleges 1995, 3. Who's Who among Student in American Jr. Colleges 1994-95, 4. 3rd Place Essay Contest, Gainesville College, 1995, 5. Foundation Scholarship, 1993-95, 6. English Scholarship, Gainesville College, 1994-95, 7. Merit List, 1993-94, 8. Dean's List 1994-95; [oth. writ.] Several poems published in other publications, several essays published in school literary publication Ho: Pollo, poem published in school literary publication perceptions; [a.] Gainesville, GA

MCDOUGALL, GARY
[b.] April 10, 1960, Jamaica; [m.] February 11, 1986; [ch.] Jean & Kim; [occ.] Building Supervisor; [memb.] SAW, ASCAP; [pers.] This life, this world is real and so are my tears, my laughter & my happiness.

MCDUFFEY, ARGUSTA
[b.] April 2, 1962, Newhebron, MS; [p.] RJ and Tressie L. McDuffey; [m.] Kimberly K. McDuffey, June 25, 1989; [ch.] Christian A. and Jared M. McDuffey; [ed.] BSEE Electrical Engineering, Mississippi State University, New Hebron, MS High School; [occ.] Naval Oceanographic office, Stennis Space Center, Electronics Engineer; [a.] Slidell, LA

MCGILL, WANDA
[b.] April 5, 1936, Los Angeles; [p.] Victor and Emily Wirt; [m.] Maurice McGill, February 2, 1957; [ch.] Melany, Melinda and Shannon; [ed.] B.S. in Ele. Ed. and Lib Sc. from University of Missouri; [occ.] Retired Librarian and Music Teacher; [memb.] A.A.V.W., Christian Church International Society of Poets, The National Library of Poetry, Am Cancer Society - Volunteer Mesquite Symphony Orchestra Preston Road Literary Society; [hon.] 1993 Poet of Merit Award, 1994 Editors Choice Award from the National Library of Poetry; [oth. writ.] Several poems and articles published in local publications; [pers.] My writing usually reflects day to day happenings and observations.; [a.] Garland, TX

MCGUIRE, JILLIAN.
[b.] December 4, 1971, Santa Cruz, CA; [p.] Daniel M. and Julianne Crowl; [m.] John P. McGuire, June 23, 1990; [ch.] Kamaron Tass McGuire; [ed.] Sparks High School, Truckee Meadows Community College, Morrison Business College; [occ.] Pre-School teacher; [pers.] The answers to tomorrows questions lie in the eyes of our children.; [a.] Sparks, NV

MCGUIRE, KATHERINE V.
[b.] January 22, 1978, Pittsburg, PA; [p.] Anna and Kevin; [ed.] Currently High School student at Kiski Area in Apollo, PA; [occ.] Student; [hon.] Publications in school newspapers literary

magazine 1994; [oth. writ.] Many poems and short stories, not yet published.; [pers.] A writer writes... always.; [a.] Apollo, PA

MCGURER, DARLET D.
[b.] February 28, 1936, Orient, OH; [p.] Kenneth Boyd, Cora Boyd; [m.] Charles McGurer, October 23, 1957; [ch.] Douglas McGurer, Curt McGurer; [ed.] Madison Mills High Schools, Fayelle County, Ohio; [occ.] retired Medical Record Technician, Currently Clerical Assistant at Local Community College.; [oth. writ.] poems published in local newspapers.; [pers.] Writing poetry is a hobby which provides an outlet to express my deepest and most sincere thoughts and feelings. I have so much to be thankful for; being able to express myself through poetry is for me a blessing.; [a.] Mocksville, NC

MCINTIRE, ELIZABETH
[pen.] Elizabeth Honabarger McIntire; [b.] May 26, 1939, Near Bakersville, OH; [p.] Edward and Lavena Honabarger; [ch.] Jeffrey McIntire, Lavena Domalewski and Raymond McIntire; [ed.] High School, Computer Classes at Vocational School; [occ.] Payroll Clerk/Sec; [memb.] Renners St. Paul United Church of Christ, Church Council Member, Superintendent of Sunday School, Ladies Guild, Treasurer of both Renners Church and Baltic Parish; [hon.] I have no formal honors my personal honor is to read my poems at different Church functions. And to pray they help others, as they have helped me heal after the loss of my beloved mother.; [oth. writ.] My first poem was "Why Didn't I?" Other have been "Mother's Gentle Kiss", "Reason for the Season", "Yesterday" and others.; [pers.] I have had my poems read at different Church functions. My hope is that my poems can in some way be instrumental in winning people to the LORD and to help mankind.; [a.] Bakersville, OH

MCINTOSH, JESSE
[b.] May 27, 1983, Pontiac; [p.] Kay and Gary McIntosh; [ed.] Attends Glengary Elementary in Walled Lake, Michigan. Jesse is in fifth grade.; [occ.] Student; [hon.] Received a state board of education certificate for achievement on the 94-95 Michigan Educational Assessment Program in Science, received green belt in Tast Karate.; [pers.] I enjoy writing stories and poems also like to draw. Hope to someday become an author.; [a.] Walled Lake, MI

MCINTURF, MARGARET KRISTINE
[b.] December 30, 1977; [p.] Don and Lynda McInturf; [ed.] I will be a Senior at Athens High School next year.; [occ.] I work at a small ice cream store in Athens, Ohio.; [hon.] Honor Roll in my High School; [pers.] Try to respect older people and listen to what they say. They have lots of wisdom to share with others. I'm proud to be a part of this book.; [a.] Athens, OH

MCINTYRE, ERIN
[b.] October 2, 1981, Voorhees, NJ; [p.] Dannette and Joe McIntyre; [ed.] Bells School and Chestnut Ridge Middle School, Washington, Twp. NJ; [occ.] Student in Washington Twp., NJ School System; [memb.] Sts. Peter and Paul Roman Catholic Church, Washington Twp. Mustang

Soccer Club; [hon.] Principals list, 8 years Presidential Physical Fitness Award, Soccer Team Captain; [a.] Turnersville, NJ

MCKEE JR., LANDRY
[b.] January 17, 1950, Indiana; [p.] Mr. and Mrs. L. B. McKee; [m.] Jamie B. McKee, June 17, 1991; [ed.] High School, New York Institute of Photography La Salle Extension of Illinois Chicago Art Institute; [occ.] Investor; [memb.] Civil Air Patrol Nevada Wing, United States Tennis Association; [oth. writ.] None published before; [pers.] Linking words with phrases to make life more meaningful and cheerful is what I wish to accomplish through poetry; [a.] Las Vegas, NV

MCKINNEY, EVER CLAIR
[b.] January 9, 1983; [p.] Mitch and Mary McKinney; [ed.] 6th grade student at Peter Muhlenberg Middle School; [memb.] Play Alto Sax, School Band; [hon.] 1st Place Daughter's of American Revolution essay contest 1993; [pers.] My poetry is written mainly to reflect the accomplishments and achievements of Egyptian Civilians. I have been influenced greatly by William Butler Yeats, the "Last Romantic"; [a.] Toms Brook, VA

MCKIRDY, DONALD H.
[pen.] Donald McKirdy; [b.] June 30, 1922, Bridge Port, CT; [p.] James and Hazel McKirdy; [m.] Jennette McKirdy, July 4, 1952; [ch.] Jean, Kathleen, Donna, Gail; [ed.] Attended Warren Harding High School, Bridge Port, CT; [occ.] Retired Radial Drill Operator; [memb.] 10th Armoured Division's Tiger Division - 3rd Army Headed by General Georges, Patton, 1942-1945, V.F.W. Post No. 1236, Served U.S. Army 1942, November 16, to January 16, 1945; [hon.] Served - With 90 Calry R.C.N. SQDN. (MECZ), 1942-1945, Plaqe's erected-Luxemburg, Fort-Gordon, GA, Arlington Cemetery and Monument Decoration's and Award's - 7,117 - 320 Certificate-of Merit. At-Entrance-to All Armored Division's including marine's; [oth. writ.] Including 101st Air Borne who served with 10th Armoured Division at Bastonge in Battle of the bulge 1944-1945.; [pers.] Men of the 10th Armoured Div. were the finest 1 served with in the world including our general's 1st Gen. Paul Neguardenang, 2nd Gen. William Morris.; [a.] Shelton, CT

MCKNIGHT, LAWRENCE J.
[pen.] Larry James; [b.] November 11, 1969, Brookhaven, NY; [p.] James L. McKnight, Betty A. Wagner; [m.] Cathleen E. McKnight, August 20, 1994; [ed.] Patchogue-Medford High, AIFL, ICS - Business Management, B.O.C.E.S. II Advertising; [occ.] Owner/President - Scorpion's Kiss Designs and S.K.D. advertising Specialists, Ltd.; [memb.] N.Y.C. Adv. Artist Exchange, AMG - American Musicians Guild; [hon.] Presidential Academic Physical Fitness Award, Suffolk Country, NY. D.W.I. Awareness/Participation Award, C.A.P.D.A. Logo Design; [oth. writ.] Several musical, lyrical compositions for self and local, professional bands.; [pers.] Live life, but always be honest and true to your innerself. My style is like those of Edgar Allen Poe, not all is as it appears.; [a.] Holbrook, NY

MCKOWN, CHRIS
[pen.] Michael Farris; [b.] May 14, 1960, Middletown, OH; [p.] Robert McKown, Evelyn McKown; [m.] Single; [ed.] Franklin H.S., Wilmington College; [occ.] Builder; [hon.] Dean's List; [oth. writ.] Several love poems; [pers.] Words that cannot be spoken orally, are often reflected in love poetry. A wonderful way to express one's true feelings.; [a.] Franklin, OH

MCLAIN, JERMEY
[b.] June 29, 1973, Huntingburg, IN; [p.] Gary McLain, Teresa Lynch; [ed.] Crawford County Jr. - Sr. High School Marengo Indiana; [occ.] Laborer; [a.] English, IN

MCLEAN, TERRI L.
[pen.] Terri Lynn; [b.] August 27, 1964, Columbus, OH; [p.] George Cochran, Barbara Cochran; [m.] Jeffrey Lee McLean, May 3, 1991; [ch.] Shanita Alexandria McLean; [ed.] Graduated Cody High School in 1983 and attended Wayne County Community College in Detroit, Michigan; [occ.] Homemaker and child care provider; [memb.] Public Television WETA Channel 26 Washington, DC; [hon.] Honor role in High School; [oth. writ.] I have other poems that have never been read by the public or friends; [pers.] I love being a wife and mother. I also enjoy teaching and telling poetry to our 2 years old daughter.; [a.] Dumfries, VA

MCMAHAN, NANCY
[b.] August 19, 1964, Hickory, NC; [m.] Donald McMahan; [ch.] Katisha Dawn, Crystal Star, David Andrew; [pers.] Dedicated to Lisa for her Encourage-ment and Support. That gave me the inspiration to keep writing.; [a.] Connellys Springs, NC

MCMANN, AMBER
[b.] October 31, 1980, Dicking Country; [p.] Judith Long and Paul McMann; [ed.] In 8th Grade going into 9th; [occ.] In School; [memb.] Track, Reader Theater and Church. Also a member in choir.; [hon.] Honor and Merit Roll, Tracks Award, National Honor Student, and Readers Theaters; [oth. writ.] I haven't had any of my poems published. I just write them for myself.; [pers.] Most of my poems are based on real life I usually write about my family or dreams I have.; [a.] Newark, OH

MCMENAMIN, EILEEN
[b.] November 27, 1972, Woodburg, NJ; [p.] Daniel J. and Barbara Burke; [m.] Padrick McMenamin, August 10, 1991; [ed.] Gateway Regional High School; [occ.] Cashier Superior, A.C. Moore Mt. Laurel, NJ; [hon.] Who's who among American High School Students 1989-1990; [oth. writ.] One poem published in my high school newsletter and many other unpublished poems.; [pers.] My writing reflects my deepest feelings of different situations in my life as they occur. I would like to take this opportunity to commemorate my most recent inspiration, my brother Chuck (passed away November 2, 1994), whom I have written much in his memory.; [a.] Wenonah, NJ

MCNABB, TUDY
[b.] June 17, 1943, New Orleans, LA; [m.] Freddie, Jr, November 20, 1965; [ch.] Frank W.

Freddie, III; [ed.] Graduate of Business College, Some College and Numerous Continuing Educational Courses; [occ.] Homemaker with strong desire to write; [memb.] Moebius Syndrome Foundation, Alcoholic Anonymous; [hon.] Full scholarship to Business College and L.S.U. based solely on merit numerous High School Awards Louisiana State University; [oth. writ.] Working on book about a very special person who has numerous handicaps but has somehow managed to overcome them; [pers.] The struggle to admit one's alcoholism with hopes of helping others.; [a.] Saint Charles, MO

MCNETT, ROSE MARIE
[b.] February 21, 1951, Salem, OH; [p.] LeRoy P. and Arvie L. Barth; [ch.] Tracy Adam, Jack J. Adam Jr., Christopher S. Adam; [ed.] Moline Senior High Moline, IL, Sawyer Secretarial College Saint Louis, MO, Black Hawk College Moline, IL; [occ.] Shipping Clerk; [pers.] I have always enjoyed writing. One day I would like to compose a novel. Poems is just something I have been toying around with.; [a.] Moline, IL

MCPHERSON, SANDRA
[pen.] Sam's; [b.] October 6, 1965, Hattisburg, VA; [p.] Guy F. Whetzel and Luvada Whetzel; [m.] Victor W. McPherson, September 29, 1991; [ch.] Amber May, Lynn, Damein Alexander, Ondreia Deloris; [ed.] Degree in Technical Engineering and Art; [occ.] Professional Artist and Home-maker; [pers.] Tomorrow's never ends they are only our door-way's into the future.; [a.] Manassas, VA

MCVEIGH, JACQUELINE A.
[pen.] Jackie McVeigh; [b.] March 18, 1965, Racine, WI; [p.] Donna Howe and Jack Eisel Sr.; [m.] John D. McVeigh, November 19, 1983; [ch.] Heather, Brandi, Kourtney, Joshua, and Jeremiah; [ed.] J.I. Case High School, Studying Medical Transcription; [a.] Menominee, MI

MEADOWS, VIRGINIA M.
[pen.] Ginny Lynn; [b.] March 29, 1937, Alleghany Co. Corengton, VA; [p.] Bishop and Nancy Meadows; [m.] Divorced; [ch.] Larry, Robin, Donald and Bonnie; [ed.] High School 12 grades, Virginia 3 years Bible College, Maryland 1 year Nursing, Maine Tech College; [occ.] Nurse; [memb.] American between Assoc, American heart assoc.; [hon.] For teaching and Nursing school, Certificate of teaching, Certificate of Nursing; [oth. writ.] Songs and poems.; [pers.] I have dedicated my life in being a blessings to man kind in every walk of life. I have collected books by Henry Wadsworth Love fellow 1885 also by Henry Van Wykie 1924 which I love.; [a.] Holiday, FL

MEATRIS, REGINA
[b.] September 27, 1967, Steubenville, OH; [p.] David Mancano and Mary Ann Mancano; [m.] John Meatris, March 27, 1991; [ed.] Steubenville High School; [pers.] With the love of God and family, my writing is able to express my thoughts and feelings. I try to, if but for one moment, capture time, fill it and release it back, richer and fuller. So all can enjoy.; [a.] Steubenville, OH

MEDEIROS, JENNIFER
[b.] February 1, 1962, Dover, OH; [p.] Paul Holderbaum, June Holderbaum; [m.] David Medeiros, January 8, 1986; [ch.] Candice June, Ashley Rene; [ed.] Lee Voc. Tech.; [occ.] Printer; [oth. writ.] Several Personal Poems; [pers.] I enjoy writing about feelings between two people whether it be lovers or family. Also about the beauty of the environment God has created.; [a.] Cape Coral, FL

MEEK, KIMBERLY
[b.] July 26, Walnutt Creek, CA; [p.] Rosanne and James Meek; [pers.] Poets find words for the unspeakable, we turn ordinary into extra ordinary. Regardless of race or religion we are all up against the same unstoppable force, which is time. So use it wisely because like words, once they are used, you can never take them back; [a.] Visalia, CA

MEHALSO, MATTHEW
[pen.] Matt Mehalso; [b.] December 16, 1983, Highland Park, IL; [p.] Robin and Jim Mehalso; [ed.] Esther Jackson Elementary Roswell, GA; [occ.] Student; [memb.] Roswell Baseball Travelling Team; [hon.] Member of the TAG (Talented and Gifted) Program; [pers.] I always want to feel and believe that I've tried by hardest and given everything I do my best shot.; [a.] Roswell, GA

MELDRUM, ABBIE
[b.] September 20, 1982, Marine City; [p.] Gail Grace and Bill Meldrum; [ed.] I'm in 7th grade; [oth. writ.] Best friends and influences to keep writing Cheyenne Stephonson, Lena Boyd, and Sammy Duchene; [pers.] Always believe in yourself and do what you think is right no matter what! Never stop writing; [a.] Marine City, MI

MELNIK, JENNIE MARIE
[b.] May 13, 1962, Bronx, NY; [p.] Louise Tetro and Vito Tetro; [m.] Thomas Paul Melnik Sr., June 13, 1982; [ch.] Thomas Jr. and Christopher Scott; [ed.] P.S. 133, P.S. 172, Martin Van Buren High School, Saint Johns University; [occ.] Dedicated wife and loving mother.; [pers.] I firmly believe that through God all things are possible - Each person, past or present, that has touched my life, has become a very important part of "The making of my soul". My own unique spirit molded gently together with love and guidance.

MENDEZ, MANUEL
[pen.] Elivan Mendez; [b.] February 28, 1963, Michigan; [p.] Mary Louise Mendez/Art Maravilla; [ed.] Baldwin Park H.S. Mtn. San Antonio Coll. John Robert powers; [occ.] Painting and badge maker, Sun Badge Co.; [memb.] Home club; [hon.] Oil painting award/three from "All Talk All Talent"; [oth. writ.] Songs like "Don't leave me from your side," "Only thing I do is cry". ... and others.; [pers.] Sometimes we long for love not realizing we have it, because God is tender powerful and unique... And we can find Him in the brightness of our eyes.; [a.] Montebello, CA

MENDEZ, MARINA R.
[pen.] Al-Mari; [b.] January 18, 1957, Hispaniola; [p.] Genero R. Mendez and Ramona Jimenez Mendez; [ch.] Maria Trinidad Sanchez; [ed.] Hostos H.S, N.Y.C, A.S.S at Hostos College, BA

in Psychology at Lehman College N.Y.C, Doctor degree in divinity of Vision University of New York; [occ.] Psychologist, writer; [memb.] Shmissonion Ass., N.Y.C. Museum of Art of Box., Christian Coalition, American Bible Society, World Vision, CUNY disable students ass.; [hon.] North Shore Annual League, Boytown, American society of prevention of cruelty for animals, 1986 - Hostos College N.Y.C., March Student of the month and best ESL student writer 1st and 2nd place, 1977 - Francis Harrstyle Academy (France) student of the year, 1981, - P.R. Council Multal service N.Y.C the best design plate student.; [oth. writ.] Hostos College City of NY, 1986 March ESL and best Composition as foreign student; [pers.] I love people. It doesn't matter color, race or religious belief. Because I see God in each human being. "With out God, love and peace we are nothing."; [a.] Bronx, NY

MENGISTU, AMDIE
[pen.] Amdie; [b.] January 12, 1979, Berkeley, CA; [p.] Berhany Mengistu, Lemlem Tsegaw; [ed.] Junior at the Norfolk Academy Norfolk Virginia; [occ.] 11th grade student; [memb.] Debate Team, Varsity Track; [hon.] Optimist International Club Oratorical Award, Honor Roll; [oth. writ.] No other published works.; [pers.] As the 16 years old son of foreign parents, I have a unique perspective and cultural outlook. Through my writing, I strive to convey the value of unique perspective and different paradigms.; [a.] Chesapeake, VA

MERCHANT, VINCENT MICHAEL
[pen.] Jim Stark; [b.] February 13, 1971, Hospital; [p.] Marjorie and Michael Merchant; [ed.] S.U.N.Y. New Paltz, W.C.C.; [occ.] Layabout/ Living Life; [memb.] Human Race, Apathy Club; [hon.] Honorable parents M and M and Brother, Nicholas; [oth. writ.] Poem in the Accordian Flyer; [pers.] Dead flowers and our love: Neither thrive nor survive. When I die, please don't cry. And don't deny that I tried.; [a.] Mohegan Lake, NY

MERCURO JR., GEORGE J.
[b.] August 21, 1966, Sumter, SC; [p.] Col. George J. Mercuro Sr, Kay Mercuro; [m.] Heidi M. Hinkamp, July 9, 1994; [ch.] TBA expected September 14, 1995; [ed.] University of Florida, Gainesville, B.S. Accounting 1989, CPA State of VA; [occ.] Accountant - Specialized. Financial Consultant; [pers.] Be thankful for everything; [a.] Woodbridge, VA

MERRITT, JACKIE GAY
[pen.] T. J. Merritt; [b.] November 23, 1942, Bristol, TN; [p.] Tressie and Ted Merritt; [pers.] This poem was written a dear friend, whose daughter died after a battle with cancer. Basically, I write for my own pleasure and as a form of communication. I have no former education in literature, and any talent is solely, God given.; [a.] Las Vegas, NV

MERRITT, LEE
[b.] December 30, 1972, Brooklyn, NY; [p.] Richard Merritt, Eileen Merritt; [ed.] Washingtonville High School (To 9th Grade only), G.E.D.; [occ.] Musician; [pers.] I only hope that other people enjoy and can gain some form of benefit from my work.; [a.] Washingtonville, NY

MERRITT, ROY B.
[b.] October 21, 1918; [p.] Deceased; [m.] Mary Henderson Merritt, June 10, 1942; [ch.] Lydia Merritt, Deborah Garfield, Kate Merritt and S/Sgt. Savre Merritt USAF; [ed.] Pelham Memorial HS, Pelham. NY College of William and Mary, B. Sc. Boston University, M. Ed. Boston University Additional Study; [occ.] Retired; [memb.] The Country Club, Brookline, MA, Sigma Pi Fraternity, First Church in Chestnuthill (Unitarian); [hon.] Several as a High School and College athlete. 1st Prize poetry, hillhoven Inc. 1994-95 in 1955-56 Who's Who in American education, signed as Pitcher by NY Yankees 1937 and in 1942; [oth. writ.] Articles in Professional journals. Poetry in various newspapers and in children's publications. Poem in National anthology of teacher poetry, 1974; [pers.] As an "Old Fogy" of the 1920's when rhymed poetry of some form and beauty was predominant, I deplore the direction taken by modern "free" verse. It is unrhymed, unmusical, uninteresting, unclear and often obscene!

MERTENS, DIANE MARIE
[b.] March 1, 1976, Marshfield, WI; [p.] Robert and Rosalie Mertens; [ed.] Thorp High School, University of WI - Oshkosh Nelson Hall Newsletter Columnist; [occ.] Student at UW-Oshkosh; [memb.] Students Educating Against Kidnapping, Nelson Hall Treasurer, University Scholars Program, Nelson Hall Newsletter Staff; [hon.] University Honor Roll; [pers.] I have loved poetry all my life. Poetry has a way of expressing thoughts and feelings in a way that makes you stop and think about the world for a moment.; [a.] Thorp, WI

MERTZ, BRIAN CHRISTOPHER
[b.] January 2, 1973, Houston, TX; [p.] Charles and Jane Mertz; [ed.] Marfa High School, Marfa Texas, East Texas State University, Commerce Texas; [occ.] Student; [memb.] Cato Institute; [pers.] "It is unethical to capitalize on another person's misery, yet it is possible for a poet to profit from their own misery."

METZ, BESSIE CATHERINE
[b.] June 12, 1975, Bouider, CO; [p.] Robert Metz and Roberta Metz; [ed.] Sandy Creek High School, Lamar Community College; [occ.] Student; [memb.] American quarter horse, National Art Honor Society; [pers.] I write what I feel at that moment. This poem is about my Grandmothers passing on. I love to write, draw and of course day dream.; [a.] Fairfield, NE

MEYER, JAMES CURTIS
[b.] December 9, 1957, Lackawanna, NY; [ed.] B.A. English Literature, Saint Bonaventure University, Olean, NY; [pers.] 'Angel Of Hope' is one of several songs I hope to publish in my life time. Thank you for taking the time to read it.; [a.] Kenmore, NY

MEYERS, KATHLEEN
[pen.] Katrina; [b.] February 19, 1960, Manhattan, NY; [p.] Marilyn and William Meyers; [ed.] Lakeland High School graduate completion of several courses in Computer Technology; [occ.]

Graphics Artist; [memb.] Peta Doris Day Animal League Green peace; [oth. writ.] Soulful Poetry: Silent man, The Profundity of one's soul personal, A dedication to my Father; [pers.] One who can see inner and outer beauty is one filled with passion. One who can taste the time and effort put into a meal is one filled with passion. One who can touch another's heart is one filled with passion. One who can hear out is also listening is one filled with passion. One who can smell the beauty of nature is one filled with passion. Without passion of the senses, life's experiences could not become poetry.

MICHAELS, DON L.
[b.] December 25, 1969, Fall River, MA; [ed.] University of Massachusetts, North Dartmouth, MA; [oth. writ.] Poem's published in The Church House Anthology, Volumes II and III, and National Collegiate Poets.; [a.] Providence, RI

MICK, FLORENCE MAE
[pen.] Mark in time; [b.] September 23, 1929, Pennsylvania; [p.] Charles L. Johnson and Iva A. Reed Johnson; [m.] Joseph R. Mick Sr. (deceased), February 7, 1956; [ch.] Joann Marie, Susan Genevieve and Lena Lucy Mick (deceased); [ed.] Little Marsh PA Elementary and God's Bible School High, Ohio. A Child Evangelist in teaching courses; [occ.] Retired N.Y.S. Employee I do some teaching as a volunteer 4th, 5th and 6th grade - in writing; [memb.] At Diven School, Vested Rights in New York State, as a N.Y.S. Retiree. Also Worked with handicapped as a Vocational development instructor.; [hon.] Two golden poets, a ruby award, emerald award, some teachers awards, lake Lomoka lake, baptist camp counselor, two scholarship in arts and crafts. I have received several news write ups in Elmira Star.; [oth. writ.] 5 Adult Poetry Book, 4 Children's Poetry Books, 3 Poetic Baletts, 10 Children's Story books some poetically written. Listing of books such as Poetry Books 1. A Mark In Time - for veterans of forgine war. 2. Time for Pleasure - for fun. 3. A Time to Remember - Poetry remembering the 30 years and 40 years. Children Books, 1. The Happy Reunion - is about two orangoutang's. 2. No Name - Children who are a abandoned with Aid. 3. The Little Black Bear - Diabetic Research; [pers.] All my works are donated to help others have a better life. 1. Juvenal Diabetic, 2. Undetectable Birth defects, 3. Children born with Aids It is my way to do something meaningful for others.; [a.] Elmira, NY

MILES, SYLVIA
[b.] October 6, 1929, Thomas Co., NE; [p.] Claude Florea, Mary Florea; [m.] Lester Miles, October 30, 1948; [ch.] 4 girls and twin sons; [ed.] Kearney State University; [occ.] Librarian and Writer; [memb.] Faith Church, Historical Society; [hon.] High School valedictorian, Editor, Youth Leader; [oth. writ.] Several poems and humorous incidents; [pers.] Children have been my interest— to help shape their pathways in life. I try to give my full attention to young and oldsters alike to brighten their day and give a listening ear when no one else hears them... They are an inspiration to me.; [a.] O'Neill, NE

MILLER, ELIZABETH MARIE
[pen.] Isabel Martin, Ruriko Mochida; [b.]
September 18, 1945, Baltimore, MD; [p.] Albert
H. and Angela Miller; [m.] Single; [ed.] Lafayette
High School, Brooklyn, NY, Staten Island
Community College, AA, 1969, Hunter College,
BA in History, 1975; [occ.] Secretary for the New
York City Housing Authority; [memb.] Esperanto
League for North America, Institute for Policy
Studies; [hon.] Hunter College Dean's List; [oth.
writ.] Several poems published in other magazines,
two published in the Housing Authority's "Focus
on Women." One poem published in "Dark Side
of the Moon", another published in "Best Poems of
1995."; [pers.] Poetry is a gift of the Goddess. I
hope to serve Her through my life and through my
poetry.; [a.] Brooklyn, NY

MILLER, JENNIFER KAY
[b.] August 3, 1980, Everett; [p.] Ducina Lin
Meek, Richard Scott Miller Jr.; [oth. writ.] This is
my first contest entry of my poems I love to write
and express my feelings through poems.

MILLER, KATHRYN
[b.] December 4, 1981, San Francisco, CA; [p.]
Eleni and Steve Miller; [ed.] I attend Ecole Bilingue
French American Middle School; [occ.] Student;
[memb.] United States Figure Skating Association;
[pers.] To be a writer is not a choice, a true writer
is obligated to write, it's not optional.; [a.] Oakland, CA

MILLER, LOIS
[b.] October 14, 1946; [p.] Jess and Josiphine
Eldridge; [m.] Paul Edward Miller (Deceased),
July 10, 1963; [ch.] Angela, Caroline, and Ashley;
[oth. writ.] Children's books and poems. I am
currently working on a novel, titled Josiphine.;
[pers.] I have always wanted to write. My husband
died of cancer January of this year. I have decided
to take the next four years for my writing.

MILLER, NICOLE
[b.] May 4, 1972, La Crosse, WI; [p.] David
Miller and Myrna Miller; [ed.] Harrah High
School, Oklahoma State University; [occ.] Receive
BFA in Graphic Design in May 1995; [memb.]
People for the Ethical Treatment of Animals,
World Wildlife Fund; [pers.] Children are gifts, not
burdens. They should be raised by parents, not by
television. I believe cats have souls and angels are
among us. There is music, art, and poetry all
around us. We need to not only hear, but listen to
it as well.; [a.] Wellston, OK

MILLER, T. C.
[b.] July 30, 1952, Gainesville, FL; [p.] Louise
Dyal Miller, Jack F. Miller Sr.; [m.] Eva Roller
Miller, April 7, 1974; [ch.] Heather 20, Dawn 18;
[ed.] Some College at Lake City Community and
Santa Fe Community Colleges; [occ.] Power
System Operator with Local R.E.A.; [memb.]
Action Committee for Rural electrification; [oth.
writ.] Several other poems mostly enjoyment and
entertainment for Family and Friends. And Fund
Raiser for the Local Volunteer Fire Dept.
(squealed with a kiss poems); [pers.] Humor and
family go along way to ease the tensions of the
day. I feel I have accomplished my goal with my
writing if I attain a smile, a laugh or a tear.; [a.]
Keystone Heights, FL

MILLER, TRACY A.
[b.] June 25, 1970, New Jersey; [p.] James and
Charlotte Hall; [m.] Xavier D. Miller, July 3,
1989; [ch.] Laural Anne Miller, Jared Isaac Miller;
[ed.] Housewife; [pers.] I enjoy writing poetry, and
playing my cello, starting when I was nine years
old. As a Christian, I know God has truly blessed
my life with a wonderful family, and with my
talents

MILLMAN, HOWARD L.
[b.] August 16, 1938, New York, NY; [p.]
Florence and Harry Weiner; [m.] Karen
McInerney, September 3, 1988; [ch.] Travis, Josh;
[ed.] B.S. City College of N.Y., Ph.d Clinical
Psychology, Adelphi Univ.; [occ.] Clinical and
consulting psychologist, author; [memb.]
American, New York and Westchester County,
Psychological Associations; [hon.] Past President,
Westchester County Psychological Assoc.; [oth.
writ.] Co-author of Therapies for Adults, Therapies
for School Behavior Problems, Goals and Behavior
in Psychotherapy and Counseling, Therapies for
Children, How To Help Children with Common
Problems, Therapies for Psychosomatic Disorders
in Children, Advances in Therapies for Children.;
[pers.] In practicing and teaching psychology and
through my books, I have helped people lead more
satisfying lives. My latest project is translating
psychological insights into poetry.; [a.] Pound
Ridge, NY

MILLS, CYNTHIA T.
[b.] March 15, 1947, Amarillo, TX; [p.] Jack and
Helen Taylor; [m.] Divorced; [ch.] David Mills;
[ed.] BFA-Southern Meth. Univ., MA-Southern
Meth. Univ.; [occ.] Art Historian; [oth. writ.]
Short stories, novel, and screenplay in progress,
other poems; [pers.] I am interested in the art of
living.; [a.] Dallas, TX

MILLS, JACELYN R.
[pen.] J. R. Mills; [b.] September 9, 1948; [p.]
Geneva Calloway and Norris Turner; [ch.] Mark,
Amy, Roosevelt, Genalyn and Rita; [ed.] Belle
Vernon Area Aenon Academy '87; [occ.] Pastor
First Christian Church, Wickhaven; [pers.] All of
my writings are spiritual, for this is my life.

MINES, ROSETTE
[b.] April 1, 1929, Brooklyn, NY; [p.] Samuel
Mines, Esther Mines; [ed.] Erasmus High School
Brooklyn College night school Owns Bus Cust.
Serv. Inc. Printers; [memb.] Artist League of
Brooklyn; [hon.] Honorable mention World of
Poetry National Library of Poetry Editors choice
Artist League of Brooklyn Honorable mention
Artist League of Brooklyn Honorable mention,
Editor's choice; [oth. writ.] National Library of
Poetry Poetic Eloquence Feeling World of Poetry
Anthology Honorable Mention; [pers.] Creating
through writing or painting is my love sensing life,
feelings air nature people bowling music the
summary's being part of life.; [a.] New York, NY

MIRABAL, LUZ MARIA
[b.] August 18, 1967; [p.] Marco P. Mirabal,
Lourdes Mirabal; [ed.] Taylor Business Institute
Technology; [occ.] Executive Secretary; [pers.]
Nothing lasts forever.; [a.] North Bergen, NJ

MITCHELL, ARTHUR
[b.] Oregon; [p.] Maxwell G. Mitchell, Connie
Mitchell (French); [memb.] Zero Population
Growth; [oth. writ.] "Ground Zero," a techno-
ambient music and spoken word album of mine in
progress including "Desiderata" "The Book of
Life" is my vocal-poem on vanishing rain forests
which I recorded for jazz saxophonist YIL, on his
recent (1995) album "Pages from: The Book of
Love;" [pers.] I explore man's place in nature and
our relationship between worlds we apprehend and
the unseen worlds that hold timeless wisdom. I
want to recover some of the lost worlds that man
has plundered, to protect the planet and insure that
the miracle of life continues in all its diversity.; [a.]
San Francisco, CA

MITCHELL, BRIAN
[pen.] Brian Taylor Mitchell; [b.] October 11,
1961, Pittsburgh, PA; [p.] Robert Mitchell, Mary
Dale Mitchell, (Grandparents) J. T. Mitchell,
Naomi Mitchell; [ed.] Severn High School, MD
Towson State University, MD; [occ.] Customer
Relations Communication Systems; [memb.]
Benevolent Protective Orders of the Elks; [hon.]
Electronics and Aerospace Conference Program
Assistance Award; [oth. writ.] Starting on my first
novel - look for best seller New York Times 1996.;
[pers.] At times man and nature can fit so well
together. Your not out of place, but in place as
part of your surroundings. Wether your alone,
with friends at the ocean, mountains or desert.; [a.]
Springfield, VA

MITCHELL, PEARL E.
[pen.] P. M.; [b.] March 30, 1913, Leeton, MO;
[p.] Jesset, Rose, Pilgrim; [m.] Buell F. Mitchell,
(deceased), December 24, 1938; [ch.] Evelyn and
Earlene; [ed.] BS, SP, ED, Grad, Kirksville MO;
[occ.] Teacher 31 years, Retired; [memb.] ME,
Church Mo. Retired Teachers; [oth. writ.] none
published; [pers.] I'm very independent and
honest, too trusting. All should be free to do what
they can for the good of all."; [a.] Humble, TX

MITTELSTEADT, HELENE
[b.] October 15, 1915, Gillet, WI; [p.] J. P. Jensen
- Emma Jensen; [m.] Walter Benz, June 10, 1936,
(deceased), Otto Mittelsteadt, April 3, 1990
(deceased); [ch.] Paulette Benz Baehman; [ed.]
Bachelors Degree in Elementary Education, Taught
School - 30 Complete years in Wisconsin 6 part-
years; [occ.] Retired widow; [memb.] Grace
Lutheran Church-Oconto Falls Our Savior's
Lutheran Church. Hendersonville, NC, AARP,
President of Ladies Guild in Rhineland, Wis. -
Lutheran Church; [hon.] Attended Elementary
School in Wis. Graduated from 8th grade when I
was 11 years old. Graduated from High School 15
years old, enrolled in County Normal Shawano,
Wis-15 years old Graduated 1 year Teacher's
Training 16 years old.; [oth. writ.] Religious
poems and articles for my own use. Inspired by
God.; [pers.] My greatest desire was to be a
teacher, as I love little children and want to help
them learn. I am nearly 80 years old and with
God's help I have achieved my goal.; [a.]
Weaverville, NC

696

MOBLEY, DOLLY A.
[b.] February 9, 1946, Austell, GA; [p.] E. D. Henry, Amy Henry; [m.] Russell Mobley Jr.; [occ.] Homemaker; [oth. writ.] Poem featured in High School Yearbook, a number of poems and short stories published in local newspapers; [pers.] I enjoy writing words which, by forming pictures in the mind of the reader, produce understanding and pleasure; [a.] Cartersville, GA

MOLENDA, JOAN
[b.] February 26, 1962, WY; [p.] Maureen and Lloyd Wood, Emil Styke; [ch.] Andrew Charles, Kathryn Joan; [ed.] Beaverhead Country High, Western Montana College, University of Montana; [occ.] Title Clerk; [memb.] Dillon Jaycees, WIBC, YABC; [hon.] Montana State Jaycee Secretary of the year, Dean's List; [pers.] My writings tend to reflect events in my children's lives.; [a.] Dillon, MT

MOLLOY, ERIKA
[b.] April 13, 1935, Wurzburg, Germany; [p.] George Seubert, Anny Seubert; [ch.] Daughter: Maria Elisabeth and 3 grand daughters: Courtney, Erin, Aly, Son: Edward and Grandson: Sean Michael; [ed.] MPA - American University; [occ.] Financial MGR - Government; [memb.] Westmister Presb. Church Woodmoor Country Club American Society of Military Comptroullers; [hon.] FWE Woman of the Year - 1984, Meritorious Civil Svs. Award - 1989 Pi Alpha Alpha; [oth. writ.] Other unpublished poems: The tree, etc.; [pers.] My focus is on relationship. (Man to Man, to Nature and to God), on human development and spiritual growth. My writings reflect my own personal experiences and dreams.; [a.] Alexandria, VA

MOLLOY, MICHELE STEVENS
[pen.] Ursula Swanson Stillwell; [b.] October 31, 1949, Kalgoorlie, W. Australia; [p.] Ben E. and Mary T. Stevens; [m.] Annullment, 1971; [ch.] two girls; [ed.] B.A. El. Education/ Soc. Science, High School, Graduate credits; [occ.] Teacher / child care service / writer; [memb.] Hell gate writers, A. Med. Assoc. Associate, Symphony Assoc., MT Arts Assoc.; [hon.] Hopefully - near future; [oth. writ.] Not yet published but which are outlined and in process, poetry and children's lit; [pers.] Man's existence is mainly definitive through that which is created by this essence called spirit self - captured only by the silence found in leisure moments; [a.] Missoula, MT

MONIZ, KIMBERLY A.
[pen.] Kim Moniz; [b.] March 21, 1973, Providence, RI; [p.] David and Donna Moniz; [ed.] Joseph Case High School, Bristol Community College, University of Louisville, KY; [occ.] Specialist in the United States Army; [hon.] Deans List, Army Achievement Medal; [oth. writ.] "Life Goes On" published in "Echoes of Yesterday" by the National Library of Poetry. Several others that have not been published.; [pers.] My poems reflect my deepest and innermost thoughts and feelings, these that express the Humanity of my own being and my love of life itself.; [a.] Swansea, MA

MONTELEONE, ANTHONY
[b.] June 13, 1930, North of Boston, MA; [m.] Paula Monteleone, September 9, 1965; [ch.] Lucia, Conceta, Annette; [ed.] High School, Boston Industrial Tech.; [occ.] Retired; [oth. writ.] Other poems, and a published subsidized novel trying to attract a publisher for a possible reprint. Accepted by Boston Public Library as part of permanent collection excellent blending of history and fiction. Book title "Gina"; [pers.] To ever try to be an asset to humanity by artistic achievement; [a.] Winthrop, MA

MONTPETITE, RENEE D.
[pen.] Renee Dianne; [b.] June 26, 1949, Stillwater, MN; [ch.] Chad Alan, Amie Jo; [ed.] Stillwater Senior High; [pers.] I have written many poems and would like an opportunity to get some of them published.; [a.] Stillwater, MN

MOORE, AMY
[pen.] Amey Moore; [b.] July 31st, Springfield, MO; [p.] Boyd and Susie Gray; [ed.] 8th Norwood, Middle School; [occ.] Fulltime Student; [memb.] Macomb Baptist Church; [hon.] Math Contest; [oth. writ.] Marrissa, Between, Lessons For Life, Granny, Transition, Sisters, That's What Families Are For; [pers.] I look at life as there should be no drugs, no abuse, and especially I don't think people should drop-out of school because you can get a lot more jobs then when you don't drop-out.; [a.] Norwood, MO

MOORE, AMY LYNN
[b.] August 14, 1979, Silver Spring, MD; [p.] Ralph and Debra Moore; [ed.] Currently sophomore attending Frederick High School, Frederick, MD; [oth. writ.] Several poems yet to be published.; [a.] Frederick, MD

MOORE, BARBARA
[pen.] Moore Pickens A. Barbara; [b.] December 12, 1957, Cross Country; [p.] Earleaer Kyles; [m.] Divorced, June 27, 1991; [ch.] Melody Pickens, Dee De Pickens Brittany Smith; [ed.] 12th McCrory High School graduate 1976; [occ.] Disable Mother; [hon.] I write poem to keep me from being sad and lonely made me forget about all my troubles and pain so sometimes I feel like I'm in a dream about the waker in up five or six of poems have been put in McCrory; [oth. writ.] Leader, Monitor IH; [pers.] The reason I start writing poems because I'm are should I said I have Kidney failure I have treatment their days a week for four hour.; [a.] McCrory, AK

MOORE, DOROTHY
[pen.] Drotty; [b.] October 9, 1937, New Jersey; [p.] Mr. and Mrs. A. Eiflander; [m.] Larry N. Moore, June 9, 1959; [ch.] Bryan 1960, Hugh 1963, Lawrence 1964; [ed.] High School 1957, NJ AirForce 27 mouths ACW operator, Allan Hancock 1 1/2 years GI bill, CETA 6 mos. welfare dept.; [memb.] "National Library of Poetry"; [hon.] Certificate 1994 poems; [oth. writ.] "I have about ten good poems."; [pers.] I took a plane and went to another place. New Mexico I stayed there and worked I was working at Cannon AFB. I started my poetry in that place the year was 1980.; [a.] Lompoc, CA

MOORE, GREGORY W.
[b.] February 4, 1973, Houston, TX; [p.] Paul and Toni Moore; [ed.] Shadow Oaks Elementary, Spring Oaks Jr. High, Spring Woods High HCC, ITT Tech.; [occ.] Randall's Sacker; [memb.]

Central Baptist Church N.W., Higher Ground (Gospel Group); [oth. writ.] "The Flying, Racing, Thrilling, Falling, Flipping Ride Of Your Life" published in the 1991 chrysalis magazine.; [pers.] John 3:16-18, John 11:27-30, Thessalonians 5:16-17, of the old King James Bible.; [a.] Houston, TX

MOORE, SANDRA L.
[b.] August 20, 1940, Princess Anne, MD; [p.] McKelery (Deceased) and Frances Bailey; [ch.] Gentry Moore, Sheila Deshiell, Billie Cornish, DeAndra Martin; [ed.] Somerset High School, Princess Anne, MD, Wor-Wic Community College; [memb.] High School Quill and Scroll Member, Humor Editor of Somerset Recorder, Author of Class Poem. Church Clerk Choir member Sunday School Teacher. Mount Zion U.M. Church; [oth. writ.] Poems for my own pleasure.; [pers.] Beauty is everywhere. I try to help people see it, and remind them. That laughter is the substance that keeps hope alive in every soul.; [a.] Princess Anne, MD

MOREL, GUY HENRI
[pen.] Guy H. Morel; [b.] March 25, 1921, Toronto; [p.] D'Avignon and Blanche (Lajoie) Morel; [m.] Estelle Mae (Breivogel) Morel, December 26, 1949; [ed.] B.A. Universite de Montreal, 1939, M.A. Wayne (now State) University, Detroit; [occ.] Retired school teacher Detroit Public Schools, Bloomfield Hills Public Schools, Brother Rice H.S.; [memb.] St. Gerald Parish, Farmington. Catholic Theater of Detroit, Royal Oak Civic Theater, Farmington Players, Presentation Players, National Retired Teacher's Life Association; [hon.] Row Peterson Award for best pictures of the set of a play, one character, or a scene. First, second and third several consecutive years. "MY FAVORITE TEACHER" DETROIT NEWS, 1968, school winner Bloomfield Hills, Jr. H.S.; [oth. writ.] One short story, Catholic Digest entitled "The Halfpenny Club"; [pers.] The country will recapture its place in the world when it rediscovers its respect for life.; [a.] Farmington Hills, MI

MORGAN, BERNICE ANN
[pen.] Bea Morgan; [b.] March 15, 1933, Cairo, IL; [p.] Rosa and John Schaffer; [m.] Caluin C. Morgan (Deceased), October 29, 1955; [ch.] Calvin C. Morgan Jr. and Wayne E. Morgan; [ed.] Carterville, Illinois, Elementary and High School; [occ.] Home Health Care Nurse; [memb.] Five Points Community Church; [hon.] Editors Choice Awards, National Anthology; [oth. writ.] Poems and gospel music articles in church news letters news papers - Readers digest. Poems appearing in books after the storm outstanding poets 1994 - Whispers in the Wind-on the threshold of and Dream; [pers.] I have always loved writing about special people or events in my life and I love to share my thoughts with others. This poem is dedicated to my Grandmother Kathryn Morgan.; [a.] Rochester Hills, MI

MORGAN, JOSHUA S.
[pen.] Josh Morgan; [b.] December 26, 1980, Beckley, WV; [p.] Stephanie Morgan; [ed.] Currently attending 8th grade; [occ.] Student; [pers.] "The kids of the world today have a lot on their minds. Adults could learn a lot from us." [a.] Beckley, WV

MORGAN, SHANE
[b.] December 18, 1975, Man, WV; [p.] Dorsey and Bonnie Morgan; [pers.] "Poetry is a talent, a blessing from God to a certain few. In this, we must work and wait. For someday our dreams will come true". My influences are songwriters. But I thank God for the gift.; [a.] Davin, WV

MORGAN, SHARON GRIGGS
[pen.] Sharon Griggs Morgan; [b.] March 21, 1957, Poplar Bluff, MO; [p.] Joe and Hazel Griggs; [m.] Allen Morgan, July 31, 1993; [ch.] Kevin Morgan (Step-son); [ed.] Greenville High; [occ.] City of Poplar Bluff for 14 years in tax department; [oth. writ.] This is the first time I have ever submitted any of my work, and this is my first publication.; [pers.] This poem is dedicated to my parents, who are always there for me. I love you both.; [a.] Poplar Bluff, MO

MORGAN, THOMAS T.
[b.] April 18, 1942, Los Angeles, CA; [m.] Divorced two times; [ch.] 2 Daughters and 2 ex-step-daughters; [ed.] B.A., V.C. Berkeley, 1970, Anthropology; [memb.] Amnesty International, ACLU, Institute Of Human Origins; [oth. writ.] Screen Play - 26 Hour's, A Day In The Life, Poetry, I also make Paper-Mache Masks.; [pers.] After a 17 yrs. drunk and a Heroin run for the same number of years, I've been sober for almost 5 yrs. I want to dedicate this poem to my 3 daughters, both living and dead and to my 2 ex-step-daughters; [a.] Kensington, CA

MORGERA, SALVATORE J.
[pen.] Salvatore J. Morgera; [b.] November 19, 1965, Stanford, CT; [p.] John Morgera, Marie Morgera; [m.] Debbie Schmitz; [ed.] Stamford Catholic High; [occ.] Manager of an Art Gallery; [memb.] National Wildlife Assoc. Dolphin Sponsorship; [oth. writ.] Several poems published in local magazines just finished writing my first novel "The Ridges"; [pers.] I do not believe in writer's block, I find that there is always something to write about

MORRIS, DANA PURCELL
[pen.] Dana Purcell Morris; [b.] May 5, 1942, Childress, TX; [p.] Bill and Bess Purcell; [m.] Jim V. Morris, December 3, 1960; [ch.] Jay Von Morris, Clay Purcell Morris; [ed.] Childress High School-1960, AHIMA-Accredited Record Technician; [occ.] Family Clinic, Billing Mgr; [memb.] AHIMA TX Medical Record Assn., First United Methodist Church; [oth. writ.] Various-poetry several poems in local contest at County Museum (Childress County Heritage Museum Poetry Festival); [pers.] "Treat everyone you meet-as though their heart were breaking."; [a.] Childress, TX

MORRIS, GABRIEL DOUGLAS
[b.] January 25, 1975, Denver, CO; [p.] Alan D. Morris and Ramona K. Faust; [m.] Elizabeth A. Morris; [ch.] October 7, 1994; [ed.] Ponderosa High, and Defense Language Institute at Monterey, CA; [occ.] Naval Linguist; [hon.] Defense Language Institute - Dean's List/Provost Award, Best Actor - 1993 Harvey Awards; [pers.] A philosopher, I'm definitely not, but I can honestly say, that my incredible wife is the blood that flows

through the veins of my poetry. Without her influence, they would just be words straining to rhyme.; [a.] Wahiawa, HI

MORRIS, NANCY
[pen.] Nancy Laline; [b.] February 8, 1938, La Jolla, CA; [p.] Stephen and Anna Tranbsky Bradaric; [ch.] Candice, Melanie, Jan and John; [ed.] Pasadena Jr. College, Beirut University College, London Film Academy; [occ.] Sr. Technical Writer, Consultant; [memb.] Authors Guild Society of Technical Communications; [oth. writ.] Columnist, Copywriter, Technical Articles, Short Stories, etc. Anything and Everything!; [pers.] Poetry speaks from the heart; [a.] Hamilton, MT

MORRISSETTE, SCOTT ALAN
[b.] May 7, 1967, Fall River, MA; [p.] Nancy Olival, Robert Morrissette (deceased); [m.] Single; [ed.] Completed High School at Westport High, 1 1/2 semesters at U-mass Dartmouth (Biology); [occ.] Look-Bayside Rest, Westport, MA; [memb.] World Wildlife Fund Smithsonian Institute, National Association of Weathercaster, AAA Auto Club; [oth. writ.] No other published writings, have written other poems and short stories; [pers.] Interested in becoming a meteorologist. I've been looking for Mrs. Right, but I keep finding Mrs. Wrong, I've been influenced by my own life experience, both good and bad; [a.] Westport, MA

MORROW, MR. ROBERT J.
[pen.] Rabboni Makar; [b.] August 29, 1951, Westerly, RI; [p.] Joseph R. and Priscilla S.; [ed.] Chaminade College, La Salle Univ.; [occ.] Entrepreneurial; [memb.] Highlander Club, American Legion; [hon.] Military - High Academic Award; [oth. writ.] Poems and articles published in local newspapers. Self published "mind the master" series books 1-4 (included in the Regan Presidential Library) also an unpublish screenplay called "The Fifth Street Murders"; [pers.] A friend from Switzerland put it best and I quote... "In my simple way of thinking, every single one of your poems is extraordinarily beautiful in its human sensibility" Barsey Calvary, Locarno; [a.] Orlando, FL

MORSE, CHRISTIAN A.
[pen.] Allen Christian; [b.] April 12, 1970, Attleboro, MA; [p.] George, Elizabeth; [ed.] North Attleboro High, Hall Institute; [occ.] Drafter; [memb.] Masspirg; [oth. writ.] Several poems not yet published; [pers.] I write by my heart. I know when I write a poem and before I even get to the next line. I know what I want to say, then that's my best work.; [a.] North Attleboro, MA

MORSE, TAMMY
[b.] February 21, 1979, Manchester, NH; [p.] Ron and Mona Morse; [ed.] Still in Goffstown High School; [occ.] Student; [oth. writ.] I have written many of other poems. I get my ideals from the people and the surrounding around me.; [pers.] It is always hard to say how you feel. But for me I find it a little easier writing poems to show my feelings.

MOSS, TAMARA L.
[pen.] Tamara L. Moss; [b.] October 29, 1974, Dublin, GA; [p.] Roosevelt and Delois Moos; [m.]

Single; [ed.] Dublin High, Middle Georgia College; [occ.] Student, Education Major; [memb.] Wabash C.O.G. (Church Of God), Middle Georgia College Newspaper Staff; [oth. writ.] Poems Published in local newspaper, several short stories; [pers.] I want to remind people that, we are the future and if we don't take care of our world there won't be a future. The children are our biggest investment, love them.; [a.] Dublin, GA

MRKVICKA, KELLY HELEN
[b.] March 4, 1977, Woodstock, IL; [p.] Edward F. Mrkvicka Jr., Madelyn H. Mrkvicka; [ed.] 1995 Graduate Marian Central Catholic HS. Woodstock, IL; [occ.] Student; [hon.] All American Scholar, Outstanding Science Award, Math Achievement Award, Anthology of Poetry by Young Americans, Spanish National Honors Society, Composition Writing Award, Presidential Academic Fitness Award, Top 10% of Class Awards, Presidential Physical Fitness Awards; [pers.] You learn what you live, and you live what you learn; [a.] Marengo, IL

MUELLER, MARC C.
[b.] August 23, 1949, Bluffs, IL; [p.] Coin and Aliene Mueller and Ellen Bernadine Wilcox Mueller; [m.] Judy Graves Mueller, November 13, 1971; [ch.] Marc Christopher and Maryon Colleen; [ed.] Bluffs High, Illinois College, Lincoln Land College; [occ.] Poet, Novelist; [pers.] To worry about what one can not change is a waste of valuable time and energy. We should all strive to improve this world for our children's future in whatever way we can.; [a.] Bluffs, IL

MUHAMMAD, MARZUQ
[pen.] Marcus Charlton; [b.] July 6, 1970, Fort Wayne, IN; [p.] Debra Charlton; [ch.] Marcus Jr., Marquavis, Marquanitta; [ed.] Norcoss High, DeKalb Tech, Mercer University; [occ.] Chef, Head cook; [oth. writ.] Several poems and songs; [pers.] I truly enjoy writing poems. I write from life experiences and my own feelings. I hope to become a poem writer to inspire the world. I want to thank God for this wonderful talent.; [a.] Doraville, GA

MUKHERJEE, SONJIT
[b.] February 22, 1968, Jacksonville, IL; [p.] Subhash Chandra Mukherjee, (Father), Bharoti Mukherjee, (Mother); [ed.] Central Catholic High School, Lawrence, MA, Boston College, Bachelor's Degree, Chestnut Hill, MA, Boston University Graduate School of Social Work, M.S.W. degree, Boston, MA; [occ.] Social Worker; [hon.] Billy Sansoucie Literary Award, Robert Gallagher Award Scholarship, Youth Of The Month Award (The Ladies Exchange Club), Youth Of The Year Award (April 1986, from The Ladies Exchange Club), Presidential Scholar; [oth. writ.] Poetry and Prose in personal collection.; [pers.] Never speak ill or look with scorn upon any person or creature. Cogitate and feel with the heart. Reflect the prism of life through your senses and intellect. Recreate these feelings with passion in your writings.; [a.] North Andover, MA

MULLINAX, JENNY LYNNE
[pen.] Jen; [b.] August 11, 1958, San Bernardino, CA; [p.] Charles Moore, Marcella Moore; [m.]

William Everett Mullinax, October 25, 1992; [ch.] Jimmy Lee, Cindy Lynne, Richard Lee, Shawna Dee; [occ.] Housewife, poet; [memb.] First Church of the Nazarene; [hon.] Honor Roll 3 yrs. Pacific High School; [oth. writ.] One of my Poems that was entered at A.B. Miller High Library Contest won a special recognition ribbon, which goes on to the states finalist contest.; [pers.] Thanks to my wonderful husband and children who have greatly inspired my talent for my love of reading and writing my poetry; [a.] Fontana, CA

MULLINAX, XEMENIA
[pen.] Xemenia; [b.] January 8, 1958, Des Arc, AR; [p.] John M. Willis and Ora Mae Bridges; [m.] Larry Mullinax, January 21, 1985; [ch.] Nick Stacy, Matthew Mullinax; [ed.] Des Arc High; [occ.] Housekeeper; [memb.] Glad Tidings Church of God. National Rifle Association; [hon.] Receiving a response letter from President Clinton; [oth. writ.] Seven Years, God Can Comfort, It Happened One Easter, all poems written for a special person or family member.; [pers.] I love to make people laugh and touch their hearts through my poems; [a.] Phillipsburg, MO

MULVANEY, DARYL J.
[b.] July 26, 1974, Easton, PA; [p.] James Mulvaney, Marsha Mulvaney; [m.] Single; [ed.] Graduates of Easton Area High School; [occ.] Cook; [oth. writ.] Have written numerous poems and prose which are not available to the public (not published).; [pers.] It's not the one big event in life, but the sum of all the little one's that count.; [a.] Nazareth, PA

MULVIHILL, IRENE
[b.] December 23, 1975, Smithtown; [p.] Olives Mulvihill, Helen Mulvihill; [ed.] Sachem High School; [occ.] Student; [memb.] National Honor Society Dimensions (Sachem's Literary mag) Girl Scouts Wonderful Outdoor Women; [hon.] Gold Award in Girl Scouts, Silver Award in Girl Scouts; [a.] Holbrook, NY

MUNSON, JOSETTE ROSE
[b.] July 19, 1979, Toledo, OH; [p.] Luther Munson - Jennifer Knoblach; [ed.] Now in 10th grade Tylertown High School Tylertown, MS; [occ.] Student; [oth. writ.] 2 poems published previously by the National Library of Poetry plus 200 unpublished; [pers.] Have been writing poems since 11 years old, I show my dreams, feelings and emotions in my poems and try to make others see in life what I see.; [a.] Tylertown, MS

MURILLO, YESSENIA
[pen.] Jessie Franco; [b.] July 1, 1978, New York, NY; [p.] Lester E. Murillo Sr. and Maria Murillo; [ed.] High School Jr.; [hon.] Honorable Mention in Iliad Literary Awards Program; [oth. writ.] One poem published in remembrances.; [pers.] Don't let life's hardships bring you down, just sit down and write about them. And always do what your heart desires.; [a.] New York, NY

MURKLEY, LESLEY ANN
[b.] April 5, 1982, Fairfield, CA; [p.] Dale and Wanda Murkley; [ed.] Currently in 7th grade at McKenzie High School; [occ.] Student (Jr. High);

[hon.] Honor Roll Student, Student of the Month; [pers.] I like to write about whales to hopefully send peaceful thought's through a reader's mind and let them know about whales' existence.; [a.] Blue River, OR

MURPHY, ELIZABETH L.
[b.] January 11, 1943, Bronx, NY; [p.] Henry C. Scherf/Eleanor Mergner; [m.] Michael F. Murphy Jr., October 20, 1962; [ch.] Michael Charles, Karen Ann, Christopher James, (grandchildren) Brian Michael, Christina Marie, Jessica Ann, (brothers) Henry Scherf, Michael Scherf; [ed.] Cathedral H.S. Thorde Secretarial Quecsborough College; [occ.] Self-employed; [pers.] Influenced by motherhood. Devotion to children, Spouse, grandchildren and all family members.; [a.] Bronx, NY

MURRAY, RETHA SLOTER
[b.] January 17, 1941, Newark, OH; [p.] William Clifford Sloter and Shirley Mildred Wehr Sloter; [m.] Patrick William Murray (div.), September 1962 div July 1991; [ch.] Corinna, Karen, Lonnie, Russell, Daniel, Wade, Sheila, Shirla, and Jason; [ed.] Associates Degree Ohio State, Bachelor's Degree in Education, I graduate June 9, 1995; [occ.] Student at Ohio State University Library assistant at Ohio State; [hon.] National Dean Lists 1991/1992 and 1994/1995; [oth. writ.] Poem When You Get Home published in Treasured Poems of America by Sparrow grass Poetry Forum.

MUSIC, KAYLA LEE
[b.] August 19, 1983, Prestonsburg, KY; [p.] Debra Kay (Blanton) Music; [ch.] Katlin Music (brother); [occ.] Student (6th grade) Metro North Elementary School Wabash, Indiana; [a.] Wabash, IN

MYERS, RACHEL A.
[pen.] Rap; [b.] November 8, 1960, Alton, IL; [p.] Joe and Carol Powell; [m.] Geffrey A. Myers, December 24, 1989; [ch.] Sara Ann, Sandy Renee, Shelly Jean, Step children, Olivia M., Patrick J., Elaine C.; [ed.] High School; [occ.] Mother and Housewife; [oth. writ.] A collection of poetry written since 1978; [pers.] It delights me to know that someone will enjoy reading my poetry as much as I enjoyed writing it.; [a.] Brighton, IL

NANNI, VINCENT
[b.] February 9, 1926, Franklin, MA; [p.] Dominick and Josephine (deceased); [m.] Maria, June 25, 1950; [ch.] Josephine, D. James, Carmela, Mark, Daniel; [ed.] High School, Navy Gunnery and Air Recognize School; [occ.] Retired; [memb.] American Legion; [hon.] WW II European Theatre Awards and two Victory Medals; [oth. writ.] "Within The Darkest Shadows", "In Name Alone, The Wartburg Home", "Of The Heart And Mind".; [a.] Yonkers, NY

NARDO, RITA A.
[b.] October 3, 1953; [p.] Joseph and Genevieve Nardo; [ed.] Our Lady of Mt. Carmel, William McKinley High, Y.S.U., North Central Tech. College, Ohio State School of Cosmetology; [occ.] Nursing-public service; [hon.] N.C.T.C. Dean's List, several poems published in the college's Literary-magazine called Transitions published at

N.C.T.C. College-Mansfield, OH 44906; [oth. writ.] I have written many other poems and short stories.; [pers.] I believe that genuine love is the strongest force in the universe. I believe genuine love can conquer all and I work hard to express the feeling of genuine love in my writing. I'm an incurable romantic at heart who loves humanity dearly.; [a.] Mansfield, OH

NATAL, MELISSA
[b.] May 24, 1982, San Juan, PR; [p.] Carmen D. Lugo and Santiago Natal; [ed.] St. Mary Immaculate Conception Grammar School; [occ.] Student; [a.] Lawrence, MA

NATURAL, LENNY
[pen.] Leonardo Naturale; [b.] June 25, 1961, Niles, OH; [p.] Mr. and Mrs Angelo Natural; [ed.] G.E.D. and to date 34 of a year of college; [occ.] Exotic dancer, construction work; [memb.] Tropical gym in Pompano Beach, FL; [hon.] This is my first publication.; [oth. writ.] Currently editing a book of philosophical thoughts a compulation due out in the end of the year 1996; [pers.] My poetry and writings are directed towards people who feel poetry is boring. And to those who enjoy a change though I am new I have many books (notebooks) for years of thought; [a.] Pompano Beach, FL

NAVAL, APRIL
[pen.] April Johnson or AJ; [b.] January 21, 1971, CA; [p.] Grace Johnson, James Johnson; [m.] July Naval, May 24, 1992; [ch.] Benigno J. Naval II; [ed.] Tennyson High, Valecitos C.E.T.; [occ.] Housewife and Manager of Naval Properties; [memb.] Second Chance Center. Project Open Hand.; [hon.] Top five computer tech. from Valecitos C.E.T. Honor student of Tennyson High; [oth. writ.] Night of Violence, A Fool's Advice, People of the Streets, A Friend Like You, My Little One. Which I'm waiting to be published.; [pers.] To my son Ben: Lonely is the heart. The heart which has no knowledge of love. Love that comes from another spirit, without spirit there isn't soul. Soul leads to life. The meaning of life is love from the heart towards the spirit of the soul.; [a.] Stockton, CA

NEAL, MARQUITA D.
[b.] January 14, 1977, Philadelphia, PA; [p.] Evelyn Neal; [ed.] Germantown High School, Temple University-freshman; [occ.] Student; [memb.] Gospel Light Church, Phi Sumga Pi Honor Fraternity, Outstanding Achievement Scholarship Steering Committee; [hon.] National Honor Society, National Spanish Honor Society, Valedictorian, Outstanding Achievement Scholarship Recipient; [pers.] In my writings I attempt to reflect what so many young people face growing up in the cities of America.; [a.] Philadelphia, PA

NELSON, DEBRA A.
[b.] June 15, 1955, CT; [p.] Marion and Homer Cobb; [ed.] New Bedford HS, New Bedford, MA; [occ.] Internat'l A/P-Johnson Worldwide Assoc.; [memb.] I.D.M.R.; [pers.] Special thanks to those I love, your love and belief in me is my inspiration.; [a.] Binghamton, NY

NESS, GERTRUDE J.
[pen.] Gee-Jaye; [b.] January 8, 1923, Wolverine, MI; [ch.] Darryl, Philip, Ness, James, Janet Wood; [ed.] High School; [occ.] Retired; [oth. writ.] None, first attempt at writing poetry.; [pers.] Poetry makes me aware of Life around me. It encompasses everything good and bad.; [a.] Calumet, MI

NEUMAN, LILLIAN
[b.] October 13, 1957, NY; [p.] William Neuman, Brenda Neuman; [ch.] Ashley and Michael; [ed.] Christopher Columbus H.S., Iona College; [occ.] Certified Alcoholic Counselor; [pers.] My experiences in my life have made me a stronger and richer person, my poems reflect those experiences and what I have gained from them.; [a.] Harrison, NY

NEVILLE, ANDREW THOMAS
[pen.] TTG; [b.] August 26, 1938, Rocky Mount, NC; [p.] Leonard and Bertha Neville; [ch.] Andy Neville, Grandson Andrew; [ed.] Enfield High School, NC Wesleyan College; [occ.] Store proprietor and US Postal Carrier; [memb.] Eden United Methodist Church, Church choir, postal union, Enfield Lions Club; [hon.] Church treasurer, President PTA; [oth. writ.] Poems used in church newspaper-local library and poems published in Treasured Poems of America; [a.] Enfield, NC

NEVILLE, NICHOLAS
[pen.] Nick Neville; [b.] January 16, 1980, Los Angeles, CA; [p.] Debra and Richard; [ed.] Elkin Academy; [occ.] Student; [hon.] Honor Roll, Editors Choice Award; [oth. writ.] Earth a poem; [pers.] My writing comes from the feeling I have from life. I write for the fun of it and the joy it gives me and others.; [a.] Los Angeles, CA

NEWBY, YASHICA
[pen.] Shica; [b.] February 13, 1981, Detroit, MI; [p.] Wanda and Alfred Newby; [ed.] I attend Durfee Middle School. I'm in the 8th grade and plan on going to Murry Wright High School after completing 8th grade.; [memb.] I'm the co-captain on the Cheer Squad. And have a membership to the Vision Club, and Science Club.; [hon.] I have a award for Outstanding Achievement and have a award for cheering. I also have an 8th grade diploma. And have a grade point average of 3.3.; [pers.] I want to encourage young writers that in order to succeed their dreams they must stay in school and become anything they want to be. Reading is the key to success.; [a.] Detroit, MI

NEWSOM, MARJORIE BRUNTON
[b.] January 20, 1909, Cape Breton Island, Canada; [p.] John and Ruby Brunton; [m.] Stugh Newsom (deceased), August 23, 1937; [ed.] High School, 5 years New England Conservatory of Music, where graduated as concert baptist and pianist. Study by self: Literature and Mandarin, Chinese.; [occ.] Writing classical pieces for the harp, 2 volumes complete and painting in oils.; [memb.] For some years member of the American Harp Society, otherwise not a joiner.; [hon.] Some poetry awards - some acclaim as a concert harpist for 4 years, U.S., Canada, Mexico.; [oth. writ.]

Short stories, essays, unfinished novel in Chaucerian English. Edited and placed in libraries all late husband's (Hugh Newsom) oratories and concert songs, harp and piano words.; [pers.] To make utmost possible use of whatever talents one has been given to live as honorably as possible in a corrupt world-to appreciate and reverence all beauty and goodness.; [a.] Hollywood, FL

NGUYEN, VIEN MINH
[pen.] Minh-Vien; [b.] January 18, 1940, Vietnam; [m.] Huong Ngo Nguyen, 1969; [ch.] Khoi Nguyen (son), An Nguyen (daughter), Daisy Nguyen (daughter); [ed.] Saigon University, Vietnam; [memb.] Vietnam, P.E.N. Center, Association of Free Vietnamese Writers and Artists, The International Society of Poets; [hon.] Editor's Choice Award (1994), The International Poet of Merit Award (1994); [oth. writ.] Published works of poetry: The Moon, Vietnam: A Nightmare War, Blue Rain, Saigon: The Unhealed Wound, etc.; [pers.] Poetry is the mirror reflecting human life.; [a.] San Francisco, CA

NICHOLS, JESSICA R.
[b.] November 20, 1981, Flagstaff, AR; [p.] Heidi and Art Nichols; [ed.] Currently in 7th grade at Mt. Elden Middle School (April 1995); [occ.] Student, babysitter, flutist; [memb.] Nazarene Church Youth Group, School band, 7th grade Volleyball team.; [hon.] 4.0 G.P.A. 1st sem, 7th grade, still on honor roll. Winner of Cromer School Spelling Bee, 6th grade (1994). Certificate of Merit for flute duet.; [pers.] In the future, I hope to finish school, go to college, and become an interior designer. Dolphins are my favorite animal and I love to babysit.; [a.] Flagstaff, AZ

NICOL, DAVID W.
[b.] November 3, 1966, Putnam, CT; [p.] Arthur and Irene Nicol; [ed.] St. Bernard High; [oth. writ.] Poem 'Love' and Between the Raindrops; [pers.] Power is all around us it is up to all to take and use for the good of all LIFE; [a.] Plainfield, CA

NINNESS, BARBARA SHOTTER
[b.] London, England; [p.] George Frederick and Alice Shotter; [m.] Widowed; [ed.] Crouch End College, London U.K. Royal Society of Arts; [occ.] Paralegal; [hon.] Diplomas: Royal Academy of Music, Royal Drawing Society, Scholarship to Slade School of Art; [oth. writ.] Children's verses, short stories and all forms of poetry; [pers.] To express ones love of writing, music and art reflects the deepest and most intimate part of ones self the soul.; [a.] Gloucester, MA

NOEL, HARRY
[pen.] Neil Richards; [b.] November 25, 1935, Wellsville, MO; [p.] Richard and Geneva Noel; [ed.] Graduate of High School-Soldan High St. Louis, MO, two years College; [oth. writ.] Mostly political editorials. First poem to be published.; [pers.] I have been influenced much by the writings of William James.

NOLLER, MARIANN
[pen.] Marianna DeFrank Hancock Noller; [b.] May 15, 1945; [ch.] Heath, Eddie; [occ.] Woodcrafts; [pers.] "To my guardian angel" is

dedicated to the loving memory of my son Eddie Hancock.; [a.] Brookfield, NY

NORRIS, KRISTEN
[b.] December 27, 1978, Cincinnati, OH; [p.] Paul Norris, Rosemary Norris; [ed.] I am a sophomore at Hughes Center High School; [hon.] B-honors and perfect attendance from school; [oth. writ.] Short stories and other poems that haven't been submitted.; [pers.] I want to give a special thanks to my new mother and great friend, Michele Norris.; [a.] Cincinnati, OH

NOSSER, DOLORES P.
[pen.] Dee Dee; [b.] August 8, 1931, Vicksburg, MS; [p.] Sara J. Duck and Toufic Nosser; [m.] Divorced, April 1951; [ch.] Vicki Ariatti, Micki Brooks, Kathy Haach, Sheila McInnis; [ed.] High School; [occ.] Retired-disability (over 30 years of racehorse groom and training) also gourmet chef, Shortorder cook, waitress and carhop.; [memb.] YMCA-joining for water aerobics and other exercises; [hon.] National Library of Poetry (award for poetry). Most enthusiastic Award for Wall plagues of Poetry (club house) at Rockingham Park-Art Exhibit (race track) Salem, NH 1993. Name of winning title for no. 1 line, "Memories of the Past".; [oth. writ.] I have over 300 poems (folder of love poems) to publish. I also have a folder of on and off duty (in humor) of life at (Rock Park) horse training, employees, owners and trainers. Also a beautiful true story of a great racehorse is included.; [pers.] I strive to publish my race horse poetry into a paper-back book. I also may publish many true stories of many unusual incidents in my lifetime.; [a.] Jackson, MS

NOVAK, AMBER
[b.] August 22, 1981, IA; [p.] Cindy and Jeff Novak; [ed.] I am in the 7th grade at Nashville Jr. High; [occ.] Student; [memb.] I am in the F.B.L.A. Chapter at school and am in 4-H club and have the job of historian. I play the trumpet in the school band.; [oth. writ.] 4-H Articles published in the newspaper.; [pers.] I wouldn't have even written this poem if it hadn't been for my English teacher Mrs. Davis and I want to thank her.; [a.] Nashville, AR

NYBO, JENNIFER L.
[b.] January 9, 1979, Tracy Hospital; [p.] Cynthia E. Nybo, Thomas H. Nybo; [ed.] I'm in tenth grade in Tracy High School; [occ.] Student; [memb.] United Methodist Youth Group; [hon.] I lettered in choir; [oth. writ.] I have over a hundred poems but none of them are published.; [pers.] I just write what I feel and out it all together.; [a.] Tracy, MN

O'BRIEN III, PHILIP G.
[pen.] Phillie; [b.] June 3, 1968, Ellsworth, ME; [p.] Philip O'Brien Jr., Shirley Gulowsen; [m.] Stephanie "Wiley" O'Brien, December 27, 1989; [ed.] Bucksport High School, University of Maine, Bob Jones University Biblical Education-Applied Theology; [occ.] P.O.W. Maine State Prison; [memb.] Jaycees, Amnesty Int'l Wiccan Community, Tattoo America, Coalition for Prisoners Rights, NAACP, The Amherst Society, Crystal Star, Recovering Addicts, A.A.; [hon.] Editors

Choice Award N.L.P., Certificate of Poetic Achievement-Amherst Society, Loves Lost Donna Skillins, Roxanne Hardie, My Family "Lamh Laidir An Uachtar", all those in prison, may they be free behind the walls, peace.; [oth. writ.] Of The Sky, The River, Forgive Me, Your Love, Between The World of Dawn, Leo's Pride, Amanda, Battle of the Bulge, Yesterday, Dream State, With a Witch, To Roxie, In Memory of, Suicide Solutions, Unforgiven, Lamh Laidir An Uachtar; [pers.] Thanks again to all those in my life, they know who they are. I wish I had learned long ago what I know today. For I love more today than ever before. And I have become a better person having been in hell. I know If I love, if I try harder, I will make it.; [a.] Thomaston, ME

O'BRIEN, LACEY
[b.] April 21, 1981, Cleburne, TX; [p.] Tim and Mary Ann O'Brien; [ed.] Eight grade student at Whittemore Park Middle School; [memb.] Cheerleader dancer, Gymnast National Show Stoppers; [hon.] 3rd place winner Horry County S.C. Library Short Stories Talent Identification Program, Duke Univ.

O'DELL, JAIME D.
[pen.] J. D. O'Dell; [b.] September 22, 1978, Santa Rosa; [p.] Katherine S. O'Dell; [pers.] When I started writing, it was long me. I never expected to enter a contest, or get published. At 16, I find writing the best expression of myself. If you like writing, never stop. Something unexpected may occur.; [a.] Chula Vista, CA

O'FARRELL, SANDRA LEE
[pen.] Sandra O'Farrell; [b.] February 9, 1943, New Orleans, LA; [p.] Daisy and Paul Green; [m.] Donald D. O'Farrell, February 23, 1963; [ch.] Beth and Bart O'Farrell; [ed.] Middle School-also high school grad. and Secretary College; [occ.] Teaches children and adults to swim and writes; [memb.] Board of Director's for the Krewe of Columbus Poet's Society; [hon.] Girl's Softball Letter, seven poems-all published Poets Award-1993, High School Poetry Award 1961, Cooking Awards 4 ribbons won; [oth. writ.] The 3rd Voyage 1995, Nixon Peacemaker 1994, Tears 1994, "My Beth" 1994, Santa Fe 1994, The Poet 1995, Far and Away 1995; [pers.] This poem "Mother Dear" is dedicated to my precious mother, Mrs. Daisy Bedell Green. She worked very hard all of her life and raised 6 children. She lives in Louisiana.; [a.] Navarre, FL

O'HAIR, SUSAN E.
[b.] July 13, 1939, San Francisco, CA; [p.] Donald L. O'Hair, Jane Larsen Hudkins; [ed.] Burlingame High School, Sacramento State College; [occ.] Retired Educator; [memb.] AAUW, Eugene O'Neill Foundation, Life Member NEA-CTA California Writer's Club, Society of Children's Book Writers and Illust. Library of Congress, Romance Writers of America; [hon.] 1989 Teacher of the Year San Ramon Valley, U.S.D., WHO (We Honor Ours) from local CTA, Mentor Teacher 3 years. Who's Who in Education 1992.; [oth. writ.] Poems in books and magazines, working on children's novel; [a.] San Ramon, CA

O'MEARA, SHANNAH
[b.] December 3, 1982, Valparaiso, IN; [p.] Kurt and Patty Moldenhauer; [ed.] Now in 6th grade at Galena Elementary; [pers.] She is her mothers pride and joy!; [a.] Rolling Prairie, IN

O'NEAL, RAY N.
[b.] January 11, 1932, Tryssville, AL; [p.] James and Pearl O'Neal; [m.] Divorced; [ch.] Teresa, Winifred, Peggy and Fred; [ed.] City College San Diego, CA; [occ.] Retired; [memb.] Christian Faith and The International Society of Poets; [hon.] Dean's List; [oth. writ.] Published in four books-River of Dream, Best Poems of 1995, East Of The Sunrise, at Water's Edge. Recorded in the "Sound of Poetry" and "Visions". Other poems pending.; [pers.] Listen to the song of life and share discreetly.; [a.] San Diego, CA

ODELL, HAZEL
[b.] June 5, 1922, Sevierville, TN; [p.] James and Susan Benson; [m.] James Odell, December 15, 1942; [ch.] Carolyn, James, Mary, John, David, Ethel; [ed.] 9th grade; [occ.] Housewife; [memb.] Piney Level Baptist Church; [oth. writ.] I have helped raise 4 grandchildren, Justin Hurst owe the poem is about the others are working now. I have 9 grandchildren. I love them all.; [pers.] My husband and I celebrated our 50th Wedding Anniversary 2 years ago. We have had a happy marriage; [a.] TN

ODOM, CINDY
[b.] February 28, 1951, Elwood, IN; [p.] Robert and Lola Benedict; [m.] Steve, January 5, 1969; [ch.] Lisa, Bradley and Brett; [ed.] Currently enrolled-IUPUI Nursing Program; [occ.] Working with Autistic teenage boys; [pers.] Writing is an important part of my chosen profession. I have to be able to write about the prevailing needs of convalescents-as well as their state of health, in a pertinent and satisfactory manner. I enjoy being outside, therefore my poetry reflects things of nature, scenery, animals, etc. Along with poetry writing, I enjoy photography. I often write about a picture I have taken. I would like to be successful with both. I hope whoever reads my poems, enjoys them as much as I enjoyed creating them.; [a.] Franklin, IN

OGBUIKE, CHINEDU DEAN
[pen.] Chin, Dean; [b.] April 21, 1974, Roxbury, MA; [p.] Felicia and Gregory Ogbuike; [ed.] Boston Latin School (H.S.) September 1989-June 1992, Boston University (college) September 1992-December 1993, University of Massachusetts Amherst January 1994 present anticipated graduation May 1996; [occ.] Resident Assistant; [memb.] Black Student Union, Daily Collegian, CCEBMS all at UMASS Amherst; [hon.] National Library of Poetry's Editor's Choice Award 1994, ALANA Honors Society at UMASS campus Center Print Shop, Certificate of Appreciation Group III First Prize May 20, 1990, age 15, copyright June 13, 1994, Dean's List.; [oth. writ.] Copyright for 55 poems of my one hundred poems last year.; [pers.] If I can't help myself that there is no way I can possible help someone else. My poems reflect my true feelings inside along with my personal experiences.; [a.] Roxbury, MA

OKPE, SOLACE
[pen.] Solace Ogechukwu; [b.] June 24, 1967, Lagos; [p.] Benjamin and Love Okde (deceased); [ch.] Chizomam Okpe; [ed.] Under-grad. degree, Electronic Technology-Engineering, New York, NY; [occ.] Auto-Technician; [oth. writ.] Unpublished; [pers.] I have found out that the knowledge of God Almighty and the things about Him are the greatest control and standard for all humanity; [a.] Jersey City, NJ

OLDHAM, AUDREY
[pen.] Sam Leavitt; [b.] November 16, 1981, Reno, NV; [p.] Dale and Linda Oldham; [ed.] At present, a 7th grader; [occ.] Student; [memb.] Track, choir, G/T; [hon.] Honor Student; [oth. writ.] "Envy" and "My Special Place", both published poems; [pers.] I find writing to be a wonderful source of release from the stress of daily life.; [a.] Blackfoot, ID

OLIVER, GRACE G.
[b.] Murphy, NC; [m.] Felix "Red" Oliver (deceased); [ch.] One son; [ed.] BS Degree Elementary Education, University of Tennessee at Chattanooga; [occ.] Retired Math and Science teacher from the Chattanooga Public Schools. A team leader for three years in a middle school from which I retired.; [memb.] Life member of the Tennessee P.T.A., Brainerd United Methodist Church, Who's Who Among America's Teachers and Outstanding Elementary Teacher of America.; [hon.] Past President of International Reading Association of Chattanooga Council and past Secretary for the Tennessee State Dixie Youth Baseball for which I was given a plaque for each.

OLIVERI, NAT
[b.] April 28, 1955, Brooklyn, NY; [p.] Carl Oliveri, Mary Oliveri; [ed.] Connecticut High School, St. John's University; [oth. writ.] Poems, and songs dealing with sensitivity and passion; [pers.] Life's experience is my inspiration and motivation; [a.] Oakdale, NY

OLIVIER, COURTNEY
[b.] November 28, 1981, New Orleans; [p.] Edward and Cynthia; [ed.] 8th student; [memb.] Drama Club; [a.] Paris, TN

OLSEN, ANGELA MANE
[pen.] A.M.O.; [b.] December 6, 1968, Iran Mountain, MI; [p.] Patricia S. Olsen, Jerry E. Olsen; [ed.] Hamilton College-B.A., Georgetown University, Catholic University of America-M.S.; [memb.] International Society of Poets; [hon.] Editor's Choice Award, Journey of the Mind-1994; [oth. writ.] "The Rosebud" published in Journey of the Mind. "The Raven's Rape" published in East of the Sunrise; [pers.] I have been strongly influenced by the Asian styles of writing, and by my studies of analytical symbolism in Hong Kong. The existential slant of my works blows life and spirit into my symbols. Their existence is an embodiment of powerful emotion.

OPARAH, BERNARD I.
[pen.] Ijedimma Bernard Oparah; [b.] April 9, 1945, Umuaka, Imo Nigeria; [p.] Boniface A. and Cecelia Oparah; [m.] Dawn C. Oparah, May 26, 1978; [ch.] Chinenye, Kelechukwu Ogechi, Chinonso; [ed.] Bishop Shanahan College Orlu Nigeria, Indiana University of Pennsylvania, Miami University, OH; [occ.] School Psychologist; [memb.] Phi Delta Kappa Professional Fraternity in Education, National Association of School Psychologists, Georgia Association of School Psychologists, American Counseling Association; [hon.] Distinguished Dissertation Award (Phi Delta Kappa), Outstanding Faculty Annual Award; [oth. writ.] Wings of Love: selected poems by Ijedimma B. Oparah (1995). Article for the Dialogue.; [pers.] People are spiritual beings having a human experience. We are called to love!; [a.] Peachtree City, GA

OPRIS, GIANINA
[b.] September 30, 1963, Peru; [p.] David and Raquel Corrales; [m.] Petru Opris, September 24, 1982; [ch.] David and Jamie; [ed.] Colegio Rosa De America (Peru), Queensborough Community College; [occ.] Bilingual Teacher's Assistant and Receptionist Support Staff Marin Community Foundation; [memb.] Bilingual School Advisory Committee (Coronado School), MCF Arts Committee; [hon.] Chairperson Bilingual Advisory Committee; [oth. writ.] A poem published in a local paper "Artists Dialogue". An article in Spanish in a local Spanish paper.; [pers.] I bring in my writing all the respect and values from my background. I feel fortunate to have most of my inspirations based on good role models from my childhood and from the history of life!; [a.] Albany, CA

OSEGUERA, ELVIRA CEJA
[b.] March 19, 1969, Mexico; [p.] Enrique and Juana Ceja; [ed.] BA Child Development from California State, L.A.; [occ.] Elementary School Teacher; [hon.] Nominated poet of the year for 1995 by National Library of Poetry. Received Editor's Choice Award for "Riddle".; [oth. writ.] In Journey of the Mind, Alchemy, Statement Magazine, River Sedge, Untitled and Inspirations.; [a.] Huntington Park, CA

OSHER, REGINA LYNN
[pen.] Gina Osher; [b.] February 11, 1951, Topeka, KS; [ed.] El Cerrito High School, El Cerrito, CA. University of Oregon, Eugene, OR; [occ.] Employment Counselor Alameda County Social Services Agency Oakland, CA; [oth. writ.] I have authored approximately 70 poems to date. I have also written three children's stories: The Legend of Greenhorn, The Barefoot Boy and Sky and Cloud Together, as well as an article, "Journal of a Californian" about my experiences, observations, thoughts and responses in regard to the 1989 Bay Area Earthquake.; [pers.] I believe people should be connected by the down-to-earth aspects of life and I revere Mother Earth. I try to reflect this in my poetry. I try to create poetry that will promote peace on earth and peace of mind and which is timeless and enjoyable to all.; [a.] Alameda, CA

OSTRANDER, SARAH J.
[pen.] Sis; [b.] June 4, 1981, Albany, NY; [p.] Michael and Pam Ostrander; [ed.] 8th student, Ravena Coeymans-Selkirk Middle School; [occ.] Student; [hon.] Honor Roll, 7th/8th grade, highest average Bowling '93, All Star Team Softball '93, Highest High Series Bowling '94; [pers.] Enjoys soccer, bowling and softball.

OSTROFF, BENJAMIN
[b.] November 24, 1978, NY; [p.] Dr. James Ostroff and Cynthia Ostroff; [occ.] 16 year old student; [oth. writ.] Mostly worked dark poems about my life and experiences.; [pers.] Every second lived is a second passed, a second you'll never have again, so live life how you want to and not how others want you to.; [a.] San Francisco, CA

OSWEILER, GREG
[b.] January 10, 1970, Tucson, AZ; [p.] George and Sue Osweiler; [m.] Laura Hosch, June 14, 1995; [ed.] Valley High School, Las Vegas, NV, University of Nevada Las Vegas; [memb.] U.N.L.V.'s Honors Program, Golden Key National Honors Society; [hon.] Graduated from U.N.L.V. with honors, recipient of Mildred P. Cotner Alumni Scholarship, Dean's List; [oth. writ.] "Out of Gas" is the first piece I've tried to publish. Writing poetry is my first love, but I enjoy writing prose as well - mainly short stories. Someday, I hope soon, I can publish more of my work.; [pers.] Good writing, especially literature, allows us to explore and map the undisclosed diversity of experience. In doing so, we manifest the potentials obscured by limiting familiarity and champion all of our faculties.; [a.] Las Vegas, NV

OTOSHI, YOSHIYUKI
[b.] July 23, 1920, Hiroshima, Japan; [p.] Asazo Otoshi, Tamano Otoshi; [m.] Betty Kiyoko Otoshi; [ch.] Grant Yukio and Beverly Yukino; [ed.] McKinley High School (Honolulu), American Institute of Banking (Standard Certificate); [occ.] Retired since 1985, after working 43 years with First Hawaiian Bank as an accountant; [memb.] Honolulu Japanese Chamber of Commerce, Hawaii Economic Study Club, Honpa Hongwanji Mission of Hawaii, Japanese Cultural Center of Hawaii; [hon.] Distinguished Member, International Society of Poets, Editor's Choice Award presented by The National Library of Poet; [oth. writ.] My poem, "Of Tassels in the Wind" printed in anthology Journey of the Mind, "Bits of Beauty" in anthology A Moment in Time, "A Place on Earth I love to Be" in anthology East of the Sunrise, "The Four winds of Time and Ozymandias" in anthology The Garden Of Life; [pers.] I became a naturalized citizen of the United States of America on February 26, 1953. It was a very proud and happy moment of my life. To my Senior Class (1938). Core Studies teacher, Mrs. Mary Robey Harris, I am deeply grateful for first opening my eyes and mind into the world of literature and poetry. With thoughts and deeds, however puny they may be, I am striving to make our world a bit more beautiful.; [a.] Honolulu, HI

OTTE, ELMER
[pen.] Elmer Otte; [b.] July 31, 1910, Kaukauna, WI; [p.] Andrew and Anne Otte; [m.] Margaret Peters Otte, October 27, 1934; [ch.] Cecile Otte Pernica, L. David Otte; [ed.] Attended Lawrence University Appleton, Wi. Also attended (special courses): Grand Central School of Art, Columbia University; [occ.] Author, Lecturer. Retired from Advertising Agency creative director and partner; [memb.] Council for Wisconsin Writers, Wisconsin Regional Writers, Wisconsin Fellowship of Poets, International Society Retirement Planners, Community Foundation of Fox Valley Region, American Society of Aging; [hon.] Outstanding Service Award, Lawrence Univ. Appleton, WI. Four time: Jade Ring Award Winner (Wisconsin Regional Writers Assn.), Jade Rings: Juvenile Fiction, Articles, Essays, Poetry. Presented Paper: International of Social Gerontology, 1984 in Rome.; [oth. writ.] Six published books: Rehearse Before You Retire, Retirement Rehearsal Guidebook, Welcome Retirement, Retirement Planning System Kit, Inherit Your Own Money, Engaging The Aging In Ministry; [pers.] I have been blessed in being a lifelong student, both in advertising and news work, and in a life of free lance and published writing. I cannot remember when I was not writing, selling first modest work at age 15. Writing is like breathing to me for which I am grateful. My family, my associates and friends almost always encouraged me. When they did not, I ignored them and wrote something else-anyway.; [a.] Appleton, WI

OUEDRAOGO, BOUREIMA
[pen.] Ibrahim Burkina; [b.] June 30, 1959, Cote D' Ivoire; [p.] Signissida and Fatouma; [m.] Awa, November 1990; [ch.] Azur, Cristal, Symphony, and Perspective; [ed.] University of Ouagadougou (Burkina Faso): Law, National School of Administration (Burkina Faso): Economics and Finance, University of Maryland: International Management, LaSalle University: Law.; [occ.] Financial Manager, Embassy of Burkina Faso; [memb.] Art Phare (France), Institute of Neotic Sciences, World Future Society; [hon.] Several awards in poetry and essay; [oth. writ.] Several unpublished poems and essays in French and English.; [pers.] I always feel like changed with a mission to remind to my fello human beings that life is a game that can be won and that we must win in order to merit the title of "Children Of God".; [a.] Silver Spring, MD

OUELLETTE, CHANCTETINYEA
[pen.] Chalona Oueles, Jacqueline Hill; [b.] September 10, 1969, Oak Grove, LA; [m.] Separated; [ch.] Torrese Arquee, Ondrelique Cemone, Dauriauna Majestique; [ed.] Attended two years at Phillips' Exeter Academy, graduated from Oak Grove High School, went on to Trinity College of Vermont from which I transferred to Middlebury College of Vermont; [occ.] Beginning writer; [memb.] First Baptist Church of Charlottesville; [hon.] Who's Who in America (1982-83); [pers.] Writing for me is not only an outlet for emotions or opinions but also the most powerful and provocative way to ignite the minds of others. It is my ambition as a writer to make a true and profound difference in this world.; [a.] Charlottesville, VA

OVERTON, RANDY
[pen.] Bart Bundy; [b.] January 13, 1961, Elizabeth City, NC; [p.] Jan and Grace Overton;

[m.] Irene Overton, May 19, 1984; [ed.] North-eastern High School, College of the Albermarle; [occ.] Retail Mgmt; [oth. writ.] Stories in local magazine; [pers.] Thank-you Sunshine for adding a hint of fantasy in your recipe of life. Keep "Shining"; [a.] Elizabeth City, NC

OWEN, DAVID

[pen.] H. M. Hollis; [b.] January 8, 1958, Jacksonville, TX; [p.] Mr. and Mrs. Kenneth Owen; [ed.] Certificate of Technology in Horticulture; [occ.] Nursery Salesman; [memb.] Houston Orchid Society; [hon.] Phi Beta Lambda State Competition in Parliamentary Procedures 1st place; [oth. writ.] Dreamland, Autumn, Power, Worry Not, The Reasons for the Seasons, 24 Hours, and Bow Legs and Buck Teeth; [pers.] I wish to dedicate "To A Friend" to Simcha Todd and her family; [a.] Frankston, TX

OWENS, COLLETTE

[b.] February 17, 1938, Denver, CO; [p.] Deceased; [ch.] Andy Owens, Kelly Deford, Kevin Owens; [ed.] St. Francis De Sales High; [occ.] Quality Management Coordinator; [memb.] (ICSA) International Customer Service Assoc., (ASTD) Amer. Society for Training and Development, (ASQG) Amer. Society for Quality Control; [hon.] Certified Customer Service Executive, Certified Master Trainer; [oth. writ.] Sequel to this poem which was written 10 years later.; [pers.] This poem was written during a transition in my life when I realized my 3 children were growing up and didn't need me as much as I needed them.; [a.] Lakewood, CO

PACCIONE, SALVOTONE P.

[pen.] Sal; [b.] January 23, 1960, New York, NY; [p.] Elvira (living), Nicholas (deceased); [m.] Elba Patricia, September 3, 1993; [ch.] Rebecca Patricia, Omar; [ed.] La Salle Academy (High School); [occ.] Unemployed; [hon.] Sea Service Nibboi (Navy); [pers.] Jesus Christ is the way, the truth and the life; [a.] Chula Vista, CA

PADDOCK, MARIA A.

[pen.] Maria A. Boyd Paddock; [b.] March 19, 1967, Honolulu, HI; [p.] Donna M. Boyd [m.] Rodney J. Paddock, December 26, 1992; [ch.] Silly (our cat), Harriet (our turtle) and Candy (our horse) - human children are still a few years away; [ed.] Marin Catholic High School University of Puget Sound - B.S. in Psychology U. of Washington -B.S. in Zoology Seattle U. - MBA in progress; [occ.] Environmentalist, Artist, Author, and Student; [memb.] Wilderness Society, National Wildlife Federation, Nature conservancy, World Wildlife Fund, National Wildlife Rehabilitators Association, Natural Resources Defense Council; [pers.] I hope my writing will appeal to the hearts and minds of those who read it and that it will inspire them to make the world a healthier, happier place for all living things.; [a.] Federal Way, WA

PALMER, CHANELLE

[pen.] Col-Co; [b.] July 2, 1974; [p.] James D. Palmer, Vivian Palmer; [ed.] Mifflin High, Ohio State University, now attending University of Cincinnati major Physical Thern; [occ.] Lab Asst., Providence Hospital; [memb.] D.A.R.E., Aids

Foundation and Helping Kid of Tomorrow; [hon.] Entering my first poem contest and having it publish.; [pers.] Jesus, gave me the talent to write. I believe thru Him all good things are possible. If any of my poems can make a person change or even think about their life, that its self is worth a million.; [a.] Cincinnati, OH

PAMIN, DIANA DOLHANCYK

[pen.] Diana Dolhancyk; [b.] December 13, Cleveland OH; [p.] Peter Dolhancyk, Diana Dribus Dolhancyk; [m.] Leonard Pamin; [ch.] Diana Anne, Louis Peter; [ed.] West Tech High, Titus College of Cosmetology; [memb.] I've sponsored a young girl in India for 15 years. Arthritis Foundation; [hon.] "Editors Choice Award" for outstanding achievement in poetry. Poem - "The Parting" in "Journey of the Mind," published by The National Library of Poetry; [oth. writ.] Poem - "Stormy" in "Songs on the Wind", "Burnt by Love" in "East of the Sunrise," and "Shadow Side" in this anthology; [pers.] Always give someone a smile, you'll never know who's heart your might lighten. I wrote my first poem at age twelve. My roots begin in Russia, Maybe that's why I have a passion for poetry.; [a.] North Royalton, OH

PANCOL, LEE JAMES

[b.] December 15, 1968, Anderson; [p.] James and Demetra Pancol; [m.] Lori Sue Pancol, October 2, 1993; [ed.] Anderson High School 1 year Ball State University; [occ.] Manager: Dunkin Donuts; [memb.] Green Orthodox, Church of "The Holy Trinity", Order of Ahepa: Chapter #198 District #12; [hon.] DECA - Distributive Education Clubs of America: "Outstanding Service Award" - May 14, 1988, and other different awards; [oth. writ.] "All About snakes", "A Bare Bear Story", "The Buffalo", "Rabbits", and various others! (mostly in high school).; [pers.] I would like to dedicate this poem "Born Free", for two special people in my life, my wife Lori, and my Godchild Stephanie! And to my family and friends, I love you!!; [a.] Anderson, IN

PANYKO, VERONICA

[b.] December 16, 1979, Hacken-Sack; [p.] Sharon Siegrist and Mr. Ronald Panyko; [ed.] I am a good student, with good grades, and take honors classes; [hon.] I enjoy my art classes, and am currently participating in "teen Arts" and am in the Gifted and Talented Program at my school.; [oth. writ.] I have been writing short stories, poems and enjoy painting and drawing images to go along with my work.; [pers.] I think if you express your self, it's the key to open up, your heart and mind. Fear not, for what is here today, can be gone tomorrow.; [a.] Little Ferry, NJ

PAQUET, BILL

[pen.] Bill Paquet; [b.] October 13, 1931, Fall River, MA; [p.] Ernest and Elizabeth; [m.] Yvette, March 25, 1977; [ch.] Three, Nine stepchildren; [ed.] 1950 graduate of Muagu Tames Coyle High, Taunton, MA, Johnson and Wales College, 1 yr. business course; [occ.] Semi-retired - part time Prop. Mngr.; [memb.] Life Member - Sayles Hill Rod and Gun Club - No. Smithfield, RI, VFW Post-Cumberland, RI; [hon.] All state in Massachu-setts High School Basketball 1948, Korean Won

Medals; [oth. writ.] Essay - "I Don't Want to Be An Angel, Especially a Guardian Angel and many more; [pers.] Life is worth living. Fulton J. Sheehan; [a.] Narragansett, RI

PAQUETTE, MEGHAN FAITH

[pen.] Faith Anne Quinn; [b.] November 13, 1977, Pawt, RI; [p.] James and Elizabeth Paquette; [ed.] St. Raphael Academy 1995, I will be attending Rhode Island College in the Fall of 1995; [occ.] Student - Education Major; [hon.] Feinstein Scholar, People to People Student Ambassador to Northern Europe; [oth. writ.] I have written a small collection of poetry for my own personal pleasure I am very pleased that "A Child's Tear" will be my first published piece.; [a.] Seekonk, MA

PARA, BEVERLY

[pen.] Beverly Para; [b.] October 27, 1947, Penna; [p.] Henry and Geraldine Miller; [m.] Girard A. Para, June 26, 1967; [ch.] Amy, Aileen, Greg, Ryan; [ed.] Blakely High School, Keystone Jr. College, Marywood College; [occ.] Manager Sports Arena; [memb.] First Presbyterian Church of Peckville, Elder, Deacon. Superintendent of Sunday School.; [pers.] Reading has been my favorite past time. I would like to write both poetry and short stories. The written word is a prized possession of all people.; [a.] Blakely, PA

PARBERRY, HELEN P.

[pen.] Helen Connor; [b.] August 25, 1912, Nooksack, WA; [p.] Robert and Emma Connor; [m.] Floyd L. Parberry (Deceased), November 12, 1929; [ch.] Glenetta Crowell, Annette, Wells; [ed.] High School; [occ.] Retired; [hon.] Poems published in National High School Anthology; [oth. writ.] Wrote songs for several High School Occasions (Graduation Classes etc.); [pers.] As can be seen from marriage and birth dates, I was married at age of seventeen. As I had a very busy life after marriage as a farmer's wife, and raising of a family I had nothing published, but kept writing; [a.] Sedro-Woolley, WA

PARKER, CHRISTOPHER BLAKE

[pen.] Chris; [b.] April 18, 1975, El Dorado, AR; [p.] Marsha Shryock-Gary Hughes; [m.] Single; [ed.] Norphlet School Ark El Dorado Ark Public School, GED; [occ.] Unemployed is going into the army soon; [memb.] American Red Cross has donated I gallon of blood life guard qualified American Heart Association; [oth. writ.] Has written several poems. Including "As A Rosetrapped Under Glass"; [pers.] Believes in God and that people should be treated fair and equal. That you can't judge people by how they look.; [a.] El Dorado, AR

PARKER, TANISHA RASHANA

[b.] May 12, 1977, Detroit, MI; [p.] Joe Ann Williams, Sylvester Rushing, Thomas Williams (step father); [ed.] Osborn High School, Nolan Middle School, and Marshall Elementary, School; [oth. writ.] Is it Love, He's not just Anyone, Now I Speak Out, Heartbreak, My Best Friend, Where Can I Go? Beauty is Blackness, Love Never Dies, Me, and As I Grow Up; [pers.] No matter how many people you are with, if you can't find company in yourself, you will always be alone.; [a.] Detroit, MI

PARKER, VIRGINIA
[pen.] Patience; [b.] October 15, 1941, Winchester, VA; [p.] Charles Avery, Edna Mae Avery; [m.] Charles Parker; [ch.] Tonya Cherie Charles Anthony; [ed.] Estern High Fashion International, University of the District of Columbia; [occ.] Administrative Secretary National Rehabilitation Hospital; [memb.] National Bridal Association (Wedding's Beautiful); [pers.] Circumstances that have happened in my life and my surroundings have led me to express myself in poetry.; [a.] Cheverly, MD

PARKS, VIOLA K.
[b.] April 26, 1922, Booneville, AR; [p.] Walter and Cora Elizabeth, Blewer Parks; [ed.] Wichita Business College, Wichita KS, Baylor University, Waco, TX, Columbia Bible College, Columbia, SC; [occ.] Retired Medical Secretary; [hon.] H.S. Valedictorian medals in Science and, Scholarship, Top Secret Clearance, Secretary to command Surgeon at USAF Academy in Col. Springs, Certificate of Excellence from Juried Section of Colo. Spgs. Art Guild for Oil Painting; [oth. writ.] Several poems in book of memories entitled "-And so it was" and it's sequence "Dear Diary, P.S." from which this poem was taken; [pers.] I am a born-again Christian through faith in Jesus Christ as the Son of God and my personal Saviour, and seek to glorify God in my writing and in my life.; [a.] Colorado Springs, CO

PARNELL, JENNIE
[b.] October 1, 1976, Oakland, CA; [p.] Erika Parnell; [ed.] North Stafford High School in Stafford, VA; [occ.] I work at Cards and cones in Fredericksburg, VA; [hon.] "Best Writer" award in eighth grade; [oth. writ.] Two poems and a short story in the literary magazine, The North Wind, at North Stafford High School.; [pers.] Poetry is the only type of literature with an infinite number of meanings and possibilities.; [a.] Fredericksburg, VA

PARSON, GEISELA
[b.] February 16, 1978, Boston, MA; [p.] Terry and Cecil Parson; [ed.] Emily A. Field School (Boston), Beaumont Middle School (Kissimmee, FL) Cypress Creek High School, Orlando, FL; [occ.] Student; [memb.] Gym, Beta Club, Science Club, Drama Club, Lisa Maile Modeling and Image; [hon.] High Honor Award (9 and 10), Honor Award (11), USAA Science Award, Alice Casey Award Beta Club Certificate; [oth. writ.] The Voice, The Warmth Inside, My Special Friend, Uncertainty, Eyes, The Gift, Goodnight, A Peak, Who Are You?, Mislead, Dreams, A Second Chance, Beyond Reality, Mother Earth, Everlasting Peace, I Love You, etc. (None of my poems have ever been published.); [pers.] Poetry is an expression that is only as deep as the person reading it.; [a.] Orlando, FL

PATTERNSON, CELESTINE J.
[pen.] Tina Jay; [b.] April 29, 1939, Chicago, IL; [p.] Wardell Sutton, Opral Sutton; [ch.] Michael, Michelle, Crystal, Jacquelynne, and Steven; [ed.] Corpus Christi High, Some College Course; [occ.] Office Manager Nursing Administration Mount Sinai Hospital; [memb.] Professional Secretaries International (PSI) Executive Associates Forum;

[oth. writ.] Personal writing inspirational and speeches on request; [pers.] My goal is to acknowledge God's generosity in the gift of writing and to reflect love and humility in that gift writing is a joy. It is like putting a hug on paper; [a.] Chicago, IL

PATTERSON, ALICE
[b.] July 5, 1931, Westland, PA; [p.] Ernest and Beatrice Mosley; [m.] Charles, August 4, 1950; [ch.] Gary, Darrell, Dottie; [ed.] Canonsburg High School, California St. University - PA, "B.S. in Elementary Ed."; [occ.] Retired teacher, now Therapeutic Support Services, children and youth, (Mental Health); [memb.] Central Assembly of God Church, Sweet Lorraine's Club, Women's Ministry of Central Assembly; [hon.] California St. University Honors Convocation, Presidential Scholars; [oth. writ.] Silent Plea of the Unborn Child, Crossroads of Life, The Wonders of a Storm, Who is On the Lord's Side, The Children and many more; [pers.] My inspirations are God's gifts to me. I enjoy writing hoping to bring comfort not only to myself, but to others also.; [a.] Canonsburg, PA

PATTERSON, MARYJO LORENA
[pen.] Lorena Patterson; [b.] March 7, 1978, Columbia, SC; [p.] Betty Patterson - William Grodhaus; [ed.] Caldwell High School, Caldwell, Ohio, 1 yr., Muskingum-Perry Career Center, Zanesville Ohio; [occ.] Student; [memb.] Jr. High and High School Choir, Business Professionals of America; [hon.] Voted Best Personality in Banking and Finance I, Jr. Class Historian; [oth. writ.] School Contests; [pers.] I struggle to put my true feelings in my writing, I've been greatly influenced by events in my own life.; [a.] Caldwell, OH

PATTERSON, PAULINE NIX
[pen.] Pauline Nix Patterson; [b.] May 20, 1913, Cleveland; [p.] E.B. Emma Nix; [m.] Clarence Patterson, February 25, 1942; [ch.] Rosemary; [ed.] High School; [occ.] Volunteer Veterans Hospital; [memb.] Brookhaven Baptist Church, Veterans of Foreign War's Aux.; [pers.] Love for all people, inspires me to live my life through poetry; [a.] Atlanta, GA

PATTON, MONTFORD C.
[pen.] Monty Patton; [b.] April 5, 1926; [m.] Irene Patton, April 14, 1950; [ch.] Four; [occ.] Retired Rural mail Carrier; [a.] Hopedale, OH

PAUL, WILLIAM C.
[b.] May 31, 1974, Harrison, NY; [p.] Chades and Nancy Paul; [ed.] Currently a junior attending the State University of New York at Oswego; [memb.] Delta Kappa Kappa Fraternity; [pers.] I write about experiences, emotions, sights and sounds, all of which have, at one time or another influenced me in some degree, either positively or negatively.; [a.] West Harrison, NY

PAYEUR, KERI
[b.] August 22, 1977, Portland, ME; [p.] Richard and Sylvia Payeur; [ed.] Westbrook High School - class of 1995, planning to attend Ithaca College in the fall, majoring in Journalism; [occ.] Student; [memb.] Key Club, Youth Ministry, Soccer, Softball, Swim Team, Project Graduation Committee, National Honor Society, French

National Honor Society; [hon.] Salutatorian of the class of 1995, Scholar athlete awards, all-Westbrook student, high honors-honor roll, celebration of writing-sophomore winner/junior commendation, mea reading/writing awards, outstanding chemistry, Latin I, food and fitness student (junior year), Girls' Varsity soccer-coach's award Girls' soccer all-stars-honorable mention, outstanding achievement-National latin exam, Wgan-Tu Scholar Athlete of the week, Horatio Alger National Scholar!; [oth. writ.] Poem published in "The Sanford News."; [pers.] My writing stems from personal experience. Under the seemingly plain words is a message I strive to portray by delving into personal feelings.; [a.] Westbrook, ME

PAYNE, JENNIFER
[pen.] Jen only; [b.] April, 1972, Chicago, IL; [p.] William H. and Dolores Y. Payne; [m.] Not married; [ed.] St. Michaels, St. Agnas and Richer High, University of Illinois; [occ.] Builders Square, Front End Supervisor, Chicago; [memb.] Girl Scouts of America; [hon.] Girl Scouts of America, Most Outstanding Basketball Player at St. Michaels, St. Michael Tigers Major Softball of 1983; [oth. writ.] I have written several poems in the past. It is a hobby I enjoy very much. My family and friends enjoy them also.; [pers.] I believe everyone has a talent and that it should be used to make others happy. My poems are my expressions of love. Loving ourselves and loving others.; [a.] Chicago, IL

PEDOTTO, KELLY
[b.] May 10, 1977, Canon City, CO; [p.] David and Carol Pedotto; [m.] Not married; [ed.] Graduated from Olathe East high school in 1995; [occ.] Full time student at Northwest Missouri State University; [a.] Overland Park, KS

PEIFFER, THERESA
[b.] December 20, 1958, Manchester, IA; [p.] Robert Peiffer, Mary Peiffer; [ch.] Nicholas Seth; [ed.] Maquoketa Valley High School, Hamilton Business College; [occ.] Assembler, Cascade Die Mold, Monticello, IA; [memb.] Former Thespian, former member of the National Federation of Students of German, formerly acted in several plays at Church (5 years ago); [hon.] High honors, Hamilton Business College, 1984; [oth. writ.] This is my first time being published I have written songs, poems, stories.; [pers.] I strive to reflect the Christian perspective in my writing. Uplifting material about overcoming difficulties inspires me.; [a.] Monticello, IA

PENDERGAST JR., DONALD
[b.] September 15, 1959, New York, NY; [p.] Donald and Ann Pendergast; [ed.] Graduate, St. Pius X H.S. Albuquerque, NM 1977, National Tax Training School 1994; [occ.] Concert Tour Transportation; [oth. writ.] Several short stories and poems, unpublished thus far.; [pers.] This poem attempts to capture some as the elegant glory and sorrowful despair that characterize the city of New York, a unique and important place. More than anywhere, New York is truly home, no matter where I go.; [a.] Canonsburg, PA

PENIX, MARTIA COX
[pen.] Martia C. Penix; [b.] July 21, 1923, Proctorville, OH; [p.] Earl Cox and Mary Lunsford Cox; [m.] Roscoe Harland Penix, June 23, 1947; [ch.] Ross, Randy and Rick Penix; [ed.] Decatur High, Wiseman Business School, Cabell County (WV) Career Center LPN School; [occ.] LPN (nursing), Freelance Writer and Homemaker; [memb.] Lawrence Co. Historical Society, Huntington Museum of Art, Union Missionary Baptist Church; [hon.] Honored by Regional Authors' Council for Poetry Column And other articles, 1st Place Winner in Christmas Story Contest 1991. Ironton Ohio Tribune. Honorable Mention for poem, HONOR, in 1988 World of Poetry Contest; [oth. writ.] Frontpage feature articles in The WEST VA. HILLBILLY weekly news-paper, The Hungtington Herrald Advertiser SUNDAY Magazine, Poems: In The DREAMSHOP Magazine, of Verse Published by Verse Writers' Guild of Ohio, ECHOES OF WVA, OHIO WOODLANDS (Story); [pers.] I am thankful for a wonderful life and precious family and friends. I find great joy in simple things, sunsets, nature, springtime, love. God is my strength and comfort.; [a.] Chesapeake, OH

PENN, JAIMIE
[pen.] Jaimie; [b.] October 7, 1975, Washington, DC; [p.] Cheri Welk, John Penn; [ed.] High school diploma, Hayfield high school, Fairfax County; [oth. writ.] I like to write short stories also I also draw from time to time.; [pers.] Here is a special quote that I wrote in 10th Grade. "To know yourself, is to love yourself, but it's hard enough to be yourself"; [a.] Burke, VA

PENSO, KATHRYN
[b.] September 22, 1967, Redondo Beach, CA; [p.] Phil and Lynn Roberts; [m.] Kemal Penso; [ch.] Kassidy Jane; [ed.] B.A., Mills College; [hon.] Mary Merrit Henry Award for poetry - Mills College; [a.] Hayward, CA

PERAK, KELLY A.
[b.] January 10, 1975, Los Angeles, CA; [p.] John Perak, Darlene Perak; [ed.] Notre Dame High School, California State University, Fullerton; [occ.] Student; [hon.] English honor St. John the Baptist De La Salle, Bank Of America Business award, Cal State Fullerton School of Business, Dean's List; [pers.] Creating is my key to self knowledge. I have been greatly influenced by John, Kleats, D.H. Lawrence, Edgar Allen Poe, and romantic poets; [a.] Brea, CA

PEREZ, CLAUDIA ASHLEY
[b.] April 30, 1983, North Bergen, NJ; [p.] Jose and Michaline Perez; [ed.] 6 Grader At Village Pines School; [hon.] Medal for academic excellence in Language and Social Studies. My experiences of Hurricane Andrew published in The Miami Herald Hurricanes (How To Prepare and Recover) guide book.; [oth. writ.] Poem published in Creative Exchange Children's Magazine.; [pers.] I express myself through poems, and hope one day soon to publish all my poems in "My Own Book of Poetry". Thank you, Ms. Kohler, for all your encouragement!; [a.] Miami, FL

PERRY, JOHN W.
[b.] April 18, 1912, Hot Springs, AR; [p.] John Riley and Eva Perry, Deceased 1991; [m.] Deceased, 1936; [ch.] John Windsor Perry, Sandra Perry, John W. Perry; [ed.] High School, graduate and Valedictorian I am the author of the poems listed; [occ.] Retired 36 years, Auditor, D.R.S. Present age 82 will be 83 come April 18th this year.; [hon.] PHD, University Tex. Austin TX, PHD, University, Tex, Austin, TX; [oth. writ.] My Star, Life's Highway, Fire, all of these poems, were written about the same time in 1930, 1931 and, Tomorrow which you have now.; [pers.] I am enclosing the fee of 20.00 as mentioned above and request the book when published," The Garden Of Life" to be published in the fall of 1995. I would be happy if you can published the additional poems written about the same time.; [a.] Little Rock, AR

PERRY JR., LAWRENCE E.
[b.] September 23, 1942, Louisville, KY; [p.] Lawrence E. Perry Sr., Eleanor Perry; [ed.] Walton N.Y. Central High School I'; [memb.] American Contract Bridge League; [oth. writ.] Limericks Flomorus and serious poetry, essays, numbering in the hundreds all unpublished; [pers.] I try to see both sides of a story if one can not find humor in most situations, you aren't looking hard enough. Odenen Nash is my inspiration; [a.] Washington, DC

PERZI, HELMUT G.
[b.] March 4, 1977, West Chester, PA; [p.] Gunter Perzi, Edeltraud Perzi; [ed.] Malvern Preparatory School; [memb.] Amnesty International, Student Government; [hon.] St. Agustine Christian Leadership Award, Academic Excellence in Art; [oth. writ.] Personal Reflections of life situations; [pers.] "Dreams are only dreams until you set your imagination to a fairy tale book that never wants to be closed"; [a.] Honey Brook, PA

PETERMAN, JASON
[pen.] Jaysen True Blood; [b.] June 4, 1974, Fairfax, MO; [p.] Alfred D. and Charlotte Peterman; [ed.] High School, (Sidney Comm. Schools); [occ.] Song Writer, Singer, Novelist, Waiter; [memb.] TRSA, (Top Records Song Writing Association), Song Writers' Club of America, ASCAP and BMI (pending); [oth. writ.] Free, Valley of Death, Hall of Kings, Vampire, Swanson, Turnus Loose, Too Lotto Touch, Jessica, Keep me Alive, Keep on Walkin', Gypsie Road, Enough is Enough, Summer Time Blues (p.2) (songs); [pers.] Versatility is essential as is the willingness to change constantly. Remember... A song unsung or a poem unwritten is a masterpiece unpainted.; [a.] Sidney, IA

PETERS, ANNETTE
[b.] April 24, 1913, Texas; [p.] Tammen; [m.] A. Lee Peters, November 14, 1937; [ch.] Wally Lew, Sally Sue, Polly Eileen; [ed.] 1-7 Lutheran School 8 Public School, 9-12 Broken Arrow High School; [occ.] Housewife; [memb.] Trinity Lutheran Church, Craft Circle, Prime Timers, Pioneer of Broken Arrow; [hon.] At least six "Greatest Grandma" awards that I'm proud of.; [oth. writ.] "Fall Beauty," "Fishing," "Life's Journey," "Our Birds," "Contest Day," "Gary Lee's Snowman," "To Lee," "Snow Time," "To Scott;" [pers.] I love people the way they are. I've lived in Broken Arrow since 1914; [a.] Broken Arrow, OK

PETERSON, MATTHEW
[b.] May 25, 1973, Winfield, IL; [p.] Kenneth Peterson, Janet Peterson; [ed.] College Of DuPage, Western Illinois University; [occ.] Law Enforcement Administration Student; [memb.] WIU Investigators Club, Lambda Alpha Epsilon, Western Emergency Medical Service; [hon.] Phi Theta Kappa, Dean's List; [pers.] A man sleeps and dreams. He does not realize that he is only a dream himself, existing for a brief flicker of time, only to be forgotten as the next moment passes.; [a.] Winfield, IL

PETERSON, RANDALL W.
[pen.] Randall Peterson; [b.] October 18, 1978; [p.] Dorothy F. Peterson; [ed.] 11th Grade; [occ.] Deceased; [hon.] A Randall Peterson Poets award has been established at Blacksburg High and will be awarded to a member of the Jr. class every year - first one May 17, 1995; [oth. writ.] Randall had written about 100 poems at the time of his death - December 19, 1994. Hopefully all his poems will be published in hard back one day soon.; [pers.] Randall was a good student at Blacksburgh High School, he was in a car wreck and killed December 19, 1994, on his way to school. He was kind and loved by many.; [a.] Goffrey, SC

PETERSON, SANDRA
[b.] February 25, 1963, Clinton, MA; [p.] Arther G. and Constance A. Therrien; [m.] Eric V. Peterson, November 27, 1982; [ch.] Mandy Therrien, Eric Peterson, David Peterson, Ashley Peterson; [ed.] McCann Tech.; [occ.] Home Maker; [pers.] The poem I wrote was in memory of my only Brother David A. Therrien born June 18, 1957-died 1994. He was killed in a tragic construction accident IW Albany N.Y. November 10, 1994. It was my first poem that I ever wrote.; [a.] North Adams, MA

PETERSON, SHARAI
[b.] January 3, 1951, Washington, D.C.; [p.] Honey and Morrie Cohen; [m.] Jeffrie Edward Peterson; [ed.] B. Ed., University of Miami, 1972; [memb.] Haiku Poets of Northern California; [pers.] My inspiration for writing derives from many facets of life. I dedicate this poem to my mother, in heaven above, who I think of when "my feet touch the clouds;" [a.] San Francisco, CA

PETRACCO, CARIN
[pen.] Carin Petracco; [b.] July 16, 1972, Jacksonville, AL; [p.] Angelo and Joyce Petracco; [ed.] Summit High School, Summit, NJ - Art Instruction School Minnesota; [oth. writ.] Write several poems, but never sent them in.; [pers.] I love writing poetry, I was influenced to continue writing by someone very dear to me.; [a.] Summit, NJ

PETTIT, CLAIRE FELICE
[pen.] Golden Felice; [b.] November 25, 1959, Pittsburgh, PA; [p.] Harry William and Jeanne Claire Seamon; [pers.] My writings are dedicated to the memory of my father who taught me so subtly how to love so deeply.; [a.] Washington, PA

PHELAN, ELIZABETH
[pen.] Liz Phelan; [b.] December 26, 1980, Los Angeles, CA; [p.] Donna Phelan, Geoff Phelan; [ed.] 8th grade; [occ.] Student; [memb.] Basketball team, Volleyball team, Track Team; [hon.] Principal's List, Honor roll; [oth. writ.] Several poems, not published; [pers.] I try to show my love for God and His creations in my writing.; [a.] Leona Valley, CA

PHELPS, ELEANOR
[pen.] Eleanor Phelps; [b.] September 8, 1907, Balto, MD; [p.] Alma Turner Phelps, John Phelps; [m.] Halfdan Hebo, August 1939; [ch.] Lisa Hebo; [ed.] AB- Vassar College close of (1928); [memb.] Actor's Equity Association, Dramatist's Guild, Screen Actor's Guild, American Federation of Television and Radio Artists

PHILLIPS, CALLIE L.
[pen.] Bonnie Phillips; [b.] June 26, 1940, Indiana; [p.] Willis Cook, Nettie Cook; [m.] Dale E. Phillips, April 8, 1961; [ch.] Kim, Mike, Karen, Sherry, Kent; [ed.] Edinburgh High; [occ.] Home Maker; [hon.] World Of Poetry, Honorable Mention 1987 and 1990, Golden Poet 1988, Silver Poet Award 1989, The National Library of Poetry Editors Choice Award 1994; [oth. writ.] Several Poems Published in local Newspaper sheaves: A journal for the Arts, Published National Library of Poetry, seasons to come 1995; [pers.] I enjoy writing and sharing my thought's with other's.; [a.] Edinburgh, IN

PHILLIPS, CRISTINA M.
[b.] October 16, 1980, Elmira, NY; [p.] Richard and Susan Phillips; [ed.] Eighth grade; [occ.] Student; [memb.] Oddesey of the Mind Barnstable Middle School: Softball and Tennis Team; [hon.] Honor roll status for last 2 years; [oth. writ.] Non published; [pers.] I write mainly about life, our world in hope that someday my poems will influence others. Favorite poet: Emily Dickinson; [a.] Hyannis, MA

PHILLIPS, JENNIFER J.
[b.] June 21, 1976, Destin, FL; [ed.] Currently working on a masters degree in Social Work; [oth. writ.] I have literally hundreds of poems that I hope will be published in the near future; [pers.] Every form of thought was meant to be interpreted. It is the author who expresses the fantastic ideals of reality and its meaning.; [a.] Largo, FL

PHIPPS, CONSTANCE
[pen.] Constance Kaye; [b.] November 29, 1946, Hamilton, OH; [p.] Gordon and Janice Baker; [m.] Dale Phipps, May 22, 1965; [ch.] Wendy Ann and Dana Dale; [ed.] Hamilton Garfield High Miami University; [occ.] Receptionist American Fan Co; [pers.] Until now, my poems have personal messages to family and close friends. Their support has greatly increased my ability; [a.] Fairfield, OH

PIERCE, MACHELLE RENEE
[b.] April 10, 1965, Oneida, TN; [p.] Jim and Linda Lewis; [m.] E. Wayne Pierce, July 29, 1981; [ch.] Dawn Rachelle, Miranda Rae, Anthony Wayne; [ed.] South Louisville Christian Jefferson State; [memb.] Church of Pentecost (Orchestra

Director); [hon.] Highest GPA for nursing program to date 1982; [oth. writ.] None published; [pers.] From personal journal just as families share your joy they also divide your grief. (Machelle lays in rest at Brookland Cemetery Sheperdsville, Ky.); [a.] Jacksonville, FL

PIERCE, SHELLY LYNN
[b.] June 16, 1973, Chehalis; [p.] Linda and Gary Pierce; [ed.] Graduated Rochester High School - Rochester WA, AA. at Centralia College - Cent. WA., Currently attending Evergreen State College - Olympia WA; [memb.] America Northwest Repertory Theater; [hon.] Received several awards in horse 4-H and United States Pony Club. Such as 4-H horse State fitting, showing champion, United States Pony Championship West, Dressage Team Champion. Received an Honorable mention in the National College Poetry Contest for my poem titled good-bye; [oth. writ.] My poem - Good Bye - was published in - American Collegiate Poets - Fall conquers 1993; [pers.] I am a peaceful person. I love to listen to music and pick flowers. My poems are inspired by pictures, sounds, and life, and life.; [a.] Rochester, WA

PILE, PHOEBE R.
[b.] May 29, 1983, Boston, MA; [p.] Debbie Pile, Wells Pile; [ed.] Cunningham School, Medway Middle School; [occ.] Sixth Grader; [hon.] High Honors, 6th Grade (twice), Von Orton Language Arts Award, (5th Grade, most avid reader); [pers.] Don't force yourself. It will come to you.; [a.] Medway, MA

PILE, TAMMY
[b.] July 17, 1961, Kansas City, KS; [p.] Gerald and Joyce Corp; [m.] Piandy Pile, October 2, 1980; [ch.] Jennifer Michelle and Jessica Renee; [ed.] J. C. Harmon High School; [occ.] Certified Medication Aide; [oth. writ.] Several poems I'm writing to publish my own book.; [pers.] I find writing to be very relaxing and fulfilling to the soul; [a.] Topeka, KS

PILGRIM, ANGELA DAWN
[b.] October 20, 1973, Fayetteville, AR; [p.] Eugene Pilgrim, Sherrion Pilgrim; [ed.] Gaffney High School; [occ.] Blow Mold Operator, Pet Dairy Spartanburg SC; [memb.] Cherokee Tribe Tahlequah, OK; [hon.] Art awards - Pointalism and Model Clay and Abstract, Senior Captain Award - Softball, American Academic Physical Fitness Award; [oth. writ.] Haiku's published in our school art pamphlet.; [pers.] In my poetry, I wish to enable my readers to feel the emotion and touch the imagination of each and every line.; [a.] Gaffney, SC

PILGRIM, NATHAN LEE
[pen.] BI; [b.] September 1, 1967, North Carolina; [p.] Brenda Hodge; [m.] Single; [ed.] G.E.D., College Courses, Electrical 1, Arc Welding, Science Creation, Typing 1, Bible College Courses; [memb.] The Body of Christ of God's Church. Denomination is (Independent Bible Believer.); [hon.] Creation Science Certificate, I Corinthians 10:31; [oth. writ.] Religion or Salvation Which Do you Have, Christmas What We As Christians Believe, Who is the Whore of Babylon Revelation 17:9; [pers.] All praise and honor to my Lord Jesus Christ who worked this

work through me. I Corinthians 15:10, Ephesians 2:8-10, Titus 3:5-7, Jeremiah 18:1-6, John 6:28-40; [a.] Kings Mountain, NC

PIMENTEL, HANSER DIONIS
[b.] June 4, 1980, New Jersey; [p.] Dionis and Leslie Pimentel; [ed.] Freshman at Bergen Catholic High School in Oradell, New Jersey; [occ.] Student; [memb.] Bally's Health/Jack LaLanne; [hon.] Principal's List, Bronze Medal won at Science Fair in elementary school; [oth. writ.] Small poems written while in elementary school and published in the school bulletin; [pers.] "Anything is possible."; [a.] Palisades Park, NJ

PINEDA, RITA M.
[b.] May 21, 1940, Pueblo, CO; [p.] Jose and Josephine Gama; [m.] Lee, December 9, 1961; [ch.] Gina; [ed.] Central High School, Pueblo, CO; [occ.] Workers Compensation Specialists; [hon.] Exceptional Achievement Award. Best Xmas Decoration for Home or Apartment (1st Prize); [oth. writ.] "Memories Of Days Gone By", "Today, tomorrow, and yesterday." "Chances", I Must Be Dreaming," "My Mom's The Best", "Love can Be Forever," and many more.; [pers.] I've always loved poetry and verses, all my poetry is based on the person's personality and their influence in my life.; [a.] Walsenburg, CO

PIPER, JO
[b.] April 5, 1929, Lake City, IA; [p.] Wilber and Ella Chase; [m.] Charles M. Piper, Marcy 23, 1951; [ch.] Steven, Kevin, Alan; [ed.] Lake City HS, U of North Iowa, Rebuilding Seminars, Writing seminars, Volunteer Instruction, Seminars on Aging; [occ.] Writer, volunteer, Office Assistant, Sub In Chapel; [memb.] College Honor Societies, Church Of Christ, RSUP, International Society of Poets, Board Of Senior Transportation, Serendipity Singles; [hon.] International Society Poets, 4 Editor's choice awards from National Library of Poetry, Torch and Tassel, Pi Tau Phi; [oth. writ.] Sparrow Grass Poetry Forum, "Intruded," "Verses", "Prodigal Found," "Farewell Visit", "A Daughter Writes Home." NLB, "The Gift", "The Candle", "Tribute", "Simplicity Is Child", Quill Books, "Love Letter"; [pers.] My poetry muse guides me every day and I am my own person. Writing keeps me structured but when I am not writing, I love shopping and talking. My volunteers worn keeps me whole.; [a.] Loveland, CO

PLIMPTON, LESLIE
[b.] September 24, 1959, Chicago; [p.] Charles and Bonnie Plimpton; [ed.] Glenbrook South High, Western Illinois Univ, Defaul Univ., Loyola Univ., Columbia College; [occ.] Producer-Film, Video and Television, Chromosohn Media, Inc.; [oth. writ.] Currently writing a book on the life and teachings of Rev. Mike Matoin, Unity Minister in Chicago.; [a.] Ojai, CA

PLUMMER, WINOKA JONES
[pen.] Winoka Jones Plummer; [b.] August 24, 1947, Winston-Salem, NC; [p.] Clifton and Etta Mae Jones; [m.] Ronald Lee Plummer, June 12, 1966; [ch.] Todd Eric, Rusty Lee, Jamie Jones, Christy Dawn; [ed.] East Forsyth High, Forsyth Technical Community College, Guilford Technical

Community College; [occ.] Registered Nurse Hospice of Davidson County Lexington, North Carolina; [memb.] CPR Instructor - American Heart Association. Founder and Coordinator of Hearts and Hands Support Group (for rare or undiagnosed illnesses); [hon.] Graduated with honors from Nursing School; [oth. writ.] Have written articles on rare diseases and other medical articles for Med-Text, a Home Health Care Newsletter for Advanced Home Care in North Carolina; [pers.] My poem, "Keeping Up With The Joneses" was written for my parents, Clifton and Etta Mae Jones, who are not wealthy as far as possessions, but are rich in blessings; [a.] Winston-Salem, NC

PLUMPTON, JILL
[b.] October 23, 1979, Dover, NH; [p.] Sharon and Robert Plumpton; [ed.] Freshman at Somersworth High School; [occ.] Student; [memb.] Member of the Women's NH Select Ice Hockey Team and the Somersworth Varsity Ice Hockey and Field Hockey Team; [a.] Somersworth, NH

POE, ZYANGQUELYN A.
[b.] October 4, 1946, Sallisburg, NC; [p.] Leon and Aleese Witherspoon; [m.] Gerald F. Poe, Sr.; [ch.] Rocquelia, Jamont, Stepchildren Gerald Sr., Shawn; [ed.] Dunbar High School, Livingstone College; [occ.] Teacher/Director of Educational Technology; [memb.] Nat. Assoc. of Women in Media and Film, Assoc. for Supervision and Curriculum Development, Assoc. of American, Univ. Women Nat. Assoc. of Female Exec., Delta Sigma Theta Sorority, Inc.; [hon.] NASA Teacher in Space Candidate, Third-Place in City-Wide Media Festival, Who's Who in American Education; [oth. writ.] Deah Johnson Janes-Greeting Cards, "From Magic Pencils Come Magic Thoughts"- Poetic Forms.; [pers.] "They can, because they think it."; [a.] Takoma Park, MD

POHLMANN, DOTTIE
[b.] December 30, 1967, San Francisco, CA; [p.] Dorothy Pohlmann, Theodore Pohlmann; [ed.] San Jose State University, University of Metaphysics, Certified Phlebotomist, Certified Electrocardiograph Tech. and Certified Laboratory Assistant; [occ.] Currently expanding my medical education with emphasis in areas of Psychological understanding; [oth. writ.] I have a variety of other collections of my innermost thoughts I've held onto over the years. This I am flattered to say is my first poem to ever be published and first attempt at doing so.; [pers.] For you Mom, was called upon to soon to be released of her earthly existence. I try to look deep inside to feel the connection of the soul. A helpful guide enabling us to see through stone walls, which seems impossible, I've done the impossible. Personal thought: To be able to reflect on the goodness and meaning each and everyone of has to offer, with emphasis focused on those actions or intentions could very well deteriorate and fill up that black hole in heart with a sweet raw new beginning.; [a.] Milpitas, CA

POLANCIC, FRANK P.
[pen.] Frank Polancic; [b.] August 27, 1969, Ottawa; [p.] Frank and Patricia Polancic; [ed.] Ottawa Township High School University of Illinois-Champaign, Urbana the players workshop-

acting and improvisation david gaschen-opera instructor; [occ.] Realtor, Singer/Songwriter/ Lyricist/Poet. Chicago; [hon.] Dean's List; [oth. writ.] Completed between 400-500 poems, and song lyrics in 1993 and 1994. A myriad of subjects ranging from love, feelings, experiences to evolution, art and people.; [pers.] I concentrate on the abstract in order to engender simplify, and magnify the obvious.; [a.] Chicago, IL

POLAND JR., ERNEST L.
[b.] November 27, 1958, Keyser, WV; [p.] Ernie and 'Wid' Poland; [m.] Karen L. Poland, December 11, 1993; [ch.] Jamie - 18, Paul - 15; [ed.] Frostburg State College - BS Ball State University - MA; [occ.] High school teacher, Earth and Environmental Sciences; [memb.] Epilepsy Association of MD, NEA, MSTA; [hon.] Gamma Theta Upsilon; [pers.] Never say die! Give up only with your last breath.; [a.] Poolesville, MD

POLLITT, KATHERINE
[pen.] Diana; [b.] October 5, 1949, Camden, NJ; [p.] Katherine and Heubert McKinney; [m.] Maurice Pollitt Sr.; [ch.] Maurice Anthony, Shyra, daughter in laws - Janell and Yvonne; [ed.] Somerdale Elementary School, Sterling High School; [pers.] Poetry is not for everyone but take the time to read, this gifted art ... it might be for you!

POLLOCK, JOSEPH L.
[pen.] Joe Pollock, Joseph L. Pollock; [b.] March 7, 1922, Philadelphia, PA; [p.] Rose and Samuel George; [m.] Adella, October 10, 1949; [ch.] Stephen George, Marjorie (daughter-in-law), Meredith Jill and Lauren Beth (grand daughters); [ed.] West Phila. high school, State Teachers College, West Chestey PA, B.S. University of Pennsylvania '49 M.S. certification as Sunt. of School LeHigh Univ. Bethlehem, PA - studies; [occ.] Executive Director, Denna. Conference of Public Alumni Assn. Ex. Dir, Matrayal Chearinghouse for Public Alumni Association; [memb.] Past Master, Equity Lodgo Thp. A.M., Phib. PA, Valley of Reading, 320 Noble, Award Shrine, West Palm Beach, FL, Past Pres. Master Mascus of Kings Houcuzuy, Pres. West Phila. H.S. Alumni Ass., Past Pres. The Chapter Phi Delta Kapp Exec. Div. citizen for a free city college, Executive Director, Youth and Young Adult Division A.J.A. CHR. Liberty Bell Speakers Bureau, Scholarship Fund of W.P.H.S. is named in my hover.; [hon.] Outstanding Alumni Award West Phila H.S. 1987, Bronze Star World War II, E.T.O. 63rd Infantry Division; [oth. writ.] Student Life, Magazine, "Youth's Voice in Civic Affairs" 1947 various magazine and necessary articles. Lecture on "Life of Red Skelten 220" various plats at Nelwes Jr. High W.P.N.S., U.S. Army and West Chester University; [pers.] My Epitaph will read: "Mr. Alumni" his voice and zeal brought people together. "No two people in the world are exactly alike"; [a.] Delray Beach, FL

POOLE, VEONNE
[b.] November 17, 1966, Meridian, MS; [p.] Mr. and Mrs. Clayton Poole; [ed.] MS at Univ. of So. MS (Masters in English), West Lauderdale High School; [occ.] English Teacher and Instructor; [memb.] USM Alumni Association; [hon.] High School Valedictorian, Junior Miss Scholarships, Summer Missions Projects in Taiwan, R.O.C.;

[oth. writ.] "Fireside Poetry," "Drifting Away," "Carousel," "Calling Me," "Leaves in the Autumn," "If Dreams Became Reality," "Burning to Give," "Take Some Time," "Call of the Wild," "Make it Right," "Choice is Up to You," "Rainbow in My Sight", "You and Me".; [pers.] "Writing songs and poetry is drug-free therapy....."; [a.] Collinsville, MS

POWELL, ELAINE S.
[pen.] ESP; [b.] July 20, 1936, Chicago, IL; [p.] John and Hattie Henley; [m.] Divorced; [ch.] Regina, William, Beverly; [ed.] Phillips, H.S. - Wilson College; [occ.] Retired; [memb.] AARP, A.M.E. Church, Arthritis Foundation, Maryland Chapter of Secretaries; [hon.] Howard University Supporting Staff Award, Volunteer Award for Maryland Mental Health, Volunteer Award for Senior Citizens; [oth. writ.] Several poems published in local magazines and newspapers. Poetry used in soon to be released album. Readings at coffee houses in Chicago and D.C. areas.; [pers.] I write from my heart about daily situation in these trying times and keeping the faith to stay positive and make the best of life for yourself and others. My idol is the poet favorite of Illinois, Ms. Gwendolyn Brooke.; [a.] Riverdale, MD

POWERS, CORINE ELIZABETH
[pen.] Cory Sun; [b.] January 12, 1959, Mount Vernon, NY; [p.] Arthur and Evelyn Powers; [m.] Dr. Ibraheim Yassein, D.D.S., October 25, 1993; [ed.] Graduated Horace Greeley, H.S. Chappaqua, N.Y. 1977 went on to the School of Visual Arts, N.Y.C. transferred to: S.U.N.Y. Purchase, N.Y.; [occ.] Musicians-Songwriter and Spiritual Counselor; [memb.] ASCAP - (Assoc. of Songwriters, Composers and Pub.) Amherst Society of Poets; [hon.] Recently selected out of 1,500 applicants to be on Rodell Records Compilation Disc. "Music Menagerie V" "they felt my talent was far superior to the majority." Poem "Seal" selected to be published in the Amherst Society - Annual 1995.; [pers.] My writings reflect the sincerity of my soul, my life experiences and my compassion for others. I hope to bring a positive message, on a universal level through my music.; [a.] Butler, NJ

POWERS, THOMAS M.
[b.] February 5, 1963, Framingham, MA; [p.] James P. and Irene T. Powers; [ed.] Natick High, Boston University, Fisher College

PRATT, KENNETH DWAYNE
[pen.] K. D. Pratt; [b.] April 23, 1973, Tallahassee, FL; [p.] Dr. and Mrs. L.H. Pratt; [ed.] B.A. Morehouse College, Atlanta, GA Developmental Research School, Tallahasee, Fl; [memb.] President, Morehouse English Majors Club, (1993-95) Morehouse Pre-Law Society (1991-95), Member Bethel Missionary Baptist Church; [hon.] National Dean's List (1993-94, 1994-95), Honor Roll, Morehouse College (1991-1995), Morehouse English Departmental Honors; [oth. writ.] Western Reading Services ("Time Machine") and other local newspapers and anthologies; [pers.] Effects us all, no matter what our fields or interests. It's boundaries are limitless.; [a.] Tallahassee, FL

PRESLEY, PRESTON E.
[b.] July 8, 1954, Fort Campbell, KY; [p.] Preston and Mable Joyce Presley; [ed.] BA University of Tenn. Studied Music Under Timothy Coetz. Lebanon High; [occ.] Social Worker; [memb.] Sons of the Confederacy; [hon.] Have won 3 poetry contest not worth mention; [oth. writ.] Currently write music; [pers.] I love being alive take love where I find it, give to anyone who'll accept it. Learn from those wiser, teach to anyone who'll listen to me.; [a.] Lebanon, TN

PRETZER, RYAN
[b.] March 24, 1982, Washington, DC; [p.] William Pretzer, Terry Moores; [occ.] 7th grade student, Allen Park Middle School; [memb.] National Junior Honor Society, Student Council, Dearborn Recreation Dolphins Swim Team (Member of State Swim Team at Michigan Swimming State Champion shipments '94 and '95); [hon.] Local Literature winner Michigan PTA's Reflections Contest '93, '94 and '95, photography winner '93 reflections, honor roll student; [a.] Allen Park, MI

PRIBBLE, NANCY GALLIER
[b.] February 13, 1946, Lynchburg, VA; [p.] William and Beulah Gallier; [m.] Clarence Thomas Pribble, May 16, 1964; [ch.] Sheila Marie and Clarence Thomas Jr.; [ed.] E. C. Class High; [occ.] Minister, Lynchburg VA; [oth. writ.] Have over 250 other poems.; [pers.] I only write when I feel inspiration from God.; [a.] Forest, VA

PRICE, GREGORY L.
[pen.] Greg Price; [b.] January 16, 1953, Washington, DC; [p.] Edward and Vernell Price; [m.] Dorothy D. Price, April 30; [ed.] Post secondary education at Prince Georges Comm. College, Prince Georges, MD; [occ.] Chief Engineer; [memb.] Naval Memorial Society, National Association of Power Engineers; [hon.] Letter of Appreciation Naval District Washington, DC; [oth. writ.] Forever, Dreamer, Why Love Hurts, Distant Shore, A Lover's Love; [pers.] The goal of every human who has lived, is to leave a permanent foot print upon the earth so that they will never be forgotten. I feel with honor, you have given me my foot print.; [a.] Washington, DC

PRICE, MATT
[b.] June 9, 1982, Grand Junction, CO; [p.] Kevin Price, Shari Price; [ed.] 6th Grade student at The Connect School, Pueblo, CO; [occ.] Student; [oth. writ.] This is my first published work.; [a.] Pueblo, CO

PRIDE, MELODY
[pen.] Amber; [b.] August 20, 1955, Utah; [p.] Oscar and Teressa Pride; [m.] Thad Bonduris, December 31, 1994; [ch.] Heather and Nicole; [occ.] Environmental Lab Tech; [memb.] World Wildlife, The Nature Conservancy, National Audubon Society, PETA, EDF, Doris Day Animal, ASPCA; [pers.] The Sadness I have seen in so many people and animals inspires me to write in hopes to have all of us stop for just a few minutes a day and perhaps be kind to those around us!; [a.] Denton, TX

PRINCE, OLA LEE
[pen.] Ola; [b.] September 22, 1925, Konawa, OK; [p.] Arthur anf Callie Williams; [m.] Virgil Owen Prince D., June 16, 1946; [ch.] Jon Patrick, Kathryn Lee, Terrence Owen; [ed.] 12th Grade

PRINGLE, FRONCINE R.
[pen.] Sunshine and Honey Bear; [b.] May 10, 1963, Philadelphia, PA; [p.] John B. and Paulina V. Young, Sr.; [ch.] Daniel David III, DaYona Danielle and KaVona Victoria Pringle; [ed.] Martin Luther King High, Berean Institute - Cosmetology, Ralph Amedei - Barber School; [occ.] Mail Processor, U.S. Postal Service; [memb.] American Entrepreneurs Association, American Cancer Society Foundation, Home and School Association of Philadelphia APWU, AFL - CIO; [hon.] Awards for Acting, various sports and hair styling; [oth. writ.] 1st book to be published fall of '95, for children Tiny Bops, "Wee Bop Out Alone" with a series to follow....; [pers.] Life have so much to offer so shoot for the stars and stick to your guns for your life is only one.; [a.] Philadelphia, PA

PROESL, LINDA MARIE
[pen.] Lynne Prizle; [b.] July 28, 1963, Springfield, MA; [p.] Donald and Carmen Proesl; [m.] Divorced; [ch.] 2 girls Nicole age 13, Natalie age 9; [ed.] Martin County High Graduate Sophomore College student, previous 4 years financial planning - 8 years nursing experience; [occ.] Tractor-Trailer Driver; [hon.] 1990 - National Sales Achievement, 1977 American Legon Award, Miscellaneous Sales activity awards; [oth. writ.] "But One Rose..." At The Top" Peg O' My Heart other short stories and poetry; [pers.] I strive to make each day the best day, in the event it should be my last - I live to share my thoughts and desires to hopefully influence others; [a.] Port Saint Lucie, FL

PROPER, AMANDA
[pen.] Kayla Austin; [b.] July 25, 1979, Arkansas; [p.] John and Cindy Proper; [ed.] Akron Fairgrove High School; [pers.] I dedicate my first published poem to the person who has inspired me the most. I hope I can make your dreams come true in me. "GM"; [a.] Akron, MI

PROPST, RUBY
[pen.] Ruby Adkins Propst; [b.] September 5, 1913, Durango, CO; [p.] Ed and Frances Stoddard; [m.] Harry Propst, May 2, 1974; [ch.] Steven Adkins, Ted Adkins; [ed.] High School, Three College Courses in writing; [occ.] Retired; [memb.] Poetry Society of Colo, Quill Club (Denver, Co.); [oth. writ.] About 50 Poems four journals a number of articles a few short stories; [pers.] I have always loved to write both prose and poetry. During the long illness of my husband with Alzheimers Disease I kept a journal. I would like to have my poems published in a book; [a.] Independence, MO

PRUNTY, JOSEPH N.
[b.] December 29, 1973, Sewickley, PA; [p.] Joseph R. Prunty, Penelope M. Prunty; [ed.] Current College Student; [occ.] Full-time College Student; [oth. writ.] Other poems are not published.; [pers.] I love, therefore, I write to fill the emptiness inside myself.; [a.] Ambridge, PA

PUGH, WANDA
[pen.] Wanda; [b.] March 11, 1963, West Monroe, LA; [p.] Richard and Billie Muirhead; [m.] Wendell E. Pugh, September 6, 1986; [ch.] Natasha Kay Pugh, Joshua Caleb Pugh; [ed.] High School; [occ.] Homemaker and Beauty School; [memb.] Arbor Foundation Day, Trinity Assembly of God; [oth. writ.] The reason published in The Arcadia Poetry Anthology of Summer 1994 and Sparrow grass Poetry of 1995. Also Daddy's Star to be published this summer in the sparrow grass forum this summer 1995; [pers.] Poetry is the beauty of words coming from the heart and soul. Poetry is the art of words.; [a.] Bastrop, LA

PULCHTOPEK, JOSEPH
[b.] April 18, 1971, Springfield; [p.] Christine May Watt; [m.] Lori Donohue (Fiancee); [ch.] Not set yet; [ed.] High school grad. of Business; [occ.] Sales P/T F/T Laborer; [oth. writ.] I have many poems.; [pers.] I wrote the poem just thinkin' of my beautiful lady, Lori, my heart belongs to her and I'd like to say "I Love You".; [a.] Springfield, MA

QUEENAN, MARK RICHARD
[pen.] Mark Richard Queenan; [b.] June 6, 1963, Medford, MA; [p.] James Queenan and Cynthia Weightman; [ch.] Amanda Lynne Queenan, Melanie Dawn Queenan; [ed.] Triton Regional High, Salem St. College; [occ.] Manager, Alden Merrell Corp.; [hon.] Greatest honors and awards are my two priceless daughters of whom I love madly.; [oth. writ.] None. This is my first entry and first publication.; [pers.] I am honored to be published in your anthology, thank you.; [a.] Newburyport, MA

QUIGG, ERIC
[b.] June 6, 1977; [ed.] Spring-Ford High; [occ.] Student; [oth. writ.] Poem in school publishing; [pers.] "Now we must have the strength to mend." - R. S.; [a.] Royersford, PA

RADEBE-MBATA, BUSISIWE
[b.] South Africa; [ch.] Five; [ed.] Cornell University in 1988; [occ.] Mother of five, revolutionary, warrior and emancipated woman; [oth. writ.] I began work as a writer in South Africa where the political system denied me the opportunity for publication or performance. As I continued my writing in the U.S.A., I was encouraged by a good friend.; [pers.] I believe that even though we are different and come from different backgrounds, we are all tied together by one common thread-our HUMANITY!; [a.] Tompkins County

RADER, JEFFERY TODD
[pen.] Stephen Todd; [b.] June 5, 1969; [p.] Stan Rader, Sandra Giancola; [ed.] Crystal Lake South High School, Northern Illinois University (1 year) in Tech. Institute; [occ.] Technical Support; [oth. writ.] None published; [pers.] Never be afraid to be different, or to follow the dream.; [a.] Crystal Lake, IL

RAE, DORIS ELIZABETH
[b.] February 10, 1932, Aldershot, England; [p.] Jane and Samuel Didsbury; [m.] James M. Rae, October 12, 1952; [ch.] Iain Muir-Stuart McAllan,

Lesley Ann-Sandra Lynn; [ed.] Peterhead Academy High School-2 yrs. Buffalo General Nursings School; [occ.] Retired; [memb.] London Club, Geneva Presbyterian Church Art Club; [hon.] Had this poem published in the church magazine, Dean's List, Travel and Tourism Bryant and Stratton Business College; [pers.] I was moved by the Holy Spirit to write this poem when I visited Yosemite Park last year; [a.] Laguna Hills, CA

RAGAN, GALE
[b.] April 5, 1956, Miami, FL; [p.] Jerry and Mae Ragan (both are deceased); [ch.] Melvin Ted Reid, David John Alexander Reid; [ed.] University of Miami; [occ.] Math Curriculum Specialist, College Professor; [memb.] Book Review Club "Between Friends", National Council of Teachers of Math (NCTM), Florida Council of Teachers of Mathematics.; [hon.] Fulbright scholar, Teachers for Africa, Leadership Miami, Teacher Quest Scholarship Program, Alpha Kappa Alpha Sorority, Inc., Board of Director, University of Miami, College of Arts and Sciences Alumni Association.; [oth. writ.] Books "Divine" family story (being published Winston-Derek Publishers, Inc.), "Lemonade and Teardrops" fairy tale (to be published- submitted to Winston-Derek, Game-Invention, "Game of Hearts" (to be submitted to Winston- Derek.); [pers.] I enjoy writing and creating educational materials. I have been influenced by my mother, a country school teacher.; [a.] Miami, FL

RAINWATER, JOAN
[b.] March 5, 1943, Chattanooga, TN; [p.] Bob and Lucille Morse; [m.] Divorced; [ch.] Linda, Karen, Steve and Robin; [occ.] Artist; [pers.] "I look at life as a journey and treasure each moment, the good and the bad, for each brings its own gift."; [a.] Occoquan, VA

RAK, VICTORIA L.
[pen.] Vicki Rak; [b.] January 7, 1967, Chicago, IL; [p.] William and Olga Bake; [m.] Larry Rak, July 11, 1987; [ch.] Aileen - Amy Rak and Alyssa Lynn Rak; [ed.] Alan B Sheppard High School; [occ.] Homemaker; [memb.] Sts. Peter and Paul Ukrainian Orthodox Church Sunday School; [oth. writ.] Many other personal poems not published.; [pers.] I use my writing to help with either and my own tragedies and accomplishments. I enjoy to show my feelings in writing.; [a.] Hazel Crest, IL

RAMIREZ, PAUL
[b.] October 12, 1956, Bronx, NY; [p.] Thomas D. and Carmen Ramirez; [m.] Jean Victory-Ramirez, January 23, 1988; [ch.] Gabriel Ramirez, Olivia Ramirez; [ed.] Currently attending Lehman College (C.U.N.Y.); [occ.] Asst. Mgr., Credit and Collections, Covington Fabrics; [memb.] Civil War Re-enactment Organization, the 88th New York Volunteer Infantry, 2nd Rgt., Irish Brigade (rank, Corporal); [hon.] Golden Key National Honor Society, Dean's List; [pers.] The greatest tragedy is to pass through life without ever having dreamt or hoped of a better existence than this one.; [a.] New York City, NY

RAMIREZ, ROSEMARY
[b.] May 28, 1966, Denver, CO; [p.] Dorothy Almaguer, Joe DeHerrera; [m.] Chris Ramirez,

February 8, 1991; [ch.] Vicente C. Ramirez; [ed.] 9th Grade; [occ.] Housewife, Poet, Children Fiction; [memb.] Golden Triangle Writers Guild; [oth. writ.] Several poems published in newspapers, and one other in a different anthology.; [pers.] I've learned that live's are patterned by the decisions that are made, so I try to weigh consequences before I have to pay them.; [a.] Kerrville, TX

RANAWEERA, TANYA
[b.] April 14, 1947, Moscow, Russia; [p.] Wassily and Valentina Ignatenko; [m.] Thilak Ranaweera, April 14, 1966; [ch.] Asoka and Olga Ranaweera; [ed.] Bachelor of Science in Printing and Publishing. Diploma in Journalism.; [occ.] Teaching Russian Language to IMF Spouses.; [oth. writ.] Poems and short stories.; [pers.] "Once more in my life I realized that the ways of the Lord are imponderable, that we ourselves never know what we want, and how many times in life I passionately sought what I did not need and felt despondent over families which were successes."; [a.] Germantown, MD

RANQUIST, MAUREEN
[b.] March 19, 1944, New London, CT; [p.] Catherine and Arthur Parenteau; [m.] Carlton Ranquist, August 17, 1963; [ch.] Deborah 30, Patrick 27, Raymond 20; [ed.] Graduated New London High School 1962; [occ.] Seamstress; [hon.] Photo Contest Post Card Composite for City of Norwich, CT 1993; [oth. writ.] Essay for contest most romantic person.; [pers.] This poem was wrote in a few minutes on the spur of the moment as I thought about my daughters return home from a great distance after many years separation.; [a.] Bozrah, CT

RAPKIN, AMIDO
[b.] November 27, 1952, Remscheid, Germany; [p.] Kurt and Gertrud Somborn; [ed.] High School and Abitur in Wuppertal/Germany 5 years University Bonn Geographic/Biologie; [occ.] Tour Guide; [memb.] San Francisco, Tour Guide Guild; [pers.] The older I grow the less I know and have to say. Inspired thou you ad I wanted to give it another boy - what do I have to say... can I communicate...? Thanks to Jim for love and inspiration.; [a.] Sausalito, CA

REASON, BETTE V.
[pen.] Bette V. Reason; [b.] August 18, 1926, Peoria, IL; [p.] Alice A. and Roy Crawford; [m.] Tinker Reason, November 15, 1965; [ch.] Gary Shaffer (son); [ed.] Jefferson Center High School graduate, 2 yrs. Creative Writing Vo-Tech; [occ.] Security Desk Employee Computer Operator; [memb.] Board of Directors Sarasota Co. Recreational Club, Jazz Club of Sarasota, Red Cross Association, The Players Theatre; [hon.] Pres. Jefferson Center Assoc., Editor Jeffersonian TV Personality with husband musical duo named "The Tinkers"; [oth. writ.] Short stories of experiences traveling as musician for 20 years. None published "Bargain of Lifetime", "The Blizzard", "The Rev. Mr. Black", etc. I'm writing a novel called "The Gambit."; [pers.] Never give up and don't be afraid to start something new.; [a.] Sarasota, FL

REDELS, JANE ALICE
[b.] February 23, 1951, Holdenville, OK; [p.] James and Maxine Cowherd; [m.] S., Lynn Redels D.O., August 10, 1973; [ch.] Jennifer Gail Redels, Rebecca Dawn Redels; [ed.] B.S.E. Home Economics, Oklahoma Christian College, 1972 Lifetime Texas Teacher Certificate; [occ.] Housewife; [memb.] Church of Christ South, Corpus Christi, TX; [hon.] Magna Cum Laude OCC, 1972; [pers.] To raise a family in service to the Lord is the most valuable contribution a mother can make to a family. To live knowing where you are going is the greatest confidence.; [a.] Corpus Christi, TX

REHIL, RUSSELL E.
[b.] October 19, 1916, Hale, MI; [p.] Henry and Mary Rehil; [m.] Irene Rehil, October 5, 1943; [ch.] 1 Son Dayna Layne Rehil; [ed.] Graduated from 10th Grade on May 18th in 1933 from Hale High School; [occ.] Retired April 8th 1979 was Production manager at Adelphian Mills in Holly Michigan.; [memb.] Member of the 7th day Adventists Church for 42 years. Was in the army almost 4 years in World War 2; [hon.] I received several medals and was Sergeant in the Army.; [oth. writ.] I have written about 150 poems about all kinds of occasions I just finished one about the awful disaster in Oklahoma City.; [pers.] I like to paint pictures with words and I like to write about my Lord and Saviour. He has been so good to me, He gave me the talent, so O feel I should use it.; [a.] Hale, MI

REICH, JESSICA
[b.] June 27, 1974, Coosbay, OR; [p.] Candice Reich, Curtis Reich; [ed.] Received my GED from C.A.E.C. in Caldwell, ID 1991; [occ.] Assistant Office Manager for Marca Electric and Electrical Contracting Co.; [hon.] Previous publication in "Seasons to Come." Special Olympics Award. Editors Choice Award; [oth. writ.] Half way, published in "Seasons to Come." Professional recording for "The Sound of Poetry."; [pers.] Do not label another "crazy" because their views are not as yours. For if you do, only your fear and ignorance shows.; [a.] Coquille, OR

REID, NORMAN M.
[pen.] Norman M. Reid; [b.] May 19, 1929, Belfast, North Ireland; [p.] William A. and Mary Shaw Reid; [m.] Erna H. Reid, June 21, 1957; [ch.] Heidi; [ed.] Methodist College, Belfast, North Ireland; [occ.] Retired; [pers.] I am a Christian and I just started writing poetry. I strive to communicate my faith in such a way that it will help other people strengthen theirs.; [a.] Granada Hills, CA

REIL, NANCY L.
[b.] June 11, 1947, MA; [p.] Joseph and Irene Sylvain; [m.] Divorced; [ch.] John, Robin, Sherry, Patrick; [ed.] Brown Elem. Case High Swansea Mass. School Illinois Hawthorn Univ. Candidate for Ass. Degree Stratham Vo. Tech. Phlibotany; [occ.] CNA, Phlibotanist; [hon.] 3 Science Deplomas World of Poetry Gold Award 1986; [oth. writ.] Mighty Man (song) published, Heavenly Manner, The Blind Man, Gods Flower Never Pretend, Empty Nest; [pers.] As God tries even the eyelids of the righteous there's a reason for everything even life short lived had its purpose, there is a light on every life, there is a light on every life, and a great value; [a.] Farmingtan, NH

REINACHER, RANDY LEE
[b.] January 25, 1957, UT; [p.] Robert W. and Phoebe K.; [ch.] Jesse Lee, Brian Robert and Jeffery Michael; [ed.] Graduated Washington High School; [oth. writ.] "The Final Battlefield" a poem about nuclear war "The Old Man and the Mountain" an unpublished short story for children about racial and sexual prejudice; [pers.] Most of my writing is geares towards pointing out the wrongs in our society; [a.] Ogden, UT

RELL, JOE
[pen.] Giuseppe Rella; [b.] Grumo Appula, Bari, Italy; [p.] Michele Rella and Lucia Raguso; [ed.] Average; [occ.] On call; [memb.] Knights of Columbus; [hon.] Bronze Medal from Grand Union, American Citizen from 1990, blood donor of New York Blood Center; [oth. writ.] One poem in the book of dark side of the moon 1994 from the National Library of Poetry with name: Giuseppe Rella.; [pers.] I believe in God and for he is on the top of everything seen and unseen; [a.] Brewster, NY

REMBECKI, ROBERT
[pen.] Robert Henry; [b.] December 13, 1965, Detroit, MI; [p.] Henry and Louise Rembecki; [oth. writ.] Several poems, short stories and a personal diary, as yet unpublished.; [pers.] Through my writing, I wish to expand the way people view the world around them.; [a.] Warren, MI

RESCHKE, VALERIE J.
[pen.] Andre'; [b.] February 5, 1934, NY; [p.] Michel Audroue, Julia Audroue'; [m.] William Reschke, June 5, 1960; [ch.] Julie, Michele, William III; [ed.] Degree - Biology, Chemistry, Math, BA; [occ.] Broker, Author; [memb.] National Association for female Executives, Leukemia Society Scholarship President CCAR; [hon.] Phi Beta Kappa; [oth. writ.] Mendel and the Pea, the true road to profitability; [pers.] My ultimate goal is to bring joy with word images. One who gives through the written word - lives forever.; [a.] Danville, CA

REYNAUD, RALPH
[pen.] Kahlil Opio Lasana; [b.] September 30, 1943, Lake Charles, LA; [p.] Prof. Ralph Reynaud Sr., Liora B. Reynaud; [m.] Onida Claire Reynaud, November 25, 1965; [ch.] Lora Reynaud Griffin, Austin Reynaud, Michael Reynaud; [ed.] W.O. Boston High Fisk University - B.A. in Soc. The American Univ. - M.A. in African Studies; [occ.] Parole Officer (youth) Washington, DC; [memb.] St. Stephen and The Incarnation Episcopal Church, The Omega Psi Phi Fraternity, The Ex-Offender Task Force.; [hon.] Scholarship for African studies from the United Church of Christ, various job related awards.; [oth. writ.] Poems published in student publication at fisk University, poems published in newsletters "bread" at SSI Church and "Parole Works" on the job.; [pers.] Encompassing Challenges and obstacles, life is an enlightening spiritual journey of discovery and discernment linking human and divine within one's true-self and through one's relationships in the I am ness of the life force of being!; [a.] Washington, DC

RHINEBERGER, JANICE
[b.] June 14, 1943, Greenwich, OH; [p.] John and Ruth Laser (both deceased); [m.] Robert Rhineberger, September 17, 1966; [ch.] Thomas, Roberta, Kevin, Rebecca and Brian; [ed.] High School Graduate, Graduated 6-2-61 from Willard High School Willard, Ohio; [occ.] Housewife disabled with multiple sclerosis in 1987; [memb.] Sandusky country multiple sclerosis society secretary for two years Harvest Temple Church since 1-1-67 S.S. Secretary for 8 1/2 years.; [hon.] My husband I received a framed certificate for 10 years in the bus ministry. (Husband (over 15 years) me 12 years-total); [oth. writ.] Another poem printed in our church bulletin.

RHODES SR., DONNIE RAY
[b.] April 29, 1948; [p.] Delma Talton, Jesse J. Rhodes; [m.] Brenda Jackson Rhodes, December 31, 1964; [ch.] Brenda Dianne, Donna Faye, Donnie Jr.; [ed.] Smithfield, NC; [occ.] Writer; [memb.] D.A.V.; [oth. writ.] Romance Novel - Almost finished - "Joe Jones and his True Love."; [pers.] You can take a pencil and paper and your mind, and go anyplace, anywhere, at anytime.; [a.] Gloucester, NC

RICE, JOYCE A.
[pen.] Cricket; [b.] February 1, 1933, Ohio; [p.] Earsie and James Poe; [m.] Manford Rice (Deceased), November 11, 1953; [ch.] 4; [ed.] 12th grade; [occ.] Housewife

RICE, SHELDON W.
[b.] August 3, 1961, McConnell AFB, KS; [p.] Emanuel Rice Jr., Ellen Virginia Rice; [m.] Carolyn Jean Tolbert-Rice, March 18, 1988; [ed.] R.A.F. Lakenheath High School, Suffolk, England, University of Maryland (Europe) Wichita State University, KS. University of South Carolina; [occ.] Security Officer; [memb.] Sisters of the Nineties, The Amy Biehl Foundation, Fund For a Free South Africa, The Africa Fund; [oth. writ.] Journalism Fellowship (USC) Several OP-Ed pieces in newspapers in Germany, Virginia, Florida and South Carolina. OP-Ed piece for Ebony magazine. Several article for the New Reporter (USC).; [pers.] I thank God, my parents and my wife who are my inspiration and sisters of the nineties for belief in me.; [a.] Columbia, SC

RICHARDS, JEANETTE HAMMOND
[b.] July 23, 1953, Houston, TX; [p.] Richard W. and Patricia Flippen; [m.] Dr. Clifford W. Hammond Jr. (Deceased), Jake Richards; [ch.] Daughter 16, Dijeanait Hammond; [ed.] Graduated from Tomball High School 1971 Southwestern Business College 1972, Bryman Medical School 1976, Champions School of Real Estate 1991, Currently a student of Liberty University of Lynchburg, VA; [occ.] Student, Homemaker; [memb.] Dolen Baptist Church; [hon.] Former President of Harris County Chapter 6 Auxiliary of American Osteopathic Physicians 1985; [oth. writ.] None published various medical articles; [pers.] I was inspired to write the poem. Attitude checked, by God, to honor my very special cousin, Ann Hammond Parisoe of Lessburgh, Florida, who has such a remarkable attitude, like the Apostle Paul.; [a.] Shepherd, TX

RIDGWAY, CAULETTE
[b.] March 9, 1965, Jamaica; [p.] Mr. Edison and Mrs. Gwendolyn Ridgway; [ed.] White Plains High, Pace Business Institute; [occ.] Advertising Representative; [memb.] Bethel Baptist Church; [pers.] To have faith always can bring things hoped, for that's not yet seen. Believe in yourself.

RILEY, DAVID P.
[b.] January 21, 1957, Hot Springs, AR; [p.] Kenneth and Patsy Riley; [m.] Connie Sue Riley, July 11, 1975; [ch.] Jeremy Clyde and Jennifer Nicole; [ed.] Hot Springs High School; [occ.] Self-employed contractor; [hon.] National Library of Poetry; [oth. writ.] Published in local newspaper, The Sentinel Record; [pers.] I find the instilled infallible values of my past youth inspire my thoughts in regards to this rapid changing present world!; [a.] Royal, AR

RILEY, DEAN WAYNE
[pen.] Dean Wayne; [b.] March 28, 1961, Clinton, OK; [p.] Royce Riley, Deanna Brownell; [m.] Divorced; [ch.] Shannon Paige Riley; [ed.] Oliver Wendell Holmes High School, San Antonio, TX, Platt Technical College, Tulsa, OK; [hon.] Platt College Student of the Year, 1987; [pers.] I write positive poetry for people of all ages who go through divorce. Especially for children, so they can keep high self-esteem, through separation from parents.; [a.] Tulsa, OK

RIORDAN, MELISSA ANN
[b.] November 19, 1975, Louisville, KY; [p.] Danny Riordan, Jean Miller; [ed.] Henry Co. High, Jefferson Community College, The Hair Design School; [occ.] Buffet attendant at Ponderosa, attending Hair Design School; [pers.] I really haven't been influenced by any early poets. I just write when a thought comes to my mind, and a poem becomes of it.; [a.] Louisville, KY

RIOS, ELIZABETH
[b.] May 26, 1978, Sangandro, CA; [p.] Magdalena and Rafael Rios; [ed.] Independent Study in 11th Grade - Armiyo High School; [occ.] Student; [hon.] Honor Student; [oth. writ.] Have written many poems and couple of stories, but this is first publication.; [a.] Fairfield, CA

RIOS, KATHLEEN H.
[b.] April 26, 1918, Shellman, GA; [p.] P. J. Hilton, Jannie Edwards; [m.] Raymond Rios, July 20, 1941; [ch.] Ray 2, Ramona, Georgia, Susie; [ed.] High School, Columbus GA; [occ.] Housewife

RIVERA, STEPHANIE
[b.] May 17, 1984, Fort Belvoir, VA; [p.] Mike and Gloria Rivera; [ed.] Currently in 5th grade, Meadow Park Elementary School, Port Charlotte, FL; [occ.] Student; [memb.] Meadow Park Student Council; [a.] Port Charlotte, FL

ROACHELL, ORETHA HELEN JACKSON
[b.] October 30, 1934, Van Alstyne, TX; [p.] John Lester and Martha Jane (Burk) Jackson; [m.] Mickey Lee Roachell, December 3, 1983; [ch.] Pamela Jane Doy, Larry Don Ervin, Glenn Ray Ervin, Rickey DeWayne Ervin Deborah Dianne Collins, Celesta Eileen Douglas; [ed.] Van Alstyne

High School and Anna High School Texas, Data Processing; [occ.] Housewife and Pastor's Wife; [memb.] Florence Assembly Full Gospel, Arkansas; [hon.] Texas Instruments, H and R Block Tax, Data Processing and Senior Year, too many things to mention; [oth. writ.] I have written other songs, poems, stories, and books, but nothing has been published.; [pers.] I love to write poems, songs and children stories, but only write when God lays something on my heart to write about.; [a.] Wilmar, AR

ROBERT, AYANNA MONIQUE
[b.] August 15, 1973, New Orleans, LA; [p.] Earline T. Robert and Adam W. Robert Jr.; [ed.] High School graduate of West Jefferson High, Harrey, LA pursuing Bachelors of Bus. Administration, Accounting at University of Texas San Antonio; [occ.] Student, model and part-time substitute teacher; [memb.] Data Processing Management Association, Circle K, Baptist Student Union, Phyllis Nelson's Performing Arts Academy and Ebene (Urban Contemporary singing trio); [hon.] Honors in Physics and English, Marine Corps Scholarship award; [oth. writ.] "The Existing Black Woman", "No Longer a Little Girl", "Freedom Cries", "Money and Live", "Christmas", "Satisfaction", "Once in a Lifetime", "Spring", "Missing You", "Give A Smile", "Sun Vs. Moon", and many other writings.; [pers.] Honesty is the best policy. You must be true to yourself first, then to others.; [a.] San Antonio, TX

ROBERTS, CHARLES EDWARD
[pen.] Chas; [b.] September 16, 1946, New Haven, CT; [p.] Helen and Raymond Roberts; [m.] Donna M. Roberts, October 20, 1989; [ch.] Step children Lorrinda, Gerald, Janna; [ed.] Derby High School, Mattatuck Community College-Association Degree Police Science and Business; [occ.] Limousine and Bus Driver Conn. Limo Inc.; [memb.] Storm Engine Co. 2 21 yrs., Army reserves (24 yrs), American Legion; [hon.] All-state Football 1962, numerous safety awards, Army Achievement Award, Army Recommendation Award Medal; [pers.] I believe that great achievement should be recognized and documented for all to see and cherish forever! Special people touch our life's for a short time and they should never be forgotten.; [a.] Ansonia, CT

ROBERTS, DAVID
[b.] October 5, 1968, Marin County, CA; [p.] Cathy and George Dray; [occ.] Sports Instructor Gallinas Child-Care; [pers.] Either a poem of love for a woman or the chaos that draws near. It is all indicative of freedom in letting it out on paper.; [a.] San Rafael, CA

ROBERTS, EARNESTEEN
[pen.] Et Roberts; [b.] April 7, 1925, AR; [p.] Rev. Ira and Ella Jones; [m.] 1940, Divorced 1964; [ch.] Ira Van Byron Roberts, Trecia Roberts Chedister and Virgil Ray Roberts; [ed.] Only Jr. College; [occ.] Home keeper writing often in early hours.; [oth. writ.] None published but I do write essays, short stories, my opinions often, most of my work though is poetry and essays seldom kept.; [pers.] No town or country can ever be better than the quality of it's citizens. You are never defeated until you admit it, and never old until you want to be!

ROBERTS, JOSEPH M.
[pen.] J. Michael Roberts; [b.] May 12, 1977, Wareham, MA; [p.] George and Patricia Roberts; [ed.] High School - Wareham High School Class of 1995; [pers.] "I always look for the burning star in any situation."; [a.] Wareham, MA

ROBERTS, LISA MICHELLE
[b.] March 25, 1971, Ravenna, OH; [p.] Linda M. Seguin; [ch.] Billy Joe Beard, Bethany Leanne Turner, Kimber Lynn Roberts; [occ.] Full-time mom; [pers.] I write from what I feel inside.; [a.] Branford, FL

ROBERTSON, JADA
[b.] February 6, 1970, Lyndonville, NY; [p.] Arlene O'Brien, Hubert Tuttle; [ed.] L.A. Webber, Daeman College; [occ.] Secretary, Doan and Co. Rochester, NY; [memb.] Social Sciences Honor Society; [hon.] Cum Laude, Dean's List; [oth. writ.] Co-Editor L.A. Webber Year Book Staff a poem published through a Literary magazine, 1989.; [pers.] Many thanks to Ed and Doreen for giving me a start in life, to Ron and Kathy for always believing in me and to Ben for taking the time to listen. The greatest gifts are felt within your heart-thank you for giving me the greatest gift of all: Friendship; [a.] Lyndonville, NY

ROBINS, JENNIFER
[b.] February 16, 1975, Walnut Creek, CA; [p.] William and Sharon Robins; [ed.] Meridian High School, Meridian Idaho. Whitman College Walla Walla, Washington; [occ.] Student; [memb.] Delta Delta Delta Theta Omicron Chapter; [hon.] Presidential Academic Fitness Award. 1989, 1993; [oth. writ.] 50-60 poems, 10 short stories.; [pers.] My poetry reflects events in my life that have affected me.; [a.] Walla Walla, WA

ROBINSON, ANDREA LAWSON
[b.] March 16, 1955, Manhattan, NY; [p.] Horance H. Lawson, Frieda O. Lawson; [m.] Divorced; [ed.] B.A. SUNY College Old Westbury, Adelphi Univ. Garden City, NY Certified Paralegal; [occ.] Certified NY State Teaching Assistant; [memb.] Independent Musicians Association; [hon.] 4 year undergrad college scholarship United Christian Evangelistic Association 4140 Broadway New York; [oth. writ.] Six articles ready for publication: How Do You Treat Your Glory, Our Heavenly Credit Card, A Seduced Society, The Submission Question, The Heartbeat of a Marriage; [pers.] I want my writings to be thought provoking and make a positive difference in someone's life.; [a.] Hempstead, NY

ROBINSON, ANNA MARIE
[b.] July 30, 1960, Baltimore, MD; [p.] June R. Sommers; [m.] David Wells Robinson, May 3, 1980; [ch.] Lindsay Elizabeth, Kelsey, Rebecca; [ed.] Perry Hall High School, Life - The Best School; [occ.] Homemaker, Wife and Mother; [memb.] Active on Local PTA and School Council; [oth. writ.] Poems, short stories and Christian music. None have been published at this time. Some seuss-like rhymes for family friends and party events.; [pers.] I write as I am inspired, although some what slowly and methodically I'm only on this earth once and I hope to express all the aspects of life, love and disappointment. With God's and my families help I will.; [a.] Richmond, VA

ROBINSON, BRANDI E.
[b.] February 13, 1973, Lynn, MA; [p.] Barbara and Fornest Dyer; [ed.] Lasell Collegem Newton, MA., A.A. Human Service; [occ.] Special needs direct care manager; [oth. writ.] Several poems, poem published in sparrow grass poetry forum anthology.; [pers.] This poem is dedicated to my closest friend Lanni, who has been there for me through and through and has never asked for anything in return.; [a.] Salem, MA

ROBINSON, CARRIE LYNN
[pen.] Care Bear; [b.] December 5, 1981, Warren, OH; [p.] Drew A. and Carol L. Robinson; [ed.] Sixth Grade Student at Three Oaks Middle School, Ft. Myers, FL; [occ.] Student; [memb.] Bear-A-Tones Choir, Collier County Softball League (Red Sox) and Blue Heron Band; [hon.] Three Oaks Middle School Student of the Week and Student of the Month; [pers.] I enjoy playing the piano and writing. Do your best at whatever you do. Live each day as if it was your last.; [a.] Fort Myers, FL

ROBINSON, ELIZABETH L.
[pen.] Lady McBeth/Miss Beth; [b.] August 16, 1969, Onemia, MN; [p.] Patrick and Mary Marrs; [m.] (Divorced), July 25, 1989; [ch.] Kirsten E. Robinson (Father), Cory Robinson; [ed.] Mat-Su Alternative School Graduate '87, Mat-Su Community College '87-89; [occ.] Poet/Mother; [memb.] Home Business, Assco. TSN Tee-Shirt Distributorship; [oth. writ.] This is my first published work, but there are several promising works yet to come.; [pers.] I splash my emotions on paper as the ink spills from my pen. My writings are inspired by my mentors and close friends.; [a.] Wasilla, AK

ROBINSON, GWENDOLYN
[pen.] Amber Nelson; [b.] May 4, 1943, Philadelphia, PA; [p.] Edison Nelson, Leola Nelson; [m.] Caldwell Robinson, June 19, 1962; [ch.] Caldwell Buzzy and Darren Amina, Gabrielle; [ed.] William Penn High, Pierce Business School; [occ.] Pedestrian Traffic Director; [memb.] Metropolitan Baptist Church Sunday School Committee; [pers.] I strive to bring man and woman, boy and girl into the knowledge of Jesus Christ, through my poetry.; [a.] Philadelphia, PA

ROBINSON, ISABEL
[pen.] Miss Bell; [b.] December 28, 1939, Mound Bayou, MS; [p.] Bernadine Murry, Richard Gattin; [m.] Freddie Robinson, December 24, 1982; [ed.] Southwest Mississippi Community College, Summit, MS, Delgado Community College Summit, MS and South Eastern Louisiana University Hammond, LA; [occ.] Private duty nursing, and quilter; [hon.] Honorable mention received an Award of Merit, Certificate from the World of Poetry September 21, 1990 poem was "Yesteryears"; [oth. writ.] Wrote first poem when I was twelve English teacher and I copied it from somewhere, but I did not. I was discouraged and shy from then on.; [pers.] A deep desire to let the world know that God is alive and will soon make his final appearance to claim his own.; [a.] Magnolia, MS

ROBINSON, JACK K.
[pen.] Jack Robinson; [b.] September 1, 1907; [p.] Ella, Daniel; [m.] Ellen, May 14, 1938; [ch.] U.S.A; [ed.] High School Grad.; [occ.] Retired; [hon.] Poem published in "Seasons to Come"; [oth. writ.] About 50 poems

ROBINSON, MESHELLE A.
[pen.] Meshelle A. Robinson; [b.] October 29, 1970, Lafayette, IN; [p.] Nelson and Beverly Robinson; [ed.] Elementary-Mayflower Mill Jr High, Southwestern High School, McCutheon High Vocational College-Ivy Tech; [occ.] Medical Assistant, Arnett Clinic of Lafayette, IN; [memb.] Alumni Associate of Medical Assistants of Ivy Tech; [pers.] No one asks for the life they get, and many times it's unfair. But as Matthew 7:7 says - "if you keep seeking, you will find." So you can't give up, as long as you try, you'll succeed.; [a.] Lafayette, IN

ROBINSON, NATALIE
[b.] January 24, 1978, Pennsylvania; [p.] Mr. and Mrs. Burnell Robinson; [ed.] Monessen Sr. High School, plan on attending the University of Pittsburgh; [memb.] Mentoring young minds Monessen High School Band, Group of the Performing Arts; [hon.] Black History Month Essay Contest Winner (Honorable Mention), Lions Club Student of the month, Achieved Captain of Majorettes, 1st Clarinetist in Concert Band; [oth. writ.] I would like to thank God for giving me this talent as well as others and I would like to thank my mother Mrs. Evelyn Robinson for encouraging me to show those talents.; [pers.] Monessen, PA

ROBINSON SR., DONALD
[b.] September 14, 1945, Washington, LA; [p.] Thonius Robinson Sr., Hinda Robinson; [m.] Jacqueline Robinson; [ch.] Kevin Duane, Dona Inez, Donald II Hinda Rasheda; [ed.] Paul L. Dunbar High, Southern University, (B.A.) Southern Univ. Law School (J.D., Juris Doctor); [occ.] County Administrator-Human Services Agency, Opelousas, LA; [memb.] NACAA, LSU-E Bd. of Advisors, St. Landry Bank Adv. Bd., Wash. Museum and Tourist Commission, Am. Society of Notary Publics, Nat'l Bar Assn. LACSO, Project Independence, Advisory Comm., Chairman, Wash. Vo-Ed Center, Drs. Hosp. Bd. of Dir., CEO St. Landry Parish CAA Foundation, Inc., Gov. Policy Adv. Com. (State-wide) Supt. SS Shiloh Bapt. Church, Deacon Bd. Sec., Teacher; [hon.] Am. Leg, Who's Who, South and Southwest, 7th Ed., DOE, Frontiers Intl., Gov. State of LA, SLPCAA BOD and Staff, U.S. Civil Ser. Comm., CSA, Salutatorian, All-Around Boy, Music, Drama, Speech, English, Science, SGA (Pres.); [oth. writ.] Two poems published in Spring and Fall Anthologies of College Poetry (Nat'l P. Press, LA, Calif.). One poem re-printed in "Pegasus", 30 poems written, 3-plays, 2-Novels (unfinished).; [pers.] I live to lift, one, let, one, lead one to external joy, and life. My parents influenced, taught and nurtured profoundly.; [a.] Washington, LA

RODGERS, ROBERT HOMER
[pen.] Bob Rodgers; [b.] November 8, 1926, Cleveland, OH; [p.] Mr. and Mrs. Samuel Homer Rodgers; [m.] Mary Patricia (Brady) Rodgers, November 27, 1947; [ch.] Robert T., Mary Denise - Beth Ann - Ann Marie - Mary Pat.,; [ed.] 2 Years College; [occ.] Retired; [pers.] I spent 34 years on the Lakewood Fire Dept. The last eleven as Asst. Fire Chief. I loved it and would start all over again if I could. I've been married to Pat almost 48 years and I'd love to repeat those years also.; [a.] Lakewood, OH

RODRIGUEZ JR., DANIEL E.
[b.] July 27, 1967, CA; [p.] Dan and Sheila Rodriguez; [ed.] Simi Valley High School Grad. 1987, Moorpark College Grad. 1992; [occ.] Sales Associate; [hon.] Certificates of Apreciation Disabled Student of the Year, Best Poet; [oth. writ.] Defending the Throne, Reflections/over 550 call for list (805) 584 9060; [pers.] We are more held by love than love is by us; [a.] Simi Valley, CA

ROFFLER, ILSE
[b.] February 28, 1940, Switzerland; [p.] Hans and Ida Schoedler; [m.] Hans Roffler, June 24, 1961; [ch.] Kathrin, Robert and Jean; [ed.] College and Trade School in Switzerland; [memb.] San Pedro Writer's Guild; [pers.] In my writings I like to capture the essence and values of life. I have lived in New York for 14 years, and in Los Angeles since 6 years. I do write in German and in English.; [a.] San Pedro, CA

ROGERS, BRIAN K.
[pen.] BRI, Nick Moore, Michael Donavan; [b.] August 17, 1970, Cincinnati, OH; [p.] Don Rogers, June Rogers; [ed.] Lemon-Monroe High School; [occ.] Slave to Industrial Routine; [oth. writ.] Various poems in various arts and entertainment newspapers; [pers.] The diversity of my poetry stems from melodramatic episodes in my life. I'll continue to be somewhere…writing something.; [a.] Middletown, OH

ROGERS, BRON LEE
[b.] July 31, 1978, Harrison, AR; [p.] Lonnie and Sharon Rogers; [ed.] Senior in fall 1995; [occ.] Student; [memb.] None I wish to share; [oth. writ.] "A Guilty Soul" (a sonnet); [pers.] I've always believed that when I'm writing a piece of poetry, I'm pouring part of my spirit into the poem and onto the paper… This is why I've always called poetry, or any writings that express feelings, "Paper Spirits…"; [a.] Harrison, AR

ROGERS, LINDA
[b.] February 5, 1966, Nisayuna, NY; [p.] Joseph and Penny Costello; [m.] Joseph G. Rogers Sr., November 14, 1987; [ch.] Kimberly Marie Rogers, Joseph Gary Rogers Jr., Johnathan Michael Rogers; [ed.] Grade 12. High School Diploma; [occ.] Mother, Housewife; [oth. writ.] I have put together a large notebook collection of 70 poems that I have written over the years and yes, they are all mine.; [pers.] My dream is to eventually put together and publish all the poems I have written. And maybe touch the hearts of many people. I would also like to maybe have some of my poems turned into music. That how I would like to make my living.; [a.] Annapolis, MD

ROGERS, NEIL G.
[b.] September 21, 1944, Cochrane, Ontario, Canada; [p.] Fred Rogers, (Mother deceased); [ed.] B.A. Psychology and Economics Ripon College, Ripon Wisconsin; [occ.] Senior Consultant Technology Planning and Management Corp. RTP, NC; [memb.] Still a number in good standing with my friends and family which might also be considered an honor perhaps.; [hon.] All too old and tarnished for "reflection" here upon; [oth. writ.] I have written several of these (3 in 1 poems for personal friends and family but none have been written for publication. They have been for weddings and for the passing of family and friends for the most part.; [pers.] These poems are based on the belief that two separate and distinct entities can be joined in the heart, the spirit or the mind to form yet a third entity with its own identity or essence; [a.] Apex, NC

ROGERS, STEVE
[b.] August 9, 1950, Stamford, TX; [p.] Clinton and Betty Rogers; [ch.] Mason and Maylee Rogers; [ed.] Angelo State University, San Angelo, TX; [occ.] Park Ranger for the Texas Parks and Wildlife Dept.; [memb.] Texas Poets Assoc.; [hon.] Poet Lariat of 1st and 2nd Cowboy gathering of Buffalo Gap, TX; [oth. writ.] Book of poetry-country and cowboy poetry. Articles published in Abilene Reporter News.; [pers.] I am dedicated to preserving the heritage of the American Cowboy through poetry and interpretive programs.; [a.] Buffalo Gap, TX

ROLL, DORIS M.
[pen.] Doris M. Roll; [b.] August 16, 1943, Kansas City, KS; [p.] Arthur Keightley, Mabel Keightley; [m.] Robert D. Roll, June 6, 1960; [ch.] Roberta DeAnn-Stephanie Michelle, Jason Matthew Roll Sr.; [ed.] 11th; [occ.] Raising 3 grand children; [memb.] First Christian Church, Co. Camp Fire Girls and Boys Leader; [hon.] Life; [oth. writ.] This is my first one; [pers.] This publication of my poem brightens a corner in my life. My husband passed away May 2, 1995.; [a.] Kansas City, KS

ROLLINGS, BONNIE
[b.] May 3, 1951, Baltimore, MD; [ed.] B.A. 1975 Univ. of Florida; [occ.] Secretary at the National Institutes of Health; [memb.] Altar Guild-Grace Episcopal Church, Assistant Director 1975-1977 Santa Fe Dance Co., Apprentice 1977 Polish Dance Theatre Poznan Poland, Artistic Director Spring 1988 Central, MD Ballet Theatre; [hon.] Dean's List; [oth. writ.] Much poetry

ROMAN, ABIMELETH
[b.] June 6, 1963, Las Piedras, PR; [p.] Angel Roman, Francisca Martinez; [m.] Mercedes Natalia Roman, September 25, 1992; [ch.] Abieser Roman; [ed.] A. Dias Lebron High School, P.R. Humacao University, P.R.; [occ.] Utilities Operator; [memb.] International Churches Of Christ; [oth. writ.] Several poems written in Spanish and some other compositions.; [pers.] My writings reflect my own deep emotions and those of all people striving to conquer love. I've been greatly influenced by nature itself and by the beauty of being, at times, in peace with myself.; [a.] Haverhill, MA

ROMO, MONICA
[b.] August 16, 1977, California; [p.] Maria Romo; [ed.] Montgomery High School; [oth. writ.] Several poems and short stories, none of which

have been published.; [pers.] All I write comes straight from my soul and personal experience. I am especially influenced by the beat writers such as Jack Kerouac, and by Sylvia Plath; [a.] Imperial Beach, CA

RONNBACK, GUNNAR
[pen.] Gunnar Lindh; [b.] October 29, 1920; [m.] Sweden, Disolved; [ch.] Tora and Leif; [ed.] Stockholm Tech Furniture Design entered U.S. Aug. 7 1940, U.S. Army 3 1/2 years; [occ.] Retired, cabinet maker; [oth. writ.] None published; [a.] Sacramento, CA

ROSARIO, B. J.
[pen.] B. J.; [b.] December 27, 1947, Miami, FL; [p.] Mrs. Pauline Plummer; [m.] Mr. Jesus Rosario, April 26, 1987; [ch.] Kenneth M. Adams, Robert L. Anderson Jr., Kameron G. Anderson; [ed.] Miami Northwestern High, UDC University (University of the District of Columbia) Philosophy Major BA 1990; [occ.] Housewife; [memb.] International Biographical Centre; [hon.] International Who's Who, 1992-93 Platinum Edition of Who's who Registry; [oth. writ.] Several new stories and poems not yet submitted for publication.; [pers.] Writing is a gift that I did not know I had. Thanks to the Chairman (Dr. Terry Smith), of my dept. at the University who encouraged my writing skills. It was his suggestion, that I write for publication.; [a.] Alexandria, VA

ROSINI, LISA MARIE
[b.] December 9, 1970, Alabama; [p.] Maria and Kasimir Rosini; [ed.] Northport High School, Northport, NY; [hon.] Semi-finalist in the 1995 North American Open Poetry Contest.; [pers.] Thank you, Grandpa; [a.] East Northport, NY

ROSS, DOROTHY J.
[pen.] Gracie Welldon; [b.] Vicksburg, MS; [p.] Willis Ross Sr., Attean (Atlean) Ross; [ed.] Rosa A. Temple High, Vicksburg, MS, Jackson State University, Jackson, MS, Institute of Children Literature, CT, Utica Junior College, Utica, MS; [occ.] Administrative Clerk-US Postal Service; [memb.] Greater Bethlehem Temple Apostolic Church-Sunday School Teacher, Education Committee, Reporter for National Organization Magazine; [hon.] Who's Who Among American Junior Colleges and Universities, Honor Student; [oth. writ.] A collection a poetry not yet published, also do short stories, prose, hears words in music and can match words with moods, a lyricist, a few pieces of poetry have been published in my church National Organization Magazine, "The Voice In The wilderness.; [pers.] In poetry I touch hearts, sharpen insight, build character, alert the mind, mend spirits, inspire, my natural love for people inclines me to offer them the best of me, those things that have been the best for me, "Doing good is the spice of life, sew and live."; [a.] Jackson, MS

ROSSETER, L. GEORGIA
[b.] Before Prohibition, MN; [p.] Lillian, George Tate; [m.] George Rosseter; [ed.] B.S. South Dakota State; [occ.] Retired art teacher; [hon.] Cum Laude; [oth. writ.] Purple Wins (my own) and poems in magazines; [pers.] "What's comin' to ye won't pass ye by" an old Scotch saying.; [a.] Madison, WI

ROWE, DARLENE E.
[b.] January 10, 1966, McConnelsburg, PA; [m.] Donnie Rowe Jr., August 15, 1987; [occ.] Administrative Specialist-Frederick Cancer Research and Development Center; [oth. writ.] Several poems for friends and family members, publications in Frederick News Post; [pers.] I write poems to comfort and bring happiness to those who are special to me.; [a.] Knoxville, MD

ROWLAND, JODIE THERESA
[b.] August 21, 1984, Queens; [p.] Sharon and Peter Rowland; [ed.] P.S. 183 Astre Program for Gifted Children; [occ.] Student; [hon.] Achievement for Reading, Math and Social Studies, Federal Aviation Administration, Aviation Medical Division for excellent performance in a Essay contest about drugs.; [oth. writ.] Echoes of Yesterday; [pers.] I wrote this poem to let people know we have to save the forests and animals.; [a.] Arverne, NY

ROWLEY, ERIN
[b.] May 14, 1983, Elyria, OH; [p.] Frank and Celine Rowley; [ed.] Avon East Elementary; [occ.] Student; [hon.] Semi Finalist Ribbon for Young Authors; [oth. writ.] Three young authors book.; [a.] Avon, OH

ROYCHOWDHURY, SANGHAMITRA
[b.] December 20, 1976, New York, NY; [p.] Samar Roychowdhury, Shipra Roychowdhury; [ed.] United Nations International School, Brooklyn Technical High School; [hon.] Certificates of Excellence received in several academic subjects, Medals received for Math and English in Eleventh grade have been in Math and Science honor roll.; [oth. writ.] Several poems published in an anthologies and High School literary magazines. "Self-Portrait" Published in 1992's "A Different Light"; [pers.] I write poetry simply for inner satisfaction and self-fulfillment. I am grateful to my friends, teachers, and parents. Without their support and encouragement, my success would not have been possible.; [a.] New York, NY

RUDOLPH, HEATHER J.
[b.] April 30, 1975, New Jersey; [p.] Carol Crystal and Frank Rudolph; [ed.] Rollins College, Orlando!; [occ.] Student; [pers.] Our sadness is sometimes the only way to connect to another soul. Our joy surfaces after the connection.; [a.] Indian Rocks Beach, FL

RUEL, LINDA
[b.] May 30, 1953, New Britain, CT; [p.] John and Martha (Field) Cheskus; [m.] Dennis Ruel, August 1, 1970; [ch.] Lori Ann, Douglas, Joseph; [oth. writ.] Several poems published in magazine and book form.; [pers.] My family, my love, my life; [a.] Plainville, CT

RULE, ALEXANDER JAMES WAISH
[b.] August 21, 1970, Wisconsin; [p.] Alan and Beverly Rule; [m.] Allison L. Rule, June 19, 1993; [oth. writ.] In the process of writing a novel.; [pers.] Has traveled to Ireland Germany, Austria, England, Japan and lived several years in Alaska.; [a.] Savannah, GA

RUNGE, ROBERT
[pen.] Fredrick LeMore; [b.] February 28, 1972, Elkhorn, WI; [p.] Sheila Tharp, Shirley Brockwell (grandparent); [ed.] Sharon Community, Beloit Catholic High School, Nova; [occ.] Yeoman, USN; [memb.] Historical Society, American Red Cross; [hon.] National Defense Medal, National Forensics Finalist; [oth. writ.] Magazines and local papers; [pers.] "Carp diem". Live for the day and always be free for death my knock tomorrow.; [a.] Churchton, MD

RUSSELL, SARAH M.
[b.] January 11, 1967, Sylva, NC; [p.] David and Margaret Mathewes; [m.] Henry T. Russell, August 1, 1992; [ch.] Alia Roanne, Boothby Taylor; [ed.] St. Andrews-Sewanee Episcopal School Sewanee, TN; [oth. writ.] 'Forever and Always' only published work.; [a.] Mount Airy, NC

RUSSEY, STEVE
[pen.] Doc LaTrec; [b.] February 14, 1963, Santa Rosa, CA; [p.] Marcy and James Russey; [ed.] B.A. Clinical Psychology San Francisco State University; [occ.] Graduate Student, Music Therapy-University of the Pacific; [oth. writ.] Countless lyrics and poems; [pers.] I cannot accurately define what I do aside from saying that this is the only form of expression I am truly comfortable, and at ease with. I would also like to stress to other writers and artists to not be afraid to share and express their art.; [a.] Stockton, CA

RUTON, MILDRED K.
[pen.] Mildred Marsh Ruton; [b.] November 2, 1906, Kirkwood, OH; [p.] Jos. Clarence and Pearl Marsh; [m.] Edgar "Eddie" Ruton, October 15, 1947; [ch.] William Beckford (deceased), Lawrence "Larry" Oliver (previous marriages husbands deceased); [ed.] Wheeling, WV High School and traveling all around in show business.; [occ.] Retired and do some stand up comedy entertaining.; [memb.] International Society of Poets distinguished member. Member of AARP, Ohio Auto Club, Newark Chapter No. 305 Order of Eastern Star, Silver Club; [hon.] 1994 Editor's Choice Award from the National Library of Poetry, Silver Club Zerger Hall, Past President; [oth. writ.] Poem published by N.L.P. I am in the process of writing a children's book and some short stories. A few poems printed in the Zerger Times, which is a newsletter (monthly) for L.C.A.P Senior citizens; [pers.] Anything worth doing is worth doing well (or the best you can) and keep them laughing, it's the best medicine in our troubled world. Be thankful for what you have; [a.] Newark, OH

RUZGA, TONI
[b.] October 3, 1979, Valparaiso, IN; [p.] Amy Billups and Don Ruzga; [ed.] So far I am in High School, but plan to continue through College; [occ.] Student; [oth. writ.] Nothing published; [pers.] My writing reflects what is going on around me or to me.; [a.] Valparaiso, IN

RUZZENE, MARILYN A.
[b.] July 13, 1951, England; [p.] Stanley and Vera MacLeish; [ch.] John Jason and Rosann; [ed.] Convent of Our Lady of Mercy, Weymouth, Dorset, England; [memb.] John XXIII; [a.] Knoxville, TN

713

RYDER, KATHERINE
[b.] June 23, 1953, Sewanee, TN; [p.] Harold and Johnie Mae Hawkins; [m.] Donald, May 12, 1973; [ch.] Benjamin, Brad; [ed.] Stonewall Jackson High; [oth. writ.] Ask Somer (published in PIE Newsletter) sometimes, Ben's Reflection; [pers.] Personal thoughts, experiences, and events are the sources of my writing. Therefore, I find writing to be the most rewarding means of becoming acquainted with myself.; [a.] Manassas, VA

SAAVEDRA, MARCIAL ROSSY
[pen.] Marchello Rochetto; [b.] April 28, 1938, Puerto Rico; [p.] Americo Rossy, Antonia Saavedra; [m.] Andrea Saavedra, August 5, 1959; [ch.] 5 children, Frank, Marina, Ramon E. - Cruz Ivon and Maria Magdalena; [ed.] 2nd year University Social Worker; [memb.] I'm member of the Saint Mary Church Catholic.; [hon.] U.S. Veteran awards of good Conduct National Guard 11 Conduct State award, good conduct; [oth. writ.] Yes I have some more.; [a.] New Britain, CT

SACHARA, BETTY JANE
[b.] March 29, 1924, Cleveland, OH; [p.] Myron and Elizabeth Walzak (Deceased); [m.] Eugene, August 7, 1948; [ch.] Lance, Lynette, Mark; [ed.] James Ford Rhodes H. S. Notre Dame College of Ohio—BA, Master's Work—Western Reserve U and Colorado U — Taught languages and journalism; [occ.] Writing; [memb.] CA Federation of Chaparral Poets—20 yrs. World Poetry Society International—14 yrs. Poetry Society of America, Academy of American Poets; [hon.] Too many to count.; [oth. writ.] Editorial commentator for Gilroy Dispatch—3 yrs. self-published Pope of Peace 72 sonnets based upon trips and philosophy of John Paul II, given as gift to Holy Father when he visited Carmel in 1987.; [pers.] Man's Serape, God's Agape.; [a.] Gilroy, CA

SAENZ, IRASEMA
[b.] January 17, 1978, Laredo, TX; [p.] Eloisa Saenz; [ed.] Zapata High School; [occ.] High School Student; [pers.] I try to reflect the importance and good will of all humanity in good and in bad in the heart of mind in my writing. I have greatly been influenced by many good poets from the past and the present.; [a.] Zapata, TX

SAEPHAN, NAIHIN
[pen.] Nadja; [b.] January 26, 1981, Richmond, CA; [p.] Sanghin Saephan, Farmluang Saephan; [ed.] Elizabeth Stewart Middle School in Pinole, CA and Juan Crespi Junior High School in El Sobrante, CA; [occ.] Eighth grade student at Juan Crespi Junior High School in El Sobrante, CA; [hon.] Straight a student since fourth grade; [pers.] May I simply explain ... friends among "friends" are the best to form a - CIRCLE, friends -... they shall always shine the light within your eyes.; [a.] Pinole, CA

SAGGESE, CHARLES MATTHEW
[pen.] Charles Matthews, Chaz Sajaze; [b.] September 30, 1959, Darby; [p.] Charles Saggese, Rita Saggese; [m.] Karen Sroke-Saggese, August 18, 1990; [ed.] Grad. Lansdowne Ablan H.S.; [occ.] Musician, Writer; [memb.] American Museum of Natural History and LiSetim Fellow-

ship (highlander Club); [oth. writ.] Several poems, songs, and novels. Some published.; [pers.] I always try to reflect my personality and feelings in my work. Writing is a passion and I am honored that it can also be a career. My songs, poems, and other work are dedicated to my family. And mostly the memory of my mom....; [a.] Aldan, PA

SAINT GERAUD, REBECCA
[pen.] Regina Dauphin; [b.] February 6, 1979, Brooklyn, NY; [p.] Ferna And Rosario Saint Geraud; [ed.] I attend Culver City High School currently. I am in the 10th grape; [occ.] Student; [memb.] I am a member of a High School Sorority Ja-ketts.; [oth. writ.] I have written many other poems and short stories. Which will soon be recognized in the eye of the public.; [pers.] Never stop trying; [a.] Culver City, CA

SAJA, GIAN ENZO
[pen.] Gian Saja; [b.] February 11, 1973, Cleveland, OH; [p.] Vincint Saja, Antonia Saja Fitzwater; [ed.] Kent State University, BA. 1995 (with honors); [occ.] Student; [hon.] Young authors award 1986 Cuyahoga county, Ohio Partial scholarship to KSU. High School Academic Achievement award; [oth. writ.] Many short stories, poems, and is also a composer and has written many contemporary songs.; [pers.] I have been greatly influenced by the lyrics and music of the beattles...who rank among my all time favorites.; [a.] Cleveland, OH

SALAVARRIETA, JENNIFER P.
[b.] May 2, 1986, Piscataway, NJ; [p.] Manuel and Carmen Salavarrieta; [ed.] 3rd grade; [occ.] Student at Our Lady of Fatima, Piscataway, NJ; [memb.] Piscataway Soccer Club, South Plainfield Tiger Sharks Swimming Team; [pers.] Thanks to my brother Chris for telling me about this contest.; [a.] Piscataway, NJ

SALAZAR, ANASTASIA
[pen.] Anastasia Salazar; [b.] August 9, 1971, Seattle; [p.] Judy Tamerlaine, Alejos Salazar; [ch.] Hope, William, and Goldfinger (goldfish); [ed.] Thomas Jefferson High; [occ.] Amtrak Passenger Railroad; [memb.] Member of generation X; [oth. writ.] Writing is a personal Hobby I have a book at home unpublished.; [pers.] Freedom is a state of mind and no one can take that from you; [a.] Kent, WA

SALAZAR, JANETT
[b.] September 20, 1950, Gainesville, TX; [p.] Bennett and Joan Arthur; [ch.] Jody Alonn and Derek Jaron; [ed.] Copperas Cove High; [occ.] Banker, First Nat'l and Trust Co., Ardmore, OK; [memb.] Oklahoma Municipal League, Inc. and Oklahoma Rural Water Assn.; [hon.] H.S. Valedictorian; [pers.] I try to express my emotions with strong words and phrases, so that when others read them they may be able to feel what I feel.; [a.] Leon, OK

SALISBURY III, THOMAS M.
[b.] May 30, 1946, Long Branch, NJ; [p.] Tom and Sadie Salisbury; [ed.] Virginia Military Institute; [occ.] Research Specialist; [memb.] Order of Indian Wars (first Companion), Society of Friends of Historic Fort Haya (Life member); [oth.

writ.] Professional articles in Military Review 1977 and Aviation Digest 1980; [pers.] To me, historical settings frame on paper our human senses best and can convey depth in feelings at times lost in contemporary settings.; [a.] Arlington, VA

SALMON, LOUISA
[b.] October 13, 1938, Columbus, OH; [p.] Angileen G. Neil, Thomas J. Potts; [m.] James H. Salmon MD, October 14, 1967; [ch.] Rebecca H. Salmon, James T. Salmon; [ed.] Middlebury College AB, The Ohio State University MA; [occ.] Substitute teacher; [memb.] Glenwood United Methodist Church Kappa Kappa Gamma; [hon.] PTA Honorary Life Membership; [oth. writ.] Numerous poems and limericks for family and friends. Several published "letters to the editor."; [pers.] Written in the late 60's, my poem reflects my restless heart and the turbulent times. I have since found fulfillment in my family, church, work, and community service. May today's "searchers" find their "something of value!"; [a.] Erie, PA

SALMONSON, BRETT LEE
[b.] April 3, 1981, Worcester, MA; [p.] Denise and Robert; [ed.] Entering Auburn High School in the fall of '95; [memb.] Trinity Lutheran Church, Auburn Youth Soccer, Junior Youth Group of Auburn Massachusetts; [hon.] National Junior Honor Society, Trinity Lutheran Youth Advisory Council, Auburn Middle School Student of the month, distinguished Expert Light Rifle Course, (NRA), "Hands" award from "4-H" Camp Marshall Spencer MA, and High Honors Auburn Middle School all three years.; [pers.] I enjoy writing and reading about human feelings and that is what influences my writings. One of my philosophies is: "Express and love being yourself".; [a.] Auburn, MA

SALOUR, ELSIE MARIE
[pen.] Elsie Salour; [b.] July 9, 1953, Saint Louis, MO; [p.] William and Josephine Green; [m.] Ali Salour; [ch.] Ninaz, Shireen; [ed.] McKinley High Saint Louis, MO; [occ.] Home maker Management and own 3 condos; [oth. writ.] Little town, upon the shelf, as sky is to Sea, Harvest Red, Tommy, and others.; [pers.] I dedicate my poems to: Ali, Ninaz, and Shireen.; [a.] Fenton, MO

SAMMONS, THOMAS R.
[b.] April 12, 1920, Whiteville, TN; [p.] Thomas and Lois Sammons; [m.] Anna Sammons (Deceased), January 22, 1942; [ch.] Ronald and Michael Sammons, Michael Key; [ed.] BA Degree; [occ.] Retired Lt/Col. USAF; [memb.] The distinguished flying cross society, 409 Bomb GP Ass'n 9th airforce assoc., retired officers assoc..; [hon.] All military distinguished flying cross, 12 air medals, purple heart; [oth. writ.] Personal poems to my children and on my wife's death; [a.] Las Vegas, NV

SAMPLES, DORIS REEVES
[pen.] Doris R. Samples; [b.] Alcoa, TN; [m.] Harold F. Samples, July 3, 1947; [ch.] Stephen T. Samples; [occ.] Retired from Unisys Corporation 1986; [pers.] The poems I compose are closely related to the deep faith I have in God.; [a.] Louisville, TN

SAMPSON, HAROLD L.
[b.] December 25, 1928, Chicago; [m.] Terry Lee Sampson, June 24, 1952; [ch.] Roberta Swidersky, Debra Boogaard, Arthur Sampson; [ed.] 2 yrs. College; [occ.] Eng. Tech.; [pers.] If my poetry evokes thoughtful moments, then my labors in pleasure, have not been in vain.

SANDEGREN, JAMES J.
[pen.] James J. Sandegren; [b.] December 25, 1937, Johnston, IA; [p.] Rudolph E., Esther L.; [m.] Suzanne L., May 18, 1963; [ch.] Jill K., Jana L.; [ed.] Des Moines Tech H.S. Drake University, D.M. IA Sinclair Com. College, Dayton, OH; [occ.] Horticulturist; [memb.] Kiwanis Downtown Dayton, First Lutheran - Dayton, Ohio Assn. Cemetery Supts and officials, Amer. Assn. Botanical Gardens and Arboreta; [a.] Dayton, OH

SANDERS, LOIS H.
[b.] December 31, 1971, Salisbury, NC; [p.] David and Bobbie Sanders; [ch.] Dylan Mackenzie; [ed.] Needham B. Broughton High School, Alvernia College; [occ.] Waitress-reading, Country Club, Student, mother; [memb.] Kappa Delta Sorority, Trinity Lutheran Church; [pers.] With my writing, I want to touch people's lives and make 2 difference in the way they live, believe, and think about life.; [a.] Reading, PA

SANDERS, RAVEN
[pen.] Raven-Marie; [b.] November 27, 1979, Indianapolis, IN; [p.] Karl and Barbara Sanders; [ed.] I am a Sophomore at Scecina Memorial High School; [memb.] I am in SAY (Students Assisting Youth), SADD (Students Against Drunk Driving), Pride, Service Program, and Crusader Girls (a dance squad at Scecina).; [hon.] In grade school I received honors for reading and academic skills.; [oth. writ.] I have written short stories and poetry since I was at the age of eight.; [pers.] "Shining Star" is the very first poem that I had written, I was eight years old at that time. I plan to be a journalist and/or a creative writer.; [a.] Indianapolis, IN

SANDERS SR., REV. WILKIE L.
[pen.] Wilkie Sanders; [b.] April 29, 1951, Louisiana; [p.] J. D. and Dorothy Sanders Holt; [m.] Mrs. Florence K. Sanders, March 26, 1994; [ch.] Wilkie L. Sanders Jr. and DeCarlos R. Sanders; [ed.] Master Of Science in Management Of Human Resources from Southern Nazarene University, Bachelors Of Arts Degree from Southern Nazarene University in Bethany, OK; [occ.] Ordained Minister, Founder and President of Disciples For Christ Min.; [memb.] Life Memberships in Disabled Americans Veterans, The American Legion, Toastmasters International, Laubauch Literacy Council, Martial Arts Instructor, Weight Trainer and Body Builder at Tinker Air Force Base Gerrity Gymnasium.; [hon.] Graduated Most likely to Succeed and in the top 10 of my class, Viet-Nam Service Medal, Army Accommodation Army Meritorious Service Medal, Presidential Unit Medal, Army Achievement Medal.; [oth. writ.] Over 60 publications and poems in the Disciples For Christ Christian News Letter, soon to be published book titled "Poetry of A Prisoner," Published Poem in the book titled "At Water's Edge, Publish Poem in "The Garden Of Life Anthology"; [pers.] I strive to reflect the times of

now in my poetry as they represent the Word of God which stresses the importance of man adhering to the wisdom of God's Word that has lasted throughout the centuries and is still alive in the heart of the Christian believer. The ultimate peace and joy the world seeks will only come when we learn to love and respect one another as God has so commanded us to do.; [a.] Midwest City, OK

SANDFORD, HERMAN P.
[pen.] Pat Sandford; [b.] December 7, 1963, New York, NY; [p.] Lelia E. Williams; [ed.] Dwight Morrow High, Rutgers University - Livingston College; [occ.] Counselor, Charles Nechtem Associates, Jersey City, NJ; [memb.] Phi Beta Sigma Fraternity, Rutgers African American Alumni Alliance, The Livingston Alumni Association, Big Brothers of Hudson County; [oth. writ.] Several articles for the News-Record of Marlewood and South Orange, The Independent Press of Bloomfield.; [pers.] Writing is one of the purest elements to explore new horizons and impetus to the ideas for creative thought and expression.; [a.] Jersey City, NJ

SANDY, WALTER A.
[b.] August 31, 1924, Taylor Co, WI; [p.] Bert and Elsie Sandy; [m.] Clista Mae Sandy, September 18, 1945; [ch.] Three daughters and two sons; [ed.] I went to a one room school to the six grade and High School at Bridgeport 1942; [occ.] Retired Coal Miner; [pers.] I never wrote a poem in my life until my wife past away I haved her so. Then I couldn't sleep that when I started writing.; [a.] Bridgeport, WV

SANETRA, FAYELLEN
[pen.] Fayellen Krejci Sanetra; [b.] June 29, 1945, Savanna, IL; [p.] Robert H. Krejci and Grace Winters Krejci; [m.] Divorced, 1965 to 1975; [ch.] Rea Sanetra, Nico Sanetra; [ed.] Several elementary Schools and High School in Savanna, IL, Cosmetology school, Clinton, IA. Bank, Art, Typing, Waubonsee College, Sugar Grove, IL; [occ.] Beautician, Clown, grandmother, folk singer, story teller; [memb.] Fox Valley Folk Society, presently 1995; [hon.] From the world of poetry, I received certificates of golden poet and silver poet. Certificate of being a clown. Several awards in school.; [pers.] This poem was written to be sung. It is scenes I saw growing up in the hills and pasteurs and creeks with fairy steps and getting the cows for milking. The sweetness of the soul comes out in music. The heart pens to words.; [a.] Aurora, IL

SANFORD, SHALONDRA MARIE
[b.] October 24, 1979, Calver City, CA; [p.] Alisa Stephens, Robert Sanford, Sr.; [ed.] Saturn street Elementary School in Los Angeles, Culver City Middle School and Culver City High School in Culver City; [occ.] Sophomore at Culver city High School; [memb.] Soroptomists club, a club which involves young women in community service; [hon.] Honor roll, student of the month award, certificate of promotion eight grade; [oth. writ.] Essays for (CAS) 2 on which I have previously received a rhetorical score of 6, articles for school newspaper in 8th grade, poetry in my diary; [pers.] I love writing because I get the chance to use my imagination and convey my feelings about different

subjects I hope that through my writing I can touch I can touch people and make an imprint on their lives.; [a.] Culver City, CA

SANTORELLI, LANA DE GEORGE
[b.] February 11, 1948, New York City; [p.] Angelo and Anna De George; [m.] Leonard Santorelli, June 1, 1968; [ch.] Claudia, Francesca Lana-Jeanne, Angelo, Anthony and Gabriella; [ed.] Long Island City High, Nursing School, Stone Brook University; [occ.] Business Exect.; [memb.] St. Philip and James Church. Religion Teacher, Eucharistic Minister Cystic Fibrosis Foundation, American Ballet, Boy Scouts of America; [hon.] S.S. Calleope poetry award prairie Dog Press Award The America Poetry Society Award; [oth. writ.] Cook book in Third printing History in the making. Lessons of a life time things that make me happy short stories; [pers.] There is a piece of this world that belongs solely to me and it is up to me to transform that place into the best place it can possibly be.; [a.] Nissequogue, NY

SARACENO, ALBERT
[b.] August 30, 1968, IL; [p.] Bobby Anne and Fritz; [ed.] 3 yrs. college and working on more; [occ.] Student; [pers.] I am asking that my work stand on it's own merit.

SARAUER, DAVID HENRY
[b.] October 16, 1950, Royal Oak, MI; [occ.] Machinist; [oth. writ.] Over 1,000 poems and songs written, 3 major plays and numerous other writings. Some are secular, some are spiritual. I am waiting on a wonder!; [pers.] There is no goodness in mankind, only in Jesus and Father God. I am anti humanistic and it reflects in my writing.; [a.] Utica, MI

SARBAUGH, L. E.
[pen.] Larry Sarbaugh; [b.] May 17, 1921, Dresden, OH; [p.] Grover and Nellie Sarbaugh; [m.] Dorothy (Deceased), September 27, 1942; [ch.] Marjorie Ellen, Stephen, Debbie; [ed.] Jefferson High School, Dresden, OH, B.S. Agr. Educ., OH State Univ. M.S. Journalism and Communication University of Illinois Ph.D Communication, Mich. State Univ.; [occ.] Retired Prof., Mich. State University Grow Christmas trees; [oth. writ.] Books — (1) Teaching Speech Communication, and (2) Intercultural Communication; [pers.] I believe that to live is to grow, when we stop growing, we begin to deteriorate. We should balance our growth among the mental, physical and religious aspects of life. We observe only a small fraction of beauty in nature.; [a.] Adamsville, OH

SARIAN, ROSE NEVART
[b.] January 11, 1947; [ed.] BA at UCLA, MS at USC; [occ.] Speaker, Home Business Consultant; [memb.] Women's Leadership Network, Professional Speakers Association Children's Museum Guild; [hon.] Dean's Honor Roll Speech Contest Winner International Speech Contest; [pers.] My mother came to this country leaving everything she knew. From her I learned courage, determination, nurturing others and playfulness. My writings that reflect deep emotions, women's issues and nurturing are dedicated to her.; [a.] Whittier, CA

SAUCEDA, CRAIG STUART
[pen.] Stuart Marlowe; [b.] June 24, 1969, Claire Co., MI; [p.] Linda R. Marlowe/unknown; [m.] single; [ed.] Boonville High School, 3rd year Literature Major at University of Southern Indiana; [occ.] Sales Manager/Part Time Writer, writing a book titled "Standing Alone in the Stream of Love;" [memb.] Sigma Pi Fraternity, Greek Council; [hon.] Travis Fuller Award, Several Booster Club and Athletic Award, Cinderman of the year for Warrick W. 87, 88. [oth. writ.] Published several poems in school newspapers and collegiate collections and 1 short story at ISU; [pers.] Influenced by Robert Frost, Early Romantic Poets, Mr. D. Stilwell and the love of Life. Statement: I try to live each day brailing life. [a.] Newburgh, IN

SAUPAN, JAMES FRANCIS
[b.] October 10, 1959, Honolulu, HI; [p.] Roberto Saupan Sr., Dolores Saupan; [ch.] Briana Marie Loleina Saupan; [ed.] Radford High; [occ.] Flight Attendant; [memb.] International Society of Poets 1994-1995; [hon.] Editor's Choice Award 1994, The National Library of Poetry, Nominee Poet of the Year 1995, International Society of Poets, International Poet of Merit 1995, International Society of Poets; [oth. writ.] Published poem in anthology "Journey Of The Mind" pg. 285, The National Library of Poetry, published poem in anthology "Dusting Off Dreams" pg. 62, Quill Books, "Words From The Heart" a collection of my poems also to be translated in Spanish version, unpublished, poetry written in song, translated in Spanish and arranged to music, unpublished.; [pers.] I write from my heart with inspiration from my family, friends and everyday life occurances.; [a.] San Juan, PR

SAWYER, VERA H.
[pen.] August Hope; [b.] May 27, 1940, Clendenin, WV; [p.] Austin and Wavy Violet Donohoe; [ch.] Pamela Kay (deceased) and John Edward; [ed.] Nitro High School, WV P.B. Jr. College, FL; [occ.] Fitness Inst., Self Employee; [memb.] Past: Organized and 1st Pres. of Palm Beach Co. Foster Parents; [hon.] Past: Speaker at many Club, Organizations and Seminars - on child Abuse; [oth. writ.] Current - Foxfire 100th issue - Summer 1992, Past - Newspaper Articles on Child Abuse and foster care; [pers.] Every adversity is a learning experience. We grow in the valleys of our living - the mountain top experiences are the rewards - expect a fair amount of both; [a.] Tiger, GA

SAWYER, WARREN DAVID
[pen.] Warren Sawyer; [b.] January 18, 1969, Dallas, TX; [p.] Jim and Rita Sawyer; [m.] Dawn Sawyer, September 26,1992; [ed.] Lewisville HS, grad. 1987; [occ.] Computer Technician; [oth. writ.] I've written many poems but none have been published.; [pers.] I like to write on Social issues, because it is about every day life. We see many good and bad things and this is my way of expression on them; [a.] Lewisville, TX

SAXON, SANDRA LEE
[pen.] Sandie; [b.] April 15, 1959, West Palm Beach, FL; [p.] Harry Saxon - Glenese Oppel Ken Oppel; [ch.] Kevin 18, Sheila 16, and Kelly 7; [ed.] Western High, Las Vegas NV, Clark County Community College, LV, NV Fashion Merchandis-ing institute of NV; [occ.] Public Relations, Saxon Creative Services, Inc.; [pers.] I write only from my heart.; [a.] Sherman Oaks, CA

SCAMPINI, AMANDA
[b.] March 31, 1977, Hazel Crest, IL; [p.] Allan and Marilyn Scampini; [ed.] Bloom Township High School; [hon.] Illinois State Scholar Salutatorian of class of '95; [oth. writ.] Article in Illinois History magazine; [pers.] "Dear Jimmy" is dedicated to the late James A. Salyer, Jr. and the rest of the Spanos gang.; [a.] Glenwood, IL

SCANLON, JOSEPH
[b.] April 3, 1960, Philadelphia; [p.] William Scanlon and Mary Scanlon; [m.] Divorced; [ch.] Lindsay Anne Scanlon; [ed.] Father Judge H.S., La Salle University, University of Fribourg (Switzerland); [occ.] Direct Mail "Letter Writer"; [pers.] I hope that my poetry can touch people and hopefully inspire others to write their own poetry.; [a.] Philadelphia, PA

SCAPPATICCI, GINA
[b.] June 3, 1981, Dearborn, MI; [ed.] attending Sacred Heart School, Dearborn, Michigan; [hon.] D.A.R.E. Program Essay Award (1992), 1st place tap dance Award (1991), Yearly Poem Contest Awards at school, 1st and 2nd place 1992-1995 Science Fair Awards; [pers.] I enjoy reciting and writing poetry; [a.] Dearborn, MI

SCEARCE, RUTH ANN VAUGHAN
[pen.] Ruth Vaughan-Scearce; [b.] May 6, 1941, Springboro, OH; [p.] Martha Click; [m.] Bobby D. Scearce, October 26, 1974; [ch.] Craig Mercer, Renee Mercer, Marla Rogers; [ed.] Fairmont High, Miami University, Middletown, OH, Ohio Real Estate Institute, Inc.; [occ.] Real Estate Sales Agent, REMI; [memb.] Springboro Christian Church, Moore's Nautilaus Health Club, AARP, International Society of Poets, Warren County Battered Women's Ass., Centerville Writer's Group, Dayton Area Board of Realtors; [hon.] An award-winning poet, is included in Who's Who in Poetry. Her work has appeared in Poet Magazine, in A Break in the Clouds, and Whispers in the Wind (National Library of Poetry), in Today's Best Poems and Great Poems of the Western World, (World of Poetry Press), and in The American Poetry Anthology, (American Poetry Assoc). A member of the International Society of Poets, her poem "Mother of War" won first runner-up honors at the 1991 Annual Meeting of the Society, and her poem "Three Squeezes" was a semi-finalist at the 1994 Meeting. Reflections of Ruth is a collection of her poems now being edited for publication. A graduate of Miami University majoring in English and History, she was a winner at Miami of the Malcolm Sadam Writing Award for excellence in short story writing. Dean's List-Miami University, Malcolm Sadam short story award.; [oth. writ.] 1st runner up ISP, 1991 semi-finalist ISP, 1994. Many Golden Poet awards. Winner of Poetry Contest, words and things, 1994. Several poems published in local newspapers. Book of poems Reflection's of Ruth in making.; [pers.] I have loved poetry all of my life, having been greatly influenced by Edgar Guest and Emily Dickinson, and the Bible. In my writing, I strive to arouse human compassion and love, and reflect the good of mankind.; [a.] Centerville, OH

SCHELOSKY, VIRGINIA
[pen.] Virginia Schelosky; [b.] April 24, 1921, Detroit, MI; [p.] Marie and William Scurlock; [m.] Edgar Schelosky, September 9, 1943; [ch.] David A. Schelosky; [ed.] 12 yrs. in Public Schools, 1 yr Det. Bus. Institute; [occ.] Retired; [pers.] My sister, Rosemary, was very close to me. We were the youngest of 6 children. Joseph, Margaret, Barbara Dorothy, Myself and Rosemary. My poem speaks for itself.; [a.] Allen Park, MI

SCHETTLER, BIRGIT
[ed.] M.A. Stanford University, B.A. California State University; [occ.] Teacher, IBM Almader Research Center, San Jose, California; [memb.] Phi Kappa Phi Honor Society; [hon.] B.A. with great distinction, Phi Kappa Phi Award for Faculty Excellence, Mission College, Santa Clara, California; [oth. writ.] Award for excellence in teaching, Fraunhofer Institute, Erlangen, Germany

SCHLEGEL, SUSAN M.
[b.] November 14, 1954, Philadelphia; [m.] Harry W. Schlegel, October 8, 1983; [ch.] Seven lost to God Above; [ed.] Abington South Campus H.S. Gwynedd Mercy College; [occ.] Nurse/School Teacher; [hon.] Dean's List, Cum Laude; [oth. writ.] Scholastic Weekly leader 5/6 grade title wonderful flight of the arrow heads. Local newspaper charity work and donation through my 1st graders. Short poem: Big On Little Hearts.; [pers.] Life is poetry, dare to compose what strikes to compose what strikes at your heart, for words are but a passage in to ones soul.; [a.] Woodbridge, VA

SCHLEUPNER, LISA
[b.] June 21, 1976, Annapolis, MD; [p.] Sharon and Andrew Schleupner; [ed.] Chesapeake High School, Anne Arindel Community College; [occ.] Sales; [memb.] Abundant Life Church; [oth. writ.] My first publication; [pers.] My poems reflect my spirit and strength, and give me a philosophical comfort.; [a.] Pasadena, MD

SCHNEIDER, PATRICIA
[pen.] P. C. Schneider; [b.] March 23, 1952, Alliance, OH; [p.] Will and Margaret Clunen; [m.] Deceased; [ed.] High School - Electronics; [occ.] Disabled; [oth. writ.] Many yet to be published; [pers.] I express the passion and pain of my life through my writings, each reflects a piece of my life or an experience that I have tasted; [a.] Granada Hills, CA

SCHOCK, JANICE
[pen.] "Jan" Schock; [b.] September 3, 1940, Harvey, ND; [p.] Albert and Bertha Pfaff; [m.] Rudy Schock, March 3, 1983; [ch.] Tamra-Mitch-Lori-April, Shirley-Karl-Kenny (desc) Twin Sister Jeanette; [ed.] High School; [occ.] "Certified" Nursing Assistant; [memb.] American Heart Association North Dakota Department of Health and Laboratories, Trinity Lutheran Church; [hon.] Volunteer of the year award 1991-1992 at Garrison Nursing Center; [oth. writ.] I read alot of my poetry at senior citizen clubs and hospitals, for the sink and elderly my husband and I do alot of volunteer work.; [pers.] I get all my inspirations from the Lord. (I simply write them down on paper.); [a.] Underwood, ND

SCHONVISKY, JENNIFER A.
[b.] August 31, 1979, New Britain, CT; [p.] Gary and Penny Schonvisky; [ed.] East Hampton Elementary Schools East Hampton High School; [occ.] High School Student, Sophomore; [memb.] GLOBE (environmental club), Visions (art and literary magazine committee), CCD, Participant in East Hampton High School Honors Program; [hon.] Young Author Award, Reading Achievement Award, Honor Roll throughout High School, Civic Achievement Award, Student of the Month (1989), 7th in my school on American Junior High Math Exam, 2 Merit Diploma Certificates and Achievement Award in Junior Great Books (2); [oth. writ.] Several poems published in school magazine, and several newspaper articles in school newspaper.; [pers.] I dedicate my accomplishments in the 1995 N. American Open Poetry Contest to my grandmother, Roxanne Xenos, who showed me the articles about the contest and encouraged me to enter.; [a.] East Hampton, CT

SCHOTT, APRIL
[b.] May 25, 1980, Korea; [p.] Antoinette and Newton; [ed.] Montclair Kimberly Academy (Primary, Middle, and High); [hon.] High honors (grades), Hardest working Gymnast, 2nd and 3rd place standings at Gymnastics competitions; [oth. writ.] Do You Hear? Ruiner, Light Of Trees; [pers.] Believe in yourself and say to others what you believe.; [a.] Upper Montclair, NJ

SCHRADE, CARL G.
[b.] April 1, 1922, Germany; [p.] Gottlieb and Marie Schrade; [m.] Helga (died in 1991), October 20, 1951; [ch.] Karen Lessig, Susan Gift; [ed.] In Phila. PA. Gratz H.S. Strayer's Business College and Classes in Eng. At temple and Villa Nova Univ.; [occ.] Retired, formerly, Mech. Eng. and Syst. Analyst; [memb.] Member of the new apostolic church in limerick, PA; [oth. writ.] First book of poetry titled "Fire side treasures" published by Carlton Press NY. Due out Spring 1995. While employed, Authored Various Company Procedure Manuals.; [pers.] My love for and for poetry goes back to my mother and my Third Grade Teacher, Mrs. Hansen.; [a.] Sanatoga, PA

SCHUETTER, LARRY JOSEPH
[b.] October 27, 1947, Jasper IN; [p.] Clarence and Mary Alice Schuetter; [m.] Veronica J. D. Schuetter, August 31, 1976; [ch.] Louis Jasper, Christopher Clarence Verna Leigh, Schuetter; [ed.] Associate Degrees in law enforcement, corrections-Solano Community College, Military Science-Community College United States Air Force Major in Engineering, Computer Art Media, Wireless T.V. productions.; [occ.] Police Officer, Department of Defense, Tracy Depot; [memb.] NRA - National Rifle Association Fil-AM Fairfield CA. Fraternal Order of Police, Northern CA. Education Historical. Graduated 10th Street School - 1961 Jasper Indiana Jasper High School-1965-Jasper Indiana (Industrial Arts Curriculum.) Occupations, Baker-Usaf, and Hallers, 1965-1987, Meat Cutter-Iga-1971-1972-Iga Jasper Indiana. Vincennes University-1970-71; [hon.] Numerous Military Service awards, Meritorious Service Award 1987. Top 10-Aircrew Life Support 1982 Graduates,

United States Air Force; [oth. writ.] Planet orange-science fiction of planet life behind Mars. Fantasia as planet earth euthanism turned up side down.

SCHULMAN, SAMUEL
[b.] April 21, 1915, Chicago; [p.] Phillip and Sarah Schulman; [m.] Stephanie T. Schulman, December 31, 1938; [ch.] Barbara J. Schulman, Philip Schulman; [ed.] Bachelor of Arts, University of Chicago; [occ.] Retired; [memb.] Council of Former Federal Executives; [hon.] Dept. of the Navy Distinguished Civilian Service Award; [oth. writ.] Articles in the Magazine of the Federal Managers Association; [pers.] I write for my own amusement.; [a.] Arlington, VA

SCHULTZE, CHESTER L.
[b.] March 5, 1968, Whitefish, MT; [p.] Rev. Reimar and Marcia Schultze; [ed.] Dayspring Academy, Kokomo High School, Indiana Vocational Technical State College; [occ.] Soda Fountain Worker; [memb.] Kokomo Christian Fellowship; [oth. writ.] Several writings but none so far published; [pers.] I believe that God can be seen in all things. And if you are adopted as I was, don't let anyone try to kill your dreams.; [a.] Kokomo, IN

SCHUTTE, MARK SAMUEL
[b.] December 26, 1979, Stamford, CT; [p.] Mark L. Schutte, Doria A. Schutte; [a.] Ridgefield, CT

SCHUYLER, KRISTIN
[pen.] Gigler; [b.] December 31, 1979, Lompoc, CA; [p.] Sue and Lester Schuyler; [ed.] I'm in the 9th grade and go to Cabrillo High School; [occ.] Native American Reinactor.; [memb.] I belong to the boy scouts of American in the Indian explorer post and FHA at School; [hon.] I made this contest and I won a contest in Camp fire and I win alot of reading awards; [oth. writ.] I have a book of poems and I write during school and for school functions.; [pers.] I think that we all should treat each other with respect and be loyal to the one you love. We all deserve the best.; [a.] Lompoc, CA

SCHWAB, JASON W.
[b.] July 13, 1969, Concordia, KS; [p.] William L. and Eva L. Schwab; [m.] Dana J. Schwab, July 11, 1992; [ch.] Jack William Schwab; [ed.] High School diploma from Clifton - Clyde High School Clyde KS; [occ.] Assistant well-driller; [memb.] American Legion Member; [hon.] Served 4 years in the United States Marine Corps. Because a father January 17, 1994; [oth. writ.] Nothing published just a book of words and thoughts.; [pers.] I started writing at a time in my life, when, the hardest thing I had to deal with were my thoughts. I really appreciate the thought that others find interest in them now.; [a.] Clifton, KS

SCHWAGER, ELAINE
[b.] August 3, 1949, Pittsburgh, PA; [p.] Carl Schwager, Ihge Schwager; [m.] Marvin Hurvich, November 1, 1981; [ch.] Carl Hurvich, Julia Hurvich; [ed.] C.C.N.Y. - BA S. U. of Storybrook MA Englit L.I.U. Ph.D. Clinical Psychology NYC - analytic training; [occ.] Psychologist; [memb.] American Psychological Association, International Psychoanalytic Association, Poetry Peer Group at The Writer's Voice; [hon.] McDowell, Writing

Residency Poetry Prize, City College International Psychoanalytic Assoc.; [oth. writ.] Poems published in journals-Inc. WRIT, The World, Armadillo, Co-author of Book "Transference in Short Term Therapy."; [pers.] There's no one way and only one way; [a.] New York, NY

SCHWENN, JANET M.
[b.] December 29, 1963, Oaklawn; [p.] Robert and Madeline Aitchison; [m.] William R. Schwenn, November 9, 1986; [ch.] Amanda and Samantha Schwenn; [ed.] Moraine Valley Community College; [occ.] Florist; [hon.] MVCC Faculty Scholarship and Saint Xavier's Presidential Scholarship Presidential Scholar and MVCC Faculty Scholarship Award; [oth. writ.] Several poems published in local and international journals.; [pers.] I strive to reflect the goodness of God in my writing. James Joyce and Sylvia Plath are my favorite writers.; [a.] Oak Lawn, IL

SCHWERIN, LE ROY F.
[b.] May 24, 1924, Chicago, IL; [p.] Arthur and Margaret; [m.] Rita A. Schwerin, August 26, 1950; [ch.] Lee Schwerin, Merry Lee Streich; [ed.] The school of the Art Institute Of Chicago and University of Chicago College 1945-1949. BFA Degree; [occ.] Retired; [memb.] 94th Bomb Group Memorial Association Corvallis, OR., Church of Holy Spirit EGV, IL; [hon.] European - African - Middle Eastern Thester Ribbon With 4 Bronze Battle Stars, 2 Overseas Service Bars, Good Conduct Medal, Air Medal, Go 714 HQ HQ 3rd Bb. Div. 44, 1st and 2nd Bronze Oak Leaf Cluster, AAF Gunnery Instructor 938, 1942-45.; [a.] Elk Grove Village, IL

SCOTT, CECELIA E.
[pen.] Bobo; [b.] October 26, 1934, Rockaway, NJ; [p.] Arthur and Ethel Daniel; [m.] William T. Scott Jr., October 4, 1953; [ch.] 1 Daughter Teala Lee Vargas 2 Grandchildren Christopher and William; [ed.] Graduated High School Went to Hurdtown Grammar School till 8th grade. Attened Roxbury High School and graduated there in 1952. Business Course.; [occ.] Self-employed with husband in a sharpening business called Scotty's Sharpening service for 15 years now.; [memb.] Hurdtown United Methodist Church, Life Member of the Jefferson Twp. Ladies Auxiliary. Member of the Mended Hearts, Inc. and the local Chapter in Morris County. Alumni of roxbury High School. Member of the Circle of Light prayer group which I started 1989.; [hon.] 10 yearly awards for outstanding services to The Mended Hearts, Inc. for outstanding service and devotion to the organization. Given life membership in the Ladies Aux. of the Fire Company #2 of Jefferson for outstanding service and devotion to the group and fire men. of same twp. first adult to have this operation. Had open heart surgery to repair IA Septa defect 1960 March 2.; [oth. writ.] Wrote articles for our local newspaper on the happenings of the community and events 1964-1974. (Daily Advance) Wrote several articles for a local Paper called the shoppers' friend. Wrote for our church newsletter The Crier, 1964 to 1970. Chapter of Mended Newsletter 1969 till 1979.; [pers.] It's great to be alive and help others. To encourage others and give everyone you meet a big friendly smile.; [a.] Hurdtown, NJ

SCRIBNER, ELETA S.
[pen.] Eleta S. Scribner; [b.] April 6, 1916, Middlebury, VT; [p.] Carroll and Claribel Sargent (Deceased); [m.] Gerald W. Scribner (Deceased), July 33, 1934; [ch.] Five; [ed.] Graduation High School, 1934; [occ.] Retired

SEABORG, DAVID M.
[b.] April 22, 1949, Berkeley, CA; [p.] Glenn T. and Helen L. Seaborg; [m.] Adele Seaborg, June 17, 1980; [ed.] Bachelor of Science, Univ. of Calif. at Davis, Zoology, 1972, Master of Arts, Univ. of Calif, at Berkeley, Zoology, 1974; [occ.] President, Foundation for Biological Conservation and Research; [memb.] World Wildlife Fund, Sierra Club, Earth Island Institute, Club of Rome, Nature Conservancy, Natural Resources Defense Council, Lafayette Langeac Society, Calif. Academy of Sciences, Calif. Alumni Assoc. Cal Aggie Alumni Assoc, East Bay astronomical society.; [hon.] Listed in Who's Who in the West and Who's Who of Emerging leaders in America, 1 of only 300 elected to U.S. brandy Club of Rome, 2 Photography awards, Meritorious service award, Smithsonian Institution.; [oth. writ.] Scientific Articles.; [pers.] Science has implications for the great philosophical questions that humans are concerned with. We need a strengthened relationship to the earth, and a commitment to save its biodiversity.; [a.] Walnut Creek, CA

SEAMAN, DEANA
[p.] Shelby Bramlett, Lucy Earnest; [m.] John Seaman, July 13, 1968; [ch.] Christina, John Jr., Heather, Dustin; [ed.] Pennsville High, Salem Community College studying social work; [occ.] Owner - J and D painting Co.; [hon.] Dean's list; [pers.] I was inspired to write "Lost Ones" while working at our local youth shelter.; [a.] Woodstown, NJ

SEATON, REV. CLYDE C.
[pen.] Clyde C. Seaton; [b.] January 13, 1943, T, Dad; [p.] Roy and Thelma Seaton; [m.] Sadie D. Seaton, March 17, 1976; [ch.] Jermaine Tyrone Seaton; [ed.] Buniwick High School and PS 3; [occ.] Security Officer.; [memb.] Trinity Community Assembly of God; [hon.] Berean College; [oth. writ.] Several Articles Written on me. The propector and the queens tribune.; [pers.] I liked to write poetry, to calm the hearts and soul of people.; [a.] Bronx, NY

SEELEY, MARIE
[b.] April 5, 1921, New York City; [p.] Henry and Victoria Restel; [m.] Alexander Seeley, October 4, 1938; [ch.] Dorothy, Alex, Victoria; [ed.] High School and Self taught reading 1,000s of books; [occ.] Retired; [memb.] Too old for memberships now; [hon.] Silver medal, P.S. 11-20 and 21 New York City, were all verbal; [oth. writ.] 7 books unpublished and 2 books of poetry. Unpublished got nice notices etc., etc.; [pers.] Grandmother Marie, grandfather F. Barile wrote poetry. No published but used in shop window if old king tot were alive today); [a.] Village, NY

SEITZ, MARJORIE
[pen.] Hannah Glennah Wray; [b.] March 14, 1917, York, NE; [p.] Judge Arthur G. and Clara R. Wray; [m.] John K. Seitz, August 28, 1936; [ch.] Dr. James F. Seitz (wife Moree) Capt.

Donald Donald W. Seitz (wife Charron) and 5 grandchilren Amber, Adam, Jason, Kylee and Kory; [ed.] Whittier, CA High School and College courses, Psychology and writing - and religion.; [occ.] Home - retired; [memb.] 1st Baptist Church since 1923 Whittier, Whittier Historical Society, Founding member - Whittier CA, Art Association and Child Guidance, Association founding member.; [hon.] By City of Whittier, CA for civic service.; [oth. writ.] Historical articles - for news papers and historical societies.; [pers.] This moment in time is not all that we have! Our most treasured possessions can be memories, the joys, the sorrows, the lessons of life. One guest is to find our God given talent and gift. Could one of mine by writing?; [a.] San Diego, CA

SELBY, SPRING MAE
[b.] April 13, 1955, Cleveland, OH; [p.] Henry E. Selby and Carmela D. Mesiani; [m.] B. J. Hansen, February 16, 1992; [ed.] Cornish School, or Allied Arts, Seattle, WA; [occ.] Herbalife Independent distributor; [memb.] "19-10-1 Society"; [oth. writ.] Hundreds of other poems and lyrics to my own, and other peoples musical compositions.; [pers.] The power of the mind is awesome, every thought creates reality. Therefore I am goal specific and come from the space of abundance, acceptance and love.; [a.] Seattle, WA

SELIQUINI, ANTHONY
[b.] July 27, 1978; [p.] Dennis M. Seliquini, Doreen A. Leigh; [ed.] Book, especially Ayn Rand, Ray Bradbury, Aldous Huxley, William Shakespeare, and George Orwell. Music, especially Rush, Supertramp, and Styx. Life; [oth. writ.] Lyrics for band of musicians "Napalm Sicarians", including Closet, Aquae Aeternarum, and Beyond Dream's Horizon; [pers.] "I swear — by my life and my love of it — that I will never live for the sake of another man, nor ask another man to live for mine." — Ayn Rand, Atlas Shrugged.

SEN, LEILA
[b.] May 12, 1945, Calcutta, India; [p.] Father: From West Bengal, India, Mother: Greek, Armenian from Turkey; [m.] Childhood friend - Ronjon Sen; [ed.] Senior Cambridge (first division) Cambridge university and Bachelor of Arts (first division) Loreto Convent Calcutta University in English and Education; [hon.] Best of America 1994 award; [oth. writ.] "Four Maids Fair" is from a collection of poems titled "Canticles". I have also written a collection of fantasies titled "Faerie Gossip and Faerie Song." And a narrative in verse titled "Lor' O' Lei"; [pers.] My work is spun out of the magic and laughter of childhood, a tapestry woven from the song and dance of nature, a pennant raised in belief and flown in honour of the inherent goodness to be found within all around this world of ours; [a.] San Francisco, CA

SENGER, JOHN J.
[pen.] Johnny Jay; [b.] October 5, 1917, Dayton, KY; [p.] Lewis and Mae Senger; [m.] Julia Inez Senger, October 23, 1945; [ed.] Dayton High School (10th grade), GED-Auburn Coll Ge-Lee County, AL, Parachute School U.S. Army; [occ.] Retired U.S. Army 24 yrs. Retired Government Civil Service 17 1/2 yrs.; [memb.] Veterans of

Foreign Wars, National Rifle Association, Canadian/American First Special Service Force Association WW II; [hon.] Bronze Star Medal with "V" device for Valor in Korean War; [oth. writ.] Several songs copyrighted, approximately 68 poems written since 1938 but not published.; [pers.] I try to reflect my feeling of persons or places I have been, with a light touch of romance.; [a.] Anniston, AL

SENSEBE, GINA
[pen.] Rise Alice; [b.] January 20, 1979, New Orleans; [p.] Beverly and Eddie Sensebe; [ed.] Andrew Jackson High School; [occ.] Cashier; [memb.] I belong to save the blackbears and dolphins.; [pers.] True love never dies, but it doesn't wait either; [a.] New Orleans, LA

SEPELAK, JUDITH L.
[pen.] Judith L. Sepelak; [b.] June 3, 1941, Bridgeport, CT; [p.] Thomas C. Dumas and Marion Brunn Dumas; [m.] John M. Sepelak (deceased, July 9, 1992), January 22, 1992; [ch.] Thomas S. Murray and Todd R. Leveen, (grandchildren) Tricia Ann and John T. Murray; [ed.] Newton High, Housatonic Community College and Sacred Heart University; [occ.] Staff Accountant Country Home Bakers, Inc.; [memb.] Grace Lutheran Church, Genesis, A.A.R.P. Shelton Land Conservation Trust, National Wildlife Federation A.I.C.R.; [hon.] Alpha Beta Gamma, Dean's List, State CT Essay Award "Hiring the Handicap", 1959; [pers.] The journey of life leads us up many paths and up to many crossroads, hopefully we take the right turn....; [a.] Shelton, CT

SERGENT, IRENE M. THOMPSON
[pen.] Daisy Charles; [b.] April 4, 1929, KY; [p.] Daisy and Charles F. Thompson; [m.] Roy C. Sergent, May 31, 1947; [ch.] John F. W. - Diana Gail, Keith David; [ed.] Ashland High - Ash. Beauty College - Nursing Home Adm. Ohio State; [occ.] Retired; [memb.] Holy Family Church; [hon.] Legionaries Award "Outstanding Sales"; [oth. writ.] Poems published in local paper - commercials for local recording studio, songs, short stories for children.; [pers.] Internal happiness is a bubbling brook of contentment, when the heart and spirit unite to become one, with it's creator.; [a.] Ashland, KY

SERRANO, AMELIA
[pen.] Amelia Chevremont; [b.] June 20, 1908, Puerto Rico; [p.] Anselmo and Anna Serrano; [m.] Carlos Chevremont, May 3, 1978; [ch.] Annetteo Liveira, Sylvia Walshe; [occ.] Writing; [memb.] American Society of composer, authors and publishers (ASCAP) that United Hospital fund; [hon.] My honors is when I write a poem or a writing that the people like to hear again or read; [oth. writ.] Some poems and writings for unions and some centers that they keep them in their files. I go far away when I am writing a poem or any other article that amuse me so much because it brings me a lot of thoughts and beautiful places to describe and put into writing; [a.] New York, NY

SERRANO, DEAN CHRIST PRE
[pen.] DC; [b.] November 30, 1976, Ilocos Sur, Philippines; [p.] Danny and Leticia Serrano; [ed.] St. Lawrence Academy; [occ.] Student; [pers.] In Dedication to all those who have terminal disease

that mankind may someday come to understand the pain and suffering one endures day by day...; [a.] San Jose, CA

SEWER, IHSAN
[pen.] Banton, Shambi; [b.] November 11, 1977, New York; [p.] Vancito and Sylvia Sewer; [ed.] Graduated from All Saints School St. Thomas. I have been accepted to Rutgers University in New Jersey.; [occ.] Student; [memb.] I'm a member and junior instructor of the kids and the sea program (a local boating class).; [hon.] Highlights Magazine 6/93 issue-Tutu Archaelogical Village Project-Volunteer (age 13), Rolex Regatta 1992, 1994 Governors Cup bot Races 1992, 1993, 1994; [oth. writ.] Old man crow, My hero?, A gift?, Being a poet poverty, the trials of life, staying up, I was born an American Slave Sonnet II, An Evil Sterotype There was a River, bein Po Aint Nice etc.; [pers.] Poetry is life distilled - G. Brooks Poetry is a way of explaining poetry is a way of explaining complex things in their simplest form and simple things in an even simpler form. Ihsan Sewer; [a.] Saint Thomas, VI

SHABANOV, YURI
[pen.] Rossiander; [b.] February 23, 1930, Rostov-on-Don Region, Cossack City, Proletarsk; [ed.] Bachelor's Degree, Teacher of Russian and Western Literature University of Taganrog, 1961., University of Novosibirsk, Diploma of Philosophy, 1968-1971., Diploma of Patent Expert, Moscow Patent Institute, 1968-1971; [memb.] San Francisco Bar Association, Translator Patent Institute; [oth. writ.] Crimes are not to be forgotten, If the politics would go wrong, I blame, Crimes are not to be forgiven; [pers.] I blame. I, Yuri Shabanov, citizen of USA and Russia, at present time write personal histories lof holocaust victims at Russian Law Firm in San Francisco. I used to be political and legal correspondent for Russian Newspaper Vzglyad. Before coming to this country, I was a teacher of Russian Literature, Philosophy, Ethics and Esthetics in Colleges and Institutes in Russia.

SHADDEN, RICKY W.
[b.] February 16, 1979, Crane, TX; [p.] Keats and Iva Dunn (grandparents); [ed.] Comanche High School, 9th Grade; [memb.] Columbia House Music; [oth. writ.] Just starting out; [pers.] I want to make the world aware of all our troubles that deal with suicide, gangs, violence, and sometimes love.; [a.] Comanche, TX

SHAMMAMI, FRANCINE MARY
[b.] September 8, 1986, Royal Oak, MI; [p.] Jalal and Salwa Shammami; [ed.] Brookefield Academy, formerly Montessori Center, January 1989 - June 1993, Our Lady of Refuge August 1993 - Present; [occ.] Student; [memb.] Participated in Anthology of Poetry by Young Americans; [hon.] 1994-95 Principal's List October 1994 Student of the Month, 1994-95 State Board of Education, Certificate of Recognition; [a.] West Bloomfield, MI

SHANK, M. JOYCE
[b.] December 8, 1927, Manheim, PA; [occ.] Retired! Part-time Artist and Card Player.; [memb.] Unitarian Church of Lancaster, PA., American Business Women's Assoc., Manheim Historical Society, General Hospital Aux. AARP-National and local chapter #4458; [hon.] Art

awards Abwa woman of the year; [pers.] "My favorite poet is Emily Dickenson but I also like the wit of Dorothy Parker."; [a.] Manheim, PA

SHANKS, FLORENCE
[pen.] Fes, Florence Eva Shanks; [b.] August 4, 1910, Bayard, NE; [p.] James Cadwell, Lulu Cadwell; [m.] Howard Shanks, December 26, 1931; [ch.] Harold Asa Shanks, Cyrilla Maxine Shanks; [ed.] Bayard High School, 1928 Secy. "Great Western Sugar Factory." Bookkeeper - "Abbott's Laboratories," North Chicago, Illinois; [occ.] Retired Housewife; [memb.] Methodist Church (Lady Deacon) Federated Garden Club, AARP, Christian Women's Association, Order of Easter Stav. Job's Daughter Women's Golf Ass'n. Boy Scout Den Mother; [hon.] Past Matron O.E.S. Past President Toastmistress. Lay Ministry, June 1984, Arid Golfer. ("Two Aces," "Hole-in-One," 1964-1969.) Artists Guild, Portraits, oils; [oth. writ.] "Poetry," "Dancing," "Sabotage," words and Music. "Every Season Of Life," "A marathon with you," "Values," "Attitude" and "Behavior," "I'm Thankful."; [pers.] Time and tide waits for no man, and we need to do what we can, while we can as another yearly cycle of life will pass.; [a.] Scottsbluff, NE

SHARPE, CASSANDRA
[pen.] Cassie; [b.] September 8, 1982; [p.] Marjorie Lisa; [ed.] Burnet Middle School; [memb.] Boys and Girls Club of Union, Middle School track team; [hon.] Second honor roll, Cross-country and track trophies and medals, and medals, Bowling trophies, Cooking-baking trophies; [a.] Union, NJ

SHAW, JOYCE B.
[b.] September 19, 1930, Knoxville, TN; [p.] Ira and Maggie Capps; [m.] T. J. Shaw, September 13, 1969; [ch.] Donald Ray Baker; [ed.] Rule High School; [occ.] Retired (from University of Tennessee); [memb.] American Association of Retired persons (AARP) Knox County Humane Society Doris Day Animal League; [hon.] National Honor Society (High School); [pers.] I strive to reflect all of Nature's beauty in my poems, so that in reading them, others may also see that Beauty.; [a.] Knoxville, TN

SHEFFIELD, LEON
[pen.] L. T. Sheffield or Luv Hunter; [b.] December 5, 1975, Livingston, AL; [p.] Mayola Robinson; [ed.] Graduated from the Alabama school of Math and Science. I am presently a Freshman at Xavier Univ. in New Orleans, LA; [occ.] College Student and phone Ambassador at the house of blues in New Orleans.; [memb.] I am a member of NAACP, Xavier's Biomedical Honors program and biology club; [hon.] National honors society, Dean's List, Xavier Merit Scholarship; [oth. writ.] I have entered poetry to contests held by Quill books and the Iliad press, also for publication.; [pers.] "My writing comes from the heart. When I write a piece of myself is being placed on paper, and I want my work to provoke thought and discussion.; [a.] New Orleans, LA

SHEK, JOHNNY
[b.] August 12, 1928, China; [m.] Chun-Chun Shek, February 17, 1968; [ch.] Byzan Shek; [ed.] B.F.A. School of the Art Institute of Chicago,

1966. M.F.A. University of Chicago, 1968; [occ.] Professional Artist; [hon.] Interjacent, Mixed media, Water Course, Mixed media, City Lights, Mixed media, Kailua Bay, O'ahu, Oil, Wailua River, Kaua'i, Oil, Sunset Beach, O'ahu, Acrylic, Sandy Beach, O'ahu #1, Mixed media, Sandy Beach, O'ahu #2, Mixed media, Ala Wai Boat Harbor #1, Watercolor, Ala Wai Boat Harbor #2, Watercolor, Ala Wai Boat Harbor #3, Oil, Lumahai Beach, Kaua'i, Acrylic; [oth. writ.] An eight-verse poem published in Wen Hue Daily newspaper, April 20, 1966. Two poems published in Honolulu local Chinese newspaper, January 16, 1964. For more important writings please see the Catalogue under the Publications.; [a.] Honolulu, HI

SHEPARD, MARTHA I.
[pen.] Martha I. Shepard; [b.] November 1, 1922, Battle Creek, MI; [p.] Leslie and Alta Gibson; [m.] Douglas A. Shepard, December 18, 1948; [ch.] David, Daniel, and Linda (Linda Po lar now); [ed.] Mine - High School, it was battle creek central class 1941.; [occ.] Retired, was Central National Bank, also Mishawaka, Ind. Bank; [memb.] Churches United Missionary in Battle Creek, California Rd. Church in Elkhart, Indiana - Husband was pastor there. Now it is Faith United Methodist Church Elkhart, Indiana; [hon.] National Honor Society - in High school. Poetry Award later.; [oth. writ.] Have many to family, friends, and special times for church. Also one is Sunday School Song. Very many of them.; [pers.] I had a very happy marriage for over 40 yrs. I am now a widow, and wrote this poem for my daughter's wedding and young man to marry her, I call him my new son, Mike.; [a.] Elkhart, IN

SHEPARD, NANCY BAYLIS
[pen.] Nancy Baylis Shepard; [b.] April 13, 1942, Farmerville, LA; [p.] Elizabeth and Otha Baylis; [m.] Wilbert M. Shepard, November 26, 1966; [ch.] Sabrina Faye Shepard; [ed.] B.S. Grambling State University, Masters and Specialist degrees McNeese State University; [occ.] Author and poet director of Calcasieu community Detox Center; [memb.] Top ladies of Distinction, Inc., Zete Phi Beta Sorority, Inc. Deep South Writers Club, Calcasieu Arts' Council Pannel Member, NAACT, Nic-Acorn and Louisiana Minority Arts and Humanities, Council; [hon.] Top Lady of the year, Zeta of the Year, Honorary Governor of Louisiana, Honorary Secretary of Louisiana, Honored by women's Pavillion world fair exposition 1884-1984 Who's Who in the South, Semi-finalist National Library of Poetry contest, who's Who of Louisiana, Zeta of the year Achievement Award; [oth. writ.] Books - my sister, my friend, shared gifts, with love, Rhythmic Alphabets, first step Arithmetic, many articles moments thoughts and deeds; [pers.] "If a man has a talent to write and shares it with others, he helps to build God's Kingdom through his words."; [a.] Lake Charles, LA

SHEPHERD, BEVERLY RENEE JOHNSON
[b.] August 5, 1959, Waco, TX; [p.] Loreen and James Johnson; [m.] Ronald Shepherd, August 7, 1993; [ch.] (1) De Aundrae Johnson; [ed.] High School graduate of Evan E. Worthing; [occ.] Insurance Biller of St. Joseph Hospital; [memb.] St. Agnes Baptist Church; [oth. writ.] Several unpublished poems.; [pers.] A smile may be all the words needed.; [a.] Houston, TX

SHEPHERD, LEE
[pen.] Annastacia; [b.] May 28, 1965, Hammond, IN; [p.] Clarence & Martha Pointer; [m.] divorced; [ch.] Anthony Shepherd, Abagail Nicole Speidel; [ed.] High school grad, 2½ yrs comm. college, night classes for French, Ancient History, English Comp II, Archeology, Comp. Science; [occ.] Vagabond on life's road; [memb.] I don't belong to any groups, unless you count AAA. I am in the class where no one is understood, I am a dreamer; [hon.] Drafting, Auto Mech., Hunter Safety; [oth. writ.] Poems in Community College papers; [pers.] "Centuries have taught me that wise men will turn coldly away, when faced with hardships never-ending, day after endless day. With my centuries of searched for knowledge..., I have learned immortal I may be, I will never be wise." ...Another thousand years, Shepherd, Lee. [a.] TN

SHEPPARD, MARK J.
[b.] December 11, 1971, Rochester, NY; [p.] Ronald J. Sheppard, Shirl C. Sheppard; [ed.] Sylvania Southview High, Sylvania OH, University of Toledo B.A. Honors in Political Science, Student at Univ. of Cincinnati College of Law; [occ.] Summer Associate Law Clerk at Taft Stettinius and Hollister; [memb.] Golden Key National Honors Society, Phi Sigma Alpha, Black Law Student Association; [hon.] Won prize for poem "A Sister's Love" in H.S., Honors Award from University of Toledo, Full Scholarship to University Cincinnati College of Law; [oth. writ.] Published empirical studies in the National Conference for Undergraduate research Anthologies 1992 and 1993; [pers.] Through poetry, I am searching for the meeting point where nature, culture, and the introspective mind meet in fascinating, unsettling moments. I am driven by a fresh outlook and an active imagination.; [a.] Cincinnati, OH

SHIELDS, IVORY J.
[pen.] Jazz; [b.] October 28, 1955, Oscar, LA; [p.] Mr. and Mrs. Albert and Selma Shields; [m.] Gwendolyn Manning Shields, March 31, 1984; [ed.] AA Marketing Barber College, Real Estate School; [occ.] Barber Stylist, Direct care worker - freelance photographer - Real Estate Agent; [memb.] Great Lake Christain Center; [hon.] Honorable Discharge USAF; [oth. writ.] Over 400 poems writing - unpublish today - short stories; [pers.] God has created me to express love and kindness to others and upon doing so I will be honor both on earth and in heaven.; [a.] Pontiac, MI

SHINE, NAOMI
[pen.] Nermal; [b.] August 27, 1979, Weaverville, CA; [p.] Jacquelyne Shine and James J. Shine; [ed.] Trinity High School; [occ.] Student; [memb.] Bad Youth Group; [oth. writ.] Many other poems. (Unpublished); [pers.] Keep the faith - live your life to its fullest its not as bad as it seems; [a.] Weaverville, CA

SHIPLEE, WALTER HOGUET
[b.] December 15, 1918, Philadelphia, PA; [m.] Divorced, 1946; [ch.] Three great kids, now grown and doing well.; [ed.] GED - 2 yrs. Jax. Jr. College Jacksonville, FL, '46-'48.'; [occ.] Retired; [memb.] VFW-4th Mar. Divn. Ass'n. and all organizations claiming to get you great discounts at fine hotels and restaurants, but don't.; [hon.] Cards on Father's Day.; [oth. writ.] Many 'Letters to the Editor.' (published), Colorful letters to our disgraceful professional politicians. (not published), Dozens of efforts of 60 to 80 pages which, so far, have ended up in the round file.; [pers.] Remember, the History books are always written by the winner.!; [a.] Sicklerville, NJ

SHIRINIAN, EMELDA DARLENE
[b.] Fresno, CA; [ch.] Renee, Cynthia, Gregory and Monica; [ed.] Calif. State University, Fresno College of the Sequoias, Visalia, Montery Peninsula College, Montery; [occ.] Artist Owner/ Shirinian Studio and Gallery; [memb.] The National Author's Registry, Carmel Business Assoc.; [hon.] "Editor's Choice Award," "International Poet of Merit Award, Selected for the recording, "the sound of poetry, "National Library of Poetry" Honorable mention," "President's Award," Illiad Press '95; [oth. writ.] Published in "Treasured Poems of America" winter 94, spring, summer and fall winter 95, Sparrowgrass Forum, "Seasons to come", The National Library of Poetry, "Celebration of Nature," "Musings", "Celebrating Excellence, Illiad Press; [pers.] I feet that "Art is all of life and an expression of the creative ` faces, a visual and written statement of the world within." I am in constant pursuit of portraying the feelings of love hope and the peaceful union of all life on earth.; [a.] Carmel by the Sea, CA

SHORS II, JOHN
[b.] March 4, 1969, Des Moines, IA; [p.] John and Patricia Shors; [ed.] Colorado College B.A. in English; [occ.] Writer, Photographer; [oth. writ.] My first book, Moonset Over DryJen, is an epic fantasy novel devoted to the conflict between good and evil. The culmination of several years work, moonset over DryJen is intricate and gripping, filled with unrelenting action and drama.; [pers.] Since graduating from college in 1991 I have spent the majority of my life working and traveling throughout Asia. Recently I completed chance encounters: Tales of Asia, which is a compilation of exotic stories and photographs that tells of those I met and the environs in which they flourished. My agent is currently looking for a publisher.; [a.] Des Moines, IA

SHOSHANI, SAMUEL
[pen.] Shaham; [b.] March 8, 1926, Jerusalem; [p.] Yosef-Rivka; [m.] Farokh, December 31, 1947; [ch.] Ilana-Edna and Amir; [ed.] College; [occ.] Writing and poetry and translations; [memb.] Dix Hills Jewish Center, Ritual Committee; [hon.] National Library of Poetry. Royal-Air Force, WW II demobilized with special appreciations. Member of Haganah, Jewish Defense Forces in Palestine.; [oth. writ.] Translations of Persian Poetry Post Islamic Revolution into English and Hebrew. Biography in making and a novel in hand.; [pers.] When decided to do anything. Do it, do not hesitate nor postpone. Do not expect others to do for you. Be original in your writing, express your thought plainly.; [a.] Huntington, NY

SHRAMEK, RUTH
[pen.] Ruth M. Shramek; [b.] May 22, 1977, Glennallen, AK; [p.] Gerry and Jan Shramek; [ed.] Calvert Correspondence, grades K-7, Kenny Lake School, grades 8-12; [occ.] High School Senior; [hon.] High Honor Roll, Who's Who in American High School Students, writing award; [oth. writ.] Articles for school and local newspaper, short story published, one poem published, poems published in another anthology, honorable mention in voices; [pers.] The sky's not the limit. Aim for the stars!; [a.] Copper Center, AK

SHULER, TERESA D.
[b.] January 24, 1959, Columbia, SC; [p.] Barbara and James Shuler; [ch.] Elizabeth Cheyenne and James Ryan; [ed.] Irmo, High School BMCC School of Radiology; [occ.] Home Schooling Parent; [pers.] My love of children has taught me that each and every child is special in their own way no matter what!; [a.] Columbia, SC

SHULTS, TINA MARIE
[b.] May 5, 1980, Spartanburg, SC; [p.] (grand-mother) Judy Hale; [ed.] up to 9th grade in High School Southside Christian School; [occ.] High School Student; [memb.] Taek-Won-do/ National Federation of Tae-kwon-do, The World of Tae-kwon-do Federation; [hon.] Southside Christian School Sabre Award - most outstanding Middle School band player 1993-94, SC Band Directors and Music Educators Assoc. Award - Superior rating for solo and Ensemble 1994, Taek-won-do Gup (belt) - 8th yellow gup '94 and 6th green gup - '95.; [oth. writ.] Nothing published - just for school and my pleasure; [pers.] I like writing poetry in my spare time. I write them if I am angry or when I am alone. I relieve my anger on paper instead of fighting with someone.; [a.] Greer, SC

SHULTZMAN, BONNIE
[b.] January 21, 1945; [p.] Walter-Sylvia Reeves; [m.] Terry, August 6, 1966; [ch.] Kendra Lane, Aaron David; [ed.] Northwestern High, Grace College, Bethel Bible Institute, Indiana University, Ashland University; [occ.] 3rd grade teacher Apple Creek Elem, Apple Creek OH; [oth. writ.] Compilation of approximately 50 other poems, (unpublished) personnel journal.; [pers.] My writing began two years ago with the sudden death of our beautiful 20-year old daughter. I have found writing to be great therapy. It has helped me with my journey through grief. It is my desire to comfort others in their pain.; [a.] Wooster, OH

SIEIRA, ANTONIO
[pen.] "Antonio Ramon Sieira"; [b.] November 30, 1949, Detroit; [p.] Ramon and Carmen Sieira; [m.] Divorced (single); [ch.] Tiffany Dionne 26, Antonio Ainsley 23; [ed.] Eastern Mich. University Wayne State University Michigan State University B.S. 1972, M.A. 1973; [occ.] Mental Health Professional; [oth. writ.] Numerous poems and writings (unpublished), a few, published; [pers.] Always carry a pen and paper. Words may come to you at any moment. How sad to think. They could be lost forever, simply for lack of pen and paper!; [a.] Detroit, MI

SIFORD, SANDRA, L.
[b.] January 16, 1952, Indiana, PA; [p.] John Menoskey and Helen Gromley; [m.] Paul O. Siford, September 24, 1980; [ch.] Nicole Marie, Paula Jo; [ed.] Purchase Line HS, Class of '70;

[occ.] Housewife; [memb.] National Library of Poetry; [hon.] Editors Choice Award 1994, National Library of Poetry; [oth. writ.] Had a poem published in our local paper "The Barnesboro Star", Name of the poem was "PALS" dedicated to my brother and to of his close friends-all of whom have passed away.; [pers.] Writing poetry is very scare, I have never written a poem during the day. They come to me late at night. But I do enjoy the finished product. And seeing it down on paper.; [a.] Cherry Tree, PA

SIGMON, DONNA KAY
[pen.] Donna Kay; [b.] August 4, 1956, Lancaster, SC; [p.] Sarah and James Reid; [m.] Henry Alan Sigmon, December 26, 1988; [ch.] Robert Starnes Gibson; [occ.] Author retired nurse; [hon.] Editor's choice award; [oth. writ.] My Best Friend; [pers.] Through good times and bad times I believe.; [a.] Lancaster, SC

SILVA, THERESA
[b.] August 4, 1960, Taos, NM; [p.] Vic and Viola Silva; [ed.] My travels; [occ.] Gallery - Art Consultant (Bryan Gallery, Taos, NM); [oth. writ.] Mystical, Prayerful, Humorous, Spanish, Cultural, Suffered. Several Spanish poems published by the Spanish section, "El Crepusculo", of the local weekly newspaper, The Taos News.; [pers.] My gift is a reflection from the profound, in which the world shows me to love without limitations. To love with the beauty of the creations.; [a.] Taos, NM

SIMMONS, JOYCE NICOLE
[b.] June 14, 1981, Fort Riley, KS; [p.] Gerald J. Simmons and Monique; [ch.] I have no children, but I have a brother Sean Micheal and sister, Hillary Rodcliff.; [ed.] Currently in the 7th grade at Tri-North Middle School.; [occ.] Student; [hon.] 6th Grade Honor Roll twice; [pers.] I hope to influence myself and others. I like to be imaginative and creative. Hey that's my job as a teenage!; [a.] Bloomington, IN

SIMO, WILLIAM D.
[b.] November 22, 1945, Ishpeming, MI; [p.] Father deceased, Mother Mrs. Ann F. Simo; [m.] Yvonne B. Simo, November 10, 1978; [ch.] Jamie Lea and Janelk Lesley (Simo); [ed.] BIS Degree Geo. Mason Univ. Fairfax, Va., AS Education degree Northern Va. Community College, Alex, VA; [occ.] Logistics Manager for Dept. of Navy.; [memb.] Navy League of U.S., American Legion. Retired from U.S. Navy Veteran - Vietnam service.; [hon.] Magma Cum Laude No. Va Comm. College 1975, Golden Key Honor Society Geo. Mason University, 1989; [oth. writ.] Acquisition documents, poems as a hobby and personal satisfaction.; [pers.] We search for love which we can't define, but we hope we know it when we find it. Our hearts should always be filled with hope. Poetry's power lies in the emotions it creates in the reader.; [a.] Fairfax, VA

SINCERBEAUX, KAREN WILSER
[pen.] Luigi; [b.] January 24, 1957, New Rochelle, NY; [m.] Robert Kingsley Sincerbeaux, July 7, 1979; [ch.] Jesse, Genevieve, Joshua; [ed.] BSN at Storybrook (State University of N.Y.); [occ.] Childbirth educator; [memb.] Girl Scouts; [oth.

writ.] Childbirth poem "A baby's touch can give so much to the love you hold inside you'll never know how love can grow until a miracle takes place before your eyes you have the strength and courage. Hold them close and they will see you through for it won't be very long now before your baby will be gazing back at you."; [pers.] I am truly thankful for the compassion that breathes within me, the lives that surround me, and the love that embraces me daily.; [a.] Westford, VT

SIZEMORE, MICHELE
[pen.] Shelley Sizemore; [b.] April 21, 1949, Hamilton, OH; [p.] Stanley and Mildred Clark; [m.] James Sizemore, April 13, 1974; [ed.] Stephen T. Badin High School, Miami University, Oxford, Ohio BS in Education 1972, Miami University, Oxford Oh Masters ongoing; [occ.] Instructor - Fitton Center for Creative Arts, Hamilton, Ohio Artist Animal Portrait Artist; [memb.] Hamilton - Fairfield Arts Association, Middletown Fine Arts Center, Middletown Dog Training Club, PETA (People for the Ethical Treatment of animals, Dog Lovers of America; [hon.] Dean's List Miami University, Best of Show - Butler County Fair - Art 1987, 1st Place Watercolor Area Art Show 1990, Numerous Art Awards, Two "one Woman Shows" Sinclair Community College, Annual writing awards 2nd place - non-fiction, 3rd place - non-fiction; [oth. writ.] "Sunlight and shadows" non-fiction, 2nd place winner in Sinclair Community College, Dayton Ohio Annual writing awards 1993, "The Swing" non-fiction 3rd place in Sinclair Community College Dayton, OH awards 1986; [pers.] Some ideas are best expressed visually as in my paintings, and others literally as in my writings. Each is a kind of impressionism of nature's intertwining in the workings of man.; [a.] Middletown, OH

SKAGGS, RUBY
[pen.] Ruby Farnham Skaggs; [b.] January 16, 1912, Commercial Point, OH; [p.] Pearl and Alice Farnham; [m.] William P. Skaggs, November 21, 1935; [ch.] David, Keith, Kenneth, Wayne, Elaine, Maxine, Nancy, Joy (8 Children); [ed.] 10 yrs. High School Corresponding art course (Famous Arts); [occ.] Housewife, retired Sales; [memb.] Member of Happy Valley Church as of Christian Christian Union. Some song under promotion at top records; [hon.] Retired with high sales ability in Amway and Rawleegh business. Several anthologist of poems by The National Library of poetry contain Ruby's poems. Also poems in quills several book publications. Recognized for her oil painting, painted original picture. "Three Crosses" for Easter 94 at Happy Valley Church. Along with original poem read as picture was shown.; [oth. writ.] During stay in Reversed Hosp. March 15 thru April 1 she wrote "Hospital Praise" in appreciation for their wonderful care and was talk her contribution was the first they'd knowing all their. Hospital service poem was on bulliten; [pers.] During the 12 days which Ruby recognized no one, then wonderfully is recovering. God has been so good to me. He must still have work for me, since he spared my life from pneumonia and viral sickness (Mar. - April 95) He has given me a song and a painting already.; [a.] Chillicothe, OH

SKIBICKI, RONALD
[pen.] Ron Skibicki; [b.] August 10, 1945, Chicago; [p.] Mrs. Belle Skibicki; [m.] Mary (Keejan) Skibicki, May 10, 1980; [ch.] Ann - 13, Sarah 10; [ed.] St. Josephat Sc, Grade K Trough 6, St. Priscilla 7 and 8th St. Benedict H.S. 9-19th all in Chicago; [occ.] V.S. Postal Service "Letter Carrier"; [memb.] Mount Olive Church, National Ass'n of Letter Carriers Union former President of St. Priscilla Holy name Society; [oth. writ.] Another poem about springtime. My family is very supportive of my poetry my wife Mary daughters Ann 14, Sarah 10; [pers.] Served 2 years in U.S. army 1965-67. I help coach my daughters soft ball team. My writings so far have been about the seasons.; [a.] Chicago, IL

SLATER, DONNA L.
[b.] June 2, 1959, Winchester, VA; [p.] Frank and Vernie Lockhart; [m.] David W. Slater, December 6, 1980; [ch.] Heidi Lynn Slater; [ed.] James Wood High School; [occ.] Factory worker-Henkel-Harris; [oth. writ.] None-life goes on! is my 1st poem; [a.] Gore, VA

SLAY, TABETHA M.
[pen.] Kitty Marie; [b.] April 20, 1975, Sacramento, CA; [p.] Patrick Murray and Karen Slay; [ch.] Sebastian, David, Alexander, Bullington; [pers.] If you want the rainbow, you gotta put up with the rain!; [a.] Santa Rosa, CA

SLOAN, CHARLOTTE P.
[b.] April 27, 1956, Huntington, WV; [p.] Charlotte DeGroff, Raymond Sloan, Jr.; [m.] Divorced; [ch.] Philip Hardy, Rowan Hardy; [ed.] AAS - Nursing Registered Professional Nurse, Registered Clinical Hypnotherapist; [occ.] RW-Hypnotherapist; [memb.] NY Society of Clinical Hypnotherapy - Mental Health Ass. of Dutchess County, ICAW of Ulstres County; [oth. writ.] "What love", "To Me", numerous poems; [pers.] Began writing to take care of myself. Have found it in valuable as a tool in my healing work. Love is the answer to all our problems.; [a.] Kingston, NY

SMILES, LISA MARIE
[b.] June 5, 1973, Middletown, NY; [p.] Frank and Sharon Krom; [m.] Christ Smiles, December 5, 1993; [ch.] Amanda Marie Smiles; [ed.] High School Diploma; [occ.] Homemaker; [oth. writ.] Personal poems, written for myself reflecting the many joys and sorrows one goes through.; [pers.] This particular poem was written for my mother who battled with cancer and beat it. The love of my family is worth more to me than all the money in the world.; [a.] Summitville, NY

SMITH, ALONDA MARIE
[b.] January 30, 1961, Chicago, IL; [p.] Geraldine Wilson, Norman Wilson; [m.] Jeffery Smith, September 5, 1985; [ch.] Natasha and Reggie Smith; [ed.] Fermi Elementary Hircsh High School; [occ.] Housewife; [pers.] In Honor of my father Norman Wilson Sr., Grandmother Margie Wynn Step mother Minnie Steele who is no longer with us God Bless; [a.] Chicago, IL

SMITH, BRENDA DUTTON
[b.] August 12, 1956, Philadelphia, PA; [p.] Clinton and Lois Dutton; [m.] Ernest Smith Jr., September 7, 1985; [ch.] Zerrick Isiah; [ed.] New Hanover High School, Fayetteville State University; [hon.] The national Dean's List; [a.] Virginia Beach, VA

SMITH, DEE DEE
[b.] January 11, 1973, Fairfax, VA; [p.] Jim and Caroll Smith; [m.] Greg Yeck (Fiance), October 14, 1995; [ed.] Falls Church High School, Washington Business School - Legal Secretary Program; [occ.] Accounts Payable at Executone Info. Systems, Inc.; [pers.] I have found that you don't have to be gifted and talented to be a writer. When you open your mind and your heart you can accomplish anything.; [a.] Falls Church, VA

SMITH, ELIZABETH J.
[b.] March 3, 1937, Pennsylvania; [p.] Dorothy and William Schiebel; [m.] Richard C. Smith, December 1, 1962; [ch.] Christina (Tina), Theresa (Terri), Richard (Rick), Tammi and 11 Grandkids.; [ed.] Brookline Elementary, South Hills High; [occ.] Housewife and formerly Computer Operator; [oth. writ.] Several poems for my family and friends on special occassions such as my parents 50th wedding anniversary or birth of a child and for each of my children to show how special each of their lives are to us.; [pers.] This poem was written as a tribute to my wonderful mother who passed away in September 1993.; [a.] Andover, OH

SMITH, GREG
[pen.] Greg Smith; [b.] November 6, 1977, Arlington Heights, IL; [p.] Karen Smith, Donald Smith; [ed.] Junior at William Frend High School; [occ.] Student; [memb.] Frend Lacrosse Team; [pers.] Writing poetry helps me to express my feelings, when I can't verbally acknowledge them to others. It gives me inner peace.; [a.] Palatine, IL

SMITH, JIMMY R.
[pen.] Jimmy Smith; [b.] April 8, 1951, Jonesboro, AK; [p.] Irene Grissom; [ed.] College - University of Memphis; [occ.] Electrician; [pers.] I write songs and poems. Would like to have some of my songs recorded someday.; [a.] Memphis, TN

SMITH JR., SYLVESTER
[pen.] Skip; [b.] August 23, 1951, Rock Hill, SC; [p.] Mr. Sylvester Smith and Mrs. Mary L. Smith; [m.] Dr. Connie Smith, November 15, 1975; [ch.] Cynthia Lynn Smith, Christine Shreen Smith; [pers.] Poetry is a surrounding message, our sight of vision that translate beauty into words of color, my journey, that reflect harmony.; [a.] Philadelphia, PA

SMITH, KYLE A.
[pen.] Kyle A. Smith; [b.] February 7, 1970, West Chester, PA; [p.] Marianne F. Smith and Gordon W. Smith; [ed.] East High School; [occ.] Notary Public Wiggins Auto Tags, Kennett Square, PA; [memb.] Fraternal Order of Police (FOP) Masonic Blue Lodge (F&AM), Benevolent and Protective Order of Elks (BPOE); [oth. writ.] Many poems, but nothing ever published; [pers.] I would say to

always keep a positive attitude and never take away somebody's hope! It may be all they have. Dreams do come true!; [a.] Kennett Square, PA

SMITH, LARRY
[pen.] Larry Smith; [b.] March 25, 1938, Clearfield, PA; [p.] Clark Smith, Irene Smith; [m.] Shirley Smith, September 19, 1964; [ch.] Polly Ann, Hal Mark, Dean Wayne; [ed.] Clearfield Area High School; [occ.] Heavy Equipment Operator, Coal Striping, Clearfield PA; [oth. writ.] Collection of poems, non-published; [pers.] I write poems to bring a smile, chuckle or a happy tear from the reader. I feel laughter and humor helps break tension and lets you live longer.; [a.] Clearfield, PA

SMITH, LAUREN N.
[pen.] Linda Star; [b.] August 9, 1980, Greenville, NC; [p.] Charlie Smith, Cena Smith; [m.] Not married; [ed.] Currently attending D.H. Conley High School as a freshman; [occ.] I am not currently employed.; [memb.] Mariah Carey fan club; [hon.] Good Citizenship Award Principal's List Award; [oth. writ.] 1st prize in 5th grade for a clarification paper, 1 of 2 out of 120 students to make a 4.0 on last year's writing test.; [pers.] I feel that writing poetry is a great way to express your feelings without being mean or crude. I have strong personal beliefs and poetry helps me express them.; [a.] Greenville, NC

SMITH, LILLIE MARIE
[pen.] Christon Reed; [b.] February 9, 1968, Indiana; [p.] Helen M. Smith; [ed.] St. Anne Community High School; [occ.] Baker and Taylor Books; [pers.] I strive to make the most out of all that comes. And the least out of all that goes. And to those who have loved me without demand or change I am forever thankful. I have been taught to love.; [a.] Momence, IL

SMITH, LOIS BEAVER
[b.] October 15, 1908, Hico, TX; [p.] Mikiel E. and Samintha A. Beaver [m.] John Holman Smith (Deceased), May 24, 1929; [ch.] Robert Don, Daniel Polk; [ed.] Girard High School North Texas State Teachers' College Texas Technological University. Lubbock Taught elementary school for 7 years.; [occ.] Retired after 15 years with the Army Corps of Engineers.; [memb.] The Church of Christ. The National Association of Retired Federal Employees (NARFE). Public Broadcasting Station. Cemetery Association. Senior Citizens' Clubs.; [hon.] A birthstone ring at age 8 for publicly reciting a lengthy poem. I still have the little ring after 78 years. Valedictorian of my class. A cash award for a suggestion. Numerous certificates of honor throughout.; [oth. writ.] I researched, compiled and wrote a book of my family genealogy. I wrote a eulogy for my sister's memorial. I wrote a golden anniversary poem that was published in a County History book. I was contributing editor for two church publications.; [pers.] A dream was realized when I saw and read original manuscript in the British museum of works by the great English writers who have forever enriched my life.; [a.] Albuquerque, NM

SMITH, MARK WILLIAM
[b.] July 25, 1962, Miles City, MT; [p.] Melvin W. Smith, Lola "Chic" Reser; [m.] Brenda J. Smith, March 19, 1986; [ch.] Marlena J. Smith, Miranda Rose Smith; [ed.] Huntley Project High, University of Maryland, Asian Div.; [occ.] Student; [oth. writ.] Three non-fiction articles and one fiction short story published in various English publications on Okinawa, Japan.; [pers.] When considering our current ecological desperations, let's not forget that humans, with all of their confusion, are part of that ecosystem.; [a.] Fayetteville, NC

SMITH, MARY R.
[b.] January 17, 1945, Fairfield, IL; [p.] Bernard and Ruth Simpson (Deceased); [m.] Larry L. Smith, November 27, 1964; [ch.] Pamela Lyn; [ed.] Fairfield Community High School; [occ.] Payroll Clerk; [pers.] The teachings in the Bible are my daily guidance. I enjoy life in all it's beauty. Though I have been through a few tough times, I believe in the basic goodness of mankind.; [a.] Dickinson, TX

SMITH, MAXINE H.
[b.] July 14, 1929, Ogden, UT; [p.] Frances and Percy Turner; [m.] Bill M. Smith (Deceased) May 29, 1946; [ch.] David Smith, Starrlette Howard, Fawn Carlin; [ed.] Graduated Ogden High School, attended Weber State University; [occ.] Retired; [memb.] "Country Western Bands and Fans" "Daughters of the Utah Pioneers," "Open Door Shutins"; [hon.] "Citizen's Award for work with Shutins" zero Defects Award, Procurement HAFB, Award for work with shutins; [oth. writ.] Articles and poems published in various magazines and papers.; [pers.] I believe in the "Golden Rule," that people should be accountable for their own actions and the results thereof, and the strongest influence in life is love.; [a.] Ogden, UT

SMITH, MELANIE A.
[pen.] "Meya"; [b.] June 16, 1979, Flint, MI; [p.] Arlivia (Henry) (Smith) White (mom), Jerome Smith (father); [m.] Single; [ed.] Completed Elementary through middle School in gifted program, High School - Kingdom Academy Christian and currently at Southwestern Academy, Flint, MI; [occ.] High School Student; [memb.] Flint Southwestern Academy Cheerleading team, verse by verse Christian center, girl scouts of America, Urban league; [hon.] 1st place poetry - Martin Luther King Jr. National Youth Assembly 1992 Radio spot on Christian Station, 1993 numerous Leadership and Participation Honors and Awards (workshops, Camps, and programs); [oth. writ.] About (20) other writings including "Let It Begin Today With Me", "I'm a Black Woman", and "Success," published in local newspapers, several plays performed at University of Michigan - Flint and Kingdom Academy Christian School - Flint; [pers.] My writing project spiritual and moral virtues. My philosophy is "To give God the credit for everything that he allows me to do." [a.] Flint, MI

SMITH, MINETTE
[pen.] "The Missionary Poet" [b.] December 16, 1949, Saint Louis, MO; [p.] Fred and Clendell

Henry; [m.] Divorced twice; [ch.] Johnny Johnson Jr., Melodie Smith-Wells and Michelle Smith; [ed.] 1967 Graduate of O'Fallon High Westside Leadership Training School; [occ.] Homemaker; [memb.] Mt. Airy M.B. Church, Mt. Airy Mission Society, Mt. Airy Adult Sunday School, Mt. Airy Bible Study Class, Berean Dist. Missionary Baptist Assoc., Berean Dist. Women's Mission Union, Poet's Alley Workshop, The International Society of Poets; [hon.] Substitute Sunday School Teacher Award, Editor's Choice Award, International Society of Poets Award, The International Society of Poets Distinguished Member Awarded Member Award, and the Poet of Merit Award; [oth. writ.] "Jesus Christ," published. "The Christmas Story," a play, and other unpublished short stories and poems.; [pers.] In order to cope with the stress and problems of daily living, I trust Jesus to solve them. I am his. He said, "I am with with you always, even unto the end of the world. Jesus said it and I believe it.; [a.] St. Louis, MO

SMITH, NELSON E.
[b.] March 7, 1951, Martinsville, VA; [p.] Robert and Eula Smith; [m.] Terry S. Smith, April 18, 1987; [ch.] Christy Elaine, Kenneth Robert and Jeffrey Brandon; [ed.] Martinsville High, Tidewater Community College; [occ.] Supply Officer Naval Base Norfolk; [memb.] President, Bromley civic league, life member national R. Fle Association, American Legion; [a.] Norfolk, VA

SMITH, PAMELA LINETTE
[b.] June 9, 1972, Fort Lee; [p.] William E. and Dorothy B. Smith; [ch.] Tyrone Bullock, Cheyenne Bullock, Cindy Bullock, Vanessa Bullock, Darrell Bullock, Cathy Smith; [ed.] Petersburg High School Richard Bland College; [occ.] Customer Representative at JC Penney Telemarketing Catalog Co.; [memb.] March of Dimes; [hon.] Alpha Beta Psi, (Pledge Mistress, Historian, Chaplin) Editor's Choice Award from the "National Library of Poetry.; [oth. writ.] Richard Bland Memy. "Rising Beauty," Seasons to Come "Marbles"; [pers.] A vine of description grows within me, each bloom a thought of uniqueness. Furthermore, I would to thank my best friend Kristin Rodman for taking time out to read and listen to my poems, and my family for staying by me.; [a.] Petersburg, VA

SMITH, PATRICIA M.
[p.] Annette M. Monroe; [ed.] Villa Julie College; [occ.] Management Associate North Baltimore Center, Baltimore, MD 21218; [hon.] Who's Who of Black students villa Julie College; [pers.] I write about the inner beauty I perceive in things and people.; [a.] Stevenson, MD

SMITH, RAY
[b.] March 4, 1918, Philadelphia, PA; [m.] Sophie Smith; [ch.] Carol Smith; [ed.] Southorn High, Govern Schools for Electronic Studies; [occ.] Retired: 15 years volunteer, RSVP, Setting up small volunteer news papers; [oth. writ.] Writing poetry effects me deeply. I write only to myself and, if the result is pleasing to others, I have succeeded.

SMITH, WILLIAM B.
[pen.] William B. Smith; [b.] January 24, 1952, Brooklyn, NY; [p.] Richard A. Smith, Viola Smith; [oth. writ.] Extensive but no attempt made at publication; [pers.] As a Christian and one who loves and writes poetry, my interest lies primarily in the sacred. God, heaven, the immortal truths of scripture, the mysteries of life and death goodness, virtue, beauty and purity. Whenever I see these divine aspects, wether in music or literature, I cling to them and aspire toward them in so much as they bring glory to God. I see it as the poets job to capture and express these qualities that are so elusive and identifiable, to help one to see, feel, and appreciate the wonder and glory of life, while at the same time being moved along by the majesty and grandeur of poetic verse. To this end, I have been inspired many times in the past.; [a.] Fishkill, NY

SNEAD, BERNADETTE
[pen.] Bernie; [b.] September 12, 1977, Washington; [p.] Terrill and Modestine Snead; [ed.] Archbishop Carroll High School; [occ.] Clerk at the Library of Congress; [memb.] Children's International Summer Village Program (CISV); [hon.] Who's Who Among American High School Students Honor roll student, 1 poem published in neighborhood newspaper, United States, Achievement Academy, National Merit Scholar; [oth. writ.] Publication of a children's coloring book; [pers.] My writings reflect my personal experiences and emotions. I truly thank God Almighty and a ambitious mind to write; [a.] Washington, DC

SNELLGROSE, RENI
[b.] September 18, 1962, Kalamazoo, MI; [p.] Raymond Snellgrose, Anna Logan, (Step Dad) Russell Logan; [ed.] Gladstone High School; [occ.] Nanny; [memb.] Redwings Sanctuary, National Marfans Foundation, New Apostolic Church and young group and Choir; [oth. writ.] 1 poem published in journey of the mind.; [pers.] I hope that one day soon, all people will see each other for who they are, instead of what they are, and that they will let "God" back into their lives.; [a.] LaVerne, CA

SNYDER, LINDA MARIE
[b.] April 20, 1960, Cleveland, OH; [p.] Lawrence Snyder, Mavis Snyder; [ed.] Victory Park Elementary School Memorial Jr. High School, Charles F. Brush High School (graduate 1978); [occ.] Avon Representative; [pers.] Always keep the hope that - Life will get better!"; [a.] South Euclid, OH

SOLIS, DEBBIE
[pen.] Debra Dowdey; [b.] October 4, 1957, Mineral Wells, TX; [p.] Lloyd A. and Janie E. Dowdey; [m.] Charles E. Solis, Sept. 3, 1982; [ch.] David Shawn Dowdey - Amy Rene' Solis; [ed.] Bryan Adams High Dallas Texas; [memb.] Shiloh Terrace Baptist Church; [oth. writ.] Poems I have given to family and friends as gifts. And a scrapbook of poems and writings about life, love and the world around me.; [pers.] Learn to look at life through the eyes of your children there are so many great wonders to be seen. Children are a true gift from God, and one of the sweetest joys a mother could know. "Gift from God" is dedicated to my son David; [a.] Mesquite, TX

SOLTAN, BARBARA ANN
[pen.] Barb; [b.] March 13, 1946, Long Island City Queens, NY; [p.] Walter C. Soltan, Rosetta (Hoy) Soltan; [m.] Divorce, November 12, 1967; [ch.] Frank Victor Fiume and Donna Ann Fiume; [ed.] St Patrick's LIC, NY Long Island City H.S. NY; [occ.] Treasurer of "ABA" Amateur Ballplayers Association; [oth. writ.] My book "Micky" and numerous poems nevertheless, I haven't published; [pers.] My compassion for writing was influence by family friends and others; [a.] NY

SOPKO, SHERRY LYNNE
[pen.] Sherry Lynne Sopko; [b.] January 17, 1960, Lakeland, FL; [p.] James Kuh, Margaret Crews Kuhn; [m.] James Joseph Sopko, December 27, 1981; [ch.] Alison Lynne, Lindsay Diane and Joseph Aaron; [ed.] Kathleen Sr. High; [occ.] Homemaker/home schooler (Teach own children); [hon.] Nat'l Honor Society, Who's Who (among Amer, High School Students); [oth. writ.] Submitted short story to The Institute of Children's Literature/ gained acceptance/(course not taken yet)

SORG, MICHAEL E.
[b.] December 14, 1950, Arkansas; [p.] Edward and Sara Sorg; [ed.] Ball State University; [pers.] To explore: The psychological web within the cosmic unity the interplay of the particular and universal - the humanness at the heart of consciousness isn't this essential?; [a.] Anderson, IN

SOULE', JO ANN
[b.] January 23, 1936, Kirksville, MO; [p.] Dorothy K. Bell and Jack A. Webb; [m.] Douglas A. Soule, September 4, 1970; [ch.] Jamie Lynn Soule; [ed.] University of Nevada, Las Vegas, Bachelor's Degree, National University, Mater's Degree (Business Administration); [occ.] Sr. Management Analyst, Department of Finance, Clark County; [memb.] American Society of public Administration; [hon.] Leadership-Chamber of Commerce, Leadership (scholarship) National University; [oth. writ.] Personal collection only; [pers.] Nature's Beauty inspires me to put my thoughts on paper. It calms the mind and heals the soul.; [a.] Las Vegas, NV

SPADIDEAS, DEMY D.
[pen.] The Kikster; [b.] September 18, 1973, New York; [p.] Costas and Aglaia Spadideas; [ed.] Drake Business Schools Benjamin Cardozo High School; [occ.] Retail Management; [oth. writ.] Poems publishes in two anthologies, "Dance on the horizon" and "Best poets '95"; [pers.] Nothing brings out the true color of the spirit then the written word...; [a.] New York, NY

SPENCE, REBECCA A.
[b.] April 16, 1960, Rochester, NY; [m.] Michael K. Mooney, October 3, 1992; [ed.] B.A. Cornell University, M.A. University of Michigan, M.B.A. Harvard Business School; [occ.] Director, Policy and Business Development, CBA Pharmaceuticals; [hon.] Dean's List; [pers.] My poetry is inspired predominantly by nature. I strive to convey the beauty and emotional impact of what I see and feel, to pray equal attention to the sound and rhythm of my poems a to the content of the message.; [a.] Summit, NJ

SPENCER, JOANNE
[m.] Samuel Spencer Sr.; [ch.] Samuel Jr., Josiah and Susanna; [occ.] A minister of Refuge of Hope Mission, Newark, NJ, Tax controller for an accounting firm in Livingston, NJ; [memb.] School Board Member - Refuge of Hope Inst. of Learning, Newark, NJ; [hon.] Essex/Hudson County winner of the 1993 New Jersey Library Association poetry award; [oth. writ.] Many poems, including "How The Library Changed My Life" published by the Maplewood Public Library, Maplewood, NJ; [pers.] My writings reflect personal experience - mine and those of others. As a Born-again Christian, I've found that whether the circumstances of life are joyful or tragic, the antidote for handling every situation can be found in God's Word.; [a.] Caldwell, NJ

SPERRY, RICHARD R.
[b.] May 20, 1964, Elmhurst, IL; [p.] Bonnie (Rouse) Sperry, Kenneth Sperry; [m.] Donald E. Van Duyse, May 15, 1986; [ed.] College of Dupage Kishwakee College, College of Art Institute of Chicago; [occ.] Aspiring Artist Painter, Writer; [memb.] Unitarian Universalist Church Fox Valley Gay Lesbian Assoc.; [pers.] I am keenly aware of the details and constantly in all of the delicate balance and nature of being - thou.; [a.] IL

STACK, BRIAN
[b.] March 25, 1970, Medford; [p.] Paul and Joyce Stack; [ed.] Woburn High School, Middlesex Community College Petersun School or Engineering; [occ.] Cleaning and Resturation Specialist; [hon.] Journalism Award at Community College for School paper.; [oth. writ.] Writer at least 50 poems none published.; [pers.] I feel that poetry can be anything that grabs attention. Anything written that can cause even one person to stop and reflect on something is poetry, regardless of the poems intention.; [a.] Woburn, MA

STAIRS, LAURA
[b.] November 13, 1939, Searsport, ME; [p.] Charles and Isabel Stairs; [ed.] High School; [occ.] Accountant, State of Maine; [memb.] Attend Belfast United Methodist Church - Belfast, ME, Midcoast Christian Fellowship, Belfast, ME; [oth. writ.] Several in Binder written for personal use. None published.; [a.] Belfast, ME

STAMM, M. SUZIE
[b.] March 9, 1957, Mohrsville, PA; [p.] Adam C. Stamm, Miriam T. Stamm; [ch.] Keith Allen Stamm; [ed.] Schuylkill Valley High and Writers Institute. NY; [occ.] Accounts payable and Receivable clerk; [memb.] Grace Fellowship, Green Peace, Defenders of Wildlife and WWF; [pers.] I write to express myself and to pass good feelings unto others.; [a.] Shillington, PA

STANDFIELD, NADINE
[b.] February 3, 1931, Minneapolis, MN; [p.] Archie and Alice Austin; [ch.] Kathleen Craig Duane Randy Kevin and Donette; [ed.] High School Institute of Children's Literature; [occ.] Retired; [memb.] International Society of poets American Legion; [oth. writ.] Poem published 1995 short stories for children; [pers.] My hand is a personal messenger for my heart and soul. May God continue to bless me with the ability to continue my writings.; [a.] Mounds View, MN

STANFORD, CHERI
[pen.] Cheri; [b.] November 2, 1978, Iowa City, IA; [p.] Wilbur Dean and Paula Stanford; [ed.] Heritage Institute, home schooling; [occ.] Student, Sophomore; [hon.] Pioneer Scholarship for 1st year of college; [oth. writ.] Many poems, but no others published.; [pers.] When things get bad, it's time to go bad to the Lord Jesus.; [a.] Harrison, AR

STANLEY, KEITH L.
[b.] June 4, 1973, Worcester, MA; [p.] Alden Stanley, Linda Stanley; [ed.] David Prouty H.S.; [occ.] U.S. Army 1st Ranger Battalion, Savannah, GA; [hon.] High School Honor Grad, Airborne Wings, Ranger Tab, Sargent Stripes; [oth. writ.] This is my 1st writing that I ever tried to get published; [pers.] Most all of my writing comes from my mood, and this particular poem comes from a time when I was in love with this woman who I let slip away!; [a.] Spencer, MA

STARKEY, ANN MARIE
[pen.] Annie; [b.] March 21, 1973, Hammond; [p.] Ronald and Phyllis Starkey; [ed.] Graduated at Highland High School by GED in 1993. In my first year of college at calumet college transferring to Lincoln Christian college.; [occ.] Cashier at Highland Pharmacy; [memb.] Red Cross Blood Donor, member at Black Oak Church of Christ.; [hon.] Received a scholarship for my GED score which paid half of my tuition.; [oth. writ.] This is the very first writing I've ever sent in. My poem has been published in my church bulletin.; [pers.] My only inspiration with writing poetry is from my Lord, Jesus Christ. I love the Lord with all my heart, soul, and mind, I have truly been blessed by the Lord! I love you, Jesus!; [a.] Highland, IN

STARKS, SANDRA J.
[b.] October 17,1942, Sacramento, CA; [p.] Marion S. Smith, Esther L. Smith; [m.] Dan Starks, July 28, 1990; [ch.] (son) Kip J. Mussatt, (daughter) Zanet S. Camino; [ed.] Grants High, Grants, NM; [occ.] Artist; [hon.] Poem accepted for publication in Treasured Poems of America to be published Fall 1995.; [oth. writ.] I have written since childhood, only recently submitting poems in competition, and to my amazement, both have been selected for publication.; [pers.] Nature and the normal flow of life are full of knowledge and wisdom, and are a free gift if we take the time to observe and absorb; [a.] Hutchinson, KS

STAYER, JERRI
[b.] December 19, 1924, Jasper, NY; [p.] Ernest and Mary Vergason; [m.] Edgar Stayer, Jr., August 3, 1963; [ch.] Two boys, two girls; [occ.] Retired; [memb.] Irvington Baptist Church; [oth. writ.] Published in Montana - two songs: Montana is Heaven to Me and The Montana Waltz.; [pers.] I have written many ballad type songs and many poems reflecting God's love for mankind. Poetry is in narrative form.; [a.] Irvington, KY

STAZENSKI, CHRISTINA ALISON
[pen.] Alison Mack-Stazenski; [b.] March 10, 1964, San Francisco; [p.] Sandy and Anne McCurdy; [m.] Derek Stazenski, July 4, 1992; [oth. writ.] Have had a couple letters published in the local paper; [pers.] May we always learn from our past. So we may have a better future.; [a.] Las Vegas, NV

STEALEY, ALY
[b.] February 15, 1980, Princeton, NJ; [p.] John W. Stealey, Laura Stealey; [ed.] So far, only through public school. I hope to attend Yale or Rice. (Hereford Middle and High, and Sparks Elem.); [oth. writ.] I've had numerous writings published in Merlyn's pen.; [pers.] I wish to thank my 7th and 8th grade English teacher, Mrs. Sue Ellen Winter for making me the writer I am today and my mother for he unceasing, encouragement.; [a.] Sparks, MD

STEBBINS, BONNIE
[pen.] Bonnie Elaine Stuart Ransom Stebbins; [b.] January 20, 1951, Detroit, MI; [p.] Boris Dave Miller, Elaine Stuart Stebbins; [ch.] Shawn Charles Harris, Ayrianna Dawn Harris, grand child- Meric Bruce Ransom Harris; [ed.] BA Psychology and 12 PhD Credits from University of Detroit Mercy; [occ.] Student; [hon.] Published Poetry Award for Bravery from Berkley Fire and Police Community Service; [oth. writ.] In a moment of an instant, we, Blue Embers, As the way that I feel for you.; [pers.] With sharpness of mind - conquer those who would enslave thee. B Stebbins; [a.] Detroit, MI

STEELE, GORDON
[m.] Marion; [ch.] Carolyn and Alissa; [ed.] USMA, West Point; [occ.] Artist; [memb.] Association of Graduates USMA; [hon.] DFC, PH (OLC), AM (IOLC); [pers.] The pedigree of certainty is shot through with the mongrel blood of fallacy The Fighter Pilot's Tale with Apologies to Chaucer (a manuscript in progress).

STENDER, BARBARA JEAN
[b.] October 17, 1976, Randolph, VT; [p.] Youngsun Stender, Dale Stender; [ed.] Hartford High School; [occ.] Student at Western Maryland College; [oth. writ.] Poems published in Echoes from the silence and college magazine.; [pers.] Although I am first and foremost a visual artist, I also like to express myself through the words of poetry. It is my hope that someone out there will be as moved by my poems as I was when I wrote them.; [a.] Hartford, VT

STEPHENS II, BENJAMIN J.
[b.] June 7, 1952, Panama City, FL; [p.] Ben and Catherine Stephens; [ch.] Benjamin III, Astra, Crystal; [ed.] Bay County High, Embry-Riddle Aeronautical Univ., Navy Senior Enlosted Academy; [occ.] Equal Opportunity Specialist (Senior Chief Petty Official); [memb.] US Navy; [oth. writ.] Two Article For "Reflections" defense equal opportunity management Inst. Magazine, one poem for home town paper.; [pers.] Wisdom: Lessons Learned from survived experiences. The quest of knowledge is life.; [a.] Largo, MD

STEPHENSON, ESSIE P.
[pen.] Essie P. Stephenson; [b.] June 15, 1945, Ravenswood, WV; [p.] Raymond and Esther Sams; [m.] Howard E. Stephenson, August 1, 1964; [ch.] April E. Riggs, Howard E. Stephenson Jr, Janie Lynn Muluahill, Jeffrey A. Stephenson; [ed.] Ravenswood High School, Ravenswood WV; [occ.] Housewife; [memb.] Church of God in Mans.; [hon.] Won awards in Art, Spelling, writing in high school; [oth. writ.] The promise, things we take for granted summer is gone, my special love; [pers.] My poetry was influenced by my parents

and by God and life. My parents were well respected in their community. And I love them very much. The love of my life, my husband was also an inspiration in my poetry.; [a.] Mansfield, OH

STERN, ALEXANDRA
[b.] August 28, 1980, New York City; [p.] Caria Stern, Paul Stern; [ed.] Presently a freshman at Livingston High School; [occ.] Student; [memb.] FBLA (future business leaders of America) for my High School; [oth. writ.] This is the first of my many poems to be published.; [pers.] The time we have in this life is short. I find no purpose in attempting to hide your true self to the world in fear. I feel everyone has a unique beliefs and they should express them, no matter what the consequences may be.; [a.] Livingston, NJ

STEVENS, GERTRUDE C.
[pen.] Trudy Stevens; [b.] April 2, 1923, Derby Line, VT; [p.] Lillian and Cyril Cargill; [m.] James E. Stevens (deceased), November 29, 1944; [ch.] Sons Lynn, Barry and Timothy; [ed.] High School; [occ.] Homemaker; [memb.] First University Parish (UU) North Country Swingers Square Dance Club, Community circle, AARP, Orleans County and Derby, VT, Historical Metropolitan Museum of Arts - Boston, MA North Country Hospital Auxiliary, Newport, VT; [pers.] I believe in the supreme worth of every human personality and the inherent goodness in everyone and that love will prevail.; [a.] Derby Line, VT

STEVENS, JOHN R.
[b.] May 6, 1925, Moberly, MO; [p.] Frank E. and Jewell Stevens; [ch.] Timothy Jon, Jeffrey Ronald; [ed.] Moberly Junior College; [occ.] Electrical Engineer, (Retired); [memb.] V.F.W. Masonic Lodge; [oth. writ.] Numerous poems mostly attempting colloquial humor, none of which has ever been submitted for publication.; [pers.] Humor often widens the gateway to understanding life's complexity.; [a.] Warsaw, MO

STEVENS, SCOTT SHORETTE
[b.] July 7, 1985, Bangor, ME; [p.] Myrle and Daniel Stevens; [ed.] Newport Elementary Mrs. Currier's 4th Grade Class; [occ.] Student; [hon.] Basketball League Champion 1995; [oth. writ.] Several short stories published at school.; [pers.] I enjoy writing poetry and short stories about family, friends and the great outdoors, writing gives me the chance to express my thoughts in more detail than talking.; [a.] Newport, ME

STEWART, LATOSHIA
[pen.] Rhythm of Love; [b.] March 4, 1978, St. Petersburg, FL; [p.] Irene Cook & Aurthur Shannon Jr.; [ch.] No children but I have a godson (Donte' Ware Jr.); [ed.] Eastlake High School; [occ.] Student; [memb.] St. Luke Apostolic #2 Choir Director's assistant! [hon.] I have received several choral awards; [pers.] I try to be the best person that I can be by writing lovely poems. I have been influenced by my English teachers and friends and also my family. [a.] Clearwater, FL

STEWART, STACI
[b.] May 22, 1980, Arleta, CA; [p.] Ray Stewart, Vicki Stewart; [ed.] Attending Granada Hills High School; [pers.] Writing for me is my own immunity

to the world. With words I can create mental freedom... anything.; [a.] Arleta, CA

STILLMAN, JANE E.
[b.] July 13, 1933, Van Buren, MO; [p.] Isabel and Earl Labeau; [m.] Henry R. Stillman, June 12, 1953; [ch.] Dennis, Jon, Debra, Patti, Richard, Karen, Mark; [ed.] Grade 10; [occ.] Disabled; [memb.] Member of St. Mark's Methodist Church former Cub Scout Den Mother, Demolee and Jobs daughter mother's club. Active with girl scouts, Khoury League and P.T.A.; [hon.] Received commendation for quick emergency action as a switchboard operator when employed by S.W.B.T. Co.; [oth. writ.] Sight, sound and praise. Wave on old glory. Many personal works to family and friends for special occasions.; [pers.] Loved poetry as a child. Wrote first poem to my brother who was serving in the air force during Wm. II at age 9. Liked the work of Longfellow and POE.; [a.] St. Louis, MO

STINER, LOIS
[m.] Nicholas; [ch.] Craig Stiner, Pamela Kasch, Doreen Byrnes; [ed.] Morristown, New Jersey High School - some college Morris County Junior College; [occ.] Retired; [memb.] Attend United Methodist Church - and circle group. Volunteer work for WORC, (Work Oriented Rehabilitation Center); [hon.] Roller Skating Costume Contest - Design and creativity; [oth. writ.] Tooth Fairy Booklet (for my original Tooth Fairy pillow); [pers.] My goal is aimed at helping others face reality thru pleasurable reading.; [a.] Daytona Beach, FL

STINSON, JUDITH E. SELLERS
[pen.] Judith E; [b.] March 30, 1961, Upland, PA; [p.] Shirley and Everett Sellers; [m.] Divorced; [ch.] Amanda Judith Stinson; [ed.] High School ICU - correspondence, DCCC - classes, Career track tapes, skill path seminars; [occ.] Production manager/Office manager; [memb.] 1st Baptist Church of Aston; [pers.] I've always written theologically (this means I write poems during church - sometimes about the sermon!) Poems have just always been my way of expressing my heart. I seem to always rhyme. My life rhymes, too. God does that one.; [a.] Upland, PA

STIRITZ, JAMES B.
[b.] October 14, 1961, Los Angeles; [p.] Hurry and Sharron Stiritz; [m.] Suzanne, April 3, 1993; [ch.] Three by Marriage (step); [ed.] High School (partial); [occ.] Floorcovering Sales; [memb.] None to speak of (I am a Trekker); [oth. writ.] I've never written professionally, but when I saw your ad, I sat down and dreamed up this submission. From Magazine to mailing IT took about 45 minutes.; [pers.] Thank you for considering my poem. Be kind to one another.; [a.] Prescott Valley, AZ

STIRSMAN, CHARLES H.
[b.] December 22, 1925, Bremen, KY; [p.] William and Susan Stirsman; [m.] Helen Harmon Stirsman (Deceased), November 24, 1948; [ch.] Allen, Brian, Janet; [ed.] High School; [occ.] Retired Chemical operator; [memb.] Beulah Presbyterian Church Masonic Lodge F. and A.M.;

[oth. writ.] Unpublished poems some Masonic writings; [pers.] I believe there is beauty and art in everyone and everything and it is the purist pursuit of art to find and express this. Poetry, to me, is the ultimate expression of one's innermost feelings.; [a.] Louisville, KY

STOCKTON, EUGENE
[pen.] Antonio; [b.] February 12, 1924, Statesville, NC; [p.] Eugene Stockton, Ida Stockton; [m.] Colleen M. Stockton, January 15, 1955; [ch.] Andrea Barton, Eugene Stockton; [ed.] Morningside High, Johnson C. Smith University, Coulter Jr. College, Shaw University; [occ.] Retired from Health, Education and Welfare. As Investigator; [memb.] Alpha Phi Alpha, 32 Degree Mason, member of VFW, member of Coulter Alumni, Member of Israel Baptist Church; [hon.] Superior Performance Award, honored for dedication to blood bank; [oth. writ.] "So Great To Be Alive," "Remembering When," "The Plan" (Master Plan).; [pers.] To God Be The Glory.

STOKES, TIFFANY
[b.] November 3, 1981, Manhattan, NY; [p.] Mother: Cynthia Stokes; [ed.] DeWitt Clinton High School; [occ.] student; [hon.] Merit Awards since 1992 to 1995, Music Awards in 1992, S.P.E.C.D.A. Award in 1992; [oth. writ.] Poems published in year books (school); [pers.] When I write my poetry, I want people to know how I feel... like Maya Angelou does; [a.] Bronx, NY

STONE, AMY O.
[pen.] "Amy O."; [b.] July 17, 1920, Carter County, MO; [p.] Doyle and Lura Coleman (nee' Kelly); [m.] James Campbell Stone, December 20, 1946; [ch.] (Son) Jan Coleman Stone (Daughter) Jill Christy (nee' Stone) Leake; [ed.] 12 years - graduated from Central High - St. Louis, MO 6/39; [occ.] Retired from Secretarial type work '74; [memb.] Ascension Lutheran Church; [oth. writ.] Other poems published in church newsletter. Skits written for use at church. Conventional poems for personal friends and/or events.; [pers.] Japanese writers of HAIKU have influenced my style of poetry composing since I first saw them in a library at the national educational laboratory I worked at in the late 60's. I enjoy all styles of poetry, but have concentrated on Haiku style since I learned the simplicity and beauty of it. My senior years have brought much pleasure to me and I have been encouraged by many knowledgeable people in education and the arts to continue my Haiku efforts.; [a.] Saint Louis, MO

STOUFFER, ESSIE C.
[b.] February 4, 1975, Winchester, VA; [p.] Stephanie Butler and Covey Stouffer; [ch.] Lucas D. Logan; [ed.] Completed High School 1992 one quarter college; [occ.] Waitress; [hon.] Selected by friendship Caravan as Student ambassador to Russia Nominated for Miss Teen USA, Included in 1992 Who's Who in America High School Students; [oth. writ.] The ocean published in on the threshold of a dream; [pers.] The only real thing we have is our friends and family. Everything else can be lost or stolen. Everything else is expendable.; [a.] Fort Jones, CA

STOUT, SHELDON
[pen.] Sheldon S. Stout; [b.] November 16, 1971, Enid, OK; [p.] Jerry and Chris Stout; [m.] Ansela Stout, December 31, 1994; [ch.] April Dawn, Amber Renea; [ed.] Medford High School, OSU/ Okmulgee; [occ.] Student; [oth. writ.] Nothing published as of yet.; [pers.] I write about what I see around me everyday. My environment influences my work greatly. Some of my poems may not be pretty but poetry can't always be love and roses.; [a.] Medford, OK

STRADTMAN, ELIZABETH C.
[b.] January 7, 1917, Brooklyn, NY; [p.] Royal A. and Elizabeth V.D. Curtis; [m.] John F. Stradtman (deceased), December 28, 1946; [ch.] Paul Curtis Stradtman, Stephan Carl Stradtman; [ed.] Erasmus Hall H.S. Business College, A. D'Annunzio Painting Class; [occ.] Retired; [memb.] Lions Club (Ft. Vancouver Club), Save the children, St Anne's Episcopal church, Oxford Athletic Club; [hon.] Palo Alto (CA) Art Club 1st in show for thread "painting"; [oth. writ.] Several other poems on different occassions and subjects. Rereading them, some are refined and some discarded.; [pers.] This is the first submission of my poetry for possible publication. I wrote for my own pleasure and satisfaction. I love the beauty of this world and try now again to add my small bit to it and sometimes succeed to free imagination.; [a.] Vancouver, WA

STREET, JEANNETTE
[b.] April 4, 1980; [p.] Homer and Myrtle Street; [ed.] Garden Elementary-Middle Schools, Smiths Middle-Junior High Schools, current - Smiths High School; [hon.] Honor student-Garden Middle School, Honor student-Smiths High School, Presidential Fitness Award; [oth. writ.] Several poems that have never been published-not to mention the occasional short story.; [pers.] I always wrote things out of boredom. Then one day a teacher made me write a poem for class and I've been writing since.; [a.] Smiths, AL

STREET, RICHARD L.
[b.] August 19, 1959, Zanesville, OH; [m.] Never wed; [ed.] Graduated from Newark, (Ohio) High School 1975 At age 15; [occ.] I was formerly an actor; [oth. writ.] A few screen plays, A few songs.; [pers.] It is a hard life. There are not always happy endings. I see the dark side, more often than not.; [a.] Newark, OH

STRINGER, DARRELL
[b.] October 3, 1955, Detroit, MI; [p.] James and Minnie Carr; [ch.] Toi, Stephanie, Darrell, and Brittany; [ed.] Murray-Wright High School Lawton School of Business; [occ.] Bible student; [memb.] Hebron Church of Truth Deacons Board; [oth. writ.] Do You Remember, My Song to Mother, I'm Missing You, In The Garden of God, Ect....; [pers.] I thank God for my gift of writing and to Tawana L. Mullins for being the inspiration and the fulfillment of that vision and to tell the world that I love her...(the lovely); [a.] Detroit, MI

STRONG, RON
[pen.] Ronald A. Strong; [b.] November 20, 1960, Indiana, PA; [p.] Clarence Strong, Verla Strong; [ch.] Ronald Arthur Jr., Roger Alan; [ed.]

Saltsburg High School; [memb.] American Legion; [oth. writ.] Several Poems written but not published at this time; [pers.] I enjoy sharing my personal thoughts, feeling and experience with other; [a.] Daytona Beach, FL

STUDDARD, DANIELLE LEIGH-ANNE
[b.] August 22, 1982, Lagrange, GA; [p.] Ramona D. Parlier-mom, Eddie M. Studdard-dad; [ed.] In 7th grade at East Coweta Middle School; [hon.] Academic and achievement, all A's and all A's and B's honor roll, behavior awards at school also.; [oth. writ.] Many unpublished poems; [pers.] I love the beauty and magic in life so I express it through poems, I also write about disabilities; [a.] Grantville, GA

STUDEBAKER, KRISTINA RENA
[pen.] Nina; [b.] July 1, 1979, Lafayette, IN; [p.] Larry Turner, Terri Turner; [m.] Greg Studebaker; [ed.] Fairmont High School; [hon.] Honor Roll, 4 yrs. in a row; [oth. writ.] Poem "Flying Away"; [pers.] My dream is to be a veterinarian and to live in the country which has inspired my poetry.; [a.] Kettering

STULTZ, PATRICIA
[pen.] Patt; [b.] July 29, 1931, Roanoke, VA; [p.] Hubert and Edna Walters; [m.] Divorced; [ch.] 2 Daughters, 2 Granddaughters, 4 Grandsons, 1 Great-Grandson; [ed.] Old Dominion University, Norfolk, VA, Elizabeth City State University Elizabeth City, NC; [occ.] Medical Technology (Ret.); [memb.] Clinical Laboratory Scientist (N.C.A.), Medical Technologist (H.H.S.) Medical Technologist (A.M.T.), Medical Technician (A.S.C.P.) Can be abbreviated As: CLS (N.C.A.), M.T. (H.H.S) M.T, (AMT) MT (ASCP); [hon.] Diplomas (4) for courses at C.D.C. in Atlanta, GA; [oth. writ.] Christmas cinquains published in Virginian-pilot newspaper Dec. 1958. Letters-to-the-editor published in V/P newspaper 1994-1995.; [pers.] I am inspired by the beauty of all living organisms that turn with us in our circles of life. As science describes our DNA Sequence, I see the poet's ribbons revolve to reveal the beauty of the Helix.; [a.] Norfolk, VA

STURGILL, HEATHER D.
[b.] April 6, 1975, Atlanta, GA; [p.] Francis L. Sturgill, Sharon Donkle; [ed.] Beaver creek High School; [oth. writ.] Several unpublished poems and short stories.; [pers.] I am stimulated by challenges and I thrive on unconventional endeavors.; [a.] Beavercreek, OH

SUAREZ, SABRINA TERESA
[b.] February 24, 1981, NC; [p.] Angela and Johnnie Green; [oth. writ.] Realizing and Forever Friends and My Mother; [pers.] I've worked really hard on these I hope you like them.; [a.] Hope Mills, NC

SUITERS, CLOAMAE
[pen.] Corkey; [b.] August 24, 1932, Indianapolis; [p.] Don and Edith Hollowell; [m.] William Suiters Sr., March 15, 1952; [ch.] William Jr., Harry, Don, Paul, Phil, Kenny, Rosemarie Russo, Dianna McMunus; [ed.] Ben Davis High School 1 short class during summer of 51 at IBS; [occ.] Retired;

[oth. writ.] Several short stories in grade school paper and Indianapolis Times when I was 10 years old. Two poems published this year; [pers.] Most of my writing are done in Hosp. waiting room when my husband was in ICCU. After heart surgery 6 months, now mostly, when I need to relax.; [a.] Indianapolis, IN

SULLIVAN, GENTRY C.
[pen.] Isham Caheen; [b.] February 5, 1947, Detroit, MI; [p.] Isham C. and Lillie M. Sullivan; [ch.] Monseille, Shavonne, Genique, Maleece, Ashley; [ed.] Central High, Ferris State University, Shaw College; [occ.] Internal Auditor, AAA Michigan-retired; [memb.] Word of Faith International Christian Center, WOFICC Outreach Ministry, Christian Leadership Ministries, International Society of Poets, North Shore Animal League; [hon.] Editor's Choice Award; [oth. writ.] Several poems published, and recorded professionally on tape; [pers.] As a Christian, and a Christian Soldier through Jesus Christ, I strive to make people aware of the existence, and evil being of satan while acquainting them with the Lord, Jesus Christ, for He is definitely the Way, the Truth, and the Life. And the Truth will set you free from the wiles of satan.; [a.] Detroit, MI

SULLIVAN, MARY JANE
[b.] September 12, 1955, Memphis, TN; [p.] Don Carter (deceased), Betty Garrison; [m.] Divorced; [ch.] John Derek - 20, Frank Jr. - 19, Donald W - 17; [ed.] 12th grade; [occ.] Secretary; [hon.] Co-wrote a poem last year with a friend, that was published in the book, The Space Between.; [oth. writ.] Wrote other poems, just as a past time; [pers.] Enjoy writing poems that have a meaning or that seems to help brighten up a gloomy day, or turn a frown into a smile.; [a.] Batesville, AR

SULLIVAN, MARY L.
[pen.] Mary L. Sullivan; [b.] August 12, 1940, Winthrop, MA; [p.] Leah and Joseph Sullivan; [m.] Deceased, February 23, 1957; [ch.] Tom, Mary, Joan, Jackie, Patti, Laverne, Shawn; [ed.] Associate in Science with Drug and Alcohol Counselor BA Human Service with Specialty Counseling Psychology; [occ.] CHHA, Clerk; [pers.] Learning how to put my feelings and thought into words of poetry; [a.] Gloucester, MA

SUTHERLAND, NANCY HOPKINS
[b.] April 26, 1928, Los Angeles, CA; [p.] Leon and Bessye Hopkins; [m.] Leland M. Sutherland (Deceased); [ed.] Graduate of Glendale (CA) (Jr.) College, Majored in English and Journalism; [occ.] Retired travel Consultant, Manager; [oth. writ.] Wrote a column called "Counter Intelligence" for a short time for `Travel Age West' magazine. Received "Golden Poet" award in 1989 for my poem "Cherish" from (And Published by) `World of Poetry'."; [pers.] Love to read, golf, play card games and travel. Have 3 persian cats, top gun, clipper and shadow who are a great inspiration to me in my writing. Am working on my first children's book (it's never too late!); [a.] Escondido, CA

SUZEL, TANYA M.
[pen.] Zekeya Royal; [b.] December 8, 1979, Middletown; [p.] Martin and Debra Suzel; [ed.] I

am now in 9th grade at Monticello High School; [hon.] I was honor roll in school for 3 years; [pers.] I enjoy my schoolwork, my vacations, reading and writing notes and poems to my friends.; [a.] Wurtsboro, NY

SWANN, WILLIAM
[b.] July 7, 1924, Fellowsville, WV; [p.] Louis "Smoky" Swann Madeline Harvey Swann; [m.] Maggie Grey Smithwick, December 25, 1948; [ch.] Rita Y. Spangler (Adopted); [ed.] Attended Fairmont State College, Fairmont, W.V. Graduated Fellowsville, High; [occ.] Retired - Part Time Restaurant Mgr.; [memb.] Zeta Sigma Frat in College National Rifle Assn, World War II Air Force Veteran; [pers.] I try to treat my fellow man as I would have them treat me, always looking for good instead of evil.; [a.] Chesapeake, VA

SWAYZE, RUBY
[b.] October 1, 1942, North Platte, NE; [p.] George and Nellie Swayze; [ch.] Five-Chris, Ed, Bryan, Nellie and Joseph Kinney; [ed.] College; [occ.] Owner of Prairie Crafts and Etc.; [memb.] Central Idaho Art Association; [oth. writ.] Writer for Idaho County Free Press; [pers.] Every person is born with a unique combination of gifts, talents and abilities, therefore each is of great value to our father in heaven.; [a.] Cottonwood, ID

SWEENEY, MARTHA
[b.] February 22, 1897, Albany, NY; [p.] William and Ann Goelz; [m.] William J. Sweeney, February, 1917; [ch.] Helen and Mary; [ed.] Albany High School; [occ.] Retired; [pers.] A long time admirer of long fellow.; [a.] Las Vegas, NV

SWEENEY, STEVEN
[pen.] Steven Sweeney; [b.] October 16, 1973, Wichita, KS; [p.] Stephen/Suzanna Sweeney; [ed.] Still in High School; [hon.] General School awards; [a.] Wichita, KS

SWIES, ANN
[pen.] Annie; [b.] April 6, 1960, Chicago, IL; [p.] Bob and Donna Loszach; [ch.] Angel, Donna, Tony; [ed.] Curie High School; [occ.] Customer Service, Tilecera-Mid Atlantic; [memb.] National Honor Society; [pers.] I write from my heart and encourage others if it's in their hearts but can't say it, put it in writing. Our home was full of love as growing up and I want to share that with all.; [a.] Justice, IL

SZACH, EDWARD J.
[pen.] Eddie; [b.] July 8, 1960, Detroit; [p.] Edward and Alexandria Szach; [m.] Diane L. Szach; [ch.] May 21, 1988; [ed.] High School, Rets Electronics; [occ.] Electrician; [memb.] NRA, MUCC, World Bow Hunter's; [pers.] With a little common sense we have a constitution that will last an eternity.; [a.] Ortonville, MI

SZASZ, PETER
[b.] March 27, 1941, Budapest, Hungary; [p.] Elisabeth and Frank Szasz; [m.] Divorced; [ch.] Eli, Ame and Moira; [ed.] Washington University, St. Louis School of Architecture, BA in Architecture and Minor in Fine Arts; [occ.] Architectural Illustrator and Graphic Design; [memb.] American Society of Architectural Illustrators (ASAP); [hon.]

Had one man shows of paintings and poetry combined in St. Louis, San Francisco and Los Angeles. Has been giving poetry readings on the West Coast, SF area for the past ten years.; [oth. writ.] Recently finished a children's book, Prince John, and currently working on the illustrations and looking for a publisher - any ideas?; [pers.] Poetry should be an aid toward transformation and inner growth through connecting us with ourselves and others in a new way. A prime example would be the world of Rilke.; [a.] San Francisco, CA

SZETO, ALEX
[b.] March 14, 1971, San Francisco, CA; [p.] Yin Szeto, Miu Lin Szeto; [ed.] Galileo High School, City College of San Francisco; [occ.] Student; [pers.] In today's world as I see it, I can't help but dream about the moments. What brings you joy? The moments in which we glorify? Doesn't it?.... (As it only comes around once in a life-time.); [a.] San Francisco, CA

TABACZYNSKI, JOSEPH F.
[b.] February 13, 1968, Pontiac; [p.] Frank Tabaczynski, Elaine Tabaczynski; [ed.] Avondale High; [occ.] Administrative Assistant; [pers.] I wish to dedicate this to Jennifer Goodale, the inspiration behind it, the one person who taught me to believe in my dreams, and to strive to make them all come true.; [a.] Auburn Hills, MI

TALLCHIEF, CLIFTON J.
[pen.] Chief; [b.] February 10, 1946, Steubenville, OH; [ed.] B.S. Degree Political Science Minor in European History 24 Semester hours of education classes 21 semester hours towards a Masters Degree in Political Science taught introduction to Political Science Constitutional Law and Comparative Governments of Europe as a graduate student at Eastern N.M. University

TALLENT, LISA D.
[b.] August 12, 1963, Greensboro, NC; [p.] Donald Dennis, Barbara Dennis; [m.] Timothy Wayne Tallent, March 28, 1992; [ch.] Sandy Faye Tallent, Victoria Lynn Tallent, Jessica Diane Tallent; [ed.] Northeast High; [occ.] Guilford Mills, Inc. Greensboro, NC; [a.] Brown Summit, NC

TALLMAN, EVELYN T.
[b.] November 13, 1922, South Westerlo, NY; [p.] Mrs. Hazel F. Mabie; [m.] Deceased, January 23, 1940; [ch.] One; [ed.] Greenville, Central High School and National Bakers School; [occ.] Retired and write; [memb.] Alban Co Social Service, Social Security Benefits; [oth. writ.] International Society of Poets

TAO, JENNIFER
[pen.] Samantha J. Kyles; [b.] February 14, 1978, Taiwan; [p.] Allen Tao and Gina Tao; [ed.] Currently attending High School in Edison; [oth. writ.] Assorted writings such as plays, poem, and short stories. I have a recent poem published called "love's prisoner." It's the first of my published work.; [pers.] Always strive for what you believe it, if you have a dream, go for it. You'll never know if you succeed if you never try. Always follow your dreams.; [a.] Edison, NJ

TASSINARI, CLAIRE JUNE
[pen.] Claire June Cardon Tassinari; [b.] October 14, 1938, Plymouth, MA; [p.] Raymond A. Cardon; [m.] Vincent P. Tassinari Jr., June 18, 1955; [ch.] Paul - Marianne; [ed.] Plymouth High School La Salle - Interior Design, Oil Painting - Plymouth High Private and Instructor; [occ.] Homemaker; [memb.] Century Club - St. Labre Indian School Educational Assoc.; [pers.] I feel in writing a poem I am creating a picture with words in place of my paints ect.; [a.] Plymouth, MA

TATE, TAMMY R.
[b.] September 27, 1965, Atlanta, GA; [p.] Rev. and Mrs. Gerral Richards; [m.] Charles B. Tate, April 9, 1994; [ed.] Cherokee High School, Shorter College (undergraduate), West Georgia College (graduate); [occ.] Sixth Grade teacher, Sixes Elementary School, Canton, GA; [memb.] Long Street Baptist Church, PAGE; [hon.] Named Outstanding Young Educator in Cherokee County, Teacher of the Year at Sixes Elem., Named Outstanding Young Woman of America, Who's Who Among Colleges and Universities; [pers.] With God's help and my family's love and support, I strive to instill the love of learning and writing in my students. My desire is that others will see a glimmer of God's Love shining through my writing and me.; [a.] Canton, GA

TEDEROUS, KYLE G.
[b.] April 13, 1964, Dunkirk, NY; [p.] George P. and Sheila C. Tederous; [ed.] Graduate of Dunkirk High School with a Regents Diploma; [occ.] Entrepreneur; [oth. writ.] Various other non-published poems.; [pers.] "A lonely soul, in constant need of friends, has no friend in any mirror" special thanks to Mom and Dad, Tom N. and Shelley K. to whom the inspiration of this poem was derived.; [a.] Dunkirk, NY

TENORE-GRIFFIN, GINA
[pen.] Gina Tenore; [b.] December 23, 1955, Ft Sill, OK; [p.] Jack and Gwendolyn Tenore; [m.] Jeff Griffin, May18, 1985; [ch.] none; [ed.] Radford High School, Honolulu Hawaii, B.S. Psychology, Towson State University, Baltimore, MD; Peabody Conservatory of Music-Voice, Baltimore, MD; No. VA Community College-Commercial Art & Illustration Degree, Alexandria, VA; [occ.] Singer/songwriter; [memb.] S.A.W. (Songwriter's Assoc. of Washington, D.C.), W.A.M.A. (Washington Area Music Assoc.), P.E.T.A. (People for the Ethical Treatment of Animals); [hon.] Magna Cum Laude - No. VA Comm. College Art School, Music City Song Festival Contest-1987 Top 10% Award for song Lyrics "Does She," Nashville, TN, 7th Annual Mid-Atlantic Song Contest-honorable mention for "Just Say No" song-(S.A.W.), Music City Song Festival Contest 1989 Top 10% for songs "Work Ethic" and "Just Say No," Nashville, TN;[oth. writ.] Lyrics in Music Paper Magazine 1989 - National Publication; [pers.] I hope that through my writing I can bring out someone's emotions, and make them feel deeply. If I can strike some universal chord with my writing, to add to others' lives, in even a small way, what I have left behind will have made my life worth living. [a.] Asheville, NC

THACKER, BRENDA K.
[b.] July 26, 1949, Exter, VA; [p.] Sam and Omea Cress,; [m.] William Thacker, January 11, 1967; [ch.] William Jr. and Kenneth; [ed.] High School graduate and Courses through Piedmont VA. Community College, Licensed Cosmetologist; [occ.] Vice President of Thacker Builders, Inc.; [memb.] Blue Ridge Doll Club Greene County Chamber of Commerce First Bible Baptist Church; [oth. writ.] None published I have written several poems and short stories. I would like to put them into a book and give them to my family and friends as gifts.; [pers.] I thank the Lord Jesus Christ, my Lord and Savior, for the talent he has given to me. I pray that through my writing, I may lift up His name and reveal to others His goodness and love. He is my inspiration. Galatians 2:20; [a.] Stanardsville, VA

THAMES, KATHI L.
[pen.] Kat; [b.] March 11, 1959, Chicago, IL; [p.] Carol Frazier; [ch.] Domonique, Eric; [ed.] Corliss H.S. Malcolm X, Olive Harvey South Suburban College, Chicago City Wide College; [occ.] Paramedic Chicago Fire Dept.; [memb.] Christ Universal Temple, American Heart Association State of Illinois Dept. of Public Health; [hon.] American Heart Association; [oth. writ.] Many other poems; [pers.] Working on the streets of Chicago has made me see things differently some things seem to happen in slow motion in my mind's eye, allowing me to tell and write all about it.; [a.] Chicago, IL

THAYER, ANDY SCOTT
[b.] April 7, 1979, Lafayette, IN; [p.] Steve and Carol Thayer; [oth. writ.] Working on several novels; [pers.] Underneath all of these clothes, we are all naked; [a.] Cedar Rapids, IA

THERIAULT, MARK
[b.] June 17, 1977, Fort Kent, ME; [p.] John and Ann Theriault; [ed.] Graduate of Fort Kent Community High School. Going to College for a degree in pharmacy.; [occ.] Student; [hon.] Eagle Scout, placed sixth in my class, Maine Scholars Achievement Award; [pers.] I dedicate "Remembrance to Tracy A. Love. Though it pains me to remember, I'll never forget you.; [a.] Fort Kent, ME

THOMAS, ANNA F.
[pen.] Sandy Light; [b.] May 20, 1948; [m.] Vinson D. Thomas, December 21, 1966; [ed.] High School, Nursing School, graduated as Licensed Practical Nurse; [oth. writ.] "We Stand On Faith" poem "Hear Us" Article "What's It Like for Me" Article "Hey! What About Us Spouses"; [pers.] Thank you for accepting my poem "Little Girl". I just want to relate how this came to be, as well as my other writings. Five years ago I was diagnosed having Dissociative Identity Disorder (Multiple Personality). One of the many people inside, name Sandy, writes about the feelings of the abuse we went through as a child. "Little Girl" is based on one of my child alters. As an adult, I know exactly what it's like to look into a child's mind, to be a child that I was never allowed to be years ago. Our articles and poetry are about the struggles of the past, releasing the feelings through therapy, talking and writing. Our articles also

reflects how my husband and I stand on faith, that GOD will bring us through the journey we are now on. Every article and poem stems from the feelings within. I have never written anything before, had no desire until five years ago. I want my writing to give encouragement to others, reflect faith, hope and healing. To reflect GOD'S love, the strength He gives in the mist of a storm. What is my philosophical statement? To live a life that show's GOD'S love for all of mankind. To use what I've learned from life experiences to help others who are hurting.; [a.] Dumfries, VA

THOMAS, ESTHER MERLENE
[pen.] Sally Charles; [b.] October 16, 1945, San Diego, CA; [p.] Merton Thomas, Nellie Thomas; [ed.] AA, Grossmont College, 1966, BA, San Diego State University, 1969, MA University of Redlands, 1977. Cert. Elem. and adult edn. tchr.; [occ.] Educator, teacher Cajon Valley Union School District, El Cajon, CA. 1969; [memb.] Mem. U.S. Senatorial Club, Washington, D.C., 1984, Conservative Caucus, Inc., Washington, 1988, Ronald Reagan Commn., 1989, Rep. Platform Planning Com., CA., 1992, at-large del. representing dist. #45, Lakeside, CA, 1992; [hon.] Recipient of the outstanding service award P.T.A., 1972-1974, Hats Off to Teachers, Nomination Award, San Diego Board of Education 1989, Recognized by Marine Corps, Commdg. Post Gen., for various contributions 1989, Who's Who in American Education 1994-1995; [oth. writ.] Author: Individualized Curriculum in the Affective Domain, contbg. author: Campbell County, The Treasured Years, 1990, Legends of Lakeside, conbtr. articles to newspapers, column, lakeside portraits - 1963-1964; [a.] Lakeside, CA

THOMAS, KIMBERLY ANN
[pen.] Ana Kin; [b.] July 28, 1979, Peoria, IL; [p.] Grace and Charles Thomas; [ed.] Starlight Park Elementary Estrella Jr. High and Trexoe G Browne High School; [hon.] 1st place ribbon for story awarded by school district; [oth. writ.] "Dream Catchers" Estrella Jr High, Mrs. O'Dowd - Burkard's Class; [a.] Phoenix, AZ

THOMAS, MRS. ANNIE D.
[pen.] Mendiza Shangy; [b.] September 26, 1942, Chatta, TN; [p.] Mary and William Hughes (Both deceased); [m.] Divorced, April 24, 1960; [ch.] Melvin Thomas Jr., Lisa Smith, Lori Barber, Lydia Thomas, Letoya Peters; [ed.] Howard Chatta High, TN Voc. Tech. Rehab. Center (Smyrna, TN), Goodwill Voc. Rehab. Training Center (Atlanta, GA); [occ.] Social Security Administration - personal Assistant; [memb.] Southern Organizing Committee, Tennessee Hunger Coalition (founded the Chatta Chapter), former representator of cromwell Hills Tenant Association (Chatta); [hon.] Community Service from TN State Institute legislative Congressional Blackcaucus, Nation of Islam (Chatta) Chatta Urban league. Secretary for student council award, appreciation for founding Chatta Chapter TN Hunger Coalition; [oth. writ.] Poetry - up and Down Road of Life, Cross in the Road, don't turn me away, homelessness, Meleya, the T.V. is my shepherd.; [pers.] Life is a journey, we learn from experience and should be willing to share that wisdom with our children, for one day

will come to realize that God is the source of all our endeavors.; [a.] Stone Mountain, GA

THOMAS, ROSE
[b.] August 13, 1943, Dahlgren, IL; [p.] Albert and Maude (Apgar) Kelly; [m.] Robert E. Thomas, July 29, 1961; [ch.] Cynthia and Christopher; [ed.] High School; [occ.] Housewife - Mother and Grandma; [memb.] Member of St. Charles Parish, Parish Council, Song Leader, Lector, Eucharistic Minister and CCD Teacher; [oth. writ.] I have written many poems some of which has appeared in local newspapers.; [pers.] When we count our many blessings. It isn't hard to see that the best things in life are free.; [a.] Cunningham, KY

THOMES, CHARLES J.
[pen.] Champy; [b.] March 27, 1966; [p.] Susan P. Schofield and Ret. Col. (USAF) James T. Thomes; [ed.] The question of higher learning in relation to my level of creativity, to me, is irrelevant. Universities mostly teach us the essentials. Expanding from those basic teachings and utilizing logic, life's experiences and talent, that in itself forms knowledge. Doesn't it?; [oth. writ.] I have an ongoing library of poems, Art pieces, short stories and journals, all that have not yet been published or sold.; [pers.] Many times have I tried to convey my thoughts and to channel my vision, only to run into that same old channel end. I now have the chance to let go of a piece and I thank you dearly. Dreams do come true.

THOMPSON, JUDITH CLARK
[b.] September 28, 1962, Hartford, CT; [p.] Robinson and Nancy Clark; [m.] Michael N. Thompson, August 17, 1993; [ch.] Justin 13, Jordan 12; [occ.] Owner, operator Thompson Irrigation and Thompson Cleaning Service; [memb.] Marco Island Church of God Marco Church of God Choir Teacher Bluebelles Girls Club; [oth. writ.] Poems, songs, short stories; [pers.] Humble yourselves in the sight of the Lord and He will lift you up. James 4:10 Humble yourself and you will find that love is spreading a carpet of flowers; [a.] Marco Island, FL

THOMPSON, MICHAEL A.
[pen.] Seville Anthony; [b.] September 4, 1955, Brooklyn, NY; [p.] Leon and Sadie Thompson; [ch.] Kia A. Thompson; [ed.] TAE Gilbert School, New York City, Center for Media Arts, New York City, B.M.C. College, New York City; [occ.] Musician, poet, writer; [memb.] ASCAP, Believer gateway to Freedom Church, American Red Cross, the Band Bad poets Society; [hon.] Awards for Community Service; [oth. writ.] Several poems published with music, I found out, and it's no secret! No secret to me; [pers.] My write come from a deep spiritual source with in with self experience, love truth reality of feelings and social problems; [a.] Douglasville, GA

THOMPSON, REBECCA L.
[b.] June 2, 1982, Front Royal, VA; [p.] William Thompson, Nancy Thompson; [ed.] Leslie Fox Keyser Elementary School, 7th grade student at Warren Co. Middle School; [occ.] 7th grade student - Middle School; [memb.] Warren C. Middle School Basketball Team; [hon.] 2nd place

winner in Lord Fairfax Community College essay contest, Honor roll student - Warren Co. Middle School, Student of the Month Warren Co. Middle School, Honorable Mention in Apple Valley Reading Council Writing Contest; [oth. writ.] Many poems, some of which have been published in the school newspaper and a church newsletter; [pers.] My poetry helps me express myself, my feelings, and thoughts on issues, both current and past.; [a.] Front Royal, VA

THOMPSON, STEVEN R.
[pen.] Steve; [b.] February 18, 1941, Glendale, CA; [p.] Richard Johnathon and Margot M. Haukaas-Thompson; [m.] Patricia Kay Wasson, December 30, 1963; [ch.] Richard Jonathon, Brenda Kay, granddaughters: Anna Nicole, Carrie Michelle, Taylor Kay; [ed.] Eagle Rock High School, Los Angeles California, graduated 1959, Associate of Arts in Horticulture 1975; [oth. writ.] Steve stays busy writing letters of encouragement to politicians. The poem in this book is his first attempt at poetry, and with equal inspiration he may write more poems in the future.; [a.] Silt, CO

THOMSON, CHRISSY
[b.] October 28, 1978, Portland, OR; [p.] Chatherine and Toshi Thomson; [ed.] Newberg High; [pers.] I believe that everyone has their own special way of releasing the stress of their problems, whether it's sports, drawing, or talking about it, mine is through poetry. I write what I feel from the heart, a pen and paper can save you from a lot of extended hurt.; [a.] Newberg, OR

THORNTON, CYNTHIA A.
[b.] April 24, 1960, Illinois; [p.] Mr. and Mrs. Wm. P. Hutchcraft; [m.] George Henry Thornton Jr., January 17, 1982; [ch.] My dogs: Chingu (Korean keys) and Cera (West High Land Terrior); [ed.] Winchester High Childcare and Development Courses; [occ.] Security person for Eli Bridge Co., housewife and Day Care Provider; [memb.] United Methodist Church, David Winter's Collector Guild; [hon.] Presidential Meritorious Award for volunteering and moral support to troops and their dependents during operation desert shield and desert storm.; [oth. writ.] Several columns published in hometown newspaper. Self published newsletter during operation Desert Storm.; [pers.] I strive to reflect on the feelings and attitudes of people of all ages in my writing. I am greatly influenced by the love of Jesus Christ and the moral values of society.; [a.] Jacksonville, IL

THORPE, BOBBY
[b.] June 26, 1973, Elmira, NY; [p.] Nedra Thorpe, Robert M. Thorpe; [ed.] Graduated from Yucaipa High School 1991; [occ.] I work at an environmental Camp for kids.; [hon.] I have several art awards; [oth. writ.] I have also written screenplays and short stories but have not published them yet.; [pers.] My poetry is mostly about the darker side of Life, they are also my feelings at that moment. I feel great poetry comes from experience and true feeling. Edgar Allan Poe and Sylvia Plath have influenced me the most.; [a.] Yucaipa, CA

THUNELL, KELLI
[b.] August 31, 1977, Utah; [p.] Patricia and Steven Thunell; [ed.] I passed my G.E.D.'s at Benjamin Franklin Academy and am now attending Salt Lake Community College; [hon.] I have never won any honors or awards but am working for that in my writing.; [pers.] I write what's in my heart and I write about what I see in this world. Right now I am working on writing a book. I write songs in my poetry. It's all musical to me.; [a.] Salt Lake City, UT

TILLETT, ASHLEY BROOKS
[pen.] Ashley B. Tillett; [b.] October 31, 1981, Goldsboro, NC; [p.] Robert Tillett, Becky Grady; [ed.] 3 yrs. Pre-School, the Protestant School, K-4 St. Mary's Catholic School, 5-7 grade - Wayne Co. Public Schools; [memb.] National Junior Beta Club, Peer Mediator, Technology Student Association; [hon.] 4 times B-Honor Roll, 3 times A-Honor Roll; [oth. writ.] Articles about school field trips published in local newspaper.; [pers.] Poetry is a way of release my inner feelings. I help my friends release their feelings through peer mediation. I wrote the poem "I Do" when my Mother and Step Father got married. I felt it expressed her feelings to her husband to be.; [a.] Goldsboro, NC

TILLMAN, CARRIE L. BROWN
[b.] October 15, 1956, Marianna, AR; [p.] Joe E. Ward, Kather L. Ward; [m.] John J. Tillman Jr., January 4, 1977; [ch.] Ranier S. Brown; [ed.] Christian Fencer High, Olive-Harvey Jr. College; [occ.] Housewife; [memb.] The Humane Society of the United States, American Diabetes Assoc.; [pers.] Good books, good food, good friends and a loving family are the key to a good life; [a.] Harvey, IL

TIPTON, PEGGY A.
[b.] November 22, 1932, Fairmont, WV; [p.] Arley and Genevieve Bradley; [m.] John L. Tipton (Deceased), May 28, 1953; [ch.] Melanie Wheeler, Tracie Monreal, Grandchildren - Cori, Keri, John, Katie; [ed.] Rushcreek Memorial High School; [occ.] Retired Medical Secretary; [memb.] Garden Acres Baptist Church - Heart Association, Cancer Association; [oth. writ.] I have written both words and music to eighty five gospel songs and I am in the process of writing a spiritual book about faith and courage; [pers.] I learned early from a birth defect to reach out to people with love, and through my writings, I try to instill faith in God and our fellow man.; [a.] Bremen, OH

TITUS, CHERYL
[b.] April 18, 1958; [p.] Donald G. Crawford and Doris M. Crawford; [m.] Gerald A. Titus, December 2, 1991; [ch.] Adam Slee; [ed.] Karns City HIgh School Graduate (1977); [occ.] Nurse's Aide; [oth. writ.] (Unpublished poems) Reflections of life and nature (A collection of poems reflecting peoples problems in society and the beauty of nature) Approx 30 poems; [pers.] Children are the future of the world. How they are raised and influenced by society reflects on our world's future. I strive to address this in my writing.; [a.] Kittanning, PA

TOBIN, BRAD E.
[b.] May 29, 1974, Long Island, NY; [p.] Robert and Vangela; [ed.] Currently studying at University of NC at Chapel Hill, studied a semester in St. Petersburg, Russia; [occ.] Student; [hon.] Dean's List

TOBOLT, ROBYN
[b.] December 19, 1964, Mansfield; [p.] James and Lavonna Lewis; [m.] Randy Tobolt, March 8, 1986; [ch.] Crystal Rose Tobolt (9); [occ.] Nurse Assistant; [pers.] I would like to give my mother alot of the credit for my ability to write poems. She always told me there is beauty in everyone if you look deep enough and that's where my poems come from deep in my heart, thanks Mom, I'm proud to be your daughter, I'm glad to be your friend.

TOLEDO, MICHELLE B.
[b.] August 1, 1977, Puerto Rico; [p.] Raquel Coinas, Cesar Toledo; [ed.] High School graduate (6-14-95) from Southwest High School, Florida attending the University of Alaska, Southeast; [occ.] Student; [memb.] Greenpeace, Future Homemakers of America; [hon.] Leadership Award, Editors Choice Award; [oth. writ.] Poem published in the National Library of Poetry and school newspaper.; [pers.] Never quite, for you're never a loser if you try.; [a.] Miami, FL

TOLSON, FRANCES E.
[b.] September 15, 1913, Licking Co, OH; [p.] Harrison and Mary Hoover; [m.] Melvin L. Tolson (Deceased), November 8, 1953; [ch.] Dawn Brennan (Deceased), 4 grandchildren, 4 great grandchildren; [ed.] Ohio State University, Master's Art Education, Kent State University; [occ.] Retired Art Teacher; [memb.] Ohio State Retired Teachers; [hon.] Who's Who in American Education, Who's Who in the Arts 1971-72; [oth. writ.] Christian Life letters, The Lookout Free Press Standard, The Evangelist World of Poetry; [pers.] I have tried to put feelings and values into words.; [a.] Carrollton, OH

TOMMASELLI, DEANA
[b.] June 9, 1972, Pittston, PA; [p.] William and Margaret Tommaselli; [ed.] Penn State University and Kings College; [hon.] Dean's List and President's Freshman Award; [oth. writ.] An article in the Crown (Kings College Newspaper); [pers.] When I was younger I used to write short stories and my Dad would proofread them and give me suggestions. I've always love to write, it's inner peace.; [a.] Las Vegas, NV

TOOLE, LAWRENCE
[b.] April 1, 1970, Buffalo, NY; [p.] Lawrence and Georgina; [ed.] South Park High Buffalo State College; [occ.] Student, Traveler; [memb.] Involved extensively with the Battle against homelessness.; [hon.] Sherman F. Fyler Award, Dean's List; [pers.] As an individual I'm constantly striving to better our human condition on every possible level. I'm driven by what Dr. King has said "The Time is always right, to do what is right."; [a.] Buffalo, NY

TOOMBS, SABRINA M.
[pen.] Monique Walker; [b.] August 29, 1954, Nyack, NY; [p.] John and Lavenia Pervis; [m.] Willie Toombs, June 24, 1992; [ed.] High School grad. Theodore Roosevelt High School Bronx, NY; [occ.] Housewife; [memb.] Dale City Christian Church Music Committee; [hon.] World of Poetry 1991 Award; [oth. writ.] The Beauty of You; [pers.] I thank the Lord for my talent, my husband for the Love, my mother for the strength and my father for the laughter.

TOTER, TANYA E.
[pen.] Tanjuska; [b.] October 30, 1966, Waverly, NY; [p.] Karen and Bronco Toter (father is of Slovenian descent); [ed.] B.S. Indiana University of PA; [occ.] Medical writer; [oth. writ.] 'Senior Fitness Digest', a medical newsletter published for participants of a research project funded by the National Institute of Aging.; [pers.] Many thanks to 'Mama' for living in my heart and providing me with her unique knowledge. A compilation of Mama's stories is in the works, and we hope she makes it to print. I also thank Patrick Smallwood, who brought 'Jimmi' to life, and gave 'Mama' inspiration. [a.] Mill Valley, CA

TOWERS, BRANDIE L.
[pen.] Brandie; [b.] August 10, 1980, Easton, MD; [p.] Nancy Moran and Jeff Towers; [ed.] 9th grade at North Caroline High School; [occ.] Baby sitter; [memb.] North Caroline Marching Band of Blue Flag Corp, Mannaquin Club (modeling club), Roni Brandt Dance Studio (Jazz and ballet); [pers.] "If you put your mind to it you can do anything"; [a.] Denton, MD

TOWNEND, MARION
[pen.] Sis; [b.] November 7, 1956, Taylor, PA; [p.] Raymond A. Herron Sr. and Marion Vosborg Herron; [m.] David P. Townend, June 9, 1984; [ch.] Angela, Kenin, Heather and Felicia; [ed.] Graduate Riverside High Class of '74, attended Lackawmuna Jr.College; [occ.] Team Member of Ceasar's Cove Haven; [memb.] Maplewood Fire House Lady's Axili, N.R.A. Trinity Baptist Church; [oth. writ.] A collection of poems not yet published.; [pers.] With Confidence, positive attitude, and prayer all things are possible. My poem "A Dream" is dedicated in memory of my father.; [a.] Lake Ariel, PA

TRASVINA, CARMEN P.
[m.] Juan J. Trasvina NBC Engineer; [ch.] Jeannine, Nicole, and John, a teacher, an engineer, and a lawyer; [ed.] BA - Social Work - Cum Laude M.A. Education Administration Univ. of San Francisco; [occ.] Retired - School Administration High School; [memb.] President, Delta Kappa Gamma San Francisco Chapter, Commissioner, Deliquency Prevention Commission, Mayor's Council on Child Care San Francisco, California; [oth. writ.] THE TORCH HAS BEEN PASSED an adaption of President Kennedy's Inaugural Address, 1961. Where is it! I have sent you two copies already and have not received a response since February 12, 1995.; [pers.] Nothing more precious than children.

TREADWAY, G. HELENE
[p.] George Lester, Sadie Lester; [m.] C. James Treadway; [ch.] Bonita Lester Phillips; [m.] 1st Baptist Church - Erwin, AARP, PTO; [oth. writ.] Numerous poems many used in special church services and social gatherings. A few children's stories (used at school.); [pers.] My poems address the greatest influences in my life. My love for God family, country friends. It is my way of expressing my appreciation for each of the above. I cannot ever remember not loving poetry. It has always been a vital part of my being (G.H.T.); [a.] Erwin, NC

TREAKLE, MARSHA
[b.] July 3, 1976, Kalamazoo, MI; [p.] Bob and Carol Treakle; [ed.] Climax - Scotts High School, attending Western Michigan University majoring in Elementary Education; [hon.] Alpha Omega Award, Social Studies - Student of the Departmental year, Music - Student of the year, John Philip Sousa band award; [pers.] I strive to reflect my inner most feelings in my writing; [a.] Scotts, MI

TRIBO, TONY
[b.] August 30, 1980, Memphis; [p.] David and Theresa Tribo; [ed.] K-8, currently in 9th Grade; [occ.] Student at Bartlett High School; [memb.] National Geographic Society, Young Astronauts Club, St. Ann Catholic Church Youth Group; [hon.] Third place in Shelby County Cultural Arts Contest, second place in Ellendale School Cultural Arts Contest, 8 honorable mentions for Science Projects, and Honor Roll for grades; [oth. writ.] Poem entitled "No More" published in Commercial Appeal talking about the baseball strike. Entry and Finalist in "Imagine That" poetry contest.; [pers.] I think I write, I write how I think.; [a.] Memphis, TN

TRUITT, JOSHUA
[b.] June 3, 1976; [pers.] Open mindedness is a path of fullness constantly directed toward the growth of living internally.

TSAI, EDWARD
[b.] June 2, 1980, Daly City, CA; [p.] Raymond Tsai, Anita Tsai; [ed.] 9th Grade High School; [occ.] Student; [memb.] Home of Christ; [hon.] Principal's Honor Roll, School Award in History, School Award in Spanish, CCS Science Bowl 1st place; [pers.] Just trust and obey God all your life. For He is good.; [a.] Union City, CA

TUDMAN, COLLEEN
[b.] January 1, 1980, Fresno; [p.] Cathi Graves Tudman, Dennis Tudman; [ed.] Sophomore - C.L. McLane High School (Class of '97); [occ.] Student; [memb.] Chafee Zoological Gardens, California Scholarship Federation, M. de Young Museum Society; [hon.] 1992 AAUW - "Real Women Make A Difference" 3rd place winner, 1993 - Disney Corp. - History Day Regional Finalist - Graffiti Project, 1988-1995 - Fresno - Madera Counties, Honor Bands and Orchestras 1993 Principal Trumpet, 1993 and 1994 - Calif. Golden State Exams - Honorable Mention - Algebra, School Recognition - Geometry, 1994-95 Fresno City College Orchestra Principal Trumpet, 1995 Fresno Zoological Gardens Junior Docent, 1995 Calif. State Scholar Federation 1993-94 C.L. McLane Honor Roll 1994-95 Academic Excellence School Letter - Principal's Lucheon; [oth. writ.] 1992 - "Real Women A Difference" Essay on

Helen Keller, 1993 - Tioga Tomahawk Newsletter "What Is A Middle School Student?", 1994 - "Sass" Teen Temp - Fresno Bee Reader Response; [a.] Fresno, CA

TULLOCK, TINA
[b.] August 12, 1969, Hartford, CT; [p.] Patricia Duorg, William Tullock; [ch.] Elizabeth Marie; [hon.] Editor's Choice Award - 1994, National Library of Poetry; [oth. writ.] Poem - Famous Poets Anthology, Poem - Echoes of Yesterday, Poem - Best Poems of 1995; [a.] Winsted, CT

TURLEY, TOM
[b.] December 19, 1945, FL; [p.] W. T. Turley (Deceased), Melonee Turley; [ch.] Rachel, Heather; [occ.] Field Engineer; [oth. writ.] Several poems and short prose items, non of which have been sent for publication.; [a.] Fairfield, CA

TURNER, GRACE TAYLOR
[b.] October 23, 1920, New Bern, NC; [p.] Charles Kinchen Taylor and Mary Rebecca Sermons Taylor; [m.] Marvin Hoyle Turner (Deceased October 25, 1990), December 28, 1946; [ch.] Marvin Jr., Mary Grace, Marcia Helen; [ed.] Winterville, N.C. High School, James Walker Memorial School of Nursing, East Carolina University 1 year, N.C. Broker, Real Estate; [occ.] Semi-retired private Duty Registered Nurse; [memb.] Past memberships (for many years) in American Nurses Assn., American Red Cross, Business and Professional Women, Benjamin May Chapter DAR. Presently, Jarvis Methodist Church; [hon.] High School Class Poet, Second highest on N.C., Nurse State Board Exam (in the state) in 1944 represented Nurse Cadets in N.C. at N.C. Nurse Convention 1944; [oth. writ.] Play published in National Beta Club Magazine in 1937. Poem published in "Progressive Farmer", poem published in Vol. of the Clover Collection of Verse by Clover publishing Co., Washington D.C., 2 Hymns copyrighted.; [pers.] My philosophy is quoting from H.W. Beechen, "We should so live and labor in our time that what came to us as seed may go to the next generation as blossoms, and what came to us as blossoms go to them as fruit."; [a.] Greenville, NC

TURNER, JEANNE C.
[pen.] Jeanne C. Goil or Turner; [b.] October 13, 1917, Philadelphia, PA; [p.] Mary Kelly and Joseph Cruice; [m.] Charles Whitney, Goit June 14, 1941 and Edward Turner, October 27, 1964; [ch.] Whitney Goit II and Tony Goit; [ed.] High School and Art School; [occ.] Painting and Poetry

TURNER, MICHELLE
[b.] January 19, 1974, Waynesville, MO; [p.] Susan and Ed Weaver; [ed.] Cole B-5 High School, Central Missouri State University; [occ.] Student; [memb.] Zeta Tau Alpha, Sigma Tau Delta, Photographic Society, Rhetor Yearbook, Pi Omicron Delta; [hon.] Sigma Tau Delta (English Honors Pen); [pers.] English is the greatest art form, constantly changing and evolving towards perfection.; [a.] Warrensburgh, MO

UEBEL, JON JAY
[b.] May 25, 1964, West Islip, NY; [p.] Robert K. Uebel, Muriel B. Uebel; [ed.] St. John the Baptist,

High School West Islip, NY, B.S. in Mechanical Engineering, M.S. of Environmental Technology (New York Institute of Technology, Old Westbury, NY); [occ.] Environmental Engineer, Captain - U.S. Army; [memb.] Ancient Order of Hibernians, American Society of Mechanical Engineers, National Guard Association of the United States, New York Militia Association, Squadron "C" 101st Cavalry Association; [hon.] Graduated "with distinction" Master of Science Degree - Environmental Technology, Army Commendation Metals, Numerous Physical Fitness Awards; [oth. writ.] Several poems and short stories published through the academia setting. Presently working/research on a video documentary "The Gaelic Language (History of) in America". - Ancient Order of Hibernians.; [pers.] A dream gives hope. A goal is a dream made into reality. Never give up on life's endeavors - no matter the odds. Live your life "To The Utmost".; [a.] North Brentwood, NY

ULM, HELEN W.
[pen.] Helen Ulm; [b.] January 5, 1916, Carlinville, IL; [p.] James and Waneta Brickey; [m.] Chris Ulm, October 17, 1933; [ch.] Lloyd D. Ulm, Patricia L. Von De Bur, Chris E. Ulm; [ed.] 8th grade and High School; [occ.] Was a beautician now retired; [memb.] Knox Presbyterian Church, Sr. Center Chatham, Kitchen Band Chatham, Card Clubs; [hon.] Wrote an article in our newspaper. In Springfield, IL - #2 an article in Sr. Voice - Peoria; [a.] Chatham, IL

URQUHART, BARBARA
[b.] September 1, 1977, Harrisburg, PA; [p.] Rita Urquhart; [ed.] Home School High School; [memb.] USA Gymnastics; [hon.] Girl Scout Silver Award, Girl Scout Gold Award; [pers.] I try to give an idea of what I have seen of this world.; [a.] Rogersville, TN

VALEU, MARY MARGARET
[pen.] St Jo Mary; [b.] March 30, 1960, Burlington, IA; [p.] Elsie and Lindy VaLeu; [m.] Not married; [ed.] High School (G.E.D.); [pers.] I've been writing poems ever since I was a little girl. This is the first one I ever sent in to anyone.; [a.] Saint Joseph, MO

VALICENTI, ELIZABETH
[b.] Canton, NY; [p.] Samuel and Ida Kaplan; [m.] Pasquale W. Valicenti (Deceased), June 21, 1952; [ed.] Graduate, Rogers High, Newport, RI, Courses at George Washington, U., Washington, DC, Poetry and writing by teacher from Georgetown U.; [occ.] Retired from business, now occupied with the arts — Japanese Brush Painting at the Smithsonian, Voice at Levine School of Music, Poetry and writing; [memb.] Smithsonian, Washington Opera, Washington Performing Arts Society, Kennedy Center, Hebrew Home of DC; [hon.] First Place for Poetry, Creative Writing Festival 1989, $75.00 Washington, DC; [oth. writ.] "Safari in Kenya, East Africa" submitted for possible publication, brief stories about people and things (School Assignments and Local publication); [pers.] My love of nature and interest in people seem to pull my poems in that direction.; [a.] Washington, DC

VALLEYFIELD, BOB
[pen.] Chief; [b.] December 13, 1931, Chicago, IL; [ed.] High School; [occ.] Retired Police Officer; [oth. writ.] Several

VANDERHOOF, VICKIE L.
[b.] April 10, 1954, Indiana, PA; [p.] Russell J. and Myra B. Vanderhoof; [ed.] University of Pittsburgh - Bachelor of Arts; [occ.] Part-time clerical work seeking to establish home-based self-employment computerized clerical work; [oth. writ.] Poetry, essays and editorials still knocking on publisher's doors; [pers.] Life is tough. Love is tougher. Faith is the toughest of all. God's "Retirement" benefits are worth it!; [a.] Fairview, PA

VANDERHORST, JAMES
[pen.] Jim Vanderhorst; [b.] January 5, 1945, Philadelphia, PA; [p.] Queen and Issac Vanderhorst; [m.] Sheree Vanderhorst, June 2, 1994; [ed.] Achievement in Christian Service Downington, PA, Full Gospel of Christ Fellowship College, Richmond, VA; [occ.] I am a disabled person, everyday I devote to the work; [memb.] Calvary Baptist Church, Friendship Ame Church, Friendship Committee; [hon.] Good Fellowship Award, Minister of Gospel Award, Certificate of Association of Bachelor Degree; [oth. writ.] License of Minister, many of poems, just waiting to be published, by someone, of "The Lord"!; [pers.] Always keep faith and hope and have charity in your heart. I pray for a publisher, to contact me about my work, bless you. AMEN!; [a.] Yeadon, PA

VARNEDOE, PATRICK J.
[b.] May 25, 1970, Baltimore, MD; [p.] Richard and Gail Varnedoe; [m.] Shawn Marie Varnedoe, October 8, 1995; [occ.] Dept. of Defense; [oth. writ.] One published poem, working on a personal anthology.; [pers.] Thank you Shawn. A love like ours comes once in a lifetime. You are my eternal inspiration. Thanks for coming to me, out of the blue.; [a.] Pasadena, MD

VARTOUKIAN, JOHN
[b.] March 23, 1934, New York; [m.] Juno Vartoukian; [ed.] Masters Degree in Literature, New York University; [occ.] Writing Specialist Howard University School of Law; [oth. writ.] Occasional poems and stories published, most recently in Ararat, a Literary Quarterly

VASQUEZ, JIMMIE
[b.] September 9, 1946, Orange, CA; [p.] James and Fena Vasquez; [ed.] 10th Grade, San Bernardino High School; [occ.] Unemployed; [oth. writ.] Several non-published poems and a children's story; [pers.] I began attending the San Bernardino Library Literacy Program in 1992 at the age of 45 to learn to read and write. My tutors have given me encouragement and a life-line to open doors and to express myself through my long hidden thoughts and ideas. I have discovered that I don't lose by not trying, but I win by learning.; [a.] San Bernardino, CA

VAUGHAN, REBECCA A.
[b.] January 15, 1942, Huntington, WV; [p.] Edna L. Broughton and Ralph Broughton; [ch.] Terri Lane, Robert Lane II, Catherine Lane; [ed.]

Ashland High, going to Ohio University - majoring in Criminal Justice; [memb.] Friends of some, Los Amigos International; [hon.] Dean's List, Honorary Mention - ARMCO Photo Contest; [oth. writ.] Several poems published in College Literary Publications; [pers.] I owe my inspiration to Joseph Petitt, my friend through life.; [a.] Portsmouth, OH

VAZQUEZ, ANITA
[pen.] Anita Vazquez; [b.] September 11, 1980, Brooklyn; [p.] Tony and Rita Vazquez; [ed.] Shallow I.S. 227; [occ.] Full time student; [oth. writ.] 1 poem which I won last year.; [pers.] I write down how I feel. I express my feelings through poetry.; [a.] Brooklyn, NY

VEILLEUX, NICOLE M.
[b.] November 28, 1978, Brunswick, ME; [p.] Andrew and Mary Veilleux; [ed.] Currently attending Hall-Dale High School in the town of Farmingdale, ME; [occ.] Student; [oth. writ.] Several none published poems; [pers.] I enjoy writing poetry because it helps me express how I'm feeling and it's also a hobby.; [a.] Farmingdale, ME

VELA, ALYSSA AIDE
[b.] January 14, 1980, McAllen, TX; [p.] Antonio and Corina Vela; [ch.] Ariel Adan Vela (Brother); [ed.] 1 thru 8th, Immaculate Concepcion School - Rio Grande City, TX, 9th, Rio Grande City High School; [occ.] Student; [memb.] Rio Grand City High School Band, Drama - one Act Play, VIL - Poetry; [hon.] 1st place - VIL, University Intersc League - on Poetry; [pers.] Live today as if there is no tomorrow.; [a.] Rio Grande City, TX

VELAZQUEZ, BIANCA
[b.] August 19, 1979, Ohio; [p.] Jacqueline Velazquez; [ed.] South View High School; [occ.] St. Vince de Paul; [oth. writ.] Poems in my poems book; [pers.] I write about what I think in my heart and what's going on in the world today and feelings.; [a.] Lorain, OH

VELINSKIE, JENNIFER
[b.] November 4, 1968, Brooklyn, NY; [p.] Laverne Barrett; [ed.] Milpitas High, Central County Occupational Center; [occ.] Accountant; [pers.] I would like to thank the Great Spirit for the gifts I have been given and Michael for all his loving support. May all see what great miracles can come about when spiritually is true.; [a.] Milpitas, CA

VELKOFF, MS. SYLVIA
[pen.] Ms. Sylvia Velkoff; [b.] August 23, 1914, Manhattan, NY; [p.] Lena and David Black; [m.] H. Y. Velkoff (Deceased), June 12, 1938; [ch.] Jan Simone, Kenneth Douglas; [ed.] High School; [occ.] Volunteering Theatre-Mental Health; [memb.] O.R.T. - Life Member - Brandies University National Women's Committee - Life Member; [hon.] Life Membership of P.T.A. for "Sex Heigene and Social Growth", Almost became an M.G.M. actress at 17 - Lost voice at audition; [oth. writ.] Local poetry publishing's; [pers.] With it's Trials and Tribulations. Life is an exciting adventure, especially if you've been loved unconditionally.; [a.] New York, NY

VENNEBUSH, JO ANN
[pen.] Jo Ann Vennebush; [b.] May 19, 1936, Kiamichi, OK; [p.] Roland and Alice Sutton; [m.] Jos A. Vennebush, July 2, 1955; [ch.] Barbette Elaine, Roland Anthony, Robert Michael, David Lee; [ed.] Delhaas High School, Lamar University; [occ.] Housewife; [oth. writ.] Several poems and articles published in local newspapers; [pers.] Most of my writings reflect on some aspect of my life, my family's lives and your reflections of life.; [a.] Dickinson, TN

VENTURA, FLORIDA V.
[pen.] Florie; [b.] August 15, 1950, Philippines; [p.] Steve S. Vicuna and Lydia L. Lindain; [m.] Honorio C. Ventura, January 2, 1971; [ch.] Veejay and Helen (Both in College); [ed.] Bachelor of Music Ed. - SJC, Real Estate, Notary Public, Int'l. Banking; [occ.] Music Teacher, Real Estate Agent, Notary Public; [memb.] Music Teachers Assoc. of California, CAPMT, MTNA; [hon.] Dean's List, Scholarship Recipient Top Producer, Real Estate Community Service Award - Music; [oth. writ.] Love Me in Your Dreams, Lord, I Want to Talk to You, My Children, A Mother's Song, Christmas in My Hometown and many more unpublished poems and songs.; [pers.] Despite its imperfection, there world and everyone that dwells on it deserves to be loved. From love springs out all good things that make man live.; [a.] South San Francisco, CA

VERNON, MARY LEE
[b.] October 3, 1970, Bakersfield, CA; [p.] Ron Vernon and Clara Vernon, Stepfather: Richard Stowers; [ch.] Ricky Lee Blackman Jr.; [ed.] Class of 1988 Arvin High School, Arvin California; [occ.] Care Provider, Secretary working for temporary service; [hon.] In 1991 won an Award of Merit Certificate for poem "Thorn of Pain"; [oth. writ.] I have wrote several non-published poems and short stories.; [pers.] My poetry is an expression from my soul that has touched my heart in ways I can only express in words.; [a.] Bakersfield, CA

VICK, ELIZABETH DAUB
[pen.] Beth Vick; [b.] New Jersey; [m.] Gerald Allen Vick, Colonel; [ch.] Elizabeth and Marjorie; [ed.] B.S. Education; [occ.] Programmer; [memb.] American Association of University Women, D.C. Cares, Kappa KAPPA Gamma National Fraternity - Alumni; [hon.] Dean's List; [oth. writ.] Other poems previously published; [a.] Arlington, VA

VIEIRA, DOMITRIA A.
[pen.] Angelina; [b.] July 21, 1970, Washington, DC; [p.] Jennifer Ann Smith and William Monk; [m.] Anthony Wilfred Vieira Sr., April 4, 1990; [ch.] Anthony Wilfred Jr., India Shareka; [ed.] Parkdale High, P.G. Community College; [occ.] Cosmetologist, The Hair Salon Largo, MD; [oth. writ.] I've been inspired by many writers mainly Maya Angelou. Also, Oprah Winfrey has been a great inspiration to me. I'm currently working on two short stories entitled: Deep in the Ghetoo and Color Blind in which I wish to dedicate to Oprah Winfrey if she would except. In addition to that I'm in continued pursuit of circulating my work for publications.; [pers.] I've been writing since High School and since then my work has matured into

the realities of the world and its people's indifference. A QUOTE TO REMEMBER: "For we are from the same creator, who displayed a love for life, an array of rainbows and it's colors..."

VIELOT, ALAIN J.
[b.] April 20, 1957, Haiti; [p.] Kleber Vielot, Marie Claire Vielot; [ed.] Woodrow Wilson High, Ecole Nouvelle Lausanne Switzerland, Howard University Washington, DC; [occ.] Sociologist, Teacher, North Miami Elementary; [memb.] International Club, Carsdale, Dade County Teacher Association; [hon.] Dean's List - Lausanne Switzerland, 1st place Winner, French Writing Contest, Switzerland, National Poetry Contest, 2nd place winner for 15-18 years old; [oth. writ.] Music critic, essayist, I have also written a treatise education - how students learn. Several articles published in school newspaper.; [pers.] I describe myself as a humanist and absentist, an existentialist, whose sole and primary concern is the betterment of the human condition.; [a.] Miami, FL

VIRAY, CONCEPCION GERONIMO
[b.] Philippines; [p.] Deceased; [m.] Clarito Viray, March 19, 1961; [ch.] Rose Virginia, Jose Carlito, Rowena Joy, Ma. Rica, Rossana Leah, and Rene Clarito; [ed.] Far Eastern University - Philippines, University of Portland - Oregon, USA; [occ.] Teacher; [memb.] American Federation of Teachers, Filipino Educators Association of Guam, Faculty Council - Dededo Middle School National Junior Honor Society; [hon.] Merit Awards; [oth. writ.] Poems published in school papers; [pers.] I nurture a deep faith in an Almighty Being who charts man's destiny, and a fervent hope of a promising future for a new mankind emerging— from the ashes of war and fires, the turmoils of earthquakes and floods, the pangs of famine and hunger, the snares of oppression and greed... the unkindness of man to another man.; [a.] Tamuning, Guam

VIRGO, DEBORAH KATHERINE
[b.] October 27, 1955, Oswego, NY; [p.] Burton and Katherine Rose; [m.] Samuel Virgo, October 27, 1984; [ch.] Derrick, Brandi, Sammy, Pamela, Bobby and Becky; [ed.] Oswego High School; [occ.] Housewife; [a.] Oswego, NY

VLACHOS, NICK A.
[b.] November 21, 1950, Chicago, IL; [p.] Alex and Catherine Vlachos; [ch.] Andren William Vlachos, Alex Donald Vlachos; [ed.] Morgan Park High School, University of Idaho, Athens Medical School, University of Illinois Medical School - Peoria; [occ.] Physician; [memb.] American Medical Association, ACDEM, McLean County Medical Society, Illinois Medical Society; [pers.] Promise only what you can deliver, then deliver more than you promised; [a.] Bloomington, IL

VOIE, MAGNUS O.
[b.] October 7, 1977, Kirkenes, Norway; [p.] Margareth Voie and Waling Gorter; [ed.] Second year in Namsos, Norway Gymnas; [occ.] Benefactor of teaching; [oth. writ.] Some freelance for local newspaper; [pers.] Everything thrieves on balance. This is a simple truth in our complex society.; [a.] Gilbertown, AL

VOLLNER, JENNIFER
[b.] June 7, 1980, Cincinnati, OH; [p.] Leigh and Roger Dick; [ed.] South Western High School; [pers.] Don't let your life happen to you, let it happen to your life.; [a.] Nancy, KY

VOTAPKA, KEN
[pen.] Kenneth Scott; [b.] September 21, 1976, Vero Beach, FL; [p.] Richard and Linda Votapka; [ed.] Vero Beach High, Indian River Community College; [occ.] Student at I.R.C.C.; [hon.] High School graduate with Honors, top 10% of class; [oth. writ.] With this poem, I have taken another forward on the path to my future, it stretches before me with marvelous opportunities.; [a.] Vero Beach, FL

VOYLES, PAMELA K.
[b.] February 5, 1965; [p.] Mr. and Mrs. L. Wallace and B. Regmund; [m.] Robert Voyles, December 27, 1987; [ch.] Katherine Voyles; [ed.] Bachelors of Science; [occ.] School Teacher; [pers.] I enjoy the thrill that overcomes me when I write poetry.

VUJOSEVIC, NEVENA
[pen.] Nev; [b.] July 16, 1978, Belgrade; [p.] Miroslav and Dobrila Vujosevic; [ed.] West-Windsor Plainsboro High School, New Jersey; [occ.] Student; [memb.] Human Relations Steering Committee in School (2 years), 4 yrs. Member of the Princeton Skating Club; [hon.] 1 second place and 1 third place medals in the Princeton Club Competitions, 1 third and 1 fourth place in Princeton Open Competitions, various awards for band and orchestra, 2 honors awards from NJ Music Teachers Assoc. Inc. - PIANO, won poetry contest in school, won Shakespeare Recitation contest in school, Nat. Youth Leadership Council; [pers.] I write to bring out all that makes me live to the world. It is one of my ways of being honest with it. What else is life but a chance to experience as much as one can. However, in order to do that, one must share a little bit of their own.; [a.] Princeton, NJ

WADLEY, DAMON
[b.] September 27, 1976, Detroit; [p.] Lolita Wadley; [ed.] Lutheran High School East. Indiania Institute of Technology; [occ.] Librarian Assistant; [memb.] Sigma Phi Epsilon Fraternity; [hon.] Dean List's Two letters in track and cross-country U.S. Academic Achievement Award; [oth. writ.] Girl with the black hair. Please don't go. You hurt me.; [a.] Fort Wayne, IN

WAITS, EMILY C.
[b.] October 23, 1974; [p.] Paula Jones, Richard Jones; [ed.] St. Michaels High School, Menlo College; [occ.] Student, part-time Bank Teller at First Interstate Bank; [memb.] Founder and President of the Poetry, Art and Music Club, Roteract Club Member; [hon.] Dean's List; [oth. writ.] Numerous poems and short stories never published; [pers.] I am a firm believer that everyone's soul needs to be exposed at least once, and my time is now.; [a.] Atherton, CA

WALKER, JACQUELYN E.
[pen.] Jacque Walker; [b.] November 6, 1949, Downey, CA; [p.] Robert & Sallye Walker; [m.] Chris Holm, May 10, 1977 (Dissolution of Marriage Nov. 1988); [ch.] Cerissa Holm (Age 17) My beautiful child turned into an absolutely charming young lady, inherent of all my talents and more! [ed.] A different school every year of H.S. From High School 1967 I entered USAF with intentions to go to Viet Nam as a photographer/ writer but Uncle Sam made me a medical tech. specialist and sent me to Travis/After discharged from service, received AA Accreditation St. Luke's School of Nursing, currently interested in returning to school for Master's Degree in Nutrition; [occ.] disabled for 3 years, Business owner-operator, masseuse, healer, nurse, musician, songwriter, editor, illustrator, writer; [memb.] American Legion/Vocational Nursing/ Veteran of Foreign Wars/Crohn's Colitis Foundation of America/ Women's Small Business/Local Recording Studios; [hon.] High School safety poster 1966, Merited Woman of the Month Sheppard AFB 1968/ multi-merits through 14 years hospital OB, Neonatal nursing/studio recordings with multi songwriter artists and groups/ chosen top female vocalist electric symphony composits/illustration and design team and business logos/posters advertising musicals/illustrations of monumental town structure implicated for restoration/co-authored book to be transformed into a screenplay "Ruben's Ritual;" [oth. writ.] Too many to name, all quaintly titled, song lyrics in excess of 200, completed melodies 90 some, multiple short stories-fiction, non-fiction, philosophical. Co-authored civil war drama, children's prose and illustration, satirical autobiography. Illustrated Children's series "Choices: The Game of Life"; [pers.] I've never submitted any of my works for publication or commercialization but with so much to say, this is for you... It's about time! I've been haunted by friends and strangers alike for over 2 decades. This is my first step; [a.] Placerville, CA

WALKER, JO ANN
[b.] June 22nd, Mobile, AL; [p.] Joe N. Walker, Daisy D. Walker; [ed.] Central High, 20th Century Bus. College, Univ. of So. Alabama; [occ.] Senior Secretary, Alabama Power Company, Mobile, AL; [memb.] National Assn. of Female Executives, Alabama Fellowship Mass Choir Scholarship Committee, Mt. Zion Baptist Church, Port City United Voices, Gospel Music Workshop of America, Alabama Power Service Organization Board of Directors; [hon.] Golden Poet; Certificate of Merit, TNLB; Distinguished Member, International Society of Poets; [oth. writ.] poem "No Dust On The Cross" published in early 1995; [pers.] There is no failure in God. [a.] Mobile, AL

WALKER, JOAN P.
[pen.] Jo Ann Walker; [b.] July 8, 1947; [p.] Earl H. and Lillie Mae Payne; [m.] Blaine H. Walker, November 29, 1963; [ch.] Connie Laverne Travis, Michael Blaine Walker, Jamey D. Walker, 3 grandchildren; [ed.] 12th grade education; [occ.] Gospel writer and Gospel singer; [hon.] Poem in "Best Poems of 1995 also Editors Choice Award in 1994 for poem titled "Hallelujah Mothers Back"

presented by National Library of Poetry, Award of Merit Certificate form "World of Poetry" for Poem "My Son, My Son"; [oth. writ.] 1 Poem published in "A Far Off Place" one poem published in "Best Poems of 1995" by National Library of Poetry; [pers.] My greatest desire is to do the service of my great creator, to work while there is day, for the night cometh when no man can work.; [a.] Maryville, TN

WALKER, LILLIAN
[pen.] Grama; [b.] April 15, 1910, Chicago, IL; [p.] Deceased; [m.] Nathaniel Walker (Deceased), October 21, 1933; [ch.] 2 sons Robert and Larry Walker, 7 Grandchildren - all married, 4 great grandchildren; [ed.] I- Catholic Grade School, graduate July, 1924; [occ.] Housewife, grand and great grandma; [hon.] Sent in poem called "This Child is Mine" in 1990. Received Honorable Mention from World of Poetry Eddie Lou Cole - editor, Sacramento, Calif.; [oth. writ.] Many of my poems relate to true happenings in family life. Birthdays, weddings, true friendships, children growing up, a farewell to those who left us.; [pers.] I am a widow - 85 yrs old. 14 grandchildren, 4 great grandchildren. Have written many many poems, in my life time.; [a.] Chicago, IL

WALKER, WILLIAM BOTTS
[b.] October 4, 1950, Barren Co; [p.] Johnny and Merlene Walker; [m.] Loretta Gaye Walker, June 7, 1969; [ch.] Robbie Ellison Walker, Angela Gaye Walker; [ed.] High School; [occ.] Truck driver, horse trainer, carpenter, plays and sings in country band; [memb.] 4-H-Board, AQHA - American Quarter Horse Assoc.; [hon.] 1994/4-H Conrad Feltner Leadership Award, several awards when we had dairy cattle and show at state fairs

WALL, DONALD
[pen.] Joseph; [b.] September 3, 1948, Wyandotte Hospital; [p.] Mr. and Mrs. John M. Wall; [m.] Single; [ed.] Theodore Roosevelt High School. Special Education Program, Receive Certificate. Someday Receive a certificate from Liberty Home Bible Institute.; [memb.] Of a local church; [hon.] Having my poem chosen. "By God's Hand" By the National Library of Poetry, this is an honor to me. One certificate from my poem days or nights. Church for the poem is of little children.; [oth. writ.] Only had a poem published in Cadiz record newspaper in Cadiz KY.; [pers.] I use the gift that God has given me the best way I can with Him there is no such word as I can't but I will keep on trying to write.; [a.] Wyandotte, MI

WALLACE, DOROTHY A.
[b.] September 11, 1942, Wright County, MO; [p.] Stephen Foster Dudley, Lois Breman Dudley; [ch.] Michael Huckaby, David Wallace; [ed.] Mansfield High School, Mansfield, MO Drury College and Southwest Missouri State University, Springfield, MO; [occ.] Director of Special Services, Mansfield Schools, Mansfield, MO; [memb.] Missouri State Teachers Association, Council of Administrators of Special Education, American Salers Association, International Society of Poets; [oth. writ.] Several poems published, articles for local newspapers, family histories for County History Books; [a.] Mansfield, MO

WALLACE, SHIRLEY
[pen.] Wallace Brade; [b.] March 4, 1947, N. Hollywood, CA; [p.] Constanee Edwards and Harold Patterson; [m.] William Wallace, June 4, 1986; [ch.] John and Kelly; [ed.] Hawthorne High, Hawthorne, CA - St. Simon and St. Jude Southport, England Clark College, Vancouver WA; [occ.] Secretary; [oth. writ.] Several articles published in local newspapers, articles for Tekweek Business newsletter.; [pers.] My outlook on life has been greatly influenced by my late English grandmother. I spent my youth traveling between two cultures, and I was truly enriched by this experience.; [a.] Washougal, WA

WALLEN, IRENE B.
[pen.] Irene B. Wallen; [b.] August 22, 1907, Helsingor, Denmark; [p.] Jens and Anna Boeholt; [m.] Jarvis A. Wallen (Deceased), February 11, 1933; [ch.] Joanne L. and Lance A., six grandchildren - Brant, Kathy, Morgan, Garth, Kristin, two great grandsons - Ryan and Garrett, more grandchildren - Margot Wallen and Kaleg Wallen; [ed.] About two months in 1st grade in Denmark and my parents immigrated to America and 7 children; [occ.] Not retired yet when I have time, I will retire!; [memb.] A Senior Club, "Jet Set", Maple Leaf Garden Club and song, "The Mother Singers", PTA, been in a few style shows and skits; [hon.] 10 years volunteer at a Senior Center two times per week. Charter Member of Knute Rockne (Sons of Norway); [oth. writ.] Oil paint a little and water color (volunteer for seniors and cooks and clean and knit, crochet and I also bake "A Chocolate Cherry Cake" now and then. I love my family all!; [pers.] Forget "age" and it goes elsewhere.

WALLER, DOLORES K.
[b.] May 10, 1944, Oregon; [p.] Lloyd Cox and Eva Anderson; [m.] George C. Waller, November 17, 1976; [ch.] I have three, husband has three total six; [ed.] High School with GED Massey Business College 1988, at present taking writing course and studying for ASB - major in Accounting; [occ.] Correctional Officer at Texas Dept. of Criminal Justice; [memb.] Nat'l. Cancer Institute - Research National Park Trust, National Arbor Day Foundation, National Humane Education Society, Father Flangan's Boys' Home; [hon.] Directors Club for highest achievement. National Honor Society, Alpha Beta Kappa; [pers.] My husband inspired this poem and does all that is mentioned in the poem.; [a.] Trinity, TX

WALLER, MONICA RENEE
[pen.] "Thunder" Moon; [b.] September 5, 1960, Washington, DC; [p.] Joseph Bowman, Rose Poole; [m.] Glenwood Waller, October 28, 1988; [ch.] Vincent Langston Waller, Victoria Bobbie Waller; [ed.] GED, Lincoln Univ. Substitute Teachers Aide for the Enterprise Children's Ctr.; [occ.] Counselor for the Mental Retardation; [memb.] I take pride in being a native American. My tribe is "Meherrin Indians. Meherrin means "People of the muddy water" or the muddy water people."; [hon.] I'm a Eucharist Minister for Mt. Calvary Catholic Church.; [oth. writ.] I've written several short stories, that I'm in the process of getting published; [pers.] I write what I feel that's in my heart.; [a.] District Heights, MD

WALLING, SAMANTHA LEIGH SANDERS
[b.] April 25, 1975, San Diego, CA; [p.] James
Lloyd Sanders and Patricia Ann Sanders; [m.]
Roger Wade Walling, December 18, 1994; [ed.]
Lee High School, Satellite Education Resources
Consortium, University of AL in Huntsville; [occ.]
Technical Support Dispatcher, Adtran, Huntsville,
AL; [memb.] Holmes Street United Methodist
Church; [oth. writ.] Teen Correspondent for the
Huntsville Times, 1992-93, Several poems
published in the LHS literary magazine, expres-
sions; [a.] Gurley, AL

WALLIS, ELIZABETH JOAN
[pen.] Joan Wallis; [b.] July 10, 1940, Winchester,
VA; [p.] Eugene Miller and Julia Miller; [m.]
Thomas Lee Wallis, June 27, 1964; [ch.] Julie
Marie, Thomas Lee, Jr. Kimberly Ann and David
Randolph; [ed.] Handley High School James
Madison University Bachelor of Science in
Education; [occ.] Homemaker and educator in the
Alexandria schools and Browne Academy; [memb.]
St. Louis Catholic church Hayfield Citizens
Association; [hon.] Sigma Phi Lambda Kappa
Delta Pi; [oth. writ.] Poetry short stories children's
stories; [pers.] I am very concerned about quality
education and family life. I have a strong faith and
a love of nature which are reflected in my writing.;
[a.] Alexandria, VA

WALSER, ESTHER
[b.] September 16, 1897, Kishinev, Russia; [p.]
Maxwell and Sarah Gealt; [m.] Norbert Walser;
[occ.] English Teacher (retired); [pers.] This poem
was written on December 12, 1988 following a
visit by my great grand - Nephew, Daniel Marcus -
Toll (then two years old), who played with my cane.

WALSH, HERBERT JAMES
[pen.] Herb Walsh; [b.] August 18, 1918, Chicago,
IL; [ed.] H.S. Graduate; [occ.] Retired Musician;
[memb.] Musicians Union - Local #47

WALSH, MELANIE
[b.] September 13, 1975, Aurora, IL; [p.] Tim and
Jackie Walsh; [ed.] Sophomore at Wawbonsce
Community College; [occ.] Cashier; [hon.] Who's
who among American High School Students '90-
'91; [oth. writ.] Death's door published in tears of
fire almighty love "Spirit" of world wide marriage
encounter

WALTERS, KELLIE
[b.] April 20, 1977, Illinois; [p.] Sharen Pierce,
Arvin Walters; [pers.] Youth Against Fascism; [a.]
Libertyville, IL

WAMMES, HELEN V.
[b.] September 15, 1924, Findlay, OH; [p.] Carl
and Leida Basye; [m.] William E. Wammes, June
15, 1946; [ch.] William C., Michael P., Janeen;
[ed.] High school, Findlay, OH; [occ.] Retired;
[memb.] Calvary United Methodist Church,
American Legion Auxiliary, 8 Et 40 International
Society of Poets, WIBC; [hon.] Hall of Fame
Bowling Association; [oth. writ.] Write and direct a
historical pageant each year in my community
(Tontogany, Ohio) pageant called "Feast of Ton
Doganie", also have some poems published in local
newspapers, and write personal honorary poetry on
request. Poem published NLP after the storm;
[pers.] In my poetry I try to reflect my outlook on
life and give a message.; [a.] Bowling Green, OH

WATERHOUSE, LOIS VIVIAN
[pen.] Lois Waterhouse; [b.] Tarboro, NC; [p.]
Arthur Tillery, Ada Tillery; [m.] Robert
Waterhouse; [ed.] Huntington High, North
Carolina Central University, Christopher Newport
University.; [occ.] Chief, Procurement Division
US International Trade Commission; [memb.]
BWUFA, Detroit Writer's Guild; [oth. writ.] Other
poems published in local papers and special
programs.; [pers.] Each of us is given a gift to use,
and the fruits obtained are fulfillment and joy.
Influenced by James Weldon Johnson.; [a.] Fort
Washington, MD

WATERS, ANN
[pen.] Ramouth Ann Carr; [b.] February 28, 1945,
Dalton, GA; [m.] Widow; [ch.] Ray, Mark, Johnny
Stanley, 3 grown sons, 10 grandchildren; [ed.]
LPN Nurse for 1 yr after High School GED; [occ.]
Retired; [oth. writ.] Have been writing poetry and
short stories since Jr. High School. Have had
published poems in local paper.; [pers.] I write
from my heart. I just let my feeling and emotions
go down on paper, I love romantic poems and
children poems.; [a.] Rocky Face, GA

WATKINS, DIANE
[b.] December 20, 1948, North Carolina; [p.]
Nelson John and Beatrice Watkins; [m.] Deceased,
September 9, 1969; [ch.] Kimberly Lau and
Catherine (Betsy) Watkins; [ed.] Middletown
Township High School, Middletown NJ; [occ.]
Seafood Manager for Winn Dixie in FL; [memb.]
Amvets Ladies Aux., Post 7674 Ladies Aux. Ft.
Walton, FL; [oth. writ.] Write poems in spare
time. No other ones published so far.; [pers.] I
enjoy writing about any subject and try to help
others. And relate within,; [a.] Navarre, FL

WATKINS, RUTH J.
[pen.] Ruth J. Watkins; [b.] April 16, 1909,
Prestonsburg, KY; [p.] Rose and Wade Burchett;
[m.] Clarence M. Watkins, December 30, 1929;
[ch.] 4 (1 living) John M. Watkins, Falls Church
VA; [ed.] Stroger Bus College Wash. DC (Grad);
[occ.] Retired Registrer Wash - Lee High, Arl,
VA; [memb.] Christ Methodist, several PTAs, Past
Motron Acacia Chapter #51, Eastern Star Falls
Church, VA, Grand Rep. to South Carolina; [hon.]
Kentucky Colonels Editors Choice Award, among
best 3% - Dark Side of the Moon; [oth. writ.] Me
Too Mom published in Dark Side of the Moon.

WATSON, ALICE
[b.] July 4, 1979, Dallas, TX; [p.] Gene and Anne
Watson; [ed.] West Wood Junior High; [occ.]
Student; [hon.] Best of Texas 1992 (poetry
contest); [pers.] I write by whim and intuition, I am
inspired by offbeat experiences and situations.; [a.]
Dallas, TX

WATSON, MARIE
[b.] December 19, 1930, Clark County, Indiana;
[p.] Mr. and Mrs P. M. Kemp; [m.] Jerry K.
Watson Sr., August 15, 1953, (Divorced June 24,
1977); [ch.] Jerry Kenneth Watson II and Mettie;
[ed.] I was graduated from New Washington High
School, 1948. I attended in Louisville, KY, My
elementary schooling was in a one room rural
school house in Owen Township. It was called
Shiloh School.; [occ.] Retired; [memb.] Local Red

Cross Chapter, Light house Church of God; [oth.
writ.] Numerous items in Church paper and local
newspaper.; [pers.] I love human of all kinds, I
believe laughter is great therapy

WATTEL, JEANNE-HELENE
[pen.] Jeanne-Helene Wattel; [b.] January 18th,
Los Angeles, CA; [p.] Leona and Aymar Jules
Wattel; [m.] Divorced; [ed.] Three years college
units. Perpetual Student UCLA (Univ. of Call at
L.A.) USC (Univ. of South California) Columbia
Univ. Studied voice, appeared musical comedies.
Studied creative writing UCLA and Columbia.
Studied all religions at USC. Graduated from
Rhema Bible School, Tulsa, OK, 1991.; [occ.] I
am a Prayer Counselor on phones in the Prayer
Tower at Oral Roberts University, Tulsa, OK;
[memb.] Tulsa Christian Writers, Sierra Club,
Rhema Alumi Association; [hon.] 1993 Winner
Tulsa Christian Writers contest for inspirational
category, 1994 Hon. Mention Poetry in TCW
contest; [oth. writ.] Poetry accepted in "Apogee",
a publication by the late James Irwin, the astronaut,
after his return from moon. "Freedom Speaks" a
poetic commentary on freedom's view of America
from 1600's to present. I performed this at
preview of film "Executive Action" with Burt
Lancaster. It was film on political intrigue in
America. Volumes of writings and poetry never
submitted for publication as yet.; [pers.] Driven by
personal goal to help make a better world for
mankind by inspiring via my writings and prayers.
Goal is to encourage young poeple to believe God
does exist and speaks to us personally via the Holy
Spirit as sent by Jesus Christ. He speaks via "inner
voice" into our mind with scripture numbers giving
us His love, warnings and guidance. I trust my
books will inspire youth of the future society) to
assure them there was and is a God who loves us
and speaks into our mind. I am inspired by
writings of French author Jeanne Guyon of 1600's
France.; [a.] Tulsa, OK

WAUGH, VENICE G.
[b.] September 27, 1923, AL; [p.] John C. and
Mary Johnson; [m.] W. A. Waugh, August 7,
1942; [ch.] Two; [ed.] High School; [occ.]
Retired; [pers.] I love all books my favorite poems;
[a.] Oxford, AL

WAWRZYNIAK, PATTIE
[b.] April 9, 1981, Doylestown, PA; [p.] Joseph
and Sharon; [ed.] Schmucker Middle School; [oth.
writ.] The Killer Among Us, The Choice, The
Pain, Lost Love, Death; [a.] Mishawaka, IN

WEAR, DANIEL
[pen.] Hugh Daniels; [b.] October 26, 1971, Flint,
MI; [p.] Hugh Ronald Wear II, Jane Carol Wear;
[ed.] Flushing Senior High School, currently
attending the University of Michigan; [pers.]
"Poetry is the most beautiful thing a person can
create. It is the language of the soul, inspired by
love and written with passion. Without it, this
world would be a dark and dismal place."; [a.]
Flushing, MI

WEAVER, JUDY CAROL
[pen.] Judy; [b.] April 19, 1952, Rowan County;
[p.] Bennie E. and Ruth P. Lefler; [m.] Charles L.
Weaver, January 17, 1982; [ch.] Charles Leon,

Michael Everette and Willie Marvin; [ed.] East Rowan High School Salisbury, NC. 28144, Granite Quarry Elementary Granite Quarry, NC. 28072; [occ.] Homemaker Landis, NC; [memb.] Faith Missionary Baptist Church Rockwell, NC. 28138; [oth. writ.] I've entered different poems into many contest; [pers.] I write my poems as God instill in me to write them, as a means to get his word and marvelous grace he has shown me, to others. About this Lost and dying world in hope that many will gain salvation; [a.] Landis, NC

WEAVER, KRISTINA
[b.] January 11, 1981, Long Beach, CA; [p.] Donn and Jeanne Weaver; [ed.] Presently in 8th grade at Franklin Middle School; [occ.] Student; [memb.] National Junior Honor Society; [hon.] Academic awards including school team Student of the Month, Excellence in Writing, Excellence in Academics, "All A Award, National Junior Honor Society; [oth. writ.] Poems published in school literary magazine; [pers.] The wonderful thing about a poem is that it cuts the square corners of factual truth to create a circle. A circle means something different to everyone and includes anyone.; [a.] Herndon, VA

WEBB, EUGENE C.
[b.] January 4, 1927, Whitesville, WV; [p.] Dayton and Madeline Webb; [m.] Wilnia L. Webb, October 25, 1972; [ch.] Deborah Lynn (daughter), Larry, Gina, Kenneth, Nancy, Donna and Mark (step children); [ed.] 8 years elementary GED also served 4 yrs Machinist apprenticeship; [occ.] Retired Machinist 27 years as US Gov't employee; [memb.] Veteran of Foreign Wars American Legion; [oth. writ.] A number of poems none published.; [pers.] I have written a number of poems for my personal enjoyment. I have never tried to have one published before. Most of my poems are based on real happenings.; [a.] Browsville, TX

WEBER, ROELA OVING
[pen.] Roela Oving-Weber; [b.] July 6, 1922, Netherlands; [p.] Harm Oving, Hillechien Brouwer; [m.] Nicholas Alexander Weber, January 5, 1952; [ch.] George Alexander Weber; [ed.] Rosenburg High, MULO High Danckaerts Industrial College (Netherlands), J-College and David Wolcott Kendall College Gr Rapids Mt., USA; [occ.] Retired, hobbies-writing, painting, doll making; [memb.] Netherlands Cultural Society; [hon.] Graduated with high honors from Danckaerts Industrial College. Received a certificate (continuing education) of the David Wolcott Kendall School of Design.; [oth. writ.] Poem (Messengers of Spring) published in a College Arts magazine, Spring 1982, unpublished, poems and short stories.; [pers.] Emigrated to the USA in 1952, by reading and memorizing Shakespeare and other famous poets, I got inspired to write poetry.; [a.] Brookeville, MD

WEBSTER, DAISY L.
[b.] April 11, 1955; [p.] Tom Webster and Lannie Webster; [ch.] Sabrina D., Antonio D., Andre L.; [ed.] Carver High Montgomery Alabama; [pers.] In my work I always think or mankinds love and care for family and mankind toward each other; [a.] Montgomery, AL

WECHTER, AMANDA
[pen.] Sky; [b.] May 21, 1979, Edison, NJ; [p.] Mark and Trish Wechter; [ed.] Edison High School, Summer Arts Institute, Rutgers; [occ.] Honors Student at Edison High School; [memb.] Animal Rescue Force, Acrodanse Theatre Jr. Company; [oth. writ.] Selection of poetry and several abstract pieces; [pers.] Life is poetry is life. Although it many not always rhyme, it is nonetheless explosive. Thank you for my being inspiration, blue eyes.; [a.] Edison, NJ

WEISS, MRS. SALLY
[pen.] Sally Weiss; [b.] September 14, 1908, Chicago, IL; [p.] Deceased; [m.] Deceased; [ch.] Rebecca Jean Knettel, Five Grand children; [ed.] Four years High School by home study one year at Brunch of Wheaton College in Chicago, IL; [occ.] Retired; [memb.] Life member of Chinese Hospital in San Francisco, CA; [hon.] Received a plack of award for ten year of volunteer service at UC San Francisco in Pediatrics children's Dept., In Ukiah in Schools, also 5 yrs. volunteers foster grandma.; [oth. writ.] Yes. Poem published in wings of Faith entitled Hebrews Inspiration

WELCH, PATRICIA J.
[b.] December 5, 1958, Mt. Pleasant, PA; [p.] Harry Welch and Josephine Welch; [ch.] Jason Michael, Justin Matthew; [ed.] South Huntingdon High School; [occ.] Machine Operator at Constar Plastic; [oth. writ.] Several poems written to read in church. One poem published in the Constar Report. (The Winds of Change). He Cares For You, My Dreams, Thank You, Lord. (Now Published); [pers.] God has given me a special talent to write. Through my writings, I pray, the Lord is glorified. I enjoy writing about the Lord and his goodness toward us.; [a.] Wyano, PA

WELLS, FLOYD EUGENE
[b.] 1923, Chippewa Falls, WI; [hon.] The last survivor of the original Pilgrims to receive the Puritan Liturgy. Became one of the nation's youngest pilots. With his younger brother, built a boat that took first place at the State Fair. At middle age he drove "Formula" race cars under the auspices of the S.C.C.A. He painted landscapes in acrylic for twelve years.; [pers.] "After many years, through poetry, I have gained my first acknowledgments." Philosophy! "Life is a maze. Search until you find your niche and vigorously pursue your dream."

WELLS, KRISTY
[b.] May 23, 1979, Dearborn, MI; [p.] Robert and Mary Wells; [ed.] Annapolis High School; [occ.] Student; [memb.] National Honor Society S.A.D.D. (Students Against Drunk Driving); [pers.] I love to read, to write, and to draw. My favorite places in the whole world are bookstores and museums.; [a.] Dearborn Heights, MI

WEST, CORA MAE
[pen.] Cora Ma'el; [b.] October 1, Greenville, AL; [ed.] Southern Illinois University 2 years University Science and Philosophy 1 year certificate; [occ.] American Cancer Society, Illinois Div. I, Creative Writer, Secretary, Lecturer, Poet; [oth. writ.] 'Murder on The Whitehouse Lawn,' 'Charisma,' 'Love's Thrashing Floor,' 'I'll Show

You God,' 'Suppose This Is The Way It Was,' which is the pieces of the creation story pieced together as never before. Kitty Kitaby, odd stories, Unaware, autobiography.; [pers.] I write to share myself with the world through my many experiences. If I didn't have to write, I would not, but write I must! In 1981 I had the experience of becoming universal LOVE—I have to spread it through my writings and my personal contacts. I am influenced by the awakened spirit within me; [a.] Batavia, IL

WEST, TRESSA (PRICE)
[b.] July 10, 1964, Sparta, TN; [p.] Billy and JoAnn Price; [m.] James Stevens (Steve) West, April 15, 1995; [ed.] Tennessee Technological University, White County High School; [occ.] Marketing and Sales; [pers.] To my special friend and my love of a lifetime, Steve.; [a.] Nashville, TN

WESTER, MARK W.
[b.] January 23, 1969, Birmingham, AL; [p.] Jerry and Jane Wester; [m.] Kimberly Wester, December 23, 1989; [ch.] Aaron Mitchell Wester; [ed.] Indian River Academy Indian River Community College; [occ.] Owner of Grove Caretaking Business; [memb.] Community United Methodist Church; [oth. writ.] "A Blessing" published in local paper; [pers.] Written by Mark W. Wester, inspired by God.; [a.] Fort Pierg, FL

WHEELER, LILLY
[pen.] Fhransescka Lilly Perdomo; [b.] May 2,; [ch.] Esther Georgine; [ed.] Bachelor of Science, Letter and Mathematics, Cervantes College, El Salvador, Industrial Engineering, University National of El Salvador, Commercial Secretarial Studies, Our Lady of Guadalope, El Salvador, Clerical Office Procedures, Job Preparation, S.E.R., Los Angeles, CA, Commercial Fashion Modeling, Human Robots, Faces International, Hollywood, CA, Real Estate Principles, Century 21 Real Estate, Los Angeles, CA; [oth. writ.] Several poems; [pers.] I want to make public, my thanks to my friend who is my inspiration: Alex Justice; [a.] Los Angeles, CA

WHITE, AMANDA
[pen.] Faith Eubanks; [b.] February 9, 1979, Redding, CA; [p.] Linda Eubanks-White, Paul White; [ed.] Sophomore at Red Bluff Union High School, Red Bluff, CA; [occ.] Odd jobs, work at Lassen National Park last summer; [hon.] Tehama County Reading Council Writing Contest, competition of I-220 Basic ICS, and VIP for the National Park Service; [oth. writ.] A poem published in 1993 writing contest of Tehama County.; [pers.] With integrity, leadership and imagination, achievement knows no boundaries, I love you Mom.; [a.] Paynes Creek, CA

WHITE, ANISA
[b.] August 16, 1977, Birmingham, AL; [p.] Terry White, Diann White; [ed.] J.B. Pennington High School; [occ.] Student; [memb.] Future Business Leaders of America Future Homemakers of America; [pers.] Everyone hurts no matter how we deceive ourselves or others. However, we must live our lives to the fullest and deal with the pain within.; [a.] Blountsville, AL

WHITE, CARRIE W.
[b.] May 9, 1923, North Carolina; [p.] Melvin and Dessie Wilson; [m.] Ralph O. White, August 30, 1981; [ch.] Carolyn and Jane; [ed.] Lattimore High School 1941; [occ.] Retired; [memb.] Sharon Methodist Church in past have been Girl Scout Leader, Leader of children in church, Pink Lady in hospital etc.; [oth. writ.] I write what I feel for my own pleasure.; [pers.] I have always loved nature. Mother, taught us the roots, herbs, tree bark to use for medicine and food etc. Grape vines and swimming holes our play ground.; [a.] Shelby, NC

WHITE, KATRINA NICOLE
[pen.] Nicki Hardwick White; [b.] January 22, 1973, Jacksonville, IL; [p.] Marcia and Alan Hardwick; [m.] Donnie E. White, July 23, 1993; [ch.] None just one pet cat, Monique, my "baby;" [ed.] Basic, no special training, writing comes naturally, like breathing; [occ.] Wigsty List, Hestess at Banquet Hall; [oth. writ.] "Daddy", dedicated to Dionne, "Where is Jennifer Today?", "Love Conquers All", "A Mother's Memories", "Mommy of Mine"; [pers.] "Believe you can achieve anything, especially in the face of adversity."; [a.] Jacksonville, IL

WHITE, KEVIN
[b.] January 19, 1979, Woodbury, NJ; [p.] David and Cheryl White; [occ.] Sophomore Lake Mary High School; [memb.] Spinabifida Assoc. of South Jersey; [pers.] I'd like to thank you family and friends for all of their support and help. And most of all my parents for being there when I needed them most. I'd also like to thank my favorite cousin Stacie White for always being my friend.; [a.] Lake Mary, FL

WHITE, MELISSA
[b.] January 17, 1972, Tribune, KS; [p.] Kenneth and Linda Bieker; [m.] Arlyn White, January 5, 1990; [ch.] Brittany, John, Rebekka, and Levi; [occ.] Homemaker and farm wife; [pers.] I've written many poems, but have never had the courage to submit any. I'm grateful I took that first step. To others have courage and don't be afraid to try.; [a.] Weskan, KS

WHITLOCK, BRENDA
[pen.] B. Whitlock; [b.] May 14, 1949, Bruce, MS; [p.] Robert Lambert, Inez Lambert; [m.] Sidney Whitlock, September 1, 1966; [ch.] Sidney Wade Whitlock; [ed.] Okolona High School and Vaughn's Beauty College; [memb.] Church of God of Prophecy, Verona, MS; [oth. writ.] Many poems published in local papers and personal request for special occasions poems; [pers.] I feel that I have been greatly inspired all through my life and this can only come from my creator in which I give Him all the credit.; [a.] Okolona, MS

WHITSON, MALINDA SUE
[b.] July 10, 1973, Madison Height, MI; [p.] Darryl and Lorraine Whitson; [ed.] Mountain Heritage High, University of North Carolina-Asheville, Asheville-Buncombe Technical Community College; [occ.] Loam Officer, Mitchell Credit Co., Inc., Spruce Pine, NC; [memb.] National Restaurant Association, Beta Club, National Vocational Honors Society; [hon.] Honor Student, Phi Theta Kappa, 1st in state and 7th in

National's VICA, 2nd in State FHA, NVP Softball, Math and Home Ec. Awards; [pers.] This goes out in thanks to my mother for always praising my writings. It has given me the confidence I need to believe in myself and my poems.; [a.] Burnsville, NC

WHITT, SHARON
[b.] September 10, 1968, Marble Falls, TX; [p.] Gordon and Goldia King; [m.] Frank Whitt, November 20, 1989; [ch.] John, Walter, Christopher, Franklin and Amy; [ed.] Mayo - GED; [occ.] Production Line - Warsaw Coil; [memb.] Vets of America; [oth. writ.] I am striving to finish my first science - fiction novel.; [pers.] I firmly believe everyone should try and fulfill their dreams. Life is full of happiness if one would only open their eyes and see it.; [a.] Warsaw, IN

WIDDOWSON, SUSANNE A.
[b.] April 10, 1954, Lincoln, NE; [p.] Ed and Verneta Itzen; [m.] Ex-Richard C. Widdowson, February 23, 1974 (Divorced October 1, 1991); [ch.] Heath, December 18, 1973, Katrina, June 18, 1975; [ed.] G.E.D., 1/2 yr. College (Archaeology); [occ.] Displaced Home Maker (living in past, working on future).; [memb.] National Audubon Society, National Parks and Conservation Association, National Arbor Day Foundation, Defenders of Wild Life, National Wildlife Federation; [oth. writ.] "We the Creatures," published by World of Poetry, 1988, Golden Poet Award, 1989, Silver Poet Award.; [pers.] I don't understand life, and I'm not sure I ever will. But we need to keep more families together, and make the land and environment safer, not only for our children, but, for our distant relatives, the animals.; [a.] Lincoln, NE

WIDNER, EVELYN COPPLE
[b.] January 4, 1911, Jefferson County, IL; [p.] Birthel and Mayme (Dickinson) Copple; [m.] Eldon L. Widner, November 7, 1980; [ed.] Centralia High School, Centralia, IL, B.A. Degree-Monmouth College, Monmouth, IL, other additional credits for special K-14 Teaching and Supervising Instructional; [occ.] Retired. Materials former School Teacher and Learning Center Director (Media Specialist); [memb.] NRTA, IRTA, Tri-County Retired Teacher's Assoc., Delta Kappa Gamma Professional Society International, International Society of Poets (lifetime member), Jacksonville, Area Genealogy and Historical Society, AARP, Central Christian Church; [hon.] High Honor Student in High School, Teacher Emeritus - Galesburg, IL, Editor's Choice Awards - National Library of Poetry, "International Poet of Merit" Award - International Society of Poets, Poems published in The National Library of Poetry Anthologies, Poem in "The World's Largest Poem for Peace"; [oth. writ.] Have written many poems for various occasions and celebrations- birthdays, anniversaries, school days, travels, the seasons, etc. For many years, I have composed my own Christmas greetings in the form of acrostics. 30 of these are now published in book form. Some of my poems have been published in news letters bulletins, and The National Library of Poetry anthologies. Some read on "Sound of Poetry" and "Impressions" cassettes. Have had more copy righted and ready for publication.; [pers.] I enjoy expressing my thoughts and feelings in poetry. It

helps fulfill my desire to promote love, peace, and understanding throughout our beautiful world. My hope is that my poetry will be an inspiration to anyone who reads it. All these things continue to be important to me; [a.] Jacksonville, IL

WIDUCH, BEATRICE ANNE SCHOELLER
[pen.] Tris Widuch; [b.] August 2, 1952, Waterbury, CT; [p.] George Schoeller, Catherine Buckgowski; [m.] James S. Widuch, Deceased, May 2, 1969; [ch.] David, Karen, Gordon, Patty; [ed.] High School Southbury, CT, Graduate at Naugatuck Valley Tech College In Waterbury, CT; [occ.] Trained for private duty home health aide training, CNA also 1972; [oth. writ.] Re:Beware you shall hear us three day. Have written 70 poems, in total. Have just recently shown a few of them. Writing for the last 10 or 15 years. Have written stories as well in "Conflict" and "Love Blooms Summer." Someday I wish them to become novels.; [pers.] I want to share all my feelings and views from the heart with many to reflect on, to stir up the mind and the soul.; [a.] Naugatuck, CT

WIECZOREK, TRACEY
[b.] February 26, 1977, New Britain; [p.] Ronald and Jean Wieczorek; [ed.] Newington High School; [hon.] Music awards from school, honor roll; [oth. writ.] I write poems with all different meanings and topics. Also my 3 dogs Sharon, Mona, and Casey influence some of my writings.; [pers.] I give my love to my parents and brother for all their encouragement. Poems are the words of life; [a.] Newington, CT

WIGHT, CATHERINE
[pen.] Cathy Car; [b.] June 14, 1958, San Diego; [p.] Larry and Maria Weir; [ch.] Elizabeth 12 years, Laura 8 years; [ed.] Oxnard H.S. and Poway H.S. Oak Groves School of Music, Claude Trumpt, Private Vocal, Instructions; [occ.] Soloist; [memb.] BMI Songwriter AFTRA (American Federation of Theatre and Radio Artists) St. Sebastian's Church Music Director and Music Minister; [oth. writ.] Songs "Get Up And Move" and "Dream Lover" and have completed a children's book but has not been published yet.; [pers.] Remain positive despite the negative forces. Smile and love one another with sincerity.; [a.] West Lost Angeles, CA

WILCOX, CHRIS
[pen.] Bean; [b.] March 31, 1964, Ohio; [p.] Kenneth Havezy, Donna Havezy; [m.] Tony Wilcox, November 1, 1985; [ch.] Anthony Ryan, Adam Ray; [ed.] Reyn. High, Col. State, ICS - Computer Specialist; [occ.] Cashier, Writer; [memb.] Sterra Club, Church Of Christ; [hon.] Honorable Certificates for several poems, three poems published; [oth. writ.] I have written over 150 poems; [pers.] I write to free myself and to help others attain freedom. I want others to be aware of the silence of abuse.; [a.] Gahanna, OH

WILHELMY, GUS
[b.] February 17, 1935, Saint Paul, MN; [p.] George Wilhelmy, Emily Wegner; [m.] Mary Rose Valley, September 1, 1990; [ch.] Rochelle Marie, Todd Jerome, Rebecca Ann; [ed.] B.A. and M.A.'S University of Michigan, Ann Arbor; [occ.]

Fund Raising Executive; [memb.] American Marketing Association, American Management Association, National Society of Fund Raising Executives; [hon.] Martin Luther King Community Service Award, Outstanding Youth Man of America, Founder's Award: Safer Foundation Editor's Choice Award from National Library of Poetry; [oth. writ.] Numerous articles published in magazines and newspapers... poetry in other magazines; [pers.] I seemingly write best about the pain, the struggle, the weakness of all of us... yet my view is hopefully romantic and touches the light within.; [a.] Chicago, IL

WILKERSON, CINDY
[b.] May 8, 1959, Marshalltown, IA; [p.] Theron Wilkerson, Elaine Wilkerson; [ed.] Gladbrook High, A.I.B. (American Institute of Business); [occ.] Computer Consultant and Business Owner; [memb.] American Business Women's Association; [hon.] State of Iowa Scholar, Dean's List; [oth. writ.] Several poems unpublished.; [pers.] "As if I walk with one breath, I take it to it's depth, I ask the question why, and always try, to find the truth in living and have a heart that's giving."; [a.] Lakewood, CO

WILKES, EDWARD
[pen.] Ed Wilkes/Blake Edwards; [b.] October 19, 1959, Niagara falls, NY; [p.] James Wilkes, Joan Heartbridge; [m.] Divorced; [ch.] Kelly Marie, Shelly Lynn, Edward Blake Jr., Eric Patrick, Billie Jean Marie; [ed.] Attended Mohawk Valley Community College, currently enrolled in Emmaus Bible correspondence; [occ.] Painter; [memb.] Inventors Club, S.U.N.Y., Marcy NY, Moose Lodge Rome, NY; [oth. writ.] Lonely is the night, plus others soon to be published.; [pers.] Most of my writings are derived from personal experiences, the experiences of others as well as from my own experiences. Since age 13 my writings have mostly centered on real life experiences, they tell a story.; [a.] Rome, NY

WILKIE, HELEN SHELLY
[b.] February 24, 1918, Mt. Kisco, NY; [m.] Paul Wilkie, December 27, 1970; [ed.] Mt. Kisco High School, NY, Skidmore College, Saratoga Springs, NY C.W. Post, Westbury, NY; [occ.] Retired from careers as pathologist, dental educator, later proprietor Art and Gift Shop... Walpole, NH; [memb.] Smithsonian Associates, Hoper Golf Club, Walpole, NH; [oth. writ.] After publishing my book of poetry "Yours Truly", my original poems and several short stories were published weekly in The Walpole Gazette for several years.; [pers.] My New England oil paintings have been well-received and carry over to my feeling that writing poetry is not only spontaneous but like looking at a blank canvas, then painting a picture....with words. The words bare the very being and fiber of the poet.; [a.] Walpole, NH

WILKINS, DREW M.
[b.] July 15, 1986, California; [p.] Mac and Fran Wilkins; [ed.] 3rd grader in the prism program for gifted children; [occ.] Student; [hon.] 1st place for children's poetry writing contest. "Island Books" on Mercer Island, WA; [oth. writ.] Other poem published in Montessori Magazine; [pers.] My

dream 18 to someday become a scientist and hopefully contribute something to help make our world a better place. This poem was written for my 2nd grade teacher, Mrs. Moe.; [a.] Belleyuc, WA

WILKINS, EDWARD L.
[pen.] Ghost; [b.] July 31, 1952, Port Clinton, OH; [ch.] Crystal Nicole and Jessica Renee; [ed.] Oak, Harber High, Hocking College, and Terra Tech. College; [occ.] Self-employed - several business; [memb.] Several Literary Clubs; [oth. writ.] Short fiction (i.e. Horror, Adult, Adventure, Poetry, etc.); [pers.] My Prayer: Lord, give me the strength for 'one more shot' - there are people worse off than I - I will make my own - don't fret, then you and I will help the rest. Amen; [a.] Port Clinton, OH

WILLETTE, ELIZABETH A.
[pen.] David E. Willette; [b.] July 7, 1968, Bingham, ME; [p.] George and Frances Tatakis; [m.] David E. Willette, July 15, 1992; [ch.] Anthony Keith Willette; [ed.] U.K.V. High School - Bingham, ME. Skowhegan Vocational School, Skowhegan, ME; [occ.] Home Teacher and Home Maker; [pers.] My poems bring out the spirits and souls of every living thing. Many people has forgotten to let their minds fly to human beingness.; [a.] Wasilla, AK

WILLIAMEE, BEATRICE C.
[pen.] Beatrice Eleanor Callahan; [b.] August 4, 1908, Wellsboro, PA; [p.] John W. and Mae E. Callahan; [m.] Goron Coolidge (deceased September 1936), Irvin L. Williamee (deceased November 2, 1985); [ch.] Ronald G. Coolidge, Garth C. Coolidge; [ed.] Graduate Wellsboro, PA, High School June 1927, Wellsboro, PA; [occ.] Retired Legal Secretary; [memb.] Mary Wells Chapter, O.E. Star - First Baptist Church, Wellsboro, PA - Penna, Society Prevention of Cruelty to Animals - Women of the Moose; [hon.] Order Eastern Star 50 years - Baptist Church - 70 years - Moose 20 years, Valentine Week 2-1982, Wellsboro, PA Gazette; [oth. writ.] 1927 Rambler; [pers.] Began working Law Office December 23, 1926, worked 59 years, retired at age 74.; [a.] Wellsboro, PA

WILLIAMS, APRIL M.
[pen.] Akilah Kamau; [b.] December 18, 1958, San Francisco; [p.] Boy L. Williams/Sarah E. Porter; [m.] none; [ch.] Reginald Lawrence, II; [ed.] B.A. Black Studies, San Francisco State University; [occ.] Legal Secretary; [memb.] National Golden Key Honor Society; [hon.] Graduated 1994 Summa Cum Laude (SFSU), Golden Key Honor Society, IBWA (International Black Writer's Association) Award winner, Dean's List; [oth. writ.] "How Can I Believe in the Rainbow," several poems ("Two Minutes to Hell," "Shadows Don't Die," "Black History Rhyme For Children," "Nostalgia," "Wading in the Water") and others.

WILLIAMS, BARBARA K.
[pen.] Boo-Boo - Turtle; [b.] Local Hospita, Pittston, PA; [p.] Pred C. and Marion M. Williams; [m.] September 8, 1973; [ch.] Five nieces and nephews, two brothers; [ed.] Finished

High School 1969, Wyoming Area High School, West Pittston, Pa., one year, pre-special ed. curriculum, Mansfield State College, Mansfield Pa. (No formal Lit. Education); [occ.] Dis. Soc. Sec. and SSI, Primary caregiver for ill mother; [memb.] Methodist Youth Fellowship, High School Band (Clarinet); [hon.] Mississippi river boat "Caliope Playing" award (certificate), Blood donor when allowed (on medication); [oth. writ.] Many unpublished, but read, and critiqued by poetry teachers - told had promising talent and to further pursue my writing, (Doing so, hoping to publish a book) poetry on life's experiences (death, friendship, love, family); [pers.] "Live is but a dream, unforgettably blended with happy and sad times, both, leading us, day to day, (minute by minute), to the final "wake-up call" of eternity.; [a.] West Wyoming, PA

WILLIAMS, C. SCOTT
[b.] September 24, 1968, Decatur, AL; [p.] Clint and Cecelia Williams; [ed.] 4th year Medical Student at Univ. of Alabama at Birmingham, undergraduate: BAC Clemson Univ.; [occ.] Medical Student; [memb.] Bare "Somerset Maugham The Summing Up;" [hon.] ACC Champion in Wrestling in 1992, 6th in "U.S. National Open" in Wrestling, 1991; [oth. writ.] "Christmas," Published in Aura of the Univ. of Alabama at Birmingham, Vol. 2, Number 1, 1994; [pers.] "I do not know a better training for a writer than to spend some years in the medical profession - The doctor, especially the hospital doctor sees (Human Nature).; [a.] Birmingham, AL

WILLIAMS, EDWARD MACON
[pen.] Eddie Macon; [b.] February 11, 1931, Rose Hill, NC; [p.] Samuel P. Williams and Laura A. Williams; [ed.] I have acquired much through private studies and from the book of nature.; [occ.] Missionary, Writer; [memb.] National Writers Asso., Seventh Day Adventist Church; [oth. writ.] Child of Paradise, Heaven Rejoices, Three Angels, Mother Love, Beautiful Rose of Sharron, New Jerusalem; [pers.] In my writings I try to dwell upon the good qualities of my fellow beings as taught by our Lord in the sermon on the mount that those who are wise in heart might see the light of eternal truth as taught in the holy scriptures.; [a.] Raleigh, NC

WILLIAMS, ELIZABETH WILSON
[pen.] "Elka"; [b.] October 21, 1923, Canada; [p.] Mother - Stamford, CT, USA, Father - New Hampshire, USA; [m.] Divorced, 1970; [ch.] Three daughters, Two sons; [ed.] State of California Teaching Served on Faculty of Credential Art. Le Lycee' Francaise de Los Angeles, Calif. USA (International Private Schools) Sunny Hill Hospital for Children - Vancouver, BC, Canada, Taught "art therapy"; [occ.] Writer - Poet Artist; [hon.] Medical Terminology - Achievement Award - Cedars Sini, Beverly Hills, CA, USA; [oth. writ.] Poetry 5 poems to publisher. Novel broken promises under contract with agent. Currently preparing how to art book with illustrations "The World of Light."; [pers.] "I am inspired by the unlimited possibilities of abstract thought opening the doors to higher creativity."; [a.] Las Vegas, NV

WILLIAMS, JANET R.
[pen.] Marilyn; [b.] May 1, 1969, Montgomery, AL; [p.] Robert and Joyce Williams; [ed.] Prattville High; [occ.] Courtroom Deputy, US Bankruptcy Court; [memb.] Winner of two National Speech Competitions, Miss Prattville Lion 1987; [oth. writ.] Have a collection of twenty other poems; [pers.] Count each day as a special gift from above. Your heart will be light, and your days filled with love.; [a.] Montgomery, AL

WILLIAMS, KAREN PATRICE
[b.] London, England; [p.] Barbara Jean and Marcus; [m.] Michael Robert; [ed.] St. Clement Danes Primary. Parliament Hill Girls High London England; [memb.] American NAFE and British Equity; [oth. writ.] Poem published in "Dusting off Dreams" also published in the "Vegas Times."; [pers.] Encouraged by my husband Michael inspired by my mother Barbara influenced to begin writing after reading W.S. Merwin's Winning poem Sept. 1994 Winner of American Poets tanning and previous Pulitzer prize winner being surrounded by nature and the rugged Beauty of America, I got started!.; [a.] Las Vegas, NV

WILLIAMS, KIRRA CHARISSE
[b.] March 21, 1976, Asheville, NC; [p.] Robert and Mary Thomas; [ed.] Lathrop High School, freshman at University of Alaska Fairbanks; [memb.] Young American Bowlers Association, President for 2 years of Bowling League; [pers.] I have always been a lover of poetry and I find writing poetry relaxes me. It seems to bring out my feelings through my poems.; [a.] Fort Wainwright, AK

WILLIAMS, PEARLIE L.
[pen.] Pearl Williams; [b.] July 22, 1925, Houston, TX; [p.] Pearlie Mullen, Letitia Mullen; [m.] Clarence J. Williams (deceased), April 4, 1945; [ch.] Letitia Williams Shelby, Phyllis Williams Sheed, Clarence Williams Jr.; [ed.] Robinson High, Laney Jr. College; [occ.] Retired Library Assistant; [memb.] Allen Temple Baptist Church Library Committee; [oth. writ.] A collection of mini-biographies: How They Got Over published by the Aller Temple Church Press; [a.] Oakland, CA

WILLIAMS, STEPHANIE LYNN
[b.] March 26, 1969, Wilkes Co, NC; [p.] Jack and Neta Williams; [ch.] Karye Jeanette Williams and Dustin Clinton Call; [ed.] 10th Grade Wilkes East High; [occ.] Poultry Tyson Foods, Inc. (fresh plant); [oth. writ.] Several poems that have not been published. I'm waiting for anyone who is interested in my work to contact me at: Stephanie Lynn Williams c/o Angie Brown P.O. Box 133 Taylorsville, N.C. 28681; [pers.] Poems we're wrote from experience and feelings from my own life and from the love of both my deceased parents of whom I'll always respect and love; [a.] Wilkesboro, NC

WILLIAMS, SUSAN A.
[pen.] S. A. S. or S. A. W.; [b.] February 9, 1959, Lebanon, PA; [p.] Joan and Frank Swanger; [m.] John, October 10, 1986; [ch.] Joanne Marie; [ed.] Theodore Roosevelt High; [occ.] Self-employed; [pers.] I have always been a day dreamer, with an active imagination that lets me see things most people don't notice. Always enjoy earths beauty and see the flowers.; [a.] San Antonio, TX

WILLIAMS, SYLVESTER
[b.] March 13, 1954, San Francisco, CA; [p.] John Q. Williams, Naomi Williams; [ed.] Woodrow Wilson High San Francisco State University; [occ.] Medical Laboratory Technologist; [oth. writ.] Unpublished novel; [pers.] Happiness is based on happiness on the outside. Joy is based upon what is happening on the inside.; [a.] Hayward, CA

WILLIAMS, WILLIE C.
[pen.] Willie C. Williams; [b.] January 30, 1938, Coolidge, TX; [p.] Edward and Dollie Mae Williams; [ed.] Waco High School-TSTI (TSTI changed to TSTC); [occ.] Semi-Retired; [memb.] International Society of Poets; [hon.] I feel it's an honor to published by the "National Library of Poetry". Award for waiting essay East Jr., High School; [oth. writ.] Poems (published) Love-War; [pers.] Hopefully someone will gain from each of my poems.; [a.] Waco, TX

WILLS, AMANDA KAY
[b.] July 17, 1979, Indianapolis, IN; [p.] W. Bryan and Patty Wills; [ed.] Frank W. Cox High School, currently enrolled; [occ.] High School Sophomore; [memb.] The National Junior Beta Club; [hon.] Outstanding Omer Award for Creativity in Odyssey of the Mind, Presidential Academic Fitness Award; [pers.] I write about my personal experiences and emotions. I have been influenced by such poets as Shanna Flipse, Lord Byron, and John Bennett; [a.] Virginia Beach, VA

WILMORE, LINDA MORROW
[pen.] Linda Morrow-Wilmore; [b.] December 27, 1957, Houston, TX; [p.] Mr. and Mrs. N. C. Morrow; [m.] Joe Wilmore, July 4, 1992; [ed.] 1 year College, Real Estate; [hon.] Scholastic Honors Grades 3-12, accelerated in artistry; [oth. writ.] Published in National Literary Cavalcade, 1 Haiku, 1 Tonka in 8th grade; [pers.] Each individual's writing achieves expression with versatility for a singular viewpoint making life full and interesting.; [a.] Houston, TX

WILSEY, ROCHELLE ANN
[pen.] Dawn Nichole; [b.] July 6, 1944, New Orleans, LA; [p.] Hazel and Buddy Blackman; [m.] Miles Stephen Wilsey, May 19, 1972; [ch.] Christopher Miles Wilsey; [ed.] Abraham Lincoln H.S., Miami Dade Community College, Clayton State College; [occ.] Realtor and Student; [memb.] Southern Stampede, Clogging Team; [hon.] Phi Theta Kappa, National Honor Fraternity; [pers.] To touch as many lives as possible. To be an open vessel and to channel through as much information as I can. To know that God in his wisdom gives us more than one crack at getting it right.; [a.] Fayetteville, GA

WILSON, CATHY
[b.] November 25, MD; [p.] Roger and Grace Funk; [m.] Nolan M. Wilson, May 25; [ch.] Marsha, Dana, Blaine, Dion, Clay; [ed.] High School; [occ.] Homemaker; [oth. writ.] Poems and songs I have at home not published; [pers.] Hold on to your dreams, someday they may come true.; [a.] Manassas Park, VA

WILSON, JULIA F.
[pen.] J. Fowler Wilson; [b.] June 7, 1941, Lyme, NH; [p.] David and Olive Fowler; [m.] Ralph Wilson (Deceased), December 7, 1968; [ch.] Darryl, Mahlon, and Joshua; [ed.] Class of 1959 Orford High School, Orford NH, 2 year Business College, Nathaniel Howthorne; [occ.] Industrial Mechanical Inspector; [memb.] United Methodist Church, Lebanon NH, AARP; [hon.] Volume 1978 Outstanding Young Women of America, Orford High School Class of 1959 Co-valedictorian.; [oth. writ.] Several poems published in company newsletter and (Local School District) Federal "Follow Through" Responsive Education Program in 1975-76 news letter.; [pers.] My writing is a gift. In it I try to reflect my love and respect for my world, myself, my family, and all of life. My writing is strongly influenced by Emily Dickinson, Elizabeth Browning, and Robert Frost, My Love of The Language and Methods are influenced by Judson Jerome and my first H.S. English Teacher, E.B. Fulton High School.; [a.] Lebanon, NH

WILSON, LINDA B.
[b.] July 31, 1951, Baytown, TX; [p.] Murphy Travis Beverly, Trevia Josephine Wooster Beverly; [m.] LTC Gary M. Wilson, April 30, 1983; [ch.] Heather Leigh Wilson, Mackenzie Travis Wilson; [ed.] Spring Branch High School, East Texas Baptist College (1 yr); [occ.] Homemaker, Small Business Owner (Business services); [memb.] National Society Magna Charta Dames, United Daughters of the Confederacy, Mayflower Society; [hon.] JC Penney Golden Rule Award, Honorable Order of Molly Pitcher Dept. of Army Commanders Award for Public Service, United Way of El Paso Certificate of Recognition, LDAT Certificate of Excellence; [oth. writ.] Article on "Whig Hill", an old (previously owned by family) estate dating back to the early 1700's published in the Beverly Family Records No. 4 July 1989, and several other non-published poems.; [pers.] God and His word are what we will be ultimately judged by (believers and unbelievers alike) - therefore, it behooves us to live by His word. I hope that I am thought well of and remembered for my heart attitude, sincerity of my beliefs, and desire to do good and what is right. I want to be remember as a good mother and wife.; [a.] Roswell, NM

WILSON, MICHELLE LEE
[pen.] Michelle Wilson; [b.] November 4, 1975, Natrona Heights; [p.] Ronald and Carol Wilson; [ed.] I'm currently attending Pittsburgh Beauty Academy in New Kensington; [occ.] Student Hairdresser; [memb.] I am on honor roll at my beauty school; [hon.] I haven't has any other poems published, but I wrote a poem when a close friend of mine passed away that everyone took a copy of.; [oth. writ.] Whenever you say you can't do something then you can't, but when you believe in who you are and what you do the world will come to you.; [pers.] Apello, PA

WILSON, PATRICIA
[pen.] Tricia Wilson; [b.] March 21, 1954, El Paso, TX; [p.] Harold and Marjorie Wilson; [m.] Roy Glenn Wilson, September 10, 1979; [ch.] Christopher McFarland, Tricia Twonsend; [ed.] Robert E. Lee High School Tyler, TX; [occ.] Housewife; [memb.] God's storehouse Church, Founded the Women's Auxiliary, American Cancer Society, North Shore Animal League; [pers.] I have two grandson's Dylan McFarland Aaron Townsend all my work has been given to me

through Jesus. Without him I am nothing. My Dad and husband have continually supported my work Dad however passed away on Jan 22 1995; [a.] Pittsburg, TX

WILSON, STEVEN R.
[pen.] Steven Wilson; [b.] January 11, 1965, Philadelphia; [p.] Josephine and Calvin Wilson; [occ.] Line and Prep Cook Ruby Tuesdays; [oth. writ.] Poems: Lies published in National Library 1994 book "Seasons To Come" Unpublished short stories, screenplays; [pers.] The power of film can create joy, pain, fear, suspense. I am hoping that film and art school can move me up to the next level and give me a shot at working with the Hollywood big boys.; [a.] Dover, DE

WINHAM, MARY
[b.] January 11, 1943; [p.] Cecil and Ruth Grady; [m.] Harry Winham, September 30, 1966; [ch.] Anthony Winham, Michael Winham; [ed.] Gainesville High School; [memb.] I am a member of the national library of poetry, I work in Denton Texas, my husband is a cabinet maker; [oth. writ.] I written "The Indian Woman" and also other poems.; [pers.] I hope to continue to write poems.

WINSLOW, ELIZABETH ANN
[pen.] E. A. Winslow; [b.] February 29, 1976, Tewksbury; [p.] Shirley and Robert Winslow; [ed.] Tewksbury Memorial High School, Cornell University; [occ.] Student; [hon.] NFAA Arts Recognition and Talent Search 1994 Honorable Mention Recepient in poetry; [pers.] I have no famous last words at this time. Hopefully I will have more time to come up with some.; [a.] Ithaca, NY

WINSTON JR., JOHN
[b.] December 2, 1947, Thibodaux; [p.] Mrs. Eleana O. Winston, Father (Deceased) November '92; [m.] Carol A. Winston (Deceased) January '91, October 16, 1972; [ch.] Nicholtte, Tamara, Keishia and John III; [ed.] C.M. Washington High School currently enrolled at Nicholls University; [occ.] Janitor for Lafourche Parish School Board (Pupil Appraisal Center); [memb.] American Legion Post #513; [hon.] U.S. Army November 66-69; [oth. writ.] I had a poem published in the Nicholls State University (Nicholls Worth) February 2, 1995 "Anyone can"; [pers.] I am a single parent with two children since my wife's death January 8, 1991, working, and attending Nicholls State University.; [a.] Thibodaux, LA

WINTERS, BETTY J.
[pen.] Winifred; [b.] March 22, Los Angeles, CA; [p.] Deceased; [m.] Married 10 years; [ch.] 2 Sons (adults); [ed.] Jr. College; [occ.] Housewife; [memb.] Charity Club for Scholarships; [hon.] Leadership,; [oth. writ.] Poems for myself; [pers.] I have always written poems since I was a teenager. I love to read romantic novels. Poetry is a way of expressing your inter feelings; [a.] Panorama City, CA

WIRT, DYAN MARIE
[b.] October 23, 1957; [ed.] University of Florida; [pers.] Poetry is the primordial in us—the magic filling our veins put to music. It is the fertile language of truth and dreams. Good poetry is the convergence of sound, image, content, meaning

and self: each well-crafted work a unique vessel riding the swell of our internal rhythms and exploring infinite seas.; [a.] Santa Barbara, CA

WISWELL, JASON
[pen.] Victor Jobe Blackman; [p.] Eileen Blackman, Don Wiswell; [pers.] Though my writings are of the dark nature in our minds, believe when I say to strive for love. Only death awaits the lonely; [a.] The Colony, TX

WITHEE, BEVERLY
[b.] December 26, 1967, St. Thomas, VI; [p.] David F. Withee Sr., Pamela B. Withee; [ed.] University Of New Orleans and Delgado Community College; [occ.] Rehabilitation Technician for (Rehability Corporation); [memb.] Symphony Chorus of New Orleans, Concert choir of New Orlenas, Aurora United Methodist Church, and International Society of Poets; [hon.] "World of Poetry" - Golden Poet (1992), "International Society of Poets" - International Poet of Merit Award (1993, 1994, 1995) "The National Library of Poetry" - Editor's Choice Award (1993, 1994, 1995); [oth. writ.] Poems published in Anthologies, through "The National Library of Poetry" - "Whispers In The Wind" (1993), "Outstanding poet of 1994 (1994), "Best Poems Of 1995' (1995); [pers.] It was best said, by a very special person, "We judge ourselves by our intentions, and others by their actions." "It is only by truly loving ourselves, that we are able to love others unconditionally, free of all expectations.; [a.] Harvey, LA

WITHERSPOON, LOUISE
[b.] July 10, 1913, West Alexander, PA; [p.] Jacob and Lelle Smith (Deceased); [m.] Norman Witherspoon (Deceased), September 9, 1936; [ch.] Kay Greenlee, Linda Snyder; [ed.] Claysville High School (Penn.), Nursing and Business Training, owned and operated jewelry business; [occ.] Homemaker; [memb.] First Methodist Church, New Philadelphia, Ohio - formerly active in numerous community and service organizations; [oth. writ.] Compilation of several hundred poems in book form (non-published), Booklet in story-form of my mother's 100 years of life in honor of her 100th birthday (non-published); [pers.] My degrees are in Life. The varied and interesting people and wonderful experiences in 82 years of living have provided me with a wide and rewarding education. Poetry is a form of therapy, a soothing balm to the soul, portraying beauty and melody beyond the spoken word.; [a.] New Philadelphia, OH

WOHLERS, LINDSAY
[b.] May 2, 1985, Syracuse, NY; [p.] Kathleen and David Wohlers; [ed.] 4th grade Van Buren Elementary School Baldwinsville, NY 13027; [occ.] Student; [oth. writ.] A story published in Kaleidoscope-a CIMS language Arts literary magazine in 1993 second grade; [pers.] I started writing poetry in kinder garden and continue to enjoy it; [a.] Baldwinsville, NY

WOLF, JOYCE VENNE CARTER
[b.] January 19, 1939, Saranac, NY; [p.] Irene and Eldric Venne; [m.] Lawrence E. Wolf, June 11, 1988; [ch.] Ricky Carter, Stephen Carter, Laura Conte, DJ Carter; [ed.] Bachelor's Degree - Bus.

Admin.; [occ.] Housewife, past Procurement Admin.; [memb.] Toast Masters, Women of the Moose; [hon.] Raising 4 wonderful, productive children.; [oth. writ.] They don't have a clue and newspaper articles.; [pers.] You are never alone.; [a.] Palm Bay, FL

WOLFSON, BEN
[pen.] Ben Wolfson; [b.] March 1, 1982, Kansas City; [p.] Irma and Bill Wolfson; [ed.] In Junior High School; [occ.] Student; [pers.] Things are how you perceive them to be.; [a.] Irvine, CA

WOOD, DAVID H.
[pen.] David H. Wood; [b.] March 30, 1925, VA; [p.] Raymond and Edna Wood; [m.] Dorothy Weisiger, October 9, 1944; [ch.] Linda, Martha, Patti, Nancy and Betsy; [ed.] George Washington High, Alexandria, VA, Bus. Adm. Washington Bus. School; [occ.] Retired Builder; [memb.] Civitan Club, member of United Methodist Church; [hon.] U.S. Marine Corp. 4 yrs. ordained deacon (S. Baptist); [oth. writ.] First try at writing; [pers.] In still family values and marital commitment to future generation. Show young people the importance of loving and sharing life.; [a.] Luray, VA

WOOD, MARY C.
[b.] June 27, 1920, Ruxton, MD; [p.] Even and Ethel Fisher; [m.] Gilbert W. Wood Sr., June 15, 1940; [ch.] Ellen, Ethel and Gilbert Jr.; [ed.] Minimal started age 9, graduated School #1 9th Gr. age 15 rec. GED 11/60; [occ.] Clerk (Secretarial); [memb.] Order of Eastern Star, Order of Amaranth, Cedarettes, Ladies Council: UCC of E., Marley U.M. Church, U.M.W. of Marley, Glen Burnie Chapter 1519 NARFE. (Hold office in all but one.); [oth. writ.] Several poems published in other anthologies, church papers, stories for children.; [pers.] Mother died at age 9 mo. and was raised in home for children 'til age 10. Went to live with father and received instructions in living. Have enjoyed my life and still do. At present time have 33 volunteer jobs.; [a.] Glen Burnie, MD

WOODS, CHRISTOPHER
[b.] May 7, 1977, Detroit, MI; [p.] Mary Woods, Eugene Matthews; [ed.] Denby High School, Macomb College, Art Instruction School; [occ.] Senior High School Student; [memb.] Southeastern Michigan Tennis Association, Vocational Industrial Clubs of America; [hon.] Academic Excellence, Nominee for Scholar Athlete 1st Place Trophy's Candy Sale and Tennis; [oth. writ.] Poems published in school paper.; [pers.] Don't look at each day as the first day of the rest of your life, look at it as the first day of a new beginning.; [a.] Detroit, MI

WOODS, NINA FAITH
[pen.] Sissca; [b.] August 17, 1964, Wichita, KS; [p.] Yvonne Washington, Charlie Phillips; [m.] Divorce; [ch.] Sheena, Rickena, Krystina, Reginald and Retiya; [ed.] HSG; [occ.] Civil Service Employee; [oth. writ.] The Man of My Dreams and A Mother's Love; [pers.] Learn from things that happen in life, to have strength to go on and to survive. God thank you for blessing me with my loving children Sheena, Rickena, Krystina, Reginald and Retiya; [a.] Pensacola, FL

WOODUM, SHELLY A.
[b.] August 27, 1959, Georgia; [p.] Eddie James and Bernice Wallace; [m.] Keith B. Woodum, August 30, 1986; [ch.] Rosalynn and Justin; [ed.] Lanier County High School; [occ.] Medical Biller; [memb.] 20th Street Church of Christ Share Committee and Blood Drive; [hon.] President of Phi Beta Lambda Club; [oth. writ.] September 30, 1985 given an award certificate for a poem written, titled Jesus is the source of power. In 1986 I was also issued a golden poet certificate from The World of poetry.; [pers.] I focus on reality, love and humor in my writing, because I think it helps to bring out the best in mankind. Writing is what I enjoy doing the best.; [a.] Saint Petersburg, FL

WOODWARD, HOWARD H.
[pen.] Howard H. Woodward; [b.] January 4, 1951, Glendale, CA; [p.] Florence and Walter Woodward; [ch.] Joshua Jamin and Anna Rachelle Woodward; [ed.] MBA Pepperdine "81", B.S. Bus. Adm CSUCHICO "76", A.A. Shasta College "74"; [occ.] Market Manager; [hon.] Recognition for work with "DARE", ASB life member H.S.; [oth. writ.] "Chunks of Gold"; [a.] Moorpark, CA

WOOLEY, GERALDINE H.
[pen.] "God Sends His Own"; [b.] February 15, 1942, Idlewild, MI; [p.] Charles L. Hamilton, Alice Smith Hamilton; [m.] Divorce, June 11, 1961; [ch.] Vickie M. Houston, Monica L. Roberts, Deborah J. Wooley; [ed.] Nothern High, Jordan College; [occ.] Disabled Poem and Song Writer. Study the organ.; [memb.] Faith Baptist Temple, Flint, MI. Rev. Freelon Threlkeld Jr. Pastor; [oth. writ.] Collection of Poems and Songs. Poems used for sermon by the Rev. Edward C. Roberts, Charlotte, N.C. "You are not Feeding my Soul" Poem in Anthology. Between the Raindrops "It is the Fruit of My Suffering; [pers.] Dedicated to the memory of the late, Thomas A. Robinson; [a.] Mount Morris, MI

WORTHAM, TOYIA PATRICE
[b.] December 27, 1965, San Francisco, CA; [p.] T. O. and Grace Wortham; [ed.] Lowell High, San Francisco State University, Long Ridge Writer's Group; [occ.] Special Events Coordinator; [memb.] S.F. Arc, Glide Memorial Church, SF. Aids Foundation, S.F. SPCA; [hon.] Dean's List, victoria sinclair award of merit, youth search light scholarship recipient; [oth. writ.] "Beacon", "Toast of the town" - screenplays, several poems, short stories, editorial satires, and contemporary songs; [pers.] In swahili, nia means purpose my inspiration for this poem were my mother, grandmother, sister, niece, and my sisters in prose - Maya Angelou, Toni Morrison, Isabel Allende, Amy Tan, and Janice Mirikitani.; [a.] San Francisco, CA

WRIGHT, CHERYL
[pen.] T. Bell; [b.] San Diego; [ed.] San Diego; [occ.] Designer, Writer; [memb.] Professional Member of American Center for Design, The Museum Society (Advocate) Voices for children MCA; [hon.] My greatest honor is volunteering with children affairs others pale; [pers.] Poetry is in my family line - 1 grew up with readings - my great Uncle was the well known poet James Whitcomb Reilley; [a.] San Diego, CA

WRIGHT, DORIS F.
[pen.] Doris F. Wright; [b.] March 8, 1923, Marion, IN; [p.] Nellie and Courtney Farr; [m.] Norman Wright, July 18, 1993; [ch.] Janean, George, Ronada, Doris Ann, Michel and Patricia; [ed.] Pasadena, TX High, San Jacinto College; [occ.] Retired Housewife; [memb.] Pine River Valley Baptist Church; [hon.] Eight Grandchildren Cortney, Christopher, Jolie, Matthew, Charlotte, Daniel, Bradley and Emily; [pers.] My husband is the poet, I was moved by the death of our dear friend's wife taken by alzhiemers to write this one and only poem.; [a.] Ignacio, CO

WRIGHT, LINDA S.
[pen.] "Ellis"; [b.] August 31, 1952, El Paso, TX; [p.] Bill and Nina Long; [m.] Craig E. Wright, July 2, 1972; [ch.] Dana LeAnn (21), Austin Evan (16); [ed.] Highland Park High School, Kansas State Teacher's College; [occ.] Administrative Secretary Legislative Relations, BCBS of Kansas; [memb.] Lake Perry Country Club International Association of Turtles, Inc.; [hon.] 1995 National Library of Poetry Semi-Finalist; [oth. writ.] Special Occasion Poetry produced under "Just The Wright Touch" and Two Children's books still looking for a publisher.; [pers.] People are always telling me that my poetry makes them cry, I suppose that's the magic of poetry - touching someone's emotions with words.; [a.] Topeka, KS

WRISBON, JAMEKA
[b.] December 29, 1978, Wilmington, NC; [p.] James and Hazel Wrisbon; [ed.] Forest Hills Elementary, D.C. Virgo Middle School New Hanover High School; [memb.] New Hanover Regional Medical Center Volunteers, Keywanettes, Prisms Literacy Magazine, Math Team; [hon.] New Hanover High School Masters Award, New Hanover Regional Medical Center Auxiliary Volunteer Award, North Carolina School of Science and Mathematics Semi-finalist; [pers.] Poetry is the window to the soul, it expresses one's thoughts in a way no other form of writing can. In my poetry I try to convey a message without making one word more important than any other. This makes it a true form of art.; [a.] Wilmington, NC

WUNSCH, FRIEDRICH HAGEN
[b.] July 14, 1971, Decatur, AL; [p.] Pete and Barbara Wunsch; [ed.] A.P. Brewer High School, Freed Hardiman University, University of North Alabama (Florence); [occ.] Sound Engineer; [memb.] Alpha Tau Lambda; [pers.] My poetry is the interpretation of the music that flows through all of nature.; [a.] Falkville, AL

WYATT, JULIA L.
[b.] May 1, 1983; [p.] Michael K. Wyatt, Karen A. Wyatt; [hon.] Represented Haycock School at Fairfax Video '95 Student Documentary Competition; [oth. writ.] Being published in this anthology!; [pers.] Though this is the very beginning of my writing career and I am young, I think my poetry has considerable style and quality.; [a.] Falls Church, VA

WYCOFF, ANGELA JEAN
[b.] May 18, 1974, Tacoma, WA; [p.] Gregory Wycoff, Colleen Wycoff; [ed.] Emmanuel Holiness Academy; [pers.] My poem was inspired by the tragedy of America's aborted children. I wanted to dedicate something to those whose lives were so sadly ended.; [a.] Burley, WA

XAVER, CHERI ALLYSE BOSELL
[pen.] Cherie Xaver; [b.] South Bend, IN; [p.] Larry Evelyn Bosell; [ed.] James Whitcomb Riley, Indiana University; [occ.] Manager Al's Formal Wear, Bridal Couture, Designer, Dallas, TX; [memb.] 1. I society of Spiritual Prose Logan Center for Children, 2. National Executive Woman Writers, Assoc.; [hon.] National President, Emeritus of Vica and DCE Speaker for Student Entrepreneurs. Top marketing/special event for formal Russell's Wear, Dean's List; [oth. writ.] Children poem's, Prose of Children's Spirits, Short Stories of Children's Memories.; [pers.] Nothing is Forever, but our lives from the beginning strives for a balance. My purpose is to share a memory of much goodwill between our spirits.; [a.] Dallas, TX

YASPARRO, ROSEMARY MUNTZ
[b.] October 18, Cynthiana, KY; [p.] Florence and Doan Muntz; [m.] Joseph Yasparro, October 4, 1969; [ed.] Buena Vista High School - Georgetown College; [memb.] International Society of Poets; [hon.] Editor's Choice Awards; [oth. writ.] Several other poems published; [pers.] It is my wish to bring beauty into people's lives, also I would like to leave a little piece of myself behind.; [a.] Lynbrook, NY

YEFRAIMOV, GOLDA
[b.] December 16, 1981, Russia; [p.] Boris and Zoya Yefraimov; [ed.] Student in 8th grade of Brighton Middle School; [occ.] Student; [pers.] The minute I step outside, the beautiful, rhyming words enter my mind, rhyming words enter my mind, describing the beautiful view of todays day.; [a.] Rochester, NY

YOSHA, HOWARD
[b.] March 27, 1972, Hollywood, CA; [p.] Asher and Milliscent Yosha; [ed.] UCLA student, senior graduating June 1995 from the School of English. Theatre writing major; [occ.] UCLA student; [memb.] UCLA Marching Band; [oth. writ.] Unpublished poems, 3 plays, and short stories.; [a.] Santa Monica, CA

YOST, JOANNE E.
[pen.] Jey; [b.] October 3, 1954, Gardena, CA; [m.] Daniel, May 11, 1979; [ed.] Torrance High and Los Amigos High, Orange Coast College; [occ.] Diet. Technician by Trade - taking time off to devote to writing; [memb.] Inland Valley Dietetic Association; [oth. writ.] Many poems one published by National Library of Poetry in Journey of the Mind, also currently working on two novels.; [pers.] I write from personal experience, hoping to touch others in some small way. I believe poetry is a reflection of one's soul.; [a.] Perris, CA

YOUNGBAR, LORRAINE
[b.] May 11, 1937, Baltimore, MD; [p.] Michael and Edna Quasney; [m.] William Youngbar, November 29, 1952; [ch.] Darlene Maria Youngbar, Jason Scott Youngbar; [ed.] High School Graduate; [occ.] Housewife; [memb.] AARP National and Local Chapter 4222, Volunteer

Instructor for 55 Alive (AARP), Arthritis Foundation; [pers.] I like to write poems in words that come from my heart and enjoy sharing my feelings with others.; [a.] Onancock, VA

YOUNGBLOOD, JEFF
[b.] September 10, 1973, CA; [p.] William T. and Cynthia R. Youngblood; [ed.] Student at Louisiana State University in Chemistry and Physics; [memb.] Tae Kwon Do at L.S.U.; [pers.] A self-proclaimed neo-romantic, I like my verse as well as my music to flow and harmonize as one.; [a.] Baton Rouge, LA

YOUNGER, PATRICK ALLEN
[b.] September 5, 1952, Fort Chaffee, AR; [p.] John and DeWayne Younger; [m.] Fe De La Cerna Younger, April 22, 1988; [ch.] John Lawrence Younger; [ed.] B.S. Pharmacy, Southwestern Oklahoma State University, P.A.D.I. Dive Instructor; [occ.] Pharmacist, Southwest Florida Regional Medical Center; [memb.] Gulf Coast Society of Hospital Pharmacists, Florida Society of Hospital Pharmacists P.A.D.I.; [hon.] Eagle Scout, Dean's List; [oth. writ.] "In Search Of Silence" Travel Article in "Florida Journal" 2. Diver's Poem - to be published in Fall 1995, 3. Poems - Pele's Tear's Pilgrims of the Sea, Mirage? Soon will be submitted for publication.; [pers.] I have lived in Hawaii and traveled to the Islands, in the South Pacific. They are the inspiration for my Poetry.; [a.] Cape Coral, FL

YOVICH, ERIN
[b.] July 8, 1976, Rochester, PA; [p.] Ken and Linda Yovich; [ed.] Beaver High., CCBC, Waynesburg College; [memb.] Church of Jesus Christ of Latter-day Saints, Leukemia Society; [pers.] Always look for the best.; [a.] Beaver, PA

YRIART, MONICA COLLETE
[b.] April 7, 1960, Montevideo, Uruguay; [p.] Juan Felipe Yriart, Riley Moore Yriart; [ed.] Swarthmore College, BA, George Washington University National Law Center, J.D.; [occ.] Writer, Comparative Constitutional Legal History, Lawyer; [hon.] Swarthmore College B.A. Honors, George Washington U. Nat'l Law Center Full Scholarship for Juris Doctor, Equal Justice Foundation Grant for public interest legal users in progress book; [oth. writ.] Patterns in Constitutionalism and Dictatorship in Uruguay, Argentina, and Chile. Previous article "Trading In Trouble" in Multinational Monitor. Legal Educational booklet, Framing Legal Issues in Light of the Logical Structure of Judicial Rules; [pers.] Hope and idealism form a deep source of growth and creation. Use it carefully, but never leave.; [a.] McLean, VA

YTURRALDE, LYNN M.
[pen.] Rebeccah J. Roberts; [b.] June 19, 1974, New London, CT; [p.] Joyce Thomas, Michael Hull; [m.] Stephen Yturralde II; [ch.] Moira Elisabeth; [ed.] Chino High, Chaffey College; [memb.] World Wildlife Fund, Environmental Defense Fund, National Geographic Society.; [oth. writ.] "Deluge" and "Mindspider", both unpublished collections of my poetry.; [pers.] "An' it harm none, do as ye will" the Wiccan rede.

YVONNE, WILSON CHERYL
[pen.] Cheryl Wilson; [b.] September 25, 1958, Dayton, OH; [p.] Samuel Wilson Sr. and Hazel Lattimore Wilson; [m.] Henry Heard Cofield Jr., July 27, 1985; [ed.] Middletown Senior High 1976, Miami University, Oxford, Ohio, Associates in Arts Degree 1987 and NRI non fiction writing student; [occ.] Mailroom Clerk, Butler County Printing Company, Hamilton, Ohio; [memb.] Ohio Association of Historical Societies and Museums, Middletown Historical Society, the National Assn of the Advancement of Colored People; [hon.] NRI Achievement Award with high honors; [oth. writ.] "Loves' Lonely Silence" and "Love Is..." are parts of two poems that make up my poem that is in the semi finalist competition for the publication, "At Water's Edge" titled "Loves' Lonely Silence", as a city bicenntinial song for African-American heritage.; [pers.] I am a curator for local African-American history. I will always remember what my father said, the first law of nature is self-preservation. I enjoy researching, family genealogy and photography.; [a.] Middletown, OH

ZABLAN, WANDA
[pen.] Tiera James; [b.] July 18, 1950, Honolulu, HI; [p.] William Kahapea Sr., Miriam McCabe; [ch.] Tiera Kahapea, James Kaholo; [ed.] Kailua High, University of Hawaii, Honolulu; [occ.] Personnel Management Specialist, HI State Human Services Dept.; [oth. writ.] Poems for local school and community publication; [pers.] I choose to act upon scripture which states: Use the talents (gifts) you have been given or lose it.; [a.] Honolulu, HI

ZAHARCHUK, DAVID R.
[b.] November 16, 1971, Lebanon, NH; [p.] Peter and Joan Zaharchuk; [ed.] BS Accounting - Bentley College Waltham, MA, Graduate Student - George Mason Univ. (current); [occ.] Officer, U.S. Army, Ft. Belvoir, VA; [hon.] Beta Alpha Psi; [pers.] There is no greater joy than watching your thoughts come alive on a page.; [a.] Alexandria, VA

ZEH, LYNDA R.
[b.] May 17, 1949, La Harpe, IL; [p.] Eldon E. Snyder and Audrey M. Cludray; [m.] Jack B. Zeh, September 17, 1978; [ch.] Tabitha J. Martin, Dustin D. Wamsley; [ed.] Nauvoo-Colusa High, Cloud County Community College; [occ.] Housewife, Student, Evangelist; [hon.] Abilene Foursquare FWI Plaque; [oth. writ.] Poem, article pending publication with Foursquare World Advance Magazine, Songs composed with husband (not published); [pers.] My greatest influence has been King David, author of the Book of Psalms in the Holy Bible. All my poetry and songs are inspirations of God.; [a.] Abilene, KS

ZIEGELBAUER, AMANDA M.
[b.] October 22, 1983, West Bend, WI; [p.] Gary and Glennis Ziegelbauer; [ed.] Presently in the 6th grade at Slinger Middle School; [occ.] Student; [memb.] Slinger Middle School Band (Flute); [hon.] D.A.R.E. (Drug Abuse Resistance Education) Essay Contest, 1st place in 6th grade, Creative Writing Contest, Creative Writing Award (4th and 5th grade), Presidential Academic Fitness Award (5th grade), High Honor Roll (6th grade); [pers.] I have always enjoyed writing. I have written a number of short stories and poems since I was in first grade. I hope to someday write a novel; [a.] Slinger, WI

ZUBER, KATHI
[b.] September 8, 1978, Colorado Springs, CO; [p.] Col. Richard Zuber and Ann Zuber; [ed.] High School, DOD Schools in Europe; [occ.] High School Student; [hon.] Excellence in acting (at the Folger Shakespeare Library in D.C.), Honor student for all school years; [oth. writ.] Poems, short stories, and songs but none published; [pers.] My writings are inspired by the negative aspects of life.; [a.] Burke, VA

ZWEIG, ROBERT M.
[b.] September 16, 1920, New York, NY; [p.] Rebecca Zweig, Pinkus Zweig; [m.] Estelle Mishler Zweig, August 23, 1947; [ch.] Paul Ronald Zweig, Michael Kevin Zweig; [ed.] B.A. Queens College, E.E. West Virginia Univ.; [occ.] Consultant; [hon.] Standard and Poor's Who's Who 1980 - Past President John Chatillen and Sons Inc.; [oth. writ.] Poems for local magazines; [pers.] However dismal the state of society may be, the laser light of hope will always penetrate its darkest recess.; [a.] Boca Raton, FL

Index
of
Poets

Leftwich, Charles 433
Leinberger, Joela 446
Leistner, David 446
Leith, Justin 230
Lelaina, Victoria 82
Lembo, Allison 102
Lemieux, Christopher 309
Lentz, Teresa 274
Lenz, Harry E. 332
Leon, Nuccia Giacalone 482
Leonard, Edward T. 242
Leonard, Laura 380
Lerner, Amy 294
Lesene, Cheryl 148
Leslie, M. J. 388
Lester, Gordon 451
Lester, Rosemary 95
Letulle, Leona 600
Leuang, Laura 280
Levendis, Margaret M. 216
Levine, Laurence 209
Lewandowski, Nancy 58
Lewellen, John 341
Lewis, Amanda 141
Lewis, Bette F. 465
Lewis, Danielle 544
Lewis, Jeannie 132
Lewis, Johnnie 320
Lewis, Kimberly 366
Lewis, Michelle 272
Lewis, Queen E. 474
Lewis, Richard K. 279
Lewis, Sharon G. 275
Li, Velvet 366
Liao, Xiaosheng 97
Lievense, Kathleen Bigge 273
Liewald, Cleda D. 335
Lifto, Marge 583
Light, Erin 512
Light, Forrest L. 554
Lijoi, Heather 443
Lilley, Leona C. 399
Lillibridge, Freda R. 159
Lillibridge, Linda 73
Lillie, Rosalie Ringer 573
Lilly, Thomas 55
Lim, K. C. 364
Lim, Michael 61
Limbach, Randall S. 375
Liming, Josie 419
Lin, Paul 369
Linden Jr., Richard G. 220
Linden, Petra 288
Lindsay, Irene H. Courreges 335
Lindsey, Beverly Pettiford 556
Lindsey, Doris 616
Lindsey, Sylvia 364
Lindstrom, Lisa 286
Linet, Crystal 316
Lingren, Judy M. 527
Linn, Amy 529
Linstrum, Erin 455
Linton, Heidi A. 329
Linton, Stefani 495
Linzner, Terra 365
Lipscomb, Audrey 107
Lisowski, Katherine 363
Litsch, April 525
Little, Brandy 297
Little, Janet 449
Little, Nancy L. 587

Little, Sherry 210
Litz, Peggy 53
Livingston, Ann Everett 444
Llewellyn, Holly R. 508
Llinas, Rita 68
Lloyd, Kelly 588
Lloyd Sr., William E. 200
LoBue, Chris 326
Locantore, Joshua 226
Locher, Nichole 580
Lockard, James William 240
Locklear, Ethel S. 329
Lockwood, Don 35
Lockwood, Rena 571
Loebach, Paul 472
Loerzel, Sister Mary Cabrini 282
Logan, Ashley 224
Logan, Sandra 590
Lohr, Katanya 375
Lomas, Michelle Lynn 489
Lomax, Mark S. 415
Lombardi, Amanda B. 548
Lombardo, Lawrence 396
Loncharich, Anthony B. 197
Long, Jane M. 319
Long, Jennifer 135
Long, Kathryn 49
Long, Margaret Demanett 358
Long, Shirley J. 209
Longmire, Jerry Walters 362
Longo, Brenda L. 434
Longstaff, Michelle 598
Loomis, Robert 575
Looney, Nita 411
Lopez, Reginaldo P. 282
Lopez, Steven 42
Lopp, Bettye 156
Loprieno, John 336
Lor, Rosy 181
Loraine 509
Lord, Brian J. 463
Lord, Helen 430
Lordo, Carl B. 608
Lotz, John M. 416
Loupé, Gladys B. 300
Loutzenhiser, Shelly L. 81
Love, Johnnie 520
Love, Jonathan 453
Love, Samantha 589
Lowe, Brenda 131
Lowe, Max K. 200
Lowther, Helen L. 324
Lucas, Rebecca 394
Lucia, Kristy Marie 60
Luciano, Toni Anne 414
Luckenbill, Richard S. 400
Lugo, Noed B. 91
Lum, James 324
Lumetta, Lawrence C. 410
Lundstrom, Susan L. 90
Luscombe, Jason Lin 445
Lute, Katherine M. 395
Luther, Karl 262
Lutze, Debbra A. 334
Lux, Dorothea Ruth 350
Luxardo, Adalcinda Camarao 305
Lynar-Cohen, Eleanor 514
Lynch, Jean B. 532
Lynn, Audra 223
Lyon, Tiffany A. 383
Lyons, Daniel 549

Lyons, Vicky 212

M

Mabroucky, Opanga 356
Macabeo, Carolyn D. 300
Macdonald, David A. 449
Mack, Jon Oliver 543
Mack, Robin 415
Mack-Stazenski, Alison 540
Mackanic, Kimberly 612
MacKenzie, Joan 129
Mackowski, Sandra Lee 619
MacLean, Carole A. 437
MacNair, Donald J. 525
MacRae, Heidi 533
Mader, Connie Kay 338
Madewell, Colleen 456
Magnus, Marcy 60
Magtira, Jasmine 115
Mahaffey, Sharon 51
Maher, Brian Thomas 33
Mahoney, Sean P. 184
Maier, Susanna 45
Maille, Nicole L. 561
Majid, Mariam Al 173
Makela, Jason 136
Malanga, Jenean R. 458
Malar, Kari Sue 498
Malcolm, Tracy 477
Male, Shirley 101
Mallow, Amy M. 250
Malloy, Jason 311
Malone, Elizabeth D. 138
Malone, JoAnn 142
Malonn, Marcella 204
Maloomian, Diana 344
Malsom, Donna 107
Manasa, Morgan L. 382
Mancheno 367
Mancini, Patricia Flynn 507
Mandich, Max 392
Mangini, Brighton 108
Manifold, Cindy 155
Manix, Patricia 273
Mann, Celeta 130
Mann, Hilary Clark 450
Manning, Dee 558
Manning, Judi 531
Manning, Kevin D. 614
Manning, Lindsay A. 190
Manor, Cyndia 134
Mantoen, Hope 417
Manuel, Carrie 5
Manuel, Eduardo G. 298
Manzo, Joanne 301
Manzo, Sandra 579
Maples, Virginia F. 600
Maranon, Andrea 142
Marchalonis, Lisa 572
Marchant, Lillian 84
Marcus, Bernice 453
Maria, Annette 158
Marie, A. 266
Marigliano, Mary 215
Marion, Chanda R. 313
Market, Megan 610
Markidis, Despina 345
Markle, Roger 351
Markowitz, David S. 426
Marks, Jessica 13

Marlow, Roberta 389
Marouf, David 252
Marques, Walter 271
Marquis, Carolyn F. 424
Marquis, Helen Hunt 526
Mars, Rosie L. Miller 621
Marshall, Andrea 426
Marshall, Gloria J. 233
Marshall, Victoria 498
Martens, Lucille 53
Martensen, Mindy 390
Martin, Adrian 197
Martin, Amanda 241
Martin, Amelia 38
Martin, Bonita S. 123
Martin, Edouard 304
Martin, Emily 458
Martin, Glenda 549
Martin, Isabel 427
Martin, Laura Belle 99
Martin, Liz 207
Martin, Margaret E. 270
Martin, Meredith 569
Martin, Meryl L. 52
Martin, Morris 166
Martin, Sandra B. 261
Martin, Stacy 66
Martin, Stephanie Elizabeth 260
Martin, Terry L. 88
Martineau, Katie 94
Martinelli, Jacquelyn 545
Martinez, Bob G. 112
Martinez, Isidro A. 245
Martinez, Madeline 44
Martinez, Rebecca 566
Martinez, Roger D. 361
Martinez, Sharon 91
Martino, Josephine 14
Martinus, Sarah E. 85
Martorelli, Mary 568
Martyn, Lisa 568
Masi, Barbara L. 103
Maslowski, Larry 208
Mason, Ada Hall 516
Mason, Betty D. 460
Mason, Doug 333
Mason, Janice 301
Mason, Mandy 360
Mason, Michal Jon 352
Mason, Mildred H. 269
Mason, Shirley J. 100
Mason, Wendy K. 586
Massman, Kristen 97
Mastainich, Joseph A. 521
Mastantuono, Janine 517
Mastel, Ellen 253
Masters, Scott 362
Mastrantonis, Vivian Parris 615
Mastropolo, Peter 72
Mata, Anthony 32
Mates, Annette 549
Mathews, Charles 438
Mathis, Audrey M. 544
Mathis, Jean K. 30
Mathys, Dianne 418
Matlack, Jennifer C. 154
Matsunaga, Ernest Michio 325
Mattei, Regina 180
Matteis, Justine 471
Matteo, Lisa Ann 191
Matthews, Eileen 232

Williamson, Loveniar A. 193
Willoughby, William E. 561
Wills, Amanda 422
Wills, Nicole 202
Wilmeth, Eva Nell 33
Wilmore, Charles A. 156
Wilsey, Rochelle Ann 97
Wilson, Amanda 444
Wilson, Cathy 417
Wilson, Cheryl 253
Wilson, Daniel J. 322
Wilson, Donna 119
Wilson, Donna 158
Wilson IX, Thomas 581
Wilson, J. Fowler 144
Wilson, Kathryn Marie 70
Wilson, Lee 87
Wilson, Linda B. 357
Wilson, Michelle 98
Wilson, Patricia 603
Wilson, Stephanie 205
Wilson, Steven 70
Wilson, Tiffany 594
Wilson-Smith, Barbara 347
Wiltse, Trisha 503
Winburn, Nichole 412
Winham, Mary 355
Winslow, E. A. 488
Winston Jr., John 426
Winter, Daniel 157
Winters, Betty J. 320
Wirt, Dyan 433
Wise, Heather 311
Wise, Katie L. 591
Wiswell, Jason Michael 7
Withee, Beverly 136
Witherow, Leona Z. 180
Witherspoon, Louise 78

Wittenberg, Paul M. 356
Woessner, Kim 490
Wohlers, Lindsay 360
Wojczyk, Michelle 209
Wolf, Joyce C. 618
Wolf, Priscilla 268
Wolfe, Amy Rana 28
Wolfe, Franchesa 455
Wolfe, Paula J. 98
Wolfe, Whitney 601
Wolfson, Ben 122
Womack, Lucas 211
Wong, Dora 238
Wong, Helen S. 343
Wood, Candy 144
Wood, David H. 441
Wood, Lyndsey S. 357
Wood, Mary C. 211
Wood, Miranda 373
Wood, Sharon 586
Wood, Val 359
Woodburn, Tabitha Deloris 351
Wooderson, Shelley-Anne 360
Woodfin, Suzanne 612
Woodhall, Gabriele C. 117
Woodland, Tonya 568
Woods, Angel 103
Woods, Christopher A. 466
Woods, Jeff 148
Woods, Jennifer K. 452
Woods, Nina Faith 97
Woodum, Shelly A. 273
Woodward, Howard 108
Wooley, Geraldine 246
Woolson, Barbara A. 520
Wooten, Amanda 153
Wortham, Toyia 261

Woss, Sharon A. 52
Wright, Angela L. 550
Wright, Carolyn 455
Wright, Doris F. 245
Wright, Linda S. 505
Wright, Paul 212
Wright, Phyrne Harper 457
Wrisbon, Jameka 24
Wroblewski, Marie Baia 190
Wu, Lisa 507
Wunsch, Friedrich 542
Wyatt, Julia 142
Wycoff, Angela 329
Wynn, Karen P. 501

X

X, Lawrence 369
Xaver, Cheri Allyse 228

Y

Yalin, Debra Carter 115
Yarnell, Bruce 145
Yasparro, Rosemary Muntz 200
Yates, Kathryn M. 613
Yates, Ruth 169
Yeager, Michael Raymond 174
Yefraimov, Golda 435
Yim, Jennifer 77
Yocom, Dennis R. 4
Yoder, Danielle 337
Yore, Patrick E. 50
York, ReAnna Nicole 221
Yosha, Howard 439
Yost, JoAnne E. 334
Young, Deborah (Hively) 326
Young, Dianne M. 452

Young, Jean 511
Young, Katherine M. 220
Young, Kenneth E. 397
Young, Pauline 188
Young, Shirley 55
Young, Stacy 413
Young, Vivian 54
Young-Burns, Karen 99
Youngbar, Lorraine M. 71
Youngblood, Jeff P. 325
Younger, P. A. 364
Yovich, Erin 154
Yriart, Monica Collette 173

Z

Zabadal, Richard J. 566
Zabaldo, Joel Thomas 438
Zablan, Wanda 289
Zagrebin, Alexei 324
Zaharchuk, David R. 429
Zampelli, Barbara 146
Zanger, Jennifer A. 295
Zarychta, Nikole 365
Zee, Scott 606
Zeh, Lynda R. 209
Zehrung, Linda 194
Zepeda, D. B. 412
Zetina, Paul 564
Zetty, Jenny 437
Zidarevich, Amber 146
Ziebart, Sandra 414
Ziegelbauer, Amanda 515
Zier, Kristen 381
Zimarowski, Katy 210
Zlakovski, Patzi 216
Zook, Jon V. 36
Zook, Lara Headlee 569
Zuber, Kathi 497
Zweig, Robert M. 482